Environmental Encyclopedia

Environmental Encyclopedia

Second Edition

William P. Cunningham, Terence H. Cooper,
Eville Gorham, Malcolm T. Hepworth,

Editors

GALE

DETROIT · NEW YORK · TORONTO · LONDON

William P. Cunningham, Terence H. Cooper, Eville Gorham, Malcolm T. Hepworth, *Editors*

Gale Research Staff

Kimberley A. McGrath, *Project Coordinator*

Nicole Beatty, *Associate Editor*

Susan Trosky, *Permissions Manager*
Margaret A. Chamberlain, *Permissions Specialist*
Shalice Shah, *Permissions Associate*

Jeffrey Muhr, *Editorial Technical Consultant*

Mary Beth Trimper, *Production Director*
Evi Seoud, *Assistant Production Manager*
Shanna Heilveil, *Production Assistant*

Cynthia D. Baldwin, *Product Design Manager*
Barbara Yarrow, *Graphic Services Manager*
Randy Bassett, *Image Database Supervisor*
Pamela A. Reed, *Photography Coordinator*

Bernadette M. Gornie, *Page Designer*
Tracey Rowens, *Cover Designer*

Electronic illustrations provided by Hans Neuhart, of Fountain Hills, Arizona

The paper used in this publication meets the minimum requirements of American National Standard for Information Sciences—Permanence Paper for Printed Library Materials, ANSI Z39.48-1984.

ISBN 0-8103-9314-X
ISSN 1072-5083

Printed in the United States of America
10 9 8 7 6 5 4 3 2 1

Table Of Contents

Acknowledgments vii

Advisors xiii

Contributors xv

How to Use This Book xix

Introduction xxi

A-Z 1

Historical Chronology 1147

Environmental Legislation in the United States 1151

Index 1155

Acknowledgments

The editors wish to thank the copyright holders of the excerpted text included in this edition and the permissions managers of many book and magazine publishing companies for assisting us in securing reproduction rights. We are also grateful to the staffs of the Detroit Public Library, the Library of Congress, the University of Detroit Mercy Library, Wayne State University Purdy/Kresge Library Complex, and the University of Michigan Libraries for making their resources available to us. Following is a list of the copyright holders who have granted us permission to reproduce material in this edition of *EE-2*. Every effort has been made to trace copyright, but if omissions have been made, please let us know.

COPYRIGHTED EXCERPTS IN *EE*, SECOND EDITION, WERE REPRODUCED FROM THE FOLLOWING BOOKS:

Callicott, J. Baird. From "Conservation Values of Ethics," in *Principles of Conservation Biology*. Sinauer Associates, Inc., 1994. © 1994 by Sinauer Associates, Inc. All rights reserved. Reproduced by permission

PHOTOGRAPHS AND ILLUSTRATIONS APPEARING IN *EE-2* WERE RECEIVED FROM THE FOLLOWING SOURCES:

Acid deposition, illustration. Wadsworth, Inc. Reproduced by permission: p. 4; Acid rain damage, Chicago, photograph by Richard P. Jacobs. JLM Visuals. Reproduced by permission: p. 6; Africanized bee, photograph by Scott Camazine. Photo Researchers, Inc. Reproduced by permission: p. 13; Agent Orange, photograph by AP/Wide World Photos. Reproduced by permission: p. 15; Air Pollution, diagram of a temperature inversion, line drawing by Robert L. Wolke. Reproduced by permission: p. 24; Alaska Highway, map, line drawing by Laura Gritt Lawson. Reproduced by permission: p. 29; *Amoco Cadiz* tanker, its oil spill being contained, photograph by Leonard Freed. Magnum Photos. Reproduced by permission: p. 41; Amory, Cleveland, holding a cat, photograph: p. 42; Animal rights, people dressed in prison suits wearing monkey masks, photograph. Corbis-Bettmann. Reproduced by permission: p. 46; Aquifer restoration, shown between layers of rock and clay, illustration. McGraw-Hill, Inc. Reproduced by permission: p. 57; Arctic National Wildlife Refuge, the shaded area on map of Alaska. World Management Credit. Reproduced by permission: p. 61; Asbestos, two men removing asbestos from a pipe, by Eugene Smith. Black Star Publishing Co., Inc. Reproduced by permission: 65; Aswan, U.A.R., dam, photograph. Corbis-Bettmann. Reproduced by permission: 71; Atmosphere, composition and structure of, line drawing. Gale Research: p. 72; Audubon, John James (sitting on stump), engraving. Corbis-Bettmann. Reproduced by permission: p. 75; Avalanche, photograph by Ned Gillette. Stock Market. Reproduced by permission: p. 80; Bacon, Francis, painting by Paul van Somer. Corbis-Bettmann. Reproduced by permission: p. 85; Baghouse, a graph showing a control device for air pollution. McGraw-Hill, Inc. Reproduced by permission: p. 85; Bald eagle, white head, brown shoulders, right profile, photograph by Robert J. Huffman. Field Mark Publications. Reproduced by permission: p. 87; Barrier island, Cape Hatteras, North Carolina, photograph. JLM Visuals. Reproduced by permission: p. 88; Bhopal, India, farmer walking his cattle past the Union Carbide plant, photograph. Corbis-Bettmann. Reproduced by permission: p. 95; Biodiversity, chart with headings of known and estimated diversity of life on earth, line drawing. Beacon Press. Reproduced by permission: p. 100; Biomagnification, birds and fish swimming, graph showing the pesticide DDT in the food chain, illustration. McGraw-Hill, Inc. Reproduced by permission: p. 111; Bioremediation, system showing its Raymond process, photograph. Reproduced by permission: p. 117; Biosphere reserve, schematic plan of, line drawing. Beacon Press. Reproduced by permission: 120; Bison, photograph by Yoav Levy. Phototake NYC. Reproduced by permission: p. 126; Black-footed ferret, photograph. Visuals Unlimited. Reproduced by permission: p. 127; Bookchin, Murray, photograph by Debbie Bookchin. Reproduced by permission: p. 131; Borlaug, Norman Ernest (standing in wheat field with right hand on hip), photograph. Corbis-Bettmann. Reproduced by permission: p. 132; Boulding, Kenneth E., photograph by Ken Abbott. University of Colorado at Boulder. Reproduced by permission: p. 136; Brower, David (looking into distance), photograph. Corbis-Bettmann. Reproduced by permission: p. 138; Brown, Lester (with book "State of the World"), photograph. Corbis-Bettmann. Reproduced by permission: 139; Browner, Carol (at microphones), photograph. Corbis-Bettmann. Reproduced by permission: p. 141; Bruntland, Gro Harlem (wearing pearl necklace and earrings), photograph. Corbis-Bettmann. Reproduced by permission: p.

143; Burroughs, John and John Muir (seated on large rocks), photograph. Corbis-Bettmann. Reproduced by permission: p. 146; Caldicott, Helen (standing at podium), photograph. Corbis-Bettmann. Reproduced by permission: p. 149; California condor, photograph by Roy Toft. Tom Stack & Associates. Reproduced by permission: p. 151; Captive propagation, Peter Noyes releasing baby Kemp's Ridley sea turtles, on the shoreline in Tamaulipas, Mexico, illustration by Allan Morgan. Peter Arnold Inc. Reproduced by permission: p. 155; Carbon cycle, outdoors, photograph by Hans & Cassidy. Gale Research: p. 157; Carson, Rachel, (with microscope), photograph. Corbis-Bettmann. Reproduced by permission: p. 165; Catalytic Converter, at Petro-Chemical Plant, photograph by Tom Carroll. Phototake. Reproduced by permission: p. 166; Chain reaction, graph showing and explaining how neutron travels, illustration by Laura Gritt Lawson. Reproduced by permission: p. 171; Chernobyl Nuclear Power Station with reactor #4 in foreground, photograph. Corbis-Bettmann. Reproduced by permission: p. 176; Clear-cutting, aerial view of forest in S. Africa, photo by F. Bouillot. Phototake. Reproduced by permission: p. 194; Coal gasification, graph showing the elements that are used to give off power to electric generators. McGraw-Hill, Inc. Reproduced by permission: p. 200; Commoner, Barry (speaking to protestors), photograph. Corbis-Bettmann. Reproduced by permission: p. 211; Composting, man wetting mushroom compost, photograph by Holt Confer. Phototake. Reproduced by permission: p. 218; Contour plowing, aerial view in S.E. Penna, photograph by Jerry Irwin. Photo Researchers, Inc. Reproduced by permission: p. 230; Coral reef, two yellow tropical fish, swimming around coral reef, photograph. Phototake. Reproduced by permission: p. 235; Cousteau, Jacques (arms crossed in front of him), photograph. Corbis-Bettmann. Reproduced by permission: p. 240; Crocodile in Florida, photograph by Tom & Pat Leeson. Photo Researchers, Inc. Reproduced by permission: p. 243; Cultural euthropication, a graph showing oxygen going downstream, illustration. McGraw-Hill, Inc. Reproduced by permission: p. 246; Cyclone collector, line drawing. McGraw-Hill, Inc. Reproduced by permissiona: p. 248; Darwin, Charles Robert, photograph. Photo Researchers, Inc. Reproduced by permission: p. 251; Defoliation, deforestation of the jungle in Brazil. AP/Wide World Photos. Reproduced by permission: p. 258; Desert tortoise, photograph by Dan Suzio. Reproduced by permission: p. 262; Desertification, line art, McGraw Hill, Inc. Reproduced with permission: p. 264; Dodo, illustration by George Bernard/Science Photo Library. Photo Researchers, Inc. Reproduced by permission: p. 272; Drift net, two fishermen with a drift net, photograph by Dan Guravich. Photo Researchers, Inc. Reproduced by permission: p. 278; Dubos, Rene Jules (in laboratory), photograph. Corbis-Bettmann. Reproduced by permission: p. 283; Dust bowl effect in Oklahoma (iron wheel seen poking up through dust), photograph. Corbis-Bettmann. Reproduced by permission: p. 286; Earth Day, street filled with people carrying a dead tree, photograph. Corbis-Bettmann. Reproduced by permission: p. 291; Earth First!, two women hold sign in front of the Lincoln memorial, photograph.

Corbis-Bettmann. Reproduced by permission: p. 293; Ecosystem, underwater, illustration by Hans & Cassidy. Gale Research: p. 313; Ecotourism, tourist looking out at the Galapagos Island, photograph by Anthony Wolff. Phototake NYC. Reproduced by permission: p. 317; Electrostatic precipitation, illustration. McGraw-Hill, Inc. Reproduced by permission: p. 325; Environmental Protection Agency (EPA), Organizational chart. photograph by Tom Pantages. Reproduced by permission: p. 374; Erosion, soil erosion on the trail, Adirondack by Yoav Levy. Phototake. Reproduced by permission: p. 384; Everglades, view of swampy area, photograph by Gerald Davis. Phototake. Reproduced by permission: p. 388; *Exxon Valdez* accident, photograph. AP/Wide World Photos. Reproduced by permission: p. 397; Florida panther, standing in between weeds and trees, photograph by Tom & Pat Leeson. Photo Researchers, Inc. Reproduced by permission: p. 415; Fludized bed combustion, a graph showing the direction of how fuel flows, illustration. McGraw-Hill, Inc. Reproduced by permission: p. 417; Food chain/web, drawing showing how wildlife and how interconnected to form food webs, illustration by Hans Neuhart. Gale Research: p. 421; Fossey, Dian, photograph. AP/Wide World Photos. Reproduced by permission: p. 430; Frog, lesser gray treefrog, photograph by Robert J. Huffman. Reproduced by permission: p. 439; Galapagos Islands, shoreline, photograph by Anthony Wolff/Phototake NYC. Reproduced by permission: p. 446; Genetic engineering, DNA injected into a mouse embryo, photograph by Jon Gordon. Phototake. Reproduced by permission: p. 455; Giardia, cells shown through a microscope, photograph by J. Paulin. Reproduced by permission: p. 461; Gibbs, Lois (at desk), photograph. Corbis-Bettmann. Reproduced by permission: p. 462; Goodall, Jane, photograph. The Library of Congress: p. 468; Gore, Al (hand gesturing), photograph. Corbis-Bettmann. Reproduced by permission: p. 471; Green Seal symbol, photograph by Tom Pantages. Reproduced by permission: p. 483; Greenhouse effect, illustration by Hans Neuhart. Gale Research: p. 485; Greenpeace, Rainbow Warrior, photograph. Greenpeace. Reproduced by permission: p. 487; Groundwater pollution, a graph, illustration. McGraw-Hill, Inc. Reproduced by permission: p. 495; Gully erosion in Australia, photograph by A. B. Joyce. Photo Researchers, Inc. Reproduced by permission: p. 495; Gypsy moth, female moths, laying eggs, photograph by Michael Gadumski. Photo Researchers, Inc. Reproduced by permission: p. 496; Haeckel, Ernst Heinrich Phillip August, photograph. Corbis-Bettmann. Reproduced by permission: p. 500; Hayes, Denis, photograph. Corbis-Bettmann. Reproduced by permission: p. 504; Hazardous substances that affects our health, chart. Beacon Press. Reproduced by permission: p. 505; Heilbroner, Robert, photograph by Jose Pelaez. W.W. Norton. Reproduced by permission: p. 514; Hiroshima, painting by Yasuko Yamagata: p. 521; Human-powered vehicles, four different bicycle illustrations. McGraw-Hill, Inc. Reproduced by permission: p. 529; Hydrologic cycle, a graph showing the circulation of water on earth, illustration. McGraw-Hill, Inc. Reproduced by permission: p. 534; Incinerator, diagram of a municipal facility, illustration. McGraw-Hill, Inc.

Reproduced by permission: p. 539; Indoor air pollutants, a graph of house, illustration. Wadsworth, Inc. Reproduced by permission: p. 542; Ivory-billed woodpecker, sitting on a man back, photograph by James Tanner. Photo Researchers, Inc. Reproduced by permission; p. 566; Kesterson National Wildlife Refuge, American coots, photograph by Leonard Lee Rue III. Visuals Unlimited. Reproduced by permission: p. 575; Krill, illustration. McGraw-Hill, Inc. Reproduced by permission: p. 579; Lake Baikal, Russia, view of the Strait of Olkhon, on the west coast of, photograph by Novosti Press Agency/Science Photo Library. Photo Researchers, Inc. Reproduced by permission: p. 584; Land use, graph, illustration. McGraw-Hill, Inc. Reproduced by permission: p. 591; Landfill, graph showing the different levels of, illustration. McGraw-Hill, Inc. Reproduced by permission: p. 593; Leakey, Mary, photograph. AP/Wide World Photos. Reproduced by permission: p. 602; Leakey, Richard, photograph. The Library of Congress: p. 605; Lepold, Aldo, examining a gray partridge, photograph by Robert Oetking. University of Wisconsin-Madison Archives. Reproduced by permission: p. 607; Liquid metal fast breeder reactor, illustration. McGraw-Hill, Inc. Reproduced by permission: p. 612; Love Canal, weeds grow around boarded up house (street signs in foreground), photograph. Corbis-Bettmann. Reproduced by permission: p. 616; Lovelock, James, (pictured with a device that measures fluorocarbons in the Antarctic atmosphere), photograph by Anthony Howarth. Photo Researchers, Inc. Reproduced by permission: p. 617; Lovins, Amory, photograph. Rocky Mountain Institute. Reproduced by permission: p. 618; Manatee and a researcher, in the water in Homosassa Springs, FL, photograph by Douglas Faulkner. Photo Researchers, Inc. Reproduced by permission: p. 626; Mangrove swamp, Mangrove creek in the Everglades National Park, photograph by Max & Bea Hunn. Visuals Unlimited. Reproduced by permission: p. 627; Mass extinction, graph, line drawing by Hans Neuhart. Gale Research: p. 636; Mendes, Francisco (touching face with left hand), photograph. Corbis-Bettmann. Reproduced by permission: p. 646; Mexico City, smog, over the buildings in Mexico City, photograph by A.J. Copley. Visuals Unlimited. Reproduced by permission: p. 651; Minamata, Tomoko Eumura being bathed by her mother, photograph by Eugene Smith. Black Star. Reproduced by permission: p. 656; Mono Lake, in California, photograph by R. Rowan. Photo Researchers, Inc. Reproduced by permission: p. 662; Monsoon, map of where the rain falls in Western Ghats and the Himalayas, illustration. McGraw-Hill, Inc. Reproduced by permission: p. 663; Mt. St. Helens erupting, May 18, 1980, photograph. UPI/Bettmann Newsphotos. Reproduced by permission: p. 666; Muir, John (with dog), photograph. Corbis-Bettmann. Reproduced by permission: p. 667; Mutation, six-legged frog, photograph. JLM Visuals. Reproduced by permission: p. 671; Nagasaki in the aftermath of the Atom Bomb, photograph. UPI/Corbis-Bettmann. Reproduced by permission: p. 675; National Lakeshore, Grand Sable Dunes, photograph by Rod Planck. Tom Stack & Associates. Reproduced by permission: p. 675; National Lakeshore, Indiana Dunes, photograph by Robert J. Huffman. Reproduced by

permission: p. 687; National Park, Grand Canyon, photograph by Robert J. Huffman/Field Mark Publications. Reproduced by permission: p. 690; Nitrogen cycle, environment, photograph by Hans & Cassidy. Gale Research: p. 706; Nonpoint source, farm, city, photograph by Hans & Cassidy. Gale Research: p. 711; Northern spotted owl, photograph by John & Karen Hollingsworth. U.S. Fish & Wildlife Service. Reproduced by permission: p. 718; Nuclear fission, the process of a nuclear fission, illustration. McGraw-Hill, Inc. Reproduced by permission: p. 719; Ocean dumping, dumping jarosite waste at sea off the Australian coast, photograph by Hewetson. Greenpeace. Reproduced by permission: p. 729; Ocean thermal energy conversion, the Open Cycle Ocean Thermal Electric Generator, a graph showing the water flow, illustration. McGraw-Hill, Inc. Reproduced by permission: p. 734; Off-road vehicles, person riding a three-wheeler in the sand dunes, photograph by Inga Spence. Tom Stack & Associates. Reproduced by permission: p. 739; Ogallala Aquifer, line drawing by Laura Gritt. U.S. Geological Survey Water Resource Investigations Report: p. 740; Oil embargo, cars lined up for gas at the Exxon station, along Route 4, in Fort Lee, NJ, photograph. AP/Wide World Photos. Reproduced by permission: 742; Oil spill, worker uses a giant pompon to absorb oil on Huntington Beach, CA, photograph. Corbis-Bettmann. Reproduced by permission: p. 744; Old growth forest, Douglas firs, photograph by Tom and Pat Lesson. National Audubon Society Collection/ Photo Researchers, Inc. Reproduced by permission: p. 746; Oregon Silverspot butterfly, resting on a leaf, photograph by Paul A. Opler. Reproduced by permission: p. 750; Ozone depletion from October 1979 to October 1990, photograph. NASA. Reproduced by permission: p. 762; Passenger Pigeon, sitting in trees, photograph by John D. Cunningham. Visuals Unlimited. Reproduced by permission: p. 771; People for the Ethical Treatment of Animals (PETA), animal rights activists protesting, photograph. Corbis-Bettmann. Reproduced by permission: p. 776; Peregrine falcon with babies on a building ledge in downtown Detroit, photograph by David Kenyon. Reproduced by permission: p. 777; Pesticide chart explaining the different types, illustration. McGraw-Hill, Inc. Reproduced by permission: p. 783; Petroleum, map of United States natural gas and oil deposits, illustration. Council on Environmental Quality. pH scale, illustration. McGraw-Hill, Inc. Reproduced by permission: p. 789; pH Scale, McGraw-Hill, Inc. Reproduced by permission: p. 790; Photosynthesis, a chart, illustration. McGraw-Hill, Inc. Reproduced by permission: p. 794; Photovoltaic cell, operation of, illustration. McGraw-Hill, Inc. Reproduced by permission: p. 795; Pinchot, Gifford (coat over right arm), photograph. Corbis-Bettmann. Reproduced by permission: p. 798; Plate tectonics, plates of the Earth, illustration. United States Geological Survey: p. 803; Poaching, Black Rhinoceros, photograph by Warren and Jenny Garst. Tom Stack & Associates. Reproduced by permission: p. 805; Point source, illustration by Hans & Cassidy. Gale Research: p. 806; Population growth, chart, line drawing by Hans Neuhart. Electronic Illustrations Group: 817; Powell, John Wesley, photograph. Corbis-Bettmann. Reproduced by permission: p. 821; Prairie, photograph by Robert J. Huffman. Field Mark Publications. Reproduced by permission: p. 823; Prescribed burn, controlled burning of prairie, photograph by Stephen J. Krasemann. National Audubon Society Collection/Photo Researchers, Inc. Reproduced by permission: p. 826; Purple Loosestrife (*Lythrum salicaria*), in sunlight, photograph by John Dudak. Phototake. Reproduced by permission: p. 839; Rabbits in Australia, western Australia, photograph by Ulrike Welsch. Reproduced by permission: p. 841; Radioactive waste, map of the United States, showing where there is radioactive waste disposal sites, illustration. McGraw-Hill, Inc. Reproduced by permission: p. 849; Radioisotope, line drawing. McGraw-Hill, Inc. Reproduced by permission: p. 852; Radon, map of the United States, showing where high levels of uranium and radon, illustration. McGraw-Hill, Inc. Reproduced by permission: p. 853; Rain forest in Brazil, photograph by David Julian. Phototake NYC. Reproduced by permission: p. 854; Rain shadow in Mount Waialeale in Hawaii, illustration. McGraw-Hill, Inc. Reproduced by permission: p. 857; Recycling, truck with receptacles, photograph by Robert J. Huffman. Field Mark Publications. Reproduced by permission: p. 862; Redwood trees, photograph by Jack Dermid. Photo Researchers, Inc. Reproduced by permission: p. 865; Reilly, William (at podium with chart), photograph. Corbis-Bettmann. Reproduced by permission: p. 870; Rhinoceroses, feeding on grass, photograph by Gerald Davis. Phototake. Reproduced by permission: p. 885; River blindness, victim of Onchocerciasis disease, photograph by Ray Witlin. United Nations. Reproduced by permission: p. 894; Rolston, Holmes, photograph. Colorado State University Photographic Archives. Reproduced by permission: p. 899; Roosevelt, Theodore (with John Muir on Glacier Point above Yosemite Valley, California), photograph. Archive/Corbis-Bettmann. Reproduced by permission: p. 900; Saltwater intrusion, illustration by Hans Neuhart. Gale Research: p. 913; Sand dunes engulf a forest, photograph by Jack Dermid. National Audubon Society Collection/Photo Researchers, Inc. Reproduced by permission: p. 915; Schistosomiasis, tropical disease, spread through water, photograph by Hans & Cassidy. Gale Research: p. 922; Sea otter, eating squid, photograph by Karl W. Kenyon. National Audubon Society/Photo Researchers, Inc. NYC. Reproduced by permission: p. 925; Sea turtle, Loggerhead, covered with sand on beach, photograph. Corbis-Bettmann. Reproduced by permission: p. 927; Seabrook Nuclear Reactor, photograph by Tom Pantages. Reproduced by permission: p. 929; Secchi disk, a gentleman in a boat, using this instrument to test the water clarity, photograph by W.A. Banaszewski. Visuals Unlimited. Reproduced by permission: p. 932; Serengeti National Park, Ngorongoro Crater, Tanzania by Carolina Biological Supp. Phototake. Reproduced by permission: p. 939; Sewage treatment system, schematic representation, illustration. McGraw-Hill, Inc. Reproduced by permission: p. 941; Shanty town, two women along with others have all of their belongings outdoors in New Delhi. Visuals Unlimited. Reproduced by permission: p. 943; Slash and burn agriculture in the jungle, photograph by George Holton. Photo Researchers, Inc. Reproduced by

permission: p. 950; Smog, New York City, photograph by Yoav Levy. Phototake. Reproduced by permission: p. 955; Snail darter, photograph by J.R. Shute. Visuals Unlimited. Reproduced by permission: p. 957; Soil profile, showing the horizons in a soil in cross-section. McGraw-Hill, Inc. Reproduced by permission: p. 965; Soil texture, graph, line drawing. McGraw-Hill, Inc. Reproduced by permission: p. 967; Solar energy, a solar furnace, reflector and tower by Mark Antman. Phototake, NYC. Reproduced by permission: p. 969; Strategic minerals, graph showing the flow of global mineral trade, line drawing. McGraw-Hill, Inc. Reproduced by permission: p. 987; Succession, five stages of primary succession on a terrestrial site, illustration. McGraw-Hill, Inc. Reproduced by permission: p. 993; Sudbury, Ontario, Canada, nickel smelter and forest destruction by A.J. Copley. Visuals Unlimited. Reproduced by permission: p. 994; Sulfur cycle, environment, illustration by Hans & Cassidy. Gale Research: p. 996; Surface mining, view of the open-pit Copper Mine, in Santa Rita, NM, photograph by Paul Logsdon. Phototake. Reproduced by permission: p. 998; Symbiosis, Javanese moray eel, in the Great Barrier Reef in Australia, photograph by Fred McConnaughey. Photo Researchers, Inc. Reproduced by permission: p. 1007; Taiga, aerial view of a valley of White Spruce trees in Alaska, photograph by Charlie Ott. Photo Researchers, Inc. Reproduced by permission: p. 1011; Terracing, Ifugo rice terraces, phot by Jules Bucher. Photo Researchers, Inc. Reproduced by permission: p. 1016; Thermal stratification of a deep lake, graph from the mud bottom to the top, illustration. McGraw-Hill, Inc. Reproduced by permission: p. 1018; Thoreau, Henry David, drawing. The Library of Congress: p. 1023; Three Mile Island Nuclear Generating Plant, near Harrisburg, PA, photograph. AP/Wide World Photos. Reproduced by permission: p. 1025; Tragedy of the Commons, sheep grazing in field, photograph. © Richard Dibon-Smith, National Audubon Society Collection/Photo Researchers, Inc. Reproduced with permission: p. 1038; Trans-Alaska pipeline, map of route from Prudoe Bay to the part of Valdez, illustration. McGraw-Hill, Inc. Reproduced by permission: 1042; Tropical rain forest, layered communities, illustration by Hans Neuhart. Gale Research: p. 1047; Waste Isolation Pilot Plant, WIPP Layout, line drawing. US Dept of Energy: p. 1078; Water hyacinth, photograph by Ray Coleman. Photo Researchers, Inc. Reproduced by permission: p. 1085; Water pollutants affecting U.S. Coastal waters, chart. Beacon Press. Reproduced by permission: p. 1087; Wetlands, two Snow and Blue Geese, standing in wetland, photograph by Judd Cooney. Phototake NYC. Reproduced by permission: p. 1101; Whale, humpback, photograph by Glenn Oliver. Visuals Unlimited. Reproduced by permission: p. 1103; Whaling, Japanese delegate from International Whaling Commission, protestors behind him, photograph. Greenpeace. Reproduced by permission: p. 1105; Wild River, Klamath River, North Carolina photograph. Visuals Unlimited. Reproduced by permission: p. 1108; Wildfire, Grand Teton National Forest, Wyoming with dead trees and firefighter, photograph. Reproduced by permission: p. 1114; Wilson, Edward O., sitting at the table, with a insect sculpture in front of him, photograph. Reproduced by permission: p. 1121; Wind turbines at Tehachapi Pass, California, photograph. U. S. Department of Energy, Washington DC: p. 1122; Wolman, Abel, photograph. The Ferdinand Hamburger Jr. Archives of Johns Hopkins University. Reproduced by permission: p. 1125; Wolves, Red wolf in the Great Smoky Mountain National Park, photograph by Tim Davis. Photo Researchers, Inc. Reproduced by permission: p. 1127; Yellowstone, map of complex ecosystem, line drawing. McGraw-Hill, Inc. Reproduced by permission: p. 1136; Zebra mussel, photograph. Michigan Sea Grant Society. Reproduced by permission: p. 1141.

Advisors

A number of recognized experts in the library and environmental communities provided invaluable assistance in the preparation of this book. Our panel of advisors helped us shape this publication into its final form, and we would like to express our sincere appreciation to them:

Dean Abrahamson
Hubert H. Humphrey Institute of Public Affairs
University of Minnesota
Minneapolis, Minnesota

Maria Jankowska
Library
University of Idaho
Moscow, Idaho

Terry Link
Library
Michigan State University
East Lansing, Michigan

Holmes Rolston
Department of Philosophy
Colorado State University
Fort Collins, Colorado

Frederick W. Stoss
Science and Engineering Library
State University of New York - Buffalo
Buffalo, New York

Hubert J. Thompson
Conrad Sulzer Regional Library
Chicago, Illinois

Contributors

William G. Ambrose, Jr.
Department of Biology
East Carolina University
Greenville, North Carolina

James L. Anderson
Soil Science Department
University of Minnesota
St. Paul, Minnesota

Terence Ball
Department of Political Science
University of Minnesota
Minneapolis, Minnesota

Brian R. Barthel
Department of Health, Leisure
and Sports
The University of West Florida
Pensacola, Florida

Stuart Batterman
School of Public Health
University of Michigan
Ann Arbor, Michigan

Eugene C. Beckham
Department of Mathematics and
Science
Northwood Institute
Midland, Michigan

Milovan S. Beljin
Department of Civil Engineering
University of Cincinnati
Cincinnati, Ohio

Lawrence J. Biskowski
Department of Political Science
University of Georgia
Athens, Georgia

E. K. Black
University of Alberta
Edmonton, Alberta, Canada

Paul R. Bloom
Soil Science Department
University of Minnesota
St. Paul, Minnesota

Gregory D. Boardman
Department of Civil Engineering
Virginia Polytechnic Institute and
State University
Blacksburg, Virginia

Marci L. Bortman
Waste Management Institute
Marine Sciences Research Center
State University of New York
Stony Brook, New York

Peter Brimblecombe
School of Environmental Sciences
University of East Anglia
Norwich, United Kingdom

Kenneth N. Brooks
College of Natural Resources
University of Minnesota
St. Paul, Minnesota

Ted T. Cable
Department of Horticulture,
Forestry and Recreation
Resources
Kansas State University
Manhattan, Kansas

John Cairns, Jr.
University Center for
Environmental and Hazardous
Materials Studies
Virginia Polytechnic Institute and
State University
Blacksburg, Virginia

Liane Clorfene Casten
Freelance Journalist
Evanston, Illinois

Ann S. Causey
Prescott College
Prescott, Arizona

Ann N. Clarke
Eckenfelder Inc.
Nashville, Tennessee

David Clarke
Freelance Journalist
Bethesda, Maryland

Sally Cole-Misch
Freelance Writer
Bloomfield Hills, Michigan

Edward J. Cooney
Patterson Associates, Inc.
Chicago, Illinois

Terence H. Cooper
Soil Science Department
University of Minnesota
St. Paul, Minnesota

Neil Cumberlidge
Department of Biology
Northern Michigan University
Marquette, Michigan

John Cunningham
Freelance Writer
St. Paul, Minnesota

Mary Ann Cunningham
Environmental Writer
St. Paul, Minnesota

William P. Cunningham
Department of Genetics and Cell
Biology
University of Minnesota
St. Paul, Minnesota

Richard K. Dagger
Department of Political Science
Arizona State University
Tempe, Arizona

Frank M. D'Itri
Institute of Water Research
Michigan State University
East Lansing, Michigan

Teresa C. Donkin
Freelance Writer
Minneapolis, Minnesota

David A. Duffus
Department of Geography
University of Victoria
Victoria, British Columbia,
    Canada

Cathy M. Falk
Freelance Writer
Portland, Oregon

George M. Fell
Freelance Writer
Inver Grove Heights, Minnesota

Gordon R. Finch
Department of Civil Engineering
University of Alberta
Edmonton, Alberta, Canada

Bill Freedman
School for Resource and
    Environmental Studies
Dalhousie University
Halifax, Nova Scotia, Canada

Cynthia Fridgen
Department of Resource
    Development
Michigan State University
East Lansing, Michigan

Andrea Gacki
Freelance Writer
Bay City, Michigan

Brian Geraghty
Ford Motor Company
Dearborn, Michigan

Robert B. Giorgis, Jr.
Air Resources Board
Sacramento, California

Debra Glidden
Freelance American Indian
    Investigative Journalist
Syracuse, New York

Eville Gorham
Department of Ecology, Evolution
    and Behavior
University of Minnesota
St. Paul, Minnesota

Malcolm T. Hepworth
Department of Civil and Mineral
    Engineering
University of Minnesota
Minneapolis, Minnesota

Richard A. Jeryan
Ford Motor Company
Dearborn, Michigan

Barbara J. Kanninen
Hubert H. Humphrey Institute of
    Public Affairs
University of Minnesota
Minneapolis, Minnesota

Christopher McGrory Klyza
Department of Political Science
Middlebury College
Middlebury, Vermont

John Korstad
Department of Natural Science
Oral Roberts University
Tulsa, Oklahoma

Royce Lambert
Soil Science Department
California Polytechnic State
    University
San Luis Obispo, California

William E. Larson
Soil Science Department
University of Minnesota
St. Paul, Minnesota

Ellen E. Link
Freelance Writer
Laingsburg, Michigan

James P. Lodge, Jr.
Consultant in Atmospheric
    Chemistry
Boulder, Colorado

William S. Lynn
Department of Geography

University of Minnesota
Minneapolis, Minnesota

Alair MacLean
Environmental Editor
OMB Watch
Washington, D.C.

Alfred A. Marcus
Carlson School of Management
University of Minnesota
Minneapolis, Minnesota

Cathryn McCue
Freelance Journalist
Roanoke, Virginia

Jennifer L. McGrath
Freelance Writer
South Bend, Indiana

Robert G. McKinnell
Department of Genetics and Cell
    Biology
University of Minnesota
St. Paul, Minnesota

Nathan H. Meleen
Engineering and Physics
    Department
Oral Roberts University
Tulsa, Oklahoma

Muthena Naseri
Moorpark College
Moorpark, California

B. R. Niederlehner
University Center for
    Environmental and Hazardous
    Materials Studies
Virginia Polytechnic Institute and
    State University
Blacksburg, Virginia

David E. Newton
Instructional Horizons, Inc.
San Francisco, California

Robert D. Norris
Eckenfelder Inc.
Nashville, Tennessee

Stephanie Ocko
Freelance Journalist
Brookline, Massachusetts

Kristin Palm
Freelance Writer
Royal Oak, Michigan

James W. Patterson
Patterson Associates, Inc.
Chicago, Illinois

Paul Phifer
Freelance Writer
Minneapolis, Minnesota

Jeffrey L. Pintenich
Eckenfelder Inc.
Nashville, Tennessee

Douglas C. Pratt
University of Minnesota
Department of Plant Biology
St. Paul, Minnesota

Jeremy Pratt
Institute for Human Ecology
Santa Rosa, California

Klaus Puettman
University of Minnesota
St. Paul, Minnesota

Stephen J. Randtke
Department of Civil Engineering
University of Kansas
Lawrence, Kansas

Lewis G. Regenstein
Author and Environmental Writer
Atlanta, Georgia

Linda Rehkopf
Freelance Writer
Marietta, Georgia

Paul E. Renaud
Department of Biology
East Carolina University
Greenville, North Carolina

Marike Rijsberman
Freelance Writer
Chicago. Illinois

L. Carol Ritchie
Environmental Journalist
Arlington, Virginia

Linda M. Ross
Freelance Writer
Ferndale, Michigan

Mark W. Seeley
Department of Soil Science
University of Minnesota
St. Paul, Minnesota

James H. Shaw
Department of Zoology
Oklahoma State University
Stillwater, Oklahoma

Judith Sims
Utah Water Research Laboratory
Utah State University
Logan, Utah

Douglas Smith
Freelance Writer
Dorchester, Massachusetts

Lawrence H. Smith
Department of Agronomy and
    Plant Genetics
University of Minnesota
St. Paul, Minnesota

Carol Steinfeld
Freelance Writer
Concord, Massachusetts

Paulette L. Stenzel
Eli Broad College of Business
Michigan State University
East Lansing, Michigan

Les Stone
Freelance Writer
Ann Arbor, Michigan

Max Strieb
Freelance Writer
Huntington, New York

Amy Strumolo
Freelance Writer
Beverly Hills, Michigan

Edward Sucoff
Department of Forestry Resources
University of Minnesota
St. Paul, Minnesota

Deborah L. Swackhammer
School of Public Health
University of Minnesota
Minneapolis, Minnesota

Ronald D. Taskey
Soil Science Department
California Polytechnic State
    University
San Luis Obispo, California

Usha Vedagiri
IT Corporation
Edison, New Jersey

Donald A. Villeneuve
Ventura College
Ventura, California

Nikola Vrtis
Freelance Writer
Kentwood, Michigan

Eugene R. Wahl
Freelance Writer
Coon Rapids, Minnesota

Roderick T. White, Jr.
Freelance Writer
Atlanta, Georgia

T. Anderson White
University of Minnesota
St. Paul, Minnesota

Kevin Wolf
Freelance Writer
Minneapolis, Minnesota

Gerald L. Young
Program in Environmental Science
    and Regional Planning
Washington State University
Pullman, Washington

How to Use This Book

The *Environmental Encyclopedia* has been designed with ease-of-use and ready reference in mind.

Entries are arranged alphabetically in a single sequence, rather than by scientific field.

Boldfaced terms within each entry direct the reader to related entries in the book.

Contact information is given for each organization profiled in the book.

Cross-references at the end of entries alert the reader to related entries not specifically mentioned in the body of the text.

Further Reading lists appended to many entries guide the reader to sources of additional information on the topic.

Two appendices provide the reader with a chronology of environmental events and a summary of environmental legislation.

A **comprehensive general index** guides the reader to all topics and persons mentioned in the book. Bolded page references indicate the main entry for term.

Introduction

Welcome to the second edition of the Gale *Environmental Encyclopedia*! We hope that you will find the definitions and articles here interesting and useful. As you might imagine, choosing what to include and what to exclude from this collection has been challenging. Almost everything in the world has some environmental significance, so our task has been to select a limited number of topics we think are of greatest importance in understanding our environment and our relation to it. Undoubtedly, we have neglected some topics that interest you and included some that you may consider irrelevant, but we hope that overall you will find this edition helpful and worthwhile.

The word environment is derived from the French *environ*, which means to "encircle" or "surround." Thus, our environment can be defined as the physical, chemical, and biological world that surrounds us, as well as the complex of social and cultural conditions affecting an individual or community. This broad definition includes both the natural world and the "built" or technological environment, as well as the cultural and social contexts that shape human lives. You will see that we have used this comprehensive meaning in choosing the articles and definitions contained in this volume.

Among the central concerns of environmental science are: (1) how did the natural world on which we depend come to be as it is, and how does it work? (2) what have we done and what are we now doing to our environment—both for good and ill, and (3) what can we do to ensure a sustainable future for ourselves, future generations, and the other species of organisms on which—although we may not be aware of it—our lives depend? The articles in this volume attempt to answer those questions from a variety of different perspectives.

Historically, environmentalism is rooted in natural history, a search for beauty and meaning in nature. Modern environmental science expands this concern, drawing on almost every area of human knowledge—from social sciences, humanities, and the physical sciences. Its strongest roots, however, are in ecology, the study of interrelationships among and between organisms and their physical or nonliving environment. A particular strength of the ecological approach is that it studies systems *holistically*; that is, it looks at interconnections that make the whole greater than the mere sum of its parts. You will find many of those interconnections reflected in this book. Although the entries are presented individually so that you can find topics easily, you will notice that many refer to other topics that, in turn, can lead you on through the book if you have time to follow their trail. This series of linkages reflects the multilevel associations in environment issues.

Many current environmental issues clamor for our attention. If you read a newspaper or watch television news, even occasionally, you undoubtedly are aware of some of the issues of long-term concern with regard to the sustainability of the world's resources. For many environmentalists the rapid growth of human populations is of overriding importance. In 1997, the world population reached some 5.8 billion people, and more are being added to an increasingly overcrowded world at a rate of about 90 million per year. Most demographers predict that the world population will double, or even triple, before stabilizing sometime in the twenty-first century. The adverse environmental impacts of a population that large are of great concern.

Availability of resources to support future human populations also is questionable. Already there are signs that we are exhausting our supplies of fertile soil, clean water, energy, and biodiversity that are essential for life. Furthermore, pollutants released into the air and water, along with increasing amounts of toxic and hazardous wastes created by our industrial society, threaten to damage the ecological life support systems on which all organisms—including humans—depend. Even without additional population growth, we may need to drastically rethink our patterns of production and disposal of materials if we are to maintain a habitable environment for ourselves and our descendants.

There has been an interesting and significant shift in our awareness of environmental problems in the last twenty years. Although worldwide radioactive fallout and pesticide pollution had been on the environmental agenda since the 1950s, the environmental problems on which most of us focused on the first Earth Day in 1970 were issues of local pollution or resource depletion. Citizen groups campaigned to stop air and water pollution in their local neighborhoods. River clean-up projects or soil erosion-control efforts "in our own backyards" tended to be the focal point. Although those efforts have been effective both in activating people and in bringing about protection of local environments, there are worries that NIMBYism (Not In My Back Yard) may create a gridlock in which citizens become so self-centered and suspicious of change that initiating needed environmental projects will be impossible.

Recently, the emphasis for many environmentalists has shifted to global issues. At the United Nations Conference on Environment and Development (the Earth Summit) at Rio de Janeiro in 1992, for instance (as well as at the follow-up meetings on women, habitat, and climate that followed it) world attention concentrated on our impacts on large-scale environmental systems. With increased transportation and communication around the globe, we now are aware of the environmental effects of human actions worldwide. For the first time in our history, we have the ability to bring about both detrimental and beneficial environmental modifications on a global scale.

Carbon dioxide, methane, and other *greenhouse gases* added to the atmosphere through human activities now appear to be setting into motion global climate changes that may well have disastrous effects. For example, sulfuric and nitric acids created by burning fossil fuels can be transported thousands of miles by air currents to form acid rain that damages aquatic life and forests in far distant places. Chlorofluorocarbons (CFCs) used as refrigerants, cleaning solutions, aerosol propellants, and foam-blowing agents migrate into the stratosphere where they destroy the protective ozone layer that shields the Earth from destructive ultraviolet rays in solar radiation. These halogenated hydrocarbons also are potent greenhouse gases.

An important lesson to be learned from these crises is that solving one problem often creates another. Chlorofluorocarbons, for instance, were once lauded as a wonderful discovery because they replaced toxic or explosive chemicals then in use as refrigerants and solvents. No one thought to ask what CFCs might do to stratospheric ozone. Similarly, the building of tall smokestacks on power plants and smelters lessened local air pollution, but spread acid rain over broad areas of the countryside. Because of our lack of scientific understanding of complex systems, we are continually subjected to surprises. How to plan for "unknown unknowns" is an increasing challenge as our world becomes more tightly interconnected and our ability to adjust to mistakes decreases.

After global climate change, perhaps the greatest environmental concern for most biologists is the worldwide loss of biological diversity. Research studies suggest we are losing species hundreds or perhaps thousands of times faster than would normally result from natural processes. Habitat destruction, pollution, introduction of exotic species, and excessive harvesting of commercially important species all contribute to these losses. Millions of species—most of which have never even been named by science, let alone examined for potential usefulness in medicine, agriculture, science, or industry—may disappear in the next century as a result of our actions. We know little about the biological roles of these organisms in the ecosystems and their loss could result in an ecological tragedy.

In 1997, a group of ecological economists attempted to put a price on the goods and services provided by natural ecosystems. Although many ecological processes have no direct market value, we can estimate replacement costs, contingent values, shadow prices, and other methods of indirect assessment to determine a rough value. For instance, we now dispose of much of our wastes by letting nature detoxify them. How much would it cost if we had to do this ourselves? In their study, the economists looked at everything from recreational beaches to forest lumber to hidden services (such as the ocean's regulation of atmospheric carbon dioxide) to pollination of crops by insects.

What they found was the estimated annual value of all ecological goods and services provided by nature ranged from $16 trillion to $54 trillion, with a median worth of $33 trillion, or about twice the annual GNPs of all national economies in the world. These estimates are probably understated because they ignore ecosystem services from several biomes, such as deserts and tundra, that have not yet been studied for their economic contributions. The most valuable ecosystems in terms of biological processes are wetlands and coastal estuaries because of their high level of biodiversity and their central role in many biogeochemical cycles.

Not all is discouraging, however, in the field of environmental science. Although many problems beset us, there are also encouraging signs of progress. Some dramatic successes have occurred in wildlife restoration and habitat protection programs, for instance. In 1996, an estimated 90 million ducks flew south from their breeding grounds in North America. This number is up nearly ten-fold from populations early in this century. Hunting regulations, better weather, and conservation and restoration of millions of acres of wetlands are largely responsible for this success. On a smaller scale, some 230 whooping cranes now winter in three separate populations in Texas, Florida, and Arizona. In the 1940s, only 16 of these huge birds remained in the wild and survival of the species was doubtful. Banning of DDT in the 1970s has enabled bald eagle populations to rebound sufficiently for this national symbol to be moved from the endangered to the threatened list over much of its range in the United States.

As a result of citizen activism, government intervention, and private sector investment in pollution control devices, ambient air quality in most American cities has improved substantially in the past few decades. New air pollution regulations have resulted in the significant reduction of acid precipitation as well as decreased levels of toxic air contaminants in most parts of the United States. Water clean-up efforts have had promising effects on water quality in many areas. Salmon and other pollution-sensitive fish have returned to the Thames River in London, England, after being absent for more than two centuries. Mayfly hatches once again occur on the upper Mississippi, a sign that oxygen levels are reaching healthy concentrations, as a result of building sewage treatment plants and restricting toxic outfalls from factories.

Solutions for many of our pollution problems can be found in either improved technology, more personal responsibility, or better environmental management. The question is often whether we have the political will to enforce pollution control programs and whether we are willing to sacrifice short-term convenience and affluence for long-term ecological stability. We in the richer countries of the world have become accustomed to a highly consumptive lifestyle of instant gratification and great luxury. Ecologists estimate that humans either use directly, destroy, co-opt, or alter almost 40% of terrestrial plant productivity, with unknown consequences for the biosphere. Whether we will be willing to leave some resources for other species and future generations is a central question of environmental policy.

The inequitable distribution of resources between wealthy and poor countries is a matter of ethical concern given far too little consideration by most of us. The United States is perhaps the preeminent example of excessive consumption. With only 5% of the world population, we consume about one-quarter of all commercial energy and one-fifth of most commercial metals. At the same time, we produce about half of all toxic wastes and approximately a quarter of all nitrogen oxides, sulfur oxides, chlorofluorocarbons, and carbon dioxide released through human activities. To get an average American through the day takes about 1,000 lb (nearly 450 kg) of raw materials, including 40 lb (18 kg) of fossil fuels, 29 lb (13 kg) of minerals, 26.5 lb (12 kg) of food and fiber from farm products, 22 lb (10 kg) of wood and paper pulp, and 30 gal (450 l) of water. We use more than 100 times as much energy, paper, and metal per capita as the residents of the poorest countries such as Bangladesh, Haiti, Mali, and Nepal. Is this an equitable distribution of resources? Are we willing to give up some of our affluence so that others can enjoy a higher standard of living?

Rather than cut our consumption, another approach to extending resources is to increase efficiency and recycling of the items we use. Automobiles have already been designed, for example, that get more than 100 mi/gal (42 km/l) of diesel fuel and are completely recyclable when they reach the end of their designed life. Although recycling rates in the United States have increased in recent years, we could probably double our current rate with very little sacrifice in economics or convenience. Similarly, fossil fuel-fired electric power plants currently convert less than 40% of the energy in their fuel into usable energy. Cogeneration—simultaneous production of heating steam and electricity—can double that yield. Even better would be conversion to renewable energy sources such as solar or wind power.

Questions about poverty and lack of access to resources are more than issues of fairness and compassion; the desperate circumstances in which many people live are a major source of environmental problems as well. In many cases, the poor are both victims and agents of environmental damage. Without access to land, for instance, poor rural people are forced to try to grow crops on unstable hillsides, frequently flooded lowlands, or to move into virgin areas where they convert forests or native grasslands to farm fields. In many cases these lands are unsuitable for continuous agriculture. After a few years of growing crops, the soil is exhausted and farmers are forced to move farther into the forest in search for land. This dismal cycle impoverishes both the people and the ecosystems they invade. Having to meet urgent short-term needs, impoverished people are forced to "mine" natural

capital through excessive tree cutting, failure to replace soil nutrients, and cultivation of erosion-prone hillsides.

The poverty/environment connection affects billions of people and entails serious geopolitical consequences. The United Nations estimates that nearly one-third of the world's population has inadequate sanitation and one-quarter is exposed to dangerous levels of air pollution on a regular basis. More than one billion people suffer from malnourishment, lack access to clean drinking water, and live in what the World Bank categorizes as absolute poverty. All of these factors contribute to chronic diseases, improper childhood development, premature death, and other tragic social consequences that retard human development and environmental protection. People who are chronically malnourished and ill are unable to work regularly. Without a dependable income, they are unable to purchase the food, shelter, and medicine they need for a healthy life. Caught in a desperate struggle for survival, they are unable to protect their environment, preserve wildlife, or invest in pollution control and efficient technology necessary to conserve resources.

One of the solutions widely advocated for breaking this link between poverty and environmental damage is an improved standard of living for all people, generally called *sustainable development*. A commonly used definition of this term is given in *Our Common Future*, the report of the World Commission on Environment and Development (generally called the Brundtland Commission after the prime minister of Norway, who chaired it), described sustainable development as: development that "meets the needs of the present without compromising the ability of future generations to meet their own needs." This implies improving health, education, and equality of opportunity, as well as ensuring political and civil rights through jobs and programs based on sustaining the ecological base, living on renewable resources rather than nonrenewable ones, and living within the carrying capacity of supporting ecological systems.

Several important ethical considerations are embedded in environmental questions. One of these is intergenerational justice: what responsibilities do we have to leave resources and a habitable planet for future generations? Is our profligate use of fossil fuels, for example, justified by the fact that we have technology to extract fossil fuels and enjoy their benefits? Will human lives in the future be impoverished by the fact that we have used up most of the easily available oil, gas, and coal? Author and social critic Wendell Berry suggests that our consumption of these resources constitutes a theft of the birthright and livelihood of posterity. Philosopher John Rawls advocates a "just savings principle" in which members of each generation may consume no more than their fair share of scarce resources.

How many generations are we obliged to plan for and what is our "fair share?" It is possible that our use of resources now—inefficient and wasteful as it may be—represents an investment that will benefit future generations. The first computers, for instance, were huge clumsy instruments that filled rooms full of expensive vacuum tubes and consumed inordinate amounts of electricity. Critics complained that it was a waste of time and resources to build these enormous machines to do a few simple calculations. And yet if this technology had been suppressed in its infancy, the world would be much poorer today. Now nanotechnology promises to make machines and tools in infinitesimal sizes that use minuscule amounts of materials and energy to carry out valuable functions. The question remains whether future generations will be glad that we embarked on the current scientific and technological revolution or whether they will wish that we had maintained a simple agrarian, Arcadian way of life.

Another ethical consideration inherent in many environmental issues is whether we have obligations or responsibilities to other species or to the Earth as a whole. An *anthropocentric* (human-centered) view holds that humans have rightful dominion over the earth and that our interests and well-being take precedence over all other considerations. Many environmentalists criticize this perspective, considering it arrogant and destructive. *Biocentric* (life-centered) philosophies argue that all living organisms have inherent values and rights by virtue of mere existence, whether or not they are of any use to us. In this view, we have a responsibility to leave space and resources to enable other species to survive and to live as naturally as possible. This duty extends to making reparations or special efforts to encourage the recovery of endangered species that are threatened with extinction as a result of human activities.

Some environmentalists claim that we should adopt an *ecocentric* (ecologically centered) outlook that respects and values nonliving entities such as rocks, rivers, mountains—even whole ecosystems—as well as other living organisms. In this view, we have no right to break up a rock, dam a free-flowing river, or reshape a landscape simply because it benefits us. More importantly, we should conserve and maintain the major ecological processes that sustain life and make our world habitable.

Others argue that our existing institutions and understandings, while they may need improvement and reform, have provided us with many advantages and amenities. Our lives are considerably better in many ways than those of our ancient ancestors, whose lives were, in the words of British philosopher Thomas Hobbes: "nasty, brutish, and short." Although science and technology have introduced many problems, they also have provided answers and possible alternatives as well.

It may be that we are at a major turning point in human history. Young people today are in a unique position to address the environmental problems described in this encyclopedia. For the first time, we now have the resources, motivation, and knowledge to protect our environment and to build a sustainable future for ourselves and our children. Until recently, we didn't have these opportunities, or there was not enough clear evidence to inspire people to change their behavior and invest in environmental protection; now the need is obvious to nearly everyone. Unfortunately, this also may be the last opportunity to act before our problems become irreversible.

We hope that an interest in preserving and protecting our common environment is the reason that you are reading this encyclopedia and that you will find information here to help you in that quest.

William P. Cunningham
Managing Editor
Environmental Encyclopedia

Environmental Encyclopedia

A

Abbey, Edward (1927-1989)

American environmentalist and writer

Novelist, essayist, white-water rafter, and self-described "desert rat," Abbey wrote of the wonders and beauty of the American West that was fast disappearing in the name of "development" and "progress." Often angry, frequently funny, and sometimes lyrical, Abbey recreated for his readers a region that was unique in the world. The American West was perhaps the last place where solitary selves could discover and reflect on their connections with wild things and with their fellow human beings.

Abbey was born in Home, Pennsylvania, in 1927. He received his B.A. from the University of New Mexico in 1951. After earning his master's degree in 1956, he joined the **National Park Service**, where he served as park ranger and fire fighter. He later taught writing at the University of Arizona.

Abbey's books and essays, such as *Desert Solitaire* (1968) and *Down the River* (1982), had their angrier fictional counterparts—most notably, *The Monkey Wrench Gang* (1975) and *Hayduke Lives!* (1990)—in which he gave voice to his outrage over the destruction of **desert**s and rivers by dam-builders and developers of all sorts. In *The Monkey Wrench Gang* Abbey weaves a tale of three "ecoteurs" who defend the wild west by destroying the means and machines of development—dams, bulldozers, logging trucks—which would otherwise reduce forests to lumber and raging rivers to **irrigation** channels.

This aspect of Abbey's work inspired some radical environmentalists, including **Dave Foreman** and other members of **Earth First!**, to practice "**monkey-wrenching**" or "ecotage" to slow or stop such environmentally destructive practices as **strip mining**, the **clear-cutting** of **old-growth forest**s on **public land**, and the damming of wild rivers for flood control, hydroelectric power, and what Abbey termed "industrial tourism." Although Abbey's description and defense of such tactics has been widely condemned by many mainstream environmental groups, he remains a revered figure among many who believe that gradualist tactics have not succeeded in slowing, much less stopping, the destruction of North American **wilderness**. Abbey is unique among environmental writers in having an oceangoing ship named after him. One of the vessels in the fleet of the militant **Sea Shepherd Conservation Socie-**ty, the *Edward Abbey*, rams and disables whaling and drift-net fishing vessels operating illegally in international waters. Abbey would have welcomed the tribute and, as a white-water rafter and canoeist, would doubltess have enjoyed the irony.

Abbey died on March 14, 1989. He is buried in a desert in the southwestern United States.

[*Terence Ball*]

FURTHER READING

Abbey, E. *Desert Solitaire.* New York: McGraw-Hill, 1968.

———. *Down the River.* Boston: Little, Brown, 1982.

———. *Hayduke Lives!* Boston: Little, Brown, 1990.

———. *The Monkey Wrench Gang.* Philadelphia: Lippincott, 1975.

Berry, W. "A Few Words in Favor of Edward Abbey." In *What Are People For?* San Francisco: North Point Press, 1991.

Bowden, C. "Goodbye, Old Desert Rat." In *The Sonoran Desert,* by Charles Bowden. New York: Abrams, 1992.

Manes, C. *Green Rage: Radical Environmentalism and the Unmaking of Civilization.* Boston: Little, Brown, 1990.

Absorption

Absorption, or more generally "sorption," is the process by which one material (the sorbent) takes up and retains another (the sorbate) to form a homogenous concentration at equilibrium.

The general term is "sorption," which is defined as adhesion of gas molecules, dissolved substances, or liquids to the surface of solids with which they are in contact. In soils, three types of mechanisms, often working together, constitute sorption. They can be grouped into physical sorption, chemiosorption, and penetration into the solid mineral phase. Physical sorption (also known as adsorption) involves the attachment of the sorbent and sorbate through weak atomic and molecular forces. Chemiosorption involves chemical bonds similar to holding atoms in a molecule. Electrostatic forces operate to bond minerals via ion exchange, such as the replacement of sodium, magnesium, potassium, and aluminum cations (+) as exchangeable bases with acid (-) soils. While cation (positive ion) exchange is the dominant exchange process occurring in soils, some soils have the ability to retain anions (negative ions) such as nitrates, chlorine and, to a larger extent, oxides of sulfur.

Absorption and Wastewater Treatment

In on-site wastewater treatment, the **soil** absorption field is the land area where the **wastewater** from the septic tank is spread into the soil. One of the most common types of soil absorption field has porous plastic pipe extending away from the distribution box in a series of two or more parallel trenches, usually 1.5-2 ft (30.5-61 cm) wide. In conventional, below-ground systems, the trenches are 1.5-2 ft deep. Some absorption fields must be placed at a shallower depth than this to compensate for some limiting soil condition, such as a hardpan or high water table. In some cases they may even be placed partially or entirely in fill material that has been brought to the lot from elsewhere.

The porous pipe which carries wastewater from the distribution box into the absorption field is surrounded by gravel that fills the trench to within a foot or so of the ground surface. The gravel is covered by fabric material or building paper to prevent plugging. Another type of drainfield consists of pipes that extend away from the distribution box, not in trenches but in a single, gravel-filled bed that has several such porous pipes in it. As with trenches, the gravel in a bed is covered by fabric or other porous material.

Usually the wastewater flows gradually downward into the gravel-filled trenches or bed. In some instances, such as when the septic tank is lower than the drainfield, the wastewater must be pumped into the drainfield. Whether gravity flow or pumping is used, wastewater must be evenly distributed throughout the drainfield. It is important to ensure that the drainfield is installed with care to keep the porous pipe level, or at a very gradual downward slope away from the distribution box or pump chamber, according to specifications stipulated by public health officials. Soil beneath the gravel-filled trenches or bed must be permeable so that wastewater and air can move through it and come in contact with each other. Good aeration is necessary to ensure that the proper chemical and microbiological processes will be occurring in the soil to cleanse the percolating wastewater of contaminants. A well-aerated soil also ensures slow travel and good contact between wastewater and soil.

How Common Are Septic Systems with Soil Absorption Systems?

According to the 1990 U.S. Census, there are about 24.7 million households in the United States that use **septic tank** systems or cesspools (holes or pits for receiving sewage) for wastewater treatment. This figure represents roughly 24% of the total households included in the census.

According to a review of local health department information by the National Small Flows Clearinghouse, 94% of participating health departments allow or permit the use of septic tank and soil absorption systems. Those that do not allow septic systems have sewer lines available to all residents. The total volume of waste disposed of through septic systems is more than one trillion gallons (3.8 trillion l) per year, according to a study conducted by the **U.S. Environmental Protection Agency**'s Office of Technology Assessment, and virtually all of that waste is discharged directly to the subsurface, which affects groundwater quality.

[*Carol Steinfeld*]

FURTHER READING

Elliott, L.F., and F. J. Stevenson, *Soils for the Management of Wastes and Waste Waters.* Madison, Wisconsin: Soil Science Society of America, 1977.

Fact Sheet SL-59, a series of the Soil and Water Science Department, Florida Cooperative Extension Service, Institute of Food and Agricultural Sciences, University of Florida. February 1993.

Acaricide
See **Pesticide**

Acceptable risk
See **Risk analysis**

Acclimation

Acclimation is the process by which an organism adjusts to a change in its environment. It generally refers to the ability of living things to adjust to changes in **climate**, and usually occurs in a short time of the change.

Scientists distinguish between acclimation and acclimatization because the latter adjustment is made under natural conditions when the organism is subject to the full range of changing environmental factors. Acclimation, however, refers to a change in only one environmental factor under laboratory conditions.

In an acclimation experiment, adult frogs (*Rana temporaria*) maintained in the laboratory at a temperature of either 50°F (10°C) or 86°F (30°C), were tested in an **environment** of 32°F (0°C). It was found that the group maintained at the higher temperature was inactive at freezing. The group maintained at 50°F (10°C), however, was active at the lower temperature; it had acclimated to the lower temperature.

Acclimation and acclimatization can have profound effects upon behavior, inducing shifts in preferences and in mode of life. The golden hamster (*Mesocricetus auratus*) prepares for hibernation when the environmental temperature drops below 59°F (15°C). Temperature preference tests in the laboratory show that the hamsters develop a marked preference for cold environmental temperatures during the pre-hibernation period. Following arousal from a simulated period of hibernation, the situation is reversed, and the hamsters actively prefer the warmer environments.

An acclimated microorganism is any microorganism that is able to adapt to environmental changes such as a change in temperature or a change in the quantity of oxygen or other gases. Many organisms that live in environments with seasonal changes in temperature make physiological adjustments that permit them to continue to function normally, even though their environmental temperature goes through a definite annual temperature cycle.

Acclimatization usually involves a number of interacting physiological processes. For example, in acclimatizing to high altitudes, the first response of human beings is to increase their breathing rate. After about 40 hours, changes have occurred in the oxygen-carrying capacity of the blood, which makes it more efficient in extracting oxygen at high altitudes. As this occurs, the breathing rate returns to normal. *See also* Adaptation; Biotic community; Habitat

[*Linda Rehkopf*]

Further Reading

Ford, M. J. *The Changing Climate: Responses of the Natural Fauna and Flora.* Boston: G. Allen and Unwin, 1982.

McFarland, D., ed. *The Oxford Companion to Animal Behavior.* Oxford, England: Oxford University Press, 1981.

Stress Responses in Plants: Adaptation and Acclimation Mechanisms. New York: Wiley-Liss, 1990.

Accounting for nature

A new approach to national income accounting in which the degradation and depletion of natural resource stocks and environmental amenities are explicitly included in the calculation of net national product (NNP). NNP is equal to gross national product (GNP) minus capital depreciation, and GNP is equal to the value of all final goods and services produced in a nation in a particular year. It is recognized that **natural resources** are economic assets that generate income, and that just as the depreciation of buildings and capital equipment are treated as economic costs and subtracted from GNP to get NNP, depreciation of *natural capital* should also be subtracted when calculating NNP. In addition, expenditures on environmental protection, which at present are included in GNP and NNP, are considered defensive expenditures in accounting for nature which should not be included in either GNP or NNP. *See also* Environmental economics

Acid and base

According to the definition used by environmental chemists, an acid is a substance that increases the **hydrogen** ion (H⁺) concentration in a solution and a base is a substance that removes hydrogen **ion**s (H⁺) from a solution. In water, removal of hydrogen ions results in an increase in the hydroxide ion (OH⁻) concentration. Water with a **pH** of 7.0 is neutral, while lower pH values are acidic and higher pH values are basic. *See also* Acidification; Buffer

Acid deposition

Acid precipitation from the **atmosphere**, whether in the form of dryfall (finely divided acidic salts), rain, or snow. Naturally occurring carbonic acid normally makes rain and snow mildly acidic (approximately 5.6 **pH**). Human activities often introduce much stronger and more damaging acids. Sulfuric acids formed from sulfur oxides released in **coal** or oil **combustion** or smelting of sulfide ores predominate as the major atmospheric acid in industrialized areas. Nitric acid created from **nitrogen oxides**, formed by oxidizing atmospheric **nitrogen** when any fuel is burned in an oxygen-rich environment, constitutes the major source of acid precipitation in cities such as **Los Angeles** with little industry, but large numbers of trucks and **automobile**s. The damage caused to building materials, human health, crops, and natural **ecosystem**s by atmospheric acids amounts to billions of dollars per year in the United States. *See also* Acid rain

Acid mine drainage

The process of mining the earth for **coal** and metal ores has a long history of rich economic rewards—and a high level of environmental impact to the surrounding aquatic and terrestrial **ecosystem**s. Acid mine drainage is the highly acidic, sediment-laden **discharge** from exposed mines that is released into the ambient aquatic **environment**. In large areas of Pennsylvania, West Virginia, and Kentucky, the bright orange seeps of acid mine drainage have almost completely eliminated aquatic life in streams and ponds that receive the discharge. In the Appalachian coal mining region, almost 7,500 miles (over 12,000 km) of streams and almost 30,000 acres (over 12,000 hectares) of land are estimated to be seriously affected by the discharge of uncontrolled acid mine drainage.

In the United States, coal-bearing geological strata occur near the surface in large portions of the Appalachian mountain region. The relative ease with which coal could be extracted from these strata led to a type of mining known as **strip mining** that was practiced heavily in the nineteenth and early twentieth centuries. In this process, large amounts of earth, called the **overburden**, were physically removed from the surface to expose the coal-bearing layer beneath. The coal was then extracted from the rock as quickly and cheaply as possible. Once the bulk of the coal had been mined, and no more could be extracted without a huge additional cost, the sites were usually abandoned. The remnants of the exhausted coal-bearing rock and soil are called the **mine spoil waste**.

The basic mechanisms of acid deposition.

Acid mine drainage is not generated by strip mining itself but by the nature of the rock where it takes place. Three conditions are necessary to form acid mine drainage: pyrite-bearing rock, oxygen, and iron-oxidizing bacteria. In the Appalachians, the coal-bearing rocks usually contain significant quantities of pyrite (iron). This compound is normally not exposed to the atmosphere because it is buried underground within the rock; it is also insoluble in water. The iron and the sulfide are said to be in a reduced state, i.e. the iron atom has not released all the electrons that it is capable of releasing. When the rock is mined, the pyrite is exposed air. It then reacts with oxygen to form ferrous iron and sulfate **ions**, both of which are highly soluble in water. This leads to the formation of sulfuric acid and is responsible for the acidic nature of the drainage. But the oxidation can only occur if the bacteria *Thiobacillus ferrooxidans* are present. These activate the iron-and-sulfur oxidizing reactions, and use the energy released during the reactions for their own growth. They must have oxygen to carry these reactions through. Once the maximum oxidation is reached, these bacteria can derive no more energy from the compounds and all reactions stop.

The acidified water may be formed in several ways. It may be generated by rain falling on exposed mine spoils waste or when rain and surface water (carrying **dissolved oxygen**) flow down and seep into rock fractures and mine shafts and thus come into contact with pyrite-bearing rock. Once the acidified water has been formed, it leaves the mine area as seeps or small streams.

Characteristically bright orange to rusty red in color due to the iron, the liquid may be at a **pH** of 2 to 4. These are extremely low pH values and signify a very high degree of acidity. Vinegar, for example, has a pH of about 4.7 and the pH associated with **acid rain** is in the range of 4 to 6. Thus, acid mine drainage with a pH of 2 is more acidic than almost any other naturally occurring liquid release in the environment (with the exception of some volcanic lakes that are pure acid). Usually, the drainage is also very high in dissolved iron, manganese, aluminum, and suspended solids.

The acidic drainage released from the mine spoil wastes usually follows the natural topography of its area and flows into the nearest streams or **wetlands** where its effect on the **water quality** and **biotic community** is unmistakable. The iron coats the stream bed and its vegetation as a thick orange coating that prevents sunlight from penetrating leaves and plant surfaces. **Photosynthesis** stops and the vegetation (both vascular plants and algae) dies. The acid drainage eventually also makes the receiving water acid. As the pH drops, the fish, the invertebrates, and algae die when their **metabolism** can no longer adapt. Eventually, there is no life left in the stream with the possible exception of some bacteria that may be able to tolerate these conditions. Depending on the number and volume of seeps entering a stream and the volume of the stream itself, the area of impact may be limited and improved conditions may exist downstream, as the acid drainage is diluted. Abandoned mine spoil areas also tend to remain barren, even after decades. The colonization of the acidic mineral soil by plant species is a slow and difficult process, with a few **lichens** and aspens being the most hardy species to establish.

While many methods have been tried to control or mitigate the effects of acid mine drainage, very few have been successful. Federal mining regulations (**Surface Mining Control and Reclamation Act** of 1978) now require that when mining activity ceases, the mine spoil waste should be buried and covered with the overburden and vegetated top-soil. The intent is to restore the area to premining condition and to prevent the generation of acid mine drainage by limiting the exposure of pyrite to oxygen and water. Although some minor seeps may still occur, this is the single-most effective way to minimize the potential scale of the problem. Mining companies are also required to monitor the effectiveness of their restoration programs and must post bonds to guarantee the execution of abatement efforts, should any become necessary in the future.

There are, however, numerous abandoned sites exposing pyrite-bearing spoils. Cleanup efforts for these sites have focused on controlling one or more of the three conditions necessary for the creation of the acidity: pyrite, bacteria, and oxygen. Attempts to remove bulk quantities of the pyrite-bearing mineral and store it somewhere else are extremely expensive and difficult to execute. Inhibiting the bacteria by using **detergents**, solvents, and other bactericidal agents are temporarily effective, but usually require repeated application. Attempts to seal out air or water are difficult to implement on a large scale or in a comprehensive manner.

Since it is difficult to reduce the formation of acid mine drainage at abandoned sites, one of the most promising new methods of mitigation treats the acid mine drainage after it exits the mine spoil wastes. The technique channels the acid seeps through artificially created **wetlands**, planted with cattails or other wetland plants in a bed of gravel, limestone or compost. The limestone neutralizes the acid and raises the pH of the drainage while the mixture of oxygen-rich and oxygen-poor areas within the wetland promote the removal of iron and other metals from the drainage. Currently, many agencies, universities, and private firms are working to improve the design and performance of these artificial wetlands. A number of additional treatment techniques may be strung together in an interconnected system of anoxic limestone trenches, settling ponds, and planted wetlands. This provides a variety of physical and chemical microenvironments so that each undesirable characteristic of the acid drainage can be individually addressed and treated, e.g., acidity is neutralized in the trenches, suspended solids are settled in the ponds, and metals are precipitated in the wetlands. In the United States, the research and treatment of acid mine drainage continues to be an active field of study in the Appalachians and in the metal-mining areas of the Rocky Mountains. *See also* Acidification; Bureau of Mines; Clean coal technology

[*Usha Vedagiri*]

FURTHER READING

Clay, S. "A Solution to Mine Drainage?" *American Forests* 98 (July-August 1992): 42-43.

Hammer, D. A. *Constructed Wetlands for Wastewater Treatment: Municipal, Industrial, Agricultural.* Chelsea, MI: Lewis, 1990.

Schwartz, S. E. "Acid Deposition: Unraveling a Regional Phenomenon." *Science* 243 (10 February 1989): 753-763.

Welter, T. R. "An 'All Natural' Treatment: Companies Construct Wetlands to Reduce Metals in Acid Mine Drainage." *Industry Week* 240 (5 August 1991): 42-43.

Acid rain

Acid rain is the term used in the popular press that is equivalent to acidic deposition as used in the scientific literature. **Acid deposition** results from the deposition of airborne acidic pollutants on land and in bodies of water. These pollutants can cause damage to forests as well as to lakes and streams.

The major pollutants that cause acidic deposition are **sulfur dioxide** (SO_2) and **nitrogen oxides** (NO_x) produced during the **combustion** of **fossil fuels**. In the **atmosphere** these gases oxidize to sulfuric acid (H_2SO_4) and nitric acid (HNO_3) which can be transported long distances before being returned to the earth dissolved in rain drops (wet deposition), deposited on the surfaces of plants as cloud droplets, or directly on plant surfaces (dry deposition). Electrical utilities contribute 70 percent of the 20 million tons (21 million metric tons) of SO_2 that are annually added to the atmosphere (1985 data). Most of this is from the combustion of **coal**. Electric utilities also contribute 30 percent of the 19 million tons of NO_x added to the atmosphere, and internal combustion engines used in **automobile**s, trucks and buses contribute more than 40 percent. Natural sources such as forest fires, swamp gases, and **volcano**es only contribute 1-5 percent of atmospheric SO_2. Forest fires, lightning, and microbial processes in **soil**s contribute about 11 percent to atmospheric NO_x. In response to air quality regulations, electrical utilities have switched to coal with lower sulfur content and installed scrubbing systems to remove SO_2. This has resulted in a steady decrease in SO_2 emissions in the United States since 1970, with a 18-20 percent decrease between 1975 and 1988. Emissions of NO_x have also decreased from the peak in 1975, with a 9-15 percent decrease from 1975 to 1988.

A commonly used indicator of the intensity of acid rain is the **pH** of this rainfall. The pH of non-polluted rainfall in forested regions is in the range 5.0 -5.6. The upper limit is 5.6, not neutral (7.0), because of carbonic acid that results from the dissolution of atmospheric **carbon dioxide**. The contribution of naturally occurring nitric and sulfuric acid, as well as organic acids, reduces the pH somewhat to less than 5.6. In arid and semi-arid regions, rainfall pH values can be greater than 5.6 due the effect of alkaline soil dust in the air. Nitric and sulfuric acids in acidic rainfall (wet deposition) can result in pH values for individual rainfall events of less than 4.0.

In North America, the lowest acid rainfall is in the northeastern United States and southeastern Canada. The lowest mean pH in this region is 4.15. Even lower pH values are observed in central and northern Europe. Generally, the

Acid rain in Chicago is eroding the sculptures adorning historical buildings.

greater the population density and density of industrialization the lower the rainfall pH. Long distance transport, however, can result in low pH rainfall even in areas with low population and low density of industries, as in parts of New England, eastern Canada and in Scandinavia.

A very significant portion of acid deposition occurs in the dry form. In the United States, it is estimated that 30-60 percent of acidic deposition occurs as dry fall. This material is deposited as sulfur dioxide gas and very finely divided particles (**aerosol**s) directly on the surfaces of plants (needles and leaves). The rate of deposition depends not only on the concentration of acid materials suspended in the air, but on the nature and density of plant surfaces exposed to the atmosphere and the atmospheric conditions(e.g. wind speed and humidity).

Direct deposition of acid cloud droplets can be very important especially in some high altitude forests. Acid cloud droplets can have acid concentrations of 5 to 20 times that in wet deposition. In some high elevation sites that are frequently shrouded in clouds, direct droplet deposition is three times that of wet deposition from rainfall.

Acid deposition has the potential to adversely affect sensitive forests as well as lakes and streams. Agriculture is generally not included in the assessment of the effects of acidic deposition because experimental evidence indicates that even the most severe episodes of acid deposition do not adversely affect the growth of agricultural crops, and any long-term soil **acidification** can readily be managed by addition of agricultural lime. In fact, the acidifying potential of the **fertilizer**s normally added to cropland is much greater than that of acidic deposition. In forests, however, long-term

acidic deposition on sensitive soils can result in the depletion of important **nutrient** elements (e.g., calcium, magnesium and potassium) and in soil acidification. Also, acidic pollutants can interact with other pollutants (e.g. **ozone**) to cause more immediate problems for tree growth. Acid deposition can also result in the acidification of sensitive lakes and with the loss of biological productivity.

Long-term exposure of acid sensitive materials used in building construction and in monuments (e.g.. zinc, marble, limestone and some sandstones) can result in surface corrosion and deterioration. Monuments tend to be the most vulnerable because they are usually not as protected from rainfall as most building materials. Good data on the impact of acidic deposition on monuments and building material is lacking.

Nutrient depletion due to acid deposition on sensitive soils is a long-term (decades to centuries) consequence of acidic deposition. Acidic deposition greatly accelerates the very slow depletion of soil nutrients due to natural weathering processes. Soils that contain less plant-available calcium, magnesium and potassium are less **buffer**ed with respect to degradation due to acidic deposition. The most sensitive soils are shallow sandy soils over hard bedrock. The least vulnerable soils are the deep clay soils which are highly buffered against changes due to acidic deposition.

The more immediate possible threat to forests is the **forest decline** phenomenon that has been observed in forests in northern Europe and North America. Acidic deposition in combination with other stress factors such as ozone, disease and adverse weather conditions can lead to decline in forest productivity and, in certain cases, to **dieback**. Acid deposition alone cannot account for the observed forest decline, and acid deposition probably plays a minor role in the areas where forest decline has occurred. Ozone is a much more serious threat to forests, and it is a key factor in the decline of forests in the Sierra Nevada and San Bernardino mountains in California.

The greatest concern for adverse effects of acidic deposition is the decline in biological productivity in lakes. When a lake has a pH less than 6.0, several species of minnows, as well as other species that are part of the **food chain** for many fish, cannot survive. At pH values less than about 5.3, lake trout, walleye and smallmouth bass cannot survive. At pH less than about 4.5, most fish cannot survive (largemouth bass is an exception).

Many small lakes are naturally acid due to organic acids produced in acid soils and acid bogs. These lakes have chemistries dominated by organic acids, and many have brown colored waters due to the organic acid content. These lakes can be distinguished from lakes acidified by acidic deposition, because lakes strongly affected by acidic deposition are dominated by sulfate.

Lakes that are adversely affected by acidic deposition tend to be in steep terrain with thin soils. In these settings the path of rainwater movement into a lake is not influenced greatly by soil materials. This contrasts to most lakes where much of the water that collects in a lake flows first into the ground water before entering the lake via subsurface flow.

Due to the contact with soil materials, acidity is neutralized and the capacity to neutralize acidity is added to the water in the form of bicarbonate **ion**s (bicarbonate alkalinity). If more than 5 percent of the water that reaches a lake is in the form of ground water a lake is not sensitive to acid deposition.

An estimated 24 percent of the lakes in the Adirondack region of New York are devoid of fish. In one third to one half of these lakes this is due to acidic deposition. Approximately 16 percent of the lakes in this region may have lost one or more species of fish due to acidification. In Ontario, Canada, 115 lakes are estimated to have lost populations of lake trout. Acidification of lakes, by acidic deposition, extends as far west as Upper Michigan and northeastern Wisconsin, where many sensitive lakes occur and there is some evidence for acidification. However, the extent of acidification is quite limited. *See also* Acid and base; Adirondack Mountains; Experimental Lakes Area

[*Paul R. Bloom*]

FURTHER READING

Bresser, A. H., ed. *Acid Precipitation.* New York: Springer-Verlag, 1990.

Mellanby, K., ed. *Air Pollution, Acid Rain and the Environment.* New York: Elsevier, 1989.

Turck, M. *Acid Rain.* New York: Macmillan, 1990.

Wellburn, A. *Air Pollution and Acid Rain: The Biological Impact.* New York: Wiley, 1988.

Young, P. M. *Acidic Deposition: State of Science and Technology. Summary Report of the U. S. National Acid Precipitation Program.* Washington, DC: U. S. Government Printing Office, 1991.

Acidification

The process of becoming more acidic due to inputs of an acidic substance. The common measure of acidification is a decrease in **pH**. Acidification of **soil**s and natural waters by **acid rain** or acid wastes can result in reduced biological productivity if the pH is sufficiently reduced. *See also* Acid and base; Buffer

Acidity

See **pH**

Acoustics

See **Noise pollution**

Activated sludge

The activated sludge process is an **aerobic** (oxygen-rich), continuous-flow biological method for the treatment of domestic and biodegradable industrial **wastewater**, in which organic matter is utilized by microorganisms for life-sustaining processes, that is, for energy for reproduction,

digestion, movement, etc. and as a food source to produce cell growth and more microorganisms. During these activities of utilization and degradation of organic materials, degradation products of **carbon dioxide** and water are also formed. The activated sludge process is characterized by the suspension of microorganisms in the wastewater, a mixture referred to as the mixed liquor. Activated sludge is used as part of an overall treatment system, which includes primary treatment of the wastewater for the removal of **particulate** solids before the use of activated sludge as a secondary treatment process to remove suspended and dissolved organic solids.

The conventional activated sludge process consists of an **aeration** basin, with air as the oxygen source, where treatment is accomplished. Soluble (dissolved) organic materials are absorbed through the cell walls of the microorganisms and into the cells, where they are broken down and converted to more microorganisms, carbon dioxide, water and energy. Insoluble (solid) particles are adsorbed on the cell walls, transformed to a soluble form by **enzyme**s (biological catalysts) secreted by the microorganisms, and absorbed through the cell wall, where they are also digested and used by the microorganisms in their life-sustaining processes.

The microorganisms that are responsible for the degradation of the organic materials are maintained in suspension by mixing induced by the aeration system. As the microorganisms are mixed, they collide with other microorganisms and stick together to form larger particles called *floc*. The large flocs that are formed settle more readily than individual cells. These flocs also collide with suspended and colloidal materials (insoluble organic materials), which stick to the flocs and cause the flocs to grow even larger. The microorganisms digest these adsorbed materials, thereby re-opening sites for more materials to stick.

The aeration basin is followed by a secondary clarifier (settling tank), where the flocs of microorganisms with their adsorbed organic materials settle out. A portion of the settled microorganisms, referred to as **sludge**, are recycled to the aeration basin to maintain an active population of microorganisms and an adequate supply of biological solids for the adsorption of organic materials. Excess sludge is wasted by being piped to separate sludge-handling processes. The liquids from the clarifier are transported to facilities for disinfection and final **discharge** to receiving waters, or to tertiary treatment units for further treatment.

Activated sludge processes are designed based on the mixed liquor suspended solids (MLSS) and the organic loading of the wastewater, as represented by the **biochemical oxygen demand (BOD)** or **chemical oxygen demand (COD)**. The MLSS represents the quantity of microorganisms involved in the treatment of the organic materials in the aeration basin, while the organic loading determines the requirements for the design of the aeration system.

Modifications to the conventional activated sludge process include:

1. *Extended aeration.* The mixed liquor is retained in the aeration basin until the production rate of new cells is the same as the decay rate of existing cells, with no excess sludge production. In practice, excess sludge is

produced, but the quantity is less than that of other activated sludge processes. This process is often used for the treatment of industrial wastewater that contains complex organic materials requiring long detention times for degradation.

2. *Contact stabilization*. A process based on the premise that as wastewater enters the aeration basin (referred to as the contact basin), colloidal and insoluble organic biodegradable materials are removed rapidly by biological **sorption**, synthesis, and flocculation during a relatively short contact time. This method uses a reaeration (stabilization) basin before the settled sludge from the clarifier is returned to the contact basin. The concentrated flocculated and adsorbed organic materials are oxidized in the reaeration basin, which does not receive any addition of raw wastewater.

3. *Plug flow*. Wastewater is routed through a series of channels constructed in the aeration basin; wastewater flows through and is treated as a plug as it winds its way through the basin. As the "plug" passes through the tank, the concentrations of organic materials are gradually reduced, with a corresponding decrease in oxygen requirements and microorganism numbers.

4. *Step aeration*. Influent wastewater enters the aeration basin along the length of the basin, while the return sludge enters at the head of the basin. This process results in a more uniform oxygen demand in the basin and a more stable environment for the microorganisms; it also results in a lower solids loading on the clarifier for a given mass of microorganisms.

5. *Oxidation ditch*. A circular aeration basin (race-track-shaped) is used, with rotary brush aerators that extend across the width of the ditch. Brush aerators aerate the wastewater, keep the microorganisms in suspension, and drive the wastewater around the circular channel. *See also* Industrial waste treatment; Sludge; Sludge treatment and disposal; Slurry; Waste management

[*Judith Sims*]

FURTHER READING

Corbitt, R. A. "Wastewater Disposal." In *Standard Handbook of Environmental Engineering*, edited by R. A. Corbitt. New York: McGraw-Hill, 1990.

Junkins, R., K. Deeny, and T. Eckhoff. *The Activated Sludge Process: Fundamentals of Operation*. Boston: Butterworth Publishers, 1983.

Acute effects

Effects that persist in a biologic system for only a short time, generally less than a week. The effects might range from behavioral or color changes to death. Tests for acute effects are performed with humans, animals, plants, insects, and microorganisms. Intoxication and a hangover resulting from the consumption of too much alcohol, the common cold, and parathion poisoning are examples of acute effects. Generally, little tissue damage occurs as a result of acute effects. The term acute effects should not be confused with acute toxicity studies or acute dosages, which respectively refer to short-term studies (generally less than a week) and short-term dosages (often a single dose). Both chronic and acute exposures can initiate acute effects. *See also* Chronic effects

Adams, Ansel (1902-1984)

American photographer and conservationist

Ansel Adams is best known for his stark black-and-white photographs of nature and the American landscape. He was born and raised in San Francisco. Schooled at home by his parents, he received little formal training except as a pianist. A trip to Yosemite Valley as a teenager had a profound influence on him, and **Yosemite National Park** and the Sierra "range of light" attracted him back many times and inspired two great careers: photographer and conservationist. As he observed, "Everybody needs something to believe in [and] my point of focus is **conservation**." He used his photographs to make that point more vividly and turned it into an enduring legacy.

Adams was a painstaking artist, and some critics have chided him for an overemphasis on technique and for creating in his work "a mood that is relentlessly optimistic." Adams *was* a careful technician, making all of his own prints (reportedly hand-producing over 13,000 in his lifetime), sometimes spending a whole day on one print. He explained: "I have made thousands of photographs of the natural scene, but only those images that were most intensely felt at the moment of exposure have survived the inevitable winnowing of time."

He did winnow, ruthlessly, and the result was a collection of work that introduced millions of people to the majesty and diversity of the American landscape. Not all of Adams's pictures were "uplifting" or "optimistic" images of scenic wonders; he also documented scenes of **overgrazing** in the **arid** Southwest and of incarcerated Japanese-Americans in the Manzanar internment camp.

From the beginning, Adams used his photographs in the cause of conservation. His pictures played a major role in the late 1930s in establishing Kings Canyon National Park. Throughout his life, he remained an active, involved conservationist; for many years he was on the Board of the **Sierra Club** and strongly influenced the Club's activities and philosophy.

Ansel Adams's greatest bequest to the world will remain his photographs and advocacy of **wilderness** and the **national park** ideals. Through his work he not only generated interest in environmental conservation, he also captured the beauty and majesty of nature for all generations to enjoy.

[*Gerald L. Young*]

FURTHER READING

Adams, Ansel. *Ansel Adams: An Autobiography*. New York: New York Graphic Society, 1984.

Cahn, R. "Ansel Adams, Environmentalist." *Sierra* 64 (May-June 1979): 31-49.

Grundberg, A. "Ansel Adams: The Politics of Natural Space." *The New Criterion* 3 (1984): 48-52.

Adaptation

All members of a population share many characteristics in common. For example, all finches in a particular forest are alike in many ways. But if many hard-to-shell seeds are found in the forest, those finches with stronger, more conical bills will have better rates of reproduction and survival than finches with thin bills. Therefore, a conical, stout bill can be considered an adaptation to that forest environment. Any specialized characteristic that permits an individual to survive and reproduce is called an adaptation. Adaptations may result either from an individual's genetic heritage or from its ability to learn. Since successful genetic adaptations are more likely to be passed from generation to generation through the survival of better adapted organisms, adaptation can be viewed as the force that drives biological **evolution**.

Adirondack Mountains

A range of mountains in northeastern New York, containing Mt. Marcy (5,344 feet; 1,644 m), the state's highest point. Bounded by the Mohawk Valley on the south, the St. Lawrence Valley on the northeast, and by the **Hudson River** and Lake Champlain on the east, the Adirondack Mountains form the core of Adirondack Park. This park is one of the earliest and most comprehensive examples of regional planning in the United States. The regional plan attempts to balance conflicting interests of many users at the same time as it controls environmentally destructive development. Although the plan remains controversial, it has succeeded in largely preserving one of the last and greatest **wilderness** areas in the East.

The Adirondacks serve a number of important purposes for surrounding populations. Vacationers, hikers, canoeists, and anglers use the area's 2,300 wilderness lakes and extensive river systems. The state's greatest remaining forests stand in the Adirondacks, providing animal **habitat** and serving recreational visitors. Timber and mining companies, employing much of the area's resident population, also rely on the forests, some of which contain the East's most ancient old-growth groves. Containing the headwaters of numerous rivers, including the Hudson, Adirondack Park is an essential source of clean water for farms and cities at lower elevations.

Adirondack Park was established by the New York State Constitution of 1892, which mandates that the region shall remain "forever wild." Encompassing six million acres (2.4 million hectares), this park is the largest wilderness area in the eastern United States—nearly three times the size of **Yellowstone National Park**. Only a third of the land within park boundaries, however, is owned by the state of New York. Private mining and timber concerns, public agencies, several towns, thousands of private cabins, and 107 units of local government occupy the remaining property.

Because the development interests of various user groups and visitors conflict with the state constitution, a comprehensive regional **land use** plan was developed in 1972-73. The novelty of the plan lay in the large area it covered and in its jurisdiction over land uses on private land as well as **public land**. According to the regional plan, all major development within park boundaries must meet an extensive set of environmental safeguards drawn up by the state's Adirondack Park Agency. Stringent rules and extensive regulation frustrate local residents and commercial interests, who complain about the plan's complexity and resent "outsiders" ruling on what Adirondackers are allowed to do. Nevertheless, this plan has been a milestone for other regions trying to balance the interests of multiple users. By controlling extensive development the park agency has preserved a wilderness resource that has become extremely rare in the eastern United States. The survival of this century-old park, surrounded by extensive development, demonstrates the value of preserving wilderness in spite of ongoing controversy.

In recent years forestry and **recreation** interests in the Adirondacks have encountered a new environmental problem in acid precipitation. Evidence of deleterious effects of **acid rain** and snow on aquatic and terrestrial vegetation began to accumulate in the early 1970s. Studies revealed that about half of the Adirondack lakes situated above 3,300 feet (1,000 m) have **pH** levels so low that all fish have disappeared. Prevailing winds put these mountains directly downstream of urban and industrial regions of western New York and southern Ontario. Because they form an elevated obstacle to weather patterns, these mountains capture a great deal of precipitation carrying acidic sulfur and **nitrogen oxides** from upwind industrial cities. *See also* Land-use control; National park; Old-growth forest; Wilderness Act (1964)

[*Mary Ann Cunningham*]

FURTHER READING

Ciroff, R. A., and G. Davis. *Protecting Open Space: Land Use Control in the Adirondack Park.* Cambridge, MA: Ballinger, 1981.

Davis, G., and T. Duffus. *Developing a Land Conservation Strategy.* Elizabethtown, NY: Adirondack Land Trust, 1987.

Graham, F. J. *The Adirondack Park: A Political History.* New York: Knopf, 1978.

Popper, F. J. *The Politics of Land Use Reform.* Madison, WI: University of Wisconsin Press, 1981.

Adsorption

The removal of **ion**s or molecules from solutions by binding to solid surfaces. **Phosphorus** is removed from water flowing through **soil**s by adsorption on soil particles. Some **pesticide**s adsorb strongly on soil particles. Adsorption by suspended solids is also an important process in natural waters.

Aeration

In discussions of plant growth, aeration refers to an exchange that takes place in **soil** or another medium allowing oxygen to enter and **carbon dioxide** to escape into the **atmosphere**. Crop growth is often reduced when aeration is poor. In geology, particularly with reference to **groundwater**, aeration is the portion of the earth's crust where the pores are only partially filled with water. In relation to **water treatment**, aeration is the process of exposing water to air in order to remove such undesirable substances in drinking water as iron and manganese. *See also* Soil compaction; Vadose zone; Zone of saturation

Aerobic

Refers to either an environment that contains molecular oxygen gas (O_2); an organism or tissue that requires oxygen for its metabolism; or a chemical or biological process that requires oxygen. Aerobic organisms use molecular oxygen in **respiration**, releasing **carbon dioxide** (CO_2) in return. These organisms include mammals, fish, birds, and green plants, as well as many of the lower life forms such as **fungi**, algae, and sundry bacteria and actinomycetes. Many, but not all, organic **decomposition** processes are aerobic; a lack of oxygen greatly slows these processes.

Aerobic/anaerobic systems

Most living organisms require oxygen to function normally, but a few forms of life exist exclusively in the absence of oxygen and some can function both in the presence of oxygen (aerobically) and in its absence (anaerobically). Examples of anaerobic organisms are found in bacteria of the genus *Clostridium*, in parasitic protozoans from the gastrointestinal tract of humans and other vertebrates, and in ciliates associated with sulfide-containing sediments. Organisms capable of switching between aerobic and anaerobic existence are found in forms of fungi known as yeasts. The ability of an organism to function both aerobically and anaerobically increases the variety of sites in which it is able to exist and conveys some advantages over organisms with less adaptive potential.

Microbial decay activity in nature can occur either aerobically or anaerobically. Aerobic **decomposers** of compost and other organic substrates are generally preferable because they act more quickly and release fewer noxious odors. Large sewage treatment plants use a two-stage digestion system in which the first stage is anaerobic digestion of sludge that produces flammable methane gas that may be used as fuel to help operate the plant. Sludge digestion continues in the aerobic second stage, a process which is easier to control but more costly because of the power needed to provide aeration. Although most fungi are generally aerobic organisms, yeasts used in bread making and in the production of fermented beverages such as wine and beer can metabolize anaerobically. In the process, they release ethyl alcohol and the carbon dioxide which causes bread to rise.

Tissues of higher organisms may have limited capability for anaerobic metabolism, but they need elaborate compensating mechanisms to survive even brief periods without oxygen. For example, human muscle tissue is able to metabolize anaerobically when blood cannot supply the large amounts of oxygen needed for vigorous activity. Muscle contraction requires an energy-rich compound called adenosine triphosphate (ATP). Muscle tissue normally contains enough ATP for 20-30 seconds of intense activity. ATP must then be metabolically regenerated from glycogen, the muscle's primary energy source. Muscle tissue has both aerobic and anaerobic metabolic systems for regenerating ATP from glycogen. Although the aerobic system is much more efficient, the anaerobic system is the major energy source for the first minute or two of exercise. The carbon dioxide released in this process causes the heart rate to increase. As the heart beats faster and more oxygen is delivered to the muscle tissue, the more efficient aerobic system for generating ATP takes over. A person's physical condition is important in determining how well the aerobic system is able to meet the needs of continued activity. In fit individuals who exercise regularly, heart function is optimized, and the heart is able to pump blood rapidly enough to maintain aerobic metabolism. If the oxygen level in muscle tissue drops, anaerobic metabolism will resume. Toxic products of anaerobic metabolism, including lactic acid, accumulate in the tissue, and muscle fatigue results.

Other interesting examples of limited anaerobic capability are found in the animal kingdom. Some diving ducks have an adaptation that allows them to draw oxygen from stored oxyhemoglobin and oxymyoglobin in blood and muscles. This adaptation permits them to remain submerged in water for extended periods. To prevent desiccation, mussels and clams close their shells when out of the water at low tide, and their metabolism shifts from aerobic to anaerobic. When once again in the water, the animals rapidly return to aerobic metabolism and purge themselves of the acid products of anaerobiosis accumulated while they were dry.

[*Douglas C. Pratt*]

FURTHER READING

Klass, D. L. "Methane from Anaerobic Fermentation." *Science* 223 (1984): 1021.

Lea, A.G.H., and Piggott, J.R. *Fermented beverage production.* New York: Blackie, 1995.

McArdle, W. D. *Exercise Physiology: Energy, Nutrition, and Human Performance.* 4th ed. Baltimore: Williams & Wilkins, 1996.

Stanbury, P. F., Whitaker, A., and Hall, S. J. *Principles of Fermenentation Technology.* 2nd ed. Tarrytown, N.Y.: Pergamon, 1995.

Aerobic sludge digestion

Wastewater treatment plants produce organic **sludge** as **wastewater** is treated; this sludge must be further treated before ultimate disposal. Sludges are generated from primary settling tanks, which are used to remove settleable, **particulate** solids, and from secondary clarifiers (settling basins), which are used to remove excess **biomass** production generated in secondary biological treatment units.

Disposal of sludges from wastewater treatment processes is a costly and difficult problem. The processes used in sludge disposal include: (1) reduction in sludge volume, primarily by removal of water, which constitutes 97-98 percent of the sludge; (2) reduction of the volatile (organic) content of the sludge, which eliminates nuisance conditions by reducing putrescibility and reduces threats to human health by reducing levels of microorganisms; and (3) ultimate disposal of the residues.

Aerobic sludge digestion is one process that may be used to reduce both the organic content and the volume of the sludge. Under **aerobic** conditions, a large portion of the organic matter in sludge may be oxidized biologically by microorganisms to **carbon dioxide** and water. The process results in approximately 50 percent reduction in solids content. Aerobic sludge digestion facilities may be designed for batch or continuous flow operations. In batch operations, sludge is added to a reaction tank while the contents are continuously aerated. Once the tank is filled, the sludges are aerated for two to three weeks, depending on the types of sludge. After **aeration** is discontinued, the solids and liquids are separated. Solids at concentrations of two to four percent are removed, and the clarified liquid supernatant is decanted and recycled to the wastewater treatment plant. In a continuous flow system, an aeration tank is utilized, followed by a settling tank.

Aerobic sludge digestion is usually used only for biological sludges from secondary treatment units, in the absence of sludges from primary treatment units. The most commonly used application is for the treatment of sludges wasted from extended aeration systems (which is a modification of the **activated sludge** system). Since there is no addition of an external food source, the microorganisms must utilize their own cell contents for metabolic purposes in a process called endogenous respiration. The remaining sludge is a mineralized sludge, with remaining organic materials comprised of cell walls and other cell fragments that are not readily **biodegradable**.

The advantages of using aerobic digestion, as compared to the use of **anaerobic** digestion include: (1) simplicity of operation and maintenance; (2) lower capital costs; (3) lower levels of **biochemical oxygen demand (BOD)** and **phosphorus** in the supernatant; (4) fewer effects from upsets such as the presence of toxic interferences or changes in loading and **pH**; (5) less odor; (6) nonexplosive; (7) greater reduction in grease and hexane solubles; (8) greater sludge **fertilizer** value; (9) shorter retention periods; and (10) an effective alternative for small wastewater treatment plants.

Disadvantages include: (1) higher operating costs, especially energy costs; (2) highly sensitive to ambient temperature (operation at temperatures below 59°F (15°C) may require excessive **retention time**s to achieve stabilization; if heating is required, aerobic digestion may not be cost-

effective); (3) no useful byproduct such as **methane** gas that is produced in anaerobic digestion; (4) variability in the ability to dewater to reduce sludge volume; (5) less reduction in volatile solids; and (6) unfavorable economics for larger wastewater treatment plants. *See also* Bioremediation; Sewage treatment; Toxic substance

[*Judith Sims*]

FURTHER READING

Corbitt, R. A. "Wastewater Disposal." In *Standard Handbook of Environmental Engineering*, edited by R. A. Corbitt. New York: McGraw-Hill, 1990.

Gaudy, A. F., Jr., and E. T. Gaudy. *Microbiology for Environmental Scientists and Engineers*. New York: McGraw-Hill, 1980.

Peavy, H. S., D. R. Rowe, and G. Tchobanoglous. *Environmental Engineering*. New York: McGraw-Hill, 1985.

Aerosol

A suspension of particles, liquid or solid, in a gas. The term implies a degree of permanence in the suspension, which puts a rough upper limit on particle size at a few tens of micrometers at most (1 micrometer = 0.00004 inch). Thus in proper use the term connotes the ensemble of the particles and the suspending gas.

The atmospheric aerosol has two major components, generally referred to as coarse and fine particles, with different sources and different composition. Coarse particles result from mechanical processes, such as grinding. The smaller particles are ground, the more surface they have per unit of mass. Creating new surface requires energy, so the smallest average size that can be created by such processes is limited by the available energy. It is rare for such mechanically-generated particles to be less than 1 μm (0.00004 in.) in diameter. Fine particles, on the other hand, are formed by condensation from the vapor phase. For most substances, condensation is difficult from a uniform gaseous state; it requires the presence of pre-existing particles on which the vapors can deposit. Alternatively, very high concentrations of the vapor are required, compared with the concentration in equilibrium with the condensed material.

Hence fine particles form readily in **combustion** processes when substances are vaporized. The gas is then quickly cooled. These can then serve as nuclei for the formation of larger particles, still in the fine particle size range, in the presence of condensible vapors. However, in the **atmosphere** such particles become rapidly more scarce with increasing size, and are relatively rare in sizes much larger than a few micrometers. At about 2 μm (0.00008 in.), coarse and fine particles are about equally abundant.

Using the term strictly, one rarely samples the atmospheric aerosol, but rather the particles out of the aerosol. The presence of aerosols is generally detected by their effect on light. Aerosols of a uniform particle size in the vicinity of the wavelengths of visible light can produce rather spectacular optical effects. In the laboratory, such aerosols can be produced by condensation of the heated vapors of certain oils on nuclei made by evaporating salts from heated filaments. If the suspending gas is cooled quickly, particle size is governed by the supply of vapor compared with the supply of nuclei, and the time available for condensation to occur. Since these can all be made nearly constant throughout the gas, the resulting particles are quite uniform. It is also possible to produce uniform particles by spraying a dilute solution of a soluble material, then evaporating the solvent. If the spray head is vibrated in an appropriate frequency range, the drops will be uniform in size, with the size controlled by the frequency of vibration and the rate of flow of the spray. Obviously, the final particle size is also a function of the concentration of the sprayed solution. *See also* Condensation nuclei; Particulate

[*James P. Lodge, Jr.*]

FURTHER READING

Jennings, S. G., ed. *Aerosol Effects on Climate.* Tucson, AZ: University of Arizona Press, 1993.

Monastersky, R. "Aerosols: Critical Questions for Climate." *Science News* 138 (25 August 1990): 118.

Reist, P. *Aerosol Science and Technology.* New York: McGraw-Hill, 1992.

Sun, M. "Acid Aerosols Called Health Hazard." *Science* 240 (24 June 1988): 1727.

Aflatoxin

Toxic compounds produced by some **fungi** and among the most potent naturally occurring **carcinogen**s for humans and animals. Aflatoxin intake is positively related to high incidence of liver **cancer** in humans in many developing countries. In many farm animals aflatoxin can cause acute or chronic diseases. Aflatoxin is a metabolic by-product produced by the fungi *Aspergillus flavus* and the closely related species *Aspergillus parasiticus* growing on grains and decaying organic compounds. There are four naturally occurring aflatoxins: B_1, B_2, G_1, and G_2. All of these compounds will fluoresce under a UV (black) light around 425-450 nm providing a qualitative test for the presence of aflatoxins. In general, starch grains, such as corn, are infected in storage when the moisture content of the grain reaches 17 to 18 percent and the temperature is 79 to 99°F (26 to 37°C). However, the fungus may also infect grain in the field under hot, dry conditions.

African Wildlife Foundation (Washington, D.C.)

The African Wildlife Foundation (AWF) was established in 1961 to promote the protection of the animals native to Africa. The group maintains offices in both Washington, D.C., and Nairobi, Kenya. The African headquarters promotes the idea that Africans themselves are best able to protect the **wildlife** of their continent. AWF also established two colleges of **wildlife management** in Africa (Tanzania and Cameroon), so that rangers and park and reserve wardens can be professionally trained. **Conservation** education, especially as it relates to African wildlife, has

always been a major AWF goal—in fact, it has been the association's primary focus since its inception.

AWF carries out its mandate to protect Africa's wildlife through a wide range of projects and activities. Since 1961, AWF has provided a radio communication network in Africa, as well as several airplanes and jeeps for anti-poaching patrols. These were instrumental in facilitating the work of Dr. Richard Leakey in the Tsavo National Park, Kenya. The AWF project, Protected Areas: Neighbors as Partners, attempts to involve people who live adjacent to protected wildlife areas, such as the **Serengeti National Park**, by asking them to take joint responsibility for **natural resources**. The program demonstrates that land conservation and the needs of neighboring people and their livestock can be balanced, and the benefits shared.

Another highly successful AWF program is the Elephant Awareness Campaign. Its slogan, "Only Elephants Should Wear Ivory," has become extremely popular, both in Africa and in the United States, and is largely responsible for bringing the plight of the African elephant (*Loxodonta africana*) to public awareness. In 1990 AWF and the **World Wildlife Fund** began a three-year Planning and Assessment for Wildlife Management Project to provide technical assistance to Tanzania's Ministry of Lands, Natural Resources, and Tourism, and to help upgrade the Tanzanian Wildlife Division.

Although AWF is concerned with all the wildlife of Africa, in recent years the group has focused on saving African **elephants**, black **rhinoceroses** (*Diceros bicornis*), and mountain **gorillas** (*Gorilla gorilla berengei*). These species are seriously endangered, and are benefitting from AWF's Critical Habitats and Species Program, which works to aid these and other animals in critical danger.

From its inception, AWF has supported education centers, wildlife clubs, **national park**s and reserves. It recently introduced a new course at the College of African Wildlife Management in Tanzania which allows students to learn community conservation activities and helps park officials learn to work with residents living adjacent to protected areas. AWF also involves teachers in its endeavors with a series of publications, *Let's Conserve Our Wildlife*. Written in Swahili, the series includes teacher's guides and has been used in both elementary schools and adult literacy classes in African villages. AWF also publishes the quarterly magazine *Wildlife News*. Contact: African Wildlife Foundation, 1717 Massachusetts Avenue, NW, Washington, DC 20036. Internet: http://www.awf.org/.

[*Cathy M. Falk*]

Africanized bees (*Apis mellifera scutellata*)

The Africanized bee, or "killer bee," is an extremely aggressive honeybee. This bee developed when African honeybees were brought to Brazil to mate with other bees to increase honey production. The imported bees were accidentally

An Africanized bee collecting grass pollen in Brazil.

particularly for those bees that display European-style physiques and African behaviors, or vice versa.

When Africanized bees first appeared in southern Texas, researchers from the USDA's Honeybee Research Laboratory in Weslaco, Texas, destroyed the colony, estimated at 5,000 bees. Some of the members of the three-pound colony were preserved in alcohol and others in freezers for future analysis. Researchers are also developing management techniques, including the annual introduction of young mated European queens into domestic hives, in an attempt to maintain gentle production stock and ensure honey production and pollination.

[*Linda Rehkopf*]

FURTHER READING

"African Bees Make U.S. Debut." *Science News* 138 (27 October 1990): 261.

Barinaga, M. "How African Are 'Killer' Bees?" *Science* 250 (2 November 1990): 628-629.

Hubbell, S. "Maybe the 'Killer' Bee Should Be Called the 'Bravo' Instead." *Smithsonian* 22 (September 1991): 116-124.

White, W. "The Bees From Rio Claro." *The New Yorker* 67 (16 September 1991): 36-53.

Winston, M. *Killer Bees: The Africanized Honey Bee in the Americas.* Cambridge: Harvard University Press, 1992.

released and they have since spread northward, traveling at a rate of 300 miles (483 km) per year. The bees first appeared in the United States at the Texas-Mexico border in late 1990.

The bees get their "killer" title because of their vigorous defense of colonies or hives when disturbed. Aside from temperament, they are much like their counterparts now in the United States, which are European in lineage. Africanized bees are slightly smaller than their more passive cousins.

Honeybees are social insects and live and work together in colonies. When bees fly from plant to plant, they help pollinate flowers and crops. Africanized bees, however, seem to be more interested in reproducing than in honey production or pollination. For this reason they are constantly swarming and moving around, while domestic bees tend to stay in local, managed colonies. Because Africanized bees are also much more aggressive than domestic honey bees when their colonies are disturbed, they can be harmful to people who are allergic to bee stings.

More problematic than the threat to humans, however, is the impact the bees will have on fruit and vegetable industries in the southern parts of the United States. Many fruit and vegetable growers depend on honey bees for pollination, and in places where the Africanized bees have appeared, honey production has fallen by as much as 80 percent. Beekeepers in this country are experimenting with "requeening" their colonies regularly to ensure that the colonies reproduce gentle offsprings.

Another danger is the propensity of the Africanized bee to mate with honey bees of European lineage, a kind of "infiltration" of the **gene pool** of more domestic bees. Researchers from the **U.S. Department of Agriculture** (USDA) are watching for the results of this interbreeding,

Agency for Toxic Substances and Disease Registry

The Agency for Toxic Substances and Disease Registry (ATSDR) studies the health effects of hazardous substances in general and at specific locations. As indicated by its title, the Agency maintains a registry of people exposed to toxic chemicals. Along with the **Environmental Protection Agency (EPA)**, ATSDR prepares and updates profiles of **toxic substance**s. In addition, ATSDR assesses the potential dangers posed to human health by exposure to hazardous substances at Superfund sites. The Agency will also perform health assessments when petitioned by a community. Though ATSDR's early health assessments have been criticized, the Agency's later assessments and other products are considered more useful.

ATSDR was created in 1980 by the **Comprehensive Environmental Response, Compensation, and Liability Act (CERCLA)**, also known as the Superfund, as part of the **U.S. Department of Health and Human Services**. As originally conceived, ATSDR's role was limited to performing health studies and examining the relationship between toxic substances and disease. The **Superfund Amendments and Reauthorization Act (SARA)** of 1986 codified ATSDR's responsibility for assessing health threats at Superfund sites. ATSDR, along with the national **Centers for Disease Control** and state health departments, conducts health surveys in communities near locations that have been placed on the Superfund's **National Priorities List** for clean up. ATSDR has preformed 951 health assessments in the two years after the law was passed. Approximately one quarter of these assessments were memos or reports that had been completed prior to 1986 and were simply relabeled as health assessments.

These first assessments have been harshly criticized. The General Accounting Office (GAO), a congressional agency that reviews the actions of the federal administration, charged that most of these assessments were inadequate. Some argued that the agency was underfunded and poorly organized. Recently, ATSDR received less than five percent of the $1.6 billion appropriated for the Superfund project.

Subsequent health assessments, more than 200 of them, have generally been more complete, but they still may not be adequate in informing the community and the EPA of the dangers at specific sites. In general, ATSDR identifies a local agency to help prepare the health surveys. Unlike many of the first assessments, more recent surveys now include site visits and face-to-face interviews. However, other data on environmental effects are limited. ATSDR only considers environmental information provided by the companies that created the hazard or data collected by the EPA. In addition, ATSDR only assesses health risks from illegal **emission**s, not from "permitted" emissions. Some scientists contend that not enough is known about the health effects of exposure to hazardous substances to make conclusive health assessments.

Reaction to the performance of ATSDR's other functions has been generally more positive. As mandated by SARA, ATSDR and the EPA have prepared hundreds of toxicological profiles of hazardous substances. These profiles have been judged generally helpful, and the GAO praised ATSDR's registry of people who have been exposed to toxic substances.

[Alair MacLean]

FURTHER READING

Environmental Epidemiology: Public Health and Hazardous Wastes. National Research Council. Committee on Environmental Epidemiology. Washington, DC: National Academy Press, 1991.

Lewis, S., B. Keating, and D. Russell. *Inconclusive by Design: Waste, Fraud and Abuse in Federal Environmental Health Research*. Boston: National Toxics Campaign Fund; and Harvey, LA: Environmental Health Network, 1992.

Superfund: Public Health Assessments Incomplete and of Questionable Value. Washington, DC: General Accounting Office, 1991.

Agent Orange

Agent Orange is a **herbicide** recognized primarily for its use during the Vietnam War. It is composed of equal parts of two chemicals: **2,4-D** and **2,4,5-T**. The herbicide has also been used for clearing heavy growth on a commercial basis for a number of years. On a commercial level, Agent Orange was used in forestry control as early as the 1930s. In the 1950s through the 1960s, Agent Orange was also exported. For example, New Brunswick, Canada, was the scene of major

Agent Orange spraying to control forests for industrial development. In Malaysia in the 1950s, the British used compounds with the chemical mixture 2,4,5-T to clear communication routes.

In the United States, herbicides were considered for military use towards the end of the second World War, during the action in the Pacific. However, the first American military field tests were actually conducted in Puerto Rico, Texas, and Fort Drum, New York, in 1959.

That same year—1959—the Crops Division at Fort Detrick, Maryland initiated the first large-scale military defoliation effort. The project involved the aerial application of Agent Orange to about four square miles (10.4 sq km) of vegetation. The experiment proved highly successful; the military had found an effective tool. By 1960, the South Vietnamese government, aware of these early experiments, had requested that the United States conduct trials of these herbicides for use against guerrilla forces. The United States military was ready when President Diem made his request.

Spraying of Agent Orange in Southeast Asia began in 1961. South Vietnam President Diem stated that he wanted this "powder" in order to destroy the rice and the food crops that would be used by the Viet Cong. Thus began the use of herbicides as a weapon of war.

The United States military became involved, recognizing the limitations of fighting in foreign territory with troops that were not accustomed to jungle conditions. The military wanted to clear communication lines and open up areas of visibility in order to enhance their opportunities for success. Eventually, the United States military took complete control of the spray missions.

Initially, there were to be restrictions: the spraying was to be limited to clearing power lines and roadsides, railroads and other lines of communications and areas adjacent to depots. Eventually, the spraying was used to defoliate the thick jungle brush, thereby obliterating enemy hiding places.

Once under the authority of the military, and with no checks or restraints, the spraying continued to increase in intensity and abandon, escalating in scope because of military pressure. It was eventually used to destroy crops, mainly rice, in an effort to deprive the enemy of food. Unfortunately, the civilian population—Vietnamese men, women, and children—was also affected.

The spraying also became useful in clearing military base perimeters, cache sites, and waterways. Base perimeters were often sprayed more than once. In the case of dense jungle growth, one application of spray was made for the upper and another for the lower layers of vegetation. Inland forests, mangrove forests, and cultivated lands were all targets.

Through Project Ranch Hand—the Air Force team assigned to the spray missions—Agent Orange became the most widely produced and dispensed defoliant in Vietnam.

Military requirements for herbicide use were developed by the Army's Chemical Operations Division, J-3, Military Assistance Command, Vietnam, (MACV). With Project Ranch Hand underway, the spray missions increased monthly after 1962, with Project Ranch Hand. This increase was made possible by the continued military promises to stay

Deforestation of the Viet Cong jungle in Vietnam.

away from the civilians or to re-settle those civilians and re-supply the food in any areas where herbicides destroyed the food of the innocent. These promises were never kept. The use of herbicides for crop destruction peaked in 1965 when 45 percent of the total spraying was designed to destroy crops.

Initially, the aerial spraying took place near Saigon. Eventually the geographical base was widened. During the 1967 expansion period of herbicide procurement, when requirements had become greater than the industries' ability to produce, the Air Force and Joint Chiefs of Staff become actively involved in the herbicide program. All production for commercial use was diverted to the military, and the Department of Defense (DOD) was appointed to deal with problems of procurement and production. Commercial producers were encouraged to expand their facilities and build new plants, and the DOD made attractive offers to companies which might be induced to manufacture herbicides. A number of companies were awarded contracts. Working closely with the military, certain chemical companies sent technical advisors to Vietnam to instruct personnel on the methods and techniques necessary for effective use of the herbicides.

During the peak of the spraying, approximately 129 sorties were flown per aircraft. Twenty-four UC-123B aircraft were used, averaging 39 sorties per day. In addition, there were trucks and helicopters that went on spraying missions, backed up by such countries as Australia. C-123 cargo planes and helicopters were also used. Helicopters flew without cargo doors so that frequent ground fire could be returned. But the rotary blades would kick up gusts of spray, thereby delivering a powerful dose onto the faces and bodies of the men inside the plane.

The dense Vietnamese jungle growth required two applications to defoliate both upper and lower layers of vegetation. On the ground, both enemy troops and Vietnamese civilians came in contact with the defoliant. American troops were also exposed. They could inhale the fine misty spray or splash in the sudden and unexpected deluge of an emergency dumping. Readily absorbing the **chemicals** through their skin and lungs, hundreds of thousands of United States military troops were exposed as they lived on the sprayed bases, slept near empty drums, and drank and washed in water in areas where defoliation had occurred. They ate food that had been brushed with spray. Empty herbicide drums were indiscriminately used and improperly stored. Volatile fumes from these drums caused damage to shade trees and to anyone near the fumes. Those handling the herbicides in support of a particular project goal had the unfortunate opportunity of becoming directly exposed on a consistent basis.

Nearly three million veterans served in Southeast Asia. There is growing speculation that nearly everyone who was in Vietnam was eventually exposed to some degree—far less a possibility for those stationed in urban centers or on the waters.

According to official sources, in addition to the Ranch Hand group at least three groups were exposed:

(1) A group considered secondary support personnel. This included Army pilots who may have been involved in helicopter spraying, along with the Navy and even the Marine pilots.

(2) Those who transported the herbicide to Saigon, and from there to Bien Hoa and Da Nang. Such personnel transported the herbicide in the omnipresent 55-gallon (203 l) containers.

(3) Specialized mechanics, electricians, and technical personnel assigned to work on various aircraft. Many of this group were not specifically assigned to Ranch Hand but had to work in aircraft that were repeatedly contaminated.

Above all, the herbicides were effective. Agent Orange was used in Vietnam in undiluted form at the rate of three to four gallons (11.4-15.2 l) per acre. 13.8 pounds (6.27 kg) of the chemical 2,4,5-T were added to 12 pounds (5.5 kg) of 2,4-D per acre, a nearly 50-50 ratio. This intensity is 13.3 pounds (6.06 kg) per acre more than was recommended by the military's own manual. Computer tapes (HERBS TAPES) now available show that some areas were sprayed as much as 25 times in just a few short months, thereby dramatically increasing the exposure to anyone within those sprayed areas.

Evaluations show that the chemical had killed and defoliated 90 percent to 95 percent of the treated vegetation. Thirty six percent of all mangrove forest areas in South Vietnam were destroyed. Viet Cong tunnel openings, caves and above ground shelters were revealed to the aircraft after the herbicides were shipped in drums identified by an orange stripe and a contract identification number that enabled the government to identify the specific manufacturer. The drums were sent to a number of central transportation points for shipment to Vietnam.

Agent Orange is contaminated by the chemical **dioxin**. In Vietnam, the dioxin concentration in Agent Orange varied from **parts per billion** to **parts per million**, depending on each manufacturer's production methods. The **Environmental Protection Agency** (EPA) evacuated **Times Beach, Missouri** when tests revealed soil samples there with two parts per billion of dioxin. The EPA has stated that one p.p.b. is dangerous to humans.

Today, the use of 2,4,5-T has been phased out in the United States, but the use of 2,4-D—with the dioxin contaminant—is still permitted and is used in agriculture and by lawn care companies to control weeds.

[*Liane Clorfene Casten*]

FURTHER READING

Gough, M. "Agent Orange: Exposure and Policy." *American Journal of Public Health* 81 (March 1991): 289-90.

Husar, R. B. *Biological Basis for Risk Assessment of Dioxins and Related Compounds*. Cold Spring Harbor, NY: Cold Spring Harbor Laboratory Press, 1991.

———. *The Health Risks of Dioxin*. Hearing Before the Human Resources and Intergovernmental Relations Subcommittee on Government Operations, House of Representatives, One Hundred Second Congress, June 10, 1992. Washington, DC: U. S. Government Printing Office, 1993.

———, and M. Gough. *Dioxin, Agent Orange: The Facts*. New York: Plenum, 1986.

"A Review of the Scientific Literature: Human Health Effects Associated with Exposure to Herbicides and/or Their Associated Contaminants—Chlorinated Dioxins: Agent Orange and the Vietnam Veteran." Compiled by the Agent Orange Scientific Task Force, working with The American Legion, Vietnam Veterans of America, The National Veterans Legal Services Project. April 1990.

Schmidt, K. F. "Dioxin's Other Face: Portrait of an 'Environmental Hormone'." *Science News* 141 (11 January 1992): 24-7.

Tschirley, F. "Dioxin." *Scientific American* 254 (February 1986): 29-35.

Zumwalt, Admiral Elmo R. Jr. USN (Ret.) "Report to the Secretary of Veterans Affairs, The Hon. Edward J. Derwinski. From the Special Assistant: Agent Orange Issues." First Report, May 5, 1990.

Agglomeration

Any process by which a group of individual particles is clumped together into a single mass. The term has a number of specialized uses. Some types of rocks are formed by the agglomeration of particles of sand, clay or some other material. In geology, an agglomerate is a rock composed of volcanic fragments. One technique for dealing with **air pollution** is ultrasonic agglomeration. A source of very high frequency sound is attached to a smokestack, and the ultrasound produced by this source causes tiny **particulate** matter in waste gases to agglomerate into particles large enough to be collected.

Agricultural chemicals

The term agricultural chemical refers to any substance involved in the growth or utilization of any plant or animal of economic importance to humans. An agricultural chemical may be a natural product, such as urea, or a synthetic chemical, such as **DDT**. The agricultural **chemicals** now in use include **fertilizer**s, **pesticide**s, growth regulators, animal feed supplements, and raw materials for use in chemical processes.

In the broadest sense, agricultural chemicals can be divided into two large categories, those that promote the growth of a plant or animal and those that protect plants or animals. To the first group belong plant fertilizers and animal food supplements, and to the latter group belong pesticides, **herbicide**s, animal vaccines, and antibiotics.

In order to stay healthy and grow normally, crops require a number of **nutrient**s, some in relatively large quantities called macronutrients, and others in relatively small quantities called micronutrients. **Nitrogen**, **phosphorus**, and potassium are considered macronutrients, and boron, calcium, **chlorine**, **copper**, iron, magnesium, manganese among others are micronutrients.

Farmers have long understood the importance of replenishing the **soil**, and they have traditionally done so by natural means, using such materials as manure, dead fish, or compost. Synthetic fertilizers were first available in the early twentieth century, but they became widely used only after World War II. By 1990 farmers in the United States were using about 20 million tons (20.4 million metric tons) of these fertilizers a year.

Synthetic fertilizers are designed to provide either a single nutrient or some combination of nutrients. Examples of single-component or "straight" fertilizers are urea (NH_2CONH_2), which supplies nitrogen, or potassium chloride (KCl), which supplies potassium. The composition of "mixed" fertilizers, those containing more than one nutrient, is indicated by the analysis printed on their container. An 8-10-12 fertilizer, for example, contains 8 percent nitrogen by weight, 10 percent phosphorus, and 12 percent potassium.

Synthetic fertilizers can be designed to release nutrients almost immediately ("quick-acting") or over longer periods of time ("time-release"). They may also contain specific amounts of one or more trace nutrients needed for particular types of crops or soil. Controlling micronutrients is one of the most important problems in fertilizer compounding and use; the presence of low concentrations of some elements can be critical to a plant's health, while higher levels can be toxic to the same plants or to animals that ingest the micronutrient.

Plant growth patterns can also be influenced by direct application of certain chemicals. For example, the gibberellins are a class of compounds that can dramatically affect the rate at which plants grow and fruits and vegetables ripen. They have been used for a variety of purposes ranging from the hastening of root development to the delay of fruit ripening. Delaying ripening is most important for marketing agricultural products because it extends the time a crop can be transported and stored on grocery shelves. Other kinds of chemicals used in the processing, transporting, and storage of fruits and vegetables include those that slow down or speed up ripening (maleic hydrazide, ethylene oxide, potassium permanganate, ethylene, and acetylene are examples), that reduce weight loss (chlorophenoxyacetic acid, for example), retain green color (cycloheximide), and control firmness (ethylene oxide).

The term agricultural chemical is most likely to bring to mind the range of chemicals used to protect plants against competing organisms: pesticides and herbicides. These chemicals disable or kill bacteria, **fungi**, rodents, worms, snails and slugs, insects, mites, algae, termites, or any other **species** of plant or animal that feeds upon, competes with, or otherwise interferes with the growth of crops. Such chemicals are named according to the organism against which they are designed to act. Some examples are **fungicide**s (designed to kill fungi), insecticides (used against insects), nematicides (to kill round worms), avicides (to control birds), and herbicides (to combat plants). In 1990, 393 million tons of herbicides, 64 million tons of insecticides, and 8 million tons of other pesticides were used on American farmlands.

The introduction of synthetic pesticides in the years following World War II produced spectacular benefits for farmers. More than 50 major new products appeared between 1947 and 1967, resulting in yield increases in the United States ranging from 400 percent for corn to 150 percent for sorghum and 100 percent for wheat and soybeans. Similar increases in **less developed countries**, resulting from the use of both synthetic fertilizers and pesticides, eventually became known as the Green Revolution.

By the 1970s, however, the environmental consequences of using synthetic pesticides became obvious. Chemicals were becoming less effective as pests developed resistances to them, and their toxic effects on other organisms had grown more apparent. Farmers were also discovering drawbacks to chemical fertilizers as they found that they had to use larger and larger quantities each year in order to maintain crop yields. One solution to the environmental hazards posed by synthetic pesticides is the use of natural chemicals such as juvenile hormones, sex attractants, and anti-feedant compounds. The development of such natural **pest**-control materials has, however, been relatively modest; the vast majority of agricultural companies and individual farmers continue to use synthetic chemicals that have served them so well for over a half century.

Chemicals are also used to maintain and protect livestock. At one time, farm animals were fed almost exclusively on readily available natural foods. They grazed on **rangelands** or were fed hay or other grasses. Today, carefully blended chemical supplements are commonly added to the diet of most farm animals. These supplements have been determined on the basis of extensive studies of the nutrients that contribute to the growth or milk production of cows, sheep, goats, and other types of livestock. A typical animal supplement diet consists of various vitamins, minerals, amino acids, and nonprotein (simple) nitrogen compounds. The precise formulation depends primarily on the species; a vitamin supplement for cattle, for example, tends to include A, D, and E, while swine and poultry diets would also contain Vitamin K, riboflavin, niacin, pantothenic acid, and choline.

A number of chemicals added to animal feed serve no nutritional purpose but provide other benefits. For example, the addition of certain hormones to the feed of dairy cows can significantly increase their output of milk. **Genetic engineering** is also becoming increasingly important in the modification of crops and livestock. Cows injected with a genetically modified chemical, bovine somatotropin, produce a significantly larger quantity of milk.

It is estimated that infectious diseases cause the death of 15 to 20 percent of all farm animals each year. Just as plants are protected from pests by pesticides, so livestock are protected from disease organisms by immunization, antibiotics, and other techniques. Animals are vaccinated against species-specific diseases, and farmers administer antibiotics, sulfanamides, nitrofurans, arsenicals, and other chemicals that protect against disease-causing organisms.

The use of chemicals with livestock can have deleterious effects, just as crop chemicals have. In the 1960s, for example, the hormone diethylstilbestrol (DES) was widely used to stimulate the growth of cattle, but scientists found that detectable residues of the hormone remained in meat sold from the slaughtered animals. DES is now considered a **carcinogen**, and the U.S. **Food and Drug Administration** has banned its use in cattle feed since 1979. *See also* Agricultural pollution; Agricultural revolution; Agricultural technology; Feedlot runoff; Organic gardening and farming; Sustainable agriculture

[David E. Newton]

FURTHER READING

Benning, L. E. *Beneath the Bottom Line: Agricultural Approaches to Reduce Agrichemical Contamination of Groundwater.* Washington, DC: Office of Technology Assessment, 1990.

———, and J. H. Montgomery. *Agrochemicals Desk Reference: Environmental Data.* Boca Raton, FL: Lewis, 1993.

———, and T. E. Waddell. *Managing Agricultural Chemicals in the Environment: The Case for a Multimedia Approach.* Washington, DC: Conservation Foundation, 1988.

Chemistry and the Food System, A Study by the Committee on Chemistry and Public Affairs of the American Chemical Society. Washington, DC: American Chemical Society, 1980.

Agricultural pollution

The development of modern agricultural practices is one of the great success stories of applied sciences. Improved plowing techniques, new **pesticide**s and **fertilizer**s, and better strains of crops are among the factors that have resulted in significant increases in agricultural productivity.

Yet these improvements have not come without cost to the **environment** and sometimes to human health. Modern agricultural practices have contributed to the pollution of air, water, and land. **Air pollution** may be the most memorable, if not the most significant, of these consequences. During the 1920s and 1930s, huge amounts of fertile **topsoil** were blown away across vast stretches of the Great Plains, an area that eventually became known as the **Dust Bowl**. The problem occurred because farmers either did not know about or chose not to use techniques for protecting and conserving their **soil**. The soil then blew away during droughts, resulting not only in the loss of valuable farmland, but also in the pollution of the surrounding **atmosphere**.

Soil conservation techniques developed rapidly in the 1930s, including **contour plowing**, strip cropping, crop rotation, windbreaks, and minimum- or no-tillage farming, and thereby greatly reduced the possibility of **erosion** on such a scale. However, such events, though less dramatic, have continued to occur, and in recent decades they have presented new problems. When top soils are blown away by winds today, they can carry with them the pesticides, **herbicide**s, and other crop **chemicals** now so widely used. In the worst cases, these chemicals have contributed to the collection of air pollutants that endanger the health of plants and animals, including humans. Ammonia, released from the decay of fertilizers, is one example of a compound that may cause minor irritation to the human respiratory system and more serious damage to the health of other animals and plants.

A more serious type of agricultural pollution are the **solid waste** problems resulting from farming and livestock practices. Authorities estimate that slightly over half of all the solid wastes produced in the United States each year—a total of about 2 billion tons (2 billion metric tons)—come from a variety of agricultural activities. Some of these wastes pose little or no threat to the environment. Crop residue left on cultivated fields and animal manure produced on **rangelands**, for example, eventually decay, returning valuable **nutrient**s to the soil.

Some modern methods of livestock management, however, tend to increase the risks posed by animal wastes. Farmers are raising a larger variety of animals, as well as larger numbers of them, in smaller and smaller areas such as **feedlots** or huge barns. In such cases, large volumes of wastes are generated in these areas. Many livestock managers attempt to sell these waste products or dispose of them in a way that poses no threat to the environment. Yet in many cases the wastes are allowed to accumulate in massive dumps where soluble materials are leached out by rain. Some of these materials then find their way into **groundwater** or surface water, such as lakes and rivers. Some are harmless to the health of animals, though they may contribute to the eutrophication of lakes and ponds. Other materials, however, may have toxic, **carcinogen**ic, or genetic effects on humans and other animals.

The **leaching** of **hazardous material**s from **animal waste** dumps contributes to perhaps the most serious form of agricultural pollution: the contamination of water supplies. Many of the chemicals used in agriculture today can be harmful to plants and animals. Pesticides and herbicides are the most obvious of these; used by farmers to disable or kill plant and animal pests, they may also cause problems for beneficial plants and animals as well as humans.

Runoff from agricultural land is another serious environmental problem posed by modern agricultural practices. Runoff constitutes a **nonpoint source** of pollution. Rainfall leaches out and washes away pesticides, fertilizers, and other agricultural chemicals from a widespread area, not a single source such as a sewer pipe. Maintaining control over nonpoint sources of pollution is an especially difficult challenge. In addition, agricultural land is more easily leached out than is non-agricultural land. When lands are plowed, the earth is broken up into smaller pieces, and the finer the soil particles, the more easily they are carried away by rain. Studies have shown that the **nitrogen** and **phosphorus** in chemical fertilizers are leached out of croplands at a rate about five times higher than from forest woodlands or idle lands.

The accumulation of nitrogen and phosphorus in waterways from chemical fertilizers has contributed to the acceleration of eutrophication of lakes and ponds. Scientists believe that the addition of human-made chemicals such as those in chemical fertilizers can increase the rate of eutrophication by a factor of at least ten. A more deadly effect is the poisoning of plants and animals by toxic chemicals leached off of farmlands. The biological effects of such chemicals are commonly magnified many times as they move up a **food chain/web**. The best known example of this phenomenon involved a host of biological problems—from reduced rates of reproduction to malformed animals to increased rates of death—attributed to the use of **DDT** in the 1950s and 1960s.

Sedimentation also results from the high rate of erosion on cultivated land, and increased sedimentation of waterways poses its own set of environmental problems. Some of these are little more than cosmetic annoyances. For example, lakes and rivers may become murky and less attractive, losing potential as recreation sites. However, sedimentation can block navigation channels, and other problems may have fatal results for organisms. Aquatic plants may become covered with sediments and die; marine animals may take in sediments and be killed; and cloudiness from sediments may reduce the amount of sunlight received by aquatic plants so extensively that they can no longer survive.

Environmental scientists are especially concerned about the effects of agricultural pollution on groundwater. Groundwater is polluted by much the same mechanisms as is surface water, and evidence for that pollution has accumulated rapidly in the past decade. Groundwater pollution tends to persist for long periods of time. Water flows through an **aquifer** much more slowly than it does through a river, and agricultural chemicals are not flushed out quickly.

Many solutions are available for the problems posed by agricultural pollution, but many of them are not easily implemented. Chemicals that are found to have serious toxic effects on plants and animals can be banned from use, such as DDT in the 1970s, but this kind of decision is seldom easy. Regulators must always assess the relative benefit of using a chemical, such as increased crop yields, against its environmental risks. Such as a risk-benefit analysis means that some chemicals known to have certain deleterious environmental effects remain in use because of the harm that would be done to agriculture if they were banned.

Another way of reducing agricultural pollution is to implement better farming techniques. In the practices of minimum- or no-tillage farming, for example, plowing is reduced or eliminated entirely. Ground is left essentially intact, reducing the rate at which soil and the chemicals it contains are eroded away.

[*David E. Newton*]

FURTHER READING

Benning, L. E. *Agriculture and Water Quality: International Perspectives.* Boulder, CO: L. Rienner, 1990.

——, and L. W. Canter. *Environmental Impacts of Agricultural Production Activities.* Chelsea, MI: Lewis, 1986.

——, and M. W. Fox. *Agricide: The Hidden Crisis That Affects Us All.* New York: Shocken Books, 1986.

Crosson, P. R. *Implementation Policies and Strategies for Agricultural Non-Point Pollution.* Washington, DC: Resources for the Future, 1985.

Agricultural Research Service

A branch of the **U.S. Department of Agriculture** charged with the responsibility of agricultural research on a regional or national basis. The Agricultural Research Service (ARS) has a mission to develop new knowledge and technology needed to solve agricultural problems of broad scope and high national priority in order to ensure adequate production of high quality food and agricultural products for the United States. The national research center of the ARS is located at Beltsville, Maryland, consisting of laboratories, land, and other facilities. In addition, there are many other research centers located throughout the United States, such as the U.S. Dairy/Forage Research Center at Madison, Wisconsin.

Scientists of the ARS are also located at Land Grant Universities throughout the country where they conduct cooperative research with state scientists.

Agricultural revolution

The development of agriculture has been a fundamental part of the march of civilization. It is an ongoing challenge, for as long as **population growth** continues, mankind will need to improve agricultural production.

The agricultural revolution is actually a series of four major advances, closely linked with other key historical periods. The first, the *Neolithic* or New Stone Age, marks the beginning of sedentary (settled) farming. Much of this history is lost in antiquity, dating back perhaps 10,000 years or more. Still, humans owe an enormous debt to those early pioneers who so painstakingly nourished the best of each year's crop. Archaeologists have found corn cobs a mere two inches long, so different from today's giant ears.

The second major advance came as a result of Christopher Columbus' voyages to the New World. Isolation had fostered the development of two completely independent agricultural systems in the New and Old Worlds. A short list of interchanged crops and animals clearly illustrates the global magnitude of this event; furthermore, the current population explosion began its upswing during this period. From the New World came maize, beans, the "Irish" potato, squash, peanuts, tomatoes, and tobacco. From the Old World came wheat, rice, coffee, cattle, horses, sheep, and goats. Maize is now a staple food in Africa. Several Indian tribes in America adopted new lifestyles, notably the Navajo as sheepherders, and the Cheyenne as nomads using the horse to hunt buffalo.

The Industrial Revolution both contributed to and was nourished by agriculture. The greatest agricultural advances came in transportation, where first canals, then railroads and steamships made possible the shipment of food from areas of surplus. This in turn allowed more specialization and productivity, but most importantly, it reduced the threat of starvation. The steamship ultimately brought refrigerated meat to Europe from distant Argentina and Australia. Without these massive increases in food shipments the exploding populations and greatly increased demand for labor by newly emerging industries could not have been sustained.

In turn the Industrial Revolution introduced major advances in farm technology, such as the cotton gin, mechanical reaper, improved plows, and, in this century, tractors and trucks. These advances enabled fewer and fewer farmers to feed larger and larger populations, freeing workers to fill demands for factory labor and the growing service industries.

Finally, agriculture has fully participated in the scientific advances of the twentieth century. Key developments include hybrid corn, the high responders in tropical lands, described as the "Green Revolution," and current genetic research. Agriculture has benefitted enormously from scientific advances in biology, and the future here is bright for applied research, especially involving genetics. Great potential exists for the development of crop strains with greatly improved dietary characteristics, such as higher protein or reduced fat.

Growing populations, made possible by these food surpluses, have forced agricultural expansion onto less and less desirable lands. Because agriculture radically simplifies **ecosystem**s and greatly amplifies soil **erosion**, many areas such as the Mediterranean Basin and tropical forest lands have suffered severe degradation.

Major developments in civilization are directly linked to the agricultural revolution. A sedentary lifestyle, essential to technological development, was both mandated and made possible by farming. Urbanization flourished, which encouraged specialization and division of labor. Large populations provided the energy for massive projects, such as the Egyptian pyramids and the colossal engineering efforts of the Romans.

The plow represented the first lever, both lifting and overturning the **soil**. The draft animal provided the first in a long line of nonhuman energy sources. Plant and animal selectivity are likely the first application of science and technology toward specific goals. A number of important crops bear little resemblance to the ancestors from which they were derived. Animals such as the fat-tailed sheep represent thoughtful cultural control of their lineage.

Climate dominates agriculture, second only to **irrigation**. Farmers are especially vulnerable to variations, such as late or early frosts, heavy rains, or **drought**. Rice, wheat, and maize have become the dominant crops globally because of their high caloric yield, versatility within their climate range, and their cultural status as the "staff of life." Many would not consider a meal complete without rice, bread, or tortillas. This cultural influence is so strong that even starving peoples have rejected unfamiliar food. China provides a good example of such cultural differences, with a rice culture in the south and a wheat culture (noodles) in the north.

These crops all need a wet season for germination and growth, followed by a dry season to allow spoilage-free storage. Rice was domesticated in the **monsoon**al lands of Southeast Asia, while wheat originated in the Fertile Crescent of the Middle East. Historically, wheat was planted in the fall, and harvested in late spring, coinciding with the cycle of wet and dry seasons in the Mediterranean region. Maize needs the heavy summer rains provided by the Mexican highland climate.

Other crops predominate in areas with less suitable climates. These include barley in semiarid lands; oats and potatoes in cool, moist lands; rye in colder climates with short growing seasons; and dry rice on hillsides and drier lands where paddy rice is impractical.

Although food production is the main emphasis in agriculture, more and more industrial applications have evolved. Cloth fibers have been a mainstay, but paper products and many **chemicals** now come from cultivated plants.

The agricultural revolution is also associated with some of mankind's darker moments. In the tropical and subtropical climates of the New World, slave labor was extensive. Close, unsanitary living conditions have fostered plagues of Biblical proportions. And the desperate dependence on agriculture is all too vividly evident in the records of historic and contemporary famine. As a world, people are never more than one harvest away from global starvation, a fact amplified by the growing understanding of cosmic catastrophes.

Some argue that the agricultural revolution masks the growing hazards of an overpopulated, increasingly contaminated earth. Since the agricultural revolution has been so productive it has more than compensated for the population explosion of the last two centuries. Some appropriately labeled "cornucopians" believe there is yet much potential for increased food production, especially through scientific agriculture and **genetic engineering**. There is much room for optimism, and also for a sobering assessment of the environmental costs of agricultural progress. We must continually strive for answers to the challenges associated with the agricultural revolution. *See also* Agricultural technology; Arable land; Pesticide; Sustainable agriculture

[*Nathan H. Meleen*]

FURTHER READING

Anderson, E. "Man as a Maker of New Plants and New Plant Communities." In *Man's Role in Changing the Face of the Earth,* edited by W. L. Thomas, Jr. Chicago: The University of Chicago Press, 1956.

Crosson, P. R., and N. J. Rosenberg. "Strategies for Agriculture." *Scientific American* 261 (September 1989): 128-32+.

Doyle, J. *Altered Harvest: Agriculture, Genetics, and the Fate of the World's Food Supply.* New York: Penguin, 1985.

Gliessman, S. R., ed. *Agroecology: Researching the Ecological Basis for Sustainable Agriculture.* New York: Springer-Verlag, 1990.

Jackson, R. H., and L. E. Hudman. *Cultural Geography: People, Places, and Environment.* St. Paul, MN: West, 1990.

Narr, K. J. "Early Food-Producing Populations." In *Man's Role in Changing the Face of the Earth,* edited by W. L. Thomas, Jr. Chicago: The University of Chicago Press, 1956.

Simpson, L. B. "The Tyrant: Maize." In *The Cultural Landscape,* edited by C. Salter. Belmont, CA: Wadsworth, 1971.

Agriculture, drainage

See **Runoff**

Agricultural Stabilization and Conservation Service

For the past half century, agriculture in the United States has faced the somewhat unusual and enviable problem of overproduction. Farmers have produced more food than U.S. citizens can consume, and, as a result, per capita farm income has decreased as the volume of crops has increased. To help solve this problem, the Secretary of Agriculture established the Agricultural Stabilization and Conservation Service on June 5, 1961. The purpose of the service is to administer commodity and **land-use** programs designed to control production and to stabilize market prices and farm income. The service operates through state committees of three to five members each and committees consisting of three farmers in approximately 3,080 agricultural counties in the nation. *See also* Agricultural Research Service; U.S. Department of Agriculture

Agriculture, sustainable
See **Sustainable agriculture**

Agroecology

Agroecology is an interdisciplinary field of study that applies ecological principles to the design and management of agricultural systems. Agroecology concentrates on the relationship of agriculture to the biological, economic, political, and social systems of the world.

The combination of agriculture with ecological principles such as **biogeochemical cycles**, **energy conservation**, and **biodiversity** has led to practical applications that benefit the whole **ecosystem** rather than just an individual crop. For instance, research into **integrated pest management** has developed ways to reduce reliance on **pesticide**s. Such methods include biological or biotechnological controls such as **genetic engineering**, cultural controls such as changes in planting patterns, physical controls, such as quarantines to prevent entry of new **pest**s, and mechanical controls such as physically removing weeds or pests.

Sustainable agriculture is another goal of agroecological research. Sustainable agriculture views farming as a total system and stresses the long-term **conservation** of resources. It balances the human need for food with concerns for the environment and maintains that agriculture can be carried on without reliance on pesticides and **fertilizer**s.

Agroecology advocates the use of biological controls rather than pesticides to minimize agricultural damage from insects and weeds. Biological controls use natural enemies to control weeds and pests, such as ladybugs that kill aphids. Biological controls include the disruption of the reproductive cycles of pests and the introduction of more biologically diverse organisms to inhibit overpopulation of different agricultural pests.

Agroecological principals shift the focus of agriculture from food production alone to wider concerns, such as environmental quality, food safety, the quality of rural life, humane treatment of livestock, and conservation of air, **soil** and water. Agroecology also studies how agricultural processes and technologies will be impacted by wider environmental problems such as global warming, **desertification**, or **salinization**.

The entire world population depends on agriculture, and as the number of people continues to grow agroecology is becoming more important, particularly in developing countries. Agriculture is the largest economic activity in the world, and in areas such as sub-Saharan Africa about 75 percent of the population is involved in some form of it. As population pressures on the world food supply increase, the application of agroecological principles is expected to stem the ecological consequences of traditional agricultural practices such as pesticide poisoning and **erosion**. *See also* Agricultural chemicals; Agricultural pollution; Agricultural technology; Agroforestry; Conservation tillage; Pesticide residue

[*Linda Rehkopf*]

FURTHER READING

Altieri, M. A. *Agroecology: The Scientific Basis of Alternative Agriculture.* Boulder, CO: Westview Press, 1987.

Carroll, D. R. *Agroecology.* New York: McGraw-Hill, 1990.

Gliessman, S. R., ed. *Agroecology.* New York: Springer-Verlag, 1991.

Norse, D. "A New Strategy for Feeding a Drowned Planet." *Environment* 34 (June 1992): 6-19.

Agroforestry

Agroforestry is a **land use** system in which woody perennials (trees, shrubs, vines, palms, bamboo, etc.) are intentionally combined on the same **land management** unit with crops and sometimes animals, either in a spatial arrangement or a temporal sequence. It is based on the premise that woody perennials in the landscape can enhance the productivity and sustainability of agricultural practice. The approach is especially pertinent in tropical and subtropical areas where improper land management and intensive, continuous cropping of land have led to widespread devastation. Agroforestry recognizes the need for an alternative agricultural system that will preserve and sustain productivity. The need for both food and forest products has led to an interest in techniques that combine production of both in a manner that can halt and may even reverse the ruin caused by existing practices.

Although the term agroforestry has come into widespread use only in the last 15-20 years, environmentally sound farming methods similar to those now proposed have been known and practiced in some tropical and subtropical areas for many years. As an example, one type of intercropping found on small rubber plantations (less than 25 acres/10 hectares), in Malaysia, Thailand, Nigeria, India, and Sri Lanka involves rubber plants intermixed with fruit trees, pepper, coconuts, and arable crops such as soybeans, corn, banana, and groundnut. Poultry may also be included. Unfortunately, in other areas the pressures caused by expanding human and animal populations have led to increased use of destructive farming practices. In the process, inhabitants have further reduced their ability to provide basic food, fiber, fuel, and timber needs and contributed to even more **environmental degradation** and loss of soil fertility.

The successful introduction of agroforestry practices in problem areas requires the cooperative efforts of experts from a variety of disciplines. Along with specialists in forestry, agriculture, meteorology, **ecology**, and related fields, it is often necessary to enlist the help of those familiar with local culture and heritage to explain new methods and their advantages. Usually, techniques must be adapted to local circumstances, and research and testing are required to develop viable systems for a particular setting. Intercropping combinations that work well in one location may not be appropriate for sites only a short distance away because of important meteorological or ecological differences. Despite apparent difficulties, agroforestry has great appeal as a means of arresting problems with **deforestation** and declining agricultural yields in warmer climates. The practice is expected to grow significantly in the next several decades. Some areas of special interest include intercropping with coconuts as the woody component, and mixing tree legumes with annual crops.

Agroforestry does not seem to lend itself to mechanization as easily as the large-scale grain, soybean, and vegetable cropping systems used in industrialized nations because practices for each site are individualized and usually labor-intensive. For these reasons they have had less appeal in areas like the United States and Europe. Nevertheless, temperate zone applications have been developed or are under development. Examples include small scale **organic gardening and farming**, mining wasteland reclamation, and **biomass** energy crop production on marginal land. *See also* Agricultural Stabilization and Conservation Service; Agricultural technology; Agroecology; Arable land

[*Douglas C. Pratt*]

FURTHER READING

Huxley, P. A., ed. *Plant Research and Agroforestry*. Edinburgh, Scotland: Pillans & Wilson, 1983.

Reifsnyder, W. S., and T. O. Darnhofer, eds. *Meteorology and Agroforestry*. Nairobi, Kenya: International Council for Research in Agroforestry, 1989.

Zulberti, E., ed. *Professional Education in Agroforestry*. Nairobi, Kenya: International Council for Research in Agroforestry, 1987.

AIDS

AIDS (acquired immune deficiency syndrome) is an infectious and fatal disease of apparently recent origin. AIDS is *pandemic*, which means that it is worldwide in distribution. A sufficient understanding of AIDS can be gained only by examining its causation (etiology), symptoms, treatments, and the risk factors for transmitting and contracting the disease.

AIDS occurs as a result of infection with the HIV (human immunodeficiency virus). HIV is a ribonucleic acid (**RNA**) virus that targets and kills special blood cells, known as helper T-lymphocytes, which are important in immune

protection. Depletion of helper T-lymphocytes leaves the AIDS victim with a disabled immune system and at risk for infection by organisms that ordinarily pose no special hazard to the individual. Infection by these organisms is thus opportunistic and is frequently fatal.

The initial infection with HIV may entail no symptoms at all or relatively benign symptoms of short duration which may mimic infectious mononucleosis. This initial period is followed by a longer period (from a few to as many as ten years) when the infected person is in apparent good health. The HIV infected person, despite the outward image of good health, is in fact contagious, and appropriate care must be exercised to prevent spread of the virus at this time. Eventually the effects of the depletion of helper T cells become manifest. Symptoms include weight loss, persistent cough, persistent colds, diarrhea, periodic fever, weakness, fatigue, enlarged lymph nodes, and malaise. Following this, the AIDS patient becomes vulnerable to chronic infections by opportunistic pathogens. These include, but are not limited to oral yeast infection (thrush), pneumonia caused by the fungus *pneumocystis carinii*, and infection by several kinds of herpes viruses. The AIDS patient is vulnerable to Kaposi's sarcoma which is a **cancer** seldom seen except in those individuals with depressed immune systems. Death of the AIDS patient may be accompanied by confusion, dementia, and coma.

There is no cure for AIDS. Opportunistic infections are treated with antibiotics, and drugs such as AZT (azidothymidine), which slow the progress of the HIV infection, are available. But viral diseases in general, including AIDS, do not respond well to antibiotics. Thus, the future for an AIDS cure seems bleak. Vaccines, however, can provide protection against viral diseases. Research to find a vaccine for AIDS has not yet yielded satisfactory results, but scientists have been encouraged by the development of a vaccine for feline leukemia—a viral disease that has similarities to AIDS. Unfortunately, this does not provide hope of a cure for those already infected with the HIV virus.

Prevention is crucial for a lethal disease with no cure. Thus, modes of transmission must be identified and avoided. Who is at risk? Homosexual males who practice unprotected sex with multiple sexual partners were originally the group most likely to contract AIDS. They constituted about 58 percent of AIDS cases in the United States in 1991. At that time, intravenous drug abusers who share needles (particularly those who "boot" their drug, i.e., draw blood into the syringe to mix with the remaining drug followed by re-injection) made up another 23 percent of cases. About 6 percent of AIDS cases were homosexual males who also abused drugs. The remainder of cases were babies of mothers who had AIDS and patients, such as hemophiliacs, who received human blood clotting factors prior to the mid 1980s. However, donor blood is now carefully screened and heat treated and the risk from HIV-contaminated blood is considered to be extremely low.

AIDS cases in heterosexual males and women are on the increase, and no sexually active person can be considered "safe" from AIDS any longer. Therefore, everyone who is sexually active should be aware of the principal modes of transmission of the HIV virus—infected blood, semen from the male and genital tract secretions of the female—and use appropriate means to prevent exposure. While the virus has been identified in tears, saliva, and mother's milk, contagions by exposure to those substances seems to be significantly less.

[*Robert G. McKinnell*]

FURTHER READING

Alcamo, I. E. *AIDS, the Biological Basis*. Dubuque, Iowa: William C. Brown, 1993.

Fan, H., R. F. Connor, L. P. Villarreal. *The Biology of AIDS*. 2nd edition. Boston: Jones and Bartlett, 1991.

HIV/AIDS Surveillance Report (Published Quarterly). Atlanta, GA: National Center for Infectious Diseases, Centers for Infectious Diseases. (Single copies available free from National AIDS Information Clearing House, PO Box 6003, Rockville, MD 20849-6003).

Rhame, F. S. "Acquired Immunodeficiency Syndrome." In *Infectious Diseases*, edited by P. D. Hoeprich and M. C. Jordan. Philadelphia: Lippincott, 1989.

Air and Waste Management Association (Pittsburgh, Pennsylvania)

Founded in 1907 as the International Association for the Prevention of Smoke, this group changed its name several times as the interests of its members changed, becoming the Air and Waste Management Association (A&WMA) in the late 1980s. Although an international organization for environment professionals in more than 50 countries, the association is most active in North America and most concerned with North American environmental issues. Among its main concerns are **air pollution** control, environmental management, and waste processing and control.

A nonprofit organization that promotes the basic need for a clean **environment**, A&WMA seeks to educate the public and private sectors of the world by conducting seminars, holding workshops and conferences, and offering continuing education programs for environmental professionals in the areas of **pollution control** and **waste management**. One of its main goals is to provide "a neutral forum where all viewpoints of an environmental management issue (technical, scientific, economic, social, political and public health) receive equal consideration." Approximately ten to twelve specialty conferences are held annually, as well as five or six workshops. The topics continuously revolve and change as new issues arise.

Education is so important to A&WMA that it funds a scholarship for graduate students pursuing careers in fields related to waste management and pollution control. Although A&WMA members are all professionals, they seek to educate even the very young by sponsoring essay contests, science fairs, and community activities, and by volunteering

to speak to elementary, middle school, and high school audiences on environmental management topics.

The association's 12,000 members, all of whom are volunteers, are involved in virtually every aspect of every A&WMA project. There are 21 association sections across the United States, facilitating meetings at regional and even local levels to discuss important issues. Training seminars are an important part of A&WMA membership, and members are taught the skills necessary to run public outreach programs designed for students of all ages and the general public.

A&WMA's publications deal primarily with air pollution and waste management, and include the *Journal of the Air & Waste Management Association*, a scientific monthly; a bimonthly newsletter; a wide variety of technical books; and numerous training manuals and educational videotapes. Contact: Air and Waste Management Association, PO Box 2861, Pittsburgh, PA 15230.

[*Cathy M. Falk*]

Air pollution

A general term that covers a broad range of contaminants in the **atmosphere**. Pollution can occur from natural causes or from human activities. Discussions about the effects of air pollution have focused mainly on human health but attention is being directed to environmental quality and amenity as well. Air pollutants are found as gases or particles, and on a restricted scale they can be trapped inside buildings as indoor air pollutants. Urban air pollution has long been an important concern for civic administrators, but increasingly, air pollution has become an international problem.

The most characteristic sources of air pollution have always been **combustion** processes. Here the most obvious pollutant is **smoke**. However, the widespread use of **fossil fuels** have made sulfur and **nitrogen oxides** pollutants of great concern. With increasing use of petroleum-based fuels, a range of organic compounds have become widespread in the atmosphere.

In urban areas, air pollution has been a matter of concern since historical times. Indeed, there were complaints about smoke in Ancient Rome. The use of **coal** throughout the centuries have caused cities to be very smoky places. Along with smoke, large concentrations of **sulfur dioxide** were produced. It was this mixture of smoke and sulfur dioxide that typified the foggy streets of Victorian London, paced by such figures as Sherlock Holmes and Jack the Ripper, whose images remain linked with smoke and fog. Such situations are far less common in the cities of North America and Europe today. However, until recently, they have been evident in other cities, such as Ankara, Turkey, and Shanghai, China, that rely heavily on coal.

Coal is still burnt in large quantities to produce electricity or to refine metals, but these processes are frequently undertaken outside cities. Within urban areas, fuel use has shifted towards liquid and gaseous **hydrocarbons** (petrol

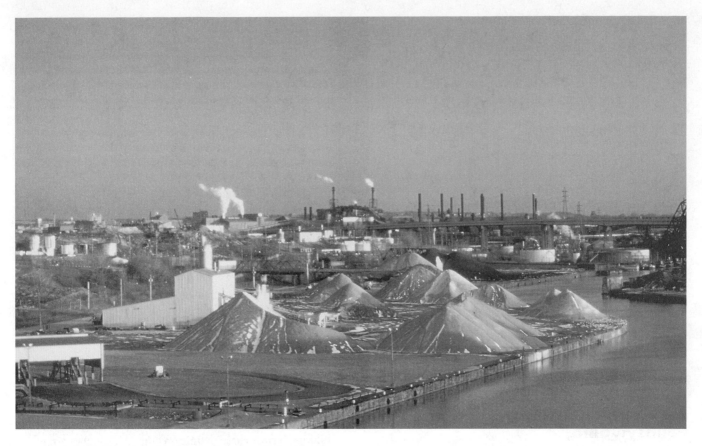

An industrial complex releasing smoke from multiple chimneys.

and **natural gas**). These fuels typically have a lower concentration of sulfur, so the presence of sulfur dioxide has declined in many urban areas. However the widespread use of liquid fuels in **automobile**s has meant increased production of **carbon monoxide**, nitrogen oxides, and **volatile organic compound**s.

Primary pollutants such as sulfur dioxide or smoke are the direct **emission** products of the combustion process. Today, many of the key pollutants in the urban atmospheres are secondary pollutants, produced by processes initiated through **photochemical reaction**s. The Los Angeles, California, type **photochemical smog** is now characteristic of urban atmospheres dominated by secondary pollutants.

Although the automobile is the main source of air pollution in contemporary cities, there are other equally significant sources. Stationary sources are still important, and the oil-burning furnaces that have replaced the older coal-burning ones are still responsible for a range of gaseous emissions and **fly ash**. **Incineration** is also an important source of complex combustion products, especially where this incineration burns a wide range of refuse. These emissions can include **chlorinated hydrocarbons** such as **dioxin**. When **plastics**, which often contain **chlorine**, are incinerated, hydrochloric acid results in the waste gas stream. Metals, especially where they are volatile at high temperatures, can migrate to smaller, respirable particles. The accumulation of toxic metals, such as **cadmium**, on fly ash gives rise to concern over harmful effects from incinerator emissions.

In specialized incinerators designed to destroy toxic compounds such as **PCB**s, many questions have been raised about the completeness of this destruction process. Even under optimum conditions where the furnace operation has been properly maintained, great care needs to be taken to control leaks and losses during transfer operations (**fugitive emissions**).

The enormous range of compounds used in modern manufacturing processes have also meant that there has been an ever-widening range of emissions from both from the industrial processes and the combustion of their wastes. Although the amounts of these exotic compounds are often rather small, they add to the complex range of compounds found in the urban atmosphere. Again, it is not only the deliberate loss of **effluent**s through **discharge** from pipes and chimneys that needs attention. Fugitive emissions of volatile substances that leak from valves and seals often warrant careful control.

Air pollution control procedures are increasingly an important part of civic administration, although their goals are far from easy to achieve. It is also noticeable that although many urban concentrations of primary pollutants, for example, smoke and sulfur dioxide, are on the decline in developed countries, this is not always true in the developing countries. Here the desire for rapid industrial growth has often lowered urban **air quality**. Secondary air pollutants are generally proving a more difficult problem to eliminate than primary pollutants like smoke.

Urban air pollutants have a wide range of effects, with health problems being the most enduring concern. In the classical polluted atmospheres filled with smoke and sulfur dioxide, a range of bronchial diseases were enhanced. While **respiratory diseases** are still the principal problem, the issues are somewhat more subtle in atmospheres where the air pollutants are not so obvious. In photochemical smog, eye irritation from the secondary pollutant **peroxyacetyl nitrate (PAN)** is one on the most characteristic direct effects of the smog. High concentrations of carbon monoxide in cities where automobiles operate at high density means that the human heart has to work harder to make up for the oxygen displaced from the blood's hemoglobin by carbon monoxide. This extra stress appears to reveal itself by increased incidence of complaints among people with heart problems. There is a widespread belief that contemporary air pollutants are involved in the increases in **asthma**, but the links between asthma and air pollution are probably rather complex and related to a whole range of factors. **Lead**, from automotive exhausts, is thought by many to be a factor in lowering the IQs of urban children.

Air pollution also affects materials in the urban environment. Soiling has long been regarded as a problem, originally the result of the smoke from wood or coal fires, but now increasingly the result of fine black soot from diesel exhausts. The acid gases, particularly sulfur dioxide, increase the rate of destruction of building materials. This is most noticeable with calcareous stones, which are the predominant building material of many important historic structures. Metals also suffer from atmospheric acidity. In the modern photochemical smog, natural rubbers crack and deteriorate rapidly.

Health problems relating to indoor air pollution are extremely ancient. Anthracosis, or **black lung disease**, has been found in mummified lung tissue. Recent decades have witnessed a shift from the predominance of concern about outdoor air pollution into a widening interest in **indoor air quality**.

The production of energy from combustion and the release of solvents is so large in the contemporary world that it causes air pollution problems of a regional and global nature. **Acid rain** is now widely observed throughout the world. The sheer quantity of carbon dioxide emitted in combustion process is increasing the concentration of carbon dioxide in the atmosphere and enhancing the **greenhouse effect**. Solvents, such as carbon tetrachloride and **aerosol** propellants (such as **chlorofluorocarbons**) are now detectable all over the globe and responsible for such problems as **ozone layer depletion**.

At the other end of the scale, we need to remember that gases leak indoors from the polluted outdoor environment, but more often the serious pollutants arise from processes that take place indoors. Here there has been particular concern with indoor air quality as regards to the generation of nitrogen oxides by sources such as gas stoves. Similarly formaldehyde from insulating foams causes illnesses and adds to concerns about our exposure to a substance that may induce **cancer** in the long run. In the last decade it

has become clear that **radon** leaks from the ground can expose some members of the public to high levels of this radioactive gas within their own homes. Cancers may also result from the emanation of solvents from consumer products, glues, paints, and mineral fibers (**asbestos**). More generally these compounds and a range of biological materials, animal hair, skin and pollen spores, and dusts can cause allergic reactions in some people. At one end of the spectrum these simply cause annoyance, but in extreme cases, such as found with the bacterium *Legionella*, a large number of deaths can occur.

There are also important issues surrounding the effects of indoor air pollutants on materials. Many industries, especially the electronics industry, must take great care over the purity of indoor air where a speck of dust can destroy a microchip or low concentrations of air pollutants change the composition of surface films in component design. Museums must care for objects over long periods of time, so precautions must be taken to protect delicate dyes from the effects of photochemical **smog**, paper and books from sulfur dioxide, and metals from sulfide gases.

[*Peter Brimblecombe*]

FURTHER READING

Bridgman, H. *Global Air Pollution: Problems for the 1990s.* New York: Columbia University Press, 1991.

Elsom, D. M. *Atmospheric Pollution.* Oxford: Blackwell, 1992.

Kennedy, D., and R. R. Bates, eds. *Air Pollution, the Automobile, and Public Health.* Washington, DC: National Academy Press, 1988.

MacKenzie, J. J. *Breathing Easier: Taking Action on Climate Change, Air Pollution, and Energy Efficiency.* Washington, DC: World Resources Institute, 1989.

Smith, W. H. *Air Pollution and Forests.* 2nd ed. New York: Springer-Verlag, 1989.

Air pollution control

The need to control **air pollution** was recognized in the earliest cities. In the Mediterranean at the time of Christ, laws were developed to place objectionable sources of odor and **smoke** downwind or outside city walls. The adoption of **fossil fuels** in thirteenth century England focused particular concern on the effect of **coal** smoke on health, with a number of attempts at regulation with regard to fuel type, chimney heights, and time of use. Given the complexity of the air pollution problem it is not surprising that these early attempts at control met with only limited success.

The nineteenth century was typified by a growing interest in urban public health. This developed against a background of continuing industrialization, which saw smoke abatement clauses incorporated into the growing body of sanitary legislation in both Europe and North America. However, a lack of both technology and political will doomed these early efforts to failure, except in the most blatantly destructive situations (for example, industrial settings such as those around Alkali Works in England).

The rise of environmental awareness in the current century has reminded us that air pollution ought not to be seen as a necessary product of industrialization. This has redirected responsibility for air pollution towards those who create it. The notion of "making the polluter pay" is seen as a central feature of air pollution control. The century has also seen the development of a range of broad air pollution control strategies, among them: (1) **Air quality** management strategies that set **ambient air** quality standards so that **emission**s from various sources can be monitored and controlled; (2) **Emission standards** strategy that sets limits for the amount of pollutant that can be emitted from a given source. These may be set to meet air quality standards, but the strategy is optimally seen as one of adopting best available techniques not entailing excessive costs (BATNEEC); (3) Economic strategies that involve charging the party responsible for the pollution. If the level of charge is set correctly, some polluters will find it more economical to install air pollution control equipment than continue to pollute. Other methods utilize a system of tradable pollution rights; (4) **Cost-benefit analysis**, which attempts to balance economic benefits with environmental costs. This is an appealing strategy but difficult to implement because of its controversial and imprecise nature.

In general air pollution strategies have either been air quality- or emission-based. In the United Kingdom, emission strategy is frequently used; for example the Alkali and Works Act of 1863 specifies permissible emissions of hydrochloric acid. By contrast, the United States has aimed to achieve air quality standards, as evidenced by the **Clean Air Act**. One criticism of using air quality strategy has been that while it improves air in poor areas it leads to degradation in areas with high air quality. Although the emission standards approach is relatively simple, it is criticized for failing to make explicit judgments about air quality and assumes that good practice will lead to an acceptable atmosphere.

Until the mid-twentieth century, legislation was primarily directed towards industrial sources, but the passage of the United Kingdom Clean Air Act (1956), which followed the disastrous **smog** of December 1952, directed attention towards domestic sources of smoke. While this particular act may have reinforced the improvements already under way, rather than initiating improvements, it has served as a catalyst for much subsequent legislative thinking. Its mode of operation was to initiate a change in fuel, perhaps one of the oldest methods of control. The other well-tried aspects were the creation of smokeless zones and an emphasis on tall chimneys to disperse the pollutants.

As simplistic as such passive control measures seem, they remain at the heart of much contemporary thinking. Changes from coal and oil to the less polluting gas or electricity have contributed to the reduction in smoke and **sulfur dioxide** concentrations in cities all around the world. Industrial zoning has often kept power and large manufacturing plants away from centers of human population, and "superstacks," chimneys of enormous height are now quite common. Successive changes in automotive fuels—lead-free **gasoline**, low volatility gas, **methanol**, or even the interest in the electric **automobile**—are further indications of continued use of these methods of control.

There are more active forms of air pollution control that seek to clean up the exhaust gases. The earliest of these were smoke and grit arrestors that came into increasing use in large electrical stations during the twentieth century. Notable here were the **cyclone collector**s that removed large particles by driving the exhaust through a tight spiral that threw the grit outward where it could be collected. Finer particles could be removed by **electrostatic precipitation**. These methods were an important part of the development of the modern pulverized fuel power station. However they failed to address the problem of gaseous emissions. Here it has been necessary to look at burning fuel in ways that reduce the production of **nitrogen oxides**. Control of sulfur dioxide emissions from large industrial plants can be achieved by desulfurization of the **flue gas**es. This can be quite successful by passing the gas through towers of solid absorbers or spraying solutions through the exhaust gas stream. However, these are not necessarily cheap options.

Catalytic converters are also an important element of active attempts to control air pollutants. Although these can considerably reduce emissions, they have to be offset against the increasing use of the automobile. There is much talk of the development of zero pollution vehicles that do not emit any pollutants.

Legislation and control methods are often associated with monitoring networks that assess the effectiveness of the strategies and inform the general public about air quality where they live. A balanced approach to the control of air pollution in the future may have to look far more broadly than simply at technological controls. It will become necessary to examine the way we structure our lives in order to find more effective solutions to air pollution.

See also Baghouse; Filters; Raprenox; Scrubbers; Tall stacks; Wet scrubber

[*Peter Brimblecombe*]

FURTHER READING

Elsom, D. M. *Atmospheric Pollution.* Oxford: Blackwell, 1992.

Luoma, J. R. *The Air Around Us: An Air Pollution Primer.* Raleigh, NC: The Acid Rain Foundation, 1989.

Wark, K., and C. F. Warner. *Air Pollution: Its Origin and Control.* 3rd ed. New York: Harper & Row, 1986.

Air pollution index

The air pollution index is a value derived from an **air quality** scale which uses the measured or predicted concentrations of several **criteria pollutant**s and other air quality indicators, such as coefficient of **haze** (COH) or **visibility**. The best known index of **air pollution** is the pollutant standard index (PSI).

The PSI has a scale that spans from 0 to 500. The index represents the highest value of several subindices; there is a subindex for each pollutant, or in some cases, for a product of pollutant concentrations and a product of pollutant concentrations and COH. If a pollutant is not monitored, its subindex is not used in deriving the PSI. In general, the subindex for each pollutant can be interpreted as follows:

Air Pollution Stages	
Index Value	**Interpretation**
0	No concentration
100	National Ambient Air Quality Standard
200	Alert
300	Warning
400	Emergency
500	Significant harm

The subindex of each pollutant or pollutant product is derived from a PSI nomogram which matches concentrations with subindex values. The highest subindex value becomes the PSI. The PSI has five health-related categories:

PSI Range	Category
0 to 50	Good
50 to 100	Moderate
100 to 200	Unhealthful
200 to 300	Very Unhealthful
300 to 500	Hazardous

See also Air Quality Control Region; Air quality criteria; Attainment area; Nonattainment area; Smog

Air quality

Air quality is determined with respect to the total **air pollution** in a given area as it interacts with meteorological conditions such as humidity, temperature and wind to produce an overall atmospheric condition. Poor air quality can manifest itself aesthetically (as a displeasing odor, for example), and can also result in harm to plants, animals, people and even damage to objects.

As early as 1881, cities such as Chicago, Illinois and Cincinnati, Ohio had passed laws to control some types of pollution, but it wasn't until several air pollution catastrophes occurred in the twentieth century that governments began to give more attention to air quality problems. For instance, in 1930, **smog** trapped in the Meuse River Valley in Belgium caused 60 deaths. Similarly, in 1948, smog was blamed for 20 deaths in Donora, Pennsylvania. Most dramatically, in 1952 a sulfur-laden fog enshrouded London for five days and caused as many as 4,000 deaths over two weeks.

Disasters such as these prompted governments in a number of industrial countries to initiate programs to protect air quality. The year of the London tragedy, the United States passed the Air Pollution Control Act granting funds to assist the states in controlling airborne pollutants. In 1963, the **Clean Air Act**, which began to place authority for air quality into the hands of the federal government, was established. Today the Clean Air Act, with its 1970 and 1990 amendments, remains the principal air quality law in the United States.

The Act established a **National Ambient Air Quality Standard** under which federal, state and local monitoring stations at thousands of locations, together with temporary stations set up by the **Environmental Protection Agency (EPA)** and other federal agencies, directly measure pollutant concentrations in the air and compare those concentrations with national standards for six major pollutants: **ozone, carbon monoxide, nitrogen oxide**s, **lead, particulate**s, and **sulfur dioxide**. When the air we breathe contains amounts of these pollutants in excess of EPA standards, it is deemed unhealthy, and regulatory action is taken to reduce the pollution levels.

In addition, urban and industrial areas maintain an **air pollution index**. This scale, a composite of several pollutant levels recorded from a particular monitoring site or sites, yields an overall air quality value. If the index exceeds certain values public warnings are given; in severe instances residents might be asked to stay indoors and factories might even be closed down.

While such air quality emergencies seem increasingly rare in the United States, developing countries, as well as Eastern European nations, continue to suffer poor air quality, especially in urban areas such as Bangkok, Thailand and **Mexico City, Mexico**. In Mexico City, for example, seven out of ten newborns have higher lead levels in their blood than the World Health Organization considers acceptable. At present, many **Third World** countries place national economic development ahead of **pollution control**—and in many countries with rapid industrialization, high population growth, or increasing per capita income, the best efforts of governments to maintain air quality are outstripped by rapid proliferation of automobiles, escalating factory emissions, and runaway urbanization.

For all the progress the U.S. has made in reducing **ambient air** pollution, *indoor* air pollution may pose even greater risks than all of the pollutants we breathe outdoors. The Radon Gas and Indoor Air Quality Act of 1986 directed the EPA to research and implement a public information and technical assistance program on indoor air quality. From this program has come monitoring equipment to measure an individual's "total exposure" to pollutants both in indoor and outdoor air. Studies done using this equipment have shown indoor exposures to toxic air pollutants far exceed outdoor exposures for the simple reason that most people spend 90 percent of their time in office buildings, homes, and other enclosed spaces. Moreover, nationwide energy conservation efforts following the oil crisis of the 1970s led to building designs that trap pollutants indoors, thereby exacerbating the problem. *See also* Air Quality Control Region; Air quality criteria; Attainment area; Eastern European pollution; Indoor air quality; Nonattainment area; Radon

[*David Clarke and Jeffrey Muhr*]

FURTHER READING

Brown, Lester, ed. *The World Watch Reader On Global Environmental Issues.* Washington, DC: Worldwatch Institute, 1991.

Council on Environmental Quality. *Environmental Trends.* Washington, DC: U. S. Government Printing Office, 1989.

Environmental Progress and Challenges: EPA's Update. Washington, DC: U. S. Environmental Protection Agency, 1988.

Air Quality Control Region (AQCR)

The **Clean Air Act** defines an Air Quality Control Region as a contiguous area where **air quality**, and thus **air pollution**, is relatively uniform. In those cases where **topography** is a factor in air movement, AQCRs often correspond with **airshed**s. AQCRs may consist of two or more cities, counties or other governmental entities, and each region is required to adopt consistent **pollution control** measures across the political jurisdictions involved. AQCRs may even cross state lines and, in these instances, the states must cooperate in developing pollution control strategies. Each AQCR is treated as a unit for the purposes of pollution reduction and achieving **National Ambient Air Quality Standards**. As of 1993, most AQCRs had achieved national air quality standards; however the remaining AQCRs where standards had not been achieved were a significant group, where a large percentage of the United States population dwelled. AQCRs involving major metro areas like Los Angeles, New York, Houston, Denver, and Philadelphia were not achieving air quality standards because of **smog**, motor vehicle emissions, and other pollutants.

Air quality criteria

The relationship between the level of exposure to air pollutant concentrations and the adverse effects on health or public welfare associated with such exposure. Air quality criteria are critical in the development of **ambient air** quality standards which define levels of acceptably safe exposure to an air pollutant. *See also* Air pollution; Clean Air Act; National Ambient Air Quality Standard

Air-pollutant transport

Air-pollutant transport is the advection or horizontal convection of air pollutants from an area where **emission** occurs to a downwind receptor area by local or regional winds. It is sometimes referred to as atmospheric transport of air pollutants. This movement of **air pollution** is often simulated with computer models for **point source**s as well as for large diffuse sources such as urban regions.

In some cases, strong regional winds or low-level nocturnal jets can carry pollutants hundreds of miles from source areas of high emissions. The possibility of transport over such distances can be increased through topographic channelling of winds through valleys. Air-pollutant transport over such distances is often referred to as long-range transport.

Air-pollutant transport is an important consideration in **air quality** planning. Where such impact occurs, the success of an air quality program may depend on the ability of air **pollution control** agencies to control upwind sources. *See also* Air pollution index; Air Quality Control Region; Air quality criteria; Atmospheric inversion

Airshed

A geographical region, usually a topographical basin, that tends to have uniform air quality. The **air quality** within an airshed is influenced predominantly by **emission** activities native to that airshed, since the elevated **topography** around the basin constrains horizontal air movement. Pollutants move from one part of an airshed to other parts fairly quickly, but are not readily transferred to adjacent airsheds. An airshed tends to have a relatively uniform climate and relatively uniform meteorological features at any given point in time. *See also* Watershed

Alar

Alar is the trade name for the chemical compound daminozide, manufactured by the Uniroyal Chemical Company. The compound has been used since 1968 to keep apples from falling off trees before they are ripe and to keep them red and firm during storage. As late as the early 1980s, up to 40 percent of all red apples produced in the United States were treated with Alar.

In 1985, the **Environmental Protection Agency (EPA)** found that UDMH (N,N-dimethylhydrazine), a compound produced during the breakdown of daminozide, was a **carcinogen**. UDMH was routinely produced during the processing of apples, as in the production of apple juice and apple sauce, and the EPA suggested a ban on the use of Alar by apple growers. An outside review of the EPA studies, however, suggested that they were flawed, and the ban was not instituted. Instead, the agency recommended that Uniroyal conduct further studies on possible health risks from daminozide and UDMH.

Even without a ban, Uniroyal felt the impact of the EPA's research well before its own studies were concluded. Apple growers, fruit processors, legislators, and the general public were all frightened by the possibility that such a widely used chemical might be carcinogenic. Many growers, processors, and store owners pledged not to use the compound nor to buy or sell apples on which it had been used. By 1987, sales of Alar had dropped by 75 percent.

In 1989, two new studies again brought the subject of Alar to the public's attention. The consumer research organization Consumers' Union found that, using a very sensitive test for the chemical, 11 of 20 red apples they tested contained Alar. In addition, 23 of 44 samples of apple juice tested contained detectable amounts of the compound. The **Natural Resources Defense Council** (NRDC) announced their findings on the compound at about the same time. The NRDC concluded that Alar and certain other **agricultural chemicals** pose a threat to children about 240 times higher than the one-in-a-million risk traditionally used by the EPA to determine the acceptability of a product used in human foods.

The studies by the NRDC and the Consumers' Union created a panic among consumers, apple growers, and apple processors. Many stores removed all apple products from their shelves, and some growers destroyed their whole crop of apples. The industry suffered millions of dollars in damage. Representatives of the apple industry continued to question how much of a threat Alar truly posed to consumers, claiming that the carcinogenic risks identified by the EPA, NRDC, and Consumers' Union were greatly exaggerated. But in May of that same year, the EPA announced interim data from its most recent study, which showed that UDMH caused blood-vessel tumors in mice. The agency once more declared its intention to ban Alar, and within a month, Uniroyal announced it would end sales of the compound in the United States. *See also* Agricultural technology; Cancer; Herbicide; Organic gardening and farming; Pesticide; Pesticide residue

[*David E. Newton*]

FURTHER READING

"Alar: Not Gone, Not Forgotten." *Consumer Reports* 52 (May 1989): 288-292.

Roberts, L. "Alar: The Numbers Game." *Science* 243 (17 March 1989): 1430.

———. "Pesticides and Kids." *Science* 243 (10 March 1989): 1280-1281.

Alaska Highway

The Alaska Highway, sometimes referred to as the Alcan (*Al*aska-*Can*ada) Highway, is the final link of a binational transportation corridor that provides an overland route between the lower United States and Alaska. The first, all-weather, 1,522-mile (2,451 km) Alcan Military Highway was hurriedly constructed during 1942-43 to provide land access between Dawson Creek, a Canadian village in northeastern British Columbia, and Fairbanks, a town on the Yukon River in central Alaska. Construction of the road was motivated by perception of a strategic, but ultimately

The route of the Alaska (or Alcan) Highway.

unrealized, Japanese threat to maritime supply routes to Alaska during the Second World War.

The route of the Alaska Highway extended through what was then a **wilderness**. An aggressive technical vision was supplied by the United States **Army Corps of Engineers** and the civilian U.S. Public Roads Administration and labor by approximately 11,000 American soldiers and 16,000 American and Canadian civilians. In spite of the extraordinary difficulties of working in unfamiliar and inhospitable terrain, the route was opened for military passage in less than two years. Among the formidable challenges faced by the workers was a need to construct 133 bridges and thousands of smaller culverts across energetic watercourses, the infilling of alignments through a boggy muskeg capable of literally swallowing bulldozers, and working in winter temperatures that were so cold that vehicles were not turned off for fear they would not restart (steel dozer-blades became so brittle that they cracked upon impact with rock or frozen ground).

In hindsight, the planning and construction of the Alaska Highway could be considered an unmitigated environmental debacle. The enthusiastic engineers were almost totally inexperienced in the specialized techniques of arctic construction, especially about methods dealing with **permafrost**, or permanently frozen ground. If the integrity of permafrost is not maintained during construction, then this underground, ice-rich matrix will thaw and become unstable, and its water content will run off. An unstable morass could be produced by the resulting **erosion**, mudflow, slumping, and thermokarst-collapse of the land into subsurface voids left by the loss of water. Repairs were very difficult, and reconstruction was often unsuccessful, requiring abandonment of some original alignments. Physical and biological disturbances caused terrestrial landscape scars that persist to this day and will continue to be visible (especially from the air) for centuries. Extensive reaches of aquatic **habitat** were secondarily degraded by erosion and/or **sedimentation**. The much more careful, intensively scrutinized, and ecologically sensitive approaches used in the Arctic today, for example during the planning and construction of the **trans Alaska pipeline**, are in marked contrast with the unfettered and free-wheeling engineering associated with the initial construction of the Alaska Highway.

The Alaska Highway has been more-or-less continuously upgraded since its initial completion and was opened to unrestricted traffic in 1947. Non-military benefits of the Alaska Highway include provision of access to a great region of the interior of northwestern North America. This access fostered economic development through mining, forestry, trucking, and tourism, as well as helping to diminish the perception of isolation felt by many northern residents living along the route.

Compared with the real dangers of vehicular passage along the Alaska Highway during its earlier years, today the route safely provides one of North America's most spectacular **ecotourism** opportunities. Landscapes range from alpine **tundra** to expansive boreal forest, replete with abundantly cold and vigorous streams and rivers. There are abundant opportunities to view large mammals such as moose (*Alces alces*), caribou (*Rangifer tarandus*), and bighorn sheep (*Ovis canadensis*), as well as charismatic smaller mammals and birds and a wealth of interesting arctic, boreal, and alpine species of plants.

[*Bill Freedman*]

FURTHER READING

Alexandra, V., and K. Van Cleve. "The Alaska Pipeline: A Success Story." *Annual Review of Ecological Systems* 14 (1983): 443-63.

Christy, J. *Rough Road to the North*. Markham, ON: Paperjacks, 1981.

Alaska National Interest Lands Conservation Act (1980)

Commonly known as the Alaska Lands Act, this law protected 104 million acres (42 million ha), or 28 percent, of the state's 375 million acres (152 million ha) of land. The law added 44 million acres (18 million ha) to the **national park** system, 55 million acres (22.3 million ha) to fish and **wildlife refuge** system, 3 million acres (1.2 million ha) to **national forest** system, and made 26 additions to national wild and scenic rivers system. The law also designated 56.7 million acres (23 million ha) of land as **wilderness**, with the stipulation that 70 million acres (28.4 million ha) of additional land be reviewed for possible wilderness designation.

The genesis of this act can be traced to 1959, when Alaska became the forty-ninth state. As part of the statehood act, Alaska could choose 104 million acres (42.1 million ha) of federal land to be transferred to the state. This selection process was halted in 1966 to clarify land claims made by Alaskan **indigenous peoples**. In 1971, the Alaska Native Claims Settlement Act was passed to satisfy the native land claims and allow the state selection process to continue. This act stipulated that the Secretary of the Interior could withdraw 80 million acres (32.4 million ha) of land for protection as national parks and monuments, fish and wildlife refuges,

and national forests, and that these lands would not be available for state or native selection. Congress would have to approve these designations by 1978. If Congress failed to act, the state and the natives could select any lands not already protected. These lands were referred to as national interest or d(2) lands.

Secretary of the Interior Rogers Morton recommended 83 million acres (33.6 million ha) for protection in 1973, but this did not satisfy environmentalists. The ensuing conflict over how much and which lands should be protected, and how these lands should be protected, was intense. The environmental community formed the Alaska Coalition, which by 1980 included over 1500 national, regional, and local organizations with a total membership of 10 million people. The state of Alaska and development-oriented interests launched a fierce and well-financed campaign to reduce the area of protected land. In 1978, the House, under the leadership of Morris Udall of Arizona, passed a bill protecting 124 million acres (50.2 million ha). The Senate passed a bill protecting far less land, and House-Senate negotiations over a compromise broke down in October. Thus, Congress would not act before the December 1978 deadline. In response, the executive branch acted. Department of the Interior Secretary Cecil Andrus withdrew 110 million acres (44.6 million ha) from state selection and mineral entry. President Jimmy Carter then designated 56 million acres (22.7 million ha) of these lands as national monuments under the authority of the Antiquities Act. Forty million additional acres (16.2 million ha) were withdrawn as fish and wildlife refuges, and 11 million acres (4.5 million ha) of existing national forests were withdrawn from state selection and mineral entry. Carter indicated that he would rescind these actions once Congress had acted.

In 1979, the House passed a bill protecting 127 million acres (51.4 million ha). The Senate passed a bill designating 104 million acres (42.1 million ha) as national interest lands in 1980. Environmentalists and the House were unwilling to reduce the amount of land to be protected. In November, however, Ronald Reagan was elected President, and the environmentalists and the House decided to accept the Senate bill rather than face the potential for much less land under a President who would side with development interests. President Carter signed the bill into law on December 2, 1980.

[*Christopher McGrory Klyza*]

FURTHER READING

Allin, C. W. *The Politics of Wilderness Preservation*. Westport, CT: Greenwood Press, 1982.

Nash, R. *Wilderness and the American Mind*. 3rd ed. New Haven, CT: Yale University Press, 1982.

Alaska pipeline

See **Trans Alaska pipeline**

Albedo

The reflecting power of a surface, expressed as a ratio of reflected radiation to incident or incoming radiation; it is sometimes expressed as a percentage. Albedo is also called the "reflection coefficient" and derives from the Latin root word *albus*, which means whiteness. Sometimes expressed as a percentage, albedo is more commonly measured as a fraction on a scale from zero to one, with a value of one denoting a completely reflective, white surface, while a value of zero would describe an absolutely black surface that reflects no light rays.

Albedo varies with surface characteristics such as color and composition, as well as with the angle of the sun. The albedo of natural earth surface features such as oceans, forests, **desert**s, and crop canopies varies widely. Some measured values of albedo for various surfaces are shown below:

Type of Surface	Albedo
Fresh, dry snow cover	0.80-0.95
Aged or decaying snow cover	0.40-0.70
Oceans	0.07-0.23
Dense clouds	0.70-0.80
Thin clouds	0.25-0.50
Tundra	0.15-0.20
Desert	0.25-0.29
Coniferous forest	0.10-0.15
Deciduous forest	0.15-0.20
Field crops	0.20-0.30
Bare dark soils	0.05-0.15

The albedo of clouds in the **atmosphere** is important to life on earth because extreme levels of radiation absorbed by the earth would make the planet uninhabitable; at any moment in time about 50 percent of the planet's surface is covered by clouds. The mean albedo for the earth, called the planetary albedo, is about 30 to 35 percent.

[*Mark W. Seeley*]

Algal bloom

Algae are simple, single-celled, filamentous aquatic plants; they grow in colonies and are commonly found floating in ponds, lakes, and oceans. Populations of algae fluctuate with the availability of **nutrient**s, and a sudden increase in nutrients often results in a profusion of algae known as algal bloom.

The growth of a particular algal **species** can be both sudden and massive. Algal cells can increase to very high densities in the water, often thousands of cells per milliliter,

and the water itself can be colored brown, red, or green. Algal blooms occur in freshwater systems and in marine environments, and they usually disappear in a few days to a few weeks. These blooms consume oxygen, increase turbidity, and clog lakes and streams. Some algal species release water-soluble compounds that may be toxic to fish and shellfish, resulting in **fish kills** and poisoning episodes.

Algal groups are generally classified on the basis of the pigments that color their cells. The most common algal groups are blue-green algae, green algae, red algae, and brown algae. Algal blooms in freshwater lakes and ponds tend to be caused by blue-green and green algae. The excessive amounts of nutrients that cause these blooms are often the result of human activities. For example, **nitrates** and phosphates introduced into a lake from fertilizer runoff during a storm can cause rapid algal growth. Some common blue-green algae known to cause blooms as well as release nerve toxins are *Microcystis, Nostoc,* and *Anabaena.*

Red tides in coastal areas are a type of algal bloom. They are common in many parts of the world, including the **New York Bight**, the Gulf of California, and the Red Sea. The causes of algal blooms are not as well understood in marine environments as they are in freshwater systems. Although human activities may well have an effect on these events, weather conditions probably play a more important role: turbulent storms which follow long, hot, dry spells have often been associated with algal blooms at sea. Toxic red tides most often consist of genera from the dinoflagellate algal group such as *Gonyaulax* and *Gymnodinium.* The potency of the toxins has been estimated to be 10 to 50 times higher than cyanide or curare, and people who eat exposed shellfish may suffer from paralytic shellfish poisoning within 30 minutes of consumption. A **fish kill** of 500 million fish was reported from a red tide in Florida in 1947. A number of blue-green algal genera such as *Oscillatoria* and *Trichodesmium* have also been associated with red blooms, but they are not necessarily toxic in their effects. Some believe that the blooms caused by these genera gave the Red Sea its name.

The economic and health consequences of algal blooms can be sudden and severe, but the effects are generally not long lasting. There is little evidence that algal blooms have long-term effects on **water quality** or **ecosystem** structure. *See also* Algicide; Nitrogen cycle

[*Usha Vedagiri and Douglas Smith*]

FURTHER READING

Culotta, E. "Red Menace in the World's Oceans." *Science* 257 (11 September 1992): 1476-77.

Lerman, M. *Marine Biology: Environment, Diversity and Ecology.* Menlo Park, CA: Benjamin/Cummings, 1986.

Mlot, C. "White Water Bounty: Enormous Ocean Blooms of White-Plated Phytoplankton Are Attracting the Interest of Scientists." *Bioscience* 39 (April 1989): 222-24.

Algicide

The presence of nuisance algae can cause unsightly appearance, odors, slime, and coating problems in aquatic media. Algicides are chemical agents used to control or eradicate the growth of algae in aquatic media such as industrial tanks, swimming pools and lakes. These agents used may vary from simple inorganic compounds such as copper sulphate which are broad-spectrum in effect and control a variety of algal groups to complex organic compounds that are targeted to be species-specific in their effects. Algicides usually require repeated application or continuous application at low doses in order to maintain effective control.

Allelopathy

Derived from the Greek words *allelo* (other) and *pathy* (causing injury to), allelopathy is a form of **competition** among plants. One plant produces and releases a chemical into the surrounding **soil** that inhibits the germination or growth of other species in the immediate area. These chemical substances are both acids and bases and are called secondary compounds. For example, black walnut (*Jugans nigra*) trees release a chemical called juglone which prevents other plants such as tomatoes from growing in the immediate area around each tree. In this way, plants such as black walnut reduce competition for space, **nutrient**s, water, and sunlight.

Allergen

Any substance that can bring about an allergic response in an organism. Hay fever and **asthma** are two common allergic responses. The allergens that evoke these responses include pollen, **fungi**, and dust. Allergens can be described as host-specific agents in that a particular allergen may affect some individuals, but not others. A number of air pollutants are known to be allergens. Formaldehyde, thiocyanates, and epoxy resins are examples. People who are allergic to natural allergens, such as pollen, are more inclined to be sensitive also to synthetic allergens, such as formaldehyde. *See also* Air pollution

All-terrain vehicle
See **Off-road vehicle**

Alligator, American (*Alligator mississippiensis*)

The American alligator is a member of the reptilian family Crocodylidae, which consists of 21 **species** found in tropical and subtropical regions throughout the world. It is a species which has been reclaimed from the brink of **extinction**.

Historically, the American alligator ranged in the Gulf and Atlantic coast states from Texas to the Carolinas, with rather large populations concentrated in the swamps and river bottomlands of Florida and Louisiana. From the late nineteenth century into the middle of the twentieth century, the population of this species decreased dramatically. With no restrictions on their activities, hunters killed alligators as **pest**s or to harvest their skin, which was highly valued in the leather trade. The American alligator was killed in such great numbers that biologists predicted its probable extinction. It has been estimated that about 3.5 million of these reptiles were slaughtered in Louisiana between 1880 and 1930. The population was also impacted by the fad of selling young alligators as pets, principally in the 1950s.

States began to take action in the early 1960s to save the alligator from extinction. In 1963 Louisiana banned all legalized trapping, closed the alligator hunting season, and stepped up enforcement of game laws against poachers. By the time the **Endangered Species Act** was passed in 1973, the species was already experiencing a rapid recovery. Because of the successful re-establishment of alligator populations, its endangered classification was downgraded in several southeastern states, and there are now strictly regulated seasons that allow alligator trapping. Due to the persistent demand for its hide for leather goods and an increasing market for the reptile's meat, alligator farms are now both legal and profitable.

Human fascination with large, dangerous animals, along with the American alligator's near extinction, have made it one of North America's best studied reptile species. Population pressures, primarily resulting from being hunted so ruthlessly for decades, have resulted in a decrease in the maximum size attained by this species. The growth of a reptile is indeterminate, and they continue to grow as long as they are alive, but old adults from a century ago attained larger sizes than their counterparts do today. The largest recorded American alligator was an old male killed in January, 1890, in Vermilion Parish, Louisiana, which measured 19 feet 2 inches (6 m) long. The largest female ever taken was only about half that size.

Alligators do not reach sexual maturity until they are about 6 feet long (1.3 m) and are nearly 10 years old. Females construct a nest mound in which they lay an average of about 40 eggs. The nest is usually 5 to 7 feet (1.5-2.1 m) in diameter and 2 to 3 feet (0.6-0.9 m) high, and decaying vegetation produces heat which keeps the eggs at a fairly constant temperature during incubation. The young stay with their mother through their first winter, striking out on their own when they are about one and a half feet (0.5 m) in length.

[*Eugene C. Beckham*]

FURTHER READING

Crocodiles. Proceedings of the 9th Working Meeting of the IUCN/SSC Crocodile Specialist Group, Lae, Papua New Guinea. Vol. 2. Gland, Switzerland: IUCN-The World Conservation Union, 1990.

Dundee, H. A., and D. A. Rossman. *The Amphibians and Reptiles of Louisiana.* Baton Rouge: LSU Press, 1989.

Webb, G. J. W., S. C. Manolis, and P. J. Whitehead, eds. *Wildlife Management: Crocodiles and Alligators.* Chipping Norton, Australia: Surrey Beatty and Sons, 1987.

Alpha particle

A particle emitted by certain kinds of radioactive materials. An alpha particle is identical to the nucleus of a helium atom, consisting of two protons and two **neutron**s. Some common alpha-particle emitters are **uranium**-235, uranium-238, radium-226, and **radon**-222. Alpha particles have relatively low penetrating power. They can be stopped by a thin sheet of paper or by human skin. They constitute a health problem, therefore, only when they are taken into the body. The inhalation of alpha-emitting radon gas escaping from bedrock into houses in some areas is thought to constitute a health hazard. *See also* Radioactivity

Alternative energy sources

Coal, oil, and **natural gas** provide over 85% of the total primary energy used around the world. Although figures differ in various countries, nuclear reactors and hydroelectric power together produce less than 10% of the total world energy. Wind power, active and passive solar systems, and **geothermal energy** are examples of alternative energy sources. Collectively, these make up the final small fraction of total energy production.

The exact contribution alternative energy sources make to the total primary energy used around the world is not known. Conservative estimates place their share at 3-4%, but some energy experts dispute these figures. **Amory Lovins** has argued that the statistics collected are based primarily on large **electric utilities** and the regions they serve. They fail to account for areas remote from major power grids, which are more likely to use **solar energy**, **wind energy**, or other sources. When these areas are taken into consideration, Lovins claims, alternative energy sources contribute as much as 11% to the total primary energy used in the United States. Animal manure, furthermore, is widely used as an energy source in India, parts of China, and many African nations, and when this is taken into account the percentage of the worldwide contribution alternative sources make to energy production could rise as high as 10-15%.

Now an alternative energy source, wind power is one of the earliest forms of energy used by humankind. Wind is caused by the uneven heating of the earth's surface, and its energy is equal to about 2% of the solar energy that reaches the earth. In quantitative terms, the amount of kinetic energy within the earth's **atmosphere** is equal to about 10,000 trillion kilowatt hours.

The kinetic energy of wind is proportional to the wind velocity, and the ideal location for a windmill generator is an area with constant and relatively fast winds and no obstacles such as buildings or trees. An efficient windmill can produce 175 watts per square meter of propeller blade area at a height of 75 feet (25 m). The estimated cost of generating one kilowatt hour by wind power is about eight cents, as compared to five cents for hydropower and fifteen cents for **nuclear power**. The largest two utilities in California purchase wind-generated electricity, and though this state leads the country in the utilization of wind power, Denmark leads the world. The Scandinavian nation has refused to use nuclear power, and by the turn of the century it expects to obtain 10% of its energy needs from windmills.

Solar energy can be utilized either directly as heat or indirectly by converting it to electrical power using **photovoltaic cell**s. Greenhouses and solariums are the most common examples of the direct use of solar energy, with glass windows concentrating the visible light from the sun but restricting the heat from escaping. Flatplate collectors are another direct method, and mounted on rooftops they can provide one third of the energy required for space heating. Windows and collectors alone are considered passive systems; an active solar system uses a fan, pump, or other machinery to transport the heat generated from the sun.

Photovoltaic cells are made of semiconductor materials such as silicon. These cells are capable of absorbing part of the solar flux to produce a direct electric current with about 14% efficiency. The current cost of producing photovoltaic current is about four dollars a watt. However, a thin-film technology is being perfected for the production of these cells, and the cost per watt will eventually be reduced because less materials will be required. Photovoltaics are now being used economically in lighthouses, boats, rural villages, and other remote areas. Large solar systems have been most effective using trackers that follow the sun or mirror reflectors that concentrate its rays.

Geothermal energy is the natural heat generated in the interior of the earth, and like solar energy it can also be used directly as heat or indirectly to generate electricity. Steam is classified as either dry (no water droplets), or wet (mixed with water). When it is generated in certain areas containing corrosive sulfur compounds, it is known as "sour steam," and when generated in areas that are free of sulfur it is known as "sweet steam." Geothermal energy can be used to generate electricity by the flashed steam method, in which high temperature geothermal brine is used as a heat exchanger to convert injected water into steam. The produced steam is used to turn a turbine. When geothermal wells are not hot enough to create steam, a fluid which evaporates at a much lower temperature than water, such as isobutane or ammonia, can be placed in a closed system where the geothermal heat provides the energy to evaporate the fluid and run the turbine.

There are 20 countries worldwide that utilize this energy source, and they include the United States, Mexico, Italy, Iceland, Japan, and the former Soviet Union. Unlike solar energy and wind power, geothermal energy is not free of environmental impact. It contributes to **air pollution**, it can emit dissolved salts and, in some cases, toxic heavy metals such as **mercury** and **arsenic**.

Though there are several ways of utilizing energy from the ocean, the most promising are the harnessing of **tidal power** and **ocean thermal energy conversion**. The power of ocean tides is based on the difference between high and low water. In order for tidal power to be effective the differences in height need to be very great, more than three meters or fifteen feet, and there are only a few places in the world where such differences exist. These include the Bay of Fundy and a few sites in China. Ocean thermal energy conversion utilizes temperature changes rather than tides. Ocean temperature is stratified, especially near the tropics, and the process takes advantage of this fact by using a fluid with a low boiling point, such as ammonia. The vapor from the fluid drives a turbine, and cold water from lower depths is pumped up to condense the vapor back into liquid. The electrical power generated by this method can be shipped to shore or used to operate a floating plant such as a cannery.

Other sources of alternative energy are currently being explored, some of which are still experimental. These include harnessing the energy in **biomass** through the production of wood from trees or the production of **ethanol** from crops such as sugar cane or corn. **Methane** gas can be generated from the **anaerobic** breakdown of **organic waste** in sanitary **landfill**s and from **wastewater** treatment plants. With the cost of **garbage** disposal rapidly increasing, the burning of garbage is becoming a viable option as an energy source. Adequate **air pollution control**s are necessary, but trash can be burned to heat buildings, and municipal garbage is currently being used to generate electricity in Hamburg, Germany. In an experimental method known as *magnetohydrodynamics*, hot gas is ionized (potassium and sulfur) and passed through a strong magnetic field where it produces an electrical current. This process contains no moving parts and has an efficiency of 20-30%.

Ethanol and **methanol** can be produced from **biomass** and used in transportation; in fact, methanol currently powers Indianapolis race cars. Hydrogen could be valuable if problems of supply and storage can be solved. It is very clean-burning, forming water, and may be combined with oxygen in **fuel cells** to generate electricity. Also, it is not nearly as explosive as **gasoline**.

Of all the alternative sources, **energy conservation** is perhaps the most important, and improving **energy efficiency** is the best way to meet energy demands without adding to air and **water pollution**. One reason the United States survived the energy crises of the 1970s was that we were able to curtail some of our immense waste. Relatively easy lifestyle alterations, vehicle improvements, building insulation, and more efficient machinery and appliances have significantly reduced our potential energy demand. Experts have estimated that it is possible to double the efficiency of electric motors, triple the intensity of light bulbs, quadruple the efficiency of refrigerators and air conditioners, and quintuple the **gasoline** mileage of **automobile**s. Several automobile manufacturers in Europe and Japan have already produced prototype vehicles with very high gasoline mileage. Volvo has developed the LCP 2000, a passenger sedan that holds four to five people, meets all United States safety standards, accelerates from 0-50 MPH (0-80.5 km/hr) in eleven seconds, and has a high fuel efficiency rating. Alternative fuels will be required to meet future energy needs. Enormous investments in new technology and equipment will be needed, and potential supplies are uncertain, but there is clearly hope for an energy-abundant future. *See also* Energy and the environment; Energy policy; Fossil fuels; Fuel-

switching; Gasohol; Nuclear energy; Renewable resources; Synthetic fuels; Wave power; Wind energy

[*Muthena Naseri and Douglas Smith*]

FURTHER READING

Alternative Energy Handbook. Englewood Cliffs, NJ: Prentice Hall, 1993.

Brower, M. *Cool Energy: Renewable Solutions to Environmental Problems.* Cambridge: MIT Press, 1992.

Brown, Lester R., ed. *The World Watch Reader on Global Environmental Issues.* New York: W. W. Norton, 1991.

Goldemberg, J. *Energy for a Sustainable World.* New York: Wiley, 1988.

Schaeffer, J. *Alternative Energy Sourcebook: A Comprehensive Guide to Energy Sensible Technologies.* Ukiah, CA: Real Goods Trading Corp., 1992.

Shea, C. P. *Renewable Energy: Today's Contribution, Tomorrow's Promise.* Washington, DC: Worldwatch Institute, 1988.

Stein, J. "Hydrogen: Clean, Safe, and Inexhaustible." *Amicus Journal* 12 (Spring 1990): 33-36.

Aluminum

Aluminum, a light metal, comprises about 8 percent of the earth's crust, ranking as the third-most abundant element after oxygen (47 percent) and silicon (28 percent). Virtually all environmental aluminum is present in mineral forms that are almost insoluble in water, and therefore not available for uptake by organisms. Most common among these forms of aluminum are various aluminosilicate minerals, aluminum clays and sesquioxides, and aluminum phosphates.

However, aluminum can also occur as **chemical** species that are available for biological uptake, sometimes causing toxicity. In general, bio-available aluminum is present in various water-soluble, ionic or organically complexed chemical species. Water-soluble concentrations of aluminum are largest in acidic environments, where toxicity to non-adapted plants and animals can be caused by exposure to Al^{3+} and $Al(OH)^{2+}$ ions, and in alkaline environments, where $Al(OH)_4^-$ is most prominent. Organically bound, water-soluble forms of aluminum, such as complexes with fulvic or humic acids, are much less toxic than ionic species. Aluminum is often considered to be the most toxic chemical factor in acidic **soil**s and aquatic **habitat**s.

Amazon basin

The Amazon basin, the region of South America drained by the Amazon River, represents the largest area of **tropical rain forest** in the world. Extending across nine different countries and covering an area of 2.3 million square miles (6 million sq. km), the Amazon basin contains the greatest abundance and diversity of life anywhere on earth. Tremendous numbers of plant and animal **species** that occur there have yet to be discovered or properly named by scientists, as this area has only begun to be explored by competent researchers.

It is estimated that the Amazon basin contains over 20 percent of all higher plant species on earth, as well as about 20 percent of all birdlife and 10 percent of all mammals. More than 2,000 known species of freshwater fishes live in the Amazon river and represent about eight percent of all fishes on our planet, both freshwater and marine. This number of species is about three times the entire ichthyofauna of North America and almost ten times that of Europe. The most astonishing numbers, however, come from the **river basin**'s insects. Every expedition to the Amazon basin yields countless new species of insects, with some individual trees in the tropical forest providing scientists with hundreds of undescribed forms. Insects represent about three-fourths of all animal life on earth, yet biologists believe that the 750,000 species which have already been scientifically named account for less than 10 percent of all insect life that exists.

However incredible these examples of **biodiversity** are, they may soon be destroyed as the rampant **deforestation** in the Amazon basin continues. Much of this destruction is directly attributable to human **population growth**. The number of people who have settled in the Amazonian uplands of Colombia and Ecuador has increased by 600 percent over the past forty years, and this has led to the clearing of over 65 percent of the region's forests for agriculture.

In Brazil, up to 70 percent of the deforestation is tied to cattle ranching. In the past large governmental subsidies and tax incentives have encouraged this practice, which had little or no financial success and caused widespread environmental damage. Tropical **soil**s rapidly lose their fertility, and this allows only limited annual meat production. It is often only 300 pounds (136 kg) per acre, compared to over 3,000 pounds (1360 kg) per acre in North America.

Further damage to the tropical forests of the Amazon basin is linked to commercial logging. Although only five of the approximately 1,500 tree species of the region are extensively logged, tremendous damage is done to the surrounding forest as these are selectively removed. When loggers build roads move in heavy equipment, they may damage or destroy half of the trees in a given area.

The deforestation taking place in the Amazon basin has a wide range of environmental effects. The clearing and burning of vegetation produces **smoke** or **air pollution**, which at times has been so abundant that it is clearly visible from space. Clearing also leads to increased soil **erosion** after heavy rains, and can result in **water pollution** through **siltation** as well as increased water temperatures from increased exposure. Yet the most alarming, and definitely the most irreversible, environmental problem facing the Amazon basin is the loss of biodiversity. Through the irrevocable process of **extinction**, this may cost humanity more than the loss of species. It may cost us the loss of potential discoveries of medicines and other beneficial products derived from these species. *See also* Decline spiral; Greenhouse effect; Mendes, Chico; Rain forest; Rainforest Action Network; Selection cutting; Soil fertility; Watershed

[*Eugene C. Beckham*]

FURTHER READING

Caufield, C. *In the Rainforest: Report From a Strange, Beautiful, Imperiled World.* Chicago: University of Chicago Press, 1986.

Cockburn, A., and S. Hecht. *The Fate of the Forest: Developers, Destroyers, and Defenders of the Amazon.* New York: Harper/Perennial, 1990.

Collins, M. *The Last Rain Forests: A World Conservation Atlas.* London: Oxford University Press, 1990.

Cowell, A. *Decade of Destruction: The Crusade to Save the Amazon Rain Forest.* New York: Doubleday, 1991.

Holloway, M. "Sustaining the Amazon." *Scientific American* 269 (July 1993): 90-96+.

Margolis, M. *The Last New World: The Conquest of the Amazon Frontier.* New York: Norton, 1992.

Wilson, E. O. *The Diversity of Life.* Cambridge, MA: Belknap Press, 1992.

Aline, Tundra

See **Tundra**

Ambient air

The air, external to buildings and other enclosures, found in the lower **atmosphere** over a given area, usually near the surface. **Air pollution** standards normally refer to ambient air. *See also* National Ambient Air Quality Standard

Amenity value

The idea that something has worth because of the pleasant feelings it generates to those who use or view it. This value is often used in benefit-costs analysis, particularly in **shadow pricing**, to determine the worth of **natural resources** that will not be harvested for economic gain. A virgin forest will have amenity value, but its value will decrease if the forest is harvested, thus the amenity value is compared to the value of the harvested timber.

American Box Turtle

Box turtles are in the Order Chelonia, Family Emydidae, and genus *Terrapene*. There are two major species in the United States: *carolina* (Eastern Box Turtle) and *ornata* (Western or Ornate Box Turtle).

Box turtles are easily recognized by their dome-shaped upper shell (carapace) and by their lower shell (plastron) which is hinged near the front. This hinging allows them to close up tightly into the "box" when in danger (hence their name).

Box turtles are fairly small, having an adult maximum length of 4-7 in (10-18 cm). Their range is restricted to North America, with the Eastern species located over most of the eastern U.S. and the Western species located in the Central and Southwestern United States and into Mexico, but not as far west as California. Both species are highly variable in coloration and pattern, ranging from a uniform tan to dark brown or black, with yellow spots or streaks. They prefer a dry habitat such as woodlands, open brush lands, or prairie. They typically inhabit sandy soil, but are sometimes found in springs or ponds during hot weather where they aestivate. During the winter, they hibernate in the soil below the frost line, often as deep as 2 ft (60 cm). Their home range is usually fairly small, and they often live within areas less than 300 yd² (300 m²).

Box turtles are omnivorous, feeding on living and dead insects, earthworms, slugs, fruits, berries (particularly blackberries and strawberries), leaves, and mushrooms. They have been known to ingest some mushrooms which are poisonous to humans, and there have been reports of people eating box turtles and getting sick. Other than this, box turtles are harmless to humans and are commonly collected and sold as pets (although this should be discouraged because they are now a threatened species). They can be fed raw hamburger, canned pet food, or leafy vegetables.

Box turtles normally live as long as 30-40 years. Some have been reported with a longevity of more than one hundred years, and this makes them the longest-lived land turtle. They are active from March until November and are diurnal, usually being more active in the early morning. During the afternoons they typically seek shaded areas. They breed during the spring and autumn, and the females build nests from May until July, typically in sandy soil where they dig a hole with their hind feet. The females can store sperm for several years. They typically hatch 3-8 eggs which are elliptically-shaped and about 1.5 in (4 cm) in diameter. Male box turtles have a slight concavity in their plastron which aids in mounting females during copulation. All four toes on the male's hind feet are curved, which aids in holding down the posterior portion of the female's plastron during copulation. Females have flat plastrons, shorter tails, and yellow or brown eyes. Most males have bright red or pink eyes. The upper jaw of both sexes ends in a down-turned beak.

Predators of box turtles include skunks, raccoons, foxes, snakes, and other animals. Native American Indians used to eat box turtles and incorporated their shells into their ceremonies as rattles.

[*John Korstad*]

FURTHER READING

Conant, R. *A Field Guide to Reptiles and Amphibians of Eastern and Central North America.* 2nd ed. Boston: Houghton Mifflin, 1975.

Tyning, T. F. *A Guide to Amphibians and Reptiles.* Boston: Little, Brown and Co., 1990.

American Cetacean Society (San Pedro, California)

The American Cetacean Society (ACS) is dedicated to the protection of **whales** and other cetaceans, including **dolphins** and porpoises. Principally an organization of scientists and teachers (though its membership does include students and laypeople) the ACS was founded in 1967 and claims to be the oldest whale **conservation** group in the world.

The ACS believes the best protection for whales, dolphins, and porpoises is better public awareness about "these remarkable animals and the problems they face in their increasingly threatened **habitat**." The organization is committed to political action through education, and much of its work has been in improving communication between marine scientists and the general public.

The ACS has developed several educational resource materials on cetaceans, making such products as the "Gray Whale Teaching Kit," "Whale Fact Pack," and "Dolphin Fact Pack," which are widely available for use in classrooms. There is a cetacean research library at the national headquarters in San Pedro, California, and the organization responds to thousands of inquiries every year. The ACS supports marine mammal research and sponsors a biennial conference on whales. It also assists in conducting whale-watching tours.

The organization also engages in more traditional and direct forms of political action. A representative in Washington monitors legislation that might affect cetaceans, attends hearings at government agencies, and participates as a member of the International Whaling Commission. The ACS also networks with other conservation groups. In addition, the ACS directs letter-writing campaigns, sending out "Action Alerts" to citizens and politicians. The organization is currently emphasizing the threats to marine life posed by **oil spills**, toxic wastes from industry and agriculture, and particular fishing practices (including commercial whaling).

The ACS publishes a quarterly newsletter on whale research, conservation, and education, called *WhaleNews*, and a quarterly journal of scientific articles on the same subjects, called *Whalewatcher*. Contact: American Cetacean Society, PO Box 2639, San Pedro, CA 90731. Internet: http://www.acsonline.org/acs/.

[*Douglas Smith*]

American Committee for International Conservation (Washington, D.C.)

The American Committee for International Conservation (ACIC) is an association of **nongovernmental organizations** (NGOs) that is concerned about international **conservation** issues. The ACIC, founded in 1930, includes 21 member organizations. It represents conservation groups and individuals in 40 countries. While ACIC does not fund conservation research, it does promote national and international conservation research activities. Specifically, ACIC promotes conservation and preservation of **wildlife** and other **natural resources**, and encourages international research on the ecology of **endangered species**.

Formerly called the American Committee for International Wildlife Protection, ACIC assists **IUCN—The World Conservation Union**, an independent organization of nations, states, and NGOs, in promoting natural resource conservation. ACIC also coordinates its members' overseas research activities.

Member organizations of the ACIC include the African Wildlife Leadership Foundation; **National Wildlife Federation**; **World Wildlife Fund** (US)/RARE; Caribbean Conservation Corporation; **National Audubon Society**; **Natural Resources Defense Council**; **Nature Conservancy**; International Association of Fish and Wildlife Agencies; and **National Parks and Conservation Association**. Members also include The Conservation Foundation; International Institute for Environment and Development; Massachusetts Audubon Society; Chicago Zoological Society; Wildlife Preservation Trust; Wildfowl Trust; School of Natural Resources, University of Michigan; World Resources Institute; **Global Tomorrow Coalition**; and The Wildlife Society, Inc.

ACIC holds no formal meetings or conventions, nor does it publish magazines, books, or newsletters. Contact: American Committee for International Conservation, c/o Center for Marine Conservation, 1725 DeSales Street, NW, Suite 500, Washington, DC 20036.

[*Linda Rehkopf*]

American Farmland Trust (Washington, D.C.)

The American Farmland Trust (AFT) is an advocacy group for farmers and farmland. It was founded in 1980 to help reverse or at least slow the rapid decline in the number of productive acres nationwide, and it is particularly concerned with protecting land held by private farmers. The principles that motivate the AFT are perhaps best summarized in a line from William Jennings Bryan that the organization has often quoted: "Destroy our farms, and the grass will grow in the streets of every city in the country."

Over one million acres of farmland in the United States is lost each year to development, according to the AFT, and in Illinois one and a half bushels of **topsoil** are lost for every bushel of corn produced. The AFT argues that such a decline poses a serious threat to the future of the American economy. As farmers are forced to cultivate increasingly marginal land, food will become more expensive, and the United States could become a net importer of agricultural products, damaging its international economic position. The organization believes that a declining farm industry would also affect American culture, depriving the country of traditional products such as cherries, cranberries, and oranges and imperiling a sense of national identity that is still in many ways agricultural.

The AFT works closely with farmers, business people, legislators, and environmentalists "to encourage sound farming practices and wise use of land." The group directs lobbying efforts in Washington, working with legislators and policymakers and frequently testifying at congressional and public hearings on issues related to farming. In addition to mediating between farmers and state and federal government, the trust is also involved in political organizing at the grassroots level, conducting public opinion polls, contesting proposals for incinerators and toxic waste sites, and drafting model **conservation** easements. They conduct workshops and seminars across the country to discuss farming methods and **soil conservation** programs, and they worked with the

State of Illinois to establish the Illinois Sustainable Agriculture Society. The group is currently developing kits for distribution to schoolchildren in both rural and urban areas called "Seed for the Future," which teach the benefits of agriculture and help each child grow a plant.

The AFT has a reputation for innovative and determined efforts to realize its goals, and former Secretary of Agriculture John R. Block has said that "this organization has probably done more than any other to preserve the American farm." Since its founding the trust has been instrumental in protecting nearly 30,000 acres of farmland in nineteen states. In 1989, the group protected a 507-acre cherry farm known as the Murray Farm in Michigan, and it has helped preserve 300 acres of farm and **wetlands** in Virginia's Tidewater region. The AFT continues to battle **urban sprawl** in areas such as California's Central Valley and Berks County, Pennsylvania, as well as working to support farms in states such as Vermont, which are threatened not so much by development but by a poor agricultural economy. The AFT promotes a wetland policy that is fair to farmers while meeting environment standards, and it recently won a national award from the Soil and Water Conservation Society for its publication *Does Farmland Protection Pay?*

The AFT has 20,000 members and an annual budget of $3,850,000. The trust publishes a quarterly magazine called *American Farmland*, a newsletter called *Farmland Update*, and a variety of brochures and pamphlets which offer practical information on soil **erosion**, the cost of community services, and estate planning. They also distribute videos, including *The Future of America's Farmland*, which explains the sale and purchase of development rights. Contact: American Farmland Trust, 1920 N Street, NW, Suite 400, Washington, DC 20036. Internet: http://www.farmland.org/.

[*Douglas Smith*]

American Forestry Association (Washington, D.C.)

The American Forestry Association (AFA) was founded in 1875, during the early days of the American **conservation** movement, to encourage **forest management**. The group is dedicated to promoting the wise and careful use of all **natural resources**, including **soil**, water, and **wildlife**, and it emphasizes the social and cultural importance of these resources as well as their economic value.

Although benefitting from increasing national and international concern about the environment, the AFA takes a balanced view on preservation, and it has worked to set a standard for the responsible harvesting and marketing of forest products. The AFA sponsors the Trees for People program, which is designed to help meet the national demand for wood and paper products by increasing the productivity of private woodlands. It provides educational and technical information to individual forest owners, as well as making recommendations to legislators and policymakers in Washington.

To draw attention to the **greenhouse effect**, the AFA inaugurated their Global ReLeaf program in October 1988. Global ReLeaf is what the AFA calls "a tree-planting crusade." The message is, "Plant a tree, cool the globe," and Global ReLeaf has organized a national campaign, challenging Americans to plant millions of trees. The AFA has gained the support of government agencies and local conservation groups for this program, as well as many businesses, including such Fortune-500 companies as Texaco, McDonald's, and Ralston-Purina. Global ReLeaf has recently launched a cooperative effort with the **American Farmland Trust** called Farm ReLeaf, and it has also participated in the campaign to preserve Walden Woods in Massachusetts. In 1991 the AFA brought Global ReLeaf to Eastern Europe, running a workshop in Budapest, Hungary, for environmental activists from many former communist countries.

The AFA has been extensively involved in the controversy over the preservation of **old-growth forest**s in the American Northwest. They have been working with environmentalists and representatives of the timber industry, and consistent with the history of the organization, the AFA is committed to a compromise that both sides can accept: "If we have to choose between preservation and destruction of old-growth forests as our only options, neither choice will work." The AFA supports an approach to forestry known as *New Forestry*, where the priority is no longer the quantity of wood or the number of board feet that can be removed from a site, but the vitality of the **ecosystem** the timber industry leaves behind. The organization advocates the establishment of an Old Growth Reserve in the Pacific Northwest, which would be managed by the principles of New Forestry under the supervision of a Scientific Advisory Committee.

The AFA publishes the *National Registry of Champion Big Trees and Famous Historical Trees,* which celebrated its fiftieth anniversary in 1990. The registry is designed to encourage the appreciation of trees, and it includes such trees as the recently fallen Dyerville Giant, a **redwood** tree in California, the General Sherman, a giant sequoia in Texas, and the Wye Oak in Maryland. The group also publishes *American Forests,* a bimonthly magazine, and *Resource Hotline,* a biweekly newsletter, as well as *Urban Forests: The Magazine of Community Trees.* It presents the Annual Distinguished Service Award, the John Aston Warder Medal, and the William B. Greeley Award, among others. The AFA has over 35,000 members, a staff of 21, and a budget of $2,725,000. Contact: American Forestry Association, 1516 P Street, NW, Washington, DC 20005.

[*Douglas Smith*]

American Indian Environmental Office (Washington, D.C.)

The American Indian Environmental Office (AIEO) was created to increase the quality of public health and environmental protection on Native American land and to expand tribal involvement in running environmental programs.

Native people are the second-largest landholders besides the government. Their land is often threatened by environmental degradation such as **strip mining**, **clear-cutting**, and toxic storage. The AIEO, with the help of the President's Federal Indian Policy (January 24, 1983), works closely with the **U.S. Environmental Protection Agency (EPA)** to prevent further degradation of the land. The AIEO has received grants from the EPA for environmental clean-up and obtained a written policy that requires the EPA to continue with the trust responsibility, a clause expressed in certain treaties that requires the EPA to notify the Tribe when performing any activities that may affect reservation lands or resources. This involves consulting with tribal governments, providing technical support, and negotiating EPA regulations to ensure that tribal facilities eventually comply.

The pollution of Dine Reservation land is an example of an environmental injustice that the AIEO wants to prevent in the future. The reservation has over 1,000 abandoned uranium mines that leak radioactive contaminants and is also home to the largest coal strip mine in the world. The cancer rate for the Dine people is 17 times the national average. To help tribes with pollution problems similar to the Dine, several offices now exist that handle specific environmental projects. They include the Office of Water, Air, Environmental Justice, Pesticides and Toxic Substances; Performance Partnership Grants; Solid Waste and Emergency Response; and the Tribal Watershed Project. Each of these offices reports to the National Indian Headquarters in Washington, D.C.

At the Rio Earth Summit in 1992, the Biodiversity Convention was drawn up to protect the diversity of life on the planet. Many Native American groups believe that the convention also covered the protection of indigenous communities, including Native American land. In addition, the groups demand that prospecting by large companies for rare forms of life and materials on their land must stop.

Tribal Environmental Concerns

Tribal governments face both economic and social problems dealing with the demand for jobs, education, health care, and housing for tribal members. Often the reservations' largest employer is the government, which owns the stores, gaming operations, timber mills, and manufacturing facilities. Therefore, the government must deal with the conflicting interests of protecting both economic and environmental concerns. Many tribes are becoming self-governing and manage their own natural resources along with claiming the reserved right to use natural resources on portions of public land that border their reservation. As a product of the reserved treaty rights, Native Americans can use water, fish, and hunt anytime on nearby federal land.

Robert Belcourt, Chippewa-Cree tribal member and director of the Natural Resources Department in Montana stated:

"We have to protect nature for our future generations. More of our Indian people need to get involved in natural resource management on each of our reservations. In the long run, natural resources will be our bread and butter by our developing them through tourism and recreation and just by the opportunity they provide for us to enjoy the outdoor world."

Belcourt has fought to destroy the negative stereotypes of conservation organizations that exist among Native Americans who believe, for example, that conservationists are extreme tree-huggers and insensitive to Native American culture. These stereotypes are a result of cultural differences in philosophy, perspective, and communication. To work together effectively, tribes and conservation groups need to learn about one another's cultures, and this means they must listen both at meetings and in one-on-one exchanges.

The AIEO also addresses the organizational differences that exist in tribal governments and conservation organizations. They differ greatly in terms of style, motivation, and the pressures they face. Pressures on the Wilderness Society, for example, include fending off attempts in Washington, D.C. to weaken key environmental laws or securing members and raising funds. Pressures on tribal governments more often are economic and social in nature and have to do with the need to provide jobs, health care, education, and housing for tribal members. Because tribal governments are often the reservations' largest employers and may own businesses like gaming operations, timber mills, manufacturing facilities, and stores, they function as both governors and leaders in economic development.

Native Americans currently occupy and control over 52 million acres (21.3 million ha) in the continental United States and 45 million more acres (18.5 million ha) in Alaska, yet this is only a small fraction of their original territories.

In the nineteenth century, many tribes were confined to reservations that were perceived to have little economic value, although valuable natural resources have subsequently been found on some of these land. Pointing to their treaties and other agreements with the federal government, many tribes assert that they have reserved rights to use natural resources on portions of public land.

In previous decades these natural resources on tribal lands were managed by the Bureau of Indian Affairs (BIA). Now many tribes are becoming self-governing and are taking control of management responsibilities within their own reservation boundaries. In addition, some tribes are pushing to take back management over some federally managed lands that were part of their original territories. For example, the Confederated Salish and Kootenai tribes of the Flathead Reservation are taking steps to assume management of the National Bison Range, which lies within the reservation's boundaries and is currently managed by the U.S. Fish and Wildlife Service.

Another issue concerns Native American rights to water. There are legal precedents that support the practice of reserved rights to water that is within or bordering a reservation. In areas where tribes fish for food, mining pollution has been a continues threat to maintaining clean water. Mining pollution is monitored, but the amount of fish that Native Americans consume is higher than the government acknowledges when setting health guidelines for their consumption. This is why the AIEO is asking that stricter regulations be imposed on mining companies. As tribes increasingly exer-

cise their rights to use and consume water and fish, their roles in natural resource debates will increase.

Many tribes are establishing their own natural resource management and environmental quality protection programs with the help of the AIEO. Tribes have established fisheries, wildlife, forestry, water quality, waste management, and planning departments. Some tribes have prepared comprehensive resource management plans for their reservations while others have become active in the protection of particular species. The AIEO is uniting tribes in their strategy and involvement level with improving environmental protection on Native American land. Contact: American Indian Environmental Office, 401 M. St., SW, Washington, D.C. 20460.

[*Nicole Beatty*]

American Oceans Campaign (Santa Monica, California)

The American Oceans Campaign (AOC) was founded in 1987 as a political interest group dedicated primarily to the restoration, protection, and preservation of the health and vitality of coastal waters, **estuaries**, bays, **wetlands**, and oceans. More national and conservationist (rather than international and preservationist) in its focus than other groups with similar concerns, the AOC tends to view the oceans as a valuable resource whose use should be managed carefully. As current president Ted Danson puts it, the oceans must be regarded as far more than a natural preserve by environmentalists; rather, healthy oceans "sustain biological diversity, provide us with leisure and recreation, and contribute significantly to our nation's GNP."

The AOC's main political efforts reflect this focus. Central to the AOC's lobbying strategy is a desire to build cooperative relations and consensus among the general public, public interest groups, private sector corporations and trade groups, and public/governmental authorities around responsible management of ocean resources. The AOC is also active in grassroots public awareness campaigns through mass media and community outreach programs. This high-profile media campaign has included the production of a series of informational bulletins (Public Service Announcements) for use by local groups, as well as active involvement in the production of several documentary television series that have been broadcast on both network and public television. The AOC also has developed extensive connections with both the news and entertainment industries, frequently scheduling appearances by various celebrity supporters such as Jamie Lee Curtis, Whoopi Goldberg, Leonard Nimoy, Patrick Swayze, Lloyd Bridges, and Beau Bridges.

As a lobbying organization, the AOC has developed contacts with government leaders at all levels from local to national, attempting to shape and promote a variety of legislation related to clean water and oceans. It has been particularly active in lobbying for strengthening various aspects of the **Clean Water Act**, the **Safe Drinking Water Act**, the **Oil Pollution Act**, and the **Ocean Dumping Ban Act**. The AOC regularly provides consultation services, assistance in drafting legislation, and occasional expert testimony on matters concerning ocean ecology. Recently this has included AOC Political Director Barbara Polo's testimony before the U.S. House of Representatives Subcommittee on Fisheries, Conservation, Wildlife, and Oceans on the substance and effect of legislation concerning the protection of coral reef ecosystems.

Also very active at the grassroots level, AOC has organized numerous "cleanup" operations which both draw attention to the problems caused by ocean dumping and make a practical contribution to reversing the situation. Concentrating its efforts in California and the Pacific Northwest, the AOC launched its "Dive for Trash" program in 1991. As many as one thousand divers may team up at AOC-sponsored events to recover garbage from the coastal waters. In cooperation with the U.S. Department of Commerce's National Maritime Sanctuary Program, the AOC is planning to add a marine environmental assessment component to this diving program, and to expand the program into Gulf and Atlantic coastal waters.

Organizationally, the AOC divides its political and lobbying activity into three separate substantive policy areas: "Critical Oceans and Coastal Habitats," which includes issues concerning estuaries, watersheds, and wetlands; "Coastal Water Pollution," which focuses on beach water quality and the effects of storm water runoff, among other issues; and "Living Resources of the Sea," which include coral reefs, fisheries, and marine mammals (especially dolphins). Activities in all these areas have run the gamut from public and legislative information campaigns to litigation.

The AOC has been particularly active along the California coastline and has played a central role in various programs aimed at protecting coastal wetland ecosystems from development and pollution. It has also been active in the Santa Monica Bay Restoration Project, which seeks to restore environmental balance to Santa Monica Bay. Typical of the AOC's multi-level approach, this project combines a program of public education and citizen (and celebrity) involvement with the monitoring and reduction of private-sector pollution and with the conducting of scientific studies on the impact of a various activities in the surrounding area. These activities are also combined with an attempt to raise alternative revenues to replace funds recently lost due to the reduction of both federal (National Estuary Program) and state government support for the conservation of coastal and marine ecosystems. In addition, the AOC has been involved in litigation against the County of Los Angeles over a plan to build flood control barriers along a section of the Los Angeles River. AOC's major concern is that these barriers will increase the amount of polluted storm water runoff being channelled into coastal waters. The AOC contends that prudent management of this storm water would be better used in recharging Southern California's scant water resources via storage or redirection into underground aquifers before this runoff becomes polluted. Contact: American Oceans Campaign, 725 Arizona St., Ste. 102, Santa Monica, CA 90402.

[*Lawrence J. Biskowski*]

American Wildlands (Lakewood, Colorado)

American Wildlands (AWL) is a nonprofit wildland resource **conservation** and education organization founded in 1977. AWL is dedicated to protecting and promoting proper management of America's publicly owned wild areas and to securing **wilderness** designation for public land areas. The organization has played a key role in gaining legal protection for many wilderness and river areas in the U.S. interior west and in Alaska.

Founded as the American Wilderness Alliance, AWL is involved in a wide range of wilderness resource issues and programs including timber management policy reform, **habitat** corridors, **rangeland** management policy reform, riparian and **wetlands** restoration, and **public land** management policy reform. AWL promotes ecologically sustainable uses of public wildlands resources including forests, wilderness, wildlife, fisheries and rivers. It pursues this mission through grassroots activism, technical support, public education, litigation and political advocacy.

AWL maintains three offices: the central Rockies office in Lakewood, Colorado; the northern Rockies office in Bozeman, Montana; and the Sierra-Nevada office in Reno, Nevada. The organization's annual budget of $350,000 has been stable for many years, but with programs that are now being considered for addition to its agenda, that figure is expected to increase over the next few years.

The Central Rockies office in Bozeman considers its main concern timber management reform. It has launched the Timber Management Reform Policy Program, which monitors the U.S. **Forest Service** and works toward a better management of public forests. Since initiation of the program in 1986, the program includes resource specialists, a wildlife biologist, forester, water specialist, and an aquatic biologist who all report to an advisory council. A major victory of this program was stopping the sale of 4.2 million board feet (1.3 million m) of timber near the Electric Peak Wilderness Area.

Other programs coordinated by the Central Rockies office include: 1) *Corridors of Life Program* which identifies and maps **wildlife** corridors, land areas essential to the genetic interchange of wildlife that connect roadless lands or other wildlife habitat areas. Areas targeted are in the interior West, such as Montana, North and South Dakota, Wyoming, and Idaho; 2) The *Rangeland Management Policy Reform Program* monitors grazing allotments and files appeals as warranted. An education component teaches citizens to monitor grazing allotments and to use the appeals process within the U.S. Forest Service and **Bureau of Land Management**; 3) The *Recreation-Conservation Connection*, through newsletters and travel-adventure programs, teaches the public how to enjoy the outdoors without destroying **na-**

ture. Six hundred travelers have participated in **ecotourism** trips through AWL.

AWL is also active internationally. The AWL/Leakey Fund has aided Dr. Richard Leakey's wildlife habitat conservation and **elephant** poaching elimination efforts in Kenya. A partnership with the Island Foundation has helped fund wildlands and river protection efforts in Patagonia, Argentina. AWL also is an active member of Canada's Tatshenshini International Coalition to protect that river and its 2.3 million acres of wilderness. Contact: American Wildlands, 3609 S. Wadsworth Boulevard, Suite 123, Lakewood, CO 80235. Internet:http://dns.mcn.net/~amwild/.

[*Linda Rehkopf*]

Ames test

A laboratory test developed by biochemist Bruce N. Ames (1928-) to determine the possible carcinogenic nature of a substance. The Ames test involves using a particular strain of the bacteria *Salmonella typhimurium* that lacks the ability to synthesize histidine and is therefore very sensitive to **mutation**. The bacteria are inoculated into a medium deficient in histidine but containing the test compound. If the compound results in **DNA** damage with subsequent mutations, some of the bacteria will regain the ability to synthesize histidine and will proliferate to form colonies. The culture is evaluated on the basis of the number of mutated bacterial colonies it produced. The ability to replicate mutated colonies leads to the classification of a substance as probably carcinogenic.

The Ames test is a test for mutagenicity not carcinogenicity. However, approximately nine out of ten **mutagen**s are indeed carcinogenic. Therefore, a substance that can be shown to be mutagenic by being subjected to the Ames test can be reliably classified as a suspected **carcinogen** and thus recommended for further study.

[*Brian R. Barthel*]

FURTHER READING

Taber, C. W. *Taber's Cyclopedic Medical Dictionary*. Philadephia: F. A. Davis, 1990.

Turk J., and A. Turk. *Environmental Science*. Philadelphia: W. B. Saunders, 1988.

Amoco Cadiz

This shipwreck in March 1978 off the Brittany coast was the first major supertanker accident since the *Torrey Canyon* eleven years earlier. Ironically, this spill, more than twice the size of the *Torrey Canyon*, blackened some of the same shores and was one of four substantial **oil spills** there since 1967. It received great scientific attention because it occurred near several renowned marine laboratories.

The cause of the wreck was a steering failure as the ship entered the English Channel off the northwest Brittany coast, and failure to act swiftly enough to correct it. During

The *Amoco Cadiz* oil spill being contained.

the next twelve hours, the *Amoco Cadiz* could not be extricated from the site. In fact, three separate lines from a powerful tug broke trying to remove the tanker before it drifted onto rocky shoals. Eight days later the *Amoco Cadiz* split in two.

Seabirds seemed to suffer the most from the spill, although the oil devastated invertebrates within the extensive, 20 to 30 feet (6-9 m) high intertidal zone. Thousands of birds died in a bird hospital described by one oil spill expert as a bird morgue. Thirty percent of France's seafood production was threatened, as well as an extensive kelp crop, harvested for **fertilizer**, **mulch**, and livestock feed. However, except on oyster farms located in inlets, most of the impact was restricted to the few months following the spill.

In an extensive journal article, Erich Grundlach and others reported studies on where the oil went and summarized the findings of biologists. Of the 223,000 metric tons released, 13.5 percent was incorporated within the water column, 8 percent went into subtidal **sediment**s, 28 percent washed into the intertidal zone, 20-40 percent evaporated, and 4 percent was altered while at sea. Much research was done on chemical changes in the hydrocarbon fractions over time, including that taken up within organisms. Researchers found that during early phases, biodegradation was occurring as rapidly as evaporation.

The cleanup efforts of thousands of workers were helped by storm and wave action which removed much of the stranded oil. High energy waves maintained an adequate supply of **nutrient**s and oxygenated water, which provided optimal conditions for biodegradation. This is important because most of the biodegradation was done by **aerobic** organisms. Except for protected inlets, much of the impact was gone three years later, but some effects were expected to last a decade. *See also* Clean Water Act; Environmental degradation; *Exxon Valdez*; Hydrocarbons; Marine pollution; Water pollution

[*Nathan H. Meleen*]

FURTHER READING

Grove, N. "Black Day for Brittany: *Amoco Cadiz* Wreck." *National Geographic* 154 (July 1978): 124-135.

Grundlach, E. R., et al. "The Fate of *Amoco Cadiz* Oil." *Science* 221 (8 July 1983): 122-129.

Schneider, E. D. "Aftermath of the *Amoco Cadiz*: Shorline Impact of the Oil Spill." *Oceans* 11 (July 1978): 56-9.

Spooner, M. F., ed. *Amoco Cadiz Oil Spill.* New York: Pergamon, 1979. (Reprint of *Marine Pollution Bulletin*, v. 9, no. 11, 1978)

Amory, Cleveland (1917-)

American author, humorist, and defender of animals

Amory is known both for his series of classic social history books and his work with the **Fund for Animals**. Born in Nahant, Massachusetts, to an old Boston family, Amory attended Harvard University, where he became editor of *The Harvard Crimson*. This prompted his well-known remark, "If you have been editor of *The Harvard Crimson* in your senior year at Harvard, there is very little, in after life, for you."

Amory was hired by *The Saturday Evening Post* after graduation, becoming the youngest editor ever to join that publication. He worked as an intelligence officer in the United States Army during World War II, and in the years after the war, wrote a trilogy of social commentary books, now considered to be classics. *The Proper Bostonians* was published to critical acclaim in 1947, followed by *The Last Resorts* (1948), and *Who Killed Society?* (1960), all of which became best sellers.

Beginning in 1952, Amory served for eleven years as social commentator on NBC's "The Today Show." The network fired him after he spoke out against cruelty to animals used in biomedical research. From 1963 to 1976, Amory served as a senior editor and columnist for *Saturday Review* magazine, while doing a daily radio commentary, entitled "Curmudgeon-at-Large." He was also chief television critic for *TV Guide*, where his biting attacks on sport hunting angered hunters and generated bitter but unsuccessful campaigns to have him fired.

In 1967, Amory founded The Fund for Animals "to speak for those who can't," and he still serves as its unpaid president. Animal protection has become his passion and his life's work, and he is considered one of the most outspoken and provocative advocates of animal welfare. Under his leadership, the Fund has become a highly activist and controversial group, engaging in such activities as confronting hunters of **whales** and **seals**, and rescuing wild horses, burros, and goats. The Fund, and Amory in particular, are well known for their campaigns against sport hunting and trapping, the fur industry, abusive research on animals, and

Cleveland Amory with his cat.

other activities and industries that engage in or encourage what they consider cruel treatment of animals.

In 1975, Amory published *ManKind? Our Incredible War on Wildlife*, using humor, sarcasm, and graphic rhetoric to attack hunters, trappers, and other exploiters of wild animals. The book was praised by *The New York Times* in a rare editorial. His next book, *AniMail*, (1976) discussed animal issues in a question-and-answer format. In 1987, he wrote *The Cat Who Came for Christmas*, a book about a stray cat he rescued from the streets of New York, which became a national best seller. This was followed in 1990 by its sequel, also a best seller, *The Cat and the Curmudgeon*. Amory has been a senior contributing editor of *Parade* magazine since 1980, where he often profiles famous personalities. *See also* Animal Legal Defense Fund; Animal rights; People for the Ethical Treatment of Animals; Singer, Peter; Speciesism

[*Lewis G. Regenstein*]

FURTHER READING

Amory, C. *The Cat and the Curmudgeon.* New York: G. K. Hall, 1991.

———. *The Cat Who Came for Christmas.* New York: Little Brown, 1987.

Pantridge, M. "The Improper Bostonian." *Boston Magazine* 83 (June 1991): 68-72.

Anaerobic

Without oxygen. This term refers to an environment lacking in molecular oxygen (O_2), or to an organism, tissue, chemical reaction, or biological process that does not require oxygen. Anaerobic organisms can use a molecule other than O_2 as the terminal electron acceptor in **respiration**. These organisms can be either obligate, meaning that they cannot use O_2, or facultative, meaning that they do not require oxygen but can use it if it is available.

Organic matter **decomposition** in poorly aerated environments, including water-logged **soils**, **septic tank**s, and anaerobically-operated **waste treatment** facilities, produces large amounts of **methane** gas. The methane can become an atmospheric pollutant, or it may be captured and used for fuel, as in "biogas"-powered electrical generators. Anaerobic decomposition produces the notorious "swamp gases" that have been reported as unidentified flying objects (UFOs).

Anaerobic digestion

Refers to the biological degradation of either **sludge**s or **solid waste** under **anaerobic** conditions, meaning that no oxygen is present. In the digestive process, solids are converted to noncellular end products.

In the anaerobic digestion of sludges, the goals are to reduce sludge volume, insure the remaining solids are chemically stable, reduce disease-causing **pathogen**s, and enhance the effectiveness of subsequent dewatering methods, sometimes recovering **methane** as a source of energy. Anaerobic digestion is commonly used to treat sludges that contain primary sludges, such as that from the first settling basins in a **wastewater** treatment plant, because the process is capable of stabilizing the sludge with little **biomass** production, a significant benefit over **aerobic sludge digestion**, which would yield more biomass in digesting the relatively large amount of **biodegradable** matter in primary sludge.

The microorganisms responsible for digesting the sludges anaerobically are often classified in two groups, the acid formers and the methane formers. The acid formers are microbes that create, among others, acetic and propionic acids from the sludge. These chemicals generally make up about a third of the by-products initially formed based on a **chemical oxygen demand (COD)** mass balance, and some of the propionic and other acids are converted to acetic acid.

The methane formers convert the acids and by-products resulting from prior metabolic steps (e.g., alcohols, **hydrogen**, **carbon dioxide**) to methane. Often, approximately 70 percent of the methane formed is derived from acetic acid, about 10 to 15 percent from propionic acid.

Anaerobic digesters are designed as either standard- or high-rate units. The standard-rate digester has a solids retention time of 30 to 90 days, as opposed to 10 to 20 days for the high-rate systems. The volatile solids loadings of the standard- and high-rate systems are in the area of 0.5 - 1.6 and 1.6 - 6.4 $Kg/m^3/d$, respectively. The amount of sludge introduced into the standard-rate is therefore generally much less than the high-rate system. Standard-rate digestion is accomplished in single-stage units, meaning that sludge is fed into a single tank and allowed to digest and

settle. High-rate units are often designed as two-stage systems in which sludge enters into a completely-mixed first stage that is mixed and heated to approximately 98 degrees F (35 degrees C) to speed digestion. The second-stage digester, which separates digested sludge from the overlying liquid and scum, is not heated or mixed.

With the anaerobic digestion of solid waste, the primary goal is generally to produce methane, a valuable source of fuel that can be burned to provide heat or used to power motors. There are basically three steps in the process. The first involves preparing the waste for digestion by sorting the waste and reducing its size. The second consists of constantly mixing the sludge, adding moisture, **nutrient**s, and **pH** neutralizers while heating it to about 143 degrees F (60 degrees C) and digesting the waste for a week or longer. In the third step, the generated gas is collected and sometimes purified, and digested solids are disposed of. For each pound of undigested solid, about 8 - 12 ft^3 of gas is formed, of which about 60 percent is methane. *See also* Methane digester; Sewage treatment; Sludge treatment and disposal; Volatile organic compound

[*Gregory D. Boardman*]

FURTHER READING

Corbitt, R. A. *Standard Handbook of Environmental Engineering.* New York: McGraw-Hill, 1990.

Davis, M. L., and D. A. Cornwell. *Introduction to Environmental Engineering.* New York: McGraw-Hill, 1991.

Viessman, W., Jr., and M. J. Hammer. *Water Supply and Pollution Control.* 5th ed. New York: Harper Collins, 1993.

Anemia

Anemia is a medical condition in which the red cells of the blood are reduced in number or volume or are deficient in hemoglobin, their oxygen-carrying pigment. Almost 100 different varieties of anemia are known. Iron deficiency is the most common cause of anemia worldwide. Other causes of anemia include **ionizing radiation**, **lead** poisoning, vitamin B_{12} deficiency, folic acid deficiency, certain infections, and **pesticide** exposure. Some 350 million people worldwide—mostly women of child-bearing age—suffer from anemia.

The most noticeable symptom is pallor of the skin, mucous membranes, and nail beds. Symptoms of tissue oxygen deficiency include pulsating noises in the ear, dizziness, fainting, and shortness of breath. The treatment varies greatly depending on the cause and diagnosis, but may include supplying missing nutrients, removing toxic factors from the environment, improving the underlying disorder, or restoring blood volume with transfusion.

Aplastic anemia is a disease in which the bone marrow fails to produce an adequate number of blood cells. It is usually acquired by exposure to certain drugs, to toxins such as **benzene**, or to ionizing radiation. Aplastic anemia from **radiation exposure** is well-documented from the **Chernobyl** experience. Bone marrow changes typical of aplastic anemia can occur several years after the exposure to the offending agent has ceased.

Aplastic anemia can manifest itself abruptly and progress rapidly; more commonly it is insidious and chronic for several years. Symptoms include weakness and fatigue in the early stages, followed by headaches, shortness of breath, fever and a pounding heart. Usually a waxy pallor and hemorrhages occur in the mucous membranes and skin. Resistance to infection is lowered and becomes the major cause of death. While spontaneous recovery occurs occasionally, the treatment of choice for severe cases is bone marrow transplantation.

Marie Curie, who discovered the element radium and did early research into **radioactivity**, died in 1934 of aplastic anemia, most likely caused by her exposure to ionizing radiation.

While lead poisoning, which leads to anemia, is usually associated with occupational exposure, toxic amounts of lead can leach from imported ceramic dishes. Other environmental sources of lead exposure include old paint or paint dust, and drinking water pumped through lead pipes or lead-soldered pipes.

Cigarette smoke is known to cause an increase in the level of hemoglobin in smokers, which leads to an underestimation of anemia in smokers. Studies suggest that **carbon monoxide** (a by-product of smoking) chemically binds to hemoglobin, causing a significant elevation of hemoglobin values. Compensation values developed for smokers can now detect possible anemia. *See also* Radiation sickness

[*Linda Rehkopf*]

FURTHER READING

Harte, J., et. al. *Toxics A to Z.* Berkeley: University of California Press, 1991.

Nordenberg, D., et al. "The Effect of Cigarette Smoking on Hemoglobin Levels and Anemia Screening." *Journal of the American Medical Association* (26 September 1990): 1556.

Stuart-Macadam, P., ed. *Diet, Demography and Disease: Changing Perspectives on Anemia.* Hawthrone: Aldine de Gruyter, 1992.

Animal cancer tests

Cancer causes more loss of life-years than any other disease in the United States. At first reading, this statement seems to be in error. Does not cardiovascular disease cause more deaths? The answer to that rhetorical question is "yes." However, many deaths from heart attack and stroke occur in the elderly. The loss of life-years of an 85 year old person (whose life expectancy at the time of his/her birth was between 55 and 60) is, of course, zero. However, the loss of life-years of a child of 10 who dies of a pediatric leukemia is between 65 to 70 years. This comparison of youth with the elderly is not meant in any way to demean the *value* that reasonable people place on the lives of the elderly. Rather, the comparison is made to emphasize the great loss of life due to malignant tumors.

The chemical causation of cancer is not a simple process. Many, perhaps most, chemical **carcinogen**s do not

in their usual condition have the potency to cause cancer. The non-cancer causing form of the chemical is called a "procarcinogen." Procarcinogens are frequently complex organic compounds which the human body attempts to dispose of when ingested. Hepatic **enzyme**s chemically change the procarcinogen in several steps to yield a chemical that is more easily excreted. The chemical changes result in modification of the procarcinogen (with no cancer forming ability) to the ultimate carcinogen (with cancer causing competence). Ultimate carcinogens have been shown to have a great affinity for **DNA**, **RNA**, and cellular proteins, and it is the interaction of the ultimate carcinogen with the cell macromolecules that causes cancer. It is unfortunate indeed that one cannot look at the chemical structure of a potential carcinogen and predict whether or not it will cause cancer. There is no computer program that will predict what hepatic enzymes will do to procarcinogens and how the metabolized end product(s) will interact with cells.

Great strides have been made in the development of chemotherapeutic agents designed to cure cancer. The drugs have significant efficacy with certain cancers (these include but are not limited to pediatric acute lymphocytic leukemia, choriocarcinoma, Hodgkin's disease, and testicular cancer), and some treated patients attain a normal life span. While this development is heartening, the cancers listed are, for the most part, relatively infrequent. More common cancers such as colorectal carcinoma, lung cancer, breast cancer, and ovarian cancer remain intractable with regard to treatment.

These several reasons are why animal testing is used in cancer research. The majority of Americans support the effort of the biomedical community to use animals to identify potential carcinogens with the hope that such knowledge will lead to a reduction of cancer prevalence. Similarly, they support efforts to develop more effective chemotherapy. Animals are used under terms of the Animal Welfare Act of 1966 and its several amendments. The act designates that the **U. S. Department of Agriculture** is responsible for the humane care and handling of warm-blooded and other animals used for biomedical research. The act also calls for inspection of research facilities to insure that adequate food, housing, and care are provided. It is the belief of many that the constraints of the current law have enhanced the quality of biomedical research. Poorly maintained animals do not provide quality research. The law also has enhanced the care of animals used in cancer research. *See also* Animal Legal Defense Fund; Animal rights; Animal Welfare Institute; Humane Society of the United States; People for the Ethical Treatment of Animals

[*Robert G. McKinnell*]

FURTHER READING

Abelson, P. H. "Tesing for Carcinogens With Rodents." *Science* 249 (21 September 1990): 1357.

Donnelly, S., and K. Nolan. "Animals, Science, and Ethics." *Hastings Center Report* 20 (May-June 1990): suppl 1-32.

Marx, J. "Animal Carcinogen Testing Challenged: Bruce Ames Has Stirred Up the Cancer Research Community." *Science* 250 (9 November 1990): 743-5.

Animal Legal Defense Fund (San Rafael, California)

Originally established in 1979 as Attorneys for Animal Rights, this organization changed its name to Animal Legal Defense Fund (ALDF) in 1984, and is known as "the law firm of the **animal rights** movement." Their motto is "we may be the only lawyers on earth whose clients are all innocent." ALDF contends that animals have a fundamental right to legal protection against abuse and exploitation. Over 350 attorneys work for ALDF, and the organization has more than 50,000 supporting members who help the cause of animal rights by writing letters and signing petitions for legislative action. The members are also strongly encouraged to work for animal rights at the local level.

ALDF's work is carried out in many places including research laboratories, large cities, small towns, and the wild. ALDF attorneys try to stop the use of animals in research experiments, and continue to fight for expanded enforcement of the Animal Welfare Act. ALDF also offers legal assistance to humane societies and city prosecutors to help in the enforcement of anti-cruelty laws and the exposure of veterinary malpractice. The organization attempts to protect wild animals from exploitation by working to place controls on trappers and sport hunters. Recently, in California, ALDF successfully stopped the hunting of mountain lions and black bears. ALDF is also active internationally bringing legal action against elephant poachers as well as against animal dealers who traffic in **endangered species**.

ALDF's clear goals and swift action have resulted in many court victories. In 1992 alone, the organization won cases involving cruelty to **dolphins**, dogs, horses, birds, and cats. It has also recently blocked the importation of over 70,000 monkeys from Bangladesh for research purposes, and has filed suit against the National Marine Fisheries Services to stop the illegal gray market in dolphins and other marine mammals.

The organization has also entered the classroom in its fight against animal abuse. In 1989 it started a toll-free national Dissection Hotline (1-800-922-FROG), through which it offers legal counsel to students who object to dissecting animals as part of their required coursework. ALDF also publishes a quarterly magazine, *The Animals' Advocate*. Contact: Animal Legal Defense Fund, 1363 Lincoln Avenue, San Rafael, CA 94901. Internet: http://aldf.org/.

[*Cathy M. Falk*]

Animal rights

Recent concern about the way humans treat animals has spawned a powerful social and political movement driven by the conviction that humans and certain animals are similar in morally significant ways, and that these similarities oblige humans to extend to those animals serious moral consideration, including rights. Though animal welfare movements, concerned primarily with humane treatment of pets, date back to the 1800s, modern animal rights activism has developed primarily out of concern about the use and treatment of domesticated animals in agriculture and in medical, scientific, and industrial research. The rapid growth in membership of animal rights organizations testifies to the increasing momentum of this movement. The leading animal rights group today, **People for the Ethical Treatment of Animals** (PETA), was founded in 1980 with 100 individuals; today, it has over 300,000 members. The animal rights activist movement has closely followed and used the work of modern philosophers who seek to establish a firm logical foundation for the extension of moral considerability beyond the human community into the animal community.

The nature of animals and appropriate relations between humans and animals have occupied Western thinkers for millennia. Traditional Western views, both religious and philosophical, have tended to deny that humans have any moral obligations to nonhumans. The rise of Christianity and its doctrine of personal immortality, which implies a qualitative gulf between humans and animals, contributed significantly to the dominant Western paradigm. When seventeenth century philosopher René Descartes declared animals mere biological machines, the perceived gap between humans and nonhuman animals reached its widest point. Jeremy Bentham, the father of ethical , challenged this view when he insisted that "The question is not, Can they *reason?*, nor Can they *talk?* but Can they *suffer?*", thus establishing sentience, or the ability to feel, as the sole criterion for membership in the moral community. This fostered a widespread anticruelty movement and exerted powerful force in shaping our legal and moral codes. Its modern legacy, the animal welfare movement, is reformist in that it continues to accept the legitimacy of sacrificing animal interests for human benefit, provided animals are spared any suffering which can conveniently and economically be avoided.

In contrast to the conservatively reformist platform of animal welfare crusaders, a new radical movement began in the late 1970s. This movement, variously referred to as animal liberation or animal rights, seeks to put an end to the routine sacrifice of animal interests for human benefit, even where the sacrifice is executed humanely. Added to the old language of anticruelty and humaneness is the new language of rights, justified in terms of tradition, nature, or fundamental moral principles. The rights of any entity, whether human or nonhuman, impose on humans certain obligations which we, as responsible moral agents, are necessarily compelled to meet.

In seeking to redefine the issue as one of rights, some animal protectionists organized around the well-articulated and widely disseminated utilitarian perspective of Australian philosopher **Peter Singer**. In his 1975 classic *Animal Liberation*, Singer argued that because some animals can experience pleasure and pain, they deserve our moral consideration. While not actually a rights position, Singer's work nevertheless uses the language of rights and was among the first to abandon welfarism and to propose a new ethic of moral considerability for all sentient creatures.

Animal rights activists, dressed as monkeys in prison suits, block the entrance to the Department of Health and Human Services in Washington, D.C. They are protesting the use of animals in laboratory research.

To assume that humans are inevitably superior to other species simply by virtue of their species membership is an injustice which Singer terms **speciesism**, an injustice parallel to racism and sexism.

Singer does not claim all animal lives to be of equal worth, nor that all sentient beings should be treated identically. In some cases, human interests may outweigh those of nonhumans, and Singer's utilitarian calculus would allow us to engage in practices which require the use of animals in spite of their pain, where those practices can be shown to produce an overall balance of pleasure over suffering.

Some animal advocates thus reject utilitarianism on the grounds that it allows the continuation of morally abhorrent practices. Lawyer Christopher Stone and philosophers Joel Feinberg and **Tom Regan** have focused on developing cogent arguments in support of rights for certain animals. Regan's 1983 book *The Case For Animal Rights* developed an absolutist position which criticized and broke from utilitarianism. It is Regan's arguments, not reformism or the pragmatic principle of utility, which have come to dominate the rhetoric of the animal rights crusade.

The question of which animals possess rights then arises. Regan asserts it is those who, like us, are subjects experiencing their own lives. By "experiencing" Regan means conscious creatures aware of their **environment** and with goals, desires, emotions, and a sense of their own identity. These characteristics give an individual inherent value, and

this value entitles the bearer to certain inalienable rights, especially the right to be treated as an end in itself, and never merely as a means to human ends.

The environmental community has not embraced animal rights; in fact, the two groups have often been at odds. A rights approach focused exclusively on animals does not cover all the entities such as **ecosystem**s that many environmentalists feel ought to be considered morally. Yet a rights approach that would satisfy environmentalists by encompassing both living and nonliving entities may render the concept of rights philosophically and practically meaningless. Regan accuses environmentalists of environmental fascism, insofar as they advocate the protection of species and ecosystems at the expense of individual animals. Most animal rightists advocate the protection of ecosystems only as necessary to protect individual animals, and assign no more value to the individual members of a highly **endangered species** than to those of a common or domesticated species. Thus, because of its focus on the individual, animal rights can offer no realistic plan for managing natural systems or for protecting ecosystem health, and may at times hinder the efforts of resource managers to effectively address these issues.

For most animal activists, the practical implications of the rights view are clear and uncompromising. The rights view holds that all animal research, factory farming, and commercial or sport hunting and trapping should be abolished. This change of moral status necessitates a fundamental change in contemporary Western moral attitudes towards animals, for it requires humans to treat animals as inherently valuable beings with lives and interests independent of human needs and wants. While this change is not likely to occur in the near future, the efforts of animal rights advocates may ensure that wholesale slaughter of these creatures for unnecessary reasons that is no longer routinely the case, and that when such sacrifice is found to be necessary, it is accompanied by moral deliberation. *See also* Animal cancer tests; Animal Legal Defense Fund; Animal Welfare Institute; Commercial fishing; Humane Society of the United States; Overhunting; Wildlife

[*Ann S. Causey*]

FURTHER READING

Hargrove, E. C. *The Animal Rights/Environmental Ethics Debate.* New York: SUNY Press, 1992.

Regan, T. *The Case For Animal Rights.* Los Angeles: University of California Press, 1983.

———, and P. Singer. *Animal Rights and Human Obligations.* 2nd ed. Englewood Cliffs, NJ: Prentice-Hall, 1989.

Singer, P. *Animal Liberation.* New York: Avon Books, 1975.

Zimmerman, M. E., et al, eds. *Environmental Philosophy: From Animal Rights To Radical Ecology.* Englewood Cliffs, NJ: Prentice-Hall, 1993.

Animal waste

Animal wastes are commonly considered the excreted materials from live animals. However, under certain production conditions, the waste may also include straw, hay, wood shavings, or other sources of organic debris. It has been estimated that there may be as much as 2 billion tons of animal wastes produced in the United States annually. Application of excreta to **soil** brings benefits such as improved soil **tilth**, increased water-holding capacity, and some plant **nutrient**s. Concentrated forms of excreta or high application rates to soils without proper management may lead to high salt concentrations in the soil and cause serious on- or off-site **pollution**.

Animal Welfare Institute (Washington, D.C.)

Founded in 1951, the Animal Welfare Institute (AWI) is a non-profit organization that works to educate the public and to secure needed action to protect animals. AWI is a highly respected, influential, and effective group that works with Congress, the public, the news media, government officials, and the **conservation** community on animal protection programs and projects. Its major goals include improving the treatment of laboratory animals and a reduction in their use; eliminating cruel methods of trapping **wildlife**; saving **species** from **extinction**; preventing painful experiments on animals in schools and encouraging humane science teaching; improving shipping conditions for animals in transit;

banning the importation of parrots and other exotic wild birds for the pet industry; and improving the conditions under which farm animals are kept, confined, transported, and slaughtered.

In 1971 AWI launched the Save the Whales Campaign to help protect **whales**. The organization provides speakers and experts for conferences and meetings around the world, including Congressional hearings and international treaty and commission meetings. Each year, the institute awards its prestigious Albert Schweitzer Medal to an individual for outstanding achievement in the advancement of animal welfare. Its publications include *The AWI Quarterly*; books such as *Animals and Their Legal Rights*; *Facts about Furs*; and *The Endangered Species Handbook*; booklets, brochures, and other educational materials, which are distributed to schools, teachers, scientists, government officials, humane societies, libraries, and veterinarians.

AWI works closely with its associate organization, The Society for Animal Protective Legislation (SAPL), a lobbying group based in Washington, D.C. Founded in 1955, SAPL devotes its efforts to supporting legislation to protect animals, often mobilizing its 14,000 "correspondents" in letter-writing campaigns to members of Congress. SAPL has been responsible for the passage of more animal protection laws than any other organization in the country, and perhaps the world, and it has been instrumental in securing the enactment of 14 federal laws.

Major federal legislation which SAPL has promoted includes the first federal Humane Slaughter Act in 1958 and its strengthening in 1978; the 1959 Wild Horse Act; the 1966 Laboratory Animal Welfare Act and its strengthening in 1970, 1976, 1985, and 1990; the 1969 Endangered Species Act and its strengthening in 1973; a 1970 measure banning the crippling or "soring" of Tennessee Walking Horses; measures passed in 1971 prohibiting hunting from aircraft, protecting wild horses, and resolutions calling for a moratorium on commercial **whaling**; the 1972 **Marine Mammal Protection Act**; negotiation of the 1973 **Convention on International Trade in Endangered Species of Fauna and Flora (CITES)**; the 1979 Packwood-Magnuson Amendment protecting whales and other ocean creatures; the 1981 strengthening of the Lacey Act to restrict the importation of illegal wildlife; the 1990 Pet Theft Act; and, in 1992, The Wild Bird Conservation Act, protecting parrots and other exotic wild birds; the International Dolphin Conservation Act, restricting the killing of **dolphins** by tuna fishermen; and the Driftnet Fishery Conservation Act, protecting whales, sea birds, and other ocean life from being caught and killed in huge, 30-mile-long nets.

Major goals of SAPL include enacting legislation to end the use of cruel steel-jaw leg-hold traps and to secure proper enforcement, funding, administration, and reauthorization of existing animal protection laws. Both AWI and SAPL have long been headed by their chief volunteer, Christine Stevens, a prominent Washington, D.C. humanitarian and community leader. Contact: Animal Welfare Institute, PO Box 3650, Georgetown Station, Washington, DC 20007. Society for Animal Protective Legislation,

PO Box 3719, Georgetown Station, Washington, DC 20007. Internet: http://www.animalwelfare.com/.

[*Lewis G. Regenstein*]

Anion
See **Ion**

Antarctic Treaty (1961)

The Antarctic Treaty, signed in 1961, established an international administrative system for the continent. The impetus for the treaty was the International Geophysical Year, 1957-1958, which had brought scientists from many nations together to study **Antarctica**. The political situation in Antarctica was complex at the time, with seven nations having made sometimes overlapping territorial claims to the continent: Argentina, Australia, Chile, France, New Zealand, Norway, and the United Kingdom. Several other nations, most notably the former U.S.S.R. and the United States, had been active in Antarctic exploration and research and were concerned with how the continent would be administered.

Negotiations on the treaty began in June 1958 with Belgium, Japan, and South Africa joining the original nine countries. The treaty was signed in December 1959 and took effect in June 1961. It begins by "recognizing that it is in the interest of all mankind that Antarctica shall continue forever to be used exclusively for peaceful purposes." The key to the treaty was the nations' agreement to disagree on territorial claims. Signatories of the treaty are not required to renounce existing claims, nations without claims shall have an equal voice as those with claims, and no new claims or claim enlargements can take place while the treaty is in force. This agreement defused the most controversial and complex issue regarding Antarctica, and in an unorthodox way. Among the other major provisions of the treaty are: the continent will be demilitarized; nuclear explosions and the storage of nuclear wastes are prohibited; the right of unilateral inspection of all facilities on the continent to ensure that the provisions of the treaty are being honored is guaranteed; and scientific research can continue throughout the continent.

The treaty runs indefinitely and can be amended, but only by the unanimous consent of the signatory nations. Provisions were also included for other nations to become parties to the treaty. These additional nations can either be "acceding parties," which do not conduct significant research activities but agree to abide by the terms of the treaty, or "consultative parties," which have acceded to the treaty and undertake substantial scientific research on the continent. Twelve nations have joined the original twelve in becoming consultative parties: Brazil, China, Finland, Germany, India, Italy, Peru, Poland, South Korea, Spain, Sweden, and Uruguay.

Under the auspices of the treaty, the Convention on the Conservation of Antarctic Marine Living Resources was adopted in 1982. This regulatory regime is an effort to protect the Antarctic marine **ecosystem** from severe damage due to **overfishing**. Following this convention, negotiations began on an agreement for the management of Antarctic mineral resources. The Convention on the Regulation of Antarctic Mineral Resource Activities was concluded in June 1988, but in 1989 Australia and France rejected the convention, urging that Antarctica be declared an international **wilderness** closed to mineral development. In 1991 the Protocol on Environmental Protection, which included a 50-year ban on mining, was drafted. At first the United States refused to endorse this protocol, but it eventually joined the other treaty parties in signing the new convention in October 1991.

[*Christopher McGrory Klyza*]

FURTHER READING

Shapley, D. *The Seventh Continent: Antarctica in a Resource Age.* Baltimore: Johns Hopkins University Press for Resources for the Future, 1985.

Antarctica

The earth's fifth largest continent, centered asymmetrically around the South Pole. Ninety-eight percent of this land mass, which covers approximately 5.4 million square miles (13.8 million sq km), is covered by snow and ice sheets to an average depth of 1.25 miles (2 km). This continent receives very little precipitation, less than 5 inches (12 cm) annually, and the world's coldest temperature was recorded here, at -128° F (-89° C). Exposed shorelines and inland mountain tops support life only in the form of **lichens**, two **species** of flowering plants, and several insect species. In sharp contrast, the ocean surrounding the Antarctic continent is one of the world's richest marine **habitat**s. Cold water rich in oxygen and **nutrient**s supports teeming populations of **phytoplankton** and shrimp-like Antarctica **krill**, the food source for the region's legendary numbers of **whales**, **seals**, penguins, and fish. During the nineteenth century and early twentieth century, whalers and sealers severely depleted Antarctica's marine mammal populations. In recent decades the whale and seal populations have begun to recover, but interest has grown in new resources, especially oil, minerals, fish, and tourism.

The Antarctic's functional limit is a band of turbulent ocean currents and high winds that circle the continent at about 60 degrees South latitude. This ring is known as the Antarctic convergence zone. Ocean turbulence in this zone creates a barrier marked by sharp differences in **salinity** and water temperature. Antarctic marine habitats, including the limit of krill populations, are bounded by the convergence.

Since 1961 the **Antarctic Treaty** has formed a framework for international cooperation and compromise in the use of Antarctica and its resources. The treaty reserves the Antarctic continent for peaceful scientific research and bans all military activities. Nuclear explosions and **radioactive waste** are also banned, and the treaty neither recognizes nor establishes territorial claims in Antarctica. However, neither does the treaty deny pre-1961 claims, of which seven exist. Furthermore, some signatories to the treaty, including the

United States, reserve the right to make claims at a later date. At present the United States has no territorial claims, but it does have several permanent stations, including one at the South Pole. Questions of territorial control could become significant if oil and mineral resources were to become economically recoverable. The primary resources currently exploited are fin fish and krill fisheries. Interest in oil and mineral resources has risen in recent decades, most notably during the 1973 "oil crisis." The expense and difficulty of extraction and transportation has so far made exploitation uneconomical, however.

Human activity has brought an array of environmental dangers to Antarctica. Oil and mineral extraction could seriously threaten marine habitat and onshore penguin and seal breeding grounds. A growing and largely uncontrolled fishing industry may be depleting both fish and krill populations in Antarctic waters. The parable of the **Tragedy of the Commons** seems ominously appropriate to Antarctica fisheries, which have already nearly eliminated many whale, seal, and penguin species. **Solid waste** and **oil spills** associated with research stations and with tourism pose an additional threat. Although Antarctica remains free of "permanent settlement," forty year-round scientific research stations are maintained on the continent. The population of these bases numbers nearly 4,000. In 1989 the Antarctic had its first oil spill when an Argentine supply ship, carrying 81 tourists and 170,000 gallons (643,500 liters) of diesel fuel, ran aground. Spilled fuel destroyed a nearby breeding colony of Adele penguins (*Pygoscelis adeliae*). With more than 3,000 cruise ships visiting annually, more spills seem inevitable. Tourists themselves present a further threat to penguins and seals. Visitors have been accused of disturbing breeding colonies, thus endangering the survival of young penguins and seals. *See also* Ecotourism

[*Mary Ann Cunningham*]

FURTHER READING

Child, J. *Antarctica and South American Geopolitics.* New York: Praeger, 1988.

Parsons, A. *Antarctica: The Next Decade.* Cambridge: Cambridge University Press, 1987.

Shapely, D. *The Seventh Continent: Antarctica in a Resource Age.* Baltimore: Johns Hopkins University Press for Resources for the Future, 1985.

Suter, K. D. *World Law and the Last Wilderness.* Sydney: Friends of the Earth, 1980.

Antarctica Project (Washington, D.C.)

The Antarctica Project, founded in 1982, is an organization designed to protect **Antarctica** and educate the public, government, and international groups about its current and future status. The group monitors activities that affect the Antarctic region, conducts policy research and analysis in both national and international arenas, and maintains an impressive library of books, articles, and documents about Antarctica. It is also a member of the Antarctic and Southern Ocean Coalition (ASOC), which has 200 member organizations in 35 countries.

In 1988, ASOC received a limited observer status to the Convention on the Conservation of Antarctic Marine Living Resources (CCAMLR). So far, the observer status continues to be renewed, providing ASOC with a way to monitor CCAMLR and to present proposals. In 1989, the Antarctica Project served as an expert adviser to the U.S. Office of Technology Assessment on its study and report of the Minerals Convention. The group prepared a study paper outlining the need for a comprehensive environmental protection convention. Later, a **conservation** strategy on Antarctica was developed with **IUCN—The World Conservation Union**.

Besides continuing the work it has already begun, the Antarctica Project has several goals for the future. One calls for the designation of Antarctica as a world park. Another focuses on developing a bilateral plan to pump out the oil and salvage the *Bahia Parasio*, a ship which sank in early 1989 near the U.S. Palmer Station. Early estimated salvage costs ran at $50 million.

Three to four times a year, The Antarctica Project publishes *ECO*, an international publication which covers current political topics concerning the Antarctic Treaty System (provided free to members). Other publications include briefing materials, critiques, books, slide shows, videos, and posters for educational and advocacy purposes. Contact: The Antarctica Project, 218 D Street, SE, Washington, DC 20003.

[*Cathy M. Falk*]

Anthracite coal

See **Coal**

Anthropocentrism

See **Environmental ethics**

Anthropogenic

Refers to changes in the natural world due to the activities of people. Such changes may be positive or negative. For example, anthropogenic changes in **soil**s can occur due to plowing, fertilizing, using the soil for construction, or long continued manure additions. When manure is added to soils, the change is considered beneficial, but when soils are compacted for use as parking lots, the change is considered negative. Other examples of anthropogenic effects on the environment include **oil spills**, **acid rain**, logging of **old-growth forest**s, creation of **wetlands**, preservation of **endangered species**, among others.

Ants

See **Fire ants**

Aquaculture

Aquaculture is the husbandry or rearing of aquatic organisms under controlled or semi-controlled conditions. Stated another way, it is the art of cultivating natural plants and animals in water for human consumption or use. It can be considered aquatic agriculture, or as some people wish to call it, underwater agriculture. It is sometimes incorrectly termed aquiculture. Aquaculture involves production in both fresh and salt water. Mariculture is aquaculture in saline (brackish and marine) water. **Hydroponics** is the raising of aquatic plants in water. Organisms that are grown in aquaculture include fish, shellfish (crustaceans such as crawfish and shrimp, and molluscs such as oysters and clams), algae, and aquatic plants. More people are eating seafood for their added health benefit. Not only can these organisms be raised for human consumption, but they can also be reared for the lucrative baitfish, health food, aquarium, and home garden-pond industries.

Aquaculture dates back more than 3,500 years ago when carp were spawned and reared in China. There have also been records of aquaculture practices being performed in Egypt and Japan nearly that long ago. Mariculture is thought to have been brought to Hawaii about 1,500 years ago. Modern aquaculture finds its roots in the 1960s in the culturing of catfish in the United States and salmon in Europe.

There are two general methods used in aquaculture, extensive and intensive. Extensive aquaculture involves the production of low densities of organisms. For example, fingerling fish can be raised in ponds where they feed on the natural foods such as phytoplankton and zooplankton, and the matured fish are harvested at the end of the growing season. These ponds can also be fertilized to enhance the **food chain**, thus increasing fish or shellfish production. Typically, several hundred to several thousand pounds of fish are raised per acre annually. Intensive practices utilize much higher densities of organisms. This requires better water quality, which necessitates circulation, oxygenation, added commercial foods, and biological filters (with bacteria) to remove toxic wastes. These systems can produce more than a million pounds of fish per acre. Intensive aquaculture often utilizes tanks to grow the fish or shellfish, either indoor or outdoor. The water can be recirculated as long as toxic wastes such as ammonia are removed. Some processors run the effluent from the fish tanks through greenhouses with plants raised hydroponically to remove these chemicals. In this way, added revenue is gained. Some aquaculture operations raise only one type of organism (called monoculture) while others grow several species together (termed polyculture). An example of polyculture would be growing tilapia and catfish together.

About 86% of the world's aquaculture production (about 22 million tons in 1993) comes from Asia. China is the leading producer nation, with most of their production coming from carp, and secondarily shrimp. India is the second largest producer nation, followed by Japan, Taiwan, and the Philippines. For example, 1991 shrimp production in China reached nearly 250,000 tons. (Note: One English ton equals approximately one metric ton, so they can be thought of as equivalents). Only Taiwan exceeded this with 350,000 tons of shrimp produced. Ecuador produced 100,000 tons. In contrast, total shrimp production for the United States was only 1,600 tons. Salmon is another major fish produced by aquaculture, with most coming from Norway. Nearly 300,000 tons were produced in 1990. Great Britain, Canada, Chile, and Iceland are also major producers of farm-raised salmon. Other important aquaculture species and some of the countries where they are raised include: tilapia (Caribbean countries, Egypt, India, Israel, the Philippines); milkfish (the Philippines); Nile perch (Egypt); sea bass and sea bream (Egypt, Israel); mullet (Egypt, India, Israel); dolphin fish (also known as mahi-mahi; Egypt); grass and silver carp (Israel); halibut and other flatfishes (France, Norway); prawns (Caribbean countries, Israel, the Philippines); mussels and oysters (the Philippines); crabs (India); seaweeds (India, Japan); *Spirulina* (a blue-green algae; India); and many other examples.

Although people in the United States consume less fish and shellfish than people in other parts of the world, each year we spend billions of dollars importing edible fish. Total production from aquaculture in the United States in 1991 was about 540,000 tons, which earned about $750 million. This comprises only about 3% of the world's total aquaculture production. Domestically, catfish is our major aquaculture species ($200 million per year in 1991). Trout (primarily raised in Idaho) is the number two species raised in aquaculture and accounts for a $55 million per year industry. Shrimp, hybrid-striped bass, and tilapia are other species commonly raised in the United States. Of the 16,000 tons of crawfish (more appropriately called crayfish) collected in 1990 in the United States, about 60% came from aquaculture ponds.

In 1986 the U.S. Congress placed aquaculture under the jurisdiction of the U.S. Department of Agriculture appropriated $3 million to establish four regional aquaculture centers. These centers are located at the University of Washington, Southeastern Massachusetts University, Mississippi State University, and a Center for Tropical and Subtropical Aquaculture jointly administered by the University of Hawaii and the Oceanic Institute. The following year Congress created a fifth center at Michigan State University. The mandate for these centers was, and still is, to promote aquaculture in their region and to solve some of the problems facing this industry. More recent legislation has created mariculture research centers under the Sea Grant Program within the Department of Commerce.

Aquaculture is an appealing industry because it can help supplement what is caught in natural fisheries and what is produced through agriculture. This has tremendous implications in terms of the growing future dilemma with human over-population, decreased fisheries captured from the oceans, and stabilized agriculture production. Aquaculture is a growing industry in the world, which not only translates into more food, but also more revenue and jobs. This fulfills the old Chinese proverb that you can give a person a fish and feed them for a day, or you can teach a person to fish (or do aquaculture) and feed them for a lifetime.

It is particularly important to look at aquaculture development in third-world countries where protein sources are scarce. Since many of these countries lie in equatorial regions, tilapia (also called St. Peter's fish because they are the likely fish caught by the disciples in the Sea of Galilee) are one of the best prospects to grow because of their tolerance of high temperatures and poor water quality (i.e., high ammonia levels). They are also omnivorous filter feeders and thrive on blue-green algae. One alternative to the deforestation of our precious rain forests might be to encourage indigenous people to construct earthen ponds and raise tilapia on the fringes of the forests, thus producing not only a protein source, but also a cash crop. An advantage of aquaculture over agriculture is that fish can be grown in ponds overlying soil that may be toxic to plants (for example, with high concentrations of sulphur, aluminum, or salt). In addition, aquaculture species can often be held longer if there is a glut on the market, thus allowing more flexible selling times. Despite these positive attributes, there are serious problems involved in aquaculture. These include release of waste into the water (adversely affecting water quality); spread of diseases and parasites through concentrated growing conditions; disfavorable taste through chemicals like geosmin in the water being taken up by the fish (termed "off-flavor" in catfish); release of hybrid strains into the natural population which can result in mixed genetics with natural populations; obstruction of the aesthetics along coastlines; and overproduction, which can result in depressed market prices. For example, both the catfish and salmon industries experienced a tremendous drop in their market prices due to overproduction in 1990 and 1991.

Aquaculture seems to have a bright future as long as we address some of the above-mentioned problems. One example of an enterprising solution to one of these problems is that of releasing wrasse (marine parasite-feeding fish) into aquaculture tanks and cages to remove fish lice from salmon. This not only solves the problem of parasites, but also eliminates the need to add chemicals to the water that kill parasites, stress the fish, and pollute the environment. The same pitfalls that have plagued agriculture must be avoided in aquaculture. A key concern is that of sustainability—concern for the culture environment and non-crop organisms in measuring the success of the aquaculture industry (discussed in the June 1996 issue of "World Aquaculture"). There is no need for agriculture farmers to feel threatened by aquaculture; on the contrary, it seems that these two areas can actually be brought together, particularly with small local farms in underdeveloped countries supplementing their terrestrial crops with aquatic production. This has already been done quite well in Norway, which has more than 700 fish farms in a country with only 4.2 million people. Aquaculture is evolving from an art, with trial-and-error learning, to more of a science with ongoing research. Countries such as Japan, the United States, Israel, and Norway are developing new technology to bring this field to higher levels. Recent predictions suggest that aquaculture will be able to meet at least 40% of the global demand for fish and shellfish over the next 15 years if current trends prevail. Government, academic institutions, and industry must work hand-in-hand to see that these predictions come to fruition with minimal environmental damage.

[*John Korstad*]

FURTHER READING

Bardach, J. "Aquaculture." *BioScience* 37 (1987): 318-19.

Hopkins, J. S. "Aquaculture Sustainability: Avoiding the Pitfalls of the Green Revolution." *World Aquaculture* 27 (1996): 13-5.

Lee, J. S., and M. E. Newman. *Aquaculture Today—An Introduction*. Illinois: Interstate Publishers, 1992.

Parker, N. C. "History, Status, and Future of Aquaculture in the United States." *CRC Critical Reviews in Aquatic Science*. 1 (1989): 97-109.

Stickney, R. R. *Principles of Aquaculture*. New York: Wiley, 1994.

World Aquaculture Society. "World Aquaculture—A Special Section on Aquaculture Research and Development Around the World." *World Aquaculture* 27 (1996): 7-30.

Aquarium trade

International trade in live fish and other marine species for international aquarium hobby market. Most fish, corals, and other marine aquarium species traded internationally are collected live from tropical and subtropical **coral reef**s, especially in the Philippines, Indonesia, and other Asian countries. Nearly half the world aquarium fish market is in the United States. Although the capture and marketing of live reef species provides a significant income source in remote communities, international trade has alarmed conservationists and environmentalists because of harmful collecting methods. A majority of live tropical fish are captured with sodium cyanide (NaCN), a highly toxic and inexpensive powdered poison. Divers use squirt bottles containing a cyanide solution or drop cyanide tablets into reef crevices where fish hide. The poison stuns the fish, making them easy to capture, and the fish usually recover after a few minutes. Fish are transferred to holding tanks on ships and then transported to international wholesalers. From 70-90% of fish captured with cyanide die later, however, due to damage to the liver, stomach and other tissues. Another problem common in salt water aquaria is "sudden death syndrome," when fish inexplicably die soon after they are introduced to the aquarium. Some researchers attribute the syndrome to cyanide, which is stored in tissues during transport. Fish are often not fed during storage, but when they begin to eat in their new aquarium, or if they undergo even mild shock, the cyanide is released into the blood stream and kills the fish. Although solid figures are impossible to establish, estimates of the proportion of tropical live fish caught with cyanide are 75% or higher worldwide, and 90% in some countries.

The reefs where fish are captured fare as badly as the fish: one study found all cyanide-treated corals dead within three months after treatment. Coral reefs also suffer physical damage as divers break off chunks of coral to retrieve stunned fish. Despite harm to reefs and high fish mortality rates, cyanide is considered the most cost effective method to capture popular species such as angel fish and trigger fish.

Peter Rubec, a researcher with the International Marinelife Alliance, reports that an exporter operating from Manila initiated the export of marine fish from the Philippines in 1957. With almost 2,200 fish species, the Philippines has the highest reef fish diversity in the world, including 200 species that are commonly exported for the marine pet fish industry. In 1986 Filipino reefs provided as much as 80% of the world's tropical marine fish, a number that fell only to 70% by 1997. From 1970-1980 exports rose from 1,863,000 lbs (845,000 kg) of live fish packed in water to 4.41 million lbs (2 million kg) worth $2 billion dollars. Since then export numbers have fallen in the Philippines, as stocks have thinned and the trade has diversified to other countries, but in 1986 the country's marine tropical fish trade was worth $10 million dollars. Worldwide the value of aquarium fish was $100 million dollars, plus corals and other supplies.

Cyanide fishing was first introduced in the Philippines in about 1962. The technique has since spread to Indonesia, New Guinea, and other regions where live fish are caught. Cyanide has since been banned in the Philippines and Indonesia, but enforcement is difficult because fishing vessels are dispersed, often in hard-to-reach sections of remote islands. Despite legal bans, an estimated 375,000 lbs (170,000 kg) of cyanide is still used each year in the Philippines. Cyanide fishing boats have even exploited established marine preserves and parks, such as Indonesia's Take Bone Atoll. Furthermore, as enforcement mechanisms develop, cyanide fishing can quickly spread to other countries, where laws are still weak or lacking.

The greatest problems of the live reef fish trade result from its mobility. The frontier of cyanide fishing has moved steadily through Southeast Asia to tropical Pacific islands and even across the Indian Ocean to the Seychelles and Tanzania, as fertile reefs have disappeared and as governments caught on to their fishing practices and began to impose laws restricting the use of cyanide and explosives. Since the market is international and lucrative, it does not matter where the fish are caught. Furthermore, fish exporters succeed best if they continually explore new, unexploited reefs where more unusual and exotic fish can be found. The migratory nature of the industry makes it easy for fishing vessels to move on as soon as a country begins to enact or enforce limits on their activities.

Starting in 1984 international conservation groups have worked to introduce net fishing as a less harmful fishing alternative that still allows divers to retain their income from live fish. To catch fish with nets, divers may use a stick to drive fish from their hiding places in the reef and then trap the fish with a fine mesh net. Reports indicate that long-term survival rates of net-caught fish may be as high as 90%, compared to as little as 10% among cyanide-caught fish. In Hawaii and Australia, where legal controls are more effective than in Southeast Asia, nets are used routinely. Although the

aquarium industry has provided little aid in the effort to increase net-fishing, local communities in the Philippines and Indonesia, with the aid of international conservationist organizations, have worked to encourage net fishing. Increased local control of reef fisheries is also important in helping communities to control cyanide fishing in their nearby reefs. Local communities that have depended on reefs and their fish for generations understand that sustainable use is both possible and essential for their own survival, so they often have a greater incentive to prevent reef damage than either state governments or transient fishing enterprises. In an effort to help coastal villages help themselves, the government of the Philippines has recently granted villagers greater rights to patrol and control nearby fishing areas.

Another step toward the control of cyanide fishing is the development of cyanide detection techniques that allow wholesalers to determine whether fish are tainted with residual cyanide. Simply by sampling the water a fish is carried in, the test can detect if the fish is releasing cyanide from its tissues or metabolizing cyanide. Ideally this test could help control illegal and harmful fish trade, but thus far it is not widely used. Attempts have also begun to establish cyanide-free certification, but this has been slow to take effect because the market is dispersed and there are many different exporters.

Coastal villages also suffer from reef damage. Most coastal communities in coral reef regions have traditionally relied on the rich fishery supported by the reef as a principal protein and food source. As reefs suffer, fisheries deteriorate. Some researchers estimate that just 1,300 feet (400 m) of healthy reef the can support 800 people, while the same amount of damaged reef can support only a quarter that many people. Other ecological benefits also disappear as reefs deteriorate, since healthy coral reefs perform critical water clarification functions. Corals, along with sea anemones and other life forms they shelter, filter floating organic matter from the water column, cycling it into the food chain that supports fish, crustaceans, birds, and humans. By breaking ocean waves offshore, healthy and intact corals also control beach erosion and reduce storm surges, the unusually large waves and tides associated with storms and high winds.

Divers collecting the fish suffer as well. Exposure to cyanide and inadequate or unsafe breathing hoses are common problems. In addition divers must search deeper waters as more accessible fish are depleted. In 1993, 40 divers in a single small village were reported to have been injured and 10 killed by the bends, which results from rapid changes of pressure as divers rise from deep water; ten of these fishermen died.

Unfortunately there has been relatively little breeding of tropical fish in aquaria, at least in part because these fish often have specialized habitat needs and life style requirements that are difficult to produce under controlled or domestic conditions. In addition the aquarium trade is specialized and limited in volume, and gearing up to produce fish can be an expensive undertaking for which a reliable market must be assured. Equally unfortunate is the fact that American and European dealers in aquarium products tend to be elusive about the details of where their fish came from and how they were caught. If pet shops do not mention the source, many aquarium owners are able to ignore the implications of the fish trade they are participating in.

In addition to aquarium fishing, cyanide has now been introduced to the live food-fish market, especially in Asia, where live fish are an expensive delicacy. The live food/fish trade, centered in China and Hong Kong, is estimated to exceed $1 billion per year. The Hong Kong cyanide fleet alone has hundreds of vessels, each employing up to 25 divers to catch fish with cyanide for the Chinese and Hong Kong restaurant market.

Another harmful fishing technique is blast fishing—releasing a small bomb that breaks up coral masses in which fish hide. A single explosive might destroy corals in a circle from 10-33 feet (3-10 m) wide. The fish, briefly stunned by the blast, are easily retrieved from the rubble. Half the countries in the South Pacific have seen coral damage from blasting, including Guam, Indonesia, Malaysia, and Thailand. The technique has also spread to Africa, where it is used in Tanzania and other countries bordering the Indian Ocean.

Some environmentalists stress that simply eliminating the live fish trade is not an adequate solution. Because live fish are so lucrative, much more valuable than the same weight in dead fish, fishermen may be able to produce a better income with fewer fish when they catch live fish. Steering the fish capture methods to a safer alternative, especially the use of nets, could do more to save reef communities than eliminating the trade altogether.

[*Mary Ann Cunningham*]

FURTHER READING

Ariyoshi, R. "Halting a coral catastrophe." *Nature Conservancy* 47, no.1 (1997): 20-25.

Robinson, S. "A Proposal for the Marine Fish Industry: Converting Philippine Cyanide Users into Netsmen." *Greenfields* 15, no. 9 (1985): 39-45.

Rubec, P.I. "The Effects of Sodium Cyanide on Coral Reefs and Marine Fish in the Philippines". *The First Asian Fisheries Forum*. Manila, Philippines: Asian Fisheries Society, 1986.

Aquatic chemistry

Water can exist in various forms within the **environment**, including: (1) liquid water of oceans, lakes and ponds, rivers and streams, soil interstices, and underground **aquifers**; (2) solid water of glacial ice and more-ephemeral snow, rime, and frost; and (3) vapour water of cloud, fog, and the general **atmosphere**. More than 97 percent of the total quantity of water in the hydrosphere occurs in the oceans, while about two percent is glacial ice, and less than one percent is **groundwater**. Only about 0.01 percent occurs in freshwater lakes, and the quantities in other compartments are even smaller.

Each compartment of water in the hydrosphere has its own characteristic chemistry. Seawater has a relatively large concentration of inorganic solutes (about 3.5 percent), dominated by the **ion**s chloride (1.94 percent), sodium (1.08 percent), sulfate (0.27 percent), magnesium (0.13 percent),

calcium (0.041 percent), potassium (0.049 percent), and bicarbonate (0.014 percent).

Surface waters such as lakes, ponds, rivers, and streams are highly variable in their chemical composition. Saline and soda lakes of **arid** regions have total salt concentrations that can substantially exceed that of seawater. Lakes such as Great Salt Lake in Utah and the Dead Sea in Israel can have salt concentrations that exceed 25 percent. The shores of such lakes are caked with a crystalline rime of evaporite minerals, which are sometimes mined for industrial use.

The most chemically dilute surface waters are lakes in **watershed**s with hard, slowly weathering bedrock and **soil**s. Such lakes can have total salt concentrations of less than 0.001 percent. For example, Beaverskin Lake in Nova Scotia has very clear, dilute water that is chemically dominated by chloride, sodium, and sulfate, in concentrations of two-thirds of the norm for surface water or less, with only traces of calcium, usually most abundant, and no silica. A nearby body of water, Big Red Lake, has a similarly dilute concentration of inorganic ions but, because it receives drainage from a bog, its chemistry also includes a large concentration of dissolved organic **carbon**, mainly comprised of humic/fulvic acids that stain the water a dark brown and greatly inhibit the penetration of sunlight.

The water of precipitation is considerably more dilute than that of surface waters, with concentrations of sulfate, calcium, and magnesium of one-fortieth to one-hundredth of surface water levels, but adding small amounts of **nitrate** and ammonium. Cloride and sodium concentrations depend on proximity to salt water. For example, precipitation at a remote site in Nova Scotia, only 31 miles (50 km) of the Atlantic Ocean, will have six to ten times as much sodium and chloride as a similarly remote location in northern Ontario.

Acid rain is associated with the presence of relatively large concentrations of sulfate and nitrate in precipitation water. If the negative electrical charges of the sulfate and nitrate anions cannot be counterbalanced by positive charges of the cations sodium, calcium, magnesium, and ammonium, then hydrogen ions go into solution, making the water acidic. **Hubbard Brook Experimental Forest**, New Hampshire, within an airshed of industrial, **automobile**, and residential **emission**s from the northeastern United States and eastern Canada, receives a substantially acidic precipitation, with an average **pH** of about 4.1. At Hubbard Brook, sulfate and nitrate together contribute 87 percent of the anion-equivalents in precipitation. Because cations other than the **hydrogen** ion can only neutralize about 29 percent of those anion charges, hydrogen ions must go into solution, making the precipitation acidic.

Fogwaters can have much larger chemical concentrations, mostly because the inorganic **chemicals** in fogwater droplets are less diluted by water than in rain and snow. For example, fogwater on Mount Moosilauke, New Hampshire, has average sulfate and nitrate concentrations about nine times more than in rainfall there, with ammonium eight times more, sodium seven times more, and potassium and the hydrogen ion three times more.

The above descriptions deal with chemicals present in relatively large concentrations in water. Often, however, chemicals that are present in much smaller concentrations can be of great environmental importance.

For example, in freshwaters phosphate is the **nutrient** that most frequently limits the productivity of plants, and therefore, of the aquatic **ecosystem**. If the average concentration of phosphate in lakewater is less than about 10 µg/L, then the algal productivity will be very small, and the lake is classified as oligotrophic. Lakes with phosphate concentrations ranging from about 10 to 35 µg/L are mesotrophic, those with 35 to 100 µg/L are eutrophic, and those with more than 100 µ/L are very productive, and very green, hypertrophic waterbodies. In a few exceptional cases, the productivity of freshwater may be limited by **nitrogen**, silica, or carbon, and sometimes by unusual **micronutrient**s. For example, the productivity of **phytoplankton** in Castle Lake, California, has been shown to be limited by the availability of the trace metal, molybdenum.

Sometimes, chemicals present in trace concentrations in water can be toxic to plants and animals, causing substantial ecological changes. An important characteristic of acidic waters is their ability to solubilize **aluminum** from minerals, producing ionic aluminum. In non-acidic waters, ionic aluminum is generally present in minute quantities, but in very acidic waters when pH is less than 2, attainable by **acid mine drainage**, soluble-aluminum concentrations can rise drastically. Although some aquatic biota are physiologically tolerant of these aluminum ions, other species, such as fish, suffer toxicity and may disappear from acidified waterbodies. Many aquatic species cannot tolerate even small quantities of ionic aluminum. Many ecologists believe that aluminum ions are responsible for most of the toxicity of acidic waters and also of acidic soils.

Some chemicals can be toxic to aquatic biota even when present in ultra trace concentrations. Many species within the class of chemicals known as **chlorinated hydrocarbons** are insoluble in water but are soluble in biological lipids such as animal fats. These chemicals often remain in the environment because they are not easily metabolized by microorganisms or degraded by **ultraviolet radiation** or other inorganic processes. Examples of chlorinated hydrocarbons are the insecticides **DDT**, DDD, dieldrin, and methoxychlor, the class of dielectric fluids known as **PCBs**, and the chlorinated **dioxin**, TCDD.

These chemicals are so dangerous because they collect in biological tissues, and accumulate progressively as organisms age. They also accumulate into especially large concentrations in organisms at the top of the ecosystem's **food chain/web**. In some cases, older individuals of top predator species have been found to have very large concentrations of chlorinated hydrocarbons in their fatty tissues. The toxicity caused to raptorial birds and other predators as a result of their accumulated doses of DDT, PCBs, and other chlorinated hydrocarbons is a well-recognized environmental problem.

Water pollution can also be caused by the presence of **hydrocarbons**. Accidental spills of **petroleum** from disabled tankers are the highest profiled causes of oil pollution, but smaller spills from tankers disposing of oily bilge waters and chronic **discharge**s from refineries and **urban runoff** are also significant sources of oil pollution. Hydrocarbons can also be present naturally, as a result of the release of chemicals synthesized by algae or during decomposition processes in **anaerobic** sediment. In a few places, there are natural **seepage**s from near-surface petroleum reservoirs, as occurs in the vicinity of Santa Barbara, California. In general, the typical, naturally-occurring concentration of hydrocarbons in seawater is quite small. Beneath a surface slick of spilled petroleum, however, the concentration of soluble hydrocarbons can be multiplied several times, sufficient to cause toxicity to some biota. This dissolved fraction does not include the concentration of finely suspended droplets of petroleum, which can become incorporated into an oil-in-water emulsion toxic to organisms that become coated with it. In general, within the very complex mix of hydrocarbons found in petroleum, the smallest molecules are the most soluble in water. *See also* Bioaccumulation; Biomagnification; Oil spills

[*Bill Freedman*]

FURTHER READING

Bowen, H. J. M. *Environmental Chemistry of the Elements*. San Diego: Academic Press, 1979.

Freedman, B. *Environmental Ecology*. San Diego: Academic Press, 1989.

Aquatic microbiology

Aquatic microbiology is the science that deals with microscopic living organisms in fresh or salt water systems. While aquatic microbiology can encompass all microorganisms, including microscopic plants and animals, it more commonly refers to the study of bacteria, viruses, and fungi and their relation to other organisms in the aquatic **environment**.

Bacteria are quite diverse in **nature**. The scientific classification of bacteria divides them into 19 major groups based on their shape, cell structure, staining properties (used in the laboratory for identification), and metabolic functions. Bacteria occur in many sizes as well ranging from 0.1 micrometer to greater than 500 micrometers. Some are motile and have flagella, which are tail-like structures used for movement.

Although **soil** is the most common habitat of fungi, they are also found in aquatic environments. Aquatic fungi are collectively called *water molds* or *aquatic Phycomycetes*. They are found on the surface of decaying plant and animal matter in ponds and streams. Some fungi are parasitic and prey on algae and protozoa.

Viruses are the smallest group of microorganisms and usually are viewed only with the aid of an electron microscope. They are disease-causing organisms that are very different than bacteria, fungi, and other cellular life-forms. Viruses are infectious **nucleic acid** enclosed within a coat of protein. They penetrate host cells and use the nucleic acid of other cells to replicate.

Bacteria, viruses, and fungi are widely distributed throughout aquatic environments. They can be found in fresh water rivers, lakes, and streams, in the surface waters and sediments of the world's oceans, and even in hot springs. They have even been found supporting diverse communities at hydrothermal vents in the depths of the oceans.

Microorganisms living in these diverse environments must deal with a wide range of physical conditions, and each has specific adaptations to live in the particular place it calls home. For example, some have adapted to live in fresh waters with very low salinity, while others live in the saltiest parts of the ocean. Some must deal with the harsh cold of arctic waters, while those in hot springs are subjected to intense heat. In addition, aquatic microorganisms can be found living in environments where there are extremes in other physical parameters such as pressure, sunlight, organic substances, dissolved gases, and water clarity.

Aquatic microorganisms obtain nutrition in a variety of ways. For example, some bacteria living near the surface of either fresh or marine waters, where there is often abundant sunlight, are able to produce their own food through the process of **photosynthesis**. Bacteria living at hydrothermal vents on the ocean floor where there is no sunlight can produce their own food through a process known as chemosynthesis, which depends on preformed organic carbon as an energy source. Many other microorganisms are not able to produce their own food. Rather, they obtain necessary nutrition from the breakdown of organic matter such as dead organisms.

Aquatic microorganisms play a vital role in the cycling of **nutrient**s within their environment, and thus are a crucial part of the **food chain/web**. Many microorganisms obtain their nutrition by breaking down organic matter in dead plants and animals. As a result of this process of decay, nutrients are released in a form usable by plants. These aquatic microorganisms are especially important in the cycling of the nutrients **nitrogen**, **phosphorus**, and **carbon**. Without this **recycling**, plants would have few, if any, organic nutrients to use for growth.

In addition to breaking down organic matter and recycling it into a form of nutrients that plants can use, many of the microorganisms become food themselves. There are many types of animals that graze on bacteria and fungi. For example, some deposit-feeding marine worms ingest sediments and digest numerous bacteria and fungi found there, later expelling the indigestible sediments. Therefore, these microorganisms are intimate members of the food web in at least two ways.

Humans have taken advantage of the role these microorganisms play in nutrient cycles. At sewage treatment plants, microscopic bacteria are cultured and then used to break down human wastes. However, in addition to the beneficial uses of some aquatic microorganisms, others may cause problems for people because they are pathogens, which can cause serious diseases. For example, viruses such as *Salmonella typhi*, *S. paratyphi*, and the Norwalk virus are found in water contaminated by **sewage** can cause illness. Fecal coliform (*E. coli*) bacteria and Enterococcus bacteria are two types of microorganisms that are used to indicate the presence of disease causing microorganisms in aquatic environments.

[*Marci L. Bortman*]

Aquatic toxicology

Aquatic toxicology is the study of the adverse effects of toxins and their activities on aquatic **ecosystem**s. Aquatic toxicologists assess the condition of aquatic systems, monitor trends in conditions over time, diagnose the cause of damaged systems, guide efforts to correct damage, and predict the consequences of proposed human actions so the ecological consequences of those actions can be considered before damage occurs. Aquatic toxicologists study adverse effects at different spatial, temporal, and organizational scales. Because aquatic systems contain thousands of species, each of these species can respond to toxicants in many ways, and interactions between these species can be affected.

Consequently, a virtually unlimited number of responses could be produced by chemicals. Scientists study effects as specific as a physiological response of an important fish species or as inclusive as the biological diversity of a large **river basin**. Generally, attention is first focused on responses that are considered important either socially or biologically. For example, if a societal goal is to have fishable waters, responses to toxicants of game fishes and the organisms they depend on would be of interest.

The two most common tools used in aquatic toxicology are the field survey and the toxicity test. A field survey characterizes the indigenous biological community of an aquatic system or **watershed**. Chemistry, geology, and land use are also essential components of field surveys. Often, the characteristics of the community are compared to other similar systems that are in good condition. Field surveys provide the best evidence of the existing condition of natural systems. However, when damaged communities and chemical contamination co-occur, it is difficult to establish a cause-and-effect relationship using the field survey alone. Toxicity tests can help to make this connection. The toxicity test excises some replicable piece of the system of interest, perhaps fish or microbial communities of lakes, and exposes it to a chemical in a controlled, randomized, and replicable manner. The most common aquatic toxicity test data provide information about the short-term survival of fish exposed to one chemical. Such tests demonstrate whether a set of chemical conditions can cause a specified response. They also provide information about what concentrations of the chemical are of concern. Toxicity tests can suggest a threshold chemical concentration below which the adverse effect is not expected to occur; they can also present an index of relative toxicity used to rank the toxicity of two chemicals. By using information from the field survey and toxicity tests, along with other tools such as tests on the fate of chemicals released into aquatic systems, aquatic toxicologists can develop models predicting the effects of proposed actions.

The most important challenge to aquatic toxicology will be to develop methods that support sustainable use of the aquatic and other ecosystems. Sustainable use is intended to ensure that those now living do not deprive future generations of the essential natural resources necessary to maintain a quality lifestyle. Achieving the goal of sustainable use will require aquatic toxicologists to have a much longer temporal perspective than we now have. Additionally, in a more crowded and increasingly affluent world, cumulative effects will become extremely important.

[John Cairns Jr.]

Aquatic weed control

A simple definition of an aquatic weed is a plant that grows (usually too densely) in an area such that it hinders the usefulness or enjoyment of that area. Some common examples of aquatic plants that can become weeds are the water milfoils, ribbon weeds, and pondweeds. They may grow in ponds, lakes, streams, rivers, navigation channels, and seashores, and the growth may be due to a variety of factors such as excess **nutrient**s in the water or the introduction of rapidly-growing **exotic species**. The problems caused by aquatic weeds are many, ranging from unsightly growth and nuisance odors to clogging of waterways, damage to shipping and underwater equipment, and impairment of **water quality**.

It is difficult and usually unnecessary to eliminate weeds completely from a lake or stream. Therefore, aquatic weed control programs usually focus on controlling and maintaining the prevalence of the weeds at an acceptable level. The methods used in weed control may include one or a combination of the following: physical removal, mechanical removal, **habitat** manipulation, biological controls, and chemical controls.

Physical removal of weeds involves cutting, pulling, or raking weeds by hand. It is time-consuming and labor-intensive and is most suitable for small areas or for locations that cannot be reached by machinery. Mechanical removal is accomplished by specialized harvesting machinery equipped with toothed blades and cutting bars to cut the vegetation, collect it, and haul it away. It is suitable for off-shore weed removal or to supplement chemical control. Repeated harvesting is usually necessary and often the harvesting blades may be limited in the depth or distance that they can reach. Inadvertent dispersal of plant fragments may also occur and lead to weed establishment in new areas. Operation of the harvesters may disturb fish habitat.

Habitat manipulation involves a variety of innovative techniques to discourage the establishment and growth of aquatic weeds. Bottom liners of **plastic** sheeting placed on lake bottoms can prevent the establishment of rooted plants. Artificial shading can discourage the growth of shade-intolerant **species**. Drawdown of the water level can be used to eliminate some species by desiccation. **Dredging** to remove accumulated **sediment**s and organic matter can also delay colonization by new plants.

Biological control methods generally involve the introduction of weed-eating fish, insects, competing plant species or weed **pathogen**s into an area of high weed growth. While there are individual success stories (for example, stocking lakes with grass carp), it is difficult to predict the long-term effects of the **introduced species** on the native species and **ecology** and therefore, biological controls should be used with caution.

Chemical control methods consist of the application of **herbicide**s that may be either systemic or contact in nature. Systemic herbicides are taken up into the plant and cause plant death by disrupting its **metabolism** in various ways. Contact herbicides only kill the directly exposed portions of the plant, such as the leaves. While herbicides are convenient and easy to use, they must be selected and used with care at the appropriate times and in the correct quantities. Sometimes, they may also kill non-target plant species and in some cases, toxic residues from the degrading herbicide may be ingested and transferred up the **food chain**.

[Usha Vedagiri]

FURTHER READING

Schmidt, J. C. *How to Identify and Control Water Weeds and Algae.* Milwaukee, WI: Applied Biochemists, 1987.

Aquifer

Natural zones below the surface that yield water in sufficient quantities to be economically important for industrial, agricultural, or domestic purposes. Aquifers can occur in a variety of geologic materials, ranging from glacial-deposited outwash to sedimentary beds of limestone and sandstone, and fractured zones in dense igneous rocks. Composition and characteristics are almost infinite in their variety.

Aquifers can be confined or unconfined. Unconfined aquifers are those where direct contact can be made with the **atmosphere**, while confined aquifers are separated from the atmosphere by impermeable materials. Confined aquifers are also artesian aquifers. Though originally artesian was a term applied to water in an aquifer under sufficient pressure to produce flowing wells, the term is now generally applied to all confined situations. *See also* Aquifer restoration; Artesian well; Drinking-water supply; Groundwater; Ogallala Aquifer

Aquifer restoration

Once an **aquifer** is contaminated, the process of restoring the quality of water is generally time-consuming and expensive, and it is often more cost effective to locate a new source of water. For these reasons, the restoration of an aquifer is usually evaluated on the basis of these criteria: 1) the potential for additional contamination; 2) the time period over which the contamination has occurred; 3) the type of contaminant; and 4) the **hydrogeology** of the site. Restoration tech-of in-situ degradation fall into three general categories: 1) injection of neutralizing agents for acid or caustic compounds; 2) addition of **oxidizing agent**s such as **chlorine** or **ozone** to destroy organic compounds; and 3) introduction of amino acids to reduce PCBs (**polychlorinated biphenyl**s).

There are also methods for stabilizing an aquifer and preventing a contaminant **plume** from extending. One stabilizing alternative is the conversion of a contaminant to an insoluble form. This method is limited to use on inorganic salts, and even those compounds can dissolve if the physical or chemical properties of the aquifer change. A change in **pH**, for instance, might allow the contaminant to return to solution. Like other methods of in-situ restoration, conversion requires the contaminant to be contained within a workable area.

The other important stabilizing alternatives are containment methods, which enclose the contaminant in an insoluble material and prevent it from spreading through the rest of the aquifer. There are partial and total containment methods. For partial containment, a clay cap can be applied to keep rainfall from moving additional contaminants into the aquifer. This method has been used quite often where there are sanitary **landfill**s or other types of hazardous waste sites. Total containment methods are designed to isolate the area of contamination through the construction of some kind of physical barrier, but these have limited usefulness. These barriers include **slurry** walls, grout curtains, sheet steel and floor seals. Slurry walls are usually made of concrete, and are put in place by digging a trench, which is then filled with the slurry. The depth at which these walls can be use is limited to 80-90 ft (24-27 m). Grout curtains are formed by injecting a cement grout under pressure into the aquifer through a series of injection wells, but it is difficult to know how effective a barrier this is and whether it has uniformly penetrated the aquifer. Depth is again a limiting factor, and this method has a range of 50-60 ft (15-18 m). Steel sheets can be driven to a depth of 100 ft (30 m) but no satisfactory technique for forming impermeable joints between the individual sheets has been developed. Floor seals are grouts installed horizontally, and they are used where the contaminant plume has not penetrated the entire depth of the aquifer. None of these methods offers a permanent solution to the potential problems of contamination, and some type of continued monitoring and maintenance is necessary.

Conventional methods of restoration involve removal of the contaminant followed by withdrawal of the water, and final treatment and disposal. Site characteristics that are important include the topography of the land surface, characteristics of the soil, depth to the **water table** and how this depth varies across the site, and depth to impermeable layers. The options for collection and withdrawal can be divided into five groups: 1) collection wells; 2) subsurface gravity collection drains; 3) impervious grout curtains (as described above); 4) cut-off trenches; or 5) a combination of these options. Collection wells are usually installed in a line, and are designed to withdraw the contaminant plume and to keep movement of other clean water into the wells at a minimum.

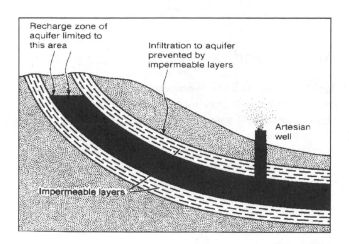

The aquifer shown here is contained between impermeable layers of rock or clay, and is bent by geologic forces creating hydrostatic pressure. An artesian well or spring occurs at a break in the overlying layer.

niques fall into two major categories, in-situ methods and conventional methods of withdrawal, treatment, and disposal.

Remedies undertaken within the aquifer involve the use of chemical or biological agents which either reduce the toxicity of the contaminants or prevent them from moving any further into the aquifer, or both. One such method requires the introduction of biological cultures or chemical reactants and sealants through a series of **injection well**s. This action will reduce the toxicity, form an impervious layer to prevent the spread of the contaminant, and clean the aquifer by rinsing. However, a major drawback to this approach is the difficulty and expense of installing enough injection wells to assure a uniform distribution throughout the aquifer.

In-situ degradation, another restoration method, can theoretically be accomplished through either biological or chemical methods. Biological methods involve placing microorganisms in the aquifer that are capable of utilizing and degrading the hazardous contaminant. A great deal of progress has been made in the development of microorganisms which will degrade both simple and complex organic compounds. It may be necessary to supplement the organisms introduced with additional **nutrient**s and substances to help them degrade certain insoluble organic compounds. Before introduction of these organisms, it is also important to evaluate the intermediate products of the degradation to **carbon dioxide** and water for toxicity. Chemical methods

Various sorts of drains can be effective in intercepting the plume, but they do not work in deep aquifers or hard rock. Cut-off trenches can be dug if the contamination is not too deep, and water can then be drained to a place where it can be treated before final **discharge** into a lake or stream.

Water taken from a contaminated aquifer requires treatment before final discharge and disposal. To what degree it can be treated depends on the type of contaminant and the effectiveness of the available options. Reverse **osmosis** uses pressure at a high temperature to force water through a membrane that allows water molecules, but not contaminants, to pass. This process removes most soluble organic chemicals, heavy metals, and inorganic salts. Ultrafiltration also uses a pressure-driven method with a membrane. It operates at lower temperatures and is not as effective for contaminants with smaller molecules. An **ion exchange** uses a bed or series of tubes filled with a resin to remove selected compounds from the water and replace them with harmless **ion**s. The system has the advantage of being transportable, depending on the type of resin, it can be used more than once by flushing the resin with either an acid or salt solution. Both organic and inorganic substances can be removed using this method.

Wet-air oxidation is another important treatment method. It introduces oxygen into the liquid at a high temperature, which effectively treats inorganic and organic contaminants.Combined ozonation/ultraviolet radiation is a chemical process in which the water containing toxic chemicals is brought into contact with ozone and **ultraviolet radiation** to break down the organic contaminants into harmless parts. Chemical treatment is a general name for a variety of processes that can be used to treat water. They often result in the precipitation of the contaminant, and will not remove soluble organic and inorganic substances. **Aerobic** biological treatments are processes that employ microorganisms in the presence of **dissolved oxygen** to convert organic matter to harmless products. Another approach uses activated **carbon** in columns—the water is run over the carbon and the contaminants become attached to it. Contaminants begin to cover the surface area of the carbon over time, and these filters must be periodically replaced.

These treatment processes are often used in combination. The methods used depend on the ultimate disposal plan for the end products. The three primary disposal options are: 1) discharge to a sewage treatment plant; 2) discharge to a surface water body; and 3) land application. Each option has positive and negative aspects. Any discharge to a municipal treatment plant requires pre-treatment to standards that will allow the plant to accept the waste. Land application requires an evaluation of plant nutrient supplying capability and any potentially harmful side-effects on the crops grown. Discharge to surface water requires that the waste be treated to the standard allowable for that water. For many organics the final disposal method is burning. *See also* Contaminated soil; Deep-well injection; Drinking-water supply; Safe Drinking Water Act; Water quality; Water quality standards; Water table draw-down; Water treatment

[*James L. Anderson*]

FURTHER READING

Freeze, R. A., and J. A. Cherry. *Ground Water*. Englewood Cliffs, NJ: Prentice-Hall, 1979.

Pye, V. I., R. Patrick, and J. Quarles.*Ground Water Contamination in the United States*. Philadelphia: University of Pennsylvania Press, 1983.

Arable land

Arable land has **soil** and **topography** suitable for economical and practical cultivation of crops. These range from grains, grasses, and legumes to fruits and vegetables. Permanent pastures and **rangelands** are not considered arable. Forested land is also nonarable, although it can be farmed if the area is cleared and the soil and topography are suitable for cultivation.

Aral Sea

The Aral Sea is a large, shallow, saline lake hidden in the remote deserts of the republics of Uzbekistan and Kazakhstan in the south-central region of the former Soviet Union. Once the world's fourth largest lake in area (smaller only than America's Lake Superior, Siberia's **Lake Baikal**, and East Africa's Lake Victoria), in 1960 the Aral Sea had a surface area of 68,000 sq km (26,250 sq mi), and a volume of 1,090 cu km (260 cu mi). Its only water sources are two large rivers, the Amu Darya and the Syr Darya. Flowing northward from the Pamir Mountains on the Afghan border, these rivers pick up salts as they cross the Kyzyl Kum and Kara Kum **desert**s. Evaporation from the landlocked sea's surface (it has no outlet) makes the water even saltier.

The Aral Sea's destruction began in 1918 when plans were made to draw off water to grow cotton, a badly needed **cash crop** for the newly formed Soviet Union. The amount of irrigated cropland in the region was expanded greatly (from 2.9 to 7.6 million ha; from 7.2 to 18.8 million acres) in the 1950s and 1960s with the completion of the Kara Kum canal. Annual water flows in the Amu Darya and Syr Darya dropped from about 55 cu km (13 cu mi) to less than 5 cu km (1 cu mi). In some years the rivers were completely dry when they reached the lake.

Soviet authorities were warned that the sea would die without replenishment, but sacrificing a remote desert lake for the sake of economic development seemed an acceptable tradeoff. Inefficient **irrigation** practices drained away the lifeblood of the lake. Dry years in the early 1970s and mid-1980s accelerated water shortages in the region. Now, in a disaster of unprecedented magnitude and rapidity, the Aral Sea is disappearing as we watch.

Until 1960 the Aral Sea was fairly stable, but by 1990, it had lost 40 percent of its surface area and two-thirds of its volume. Surface levels dropped 14 m (42 ft), turning 30,000 sq km (11,580 sq mi, about the size of the state of Maryland) of former seabed into a salty, dusty desert. Fishing villages that were once at the sea's edge are now 40 km (25 mi) from water. Boats trapped by falling water levels lie abandoned in the sand. **Salinity** of the remaining water has tripled and almost no aquatic life remains. **Commercial fishing** that brought in 48,000 metric tons in 1957 was completely gone in 1990.

Winds whipping across the dried-up seabed pick up salty dust, poisoning crops and causing innumerable health problems for residents. An estimated 43 million metric tons of salt are blown onto nearby fields and cities each year. Eye irritations, intestinal diseases, skin infections, **asthma**, **bronchitis**, and a variety of other health problems have risen sharply in the past 20 years, especially among children. Infant mortality in the Kara-Kalpak Autonomous Region adjacent to the Aral Sea is 60 per 1,000, twice as high as in other former Soviet Republics.

Among adults, throat **cancer**s have increased five fold in 30 years. Many physicians believe that heavy doses of **pesticide**s used on the cotton fields and transported by **runoff** water to the lake **sediment**s are now becoming airborne in dust storms. Although officially banned, **DDT** and other persistent pesticides have been widely used in the area and are now found in mothers' milk. More than 35 million people are threatened by this disaster.

A report by the Institute of Geography of the Russian Academy of Sciences predicts that without immediate action, the Aral Sea will vanish by 2010. It is astonishing that such a large body of water could dry up in such a short time. Philip P. Micklin of Western Michigan University, an authority on water issues says this may the world's largest ecological disaster.

What can be done to avert this calamity? Clearly, one solution would be to stop withdrawing water for irrigation, but that would compound the disastrous economic and political conditions in the former Soviet Republics. More efficient irrigation might save as much as half the water now lost without reducing crop yields, but lack of funds and organization in the newly autonomous nations makes new programs and improvements almost impossible. Restoring the river flows to about 20 cu km (5 cu mi) per year would probably stabilize the sea at present levels. It would take perhaps twice as much to return it to 1960 conditions.

Before the dissolution of the Soviet Union, there was talk of grandiose plans to divert part of the northward-flowing Ob and Irtysh rivers in Western Siberia. In the early 1980s a system of **dams**, pumping stations, and a 2,500 km (1,500 mi) canal was proposed to move 25 cu km (6 cu mi) of water from Siberia to Uzbekistan and Kazakhstan. The cost of 100 billion rubles ($150 billion) and the potential adverse environmental effects led President Mikhail Gorbachev to cancel this scheme in 1986.

Perhaps more than technological fixes, what we all need most is a little foresight and humility in dealing with **nature**. The words painted on the rusting hull of an abandoned fishing boat lying in the desert might express it best, "Forgive us Aral. Please come back." *See also* Salinization of soils

[*William P. Cunningham*]

FURTHER READING

Ellis, M. S. "A Soviet Sea Lies Dying." *National Geographic* 177 (February 1990): 73-93.

Micklin. P. P. "Dessication of the Aral Sea: A Water Management Disaster in the Soviet Union." *Science* 241 (2 September 1988): 1170-1176.

Agriculture and Energy Conservation
See **Environmental Engineering**

Arco, Idaho

"Electricity was first generated here from Atomic Energy on December 20, 1951. On December 21, 1951, all of the electrical power in this building was supplied from Atomic Energy."

Those words are written on the wall of a nuclear reactor in Arco, Idaho, a site now designated as a Registered National Historic Landmark by the **U.S. Department of the Interior**. The inscription is signed by sixteen scientists and engineers responsible for this event.

The production of electricity from **nuclear power** was truly a momentous occasion. Scientists had known for nearly two decades that such a conversion was possible. Use of nuclear energy as a safe, efficient energy source of power was regarded by many people in the United States and around the world as one of the most exciting prospects for the "world of tomorrow."

Until 1945, scientists' efforts had been devoted to the production of **nuclear weapons**. The conclusion of World War II allowed both scientists and government officials to turn their attention to more productive applications of nuclear energy. In 1949, the United States **Atomic Energy Commission (AEC)** authorized construction of the first nuclear reactor designed for the production of electricity. The reactor was designated Experimental Breeder Reactor No. 1 (EBR-I).

The site chosen for the construction of EBR-I was a small town in southern Idaho named Arco. Founded in the late 1870s, the town had never grown very large. Its population in 1949 was 780. What attracted the AEC to Arco was the 400,000 acres of lava-rock-covered wasteland around the town. The area provided the seclusion that seemed appropriate for an experimental nuclear reactor. In addition, AEC scientists considered the possibility that the porous lava around Arco would be an ideal place in which to dump wastes from the reactor.

On December 21, 1951, the Arco reactor went into operation. Energy from a **uranium** core about the size of a football generated enough electricity to light four 200-watt light bulbs. The next day its output was increased to a level where it ran all electrical systems in EBR-I. In July 1953, EBR-I reached another milestone. Measurements showed that breeding was actually taking place within the reactor. The dream of a generation had become a reality.

The success of EBR-I convinced the AEC to expand its breeder experiments. In 1961, a much larger version of the original plant, Experimental Breeder Reactor No. 2 (EBR-II) was also built near Arco on a site now designated as the Idaho National Engineering Laboratory of the **U.S. Department of Energy**. EBR-II produced its first electrical power in August of 1964. *See also* Nuclear winter; Radioactive waste management; Radioactivity

[*David E. Newton*]

FURTHER READING

Crawford, M. "Third Strike for Idaho Reactor." *Science* 251 (18 January 1991): 263.

Elmer-DeWitt, P. "Nuclear Power Plots a Comeback." *Time* 133 (2 January 1989): 41.

Schneider, K. "Idaho Says No." *The New York Times Magazine* 139 (11 March 1990): 50.

U.S. Congress, Office of Technology Assessment. *The Containment of Underground Nuclear Explosions.* OTA-ISC-414. Washington, DC: U.S. Government Printing Office, 1989.

"A Village Wakes Up." *Life* (9 May 1949): 98-101.

Arctic Council (Oslo, Norway)

The Arctic Council is a cooperative environmental protection council composed of eight governments whose goal is to protect the Arctic's fragile environment while continuing economic development. Established in 1996, the Council plans to protect the environment by protecting **biodiversity** in the Arctic region and maintaining the sustainable use of its natural resources.

The Arctic Council was formed on September 19, 1996, when representatives from Canada, Denmark, Finland, Iceland, Norway, the Russian Federation, Sweden, and the United States signed a *Declaration on the Establishment of the Arctic Council.* The work and programs founded under the former Arctic Environmental Protection Strategy (AEPS) have become integrated into the new Arctic Council, which provides for indigenous representation—including the Inuit Circumpolar Conference, the Saami Council (Scandinavia, Finland, and Russia) for the Nordic areas and the Association of Indigenous Minorities of the North, Siberia, and the Far East of the Russian Federation—at all meetings. The indigenous people cannot vote but may provide knowledge of traditional practices for research and a collective understanding of the Arctic. As members of the Council's board, they can recomended ways to spread the work and benefits of oil drilling and mining businesses among indigenous communities while minimizing the negative effects on their land.

The **World Wildlife Fund** oversees the Council's work on protecting the Arctic's wildlife and vegetation from various destructive activities, such as diamond mining and **clear-cutting**. There is also evidence that the Arctic area receives a disproportionate amount of pollution, as witnessed in the overall land and water degradation.

Canadian Environment Minister Sergio Marchi is a supporter of the Council's work, emphasizing "The Arctic is an environmental early warning system for our globe. The Arctic Council will help deliver that warning from pole to pole." Contact: Arctic Council, 333 River Rd., Ottawa, ON K1A0G2, Canada.

[*Nicole Beatty*]

Arctic haze

The dry **aerosol** present in arctic regions during much of the year and responsible for substantial loss of **visibility** through the **atmosphere**. The arctic regions are, for the most part, very low in precipitation, qualifying on that basis as **desert**s. Ice accumulates because even less water evaporates than is deposited. Hence, particles that enter the arctic atmosphere are only very slowly removed by precipitation, a process that removes a significant fraction of particles from the tropical and temperate atmospheres. Thus, relatively small sources can lead to appreciable final atmospheric concentrations.

A succession of studies has been conducted on the chemistry of the particles in that **haze**, and those trapped in the snow and ice. Much of the time the mix of **trace element**s in the particles is very close to that found in the industrial **emission**s from northern Europe and Siberia and quite different from that in such emissions from northern North America. Concentrations decrease rapidly with depth in the ice layers, indicating that these trace elements began to enter the atmosphere within the past few centuries. It is now generally conceded that most of the haze particles are derived from human activities, primarily—though not exclusively—in northern Eurasia.

Since the haze scatters light, including sunlight, it decreases the **solar energy** received at the ground level in polar regions and may, therefore, have the potential to decrease arctic temperatures. Arctic haze also constitutes a nuisance because it decreases visibility. The trace elements found in arctic haze apparently are not yet sufficiently concentrated in either atmosphere or precipitation to constitute a significant toxic hazard.

[*James P. Lodge, Jr.*]

FURTHER READING

Nriagu, J. O., et al. "Origin of Sulfur in Canadian Arctic Haze From Isotope Measurements." *Nature* 349 (10 January 1991): 142-5.

Soroos, M. S. "The Odyssey of Arctic Haze: Toward a Global Atmospheric Regime." *Environment* 36 (December 1992): 6-11+.

Arctic National Wildlife Refuge, Alaska

The Arctic National Wildlife Refuge is an 18-million-acre (7.3-million-ha) tract of land in northeastern Alaska. It is the northern-most unit of the **National Wildlife Refuge** System and is administered by the United States **Fish and**

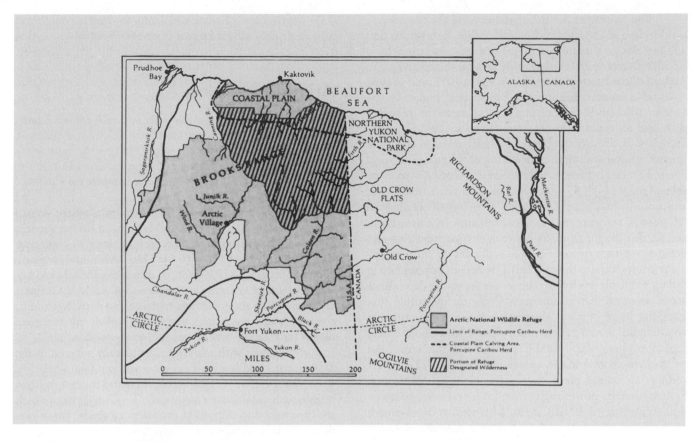

The Arctic National Wildlife Refuge, Alaska.

Wildlife Service. The 8 million acres (3.2 million ha) designated as **wilderness** is the second largest wilderness area in the United States and the largest in the National Wildlife Refuge System. The primary purpose of the refuge is to conserve the fish and **wildlife** populations and **habitat**s found there.

This refuge has unique scenic and ecological values found nowhere else in the United States. The spectacular Brooks Range bisects the refuge creating a natural north-south division. The south slope is sub-arctic boreal forest, while the north slope descends in a **tundra**-covered plain to the Arctic Ocean. The close proximity of the Brooks Range to the ocean accounts for the tremendous diversity of habitats found within the refuge. Moreover, because of its large size, it is considered to be one of the few protected **ecosystem**s large enough to be self-sustaining. It is truly natural in that there are few signs of humans, and it is one of the few places on the continent where there are no non-native species.

The refuge teems with wildlife, particularly in the short but intense summer (sunlight 24 hours per day). Two herds of caribou (*Rangifer tarandus*) use the refuge, the Porcupine herd (180,000 animals) and the Central Arctic herd (18,000-20,000 animals). Other large mammals in the refuge include: black bear (*Ursus americanus*) (south slope only), **grizzly bear** (*Ursus arctos*), polar bear (*Ursus maritimus*), Dall's sheep (*Ovis dalli*), and muskox (*Ovibos moschatus*). The latter species was extirpated in the 1800s, but was reintroduced in 1969 and 1970. The north slope population is now over 500 animals. Thousands of ducks, geese, and swans nest on the coastal plain, and in the fall 100,000 to 300,000 snow geese (*Chen caerulescens*) use the site as a staging area prior to migration. Besides waterfowl, 70 other bird species use the coastal plain.

This refuge has a history of controversy. In 1949, the **National Park Service** began a recreational survey in Alaska to determine areas deserving formal protection. Five years later they recommended preservation of the northeast corner of Alaska as a unique ecosystem. In 1957, at the urging of many **conservation** groups and prominent conservationists, the **U. S. Department of the Interior** announced plans to seek legislation establishing an 8,000-square-mile (20,700-square-km) **wildlife refuge** in the area identified by the National Park Service. After much debate, Congress failed to pass the legislation establishing the refuge. However, on December 6, 1960, the Secretary of the Interior signed a Public Land Order creating an 8.9-million-acre (3.6-million-ha) Arctic National Wildlife Range. Twenty years later, on December 2, 1980, Congress established the Arctic National Wildlife Refuge as part of the **Alaska National Interest Lands Conservation Act** (ANILCA). ANILCA set aside 18 million acres (7.3 million ha) for the refuge and officially designated 8 million acres (3.2 million ha) as wilderness. In 1983, the state of Alaska donated an adjacent 971,800 acres (393,600 ha) of land to the refuge and in 1988 Congress enacted legislation that added about 325,000 acres (131,625 ha) to the refuge.

The passing of ANILCA did not end the controversy surrounding the Arctic National Wildlife Refuge. Section 1002 of the Act mandated an oil and gas assessment of a 1,550,000-acre (627,750-ha) study area on the coastal plain. An initial base line report was published in 1982, and in 1983 eight oil companies began surface geological studies on the Section 1002 lands. Seismic exploration began the following year, and all exploration was completed in 1985. In 1987 Secretary of the Interior Donald Hodel released the 1002 Report recommending the full leasing of the refuge's coastal plain. The current mean estimate of economically recoverable oil reserves is 3.55 billion barrels, with the probability of an economic find being 46 percent. The issue of opening the refuge to oil and gas extraction has been one of the most bitter and fiercely fought conflicts between environmentalists and pro-development groups. People representing oil development interests claim they are being denied an opportunity to make a profitable investment and reduce America's dependance on oil imports. Environmentalists counter by noting that installing more efficient shower heads (or redesigning car door handles to make them more aerodynamic) alone would save more energy than could be produced on the refuge, and without the economic and environmental costs. They prefer adding the coastal plain area to the National Wilderness System, thereby protecting it from future oil and gas activities. According to ANILCA, no **petroleum** development can occur on the plain until Congress specifically allows it. Congress has yet to pass legislation on this issue, although bills have been introduced to allow such development. In the meantime the battle continues over what many believe has been the dominant **public lands** issue of the 1980s and early 1990s.

[*Ted T. Cable*]

FURTHER READING

Miller, D. S. *Midnight Wilderness: Journeys in Alaska's Arctic National Wildlife Refuge.* San Francisco: Sierra Club Books, 1990.

Tracking Arctic Oil: The Environmental Price of Drilling in the Arctic National Wildlife Refuge. New York: Natural Resources Defense Council, 1991.

U. S. Fish and Wildlife Service. *Arctic National Wildlife Refuge.* Washington, DC: U. S. Government Printing Office, 1992.

Arid

Arid lands are dry areas or **desert**s where a shortage of rainfall prevents permanent rain-fed agriculture. They are bordered by, and interact with, marginal or semi-arid lands where the annual rainfall (still only 10-15 inches or 25-38 cm) allows limited agriculture and light grazing. However, in many parts of the world human mismanagement, driven by increasing populations, has degraded these areas into unusable arid lands. For example, clearing natural vegetation and overgrazing have led to soil **erosion**, reduced land productivity, and ultimately reduced water availability in the region.

This degradation of semi-arid lands to deserts, which can also occur naturally, is known as **desertification**.

Arid landscaping

Arid landscaping, or xeriscaping (from the Greek word *xeros*, meaning dry), is the integration of practicality and beauty in **drought**-prone public and private gardens. Xeriscaping is part of a larger trend among environmentalist gardeners to incorporate native rather than imported **species** within local **ecosystems**.

In drought-prone areas like California, where **water conservation** is imperative and lawns and flower gardens are at risk, gardeners have taken several steps to cope with drought. A 20-by-40-foot (6-by-12 m) green lawn requires about 2,500 gallons (9,475 liters) of water a month, enough for a four-member family for ten days. Some arid landscapers eliminate lawns altogether and replace them with flagstone or concrete walkways; others aerate the **soil** or cut the grass higher for greater water retention. More popular is replacing imported grasses with native grasses, already adapted to the local climate, and letting them grow without being cut.

Some big trees, such as oak, do better in drought than others, such as birches or magnolias. To save big trees which are expensive and important providers of shade, some gardeners place "soaker" hoses, in which water flows out through holes in the length of the hose in concentric circles at the base of trees and water them deeply once or twice a season.

More commonly, arid landscapers replace water-loving shrubs and trees with those best adapted to drought conditions. These include some herbs, such as rosemary, thyme, and lavender, and shrubs like the silvery santolina, which are important in color composition of gardens.

Other plants that grow well in semi-arid and **arid** conditions are legumes (Leguminosae), poppies (Papaveraceae), daisies (Compositae), black-eyed susans (*Rudbeckia fulgida*), goldenrod (*Solidago*), honeysuckle (*Lonicera*), sunflowers (*Helianthus*), daylilies (*Hemerocallis*), and eucalyptus. Generally, drought-resistant plants have silvery leaves that reflect sunlight (*argentea*); hairy (*tomentosum*) or stiff haired (*hirsuta*) leaves that help retain moisture; long narrow leaves (*angustifolia*), threadlike leaves (*filimentosa*), and aromatic leaves (*aromatica*) that provide a moisture-protecting haze in heat.

Drip irrigation, hoses with small regular holes, whose amount is regulated by timers, is the most efficient xeriscape watering technique. Mulching with dead leaves, pine bark, straw, and other organic matter helps retain soil moisture. Soil types are a critical part of arid landscaping: one inch (2.5 cm) of water, for example, will penetrate 6-8 in (15-20 cm) into loam (a sand, peat, and clay mixture), but only 4-5 in (10-13 cm) into dense clay.

Arid landscapers monitor plant health and soil dryness only when necessary, often in the early morning or in the evening to avoid evaporation by the sun. **Recycling** "gray" water, **runoff** from household sinks and washing machines, is best if the water is used quickly before bacteria collects and if laundry **detergents** are **biodegradable**. Arid landscapers, using native and drought-resistant plant species in conjunction with stone and concrete walkways and **mulch**, create gardens that are not only aesthetically pleasing but ecologically healthy.

[*Stephanie Ocko*]

FURTHER READING

Ball, K. *Xeriscape Programs for Water Utilities.* Denver: American Water Works Association, 1990.

Ball, K., and G. O. Robinette. "The Water-Saving Garden Landscape." *Country Journal* (Sept-Oct 1990): 62-69.

Sunset Magazine, May 1991. (Note: The issue is devoted to drought, with a large section on arid landscaping.)

Army Corps of Engineers

The United States Army Corps of Engineers, headquartered in Washington, D.C., is the world's largest engineering organization. The Corps was founded on June 16, 1775, the eve of the Battle of Bunker Hill, as the Continental Army fought cannon bombardments from British ships.

From early in the history of the Corps, the organization has handled both military and civil engineering needs of the United States. In earlier times those needs included coastal fortifications and lighthouses, surveying and exploring the frontier, construction of public buildings, snagging and clearing river channels, and operating early **national parks** such as **Yellowstone**. Under Corps' direction, the Panama Canal and **St. Lawrence Seaway** were built, and the Corps administered the Manhattan Project which led to the development of the atomic bomb during World War II.

Today, the Corps of Engineers provides engineering and related services in four areas: water and **natural resource** management (civil works), military construction and support, engineering research and development, and support to other government agencies.

In its military role, the Corps of Engineers provides support on the battlefield, enhancing movement and operations of American forces while impeding or delaying enemy actions. Corps engineers also plan, design, and supervise construction of military facilities and operate and maintain Army installations worldwide.

In its civil role, the Corps is responsible for the development of the nation's **water resources** and the operation and maintenance of completed water resource projects. Emerging engineering needs include renewal of infrastructure, management and control of **wetlands** development and **ocean dumping**, **waste management**, including hazardous and toxic waste, **solid waste**, and **nuclear waste**, and disaster response and preparedness.

The Corps is currently undertaking the task of "unstraightening" the Kissimmee River in south Florida. The river had been straightened into a canal for flood control between 1961 and 1971, losing half its length and most of its marshes. In the first reversal of a Corps' project, the river is slated to regain its curves. The restoration is expected to bring back **wildlife** and stave off development in south Florida.

The Corps employees more than 48,000 military and civilian members, has 13 regional headquarters, 39 district offices, and four major laboratories and research centers throughout the country.

[*Linda Rehkopf*]

FURTHER READING

Duplaix, N. "Paying the Price." *National Geographic* 178 (July 1990): 96.

Historical Highlights of the United States Army Engineers. Publication EP 360-1-13. Washington, DC: U. S. Government Printing Office, March, 1978.

Arsenic

An element having an atomic number of 33 and an atomic weight of 74.9216 which is listed by the U. S. **Environmental Protection Agency** as a hazardous substance (Hazardous waste numbers P010, P012) and as a **carcinogen**. *The Merck Index* states that the symptoms of acute poisoning following arsenic ingestion are irritation of the gastrointestinal tract, nausea, vomiting, and diarrhea which can progress to shock and death. Chronic poisoning can result in exfoliation and pigmentation of the skin, herpes, polyneuritis and degeneration of the liver and kidneys. Since arsenic compounds are amphoteric, (i. e. soluble in **acids and bases**) they are not readily removed by upward adjustment of **pH**. Arsenic is still used in insecticides and rodenticides, although much less widely than it once was due to its toxicity. *See also* Pesticide

Artesian well

A well that discharges water held in a confined **aquifer**. Artesian wells are usually thought of as wells whose water is free flowing at the land surface. However, there are many other natural systems that can result in such wells. The classic concept of artesian flow involves a basin with a water-intake area above the level of **groundwater** discharge. These systems can include stabilized sand dunes; fractured zones along bedrock faults; horizontally layered rock formations; and the intermixing of **permeable** and impermeable materials along glacial margins.

Asbestos

Asbestos is a fibrous mineral silicate, occurring in numerous forms, of which amosite [$Fe_5Mg_2(Si_8O_{22})(OH)_2$] has been shown to cause mesothelioma, squamous cell carcinoma and adenocarcinoma of the lung after long exposure times. This substance has been listed by the **Environmental Protection Agency**. Lung **cancer** is most likely to occur in those individuals who are exposed to high air-borne doses of asbestos and who also smoke. The pathogenic potential of asbestos appears to be related to its aspect ratio (length-to-diameter ratio), size (particles less than 2 micrometers in length are the most hazardous), and to its surface reactivity.

Asbestos exposure causes thickening of and calcified plaques on the lining of the chest cavity. When inhaled it forms "asbestos bodies" in the lungs, yellowish-brown particles created by reactions between the fibers and lung tissue. This disease was first described by W. E. Cooke in 1921 and given the name **asbestosis**. The latency period is generally longer than 20 years—the heavier the exposure, the more likely and the earlier is the onset of the disease. In 1935 an association between asbestos and cancer was noted by Kenneth M. Lynch. However, it was not until 1960 that Christopher Wagner demonstrated a particularly lethal association between cancer of the lining of the lungs and asbestos. By 1973 the **National Institute of Occupational Safety and Health** recommended adoption of an occupational standard of two asbestos fibers per cubic centimeter of air.

During this time, many cases of lung cancer began to surface, especially among asbestos workers who had been employed in shipbuilding during World War II. The company most impacted by lawsuits was the Manville Corporation which had been the supplier to the United States government. Manville Corporation eventually sought Title 11 Federal Bankruptcy protection as a result of these law suits.

More recently, the Reserve Mining Company, a taconite (iron ore) mining operation in **Silver Bay, Minnesota**, was involved in litigation over the dumping of **tailings** (wastes) from their operations into Lake Superior. These tailings contained amositic asbestos particles which appeared to migrate into the Duluth, Minnesota water supply. In an extended law suit, Reserve Mining Company was ordered to shut down their operations. One controversial question raised during the legal action was whether cancer could be caused by from drinking water containing asbestos fibers. In other cancer cases related to asbestos, the asbestos was inhaled rather than ingested. Federal courts held that there is reasonable cause to believe that asbestos in food and drink is dangerous—even in small quantities—and ordered Reserve Mining to stop dumping tailings in the lake.

A significant industry has developed for removing asbestos materials from private and public buildings as a result of the tight standards placed on asbestos concentrations by the **Occupational Safety and Health Administration**. At one time, many steel construction materials, especially horizontal beams, were sprayed with asbestos to enhance their resistance to fires. Wherever these materials are now exposed to **ambient air** in buildings, they have the potential to create a hazardous condition. The asbestos must either be covered or removed, and another insulating material substituted as great cost. Removal, however, causes its own problems, releasing high concentrations of fibers into the air. Many experts regard covering asbestos in place with a plastic covering to be the best option in most cases. What was once considered a life-saving material for its flame retardancy, now has become a hazardous substance which must be removed and sequestered in sites specially certified for holding asbestos building materials. *See also* Respiratory diseases

[*Malcolm T. Hepworth*]

FURTHER READING

Bartlett, R. V. *The Reserve Mining Controversy: Science, Technology, and Environmental Quality.* Bloomington: Indiana University Press, 1980.

Brodeur, P. *Asbestos and Enzymes.* New York: Ballantine Books, 1972.

Asbestos removal

Asbestos is a naturally occurring mineral, used by humans since ancient times but not extensively until the 1940s. After World War II and for the next 30 years, it was widely used as a construction material in schools and other public buildings. The United States **Environmental Protection Agency** (EPA) estimates that there are asbestos-containing materials in most of the primary and secondary schools as well as in most public and commercial buildings in the nation. It is estimated that 27 million Americans had significant occupational exposure to asbestos between 1940 and 1980. Asbestos has been popular because it is readily available, low in cost, and has very useful properties. It does not burn, conducts heat and electricity poorly, strengthens concrete products into which it is incorporated, and is resistant to chemical corrosion. It has been used in building materials as a thermal and electrical insulator and has been sprayed on steel beams in buildings for protection from heat in fires. Asbestos has also been used as an acoustical plaster. In 1984, an EPA survey found that approximately 66% of those buildings containing asbestos had damaged asbestos-containing materials in them. The EPA distinguishes between two types of asbestos damage. If the material, when dry, can be crumbled by hand pressure, it is called "friable." If not, it is called "non-friable." The friable form is much more likely to release dangerous fibers into the air. Fluffy, spray-applied asbestos fireproofing material is an example of friable asbestos. Vinyl-asbestos floor tile is an example of a non-friable material, although it too can release fibers when sanded, sawed, or aggressively disturbed.

Growing recognition that asbestos dust is a dangerous air pollutant has led to government regulation of its use and provisions for removal of asbestos and asbestos-containing products from dwellings, schools, and the workplace. In the United States, the Federal Government has taken steps to prevent unnecessary exposure to asbestos since the 1970s. Six different agencies have authority to regulate some aspect of asbestos use in the U.S. The authorized agencies are the EPA, **Occupational Safety and Health Administration** (OSHA), **Food and Drug Administration**, **Consumer Product Safety Commission**, Department of Transportation, and the Mine Safety and Health Administration.

The EPA has authority to oversee use of asbestos in commerce and has developed standards controlling its handling and use. It administers the Asbestos Hazard Emergency Response Act (AHERA) of 1986 which regulates asbestos in schools. The Act prescribes management practices and abatement standards for both public and private schools, and it follows a 1979 rule that launched a technical assistance program to aid schools in efforts to identify asbestos-containing materials. AHERA requires schools to develop a

Removal of asbestos from a building.

management plan concerning their asbestos-containing materials. Schools must appoint an asbestos manager to be responsible for a number of activities, which include implementing a plan to manage asbestos-containing building materials and ensuring compliance with federal asbestos regulations. AHERA also requires local officials to carry out inspections to identify asbestos-containing materials in public and private elementary and secondary schools, and to comply with AHERA's record keeping requirements. The emphasis on asbestos abatement in schools arises from the recognition that children are especially vulnerable to a virulent form of lung cancer called mesothelioma caused by asbestos.

The EPA also administers the Asbestos School Hazard Abatement Reauthorization Act (ASHARA) of 1990 which requires that accredited personnel be used to work with asbestos in schools and in public and commercial buildings. The Act sets training requirements for asbestos professionals, contractors, and abatement workers. It is estimated that 733,000 public buildings in the United States (about 20% of the total) have some type of defective or deteriorating asbestos-containing material in them. Asbestos is frequently found in pipe and boiler insulation, caulking putties, joint compounds, linoleum, acoustical plaster, ceiling tiles, and other building components. ASHARA does not require owners of public and commercial buildings to conduct inspections for asbestos-containing materials, but it does require owners who opt for inspections to use accredited

inspectors. To obtain accreditation, asbestos workers must take a 4-day, 32-hour EPA-approved training course covering topics such as potential health effects of asbestos exposure, the use of personal protective equipment, and up-to-date work practices. Detached single-family homes and residential apartment buildings of fewer than 10 units are not covered by the Act.

The EPA is also responsible for the 1989 Asbestos Ban and Phase out Rule that was partially overturned by a Federal Court in 1991. Originally, the ban applied to a wide variety of asbestos-containing products including roof coatings, floor tile, brake pads and linings, and pipeline wrap. Although these products and many others were removed from the ban, it still applies to all new uses of asbestos. The ban remains in effect for the sprayed-on asbestos fireproofing that has been prohibited since 1978.

Individual home owners may seek advice from local health officials concerning potential asbestos problems in or on their dwelling. State agencies often publish pamphlets or brochures that offer help in identifying and correcting problems. Common places to find asbestos in homes include wall, ceiling, and pipe insulation in structures built between 1930 and 1950, and in sheet vinyl, vinyl tile, and vinyl adhesive used in floor coverings. These materials are considered safe, and need not be removed unless they are damaged or disturbed. Wall and ceiling surfaces may contain troweled-on or sprayed-on surface material containing asbestos. If the material is hard, firmly attached, and does not produce a powder or dust when hand pressure is applied, it is probably not hazardous. On the exterior of many older homes, a cement asbestos board called Transite™ has been used as sheet or lap siding and has sometimes been shaped to mimic wood shingles. This material, too, is considered safe unless it has been damaged or disturbed. Other asbestos-containing objects in the home include older electrical lamp socket collars, switch and receptacle boxes, fuse boxes, and old-fashioned "knob and tube" wiring. Asbestos is found in insulation blankets of older ovens, dishwashers, water heaters, and freezers. These items need not be removed if they are intact and not damaged.

There is no safe and reliable way for an untrained individual to identify asbestos except to have it analyzed by a competent testing laboratory. In taking a sample for laboratory analysis, it is important that one not release fibers into the air or get them into one's clothes. To avoid this, it is often helpful to spray the material with a fine mist of water before sampling. The material should not be disturbed more than necessary, and the sample for testing should be enclosed in a sealed plastic or glass vial. If asbestos-containing materials must be removed, they should not be placed with other household trash. Local health officials should be contacted for instructions on safe disposal.

Most public buildings with asbestos-containing materials do not pose an immediate risk to the occupants. As long as the asbestos is sealed and not releasing fibers, there is no health threat. Since asbestos is easily disturbed during building alterations, routine maintenance, and even normal use, it is wise to take precautions to control or eliminate exposure. When asbestos-containing objects are identified, removal, encapsulation, and containment may be used to protect occupants. If the objects are damaged or in poor condition, they should be removed. Proper removal techniques must be strictly followed to avoid spreading contamination. Encapsulation is accomplished by sealing objects with an approved chemical sealant. Containment can be accomplished by constructing suitable physical barriers around the objects to contain any fibers that may be released. Air monitoring and inspection of buildings with asbestos-containing material should be performed regularly to be sure that fiber releases have not occurred. Maintenance and operations crews should be notified of an asbestos threat in their building, and they should be taught proper precautions to avoid accidental disturbance.

The Occupational Safety and Health Administration (OSHA), under the jurisdiction of the United States Department of Labor, is charged with protection of worker safety on the job. OSHA estimates that 1.3 million employees in construction and general industry face significant asbestos exposure in the workplace. Greatest exposure occurs in the construction industry, especially while removing asbestos during renovation or demolition. Workers are also apt to be exposed during the manufacture of asbestos products and during automobile brake and clutch repair work. OSHA has set standards for maximum exposure limits, protective clothing, exposure monitoring, hygiene facilities and practices, warning signs, labeling, record keeping, medical exams, and other aspects of the workplace. Workplace exposure for workers in general industry and construction must be limited to 0.2 asbestos fibers per .061 cu in. of air (0.2 f/cc), averaged over an eight-hour shift, or 1 fiber per .3 cu in. of air (1 f./5cc) over a standard 40-hour work week.

[*Douglas C. Pratt*]

FURTHER READING

U.S. Environmental Protection Agency. *How to Manage Asbestos in School Buildings:*

AHERA Designated Person's Self Study Guide. Washington, D.C., 1996.

U.S. Environmental Protection Agency. *Asbestos in the Home: A Homeowner's Guide.*

Washington, D.C., 1992.

U.S. Environmental Protection Agency. *Managing Asbestos in Place: A Building Owners*

Guide to Operations and Maintenance Programs for Asbestos-Containing Materials,

Washington, D.C., 1990: 207-2003.

U.S. Department of Labor, Occupational Safety and Health Administration. *Better Protection*

Against Asbestos in the Workplace: *Fact Sheet No. OSHA 92-06.* Washington, D.C.: GPO, 1992.

Yang, C. S. and F. W. Piecuch. "Asbestos: A Conscientious Approach." *Enviros* 01,

no. 11 (November 1991).

Asbestosis

Asbestos is a fibrous, incombustible form of magnesium and calcium silicate used in making insulating materials. By the late 1970s, over 6 million tons of asbestos were being produced worldwide. About two-thirds of the asbestos used in the United States is used in building materials, brake linings, textiles, and insulation, while the remaining one-third is consumed in such diverse products as paints, plastics, caulking compounds, floor tiles, cement, roofing paper, radiator covers, theater curtains, fake fireplace ash, and many other materials.

It has been estimated that of the eight to eleven million current and retired workers exposed to large amounts of asbestos on the job, 30 to 40 percent can expect to die of **cancer**. Several different types of asbestos-related diseases are known, the most significant being asbestosis. Asbestosis is a chronic disease characterized by scarring of the lung tissue. Most commonly seen among workers who have been exposed to very high levels of asbestos dust, asbestosis is an irreversible, progressively worsening disease. Immediate symptoms include shortness of breath after exertion, which results from decreased lung capacity. In most cases, extended exposure of 20 years or more must occur before symptoms become serious enough to be investigated. By this time the disease is too advanced for treatment. That is why asbestos could be referred to as a silent killer.

Exposure to asbestos not only affects factory workers working with asbestos, but individuals who live in areas surrounding asbestos emissions. In addition to asbestosis, exposure may result in a rare form of cancer called mesothelioma, which affects the lining of the lungs or stomach. Approximately 5 to 10 percent of all workers employed in asbestos manufacturing or mining operations die of mesothelioma.

Asbestosis is characterized by dyspnea (labored breathing) on exertion, a nonproductive cough, hypoxemia (insufficient oxygenation of the blood), and decreased lung volume. Progression of the disease may lead to respiratory failure and cardiac complications. Asbestos workers who smoke have a marked increase in the risk for developing bronchogenic cancer.

Increased risk is not confined to the individual alone, but there is an extended risk to workers' families, since asbestos dust is carried on clothes and in hair. Consequently, in the fall of 1986, President Reagan signed into law the Asbestos Hazard Emergency Response Act (AHERA), requiring that all primary and secondary schools be inspected for the presence of asbestos; if such materials are found, the school district must file, and carry out an asbestos abatement plan. The **Environmental Protection Agency** (EPA) was charged with the oversight of the project. *See also* Respiratory diseases

[*Brian R. Barthel*]

FURTHER READING

Agency for Toxic Substances and Disease Registry. Annual Report. Atlanta, GA: U. S. Department of Health and Human Services, 1989 and 1990.

Mossman, B. T., and J. B. L. Gee. "Asbestos-Related Diseases." *New England Journal of Medicine* 320 (29 June 1989): 1721-30.

Nadakavukaren, A. *Man & Environment: A Health Perspective.* Prospect Heights, IL: Waveland, 1990.

Ash, fly

See **Fly ash**

Ashio, Japan

Much could be learned from the Ashio, Japan, mining and smelting operation concerning the effects of **copper** poisoning on human beings, rice paddy **soils**, and the **environment**, including the comparison of long term costs and short term profits.

Copper has been mined in Japan since A.D. 709, and **pollution** has been reported since the sixteenth century. Copper leached from the Ashio Mine pit and tailings flowed into the Watarase River killing fish and contaminating rice paddy soils in the mountains of central Honshu. The refining process also released large quantities of sulfur oxide and other waste gases, which killed the vegetation and life in the surrounding streams. In 1790 protests by local farmers forced the mine to close, but it became the property of the government and was reopened to increase the wealth of Japan after Emperor Meiji came to power in 1869. The mine passed into private ownership in 1877, and new technological innovations were introduced to increase the mining and smelting output. A year later, signs of copper pollution were already appearing. Rice yields decreased and people who bathed in the river developed painful sores, but production expanded.

A large vein of copper ore was discovered in 1884, and by 1885 the Ashio Copper mine produced 4100 tons, about 40 percent of the total national output per year. **Arsenic** was a byproduct. The piles of slag mounted, and more waste **runoff** polluted the Watarase River and local farmlands. As the crops were damaged and the fish polluted, many people became ill. Consequently, a stream of complaints was heard, and some agreements were made to pay money, not for damages as such but just to "help out" the farmers. Meanwhile, mining and smelting continued as usual. In 1896 a **tailings pond** dam gave way and the deluge of **mine spoil waste** and water contaminated 59,280 acres (24,000 ha) of farm land in six prefectures from Ashio nearly to Tokyo 93 miles (150 km) away. Then the government ordered the Ashio Mining Company to construct facilities to prevent damage by pollutants, but in times of **flooding** these were largely ineffectual. In 1907 the government forced the inhabitants of the Yanaka Village, who had been the most affected by poisoning, to move to Hokkaido, making way for a flood control project.

In 1950, as a result of the Korean War, the Ashio Copper Mine expanded production and upgraded the smelting plant to compete with the high grade ores being processed from other mines. When the Gengorozawa slag pile, the smallest of 14, collapsed and introduced 2,614 cubic yards (2,000 cubic meters) of slag into the Watarase River in 1958, it contaminated 14,820 acres (6,000 ha) of rice fields. No remedial action was taken, but in 1967 a maximum average yearly standard of 0.06 mg/l copper in the river water was set. This was meaningless because most of the contamination occurred when large quantities of slag were **leaching** out during the rainy periods and floods. Japanese authorities also set 125 mg Cu/kg in paddy soil as the maximum allowable limit alleged not to damage rice yields, twice the minimum effect level of 56 mg Cu/kg.

In 1972 the government ordered that rice from this area be destroyed, even as the Ashio Mining Company still denied responsibility for its contamination. Testing showed that the soil of the Yanaka Village up to 10 feet (3 m) below the surface still contained 314 mg/kg of copper, 34 mg/kg of lead, 168 mg/kg of zinc, 46 mg/kg of arsenic, 0.7 mg/kg of cadmium, and 611 mg/kg of manganese. This land drains into the Watarase River, which now provides drinking water for the Tokyo metropolitan area and surrounding prefectures.

That same year the Ashio Mine announced that it was closing due to reduced demand for copper ore and worsening mining conditions; however, smelting continued with imported ores, so the slag piles still accumulated and minerals percolated to the river, especially during spring flooding. In August 1973, the Sabo dam collapsed and released about 2,000 tons of tailings into the river. Later that year the Law Concerning Compensation for Pollution Related Health Damage and Other Measures was passed, and it prompted the Environmental Agency's Pollution Adjustment Committee to begin reviewing the farmers' claims more seriously. For the first time, the company was required to admit being the source of pollution. The farmers' suit was litigated from March 1971 until May 1974, and the plaintiffs were awarded $5 million, much less than they asked for.

As major floods have been impossible to control, some efforts are being made to reforest the mountains. After they were washed bare of soil, the rocks fell and eroded, adding another hazard. So far, large expenditures have produced few results either in flood control or reforestation. The town of Ashio is now trying to attract tourism by billing the denuded mountains as the Japanese Grand Canyon, and the pollution continues. *See also* Air pollution; Biomagnification; Contaminated soil; Environmental law; Heavy metals and heavy metal poisoning; Percolation; Smelter; Water pollution; Xenobiotic

[*Frank M. D'Itri*]

FURTHER READING

Huddle, N., and M. Reich. *Island of Dreams: Environmental Crisis in Japan.* New York: Autumn Press, 1975.

Morishita, T. "The Watarase River Basin: Contamination of the Environment with Copper Discharged from Ashio Mine." In *Heavy Metal Pollution in Soils of Japan*, edited by K. Kitagishi and I. Yamane. Tokyo: Japan Scientific Societies Press. 1981.

Shoji, K., and M. Sugai. "The Ashio Copper Mine Pollution Case: The Origins of Environmental Destruction." In *Industrial Pollution in Japan.* Edited by J. Ui. Tokyo: United Nations University Press. 1992.

Asiatic black bear

The Asiatic black bear or moon bear (*Ursus thibetanus*) ranges through southern and eastern Asia, from Afghanistan and Pakistan through the Himalayas to Indochina, including most of China, Manchuria, Siberia, Korea, Japan, and Taiwan. The usual habitat of this bear is angiosperm forests, mixed hardwood-conifer forests, and brushy areas. It occurs in mountainous areas up to the tree-line, which can be as high as 13,000 ft (4,000 m) in parts of their Himalayan range.

The Asiatic black bear has an adult body length of 4.3-6.5 ft (1.3-2.0 m), a tail of 2.5-3.5 ft (75-105 cm), a height at the shoulder of 2.6-3.3 ft (80-100 cm), and a body weight of 110-440 lb. (50-200 kg). Male animals are considerably larger than females. Their weight is greatest in late summer and autumn, when the animals are fat in preparation for winter. Their fur is most commonly black, with white patches on the chin and a crescent- or Y-shaped patch on their chest. The base color of some individuals is brownish rather than black.

Female Asiatic black bears, or sows, usually give birth to two small cubs 12-14 oz. (350-400 g) in a winter den, although the litter can range from one to three. The gestation period is 6-8 months. After leaving their birth den, the cubs follow their mother closely for about 2.5 years, after which they are able to live independently. Asiatic black bears become sexually mature at an age of 3-4 years, and they can live for as long as 33 years. These bears are highly arboreal, commonly resting in trees, and feeding on fruits by bending branches towards themselves as they sit in a secure place. They may also sleep during the day in dens beneath large

logs, in rock crevices, or in other protected places. During the winter Asiatic black bears typically hibernate for several months, although in some parts of their range they only sleep deeply during times of particularly severe weather.

Asiatic black bears are omnivorous, feeding on a wide range of plant and animal foods. They mostly feed on sedges, grasses, tubers, twig buds, conifer seeds, berries and other fleshy fruits, grains, and mast (i.e., acorns and other hard nuts). They also eat insects, especially colonial types such as ants. Because their foods vary greatly in abundance during the year, the bears have a highly seasonal diet. Asiatic black bears are also opportunistic carnivores, and will also scavenge dead animals that they find. In cases where there is inadequate natural habitat available for foraging purposes, these bears will sometimes kill penned livestock, and they will raid bee hives when available. In some parts of their range, Asiatic black bears maintain territories in productive, lowland forests. In other areas they feed at higher elevations during the summer, descending to lower habitats for the winter.

All the body parts of Asiatic black bears are highly prized in traditional Chinese medicine, most particularly the gall bladders. Bear-paw soup is considered to be a delicacy in Chinese cuisine. Most bears are killed for these purposes by shooting or by using leg-hold, dead-fall, or pit traps. Some animals are captured alive, kept in cramped cages, and fitted with devices that continuously drain secretions from their gall bladder, which are used to prepare traditional medicines and tonics.

Populations of Asiatic black bears are declining rapidly over most of their range. These damages are being caused by overhunting of the animals for their valuable body parts (much of this involves illegal hunting, or poaching),disturbance of their forest habitats by timber harvesting, and permanent losses of their habitat through its conversion into agricultural land-use. These stresses and ecological changes have caused Asiatic black bears to become endangered over much of their range.

[*Bill Freedman*]

FURTHER READING

Grzimek, B (ed.) *Grzimek's Encyclopedia of Mammals.* London: McGraw Hill, 1990.

Nowak, R.M. *Walker's Mammals of the World,* 5th ed. Baltimore, MD: The John Hopkins University Press, 1991.

Assimilative capacity

Assimilative capacity refers to the ability of the **environment** or a portion of the environment (such as a stream, lake, air mass, or soil layer) to carry waste material without adverse effects on the environment or on users of its resources. **Pollution** occurs only when the assimilative capacity is exceeded. Some environmentalists argue that the concept of assimilative capacity involves a substantial element of value judgement, i.e. pollution **discharge** may alter the flora and fauna of a body of water, but if it does not effect organisms we value (e.g. fish) it is acceptable and within the assimilative capacity of the body of water.

A classical example of assimilative capacity is the ability of a stream to accept modest amounts of **biodegradable** waste. Bacteria in a stream utilize oxygen to degrade the organic matter (or **biochemical oxygen demand**) present in such a waste, causing the level of **dissolved oxygen** in the stream to fall; but the decrease in dissolved oxygen causes additional oxygen to enter the stream from the **atmosphere**, a process referred to as reaeration. A stream can assimilate a certain amount of waste and still maintain a dissolved oxygen level high enough to support a healthy population of fish and other aquatic organisms. However, if the assimilative capacity is exceeded, the concentration of dissolved oxygen will fall below the level required to protect the organisms in the stream.

Two other concepts are closely related: 1) critical load; and 2) self purification. The term critical load is synonymous with assimilative capacity and is commonly used to refer to the concentration or mass of a substance which, if exceeded, will result in adverse effects, i.e., pollution. Self purification refers to the natural process by which the environment cleanses itself of waste materials discharged into it. Examples include biodegradation of wastes by natural bacterial populations in water or soil, oxidation of organic chemicals by **photochemical reaction**s in the atmosphere, and natural **die-off** of disease causing organisms.

Determining assimilative capacity may be quite difficult, since a substance may potentially affect many different organisms in a variety of ways. In some cases, there is simply not enough information to establish a valid assimilative capacity for a pollutant. If the assimilative capacity for a substance can be determined, reasonable standards can be set to protect the environment and the allowable waste load can be allocated among the various dischargers of the waste. If the assimilative capacity is not known with certainty, then more stringent standards can be set, which is analogous to buying insurance (i.e., paying an additional sum of money to protect against potential future losses). Alternatively, if the cost of control appears high relative to the potential benefits to the environment, a society may decide to accept a certain level of risk.

The Federal Water Pollution Control Amendments of 1972 established the elimination of **discharge**s of pollution into navigable waters as a national goal. More recently, pollution prevention has been heavily promoted as an appropriate goal for all segments of society. Proper interpretation of these goals requires a basic understanding of the concept of assimilative capacity. The intent of Congress was to prohibit the discharge of substances in amounts that would cause pollution, not to require a concentration of zero. Similarly, Congress voted to ban the discharge of **toxic substance**s in concentrations high enough to cause harm to organisms.

Well meaning individuals and organizations sometimes exert pressure on regulatory agencies and other public and private entities to protect the environment by ignoring the concept of assimilative capacity and reducing waste discharges to zero or as close to zero as possible. Failure to utilize the natural assimilative capacity of the environment not only increases the cost of **pollution control** (the cost to the discharger and the cost to society as a whole); more importantly, it results in the inefficient use of limited resources and, by expending materials and energy for something that nature provides free of charge, results in an overall increase in pollution. *See also* Clean Water Act

[*Stephen J. Randtke*]

Asthma

Asthma is a condition characterized by unpredictable and disabling shortness of breath. It features episodic attacks of bronchospasm (prolonged contractions of the bronchial smooth muscle), and is a complex disorder involving biochemical, autonomic, immunologic, infectious, endocrine, and psychological factors to varying degrees in different individuals.

Asthma occurs in families suggesting that there is a genetic predisposition for the disorder, although the exact mode of genetic transmission remains unclear. The **environment** appears to play an important role in the expression of the disorder. For example, asthma can develop when *predisposed* individuals become infected with **virus**es or are exposed to **allergen**s or pollutants. On occasion foods or drugs may precipitate an attack. Psychological factors have been investigated but have yet to be identified with any specificity.

The severity of asthma attacks varies among individuals, over time, and with the degree of exposure to the triggering factors. Approximately half of all cases of asthma develop during childhood. Another third develop before the age of 40. There are two basic types of asthma—intrinsic and extrinsic. Extrinsic asthma is triggered by allergens while intrinsic asthma is not. Extrinsic asthma, or allergic asthma, is classified as Type I or Type II, depending on the type of allergic response involved. Type I extrinsic asthma is the classic allergic asthma which is common in children and young adults who are highly sensitive to dust and pollen, and is often seasonal in nature. It is characterized by sudden, brief, intermittent attacks of bronchospasms that readily respond to bronchodilators. Type II extrinsic asthma, or allergic alviolitis, develops in adults under age 35 after long exposure to irritants. Attacks are more prolonged than Type I and are more inflammatory. Fever and infiltrates which are visible on chest **x-ray**s often accompany bronchospasm.

Intrinsic asthma has no known immunologic cause and no known seasonal variation. It usually occurs in adults over the age of 35, many of whom are sensitive to aspirin and have nasal polyps. Attacks are often severe and do not respond well to bronchodilators.

A third type of asthma which occurs in otherwise normal individuals is called exercise induced asthma. Individuals with exercise induced asthma experience mild to severe bronchospasms during or after moderate to severe exertion. They have no other occurrences of bronchospasms when not involved in physical exertion. Although the cause of this type of asthma has not been established it is readily controlled by using a bronchodilator prior to beginning exercise. *See also* Respiratory diseases; Yokkaichi asthma

[Brian R. Barthel]

FURTHER READING

Berland, T. *Living With Your Allergies and Asthma.* New York: St. Martin's Press, 1983.

Lane, D. J. *Asthma: The Facts.* New York: Oxford University Press, 1987.

McCance, K. L. *Pathophysiology: The Biological Basis for Disease in Adults and Children.* St. Louis: Mosby, 1990.

Aswan High Dam, Egypt

A heroic symbol and an environmental liability, this dam on the Nile River was built as a central part of modern Egypt's nationalist efforts toward modernization and industrial growth. Begun in 1960 and completed by 1970, the High Dam lies near the town of Aswan, which sits at the Nile's first cataract, or waterfall, 200 river miles (322 km) from Egypt's southern border. The dam generates urban and industrial power, controls the Nile's annual **flooding**, ensures year-round, reliable **irrigation**, and has boosted the country's economic development as its population climbed from 20 million in 1947 to 58 million in 1990. The Aswan High Dam is one of a generation of huge dams built on the world's major rivers between 1930 and 1970 as both functional and symbolic monuments to progress and development. It also represents the hazards of large-scale efforts to control **nature**. Altered flooding, irrigation, and **sediment** deposition patterns have led to the displacement of villagers and farmers, a costly dependence on imported **fertilizer**, **water quality** problems and health hazards, and **erosion** of the Nile Delta.

Aswan attracted international attention in 1956, when planners pointed out that flooding behind the new dam would drown a number of ancient Egyptian tombs and monuments. A worldwide plea went out for assistance in saving the 4000-year old monuments, including the tombs and colossi of Abu Simbel and the temple at Philae. The United Nations Educational and Scientific Organization (UNESCO) headed the epic project, and over the next several years the monuments were cut into pieces, moved to higher ground, and reassembled above the water line.

The High Dam, built with international technical assistance and substantial funding from the former Soviet Union, was the second to be built near Aswan. English and Egyptian engineers built the first Aswan dam between 1898 and 1902. Justification for the first dam was much the same as that for the second, larger dam, namely flood control and irrigation. Under natural conditions the Nile experienced annual floods of tremendous volume. Fed by summer rains on the Ethiopian Plateau, the Nile's floods could reach sixteen times normal low season flow. These floods carried terrific **silt** loads, which became a rich fertilizer when flood waters overtopped the river's natural banks and sediments settled in the lower surrounding fields. This annual soaking and fertilizing kept Egypt's agriculture prosperous for thou-

sands of years. But annual floods could be wildly inconsistent. Unusually high peaks could drown villages. Lower than usual floods might not provide enough water for crops. The dams at Aswan were designed to eliminate the threat of high water and ensure a gradual release of irrigation water through the year.

Flood control and regulation of irrigation water supplies became especially important with the introduction of commercial cotton production. Cotton was introduced to Egypt by 1835, and within 50 years it became one of the country's primary economic assets. Cotton required dependable water supplies, but with reliable irrigation up to three crops could be raised in a year. Full-year commercial cropping was an important economic innovation, vastly different from traditional seasonal agriculture. By holding back most of the Nile's annual flood, the first dam at Aswan captured 65.4 billion cubic yards (50 billion cubic meters) of water each year. Irrigation canals distributed this water gradually, supplying a much greater acreage for a much longer period than did natural flood irrigation and small, village-built water works. But the original Aswan dam allowed 39.2 billion cubic yards (30 billion cubic meters) of annual flood waters to escape into the Mediterranean. As Egypt's population, agribusiness, and development needs grew, planners decided this was a loss that the country could not afford.

The High Dam at Aswan was proposed in 1954 to capture escaping floods and to store enough water for long-term **drought**, something Egypt had seen repeatedly in history. Three times as high and nearly twice as long as the original dam, the High Dam increased the reservoir's storage capacity from an original 6.5 billion cubic yards (5 billion cubic meters) to 205 billion cubic yards (157 billion cubic meters). The new dam lies 4.3 miles (7 km) upstream of the previous dam, stretches 2.2 miles (3.6 km) across the Nile and is 0.6 m (1 km) wide at the base. Because the dam sits on sandstone, gravel, and comparatively soft sediments, an impermeable screen of concrete was injected 590 feet (180 m) into the rock, down to a buried layer of granite. In addition to increased storage and flood control, the new project incorporates a hydropower generator. The dam's turbines, with a capacity of 8 billion kilowatt hours per year, doubled Egypt's electricity supply when they began operation in 1970.

Lake Nasser, the reservoir behind the High Dam, now stretches 311 miles (500 km) south to the Dal cataract in Sudan. Averaging 6.2 miles (10 km) wide, this reservoir holds the Nile's water at 558 feet (170 m) above sea level. Because this reservoir lies in one of the world's hottest and driest regions, planners anticipated evaporation at the rate of 13 cubic yards (10 billion cubic meters) per year. Dam engineers also planned for **siltation**, since the dam would trap nearly all the sediments previously deposited on downstream **flood plain**s. Expecting that Lake Nasser would lose about 5 percent of its volume to siltation in 100 years, designers anticipated a volume loss of 39.2 billion cubic yards (30 billion cubic meters) over the course of five centuries.

An ambitious project, the Aswan High Dam has not turned out exactly according to sanguine projections. Actual

An aerial view of the Aswan High Dam, Egypt.

evaporation rates today stand at approximately 15 billion cubic meters per year, or half of the water gained by constructing the new dam. Another one to two billion cubic meters are lost each year through **seepage** from unlined irrigation canals. Siltation is also more severe than expected. With 60 to 180 million tons of silt deposited in the lake each year, current projections suggest that the reservoir will be completely filled in 300 years. The dam's effectiveness in flood control, water storage, and power generation will decrease much sooner. With the river's silt load trapped behind the dam, Egyptian farmers have had to turn to chemical fertilizer, much of it imported at substantial cost. While this strains commercial **cash crop** producers, a need for fertilizer application seriously troubles local food growers who have less financial backing than agribusiness ventures.

A further unplanned consequence of silt storage is the gradual disappearance of the Nile Delta. The Delta has been a site of urban and agricultural settlement for millennia, and a strong local fishing industry exploited the large schools of sardines that gathered near the river's outlets to feed. Longshore currents sweep across the Delta, but annual sediment deposits counteracted the erosive effect of these currents and gradually extended the delta's area. Now that the Nile's sediment load is negligible, coastal erosion is causing the Delta to shrink. The sardine fishery has collapsed, since river discharge and **nutrient** loads have been so severely depleted. Decreased fresh water flow has also cut off water supply to a string of fresh water lakes and underground **aquifer**s near

the coast. Salt water **infiltration** and **soil salinization** have become serious threats.

Water quality in the river and in Lake Nasser have suffered as well. The warm, still waters of the reservoir support increasing concentrations of **phytoplankton**, or floating water plants. These plants, most of them microscopic, clog water intakes in the dam and decrease water quality downstream. Salt concentrations in the river are also increasing as a higher percentage of the river's water evaporates from the reservoir.

While the High Dam has improved the quality of life for many urban Egyptians, it has brought hardship to much of Egypt's rural population. Most notably, severe health risks have developed in and around irrigation canal networks. These canals used to flow only during and after flood season; once the floods dissipated the canals would again become dry. Now that they are full year round, irrigation canals have become home to a common tropical snail that carries **schistosomiasis**, a debilitating disease that severely weakens its victims. **Malaria** may also be spreading, since moist mosquito breeding spots have multiplied. Farm fields, no longer washed clean each year, are showing high salt concentrations in the soil. Perhaps most tragic is the displacement of villagers, especially Nubians, who are ethnically distinct from their northern Egyptian neighbors and who lost most of their villages to Lake Nasser. Resettled in apartment blocks and forced to find work in the cities, Nubians are losing their traditional culture.

The Aswan High Dam was built as a symbol of national strength and modernity. By increasing industrial and agricultural output the dam generates foreign exchange for Egypt, raises the national standard of living, and helps ensure the country's high status and profile in international affairs. For all its problems, Lake Nasser now supports a fishing industry that partially replaces jobs lost in the delta fishery, and tourists contribute to the national income when they hire cruise boats on the lake. Most important, the country's expanded population needs a great deal of water. The Egyptian population is projected at 70 million by the year 2000, and neither the people nor their necessary industrial activity could survive on the Nile's natural meager water supply in the dry season. The Aswan dam was built during an era when dams of epic scale were appearing on many of the world's major rivers. Such projects were a cornerstone of development theory at the time, and if most rivers were not already dammed today, huge dams might still be central to development theory. Like other countries, including the United States, Egypt experiences serious problems and threats of future problems in its dam, but the Aswan dam is a central part of life and planning in modern Egypt. *See also* Commercial fishing; Salinization of soils; Saltwater intrusion; Water resources

[*Mary Ann Cunningham*]

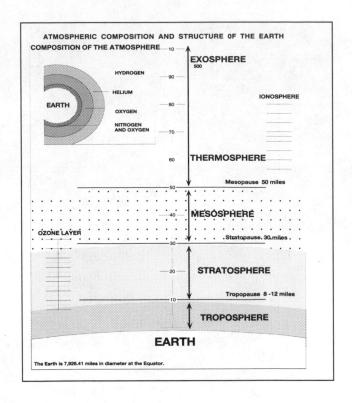

FURTHER READING

Driver, E. E., and W. O. Wunderlich, eds. *Environmental Effects of Hydraulic Engineering Works.* Proceedings of an International Symposium Held at Knoxville, TN, Sept. 12-14, 1978. Knoxville: Tennessee Valley Authority, 1979.

Little, T. *High Dam at Aswan—the Subjugation of the Nile.* London: Methuen, 1965.

Säve-Söderbergh, T. *Temples and Tombs of Ancient Nubia: The International Rescue Campaign at Abu Simbel, Philae, and Other Sites.* London: (UNESCO) Thames and Hudson, 1987.

Atmosphere

The atmosphere is the envelope of gas surrounding the earth, which is for the most part permanently bound to the earth by the gravitational field. It is composed primarily of **nitrogen** (78 percent by volume) and oxygen (21 percent). There are also small amounts of argon, **carbon dioxide**, and water vapor, as well as trace amounts of other gases and **particulate** matter.

Trace components of the atmosphere can be very important in atmospheric functions. **Ozone** accounts on average for 2 **parts per million** of the atmosphere but is more concentrated in the **stratosphere**. This stratospheric ozone is critical to the existence of terrestrial life on the planet. Particulate matter is another important trace component. **Aerosol** loading of the atmosphere, as well as changes in the tiny carbon dioxide component of the atmosphere, can be responsible for significant changes in climate.

The composition of the atmosphere changes over time and space. Outside of water vapor (which can vary from 0-4 percent in the local atmosphere) the concentrations of the major components varies little in time. Above 31 mi (50 km) from sea level, however, the relative proportions of component gases change significantly. As a result, the atmosphere is divided into two compositional components: Below 31 mi (50 km) is the homosphere and above 31 mi (50 km) is the heterosphere.

The atmosphere is also divided according to its thermal behavior. By this criteria, the atmosphere can be divided into several layers. The bottom layer is the *troposphere*; it contains most of the atmosphere and is the domain of weather. Above the troposphere is a stable layer called the stratosphere. This layer is important because it contains much of the ozone which filters ultraviolet light out of the incident solar radiation. The next layer, is the *mesosphere*, which is much less stable. Finally, there is the *thermosphere*; this is another very stable zone, but its contents are barely dense enough to cause a visible degree of solar radiation scattering. *See also* Greenhouse effect; Ozone layer depletion; Ultraviolet radiation

[*Robert B. Giorgis, Jr.*]

FURTHER READING

Anthes, R. A., et al. *The Atmosphere.* 3rd ed. Columbus, OH: Merrill, 1981.

Graedel, T. E., and P. J. Crutzen. "The Changing Atmosphere." *Scientific American* 261 (September 1989): 58-68.

Schaefer, V., and J. Day. *A Field Guide to the Atmosphere.* New York: Houghton Mifflin, 1981.

Atmospheric (air) pollutants

Atmospheric pollutants are substances that accumulate in the air to a degree that is harmful to living organisms or to materials exposed to the air. Common air pollutants include **smoke**, **smog**, and gases such as **carbon monoxide**, **nitrogen** and sulfur oxides, and hydrocarbon fumes. While gaseous pollutants are generally invisible, solid or liquid pollutants in smoke and smog are easily seen. One particularly noxious form of **air pollution** occurs when oxides of sulfur and nitrogen combine with atmospheric moisture to produce sulfuric and nitric acid. When the acids are brought to earth in the form of acid rain, damage is inflicted on lakes, rivers, vegetation, buildings, and other objects. Because sulfur and nitrogen oxides can be carried for long distances in the atmosphere before they are removed in precipitation, damage may occur far from pollution sources.

Smoke is an ancient environmental pollutant, but increased use of fossil fuels in recent centuries has increased its severity. Smoke can aggravate symptoms of **asthma**, **bronchitis**, and **emphysema**, and long term exposure can lead to lung **cancer**. Smoke toxicity increases when fumes of sulfur dioxide, commonly released by coal combustion, are inhaled with it. One particularly bad air pollution incident occurred in London in 1952 when approximately 4,000 deaths resulted from high smoke and sulfur dioxide levels that accumulated in the metropolitan area during an atmospheric inversion.

Sources of air pollutants are particularly abundant in modem, industrial population centers. Major sources include power and heating plants, industrial manufacturing plants, and transportation vehicles. **Mexico City** is a particularly bad example of a very large metropolitan area that has not adequately controlled harmful emissions into the atmosphere, and as a result many area residents suffer from respiratory ailments. The Mexican government has been forced to shut down a large oil refinery and ban new polluting industries from locating in the city. More difficult for the Mexican government to control are the emissions from over 3.5 million automobiles, trucks, and buses.

Smog (a combination of smoke and fog) is formed from the condensation of moisture (fog) on particulate matter (smoke) in the atmosphere. Although smog has been present in urban areas for a long time, photochemical smog is an exceptionally harmful and annoying form of air pollution found in large urban areas. It was first recognized as a serious problem in Los Angeles in the late 1940s. Photochemical smog forms by the catalytic action of sunlight on some atmospheric pollutants including unburned hydrocarbons evaporated from automobile and other fuel tanks. Products of the photochemical reactions include **ozone**, aldehydes, ketones, peroxyacetyl nitrate, and organic acids. Photochemical smog causes serious eye and lung irritation and other health problems.

Because of the serious damage caused by atmospheric pollution, control has become a high priority in many countries. Several approaches have proven beneficial. An immediate control measure involves a system of air alerts announced when air pollution monitors disclose dangerously high levels of contamination. Industrial sources of pollution are forced to curtail activities until conditions return to normal. These emergency situations are often caused by atmospheric inversions that limit the upward mixing of pollutants. Wider dispersion of pollutants by taller smokestacks can alleviate local pollution. However, dispersion does not lessen overall amounts; instead, it can create problems for communities downwind from the source. Greater energy efficiency in vehicles, homes, electrical power plants, and industrial plants, lessens pollution from these sources. This reduction in fuel use also reduces pollution created when fuels are produced, and as an added benefit, more energy efficient operation reduces costs. Efficient and convenient mass transit also helps to mitigate urban air pollution by cutting the need for personal vehicles.

[*Douglas C. Pratt*]

FURTHER READING

Georgii, H. W., ed. *Atmospheric Pollutants in Forest Areas: Their Deposition and Interception.*

Boston: Kluwer Academic Publishers, 1986.

Graedel, T. E., and P. J Crutzen. "The Changing Atmosphere." *Scientific American* 261, no. 3 (Sept 1989): 58-59.

Hutchinson, T.C., and K. M. Meema, eds. *Effects of Atmospheric Pollutants on Forests,*

Wetlands, and Agricultural Ecosystems. New York: Springer-Verlag, 1987.

Restelli, G., and G. Angeletti, eds. *Physico-Chemical Behaviour of Atmospheric Pollutants.*

Boston: Kluwer Academic Publishers, 1990.

Atmospheric inversion

Atmospheric inversions are horizontal layers of air that increase in temperature with height. Such warm, light air often lies over air that is cooler and heavier. As a result the air has a strong vertical stability, especially in the absence of strong winds.

Atmospheric inversions play an important role in **air quality**. They can trap air pollutants below or within them, causing high concentrations in a volume of air that would otherwise be able to dilute air pollutants throughout a large portion of the troposphere.

Atmospheric inversions are quite common, and there are several ways in which they are formed. Surface inversions can form during the evening when the radiatively cooling ground becomes a heat sink at the bottom of an air mass immediately above it. As a result heat flows down through the air which sets up a temperature gradient that coincides with an inversion. Alternatively, relatively warm air may flow over a cold surface with the same results.

Elevated atmospheric inversions can occur when vertical differences in wind direction allow warm air to set up over cold air. However, it is more common in near-subtropical latitudes, especially on the western sides of continents, to get subtropical subsidence inversions. Subtropical subsidence inversions often team with mountainous topography to trap air both horizontally and vertically. This is the situation on the coast of southern and central California. *See also* Air pollution; Air quality criteria; Mexico City, Mexico; Nonattainment area

Atmospheric pollutants

See **Carbon monoxide; Nitrogen oxides; Particulates; Smog; Sulfur dioxide; Volatile organic compound**

Atomic bomb

See **Nuclear weapons**

Atomic bomb testing

See **Bikini Atoll; Nevada Test Site**

Atomic energy

See **Nuclear energy**

Atomic Energy Commission (AEC)

The Atomic Energy Commission (AEC) was established by act of the United States Congress in 1946. It originally had a dual function: to promote the development of **nuclear power** and to regulate the nuclear power industry. These two functions were occasionally in conflict, however. Critics of the AEC claimed that the Commission sometimes failed to apply appropriate safety regulations, for example, because doing so would have proved burdensome to the industry and hindered its growth. In 1975, the AEC was dissolved. Its regulatory role was assigned to the **Nuclear Regulatory Commission** and its research and development role to the **Energy Research and Development Administration**.

Atomic fission

See **Nuclear fission**

Atomic fusion

See **Nuclear fusion**

Atrazine

Atrazine is used as a selective preemergent **herbicide** on crops, including corn, sorghum, and sugar cane, and as a

nonselective herbicide along fence lines, right-of-ways, and road sides. It is used in a variety of formulations, both alone and in combination with other herbicides. In the United States it is the single most widely used herbicide, accounting for about 15 percent of total herbicide application by weight. Its popularity stems from its effectiveness, its selectivity (it inhibits **photosynthesis** in plants lacking a **detoxification** mechanism), and its low mammalian toxicity (similar to that of table salt). Concern over its use stems from the fact that a small percentage of the amount applied can be carried by rainfall into surface waters (stream and lakes), where it may inhibit the growth of plants and algae or contaminate **drinking-water supply**. Because atrazine is classified as a possible human **carcinogen**, the United States **Environmental Protection Agency (EPA)** has limited its concentration in drinking water to 3 µg/L.

Attainment area

An attainment area is a politically or geographically defined region that is in compliance with the **National Ambient Air Quality Standard**s, as set by the **Environmental Protection Agency (EPA)**. A region is considered to be an attainment area if it does not exceed the specified thresholds for air pollutants that may be a threat to public health. The standards are set for a variety of **ambient air** pollutants, including **particulate**s, **ozone**, **carbon monoxide**, sulfur oxides, and **nitrogen oxides**. A region can be an attainment area for one pollutant and a **nonattainment area** for another. *See also* Air pollution; Air quality criteria

Audubon, John James (1785-1851)

American artist and naturalist

John James Audubon, the most renowned artist and naturalist in nineteenth century America, left a legacy of keenly observant writings as well as a portfolio of exquisitely rendered paintings of the birds of North America.

Born April 26, 1785, Audubon was the illegitimate son of a French naval captain and a domestic servant girl from Santo Domingo (now Haiti). Audubon spent his childhood on his father's plantation in Santo Domingo and most of his late teens on the family estate in Mill Grove, Pennsylvania—a move intended to prevent him from being conscripted into the Napoleonic army.

Audubon's early pursuits centered around natural history, and he was continuously collecting and drawing plants, insects, and birds. His habit of keeping meticulous field notes of his observations at a young age. It was at Mill Grove that Audubon, in order to learn more of the movements and habits of birds, tied bits of colored string onto the legs of several Eastern Phoebes and so proved that these birds returned to the same nesting sites the following year. Audubon was the first to use banding to study the movement of birds.

John James Audubon

While at Mill Grove, Audubon began courting their neighbor's eldest daughter, Lucy Bakewell, and they were married in 1808. They made their first home in Louisville, Kentucky, where Audubon tried being a storekeeper. He could not stand staying inside, and so he spent most of his time afield to "supply fowl for the table," thus dooming the store to failure.

In 1810, Audubon met by chance Alexander Wilson, who is considered the father of American ornithology. Wilson had finished much of his nine volume *American Ornithology* at this time, and it is believed that his work inspired Audubon to embark on his monumental task of painting the birds of North America.

The task that Audubon undertook was to become *The Birds of America*. Because Audubon decided to depict each species of bird life-size, thus rendering each on a 36 1/2 in by 26 1/2 in (93 cm by 67 cm) page, this was the largest book ever published up until that time. He was able to draw even larger birds such as the **whooping crane** life-size by depicting them with their heads bent to the ground. Audubon pioneered the use of fresh models instead of stuffed museum skins for his paintings. He would shoot birds and wire them into life-like poses to obtain the most accurate drawings possible. Even though his name is affixed to a modern conservation organization, the **National Audubon Society**, it must be remembered that little thought was given to the **conservation** of birds in the early nineteenth century. It was not uncommon for Audubon to shoot a dozen or more individuals of a species to get what he considered the perfect one for painting.

Audubon solicited subscribers for his *Birds of America* to finance the printing and hand-coloring of the plates. The project took nearly twenty years to complete, but the resulting double elephant folio, as it is known, was truly a work of art, as well as the ornithological triumph of the time.

Later in his life, Audubon worked on a book of the mammals of North America with his two sons, but failing health forced him to let them complete the work. He died in 1851, leaving behind a remarkable collection of artwork that depicted the natural world he loved so much.

[*Eugene C. Beckham*]

FURTHER READING

Audubon, J. J. *Audubon's Western Journal: 1849-1850*. Irvine: Reprint Services, 1992.

———. *Life of John James Audubon: The Naturalist*. Irvine: Reprint Services, 1993.

Gopnik, A. "Audubon's Passion." *The New Yorker* 67 (25 February 1991): 96-104.

Running Press Staff, eds. *Audubon Journal*. Philadelphia: Running Press, 1993.

Audubon Society
See **National Audubon Society**

Australia

The Commonwealth of Australia, a country in the South Pacific Ocean, occupies the smallest continent and covers an area of 2,966,200 mi² (7,682,000 km²). Along the northeast coast of Australia, for a distance of 1,200 mi (2,000 km) in length and offshore as much as 100 mi (160 km) into the Pacific Ocean, lies the Great Barrier Reef, the greatest assemblage of **coral reef**s in the world. The island of Tasmania, which is a part of Australia, lies off the southeast coast of the mainland. Australia consists mainly of plains and plateaus, most of which average 2,000 ft (600 m) above sea level. There are several low mountain ranges in the country. Only about 16,000,000 people live in Australia, of whom about 150,000 are native people, the Aborigines.

More than a third of Australia receives under 10 in (25 cm) of annual rainfall, while less than a third receives over 20 in (51 cm). Many areas experience prolonged **drought** and frequent heat waves. The Outback is one such area. It is comprised of dry, barren land and vast interior deserts. **Soil**s generally are poor, with fertile land found only in the lowlands and valleys near the east and southeast coast. The largest river is the Murray River in southeastern Australia. In the inland area, few rivers have much water due to the lack of rainfall. In areas with coastal highlands, rivers flow only a short distance to the sea. Lakes frequently dry up and become beds of salt. In contrast, there are lush **rain forest**s in the north and snowy mountains in the southeastern Blue Range.

The most common tree is the eucalyptus, of which there are at least 600 different kinds. Since Australia is the driest of the inhabited continents, there are few forests. The acacia, or wattle, is Australia's national flower. Many of the mammals of Australia (kangaroos, wallabies, and koala bears)

are marsupials, unlike those found anywhere else in the world. The young of marsupials are born premature and require continued development outside the womb in pouches on the parent's body. The egg-laying mammal, or monotreme, is also only found in Australia. There are two species of monotreme: the duck-billed platypus and the echidna, or spiny anteater. The most famous Australian bird is the kookaburra. There are no hoofed animals in Australia. Two flightless birds, the emu and the cassowary, also are found only in Australia. Snakes are common and include many poisonous species. Two kinds of crocodiles are found in the northern part of Australia. All of these unique fauna and flora species have evolved due to the long separation of the Australian continent from southeast Asia and a general lack of predators.

The goal of environmental protection and management in Australia is integration of the principles of ecologically **sustainable development** into policies and programs encompassing all aspects of environmental issues.

Australia's land resources form the basis of its unique natural heritage and its agricultural industry. However, problems of land degradation are widespread. Land degradation due to dryland salinity is a national problem that threatens both biodiversity and agricultural productivity. Dryland salinity affects about 5,434,000 acres (2.2 million ha) of once-productive agricultural land and costs an estimated $243 million per year in lost agricultural production. Dryland salinity originates from salt deposited in the landscape over millions of years due to marine sedimentation. Land clearing over the last two hundred years and the replacement of deep-rooted perennial native vegetation with shallow-rooted annuals have caused water tables to rise, bringing saline water close to the surface into the root zones of plants. Excessive irrigation has also led to increases in levels of water tables. Strategies to address this problem include research for the prediction, prevention, and reversal of dryland salinity. An example of a research effort to ameliorate the effects of salinity is a project that addresses the identification of salt-tolerant plant species and development of appropriate establishment and growth management techniques to ensure their survival. Australia's naturally fire-adapted **ecosystem** has frequent brushfires that now threaten many new developments and even major cities. Other land degradation problems being addressed include the rehabilitation of mining sites and **remediation** of sites contaminated by railway operations.

Australia contains about 10 % of the world's biological diversity. The Commonwealth is addressing the issues of loss of **biodiversity** through a program referred to as the National Vegetation Initiative (NVI). About 988 million acres (40 million ha) of land is protected within a terrestrial reserves system, but 1,235 million acres (500 million ha), or more than two-thirds of Australia's land area, are managed by private landholders. Biodiversity outside the reserves has been affected by vegetation clearance and modification. The NVI will attempt to reverse the long-term decline in the quality and extent of Australia's native vegetation by developing programs and incentives to conserve, enhance, and mana-ge remnant native vegetation; to increase revegetation activities; and to encourage the integration of native vegetation into conventional farming systems.

The state of Australia's rivers and other aquatic systems has been declining due to a range of factors. Unsustainable water extractions for agricultural production have resulted in reduced flows in rivers that result in blue-green algae outbreaks, declines in native fish populations, increases in salinity, loss of wetlands, and loss of the beneficial aspects of small floods. Research is being conducted to define environmental flow requirements so that water allocations or entitlements will include environmental needs as a legitimate use. Other factors affecting the decline in aquatic systems include poor land and vegetation management, agricultural and urban **pollution**, salinity, destruction of native habitat, and spread of exotic pests such as the European carp and the water weed *Salvinia*.

In a 1997 Australian Bureau of Statistics survey, the Australian people identified **air pollution** as their greatest environmental concern. The government's primary **air quality** objective is to provide all Australians with equivalent protection from air pollution, which will be achieved by the development of national air quality strategies and standards that minimize the adverse environmental impacts of air pollution. Since over 60% of the Australian population lives in cities, the Government's first priority is to develop measures to reduce the impact of air pollution on urban areas.

The government of Australia considers **climate** changes as another of its most important environmental issues. A National Greenhouse Response Strategy was adopted in 1992 to respond to the need for **greenhouse gas** emission mitigation. The major thrust of the program is to develop cooperative agreements with industry to abate and reduce greenhouse gas emissions. In addition, large scale vegetation plantings for improvement of land resources will reduce **carbon dioxide**, a major greenhouse gas, in the **atmosphere**. **Methane** emission from intensive agriculture will be reduced through livestock waste treatment. The use of alternative transport fuels such as liquefied **petroleum** gas, compressed **natural gas**, **ethanol**, and other alcohol blends will be encouraged through the use of a fuel excise exemption.

Although **ozone layer depletion** in the atmosphere occurs over most of the Earth, the most dramatic changes are seen when an ozone "hole" forms over Antarctica each spring. The ozone layer protects life on Earth from harmful **ultraviolet radiation** from the sun, but it can be depleted by the use of some widely used ozone-depleting chemicals. The ozone hole sometimes drifts over Australia and exposes residents to dangerous levels of UV radiation. Australia, because of its proximity to Antarctica, has taken a leading role in ozone protection and has been influential in the development and implementation of cost-effective mechanisms to ensure the phase-out of use of ozone-depleting substances by all countries. The government also monitors solar ultraviolet radiation levels and assesses the consequences for public health.

Australia's marine and coastal environments are rich in natural and cultural resources, are adjacent to most of the nation's population (about 86%), and are a focus of much of Australia's economic, social, tourism, and recreational activity. Australia's Exclusive Economic Zone (EEZ) is one of the largest in the world, comprising 4.25 million mi^2 (11 million km^2) of marine waters. Uncoordinated and ad hoc development has been identified as a major contributing factor to the decline of coastal water quality and marine and estuarine habitats. Programs that include cooperation of the Commonwealth government with state and local governments, industry groups, nongovernmental organizations, and the community have been developed to protect and rehabilitate these environments. These programs include addressing threats to coastal water quality and marine biodiversity from land-based and marine pollution; developing integrated management plans for the conservation and sustainable use of coastal resources, including fisheries resources; supporting capital works and improvement of technologies to reduce the impacts of sewage and stormwater; controlling the introduction and spread of exotic marine pests in Australian waters; protecting and restoring fish habitats; and supporting comprehensive and consistent coastal monitoring.

The Great Barrier Reef is facing growing pressures from the reef-based tourism industry, commercial and recreational fishing (which is worth about $1.3 billion per year), expanding coastal urban areas, and downstream effects of land use from agricultural activities. Several programs are being developed and implemented to ensure that activities can continue on an ecologically sustainable basis. For example, tourist and recreational impacts are being reduced while providing diverse tourist activities. Fishing catches and efforts are being monitored, major or critical habitats are being identified, and fishing by-catch is being reduced through the development of new methods. Sediment, nutrient, and other land-based runoff that impacts the health of adjacent marine areas are being controlled in coastal developments. Also, spill contingency planning and other responses to prevent pollution from ships, navigational aids, and ship reporting systems are all being improved. In addition, the state of water quality is being monitored in long-term programs throughout the Reef and threats from pollution are being assessed. Finally, all planning exercises include consultation with Aboriginal and Torres Strait Islander (ATSI) communities to ensure that their interests are considered.

The Commonwealth, through its National and World Heritage programs, is protecting elements of Australia's natural and cultural heritage that are of value for this and future generations. The National Estate comprises natural, historic, and indigenous places that have aesthetic, historic, scientific or social significance or other special value. The Register of the National Estate by 1997 had 11,000 places listed. The Register educates and alerts Australians to places of heritage significance. World Heritage properties are areas of outstanding universal cultural or national significance that are included in the UNESCO World Heritage List. In 1997, there were 11 Australian properties on the World Heritage List, including the Great Barrier Reef.

[*Judith L. Sims*]

FURTHER READING

Hill, R. *Investing in Our Natural Heritage*. Canberra, Australia: Annual Report on the Commonwealth's Environment Expenditure, Minister for the Environment, 1997.

Autecology

A branch of **ecology** emphasizing the interrelationships among individual members of the same species and their environment. Autecology includes the study of the life history and/or behavior of a particular species in relation to the environmental conditions that influence its activities and distribution. Autecology also includes studies on the tolerance of a species to critical physical factors (e.g., temperature, salinity, oxygen level, light) and biological factors (e.g., predation, symbiosis) thought to limit its distribution. Such data are gathered from field measurement or from controlled experiments in the laboratory. Autecology contrasts with *synecology*, the study of interacting groups (i.e., communities) of species.

Automobile

The development of the automobile at the end of the nineteenth century fundamentally changed the structure of society in the developed world and has had wide-ranging effects on the **environment**, the most notable being the increase of **air pollution** in cities. The piston-type internal **combustion** engine is responsible for the peculiar mix of pollutants that it generates. There are a range of other engines suitable for automobiles, but they have yet to displace engines using rather volatile **petroleum** derivatives.

The simplest and most successful way of improving gaseous **emissions** from automobiles is to find **alternative fuels**. Diesel fuels have always been popular for larger vehicles, although a few private vehicles in Europe are also diesel-powered. Compressed **natural gas**es have been widely used as fuel in some countries (e.g. New Zealand), while **ethanol** has had a limited success in places such as Brazil, where it can be produced relatively cheaply from sugar cane. There is some enthusiasm for the use of **methanol** in the United States, but it has yet to be seen if this will be widely adopted as a fuel.

Others have suggested that fundamental changes to the engine itself can lower the impact of automobiles on **air quality**. The Wankel rotary engine is a promising power source that offers both low vibration and pollutant emissions from a relatively lightweight engine. Although Wankel engines are found on a number of exotic cars, there are still doubts about long-term engine performance and durability in the urban setting. Steam and gas turbines have many of the advantages of the Wankel engine, but questions of their expense and suitability for automobiles have restricted their use. Electric vehicles have had some impact for special sectors of the market. They have proved ideal for small vehicles within cities where frequent stop-start operation is required (e.g., delivery vans). A few small, one-seat vehicles have been available at times, but they have failed to achieve any enduring popularity. The electric vehicle suffers from low range, low speed and acceleration, and needs heavy batteries. However these vehicles produce none of the conventional combustion-derived pollutants during operation, although the electricity to recharge the batteries requires the use of an electricity generating station. Still, electricity generation can be sited away from the urban center and employ **air pollution controls**. **Fuel cells** are an alternate source of electricity for electric automobiles. It is also possible to power automobiles through the use of flywheels. These are driven up to high speeds by a fixed, probably electric, motor, then the vehicle can be detached and powered using the stored momentum, although range is often limited.

Although **automobile emissions** are of great concern, the automobile has a far wider range of environmental impacts. Large amounts of material are used in their construction, and discarded automobiles can litter the countryside and fill waste dumps. Through much of the twentieth century the vehicles have been made of steel. Increasingly, other materials, such as **plastics** and fiberglass, are used as construction materials. A number of projects, most frequently on the European continent, have tried **recycling** automobile components. Responsible automobile manufacturers are aiming to build vehicles with longer road lives, further aiding **waste reduction**.

The high speeds now possible for automobiles lead to sometimes horrendous accidents, which can involve many vehicles on crowded highways. The number of accidents have been reduced through anti-lock braking systems, thoughtful road design, and imposing harsh penalties for drunk driving. In the future, on-board radar may give warning of impending collisions. Safety features such as seat belts, padding, and collapsible steering columns have helped lower injury during accidents.

The structure of cities has changed with widespread automobile ownership. It has meant that people can live further away from where they work or shop. The need for parking has led to the development of huge parking lots within the inner city. Reaction to crowding in city centers are seen in the construction of huge shopping centers out-of-town, where parking is more convenient (or strip development of large stores along highways). These effects have often caused damage to inner city life and disenfranchised non-car owners, particularly because a high proportion of car ownership often works against the operation of an effective **mass transit** system. For people who live near busy roads, **noise pollution** can be a great nuisance. The countryside has also been transformed by the need for super highways that cope with a large and rapid traffic flow. Such highways have often been built on valuable agricultural land or natural **habitat**s, and once constructed, create both practical and aesthetic nuisances.

[*Peter Brimblecombe*]

FURTHER READING

Environmental Effects of Automotive Emissions. Paris: OECD Compass Project, 1986.

Automobile emissions

The **automobile**, powered by piston-type internal **combustion** engine, is so widely used that it has become the dominant source of air pollutants, particularly of **photochemical smog**, in large, urban cities.

Modern internal combustion engines operate through the Otto cycle, which involves rapid batch-burning of **petroleum** vapors. The combustion inside the cylinder is initiated by a spark and proceeds outward through the gas volume until it reaches the cylinder walls where it is cooled. Close to the cylinder wall, where combustion is quenched, a fraction of the fuel remains unburnt. In the next cycle of the engine the hot combusted gases and unburnt fuel vapor are forced out through the exhaust system of the automobile.

Automotive engines generally operate on "fuel rich" mixtures, which means that there is not quite enough oxygen to completely burn the fuel. As a result there is an excess of unburnt **hydrocarbons**, particularly along the cylinder walls, and substantial amounts of **carbon monoxide**. This efficient production of carbon monoxide has made automobiles the most important source of this poisonous gas in the urban atmosphere.

The high **emission** levels of hydrocarbons and carbon monoxide have caused some engineers to become interested in "lean burn" engines that make more oxygen available during combustion. While such an approach is possible, the process also produces high concentrations of nitric oxide in the exhaust gases.

When the fuel enters the cylinder of an automobile engine in the gaseous form, it generally does not produce **smoke**. However in diesel engines where the fuel is sprayed into the combustion chamber, it will become dispersed as tiny droplets. Sometimes, especially under load, these droplets will not burn completely and are reduced to fine **carbon** particles, or soot, that are easily visible from diesel exhausts. In many cities this diesel smoke can represent the principle soiling agent in the air. In addition, soot, particularly those from diesel engines, contain small amounts of carcinogenic material.

Many of the **carcinogen**s found in the exhaust from diesel engines are **polycyclic aromatic hydrocarbons (PAH)** and are archetypical carcinogens. Best known of these is **benzo-a-pyrene**, which was tentatively recognized as a carcinogen in the eighteenth century from observations of chimney sweepers who had high incidence of **cancer**. Some of the PAH can become nitrated during combustion and these may be even more carcinogenic than the un-nitrated PAH. Diesel emissions may pose a greater cancer risk than the exhaust gases from **gasoline** engines. There are a number of emissions from gasoline engines that are potentially carcinogenic. **Benzene** represents a large part of the total volatile organic emissions from automobiles. Yet the compound is also recognized by many as imposing a substantial carcinogenic risk to modern society. Toluene, although by no means as carcinogenic as benzene, is also emitted in large quantities. Toluene proves a very effective compound at initiating photochemical smog and also reacts to form the eye irritant peroxybenzoyl nitrate. The highly dangerous compound **dioxin** can be produced in auto exhausts where **chlorine** is present (anti-knock agents often contain chlorine). Formaldehyde, a suspected carcinogen, is produced in photochemical smog but may also be an enhanced risk from engines burning the otherwise less polluting **methanol** as a fuel.

Many exotic elements that are added to improve the performance of automotive fuels produce their own emissions. The best known is the anti-knock agent **tetraethyl lead**, which was added in such large quantities that it became the dominant source of **lead** particles in the air. A wide range of long-term health effects, such as lowering IQ, have been associated with exposure to lead. Although lead in urban populations are still rather high, the use of unleaded gasoline have decreased the problem somewhat.

Most attention usually focuses on the engine as a source of automobile emissions, but there are other sources. Evaporative loss of volatile materials from the crank case, carburetion system, and fuel tank represent important sources of hydrocarbons for the urban atmosphere. The wear of tires, brake linings, and metal parts contribute to particles being suspended in the air of the near roadside environment. The presence of **asbestos** fibers from brake linings in the urban air has often been discussed, although health threats from this source is less serious than from other sources.

There have been relatively few studies of the pollutants inside automobiles, but there has been some concern about the potential hazard of the build-up of automobile emissions from malfunctioning units and from "leaks." These can be from the evaporation of fuel, especially leaded fuels where the volatile tetraethyl lead is present. Carbon monoxide, from the exhaust system, can cause drowsiness and impair judgment. However in many cases the interior of a properly functioning automobile, without additional sources such as smoking, can have somewhat better air quality than the air outside. In general, pedestrians, cyclists, and those who work at road sites are likely to experience the worst of automotive pollutants such as carbon monoxide and potentially carcinogenic hydrocarbons.

Although huge quantities of **fossil fuels** are burnt in power generation and a range of industrial processes, automobiles make a significant and growing contribution to **carbon dioxide** emissions which enhance the **greenhouse effect**. **Ethanol**, made from sugar cane, is a renewable source and has the advantage of not making as large a contribution to the **greenhouse gases** as gasoline. Automobiles are not large emitters of **sulfur dioxide** and thus do not contribute greatly to the regional **acid rain** problem. Nevertheless, the **nitrogen oxides** emitted by automobiles are ultimately converted to nitric acid and these are making an increasing contribution to rainfall acidity. Diesel-powered vehicles use fuel of a higher sulfur content and can contribute to the sulfur compounds in urban air.

Despite the enormous problems created by the automobile, few propose its abolition. The ownership of a car carries with it powerful statements about personal freedom and power. Beyond this, the structure of many modern cities requires the use of a car. Thus while air pollution problems might well be cured by a wide range of sociological changes, a technological fix has been favored, such as the use of **catalytic converter**s. Despite this and other devices, cities still face daunting air quality problems. In some areas, most notably the **Los Angeles Basin**, it is clear that there will have to be a wide range of changes if air quality is to improve. Although much attention is being given to lowering emissions of **volatile organic compound**s, it is likely that non-polluting vehicles will have to be manufactured and better a **mass transit** system created.

[*Peter Brimblecombe*]

FURTHER READING

Environmental Effects of Automotive Emissions. Paris: OECD Compass Project, 1986.

Kennedy, D., and R. R. Bates, eds. *Air Pollution, the Automobile, and Public Health.* Washington, DC: National Academy Press, 1988.

Renner, M. G. "Car Sick." *World Watch* (November-December 1988): 36-43.

Autotroph

An organism that derives its **carbon** for building body tissues from **carbon dioxide** (CO_2) or carbonates and obtains its energy for bodily functions from radiant sources, such as sunlight, or from the oxidation of certain inorganic substances. The leaves of green plants and the bacteria that oxidize sulfur, iron, ammonium, and nitrite are examples of autotrophs. The oxidation of ammonium to nitrite, and of nitrite to nitrate, a process called nitrification, is a critical part of the **nitrogen cycle**. Moreover, the creation of food by photosynthetic organisms is largely an autotrophic process.

Avalanche

A sudden slide of snow and ice, usually in mountainous areas where there is heavy snow accumulation on moderate to steep slopes. Snow avalanches flow at an average speed of 80 MPH (130 km/hr), and their length can range from less than 300 ft. (100 m) to 2 mi (3.2 km) or more. Generally the term "avalanche" refers to sudden slides of snow and ice, but it can also be used to describe catastrophic debris slides consisting of mud and loose rock. Debris avalanches are especially associated with volcanic activity in which melted snow, earthquakes, and clouds of flowing ash can trigger movement of rock and mud. Snow avalanches generally consist either of loose, fresh snow or of slabs of accumulated snow and ice that move in large blocks. Snow avalanches occur most often where the snow surface has melted under the sun and then refreezes, forming a smooth surface of snow. Later snow

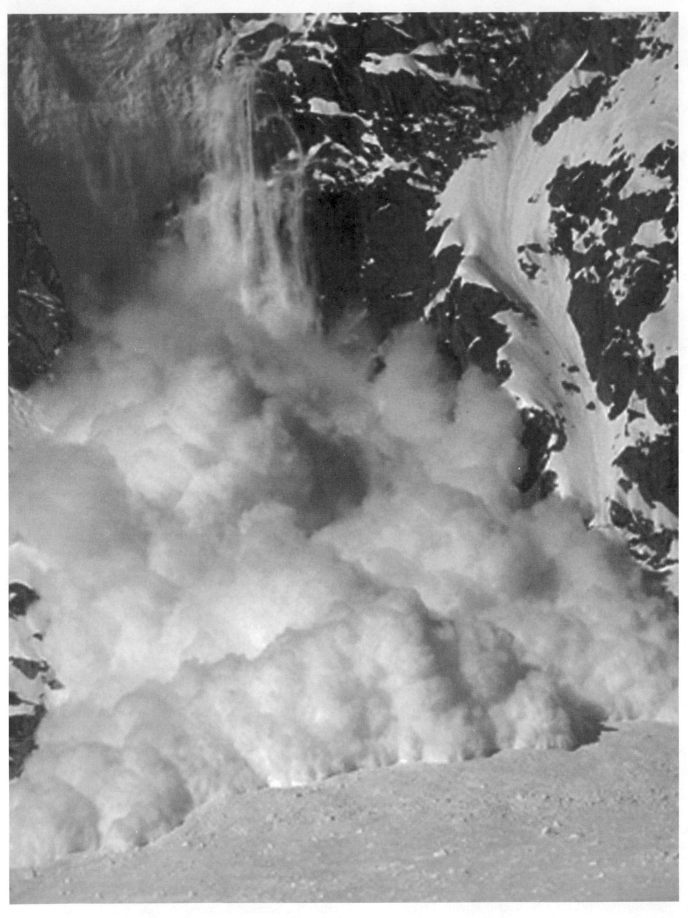

An avalanche crashes down the mountainside.

falling on this smooth surface tends to adhere poorly, and it may slide off the slick plane of recrystallized snow when it is shaken by any form of vibration—including sound waves, earthquakes, or the movement of skiers.

Several factors contribute to snow avalanches, including snow accumulation, hill slope angle, slope shape (profile), and weather. Avalanches are most common where there is heavy snow accumulation on slopes of 25°-65°, and they occur most often on slopes between 30°-45°. On slopes steeper than 65° snow tends to sluff off rather than accumulate. On shallow slopes avalanches are likely to occur only in wet (melting) conditions, when accumulated snow may be heavy, and when snow melt collecting along a hardened old snow surface within the snowpack can loosen upper layers, allowing them to release easily. Slab avalanches may be more likely to start on convex slopes, where snow masses can be fractured into loose blocks, but they rarely begin on tree-covered slopes. However, loose snow avalanches often start among trees, gathering speed and snow as they cross open slopes. Weather can influence avalanche probability by changing the stability and cohesiveness of the snow pack. Many avalanches occur during storms when snow accumulates rapidly, or during sustained periods of cold weather when new snow remains loose. Like snow melt, rainfall, can increase chances of avalanche by lubricating the surface of hardened layers within the snow pack. Sustained winds increase snow accumulation on the leeward side of slopes, producing snow masses susceptible to slab movement. When conditions are favorable, an avalanche can be triggered by the weight of a person or by loud noises, earthquakes, or other sources of vibration. Avalanches tend to be most common in mid-winter, when snow accumulation is high, and in late spring, when melting causes instability in the snow pack.

Avalanches play an ecological role by keeping slopes clear of trees, thus maintaining openings vegetated by grasses, forbs, and low brush. They are also a geomorphologic force, since they maintain bare rock surfaces, which are susceptible to erosion.

Most research into the dynamics and causes of avalanches has occurred in populous mountain regions such as the Alps, the Cascades, and the Rocky Mountains, where avalanches cause damage and fatalities by crushing buildings and vehicles. Avalanches are very powerful: they can crush buildings, remove full-grown trees from hillsides, and even sweep railroad trains from their tracks. One of the greatest avalanche disasters on record occurred in 1910 in the Cascades near Seattle, Washington, when a passenger train, trapped in a narrow valley in a snow storm for several days, was caught in an avalanche and swept to the bottom of the valley. Ninety-six passengers died as the cars were crushed with snow. Although avalanches are among the more dangerous natural hazards, they have caused fewer than 200 recorded mortalities in North America, and most avalanche victims in North America are caught in slides they triggered themselves by walking or skiing across open slopes with accumulated snow.

[*Mary Ann Cunningham*]

FURTHER READING

Brugnot, G., ed. *Snow and Avalanches*. Conference proceedings, Chamonix, Switzerland, 1992. Zurich: Cemagret, 1995.

Salm, B., and H. Gubler. *Avalanche Formation, Movement, and Effects.* Wallingford, Oxfordshire, UK: IAHS Press, 1987.

United States Forest Service. "Snow Avalanche: General rules for Avoiding and Surviving Snow Avalanches." Portland, OR: USDA Forest Service, 1982.

B

Bacillus thuringiensis

Bacillus thuringiensis, or *B.t.*, is a family of bacterial-based, biological insecticides. Specific strains of *B.t.* are used against a wide variety of leaf-eating lepidopteran **pest**s such as European corn borer, tomato hornworms, and tobacco moths, and some other susceptible insects such as blackflies and mosquitoes. The active agent in *B.t.* is toxic organic crystals that bind to the gut of an insect and poke holes in cell membranes, literally draining the life from the insect. *B.t.* can be applied using technology similar to that used for chemical insecticides, such as high-potency, low-volume sprays of *B.t.* spores applied by aircraft. The efficacy of *B.t.* is usually more variable and less effective than that of chemical insecticides, but the environmental effects of *B.t.* are considered to be more acceptable because there is little non-target toxicity.

Background radiation

Ionizing radiation has the potential to kill cells or cause somatic or germinal **mutation**s. It has this ability by virtue of its power to penetrate living cells and produce highly reactive charged **ion**s. It is the charged ions which cause cell damage. Radiation accidents and the potential for radiation from nuclear (atomic) bombs create a fear of radiation release due to human activity. Many people are subjected to diagnostic and therapeutic radiation, and older Americans were exposed to **radioactive fallout** from atmospheric testing of **nuclear weapons**. There is some environmental contamination from nuclear fuel used in **power plants**. Accordingly, there is considerable interest in radiation effects on biological systems and the sources of radiation in the **environment**.

Concern for radiation safety is certainly justified and most individuals seek to minimize their exposure to human-generated radiation. However, for most people, exposure levels to radiation from natural sources far exceed exposure to radiation produced by humans. Current estimates of human exposure levels of ionizing radiation suggest that only about 18 percent is of human origin. The remaining radiation (82 percent) is from natural sources and is referred to as "background radiation." While radiation doses vary tremendously from person to person, the average human has an annual exposure to ionizing radiation of about 360 millirem. (Millirem or mrem is a measure of radiation absorbed by tissue multiplied by a factor that takes into account the biological effectiveness of a particular type of radiation and other factors such as the competence of radiation repair. One mrem is equal to 10 μSv; μSv is an abbreviation for microSievert, a unit that is used internationally.)

Some radiation has little biological effect. Visible light and infrared radiation do not cause ionization, are not mutagenic and are not carcinogenic. Consequently, background radiation refers to ionizing radiation which is derived from cosmic radiation, terrestrial radiation, and radiation from sources internal to the body. (Background radiation has the potential for producing inaccurate counts from devices such as a Geiger counter. For example, cosmic rays will be recorded when measuring the radioactive decay of a sample. This background "noise" must be subtracted from the indicated count level to give a true indication of activity of the sample.)

Cosmic rays are of galactic origin, entering the earth's **atmosphere** from outer space. Solar activity in the form of sunflares and sunspots affects the intensity of cosmic rays. The atmosphere of the earth serves as a protective layer for humans and anything that damages that protective layer will increase the **radiation exposure** of those who live under it. The dose of cosmic rays doubles at 4,920 ft (1,500 m) above sea level. Because of this, citizens of Denver, near the Rocky Mountains, receive more than twice the dose of radiation from cosmic rays as do citizens of coastal cities such as New Orleans. The aluminum shell of a jet airplane provides little protection from cosmic rays, and for this reason passengers and crews of high flying jet airplanes receive more radiation than their earth traveling compatriots. Even greater is the cosmic radiation encountered at 60,000 ft (18,300 m) where supersonic jets fly. The level of cosmic radiation there is 1,000 times that at sea level. While the cosmic ray dose for occasional flyers is minimal, flight and cabin crews of ordinary jet airliners receive an additional exposure of 160 mrem per year, an added radiation burden to professional flyers of more than 40 percent. Cosmic sources for non-flying citizens at sea level are responsible for about 8 percent (29-30 mrem) of background radiation exposure per annum.

Another source of background radiation is terrestrial **radioactivity** from naturally occurring minerals, such as **uranium**, thorium, and cesium, in soil and rocks. The abundance of these minerals differs greatly from one geographic area to another. Residents of the Colorado plateau receive approximately double the dose of terrestrial radiation as those who live in Iowa or Minnesota. The geographic variations are attributed to the local composition of the earth's crust and the kinds of rock, soil and minerals present. Houses made of stone are more radioactive than houses made of wood. Limestones and sandstones are low in radioactivity when compared with granites and some shales. Naturally occurring radionuclides in soil may become incorporated into grains and vegetables and thus gain access to the human body. **Radon** is a radioactive gas produced by the disintegration of radium (which is produced from uranium). Radon escapes from the earth's crust and becomes incorporated into all living matter including humans. It is the largest source of inhaled radioactivity and comprises about 55 percent of total human radiation exposure (both background and human generated). Energy efficient homes, which do not leak air, may have a higher concentration of radon inside than is found in outside air. This is especially true of basement air. The radon in the home decays into radioactive "daughters" that become attached to **aerosol** particles which, when inhaled, lodge on lung and tracheal surfaces. Obviously, the level of radon in household air varies with construction material and with geographic location. Is radon in household air a hazard? Many people believe it is, since radon exposure (at a much higher level than occurs breathing household air) is responsible for lung **cancer** in non-smoking uranium miners.

Naturally occurring radioactive **carbon** (carbon-14) similarly becomes incorporated into all living material. Thus, external radiation from terrestrial sources often becomes internalized via food, water, and air. Radioactive atoms (radionuclides) of carbon, uranium, thorium, and actinium and radon gas provide much of the terrestrial background radiation. The combined annual exposure to terrestrial sources, including internal radiation and radon, is about 266 mrem and far exceeds other, more feared sources of radiation.

Life on earth evolved in the presence of ionizing radiation. It seems reasonable to assume that mutations can be attributed to this chronic, low level of radiation. Mutations are usually considered to be detrimental, but over the long course of human and other organic **evolution**, many useful mutations occurred, and it is these mutations that have contributed to the evolution of higher forms.

Nevertheless, it is to an organism's advantage to resist the deleterious effects associated with most mutations. The forms of life that inhabit the earth today are descendants of organisms that existed for millions of years on earth. Inasmuch as background ionizing radiation has been on earth longer than life, humans and all other organisms obviously cope with chronic low levels of radiation. Survival of a particular species is not due to a lack of genetic damage by background radiation. Rather, organisms survive because of a high degree of redundancy of cells in the body, which enables organ function even after the death of many cells (e.g., kidney and liver function, essential for life, does not fail with the loss of many cells; this statement is true for essentially all organs of the human body). Further, stem cells in many organs replace dead and discarded cells. Naturally occurring antioxidants are thought to protect against free radicals

produced by ionizing radiation. Finally, repair mechanisms exist which can, in some cases, identify damage to the double helix and effect **DNA** repair. Hence, while organisms are vulnerable to background radiation, mechanisms are present which assure survival. *See also* Radiation sickness

[*Robert G. McKinnell*]

FURTHER READING

Benarde, M. A. *Our Precarious Habitat: 15 Years Later.* New York: Wiley, 1989.

Hall, E. J. "Principles of Carcinogenesis: Physical." In *Cancer: Principles and Practice of Oncology,* edited by V. T. DeVita, et al. 4th ed. Philadelphia: Lippincott, 1993.

Knoche, H. W. *Radioisotopic Methods for Biological and Medical Research.* New York: Oxford University Press, 1991.

Bacon, Sir Francis (1561-1626)

English philosopher

Sir Francis Bacon, philosopher and Lord Chancellor of England, was one of the key thinkers involved in the development of the procedures and epistemological standards of modern science. Bacon thus has also played a vital role in shaping modern attitudes towards **nature**, human progress, and the **environment**. He inspired many of the great thinkers of the Enlightenment, especially in England and France. Moreover, Bacon laid the intellectual groundwork for the mechanistic view of the universe characteristic of eighteenth and nineteenth century thought and for the explosion of technology in the same period.

In *The Advancement of Learning* (1605) and *Novum Organum* (1620), Bacon attacked all teleological ways of looking at nature and natural processes (i.e., the idea found in Aristotle and in medieval scholasticism that there is an end or purpose which somehow guides or shapes such processes). For Bacon, this way of looking at nature resulted from the tendency of human beings to make themselves the measure of the outer world, and thus to read purely human ends and purposes into physical and biological phenomena. Science, he insisted, must guard against such prejudices and preconceptions if it was to arrive at valid knowledge.

Instead of relying on or assuming imaginary causes, science should proceed empirically and inductively, continuously accumulating and analyzing data through observation and experiment. Empirical observation and the close scrutiny of natural phenomena allow the scientist to make inferences, which can be expressed in the form of hypotheses. Such hypotheses can then be tested through continued observation and experiment, the results of which can generate still more hypotheses. Advancing in this manner, Bacon proposed that science would come to more and more general statements about the laws which govern nature and, eventually, to the secret nature and inner essence of the phenomena it studied.

As Bacon rather famously argued, "Knowledge is power." By knowing the laws of nature and the inner essence of

Sir Francis Bacon.

Baghouse.

the phenomena studied, human beings can remake things as they desire. All knowledge is for use, and the underlying motivation of science is technical control of nature. Bacon believed that science would ultimately progress to the point that the world itself would be, in effect, merely the raw material for whatever future ideal society human beings decided to create for themselves.

The possible features of this future world are sketched out in Bacon's unfinished utopia, *The New Atlantis* (1627). Here Bacon developed the view that the troubles of his time could be solved through the construction of a community governed by natural scientists and the notion that science and technology indeed could somehow redeem mankind. Empirical science would unlock the secrets of nature thus providing for technological advancement. With technological development would come material abundance and, implicitly, moral and political progress. Bacon's utopia is ruled by a "Solomon's House"—an academy of scientists with virtually absolute power to decide which inventions, institutions, laws, practices, and so forth will be propitious for society. Society itself is dedicated to advancing the human mastery of nature: "The End of Our Foundation is the Knowledge of Causes and secret motions of things; and the enlarging of the bounds of the human empire, to the effecting of all things possible."

[*Lawrence J. Biskowski*]

FURTHER READING

Bacon, F. *The Advancement of Learning*, 1605.

——. *Novum Organum*, 1620.

——. *The New Atlantis*, 1627.

Sibley, M. Q. *Nature and Civilization*. Itasca, IL: Peacock, 1977.

Baghouse

An **air pollution** control device normally using a collection of long, cylindrical, fabric **filters** to remove **particulate** matter from an exhaust air stream. The filter arrangement is normally designed to overcome problems of cleaning and handling large exhaust volumes. In most cases, exhaust gas enters long (usually 33-50 ft [10-15 m]), vertical, cylindrical filters on the inside from the bottom. The bags are sealed at the top. As the exhaust air passes through the fabric filter, particles are separated from the air stream by sticking either to the filter fabric or to the cake of particles previously collected on the inside of the filter. The exhaust then passes to the **atmosphere** free of most of its original particulate-matter loading; collection efficiency usually increases with particle size.

The buildup of particles on the inside of the bags is removed periodically by various methods, such as rapping the bags, pulsing the air flow through the bags, or shaking. The particles fall down the long cylindrical bags and are normally caught in a collection bin, which is unloaded periodically. A baghouse system is usually much cheaper to install and operate than a system using **electrostatic precipitation** to remove particulates. *See also* Cyclone collector; Wet scrubber

Balance of nature

The ideal of a balance of nature is based on a view of the natural world that is largely an artifact created by the temporal, spatial, and cultural filters through which humans respond to the natural world. For a variety of reasons we have interpreted the natural course of events in the world around us to maintain equilibrium, and seek to return it to equilibrium when disturbed.

There are three components to nature's balance: ecological, evolutionary, and population. In an ecological sense, communities were thought to proceed through successional stages to a steady state climax. When disturbed, the community would return to that climax state. Stability was an endpoint, and once reached the community became a partly closed homeostatic system. In an evolutionary sense, the current compliment of species is interpreted as the ultimate product of evolution, rather than a temporary expression of a continually changing global taxa. In the population sense, concepts like carrying capacity and the constant interplay between environmental resistance and biotic potential is interpreted as creating a balance of numbers in a population, and between the population and its environment. Three ideas are fundamental to the above; that nature undisturbed is constant, when disturbed nature returns to the constant condition, and constancy in nature is the desired endpoint.

This interpretation of nature may be so strongly filtered by our cultural interpretation and idealization of balance, that we tend to produce conclusions not in keeping with our observations of nature. Assumptions of human centrality may be sufficiently strong to bend the usually clear lens supplied by science in this case. Although the theme of balance in nature has been formally criticized in ecology for over 60 years (since Frederick Clements and Henry Gleason focused the argument in the 1920s) the core of the science did not change until about 20 years ago. Since that time, a dynamic approach that pays no special attention to equilibrium processes has taken center stage in ecological theorizing.

The primary alternatives are part of the group of ideas termed intermediate disturbance hypotheses. These ideas offer a different view of how communities assemble, suggesting that disturbance is more frequent and/or more influential than performing a routine return to an equilibrium state. Furthermore, disturbance and non-equilibrium situations are responsible for the most diverse communities, tropical rain forests and coral reefs, through the reduction in competition caused by disturbance factors.

Few theorists, however, suggest that non-equilibrium settings are the single most powerful explanation, or are mutually exclusive with communities that do have an equilibrium. There are situations that seem to seek equilibrium, and smaller subsystems that appear virtually closed. In local situations, certain levels of resources and disturbance may create long term stability and niche differentiation or other mechanisms may be the principal cause of a species diverse situation.

Although theorists have been working to verify, revise, and examine new developments in ecology, very little attention has been given to alternative, more complex theoretical interpretations of nature, in terms of time, space, and dynamism in resource and environmental management. The implications of accepting a non-equilibrium orientation for environmental management are significant. Most of the underpin-

nings of resource management include steady state carrying capacity, succession, predator-prey balance, and community equilibrium as foundations.

There are three major implications of the shift from equilibrium to non-equilibrium approaches to the environment. First, until a more realistic theory is used, the rate of resource extraction from nature will be subject to considerably higher uncertainty than we currently suspect. Since we expect communities to seek equilibrium, we believe we can predict populations and species numbers to a greater degree than may be warranted. Second, we perceive that areas of high biodiversity are due to long and short term stability, when in fact the forces may be just the opposite. Therefore, management that attempts to maintain stability is the reverse of what is actually needed. Third, the kinds of disturbance we create in these diverse communities (deforestation, introduction of non-native species, or oil pollution) may not mimic anything natural and a species may have little defense against them. A characteristic of communities with high species diversity is small population size, thus human disturbance may cause exceptionally high rates of extinction. A central facet of the burgeoning practice of ecological restoration should be an ability to accurately mimic disturbance regimes.

Balance in nature has a strong appeal to our sensibilities and has anchored natural resource management practices. Now practice stands well behind theoretical developments and increased integration of more modern ecological science is required to avoid costly resource management mistakes.

[*Dave Duffus*]

FURTHER READING

Botkin, D. E. *Discordant Harmonies: A New Ecology for the Twenty First Century.* New York: Oxford University Press, 1990.

Gleason, H. A. "The Individualistic Concept of Plant Association." *Bulletin of the Torrey Botanical Club* 53 (1926): 7-26.

Ehrenfeld, D. *The Arrogance of Humanism.* New York: Oxford University Press, 1981.

Pickett, S. T. A., V. T. Parker and P. L. Fiedler. "The New Paradigm in Ecology: Implications for Conservation Biology Above the Species Level." In *Conservation Biology*, edited by P. L. Fiedler and S. K. Jain. New York: Chapman and Hall, 1992.

Bald eagle (*Haliaeetus leucocephalus*)

The bald eagle, one of North America's largest birds of prey with a wingspan of up to 7.5 ft (2.3 m), is a member of the family Accipitridae. Adult bald eagles are dark brown to black with a white head and tail; immature birds are dark brown with mottled white wings and are often mistaken for golden eagles (*Aquila chrysaetos*). Bald eagles feed primarily on fish, but also eat rodents, other small mammals and carrion. The bald eagle is the national emblem for the United States, adopted as such in 1782 because of its fierce, independent appearance. This characterization is unfounded, however, as this species is usually rather timid.

Formerly occurring over most of North America, the bald eagle's range, particularly in the lower 48 states, has been

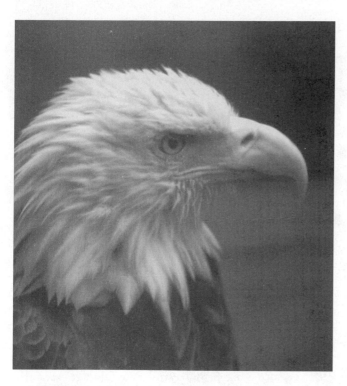

Bald eagle.

drastically reduced by a variety of reasons. It is currently listed as endangered by the U. S. **Fish and Wildlife Service** in all the 48 contiguous states except Washington, Oregon, Minnesota, Wisconsin, and Michigan, where it is listed as threatened. One reason for this bird's decline was its exposure to **DDT** and related **pesticide**s, which are magnified in the **food chain/web**. This led to reproductive problems, in particular, thin-shelled eggs which were crushed during incubation. The banning of DDT use in the United States in 1972 may have been a turning point in the recovery of the bald eagle. Eagle populations also have been depleted due to **lead** poisoning. Estimates are that for every bird that hunters shot and carried out with them, they left behind about a half pound of **lead shot**, which affects the **wildlife** in that **ecosystem** long after the hunters are gone. Since 1980, more than 60 bald eagles have died from lead poisoning. Other threats facing their populations include **habitat** loss or destruction, human encroachment, collisions with high power lines, and shooting.

These threats remain most severe in the lower 48 states. In 1982 the population in those states had fallen to less than 1,500 pairs, but by 1988 their numbers had risen to about 2,400 pairs. The bald eagle is not endangered in the state of Alaska, since a large, healthy population of about 30,000 birds exists there. During the annual salmon run, up to 4,000 bald eagles congregate along the Chilkat River in Alaska to feed on dead and dying salmon. This area, the Chilkat Bald Eagle Preserve, near Glacier National Park, is currently threatened, however, by a proposed copper mine.

Bald eagles, which typically mate for life and build huge platform nests in tall trees or cliff ledges, have been aided by several recovery programs, including the construc-

tion of artificial nesting platforms. They will reuse, add to, or repair the same nest annually, and some pairs have been known to use the same nest for over 35 years. Because the bald eagle is listed as either endangered or threatened throughout most of the United States, the federal government provides some funding for its **conservation** and recovery projects. In 1989, the federal government spent $44 million on the conservation of threatened and endangered species. Of the 554 species listed, $22 million, half of the total allotment, was spent on the top 12 species on a prioritized list. The bald eagle was at the top of that list and received $3 million of those funds. *See also* Carson, Rachel

[*Eugene C. Beckham*]

FURTHER READING

Dunstan, T. C. "Our Bald Eagle: Freedom's Symbol Survives." *National Geographic* 153 (1978): 186-99.

Ehrlich, P., D. Dobkin, and D. Wheye. *Birds in Jeopardy.* Stanford, CA: Stanford University Press, 1992.

Temple, S., ed. *Endangered Birds: Management Techniques for Preserving Threatened Species.* Madison: University of Wisconsin Press, 1977.

Barrier island

An elongated island that lies parallel to, but mostly separate from, a coastline. Barrier islands are composed of **sediment**s, mainly sand, deposited by longshore currents, wind, and wave action. Both marine and terrestrial plants and animals find **habitat** on barrier islands or along their sandy beach shorelines. These islands also protect coastal **lagoon**s from ocean currents and waves, providing a warm, quiet **environment** for species that cannot tolerate more violent wind and wave conditions. In recent decades these linear, sandy islands, with easy access from the mainland, have proven a popular playground for vacationers. These visitors now pose a significant threat to breeding birds and other coastal **species**. Building houses, roads, and other disruptive human activities can destabilize dunes and expose barrier islands to disastrous storm damage. In some cases, whole islands are swept away, exposing protected lagoons and delicate **wetlands** to further damage. Major barrier island formations in North America include those along the eastern coasts of the mid-Atlantic states, Florida, and the Gulf of Mexico.

Basel Convention

The Basel Convention on the Control of Transboundary Movements of Hazardous Wastes and their Disposal is a global treaty that was adopted in 1989 and became effective on May 5, 1992. The Basel Convention represents a response by the international community to problems caused by the international shipment of wastes. Of the over 400 million tons of hazardous wastes generated globally every year, an unknown amount is subject to transboundary movement.

Barrier islands lie parallel to coastlines. These lovely areas attract visitors that now pose a significant threat to the birds and other coastal species living there.

(U.S. companies were estimated to export about 140,000 tons of hazardous waste in 1993). In the 1980s, several highly publicized "toxic ships" were accused of trying to dump hazardous wastes illegally in developing countries. The uncontrolled movement and disposal of hazardous waste, especially in developing countries which often lacked the know-how and equipment to safely manage and treat hazardous wastes, became a significant problem due to high domestic costs of treating or disposing of wastes.

Through its Secretariat in the **United Nations Environment Programme**, the Convention aims to control the transboundary movement of wastes, monitor and prevent illegal traffic, provide technical assistance and guidelines, and promote cooperation. The Convention imposes obligations on treaty signatories to ensure that wastes are managed and disposed of in an environmentally sound manner. The main principles of the Basel Convention are to (1) reduce transboundary movements of hazardous wastes to a minimum consistent with environmentally sound management; (2) treat and dispose of hazardous wastes as close as possible to their source of generation; and (3) reduce and minimize the generation of hazardous waste. The Convention generally prohibits Parties to the Convention from importing or exporting hazardous wastes or other wastes from or to a non-contracting party. However, a Party to the convention may allow such import or export if the Party has a separate bilateral or multilateral agreement regarding the transboundary movement of hazardous wastes with a non-party and that agreement provides for "environmentally sound management." To date, the Convention has defined environmentally sound management practices for a number of wastes and technologies, including organic solvents, waste oils, pentachloraphenol (PCBs), household wastes, **landfill**s, incinerators, and oil recycling.

The Conference of the Parties (COP) is the governing body of the Basel Convention and is composed of all governments that have ratified or acceded to it. The COP has met three times since the Convention entered into force in May 1992 (in Piriapolis, Uruguay, on December 4, 1992; Geneva, Switzerland, on March 25, 1994; and Geneva, Switzerland, September 18-22, 1995). In the most recent meeting, the Parties adopted an amendment to the Convention that will ban the export of hazardous wastes from developed countries to developing ones. The Fourth Meeting of the Conference of the Parties, to be held in Kuala Lumpur in October 1997, will incorporate work on lists of wastes into the system of the Basel Convention. These lists should help to mitigate practical difficulties in determining exactly what is a waste, a problem that has been encountered by a number of Parties.

Currently (1997), the European Community and 108 States are Party to the Basel Convention. Though the U.S. was among the original signatories to the Basel Convention in 1989, the U.S. is still not a party to the Convention since Congress has yet to pass implementing legislation. The U.S.

does participate in planning and technical aspects of the Convention.

[*Stuart Batterman*]

Bats

Bats, the only mammals that fly, are among **nature**'s least understood and unfairly maligned creatures. They are extremely valuable animals, responsible for consuming huge numbers of insects and pollinating and dispersing the seeds of fruit-bearing plants and trees, especially in the tropics. Yet, superstitions about and fear of these nocturnal creatures have led to their persecution and elimination from many areas, and several **species** of bats are now threatened with **extinction**.

There are over 900 species of bats, representing almost a quarter of all mammal species, and they are found on every continent except Antarctica. Most types of bats live in the tropics, and some 40 species are found in the United States and Canada. The largest bats, flying foxes, found on Pacific islands, have wingspreads of 5 ft (1.5 m). The smallest bats, bamboo bats, are the size of the end of a person's thumb.

Bats commonly feed on mosquitoes and other night-flying insects, especially over ponds and other bodies of water. Some bats consume half of their weight in insects a night, eating up to 5,000 gnat-sized mosquitoes an hour, thus helping to keep insect population under control. Some bats hunt ground-dwelling species, such as spiders, scorpions, large insects, and beetles, and others prey on frogs, lizards, small birds, rodents, fish, and even other bats. The infamous vampire bat of Central and South America does actually feed on blood, daily consuming about a tablespoon from cattle and other animals, but it does not generally molest humans.

Bats that live in tropical areas, such as fruit bats (also called flying foxes), often feed on and pollinate plants. Bats are thus extremely important in helping flowers and fruit-bearing plants to reproduce. In **tropical rain forest**s, for example, bats are responsible for pollinating most of the fruit trees and plants.

Bats are usually social animals. Some colonies consist of millions of bats and use the same roost for centuries. Bat manure (**guano**) is often collected from caves and used as **fertilizer**. Most bats come out only at night and spend their days in dark roosts, hanging upside down, sleeping, nursing and tending their young, or grooming their wings and fur. Bats become active an hour or so before dark, and at dusk they leave their roosting areas and fly out to feed, returning home before dawn. Many bats flying at night navigate and locate food, such as flying insects, by echolocation, emitting continuous high frequency sounds that echo or bounce off of nearby objects. Such sounds cannot be heard by humans. Most bats have just one or two young a year, though some have up to four offsprings at a time. The newborn must hold onto its mother, sometimes for several weeks, and be nursed for six to eight weeks. Some species of bats live up to twenty-five years. Most bats in North America migrate or hibernate in caves during the winter, when food is scarce and temperatures reach freezing point. Superstitions about and prejudice against bats have existed for hundreds of years, but most such tales are untrue. Bats do not carry bedbugs or become entangled in women's hair; they are not blind and indeed do not even have poor vision. In fact, except for the occasional rabid bat, these creatures are not dangerous to humans and are quite timid and will try to escape if confronted. In recent years, public education programs and conservationists, such as Dr. Merlin Tuttle, head of Bat Conservation International in Austin, Texas, have helped correct these misconceptions about bats and have increased appreciation for the valuable role these creatures play in destroying pests and pollinating crops. Bracken Cave, located between San Antonio and Austin, is owned by Bat Conservation International and with some 20 million Mexican freetailed bats residing there in the spring and summer, the cave is said to shelter the world's largest bat colony and the largest collection of mammals anywhere on the planet. The pregnant females migrate there in early March from central Mexico to nurse and raise their young, and the colony can consume 250 tons of insects a night.

According to Dr. Tuttle, a colony of just 150 big brown bats can eat almost 40,000 cucumber beatles in a summer, which "means that they've protected local farmers from 18 million root worms, which cost American farmers $1 billion a year," including crop damage and **pesticide** costs. Dr. Tuttle and his organization suggest that people attract the creatures and help provide **habitat** for them by constructing or buying bathhouses, which his groups sell. Nevertheless, bats continue to be feared and exterminated throughout the world. Major threats to the survival of bats include intentional killing, loss of habitat (such as old trees, caves, and mines), eviction from barns, attics, and house eaves, pesticide poisoning, and vandalism and disturbance of caves where they roost. According to Dr. Tuttle, "Bats are among the most endangered animals in America. Nearly 40 percent of America's 43 species are either endangered or candidates for the list."

Over a dozen species of bats worldwide are listed by the **U.S. Department of the Interior** as **endangered species**, including the gray bat (*Myotis grisescens*) of central and southeastern United States; the Hawaiian hoary bat (*Lasiurus cenereus semotus*); the Indiana bat (*Myotis sodalis*) of the eastern and midwestern United States; the Ozark big-eared bat (*Plecotus townsendii ingens*) found in Missouri, Oklahoma, and Arkansas; the Mexican long-nosed bat (*Leptonycteris nivalis*) of New Mexico, Texas, Mexico, and Central America; Sanborn's long-nosed bat (*Leptonycteris sanborni*) of Arizona, New Mexico, Mexico, and Central America; and the Virginia big-eared bat (*Plecotus townsendii virginianus*) found in Kentucky, North Carolina, West Virginia, and Virginia.

[*Lewis G. Regenstein*]

FURTHER READING

Raver, Anne. "Batman Returns (The Real One)." *The New York Times* (23 May 1993): 18.

Tuttle, Merlin D. *America's Neighborhood Bats.* Austin: University of Texas Press, 1988.

Batteries
See **Lead**

Bear
See **Grizzly bear**

Beattie, Mollie (1947-1996)
Former Director of Fish and Wildlife Service

Mollie Hanna Beattie was trained as a forester, worked as a land manager and administrator, and ended her brief career as the first woman to serve as director of the U.S. **Fish and Wildlife Service**. Beattie's bachelor's degree was in philosophy, followed by a master's degree in forestry from the University of Vermont in 1979. Later (in 1991), she used a Bullard Fellowship at Harvard University to add a master's degree in public administration.

Early in her career, Mollie Beattie served in several **conservation** administrative posts and land management positions at the state level. She was commissioner of the Vermont Department of Forests, Parks, and Recreation (1985-1989), and deputy secretary of the state's Agency of Natural Resources (1989-1990). She also worked for private foundations and institutes: as program director and lands manager (1983-1985), for the Windham Foundation, a private, nonprofit organization concerned with critical issues facing Vermont, and later (1990-1993), as executive director of the Richard A. Snelling Center for Government in Vermont, a public policy institute.

Before becoming director of the Fish and Wildlife Service, Beattie was perhaps most widely known (especially in New England) for the book she co-authored on managing woodlots in private ownership, an influential guide reissued in a second edition in 1993. As a reviewer noted about the first edition, for the decade it was in print "thousands of landowners and professional foresters [recommended the book] to others." Especially noteworthy is the book's emphasis on the responsibility of private landowners for effective stewardship of the land. This background was reflected in her thinking as Fish and Wildlife director by making the private lands program—conservation in partnership with private land-owners—central to the agency's conservation efforts.

As director of the Fish and Wildlife Service, Beattie quickly became nationally known as a strong voice for conservation and as an advocate for thinking about land and **wildlife management** in **ecosystem** terms. One of her first actions as director was to announce that "the Service [will] shift to an ecosystem approach to managing our fish and wildlife resources." She emphasized that people use natural ecosystems for many purposes, and "if we do not take an ecosystem approach to conserving **biodiversity**, none of [those uses] will be long lived."

Her philosophy as a forester, conservationist, administrator, and land manager was summarized in her repeated insistence that people must start making better connections—between **wildlife** and **habitat** health and human health; between their own actions and "the destiny of the ecosystems on which both humans and wildlife depend"; and between the well-being of the environment and the well-being of the economy." She stressed "even if not a single job were created, wildlife must be conserved" and that the diversity of natural systems must remain integral and whole because "we humans are linked to those systems and it is in our immediate self interest to care" about them. She reiterated that in any frame greater than the short-term, the economy and the environment are "identical considerations."

Though Beattie's life was relatively short, and her tenure at the Fish and Wildlife Service cut short by illness, her ideas were well received in conservation circles and her influence continues after her death, helping to create what she called "preemptive conservation," anticipating crises before they appear and using that foresight to minimize conflict, to maintain biodiversity and sustainable economies, and to prevent extinctions.

[*Gerald L. Young*]

FURTHER READING

Beattie, M. "A Broader View," *Endangered Species Update* 12, nos. 4/5 (April/May, 1995): 4-5.

———. "An Ecosystem Approach to Fish and Wildlife Conservation," *Ecological Applications,* 6, no. 3 (August 1996): 696-699.

———. "Biodiversity Policy and Ecosystem Management," *Biodiversity and the Law,* W.J. Snape III, ed. Washington, D.C.: Island Press, 1996.

———. "The Missing Connection: Remarks to Natural Resources Council of America," *Land and Water Law Review* 29, no. 2 (1994): 407-415.

Beattie, M., C. Thompson, and L. Levine. *Working With Your Woodland: A Land-Owner's Guide.* Rev. ed. Hanover, N.H.: University Press of New England, 1993.

Cohn, J. P. "Wildlife Warrior," *Government Executive* 26, no. 2 (February 1994): 41-43.

Gup, T. "Beattie's Battle," *Audubon* 96, no. 2 (March-April 1994): 64-68.

Walsh, B. W. "The Ecosystem Thinking of Mollie Hanna Beattie," *American Forests* 100, nos. 5/6 (May/June 1994): 13-16.

Bees
See **Africanized bees**

Below Regulatory Concern

Large populations all over the globe continue to be exposed to low-level radiation. Sources include natural **background**

radiation, widespread medical uses of **ionizing radiation**, releases and leakages from **nuclear power** and weapons manufacturing plants and waste storage sites. An added potential hazard to public health in the United States stems from government plans to deregulate **low-level radioactive waste** generated in industry, research, and hospitals and allow it to be mixed with general household trash and industrial waste in unprotected dump sites.

The **Nuclear Regulatory Commission** (NRC) plans to deregulate some of this **radioactive waste** and treat it as if it were not radioactive. The makers of radioactive waste have asked the NRC to treat certain low levels of **radiation exposure** with no regulations. The NRC plan, called Below Regulatory Concern (BRC), will categorize some of this waste as acceptable for regular dumping or **recycling**. It will deregulate radioactive consumer products, manufacturing processes and anything else that their computer models project would, on a statistical average, cause radiation exposures within the acceptable range. The policy sets no limits on the cumulative exposure to radiation from multiple sources or exposures or multiple human use.

In July 1991 the NRC responded to public pressure and declared a moratorium on the implementation of BRC policy. This was a temporary move, leaving the policy intact. The **U. S. Department of Energy** (DoE) has already dumped radioactive trash on unlicensed incinerators. Although DoE is not regulated by the NRC, this action reflects an adoption of the BRC concept. If the BRC plan is eventually approved, radioactive waste will end up in local **landfill**s, sewage systems, incinerators, recycling centers, consumer products and building materials, **hazardous waste** facilities and farmland (through sludge spreading).

Some scientists maintain that there are acceptable low levels of radiation exposure (in addition to natural background radiation) that do not pose a threat to public health. Other medical studies conclude that there is no safe level of radiation exposure. Critics claim BRC policy is nothing more than linguistic detoxification and will, if implemented, inevitably lead to increased radiation exposure levels to the public, and increased risk of **cancer**, **birth defects**, reduced immunity, and other health problems. Implementation of BRC may also mean that efficient cleanup of contaminated **nuclear weapons** plants (**Oak Ridge**, **Savannah River**, Fernald), nuclear reactors, and other radioactive facilities might not be completed.

Its critics contend that BRC is basically a financial, not a public health, decision. The nuclear industry has projected that it will save hundreds of millions of dollars if BRC is implemented. *See also* Radioactive waste management

[*Liane Clorfene Casten*]

FURTHER READING

Below Regulatory Concern: A Guide to the Nuclear Regulatory Commission's Policy on the Exemption of Very Low-Level Radioactive Materials, Wastes and Practices. Washington, DC: U. S. Government Printing Office, 1990?.

Below Regulatory Concern, But Radioactive and Carcinogenic. Washington, DC: U. S. Public Interest Research Group, 1990.

Low-Level Radioactive Waste Regulation—Science, Politics and Fear. Chelsea, MI: Lewis, 1988.

Bennet, Hugh Hammond (1881-1960)

American soil conservationist

Dr. Bennett, a noted conservationist, is often called the father of **soil conservation** in the United States. He was born on April 13, 1881, in Anson County, North Carolina, and died July 7, 1960. He is buried in Arlington National Cemetery.

Dr. Bennett graduated from the University of North Carolina in 1903. After completing his university education, he became a **soil** surveyor in the Bureau of Soils of the **U.S. Department of Agriculture**. He recognized early the degradation to the land from soil **erosion** and in 1929 published a bulletin entitled "Soil Erosion, A National Menace." Soon after that, the nation began to heed the admonitions of this young scientist.

In 1933, the U.S. Department of Interior set up a Soil Erosion Service to conduct a nation-wide demonstration program of soil erosion, with Bennett as its head. In 1935, the **Soil Conservation Service** was established as a permanent agency of the U.S. Department of Agriculture, and Bennett became its head, a position he retained until his retirement in April 1951. He was the author of several books and many technical articles on soil **conservation**. He received high awards from many organizations and several foreign countries.

Dr. Bennett traveled widely as a crusader for soil conservation, and was a forceful speaker. Many colorful stories about his speeches exist. Perhaps the most widely quoted concerns the dust storm that hit Washington D.C. in the spring of 1935 at a critical moment in Congressional hearings concerning legislation that, if passed, would establish the Soil Conservation Service. A hugh dust cloud that had started in the Great Plains was steadily moving toward Washington. As the storm hit the district, Dr. Bennett, who had been testifying before members of the Senate **public lands** committee, called the committee members to a window and pointed to the sky, darkened from the dust. It made such an impression that legislation was promptly approved, establishing the Soil Conservation Service.

Dr. Bennett was an outstanding scientist and crusader, but he was also an able administrator. He visualized that if the Soil Conservation Service was to be effective, it must have grass roots support. He laid the foundation for the establishment of the local soil conservation districts with locally elected officials to guide the program and Soil Conservation Service employees to provide the technical support. Currently there are over 3,000 districts (usually by county). The National Association of Conservation Districts is a powerful voice in matters of conservation. Because of Dr. Bennett's leadership in the United States, soil erosion was increasingly recognized worldwide as a serious threat to the long-term welfare of humans. Many other countries then followed the

United States' lead in establishing organized soil conservation programs. *See also* Environmental degradation; Environmental policy

[*William E. Larson*]

FURTHER READING

Bennett, H. H. Soil Conservation. Manchester: Ayer, 1970.

Benzene

A **hydrocarbon** with chemical formula C_6H_6, benzene contains six carbon atoms in a ring structure. A clear volatile liquid with a strong odor, it is one of the most extensively used hydrocarbons. Because it is an excellent solvent and a necessary component of many industrial chemicals, including **gasoline**, benzene is classified by United States federal agencies as a known human **carcinogen** based on studies that show an increased incidence of nonlymphocytic **leukemia** from occupational exposure and increased incidence of neoplasia in rats and mice exposed by inhalation and gavage. Because of these cancer-causing properties, benzene has been listed as a hazardous air pollutant under Section 112 of the **Clean Air Act**.

Benzo(a)pyrene [B(a)P]

B(a)P is a **polycyclic aromatic hydrocarbon (PAH)** having five aromatic rings in a fused, honeycomb-like structure. Its formula and molecular weight are $C_{20}H_{12}$ and 252.30, respectively. It is a naturally occurring and man-made organic compound formed along with other PAH in incomplete **combustion** reactions, including the burning of **fossil fuels**, motor vehicle exhaust, wood products, and cigarettes. It is classified as a known human **carcinogen** by the EPA, and is considered to be one of the primary carcinogens in **tobacco smoke**. Synthesized in 1933, it was the first carcinogen isolated from coal tar and often serves as a surrogate compound for modeling PAHs.

Berry, Wendell (1934 -)

American environmental writer

A Kentucky farmer, poet, novelist, essayist and conservationist, Berry has been a persistent critic of large-scale industrial agriculture—which he believes to be a contradiction in terms—and a champion of environmental stewardship and **sustainable agriculture**. Wendell Erdman Berry was born on August 5, 1934 in Henry County, Kentucky, where his family had farmed for four generations. Although he learned the farmer's skills, he did not wish to make his living as a farmer but as a writer and teacher. He earned his B.A. in English at the University of Kentucky in 1956 and an M.A. in 1957. He was awarded a Wallace Stegner writing fellow at Stanford University (1958-1959), where he remained to teach in the English Department (1959-1960). He spent the following year in Italy on a Guggenheim fellowship. In 1962 Berry joined the English faculty at New York University.

Dissatisfied with urban life and feeling disconnected from his roots, in 1965 Berry resigned his professorship of English at New York University to return to his native Kentucky to farm, to write, and to teach at the University of Kentucky. His recurring themes—love of the land, of place or region, and the responsibility to care for them—appear in his poems and novels and in his essays. Many modern farming practices, as he argues in *The Unsettling of America* (1977) and *The Gift of Good Land* (1981) and elsewhere, deplete the soil, despoil the environment, and deny the value of careful husbandry. In relying on industrial scales, techniques and technologies, they fail to appreciate that agriculture is agri-culture—that is, a coherent way of life that is concerned with the care and cultivation of the land—rather than agri-business concerned solely with maximizing yields, efficiency, and short-term profits to the long-term detriment of the land, of family farms, and of local communities. A truly sustainable agriculture, as Berry defines it, "would deplete neither soil, nor people, nor communities."

Berry believes that too few people now live on and farm the land, leaving it to the less-than-tender mercies of corporate "managers" who know more about accounting than about agricultural stewardship. The so-called miracle of modern agriculture has been purchased by selling our birthright, the God-given gift of good land that Americans have heedlessly traded for the ease, convenience and affluence of urban and suburban living. As a consequence we have become disconnected from our cultural roots and have lost a sense of place and purpose and pleasure in work well done. We have also lost a sense of connection with the land and the lore of those who work on and care for it. Instead of food from our own fields, water from rainfall and wells, and stories from family and friends, most Americans now get food from the grocery store, water from the faucet, and endless entertainment from television. A wasteful throwaway society produces not only material but cultural junk—throwaway farms, throwaway marriages and children, disposable communities, and a wanton disregard for the natural environment. The transition to a culture of consumption and convenience, Berry believes, does not represent progress so much as it marks a deep and lasting loss.

Although Berry does not believe it possible (or desirable) that all Americans become farmers, he holds that we need think about what we do daily as consumers and citizens and how our choices and activities affect the land. He suggests that the act of planting and tending a garden is a "complete act" in that it enables one to connect consumption with production, and both to a sense of reverence for the fertility and abundance of a world well cared for.

[*Terence Ball*]

FURTHER READING

Berry, Wendell. *A Continuous Harmony: Essays Cultural and Agricultural.* New York: Harcourt Brace Jovanovich, 1972.

———. *The Unsettling of America.* San Francisco: Sierra Club Books, 1977.

————. *The Gift of Good Land.* San Francisco: North Point Press, 1981.

————. *Home Economics.* San Francisco: North Point Press, 1987.

————. *A Place on Earth.* rev. ed. San Francisco: North Point Press, 1983.

————. *Collected Poems, 1957–1982.* San Francisco: North Point Press, 1985.

————. *What Are People For?* San Francisco: North Point Press, 1990.

————. *Sex, Economy, Freedom and Community.* New York: Pantheon Books, 1993.

————. *Another Turn of the Crank.* Washington, DC: Counterpoint Press, 1995.

Merchant, Paul, ed. *Wendell Berry.* American Authors Series. Lewiston, Idaho: Confluence Press, 1991.

Best Available Control Technology (BACT)

Best Available Control Technology (BACT) is a standard used in **air pollution control** in the prevention of significant deterioration (PSD) of **air quality** in the United States. Under the **Clean Air Act**, a major stationary new source of **air pollution**, such as an industrial plant, is required to have a permit that sets **emission** limitations for the facility. As part of the permit, limitations are based on levels achievable by the use of BACT for each pollutant.

To prevent risk to human health and public welfare, each region in the country is placed in one of three PSD areas in compliance with **National Ambient Air Quality Standards** (NAAQS). Class I areas include **national parks** and **wilderness** areas, where very little deterioration of air quality is allowed. Class II areas allow moderate increases in ambient concentrations. Those classified as Class III permit industrial development and larger increments of deterioration. Except for national parks, most of the land in the United States is set at Class II.

Under the Clean Air Act, the BACT standards are applicable to all plants built after the effective date, as well as preexisting ones whose modifications might increase emissions of any pollutant. To establish a major new source in any PSD area, an applicant must demonstrate, through monitoring and diffusion models, that emissions will not violate NAAQS or the Clean Air Act. The applicant must also agree to use BACT for all pollutants, whether or not that is necessary to avoid exceeding the levels allowed and despite its cost. The **Environmental Protection Agency (EPA)** requires that a source use the BACT standards, unless it can demonstrate that its use is infeasible based on "substantial and unique local factors." Otherwise BACT, which can include design, equipment, and operational standards, is required for each pollutant emitted above minimal defined levels.

In areas that exceed NAAQS for one or more pollutants, permits are issued only if total allowable emissions of each pollutant are reduced even though a new source is added. The new source must comply with the lowest achievable emission rate (LAER), the most stringent limitations possible for a particular plant.

Under the Clean Air Act, if a new stationary source is incapable of BACT standards, it is subject to the **New Source Performance Standard** (NSPS) for a pollutant, as determined by the EPA. NSPSs take into consideration the cost and energy requirements of emission reduction processes, as well as other health and environmental impacts. This contrasts with BACT standards, which are determined without regard to cost. Strict BACT requirements resulted in a more than 20 percent reduction in **particulate**s and **sulfur dioxide** below NSPS levels. *See also* Air quality criteria; Air quality standards

[Judith Sims]

FURTHER READING

Findley, R. W., and D. A. Farber. *Environmental Law.* St. Paul, MN: West Publishing Company, 1992.

Plater, Z. J. B., R. H. Abrams, and W. Goldfarb. *Environmental Law and Policy: Nature, Law, and Society.* St. Paul, MN: West Publishing Company, 1992.

Best Practical Technology (BPT)

Best Practical Technology (BPT) refers to any of the categories of technology-based **effluent** limitations pursuant to Section 301(b) and Sections 304(b) of the **Clean Water Act** as amended. These categories are the best practicable control technology currently available (BPT); the **best available control technology (BACT)** economically feasible; and the best conventional pollutant control technology (BCT).

Section 301(b) of the Clean Water Act specifies that "in order to carry out the objective of this Act there shall be achieved—(1)(A) not later than July 1, 1977, effluent limitations for **point source**s, other than publicly owned treatment works (i) which shall require the application of the best practicable control technology currently available as defined by the Administrator pursuant to Section 304(b) of this Act, or (ii) in the case of discharge into a publicly owned treatment works which meets the requirements of subparagraph (B) of this paragraph, which shall require compliance with any applicable pretreatment requirements and any requirements under Section 307 of this Act;..."

The BPT identifies the current level of treatment and is the basis of the current level of control for direct **discharge**s. BACT improves on the BPT, and it may include operations or processes not in common use in industry. BCT replaces BACT for the control of conventional pollutants, such as **biochemical oxygen demand (BOD)**, total suspended solids (TSS), fecal coliform, and **pH**. Details such as the amount of constituents, and the chemical, physical, and biological characteristics of pollutants, as well as the degree of effluent reduction attainable through the application of the selected technology can be found in the development documents published by the **Environmental Protection Agency (EPA)**. These development documents cover different industrial categories such as diary products processing, soap and **detergents** manufacturing, meat products, grain mills, canned and preserved fruits and vegetables processing, and **asbestos** manufacturing.

In accordance with Section 304(b) of the Clean Water Act, the factors to be taken into account in assessing the BPT include the total cost of applying the technology in relation to the effluent reductions to the results achieved from such an application, the age of the equipment and facilities involved, the process employed, the engineering aspects of applying various types of control technologies and process changes, and calculations of environmental impacts other than **water quality** (including energy requirements). As far as evaluating the BCT is concerned, the factors are mostly the same. They include consideration of the reasonableness of the relationship between the costs of attaining a reduction in effluents and the benefits derived from that reduction, and the comparison of the cost and level of reduction of such pollutants from the discharge from publicly owned treatment works to the cost and level of reduction of such pollutants from a class or category of industrial sources. Control technologies may include in-plant control and preliminary treatment, and end-of-pipe treatment, examples of which are **water conservation** and **reuse**, raw materials substitution, screening, multimedia filtration, and activated carbon absorption. *See also* Aquatic chemistry; Industrial waste treatment; Nonpoint source; Runoff; Sewage treatment; Wastewater; Water pollution; Water quality standards; Water treatment

[*James W. Patterson*]

Beta particle

An electron emitted by the nucleus of a radioactive atom. The beta particle is produced when a neutron within the nucleus decays into a proton and an electron. Beta particles have greater penetrating power than **alpha particle**s but less than x-ray or **gamma ray**s. Although beta particles can penetrate skin, they travel only a short distance in tissue. Beta rays pose relatively little health hazard, therefore, unless they are ingested into the body. Naturally radioactive materials such as potassium-40, carbon-14, and strontium-90 emit beta particles, as do a number of synthetic radioactive materials. *See also* Radioactivity

Bhopal, India

On December 3, 1984, one of the world's worst industrial accidents occurred in Bhopal, India. Along with **Three Mile Island** and **Chernobyl**, Bhopal stands as an example of the dangers of industrial development without proper attention to **environmental health** and safety.

A large industrial and urban center in the state of Madhya Pradesh, Bhopal was the location of a plant owned by the American chemical corporation, Union Carbide, Inc. and its Indian subsidiary, Union Carbide India, Ltd. The plant manufactured **pesticide**s, primarily the pesticide carbaryl (marketed under the name Sevin), which is one of the most widely used carbamate class pesticides in the United States and throughout the world. Among the intermediate chemical compounds used together to manufacture Sevin is methyl isocyanate (MIC)—a lethal substance that is reactive, toxic, volatile, and flammable. It was the uncontrolled release of MIC from a storage tank in the Bhopal facility that caused the death of 5,000 people, seriously injured another 20,000 and affected an estimated 200,000 people. The actual number of casualties remains unknown; many believe the numbers cited above to be serious underestimates.

MIC (CH3-N=C=O) is highly volatile and has a boiling point of 89°F (39.1°C). In the presence of trace amounts of impurities such as water or metals, MIC reacts to generate heat, and if the heat is not removed, the chemical begins to boil violently. If relief valves, cooling systems and other safety devices fail to operate in a closed storage tank, the pressure and heat generated may be sufficient to cause a release of MIC into the atmosphere. Because the vapor is twice as heavy as air, the vapors if released remain close to the ground where they can do the most damage, drifting along prevailing wind patterns. As set by the **Occupational Health and Safety Administration (OSHA)**, the standards for exposure to MIC are set at 0.02 ppm over an 8-hour period. The immediate effects of exposure, inhalation and ingestion of MIC at high concentrations (above 2 ppm) are burning and tearing of the eyes, coughing, vomiting, blindness, massive trauma of the gastrointestinal tract, clogging of the lungs and suffocation of bronchial tubes. When not immediately fatal, the long-term health consequences include permanent blindness, permanently impaired lung functioning, corneal ulcers, skin damage, and potential birth defects.

Many explanations for the disaster have been advanced, but the most widely accepted theory is that trace amounts of water entered the MIC storage tank and initiated the hydrolysis reaction, which was followed by MIC's spontaneous reactions. The plant was not well designed for safety, and maintenance was especially poor. Four key safety factors should have contained the reaction, but it was later discovered that they were all inoperative at the time of the accident. The refrigerator that should have slowed the reaction by cooling the chemical was shut off, and, as heat and pressure built up in the tank, the relief valve blew. A vent gas **scrubber** designed to neutralize escaping gas with caustic soda failed to work. Also, the flare tower that would have burned the gas to harmless by-products was under repair. Yet even if all these features had been operational, subsequent investigations found them to be poorly designed and insufficient for the capacity of the plant. Once the runaway reaction started, it was virtually impossible to contain.

The poisonous cloud of MIC released from the plant was carried by the prevailing winds to the south and east of the city—an area populated by highly congested communities of poorer people, many of whom worked as laborers at the Union Carbide plant and other nearby industrial facilities. Released at night, the silent cloud went undetected by residents who remained asleep in their homes, thus possibly ensuring a maximal degree of exposure. Many hundreds died in their sleep, others choked to death on the streets as they ran out to the streets in hopes of escaping the lethal cloud. Thousands more died in the following days and weeks. The Indian government and numerous volunteer agencies organized a massive relief effort in the immediate aftermath of the disaster consisting of emergency medical treatment, hospital

Union Carbide plant in Bhopal, India.

facilities, and supplies of food and water. Medical treatment was often ineffective, for doctors had an incomplete knowledge of the toxicity of MIC and the appropriate course of action.

In the weeks following the accident, the financial, legal and political consequences of the disaster unfolded. In the United States Union Carbide's stock dipped 25 percent in the week immediately following the event. Union Carbide India Ltd. (UCIL) came forward and accepted moral responsibility for the accident, arranging some interim financial compensation for victims and their families. However its parent company, Union Carbide Inc., which owned 50.9 percent of UCIL, refused to accept any legal responsibility for their subsidiary. The Indian government and hundreds of lawyers on both sides pondered issues of liability and the question of a settlement. While Union Carbide hoped for out-of-court settlements or lawsuits in the Indian courts, the Indian government ultimately decided to pursue class action suits on behalf of the victims in the United States courts in the hope of larger settlements. The United States courts refused to hear the case, and it was transferred to the Indian court system. Warren Anderson, then chairman of Union Carbide, refused to appear in Indian court. The case is still under litigation and the interim compensation set aside has reached only a fraction of the victims.

The disaster in Bhopal has had far-reaching political consequences in the United States. A number of Congressional hearings were called and the **Environmental Protec-**

tion Agency (EPA) and OSHA initiated inspections and investigations. A Union Carbide plant in McLean, Virginia, that uses processes and products similar to those in Bhopal was repeatedly inspected by officials. While no glaring deficiencies in operation or maintenance were found, it was noted that several small leaks and spills had occurred at the plant in previous years that had gone unreported. These added weight to growing national concern about workers' right-to-know provisions and emergency response capabilities. In the years following the Bhopal accident, both state and federal environmental regulations were expanded to include mandatory preparedness to handle spills and releases on land, water or air. These regulations include measures for emergency response such as communication and coordination with local health and law enforcement facilities, as well as community leaders and others. In addition, employers are now required to inform any workers in contact with **hazardous materials** of the nature and types of hazards to which they are exposed; they are also required to train them in emergency health and safety measures.

The disaster at Bhopal raises a number of critical issues and highlights the wide gulf between developed and developing countries in regard to design and maintenance standards for health and safety. Management decisions allowed the Bhopal plant to operate in an unsafe manner and for a shantytown to develop around its perimeter without appropriate emergency planning. The Indian government, like many other developing nations in need of foreign investment, appeared to sacrifice worker safety in order to attract and keep Union Carbide and other industries within its borders. While a number of environmental and occupational health and safety standards existed in India before the accident, their inspection and enforcement was cursory or non-existent. Often understaffed, the responsible Indian regulatory agencies were rife with corruption as well. The Bhopal disaster also raised questions concerning the moral and legal responsibilities of American companies abroad, and the willingness of those corporations to apply stringent U.S. safety and environmental standards to their operations in the Third World despite the relatively free hand given them by local governments.

Although worldwide shock at the Bhopal accident has largely faded, the suffering of many victims continues. While many national and international safeguards on the manufacture and handling of hazardous chemicals have been instituted, few expect that lasting improvements will occur in developing countries without a gradual recognition of the economic and political values of stringent health and safety standards. *See also* Emergency Planning and Right-to-Know Act; Hazardous Substances Act; Toxic substance; Control inventory; Toxic use reduction legislation

[*Usha Vadagiri*]

FURTHER READING

"Bhopal Report." *Chemical and Engineering News* (February 11, 1985): 14-65.

Diamond, A. *The Bhopal Chemical Leak.* San Diego, CA: Lucent, 1990.

Kurzman, D. *A Killing Wind: Inside the Bhopal Catastrophe.* New York: McGraw-Hill, 1987.

Bikini atoll

The primary objective of the Manhattan Project during World War II was the creation of a **nuclear fission** or atomic bomb. Even before that goal was accomplished in 1945, however, some nuclear scientists were thinking about the next step in the development of nuclear weapons, a fusion or hydrogen bomb.

Progress on a fusion bomb was slow. Questions were raised about the technical possibility of making such a bomb, as well as the moral issues raised by the use of such a destructive weapon. But the detonation of an atomic bomb by the Soviet Union in 1949 placed the fusion bomb in a new perspective. Concerned that the United States was falling behind in its arms race with the Soviet Union, President Harry S. Truman authorized a full-scale program for the development of a fusion weapon.

The first test of a fusion device occurred on October 31, 1952 at Eniwetok Atoll in the Marshall Islands in the Pacific Ocean. This was followed by a series of six more tests, code-named "Operation Castle," at Bikini Atoll in 1954. Two years later, on May 20, 1956, the first **nuclear fusion** bomb was dropped from an airplane over Bikini Atoll.

Bikini Atoll had been selected in late 1945 as the site for a number of tests of fission weapons, to experiment with

different designs for the bomb and to test its effects on ships and the natural environment.

At that time, 161 people belonging to 11 families lived on Bikini. Since the Bikinians have no written history, little is known about their background. According to their oral tradition, the original home of their ancestors is nearby Wotje Atoll. Until the early 1900s, they had relatively little contact with strangers and were regarded with some disdain even by other Marshall Islanders. After the arrival of missionaries early in the twentieth century, the Bikinians became devout Christians. People lived on coconuts, breadfruits, arrowroot, fish, turtle eggs, and birds, all available in abundance on the atoll. The Bikinians were expert sailors and fishermen. Land ownership was important in the culture, and anyone who had no land was regarded as lacking in dignity.

On January 10, 1946, President Truman signed an order authorizing the transfer of everyone living on Bikini Atoll to the nearly uninhabited Bongerik Atoll. The United States Government asked the Bikinians to give up their native land to allow experiments that would bring benefit to all humankind. Such an action, the Americans argued, would earn for the Bikinians special glory in heaven. The islanders agreed to the request and, along with their homes, church, and community hall, were transported by the United States Navy to Rongerik.

In June and July of 1946, two tests of atomic bombs were conducted at Bikini as part of "Operation Crossroads." More than 90 vessels, including captured German and Japanese ships along with surplus cruisers, destroyers, submarines, and amphibious craft from the United States Navy, were assembled. Following these tests, however, the Navy concluded that Bikini was too small and moved future experiments to Eniwetok Atoll.

The testing of a nuclear fusion device in Operation Castle marked the return of bomb testing to Bikini. The most memorable test of that series took place in 1954 and was code-named "Bravo." Experts expected a yield of six megatons from the hydrogen bomb used in the test, but measured instead a yield of 15 megatons, 250 percent greater. Bravo turned out to be the largest single explosion in all of human history, producing an explosive force greater than all of the bombs used in all the previous wars in history.

Fallout from Bravo was consequently much larger than had been anticipated. In addition, because of a shift in wind patterns, the fallout spread across an area of about 50,000 square miles (11.5 million ha), including three inhabited islands—Rongelap, Itrik, and Rongerik. A number of people living on these islands developed radiation burns and many were evacuated from their homes temporarily. Farther to the east, a Japanese fishing boat which had accidentally sailed into the restricted zone was showered with fallout. By the time the boat returned to Japan, 23 crew members had developed **radiation sickness**. One eventually died of infectious hepatitis, probably because of the numerous blood transfusions he received.

The value of Bikini as a test site ended in 1963 when the United States and the Soviet Union signed the Limited Test Ban Treaty which outlawed **nuclear weapons** testing in the atmosphere, the oceans, and outer space. Five years later, the United States government decided that it was safe for the Bikinians to return home. By 1971, some had once again take up residence on their home island. Their return was short-lived. In 1978, tests showed that returnees had ingested quantities of radioactive materials much higher than the levels considered to be safe. The Bikinians were relocated once again, this time to the isolated and desolate island of Kili, 500 miles from Bikini.

The primary culprit on Bikini was the radioactive **isotope cesium-137**. It had become so widely distributed in the soil, the water, and the crops on the island that no one living there could escape from it. With a half life of 30 years, the isotope is likely to make the island uninhabitable for another century.

Two solutions for this problem have been suggested. The brute-force approach is to scrape off the upper 12 in (30 cm) of soil, transport it to some uninhabited island, and bury it under concrete. A similar burial site, the "Cactus Crater," already exists on Runit Island. It holds radioactive wastes removed from Eniwetok Atoll. The cost of clearing off Bikini's 560 acres and destroying all its vegetation (including 25,000 trees) has been estimated at more then $80 million. A second approach is more subtle and makes use of chemical principles. Since potassium replaces cesium in soil, scientists hope that adding potassium-rich fertilizers to Bikini's soil will leach out the dangerous cesium-137.

At the thirtieth anniversary of Bravo, the Bikinians had still not returned to their home island. Many of the original 116 evacuees had already died. A majority of the 1300 Bikinians who then lived on Kili no longer wanted to return to their native land. If given the choice, most wanted to make Maui, Hawaii, their new home. But they did not have that choice. The United States continues to insist that they remain somewhere in the Marshall Islands. The only place there they can't go, at least within most of their lifetimes, is Bikini Atoll. *See also* High-level radioactive waste; Radiation exposure; Radioactive decay; Radioactive fallout; Radioactive pollution; Radioactive waste; Rocky Flants, Colorado

[*David E. Newton*]

FURTHER READING

Davis, J. "Paradise Regained?" *Mother Jones* 18 (March-April 1993): 17.

Delgado, J. P. "Operation Crossroads." *American History Illustrated* 28 (May-June 1993): 50-59.

Eliot, J. L., and B. Curtsinger. "In Bikini Lagoon Life Thrives in a Nuclear Graveyard." *National Geographic* 181 (June 1992): 70-83.

Lenihan, D. J. "Bikini Beneath the Waves." *American History Illustrated* 28 (May-June 1993): 60-67.

Bioaccumulation

The general term for describing the accumulation of **chemicals** in the tissue of organisms. The chemicals that bioaccumulate are most often organic chemicals that are very soluble in fat and lipids and are slow to degrade. Usually used

in reference to aquatic organisms, bioaccumulation occurs from exposure to contaminated water (e.g., gill uptake by fish) or by consuming food that has accumulated the chemical (e.g., **food chain/web** transfer). Bioaccumulation of chemicals in fish has resulted in public health consumption advisories in some areas, and has affected the health of certain fish-eating **wildlife** including eagles, cormorants, terns, and mink.

Bioaerosols

Bioaerosols are airborne particles derived from plants, animals or are living organisms, including viruses, bacteria, fungi, and mammal and bird antigens. Bioaerosols can range in size from roughly 0.01 micrometer (virus) to 100 micrometer (pollen). These particles can be inhaled and can cause many types of health problems, including allergic reactions (specific activation of the immune system), infectious disease (pathogens that invade human tissues), and toxic effects (due to biologically produced chemical toxins). The most common outdoor bioaerosols are pollens from grasses, trees, weeds, and crops. The most common indoor biological pollutants are animal dander (minute scales from hair, feathers, or skin), dust mite and cockroach parts, fungi (molds), infectious agents (bacteria and viruses), and pollen.

Bioassay

Bioassay refers to an evaluation of the toxicity of an **effluent** or other material on living organisms such as fish, rats, insects, bacteria, or other life forms. The bioassay may be used for many purposes, including the determination of: 1) permissible **wastewater** discharge rates; 2) the relative sensitivities of various animals; 3) the effects of physicochemical parameters on toxicity; 4) the compliance of **discharge**s with effluent guidelines; 5) the suitability of a drug; 6) the safety of an environment; and 7) possible synergistic or antagonistic effects.

There are those who wish to reserve the term simply for the evaluation of the potency of substances such as drugs and vitamins, but the term is commonly used as described above. Of course, there are times when it is inappropriate to use bioassay and evaluation of toxicity synonymously, as when the goal of the assay is not to evaluate toxicity.

Bioassays are conducted as static, renewal or continuous-flow experiments. In static tests, the medium (air or water) about the test organisms is not changed, in renewal tests the medium is changed periodically, and in continuous-flow experiments the medium is renewed continuously. When testing chemicals or wastewaters that are unstable, continuous-flow testing is preferable. Examples of instability include the rapid degradation of a chemical, significant losses in dissolved oxygen, problems with volatility, and precipitation.

Bioassays are also classified on the basis of duration. The tests may be short-term or acute, intermediate-term, or long-term, also referred to as chronic. In addition, aquatic toxicologists speak of partial or complete **life-cycle assessment**s. The experimental design of a bioassay is in part reflected in such labels as range-finding, which is used for preliminary tests to approximate toxicity; screening for tests to determine if toxicity is likely by using one concentration and several replicates; and definitive, for tests to establish a particular end point with several concentrations and replicates).

The results of bioassays are reported in a number of ways. Early aquatic toxicity data were reported in terms of tolerance limits (TL). The term has been superseded by other terms such as effective concentration (EC), inhibiting concentration (IC), and lethal concentration (LC). The results of tests in which an animal is dosed (fed or injected) are reported in terms of effective dosage (ED) or lethal dosage (LD). When the potency of a drug is being studied, a therapeutic index (TI) is sometimes reported, which is the dose needed to cause a certain desirable effect (ED) divided by the lethal dose (LD) or some other ED. Median doses, the amount needed to affect 50 percent of the test population, are not always used. Needless to say, an evaluation of the response of a control population of organisms not exposed to a test agent or solution during the course of an experiment is very important.

Quality assurance and quality control procedures have become a very important part of bioassay methods. For example, the U.S. **Environmental Protection Agency (EPA)** has very specifically outlined how various aquatic bioassay procedures are to be performed and standardized to enhance reliability, precision, and accuracy. Other agencies in the United States and around the world have also worked very hard in recent years to standardize and improve quality assurance and control guidelines for the various bioassay techniques. *See also* Animal cancer tests; LD$_{50}$; Tolerance level

[*Gregory D. Boardman*]

FURTHER READING

Manahan, S. E. *Toxicological Chemistry.* 2nd ed. Ann Arbor, MI: Lewis, 1992.

Rand, G. M., and Petrocelli, S. R. *Fundamentals of Aquatic Toxicology Methods and Applications.* Washington, DC: Hemisphere, 1985.

Biocentrism

See **Environmental ethics**

Biochemical oxygen demand (BOD)

The BOD test is an indirect measure of the **biodegradable** organic matter in an aqueous sample. The test is indirect because oxygen used by microbes as they degrade organic matter is measured, rather than the depletion of the organic materials themselves. Generally, the test is performed over a 5-day period (BOD$_5$) at 20°C in 300 mL bottles incubated in the dark to prevent interference from algal growth. Dissolved oxygen (DO) levels (in mg/L) are measured on day 0 and at

the end of the test. The following equation relates how the BOD$_5$ of a sample is calculated:

$$BOD_5, mg/L = \frac{(Do_{initial} - DO_{after\ 5\ days})}{mL\ sample} \times 300$$

Note that in the above equation "mL sample" refers to the amount of sample that is placed in a 300 mL BOD bottle. This is critical in doing a test because if too much sample is added to a BOD bottle, microbes will use all the DO in the water (i.e. DO$_{after\ 5\ days}$=0) and a BOD$_5$ cannot be calculated. Thus, the DO uptake at various dilutions of a given sample are made. One way of making the dilutions is to add different amounts of sample to different bottles. The bottles are then filled with dilution water which is saturated with oxygen, contains various nutrients, is at a neutral pH, and is very pure so as not to create any interferences. Researchers attempt to identify a dilution which will provide for a DO uptake of greater than or equal to 2 mg/L and a DO residual of greater than or equal to 0.5-1.0 mg/L.

In some cases compounds or ions may be present in a sample that will inhibit microbes from degrading organic materials in the sample, thereby resulting in an artificially low or no BOD. Other times, the right number and/or types of microbes are not present, so the BOD is inaccurate. Samples may be "seeded" with microbes to compensate for these problems. The absence of a required nutrient will also make the BOD test invalid.

Thus, a number of factors can influence the BOD, and the test is known to be rather imprecise (i.e., values obtained vary by 10-15 percent of the actual value in a good test). However, the test continues to be a primary index of how well waters need to be treated or are treated and of the quality of natural waters. If wastes are not treated properly and contain too much BOD, the wastes may create serious oxygen deficits in environmental waters. The saturation concentration of oxygen in water varies somewhat with temperature and pressure but is often only in the area of 8-10 mg/L or less. To serve as a reference, the BOD$_5$ of raw, domestic **wastewater** ranges from about 100-300 mg/L. The demand for oxygen by the sewage is therefore clearly much greater than the amount of oxygen that water can hold in a dissolved form. To determine allowable BOD levels for a wastewater **discharge**, one must consider the relative flows/volumes of the wastewater and receiving (natural) water, temperature, reaeration of the natural water, biodegradation rate, input of other wastes, influence of benthic deposits and algae, DO levels of the wastewater and natural water, and condition/value of the receiving water. *See also* Water quality

[*Gregory D. Boardman*]

FURTHER READING

Corbitt, R. A. *Standard Handbook of Environmental Engineering.* New York: McGraw-Hill, 1990.

Davis, M. L., and D. A. Cornwell. *Introduction to Environmental Engineering.* New York: McGraw-Hill, 1991.

Tchobanoglous, G., and E. D. Schroeder. *Water Quality.* Reading, MA: Addison-Wesley, 1985.

Viessman, W., Jr., and M. J. Hammer. *Water Supply and Pollution Control.* 5th ed. New York, Harper Collins, 1993.

Bioconcentration

See **Biomagnification**

Biodegradable

Biodegradable substances are those that can be decomposed quickly by the action of biological organisms, especially microorganisms. The term is a process by which materials or compounds are broken down to smaller components, and all living organisms participate to some degree. Foods, for instance, are degraded by living creatures to release energy and chemical constituents for growth. In the sense that the term is usually used, however, it has a more restricted meaning. It refers specifically to the breakdown of undesirable toxic and waste materials or compounds to harmless or tolerable ones. When breakdown results in the destruction of useful objects, it is referred to as biodeterioration.

Although the term has been in common use for only two or three decades, processes of biodegradation have been known and used for centuries. Some of the most familiar are **sewage treatment** of human wastes, **composting** of kitchen, garden and lawn wastes, and spreading of **animal waste** on farm fields. These processes, of course, all mitigate problems with common and ubiquitous byproducts of civilization. The variety of objectionable wastes has greatly increased as human society has become more complex. The **waste stream** now includes items such as plastic bottles, lubricants, and foam packaging. Many of the newer products are virtually non-biodegradable, or they degrade only at a very slow rate. In some instances biodegradability can be greatly enhanced by minor changes in the chemical composition of the product. Biodegradable containers and packaging have been developed that are just as functional for many purposes as their non-degradable counterparts.

Advances in the science of microbiology have greatly expanded the potential for biodegradation and have increased public interest. Examples of new developments include the discovery of hitherto unknown microorganisms capable of degrading crude oil, petroleum **hydrocarbons**, diesel fuel, **gasoline**, industrial solvents, and some forms of synthetic polymers and **plastics**. These discoveries have opened new approaches for cleansing the **environment** of the accumulating toxins and debris of human society. Unfortunately, the rate at which the new organisms attack exotic wastes is sometimes quite slow, and dependent on environmental conditions. Presumably, microorganisms have been exposed to common wastes of a very long time and have evolved efficient and rapid ways to attack and use them as food. On the other hand, there has not been sufficient time to develop equally efficient means for degrading the newer wastes.

Research continues on the surprising capabilities of the new microbes, emphasizing opportunities for genetic control and manipulation of the unique metabolic pathways that make the organisms so valuable. The potential for biodegradation can be improved by increasing the rates at which wastes are attacked, and the range of environmental conditions in which degrading organisms can thrive. The advantages of biological cleanup agents are several. Non-biological techniques are often difficult and expensive. The traditional way of removing petroleum wastes from **soil**, for instance, has been to collect and incinerate it at high temperatures. This is very costly and sometimes impossible. The prospect of accomplishing the same thing by treating the **contaminated soil** with microorganisms without removing it from its location has much appeal. It should have less destructive impact on the contaminated site and be much less expensive. *See also* Alternative energy sources; Alternative fuels; Biogeochemical cycles; Biomass; Fossil fuels; Incineration; Recycling; Solid waste

[*Douglas C. Pratt*]

FURTHER READING

King, R. B., G. M. Long and J. K. Sheldon. *Practical Environmental Bioremediation.* Boca Raton, Florida: CRC Press, Inc., 1992.

Sharpley, J. M. and A. M. Kaplan. *Proceedings of the Third International Biodegradation Symposium.* London: Applied Science Publishers, 1976.

Biodiversity

Biodiversity is an ecological notion that refers to the richness of biological types at a range of hierarchical levels, including: (1) genetic diversity within species, (2) the richness of species within communities, and (3) the richness of communities on landscapes. In the context of environmental studies, however, biodiversity usually refers to the richness of species in some geographic area, and how that richness may be endangered by human activities, especially through local or global **extinction**.

Extinction represents an irrevocable and highly regrettable loss of a portion of the biodiversity of Earth. Extinction can be a natural process, caused by: 1) random catastrophic events; 2) biological interactions such as competition, disease, and predation; 3) chronic stresses; or 4) frequent disturbance. However, with the recent ascendance of human activities as a dominant force behind environmental changes, there has been a dramatic increase in rates of extinction at local, regional, and even global levels.

The recent wave of **anthropogenic** extinctions includes such well-known cases as the **dodo**, **passenger pigeon**, great auk, and others. There are many other high-profile species that humans have brought to the brink of extinction, including the plains buffalo, **whooping crane**, eskimo curlew, **ivory-billed woodpecker**, and various marine mammals. Most of these instances were caused by an insatiable over-exploitation of species that were unable to sustain a high rate of mortality, often coupled with an intense disturbance of their habitat.

Beyond these tragic cases of extinction or endangerment of large, charismatic vertebrates, the earth's biota is experi-

Form of Life	Known Species	Estimated Total Species
Insects and other arthropods	874,161	30 million insect species, extrapolated from surveys in forest canopy in Panama; most believed unique to tropical forests.
Higher Plants	248,400	Estimates of total plant species range from 275,000 to as many as 400,000; at least 10-15 percent of all plants are believed undiscovered.
Invertebrates[1]	116,873	True invertebrate species may number in the millions; nematodes, eelworms, and roundworms each may comprise more than 1 million species.
Lower Plants[2]	73,900	Not available.
Microorganisms	36,600	Not available.
Fish	19,056	21,000, assuming that 10 percent of fish remain undiscovered; the Amazon and Orinoco rivers alone may account for 2,000 additional species.
Birds	9,040	Known species probably account for 98 percent of all birds.
Reptiles and Amphibians	8,962	Known species of reptiles, amphibians, and mammals probably comprise over 95 percent of total diversity.
Mammals	4,000	
Total	1,390,992	10 million species considered a conservative estimate; if insect estimates are accurate the total exceeds 30 million.

[1]Excludes arthropods, includes 1,273 miscellaneous chordates.
[2]Fungi and algae.

Known and estimated diversity of life on earth.

encing an even more substantial loss of biodiversity caused by the loss of **habitat**. In part, this loss is due to the conversion of large areas of tropical **ecosystem**s, particularly moist forest, to agricultural or otherwise ecologically degraded habitats. A large fraction of the biodiversity of tropical **biome**s is comprised of rare, **endemic** (i.e., with a local distribution) **species**. Consequently the conversion of **tropical rain forest** to habitats unsuitable for these specialized species inevitably causes the extinction of most of the locally endemic biota. Remarkably, the biodiversity of tropical forests is so large, particularly in insects, that most of it has not yet been identified taxonomically. We are therefore faced with the prospect of a **mass extinction** of perhaps millions of species before they have been recognized by science.

To date, about 1.7 million organisms have been identified and designated with a scientific name. About 6 percent of identified species live in boreal or polar latitudes, 59 percent in the temperate zones, and the remaining 35 percent in the tropics. The knowledge of the global richness of species is very incomplete, particularly in the tropics. If a conservative estimate is made of the number of unidentified tropical species, the fraction of global species that live in the tropics would increase to at least 86 percent.

Invertebrates comprise the largest number of described species, with insects making up the bulk of that total and beetles (*Coleoptera*) comprising most of the insects. Biologists believe that there still is a tremendous number of undescribed species of insects in the tropics, possibly as many as another 30 million species. This remarkable conclusion has emerged from experiments conducted by the entomologist Terry Erwin, in which scientists "fogged" tropical forest canopies and then collected the "rain" of dead arthropods. This research suggests that: (1) a large fraction of the insect biodiversity of tropical forests is undescribed; (2) most insect species are confined to a single type of forest, or even to particular plant species, both of which are restricted in distribution; and (3) most tropical forest insects have a very limited dispersal ability.

The biodiversity and endemism of other tropical forest biota are better known than that of arthropods. For example, a plot of only 0.1 ha in an Ecuadorian forest had 365 species of **vascular plant**s. The richness of woody plants in tropical rain forest can approach 300 species per hectare, compared with fewer than twelve to fifteen tree species in a typical temperate forest, and thirty to thirty-five species in the Great Smokies of the United States, the richest temperate forest in the world.

There have been few systematic studies of all of the biota of particular tropical communities. In one case, D. H. Janzen studied a **savanna**-like, 108-km² reserve of dry tropical forest in Costa Rica for several years. He estimated that the site had at least 700 plant species, 400 vertebrate species, and a remarkable 13,000 species of insect, including 3,140 species of moths and butterflies.

Why should one worry about the likelihood of extinction of so many rare species of tropical insects, or of many other rare species of plants and animals? There are three classes of reasons why extinctions are regrettable:

(1) There are important concerns in terms of the ethics of extinction. Central questions are whether humans have the "right" to act as the exterminator of unique and irrevocable species of **wildlife** and whether the human existence is somehow impoverished by the tragedy of extinction. These are philosophical issues that cannot be scientifically resolved, but it is certain that few people would applaud the extinction of unique species.

(2) There are utilitarian reasons. Humans must take advantage of other organisms in myriad ways for sustenance, medicine, shelter, and other purposes. If species become extinct, their unique services, be they biological, ecological, or otherwise, are no longer available for exploitation.

(3) The third class of reasons is ecological and involves the roles of species in maintaining the stability and integrity of ecosystems, i.e., in terms of preventing **erosion** and controlling **nutrient** cycling, productivity, trophic dynamics, and other aspects of ecosystem structure and function. Because we rarely have sufficient knowledge to evaluate the ecological "importance" of particular species, it is likely that an extraordinary number of species will disappear before their ecological roles are understood.

There are many cases where research on previously unexploited species of plants and animals has revealed the existence of products of great utility to humans, such as food or medicinals. One example is the rosy periwinkle (*Catharantus roseus*), a plant native to **Madagascar**. During a screening of many plants for possible anti-cancer properties, an extract of rosy periwinkle was found to counteract the reproduction of cancer cells. Research identified the active ingredients as several alkaloids, which are now used to prepare the important anti-cancer drugs vincristine and vinblastine. This once obscure plant now allows treatment of several previously incurable cancers and is the basis of a multi-million-dollar economy.

Undoubtedly, there is a tremendous, undiscovered wealth of other biological products that are of potential use to humans. Many of these natural products are present in the biodiversity of tropical species that has not yet been "discovered" by taxonomists.

It is well known that extinction can be a natural process. In fact, most of the species that have ever lived on Earth are now extinct, having disappeared "naturally" for some reason or other. Perhaps they could not cope with changes in their inorganic or biotic environment, or they may have succumbed to some catastrophic event, such as a meteorite impact.

The rate of extinction has not been uniform over geological time. Long periods characterized by a slow and uniform rate of extinction have been punctuated by about nine catastrophic events of mass extinction. The most intense mass extinction occurred some 250 million years ago, when about 96 percent of marine species became extinct. Another example occurred 65 million years ago, when there were extinctions of many vertebrate species, including the reptilian orders Dinosauria and Pterosauria, but also of many plants and invertebrates, including about one half of the global fauna that existed then.

In modern times, however, humans are the dominant force causing extinction, mostly because of: (1) overharvesting; (2) effects of introduced predators, competitors, and diseases; and (3) habitat destruction. During the last 200 years, a global total of perhaps 100 species of mammals, 160 birds, and many other taxa are known to have become extinct through some human influence, in addition to untold numbers of undescribed, tropical species.

Even pre-industrial human societies caused extinctions. Stone-age humans are believed to have caused the extinctions of large-animal fauna in various places, by the unsustainable and insatiable hunting of vulnerable species in newly discovered islands and continents. Such events of mass extinction of large animals, co-incident with human colonization events, have occurred at various times during the last ten to fifty thousand years in Madagascar, New Zealand, Australia, Tasmania, Hawaii, North and South America, and elsewhere.

In more recent times, **overhunting** has caused the extinction of other large, vulnerable species, for example the flightless dodo (*Raphus cucullatus*) of Mauritius. Some North American examples include Labrador duck (*Camptorhynchus labradorium*), passenger pigeon (*Ectopistes migratorius*), Carolina parakeet (*Conuropsis carolinensis*), great auk (*Pinguinus impennis*), and Steller's sea cow (*Hydrodamalis stelleri*). Many other species have been brought to the brink of extinction by overhunting and loss of habitat. Some North American examples include eskimo curlew (*Numenius borealis*), plains bison (*Bison bison*), and a variety of marine mammals, including **manatee** (*Trichechus manatus*), right **whales** (*Eubalaena glacialis*), bowhead whale (*Balaena mysticetus*), and blue whale (*Balaenoptera musculus*).

Island biotas are especially prone to both natural and anthropogenic extinction. This syndrome can be illustrated by the case of the **Hawaiian Islands**, an ancient volcanic archipelago in the Pacific Ocean, about 994 miles (1600 km) from the nearest island group and 2484 miles (4000 km) from the nearest continental landmass. At the time of colonization by Polynesians, there were at least sixty-eight endemic species of Hawaiian birds, out of a total richness of land birds of eighty-six species. Of the initial sixty-eight endemics, twenty-four are now extinct and twenty-nine are perilously endangered. Especially hard hit has been an endemic family, the Hawaiian honeycreepers (Drepanididae), of which thirteen species are believed extinct, and twelve endangered. More than fifty alien species of birds have been introduced to the Hawaiian Islands, but this gain hardly compensates for the loss and endangerment of specifically evolved endemics. Similarly, the native flora of the islands is estimated to have been comprised of 1,765-2,000 taxa of angiosperm plants, of which at least 94 percent were endemic. During the last two centuries, more than 100 native plants have become extinct, and the survival of at least an additional 500 taxa is threatened or endangered, some now being represented by only single individuals. The most important causes of extinction of Hawaiian biota have been the conversion of natural ecosystems to agricultural and urban landscapes, the introduction of alien predators, competitors, herbivores, and diseases, and to some extent, aboriginal overhunting of some species of bird.

Overhunting has been an important cause of extinction, but in modern times habitat destruction is the most important reason for the event of mass extinction that Earth's biodiversity is now experiencing. As was noted previously, most of the global biodiversity is comprised of millions of as yet undescribed taxa of tropical insects and other organisms. Because of the extreme endemism of most tropical biota, it is likely that many species will become extinct as a result of the clearing of natural tropical habitats, especially forest, and its conversion to other types of habitat.

The amount and rate of deforestation in the tropics are increasing rapidly, in contrast to the situation at higher latitudes where forest cover is relatively stable. Between the mid 1960s and the mid 1980s there was little change (less than 2 percent) in the forest area of North America, but in Central America forest cover decreased by 17 percent, and in South America by 7 percent (but by a larger percentage in equatorial countries of South America). The global rate of clearing of tropical rain forest in the mid 1980s was equivalent to 6-8 percent of that biome per year, a rate that if projected into the future would predict a biome half-life of only nine to twelve years. Some of the cleared forest will regenerate through secondary succession, which would ultimately produce another mature forest. Little is known, however, about the rate and biological character of succession in tropical rainforests, or how long it would take to restore a fully biodiverse ecosystem after disturbance.

The present rate of disturbance and conversion of tropical forest predicts grave consequences for global biodiversity. Because of a widespread awareness and concern about this important problem, much research and other activity has recently been directed towards the conservation and protection of tropical forests. As of 1985, several thousand sites, comprising more than 640,000 square miles (160 million ha), had received some sort of "protection" in low-latitude countries. Of course the operational effectiveness of the protected status varies greatly, depending on the commitment of governments to these issues. Important factors include: (1) political stability; (2) political priorities; (3) finances available to mount effective programs to control **poaching** of animals and lumber and to prevent other disturbances; (4) the support of local peoples and communities for biodiversity programs; (5) the willingness of relatively wealthy nations to provide a measure of debt relief to impoverished tropical countries and thereby reduce their short term need to liquidate natural resources in order to raise capital and provide employment; and (6) local population growth, which also generates extreme pressures to over exploit natural resources.

The biodiversity crisis is a very real and very important aspect of the global environmental crisis. All nations have a responsibility to maintain biodiversity within their own jurisdictions and to aid nations with less economic and scientific capability to maintain their biodiversity on behalf of the entire planet. The modern biodiversity crisis focuses on species-rich tropical ecosystems, but the developed nations of temperate latitudes also have a large stake in the outcome and will have to substantially subsidize global conservation activities if these are to be successful. Much needs to be done, but an encouraging level of activity in the conservation and protection of biodiversity is beginning in many countries, including an emerging commitment by many nations to the conservation of threatened ecosystems in the tropics. *See also* Biotic community

[*Bill Freedman*]

FURTHER READING

Ehrlich, P. R., and A. H. Ehrlich. *Extinction: The Causes and Consequences of the Disappearance of Species.* New York: Ballantyne Books, 1981.

Freedman, B. *Environmental Ecology.* San Diego, CA: Academic Press, 1989.

Janzen, D. H. "Insect Diversity in a Costa Rican Dry Forest: Why Keep It, and How." *Biological Journal of the Linnaean Society* 30 (1987): 343-356.

Peters, R. L., and T. E. Lovejoy. *Global Warming and Biological Diversity.* New Haven, CT: Yale University Press, 1992.

Wilson, E. O. *Biodiversity.* Washington, DC: National Academy Press, 1988.

———. *Biophilia: The Human Bond With Other Species.* Cambridge, MA: Harvard University Press, 1984.

Biofilms

Marine microbiology began with the investigations of marine microfouling by L. E. Zobell and his colleagues in the 1930s and 1940s. Their interests focused primarily on the early stages of settlement and growth of microorganisms, primarily bacteria on solid substrates immersed in the sea. The interest in the study of marine microfouling was sporadic from that time until the early 1960s when interest in marine bacteriology began to increase. Since 1970 the research on the broad problems of bioadhesion and specifically the early stages of microfouling has expanded tremendously.

The initial step in marine fouling is the establishment of a complex film. This film, which is composed mainly of bacteria and diatoms plus secreted extracellular materials and debris, is most commonly referred to as the "primary film" but may also be called the "bacterial fouling layer," or "slime layer." The latter name is aptly descriptive since the film ultimately becomes thick enough to feel slippery or slimy to touch. In addition to the bacteria and diatoms that comprise most of the biota, the film may also include yeasts, fungi, and protozoans.

The settlement sequence in the formation of primary films is dependent upon a number of variables which may include the location of the surface, season of the year, depth, and proximity to previously fouled surfaces and other physiochemical factors.

Many studies have demonstrated the existence of some form of ecological **succession** in the formation of fouling communities, commencing with film forming microorganisms and reaching a climax community of macrofouling organisms such as barnacles, tunicates, mussels, and seaweeds.

Establishment of primary films in marine fouling has two functions: (a) to provide a surface favoring the settlement and adhesion of animal larvae and algal cells, and (b) to provide a nutrient source that could sustain or enhance the development of the fouling community.

Formation of a primary film is initiated by a phenomenon known as "molecular fouling" or "surface conditioning." The formation of this molecular film was first demonstrated by Zobell in 1943 and since has been confirmed by many other investigators. The molecular film forms by the **sorption** to solid surfaces of organic matter dissolved or suspended in seawater. The sorption of this dissolved material creates surface changes in the surface of the substrate which are favorable for establishing biological settlement. These dissolved organic materials originate from a variety of sources such as end-products of bacterial decay, excretory products, dissolution from seaweeds, etc., and consist principally of sugars, amino acids, urea, and fatty acids.

This molecular film has been observed to form within minutes after any clean, solid surface is immersed in natural seawater. The role of this film in biofouling has been shown to modify the "critical surface tension" or wetability of the immersed surface which than facilitates the strong bonding of the microorganisms through the agency of mucopolysaccharides exuded by film-forming bacteria.

Bacteria have been found securely attached to substrates immersed in seawater after just a few hours. Initial colonization is by rod-shaped bacteria followed by stalked forms within twenty-four to seventy-two hours. As many as forty to fifty species have been isolated from the surface of glass slides immersed in seawater for a few days.

Following the establishment of the initial film of bacteria and their secreted extracellular polymer on a solid substrate, additional bacteria and other microorganisms may attach. Most significant in this population are benthic diatoms but there are also varieties of filamentous microorganisms and protozoans. These organisms, together with debris and other organic particular matter that adhere to the surface create an intensely active biochemical environment and form the primary stage in the succession of a typical macrofouling community.

Considering the enormous economic consequences of marine fouling it is not at all surprising that there continues to be intense interest in the results of recent research, particularly in the conditions and processes of molecular film formation.

[*Donald A. Villeneuve*]

FURTHER READING

Corpe, W. A. "Primary Bacterial Films and Marine Microfouling." In *Proceedings of the 4th International Congress of Marine Corrosion and Fouling*, edited by V. Romansky. 1977.

Zobell, L. E., and E. C. Allen. "The Significance of Marine Bacteria in the Fouling of Submerged Surfaces." *Journal of Bacteriology* 29 (1935): 239-251.

Biofiltration

Biofiltration refers to the removal and oxidation of organic gases (i.e., **volatile organic compound**s, or VOCs) from contaminated air by vapor phase biodegradation in beds (biofilters) of compost, **soil**, or other materials such as municipal waste, sand, bark peat, volcanic ash, or diatomaceous earth. As contaminated air (such as air from a soil vapor extraction process) flows through the biofilter, the VOCs sorb onto surfaces of the pile and are degraded by microorganisms. Nutrient blends or exogenous microbial cultures can be added to a biofilter to enhance its performance. Moisture needs to be continually supplied to the biofilter to counteract the drying effects of the gas stream. The stationary support media that make up the biofiltration bed should be porous enough to allow gas flow through the biofilter and should provide a large surface area with high wetting and sorptive capacities. This support media should also provide adequate buffering capacity and may also serve as a source of inorganic nutrients. Biofilters, also used to treat odors as well as organic contaminants, have been used in Europe for over twenty years. Compared to incineration and carbon adsorption, biofilters do not require landfilling of residuals or regeneration of spent materials.

Waste gases are moved through the units by induced or forced draft. Biofilters are capable of handling rapid air flow rates (e.g., up to 90,000 cubic ft (2,700 cubic m) per minute (cfm) in filters up to 20,000 sq ft (1,800 sq m) in wetted area) and VOC concentrations greater than 1,000 ppm. However, biofiltration removal of more highly halogenated compounds such as trichloroethylene (TCE) or carbon tetrachloride, which biodegrade very slowly under aerobic conditions, may require very long residence times (i.e., very large biofilters) or treatment of very low flow rates of air containing the contaminants.

The soil-type biofilter is similar in design to a soil compost pile. Fertilizers are preblended into the compost pile to provide nutrients for indigenous microorganisms, which accomplish the biodegradation of the VOCs. In the treatment bed type of biofilter, the waste air stream is humidified as it is passed through one or more beds of compost, municipal waste, sand, diatomaceous earth or other materials. Another type of biofilter is the disk biofilter, which consists of a series of humidified, compressed disks placed inside a reactor shell. These layered disks contain activated charcoal, nutrients, microbial cultures, and compost material.

The waste air stream is passed through the disk system. Collected water condensate from the process is returned to the humidification system for reuse.

[*Judith L. Sims*]

FURTHER READING

Baker, K. H., and D. S. Herson. *Bioremediation*. New York: McGraw-Hill, 1994.

King, B. R., G. M. Long, and J. K. Sheldon. *Practical Environmental Bioremediation*. Boca Raton, FL: Lewis Publishers, 1992.

Stoner, D. L., ed. "Organic Waste Forms and Treatment Strategies." *Biotechnology for the Treatment of Hazardous Waste*. Boca Raton, FL: Lewis Publishers, 1994.

Biofouling

The term fouling, or more specifically biofouling, is used to describe the growth and accumulation of living organisms on the surfaces of submerged artificial structures as opposed to natural surfaces. Concern over and interest in fouling arises from practical considerations including the enormous costs resulting from fouling of ships, buoys, floats, pipes, cables and other underwater man-made structures.

From its first immersion in the sea, an artificial structure or surface changes through time as a result of a variety of influences including location, season and other physical and biological variables. Fouling communities growing on these structures are biological entities and must be understood developmentally. The development of a fouling community on a bare, artificial surface immersed in the sea displays a form of **succession**, similar to that seen in terrestrial **ecosystem**s, which culminates in a community which may be considered a climax stage. Scientists have identified two distinct stages in fouling community development: 1) the primary or microfouling stage, and 2) the secondary or macrofouling stage.

Microfouling: When a structure is first submerged in seawater, microorganisms, primarily bacteria and diatoms, appear on the surface and multiply rapidly. Together with debris and other organic particulate matter, these microorganisms form a film on the surface. Although the evidence is not conclusive, it appears that the development of this film is a prerequisite to initiation of the fouling succession.

Macrofouling: The animals and plants that make up the next stages of succession in fouling communities are primarily the attached or sessile forms of animals and plants that occur naturally in shallow waters along the local coast. The development of fouling communities in the sea depends upon the ability of locally-occurring organism to live successfully in the new artificial habitat. The first organisms to attach to the microfouled surface are the swimming larvae of species present at the time of immersion. The kinds of larvae present vary with the season. Rapidly growing forms that become established first may ultimately be crowded out by others which grow more slowly. A comprehensive list of species making up fouling communities recorded from a wide variety of structures identified 2,000 **species** of animals and plants. Although the variety of organisms identified seems large it actually represents a very small proportion of the known marine species. Further, only about 50 to 100 species are commonly encountered in fouling, including bivalve mollusks (primarily oysters and mussels), barnacles, aquatic invertebrates in the phylum Bryozoa, tubeworms and other organisms in the class Polychaeta, and green and brown algae.

Control of fouling organisms has long been a formidable challenge resulting in the development and application of a wide variety of toxic paints and greases, or the use of metals which give off toxic **ion**s as they corrode. However, none of the existing methods provide permanent control. Furthermore, the recognition of the potential environmental hazards attendant with the use of materials that leach toxins into the marine **environment** has led to the ban of some of the most widely used materials. This has stimulated efforts to develop alternative materials or methods of controlling biofouling that are environmentally safe.

[*Donald A. Villeneuve*]

FURTHER READING

Melo, L. F., et al, eds. *Fouling Science and Technology*. Norwell, MA: Kluwer Academic, 1988.

Woods Hole Oceanographic Institution. *Marine Fouling and Its Prevention*. Annapolis, MD: U. S. Naval Institute, 1952.

Workshop on Preservation of Wood in the Marine Environment. *Marine Borers, Fungi and Fouling Organisms of Wood*. Paris: Organisation for Economic Cooperation and Development, 1971.

Biogeochemistry

Biogeochemistry refers to the quantity and cycling of chemicals in **ecosystem**s. Biogeochemistry can be studied at various spatial scales, ranging from communities, landscapes (or seascapes), and over Earth as a whole. Biogeochemistry involves the study of chemicals in organisms, and also in non-living components of the **environment**.

An important aspect of biogeochemistry is the fact that elements can occur in various molecular forms that can be transformed among each other, often as a result of biological reactions. Such transformations are an especially important consideration for nutrients, i.e., those chemicals that are required for the healthy functioning of organisms. As a result of biogeochemical cycling, nutrients can be used repeatedly—nutrients contained in dead biomass can be recycled through inorganic forms, back into living organisms, and so on. Biogeochemistry is also relevant to the movements and transformations of potentially toxic chemicals in ecosystems, such as **metals**, **pesticide**s, and certain gases.

Nutrient Cycles

Ecologists have a good understanding of the biogeochemical cycling of the most important nutrients. These include **carbon**, **nitrogen**, **phosphorus**, potassium, calcium, magnesium, and sulfur. Some of these can occur variously as gases in the atmosphere, as ions dissolved in water, in minerals in rocks and soil, and in a great variety of organic chemicals in the living or dead **biomass** of organisms. Ecologists study nutrient cycles by determining the quantities of the various chemical forms of nutrients in various compartments of ecosystems, and by determining the rates of transformation and cycling among the various compartments.

The nitrogen cycle is particularly well understood, and it can be used to illustrate the broader characteristics of nutrient cycling. Nitrogen is an important nutrient, being one of the most abundant elements in the tissues of organisms and a component of many kinds of biochemicals, including amino acids, proteins, and nucleic acids. Nitrogen is also one of the most common limiting factors to primary productivity, and the growth rates of plants in many ecosystems will increase markedly if they are fertilized with nitrogen. This is a fairly common characteristic of terrestrial and marine environments, and to a lesser degree of freshwater ones.

Plants assimilate most of their nitrogen from the soil environment, as nitrate (NO_3^-) or ammonium (NH_4^+) dissolved in the water that is taken up by roots. Some may also be taken up as gaseous nitrogen oxides (such as NO or NO_2) that are absorbed from the atmosphere. In addition, some plants live in a beneficial symbiosis with microorganisms that have the ability to fix atmospheric dinitrogen gas (N_2) into ammonia (NH_3) which can be used as a nutrient. In contrast, almost all animals satisfy their nutritional needs by eating plants or other animals and metabolically breaking down the organic forms of nitrogen, using the products (such as amino acids) to synthesize the necessary biochemicals of the animal. When plants and animals die, microorganisms active in the detrital cycle metabolize organic nitrogen in the dead biomass into simpler compounds, ultimately to ammonium.

The **nitrogen cycle** has always occurred naturally, but in modern times some of its aspects have been greatly modified by human influences. These include the fertilization of agricultural ecosystems, the dumping of nitrogen-containing sewage into lakes and other waterbodies, the emission of gaseous forms of nitrogen into the atmosphere, and the cultivation of nitrogen-fixing legumes. In some cases, human effects on nitrogen biogeochemistry result in increased productivity of crops, but in other cases serious ecological damages occur.

Toxic Chemicals in Ecosystems

Some human activities result in the release of toxic chemicals into the environment, which under certain conditions can pose risks to human health and cause serious damages to ecosystems. These damages are called **pollution**, whereas the mere presence of chemicals which cause no damage in the environment is referred to as contamination. Biogeochemistry is concerned with the emissions, transfers, and quantities of these potentially toxic chemicals in the environment and ecosystems.

Certain chemicals have a great ability to accumulate in organisms rather than in the non-living (or inorganic) components of the environment. This tendency is referred to as bioconcentration. Chemicals that strongly bioconcentrate include methylmercury and all of the persistent organochlorine compounds, such as **dichlorodiphenyl-trichloroethane (DDT)**, **pentachlorophenol (PCBs)**, **dioxin**s, and furans. Methylmercury bioconcentrates because it is rather tightly bound in certain body organs of animals. The organochlorines bioconcentrate because they are extremely insoluble in water but highly soluble in fats and lipids, which are abundant in the bodies of organisms but not in non-living parts of the environment.

In addition, persistent organochlorines tend to occur in particularly large concentrations in the fat of top predators, that is, in animals high in the ecological food web, such as marine mammals, predatory birds, and humans. This happens because these chemicals are not easily metabolized into simpler compounds by these animals, so they accumulate in increasingly larger residues as the animals feed and age. This phenomenon is known as food-web magnification (or **biomagnification**). Food-web magnification causes chemicals such as DDT to achieve residues of tens or more parts per million (ppm) in the fatty tissues of top predators, even though they occur in the inorganic environment (such as water) in concentrations smaller than one part per billion (ppb). These high body residues can lead to ecotoxicological problems for top predators, some of which have declined in abundance because of their exposure to chlorinated hydrocarbons.

Because a few species of plants have an affinity for potentially toxic elements, they may bioaccumulate them to extremely high concentrations in their tissues. These plants are genetically adapted ecotypes which are themselves little affected by the residues, although they can cause toxicity to animals that might feed on their biomass. For example, some plants that live in environments in which the soil contains a mineral known as serpentine accumulate nickel to concentrations which may exceed thousands of ppm. Similarly, some plants (such as locoweed) growing in semi-arid environments can accumulate thousands of ppm of selenium in their tissues, which can poison animals that feed on the plants.

[*Bill Freedman*]

FURTHER READING

Atlas, R.M., and R. Bartha. *Microbial Ecology.* Menlo Park, CA: Benjamin/Cummings, 1987.

Freedman, B. *Environmental Ecology*, 2nd ed. San Diego, CA: Academic Press, 1995.

Schlesinger, W. H. *Biogeochemistry: An Analysis of Global Change.* San Diego, CA: Academic Press, 1991.

Smith, R. P. *A Primer of Environmental Toxicology.* Philadelphia, PA: Lea & Febiger, 1992.

Biogeography

Biogeography is the study of the spatial distribution of plants and animals, both today and in the past. Developed during the course of nineteenth century efforts to explore, map, and describe the earth, biogeography asks questions about regional variations in the numbers and kinds of **species**: Where do various species occur and why? What physical and biotic factors limit or extend the range of a species? In what ways do species disperse (expand their ranges), and what barriers block their dispersal? How has species distribution changed over centuries or millennia, as shown in the fossil record? What controls the makeup of a **biotic community** (the combination of species that occur together)? Biogeography is an interdisciplinary science: many other fields, including paleontology, geology, botany, oceanography, and climatology, both contribute to biogeography and make use of ideas developed by biogeographers.

Because physical and biotic environments strongly influence species distribution, the study of **ecology** is closely tied to biogeography. Precipitation, temperature ranges, **soil** types, soil or water **salinity**, and insolation (exposure to the sun) are some elements of the physical **environment** that control the distribution of plants and animals. Biotic limits to distribution, constraints imposed by other living things, are equally important. Species interact in three general ways: **competition** with other species (for space, sunlight, water, or food), predation (e.g., an owl species relying on rodents for food), and mutualism (e.g., an insect pollenizing a plant while the plant provides nourishment for the insect). The presence or absence of a key plant or animal may function as an important control on another species' spatial distribution. Community ecology, the ways in which an assemblage of species coexist, is also important. Biotic communities have a variety of niches, from low to high **trophic level**s, from generalist roles to specialized ones. The presence or absence of species filling one of these roles influences the presence or survival of a species filling another role.

Two other factors that influence a region's biotic composition or the range of a particular species are dispersal, or spreading, of a species from one place to another; and barriers, environmental factors that block dispersal. In some cases a species can extend its range by gradually colonizing adjacent, hospitable areas. In other cases a species may cross a barrier, such as a mountain range, an ocean, or a **desert**, and establish a colony beyond that barrier. The cattle egret (*Bubulcus ibis*) exemplifies both types of movement. Late in the nineteenth century these birds crossed the formidable barrier of the Atlantic Ocean, perhaps in a storm, and established a breeding colony in Brazil. During the past one hundred years this small egret has found suitable **habitat** and gradually expanded its range around the coast of South America and into North America, so that by 1970 it had been seen from southern Chile to southern Ontario.

The study of dispersal has special significance in island biogeography. The central idea of island biogeography, proposed in 1967 by R. H. MacArthur and **Edward O. Wilson**, is that an island has an equilibrium number of species that increases with the size of the land mass and its proximity to other islands. Thus species diversity should be extensive on a large or nearshore island, with enough complexity to support large carnivores or species with very specific food or habitat requirements. Conversely, a small or distant island may support only small populations of a few species,

with little complexity or **niche** specificity in the biotic community.

Principles of island biogeography have proven useful in the study of other "island" **ecosystem**s, such as isolated lakes, small mountain ranges surrounded by deserts, and insular patches of forest left behind by clearcut logging. In such threatened areas as the Pacific Northwest and the Amazonian **rain forest**s, foresters are being urged to leave larger stands of trees in closer proximity to each other so that species at high trophic levels and those with specialized food or habitat requirements (e.g., **Northern spotted owl**s and Amazonian monkeys) might survive. In such areas as **Yellowstone National Park**, which national policy designates as an insular unit of habitat, the importance of adjacent habitat has received increased consideration. Recognition that clearcuts and farmland constitute barriers has led some planners to establish forest corridors to aid dispersal, enhance genetic diversity, and maintain biotic complexity in unsettled islands of natural habitat. *See also* Biodiversity; Biosphere; Clear-cutting; Climate; Predator-prey interactions; Territoriality

[*Mary Ann Cunningham*]

FURTHER READING

Brown, J. H., and A. C. Gibson. *Biogeography*. St. Louis: Mosby, 1983.

MacArthur, R. H., and E. O. Wilson. *The Theory of Island Biogeography*. Vol. 1, *Monographs in Population Biology*. Princeton: Princeton University Press, 1967.

Biohydrometallurgy

Biohydrometallurgy is a technique by which microorganisms are used to recover certain metals from ores. The technique was first used over three hundred years ago to extract **copper** from low-grade ores. In recent years, its use has been extended to the recovery of **uranium** and gold, and scientists believe that it will eventually be applied to the recovery of other metals such as **lead**, **nickel**, and zinc.

In most cases, biohydrometallurgy is employed when conventional mining procedures are too expensive or ineffective in recovering a metal. For example, dumps of unwanted waste materials are created when copper is mined by traditional methods. These wastes consist primarily of rock, gravel, sand, and other materials that are removed in order to reach the metal ore itself. But the wastes also contain very low concentrations (less than 0.5 percent) of copper ore.

Until recently, the concentrations of copper ore in a dump were too low to have any economic value. The cost of collecting the ore was much greater than the value of the copper extracted. But, as richer sources of copper ore are used up, low grade reserves (like dumps) become more attractive to mining companies. At this point, biohydrometallurgy can be used to leach out the very small quantities of ore remaining in waste materials.

The extraction of copper by means of biohydrometallurgy involves two types of reactions. In the first, microorganisms operate directly on compounds of copper. In the second, microorganisms operate on metallic compounds other than those of copper. These metallic compounds are then converted into forms which can, in turn, react with copper ores.

The use of biohydrometallurgical techniques on a copper ore waste dump typically begins by spraying the dump with dilute sulfuric acid. As the acid seeps into the dump, it creates an **environment** favorable to the growth of acid-loving microorganisms that attack copper ores. As the microorganisms metabolize the ores, they convert copper from an insoluble to a soluble form. Soluble copper is then leached out of the dump with sulfuric acid. It is recovered when the solution is pumped out to a recovery tank.

A second reaction occurs within the dump. Microorganisms also convert ferrous iron (Fe^{2+}) in ores such as pyrite (FeS_2) to ferric iron (Fe^{3+}). The ferric iron, in turn, oxidizes copper in the dump from an insoluble to a soluble form.

The mechanism described here is a highly efficient one. As microorganisms act on copper and iron compounds, they produce sulfuric acid as a by-product, thus enriching the environment in which they live. Ferric iron reduces and oxidizes copper at the same time, making the copper available for attack by microorganisms once again.

A number of microorganisms have been used in biohydrometallurgy. One of the most effective for the leaching of copper is *Thiobacillus ferrooxidans*. Research is now being conducted on the development of genetically engineered microorganisms that can be used in the recovery of copper and other metals.

The two other metals for which biohydrometallurgy seems to be most useful are uranium and gold. Waste dumps in South Africa and Canada have been treated to convert insoluble forms of uranium to soluble forms, allowing recovery by a method similar to that used with copper. In the treatment of gold ores, biohydrometallurgy is used in a pretreatment step prior to the conventional conversion of the metal to a cyanide-complex. The first commercial plants for the biohydrometallurgical treatment of gold ores are now in operations in South Africa and Zimbabwe. *See also* Genetic engineering; Heavy metals and heavy metal poisoning; Overburden; Strip mining; Surface mining

[*David E. Newton*]

FURTHER READING

McGraw Hill Encyclopedia of Science and Technology. 7th ed. New York: McGraw-Hill, 1992.

Rossi, G. *Biohydrometallurgy.* New York: McGraw-Hill, 1990.

Bioindicator

A bioindicator is a plant or animal **species** that is known to be particularly tolerant or sensitive to **pollution**. Based on the known association of an organism with a particular type or intensity of pollution, the presence of the organism can be used as a tool to indicate polluted conditions relative to unimpacted reference conditions. Sometimes a set of species or the structure and function of an entire **biological community** may function as a bioindicator. In assessing the impacts of pollution, bioindicators are frequently used to evaluate the "health" of an impacted **ecosystem** relative to a reference area or reference conditions. Field-based, site-specific environmental evaluations based on the bioindicator approach generally are complemented with laboratory studies of toxicity testing and **bioassay** experiments.

The use of individual species or a community structure as bioindicators involves the identification, classification and quantification of biota in the affected area. While many species are in use, the most widely used biological communities are the benthic macroinvertebrates. These are the sedentary and crawling worms and insect larvae that reside in the bottom **sediment**s of aquatic systems such as lake and river bottoms. The bottom sediments usually contain most of the pollutants introduced into an aquatic system. Since these macroinvertebrates have limited mobility, they are continually exposed to the highest concentrations of pollutants in the system. Therefore, this benthic community is an ideal bioindicator: stationary, localized and exposed to maximum pollutant concentrations within a specific location.

Often, alterations in community structure due to pollution include a change from a more diverse to a less diverse community with fewer species or taxa. The indicator community may also be composed mostly of species that are tolerant of or adapted to polluted conditions and pollution-sensitive species that are present upstream may be absent in the impacted zones. However, depending on the type of pollutant, the abundance of the pollution-tolerant species may be very high and, therefore, the size of the benthic community may be similar to or exceed the reference community upstream. This is common in cases where pollution from sewage **discharge**s adds organic matter that provides food for some of the tolerant benthic species. In the case of toxic chemical (e.g. heavy metals, organic compounds) pollution, the benthic community may show an overall reduction both in diversity and abundance.

Tubificid worms are an example of pollution-tolerant **indicator organism**s. These worms live in the bottom sediments of streams and lakes and are highly tolerant of the kind of pollution that results from sewage discharges. In a river polluted by **wastewater** discharge from a **sewage treatment** plant, it is common to see a large increase in the number of tubificid worms in the stream sediments immediately downstream of the discharge. Upstream of the discharge, the number of these worms is much lower, reflecting the cleaner conditions. Further downstream, as the discharge is diluted, the number of tubificid worms again decreases to a level similar to the upstream portions of the river. Large populations of these worms dramatically demonstrate that pollution is present, and the location of these populations may also indicate the general area where the pollution enters the environment.

Alternatively, pollution-intolerant organisms can also be used to indicate polluted conditions. The larvae of mayflies live in stream sediments and are known to be particularly sensitive to pollution. In a river receiving wastewater discharge, mayflies show a pattern opposite to that of the tubificid worms. The mayfly larvae are normally present in large numbers above the discharge point, decrease or disappear at the discharge point (just where the tubificid worms are most abundant) and reappear further downstream as the effects of the discharge are diluted. In this case, the mayflies are pollution-sensitive indicator organisms and their absence serves as the indication of pollution. Similar examples of indicator organisms can be found among plants, fishes and other biological groups. Giant reedgrass (*Phragmites australis*) is a common marsh plant that is typically indicative of disturbed conditions in **wetlands**. Among fish, disturbed conditions may be indicated by the disappearance of sensitive species like trout which require clear, cold waters to thrive.

The usefulness of indicator organisms is unquestionable but limited. While their presence or absence provides a reliable general picture of polluted conditions, it is often difficult to identify clearly the exact sources of pollution, especially in areas with multiple sources of pollution. In the sediments of New York Harbor, for example, pollution-tolerant insect larvae are overwhelmingly dominant. However, it is impossible to attribute the large larval populations to just one of the numerous possible sources of pollution in this area which include ship traffic, sewage discharge, industrial discharge, and **storm runoff**. As more is learned about the physiology and life-history of an indicator organism and its response to different types of pollution, it may be possible to draw more specific conclusions.

Although the two terms are sometimes used interchangeably, indicator organisms should not be confused with monitor organisms (also called biomonitors) which are organisms that bioaccumulate **toxic substance**s present in trace amounts in the environment. For example, when it is difficult to measure directly the low concentrations of a pollutant in water, chemical analysis of shellfish tissues from that location may show much higher, easily detected concentrations of that pollutant. In this case, the shellfish is used to monitor the level of the long-term presence of that pollutant in the area.

In the environmental field, bioindicators are commonly used in field investigations of contaminated sites to document impacts on the biological community and ecosystem. These studies are then followed up with focused laboratory tests to pinpoint the source of toxicity or stress. After clean-up and remedial actions have been implemented at a site, bioindicators are also used to track the effectiveness of the remediation activity. In the future, bioindicators may be used more widely as investigative and decision-making tools from the initial pollution and impact assessment stage to the remediation and post-remediation monitoring stages.

[*Usha Vedagiri*]

FURTHER READING

Connell, D. W., and G. J. Miller. *Chemistry and Ecotoxicology of Pollution.* New York: Wiley-Interscience, 1984.

Biological community

A biological community is an association or assemblage of populations of organisms living in a localized area or **habitat**. The community is a level of organization incorporating individual organisms, **species**, and populations. A population is an assemblage of one species, and the community is a collage of one or more populations. Communities may be large or small, ranging from the microscopic to the level of **biome** and **biosphere**.

"Community," as contrasted conceptually to **ecosystem**, does not necessarily include consideration of the physical **environment** or the habitat of a particular group of organisms, though it is of course impossible to understand fully the dynamics of a community without reference to the resources on which it exists. The term ecosystem was coined to incorporate study of a community together with its physical environment. Still, communities are adaptive systems, inseparable from and evolving in response to changing environmental conditions. So, the supply and availability of resources in the environment and also time are considerations in the dynamics of community structure and relationships. Individual communities may be relatively stable or in constant flux. Actual equilibrium may never exist but, even in approximation, it must be viewed as a dynamic state—the community in constant, subtle flux and change.

Biological communities are "interactional fields" characterized by a complicated set of interactions among complex assemblages, both within the locale and from without—including trophic relationships, the "who eats who" of energy exchanges. Interactions may be proximal or between locales (close by or quite widely separated), including intensive, extensive, or limited exchanges with the outside world. Organisms in communities interact both functionally and spatially or locationally, both "horizontally" and "vertically," interactions often independent of each other and not reducible to one or the other. Not all organisms necessarily interact with all the others, some may be almost totally uncoupled from some of the others and coexist relatively independently.

Most questions in community ecology focus on the "existence, importance, looseness, transience, and contingency of interactions." The degree to which these interactions result in meaningful biological patterns is still an open question—though particular communities are usually identified by some pattern of interactions, if only to set them off from others for the purposes of scientific study.

[*Gerald L. Young*]

FURTHER READING

Drake, J. A. "The Mechanics of Community Assembly and Succession." *Journal of Theoretical Biology* 147 (1990): 213-233.

Richardson, J. L. "The Organismic Community: Resilience of an Embattled Ecological Concept." *BioScience* 30 (1988): 465-471.

Roughgarden, J. *The Structure and Assembly of Communities.* In *Perspectives in Ecological Theory,* edited by J. Roughgarden, R. M. May, and S. A. Levin. Princeton: Princeton University Press, 1989.

Strong, D. R., Jr., et. al., eds. *Ecological Communities: Conceptual Issues and the Evidence.* Princeton: Princeton University Press, 1984.

Taylor, P. J. "Community." In *Keywords in Evolutionary Biology*, edited by E. Keller and E. Lloyd. Cambridge: Harvard University Press, 1991.

Biological fertility

The number of offspring produced by a female organism. In a population, biological fertility is measured as the general fertility rate (the birth rate multiplied by the number of sexually productive females) or as the total fertility rate (the lifetime average number of offspring per female). General dictionaries list fertility and fecundity as synonyms for reproductive fruitfulness. In **population biology**, biological fertility refers to the number of offspring actually produced, while fecundity is merely the biological ability to reproduce. Fecund individuals that fail to mate do not produce offspring (that is, are not biologically fertile), and do not contribute to **population growth**.

Biological magnification

See **Biomagnification**

Biological methylation

The process by which a methyl radical ($-CH_3$) is chemically combined with some other substance through the action of a living organism. One of the most environmentally important examples of this process is the methylation of **mercury** in the sediments of lakes, rivers, and other bodies of water. Elementary mercury and many of its inorganic compounds have relatively low toxicity because they are insoluble. However, in sediments, bacteria can convert mercury to an organic form, methylmercury, that is soluble in fat. When ingested by animals, methylmercury accumulates in body fat and exerts highly toxic, sometimes fatal, effects. *See also* Minamata disease

Biological oxygen demand

See **Biochemical oxygen demand**

Biological Resources Division (formerly National Biological Service) (Washington, D.C.)

Created to assess, monitor and research biological resources in United States, the Biological Resources Division (BRD) of the United States Geological Survey (USGS) is the non-regulatory biological research component of the United States Department of the Interior. First created in 1994 as the National Biological Survey (NBS), an independent agency within the **U.S. Department of the Interior**, the NBS was merged with the USGS (also part of the Interior Department) in 1996.

The BRD is the principal biological research and monitoring agency of the federal government. It is responsible for gathering, analyzing, and disseminating biological information in order to support sound management and stewardship of nation's biological and natural resources. It is also directed to foster understanding of biological systems and their benefits to society, and to make biological information available to the public. Although it was created mainly on the impetus of environmental and scientific organizations, the BRD also supports commercial and economic interests in that it seeks to identify opportunities for sustainable resource use. Agriculture and **biotechnology** are among the industries that stand to benefit from BRD research on new sources of food, fiber, and medicines.

Because it is independent of regulatory agencies—which are responsible for enforcing laws—the BRD has no formal regulatory, management, or enforcement roles. Therefore the BRD does not enforce laws such as the **Endangered Species Act**. Instead the BRD is responsible for gathering data that are scientifically sound and unbiased. The BRD also fosters public-private cooperation. For example it worked with the International Paper Company in Alabama to develop a management plan for two species of pitcher plants found on company land that were candidates for the Endangered Species List. If it succeeds, this management plan will both preserve the pitcher plant populations—preventing the legal complications of having it listed as a federally endangered species—and allow continued judicious use of the land and resources.

The Biological Resources Division of the USGS was created in 1994 as an independent agency with the name National Biological Survey. The Survey was established on November 11, 1994 on the recommendations of President Bill Clinton and Interior Secretary Bruce Babbit. Renamed the National Biological Service (NBS) shortly after its creation, the agency was created by combining the biological research, inventory, and monitoring programs of seven agencies within the Department of the Interior. Built on the model of the Geological Survey, the NBS was established to provide accurate baseline data about ecosystems and species in United States territory. The mission of the NBS was to provide information to support sound stewardship of natural resources on public lands under the administration of the Department of the Interior. Part of its mission was also to foster cooperation among other entities involved in managing, monitoring, and researching natural resources. On October 1, 1996 the NBS was renamed the Biological Resources Division and merged with the United States Geological Survey. The USGS-BRD retains the research and information provision mandates of the NBS. Appointed as the first NBS/BRD director was H. Ronald Pulliam, a professor and research ecologist from of the Institute of Ecology and the University of Georgia in Athens.

The National Biological Service had a predecessor in the Bureau of Biological Survey, which operated as part of the Department of Agriculture from 1885-1939. The Bureau's first director, C. Hart Merriam, revolutionized biological collection techniques and in 15 years nearly quadrupled the number of known American mammal species. In 1939, the Bureau was transferred to the Department of the Interior, where it was the predecessor to the Fish and Wildlife Service. After its transfer to the Department of the Interior, the Bureau of Biological Survey's baseline data gathering and survey functions gradually diminished. The Fish and Wildlife Service now has regulatory and management responsibilities as well as research programs.

In recent years the need for a biological survey, and especially for the production of reliable baseline data, has resurfaced. The resurgence of interest in baseline data results in part from an interest in managing **ecosystem**s, with a focus on stewardship and ecosystem restoration, in place of previous emphasis on individual species management. Managing and restoring ecosystems requires basic data and information on biological indicators, which are often unavailable. Interest in threatened and **endangered species**, and public participation in environmental organizations probably also contributed to the widespread support for establishing a biological survey.

The BRD is important because it is the only federal agency whose principal mission is to perform basic scientific, biological and ecological research. As an explicitly scientific research body, the BRD works to incorporate current ecological theory in its research and monitoring programs. Central to the BRD's mission are ideas such as long-term stewardship of resources, maintaining **biodiversity**, identifying ecological services of biological resources, anticipating climate change, and restoring populations and habitats. Because of its emphasis on basic research the BRD can address current scientific themes that pertain to public policy such as fire ecology, endocrine disruptors (chemicals such as **pentachlorophenols [PCPs]** that interfere with endocrine and reproductive functions in animals), ecological roles of **wetlands**, and **habitat** restoration. The primary purpose of this research activity is to provide land managers, especially within the Department of the Interior, with sound information to guide their management policies.

The BRD has two broad categories of research activities. One focus is on **species** for which the Department of Interior has trust responsibilities, including endangered species, marine mammals, migratory birds, and anadromous fish such as salmon. Research on these organisms involves studies of physiology, behavior, population dynamics, and mortality. The second general focus is on ecosystems. This class of research is directed at using experimentation, modeling, and observation to produce practical information concerning the complex interactions and functions of ecosystems, as well as human-induced changes in ecosystems.

In addition to these ecological research questions, the BRD is mandated to perform basic classification, mapping, and description functions. The division is responsible for classifying and mapping species within the United States, as well as prospecting for new species. It is also directed to develop a standard classification system for ecological units, biological indicators for **ecosystem health**, protocols for managing **pollution**, and guidelines for ecosystem restoration.

Part of this basic assessment function is a series of National Status and Trends Reports, to be released by the BRD every two years. These reports are to assess the health of biological resources and to report trends in their decline or improvement. The first two National Status and Trends Reports were released in 1995 and 1997. The 1995 report included more than 200 contributions on monitoring and population trends for plant, invertebrate, and vertebrate species, as well as summaries on the status of several biological communities and ecosystems. The 1997 report, published in two volumes, discusses factors such as natural processes, harvest exploitation, contaminants, **land use**, water use, nonindigenous species, and climate change that affect ecosystems in the United States. This status report also includes a major section discussing marine biological resources.

The USGS-BRD also provides a nationwide coordinated research agenda and a set of priorities for biological research. For example, it has undertaken a set of coordinated regional studies of the wide-ranging biological and ecological impacts of wetland distributions in Colorado, California, Texas, and other regions of the United States. Collectively these studies can provide a picture of nationwide trends and conditions, as well as producing coordinated information on restoration techniques, biodiversity issues, and biological indicators, at the same time as regional wetland problems are being addressed. Similar sets of coordinated studies have begun concerning the effects of endocrine-disrupting chemicals in the environment and on the use of prescribed fire as a management technique in a variety of ecosystems.

One of the principal mandates of the BRD is to distribute information. Free sharing of information is intended to maximize the usefulness of research findings. Part of the information sharing program includes substantial use of the Internet to distribute publications. Even the book-size National Status and Trends Reports are being published online to facilitate easy public access to their findings.

In addition to performing its own research the BRD provides coordination and a network of communication between federal agencies, state governments, universities, museums, and private conservation organizations. The National Partnership for Biological Survey, coordinated by the BRD, provides a network for sharing information and technology between federal, state, and other agencies. Participants in the Partnership include the United States **Forest Service**, the Natural Resources Conservation Service, the **National Oceanic and Atmospheric Administration**, the **Environmental Protection Agency**, the National Science Foundation, the Department of Defense, and the **Army Corps of Engineers**, as well as the Natural Heritage data centers and programs maintained by many states. The network of Natural Heritage programs is coordinated by the **Nature Conservancy**, a private organization dedicated to preserving habitat and species diversity. Also included in the Partnership are museums and universities nationwide that serve as repositories of information on biological resources and that conduct biological research, a range of non-governmental organizations, international conservation and research groups, Native American groups, private land holders, and resource user groups. Contact: U.S. Department of the Interior, Biological Resources Division, Office of Public Affairs, 1849 C St., NW, Washington D.C. 20240.

[*Mary Ann Cunningham*]

FURTHER READING

Biological Resources Division. *Biological Resources Strategic Science Plan.* Washington, D.C.: Government Printing Office, 1996.

Biological Resources Division Home Page, Worldwide Web, March 1997. "National Biological Information Infrastructure (NBII)." http://www.nbs.gov/nbs/whatsnew.html

National Biological Service. *Our Living Resources.* Washington, D.C.: Government Printing Office, 1995.

Biological treatment

See **Bioremediation**

Biomagnification of the pesticide DDT in the food chain.

Bioluminescence

Bioluminescence ("living light") is the production of light by living organisms through a biochemical reaction. The general reaction involves a substrate called luciferin and an enzyme called luciferase, and requires oxygen. Specifically, luciferin is oxidized by luciferase and the chemical energy produced is transformed into light energy. In nature, bioluminescence is fairly widespread among a diverse group of organisms such as bacteria, fungi, sponges, jellyfish, molluscs, crustaceans, some worms, fireflies, and fish. It is totally lacking in vertebrate animals. Fireflies are probably the most commonly recognized examples of bioluminescent organisms, using the emitted light for mate recognition.

Biomagnification

The **bioaccumulation** of **chemicals** in organisms beyond the concentration expected if the chemical was in equilibrium between the organism and its surroundings. Biomagnification can occur in both terrestrial and aquatic environments, but it is generally used in relation to aquatic situations. Most often, biomagnification occurs in the higher **trophic level**s of the **food chain/web**, where exposure to chemicals takes place mostly through food consumption rather than water uptake.

Biomagnification is a specific case of bioaccumulation and is different from bioconcentration. Bioaccumulation describes the accumulation of contaminants in the tissue of organisms. Typical examples of this include the elevated levels of many chlorinated **pesticide**s and **mercury** in fish tissue. Bioconcentration is used to describe the concentration of a chemical in an organism from water uptake alone. This is quantitatively described by the bioconcentration factor, or BCF, which is the chemical concentration in tissue divided by the chemical concentration in water, expressed in equivalent units, at equilibrium. The vast majority of chemicals that bioaccumulate are aromatic organic compounds, particularly those with **chlorine** substituents. For organic compounds, the mechanism of bioaccumulation is thought to be the partitioning or solubilization of chemical into the lipids of the organism. Thus the BCF should be proportional to the lipophilicity of the chemical, which is described by the octanol-water partition coefficient, Kow. The latter is a physical-chemical property of the compound describing its relative solubility in an organic phase and is the ratio of its solubility in octanol to its solubility in water at equilibrium. It is constant at a given temperature. If one assumes that a chemical's solubility in octanol is similar to its solubility in lipid, then we can approximate the lipid-normalized BCF as equal to the Kow. This assumption has been shown to be a reasonable first approximation for most chemicals accumulation in fish tissue.

However, animals are exposed to contaminants by other routes in addition to passive partitioning from water. For instance, fish can take up chemical from the food they eat. It has been noted in field collections that for certain chemicals, the observed fish-water ratio (BCF) is significantly greater than the theoretical BCF, based on Kow. This indicates that the chemical has accumulated to a greater extent than its equilibrium concentration. This is defined as biomagnification. This condition has been documented in aquatic animals, including fish, shellfish, **seals and sea lions**, **whales**, and otters, and in birds, mink, rodents, and humans in both laboratory and field studies.

The biomagnification factor, BMF, is usually described as the ratio of the observed lipid-normalized BCF to Kow, which is the theoretical lipid-normalized BCF. This is equivalent to the multiplication factor above the equilibrium concentration. If this ratio is equal to or less than one, then the compound has not biomagnified. If the ratio is greater than one, then the chemicals biomagnified by that factor. For instance, if a chemical's Kow were one hundred thousand, then its lipid normalized BCF should be one hundred thousand if the chemical were in equilibrium in the organism's lipids. If the fish tissue concentration (normalized to lipids) were five hundred thousand, then the chemical would be said to have biomagnified by a factor of five.

Biomagnification in the aquatic food chain often leads to biomagnification in terrestrial food chains, particularly in the case of bird and **wildlife** populations that feed on fish. Consider the following example that demonstrates the results of biomagnification. The concentrations of the insecticide dieldrin in various trophic levels are determined to be the following: water, 0.1 ng/L; **phytoplankton**, 100 ng/g lipid; **zooplankton**, 200 ng/g lipid; fish, 600 ng/g lipid; terns, 800 ng/g lipid. If the Kow were equal to one million, then the phytoplankton would be in equilibrium with the water, but the zooplankton would have magnified the compound by a factor of 2, the fish by a factor of 6, and the terns by a factor of 8.

The mechanism of biomagnification is not completely understood. To achieve a concentration of a chemical greater than its equilibrium value indicates that the elimination rate is slower than for chemicals that reach equilibrium. Transfer efficiencies of the chemical would affect the relative ratio of uptake and elimination. There are many factors that control the uptake and elimination of a chemical from the consumption of contaminated food, and these include factors specific to the chemical as well as factors specific to the organism. The chemical properties include solubility, Kow, molecular weight and volume, and diffusion rates between organism gut, blood, and lipid pools. The organism properties include the feeding rate, diet preferences, assimilation rate into the gut, rate of chemical's metabolism, rate of egestion, and rate of organism growth. It is thought that the chemical's properties control whether biomagnification will occur, and that it is the transfer rate from lipid to blood that allows the chemical to attain a lipid concentration greater than its equilibrium value. Thus it follows that the chemicals that biomagnify have similar properties. They typically are organic; they have molecular weights between 200 and 600 daltons; they have Kows between ten thousand and ten million; they are resistant to **metabolism** by the organism; they are non-ionic, neutral compounds; and they have molecular volumes between 260 and 760 cubic angstroms, a cross sectional width of less than 9.5 angstoms and a molecular surface area between 200 and 460 square angstroms. The latter dimensions allow them to more easily pass through lipid bilayers

into cells but perhaps do not allow them to leave the cell easily due to their high lipophilicity. Since this dis-equilibrium would occur at each trophic level, it results in more and more biomagnification at each higher trophic level. Because humans occupy a very high trophic level, we are particularly vulnerable to adverse health effects as a result of exposure to chemicals that biomagnify.

[*Deborah L. Swackhammer*]

FURTHER READING

Bierman, V. J., Jr. "Equilibrium Partitioning and Biomagnification of Organic Chemicals in Benthic Animals." *Environmental Science and Technology* 24 (September 1990); 1407-12.

Connell, D. W. *Bioaccumulation of Xenobiotic Compounds*. Boca Raton, FL.: CRC Press, 1990.

Sijm, D., W. Seinen, and A. Opperhuizen. "Life Cycle Biomagnification Study in Fish." *Environmental Science and Technology* 26 (November 1992): 2162-74.

Biomass

Biomass is a measure of the amount of biological substance minus its water content found at a given time and place on the earth's surface. Although sometimes defined strictly as living material, in actual practice the term often refers to living organisms, or parts of living organisms, as well as waste products or non-decomposed remains. It is a distinguishing feature of ecological systems and is usually presented as biomass density in units of dry weight per unit area. The term is somewhat imprecise in that it includes autotrophic plants, referred to as phytomass, heterotrophic microbes, and animal material, or zoomass. In most settings, phytomass is by far the most important component. A square meter of the planet's land area has, on average, about 22.05 to 26.46 pounds (10-12 kilograms) of phytomass, although values may vary widely depending on the type of **biome**. **Tropical rain forest**s average about 45 kg/m² while a **desert** biome may have a value near zero. The global average for heterotrophic biomass is approximately 0.1 kg/m², and the average for human biomass has been estimated at 0.5 g/m² if permanently glaciated areas are excluded.

The nature of biomass varies widely. Density of fresh material ranges from a low of 0.14 g/cm³ for floats of aquatic plants to values greater that 1 g/cm³ for very dense hardwood. The water content of fresh material may be as low as 5 percent in mature seeds or as high as 95 percent in fruits and young shoots. Water levels for living plants and animals run from 50 to 80 percent, depending on the **species**, season, and growing conditions. To insure a uniform basis for comparison, biomass samples are dried at 221°F (105°C) until they reach a constant weight.

Organic compounds typically constitute about 95 percent by weight of the total biomass, and nonvolatile residue, or ash, about 5 percent. **Carbon** is the principle element in biomass and usually represents about 45 percent of the total. An exception occurs in species that incorporate large amounts of inorganic elements such as silicon or calcium, in which case the carbon content may be much lower and nonvolatile residue several times higher. Another exception is found in tissues rich in lipids (oil or fat), where the carbon content may reach values as high as 70 percent.

Photosynthesis is the principle agent for biomass production. Light energy is used by chlorophyll-containing green plants to remove (or fix) carbon dioxide from the atmosphere and convert it to energy rich organic compounds or biomass. It has been estimated that on the face of the earth approximately 200 billion tons of **carbon dioxide** are converted to biomass each year. Carbohydrates are usually the primary constituent of biomass, and cellulose is the single most important component. Starches are also important and predominate in storage organs such as tubers and rhizomes. Sugars reach high levels in fruits and in plants such as sugar cane and sugar beet. Lignin is a very significant non-carbohydrate constituent of woody plant biomass. *See also* Animal waste; Biodegradable; Biogeochemical cycles; Biosphere; Carbon cycle; Ecosystem

[*Douglas C. Pratt*]

FURTHER READING

Lieth, H. F. H. *Patterns of Primary Production in the Biosphere.* Stroudsburg, PA: Dowden, Hutchinson, and Ross, distributed by Academic Press, 1978.

Smil, V. *Biomass Energies: Resources, Links, Constraints.* New York: Plenum Press, 1983.

Biomass fuel

A **biomass** fuel is an energy source derived from living organisms. Most commonly it is plant residue, harvested, dried and burned, or further processed into solid, liquid, or gaseous fuels. The most familiar and widely used biomass fuel is wood. Agricultural waste, including materials such as the cereal straw, seed hulls, corn stalks and cobs, is also a significant source. Native shrubs and herbaceous plants are potential sources. **Animal waste**, although much less abundant overall, is a bountiful source in some areas.

Wood accounted for 25 percent of all energy used in the United States at the beginning of this century. With increased use of **fossil fuels**, its significance rapidly declined. By 1976, only 1 to 2 percent of United States energy was supplied by wood, and burning of tree wastes by the forest products industry accounted for most of it. Although the same trend has been evident in all industrialized countries, the decline has not been as dramatic everywhere. Sweden, for instance, still meets 8 percent of its energy needs with wood, and Finland, 15 percent.

Globally, it is estimated that biomass supplies about 6 or 7 percent of total energy, and it continues to be a very important energy source for many developing countries. In the last 15 to 20 years, interest in biomass has greatly increased even in countries where its use has drastically declined. In the United States rising fuel prices led to a large increase in the use of wood-burning stoves and furnaces for space heating. Impending fossil fuel shortages have greatly increased research on its use in the United States and elsewhere. Because biomass is a potentially **renewable** resource, it is recognized as a possible replacement of **petroleum** and **natural gas**.

Historically, burning has been the primary mode for using biomass, but because of its large water content it must be dried to burn effectively. In the field, the energy of the sun may be all that is needed to sufficiently lower its water level. When this is not sufficient, another energy source may be needed.

Biomass is not as concentrated an energy source as most fossil fuels even when it is thoroughly dry. Its density may be increased by milling and compressing dried residues. The resulting briquettes or pellets are also easier to handle, store, and transport. Compression has been used with a variety of materials including crop residues, herbaceous native plant material, sawdust, and other forest wastes.

Solid fuels are not as convenient or versatile as liquids or gases, and this is a drawback to the direct use of biomass. Fortunately, a number of techniques are known for converting it to liquid or gaseous forms.

Partial **combustion** is one method. In this procedure, biomass is burned in an environment with restricted oxygen. **Carbon monoxide** and **hydrogen** are formed instead of **carbon dioxide** and water. This mixture is called **synthetic gas** or "syngas." It can serve as fuel although its energy content is lower than natural gas (methane). Syngas may also be converted to **methanol**, a one carbon-alcohol that can be used as a transportation fuel. Because methanol is a liquid, it is easy to store and transport.

Anaerobic digestion is another method for forming gases from biomass. It uses microorganisms, in the absence of oxygen, to convert organic materials to **methane**. This method is particularly suitable for animal and human waste. Animal **feedlots** faced with disposal problems may install microbial gasifiers to convert waste to gaseous fuel used to heat farm buildings or generate electricity.

For materials rich in starch and sugar, fermentation is an attractive alternative. Through acid hydrolysis or enzymatic digestion, starch can be extracted and converted to sugars. Sugars can be fermented to produce **ethanol**, a liquid biofuel with many potential uses.

Cellulose is the single most important component of plant biomass. Like starch, it is made of linked sugar components that may be easily fermented when separated from the cellulose polymer. The complex structure of cellulose makes separation difficult, but enzymatic means are being developed to do so. Perfection of this technology will create a large potential for ethanol production using plant materials that are not human foods.

The efficiency with which biomass may be converted to ethanol or other convenient liquid or gaseous fuels is a major concern. Conversion generally requires appreciable energy. If an excessive amount of expensive fuel is used in the process, costs may be prohibitive. Corn (*Zea mays*) has been a particular focus of efficiency studies. Inputs for the corn system include energy for production and application of **fertilizer** and **pesticide**, tractor fuel, on-farm electricity, etc., as well as those more directly related to fermentation. A recent estimate puts the industry average for energy output at

133 percent of that needed for production and processing. This net energy gain of 33 percent includes credit for co-products such as corn oil and protein feed as well as the energy value of ethanol. The most efficient production and conversion systems are estimated to have a net energy gain of 87 percent. Although it is too soon to make an accurate assessment of the net energy gain for cellulose-based ethanol production, it has been estimated that a net energy gain of 145 percent is possible.

Biomass-derived gaseous and liquid fuels share many of the same characteristics as their fossil fuel counterparts. Once formed, they can be substituted in whole or in part for petroleum-derived products. **Gasohol**, a mixture of 10 percent ethanol in **gasoline**, is an example. Ethanol contains about 35 percent oxygen, much more than gasoline, and a gallon contains only 68 percent of the energy found in a gallon of gasoline. For this reason, motorists may notice a slight reduction in gas mileage when burning gasohol. However, automobiles burning mixtures of ethanol and gasoline have a lower exhaust temperature. This results in reduced toxic **emission**s, one reason that clean air advocates often favor gasohol use in urban areas.

Biomass is called as a renewable resource since green plants are essentially solar collectors that capture and store sunlight in the form of chemical energy. Its renewability assumes that source plants are grown under conditions where yields are sustainable over long periods of time. Obviously, this is not always the case, and care must be taken to insure that growing conditions are not degraded during biomass production.

A number of studies have attempted to estimate the global potential of biomass energy. Although the amount of sunlight reaching the earth's surface is substantial, less than a tenth of a percent of the total is actually captured and stored by plants. About half of it is reflected back to space. The rest serves to maintain global temperatures at life-sustaining levels. Other factors that contribute to the small fraction of the sun's energy that plants store include Antarctic and Arctic zones where little **photosynthesis** occurs, cold winters in temperate belts when plant growth is impossible, and lack of adequate water in **arid** regions. The global total net production of biomass energy has been estimated at 100 million megawatts per year per year. Forests and woodlands account for about 40 percent of the total, and oceans about 35 percent. Approximately one percent of all biomass is used as food by humans and other animals.

Soil requires some organic content to preserve structure and fertility. The amount required varies widely depending on **climate** and soil type. In **tropical rain forest**s, for instance, most of the **nutrient**s are found in living and decaying vegetation. In the interests of preserving photosynthetic potential, it is probably inadvisable to remove much if any organic matter from the soil. Likewise, in sandy soils, organic matter is needed to maintain fertility and increase water retention. Considering all the constraints on biomass harvesting, it has been estimated that about 6 million MWyr/yr of biomass are available for energy use. This represents about 60 percent of human society's total energy

use and assumes that the planet is converted into a global garden with a carefully managed "photosphere."

Although biomass fuel potential is limited, it provides a basis for significantly reducing society's dependence on non-renewable reserves. Its potential is seriously diminished by factors that degrade growing conditions either globally or regionally. Thus, the impact of factors like global warming and **acid rain** must be taken into account to assess how well that potential might eventually be realized. It is in this context that one of the most important aspects of biomass fuel should be noted. Growing plants remove carbon dioxide from the **atmosphere** that is released back to the atmosphere when biomass fuels are used. Thus the overall concentration of atmospheric carbon dioxide should not change, and global warming should not result. Another environmental advantage arises from the fact that biomass contains much less sulfur than most fossil fuels. As a consequence, biomass fuels should reduce the impact of acid rain. *See also* Alternative energy sources; Automobile emissions; Biosphere; Carbon cycle; Environmental degradation; Enzyme; Food waste; Greenhouse effect; Methane digester; Refuse-derived fuel; Soil fertility; Soil organic matter; Sustainable agriculture; Synthetic fuels

[*Douglas C. Pratt*]

FURTHER READING

Häfele, W. *Energy in a Finite World: A Global Systems Analysis.* Great Britain: Harper & Row Ltd., Inc., 1981.

Hall, C. W. *Biomass as an Alternative Fuel.* Rockville, Maryland: Government Institutes, Inc., 1981.

Lieth, H. F. H. *Patterns of Primary Production in the Biosphere.* Stroudsburg, Pennsylvania: Dowden, Hutchinson and Ross, Inc., 1981.

Morris, D. M., & I. Ahmed, *How Much Energy Does It Take to Make a Gallon of Ethanol?* Washington D.C.: Institute for Local Self-Reliance, 1992.

Smil, V. *Biomass Energies: Resources, Links, Constraints.* New York: Plenum Press, 1983.

Stobaugh, R. & D. Yergin, eds. *Energy Future: Report of the Energy Project at the Harvard Business School.* New York: Random House, Inc., 1979.

Biome

A large terrestrial **ecosystem** characterized by distinctive kinds of plants and animals and maintained by a distinct **climate** and **soil** conditions. To illustrate, the **desert** biome is characterized by low annual rainfall and high rates of evaporation, resulting in dry environmental conditions. Plants and animals that thrive in such conditions include cacti, brush, lizards, insects, and small rodents. Special adaptations, such as waxy plant leaves, allow organisms to survive under low moisture conditions. Other examples of biomes include **tropical rain forest**, arctic **tundra**, **grasslands**, temperate **deciduous forest**, **coniferous forest**, tropical **savanna**, and Mediterranean chaparral.

Biomonitoring

See **Bioindicators**

Bioregional Project (Brixley, Missouri)

Based in the Ozark Mountains in Missouri, the Bioregional Project (BP) was founded in 1982 to promote the aims and interests of the bioregional movement in North America. Consisting primarily of a resource center designed to show people how to "come back home to Earth," the Bioregional Project is part of the international campaign to reshape culture and society according to ecological principles: "We work for the honor, protection and healing of the Earth, the Earth's people, and all the Earth's life."

A bioregion is what the group calls a "life region," an area determined by natural rather than historical or political boundaries. It is distinguished by the character of the **flora** and **fauna**, by the landforms, the types of rocks and **soil**s and the climate in general, and by human habitation as it relates to this environment. The Bioregional Project emphasizes the natural logic of these boundaries, and it promotes the development of social and political institutions that take into account the interrelatedness of everything within them. They are working to increase the awareness that bioregions are "living, self-organizing systems," and they value humanity as one **species** among many. The Bioregional Project traces the roots of the movement to native and indigenous peoples and the "oldest Earth traditions." The group believes that ecological laws and principles form the basis of society and that the future survival of humanity depends on their ability to cooperate with the environment.

The Bioregional Project and the bioregional movement as a whole have strong ties to the international Green Movement, although bioregionalists consider themselves more "ecologically-centered." The Greens are oriented to urban areas, and they work for change in traditional political structures, operating within legislative as opposed to bioregional systems. The chief organizing tool of the bioregional movement is a model known as "the bioregional congress" or "green congress," where participants share information, develop ecological strategies, and draft planning programs and platform statements. The Bioregional Project convened the first bioregional congress in 1980 as the Ozark Community Congress (OACC). This congress celebrated its tenth anniversary in 1989, and it has since influenced both bioregional and green organizing throughout North America. The Project coordinated the first North American Bioregional Congress in 1984, an international assembly attended by over 200 people representing 130 organizations.

In addition to the assistance it provides for "those organizing bioregionally," the Bioregional Project also publishes books and pamphlets on **bioregionalism** and **ecology**. The organization sponsors lectures and educational presentations on these subjects as well. It supports research and lends technical assistance in a variety of areas from community economic development to **recycling**, **sustainable agriculture**, and forest protection. It is a subsidiary of the Ozarks Resource Center. Contact: Bioregional Project, Box 3, Brixley, MO 65618.

[*Douglas Smith*]

Bioregionalism

Drawing heavily upon the cultures of **indigenous peoples**, bioregionalism is a philosophy of living that stresses harmony with **nature** and the integration of humans as part of the natural **ecosystem**. The keys to bioregionalism involve learning to live off the land, without damaging the **environment** or relying on heavy industrial machines or products. Bioregionalists believe that if the relationship between nature and humans improves the society as a whole will benefit.

Environmentalists who practice this philosophy "claim" a bioregion or area. For example, one's place might be a **watershed**, a small mountain range, a particular area of the coast, or a specific **desert**. To develop a connection to the land and a sense of place, bioregionalists try to understand the natural history of the area as well as how it supports human life. For example, they study the plants and animals that inhabit the region, the geological features of the land, as well as the cultures of the people who live or have lived in the area.

Bioregionalism also stresses community life where participation, self-determination, and local control play important roles in protecting the environment. Various bioregional groups exist throughout the United States, ranging from the Gulf of Maine to the Ozark Mountains to the San Francisco Bay area. A North American Bioregional Congress loosely coordinates the bioregional movement.

[*Christopher McGrory Klyza*]

FURTHER READING

Andruss, V., et al. *Home! A Bioregional Reader*. Philadelphia: New Society Publishers, 1990.

Sale, K. *Dwellers in the Land: The Bioregional Vision*. San Francisco: Sierra Club Books, 1985.

Snyder, G. *The Practice of the Wild*. San Francisco: North Point Press, 1990.

Bioremediation

A number of processes for remediating **contaminated soil**s and **groundwater** based on the use of microorganisms to convert contaminants to less hazardous substances. Most commercial bioremediation processes are intended to convert organic substances to **carbon dioxide** and water, although processes for addressing metals are under development. Many bacteria ubiquitously found in **soil**s and groundwater are able to biodegrade a range of organic compounds. Compounds found in nature, and ones similar to those, such as petroleum **hydrocarbons**, are most readily biodegraded by these bacteria. Bioremediation of chlorinated solvents, **polychlorinated biphenyl (PCB)**s, **pesticide**s, and many munitions compounds, while of great interest, is more difficult and has thus been much slower to reach commercialization.

In most bioremediation processes the bacteria use the contaminant as a food and energy source and thus survive and grow in numbers at the expense of the contaminant. In order to grow new cells, bacteria, like other biological **species**, require numerous minerals as well as **carbon** sources. These minerals are typically present in sufficient amounts except for

phosphorus and **nitrogen**, which are commonly added during bioremediation. If contaminant molecules are to be transformed, species called **electron acceptor**s must also be present. By far the most commonly used electron acceptor is oxygen. Other electron acceptors include nitrate, sulfate, carbon dioxide, and iron. Processes that use oxygen are called **aerobic** biodegradation. Processes that use other electron acceptors are commonly lumped together as **anaerobic** biodegradation.

The vast majority of commercial bioremediation processes use aerobic biodegradation and thus include some method for providing oxygen. The amount of oxygen that must be provided depends not only on the mass of contaminant present but also on the extent of conversion of the contaminants to carbon dioxide and water, other sources of oxygen, and the extent to which the contaminants are physically removed from the soils or groundwater. Typically, designs are based on adding two to three pounds of oxygen for each pound of biodegradable contaminant.

The processes generally include the addition of nutrient (nitrogen and phosphorus) sources. The amount of nitrogen and phosphorus that must be provided is quite variable and frequently debated. In general, this amount is less than the 100:10:1 ratio of carbon to nitrogen to phosphorus of average cell compositions. It is also important to maintain the soil or groundwater **pH** near neutral (pH 6 to 8.5), moisture levels at or above 50 percent of field capacity, and temperatures between 4°C (39°F) and 35°C (95°F), preferably between 20°C (68°F) and 30°C (86°F).

Bioremediation can be applied in situ and ex situ by several methods. Each of these processes are basically engineering solutions to providing oxygen (or alternate electron acceptors) and possibly, nutrients to the contaminated soils, which already contain the bacteria. The addition of other bacteria is not typically needed or beneficial.

In situ processes have the advantage of causing minimal disruption to the site and can be used to address contamination under existing structures. In situ bioremediation to remediate **aquifer**s contaminated with petroleum hydrocarbons such as gasoline, was pioneered in the 1970s and early 1980s by Richard L. Raymond and coworkers. These systems used groundwater recovery wells to capture contaminated water which was treated at the surface and reinjected after amendment with nutrients and oxygen. The nutrients consisted of ammonium chloride and phosphate salts and sometimes contained magnesium, manganese, and iron salts. Oxygen was introduced by sparging (bubbling) air into the reinjection water. As the injected water swept through the aquifer, oxygen and nutrients were carried to the contaminated soils and groundwater where the indigenous bacteria converted the hydrocarbons to new cell material, carbon dioxide, and water. Variations of this technology include the use of hydrogen peroxide as a source of oxygen and direct injection of air into the aquifer.

Bioremediation of soils located between the ground surface and the water table is most commonly practiced through **bioventing**. In this method, oxygen is introduced into the contaminated soils by either injecting air or extracting air from wells. The systems used are virtually the same as for vapor extraction. The major difference is in mode of operation and in the fact that nutrients are sometimes added by percolating nutrient amended water through the soil from the ground surface or buried horizontal pipes. Systems designed for bioremediation operate at low air flow rates to replace oxygen consumed during biodegradation and to minimize physical removal of volatile contaminants.

Bioremediation can be applied to excavated soils by landfarming, soil cell techniques, or in soil **slurries**. The simplest method is landfarming. In this method soils are spread to a depth of 12 to 18 inches (30 to 46 cm). Nutrients, usually commercial **fertilizer**s with high nitrogen and low phosphorous content, are added periodically to the soils which are tilled or plowed frequently. In most instances, the treatment area is prepared by grading, laying down an impervious layer (clay or a synthetic liner), and adding a six-inch layer of clean soil or sand. Provisions for treating rainwater **runoff** are typically required. The frequent tilling and plowing breaks up soil clumps and exposes the soils and thus bacteria to air. This method is more suitable for treating silty and clayey soils than are most of the other methods. It is not generally appropriate for soils contaminated with volatile contaminants such as **gasoline** because vapors can not be controlled unless the process is conducted within a closed structure.

Excavated soils can also be treated in cells or piles. A synthetic liner is placed on a graded area and covered with sand or gravel to permit collection of runoff water. The sands or gravel are covered with a permeable fabric and nutrient amended soils are added. Slotted PVC pipe is added as the pile is built. The soils are covered with a synthetic liner and the PVC pipes are connected to a blower. Air is slowly extracted from the soils and, if necessary, treated before being discharged to the **atmosphere**. This method requires less room than landfarming and less maintenance during operations, and can be used to treat volatile contaminants because the vapors can be controlled.

Excavated soils can also be treated in soil/water slurries in either commercial reactors or in impoundments or lagoons. Soils are separated from oversize materials and mixed with water, nutrients are added, and the slurry is aerated to provide oxygen. In some cases additional sources of bacteria and/or surfactants are added. These systems are usually capable of attaining more rapid rates of biodegradation than other systems but have limited throughput.

Selection and design of a particular bioremediation method requires that the site be carefully investigated to define the lateral and horizontal extent of contamination including the total mass of **biodegradable** substances. Understanding the soil types and distribution and the site **hydrogeology** is as important as identifying the contaminants and their distribution in both soils and groundwater. Designing bioremediation systems requires the integration of microbiology, chemistry, hydrogeology, and engineering.

Bioremediation is generally viewed favorably by regulatory agencies and is actively supported by the U. S. **Environmental Protection Agency (EPA)**. The mostly favor-

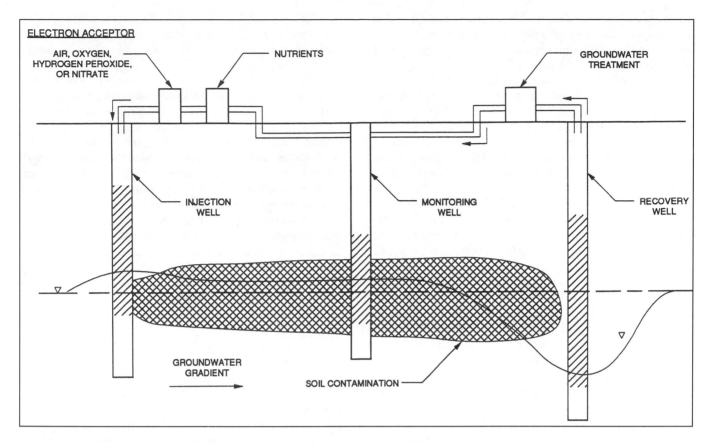

Bioremediation of the saturated zone using hydrogen peroxide in the Raymond process.

able publicity and the perception of bioremediation as a natural process has led to greater acceptance by the public compared to other technologies, such as incineration. It is expected that the use of bioremediation to treat soils and groundwater contaminated with petroleum hydrocarbons and other readily biodegradable compounds will continue to grow. Continued improvements in the design and engineering of bioremediation systems will result from the expanding use of bioremediation in a competitive market. It is anticipated that processes for treating the more recalcitrant organic compounds and metals will become commercial through greater understanding of microbiology and specific developments in the isolation of special bacteria and **genetic engineering**. *See also* Hazardous waste site remediation; Injection well; Vapor recovery system

[*Robert D. Norris*]

FURTHER READING

Chapelle, F. H. *Ground-Water Microbiology and Geochemistry.* New York: Wiley, 1993.

Hinchee, R. E., and R. F. Olfenbuttel, eds. *In Situ Bioreclamation: Applications and Investigation for Hydrocarbons and Contaminated Site Remediation.* Butterworth-Heinemann, 1991.

Hinchee, R. E., and R. F. Olfenbuttel, eds. *On-Site Bioreclamation: Processes for Xenobiotic and Hydrocarbon Treatment.* Butterworth-Heinemann, 1991.

Matthews, J. E., ed. *In Situ Bioremediation of Groundwater and Geological Materials: A Review of Technologies.* Chelsea, MI: Lewis, 1993.

National Research Council. *In Situ Bioremediation: When Does It Work?* Washington, DC: National Academy Press, 1993.

Biosequence

A sequence of **soil**s that contain distinctly different soil **horizon**s because of the influence that vegetation had on the soils during their development. A typical biosequence would be the prairie soils in a dry environment, oak-savannah soils as a transition zone, and forested soils in a wetter environment. Prairie soils have dark, thick surface horizons while forested soils have a thin, dark surface with a light-colored zone below.

Biosphere

The biosphere is the largest possible earthly organismic community. It is a terrestrial envelope of life, or the total global **biomass** of living matter. The biosphere incorporates every individual organism and **species** on the face of the earth—those that walk on the ground or live in the crevices of rock and down into the soil, those that swim in rivers, lakes and oceans, and those that move in and out of the **atmosphere**.

Bios is the Greek word for life; "sphere" is from the Latin *sphaera*, which means essentially the "circuit or range of action, knowledge or influence," the "place or scene of action or existence," the "natural, normal or proper place." Combined into biosphere, the two ideas define the normal global place of existence for all earthly life-forms and, increasingly, a global area of influence and action for humans. Thinking of the mass of life forms on the earth as the biosphere also provides an impression of circular, cyclic systems and suggests a holistic concept of integration and unity.

A *Scientific American* book on the biosphere described it as "this thin film of air and water and soil and life no deeper than ten miles, or one four-hundredth of the earth's radius [that] is now the setting of the uncertain history of man." G. E. Hutchinson in that same book asked, "What is it that is so special about the biosphere?" He suggested that the answer seems to have three parts: "First, it is a region in which liquid water can exist in substantial quantities. Second, it receives an ample supply of energy from an external source, ultimately from the sun. And third, within it there are interfaces between the liquid, the solid and the gaseous states of matter." Both of these might better describe what LaMont Cole labeled the "ecosphere," the global **ecosystem**—the biosphere plus its abiotic environment. But the significance of Hutchinson's three-part statement is that those three characteristics of the earth's surface make it possible for life to exist. They provide the conditions necessary for the abundant and diverse organisms of the biosphere to live.

Life began in a very different environment than found today: the atmosphere, for example, was mostly **methane**, ammonia, and **carbon dioxide**. As life evolved, it changed the atmosphere (and other abiotic components of the surface of the earth), transforming it into the present oxygen-rich mixture of gases vital to life as it now exists. And those life-forms maintain that critical mixture in a complex, fluctuating system of global cycles.

The diversity and complexity of the biosphere is staggering. The accumulated human knowledge of its workings is prodigious, but even more impressive is the immense ignorance of that complexity. Humans have identified about 1.5 million living members of the biosphere and thus have some knowledge of at least that many. However, conservative estimates of the actual number of species begin at 3 or 3.5 to 5 million species. Recent and less conservative estimates range up to a possible 100 million. That means humans are totally ignorant of anywhere from 50 percent to as much as 98.5 percent of the other members of the earth's biological community. Their existence is suspected, but they cannot be identified or their existence documented by even a name.

One of the concerns about large-scale human ignorance of the biosphere is that many species might be extinguished before they are even known. Human activities, especially destruction of **habitat**, are increasing the normal rate of species **extinction**. The diversity of the biosphere may be diminishing rapidly.

Taxonomically, the biosphere is organized into five kingdoms: monera, protista, **fungi**, animalia, and plantae, and a multitude of subsets of these, including the multiple millions of species mentioned above. G. Piel estimates that of the 1200 to 1800 billion tons dry weight of the biosphere,

most of it—some 99 plus percent—is plant material. All the life-forms in the other four taxons, including animals and obviously the 5 billion-plus humans alive today, are part of that less than one percent.

The biosphere can also be subdivided into **biome**s: a biome incorporates a set of **biotic communities** within a particular region exposed to similar climatic conditions and which have dominant species with similar life cycles, **adaptation**s, and structures. **Deserts**, **grasslands**, temperate **deciduous forest**s, **coniferous forest**s, **tundra**, **tropical rain forest**s, tropical seasonal forests, freshwater biomes, estuaries, **wetlands**, and marine biomes, are examples of specific terrestrial or aquatic biomes.

Another indication of the complexity of the biosphere is a measure of the processes that take place within it, especially the essential processes of **photosynthesis** and **respiration**. The sheer size of the biosphere is indicated by the amount of biomass present. Vitousek and his colleagues estimate the net primary production of the earth's biosphere as 224.5 petagrams, one petagram being equivalent to 10^{15} grams.

The biosphere interacts in constant, intricate ways with other global systems: the atmosphere, lithosphere, hydrosphere, and pedosphere. Maintenance of life in the biosphere depends on this complex network of biological-biological, physical-physical, and biological-physical interactions. All the interactions are mediated by an equally complex system of positive and negative feedbacks—and the total makes up the dynamics of the whole system. Since each and all interpenetrate and react on each other constantly, outlining a global **ecology** is a major challenge.

Normally biospheric dynamics are in a rough balance. The **carbon cycle**, for example, is usually balanced between production and **decomposition**, the familiar equation of photosynthesis and respiration. As Piel notes: "The two planetary cycles of photosynthesis and aerobic metabolism in the biomass not only secure renewal of the biomass but also secure the steady-state mixture of gases in the atmosphere. Thereby, these life processes mediate the inflow and outflow of **solar energy** through the system; they screen out lethal radiation, and they keep the temperature of the planet in the narrow range compatible with life." But human activities, especially the combustion of **fossil fuels**, contribute to increases in carbon dioxide, distorting the balance and in the process changing other global relationships such as the nature of incoming and out-going radiation and differentials in temperature between poles and tropics.

If humans are to better understand the biosphere, many more studies must be undertaken on many levels. A number of levels of biological integration must be recognized and analyzed, each with different properties and each offering scholars special problems and special insights. The totality of the biosphere can be broken down in many different ways, but life extends from the single cell to the totality of the globe. Though biologists usually define their disciplines within the bounds of one level and though they may study only one level, scholars should recognize context, the full range of levels and the interactions between them.

Humans are, of course, one of the species that make up the living biosphere. *Homo sapiens* fits into the Linnean hierarchy on the primate branch. Using that hierarchy as a connective device, humans may take a first step toward understanding how they relate to the rest of the inhabitants of the biosphere, down to the most remote known species.

Humans are without doubt the dominant species in the biosphere. The transformation of radiant energy into useable biological energy is increasingly being diverted by humans to their own use. A common estimate is that humans are now diverting huge amounts of the net primary production of the globe to their own use: perhaps 40 percent of terrestrial production and close to 25 percent of all production is either utilized or wasted through human activity. Net primary production is defined as the amount of energy left after subtracting the respiration of primary producers, or plants, from the total amount of energy. It is the total amount of "food" available from the process of photosynthesis—the amount of biomass available to feed organisms, such as humans, that do not acquire food through photosynthesis.

Humans are displacing their neighbors in the biosphere through a multitude of activities: conversion of natural systems to agriculture, direct consumption of plants, consumption of plants by livestock, harvesting and conversion of forests, **desertification**, and many, many others. The biosphere is the source of all good: humans are an integral part of the biosphere and depend on its functioning for their well-being, for their very lives.

[*Gerald L. Young*]

FURTHER READING

Bradbury, I. K. *The Biosphere.* London/New York: Belhaven Press, 1991.

Clark, W. C., and R. E. Munn, eds. *Sustainable Development of the Biosphere.* Cambridge: Cambridge University Press, 1986.

Piel, G. "The Biosphere." In *Only One World: Our Own to Make and to Keep.* New York: W. H. Freeman, 1992.

Salthe, S. N. "The Evolution of the Biosphere: Towards a New Mythology." *World Futures* 30 (1990): 53–67.

Vitousek, P. M., et al. "Human Appropriation of the Products of Photosynthesis." *BioScience* 36 (1986): 368–373.

Biosphere reserve

A biosphere reserve is an area of land recognized and preserved for its ecological significance. Ideally **biosphere** reserves contain undisturbed, natural **environment**s that represent some of the world's important ecological systems and communities. Biosphere reserves are established in the interest of preserving the genetic diversity of these ecological zones, supporting research and education, and aiding local, **sustainable development**. Official declaration and international recognition of biosphere reserve status is intended to protect ecologically significant areas from development and destruction. Since 1976 an international network of biosphere reserves has developed, with the sanction of the United Nations. Each biosphere reserve is proposed, reviewed, and established by a national biosphere reserve commission in the

home country under United Nations guidelines. Communication among members of the international biosphere network helps reserve managers share data and compare management strategies and problems.

The idea of biosphere reserves first gained international recognition in 1973, when the United Nations Educational and Scientific Organization (UNESCO)'s **Man and the Biosphere Program** (MAB) proposed that a worldwide effort be made to preserve islands of the world's living resources from logging, mining, urbanization, and other environmentally destructive human activities. The term derives from the ecological word "biosphere," which refers to the zone of air, land, and water at the surface of the earth that is occupied by living organisms. Growing concern over the survival of individual species in the 1970s and 1980s led increasingly to the recognition that **endangered species** could not be preserved in isolation. Rather, entire **ecosystem**s, extensive communities of interdependent animals and plants, are needed for threatened species to survive. Another idea supporting the biosphere reserve concept was that of genetic diversity. Generally ecological systems and communities remain healthier and stronger if the diversity of resident **species** is high. An alarming rise in species **extinction**s in recent decades, closely linked to rapid **natural resources** consumption, led to an interest in genetic diversity for its own sake. Concern for such ecological principles as these led to UNESCO's proposal that international attention be given to preserving the earth's ecological systems, not just individual species.

The first biosphere reserves were established in 1976. In that year, eight countries designated a total of 59 biosphere reserves representing ecosystems from **tropical rain forest** to temperate sea coast. The following year 22 more countries added another 72 reserves to the United Nations list, and by 1990 there was a network of 283 reserves established in 72 different countries.

Like **national park**s, **wildlife refuge**s, and other **nature** preserves, the first biosphere reserves aimed to protect the natural environment from surrounding populations, as well as from urban or international exploitation. To a great extent this idea followed the model of United States national parks, whose resident populations were removed so that parks could approximate pristine, undisturbed natural environments.

But in smaller, poorer, or more crowded countries than the United States, this model of the depopulated reserve made little sense. Around most of the world's nature preserves, well-established populations—often indigenous or tribal groups—have lived with and among the area's **flora** and **fauna** for generations or centuries. In many cases, these groups exploit local resources—gathering nuts, collecting firewood, growing food—without damaging their environment. Sometimes, contrary to initial expectations, the activity of **indigenous peoples** proves essential in maintaining **habitat** and species diversity in preserves. Furthermore, local residents often possess an extensive and rare understanding of plant habitat and animal behavior, and their skills in using resources are both valuable and irreplaceable. At the

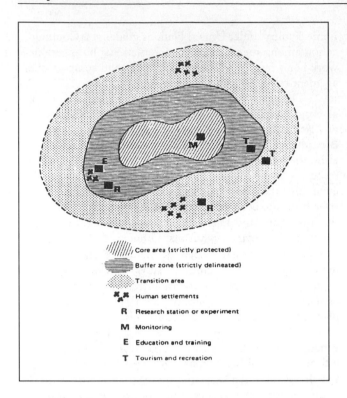

Schematic plan of a biosphere reserve.

very least, the cooperation and support of local populations is essential for the survival of parks in crowded or resource-poor countries. For these reasons, the additional objectives of local cooperation, education, and sustainable economic development were soon added to initial biosphere reserve goals of biological preservation and scientific research. Attention to humanitarian interests and economic development concerns today sets apart the biosphere reserve network from other types of nature preserves, which often garner resentment from local populations who feel excluded and abandoned when national parks are established. United Nations MAB guidelines encourage local participation in management and development of biosphere reserves, as well as in educational programs. Ideally, indigenous groups help administer reserve programs rather than being passive recipients of outside assistance or management.

In an attempt to mesh the diverse objectives of biosphere reserves, the MAB program has outlined a theoretical reserve model consisting of three zones, or concentric rings, with varying degrees of use. The innermost zone, the core, should be natural or minimally disturbed, essentially without human presence or activity. Ideally this is where the most diverse plant and animal communities live and where natural ecosystem functions persist without human intrusion. Surrounding the core is a buffer zone, mainly undisturbed but containing research sites, monitoring stations, and habitat rehabilitation experiments. The outermost ring of the biosphere reserve model is the transition zone. Here there may be sparse settlement, areas of traditional use activities, and tourist facilities.

Many biosphere reserves have been established in previously existing national parks or preserves. This is espe-

cially common in large or wealthy countries where well established park systems existed before the biosphere reserve idea was conceived. In 1991 most of the United States' 47 biosphere reserves lay in national parks or **wildlife** sanctuaries. In countries with few such preserves, nomination for United Nations biosphere reserve status can sometimes attract international assistance and funding. In some instances **debt for nature swaps** have aided biosphere reserve establishment. In such an exchange, international **conservation** organizations purchase part of a country's national debt for a portion of its face value, and in exchange that country agrees to preserve an ecologically valuable region from destruction. Bolivia's Beni Biosphere Reserve came about this way in 1987 when **Conservation International**, a Washington-based organization, paid $100,000 to Citicorp, an international lending institution. In exchange, Citicorp forgave $650,000 in Bolivian debt, loans the bank seemed unlikely to ever recover, and Bolivia agreed to set aside a valuable tropical mahogany forest. This process has also produced other reserves, including Costa Rica's La Amistad, and Ecuador's Yasuni and Galapagos Biosphere Reserves.

In practice, biosphere reserves function well only if they have adequate funding and strong support from national leaders, legislatures, and institutions. Without legal protection and long-term support from the government and its institutions, reserves have no real defense against development interests.

National parks can provide a convenient institutional niche, defended by national laws and public policing agencies, for biosphere reserves. Pre-existing wildlife preserves and game sanctuaries likewise ensure legal and institutional support. Infrastructure—management facilities, access roads, research stations, and trained wardens—is usually already available when biosphere reserves are established in or adjacent to ready-made preserves.

Funding is also more readily available when an established national park or game preserve, with a pre-existing operating budget, provides space for a biosphere reserve. With intense competition from commercial loggers, miners, and developers, money is essential for reserve survival. Especially in poorer countries, international experience increasingly shows that unless there is a reliable budget for management and education, nearby residents do not learn cooperative reserve management, nor do they necessarily support the reserve's presence. Without funding for policing and legal defense, development pressures can easily continue to threaten biosphere reserves. Logging, clearing, and destruction often continue despite an international agreement on paper that resource extraction should cease. Turning parks into biosphere reserves may not always be a good idea. National park administrators in some less wealthy countries fear that biosphere reserve guidelines, with their compromising objectives and strong humanitarian interests, may weaken the mandate of national parks and wildlife sanctuaries set aside to protect endangered species from population pressures and development. In some cases, they argue, there exists a legitimate need to exclude people if **rare species** such as **tigers** or **rhinoceroses** are to survive.

Because of the expense and institutional difficulties of establishing and maintaining biosphere reserves, about two-thirds of the world's reserves exist in the wealthy and highly developed nations of North America and Europe. Poorer countries of Africa, Asia, and South America have some of the most important remaining intact ecosystems, but wealthy countries can more easily afford to allocate the necessary space and money. Developed countries also tend to have more established administrative and protective structures for biosphere reserves and other sanctuaries. An increasing number of developing countries are working to establish biosphere reserves, though. A significant incentive, aside from national pride in indigenous species, is the international recognition given to countries with biosphere reserves. Possession of these reserves grants smaller and less wealthy countries some of the same status as that of more powerful countries such as the United States, Germany, and Russia.

Some difficult issues surround the biosphere reserve movement. One question that arises is whether reserves are chosen for reasons of biological importance or for economic and political convenience. In many cases national biosphere reserve committees overlook critical forests or endangered habitats because logging and mining companies retain strong influence over national policy makers. Another problem is that in and around many reserves, residents are not yet entirely convinced, with some reason, that management goals mesh with local goals. In theory sustainable development methods and education will continue to encourage communication, but cooperation can take a long time to develop. Among reserve managers themselves, great debate continues over just how much human interference is appropriate, acceptable, or perhaps necessary in a place ideally free of human activity. Despite these logistical and theoretical problems, the idea behind biosphere reserves seems a valid one, and the inclusiveness of biosphere planning, both biological and social, is revolutionary. *See also* Biodiversity; Biotic community; Critical habitat; Ecology; Economic growth and the environment; Environmental degradation; Environmental education; Environmental law; Environmental monitoring; Environmental policy; Environmental science; Galapagos Islands; International Geosphere-Biosphere Programme (U.N. Environmental Programme); United Nations Earth Summit; United Nations Environment Programme

[*Mary Ann Cunningham*]

FURTHER READING

Biosphere Reserves: Proceedings of the First National Symposium, Udhagamandalam, 24-26 Septemeber 1986. New Delhi: Ministry of Environment and Forests.

Dogsé, P, and B. Von Droste. *Debt-for-Nature Exchanges and Biosphere Reserves.* Paris: UNESCO, 1990.

Proceedings of the Symposium on Biosphere Reserves, Estes Park, Colorado, 14-17 September 1987. Atlanta, GA: U.S. Department of the Interior.

Biota

See **Biotic community**

Biotechnology

Few developments in science have had the potential for such profound impact on research, technology, and society in general as has biotechnology. Yet authorities do not agree on a single definition of this term. Sometimes, writers have limited the term to techniques used to modify living organisms and, in some instances, the creation of entirely new kinds of organisms.

In most cases, however, a broader, more general definition is used. The Industrial Biotechnology Association, for example, uses the term to refer to any "development of products by a biological process." These products may indeed be organisms or they may be cells, components of cells, or individual and specific chemicals. A somewhat more detailed definition is that of the European Federation of Biotechnology, which defines biotechnology as the "integrated use of biochemistry, microbiology, and engineering sciences in order to achieve technological (industrial) application of the capabilities of microorganisms, cultured tissue cells, and parts thereof."

By almost any definition, biotechnology has been used by humans for thousands of years, long before modern science existed. Some of the oldest manufacturing processes known to humankind make use of biotechnology. Beer, wine, and breadmaking, for example, all occur because of the process of fermentation. During fermentation, microorganisms such as yeasts, molds, and bacteria are mixed with natural products which they use as food. In the case of winemaking, for example, yeasts live on the sugars found in some type of fruit juice, most commonly, grape juice. They digest those sugars and produce two new products, alcohol and **carbon dioxide**.

The alcoholic beverages produced by this process have been, for better or worse, a mainstay of human civilization for untold centuries. In breadmaking, the products of fermentation are responsible for the wonderful odor (the alcohol) and texture (the carbon dioxide) of freshly-baked bread. Cheese and yogurt are two other products formed when microorganisms act on a natural product, in this case milk—changing its color, odor, texture, and taste.

Biotechnology has long been used in a variety of industrial processes also. As early as the seventeenth century, bacteria were used to remove **copper** from its ores. Around 1910, scientists found that bacteria could be used to decompose organic matter in sewage, thus providing a mechanism for dealing efficiently with such materials in **solid waste**. A few years later, a way was found to use microorganisms to produce glycerol synthetically. That technique soon became very important commercially, since glycerol is used in the manufacture of explosives and World War I was about to begin.

Not all forms of biotechnology depend on microorganisms. Hybridization is an example. Farmers long ago learned that they could control the types of animals bred by carefully selecting the parents. In some cases, they actually created entirely new animal forms that do not occur in nature. The mule, a hybrid of horse and donkey, is such an animal.

Hybridization has also been used in plant growing for centuries. Farmers found that they could produce food plants with any number of special qualities by carefully selecting the seeds they plant and by controlling growing conditions. As a result of this kind of process, the two-to-three-inch-long vegetable known as maize has evolved over the years into the foot-long, robust product we call corn. Indeed, there is hardly a fruit or vegetable in our diet today that has not been altered by long decades of hybridization.

Until the late nineteenth century, hybridization was largely a trial-and-error process. Then the work of Gregor Mendel started to become known. Mendel's research on the transmission of hereditary characteristics soon gave agriculturists a solid factual basis on which to conduct future experiments in cross-breeding.

Modern principles of hybridization have made possible a greatly expanded use of biotechnology in agriculture and many other areas. One of the greatest successes of the science has been in the development of new food crops that can be grown in a variety of less-than-optimal conditions. The dramatic increase in harvests made possible by these developments has become known as the **agricultural revolution** or green revolution.

Three decades after the green revolution first changed agriculture in many parts of the world, a number of problems with its techniques have become apparent. The agricultural revolution forced a worldwide shift from subsistence farming to cash farming, and many small farmers in developing countries lack the resources to negotiate this shift. A farmer must make significant financial investments in seed, agricultural chemicals (**fertilizer**s and **pesticide**s), and machinery to make use of new farming techniques. In developing countries, peasants do not have and cannot borrow the necessary capital. The seed, chemicals, machinery, and oil to operate the equipment must commonly be imported, adding to already crippling foreign debts. In addition, the new techniques often have harmful effects on the environment. In spite of problems such as these, however, the green revolution has clearly made an important contribution to the lessening of world hunger.

Modern methods of hybridization have application in many fields besides agriculture. For example, scientists are now using controlled breeding techniques and other methods from biotechnology to insure the survival of species that are threatened or endangered.

The nature of biotechnology has undergone a dramatic change in the last half century. That change has come about with the discovery of the role of **DNA** in living organisms. DNA is a complex molecule that occurs in many different forms. The many forms that DNA can take allow it to store a large amount of information. That information provides cells with the direction they need to carry out all the functions they have to perform in a living organism. It also provides a mechanism by which that information is transmitted efficiently from one generation to the next.

As scientists learned more about the structure of the DNA molecule, they discovered precisely and in chemical terms how genetic information is stored and transmitted.

With that knowledge, they have also developed the ability to modify DNA, creating new instructions that direct cells to perform new and unusual functions. The process of DNA modification has come to be known as **genetic engineering**. Since genetic engineering normally involves combining two different DNA molecules, it is also referred to as recombinant DNA research.

There is little doubt that genetic engineering is the best known form of biotechnology today. Indeed, it is easy to confuse the two terms and to speak of one when it is the other that is meant. However, the two terms are different in the respect that genetic engineering is only one type of biotechnology.

In theory, the steps involved in genetic engineering are relatively simple. First, scientists decide what kind of changes they want to make in a specific DNA molecule. They might, in some cases, want to alter a human DNA molecule to correct some error that results in a disease such as diabetes. In other cases, a researcher might want to add instructions to a DNA molecule that it does not normally carry. He or she might, for example, want to include instructions for the manufacture of a chemical such as insulin in the DNA of bacteria that normally lack the ability to make insulin.

Second, scientists find a way to modify existing DNA to correct errors or add new information. Such methods are now well developed. In one approach, **enzyme**s that "recognize" certain specific parts of a DNA molecule are used to cut open the molecule and then insert the new portion.

Third, scientists look for a way to insert the "correct" DNA molecule into the organisms in which it is to function. Once inside the organism, the new DNA molecule may give correct instructions to cells in humans (to avoid genetic disorders), in bacteria (resulting in the production of new chemicals), or in other types of cells for other purposes.

Accomplishing these steps in practice is not always easy. One major problem is to get an altered DNA molecule to express itself in the new host cells. That the molecule is able to enter a cell does not mean that it will begin to operate and function (express itself) as scientists hope and plan. This means that many of the expectations held for genetic engineering may not be realized for many years.

In spite of problems, genetic engineering has already resulted in a number of impressive accomplishments. Dozens of products that were once available only from natural sources and in limited amounts are now manufactured in abundance by genetically engineered microorganisms at relatively low cost. Insulin, human growth hormone, tissue plasminogen activator, and alpha interferon are examples. In addition, the first trials with the alteration of human DNA to cure a genetic disorder were begun in 1991.

The prospects offered by genetic engineering have not been greeted with unanimous enthusiasm by everyone. Many people believe that the hope of curing or avoiding genetic disorders is a positive advance. But they question the wisdom of making genetic changes that are not related to life-threatening disorders. Should such procedures be used for helping short children become taller or for making new kinds of tomatoes? Indeed, there are some critics who oppose *all*

forms of genetic engineering, arguing that humans never have the moral right to "play God" with any organism for any reason. As the technology available for genetic engineering continues to improve, debates over the use of these techniques in practical settings arc almost certainly going to continue—and to escalate—in the future.

As progress in genetic engineering goes forward, so do other forms of biotechnology. The discovery of monoclonal antibodies is an example. Monoclonal antibodies are cells formed by the combination of tumor cells with animal cells that make one and only one kind of antibody. When these two kinds of cells are fused, they result in a cell that reproduces almost infinitely and that recognizes one and only one kind of antigen. Such cells are extremely valuable in a vast array of medical, biological, and industrial applications, including the diagnosis and treatment of disease, the separation and purification of proteins, and the monitoring of pregnancy.

Biotechnology became a point of contention in 1992 during planning for the **United Nations Earth Summit** in Rio de Janeiro. In draft versions of the treaty on **biodiversity**, developing nations insisted on provisions that would force biotechnology companies in the developed world to pay fees to developing nations for the use of their genetic resources (the plants and animals growing within their boundaries). Currently, companies have free access to most of these raw materials used in the manufacture of new drugs and crop varieties. President George Bush argued that this provision would place an unfair burden on biotechnology companies in the United States, and he refused to sign the biodiversity treaty that contained this clause. For now, it seems that, for a second time, profits to be reaped from biotechnological advances will elude developing countries. (The Clinton administration subsequently endorsed the provisions of the biodiversity treaty and it was signed by Madeleine Albright, U. S. ambassador to the United Nations, on June 4, 1993.) *See also* Decomposition; Endangered species; Genetically engineered organism; Sewage treatment

[*David E. Newton*]

FURTHER READING

Fox, M. W. *Superpigs and Wondercorn: The Brave New World of Biotechnology and Where It May All Lead.* New York: Lyons and Buford, 1992.

Kessler, D. A., et al. "The Safety of Foods Developed by Biotechnology." *Science* (26 June 1992): 1747-1749+.

Kieffer, G. H. *Biotechnology, Genetic Engineering, and Society.* Reston, VA: National Association of Biology Teachers, 1987.

Marx, J., ed. *A Revolution in Biotechnology.* New York: Cambridge University Press, 1989.

Mellon, M. *Biotechnology and the Environment.* Washington, D.C.: National Biotechnology Policy Center of the National Wildlife Federation, 1988.

Weintraub, P. "The Coming of the High-Tech Harvest." *Audubon* (July-August 1992): 92-103.

Biotic community

All the living organisms sharing a common environment. The members of a biotic community are usually divided into three major categories: producers, consumers, and decomposers, based on the organisms' nutritional habits. Producers (sometimes called **autotroph**s) include plants and some forms of bacteria that use solar or chemical energy to convert simple compounds into their food. Consumers (sometimes called **heterotroph**s) obtain the energy they need by eating living plants and animals, or dead plant and animal material (detritus). Primary consumers (herbivores) eat plants, while secondary consumers (carnivores) eat other consumers. Consumers that feed on dead plant and animal material are called detrivores. There are two classes of detrivores: detritus feeders and decomposers. Detritus feeders (e.g., crabs, termites, earthworms, vultures) consume dead organisms or organic wastes, while decomposers (fungi and bacteria) feed on dead plant material, converting it into simple inorganic compounds such as carbon dioxide, water, and ammonia. Decomposers are also an important food sources for other consumers (e.g., worms and insects) living in the soil or water.

Biotic impoverishment
See **Biodiversity**

Bioventing

The process for treating environmental contaminants in the soils located between the ground surface and the **water table** by inducing **aerobic** biodegradation. Air is introduced into the **contaminated soil**s, providing oxygen for native **soil** bacteria to use in the biodegradation of organic compounds. The process is typically accomplished by extracting and/or injecting air from trenches or shallow wells which are screened within the unsaturated soils. The systems are similar to those used in vapor extraction. The main difference is that air extraction rates are low to minimize physical removal (stripping) of **volatile organic compound**s (VOCs) reducing the need for expensive treatment of the off-gases. The process may include the addition of **nutrient**s such as common **fertilizer**s, to provide **nitrogen** and phosphate for the bacteria. Bioventing is particularly attractive around buildings and actively used areas because it is relatively nonintrusive and results in minimal disturbance during installation and operation. The process is most suitable for petroleum **hydrocarbon** blends such as **gasoline**, jet fuel, and diesel oil, for petroleum distillates such as toluene, and for nonchlorinated solvents. *See also* Biodegradable; Bioremediation; Vapor recovery system

Birth control
See **Family planning**

Birth defects

Birth defects, also known as congenital malformations, are structural or metabolic abnormalities present at birth. While subtle variations from the normal, of no clinical interest, occur in about half of all individuals in the United States, significant congenital defects are found in about 3 percent of live births. Fortunately, only about half of these require medical attention.

Birth defects may result from genetic causes or environmental insult. Defective genes are not easily repaired and thus are perhaps less interesting than teratogenic substances to environmentalists. It is theoretically possible to limit exposure to **teratogen**s by elimination of the agent in the environment or by modification of behavior to prevent contact. It should be noted, however, that the causes of more than half of congenital malformations remain unknown.

Birth defects of genetic origin may be due to aberrant chromosome number or structure, or to a single gene defect. Normal humans have 46 chromosomes, and variation from this number is referred to as aneuploidy. Down's syndrome, an example of aneuploidy, is usually characterized by an extra chromosome designated number 21. The Down's individual thus has a total of 47 chromosomes, and the presence of the extra chromosome results in multiple defects. These include mental retardation and physical characteristics comprising a small round head, eyes that slant slightly upward, a large and frequently protruding tongue, low set ears, broad hands with short fingers and short stature. People with Down's syndrome are particularly vulnerable to leukemia. Children with this condition are rarely born to mothers less than 25 years of age (less than one in 1,500), but the prevalence of Down's syndrome babies increases with mothers older than 45 (about one in 25). Down's syndrome can be detected during pregnancy by chromosome analysis of fetal cells. Fetal chromosomes may be studied by chorionic villus sampling or by amniocentesis.

Other congenital abnormalities with a chromosomal basis include Klinefelter's syndrome, a condition of male infertility associated with an extra X chromosome, and Turner's syndrome, a condition wherein females fail to mature sexually and are characterized by the aneuploid condition of a missing X chromosome. Achondroplasia is a birth defect due to a dominant mutation of a Mendelian gene that results in dwarfism. Leg and arm bones are short but, the trunk is normal and the head may be large. Spontaneous **mutation** accounts for most achondroplasia. The mortality rate for affected individuals is so high that the gene would be lost if it were not for mutation. Albinism, a lack of pigment in the skin, eyes, and hair, is another congenital defect caused by a single gene, which in this case is recessive.

The developing fetus is at risk for agents which can pass the placental barrier such as infectious microbes, drugs and other **chemicals**, and ionizing radiation. Transplacental teratogens exert their effect on incompletely formed embryos or fetuses during the first three months of pregnancy. Organs and tissues in older and full term fetuses appear much as they will throughout life. It is not possible to alter the development of a fully formed structure. However, prior to the appearance of an organ or tissue, or during the development of that structure, teratogenic agents may have a profoundly deleterious effect.

Perhaps the best known teratogen is the sedative thalidomide which induces devastating anatomical abnormalities. The limb bones are either shortened or entirely lacking leading to a condition known as phocomelia. Intellectual development of thalidomide babies is unaffected. The experience with this drug, which started in 1959 and ended when it was withdrawn in 1961, emphasizes the fact that medications given to pregnant mothers generally cross the placenta and reach the developing embryo or fetus. Another drug that effects developmental abnormalities is warfarin which is used in anticoagulant therapy. It can cause fetal hemorrhage, mental retardation, and a multiplicity of defects to the eyes and hands when given to pregnant women.

The teratogenic effects of alcohol, or the life style that may accompany alcohol abuse, serve to illustrate that the term **environment** includes not only air and water but the personal environment as well. Alcoholism during pregnancy can result in "fetal alcohol syndrome" with facial, limb, and heart defects accompanied by growth retardation and reduced intelligence. The effects of alcohol may be magnified by factors associated with alcoholism such as poor diet, altered metabolism and inadequate medical care. Because neither the time of vulnerability nor the toxic level of alcohol is known, the best advice is to eschew alcohol as a dietary constituent altogether during pregnancy.

Disease of the mother during pregnancy can present an environmental hazard to the developing fetus. An example of such a hazard is the viral disease German measles, also known as rubella. The disease is characterized by a slight increase in temperature, sore throat, lethargy and a rash of short duration. Greatest hazard to the fetus is during the second and third month. Children born of mothers who had rubella during this period may exhibit cataracts, heart defects, hearing loss and mental retardation. Obviously, the virus transverses the placenta to infect the embryo or fetus and that infection may persist in the newborn. Birth defects associated with rubella infection have decreased since the introduction of a rubella vaccine.

The most common viral infection that occurs in human fetuses is that of a herpes virus known as cytomegalovirus. The infection is detected in about one or two percent of all live births. Most newborns, fortunately, do not manifest symptoms of the infection. However, for a very small minority, the effects of congenital cytomegalovirus are cruel and implacable. They include premature birth or growth retardation prior to birth, frequently accompanied by hepatitis, enlarged spleen, and reduction in thrombocytes (blood cells important for clotting). Abnormally small heads, mental retardation, cerebral palsy, heart and cerebral infection, bleeding problems, hearing loss and blindness occur. Exposure of the fetus to the virus occurs during infection of the pregnant woman or possibly from the father, since cytomegalovirus has been isolated from human semen.

Other infections known to provoke congenital defects include herpes simplex virus type II, toxoplasmosis, and syphilis.

Methylmercury is an effective fungicide for seed grain. Accidental human consumption of food made from treated seeds has occurred. Industrial pollution of sea water with organic **mercury** resulted in the contamination of fish, consumed by humans, from Minamata Bay in Japan. It has been established that organic mercury passes the placental barrier with effects that include mental retardation and a cerebral palsy-like condition due to brain damage. Anatomical birth defects, engendered by organic mercury, include abnormal palates, fingers, eyes and hearts. The toxicity of methylmercury affects both early embryos and developing fetuses. Exclusion of mercury from human food can be effected by not using organic mercury as a fungicide and by ending industrial discharge of mercury into the environment.

Of course other chemicals may be hazardous to the offspring of pregnant women. **Polychlorinated biphenyl (PCB)**s, relatively ubiquitous but low level oily contaminants of the environment, cause peculiar skin pigmentation, low birth weights, abnormal skin and nails, and other defects in offspring when accidentally ingested by pregnant woman.

Uncharacterized mixtures of toxic chemicals which contaminate the environment, are thought to be potential teratogens. Cytogenetic (chromosomal) abnormalities and increased birth defects were detected among the residents of **Love Canal, New York**. **Cigarette smoke** is the most common mixture of toxic substance to which fetuses are exposed. Tobacco smoke is associated with reduced birth weight but not specific birth anatomical abnormalities.

Much concern has arisen over the damaging effects of ionizing radiation, particularly regarding diagnostic x-rays and **radiation exposure** from nuclear accidents. The latter concern was given international attention following the explosion at the Ukraine's **Chernobyl Nuclear Power Station** in 1986. Fear that birth defects would occur as a result was fueled by reports of defects in Japanese children whose mothers were exposed to radiation at Hiroshima. Scientists believe that radiation to the fetus can result in many defects including various malformations, mental retardation, reduced growth rate and increased risk for leukemia. Fortunately, however, the risk of these effects is exceptionally low. Fetal abnormalities caused by factors other than radiation are thought to be about 10 times greater than those attributed to radiation during early pregnancy. However small the risk, most women choose to limit or avoid exposure to radiation during early pregnancy. This may be part of the reason for the increased popularity of diagnostic ultrasound as opposed to X-ray.

While concern is expressed for particular teratogenic agents or procedures, the etiology of most birth defects is unknown. Common defects, with unknown etiology, include hare lip and cleft palate, extra fingers and toes, fused fingers, extra nipples, various defects in the heart and great vessels, cerebral palsy (sometimes as a result of difficult labor and delivery but frequently for no known cause), narrowing of the entrance to the stomach, esophageal abnormalities, spina bifida, clubfoot, hip defects, and many, many others. Since the majority of birth defects are not caused by known effects of disease, drugs, chemicals or radiation, much remains to be learned. *See also* Minamata disease

[*Robert G. McKinnell*]

FURTHER READING

Brent, R. L. and J. L. Sever, eds. *Teratogen Update*. New York: Alan R. Liss, 1986.

Persaud, T. V. N., et al. *Basic Concepts in Teratology*. New York: Alan R. Liss, 1985.

Moore, K. L. *Essentials of Human Embryology*. Philadelphia: B.C. Decker, Inc., 1988.

Bison

The American bison (*Bison bison*) or "buffalo" is one of the most famous animals of the American West. Providing food and hides to the early Indians, it was almost completely eliminated by hunters, and now only remnant populations exist though its future survival seems assured.

Scientists do not consider the American bison a true buffalo (like the Asian water buffalo or the African buffalo), since it has a large head and neck, a hump at the shoulder, and 14 pairs of ribs instead of 13. In America, however, the names are used interchangeably. A full-grown American bison bull stand 5.5 to 6 ft (1.7 to 1.8 m) at the shoulder, extends 10 to 12.25 ft (3 to 3.8 m) in length from nose to tail, and weighs 1,600 to 3,000 lbs (726 to 1,400 kg). Cows usually weigh about 900 lbs (420 kg) or less. Bison are brown-black with long hair which covers their heads, necks, and humps, forming a "beard" at the chin and throat. Their horns can have a spread as large as 35 in (89 cm). Bison can live for 30 or more years, and they are social creatures, living together in herds. Bison bulls are extremely powerful; a charging bull has been known to shatter wooden blanks two inches thick and one foot wide.

The American bison is one of the most abundant animals ever to have existed on the North American continent, roaming in huge herds between the Appalachians and the Rockies as far south as Florida. One herd seen in Arkansas in 1870 was described as stretching "from six to ten miles in almost every direction." In the far West, the herds were even larger, stretching as far as the eye could see, and in 1871 a cavalry troop rode for six days through a herd of bison.

The arrival of Europeans in America sealed the fate of the American bison. By the 1850s massive slaughters of these creatures had eliminated them from Illinois, Indiana, Kentucky, Ohio, New York, and Tennessee. After the end of the Civil War in 1865, railroads began to bring a massive influx of settlers to the West and bison were killed in enormous numbers. The famous hunter "Buffalo Bill" Cody was able to bag 4,280 bison in just 18 months, and between 1854 and 1856, an Englishman named Sir George Gore killed about 6,000 bison along the lower Yellowstone River. Shooting bison from train windows became a popular recreation during the long trip west; there were contests to see who could kill

American bison.

the most animals on a single trip, and on one such excursion a group accompanying Grand Duke Alexis of Russia shot 1,500 bison in just two days. When buffalo tongue became a delicacy sought after by gourmets in the east, even more bison were killed for their tongues and their carcasses left to rot.

In the 1860s and 1870s extermination of the American bison became the official policy of the United States Government in order to deprive the Plains Indians of their major source of food, clothing, and shelter. During the 1870s, two to four million bison were shot each year, and 200,000 hides were sold in St. Louis in a single day. Inevitably, the extermination of the bison helped to eliminate not only the Plains Indians, but also the predatory animals dependent on it for food, such as plains **wolves**. By 1883, according to some reports, only one wild herd of bison remained in the West, consisting of about 10,000 individuals confined to a small part of North Dakota. In September of that year, a group of hunters set off to kill the remaining animals and by November the job was done.

By 1889 or 1890 the entire North American bison population had plummeted to about 500 animals, most of which were in captivity. A group of about 20 wild bison remained in **Yellowstone National Park**, and about 300 wood bison (*Bison bison athabascae*) survived near Great Slave Lake in Canada's Northwest Territories. At that time, naturalist William Temple Hornaday (1854-1937) led a campaign to save the species from complete extinction by the passage of laws and other protective measures. Canada enacted legislation to protect its remnant bison population in 1893 and the United States took similar action the following year.

Today, thousands of bison are found in several **national park**s, private ranches, and game preserves in the United States. About 15,000 are estimated to inhabit Wood Bison National Park and other locations in Canada. The few hundred wood bison originally saved around Great Slave Lake also continued to increase in numbers until the population reached around 2,000 in 1922. But in the following years, the introduction of plains bison to the area caused hybridization, and pure specimens of wood bison probably disappeared around Great Slave Lake. Fortunately, a small,

previously unknown herd of wood bison was discovered in 1957 on the upper North Yarling River, buffered from hybridization by 75 miles of swampland. From this herd (estimated at about 100 animals in 1965) about 24 animals were successfully transplanted to an area near Fort Providence in the Northwest Territories and 45 were relocated to Elk Island National Park in Alberta. Despite these rebuilding programs, the wood bison is still considered endangered, and is listed as such by the **U. S. Department of the Interior**. It is also listed in Appendix I of the **Convention on International Trade in Endangered Species of Fauna and Flora (CITES)** treaty.

Controversy still surrounds the largest herd of American bison (5,000 to 6,000 animals in the early 1990s) in Yellowstone National Park. The free-roaming bison often leave the park in search of food in the winter and Montana cattle ranchers along the park borders fear that the bison could infect their herds with brucellosis, a contagious disease that can cause miscarriages and infertility in cows. In an effort to prevent any chance of brucellosis transmission, the **National Park Service** (NPS) and the Montana Department of Fish, Wildlife and Parks, along with sport hunters acting in cooperation with these agencies, killed 1,044 bison between 1984 and 1992. Montana held a lottery-type hunt, and 569 bison were killed in the winter of 1988-89, and 271 were killed in the winter of 1991-92. The winter of 1996-97 was exceptionally harsh, and some 850 buffalo of the Park's remaining 3,500 starved or froze to death. In addition, the NPS, the U.S. Department of Agriculture (USDA), and the Montana Department of Livestock cooperated in a stepped-up buffalo killing program, in which some 1,080 were shot or shipped off to slaughterhouses. In all, more than half of Yellowstone's bison herd perished that winter.

Wildlife protection groups, such as the **Humane Society of the United States** and the **Fund for Animals**, have protested the hunting of these bison—which usually consists of walking up to an animal and shooting it. Animal protection organizations have offered alternatives to the killing of the bison, including fencing certain areas to prevent them from coming into contact with cattle. Conversely, Montana state officials and ranchers, as well as the USDA, have long pressured the National Park Service to eradicate many or all of the Yellowstone bison herd or at least test the animals and eliminate those showing signs of brucellosis. Such an action, however, would mean the eradication of most of the Yellowstone herd, even though no bison have not been known to infect a single local cow.

There is also a species of European bison called the wisent (*Bison bonasus*) which was once found throughout much of Europe. It was nearly exterminated in the early 1900s, but today a herd of about 1,600 animals can be found in a forest on the border between Poland and Russia. The European bison is considered vulnerable by **IUCN—The World Conservation Union**. *See also* Endangered Species Act; Endangered species; Overhunting; Rare species; Wildlife management

[*Lewis G. Regenstein*]

FURTHER READING

Grainger, D. *Animals in Peril.* Toronto: Pagurian Press, 1978.

McHugh, T. *Time of the Buffalo.* New York: Knopf, 1972.

Park, E. *The World of the Bison.* New York: Lippincott, 1969.

Turbak, G. "When the Buffalo Roam." *National Wildlife* 24 (1986): 30-35.

Bituminous coal

See **Coal**

Black-footed ferret (*Mustela nigripes*)

A member of the Mustelidae (weasel) family, the black-footed ferret is the only ferret native to North America. It has pale yellow fur, an off-white throat and belly, a dark face, black feet, and a black tail. The black-footed ferret usually grows to a length of 18 inches (46 cm) and weighs one and a half to three pounds (.68 to 1.4 kg), though the males are larger than the females. These ferrets have short legs and slender bodies, and lope along by placing both front feet on the ground followed by both back feet.

Ferrets live in prairie dog burrows and feed primarily upon prairie dogs, mice, squirrels, and gophers, as well as small rabbits and carrion. Ferrets are nocturnal animals; activity outside the burrow occurs after sunset until about two hours before sunrise. They do not hibernate and remain active all year long.

Breeding takes place once a year, in March or early April, and during the mating season males and females share common burrows. The gestation period lasts approximately six weeks, and the female may have from one to five kits per litter. The adult male does not participate in raising the young. The kits remain in the burrow where they are protected and nursed by their mother until about 4 weeks of age, usually sometime in July, when she weans them and begins to take them above ground. She either kills a prairie dog and carries it to her kits or moves them into the burrow with the dead animal. During July and early August she usually relocates her young to new burrows every three or four days, whimpering to encourage them to follow her or dragging them by the nape of their neck. At about eight weeks old the kits begin to play above ground. In late August and early September the mother positions her young in separate burrows, and by mid-September her offspring have left to establish their own territories.

Black-footed ferrets, like other members of the mustelid family, establish their territories by scent marking. They have well developed lateral and anal scent glands. The ferrets mark their territory by either wiggling back and forth while pressing their pelvic scent glands against the ground, or by rubbing their lateral scent glands against shrubs and rocks. Urination is a third form of scent marking. Males establish large territories that may encompass one or more females of the species and exclude all other males. Females establish smaller territories.

Black-footed ferret.

Historically, the black-footed ferret was found from Alberta, Canada southward throughout the Great Plains states. The decline of this species began in the 1800s with the settling of the west. Homesteaders moving into the Great Plains converted the prairie into agricultural lands, which led to a decline in the population of prairie dogs. Considering them a nuisance species, ranchers and farmers undertook a campaign to eradicate the prairie dog. The black-footed ferret is dependent upon the prairie dog: it takes 100 to 150 acres of prairie-dog colonies to sustain one adult. Because it takes such a large area to sustain a single adult, one small breeding group of ferrets requires at least 10 square miles of habitat. As the prairie dog colonies became scattered, the groups were unable to sustain themselves.

In 1954 the **National Park Service** began capturing black-footed ferrets in an attempt to save them from their endangered status. These animals were released in wildlife sanctuaries that had large prairie dog populations. Black-footed ferrets, however, are highly susceptible to canine distemper, and this disease wiped out the animals the park service had relocated.

In September 1981, scientists located the only known wild population of black-footed ferrets near the town of Meeteetse in northwestern Wyoming. The colony lived in 25 prairie dog towns covering 53 square miles. But in 1985 canine distemper decimated the prairie dog towns around Meeteetse and spread among the ferret population, quickly reducing their numbers. Researchers feared that without immediate action the black-footed ferret would become extinct. The only course of action appeared to be removing them from the wild. If an animal had not been exposed to canine distemper, it could be vaccinated and saved. Some animals from the Meeteetse population did survive in captivity.

There is a breeding program and research facility at the Sybille Wildlife Research Institute in Wyoming, and in 1987 the Wyoming Fish and Game Department implemented a plan for preserving the black-footed ferret within the state. Researchers identified habitats where animals bred in captivity could be relocated. The program began with the eighteen animals from the wild population located at Meeteetse. In 1987 seven kits were born to this group. The following year thirteen female black-footed ferrets had litters and 34 of the kits survived. Captive propagation efforts have improved the outlook for the black-footed ferret, and captive populations will continue to be used to reestablish ferrets in the wild. *See also* Endangered Species Act; Endangered species; Wildlife refuge; Wildlife rehabilitation

[*Debra Glidden*]

FURTHER READING

"Back Home on the Range." *Environment* 33 (November 1991): 23.

Behler, D. "Baby Black-Footed Ferrets Sighted." *Wildlife Conservation* 95 (November-December 1992): 7.

Boxer, S. "The Plight of the Black-Footed Ferret." *Discover* 7 (February 1986): 7.

Cohn, J. "Ferrets Return From Near Extinction." *Bioscience* 41 (March 1991): 132-5.

Richardson, L. "On The Track of the Last Black-Footed Ferrets." *Natural History* 95 (February 1986): 69-77.

Weinberg, D. "Decline and Fall of the Black-footed Ferret." *Natural History* 95 (February 1986): 92-9.

Black lung disease

Black lung disease, also known as anthracosis or **coal** workers' pneumoconiosis, is a chronic, fibrotic lung disease of coal miners. It is caused by inhaling coal dust which accumulates in the lungs, and forms black bumps or coal macules on the bronchioles. These black bumps in the lungs give the disease its common name. Lung disease among coal miners was first described by German mineralogist Georgius Agricola in the sixteenth century and it is now a widely recognized occupational illness.

Black lung disease occurs most often among miners of anthracite (hard) coal, but it is found among soft coal miners and graphite workers as well. The disease is characterized by gradual onset—the first symptoms usually appear only after 10-20 years of exposure to coal dust. The extent and severity of the disease is clearly related to the length of this exposure. The disease also appears to be aggravated by cigarette smoking. The more advanced forms of black lung disease are frequently associated with **emphysema** or chronic **bronchitis**. There is no real treatment for this disease, but it may be controlled or its development arrested by avoiding exposure to coal dust. Black lung disease is probably the best know occupational illness in the United States. In some regions, more than 50 percent of coal miners develop the disease after 30 or more years on the job. *See also* Fibrosis; Respiratory diseases

[*Linda Rehkopf*]

FURTHER READING

Holt, P. F. *Inhaled Dust and Disease.* New York: Wiley, 1988.

Moeller, D. W. *Environmental Health.* Cambridge: Harvard University Press, 1992.

Blackout/brownout

A blackout is a total loss of electrical power. A blackout is usually defined as a drop in line voltage below 80 volts (V) (the normal voltage is 120V), since most electrical equipment will not operate below these levels. A blackout may be due to a planned interruption, such as limiting of loads during power shortages by rotating power shutoffs through different areas, or due to an accidental failure caused by human error, a failure of generating or transmission equipment, or a storm. Blackouts can cause losses of industrial production, disturbances to commercial activities, traffic and transportation difficulties, disruption of municipal services, and personal inconveniences. In the summer of 1977, a blackout caused by transmission line losses during a storm affected the New York City area. About 9 million people were affected by the blackout, with some areas without power for more than 24 hours. The blackout was accompanied by looting and vandalism. A blackout in northeastern United States and eastern Canada due to a switching relay failure in November of 1965 affected 30 million people and resulted in improved electric utility power system design.

A brownout is a condition (usually temporary, but which may last longer, i.e., from periods ranging from fractions of a second to hours) when the alternating current (AC) electrical utility voltage is lower than normal. If the brownout lasts less than a second, it is called a *sag*. Brownouts may be caused by overloaded circuits, but are sometimes caused intentionally by a utility company in order to reduce the amount of power drawn by users during peak demand periods, or unintentionally when demand for electricity exceeds generating capacity. A sag can also occur when line switching is employed to access power from secondary utility sources. Equipment such as shop tools, compressors, and elevators starting up on a shared power line can cause a sag, which can adversely affect other sensitive electronic equipment such as computers. Generally, electrical utility customers do not notice a brownout except when it does affect sensitive electronic equipment.

Measures to protect against effects of blackouts and brownouts include efficient design of power networks, interconnection of power networks to improve stability, monitoring of generating reserve needs during periods of peak demand, and standby power for emergency needs. An individual piece of equipment can be protected from blackouts and brownouts by the use of an uninterruptible power source (UPS). A UPS is a device with internal batteries that is used to guarantee that continuous power is supplied to equipment even if the power supply stops providing power or during line sags. Commonly the UPS will boost voltage if the voltage drops to less than 103V and will switch to battery power at 90V and below. Some UPS devices are capable of shutting down the equipment during extended blackouts.

[*Judith L. Sims*]

FURTHER READING

Curvin, R., and B. Porter. *Blackout Looting! New York City, July 13, 1977.* New York: Gardner Press, 1979.

Dugan, R.C. *Electrical Power Systems Quality.* New York, McGraw-Hill, 1996.

Kabisama, H.W. *Electrical Power Engineering.* New York: McGraw-Hill, 1993.

Kazibwe, W.E., and M.H. Sendaula. *Electric Power Quality Control Techniques.* New York: Van Nostrand Reinhold, 1993.

Blow-out

A blow-out occurs where the **soil** is left unprotected to the erosive force of the wind. Blow-outs commonly occur as depressional areas, once enough soil has been removed. They most often occur in sandy soils, where vegetation is sparse.

Blue Angel (Germany)

The best known environmental product certification effort outside the United States, the Blue Angel program was initiated by the German government in 1978. The Blue Angel label features a stylized angel with arms outstretched encircled by a laurel wreath. Since its inception, the program has certified more than 3,000 products, including automobiles, batteries, and deodorants, as environmentally safe. Similar, government-sponsored certification programs also exist in Canada (**Environmental Choice**) and Japan (**Ecomark**). *See also* Environmental advertising and marketing; Green Cross; Green Seal

Blue-baby syndrome

Blue-baby syndrome (or infant cyanosis) occurs in infants who drink water with a high concentration of nitrate or are fed formula prepared with water containing high nitrate levels. Excess nitrate can result in methemoglobinemia, a condition in which the oxygen-carrying capacity of the blood is impaired by an **oxidizing agent** such as nitrite, which can be reduced from nitrate by bacterial **metabolism** in the human mouth and stomach. Infants in the first three to six months of life, especially those with diarrhea, are particularly susceptible to nitrite-induced methemoglobinemia.

Adults convert about 10 percent of ingested nitrates into nitrites, and excess nitrate is excreted by the kidneys. In infants, however, nitrate is transformed to nitrite with almost 100 percent efficiency. The nitrite and remaining nitrate are absorbed into the body through the intestine. Nitrite in the blood reacts with hemoglobin to form methemoglobin, which does not transport oxygen to the tissues and body organs. The skin of the infant appears blue due to the lack of oxygen in the blood supply, which may lead to asphyxia, or suffocation.

Normal methemoglobin levels in humans range from one to two percent; levels greater than three percent are defined as methemoglobinemia. Methemoglobinemia is rarely fatal, readily diagnosed, and rapidly reversible with clinical treatment.

In adults, the major source of nitrate is dietary, with only about 13 percent of daily intake from drinking water.

Nitrates occur naturally in many foods, especially vegetables, and are often added to meat products as preservatives. Only a few cases of methemoglobinemia have been associated with foods high in nitrate or nitrite. Nitrate is also found in air, but the daily respiratory intake of nitrate is small compared with other sources. Nearly all cases of the disease have resulted from ingestion by infants of nitrate in private well water that has been used to prepare infant formula. Levels of nitrate of three times the Maximum Contaminant Levels (MCLs) and above have been found in drinking water **wells** in agricultural areas. Federal MCL standards apply to all public water systems, though they are unenforceable recommendations. Insufficient data are available to determine whether subtle or chronic toxic effects may occur at levels of exposure below those that produce clinically obvious toxicity. If water has or is suspected to have high nitrate concentrations, it should not be used for infant feeding, nor should pregnant women or nursing mothers be allowed to drink it.

Domestic water supply wells may become contaminated with nitrate from mineralization of soil organic nitrogen, **septic tank** systems, and some agricultural practices, including the use of **fertilizer**s and the disposal of **animal waste**s. Since there are many potential sources of nitrates in **groundwater**, the prevention of nitrate contamination is complex and often difficult.

Nitrates and nitrites can be removed from drinking water using several types of technologies. The **Environmental Protection Agency (EPA)** has designated reverse **osmosis**, anion exchange, and electrodialysis as the **Best Available Control Technology** (BAT) for the removal of nitrate, while recommending reverse osmosis and anion exchange as the BAT for nitrite. Other technologies can be used to meet MCLs for nitrate and nitrite if they receive approval from the appropriate state regulatory agency. *See also* Chronic effects; Drinking water supply; Fertilizer runoff; Ion exchange; Oxidation reduction reactions; Water quality; Water quality standards; Water treatment

[*Judith Sims*]

FURTHER READING

Clark, R. M. "Water Supply." In *Standard Handbook of Environmental Engineering,* ed. R. A. Corbitt. New York: McGraw-Hill, 1990.

Pontius, F. W. "New Standards Protect Infants from Blue Baby Syndrome." *Opflow* 19 (1993): 5.

Lappensbusch, W. L. *Contaminated Drinking Water and Your Health.* Alexandria, VA: Lappensbusch Environmental Health, 1986.

Blue revolution (fish farming)

The blue revolution has been brought about in part by a trend towards more healthy eating which has increased the consumption of fish. Additionally, the supply of wild fish is declining, and some species such as cod, striped sea bass, **salmon**, haddock, and flounder have already been overfished. Aquaculture, or fish farming, appears to be a solution to the problems created by the law of supply and demand. Farm-raised fish currently account for about 15 percent of the market. There are 93 species of fin fish, seven species of shrimp, and six species of crawfish, along with numerous species of clams, oysters and shellfish that are currently being farm raised worldwide.

There are five central components to all fish farming operations: fish, water supply, nutrition, management and a contained method. Ideally, every aspect of the fishes' environment is scientifically controlled by the farmer. The quality of the water should be constantly monitored and adjusted for **pH** and numerous other factors, including **oxygen** content. Adequate water circulation is also necessary to insure that waste matter does not accumulate in the cages, for this can lead to outbreaks of disease. The fish are fed formulated diets that contain only enough protein for optimal growth. They are fed regulated amounts that vary according to stage of development, water temperature, and the availability of naturally occurring food in their **habitat**.

Herbicides are used on a regular basis to control any unwanted aquatic vegetation and to prevent fouling of cages. Vaccines are routinely given to the fish to prevent disease, although their effectiveness against most **pathogen**s has yet to be determined. Antibiotics are routinely placed in the food that is fed to farm raised fish, a practice which many have questioned. When given over a prolonged period of time, antibiotics can result in higher incidences of disease because bacterial strains develop resistance to them.

Fish that are raised on farms mature in rearing units that are frequently located on shore. These on shore units are typically ponds, large circular tanks or concrete enclosures. Many types of freshwater fin fish are raised in pond systems. Ponds that are easy to harvest, drain and refill are the most economical. Walleye, perch and northern pike are a few of the cool-water species that are raised in pond cultures. Warm-water species such as catfish, carp, and tilapia are also common. A few cold water species, especially trout and salmon, can also be raised in pond systems. Most pond systems are **monoculture** in nature, so only one type of fish is raised in each pond.

Silos, raceways, and circular pools are commonly used in fish farming. These are popular because they require a small land base in comparison with most other systems. Trout and salmonoid species are frequently raised in raceways, which are rectangular enclosures usually made of cement, fiberglass or metal, and positioned in a series so that water flows from one into the next. Circular pools are shallow with a center drain. They are easy to clean and maintain, since the growth of aquatic vegetation is usually minimal. Silos are very deep, circular tanks that are similar to silos used for grain storage on traditional farms.

All on shore fish farming operations use large quantities of water, and their operations are either open or closed systems. In open systems the water is used only once, flowing into a pool or through a series of pools before being discharged into a drainage ditch, creek, or river. Open systems are used whenever possible because they are relatively inexpensive. In most cases, farmers are not required to treat the water before it is discharged, which poses an environmental hazard because the organic fish wastes, the residues of

medications, and the **herbicide**s used in the operation enter the water supply unchecked.

Closed systems are not popular among fish farmers because they are very expensive to build, maintain and operate. In a closed system used water is treated and then reused in the farming operation. The treatment process can include disinfection, removal of organic wastes that have dissolved in the water, and reaeration. The closed system is more environmentally sound than the open systems.

Coastal lakes and **estuaries** are the most frequently used off-shore sites for rearing units, but it is becoming more common to see units located at sea. There are four basic types of cages used for off-shore fish-farming operations. They are fixed, floating, submersible, and submerged. Fixed cages are made of net or webbing material and supported by posts that are anchored in the river bottom. Floating cages, also known as net pens, are the most common type of cage used. Developed in Norway, they are made of net or rigid mesh and are supported by a buoyant collar. Submersible cages have a frame which enables them to hold their shape made of net or rigid mesh and are supported by a buoyant collar. Submerged cages are usually made of wood and anchored in place.

One major concern about off-shore nets and pens is that they tend to attract marine birds and mammals, which attempt to get at the fish often fatal results. Fish farmers currently use wire barriers and electrical devices to discourage predators and these devices have killed sea lions, **seals**, and birds.

Fish farms are now considered to be large-scale polluters of the **environment**. A typical four-acre salmon farm holds 75,000 fish, and the amount of **organic waste** produced is equal to that of a town with 20,000 people. Waste matter then settles on the ocean floor, where it disrupts the normal **ecosystem**. Accumulated wastes kill clams, oysters and other shellfish, and also causes a proliferation of algae, fungi, and **parasites**, as well as **plankton** bloom. Plankton bloom is dangerous to sea life and to humans. In order to control the algae and plankton farmers treat the fish and the water with numerous **chemicals** such as copper sulfate and formalin. These chemicals do not act exclusively on algae, killing many other beneficial forms of aquatic life and disrupting the ecological balance. According to the **Sierra Club** Legal Defense Fund, the pens qualify as **point source**s of **pollution** and should fall under the **Clean Water Act**. At this point in time, however, the pens do not come under the jurisdiction of the act.

Many fish on farms are raised from eggs imported from other areas. Farm-raised fish can and do escape from their pens, causing havoc with local ecosystems. The interbreeding of imported fish with indigenous species can alter the genetic traits that allow the indigenous species to survive in that particular location. Farm-raised stock that escapes and reproduces may also compete with native species, resulting in the decline of wild fish in that particular area. Off the coast of Norway for example, the offspring of escaped farm-raised salmon outnumber the indigenous species.

There are many questions about health and nutrition that may affect consumers of farm-raised fish. Fish farmers frequently use large quantities of medications to keep the fish healthy and there are concerns over the effects that these medications have on human health. Possible side effects of eating farm-raised fish on a regular basis include allergic reactions, increased incidence of infections by resistant bacterial strains, and suppressed immune system response. If eaten by pregnant women there is evidence of fetal damage, discoloration of infants teeth, and abnormal bone growth. Omega-3 fatty acids are a beneficial part of our diet and they are present in the flesh of wild salmon and in some other fish, but not in their farm-raised counterparts. Recent studies have found that farm-raised salmon and catfish contained twice the amount of fat found in wild species. Other comparative nutritional studies are currently underway.

Fish farming is a relatively new industry that shows a lot of potential, but there are many environmental and health questions that need to be addressed. Monitoring of the industry is virtually non-existent. In the United States, the Joint Subcommittee on Aquaculture (JSA) has made recommendations for additional studies of the industry including the **environmental impact** of fish farming. JSA has pointed out the need for extensive research into the life cycle of parasites and diseases that plague fish. They have recommended drug and chemical testing as well as registration procedures. In the 1983 report issued by JSA every aspect of the farming operation was cited as needing additional studies. *See also* Agricultural pollution; Algal bloom; Aquatic chemistry; Aquatic weed control; Commercial fishing; Feedlot runoff; Marine pollution; Water quality standards

[*Debra Glidden*]

Further Reading

Beveridge, M. *Cage Aquaculture.* Farham, England: Fishing News Books, 1987.

Brown, E. E. *World Fish Farming: Cultivation and Economics.* Westport, CT: Avi Publishing Company, 1983.

Fischetti, M. "A Feast of Gene-Splicing Down on the Fish Farm." *Science* 253 (2 August 1991): 512-3.

"Foods From Aquaculture." *Food Technology* 45 (September 1991): 87-92.

National Aquaculture Development Plan. Volume I and II. Joint Subcommittee on Aquaculture of the Federal Coordinating Council on Science, Engineering and Technology. Washington, DC, 1983.

BOD
See **Biochemical oxygen demand**

Bogs
See **Wetlands**

Bonn Convention
See **Convention on the Conservation of Migratory Species of Wild Animals**

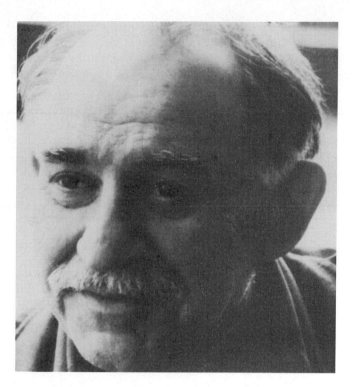

Murray Bookchin.

Bookchin, Murray (1921-)
American social critic, environmentalist, and writer

Born in New York in 1921, Bookchin is a writer, social critic, and founder of "**social ecology**." He has had a long and abiding interest in the **environment**, and as early as the 1950s he was concerned with the effects of human actions on the environment. In 1951 he published an article entitled "The Problem of Chemicals," which exposed the detrimental effects of **chemicals** on **nature** and on human health. This work predates **Rachel Carson**'s famous *Silent Spring* by over ten years.

In developing his theory of social ecology, Bookchin makes the basic point that "you can't have sound ecological practices in nature without having sound social practices in society. Harmony in society means harmony with nature." Bookchin describes himself as an anarchist, contending that "there is a natural relationship between natural ecology and anarchy."

Bookchin has long been a critic of modern cities: his widely read and frequently quoted *Crisis in Our Cities* (1965) examines urban life, questioning "the lack of standards in judging the modern metropolis and the society that fosters its growth." His *The Rise of Urbanization and the Decline of Citizenship* (1987) continues the critique by advancing green ideas as a new municipal agenda for the 1990s and the next century.

Though he is often mentioned as one of its founding thinkers, Bookchin is an ardent critic of **deep ecology**. He states: "Bluntly speaking, deep ecology, despite all its social rhetoric, has no real sense that our ecological problems have their roots in society and in social problems." Bookchin instead reaffirms a social ecology that is, first of all "social," incorporating people into the calculus needed to solve environmental problems, "avowedly rational," "revolutionary, not merely 'radical'," and "radically" green.

[*Gerald L. Young*]

FURTHER READING

Bookchin, Murray. *Toward an Ecological Society*. Montreal: Black Rose Books, 1980.

———. *The Ecology of Freedom: The Emergence and Dissolution of Hierarchy*. Palo Alto, CA: Cheshire Books, 1982.

———. *Remaking Society: Pathways to a Green Future*. Boston: South End Press, 1990.

———. "Social Ecology Versus Deep Ecology." *Socialist Review* 18 (1988): 9-29.

Clark, J. "The Social Ecology of Murray Bookchin." In *The Anarchist Moment*, pp. 201-28. Montreal: Black Rose Books, 1984.

Boreal forest

See **Taiga**

Norman Borlaug.

Borlaug, Norman E. (1914-)

American environmental activist

Borlaug, known as the father of the "green revolution," or **agricultural revolution**, was born on March 25, 1914, on a small farm near Cresco, Iowa. He received a B.S. in forestry in 1937 followed by a master's degree in 1940 and a PhD. in 1941 in plant pathology all from the University of Minnesota.

Agriculture is an activity of humans with profound impact on the environment. Traditional cereal grain production methods in some countries have led to recurrent famine. Food in these countries can be increased either by expansion of land area under cultivation or by enhancement of crop yield per unit of land. In many developing countries, little if any space for agricultural expansion remains, hence interest is focused on increasing cereal grain yield. This is especially true with regard to wheat, rice, and maize.

Borlaug is associated with the green revolution which was responsible for spectacular increases in grain production. He began working in Mexico in 1943 with the Rockefeller Foundation and the International Maize and Wheat Improvement Center in an effort to increase food crop production. As a result of these efforts, wheat production doubled in the decade after World War II, and nations such as Mexico, India, and Pakistan became exporters of grain rather than importers. Increased yields of wheat came as the result of high genetic yield potential, enhanced disease resistance (Mexican wheat was vulnerable to stem rust fungus), responsiveness to **fertilizer**s, the use of **pesticide**s, and the development of dwarf varieties with stiff straw and short blades that resist lodging, i.e., do not grow tall and topple over with the use of fertilizer. Further, the new varieties could be used in different parts of the world because they were unaffected

by different daylight periods. Mechanized threshing is now replacing the traditional treading out of grain with large animals followed by winnowing because these procedures are slow and leave the grain harvest vulnerable to rain damage. Thus, modern threshers are an essential part of the green revolution.

Borlaug demonstrated that the **famine** so characteristic of many developing countries could be controlled or eliminated at least with respect to the population of the world at that time. However, respite from famine and poverty is only temporary as the world population relentlessly continues to increase. The sociological and economic conditions which have historically precipitated famine have not been abrogated. Thus, famine will appear again if human population expansion continues unabated despite efforts of the green revolution. Further, critics of Borlaug's agricultural revolution cite the possibility of crop vulnerability because of genetic uniformity—development of crops with high-yield potential have eliminated other varieties, thus limiting **biodiversity**. High-yield crops have not proven themselves hardier in several cases; some varieties are more vulnerable to molds and storage problems. In the meantime, other, hardier varieties are now nonexistent. The environmental effects of fertilizers, pesticides, and energy-dependent mechanized modes of cultivation to sustain the newly developed crops have also provoked controversy. Such methods are expensive for poorer countries and sometimes create more problems than they solve. For now, however, food from the green revolution saves lives and the benefits currently outweigh liabilities.

At the presentation of the Nobel Peace Prize to Borlaug in 1970, the president of Norway's Lagting honored him, saying "more than any other single person of this age, he has helped to provide bread for a hungry world." His alma mater, the University of Minnesota, celebrated his career accomplishments with the award of a Doctor of Science (*honoris causa*) degree in 1984, as have many other academic institutions throughout a grateful world.

In 1992, the Agricultural Council of Experts (ACE) was formed to advise Borlaug and former President Jimmy Carter on information concerning Africa's agricultural and economic issues. They created a model that has since been incorporated into the Global 2000 program, which addresses the African food crisis by experimenting with production test plots (PTPs) in an attempt to extract greater crop yields.

[*Robert G. McKinnell*]

FURTHER READING

Transcript of Proceedings for the Nobel Prize for Peace, 1970 (Speech by Ms. Aase Lionaes, President of the Lagting, December 11, 1970 and Lecture by Norman E. Borlaug on the Occasion of the Award of the Nobel Peace Prize for 1970, Oslo, Norway, December 11, 1970).

Wilkes, H. Garrison. The Green Revolution. In: *McGraw-Hill Encyclopedia of Food, Agriculture & Nutrition*, edited by D. N. Lapedes, pp 41–47. New York: McGraw-Hill Book Company, 1977.

Boston Harbor clean up

Like many harbors near cities along the eastern seaboard, the Boston Harbor in Massachusetts has been used for centuries as a receptacle for raw and partially treated sewage from the city of Boston and surrounding towns. In the late 1800s, Boston designed a sewage and stormwater collection system. This sewage system combined millions of gallons of untreated sewage from homes, schools, hospitals, factories, and other buildings with stormwater collected from streets during periods of moderate to heavy rainfall. The combined sewage and stormwater collected in the sewage system was discharged untreated to Boston Harbor on outgoing tides. Sewage from communities surrounding Boston was also piped to Boston's collection system and discharged to Boston Harbor and the major rivers leading to it: the Charles, Mystic, and Neponset Rivers. Many of the sewage pipes, tunnels, and other infrastructure built in the late 1800s and early 1900s are still in use today.

In the 1950s, the City of Boston was concerned with growing health risks of swimming in and eating shellfish harvested from Boston Harbor as well as odors and aesthetic concerns that resulted from discharging raw sewage into Harbor waters. The city built two advanced primary **sewage treatment** plants during the 1950s and 1960s on two islands located in Boston Harbor. The first sewage treatment plant was built on Nut Island; it treated approximately 110 million gal/per day (416 million L/per day). The second sewage treatment plant was built on Deer Island; it treated approximately 280 million gal/per day (1,060 million L/per day). The two sewage treatment plants removed approximately half the total suspended solids and 25% of the biological oxygen demand found in raw sewage. The outgoing tide in Boston Harbor was still used to flush the treated

wastewater and approximately 50 tons (46 metric tons) per day of sewage **sludge** (also called biosolids), which was produced as a byproduct of the advanced primary treatment process. The sewage sludge forms from solids in the sewage settling in the bottom of tanks.

During the 1960s, the resources devoted to maintaining the City's aging sewage system decreased. As a result, the **sewage treatment** plants, pipes, pump stations, tunnels, interceptors, and other key components of Boston's sewage infrastructure began to fall into disrepair. Equipment breakdowns, sewer line breaks, and other problems resulted in the discharge of raw and partially treated sewage to Boston Harbor and the rivers leading to it. During this time, the Metropolitan District Commission (MDC) was the agency responsible for sewage collection, treatment, and disposal.

In 1972, the United States Congress enacted the **Clean Water Act**. This was landmark legislation to improve the quality of our nation's waters. The Clean Water Act required that sewage discharged to United States waters must meet secondary treatment levels by 1977. Secondary treatment of sewage means that at least 85% of total suspended solids and 85% of biological oxygen demand is removed from sewage. Instead of working towards meeting this federal requirement, the MDC requested a waiver from this new obligation from the United States **Environmental Protection Agency** (EPA). In 1983, the EPA denied the waiver request. The MDC responded by modifying its waiver request to promise that the city would construct a 9.2 mi-long (14.8 km) outfall to achieve increased dilution of the sewage by discharging to deeper, more flushed waters. As part of its waiver, MDC also promised an end to discharging sewage sludge in the harbor and initiation of a combined sewer overflow abatement project to cease flow into Boston Harbor from 88 overflow pipes. In 1985, EPA denied the second waiver request.

During EPA's consideration of Boston's waiver request, in 1982, the City of Quincy filed a lawsuit against the MDC for violating the Clean Water Act. In 1983, the Conservation Law Foundation filed two lawsuits; one was against MDC for violating the Clean Water Act and the other was against EPA for not fully implementing the Clean Water Act by failing to get Boston to comply with the law. The Massachusetts legislature responded to these pressures by replacing the MDC with the Massachusetts Water Resources Authority (MWRA) in 1984. The MWRA was created as an independent agency with the authority to raise water and sewer rates to pay for upgrading and maintaining the collection and treatment of the region's sewage. The following year, the federal court ruled that the MWRA must come into compliance with the Clean Water Act. As a result of this ruling, the MWRA developed a list of sewage improvement projects that were necessary to upgrade the existing sewage treatment system and clean up Boston Harbor.

The Boston Harbor clean up consists of $3.4 billion worth of sewage treatment improvements that include the construction of a 1,270 million-gal/per day (4,800 million-L/per day) primary sewage treatment plant, a 1,080 million-gal/per day (4,080 million-L/per day) secondary sewage treatment plant, a dozen sewage sludge digesters, disinfection basins, a sewage screening facility, an underwater tunnel, a 9.5 mi-long (15.3 km) outfall pipe, 10 pumping stations, a sludge-to-fertilizer facility, and combined sewer overflow treatment facilities.

Today, approximately 370 million-gal/per day (1,400 million L/per day) of sewage effluent from over 2.5 million residents and businesses is discharged to Boston Harbor. Almost half the total flow is stormwater **runoff** from streets and **groundwater** infiltrating into cracked sewer pipes. The combined sewage and stormwater is moved through 5,400 mi (8,700 km) of pipes by gravity and with the help of pumps. Five of the 10 pumps have already been replaced. At least two of the pumping stations that were replaced as part of the clean up effort dated back to 1895. The sewage is pumped to Nut Island where more than 10,000 gal/per day (37,800 L/per day) of floatable pollution such as grease, oil, and plastic debris are now removed by its new sewage screening facility. The facility also removes any grit, sand, gravel, or large objects. A 4.8-mi (7.7 km) long deep-rock tunnel will be used to transport screened wastewater to Deer Island for further treatment.

One of the most significant changes that has occurred as part of the Boston Harbor clean up project is the reconstruction of Deer Island. Prior to 1989, Deer Island had prison buildings, World War II army bunkers, and an aging sewage treatment plant. All the old buildings and structures have been removed and the island has been reshaped to accommodate 12 massive sewage sludge digesters, 60 acres of a new primary sewage treatment plant, and a new secondary treatment facility. The primary sewage treatment plant has reduced the amount of suspended solids discharged to Boston Harbor from 138 to 57 tons per day (126 to 52 metric tons).

The secondary sewage treatment plant on Deer Island is still under construction. It will use settling tanks, as are found in primary sewage treatment plants, as well as microorganisms, which will consume organic matter in the sewage thereby increasing treatment levels. Secondary treatment of Boston's sewage will result in an increase in removal of total suspended solids from 50-90% and biological oxygen demand from 25-90%. The first phase of the secondary treatment plant construction is expected to be completed by the end of 1997.

After the sewage is treated and disinfected to remove any remaining pathogens (disease-causing organisms), the effluent will be discharged through a 9.5 mi (15.3 km) long outfall tunnel into the waters of Massachusetts Bay. Work on the outfall has been underway since 1990. Massive tunnel boring machines are used to drill the tunnel below the ocean floor. The outfall will have 55 diffuser pipes connected at right angles to it along the last 1.25 mi (2.01 km) of the outfall. The diffuser pipes will increase dispersion of the treated sewage in the receiving waters. The outfall is expected to be completed in 1998.

The outfall has been a source of controversy for many residents of Cape Cod and for the users of Massachusetts Bay and the Gulf of Maine. There is concern about the long-term impact of contaminants from the treated sewage on the area, which is used for transportation, recreation, fishing, and tourism. Some alternatives to the sewage treatment plant and the 9.5-mi (15.3 km) long outfall pipe were developed by civil engineers at the Massachusetts Institute of Technology. The alternatives included modifications to the advanced primary treatment facility and a smaller secondary treatment facility with the effluent discharged to Boston Harbor. Because there was not enough evidence to convince EPA that water quality standards would always be met in the harbor, EPA rejected the alternatives.

As part of the Boston Harbor clean up, sewage sludge is no longer discharged to the harbor. Twelve sewage sludge digesters in Deer Island were constructed in 1991. The digesters break down the sewage sludge by using microorganisms such as bacteria. Different types of microorganisms are used in the sewage sludge digestion process than in the secondary treatment process. As the microorganisms consume the sewage sludge, methane gas is produced which is used for heat and power. Prior to 1991, all the sewage sludge was discharged to Boston Harbor. Since 1991, the sewage sludge has been shipped to a facility that converts the digested sewage sludge into **fertilizer**.

The sludge-to-fertilizer facility dewaters the sludge and uses rotating, high temperature dryers that produce fertilizer pellets with 60% organic matter, and important nutrients such as nitrogen, phosphorus, calcium, sulfur, and iron. The fertilizer is marketed in bulk and also sold as *Bay State Organic*, which is sold locally for use on golf courses and landscape.

This massive undertaking to clean up the harbor by upgrading its sewage treatment facilities is one of the world's largest public works projects. Over 80% of the Boston Harbor clean up is completed. These changes have resulted in measurable improvements to Boston Harbor. The harbor sustains a $10 million lobster fishery annually as well as flounder, striped bass, cod, bluefish, and smelt recreational fisheries. *See also* Aerobic sludge digestion

[*Marci L. Bortman*]

FURTHER READING

Aubrey, D. G., and M. S. Connor. "Boston Harbor Fallout Over the Outfall." *Oceanus* 36:1, (Spring 1993).

Levy, P. F. "Sewer Infrastructure: An Orphan of Our Times." *Oceanus* 36:1, (Spring 1993).

Massachusetts Water Resources Authority. Internet: http://www.mwra.state.ma.us/

National Research Council. *Managing Wastewater in Coastal Urban Areas.* Washington DC: National Academy Press, 1993.

Botanical garden

A botanical garden is a place where collections of plants are grown, managed, and maintained. Plants are normally labeled and available for scientific study by students and observation by the public. An arboretum is a garden composed primarily of trees, vines and shrubs. Gardens often preserve collections of stored seeds in special facilities referred to as **seed bank**s. Many gardens maintain special collections of preserved plants, known as herbaria, used to identify and classify unknown plants. Laboratories for the scientific study of plants and classrooms are also common.

Although landscape gardens have been known for as long as 4,000 years, gardens intended for scientific study have a more recent origin. Kindled by the need for herbal medicines in the sixteenth century, gardens affiliated with Italian medical schools were founded in Pisa about 1543, and Padua in 1545. The usefulness of these medicinal gardens was soon evident, and similar gardens were established in Copenhagen, Denmark (1600), London, England (1606), Paris, France (1635), Berlin, Germany (1679) and elsewhere. The early European gardens concentrated mainly on **species** with known medical significance. The plant collections were put to use to make and test medicines and to train students in their application.

In the eighteenth and nineteenth centuries, gardens evolved from traditional herbal collections to facilities with broader interests. Some gardens, notably the Royal Botanic Gardens at Kew, near London, played a major role in spreading the cultivation of commercially important plants such as coffee (*Coffea arabica*), rubber (*Hevea* spp.), banana (*Musa paradisiaca*), and tea (*Thea sinensis*) from their places of origin to other areas with an appropriate climate. Other gardens focused on new varieties of horticultural plants. The Leiden garden in Holland, for instance, was instrumental in stimulating the development of the extensive worldwide Dutch bulb commerce. Many other gardens have had an important place in the scientific study of plant diversity as well as the introduction and assessment of plants for agriculture, horticulture, forestry, and medicine.

The total number of botanical gardens in the world can only be estimated, but not all plant collections qualify for the designation because they are deemed to lack serious scientific purpose. A recent estimate places the number of botanical gardens and arboreta at 1,400. About 300 of those are in the United States. Most existing gardens are located in the North Temperate Zone, but there are important gardens on all continents except Antarctica. Although the tropics are home to the vast majority of all plant species, until recently, relatively few gardens were located there. A recognition of the need for further study of the diverse tropical **flora** has led to the establishment of many new gardens. An estimated 230 gardens are now established in the tropics.

In recent years botanical gardens throughout the world have united to address increasing threats to the planet's flora. The problem is particularly acute in the tropics, where as many as 60,000 species, nearly one-fourth of the world's total, risk extinction by the year 2050. Botanical gardens have organized to produce, adopt and implement a Botanic Gardens Conservation Strategy to help deal with the dilemma. *See also* Conservation; Critical habitat; Ecosystem; Endangered species; Forest decline; Organic gardening and farming

[*Douglas C. Pratt*]

FURTHER READING

Bramwell, D., O. Hamann, V. Heywood, H. Synge. *Botanic Gardens and the World Conservation Strategy.* London: Academic Press, 1987.

Hyams, E. S., and W. MacQuitty. *Great Botanical Gardens of the World.* New York: Macmillan, 1969.

Wyman, D. *The Arboretums and Botanical Gardens of North America.* Jamaica Plain, MA: Arnold Arboretum of Harvard University, 1947.

Boulding, Kenneth (1910-)

English-born American economist

Kenneth Boulding is a highly respected economist, educator, author, and pacifist. In an essay in *Frontiers in Social Thought: Essays in Honor of Kenneth E. Boulding* (1976), Cynthia Earl Kerman described Boulding as "a person who grew up in the poverty-stricken 'inner city' of Liverpool, broke through the class system to achieve an excellent education, had both scientific and literary leanings, became a well-known American economist, then snapped the bonds of economics to extend his thinking into wide-ranging fields—a person who is a religious mystic and a poet as well as a social scientist."

A major recurring theme in Boulding's work is the need—and the quest—for an integrated social science, even a unified science. He does not see the disciplines of human knowledge as distinct entities, but rather a unified whole characterized by "a diversity of methodologies of learning and testing." For example, Boulding is a firm advocate of adopting an ecological approach to economics, asserting that **ecology** and economics are not independent fields of study. He has identified five basic similarities between the two disciplines: 1) both are concerned not only with individuals, but individuals as members of **species**; 2) both have an important concept of dynamic equilibrium; 3) a system of exchange among various individuals and species is essential in both ecological and economic systems; 4) both involve some sort of development—**succession** in ecology and **population growth** and capital accumulation in economics; 5) both involve distortion of the equilibrium of systems by humans in their own favor.

"If my life philosophy can be summed up in a sentence," Boulding stated, "it is that I believe that there is such a thing as human betterment—a magnificent, multi-dimensional, complex structure—a cathedral of the mind—and I think human decisions should be judged by the extent to which they promote it. This involves seeing the world as a total system." Boulding's views have been influential in many fields, and he has helped environmentalists reassess and redefine their role in the larger context of science and economics.

[*Gerald L. Young*]

FURTHER READING

Boulding, K. E. "Economics As an Ecological Science." In *Economics As a Science.* New York: McGraw-Hill, 1970.

———. *Collected Papers.* Boulder: Colorado Associated University Press, 1971.

Kenneth Boulding.

Kerman, C. E. *Creative Tension: The Life and Thought of Kenneth Boulding.* Ann Arbor: University of Michigan Press, 1974.

Pfaff, M., ed. *Frontiers in Social Thought: Essays in Honor of K. E. Boulding.* Amsterdam and New York: North-Holland, 1976.

Silk, L. "K. E. Boulding: The Economics of Peace and Love." In *The Economists.* New York: Basic Books, 1976.

Wright, R. "Kenneth Boulding." In *Three Scientists and Their Gods: Looking for Meaning in an Age of Information.* New York: Times Books, 1988.

Boundary Waters Canoe Area (Minnesota)

The Boundary Waters Canoe Area (BWCA), a federally designated **wilderness** area in northern Minnesota, includes approximately 1 million acres (410,000 ha) stretching some 200 mi (322 km) along the United States-Canadian border. The BWCA contains more than 1,200 mi (1,932 km) of canoe routes and portages. The second largest expanse in the National Wilderness Preservation system, the BWCA is administered by the United States **Forest Service**. Constituting about one-third of the Superior National Forest (established in 1909), the BWCA was set apart as wilderness by an act of Congress in 1958. The 1964 **Wilderness Act** allowed limited logging in some parts of the BWCA and the use of motorboats on 60% of the water area. Under pressure from environmental groups—and over objections by developers, logging interests, and many local residents—the Congress finally passed the BWCA Wilderness Act of 1978, which outlawed all logging and limited motorboats to 33% of the water surface area (due to drop to 24% by 1999), and

added 45,000 acres (18,450 ha), bringing the total area to 1,075,000 acres (440,750 ha).

Many area residents and resort owners continue to resent and resist efforts to reduce the areas open to motorized watercraft and snowmobile traffic. They have pressed unsuccessfully for federal legislation to that effect. At the urging of Senator Paul Wellstone (D-MN), a mediation panel was convened in 1996 to consider the future of the BWCA. Environmentalists, resort owners, local residents, and representatives of other groups met for several months to try to reconcile competing interests in the area. Unable to reach agreement and arrive at a compromise, the panel disbanded in 1997. The fierce and continuing political quarrels over the future of the BWCA contrast markedly with the silence and serenity of this land of sky-blue waters and green forests.

[*Terence Ball*]

FURTHER READING

Beymer R. *The Boundary Waters Canoe Area*, vol. 1: "The Western Region" and vol. 2: "The Eastern Region." Berkeley: Wilderness Press, 1978.

Brackish

The salinity of brackish water is intermediate between seawater and fresh waters. Brackish water contains too much salt to be drinkable, but not enough salt to be considered seawater. The ocean has an average salinity of 35 **parts per thousand** (ppt), whereas freshwater contains 0.065 to 0.30 ppt of salts, primarily chloride, sodium, sulfate, magnesium, calcium, and potassium **ion**s. The salt content of brackish water ranges between approximately 0.50 and 17 ppt. Brackish water occurs where freshwater flows into the ocean, or where salts are dissolved from subsoils and percolate into freshwater basins. The gradient between salt and fresh water in **estuaries** and deltas varies from sharp distinction to gradual mixing, and different levels of vertical and horizontal mixing depend on the influence of tide, current, and rate of freshwater inflow.

Broad spectrum pesticide
See **Pesticide**

Bronchial constriction
See **Asthma**

Bronchitis

Chronic bronchitis is a persistent inflammation of the bronchial tubes, airways leading to the lungs. The disease is characterized by a daily cough that produces sputum for at least three months each year for two consecutive years, when no other disease can account for these symptoms. The diagnosis of chronic bronchitis is made by this history, rather than by any abnormalities found on a chest **X-ray** or through a pulmonary function test.

When a person breathes in, air, **smoke**, germs, **allergen**s and pollutants pass from the nose and mouth into a large central duct called the trachea. The trachea branches into smaller ducts, the bronchi and bronchioles, which lead to the alveoli. These are the tiny, balloonlike, air sacs, composed of capillaries, supported by connecting tissue, and enclosed in a thin membrane. Bronchitis can permanently damage the alveoli.

Bronchitis is usually caused by **cigarette smoke** or exposure to other irritants or air pollutants. The lungs respond to the irritation in one of two ways. They may become permanently inflamed with fluid, which swells the tissue that lines the airways, narrowing them and making them resist airflow. Or, the mucus cells of the bronchial tree may produce excessive mucus.

The first sign of excessive mucus production is usually a morning cough. As smoking or exposure to air pollutants continues, the irritation increases and is complicated by infection, as excess mucus provides food for bacteria growth. The mucus changes from clear to yellow, and the infection becomes deep enough to cause actual destruction of the bronchial wall. Scar tissue replaces the fine cells, or cilia, lining the bronchial tree, and some bronchioles are completely destroyed. Paralysis of the cilia permits mucus to accumulate in smaller airways, and air can no longer rush out of these airways fast enough to create a powerful cough.

With each pulmonary infection, excess mucus creeps into the alveoli, and on its way, totally blocking portions of the bronchial tree. Little or no gas exchange occurs in the alveoli, and the ventilation-blood flow imbalance significantly reduces oxygen levels in the blood and raises **carbon dioxide** levels. Chronic bronchitis eventually results in airway or air sac damage; the air sacs become permanently hyperinflated because mucus obstructing the bronchioles prevents the air sacs from fully emptying.

Chronic bronchitis usually goes hand-in-hand with the development of **emphysema**, another chronic lung disease. These progressive diseases cannot be cured, but can be treated. Treatment includes avoiding the inhalation of harmful substances such as polluted air or cigarette smoke. *See also* Air quality; Air pollution; Respiration; Respiratory diseases

[*Linda Rehkopf*]

FURTHER READING

Baker, Sherry and Carl Sherman. "Saving Your Lungs and Your Life." *Health* (June 1991): 63.

Haas, Francois, et. al. *The Chronic Bronchitis and Emphysema Handbook.* New York: Wiley Science Editions, 1990.

Shayevitz, Myra B., et. al. *Living Well With Emphysema and Bronchitis.* New York: Doubleday, 1985.

Brower, David Ross (1912-)

American environmentalist

David R. Brower (born in 1912, in Berkeley, California), the founder of both **Friends of the Earth** and the **Earth Island Institute**, has long been widely considered to be one of the most radical and effective environmentalists in the United States.

Joining the **Sierra Club** in 1933, Brower became a member of its Board of Directors in 1941 and then its first executive director, serving from 1952 to 1969. In this position, Brower helped transform the group from a regional to a national force, seeing the club's membership expand from 2,000 to 77,000 and playing a key role in the formation of the Sierra Club Foundation. Under Brower's leadership the Sierra Club, among other achievements, successfully opposed the **Bureau of Reclamation**'s plans to build **dams** in Dinosaur National Monument in Utah and Colorado as well as in Arizona's Grand Canyon, but lost the fight to preserve Utah's Glen Canyon. The loss of Glen Canyon became a kind of turning point for Brower, indicating to him the need to take uncompromising and sometimes militant stands in defense of the natural **environment**. This militancy has recurringly caused friction both between the groups he has led and the private corporations and governmental agencies with which they interact and also within the increasingly broad-based groups themselves. In 1969 Brower was asked to resign as executive director of the Sierra Club's Board of Directors, which disagreed with Brower's opposition to a nuclear reactor in California's Diablo Canyon, among other differences. Eventually reelected to the Sierra Club's Board in 1983 and 1986, Brower is now an honorary vice-president of the club and was the recipient, in 1977, of the John Muir Award, the organization's highest honor.

After leaving the Sierra Club in 1969, Brower founded Friends of the Earth with the intention of creating an environmental organization which would be more international in scope and concern and more political in its orientation than the Sierra Club. Friends of the Earth, which now is operating in some fifty countries, was intended to pursue a more global vision of **environmentalism** and to take more controversial stands on issues—including opposition to **nuclear weapons**—than could the larger, generally more conservative organization. But in the early 1980s, Brower again had a falling out with his associates over policy, eventually resigning from Friends of the Earth in 1986 to devote more of his time and energy to the **Earth Island Institute**, a San Francisco-based organization he founded in 1982 and of which he is presently chairman.

Over the years, Brower has played a key role in preserving **wilderness** in the United States, helping to create **national park**s and **national seashore**s in Kings Canyon, the North Cascades, the Redwoods, Cape Cod, Fire Island, and Point Reyes. He also was instrumental in protecting primeval forests in the Olympic National Park and wilderness on San Gorgonio Mountain in California and in establishing the National Wilderness Preservation System and the Outdoor Recreation Resources Review, which resulted in the Land and Water Conservation Fund.

In his youth, Brower was one of this country's foremost rock climbers, leading the historic first ascent of New Mexico's Shiprock in 1939 and making seventy other first ascents in **Yosemite National Park** and the High Sierra as well as joining expeditions to the Himalayas and the Canadian Rockies. A proficient skier and guide as well as a mountaineer, Brower served with the United States Mountain Troops from 1942-45, training soldiers to scale cliffs and navigate in Alpine areas and serving as a combat-intelligence officer in Italy. For his service, Brower was awarded both the Combat Infantryman's Badge and the Bronze Star, and rose in rank from private to captain before he left active duty. As a civilian, Brower has employed many of the same talents and abilities to show people what he has fought so long and so hard to preserve: He initiated the knapsack, river, and wilderness threshold trips for the Sierra Club's Wilderness Outings Program, and between 1939 and 1956 led some 4,000 people into remote wilderness.

Excluding his military service, Brower was an editor at the University of California Press from 1941 to 1952. Appointed to the *Sierra Club Bulletin*'s Editorial Board in 1935, Brower eventually became the *Bulletin*'s editor, serving in this capacity for eight years. He has been involved with the publication of more than fifty environmentally oriented books each for the Sierra Club and Friends of the Earth, several of which have earned him prestigious publishing industry awards. He wrote a two-volume autobiography, *For Earth's Sake* and *Work in Progress*. Brower also made several Sierra Club films, including a documentary of raft trips on the Yampa and Green Rivers designed to show people the stark beauty of Dinosaur National Monument, which at the time was threatened with flooding by a proposed dam.

Brower has been the recipient of numerous awards and honorary degrees and serves on several boards and councils, including the Foundation on Economic Trends, the Council on National Strategy, the Council on Economic Priorities, the North Cascades Conservation Council, the Fate and Hope of the Earth Conferences, Zero Population Growth, the Committee on National Security, and **Earth Day**. He has twice been nominated for the Nobel Peace Prize. Brower has promoted environmental causes around the globe, giving dozens of lectures in 17 different countries and organizing several international conferences. In 1990, Brower's life was the subject of a PBS Video Documentary entitled *For Earth's Sake*. He also was featured in the TV documentary *Green for Life*, which focused on the 1992 Earth Summit in Rio de Janeiro.

Now over eighty years old, Brower is still actively promoting environmental causes. He is currently absorbed in his duties at the Earth Island Institute, and in promoting the activities of the International Green Circle. In 1990 and 1991, he led Green Circle delegations to Siberia's **Lake Baikal** to aid in its protection and restoration. Brower is presently lecturing to companies and schools throughout the U.S. on Planetary Conservation Preservation and Restoration (CPR). His topics include land conservation, the econo-

David Ross Brower.

mics of sustainability and he meaning of wilderness to science. Brower's book, *Let the Mountains Talk, Let the Rivers Run*, includes a credo for the Earth, which reflects what Brower hopes to accomplish with his lectures and publications: "We urge that all people now determine that an untrammeled wilderness shall remain here to testify that this generation had love for the next."

[*Lawrence J. Biskowski*]

FURTHER READING

Brower, D. *For Earth's Sake.* Layton, UT: Gibbs Smith, 1990.

———. *Work in Progress.* Layton, UT: Gibbs Smith, 1991.

Foster, C. "A Longtime Gadfly Still Stings." *Christian Science Monitor* (8 April 1991): 14.

McKibben, B. "David Brower: Interview." *Rolling Stone* (28 June 1990): 59-62, 87.

Russell, D. "Nicaraguan Journey: The Archdruid at 76." *Amicus Journal* 11 (Summer 1989): 32-37.

Brown, Lester R. (1934-)

American agricultural economist and writer

The founder, president, and senior researcher of the prestigious **Worldwatch Institute**, Brown is a highly respected and influential authority on global environmental issues. Through the Worldwatch Institute, he has written or directed numerous papers and publications analyzing and discussing environmental, agricultural, and economic problems and trends.

Brown was born in Bridgeton, New Jersey, and during high school and college, he grew tomatoes with his younger brother. At this time he developed his appreciation for **nature**'s ability, if properly treated, to supply us with food on a regular and sustainable basis.

After earning a degree in agricultural science from Rutgers University in 1955, he spent six months in rural India studying and working on agricultural projects. In 1959, he joined the **U.S. Department of Agriculture**'s Foreign Agricultural Service as an international agricultural analyst. After receiving an M.S. in agricultural economics from the University of Maryland and a master's degree in public administration from Harvard, he went to work for Orville Freeman, the Secretary of Agriculture, as an advisor on foreign agricultural policy in 1964.

In 1969, Brown helped establish the Overseas Development Council and in 1974, with the support of the Rockefeller Fund, he founded the Worldwatch Institute to analyze world conditions and problems such as **famine**, overpopulation, and scarcity of **natural resources**.

In 1984, Brown launched Worldwatch's annual *State of the World* report, a comprehensive and authoritative account of worldwide environmental and agricultural trends and problems. Now published in twenty-six languages, *State of the World* may be one of the most influential and widely read reports on public policy issues. Other Worldwatch publications initiated and overseen by Brown include *Worldwatch*, a bimonthly magazine, the *Environmental Alert* book series, and the annual *Vital Signs: The Trends That Are Shaping Our Future*.

Brown has written or co-authored over a dozen books and some two dozen Worldwatch papers on various economic, agricultural, and environmental topics. He serves as a board member of **Green Seal**, which endorses environmentally responsible consumer products, and is a member of the Council on Foreign Relations. Brown has received a $250,000 "genius award" from the MacArthur Foundation, as well as the United Nation's 1989 environmental prize. *The Washington Post* has described him as "one of the world's most influential thinkers."

Brown has long warned that unless the United States and other nations adopt policies that are ecologically and agriculturally sustainable, the world faces a disaster of unprecedented proportions. In *State of the World 1992* he wrote, "The health of the planet has deteriorated dangerously during the [last] 20 years. As a result the world faces potentially convulsive change.... Building an environmentally sustainable future depends on restructuring the global economy, major shifts in human reproductive behavior, and dramatic changes in values and lifestyles." *See also* Agroecology; Population growth; Sustainable agriculture

[*Lewis G. Regenstein*]

FURTHER READING

Brown, L. R., ed. *State of the World*. New York: W. W. Norton, annual.

———, et al. *Vital Signs: The Trends That Are Shaping Our Future*. New York: W. W. Norton, annual.

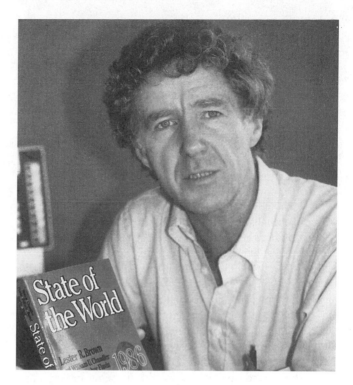

Lester R. Brown

———, ed. *The World Watch Reader on Global Environmental Issues*. New York: W. W. Norton, 1991.

Brown pelican (*Pelecanus occidentalis*)

The brown pelican is a large water bird of the family Pelicanidae that is found along both coasts of the United States, chiefly in saltwater habitats. It weighs up to 8 lbs (3.5 kg) and has a wingspan of up to 7 ft (2 m). This pelican has a light brown body, and a white head and neck often tinged with yellow. Its distinctive, long, flat bill and large throat pouch are adaptations for catching its primary food, schools of mid-water fishes. The brown pelican hunts while flying a dozen or more feet above the surface of the water, dropping or diving straight down into the water, and using its expandable pouch as a scoop or net to engulf its catch.

Both east and west coast populations, which are considered to be different subspecies, have shown various levels of decline over the past half century. It is estimated that there were 50,000 pairs of nesting brown pelicans along the Gulf coast of Texas and Louisiana in the early part of this century, but by the early 1960s, most of the Texas and all of the Louisiana populations were depleted. The main reason for the drastic decline was the use of organic **pesticide**s, including **DDT** and endrin. These pesticides poisoned pelicans directly and also caused thinning of their eggshells. This eggshell thinning led to reproductive failure, because the egg were crushed during incubation. Louisiana has the distinction of being the only state to have its state bird become extinct within its borders. In 1970 the brown pelican was listed as endangered throughout its U.S. range.

During the late 1960s and early 1970s, brown pelicans from Florida were reintroduced to Louisiana, but many of these birds were doomed. Throughout the 1970s these transplanted birds were poisoned at their nesting sites at the outflow of the Mississippi River by endrin, which was used extensively upriver. In 1972 the use of DDT was banned in the U. S., and the use of endrin was sharply curtailed. Continued reintroduction of the brown pelican from Florida to Louisiana subsequently met with greater success, and the Louisiana population had grown to more than 1,000 pairs by 1989. Although the Texas, Louisiana, and California populations are still listed as endangered, the Alabama and Florida populations of the brown pelican have been removed from the federal list due to recent increases in fledgling success.

Other problems that face the brown pelican include **habitat** loss, encroachment by humans, and disturbance by humans. Disturbances have included mass visitation of nesting colonies. This practice has been stopped on federally owned lands and access to nesting colonies is restricted. Other human impacts on brown pelican populations have had a more malicious intent. On the California coast in the 1980s there were cases of pelicans' bills being broken purposefully, so that these birds could not feed and would ultimately starve to death. It is thought that disgruntled commercial fishermen faced with dwindling catches were responsible for at least some of these attacks. The brown pelican was a scapegoat for conditions that were due to weather, pollution, or, most likely, **overfishing**.

Recovery for the brown pelican has been slow, but progress is being made on both coasts. The banning of DDT in the early 1970s was probably the turning point for this species, and the delisting of the Alabama and Florida populations is a hopeful sign for the future. *See also* Carson, Rachel; Endangered species

[*Eugene C. Beckham*]

FURTHER READING

Briggs, K. T., et al. "Brown Pelicans in Central and Northern California." *Journal of Field Ornithology* 54 (1983): 353-373.

Ehrlich, P., D. Dobkin, and D. Wheye. *Birds in Jeopardy.* Stanford, CA: Stanford University Press, 1992.

King, K. A., et al. "The Decline of Brown Pelicans on the Louisiana and Texas Gulf Coast." *Southwest Naturalist* 21 (1977): 417-431.

Schreiber, R. W. "The Brown Pelican: An Endangered Species?" *BioScience* 30 (November 1980): 742-747.

Browner, Carol (1955-)

Director of Environmental Protection Agency

Carol Browner is the current head of the **Environmental Protection Agency (EPA)** under the Clinton administration and a former aide to Vice President **Albert Gore**. According to *USA Today*, she has "a reputation for listening, negotiating and compromising [and] has critics on every side. Environmentalists suggest she may favor business; big busi-

nesses worries that she lacks corporate experience." Browner was born in Florida on December 17, 1955. Her father taught English and her mother social science at Miami Dade Community College. Browner grew up hiking in the **Everglades**, where her lifelong love for the natural world began. She was educated at the University of Florida in Gainesville, receiving both a BA in English and her law degree there.

Her political career began in 1980 as an aide in the Florida House of Representatives. Browner moved to Washington, D.C. a few years later to join the national office of Citizen Action, a grassroots organization that lobbies for a variety of issues, including the environment. She left Citizen Action to work with Florida Senator Lawton Chiles, and in 1989 she joined Senator Al Gore's staff as a senior legislative aide.

For the two years before her appointment to the EPA, Browner headed the Department of Environmental Regulation in Florida, the third-largest environmental agency in the country. She streamlined the process the department used to review permits for expanding manufacturing plants and developing **wetlands**, thus reducing the amount of money and time that process was costing businesses as well as the department. Activists have argued that this kind of streamlining interferes with the ability of government to supervise industries and assess their impact on the environment. But in Florida's business community, Browner has built a reputation as a formidable negotiator on behalf of the environment. When the Walt Disney Company filed for state and federal permits to fill in 400 acres of wetlands, she negotiated an agreement which allowed the company to proceed with their development plans in return for a commitment to buy and restore an 8,500-acre ranch near Orlando. She was also the chief negotiator in the settlement of a lawsuit the government had brought against Florida for environmental damage done to Everglades National Park. The result was the largest ecological restoration project ever attempted in the United States, a plan to purify and restore the natural flow of water to the Everglades with the cost shared by the state and the federal government, as well as Florida's sugar farmers.

Browner has often been called "a new type of environmentalist" because of her belief that environmental protection is compatible with economic development and her strong conviction that the stewardship of the environment requires accommodations with industry. "I've found that business leaders don't oppose strong environmental programs," she said in a recent interview with the *New York Times*. "What drives them crazy is a lack of certainty." As head of the EPA, she is determined to address the resistance from industry which has burdened the agency since its founding, and she remains committed to streamlining environmental regulations and increasing efficiency in the organization. Her highest priority, however, is "restoring credibility" to a demoralized and ineffective agency, underemphasized during the Reagan and Bush administrations and damaged by political conflicts.

Early in her tenure, Browner displayed her determination to reshape the agency's relationship to business by addressing the complex problem of **pesticide** food safety

Carol Browner.

laws. For many years the EPA has been caught been two conflicting statutes which have prevented the agency from approving the use of newer pesticides that cause less harm to the environment, and Browner has begun to lobby for changes in federal legislation. She also plans to improve the agency's management of the Superfund program which is consuming an increasingly large portion of the agency's budget. She recently removed herself from decisions about the testing and commercial operation of a **hazardous waste** incinerator in Ohio because the national office of Citizen Action, which continues to employ her husband, had become involved in the dispute. "You can't have environmental protection," Browner has said, "without having people believe in what you are doing."

[*Douglas Smith*]

FURTHER READING

"Greener and Browner: Environmentalists." *The Economist* 326 (January 9, 1993): 25–26.

"Babbitt, Browner Take Interior, EPA Posts." *National Parks* 67 (March-April 1993): 9.

"The Nominee for E.P.A. Sees Industry's Side Too." *New York Times* (December 17, 1992): A13.

"Agency Head Removes Herself from Decision on Ohio Incinerator." *New York Times* (February 8, 1993): A11.

Brownfields

By some estimates, as many as 450,000 urban brownfield sites may exist nationwide. These former commercial or industrial properties can be found in nearly every community where, because of real or perceived contamination, the land sits idle or under-used. Brownfield sites can be as small as a gas station with a **leaking underground storage tank** or as large as a 100-acre abandoned factory containing dumped waste on the site. The sites are not remarketed or reused because owners or operators fear that, if the properties are contaminated, the regulatory requirements to clean them up could be prohibitively time-consuming and expensive. Furthermore, even if such properties were put on the market, developers, and financial credit sources would shun them in part from concerns that dealing with contamination cleanup could raise the costs and slow the pace of reusing the properties.

But the brownfields situation has been changing as local, state, and federal government officials recognize the dire need to begin cleaning up and returning these contaminated properties to productive use. These officials point out that reusing the brownfield sites not only would reduce the phenomenon of "**urban sprawl**" but would also furnish communities with the chance to renew the economic vitality of abandoned urban centers. In many metropolitan areas urban sprawl has been recognized as a serious problem, with developers turning to rural greenfields for their projects and thereby reducing habitat for wildlife and contributing to air pollution as commuters drive longer distances to outlying greenfield locations. Moreover, environmental justice advocates point to the need for cleaning up contaminated urban sites to reduce exposure to hazardous contaminants faced by residents in these areas. Together, these factors have created momentum for a national brownfields redevelopment initiative. The promise some see in brownfields redevelopment led the Environmental Manager of Portland, Oregon, to state that "Brownfields renewal is one of the most important environmental and economic challenges facing our nation's communities, calling for partnership among our federal and local governments, business and community and environmental leaders."

Although **land use** decisions are made by local authorities, the U.S. **Environmental Protection Agency** (EPA) plays a critical role in the brownfields reuse initiative. On the one hand, the EPA's rules governing contaminated site cleanups, based on federal statutes, have played a significant part in deterring brownfields redevelopment; on the other, the Agency has been a major source of funding for brownfields pilots. In particular, the **Comprehensive Environmental Response, Compensation, and Liability Act** (CERCLA)—commonly known as Superfund—has made brownfield sites into expensive liabilities, causing businesses to avoid them because stringent cleanup standards and related costs often exceed the property's value. Under CERCLA, new property owners can be held liable for contamination created by previous owners. The **Clean Air Act** also drives businesses away from urban brownfield sites because it burdens companies in areas not attaining national air quality standards, making it more attractive for them to locate in rural regions where meeting clean air standards may be easier than in the city.

The EPA began its brownfields pilot program in 1993 by supporting pilot projects—each funded up to $200,000 over two years—at eight separate locations. The goal was to learn about brownfields, which the Agency saw as a new and complex territory in which it had little experience. The EPA awarded its first pilot in November 1993 to Cuyahoga County, Ohio, where the county planning commission had formed a broad effort to involve stakeholders in addressing brownfields reuse. The EPA described Cuyahoga County's report on its brownfields initiative as the most complete known to the Agency on the problems urban areas faced in reusing brownfields. Two additional pilots were awarded in 1994 to Bridgeport, Connecticut, and Richmond, Virginia. By October 1996 the EPA had funded 76 brownfields pilots, 39 under its "National Pilots" selected by the EPA Headquarters in Washington, D.C., and 37 under its "Regional Pilots" selected by the EPA's regional offices. An additional 25 National Pilots were scheduled for selection by March 1997.

In addition to funding pilot projects, the EPA took other actions to underscore its commitment to a Brownfields Economic Redevelopment Initiative, intended to help communities revitalize brownfields properties both environmentally and economically. In January 1995, the EPA Administrator **Carol Browner** announced a Brownfields Action Agenda, stating, "We at EPA firmly believe that environmental cleanup is a building block to economic development, not a stumbling block—that identifying and cleaning up contaminated property must go hand-in-hand with bringing life and vitality back to a community." The Brownfields Action Agenda included the Agency's pilots; joint efforts by EPA, states, and local governments to develop guidance documents to clarify burning liability issues; partnership and outreach endeavors with states, cities, and communities; and job training and development activities, including funding towards an environmental education program at Cuyahoga Community College in Cleveland, Ohio.

The National Environmental Justice Advisory Council (NEJAC), chartered in September 1993 as a federal advisory committee to the EPA, in a December 1996 report expressed hope that the Agency's brownfields initiative would stem the "ecologically untenable" and "racially divisive" phenomenon of urban sprawl, in which urban areas were left to stagnate while greenfields were subjected to increasing development. NEJAC also emphasized that the brownfields problem is "inextricably linked to environmental justice" through, for instance, the deterioration of the nation's urban areas. NEJAC reached its hopeful evaluation of the prospects for the brownfields initiative despite misgiving by some NEJAC members that the initiative might be a "smoke screen" for gutting cleanup standards and liability safeguards.

The liability issues addressed under the EPA's Brownfields Action Agenda are among the most important factors affecting these sites. According to the Agency, the fear of inheriting cleanup liabilities for contamination they did not create affects communities, lenders, property owners, municipalities, and others. To help assuage liability concerns, in February 1995 the EPA removed 24,000 of the 40,000 sites listed in its Comprehensive Environmental Response, Compensation and Liability Information System (CERCLIS), a Superfund tracking system. These sites had been screened out of the "Active Investigations" category and designated "No Further Remedial Action Planned," either because they were found to be clean or were being addressed by state cleanup programs. By taking the sites off the CERCLIS list, the EPA hoped to remove any stigma resulting from federal involvement at the sites and thereby to overcome obstacles to their cleanup and reuse.

In May 1995 the EPA issued guidance on "Agreements with Prospective Purchaser of Contaminated Property." The guidance indicated the situations under which the Agency may enter into an agreement to not file a lawsuit against a prospective contaminated property buyer for contamination present at the site before the purchase. Also in May 1995 the EPA issued guidance regarding "Land Use in the CERCLA Remedy Selection Process" to ensure that the Agency considers land use during Superfund cleanups. Land designated for reuse as an industrial site would require less strict cleanup than land designated for a park or school, a recognition that not all contaminated sites should be regarded as equally befouled. In September 1995 the EPA issued guidance that, among other things, released from CERCLA liability governmental units such as municipalities that involuntarily take ownership of property under federal, state, or local law. The EPA hoped this guidance would encourage municipalities to start cleaning up sites without fear of the Superfund liability predicament. These and other guidance documents issued under the Brownfields Action Agenda helped to clarify liabilities facing prospective new owners of private and federally owned contaminated sites.

But the EPA's guidance documents are regarded as only partial solutions to the brownfields problem. A report released February 1997 by the National Association of Local Government Environmental Professionals (NALGEP), representing 50 cities nationwide, stresses that the EPA's ability to "further clarify and reduce environmental liability for brownfields activity is limited," and therefore "legislative solutions" are required to make further progress on the brownfields agenda. Noting that the U.S. House and Senate introduced "numerous brownfields bills" during the 104th Congress and that brownfields legislation is likely in the 105th Congress, NALGEP's report suggests federal law should empower the EPA to delegate authority to the states with cleanup programs that meet minimum requirements to protect health and the environment. The EPA would be empowered to authorize qualifying states to limit liability and issue "no action assurances" for less contaminated brownfield sites. Those sites would be clearly differentiated from more seriously contaminated properties that warrant management under the federal Superfund **National Priorities List** of sites.

Going into the 105th Congress, federal lawmakers and President Bill Clinton agreed that brownfields legislation ought to be a priority. Underscoring the close link between brownfields and economic revitalization, Senator Max Baucus (D-Montana), the Ranking Democrat of the Senate Environment and Public Works Committee, said at a press conference in January 1997 that passage of a brownfields bill—apart from Superfund reauthorization legislation—would be a step towards helping create jobs where they are really needed. Welfare reform added to the growing momentum for urban renewal and job opportunities. Representative Michael Oxley (R-Ohio), who proposed Superfund amendments in the 103rd Congress to direct the EPA to help states set up "voluntary cleanup programs" aimed at brownfields sites, compared the federal Superfund liability scheme to the Berlin Wall and said that it should be torn down. The chorus of voices joining Oxley has grown substantially since 1993, and today not only the EPA but also the U.S. Department of Housing and Urban Development, the U.S. Department of Labor, and other federal agencies have joined states and local governments in promoting brownfields redevelopment.

[*David Clarke*]

FURTHER READING

Powers, C. *State Brownfields Policy and Practice.* Boston: Institute for Responsible Management, 1994.

U.S. Environmental Protection Agency. *The Brownfields Action Agenda.* Washington, D.C.: GPO, 1995.

U.S. Environmental Protection Agency. National Environmental Justice Advisory Council. *Environmental Justice, Urban Revitalization, and Brownfields: The Search for Authentic Signs of Hope.* Washington, D.C.: GPO, 1996.

National Association of Local Government Environmental Professionals. *Building a Brownfields Partnership from the Ground Up.* Washington, D.C., 1997.

Gro Harlem Brundtland.

Brundtland, Gro Harlem (1939-)

Norwegian Prime Minister

Gro Harlem Brundtland has been instrumental in promoting political awareness of the importance of environmental issues. In her view, the world shares one economy and one **environment**. Her writings and speeches emphasize the need to adopt global solutions to environmental problems.

Brundtland began her political career as Oslo's parliamentary representative in 1977. She became the leader of the Norwegian Labor Party in 1981, when she first became prime minister. At 42, she was the youngest person ever to lead the country and the first woman to do so. She regained the position in 1986 and held it until 1989; in 1990 she was again elected prime minister.

Brundtland earned a degree in medicine from the University of Oslo in 1963 and a Master's Degree in Public Health from Harvard in 1965. She served as a medical officer in the Norwegian Directorate of Health and as medical director of the Oslo Board of Health. In 1974 she was appointed Minister of the Environment, a position she held for four years. This appointment came at a time when environmental issues, especially **pollution**, were becoming increasingly important, not only locally but nationally. She

gained international attention and in 1983 was selected to chair the United Nation's World Commission on Environment and Development. The commission published *Our Common Future* in 1987, calling for **sustainable development** and intergenerational responsibility as guiding principles for economic growth. The report states that the present economic development depletes **nonrenewable resources** that must be preserved for **future generations**. The commission strongly warned against **environmental degradation** and urged nations to reverse this trend.

Aside from her involvement in the environmental realm, Brundtland has promoted equal rights and a larger role in government for women. In her second cabinet, 8 of the 18 positions were filled by women; in her 1990 government, 9 of 19 ministers were women. Since other government positions are also held by women, some speculate that Norway may be evolving into Europe's first state matriarchy.

Brundtland has been recognized often for her work, receiving the Third World Prize; the Indira Ghandi Prize for Peace, Disarmament, and Development; and the Scandinavian of the Year Award, all in 1988. Like any politician, however, she has also been criticized, most recently for her support of **whaling** along Norway's coast. Bruntland resigned her position as prime minister in October 1996. There were many factors that contributed to her decision, including the 1992 suicide of her son and a chance for the position of United Nations Secretary General. Brundtland continues to maintain her international visibility while championing sustainable development and empowering women in all realms of society.

[*William G. Ambrose, Jr. and Paul E. Renaud*]

FURTHER READING

Anonymous. *Authorized Biographical Sketch of Gro Harlem Brundtland.* Norwegian Department of State, 1992.

Brady, M. "Gro Harlem Brundtland, Scandinavian of the Year." *Scanorama* 18 (1988).

Brundtland, G.H. "Global Change and Our Common Future." *Environment* 31 (1989): 16-34.

Brundtland Report

*See **Our Common Future***

Btu

Abbreviation for "British Thermal Unit," the amount of energy needed to raise the temperature of one pound of water by one degree Fahrenheit. One Btu is equivalent to 1,054 joules or 252 calories. To gain an impression of the size of a Btu, the **combustion** of a barrel of oil yields about 5.6×10^6 joule. A multiple of the Btu, the quad, is commonly used in discussions of national and international energy issues. The term quad is an abbreviation for one quadrillion, or 10^{15}, Btu.

Buffer

A term in environmental chemistry that refers to the capacity of a system to resist chemical change. Most often it is used in reference to the ability to resist change in **pH**. A system that is strongly pH buffered will undergo less change in pH with the addition of an acid or a base than a less well buffered system. A well buffered lake contains higher concentrations of bicarbonate ions that react with added acid. This kind of lake resists change in pH better than a poorly buffered lake. A highly buffered **soil** contains an abundance of **ion exchange** sites on **clay minerals** and organic matter that react with added acid to inhibit pH reduction. *See also* Acid and base

Bulk density

The mass of **soil** per unit bulk volume. The bulk volume consists of mineral and organic materials, water, and air. Bulk density is affected by external pressures (e.g. weight of tractors and harvesting equipment, mechanical pressures from cultivation machines) and by internal pressures (e.g. swelling and shrinking due to water-content changes, freezing and thawing, and by plant roots). The bulk density of cultivated mineral soils ranges from 1-1.6 mg/m^3.

Burden of proof

The current regulatory system, following traditional legal processes, generally assumes that **chemicals** are innocent, or not harmful, until proven guilty. Thus, the burden to show proof that a chemical is harmful to human and/or **ecosystem** health falls on those who regulate or are affected by these chemicals. As evidence increases that many of the more than 70,000 chemicals in the marketplace today—and the 10,000 more introduced each year—are causing health effects in various species, including humans, new regulations are being proposed that would reverse this burden to the manufacturer, importer or user of the chemical and its byproducts. They would then have to prove before its production and distribution that the chemical will not be harmful to human health and the environment.

Bureau of Land Management (BLM)

The Bureau of Land Management (BLM), in the **U. S. Department of the Interior**, was created by executive reorganization in June 1946. The new agency was a merger of the Grazing Service and the General Land Office (GLO). The GLO was established in the Treasury Department by Congress in 1812 and charged with the administration of the **public land**s. The agency was transferred to the Department of the Interior when it was established in 1849. Throughout the 1800s and early 1900s, the GLO played the central role in administering the disposal of public lands under a multitude of different laws. But, as the nation began to move from disposal of public lands to retention of them, the services of the GLO became less needed, which helped to pave the way for the creation of the BLM. The Grazing Service was created in 1934 (as the Division of Grazing) to administer the **Taylor Grazing Act**.

In the 1960s, the BLM began to advocate for an organic act that would give it firmer institutional footing, would declare that the federal government planned to retain the BLM lands, and would grant the agency statutory authority to professionally manage these lands (like the **Forest Service**). Each of these goals was achieved with the passage of the **Federal Land Policy and Management Act** (FLPMA) in 1976. The agency was directed to manage these lands and undertake long-term planning for the use of the lands, guided by the principle of multiple use.

The BLM manages 272 million acres of land, primarily in the western states. This land is of three types: Alaskan lands (92 million acres), which is virtually unmanaged; the Oregon and California lands (2.6 million acres), prime timber land in western Oregon that reverted back to the government in the early 1900s due to land grant violations; and the remaining land (177 million acres), approximately 70 percent of which is in grazing districts. As a multiple use agency, the BLM manages these lands for a number of uses: fish and wildlife, forage, minerals, recreation, and timber. Additionally, FLPMA directed that the BLM review all of its lands for potential **wilderness** designation, a process that is now well underway. (BLM lands were not covered by the **Wilderness Act** of 1964). In addition to these general land management responsibilities, the BLM also issues leases for mineral development on all public lands. FLPMA also directed that all mineral claims under the 1872 Mining Law be recorded with the BLM.

The BLM is headed by a director, appointed by the President and confirmed by the Senate. The chain of command runs from the Director in Washington to state directors in eleven western states (all but Hawaii and Washington), to district managers, who administer grazing or other districts, to resource area managers, who administer parts of the districts.

The BLM has often been compared unfavorably to the Forest Service. It has received less funding and less staff than its sibling agency, has been less professional, and has been characterized as captured by livestock and mining interests. Recent studies suggest that the administrative capacity of the BLM has improved. *See also* Land use; Public trust

[*Christopher McGrory Klyza*]

FURTHER READING

Culhane, P. J. *Public Lands Politics: Interest Group Influence on the Forest Service and the Bureau of Land Management.* Baltimore: Johns Hopkins University Press for Resources for the Future, 1981.

Dana, S. T., and Fairfax, S. K. *Forest and Range Policy.* 2nd ed. New York: McGraw-Hill, 1980.

Public Land Statistics 1990. U.S. Department of the Interior, Bureau of Land Management. Washington, DC: Government Printing Office, 1991.

Bureau of Mines

The U. S. Bureau of Mines was founded in 1910 after a series of **coal** mine disasters took more than 3,000 lives within the prior three years. Congress established this Bureau under the **U. S. Department of the Interior** to promote mineral technology and mine safety. The Bureau opened an experimental coal mine near Pittsburgh, where it conducted tests with coal dust and ultimately prompted rescue stations and first aid training for miners. In addition to mine safety, the Bureau has been active in research and development of technology to extinguish underground coal mine fires and also to remediate mine **tailings** and waste streams. These latter studies have included the development of stabilization **chemicals** and ground cover to minimize air-borne transport of dusts from mine wastes, as well as the use of a product made from peat to absorb **heavy metals** from mine drainage.

In the mid 1970s the Bureau of Mines at several of their research laboratories conducted pioneer studies on methods of reclaiming wastes, including the manufacture of construction bricks from mining wastes, the pyrolysis of **garbage** to form **petrochemical**s, and the separation and recovery of valuable metals, **plastics**, and glass products from municipal trash. These studies were undertaken as part of a program to look upon waste as a substitute for mined materials . Also, the Bureau was active in developing processes for removing sulfur from **smelter** stack gases, a process which also has applicability in the burning of high-sulfur utility coal. The Bureau has also been custodian of our helium reserves. This inert gas is associated with the production of natural gas and is found in relatively high concentrations in

North America, where it has unique properties with respect operation of processes at very low temperatures, (e.g. superconductors).

Currently the Bureau continues to strongly emphasize mine safety, and to develop processes for in situ mining. In this method of mining, acids are injected into an ore body selectively to dissolve (leach) the valuable constituent (e.g. copper) and bring it to the surface as a solution. The copper is then removed and replaced with acid and the solutions are reused. If properly conducted, this mining method has minimum impact upon the land surface, although, careful monitoring of subsurface conditions is required to prevent migration of the leach solutions into **aquifer**s.

[*Malcolm T. Hepworth*]

FURTHER READING

Utley, R., and B. MacKintosh. *The Department of Everything Else, Highlights of Interior History.* Washington, DC: U.S. Government Printing Office, 1989.

Bureau of Oceans and International Environmental and Scientific Affairs (OES)

The Bureau of OES was established in 1974 under Section 9 of the Department of State Appropriations Act. It is the lead office in Department of State in the formulation of foreign policy in four areas: 1) International Science and Technology (S&T) Affairs; 2) Environmental, Health, Natural Resource Protection and Global Climate Change; 3) Nuclear Energy and Energy Technology Affairs; and 4) Oceans and Fisheries Affairs. Each area is headed by a Deputy Associate Secretary of State. A Bureau coordinator oversees the Office of World Population Affairs. OES provides support and guidance to U. S. Embassy science counselors and attaches in reporting and negotiations. It has responsibility for the International Fisheries Commissions, the Fisherman's Guarantee Fund and the U.S. Secretariat for the **Man and the Biosphere Program**. The bureau prepares an annual Presidential report (the title V Report) on international "Science, Technology and American Foreign Policy.

Bureau of Reclamation

The U. S. Bureau of Reclamation was established in 1902 and is part of the **U. S. Department of the Interior**. It is primarily responsible for the planning and development of **dams, power plants,** and water transfer projects, such as Grand Coulee Dam on the Columbia River, the Central Arizona Project, and Hoover Dam on the Colorado River. This latter dam, completed in 1935 between Arizona and Nevada, is the highest arch dam in the Western Hemisphere and is part of the Boulder Canyon Project, the first great multipurpose water development project, providing **irrigation**, electric power, and flood control. It also created Lake Mead, which is supervised by the **National Park Service**

John Burroughs (left) with naturalist John Muir.

to manage boating, swimming, and camping facilities on the 115 mile-long **reservoir** formed by the dam. The dams on the **Colorado River** are intended to reduce the impact of the destructive cycle of floods and **drought**s which makes settlement and farming precarious and to provide electricity and **recreation**al areas; however, the deep canyons and free-flowing rivers with their attendant **ecosystem**s are substantially altered. Along the Columbia River, efforts are made to provide "fish ladders" adjacent to dams to enable **salmon** and other **species** to bypass the dams and spawn up river; however, these efforts have not been as successful as desired and many native species are now endangered.

Problems faced by the Bureau relate to creating a balance between its mandate to provide hydropower, water control for irrigation, and by-product recreation areas, and the conflicting need to preserve existing ecosystems. For example, at the **Glen Canyon Dam** on the Colorado River, controls on water releases are presently being imposed (February 1992) while studies are completed on the best manner of protecting the **environment** downstream in the Grand Canyon National Park and the Lake Mead National Recreation Area.

[*Malcolm T. Hepworth*]

FURTHER READING

The United States Government Manual, 1992/93. Washington, DC: U. S. Government Printing Office, 1992.

Buried soil

Buried soil is **soil** that appeared on the surface of the earth and sustained plant life but because of a geologic event has been covered by a layer of **sediment**. Sediments can result from **volcano**es, rivers, dust storms, or blowing sand or **silt**.

Burroughs, John (1827-1921)

American naturalist

A follower of both **Henry David Thoreau** and Ralph Waldo Emerson (1803-1882), Burroughs more clearly defined the nature essay as a literary form. His writings provided vivid descriptions of outdoor life and gained popularity among a diverse audience.

Burroughs spent his boyhood exploring the lush countryside surrounding his family's dairy farm in the valleys of the Catskill Mountains, near Roxbury, New York. He left school at age sixteen and taught grammar school in the area until 1863, when he left for Washington, D.C. for a position as a clerk in the U. S. Treasury Department. While in Washington, Burroughs met poet Walt Whitman (1819-1892), through whom he began to develop and refine his writing style. His early essays were featured in the *Atlantic Monthly*. These works, including "With the Birds" and "In the Hemlocks", detailed Borroughs's boyhood recollections as well as recent observations of nature. In 1867 Burroughs published his first book, *Notes on Walt Whitman as a Poet and Person*, to which Whitman himself contributed significantly. Four years later, Burroughs produced *Wake-Robin* independently, followed by *Winter Sunshine* in 1875, both of which solidified his literary reputation.

By the late 1800s, Burroughs had returned to New York and built a one-room log cabin house he called "Slabsides," where he philosophized with such guests as **John Muir**, **Theodore Roosevelt**, Thomas Edison, and Henry Ford. Burroughs accompanied Roosevelt on many adventurous expeditions and chronicled the events in his book, *Camping and Tramping with Roosevelt* (1907).

Burroughs's later writings took new directions. His essays became less purely naturalistic and more philosophical and deductive. He often sought to reach the levels of spirituality and vision he found in the works of Whitman, Emerson, and Thoreau. Borroughs explored poetry, for example, in *Bird and Bough* (1906), and *The Summit of the Years* (1913), which searched for a less scientific explanation of life, while *Under the Apple Trees* (1916) examined World War I.

Although Burroughs's enthusiastic inquisitiveness prompted travel abroad, he travelled primarily within the United States. He died in 1921 en route from California to his home in New York. Following his death, the John Burroughs Association was established through the auspices of the American Museum of Natural History. The association remains active and continues to maintain an exhibit at the museum.

[*Kimberley A. Peterson*]

FURTHER READING

Burroughs, J. *In the Catskills: Selections from the Writings of John Burroughs.* Marietta: Cherokee Publishing Co., 1990.

Kanze, E. *The World of John Burroughs.* Bergenfield: Harry N. Abrams, 1993.

McKibben, B., ed. *Birch Browsings: A John Burroughs Reader.* New York: Viking Penguin, 1992.

Renehan, E. J., Jr. *John Burroughs: An American Naturalist.* Post Mills: Chelsea Green, 1992.

Bycatch Reduction Devices (BRDs)

Seabirds, seals, **whales**, **sea turtles**, dolphins, and non-targeted fish can be unintentionally caught and killed or maimed by modern fish and shrimp catching methods. This phenomenon is called "bycatch" or the unintended capture or mortality of living marine resources as a result of fishing. It is managed under such laws as the Migratory Bird Treaty Act, the **Endangered Species Act** of 1973, the **Marine Mammals Protection Act** of 1972 (amended in 1994), and, most recently, the Magnuson-Stevens Fishery Conservation and Management Act of 1996. The 1995 United Nations Code of Conduct for Responsible Fisheries, to which the United States is a signatory, also emphasizes the importance of bycatch reduction. Bycatch occurs because most fishing methods are not perfectly "selective," (i.e., they do not catch and retain only the desired size, sex, quality and quantity of target

species). It also occurs because fishermen often have incentive to catch more fish than they will keep.

Although the exact extent of bycatch-related mortality is uncertain, public awareness of the problem has grown in the 1990s, leading to a deepening public perception that commercial fisheries are wasteful of the world's finite marine resources. According to a 1994 estimate of the United Nations' **Food and Agriculture Organization**, worldwide **commercial fishing** operations discarded 30 million tons (27 million metric tons) of fish, approximately one-fourth of the world catch, because they were the wrong type, sex, or size. In United States fisheries, a total of 149 species groups have been identified as bycatch, 67% of them finfish, crustaceans, or mollusks, and 37% of them protected marine mammals, turtles, or seabirds.

To address this problem, numerous research programs have been established to develop BRDs and other means to reduce bycatch. Much of this research, and the nation's bycatch reduction activities overall, is centered in the Department of Commerce's National Marine Fisheries Service (NMFS), which leads and coordinates the United States' collaborative efforts to reduce bycatch. In March 1997, NMFS proposed a draft long-term strategy, *Managing the Nation's Bycatch*, that seeks to provide structure to the service's diverse bycatch-related research and management programs. These include gear research, technology transfer workshops, and the exploration of new management techniques. NMFS's Bycatch Plan was intended to as a guide for its own programs and for its "cooperators" in bycatch reduction, including eight regional fishery management councils, states, three interstate fisheries commissions, the fishing industry, the conservation community, and other parties. In pursuing its mandate of conserving and managing marine resources, NMFS relies on the direction for bycatch established by the 104th Congress under the new National Standard 9 of the Magnuson-Stevens Act, which states: "Conservation and management measures shall, to the extent practicable, (A) minimize bycatch and (B) to the extent bycatch cannot be avoided, minimize the mortality of such bycatch."

But, although the national bycatch standard applies across all regions, bycatch issues are not uniform for all fisheries. Indeed, bycatch is not always a problem and can sometimes be beneficial, (e.g., when bycatch species are kept and used as if they had been targeted species). But where bycatch is a problem, the exact nature of the problem and potential solutions will differ depending on the region and fishery. For instance, in the U.S. Gulf of Mexico shrimp fishery, which contributes about 70% of the annual U.S. domestic shrimp production, bycatch of juvenile red snapper (*Lutjanus blackfordi*) by shrimp trawlers reduces red snapper stocks for fishermen who target those fish. According to NMFS, "In the absence of bycatch reduction, red snapper catches will continue to be a fraction of maximum economic or biological yield levels." To address this problem, the Gulf of Mexico Fishery Management Council prepared an amendment to the shrimp fishery management plan for the Gulf of Mexico requiring shrimpers to use BRDs in their nets. But

BRD effectiveness differs, and devices often lose significant amounts of shrimp in reducing bycatch. For instance, one device called a "30-mesh fisheye" reduced overall shrimp catches, and revenues, by 3%, an issue that must be addressed in any analysis of the costs and benefits of requiring BRDs, according to NMFS. In Southern New England, the yellowtail flounder (*Pleuronectes ferrugineus*) has been important to the New England groundfish fisheries for several decades. But the stock has been depleted to a record low because, from 1988-1994, most of the catch has been discarded by trawlers. Reasons for treating the catch as bycatch were that most of the fish were either too small for marketing or were smaller than the legal size limit. Among the solutions to this complex problem an increase in the mesh size of nets so smaller fish would not be caught and a redesign of nets to facilitate the escape of undersized yellowtail flounder and other bycatch species.

Although fish bycatch exceeds that of other marine animals, it is by no means the only significant bycatch problem. Sea turtle bycatch has received growing attention in recent years, most notably under the Endangered Species Act Amendments of 1988, which mandated a study of sea turtle conservation and the causes and significance of their mortality, including mortality caused by commercial trawlers. That study, conducted by the **National Research Council** (NRC), found that shrimp trawls accounted for more deaths of sea turtle juveniles, subadults, and breeders in coastal waters than all other human activities combined. According to the NRC's 1990 report, some 5,000-50,000 loggerhead turtles (*Caretta caretta*) and 500-5,000 Kemp ridleys (*Lepidochelys kempi*) a year are killed by shrimping operations from Cape Hatteras, North Carolina, to the Mexican border in the Gulf of Mexico. Deaths from drowning increase when trawlers tow their catch for longer than 60 minutes. Winter flounder trawling north of Cape Hatteras, Chesapeake Bay passive-gear fishing, and other fisheries were also found to be responsible for some turtle mortality.

To address the turtle bycatch problem, NMFS, numerous Sea Grant programs, and the shrimping industry conducted research that led to the development of several types of net installation devices that were called "**turtle excluder device**s" (TEDs) or "trawler efficiency devices." In 1983, the only TED approved by NMFS was one developed by the service itself. But in the face of industry concerns about using TEDs, the University of Georgia and NMFS tested devices developed by the shrimping industry, resulting in NMFS certification of new TED designs. Each design was intended to divert turtles out of shrimp nets, excluding the turtles from the catch without reducing the shrimp intake. Over a decade of development, these devices have been made lighter and today at least six kinds of TEDs have NMFS's approval. Early in the development of TEDs, NMFS tried to obtain voluntary use of the devices, but shrimpers considered them an expensive, time-consuming nuisance and feared they could reduce the size of shrimp catches. But NMFS, and environmental groups, countered that the best TEDs reduced turtle bycatch by up to 97% with slight or no loss of shrimp. By 1985, NMFS faced threats of lawsuits to shut down the shrimping industry because trawlers were not using TEDs. In response, NMFS convened mediation meetings that included environmentalists and shrimpers. The meetings led to an agreement to pursue a "negotiated rulemaking" to phase in mandatory TED use, but negotiations fell apart after state and federal legislators, under intense pressure, tried to delay implementation of TED rules. After intense controversy, NMFS published regulations June 28, 1987, on the use of TEDs by shrimp trawlers.

Dolphins are another marine animal that has suffered significant mortality levels as a result of bycatch associated with the eastern tropical Pacific Ocean tuna fishery. Several species of tuna are often found together with the most economically important tuna species, the yellowfin (*Thunnus albacares*). As a result, tuna fishermen have used a fishing technique—called "dolphin fishing," in which they set their nets around herds of dolphins to capture the tuna that are always close by. The spotted dolphin (*Stenella attenuata*) is most frequently associated with tuna. Spinner dolphin (*Stenella longirostris*), and the common dolphin (*Delphinus delphis*) also travel with tuna. According to one estimate, between 1960-1972 the U.S. fleet in the eastern tropical Pacific Ocean fishery killed more than 100,000 dolphins a year. That number dropped to an estimated 20,000 after 1972, when the Marine Mammals Protection Act was passed. By 1989, the number was estimated at 12,643, largely because the number of boats in the U.S. tuna fishing fleet declined and those that were in operation killed fewer dolphins. U.S. fishing boats are now required to use techniques that allow dolphins to escape from tuna nets before the catch is hauled in. These include having fishermen jump into the ocean to hold the lip of the net below the water surface so the dolphin can jump out.

[*David Clarke*]

FURTHER READING

Decline of the Sea Turtles, Causes and Prevention. Washington, D.C.: National Academy Press, 1990.

Dolphins and the Tuna Industry. Washington, D.C.: National Academy Press, 1992.

Managing the Nation's Bycatch: Priorities, Programs and Actions for the National Marine Fisheries Service. Washington, D.C.: National Marine Fisheries Service, National Oceanic and Atmospheric Administration, U.S. Department of Commerce, March 20, 1997, Draft.

C

Cadmium

A metallic element that occurs most commonly in nature as the sulfide, CdS. Cadmium has many important industrial applications. It is used to electroplate other metals, in the production of paints and **plastics**, and in **nickel**-cadmium batteries. The metal also escapes into the environment during the burning of **coal** and **tobacco**. Cadmium is ubiquitous in the environment, with detectable amounts present in nearly all water, air, and food samples. In high doses, cadmium is toxic. In lower doses, it may cause kidney disease, disorders of the circulatory system, weakening of bones, and, possibly, **cancer**. *See also* Itai-Itai disease

CAFE

See **Corporate Average Fuel Economy**

Calcareous soil

A calcareous soil is **soil** that has calcium carbonate ($CaCO_3$) in abundance. If a calcareous soil has hydrochloric acid added to it, the soil will effervesce and give off **carbon dioxide** and form bubbles because of the chemical reaction. Calcareous soils are most often formed from limestone or in dry environments where low rainfall prevents the soils from being leached of carbonates. Calcareous soils frequently cause **nutrient** deficiencies for many plants.

Caldicott, Helen (1938 -)

Australian physician and activist

Dr. Helen Caldicott is a pediatrician, mother, antinuclear activist, and environmental activist. Born Helen Broinowski in Melbourne, Australia on August 7, 1938, she is known as a gifted orator and a tireless public speaker and educator. She traces her activism to age 14 when she read Nevil Shute s *On the Beach*, a chilling novel about nuclear holocaust. In 1961 she graduated from the University of Adelaide Medical School with bachelor of medicine and bachelor of surgery degrees, which are the equivalent of an American M.D. She

Dr. Helen Caldicott

married Dr. William Caldicott in 1962, and returned to Adelaide, Australia to go into general medical practice. In 1966 she, her husband, and their three children moved to Boston, Massachusetts, where she held a fellowship at Harvard Medical School. Returning to Australia in 1969, she served first as a resident in pediatrics and then as an intern in pediatrics at Queen Elizabeth Hospital. There, she set up a clinic for cystic fibrosis, a genetic disease in children.

In the early 1970s, Caldicott led a successful campaign in Australia to ban atmospheric nuclear testing by the French in the South Pacific. Her success in inspiring a popular movement to stop the French testing has been attributed to her willingness to reach out to the Australian people through letters and television and radio appearances, in which she explained the dangers of **radioactive fallout**. Next, she led a successful campaign to ban the exportation of **uranium** by Australia. During that campaign she met strong resistance from Australia's government, which had responded to the 1974 international **oil embargo** by offering to sell uranium on the world market. (Uranium is the raw material for nuclear technology.) Caldicott chose to go directly to mine workers, explaining the effects of radiation on their bodies and their genes and talking about the effects of nuclear war on them and their children. As a result, the Australian Council of Trade Unions passed a resolution not to mine, sell, or transport uranium. A ban was instituted from 1975 to 1982, when Australia gave in to international pressure to resume the exportation.

In 1977 Dr. Caldicott and her husband immigrated to the United States, accepting appointments at the Children's Hospital Medical Center and teaching appointments at Harvard Medical School in Boston, Massachusetts. She was a co-founder of Physicians for Social Responsibility (PSR), and she was its president at the time of the March 28, 1979 nuclear accident at the **Three Mile Island Nuclear Reactor** in Pennsylvania. At that time, PSR was a small group of concerned medical specialists. Following the accident, the organization grew rapidly in membership, financial support, and influence. As a result of her television appearances and statements to the media following the Three Mile Island accident, Caldicott became a symbol of the movement to ban all **nuclear power** and oppose **nuclear weapons** in any form. Ironically, she resigned as president of PSR in 1983, when the organization had grown to over 20,000 members. At that time, she began to be viewed as an extreme radical in an organization that had become more moderate as it came to represent a wide, diversified membership.

She also founded Women's Action for Nuclear Disarmament (WAND). WAND has been an effective group lobbying Congress against nuclear weapons.

Throughout her career, Caldicott has considered her family to be her first priority. She has three children and she emphasizes the importance of building and maintaining a strong marriage, believing that good interpersonal relationships are essential before a socially-minded person can work effectively for broad social change.

Caldicott has developed videotapes and films and has written over one hundred articles which have appeared in major newspapers and magazines throughout the world. She has written four books. Her first, *Nuclear Madness: What You Can Do* (1978) is considered important reading in the anti-nuclear movement. Her second, entitled *Missile Envy*, was published in 1986. In *If You Love This Planet: A Plan to Heal the Earth* (1992), Caldicott discusses the race to save the planet from environmental damage resulting from excess energy consumption, **pollution, ozone layer depletion**, and global warming. She urges citizens of the United States to follow the example set by the Australians, who have adopted policies and laws designed to move their society toward greater corporate and institutional responsibility. She urges the various nations of the world to strive for a "new legal world order" by moving toward a sort of transnational control of the world's **natural resources**. Her most recent book, *A Desperate Passion* (1996), is an autobiography in which she reflects upon crucial events that have influenced her and talks about people who have inspired her in her life and work.

Caldicott is the recipient of many awards and prizes including the SANE Peace Prize, the Ghandi Peace Prize, the John-Roger Foundation's Integrity Award (which she shared with Bishop Desmond Tutu), the Norman Cousins Award for Peace-making, the Margaret Mead Award, and many others.

[*Paulette L. Stenzel*]

FURTHER READING

Caldicott, H. *A Desperate Passion.* New York: Bantam Books, 1996.

Caldicott, H. *If You Love This Planet: A Plan to Heal the Earth.* New York: W. W. Norton, 1992.

———. *Missle Envy.* New York: Bantam Books, 1986.

_ *Nuclear Madness: What You Can Do.* New York: Bantam Books, 1981.

Nixon, W. "Helen Caldicott: Practicing Global Preventive Medicine." *E Magazine* (September-October 1992): 12-5.

Caldwell, Lynton Keith (1913-)

American scholar and environmentalist

Lynton Caldwell has been a key figure in the development of **environmental policy** in the United States. A longtime advocate for adding an environmental amendment to the Constitution, Caldwell has insisted that the federal government has a duty to protect the environment that is akin to the defense of civil rights or freedom of speech.

Caldwell was born November 21, 1913 in Montezuma, Iowa. He received his bachelor of arts from the University of Chicago in 1935 and completed a master of arts at Harvard University in 1938. The same year, Caldwell accepted an assistant professorship in government at Indiana University in Bloomington. In 1943, he attained his doctorate from the University of Chicago and began publishing academic works the following year. The subjects of his early writings were not environmental; he published a study of administrative theory in 1944 and a study of New York state government in 1954. By 1964, however, Caldwell had shifted his emphasis, and he began to receive wide recognition for his work on environmental policy. In that year, he was presented with the William E. Mosher Award from the American Society for Public Administration for his article "Environment: A New Focus for Public Policy."

Caldwell's most important accomplishment was his prominent role in the drafting of the **National Environmental Policy Act (NEPA)** in 1969. As a consultant for the Senate Committee on Interior and Insular Affairs in 1968, he prepared *A Draft Resolution on a National Policy for the Environment*. His special report examined the constitutional basis for a national environmental policy and proposed a statement of intent and purpose for Congress. Many of the concepts first introduced in this draft resolution were later incorporated into the act. As consultant to that committee, Caldwell played a continuing role in the shaping of the NEPA, and he was involved in the development of the **environmental impact statement**.

In recent years Caldwell has strongly defended the NEPA, as well as the regulatory agency it created, claiming that they represent "the first comprehensive commitment of any modern state toward the responsible custody of its environment." Although the act has influenced policy decisions at every level of government, the enforcement of its provisions have been limited. Caldwell argues that this is because environmental regulations have no clear grounding in the law. Statutes alone are often unable to withstand the pressure of economic interests. He has proposed an amendment to the Constitution as the best practical solution to this problem and he maintains that without such an amendment, environmental issues will continue to be marginalized in the political arena.

In addition to advising the Senate during the creation of the NEPA, Caldwell has done extensive work on international environmental policy. He has advised the Central Treaty Organization and served on special assignments in countries including Colombia, India, the Philippines, and Thailand. Currently, Caldwell serves as the Arthur F. Bentley Professor of Political Science emeritus and professor of public and environmental affairs at Indiana University in Bloomington, Indiana.

[*Douglas Smith*]

FURTHER READING

Caldwell, L. K. "20 Years with NEPA Indicate the Need." *Environment* 31 (December 1989): 6-11, 25-28.

Metzger, L., ed. "Caldwell, Lynton." In *Contemporary Authors New Revision Series*. Vol. 12. Detroit: Gale Research, 1984.

California condor (*Gymnogyps californianus*)

With a wingspan of over nine feet (about 3 m), the California condor is the largest North American member of the vulture family. It is also an **endangered species** barely clinging to existence, though its decline may be as much a result of natural forces as human influence.

The California condor is a **relict species** that was once distributed over much of North America: fossil records indicate its occurrence from Florida to New York in the east and British Columbia to Mexico in the west. Its distribution has dwindled steadily in recent history as its numbers have declined. The condor had begun its retreat westward by the time Columbus had arrived in North America. At the beginning of the twentieth century it could still be found in California and Baja California, but by World War II its range had been reduced to a strip of about 150 miles (241 km), across the southern end of the San Joaquin Valley.

All of the other large birds and mammals of this region from the late Pleistocene period have become extinct, and this same fate probably awaits the California condor. In the 1940s the **National Audubon Society** initiated a census of the birds' population and found approximately 60 condors. In

California condor.

the early 1960s the population was found to be 42 birds. A 1966 survey revealed 51 condors, an increase that may have been due to the sampling systems employed. By the end of 1986 there were 24 condors alive, 21 of which were in captivity.

Human activities have accelerated the decline of the condor in this century. California condors have been shot by hunters and poisoned by bait set out to kill coyotes. Their food has been contaminated with **pesticide**s, notably **DDT**, as well as lead, primarily from **lead shot** found in animal carcasses shot and lost by hunters. Their rarity has made their eggs a valuable commodity for unscrupulous collectors. Their original food sources, mammoths and giant camels of the Pleistocene, have disappeared, leaving little carrion to support much of a population. However, **habitat** destruction and general harassment have compacted their range and population size to a point where some intervening action was necessary to halt its rapid decline to extinction.

After much heated debate, the decision was made to remove all California condors from the wild and initiate a **captive propagation and reintroduction** program. The **Fish and Wildlife Service** together with the California Fish and Game Commission captured the last wild condor in April 1987.

The captive breeding program has thus far increased the population to over 50 birds. Condors nest only once every two years and typically lay only one egg. By removing the egg from the nest for laboratory incubation, the female can be tricked into laying a replacement egg, thus allowing for an accelerated population increase.

In January 1992, a pair of California condors were released into the wild. In October the male was found dead of kidney failure after apparently drinking from a pool of antifreeze in a parking lot near their sanctuary. Six additional condors were released at the end of 1992. Although the planned capture and release of this species is working, the survival of the California condor in the wild is still very much in doubt. *See also* Endangered Species Act; Extinction; Wildlife management

[*Eugene C. Beckham*]

FURTHER READING

Darlington, D. *In Condor Country: A Portrait of a Landscape, Its Denizens and Its Defenders*. New York: Henry Holt, 1991.

Jurek, R. M. "An Historical Review of California Condor Recovery Programmes." *Vulture News* 23 (1990): 3-7.

Kiff, L. "To the Brink and Back: The Battle to Save the Calfornia Condor." *Terra* 28 (1990): 6-18.

Snyder, N. F. R., and H. A. Snyder. "Biology and Conservation of the California Condor." In *Current Ornithology*, Vol. 6, edited by D. M. Power. New York: Plenum, 1989.

Willwerth, J. "Can They Go Home Again?" *Time* 139 (27 January 1992): 56-57.

Callicott, John Baird (1941-)

American environmental philosopher

J. Baird Callicott is a founder and seminal thinker in the modern field of environmental philosophy. He is best known as the leading contemporary exponent of **Aldo Leopold**'s **land ethic**, not only interpreting Leopold's original works but also applying the reasoning of the land ethic to modern resource issues such as **wilderness** designation and **biodiversity** protection.

Callicott's 1987 edited volume, *Companion to A Sand County Almanac*, is the first interpretive and critical discussion of Leopold's classic work. His 1989 collection of essays, *In Defense of the Land Ethic*, explores the intellectual foundations and development of Leopold's ecological and philosophical insights and their ultimate union in his later works. In 1991 Callicott, with Susan L. Flader, introduced to the public the best of Leopold's remaining unpublished and uncollected literary and philosophical legacy in a collection entitled *The River of the Mother of God and Other Essays* by Aldo Leopold.

Since his contribution to the inaugural issue of the journal *Environmental Ethics* in 1979, Callicott's articles and essays have appeared not only in professional philosophical journals and a variety of scientific and technical periodicals, but in a number of lay publications as well. He has contributed chapters to more than twenty books and is internationally known as an author and speaker. Born in Memphis, Tennessee, Callicott completed his Ph.D. in philosophy at Syracuse University in 1971, and has since held visiting professorships at a number of American universities. In 1971, while teaching at the University of Wisconsin-Stevens Point, Callicott designed and taught what is widely acknowledged as the nation's first course in **environmental ethics**. He is currently associate professor of Philosophy and Religion at the University of North Texas. With respect to the major value questions today in environmental ethics, Callicott's position can best be illustrated by his claim that there can be no value without valuers. He thus recognizes the legitimacy of both instrumental and intrinsic valuation on the part of a democracy of valuers, human and nonhuman.

Callicott perceives that we live today on the verge of a profound paradigm shift concerning human interactions with and attitudes toward the natural world. Much of his current work aims at distilling and giving voice to this shift and at articulating an ecologically accurate and philosophically valid concept of sustainability. This concept abandons dualistic (man versus nature), ethnocentric (modern Euroamerican), and static (e.g., wilderness frozen in time) elements of current thought in sustainability in favor of those emphasizing dynamic human/nonhuman mutualism, both in ecosystem **conservation** and in restoration. Through careful management consistent with the best ecological information and theories, Callicott believes, humans can not only protect but can and should enhance **ecosystem** health. His ideas challenge modern conventional wisdom and could radically alter much current theory in environmental philosophy as well as affect practice in wilderness management and economic development planning.

As one of a handful of scholars who launched the field of environmental ethics as we know it today, and as one of even fewer philosophers who have made their works accessible and pertinent not only to other academicians but to the general public, J. Baird Callicott occupies an important place in the history of modern philosophy. His work will undoubtedly continue to shape thinking on the ethical dimensions of resource management decisions for generations to come. *See also* Environmental economics; Environmental education; Forest management; Speciesism; Wildlife management

[*Ann S. Causey*]

FURTHER READING

Callicott, J. B. *Companion to A Sand County Almanac*. Madison: University of Wisconsin Press, 1987.

———. *In Defense of the Land Ethic: Essays in Environmental Philosophy*. Albany: State University of New York Press, 1989.

———. *Nature in Asian Tradition of Thought: Essays in Environmental Philosophy*. Albany: State University of New York Press, 1989.

Canadian Parks Service

The Canadian Parks Service (CPS) is the government agency charged with fulfilling the statutes and policies of Canada's **national park**s. The first national park was established in Banff, Alberta, in 1885, although parks were not institutionalized in Canada until 1911. The original policy and program established national parks to protect characteristic aspects of Canada's natural heritage, and, at the same time, cater to the benefit, enjoyment, and education of its people.

The National Parks Act of 1930 required parliamentary approval of parks, prohibited hunting, mining, and exploration, and limited forest harvesting. Other federal statutes gave control over lands and resources to the provinces, which meant land assembly for park development could not proceed without intergovernmental agreement. An amendment to the Parks Act increased the Park Service's ability to enforce regulations and levy meaningful penalties.

In 1971 the park system was expanded to include examples of all 39 terrestrial natural regions of Canada.

Currently, 21 regions are represented by 34 parks. The Canadian government has pledged to develop sites in the remaining 18 regions by the year 2000. The CPS hopes that national parks willl eventually encompass 12 percent of Canada's land base; they currently occupy only 1.8 percent.

Canada's four marine coasts have been classified into 29 regions, all of which are to be represented in a marine parks program. One site has been formally established, while four others are being considered. The CPS mandate was amended in 1986 to share control of marine parks with two other federal agencies, which manage fisheries and marine transportation.

Current park policy emphasizes the maintenance of ecological integrity over tourism and **recreation**. Much conflict, however, has centered on development within park boundaries. Townsites, highways, ski resorts, and golf courses provide public enjoyment, but conflict with the protective mandate of the parks' charter. Commercial and recreational fishing, logging, and trapping have also been allowed, despite legal prohibitions. In 1992, the Canadian Parks and Wilderness Society and the Sierra Legal Defense Fund successfully sued the Canadian government to stop logging in Wood Buffalo National Park, a protected **habitat** for both the endangered **whooping crane** and wood **bison**. *See also* Canadian Wildlife Service

[*David A. Duffus and Amy Strumolo*]

Canadian Wildlife Service

The Canadian Wildlife Service (CWS) was established in 1947. Until 1971 it was governed by the federal government's Parks Branch in the Department of Indian and Northern Development. Since 1971 it has been a branch of **Environment Canada**, most recently under the Conservation and Protection division. The Service is served by five regional offices across Canada and is headquartered in Hull, Quebec. There are four branches within the CWS: the Migratory Birds and Conservation Branch; the North American Waterfowl Management Plan Implementation Branch; the Wildlife Toxicology and Surveys Branch/National Wildlife Research Centre; and the Program Analysis and Co-ordination Branch.

Wildlife matters were delegated to the provinces by the Canadian constitution, and responsibility is generally in the hands of provincial administrations. Federal-provincial cooperation was facilitated through meetings of the Federal-Provincial Wildlife Ministers Conferences, ongoing since 1922 and an annual event since 1945. Through those ongoing discussions, federal wildlife policy has developed mainly around areas of transboundary issues and problems deemed in the national interest. Currently, the CWS's primary responsibility is to enforce the Migratory Birds Convention Act, the Canada Wildlife Act, the **Convention on International Trade in Endangered Species of Fauna and Flora (CITES)**, and the Ramsar **Convention on Wetlands of International Importance**. Furthermore, it has in-

creased responsibility on federal lands, north of 60°N latitude, although in recent years much responsibility has been delegated to the territorial wildlife services and local co-management agreements with aboriginal peoples.

Within those statutes and agreements CWS is responsible for policy and strategy development, enforcement, research, public relations, education and interpretation, **habitat** classification, and the management of about 82 sanctuaries and 39 wildlife areas. The combination of a national and international mandates and diverse landscapes of Canada make CWS the pivotal **wildlife management** institution in Canada. However, CWS's increasing reliance on cooperative measures with provincial governments and **nongovernmental organizations**, including **Ducks Unlimited** Canada and **World Wildlife Fund** Canada, has led the organization to less direct management and more coordination activities. Critics of Canada's wildlife management direction have suggested that the once world-renowned repository of research expertise in CWS has suffered in recent years. *See also* Canadian Parks Service; Environmental policy

[*David A. Duffus*]

Cancer

A malignant tumor, cancer comprises a broad spectrum of malignant neoplasms classified as either carcinomas or sarcomas. Carcinomas originate in the epithelial tissues, while sarcomas originate from connective tissues and structures that have their origin in mesodermal tissue. Cancer is an invasive disease that spreads to various parts of the body. It spreads directly to those tissues immediately surrounding the primary site of the cancer and may spread to remote parts of the body through the lymphatic and circulatory systems.

Cancer occurs in most, if not all, multicellular animals. Evidence from fossil records reveal bone cancer in dinosaurs, and sarcomas have been found in the bones of Egyptian mummies. Hippocrates (460-375 B.C.) is credited with coining the term *carcinoma*, the Greek word for crab. Why the word for crab was chosen enjoys much speculation, but may have had to do with the sharp, biting pain and invasive, spreading nature of the disease.

A **carcinogen** is any substance or agent that produces or induces the development of cancer. Carcinogens are known to affect and initiate metabolic processes at the level of **DNA** (the information-storing molecules in cells). DNA damage (**mutation**) is the development of cancer after exposure to a carcinogen. This kind of mutation is actually reversible; our bodies continually experience DNA damage, which is continually being corrected. It is only when promoter cells intervene during cell proliferation that tumors begin to develop. Although several agents can induce cell division, only promoters induce tumor development.

An example of this process would be what happens in an epidermal cell, when its DNA undergoes rapid, irreversible alteration or mutation after exposure to a carcinogen.

The cell undergoes proliferation, producing altered progeny, and it is at this point that the cell may proceed on one of two pathways. The cell may undergo interrupted exposure to promoters and experience early reversible precancerous lesions. Or it may experience continuous exposure to the promoters, thereby causing malignant cell changes. During the late phase of promotion, the primary epidermal cell becomes tumorous and begins to invade normal cells; then it begins to spread. It is at this stage that tumors are identified as malignant.

The spread of tumors throughout the body is believed to be governed by several processes. One possible mechanism is direct invasion of contiguous organs. This mechanism is poorly understood, but it involves multiplication, mechanical pressure, release of lytic **enzyme**s, and increased motility of individual tumor cells. A second process is metastasis. This is the spread of cancer cells from a primary site of origin to a distant site, and it is the life-threatening aspect of malignancy. At present there are many procedures available to surgeons for successfully eradicating primary tumors; however, the real challenge in reducing cancer mortality is finding ways to control metastasis.

Clinical manifestations of cancer take on many forms. Usually little or no pain is associated with the early stages of malignant disease, but pain does affect 60 to 80 percent of those terminally ill with cancer. General mechanisms causing pain associated with cancer include pressure, obstruction, invasion of a sensitive structure, stretching of visceral surfaces, tissue destruction, and inflammation. Abdominal pain is often caused by severe stretching from the tumor invasion of the hollow viscus, as well as tumors that obstruct and distend the bowel. Tumor compression of nerve endings against a firm surface also creates pain. Brain tumors have very little space to grow without compressing blood vessels and nerve endings between the tumor and the skull. Tissue destruction from infection and necrosis can also cause pain. Frequently infection occurs in the oral area, in which a common cause of pain is ulcerative lesions of the mouth and esophagus.

Cancer treatments involve chemotherapy, radiotherapy, surgery, immunotherapy, and combinations of these modalities. Chemotherapy and its efficacy is related to how the drug enters the cell cycle; the design of the therapy is to destroy enough malignant cells so that the body's own immune system can destroy the remaining cells naturally. Smaller tumors with rapid growth rates seem to be most responsive to chemotherapy. Radiation therapy is commonly used to eradicate tumors without excessive damage to surrounding tissues. Radiation therapy attacks the malignant cell at the DNA level, disrupting its ability to reproduce. Surgery is the treatment of choice when it has been determined that the tumor is intact and has not metastasized beyond the limits of surgical excision. Surgery is also indicated for benign tumors that could progress into malignant tumors. Premalignant and in situ tumors of epithelial tissues, such as skin, mouth, and cervix, can be removed.

Chemotherapy and radiation treatments are the most commonly used therapies for cancer. Unfortunately, both methods produce unpleasant side effects; they often suppress the immune system, making it difficult for the body to destroy the remaining cancer even after the treatment has been successful. In this regard, immunotherapy holds great promise as an alternative treatment, because it makes use of the unique properties of the immune system.

Immunotherapies for the treatment of cancer are generally referred to as biological response modifiers (BRMs). BRMs are defined as mammalian gene products, agents, and clinical protocols that affect biologic responses in host-tumor interactions. Immunotherapies have a direct cytotoxic effect on cancer cells, initiation or augmentation of the host's tumor-immune rejection response, and modification of cancer cell susceptibility to the lytic or tumor static effects of the immune system. As with other cancer therapies immunotherapies are not without their own side effects. Most common are flu-like symptoms, skin rashes, and vascular-leak syndrome. At their worst, these symptoms are usually less severe than those of current chemotherapy and radiation treatments. *See also* Hazardous material; Hazardous waste; Leukemia; Radiation sickness

[*Brian R. Barthel*]

FURTHER READING

Agency for Toxic Substances and Disease Registry. *Annual Report.* Atlanta: U.S. Department of Health and Human Services, 1989 and 1990.

Aldrich, T., and J. Griffith. *Environmental Epidemiology.* New York: Van Nostrad Reinhold, 1993.

Cunningham, W. P., and B. W. Saigo. *Environmental Science: A Global Concern.* Dubuque, IA: William C. Brown, 1990.

McCance, K. L. *Pathophysiology: The Biological Basis for Disease in Adults and Children.* St. Louis: Mosby, 1990.

Taber, C. W. *Taber's Cyclopedic Medical Dictionary.* Philadelphia: F.A. Davis, 1990.

Captive propagation and reintroduction

Captive propagation is the deliberate breeding of wild animals in captivity in order to increase their numbers. Reintroduction is the deliberate release of these **species** into their native habitat. The Mongolian wild horse, Pere David's deer, and the American **bison** would probably have become extinct without captive propagation. Nearly all cases of captive propagation and reintroduction involve threatened or **endangered species**. **Zoo**s are increasingly involved in captive propagation, sometimes using new technologies. One of these, embryo transfer, allows a relatively common species of antelope to act as a surrogate mother and give birth to a **rare species**.

Once suitable sites are selected, a reintroduction can take one of three forms. *Reestablishment reintroductions* take place in areas where the species once occurred but is now entirely absent. Recent examples include the red wolf, the

The release of baby Kemp's ridley sea turtles on a beach in Mexico.

black-footed ferret, and the **peregrine falcon** east of the Mississippi River. Biologists use *augmentation reintroduction* to release captive-born wild animals into areas in which the species still occurs but only in low numbers. These new animals can help increase the size of the population and enhance genetic diversity. Examples include a small Brazilian monkey called the golden lion tamarin and the peregrine falcon in the western United States. A third type, *experimental reintroduction*, acts as a test case to acquire essential information for use on larger-scale permanent reintroductions. The red wolf was first released as an experimental reintroduction. A 1982 amendment to the **Endangered Species Act** facilitates experimental reintroductions, offering specific exemptions from the Act's protection, allowing managers greater flexibility should reintroduced animals cause unexpected problems.

Yet captive propagation and reintroduction programs have their drawbacks, the chief one being their high cost. Capture from the wild, food, veterinary care, facility use and maintenance all contribute significant costs to maintaining an animal in captivity. Other costs are incurred locating suitable reintroduction sites, preparing animals for release, and monitoring the results. Some conservationists have argued that the money would be better spent acquiring and protecting **habitat** in which remnant populations already live.

There are also other risks associated with captive propogation programs such as disease, but perhaps the greatest biological concern is that captive populations of endangered species might lose learned or genetic traits essential to their survival in the wild. Animals fed from birth, for example, might never pick up food-gathering or prey-hunting skills from their parents as they would in the wild. Consequently, when reintroduced such animals may lack the skill to feed themselves effectively. Furthermore, captive breeding of animals over a number of generations could affect their **evolution**. Animals that thrive in captivity might have a selective advantage over their "wilder" cohorts in a zoo, but might be disadvantaged upon reintroduction by the very traits that aided them while in captivity.

Despite these shortcomings, the use of captive propagation and reintroduction will continue to increase in the decades to come. Biologists learned a painful lesson about the fragility of endangered species in 1986 when a sudden outbreak of canine distemper decimated the only known group of black-footed ferrets. The last few ferrets were taken into captivity where they successfully bred. Even as new ferret populations become established through reintroduction, some ferrets will remain as captive breeders for insurance against future catastrophes. Biologists are also steadily improving their methods for successful reintroduction. They have learned how to select the combinations of sexes and ages that offer the best chance of success and have developed systematic ways to choose the best reintroduction sites.

Captive propagation and reintroduction will never become the principal means of restoring threatened and endangered species, but it has been proven effective and will continue to act as insurance against sudden or catastrophic losses in the wild. *See also* Biodiversity; Extinction; Wildlife management; Wildlife rehabilitation

[*James H. Shaw*]

FURTHER READING

Jones, Suzanne R., ed. "Captive Propagation and Reintroduction: A Strategy for Preserving Endangered Species?" *Endangered Species Update* 8 (1) (1990): 1-88.

Lindburg, Donald G. "Are Wildlife Reintroductions Worth the Cost?" *Zoo Biology* 11 (1992): 1-2.

Carbamates

See **Pesticide**

Carbon

The seventeenth most abundant element on earth, carbon occurs in at least six different allotropic forms, the best known of which are diamond and graphite. It is a major component of all biochemical compounds that occur in living organisms: carbohydrates, proteins, lipids, and **nucleic acid**s. Carbon-rich rocks and minerals such as limestone, gypsum, and marble often are created by accumulated bodies of aquatic organisms. Plants, animals, and microorganisms cycle carbon through the **environment**, converting it from simple compounds like **carbon dioxide** and **methane** to more complex compounds like sugars and starches, and then, by the action of decomposers, back again to simpler compounds. One of the most important **fossil fuels**, **coal**, is composed chiefly of carbon.

Carbon cycle

Carbon makes up no more than 0.27 percent of the mass of all elements in the universe and only 0.0018 percent by weight of the elements in the earth's crust. Yet, its importance to living organisms is far out of proportion to these figures. In contrast to its relative scarcity in the **environment**, it makes up 19.4 percent by weight of the human body. Along with **hydrogen**, carbon is the only element to appear in every organic molecule in every living organism on earth.

The series of chemical, physical, geological, and biological changes by which carbon moves through the earth's air, land, water, and living organisms is called the carbon cycle.

In the **atmosphere**, carbon exists almost entirely as gaseous **carbon dioxide**. The best estimates are that the earth's atmosphere contains 740 billion tons of this gas. Its global concentration is about 350 **parts per million** (ppm),

or 0.035 percent by volume. That makes carbon dioxide the fourth most abundant gas in the atmosphere after **nitrogen**, oxygen and argon. Some carbon is also released as **carbon monoxide** to the atmosphere by natural and human mechanisms. This gas reacts readily with oxygen in the atmosphere, however, converting it to carbon dioxide.

Carbon returns to the hydrosphere when carbon dioxide dissolves in the oceans, as well as in lakes and other bodies of water. The solubility of carbon dioxide in water is not especially high, 88 milliliters of gas in 100 milliliters of water. Still, the earth's oceans are such a vast reservoir that experts estimate that approximately 36,000 billion tons of carbon are stored there. They also estimate that about 93 billion tons of carbon flows from the atmosphere into the hydrosphere each year.

Carbon moves out of the oceans in two ways. Some escapes as carbon dioxide from water solutions and returns to the atmosphere. That amount is estimated to be very nearly equal (90 billion tons) to the amount entering the oceans each year. A smaller quantity of carbon dioxide (about 40 billion tons) is incorporated into aquatic plants.

On land, green plants remove carbon dioxide from the air through the process of **photosynthesis**—a complex series of chemical reactions in which carbon dioxide is eventually converted to starch, cellulose, and other carbohydrates. About 100 billion tons of carbon are transferred to green plants each year, and a total of 560 billion tons of the element is thought to be stored in land plants alone.

The carbon in green plants is eventually converted into a large variety of organic (carbon-containing) compounds. When green plants are eaten by animals, carbohydrates and other organic compounds are used as raw materials for the manufacture of thousands of new organic substances. The total collection of complex organic compounds stored in all kinds of living organisms represents the reservoir of carbon in the earth's **biosphere**.

The cycling of carbon through the biosphere involves three major kinds of organisms. Producers are organisms with the ability to manufacture organic compounds such as sugars and starches from inorganic raw materials such as carbon dioxide and water. Green plants are the primary example of producing organisms. Consumers are organisms that obtain their carbon (that is, their food) from producers: all animals are consumers. Finally, decomposers are organisms such as bacteria and **fungi** that feed on the remains of dead plants and animals. They convert carbon compounds in these organisms to carbon dioxide and other products. The carbon dioxide is then returned to the atmosphere to continue its path through the carbon cycle.

Land plants return carbon dioxide to the atmosphere during the process of **respiration**. In addition, animals that eat green plants exhale carbon dioxide, contributing to the 50 billion tons of carbon released to the atmosphere by all forms of living organisms each year. Respiration and **decomposition** both represent, in the most general sense, a reverse of the process of photosynthesis. Complex organic compounds are oxidized with the release of carbon dioxide and water—the raw materials from which they were originally produced.

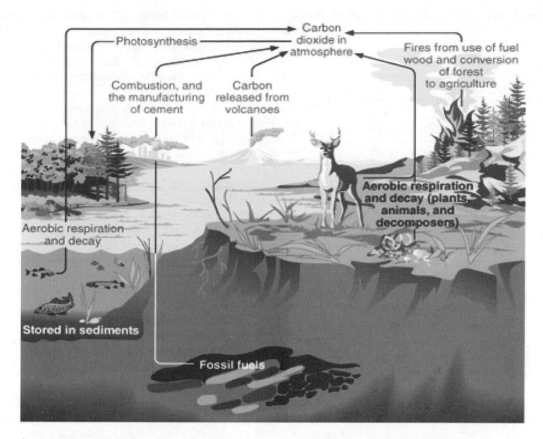

Carbon cycle.

At some point, land and aquatic plants and animals die and decompose. When they do so, some carbon (about 50 billion tons) returns to the atmosphere as carbon dioxide. The rest remains buried in the earth (up to 1,500 billion tons) or on the ocean bottoms (about 3,000 billion tons). Several hundred million years ago, conditions of burial were such that organisms decayed to form products consisting almost entirely of carbon and hydrocarbons. Those materials exist today as pockets of the **fossil fuels—coal**, oil, and **natural gas**. Estimates of the carbon stored in fossil fuels range from 5,000 to 10,000 billion tons.

The processes that make up the carbon cycle have been occurring for millions of years, and for most of this time, the systems involved have been in equilibrium. The total amount of carbon dioxide entering the atmosphere from all sources has been approximately equal to the total amount dissolved in the oceans and removed by photosynthesis. However, a hundred years ago changes in human society began to unbalance the carbon cycle. The Industrial Revolution initiated an era in which the burning of fossil fuels became widespread. In a short amount of time, large amounts of carbon previously stored in the earth as coal, oil, and natural gas were burned up, releasing vast quantities of carbon dioxide into the atmosphere.

Between 1900 and 1992, measured concentrations of carbon dioxide in the atmosphere increased from about 296 ppm to over 350 ppm. Scientists estimate that fossil fuel combustion now released about five billion tons of carbon

dioxide into the atmosphere each year. In an equilibrium situation, that additional five billion tons would be absorbed by the oceans or used by green plants in photosynthesis. Yet this appears not to be happening: measurements indicate that about 60 percent of the carbon dioxide generated by fossil fuel combustion remains in the atmosphere.

The problem is made even more complex because of **deforestation**. As large tracts of forest are cut down and burned, two effects result: carbon dioxide from forest fires is added to that from other sources, and the loss of trees decreases the worldwide rate of photosynthesis. Overall, it appears that these two factors have resulted in an additional one to two billion tons of carbon dioxide in the atmosphere each year.

No one can be certain about the environmental effects of this disruption of equilibria in the carbon cycle. Some authorities believe that the additional carbon dioxide will augment the earth's natural **greenhouse effect**, resulting in long-term global warming and **climate** change. Other argue that we still do not know enough about the way oceans, clouds, and other factors affect climate to allow such predictions.

This controversy involves a difficult choice. Should actions that could potentially cost billions of dollars be taken to reduce the emission of carbon dioxide when evidence for climate change is still uncertain? Or should governments wait until that evidence becomes more clear, with the risk that needed actions may then come too late. *See also* Energy policy; Greenhouse gases; Nitrogen cycle; Pollution; Pollution control

[*David E. Newton*]

FURTHER READING

Clapham, W. B., Jr. *Natural Ecosystems*. 2nd ed. New York: Macmillan, 1983.

Kupchella, C. E. *Environmental Science: Living within the System of Nature*. 3rd ed. Boston: Allyn and Bacon, 1993.

McGraw-Hill Encyclopedia of Science & Technology. 7th ed. New York: McGraw-Hill, 1992.

Carbon dating

See **Radiocarbon dating**

Carbon dioxide

The fourth most abundant gas in the earth's atmosphere, carbon dioxide occurs in an abundance of about 350 **parts per million**. The gas is released by **volcano**es and during **respiration**, **combustion**, and decay. Plants convert carbon dioxide into carbohydrates by the process of **photosynthesis**. Carbon dioxide normally poses no health hazard to humans. An important factor in maintaining the earth's climate, molecules of carbon dioxide capture heat radiated from the earth's surface, raising the planet's temperature to a level at which life can be sustained, a phenomenon known as the **greenhouse effect**. Some scientists believe that increasing levels of carbon dioxide resulting from human activities are now contributing to a potentially dangerous global warming.

Carbon monoxide

A colorless, odorless, tasteless gas that is produced in only very small amounts by natural processes. By far the most important source of the gas is the incomplete **combustion** of **coal**, oil, and **natural gas**. In terms of volume, carbon monoxide is the most important single component of **air pollution**. Environmental scientists rank it behind sulfur oxides, **particulate** matter, **nitrogen oxides**, and **volatile organic compound**s, however, in terms of its relative hazard to human health. In low doses, carbon monoxide causes headaches, nausea, fatigue, and impairment of judgment. In larger amounts, it causes unconsciousness and death.

Carbon offsets (CO₂-emission offsets)

Many human activities result in large emissions of **carbon dioxide** (CO₂) and other so-called **greenhouse gases** into the atmosphere. Especially important in this regard are the use of **fossil fuels** such as **coal**, oil, and natural gas to generate electricity, to heat spaces, and as a fuel for vehicles. In addition, the disturbance of forests results in large emissions of CO_2 into the atmosphere. This can be caused by the conversion of forests into agricultural or urbanized land uses, and also by the harvesting of timber.

During the past several centuries, human activities have resulted in large emissions of CO_2 into the atmosphere, causing substantial increases in the concentrations of that gas. Prior to 1850 the atmospheric concentration of CO_2 was about 280 ppm, while in 1997 it was about 360 ppm. Other greenhouse gases (these are also known as radiatively active gases) have also increased in concentration during that same period: **methane** (CH_4) from about 0.7 ppm to 1.7 ppm, nitrous oxide (N_2O) from 0.285 ppm to 0.304 ppm, and **chlorofluorocarbons (CFCs)** from zero to 0.7 ppb.

Many climatologists and environmental scientists believe that the increased concentrations of radiatively active gases are causing an increase in the intensity of Earth's greenhouse effect. The resulting climatic warming could result in important stresses for both natural ecosystems and those that humans depend on for food and other purposes (agriculture, forestry, and fisheries). Overall, CO_2 is estimated to account for about 60% of the potential enhancement of the **greenhouse effect**, while CH_4 accounts for 15%, CFCs for 12%, **ozone** (O_3) for 8%, and N_2O for 5%.

Because an intensification of Earth's greenhouse effect is considered to represent a potentially important environmental problem, planning and other actions are being undertaken to reduce the **emission**s of radiatively active gases. The most important strategy for reducing CO_2 emissions is to lessen the use of fossil fuels. This will mostly be accomplished by reducing energy needs through a variety of conservation measures, and by switching to non-fossil fuel sources. Another important means of decreasing CO_2 emissions is to prevent or slow the rates of deforestation, particularly in tropical countries. This strategy would help to maintain organic carbon within **ecosystem**s, by avoiding the emissions of CO_2 through burning and decomposition that occur when forests are disturbed or converted into other land uses.

Unfortunately, fossil-fuel use and deforestation are economically important activities in the modern world. This circumstance makes it extremely difficult for society to rapidly achieve large reductions in the emissions of CO_2. An additional tactic that can contribute to net reductions of CO_2 emissions involves so-called CO_2 offsets. This involves the management of ecosystems to increase both the rate at which they are fixing CO_2 into plant **biomass** and the total quantity stored as organic **carbon**. This biological fixation can offset some of the emissions of CO_2 and other greenhouse gases through other activities.

Offsetting CO₂ Emissions By Planting Trees

As plants grow, their rate of uptake of atmospheric CO_2 through **photosynthesis** exceeds their release of that gas by **respiration**. The net effect of these two physiological processes is a reduction of CO_2 in the atmosphere. The biological fixation of atmospheric CO_2 by growing plants can be considered to offset emissions of CO_2 occurring elsewhere—for example, as a result of **deforestation** or the combustion of fossil fuels.

The best way to offset CO_2 emissions in this way is to manage ecosystems to increase the biomass of trees in places where their density and productivity are suboptimal. The carbon-storage benefits would be especially great if a forest is established onto poorer-quality farmlands that are no longer profitable to manage for agriculture (this process is known as afforestation, or conversion into a forest). However, substantial increases in carbon storage can also be obtained whenever the abundance and productivity of trees is increased in "low-carbon ecosystems," including urban and residential areas.

Over the longer term, it is much better to increase the amounts of organic carbon that are stored in terrestrial ecosystems, especially in forests, than to just enhance the rate of CO_2 fixation by plants. The distinction between the amount stored and the rate of fixation is important. Fertile ecosystems, such as marshes and most agroecosystems, achieve high rates of net productivity, but they usually store little biomass and therefore over the longer term cannot sequester much atmospheric CO_2. A less extreme example involves second-growth forests and plantations, which have higher rates of net productivity than do older-growth forests. Averaged over the entire cycle of harvest and regeneration, however, these more-productive forests store smaller quantities of organic carbon than do older-growth forests, particularly in trees and large-dimension woody debris.

Both the greenhouse effect and emissions of CO_2 (and other radiatively active gases) are global in their scale and effects. For this reason, projects to gain CO_2 offsets can potentially be undertaken anywhere on the planet, but tallied as carbon credits for specific utilities or industrial sectors elsewhere. For example, a fossil-fueled electrical utility in the United States might choose to develop an afforestation offset in a less-developed, tropical country. This might allow the utility to realize significant economic advantages, mostly because the costs of labor and land would be less and the trees would grow quickly due to a relatively benign climate and long growing season. This strategy is known as a joint-implementation project, and such projects are already underway. These involve United States or European electrical utilities supporting afforestation in tropical countries as a means of gaining carbon credits, along with other environmental benefits associated with planting trees. Although this is a valid approach to obtaining carbon offsets, it can be controversial because some people would prefer to see industries develop forest-carbon offsets within the same country where the CO_2 is being emitted.

Afforestation in Rural Areas

An estimated 5-8 billion acres (2-3 billion ha) of deforested and degraded agricultural lands may be available world-wide to be afforested. This change in land use would allow enormous quantities of organic carbon to be stored, while also achieving other environmental and economic benefits. In North America, millions of acres of former agricultural land have reverted to forest since about the 1930s, particularly in the eastern states and provinces. There are still extensive areas of economically marginal agricultural

lands that could be afforested in parts of North America where the climate and soils are suitable for supporting forests.

Agricultural lands typically maintain about one-tenth or less of the plant biomass of forests, while agricultural soils typically contain 60-80% as much organic carbon as forest soils. Because agricultural sites contain a relatively small amount of organic carbon, reforestation of those lands has a great potential for providing CO_2 offsets.

It is also possible to increase the amounts of carbon stored in existing forests. This can be done by allowing forests to develop into an old-growth condition, in which carbon storage is relatively great because the trees are typically big, and there are large amounts of dead biomass present in the surface litter, dead standing trees, and dead logs lying on the forest floor. Once the old-growth condition is reached, however, the ecosystem has little capability for accumulating "additional" carbon. Nevertheless, **old-growth forest**s provide an important ecological service by tying up so much carbon in their living and dead biomass. In this sense, maintaining old-growth forests represents a strategy of CO_2-emissions deferral, because if those "high-carbon" ecosystems were disturbed by timber harvesting or conversion into another kind of land use, a result would be an enormous emission of CO_2 into the atmosphere.

Dixon *et al.* (1993) examined carbon-offset projects in various parts of the world, most of which involved afforestation of rural lands. The typical costs of the afforestation projects were $1-10 per ton of carbon fixed. These are only the costs associated with planting and initial tending of the growing trees; there might also be additional expenses for land acquisition and stand management and protection.

Of course, even while rural afforestation provides large CO_2-emission offsets, other important benefits are also provided. In some cases, the forests might be used to provide economic benefits through the harvesting of timber (although the resulting disturbance would lessen the carbon-storage capability). Even if trees are not harvested from the CO_2-offset forests, it would be possible to hunt animals such as deer, and to engage in other sorts of economically valuable outdoor recreation. Increasing the area of forests also provides many non-economic benefits, such as providing additional habitat for native species, and enhancing ecological services related to clean water and air, erosion control, and climate moderation.

Urban Forests

Urban forests consist of trees growing in the vicinity of homes and other buildings, in areas where the dominant character of land use is urban or suburban. Urban forests may originate as trees that are spared when a forested area is developed for residential land use, or they may develop from saplings that are planted after homes are constructed. Urban forests in older residential neighborhoods generally have a relatively high density and extensive canopy cover of trees. These characters are less well developed in younger neighbourhoods and where land use involves larger buildings used by institutions, business, or industry.

There are about 70 million acres (28-million ha) of urban land in the United States. Its urban forest supports an average density of 20 trees/acre (52 trees/ha), and has a canopy cover of 28%. Nowak *et al.* (1994) estimated that urban areas of the United States contain about 225 million tree-planting opportunities, in which suboptimal tree densities could be subjected to fill-planting.

Urban forests achieve carbon offsets in two major ways. First, as urban trees grow they sequester atmospheric CO_2 into their increasing biomass. The average carbon storage in urban trees in the United States is about 13 tons per acre (33 tonnes per ha). On a national basis that amounts to 0.8 billion tonnes of organic carbon, and an annual rate of uptake of 6 million tonnes.

In addition, urban trees can offset some of seasonal use of energy for cooling and heating the interior spaces of buildings. Large, well-positioned trees provide a substantial cooling influence through shading. Trees also cool the ambient air by evaporating water from their foliage (a process known as **transpiration**). Trees also decrease wind speeds near buildings. This results in decreased heating needs during winter, because less indoor warmth is lost by the infiltration of outdoor air into buildings. Over most of North America larger energy offsets associated with urban trees are due to decreased costs of cooling than with decreased heating costs. In both cases, however, much of the energy conserved represents decreased CO_2 emissions through the combustion of fossil fuels.

It is considerably more expensive to obtain CO_2-offset credits using urban trees than with rural trees. This difference is mostly due to urban trees being much larger than rural trees when planted, while also having larger maintenance expenses. In the survey of Dixon *et al.* (1993), the typical costs of rural CO_2-offset projects were $1-10 per ton of carbon fixed, compared with $15-30 per ton for urban trees.

Another study estimated the carbon savings associated with planting 100-million trees in urban areas in the United States (Nowak *et al.*, 1994). In this case, the total CO_2-emission offsets were estimated to be 58.2 kg C per tree per year (for trees at least ten years old). About 90% of the total CO_2 offsets was associated with indirect savings of energy for cooling and heating buildings, and 10% with carbon sequestration into the growing biomass of the trees. The estimated costs of the carbon offsets were $6.6-$27.5 per ton of carbon, but these costs would decrease considerably as the trees grew larger. This study estimated that planting trees in urban areas of the United States could potentially offset as much as 2% of this country's emissions of CO_2.

[*Bill Freedman*]

FURTHER READING

Dixon, R.K., et al. "Forest Sector Carbon Offset Projects: Near-term Opportunities To Mitigate Greenhouse Gas Emissions." *Water, Air, & Soil Pollution* 70 (1993): 561-577.

Freedman, B., and T. Keith, "Planting Trees For Carbon Credits. A Discussion Of Context, Issues, Feasibility, and Environmental Benefits, With Particular Attention To Canada." *Environmental Review* 4 (1996): 100-111.

Heisler, G.M. "Energy Savings With Trees." *Journal of Arboric* 12 (1986): 113-125.

Kinsman, J.D., and M.C. Trexler. "Terrestrial Carbon Management And Electric Utilities." *Water, Air, Soil Pollution* 70 (1993): 545-560.

McPherson, E.G. "Using Urban Forests For Energy Efficiency And Carbon Storage." *Journal of Forestry* 94 (1994): 36-41.

Nowak, D.J., E.G. McPherson, and R.A. Rowntree, eds. *Chicago's Urban Forest Ecosystem. Results of The Chicago Urban Forest Climate Project.* General Technical Report NE-186, U.S.D.A. Forestry Service, Northeastern Forest Experiment Station, Radnor, PA, 1994.

Sampson, R.N., et al. "Biomass Management and Energy." *Water, Air, Soil Pollution* 70 (1993): 139-159.

Trexler, M.C., and C. Haugen. *Keeping It Green: Tropical Forestry Opportunities for Mitigating Climate Change.* Washington, D.C.: World Resources Institute, 1995.

Carbon tax

To limit and control the amount of **carbon dioxide** (CO_2) added to the **atmosphere**, special taxes, called carbon taxes, have been proposed and in some cases adopted, on fuels containing carbon. Fuels such as **coal**, **gasoline**, heating oil, and **natural gas**, release energy by combining the carbon they contain with oxygen in the air, to produce carbon dioxide. Increased use of carbon-containing **fossil fuels** in modern times has greatly increased the rate at which carbon dioxide is entering the atmosphere. Measurable increases in atmospheric levels of the gas have been detected. Since carbon dioxide is the principle component of so-called **greenhouse gases**, changes in its concentration in the Earth's atmosphere are a concern. Increases in the level of carbon dioxide, and other greenhouse gases such as **methane**, nitrous oxide, **ozone**, and man-made **chlorofluorocarbons** can be expected to result in warmer temperatures on the surface of the Earth, and wide-ranging changes in the global climate. Greenhouse gases permit radiation from the Sun to reach the Earth's surface but prevent the infrared or heat component of sunlight from re-irradiating into space.

The wide spread concern over the possible climatic effects of increases in heat-trapping gases in the atmosphere was exemplified by a 1994 report of the Intergovernmental Panel on Climate Change (IPCC) which concluded that unless greenhouse gas **emissions** were curtailed, average global temperatures would rise 2.5 to 8.1° F (1.4 to 4.5° C) by the year 2100. A 20% reduction in emissions over 20 years was recommended and considered feasible in developed countries. It was recognized that the rapidly expanding economies of many developing countries makes similar reductions less likely.

While limiting the buildup of heat-trapping gases in the atmosphere has been a goal of natural scientists for some time, many economists have now joined the effort. In 1997, two thousand prominent economists, including six Nobel Laureates, signed the "Economists' Statement on Climate Change" stating that policies to slow global warming are needed and are economically viable. The economists agreed with a review conducted by a distinguished international panel of scientists under the auspices of the IPCC that, "The balance of evidence suggests a discernible human influence on global climate." They further stated that, "As economists, we believe that global climate change carries with it significant environmental, economic, social, and geopolitical risks, and that preventive steps are justified." They state that economic studies have found that potential policies to reduce greenhouse-gas emissions can be designed so that benefits outweigh costs, and living standards would not be harmed. They claim that U.S. productivity may actually improve as a result. The statement goes on to claim that, "the most efficient approach to slowing climate change is through market-based policies" rather than limits or regulations. The economists also suggest that, "A cooperative approach among nations is required, such as an international emissions trading agreement." They recommend, "market mechanisms such as carbon taxes or the auction of emissions permits." Their statement goes on to suggest that, "Revenues generated from such policies can effectively be used to reduce budget deficits or lower existing taxes." New taxes are never popular, but are more apt to be accepted when the revenue is used to replace other taxes or to aid the environment.

As in any public policy debate, views of even well-qualified experts are often sharply divided. Some industry representatives and scientists are unwilling to accept the premise that greenhouse gas emissions represent a serious threat. Industrial spokesmen continue to claim that efforts to reduce greenhouse gas emissions through taxation or other economic means are not cost effective, and would devastate the economy, cost jobs, and reduce living standards. Individual countries worry about the impacts on their competitiveness if other countries do not adopt similar measures. The potential impact on low-income groups must also be considered. Some are concerned that the taxes have to be high to be effective. The amount of year to year variation in climate and temperature throughout the globe, provide ample room for differences of opinion.

International attention was focused on the need to reduce greenhouse gases at the United Nations sponsored Earth Summit held in Rio de Janeiro in 1992. The conference was held to attempt to reconcile worldwide economic development with the need to preserve the environment. Representatives of 178 nations attended, including 117 heads of state, making it the largest gathering of world leaders in history. Documents and treaties were signed committing most of the world's nations to the economic development in ways that were compatible with a healthy environment. A binding treaty called "The Framework Convention on Climate Change, or Global Warming Convention" was adopted, requiring nations to reduce emissions of greenhouse gases. The treaty failed to set binding targets for emission reductions, however. Agreement was hampered by discord between industrialized nations of western Europe, and North America and developing nations in Africa, Latin America, the Middle East and Asia. Developing countries were concerned that environmental restrictions would hamper economic growth unless they received increased aid from developed nations to enable them to grow in an environmentally sound way.

National and regional efforts to limit greenhouse gas have been most evident in western Europe, although disagreements between countries have prevented a unified approach among members of the European Community (EC). Britain has refused to accept a proposed carbon and energy tax, favored by several nations. Spokesmen for Britain expressed doubt that the tax would achieve desired reductions, and claimed that the two-thirds reduction in emissions to which Britain was committed would result from a planned enactment of a value-added tax (VAT) on fuel and energy. Critics of Britain's position argued that their plan was not sufficiently focused because it did not specially target fuels that increase atmospheric carbon dioxide. A 1996 report from the European Environmental Agency (EEA) in Copenhagen concluded that "**green taxes**" adopted by individual European countries in the last decade have been successful. So-called green taxes are a variety of environmentally friendly tax measures intended to reduce **pollution** and toxic wastes and encourage efficient resource use. Carbon taxes, such as those enacted in Norway and Sweden in 1991, are one example. Other examples include taxes on sulfur and nitrogen oxide emissions, **water pollution** charges, and charges for household waste. The carbon dioxide tax in Norway was reported to have reduced CO_2 emissions by 3-4%. The goal in the Scandinavian countries and the Netherlands has been to move away from taxes on labor or capital to those on **energy and the environment**. The consensus in western Europe seems to be that current environmental policies are weighted too much in the direction of regulation, and that there is a need to provide economic incentives in the form of well-designed environmental taxes.

Although eastern European countries have moved forward more slowly than in the rest of the continent, Poland, Hungary, and Estonia are beginning to adopt environmental charges and taxes. In the far-east, the Japanese Environmental Agency has reported that Japan might be able to keep per capita emissions of carbon dioxide at 1990 levels, which would result in a small increase in total emissions because of population growth.

The effectiveness of green taxes, including carbon taxes, is not universally accepted. Some argue that goals need to be defined more carefully with specified amounts or percentages of reduction in targeted pollutants. The EEA report acknowledges that the evaluation of the effectiveness is difficult and that, "Judgments about the performance of green taxes remain at the level of best guesses." Although theoretical evaluation of environmental taxation is well-developed, adequate evaluation of practical experience with such taxes is still relatively rare. Proper evaluation must separate the effects of green taxes from other factors, and assess what would have happened without the taxes. It is also recognized that it may take as much as a decade for a tax to have the desired effect.

In the United States, the Clinton administration, in 1993, published a 50-point plan to reduce greenhouse gas emissions by 100 million tons through a number of voluntary measures. Among the steps recommended were greater **energy efficiency** in homes and electrical appliances, reduced emissions from **power plants**, greater reliance on hydroelectric power, and increased tree planting. Some observers believe that the prospects for "green taxes" are less favorable in the United States than in Europe because of difficulty of passing legislation through two houses of Congress, which may be controlled by different parties, and obtaining approval by the president. Some individual states, however, have enacted measures that create economic incentives for environmental protection. Louisiana, which has many petrochemical companies within its borders, created an "environmental scorecard" in 1991, to keep a tally of companies' toxic discharges, waste volumes, and compliance with environmental laws. Graded exemptions from property taxes are granted to companies with good scores. Oregon's Energy Facility Siting Task Force recommended establishment of a standard to reduce emissions of carbon dioxide, with provisions for offsets for planting trees (which remove CO_2 from the air), and for the use of renewable energy sources.

[*Douglas C. Pratt*]

FURTHER READING

Burke, M. "Environmental Taxes Gaining Ground in Europe." *Environmental Science & Technology* 31 (1997): 84-88.

Environmental Taxes: Implementation and Environmental Effectiveness. *Environmental Issue Series No. 1.* Copenhagen: European Environment Agency, 1996.

MacKenzie, J. J. *Toward a Sustainable Energy Future: The Critical Role of Rational Energy Pricing.* Washington, D.C.: World Resources Institute, 1991.

Repetto, R. C. *Green Fees: How a Tax Shift Can Work for the Environment and the Economy.* Washington, D.C.: World Resources Institute, 1992.

Carcinogen

A carcinogen is any substance or agent that produces or induces the development of **cancer**. Carcinogens are known to affect and initiate metabolic processes at the level of cellular **DNA**.

Cancer accounts for slightly over 20 percent of all deaths each year. It is estimated that one out of every four Americans will develop cancer eventually and that six out of ten in this group will die from the disease itself or complications arising from the disease. Half of all cancer deaths occur before the age of 65. Among women between 30-40 and children between 3-14, cancer is the leading cause of death next to accidents. It is the most frequent cause of death among Americans under 35 years of age.

The testing of **chemicals** as cancer-producing agents began with the observation of Sir Percival Pott in 1775 that scrotal cancer in young chimney sweeps resulted from the lodgement of soot in the folds of their scrotums. Pott was the first to link an environmental agent, **coal** tar, to cancer growth. In 1918 scientists began to test chemical derivatives for their cancer-causing efficacy. These first experiments looked at polycyclic hydrocarbons, specifically **benzo(a)pyrene** found in coal tar, and they demonstrated that a certain degree of exposure to coal tar produced cancer in laboratory rats. In 1908, Vilhelm Ellerman and Oluf Bang of Denmark reported that an infectious agent could cause cancer, after they found that a **leukemia**-like blood disease was transmitted among domestic fowl via a **virus**. In 1911, Peyton Rous established a viral cause for a cancer called sarcoma in domestic fowl, and he was awarded a Nobel Prize for this discovery some 55 years later. In 1932, Lacassagne reported that estrogen injections caused mammary cancer in mice. This opened up investigation into the role hormones played in the development of various types of cancers.

In 1896, Wilhelm Roentgen discovered the **X-ray**, a radioactive emission capable of penetrating many solid materials including the human body. X-rays quickly found use as a diagnostic tool in medicine; but operators of X-ray devices, unaware of their harmful effects, determined the proper intensity of the beams by repeatedly exposing their hands to the rays. Many operators of X-ray equipment began to suffer from cancer of the hand, and Roentgen himself died of cancer. The most dramatic environmental link to cancer induced by radioactivity was observed after the bombing of **Hiroshima, Japan** when there was a radical increase in leukemia-type cancers among people exposed to the atomic blast.

Environmental agents such as toxic chemicals and radiation are considered responsible for about 85 percent of all cancer cases. A great many environmental agents such as synthetic chemicals, sunlight (exposure to UV and UVB rays), air pollutants, **heavy metals**, X-rays, high-fat diet, chemical **pesticides**, and cigarette smoking are known to be carcinogenic. Surveys carried out on the geographic incidence of cancer indicate that certain types of cancer are far more common in heavily industrialized areas. New Jersey, the site of approximately 1,200 chemical plants and related industries, has the highest overall cancer rate in the United States.

Tobacco use, particularly cigarette smoking, is now recognized as the leading contributor to cancer mortality in the United States. Currently one third of all cancer deaths are due to lung cancer, and of the 130,000 new lung cancer victims diagnosed each year, 80 percent are cigarette smokers. Several years ago, the primary cause of cancer among women was breast cancer—but by the late 1980s, lung cancer had surpassed breast cancer as the leading cause of death among women. Current controversy rages over the role of secondary smoke as a contributing cause of cancer among nonsmokers exposed to **cigarette smoke**.

Dietary factors have been extensively investigated, and experiments have implicated everything from coffee to charcoal broiled meat to peanut butter as possible carcinogens. A major concern among meat producers was the use of diethylstilbestrol (DES) as a source for beefing up cattle. DES is a synthetic hormone that increases the rate of growth in cattle. In the 1960s, DES was fed to about three fourths of all the cattle raised in the United States. It was also used to prevent miscarriages in women until 1966, when it was shown to be carcinogenic in mice. DES is now linked to vaginal and cervical cancers in women born between 1950 and 1966 whose mothers took DES during their pregnancies.

In 1971, DES was banned for use in cattle by the **Food and Drug Administration (FDA)**, but the federal courts reversed the ban, contending that DES posed no danger since it was not directly added to foods but was administered only to cattle. When the FDA subsequently showed that measurable quantities remained present in slaughtered cattle, the courts reinstated the ban. But the issue of using growth additives in meat production remains unresolved today. Environmentalists are still concerned that known carcinogenic chemicals used to "beef up" cattle are being consumed by humans in various meat products, though no direct links have yet been established. In addition, various food additives, such as coal tar dyes used for artificial coloring and food preservatives, have produced cancer in laboratory animals. As yet there is no evidence indicating that human cancer rates are rising because of these substances in food.

Air pollution has been extensively investigated as a possible carcinogen and it is known that people living in cities larger than 50,000 run a 33 percent higher risk of developing lung cancer than people who live in other areas. The reasons behind this phenomenon, referred to as the "urban factor," have never been conclusively determined. Areas with populations exceeding 50,000 tend to have more industry, and air pollutants can have a profound effect in regions such as New Jersey where they are highly concentrated.

Occupational exposure to carcinogenic substances accounts for an estimated two to eight percent of diagnosed cancers in the United States. Until passage of the **Toxic Substances Control Act** in 1976, which gave the federal government the power to require testing of potentially hazardous substances before they go on the market, hundreds of new chemicals with unknown side effects came into industrial use each year. Substances such as **asbestos** are estimated to cause 30-40 percent of all deaths among workers who have been exposed to it. **Vinyl chloride**, a basic ingredient in the production of **plastics**, was found in 1974 to induce a rare form of liver cancer among exposed workers. Anaesthetic gases used in operating rooms have been traced as the reason nurse anesthetists develop leukemia and lymphoma at three times the normal rate with an associated higher rate of miscarriage and birth defects among their children. **Benzene**, an industrial chemical long known as a bone-marrow poison, has been shown to induce leukemia as well. A major step forward in the regulation of these potential cancer causing agents is the implementation by the **Occupational Safety and Health Administrations (OSHA)** of the Hazard Communication Standard in 1983, intended to provide employees in manufacturing industries access to information concerning hazardous chemicals encountered in the workplace.

With the erosion of the ozone layer of our atmosphere, increased concern about over-exposure to **ultraviolet radiation** and its subsequent effect on the formation of skin cancer has developed. The EPA estimates that a five percent **ozone** depletion in the stratosphere would result in a substantial increase in a variety of skin cancers. This would include an average of two million extra cases of basal-cell and squamous-cell skin cancers a year and an additional 30,000 cases of the often fatal melanoma skin cancer, which currently kills 9,000 Americans per year. *See also* Hazardous waste

siting; Love Canal, New York; Ozone layer depletion; Radiation exposure; Radiation sickness; Radon; Toxic substance

[*Brian R. Barthel*]

FURTHER READING

Agency for Toxic Substances and Disease Registry. *Annual Report*. Atlanta: U. S. Department of Health and Human Services, 1989 and 1990.

Aldrich, T., and J. Griffith. *Environmental Epidemiology*. New York: Van Nostrand Reinhold, 1993.

McCance, K. L. *Pathophysiology: the Biological Basis for Disease in Adults and Children*. St. Louis: Mosby, 1990.

National Academy of Sciences. *Ozone Depletion, Greenhouse Gases and Climate Change*. Washington, DC: U. S. Environmental Protection Agency, 1989.

Taber, C. W. *Taber's Cyclopedic Medical Dictionary*. Philadephia: F. A. Davis, 1990.

U. S. Environmental Protection Agency. *The Potential Effects of Global Climate Change on the United States*. Washington, DC: U. S. Government Printing Office, 1988.

Carrying capacity

Carrying capacity is a general concept based on the idea that every **ecosystem** has a limit for use that cannot be exceeded without damaging the system. Whatever the specified use of an area might be, whether for grazing, wildlife **habitat**, **recreation**, or economic development, there is a threshold that cannot be breached, except temporarily, without degrading the ability of the **environment** to support that use. Examinations of carrying capacity attempt to determine, with varying degrees of accuracy, where this threshold lies and what the consequences of exceeding it might be.

The concept of carrying capacity was pioneered early this century in studies of range management and **wildlife management**. Range surveys of what was then called "grazing capacity" were carried out on the **Kaibab Plateau** in Arizona as early as 1911, and this term was used in most of the early bulletins issued by the **U.S. Department of Agriculture** on the subject. In his 1923 classic, *Range and Pasture Management*, Sampson defined grazing capacity as "the number of stock of one or more classes which the area will support in good condition during the time that the forage is palatable and accessible, without decreasing the forage production in subsequent seasons." Sampson was quick to point out that the "grazing capacity equation has not been worked out on any range unit with mathematical precision." In fact, because of the number of variables involved, especially variables stemming from human actions, he did not believe that the "grazing-capacity factor will ever be worked out to a high degree of scientific accuracy." Sampson also pointed out that "grazing the pasture to its very maximum year after year can produce only one result—a sharp decline in its carrying capacity," and he criticized the stocking of lands at their maximum instead of their optimum capacity. Similar discussions of carrying capacity can be found in books about wildlife management from the same period, particularly *Game Management* by **Aldo Leopold**, published in 1933.

Practitioners of applied **ecology** have calculated the number of animal-unit months that any given land area can carry over any given period of time. But there have been some controversies over the application of the concept of carrying capacity. The concept is commonly employed without considering the factor of time, neglecting the fact that carrying capacity refers to **land use** that is sustainable. Another common mistake is to confuse or ignore the implicit distinctions between maximum, minimum, and optimum capacity. In discussions of land use and environmental impact, some officials have drawn graphs with curves showing maximum use of an area and claimed that these figures represent carrying capacity. Such representations are misleading because they assume a perfectly controlled population, one without fluctuation, which is not likely. In addition, the maximum allowable population can almost never be the carrying capacity of an area, because such a number can almost never be sustained under all possible conditions. A population in balance with the environment will usually fluctuate around a mean, higher or lower, depending on seasonal habitat conditions, including factors critical to the support of that particular **species** or community.

The concept of carrying capacity has important ramifications for **human ecology** and **population growth**. Many of the essential systems on which humans depend for sustenance are showing signs of stress, yet demands on these systems are constantly increasing. William R. Catton has formulated an important axiom for carrying capacity: "For any use of any environment there is a use intensity that cannot be exceeded without reducing that environment's suitability for that use." He then defined carrying capacity for humans on the basis of this axiom: "The maximum human population equipped with a given assortment of technologies and a given pattern of organization that a particular environment can support indefinitely."

The concept of carrying capacity is the foundation for recent interest in **sustainable development**, an environmental approach which identifies thresholds for economic growth and increases in human population. Sustainable development calculates the carrying capacity of the environment based on the size of the population, the standard of living desired, the overall quality of life, the quantity and type of artifacts created, and the demand on energy and other resources. With his calculations on sustainable development in Paraguay, Herman Daly has illustrated that it is possible to work out rough estimates of carrying capacity for some human populations in certain areas. He based his figures on the ecological differences between the country's two major regions, as well as on differences among types of settlers, and differences between developed good land and undeveloped marginal lands.

If ecological as well as economic and social factors are taken into consideration, then any given environment has an identifiable tolerance for human use and development, even if that number is not now known. For this reason, many environmentalists argue that carrying capacity should always be the basis for what has been called "demographic accounting."

[*Gerald L. Young and Douglas Smith*]

FURTHER READING

Budd, W. W. "What Capacity the Land?" *Journal of Soil and Water Conservation* 47 (January-February 1992): 28-31.

Catton, W. R., Jr. "The World's Most Polymorphic Species: Carrying Capacity Transgressed Two Ways." *BioScience* 37 (June 1987): 413-419.

Edwards, R. Y., and C. D. Fowle. "The Concept of Carrying Capacity." In *Readings in Wildlife Management,* edited by J. A. Bailey, W. Elder, and T. D. McKinney. Washington, DC: The Wildlife Society, 1974.

Graefe, A. R., J. V. Vaske, and F. R. Kuss. "Social Carrying Capacity: An Integration & Synthesis of Twenty Years of Research." *Leisure Sciences* 6 (December 1984): 395-431.

Nilsson, S. "The Carrying Capacity Concept." *Interdisciplinary Science Reviews* 9 (June 1984): 137-148.

Carson, Rachel (1907-1964)

American biologist

Rachel Carson was a university-trained biologist, a longtime United States government employee, and a best-selling author of such books as *Edge of the Sea, The Sea Around Us* (a National Book Award winner), and *Silent Spring.*

Her book on the dangers of misusing **pesticides**, *Silent Spring,* has become a classic of environmental literature and resulted in her recognition as the fountainhead of modern **environmentalism**. *Silent Spring* was reissued in a twenty-fifth anniversary edition in 1987, and remains standard reading for anyone concerned about environmental issues.

Carson grew up in the Pennsylvania countryside and reportedly developed an early interest in **nature** from her mother and from exploring the woods and fields around her home. She was first an English major in college, but a required course in biology rekindled that early interest in the subject and she graduated in 1928 from Pennsylvania College for Women with a degree in zoology and went on to earn a master's degree at Johns Hopkins University. After the publication of *Silent Spring,* she was often criticized for being a "popular science writer" rather than a trained biologist, making it obvious that her critics were unaware of her university work, including a master's thesis entitled "The Development of the Pronephros During the Embryonic and Early Larval Life of the Catfish (*Ictalurus punctatus*)."

Summer work also included biological studies at Woods Hole Marine Biological Laboratory in Massachusetts, where she became more interested in the life of the sea. After doing a stint as a part-time scriptwriter for the Bureau of Fisheries, she was hired full-time as a junior aquatic biologist. When she resigned from the United States **Fish and Wildlife Service** in 1952 to devote her time to her writing, she was biologist and chief editor there. First, as a biologist and writer with the Bureau and then as a free-lance writer and biologist, she successfully combined professionally the two great loves of her life, biology and writing.

Often described as "a book about death which exalts life," *Silent Spring* is the work on which Carson's position as the modern catalyst of a renewed environmental movement rests. The book begins with a shocking fable of one composite town's "silent spring" after pesticides have decimated insects and the birds that feed upon them. The main part of

Rachel Carson.

the book is a massive documentation of the effects of organic pesticides on all kinds of life, including birds and humans. The final sections are quite restrained, drawing a hopeful picture of the future, if feasible alternatives to the use of pesticides—such as biological controls—are used in conjunction with and as a partial replacement of chemical sprays.

Carson was quite conservative throughout the book, being careful to limit examples to those that could be verified and defended. In fact, there was very little new in the book; it was all available earlier in a variety of scientific publications. But her science background allowed her to judge the credibility of the facts she uncovered and provided sufficient knowledge to synthesize a large amount of data. Her literary skills made that data accessible to the general public.

Silent Spring was not a polemic against all use of pesticides but a reasoned argument that potential hazards be carefully and sufficiently considered before any such chemical was approved for use. Many people date modern concern with environmental issues from her argument in this book that "future generations are unlikely to condone our lack of prudent concern for the integrity of the natural world that supports all life." It is not an accident that her book is dedicated to **Albert Schweitzer**, because she wrote it from a shared philosophy of reverence for life.

Carson provided an early outline of the potential of using biological controls in place of **chemicals**, or in concert with smaller doses of chemicals, an approach now called **integrated pest management**. She worried that too many specialists were concerned only about the effectiveness of chemicals in destroying pests and "the overall picture" was being lost, in fact not valued or even sought. She pointed out the false safety of assuming that products considered indi-

vidually were safe, when in concert, or synergistically, they could lead to human health problems.

Her holistic approach was one of the real, and unusual, strengths of the book. Prior to the publication of *Silent Spring*, she even refused to appear on a National Audubon Society panel on pesticides because such an appearance could provide a forum for only part of the picture and she wanted her material to first appear "as a whole." She did allow it to be partially serialized in *The New Yorker*, but articles in that magazine are long and detailed.

The book was criticized early and often, and often viciously and unfairly. One chemical company, reacting to that pre-publication serialization, tried to get Houghton Mifflin not to publish the book, citing Carson as one of the "sinister influences" trying to reduce the use of **agricultural chemicals** so that United States food supplies would dwindle to the level of a developing nation. The chemical industry apparently united against Carson, distributing critical reviews and threatening to withdraw magazine advertisements from journals deemed friendly to her. Words and phrases used in the attacks included "ignorant," "biased," "sensational," "unfounded," "distorted," "not written by a scientist," "littered with crass assumptions and gross misinterpretations," to name but a few.

Some balanced reviews were also published, most noteworthy one by Cornell University ecologist LaMont Cole in *Scientific American*. Cole identified errors in her book, but finished by saying "errors of fact are so infrequent, trivial and irrelevant to the main theme that it would be ungallant to dwell on them," and went on to suggest that the book be widely read in the hopes that it "may help us toward a much needed reappraisal of current policies and practices." That was the spirit in which Carson wrote *Silent Spring* and reappraisals and new policies were indeed the result of the myriad of reassessments and studies spawned by its publication. To its credit, it did not take the science community long to recognize her credibility; the President's Science Advisory Committee issued a 1963 report that the journal *Science* suggested "adds up to a fairly thorough-going vindication of Rachel Carson's *Silent Spring* thesis."

While it is important to recognize the importance of *Silent Spring* as a landmark in the environmental movement, one should not neglect the significance of her other work, especially her three books on oceans and marine life and the impact of her writing on people's awareness of one of earth's great natural **ecosystem**s.

Under the Sea Wind (1941) was Carson's attempt "to make the sea and its life as vivid a reality [for her readers] as it has become for me." And readers are given vivid narratives about the shore, including vegetation and birds, on the open sea, especially by tracing the movements of the mackerel, and on the sea bottom, again by focusing on an example, this time the eel. *The Sea Around Us* (1951) continues Carson's treatment of marine biology, adding an account of the history and development of the sea and its physical features such as islands and tides. She also includes human perceptions of and relationships with the sea. *The Edge of the Sea* (1955) was written as a popular guide to beaches and sea shores, but focusing on rocky shores, sand beaches, and coral and mangrove coasts, it complemented the physical descriptions in *The Sea Around Us* with biological data.

Carson was a careful and thorough scientist, an inspiring author, and a pioneering environmentalist. Her groundbreaking book, and the controversy it generated, was the catalyst for much more serious and detailed looks at environmental issues, including increased governmental investigation that led to creation of the **Environmental Protection Agency (EPA)**. Her work will remain a hallmark in the increasing awareness modern people are gaining of how humans interact with and impact the environment in which they live and on which they depend.

[*Gerald R. Young*]

FURTHER READING

Bonta, M. M. "Rachel Carson, Pioneering Ecologist." In *Women in the Field: America's Pioneering Naturalists*. College Station, TX: Texas A & M University Press, 1991.

Brooks, P. *The House of Life: Rachel Carson at Work*. Boston: Houghton Mifflin, 1972.

Carson, Rachel. *Silent Spring*. Boston: Houghton Mifflin, 1962.

Downs, R. B. "Upsetting the Balance of Nature: Rachel Carson's *Silent Spring*." In *Books That Changed America*. New York: Macmillan, 1970.

Graham, F., Jr. "Rachel Carson." *EPA Journal* 4 (November-December 1978): 5-7+.

Hynes, H. P. *The Recurring Silent Spring*. New York: Pergamon Press, 1989.

Marco, G. J., R. M. Hollingworth, and W. Durham. *Silent Spring Revisited*. Washington, DC: American Chemical Society, 1987.

Cash crop

A crop that is produced for the purpose of exporting or selling rather than for consumption by the person who grows it. In many **Third World** countries, cash crops often replace the production of basic food staples such as rice, wheat, or corn in order to generate foreign exchange. For example, in Guatemala, much of the land is devoted to the production of bananas and citrus fruits (97 percent of the citrus crop is exported), which means that majority of the basic food products needed by the native people are imported from other countries. Often these foods are expensive and difficult for many poor people to obtain. Cash crop agriculture also forces many subsistence and tenant farmers to give up their land in order to make room for industrialized farming.

Catalytic converter

Catalytic converters are devices which employ a catalyst to facilitate a chemical reaction. (A catalyst is a substance that changes the rate of a chemical reaction, but whose own composition is unchanged by that reaction.) For **air pollution control** purposes, such reactions involve the reduction of nitric oxide to molecular oxygen and **nitrogen** or oxidation of **hydrocarbons** and **carbon monoxide** to **carbon dioxide** and water. Using the catalyst, the activation energy of the desired chemical reaction is lowered. Therefore, exo-

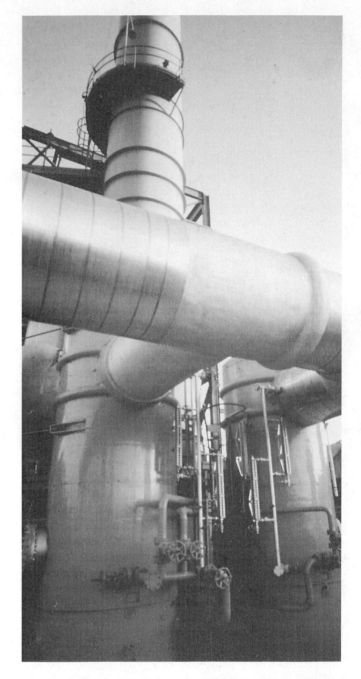

A catalytic converter at a large petrochemical plant.

thermic chemical conversion will be favored at a lower temperature.

Traditional catalysts have normally been metallic, although nonmetallic materials, such as ceramics, have been coming into use in recent years. Metals used as catalysts may include noble metals, such as platinum, or base metals, including **nickel** and **copper**. Some catalysts are more effective in oxidation, others are more effective in reduction. Some metals are effective in both kinds of reactions. The catalyst material is normally coated on a porous, inert support structure of varying design. Examples include honeycomb ceramic structures with long channels and pellet beds. The goal is to channel exhaust over a large surface area of catalyst without an unacceptable pressure drop.

In some cases, reduction and oxidation catalysts are combined to control oxides of nitric oxide, carbon monoxide, and hydrocarbon emissions in exhaust from internal **combustion** engines. The reduction and oxidation processes can be conducted sequentially or simultaneously. Dual catalysts are used in sequential reduction-oxidation. In this case, the exhaust gas from a rich-burn engine initially enters the reducing catalyst to reduce nitric oxide. Subsequently, as the exhaust enters an oxidation catalyst, it is diluted with air to provide oxygen for oxidation. Alternatively, three-way catalysts can be used for simultaneous reduction and oxidation. Engines exhausting to such catalysts run slightly rich and require tight regulation of air-fuel ratio.

Reducing catalysts can be made more efficient using a reducing agent, such as ammonia. This method of control, referred to as selective catalytic reduction, has been employed successfully on large turbines. In this case, a reducing agent is introduced upstream of a reducing catalyst, allowing for greater rates of nitric oxide reduction. *See also* Automobile emissions

[*Robert B. Giorgis, Jr.*]

FURTHER READING

Amato, I. "Catalytic Conversion Could Be a Gas." *Science* 259 (15 January 1993): 311.

Silver, R. G., ed. *Catalytic Control of Air Pollution: Mobile and Stationary Sources.* Washington, DC: American Chemical Society, 1992.

Yaverbaum, L. H. *Nitrogen Oxides Control and Removal: Recent Developments.* Park Ridge, NJ: Noyes Data Corp., 1979.

Cation

See **Ion**

Cation exchange

See **Ion exchange**

Center for Environmental Philosophy (Denton, Texas)

The Center for Environmental Philosophy was established in 1989 as an organization dedicated to furthering research, publication, and education in the area of environmental philosophy and ethics. Based at the University of North Texas since 1990, the primary activities of the center are the publication of the journal *Environmental Ethics*, the reprinting of significant books on **environmental ethics** under its own imprint, the sponsorship of various workshops and conferences dedicated to training and the furthering of research in environmental ethics, and the promotion of graduate education, postdoctoral research, and professional development in the field of environmental ethics.

The Center is best known for its journal, which virtually established the field of environmental ethics and remains perhaps the leading forum for serious philosophical work in environmental philosophy. Inspired in part by **Aldo Leopold**'s contention in "A Sand County Almanac" that the roots of most ecological problems were philosophical, Eugene C. Hargrove founded *Environmental Ethics* in 1978. The journal was originally concerned primarily with whether the attribution of rights to animals and to nature itself could be coherently defended as a philosophical doctrine. While remaining true to its central preoccupation with ethics, the journal's interests have more recently broadened to include significant essays on such topics as **deep ecology**, **ecofeminism**, **social ecology**, economics, and public policy. Under Hargrove's editorial leadership, the journal has brought environmental ethics to increasing acceptance as a serious field by mainstream academic philosophers. *Environmental Ethics* also is now widely read by researchers concerned with the environment in the fields of biological science, economics, and policy science. It also is developing a small but growing following among environmental professionals such as conservation biologists.

The Center also helps to sponsor, in conjunction with the Department of Philosophy and Religious Studies at the University of North Texas, programs in which graduate students may take courses and specialize in the field of environmental ethics. Contact: Center for Environmental Philosophy, University of North Texas, P.O. Box 13496, Denton, TX 76203-6496. Tel: 817/565-2727; Fax: 817/565-4448; E-Mail: cep@unt.edu.

[*Lawrence J. Biskowski*]

Center for Marine Conservation (Washington, D.C.)

"The will to understand, conserve, and protect ocean life is at the very core of the Center for Marine Conservation's mission. To fulfill this mission, the Center seeks to: protect marine **ecosystem**s, prevent **marine pollution**, protect endangered marine species, manage fisheries for **conservation**, and conserve marine **biodiversity**." Since its founding in 1972, the Center for Marine Conservation (CMC) has worked toward these goals. The **endangered species** the group helps to protect include, among many others, **whales**, **dolphins**, seabirds, **seals and sea lions**, and **sea turtles**.

Over 110,000 CMC members nationwide volunteer their time in many different ways, including writing to Congress asking for support of marine conservation, and organizing or participating in beach cleanups across the country. In 1988, for example, more than 16,000 people took part in beach cleanups in Florida and Texas. In October 1991, CMC received an Environment and Conservation Challenge Award from President George Bush for its efforts coordinating coastal cleanups worldwide. Nearly 150,000 people from thirteen countries on four continents had participated that year. The following year, new countries, including Nigeria, Tasmania, and New Zealand, joined the cleanup.

Because of human actions and the ever-changing **environment**, CMC's goals constantly grow and change. Over the years they have challenged formidable opponents, including Exxon. After the ***Exxon Valdez*** oil spill, CMC participated in the cleanup and forced Exxon to step up the rescue and rehabilitation of **sea otter**s (*Enhydra lutris*) and other mammals and birds injured by the accident.

Another important CMC activity is the Marine Habitat Program. Through this program, CMC has played a pivotal role in establishing six marine sanctuaries in the United States (there are only eight total), as well as in other countries. One of these, the Silver Back Humpback Whale Sanctuary, protects humpback whales (*Megaptera novaeangliae*) near the Dominican Republic. Established in 1986, it was the world's first whale sanctuary.

Research is an important component of all CMC programs. The group's ongoing research and advocacy has resulted in the adoption of stricter regulations on commercial whaling by the International Whaling Commission. CMC has also helped to pass federal and state regulations requiring the use of **turtle excluder device**s (TEDs) on shrimp nets to help protect thousands of endangered sea turtles. Turtles have also benefitted from CMC's research in artificial lighting. The group convinced counties and cities throughout Florida to control the use of artificial light on the state's beaches after proving that it prevents turtles from nesting and lures baby turtles away from their natural **habitat**.

In 1988 CMC established a database on marine debris and, subsequently, the group created two Marine Debris Information offices, one in Washington, D.C. and one in San Francisco. These offices provide information on marine debris, especially **plastics**, to scientists, policy makers, teachers, students, and the general public. While many of CMC's projects are exemplary, one has received so much attention that it has been used as a model by other environmental groups, including the **Environmental Protection Agency (EPA)**. The California Marine Debris Action Plan, scheduled for full implementation in 1994, is a comprehensive strategy for combating marine debris, and a collaborative effort of CMC and a wide network of public and private organizations. Contact: Center for Marine Conservation, 1725 DeSales Street, NW, Washington, DC, 20036.

[*Cathy M. Falk*]

Center for Respect of Life and Environment (Washington, D.C.)

Formed in 1986, the Center for Respect of Life and Environment (CRLE) is a nonprofit group based in Washington, D.C., that works to promote humane and **environmental**

ethics, particularly within the academic and religious communities with an emphasis on the links between **ecology**, spirituality, and sustainability.

CRLE describes itself as being committed to "encourage the well-being of life and living systems—plant, animal, and human relationships..." The work of the Center is "to awaken the public's ecological sensibilities, and to transform lifestyles, institutional practices, and social policies to support the community of life..." In order to accomplish these goals, CRLE sponsors conferences of professionals and experts in various fields and puts out a variety of publications, including a quarterly journal, *Earth Ethics*.

Through workshops and conferences, CRLE's Higher Education Project brings together educators from various institutions to discuss greening policies. The Center's Greening of Academia program works with colleges and universities to make the academic curricula, food services, and other campus policies "ecologically sound, socially just, and humane." CRLE also publishes a *Green Guide to Higher Education*, which describes the availability and ecological orientation of courses at various institutions of higher learning.

The Center's Religion in the Ecological Age program focuses on "ecospirituality," stressing that today's religious leaders and institutions must take the responsibility for addressing the issues of environmental justice, the human population explosion, over-consumption of **natural resources**, and other environmental problems that threaten the well-being of the natural environment and of the humans and wildlife dependent on it. CRLE sponsors conferences and publications on such issues, including a series of international conferences in Assisi, Italy (home of **St. Francis of Assisi**, the thirteenth century lover of animals and patron saint of nature).

Another program, Theological Education to Meet the Environmental Challenge (TEMEC)—funded by the Global Stewardship Initiative of the Pew Charitable Trusts—works with seminaries, theological academies, and other religious institutions to "make **ecojustice** central to their curricula and practices."

Fundamental to the Center's mission is "creating a global earth ethic...grounded in an appreciation of the sentience and spiritual depth in all life," and seeking to "establish the ethical foundations of a just and sustainable future." The program includes plans to develop an **Earth Charter** by the year 2000, as called for in 1987 by the United Nations World Commission on Environment and Development, which will "prescribe new norms for state and interstate behavior needed to maintain livelihoods and life on our shared planet." CRLE says that the main purpose of the Earth Charter Project is to "create a 'soft law' document that sets forth the fundamental principles of this emerging new ethics, principles that include respect for human rights, peace, economic equity, environmental protection and sustainable living... It is hoped that the Charter will become a universal code of conduct for states and people..."

Other activities of the Global Earth Ethic project include sponsoring conferences and publications focusing on ethics as they relate to agriculture, development, the environment, and "the appropriate use of animals in research, education, and agriculture..." This effort to raise consciousness includes a three-year project focused on establishing a new principle for agriculture explained in the "Soul of Agriculture: a Production Ethic for the 21st Century."

CRLE's Sustainable Livelihoods in Sustainable Communities program works with U.N. agencies and other regional and international organizations to promote environmentally sustainable developmental and agricultural practices through publications, conferences and meetings, with particular emphasis on **indigenous peoples** and rural communities.

CRLE's quarterly journal, *Earth Ethics*, offers book reviews and a calendar of upcoming events, and it provides a forum for scholarly and provocative feature articles discussing and debating sustainability and other environmental topics as they affect the fields of religion, agriculture, education, business, and the arts, often "challenging current economic and developmental practices."

The Center is affiliated with and supported by the **Humane Society of the United States**, the nation's largest animal protection organization. Contact: Center for Respect of Life and Environment, 2100 L St., NW, Washington, D.C. 20037.

[*Lewis G. Regenstein*]

FURTHER READING

Berry, T. *The Dream of the Earth.* San Francisco: Sierra Club Books, 1988.

Cobb, J. *Is It Too Late? A Theology of Ecology.* Environmental Ethics Books, 1995.

Fox, M.W. *The Boundless Circle: Caring for Creatures and Creation.* Wheaton, IL: Quest Books, 1996.

Gore, A. *Earth in the Balance: Ecology and the Human Spirit.* New York: Houghton Mifflin, 1992.

Regenstein, L.G. *Replenish the Earth: The Teachings of the World's Religions on Protecting Animals and Nature.* New York: Crossroads, 1991.

Earth Ethics. Washington, D.C.: Center for the Respect for Life and Environment.

Center for Rural Affairs (Walthill, Nebraska)

The Center for Rural Affairs (CRA) is a nonprofit organization dedicated to the social, economic and environmental health of rural communities. Founded in 1973, the Center for Rural Affairs includes among its participants farmers, ranchers, business people, and educators concerned with the decline of the family farm.

CRA works to provoke public thought on issues and government policies that affect rural Americans, especially in the Midwest and Plains regions of the country. It sponsors research, education, advocacy, organizing and service projects aimed to improve the life of rural dwellers. CRA's **sustainable agriculture** policy is designed to analyze,

propose, and advocate public policies that reward environmental stewardship, promote family farming, and foster responsible technology. CRA assists beginning farmers design and implement on-site research that helps to make these farms environmentally sound and economically viable. CRA's conservation and education programs address the environmental problems caused by agricultural practices in the North Central United States.

Through a rural enterprise assistance program, CRA teaches rural communities to support self-employment, and it provides business assistance and revolving loan funds for the self-employed. It also provides professional farm management and brokerage service to landowners who are willing to rent or sell land to beginning farmers. CRA promotes fair competition in the agriculture marketplace by working to prevent monopolies, encouraging enforcement of laws restricting corporate farming in the U. S., and advocating for the role of U. S. farmers in international markets.

Publications offered by CRA include the *Center for Rural Affairs Newsletter*, a monthly report on policy issues and research findings; the *Rural Enterprise Reporter*, which provides information about developing small local enterprises; and a variety of special reports on topics such as small farm technology and business strategy. Contact: Center for Rural Affairs, Box 406, Walthill, NE 68067.

[*Linda Rehkopf*]

Center for Science in the Public Interest (Washington, D.C.)

The Center for Science in the Public Interest (CSPI) was founded in 1971 by Michael Jacobson, who remains its executive director. It is a consumer advocacy organization principally concerned with nutrition and food safety, and its membership consists of scientists, nutrition educators, journalists, and lawyers.

CSPI has campaigned on a variety of health and nutrition issues, particularly nutritional problems on a national level. It is the purpose of the group to address "deceptive marketing practices, dangerous food additives or contaminants, conflicts of interests in the academic community, and flawed science propagated by industries concerned solely with profits." It monitors current research on nutrition and food safety, as well as the federal agencies responsible for these areas. CSPI maintains an office for legal affairs and special projects. It has initiated legal actions to restrict food contaminants and to ban food additives that are either unsafe or poorly tested. The special projects the group has sponsored include: Americans for Safe Food, the Nutrition Project, and the Alcohol Policies Project. The center publishes educational materials on food and nutrition, and it works to influence policy decisions affecting health and the national diet.

CSPI has made a significant impact on food marketing in the past ten years, and they have successfully contested food labelling practices in many sectors of the industry. They were instrumental in forcing fast-food companies to disclose ingredients, and they have recently pressed the **Food and Drug Administration** to improve regulations for companies which make and distribute fruit juice. Many brands do not reveal the actual percentages of the different juices used to make them, and certain combinations of juices are often misleadingly labelled as cherry juice or kiwi juice, for instance, when they may be little more than a mixture of apple and grape juice. The organization has also taken action against deceptive food advertising, particularly advertising for children's products. It has recently demanded further testing of a sweetener called sucralose, in the wake of studies that have suggested that it could cause shrinkage of the thymus, a gland affecting cellular immune responses.

CSPI is funded mainly by foundation grants and subscriptions to its *Nutrition Action Newsletter*. The newsletter is published ten months out of the year and is intended to increase public understanding of food safety and nutrition issues. It frequently examines the consequences of legislation and regulation at the state and federal level; it has explored the controversy over organic and chemical farming methods, and it has studied how agribusiness has changed the way Americans eat. CSPI also distributes posters, videos, and computer software, and it offers a directory of mail-order sources for organically-grown food. Its brochures and reports include: *Guess What's Coming to Dinner: Contaminants in Our Food* and *Organic Agriculture: What the States Are Doing*. It has a staff of 45, a membership of 800,000, and an annual budget of $10,000,000. Contact: Center for Science in the Public Interest, 1875 Connecticut Avenue, NW, No. 300, Washington, DC 20009. Internet: http://www.cspinet.org/.

[*Douglas Smith*]

Centers for Disease Control and Prevention

The Centers for Disease Control and Prevention (CDC) is the Atlanta, Georgia-based agency of the **Public Health Service** that has led efforts to prevent diseases such as **malaria**, polio, smallpox, tuberculosis, and acquired immunodeficiency syndrome (**AIDS**). As the nation's prevention agency, the CDC's responsibilities have expanded, and it now addresses contemporary threats to health such as injury, environmental and occupational hazards, behavioral risks, and chronic diseases.

Divisions within the CDC use surveillance, epidemiologic and laboratory studies, and community interventions to investigate and prevent public health threats.

The Center for Chronic Disease Prevention and Health Promotion designs programs to reduce death and disability from chronic diseases—cardiovascular, kidney, liver and lung diseases, and **cancer** and diabetes.

The Center for Environmental Health and Injury Control assists public health officials at the scene of natural or artificial disasters such as **volcanic** eruptions, forest fires,

hazardous **chemical spills**, and nuclear accidents. Scientists study the effects of **chemicals** and **pesticide**s, reactor accidents, and health threats from **radon**, among others. The **National Institute for Occupational Safety and Health** helps identify chemical and physical hazards that lead to occupational diseases.

Preventing and controlling infectious diseases has been a goal of the CDC since its inception in 1946. The Center for Infectious Diseases investigates outbreaks of infectious disease locally and internationally. The Center for Prevention Services provides financial and technical assistance to control and prevent diseases. Disease detectives in the Epidemiology Program Office investigate outbreaks around the world.

Prevention of **tobacco** use is a critical health issue for CDC because cigarette smoking is the leading preventable cause of death in this country. The Office on Smoking and Health conducts research on the effects of smoking, develops health promotion and education campaigns, and helps health departments with smoking education programs.

CDC researchers have improved technology for **lead** poisoning screening, particularly in children. CDC evidence on environmental lead **pollution** was a key in **gasoline** lead content reduction requirements. The CDC also coordinated and directed health studies of **Love Canal, New York**, residents in the 1980s. The director of the CDC administers the **Agency for Toxic Substances and Disease Registry**, the public health agency created to protect the public from exposure to **toxic substance**s in the **environment**. In 1990, CDC became responsible for energy-related epidemiologic research for the **U.S. Department of Energy** nuclear facilities. This includes studies of people who have been exposed to radiation from materials emitted to the air and water from plant operations.

The CDC today carries out an ever-widening agenda with studies on adolescent health, dental disease prevention, the **epidemiology** of violence, and categorizing and tracking birth abnormalities and infant mortality. Centers for Disease Control and Prevention, 1600 Clifton Rd., NE, Atlanta, GA 30333. Internet: http://www.cdc.gov:80/cdc.htm. *See also* Air pollution; Birth defects; Cigarette smoke; Communicable diseases; Heavy metals and heavy metal poisoning; Radiation exposure; Sick building syndrome

[*Linda Rehkopf*]

FURTHER READING

Cotton, P. "CDC Nears Close of First Half-Century." *Journal of the American Medical Association* (16 May 1990): 2579.

Cotton, P. "In the Ballpark Not Good Enough." *Journal of the American Medical Association* (16 May 1990): 2598.

Etheridge, E. W. *Sentinel for Health: A History of the Centers for Disease Control*. Berkeley, CA: University of California Press, 1991.

CERCLA

See **Comprehensive Environmental Response, Compensation and Liability Act**

NEUTRON **CHAIN REACTION**

The neutron strikes nucleus and liberates two neutrons

These liberated neutrons strike a nucleus and liberate four more neutrons

These liberated neutrons strike a nucleus and liberate eight more neutrons

These liberated neutrons strike a nucleus and etc...

A chain reaction.

CERES Principles

See **Valdez principles**

Cesium 137

A radioactive **isotope** of the metallic element cesium. Cesium-137 is one of the major products formed when **uranium** undergoes **nuclear fission**, as in a nuclear reactor or **nuclear weapons**. During atmospheric testing of nuclear weapons after World War II, cesium-137 was a source of major concern to health scientists. Researchers found that the isotope settled to the ground, where it was absorbed by plants and eaten by animals, ultimately affecting humans. Once inside the human body, the isotope releases **beta particle**s, which are **carcinogen**s, **teratogen**s, and **mutagen**s. Large quantities of cesium-137 were released when the **Chernobyl** nuclear reactor exploded in 1986.

Chain reaction

A situation in which one action causes or initiates a similar action. In a nuclear chain reaction, for example, a **neutron** strikes a **uranium**-235 nucleus, causing the nucleus to undergo fission, which in turn produces a variety of products. Among these products is one or more neutrons. Thus, the particle needed to initiate this reaction (the neutron) is itself produced as a result of the reaction. Once begun, the reaction continues as long as uranium-235 nuclei are available. Nuclear chain reactions are important sources of fission and fusion energy. *See also* Nuclear fission; Nuclear fusion; Nuclear power

CFCs

See **Chlorofluorocarbons**

Chelate

A chemical compound in which one atom is enclosed within a larger cluster of atoms that surrounds it like an envelope. The term comes from the Greek word *chela*, meaning "claw." Chelating agents—compounds that can form chelates with other atoms—have a wide variety of environmental applications. For example, the compound ethylenediaminetetraacetic acid (EDTA) is used to remove **lead** from the blood. EDTA molecules surround and bind to lead atoms, and the chelate is then excreted in the urine. EDTA can also be used to soften hard water by chelating the calcium and magnesium **ion**s that cause hardness.

Chelyabinsk, Russia

Chelyabinsk is the name of a province and its capital city in west-central Russia. It covers an area of about 34,000 square miles (88,060 km²) and has a population of about 3.6 million. Chelyabinsk city lies on the Miass River on the eastern side of the Ural Mountains. Its population in 1990 was about 1.2 million.

Chelyabinsk is best known today as the home of Mayak, a 77-square-mile (200 km²) complex where **nuclear weapons** were built for the former Soviet Union. Because of intentional policy decisions and accidental releases of radioactive materials, Mayak has been called the most polluted spot on Earth.

Virtually nothing was known about Mayak by the outside world, the Russian people, or even the residents of Chelyabinsk themselves until 1991. Then, under the new philosophy of *glasnost*, Soviet president Mikhail Gorbachev released a report on the complex. It listed 937 official cases of chronic **radiation sickness** among Chelyabinsk residents. Medical authorities believe that the actual number is many times larger.

The report also documented the secrecy with which the Soviet government shrouded its environmental problems at Mayak. Physicians were not even allowed to discuss the cause or nature of the radiation sickness. Instead, they had to refer to it as the "ABC disease."

Chelyabinsk's medical problems were apparently the result of three major "incidents" involving the release of radiation at Mayak. The first dated from the late 1940s to the mid-1950s, when **radioactive waste** from nuclear weapons research and development was dumped directly into the nearby Techa River. People downstream from Mayak were exposed to radiation levels 57 times greater than those at the better-known **Chernobyl** accident in 1986. The Gorbachev report admitted that 28,000 people received radiation doses of "medical consequence." Astonishingly, almost no one was evacuated from the area.

The second incident occurred in 1957, when a nuclear waste dump at Mayak exploded with a force equivalent to a five to ten kiloton atomic bomb. The site had been constructed in 1953 as an alternative to simply disgorging radioactive wastes into the Techa. When the automatic cooling system failed, materials in the dump were heated to a temperature of 662°F (350°C). In the resulting explosion, 20 million curies of radiation were released, exposing 270,000 people to dangerous levels of **radioactivity**. Neither the Soviet Union nor the United States government, which had detected the accident, revealed the devastation at Mayak.

The third incident happened in 1967. In their search for ways to dispose of radioactive waste, officials at Mayak decided in 1951 to use Lake Karachay as a repository. They realized that dumping into the Techa was not a satisfactory solution, and they hoped that Karachay—which has no natural outlet—would be a better choice.

Unfortunately, radioactive materials began **leaching** into the region's water supply almost immediately. Radiation was eventually detected as far as two miles (3 km) away. The 1967 disaster occurred when an unusually dry summer diminished the lake significantly. A layer of radioactive material, deposited on the newly-exposed shoreline, was spread by strong winds that blew across the area. This released radiation equivalent to the amount contained in the first atomic bomb explosion over **Hiroshima**. According to the Gorbachev report, 436,000 people were exposed to dangerous levels of radiation. As with the first two incidents, however, few people were evacuated from the area and relatively little medical treatment was available to those exposed. *See also* Nuclear power; Radioactive fallout; Radioactive pollution; Radioactive waste management

[*David E. Newton*]

FURTHER READING

Cochran, T. B., and R. S. Norris. "A First Look at the Soviet Bomb Complex." *Bulletin of the Atomic Scientists* 47 (May 1991): 25-31.

Hertsgaard, M. "From Here to Chelyabinsk." *Mother Jones* 17 (January-February 1992): 51-55+.

Perea, J. "Soviet Plutonium Plant 'Killed Thousands'." *New Scientist* 134 (20 June 1992): 10.

Wald, M. L. "High Radiation Doses Seen for Soviet Arms Workers." *New York Times* (16 August 1990): A3.

Chemical bond

A chemical bond is any force of attraction between two atoms strong enough to hold the atoms together for some period of time. At least five primary types of chemical bonds are known, ranging from very strong to very weak. They are covalent, ionic, metallic, and hydrogen bonds, and London forces.

In all cases, a chemical bond ultimately involves forces of attraction between the positively-charged nucleus of one atom and the negatively-charged electron of a second atom. Understanding the nature of chemical bonds has practical significance since the type of bonding found in a substance explains to a large extent the macroscopic properties of that substance.

An ionic bond is one in which one atom completely loses one or more electrons to a second atom. The first atom becomes a positively charged **ion** and the second, a negatively charged ion. The two ions are attracted to each other because of their opposite electrical charges.

In a covalent bond, two atoms share one or more pairs of electrons. For example, a **hydrogen** atom and a fluorine atom each donate a single electron to form a shared pair that constitutes a covalent bond between the two atoms. Both electrons in the shared pair orbit the nuclei of both atoms.

In most cases, covalent and ionic bonding occur in such a way as to satisfy the Law of Octaves. Essentially that law states that the most stable configuration for an atom is one in which the outer energy level of the atom contains eight electrons or, in the case of smaller atoms, two electrons.

Ionic and covalent bonds might appear to represent two distinct limits of electron exchange between atoms, one in which electrons are totally gained and lost (ionic bonding) and one in which electrons are shared (covalent bonding). In fact, most chemical bonds fall somewhere between these two extreme cases. In the hydrogen-fluorine example mentioned above, the fluorine nucleus is much larger than the hydrogen nucleus and, therefore, exerts a greater pull on the shared electron pair. The electrons spend more time in the vicinity of the fluorine nucleus and less time in the vicinity of the hydrogen nucleus. For this reason, the fluorine end of the bond is more negative than the hydrogen end, and the bond is said to be a polar covalent bond. A non-polar covalent bond is possible only between two atoms with equal attraction for electrons as, for example, between two atoms of the same element.

Metallic bonds are very different from ionic and covalent bonds in that they involve large numbers of atoms. The outer electrons of these atoms feel very little attraction to any one nucleus and are able, therefore, to move freely throughout the metal.

Hydrogen bonds are very weak forces of attraction between atoms with partial positive and negative charges. Hydrogen bonds are especially important in living organisms since they can be broken and reformed easily during biochemical changes.

London forces are the weakest of chemical bonds. They are forces of attraction between two uncharged molecules. The force appears to arise from the temporary shift of electrical charges within each molecule. *See also* Biogeochemical cycles; Chemicals; Cloud chemistry; Photochemical reaction

[*David E. Newton*]

FURTHER READING

Giddings, J. Calvin. *Chemistry, Man, and Environmental Change: An Integrated Approach.* San Francisco: Canfield Press, 1973.

Joesten, M. D., et al. *World of Chemistry.* Philadelphia: Saunders College Publishing, 1991.

Chemical oxygen demand

Chemical oxygen demand (COD) is a measure of the ability of chemical reactions to oxidize matter in an aqueous system. The results are expressed in terms of oxygen so that they can be compared directly to the results of **biochemical oxygen demand** (BOD) testing. The test is performed by adding the oxidizing solution to a sample, boiling the mixture on a refluxing apparatus for two hours and then titrating the amount of dichromate remaining after the refluxing period. The titration procedure involves adding ferrous ammonium sulfate (FAS), at a known normality, to reduce the remaining dichromate. The amount of dichromate reduced during the test—the initial amount minus the amount remaining at the end—is then expressed in terms of oxygen. The test has

nothing to do with oxygen initially present or used. It is a measure of the demand of a solution or suspension for a strong oxidant. The oxidant will react with most organic materials and certain inorganic materials under the conditions of the test. For example, Fe^{2+} and Mn^{2+} will be oxidized for Fe^{3+} and Mn^{4+}, respectively, during the test.

Generally, the COD is larger than the BOD exerted over a five-day period (BOD_5), but there are exceptions in which microbes of the BOD test can oxidize materials that the COD reagents cannot. For a raw, domestic **wastewater**, the COD/BOD_5 ratio is in the area of 1.5-3.0/1.0. Higher ratios would indicate the presence of toxic, non-biodegradable or less readily **biodegradable** materials.

The COD test is commonly used because it is a relatively short-term, precise test with few interferences. However, the spent solutions generated by the test are hazardous. The liquids are acidic, and contain chromium, silver, **mercury**, and perhaps other toxic materials in the sample tested. For this reason laboratories are doing fewer or smaller COD tests in which smaller amounts of the same reagents are used. *See also* Sewage treatment; Waste management

[*Gregory D. Boardman*]

FURTHER READING

Corbitt, R. A. *Standard Handbook of Environmental Engineering.* New York: McGraw-Hill, 1990.

Davis, M. L., and D. A. Cornwell. *Introduction to Environmental Engineering.* New York: McGraw-Hill, 1991.

Peavy, H. S., D. R. Rowe, and G. Tchobanoglous. *Environmental Engineering.* New York: McGraw-Hill, 1985.

Tchobanoglous, G., and E. D. Schroeder. *Water Quality.* Reading, MA: Addison-Wesley, 1985.

Viessman, W., Jr., and M. J. Hammer. *Water Supply and Pollution Control.* 5th ed. New York: Harper Collins, 1993.

Chemical spills

Chemical spills are any accidental releases of synthetic chemicals that pose a risk to the **environment**.

Spills occur at any of the steps between the production of a chemical and its use. A railroad tank car may spring a leak; a pipe in a manufacturing plant may break; or an underground storage tank may corrode allowing its contents to escape into **groundwater**. These spills are often classified into four general categories: the release of a substance into a body of water; the release of a liquid on land; the release of a solid on land; and the release of a gas into the **atmosphere**. The purpose of this method of classification is to provide the basis for a systematic approach to the control of any type of chemical spill.

Some of the most famous chemical spills in history illustrate these general categories. For example, seven cars of a train carrying the **pesticide** metam sodium fell off the tracks near Dunsmuir, California, in August 1991, breaking open and releasing the **chemicals** into the Sacramento River. Plant and aquatic life for 43 miles (70 km) downriver died as a result of the accident. The pesticide eventually formed a band 225 feet (70 m) wide across Lake Shasta before it could be contained.

In 1983, the **Environmental Protection Agency (EPA)** purchased the whole town of **Times Beach, Missouri**, and relocated more than 2,200 residents because the land was so badly contaminated with highly toxic **dioxin**s. The concentration of these compounds, a by-product of the production of **herbicide**s, was more than a thousand times the maximum recommended level.

In December 1984, a cloud of poisonous gas escaped from a Union Carbide chemical plant in **Bhopal, India**. The plant produced the pesticide Sevin from a number of chemicals, many of which were toxic. The gas that accidentally escaped probably contained a highly toxic mixture of phosgene, methyl isocyanate (MIC), **chlorine, carbon monoxide**, and hydrogen cyanide, as well as other hazardous gases. The cloud spread over an area of more than 15 square miles (40 sq km), exposing more than 200,000 people to its dangers.

Chemists have now developed a sophisticated approach to the treatment of chemical spills, which involves one or more of five major steps: containment, physical treatment, chemical treatment, biological treatment, and disposal or destruction. Soil sealants, which can be used to prevent a liquid from sinking into the ground, are an example of containment. One of the most common methods of physical treatment is activated charcoal, because it has the ability to adsorb toxic substances on its surface, thus removing them from the environment. Chemical treatment is possible because many **hazardous material**s in a spill can be treated by adding some other chemical that will neutralize them, and biological treatment usually involves microorganisms that will attack and degrade a toxic chemical. Open burning, **deep-well injection**, and burial in a **landfill** are all methods of ultimate disposal. *See also* Agricultural chemicals; Contaminated soil; Hazardous Materials Transportation Act; Hazardous Substances Act; Hazardous waste site remediation; Oil spills; Storage and transport of hazardous material

[*David E. Newton*]

FURTHER READING

Bowonder, B., et al. "Avoiding Future Bhopals." *Environment* 27 (September 1985): 6-13+.

Lepkowski, W. "Bhopal." *Chemical & Engineering News* (2 December 1985): 18-32.

Unterberg, W., et al. *How to Respond to Hazardous Chemical Spills.* Park Ridge, N.J.: Noyes Data Corporation, 1988.

Chemicals

The general public often construes the word "chemical" to mean a harmful synthetic substance. In fact, however, the term applies to any element or compound, either natural or synthetic. The thousands of compounds that make up the human body are all chemicals, as are the products of scientific research. A more accurate description, however, can be found in the dictionary. Thus, aspirin is a chemical by this definition, since it is the product of a series of chemical reactions.

The story of chemicals began with the rise of human society. Indeed, early stages of human history, such as the Iron, Copper, and Bronze Ages reflect humans' ability to produce important new materials. In the first two eras, people learned how to purify and use pure metals. In the third case, they discovered how to combine two to make an alloy with distinctive properties.

The history of ancient civilizations is filled with examples of men and women adapting **natural resources** for their own uses. Egyptians of the eighteenth dynasty (1700-1500 B.C.), for example, knew how to use cobalt compounds to glaze pottery and glass. They had also developed techniques for making and using a variety of dyes.

Over the next 3,000 years, humans expanded and improved their abilities to manipulate natural chemicals. Then, in the 1850s, a remarkable breakthrough occurred. A discovery by young British scientist William Henry Perkin led to the birth of the synthetic chemicals industry.

Perkin's great discovery came about almost by accident, an occurrence that was to become common in the synthetics industry. As an 18-year-old student at England's Royal College of Chemistry, Perkin was looking for an artificial compound that could be used as a quinine substitute. Quinine, the only drug available for the treatment of **malaria**, was itself in short supply.

Following his teacher's lead, Perkin carried out a number of experiments with compounds extracted from coal tar, the black, sticky sludge obtained when **coal** is heated in insufficient air. Eventually, he produced a black powder which, when dissolved in alcohol, created a beautiful purple liquid. Struck by the colorful solution, Perkin tried dyeing clothes with it.

His efforts were eventually successful. He went on to mass produce the synthetic dye—mauve, as it was named—and to create an entirely new industry. The years that followed are sometimes referred to as The Mauve Decade because of the many new synthetic products inspired by Perkin's achievement. Some of the great chemists of that era have been memorialized in the names of the products they developed or the companies they established: Adolf von Baeyer (Bayer aspirin), Leo Baekeland (Baekelite plastic), Eleuthère Irénée du Pont (DuPont Chemical), George Eastman (Eastman 910 adhesive and the Eastman Kodak Company), and Charles Goodyear (Goodyear Rubber).

Chemists soon learned that from the gooey, ugly by-products of coal tar, a whole host of new products could be made. Among these products were dyes, medicines, fibers, flavorings, **plastics**, explosives, and **detergents**. They found that the other **fossil fuels—petroleum** and **natural gas**—could also produce synthetic chemicals.

Today, synthetic chemicals permeate our lives. They are at least as much a part of the **environment**, if not more, than are natural chemicals. They make life healthier, safer, and more enjoyable. People concerned about the abundance of "chemicals" in our environment should remember that everyone benefits from anti-**cancer** drugs, pain-killing anesthetics, long-lasting fibers, vivid dyes, sturdy synthetic rubber tires, and dozens of other products. The world would be a much poorer place without them.

Unfortunately, the production, use, and disposal of synthetic chemicals can create problems because they may be persistent and/or hazardous. Persistent means that a substance remains in the environment for a long time: dozens, hundreds, or thousands of years in many cases. Natural products such as wood and paper degrade naturally as they are consumed by microorganisms. Synthetic chemicals, however, have not been around long enough for such microorganisms to evolve.

This leads to the familiar problem of **solid waste** disposal. **Plastics** used for bottles, wrappings, containers, and hundreds of other purposes do not decay. As a result, **landfill**s become crowded and communities need new places to dump their trash.

Persistence is even more of a problem if a chemical is hazardous. Some chemicals are a problem, for example, because they are flammable. More commonly, however, a hazardous chemical will adversely affect the health of a plant or animal. It may be (1) toxic, (2) carcinogenic, (3) teratogenic, or (4) mutagenic.

Toxic chemicals cause people, animals, or plants to become ill, develop a disease, or die. **DDT**, **chlordane**, heptachlor, and aldrin are familiar, toxic **pesticide**s. **Carcinogen**s cause **cancer**; **teratogen**s produce **birth defects**. **Mutagen**s, perhaps the most sinister of all, inflict genetic damage.

Determining these effects can often be very difficult. Scientists can usually determine if a chemical will harm or kill a person. But how does one determine if a chemical causes cancer twenty years after exposure, is responsible for birth defects, or produces genetic disorders? After all, any number of factors may have been responsible for each of these health problems.

As a result, labeling any specific chemical as carcinogenic, teratogenic, or mutagenic can be difficult. Still, environmental scientists have prepared a list of synthetic chemicals that they believe fall into these categories. Among them are **vinyl chloride**, trichloroethylene, tetrachloroethylene, the nitrosamines, and chlordane and heptachlor.

Another class of chemicals are hazardous because they may contribute to the **greenhouse effect** and **ozone layer depletion**. The single most important chemical in determining the earth's annual average temperature is a naturally-occurring compound, **carbon dioxide**. Its increased production is believed to be responsible for a gradual increase in the planet's annual average temperature.

But synthetic compounds may also play a role in global warming. **Chlorofluorocarbons** (CFCs) are widely used in industry because of their many desirable properties, one of which is their chemical stability. This very property means, however, that when released into the **atmosphere**, they remain there for many years. Since they capture heat radiated from the earth in much the way carbon dioxide does, they are probably important contributors to global warming.

These same chemicals, highly unreactive on earth, decompose easily in the upper atmosphere. When they do so, they react with the **ozone** in the **stratosphere**, converting it to ordinary oxygen. This may have serious consequences, since stratospheric ozone shields the earth from harmful **ultraviolet radiation**.

There are two ways to deal with potentially hazardous chemicals in the environment. One is to take political or legal action to reduce the production, limit the use, and/or control the disposal of such products. A treaty negotiated and signed in Montreal by more than forty nations in 1987, for example, calls for a gradual ban on CFC production. If the treaty is honored, these chemicals will eventually be phased out of use.

A second approach is to solve the problem scientifically. Synthetic chemicals are a product of scientific research, and science can often solve the problems these chemicals produce. For example, scientists are exploring the possibility of replacing CFCs with related compounds called fluorocarbons (FCs) or **hydrochloroflurocarbons** (HCFCs). Both are commercially appealing, but they have fewer harmful effects on the environment. *See also* Biodegradable; Environmental science; Hazardous material; Hazardous waste; Recycling; Toxic substance

[*David E. Newton*]

FURTHER READING

Giddings, J. Calvin. *Chemistry, Man, and Environmental Change: An Integrated Approach*. San Francisco: Canfield Press, 1973.

Joesten, M. D., et al. *World of Chemistry*. Philadelphia: Saunders College Publishing, 1991.

Newton, David E. *The Chemical Elements*. New York: Franklin Watts, 1994.

Chernobyl Nuclear Power Station (Ukraine)

On April 26, 1986, at precisely 1:24 A.M., the Chernobyl nuclear power plant exploded, releasing large amounts of **radioactivity** into the environment. The power station is located nine miles (14.5 km) northwest of the town of Chernobyl, with a population of 12,500, and less than two miles (3.2 km) from the town of Pripyat, which contains 45,000 inhabitants. The explosion and its aftermath, including the manner in which the accident was handled, have raised questions about the safety and future of **nuclear power**.

The Chernobyl accident resulted from several factors: flaws in the engineering design, which were compensated by a strict set of procedures; failure of the plant management to enforce these procedures; and finally the decision of the engineers to conduct a risky experiment. They wanted to test whether the plant's turbine generator—from its rotating inertia—could provide enough power to the reactor in case of a power shutdown. This experiment required disconnecting the reactor's emergency core cooling pump and other safety devices.

The series of critical events, as described by Richard Mould in *Chernobyl, The Real Story*, are as follows: At 1:00

A general view of the Chernobyl Nuclear Power Station. Lighter areas of the building are part of the original structure, while darker areas are the steel and concrete "sarcophagus" that was added to contain radioactivity leaking from the faulty reactor.

A.M. on April 25, power reduction was started in preparation for the experiment. At 1:40 A.M. the reactors's emergency core cooling system was turned off. At 11:10 P.M. power was further reduced, resulting in a nearly unmanageable situation. At 1:00 A.M. on April 26, power was increased in an attempt to stabilize the reactor; however, cooling pumps were operating well beyond their rated capacity, causing a reduction in steam generation and a fall in stream pressure. By 1:19 A.M., the water in the cooling circuit had approached the boiling point. At 1:23 A.M., the operators tried to control the reaction by manually pushing control rods into the core; however, the rods did not descend their full length into the reactor since destruction of the graphite core was already occurring. In 4.5 seconds, the power level rose two thousand-fold. At 1:24 A.M., there was an explosion when the hot reactor fuel elements, lacking enough liquid for cooling, decomposed the water into **hydrogen** and oxygen. The generated pressures blew off the 1000-ton concrete roof of the reactor, and burning graphite, molten **uranium**, and radioactive ashes spilled out to the **atmosphere**.

The explosion that occurred was not a nuclear explosion such as would occur with an atomic bomb but its effects were just as devastating. In order to put the expulsion of radioactive material from the Chernobyl reactor into perspective, almost 50 tons of fuel went into the atmosphere plus an additional 70 tons of fuel, and 700 tons of radioactive reactor graphite settled in the vicinity of the damaged unit.

Some 50 tons of nuclear fuel and 800 tons of reactor graphite remained in the reactor vault, with the graphite burning up completely in the next several days after the accident. The amount of radioactive material which went into the atmosphere was equivalent to 10 Hiroshima bombs.

Officials at first denied that there had been a serious accident at the power plant. The government in Moscow was led to believe for several hours after the explosion and fire at Chernobyl that the reactor core was still intact. This delayed the evacuation for a critical period during which local citizens were exposed to high radiation levels. The evacuation of Chernobyl and local villages was spread out over eight days. A total of 135,000 persons were evacuated from the area, with the major evacuation at Pripyat starting at 2:00 P.M, the day after the explosion. Tests showed that air, water, and **soil** around the plant had significant contamination. Children, in particular, were a matter of concern and were evacuated to the southern Ukraine, the Crimea, and the Black Sea coast.

At the time of the accident, and for several days thereafter, the winds carried the **radioactive waste** to the north. The radioactive cloud split into two lobes, one spreading west and then north through Poland, Germany, Belgium, and Holland, and the other through Sweden and Finland. By the first of May, the wind direction changed and the **radioactive fallout**—at a diminished rate—went south over the Balkans and then west through Italy. Large areas of Europe were affected, and many farmers destroyed their crops for fear of contamination. Forests have been cleared and large amounts of earth were removed in order to clean up radioactivity. Plastic film has been laid in some areas in an effort to contain radioactive dust.

Officially 31 persons were reported to have been killed at the reactor site by a combination of the explosion and **radiation exposure**; another 174 were exposed to high doses of radiation which resulted in **radiation sickness** and long-term illnesses. The maximum permissible dose of radiation for a nuclear power operator is 5 roentgens per year and for the rest of the population, 0.5 roentgens per year. At the Chernobyl plant, the levels of radiation ranged from 1000 to 20,000 roentgens *per hour*. One British report estimates that worldwide, the number of persons afflicted with **cancer** which can be attributed to the Chernobyl accident will be about 2300. Others argued that the number will be much higher. In Minsk, the rate of **leukemia** has doubled from 41 per million in 1985 to 93 per million in 1990.

Many heroic deeds were reported during this emergency. Fire fighters exposed themselves to deadly radiation while trying to stop the inferno. Every one eventually died from radiation exposure. Construction workers volunteered to entomb the reactor ruins with a massive concrete sarcophagus. And bus drivers risked further exposure by making repeated trips into contaminated areas in order to evacuate villagers. Over 600,000 people were involved in the decontamination and clean up of Chernobyl. The health effects on them from their exposure are not completely known. The Chernobyl accident focused international attention on the risks associated with operating a nuclear reactor for the generation of power. Public apprehension has forced some governments to review their own safety procedures and to compare the operation of their nuclear reactors with Chernobyl's. In a review of the Chernobyl accident by the Atomic Energy Authority of the United Kingdom, an effort was made to contrast the design of the Chernobyl reactor and management procedures with those in practice in the United States and the United Kingdom.

Three design drawbacks were noted of the Chernobyl nuclear power plant:

(1) The reactor was intrinsically unstable below 20 percent power and never should have been operated in that mode. (U.S. and UK reactors do not have this design flaw).

(2) The shut-down operating system was inadequate and contributed to the accident rather than terminating it. (U.S. and UK control systems differ significantly).

(3) There were no controls to prevent the staff from operating the reactor in the unstable region or preventing the disabling of existing safeguards.

In addition, the Chernobyl management had no effective watchdog agency to inspect procedures and order closure of the facility. Also in years prior to the accident there was a lack of information given the public of prior nuclear accidents, typical of the press censorship and news management occurring in the period before *glasnost*. The operators were not adequately trained nor were they themselves fully aware of prior nuclear power accidents or near accidents which

would have made them more sensitive to the dangers of a runaway reactor system.

Unfortunately there are in the former Soviet block nations several nuclear reactors which are potentially as hazardous as Chernobyl but which must continue operation to maintain power requirements; however, the operational procedures are under constant review to avoid another accident. Clearly the Western world will have to assist the former Soviet block to bring reactor operating equipment and standards up to a much higher level of safety to avoid a similar and possibly more disastrous accident. *See also* Radioactive decay; Radioactive pollution; Radioactive waste management; Three Mile Island Nuclear Reactor

[*Malcolm T. Hepworth*]

FURTHER READING

Feshbach, M., and A. Friendly, Jr. *Ecocide in the USSR*. New York: Basic Books, 1992.

Gale, R. P., and T. Hauser. *Final Warning: The Legacy of Chernobyl*. New York: Warner Books, 1988.

Medvedev, G. *No Breathing Room: The Aftermath of Chernobyl*. New York: Basic, 1993.

Mould, R. E. *Chernobyl: The Real Story*. New York: Pergamon, 1988.

Chesapeake Bay

The Chesapeake Bay is the largest **estuary** (186 mi; 300 km long) in the United States. The bay was formed 1500 years ago by the retreat of glaciers and the subsequent sea level rise that inundated the lower Susquehanna River valley. The bay has a drainage basin of 64,076 square miles (166,000 sq km) covering six states and running through Pennsylvania, Maryland, the District of Columbia, and Virginia before entering the Atlantic Ocean. While 150 rivers enter the bay, a mere eight account for 90 percent of the freshwater input, with the Susquehanna alone contributing nearly half. Chesapeake Bay is a complex system, encompassing numerous **habitat**s and environmental gradients.

Chesapeake Bay's abundant **natural resources** attracted native Americans who first settled its shores. The first European record of the bay was in 1572 and the area surrounding Chesapeake Bay was rapidly colonized by Europeans. In many ways, the United States grew up around Chesapeake Bay. The colonists harvested the bay's resources and used its waterways for transportation. Today 10 million people live in the Chesapeake Bay's drainage basin, and many of their activities affect the environmental quality of the bay as did the activities of their ancestors.

The rivers emptying into the bay were also used by the colonists to dispose of raw sewage. By the middle 1800s some of the rivers feeding the bay were polluted: the Potomac was recorded as emitting a lingering stench. The first sewer was constructed in Washington, D.C., and it pumped untreated waste into the bay. It was recognized in 1893 that the diseases suffered by humans consuming shellfish from the bay were directly related to the **discharge** of raw sewage into the bay.

Despite this recognition, efforts in 1897 by the mayor of Baltimore to oppose the construction of a sewage system which discharged sewage into the bay in favor of a "land filtration technique" failed. Ultimately, a secondary treatment system discharging into the bay was constructed. In the mid-1970s, a $27 million government-funded study of the bay's condition concluded that the deteriorating quality of the Chesapeake Bay was a consequence of human impacts. But it was not until the early 1980s that an **Environmental Protection Agency (EPA)** report on the Chesapeake focused interest on saving the bay, and $500 million was spent on cleanup and construction of **sewage treatment** plants.

While the Chesapeake Bay is used primarily as a transportation corridor, its natural resources rank a close second in importance to humans. The most commercially important fisheries in the bay are oyster (*Crassostrea virginica*), blue crab (*Callinectes sapidus*), American shad (*Alosa sapidissima*), and striped bass (*Marone saxatilis*). Fisherman first began to notice a decline in fish populations in the 1940s and 1950s, and since then abundances have declined even further. Since the turn of the century, the oyster catch has declined 70 percent, shad 85 percent and striped bass 90 percent. In the late 1970s the EPA began to study the declining oyster and striped bass populations and concluded that their decline was due to a combination of overharvesting and **pollution**.

Work by the EPA and other federal and state agencies has identified six areas of environmental concern for the bay: 1) excess **nutrient** input from both sewage treatment plants discharging into the bay and **runoff** from agricultural land, 2) low oxygen levels as a result of increased **biochemical oxygen demand** which increases dramatically with loading of organic material, 3) loss of submerged aquatic vegetation due to an increase in turbidity, 4) presence of large amounts of chemical toxins, 5) loss to development of **wetlands** surrounding the bay which serve as nurseries for juvenile fish and shellfish and as buffers for runoff of nutrients and toxic **chemicals**, and 6) increasing acidity of water in streams that feed the bay caused by **acid rain**. These streams are also nursery areas for larval fish which may not be able to survive the increasingly acid conditions.

The increasing growth of **phytoplankton**, free-floating plants, in the bay is generally considered to be the main cause of the decline in the environmental quality of the Chesapeake Bay. The number of **algal bloom**s has increased 250 fold since the 1950s, and this explosion is attributed to the high levels of the plant nutrients **nitrogen** and **phosphorus** discharged into the bay. It is estimated that discharge from sewage treatment plants and agricultural runoff accounts for 65 percent of the nitrogen and 22 percent of the phosphorus found in the bay. Acid rain, formed from discharges from industrial plants in Canada and the northeast United States, contributes 25 percent of the nitrogen found in the bay. These excess nutrients encourage phytoplankton growth, and as the large number of phytoplankton die and settle to the bottom their **decomposition** robs the water of oxygen needed by fish and other aquatic organisms. When oxygen levels fall too low these organisms die and their decomposition further reduces the concentration of oxygen. Finfish and shellfish kills have been increasingly common in the bay in recent decades.

Phytoplankton blooms and the increase in suspended **sediment** resulting from shoreline development and poor agricultural practices have resulted in increased turbidity, which has led to a decline in submerged aquatic vegetation (SAVs). SAVs are extremely important as **erosion** buffers and critical habitat spaces for commercially important fish and shellfish.

Numerous chemicals introduced into the bay from several sites have contributed to the decline in the bay's marine fish and birds. The **pesticide Kepone** was leaked or dumped into the James River in 1975 and poisoned fish and shellfish. Harvests of some **species** are still restricted in the area of this spill. **Chlorine** biocides, used in **wastewater** treatment plants and **power plants** which discharge into the bay, are known human **carcinogen**s and toxic to aquatic organisms. **Polycyclic aromatic hydrocarbons (PAH)** have caused dermal lesions in fish populations in the Elizabeth River. PAHs also affect shellfish populations. Recent public concern has focused on tributyltin (TBT) which is used in anti-fouling paint on recreational and commercial boats. TBTs belong to a family of non-regulated chemicals known as organotins, which are known to damage shellfish. The diversity of chemical pollutants found in the bay is exemplified by the results of research which identified 100 inorganic and organic contaminants in striped bass caught in the bay.

In recent years, work by private and governmental agencies has begun to turn the tide of declining environmental quality of the Chesapeake Bay. In 1983 Maryland, Virginia, Pennsylvania, the District of Columbia, the Chesapeake Bay Commission, and the EPA signed the Chesapeake Bay Agreement, which outlined procedures to correct many of the bay's ecological problems, particularly nutrient enrichment. In 1987 the agreement was significantly expanded and required that the signatories adopt a strategy that would result in at least a 40 percent reduction in nitrogen and phosphorus entering the bay by the year 2000. Since 1985, increasing compliance with discharge permits, prohibiting the sale of phosphate-based **detergents**, and upgrading wastewater plants has resulted in a 2 percent reduction in the discharge of nitrogen and a 39 percent reduction of phosphorous from **point source**s of pollution. Controls on agriculture and urban development have resulted in approximately 7 percent reductions in the amount of both nitrogen and phosphorus entering the bay from **nonpoint source**s. The amount of toxins entering the bay have also been reduced. Tributyltin has been banned for use in anti-fouling paints, pesticide runoff has been reduced by using alternate strategies for pest control, and toxic emissions from industrial sources have declined more than 40 percent since 1987. At the same time some of the bay's critical habitats are recovering: 22,000 more acres of SAVs are now growing than in 1984, although the total amount of 60,000 acres is still a fraction of the estimated 600,000 acres the bay should have, man-made oyster reefs are being created to expand suitable habitat for oysters, and rivers are being cleared to provide access to spawning areas by migratory fish.

Progress on arresting the decline of environmental quality of the Chesapeake Bay and restoring some of its natural resources is evidence that citizens, government, and industry can work cooperatively. The Chesapeake Bay program is a national model for efforts to restore other degraded ecosystems.

[*William G. Ambrose, Jr. and Paul E. Renaud*]

FURTHER READING

Brown, L. R. "Maintaining World Fisheries." In *State of the World*, edited by L. Starke. New York: Norton, 1985.

D'Elia, C. "Nutrient Enrichment of the Chesapeake Bay." *Environment* 29 (1987): 6-11.

Majumdar, S., et al. *Contaminant Problems and Management of Living Chesapeake Bay Resources.* Easton, NJ: Typehouse of Easton, 1987.

Child survival revolution

Every year in the developing countries of the world, some 14 million children under the age of five die of common infectious diseases. Most of these children could be saved by simple, inexpensive, preventative medicine. Many public health officials argue that it is as immoral and unethical to allow children to die of easily preventable diseases as it would be to allow them to starve to death or to be murdered. In 1986, the United Nations announced a worldwide campaign to prevent unnecessary child deaths. Called the "child survival revolution," this campaign is based on four principles, designated by the acronym GOBI.

"G" stands for growth monitoring. A healthy child is considered a growing child. Underweight children are much more susceptible to infectious diseases, retardation, and other medical problems than children who are better nourished. Regular growth monitoring is the first step in health maintenance.

"O" stands for oral rehydration therapy (ORT). About one-third of all deaths under five years of age are caused by diarrheal diseases. A simple solution of salts, glucose or rice powder, and boiled water given orally is almost miraculously effective in preventing death from dehydration shock in these diseases. The cost of treatment is only a few cents per child. The British medical journal *Lancet*, called ORT "the most important medical advance of the century."

"B" stands for breast-feeding. Babies who are breast-fed receive natural immunity to diseases from antibodies in their mothers' milk, but infant formula companies have been persuading mothers in many developing countries that bottle-feeding is more modern and healthful than breast-feeding. Unfortunately, these mothers usually do not have access to clean water to combine with the formula and they cannot afford enough expensive synthetic formula to nourish their babies adequately. Consequently, the mortality among bottle-fed babies is much higher than among breast-fed babies in developing countries.

"I" is for universal immunization against the six largest, preventable, **communicable diseases** of the world: measles, tetanus, tuberculosis, polio, diphtheria, and whooping cough. In 1975, less than 10 percent of the developing world's children had been immunized. By 1990, this number had risen to over 50 percent. Although the goal of full immunization for all children has not yet been reached, many lives are being saved every year. In some countries, yellow fever, typhoid, meningitis, **cholera**, and other diseases also urgently need attention.

Burkina Faso provides an excellent example of how a successful immunization campaign can be carried out. Although this West African nation is one of the poorest in the world (annual gross national product per capita of only $140), and its roads, health care clinics, communication, and educational facilities are either nonexistent or woefully inadequate, a highly successful "vaccination commando" operation was undertaken in 1985. In a single three-week period, one million children were immunized against three major diseases (measles, yellow fever, and meningitis) with only a single injection. This represents 60 percent of all children under age fourteen in the country. The cost was less than $1 per child.

In addition to being an issue of humanity and compassion, reducing child mortality may be one of the best ways to stabilize world **population growth**. There has never been a reduction in birth rates that was not preceded by a reduction in infant mortality. When parents are confident that their children will survive, they tend to have only the number of children they actually want, rather than "compensating" for likely deaths by extra births. In Bangladesh, where ORT was discovered, a children's health campaign in the slums of Dacca has reduced infant mortality rates 21 percent since 1983. In that same period, the use of birth control increased 45 percent and birth rates decreased 21 percent.

Sri Lanka, China, Costa Rica, Thailand, and the Republic of Korea have reduced child deaths to a level comparable to those in many highly developed countries. This child survival revolution has been followed by low birth rates and stabilizing populations. The United Nations Children's Fund estimates that if all developing countries had been able to achieve similar birth and death rates, there would have been nine million fewer child deaths in 1987, and nearly 22 million fewer births. *See also* Demographic transition

[*William P. Cunningham*]

FURTHER READING

UNICEF. *The State of the World's Children*. New York: Oxford University Press, 1987.

Chimpanzees

Common chimpanzees (*Pan troglodytes*) are widespread in the forested parts of West, Central, and East Africa. Pygmy chimpanzees, or bonobos (*P. paniscus*), are restricted to the swampy lowland forests of the Zaire basin. Despite their names, common chimpanzees are no longer common, and pygmy chimpanzees are no smaller than the other species.

Chimpanzees are partly arboreal and partly ground-dwelling. They feed in fruit trees by day, nest in other trees at night, and can move rapidly through treetops. On the ground chimpanzees usually walk on all fours (knuckle walking), since their arms are longer than their legs. Their hands have fully opposable thumbs and, although lacking a precision grip, can manipulate objects dexterously. Chimpanzees make and use a variety of tools: they shape and strip "fishing sticks" from twigs to poke into termite mounds, and they chew the ends of shoots to fashion fly whisks. They also throw sticks and stones as offensive weapons and hunt and kill young monkeys.

These apes live in small nomadic groups of 3-6 animals (common chimpanzee) or 6-15 animals (pygmy chimpanzee) which make up a larger community (30-80 individuals) that occupies a territory. Adult males cooperate in defending their territory against predators. Chimpanzee society consists of fairly promiscuous mixed-sex groups. Female common chimpanzees are sexually receptive for only a brief period in mid-month (estrous), while female pygmy chimpanzees are sexually receptive for most of the month. Ovulating females capable of fertilization have swollen pink hind quarters and copulate with most of the males in the group. Female chimpanzees give birth to a single infant after a gestation period of about 8 months.

Jane Goodall has studied common chimpanzees for almost 30 years in the Gombe Stream National Park of Tanzania. She found that chimpanzee personalities are as variable as those of humans, that chimpanzees form alliances, have friendships, have personal dislikes, and run feuds. Chimpanzees also have a cultural tradition, that is, they pass learnt behavior and skills from generation to generation. Chimpanzees have been taught complex sign language (the chimpanzee larynx won't allow speech) through which abstract ideas have been conveyed. These studies show that chimpanzees can develop a large vocabulary and that they can manipulate this vocabulary to frame new thoughts.

Humans share 98.4 percent of their genes with chimpanzees, so only 1.6 percent of human **DNA** is responsible for all the differences between the two species. The DNA of **gorillas** differs 2.3 percent from chimpanzees, which means that the closest relatives of chimpanzees are humans, not gorillas. Further studies of our closest relatives would undoubtedly help us better understand the origins of human social behavior and human **evolution**. Despite this special status, both species of chimpanzees are threatened by the destruction of their forest **habitat** by hunting and by capture for research.

[*Neil Cumberlidge*]

FURTHER READING

Diamond, J. M. *The Third Chimpanzee: The Evolution and Future of the Human Animal.* New York: Harper Collins, 1992.

Ghiglieri, M. P. *The Chimpanzees of Kibale Forest: A Field Study of Ecology and Social Structure.* New York: Columbia University Press, 1984.

Goodall, J. *The Chimpanzees of Gombe: Patterns of Behavior.* Cambridge, MA: Harvard University Press, 1986.

———. *Through a Window: My Thirty Years With the Chimpanzees of Gombe.* Boston: Houghton Mifflin, 1990.

Van Lawick, H. *In the Shadow of Man.* Boston: Houghton Mifflin, 1971.

Chipko Andolan movement

India has a long history of non-violent, passive resistance in social movements rooted in its Hindu concept of *ahimsa*, or "no harm." During the British occupation of India in the early twentieth century, Indian leader **Mohandas K. Gandhi** began to employ a method of resistance against the British that he called *satyagraha* (meaning "force of truth"). Synthesized from his knowledge of **Henry David Thoreau**, Leo Tolstoy, Christianity and Hinduism, Gandhi's concept of satyagraha involves the absolute refusal to cooperate with a perceived wrong and the use of nonviolent tactics in combination with complete honesty to confront, and ultimately convert, evil.

During the occupation, the rights of peasants to gather products, including forest materials, was severely curtailed. New land ownership systems imposed by the British transformed what had been communal village resources into the private property of newly created landlords. Furthermore, policies that encouraged commercial exploitation of forests were put into place. Trees were felled on a large scale to build ships for the British Royal Navy or to provide ties for the expanding railway network in India, severely depleting forest resources on which traditional cultures had long depended.

In response to British rule with its forest destruction and impoverishment of native people, a series of non-violent movements utilizing satyagraha spread throughout India. The British and local aristocracy suppressed these protests brutally, massacring unarmed villagers by the thousands, and jailing Gandhi a number of times, but Gandhi and his allies remained steadfast in their resistance. The British, forced to comprehend the horror of their actions and unable to scapegoat the nonviolent Indians, at last withdrew from India.

After India gained independence, two of Gandhi's disciples, Mira Behn and Sarala Behn, moved to the foothills of the Himalayas to establish *ashramas* (spiritual retreats) dedicated to raising women's status and rights. Their project was dedicated to four major goals: 1) organizing local women, 2) campaigning against alcohol consumption, 3) fighting for forest protection, and 4) setting up small, local, forest-based industries.

During the 1970s, commercial loggers began large-scale tree felling in the Garhwal region in the state of Uttar Pradesh in northern India. **Landslide**s and floods resulted from stripping the forest cover from the hills. The firewood on which local people depended was destroyed, threatening the way of life of the traditional forest culture.

In April, 1973, village women from the Gopeshwar region who had been educated and empowered by the principles of non-violence devised by the Behns began to confront loggers directly, wrapping their arms around trees to protect them. The outpouring of support sparked by their actions was dubbed the *Chipko Andolan* movement (literally, "movement to hug trees"). This crusade to save the forests eventually prevented logging on 4,633 square miles (12,000 sq km) of sensitive **watershed**s in the Alakanada basin. Today, the Chipko Andolan movement has grown to more than four thousand groups working to save India's forests. Their slogan is: "What do the forests bear? Soil, water, and pure air."

The successes of this movement, both in empowering local women and in saving the forests on which they depend, are inspiring models for grassroots green movements around the world.

[*William P. Cunningham and Jeffrey Muhr*]

FURTHER READING

Bandyopadhyay, J., and V. Shiva. "Chipko: Rekindling India's Forest Culture." *Ecologist* 17 (1987): 26-34.

———. "Development, Poverty and the Growth of the Green Movement in India." *Ecologist* 19 (1989): 111-17.

Durning, A. B. "Environmentalism South." *Amicus Journal* 12 (Summer 1990): 12-18.

Chisel plow

See **Conservation tillage**

Chisso Chemical Company

See **Minamata disease**

Chlordane

Chlordane and a closely related compound, heptachlor, belong to a group of chlorine-based **pesticide**s known as cyclodienes. They were among the first major chemicals to attract national attention and controversy, mainly because of their devastating effects on **wildlife** and domestic animals. By the 1970s, they had become two of the most popular pesticides for home and agricultural uses (especially for termite control), despite links between these chemicals and the poisoning of birds and other wildlife, pets and farm animals, as well as links to **leukemia** and other **cancer**s in humans.

In 1975, environmentalists finally persuaded **Environmental Protection Agency (EPA)** to issue an immediate temporary ban on most uses of chlordane and heptachlor based on an "imminent hazard of cancer in man." In 1978, when the EPA agreed to phase out most remaining uses of chlordane and heptachlor, the agency stated that "virtually every person in the United States has residues. . .in his body

tissues." Chlordane has now been banned, at least temporarily, for sale or use in the U.S. But potentially dangerous levels of the chemical are still found occasionally in foodstuffs, homes, and the **environment**. *See also* Pesticide residue

Chlorinated hydrocarbons

Chlorinated hydrocarbons are compounds made of **carbon**, **hydrogen**, and **chlorine** atoms. These compounds can be aliphatic, meaning they do not contain **benzene**, or aromatic, meaning they do. The chlorine functional group gives these compounds a certain character; for instance, the aromatic organochlorine compounds are resistant to microbial degradation; the aliphatic chlorinated solvents have certain anesthetic properties (e.g. chloroform); some are known for their antiseptic properties (e.g. hexachloraphene). The presence of **chlorine** imparts toxicity to many organochlorine compounds (e.g. chlorinated **pesticide**s).

Chlorinated hydrocarbons have many uses, including chlorinated solvents, organochlorine pesticides, and industrial compounds. Common chlorinated solvents are dichloromethane (methylene chloride), chloroform, carbon tetrachloride, trichloroethane, trichloroethylene, tetrachloroethane, tetrachloroethylene. These compounds are used in drycleaning solvents, degreasing agents for machinery and vehicles, paint thinners and removers, laboratory solvents, and in manufacturing processes, such as coffee decaffeination. These solvents are hazardous to human health and exposures are regulated in the workplace. Some are being phased out for their toxicity to humans and the **environment**, as molecules have the potential to react with and destroy stratospheric **ozone**.

The organochlorine pesticides include several subgroups, including the cyclodiene insecticides (e.g. **chlordane**, heptachlor, dieldrin), the **DDT** family of compounds and its analogs, and the hexachlorocyclohexanes (often incorrectly referred to as BHCs, or benzene hexachlorides). These insecticides were developed and marketed extensively after World War II, but due to their toxicity, persistence, widespread environmental contamination, and adverse ecological impacts, most were banned or restricted for use in the United States in the 1970s and 80s. These insecticides generally have low water solubilities, a high affinity for organic matter, readily bioaccumulate in plants and animals, particularly aquatic organisms, and have long environmental half-lives compared to the currently-used insecticides.

There are many chlorinated industrial products and reagent materials. Examples include **vinyl chloride**, which is used to make PVC (**polyvinyl chloride**) **plastics**; chlorinated benzenes, including hexachlorobenzene; PCB (**polychlorinated biphenyl**), used extensively in electrical transformers and capacitors; chlorinated phenols, including **pentachlorophenol (PCP)**; chlorinated naphthalenes; and chlorinated diphenylethers. They represent a diversity of applications, and are valued for their low reactivity and high insulating properties.

There are also chlorinated byproducts of environmental concern, particularly the polychlorinated dibenzo-p-**dioxin**s (PCDDs) and the polychlorinated dibenzofurans (PCDFs). These families of compounds are products of incomplete **combustion** of organochlorine-containing materials, and are primarily found in the **fly ash** of **municipal solid waste** incinerators. The most toxic component of PCDDs, 2,3,7,8-tetrachlorodibenzo-p-dioxin (2,3,7,8-TCDD), was a trace contaminant in the production of the **herbicide 2,4,5-T** and is found in trace amounts in 2,4,5-trichlorophenol and technical grade pentachlorophenol. PCDDs and PCDFs can also be formed in the chlorine bleaching process of **pulp and paper mills**, and have been found in their **effluent** and in trace amounts in some paper products. *See also* Bioaccumulation; Chemicals; Hazardous material; Hazardous waste; Organochloride

[*Deborah L. Swackhammer*]

FURTHER READING

Brooks, G. T. *Chlorinated Insecticides.* Cleveland, OH: CRC Press, 1974.

Chau, A. S. Y., and B. K. Afghan. *Analysis of Pesticides in Water,* Vol. II. Boca Raton, FL: CRC Press, 1982.

Fleming, W. J., D. R. Clark, Jr. and C. J. Henny. *Organochlorine Pesticides and PCBs: A Continuing Problem for the 1980s.* Washington, DC: U. S. Fish and Wildlife Service, 1985.

Manahan, S. E. *Environmental Chemistry,* 5th ed. Ann Arbor, MI: Lewis Publishers, 1991.

Chlorination

Chlorination refers to the application of **chlorine** for the purposes of oxidation. The forms of chlorine used for chlorination include: chlorine gas, hypochlorous acid (HOCl), hypochlorite **ion** (OCl), and chloramines or combined chlorine (Mono-, di-, and tri-chloramines). The first three forms of chlorine are known as free chlorine.

Chlorine (Cl) has three valences under normal environmental conditions, -1, 0 and +1. Environmental scientists often refer only to the chlorine forms having 0 and +1 valences as chlorine; they refer to the -1 form as chloride. Chlorine with a valence of 0 (Cl_2) and chlorine with a valence of +1 (HOCl) both have the ability to oxidize materials, whereas chlorine at a -1 valence, chloride, is already at its lowest oxidation state and has no oxidizing power.

The functions of chlorination are to disinfect water or **wastewater**, decolorize waters or fabrics, sanitize and clean surfaces, remove iron and manganese, and reduce odors. The fundamental principle of each application is that due to its oxidizing potential, chlorine is able to effect many types of chemical reactions. Chlorine can cause alterations in **DNA**, cell-membrane porosity, **enzyme** configurations, and other biochemicals; the oxidative process can also lead to the death of a cell or **virus**. **Chemical bond**s, such as those in certain dyes, can be oxidized, causing a change in the color

of a substance. Textile companies sometimes use chlorine to decolorize fabrics or process waters. In some cases, odors can be reduced or eliminated through oxidation. However, the odor of certain compounds, such as some phenolics, is aggravated through a reaction with chlorine. Certain soluble metals can be made insoluble through oxidation by chlorine (soluble Fe^{2+} is oxidized to insoluble Fe^{3+}), making the metal easier to remove through sedimentation or filtration.

Chlorine is commercially available in three forms; it can also be generated on-site. For treating small quantities of water, calcium hypochlorite ($Ca(OCl)_2$), commonly referred to as high test hypochlorite (HTH) because one mole of HTH provides two OCl^- ions, is sometimes used. For large applications, chlorine gas (Cl_2) is the most wide used source of chlorine. It reacts readily with water to form various chlorine species and is generally the least expensive source. There are, however, risks associated with the handling and transport of chlorine gas, and these have convinced some to use sodium hypochlorite (NaOCl) instead. Sodium hypochlorite is more expensive than chlorine gas, but less expensive than calcium hypochlorite. Some utilities and industries have generated chlorine on-site for many years, using electrolysis to oxidize chloride ions to chlorine. The process is practical in remote areas where brine, a source of chloride ions, is readily available.

Chlorine has been used in the United States since the early 1900s for disinfection. It is still commonly used to disinfect wastewater and drinking water, but the rules guiding its use are gradually changing. Until recently, chlorine was added to wastewater **effluent**s from treatment plants without great concern over its effects on the **environment**. The environmental impact was thought to be insignificant since chlorine was being used in such low concentrations. However, evidence has accumulated showing serious environmental consequences from the **discharge** of even low levels of various forms of chlorine and chlorine compounds, and many plants now dechlorinate their wastewater after allowing the chlorine to react with the wastewater for 30-60 minutes.

The use of chlorine to disinfect drinking water is undergoing a similar review. Since the 1970s, it has been suspected that chlorine and some by-products of chlorination are carcinogenic. Papers published in 1974 indicated that halogenated **methane**s are formed during chlorination. During the mid-1970s the **Environmental Protection Agency (EPA)** conducted two surveys of the **drinking-water supply** in the United States, the National Organics Reconnaissance Survey and the National Organics Monitoring Survey, to determine the extent to which **trihalomethanes** (THMs) (chloroform, bromodichloromethane, dibromochloromethane, bromoform) and other halogenated organic compounds were present. The studies indicated that drinking water is the primary route by which humans are exposed to THMs and that THMs are the most commonly detected synthetic organic **chemicals** in United States' drinking water.

Chloroform was the THM found in the highest concentrations during the surveys. The risks associated with drinking water containing high levels of chloroform are not clear. It is known that 0.2 quarts (200 mL) of chloroform is usually fatal to humans, but the highest concentrations in the drinking water surveyed fell far below (311 ug/L) this lethal dose. The potential carcinogenic effects of chloroform are more difficult to evaluate. It does not cause *Salmonella typhimurium* in the **Ames test** to mutate, but it does cause **mutation**s in yeast and has been found to cause tumors in rats and mice. However, the ability of chloroform to cause **cancer** in humans is still questionable, and the EPA has classified it and other THMs as probable human **carcinogen**s. Based on these data, the maximum contaminant level for THMs in drinking water is now 100 ug/L. This is an enforceable standard and requires the monitoring and reporting of THM concentrations in drinking water.

There are several ways to test for chlorine, but among the more common methods are iodometric, DPD (N,N-Diethyl-p-phenylenediamine) and amperometric. DPD and amperometric methods are generally used in the water and wastewater treatment industry. DPD is a dye which is oxidized by the presence of chlorine, creating a reddish color. The intensity of the color can then be measured and related to chlorine level; the DPD solution can be titrated with a reducing agent (ferrous ammonium sulfate) until the reddish color dissipates. In the amperometric titration method, an oxidant sets up a current in a solution which is measured by the amperometric titrator. A reducing agent (phenylarsine oxide) is then added slowly until no current can be measured by the titrator. The amount of titrant added is commonly related to the amount of chlorine present.

To minimize the problem of chlorinated by-products, many cities in the United States, including Denver, Portland, St. Louis, Boston, Indianapolis, Minneapolis, and Dallas, use chloramination rather than simple chlorination. Chlorine is still required for chloramination, but ammonia is added before or at the same time to form chloramines. Chloramines do not react with organic precursors to form halogenated by-products including THMs. The problem in using chloramines is that they are not as effective as the free chlorine forms at killing **pathogen**s.

Questions still remain about whether the levels of chlorine currently used are dangerous to human health. The level of chlorine in most water supplies is approximately 1 mg/L, and some scientists believe that the chlorinated by-products formed are not hazardous to humans at these levels. There are some risks, nevertheless, and perhaps the most important question is whether these outweigh the benefits of using chlorine. The final issue concerns the short-term and long-term effects of discharging chlorine into the environment. Dechlorination would be yet another treatment step, requiring the commitment of additional resources. At the present time, the general consensus is that chlorine is more beneficial than harmful. However, it is important to note that a great deal of research is now underway to explore the benefits of using alternative disinfectants such as **ozone**, chlorine dioxide, and ultraviolet light. Each alternative poses some problems of its own, so despite the current availability of a great deal of research data, the selection of an alternative

is difficult. *See also* Aquatic chemistry; Drinking-water supply; Industrial waste treatment; Odor control; Sewage treatment; Water pollution; Water quality; Water quality standards; Water treatment

[*Gregory D. Boardman*]

FURTHER READING

American Water Works Association. *Water Quality and Treatment.* 4th ed. New York: McGraw-Hill, 1990.

Davis, M. L., and D. A. Cornwell. *Introduction to Environmental Engineering.* New York: McGraw-Hill, 1991.

Moberg, D. "Sunset for Chlorine?" *E Magazine* 4 (July-August 1993): 26-31.

National Academy of Sciences. *Drinking Water and Health.* Vol. 7. Washington, DC: National Academy Press, 1987.

Pojasek, R. J., ed. *Drinking Water Quality Enhancement Through Source Protection.* Ann Arbor, MI: Ann Arbor Science, 1977.

Tchobanoglous, G., and E. D. Schroeder. *Water Quality.* Reading, MA: Addison-Wesley, 1985.

Viessman, W., Jr., and M. J. Hammer. *Water Supply and Pollution Control.* 5th ed. New York: Harper Collins, 1993.

Williams, R. B., and G. L. Culp, eds. *Handbook of Public Water Systems.* New York: Van Nostrand Reinhold, 1986.

Chlorine monoxide

One of two oxides of **chlorine**, either Cl_2O or ClO. When used in environmental science, it usually refers to the latter. Chlorine monoxide (ClO) is formed in the **atmosphere** when free chlorine atoms react with **ozone**. In the reaction, ozone is converted to normal, diatomic oxygen (O_2). This process appears to be a major factor in the destruction of ozone in the **stratosphere** observed by scientists in recent years. The most important sources of chlorine by which this reaction is initiated appear to be **chlorofluorocarbons** and other synthetic chlorine compounds released by human activities. *See also* Ozone layer depletion

Chlorofluorocarbons (CFCs)

The chlorofluorocarbons (CFCs) are a family of organic compounds containing **carbon**, **hydrogen** (usually), and either **chlorine** or fluorine, or both. The members of this family can be produced by replacing one or more hydrogen atoms in **hydrocarbons** with a chlorine or fluorine atom. In the simplest possible case, treating **methane** (CH_4) with chlorine yields chloromethane, CH_3Cl. Treating this product with fluorine causes the replacement of a second hydrogen atom with a fluorine atom, producing chlorofluoromethane, CH_2ClF.

This process can be continued until all hydrogen atoms have been replaced by chlorine and/or fluorine atoms. By using larger hydrocarbons, an even greater variety of CFCs can be produced. The compound known as CFC-113, for example, is made from ethane (C_2H_6) and has the formula $C_2F_3Cl_3$.

Over the last three decades, the CFCs have become widely popular for a number of commercial applications. These applications fall into four general categories: refrigerants, cleaning fluids, propellants, and blowing agents. As refrigerants, CFCs have largely replaced more harmful gases such as ammonia and **sulfur dioxide** in refrigerators, freezers, and air conditioning systems. Their primary application as cleaning fluids has been in the computer manufacturing business where they are used to clean circuit boards. CFCs are used as propellants in hair sprays, deodorants, spray paints, and other types of sprays. As blowing agents, CFCs are used in the manufacture of fast-food take-out boxes and similar containers. By the early 1990s, CFCs had become so popular that their production was a multi-billion dollar business worldwide.

For many years, little concern was expressed about the environmental hazards of CFCs. The very qualities that made them desirable for commercial applications—their stability, for example—appeared to make them environmentally benign.

However, by the mid-1970s, the error in that view became apparent. Scientists began to find that CFCs in the **stratosphere** decomposed by sunlight. One product of that **decomposition**, atomic chlorine, reacts with **ozone** (O_3) to form ordinary oxygen (O_2). The apparently harmless CFCs turned out, instead, to be a major factor in the loss of ozone from the stratosphere.

By the time this discovery was made, levels of CFCs in the stratosphere were escalating rapidly. The concentration of these compounds climbed from 0.8 **part per billion** in 1950 and 1.0 part per billion in 1970 to 3.5 parts per billion in 1987.

A turning point in the CFC story came in the mid-1980s when scientists found that a large hole in the ozone layer was opening up over the Antarctic each year. This discovery spurred world leaders to act on the problem of CFC production. In 1987, about 40 nations met in Montreal to draft a treaty that will reduce the production of CFCs worldwide.

This action is encouraging, but it hardly solves the CFC problem. These compounds remain in the **atmosphere** for long periods of time (about 77 years for CFC-11 and 139 years for CFC-12), so they will continue to pose a threat to the ozone layer for many decades to come. *See also* Air pollution; Air pollution control; Hydrochloroflurocarbons; Montreal Protocol on Substances that Deplete the Ozone Layer; Ozone layer depletion; Ultraviolet radiation

[*David E. Newton*]

FURTHER READING

Monastersky, R. "Decline of the CFC Empire." *Science News* 133 (9 April 1988): 234-36.

Moore, T. "The Challenge of Doing Without." *EPRI Journal* (September 1989): 4-13.

O'Sullivan, D. A. "International Gathering Plans Way to Safeguard Atmospheric Ozone." *Chemical & Engineering News* (26 June 1989): 33-36.

Pool, R. "The Elusive Replacements for CFCs." *Science* 242 (4 November 1988): 666-68.

Selinger, B. *Chemistry in the Marketplace.* 4th ed. Sydney: Harcourt Brace Jovanovich Publishers, 1989.

Zurer, P. S. "Producers Grapple with Realities of CFC Phaseout." *Chemical & Engineering News* (24 July 1989): 7-13.

Cholera

Cholera is one of the most severe and contagious diseases transmitted by water. It is marked by severe diarrhea, resulting in fluid loss and dehydration, sometimes followed by shock and death. If not treated, mortality occurs in over 60 percent of cases. The Latin American cholera epidemic claimed 4002 lives in 1991, and resulted in 391,742 reported cases that year, mostly in Peru and Ecuador. Cholera is caused by the bacillus *Vibrio cholerae*, a member of the family Vibrionaceae, which are described as Gram negative, non-sporulating rods that are slightly curved, motile, and have a fermentative metabolism.

The natural **habitat** of *V. cholerae* is human feces, but some studies have indicated that natural waters may also be a habitat of the organism. Fecal contamination of water is the most common means by which *V. cholerae* is spread, however, food, insects, soiled clothing, or person-to-person contact may also transmit sufficient numbers of the **pathogen** to cause cholera.

The ability of *V. cholerae* to survive in water is dependent upon the temperature and water type. *V. cholerae* reportedly survive longer at low temperatures, and in seawater, sterilized water, and **nutrient** rich waters. Also, the particular strain of *V. cholerae* affects the survival of the organism in water, since some strains or types are hardier than others. Most methods to isolate *V. cholerae* from water include concentration of the sample, by filtration, exposure to high **pH** and selective media. Identification of pathogenic strains of *V. cholerae* is dependent upon agglutination tests. Final confirmation of the strain or type must be done in a specialized laboratory.

Persons infected with *V. cholerae* produce 10^7 to 10^9 organisms per milliliter in the stool at the height of the disease, but the number of excreted organisms drops off quickly as the disease progresses. Asymptomatic carriers of *V. cholerae* excrete 10^2 to 10^5 organisms per gram of feces. The mild form of the illness lasts for 5 to 7 days. Hydration therapy is the treatment of choice for cholera. It is suggested that antibiotics not be used, following the emergence of multiple antibiotic resistant strains in many areas. Vaccines exist to prevent cholera, however, they do not prevent the acquisition of the bacteria in the gastrointestinal tract, do not diminish symptoms in persons already infected, and are effective for well less than a year. Proper **water treatment** should eliminate *V. cholerae* from drinking water, however, the most effective control of this pathogen is dependent upon good sanitary practices.

[*E. K. Black and Gordon R. Finch*]

FURTHER READING

Christie, A. B. *Infectious Diseases: Epidemiology and Clinical Practice.* 4th ed. Edinburgh, Scotland: Churchill Livingstone, 1987.

Feachem, R. G., et al. *Sanitation and Disease: Health Aspects of Excreta and Wastewater Management.* New York: Wiley, 1983.

Foliguet, J. M., P. Hartemann, and J. Vial. "Microbial Pathogens Transmitted by Water." *Journal of Environmental Pathology, Toxicology, and Oncology* 7 (1987): 39-114.

Mitchell, R., ed. *Environmental Microbiology.* New York: Wiley-Liss, 1992.

Cholinesterase inhibitor

Insecticides kill their target insect **species** in a variety of ways. Two of the most commonly used classes of insecticide are the **organophosphate**s (nerve gases) and the carbamates. These compounds act quickly (in a matter of hours), are lethal at low doses (**parts per billion**), degrade rapidly (in hours to days) and leave few toxic residues in the **environment**. Organophosphates kill insects by inducing loss of control of the peripheral nervous system, leading to uncontrollable spasms followed by paralysis and, ultimately, death. This is often accomplished by a biochemical process called cholinesterase inhibition.

Most animals' nervous systems are composed of individual nerve cells called neurons. Between any two adjacent neurons there is always a gap, called the synaptic cleft; the neurons do not actually touch each other. When an animal senses something—for example, pain—the sensation is transmitted chemically from one neuron to another until the impulse reaches the brain or central nervous system. The first neuron (pre-synaptic neuron) releases a substance, known as a transmitter, into the synaptic cleft. One of the most common chemical transmitters is called acetylcholine. Acetylcholine then diffuses across the gap and binds with receptor sites on the second neuron (post-synaptic neuron). Reactions within the target neuron triggered by occupied receptors result in further transmission of the signal. As soon as the impulse has been transmitted, the acetylcholine in the gap is immediately destroyed by an **enzyme** called cholinesterase; the destruction of the acetylcholine is an absolutely essential part of the nervous process. If the acetylcholine is not destroyed, it continues to stimulate indefinitely the transmission of impulses from one neuron to the next, leading to loss of all control over the peripheral nervous system. When control is lost, the nervous system is first overstimulated and then paralyzed until the animal dies. Thus, organophosphate insecticides bind to the cholinesterase enzyme, preventing the cholinesterase from destroying the acetylcholine and inducing the death of the insect.

Some trade names for organophosphate insecticides are malathion and parathion. Carbamates include aminocarb and carbaryl. The carbamates produce the same effect of cholinesterase inhibition as the organophosphates, but the chemical reaction of the carbamates is more easily reversible. The potency or power of these compounds is usually measured in terms of the quantity of the pesticide (or inhibitor) that will produce a 50 percent loss of cholinesterase activity. Since acetylcholine transmission of nervous impulses is com-

mon to most vertebrates as well as insects, there is a great potential for harm to non-**target species** from the use of cholinesterase-inhibiting insecticides. Therefore the use of these insecticides is highly regulated and controlled. Access to treated areas and contact with the compounds is prohibited until the time period necessary for the breakdown of the compounds to non-toxic endproducts has elapsed. *See also* Pesticide

[*Usha Vedagiri*]

FURTHER READING

Connell, D. W., and G. J. Miller. *Chemistry and Ecotoxicology of Pollution.* New York: Wiley, 1984.

Keeton, W. T. *Biological Science.* New York: Norton, 1980.

Chromatography

Chromatography is the process of separating mixtures of **chemicals** into individual components as a means of identification or purification. It derives from the Greek words *chroma,* meaning color, and *graphy,* meaning writing. The word was coined in 1906 by the Russian chemist Mikhail Tsvett who used a column to separate plant pigments. Currently chromatography is applied to many types of separations far beyond those of just color separations. Common chromatographic applications include gas-liquid chromatography (GC), liquid-solid chromatography (LC), thin layer chromatography (TLC), **ion** exchange chromatography, and gel permeation chromatography (GPC). All of these methods are invaluable in analytical environmental chemistry, particularly GC, LC, and GPC.

The basic principle of chromatography is that different compounds have different retentions when passed through a given medium. In a chromatographic system, one has a mobile phase and a stationary phase. The mixture to be separated is introduced in the mobile phase and passed through the stationary phase. The compounds are selectively retained by the stationary phase and move at different rates which allows the compounds to be separated.

In gas chromatography, the mobile phase is a gas and the stationary phase is a liquid fixed to a solid support. Liquid samples are first vaporized in the injection port and carried to the chromatographic column by an inert gas which serves as the mobile phase. The column contains the liquid stationary phase, and the compounds are separated based on their different vapor pressures and their different affinities for the stationary phase. Thus different types of separations can be optimized by choosing different stationary phases, and by altering the temperature of the column. As the compounds elute from the end of the column, they are detected by one of a number of methods that have specificity for different chemical classes.

Liquid chromatography consists of a liquid mobile phase and a solid stationary phase. There are two general types of liquid chromatography: column chromatography and high pressure liquid chromatography (HPLC). In column chromatography, the mixture is eluted through the column containing stationary packing material by passing successive volumes of solvents or solvent mixtures through the column. Separations result as a function of both chemical-solvent interactions as well as chemical-stationary phase interactions. Often this technique is used in a preparative manner to remove interferences from environmental sample extracts. HPLC refers to specific instruments designed to perform liquid chromatography under very high pressures to obtain a much greater degree of resolution. The column outflow is passed through a detector and can be collected for further processing if desired. Detection is typically by ultraviolet light or fluorescence.

A variation of column chromatography is gel permeation chromatography (GPC), which separates chemicals based on size exclusion. The column is packed with porous spheres, which allow certain size chemicals to penetrate the spheres and excludes larger sizes. As the sample mixture traverses the column, larger molecules move more quickly and elute first while smaller molecules require longer elution times. An example of this application in environmental analyses is the removal of lipids (large molecules) from fish tissue extracts being analyzed for **pesticide**s (small molecules).

[*Deborah L. Swackhammer*]

FURTHER READING

McNair, H. M., and E. J. Bonelli. *Basic Gas Chromatography*. Palo Alto, CA: Varian Instruments, 1969.

Peters, D. G., J. M. Hayes, and G. M. Hieftje. *Chemical Separations and Measurements*. Philadelphia: Saunders, 1974.

Chronic effects

Chronic effects occur over a long period of time. The length of time termed "long" is dependent upon the life cycle of the organism being tested. For some aquatic **species** a chronic effect might be seen over the course of a month. For animals such as rats and dogs, chronic would refer to a period of several weeks to years.

Chronic effects can be either caused by chronic or acute exposures. Acute exposure to some metals and many **carcinogen**s can result in chronic effects. With certain toxicants, such as cyanide, it is difficult, if not impossible, to cause a chronic effect. However, at a higher dosage, cyanide readily causes **acute effects**. Examples of chronic effects include pulmonary tuberculosis and, in many cases, **lead** poisoning. In each disease the effects are long-term and cause damage to tissues; acute effects generally result in little tissue reaction. Thus, acute and chronic effects are frequently unrelated, and yet it is often necessary to predict chronic toxicity based on acute data. Acute data are more plentiful and easier to obtain. To illustrate the possible differences between acute and chronic effects, consider the examples of halogenated solvents, **arsenic**, and lead.

In halogenated solvents, acute exposure can cause excitability and dizziness, while chronic exposure will result in liver damage. Chronic effects of arsenic poisoning are in blood formation and liver and nerve damage. Acute poisoning affects the gastro-intestinal tract. Lead also effects blood formation in chronic exposure, and damages the gastro-intestinal tract in acute exposure. Other chronic effects of exposure to lead include changes in the nervous system and muscles. In some situations, given the proper combination of dose level and frequency, those exposed will experience both acute and chronic effects.

There are **chemicals** that are essential and beneficial for the functions and structure of the body. The chronic effect is therefore better health, although people generally do not refer to chronic effects as being positive. However, vitamin D, fluoride, and sodium chloride are just a few examples of agents that are essential and/or beneficial when administered at the proper dosage. Too much of any of the three or too little, however, could cause acute and/or chronic toxic effects.

In aquatic toxicology, chronic toxicity tests are used to estimate the effect and no-effect concentrations of a chemical that is continuously applied over the reproductive life cycle of an organism; for example, the time needed for growth, development, sexual maturity, and reproduction. The range in chemical concentrations used in the chronic tests is determined from acute tests. Criterion for effects might include the number and percent of embryos that develop and hatch, the survival and growth of larvae and juveniles, etc.

The maximum acceptable toxicant concentration (MATC) is defined through chronic testing. The MATC is a hypothetical concentration between the highest concentration of chemical that caused no observed effect (NOEC) and the lowest observed effect concentration (LOEC). Therefore,

$$LOEC > MATC > NOEC$$

Furthermore, the MATC has been used to relate chronic toxicity to acute toxicity through an application factor (AF). AF is defined as follows:

$$AF = \frac{MATC}{LD_{50}}$$

The AF for one aquatic species might then be used to predict the chronic toxicity for another species, given the acute toxicity data for that species.

The major limitations of chronic toxicity testing are the availability of suitable test species and the length of time needed for a test. In animal testing, mice, rats, rabbits, guinea pigs, and/or dogs are generally used; mice and rats being the most common. With respect to aquatic studies, the most commonly used vertebrates are the fathead (fresh water) and sheepshead (saltwater) minnows. The most commonly used invertebrates are freshwater water fleas (*Daphnia*) and the saltwater mysid shrimp (*Mysidopsis*). *See also* Aquatic chemistry; Detoxification; Dose response; Heavy metals and heavy metal poisoning; LD₅₀; Plant pathology; Toxic substance

[*Gregory D. Boardman*]

FURTHER READING

Hodgson, E., R. B. Mailman, and J. E. Chambers. *Dictionary of Toxicology*. New York: Van Nostrand Reinhold, 1988.

Lu, F. C. *Basic Toxicology Fundamentals, Target Organs, and Risk Assessment.* Washington, DC: Hemisphere, 1985.

Manahan, S. E. *Toxicological Chemistry.* 2nd ed. Ann Arbor, MI: Lewis Publishers, 1992.

Rand, G. M., and S. R. Petrocelli. *Fundamentals of Aquatic Toxicology Methods and Applications.* Washington, DC: Hemisphere, 1985.

Cigarette smoke

Cigarette smoke contains more than 4,000 identified compounds. Many are known irritants and **carcinogen**s. Since the first Surgeon General's Report on smoking and health in 1964, evidence linking the use of **tobacco** to illness, injury, and death has continued to mount. Many thousands of studies have documented the adverse health consequences of any type of tobacco, including cigarettes, cigars, and smokeless tobacco.

Specific airborne contaminants from cigarette smoke include respirable particles, nicotine, **polycyclic aromatic hydrocarbons**, **arsenic**, **DDT**, formaldehyde, hydrogen cyanide, **methane**, **carbon monoxide**, acrolein, and nitrogen dioxide. Each one of these compounds impacts some part of the body. Irritating gases like ammonia, hydrogen sulfide and formaldehyde affect the eyes, nose and throat. Others, like nicotine, impact the central nervous system. Carbon monoxide reduces the oxygen-carrying capacity of the blood, starving the body of energy. Carcinogenic agents come into prolonged contact with vital organs and with the delicate linings of the nose, mouth, throat, lungs and airways.

Cigarette smoke is one of the six major sources of indoor air pollution, along with combustion by-products, microorganisms and allergens, formaldehyde and other organic compounds, asbestos fibers, and **radon** and its airborne decay products. The carbon monoxide concentration in cigarette smoke is more than 600 times the level considered safe in industrial plants, and a smoker's blood typically has 4 to 15 times more carbon monoxide in it than that of a nonsmoker. Airborne particle concentrations in a home with several heavy smokers can exceed ambient **air quality** standards.

Sidestream, or second-hand, smoke actually has higher concentrations of some toxins than the mainstream smoke the smoker inhales. Second-hand smoke carries more than 30 known carcinogens. According to a study by the **Centers for Disease Control and Prevention** (CDC) released in 1996, nearly 9 out of 10 nonsmoking Americans are exposed to environmental tobacco smoke as measured by the levels of cotinine in their blood. The presence of cotinine, a chemical the body metabolizes from nicotine, is documentation of exposure to cigarette smoke. On the basis of health hazards of second-hand smoke, the **Environmental Protection Agency** has classified second-hand smoke as a Group A carcinogen, known to cause cancer in humans.

Cigarettes probably represent the single greatest source of **radiation exposure** to smokers in the United States today. Two naturally occurring radioactive materials, **lead**-210 and polonium-210, are present in tobacco. Both of these long-lived decay products of radon are deposited and retained on the large, sticky leaves of tobacco plants. When the tobacco is made into cigarettes and the smoker lights up, the radon decay products are volatilized and enter the lungs. The resulting dose to small segments of the bronchial epithelium of the lungs of about 50 million smokers in the United States is about 160 mSv per year. (One Sv = 100 rem of radiation.) The dose to the whole body is about 13 mSv, more than 10 times the long-term dose rate limit for members of the public.

The **U. S. Department of Health and Human Services** reported in 1996 that more than 400,000 Americans die each year from smoking. One in every five deaths in the U.S. is smoking related, the largest preventable cause of illness and premature death in the U.S. About 10 million people in the U.S. have died from causes attributed to smoking, including heart disease, emphysema, and other respiratory disease, since the first Surgeon General's report on smoking and health in 1964. Death is caused primarily by heart disease, lung **cancer**, heart disease, and chronic obstructive lung diseases such as **emphysema** or chronic **bronchitis**. In addition, the use of tobacco has been linked to cancers of the larynx, mouth and esophagus, and as a contributory factor in the development of cancers of the bladder, kidney, pancreas, and cervix. Cigarette smoke aggravates **asthma**, triggers allergies, and causes changes in bodily tissues that can leave smokers and nonsmokers prone to illness, especially heart disease.

About 180,000 Americans will die prematurely of coronary heart disease every year due to smoking. The risk of a stroke or heart attack is greatly increased by nicotine, which impacts the platelets which enable the blood to clot. Nicotine causes the surface of the platelets to become stickier, thereby increasing the platelets' ability to aggregate. Thus, a blood clot or thrombus forms more easily. A thrombus in an artery of the heart results in a heart attack; in an artery of the brain it results in a stroke.

Epidemiological studies reveal a direct correlation between the extent of maternal smoking and various illnesses in children. Also, studies show significantly lower heights and weights in 6- to 11-year olds whose mothers smoke. A pregnant woman who smokes faces increased risks of miscarriage, premature birth, stillbirth, infants with low birth weight, and infants with physical and mental impairments. Cigarette smoking also impairs fertility in women and men, contributes to earlier menopause, and increases a woman's risk of osteoporosis.

Cigarette smoke contains **benzene** which, when combined with the radioactive toxins, can cause **leukemia**. Although smoking does not cause the disease, smoking may boost a person's risk of getting leukemia by 30 percent.

A long-time smoker increases his risk of lung cancer by 1,000 times. In 1986, according to the CDC, about 117,000 people died of lung cancer directly attributed to cigarette smoke. More than 3,000 people each year develop lung cancer from second-hand smoke. Between 1960 and 1990, deaths from lung cancer among women have increased by more than 400 percent—exceeding breast cancer deaths.

The addiction to nicotine in cigarette smoke, a chemical and behavioral addiction as powerful as that of heroin, is well documented. The immediate effect of smoking a cigarette can range from tachycardia (an abnormally fast heartbeat) to arrhythmia (an irregular heartbeat). Deep inhalations of smoke lower the pressure in a smoker's chest and pulmonary blood vessels, which increases the amount of blood flow to the heart. This increased blood flow is experienced as a relaxed feeling. Seconds later, nicotine enters the liver and causes that organ to release sugar, which leads to a "sugar high." The pancreas then releases insulin to return the blood sugar level to normal, but it makes the smoker irritable and hungry, stimulating a desire to smoke and recover the relaxed, high feeling.

Nicotine also stimulates the nervous system to release adrenaline, which speeds up the heart and respiratory rates, making the smoker feel more tense. Lighting the next cigarette perpetuates the cycle. The greater the number of behaviors linked to the habit, the stronger the habit is and the more difficult to break. Quitting involves combating the physical need and the psychological need, and complete physical withdrawal can take up to two weeks.

From an economic point of view, the Department of Health and Human Services estimates that smoking costs the United States $50 billion in health expenses. That figure is most likely conservative because the medical costs attributable to burn care from smoking-related fires, perinatal care for low birth weight infants of mothers who smoke, and treatment of disease caused by second-hand smoke were not included in the calculation. *See also* Indoor air quality

[*Linda Rehkopf*]

FURTHER READING

Baker, S., and S. Carl. "Saving Your Lungs and Your Life." *Health* (June 1991): 64.

Haas, F., and S. Haas. *The Chronic Bronchitis and Emphysema Handbook.* New York: Wiley, 1990.

Moeller, D. W. *Environmental Health.* Cambridge, MA: Harvard University Press, 1992.

National Academy of Sciences. *Environmental Tobacco Smoke: Measuring Exposures and Assessing Health Effects.* Washington, DC: National Academy Press, 1986.

Sonnett, S. *Smoking.* New York: Franklin Watts, 1988.

CITES

See **Convention on International Trade in Endangered Species of Fauna and Flora**

Citizen's Clearinghouse for Hazardous Waste

See **Gibbs, Lois Marie**

Citizens for a Better Environment (Chicago, Illinois)

Citizens for a Better Environment (CBE) is an organization that works to reduce exposure to **toxic substance**s in land, water, and air. Founded in 1971, CBE has 30,000 members and operates with a $1.8 million budget. The organization also maintains regional offices in Minnesota and in Wisconsin.

CBE staff and members focus on research, public information, and advocacy to reduce toxic substances. They also meet with policy-makers on state, regional and national levels. A staff of scientists, researchers and policy analysts evaluate specific problems brought to the attention of CBE, testify at legislative and regulatory agency hearings, and file lawsuits in state and federal courts. The organization also conducts public education programs, and provides technical assistance to local residents and organizations that attempt to halt toxic chemical exposures.

The Chicago office currently is fighting the construction of an **incinerator** in a low-income neighborhood in the Chicago area; and is researching the issues on volume-based garbage for suburban Chicago areas. In Minnesota, the staff has developed a "Good Neighbor" program of agreements between community groups, environmental activists, businesses and industries along the Mississippi River to reduce **pollution** of the river. In Wisconsin, transportation issues under study include selling ride-sharing credits to meet **Clean Air Act** standards. Selling and buying of credits between and among individuals, businesses and polluting industries has become a lucrative way for polluters to continue their practices. CBE is attempting to close the legislative loopholes that allows this practice to continue.

The Chicago office maintains a library of books, reports, and articles on environmental pollution issues. Publications include CBE's *Environmental Review*, a quarterly journal on the public health effects of pollution; it includes updates of CBE activities and research projects. Contact: Citizens for a Better Environment, 407 S. Dearborn, Suite 1775, Chicago, IL 60605.

[*Linda Rehkopf*]

Clay minerals

Clay minerals contribute to the physical and chemical properties of most **soil**s and **sediment**s. At high concentrations they cause soils to have a sticky consistency when wet. Individual particles of clay minerals are very small with diameters less than two micrometers. Because they are so finely divided, clay minerals have a very high surface area per unit weight, ranging form 5 to 800 square meters per gram. They are much more reactive than coarser materials in soils and sediments such as silt and sand, and clay minerals account for much of the reactivity of soils and sediments with respect to **adsorption** and **ion exchange**.

Mineralogists restrict the definition of clay minerals to those aluminosilicates (minerals predominantly composed of **aluminum**, silicon, and oxygen) which in nature have particle sizes two micrometers or less in diameter. These minerals have platy structures made up of sheets of silica, composed of silicon and oxygen, and alumina, which is usually composed of aluminum and oxygen, but often has iron and magnesium replacing some or all of the aluminum.

Clay minerals can be classified by the stacking of these sheets. The one to one clay minerals have alternating silica and alumina sheets; these are the least reactive of the clay minerals, and kaolinite is the most common example. The two to one minerals have layers made up of an alumina sheet sandwiched between two silica sheets. These layers have structural defects that result in negative charges, and they are stacked upon each other with interlayer cations between the layers to neutralize the negative layer charges. Common two to one clays are illite and smectite.

In smectites, often called montmorillonite, the interlayer ions can undergo cation exchange. Smectites have the greatest ion exchange capacity of the clay minerals and are the most plastic. In illite, the layer charge is higher than for smectite, but the cation exchange capacity is lower because most of the interlayer ions are potassium ions that are trapped between the layers and are not exchangeable.

Some **iron minerals** also can be found in the clay-sized fraction of soils and sediments. These minerals have a low capacity for ion exchange but are very important in some adsorption reactions. Gibbsite, an aluminum hydroxide mineral, is also found in the clay-sized fraction of some soils and sediments. This mineral has a reactivity similar to the iron minerals. *See also* Soil compaction; Soil conservation; Soil consistency

[*Paul R. Bloom*]

Clay-hard pan

A compacted subsurface **soil** layer. Hard pans are frequently found in soils that have undergone significant amounts of weathering. Clay will accumulate below the surface and cause the **subsoil** to be dense, making it difficult for roots and water to penetrate. Soils with clay pans are more susceptible to water **erosion**. Clay pans can be broken by cultivation, but over time they will re-form.

Clean Air Act (1963, 1970, 1990)

The 1970 Clean Air Act and major amendments to the act in 1977 and 1990 serve as the backbone of efforts to control **air pollution** in the United States. This law established one of the most complex regulatory programs in the country. Efforts to control air pollution in the United States date back to 1881, when Chicago and Cincinnati passed laws to control **smoke** and soot from factories in the cities. Other municipalities followed suit and the momentum continued to build. In 1952 Oregon became the first state to adopt a significant program to control air pollution, and three years later, the federal government became involved for the first time, when

the Air Pollution Control Act was passed. This law granted funds to assist the states in their **air pollution control** activities.

In 1963, the first Clean Air Act was passed. This act provided permanent federal aid for research, support for the development of state pollution control agencies, and federal involvement in cross-boundary air pollution cases. An amendment to the act in 1965 directed the Department of Health, Education and Welfare to establish federal **emission standards** for motor vehicles. (At this time, HEW administered air pollution laws. The **Environmental Protection Agency (EPA)** was not created until 1970.) This represented a significant move by the federal government from a supportive to an active role in setting air pollution policy. The 1967 Air Quality Act provided additional funding to the states, required the states to establish **Air Quality Control Region**s, and directed HEW to obtain and make available information on the health effects of air pollutants and to identify **pollution control** techniques. All of these components of the law were designed to assist the states, but they further demonstrated increasing federal involvement in the issue.

The Clean Air Act of 1970 marked a dramatic change in air pollution policy in the United States. Following the passage of this law, the federal government, not the states, would be the focal point for air pollution policy. This act established the framework that continues to be the foundation for air pollution control policy. The impetus for this change was the belief that the current state-based approach was not working and the pressure from rising environmental consciousness across the country. Public sentiment was growing so significantly that environmental issues demanded the attention of high-ranking officials. In fact, the leading policy entrepreneurs on the issue were President Richard Nixon and Senator Edmund Muskie of Maine.

These men and other leaders devised a plan with four key components. First, **National Ambient Air Quality Standards** (NAAQSs) were established for six major pollutants: **carbon monoxide**, **lead** (in 1977), nitrogen dioxide, ground-level **ozone** (a key component of **smog**), **particulate** matter, and **sulfur dioxide**. For each of these pollutants, sometimes referred to as **criteria pollutant**s, primary and secondary standards were set. The **primary standards** were designed to protect human health, the **secondary standards** were based on protecting crops, forests, and buildings if the primary standards were not capable of doing so. The Act stipulated that these standards must apply to the entire country and be established by the EPA, based on the best available scientific information. The costs of attaining these standards were not among the factors considered. Relatedly, the EPA was to establish standards for less common toxic air pollutants.

Second, **New Source Performance Standards** (NSPSs) would be established by the EPA. These standards would determine how much air pollution would be allowed by new plants in the various industrial sectors. The standards are to be based on the best affordable technology available for the control of pollutants at such sources as **power plants**, steel factories, and chemical plants.

Third, mobile source emission standards were established to control **automobile emissions**. These standards were specified in the statute (rather than left to the EPA), and schedules for meeting these standards were also written into the law. It was thought that such an approach was crucial in having success with the powerful auto industry. The pollutants regulated were carbon monoxide, **hydrocarbons**, and **nitrogen oxides**, with goals of reducing the first two pollutants by 90 percent by 1975, and nitrogen oxides by 82 percent by 1975.

The final component of the **air quality** protection framework involved the implementation of the above procedures. Each state would be encouraged to devise a state implementation plan (SIP), which would indicate how the state would achieve the national standards. This gave each state some flexibility while still maintaining national standards. These plans had to be approved by the EPA; if a state did not have an approved SIP, the EPA would administer the Clean Air Act in that state. However, since the federal government is in charge of establishing pollution standards for new mobile and stationary sources, even the states with an SIP have limited flexibility. The main focal point for the states was the control of existing stationary sources, and if necessary, mobile sources. The states had to set limits in their SIPs that allowed them to achieve the NAAQSs by a statutorily determined deadline (originally 1975, but subsequently delayed). One problem with this approach was the construction of tall smokestacks, which helped move pollution out of a particular **airshed** but did not reduce overall pollution levels. The states are also charged with monitoring and enforcing the Clean Air Act.

The 1977 amendments to the Clean Air Act dealt with three main issues: nonattainment, auto emissions, and the prevention of air quality deterioration in areas where the air was already relatively clean. The first two issues were resolved primarily by delaying deadlines and increasing penalties. Largely in response to a court decision in favor of environmentalists (**Sierra Club** v. Ruckelshaus, 1972), the 1977 amendments included a program for the prevention of significant deterioration (PSD) of air that was already clean. This program would prevent polluting the air up to the national levels in areas where the air was cleaner than the standards. In Class I areas, areas with near pristine air quality, no new significant air pollution would be allowed. Class I areas are airsheds over larger **national park**s and **wilderness** areas. In Class II areas a moderate degree of air quality deterioration would be allowed. And finally, in Class III areas, air deterioration up to the national secondary standards would be allowed. Most of the country that had air cleaner than the NAAQSs was classified as Class II. Related to the prevention of significant deterioration is a provision to protect and enhance visibility in national parks and wilderness areas even if the air pollution is not a threat to human health. The impetus of this section of the bill was the growing visibility problem in parks, especially in the Southwest.

Throughout the 1980s efforts to further amend the Clean Air Act were stymied. President Ronald Reagan was opposed to any strengthening of the act, which he argued would hurt the economy. In Congress, the controversy over **acid rain** between members from the Midwest and the Northeast further contributed to the stalemate. Gridlock on the issue broke with the election of George Bush, who supported amendments to the act, and the rise of Senator George Mitchell of Maine to Senate Majority Leader. Over the next two years, the issues were hammered out between environmentalists and industry and between different regions of the country. Major players in Congress were Representatives John Dingell of Michigan and Henry Waxman of California and Senators Robert Byrd of West Virginia and Mitchell.

Major amendments to the Clean Air Act were finally passed in the fall of 1990. These amendments addressed four major topics: (1) acid rain, (2) toxic air pollutants, (3) **nonattainment area**s, and (4) **ozone layer depletion**. To address acid rain, a 10 million ton reduction in annual sulfur dioxide emissions (a 40 percent reduction based on 1980 levels) and a 2 million ton annual reduction in nitrogen oxides by the year 2000 will be required. Most of this reduction will come from old utility power plants. The law also creates marketable pollution allowances, so that a utility that reduces emissions more than required can sell those pollution rights to another source. Economists argue that such an approach should become more widespread for all pollution control, to increase efficiency. Due to the failure of the toxic air pollutant provisions of the 1970 Clean Air Act, new, more stringent provisions were adopted requiring regulations for all major sources of 189 varieties of toxic air pollution within ten years. Areas of the country still in nonattainment for criteria pollutants will be given from three to twenty years to meet these standards. These areas are also required to impose tighter controls to meet these standards. To help these areas and other parts of the country, the Act requires stiffer motor vehicle emissions standards and cleaner **gasoline**. Finally, three chemical families that contribute to the destruction of the stratospheric ozone layer (**chlorofluorocarbons** (CFCs), **hydrochlorofluorocarbons** (HCFCs), and methyl chloroform) are to be phased out of production and use.

The Clean Air Act has met with mixed success. The national average pollutant levels for the criteria pollutants have decreased. Nevertheless, many localities have not achieved these standards and are in perpetual nonattainment. Not surprisingly, major urban areas are those most frequently in nonattainment. The pollutant for which standards are most often exceeded is ozone, or smog. The greatest successes have come with lead, which has been reduced by 96 percent (largely due to the phase-out of leaded gasoline), and particulates, which were reduced by over 60 percent. Additionally, despite numerous delays, the carbon monoxide, hydrocarbon, and nitrogen oxides pollution from new cars has decreased by 96 percent, 96 percent, and 76 percent over the period from 1967 to 1990. A final point of caution concerning evaluating the Clean Air Act: due to the tremendous complexity of air quality, we cannot conclude that all change in pollutant levels is due to the law. These changes may be due to shifts in the economy at large, changes in weather patterns, or other such variables. *See also* Air quality criteria; Best Available Control Technology; Chemicals; Environmental economics; Environmental law; Environmental policy; Trade in pollution permits

[*Christopher McGrory Klyza*]

FURTHER READING

Bryner, G. C. *Blue Skies, Green Politics: The Clean Air Act of 1990.* Washington, DC: CQ Press, 1993.

Melnick, R. S. *Regulation and the Courts: The Case of the Clean Air Act.* Washington, DC: Brookings Institution, 1983.

Moyer, C. A. *Clean Air Act Handbook: A Practical Guide to Compliance.* New York: Clark Boardman Callaghan, 1992.

Portney, P. R. "Air Pollution Policy." In *Public Policies for Environmental Protection,* edited by P. R. Portney. Washington, DC: Resources for the Future, 1990.

Clean coal technology

Coal is rapidly becoming the world's most popular fuel. Today in the United States, more than half of the electricity produced comes from coal-fired **power plants**. The demand for coal is expected to triple by the middle of the next century, making it more widely used than **petroleum** or **natural gas**.

The unpleasant aspect of this trend is that coal is a relatively dirty fuel. When burned, it releases **particulate**s and pollutants such as **carbon monoxide**, **nitrogen** and sulfur oxides into the **atmosphere**. If the use of coal is to expand continually, something must be done to reduce the hazard its use presents to the **environment**.

Over the past two decades, therefore, there has been an increasing amount of research on clean coal technologies, methods by which the combustion of coal releases fewer pollutants to the atmosphere. As early as 1970, the United States Congress acknowledged the need for such technologies in the **Clean Air Act** of that year. One provision of that Act required the installation of **flue gas** desulfurization (FGD) systems ("**scrubbers**") at all new coal-fired plants.

More than a dozen different technologies are now available on at least an experimental basis for the cleaning of coal. Some of these technologies are used on coal before it is even burned. Chemical, physical, and biological methods have all been developed for pre-combustion cleaning. For example, pyrite (FeS_2) is often found in conjunction with coal when it is mined. When the coal is burned, pyrite is also oxidized, releasing **sulfur dioxide** to the atmosphere. Yet pyrite can be removed from coal by rather simple, straightforward physical means because of differences in the densities of the two substances.

Biological methods for removing sulfur from coal are also being explored. The bacterium *Thiobacillus ferrooxidans* has the ability to change the surface properties of pyrite particles, making it easier to separate them from the coal itself. The bacterium may also be able to extract sulfur that is chemically bound to carbon in the coal.

A number of technologies have been designed to modify existing power plants to reduce the release of pollu-

tants produced during the combustion of coal. In an attempt to improve on traditional **wet scrubbers**, researchers are now exploring the use of dry injection as one of these technologies. In this approach, dry compounds of calcium, sodium, or some other element are sprayed directly into the furnace or into the ducts downstream of the furnace. These compounds react with non-metallic oxide pollutants, such as **sulfur dioxide** and nitrogen dioxide, forming solids that can be removed from the system. A variety of technologies are being developed especially for the release of oxides of nitrogen. Since the amount of this pollutant formed is very much dependent on **combustion** temperature, methods of burning coal at lower temperatures are also being explored.

Some entirely new technologies are also being developed for installation in power plants to be built in the future. **Fluidized bed combustion**, integrated gasification combined cycle, and improved coal pulverization are three of these. In the first of these processes, coal and limestone are injected into a stream of upward-flowing air, improving the degree of oxidation during combustion. In the second process, coal is converted to a gas that can be burned in a conventional power plant. The third process involves improving on a technique that has long been used in power plants, reducing coal to very fine particles before it is fed into the furnace. *See also* Coal gasification; Coal washing; Dry alkali injection; Flue-gas scrubbing; Nitrogen oxides

[*David E. Newton*]

FURTHER READING

Cruver, P. C. "What Will Be the Fate of Clean-Coal Technologies?" *Environmental Science & Technology* (September 1989): 1059-1060.

Douglas, J. "Quickening the Pace in Clean Coal Technology." *EPRI Journal* (January-February 1989): 4-15.

Shepard, M. "Coal Technologies for a New Age." *EPRI Journal* (January-February 1988): 4-17.

Clean Water Act (1972, 1977, 1987)

Federal involvement in protecting the nation's waters began with the Water Pollution Control Act of 1948, the first statute to provide state and local governments with the funding to address **water pollution**. During the 1950s and 1960s, awareness grew that more action was needed and federal funding to state and local governments was increased. In the Water Quality Act of 1965 **water quality standards**, to be developed by the newly-created Federal Water Pollution Control Administration, became an important part of federal water **pollution control** efforts.

Despite these advances, it was not until the Water Pollution Control Amendments of 1972 that the federal government assumed the dominant role in defining and directing water **pollution** control programs. This law was the outcome of a battle between Congress and President Richard M. Nixon. In 1970, facing a presidential re-election campaign, Nixon responded to public outcry over pollution problems by resurrecting the Refuse Act of 1899, which authorized the **Army Corps of Engineers** to issue **discharge** permits. Congress felt its prerogative to set national policy had been challenged. It debated for nearly 18 months to resolve differences between the House and Senate versions of a new law, and on October 18, 1972, Congress overrode a presidential veto and passed the Water Pollution Control Amendments.

Section 101 of the new law set forth its fundamental goals and policies, which continue to this day "to restore and maintain the chemical, physical, and biological integrity of the Nation's waters." This section also set forth the national goal of eliminating discharges of pollution into navigable waters by 1985 and an interim goal of achieving **water quality** levels to protect fish, shellfish, and **wildlife**. As national policy, the discharge of toxic pollutants in toxic amounts was now prohibited; federal financial assistance was to be given for constructing publicly-owned waste treatment works; areawide pollution control planning was to be instituted in states; research and development programs were to be established for technologies to eliminate pollution; and **nonpoint source** pollution—**runoff** from urban and rural areas—was to be controlled. Although the federal government set these goals, states were given the main responsibility for meeting them, and the goals were to be pursued through a permitting program in the new national pollutant discharge elimination system (NPDES).

Federal grants for constructing publicly owned treatment works (POTWs) had totalled $1.25 billion in 1971, and they were increased dramatically by the new law. The act authorized five billion dollars in fiscal year 1973, six billion for fiscal year 1974, and seven billion for fiscal year 1975, all of which would be automatically available for use without requiring Congressional appropriation action each year. But along with these funds, the act conferred the responsibility to achieve a strict standard of secondary treatment by July 1, 1977. The **Environmental Protection Agency (EPA)** was mandated to publish guidelines on secondary treatment within 60 days after passage of the law. POTWs also had to meet a July 1, 1983, deadline for a stricter level of treatment described in the legislation as "best practicable **wastewater** treatment." In addition, pretreatment programs were to be established to control industrial discharges that would either harm the treatment system or, having passed through it, pollute receiving waters.

The act also gave polluting industries two new deadlines. By July 1, 1977, they were required to meet limits on the pollution in their discharged **effluent** using **Best Practicable Technology** (BPT), as defined by EPA. The **conventional pollutant**s to be controlled included **organic waste, sediment**, acid, bacteria and **virus**es, **nutrient**s, oil and grease, and heat. Stricter state water quality standards would also have to be met by that date. The second deadline was July 1, 1983, when industrial dischargers had to install **Best Available Control Technology** (BAT), to advance the goal of eliminating all pollutant discharges by 1985. These BPT and BAT requirements were intended to be "technology forcing," as envisioned by the Senate, which

wanted the new water law to restore water quality and protect ecological systems.

On top of these requirements for conventional pollutants, the law mandated the EPA to publish a list of toxic pollutants, followed six months later by proposed effluent standards for each substance listed. The EPA could require **zero discharge** if that was deemed necessary. The zero discharge provisions were the focus of great controversy when Congress began oversight hearings to assess implementation of the law. Leaders in the House considered the goal a target and not a legally binding requirement. But Senate leaders argued that the goal was literal and that its purpose was to ensure rivers and streams ceased being regarded as components of the waste treatment process. In some cases, the EPA has relied on the Senate's views in developing effluent limits, but the controversy over what zero discharge means continues to this day.

The law also established provisions authorizing the Army Corps of Engineers to issue permits for discharging dredge or fill material into navigable waters at specified disposal sites. In recent years this program, a key component of federal efforts to protect rapidly diminishing **wetlands**, has become one of the most explosive issues in the Clean Water Act. Farmers and developers are demanding that the federal government cease "taking" their private property through wetlands regulations, and recent sessions of Congress have been besieged with demands for revisions to this section of the law.

In 1977, Congress completed its first major revisions of the Water Pollution Control Amendments, responding to the fact that by July 1, 1977 only 30 percent of major municipalities were complying with secondary treatment requirements. Moreover, a National Commission on Water Quality had issued a report which recommended that zero discharge be redefined to stress **conservation** and **reuse** and that the 1983 BAT requirements be postponed for five to ten years. The 1977 Clean Water Act endorsed the goals of the 1972 law, but granted states broader authority to run their construction grants programs. The act also provided deadline extensions and required EPA to expand the lists of pollutants it was to regulate.

In 1981, Congress found it necessary to change the construction grants program; thousands of projects had been started, with $26.6 billion in federal funds, but only 2,223 projects worth $2.8 billion had been completed. The Construction Grant Amendments of 1981 restricted the types of projects that could use grant money and reduced the amount of time it took for an application to go through the grants program.

The Water Quality Act of 1987 phased out the grants program by fiscal year 1990, while phasing in a state revolving loan fund program through fiscal year 1994, and thereafter ending federal assistance for wastewater treatment. The 1987 act also laid greater emphasis on **toxic substance**s; it required, for instance, that the EPA identify and set standards for toxic pollutants in sewage **sludge**, and it phased in requirements for stormwater permits. The 1987 law also established a new toxics program requiring states to identify "toxic hot spots"—waters that would not meet water quality standards even after technology controls have been established—and mandated additional controls for those bodies of water.

These new mandates have greatly increased the number of NPDES permits that the EPA and state governments must issue, stretching budgets of both to the limit. Moreover, states have billions of dollars worth of wastewater treatment needs that remain unfunded, contributing to continued violations of water quality standards. Together, the new permit requirements for stormwater, together with sewer overflow, sludge, and other permit requirements, as well as POTW construction needs, have led to a growing demand for more state flexibility in implementing the clean water laws and for continued federal support for wastewater treatment. State and local governments insist that they cannot do everything the law requires; they argue that they must be allowed to assess their particular problems and decide their own priorities.

Yet despite these demands for less prescriptive federal mandates, on May 15, 1991, a bipartisan group of senators introduced the Water Pollution Prevention and Control Act to expand the federal program. The proposal was eventually set aside after intense debate in both the House and Senate over controversial wetlands issues, but nevertheless the proposal points to the increasing focus on toxic pollution as a national priority. For instance, it would have enhanced the authority of regulators to force changes in industrial processes to prevent toxic pollution.

As the Federal Water Pollution Control Act enters its third decade, state and federal regulators are increasingly recognizing the need for a more comprehensive approach to water pollution problems than the current system, which focuses predominantly on POTWs and industrial facilities. Runoff pollution, caused when rain washes pollution from farmlands and urban areas, is the largest remaining source of water quality impairment, yet the problem has not received a fraction of the regulatory attention addressed to industrial and municipal discharges. *See also* Agricultural pollution; Environmental policy; Industrial waste treatment; Sewage treatment; Storm runoff; Urban runoff

[*David Clarke*]

FURTHER READING

The Clean Water Act of 1987. Alexandria, VA: Water Pollution Control Federation, 1987.

Knopman, D. S., and R. A. Smith. "20 Years of the Clean Water Act." *Environment* 35 (January-February 1993): 16-20+.

Patrick, R. *Surface Water Quality: Have the Laws Been Successful?* Princeton, NJ: Princeton University Press, 1992.

Clear-cutting

Webster's Dictionary defines clear-cutting as "removal of all the trees in a stand of timber." This **forest management** technique has been used in a variety of forests around the world. For many years, it was considered the most economi-

cal and environmentally sound way of harvesting timber. Since the 1960s and 1970s, the practice has been increasingly called into question as more has been learned about the ecological benefits of old growth timber especially in the Pacific Northwest of the United States and the global ecological value of **tropical rain forests**.

Foresters and loggers point out that there are practical economic and safety reasons for the practice of clear-cutting. For example, in the Pacific Northwest, these reasons revolve around the volume of wood that is present in the **old growth forests**. This volume can actually be an obstacle at times to harvesting, so that the most inexpensive way to remove the trees is to cut everything.

During the post-World War II housing boom in the 1950s, clear-cutting overtook selective cutting as the preferred method for harvesting in the Pacific Northwest. Since that time, worldwide demand for lumber has continued to rise. Practical arguments that the practice should continue despite its ecological implications are tied directly to the volume and character of the forest itself. Wood in temperate climates decays slowly, resulting in a large number of fallen logs—making even walking difficult, much less dragging cut trees to areas where they can be hauled to mills. Tall trees with narrow branch structures produce a lot of stems in a small area, therefore, the total **biomass** (or total input of living matter) in these temperate forests is typically four times that of the densest tropical rain forest. Some redwood forest groves in California have been measured with twenty times the biomass of similar sites in the tropics. Those supporting the harvest of these trees and clear-cutting point out that if we don't use these trees, it will put increased pressure on other timber producers throughout the world to supply this wood. This could have high environmental costs globally, since it could take 10-30 acres (4-12 ha) of **taiga** forest in northern Canada, Alaska, or Siberia to produce the wood obtainable from one acre in the state of Washington.

Clear-cutting makes harvesting these trees very lucrative. The number of trees and downed logs makes it difficult to cut only some of the trees, and falling trees can damage the survivors; in addition, they can be damaged when dragged across the ground to be loaded onto trucks. This is made more expensive and time consuming by working around the standing trees. In areas that have been selectively logged, the trees left standing are may be knocked down by winds or may drop branches, presenting a considerable safety risk to loggers working in the area.

Old growth forests leave so much woody debris and half-decayed logs on the ground that it can be difficult to walk through a harvested patch to plant seedlings. This is why an accepted part of the clear-cut practice in the past has been to burn the leftover slash, after which seedlings are planted. Brush that grows on the site is treated with **herbicide** to allow the seedlings time to grow to the point at which they can compete with other vegetation.

Supporters of clear-cutting contend that it has unique advantages: burning consumes fuel that would otherwise be available to feed forest fires; logging roads built to haul the trees out open the forests to recreational uses and provide

193

Aerial view of a South African forest with a clear-cut area.

firebreaks; clear-cutting leaves no snags or trees to interfere with reseeding the forest, and allows use of helicopters and planes to spray herbicides—the brush that grows up naturally in the sunlight and provides browse for big-game species such as deer and elk.

Detractors point to a number of very negative environmental and economic consequences that need to be considered: particularly where clear cuts have been done near urban areas, plumes of smoke produced by burning slash have polluted cities; animal browse is choked out after a few years by the new seedlings, creating a darkened forest floor that lacks almost any vegetation or wildlife for at least three decades; herbicides applied to control vegetation contribute to the degradation of surface **water quality**; mining the forest causes declines in species diversity and loss of habitats (declaration of the **northern spotted owl** as an **endangered species** and the efforts to preserve its habitat is an example of the potential loss of diversity); new microclimates appear that promote less desirable species than the trees they replace; so much live and rotting wood is harvested or burned that the soil fertility is reduced, affecting the potential for future tree growth.

Critics also point out that **erosion** and **flooding** increases from clear-cut areas have significant economic impact downstream in the **watersheds**. Studies have shown that since the clear-cut practice increased following World War II, landslides have increased to six times the previous rate. This has resulted in increased sediment delivery to rivers and streams where it has a detrimental impact on the stream fishery.

Loss of **critical habitat** for endangered species such as the spotted owl and the impact of sediment on the **salmon** fishery have resulted in government efforts to set aside old growth forest wilderness to preserve the unique forest ecosystem. The practice of clear-cutting with its pluses and minuses, however, continues not only in the Pacific Northwest, but in other forests in the United States and in other areas of the world.

Clear-cutting and Rain Forests

Another area where clear-cutting has become the focus of ecological debate is in the tropical rain forests. Many of the same economic pressures that make clear-cutting a lucrative practice in the United States make it equally attractive in the rain forest, but there are significant environmental consequences.

Since 1960, the world demand for wood has increased by 90%, and as indicated above, the pressure to supply lumber to meet this demand has also increased. Nearly one-half of the Earth's rain forests have been cut in the last 30 years. Besides the demand for building material or fuel, these forests are also subject to significant clearing to later be worked to produce food in new agricultural areas and to facilitate the exploration for oil and minerals. If this loss continues at present estimated rates, the rain forests will be totally harvested by the year 2040.

Rain forest activists continually work to remind the world of the importance of the forests. Locally, for instance, the presence or absence of the rain forest can change the climate and the local water budget. For example, times of **drought** are more severe and when the rains come, flooding is increased. As well, rain forests can have a major impact on the global climate. When they are cut and the slash burned, significant amounts of **carbon dioxide** are released into the atmosphere, which may contribute to the overall **greenhouse effect** and general warming of the Earth.

The biological diversity of these forest ecosystems is vast. Rain forests contain about one-half the known plant and animal species in the world and very few of these species have ever been studied by scientists for their potential benefits. (More that 7,000 medicines have already been derived from tropical plants. It is uncertain how many more such uses are yet to be found.)

Most rain forests occur in **less-developed countries** where it is difficult to meet the expanding needs of rapidly increasing populations for food and shelter. They need the economic benefits that can be derived from the rain forest for their very survival. Any attempt at stopping the clear-cutting practice must provide for their needs to be successful. Until a better practice is developed, clear-cutting will remain an environmental issue on a global scale for the next several decades.

[*James L. Anderson*]

FURTHER READING

Dietrich, W. *The Final Forest*. New York: Simon and Schuster, 1992.
Gallant, R.A. *Earth's Vanishing Forests*. New York: MacMillan, 1991.
Harris, D. *The Last Stand: The War between Wall Street and Main Street*. Times Books, Random House, 1995.

Climate

Climate is the general, cumulative pattern of regional or global weather patterns. The most apparent aspects of climate are trends in air temperature and humidity, wind, and precipitation. These observable phenomena occur as the **atmosphere** surrounding the earth continually redistributes, via wind and evaporating and condensing water vapor, the energy that the earth receives from the sun.

Although the climate remains fairly stable on the human time scale of decades or centuries, it fluctuates continuously over thousands or millions of years. A great number of variables simultaneously act and react to create stability or fluctuation in this very complex system. Some of these variables are atmospheric composition, rates of **solar energy** input, **albedo** (the earth's reflectivity), and terrestrial geography. Extensive research helps explain and predict the behavior of individual climate variables, but the way these variables control and respond to each other remains poorly understood. Climate behavior is often likened to "chaos," changes and movements so complex that patterns cannot be perceived in them, even though patterns may exist. Nevertheless, studies indicate that human activity may be disturbing larger climate trends, notably by causing global warming. This prospect raises serious concern because rapid **anthropogenic** climate change could severely stress **ecosystems** and **species** around the world.

Solar Energy and Climate

Solar energy is the driving force in the earth's climate. Incoming radiation from the sun warms the atmosphere and raises air temperatures, warms the earth's surface, and evaporates water, which then becomes humidity, rain, and snow. The earth's surface reflects or re-emits energy back into the atmosphere, further warming the air. Warming air expands and rises, creating convection patterns in the atmosphere that reach over several degrees of latitude. In these convection cells, low pressure zones develop under rising air, and high pressure zones develop where that air returns downward toward the earth's surface. Such differences in atmospheric pressure force air masses to move, from high to low pressure regions. Movement of air masses creates wind on the earth's surface. When these air masses carry evaporated water, they may create precipitation when they move to cooler regions.

The sun's energy comes to the earth in a spectrum of long and short radiation wavelengths. The shortest wavelengths are microwaves and infrared waves. We feel infrared radiation as heat. A small range of medium wavelength radiation makes up the spectrum of visible light. Longer wavelengths include **ultraviolet (UV) radiation** and radio waves. These longer wavelengths cannot be sensed, but UV radiation can cause damage as organic tissues (such as skin) absorb them. The difference in wavelengths is important because long and short wavelengths react differently when they encounter the earth and its atmosphere.

Solar energy approaching the earth encounters filters, reflectors, and absorbers in the form of atmospheric gases, clouds, and the earth's surface. Atmospheric gases filter incoming energy, selectively blocking some wavelengths and allowing other wavelengths to pass through. Blocked wavelengths are either absorbed and heat the air or scattered and reflected back into space. Clouds, composed of atmospheric water vapor, likewise reflect or absorb energy but allow some wavelengths to pass through. Some energy reaching the earth's surface is reflected; a great deal is absorbed in heating the ground, evaporating water, and conducting **photosynthesis**. Most energy that the earth absorbs is re-emitted in the form of short, infrared wavelengths, which are sensed as heat. Some of this heat energy circulates in the atmosphere for a time, but eventually it all escapes. If this heat did not escape, the earth would overheat and become uninhabitable.

Variables in the Climate System

Climate responds to conditions of the earth's energy filters, reflectors, and absorbers. As long as the atmosphere's filtering effect remains constant, the earth's reflective and absorptive capacities do not change, and the amount of incoming energy does not vary, climate conditions should stay constant. Most of the time, though, some or all of these elements fluctuate. The earth's reflectivity changes as the shapes, surface features, and locations of continents change. The atmosphere's composition changes from time to time, so that different wavelengths are reflected or pass through. The amount of energy the earth receives also shifts over time.

During the course of a decade the rate of solar energy input varies by a few watts per square meter. Changes in energy input can be much greater over several millennia. Energy intensity also varies with the shape of the earth's orbit around the sun. In a period of 100 million years the earth's elliptical orbit becomes longer and narrower, bringing the earth closer to the sun at certain times of year, then rounder again, putting the earth at a more uniform distance from the sun. When the earth receives relatively intense energy, heating and evaporation increase. Extreme heating can set up exaggerated convection currents in the atmosphere, with extreme low pressure areas receiving intensified rains and high pressure areas experiencing extreme **drought**.

The earth's albedo depends upon surface conditions. Extensive dark forests absorb a great deal of energy in heating, evaporation of water, and photosynthesis. Light, colored surfaces, such as **desert** or snow, tend to absorb less energy and reflect more. If highly reflective continents are large or are located near the equator, where energy input is great, then they could reflect a great deal of energy back into the atmosphere and contribute to atmospheric heating. However, if those continents are heavily vegetated, their reflective capacity might be lowered.

Other features of terrestrial geography that can influence climate conditions are mountains and glaciers. Both rise and fall over time and can be high enough to interrupt wind and precipitation patterns. For instance, the growth of the Rocky Mountains probably disturbed the path of upper atmospheric winds known as the jet stream. In southern Asia, the Himalayas block humid air masses flowing from the south. Intense precipitation results on the windward side of these mountains, while the downwind side remains one of the driest areas on earth.

Atmospheric composition is a climate variable that began to receive increased attention during the 1980s. Each type of gas molecule in the atmosphere absorbs a particular range of energy wavelengths. As the mix of gases changes, the range of wavelengths passing through the filter shifts. For instance, the gas **ozone** (O_3) selectively blocks long wave UV radiation. A drop in upper atmospheric ozone levels discovered in the late 1980s has caused alarm because harmful UV rays are no longer being intercepted as effectively before they reach the earth's surface. Water vapor and solid **particulate**s (dust) in the upper atmosphere also block incoming energy. Atmospheric dust associated with ancient meteor impacts is widely thought responsible for climatic cooling that may have killed the earth's dinosaurs 65 million years ago. Climate cooling could occur today if bombs from a nuclear war threw high levels of dust into the atmosphere. With enough radiation blockage, global temperatures could fall by several degrees, a scenario known as **nuclear winter**.

A human impact on climate that is more likely than nuclear winter is global warming caused by increased levels of **carbon dioxide** (CO_2) in the upper atmosphere. Most solar energy enters the atmospheric system as long wavelengths and is reflected back into space in the form of short

wavelength (heat) energy. Carbon dioxide blocks these short, warm wavelengths as they leave the earth's surface. Unable to escape, this heat energy remains in the atmosphere and keeps the earth warm enough for life to continue. However, many studies suggest that the burning of **fossil fuels** and **biomass** have raised atmospheric carbon dioxide levels. Rising CO_2 levels could trap excessive amounts of heat and raise global air temperatures to dangerous levels. This scenario is popularly known as the **greenhouse effect**. Extreme amounts of trapped heat could disturb precipitation patterns. Ecosystems could overheat, killing plant and animal species. Polar ice caps could melt, raising global ocean levels and threatening human settlements.

Increased anthropogenic production of other gases such as **methane** (CH_4) also contributes to atmospheric warming, but carbon dioxide has been a focus of concern because it is emitted in much greater volume.

No one knows how seriously human activity may be affecting the large and turbulent patterns of climate. Sometimes a very subtle event can have magnified repercussions in larger wind, precipitation, and pressure systems, disturbing major climate patterns for decades. In many cases the climate appears to have a self-stabilizing capacity—an ability to initiate internal reactions to a destabilizing event that return it to equilibrium. For example, extreme greenhouse heating should cause increased evaporation of water. Resulting clouds could block incoming sunlight, producing an overall cooling effect to counteract heating.

Furthermore, human influences work on climate within a context of continually changing natural conditions and events. On a geologic time scale, temperatures, precipitation, and ocean levels have fluctuated enormously. A long series of **ice age**s and warmer interglacial periods began 2.5 million years ago and may still be going on. The last glacial maximum, with low sea levels because of extreme ice volumes, ended only 18,000 years ago—an instant in the earth's climate history.

Natural fluctuations occur on a more human time scale, as well. A summer of extreme drought and high temperatures in the United States in 1988 brought threats of global warming to the public's attention, but the drought itself resulted from a temporary aberration in high altitude wind patterns that centered an unusually stable high pressure zone over the Midwest. This temporary departure from normal conditions was simply part of the continual fluctuation within the chaotic climate system. Terrestrial events, such as the 1991 eruption of **Mount Pinatubo** in the Philippines, also cause large, natural disturbances in climate. Dust from its eruption reached the upper atmosphere and was distributed around the globe, blocking enough incoming solar radiation to temporarily cool global temperatures by about 1.8°F (1°C).

No one can yet predict with precision how climate variables will respond to human activity. The earth's climate is so complex that human alterations to the atmosphere (such as those caused by carbon dioxide emission) amount to an "experiment" having an unknown—and possibly life-threatening—outcome. *See also* Cloud chemistry; Environmental stress; Ozone layer depletion; Rain shadow; Smog; Stratosphere; Sustainable biosphere; Troposphere; Weather modification; Volcano

[*Mary Ann Cunningham*]

FURTHER READING

Henderson-Sellers, A., and P. J. Robinson. *Contemporary Climatology.* London: Longman Scientific and Technical, 1986.

Ingersoll, A. P. "The Atmosphere." *Scientific American* 249 (1983): 162-74.

Schneider, S. H. "Climate Modelling." *Scientific American* 256 (1987): 72-80.

Climax (ecological)

Referring to a community of plants and animals that is relatively stable in its **species** composition and **biomass**, ecological climax is the apparent termination of directional **succession**—the replacement of one community by another. That the termination is only apparent means that the climax may be altered by periodic disturbances such as **drought** or stochastic disturbances such as volcanic eruptions. It may also change extremely slowly owing to the gradual immigration and emigration—at widely differing rates—of individual species, for instance following the retreat of ice sheets during the postglacial period. Often the climax is a shifting mosaic of different stages of sucession in a more or less steady state overall, as in many climax communities that are subject to frequent fires. Species that occur in climax communities are mostly good competitors and tolerant of the effects (e.g., shade, root competition) of the species around them, in contrast to the opportunistic colonists of early successional communities. The latter are often particularly adapted for wide dispersal and abundant reproduction, leading to success in newly opened habitats where competition is not severe.

In a climax community, productivity is in approximate balance with **decomposition**. **Biogeochemical cycling** of inorganic **nutrient**s is also in balance, so that the stock of **nitrogen, phosphorus**, calcium, etc., is in a more or less steady state.

Frederic E. Clements was the person largely responsible in the early twentieth century for developing the theory of the climax community. Clements regarded **climate** as the predominant determining factor, though he did recognize that other factors—for instance, fire—could prevent the establishment of the theoretical "climatic climax." Later ecologists placed more stress on interactions among several determining factors, including climate, **soil** parent material, **topography**, fire, and the **flora** and **fauna** able to colonize a given site.

[*Eville Gorham*]

FURTHER READING

Hagen, J. B. *An Entangled Bank: The Origins of Ecosystem Ecology.* New Brunswick, NJ: Rutgers University Press, 1992.

Clod

A compact, coherent mass of **soil** varying in size from 10 to 250 millimeters (0.39-9.75 in). Clods are produced by operations like plowing, cultivation, and digging, especially on soils that are too wet or too dry. They are usually formed by compression, or by breaking off from a larger unit. Tractor attachments like disks, spike-tooth harrows, and rollers are used to break up clods during seedbed preparation. *See also* Conservation tillage

Cloud chemistry

One of the exciting new fields of chemical research in the past half century involves chemical changes that take place in the **atmosphere**. Scientists have learned that a number of reactions are taking place in the atmosphere at all times. For example, oxygen (O_2) molecules in the upper **stratosphere** absorb **solar energy** and are converted to **ozone** (O_3). This ozone forms a layer that protects life on earth by filtering out the harmful **ultraviolet radiation** in sunlight. **Chlorofluorocarbons** and other chlorinated solvents (e.g. carbon tetrachloride and methyl chloroform) generated by human activities also trigger chemical reactions in the upper atmosphere including the break up of ozone into the two-atom form of oxygen. This reaction depletes the earth's protective ozone layer.

Clouds are often an important locus for atmospheric chemical reactions. They provide an abundant supply of water molecules that act as the solvent required for many reactions. An example is the reaction between **carbon dioxide** and water, resulting in the formation of carbonic acid. The abundance of both carbon dioxide and water in the atmosphere means that natural rain will frequently be somewhat acidic. Although conditions vary from time to time and place to place, the **pH** of natural, unpolluted rain is normally about 5.6. (The pH of pure water is 7.0). Other naturally occurring components of the atmosphere also react with water in clouds. In regions of volcanic activity, for example, **sulfur dioxide** released by outgassing and eruptions is oxidized to sulfur trioxide, which then reacts with water to form sulfuric acid.

The water of which clouds are composed also acts as solvent for a number of other chemical species blown into the atmosphere from the earth's surface. Among the most common **ion**s found in solution in clouds are sodium (Na^+), magnesium (Mg^{2+}), chloride (Cl^-), and sulfate (SO_4^{2-}) from sea spray; potassium (K^+), calcium (Ca^{2+}), and carbonate (CO_3^{2-}) from soil dust; and ammonium (NH_4^+) from organic decay.

The nature of cloud chemistry is often changed as a result of human activities. Perhaps the best known and most thoroughly studied example of this involves **acid rain**. When **fossil fuels** are burned, sulfur dioxide and **nitrogen oxides** (among other products) are released into the atmosphere. Prevailing winds often carry these products for hundreds or thousands of miles from their original source. Once deposited in the atmosphere, these oxides tend to be absorbed by water molecules and undergo a series of reactions by which they are converted to acids. Once formed in clouds by these reactions, sulfuric and nitric acids remain in solution in water droplets and are carried to earth as fog, rain, snow, or other forms of precipitation.

[*David E. Newton*]

FURTHER READING

Harrison, R. M., ed. *Pollution: Causes, Effects, and Control.* Cambridge: Royal Society of Chemistry, 1990.

Club of Rome

In April of 1968, 30 people, including scientists, educators, economists, humanists, industrialists, and government officials, met at the Academia dei Lincei in Rome. The meeting was called by Dr. Aurelio Peccei, an Italian industrialist and economist. The purpose of this meeting was to discuss "the present and future predicament of man." The "Club of Rome" was born from this meeting as an informal organization that has been described as an "invisible college." Its purpose, as described by Donella Meadows, is to foster understanding of the varied but interdependent components—economic, political, natural and social—that make up the global system in which we all live; to bring that new understanding to the attention of policy-makers and the public worldwide; and in this way to promote new policy initiatives and action. The original list of members is listed in the preface to Meadows's book entitled *The Limits to Growth*, in which the basic findings of the group are eloquently explained.

This text is a modern-day equivalent to the hypothesis of **Thomas Malthus**, who postulated that since increases in food supply cannot keep pace with geometric increases in human population, there would therefore be a time of **famine** with a stabilization of the human population. This eighteenth century prediction has, to a great extent, been delayed by the "green revolution" in which agricultural production has been radically increased by the use of **fertilizers** and development of special genetic strains of agricultural products. The high cost of **agricultural chemicals** which are generally tied to the price of oil has, however, severely limited the capability of developing nations to purchase them.

The development of the Club of Rome's studies is most potently presented by Meadows in the form of graphs which plot on a time axis the supply of **arable land** needed at several production levels (present, double present, quadruple present, etc.) to feed the world's population based upon growth models.

She states that 3.2 billion hectares (7.9 billion acres) of land are potentially suitable for agriculture on the earth; half of that land, the richest and most accessible half, is under cultivation today. She further states that the remaining land will require immense capital inputs to reach, clear, irrigate, or fertilize before it is ready to produce food. One can imagine the impact such conversion will have on the **environment**.

The Club of Rome's studies were not limited to food supply but also considered industrial output per capita, **pollution** per capita, and general resources available per capita. The key issue is that the denominator, per capita, keeps increasing with time, requiring ever more frugal and careful use of the resources; however, no matter how carefully the resources are husbanded, the inevitable result of uncontrolled population growth is a catastrophe which can only be delayed. Therefore stabilizing the rate of world population growth must be a continuing priority.

As a follow-up to the Club of Rome's original meeting, a global model for growth was developed by Jay Forrester of the Massachusetts Institute of Technology. This model is capable of update with insertion of information on population, agricultural production, **natural resources**, industrial production, and pollution. Meadows's report *The Limits to Growth* represents a readable summary of the results of this modelling. *See also* Agricultural revolution; Population growth

[*Malcolm T. Hepworth*]

FURTHER READING

Forrester, J. W. *World Dynamics.* Cambridge, MA: Wright-Allen Press, 1971.

Meadows, D. H. *The Dynamics of Commodity Production Cycles.* Cambridge, MA: Wright-Allen Press, 1970.

———, et al. *The Limits to Growth: A Report for the Club of Rome's Project on the Predicament of Mankind.* New York: Universe Books, 1974.

Randers, J., and D. H. Meadows. "The Carrying Capacity of Our Global Environment: A Look at the Ethical Alternatives." *Western Man and Environmental Ethics*, edited by Ian Barbour. Reading MA: Addison-Wesley, 1982.

C:N ratio

Organic materials are composed of a mixture of carbohydrates, lignins, tannins, fats, oils, waxes, resins, proteins, minerals, and other assorted compounds. With the exception of the mineral fraction, the organic compounds are composed of varying ratios of **carbon** and **nitrogen**. This is commonly abbreviated to the C:N ratio. Carbohydrates are composed of carbon, **hydrogen**, and oxygen and are relatively easily decomposed to **carbon dioxide** and water, plus a small amount of other by-products. Protein-like materials are the prime source of nitrogen compounds as well as sources of carbon, hydrogen, and oxygen and are important to the development of the C:N ratio and the eventual **decomposition** rate of the organic materials.

The **aerobic** heterotrophic bacteria are primarily responsible for the decay of the large amount of organic compounds generated on the earth's surface. These organisms typically have a C:N ratio of about 8:1. When organic residues are attacked by the bacteria under appropriate **habitat** conditions, some of the carbon and nitrogen are assimilated into the new and rapidly increasing microbial population, and copious amounts of carbon dioxide are released to the atmosphere. The numbers of bacteria are highly controlled by the C:N ratio of the organic substrate.

As a rule, when organic residues of less than 30:1 ratio are added to a **soil**, there is very little noticeable decrease in the amount of mineral nitrogen available for higher plant forms. However as the C:N ratio begins to rise to values of greater than 30:1, there may be competition for the mineral nitrogen forms. Bacteria are lower in the **food chain/web** and become the immediate beneficiary of available sources of mineral nitrogen, while the higher species may suffer a lack of mineral nitrogen. Ultimately, when the carbon source is depleted, the organic nitrogen is released from the decaying microbes as mineral nitrogen.

The variation in the carbon content of organic material is reflected in the constituency of the compound. Carbohydrates usually contain less than 45 percent carbon, while lignin may contain more than 60 percent carbon. The C:N ratio of plant material may well reflect the kind and stage of growth of the plant. A young plant typically contains more carbohydrates and less lignin, while an older plant of the same species will contain more lignin and less carbohydrate. Ligneous tissue such as found in trees may have a C:N ratio of up to 1000:1.

The relative importance of the C:N ratio addresses two concerns: one, the rate of the organic matter decay to the low C:N ratio of **humus**, (approximately 10:1), and secondly the immediate availability of mineral nitrogen (NH_4^+) to meet the demand of higher plant needs. The addition of mineral nitrogen to organic residues is a common practice to enhance the rate of decay and to reduce the potential for nitrogen deficiency developing in higher plants where copious amounts of organic residue which has a C:N ratio of greater than 30:1 have been added to the soil.

Composting of organic residues permits the breakdown of the residues to occur without the **competition** of higher plants for the mineral nitrogen and also reduces the C:N ratio of the resulting mass to a C:N value of less than 20:1. When this material is added to a soil, there is little concern about the potential for nitrogen competition between the micro-organisms and the higher plants.

[*Royce Lambert*]

FURTHER READING

Brady, N. C. "Soil Organic Matter and Organic Soils." In *The Nature and Properties of Soils*. 10th ed. New York: Macmillan, 1990.

Millar, R. W., and R. L. Donahue. "Organic Matter and Container Media." In *Soils: An Introduction to Plant Growth*. 6th ed. Englewood Cliffs, NJ: Prentice Hall, 1990.

Coagulation

See **Water treatment**

Coal

Consisting of altered remains of plants, coal is a widely used **fossil fuel**. Generally, the older the coal, the higher the **carbon** content and heating value. Anthracite coal ranks highest in carbon content, then bituminous coal, subbituminous coal, and lignite (as determined by the American Society for Testing Materials). Over 80 percent of the world's vast reserves occur in the former Soviet Union, the United States, and China. Though globally abundant, it is associated with many environmental problems, including acid drainage, degraded land, sulfur oxide **emissions**, **acid rain**, and heavy **carbon dioxide** emissions. However, clean coal-burning technologies, including liquified or gasified forms, are now available.

Anthracite, or "hard" coal, differs from the less altered bituminous coal by having more than 86 percent carbon and less than 14 percent volatile matter. It was formerly the fuel of choice for heat purposes because of high **Btu (British Thermal Unit)** values, minimally 14,500, and low ash content. In the United States, production has dropped from 100 million tons in 1917 to about 7 million tons as anthracite has been replaced by oil, **natural gas**, and electric heat. Predominantly in eastern Pennsylvania's Ridge and Valley Province, anthracite seams have a wavelike pattern, complicating extraction. High **water table**s and low demand are the main impediments to expansion.

Bituminous coal, or "soft" coal, is much more abundant and easier to mine than anthracite but has lower carbon content and Btu values and higher volatility. Historically dominant, it energized the Industrial Revolution, fueling steam engines in factories, locomotives, and ships. Major coal regions became steel centers because two tons of coal were needed to produce each ton of iron ore. This is the only coal suitable for making coke, needed in iron smelting processes. Major deposits include the Appalachian Mountains and the Central Plains from Indiana through Oklahoma.

Subbituminous coal ranges in Btu values from 10,500 (11,500 if agglomerating) down to 8,300. Huge deposits exist in Wyoming, Montana, and North Dakota with seams 70 feet (21.4 m) thick. Though distant from major utility markets, it is used extensively for electrical power generation and is preferred because of its abundance, low sulfur content, and good grinding qualities. The latter makes it more useful than the higher grade, but harder, bituminous coal because modern plants spray the coal into **combustion** chambers in powder form. Demand for this coal skyrocketed following the 1973 OPEC **oil embargo** and subsequent restrictions on natural gas use in new plants.

Lignite, or "brown" coal, is the most abundant, youngest, and least mature of the coals, with some plant texture still visible. Its Btu values generally range below 8,300. Although over 70 percent of the deposits are found in North America, mainly in the Rocky Mountain region, there is little production there. It is used extensively in many eastern European countries for heating and steam production. Russian scientists have successfully burned lignite *in situ*, tapping the resultant coal gas for industrial heating. If concerns over global warming are satisfied, future liquefying and gasifying technologies could make lignite a prized resource. *See also* Black lung disease; Clean coal technology; Coal gasification; Coal washing;

[*Nathan H. Meleen*]

FURTHER READING

Hartshorne, T., and J. W. Alexander. *Economic Geography*. 3rd ed. Englewood Cliffs, NJ: Prentice-Hall, 1988.

1992 Annual Book of ASTM Standards, Section 5: Petroleum Products, Lubricants, and Fossil Fuels. Volume 05.05, Gaseous Fuels; Coal and Coke. Philadelphia: American Society for Testing Materials, 1992.

Perry, H. "Coal in the United States: A Status Report." *Science* 222 (28 October 1983): 377-94.

Schobert, H. H. *Coal: The Energy Source of the Past and Future*. Washington, DC: American Chemical Society, 1987.

Young, G. "Will Coal Be Tomorrow's Black Gold?" *National Geographic* 148 (August 1975): 234-259.

Coal gasification

The term coal gasification refers to any process by which **coal** is converted into some gaseous form that can then be burned as a fuel. Coal gasification technology was relatively well known before World War II, but it fell out of favor after the war because of the low cost of oil and **natural gas**. Beginning in the 1970s, utilities showed renewed interest in coal gasification technologies as a way of meeting more stringent environmental requirements.

Traditionally, the use of **fossil fuels** in **power plants** and industrial processes has been fairly straight-forward. The fuel—coal, oil, or natural gas—is burned in a furnace and the heat produced is used to run a turbine or operate some industrial process. The problem is that such direct use of fuels results in the massive release of oxides of **carbon**, sulfur, and **nitrogen**, of unburned **hydrocarbons**, of **particulate** matter, and of other pollutants. In a more environmentally-conscious world, such reactions are no longer acceptable.

This problem became much more severe with the shift from oil to coal as the fuel of choice in power generating and industrial plants. Coal is "dirtier" than both oil and natural gas and its use, therefore, creates more serious and more extensive environmental problems.

The first response of utilities and industries to new **air pollution** standards was to develop methods of capturing pollutants after **combustion** has occurred. **Flue gas** desulfurization systems, called **scrubbers**, were one approach strongly favored by the United States government. But such systems are very expensive, and utilities and industries rapidly began to explore alternative approaches in which coal is cleansed of material that produce pollutants when burned. One of the most promising of these clean-coal technologies is coal gasification.

A variety of methods are available for achieving coal gasification, but they all have certain features in common. In the first stages, coal is prepared for the reactor by crushing and drying it and then pre-treating it to prevent caking. The pulverized coal is then fed into a boiler where it reacts with a hot stream of air or oxygen and steam. In the boiler, a complex set of chemical reactions occur, some of which are exothermic (heat releasing) and some of which are endothermic (heat-absorbing).

Coal gasification by heating a coal-and-water slurry in a low-oxygen environment. After contaminants are removed, the carbon monoxide and hydrogen produced are burned to power electric generators.

An example of an exothermic reaction is the following.

$$2\ C + {}^3/_2\ O_2 \rightarrow CO_2 + CO$$

The **carbon monoxide** produced in this reaction may then go on to react with **hydrogen** released from the coal to produce a second exothermic reaction.

$$CO + 3\ H_2 \rightarrow CH_4 + H_2O$$

The energy released by one or both of the reactions is then available to initiate a third reaction that is endothermic.

$$C + H_2O \rightarrow\ > CO + H_2$$

Finally, the mixture of gases resulting from reactions such as these, a mixture consisting most importantly of carbon monoxide, **methane**, and hydrogen, is used as fuel in a boiler that produces steam to run a turbine and a generator.

In practice, the whole series of exothermic and endothermic reactions are allowed to occur within the same vessel, so that coal, air or oxygen, and steam enter through one inlet in the boiler, coal enters at a second inlet, and the gaseous fuel is removed through an outlet pipe.

One of the popular designs for a coal gasification reaction vessel is the Lurgi pressure gasifier. In the Lurgi gasifier, coal enters through the top of a large cylindrical tank. Steam and oxygen are pumped in from the bottom of the tank. Coal is burned in the upper portion of the tank at relatively low temperatures, initiating the exothermic reactions described above. As unburned coal flows downward in the tank, heat released by these exothermic reactions raises the temperature in the tank and brings about the endothermic reaction in which carbon monoxide and hydrogen are produced. These gases are then drawn off from the top of the Lurgi gasifier.

The exact composition of the gases produced is determined by the materials introduced into the tank and the temperature and pressure at which the boiler is maintained. One possible product, chemical synthesis gas, consists of carbon monoxide and hydrogen. It is used primarily by the chemical industry in the production of other **chemicals** such as ammonia and methyl alcohol. A second possible product is medium-Btu gas, made up of hydrogen and carbon monoxide. Medium-Btu gas is used as a general purpose fuel for utilities and industrial plants. A third possible product is substitute natural gas, consisting essentially of methane. Substitute natural gas is generally used as just that, a substitute for natural gas.

Coal gasification makes possible the removal of pollutants before the gaseous products are burned by a utility or industrial plant. Any ash produced during gasification, for example, remains within the boiler, where it settles to the bottom of the tank, is collected, and then removed. **Sulfur dioxide** and **carbon dioxide** are both removed in a much smaller, less expensive version of the scrubbers used in smokestacks.

Perhaps the most successful test of coal gasification technology has been going on at the Cool Water Integrated Gasification Combined Cycle plant near Barstow, California. The plant has been operating since June 1984 and is now capable of generating 100 **megawatt**s of electricity. The four basic elements of the plant are a gasifier in which combustible gases are produced, a particulate and sulfur removal system, a combustion turbine in which the synthetic gas is burned, and a stem turbine run by heat from the combustion turbine and the gasifier.

The Cool Water plant has been an unqualified environmental success. It has easily met federal and state standards for effluent sulfur dioxide, oxides of nitrogen, and particulates, and its solid wastes have been found to be non-hazardous by the California Department of Health.

Waste products from the removal system also have commercial value. Sulfur obtained from the reduction of sulfur dioxide is 99.9 percent pure and has been selling for about $100 a ton. Studies are also being made to determine the possible use of slag for road construction and other building purposes.

Coal gasification appears to be a promising energy technology for the twenty-first century. One of the intriguing possibilities is to use sewage or **hazardous waste**s in the primary boiler. In the latter case, hazardous elements could be fixed in the slag drawn off from the bottom of the boiler, preventing their contaminating the final gaseous product.

The major impediment in the introduction of coal gasification technologies on a widespread basis is their cost. At the present time, a plant operated with synthetic gas from a coal gasification unit is about three times as expensive as a comparable plant using natural gas. Further research is obviously needed to make this new technology economically competitive with more traditional technologies.

Another problem is that most coal gasification technologies require very large quantities of water. This can be an especially difficult problem since gasification plants should be built near mines to reduce shipping costs. But most mines are located in Western states, where water supplies are usually very limited.

Finally, coal gasification is an inherently less efficient process than the direct combustion of coal. In most approaches, between 30 and 40 percent of the heat energy stored in coal is lost during its conversion to synthetic gas. Such conversions would probably be considered totally unacceptable except for the favorable environmental trade-offs they provide.

One possible solution to the problem described above is to carry out the gasification process directly in underground coal mines. In this process, coal would be loosened by explosives and then burned directly in the mine. The low-grade synthetic gas produced by this method could then be piped out of the ground, upgraded and used as a fuel. Underground gasification is an attractive alternative for many reasons. By some estimates, up to 80 percent of all coal reserves cannot be recovered through conventional mining techniques. They are either too deep underground or dispersed too thinly in the earth. The development of methods for gasification in coal seams would, therefore, greatly increase the amount of this fossil fuel available for our use.

A great deal of research is now being done to make coal gasification a more efficient process. A promising breakthrough involves the use of potassium hydroxide or potassium carbonate as a catalyst in the primary reactor vessel. The presence of a catalyst reduces the temperature at which gasification occurs and reduces, therefore, the cost of the operation.

Governments in the United States and Europe, energy research institutes, and major energy corporations are actively involved in research on coal gasification technologies. The Electric Power Research Institute, Institute of Gas Technology, **U.S. Department of Energy**, Texaco, Shell, Westinghouse, and Exxon are all studying modifications in the basic coal gasification system to find ways of using a wide range of raw materials, to improve efficiency at various stages in the gasification process, and, in general, to reduce the cost of plant construction. *See also* Alternative fuels; Air pollution control; Air quality; Coal washing; Flue-gas scrubbing; Strip mining; Surface mining

[*David E. Newton*]

FURTHER READING

Douglas, J. "Quickening the Pace in Clean Coal Technologies." *EPRI Journal* (January-February 1989): 12-15.

Joesten, M. D., et al. *World of Chemistry*. Philadelphia: Saunders, 1991.

Shepard, M. "Coal Technologies for a New Age." *EPRI Journal* (January-February 1988): 12-17.

Coal mining

See **Black lung disease; Strip mining; Surface mining**

Coal washing

Coal that comes from a mine is a complex mixture of materials with a large variety of physical properties. In addition to the coal itself, pieces of rock, sand, and various minerals are contained in the mixture. Thus, before coal can be sold to consumers, it must be cleaned. The cleaning process consists of a number of steps that results in a product that is specifically suited to the needs of particular consumers. Among the earliest of these steps is crushing and sizing, two processes that reduce the coal to a form required by the consumer.

The next step in coal preparation is a washing or cleaning step. This step is necessary not only to meet consumer requirements, but also to ensure that its combustion will conform to environmental standards.

Coal washing is accomplished by one of two major processes, by *density separation* or by *froth flotation*. Both processes depend on the fact that the particles of which a coal sample are made have different densities. When water, for example, is added to the sample, particles sink to various depths depending on their densities. The various components of the sample can thus be separated from each other.

In some cases, a liquid other than water may be used to achieve this separation. In a heavy medium bath, for example, a mineral such as magnetite or feldspar in finely divided form may be mixed with water, forming a liquid medium whose density is significantly greater than that of pure water.

A number of devices and systems have been developed for extracting the various components of coal once they have been separated with a water or heavy medium treatment. One of the oldest of these devices is the *jig*. In a jig, the column of water is maintained in a constant up-and-down movement by means of a flow of air. Clean coal particles are carried to the top of the jig by this motion, while heavier refuse particles sink to the bottom.

Another method of extraction, the *cyclone*, consists of a tank in which the working fluid (water or a heavy medium) is kept in a constant circular motion. The tank is constructed so that lighter clean coal particles are thrown out of one side, while heavier refuse particles are ejected through the bottom.

Shaking tables are another extraction method. As the table shakes back and forth, particles are separated by size, producing clean coal at one end and waste products at the other.

In cylindrical separators, a coal mixture is fed into a spinning column of air that throws the heavier waste particles outward. They coat the inner wall of the cylinder and fall to the bottom, where they are drawn off. The clean coal particles remain in the center of the air column and are drawn off at the top of the cylinder.

Froth flotation processes depend on the production of tiny air bubbles to which coal particles adhere. The amount of absorption onto a bubble depends not only on a particle's density, but also on certain surface characteristics. Separation of clean coal from waste materials can be achieved in froth flotation by varying factors, such as **pH** of the solution, time of treatment, particle size and shape, rate of **aeration**, solution density, and bubble size.

[*David E. Newton*]

FURTHER READING

Ward, C. R. *Coal Geology and Coal Technology.* Melbourne, Australia: Blackwell Scientific Publications, 1984.

Coalition for Environmentally Responsible Economies (CERES)
See **Valdez Principles**

Coase theorem

An economic theorem that is sometimes used in discussions of external costs in environment-related situations. The standard welfare economic view states that in order to make the market efficient, external costs—such as **pollution** produced by a company in making a product—should be internalized by the company in the form of taxes or fees for producing the pollution. Coase theorem, in contrast, states that the responsibility for the pollution should fall on both the producer and recipient of the pollution. For example, people who are harmed by the pollution can pay companies not to pollute, thereby protecting themselves from any potential harm.

Ronald Coase, the economist who proposed the theorem, further states that government should intervene when the bargaining process or transaction costs between the two parties is high. The government's role, therefore, is not to address external costs which harm bystanders but to help individuals organize for their protection. *See also* Externality; Internalizing costs

Coastal Society, The (Gloucester, Massachusetts)

The Coastal Society (TCS), founded in 1975, is an international, nonprofit organization which serves as a forum for individuals concerned with problems related to coastal areas. Its members, drawn from university settings, government, and private industry, agree that the **conservation** of coastal resources demands serious attention and high priority.

TCS has four main goals: 1) to foster cooperation and communication among agencies, groups, and private citizens; 2) to promote conservation and intelligent use of coastal resources; 3) to strengthen the education and appreciation of coastal resources; and 4) to help government, industry, and individuals successfully balance development and protection along the world's coastlines. Through these goals, TCS hopes to educate the public and private sectors on the importance of effective coastal management programs and clear policy and law regarding the coasts.

Since its inception, TCS has sponsored numerous conferences and workshops. Individuals from various disciplines are invited to discuss different coastal problems. Past conferences have covered such topics as "Energy Across the Coastal Zone," "Resource Allocation Issues in the Coastal Environment," "The Present and Future of Coasts," and "Gambling with the Shore." Workshops are sponsored in conjunction with government agencies, universities, professional groups, and private organizations. Conference proceedings are subsequently published. TCS also publishes a quarterly magazine, *TCS Bulletin*, which features articles and news covering TCS affairs and the broader spectrum of coastal issues.

TCS representatives present congressional testimony on coastal management, conservation, and water quality. Recently the organization drafted a policy statement and it plans to take public positions on proposed policies affecting coastal issues. Contact: The Coastal Society, P.O. Box 2081, Gloucester, MA 01930-2081.

[*Cathy M. Falk*]

Coastal Zone Management Act (1972)

The Coastal Zone Management Act (CZMA) of 1972 established a federal program to help states in planning and managing the development and protection of coastal areas. This is primarily a planning act, rather than an environmental protection or regulatory act. Under its provisions, states can receive grants from the federal government to develop and implement coastal zone programs, as long as the programs meet with federal approval. State participation in the program is voluntary, and the authority is focused in state governments. A major criticism of the CZMA is that the law recognized the interdependence in coastal zones, but this recognition has not translated into coherent management within states or across state lines.

In the 1960s, public concern began to focus on **dredging** and filling, industrial siting, offshore oil development, and second home developments in the coastal zone. The coastal zone law was developed in the context of increased development of marine and coastal areas, need for more coordinated and consistent governmental efforts, an increase in general environmental consciousness and public **recreation** demands, and a focus on **land-use control** nationally. In 1969, a report by the Commission on Marine Sciences, Engineering, and Resources (the Stratton Commission) recommended a federal grant program to the states to help them deal with coastal zone management. The Commission found

that coastal areas were of prime national interest, but development was taking place there without proper consideration of environmental and resource values.

During congressional debate over coastal zone legislation, support came primarily from marine scientists and affected state government officials. The opposition came from development and real estate interests and industry, who were also concerned with national **land use** bills. The major difference between House and Senate versions of the legislation that passed was which department would administer the program. The House favored the **U.S. Department of the Interior**, the Senate the **National Oceanic and Atmospheric Administration** (NOAA). The Senate position was adopted in conference. The congressional committees and executive branch agency involved in coastal zone management are greatly varied. In Congress, the House Merchant Marine and Fisheries Committee and the Senate Commerce Committee have jurisdiction over the legislation. At the executive level, the Office of Coastal Zone Management (OCZM) in NOAA, located in the Department of Commerce, was placed in charge of the program.

The CZMA declared that "there is a national interest in the effective management, beneficial use, protection, and development of the coastal zone." The purpose of the law is to further the "wise use of land and water resources for the coastal zone giving full consideration to ecological, cultural, historic and aesthetic values as well as to needs for economic development." The program is primarily a grant program, and the 1972 act authorized the spending of $186 million through 1977. The Secretary of Commerce was authorized to make grants to the states with coastal areas, including the **Great Lakes**, to help them develop the coastal zone management programs required by federal standards. The grants would pay for up to two-thirds of a state's program and could be received for no more than three years. In addition to these planning grants, the federal government could also make grants to the states for administering approved coastal zone plans. Again, the grants could not exceed two-thirds of the cost of the state program. With federal approval, the states could forward federal grant money to local governments or regional entities to carry out the act.

The federal government also has oversight responsibilities, to make sure that the states are following the approved plan and administering it properly. The key components of a state plan are to: (1) identify the boundaries of the coastal zone; (2) define the permissible uses in the coastal zone that have a significant effect; (3) inventory and designate areas of particular concern; (4) develop guidelines to prioritize use in particular areas; (5) develop a process for protection of beaches and public access to them; (6) develop a process for energy facility siting; and (7) develop a process to control shoreline **erosion**. The states have discretion in these stages. For instance, some states have opted for coastal zones very close to the water, others have drawn boundaries further inland. The states determine what uses are to be allowed in coastal zones. Developments in the coastal area must demonstrate coastal dependence. The plans deal primarily with private lands, though the management of federal lands within the coastal zone should be consistent with approved state plans. Indeed, this was a major incentive for states to participate in the process. Although federal agencies with management responsibility in coastal zones have input into the plans, this state-federal coordination proved to be a problem in the 1980s, especially regarding offshore oil development.

At first, states were slow to develop plans and have them approved by federal authorities. This was due primarily to the political complexity of the interests involved in the process. The first three states to have their coastal zone management plans approved were California, Oregon, and Washington, which had their final plans approved by 1978. Both California and Washington had passed state legislation on coastal zone management prior to the federal law, California by referendum in 1972 and Washington in 1971. The California program is the most ambitious and comprehensive in the country. Its 1972 act established six regional coastal commissions with permit authority and a state coastal zone agency, which coordinated the program and oversaw the development of a state coastal plan. The California legislature passed a permanent coastal zone act in 1976 based on this plan. The permanent program stemmed from local plans reviewed by the regional commissions and state agency. Any development altering density or intensity of land use requires a permit from the local government, and sensitive coastal resource areas receive additional protection. As of January 1993, of the thirty-five eligible states and territories, twenty-nine had approved coastal zone plans, four were in the planning process, and two had chosen not to participate in the program.

Three major issues arose during the state planning processes. Identifying areas of crucial environmental concern was a controversy that pitted environmentalists against developers in many states. In general, developers have proved more successful than environmentalists. A second issue is general development. States that have the most advanced coastal programs, such as California, use a permit system for development within the coastal zone. Environmental concerns and cumulative effects are often considered in these permit decisions. These permit programs often lead developers to alter plans before or during the application process. Such programs have generally served to improve development in coastal zones, and to protect these areas from major abuses. The final issue, the siting of large scale facilities, especially energy facilities, has proved to be continually controversial as states and localities seek control over such siting through their coastal zone plans, while energy companies appeal to the federal government regarding the national need for such facilities. In a number of court cases, the courts ruled that the states did have the power to block energy projects that were not consistent with their approved coastal management plans. This controversy spilled over into offshore oil development in waters under federal jurisdiction. These waters were often included in state coastal zone plans, many of which sought to prevent offshore oil development. In this case, the courts found in 1984 ruling (*Secretary of the Interior v. California*) that such development could proceed over state objections.

Major amendments to the CZMA were passed in 1976, 1980, and 1990. In 1976, the Coastal Energy Impact Fund was created to sponsor grants and loans to state and local governments for managing the problems of energy development. Other changes included an increase in the federal funding level from two-thirds to 80 percent of planning and administration, an increase in planning grant eligibility from three to four years, and the addition of planning requirements for energy facilities, shoreline erosion, and beach access. The 1980 amendments re-authorized the program through 1985 and established new grant programs for revitalizing urban water fronts and helping coastal cities deal with the effects of energy developments. The amendments also expanded the policies and objectives of the CZMA to include the protection of **natural resources**, the encouragement of states to protect coastal resources of national significance, and the reduction of state-federal conflicts in coastal zone policy. Amendments to the CZMA in 1990 were included in the budget reconciliation bill. Most importantly, the amendments overturned the 1984 decision of *Secretary of the Interior v. California*, giving states an increased voice regarding federal actions off their coasts. The law, which was strongly opposed by the Departments of Defense and Interior, gives the states the power to try to block or change federal actions affecting the coastal zones if these actions are inconsistent with adopted plans. The amendments also initiated a **nonpoint source** coastal water **pollution** grant and planning program, repealed the coastal energy impact program, and reauthorized the CZMA through 1995. *See also* Environmental law; Environmental policy; International Joint Commission; Marine pollution; National lakeshore; Water pollution

[*Christopher McGrory Klyza*]

FURTHER READING

"Coastal Zone Management Revamped." *Congressional Quarterly Almanac* 36 (1980): 380-382.

Dana, S. T., and S. K. Fairfax. *Forest and Range Policy.* 2nd ed. New York: McGraw-Hill, 1980.

Ditton, R. B., J. L. Seymour, and G. C. Swanson. *Coastal Resources Management.* Lexington, MA: D. C. Heath, 1977.

Hays, S. P. *Beauty, Health, and Permanence: Environmental Politics in the United States, 1955-1985.* New York: Cambridge University Press, 1987.

"States Get More Say in Offshore Activity." *Congressional Quarterly Almanac* 46 (1990): 288-289.

Co-composting

As a form of **waste management**, **composting** is the process whereby **organic waste** matter is microbiologically degraded under **aerobic** conditions to achieve significant volume reduction while also producing a stable, usable end product. Co-composting refers to composting two or more waste types in the same vessel or process, thus providing cost and space savings. The most common type of co-composting practiced by counties and townships in the United States involves mixing sewage **sludge** and **municipal solid waste** to speed the process and increase the usefulness of the end product. The processing and ultimate use or disposal of co-composting end products are regulated by federal and state environmental agencies.

Coevolution

Species are said to "coevolve" when their respective levels of fitness depend not only on their own genetic structure and adaptations but also the development of another species as well. The **gene pool** of one species creates selection pressure for another species. Although the changes are generally reciprocal, they may also be unilateral and still be considered coevolutionary.

The process of coevolution arises from interactions that establish structure in communities. A variety of different types of interactions can occur—symbiotic, where neither member suffers, or parasitic, predatory, and competitive relationships, where one member of a species pair suffers.

Coevolution can result from mutually positive selection pressure. For example, certain plants have in an evolutionary sense created positive situations for insects by providing valuable food sources for them. In return the insects provide a means to distribute pollen that is more efficient than the distribution of pollen by wind. Unfortunately, the plant and the insect species could evolve into a position of total dependency through increased specialization, thus enhancing the risk of **extinction** if either species declines.

Coevolution can also arise from negative pressures. Prey species will continually adapt defensive or evasive systems to avoid predation. Predators respond by developing mechanisms to surmount these defenses. However, these species pairs are "familiar" with one another, and neither of the strategies is perfect. Some prey are always more vulnerable, and some predators are less efficient due to the nature of variability in natural populations. Therefore the likelihood of extinction from this association is limited.

Several factors influence the likelihood and strength of coevolved relationships. Coevolution is more likely to take place in pairs of species where high levels of co-occurrence are present. It is also common in cases where selective pressure is strong, influencing important functions such as reproduction or mortality. The type of relationship—be it mutualistic, predator-prey, or competitor—also influences coevolution. Species that have intimate relationships, such as that of a specialist predator or a host-specific parasite, interact actively and thus are more likely to influence each other's selection. Species that do not directly encounter each other but interact through competition for resources are less likely candidates to coevolve, but the strength of the competition may influence the situation.

The result of coevolved relationships is structure in communities. Coevolution and **symbiosis** create fairly distinct relationships in communities, relationships that are mirrored in distribution, community energetics, and resistance to disturbances in species. Coevolution allows for recurring groupings of plant and animal communities. *See also* Parasites; Predator-prey interactions

[*David A. Duffus*]

FURTHER READING

Barth, F. G. *Insects and Flowers: The Biology of a Partnership.* Princeton, NJ: Princeton University Press, 1991.

Erickson, J. *The Living Earth: The Coevolution of the Planet and Life.* Blue Ridge Summit, PA: Tab Books, 1989.

Grant, Susan. *Beauty and the Beast: The Coevolution of Plants and Animals.* New York: Charles Scribner's, 1984.

Cogeneration

Cogeneration is the multiple use of energy from a single primary source. In burning **coal**, oil, **natural gas**, or **biomass**, it is possible to produce two usable forms of energy at once, such as heat and electricity. By harnessing heat or exhaust from boilers and furnaces, for example, cogeneration systems can utilize energy that is usually wasted and so operate at a higher efficiency.

The second law of thermodynamics states that in every energy conversion there is a loss of useful energy in the form of heat. It is estimated that nearly half of the energy used in the United States is wasted as heat. Energy conversion efficiencies vary in range but most systems fall below 50 percent: A **gasoline** internal **combustion** engine is 10 to 15 percent efficient, and a steam turbine operates at about 40 percent efficiency. A simple example of cogeneration would be the heater in an **automobile**, which utilizes the heat of the engine to warm the interior of the car.

Cogeneration is classified into a topping cycle or a bottoming cycle. In the topping cycle, power is generated first, then the spent heat is utilized. In the bottoming cycle, thermal energy is used first, then power is generated from the remaining heat. The basic component of a cogeneration system is the prime mover, such as an internal combustion engine or steam boiler combination, whose function is to convert chemical energy or thermal energy into mechanical energy. The other components are the generator which converts mechanical input into electrical output and a spent heat recovery system, as well as control and transmission systems. A cogeneration system utilizes the heat which the prime mover component has not converted into mechanical energy, and this can improve the efficiency of a typical gas turbine from approximately 12 to 30 percent to an overall rate of 60 percent.

In the United States, 40 percent of all electrical power is generated by burning coal, and coal-fired **power plants** lose two-thirds of their energy through the smokestack. Several large **electric utilities** have been using waste heat from their boilers for space heating in their own utility districts. This is known as district heating; zoning regulations and building locations permit this practice in New York City, New York; Detroit, Michigan; and Eugene, Oregon; among other cities. Waste heat from the generation of electricity has long been used in Europe to heat commercial and industrial buildings, and the city of Vestras, Sweden, produces all its electricity as well as all its space heating by utilizing the waste heat from industrial boilers.

In 1978, Congress passed the Public Utilities Regulatory Act, which allowed cogenerators to sell their extra power to utility companies. It has been estimated that if all waste heat generated by industry were used to cogenerate electrical power, there would be no need to construct additional power plants for the next two or three decades. The paper industry in the United States, which must produce steam for its industrial process, often uses cogeneration systems to produce electricity.

Experts maintain that half of the money consumers spend on electric bills pays not for the generation of power but for its distribution and transmission, including losses through transmission. Small, decentralized cogeneration systems that burn biomass, such as organic waste in agricultural areas, or **garbage** from large apartment buildings can minimize transmission losses and utilize waste heat for space heating. In Santa Barbara County, California, a hospital which operates a seven-**megawatt** natural gas turbine generator for its electrical power needs installed a cogeneration system to use thermal energy from the boiler to provide steam for heating and cooling. Extra steam not needed for these purposes is returned to the turbine, and excess electrical power is sold to the local utility.

A new technology for regeneration systems is **coal gasification**. Coal is heated and turned into a gas. The gas is burned to operate two turbines, one fueled by the hot gases and the other by steam generated from the burning gas. **Scrubbers** can remove 95 percent of the sulfur from the **flue gas**es, and the result is a generating facility with high efficiency and low **pollution**. *See also* Alternative energy sources; Energy conservation; Energy efficiency; Energy policy

[*Muthena Naseri and Douglas Smith*]

FURTHER READING

Aubrecht, G. *Energy*. Columbus, Ohio: Merrill Publishing Company, 1989.

Heating, Ventilating, Air-Conditioning Systems and Equipment. Atlanta: American Society of Heating, Refrigeration, and Air-Conditioning Engineers, 1992.

Kaufman, D. G., and C. M. Franz. *Biosphere 2000*. New York: Harper-Collins, 1993.

Coliform bacteria

Coliform bacteria live in the **nutrient**-rich **environment** of animal intestines. Many **species** fall into this group, but the most common species in mammals is *Escherichia coli*, usually abbreviated *E. coli*. A typical human can easily have several trillion of these tiny individual bacterial cells inhabiting his or her digestive tract. On a purely numerical basis, a human may have more bacterial than mammalian cells in his or her body. Each person is actually a community or **ecosystem** of diverse species living in a state of cooperation, **competition**, or coexistence.

The bacterial **flora** of one's gut provides many benefits. They help break down and absorb food, they synthesize and secrete vitamins such as B_{12} and K on which mammals depend, and they displace or help keep under control **pathogen**s that are ingested along with food and liquids. When the pathogens gain control, disagreeable or even potentially lethal diseases can result. A wide variety of diarrheas, dysenteries, and other gastrointestinal diseases afflict people who have inadequate sanitation. Many tourists suffer traveler's diseases known by names such as Montezuma's Revenge, La Tourista, or Cairo Crud when they come into contact with improperly sanitized water or food. Some of these diseases, such as **cholera** or food poisoning caused by *Salmonella*, *Shigella*, or *Lysteria* species, can be fatal.

Because identifying specific pathogens in water or food is difficult, time-consuming, and expensive, public health officials usually test for coliform organisms in general. The presence of any of these species, whether pathogenic or not, indicates that fecal contamination has occurred and that pathogens are likely present. *See also* Enteric bacteria

Colorado River

One of the major rivers of the western United States, the Colorado River flows for some 1500 miles (2415 km) from Colorado to northwestern Mexico. Dropping over two miles in elevation over its course, the Colorado emptied into the Gulf of California until human management reduced its water flow. Over millions of years the swift waters of the Colorado have carved some of the world's deepest and most impressive gorges, including the Grand Canyon.

The Colorado River basin supports an unusual **ecosystem**. Isolated from other drainage systems, the Colorado has produced a unique assemblage of fishes. Of the 32 **species** of native fishes found in the Colorado drainage, 21 or 66 percent, are **endemic species**—species that arose in the area and are found nowhere else.

Major projects carried out since the 1920s have profoundly altered the Colorado. When seven western states signed the Colorado River Compact in 1922, the Colorado became the first basin in which "multiple use" of water was initiated. Today the river is used to provide hydroelectric power, irrigation, drinking water, and **recreation**; over 20 **dams** have been erected along its length. The river, in fact, no longer drains into the Gulf of Colorado—it simply disappears near the Mexican towns of Tijuana and Mexicali. Hundreds of square miles of land have been submerged by the formation of **reservoir**s, and the temperature and clarity of the river's water have been profoundly changed by the action of the dams.

Alteration of the Colorado's **habitat** has threatened many of its fragile fishes, and a number are now listed as **endangered species**. The Colorado squawfish serves as an example of how river development can affect native **wildlife**. With the reservoirs formed by the impoundments on the Colorado River also came the introduction of game fishes in the 1940s. One particular species, the Channel catfish, became a prey item for the native squawfish, and many squawfish were found dead, having suffocated due to catfish lodged in their throats with their spines stiffly locked in place. Other portions of the squawfish population have succumbed to diseases introduced by these non-native fishes.

Major projects along the Colorado include the Hoover Dam and its reservoir, Lake Mead, as well as the controversial **Glen Canyon Dam** at the Arizona-Utah border, which has a reservoir extending into Utah for over one hundred miles.

[*Eugene C. Beckham and Jeffrey Muhr*]

FURTHER READING

Fradkin, P. L. *A River No More: The Colorado River and the West.* New York: Knopf, 1981.

Richardson, J. *The Colorado: A River At Risk.* Englewood, CO: Westcliffe Publishers, 1992.

Combined Sewer Overflows (CSO)

In many older coastal cities, especially in the northeastern United States, storm sewers in the street that collect stormwater **runoff** from rainfall are connected to municipal **sewage treatment** plants that process household sewage and industrial **wastewater**. Under normal, relatively dry conditions runoff and municipal waste go to a sewage treatment plant where they are treated. However, when it rains, in some cases less than an inch, the capacity of a sewage treatment plant can be exceeded; the system is overloaded. The mixed urban stormwater runoff and raw municipal sewage is released to nearby creeks, rivers, bays, estuaries or other coastal waters, completely untreated. This is a combined sewer overflow (CSO) event.

Combined sewer overflow events are not rare. In **Boston Harbor**, for example, there are 88 pipes or outfalls that discharge combined stormwater runoff and sewage. It has been estimated that CSO events occur approximately 60 times per year, discharging billions of gallons of untreated runoff and wastewater to Boston Harbor.

Materials released during these CSO events can result in serious **water quality** problems that can be detrimental to both humans and wildlife. Toxic chemicals from households and industries are released during CSO events. In addition, toxic chemicals found in rainwater runoff, such as oil and antifreeze that have dripped onto roads from cars, will wash into coastal waters during these events.

Harmful bacteria and pathogens in the water is another major problem that can result after a CSO event. Some of these bacteria (coliform), live naturally in the intestinal tracts of humans and other warm blooded animals. After heavy rainfalls, scientists have measured increased levels of coliform bacteria in coastal waters near CSO outfalls. These bacteria, which indicate that there are other bacteria and pathogens that can make people sick if they swim in the water or eat contaminated shellfish, come from both animal wastes washed

in from the streets and human wastes. The bacteria are not removed or killed because the waters have not been treated in a sewage treatment plant. Because levels of these indicator bacteria are often high after CSO events, many productive shellfish beds are closed to protect human health. This can be a serious economic hardship to the fishing industry.

Combined sewer overflow events also result in increased quantities of trash and floatable debris entering coastal waters. When people litter, the trash is washed into storm sewers with rainwater. Since sewage treatment plants cannot handle the volume of water during these rainfall events, this trash is discharged along with the stormwater and sewage directly into open waters. This floatable debris is unsightly, and can be dangerous to marine animals and birds, which eat it and choke or become entangled within it. This often results in death.

Raw sewage, animal wastes, and runoff from lawns and other fertilized areas contain very high levels of nitrogen and phosphorus, which are nutrients used by marine and aquatic plants for growth. Therefore, CSO events are major contributors of extra nutrients and organic matter to nearshore waters. These nutrients act as fertilizers for many marine and aquatic algae and plants, promoting extreme growth called blooms. When they eventually die, the bacteria decomposing the plants and algae use up vast quantities of oxygen. This results in a condition known as hypoxia or low dissolved oxygen (DO). If DO levels are too low, marine animals will not have enough oxygen to survive and they will either die or move out of the area. Hypoxia has been the cause of some major fish kills, and can result in permanent changes in the ecological community if it is persistent.

There are a number of options available to reduce the frequency and impacts of CSO events. Upgrading sewage treatment plants to handle greater flow or constructing new facilities are two of the best, although most costly options. Another possibility is to separate storm sewers and municipal sewage treatment plants. While this would not prevent discharges of stormwater runoff during rainfall events, untreated household and industrial wastewater (i.e., raw sewage) would not be released. In addition, the resulting stormwater could be minimally treated by screening out trash and disinfecting it to kill bacteria. Use of **wetlands** to filter this stormwater has also been considered as an effective alternative and is currently being used in some areas. Another option is to build large storage facilities (often underground) to hold materials that would normally be discharged during CSO events. When dry conditions return, the combined runoff and wastewater are pumped to a nearby sewage treatment plant where they are properly treated. This option is being used in several areas, including some locations in New York City. At a minimum, screening of CSO discharges would reduce the quantity of floatable debris in nearshore waters, even if it did not solve all of the other problems associated with CSOs. Of course **water conservation** is another control that reduces that volume of water treated by sewage treatment plants, and therefore the volume that would be discharged during a CSO event.

[*Max Strieb*]

FURTHER READING

National Research Council. "Managing Wastewater In Coastal Urban Areas." Washington, D.C.: National Academy Press, 1993.

Combustion

The process of burning fuels. Traditionally **biomass** was used as fuel, but now **fossil fuels** are the major source of energy for human activities. Combustion is essentially an oxidation process that yields heat and light. Most fuels are **carbon** and **hydrogen** which use oxygen in the air as an oxidant. More exotic fuels are used in some combustion processes, particularly in rockets where metals such as **aluminum** or beryllium or hydrazine (a **nitrogen** containing compound) are well known as effective fuels. As rockets operate beyond the **atmosphere** they carry their own oxidants, which may also be quite exotic.

Combustion involves a mixture of fuel and air, which is thermodynamically unstable. The fuel is then converted to stable products, usually water and **carbon dioxide**, with the release of a large amount of energy as heat. At normal temperatures fuels such as **coal** and oil are quite stable and have to be ignited by raising the temperature. Combustion is said to be spontaneous when the ignition appears to take place without obvious reasons. Large piles of organic material, such as hay, can undergo slow oxidation, perhaps biologically mediated, and increase in temperature. If the amount of material is very large and the heat cannot escape, the whole pile can suddenly burst into flame. Will-o'-the-wisps or jack-o'-lanterns (known scientifically as *ignis fatuus*) are sometimes observed over swamps where **methane** is likely to be produced. The reason these small pockets of gas ignite is not certain, but it has been suggested that small traces of gases such as phosphine that react rapidly with air could ignite the methane.

Typical solid fuels like coal and wood begin to burn with a bright turbulent flame. This forms as volatile materials are driven off and ignited. These vapors burn so rapidly that oxygen can be depleted, creating a smoky flame. After a time the volatile substances in the fuel are depleted. At this point a glowing coal is evident and combustion takes place without a significant flame. Combustion on the surface of the glowing coal is controlled by the diffusion of oxygen towards the hot surface. If the piece of fuel is too small, such as a spark from a fire, it is likely to lose temperature rapidly and combustion will stop. By contrast a bed of coals can maintain combustion because of heat storage and the exchange of radiative heat between the pieces. The most intense combustion takes place between the crevices of a bed of coal. In these regions oxygen may be in limited supply which leads to the production of **carbon monoxide**. This is subsequently oxidized to carbon at the surface of the bed of coals with a faint blue flame. The production of toxic carbon monoxide from indoor fires can occasionally represent a hazard if subsequent oxidation to carbon dioxide is not complete.

Liquid fuels usually need to be evaporated before they burn effectively. This means that it is possible to see liquid combustion and gaseous combustion as similar processes. Combustion can readily be initiated with a flame or spark. Simply heating a fuel-air mixture can cause it to ignite, but temperatures have to be high before reactions occur. A much better way is to initiate combustion with a small number of molecular fragments of radicals. These can initiate **chain reaction**s at much lower temperatures than molecular reactions. In a propane-air flame at about 2000° K, hydrogen and oxygen atoms and hydroxyl radicals account for about 0.3 percent of a gas mixture. It is these radicals that support combustion. They react with molecules and split them up into more radicals. These radicals can rapidly enter into the exothermic (heat releasing) oxidative processes that lie at the heart of combustion. The reactions also give rise to further radicals that support continued combustion. Under some situations the radicals reaction branch, such that the reaction of each radical produces two new radicals. These can enter further reactions, producing yet further increases in the number of reactions and very soon the system explodes. However the production of radicals can be terminated in a number of ways such as contact with a solid surface. In some systems, such as the internal combustion engine, an explosion is desired, but in others, such as a gas cooker flame, maintaining a stable combustion process is desirable.

In terms of **air pollution** the reaction of oxygen and nitrogen atoms with molecules in air leads to the formation of the pollutant nitric oxide through a set of reactions known as the Zeldovich cycle. It is this process that makes combustion such an important contributor of **nitrogen oxides** to the atmosphere. *See also* Oxidation reduction reactions

[*Peter Brimblecombe*]

FURTHER READING

Campbell, I. M. *Energy and the Atmosphere.* New York: Wiley, 1986.

Cometabolism

The partial breakdown of a (usually) synthetic compound by microbiological action. Synthetic **chemicals** are widely used in industry, agriculture, and in the home; many resist complete enzymatic degradation and become persistent environmental pollutants. In cometabolism, the exotic molecule is only partly modified by decomposers (bacteria or **fungi**), since they are unable to utilize it either as a source of energy, as a source of **nutrient** elements, or because it is toxic. Cometabolism probably accounts for long-term changes in **DDT**, dieldrin, and related chlorinated hydrocarbon insecticides in the **soil**. The products of this partial transformation, like the original exotic chemical, usually accumulate in the **environment**.

Commensalism

A type of symbiotic relationship. Many organisms depend on intimate physical relationship with organisms of other **spe-**

cies, a relationship called **symbiosis**. The larger organism is called the host and the smaller organism, the symbiote. The symbiote always derives some benefit from the relationship. In a commensal relationship, the host organism is neither harmed nor benefitted. The relationship that exists between the clown fish living among the tentacles of sea anemones is one example of commensalism. The host sea anemones can exist without their symbiotes, but the fish cannot exist as successfully without the protective cover of the anemone's stinging tentacles. *See also* Coevolution

Commercial fishing

On a worldwide basis humans get an average of 20 percent of their animal protein from fish and shellfish. With an ever increasing human population, the demand and market for seafood has steadily risen over the past several decades. To meet this demand the commercial fishing industry has expanded as well, and it has employed the latest in high-tech equipment for locating and harvesting enormous quantities of fish and shellfish. This expansion may be coming to an end, however, as environmental, biological, and economic woes befall this industry.

Even though the worldwide commercial fish catch is currently about 100 million tons a year, the per capita world fish catch has been steadily declining since 1970 as human population growth outdistances fish harvests. In the mid-1980s, the United States had nearly a quarter of a million commercial fishermen operating about 125,000 vessels. In 1984 alone, United States commercial fishermen landed 6.4 billion pounds of fish and shellfish valued at $2.4 billion. That same year the nation's supply of edible fish, including imports, was 8.5 billion pounds. The supply of industrial fish products was 4.1 billion pounds. Of this total amount, the United States imported $5.8 billion worth of fish products and exported about $1.1 billion worth of fish products. Over the past decade fishery imports have been one of the top five sources of the United States' trade deficit.

The commercial fisheries industry has contributed to its own problems by **overfishing** many **species** to the point where those species' populations are too low to reproduce at a rate sufficient to replace the portion of their numbers lost to harvesting. Cod and haddock in the Atlantic Ocean, red snapper in the Gulf of Mexico, and **salmon** and tuna in the Pacific Ocean have all fallen victim to this dilemma. Several factors may work against this industry at one time, as in the case of the Peruvian anchovy. Peru began fishing for anchovies off their coast in the early 1950s, and, by the late 1960s as their fishing fleet had grown exponentially, their catch made up about 20 percent of the world's annual commercial fish harvest. The Peruvian fishermen were already overfishing the anchovies when, in 1972, a strong **El Niño** struck. This phenomenon is a natural, although unpredictable, warming of the normally cool waters flowing along Peru's coast. This alters the entire food web of the region, and the Peruvian anchovy population plummeted. Along with the demise of the Peruvian anchovy came the **extinction** of Peru's anchovy

fishery. Peru has made some economic recovery since then by harvesting other species.

Environmental problems also plague commercial fishing. Near-shore **pollution** has altered **ecosystem**s and has taken its toll on all populations of fish and shellfish, not just those valued commercially. The collective actions of commercial fishermen are also creating some major environmental problems. The world's commercial fishermen annually catch, and then discard, about 20 billion pounds of non-target species of sea life. In addition to non-target species of fish and shellfish, each year about one million seabirds are caught and killed in fishermen's nets. On average more than 6,000 **seals and sea lions**, about 20,000 **dolphins** and other cetaceans, and thousands of **sea turtles** meet the same fate. Besides the slaughter, two major problems arise from this massive discarding of organisms. One is the disruption of predator-prey ratios, and the other is the tremendous overload of organic waste that has to be dealt with in this ecosystem.

In the United States, as well as foreign nations, the commercial fisheries industry is facing collapse. Severe restrictions and tight controls imposed by the federal government may be the only means of salvaging even a portion of this valuable industry.

[*Eugene C. Beckham*]

FURTHER READING

Bricklemyer, E., S. Iudicello, and H. Hartmann. "Discarded Catch in U.S. Commercial Marine Fisheries." In *Audubon Wildlife Report 1990–1991*. San Diego: Academic Press, 1990.

Lawren, B. "Net Loss." *National Wildlife* 30 (1992): 46-53.

Weber, M. "Federal Marine Fisheries Management." In *Audubon Wildlife Report 1986*. San Diego: Academic Press, 1986.

Commingled recyclables
See **Recycling**

Commission for Environmental Cooperation

The Commission for Environmental Cooperation (CEC) is a trilateral international commission established by Canada, Mexico, and the United States in 1994 to address transboundary environmental concerns in North America. The original impetus behind the CEC was the perception of inadequacies in the environmental provisions of the **North American Free Trade Agreement (NAFTA)**. A supplementary treaty, the North American Agreement for Environmental Cooperation (NAAEC) was negotiated to remedy these inadequacies, and it is from the NAAEC that the CEC derives its formal mandate.

The general goals set forth by the NAAEC are to protect, conserve, and improve the environment for the benefit of present and future generations. More specifically, the three NAFTA signatories agreed to a core set of actions and principles with regard to environmental concerns related to trade policy. These actions and principles include regular reporting on the state of the **environment**, effective and consistent enforcement of environmental law, facilitation of access to environmental information, the ongoing improvement of environmental laws and regulations, and promotion of the use of tax incentives and various other economic instruments to achieve environmental goals.

The CEC is to function as a forum for the NAFTA partners to identify and articulate mutual interests and priorities, and to develop strategies for the pursuit or implementation of these interests and priorities. The NAAEC further specifies the following priorities: identification of appropriate limits for specific pollutants; the protection of endangered and threatened species; the protection and conservation of wild flora and fauna and their habitat; the development of new approaches to environmental compliance and enforcement; strategies for addressing environmental issues that have impacts across international borders; the support of training and education in the environmental field; and promotion of greater public awareness of North American environmental issues. Central to the CEC's mission is the facilitation of dialogue among the NAFTA partners in order to prevent and solve trade and environmental disputes.

The governing body of the CEC is a Council of Ministers consisting of the environment ministers (or equivalent) from each country. The executive arm of the Commission is a Secretariat located in Montreal, consisting of a staff of about thirty members and headed by an Executive Director. The staff is drawn from all three countries and provides technical and administrative support to the Council of Ministers and to committees and groups established by the Council.

Technical and scientific advice is also provided to the Council of Ministers by a Joint Public Advisory Committee consisting of five members from each country appointed by the respective governments. This Committee may, on its own initiative, advise the Council on any matter within the scope of the NAAEC, including the annual program and budget. As a reflection of the CEC's professed commitment to participation by citizens throughout North America, the Committee is intended to represent a wide cross-section of knowledgeable citizens committed to environmental concerns who are willing to volunteer their time in the public interest. The CEC also accepts direct input from any citizen or non-governmental organization who believes that a NAFTA partner is failing to enforce effectively an existing environmental law.

The NAAEC also contains provisions for dispute resolution in cases in which a NAFTA signatory alleges that another NAFTA partner has persistently failed to enforce an existing environmental law, causing specific environmental damage or trade disadvantages to the claimant. These provisions may be invoked when a lack of effective enforcement materially affects goods ir services being traded between the NAFTA countries. If the dispute is not resolved through bilateral consultation, the complaining party may then request a special session of the CEC's Council of Ministers. If

the Council is likewise unable to resolve the dispute, provisions exist for choosing an Arbitral Panel. Failure to implement the recommendations of the Arbitral Panel subjects the offending party to a monetary enforcement assessment. Failure to pay this assessment may lead to suspension of free trade benefits.

The Council is also instructed to develop recommendations on access to courts (and rights and remedies before courts and administrative agencies) for persons in one country's territory who have suffered or are likely to suffer damage or injury caused by pollution originating in the territory of one of the other countries. In 1995, the Council created a fund of two million Canadian dollars for engaging "the energy and imagination of the people in North America in achieving the goals and objectives of the NAAEC."

The CEC has been subject to some of the same criticisms leveled at the environmental provisions of NAFTA, particularly that it serves as a kind of environmental windowdressing for a trade agreement that is generally harmful to the environment. The CEC's mandate for conflict resolution is primarily oriented towards consistent enforcement of existing environmental law in the three countries. This law is by no means uniform. By upholding the principles of free trade, and providing penalties for infringements of free trade, NAFTA establishes an environment in which private companies have an economic incentive, other considerations being equal, to locate production where environmental laws are weakest and the costs of compliance are therefore lowest. Countries with stricter environmental regulations face penalties for attempting to protect domestic industries from such comparative disadvantages.

[*Lawrence J. Biskowski*]

FURTHER READING

Kass, S. L. "First Cases Before New NAFTA Forum Suggest Its Power Will Increase." National Law Journal 18/41 (10 June 1996): C5, C7.

Commoner, Barry (1917 -)
American environmental scientist, author, and social activist

Born to Russian immigrant parents, Commoner earned a doctorate in biology from Harvard in 1941. As a biologist, he is known for his work with free radicals—**chemicals** like **chlorofluorocarbons**, which are suspected culprits in **ozone layer depletion**. Commoner led a fairly academic life at first, with research posts at various universities, but rose to some prominence in the late 1950s, when he and others protested atmospheric testing of **nuclear weapons**. He earned a national reputation in the 1960s with books, articles, and speeches on a wide range of environmental concerns, including **pollution**, **alternative energy sources**, and population. His latest book, *Making Peace with the Planet*, was published in 1990. Commoner's other works include *Science and Survival* (1967), *The Closing Circle* (1971), *Energy and Human Welfare* (1975), *The Poverty of Power* (1976), and *The Politics of Energy* (1979).

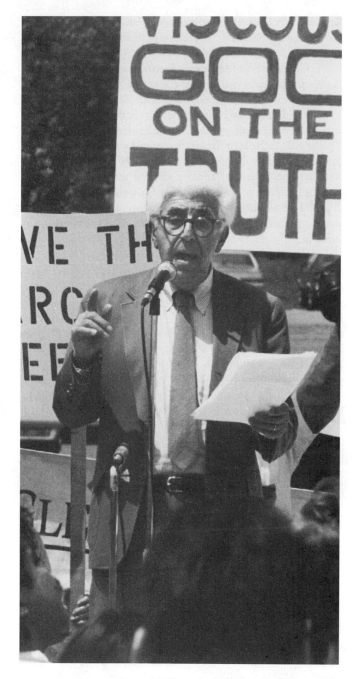

Barry Commoner speaking to a group of protestors gathered outside a New Jersey hotel where Exxon stockholders met in 1989.

Commoner believes that post-World War II industrial methods, with their reliance on nonrenewable **fossil fuels** are the root cause of modern environmental pollution. When combined with a myopic view of the bottom line, he states, the devastation is complete: "At present, economic considerations—n particular, the private desire for maximizing short-term profits—govern the choice of productive technology, which in turn determines its environmental impact, generally for the worse." The **petrochemical**s industry receives the largest share of Commoner's criticism. He refers to "the petrochemical industry's toxic invasion of the

biosphere" and states flatly that "the petrochemical industry is inherently inimical to environmental quality."

Almost as distressing as environmental pollution is our inability to clean it up. Commoner rejects attempts at environmental regulation as pointless. Far better, he says, to not produce the toxin in the first place. "When a pollutant is attacked at the point of origin—in the production process that generates it—the pollutant can be eliminated; once it is produced, it is too late. This is the simple but powerful lesson of the two decades of intense but largely futile effort to improve the quality of the **environment**."

Commoner offers radical, sweeping solutions for social and ecological ills. The most urgent of these is a renewable energy source, primarily **photovoltaic cell**s powered by **solar energy**. These would not only decentralize **electric utilities** (another target of Commoner's), but would use sunlight to fuel almost any energy need, including smaller, lighter, battery-powered cars. To ease the transition from fossil fuels to solar power, he proposes **methane**, **cogeneration** (which produces electricity from waste heat), and an organic agriculture system that would "produce enough **ethanol** to replace about 20 percent of the national demand for **gasoline** without reducing the overall supply of food or significantly affecting its price."

Commoner makes few compromises, and his environmental zeal has made him a crusader for social causes as well. Eliminating **Third World** debt, he argues, would improve life in impoverished countries and end the spiral of economic desperation that drives countries to overpopulation. "This [debt forgiveness] should be regarded not as a magnanimous gesture but as partial reparations for the damage inflicted . . . by the former colonial empires. . . . [T]he cause of poverty is the grossly unequal distribution of the world's wealth . . . we must redistribute that wealth, among nations and within them."

In 1980, Commoner made a bid for the presidency on the Citizen's Party ticket, a short-lived political attempt to combine environmental and Socialist agendas. Since 1981 he has been the director of the Center for the Biology of Natural Systems at Queens College in New York City.

[*Muthena Naseri and Amy Strumolo*]

FURTHER READING

Commoner, B. *The Closing Circle.* New York: Knopf, 1971.

———. "Ending the War Against Earth." *The Nation* 250 (30 April 1990): 589-90.

———. "The Failure of the Environmental Effort." *Current History* 91 (April 1992): 176-81.

———. *Making Peace With the Planet.* New York: New Press, 1992.

Stone, P. "The Ploughboy Interview." *Mother Earth News* (March-April 1990): 116-26.

Communicable diseases

A communicable disease is any disease that can be transmitted from one organism to another. Agents that cause communicable diseases, called **pathogen**s, are easily spread by direct or indirect contact. These pathogens include **virus**es, bacteria, **fungi**, and **parasites**. Some pathogens make toxins that harm the body's organs. Others actually destroy cells. Some can impair the body's natural immune system, and opportunistic organisms set up secondary infections that cause serious illness or death. Once the pathogens have multiplied inside the body, signs of illness may or may not appear. The human body is adept at destroying most pathogens, but the pathogens may still multiply and spread.

The pathogens responsible for some communicable diseases have been known since the mid-1800s, although they have existed for a much longer period of time. European explorers brought highly contagious diseases such as smallpox, measles, typhus and scarlet fever to the New World, to which Native Americans had never been exposed. These new diseases killed 50-90 percent of the native population. Native populations in many areas of the Caribbean were totally eliminated.

In some areas of the world, contaminated **soil** or water incubate the pathogens of communicable diseases, and contact with those agents will cause diseases to spread. In the 1800s, when Robert Koch discovered the anthrax bacillus (*Bacillus anthracis*), **cholera** bacillus (*Vibrio cholerae*), and tubercle bacillus (*Mycobacterium tuberculosis*), his work ushered in a new era of public sanitation by showing how waterborne epidemics, such as cholera and typhoid, could be controlled by water filtration.

Malaria, another communicable disease, was responsible for the decline of many ancient civilizations; for centuries, it devitalized vast populations. With the discoveries in the late 1800s of protozoan malarial parasites in human blood, and the discovery of its carrier, the *Anopheles* mosquito, malaria could be combatted by systematic destruction of the mosquitos and their breeding grounds, by the use of barriers between mosquitos and humans such as window screens and mosquito netting, and by drug therapy to kill the parasites in the human host.

Discoveries of the causes of epidemics and transmissible diseases led to the expansion of the fields of sanitation and public health. Draining of marshes, control of the water supply, widespread vaccinations, and quarantine measures improved human health. But, despite the development of advanced detection techniques and control measures to fight pathogens and their spread, communicable diseases still take their toll on human populations. For example, until the 1980s tuberculosis had been declining in the United States due in large part to the availability of effective antibiotic therapy. However, since 1985, the number of tuberculosis cases has risen steadily due to such factors as the emergence of drug-resistant strains of the tubercle bacillus, the increasing incidence of HIV infection which lowers human resistance to many diseases, poverty, and immigration.

Epidemiologists track communicable diseases throughout the world, and their work has helped to eradicate smallpox, one of the world's most deadly communicable diseases. A successful global vaccination campaign wiped out smallpox in the 1980s, and today, the virus exists only in tightly-controlled laboratories in Moscow and in Atlanta at the **Centers for Disease Control and Prevention**. Scientists are currently debating whether to destroy the viruses or preserve them for study.

Communicable diseases continue to be a major public health problem in developing countries. In the small West African nation of Guinea-Bissau, a cholera epidemic hit in 1990. Epidemiologists traced its outbreak to contaminated shellfish and managed to control the epidemic, but not before it claimed hundreds of lives in that country. Some victims had eaten the contaminated shellfish, others were infected by washing the bodies of cholera victims and then preparing funeral feasts without properly washing their hands. Proper disposal of victims' bodies, coupled with a campaign to encourage proper hygiene, helped stop the epidemic from spreading.

Communicable diseases can be prevented either by eliminating the pathogenic organism from the **environment** (as by killing pathogens or parasites existing in a water supply) or by placing a barrier in the path of its transmission from one organism to another (as by vaccination or by isolating individuals already infected). But identifying and isolating the causal agent and developing weapons to fight it is time consuming, and, as with the **AIDS** virus, thousands of people continue to become infected and many die because educational warnings about ways to avoid infection frequently go unheeded.

AIDS is caused by the human immunodeficiency virus (HIV). Spread by contact with bodily fluids of an HIV-infected person, the virus weakens and eventually destroys the body's immune system. Researchers think the virus originated in monkeys and was first transmitted to humans about 40 years ago. African chimpanzees can be infected with HIV, but don't develop AIDS. This suggests questions that are so far unanswered: Was there a genetic change in the virus, or was there simply more contact between monkeys and people as human populations encroached on their **habitat**?

Some scientists think the AIDS pandemic is just the tip of the iceberg. They worry that new diseases, deadlier than AIDS, will emerge. Virologists point out that viruses, like human populations, constantly change. Rapidly increasing human populations provide fertile breeding grounds for microbes, including viruses and bacteria. Pathogens can literally travel the globe in a matter of hours.

For example, the completion in 1990 of a major road through the Amazon **rain forest** in Brazil led to outbreaks of malaria in the region. In 1985, used tires imported to Texas from eastern Asia transported larvae of the Asian tiger mosquito, a dangerous carrier of serious tropical communicable diseases. **Deforestation** and agricultural changes can unleash epidemics of communicable diseases. Outbreaks of Rift Valley fever followed the construction of the **Aswan High Dam**, most likely because breeding grounds were created for mosquitoes which spread the disease. In Brazil, the introduction of cacao farming coincided with epidemics of Oropouche fever, a disease linked to a biting insect that thrives on discarded cacao hulls.

Continued rapid transportation of humans around the world is likely to accelerate the movement of communicable diseases. Poverty, lack of adequate sanitation and nutrition, and the crowding of people into megacities in the developing countries of the world only exacerbate the situation. The need for study and control of these disease is likely to grow in the future.

[*Linda Rehkopf*]

FURTHER READING

Jaret, P. "The Disease Detectives." *National Geographic* 179 (January 1991): 114-40.

Levine, D. "A Killer Returns." *American Health* (April 1992): 9.

Roberts, L. "Disease and Death in the New World." *Science* 246 (8 December 1989): 1245.

Community ecology

In biological **ecology**, the concept of community has been defined in various ways, each definition offering particular advantages and creating its own set of problems. As the authors of one article in a 1987 British Ecological Society symposium on community ecology noted, "Community ecology may be unique amongst the branches of science in lacking a consensus definition of the entity with which it is principally concerned." Daniel Botkin provides a summary of the major alternatives: an ecological community is "either (1) a set of interacting populations of different species found in an area, meaning that the community is the living part of an **ecosystem**; or (2) all of the species found in a local area, whether or not they actually interact; or (3) all of the species of the same kind found in a local area, as in a 'plant community' or 'animal community'." Peter Taylor describes an ecological community as consisting "of the populations of different species co-inhabiting a site—a lake, the leaf litter layer in a forest, a dung pat, and so on."

A definition of community is significant because so many different parts of the **environment** are investigated under that rubric in ecology: animal, plant, insect, primate, forest, even herbaceous plant communities. Often what is described is a component of a community rather than a *whole* community made up of many different species of plants and animals. Such a whole assemblage in community ecology has no scale, but it does denote a certain level of organization and is different from components of a community, guilds, or taxons.

Community ecology thus focuses on the living part of ecosystems, mostly on communities of interacting populations, however circumscribed. While a community can include species thrown together by locale that do not necessarily interact, community ecology generally emphasizes the wide diversity of species interactions that exist within the area.

Community ecologists investigate interactions under numerous labels and categories, including on-going studies of traditional topics such as predation, competition, trophic exchanges, and others. Borrowing concepts from other disciplines, such as physics, ecologists are also beginning to look closely at the linkages and assemblages that emerge from strong versus weak interactions, or from positive compared to negative interactions. Researchers continue to investigate the relative importance of intra-species and inter-species interactions in terms of their importance to community composition and rates of succession. One recent study, for example, analyzed the importance of interspecific interactions in the structuring of the geographical distribution and abundance of a tropical stream fish community.

The importance of trophic relationships and food web dynamics have always been recognized by ecologists, but a recent article in the journal *Ecology* can still suggest that "a step toward understanding the dynamics of communities is to describe the pathways along which feeding interactions occur." Ecologists are beginning to quantify feeding interactions, and are moving far beyond the old, linear food chain studies to recognize the complex, multiple linkages created by the feeding relationships among large assemblages of species. Current research also recognizes the composite effects that trophic interactions have on the whole community.

One example of the significance of feeding relationships is the continuing role of predation in community ecology. A study might conclude that "Alaskan kelp forests are broadly dependent on sea otter predation for protection against destructive grazing." Another might look at the timing of predation, and conclude that "temporal variability in predation by whelks can have distinctive effects on prey, create distinctive community compositions, and affect successional paths in [an] intertidal community."

Community ecologists still emphasize species interactions that have been prominent through all the decades of field research. Ecologists still claim, for example, that "assumptions about competition lie at the heart of several models of plant community organization." Other articles in the same journal *Ecology* reinforce this emphasis, stating e.g., "that competition is pervasive in the [Chihuahuan desert rodent] community." Another example, in the *Journal of Ecology* indicates that "interspecific competition may limit the growth, branching, survival and berry production by Vaccinium dwarf shrubs in a subarctic plant community."

The degree of pattern or randomness of community structure has long been an issue in community ecology. Natural communities are immensely complex and it is difficult to simplify this complexity down to useable, predictive models. Researchers continue to investigate the extent to which species' interactions can result in a unit organized enough to be considered a coherent community. The mechanics of community assembly depend heavily on invasions, rates of succession, and on changes in the physical environment, as well as a diversity of co-evolutionary patterns.

A debate still continues among community ecologists about the importance of complexity, the role of species diversity and richness in the maintenance of a community. the role of in the maintenance of a community. Community structure patterns might be dependent, in part, on factors as seemingly trivial as seed weight. Accuracy in estimations of the number of species in a given community is difficult, including the large number of microorganisms as yet unidentified and unnamed. Statistical inference can help to dilute this issue somewhat.

Disturbances and perturbations are important factors in the composition and character of communities. One study may focus on the role of fire in tall tussock **grasslands**. Another recent study of old-growth forests in British Columbia concluded that "small-scale natural disturbances involving the death of one to a few trees and creating gaps in the forest canopy are key processes in the...community ecology of many forests." In the recent "landscape view" emerging in ecology, some research indicates that natural communities may persist in patches, as long as they remain interconnected. This underlines again the importance of context in any attempt to understand community ecology.

The most significant source of disturbance and change in natural communities is human activity. Recent studies in community ecology have documented the impact of human removal and then reintroduction of a **keystone species** such as largemouth bass into a lake; have questioned the impact of "importing" an alien seaweed from Japan to expand Brittan's kelp farms; and have indicated that "human fishing pressure has influenced Caribbean **coral reef** community structure by affecting predator-herbivore relationships." Humans can also have positive effects through deliberate attempts to offset destructive impacts. A recent study published in the journal *Nature* described the deliberate modification of pH levels in lakes by adding phosphate **fertilizer**, which reversed **acidification** without "drastically altering the community structure." Such manipulations, modifications, alterations, and disruptions by humans could obviously be expanded into a very long list, but the idea should be clear.

One other type of human impact, however, is receiving a lot of attention: evidence is mounting that climate change is increasingly impacting natural communities. For example, one recent study suggested that "increased warming could change the dominant vegetation of a widespread meadow habitat, changing the competitive relationships between sagebrush and cinquefoil." Another indicated that "regional climatic warming may be altering the species composition of Alaskan arctic tundra" through changes in light, temperature and nutrients that affect community and ecosystem processes.

The information gained in community ecology studies is becoming increasingly important to achieving conservation objectives and establishing guidelines to management of the natural systems on which all humans depend. For example, clearer understanding of linkages established in communities through trophic exchanges can help predict the impacts of concentrations of toxins and pollutants. Better understanding of organismic interactions in a community context can help in comprehending the processes that lead to extinction of species, information critical to attempts to slow the loss of biological diversity. Research into community dynamics can result in better decisions about establishing preserves and refuges, and can create sustainable harvesting strategies.

The professional ecology journals do not publish research on the importance of community for the human species. Yet, few concepts are more significant in human affairs than the role of different kinds of community in establishing ties and linkages among human individuals and between humans and the locales in which they live. Equally important is the lack of community, the looseness of ties and the alienation from locale and from others that stem from failures to establish a sense of community. As in natural communities, interactions among human individuals create community and are in turn shaped by community.

[*Gerald L. Young*]

FURTHER READING

Diamond, J., and T. Case, eds. *Community Ecology*. New York: Harper & Row, 1986.
Putman, R. J. *Community Ecology*. New York: Chapman and Hall, 1994.
Taylor, P. "Community," *Keywords in Evolutionary Biology*, ed. by E.F. Keller and E.A. Lloyd. Cambridge, MA: Harvard University Press, 1992.

Community right-to-know
See **Emergency Planning and Community Right-to-Know Act**

Compaction

Compaction is the mechanical pounding of **soil** and weathered rock into a dense mass with sufficient bearing strength or impermeability to withstand a load. It is primarily used in construction to provide ground suitable for bearing the weight of any given structure. With the advent of huge earthmoving equipment we are now able to literally move mountains. However, such disturbances loosen and expand the soil. Thus soil must be compacted to provide an adequate breathing surface after it has been disturbed. Inadequate compaction during construction results in design failure or reduced service life of a structure. Compaction, however, is detrimental to crop production because it makes root growth and movement difficult, and deprives the soil of access to life-sustaining oxygen.

With proper compaction we can build enduring roadways, airports, **dams**, building foundation pads, or clay liners for secure **landfill**s. Because enormous volumes of ground material are involved, it is far less expensive to use on-site or nearby resources wherever feasible. Proper engineering can overcome material deficiencies in most cases, if rigid quality control is maintained.

Successful compaction requires a combination of proper moisture conditioning, the right placement of material, and sufficient pounding with proper equipment. Moisture is important because dry materials seem very hard, but they may settle or become permeable when wet. Because of all the variables involved in the compaction process, standardized laboratory and field testing is essential.

The American Society of State Highway Transportation Officials (ASHTO) and the American Society of Testing Materials (ASTM) have developed specific test standards. The laboratory test involves pounding a representative sample with a drop-hammer in a cylindrical mold. Four uniform samples are tested, varying only in moisture content.

The sample is trimmed and weighed, and portions oven-dried to determine moisture content.

The results are then graphed. The resultant curve normally has the shape of an open hairpin, with the high point representing the maximum density at the optimum moisture content for the compactive effort used. This curve reflects the fact that dry soils resist compaction, and overly-moistened soils allow the mechanical energy to dissipate. Field densities must normally meet 95 percent or higher of this lab result.

Because soils are notoriously diverse, several different "curves" may be needed; varied materials require the field engineer to exercise considerable judgment to determine the proper standard. Thus the field engineer and the earth-moving crew must work closely together to establish the procedures for obtaining the required densities.

In the past, density testing has required laboriously digging a hole, and comparing the volume with the weight of the material removed. Nuclear density gages have greatly accelerated this process and allow much more frequent testing if needed or desired. To take a reading, a stake is driven into the ground to form a hole into which a sealed nuclear probe can be lowered.

It is much easier to properly compact materials during construction than to try to make corrections later. A well-compacted, properly tested structure is an investment in the future, well worth the time and effort expended. *See also* Arable land; Soil compaction

[*Nathan H. Meleen*]

FURTHER READING

American Society for Testing & Materials. *Compaction of Soils.* ASTM Special Technical Publication, No. 377. Philadelphia: ASTM, 1965.

Daniel, D. P. "Summary Review of Construction Quality Control for Compacted Soil Liners." In *Waste Containment Systems: Construction, Regulation, and Performance*, edited by R. Bonaparte. New York: American Society of Civil Engineers, 1990.

Comparative risk

Initiated by the United States **Environmental Protection Agency**'s (EPA) federal Comparative Risk Project in 1986, comparative risk projects by January 1997 had been completed in 24 states and localities, with other projects underway. Furthermore, today the priority setting method had gained national attention as many members of Congress, federal professionals, and policy experts agree that environmental protection and public health agencies should, when setting priorities, consider the relative degree of risk their actions will reduce. However, while proponents tout comparative risk as a rational approach to making decisions about priorities, critics among national and grassroots environmental organizations believe that comparative risk ranking can be a "hard" technocratic approach that ignores non-risk factors in decision making, is "undemocratic," and is contrary to pollution prevention or the will of the people.

In the past, risk has not been factored into environmental priority setting and, as remarked by **William Ruckelshaus**, who twice served as EPA administrator, it "was hardly mentioned in the early years of EPA, and it does not have an important place in the Clean Air or Clean Water Acts passed in that period." But, building on Ruckelshaus's groundwork in comparative risk, EPA Administrator Lee Thomas helped thrust the concept onto the national agenda in 1986 when he asked 75 agency professionals to examine 31 environmental problems in the areas of **cancer**, non-cancer, and ecological risks as well as welfare effects (visibility impairment, damage to statuary from **acid rain**, etc.). In their 1987 report to Thomas, *Unfinished Business: A Comparative Assessment of Environmental Problems*, the professionals reported that, "Overall, EPA's priorities appear more closely aligned with public opinion than with our estimated risks." For instance, the EPA professionals regarded indoor **air pollution** and global warming as relatively high risks and contaminated hazardous waste sites as relatively low risk problems, while opinion polls showed that the public had an opposite ranking. In releasing the report, Thomas noted that EPA has finite resources and therefore must choose its priorities carefully "so that we apply those resources as effectively as possible" in reducing risks. The EPA report became the first significant study suggesting that national environmental priorities were inconsistent with the experts' sense of the most serious environmental problems, and instead the nation's priorities were guided by public perceptions of risk.

Concerns about the growing number of environmental regulations and problems demanding attention, coupled with the decline in resources to spend on these problems, kept up the pressure for EPA, states, and local governments to find a rational approach for deciding where to target finite resources. The publication of a report in 1991, *Environmental Investments: The Cost of a Clean Environment*, reinforced these concerns. That report was a first estimation of the costs that industries and municipalities must incur through compliance with federal pollution control programs. In 1991, costs were $115 billion a year—2.1% of the Gross National Product (GNP)—but were projected to rise to $185 billion or 2.8% of the GNP by the year 2000.

In late 1991, Senator Daniel Patrick Moynihan (D-N.Y.) introduced a bill (S.2132) that would have required EPA to seek the advice of experts in ranking relative risks and to use that information in managing its available resources to protect society from the greatest risks. Moynihan's bill, and its successor in the 103rd Congress, became important elements of the debate over whether risk-based "rational" priority setting should be required to ensure more efficient risk reduction.

Even before the 1991 EPA report on the rising costs of environmental protection, EPA Administrator **William K. Reilly** had taken up comparative risk as a central theme of his administration and had asked the agency's Science Advisory Board to review the report issued by the 75 agency professionals. The board's response, a 1990 report called *Reducing Risk: Setting Priorities And Strategies For Environmental*

Protection, also recommended that EPA and other government agencies "assess the range of environmental problems of concern and then target protective efforts at problems that seem to be the most serious." Far and away the greatest expenditures of EPA resources were directed at the agency's construction grants program for publicly owned **wastewater** treatment plants and the cleanup of abandoned Superfund sites—for instance, a full 70% of the agency's fiscal year 1990 budget of $6 billion went to these programs—even though other problems were deemed more serious from a scientific perspective. The science advisors also suggested that EPA should give more attention to the relatively neglected job of protecting **ecosystem**s, which faced high risks from **habitat** alteration, loss of **biodiversity**, global climate change, and **ozone layer depletion**.

Reducing Risk, and the general topic of whether "Worst Things First" should be the touchstone of environmental priority setting, was debated at a November 1992 meeting in Annapolis, Maryland, at which critics challenged its "quasi-scientific" claims and offered competing priority setting approaches, including a strategy that would make preventing pollution the fundamental criterion for environmental policy decisions founded on the public's decision that pollution is undesirable. In the critics' view, comparative risk analysis presumes that some pollution and its risk is acceptable.

Skepticism notwithstanding, EPA chose to foster development of the method. As part of its endorsement of comparative risk assessment as an important priority setting tool, EPA promoted a series of comparative risk projects in several of its regions—Region 1, New England; Region 3, the Mid-Atlantic states; and Region 10, the Pacific Northwest—and in three pilot states: Washington, Colorado, and Pennsylvania. Later, Vermont, California, Utah, Michigan, and other states joined in. Sub-state entities also developed projects, including Columbus, Ohio; Atlanta, Georgia; Elizabeth River, Virginia; Houston, Texas; and Wisconsin tribes.

Typically, comparative risk projects follow six basic steps. First, they define and analyze the risks posed by environmental problems facing the jurisdiction, usually working from a list of problems. Second, they rank the problems according to the relative severity of each, using technical information and criteria to grade the negative impacts of individual problems on health, ecosystems, or quality of life. Third, they select priorities for special attention and set goals for reducing risks posed by the problem. Fourth, they propose, analyze, and compare strategies for achieving the goals set in step three. Fifth, they implement strategies having the greatest risk-reduction promise. And, sixth, they monitor results produced by the strategies and adjust jurisdictional policies or budgets based on those results. These steps are carried out through committees composed of state or local officials, industry representatives, environmentalists, and citizens. The projects all seek to broadly incorporate public values—not merely technical scientific information—in assessing and ranking risks.

Among the more widely cited state comparative risk projects is Washington Environment 2010, which, more than any other state project, influenced legislation and state policy. It was initiated in 1988 by Washington's Department of Ecology Director Christine Gregoire and included technical committees with members from 19 state agencies and a steering committee composed of senior managers or heads of those agencies. In addition, it had a public advisory committee composed of 34 prominent legislators, representatives, and important interest groups. Resulting from this project was a ranking of 23 threats to the environment within five priority levels. Ambient air pollution, point-source discharges of pollution to water, and polluted **runoff** ranked as the top priorities, and non-ionizing radiation, materials storage in tanks, and litter ranked as the lowest priorities. Based on the project, and a statewide effort to solicit public responses that produced some 300 risk-reduction options, Washington's legislature in 1991 adopted several new environmental laws dealing with clean air, transportation demand, water conservation, recycling, growth management, and the state's energy policy. The Department of Ecology redirected $6.8 million of its budget from lower to higher risk priorities. However, in 1993 Gregoire's successor reorganized the department, dismantling an Environment 2010 planning staff that had been established and, with it, the state's institutional memory of the comparative risk project. Washington's experience in this regard, and similar experiences in other states, have made some proponents of comparative risk assessment question how deeply and lastingly its effects will be felt in environmental programs.

Despite such setbacks, the comparative risk concept has continued to find a significant place in governmental discussions of environmental policy. In 1993, the White House of Science and Technology Policy and the Office of Management and Budget invited comparative risk analysis experts to meet with federal government officials to explore how the approach could be used by federal agencies to establish broad priorities more systematically. That effort resulted in a 1996 report, *Comparing Environmental Risks: Tools for Setting Government Priorities*, that proposed a basic framework for using the method in federal agencies. Furthermore, during the 104th Congress, comparative risk analysis was one of numerous risk-related reforms that were included in the Republican Contract With America and its agenda of reducing regulatory burdens through a downsizing of government, the most far-reaching attempt to impose a "rational" risk-based priority setting system on federal agencies.

While the future of comparative risk analysis as a basis for establishing environmental priorities remains uncertain, federal, state, and local interest remains strong. Today, most practitioners and proponents of the approach recognize that comparative risk alone will not suffice to establish priorities. Public values, hard to quantify benefits, and other non-scientific elements that must be weighed in decisions about priorities have a clearly recognized role. That conclusion has been reinforced in all the state and local projects. Some recent studies suggest that the future progress of comparative risk analysis requires more research on how to better inform diverse parts of the affected public throughout the process of setting environmental priorities. Even though federal legislation that would mandate comparative risk analysis as a basis for selecting priorities may never pass, the risk-based approach enunciated in 1987 has emerged today as a central piece of environmental policy and is explicitly discussed in EPA's draft *Environmental Goals for America With Milestones for 2005*, the latest federal effort to clarify and organize environmental priorities.

[*David Clarke*]

FURTHER READING

Davies, J. C., ed. *Comparing Environmental Risks: Tools for Setting Government Priorities.* Washington, D.C.: Resources for the Future, 1996.

Finkel, A. M., and D. Golding, eds. *Worst Things First? The Debate over Risk-Based National Environmental Priorities.* Washington, D.C.: Resources for the Future, 1994.

U. S. Environmental Protection Agency. Office of Policy, Planning, and Evaluation. *Unfinished Business: A Comparative Assessment of Environmental Problems.* Washington, D.C.: GPO, 1987.

U. S. Environmental Protection Agency. Science Advisory Board. *Reducing Risk: Setting Priorities and Strategies for Environmental Protection.* Washington, D.C.: GOP, 1990.

Competition

Competition is the interaction between two organisms when both are trying to gain access to the same limited resource. When both organisms are members of the same **species**, such interaction is said to be "intraspecific competition." When the organisms are from different species, the interaction is "interspecific competition."

Intraspecific competition arises because two members of the same species have nearly identical needs for food, water, sunlight, nesting space, and other aspects of the **environment**. As long as these resources are available in abundance, every member of the community can survive without competition. When those resources are in limited supply, however, competition is inevitable. For example, a single nesting pair of bald eagles requires a minimum of 620 acres (250 ha) that they can claim as their own territory. If two pairs of eagles try to survive on 620 acres, competition will develop, and the stronger or more aggressive pair will drive out the other pair.

Intraspecific competition is also a factor in controlling plant growth. When a mature plant drops seeds, the seedlings that develop are in competition with the parent plant for water, sunlight, and other resources. When abundant space is available and the size of the community is small, a relatively large number of seedlings can survive and grow. When population density increases, competition becomes more severe and more seedlings die off.

Competition becomes an important limiting factor, therefore, as the size of a community grows. Those individuals in the community that are better adapted to gain food, water, nesting space, or some other limited resource are more likely to survive and reproduce. Intraspecific competition is thus an important factor in natural selection.

Interspecific competition occurs when members of two different species compete for the same limited resource(s).

For example, two species of birds might both prefer the same type of insect as a food source and will be forced to compete for it if it is in limited supply.

Laboratory studies show that interspecific competition can result in the **extinction** of the species less well adapted for a particular resource. However, this result is seldom, if ever, observed in nature, at least among animals. The reason is that individuals can adapt to take advantage of slight differences in resource supplies. In the **Galapagos Islands**, for example, thirteen similar species of finches have evolved from a single parent species. Each species has adapted to take advantage of some particular **niche** in the environment. As similar as they are, the finches do not compete with each other to any specific extent.

Interspecific competition among plants is a different matter. Since plants are unable to move on their own, they are less able to take advantage of subtle differences in an environment. Situations in which one species of plant takes over an area, causing the extinction of competitors, are well known.

One mechanism that plants use in this battle with each other is the release of toxic **chemicals**, known as allelochemicals. These chemicals suppress the growth of plants in other—and, sometimes, the same—species. Naturally occurring antibiotics are examples of such allelochemicals. *See also* Evolution

[*David E. Newton*]

FURTHER READING

Moran, J. M., M. D. Morgan, and J. H. Wiersma. *Environmental Science.* Dubuque, IA: William C. Brown, 1993.

Composting

Composting is a fermentation process, the break down of organic material aided by an array of microorganisms, earthworms, and other insects in the presence of air and moisture. This process yields compost (residual organic material often referred to as **humus**), ammonia, **carbon dioxide**, sulphur compounds, volatile organic acids, water vapor, and heat. Typically, the amount of compost produced is 40-60 percent of the volume of the original waste.

For the numerous organisms that contribute to the composting process to grow and function, they must have access to and synthesize components such as **carbon, nitrogen**, oxygen, **hydrogen**, inorganic salts, sulphur, **phosphorus**, and trace amounts of micronutrients. The key to initiating and maintaining the composting process is a carbon-to-nitrogen (C:N) ratio between 25:1 and 30:1. When **C:N ratio** is in excess of 30:1, the **decomposition** process is suppressed due to inadequate nitrogen limiting the evolution of bacteria essential to break the strong carbon bonds. A C:N ratio of less than 25.1 will produce rapid localized decomposition with excess nitrogen given off as ammonia, which is a source of offensive odors.

A man adds moisture to mushroom compost.

Attaining such a balance of ratio and range is possible because all organic material has a fixed C:N ratio in its tissue. For example, **food waste** has a C:N ratio of 15:1, sewage **sludge** has a C:N ratio of 16:1, grass clippings have a C:N ratio of 19:1, leaves have a C:N ratio of 60:1, paper has a C:N ratio of 200:1, and wood has a C:N ratio of 700:1. When these (and other) materials are mixed in the right proportions, they provide optimum C:N ratios for composting. Typically, nitrogen is the limiting component that is encountered in waste materials and, when insufficient nitrogen is present, the composting mixture can be augmented with agricultural **fertilizer**s, such as urea or ammonia nitrate.

In addition to **nutrient**s, the efficiency of the composting process depends on the organic material's size and surface characteristics. Small particles provide multi-faceted surfaces for microbial action. Size also influences porosity (crevices and cracks which can hold water) and permeability (circulation or movement of gases and moisture).

Moisture (water) is an essential element in the biological degradation process. A moisture level of 55-60 percent by weight is required for optimal microbial, nutrient, and air circulation. Below 50 percent moisture, the nutrients to sustain microbial activity become limited; above 70 percent moisture, air circulation is inhibited.

Air circulation controls the class of microorganisms that will predominate in the composting process: air-breathing microorganisms are collectively termed **aerobic**, while microorganisms that exist in the absence of air are called **anaerobic**. When anaerobic microorganisms prevail, the composting process is slow, and unpleasant-smelling ammonia or hydrogen sulfide is frequently generated. Aerobic microorganisms will quickly decompose organic material into its principal components of carbon dioxide, heat and water.

The role of acidity and alkalinity in the composting process depends upon the source of organic material and the predominant microorganisms. Anaerobic microorganisms generate acidic conditions which can be neutralized with the addition of lime. However, such adjustments must be done carefully or nitrogen imbalance will occur that can further inhibit biological activity and produce ammonia gas, with its associated unpleasant odor. Organic material with a balanced C:N ratio will initially produce acidic conditions, 6.0 on the **pH** scale. However, at the end of the process cycle, mature compost is alkaline, with a pH reading greater than 7.0 and less than 8.0.

The regulation and measurement of temperature is fundamental to achieving satisfactory processing of organic materials. However, the effect of ambient or surface temperatures on the process is limited to periods of intense cold when biological growth is dormant. Expeditious processing and reduction of **herbicide**s, **pathogen**s, and **pesticide**s is achieved when internal temperatures in the compost pile are maintained 120-140°F (55-60°C). If the internal temperature is allowed to reach or exceed 150°F (65°C), biological activity is inhibited due to heat stress. As the nutrient content is depleted, the internal temperature decreases to 85°F (30°C) or less—one criteria for defining mature or stabilized compost.

Mature or stabilized compost has physical, chemical, and biological properties which offer a variety of attributes when applied to a host **soil**. For example, adding compost to barren or disturbed soils provides organic and microbial resources. The addition of compost to clay soils enhances the movement of air and moisture. The water retention capacity of sandy soil is enhanced by the addition of compost and **erosion** also is reduced. Soils improved by the addition of compost also display other characteristics such as enhanced retention and exchange of nutrients, improved seed germination, and better plant root penetration. Compost, however, has insufficient nitrogen, phosphorous, and potassium content to qualify as a fertilizer. The ultimate *application* or *disposition* of compost depends upon its quality, which is a function of the type of organic material and the method(s) employed to enhance or control processing.

Compost processing can be as simple as a plastic garbage bag filled with a mixture of plant waste that has had a couple of ounces of fertilizer, some lime, and sufficient water added to make the material moist. The bag is then sealed and set aside for about 12 months. Faster processing can be achieved with the use of a 55 gallon (208 liter) drum into which half-inch holes have been drilled for air circulation. Filled with the same mixture as the garbage bag and rotated at regular intervals, this method will produce compost in two to three months. A multi-compartmentalized container is faster and increases the diversity of materials which can be processed. However, including such items as fruit and vegetable scraps, meat and dairy products, cardboard cartons, and fabrics must be undertaken with caution because they attract and breed vermin.

Such methods are designed for individual use, especially by those who can no longer dispose of garden waste with their household waste. Similarly, commercial and government institutions employ natural (low), medium, and advanced technical composting methods, depending on their motivation, i.e., diminishing **landfill** capacity, availability of fiscal resources, and commitment to **recycling**. The simplest composting method currently employed by industry and municipalities entails dumping **organic waste** on a piece of land graded (sloped) to permit precipitation and leachate (excess moisture and organics from composting) to collect in a retention pond. The pond also serves as a source of moisture for the compost process and as a system where **photosynthesis** can oxidize the leachate. The organic material is placed in piles called *windrows* (a ridge pile with a half-cone at each end). The dimensions of a windrow are typically 10-12 feet (3-3.7 m) wide at the base and about 6 feet (1.8 m) high at the top of the ridge. The length is site specific. Windrows are constructed using a front-end loader. A mature compost will be available in 12-24 months, depending on various factors including the care with which the organic material was blended to obtain optimum C:N ratio; the supplementation of the material with additional nutrients; the frequency of **aeration** (mixing and turning); and the moisture content maintained.

Using the same site layout, the next step in mechanization is the use of windrow turners. These turners can be simple aeration machines or machines with the added ability to shred material into smaller particles, while injecting supplemental moisture and/or nutrients. Optimizing the capabilities of such equipment requires close attention to temperature variation within the windrows. Typically, the operator will use a temperature probe to determine when the temperature falls in the range of 100°F (37-38°C). The equipment will then fold the outer surface of the windrow inward, replenishing air and moisture, and mixing in unconsumed or supplemental nutrients. This promotes further decomposition, which is identified by a gradual rise in temperature. Sequential turning and mixing will continue until temperatures are uniformly diminished to levels below 85°F (30°C). This method produces a mature compost in four to eight months.

Two more technologically advanced composting methods are the *in-vessel system* and the *forced-air system*. Both are capable of processing the bulk of all solid and liquid municipal wastes. However, such flexibility imposes substantial capital, technical, and operational requirements. In forced air processing, organic material is placed on top of a series of perforated pipes attached to fans which can either blow air into, or draw air through the pile to control its temperature, oxygen, and carbon dioxide needs. This system is popular for its ability to process materials high in moisture and/or nitrogen content, such as **yard waste**s. Time to produce a mature compost is measured in days, depending on the class of organic material processed. During in-vessel processing, organic material is continuously fed into an inclined rotating cylinder, where the temperature, moisture, and nutrient air and gas levels are closely controlled to achieve degradation within 24-72 hours. The composted material is then screened to remove foreign or inert materials such as glass, **plastics**, and metals and is allowed to mature for 21 days. *See also* Organic gardening and farming

[*George M. Fell*]

FURTHER READING

Appelhof, M. *Worms Eat My Garbage.* Kalamazoo, MI: Flower Press, 1982.

The Biocycle Guide to Composting Municipal Wastes. Emmaus, PA: JG Press, 1989.

The Biocycle Guide to the Art and Science of Composting. Emmaus, PA: JG Press, 1991.

The Biocycle Guide to Yard Waste Composting. Emmaus, PA: JG Press, 1989.

Kovacic, D. A., et al. "Compost: Brown Gold or Toxic Trouble?" *Environmental Science and Technology* 26 (January 1992): 38-41.

Lecard, M. "Urban Decay." *Sierra* 76 (September-October 1991): 27-8.

The Rodale Book of Composting. Emmaus, PA: Rodale Press, 1992.

Composting toilets
See **Toilets**

Comprehensive Environmental Response, Compensation, and Liability Act (CERCLA)

In response to **hazardous waste** disasters such as **Love Canal, New York**, in the 1970s, Congress passed the Comprehensive Environmental Response, Compensation, and Liability Act (CERCLA), better known as Superfund, in 1980. The law created a fund of $1.6 billion to be used to clean up hazardous waste sites and hazardous waste spills for a period of five years. The primary source of support for the fund came from a tax on chemical feedstock producers; general revenues supplied the rest of the money needed. CERCLA is different from most **environmental law**s because it deals with past problems rather than trying to prevent future **pollution**, and because the **Environmental Protection Agency (EPA)**, in addition to acting as a regulatory agency, must clean up sites itself.

Throughout the decade before the creation of Superfund, the public began to focus increasing attention on hazardous wastes. During this period, an increased number of cases involving such wastes contaminating drinking water, streams, rivers, and even homes were reported. Citizens were enraged by dangers posed by leaking **landfill**s, illegal dumping of hazardous wastes along roads or in vacant lots, and explosions and fires at some facilities.

A strong catalyst for hazardous waste regulation was the Love Canal episode near Niagara Falls, New York. In the late 1970s, chemical wastes from an abandoned dump were discovered in the basements of some homes. Studies found significant health effects, including miscarriages and low-weight newborns. Residents worried about increased **cancer** and birth defect rates. In the federal emergency declaration, a school and 200 houses were condemned. The combination of public concern and media coverage, together with EPA interest, brought national attention to this issue.

Debate soon began over proper government response to these problems. Industrial interests argued that a company should not be liable for cleaning up past hazardous waste dumps if it had not violated any law in disposing of the wastes. The industry argued that general taxes, not industry-specific taxes, should be used for the clean-up, and it sought to limit the legal liability of manufacturers in regard to the health effects of their hazardous wastes. Industrial companies also pushed for one national regulatory program, rather than a national program and several state programs to complicate the situation.

When Congress began debating a Superfund program in 1979, EPA officials argued that industry must pay the bulk of the clean-up costs. They based this argument on the philosophy that the polluter should pay, and also the pragmatic reasoning that Congress could not be relied on to continue appropriating the funds needed for such an expensive and lengthy program. The Senate focused on a comprehensive bill that included provisions for liability and victims' compensation, but these were dropped in order to secure passage of the program through the House. The act was signed by President Carter in December 1980.

Under the law, the EPA determines the most dangerous hazardous waste sites, based on characteristics like toxicity of wastes and risk of human exposure, and places them on the **National Priorities List** (NPL), which determines priorities for EPA efforts. The EPA has the authority to either force those responsible for the site to clean it up, or clean up the site itself with the Superfund money and then seek to have the fund reimbursed through court action against the responsible parties. If more than one company had dumped wastes at a site, the agency is able to hold one party responsible for all clean-up costs. It is then up to that party to recover its costs from the other responsible parties. If those identified as responsible by the EPA deny their responsibility in court and lose, they are liable for treble damages. Removal actions, emergency clean-ups, or actions costing less than $2 million and lasting less than a year, can be undertaken by the EPA for any site. For federal hazardous waste sites, the clean-up must be paid for through the appropriation process rather than through Superfund. States are required to contribute 10 to 50 percent of the cost of clean-ups within their boundaries; they are also responsible for all operation and maintenance costs once the job is finished. The EPA can also delegate lead clean-up authority to the states.

Major amendments to CERCLA were passed in 1986. As the scope of the problem grew, Congress re-authorized the Superfund through 1991 and increased its size to $8.5 billion. Plans indicated that the enlarged Superfund would be financed by taxes on **petroleum**, feedstock **chemicals**, corporate income, general revenue, interest from money in the fund, and money recovered from companies responsible for earlier clean-ups. The amendments required several areas of compliance: 1) The clean-ups must meet the applicable state and federal environmental standards; 2) The EPA must begin clean-up on at least 375 sites by 1991; 3) Negotiated settlements for clean-ups are preferred to court litigation; 4) Emergency procedures and community right-to-know standards, are required in areas with hazardous waste facilities (largely in response to the **Bhopal, India** toxic gas disaster); and 5) Federal agencies must comply with Superfund Amendments and begin the clean-up of federal facilities and sites. The 1991 **Superfund Amendments and Reauthorization Act** authorized a four-year extension of the taxes that financed Superfund, but the law was not changed significantly.

As of August 1990, 33,000 sites were listed as being potentially hazardous, 1,082 sites were on the NPL, and over 100 sites were proposed by the EPA to be added to the list. Of the sites that required preliminary EPA investigation, over 90 percent had been examined, but actual clean-up has been rather slow. In mid-1990, clean-up had been completed at only fifty-four NPL sites. However, funding had been approved for planning studies at over 1,000 sites, design work at over 400 sites, and remedial work at over 280 sites. Removal actions by the EPA or responsible parties had taken place at over 1,500 sites, most of which were not on the NPL.

Studies of Superfund implementation have been quite critical. Reports by Congressional committees, the General Accounting Office, and the Office of Technology Assessment (OTA) concluded that the EPA relied on temporary rather than permanent treatment methods, took too long to clean up sites because of poor management, too frequently opted to use the Superfund for clean-ups rather than requiring responsible parties to pay, and often lacked the expertise to oversee Superfund clean-up operations. In reality, early implementation efforts of Superfund were hampered by uncommitted EPA officials, lack of financial and staff resources, poor government coordination of policy objective, and by the complexity of identifying and exacting payment from responsible parties.

Another problem had been the amount of expensive and time-consuming litigation involved in the act. In some cases litigation costs to determine responsible parties and recover clean-up costs has exceeded the cost of clean-up itself. Between 1986 and 1988, the EPA only recovered 7 percent of what it spent on clean-up from private parties.

Implementation of CERCLA has also been marked by charges of corruption and political manipulation. Rita Lavelle, who was in charge of the Superfund program at EPA, resigned in 1983 amid charges that she was giving unduly favorable treatment to industry. She was later convicted on perjury charges. Also in 1983, EPA Administrator Anne Gorsuch Burford resigned, largely in response to the difficulties of Superfund implementation.

Thus far, CERCLA has proved to be a more complicated, costly, and time-consuming process than originally envisioned. A 1988 Congressional report estimated that between $16.7 and $23.8 billion of federal money would be needed to clean up the less than 1,000 sites then on the NPL. A 1989 OTA report estimated the cost of the program to be $500 billion in the long run, with as many as 10,000 sites eventually being placed on the NPL. *See also* Hazardous material; Hazardous Materials Transportation Act; Hazardous Substances Act; Hazardous waste site remediation; Hazardous waste siting; Toxic substances

[*Christopher McGrory Klyza*]

FURTHER READING

Davis, C. E. *The Politics of Hazardous Waste.* New York: Prentice Hall, 1993.

Dower, R. C. "Hazardous Wastes." In *Public Policies for Environmental Protection*, edited by P. R. Portney. Washington, DC: Resources for the Future, 1990.

Hays, S. P. *Beauty, Health, and Permanence: Environmental Politics in the United States, 1955-1985.* New York: Cambridge University Press, 1990.

Mazmanian, D., and D. Morell. *Beyond Superfailure: America's Toxics Policy for the 1990s.* Boulder, CO: Westview Press, 1992.

Condensation nuclei

When air is cooled below its **dew point**, the water vapor it contains tends to condense as droplets of water or tiny ice crystals. Condensation may not occur, however, in the absence of tiny particles on which the water or ice can form. These particles are known as condensation nuclei. The most common types of condensation nuclei are crystals of salt, **particulate** matter formed by the combustion of **fossil**

fuels, and dust blown up from the Earth's surface. In the process of cloud-seeding, scientists add tiny crystals of dry ice or silver iodide as condensation nuclei to the **atmosphere** to promote cloud formation and precipitation.

Condor
See **California condor**

Congenital malformations
See **Birth defects**

Coniferous forest

Coniferous forests contain trees with cones and generally evergreen needle or scale-shaped leaves. Important genera in the northern hemisphere include pines (*Pinus*), spruces (*Picea*), firs (*Abies*), redwoods (*Sequoia*), Douglas firs (*Pseudotsuga*), and larches (*Larix*). Different genera dominate the conifer forests of the southern hemisphere. Conifer forests occupy regions with cool-moist to very cold winters and cool to hot summers. Many conifer forests originated as plantations of **species** from other continents. Among conifer formations in North America are the slow-growing circumpolar **taiga** (boreal), the subalpine-montane, the southern pine, and the Pacific Coast **temperate rain forest**. Softwoods, another name for conifers, are used for lumber, panels, and paper.

Conservation

The philosophy or policy that **natural resources** should be used cautiously and rationally so that they will remain available for **future generations**. Widespread and organized conservation movements, dedicated to preventing uncontrolled and irresponsible exploitation of forests, lands, **wildlife**, and **water resources**, first developed in the United States in the last decades of the nineteenth century. This was a time at which accelerating settlement and resource depletion made conservationist policies appealing both to a large portion of the public and to government leaders. Since then, international conservationist efforts, including work of the United Nations, have been responsible for monitoring natural resource use, setting up nature preserves, and controlling environmental destruction on both public and private lands around the world.

The name most often associated with the United States' early conservation movement is that of **Gifford Pinchot**, the first head of the U.S. **Forest Service**. A populist who fervently believed that the best use of **nature** was to improve the life of the common citizen, Pinchot brought scientific management methods to the Forest Service. He also brought a strongly utilitarian philosophy, which continues to prevail in the Forest Service. Beginning as an advisor to **Theodore Roosevelt**, himself an ardent conservationist, Pinchot had extensive influence in Washington and helped to steer conservation policies from the turn of the century to the 1940s. Pinchot had a number of important predecessors, however, in the development of American conservation. Among these was **George Perkins Marsh**, a Vermont forester and geographer whose 1864 publication, *Man and Nature*, is widely held as the wellspring of American environmental thought. Also influential was the work of **John Wesley Powell**, Clarence King, and other explorers and surveyors who, after the Civil War, set out across the continent to assess and catalog the country's physical and biological resources and their potential for development and settlement.

Conservation, as conceived by Pinchot, Powell, and Roosevelt was about using, not setting aside, natural resources. In their emphasis on wise resource use, these early conservationists were philosophically divided from the early preservationists, who argued that parts of the American wilderness should be preserved for their aesthetic value and for the survival of wildlife, not simply as a storehouse of useful commodities. Preservationists, led by the eloquent writer and champion of Yosemite Valley, **John Muir**, bitterly opposed the idea that the best vision for the nation's forests was that of an agricultural crop, developed to produce only useful **species** and products. Pinchot, however, insisted that "The object of [conservationist] forest policy is not to preserve the forests because they are beautiful...or because they are refuges for the wild creatures of the wilderness...but the making of prosperous homes...Every other consideration is secondary." Because of its more moderate and politically palatable stance, conservation became, by the turn of the century, the more popular position. By 1905 conservation had become a blanket term for nearly all defense of the **environment**; the earlier distinction was lost until it began to re-emerge in the 1960s as "environmentalists" began once again to object to conservation's anthropocentric (human-centered) emphasis. More recently deep ecologists and bioregionalists have likewise departed from mainstream conservation, arguing that other species have intrinsic rights to exist outside of human interests.

Several factors led conservationist ideas to develop and spread when they did. By the end of the nineteenth century European settlement had reached across the entire North American continent. The census of 1890 declared the American frontier closed, a blow to the American myth of the virgin continent. Even more important, loggers, miners, settlers, and livestock herders were laying waste to the nation's forests, grasslands, and mountains from New York to California. The accelerating, and often highly wasteful, commercial exploitation of natural resources went almost completely unchecked as political corruption and the economic power of timber and lumber barons made regulation impossible. At the same time, the disappearance of American wildlife was starkly obvious. Within a generation the legendary flocks of **passenger pigeon**s disappeared entirely, many of them shot for pig feed while they roosted. Millions of **bison** were slaughtered by market hunters for their skins and tongues or by sportsmen shooting from passing trains. Natural land-

marks were equally threatened—Niagara Falls nearly lost its water to hydropower development, and California's Sequoia groves and Yosemite Valley were threatened by logging and grazing.

At the same time, post-Civil War scientific surveys were crossing the continent, identifying wildlife and forest resources. As a consequence of this data gathering, evidence became available to document the depletion of the continent's resources, which had long been assumed inexhaustible. Travellers and writers, including John Muir, Theodore Roosevelt, and Gifford Pinchot, had the opportunity to witness the alarming destruction and to raise public awareness and concern. Meanwhile an increasing proportion of the population had come to live in cities. These urbanites worked in occupations not directly dependent upon resource exploitation, and they were sympathetic to the idea of preserving **public land**s for recreational interests. From the beginning this urban population provided much of the support for the conservation movement.

As a scientific, humanistic, and progressive policy, conservation has led to a great variety of projects. The development of a professionally trained forest service to maintain **national forest**s has limited the uncontrolled "tree mining" practiced by logging and railroad companies of the nineteenth century. Conservation-minded presidents and administrators have set aside millions of acres public land for national forests, parks, and other uses for the benefit of the public. A corps of professionally trained game managers and wildlife managers has developed to maintain game birds, fish, and mammals for public **recreation** on federal lands. (For much of its history, federal game conservation has involved extensive predator elimination programs, however several decades of protest have led to more ecological approaches to game management in recent decades.) During the administration of Franklin D. Roosevelt, conservation projects included such economic development projects as the **Tennessee Valley Authority** (TVA), which dammed the Tennessee River for flood control and electricity generation. The Civilian Conservation Corps developed roads, built structures, and worked on **erosion** control projects for the public good. During this time the **Soil Conservation Service** was also set up to advise farmers in maintaining and developing their farmland.

At the same time, voluntary citizen conservation organizations have done extensive work to develop and maintain natural resources. The **Izaak Walton League**, **Ducks Unlimited**, and scores of local gun clubs and fishing groups have set up game sanctuaries, preserved **wetlands**, campaigned to control **water pollution**, and released young game birds and fish. Other organizations with less directly utilitarian objectives also worked in the name of conservation: the **National Audubon Society**, the **Sierra Club**, the **Wilderness Society**, the **Nature Conservancy**, and many other groups formed between 1895 and 1955 for the purpose of collective work and lobbying in defense of nature and wildlife.

An important aspect of conservation's growth has been the development of professional schools of forestry, game management, and wildlife management. When Gifford Pinchot began to study forestry, Yale had only meager resources and he gained the better part of his education at a French school of forest management in Nancy, France. Several decades later the Yale School of Forestry (financed largely by the wealthy Pinchot family) was able to produce such well-trained professionals as **Aldo Leopold**, who went on to develop the United States' first professional school of game management at the University of Wisconsin.

From the beginning, American conservation ideas, informed by the science of **ecology** and the practice of resource management on public lands, spread to other countries and regions. It is in recent decades, however, that the rhetoric of conservation has taken a prominent role in international development and affairs. The most visible international conservation organizations today is the **United Nations Environment Program (UNEP)**, the Food and Agriculture Organization of the United Nations (FAO), and the **World Wildlife Fund**. In 1980 the **International Union for the Conservation of Nature and Natural Resources (IUCN)** published a document entitled the *World Conservation Strategy*, dedicated to helping individual states, and especially developing countries, plan for the maintenance and protection of **soil**, water, forests, and wildlife. A continuation and update of this theme appeared in 1987 with the publication of the UN World Commission on Environment and Development's paper, *Our Common Future*. The idea of **sustainable development**, a goal of ecologically balanced, conservation-oriented economic development, was introduced in this 1987 paper and has since become a dominant ideal in international development programs of the 1990s.

[*Mary Ann Cunningham*]

FURTHER READING

Fox, S. *John Muir and His Legacy: the American Conservation Movement.* Boston: Little, Brown, 1981.

Marsh, G. P. *Man and Nature.* Cambridge: Harvard University Press, 1965 (originally 1864).

Meine, C. *Aldo Leopold: His Life and Work.* Madison, WI: University of Wisconsin Press, 1988.

Pinchot, G. *Breaking New Ground.* Washington, DC: Island Press, 1987 (originally 1947).

Conservation biology

Conservation biology is concerned with the application of ecological and biological science to the **conservation** and protection of Earth's **biodiversity**. Conservation biology is a relatively recent field of scientific activity, having emerged during the past several decades in response to the accelerating biodiversity crisis. Conservation biology represents an integration of theory, basic and applied research, and broader educational goals. It includes much of **ecology** but extends it with social sciences, policy, and management.

The most important cause of the biodiversity crisis is the disturbance of natural **habitat**s, particularly through the conversion of tropical forests into agricultural habitats. Biodiversity is also greatly threatened by the excessive hunting of certain species, by commercial forestry, by climate change, and by other stressors associated with human activities, such as air and water pollution. A central goal of conservation biology is to discover ways of avoiding or repairing the damages that human influences are causing to biodiversity. Important considerations include the development of science-based methods for conserving endangered populations of species on larger landscapes (or seascapes, in marine **environment**s), and of designing systems of protected areas where natural ecosystems and indigenous species can be conserved.

Biodiversity and Its Importance

Biodiversity can be defined as the total richness of biological variation. The scope of biodiversity ranges from the genetic variation of individuals within and among populations of species, to the richness of species that co-occur in ecological communities. Some ecologists also consider biodiversity to include the spatial and temporal changes of communities on the greater landscape or seascape.

About 1.7 million of Earth's species have been identified and given a scientific name. However, biologists have not yet "discovered" most species, especially those living in tropical habitats. According to some estimates, Earth may support as many as 30-50 million species, of which 90% occur in tropical ecosystems, particularly in old-growth rainforests. Biologists believe that most of the unknown species are invertebrates, especially species of beetles and other insects. Compared with invertebrates, the numbers of species of plants and vertebrate animals are relatively well known.

Biodiversity is valuable for many reasons, but these can be grouped into the following three classes:

(1) *Intrinsic value.* Regardless of its worth in terms of the needs of humans, biodiversity has its own, intrinsic value.

(2) *Utilitarian value.* Humans have an undeniable need to harvest wild and domesticated species and their communities as sources of food, materials, and energy. Although harvests of biodiversity can be conducted in ways that foster renewal, these potentially renewable resources are often harvested or managed too intensively, resulting in degradation or extinction of the resource.

(3) *Provision of ecological services.* Biodiversity provides numerous ecological services that are directly and indirectly important to human welfare. These services include biological productivity, nutrient cycling, cleansing of water and air, control of erosion, provision of atmospheric oxygen and removal of carbon dioxide, and other functions related to the health and integrity of ecosystems. According to the American biologist Peter Raven: "Biodiversity keeps the planet habitable and ecosystems functional."

Threats to Biological Diversity

Biodiversity at local, regional, continental, and global scales is critically threatened by human activities. The damages that are being caused to Earth's species and ecosystems are so severe that they are referred to by ecologists as a biodiversity crisis. Many permanent losses of biodiversity have already been caused by human influences, including the extinctions of numerous species and the losses of distinctive, natural communities. Unless there are substantial changes in the ways that humans affect ecosystems, there will be enormously greater losses of biodiversity in the near future.

Earth's natural biodiversity has always been subjected to extinction (that is, the permanent loss of species and other groups) The fossil record shows that species, families, and even entire phyla have appeared and disappeared on Earth. For example, many invertebrate phyla proliferated during an evolutionary radiation at the beginning of the Cambrian era about 570 million years ago, but most of these are now extinct.

Many of the natural extinctions occurred simultaneously, apparently as a result of an unpredictable catastrophe. For instance, about 65 million years ago a mass extinction occurred that resulted in the loss of the last of the dinosaurs and as many as 76% of the then-existing species. That catastrophe is believed to have been caused by a meteorite impacting the Earth. In other cases, natural extinctions have been caused by more gradual environmental changes, for example in climate or in the intensity of disease or predation.

More recently, however, humans have been responsible for almost all of the extinctions that are occurring. In fact, species are now being lost so quickly that the changes represent a modern mass extinction. Well-known examples of extinctions caused by humans include the dodo, passenger pigeon, and great auk. Numerous other species have been taken to the brink of extinction, including the plains bison, whooping crane, ivory-billed woodpecker, and right whale. These losses have been caused by over-**hunting** and the disturbance and conversion of natural habitats.

In addition to these famous cases involving large animals, an even more ruinous damage to Earth's biodiversity is being caused by extensive losses of tropical ecosystems, particularly the conversion of tropical **rain forest**s into agricultural habitats. Because tropical ecosystems are particularly rich in numbers of species, loss of natural tropical habitat causes extinctions of numerous species. Many of those species occurred nowhere else but in particular tropical locales.

The mission of conservation biology is to understand the causes and consequences of the modern crisis of extinction and degradation of Earth's biodiversity, and then to apply scientific principles to preventing or repairing the damages. This is largely done by conserving populations and by protecting natural areas.

Conservation at the Population Level

In some cases, **endangered species** can be enhanced by special programs that increase their breeding success and enhance the survival of their populations. Usually, a variety of actions is undertaken, along with the preservation of appropriate habitat, under a scheme that is known as a population recovery plan. Components of a population recovery plan may include such actions as (1) the careful monitoring of wild populations and the threats that they face; (2) research into the specific habitat needs of the endangered species; (3) the establishment of a captive-breeding program and the release of surplus individuals into the wild; (4) research into genetic variation within the species; and (5)

other studies of basic biology and ecology that are considered necessary for preservation of the species, particularly in its natural habitats. Unfortunately, population recovery plans have only been developed for a small fraction of endangered species, and most of these have been prepared for species that occur in relatively wealthy countries.

One example involves the whooping crane (*Grus americana*), an endangered species in North America. Because of excessive hunting and critical habitat loss, this species declined in abundance to the point where as few as only 15 individuals were alive in 1941. Since then, however, the wild population of whooping cranes has been vigorously protected in the United States and Canada, and their critical breeding, migratory, and wintering habitats have been preserved. In addition, the basic biology and behaviour of whooping cranes have been studied, and some wild birds have been taken into captivity and used in breeding programs to increase the total population of the species. Some of the captive-bred animals have been released to the wild, and whooping crane eggs have also been introduced into the nests of the closely related sandhill crane (*Grus canadensis*), which serve as foster parents. These applications of conservation biology have allowed the critically endangered population of whooping cranes to increase to more than 150 individuals in the mid-1980s, and to about 300 birds in 1997, of which about half were in captivity. Because of these actions, there is now guarded optimism for the survival of this endangered species.

Protected areas

Protected areas such as parks and ecological reserves are necessary for the conservation of biodiversity in wild, natural ecosystems. Most protected areas are established for the preservation of natural values, particularly the known habitats of endangered species, threatened ecological communities, or representative examples of widespread communities. However, many protected areas (particularly parks) are also used for human activities, as long as they do not severely threaten the ecological values that are being conserved. These uses can include **ecotourism**, and in some cases fishing, hunting, and even timber harvesting. In 1993 there were about 9,000 protected areas globally, with a total area of almost 2 million acres (792 million ha). Of this total, about 2,500 sites comprising 1.15 million acres (464 million ha) were fully protected, and could be considered to be ecological reserves.

Ideally, a national system of protected areas would provide for the longer-term conservation of all native species and their natural communities, including terrestrial, freshwater, and marine ecosystems. So far, however, no country has implemented a comprehensive system of ecological reserves to fully protect the natural biodiversity of the region. Moreover, many existing reserves are relatively small and are threatened by environmental changes and other disturbances, such as illegal hunting of animals and plants and sometimes intensive tourism.

Ecological knowledge has allowed conservation biologists to make important contributions to the optimized design of networks of protected areas. Important considerations include: (1) the need to protect areas that provide adequate representation of all types of natural ecosystems; (2) the need to preserve all endangered ecosystems and the habitats of threatened species; (3) the requirement of redundancy, so that if one example of an endangered ecosystem becomes lost through an unavoidable natural disturbance (such as a hurricane or wildfire), the type will continue to survive in another protected area; (4) the need to decide whether or not the network of protected areas should be linked by corridors, a matter of some controversy among ecologists.

Conservation biology has also made important contributions towards the spatial design of individual protected areas. Important considerations include (1) the need to make protected areas as large as possible, which will help to allow species and ecosystems to better cope with disturbances and environmental changes; (2) a preference for smaller reserves to have a minimal amount of edge, which helps to avoid damages that can be caused by certain predators and invasive species; (3) the need to take an ecosystem approach which ensues that the reserve and its surrounding area will be managed in an integrated manner.

Although conservation biology is a relatively young field, important progress is being made towards development of the effective ecological and biological tools necessary to preserve biodiversity.

[*Bill Freedman*]

FURTHER READING

Freedman, B. *Environmental Ecology*, 2nd edition. Academic Press, San Diego, 1995.

Wilson, E.O. (ed.). *BioDiversity*. Washington, D.C: National Academy Press, 1988.

Primack, R.B. *Essentials of Conservation Biology*. Sunderland, MA: Sinauer Associates, 1993.

Conservation International (Washington, D.C.)

Conservation International (CI) is a non-profit, private organization dedicated to saving the world's endangered **rain forest**s and the plants and animals that rely on these **habitat**s for survival. CI is basically a scientific organization, a fact which distinguishes it from other conservation groups. Its staff includes leading scientists in the fields of botany, ornithology, herpetology, marine biology, entomology, and zoology.

Founded in 1987 when it split off from the **Nature Conservancy**, CI now has over 55,000 members. The group, headed by Russell Mittermeier, a primatologist and field scientist, has gathered accolades since its inception. In 1991 *Outside Magazine* gave CI an A- (one of the two highest grades received) in its yearly report card rating fourteen leading environmental groups.

The high praise is well founded. CI tends to successfully implement its many projects and goals. Many CI programs focus on building local capacity for **conservation** in developing countries through financial and technical support of local communities, private organizations, and government agencies. Their "**ecosystem** conservation" approach balances conservation goals with local economic needs. CI also funds and provides technical support to local communities, private organizations, and government agencies to help build sustainable economies while protecting rain forest ecosystems.

Four broad themes underlie all CI projects: 1) a focus on entire ecosystems; 2) integration of economic interests with ecological interests; 3) creation of a base of scientific knowledge necessary to make conservation-minded decisions; and 4) an effort to make it possible for conservation to be understood and implemented at the local level.

CI is involved with conservation projects in 17 countries, including Botswana, Brazil, Canada, Colombia, Indonesia, Mexico, New Guinea, and the Philippines. Constantly seeking to broaden its horizons, CI is pursuing new projects in Ghana, Japan, the Solomon Islands, Venezuela, and Zaire, among others.

Among CI's many successful projects is the Rapid Assessment Program (RAP), which enlists the world's top field scientists to identify **wilderness** areas in need of urgent conservation attention. RAP teams have completed surveys in Bolivia, Ecuador, Belize, Peru, and Mexico, and CI plans at least 12 more surveys on four continents in the next three to five years. CI has also helped establish important **biosphere reserve**s in rain forest countries. These efforts successfully demonstrate CI's ecosystem conservation approach, and prove that the economic needs of local communities can be reconciled with conservation needs. No harvesting or hunting is allowed in the reserves, but buffer zones, which include villages and towns, are located just outside the core areas.

CI strongly supports many educational programs. In 1988, it signed a long-term assistance agreement with Stanford University which involves exchange and training of Costa Rican students and resource managers. In 1989 CI began a program with the University of San Carlos which provides financial and technical support to the research activities in northern Guatemala of the university's Center for Conservation Studies. An educational program of a different kind, the Sorcerer's Apprentice, is designed to record ethnobotanical knowledge, protect useful **species**, and pass this information on to the next generation in indigenous communities. Young men and women in forestry services learn from traditional village healers and midwives.

In the future, CI intends to focus on expanding its activities in the major wilderness areas identified as the most endangered. The organization also plans to expand its conservation efforts to new ecosystems, including marine, desert, and temperate rain forest regions. Contact: Conservation International, 1015 18th Street, NW, Suite 1000, Washington, DC 20036. Internet:http://www.conservation.org:80/.

[*Cathy M. Falk*]

Conservation tillage

Conservation tillage is any **tilth** sequence that reduces loss of **soil** or water in farmland. It is often a form of non-inversion tillage that retains significant amounts of plant residues on the surface. Thirty percent of the soil surface must be covered with plant residues at crop planting time to qualify as conservation tillage under the Conservation Technology Information Center definition. Other forms of conservation tillage include ridge tillage, rough plowing, and tillage that incorporates plant residues in the top few inches of soil.

A number of implements for primary tillage are used to retain all or a part of the residues from the previous crop on the soil surface. These include machines that fracture the soil, such as chisel plows, combination chisel plows, disk harrows, field cultivators, undercutters, and strip tillage machines. In a no-till system, the soil is not disturbed before planting. Most tillage systems that employ the moldboard plow are not considered conservation tillage because the moldboard plow leaves only a small amount of residue on the soil surface (0 to 10 percent).

When compared with conventional tillage (moldboard plow with no residue on the surface), various benefits from conservation tillage have been reported. Chief among the benefits are reduced wind and water **erosion** and improved **water conservation**. Erosion reductions from 50 to 90 percent as compared with conventional tillage are common. Conservation tillage often relies on **herbicide**s to help control weeds and may require little or no post-planting cultivation for control of weeds in row crops. Depending on the management system used, herbicide amounts may or may not be greater than the amounts used on conventionally tilled land. Yields from conservation tillage, particularly corn, may be greater or smaller than from conventional tilled soil. Crop yield problems are most frequent on wet soils in the northern United States. Costs of tillage may be lower, but not always, from conservation tillage as compared with conventional. *See also* Agricultural technology; Soil organic matter; Sustainable agriculture

[*William E. Larson*]

FURTHER READING

Little, C. E. *Green Fields Forever: The Conservation Tillage Revolution in America.* Covelo, CA: Island Press, 1987.

Consultative Group on International Agricultural Research (CGIAR) (Washington, D.C.)

The Consultative Group on International Agricultural Research (CGIAR) was founded in 1971 to improve food production in developing countries. Research into agricultural productivity and the management of **natural resources** are the two goals of this organization, and it is dedicated to making the scientific advances of industrialized nations available to poorer countries. The CGIAR emphasizes the importance of developing sustainable increases in agricultural yields and creating technologies that can be used by farmers with limited financial resources.

Membership consists of governments, private foundations, and international and regional organizations. The goals of this association are carried out by a network of International Agricultural Research Centers (IARCs). There are currently 18 such centers throughout the world, all but four of them in developing countries, and they are each legally distinct entities, over which the CGIAR has no direct authority. The group has no constitution or by-laws, and decisions are reached by consensus after consultations with its members, either informally or at their semiannual meetings. The function of the CGIAR is to assist and advise the IARCs, and to this end it maintains a Technical Advisory Committee (TAC) of scientists who review ongoing research programs at each center.

Each IARC has its own board of trustees as well as its own management, and they formulate individual research programs. The research centers pursue different goals, addressing problems in a particular sector of agriculture, such as livestock production or addressing agricultural challenges in specific parts of the world, such as crop production in the semi-**arid** regions of Africa and Asia. Some centers conduct research into integrated plant protection, and others into forestry, while some are more concerned with policy issues, such as food distribution and the international food trade. One of the priorities of the CGIAR is the **conservation** of seed and plant material, known as germplasm, and the development of policies and programs to ensure that these resources are available and fully utilized in developing countries. The International Board for Plant Genetic Resources is devoted exclusively to this goal. Besides research, the basic function of the IARCs is educational, and in the past two decades over 45,000 scientists have been trained in the CGIAR system.

The central challenge facing the CGIAR is world **population growth** and the need to increase agricultural production by nearly 50 percent in the next 20 years while preserving natural resources. The group was one of the main contributors to the so-called "Green Revolution." It helped develop new high-yielding varieties of cereals and introduced them into countries previously unable to grow the food; some of these countries now have agricultural surpluses. The CGIAR is working to increase production even further, narrowing the gap between actual and potential yields, while continuing its efforts to limit **soil erosion**, **desertification**, and other kinds of **environmental degradation**.

The **World Bank**, the Food and Agriculture Organization (FAO) and the United Nations Development Program (UNDP) are among the original sponsors of the CGIAR, and the organization has its headquarters at the offices of the World Bank, which also funds central staffing positions. Combined funding has grown from $15 million in 1971 to over $300 million in 1993, and the CGIAR has a staff of 12,000 worldwide. The group publishes a newsletter called *CGIAR Highlights.* Contact: Consultative Group on International Agricultural Research, 1818 H Street, NW, Washington, DC 20433. Internet: http://www.worldbank.org/html/cgiar/HomePage.html.

[*Douglas Smith*]

Container deposit legislation

Container deposit legislation requires payment of a deposit on the sale of most or all beverage containers and may require that a certain percentage of beverage containers be allocated for refillables. The legislation shifts the costs of collecting and processing beverage containers from local governments and taxpayers to manufacturers, retailers and consumers.

While laws vary from state to state, even city to city, container deposit legislation generally provides a monetary incentive for returning beverage cans and bottles for **recycling**. Distributors and bottlers are required to collect a deposit from the retailer on each can and bottle sold. The retailer collects the deposit from consumers, reimbursing the consumer when the container is returned to the store. The retailer then collects the deposit from the distributor or bottler, completing the cycle. Consumers who choose not to return their cans and bottles lose their deposit, which usually becomes the property of the distributors and bottlers, though in some states, unredeemed deposits are collected by the state.

Oregon implemented the first deposit law or "bottle bill" in 1972. In the 1970s and 1980s, industry opponents fought container deposit laws on the grounds that they would result in a loss of jobs, an increase in prices, and a reduction in sales. Now opponents denounce the legislation as being detrimental to curbside recycling programs. But over the past two decades, container deposit legislation has proven effective not only in controlling litter and conserving **natural resources** but in reducing the **waste stream** as well.

Recovery rates for beverage containers covered under the deposit system depend on the amount of deposit and the size of the container. The overall recovery rate for beverage containers ranges from 75 to 93 percent. The reduction in container litter after implementation of the deposit law ranges from 42 to 86 percent, and reduction in total volume ranges from 30 to 60 percent. Although beverage containers make up just over five percent by weight of all **municipal solid waste** generated in the United States, they account for nearly 10 percent of all waste recovered, according to the **Environmental Protection Agency (EPA)**. While the cans and bottles that are recycled into new containers or new products ease the burden on the **environment**, recycling is a second-best solution.

As recently as 1960, 95 percent of all soft drinks and 53 percent of all packaged beer was sold in refillable glass bottles. Those bottles required a deposit and were returned for **reuse** 20 or more times. But the centralization of the beverage industry, the increased mobility of consumers, and the desire for convenience resulted in the virtual disappearance of the reusable beverage container. Today, refillables make up less than six percent by volume of packaged soft drinks and five percent by volume of packaged beer, and these percentages

shrink every year, according to the National Soft Drink Association and the Beer Institute.

Reuse is a more environmentally responsible waste management option, and is superior to recycling in the waste reduction hierarchy established by the EPA. While the container industry has been unwilling to promote refillable bottles, new interest in container deposit legislation may move industries and governments to adopt reuse as part of their waste management practices.

Industry-funded studies have found that a refillable glass bottle used as few as eight times consumes less energy than any other container, including recycled containers. A study conducted for the National Association for Plastic Container Recovery found that the 16-ounce refillable bottle produces the least amount of waterborne waste and fewest atmospheric **emission**s of all container types.

To date, ten states and one city have enacted beverage container deposit systems, designed to collect and process beverage bottles and cans. A deposit of 5 to 10 cents per can or bottle is an economic incentive to return the container. The states that have some form of container deposit legislation and accompanying deposit system include Oregon, New York, Connecticut, Maine, Iowa, Vermont, Michigan, Massachusetts, Delaware, and California. Legislation is pending in 25 state legislatures, and on **Earth Day** 1993, a national bottle bill was introduced in the U.S. Congress by sponsors from the House of Representatives.

Despite the fact that opinion polls show the public supports bottle bills by a nearly three-to-one margin, for two decades the beverage and packaging industries have successfully blocked the passage of bottle bills in nearly 40 states and even the most successful container deposit programs have come under attack and are threatened with repeal.

Connecticut has one of the highest percentages of refillable beer bottles in the nation, according to statistics from the Beer Institute. Despite the success of the state's five-cents-per-container deposit legislation, Governor Lowell Weicker Jr. has pushed for repeal of the legislation, to be replaced by a five-cents-per-container tax to benefit the state parks system. Opponents to Weicker's plan insist that the repeal of the deposit law would result in greater numbers of bottles and cans left strewn across the state.

Others predict the repeal of the bottle bill would impact the state in other ways: about 1,000 jobs would be lost; small redemption centers would go out of business; and recycling rates for glass, **aluminum** and plastic would drop. In addition, it has been estimated that repeal would cost municipal curbside recycling programs in Connecticut between $5.4 and $12.5 million annually.

The United States has a long way to go to catch up to progressive countries such as Sweden, which does not allow aluminum cans to be manufactured or sold without industry assurances of a 75 percent recycling rate. Concerned that voluntary recycling would not meet these standards, the beverage, packaging and retail industries in Sweden have devised a deposit-refund system to collect used aluminum cans. Consumers in Sweden return their aluminum cans at a rate that has not been achieved in any other country. The 75 percent recycling rate was achieved in 1987, and industry experts expect the rate to exceed 86 percent in 1993. Most North American deposit systems rely on the distributor or bottler, but the deposit in Sweden originates with the can manufacturer or drink importer delivering cans within the country. Also, retail participation is voluntary: retailers collect the deposit but are not required to redeem the containers, though most do.

In 1991, 122 billion containers, weighing about 7.2 million tons, were produced in the United States—a 100 percent increase in packaging waste since 1960. Containers and packaging are the single largest component of the waste stream and they offer the greatest potential for reduction, reuse, and recycling, according to the EPA. Where individuals, industries, and governments will not voluntarily comply with recycling programs, container deposit legislation has decreased the amount of **recyclables** entering the waste stream.

[*Linda Rehkopf*]

FURTHER READING

Franklin, P. "Sweden's Aluminum Can Return System." *Resource Recycling* (March 1993): 66.

Langer, G. "Many Happy Returns." *Sierra* 73 (March-April 1988): 19-22.

Williams, T. "The Metamorphosis of Keep America Beautiful." *Audubon* 92 (March 1990): 124-133.

Containment structures

See **Nuclear power**

Contaminated soil

The presence of pollutants in **soil**s at concentrations above background levels that pose a potential health or ecological risk. Soils can be contaminated by many human actions including the discharge of solids and liquid pollutants at the soil surface; **pesticide** application; subsurface releases from leaks in buried tanks, pipes, and **landfill**s; and deposition of atmospheric contaminants such as dusts and particles containing **lead**. Common contaminants include volatile **hydrocarbon**s—such as **benzene**, toluene, ethylene, and xylene (BTEX compounds)—found in fuels; heavy paraffins and **chlorinated organic compounds** such as **polychlorinated biphenyl (PCB)** and **pentachlorophenol (PCP)**; inorganic compounds such as **lead**, **cadmium**, **arsenic** and **mercury**; and radionuclides such as tritium. Often, soil is contaminated with a mixture of contaminants. The nature of soil, the contaminant's chemical and physical characteristics, and environmental factors such as **climate** and **hydrology** interact to determine the accumulation, mobility, toxicity, and overall significance of the contaminant in any specific instance.

Fate of soil contaminants

Contaminants in soils may be present in solid, liquid, and gaseous phases. When liquids are released, they move downward through the soil. Some may fill pore spaces as liquids, some may partition or sorb onto mineral soil surfaces, some may dissolve into water in the soft pores, and some may volatilize. For most hydrocarbons, a multiphase system is common. When contaminants reach the **water table** (where the voids between soil particles are completely filled with water), contaminant behavior depends on its density. Light BTEX-type compounds float on the water table while dense chlorinated compounds may sink. While many hydrocarbon compounds are not very soluble, even low levels of dissolved contaminants may produce unsafe or unacceptable **groundwater** quality. Other contaminants such as inorganic salts, such as **nitrates**, may be highly soluble and move rapidly through the **environment**. Metals demonstrate a range of behaviors. Some may be chemically bound and thus quite immobile; some may dissolve and be transported by groundwater and infiltration.

Contaminated pore water, called leachate, may be transported in the groundwater flow. Groundwater travels both horizontally and vertically. A portion of the contaminant, called residual, is often left behind as the flow passes, thus contaminating soils after the major contaminant **plume** has passed. If the groundwater velocity is fast, for example, hundreds of feet per year, the zone of contamination may spread quickly, potentially contaminating extraction wells or other resources. Over years or decades, especially in sandy or porous soils, groundwater contaminants and leachate may be transported over distances of miles, producing a situation that is very difficult and expensive to remedy. In these cases, immediate action is needed to contain and clean up the contamination. In cases where soils are largely comprised of fine-grained silts and clays, contaminants may spread very slowly. Such examples show the importance of site-specific factors in evaluating the significance of soil contamination as well as the selection of a cleanup strategy.

Superfund and Other Legislation

Prior to the 1970s, inappropriate land disposal practices, such as dumping untreated liquids in **lagoon**s and landfills, were common and widespread. The presence and potential impacts of soil contamination were brought to public attention after well-publicized incidents at **Love Canal, New York** and the Valley of the Drums. Congress responded by passing the **Comprehensive Environmental Response, Compensation, and Liability Act** in 1980 (commonly known as CERCLA or Superfund) to provide funds with which to cleanup the worst sites. After five years of much litigation but little action, Congress updated this law in 1986 with the **Superfund Amendments and Reauthorization Act**. At present, about 1200 sites across the United States have been selected as **National Priorities List** (NPL) sites and are eligible under CERCLA for federal assistance for cleanup. These Superfund sites tend to be the nation's largest and worst sites in terms of the possibility for adverse human and environmental impacts and the most expensive ones to clean up. While not as well recognized, numerous other sites have serious soil contamination problems. The U.S. Office of Technology Assessment and **Environmental Protection Agency (EPA)** estimate that about 20,000 abandoned waste sites and 600,000 other sites of land contamination exist in the United States. These estimates exclude soils contaminated with lead in older city areas, the accumulation of **fertilizer**s, pesticides, and insecticides in agricultural lands, and other classes of potentially significant soil contamination. Federal and state programs address only some of these sites. Currently, CERCLA is the EPA's largest program, with expenditures exceeding $3 billion over the last decade. However, this is only a fraction of the cost to government and industry that will be needed to cleanup all waste sites. Typical estimates of funds required to mitigate the worst 9,000 waste sites reach at least $500 billion; a fifty-year time period is anticipated. The problem of contaminated soil is significant not only in the United States but in all industrialized countries.

U.S. laws such as CERCLA and the **Resource Conservation and Recovery Act** (RCRA) attempt to prohibit practices that have led to extensive soil contamination in the past. These laws restrict disposal practices; mandate financial liability to recover cleanup costs (as well as personal injury and property damage) and criminal liability to discourage willful misconduct or negligence; require record keeping to track waste; and provide incentives to reduce waste generation and improve **waste management**.

Soil Cleanups

The cleanup or remediation of contaminated soils takes two major approaches: source control and containment, or soil and residual treatment and management. Typical containment approaches include caps and covers over the waste in order to limit **infiltration** of rain and snow melt and thus decrease the leachate from the contaminated soils. Horizontal transport in near-surface soils and groundwater may be controlled by vertical **slurry** walls. Clay, cement, or synthetic membranes may be used to encapsulate soil contaminants. Contaminated water and leachate may be hydraulically isolated and managed with groundwater pump-and-treat systems, sometimes coupled with the injection of clean water to control the spread of contaminants. Such containment approaches only reduce the mobility of the contaminant, and the barriers used to isolate the waste must be maintained indefinitely.

The second approach treats the soil to reduce the toxicity and volume of contaminants. These approaches may be broken down into extractive and *in situ* methods. Extractive options involve the removal of contaminated soil, generally for treatment and disposal in an appropriate landfill or for **incineration** where contaminants are broken down by thermal oxidation. *In situ* processes treat the soil in-place. *In situ* options include thermal, biological, and separation/extraction technologies. Thermal technologies include thermal desorption and in-place vitrification (glassification). Biological treatment includes biodegradation by soil fungi and bacteria that ultimately renders contaminants into **carbon dioxide** and water. This process is called mineralization. Biodegradation may produce long-lived toxic intermediate products. Separation technologies include soil vapor extraction for **volatile organic compound**s that removes a fraction of the contaminants by enhancing volatilization by

an induced subsurface air flow; stabilization or chemical fixation that uses additives to bind organics and **heavy metals**, thus eliminating contaminated leachate; soil washing and flushing using dispersants, solvents, or other means to solubilize certain contaminants such as PCBs and enhance their removal; and finally, groundwater pump and treat schemes that purge the contaminated soils with clean water in a flushing action. The contaminated groundwater may then be treated by air stripping, steam stripping, carbon absorption, precipitation and flocculation and contaminant removal by ion exchange. A number of these approaches—*in situ* soil vitrification and enhanced bioremediation using engineered microorganisms—are experimental.

The number of potential remediation options is large and expanding due to an active research program that is driven by the need for low cost and more effective solutions. The selection of an appropriate cleanup strategy for contaminated soils requires a thorough characterization of the site and an analysis of the cost-effectiveness of suitable containment and treatment options. A site-specific analysis is required since the distribution and treatment of wastes may be complicated by variation in geology, hydrology, waste characteristics, and other factors at the site. Often, a demonstration of the effectiveness of an innovative or experimental approach may be required by governmental authorities prior to full scale implementation. In general, large sites use a combination of remediation options. Pump and treat and vapor extraction are the most popular technologies.

Cleanup Costs and Cleanup Standards

The cleanup of contaminated soils can involve significant expense and risk. In general, *in situ* containment is cheaper than soil treatment, at least in the short run. While the Superfund law establishes a preference for permanent remedies, many cleanups that have been funded under this law have used both containment and treatment options. In general, *in situ* treatment methods such as groundwater pump and treat are less expensive than extractive approaches such as soil incineration. *In situ* options, however, may not achieve cleanup goals. Like other processes, costs increase with higher removal levels. Excavation and incineration of contaminated soil can cost $1,500 per ton, leading to total costs of many millions of dollars at large sites. Superfund cleanups have averaged about $26 million (however, a substantial fraction of this is for site investigations). In contrast, small fuel spills at **gasoline** stations may be mitigated using vapor extraction at costs under $50,000.

Unlike air and water, which have specific federal laws and regulations detailing maximum allowable levels of contaminants, no levels have been set for contaminants in soils. Instead, the Environmental Protection Agency and states use several approaches to set specific acceptable contaminant levels. For Superfund sites, cleanup standards must exceed applicable or relevant and appropriate requirements (ARARs) under federal environmental and public health laws. More generally, cleanup standards may be based on achieving background levels, that is, the concentrations found in similar, nearby, and unpolluted soils. Second, soil contaminant levels may be acceptable if the soil does not produce leachate with concentration levels above drinking water standards. Such determinations are often based on a test called the Toxics Characteristic Leaching Procedure which mildly acidifies and agitates the soil. Contaminant levels in the leachate below the maximum contaminant levels (MCLs) in the federal **Safe Drinking Water Act** are acceptable. Third, soil contaminant levels may be set in a determination of health risks based on typical or worst case exposures. Exposures can include inhalation of soils as dust, ingestion of soil (generally by children), and direct skin contact with soil. In part, these various approaches response to the complexity of contaminant mobility and toxicity in soils and the difficulty of pinning down acceptable and safe levels.

[*Stuart Batterman*]

FURTHER READING

Chen, C. T. "Understanding the Fate of Petroleum Hydrocarbons in the Subsurface Environment." *Journal of Chemical Education* 5 (1992): 357-59.

Jury, W. "Chemical Movement Through Soil." In *Vadose Modeling of Organic Pollutants*, edited by S. C. Hern and S. M. Melancon. Chelsea, MI: Lewis Pub., 1988

Contour plowing

Plowing the **soil** along the contours of the land. For example, rather than plowing up-and-down the hill, the cultivation takes place around the hill. By plowing along the contour, less water runs down the hill, thereby reducing water **erosion**.

Contraceptives
See **Family planning**

Convention on the Conservation of Migratory Species of Wild Animals (1979)

The first attempt at a global approach to **wildlife management**, the Convention on the Conservation of Migratory Species of Wild Animals was held in Bonn, Germany in 1979. The purpose of the convention was to reach an agreement on the management of wild animals that migrate "cyclically and predictably" across international boundaries. Egypt, Italy, the United Kingdom, Denmark, and Sweden, among other nations, signed an accord on this issue; the treaty went into effect in 1983, but the United States and Canada, as well as the former Soviet Union, still have not agreed to it.

The challenge facing the convention was how to assist nations that did not have wildlife management programs while not disrupting those that had already established them. The United States and Canada did not believe that the agreement reached in Bonn met this challenge. Representatives from both countries argued that the definition of a migratory animal was too broad; it would embrace nearly

Contour farm in southeastern Pennsylvania.

every game bird or animal in North America, including rabbits, deer, and bear. But both countries were particularly concerned that the agreement did not sufficiently honor national sovereignty, and they believed it threatened the effectiveness of the federal-state and federal-provincial systems that were already in place.

It is widely believed that the principal failure of this convention was its inability to find language dealing with federalist systems that was acceptable to all. The agreement also came into conflict with other laws, particularly laws governing national jurisdictions and territorial boundaries at sea, but it is still considered an important advance in the process of developing international environmental agreements. *See also* Environmental law

[*Douglas Smith*]

FURTHER READING

Basic Documents of International Environmental Law. Boston: Graham & Trotman, 1992.

Effectiveness of International Environmental Agreements: A Survey of Existing Legal Instruments. Cambridge, England: Grotius, 1992.

Convention on International Trade in Endangered Species of Wild Fauna and Flora (1975)

The Convention on International Trade in Endangered Species of Wild Fauna and Flora (CITES), was signed in 1973 and came into force in 1975. The aim of the treaty is to prevent international trade in listed endangered or threatened animal and plant species and products made from them. A full-time, paid secretariat to administer the treaty was initially funded by the **United Nations Environmental Program**, but has since been funded by the parties to the treaty. By 1992, 114 nations had become party to CITES, including most of the major **wildlife** trading nations, making CITES the most widely accepted wildlife **conservation** agreement in the world. The parties to the treaty meet every two years to evaluate and amend the treaty if necessary.

The **species** covered by the treaty are listed in three appendices, each of which requires different trade restrictions. Appendix I applies to "all species threatened with **extinction**," such as African and Asian **elephants** (*Loxodonta africana* and *Elephas maximus*, the hyacinth macaw (*Anodorhynchus hyacinthinus*), and Queen Alexandria's birdwing butterfly (*Ornithoptera alexandrae*). Commercial trade is generally prohibited for the over 600 listed species. Appendix II applies to "all species which although not necessarily now threatened with extinction may become so unless trade in specimens of such species is subject to strict regulation," such as the polar bear, giant clams, and Pacific Coast mahogany. Trade in these species requires an export permit from the country of origin. Currently, over 2,300 animals and 24,000 plants (mainly orchids) are listed in Appendix II. Appendix III is designed to help individual nations control the trade of any species. Any species may be listed in Appendix III for any nation. Once listed, any export of this species from the listing country requires an export permit. Usually a species listed in Appendix III is protected within that nation's borders. These trade restrictions apply only to signatory nations, and only to trade between countries, not to practices within countries.

CITES relies on signatory nations to pass domestic laws to carry out the principles included in the treaty. In the United States, the **Endangered Species Act** and the Lacey Act include domestic requirements to implement CITES, and the **Fish and Wildlife Service** is the chief enforcement agency. In other nations, if and when such legislation is passed, effective implementation of these domestic laws is required. This is perhaps the most problematic aspect of

CITES, since most signatory nations have poor administrative capacity, even if they have strong desire for enforcement. This is especially a problem in poorer nations of the world, where monies for regulation of trade in **endangered species** is forced down the agenda by more pressing social and economic issues.

CITES can be regarded as moderately successful. There has been steady progress toward compliance with the treaty, though tremendous enforcement problems still exist. Due to the international scope and size of world wildlife trade, enforcement of CITES is estimated to be only 60-65 percent effective worldwide. International trade in endangered species is still big business; the profits from such trade can be huge. In 1988, the world market for **exotic species** was estimated to be $5 billion, $1.5 billion of which was estimated to be illegal. Among the most lucrative products traded are reptile skins, fur coats, and ingredients for traditional drugs. If violations are discovered, the goods are confiscated and penalties and fines for the violators are established by each country. Occasionally, sanctions are imposed on a nation if it flagrantly violates the convention. For example, in 1991 sanctions were imposed on the purchase of wildlife products from Thailand based on evidence that illegal traders were consistently moving goods through the country. *See also* Environmental policy; Poaching; Wildlife management

[*Christopher McGrory Klyza*]

FURTHER READING

Fitzgerald, S. *International Wildlife Trade: Whose Business Is It?* Washington, DC: World Wildlife Fund, 1989.

McCormick, J. *Reclaiming Paradise: The Global Environmental Movement.* Bloomington: Indiana University Press, 1989.

Nichol, J. *The Animal Smugglers.* New York: Facts on File, 1987.

Convention on the Law of the Sea (1982)

During the age of exploration in the seventeenth century, the Dutch lawyer Hugo Grotius (1583-1645) formulated the legal principle that the ocean was free (*Mare liberum*), which became the basis of the law of the sea. During the eighteenth century, each coastal nation was granted sovereignty over an offshore margin of three nautical miles to provide for better defense against pirates and other intruders. As undersea exploration advanced in the twentieth century, nations became increasingly interested in the potential resources of the oceans. By the 1970s, many were determined to exploit resources such as **petroleum** on the continental shelf and manganese nodules rich with metals on the deep ocean floor, but uncertainties about the legal status of these resources inhibited investment.

In 1974 the United Nations responded to these concerns and convened a Conference on the Law of the Sea, at which the nations of the world negotiated a consensus dividing the ocean among them. The participants drafted a proposed constitution for the world's oceans, including in it a number of provisions that radically altered their legal status. First, the convention extended the territorial sea from three to twenty-two nautical miles, giving nations the same rights and responsibilities within this zone that they possess over land. Negotiations were necessary to ensure that ships have a right to navigate these coastal zones when going from one ocean to another.

The convention also acknowledged a 200 nautical mile Exclusive Economic Zone (EEZ), in which nations could regulate fisheries as well as resource exploration and exploitation. By the late 1970s, over 100 nations had already claimed territorial seas extending from 12 to 200 miles. The United States, for example, claims a 200 mile zone. Today, EEZs cover about one third of the ocean, completely dividing the North Sea, the **Mediterranean Sea**, the Gulf of Mexico, and the Caribbean among coastal states. They also encompass an area that yields more than 90 percent of the ocean's fish catch, and they are considered a potentially effective means to control **overfishing** because they provide governments clear responsibility for their own fisheries.

The most heated debates during the convention, however, did not concern the EEZs, but involved provisions concerning seabed mining. Third World nations insisted that deep-sea metals were the common heritage of mankind, and that their wealth should be shared. After fierce disagreements, a compromise was reached in 1980 that would establish a new International Seabed Authority (ISA). Under the plan, any national or private enterprise could take half the seabed mining sites and the ISA would take the other half. In exchange for mining rights, industrialized nations would underwrite the ISA and sell it the necessary technology. In December 1982, 117 nations signed the Law of the Sea Convention at Montego Bay, Jamaica. President Ronald Reagan refused to sign, citing the seabed-mining provisions as a major reason for United States opposition. Two other key nations, the United Kingdom and Germany, refused, and twenty-one nations abstained. In order to become international law, sixty nations must ratify the Law of the Sea Convention, but although 159 nations have now become signatories, only forty have actually ratified it. *See also* Coastal Zone Management Act; Commercial fishing; Oil drilling

[*David Clarke*]

FURTHER READING

Law of the Sea: Protection and Preservation of the Marine Environment. New York: United Nations, 1990.

Porter, G., and J. W. Brown. *Global Environmental Politics.* Boulder, CO: Westview Press, 1991.

Simon, A. W. *Neptune's Revenge, The Ocean of Tomorrow.* New York: Franklin Watts, 1984.

Convention on Long-Range Transboundary Air Pollution (1979)

Held in Geneva in 1979 under the auspices of the United Nations, the goal of the Convention on Long-Range Transboundary Air Pollution was to reduce **air pollution**

and **acid rain**, particularly in Europe and North America. The accord went into effect in March 1983. It was signed by the United States and Canada, as well as European countries, and the signatories agreed to cooperate in researching and monitoring air pollution and to exchange information on developing technologies for **air pollution control**. This convention established the Cooperative Programme for Monitoring and Evaluating of the Long-Range Transmission of Air Pollutants in Europe, which was first funded in 1984. The countries that signed the treaty also agreed to reduce their sulfur **emission**s 30 percent by 1993. *See also* Air-pollutant transport; Environmental policy; Fossil fuels; Smog

[*Douglas Smith*]

FURTHER READING

Basic Documents of International Environmental Law. Boston: Graham & Trotman, 1992.

Effectiveness of International Environmental Agreements: A Survey of Existing Legal Instruments. Cambridge, England: Grotius, 1992.

Convention on the Prevention of Marine Pollution by Dumping of Waste and Other Matter (1972)

The 1972 International Convention on the Prevention of Marine Pollution by Dumping of Waste and Other Matter, commonly called the London Dumping Convention, entered into force on August 30, 1975. The London Dumping Convention covers "**ocean dumping**" defined as any deliberate disposal of wastes or other matter from ships, aircraft, platforms, or other human-made structures at sea. The discharge of sewage **effluent** and other material through pipes, wastes from other land-based sources, the operational or incidental disposal of material from vessels, aircraft, and platforms (such as fresh or salt water), or wastes from seabed mining are not covered under this convention.

The framework of the London Dumping Convention consists of three annexes. Annex I contains a blacklist of materials that cannot be dumped at sea. Organohalogen compounds, **mercury**, **cadmium**, oil, **high-level radioactive waste**s, warfare **chemicals**, and persistent **plastics** and other synthetic materials that may float in such a manner as to interfere with fishing or navigation are examples of substances on the blacklist. The prohibition does not apply to acid and alkaline substances that are rapidly rendered harmless by physical, chemical, or biological processes in the sea. Annex I does not apply to wastes such as sewage **sludge** or dredge material that contain blacklist substances in trace amounts.

Annex II of the convention comprises a grey list of materials considered less harmful than the substances on the blacklist. At-sea dumping of grey list wastes requires a special permit from contracting states (countries participating in the convention). These materials include wastes containing **arsenic**, **lead**, **copper**, zinc, organosilicon compounds, cyanides, **pesticide**s and radioactive matter not covered in Annex I, and containers, scrap metals, and other bulky debris that may present a serious obstacle to fishing or navigation. Grey list material may be dumped as long as special care is taken with regard to ocean dumping sites, monitoring, and methods of dumping to ensure the least detrimental impact on the **environment**. A general permit from the appropriate agencies of the contracting states to the Convention is required for ocean dumping of waste not on either list.

Annex III includes criteria that countries must consider before issuing an ocean dumping permit. These criteria require consideration of the effects dumping activities can have on marine life, amenities, and other uses of the ocean, and they encompass factors related to disposal operations, waste characteristics, attributes of the site, and availability of land-based alternatives.

The International Maritime Organization serves as Secretariat for the London Dumping Convention, undertaking administrative responsibilities and ensuring cooperation among the contracting parties. As of 1990, 65 countries have ratified the Convention, including the United States.

The London Dumping Convention covers ocean dumping in all marine waters except internal waters of the contracting states, which are required to regulate ocean dumping consistently with the convention's provisions. However, they are free to impose stricter rules on their own activities than those required by the convention. The London Dumping Convention was developed at the same time as the **Marine Protection, Research and Sanctuaries Act** of 1972 (Public Law 92-532), a law enacted by the United States. The U.S. congress amended this act in 1974 to conform with the London Dumping Convention.

Most nations using the ocean for purposes of dumping waste are developed countries. Approximately 50 permits have been issued worldwide for sewage sludge and 150 permits for industrial waste. The number of permits for dumping sewage sludge and industrial waste at sea will likely decline in the near future. The United States completely ended its dumping of sewage sludge following the passage of the **Ocean Dumping Ban Act** (1988), which prohibits ocean dumping of all sewage sludge and industrial waste (Public Law 100-688). Britain and the North Sea countries also intend to end ocean dumping of sewage sludge. During the Thirteenth Consultative Meeting of the London Dumping Convention in 1990, the contracting states agreed to terminate all industrial ocean dumping by the end of 1995.

There are some 380 permits for dredged spoils and about 50 permits for other matter such as low-level nuclear wastes and at-sea **incineration** of **chlorinated hydrocarbons**. While the volume of sewage sludge and industrial waste dumped at sea is decreasing, ocean dumping of dredged material is increasing. Incineration at sea requires a special permit and is regulated according to criteria contained in an addendum to Annex I of the convention. However, as of 1990, there have been no incinerator vessels in operation.

The International Maritime Organization convenes annual consultative and scientific meetings on ocean-dumping issues. London Dumping Convention policy has been strengthened over the years with amendments and guidelines related to emerging technologies, arbitration procedures, and knowledge gained from additional study. *See also* Marine pollution; Seabed disposal

[*Marci L. Bortman*]

FURTHER READING

Duedall, I. W. "A Brief History of Ocean Disposal." *Oceanus* 33 (Summer 1990): 29-33+.

Kitsos, T. R., and J. M. Bondareff. "Congress and Waste Disposal at Sea." *Oceanus* 33 (Summer 1990): 23-8.

U.S. House of Representatives. House Report No. 100-1090. Ocean Dumping Ban Act Conference Report, 2nd Session, 100th Congress, 1990.

Convention on Wetlands of International Importance (1971)

Also called the Ramsar Convention or Wetlands Convention, the Convention on Wetlands of International Importance is an international agreement adopted in 1971 at a conference held in Ramsar, Iran. One of the principal concerns of the agreement was the protection of migratory waterfowl, but it is generally committed, like much wetlands legislation in the United States, to restricting the loss of **wetlands** in general, because of their ecological functions as well as their economic, scientific, and recreational value. The accord went into effect in 1975, establishing a network of wetlands, primarily across Europe and North Africa.

Every country that signed the agreement was required to set aside at least one wetland reserve. Over 50 countries have done so since 1971, establishing national wetlands and training personnel to manage them. The convention has secured protection for wetlands around the world, but many environmentalists believe it has the same weakness as many international conventions on the **environment**: there is no effective mechanism for enforcement. **Population growth** continues to increase political and economic pressures to develop wetland areas around the world, and there are no provisions in the agreement strong enough to prevent nations from removing protected status from designated wetlands.

[*Douglas Smith*]

FURTHER READING

Basic Documents of International Environmental Law. Boston: Graham & Trotman, 1992.

Effectiveness of International Environmental Agreements: A Survey of Existing Legal Instruments. Cambridge, England: Grotius, 1992.

Conventional pollutant

Conventional pollutants fall into five categories; the presence of these pollutants is commonly determined by measuring **biochemical oxygen demand**, total **suspended solid**s, **pH** levels, the amount of fecal coliform, and the quantity of oil and grease.

Biochemical oxygen demand (BOD) is the quantity of oxygen required by microorganisms to stabilize five-day incubated oxidizable organic matter at 68° F (20° C). Hence, BOD is a measure of the **biodegradable** organic **carbon** and at times, the oxidizable **nitrogen**. BOD is the sum of the oxygen used in organic matter synthesis and in the endogenous respiration of microbial cells. Some industrial wastes are difficult to oxidize, and bacterial seed is necessary. In certain cases, an increase in BOD is observed with an increase in dilution. It is hence necessary to determine the detection limits for BOD.

Suspended solids interfere with the transmission of light. Their presence also affects recreational use and aesthetic enjoyment. Suspended solids make fish vulnerable to diseases, reduce their growth rate, prevent successful development of fish eggs and larvae, and reduce the amount of available food. The **Environmental Protection Agency (EPA)** restricts suspended matter to not more than ten percent of the reasonably established amount for aquatic life. This allows sufficient sunlight to penetrate and sustain **photosynthesis**. Suspended solids also cause damage to invertebrates and fill up gravel spawning beds.

The acidity or alkalinity of water is indicated by pH. A pH of seven is neutral. A pH value lower than seven indicates an acidic **environment** and a pH greater than seven indicates an alkaline environment. Most aquatic life is sensitive to changes in pH. The pH of surface waters is specified to protect aquatic life and prevent or control unwanted chemical reactions such as metal ion dissolution in acidic waters. An increase in toxicity of many substances is often observed with changes in pH. For example, an alkaline environment shifts the ammonium **ion** to a more poisonous form of un-ionized ammonia. EPA criteria for pH are 6.5 to 9.0 for freshwater life, 6.5 to 8.5 for marine organisms and 5 to 9 for domestic consumption.

Fecal **coliform bacteria** are yardsticks for detecting pathogenic or disease causing bacteria. However, this relationship is not absolute because these bacteria can originate from the intestines of humans and other warm blooded animals. Prior knowledge of **river basins** and the possible sources of these bacteria is necessary for a survey to be effective. The strictest EPA criteria for coliforms apply to shellfish, since they are often eaten without being cooked.

Common sources of oil and grease are **petroleum** derivatives and fats from vegetable oil and meat processing. Both surface and domestic waters should be free from floating oil and grease. Limits for oil and grease are based on LC_{50} values. LC_{50} is defined as the concentration at which 50 percent of an aquatic **species** population perishes. EPA criterion is for a 96-hour exposure, and during this period the concentration of individual **petrochemical**s should not exceed 0.01 of the LC_{50} median. Oil and grease contaminants vary in physical, chemical, and toxicological properties besides originating from different sources. *See also* Industrial waste treatment; Sewage treatment; Wastewater; Water pollution; Water quality

[James W. Patterson]

FURTHER READING

Viessman, W., Jr., and M. J. Hammer. *Water Supply and Pollution Control.* New York: Harper & Row, 1985.

Copper

A metallic element with an atomic number of 29. It is abbreviated Cu and has an atomic weight of 63.546. Copper is a micronutrient which is needed in many proteins and **enzyme**s. Copper has been and is frequently used in piping systems which convey potable water. Corrosive waters will leach copper from the pipelines, thereby exposing consumers to copper and possibly creating bluish-green stains on household fixtures and clothes. The staining of household fixtures becomes a nuisance when copper levels reach 2-3 mg/L. The drinking water standard for copper is 1 mg/L. It is a secondary standard based on the potential problems of staining and taste. Copper is rather toxic to aquatic life, and copper sulfate is often used to control the growth of algae in surface waters.

Copper mining

See **Ashio, Japan; Ducktown, Tennessee; Sudbury, Ontario**

Coprecipitation

Inorganic contaminants, such as **heavy metals**, which exhibit toxicity effects when present at low levels, can be difficult to treat. The level of toxicity can be well below the metal's solubility concentration, and for this reason precipitation, a common treatment method for the removal of heavy metal, does not provide the needed **effluent** quality. **Cadmium**, for instance, has a reported maximum contaminant level (MCL) of 10 µg/L, with a 5 µg/L proposed level. Based upon theoretical solubility calculations, alkaline precipitation may only reduce the level of cadmium to 140 µg/L. Hence, additional methods of **wastewater** treatment are often required to meet environmental regulations. One such treatment technique is chemical **coprecipitation**.

Coprecipitation is a process in which a solid is precipitated from a solution containing other **ion**s. These ions are incorporated into the solid by **adsorption** on the surface of the growing particles, physical entrapment in the pore spaces, or substitution in the crystal lattice. Adsorption is one of the principle mechanisms of coprecipitation. It is a process in which the solid species, or adsorbent, is added to a solution containing other ions, called adsorbates. In this case, the adsorbates are bound to the solid's surface by physical or chemical interactions between one adsorbate and the adsorbent.

In solution, coprecipitation and adsorption are thus related by the time during which an adsorbate is present. The type of adsorbent present also affects the extent of ion uptake from solution. One solid used to perform this treatment is ferric oxide. For example, iron coprecipitation of cadmium has been reported to yield a residual cadmium concentration of about 3 µg/L. Several solid and solution variables must be considered when designing and optimizing coprecipitation as a treatment option. These include the equilibrium concentration of the species in solution, the suspension **pH**, and the presence of other interacting ions. Also, the properties of the solid adsorbent are important. These include type of solid formed, surface area available, age, and surface charge. In short, coprecipitation is controlled by a number of important variables which are specific to a given system. Thus treatability studies must be performed to fully optimize this wastewater treatment process and produced the necessary effluent quality. *See also* Hazardous waste; Pollution control; Sewage treatment; Toxic substance

[*James W. Patterson*]

FURTHER READING

Anderson, M., and A. Rubin. *Adsorption of Inorganics of Solid-Liquid Interfaces.* Ann Arbor, MI: Ann Arbor Science, 1981.

Leckie, J., et al. *Adsorption/Coprecipitation of Trace Elements from Water with Iron Oxyhydroxide.* EPR5 Final Report, 1980.

A Review of Solid-Solution Interactions and Implications for the Control of Trace Inorganic Materials in Water Treatment. AWWA Committee Report. Vol. 80, 1988.

Coral reef

Coral reefs represent some of the oldest and most complex communities of plants and animals on earth. About 200-400 million years old, they cover about 231,660 sq. mi (600,000 sq. km) worldwide. (The most popular reefs range from 5,000-10,000 years old.) The primary structure of a coral reef is a calcareous skeleton formed by marine invertebrate organisms known as *cnidarians*, which are relatives of sea anemones. Corals are found in most of the oceans of the world, in deep as well as shallow seas and temperate as well as tropical waters. But corals are most abundant and diverse in relatively shallow tropical waters, where they have adapted to the constant temperatures provided by these waters. The reef-forming corals, or hermatypic corals, have their highest diversity in the Indian and Pacific Oceans, where over 700 **species** are found. By contrast, the Atlantic Ocean provides the **habitat** for less than 40 species. Other physical constraints needed for the success of these invertebrate communities are clear water, a firm substrate, high **salinity**, and sunlight. Clear water and sunlight are required for the symbiotic unicellular plants that live in the surface tissues of the coral polyps. This intimate plant-animal association benefits both participants. Corals obtain oxygen directly from the plants and avoid having to excrete nitrogenous and phosphate waste products because these are absorbed directly as **nutrient**s by the plants. **Respiration** by the coral additionally provides **carbon dioxide** to these plants to be used in the photosynthetic process.

The skeletons of hermatypic coral play a major role in the formation of coral reefs, but contributions to reef struc-

Coral reef.

ture, in the form of calcium carbonate, come from a variety of other oceanic species. Among these are red algae, green algae, foraminifers, mollusk shells, sea urchins, and the exoskeletons of many other reef-dwelling invertebrates. This limestone infrastructure provides the stability needed, not only to support and protect the delicate tissues of the coral polyps themselves, but also to withstand the constant wave action generated in the shallow, near-shore waters of the marine **ecosystem**.

There are essentially three types of coral reefs. These categories are fringing reefs, barrier reefs, and atolls. Fringing reefs form borders along the shoreline. Some of the reefs found in the **Hawaiian Islands** are fringing reefs. Barrier reefs also parallel the shoreline but are found further offshore and are separated from the coast by a lagoon. The best example of this type of reef is the Great Barrier Reef off the coast of Australia. Because the coral colonies form an interwoven network of organisms from one end of the reef to the other, this is the largest individual biological feature on earth. The Great Barrier Reef borders about 1,250 miles (2011 km) of Australia's northeast coast. The second largest continuous barrier reef is located in the Caribbean Sea off the coast of Belize, east of the Yucatan Peninsula. The third type of reef, the atoll, is typically a ring-shaped reef, from which several small, low islands may project above the surface of the ocean. The ring structure is present because it represents the remains of a fringing reef that formed around an oceanic **volcano**. As the volcano eroded or collapsed, the outwardly-growing reef is ultimately all that remains as a circle of coral. Possibly the most infamous atoll is the **Bikini Atoll**, which was the site of the United States' hydrogen bomb tests during the 1940s and 1950s.

Besides the physical structure of the coral and the reef itself, the most significant thing about these structures is the tremendous diversity of marine life that exists in, on, and around coral reefs. These highly productive marine ecosystems may contain over 3,000 species of fish, shellfish, and other invertebrates. About 33 percent of all of the fishes of the world live, and depend, on coral reefs. This tremendous diversity provides for a huge commercial fishery in countries such as the Philippines and Indonesia. With the advent and availability of SCUBA gear to the general public in this half of this century, the diversity of life exhibited on coral reefs has been a great lure for tourists to these ecosystems throughout the world.

Even with their calcium carbonate skeleton and exquisite beauty, coral reefs are being degraded and destroyed daily, not only by natural events such as constant wave action and storm surges, but, more importantly, by the actions of man. Of the 109 countries that have coral reef formations within their territorial waters, 90 are losing them because of man-induced **environmental degradation**. Most is the result of physical abuse or **pollution** which alters the narrow range of physical and chemical parameters necessary for the coral, or their plant symbionts, to remain viable and thrive. Today, 10% of the world's coral reefs are completely degraded, 30% have reached a critical stage. Scientists have determined that if degradation at this rate continues, 70% of all coral reefs could be gone in 40 years. Reefs can be salvaged however. In 1995, participants from 44 countries representing governments, nongovernmental organizations, international development agencies, and the private sector gathered to launch the International Coral Reef Initiative. In 1997, some 1,400 participants declared the year as the International Year of the Reef, a period they hoped would heighten awareness and further reef salvage activities worldwide.

These reefs, most of which are between 5,000 and 10,000 years old, and some of which have been building on the same site for over a million years, are being degraded and destroyed by a vast array of water pollutants. **Silt**, which washes into the sea from **erosion** of clearcut forests miles inland, cloud the water or smother the coral, thus prohibiting the photosynthetic process from taking place. **Oil spills** and other toxic or hazardous chemicals that find their way into the marine ecosystem through man's actions are killing off the coral and/or the organisms associated with the reefs. Mining of coral for building materials takes a massive toll on these communities. Removal of coral to supply the ever increasing demand within the aquarium trade is destroying the reefs as well. The tremendous interest in and appeal of marine aquaria has added another problem to this dilemma. In the race to provide the aquarium market with a great variety of beautiful, brilliantly-colored, and often quite rare, marine fishes, unscrupulous collectors, who are selling their catches illegally merely for the short term monetary gain, spray the coral heads with poison solutions (including cyanide) to stun the fishes, causing them to abandon the reefs. This efficient means of collecting reef fishes leaves the coral head enveloped in a cloud of poison, which ultimately kills that entire section of the reef.

An unusual phenomenon has developed within the past decade with regard to coral reefs and pollution. In the Florida Keys in the early 1980s divers began reporting that the coral, sea whips, sea fans, and sponges of the reefs, around which they had been swimming, had turned white. They also reported that the waters felt unusually warm. The same phenomenon occurred in the Virgin Islands in the late 1980s. As much as 50 percent of the reef was dying due to this bleaching effect. Scientists are still studying these occurrences; however, many feel that it is a manifestation of global warming, and that a mere change in the water temperature around the coral reefs of two to three degrees Celsius is inducing the bleaching and death of the coral.

Tourism and **recreation** are inadvertently degrading coral reefs throughout the world as well. Coral is being destroyed by the propellers of recreational boats as well as divers who unintentionally step on coral heads, thus breaking them to pieces, and degrading the very structure of the ecosystem they came to see. Many of the reefs undergoing this degradation are sections that have been set aside for protection. Even with almost a quarter of a million square miles of coral reefs in the world, and about 300 protected regions in 65 countries, ever increasing levels of near-shore pollution, coupled with other acts of man, may be destroying these extremely complex communities of marine organisms at a rate faster than we can control.

[*Eugene C. Beckham*]

FURTHER READING

Brown, B., and J. Ogdon. "Coral Bleaching." *Scientific American* 268 (January 1993): 64-70.

Derr, M. "Raiders of the Reef." *Audubon* 94 (February 1992): 48-56.

Falkner, D. *This Living Reef.* New York: The New York Times Book Co., 1974.

Corporate Average Fuel Economy standards (CAFE)

In 1975, as part of the response to the Arab **oil embargo** of 1973-1974, the U. S. Congress and President Richard Nixon passed the Energy Policy and Conservation Act. One of a number of provisions in this legislation intended to decrease fuel consumption was the establishment of fuel economy standards for passenger cars and light trucks sold in the United States. These Corporate Average Fuel Economy (CAFE) standards require that each manufacturer's entire production of cars or trucks sold in the U.S. meet a minimum average fuel economy level. Domestic and import cars and trucks are segregated into separate fleets, and each must meet the standards individually. Any manufacturer whose fleet(s) fails to meet the standard is subject to a fine, based on the CAFE shortfall times the total number of vehicles in the particular fleet. Manufacturers are allowed to generate CAFE credits for overachievement in a single year, which may be carried forward or backward up to three years to cover other shortfalls. This helps to smooth the effects of model introduction cycles or market shifts.

CAFE standards took effect in 1978 for passenger cars and 1979 for light trucks. Truck standards originally covered vehicles under 6,000 lb (2,724 kg) GVW, but, in 1980, they were expanded to trucks up to 8,500 lb (3,632 kg). Car standards were set at 18 mpg for 1978, and increased annually to 27.5 mpg for 1985 and beyond. Manufacturers responded with significant vehicle downsizing, application of new powertrain technology, and reductions in aerodynamic drag and tire friction. These actions helped improve average fuel economy of U.S.-built passenger cars from 13 mpg in 1974 to 25 mpg by 1982. The fall of **gasoline** prices following the 1980-81 oil embargo encouraged consumers to purchase larger vehicles. This mix shift slowed manufacturers' CAFE improvement by the mid-1980s, despite continued improvements in individual model fuel economy, since CAFE is based on all vehicles sold. The Secretary of Transportation has the authority to reduce the car CAFE standards from 27.5 mpg to 26 mpg. This authority was used in 1986 when it became clear that market factors would prevent CAFE compliance by a large number of manufacturers.

A separate requirement to encourage new car fuel efficiency was created through the Energy Tax Act of 1978. This act created a "Gas Guzzler" tax on passenger cars whose individual fuel economy value fell below a certain threshold, starting in 1980. The tax is progressively higher at lower fuel economy levels. This act has since been amended both to increase the threshold level and to double the tax. The Gas Guzzler tax is independent of CAFE standards.

Lawmakers are again considering raising CAFE standards to reduce **petroleum** consumption and carbon dioxide **emission**s. A new energy bill debated in the U.S. Senate in 1991 would have required each manufacturer's CAFE to increase 40 percent by 2001. The Administration subsequently requested an independent study of CAFE capability by the National Research Council, which concluded that manufacturer capability fell far short of the levels proposed in the legislation. The study also noted that "the CAFE system is increasingly at odds with market signals," and "(it) has operated to the benefit of Japanese manufacturers and the detriment of the domestics." It went on the recommend that other market demand policies be considered to reduce fuel consumption. *See also* Automobile; Automobile emissions; Energy efficiency; Energy taxes

[*Brian Geraghty*]

FURTHER READING

Gates, M. "Senate to Tackle Energy Bill, CAFE Standards." *Automotive News* (28 October 1991): 3.

"Here's What's Left of Carter's Energy Package" *U.S. News and World Report* (23 October 1978): 27-29.

Reed, D. "Government Action." *Automotive Engineering* 100 (June 1992): 65.

Corrosion and material degradation

Corrosion or degradation involves deterioration of material when exposed to an **environment** resulting in the loss of that material, the most common case being the corrosion of metals and of steel by water. The changes brought about by corrosion include weight loss or gain, material loss, or changes in physical and mechanical properties.

Metal corrosion involves **oxidation-reduction reactions** in which the metal is lost by dissolution at the anode (oxidation). The electrons travel to the cathode where the reduction takes place, while **ion**s move through a conducting solution or electrolyte. A positive and a negative pole, called the cathode and the anode respectively, are thereby created with a current flow between them. Thus the process of corrosion is basically electrochemical.

For corrosion to occur, certain conditions must be present. These are: (1) a potential difference between the cathode and the anode to drive the reaction; (2) an anodic reaction; (3) an equivalent cathodic reaction; (4) an electrolyte for the internal circuit; (5) an external circuit where electrons can travel. Sometimes, polarization of the anodic and the cathodic reactions must be taken into consideration. Polarization is a change in equilibrium electromagnetic field of a cell due to current flow. It has been reported that polarization may retard corrosion, as in the accumulation of unreacted **hydrogen** on the cathode.

In the corrosion of iron in water, the reactions differ according to whether or not oxygen is present. The common reactions that take place in a deaerated medium are essentially an oxidation reaction releasing ferrous ion into solution at the anode and a reduction reaction releasing hydrogen gas at the cathode. In the presence of oxygen, a complementary cathode reaction involves oxygen being reduced to water.

Degradation of concrete, on the other hand, depends on the composition of cement and the aggressive action of the water in contact with it. Some forms of corrosion may be visibly apparent, but some are not. Surface corrosion, corrosion at discrete areas, and anodic attack in a two-metal corrosion may be readily observed. A less identifiable form, erosion-corrosion, is caused by flow patterns that cause abrasion and wear or sweep away protective films and accelerate corrosion. Another form of corrosion which involves the selective removal of an alloy constituent requires another means of examination. Cracking, a form of corrosion which is caused by the simultaneous effects of tensile stress and a specific corrosive medium, could be verified by microscopy.

Some measures adopted to prevent corrosion in metals are cathodic protection, use of inhibitors, coating, and the formation of a passivating film. Protection of concrete, on the other hand, can be achieved by coating, avoiding corrosive **pH** of the water with which the concrete is in contact, avoiding excessive concentrations of ammonia, and avoiding deaeration in pipes. *See also* Hazardous waste sites; Seabed disposal; Waste management

[*James W. Patterson*]

FURTHER READING

Dillon, C. P. *Corrosion Control in the Chemical Process Industries.* New York: McGraw-Hill, 1986.

Fontana, M. G., and N. D. Greene. *Corrosion Engineering.* New York: McGraw-Hill, 1967.

Snoeyink, V. L., and D. Jenkins. *Water Chemistry*. New York: Wiley, 1980.

Weber, W., Jr. *Physicochemical Processes for Water Quality Control*. New York: Wiley-Interscience, 1972.

Cost-benefit analysis

Environmentalists might believe that total elimination of risk that comes with **pollution** and other forms of **environmental degradation** is possible and even desirable, but economists argue that the benefits of risk elimination have to be balanced against the costs. Measuring risk is itself very complicated. **Risk analysis** in the case of pollution, for instance, involves determining the conditions of exposure, the adverse effects, the levels of exposure, the level of the effects, and the overall contamination. Long **latency** periods, the need to draw implications from laboratory studies of animal **species**, and the impact of background contamination complicate these efforts. Under these conditions, simple cause and effect statements are out of the question.

The most that can be said in health **risk assessment** is that exposure to a particular pollutant *is likely* to cause a particular disease. Risk has to be stated in terms of probabilities, not certainties, and has to be distinguished from safety, which is a societal judgment about how much risk society is willing to bear. When assessing the feasibility of technological systems, different types of risks—from mining, radiation, industrial accidents, or **climate** impacts, for example—have to be compared. This type of comparison further complicates the judgments that have to be made.

Reducing risk involves asking to what extent the proposed methods of reduction are likely to be effective, and how much these proposed methods will cost. In theory, decision making could be left to the individual. Society could provide people with information and each person could then decide whether to purchase a product or service, depending upon the environmental and resource consequences. However, relying upon individual judgments in the market may not adequately reflect society's preference for an amenity such as **air quality**, if that amenity is a public good with no owner and no price attached to it. Thus, social and political judgments are needed.

However much science reduces uncertainty, gaps in knowledge remain. Scientific limitations open the door for political and bureaucratic biases that may not be rational. In some instances, politicians have framed legislation in ways that seriously hinder if not entirely prohibit the consideration of costs (as in the **Delaney Clause** and the **Clean Air Act**). In other instances, of which the President's Regulatory Review Council is a good example, they have explicitly required a consideration of cost factors.

There are different ways that cost factors can be considered. Analysts can carry out cost effectiveness analyses, in which they attempt to figure out how to achieve a given goal with limited resources, or they can carry out more formal risk-benefit and cost-benefit analyses in which they have to quantify both the benefits of risk reduction and the costs.

Economists admit that formal, quantitative approaches to balancing costs and benefits do not eliminate the need for qualitative judgments. Cost-benefit analysis initially was developed for water projects where the issues, while complicated, were not of the same kind as society now faces. For example, how does one assess the value of a magnificent vista obscured by **air pollution**? What is the loss to society if a given genetic strain of grass or animal species becomes extinct? How does one assess the lost opportunity costs of spending vast amounts of money on air pollution that could have been spent on productivity enhancement and global competitiveness?

The most recalcitrant question concerns the value of human life. Cost-benefit analysis requires quantifying the value of a human life in dollars, so that specific health risks can be entered into the calculations against the cost of reducing such risks. Many different methods of arriving at an appropriate figure have been undertaken, all with predictably absurd results. Estimates range from $70,000 to several million dollars a head. Although the question does not admit of a sensible answer, society must nevertheless decide how much it is willing to pay to save a given number of lives (or how much specific polluters should pay for endangering them).

Equity issues (both interpersonal and intergenerational) cannot be ignored when carrying out cost-benefit analysis. The costs of air pollution reduction may have to be borne disproportionately by the poor in the form of higher **gasoline** and **automobile** prices. The costs of **water pollution** reduction, on the other hand, may be borne to a greater extent by the rich because these costs are financed through public spending. Regions dependent on dirty **coal** may find it in their interests to unite with environmentalists in seeking pollution control technology. The pollution control technology saves coal mining jobs in West Virginia and the Midwest, where the coal is dirty, but draws away resources from the coal mining industry in the West where large quantities of clean-burning coal are located.

Intergenerational equity also plays a role. **Future generations** have no current representatives in the market system or political process. How their interests are to be taken into account ultimately amounts to a philosophical discussion about altruism: to what extent should current generations hold back on their own consumption for the sake of posterity? Should Jeremy Bentham's utilitarian ideal of "achieving the greatest good for the greatest number" be modified to read "achieving sufficient per capita product for the greatest number over time?" *See also* Environmental economics; Intergenerational justice; Pollution control costs and benefits; Risk analysis

[*Alfred A. Marcus*]

FURTHER READING

Buchholz, R., A. Marcus, and J. Post. *Managing Environmental Issues*. Englewood Cliffs, NJ: Prentice-Hall, 1992.

Mann, D., and H. Ingram. "Policy Issues in the Natural Environment." In *Public Policy and the Natural Environment*, edited by H. Ingram and R. K. Goodwin. Greenwich, CT: JAI Press, 1985.

Costle, Douglas M. (1939-)

Former director of Environmental Protection Agency

An educator and an administrator, Douglas M. Costle helped design the **Environmental Protection Agency (EPA)** under Richard Nixon and was appointed to the head of that agency by Jimmy Carter. Costle was born in Long Beach California on July 27, 1939, and spent most of his teenage years in Seattle. He received his B.A. from Harvard in 1961 and his law degree from the University of Chicago in 1964. His career as a trial attorney in the civil rights division of the Justice Department began in Washington in 1965. Later he became a staff attorney for the Economic Development Administration at the Department of Commerce.

In 1969, Costle was appointed to the position of senior staff associate of the President's Advisory Council on Executive Organization, and in this post was instrumental in the formation of the EPA. Although Costle lobbied to be appointed as assistant administrator of the new agency, his strong affiliations with the Democratic party seem to have hindered his bid. Instead he continued as a consultant to the agency for two years and an adviser to the President's Council on Environmental Quality.

The road that led Costle back to the EPA took him to Connecticut in 1972, where he became first deputy commissioner and then commissioner of the Department of Environmental Protection in that state. He proved himself an able and efficient administrator there, admired by many for his ability to work with industry on behalf of the **environment**. His most important accomplishment was the development of a structure often called the "Connecticut Plan," where fines for industrial **pollution** were calculated on the basis of the costs that business would have incurred if it had complied with environmental regulations.

Carter appointed Costle head of EPA in 1977 as a compromise candidate during a period of bitter feuding over the direction of the agency (then at the center of a debate over the economic effects of regulation). But many environmentalists believed Costle's record proved he compromised too willingly with business, and they openly questioned whether he had the political strength to support environment protection in the face of fierce political and industrial opposition.

By May of his first year in office he was able to secure funding for 600 additional staff positions in the EPA, and under him much was done to provide a rationale for the regulations he had inherited and base them wherever possible on scientific data. Among other decisions Costle made while head of the EPA, he recommended a delay on the imposition of new auto emissions standards, allowed the construction of the nuclear plant in Seabrook, New Hampshire to continue despite protests, and oversaw the formation of an agreement with U.S. Steel on the reduction of air and **water pollution**.

Throughout his tenure Costle remained a strong proponent of the view that the federal government's responsibility to the environment was not incompatible with the obligations it had to the economy. He often argued that environmental regulation actually assisted economic devel-opment. Although conflicts with lobbying groups and hostile litigation, as well as increased controversy over the inflationary effects of environmental regulation, complicated his stewardship of the EPA, Costle continued to believe in what he called a gradual and "quiet victory" for environmental protection.

[*Douglas Smith*]

FURTHER READING

Langway, L., and J. Bishop, Jr. "The EPA's New Man." *Newsweek* 89 (21 February 1977): 80-82.

Council on Environmental Quality

Until it was abolished by the Clinton Administration in 1993, the President's Council on Environmental Quality (CEQ) was the White House Office that advised the President and coordinated executive branch policy on the **environment**. CEQ was established by the **National Environmental Policy Act** (NEPA) of 1969 to "formulate and recommend national policies" to promote the improvement of the quality of the natural environment.

CEQ had three basic responsibilities: to serve as advisor to the President on environmental policy matters; to coordinate the positions of the various departments and agencies of government on environmental issues; and to carry out the provisions of NEPA. The latter responsibility included working with federal agencies on complying with the law and issuing the required regulations for assessing the environmental impacts of federal actions. (NEPA requires that all agencies of the federal government issue "a detailed statement" on "the environmental impact" of "proposals for legislation and other major federal actions significantly affecting the quality of the human environment." This seemingly innocuous provision has been used often by environmental groups to legally challenge federal projects that might damage the environment, on the grounds that the required **Environmental Impact Statement** was inadequate or had not been issued.)

CEQ also prepared and issued the annual Environmental Quality Report; administered the President's Commission on Environmental Quality, an advisory panel involved in voluntary initiatives to protect the environment; and supervised the President's Environment and Conservation Challenge Awards, which honored individuals and organizations who achieved significant environmental accomplishments. Under the Nixon and Carter administrations, CEQ had a significant impact on the formulation and implementation of **environmental policy**. But its role was greatly diminished under the Reagan and Bush administrations, which paid much less attention to environmental considerations.

Perhaps CEQ's best-known and most influential accomplishment was its landmark work, ***The Global 2000 Report to the President***, prepared with the U.S. Department of State and other federal agencies, and released in July 1980. This pioneering study was the first report by the U.S.

government—or any other—projecting long term environmental, population, and resource trends in an integrated way.

Specifically, the report projected that the world of the future would not be a pleasant place to live for much of humanity, predicting that "if present trends continue, the world in 2000 will be more crowded, more polluted, less stable ecologically and more vulnerable to disruption than the world we live in now. Serious stresses involving population, resources, and environment are clearly visible ahead....the world's people will be poorer in many ways than they are today." CEQ's *Eleventh Annual Report, Environmental Quality—1980*, further warned that "we can no longer assume, as we could in the past, that the earth will heal and renew itself indefinitely. Human numbers and human works are catching up with the earth's ability to recover...The quality of human existence in the future will rest on careful stewardship and husbandry of the earth's resources."

In the following dozen years, CEQ was much more reluctant to speak out about the ecological crisis. Early in his presidency, Bill Clinton abolished CEQ and created the White House Office on Environmental Policy to coordinate the environmental policy and actions of his administration. Clinton said this new body will "have broader influence and a more effective and focused mandate to coordinate policy" than CEQ had. Internet: http://ceq.eh.doe.gov/.

[*Lewis G. Regenstein*]

FURTHER READING

Environmental Quality: The Eleventh Annual Report of the Council on Environmental Quality. Washington, DC: Council on Environmental Quality, 1980.

The Global 2000 Report to the President. Washington, DC: Council on Environmental Quality, 1980.

"White House Environmentalists." *Buzzworm* 5 (May-June 1993): 72.

Cousteau, Jacques-Yves (1910-1997)

French oceanographer

When most people think of marine biology, the person that immediately comes to mind is Jacques-Yves Cousteau. Whether through invention, research, **conservation**, or education, Cousteau has brought the ocean world closer to scientists and the public, and it is the interest, awareness, and appreciation fostered through Cousteau's work that may ultimately save the marine **environment** from impending destruction.

Born in France in 1910, Cousteau's childhood was full of illnesses that left him anemic. His sickness, however, did not stop him from being an independent thinker, a trait that led to his strong commitment to oceanographic research. He attended the École Navale in Brest, France, the national naval academy, where his interest in marine research was sparked by a cruise around the world on the school ship *Jeanne D'Arc*. Cousteau brought his camera and filmed a rough documentary of the voyage. His fascination with pearl

Jacques Cousteau aboard *Calypso*.

and fish divers, and his ability to use a camera, would revolutionize undersea exploration.

During World War II, Cousteau, his wife, and two friends made masks and snorkles from inner tubes and garden hose. Through experimentation, they discovered that the worst enemy of a diver was the cold, and Cousteau proceeded to work on an effective diving suit. In 1943, Cousteau and Emile Paul Gagnon patented the Aqua Lung, the first self-contained underwater breathing apparatus (SCUBA). It was this invention that led to Cousteau being known as the "father of modern diving." SCUBA has opened a new world to scientific research as it is used extensively not only in marine biology, but also in marine geology, archaeology, and chemical oceanography.

Cousteau's innovations did not end with the Aqua Lung. He combined his interests in diving and photography to develop the first underwater camera housing. While stationed with the Navy in Marseilles, Cousteau continued to develop underwater photographic equipment, including battery packs and lights. In 1943, Cousteau and several friends filmed "Wrecks," a documentary of a sunken ship in the Mediterranean Sea. The French navy recognized Cousteau's talent and thought that this technology could be useful in recovering German mines and retrieving lost cargo. He was promoted to commandant and was put in charge of the Undersea Research Group, where he continued to develop diving and photographic techniques.

In 1950, Cousteau realized that the vessel donated to the Undersea Research Group was inadequate and asked the navy to furnish them with another ship. When the French navy refused, Cousteau formed a non-profit organization, Campagnes Oceanographique Françaises, and was able to raise enough money to purchase and refit an old British minesweeper. This would become the most famous and recognized scientific research vessel in the world: *Calypso.*

Cousteau first gained notoriety in the United States in the early 1950s when *Life Magazine* and *National Geographic* introduced Americans to the undersea endeavors of Cousteau and his Undersea Research Group. In 1953 Cousteau was persuaded to translate his journals into English and published them as *The Silent World*. It sold 5 million copies and was translated into twenty-two languages. It was filmed as a documentary in 1955 and won an Academy Award and the Gold Medal at the Cannes Film Festival that year. Following the commercial success of his film, Cousteau was appointed director of the world's oldest and largest marine research center, the Oceanographic Institute of Monaco. He rebuilt the deteriorating institute, adding aquariums and many live specimens collected during his travels.

While trying unsuccessfully to house **dolphins** in the facility, Cousteau developed a respect for the intelligence of these animals. This prompted him to campaign for stopping the slaughter of dolphins for use in pet foods. This was to be the first of many environmental campaigns for Cousteau, during which he discovered that the public, once educated about the environment, would be willing to try to preserve it. This theme of education has guided the **Cousteau Society**, and many other environmental organizations, ever since.

Exploring depths deeper than possible with SCUBA intrigued Cousteau and, in 1960, he tested the DS-2 diving saucer, in which he dove to over 984 ft (300 m) in the Bay of Ajaccio, near Corsica. After hundreds of successful dives, Cousteau started Continental Shelf Station Number One (Conshelf I) in the Mediterranean. This experiment not only investigated deep undersea **habitat**s, but also determined how divers would respond to life underwater for long periods of time while conducting laboratory experiments. The work performed by Cousteau and his research group not only laid the groundwork for all subsequent submersible engineering and exploration, but also was one of the first thorough investigations of hyperbaric physiology.

In 1966, Cousteau began that for which he is best known: television documentaries. With the airing of "The World of Jacques Cousteau," millions were introduced to the wonders of the sea. That same year, Cousteau signed a contract and began to film "The Undersea World of Jacques Cousteau," which ran for nearly nine years, giving Americans a glimpse of marine environments and the behaviors of the organisms that live there. The series, now in syndication, continues to fascinate generations of Americans and spawn interest in marine science and conservation.

In the early 1970s, Cousteau became frustrated with increasing marine pollution and produced a series of documentaries focusing on the destruction of marine systems. He has also expanded his explorations to riverine systems, lakes, **rain forest** destruction and the conflicts between human culture and the environment. The scope of his films demonstrates Cousteau's devotion to preserving all natural systems.

Cousteau's accomplishments are numerous. He has published more than 18 books and has contributed many articles to professional and popular journals. His documentary films have won three Academy Awards and his series, "The Undersea World of Jacques Cousteau," has won numerous Emmy Awards. Many organizations have recognized Cousteau for his work in technical fields as well as in conservation. These awards include Gold Medals from the National Geographic Society and the Royal Geographical Society, and the United Nations international environmental award. He has received honorary degrees from the University of California at Berkeley, Brandeis University, Rensselaer Polytechnic Institute, Harvard University, the University of Ghent, and the University of Guadalajara. He was named to the U.S. National Academy of Sciences in 1968.

Cousteau's devotion to the natural world has not been with out its costs. His son Philippe was killed in a diving accident and numerous financial difficulties, especially early in his career, have set back his work. He is now diving with his son, Jean-Michel, and is head of the successful Cousteau Society, which he formed in 1973. Whether it is in oceanographic research, marine engineering, the development and manufacture of diving equipment, the production of films and television specials, or environmental education, Cousteau continues to inspire and fascinate, motivating scientists and the public alike to work to preserve the ocean world.

Cousteau died in Paris on July 25, 1997, after a lengthy illness.

[*William G. Ambrose, Jr. and Paul E. Renaud*]

FURTHER READING

Cousteau, J-Y. *The Cousteau Almanac: An Inventory of Life on Our Water Planet.* New York: Doubleday, 1981.

Munson, R. *Cousteau: The Captain and His World.* New York: Morrow, 1989.

Cousteau Society, The (Chesapeake, Virginia)

The Cousteau Society is a non-profit organization dedicated to marine research, especially underwater exploration and filmmaking. Created in 1973 by **Jacques-Yves Cousteau** and his son, Jean-Michel Cousteau, the Society provides educational materials, and sponsors or cosponsors scientific, technological and environmental research studies to gauge the health of the world's marine **environment**s.

The Society's educational projects include award-winning television specials that inspire interest in the marine world. Special reports filmed and broadcast have included those on the **Exxon Valdez** oil spills, and the natural history of the great white shark (*Carcharodon charcharias*). Cousteau films are broadcast in more than 100 countries and to schools around the world. Books and filmstrips on marine and environmental issues are produced for colleges, schools, and the public. The Society produces two periodicals that explain scientific and environmental issues, the *Calypso Log* for adults and the *Dolphin Log* for youngsters.

The Society's Project Ocean Search offers field study programs under the supervision of Society educators and scientists. Presently, the Society is developing Cousteau Center sites that will provide visitors with ocean experiences through the use of film and illusion technology. The Society also sponsors research to help the scientific community better understand the nature of a region or phenomenon, as well as studies designed to provide local policy makers with guidelines to protect their environment.

Two Cousteau Society research vessels, *Calypso* and *Alcyone*, are circumnavigating the globe to take a fresh look at the planet. Four hours of television documentaries are filmed each year about those expeditions. Scientific teams aboard the two research vessels are measuring the productivity of the oceans, studying the contributions of rivers to ocean vitality, assessing the health of marine and freshwater **habitat**s, and exploring the global connections between major components of the **biosphere** such as tropical forests, rivers, the **atmosphere**, seas, oceans, and humankind.

The Society also provides assistance to the Marine Mammal Stranding Program, a network of scientists and others who study strandings of **whales** and **dolphins**. With the Smithsonian Institution, the Society sponsors the Marine Mammal Events Program, which gathers information on beach stranding reports from the United States and other parts of the world to create a centralized data base. The compilation is expected to lead to a better understanding of the phenomenon of beaching.

Currently, the Society is developing educational computer programs for young people that explore the consequences of various actions on the environment; and it is preparing environmental cartoon books for students in developing countries. It also supports the development of new technologies that will help provide solutions to environmental challenges. Contact: The Cousteau Society, 870 Greenbriar Circle, Suite 402, Chesapeake, VA 23320. Internet: http://acin.edi.fr/cousteau/.

[*Linda Rehkopf*]

Crane (bird)

See **Whooping crane**

Criteria pollutant

Criteria pollutants are air pollutants which, at certain levels of exposure, do not threaten human health, and which meet **National Ambient Air Quality Standard**s. There are two types of standards for such pollutants. National primary ambient air quality standards are levels of **air quality** with a margin of safety adequate to protect public health. National secondary ambient air quality standards are levels of air quality which are necessary to protect the public welfare from any known or anticipated adverse effects of a pollutant. *See also* Air Quality Control Region; Air quality criteria; Primary standards; Secondary standards

Critical habitat

As institutionalized in the U. S. **Endangered Species Act** of 1973, critical habitat is considered the area necessary to the survival of a **species**, and, in the case of endangered and threatened species, essential to their recovery. An animal's **habitat** includes not only the area where it lives, but also its breeding and feeding grounds, seasonal ranges, and **migration** routes. Critical habitat usually refers to the area that is essential for a minimal viable population to survive and reproduce. The Endangered Species Act is intended to conserve "the **ecosystem**s upon which **endangered species** and threatened species depend." Thus, the Secretary of the Interior is required to identify and designate critical habitats for species that are listed as endangered or threatened under this law. In some cases, areas may be excluded from such designations if the economic, social or other costs exceed the **conservation** benefits.

The listing of imperiled species and the designation of their critical habitats have become politically sensitive, since these actions can profoundly affect the development and exploitation of areas so designated, and can, under some circumstances, limit such activities as gas and **oil drilling**, timber cutting, **dam** building, mineral exploration and mining. For this and other reasons, the Department of the Interior often has been reluctant to list certain species, and has excluded species from the protected lists in order not to inconvenience certain commercial interests.

Section 7 of the Endangered Species Act requires all federal agencies and departments to ensure that the activities they carry out, fund, or authorize do not jeopardize the continued existence of listed species or adversely modify or destroy their critical habitat. This provision has proven especially significant, since federal agencies such as the **Forest Service**, **Bureau of Land Management**, and **Fish and Wildlife Service** control vast areas of land that constitute habitat for many listed species and on which a variety of commercial activities, such as logging or mining, are undertaken with federal permits.

However, Section 7 of the Endangered Species Act has been implemented in such a way as to generally not affect economic development. The U. S. Fish and Wildlife Service (and, in the case of marine species, the National Marine Fisheries Service) is directed to consult with other federal agencies and review the effects of their actions on listed species. According to a study by the **National Wildlife Federation**, over 99 percent of the more than 120,000 reviews or consultations conducted between 1979 and 1991 found that no jeopardy to a listed species was involved. In some cases, "economic and technologically feasible" alternatives and modifications, in the words of the act, were suggested that allowed the federal activities to proceed. In only 34 cases were projects cancelled because of threats to listed species. In rare situations, where the conflict between a project and the Endangered Species Act are absolutely irreconcilable, an agency can apply for an exemption from a seven-member Endangered Species Committee.

The earliest major conflict over critical habitat under the Act was the famous 1979 fight over construction of the $116 million **Tellico Dam** in Tennessee, which would have flooded and destroyed several hundred family farms as well as what was then the only known habitat of a species of minnow, the **snail darter** (*Percina tanasi*). (Since then, snail darters have been found in other areas.) Congress exempted this project from the provisions of the Endangered Species Act, and the dam was built as planned, although many consider it a political boondoggle and a huge waste of taxpayers' money.

More recently, efforts by environmentalists to save the remnants of **old-growth forest** in the Pacific Northwest to preserve habitat for the **northern spotted owl** (*Strix occidentalis caurina*) created tremendous controversy. Thousands of acres of federally-owned forests in Oregon, Washington, and California were placed off-limits to logging, costing jobs in the timber industry in those states. However, conservationists pointed out, if the federal government allowed the last of the ancient forests to be logged, timber jobs would disappear anyway, along with these unique **ecosystem**s and several species dependent upon them. In mid-1993, Interior Secretary Bruce Babbitt announced a compromise decision that allows logging of some ancient forests to continue, but also greatly decreases the areas open to this activity. As natural areas and **wildlife** habitat continue to be destroyed and degraded, conflicts and controversy over saving critical habitats for listed endangered and threatened species can be expected to continue.

[*Lewis G. Regenstein*]

FURTHER READING

Bean, M. J., et al. *Reconciling Conflicts Under the Endangered Species Act: The Habitat Conservation Planning Experience.* Washington, DC: World Wildlife Fund, 1991.

Kohm, K., ed. *Balancing on the Brink of Extinction: The Endangered Species Act and Lessons for the Future.* Covelo, CA: Island Press, 1990.

Crocodiles

The largest of the living reptiles, crocodiles inhabit shallow coastal bodies of water in tropical areas throughout the world, and they are often seen floating log-like in the water with only their eyes and nostrils showing. Crocodiles have long been hunted for their hides, and almost all **species** of crocodilians are now considered to be in danger of **extinction**. Members of the crocodile family, called crocodilians (Crocodylidae), are similar in appearance and include crocodiles, **alligator**s, caimans, and gavials. A crocodile can usually be distinguished from an alligator by its pointed snout (an alligator's is rounded), and by the visible fourth tooth on either side of its snout that protrudes when the jaw is shut.

Crocodiles prey on fish, turtles, birds, crabs, small mammals, and any other animals they can catch, including dogs and occasional humans. They hide at the shore of rivers and water holes and grab an animal as it comes to drink, seizing a leg or muzzle, dragging the prey underwater, and

American crocodile.

holding it there until it drowns. When seizing larger animals, a crocodile will thrash and spin rapidly in the water and tear its prey to pieces. After eating its fill, a crocodile may crawl ashore to warm itself and digest its food, basking in the sun in its classic "grinning" pose, with its jaws wide open, often allowing a sandpiper or plover to pick and clean its teeth by scavenging meat and **parasites** from between them.

The important role that crocodiles play in the **balance of nature** is not fully known or appreciated, but, like all major predators, their place in the ecological chain is a crucial one. They eat many poisonous water snakes, and during times of **drought**, they dig water holes, thus providing water, food, and **habitat** for fish, birds, and other creatures. When crocodiles were eliminated from lakes and rivers in parts of Africa and Australia, many of the food fish also declined or disappeared. It is thought that this may have occurred because crocodiles feed on predatory and scavenging species of fish that are not eaten by local people, and when left unchecked, these fish multiplied out of control and crowded out or consumed many of the food fish.

Crocodiles reproduce by laying eggs and burying them in the sand or hiding them in nests concealed in vegetation. Recent studies of the Nile and American crocodiles show that some of these reptiles can be attentive parents. According to these studies, the mother crocodile carefully watches over the nest until it is time for the eggs to hatch. Then she digs the eggs out and gently removes the young from the shells. After gathering the newborns together, she puts them in her mouth and carries them to the water and releases them, watching over them for some time. American crocodiles are very shy and reclusive, and disturbance during this critical period can disrupt the reproductive process and prevent successful hatchings.

In recent decades, crocodiles and other crocodilians have been intensively hunted for their scaly hides, which are used to make shoes, belts, handbags, wallets, and other fashion products. As a result, they have disappeared or have become rare in most of their former habitats. As of early 1993, 13 crocodile species have been designated endangered by the **U.S. Department of the Interior**. These species are found in Africa, the Caribbean, Central and South America, the Middle East, the Philippines, Australia, some Pacific Islands, southeast Asia, the Malay Peninsula, Sri Lanka, and Iran. They are endangered primarily due to overexploitation and habitat loss.

The American crocodile (*Crocodylus acutus*) occurs all along the Caribbean coast, including the shores of Central America, Colombia, Cuba, Hispaniola, Jamaica, Mexico, extreme south Florida, and on the Pacific coast, from Peru north to southern Mexico. The United States population of the American crocodile consists of some 200-500 individuals, with as few as 25-30 breeding females. This species breeds only in the southern part of **Everglades** National Park, mainly Florida Bay, and perhaps on nearby Key Largo, and at Florida Power and Light Company's Turkey Point plant, located south of Miami. The population is thought to be extremely vulnerable and declining, mainly due to human disturbance, habitat loss (from urbanization, especially real estate development), and direct killing such as on highways and in fishing nets. Predation of hatchlings in Florida Bay mainly by raccoons may also be a factor in the species' decline. *See also* Endangered species

[*Lewis G. Regenstein*]

FURTHER READING

Crocodiles: Their Ecology, Management and Conservation. A Special Publication of the Crocodile Specialist Group. Gland, Switzerland: IUCN-The World Conservation Union, 1989.

Ross, C. A., ed. *Crocodiles and Alligators.* New York: Facts on File, 1989.

Thorbjarnarson, J., comp. *Crocodiles. An Action Plan for Their Conservation.* Gland, Switzerland: IUCN-The World Conservation Union, 1992.

Van Meter, V. *Florida's Alligators and Crocodiles.* Miami: Florida Power and Light Company, 1987.

Cross-Florida Barge Canal

The subject of long and acrimonious debate, this attempt to build a canal across the Florida peninsula began in the 1930s and finally expired in 1990. Although it receives little attention today, the Cross-Florida Barge Canal stands as a landmark because it was one of the early cases in which the **Army Corps of Engineers**, whose primary mission has traditionally been to re-design and alter natural waterways, yielded to environmental pressure. The canal's stated purpose, aside from bringing public works funding to the state, was to shorten the shipping distances from the East Coast to the Gulf of Mexico by bypassing the long water route around the tip of Florida. Rerouting barge traffic would also bring commerce into Florida, directing trade and trans-shipment operations through Floridian hands. An additional supporting argument that persisted into the 1980s was that the existing sea route brought American commerce dangerously close to threatening Cuban naval forces.

Construction on the canal began in 1964, on a route running from the St. Johns River near Jacksonville west to the Gulf of Mexico at Yankeetown, Florida. Canal project plans included three **dams**, five locks, and 110 miles (177 km) of channel 150 feet (46 m) wide and 12 feet (3.6 m) deep.

Twenty-five miles (40 km) of this waterway, along with three locks and three dams, were complete by 1971 when President Richard Nixon, citing economic inefficiency and unacceptable environmental risks, stopped the project by executive order.

From start to finish, the canal's proponents defended the project on economic grounds. The Cross-Florida Canal was proposed as a depression-era job development program. After completion, commerce and recreational fishing would boost the state economy. The Army Corps, well-funded and actively remodelling **nature** in the 1950s and 1960s, took on the project, vastly overestimating economic benefits and essentially dismissing environmental liabilities with the argument that even modest economic gain justified any **habitat** or water loss. After work had begun, further studies concluded that most of the canal's minimal benefits would go to non-Floridian agencies and that environmental dangers were greater than first anticipated. Outcry over environmental costs eventually led to a reappraisal of economic benefits, and the state government rallied behind efforts to halt the canal.

Environmental risks were grave. Although Florida has more **wetlands** than any other state except Alaska, many of the peninsula's natural wetland and riparian habitats had already been lost to development, drainage, and channelization. Along the canal route these habitats sheltered a rich community of migratory and resident birds, crustaceans, fish, and mammals. Fifteen **endangered species**, including the red-cockaded woodpecker (*Picoides borealis*) and the Florida **manatee**, stood to loose habitat to channelized rivers and barge traffic. Specialized spring-dwelling mussels and shrimp that depend on reliable and pure water supplies in this porous limestone country were also threatened.

Most serious of all dangers was that to the Floridan **aquifer**, located in northern Florida but delivering water to cities and wetlands far to the south. Like most of Florida, the reach between Jacksonville and Yankeetown consists of extremely porous limestone full of sinkholes, springs, and underground channels. The local **water table** is high, often within a few feet of the ground surface, and currents within the aquifer can carry water hundreds of meters or more in a single day. Because the canal route was to cut through 28 miles (45 km) of the Floridan aquifer's **recharge zone**, the area in which water enters the aquifer, any pollutants escaping from barges would disperse through the aquifer with alarming speed. Even a small fuel leak could contaminate millions of gallons of drinking-quality water. In addition, a canal would expose the aquifer to extensive urban and **agricultural pollution** from the surrounding region.

Water loss presented another serious worry. A channel sliced through the aquifer would allow water to drain out into the sea, instead of remaining underground. Evaporation losses from impounded lakes were expected to reach or exceed 40 million gallons of fresh water every day. With water losses at such a rate, water tables would fall, and salt water intrusions into the fresh water aquifer would be highly probable. In 1985, 95 percent of all Floridians depended on **groundwater** for home and industrial use. The state could ill afford the losses associated with the canal.

Florida water management districts joined environmentalists in opposing the canal. By the mid-1980s the state government, eager to reclaim idle land easements for development, sale, and extension of the Ocala National Forest, put its weight against the Corps and a few local development agencies that had been resisting deauthorization for almost 20 years. In 1990 the United States Congress voted to divide and sell the land, effectively eliminating all possibility of completing the canal.

[*Mary Ann Cunningham*]

FURTHER READING

Deauthorization Hearings: The Cross-Florida Barge Canal. United States House of Representatives Committee on Public Works 1978. Washington, DC: U. S. Government Printing Office, 1978.

Hearing on the Cross-Florida Barge Canal. United States House of Representatives Committee on Public Works June 10, 1985. Washington, DC: U. S. Government Printing Office, 1985.

Hogner, R. H. "Environmentalists Lock Up Canal Development." *Business and Society Review* (Fall 1990): 74-77.

Cubatao, Brazil

Once called the "valley of death" and the "most polluted place on earth," Cubatao, Brazil, is a symbol both of severe environmental degradation and how people can work together to clean up their **environment**". A determined effort to reduce **pollution** and restore the badly contaminated air and water in the past decade has had promising results. While not ideal by any means, Cubatao is no longer among the worst places in the world to live.

Cubatao is located in the state of São Paulo, near the Atlantic coastal city of Santos, just at the base of the high plateau on which São Paulo—Brazil's largest city—sprawls. Thirty years ago, Cubatao was an agreeable, well-situated town. Overlooking Santos Bay with forest-covered mountain slopes rising on three sides around it, Cubatao was well removed from the frantic hustle and bustle of São Paulo on the hills above. Several pleasant little rivers ran through the valley and down to the sea. When the rivers were dammed to generate electricity in the early 1970s, however, the situation changed.

Cheap energy and the good location between São Paulo and the port of Santos attracted industry to Cubatao. An oil refinery, a steel mill, a **fertilizer** plant, and several chemical factories crowded into the valley, while workers and job-seekers scrambled to build huts on the hillsides and the swampy lowlands between the factories. With almost no **pollution control** enforcement, industrial smokestacks belched clouds of dust and toxic **effluent**s into the air while raw sewage and chemical waste poisoned the river. By 1981, the city had 80,000 inhabitants and accounted for three percent of Brazil's industrial output. It was called the most polluted place in the world. More than 1,000 tons of toxic gases were released into the air every day. The steaming rivers seethed with multi-hued chemical slicks, foamy suds, and debris. No birds flew in the air above, and the hills were covered with dying trees and the scars of **erosion** where rains washed dirt down into the valley.

Sulfur dioxide, which damages lungs, eats away building materials, and kills vegetation, was six times higher than World Health Organization guidelines. After a few hours exposure to sunlight and water vapor, sulfur oxides turn into sulfuric acid, a powerful and dangerous corrosive agent. Winter air inversions would trap the noxious gases in the valley for days on end. One quarter of all emergency medical calls were related to respiratory ailments. Miscarriages, still-births, and deformities rose dramatically. The town was practically uninhabitable.

The situation changed dramatically in the mid-1980s, however. Restoration of democracy allowed citizens to organize to bring about change. Governor Franco Montoro was elected on promises to do something about pollution, and his administration came through on campaign promises. Between 1983 and 1987, the government worked with industry to enforce pollution laws and to share the costs of clean-up. Backed by a **World Bank** loan of $100 million, the state and private industry invested more than $200 million for pollution control. By 1988, 250 out of 320 pollution sources were reduced or eliminated. Ammonia releases were lowered by 97 percent, **particulate emission**s were reduced 92 percent, and sulfur dioxide releases were cut 84 percent. **Ozone**-producing **hydrocarbons** and **volatile organic compound**s dropped nearly 80 percent. The air was breathable again. Vegetation began to return to the hillsides around the valley, and birds were seen once more.

Water quality also improved. Dumping of trash and industrial wastes was cut from some 64 metric tons per day to less than 6 tons. Some 780,000 tons of **sediment** were dredged out of the river bottoms to remove toxic contaminants and to improve water flow. Fish returned to the rivers after a 20-year absence. Reforestation projects are replanting native trees on hillsides where mudslides threatened the town. The government of Brazil now points to Cubatao with pride as an illustration of its concern for environmental protection. This is a heartening example of what can be done to protect the environment, given knowledge, commitment, and cooperation.

[*William P. Cunningham*]

FURTHER READING

"Cubatao: Brazil's Ecological Success." *Financial Times* (10 June 1988).

"Cubatao: New Life in the Valley of Death." *World Resources 1990-91.* Washington, DC: World Resources Institute, 1991.

Cultivation
See **Agricultural pollution**

Cultural eutrophication

One of the most important types of **water pollution**, cultural eutrophication describes human-generated fertiliza-

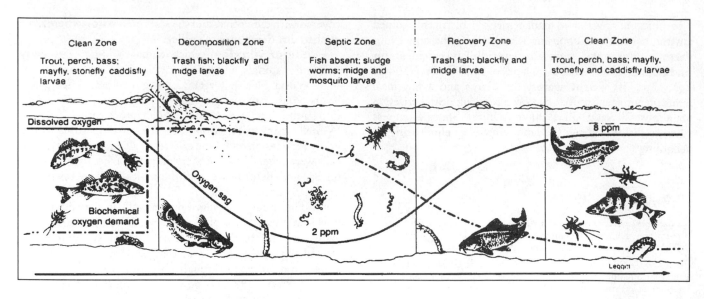

Clean Zone	Decomposition Zone	Septic Zone	Recovery Zone	Clean Zone
Trout, perch, bass; mayfly, stonefly caddisfly larvae	Trash fish; blackfly and midge larvae	Fish absent; sludge worms; midge and mosquito larvae	Trash fish; blackfly and midge larvae	Trout, perch, bass; mayfly, stonefly and caddisfly larvae

Oxygen sag downstream of a source of organic pollution.

tion of water bodies. Cultural denotes human involvement, and eutrophication means truly nourished, from the Greek word *eutrophic*. Key factors in cultural eutrophication are **nitrates** and phosphates, and the main sources are treated sewage and **runoff** from farms and urban areas. The concept of cultural eutrophication is based on **anthropocentric** values, where clear water with minimal visible organisms is much preferred over water rich in green algae and other microorganisms.

Nitrates and phosphates are the most common limiting factors for organism growth, especially in aquatic **ecosystem**s. Most **fertilizer**s are a combination of **nitrogen**, **phosphorus**, and potassium. Nitrates are key components of the amino acids, **peptides**, and proteins needed by all living organisms. Phosphates are crucial in energy transfer reactions within cells. Natural sources of nitrates (and ammonia) are more readily available than phosphates, so the latter is often cited as the crucial limiting factor in plant growth. Nitrates are supplied in limited quantities by decaying plant material and nitrogen-fixing bacteria, but phosphates must come from animal bones, organic matter, or from the breakdown of phosphate-bearing rocks. Consequently, the introduction and widespread use of phosphate **detergents**, combined with excess fertilizer in runoff, has produced a near ecological disaster in some waters.

In ecosystems, there is a continuous cycling of matter, with green algae and plants making food from **chemicals** dissolved in water via **photosynthesis**; this provides the food base needed by herbivores and carnivores. Dead plant material and animals are then decomposed by **aerobic** (oxygen using) and **anaerobic** decomposers into the simple elements they came from. Natural water bodies are usually well-suited for handling this matter cycling; however, human impacts often inject large amounts of additional **nutrient**s into the system, changing them from oligotrophic (poorly nourished) to eutrophic water bodies. Once present within a relatively closed body of water, such as a lake or

estuary, these extra nutrients may cycle numerous times before leaving the system.

Green algae and trashy fish may thrive in eutrophic water, but most people are offended by what they perceive as "scum." Nutrient-poor water is usually clear and possesses a rich supply of oxygen, but as the nutrient load increases, oxygen levels drop and turbidity rises. For example, when sewage is dumped into a body of water, the sewage fertilizes the algae, and as they multiply and die the aerobic decomposers multiply in turn. The increased demand for oxygen by the decomposers outstrips the system's ability to provide it. As a result, dissolved oxygen levels may fall or sag even below 2.0 **parts per million**, the threshold below which even trashy fish cannot a survive (trout need at least 8.0 ppm to survive). Even though the green algae are producing oxygen as a byproduct of photosynthesis, even more oxygen is consumed by decomposers breaking down the dead algae and other organisms.

As water flows downstream the waste is slowly broken down, so there is less for the decomposers to feed on. Biological oxygen demand slowly falls, while the dissolved oxygen levels rise until the river is finally back to normal levels. Most likely, the nutrients recycled by decomposers are either diluted, turned into **biomass** by trees and consumer organisms, or tied up in bottom **sediment**s. Thus a river can naturally cleanse itself of organic waste if given sufficient time. Problems arise, however, when **discharge**s are too large and frequent for the river to handle; under extreme conditions it becomes "dead" and is suited only for low-order, often anaerobic, organisms. Municipalities using river water locate their intakes upstream and their **sewage treatment** plants and storm drains downstream. If communities were required to do the reverse, the quality of river water would dramatically improve.

The major sources of nitrates and phosphates in aquatic systems are treated sewage effluent; excess fertilizer from farms and urban landscapes; and **animal waste**s from feedlots, pastures, and city streets. In some areas with pristine waters, such as **Lake Tahoe**, tertiary sewage treatment has been added; chemicals are used to reduce nitrate and phosphate levels prior to discharge.

Runoff from **nonpoint source**s is a far more difficult problem because they are harder to control and remediate than runoff from **point source**s. Point sources can be diverted into treatment plants, but the only feasible way to reduce nonpoint sources is by input reduction or by on-site control. Less fertilizer more frequently applied, especially on urban lawns, for example, would help reduce runoff. Feedlots are a major concern; runoff needs to be collected and treated in the same manner as human sewage; this may also apply to street runoff. Green cattle ponds are a sure sign of the abundant nutrients supplied by these mobile meat factories.

Phosphate **detergents** are superior cleaning agents than soap, but the resultant **wastewater** is loaded with this key limiting factor. Phosphate levels in detergents have since been reduced, but its impact is so powerful that abatement may require tertiary treatment.

The battle between Oklahoma and Arkansas over Illinois River **pollution** provides a useful case study of the debate over cultural eutrophication. This river has its headwaters in Arkansas and has become a prime tourist attraction in Oklahoma. Enthusiasts come from all over to canoe the river; summer use is especially heavy. However, economic development within the basin has resulted in a steady decline in river quality.

Arkansas started a legal war with Oklahoma when it sought and obtained **Environmental Protection Agency (EPA)** approval to dump half of the treated sewage from a new plant in Fayetteville into a tributary of the Illinois. Arkansas argued that its state-of-the-art treatment plant would produce an **effluent** having little impact on **water quality** by the time it reached the border. Oklahoma countered that it could not risk the potential economic loss if the river became polluted.

This controversy has had a salutary impact on research into the causes of cultural eutrophication within this basin. Scientists from Oklahoma State University and the University of Arkansas are collaborating on a long-term study of river quality and pollution sources. It is highly likely that nonpoint sources within both states will be identified as the key culprits, especially from livestock operations.

There is one major success story in the battle to overcome the effects of cultural eutrophication. The Thames River in England was devoid of aquatic life for centuries. Now a massive cleanup effort is restoring the river to vitality. Many fish have returned, most notably the pollution-sensitive salmon, which had not been seen in London for three hundred years. However, much work remains, especially in former Warsaw Pact countries and those in the **Third World**.

[*Nathan H. Meleen*]

FURTHER READING

Canby, T. "Water: Our Most Precious Resource." *National Geographic* 158 (August 1980): 144-179.

Harleman, D. R. F. "Cutting the Waste in Wastewater Cleanups." *Technology Review* 93 (April 1990): 60-69.

Herber, L. "Cool, Refreshing—and Filthy." In *The Human Habitat: Contemporary Readings*, edited by David L. Wheeler. New York: Van Nostrand Reinhold, 1971.

Maurits la Riviere, J. W. "Threats to the World's Water." *Scientific American* 261 (September 1989): 80-84+.

Pettyjohn, W. A. *Water Quality in a Stressed Environment*. Minneapolis: Burgess, 1972.

Cuyahoga River, Ohio

This 103-mile (166-km) long tributary of Lake Erie is a classic industrial river, with, however, one monumental distinction: it caught fire—twice. The first fire, in 1959, burned for eight days; fireboats merely spread the blaze. Typical of the times, a November 1959 article in *Fortune* seemed to glorify the industrial **pollution** here, with words and a portfolio of drawings reminiscent of Charles Dickens. Inspired by feelings of space and excitement, the artist stated: "It is a great expanse, with a smoky cast over everything, smudged with orange dust from the ore—an overall brown color." Clevelanders consoled themselves that the foul water at least symbolized prosperous times.

The second fire occurred on June 22, 1969, as several miles of river along the lowland industrial section called "the Flats" ignited, fed by bunker oil, trash, and tree limbs trapped by a bridge six miles upstream. This fire, along with the Santa Barbara oil well blowout, provided graphic television images which were projected around the world. Jack A. Seamonds's June 18, 1984 article in *U.S. News & World Report* credited the fire with lighting "the fuse that put the bang in the nationwide campaign to clean up the **environment**. Pamela Brodie described it in the September-October 1983 issue of *Sierra* as "The most infamous episode of **water pollution** in the U.S....It inspired a song...and the **Clean Water Act**."

Although the fire badly hurt Cleveland's image, steps were already underway to correct the problem. The city government had declared the river a fire hazard and won voter approval in the autumn of 1968 for major funding to correct sewage problems. After the fire, Cleveland's three image-conscious steel companies voluntarily quit dumping cyanide-laced water and two installed cooling towers. As a result of just these actions alone, the river once again began to freeze in the winter. The city of Akron banned phosphate detergents, and eventually won the lawsuits brought against it by soap companies. These and other efforts, plus completion in 1983 of the major **sewage treatment** project, brought about far more encouraging reports.

The Cuyahoga was formerly dumping 155 tons of waste per day, and was even devoid of sludge worms. But by 1978, *Business Week* could report substantial improvement: phosphates were cut in half; **chemicals** were down 20 to 40 percent; and **oil spills** went from 300 per year to 25 in 1977. For the first time, local residents saw ducks on the river. By 1984, **point source** pollution had been largely eliminated.

Cyclone collector.

The waterfront was rediscovered, with restaurants and trendy stores where once fires had burned

The water is still light brown, churned up by deep-water shipping, and Lake Erie is still polluted. Nonetheless, the Cuyahoga seems to have been largely redeemed, and thus helped revitalize the city of Cleveland. *See also* Great Lakes; Oil Pollution Act (1990); Water quality

[*Nathan H. Meleen*]

FURTHER READING

Ashworth, W. *The Late, Great Lakes: An Environmental History.* New York: Knopf, 1986.

Brodie, P. "The Clean Water Act; New Threats From Toxic Waste Demand Stronger Law." *Sierra* 68 (September-October 1983): 39-44.

Lawren, B. "Once Aflame and Filthy, A River Shows Signs of Life." *National Wildlife* 28 (February-March 1990): 24.

Seamonds, J. A. "In Cleveland, Clean Waters Give New Breath of Life." *U. S. News & World Report* 96 (18 June 1984): 68-9.

Wood, W. "Ecological Drums Along the Cuyahoga." *American Education* 9 (January 1973): 15-21.

Cyclodienes

See **Chlorinated hydrocarbons**

Cyclone

See **Tornado and cyclone**

Cyclone collector

A device that removes solids from an **effluent** stream (solid/liquid or solid/gas) using gravitational settling. The input stream enters a vertical tapered cylinder tangentially and spiral fins or grooves cause the stream to swirl. The centrifugal force created by this swirling action causes particles to settle out of the input stream. These solids are concentrated at the walls and move to the bottom of the tapered cone. The solid-free fluid or gas is removed along the center line of the collector via a vortex finder. A cyclone collector is a compact device capable of processing large volumes of effluent; however, pressure energy is expended in its operation. It removes particles from the effluent stream less effectively than bag filters or **electrostatic precipitation**. *See also* Baghouse

D

Dams (environmental effects)

Most dams are built to control flood hazards, to store water for **irrigation** or other uses, or to produce electricity. Along with these benefits come environmental costs including riparian **habitat** loss, water loss through evaporation and **seepage**, **erosion**, and declining **water quality**. Farther-reaching consequences of dams include changes in **groundwater** flow and the displacement of human populations.

Riparian, or stream–side, habitats suffer both above and below dams. Valuable ecological zones that support specialized plants, riparian **environment**s and nearby shallows provide food and breeding grounds for birds, fish, and many other animals. Upstream of a dam, impounded water drowns riparian communities. Because **reservoir**s can fill hundreds of kilometers of river channel, and because many rivers have a long sequence of dams and reservoirs, habitat drowning can destroy a great deal of river **biodiversity**. Downstream, shoreline environments dry up because of water diversions (for irrigation or urban use) or because of evaporation and seepage losses in the reservoir. In addition, dams interrupt the annual floods that occur naturally on nearly all rivers. Seasonal **flooding** fertilizes and waters flood plains and clears or redistributes debris in river channels. These beneficial effects of flooding cease once a river is dammed.

Dams and reservoirs alter **sediment** deposition in rivers. Most rivers carry large amounts of suspended **silt** and sand, and dams trap sediments normally deposited downstream. Below the dam, erosion reshapes river channels once sediment deposition ceases. If erosion becomes extreme, bridges, levees, and even river deltas can be threatened. Meanwhile, sediment piling up in the still waters of the reservoir behind the dam decrease water storage capacity. An increasingly shallow reservoir also becomes gradually warmer. Oxygen content decreases as the water temperature rises; fish populations fall, and proliferating algae and aquatic plants can begin to block the dam's water intakes. In **arid** regions a higher percentage of river water evaporates as the reservoir becomes shallower. Evaporating water leaves behind salts, which further decrease water quality in the reservoir and river.

Water losses from evaporation can be extreme: Lakes Powell and Mead on the **Colorado River** lose about 3 billion cu ft (1 billion cu m) of water to evaporation each year; Egypt's Lake Nasser, on the Nile River, loses about 45 billion cu ft (15 billion cu m). Water losses also result from seepage into bedrock. As river water enters groundwater, **water table**s usually rise around a reservoir. In arid regions increased groundwater can increase local fertility (sometimes endangering delicate dry-land plant **species**), but in moister regions excessive groundwater can cause swamping. Evaporation from exposed groundwater can leave higher salt concentrations in the **soil**. The most catastrophic results of reservoir seepage into groundwater occur when saturated rock loses its strength. In such events valley walls can collapse, causing dam failure and disastrous flooding downstream.

Perhaps the most significant environmental effect of dams results from the displacement of human populations. Because people normally settle along rivers, where water for drinking, irrigation, power, and transport are readily available, reservoir flooding can displace huge populations. The planned **Three Gorges Dam** on China's Chang Jiang (Yangtze River) will displace 1.4 million people and flood some of western China's best agricultural land. A series of dams on India's Narmada river will inundate the homes of 1.5 million people along with 600,000 acres (150,000 ha) of farm land. In both cases, people will need to find new places to live and clear new land to grow food. Such ripple effects carry a dam's influence far beyond its immediate proximity.

Where dams are needed for power, they can have a positive effect in offsetting environmental costs associated with other power sources. Hydropower is cleaner and safer than **nuclear power**. Water turbines are also cleaner than **coal**-fired generators. Furthermore, both nuclear and coal power require extensive mining, with environmental costs far more severe than those of even a large dam.

[*Mary Ann Cunningham*]

FURTHER READING

Driver, E. E., and W. O. Wunderlich, eds. *Environmental Effects of Hydraulic Engineering Works.* Proceedings of an International Symposium Held at Knoxville, Tennessee, Sept. 12-14, 1978. Knoxville: Tennessee Valley Authority, 1979.

Esteva, G., and M. S. Prakash. "Grassroots Resistance to Sustainable Development." *The Ecologist* 22 (1992): 45-51.

Goldsmith, E., and N. Hidyard, eds. *The Social and Environmental Effects of Large Dams.* (3 Vols.) New York: Wiley, 1986.

Danube River

See **Eastern European pollution**

Darling, Jay Norwood "Ding" (1876-1962)

Environmental cartoonist

Most editorial page cartoonists focus on the tough job of meeting daily deadlines, satisfied that their message will influence public opinion through their drawings. Jay Norwood "Ding" Darling, however, drew Pulitzer prize-winning cartoons, but was also immersed in **conservation** action, emerging as one of the great innovators in the conservation movement of the first half of the twentieth century.

Norwood, Michigan, was Darling's namesake birthplace, but he grew up in Elkhart, Indiana, and attended high school in Sioux City, Iowa, at a time when the area was relatively undeveloped. Wandering the prairies of nineteenth century Iowa, Nebraska, and South Dakota instilled in him a life-long love of the outdoors and wildlife.

After an uneven beginning, Darling graduated from Beloit College in Wisconsin with a degree in biology. (At one college, during one semester, biology was the only course he passed). And he was expelled from Beloit for a year for caricaturing individuals in the college faculty and administration. Building on an early interest in sketching (and the cartooning skills developed in college) Darling went on to a half-century of drawing political cartoons, including some of the most memorable conservation/environmental cartoons of the twentieth century. His first job (1900) was as a reporter (and sometimes caricaturist) in Sioux City, but six years later, he was hired by the *Des Moines Register and Leader*, where his primary task was to produce a cartoon each day for the editorial page. He retired from that same paper in 1949. Darling did spend two years as an editorial cartoonist for the *New York Globe*, but returned to Iowa at the first real opportunity.

The only other significant period away from his Des Moines newspaper position illustrates his action mode as a conservationist. Darling was active in political life generally, and this involvement often reflected his love of the outdoors and his dismay at what he felt the United States was doing to destroy its natural resource base. He helped organize the **Izaak Walton League** in Des Moines, was active in the landscaping of local parks, and worked to establish the first cooperative **wildlife** research unit at Iowa State College in Ames, a unit that served as a model for the establishment of similar units in other states.

Perhaps his greatest impact as an activist resulted from his appointment, by President Franklin Roosevelt, as head of the U.S. Bureau of Biological Survey, predecessor of the U.S. Fish and Wildlife Service. He was only in the position for two years, not being happy as a bureaucrat and not happy away from Iowa. But he was reportedly very effective in the job, "raiding" (in Roosevelt's words) the U.S. Treasury for scarce depression-era funds for waterfowl **habitat** restoration, and initiating the duck stamp program which over the years has funded the acquisition of several million acres added to the National Wildlife Refuge system. He also used his drawing skills to design the first duck stamp, as well as the flying goose that has become the signpost and symbol of the national wildlife refuge system.

Darling was also one of the founders, and then first President of the **National Wildlife Federation** in 1938. He later criticized the organization, and the proliferation of conservation organizations in general, because he first envisioned the Federation as an umbrella for conservation efforts and thought the emergence of too many groups diluted the focus on solving conservation and environmental problems. Until the end of his life, he tried, and failed, to organize a conservation clearing house that would refocus the conservation effort under one heading.

He put into all his efforts lessons of interdependence learned early from biology classes at Beloit College: "Land, water, and vegetation are [interdependent] with one another. Without these primary elements in natural balance, we can have neither fish nor game, wild flowers nor trees, labor nor capital, nor sustaining habitat for humans."

[*Gerald L. Young*]

FURTHER READING

Dudley, Joseph P. "Jay Norwood 'Ding' Darling: A Retrospective," *Conservation Biology* 7, no. 1 (March 1993): 200-203.

"Jay N. Darling: More Than a Cartoonist," *The World of Comic Art* 1, no. 1 (June 1966): 18-25.

Lendt, David L. *Ding: The Life of Jay Norwood Darling*. Ames, Iowa: Iowa State University Press, 1979.

Darwin, Charles Robert (1809-1882)

English biologist

Darwin, an English biologist known for his theory of **evolution**, was born at Shrewsbury, England, on February 12, 1809. He was born on the same day and the same year as Abraham Lincoln, a coincidence that may alert American readers to Darwin's era. He studied, traveled, and published his famous *On the Origin of Species* (1859) just prior to the American Civil War.

Darwin's father was an affluent physician and his mother the daughter of the potter Josiah Wedgwood. Charles married Emma Wedgwood, his first cousin, in 1839. Due to his family's wealth, Darwin was made singularly free to pursue his interest in science.

Darwin entered Edinburgh to study medicine, but, as he described in his autobiography, lectures were "intolerably dull," human anatomy "disgusted" him, and he experienced "nausea" in seeing surgery. He subsequently entered Christ's College, Cambridge, to prepare for Holy Orders in the Church of England. While at Cambridge, Darwin became intensely interested in geology and botany, and because of his knowledge in these sciences he was asked to join the voyage of the HMS *Beagle*. Darwin's experiences during the

Lithograph of Charles Darwin, age 40.

circumnavigational trek of the Beagle were of seminal importance in his later views on evolution.

Darwin's *On the Origin of Species* is a monumental catalog of evidence that evolution occurs, together with the description of a mechanism that explains such evolution. This "abstract" of his notions on evolution was hurried to publication because of a letter Darwin received from Alfred Russell Wallace expressing similar views. Darwin's evidence for evolution was drawn from comparative anatomy, embryology, distribution of **species**, and the fossil record. He believed that species were not immutable but evolved into other species. But how? His theory of evolution by natural selection is based on the premise that species have a great reproductive capacity. The production of individuals in excess of the number that can survive creates a struggle for survival. Variation between individuals within a species was well documented. The struggle for survival, coupled with variation, led Darwin to postulate that those individuals with favorable variations would have an enhanced survival potential and hence would leave more progeny and this process would lead to new species. This notion is sometimes referred to as "survival of the fittest." While the theory of evolution by natural selection was revolutionary for its day, essentially all biologists in the late twentieth century accept Darwinian evolution as fact.

The first edition of the *Origin* had a printing of 1,250 copies. It sold out the first day. Darwin was an extraordinarily productive author for someone who considered himself to be a slow writer. Among his other books are *Structure and Distribution of Coral Reef* (1842), *Geological Observations on Volcanic Islands* (1844), *On the Various Contrivances by which British and Foreign Orchids are Fertilized by Insects* (1862),

Insectivorous Plants (1875), and *On the Formation of Vegetable Mould through the Action of Worms* (1881). The last book, of interest to ecologists and gardeners, was published only six months prior to Darwin's death.

Darwin died at age 73 and is buried next to Sir Isaac Newton at Westminster Abbey in London.

[*Robert G. McKinnell*]

FURTHER READING

Barlow, N. *The Autobiography of Charles Darwin, 1809-1882.* With original omissions restored. Edited with appendix and notes by his granddaughter. New York: Norton, 1958.

Darwin, C. *The Voyage of the Beagle.* New York: Bantam Books, 1958.

Peckham, M., ed. *The Origin of Species by Charles Darwin.* A Variorum Text. Philadelphia: University of Pennsylvania Press, 1959.

DDT (dichlorodiphenyl-trichloroethane)

DDT is the well-known acronym for dichlorodiphenyl-trichloroethane. It can be degraded to several stable breakdown products, such as DDE and DDD. Usually DDT refers to the sum of all the DDT-related components.

DDT was first developed for use as an insecticide in Switzerland in 1939, and it was first used on a large scale on the Allied troops in World War II. Commercial, non-military use began in the United States in 1945. The discovery of its insecticidal properties was considered to be one of the great moments in public health disease control, as it was found to be effective on the carriers of many leading causes of death throughout the world including **malaria**, dysentery, dengue fever, yellow fever, filariasis, encephalitis, typhus, **cholera**, and scabies. It could be sprayed to control mosquitoes and flies or applied directly in powder form to control lice and ticks. It was considered the "atomic bomb" of **pesticide**s, as it benefited public health by direct control of more than fifty diseases and enhanced the world's food supply by agricultural pest control. It had eliminated mosquito transmission of malaria in the United States by 1953. In the first 10 years of its use, it was estimated to have saved 5 million lives and prevented 100 million illnesses worldwide.

Use of DDT declined in the mid-1960s due to increased resistance of different **species** of mosquitos and flies and other **pest**s, and to increasing concerns regarding the potential harm to **ecosystem**s and human health. Although the potential hazard from dermal absorption is small when the compound is in dry or powdered form, if the compound is in oil or an organic solvent it is readily absorbed through the skin and represents a considerable hazard.

Primarily DDT affects the central nervous system, causing dizziness, hyperexcitability, nausea, headaches, tremors, and seizures from acute exposure. Death can result from respiratory failure. It also is a liver toxin, activating microsomal **enzyme** systems and causing liver tumors. DDE is of similar toxicity. It became the focus of much public debate in the United States after the publication of *Silent Spring* by **Rachel Carson**, who effectively dramatized the harm to birds, **wildlife**, and possibly humans from the widespread use of DDT. Extensive spraying programs to eradicate Dutch elm disease and the **gypsy moth** also caused widespread songbird mortality. Its accumulation in the **food chain/web** also led to chronic exposures to certain wildlife populations. Fish-eating birds were subject to reproductive failure, due to egg shell thinning and sterility. DDT is resistant to breakdown and is transported long distances, making it ubiquitous in the world environment today. It was banned in the United States in 1972 after extensive government hearings, but is still in use in other parts of the world, mostly in developing countries, where it continues to be useful in the control of carrier-borne diseases. *See also* Acute effects; Chronic effects; Detoxification

[*Deborah L. Swackhammer*]

FURTHER READING

DDT and Its Derivatives. Environmental Health Criteria 9. Geneva, Switzerland: World Health Organization, 1979.

Toxicology of Pesticides. Copenhagen, Denmark: World Health Organization, 1982.

Dead zones

Eutrophication of estuaries and enclosed coastal seas has been observed and documented for several decades. The effect on aquatic life is also becoming clearer. The term "dead zone" specifically refers to those areas in ocean **environment**s where there is a reduction in the amount of **dissolved oxygen** in the waters. The condition is more appropriately called "hypoxia" or "hypoxic waters." A dissolved oxygen content of less than 2 parts per million (PPM) defines the term. Two PPM dissolved oxygen is generally accepted as the minimal level for most aquatic life survival and reproduction.

Factors contributing to these situations are many and complex. The timing and duration of these conditions varies from year to year and within seasons. It is certain that climatic conditions and catastrophic weather events can have a large influence on how and when oxygen becomes limiting in the different environments.

When these zones occur those species of aquatic life that can leave these zones—such as fishes and shrimp—do so. Bottom-growing plants, shellfish, and others that cannot, die creating an area that lacks aquatic life. This is the reason the term "dead zone" has been used (especially by the media) to describe these areas.

Nutrient availability, temperature, energy supply (i.e., soluble carbon for most microorganisms or light and **carbon dioxide** for plants), and oxygen status all affect the growth and sustainability of aquatic plants and animals. Conditions that perpetuate hypoxia include elevated temperatures because the ability of water to hold oxygen decreases with increasing temperature. Situations that promote consumption of oxygen such as plant and animal **respiration** can also lead to hypoxic conditions in water. Therefore, situations

that stimulate plant growth in water (i.e., algae and diatoms) can lead indirectly to hypoxic conditions. Algal growth can be accelerated with elevated levels of carbon dioxide and certain nutrients (especially **nitrogen** and **phosphorus**), provided adequate sunlight is available. Low sediment loads also support increased algal growth because the water is less turbid allowing more light to penetrate to the bottom.

Hypoxic waters occur near the mouths of most large rivers around the world and in coastal estuaries and enclosed coastal seas. In fact, over 40 hypoxic zones have been identified throughout the world. There is a general consensus among scientists that the extent of these zones has increased over the past several decades. This is based on evidence from the Baltic Sea, Kattegat, Skagerrak Dutch Wadden Sea, **Chesapeake Bay**, and northern Adriatic Sea, as well as one that occurs at the mouth of the Mississippi River in North America.

It is interesting to note that one of the largest hypoxic zones documented occurs in conjunction with the increase in ocean temperatures associated with **El Niño**. This weather event occurs periodically off the coast of South America, and influences not only the winter weather in North America, but also affects the anchovy catch in the Pacific. This in turn, affects the worldwide price for protein meal and has a direct impact on soybean farmers (since this is another major source for this product).

A large hypoxic zone occurs in the northern Gulf of Mexico where the Mississippi and Atchafalya rivers enter. The zone in recent years has exceeded 6,000 mi^2 (15,540 km^2) in size, making it one of the largest in the world.

This zone fluctuates seasonally, as do others. It can form as early as February and last until October. The most widespread and persistent conditions exist from mid-May to mid-September.

Recent research has shown a relationship between Mississippi River flow, nutrients (nitrogen and phosphorus), **plankton** productivity, and bottom water hypoxia. With increased nitrogen concentrations in the river water, massive phytoplankton blooms have occurred. As the blooms decompose they consume nearly all of the oxygen in the water. This, combined with a seasonal layering of the fresh water from the river and salt water in the Gulf, results in the zone of low-dissolved oxygen. Within the zone there are very low fish and shellfish populations. The extent of hypoxic conditions also varies during the season depending on the amount of water and nutrients discharged from the Mississippi River, water circulation patterns in the Gulf, salt and fresh water stratification, wind mixing, and tropical storms.

Changes in nutrient concentrations and ratios affect coastal **ecosystem**s in several ways. One is to influence **phytoplankton** production rates. Significant increases in nutrient concentrations and loading of nitrate and phosphorus and decreases in silicate have occurred during this century. As a result, changes have occurred in the relationship between the nutrients resulting in silica becoming more limiting than nitrogen in the production of diatoms. With this change, the type of algae produced changes. As the ratio of silica to nitrogen approaches 1:1, a level which has been documented to occur since 1993, nuisance blooms of the less desirable algae occur.

The changes in total production and types of algae affect the amount of carbon present in the water, contributing to the reduction in oxygen as the organisms decompose.

The effect of periodic events on the transport of nutrients to the Gulf, derived from areas of intensive agriculture in the upper Mississippi River Basin, have been implicated as the indirect cause. The largest amount of nutrients are delivered each year during the spring and early summer when streamflow and concentrations of nutrients, such as nitrogen are highest. During extreme high-flow events such as occurred during the floods of 1993 very high amounts of nutrients were transported to the Gulf. Levels were 100% higher than in other more normal years.

The nature of the hypoxia problem in the Gulf is complicated by the fact that some nutrient load from the Mississippi River is vital to maintain the productivity of the Gulf fisheries. Approximately 40% of the U.S. fisheries landings comes from this area including a large amount of the shrimp harvest. In addition, the area also supports a valuable sport fishing industry. The concern is that the hypoxic zone has been increasing in size since the 1960s due to human activities in the Mississippi Watershed which have increased nutrient loads, particularly nitrogen. The impacts of an expanding Gulf hypoxia include: large **algal bloom**s that affect other aquatic organisms; altered ecosystems with changes in plant and fish populations; reduced economic productivity in both commercial and recreational fisheries; and both direct and indirect impacts on fisheries such as direct mortality and altered migration patterns which may lead to declines in populations.

Studies have been conducted during the last several years on the sources of increased nutrient concentrations within the Mississippi River. Preliminary conclusions indicate that a significant amount of nutrients delivered to the Gulf come from the Upper Mississippi and Ohio River **watershed**s. The principal areas contributing nutrients are streams draining the corn belt states, particularly Iowa, Illinois, Indiana, Ohio, and southern Minnesota. About 60% of the nitrate transported by the Mississippi River comes from a land area that occupies less than 20% of the basin. These watersheds are predominantly agricultural and contain some of the most productive farmland in the world. This area produces approximately 60% of the nation's corn. Potential agricultural sources within these regions include runoff from cropland, animal grazing areas, animal waste facilities and inputs from agricultural drainage systems. How much they are a source of nutrients versus inputs from **sewage treatment** plants, atmospheric deposition, coastal **upwelling**, and industrial sources within the lower Mississippi Watershed is being evaluated. If is also unclear what effect the damming and channelization of the river for navigation has on nutrient delivery. The "dead zone" area in the Gulf will continue to be monitored to determine whether it continues to expand. In the meantime efforts to reduce nutrient loading will be undertaken in agricultural areas across the watershed. Depending on whether the zone continues to expand or

decreases as the effects of the major flooding events diminish will determine whether it remains a significant environmental problem in the Gulf of Mexico. Knowledge gained for the study of changing nutrient loads in the Mississippi River will be useful in addressing similar problems in other parts of the world.

[*James L. Anderson*]

FURTHER READING

Gulf of Mexico Information Network (GIN), World Wide Web site— http://pelican.gmpo.gov.

Rabalais, N. N., R. E. Turner, D. Justic, Q. Dortch, W. J. Wisenman, Jr., and B. K. Sen Gupta. "Nutrient changes in the Mississippi River and septum responses on the adjacent continental shelf." *Estuaries* 19, no. 2B (1996): 386-407.

Turner, R.E., and N.N. Rabalais. "Changes in Mississippi River water quality this century. Implications for coastal food webs." *Bio Science* 41 (1991): 140-147.

Debt for nature swap

Debt for nature swaps are designed to relieve developing countries of two devastating problems: spiraling debt burdens and **environmental degradation**. In a debt for nature swap, developing country debt held by a private bank is sold at a substantial discount on the secondary debt market to an environmental **nongovernmental organization (NGO)**. The NGO cancels the debt if the debtor country agrees to implement a particular environmental protection or **conservation** project. The arrangement benefits all parties involved in the transaction. The debtor country decreases a debt burden that may cripple its ability to make internal investments and generate economic growth. Debt for nature swaps may also be seen as a good alternative to defaulting on loans, which hurts the country's chances of receiving necessary loans in the future. In addition, the country enjoys the benefits of curbing environmental degradation. The creditor (bank) decreases its holdings of potentially bad debt, which may have to be written off at a loss. The NGO experiences global environmental improvement.

Debt for nature swaps were first suggested by Thomas Lovejoy in 1984. Swaps have taken place between Bolivia, Costa Rica, and Ecuador and NGOs in the United States. The first debt for nature swap was implemented in Bolivia in 1987. **Conservation International**, an American NGO, purchased $650,000 of Bolivia's foreign debt from a private bank in the United States at a discounted price of $100,000. The NGO then swapped the face value of the debt with the Bolivian government for "conservation payments-in-kind," which involved a conservation program in a 3.7 million acre tropical forest region implemented by the government and a local NGO.

Despite the benefits associated with debt for nature swaps, implementation has been minimal so far. Less than two percent of the $38 billion in debt for equity swaps have been debt for nature swaps. A lack of incentives on the part of the debtor or the creditor and the lack of well-developed supporting institutional infrastructure can hinder progress in arranging debt for nature swaps.

If a debtor country is unable to repay foreign debt, it has the option of defaulting on the loans or agreeing to a debt for nature swap. The country has an incentive to agree to a debt for nature swap if defaulting is not a viable option and if the benefits of decreasing debt through a swap outweigh the costs of implementing a particular environmental protection project. The cost of the environmental protection programs can be substantial if the developing country does not have the appropriate institutional infrastructure in place. The program will require the input of professional public administrators and environmental experts. Without institutions to support these individuals, the developing countries may find it impossible to carry out the programs they promise to undertake in exchange for cancellation of the debt. If, in addition, the debtor country is highly capital-constrained, then it might not give high priority to the benefits of an environmental investment.

Whether the creditor has an incentive to sell a debt on the secondary debt market to an NGO depends on the creditor's estimate of the likelihood of receiving payment from the developing country; on the proportion of potentially bad credit the creditor is holding; and on its own financial situation. If the NGOs are willing to pay the price demanded by private banks for developing country debt and swap it for environmental protection projects in the debtor countries, they will have the incentive to pursue debt for nature swaps.

Benefits that may be taken into account by the NGOs are those commonly associated with environmental protection. Many developing countries hold the world's richest **tropical rain forest**s, and the global community will benefit greatly from the preservation of these forests. Tropical forests hold a great deal of **carbon dioxide**, which is released into the **atmosphere** and contributes to the **greenhouse effect** when the forests are destroyed. Another benefit is known as "option value," the value of retaining the option of future use of plant or animal resources that might otherwise become extinct. Although we may not know at present of what use, if any, these **species** might be, there is a value associated with preserving them for unknown future use. Examples of future uses might be pharmaceutical remedies, scientific understanding or **ecotourism**. In addition, NGOs may attach "existence value" to environmental amenities. Existence value refers to the value placed on just knowing that natural environments exist and are being preserved. Many NGOs believe preservation is important so that future generations can enjoy the environment. This value is known as "bequest value." Finally, the NGO may be interested in decreasing hunger and poverty in developing countries, and both the reduction of external debt and the slowing of the depletion of **natural resources** in developing countries is perceived as a benefit for this purpose.

To make a swap attractive, however, the NGO must be assured that the environmental project will be carried out after the debt has been canceled. Without adequate enforcement and assistance, a country might promise to implement an environmental project without being able or willing to follow through. Again, the solution to this problem lies in the development of institutions that are committed to monitoring and giving assistance in the implementation of the programs. Such institutions might encourage long-term relationships between the debtor and NGO to facilitate a structure by which debt is canceled piecemeal on the condition that the debtor continues to comply with the agreement.

A complicating factor that may affect an NGO's **cost-benefit analysis** of debt for nature swaps in the future is that, as the number of swaps and environmental protection projects increases, the value to be derived from any additional projects will decrease, due to diminishing marginal returns.

As described above, the benefits associated with debt for nature swaps both for the debtor countries and NGOs hinge on the presence of supporting institutions in the developing countries. It is particularly important to promote the establishment of appropriate, professionally managed public agencies with adequate resources to hire and maintain environmental experts and managers. These institutions should be responsible for planning and implementing the programs.

It should be noted that, although large debt burdens and environmental degradation are both serious problems faced by many developing countries, there is no direct linkage between them. Nevertheless, debt for nature swaps are an intriguing remedy that seems to address both problems simultaneously. As the quantity and magnitude of swaps so far have been relatively small, it is impossible to say how successful a remedy it may be on a larger scale. It is clear, though, that the future of debt for nature swaps depends on the development of appropriate incentives to all parties in the swap and on the development of institutions to support the fulfillment of the agreements.

[*Barbara J. Kanninen*]

FURTHER READING

Hansen, S. "Debt for Nature Swaps: Overview and Discussion of Key Issues." *Ecological Economics* 1 (1989): 77-93.

Lovejoy, T. E. "Aid Debtor Nations' Ecology." *New York Times* (4 October 1984): A31.

Zylicz, T. "Debt-for-Environment Swaps: The Institutional Dimension." Working Paper, The Beijer International Institute of Ecological Economics. Stockholm, Sweden: The Royal Swedish Academy of Sciences, 1992.

Deciduous forest

Deciduous forests are made of trees that lose their leaves seasonally and are leafless for part of each year. The tropical deciduous forest is green during the rainy season and bare during the annual **drought**. The temperate deciduous forest is green during the wet warm summers and leafless during the cold winters with the leaves turning yellow and red before falling. Temperate deciduous forests once covered large portions of Europe, eastern United States, Japan, and eastern China. **Species** diversity is highest in Asia and lowest in

Europe. In the United States deciduous forest, 67 species of trees exist.

Decline spiral

A decline spiral is the destruction of a **species, ecosystem**, or **biosphere** in a continuing downward trend, leading to ecosystem disruption and impoverishment. The term is sometimes used to describe the loss of **biodiversity**, when a catastrophic event has led to a sharp decline in the number of organisms in a **biological community**.

In areas where the **habitat** is highly fragmented either due to human intervention or natural disaster, the loss of species is markedly accelerated. Loss of species diversity often initiates a downward spiral, as the weakening of even one plant or animal in an ecosystem, especially a **keystone species**, can lead to the malfunctioning of the biological community as a whole.

Biodiversity exists at several levels within the same community; it can include ecosystem diversity, species diversity, and genetic diversity. Ecosystem diversity refers to the different types of landscapes that are home to living organisms. Species diversity refers to the different types of species in an ecosystem. Genetic diversity refers to the range of characteristics in the **DNA** of the plants and animals of a species. A catastrophic event that affects any aspect of the diversity in an ecosystem can start a decline spiral.

Any major catastrophe that results in a decline in biospheric quality and diversity, known as an ecocatastrophe, may initiate a decline spiral. **Herbicide** and **pesticide** used in agriculture, as well as other forms of **pollution**; increased use of **nuclear power**, and exponential **population growth** are all possible contributing factors. The Lapp reindeer herds were decimated by fallout from the nuclear accident at **Chernobyl** in 1986. Similarly, the oil spill from the **Exxon Valdez** in 1989 led to a decline spiral to the Gulf of Alaska ecosystem.

The force that begins a decline spiral can also be indirect, as when **acid rain**, **air pollution**, **water pollution**, or **climate** change kill off many plants or animals in an ecosystem. Diversity can also be threatened by the introduction of non-native or **exotic species**, especially when these species have no natural predators and are more aggressive than the native species. In these circumstances, native species can enter into a decline spiral which will impact other native species in the ecosystem.

Restoration ecology is a relatively new discipline that attempts to recreate or revive lost or severely damaged ecosystems. It is a hands-on approach by scientists and amateurs alike designed to reverse the damaging trends that can lead toward decline spirals. Habitat rebuilding for **endangered species** is an example of restoration ecology. For example, the Illinois chapter of the **Nature Conservancy** has reconstructed an oak-and-grassland **savanna** in Northbrook, Illinois, and a **prairie** in the 100-acre ring formed by the underground Fermi National Accelerator Laboratory at Batavia, Illinois. Since it is easier to reintro-

duce **flora** than the **fauna** into an ecosystem, practitioners of restoration ecology concentrate on plants first. When the plant mix is right, insects, birds, and small animals return on their own to the ecosystem.

[*Linda Rehkopf*]

FURTHER READING

Ehrlich, P., and J. Roughgarden. *The Science of Ecology*. New York: Macmillian, 1987.
May, R. M. *Stability and Complexity in Model Ecosystems*. Princeton, NJ: Princeton University Press, 1973.

Decomposers

Decomposers (also called saprophages, meaning "corpse eating") are the organisms which perform the critical task of **decomposition** in nature. They include bacteria, fungi, and **detritivores** that break down dead organic matter, releasing nutrients back into the **ecosystem**. Fungi are the dominant decomposers of plant material, and bacteria primarily break down animal matter. Decomposers secrete enzymes into plant and animal material to break down the organic compounds, starting with compounds such as sugars which are easily broken down, and ending with more resistant compounds such as cellulose and lignin. Rates of decomposition are faster at higher values of moisture and temperature. Decomposers thus perform a unique and important function in the recycling process in nature.

Decomposition

The chemical and biochemical breakdown of a complex substance into its constituent compounds and elements, releasing energy, and often with the formation of new, simpler substances. Organic decomposition takes place mostly in or on the **soil** under **aerobic** conditions. Dead plant and animal materials are consumed by a myriad of organisms, from mice and moles, to worms and beetles, to **fungi** and bacteria. Enzymes produced by these organisms attack the decaying material, releasing water, **carbon dioxide**, **nutrients**, **humus**, and heat. New microbial cells are created in the process.

Decomposition is a major process in nutrient cycling, including the **carbon** and **nitrogen** cycles. The liberated carbon dioxide can be absorbed by photosynthetic organisms, including green plants, and made into new tissue in the **photosynthesis** process, or it can be used as a carbon source by autotrophic organisms.

Decomposition also acts on inorganic substances in a process called weathering. Minerals broken free from rocks by physical disintegration can chemically decompose by reacting with water and other chemicals to release elements, including potassium, calcium, magnesium, and iron. These and other elements can be taken up by plants and microorganisms, or they can remain in the soil system to react with other constituents, forming clays.

Deep ecology

The term "deep ecology" was coined by the Norwegian environmental philosopher **Arne Naess** in 1973. Naess drew a distinction between "shallow" and "deep" **ecology**. The former perspective stresses the desirability of conserving natural resources, reducing levels of air and **water pollution**, and other policies primarily for promoting the health and welfare of human beings. Deep ecologists maintain that "shallow ecology" simply accepts, uncritically and without reflection, the homocentric, or human-centered, view that humans are, or ought to be, if not the masters of **nature**, then at least the managers of nature fro human ends or purposes. Defenders of deep ecology, by contrast, claim that shallow environmentalism is defective in placing human interests above those of animals and ecosystems. Human beings, like all lower creatures, exist within complex webs of interaction and interdependency. If we insist on conquering, dominating, or merely managing nature for our own benefit or amusement, if we fail to recognize and appreciate the complex webs that hold and sustain us, we will degrade and eventually destroy the natural **environment** that sustains all life.

But, deep ecologists say, if we are to protect the environment for all **species**, now and in the future, we must challenge and change long-held basic beliefs and attitudes about our species place in nature. For example, we must recognize that animals, plants, and the ecosystems that sustain them have **intrinsic value** — that is, are valuable in and of themselves — quite apart from any use or instrumental value they might have for human beings. The genetic diversity found in insects and plants in **tropical rain forest**s is to be protected not (only or merely) because it might one day yield a drug for curing **cancer**, but also and more importantly because such **biodiversity** is valuable in its own right. Likewise, rivers and lakes should contain clean water not just because humans need uncontaminated water for swimming and drinking, but also because fish do. Like **Gandhi**, to whom they often refer, deep ecologists teach respect for all forms of life and the conditions that sustain them.

Critics complain that deep ecologists do not sufficiently respect human life and the conditions that promote prosperity and other human interests. Some go so far as to claim that they believe in the moral equivalence of human and all other life-forms. Thus, say the critics, deep ecologists would assign equal value to the life of a disease-bearing mosquito and the child it is about to bite. No human has the right to swat or spray an insect, to kill **pest**s or predators, and so on. But in fact this is a caricature of the stance taken by deep ecology. All creatures, including humans, have the right to protect themselves from harm, even if that means depriving a mosquito of a meal or even eliminating it altogether. Competition within and among species is normal, natural, and inevitable. Bats eat mosquitoes; bigger fish eat smaller fish; humans eat big fish; and so on. But for one species to dominate or destroy all others is neither natural nor sustainable. Yet human beings have, through technology, an ever-increasing power to destroy entire ecosystems and the life that they sustain. Deep ecologists hold that this power has corrupted human beings and has led them to think —quite mistakenly— that human purposes are paramount and that human interests take precedence over those of "lower" or "lesser" species. Human beings cannot exist independently from, but only interdependently with nature's myriad species. Once we recognize the depth and degree of this interdependence, deep ecologists say, we will learn humility and respect. Our species' proper place is not on top, but within nature and with nature's creatures and the conditions that nurture us all.

Some cultures and religions have long taught these lessons. Zen Buddhism, Native American religions, and other nature-centered belief systems of belief have counseled humility toward, and respect for, nature and nonhuman creatures. But the dominant Western reaction is to dismiss these teachings as primitive or mystical. Deep ecologists, by contrast, contend that considerable wisdom is to be found in these native and non-Western perspectives.

Deep ecology is at present a philosophical perspective within the environmental movement, and not a movement in itself. This perspective does, however, inform and influence the actions of some radical environmentalists. Organizations such as **Earth First!** and the **Sea Shepherd Conservation Society** are highly critical of moderate shallow environmental groups which are prepared to compromise with loggers, developers, dam builders, strip miners, and oil companies, thus putting the economic interests of some human beings ahead of all others. Such development destroys **habitat**, endangers entire species of animals and plants, and proceeds on the assumption that nature has no intrinsic value, but only instrumental value for human beings. It is this assumption, and the actions that proceed from it, that deep ecology is questioning and attempting to change. *See also* Ecosophy; Environmental ethics; Foreman, Dave; Green politics; Greens; Strip mining

[*Terence Ball*]

FURTHER READING

Devall, B., and G. Sessions. *Deep Ecology: Living as if Nature Mattered.* Salt Lake City, UT: Gibbs M. Smith, 1985.

Foreman, D. *Confessions of an Eco-Warrior.* New York: Harmony Books, 1991.

Fox, Warwick. *Toward a transpersonal Ecology: Developing New Foundations for Environmentalism.* Albany, NY: State University of New York Press, 1995.

Naess, A. "The Shallow and the Deep, Long-Range Ecology Movement," *Inquiry* 16 (1973): 95-100.

—. *Ecology, Community and Life-Style,* trans. by David Rothenberg. Cambridge and New York: Cambridge University Press, 1990.

Seed, J., J. Macy, P. Fleming, and A. Naess. *Thinking Like a Mountain.* Philadelphia, PA: New Society Publishers, 1988.

Sessions, George (ed.), *Deep Ecology for the 21st Century.* Boston and London: Shambhala, 1995.

Deep-well injection

Injection of liquid wastes into subsurface geologic formations is a technology that has been widely adopted as a waste-disposal practice. The practice entails drilling a well to a permeable, saline-bearing geologic formation that is confined above and below with impermeable layers known as confining beds. When the injection zones lie below drinking water sources at depths typically between 2,000 to 5,000 feet (610-1,525 m), they are referred to as Class I disposal wells. The liquid **hazardous waste** is injected at a pressure that is sufficient to replace the native fluid and yet not so high that the integrity of the well and confining beds is at risk. Injection pressure is a limiting factor because excessive pressure can cause hydraulic fracturing of the injection zone and confining strata, and the intake rate of most injection wells is less than 400 gallons (1500 l) per minute.

Deep-well injection of liquid waste is one of the least expensive methods of **waste management** because little waste treatment occurs prior to injection. **Suspended solids** must be removed from **wastewater** prior to injection to prevent them from plugging the pores and reducing permeability of the injection zone. Physical and chemical characteristics of the wastewater must be considered in evaluating its suitability for disposal by injection.

The principal means of monitoring the wastewater injection process is recording the flow rate, the injection and annulus pressures, and the physical and chemical characteristics of the waste. Many consider this inadequate and monitoring is still a controversial subject. The major question which arises concerns the placement of monitoring wells and whether they increase the risk that wastewater will migrate out of the injection zone if they are improperly constructed.

Deep-well injection of wastes began as early as the 1950s, and it was then accepted as a means of alleviating surface **water pollution**. Today, most **injection well**s are located along the Gulf Coast and near the Great Lakes, and their biggest users are the **petrochemical**, pharmaceutical, and steel mill industries.

As with all injection wells, there is a concern that the waste will migrate from the injection zone to the overlying **aquifer**s. *See also* Aquifer restoration; Groundwater monitoring; Groundwater pollution; Hazardous waste siting; Hazardous waste site remediation; Water quality

[*Milovan S. Beljin*]

FURTHER READING

Assessing the Geochemical Fate of Deep-Well-Injected Hazardous Wastes: Summaries of Recent Research. Washington, DC: U. S. Environmental Protection Agency, 1990.

International Symposium on Subsurface Injection of Liquid Wastes. *Proceedings of the International Symposium on Subsurface Injection of Liquid Waste.* March 3-5, 1986. Dublin, OH: National Water Well Association, 1986.

Defenders of Wildlife (Washington, D.C.)

Defenders of Wildlife was founded in 1947 in Washington, D.C. Superseding older groups such as Defenders of Furbearers and the Anti-Steel-Trap League, the organization was established to protect wild animals and the **habitat**s that support them. Today their goals include the preservation of biodiversity and the defense of **species** as diverse as gray **wolves** (*Canis lupus*), **Florida panther**s (*Felis concolor coryi*), and **grizzly bear**s (*Ursus arctos*), as well as the western yellow-billed cuckoo (*Coccyzus americanus*), the **desert tortoise** (*Gopherus agassizii*), and Kemp's Ridley **sea turtle** (*Lepidochelys kempii*).

Defenders of Wildlife employs a wide variety of methods to accomplish their goals, from research and education to lobbying and litigation. They have achieved a ban on livestock grazing on 10,000 acres of tortoise habitat in Nevada and lobbied for restrictions on the international **wildlife** trade to protect **endangered species** in other countries. In 1988 they successfully lobbied Congress for funding to expand **wildlife refuge**s throughout the country. Ten million dollars was appropriated for the Lower Rio Grande National Wildlife Refuge in Texas, $2 million to purchase land for a new preserve along the Sacramento River in California, and $1 million for additions to the **Rachel Carson** National Wildlife Refuge in Maine. They are currently seeking passage of the National Biological Diversity Conservation and Research Act and the American Heritage Trust Fund, which would support the continued acquisition of natural habitats.

The organization has been at the forefront of placing preservation on an economic foundation. In Oregon, they have overseen the establishment of a number of areas from which to view wildlife on public and private land, thus improving access to natural habitats and linking the environment with the economic benefits of the state's tourism industry. Defenders maintains a speaker's bureau, and they support a number of educational programs for children designed to nourish and expand their interest in wildlife. But the group also participates in more direct action on behalf of the environment. They coordinate grassroots campaigns through their Defenders Activist Network, which has a membership of 9,000. They work with the **Environmental Protection Agency** on a hotline called the "Poison Patrol," which receives calls on the use of **pesticide**s that damages wildlife, and they belong to the *Entanglement Network Coalition*, which works to prevent the loss of animal life through entanglement in nets and **plastic** refuse.

Restoring wolves to their natural habitats has long been one of the top priorities of Defenders of Wildlife. In 1985, they sponsored an exhibit in **Yellowstone National Park** and at Boise, Idaho, called "Wolves and Humans," which received over 250,000 visitors and won the Natural Resources Council of America Award of Achievement for Education. They have helped reintroduce red and gray wolves back into the northern Rockies. In order to assist farmers and the owners of livestock herds that graze in these areas, Defenders has raised funds to compensate them for the loss of land. They are also working to reduce and eventually eliminate the poisoning of predators, both by lobbying for stricter legislation and by encouraging Western farmers to participate in their guard dog program for livestock.

Defenders of Wildlife has 88,000 members and an annual budget of $5,200,000. In addition to wildlife viewing guides for different states, their publications include a bimonthly magazine for members called *Defenders* and *In Defense of Wildlife: Preserving Communities and Corridors.* Contact: Defenders of Wildlife, 1244 Nineteenth Street, NW, Washington, DC, 20036. Internet: http://www.defenders.org/index.html.

[*Douglas Smith*]

Defoliation

Several factors can cause a plant to lose its leaves and become defoliated. Defoliation is a natural and regular occurrence in the case of deciduous trees and shrubs that drop their leaves each year with the approach of winter. This process is aided by an abscission layer that develops at the base of the leaf petiole, weakens the attachment to the plant, and eventually causes the leaf to drop. Severe drought may also cause leaves to wilt, dry and drop from a plant. The result of severe dehydration is usually lethal for herbaceous plants, although some woody species may survive an episode of drying. Heavy infestation by leaf-eating insects can lead to partial, or complete defoliation. The gypsy moth (*Porthetria dispar*) is an important defoliator that attacks many trees, defoliating, and weakening, or killing them. Parasitic wasps that feed on the larvae can help to control gypsy moth outbreaks. Insecticide sprays have also be used to kill the larvae. Spider mites, any of the plant-feeding mites of the family Tetranychidae (subclass Acari), feed on house plants and the foliage and fruit of orchard trees. Heavy infestation can lead to serious or complete defoliation. Spider mites are controlled with pesticides, although growing resistance to chemical control agents has made this more difficult, and alternative control measures are under investigation.

Along with natural causes of defoliation, chemicals can cause plants to drop their leaves. The best known and most widely used chemical defoliators are 2,4,5 trichlorophenoxyacetic acid (2,4,5-T) and 2,4 dichlorophenoxyacetic acid (2,4-D). Both chemicals are especially toxic to broad-leaf plants. The herbicide 2,4-D is widely used in lawn care products to rid lawns of dandelions, clover, and other broad-leaf plants that interfere with robust turf development. At appropriate application rates, it selectively kills broad-leaf herbaceous plants, and has little effect on narrow-leaf grasses. The uses of 2,4,5-T are similar, although it has been more widely used against woody species.

A mixture of 2,4-D and 2,4,5-T, in a product called Agent Orange has been extensively used to control the growth and spread of woody trees and shrubs in sites earmarked for industrial or commercial development. Agent Orange saw extensive use by American forces in Southeast Asia during the Vietnam war, where it was used initially to clear for power lines, roads, railroads, and other lines of communication. Eventually, as the war continued, it was used to spray enemy hiding places, and U.S. military base perimeters to prevent surprise attack. Food crops, especially rice, were also targets for Agent Orange to deprive enemy forces of food. Although Agent Orange and other formulations containing the chlorinated phenoxy acetic acid deriva-

Deforestation of the jungle in Brazil.

tives are generally lethal to herbaceous plants, woody deciduous plants may survive one or more treatments, depending on the species treated, concentrations used, spacing of applications, and weather. In Vietnam it was found that mangrove forests in the Mekong delta were especially sensitive, and often killed by a single treatment. A member of the dioxin family of chemicals, 2,3,7,8-tetrachlorodibenzo-p-dioxin (TCDD) has been found to be an accidental but common contaminant of 2,4,5-T and Agent Orange. Dioxins are very resistant to attack by microbes in the environment, and are apt to persist in soils for a very long time. Although few disorders have been definitively proven to be caused by dioxins, their effects on laboratory animals have caused some scientists to rank them among the most poisonous substances known. The U.S. government banned some 2,4,5-T containing products in 1979 because of uncertainties regarding its safety, but its use continues in other products.

[*Douglas C. Pratt*]

FURTHER READING

Addicott, F. T. *Abscission.* Berkeley: University of California Press, 1952.

Gansner, D. A. *Defoliation potential of gypsy moth.* Radnor, Pa.: U.S. Dept. of Agriculture, Northeastern Forest Experiment Station, 1993.

Teas, H. J. *Herbicide toxicity in mangroves.* U.S. Environmental Protection Agency, Office of Research and Development, Environmental Research Laboratory, Springfield Va.: for sale by the National Technical Information Service, 1976.

Whiteside, T. *The withering rain; Americas herbicidal folly.* New York: Dutton, 1971.

Deforestation

Deforestation is the complete removal of a forest **ecosystem** and conversion of the land to another type of landscape. It differs from **clear-cutting**, which entails complete removal of all standing trees but leaves the **soil** in a condition to regrow a new forest if seeds are available. Humans destroy forests for many reasons. American Indians burned forests to convert them to **grasslands** that supported big game animals. Early settlers cut and burned forest to convert them to croplands. Between 1600 to 1909, European settlement decreased forest cover in the United States by 30 percent. Since that time, total forest acreage in the United States has actually increased. In Germany about two-thirds of the forest was lost through settlement. Food and Agriculture Organization (FAO) estimated that from 1980 to 1990, 0.9 percent of remaining tropical forests were deforested annually (169,000km^2 per year), an area equivalent to the state of Washington. FAO defines forest as land with more than 10 percent tree cover, natural understory vegetation, nature animals, natural soils, and no agriculture. Analysis of deforestation is difficult because data is unreliable and the definitions for "forest" and "deforestation" keep changing; for example, clear-cuttings which reforest within five years have been considered deforested in some studies but not in others.

The major direct causes of topical deforestation are the expansion of shifting agriculture, livestock production, and fuelwood harvest in drier regions. Forest conversion to permanent cropland, infrastructure, urban areas, and commercial fisheries also occurs. Although not necessarily resulting in deforestation, timber harvest, grazing, and fires can severely degrade the forest. The environmental costs of deforestation can include species **extinction**, **erosion**, **flooding**, reduced land productivity, **desertification**, and **climate** change and increased atmospheric **carbon dioxide**. As more **habitat** is destroyed, more species are facing extinctions. Deforestation of **watershed**s causes erosion, flooding, and **siltation**. Upstream land loses fertile **topsoil** and downstream crops are flooded, hydroelectric **reservoir**s are filled with **silt** and fisheries are destroyed. In drier areas, deforestation contributes to desertification.

Deforestation can alter local and regional climates because evaporation of water from leaves makes up as much as two-thirds of the rain that falls in some forest. Without trees to hold back surface **runoff** and block wind, available moisture is quickly drained away and winds dry the soil, sometimes resulting in desert-like conditions. Another potential effect on climate is the large scale release into the **atmosphere** of carbon dioxide stored as organic **carbon** in forests and forest soils. In 1980, tropical deforestation released between 0.4 and 1.6 billion tons of carbon into the atmosphere, an amount equal to 10 to 40 percent of that from **fossil fuels**.

As a result of misguided deforestation in the moist and dry tropics, the rural poor are deprived of construction materials, fuel, food, and cash crops harvested from the forest. Species extinctions, siltation, and flooding expand these problems to national and international levels. Despite these human and environmental costs, wasteful deforestation continues. Current actions to halt and reverse deforestation focus on creating economic and social incentives to reduce wasteful land conversion by providing for wiser ways to satisfy human needs. Other efforts are the reforestation of deforested areas and the establishment and maintenance of **biodiversity** preserves.

[*Edward Sucoff*]

FURTHER READING

Gregersen, H., S. Draper, and D. Elz. *People and Trees*. Washington, DC: World Bank, 1989.

Monastersky, R. "The Deforestation Debate." *Science News* 144 (July 10, 1993): 26-27.

Rowe, R., N. P. Sharma, and J. Browder. "Deforestation: Problems, Causes and Concerns." In *Managing the World's Forests*, edited by N. P. Sharma. Dubuque, IA: Kendall Hunt, 1992.

Delaney Clause

The Delaney Clause is a part of the Federal Food, Drug, and Cosmetic Act of 1958, Section 409, and it prohibits the addition to food of any substance that will cause **cancer** in animals or humans. The clause states "no additive will be deemed to be safe if it is found to induce cancer when ingested by man or animal, or if it is found, after tests which are appropriate for the evaluation of the safety of food additives, to induce cancer in man or animals . . ." The clause addresses the safety of food intended for human consumption and few, if any, reasonable individuals would argue with its intent.

There is however, an emerging scientific controversy over its application, and many now question the merits of the clause as it is written. For example, safrole occurs naturally as a constituent in sassafras tea and spices and thus permissibly under the Delaney Clause, but it is illegal and banned as an additive to natural root beer because it has been proven a **carcinogen** in animal tests. Coffee is regularly consumed by many individuals, yet more than 70 percent of the tested **chemicals** that occur naturally in coffee have been shown to be carcinogenic in one or more tests. Naturally occurring carcinogens are found in other foods including lettuce, apples, pears, orange juice, and peanut butter. It is important to note here that the National Cancer Institute recommends the consumption of fruits and vegetables as part of a regimen to reduce cancer risk. This is because it is widely believed that the positive effects of fruits and vegetables far outweigh the potential hazard of trace quantities of naturally occurring carcinogens.

It has been estimated that about 10,000 natural **pesticide**s of plants are consumed in the human diet. These natural pesticides protect the plants from disease and predation by other organisms. Only a few of these natural plant pesticides (less than 60) have been adequately tested for carcinogenic potential and of these about half of them tested positive. Bruce N. Ames and his associates at the University of California estimate that 99.99 percent of the pesticides ingested by humans are not residues of chemicals applied by humans but are chemicals that occur naturally and therefore legally. It has been argued that such naturally occurring chemicals are less hazardous and thus differ in their cancer-causing potential from synthetic chemicals. But this does not appear to be the case; although the mechanisms for chemical carcinogenesis are poorly understood, there seems to be no fundamental difference in how natural and synthetic carcinogens are metabolized in the body.

The Delaney Clause addresses only the issue of additives to the food supply. It is noteworthy that salt, sugar, corn syrup, citric acid and baking soda comprise 98 percent of the additives listed, while chemical additives, which many fear, constitute only a small fraction. It should also be noted that there are other significant safety issues pertaining to the food supply, including **pathogen**s which cause botulism, hepatitis, and salmonella food poisoning. Of similar concern to health are traces of environmental pollutants, such as **mercury** in fish, and cooking-induced production of carcinogens, such as benzopyrene in beef cooked over an open flame. Excess fat in the diet is also thought to be a significant health hazard.

Scientists who are rethinking the significance of the "zero risk" requirement of the Delaney Clause do not believe society should be unconcerned about chemicals added to food. They simply believe the clause is no longer consistent with current scientific knowledge, and they argue that chemicals added in trace quantities, for worthwhile reasons, should be considered from a different perspective. *See also* Agricultural chemicals; Agricultural pollution; Drinking-water supply; Food and Drug Administration

[*Robert G. McKinnell*]

FURTHER READING

Corliss, J. "The Delaney Clause: Too Much of a Good Thing?" *Journal of the National Cancer Institute* 85 (1993): 600-603.

Gold, L. S., et al. "Rodent Carcinogens: Setting Priorities." *Science* 258 (9 October 1992): 261-265.

Demographic transition

Developed by demographer Frank Notestein in 1945, this concept describes the typical pattern of falling death and birth rates in response to better living conditions associated with economic development. This idea is important, for it offers the hope that developing countries will follow the same pathway to population stability as have industrialized countries. In response to the Industrial Revolution, for example, Europe experienced a population explosion during the nineteenth century. Emigration helped alleviate overpopulation, but European couples clearly decided on their own to limit family size.

Notestein identified three phases of demographic transition: preindustrial, developing, and modern industrialized societies. Many authors add a fourth phase, labeled postindustrial. In phase one, birth rates and death rates are both high with stable populations. As development provides a better food supply and sanitation, death rates begin to plummet, marking the onset of phase two. However, birth rates remain high, as families follow the pattern of preceding generations. The gap between high birth rates and falling death rates produces a population explosion, sometimes doubling in less than twenty-five years.

After one or two generations of large, surviving families, birth rates begin to taper off, and as the population ages, death rates rise. Finally a new balance is established, phase three, with low birth and death rates. The population is now much larger yet stable. The experience of some European countries, especially in Central Europe and Russia, suggests a fourth phase where populations actually decline. This may be a response to past hardships and oppressive political systems there, however.

Historically, birth rates have always been high. With few exceptions population explosions are linked to declining death rates, not rising birth rates. As recently as the 1980s one textbook theorized that for couples in India to have a 95 percent chance of having one surviving son for old-age security, they would have to bear an average of 6.3 children. Infants and young children are especially vulnerable; sanitation and proper food are vital. Infant survival is seen by some as a threat because of the built-in momentum for population growth. However, history reveals that there has been no decline in birth rates which has not been preceded by a drop in infant mortality. In a burgeoning world this makes infant survival a matter of top priority. To this end, in 1986 the United Nations adopted a program with the acronym GOBI: Growth monitoring, Oral rehydration therapy (to combat killer diarrhea), Breast feeding, and Immunization against major communicable diseases. *See also* Child survival revolution; Population Council

[*Nathan H. Meleen*]

FURTHER READING

Cunningham, W. P., and B. W. Saigo. *Environmental Science: A Global Concern.* 2nd ed. Dubuque, IA: William C. Brown, 1992.

Keyfitz, N. "The Growing Human Population." *Scientific American* 261 (September 1989): 7-16.

Maddox, J. *The Doomsday Syndrome.* New York: McGraw-Hill, 1972.

Denitrification

A stage in the **nitrogen cycle** in which **nitrates** in the **soil** or in dead organic matter are converted into nitrite, nitrous oxide, ammonia, or (primarily) elemental **nitrogen**. The process is made possible by certain types of bacteria, known as denitrifying bacteria. Denitrification is a reduction reaction and occurs, therefore, in the absence of oxygen. For example, flooded soil is likely to experience significant denitrification since it is cut off from atmospheric oxygen. Although denitrification is an important process for the decay of dead organisms, it can also be responsible for the loss of natural and synthetic **fertilizer**s from the soil.

Department of Agriculture

See **U. S. Department of Agriculture**

Department of Energy

See **U. S. Department of Energy**

Department of Health and Human Services

See **U. S. Department of Health and Human Services**

Department of the Interior

See **U. S. Department of the Interior**

Desalinization

Desalinization, also known as "desalination," is the process of separating sea water or **brackish** water from their dissolved salts. The average salt content of the ocean water is about 3.4 percent (normally expressed as 34 parts per thousand). The range of salt content varies from 18 parts per thousand in the North Sea and near the mouths of large rivers to a high of 44 parts per thousand in locked bodies of water such as the Red Sea, where evaporation is very high. The desalination process is accomplished commercially by either distillation or reverse **osmosis** (RO).

Distillation of sea water is accomplished by boiling water and condensing the vapor. The components of the distillation system consist of a boiler and a condenser with a source of cooling water. Reverse osmosis is accomplished by forcing filtered sea water or brackish water through a reverse osmosis membrane. In a reverse osmosis process, approximately 45 percent of the pressurized sea water goes through membranes and becomes fresh water. The remaining brine (concentrated salt water) is returned to the sea.

In 1980, the United Nations declared 1981-1990 as the "International Drinking Water Supply and Sanitation Decade." The objective was to provide safe drinking water and sanitation to developing nations. Despite some progress in India, Indonesia, and a few other countries, the percentage of the world population with access to safe drinking water has not changed much since that declaration.

The World Health Organization (WHO) estimates that only two in five people in the **less developed countries (LDCs)** have access to safe drinking water. The WHO also estimates that at least 25 million people of the LDCs die each year because of polluted water and from water-born diseases such as **cholera**, polio, dysentery, and typhoid. Whether by distillation or by reverse osmosis, desalination of water can transform water that is unusable because of its **salinity** into valuable fresh water. This could be an important water source in many drought-prone areas.

Desalination Plants, Distribution, and Functions

There are approximately 7,500 desalination plants worldwide. Collectively they produce less than 0.1 percent of the world's fresh water supply. This supply is equal to about 3.5 billion gallons per day (13 million liters). The cost and the feasibility of producing desalinated water depends upon the cost of energy, labor, and relative costs of desalinated water to that of imported fresh water. It is estimated that in the United States, commercial desalinated water produced from sea water by reverse osmosis costs about $3 per thousand gallons. This price is four to five times the average price currently paid by urban consumers for drinking water and over 100 times the price paid by farmers for **irrigation** water. The current energy requirement is approximately three kilowatt hours of electricity per one gallon of fresh water extracted from sea water. Currently, using desalinated water for agriculture is cost prohibitive.

About two-thirds of the desalination water is produced in Saudi Arabia, Kuwait, and North Africa. Several small-scale reverse osmosis plants are now operating in the United States, including California (Santa Barbara, Catalina Island, and soon in Ventura and other coastal communities). Generally, desalination plants are used to supplement the existing fresh water supply in areas adjacent to oceans and seas such as southern California, the Persian Gulf region, and other dry coastal areas. Among the advantages of desalinized water are a dependable water supply regardless of rainfall patterns, elimination of **water rights** disputes, and the preservation of the fresh water supply, all of which are essential for existing natural **ecosystem**s.

Reverse Osmosis

Reverse osmosis involves forcing water under pressure through a filtration membrane that has pores small enough to allow water molecules to pass through but exclude slightly larger dissolved salt molecules. The basic parts of a reverse osmosis system include onshore and offshore components. The onshore components consist of a water pump, an electrical power source, pre-treatment filtration (to remove seaweed and debris), reverse osmosis units connected in series, **solid waste** disposal equipment, and fresh water pumps. The offshore components consist of an underwater intake pipeline, approximately 1,093 yards (one kilometer) from shore, and a second pipeline for brine discharge.

Small reverse osmosis units for home use with a few gallons-per-day capacity are available. These units use a disposable reverse osmosis membrane. Their main drawback is that they waste four to five times the volume of water they purify.

Producing potable water from sea water is an energy intensive, costly process. The high cost of producing desalinized water limits its use to domestic consumption. In areas such as the Persian Gulf and Saudi Arabia where energy is plentiful at a low cost, desalinized water is a viable option for drinking water and very limited greenhouse agriculture. The notion of using desalinized water for wider agricultural purposes is neither practical nor economical at today's energy prices and available technology.

[*Muthena Naseri*]

FURTHER READING

Kaufman, D. G., and C. M. Franz. *Biosphere 2000: Protecting Our Global Environment.* New York: Harper-Collins, 1993.

Lizarraga, S., and D. Brown. "Fresh Water from Santa Barbara Seas." Reprinted from *Desalination and Water Reuse*, 1992. Santa Barbara: Department of Water Resources.

Nebel, B. J., and R. T. Wright. *Environmental Science: The Way the World Works.* 4th Edition. Englewood Cliffs, NJ: Prentice Hall, 1993.

Desert

Six percent of the world's land surface is desert, a **biome** in which less than ten inches (25 centimeters) of precipitation occurs per year or any place where evaporation greatly exceeds precipitation, resulting in a lack of available moisture. Sometimes any area lacking the necessary conditions to support life is called a desert. Deserts occur around latitudes 30 degrees north and south where masses of dry circulating air descend to the earth's surface. There are three kinds of deserts—hot (such as Sahara), temperate (such as the Mojave), and cold (such as the Gobi). The area of global desert is increasing yearly, as marginal lands become degraded by human misuse resulting in **desertification**. Deserts are potential sites for the production of electricity using banks of solar cells or parabolic solar collectors. The lack of water and remoteness of some deserts may make them attractive places to store nuclear and other **hazardous waste**s.

Desert tortoise (*Gopherus agassizii*)

The desert tortoise is a large, herbivorous, terrestrial turtle of the family Testudinidae. It is found in both the southwestern United States and in northwestern Mexico. It is the official reptile in the states of California and Nevada. No other turtle in North America shares the extreme conditions of the **habitat**s occupied by the desert tortoise. It inhabits **desert** oases, washes, rocky hillsides, and canyon bottoms with sandy or gravelly **soil** under hot, **arid** conditions.

Desert tortoises dig into dry, gravelly soil under bushes in arroyo banks or at the base of cliffs to construct a burrow, which is their home. Climatic conditions dictate daily activity patterns of these tortoises, and they can relieve the problems of high body temperature and evaporative water loss by retreating into their burrows. Since many desert tortoises live in areas devoid of water, except for infrequent rains, they must rely on their food for their water.

The active period for the desert tortoise is from March through September, after which they enter a hibernation period. Nesting and egg laying activities extend from May through July. Desert tortoises lay an average of five moisture-proof eggs, an adaptation that helps retain water in its harsh

Desert tortoise (Desert Tortoise Natural Area, Mojave Desert, California).

environment. These tortoises reach sexual maturity at 15 to 20 years, and they have a life span of up to 80 years.

The desert tortoise is very sensitive to human disturbances, and this has led to the decimation of many of its populations throughout the desert southwest. The Beaver Dam Slope population of southwestern Utah has been studied over several decades and shows some of the general tendencies of the overall population. In the 1930s and 1940s the desert tortoise population in this area exhibited densities of about 160 adults per square mile. By the 1970s this density had fallen to less than 130 adults per square mile, and more recent studies indicate the level is now about 60 adults per square mile. In southeastern California at least one population reaches densities of 200 adults per square mile, but overall tendencies show that populations are drastically declining. Recent estimates indicate that there are about 100,000 individual desert tortoises existing in the Mojave and Sonoran deserts.

Desert tortoise populations are listed as threatened in Utah and endangered in California, Nevada, and Arizona. Numerous factors are contributing to its decline and vulnerability. Habitat loss through human encroachment and development, overcollecting for the **pet trade**, and vandalism—including shooting tortoises for target practice and flipping them over onto their backs, causing them to die from exposure—have decimated populations. Other factors contributing to their decline are grazing livestock, which trample them or their burrows, and mining operations, which also causes respiratory infections among the desert tortoises. Numerous desert tortoises have been killed or maimed by **off-road vehicles**, which also collapse the tortoises' burrows. Concern is mounting as **conservation** efforts seem to be having little effect throughout much of the desert tortoise's range.

[*Eugene C. Beckham*]

FURTHER READING

Campbell, F. "The Desert Tortoise." *Audubon Wildlife Report.* San Diego: Academic Press, 1988-89.

Ernst, C., and R. Barbour. *Turtles of the United States.* Lexington: University Press of Kentucky, 1972.

————. *Turtles of the World.* Washington, DC: Smithsonian Institute Press, 1989.

Desertification

About one billion people live in **arid** or semiarid **desert** lands that occupy about one third of the world's land surface. In these drier parts of the world, deserts are increasing rapidly from a combination of natural processes and human activities, a process known as desertification or land degradation. An annual rainfall of less than 10 inches (25 centimeters) will produce a desert anywhere in the world. In the semiarid areas along the desert margins, where the annual rainfall is around 16 inches (40 centimeters), the **ecosystem** is inherently fragile with seasonal rains supporting the temporary growth of plants. Recent changes in the climate of these regions have meant that the rains are now unreliable and the lands that were once semiarid are now becoming desert. The process of desertification is precipitated by prolonged **drought**s, causing the top layers of the **soil** to dry out and blow away. The eroded soils become unstable and compacted and do not readily allow for seeding. This means that desertified areas do not regenerate by themselves but remain bare and continue to erode. Desertification of grazing lands or croplands is accompanied, therefore, by a sharp drop in the productivity of the land.

Natural desertification is greatly accelerated by human activities that leave soils vulnerable to **erosion** by wind and water. The drier **grasslands** with too little rain to support cultivated crops have traditionally been used for grazing livestock. When semiarid land is overgrazed (by keeping too many animals on too little land), plants that could survive moderate grazing are uprooted and destroyed altogether. Since plant roots no longer bind the soil together, the exposed soil dries out and is blown away as dust. The destruction and removal of the **topsoil** means that soil productivity drops drastically. The obvious solution to desertification caused by **overgrazing** is to limit grazing to what the land can sustain, a concept that is easy to espouse but difficult to practice.

In the **Sahel** zone along the southern edge of the Sahara desert, settled agriculture and overgrazing livestock on the fragile scrublands have led to widespread soil erosion. Nomadic pastoralists, who have traditionally followed their herds and flocks in search of new pastures, are now prevented by national borders from reaching their chosen grazing grounds. Instead of migrating, the nomads have been encouraged to settle permanently and this has led to their herds overgrazing available pastures.

Other human factors leading to desertification include over-cultivation, **deforestation**, salting of the soil through **irrigation**, and the plowing of marginal land. These destructive practices are intensified in developing countries by rapid **population growth**, high population density, poverty, and poor land management. The consequences of desertification in some countries mean intensified drought and **famine** and lowered standards of living. It is estimated that desertification worldwide has claimed an area the size of Brazil (2 billion acres or 810 million hectares) in the past 50 years. Each year new deserts consume an area the size of Belgium (15 million acres or 6 million hectares), most of which is in the African Sahel.

In marginal areas throughout the world, traditional farming practices can lead to desertification. Plowing turns the top layer of the soil upside down, burying and killing weeds but exposing bare soil to erosion. In arid areas the exposed soil dries out rapidly and is easily lost through wind erosion.

The processes of erosion and soil formation vary with climate and with the composition of the parent material. In balanced ecosystems, soil lost to erosion is replaced by new soil created by natural processes. On average, new soil is formed at a rate of about 5 tons an acre (12.5 tons per hectare) per year, which is equivalent to a layer of soil about 1/64 inch (0.4 cm) thick. This means that soils can sustain an erosion rate of up to 5 tons per acre per year and still remain in balance. However, much of the world's crop and forest land is not within this balance (with erosion running at 2 to 10 times the tolerable rate). In the United States about 6 tons of topsoil are lost for every ton of grains produced.

Forests are cut down for many different reasons. Some are cleared for agriculture, some for construction, some for paper products, and some to meet cooking and heating needs. Unfortunately, deforestation results in more than just the loss of trees, for soil is eroded, nutrients are lost to the ecosystem, and the water cycle is disrupted. The roots of the trees serve to bind the soil together and to hold water in the ecosystem, while the leaves of the trees break the force of the rain and allow it to soak into the topsoil. The result is that surface **runoff** from a forested hillside is half as much as from a grass-covered slope. Additionally, water soaking into the ground (rather than running off) leads to the natural recharge of groundwater and other **water resources**. Water and soil runoff from deforested hillsides cause **flooding** and siltation of agricultural and aquatic ecosystems in adjacent lowlands. Forests are also more efficient at reabsorbing and recycling the nutrients released from decaying detritus than are grasslands. Clearing forests therefore exposes the soil to both erosion and nutrient loss and alters the recharge of water reserves in the ecosystem.

Industrialized countries experienced a period of intense deforestation during the Industrial Revolution and even today much of the land has low productivity. Fortunately, most of these countries are now reforesting faster than they are deforesting. This is possible because their population growth is low, their agricultural production per acre is high, and their need for fuelwood for cooking and heating is optional, since **fossil fuels** and electricity are widely available. All of these factors release the pressure to further deforest the land.

In developing countries, on the other hand, high population growth rates and widespread poverty put pressure on the forests. Trees are needed for firewood, charcoal, and export, and the land is needed for farmland. In some develop-

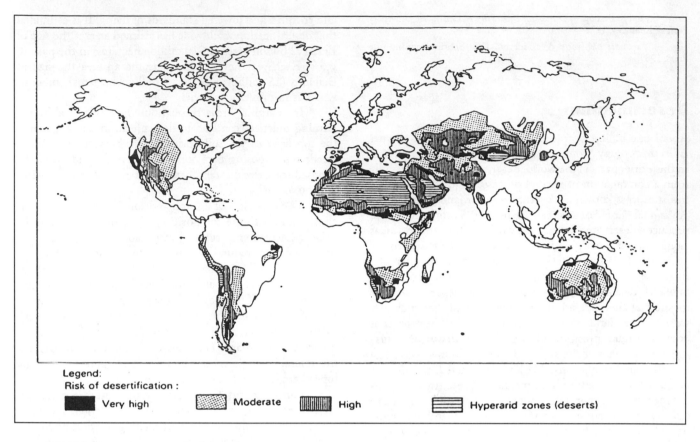

Legend:
Risk of desertification :

Very high   Moderate   High   Hyperarid zones (deserts)

World deserts and areas at risk of desertification.

ing countries deforestation exceeds replanting by five times. In Ethiopia, population and economic pressures pushed people to deforest and cultivate hillsides and marginally dry lands, and more than 1 billion tons of topsoil per year are now lost, resulting in recurrent famines. In parts of India and Africa there is so little wood available that dried animal dung is used to fuel cooking fires, an act that further robs the soil of potential nutrients. In Brazil, soil erosion and desertification have resulted from the conversion of forests to cattle ranches. In China, about one-third of its agricultural land has been lost to erosion, and the story is similar for many other countries.

The answer to erosion from deforestation is reforestation, better forest conservation, and better forest management to increase productivity. Planting trees on hillsides is particularly effective. Reforesting desertified areas first requires mulching the soil to hold moisture and the protection of the seedlings for several years until natural processes can regenerate the soil. Using these methods, Israel has achieved spectacular success in bringing desertlands (a product of past desertification) back to agriculture.

Desertification and its agents, deforestation and erosion, have been powerful shapers of human history. Agriculture had its roots in the once fertile crescent of the Middle East and in the Mediterranean lands. However, deforestation, overgrazing, and poor agricultural practices have turned once-productive pastureland and farmland into the near deserts of today. It is thought by some that deforestation and desertification may have even contributed to the collapse of the Greek and Roman Empires. Similar fates may have befallen the Harappan civilization in India's Indus Valley, the Mayan civilization in Central America, and the Anasazi civilization of Chaco Canyon, New Mexico, in what is today desertland.

[*Neil Cumberlidge*]

FURTHER READING

Dejene, A. *Environment, Famine, and Politics in Ethiopia: A View from the Village*. Boulder, CO: L. Rienner Publishers, 1990.

Grainger, A. *Desertification: How People Make Deserts, How People Can Stop, and Why They Don't*. London: International Institute for Environment and Development, 1982.

Herda, D. J., and M. L. Madden. *Land Use and Abuse*. New York: Franklin Watts, 1990.

McLeish, E. *The Spread of Deserts*. Austin, TX: Steck-Vaughn Library, 1991.

Spooner, B., and H. S. Mann, eds. *Desertification and Development: Dryland Ecology in Social Perspective*. London and New York: Academic Press, 1982.

Design for disassembly

For **recycling** to be broadly applicable, many environmentalists believe that products should be cheaper and easier to take apart so that they can be put together again and reused in other products.

Many large companies like Whirlpool, Digital Equipment, 3M, and General Electric have begun to design products in this regard. The BMW car, Z1, is considered to be the first to incorporate the concepts of disassembly. The plastic exterior of the car can be removed from the metal chassis in 20 minutes. The doors, bumpers, and front, rear, and side panels have been manufactured with recyclable plastic, and pop-in/pop-out fasteners replace screws and glues, whenever possible.

Composite materials, on the other hand, which are being used on a more widespread basis are difficult to recycle. Small juice boxes, for instance, which have become very popular are made of many layers of plastic, paper, and aluminum, which cannot be separated. *See also* Recyclables; Reuse; Waste management; Waste reduction

Detergents

A group of organic compounds that cause foaming and serve as cleansing agents based on their surface-active properties. A detergent molecule is termed surface-active because a portion of the molecule is hydrophilic and a portion is hydrophobic. It will therefore collect at the interface of water and another medium such as a gas bubble. Bubbles are stabilized by the surface-active molecules so that when the bubbles rise to the top of the bulk liquid, they maintain their integrity and form a foam. Surface-active agents can also agglomerate by virtue of their hydrophilic/hydrophobic nature to form *micelles* that can dissolve, trap, and/or envelop **soil** particles, oil, and grease. Surface-active agents are sometimes called *surfactants*. Synthetic detergents are sometimes referred to as *syndets*.

Detoxification

When many **toxic substance**s are introduced into the **environment**, they do not remain in their original form, but are transformed to other products by a variety of biological and non-biological processes. The **chemicals** and their transformation products are degraded, converted progressively to smaller molecules, and eventually utilized in various natural cycles, such as the **carbon cycle**. Toxic metals are not degraded but are interconverted between available and nonavailable forms. Some organic compounds, such as **polychlorinated biphenyl (PCB)**s, are degraded over a period of many years to less toxic compounds, while compounds such as the **organophosphate** insecticides may break down in only a few hours.

The chemical transformations that occur may either increase (referred to as intoxication, or activation if the parent compound was nontoxic) or decrease (referred to as detoxification) the toxicity of the original compound. For example, elemental **mercury**, which has low toxicity, can be converted to methylmercury, a very hazardous chemical, through **methylation**. Parathion is a fairly nontoxic insecticide until it is converted in a living system or by **photo-**

chemical reactions to paraoxon, an extremely toxic chemical. However, parathion can also be degraded to less toxic products by the process of hydrolysis.

In microbial degradation, the ultimate fate of the toxic chemicals may be mineralization (that is, the conversion of an organic compound to inorganic products), which results characteristically in detoxification; however, intermediates in the degradation sequence, which may be toxic or have unknown toxicity, may persist for a period of time, or even indefinitely. Likewise, since degradation pathways may contain many steps, detoxification may occur early in the degradation pathway, before mineralization has occurred. Detoxification may also be accomplished biologically through **cometabolism**, the **metabolism** by microorganisms of a compound that cannot be used as a **nutrient**; cometabolism does not result in mineralization, and organic transformation products remain. Studies have also shown that the structure and toxicity of many organic compounds can be altered by plants.

In modifying a toxic chemical, detoxifying processes destroy its actual or potential harmful influence on one or more susceptible animal, plant, or microbial **species**. Detoxification may be measured with the use of bioassays. A **bioassay** involves the determination of the relative toxicity of a substance by comparing its effect on a test organism with the conditions of a control. The scale or degree of response may include the rate of growth or decrease of a population, colony, or individual; a behavioral, physiological, or reproductive response; or a response measuring mortality. Bioassays can be used for environmental samples through time to determine detoxification of chemicals.

Both acute and chronic bioassays are used to assess detoxification. In an acute bioassay, a severe and rapid response to the toxic chemical is observed within a short period of time (for example, within four days for fish and other aquatic organisms and within 24 hours to two weeks for mammalian species). Detoxification of a chemical may be detected if there is a decrease in the observed toxicity of a test solution over the time of the acute test, indicating removal of the toxic chemical by degradation or other processes. Similarly, an increase in toxicity could indicate the formation of a more toxic transformation product.

Chronic bioassays are more likely to provide information on the rates of degradation, transformation, and detoxification of toxic compounds. Partial or complete life cycle bioassays may be used, with measurements of growth, reproduction, maturation, spawning, hatching, survival, behavior, and **bioaccumulation**.

Detoxification of chemicals should also be measured by toxicity testing that involves changes in different organisms and interactions among organisms, especially if the chemicals are persistent and stable and may accumulate and magnify in the **food chain/web**. Model **ecosystem**s can be used to simulate processes and assess detoxification in a terrestrial-aquatic ecosystem. A typical ecosystem could include **soil** organisms, lake-bottom **fauna**, a plant, an insect, a snail, an alga, a crustacean, and a fish species maintained under controlled conditions for a period of time.

Most major types of reactions that result in transformation and detoxification of toxic chemicals can be accomplished either by biological (enzymatic) or by non-biological (nonenzymatic) mechanisms. Although significant changes in structure and properties of organic compounds may result from non-biological processes, the biological mechanism is the major and often the only mechanism by which organic compounds are converted to inorganic products. Microorganisms are capable of degrading and detoxifying a wide variety of organic compounds; presumably, every organic molecule can be destroyed by one or more types of microorganisms (referred to as the "principle of microbial infallibility.") However, since some organic compounds do accumulate in the environment, there must be factors such as unfavorable environmental conditions that prevent the complete degradation and detoxification of these persistent compounds. There are many examples where certain microorganisms have been identified as capable of detoxifying specific organic compounds. In some cases, these microorganisms can be isolated, cultured, and inoculated into contaminated environments in order to detoxify the compounds of concern.

The major types of transformation reactions include: oxidation, ring scission, photodecomposition, **combustion**, reduction, dehydrohalogenation, hydrolysis, hydration, conjugation, and chelation. Conjugation is the only reaction mediated by **enzyme**s alone, while chelation is strictly nonenzymatic. Primary changes in organic compounds are usually accomplished by oxidative, hydrolytic, or reductive reactions.

Oxidation reactions are reactions in which energy is used in the incorporation of molecular oxygen into the toxic molecule. In most mammalian systems, a monooxygenase system is involved. One atom of molecular oxygen is added to the toxic chemical, which usually results in a decrease in toxicity and an increase in water solubility, as well as provides a reaction group that can be used in further transformation processes such as conjugation. Microorganisms use a dioxygenase system, in which oxidation is accomplished by adding both atoms of molecular oxygen to the double bond present in various aromatic (containing **benzene**-like rings) **hydrocarbons**.

Ring scission, or opening, of aromatic ring compounds also can occur through oxidation. Though aromatic ring compounds are usually stable in the environment, some microorganisms are able to open aromatic rings by oxidation. After the aromatic rings are opened, the compounds may be further degraded by other organisms or processes. The number, type, and position of substituted molecules on the aromatic ring may protect the ring from enzymatic attack and may retard scission.

Photodecomposition can also result in the detoxification of toxic chemicals in the **atmosphere**, in water, and on the surface of solid materials such as plant leaves and soil particles. The reaction is usually enhanced in the presence of water; photodecomposition is also important in the detoxification of evaporated compounds. The **ultraviolet radiation** in sunlight is responsible for most photodecomposition processes. In photooxidation, for example, photons of light provide the necessary energy to mediate the reactions with oxygen to accomplish oxidation.

Combustion of toxic chemicals involves the oxidation of compounds accompanied by a release of energy. Often combustion does not completely result in the degradation of chemicals, and may result in the production of very toxic combustion products. However, if operating conditions are properly controlled, combustion can result in the detoxification of toxic chemicals.

Under **anaerobic** conditions, toxic compounds may be detoxified enzymatically by reduction. An example of a reductive detoxifying process is the removal of halogens from halogenated compounds. Dehydrohalogenation is another anaerobic process that also results in the removal of halogens from compounds.

Hydrolysis is an important detoxification mechanism in which water is added to the molecular structure of the compound. The reaction can occur either enzymatically or nonenzymatically. Hydration of toxic compounds occurs when water is added enzymatically to the molecular structure of the compound.

Conjugation reactions involve the combination of foreign toxic compounds with endogenous, or internal, compounds to form conjugates that are water soluble and can be eliminated from the biological organism. However, the toxic compound may still be available for uptake by other organisms in the environment. Endogenous compounds used in the conjugation process include sugars, amino acid residues, phosphates, and sulfur compounds.

Many metals can be detoxified by forming complexes with organic compounds by sharing electrons through the process of chelation. These complexes may be insoluble or nonavailable in the environment; thus the toxicant can not affect the organism. **Sorption** of toxic compounds to solids in the environment, such as soil particles, as well as incorporation into **humus**, may also result in detoxification of the compounds.

Generally, the complete detoxification of a toxic compound is dependent on a number of different chemical reactions, both biological and non-biological, proceeding simultaneously, and involving the original compound as well as the transformation products formed. *See also* Biogeochemical cycles; Biomagnification; Chemical bond; Environmental stress; Incineration; Oxidation reduction reaction; Persistent compound; Water hyacinth

[*Judith Sims*]

FURTHER READING

Alexander, M. "Biodegradation of Toxic Chemicals in Water and Soil." In *Dynamics, Exposure and Hazard Assessment of Toxic Chemicals*, edited by R. Haque. Ann Arbor, MI: Ann Arbor Science, 1980.

Burnside, O. C. "Prevention and Detoxification of Pesticide Residues in Soils." In *Pesticides in Soil and Water*, edited by W. D. Guenzi. Madison, WI: Soil Science Society of America, 1974.

Dauterman, W. C., and E. Hodgson. "Chemical Transformations and Interactions." In *Introduction to Environmental Toxicology*, edited by F. E. Guthrie, and J. J. Perry. New York: Elsevier, 1980.

Rand, G. M. "Detection: Bioassay." In *Introduction to Environmental Toxicology*, edited by F. E. Guthrie, and J. J. Perry. New York: Elsevier, 1980.

Detritivores

Detritivores are organisms within an ecosystem that feed on dead and decaying plant and animal material and waste (called detritus); detritivores represent more than half of the living biomass. Protozoa, polychaetes, nematodes, Fiddler crabs, and filter-feeders are a few examples of detritivores that live in the salt marsh ecosystem. (Fiddler crabs, for instance, scoop up grains of sand and consume the small particles of decaying organic material between the grains.) While microbes would eventually decompose most material, detritivores speed up the process by comminuting, and partly digesting the dead, organic material. This allows the microbes to get at such material more readily. The continuing decomposition process is vital to the existence of an ecosystem—essential in the maintenance of nutrient cycles, as well as the natural renewal of soil fertility.

Development, sustainable
See **Sustainable development**

Dew point

An expression of humidity defined as the temperature to which air must be cooled to cause condensation of its water vapor content (dew formation) without the adding or subtracting of water vapor or changing its pressure. At this point the air is saturated and relative humidity becomes 100 percent. When the dew point temperature is below freezing it is also referred to as the frost point. The dewpoint is a conservative expression of humidity because it changes very little across a wide range of temperature and pressure, unlike relative humidity which changes with both. Dew points, however, are affected by water vapor content in the air. High dew points indicate large amounts of water vapor in the air and low dew points indicate small amounts. Scientists measure dew points in several ways: with a dew point hygrometer; from known temperature and relative humidity values; or from the difference between dry and wet bulb temperatures using tables. They use this measurement to predict fog, frost, dew and overnight minimum temperature.

Diapers
See **Disposable diapers**

Diazinon

An **organophosphate pesticide**. Malathion and parathion are other well-known organophosphate pesticides. The organophosphates inhibit the action of the **enzyme** cholinesterase, a critical component of the chain by which messages are passed from one nerve cell to the next. They are highly effective against a wide range of pests. However, since they tend to affect the human nervous system in the same way they affect insects, they tend to be dangerous to humans, wildlife, and the environment. One of the most widely-used lawn chemicals, diazinon has been implicated in killing songbirds, pet dogs and cats, and causing near fatal poisonings in humans. The EPA banned its use on golf courses and sod farms after numerous reports of its killing ducks, geese, and other birds. *See also* Cholinesterase inhibitor

Dieback

Dieback refers to a rapid decrease in numbers experienced by a population of organisms that has temporarily exceeded, or *overshot*, its **carrying capacity**. Organisms at low **trophic level**s such as rodents or deer, as well as weed species of plants, experience dieback most often. Without pressure from predators or other limiting factors, such "opportunistic" **species** reproduce rapidly, consume food sources to depletion, and then experience a population crash due chiefly to starvation (though reproductive failure can also play a part in dieback). The presence of predators—for instance, foxes in a meadow inhabited by small rodents—often results in a stabilizing effect on population numbers.

Die-off

Die-offs are the massive, sometimes unexplained but always unexpected, disappearances of plants and animals. The most well-known is probably the die-off of dinosaurs, but die-offs continue today in many regions of the world, including the United States.

Frogs and their kin are mysteriously vanishing in some areas, and scientists suspect that human alteration of **ecosystem**s is partly responsible. On five continents, scientists in nineteen countries have reported massive die-offs among amphibians. Frogs are good indicators of environmental change because of the permeability of their skin. They are extremely susceptible to **toxic substance**s on land and in water. Decreasing rainfall in some areas may be a factor in the die-offs, as is **habitat** loss due to **wetlands** drainage. Other scientists are investigating whether increased **ultraviolet radiation** due to **ozone** depletion is killing toads in the Cascade Mountain Range.

Other multiple factors—such as **acid rain**, heavy metal and **pesticide** contamination of ponds and other surface water, and human predation in some areas—may be causing the amphibians to die off. In France, for example, thousands of tons of frog legs imported from Bangladesh and Indonesia are consumed each year.

Scientists also have recorded widespread declines in the numbers of migratory songbirds in the Western Hemisphere and of wild mushrooms in Europe. The decline in these so-called **indicator organism**s is a sign of declining health of the overall ecosystems.

The decline of songbirds is attributed to the loss or fragmentation of habitat, particularly forests, throughout the songbirds' range from Canada to Central America and northern South America. **Fungi** populations in Europe are dying off, and scientists think it is more than a problem of overharvesting. The health of forests in Europe is closely linked to the fungi populations, which point to the ecological decline of the forests. Some scientists believe that **air pollution** is also playing a role in their decline.

A massive die-off of millions of starfish in the White Sea has been attributed to radioactive military waste in the former Soviet Union. French scientists have recorded growing numbers of dead **dolphins** along the Riviera, probably due to **environmental stress** which left the animals too weak to fight off a virus. This phenomenon may also explain die-offs of dolphins along the Gulf Coast in Texas, as well as the mysterious deaths of 12,000 seals washed up on the shores of the North Sea in the summer of 1988.

[*Linda Rehkopf*]

FURTHER READING

"Earth Almanac: Why Are Frogs and Toads Knee-Deep in Trouble?" *National Geographic* 183 (April 1993).

Gore, Al. *Earth in the Balance*. New York: Houghton Mifflin, 1992.

Digester

See **Wastewater**

Dillard, Annie (1945-)

American writer

Often compared to the American naturalist Henry David Thoreau, Dillard—a novelist, memoir writer, essayist, poet, and author of books about the natural world—is best known for her acute observation of the land, the seasons, the changing weather, and the wildlife within her intensely seen **environment**. Though born in Pittsburgh, Pennsylvania on April 30, 1945, Dillard's vision of nature's violence and beauty was most fully developed living in Virginia, where she received her B.A., 1967, and M.A., 1968, from Hollins College. She also lived in the Pacific Northwest from 1975-1979 as scholar-in-residence at the University of Western Washington, in Bellingham, and is adjunct professor of English and writer in residence at Wesleyan University, in Middletown, Connecticut, where she lives with her husband, Bob Richardson, and her daughter, Rosie. Since 1973, she has also been a columnist for *The Living Wilderness*, the magazine of the **Wilderness Society**, the leading organization advocating expansion of the nation's **wilderness**.

In 1975, Dillard won the Pulitzer Prize for general nonfiction for her first book of prose, *Pilgrim at Tinker Creek* (1974), subtitled "A mystical excursion into the natural world," in which she presented—quoting **Henry David Thoreau**—"a meteorological journal of the mind" based on her life in the Roanoke Valley, Virginia, where she had lived

since 1965. Her vision of "power and beauty, grace tangled in a rapture of violence," of a world in which "carnivorous animals devour their prey alive," is also an intense celebration of the things seen as she wanders the Blue Ridge mountainside, the Roanoke creek banks, observing muskrat, deer, red-winged blackbirds, and the multitude of "free surprises" her environment unexpectedly, and fleetingly, displays. *Seeing* acquires a mystical primacy in Dillard's work.

The urgency of seeing is also conveyed in Dillard's only book of essays, *Teaching A Stone To Talk* (1982), in which she writes: "At a certain point you say to the woods, to the sea, to the mountains, the world, Now I am ready. Now I will stop and be wholly attentive." Dillard suggests that, for the natural phenomena that we do not use or eat, our only task is to witness. But in witnessing, she sees cruelty and suffering, making her question at a religious level what mystery lies at the heart of the created universe, of which she writes: "The world has signed a pact with the devil . . . The terms are clear: if you want to live, you have to die."

Unlike some natural historians or writers of environmental books, Dillard is not associated with a specific program for curbing the destructiveness of human civilization. Rather, what has been described as her loving attentiveness to the phenomenal world—"nature seen so clear and hard that the eyes tear," as one reviewer commented—allies her with the broader movement of writers whose works teach some other relationship to nature than exploitation. In *Holy the Firm* (1977), her 76-page journal of several days spent in Northern Puget Sound, Dillard records such events as the burning of a seven-year-old girl in a plane crash and a moth's immolation in a candle flame to rehearse her theme of life's harshness, but at the same time, to note, "A hundred times through the fields and along the deep roads I've cried Holy." In the end, Dillard is a sojourner, a pilgrim, wandering the world, ecstatically attentive to nature's bloodiness and its beauty.

[*David Clarke*]

FURTHER READING

Dillard, A. *Pilgrim at Tinker Creek*. New York: Bantam Books, Inc., 1975.

———. *Holy the Firm*. New York: Harper & Row Publishers, 1982.

———. *Teaching A Stone To Talk: expeditions and encounters*. New York: Harper & Row Publishers, 1982.

———. *Encounters With Chinese Writers*. Connecticut: Wesleyan University Press, 1984.

———. *An American Childhood*. New York: Harper & Row Publishers, 1987.

———. *The Living*. New York: Harper Collins, 1992.

Dioxin

Dioxin is the chemical byproduct of certain manufacturing processes or products. It develops during the manufacture of two **herbicide**s known as **2,4,5-T** and **2,4-D**, which are the two components found in **Agent Orange**. Dioxin is also manufactured in several other chemical processes, including the chlorinated bleaching of pulp and paper. The issue of dioxin's toxicity is one of the most hotly debated in the scientific community, involving the federal government, industry, the press, and the general public.

While dioxin commonly refers to a particular compound known as tetrachlorodibenzo-p-dioxin, or TCDD, there are actually 75 different dioxins. TCDD has been studied in some manner since the 1940s, and the most recent information indicates that it is capable of interfering with a number of physiological systems. Its toxicity has been compared to **plutonium** and it has proven lethal to a variety of research animals, including guinea pigs, monkeys, rats, and rabbits.

TCDD is also the chemical that some scientists at the **Environmental Protection Agency (EPA)** and a broad spectrum of researchers have called the most **carcinogen**ic ever studied. During the late 1980s and early 1990s, it was linked to an increased risk of rare forms of **cancer** in humans—especially soft tissue sarcoma and non-Hodgkins lymphoma—at very high doses. Some have called dioxin "the most toxic chemical known to man." According to **Barry Commoner**, Director of the Center for the Biology of Natural Systems at Washington University, the chemical is "so potent a killer that just three ounces of it placed in New York City's water supply could wipe out the populace."

Exposure can come from a number of sources. Dioxin can be air-borne and inhaled in drifting incinerator ash, aerial spraying, or the hand spray application of weed killers. Dioxin can be absorbed through the skin as people walk through a recently sprayed area such as a backyard or a golf course. Water **runoff** and **leaching** from agricultural lands treated with **pesticide**s can pollute lakes, rivers, and underground **aquifer**s. Thus, dioxin can be ingested in contaminated water, in fish, and in beef that has grazed on sprayed lands. Residues in plants consumed by animals and humans add to the contaminated **food chain/web**. Research has shown that nursing children now receive trace amounts of dioxin in their mother's milk.

Because it bioaccumulates in the environment, TCDD continues to be found in the **soil** and waterways in microscopic quantities over 25 years after its first application. Dioxin is part of a growing family of chemicals known as organochlorines—a class of chemicals in which **chlorine** is bonded with **carbon**. These chlorinated substances are created to make a number of products such as **polyvinyl chloride**, solvents, and refrigerants as well as pesticides. Hundreds or thousands of organochlorines are produced as by-products when chlorine is used in the bleaching of pulp and paper or the disinfection of **wastewater** and when chlorinated chemicals are manufactured or incinerated. The by-products of these processes are toxic, persistent, and hormonally active. TCDD is also part of current manufacturing processes, such as the manufacture of the wood preservative, **pentachlorophenol**.

If the exposure to dioxin is intense, there can be an immediate response. Tears and watery nasal discharge have been reported, as have intense weakness, giddiness, vomiting, diarrhea, headaches, burning of the skin, and rapid heartbeat.

Usually, a weakness persists and a severe skin eruption known as chloracne develops after a period of time. The body excretes very little dioxin, and the chemical can accumulate in the body fat after exposure. Minute quantities may be found in the body years after modest exposure. Since TCDD's half-life has been estimated at as much as 10-12 years in the soil, it is possible that some TCDD—suggested to be as much as seven **parts per trillion** (ppt)—is harbored in the bodies of most Americans.

The development of medical problems may appear shortly after exposure, or they may appear 10, 12, or 20 years later. If the exposure is large, the symptoms develop more quickly, but there is a greater **latency** period for smaller exposures. This fact explains why humans exposed to TCDD may appear healthy for years before finally showing what many consider to be typical dioxin-exposure symptoms, such as cancer or immune system dysfunction. There is also a relationship between toxicology and individual susceptibility. Certain people are more susceptible to the effects of dioxin exposure than others. Once a person has become susceptible to the chemical, he or she tends to develop cross reactions to other materials that would not normally trigger any response.

Government publications and research funded by the chemical industry have questioned the relationship between dioxin exposure and many of these symptoms. But a growing number of private physicians treating people exposed to dioxins have become increasingly certain about patterns or clusters of symptoms. They have reported a higher incidence of cancer at sites of industrial accidents, including increases in rates of stomach cancer, lung cancer, soft-tissue sarcomas, and malignant lymphomas. Some reports have indicated that soft-tissue sarcomas in dioxin-exposed workers have increased by a factor of 40, and there have also been indications of psychological and personality changes and an excess of coronary disease.

Many theories about the medical effects of dioxin exposure are based on the case histories of the thousands of American military personnel exposed to Agent Orange during the Vietnam War. Agent Orange, a chemical defoliant, was used despite the fact that certain chemical companies and select members of the military knew about its toxic properties. Thousands of American ground troops were directly sprayed with the chemical. Those in the spraying planes inhaled the chemical directly when some of the herbicides were blown back by the wind into the open doors of their planes. Others were exposed to accidental dumpings from the sky, when planes in trouble had to evacuate their loads during emergency procedures.

Despite what many consider to be the obvious dangers of dioxin, industries continue to produce residues and market products contaminated with the chemical. White bleached paper goods contain quantities of TCDD because no agency has required the paper industry to change its bleaching process. Women use dioxin-tainted, bleached tampons, and infants wear bleached, dioxin-tainted paper diapers. Some scientists have estimated that every person in the United States carries a body burden of dioxin that may already be unacceptable.

Many believe that the EPA has done less to regulate dioxin than it has done for almost any other **toxic substance**. Environmentalists and other activists have argued that any other chemical creating equivalent clusters of problems within specific groups of similarly exposed victims would be considered an epidemic. Industry experts have often downplayed the problems of dioxin. A spokesman for Dow Chemical has stated that "outside of chloracne, no medical evidence exists to link up dioxin exposure to any medical problems." The federal government and federal agencies have also been accused of protecting their own interests. During congressional hearings in 1989 and 1990, the **Centers for Disease Control** was found to falsify epidemiology studies on Vietnam veterans.

In April 1991, the EPA initiated a series of studies intended to revise their estimate of dioxin's toxicity. The agency believed there was new scientific evidence worth considering. Several industries, particularly the paper industry, had also pressured the agency to initiate the studies, in the hope that public fears about dioxin toxicity could be allayed. But the first draft of the revised studies, issued in the summer of 1992, indicated more rather than fewer problems with dioxin. It appears to be the most damaging to animals exposed while still in the uterus. It also seems to affect behavior and learning ability, which suggests that it may be a **neurotoxin**. These studies have also noted the possibility of extensive effects on the immune system.

Other studies have established that dioxin functions like a steroid hormone. Steroid hormones are powerful chemicals that enter cells, bind to a receptor or protein, form a complex that then attaches to the cell's chromosomes, turning on and off chemical switches that may then affect distant parts of the body. It is not unusual for very small amounts of a steroid hormone to have major effects on the body. Newer studies conducted on **wildlife** around the **Great Lakes** have shown that dioxin has the capacity to feminize male chicks and rats and masculinize female chicks and rats. In male animals, testicle size is reduced as is sperm count.

It is likely that dioxin will remain a subject of considerable controversy both in the public realm and in the scientific community for some time to come. However, even those scientists who question dioxin's long-term toxic effect on humans, agree that the chemical is highly toxic to experimental animals. Dioxin researcher Nancy I. Kerkvliet of Oregon State University in Corvallis characterizes the situation in these terms, "The fact that you can't clearly show the effects in humans in no way lessens the fact that dioxin is an extremely potent chemical in animals—potent in terms of immunotoxicity, potent in terms of promoting cancer." *See also* Bioaccumulation; Hazardous waste; Kepone; Organochloride; Pesticide residue; Pulp and paper mills; Seveso, Italy; Times Beach, Missouri

[*Liane Clorfene Casten*]

FURTHER READING

"German Dioxin Study Indicates Increased Risk." *BioScience* 42 (February 1992): 151.

Gough, M. "Agent Orange: Exposure and Policy." *American Journal of Public Health* 81 (March 1991): 289-90.

Husar, R. B. *Biological Basis for Risk Assessment of Dioxins and Related Compounds.* Cold Spring Harbor, NY: Cold Spring Harbor Laboratory Press, 1991.

———. *The Health Risks of Dioxin.* Hearing Before the Human Resources and Intergovernmental Relations Subcommittee on Government Operations, House of Representatives, One Hundred Second Congress, June 10, 1992. Washington, DC: U. S. Government Printing Office, 1993.

———, and M. Gough. *Dioxin, Agent Orange: The Facts.* New York: Plenum, 1986.

"A Review of the Scientific Literature: Human Health Effects Associated with Exposure to Herbicides and/or Their Associated Contaminants—Chlorinated Dioxins: Agent Orange and the Vietnam Veteran." Compiled by the Agent Orange Scientific Task Force, working with The American Legion, Vietnam Veterans of America, The National Veterans Legal Services Project. April 1990.

Schmidt, K. F. "Dioxin's Other Face: Portrait of an 'Environmental Hormone'." *Science News* 141 (11 January 1992): 24-7.

Tschirley, F. "Dioxin." *Scientific American* 254 (February 1986): 29-35.

Zumwalt, Admiral Elmo R. Jr. USN (Ret.) "Report to the Secretary of Veterans Affairs, The Hon. Edward J. Derwinski. From the Special Assistant: Agent Orange Issues." First Report, May 5, 1990.

Discharge

A term generally used to describe the release of a gas, liquid, or solid to a treatment facility or the **environment**. For example, **wastewater** may be discharged to a sewer or into a stream, and gas may be discharged into the **atmosphere**.

Discount, social rate of
See **Social discount rate**

Disposable diapers

Disposable diapers were introduced by Procter & Gamble in 1961. First used as an occasional convenient substitute for cloth diapers, their popularity has since exploded. By 1990 they were the primary diapering method for 85 percent of American parents. As a result, 2.7 million tons of disposable diapers are discarded every year, a point decried by environmentalists.

Proponents of reusables argue that this accounts for only two to three percent of America's **solid waste**. Although detailed studies have examined the influence of both kinds of diapers on such variables as water consumption, **water pollution**, energy consumption, **air pollution**, and waste generation, there are no indisputable conclusions about which choice is better for the **environment**. Each study was based on different assumptions and came to different conclusions. Most were commissioned by either the disposable-diaper or reusable-diaper industry, and each side put their respective diapers slightly ahead of the other's.

Disposable diapers and their packaging create more solid waste than reusables, and because they are used only once, consume more raw materials—**petrochemical**s and wood pulp—in their manufacture. And although disposable diapers should be emptied into the **toilet** before the diapers are thrown away, many people skip this step, which puts feces (that may be contaminated with **pathogen**s) into **landfill**s and incinerators. There is no indication, however, that this practice has resulted in any increase in health problems. But cloth diapers affect the environment as well. They are made of cotton, which is watered with **irrigation** systems and treated with synthetic **fertilizer**s and **pesticide**s. They are laundered and dried up to 78 (commercial) or 180 (home) times, consuming more water and energy than disposables. In fact, home laundering is less energy efficient than commercial because it is done on a smaller scale. Diaper services make deliveries in trucks, which expends another measure of energy and generates more pollution. Human waste from cotton diapers is treated in sewer systems. Some disposable diapers are advertised as **biodegradable** and claim to pose less of a solid-waste problem than regular disposables. Their waterproof cover contains a cornstarch derivative that decomposes into water and **carbon dioxide** when exposed to water and air. Unfortunately, modern landfills are airtight and little, if any, degradation occurs. Biodegradable diapers, therefore, are not significantly different from other disposables.

[*Teresa C. Donkin*]

FURTHER READING

Lehrburger, C., J. Mullen, and C. V. Jones. *Diapers: Environmental Impacts and Lifecycle Analysis (Summary)*. Report to the National Association of Diaper Services, Philadelphia, PA. January 1991.

Poore, P. "Disposable Diapers Are OK." *Garbage* 4 (October-November 1992): 26-8+.

Raloff, J. "Reassessing Costs of Keeping Baby Dry [Cloth vs. Disposable]." *Science News* 138 (1 December 1990): 347.

Rathje, W., and C. Murphy. "Cotton vs. Disposables: What's the Damage." *Garbage* 4 (October-November 1992): 29-30.

Dissolved oxygen

Dissolved oxygen (DO) refers to the amount of oxygen dissolved in water and is particularly important in **limnology** (aquatic ecology). Oxygen comprises approximately 21 percent of the total gas in the **atmosphere**; however, it is much less available in water. The amount of oxygen water can hold depends upon temperature (more oxygen can be dissolved in colder water), pressure (more oxygen can be dissolved in water at greater pressure), and **salinity** (more oxygen can be dissolved in water of lower salinity). Many lakes and ponds have anoxic (oxygen deficient) bottom layers in the summer because of **decomposition** processes depleting the oxygen. The amount of dissolved oxygen often determines the number and types of organisms living in that body of water. For example, fish like trout are sensitive to low DO levels (less than eight parts per million) and cannot survive in warm, slow-moving streams or rivers. Decay of organic material in water caused by either chemical processes or microbial action on untreated sewage or dead vegetation can severely reduce dissolved oxygen concentration. This is the most common

cause of **fish kills**, especially in summer months when warm water holds less oxygen anyway.

Dissolved solids

Dissolved solids are minerals in solution, typically measured in parts per million (ppm) using an electrical conductance meter calibrated to oven-dried samples. In humid regions, dissolved solids are often the dominant form of sediment transport. Solution features such as caverns and **sinkholes** are common in limestone regions.

Water that contains excessive amounts of dissolved solids is unfit for drinking. Drinking water standards typically allow a maximum of 250 ppm, the threshold for tasting sodium chloride; by comparison, ocean water ranges from 33,000-37,000 ppm. Phosphates and nitrates in solution are the major cause of eutrophication (nutrient enrichment resulting in excessive growth of algae). Dissolved solids buffer acid precipitation; lakes with low levels are especially vulnerable. High levels occur in runoff from newly-disturbed landscapes, such as strip mines and road construction.

Diversity
See **Biodiversity**

DNA (deoxyribose nucleic acid)

Deoxyribose **nucleic acid** (DNA) molecules contain genetic information that is the blueprint for life. DNA is made up of long chains of subunits called nucleotides, which are nitrogenous bases attached to ribose sugar molecules. Two of these chains intertwine in the famous double helix structure discovered in 1953 by James Watson and Francis Crick.

The genetic information contained in DNA molecules is in a code spelled out by the linear sequence of nucleotides in each chain. Each group of three nucleotides makes up a codon, a unit resembling a letter in the alphabet. A string of codons effectively spells a word of the genetic message.

This message is expressed when **enzyme**s (cellular proteins) synthesize new proteins using a copy of a short segment of DNA as a template. Each nucleotide codon specifies which amino acid subunit is inserted as the protein is formed, thus determining the structure and function of the proteins. Because the chains are very long, a single DNA strand can contain enough information to direct the synthesis of hundreds of different proteins. Since these proteins make up the cell structure and the machinery (enzymes) by which cells carry out the processes of life, such as synthesizing more molecules including more copies of the DNA itself, DNA can be said to be self-replicating. When cells divide, each of the new cells receives a duplicate set of DNA molecules giving them the necessary information to live and reproduce. *See also* RNA

Dodo (*Raphus cucullatus*)

One of the best known extinct **species**, the dodo, a flightless bird native to the Indian Ocean island of Mauritius, disappeared around 1680. A member of the dove or pigeon family, and about the size of a large turkey, the dodo was a grayish white bird with a huge black-and-red beak, short legs, and small wings. The dodo did not have natural enemies until humans discovered the island in the early sixteenth century.

The dodo became extinct due to hunting by European sailors who collected the birds for food and to predation of eggs and chicks by introduced dogs, cats, pigs, monkeys, and rats. The Portuguese are credited with discovering Mauritius, where they found a tropical paradise with a unique collection of strange and colorful birds unafraid of humans: **parrots and parakeets**, pink and blue pigeons, owls, swallows, thrushes, hawks, sparrows, crows, and dodos. Unwary of predators, the birds would walk right up to human visitors, making themselves easy prey for sailors hungry for food and sport.

The Dutch followed the Portuguese and made the island a Dutch possession in 1598 after which Mauritius became a regular stopover for ships traversing the Indian Ocean. The dodos were subjected to regular slaughter by sailors, but the species managed to breed and survive on the remote areas of the island.

When the island became a Dutch colony in 1644, the colonists engaged in a seemingly conscious attempt to eradicate the birds, despite the fact that they were not **pest**s or obstructive to human living. But they were easy to kill. The few dodos in inaccessible areas that could not be found by the colonists were eliminated by the animals introduced by the settlers. By 1680, the last remnant survivors of the species were "as dead as a dodo."

Interestingly, while the dodo tree (*Calvaria major*) was once common on Mauritius, the tree seemed to stop reproducing after the dodo disappeared, and the only remaining specimens are about 300 years old. Apparently, a symbiotic relationship existed between the birds and the plants. The fruit of this tree was an important food source for the dodo. When the bird ate the fruit, the hard casing of the seed was crushed, allowing it to germinate when expelled by the dodo.

Three other related species of giant, flightless doves were also wiped out on nearby islands. The white dodo (*Victoriornis imperialis*) inhabited Reunion, 100 miles (161 kilometers) southwest of Mauritius, and seems to have survived up to around 1770. The Reunion solitaire (*Ornithoptera solitarius*) was favored by humans for eating and was hunted to **extinction** by about 1700. The "delightfully beautiful" Rodriguez solitaire (*Pezophaps solitarius*), found on the island of Rodriguez 300 miles (483 kilometers) east of Mauritius, was also widely hunted for food and disappeared by about 1780. *See also* Symbiosis

[*Lewis G. Regenstein*]

FURTHER READING

Day, David. *The Doomsday Book of Animals*. New York: Viking, 1981.
The Dodo. Philadelphia: Wildlife Preservation Trust International, 1985.

The dodo from Mauritius became extinct in the seventeenth century.

Dolphins

There are 32 **species** of dolphins, members of the cetacean family Delphinidae, that are distributed in all of the oceans of the world. These marine mammals are usually found in relatively shallow waters of coastal zones, but some may be found in open ocean. Dolphins are a relatively modern group; they evolved about ten million years ago during the late Miocene. The Delphinidae represents the most diverse group, as well as the most abundant, of all cetaceans. Among the delphinids are the bottlenose dolphins (*Tursiops truncatus*), best known for their performances in oceanaria, the spinner dolphin (*Stenella longirostris*), which have had their numbers decline due to tuna fishermen's nets, and the orca or the killer whale (*Orcinus orca*), the largest of the dolphins. Dolphins are distinguished from their close relatives, the porpoises, by the presence of a beak.

Dolphins are intelligent, social creatures, and social structure is variously exhibited in dolphins. Inshore species usually form small herds of two to twelve individuals. Dolphins of more open waters have herds comprised of up to 1,000, or sometimes more, individuals. Dolphins communicate by means of echolocation, ranging from a series of clicks to ultrasonic sounds, which may also be used to stun its prey. By acting cooperatively, dolphins can locate and herd their food using this ability. Aggregations of dolphins also have a negative aspect, however. Mass strandings of dolphins, a behavior in which whole herds beach themselves and die *en mass*, is a well-known phenomenon but little understood by biologists. Theories for this seemingly suicidal behavior include nematode parasite infections of the inner ears, which upsets their balance, orientation, or echolocation abilities; simple disorientation due to unfamiliar waters; or even perhaps magnetic disturbances.

Because of their tendency to congregate in large herds, particularly in feeding areas, dolphins have become vulnerable to large nets of commercial fishermen. **Gill nets**, laid down to catch oceanic **salmon** and capelin, also catch numerous non-target species, including dolphins and inshore species of porpoises. In the eastern Pacific Ocean, especially during the 1960s and 1970s, dolphins have been trapped and drowned in the purse seines of the tuna fishing fleets. This industry was responsible for the deaths of an average of 113,000 dolphins annually and in 1974 alone, killed over half a million dolphins in their nets. Tuna fishermen have recently adopted special nets and different fishing procedures to protect the dolphins. A panel of netting with a finer mesh, the Medina panel, is part of the net furthest from the fishing vessel. Inflatable power boats herd the tuna as the net is pulled under and around the school of fish. As the net is pulled toward the vessel many dolphins are able to escape by jumping over the floats of the Medina panel, but others are assisted by hand from the inflatable boats or by divers. The finer mesh prevents the dolphins from getting tangled in the net, unlike the large mesh which previously snared the dolphins as they sought escape. Consumer pressure and tuna boycotts were major factors behind this shift in techniques on the part of the tuna fishing industry. To advertise this new method of tuna fishing and to try to regain consumer confidence, the tuna fishing industry has begun labeling their products "dolphin safe." This campaign has been successful in that slumping sales from the boycotts have picked up over the last few years. *See also* Green advertising and marketing; Green products

[*Eugene C. Beckham*]

FURTHER READING

Dolphins, Porpoises and Whales of the World. Gland, Switzerland, IUCN—The World Conservation Union, 1991.

Evans, P. *The Natural History of Whales & Dolphins.* New York: Facts on File, 1987.

Dominance

Dominance is an ecological term that refers to the degree that a particular species is prevalent within its community, in terms of its relative size, productivity, or cover. Because of their ability to appropriate space, nutrients, and other resources, dominant species have a relatively strong or controlling influence on the structure and functions of their community, and on the fitness and productivity of other species. Ecological communities are often characterized on the basis of their dominant species.

Species may become dominant within their community if they are particularly competitive, that is, if they are relatively successful under conditions in which the availability of resources constrains ecological productivity and community structure. As such, competitive species are relatively efficient at obtaining resources. For example, competitive terrestrial plants are relatively efficient at accessing nutrients, moisture, and space, and they are capable of regenerating beneath their own shade. These highly competitive species can become naturally dominant within their communities.

Many ecological successions are characterized by relatively species-rich communities in the initial stages of recovery after disturbance, followed by the development of less-diverse communities as the most competitive species

exert their dominance. In such cases, disturbance can be an important influence that prevents the most competitive species from dominating their community. Disturbance can play this role in two ways: (1) through relatively extensive, or stand-replacing disturbances that set larger areas back to earlier stages of succession, allowing species-rich communities to occupy the site for some time, or (2) by relatively local disturbances that create gaps within late-successional stands, allowing species-rich micro-successions to increase the amount of diversity within the larger community.

Some natural examples of species-poor, late-successional communities that are dominated by only a few species include the following: (1) the rocky intertidal of temperate oceans, where mussels (e.g., *Mytilus edulis*) may occupy virtually all available substrate and thereby exclude most other species, (2) eastern temperate forests of North America, where species such as sugar maple (*Acer saccharum*) and eastern hemlock (*Tsuga canadensis*) are capable of forming pure stands that exclude most other species of trees, and (3) a few types of tropical **rain forest**s, such as some areas of Sumatra and Borneo where ironwood (*Eusideroxylon zwageri*) can dominate stands. In the absence of either stand-replacing disturbances or microdisturbances in these sorts of late-successional **ecosystem**s, extensive areas would become covered by relatively simple communities dominated by these highly competitive species.

Humans often manage ecosystems to favor the dominance of one or several species that are economically favored because they are crops grown for food, fibre, or some other purpose. Some examples include: (1) cornfields, in which dominance by *Zea mays* is achieved by plowing, **herbicide** application, insecticide use, and other practices, in order to ensure that few plants other than maize are present, and that the crop species is not unduly threatened by pests or diseases; (2) forestry plantations, in which dominance by the crop species is ensured by planting, herbicide application, and other practices; and (3) grazing lands for domestic cattle, whose dominance may be ensured by fencing lands to prevent wild herbivores from utilizing the available forage, and by shooting native herbivores and predators of cattle. In all of the above cases, continued management of the ecosystem by humans is needed to maintain the dominance of the crop species. Otherwise, natural ecological forces would result in diminished dominance or even exclusion of the crop species.

Ecologists have developed a number of quantitative indices to describe the dominance of species within communities. One of these is known as the *community dominance index* (CDI). It is calculated as the percentage of the total abundance of all species in the community that is contributed by the two most abundant species, as in:

$$CDI = 100 \times (y_1 + y_2) / Y$$

where y_1 is the abundance of the most abundant species, y_2 is that of the second-most abundant species, and Y is the total of the abundances of all species in the community. For these purposes, abundance may be estimated by **biomass**, density, cover, productivity, or another suitable measurement. In general, communities with high values of

CDI have relatively little community-level diversity. This relationship is being actively explored by ecologists who are interested in the environmental factors that control the levels of **biodiversity** in natural and managed ecosystems.

[*Bill Freedman*]

FURTHER READING

Begon, M., Harper, J.L., and Townsend, C.R. *Ecology. Individuals, Populations and Communities.* 3rd ed. London: Blackwell Sci. Pub., 1996.

Krebs, C.J. *Ecology. The Experimental Analysis of Distribution and Abundance.* San Francisco: Harper and Row, 1985.

Ricklefs, R.E. *Ecology.* New York: W.H. Freeman and Co., 1990.

Dose response

Dose response is the relationship between the effect on living things and a stimulus from a physical, chemical, or biological source. Examples of stimuli include therapeutic drugs, **pesticide**s, **pathogen**s, and radiation. A quantal response occurs when the living thing either responds or does not respond to a stimulus of a given dose. Graded responses proportional to the size of the stimulus are also found in environmental applications. Some types of responses have a significant time effect. The Effective Dose for affecting 50 percent of a population of test subjects, ED_{50}, and the Lethal Dose for killing 50 percent of a population of test subjects, LD_{50}, are commonly used parameters for reporting the toxicity of an environmental pollutant. *See also* Pollution; Radiation exposure; Toxic substance

Douglas, Marjory Stoneman (1890-)

American environmentalist and writer

A newspaper reporter, writer, and environmentalist renowned for her crusade to preserve Florida's **everglades**. Marjory Stoneman Douglas was part of the committee that first advocated formation of the Everglades National Park in 1927, and she has been an active advocate of the area's preservation ever since. Born In 1890 in Minneapolis and raised in Taunton, Massachusetts, Marjory Stoneman Douglas graduated from Wellesley College in 1912. After a brief marriage to Kenneth Douglas, a newspaper editor, she moved south to Florida in 1915 to join her father. She soon began to work as a reporter, columnist, and editor for the *Miami Herald*, founded by her father, Judge Frank Bryant Stoneman. During World War I, she left Miami to become the first female enlistee for the Naval Reserves, then joined the Red Cross, for which she worked and traveled in Europe during and after the war. Returning to Coconut Grove in 1920, Mrs. Douglas has remained there for over 75 years.

Mrs. Douglas was involved very early in efforts to preserve the everglades from agricultural and residential development, as was her father before her. Her book, *The Everglades: River of Grass* was one of the most important

statements publicizing the ecological importance and uniqueness of the area, as well as its plight in the face of drainage, filling, and water diversion. Her framing of the region as a "river of grass" effectively instilled in the general public an idea of the interconnectedness of the land, water, plants, and animals of the area, helping to raise public awareness of the urgency of preserving the entire ecosystem, not just isolated components of it.

Marjory Stoneman Douglas did not start out as a full-time environmental advocate. She wrote *The River of Grass* because she loved the history and the natural history of the area, and she was a long-time supporter of preserving the **ecosystem**, but she did not become deeply involved in the movement to save the everglades until the 1970s. Friends of Mrs. Douglas' in the **National Audubon Society**, confronted in 1969 by proposals to build an airport in the everglades, enlisted her aid and she helped organize the Friends of the Everglades, an organization that continues to defend the Park and related south Florida ecosystems.

Mrs. Douglas has proven to be an eloquent and forceful speaker and writer in the cause to save the everglades from development, and since the 1970s the everglades has become her single cause for celebrity. However she has also written poetry, short stories, histories, natural histories and novels, nearly all based in Florida. Initially her writing was popular at least in part because Florida and its history were little known, and rarely written about, when she began her literary career. Among her other publications are *Road to the Sun* (1951), *Hurricane* (1958), *Florida: the Long Frontier* (1967), and *Nine Florida Stories* (1990). She has also written an autobiography, co-authored by J. Rothchild, *Marjory Stoneman Douglas: Voice of the River*. Mrs. Douglas has remained an active public figure, speaking and writing in defense of the southern Florida environment beyond her 100th year.

[*Mary Ann Cunningham*]

FURTHER READING

Soba, D. "Still Fighting the Good Fight." *Audubon* 93 (1991): 30-39.

Douglas, M. S. *The Everglades: River of Grass.* New York: Reinhart, 1947.

Chusmir, J. "The Time and Possibilities of Marjory Stoneman Douglas." *Miami Herald*, April 6, 1975.

Drainage

The **hydrologic cycle** encompasses all movements of water molecules through the **atmosphere**, hydrosphere, and **groundwater** zones. One key part is the drainage of surface waters and groundwater back to the ocean. Natural drainage systems are well-adjusted to their climate, vegetation, and geology. Hydrologists and fluvial geomorphologists have studied these systems in great detail; human disturbances are readily apparent. Three impacts are considered here: wetland drainage and irrigation; dam construction and mining alterations; and urbanization.

Robert E. Horton identified many drainage characteristics during the 1930s and 1940s. Later researchers added other useful quantitative parameters. All of these show the predictable patterns found in natural drainage systems. Best known are stream order and drainage density. Although influenced by the detail of the maps used (commonly 1:24,000 or 1:62,500 topographic maps), stream order provides a simple system for ranking tributaries. The smallest ones are labeled first order, second-order streams have at least two first-order tributaries, third-order streams have at least two second-order tributaries, and so forth. The Mississippi River is ranked as a tenth- or twelfth-order stream, depending on the map scale used. Horton also developed a bifurcation ration between stream orders, which is generally around three; that is, on average there are three second-order streams for each third-order one.

Drainage density is a measure of channel length per unit area. This varies widely depending on the nature of the vegetation cover and **soil**. Badlands and deserts have high drainage densities compared to well-vegetated basins with permeable soils.

Stream channels are finely adjusted to their drainage requirements, and attain a state of quasi-equilibrium. Human activities disrupt this equilibrium, forcing channel adjustments. This disruption is so pervasive that essentially all channels within settled areas have been impacted.

The earliest human intrusions are wetland drainage and irrigation of arid lands for agriculture. Recent litigation has involved decisions by federal officials to deny irrigation water to farmers in order to maintain needed supplies for endangered aquatic organisms. Only recently has the tendency to drain wetlands been reversed. With the comeback of the beaver from near extinction, wetland proponents now have an efficient ally.

Many large rivers have been dammed, with direct impact on the downstream riparian environment. To counteract this, in 1996, an experimental flood was produced on the **Colorado River** through the Grand Canyon, with the desired goal of improving **habitat** for **endangered species** there. Even farm ponds, through their sheer numbers, are major drainage interrupters. Another strong impact has come from mining, through the creation of huge holes, massive sedimentation, or increased **runoff**.

Urbanization has had the greatest local impact on drainage. Channels are altered, permeable areas are covered with impervious materials, and storm drains deliver runoff more rapidly to the overwhelmed drainage network. The effect is to deliver much more water in substantial less time, a sure formula for flooding.

Tulsa, Oklahoma, is a case study in urban flooding and costly remediation. A computerized system now evaluates rain and stream-gage data in real time, and issues flood warning via sirens throughout the city. Construction is banned within the 100-year flood, and valuable land has been set aside for detention ponds so that runoff does not exceed natural conditions up to the level of a 100-year flood. Though costly, these steps have been essential in order to protect lives and reduce property damage.

Changes in the drainage network are prime indicators of human impact. If we are to work with nature rather than fight her, we must understand and reckon with the impacts of our development on this fragile and finely tuned system.

[*Nathan Meleen*]

FURTHER READING

Cooke, R.U., and J.C. Doornkamp. *Geomorphology in Environmental Management*. London: Oxford University Press, 1974.

Leopold, L.B., M.G. Wolman, and J.P. Miller. *Fluvial Processes in Geomorphology*. San Francisco: W.H. Freeman, 1964.

Strahler, A.N., and A.H. Strahler. *Modern Physical Geography* 2nd ed. New York: John Wiley & Sons, 1983.

Dredging

Dredging is a process to remove **sediment**. Dredging sediment to construct new ports and navigational waterways or maintain existing ones is essential for vessels to be able to enter shallow areas. Maintenance dredging is required because sediment suspended in the water eventually settles out, gradually accumulating on the bottom. If dredging were not done, harbors would eventually fill in and marine transportation would be severely limited. Dredging is also used to collect sediment (usually sand and gravel) for construction and other commercial uses. Hundreds of millions of cubic meters of sediment are dredged from marine bottoms annually in the United States and throughout the world.

One of the oldest types of dredging is agitation dredging, which uses a combination of mechanical and hydraulic processes and dates back over 2,000 years. An object is dragged along the bottom with the prevailing current; this suspends the sediment and the current carries the suspended material away from the area. Technology currently used to dredge sediment from a harbor, bay, or other marine bottom consists of hydraulic or mechanical devices. Hydraulic dredging involves suspending the sediment, which mixes with water to form a **slurry**, and pumping it to a **discharge** site. Mechanical dredging is typically used to dredge small amounts of material. It lifts sediment from the bottom by metal clamshells or buckets without adding significant amounts of water, and the dredged material is usually transferred to a barge for disposal at a particular site.

Most of the dredging that occurs in the United States is hydraulic dredging. Hopper dredges are vessels that employ hydraulic dredging, and they are often used in the open ocean or in areas where there is vessel traffic. The ship's hull is filled with dredged material and the ship moves the material to a designated disposal site where it is dumped through doors in the hull. Pipeline dredges use hydraulic dredging to remove sediment in nearshore areas, and the dredged material is discharged through a pipeline leading to a beach or diked area. Approximately 550 million wet metric tons of sediment are dredged from the waters of the United States each year, and an estimated one-third is disposed in the marine environment, accounting for the greatest amount of waste material dumped in the ocean. Of the dredged material dumped in the marine environment, 66 percent is disposed in **estuaries**. Two dozen marine disposal sites in the United

States receive approximately 95 percent of all of the dredged material disposed at sea.

Dredged material is typically composed of **silt**, clay, and sand, and can sometimes include gravel, boulders, organic matter, as well as chemical compounds such as sulfides, hydrous oxides, and metal and organic contaminants. The grain size of the dredged sediment will determine the conditions under which the sediment will be deposited or resuspended if disposed in the marine environment.

The choice of where the dredged material should be placed depends on whether it is uncontaminated or contaminated by pollutants. If contaminated, the level of pollutants in the dredged material can also play a role in the decision of the type and location of disposal. Because many navigational channels and ports are located in industrialized areas, and because sediments are a sink for many pollutants, dredged material may be contaminated with toxic metals, organohalogens, petrochemical by-products, or other pollutants. Dredged material can also contain contaminants from agricultural and urban sources.

Dredged material with very little contaminants can be placed in a variety of locations and beneficially reused for beach restoration, construction aggregate, fill material, cover for sanitary **landfill**s, and soil supplementation on agricultural land. The primary concerns over the disposal of uncontaminated dredged material in the marine environment are the physical impacts it can have, such as high turbidity in the water column, changes in grain size, and the smothering of bottom dwelling organisms. The ensuing alterations to the bottom habitat can lead to changes in the benthic community. Deposited dredged sediment is usually recolonized by different organisms than were present prior to the disposal of the dredged material. For example, disposal of sediment from a dredging project in Narragansett Bay, Rhode Island changed the bottom topography and sediment type, and this change in benthic habitat led to a subsequent decline in the clam and finfish fishery at the site and an increase in the lobster fishery. If the dredged material is similar to the sediment on which it is dumped, the area may be recolonized by the same **species** that were present prior to any dumping.

If dredged material is dumped in an area that has less than 197 ft (60 m) of water, most of the material will rapidly descend to the bottom as a high-density mass. A radial gradation of large-to-fine grained sediment usually occurs from the impact area of the deposition outward. Fine-grained material spreads outward from the disposal site, in some cases up to 328 ft (100 m), in the form of a fluid mud. It can range in thickness up to 3.9 in (1 dm). From one to five percent of the sediment remains suspended in the water as a plume; this sediment plume is transient in nature and eventually dissipates by dispersion and gravitational settling. The long-term fate of dredged material dumped in the marine environment depends on the location of the dumping site, its physical characteristics such as bottom topography and currents, and the nature of the sediment. Deep-**ocean dumping** of dredged material results in wider dispersal of the sediment in the water column. The deposition of the dredged material becomes more widely distributed over the ocean bottom than in nearshore areas.

Dredging contaminated sediment poses a much more severe problem for disposal. Disposing contaminated dredged material in the marine environment can result in long-term degradation to the **ecosystem**. Sublethal effects, **biomagnification** of pollutants, and genetic disorders of organisms are some examples of possible long-term effects from toxic pollutants in contaminated dredged material entering the **food chain**. However, attributing effects from placement of contaminated dredged material at a marine site to a specific cause can be very difficult if other sources of contaminants are present.

Dredged material must be tested to determine contamination levels and the best method of disposal. These tests include bulk chemical analysis, the elutriate test, selective chemical **leaching**, and **bioassay**s. Bulk chemical analysis involves measurements of volatile solids, chemical oxygen demand, oil and grease, **nitrogen**, **mercury**, **lead**, and zinc. But this chemical analysis does not necessarily provide an adequate assessment of the potential environmental impact on bottom dwelling organisms from disposal of the dredged material. The elutriate test is designed to measure the potential release of chemical contaminants from suspended sediment caused by dredging and disposal activities. However, the test does not take into account some chemical factors governing sediment-water interactions such as complexation, sorption, redox, and acid-base reactions.

Selective chemical leaching divides the total concentration of an element in a sediment into identified phases. This test is better than the bulk chemical analysis for providing information that will predict the impact of contaminants on the environment after the disposal of dredged material. Bioassay tests commonly use sensitive aquatic organisms to measure directly the effects of contaminants in dredged material as well as other waste materials. Different concentrations of wastes are measured by determining the waste dilution that results in 50 percent mortality of the test organisms. Permissible concentrations of contaminants can be identified using bioassay tests.

If dredged material is considered contaminated, special management and long-term maintenance are required to isolate it from the rest of the environment. Special management techniques can include capping dredged material disposed in water with an uncontaminated layer of sediment, a technique which is recommended in relatively quiescent, shallow water environments. Other management strategies to dispose contaminated dredged material include the use of upland containment areas and containment islands. The use of submarine burrow pits has also been examined as a possible means to contain contaminated dredged material.

There is more than one law in the United States governing dredging and disposal operations. The General Survey Act of 1824 delegates responsibility to the **Army Corps of Engineers** (ACOE) for the improvement and maintenance of harbors and navigation. The ACOE is required to issue permits for any work in navigable waters, according to the Rivers and Harbors Act of 1899. **The**

Marine Protection, Research, and Sanctuaries Act (MPRSA) of 1972 requires the ACOE to evaluate the transportation and ocean dumping of dredged material based on criteria developed by the **Environmental Protection Agency** (EPA), and to issue permits for approved non-federal dredging projects. Designating ocean disposal sites for dredged material is the responsibility of EPA. The discharge of dredged material through a pipeline is controlled by the Federal Water Pollution Control Act, as amended by the **Clean Water Act (1977)**. This act requires the ACOE to regulate ocean discharges of dredged material and evaluate projects based on criteria developed by the EPA in consultation with the ACOE. Other Federal agencies such as the U. S. **Fish and Wildlife Service** and the National Marine Fisheries Service can provide comments and recommendations on any project, but the EPA has the power to veto the use of proposed disposal sites. *See also* Agricultural pollution; Contaminated soil; Hazardous waste; LD50; Runoff; Sedimentation; Synergism; Toxic substance; Urban runoff

[*Marci L. Bortman*]

FURTHER READING

Bokunwiewicz, H. J. "Submarine Borrow Pits as Containment Sites for Dredged Sediment." *Wastes in the Ocean.* Volume 2, *Dredged Material Disposal in the Ocean,* edited by D. R. Kester, et al. New York: Wiley, 1983.

Engler, R. M. "Managing Dredged Materials." *Oceanus* 33 (1990): 63-9.

Kamlet, K. S. "Dredge-Material Ocean Dumping: Perspectives on Legal and Environmental Impacts." *Wastes in the Ocean.* Volume 2, *Dredged Material Disposal in the Ocean,* edited by D. R. Kester, et al. New York: Wiley, 1983.

Kester, D. R., et al. "The Problem of Dredged-Material Disposal." *Wastes in the Ocean.* Volume 2, *Dredged Material Disposal in the Ocean,* edited by D. R. Kester, et al. New York: Wiley, 1983.

Kester, D. R., et al. "Have the Questions Concerning Dredged-Material Disposal Been Answered?" *Wastes in the Ocean.* Volume 2, *Dredged Material Disposal in the Ocean,* edited by D. R. Kester, et al. New York: Wiley, 1983.

Office of Technology Assessment. *Wastes in Marine Environments.* OTA-O-334. Washington, DC: U.S. Government Printing Office, 1987.

Drift nets

Drift nets are used in large-scale **commercial fishing** operations. Nets are suspended from floats at various depths and set adrift in open oceans to capture fish or squid. These nets are generally of a type known as **gill nets**, because fish usually become entangled in them by their bony gill plates. The fishing industry has found these nets to be cost-effective, but their use has become increasingly controversial. They pose a severe threat to many forms of marine life, and they have long been the object of protests and direct action from a range of environmental groups. National and international policies concerning their use have only recently begun to change.

The problem with drift nets is that they are not selective; there is no way to use them to target a particular **species** of fish. Drift nets can catch everything in their path, and there are few protections for species that were never intended to be caught. Although some nets can be quite efficient in capturing only certain species, the by-catch from

drift nets can include not only non-commercial fish, but **sea turtles**, seabirds, **seals and sea lions**, porpoises, **dolphins**, and large **whales**. Nets that are set adrift from fishing vessels in the open ocean and never recovered pose an even more severe hazard to the marine **environment**. Drift nets are constructed of a light, plastic monofilament which resists rotting; lost nets can drift and kill animals for long periods of time, becoming what environmentalists have called "ghost nets."

Drift nets are favored by fishing industries in many countries because of their economic advantages. The equipment itself is relatively inexpensive; it is also less labor intensive than other alternatives, and it supplies larger yields because of its ability to capture fish over such broad areas. Drift-net fisheries can vary considerably, according to the target species and the type of fishing environment. In coastal areas, short nets can be set and recovered in an hour. The nets do not drift very far in this time and the environmental damage can be limited. But in the open ocean, where the target species may be widely dispersed, nets in excess of 31 miles (50 km) in length may be set and allowed to drift for 12 hours before they are recovered and stripped. The primary targets for drift netting include squid in the northern Pacific, **salmon** in the northeastern Pacific, tuna in the southern Pacific and eastern Atlantic, and **swordfish** in the Mediterranean.

Because of their cost-effectiveness, the **Food and Agricultural Organization of the United Nations** actively promoted the use of drift nets during the early 1980s. **Earthwatch**, **Earth Island Institute**, and other environmental groups instituted drift-net monitoring during this period and founded public education programs to pressure drift-net fishing nations. The **Sea Shepherd Conservation Society** and other direct action groups have actually intervened with drift-net fishing operations on the high seas. Organizations such as these led international awareness about the dangers of drift nets, and their efforts have affected national and international policy. In 1992, the United Nations reversed its earlier endorsement of drift-net fishing and passed a resolution totally banning the practice.

Enforcement of this ban has so far proven difficult, however, as drift-net fishing is done in open oceans, far from national jurisdictions. In reaching enforceable international agreements about drift-net fishing, the primary problem has been the large investment some nations have in this technology. Japan had 457 fishing vessels using drift-nets in 1990, and Taiwan and Korea approximately 140 vessels each. France, Italy, and other nations own smaller fleets.

Japan and many of these nations are primarily concerned with protecting their investment, despite worldwide protest. The United States and Canada have both expressed concern about ecological integrity and the rate of unintended catch in drift nets, particularly the by-catch of North American salmon. Bilateral negotiations are being pursued with Korea and Taiwan to control their drift net fleets. The International North Pacific Fisheries Commission has provided a forum for United States, Japan, and Canada to examine and discuss the economic advantages and environ-

Drift net.

mental costs of drift-net fishing. A special committee has analyzed by-catch from drift nets used in the northern Pacific. Three avenues are currently being considered to control ecological damage: the use of subsurface nets, research into the construction of **biodegradable** nets, and alternative gear types for the same species.

[*Douglas Smith*]

FURTHER READING

Bowden, C. "At Sea With the Shepherd." *Buzzworm* 3 (March-April 1991): 38-47.

McCloskey, W., and C. Wallace. "Casting Drift Nets with the Squidders." *International Wildlife* 21 (March-April 1991): 40-47.

"Net Losses." *Sierra* 76 (March-April 1991): 48-54.

"U.S. Considers Ratification of Driftnet Fishing Treaty." *U. S. Department of State Dispatch* 2 (26 August 1991): 639-40.

Drinking-water treatment

See **Water treatment**

Drinking-water supply

The **Safe Drinking Water Act**, passed in 1974, required the **Environmental Protection Agency (EPA)** to develop

guidelines for the treatment and monitoring of public water systems. In 1986, amendments to the act accelerated the regulation of contaminants, banning the future use of **lead** pipe, and requiring surface water from most sources to be filtered and disinfected. The amendments also have provisions for greater **groundwater** protection. Despite the improvement these regulations represent, only public and private systems that serve a minimum of 25 people at least sixty days a year are covered by them. Millions obtain their drinking water from privately owned wells which are not covered under the act.

Drinking water comes from two primary sources: surface water and groundwater. Surface water comes from a river or lake, and groundwater, which is pumped from underground sources, generally needs less treatment. Contaminants can originate either from the water source or from the treatment process.

The most common contaminants found in the public water supply are lead, nitrate, and **radon**—all of which pose substantial health threats. Studies indicate that substances such **chlorine** and fluoride which are added to water during the treatment process may also have adverse effects on human health. Over 700 different contaminants have been found in water supplies in the United States, yet the EPA has only established maximum containment levels for 30 of them. Drinking water enforcement has been severely limited at both the state and federal levels. In 1990, 38,000 public water systems committed over 100,000 violations of the act, yet state governments only took legal enforcement action against 1000, and the federal government took action against only 32. In only six percent of these cases were customers informed of the violations.

Chlorinated water was first used in 1908 as a means of reducing diseases in Chicago stockyards. Chlorination, which kills some disease-causing microbes, is now used to disinfect approximately 75 percent of the water supply in the United States. Numerous studies conducted over the past 20 years have found that chlorine reacts with organic products such as farm **runoff** or decaying leaves to form by-products that increase the risk of certain kinds of **cancer**. These by-products of chlorination are associated with cancer of the bladder and of the colon, probably because both store concentrated waste products. Recent research released by the Medical College of Wisconsin suggests that drinking chlorinated water increases the risk of bladder cancer by 20 percent and the risk of rectal cancer by 38 percent. Despite the correlation between chlorination by-products and these types of cancer, many still believe that the benefits of chlorine disinfection outweigh the risks. Some hope this study will prompt those in charge of public water systems to investigate other methods of disinfection, such as the use of **ozone** or exposure to ultraviolet light, both of which are currently used in Europe.

The effectiveness of fluoridated water in reducing dental cavities was first noted in communities with a naturally occurring source of fluoride in their drinking water, and controlled studies of communities where fluoride was added to the water confirmed the results. As of 1989, residents in 70 percent of all cities with populations greater than 100,000 were drinking fluoridated water. The EPA limit for fluoride in water is 4 **parts per million**(ppm), and most cities add only one ppm to their water. Fluoridated water also has adverse effects, and these may include immune system suppression, tooth discoloration, undesirable bone growth, enzyme inhibition, and carcinogenesis.

The EPA has set the acceptable level of lead in drinking water at 15 **parts per billion**(ppb), yet according to tests the agency has done, drinking water in almost 20 percent of cities in the United States exceeds that limit. The EPA has recently estimated that 25 percent of a child's lead intake comes from drinking water, and it cautions that the percentage could be much higher if the water contains high levels of lead. Depending on exposure, lead poisoning can cause permanent learning disabilities, behavioral and nervous system disorders, as well as severe brain damage and death. Service pipes made of lead and leaded solder used on copper plumbing and brass faucets are the main sources of lead in water. Acidic or soft water increases the danger of lead contamination, because it corrodes the plumbing and leeches out the lead. About 80 percent of homes have water that is moderately to highly acidic. As of January 1, 1993, EPA regulations require all large public water companies to reduce the corrosiveness of water by adding calcium oxide or other hardening agents.

Chlorination and government standards for drinking water quality have virtually eliminated the outbreak of the classic water-borne diseases such as cholera, typhoid, and **malaria**. According to *The American Journal of Public Health*, however, recent studies have shown that water which meets current drinking water standards can still contain organisms which cause gastrointestinal (GI) disease. In a 15-month study conducted by the University of Quebec in Montreal, researchers equipped 299 homes with reverse-osmosis water **filter**s, which remove bacterial and chemical contaminants. Over 600 families participated in the study, about half with the filters and half without them, and they were asked to keep records of all GI illnesses among household members. During this 15 month period, the households equipped with the water filters had 35 percent fewer incidents of GI illness and diarrhea. In 1992, *The New England Journal of Medicine* published a study showing that drinking water can harbor the bacterium that causes Legionnaire's disease. Some patients diagnosed with Legionnaire's disease were infected with the same type of *Legionella pneumophila* that was found in samples of their drinking water.

Vegetables, drinking water, and meat preservatives are the main sources of **nitrates and nitrites** in our diet. There is a definite link between nitrate and gastric cancer. Nitrate is converted to nitrite by bacteria in the mouth and stomach, and this is in turn converted into N-nitroso compounds, which have been proven highly carcinogenic in laboratory animals. Bottle-fed infants are at additional risk, because once the nitrate is converted to nitrite in the stomach it combines with fetal hemoglobin and converts to methaemoglobin. When 10 percent of the hemoglobin has been converted, cyanosis or **blue-baby syndrome** occurs; and when 70 percent of the hemoglobin is in methaemoglobin form, death occurs. According to a recent EPA report, half of the private wells in the United States contain nitrate.

Radioactivity occurs naturally and it can be present in drinking water. Preliminary studies have linked it to increased rates of leukemia and cancers of the bladder, breast, and lungs. The EPA has established 5 picocuries per liter (pCi/L) as the safe limit for radium in drinking water. An estimated 100 to 1,800 deaths per year are attributed to radon in tap water. According to EPA estimates over 8 million people have excessively high radon levels in their water supply. Unlike most contaminants found in water, radon does not have to be ingested to pose a health hazard; Dish washing, showering, or just running the faucet can agitate the water and release the radon into the air. According to EPA estimates, there are 10,000 to 40,000 lung-cancer deaths each year from radon inhalation. Radon is most frequently a problem in New England, North Carolina, and Arizona, and it is most likely to be found in well water and small water systems. Most large treatment facilities disperse radon during the treatment process.

Most water-treatment plants in the United States use chemical coagulation to remove impurities and contaminants. **Aluminum** sulfate is often added to the water, causing some contaminants to coagulate with the aluminum and precipitate out. The majority of the aluminum left in the water is removed by subsequent treatment processes, but a residual amount passes through the system to the consumer. Aluminum in drinking water has been linked with neurotoxicity, specifically Alzheimer's disease.

The organic **chemicals** that are found most frequently in drinking water are **pesticide**s, trichloreothylene, and trihalomines. Pesticides usually make their way into drinking water through seepage and runoff in agricultural areas, and in high doses they can damage the liver, the kidney, and the nervous system damage, as well as increase the risk of various cancers. Trichloroethylene are industrial wastes and the populations at highest risk from this chemical have a water supply located near **hazardous waste** sites. The health risks associated with trichloroethylene are nervous system damage and cancer. Chlorination of water that is contaminated with organic matter is responsible for the formation of **trihalomethanes** in water, and preliminary studies suggest that it may increase cancer rates.

In 1992, Americans spent over 3 billion dollars on bottled water and water purification units for their homes. The bottled water industry is not sufficiently regulated, and it does not guarantee water purity. Despite the image portrayed by advertising, studies indicate that bottled water is not any safer in most cases than tap water. Home treatment units carry labels which frequently claim they are EPA-approved, but these are not regulated either. Different types of water filters are capable of removing different contaminants, so most experts recommend that anyone planning to install a treatment system have their water tested first.

Though scientific evidence clearly demonstrates that drinking water can be a health hazard, some of the most effective measures are also the easiest to implement. Studies have found that letting tap water run for several minutes reduces the lead content of the water by up to 70 percent. Companies that supply drinking water can be monitored by requesting copies of their test results and reporting any violations to the EPA. Lobbying for more stringent regulations is widely considered an effective tool for ensuring safe drinking water. Reduction of pesticide use and additional measures implemented for the protection of groundwater and surface water would also greatly reduce many of these health risks. *See also* Carcinogen; Communicable diseases; Filtration; Groundwater pollution; Hazardous waste siting; Neurotoxin; Toxic substance; Water pollution; Water quality standards; Water resources; Water treatment

[*Debra Glidden*]

FURTHER READING

De Zuane, J. *Drinking Water Quality: Standards and Controls.* New York: Van Nostrand Reinhold, 1990.

Drinking Water and Health. Washington, DC: National Academy Press, 1980.

Felsenfield, A., and M. A. Roberts. "A Report of Fluorosis in the United States Secondary to Drinking Well Water." *Journal of the American Medical Association* 265 (23/30 January 1991): 486-8.

"Fluoridation of Community Water Systems." *Journal of the American Medical Association* 267 (24 June 1992): 3264-5.

Fuortes, L., et. al. "Leukemia Incidence and Radioactivity in Drinking Water in 59 Iowa Towns." *American Journal of Public Health* 80 (October 1990): 1261-2.

Lansing, D. "Making Water Safe to Drink." *Sunset* 189 (July 1992): 20-1.

Lloyd, B., and R. Helmer. *Surveillance of Drinking Water Quality in Rural Areas.* New York: Wiley, 1991.

Morris, R., et al. "Chlorination, Chlorination By-Products, and Cancer: A Meta-Analysis." *American Journal of Public Health* 82 (July 1992): 955-63.

Occurrence of Fluoride in Drinking Water, Food, and Air. McLean, VA: JRB Associates, 1984.

Packham, R. F. "Chemical Aspects of Water Quality and Health." *Annual Symposium of the Institution of Water and Environmental Management.* London, England: IWEM, 1990.

Pennisi, E. "Eastern Radon Ranked by Region." *Science News* 140 (14 September 1991): 173.

Stout, J., et al. "Potable Water as a Cause of Sporadic Cases of Community-Acquired Legionnaires' Disease." *New England Journal of Medicine* 326 (16 January 1992): 151-5.

Drip irrigation

Drip irrigation maximizes scarce resources by delivering water exactly where it is needed. The percolation **plume** from drip sources follows the bulb shape of the root zone, wasting little water. This also better controls **fertilizer** inputs by applying **nutrient**s with the water application. Though expensive to install, and best-suited to perennials or high-value crops, this system overcomes or minimizes problems from traditional irrigation methods. Spray irrigation maximizes evaporation; while gravity-fed systems contribute to **seepage** losses, **waterlogging**, and **salinization**. Through water budget analyses and weed control, growers can maintain the exact moisture and nutritional levels needed for optimum plant growth.

Drought

Of all natural disasters, drought is the subtlest. Often, farmers cannot tell there is going to be a drought until it is too late. Unlike flash floods, drought is slow to develop. Unlike earthquakes, with destruction to the exterior **environment**, drought does its damage underground long before dust storms rage across the plains.

Technically, drought is measured by the decrease in the amount of **subsoil** moisture that causes crops to die or yield less (agricultural drought) or by a drop in the water level in surface reservoirs and below ground **aquifer**s, causing **wells** to go dry (hydrological drought). Agricultural plus hydrological drought can lead to sociological drought. In this condition, drought effects food and water supplies to the extent that people have to rely on relief donations or are forced to migrate to another area.

Droughts are worldwide, repetitive, and unpredictable. Scientists believe there is a drought somewhere on the earth at any time. Nor are droughts recent developments; analysis of rock cores, glacial ice cores, and tree rings reveal prehistorical and historical droughts, some of which lasted for several decades. Tree rings in California, for example, record a forty-year-drought three hundred years ago.

The direct cause of drought is a continued decrease in optimal rainfall. But what causes clouds not to form over an area, or the winds to carry rain-bearing clouds elsewhere, is complex. **Climate** change will alter the location of increased and reduced rainfall, so that some places that have always been well-watered will experience drought.

Some scientists believe that the **El Niño**-La Niña events in the western Pacific Ocean are main drivers in the cause of droughts around the world. The El Niño, an eastward flow of warm surface waters, creates a high pressure zone over the equator that results in a change in the high and low pressure zones in other parts of the world. This affects the flow of the jet stream and results in a disturbed rainfall pattern, causing, for example, excessive rain in California and drought in southwestern Africa, among other places. The La Niña, which usually follows the El Niño, is an upwelling of cold deep waters in the western Pacific Ocean. It causes disturbed pressure zones that result in droughts in the Midwest, among other places.

Drought prediction is still in its infancy. Although scientists know that the El Niño-La Niña events cause droughts in specific areas, they cannot yet predict when the El Niño will occur. Weather satellites can measure subsoil moisture, a good indicator of incipient drought, but other factors also contribute to drought.

Lack of rain, for example, in the **Sahel**, is exacerbated by man-made environmental problems, such as cutting down trees for fuel and not allowing the soil to lie fallow, which conserves soil moisture. **Overgrazing** by animals such as cattle, goats, and sheep also contributes to the denuding of **topsoil**, which blows away in the wind, a condition known as **desertification**. Drought then becomes a cycle that feeds on itself: lack of trees reduces the amount of water vapor given off into the **atmosphere**; lack of topsoil reduces water retention. The result is that local rainfall is reduced, and the rain that does fall runs off and is not absorbed.

Of all the water on earth, less than 3 percent is fresh water. A lot of water is lost in evaporation, especially in **arid** climates, not only during rainfall but when it is stored in surface reservoirs. Rainwater or snowmelt that seeps into below-ground **permeable** rock channels, or aquifers, is pumped into wells in many communities. High-tech pumps have contributed to an increased drain on aquifers; if an aquifer is pumped too quickly, it collapses, and the ground above sinks. To increase water bank supplies, some communities recharge their aquifers by pumping water into them when they are low.

The only new water introduced into the **hydrologic cycle** is purified ocean water. **Desalinization** plants are expensive to build and maintain and often require burning **fossil fuels** or wood to run. Future plans include perfecting retrieving **solar energy** and **wind energy**.

Currently, farm **irrigation** uses most of the world's fresh water supply, but as city populations grow, they are expected to become the biggest consumers, and urban **conservation** measures will become imperative. Some communities already recycle **wastewater** for small farms and domestic garden use. Drought-causing industrial pollutants that "freeze" the water supply by rendering it toxic are being reduced and resolved under federal law. Reduced or low-flow shower heads and **toilets** are required in new construction in some states.

Distributing water from more to less abundant supplies by laying pipes and installing pumps within a state or a country requires money and management. If water is fed across state or international boundaries, legal and political negotiations are necessary.

During severe drought, sociologists find that people must either adapt, migrate, or die. Death, however, is usually caused by other factors such as war or poverty, as in the Sahel, where relief food supplies have been hijacked and sold at high prices, or where people in remote villages must walk to the distribution centers.

Some migrations have been permanent, as in the **migration** to California during the Midwestern **Dust Bowl** in the 1930s. Others are temporary, as in the Sahel region, where people migrate in search of food and water, crossing country lines.

Most people adapt in drought by making the most of their resources, such as building reservoirs or desalination plants or laying pipes connecting to more abundant water supplies. Farmers often invest in high-tech irrigation techniques or alter their crops to grow low-water plants, such as garbanzo beans.

Drought has also been the inspiration for inventions. The American West at the turn of the twentieth century gave rise to numerous rainmakers who used mysterious **chemicals** or noisemakers to attract rain. Most inventions failed or were unreliable, but out of the impetus to make rain grew silver iodide cloud-seeding, which now effects a 10 to 15 percent increase in local rainfall in some parts of the world. *See also* Aquifer restoration; Deforestation; Desert; Groundwater; Soil eluviation; Water conservation; Water resources

[*Stephanie Ocko*]

FURTHER READING

Hurt, R. D. *The Dust Bowl: An Agricultural and Social History*. Chicago: Nelson-Hall, 1981.

Glantz, M. H., ed. *Drought and Hunger in Africa: Denying Famine a Future*. New York: Cambridge University Press, 1987.

Rosenberg, N. J., ed. *Drought in the Great Plains: Research on Impacts and Strategies*. Littleton, CO: Water Resources Publications, 1980.

Dry alkali injection

A method for removing **sulfur dioxide** from **combustion** stack gas. A **slurry** of finely ground alkaline material such as calcium carbonate is sprayed into the **effluent** gases before it enters the smokestack. The material reacts chemically with sulfur dioxide to produce a non-hazardous solid product, such as calcium sulfate, that can then be collected by **filters** or other mechanical means. The technique is called dry injection because the amount of water in the slurry is adjusted so that all moisture evaporates while the chemical reactions are taking place and a dry precipitate results. The use of dry alkali injection can result in a 90 percent reduction in the

emission of sulfur dioxide from a stack. It is more expensive than wet alkali injection or simply adding crushed limestone to the fuel, but it is more effective than these techniques and results in a waste product that is relatively easy to dispose of. *See also* Air pollution control

Dry deposition

A process that removes airborne materials from the **atmosphere** and deposits them on a surface. Dry deposition includes the settling or falling-out of particles due to the influence of gravity. It also includes the deposition of gas-phase compounds and particles too small to be affected by gravity. These materials may be deposited on surfaces due to their solubility with the surface or due to other physical and chemical attractions. Airborne contaminants are removed by both wet deposition, such as rainfall scavenging, and by dry deposition. The sum of wet and dry deposition is called total deposition. Deposition processes are the most important way contaminants such as acidic sulfur compounds are removed from the atmosphere; they are also important because deposition processes transfer contaminants to aquatic and terrestrial **ecosystem**s. Cross-media transfers, such as transfers from air to water, can have adverse environmental impacts, and an example of this is how dry deposition of sulfur and **nitrogen** compounds can acidify poorly buffered lakes. *See also* Acid rain; Nitrogen cycle; Sulfur cycle

Dryland farming

Dryland farming is the practice cultivating crops without **irrigation** (rainfed agriculture). In the United States, the term usually refers to crop production in low-rainfall areas without irrigation, using moisture-conserving techniques such as **mulch**es and fallowing. Non-irrigated farming is practiced in the Great Plains, inter-mountain, and Pacific regions of the country, or areas west of the 23.5 inches (600 millimeters) annual precipitation line, where native vegetation was short **prairie** grass. In some parts of the world dryland farming means all rainfed agriculture.

In the western United States, dryland farming has often resulted in severe or moderate wind **erosion**. Alternating seasons of fallow and planting has left the land susceptible to both wind and water erosion. High demand for a crop sometimes resulted in cultivating lands not suitable for long-time farming, degrading the soil measurably.

Conservation tillage, leaving all or most of the previous crop residues on the surface, decreases erosion and conserves water. Methods used are stubble mulch, mulch, and ecofallow. In the wetter parts of the Great Plains, fallowing land has given over to annual cropping, or three-year rotations with one year of fallow. *See also* Arable land; Desertification; Erosion; Soil; Tilth

[*William E. Larson*]

FURTHER READING

Anderson, J. R. *Risk Analysis in Dryland Farming Systems*. Rome: Food and Agriculture Organization of the United Nations, 1992.

Dryland Agriculture. Madison, WI: American Society of Agronomy, 1983.

Resource Conservation Glossary. 3rd ed. Ankeny, IA: Soil Conservation Society of America, 1982.

Dubos, Rene (1901-1982)

American microbiologist and writer

Dubos, a French-born microbiologist, spent most of his career as a researcher and teacher at Rockefeller University in New York state. His pioneering work in microbiology, such as isolating the anti-bacterial substance *gramicidin* from a **soil** organism and showing the feasibility of obtaining germ-fighting drugs from microbes, led to the development of antibiotics.

Nevertheless, most people know Dubos as a writer. Dubos's books centered on how humans relate to their surroundings, books informed by what he described as "the main intellectual attitude that has governed all aspects of my professional life... to study things, from microbes to man, not *per se* but in their complex relationships." That pervasive intellectual stance, carried throughout his research and writing, reflected what *Saturday Review* called "one of the best-formed and best-integrated minds in contemporary civilization."

A related theme was Dubos's conviction that "the total **environment**" played a role in human disease. By total environment, he meant "the sum of the facts which are not only physical and social conditions but emotional conditions as well." Though not a medical doctor, he became an expert on disease, especially tuberculosis, and headed Rockefeller's clinical department on that disease for several years.

"Despairing optimism" also pervaded Dubos's human-environment writings, his own title for a column he wrote for *The American Scholar*, beginning in 1970. *Time* magazine even labeled him the "prophet of optimism:" "My life philosophy is based upon a faith in the immense resiliency of nature," he once commented.

Dubos held a lifelong belief that a constantly changing environment meant organisms, including humans, had to adapt constantly to keep up, survive, and prosper. But he worried that humans were too good at adapting, resulting in both his optimism and his despair: "Life in the technologized environment seems to prove that [humans] can become adapted to starless skies, treeless avenues, shapeless buildings, tasteless bread, joyless celebrations, spiritless pleasures—to a life without reverence for the past, love for the present, or poetical anticipations of the future." He stated that "the belief that we can manage the earth may be the ultimate expression of human conceit," but insisted that nature is not always right and even that humankind often improves on nature. As Thomas Berry suggested, "Dubos sought to reconcile the existing technological order and the planet's survival through

Rene Dubos.

the **resilience** of nature and changes in human consciousness." *See also* Environmental attitudes/values

[*Gerald L. Young*]

FURTHER READING

Culhane, J. "En Garde, Pessimists! Enter Rene Dubos." *New York Times Magazine* 121 (17 October 1971): 44-68.

Kostelanetz, R. "The Five Careers of Rene Dubos." *Michigan Quarterly Review* 19 (Spring 1980): 194-202.

Piel, G., and O. Segerberg, eds. *The World of Rene Dubos: A Collection from His Writings.* New York: Henry Holt, 1990.

Ward, B., and R. Dubos. *Only One Earth: The Care and Maintenance of a Small Planet.* New York: Norton, 1972.

Ducks Unlimited (Long Grove, Illinois)

Ducks Unlimited (DU) is an international (United States, Canada, Mexico, New Zealand, Australia), membership organization founded during the depression years in the United States by a group of sportsmen interested in waterfowl conservation. Ducks Unlimited was incorporated in early 1937, and Ducks Unlimited (Canada) was established later that spring. The organization was established to preserve and maintain waterfowl populations through **habitat** protection and development, primarily to provide game for sport hunting. During the **Dust Bowl** of the 1930s, the founding members of Ducks Unlimited recognized that most of the

continental waterfowl populations were maintained by breeding habitat in the **wetlands** of Canada's southern **prairie**s in Saskatchewan, Manitoba, and Alberta. The organizers established Ducks Unlimited Canada and used their resources to protect the Canadian prairie breeding grounds. Cross-border funding has since been a fundamental component of Ducks Unlimited's operation, although in recent years funds also have been directed to the northern American prairie states. In 1974 Ducks Unlimited de Mexico was established to restore and maintain wetlands south of the U.S.-Mexican border where many waterfowl spend the winter months.

Throughout most of its existence, DU has funded habitat restoration projects and worked with landowners to provide water management benefits on farmlands. But, from its inception Ducks Unlimited has been subject to criticism. Early opponents characterized it as an American intrusion into Canada to secure hunting areas. More recently, critics have suggested that DU defines waterfowl habitat too narrowly, excluding upland areas where many ducks and geese nest. The group plans to broaden its focus to encompass preservation of these upland breeding and nesting areas. Since many of these areas are found on private land, DU also plans to expand its cooperative programs with farmers and ranchers. Most commonly, however, DU is criticized for placing the interests of waterfowl hunters above **wildlife management** concerns. The organization does allow duck hunting on its preserves.

Following the fundamental principle of "users pay," duck hunters still provide the majority of Ducks Unlimited's funding. For that reason DU has not addressed some issues that have a serious effect on continental waterfowl populations. The combination of illegal hunting and liberal bag limits is blamed by some for the continued decline in waterfowl numbers. Ducks Unlimited has not addressed this issue, preferring to leave management issues to government agencies in the United States and Canada, while focusing on habitat preservation and restoration. Critics of Ducks Unlimited suggest that the organization will not act on population matters and risk offending the hunters who provide their financial support.

In North America DU has expanded its scope and activities to address ecological and **land use** problems through the work of the North American Waterfowl Management Plan (NAWMP) and the Prairie CARE (Conservation of Agriculture, Resources and Environment) program. The wetlands conservation and other habitat projects addressed in these and similar programs, not only benefit game species, but other **endangered species** of plants and animals as well. NAWMP (an agreement between the United States and Canada) alone protects over 5.5 million acres of waterfowl habitat.

On balance, Ducks Unlimited has had a major, positive impact on North American waterfowl habitat and management. Millions of acres of wetlands have been protected, enhanced, and managed in Canada, the United States, and Mexico. However, the continued decline in waterfowl populations may require the organization to redirect some of its efforts to population management and preservation issues.

Contact: Ducks Unlimited, One Waterfowl Way, Long Grove, IL 60047. Internet: http://www.ducks.org/.

[*David A. Duffus*]

Ducktown, Tennessee

Tucked in a valley of the Cherokee National Forest, on the border of Tennessee, North Carolina, and Georgia, Ducktown once reflected the beauty of the surrounding Appalachian Mountains. Instead, Ducktown and the valley known as the Copper Basin now form the only **desert** east of the Mississippi. Mined for its rich **copper** lode since the 1850s, it had become a vast stretch of lifeless, red-clay hills. It was an early and stark lesson in the devastation that **acid rain** and **soil erosion** can wreak on a landscape, one of the few man-made landmarks visible to the astronauts who landed on the moon.

Prospectors came to the basin during a gold rush in 1843, but the closest thing to gold they discovered was copper, and most went home. But by 1850, entrepreneurs realized the value of the ore, and a new rush began to mine the area. Within five years, 30 companies had dug beneath the **topsoil** and made the basin the country's leading producer of copper.

The only way to separate copper from the zinc, iron, and sulfur present in Copper Basin rock was to roast the ore at extremely high temperatures. Mining companies built giant open pits in the ground for this purpose, some as wide as 600 feet (183 m) and as deep as a 10-story building. Fuel for these fires came from the surrounding forests. The forests must have seemed a limitless resource, but it was not long before every tree, branch, and stump for 50 square miles had been torn up and burned. The fires in the pits emitted great billows of **sulfur dioxide** gas—so thick people could get lost in the clouds even at high noon—and this gas mixed with water and oxygen in the air to form **sulfuric acid**, which is main component in acid rain. Saturated by acidic moisture and choked by the remaining sulfur dioxide gas and dust, the undergrowth died and the soil became poisonous to new plants. **Wildlife** fled the shelterless hillsides. Without root systems, virtually all the soil washed into the Ocoee River, smothering aquatic life. Open-range grazing of cattle, allowed in Tennessee until 1946, denuded the land of what little greenery remained.

Soon after the turn of the century, Georgia filed suit to stop the **air pollution** which was drifting out of this corner of Tennessee. In 1907, the Supreme Court, in a decision written by Justice Oliver Wendell Holmes, ruled in Georgia's favor, and the sulfur clouds ceased in the Copper Basin. It was one of the first environmental-rights decisions in the United States. That same year, the Tennessee Copper Company designed a way to capture the sulfur fumes, and sulfuric acid, rather than copper, became the area's main product. It remains so today.

Ducktown was the first mining settlement in the area, and residents now take a curious pride not only in the town's history, but in the eerie moonscape of red hills and painted cliffs that surrounds it. Since the 1930s, Tennessee Copper Company, the **Tennessee Valley Authority**, and the **Soil Conservation Service** have worked to restore the land, planting hundreds of loblolly pine and black locust trees. Their efforts have met with little success, but new reforestation techniques such as slow-release **fertilizer** have helped many new plantings survive. Scientists hope to use the techniques practiced here on other deforested areas of the world. Ironically, many of the townspeople want to preserve a piece of the scar, both for its unique beauty and the environmental lesson of what human enterprise can do to nature, as well as what it can undo. *See also* Acid waste; Ashio, Japan; Mine spoil waste; Smelter; Sudbury, Ontario; Surface mining; Trail Smelter arbitration

[*L. Carol Ritchie*]

FURTHER READING

Barnhardt, W. "The Death of Ducktown." *Discover* 8 (October 1987): 34-6+.

"Copper Basin—Tennessee Badlands or 'Beloved Scar'?" *Tennessean* (16 September 1979).

Dunes and dune erosion

Dunes are small hills, mounds or ridges of wind-blown soil material, usually sand, that are formed in both coastal and inland areas. The formation of coastal or inland dunes requires a source of loose sandy material and dry periods during which the sand can be picked up and transported by the wind. Dunes exist independently of any fixed surface feature and can move or drift from one location to another over time. They are the result of natural erosion processes and are natural features of the landscape in many coastal areas and deserts, yet they also can be symptoms of land degradation. Inland dunes are either an expression of aridity or can be indicators of **desertification**—the result of long-term land degradation in dryland areas.

Coastal dunes are the result of marine erosion in which sand is deposited on the shore by wave action. During low tide, the beach sand dries and is dislodged and transported by the wind, usually over relatively short distances. Depending on the local topography and direction of the prevailing winds, a variety of shapes and forms can develop—from sand ridges to parabolic mounds. The upper few centimeters of coastal dunes generally contain chlorides from salt spray and wind-blown salt. As a result, attempts to stabilize coastal dunes with vegetation are often limited to salt-tolerant plants.

The occurrence of beaches and dunes together have important implications for coastal areas. A beach absorbs the energy of waves and acts as a buffer between the sea and the dunes behind it. Low lying coastlines are best defended against high tides by consolidated sand dunes. In such cases, maintaining a wide, high beach that is backed by stable dunes is desirable.

Engineering structures along coastal areas and the mouths of rivers can affect the formation and erosion of beaches and coastal dunes. In some instances it is desirable to build and widen beaches to protect coastal areas. This can require the construction of structures that trap littoral drift, rock mounds to check wave action, and sea walls that protect areas behind the beach from heavy wave action. Where serious erosion has occurred, artificial replacement of beach sands may be necessary. Such methods are expensive and require considerable engineering effort and the use of heavy equipment.

The weathering of rocks, mainly sandstone, is the origin of material for *inland dunes*. However, whether or not sand dunes form, depends on the vegetative cover condition and use of the land. In contrast to coastal dunes, that are often considered to be beneficial to coastal areas, inland dunes can be indicators of land degradation where the protective cover of vegetation has been removed as a result of inappropriate cultivation, overgrazing, construction activities, and so forth. When vegetative cover is absent, soil is highly susceptible to both water and wind erosion. The two work together in drylands to create sources of soil that can be picked up and transported either downwind or downstream. The flow of water moves and exposes sand grains and supplies fresh material that results in deposits of sand in flood plains and ephemeral drainage systems. Before dunes can develop in such areas, there must be long dry periods between periodic or episodic sediment-laden flows of water. Wind erosion occurs where such sand deposits from water erosion are exposed to the energy of wind, or in areas that are devoid of vegetative cover.

Where sand is the principle size soil particle and where high wind velocities are common, sand particles are moved by a process called saltation and creep. Sand dunes form under such conditions and are shaped by wind patterns over the landscape. Complex patterns can be formed—the result of interactions of wind, sand, the ground surface topography and any vegetation or other physical barriers that exist. These patterns can be sword like ridges, called longitudinal dunes, crescentic accumulations or barchans, turret-shaped mounds, shallow sheets of sand, or large seas of transverse dunes. The typical pattern is one of a gradual long slope on the windward side of the dune, dropping off sharply on the leeward side.

Exposed sand dunes can move up to 11 yd (10 m) annually in the direction of the prevailing wind. Such dunes encroach upon areas, covering farmlands, pasture lands, irrigation canals, urban areas, railroads and highways. Blowing sand can mechanically injure and kill vegetation in its path and can eventually bury croplands or rangelands. If left unchecked, the drifting sand will expand and lead to serious economic and environmental losses.

Worldwide, dryland areas are those most susceptible to wind erosion. For example, 22% of Africa north of the Equator is severely affected by wind erosion as is over 35% of the land area in the Near East. As a result, inland dunes represent a significant landscape component in many desert regions. For example, dunes represent 28%, 26% and 38% of the landscape of the Saharan Desert, Arabian Desert, and Australia, respectively (Heathcote 1983). In 1980, Walls estimated that 1.3 billion hectares of land were covered by sand dunes globally. Although dunes can be symptoms of land use problems, in some areas they are part of a natural dryland landscape that are considered to be features of beauty and interest. Sand dune have become popular recreational areas in parts of the United States, including the Great Sand Dune National Monument in southern Colorado with its 229-yd (210-m) high dunes that cover a 158-mi^2 (254.4-km^2) area, and the Indiana Dunes State Park along the shore of Lake Michigan.

When dune formation and encroachment represent significant environmental and economic problems, sand dune stabilization and control should be undertaken. Dune stabilization may initially require one or more of the following: applications of water, oil, bitumens emulsions, or chemical stabilizers to improve the cohesiveness of surface sands; the reshaping of the landscape such as construction of foredunes that are upwind of the dunes, and armoring of the surface using techniques such as hydroseeding, jute mats, mulching and asphalt; and constructing fences to reduce wind velocity near the ground surface. Although sand dune stabilization is the necessary first step in controlling this process, the establishment of a vegetative cover is a necessary condition to achieve long-term control of sand dune formation and erosion. Furthermore, stabilization and revegetation must be followed with appropriate land management that deals with the causes of dune formation in the first place. Where dune erosion has not progressed to a seriously degraded state, dunes can become reclaimed through natural regeneration simply by protecting the area against livestock grazing, all-terrain vehicles, and foot traffic.

Vegetation stabilizes dunes by decreasing wind speed near the ground and by increasing the cohesiveness of sandy material by the addition of organic colloids and the binding action of roots. Plants trap the finer wind-blown **soil** particles, which helps improve soil texture, and they also improve the microclimate of the site, reducing soil surface temperatures. Upwind barriers or windbreak plantings of vegetation, often trees or other woody perennials, can be effective in improving the success of revegetating sand dunes. They reduce wind velocities, help prevent exposure of plant roots from the drifting sand, and protect plantings from the abrasive action of blowing sand. Areas that are susceptible to sand dune encroachment can likewise be protected by using fences or windbreak plantings that reduce wind velocities near the ground surface. Because of the severity of sand dune environments, it can be difficult to find plant species that can be established and survive. In addition, any plantings must be protected against exploitation, for example, from grazing or fuelwood harvesting.

The expansion of sand dunes resulting from desertification not only represent environmental problems, but they also represent serious losses of productive land and a financial hardship for farmers and others who depend upon the land for their livelihood. Such problems are particularly acute in many of the poorer dryland countries of the world and deserve the attention of governments, international agencies, and nongovernmental organizations who need to direct their efforts toward the causes of soil erosion and dune formation.

[*Kenneth N. Brooks*]

Abandoned Oklahoma farm showing the disastrous effects of wind erosion.

FURTHER READING

Brooks, K .N., P .F. Folliott, H. M. Gregersen and L. F. DeBano. *Hydrology and the Management of Watersheds.* 2nd ed. Ames, Iowa: Iowa State University Press, 1997.

Folliott, P. F., K. N. Brooks, H.M. Gregersen and A.L. Lundgren. *Dryland Forestry—Planning and Management.* New York: John Wiley & Sons, 1995.

Food and Agricultural Organization (FAO) of the United Nations. *Sand Dune Stabilization, Shelterbelts, and Afforestation in Dry Zones.* Rome: FAO Conservation Guide 10, 1985.

Heathcote, R. L. *The Arid Lands: Their Use and Abuse.* London: Longman, 1983.

Hauk, F. W. "Soil Erosion and its Control in Developing Countries," *Soil Erosion and Conservation.* Ankeny, Iowa: Soil Conservation Society of America, 1985.

Walls, J. "Land, Man and Sand," *Desert Newsletter.* New York: MacMillan, 1980.

Dust Bowl

"Dust Bowl" is a term coined by a reporter for the *Washington* (D.C.) *Evening Star* to describe the effects of severe wind **erosion** in the Great Plains during the 1930s, caused by severe **drought** and lack of **conservation** practices.

For a time after World War I, agriculture prospered in the Great Plains. Land was rather indiscriminately plowed and planted with cereals and row crops. In the 1930s, the total cultivated land in the United States increased, reaching 530 million acres (215 million hectares), its highest level ever. Cereal crops, especially wheat, were most prevalent in the Great Plains. Summer fallow (cultivating the land, but only planting every other season) was practiced on much of the land. Moisture, stored in the **soil** during the fallow (uncropped) period, was used by the crop the following year. In a process called dust **mulch**, the soil was frequently clean tilled to leave no crop residues on the surface, control weeds, and, it was thought at the time, preserve moisture from evaporation. Frequent cultivation and lack of crop canopy and residues optimized conditions for wind erosion during the droughts and high winds of the 1930s.

During the process of wind erosion, the finer particles (**silt** and clay) are removed from the **topsoil**, leaving coarser-textured sandy soil. The fine particles carry with them higher concentrations of organic matter and plant **nutrient**s, leaving the remaining soil impoverished and with a lower water storage capacity. Wind erosion of the Dust Bowl reduced the productivity of affected lands, often to the point that they could not be farmed economically.

While damage was particularly severe in Texas, Oklahoma, Colorado, and Kansas, erosion occurred in all of the Great Plains states, from Texas to North Dakota and Montana, even into the Canadian Prairie Provinces. The eroding soil not only prevented the growth of plants, it uprooted established ones. **Sediment** filled fence rows, stream channels, road ditches, and farmsteads. Dirt coated the insides of buildings. Airborne dust made travel difficult because of decreased **visibility**; it also impaired breathing and caused **respiratory diseases**.

Dust from the Great Plains was carried high in the air and transported as far east as the Atlantic seaboard. In places, 3 to 4 inches (7-10 centimeters) of topsoil was blown away, forming dunes 15 to 20 feet (4.6-6.1 meters) high where the dust finally came to rest. In a 20-county area covering parts of southwestern Kansas, the Oklahoma strip, the Texas Panhandle, and southeastern Colorado, a soil-erosion survey by the **Soil Conservation Service** showed that 80 percent of the land was affected by wind erosion, 40 percent of it to a serious degree.

The droughts and resultant wind erosion of the 1930s created widespread economic and social problems. Large numbers of people migrated out of the Dust Bowl area during the 1930s. The **migration** resulted in the disappearance of many small towns and community services such as churches, schools, and local units of government.

Following the disaster of the Dust Bowl, the 1940s saw dramatically improved economic and social conditions with increased precipitation and improved crop prices. Gradually, changes in farming practices have also taken place. Much of the severely damaged and marginal land has been returned to grass for livestock grazing. Non-detrimental tillage and management practices, such as **conservation tillage** (stubble mulch, mulch, and residue tillage); use of tree, shrub, and grass windbreaks; maintenance of crop residues on the soil surface; and better machinery have all contributed to improved soil conditions. Annual cropping or a three-year rotation of wheat-sorghum-fallow has replaced the alternate crop-fallow practice in many areas, particularly in the more humid areas of the West.

While the extreme conditions of drought and land mismanagement of the Dust Bowl years have not been repeated since the 1930s, wind erosion is still a serious problem in much of the Great Plains. According to the Soil Conservation Service, the states with the most serious erosion per unit area in 1982 were Texas, Colorado, Nevada, and Montana. *See also* Arable land; Desertification; Overgrazing; Soil eluviation; Tilth; Water resources

[*William E. Larson*]

FURTHER READING

Hurt, R. D. *The Dust Bowl: An Agricultural and Social History.* Chicago: Nelson-Hall, 1981.

Sampson, R. N. *Farmland or Wasteland.* Emmaus, PA: Rodale Press, 1981.

E

Earth Charter

It is the objective of the Earth Charter to set forth an inspiring vision of the fundamental principles of a global partnership for sustainable development and environmental conservation. The Earth Charter initiative reflects the conviction that a radical change in humanity's attitudes and values is essential to achieve social, economic, and ecological well-being in the twenty-first century. The Earth Charter project is part of an international movement to clarify humanity's shared values and to develop a new global ethics, ensuring effective human cooperation in an interdependent world.

There have been repeated efforts to draft the Earth Charter since 1987. Early in 1997 an Earth Charter Commission was formed by the Earth Council and Green Cross International. The Commission is preparing an Earth Charter which it will circulate as a people's treaty beginning in 1998. The Charter will be submitted to the United Nations General Assembly in the year 2000.

Historical Background, 1945-1992

The role and significance of the Earth Charter are best understood in the context of the United Nations' ongoing efforts to identify the fundamental principles essential to world security. When the U.N. was established in 1945, its agenda for world security emphasized peace, human rights, and equitable socioeconomic development. No mention was made of the environment as a common concern, and little attention was given to ecological well-being in the U.N.'s early years. However, since the Stockholm Conference on the Human Environment in 1972, ecological security has emerged as a fourth major concern of the United Nations.

Starting with the Stockholm Declaration, the world's nations have adopted a number of declarations, charters, and treaties that seek to create a global alliance that effectively integrates and balances development and conservation. In addition, a variety of nongovernmental organizations have drafted and circulated their own declarations and people's treaties. These documents reflect a growing awareness that humanity's social, economic, and environmental problems are interconnected and require integrated solutions. The Earth Charter initiative builds on these efforts.

The World Charter for Nature, which was adopted by the U.N. General Assembly in 1982, was a progressive declaration of ecological and ethical principles for its time. It remains a stronger document than any that have followed from the point of view of environmental ethics. However, in its 1987 report, *Our Common Future*, the U.N. World Commission on Environment and Development (WCED) issued a call for "a new charter" that would "consolidate and extend relevant legal principles," creating "new norms ... needed to maintain livelihoods and life on our shared planet" and "to guide state behavior in the transition to sustainable development." The WCED also recommended that the new charter "be subsequently expanded into a Convention, setting out the sovereign rights and reciprocal responsibilities of all states on environmental protection and sustainable development."

The WCED recommendations, together with deepening environmental and ethical concerns, spurred efforts in the late 1980s to create an Earth Charter. However, before any U.N. action was initiated on the Earth Charter, the Commission on Environmental Law of the **World Conservation Union (IUCN)** drafted the convention proposed in *Our Common Future*. The IUCN Draft International Covenant on Environment and Development presents an integrated legal framework for existing and future international and national environmental and sustainable development law and policy. Even though the IUCN Draft Covenant was presented at the United Nations in 1995 official negotiations have not yet begun on this treaty which many environmentalists believe is urgently needed to clarify, synthesize, and further develop international sustainable development law.

The United Nations Conference on Environment and Development (UNCED), or **Earth Summit** held in Rio de Janeiro, Brazil, in 1992 did take up the challenge of drafting the Earth Charter. A number of governments prepared recommendations. Many nongovernmental organizations, including groups representing the major faiths, became actively involved. While the resulting Rio Declaration on Environment and Development is a valuable document, it falls short of the aspirations that many groups have had for the Earth Charter.

The Earth Charter Project, 1994-2000

A new Earth Charter initiative began in 1994 under the leadership of Maurice Strong, the former secretary general of UNCED and chairman of the newly formed Earth Council, and Mikhail Gorbachev, acting in his capacity as chairman of Green Cross International. The Earth Council was created to complete the unfinished business of UNCED and to promote implementation of Agenda 21, the Earth Summit's action plan. Jim MacNeill, former secretary general of the WCED and Prime Minister Ruud Lubbers of The Netherlands were instrumental in facilitating the organization of the new Earth Charter project. Ambassador Mohamed Sahnoun of Algeria served as the executive director of the project during its initial phase, and its first international workshop was held at the Peace Palace in The Hague in May 1995. Representatives from 30 countries and more than 70 different organizations participated in the workshop. Following this event, the secretariat for the Earth Charter project was established at the Earth Council in San José, Costa Rica.

A worldwide Earth Charter consultation process was organized by the Earth Council in connection with the Rio+5 review in 1996 and 1997. The Rio+5 review, which culminated with a special session of the United Nations General Assembly in June 1997, sought to assess progress toward sustainable development since the Rio Earth Summit and to develop new partnerships and plans for implementation of Agenda 21. The Earth Charter consultation process engaged men and women from all sectors of society and all cultures in contributing to the Earth Charter's development. A special program was created to contact and involve the world's religions, interfaith organizations, and leading religious and ethical thinkers. A special indigenous people's network was also organized by the Earth Council.

Early in 1997, an Earth Charter Commission was formed to oversee the project. The twenty-three members represent the major regions of the world and different sectors of society. The Commission issued a Benchmark Draft Earth Charter in March 1997 at the conclusion of the Rio+5 Forum in Rio de Janeiro. The Forum was organized by the Earth Council as part of its independent Rio+5 review, and it brought together more than 500 representatives from civil society and national councils of sustainable development. The Benchmark Draft reflects the many and diverse contributions received through the consultation process and from the Rio+5 Forum. The Commission extended the Earth Charter consultation until early 1998, and the Benchmark Draft has been circulated widely as a document in progress.

The Earth Charter Concept

A consensus has developed that the Earth Charter should be: a statement of fundamental principles of enduring significance that are widely shared by people of all races, cultures, and religions; a relatively brief and concise document composed in a language that is inspiring, clear, and meaningful in all tongues; the articulation of a spiritual vision that reflects universal spiritual values, including but not limited to ethical values; a call to action that adds significant new dimensions of value to what has been expressed in earlier relevant documents; a people's charter that serves as a universal code of conduct for ordinary citizens, educators, business executives, scientists, religious leaders, nongovernmental organizations, and national councils of sustainable development; and a declaration of principles that can serve as a "soft law" document when adopted by the U.N. General Assem-

bly. The Earth Charter is being designed to focus on fundamental principles with the understanding that the IUCN Covenant and other treaties will set forth the more specific practical implications of these principles.

The Earth Charter project draws upon a variety of resources, including ecology and other contemporary sciences, the world's religious and philosophical traditions, the growing literature on global ethics and the ethics of environment and development, the practical experience of people living sustainably, as well as relevant intergovernmental and nongovernmental declarations and treaties. At the heart of the new global ethics and the Earth Charter is an expanded sense of community and moral responsibiiity that embraces all people, future generations, and the larger community of life on Earth. Among the values affirmed by the Benchmark Draft are: respect for Earth and all life; protection and restoration of the health of Earth's **ecosystem**s; respect for human rights, including the right to an environment adequate for human well-being; eradication of poverty; nonviolent problem solving and peace; the equitable sharing of resources; democratic participation in decision making; accountability and transparency in administration; universal education for sustainable living; and a sense of shared responsibility for the well-being of the Earth community.

Additional information on the Earth Charter can be obtained, contact: The Earth Council, P.O. Box 2323-1002, San Jose, Costa Rica. Website: http://www.ecouncil.ac.cr.

[*Steven C. Rockefeller*]

FURTHER READING

Earth Ethics, Special Earth Charter Double Issue. Washington, D.C.: Center for Respect of Life and Environment, 7, nos. 3/4 (Spring/Summer, 1996): 1-7 and 8, nos. 2/3 (Winter/Spring, 1997): 3-8.

Rockefeller, S.C. *Principles of Environmental Conservation and Sustainable Development: Summary and Survey*. The Earth Council website, The Earth Charter Consultation page: http:\www.ecouncil.ac.cr.

Earth Day

The first Earth Day, April 22, 1970, attracted over 20 million participants in the United States. It launched the modern environmental movement, and spurred the passage of several important **environmental law**s. It was the largest demonstration in history. People from all walks of life took part in marches, teach-ins, rallies, and speeches across the country. Congress adjourned so that politicians could attend hometown events, and cars were banned from New York's Fifth Avenue.

The event had a major impact on the nation. Following Earth Day, **conservation** organizations saw their memberships double and triple. Within months, the **Environmental Protection Agency** was created; Congress also revised the **Clean Air Act**, the **Clean Water Act**, and other environmental laws.

The concept for Earth Day began with Senator Gaylord Nelson, a Wisconsin Democrat, who in 1969 proposed a

Marchers carry a tree down Fifth Avenue in New York City on the first Earth Day, April 22, 1970.

series of environmental teach-ins on college campuses across the nation. Hoping to satisfy a course requirement at Harvard by organizing a teach-in there, law student **Denis Hayes** flew to Washington, D.C., to interview Nelson. The senator persuaded Hayes to drop out of Harvard and organize the nationwide series of events that were only a few months away. According to Hayes, Wednesday, April 22 was chosen because it was a weekday and would not compete with weekend activities. It came before students would start "cramming" for finals, but after the winter thaw in the North.

Twenty years later, Earth Day anniversary celebrations attracted even greater participation. An estimated 200 million people in over 140 nations were involved in events ranging from a concert and rally of over a million people in New York's Central Park, to a festival in Los Angeles that attracted 30,000, to a rally of 350,000 at the National Mall in Washington, D.C.

Earth Day 1990 activities included planting trees; cleaning up roads, highways, and beaches; building bird houses; **ecology** teach-ins; and **recycling** cans and bottles. A convoy of garbage trucks drove through the streets of Portland, Oregon, to dramatize the lack of **landfill** space. Elsewhere, children wore gas masks to protest **air pollution**, others marched in parades wearing costumes made from recycled materials, and some even released ladybugs into the air to demonstrate alternatives to harmful **pesticide**s. The gas-guzzling car that was buried in San Jose, California, during the first Earth Day was dug up and recycled.

Abroad, Berliners planted 10,000 trees along the East-West border. In Myanmar, there were protests against the killing of **elephants**. Brazilians demonstrated against the destruction of their **tropical rain forest**s. In Japan, there were demonstrations against disposable chopsticks, and 10,000 people attended a concert on an island built on reclaimed land in Tokyo Bay.

The 1990 version was also organized by Denis Hayes, with help from hundreds of volunteers. This time, the event was well organized and funded; it was widely-supported by both environmentalists and the business community. The United Auto Workers Union sent Earth Day booklets to all of its members, the National Education Association sent information to almost every teacher in the country, and the Methodist Church mailed Earth Day sermons to over 30,000 ministers.

The sophisticated advertizing and public relations campaign, licensing of its logo, and sale of souvenirs provoked criticism that, Earth Day had become too commercial. Even oil, chemical, and nuclear firms joined in and proclaimed their love for **nature**. But Hayes defended the professional approach as necessary to maximize interest and participation in the event, to broaden its appeal, and to launch a decade of environmental activism that would force world leaders to address the many threats to the planet. He also pointed out that while foundations, corporations, and individuals had donated $3.5 million, organizers turned down over $4 million from companies that were thought to be harming the **environment**.

Hayes believes that the long-term success of Earth Day in securing a safe future for the planet depends on getting as many people as possible involved in **environmentalism**. The Earth Day celebrations he helped organize a have been a major step in that direction. *See also* Alternative energy sources; Alternative fuels; Environmental education; Green politics

[*Lewis G. Regenstein*]

FURTHER READING

Booth, W. "The Ecologist's New Climate." *The Washington Post* (20 April 1990): C1, C6.

Borrelli, P. "Can Earth Day Be Every Day?" *Amicus Journal* 12 (Spring 1990): 22-26.

Cohn, D. "Earth Takes Center Stage." *The Washington Post* (April 15, 1990): A1, A6.

Hayes, D. "Earth Day, 1990: Threshold of the Green Decade." *Natural History* 99 (April 1990): 55-60.

———. "The Green Decade." *Amicus Journal* 12 (Spring 1990): 10-21.

Southern, J. "Earth Day: 1970-1990." *Amicus Journal* 12 (Spring 1990): 5-9.

Earth First! (Missoula, Montana)

Earth First! is a radical and often controversial environmental group founded in 1979 in response to what **Dave Foreman** and other founders believed to be the increasing cooptation of the environmental movement. For Earth First! members, too much of the environmental movement has become lethargic, compromising, and corporate in its orientation. To avoid a similar fate, Earth First! members have restricted their use of traditional fund-raising techniques and have sought a non-hierarchical organization with neither a professional staff nor formal leadership.

A movement established by and for self-acknowledged environmental hardliners, Earth First!'s general stance is reflected in its slogan, "No compromise in the defense of Mother Earth." Its policy positions are based upon principles of **deep ecology** and in particular on the group's belief in the **intrinsic value** of all natural things. Its goals include preserving all remaining **wilderness**, ending environmental degradation of all kinds, eliminating major **dams**, establishing large-scale ecological preserves, slowing and eventually reversing human **population growth**, and reducing excessive and environmentally harmful consumption.

Combining biocentrism with a strong commitment to activism, Earth First! does not restrict itself to lobbying, lawsuits, and letter-writing, but also employs direct action, civil disobedience, "guerrilla theater," and other confrontational tactics, and in fact is probably best known for its various clashes with the logging industry, particularly in the Pacific Northwest. Earth First! members and sympathizers have been associated with controversial tactics including the chopping down of billboards and **monkey-wrenching**, which includes pouring sand in bulldozer gas tanks, spiking trees,

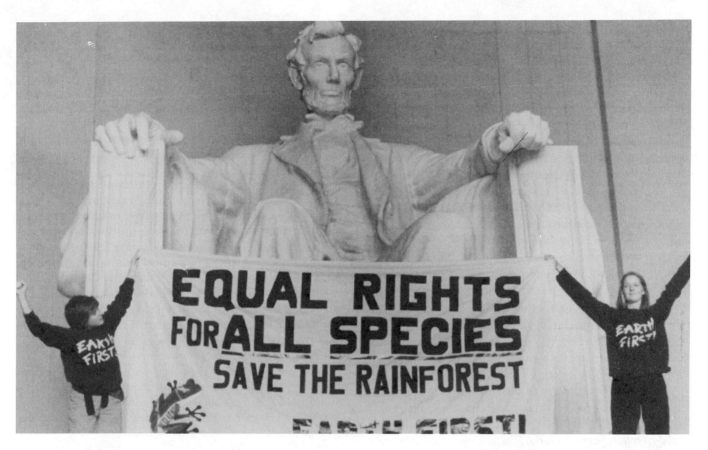

Two Earth First! members hold a sign in front of the statue of Abraham Lincoln at the Lincoln Memorial to protest the destruction of earth's rain forests. The two protestors were arrested by police.

sabotaging drilling equipment, and so forth. Officially, the organization purports neither to condone nor condemn such tactics.

Earth First! encourages people to respect **species** and wilderness, to refrain from having children, to recycle, to live simpler, less destructive lives, and to engage in civil disobedience to thwart environmental destruction. During the summer of 1990, the group sponsored its most noted event, "Redwood Summer." Activists from around the United States gathered in the Northwest to protest large-scale logging operations, to call attention to environmental concerns, to educate and establish dialogues with loggers and the local public, and to engage in civil disobedience.

Earth First! also sponsors a Biodiversity Project for protecting and restoring natural **ecosystem**s. Its Ranching Task Force educates the public about the consequences of **overgrazing** in the American West. The Grizzly Bear Task Force focuses on the preservation of the **grizzly bear** in the Rockies and the reintroduction of the species to its historical range throughout North America. Earth First!'s wider Predator Project seeks the restoration of all native predators to their respective habitats and ecological roles. Carmageddon is an anti-car campaign Earth First! sponsors in the United Kingdom. Other Earth First! projects seek to defend **redwoods** and other native forests, encourage direct action against the fur industry, intervene in government-sponsored wolf-control programs in the US and Canada, and

protest government and business decisions which have environmentally destructive consequences for **tropical rain forest**s. Contact: Earth First!, P.O. Box 5176, Missoula, MT 59806. Internet: http://www.envirolink.org/orgs/ef/.

[Lawrence J. Biskowski]

Earth Island Institute (San Francisco, California)

The Earth Island Institute (EII) was founded by **David Brower** in 1982 as a nonprofit organization dedicated to developing innovative projects for the **conservation**, preservation, and restoration of the global **environment**. In its earliest years, the Institute worked primarily with a volunteer staff and concentrated on projects like the first Conference on the Fate of the Earth, publication of *Earth Island Journal*, and the production of films about the plight of **indigenous peoples**. In 1985 and again in 1987, EII expanded its facilities and scope, opening office space and providing support for a number of allied groups and projects. Its membership now numbers approximately 35,000.

EII conducts research on, and develops critical analyses of, a number of contemporary issues. With sponsored projects ranging from saving **sea turtles** to encouraging land restoration in Central America, EII does not restrict its scope to traditionally "environmental" goals but rather pursues what it sees as ecologically-related concerns such as human rights, economic development of the **Third World**, economic conversion from military to peaceful production, and inner city poverty, among others. But much of its mission is to be an environmental educator and facilitator. In that role EII sponsors or participates in numerous programs designed to provide information, exchange viewpoints and strategies, and coordinate efforts of various groups. EII even produces music videos as part of its **environmental education** efforts.

EII is perhaps best known for its efforts to halt the use of **drift nets** by tuna boats, a practice which is often fatal to large numbers of **dolphins**. After an EII biologist signed on as a crew member aboard a Latin American tuna boat and managed to document the slaughter of dolphins in drift nets, EII brought a lawsuit to compel more rigorous enforcement of existing laws banning tuna caught on boats using such nets. EII also joined with other environmental groups in urging a consumer boycott of canned tuna. These efforts were successful in persuading the three largest tuna canners to pledge not to purchase tuna caught in drift nets. The monitoring of tuna fishing practices is an ongoing EII project.

EII also sponsors a wide variety of other projects. Its Energy Program promotes energy efficient technology. Its Friends of the Ancient Forest program aims at the protection of **old-growth forest**s on the Pacific Coast. Baikal Watch works for the permanent protection of biologically unique **Lake Baikal, Russia**. The Climate Protection Institute publishes the *Greenhouse Gas-ette* and develops public education material about changes in global **climate**. EII participates in the International Green Circle, an ecological restoration program which matches volunteers with ongoing projects worldwide. EII's Sea Turtle Restoration Project investigates threats to the world's endangered sea turtles, organizes and educates United States citizens to protect the turtles, and works with Central American sea turtle restoration projects. The Rain Forest Health Alliance develops educational materials and programs about the biological diversity of **tropical rain forest**s. The Urban Habitat Program develops multicultural environmental leadership and organizes efforts to restore urban neighborhoods.

EII administers a number of funds designed to support creative approaches to environmental conservation, preservation, and restoration to support activists exploring the use of citizen suit provisions of various statutes to enforce environmental laws and to help develop a Green political movement in the United States. EII also sponsors several international conferences, exchange programs, and publication projects in support of various environmental causes. Contact: Earth Island Institute, 300 Broadway, Suite 28, San Francisco, CA 94133. Internet: http://www.earthisland.org/ *See also* Energy efficiency; Environmental ethics; Green politics; Restoration ecology

[*Lawrence J. Biskowski*]

Earth Pledge Foundation (New York, New York)

Created in 1991 by attorney Theodore W. Kheel, the Earth Pledge Foundation (EPF) is concerned with the impact of technology on society. Recognizing the often delicate balance between economic growth and environmental protection, EPF encourages the implementation of sustainable practices, especially in community development, tourism, cuisine, and architecture.

As a result of the **United Nations Earth Summit** (Rio de Janeiro) the U.N. pledged its commitment to the principles of sustainable development—to foster "development meeting the needs of the present without compromising the ability of future generations to meet their own needs."

Created for the Summit in support of the principles, the Earth Pledge was prominently displayed throughout the event. Heads of state, ambassadors, delegates, and prominent dignitaries from around the world stood in line to sign their names on a large Earth Pledge board. Since the Summit, millions have taken the Earth Pledge:

"Recognizing that people's actions towards nature and each other are the source of growing damage to the environment and to resources needed to meet human needs and ensure survival, I pledge to act to the best of my ability to help make the Earth a secure and hospitable home for present and future generations."

In early 1996, Earth Pledge created the Business Coalition for Sustainable Cities (BCSC) to influence the development of cities as centers of commerce, employment, recreation, and settlement. By the year 2000, the number of people living in cities will surpass those living in villages for the first time in human history. Chaired by William L. Lurie, former president of The Business Roundtable, the BCSC provides business leaders a forum to address issues of major importance to our cities in ways that ensure economic viability while at the same time promoting respect for the environment. One event sponsored by the BCSC was a seven-course dinner prepared by twelve of the nation's most environmentally-conscious chefs to showing off that restaurants, one of the largest industries and employers, can practice the principles of sustainable cuisine. The BCSC hosted the event with the theme that good food can be well-prepared without adversely impacting health, culture or environment.

Founder Kheel's initial interest in technology, and its impact on society, was revisited in the Earth Pledge's latest efforts to help nonprofit organizations gain access to the World Wide Web (WWW). To facilitate this, Earth Pledge created a Division for Sustainable Media (DSM), which helps nonprofit organizations and businesses practicing sustainable development to raise funds for developing their sites on the web. The DSM offers a series of Internet seminars and sites including *Web and New Media Pricing Guide* which suggests how to develop a budget and support team for Web projects.

Earth Pledge has also formed a number of alliances to further their goals with groups such as: The Foundation for

Prevention and Resolution of Conflict (PERC—founded by Theodore Kheel); the **United Nations Environmental Programme** (UNEP); EarthKind International; the New England Aquarium.

As a joint project with the New England Aquarium, EPF sponsors a marine awareness project that educates people on the importance of coastlines and aquatic resources to the **sustainable development** of the world's cities. The project emphasizes that many countries have water shortages due to inefficient use of their water supply, degradation of their water by pollution and unsustainable usage of **groundwater** resources.

In late 1995, Earth Pledge co-sponsored the first Caribbean Conference on Sustainable Tourism with the U.N. Department for Policy Coordination and Sustainable Development, EarthKind International and UNEP. The Conference brought together officials from government and business to discuss strategies for developing a healthy tourist economy, sound infrastructure, environmental protection, and community participation.

The foundation has constructed an environmentally-sensitive building, Foundation House, to display their solutions for improving air quality and energy efficiency. Sustainable features include heating, cooling, and lighting systems that minimize consumption of **fossil fuels**; increased ventilation and use of natural daylighting; an auditorium for conferences with internet access and computer lab for training. The Foundation House will eventually house exhibits, including one on enhancing efficiency of the workplace for the benefit of the staff.

Earth Pledge continues to develop smaller organizations and promote companies that participate in sustainable practices. Contact: The Earth Pledge Foundation, 485 Madison Ave., 24th Fl., New York, NY 10022. Internet: http//www.earthpledge.org/.

[*Nicole Beatty*]

Earth Summit

See **United Nations Earth Summit**

Earthquake

See **New Madrid, Missouri**

Earthwatch (Watertown, Massachusetts)

Earthwatch is a non-profit institution that provides paying volunteers to help scientists around the world conduct field research on environmental and cultural projects. It is one of the world's largest private sponsors of field research expeditions. Its mission is "to improve human understanding of the planet, the diversity of its inhabitants, and the processes which affect the quality of life on earth" by working "to sustain the world's **environment**, monitor global change, conserve endangered **habitat**s and **species**, explore the vast heritage of our peoples, and foster world health and international cooperation."

The group carries out its work by recruiting volunteers to serve in an environmental EarthCorps and to work with research scientists on important environmental issues. The volunteers, who pay from $800 to over $2,500 to join two- or three-week expeditions to the far corners of the globe, gain valuable experience and knowledge on situations that affect the earth and human welfare.

In 1993, Earthwatch expects to sponsor 157 projects in 50 countries around the world, mobilizing 4,300 volunteers, ranging in ages from 16 to 85, on 780 research teams. They will address such topics as **tropical rain forest** ecology and **conservation**; marine studies (ocean **ecology**); geosciences (climatology, geology, oceanography, glaciology, volcanology, paleontology); life sciences (**wildlife management**, biology, botany, ichthyology, herpetology, mammalogy, ornithology, primatology, zoology); social sciences (agriculture, economic anthropology, development studies, nutrition, public health); and art and archaeology (architecture, archaeoastronomy, ethnomusicology, folklore).

Since it was founded in 1971, Earthwatch has organized over 34,000 EarthCorps volunteers, who have contributed over $22 million and more than four million hours on some 1,500 projects in 111 countries and 36 states. No special skills are needed to be part of an expedition, and anyone 16 years or older can apply. Scholarships for students and teachers are also available. Earthwatch's affiliate, The Center for Field Research, receives several hundred grant applications and proposals every year from scientists and scholars who need volunteers to assist them on study expeditions.

Earthwatch publishes *Earthwatch* magazine six times a year, describing its research work in progress and the findings of previous expeditions. The group has offices in Los Angeles, Oxford, Melbourne, Moscow, and Tokyo and is represented in all 50 American states as well as in Germany, Holland, Italy, Spain, and Switzerland by volunteer field representatives. Contact: Earthwatch, 680 Mount Auburn Street, Box 403, Watertown, MA 02172. Internet: http://gaia.earthwatch.org:80/.

[*Lewis G. Regenstein*]

Eastern European pollution

Between 1987 and 1992 the disintegration of Communist governments of Eastern Europe allowed the people and press of countries from the Baltic to the Black Sea to begin recounting tales of life-threatening **pollution** and disastrous environmental conditions in which they lived. Villages in Czechoslovakia were black and barren because of **acid rain**, **smoke**, and **coal** dust from nearby factories. Drinking water from Estonia to Bulgaria was tainted with toxic **chemicals** and untreated sewage. Polish garden vegetables were inedible because of high **lead** and **cadmium** levels in the **soil**.

Chronic health problems were endemic to much of the region, and none of the region's new governments had the spare cash necessary to alleviate their environmental liabilities.

The air, soil and water pollution exposed by new environmental organizations and by a newly vocal press had its roots in Soviet-led efforts to modernize and industrialize Eastern Europe after 1945. (Often the term "Central Europe" is used to refer to Poland, Czech Republic, Slovakia, Hungary, Yugoslavia, and Bulgaria, and "Eastern Europe" to refer to the Baltic states, Belarus, and Ukraine. For the sake of simplicity, this essay uses the latter term for all these states.) Following Stalinist theory that modernization meant industry, especially heavy industries such as coal mining, steel production, and chemical manufacturing, Eastern European leaders invested heavily in industrial buildup. Factories were often built in resource-poor areas, as in traditionally agricultural Hungary and Romania, and they rarely had efficient or clean technology. Production quotas generally took precedence over health and environmental considerations, and billowing smokestacks were considered symbols of national progress. **Emission** controls on smokestacks and waste **effluent** pipes were, and are, rare. Soft, brown lignite coal, cheap and locally available, was the main fuel source. Lignite contains up to five percent sulfur and produces high levels of **sulfur dioxide**, **nitrogen oxides**, **particulate**s, and other pollutants that contaminate air and soil in population centers, where many factories and power plants were built. The region's **water quality** also suffers, with careless disposal of toxic industrial wastes, untreated urban waste, and **runoff** from chemical-intensive agriculture.

By the 1980s the effects of heavy industrialization began to show. Dependence on lignite coal led to sulfur dioxide levels in Czechoslovakia and Poland eight times greater than those of Western Europe. The industrial triangle of Bohemia and Silesia had Europe's highest concentrations of ground-level **ozone**, which harms human health and crops. Acid rain, a result of industrial **air pollution**, had destroyed or damaged half of the forests in the former East Germany and the Czech Republic. Cities were threatened by outdated factory equipment and aging chemical storage containers and pipelines, which leaked **chlorine**, aldehydes, and other noxious gases. People in cities and villages experienced alarming numbers of **birth defects** and short life expectancies. Economic losses, from health care expenses, lost labor, and production inefficiency further handicapped hard-pressed Eastern European governments.

Popular protests against environmental conditions crystallized many of the movements that overturned Eastern and Central European governments. In Latvia, exposés on **petrochemical** poisoning and on environmental consequences of a hydroelectric project on Daugava River sparked the Latvian Popular Front's successful fight for independence. Massive campaigns against a proposed dam on the Danube River helped ignite Hungary's political opposition in 1989. In the same year, Bulgaria's Ecoglasnost group held Sofia's first non-government rally since 1945. The Polish Ecological Club, the first independent environmental organization in Eastern Europe, assisted the Solidarity movement in overturning the Polish government in the mid-1980s.

Citizens of these countries rallied around environmental issues because they had first-hand experience with the consequences of pollution. In Espenhain, of former East Germany, 80 percent of children developed chronic **bronchitis** or heart ailments before they were eight years old. Studies showed that up to 30 percent of Latvian children born in 1988 may have suffered from birth defects, and both children and adults showed unusually high rates of **cancer**, **leukemia**, skin diseases, bronchitis, and **asthma**. Czech children in industrial regions had acute **respiratory diseases**, weakened immune systems, and retarded bone development, and concentrations of lead and cadmium were found in children's hair. In the industrial regions of Bulgaria skin diseases were seven times more common than in cleaner areas, and cases of rickets and liver diseases were four times as common. Much of the air and soil contamination that produced these symptoms remains today and continues to generate health problems.

Water pollution is at least as threatening as air and soil pollution. Many cities and factories in the region have no facilities for treating **wastewater** and sewage. Existing treatment facilities are usually inadequate or ineffective. Toxic waste dumps containing old and rusting barrels of **hazardous material**s are often unmonitored or unidentified. Chemical **leaching** from poorly monitored waste sites threatens both surface water and **groundwater**, and water clean enough to drink has become a rare commodity. In Poland untreated sewage, mine drainage, and factory effluents make 95 percent of water unsafe for drinking. At least half of Polish rivers are too polluted, by government assessment, even for industrial use. According to government officials, 70 percent of all rivers in the industrial Czech region of Bohemia are heavily polluted, 40 percent of wastewater goes untreated, and nearly a third of the rivers have no fish. In Latvia's port town of Ventspils, heavy oil lies up to a meter thick on the river bottom. Phenol levels in the nearby Venta River exceed official limits by 800 percent.

Few pollution problems are geographically restricted to the country in which they were generated. Shared rivers and **aquifer**s and regional weather patterns carry both airborne and water-borne pollutants from one country to another. The **Chernobyl** nuclear reactor disaster, which spread radioactive gases and particulates from Belarus across northern Europe and the Baltic Sea to northern Norway and Sweden is one infamous example of trans-border pollution, but other examples are common. The town of Ruse, Bulgaria has long been contaminated by chlorine gas emissions from a Romanian plant just across the Danube. Protests against this poisoning have unsettled Bulgarian and Romanian relations since 1987. Toxic wastes flowing into the Baltic Sea from Poland's Vistula River continue to endanger fisheries and shoreline **habitat**s in Sweden, Germany, and Finland.

The Danube River is a particularly critical case. Accumulating and concentrating urban and industrial waste from Vienna to the Black Sea, this river supports industrial complexes of Austria, Czechia, Hungary, Croatia, Serbia, Bulgaria, and Romania. Before the Danube leaves Budapest, it is considered unsafe for swimming. Like other rivers, the Danube flows through a series of industrial cities and mining regions, each river uniting the pollution problems of several countries. Each city and farm along the way uses the contaminated water and contributes some pollutants of its own. Also like other rivers, the Danube carries its toxic load into the sea, endangering the marine **environment**.

Western countries from Sweden to the United States have their share of pollution and environmental disasters. The Rhine and the Elbe have disastrous **chemical spills** like those on the Danube and the Vistula. Like recent communist regimes, most western business leaders would prefer to disregard environmental and human health considerations in their pursuit of production quotas. Yet several factors set apart environmental conditions in Eastern Europe. Aside from its aged and outdated equipment and infrastructure, Eastern Europe is handicapped by its compressed geography, intense urbanization near factories, a long-standing lack of information and accurate records on environmental and health conditions, and severe shortages of clean-up funds, especially hard currency.

Eastern Europe's dense settlement crowds all the industrial regions of the Baltic states, Poland, the Czech and Slovak republics, and Hungary into an area considerably smaller than Texas but with a much higher population. This industrial zone lies adjacent to crowded manufacturing regions of Western Europe. In this compact region, people farm the same fields and live on the same mountains that are stripped for mineral extraction. Cities and farms rely on aquifers and rivers that receive factory effluent and **pesticide** runoff immediately upstream. Furthermore, post-1945 industrialization gathered large labor forces into factory towns more quickly than adequate infrastructure could be built. Expanding urban populations had little protection from the unfiltered pollutants of nearby furnaces. At the same time that many Eastern Europeans were eye witnesses to environmental transgressions, little public discussion about the problem was possible. Official media disliked publicizing health risks or the destruction of forests, rivers, and lakes. Those statistics that existed were often unreliable. Air and water quality data were collected and reported by industrial and government officials, who could not afford bad test results.

Now that environmental conditions are being exposed, cleanup efforts remain hampered by a shortage of funding. Poland's long-term environmental restoration may cost $260 billion, or nearly eight times the country's annual GNP in the mid-1980s. Efforts to cut just sulfur dioxide emissions to Western standards would cost Poland about $2.4 billion a year. Hungary, with a mid-1980s GNP of $25 billion, could begin collecting and treating its sewage for about $5 billion. Cleanup in the port of Ventspils, Latvia, is expected to cost 3.6 billion rubles and $1.5 billion in hard currency. East German air, soil, and water remediation get a boost from their western neighbors, but the bill is expected to run between $40 and $150 billion.

Ironically, East European leaders see little choice for raising this money aside from expanded industrial produc-

tion. Meanwhile, business leaders urge production expansion for other capital needs. Some Western investment in cleanup work has begun, especially on the part of such countries as Sweden and Germany, which share rivers and seas with polluting neighbors. Already in 1989 Sweden had begun work on water quality monitoring stations along Poland's Vistula River, which carries pollutants into the Baltic Sea. Capital necessary to purchase mitigation equipment, improve factory conditions, rebuild rusty infrastructure, and train environmental experts will probably be severely limited for decades to come, however.

Meanwhile, western investors are flocking to Eastern and Central Europe in hopes to build or rebuild business ventures for their own gain. The region is seen as one of quick growth and great potential. Manufacturers in heavy and light industries, **automobile**s, **power plants**, and home appliances are coming from Western Europe, North America, and Asia. From textile manufacturing to agribusiness, outside investors hope to reshape Eastern economies. Many Western companies are improving and updating equipment and adding pollution control devices. In a climate of uncertain regulation and rushed economic growth, however, no one knows if the region's new governments will be able or willing to enforce environmental safeguards or if the new investors will take advantage of weak regulations and poor enforcement as did their predecessors. *See also* Acid mine drainage; Agricultural chemicals; Agricultural pollution; Contaminated soil; Environmental degradation; Environmental monitoring; Fish kills; Hazardous waste; Mine spoil waste; Pesticide residue; Seepage; Sewage treatment; Stack emissions; Strip mining; Sustainable development; Toxic substance; Urban runoff; Urban sprawl; Water treatment

[*Mary Ann Cunningham*]

FURTHER READING

Feshbach, M., and A. Friendly, Jr. *Ecocide in the USSR.* New York: Basic Books, 1992.

French, H. F. "Restoring the Eastern European and Soviet Environments." In *State of the World 1991.* New York: Norton, 1991.

Hartsock, J. "Latvia's Toxic Legacy." *Audubon* 94 (1992): 27-8.

Kabala, S. J. "The Environmental Morass in Eastern Europe." *Current History* 90 (1991): 384-89.

Wallich, P. "Dark Days: Eastern Europe Brings to Mind the West's Polluted History." *Scientific American* 263 (1990): 16, 20.

Ecoanarchism

The philosophy of certain environmental or conservation groups that pursue their goals through radical political action. The name reflects both their relation to older anarchist revolutionary groups and their deep distrust of government, as well as large organizations. Nuclear issues, social responsibility, and grass-roots democracy are among the concerns of ecoanarchists.

As anarchists, ecoanarchists view mainstream political and environmental organizations as inherently flawed and those who maintain them as inevitably corrupt. Ecoanarchists may resort to direct confrontation, direct action, civil disobedience, and guerrilla theater to fight for survival of wild places.

These groups sometimes practice **monkey-wrenching**, a term for actions taken to disrupt and halt damage to the **environment**. Such actions are also called ecoterrorism. Monkeywrenchers perform sit-ins in front of bulldozers; they disable machinery in various ways including pouring sand in a bulldozer's gas tank; they ram whaling ships; and they spike trees by driving metal bars into them to prevent logging. Ecoanarchists also practice ecotage, which is sabotage for environmental ends, often of machines that alter the landscape. *See also* Earth First!; Environmental ethics; Environmentalism; Green politics; Greenpeace; Greens; Sea Shepherd Conservation Society

Ecocide

Any substance that enters an ecological system, spreads throughout that system, and kills enough members of the ecosystem to disrupt its structure and function. For example, on July 14, 1991, a freight train carrying the **pesticide** metam sodium fell off a bridge near Dunsmuir, California, spilling its contents into the Sacramento River. When mixed with water this pesticide becomes highly poisonous, and all animal life for some distance downstream of the spill site was killed.

Ecofeminism

Coined in 1974 by the French feminist Francoise d'Eaubonne, ecofeminism, or ecological feminism, is a recent movement that asserts that the **environment** is a feminist issue and that feminism is an environmental issue. The term ecofeminism has come to describe two related movements operating at somewhat different levels: (1) the grassroots, women-initiated activism aimed at eliminating the oppression of women and **nature**; and (2) a newly emerging branch of philosophy that takes as its subject matter the foundational questions of meaning and justification in feminism and **environmental ethics**. The latter, more properly termed ecofeminist philosophy, stands in relation to the former as theory stands to practice. Though closely related, there nevertheless remain important methodological and conceptual distinctions between action- and theory-oriented ecofeminism.

The ecofeminist movement developed from diverse beginnings, nurtured by the ideas and writings of a number of feminist thinkers, including Susan Griffin, Carolyn Merchant, Rosemary Radford Ruether, Ynestra King, Ariel Salleh, and Vandana Shiva. The many varieties of feminism (liberal, marxist, radical, socialist, etc.) have spawned as many varieties of ecofeminism, but they share a common ground. As described by Karren Warren, a leading ecofeminist philosopher, ecofeminists believe that there are important connections—historical, experiential, symbolic, and theoretical—between the domination of women and the domination of nature. In the broadest sense, then, ecofeminism is a distinct social movement that blends theory and practice to reveal and eliminate the causes of the dominations of women and of nature.

While ecofeminism seeks to end all forms of oppression, including racism, classism, and the abuse of nature, its focus is on gender bias, which ecofeminists claim has dominated western culture and led to a patriarchal, masculine value-oriented hierarchy. This framework is a socially constructed mindset that shapes our beliefs, attitudes, values, and assumptions about ourselves and the natural world.

Central to this patriarchal framework is a pattern of thinking that generates normative dualisms. These are created when paired complementary concepts such as male/female, mind/body, culture/nature, and reason/emotion are seen as mutually exclusive and oppositional. As a result of socially-entrenched gender bias, the more "masculine" member of each dualistic pair is identified as the superior one. Thus, a value hierarchy is constructed which ranks the masculine characteristics above the feminine (e.g., culture above nature, man above woman, reason above emotion). When paired with what Warren calls a "logic of domination," this value hierarchy enables people to justify the subordination of certain groups on the grounds that they lack the "superior" or more "valuable" characteristics of the dominant groups. Thus, men dominate women, humans dominate nature, and reason is superior to emotion. Within this patriarchal conceptual framework, subordination is legitimized as the necessary oppression of the inferior. Until we reconceptualize ourselves and our relation to nature in non-patriarchal ways, ecofeminists maintain, the continued dual denigration of women and nature is assured.

Val Plumwood, an Australian ecofeminist philosopher, has traced the roots of the development of the oppression of women and the exploitation of nature to three points, the first two points sharing historical origins, the third having its genesis in human psychology. In the first of these historical women-nature connections, dualism has identified higher and lower "halves." The lower halves, seen as possessing less or no **intrinsic value** relative to their polar opposites, are instrumentalized and subjugated to serve the needs of the members of the "higher" groups. Thus, due to their historical association and supposedly shared traits, women and nature have been systematically devalued and exploited to serve the needs of men and culture.

The second of these historical women-nature connections is said to have originated with the rise of mechanistic science before and during the Enlightenment period. According to some ecofeminists, dualism was not necessarily negative or hierarchical; however, the rise of modern science and technology, reflecting the transition from an organic to a mechanical view of nature, gave credence to a new logic of domination. Rationality and scientific method became the only socially sanctioned path to true knowledge, and individual needs gained primacy over community. On this fertile soil were sown the seeds for an ethic of exploitation.

A third representation of the connections between women and nature has its roots in human psychology.

According to this account, the features of masculine consciousness which allow men to objectify and dominate are the result of sexually-differentiated personality development. As a result of women's roles in both creating and maintaining/nurturing life, women develop "softer" ego boundaries than do men, and thus they generally maintain their connectedness to other humans and to nature, a connection which is reaffirmed and recreated generationally. Men, on the other hand, psychologically separate both from their human mothers and from Mother Earth, a process which results in their desire to subdue both women and nature in a quest for individual potency and transcendence. Thus, sex differences in the development of self/other identity in childhood are said to account for women's connectedness with, and men's alienation from, both humanity and nature.

Ecofeminism has attracted criticism on a number of points. One is the implicit assumption in certain ecofeminist writings that there is some connection between women and nature that men either do not possess or cannot experience. And, why female activities such as birth and childcare should be construed as more "natural" than some traditional male activities remains to be demonstrated. This assumption, though, has left some ecofeminists open to charges of having constructed a new value hierarchy to replace the old, rather than having abandoned hierarchical conceptual frameworks altogether. Hints of hierarchical thinking can be found in such ecofeminist practices as goddess worship and in the writings of some radical ecofeminists who advocate the abandonment of reason altogether in the search for an appropriate human-nature relationship. Rather than having destroyed gender bias, some ecofeminists are accused of merely attempting to reverse its polarity, possibly creating new, subtle forms of women's oppression. Additionally, some would argue that ecofeminism runs the risk of oversimplification in suggesting that all struggles between dominator and oppressed are one and the same and thus can be won through unity.

A lively debate is currently underway concerning the compatibility of ecofeminism with other major theories or schools of thought in environmental philosophy. For instance, discussions of the similarities and differences between ecofeminism and **deep ecology** occupy a large portion of the recent theoretical literature on ecofeminism. While deep ecologists are primarily concerned with anthropocentrism as the primary cause of our destruction of nature, ecofeminists point instead to androcentrism as the key problem in this regard. Nevertheless, both groups aim for the expansion of the concept of "self" to include the natural world, for the establishment of a biocentric egalitarianism, and for the creation of connection, wholeness, and empathy with nature.

Given the newness of ecofeminism as a theoretical discipline, it is no surprise that the nature of ecofeminist ethics is still emerging. A number of different feminist-inspired positions are gaining prominence, including feminist **animal rights**, feminist environmental ethics based on caregiving, feminist **social ecology**, and feminist **bioregionalism**. Despite the apparent lack of a unified and over-arching environmental philosophy, all forms of ecofeminism do share a commitment to developing ethics which do not sanction or encourage either the domination of any group of humans or the abuse of nature. Already, ecofeminism has shown us that issues in environmental ethics and philosophy cannot be meaningfully or adequately discussed apart from considerations of social domination and control. If ecofeminists are correct, then a fundamental reconstruction of the value and structural relations of our society, as well as a reexamination of the underlying assumptions and attitudes, is necessary.

[*Ann S. Causey*]

FURTHER READING

Adams, C., and K. Warren. "Feminism and the Environment: A Selected Bibliography." *APA Newsletter on Feminism and Philosophy* (Fall 1991).

Des Jardins, J. *Environmental Ethics: An Introduction to Environmental Philosophy.* Belmont, CA: Wadsworth, 1993.

Diamond, I., and G. Orenstein, eds. *Reweaving the World: The Emergence of Ecofeminism.* San Francisco: Sierra Club Books, 1989.

Griffin, S. *Woman and Nature: The Roaring Inside Her.* New York: Harper & Row, 1978.

Vance, Linda. "Remapping the Terrain: Books on Ecofeminism." *Choice* 30 (June 1993): 1585-93.

Warren, K. "Feminism and the Environment: An Overview of the Issues." *APA Newsletter on Feminism and Philosophy* (Fall 1991).

Ecojustice

The concept of ecojustice has at least two different usages among environmentalists. The first refers to a general set of attitudes about justice and the **environment** at the center of which is dissatisfaction with traditional theories of justice. With few exceptions (notably a degree of concern about excessive cruelty to animals), anthropocentric and egocentric Western moral and ethical systems have been unconcerned with individual plants and animals, **species**, oceans, **wilderness** areas, and other parts of the **biosphere**, except as they may be used by humans. In general, that which is non-human is viewed mainly as raw material for human uses, largely or completely without moral standing.

Relying upon holistic principles of biocentrism and **deep ecology**, the "ecojustice" alternative suggests that the value of non-human life-forms is independent of the usefulness of the non-human world for human purposes. Antecedents of this view can be found in sources as diverse as Eastern philosophy, **Aldo Leopold**'s "**land ethic**," **Albert Schweitzer**'s "reverence for life," and Martin Heidegger's injunction to "let beings be." The central idea of ecojustice is that the categories of ethical and moral reflection relevant to justice should be expanded to encompass **nature** itself and its constituent parts, and human beings have an obligation to take the inherent value of other living things into consideration whenever these living things are affected by human actions.

Some advocates of an ecojustice perspective base standards of just treatment on the evident capacity of many life-forms to experience pain. Others assert the equal inherent worth of all individual life-forms. More typically, environmental ethicists assert that all life-forms have at least some inherent worth, and thus deserve moral consideration, although perhaps not the same worth. The practical goals associated with ecojustice include the fostering of stability and diversity within and between self-sustaining **ecosystem**s, harmony and balance in nature and within competitive biological systems, and **sustainable development**.

Ecojustice can also refer simply to the linking of environmental concerns with various social justice issues. The advocate of ecojustice typically strives to understand how the logic of a given economic system results in certain groups or classes of people bearing the brunt of **environmental degradation**. This entails, for example, concern with the frequent location of polluting industries and **hazardous waste** dumps near the economically disadvantaged (i.e., those with the least mobility and fewest resources to resist).

In much the same way, ecojustice also involves the fostering of sustainable development in less-developed areas of the globe, so that economic development does not mean the export of polluting industries and other environmental problems to these less-developed areas. An additional point of concern is the allocation of costs and benefits in environmental **reclamation** and preservation—for example, the preservation of Amazonian **rain forest**s affects the global environment and may benefit the whole world, but the costs of this preservation fall disproportionately upon Brazil and the other countries of the region. An advocate of ecojustice would be concerned that the various costs and benefits of development be apportioned fairly. *See also* Biodiversity; Ecological and environmental justice; Environmental ethics; Environmental racism; Environmentalism; Holistic approach

[*Lawrence J. Biskowski*]

FURTHER READING

Devall, B., and G. Sessions, *Deep Ecology*. Salt Lake City: Peregrine Smith Books, 1985.
Miller, A. S. *Gaia Connections*. Savage, MD: Rowman and Littlefield, 1991.
Wenz, P. S. *Environmental Justice*. Albany: SUNY Press, 1988.

Ecological (biological) integrity

Ecological (or biological) integrity is a measure of how intact or complete an **ecosystem** is. Ecological integrity is a relatively new and somewhat controversial notion, however, which means that it cannot be defined exactly. Human activities cause many changes in environmental conditions, and these can benefit some species, communities, and ecological processes, while causing damages to others at the same time. The notion of ecological integrity is used to distinguish between ecological responses that represent improvements, and those that are degradations.

Challenges To Ecological Integrity

Ecological integrity is affected by changes in the intensity of **environmental stress**ors. Environmental stressors can be defined as physical, chemical, and biological constraints on the productivity of species and the processes of ecosystem

development. Many environmental stressors are associated with the activities of humans, but some are also natural factors. Environmental stressors can exert their influence on a local scale, or they may be regional or even global in their effects. Stressors represent environmental challenges to ecological integrity.

Environmental stressors are extremely complex, but they can be categorized in the following ways:

(1) Physical stressors are associated with brief but intense exposures to kinetic energy. Because of its acute, episodic nature, this represents a type of disturbance. Examples include volcanic eruptions, windstorms, and explosions; (2) **Wildfire** is another kind of disturbance, characterized by the **combustion** of much of the **biomass** of an ecosystem, and often the deaths of the dominant plants; (3) Pollution occurs when chemicals are present in concentrations high enough to affect organisms and thereby cause ecological changes. Toxic **pollution** may be caused by such gases as **sulfur dioxide** and **ozone**, **metals** such as mercury and **lead**, and **pesticide**s. Nutrients such as phosphate and nitrate can affect ecological processes such as productivity, resulting in a type of pollution known as eutrophication; (4) Thermal stress occurs when releases of heat to the environment cause ecological changes, as occurs near natural hot-water vents in the ocean, or where there are industrial discharges of warmed water; (5) Radiation stress is associated with excessive exposures to ionizing energy. This is an important stressor on mountaintops because of intense exposures to **ultraviolet radiation**, and in places where there are uncontrolled exposures to radioactive wastes; (6) Climatic stressors are associated with excessive or insufficient regimes of temperature, moisture, solar radiation, and combinations of these. Tundra and deserts are climatically stressed ecosystems, while tropical **rain forest**s occur in places where the climatic regime is relatively benign; (7) Biological stressors are associated with the complex interactions that occur among organisms of the same or different species. Biological stresses result from competition, herbivory, predation, parasitism, and disease. The harvesting and management of species and ecosystems by humans can be viewed as a type of biological stress.

All species and ecosystems have a limited capability for tolerating changes in the intensity of environmental stressors. Ecologists refer to this attribute as resistance. When the limits of tolerance to environmental stress are exceeded, however, substantial ecological changes are caused.

Large changes in the intensity of environmental stress result in various kinds of ecological responses. For example, when an ecosystem is disrupted by an intense disturbance, there will be substantial mortality of some species and other damages. This is followed by recovery of the ecosystem through the process of succession. In contrast, a longer-term intensification of environmental stress, possibly caused by chronic pollution or climate change, will result in longer lasting ecological adjustments. Relatively vulnerable species become reduced in abundance or are eliminated from sites that are stressed over the longer term, and their modified niches will be assumed by more tolerant species. Other common responses of an intensification of environmental stress include a simplification of species richness, and decreased rates of productivity, **decomposition**, and nutrient cycling. These changes represent a longer-term change in the character of the ecosystem.

Components of Ecological Integrity

Many studies have been made of the ecological responses to both disturbance and to longer-term changes in the intensity of environmental stressors. Such studies have, for instance, examined the ecological effects of air or water pollution, of the harvesting of species or ecosystems, and the conversion of natural ecosystems into managed agroecosystems. The commonly observed patterns of change in stressed ecosystems have been used to develop indicators of ecological integrity, which are useful in determining whether this condition is improving or being degraded over time. It has been suggested that greater ecological integrity is displayed by systems that, in a relative sense: (1) *are resilient and resistant to changes in the intensity of environmental stress.* Ecological resistance refers to the capacity of organisms, populations, or communities to tolerate increases in stress without exhibiting significant responses. Once thresholds of tolerance are exceeded, ecological changes occur rapidly. Resilience refers to the ability to recover from disturbance; (2) *are biodiverse.* Biodiversity is defined as the total richness of biological variation, including genetic variation within populations and species, the numbers of species in communities, and the patterns and dynamics of these over large areas; (3) *are complex in structure and function.* The complexity of the structural and functional attributes of ecosystems is limited by natural environmental stresses associated with climate, **soil**, chemistry, and other factors, and also by stressors associated with human activities. As the overall intensity of stress increases or decreases, structural and functional complexity responds accordingly. Under any particular environmental regime, older ecosystems will generally be more complex than younger ecosystems; (4) *have large species present.* The largest species in any ecosystem appropriate relatively large amounts of resources, occupy a great deal of space, and require large areas to sustain their populations. In addition, large species tend to be long-lived, and consequently they integrate the effects of stressors over an extended time. As a result, ecosystems that are affected by intense environmental stressors can only support a few or no large species. In contrast, mature ecosystems occurring in a relatively benign environmental regime are dominated by large, long-lived species; (5) *have higher-order predators present.* Top predators are sustained by a broad base of ecological productivity, and consequently they can only occur in relatively extensive and/or productive ecosystems; (6) *have controlled nutrient cycling.* Ecosystems that have recently been disturbed lose some of their biological capability for controlling the cycling of nutrients, and they may lose large amounts of nutrients dissolved or suspended in stream water. Systems that are not "leaky" of their nutrient capital are considered to have greater ecological integrity; (7) *are efficient in energy use and transfer.* Large increases in environmental stress com-

monly result in community-level **respiration** exceeding productivity, resulting in a decrease in the standing crop of biomass in the system. Ecosystems that are not losing their capital of biomass are considered to have greater integrity than those in which biomass is decreasing over time; (8) *have an intrinsic capability for maintaining natural ecological values.* Ecosystems that can naturally maintain their species, communities, and other important characteristics, without being managed by humans, have greater ecological integrity. If, for example, a population of a rare species can only be maintained by management of its habitat by humans, or by a program of captive-breeding and release, then its population, and the ecosystem of which it is a component, are lacking in ecological integrity; (9) *are components of a "natural" community.* Ecosystems that are dominated by non-native, introduced species are considered to have less ecological integrity than ecosystems composed of indigenous species.

Indicators (8) and (9) are related to "naturalness" and the roles of humans in ecosystems, both of which are philosophically controversial topics. However, most ecologists would consider that self-organizing, unmanaged ecosystems composed of native species have greater ecological integrity than those that are strongly influenced by humans. Examples of strongly human-dominated systems include agroecosystems, forestry plantations, and urban and suburban areas. None of these ecosystems can maintain their character in the absence of management by humans, including large inputs of energy and nutrients.

Indicators of Ecological Integrity

Indicators of ecological integrity vary greatly in their intent and complexity. For instance, certain metabolic indicators have been used to monitor the responses by individuals and populations to toxic stressors, as when bioassays are made of enzyme systems that respond vigorously to exposures to **dichlorodiphenyl-trichloroethane** (DDT), **pentachlorophenol**s (PCBs), and other chlorinated hydrocarbons. Other simple indicators include the populations of **endangered species**; these are relevant to the viability of those species as well as the integrity of the ecosystem of which they are a component. There are also indicators of ecological integrity at the level of landscape, and even global indicators relevant to climate change, depletion of stratospheric **ozone**, and **deforestation**.

Relatively simple indicators can sometimes be used to monitor the ecological integrity of extensive and complex ecosystems. For example, the viability of populations of spotted owls (*Strix occidentalis*) is considered to be an indicator of the integrity of the old-growth forests in which this endangered species breeds in the western United States. These forests are commercially valuable, and if plans to harvest and manage them are judged to threaten the viability of a population of spotted owls, this would represent an important challenge to the integrity of the old-growth forest ecosystem.

Ecologists are also beginning to develop composite indicators of ecological integrity. These are designed as summations of various indicators, and are analogous to such economic indices such as the Dow-Jones Index of stock markets, the Consumer Price Index, and the gross domestic product of an entire economy. Composite economic indicators of this sort are relatively simple to design, because all of the input data are measured in a common way (for example, in dollars). In ecology, however, there is no common currency among the many indicators of ecological integrity. Consequently it is difficult to develop composite indicators that ecologists will agree upon.

Still, some research groups have developed composite indicators of ecological integrity that have been used successfully in a number of places and environmental contexts. For instance, the ecologist James Karr and his co-workers have developed composite indicators of the ecological integrity of aquatic ecosystems, which are being used in modified form in many places in North America.

In spite of all of the difficulties, ecologists are making substantial progress in the development of indicators of ecological integrity. This is an important activity, because our society needs objective information about complex changes that are occurring in environmental quality, including degradations of indigenous species and ecosystems. Without such information, actions may not be taken to prevent or repair unacceptable damages that may be occurring.

Increasingly, it is being recognized that human economies can only be sustained over the longer term by ecosystems with integrity. Ecosystems with integrity are capable of supplying continuous flows of such renewable resources as timber, fish, agricultural products, and clean air and water. Ecosystems with integrity are also needed to sustain populations of native species and their natural ecosystems, which must be sustained even while humans are exploiting the resources of the **biosphere**.

[*Bill Freedman*]

FURTHER READING

Freedman, B. *Environmental Ecology,* 2nd ed. San Diego: Academic Press, 1995.

Karr, J. "Defining and assessing ecological integrity: Beyond water quality." *Environmental Toxicology and Chemistry* 12 (1993): 1521-1531.

Woodley, S., J. Kay, and G. Francis, eds. *Ecological Integrity and the Management of Ecosystems.* Boca Raton, FL: St. Lucie Press, 1993.

Ecological consumers

Organisms that feed either directly or indirectly on producers, plants that convert **solar energy** into complex organic molecules. Primary consumers are animals that eat plants directly. They are also called herbivores. Secondary consumers are animals that eat other animals. They are also called carnivores. Consumers that eat both plants and animals are omnivores. **Parasites** are a type of consumer that lives in or on the plant or animal on which it feeds. Detrivores (detritus feeders and decomposers) constitute a specialized class of

consumers that feed on dead plants and animals. *See also* Biotic community

Ecological (environmental) economics

Although ecology and economics share the common root "eco-" (from Greek *Oikos* or household), these disciplines have tended to be at odds with each other in recent years over issues such as the feasibility of continued economic growth and the value of **natural resources** and environmental services.

Economics deals with resource allocation or trade-offs between competing wants and needs. Economists ask, "what shall we produce, for whom, or for what purpose?" Furthermore, they ask, "when and in what manner should we produce these goods and services?" In mainstream, neoclassical economics, these questions are usually limited to human concerns: what will it cost to obtain the things we desire and what benefits will we derive from them?

According to classical economists, the costs of goods and services are determined by the interaction of supply and demand in the marketplace. If the supply of a particular commodity or service is high but the demand is low, the price will be low. If the commodity is scarce but everyone wants it, the price will be high. But high prices also encourage invention of new technology and substitutes that can satisfy the same demands. The cyclic relationship of scarce resources and development of new technology or new materials, in this view, allows for unlimited growth. And continued economic growth is seen as the best, perhaps the only, solution to poverty and **environmental degradation**.

Ecologists, however, view the world differently than economists. From their studies of the interactions between organisms and their **environment**, ecologists see our world as a dynamic, but finite system that can support only a limited number of humans with their demands for goods and services. Many ecological processes and the **nonrenewable natural resources** on which our economy is based have no readily available substitutes. Further, much of the natural world is being degraded or depleted at unsustainable rates. Ecologists criticize the narrow focus of conventional economics and its faith in unceasing growth, market valuation, and endless substitutability. Ecologists warn that unless we change our patterns of production and consumption to ways that protect natural resources and ecological systems, we will soon be in deep trouble.

Ecological Economics

Ecological or environmental economics is a relatively new field that introduces ecological understanding into our economic discourse. It takes a transdisciplinary, holistic, contextual, value-sensitive approach to economic planning and resource allocation. This view recognizes our dependence on the natural world and the irreplaceable life-support services it renders. Rather than express values solely in market prices, ecological economics pays attention to intangible values, nonmarketed resources, and the needs and rights of future generations and other species. Issues of equitable distribution of access to resources and the goods and services they provide need to be solved, in this perspective, by means other than incessant growth.

Where neoclassical economics sees our environment as simply a supply of materials, services, and waste sinks, ecological economics regards human activities as embedded in a global system that places limits on what we can and cannot do. Uncertainty and dynamic change are inherent characteristics of this complex natural system. Damage caused by human activities may trigger sudden and irreversible changes. The precautionary principle suggests that we should leave a margin for error in our use of resources and plan for adaptive management policies.

Natural Capital

Conventional economists see wealth generated by human capital (human knowledge, experience, and enterprise) working with manufactured capital (buildings, machines, and infrastructure) to transform raw materials into useful goods and services. In this view, economic growth and efficiency are best accomplished, by increasing the throughput of raw materials extracted from nature. Until they are transformed by human activities, natural resources are regarded as having little value. In contrast, ecological economists see natural resources as a form of capital equally important with human-made capital. In addition to raw materials such as minerals, fuels, fresh water, food, and fibers, nature provides valuable services on which we depend. Natural systems assimilate our wastes and regulate the Earth's energy balance, global **climate**, material **recycling**, the chemical composition of the **atmosphere** and oceans, and the maintenance of **biodiversity**. Nature also provides aesthetic, spiritual, cultural, scientific and educational opportunities that are rarely given a monetary value but are, nevertheless, of great significance to many of us.

Ecological economists argue that the value of natural capital should be taken into account rather than treated as a set of unimportant externalities. Our goal, in this view, should be to increase our efficiency in natural resource use and to reduce its throughput. Harvest rates for renewable resources (those like organisms that regrow or those like fresh water that are replenished by natural processes) should not exceed regeneration rates. Waste emissions should not exceed the ability of nature to assimilate or recycle those wastes. Nonrenewable resources (such as minerals) may be exploited by humans, but only at rates equal to the creation of renewable substitutes.

Accounting for Natural Capital

Where neoclassical economics seeks to maximize present value of resources, ecological economics calls for recognition of the real value of those resources in calculating economic progress. A market economist, for example, once argued that the most rational management policy for whales was to harvest all the remaining ones immediately and to invest the proceeds in some profitable business. Whales reproduce too slowly, he claimed, and are too dispersed to make much money in the long run by allowing them to remain wild. Ecologists reject this limited view of whales as only economic units of production. They see many other values in these wild, beautiful, sentient creatures. Furthermore whales may play important roles in marine ecology that we don't yet fully understand.

Ecologists are similarly critical of Gross National Product (GNP) as a measure of national progress or well-being. GNP measures only the monetary value of goods and services produced in a national economy. It doesn't attempt to distinguish between economic activities that are beneficial or harmful. People who develop cancer from smoking, for instance, contribute to the GNP by running up large hospital bills. The pain and suffering they experience doesn't appear on the balance sheets. When calculating GNP in conventional economics, a subtraction is made, for capital depreciation in the form of wear and tear on machines, vehicles, and buildings used in production, but no account is made for natural resources used up or **ecosystem**s damaged by that same economic activity.

Robert Repeto of the **World Resources Institute** estimates that **soil** erosion in Indonesia reduces the value of crop production about 40% per year. If natural capital were taken into account, total Indonesian GNP would be reduced by at least 20% annually. Similarly, Costa Rica experienced impressive increases in timber, beef, and banana production between 1970 and 1990. But decreased natural capital during this period represented by soil **erosion**, forest destruction, biodiversity losses, and accelerated water **runoff** add up to at least $4 billion, or about 25%, of annual GNP. Ecological economists call for a new System of National Accounts that recognizes the contribution of natural capital to economic activity.

Valuation of Natural Capital

Ecological economics requires new tools and new approaches to represent nature in GNP. Some categories in which natural capital might fit include:

- use values: the price we pay to use or consume a resource
- option value: preserving options for the future
- existence value: those things we like to know still exist even though we may never use or even see them
- aesthetic value: things we appreciate for their beauty
- cultural value: things important for cultural identity
- scientific and educational value: information or experience-rich aspects of nature.

How can we measure this value of natural resources and ecological services not represented in market systems? Ecological economists often have to resort to "shadow pricing" or other indirect valuation methods for natural resources. For instance, what is the worth of a day of canoeing on a wild river? We might measure opportunity costs such as how much we pay to get to the river or to rent a canoe. The direct out-of-pocket costs might represent only a small portion, however, of what it is really worth to participants. Another approach is contingent valuation in which potential resource users are asked, "how much would you be willing to pay for this experience?" or "what price would you be willing to accept to sell your access or forego this opportunity?" These approaches are controversial because people may report what they think they ought to pay rather than what they would really pay for these activities.

Carrying Capacity and Sustainable Development

Carrying capacity is the maximum number of organisms of a particular species that a given area can sustainably support. Where neoclassical economists believe that technology can overcome any obstacle and that human ingenuity frees us from any constraints on population or economic growth, ecological economists argue that nature places limits on us just as it does on any other species.

One of the ultimate limits we face is energy. Because of the limits of the second law of thermodynamics, whenever work is done, some energy is converted to a lower quality, less useful form and ultimately is emitted as waste heat. This means that we require a constant input of external energy. Many fossil fuel supplies are nearing exhaustion, and continued use of these sources by current technology carries untenable environmental costs. Vast amounts of solar energy reach the Earth, and this **solar energy** already drives the generation of all renewable resources and ecological services. By some calculations, humans now control or directly consume about 40% of all the solar energy reaching the Earth. How much more can we monopolize for our own purposes without seriously jeopardizing the integrity of natural systems for which there is no substitute? And even if we had an infinite supply of clean, renewable energy, how much heat can we get rid of without harming our environment?

Ecological economics urges us to restrain growth of both human populations and the production of goods and services in order to conserve natural resources and to protect remaining natural areas and biodiversity. This does not necessarily mean that the billion people in the world who live in absolute poverty and cannot, on their own, meet the basic needs for food, shelter, clothing, education, and medical care are condemned to remain in that state. Ecological economics calls for more efficient use of resources and more equitable distribution of the benefits among those now living as well as between current generations and future ones.

A mechanism for attaining this goal is sustainable development, that is, a real improvement in the overall welfare of all people on a long-term basis. In the words of the World Commission on Economy and Development, **sustainable development** means "meeting the needs of the present without compromising the ability of future generations to meet their own needs." This requires increased reliance on renewable resources in harmony with ecological systems in ways that do not deplete or degrade natural capital. It doesn't necessarily mean that all growth must cease. There are many human attributes such as knowledge, kindness, compassion, cooperation, and creativity that can expand infinitely without damaging our environment. While eco-

logical economics offers a sensible framework for approaches to resource use that can be in harmony with ecological systems over the long term, it remains to be seen whether we will be wise enough to adopt this framework before it is too late.

[*William P. Cunningham*]

FURTHER READING

Daly, H.E., and K.N. Townsend, eds. *Valuing the Earth: Economics, Ecology. Ethics.* Cambridge, MA: The MIT Press, 1993.

Krishnan, R., J.M. Harris, and N.R. Goodwin, eds. *A Survey of Ecological Economics.* Washington, D.C.: Island Press, 1995.

Jansson, A.M., et al., eds. *Investing in Natural Capital: the Ecological Economics Approach to Sustainability.* Washington, D.C.: Island Press, 1994.

Prugh, T. *Natural Capital and Human Economic Survival.* Solomons, MD: International Society for Ecological Economics, 1995.

Turner, R.K., D. Pearce, and I. Bateman. *Environmental Economics: an Elementary Introduction.* Baltimore: The Johns Hopkins University Press, 1993.

Ecological productivity

One of the most important properties of an **ecosystem** is its productivity, which is a measure of the rate of incorporation of energy by plants per unit area per unit time. In terrestrial ecosystems, ecologists usually estimate plant production as the total annual growth—the increase in plant **biomass** over a year. Since productivity reflects plant growth, it is often used loosely as a measure of the organic fertility of a given area.

The flow of energy through an ecosystem starts with the fixation of sunlight by green plants during **photosynthesis**. Photosynthesis supplies both the energy (in the form of **chemical bond**s) and the organic molecules (glucose) that plants use to make other products in a process known as biosynthesis. During biosynthesis, glucose molecules are rearranged and joined together to become complex carbohydrates (such as cellulose and starch) and lipids (such as fats and plant oils). These products are also combined with **nitrogen**, **phosphorus**, sulfur, and magnesium to produce the proteins, **nucleic acids**, and pigments required by the plant. The many products of biosynthesis are transported to the leaves, flowers, and roots, where they are stored to be used later.

Ecologists measure the results of photosynthesis as increases in plant biomass over a given time. To do this more accurately, ecologists distinguish two measures of assimilated light energy: gross primary production (GPP), which is the total light energy fixed during photosynthesis, and net primary production (NPP), which is the chemical energy that accumulates in the plant over time.

Some of this chemical energy is lost during plant **respiration** (R) when it is used for maintenance, reproduction, and biosynthesis. The proportion of GPP that is left after respiration is counted as net production (NPP). In an ecosystem, it is the energy stored in plants from net production that is passed up the **food chain/web** when the plants are eaten. This energy is available to consumers either directly as plant tissue or indirectly through animal tissue.

One measure of ecological productivity in an ecosystem is the production efficiency. This is the rate of accumulation of biomass by plants, and it is calculated as the ratio of net primary production to gross primary production. Production efficiency varies among plant types and among ecosystems. Grassland ecosystems which are dominated by non-woody plants are the most efficient at 60-85 percent, since grasses and annuals do not maintain a high supporting biomass. On the other end of the efficiency scale are forest ecosystems; they are dominated by trees, and large old trees spend most of their gross production in maintenance. For example, eastern **deciduous forest**s have a production efficiency of about 42 percent.

Ecological productivity in terrestrial ecosystems is influenced by physical factors such as temperature and rainfall. Productivity is also affected by air and water currents, **nutrient** availability, land forms, light intensity, altitude, and depth. The most productive ecosystems are **tropical rain forest**s, **coral reef**s, salt marshes and estuaries; the least productive are **desert**s, **tundra**, and the open sea. *See also* Ecological consumers; Ecology; Habitat; Restoration ecology

[*Neil Cumberlidge*]

Ecological risk assessment

Ecological risk assessment is a procedure for evaluating the likelihood that adverse ecological effects are occurring, or may occur, in **ecosystem**s as a result of one or more human activities. These activities may include the alteration and destruction of **wetlands** and other **habitat**s, the introduction of **herbicide**s, **pesticide**s, and other toxic materials into the **environment**, oil spills, or the cleanup of contaminated **hazardous waste** sites. Ecological risk assessments consider many aspects of an ecosystem, both the biotic plants and animals and the abiotic water, **soil**s, and other elements. Ecosystems can be as small as a pond or stretch of a river or as large as thousands of square miles or lengthy coastlines in which communities exist.

Although closely related to human health risk assessment, ecological risk assessment is not only a newer discipline but also uses different procedures, terminology, and concepts. Both human health and ecological risk assessment provide frameworks for collecting information to define a risk and to help make risk management or regulatory decisions. But human health risk assessment follows four basic steps that were defined in a 1983 by the National Research Council: hazard assessment, dose response assessment, exposure assessment, and risk characterization. In contrast, ecological risk assessment relies on a *Framework for Ecological Risk Assessment* published by **Environmental Protection Agency** in 1992 as part of a long-term plan to develop ecological risk assessment guidelines. The Framework defines three steps: problem formulation, analysis, and risk characterization.

The problems that human health risk assessments seek to address are clearly defined: **cancer**, birth defects, mortality, and the like. But the problems that ecological risk assessments tries to understand and deal with are less straightforward. For instance, a major challenge ecological risk assessors face is distinguishing natural changes in an ecosystem from changes caused by human activities and defining what changes are unacceptable. As a result, the initial problem formulation step of an ecological risk assessment requires extensive discussions between risk assessors and risk managers to define "ecological significance," a key concept in ecological risk assessment. Because it is not immediately clear whether an ecological change is positive or negative—unlike cancer or birth defects, which are known to be adverse—judgments must be made early in the assessment about whether a change is significant and whether it will alter a socially valued ecological condition. For example, Lake Erie was declared "dead" in the 1960s as a result of **phosphorous** loadings from cities and farms. But, in fact, there were more fish in the lake after it was "dead" than before; however, these fish were carp, suckers, catfish, not the walleyed pike, yellow perch, and other fish that had made Lake Erie one of the highest valued freshwater sport fishing lakes in the United States. More recently, with **pollution** inputs greatly reduced, the lake has recovered much of its former productivity. Choosing one ecological condition over the other is a social value of the kind fundamental to ecological risk assessment problem formulation. Once judgments have been made about what values to protect, analysis can proceed to examine the "stressors" that ecosystems are exposed to and a characterization can be made of the "ecological effects" likely from such stressors.

Since 1989, EPA has held workshops on "ecological significance" and other technical issues pertaining to ecological risk assessment and has published the results of its workshops in a series of reports and case studies. In 1996, EPA proposed its first ecological risk assessment guidelines, with final guidelines to be published in late 1997. To help risk managers better understand the crucial issue of defining what to protect during the problem formulation stage of and ecological risk assessment, EPA issued a "discussion draft" in March 1997 describing an initial list of "priorities for ecological protection." Overall, the direction of ecological protection priorities has been away from earlier concerns with narrow goals (e.g., use of commercially valuable natural resources) toward broader interest in protecting natural areas such as National Parks and Scenic Rivers for both present and future generations to enjoy.

[*David Clarke*]

FURTHER READING

Framework for Ecological Risk Assessment. Washington, D.C.: United States Environmental Protection Agency, Risk Assessment Forum, 1992.

Ecological Risk Assessment Issues Papers. Washington, D.C.: United States Environmental Protection Agency, Risk Assessment Forum, 1994.

Lackey, R. T. "The Future of Ecological Risk Assessment." *Human and Ecological Risk Assessment, An International Journal* 1, no. 4 (October 1995): 339-343.

Priorities for Ecological Protection: An Initial List and Discussion Document for EPA. Washington, D.C. United States Environmental Protection Agency, 1997.

Ecological Society of America (Washington, D.C.)

The Ecological Society of America (ESA), representing 7,500 ecological researchers in the United States, Canada, Mexico, and 62 other countries, was founded in 1915 as a non-profit, scientific organization and today is the nation's leading professional society of ecologists. Members include ecologists from academia, government agencies, industry, and non-profit organizations. In pursuing its goal of promoting "the responsible application of ecological principles to the solution of environmental problems," the Society publishes reports, membership research, and three scientific journals a year, and it provides expert testimony to Congress. In addition, ESA holds a conference every summer attended by more than 2,000 scientists and students at which members present the latest ecological research. The Society's three journals are: *Ecology* (eight issues per year), *Ecological Monographs* (four issues per year), and *Ecological Applications* (four issues per year). ESA also publishes a bimonthly member newsletter.

A recent milestone in the Society's development was its 1991 proposal for a Sustainable Biosphere Initiative (SBI), which was published in a 1991 issue of *Ecology* as a "call-to-arms for ecologists." Based on research priorities identified in the proposal the proposal, ESA chartered the SBI Project Office in the same year to focus on global change, **biodiversity**, and sustainable **ecosystem**s. The SBI marked a commitment by the Society to more actively convey its members' findings to the public and to policy makers, and, as such, included research, education, and environmental decision-making components. The three-pronged SBI proposal grew out of a "period of introspection" during which ESA led its members to examine "the whole realm of ecological activities" in the face of decreasing funds for research, an urgent need to set priorities, and "the need to ameliorate the rapidly deteriorating state of the environment and to enhance its capacity to sustain the needs of the world's population."

Since the SBI Project Office was chartered, it has focused on linking the ecological scientific community to other scientists and decision makers through a multi-disciplinary 12-member Steering Committee and five-member staff. For instance, in 1995, the SBI began a series of semi-annual meetings with federal government officials to discuss "overlapping areas of interest and possible collaborative opportunities." In addition, SBI has hosted discussions of key ecological topics, such as a symposium on "Ecology and the Social Sciences" that SBI and the Army Environmental Policy Institute organized at ESA's 1995 Annual Meeting and another SBI-hosted discussion on "Global Climate Change Effects on Habitat Sensitivity" at the same meeting.

In 1993 ESA chartered a Special Committee on the Scientific Basis of Ecosystem Management to establish the scientific grounds for discussing the increasingly prominent ecosystem approach to addressing land and natural resource management problems. The committee published its findings in the August 1996 issue of *Ecological Applications*. Articles discussed the emerging consensus on essential elements of **ecosystem management**, including its "holistic" nature—incorporating the biological and physical elements of an ecosystem and their interrelationships—and the concept of "sustainability" as the "essential element and precondition" of ecosystem management.

ESA's headquarters in Washington, D.C., consistent with the SBI's goal of broader public education, includes a Public Affairs Office. Its Publications Office is in Ithaca, New York. Contact: ESA, 2010 Massachusetts Ave., N.W., Ste. 400, Washington, D.C. 20035. Website: http://www.sdsc.edu/~ESA/EAS.html.

[*David Clarke*]

FURTHER READING

"Forum: Perspectives on Ecosystem Management". *Ecological Applications*, vol. 6, no. 3, (August 1996): 694-747.

"The Sustainable Biosphere Initiative: An Ecological Research Agenda". *Ecology*, vol. 72, no. 2, (1991): 371-412,

Ecological succession
See **Succession**

Ecology

The word ecology was coined in 1870 by the German zoologist **Ernst Haeckel** from the Greek words *oikos* (house) and *logos* (logic or knowledge) to describe the scientific study of the relationships among organisms and their **environment**. Biologists began referring to themselves as ecologists at the end of the nineteenth century and shortly thereafter the first ecological societies and journals appeared. Since that time ecology has become a major branch of biological science. The contextual, historical understanding of organisms as well as the systems basis of ecology set it apart from the reductionist, experimental approach prevalent in many other areas of science.

This broad ecological view is gaining significance today as modern resource-intensive lifestyles consume much of **nature**'s supplies. Although intuitive ecology has always been a part of some cultures, current environmental crises make a systematic, scientific understanding of ecological principles especially important.

For many ecologists the basic structural units of ecological organization are **species** and populations. A biological species consists of all the organisms potentially able to interbreed under natural conditions and to produce fertile offspring. A population consists of all the members of a single species occupying a common geographical area at the same time. An ecological community is composed of a number of populations that live and interact in a specific region.

This population-community view of ecology is grounded in natural history—the study of where and how organisms live—and the Darwinian theory of natural selection and **evolution**. Proponents of this approach generally view ecological systems primarily as networks of interacting organisms. Abiotic forces such as weather, **soils**, and **topography** are often regarded as external factors that influence but are apart from the central living core of the system.

In the past three decades the emphasis on species, populations, and communities in ecology has been replaced by a more quantitative, thermodynamic analysis of the processes through which energy flows and the cycling of **nutrient**s and toxins are carried out in **ecosystem**s. This process-functional approach is concerned more with the ecosystem as a whole than the particular species or populations that make it up. In this perspective, both the living organisms and the abiotic physical components of the environment are equal members of the system.

The feeding relationships among different species in a community are a key to understanding ecosystem function. Who eats whom, where, how, and when determine how energy and materials move through the system. They also influence natural selection, evolution, and species **adaptation** to a particular set of environmental conditions. Ecosystems are open systems, insofar as energy and materials flow through them. Nutrients, however, are often recycled extremely efficiently so that the annual losses to **sediment**s or through surface water **runoff** are relatively small in many mature ecosystems. In undisturbed **tropical rain forest**s, for instance, nearly 100 percent of leaves and detritus are decomposed and recycled within a few days after they fall to the forest floor.

Because of thermodynamic losses every time energy is exchanged between organisms or converted from one form to another, an external energy source is an indispensable component of every ecological system. Green plants capture **solar energy** through **photosynthesis** and convert it into energy-rich organic compounds that are the basis for all other life in the community. This energy capture is referred to as "primary productivity." These green plants form the first trophic (or feeding) level of most communities.

Herbivores (animals that eat plants) make up the next trophic level, while carnivores (animals that eat other animals) add to the complexity and diversity of the community. Detritivores (such as beetles and earthworms) and decomposers (generally bacteria and fungi) convert dead organisms or waste products to inorganic chemicals. The nutrient **recycling** they perform is essential to the continuation of life. Together, all these interacting organisms form a **food chain/web** through which energy flows and nutrients and toxins are recycled. Due to intrinsic inefficiencies in transferring material and energy between organisms, the energy content in successive trophic levels is usually represented as a pyramid in which primary producers form the base and the top consumers occupy the apex.

This introduces the problem of persistent contaminants in the food chain. Because they tend not to be broken and metabolized in each step in the food chain in the way that other compounds are, persistent contaminants such as **pesticide**s and heavy metals tend to accumulate in top carnivores, often reaching toxic levels many times higher than original environmental concentrations. This biomagnification is an important issue in **pollution control** policies. In many lakes and rivers, for instance, game fish have accumulated dangerously high levels of **mercury** and **chlorinated hydrocarbons** that present a health threat to humans and other fish-eating species.

Diversity, in ecological terms, is a measure of the number of different species in a community, while abundance is the total number of individuals. **Tropical rain forest**s, although they occupy only about five percent of the earth's land area, are thought to contain somewhere around half of all terrestrial plant and animals species, while **coral reef**s and estuaries are generally the most productive and diverse aquatic communities. Community complexity refers to the number of species at each trophic level as well as the total number of trophic levels and ecological **niche**s in a community.

Structure describes the patterns of organization, both spatial and functional, in a community. In a tropical rain forest, for instance, distinctly different groups of organisms live on the surface, at mid-levels in the trees, and in the canopy, giving the forest vertical structure. A patchy mosaic of tree species, each of which may have a unique community of associated animals and smaller plants living in its branches, gives the forest horizontal structure as well.

For every physical factor in the environment there are both maximum and minimum tolerable limits beyond which a given species cannot survive. The factor closest to the tolerance limit for a particular species at a particular time is the critical factor that will determine the abundance and distribution of that species in that ecosystem. Natural selection is the process by which environmental pressures—including biotic factors such as predation, **competition**, and disease, as well as physical factors such as temperature, moisture, soil type, and space—affect survival and reproduction of organisms. Over a very long time, given a large enough number of organisms, natural selection works on the randomly occurring variation in a population to allow evolution of species and adaptation of the population to a particular set of environmental conditions.

Habitat describes the place or set of environmental conditions in which an organism lives; niche describes the role an organism plays. A yard and garden, for instance, may provide habitat for a family of cottontail rabbits. Their niche is being primary consumers (eating vegetables and herbs).

Organisms interact within communities in many ways. **Symbiosis** is the intimate living together of two species; **commensalism** describes a relationship in which one species benefits while the other is neither helped nor harmed. **Lichens**, the thin crusty plants often seen on exposed rocks, are an obligate symbiotic association of a **fungus** and an alga. Neither can survive without the other. Some orchids and bromeliads (air plants), on the other hand, live commensally on the branches of tropical trees. The orchid benefits by having a place to live but the tree is neither helped nor hurt by the presence of the orchid.

Predation—feeding on another organism—can involve **pathogen**s, **parasites**, and herbivores as well as carnivorous predators. Competition is another kind of antagonistic relationship in which organisms vie for space, food, or other resources. Predation, competition, and natural selection often lead to niche specialization and resource partitioning that reduce competition between species. The principle of competitive exclusion states that no two species will remain in direct competition for very long in the same habitat because natural selection and adaptation will cause organisms to specialize in when, where, or how they live to minimize conflict over resources. This can contribute to the evolution of a given species into new forms over time.

It is also possible, on the other hand, for species to co-evolve, meaning that each changes gradually in response to the other to form an intimate and often highly dependent relationship either as predator and prey or for mutual aid. Because individuals of a particular species may be widely dispersed in tropical forests, many plants have become dependent on insects, birds, or mammals to carry pollen from one flower to another. Some amazing examples of **coevolution** and mutual dependence have resulted.

Ecological **succession**, the process of ecosystem development, describes the changes through which whole communities progress as different species colonize an area and change its environment. A typical successional series starts with pioneer species such as grasses or fireweed that colonize bare ground after a disturbance. Organic material from these pioneers helps build soil and hold moisture, allowing shrubs and then tree seedlings to become established. Gradual changes in shade, temperature, nutrient availability, wind protection, and living space favor different animal communities as one type of plant replaces its predecessors. Primary succession starts with a previously unoccupied site. Secondary succession occurs on a site that has been disturbed by external forces such as fires, storms, or humans. In many cases, succession proceeds until a mature "climax" community is established. Introduction of new species by natural processes, such as opening of a land bridge, or by human intervention can upset the natural relationships in a community and cause catastrophic changes for indigenous species.

Biomes consist of broad regional groups of related communities. Their distribution is determined primarily by climate, topography, and soils. Often similar niches are occupied by different but similar species (called ecological equivalents) in geographically separated biomes. Some of the major biomes of the world are **desert**s, **grasslands**, **wetlands**, forests of various types, and **tundra**.

The relationship between diversity and **stability** in ecosystems is a controversial topic in ecology. F. E. Clements, an early biogeographer, championed the concept of climax communities: stable, predictable associations towards which ecological systems tend to progress if allowed to follow natural tendencies. Deciduous, broad-leaved forests are climax communities in moist, temperate regions of the eastern United States according to Clements, while grasslands are characteristic of the dryer western plains. In this view, **homeostasis** (a dynamic steady-state equilibrium), complexity, and stability are endpoints in ecological succession. Ecological processes, if allowed to operate without external interference, tend to create a natural balance between organisms and their environment.

H. A. Gleason, another pioneer biogeographer and contemporary of Clements, argued that ecological systems are much more dynamic and variable than the climax theory proposes. Gleason saw communities as temporary or even accidental combinations of continually changing biota rather than predictable associations. Ecosystems may or may not be stable, balanced, and efficient; change, in this view, is thought to be more characteristic than constancy. Diversity may or may not be associated with stability. Some communities such as salt marshes that have only a few plant species may be highly resilient and stable while species-rich communities such as coral reefs may be highly sensitive to disturbance.

Although many ecologists now tend to agree with the process-functional view of Gleason rather than the population-community view of Clements, some retain a belief in the balance of nature and the tendency for undisturbed ecosystems to reach an ideal state if left undisturbed. The efficacy and ethics of human intervention in natural systems may be interpreted very differently in these divergent understandings of ecology. Those who see stability and constancy in nature often call for policies that attempt to maintain historic conditions and associations. Those who see greater variability and individuality in communities may favor more activist management and be willing to accept change as inevitable.

In spite of some uncertainty, however, about how to explain ecological processes and the communities they create, we have learned a great deal about the world around us through scientific ecological studies in the past century. This important field of study remains a crucial component in our ability to manage resources sustainably and to avoid or repair environmental damage caused by human actions.

[*William P. Cunningham*]

FURTHER READING

Ricklefs, R. E. *Ecology*. 3rd ed. New York: W. H. Freeman, 1990.

Smith, R. L. *Ecology and Field Biology*. 4th ed. New York: Harper and Row, 1990.

Ecology, deep
See **Deep ecology**

Ecology, human
See **Human ecology**

Ecology, restoration
See **Restoration ecology**

Ecology, social
See **Social ecology**

Ecomark

The Japanese environmental label known as "Ecomark" is a relatively new addition to a worldwide effort to designate products that are environmentally friendly. The Ecomark program was launched in February 1989. The symbol is two arms embracing the world, symbolizing the protection of the earth. The arms create the letter "e" with the earth in the center. Indicating English as the international language, the Japanese use "e" to stand for **environment**, earth, and **ecology**.

The Japanese program is entirely government funded, although a small fee is charged to applicant industries. The annual fee is based on the retail price of a product, not annual product sales as is the case for other national green labeling programs. Products ranging in price from $0-$7 are charged an annual fee of $278.00; from $7 - 70 are charged an annual fee of $417; from $70 - 700 are charged an annual fee of $556; and products priced over $700 are charged an annual fee of $700. Obviously, those products that are low in price and high in volume sold are most likely to apply for the Ecomark label.

The Ecomark program seeks to sanction products with the following four qualities: 1) minimal environmental impact from use; 2) significant potential for improvement of the environment by using the product; 3) minimal environmental impact from disposal after use; and 4) other significant contributions to improve the environment.

In addition, labeled products must comply with the following guidelines: 1) appropriate environmental **pollution control** measures are provided at the stage of production; 2) ease of treatment for disposal of product; 3) energy or resources are conserved with use of product; 4) compliance with laws, standards, and regulations pertaining to quality and safety; 5) price is not extraordinarily higher than comparable products.

The Environment Association, supervised by the Japanese Environment Agency, is in charge of the Ecomark program. All technical, research, and administrative support is provided by the government. The labeling program is guided by two committees.

The Ecomark Promotion Committee acts primarily in a supervisory capacity, approving the guidelines for the program's operation and advising on operations, including evaluation of the program categories and criteria. The promotion committee consists of nine members representing industry, marketing groups, local governments, environmental agencies, and the National Institute for Environmental Studies.

In addition to the Promotion Committee there is a committee for approval of products. This committee consists of five members with representation from the science community, the consumer protection community, and, as in the Promotion Committee, a representative each from the Environment Agency and the National Institute for Environmental Studies. The Japanese program is completely voluntary for manufacturers. Once a product is approved by the Approval Committee, a two-year renewable licensing contract for the use of the Ecomark is signed with the Japan Environment Association.

The Ecomark program is very goal-oriented and places great emphasis on overall environmental impact. The attention to production impacts, as well as use and disposal impacts, makes the program unique within the family of green labeling programs worldwide. Its primary goals are to encourage innovation by industry and elevate the environmental awareness and consumer behavior of the Japanese people in order to enhance environmental quality.

Although the Ecomark program has not been in place long enough to assess its impact, Japan's Environment Agency claims that responses from consumer and environmental organizations have been positive, while industry has been less than enthusiastic. Some scientists have voiced concern over the superficiality of the analysis procedure used to determine Ecomark products. However, despite criticisms, the Japanese Ecomark program is a strong national effort to encourage environmentally sound decisions and protect the environment for future generations in that country. *See also* Environmental policy; Green packaging; Green products; Precycling; Recycling; Reuse; Waste reduction

[*Cynthia Fridgen*]

FURTHER READING

Salzman, J. *Environmental Labeling in OECD Countries.* Paris, France: OECD Technology and Environmental Program, 1991.

EcoNet (San Francisco, California)

EcoNet is a computer network that focuses on environmental topics and, through the Institute for Global Communications, has links to the international community. Anyone can access the network by using a computer modem to dial the central computer. Users pay a one-time connect fee and then pay monthly and hourly fees based on the amount of time used. Several thousand organizations and individuals have accounts on the network. EcoNet's electronic conferences contain press releases, reports, and electronic discussions on hundreds of topics, ranging from clean air to **pesticide**s. Subscribers can also send electronic mail to other users throughout the country and around the world. Contact: EcoNet, 18 De Boom Street, San Francisco, CA 94107. Internet: http://www.igc.org/igc/econet/.

Economic growth and the environment

The issue of economic growth and the environment essentially concerns the kinds of pressures that economic growth, at the national and international level, places on the **environment** over time. The relationship between **ecology** and the economy has become increasingly significant as humans gradually understand the impact that economic decisions have on the sustainability and quality of the planet.

Economic growth is commonly defined as increases in total output from new resources or better use of existing resources; it is measured by increased real incomes per capita. All economic growth involves transforming the natural world, and it can effect environmental quality in one of three ways. Environmental quality can increase with growth. Increased incomes, for example, provide the resources for public services such as sanitation and rural electricity. With these services widely available, individuals need to worry less about day-to-day survival and can devote more resources to **conservation**. Second, environmental quality can initially worsen but then improve as the growth rate rises. In the cases of **air pollution**, **water pollution**, and **deforestation** and encroachment there is little incentive for any individual to invest in maintaining the quality of the environment. These problems can only improve when countries deliberately introduce long-range policies to ensure that additional resources are devoted to dealing with them. Third, environmental quality can decrease when the rate of growth increases. In the cases of **emission**s generated by the disposal of **municipal solid waste**, for example, abatement is relatively expensive and the costs associated with the emissions and wastes are not perceived as high because they are often borne by someone else.

In 1992, the **World Bank** estimated that, under present productivity trends and given projected population increases, the output of developing countries would be about five times higher by the year 2030 than it is today. The output of industrial countries would rise more slowly, but it would still triple over the same period. If environmental **pollution** were to rise at the same pace, severe environmental hardships would occur. Tens of millions of people would become sick or die from environmental causes, and the planet would be significantly and irreparably harmed.

Yet economic growth and sound environmental management are not incompatible. In fact, many now believe that they require each other. Economic growth will be undermined without adequate environmental safeguards, and environmental protection will fail without economic growth.

The earth's **natural resources** place limits on economic growth. These limits vary with the extent of resource substitution, technical progress, and structural changes. For example, in the late 1960s many feared that the world's supply of useful metals would run out. Yet, today, there is a glut of useful metals and prices have fallen dramatically. The demand for other natural resources such as water, however, often exceeds supply. In **arid** regions such as the Middle East and in non-arid regions such as northern China, **aquifer**s have been depleted and rivers so extensively drained that not only **irrigation** and agriculture are threatened but the local **ecosystem**s.

Some resources such as water, forests, and clean air are under attack, while others such as metals, minerals, and energy are not threatened. This is because the scarcity of metals and similar resources is reflected in market prices. Here, the forces of resource substitution, technical progress, and structural change have a strong influence. But resources such as water are characterized by open access, and there are

therefore no incentives to conserve. Many believe that effective policies designed to sustain the environment are most necessary because society must be made to take account of the value of **natural resources** and governments must create incentives to protect the environment. Economic and political institutions have failed to provide these necessary incentives for four separate yet interrelated reasons: 1) short time horizons; 2) failures in property rights; 3) concentration of economic and political power; and 4) immeasurability and institutional uncertainty.

Although economists and environmentalists disagree on the definition of sustainability, the essence of the idea is that current decisions should not impair the prospects for maintaining or improving future living standards. The economic systems of the world should be managed so that societies live off the dividends of the natural resources, always maintaining and improving the asset base.

Promoting growth, alleviating poverty, and protecting the environment may be mutually supportive objectives in the long run, but they are not always compatible in the short run. Poverty is a major cause of **environmental degradation**, and economic growth is thus necessary to improve the environment. Yet, ill-managed economic growth can also destroy the environment and further jeopardize the lives of the poor. In many poor but still forested countries, timber is a good short-run source of foreign exchange. When demand for Indonesia's traditional commodity export—**petroleum**—fell and its foreign exchange income slowed, Indonesia began depleting its hardwood forests at non-sustainable rates in order to earn export income.

In developed countries, it is competition that can shorten time horizons. Competitive forces in agricultural markets, for example, induce farmers to take short-term perspectives for financial survival. Farmers must maintain cash flow to satisfy bankers and make a sufficient return on their land investment. They therefore adopt high-yield crops, **monoculture** farming, increased **fertilizer** and **pesticide** use, salinizing irrigation methods, and more intensive tillage practices which cause **erosion**.

"The **Tragedy of the Commons**" is the classic example of property rights failure. When access to a grazing area, or commons is unlimited, each herdsman knows that grass not eaten today will not be there tomorrow. As a rational economic being, each herdsman seeks to maximize his gain and adds more animals to his herd. No herdsman has an incentive to prevent his livestock from grazing the area. Degradation follows and the loss of a common resource. In a society without clearly defined property rights, those who pursue their own interests ruin the public good.

In Indonesia, political upheaval can void property rights overnight, and so any individual with a concession to harvest trees is motivated to harvest as many and as quickly as possible. The government-granted timber-cutting concession may belong to someone else tomorrow. The same is true of some developed countries. For example, in Louisiana mineral rights revert to the state when **wetlands** become open water and there has been no mineral development on the property. Thus, the cheapest methods of avoiding loss of mineral revenues has been to hurry the development of oil and gas in areas which might revert to open water, thereby, hastening erosion and **saltwater intrusion**, or putting up levies around the property to maintain it as private property, thus interfering with normal estuarine processes.

Global or transnational problems such as **ozone layer depletion** or **acid rain** produce a similar problem. Countries have little incentive to reduce damage to the global environment unilaterally when doing so will not reduce the damaging behavior of others or when reduced fossil fuel use would leave that country at a competitive disadvantage. International agreements are thus needed to impose order on the world's nations that would be analogous to property rights.

Concentration of wealth within the industrialized countries allows for the exploitation and destruction of ecosystems in **less developed countries (LDC)** through, for example, timber harvests and mineral extraction. The concentration of wealth inside a less developed country skews public policy toward benefiting the wealthy and politically powerful, often at the expense of the ecosystem on which the poor depend. Local sustainability is dependent upon the goals of those who have power—goals which may or may not be in line with a healthy, sustainable ecosystem. Furthermore, when an exploiting party has substitute ecosystems available, it can exploit one and then move to the next. Japanese lumber firms harvest one country and then move on to another. Here the benefits of sustainability are low and exploiters have shorter time horizons than local interests. This is also an example of how the high discount rates in developed countries are imposed on the management of developing countries' assets.

Environmental policy-making is always more complicated than merely measuring the effects that a proposed policy on the environment. But because of scientific uncertainty about biophysical and geological relations and a general inability to measure a policy's effect on the environment, economic rather than ecological effects are more often relied upon to make policy. Policy-makers and institutions are often unable to grasp the direct and indirect effects of policies on ecological sustainability, nor do they know how their actions will affect other areas not under their control.

Many contemporary economists and environmentalists argue that the value of the environment should nonetheless be factored into the economic policy decision-making process. The goal is not necessarily to put monetary values on environmental resources; it is rather to determine how much environmental quality is being given up in the name of economic growth, and how much growth is being given up in the name of the environment. A danger always exists that too much income growth may be given up in the future because of a failure to clarify and minimize tradeoffs and to take advantage of policies that are good for both economic growth and the environment. *See also* Energy policy; Environmental economics; Environmental policy; Environmentally responsible investing; Exponential growth; Sustainable agriculture; Sustainable biosphere; Sustainable development

[*Kevin Wolf*]

FURTHER READING

Farber, S. "Local and Global Incentives for Sustainability: Failures in Economic Systems." In *Ecological Economics: The Science and Management of Sustainability*, edited by R. Constanza. New York: Columbia University Press, 1991.

World Bank. *World Development Report 1992: Development and the Environment*. New York: Oxford University Press, 1992.

Ecopsychology
See **Roszak, Theodore**

Eco-School, Project (Pacific Palisades, California

Project Eco-School (PES) is a nonprofit resource center designed to promote **environmental education** by serving as a link between schools and a vast library of environmental information. PES was founded in 1989 by Jayni Chase and her husband, comic-actor Chevy Chase, who were determined to foster greater environmental awareness by educating children.

Since its inception, PES has worked most closely with schools and children in California. In Inglewood, for instance, PES provided Worthington Elementary School with an environmental library. The organization has also been instrumental in developing consumer responsibility among students. It promoted the Zero Waste Lunch, in which students were encouraged to use reusable containers and avoid using the more wasteful, disposable, and prepackaged single-serving containers. The PES flyer "Guidelines for Packing a Zero Waste Lunch" provided tips on **recycling** and stressed the importance of our actions and choices on the environment.

Among PES's notable publications is *Blueprint for a Green School*, a reference book geared toward educating young people about a host of environmental issues, including recycling, **waste reduction**, and consumer alternatives. In addition, *Blueprint for a Green School* provides instruction on developing letter-writing campaigns and organizing a range of schoolchildren's activities such as field trips, community services, and fund raising.

The newsletter *Grapevine* is an important element in PES's endeavor to promote environmental awareness. A typical issue provides coverage of events and environmental activism in various schools throughout the country and reports on **environmental policy** affecting the nation and the world. The newsletter also functions as a valuable networking tool by providing readers with coverage of recent developments in **environmental law**s and publications. An "Eco-Stars" segment details events relating to recently created organizations, especially those directed to students. Contact: Project Eco-School, 881 Alma Real Drive, Suite 301, Pacific Palisades, CA 90272.

[*Les Stone*]

Ecosophy

A philosophical approach to the **environment** which emphasizes the importance of action and individual beliefs. Often referred to as "ecological wisdom," it is associated with other **environmental ethics**, including **deep ecology** and **bioregionalism**.

Ecosophy originated with the Norwegian philosopher **Arne Naess**. Naess described a structured form of inquiry he called *ecophilosophy*, which examines **nature** and our relationship to it. He defined it as a discipline, like philosophy itself, which is based on analytical thinking, reasoned argument, and carefully examined assumptions. Naess distinguished ecosophy from ecophilosophy; it is not a discipline in the same sense but what he called a "personal philosophy," which guides our conduct toward the environment. He defined ecosophy as a set of beliefs about nature and other people which varies from one individual to another. Everyone, in other words, has their own ecosophy, and though our personal philosophies may share important elements, they are based on norms and assumptions that are particular to each of us.

Naess proposed his own ecophilosophy as a model for individual ecosophies, emphasizing the **intrinsic value** of nature and the importance of cultural and natural diversity. Other discussions of ecosophy concentrate on similar issues. Many environmental philosophers argue that all life has a value that is independent of human perspectives and human uses, and that it is not to be tampered with except for the sake of survival. Human **population growth** threatens the integrity of other life systems; they argue that our numbers must be reduced substantially and that radical changes in human values and activities are required to integrate humans more harmoniously into the total system. *See also* Zero population growth

[*Gerald L. Young and Douglas Smith*]

Further Reading

Davis, D. E. *Ecophilosophy: A Field Guide to the Literature.* San Pedro, CA: R. & E. Miles, 1989.

Devall, B., and G. Sessions. *Deep Ecology: Living as if Nature Mattered.* Salt Lake City: Peregrine Smith, 1985.

Hedgpeth, J. W. "Man and Nature: Controversy and Philosophy." *The Quarterly Review of Biology* 61 (March 1986): 45-67.

Naess, A. *Ecology, Community and Lifestyle: Outline of an Ecosophy.* Translated and revised by D. Rothenberg. Cambridge: Cambridge University Press, 1989.

Naess, A. "From Ecology to Ecosophy, from Science to Wisdom." *World Futures* 27 (1989): 185-190.

Ecosystem

The term ecosystem was coined in 1935 by the Oxford ecologist Arthur Tansley to encompass the interactions among biotic and abiotic components of the **environment** at a given site. It was defined in its presently accepted form by Eugene Odum as follows: "Any unit that includes all of the organisms (i.e, the community) in a given area interacting with the physical environment so that a flow of energy leads to clearly defined trophic structure, biotic diversity, and material cycles (i.e., exchange of materials between living and non-living parts) within the system." Tansley's concept had been expressed earlier in 1913 by the Oxford geographer A.J. Herbertson, who suggested the term "macroorganism" for such a combined biotic and abiotic entity. He was, however, too far in advance of his time and the idea was not taken up by ecologists. On the other hand Tansley's concept—elaborated in terms of the transfer of energy and matter across ecosystem boundaries—was utilized within the next few years by Evelyn Hutchinson, Raymond Lindeman, and the Odum brothers, Eugene and Howard.

The boundaries of an ecosystem can be somewhat arbitrary, reflecting the interest of a particular ecologist in studying a certain portion of the landscape. However, such a choice may often represent a recognizable landscape unit such as a woodlot, a wetland, a stream or lake, or—in the most logical case—a **watershed** within a sealed geological basin, whose exchanges with the atmosphere and outputs via stream flow can be measured quite precisely. Inputs and outputs imply an open system, which is true of all but the planetary or global ecosystem, open to energy flow but effectively closed in terms of materials except in the case of large-scale asteroid impact.

Ecosystems exhibit a great deal of structure, as may be seen in the vertical partitioning of a forest into tree, shrub, herb, and moss layers, underlain by a series of distinctive **soil** horizons. Horizontal structure is often visible as a mosaic of patches, as in forests with gaps where trees have died and herbs and shrubs now flourish, or in bogs with hummocks and hollows supporting different kinds of plants. Often the horizontal structure is distinctly zoned, for instance around the shallow margin of a lake; and sometimes it is beautifully patterned, as in the vast **peatlands** of North America that reflect a very complicated **hydrology**.

Ecosystems exhibit an interesting functional organization in their processing of energy and matter. Green plants, the primary producers of organic matter, are consumed by herbivores, which in turn are eaten by carnivores that may in turn be the prey of other carnivores. Moreover, all these animals may have **parasites** as another set of consumers. Such sequences of producers and successive consumers constitute a **food chain**, which is always part of a complicated, inter-linked food web along which energy and materials pass. At each step along the food chain some of the energy is egested or passed through the organisms as feces. Much more is used for metabolic processes and—in the case of animals—for seeking food or escaping predators; such energy is released as heat. As a consequence only a small fraction (often of the order of 10 percent) of the energy captured at a given step in the food chain is passed along to the next step.

There are two main types of food chains. One is made up of plant producers and animal consumers of living organisms, which constitute a grazing food chain. The other consists of organisms that break down and metabolize dead organic matter, such as earthworms, **fungi**, and bacteria. These constitute the detritus food chain. Humans rely chiefly

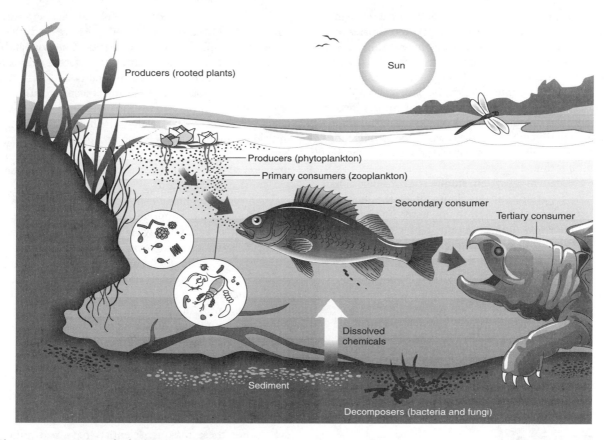

The major components of a freshwater pond ecosystem.

on grazing food chains based on grasslands, whereas in a forest it is usual for more than 90 percent of the energy trapped by **photosynthesis** to pass along the detritus food chain.

Whereas energy flows one way through ecosystems and is dispersed finally to the atmosphere as heat, materials are partially and often largely recycled. For example, **nitrogen** in rain and snow may be taken up from the soil by roots, built into leaf protein that falls with the leaves in autumn, there to be broken down by soil microbes to ammonia and nitrate and taken up once again by roots. A given molecule of nitrogen may go through this **nutrient** cycle again and again before finally leaving the system in stream outflow. Other nutrients, and toxins such as **lead** and **mercury**, follow the same pathway, each with a different **residence time** in the forest ecosystem.

Mature ecosystems exhibit a substantial degree of **stability**, or dynamic equilibrium, as the endpoint of what is often a rather orderly succession of species determined by the nature of the **habitat**. Sometimes this successional process is a result of the differing life spans of the colonizing species, at other times it comes about because the colonizing species alter the habitat in ways that are more favorable to their competitors, as in an acid moss bog that succeeds a circumneutral sedge fen that has in its turn colonized a pond as a floating mat. Equilibrium may sometimes be represented on a large scale by a relatively stable mosaic of small-scale patches in various stages of succession, for instance in fire-

dominated pine forests. On the millennial time scale, of course, ecosystems are not stable, changing very gradually owing to immigration and emigration of species and to evolutionary changes in the species themselves.

The structure, function, and development of ecosystems are controlled by a series of partially independent environmental factors: **climate**, soil parent material, **topography**, the plants and animals available to colonize a given site, and disturbances such as fire and windthrow. Each factor is, of course, divisible into a variety of components, as in the case of temperature and precipitation under the general heading of **climate**.

There are many ways to study ecosystems. Evelyn Hutchinson divided them into two main categories, holistic and meristic. The former treats an ecosystem as a "black box" and examines inputs, storages, and outputs, for example in the construction of a lake's heat budget or a watershed's chemical budget. This is the physicist's or engineer's approach to how ecosystems work. The meristic point of view emphasizes analysis of the different parts of the system and how they fit together in their structure and function, for example the various zones of a wetland or a **soil profile**, or the diverse components of food webs. This is the biologist's approach to how ecosystems work.

Ecosystem studies can also be viewed as a series of elements. The first is, necessarily, a description of the system, its location, boundaries, plant and animal communities, environmental characteristics, etc. Description may be followed by any or all of a series of additional elements, including: 1) a study of how a given ecosystem compares with others locally, regionally, or globally; 2) how it functions in terms of hydrology, productivity, and biogeochemical cycling of nutrients and toxins; 3) how it has changed over time; and 4) how various environmental factors have controlled its structure, function, and development. Such studies involve empirical observations about relationships within and among ecosystems, experiments to test the causality of such relationships, and model-building to assist in forecasting what may happen in the future.

The ultimate in ecosystem studies is a consideration of the structure, function, and development of the global or planetary ecosystem, with a view to understanding and mitigating the deleterious impacts upon it of current human activities. *See also* Biotic community

[*Eville Gorham*]

FURTHER READING

Hagen, J. B. *An Entangled Bank, the Origins of Ecosystem Ecology.* New Brunswick, NJ: Rutgers University Press, 1992.

Herbertson, A. J. "The Higher Units: A Geological Essay." *Scientia* 14 (1913): 199-212.

Tansley, A. G. "The Use and Abuse of Vegetational Concepts and Terms." *Ecology* 16 (1935): 284-307.

Ecosystem health

Ecosystem health is a new concept that ecologists are examining as a tool for use in detecting and monitoring changes in the quality of the **environment**, particularly with regard to ecological conditions.

Ecosystem health (and **ecological integrity**) is an indicator of the well-being and natural condition of **ecosystem**s and their functions. These indicators are influenced by natural changes in environmental conditions, and are related to such factors as climate change and disturbances such as **wildfire**, windstorms, and diseases. Increasingly, however, ecosystems are being affected by environmental stressors associated with human activities that cause **pollution** and disturbance, which result in many changes in environmental conditions. Some species, communities, and ecological processes benefit from those environmental changes, but others suffer great damages.

The notion of ecosystem health is intended to help distinguish between ecosystem-level changes that represent improvements and those that are considered to be degradations. In the sense meant here, ecosystem-level refers to responses occurring in ecological communities, landscapes, or seascapes. Effects on individual organisms or populations do not represent an ecosystem-level response to changes in environmental conditions.

The Notion of Health

The notion of ecosystem health is analogous to that of medical health. In the medical sense, health is a term used to refer to the vitality or well-being of individual organisms. Medical health is a composite attribute, because it is charac-

terized by a diversity of inter-related characteristics and conditions. These include blood pressure and chemistry, wounds and injuries, rational mental function and many other relevant variables. Health is, in effect, a summation of all of these characters related to vitality and well-being. In contrast, a diagnosis of unhealthiness would focus on abnormal values for only one or several variables within the diverse congregation of health-related attributes. For example, an individual might be judged as being unhealthy because they had a broken leg, or a high fever, or unusually high blood pressure, or non-normal behavioral traits, even though they are "normal" with regards to all other traits.

To compare human and ecosystem health is, however, imperfect in some important respects. Health is a relative concept. It depends on what we consider "normal" at a particular stage of development. The aches and pains that are considered normal in a human at age 80 would be a serious concern in a 20-year old. It is much more difficult, however, to say what is to be expected in an ecosystem. Ecosystems don't have a prescribed lifespan and generally don't die but rather change into some other form. Because of these problems, some ecologists prefer the notions of ecological or biological integrity rather than ecosystem health.

It should also be pointed out that many ecologists like none of these notions (that is, ecosystem health, ecological integrity, or biological integrity). The reason is that by their very nature, these concepts are imprecise and difficult to define. For these reasons, scientists have had difficulty in agreeing upon the specific variables that should be included when designing composite indicators of health and integrity in ecological contexts.

Ecosystem Health

Ecosystem health is a summation of conditions occurring in communities, **watershed**s, landscapes, or seascapes. Ecosystem health conditions are higher-level components of ecosystems, in contrast with individual organisms and their populations.

Although ecosystem health cannot be defined precisely, ecologists have identified a number of specific components that are important in this concept. These include the following indicators: (1) an ability of the system to resist changes in environmental conditions without displaying a large response (this is also known as resistance or tolerance); (2) an ability to recover when the intensity of **environmental stress** is decreased (this is known as resilience); (3) relatively high degrees of **biodiversity**; (4) complexity in the structure and function of the system; (5) the presence of large species and top predators; (6) controlled nutrient cycling and a stable or increasing content of **biomass** in the system; and (7) domination of the system by native species and natural communities that can maintain themselves without management by humans. Higher values for any of these specific elements imply a greater degree of ecosystem health, while decreasing or lower values imply changes that reflect a less healthy condition.

Ecologists are also working to develop composite indicators (or multivariate summations) that would integrate the most important attributes of ecosystem health into a single value. Indicators of this type are similar in structure to composite economic indicators such as the Dow-Jones Stock Market Index and the Consumer Price Index. Because they allow complex situations to be presented in a simple and direct fashion, composite indicators are extremely useful for communicating ecosystem health to the broader public.

[*Bill Freedman*]

FURTHER READING

Costanza, R., B.G. Norton, and B.D. Haskell. *Ecosystem Health. New Goals for Environmental Science.* Washington, D.C.: Island Press, 1992.

DiGiulio, R., and E. Monosson. *Interconnections Between Human and Ecosystem Health.* New York: Chapman and Hall, 1996.

Woodley, S., J. Kay, and G. Francis, eds. *Ecological Integrity and the Management of Ecosystems.* Boca Raton, FL: St. Lucie Press, 1993.

Ecosystem management

Ecosystem management (EM) is a new concept that has germinated within the past decade and continues to increase in popularity across the United States and Canada. It is a concept that eludes one concise definition, however, because it embodies different meanings in different contexts and for different people and organizations. This can be witnessed by the multiple variations on its title, e.g. **ecosystem**-based management or collaborative ecosystem management. The definitions that have been given for EM, though varied, fall into two distinct groups. One group emphasizes long term ecosystem integrity, while the other group emphasizes an intention to address all concerns equally, be they economic, ecological, political or social, by actively engaging and incorporating the multitude of stakeholders (literally, those who "hold a stake" in the issue) into the decision-making process.

One usable though incomplete definition of EM is provided by R. Edward Grumbine: "Ecosystem management integrates scientific knowledge of ecological relationships within a complex sociopolitical and values framework toward the general goal of protecting native ecosystem integrity over the long term." Ultimately, EM is a new way to make decisions about how we humans should live with each other and with the **environment** that supports us. And, it is best defined not only by articulating an ideal description of its contents, as Grumbine has done, but also through a rigorous analysis of actual EM examples.

EM—a New Management Style

Between the years 1992 and 1994, each of the four predominant federal land management agencies in the United States the **National Park Service**, the **Bureau of Land Management**, the **Forest Service** and the **Fish and Wildlife Service** implemented EM as their operative management paradigm. Combined, these four agencies combined control 97% of the 650 million federally-owned acres (267 million ha) in the United States, or roughly 30% of the United States' entire land area. EM has become the primary management style for these agencies because of a fact that became unavoidably apparent in the 1980s and 1990s the

traditional resource management style does not work. It is largely ineffective in addressing the loss and fragmentation of wild areas, the increasing number of threatened or **endangered species**, and the increased occurrence of environmental disputes. This ineffectiveness has been attributed to the traditional management style's focus on mainly species with economic value, its exclusion of the public from the decision-making process, and its reliance on outdated ecological beliefs. This explicit acknowledgment that the traditional management style is inadequate has coalesced within state and federal agencies, academia, and environmental organizations, and has been bolstered by advances in other relevant fields, such as **ecology** and conflict management.

If we break the traditional management style into individual components, we see that each ineffective attribute has a new or altered counterpart in EM. One of the best ways to describe what EM actually entails is to explicate this juxtaposition between traditional and new management styles.

EM, as its name makes clear, concentrates on managing at the scale of an ecosystem. Alternately, traditional resource management has tended to focus only on one or a handful of species, especially those species that have a utilitarian, or more specifically economic, value. For example, the U.S. Forest Service has traditionally managed the **national forest**s so as to produce a sustained yield of timber. This management style is often harmful to species other than timber and can have negative effects on the entire ecosystem. In EM, all significant biotic and abiotic components of the ecosystem, as well as aspects such as economic factors, are, ideally, reviewed and the important ecological data incorporated into the decision-making process. For example, review of a forest ecosystem may include an analysis of habitat for significant song birds, a description of the requirements needed to maintain a healthy black bear (*Ursus americanus*) population, *and* a discussion of acceptable levels of timber production.

A major problem associated with using an ecosystem to define one's management area is that boundaries of jurisdictional authority, or political boundaries, rarely follow ecological ones. This implies that by following political boundaries alone, ecological components may be left out of the management plan one may be forced to manage only part of an ecosystem, that part which is within one's political jurisdiction. For example, the Greater Yellowstone Ecosystem goes far beyond the boundaries of **Yellowstone National Park**. Therefore, a large scale EM project for Yellowstone would require crossing several political boundaries (e.g., **national park** lands and **national forest** lands), which is a difficult task because it entails several political jurisdictions and political entities (e.g., state and federal agencies, and county governments).

EM projects address this obstacle by forming decision teams that include, among others, representatives from all of the relevant jurisdictions. These decision-making bodies can either act as advisory committees without decision-making authority, or they can attempt to become vested with the power to make decisions. This collaborative process involves all of the stakeholders, whether that stakeholder is a logging company interested in timber production, or a private citizen concerned with water quality. Such collaboration diverges from the traditional resource management method which made most decisions "behind closed doors" asking for and receiving little public input. These agencies traditionally shied away from actively engaging the public because it is easier and faster to make decisions on one's own than to ask for input from many sources, there has often been an antagonistic and distrustful relationship between state and federal agencies and the public, and, there has been little institutional support (i.e., within the structure of the agency itself) encouraging the manager in the field to invite the public into the decision-making process.

EM's more collaborative and inclusive decision-making style ideally fosters a wiser and more effective decision. This happens because as the decision team works toward consensus, personal relationships are established, some trust may form between parties, and, ultimately, people are more likely to support a decision or plan they help create. EM attempts to transcend the traditional antagonistic relationship between agency personnel and the public. Because 70% of the United States is privately owned, many environmental issues arise on private land—land that is partially not affected by federal and state natural resource legislation. EM allows us to deal with these issues on private lands by establishing a dialogue between private and public decision makers. Finally, even though the EM decision-making style takes longer to conduct, time is saved in the end because the decision achieved is more agreeable to all interested parties. Having all parties agree to a particular management plan decreases the number of potential lawsuits which can arise and delay the plan's implementation.

Nonequilibrium Ecology and EM

A change in the dominant theories in ecology has encouraged this switch to EM and an ecosystem-level focus. The idea that environments achieve a climax state of **homeostasis** has been a significant theory in ecology since the early 1900s. This view, now discredited, was most vigorously articulated by Frederic Clements and holds that all ecosystems have a particular end point to which they each progress, and that ecosystems are closed systems. Disturbances such as fires or floods are considered only temporary setbacks on the ecosystem's ultimate progression to a final state. This theory offers a certain level of predictable stability the type of stability desired within traditional resource management. For example, if a forest is in its climax state, that condition can be maintained by eliminating disturbances such as forest fires, and a predictable level of harvestable timber can be extracted (hence, this theory contributed to the creation of "Smoky the Bear" and the national policy of stopping forest fires on public land).

This teleological view of nature has ebbed and waned in importance, but has lost favor especially within the past two decades. Ecologists, among others, have realized that from certain temporal and spatial points of view ecosystems may seem to be in equilibrium, but in the long term all ecosystems are in a state of nonequilibrium. That is, ecosystems always change. They change because their ecological

structure and function is often regulated by dynamic external forces such as storms or **drought**s and because they comprise of varied **habitat** types which change and affect one another.

This acknowledgment of a changing ecosystem means that predictable stability does not really exist and that an adaptive management style is needed to meet the changing requirements of a dynamic ecosystem. EM is adaptive. After an EM decision team has formulated and implemented a management plan, the particular ecosystem is monitored. The team watches significant biotic and abiotic factors are watched to see if and how they are altered by the management practices. For example, if logging produces changes which effect the fish in one of the ecosystem's streams, the decision team could adapt to the new data and decide to relocate the logging.

The ability to adaptively manage is a crucial aspect of EM, one that is not incorporated in traditional resource management. As stated, the traditional management style emphasizes one or a few species and believes that ecosystems are mostly stable. So, one only needs to view how a particular species fares to determine the necessary management practices little monitoring is conducted and previous management practices are rarely altered. In EM, management practices are constantly reviewed and adjusted as a result of ongoing data gathering and the goals articulated by the decision team.

The Future of EM

The future of EM in the United States and Canada looks stable, and other countries such as France are beginning to use EM. There are many impediments, though, to the successful implementation of EM. Institutions, such as the United States' federal land management agencies, are often hesitant to actually change and when they do change it happens very slowly; there are still many legal questions surrounding the legitimacy of implementing EM on federal, state and private lands; and, even though we attempt to review the entire ecosystem in EM examples, we still lack significant understanding of how even the most basic ecosystems operate. Even given these impediments, it looks as if EM will be the primary land management style of the United States and Canada well into the next century.

[*Paul Phifer*]

FURTHER READING

Grumbine, R.E. "What is ecosystem management?" *Conservation Biology* 8. (1994):27-38.

Gunderson, L.H., C.S. Holling, and S.S. Light. *Barriers and Bridges to the Renewal of Ecosystems and Institutions*. New York: Columbia University Press, 1995.

Lee, K.N. *Compass and Gyroscope: Integrating Science and Politics for the Environment*. Washington, D.C.: Island Press, 1993.

Yaffee, S.L., et al. *Ecosystem Management in the United States: An Assessment of Current Experience*. Washington, D.C.: Island Press, 1996.

Ecotage

See **Ecoanarchism; Monkey-wrenching**

Ecoterrorism

See **Ecoanarchism**

Ecotone

The boundary between adjacent **ecosystem**s is known as an ecotone. For example, the intermediary zone between a **grassland** and a forest constitutes an ecotone that has characteristics of both ecosystems. The transition between the two ecosystems may be abrupt or, more commonly, gradual. Because of the overlap between ecosystems, an ecotone usually contains a larger variety of species than is to be found in either of the separate ecosystems and often includes species unique to the ecotone. This effect is known as the edge effect. Ecotones may be stable or variable. Over a period of time, for example, a forest may invade a grassland. Changes in precipitation are an important factor in the movement of ecotones.

Ecotourism

Ecotourism is ecology-based tourism, focused primarily on natural or cultural resources such as scenic areas, **coral reef**s, caves, fossil sites, archeological or historical sites, and **wildlife**, particularly rare and **endangered species**.

The successful marketing of ecotourism depends on destinations which have **biodiversity**, unique geologic features, and interesting cultural histories, as well as an adequate infrastructure. In the United States **national park**s are perhaps the most popular destinations for ecotourism, particularly **Yellowstone National Park**, the **Grand Canyon**, the **Great Smoky Mountains** and **Yosemite National Park**. In 1989, there were 265 million recreational visits to the national parks. Some of the leading ecotourist destinations outside the United States include the **Galapagos Islands** in Ecuador, the wildlife parks of Kenya, Tanzania, and South Africa, the mountains of Nepal, and the national parks and forest reserves of Costa Rica.

Tourism is the second largest industry in the world, producing $195 billion in domestic and international receipts and accounting for 7 percent of the world's trade in goods and services. There were 390 million international tourists in 1988, creating 74 million tourism jobs. Adventure tourism, which includes ecotourism, accounts for 10 percent of this market. In developing countries tourism can comprises as much as one-third of trade in goods and services, and much of this is ecotourism. Wildlife-based tourism in Kenya, for example, generates $350 million annually, and ecotourism in the Galapagos Islands produced $180 million in foreign exchange in 1986.

Ecotourism is not a new phenomena. In the late 1800s railroads and steamship companies were instrumental in the

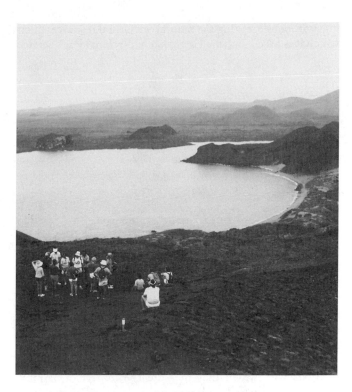
A group of tourists visit the Galapagos Islands.

establishment of the first national parks in the United States, recognizing even then the demand for experiences in nature and profiting from transporting tourists to destinations such as Yellowstone and Yosemite. However, ecotourism has recently taken on increased significance worldwide.

There has been a tremendous increase in demand for such experiences, with adventure tourism increasing at a rate of 30 percent annually. But there is another reason for the increased significance of ecotourism. It is a key strategy in efforts to protect cultural and natural resources, especially in developing countries, because resource-based tourism provides an economic incentive to protect resources. For example, rather than converting **tropical rain forest**s to farms which may be short-lived, income can be earned by providing goods and services to tourists visiting the rain forests.

Although ecotourism has the potential to produce a viable economic alternative to exploitation of the environment, it can also threaten it. **Water pollution**, litter, disruption of wildlife, trampling of vegetation, and mistreatment of local people are some of the negative impacts of poorly planned and operated ecotourism. To distinguish themselves from destructive tour companies, many reputable tour organizations have adopted environmental codes of ethics which explicitly state policies for avoiding or minimizing environmental impacts. In planning destinations and operating tours, successful firms are also sensitive to the needs and desires of the local people, for without native support efforts in ecotourism often fail.

Ecotourism can provide rewarding experiences and produce economic benefits that encourage **conservation**. The challenge upon which the future of ecotourism depends is the ability to carry out tours which the clients find rewarding, without degrading the natural or cultural resources upon which it is based. *See also* Earthwatch; National Park Service

[*Ted T. Cable*]

FURTHER READING

Boo, E. *Ecotourism: The Potentials and Pitfalls.* 2 vols. Washington, DC: World Wildlife Fund, 1990.

Ocko, Stephanie. *Environmental Vacations: Volunteer Projects to Save the Planet.* 2nd ed. Santa Fe, NM: John Muir, 1992.

Whelan, T., ed. *Nature Tourism: Managing for the Environment.* Washington, DC: Island Press, 1991.

Ecotoxicology

Ecotoxicology is a field of science that studies the effects of **toxic substance**s on **ecosystem**s. It analyzes environmental damage from **pollution** and predicts the consequences of proposed human actions in both the short and long term. With more than 100,000 **chemicals** in commercial use and thousands more being introduced each year, the scale of the task is daunting. Ecotoxicologists have a variety of methods with which they measure the impact of harmful substances on people, plants, and animals. Toxicity tests measure the response of biological systems to a substance to determine if it is toxic. A test could study, for example, how well fish live, grow, and reproduce in various concentrations of industrial **effluent**. Another could evaluate the point at which metal contaminants in **soil** damage plants' ability to convert sunlight into food. Still another could measure how various concentrations of **pesticide**s in agricultural **runoff** affect **sediment** and **nutrient** absorption in **wetlands**. Analyses of chemical fate (i.e. where a pollutant goes once it is released into the **environment**) can be combined with toxicity-test information to predict environmental response to pollution. Because toxicity is the interaction between a living system and a substance, only *living* plants, animals, and systems can be used in these experiments. There is no other way to measure toxicity.

Another tool used in ecotoxicolgy is the field survey. It describes ecological conditions in both healthy and damaged natural systems, including pollution levels. Surveys often focus on the number and variety of plants and animals supported by the ecosystem, but they can also characterize other valued attributes such as crop yield, **commercial fishing**, timber harvest, or aesthetics. Information from a number of field surveys can be combined for an overview of the relationship between pollution levels and the ecological condition.

A logical question might be: why not merely measure the concentration of a toxic substance and predict what will happen from that? The answer is because chemical analysis alone cannot predict environmental consequences in most cases. Unfortunately, interactions between toxicants and the components of ecosystems are not clear; in addition, ecotoxicologists have not yet developed simulation models that would allow them to make predictions based on chemical concentration alone. For example:

(1) An ecosystem's response to toxic materials is greatly influenced by environmental conditions. The concentration of zinc that will kill bluegill sunfish in Virginia's soft waters will not kill them in the much harder waters of Texas. Most of the relationships between environmental conditions and toxicity have not been established.

(2) Most pollution is a complex mixture of chemicals, not just a single substance. In addition, some chemicals are more harmful when combined with other toxicants.

(3) Some chemicals are toxic at concentrations and levels too small to be measured.

(4) An organism's response to toxic materials can be influenced by other organisms in the community. For example, a fish exposed to pollution may be unable to escape from its predators.

Ecotoxicologists use all three kinds of information: field surveys, chemical analyses, and toxicity tests. Field surveys prove that some important characteristic of the ecosystem has been damaged, chemical measurements confirm the presence of a toxicant, and toxicity tests link a particular toxicant to a particular type of damage.

The scope of environmental protection has broadened considerably over the years, and the types of ecotoxicological information required have also changed. Toxicity testing began as an interest in the effects of various substances on human health. Gradually this concern extended to the other organisms that were most obviously important to humans—domestic animals and crop plants—and finally spread to other organisms that are less apparent or universal in their importance. Hunters are interested in deer, fishers in fish, bird watchers in eagles or pelicans, and beachcombers in loggerhead turtles. Keeping these organisms healthy requires studying the effects of pollution on them. In addition, the toxicant must not eliminate or taint the plants and/or animals upon which they feed nor can it destroy their **habitat**. Indirect effects of toxicants, which can also be devastating, are difficult to predict. A chemical that is not toxic to an organism, but instead destroys the grasses in which it lays eggs or hides from predators, will be indirectly responsible for the death of that organism. Protecting all the **species** that people value, along with their food and habitat, is a small step toward universal protection. An ambitious goal is to prevent the loss of any existing species, regardless of its appeal or known value to human society.

Because each one of the millions of species on this planet cannot be tested before a chemical is used, ecotoxicologists tested a few "representative" species to characterize toxicity. If a pollutant could be found in rivers, testing might be done on an alga, an insect that eats algae, a fish that eats insects, and a fish that eats fish. Other representative species are chosen by their habitat: on the bottom of rivers, midstream, or in the soil. Regardless of the sampling scheme, however, thousands of organisms that will be affected by a pollutant will not be tested.

Some prediction must be made about their response, nonetheless. Statistical techniques can predict the response of organisms in general from information on a few randomly selected organisms. Another approach tests the well-being of higher levels of biological organization. Since natural communities and ecosystems are composed of a large number of interacting species, the response of the whole reflects the responses of its many constituents. The health of a large and complex ecosystem cannot be measured in the same way as the health of a single species, however. Different attributes are important. For example, examining a single species like cattle or trout might require measuring respiration, reproduction, behavior, growth, or tissue damage. The condition of an ecosystem, on the other hand, might be determined by measuring production, nutrient spiralling, or colonization. Since people depend on ecosystems for food production, waste processing, and **biodiversity**, keeping them healthy is important.

[*John Cairns, Jr.*]

FURTHER READING

Carson, R. *Silent Spring*. Boston: Houghton Mifflin, 1962.

Côté, R. P., and P. G. Wells. *Controlling Chemical Hazards*. Boston: Unwin Hyman, 1991.

Levin, S. A., et al., eds. *Ecotoxicology: Problems and Approaches*. New York: Springer-Verlag, 1989.

Wilson, E. O. *Biodiversity*. Washington, DC: National Academy Press, 1988.

Ecotype

A recognizable geographic variety, population, or ecological race of a widespread **species** that is equivalent to a taxonomic subspecies. Typically, ecotypes are restricted to one **habitat** and are recognized by distinctive characteristics resulting from **adaptation**s to local selective pressures and isolation. For example, a population or ecotype of species found at the foot of a mountain may differ in size, color, or physiology from a different ecotype living at higher altitudes, thus reflecting a sharp change in local selective pressures. Members of an ecotype are capable of interbreeding with other ecotypes within the same species without loss of fertility or vigor.

Edaphic

Refers to the concept that **soil**s have influence on living things, particularly plants. For example, soils with a low **pH** will more likely have plants growing on them that are adapted to this level of soil acidity. Animals living in the area will most likely eat these acid-loving plants. The more extreme a soil characteristic, the fewer kinds of plants and animals are able to adapt to the soil environment.

Edaphology

The ecological study of **soil**, including its role, value, and management as a medium for plant growth and as a **habitat** for animals. This branch of soil science covers physical, chemical, and biological properties, including soil fertility, acidity, water relations, gas and energy exchanges, microbial ecology, and organic decay.

Effluent

The etymological meaning of this term is "flowing forth out of." For geologists, this word refers to a wide range of situations, from lava flowing from a **volcano** to a river flowing out of a lake. However, effluent is now most commonly used by environmentalists in reference to the **Clean Water Act** of 1977. In this act, effluent is a **discharge** from a **point source**, and the legislation specifies allowable quantities of pollutants. These discharges are regulated under Section 402 of the act, and these standards must be met before these types of industrial and municipal wastes can be released into surface waters. *See also* Industrial waste treatment; Thermal pollution; Water pollution; Water quality

Effluent tax

Effluent tax refers to the fee paid by a company to **discharge** to a sewer. As originally proposed, the fee would have been paid for the privilege of discharging to the **environment**. However, there is presently no fee structure which allows a company, municipality, or person to contaminate the environment above the levels set by **water quality** criteria and **effluent** permits, unless fines levied by a regulatory agency could be deemed to be such fees.

Fees are now charged on the bases of simply being connected to a sewer and the types and levels of materials discharged to the sewer. For example, a municipality might charge all sewer customers the same rate for domestic sewage discharges below a certain flowrate. Customers discharging **wastewater** at a higher strength and/or flowrate would be assessed an incremental fee proportional to the increased amount of contaminants and/or flow. This charge is often referred to as a sewer charge, fee or surcharge.

There are cases in which wastewater is collected and tested to ensure that it meets certain criteria (e.g., required level of oil or a toxic metal, etc.) before it is discharged to a sewer. If the criteria are exceeded, the wastewater would require pretreatment. Holding the water before discharge is generally only practical when flowrates are low. In other situations, it may not be possible to discharge to a sewer because the treatment facility is unable to treat the waste; for example, many hazardous materials must be managed in a different manner. Effluent taxes force dischargers to integrate environmental concerns into their economic plans and operational procedures. The fees cause firms and agencies to re-think water **conservation** policies, waste minimization, processing techniques and additives, and **pollution control** strategies. Effluent taxes, as originally proposed, might be instituted as an alternative to stringent regulation, but the sentiment of the current public and regulatory agencies is to block any significant degradation of the environment. It appears to be too risky to allow pollution on a fee basis, even when the fees are high. Thus, in the foreseeable future, effluents to the environment will continue to be controlled by means of effluent limits, water quality criteria, and fines. However, the taxing of effluents to a sewer is a viable means of challenging industries to enhance pollution control measures and stabilizing the performance of downstream treatment facilities.

[*Gregory D. Boardman*]

FURTHER READING

Davis, M. L., and D. A. Cornwell. *Introduction to Environmental Engineering.* New York: McGraw-Hill, 1991.

Peavy, H. S., D. R. Rowe, and G. Tchobanoglous. *Environmental Engineering.* New York: McGraw-Hill, 1985.

Tchobanoglous, G., and E. D. Schroeder. *Water Quality.* Reading, MA: Addison-Wesley, 1985.

Viessman, W., Jr., and M. J. Hammer. *Water Supply and Pollution Control.* 5th ed. New York: Harper Collins, 1993.

Eggshell thinning
See **DDT**

E_H

A measure of the oxidation/reduction status of a natural water, **sediment** or **soil**. It is a relative electrical potential, measured with a potentiometer (e.g. a **pH** meter adjusted to read in volts) using an inert platinum electrode and a reference electrode (calomel or silver/silver chloride). E_H is reported in volts or millivolts, and is referenced to the potential for the oxidation of **hydrogen** gas to hydrogen **ion**s (H^+). This electron transfer reaction is assigned a potential of zero on the relative potential scale. The oxidation and reduction reactions in natural systems are pH dependent and the interpretation of E_H values requires a knowledge of the pH. At pH 7, the E_H in water in equilibrium with the oxygen in air is +0.76v. The lowest possible potential is -0.4v when oxygen and other electron acceptors are depleted and methane, **carbon dioxide**, and hydrogen gas are produced by the decay of organic matter. *See also* Electron acceptor and donor

Ehrlich, Paul (1932 -)
American ecologist and population control advocate

Born in Philadelphia, Paul Ehrlich had a typical childhood during which he cultivated an early interest in entomology and zoology by investigating the fields and woods around his home. As he entered his teen years, Ehrlich grew to be an avid reader. He was particularly influenced by ecologist William Vogt's book, *Road to Survival* (1948), in which the author was the outlined the potential global consequences of imbalance between the growing world population and level of food supplies available. This concept is one Ehrlich has

discussed and examined throughout his career. After high school, Ehrlich attended the University of Pennsylvania where he earned his undergraduate degree in zoology in 1953. He received his master's degree from University of Kansas two years later and continued at the university to receive his doctorate in 1957. His degrees led to postgraduate work on various aspects of entomological projects, including observing flies on the Bering Sea, the behavioral characteristics of parasitic mites, and (his favorite) the population control of butterfly caterpillars with ants rather than **pesticide**s. Other related field projects have taken him to Africa, Alaska, Australia, the South Pacific and South East Asia, Latin America, and Antarctica. His travels enabled him to learn first-hand the ordeals endured by those in overpopulated regions.

In 1954, he married Anne Fitzhugh Howland, biological research associate, with whom he wrote the bestselling book, *The Population Bomb* (1968). In the book, the Ehrlichs focus on a variety of factors contributing to overpopulation and, in turn, world hunger. It is evident throughout the book that the words and warnings of *The Survival Game* continued to exert a strong influence on Ehrlich. The authors warned that birth and death rates worldwide need to be "brought into line" before nature intervenes and renders (through **ozone layer depletion**, global warming, and **soil** exhaustion, among other **environmental degradation**) the human race extinct. Human reproduction, especially in highly developed countries like the United States, should be discouraged through levying taxes on diapers, baby food, and other related items; compulsory sterilization among the populations of certain countries should be enacted (the authors' feelings on *compulsory* sterilization have relaxed somewhat since 1968). Ehrlich himself underwent a vasectomy after the birth of the couple's first and only child.

In 1968, Ehrlich founded Zero Population Growth, Inc., an organization established to create and rally support for balanced population levels and the environment. He has been a faculty member at Stanford University (California) since 1959 and currently holds a full professor position there in the Biological Sciences Department. In addition, Ehrlich has been a news correspondent for NBC since 1989.

Among Ehrlich's published works are *The Population Bomb* (1968), *The Cold and the Dark: The World After Nuclear War* (1984); *The Population Explosion* (1990); and *Healing the Planet* (1991).

[*Kimberley A. Peterson*]

FURTHER READING

Dailey, G. C., and P. R. Ehrlich. "Population Sustainability and Earth's Carrying Capacity." *BioScience* 42 (November 1992): 761-71.

Ehrlich, P. R. *The Population Bomb.* New York: Ballantine Books, 1968.

———. *Healing the Planet: Strategies for Solving the Environmental Crisis.* Redding: Addison Wesley, 1992.

———, and A. H. Ehrlich. *The Population Explosion.* New York: Simon & Schuster, 1990.

———, A. H. Ehrlich, and J. Holdren. *Eco-Science: Population, Resources, and Environment.* San Francisco: W. H. Freeman, 1970.

EIS

See **Environmental Impact Statement**

El Niño

El Niño is the most powerful weather event on the earth, disrupting weather patterns across half the earth's surface. Its three- to seven- year cycle brings lingering rain to some areas and severe **drought** to others. El Niño develops when currents in the Pacific Ocean shift, bringing warm water eastward from Australia toward Peru and Ecuador. Heat rising off warmer water shifts patterns of atmospheric pressure, interrupting the high-altitude wind currents of the jet stream and causing **climate** changes.

El Niño, or "Christ child" in Spanish, tends to appear in December. The phenomenon was first noted by Peruvian fishermen in the 1700s, who saw a warming of normally cold Peruvian coastal waters and a simultaneous disappearance of anchovy schools that provided their livelihood.

The most recent El Niño began to develop in 1989, but significant warming of the Pacific did not begin until late in 1991, reaching its peak in early 1992 and lingering until 1995—the longest runing El Niño on record. Typically, El Niño results in unusual weather and short-term climate changes that cause losses in crops and **commercial fishing**. El Niño contributed to North America's mild 1992 winter, torrential **flooding** in southern California, and severe droughts in southeastern Africa. Wild animals in central and southern Africa died by the thousands, and 20 million people were plagued by **famine**. The dried **prairie** of Alberta, Canada, failed to produce wheat, and Latin America received record flooding. Droughts were felt in the Philippines, Sri Lanka, and Australia, and Turkey experienced heavy snowfall. The South Pacific saw unusual numbers of cyclones during the winter of 1992. El Niño's influence also seems to have suppressed some of the cooling effects of **Mount Pinatubo**'s 1991 explosion.

Recently, scientists mapping the sea floor of the South Pacific near Easter Island have found what may be the greatest concentration of active **volcano**es on earth. The discovery has intensified debate over whether undersea volcanic activity could change water temperatures enough to affect weather patterns in the Pacific. Some scientists speculate that periods of extreme volcanic activity underwater could trigger El Niño.

El Niño ends when the warm water is diverted toward to the North and South Poles, emptying the moving **reservoir** of stored energy. Before El Niño can develop again, the western Pacific must "refill" with warm water, which takes at least two years. *See also* Atmosphere; Desertification

[*Linda Rehkopf*]

FURTHER READING

Diaz, H. R., ed. *El Niño: Historical and Paleoclimatic Aspects of the Southern Oscillation.* New York: Cambridge University Press, 1993.

Glynn, P. W., ed. *Global Ecological Consequences of the El-Niño Southern Oscillation, 1982-1983.* New York: Elsevier Science, 1990.

Mathews, N. "The Return of El Niño." *UNESCO Courier* (July-August 1992): 44-46.

Monastersky, R. "Once Bashful El Niño Now Refuses to Go." *Science News* 143 (23 January 1993): 53.

Electric utilities

Utilities neither produce energy like oil companies nor consume it like households, but convert it from one form to another. The electricity created is attractive because it is clean and versatile, because it can be moved great distances nearly instantaneously. Demand for electricity has grown even as demand for energy as a whole has contracted, with consumption of electricity increasing from one quarter of total energy consumption in 1973 to about a third.

The major participants in the electric power industry are about 200 investor owned utilities that generate 78 percent of the power and supply 76 percent of the customers. The industry is very capital intensive and heavily regulated, and it has a large impact on other industries including **aluminum**, steel, electronics, computers, and robotics. The electrical power industry is the largest consumer of primary energy in the United States: consumes over one-third of the total national energy demand and only supplies one-tenth of that demand, losing from 65 to 75 percent of the energy in conversion, transmission, and distribution.

The electrical industry has been subjected to pressures and uncertainties which have had a profound impact on its economic viability, forcing it to reexamine numerous assumptions which previously governed its behavior. In the period after World War II, the main strategy the industry followed was to "grow and build." During this period demand increased at a rate of over seven percent per year; new construction was needed to meet the growing demand, and this yielded economies of scale, with greater efficiencies and declining marginal costs. Public utility commissions lowered prices which stimulated additional demand. As long as prices continued to fall, demand continued to rise, and additional construction was necessary. New construction also occurred because the rate of return for the industry was regulated, and the only way for it to increase profits was to expand its rate base by building new plants and equipment.

This period of industry growth came to an end in the 1970s, primarily as a result of the energy crisis. Economic growth slowed and fuel prices escalated, including the weighted average cost of all **fossil fuels** and the spot market price of **uranium** oxide. As fuel prices rose, operating costs went up, and maintenance costs also increased, including the costs of supplies and materials, labor, and administrative expenses. All this led to higher costs per kilowatt hour, and as the price of electricity went up, sales growth declined.

The financial condition of the industry was further affected as capital costs for **nuclear power** and **coal** power plants increased. As the rate of inflation accelerated during this period, interest rates escalated. The rates utilities had to pay on bonds grew, and the costs of construction rose. The average cost of new generating capacity, as well as installed capacity per kilowatt hour, went up. Net earnings and revenue per kilowatt hour went down, as both short-term and long-term debt escalated, and major generating units were cancelled and capital appropriations cut back.

During this decade, many people also came to believe that coal and nuclear power plants were a threat to the **environment**. They argued that new options had to be developed and that **conservation** was important. The federal government implemented new environmental and safety regulations which further increased utility costs. The government affected utility operations in other ways. In 1978 it deregulated interstate power sales, and required utilities to purchase alternative power such as **solar energy** from qualifying facilities at fully avoided costs. But perhaps the greatest transformation took place in the relationship electric power companies had to the public utility commissions. Once friendly, it deteriorated under the many economic and environmental changes that were then taking place. The size and number of requests for rate increases grew but the percentage of requests granted actually went down.

By the end of the 1970s, the "grow and build" strategy was no longer tenable for the electric power industry. Since then, the industry has adopted many different strategies, with different segments following different courses based on divergent perceptions of the future. Almost all utilities have tried to negotiate long-term contracts which would lower their fuel-procurement costs, and attempts have also been made to limit the costs of construction, maintenance, and administration. Many utilities redesigned their rate structures to promote use when excess capacity was available and discourage use when it was not. Multiple rate structures for different classes of customers were also implemented for this purpose.

A number of utilities (Commonwealth Edison, Long Island Lighting, Carolina Power and Light, the TVA) have pursued a modified grow and build strategy based on the perception that economic growth would recover and that conservation and renewable energy would not be able to handle the increased demand. Some utilities (Consolidated Edison, Duke Power, General Public Utilities, Potomac Electric Power) pursued an option of capital minimization. They were located in areas of the country that were not growing and where the demand for power was decreasing. In areas of rapidly growing energy demand where regulations discouraged nuclear and coal plant construction, utilities such as Southern California Edison and Pacific Gas and Electric have had no option but to rely on their strong internal research and development capabilities and their progressive leadership to explore **alternative energy sources**. They have become energy brokers, buying alternative power from third party producers. Many utilities have also diversified, and the main attraction of diversification has been that it frees these companies from the profit limitations imposed by the public utility commissions. Outside the utility business (in real-estate, banking, and energy- related services), there was more risk but no limits on making money from profitable ventures. *See also* Alternative fuels; Economic growth and the environment; Energy and the environment; Energy conservation; Energy efficiency; Energy path, hard vs. soft; Energy policy; Geothermal energy; Wind energy

[*Alfred A. Marcus*]

FURTHER READING

Anderson, D. *Regulatory Politics and Electric Utilities.* Cambridge, Massachusetts: Auburn House, 1981.

Joskow, D. "The Evolution of Competition in the Electric Power Industry." *Annual Review of Energy* (1988): 215-238.

Navarro, P. *The Dimming of America.* Cambridge, Massachusetts: Ballinger, 1985.

Thomas, S. D. *The Realities of Nuclear Power.* New York: Cambridge University Press, 1988.

Three Mile Island: A Report to the Commissioners and to the Public, Volumes I and II, Parts 1, 2, and 3. Washington, DC: U.S. Nuclear Regulatory Commission, 1980.

Three Mile Island: The Most Studied Nuclear Accident in History. Washington, DC: General Accounting Office, 1980.

Zardkoohi, A. "Competition in the Production of Electricity." In *Electric Power*, edited by J. Moorhouse. San Francisco: Pacific Research Institute, 1986.

Electromagnetic field (EMF)

Electromagnetic fields are low-level radiation generated by electrical devices, including power lines, household appliances, and computer terminals. They penetrate walls, buildings, and human bodies, and virtually all Americans are exposed to them, some to relatively high levels. Several dozen studies, conducted mainly over the last 15 years, suggest that exposure to EMFs at certain levels may cause serious health effects, including childhood leukemia, brain tumors, and damage to fetuses. But other studies show no such connections.

EMFs are strongest around power stations, high-current electric power lines, subways, movie projectors, hand-held radar guns and large radar equipment, and microwave power facilities and relay stations. Common sources of everyday exposure include electric razors, hair dryers, computer video display terminals (VDTs), television screens, electric power tools, electric blankets, cellular telephones, and appliances such as toasters and food blenders.

The electricity used in North American homes, offices, and factories is called alternating current (AC) because it alternates the direction of flow at 60 cycles a second, which is called 60 hertz (Hz) power. Batteries, in contrast, produce direct current (DC). The electric charges of 60 Hz power create two kinds of fields: electric fields, from the strength of the charge, and magnetic fields, from its motion. These fields, taken together, are called electromagnetic fields, and they are present wherever there is electric power. A typical home exposes its residents to electromagnetic fields of 1 or 2 milligauss (a unit of strength of the fields). But under a high voltage power line, the EMF can reach 100-200 milligauss.

The electromagnetic spectrum includes several types of energy or radiation. The strongest and most dangerous are **x**

rays, **gamma ray**s, and ultraviolet rays, all of which are types of **ionizing radiation**, the kind that contains enough energy to enter cells and atoms and break them apart. Ionizing radiation can cause **cancer** and even instant death at certain levels of exposure. The other forms of radiation are non-ionizing, and do not have enough energy to break up the **chemical bond**s holding cells together.

Microwave radiation constitutes the middle frequencies of the electromagnetic spectrum and includes radio frequency (RF), radar, and television waves, visible light and heat, and infrared radiation. Microwave radiation is emitted by VDTs, microwave ovens, satellites and earth terminals, radio and television broadcast stations, CB radios, security systems, and sonar, radar, and telephone equipment. Because of the pervasive presence of microwave radiation, virtually the entire American population is routinely exposed to it at some level. It is known that microwave radiation has biological effects on living cells.

The type of radiation generally found in homes is Extremely Low Frequency (ELF), and it has, until recently, not been considered dangerous, since it is non-ionizing and non-thermal . However, numerous studies over the last two decades provide evidence that the ELF range of EMFs can have serious biological effects on humans and can cause cancer and other health problems. Some scientists argue that the evidence is not yet conclusive or even convincing, but others contend that exposure to EMFs may represent a potentially serious public health problem.

After reviewing much of this evidence and data, the U. S. **Environmental Protection Agency** (EPA) released a draft report in December 1990 which determined that significant documentation exists linking EMFs to cancer in humans, and called for additional research on the matter. The study concluded that "...several studies showing leukemia, lymphoma, and cancer of the nervous system in children exposed to magnetic fields from residential 60-Hz electrical power distribution systems, supported by similar findings in adults in several occupational studies also involving electrical power frequency exposures, show a consistent pattern of response which suggests a causal link." The report went on to state that "evidence from a large number of biological test systems shows that ELF electric and magnetic fields induce biological effects that are consistent with several possible mechanisms of carcinogenesis...With our current understanding, we can identify 60-Hz magnetic fields from power lines and perhaps other sources in the home as a possible, but not proven, cause of cancer in humans."

EPA cited nine studies of cancer in children as supporting the strongest evidence of a link between the disease and EMFs stating that "these studies have consistently found modestly elevated risks (some statistically significant) of leukemia, cancer of the nervous system, and...lymphomas," with occupational studies furnishing "additional, but weaker, evidence" of EMFs raising the risk of cancer.

Concerning laboratory studies of the effects of EMFs on cells and the responses of animals to exposure, EPA found that "...there is reason to believe that the findings of carcinogenicity in humans are biologically plausible." EPA

scientists further recommended classifying EMFs as a "class B-1 carcinogen," like cigarettes and **asbestos**, meaning that they are a probable source of human cancer.

Several of the studies done on EMFs show that children living near high voltage power lines, and workers occupationally exposed to EMFs from power lines and electrical equipment, are more than twice as likely to contract cancer, especially leukemia, as are children and workers with average exposure. One study found a five-fold increase in childhood cancer among families exposed to strong EMFs, and another study even documented the leukemia rate among children increasing in direct proportion to the strength of the EMFs. There are suspicions that EMFs may also be linked to the apparent dramatic rise in fatal brain tumors over recent years, which sometimes occur in clusters near power substations and other areas where EMFs are high. There is also concern about hand-held cellular telephones, whose antennae emit EMFs very close to the brain. But none of this evidence is considered conclusive.

Fetal damage has been cited as another possible effect of EMFs with higher-than-normal rates of miscarriages reported among pregnant women using electric blankets, waterbeds with electric heaters, and VDTs for a certain number of hours a day. But, other studies have failed to establish a link between EMFs and miscarriages.

In October, 1996, the National Research Council of the National Academy of Sciences issued an important report on the feared dangers of power lines, examining and analyzing over 500 published studies conducted over the previous 17 years. In announcing the report's findings, the Council's panel of experts stressed that it could find no discernable hazard to human health from EMFs.

The announcement was hailed by the electric power industry, and widely reported in the news as disputing the alleged link between power lines and cancer. But what the report itself actually said was that there was "no conclusive and consistent evidence that shows that exposure to residential electric magnetic fields produce cancer...," a severe burden of proof indeed.

While the study did not find proof that electrical lines pose health hazards to humans, it did conclude that the association between proximity to power lines and leukemia in children was "statistically significant" and "robust." It observed that a dozen or so scientific studies had determined that children living near power lines are 1.5 times more likely to develop childhood leukemia than are other children.

Moreover, the study noted that 17 years of research had not identified any other factors that account for the increased cancer risk among children living near power lines. EMFs thus remain in the minds of many of the most likely albeit unproven cause of these cancers.

There are various theories to account for how EMFs may cause or promote cancer. Some scientists speculate that when cells are exposed to EMFs, normal cell division and **DNA** function can be disrupted, leading to genetic damage and increased cell growth and, thus, cancer. Indeed, research has shown that ELF fields can speed the growth of cancer cells, and make them more resistant to the body's immune system. The effects of EMFs on the cell membrane, on interaction and communication between groups of cells, and on the biochemistry of the brain are also being studied.

Hormones may also be involved. Weak EMFs are known to lower production of melatonin, a strong hormone secreted by the pineal gland, a tiny organ near the center of the brain. Melatonin strengthens the immune system and depresses other hormones that help tumors grow. This theory might help explain the tremendous increase in female breast cancer in developed nations, where electrical currents are so pervasive, especially the kitchen. The theory may also apply to electric razors, which operate in close proximity to the gland, and whose motors have relatively high EMFs. A 1992 study found that men with leukemia were more than twice as likely to have used an electric razor for over two-and-one-half minutes a day, compared with men who had not. The study also found weaker associations between leukemia and the use of hand-held massagers and hair dryers. Another hypothesis involves the motions of charged particles within EMFs, with calcium **ion**s, for example, accelerating and damaging the structure of cell membranes under such conditions.

With conflicting and inconclusive data being cited by scientists and advocates on both sides of the debate, it is unlikely that the controversy over EMFs wil be resolved any time soon.

In October, 1996, the National Research Council of the National Academy of Sciences issued an important report on the feared dangers of power lines, examining and analyzing over 500 published studies conducted over the previous 17 years. In announcing the report's findings, the Council's panel of experts stressed that it could find no discernable hazard to human health from EMFs.

The announcement was hailed by the electric power industry, and widely reported in the news media as disputing the alleged link between power lines and cancer. But what the report itself actually said was that there was "no conclusive and consistent evidence that shows that exposure to residential electric magnetic fields produce cancer...".

While the study did not find proof that electrical lines pose health hazards to humans, it did conclude that the association between proximity to power lines and leukemia in children was "statistically significant" and "robust." It observed that a dozen or so scientific studies had determined that children living near power lines are 1.5 times more likely to develop childhood leukemia than are other children.

Moreover, the study noted that 17 years of research had not identified any other factors that account for the increased cancer risk among children living near power lines. EMFs thus remained, in the minds of many, the most likely—albeit unproven—cause of these cancers.

And a major five-year study, by the National Cancer Institute, the University of Minnesota, and other childhood leukemia specialists, published in July 1997 in *The New England Journal of Medicine*, found no evidence linking leukemia in children to electric power lines.

[*Lewis G. Regenstein*]

FURTHER READING

Brodeur, P. *Currents of Death: Power Lines, Computer Terminals, and the Attempt to Cover Up Their Threat to Your Health.* New York: Simon & Schuster, 1989.

Savitz, D., and J. Chen. "Parental Occupation and Childhood Cancer: Review of Epidemiological Studies." *Environmental Health Perspectives* 88 (1990): 325-337.

Sugarman, E. *Warning: The Electricity Around You May Be Hazardous to Your Health.* New York: Simon & Schuster, 1992.

U.S. Environmental Protection Agency. *Evaluation of the Potential Carcinogenicity of Electromagnetic Fields.* Review Draft. Washington, DC: U. S. Government Printing Office, 1990.

Electron acceptor and donor

Electron acceptors are **ion**s or molecules that act as **oxidizing agent**s in chemical reactions. Electron donors are ions or molecules that donate electrons and are reducing agents. In the **combustion** reaction of gaseous **hydrogen** and oxygen to produce water (H_2O), two hydrogen atoms donate their electrons to an oxygen atom. In this reaction, the oxygen is reduced to an oxidation state of -2 and each hydrogen is oxidized to +1. Oxygen is an oxidizing agent (electron acceptor) and hydrogen is a reducing agent (electron donor). In **aerobic** (with oxygen) biological **respiration**, oxygen is the electron acceptor accepting electrons from organic **carbon** molecules; and as a result oxygen is reduced to -2 oxidation state in H_2O and organic carbon is oxidized to +4 in CO_2. In flooded **soil**s, after oxygen is used up by aerobic respiration, nitrate, sulfate, as well as iron and manganese oxides can act as electron acceptors for microbial respiration. Other common electron acceptors include peroxide and hypochlorite (household bleach) which are bleaching agents because they can oxidize organic molecules. Other common electron donors include antioxidants like sulfite.

Electrostatic precipitation

A technique for removing **particulate** pollutants from waste gases prior to their exhaustion to a stack. A system of thin wires and parallel metal plates are charged by a high-voltage direct current (DC) with the wires negatively charged and the plates positively charged. As waste gases containing fine particulate pollutants (i.e. **smoke** particles, **fly ash**, etc.) are passed through this system, electrical charges are transferred from the wire to the particulates in the gases. The charged particulates are then attracted to the plates within the device, where they are then shaken off the plates during short intervals when the DC current is interrupted. (Stack gases can be shunted to a second parallel device during this period). They fall to a collection bin below the plates. Under optimum conditions, electrostatic precipitation is 99 percent efficient in removing particulates from waste gases.

An electrostatic precipitator.

Elemental analysis

Chemists have developed a number of methods by which they can determine the kind of elements present in a material and the amount of each element present. Nuclear magnetic resonance (NMR), flame spectroscopy, and **mass spectrometry** are examples of elemental analysis. These methods have been improved to a point where concentrations of a few **parts per million** of an element or less can be detected with relative ease. Elemental analysis is valuable in environmental work to determine the presence of a contaminant or pollutant. As an example, the amount of **lead** in a paint chip can be determined by means of elemental analysis.

Elephants

The elephant is a large mammal with a long trunk and tusks. The trunk is an elongated nose used for feeding, drinking, bathing, blowing dust, and testing the air. The tusks are upper incisor teeth composed entirely of dentine (ivory) used for defense, levering trees, and scraping for water. Elephants are long-lived (50-70 years) and reach maturity at 12 years. They reproduce slowly (one calf every two to three years) due to a 21-month gestation period and an equally long weaning period. A newborn elephant stands three feet (one meter) at the shoulder and weighs 200 lb. (90 kg). The Elephantidae includes two living species and various extinct relatives.

Asian elephants (*Elephas maximus*) grow to 10 feet (3 meters) high and weigh four tons. The trunk ends in a single lip, the forehead is high and domed, the back convex, and the ears small. Asian elephants are commonly trained as work animals. They range from India to southeast Asia. There are four subspecies, the most abundant of which is the Indian elephant (*E. m. bengalensis*) with a wild population of about 20,000. The Sri Lankan (*E. m. maximus*), Malayan (*E. m. hirsutus*), and the Sumatran elephants (*E. m. sumatranus*) are all endangered subspecies.

In Africa, adult bush elephants (*Loxodonta africana oxyotis*) are the world's largest land mammals, growing 11 feet

(3.3 meters) tall and weighing 6 tons. The trunk ends in a double lip, the forehead slopes, the back is hollow, and the ears are large and triangular. African elephants have never been successfully trained to work. The rare round-eared African forest elephant (*L. a. cyclotis*) is smaller than the bush elephant and inhabits dense **tropical rain forest**s.

Elephants were once abundant throughout Africa and Asia, but they are now threatened or endangered nearly everywhere because of widespread ivory **poaching**. In 1970 there were about 4.5 million elephants in Africa, by 1990 there were only 600,000. Protection from poachers and the 1990 ban on the international trade in ivory (which caused a drop in the price of ivory) are slowing the slaughter of African bush elephants. However, the relatively untouched forest elephants are now coming under increasing pressure. In West Africa recent hunting has reduced forest elephants to less than 3000.

Elephants are **keystone species** in their **ecosystem**s, and their elimination could have serious consequences for other **wildlife**. For example, wandering elephants disperse fruit seeds in their dung, and the seeds of some plants must pass through elephants to germinate. Elephants are also "bulldozer herbivores," habitually trampling plants and uprooting small trees. In African forests elephants create open spaces that allow the growth of vegetation favored by **gorillas** and forest antelope. In woodland **savanna** elephants convert wooded land into **grasslands**, thus favoring grazing animals. However, large populations of elephants confined to reserves can also destroy most of the vegetation in a region. Culling exploding elephant populations in reserves has been practiced in the past to protect the vegetation for other animals that depend on it.

[*Neil Cumberlidge*]

FURTHER READING

Douglas-Hamilton, I., and O. Douglas-Hamilton. *Among the Elephants.* New York: Viking Press, 1975.

_ *Battle for the Elephants.* New York: Viking, 1992.

Martin, C. *The Rainforests of West Africa.* Boston: Birkhauser Verlag, 1991.

Moss, C. *Elephant Memories.* New York: William Morrow, 1988.

Shoshani, J., ed. *Elephants: Majestic Creatures of the Wild.* Emmaus, PA: Rodale Press, 1992.

Elton, Charles (1900-1991)

English ecologist

A factual, accurate, complete history of **ecology** as a discipline has yet to be written. When that history is finally compiled, the British ecologist Charles Sutherland Elton will stand as one of the disciplines leading mentors of the twentieth century.

Charles Elton was born March 29, 1900, in Manchester, England. His interest in what he later called "scientific natural history" was sparked early by his older brother Geoffrey. By the age of 19, Charles Elton was already investigating species relationships in ponds, streams, and sand-dune areas around Liverpool.

His formal education in ecology was shaped by an undergraduate education at Oxford University, and by his participation in three scientific expeditions to Spitsbergen in the Arctic (in 1921, 1923, and 1924), the first one as an assistant to Julian Huxley. Even though an undergraduate, he was allowed to begin an ecological survey of animal life in Spitsbergen, a survey completed on the third trip. These experiences and contacts led him to a position as biological consultant to the Hudson's Bay Company, which he used to conduct a long-term study of the fluctuations of fur-bearing mammals, drawing on company records dating back to 1736.

During this period, Elton became a member of the Oxford University faculty (in 1923), and was eventually elected a senior research fellow of Corpus Christie College. His whole academic career was spent at Oxford, from which he retired in 1967.

He applied the skills and insights gained through the Spitsbergen and Hudson Bay studies to work on the fluctuations of mice and voles in Great Britain. To advance and coordinate this work, he started the Bureau of Animal Populations at Oxford. This institution (and Elton's leadership of it) played a vital role in the shaping of research in animal ecology and in the training and education of numerous ecologists in the early twentieth century.

Elton published a number of books, but four proved to be of particular significance in ecology. He published his first book, *Animal Ecology*, in 1929, a volume now considered a classic, its author one of the pioneers in the field of ecology, especially animal ecology. In the preface to a 1966 reissue, Elton suggested that the book "must be read as a pioneering attempt to see...the outlines of the subject at a period when our knowledge [of] terrestrial communities was of the roughest, and considerable effort was required to shake off the conventional thinking of an earlier zoology and enter upon a new mental world of populations, inter-relations, movements and communities—a world [of] direct study of natural processes..." Major topics in that book remain major topics in ecology today: the centrality of trophic relationships; the significance of niche as a functional concept; ecological succession; the dynamics of dispersal; and the relationships critical to the fluctuation of animal populations, including interactions with **habitat** and physical **environment**.

His year of work on small mammals in Spitzbergen, for the Hudson's Bay Company, and in British localities accessible to Oxford, culminated in the publication, in 1942, of *Voles, Mice and Lemmings*. This work, still in print almost sixty years later, "brought together...his own work and a collection of observations from all over the world and from ancient history onward." Elton begins the book by establishing a context of "vole and mouse plagues" through history. A second section is on population fluctuations in north-west Europe, voles and mice in Britain, but also lemmings in Scandinavia. The other two sections focus on wildlife cycles in northern Labrador, including chapters on fox and marten, voles, foxes, the lemmings again, and caribou herds. In all this work, the emphasis is on the dynamics of change, on the constant interactions and subsequent fluctuations of these various populations and often stringent environments.

Elton's 1958 book, *The Ecology of Invasions by Animals and Plants*, focused on a problem that is of even more concern today—the arrival and impact of exotic species introduced from other places, sometimes naturally, increasingly through the actions of humans. As always, Elton is careful to set the historical context by showing how biological "invaders" have been moving around the globe for a long time, but he also emphasizes that "we are living in a period of the world's history when the mingling of thousands of kinds of organisms from different parts of the world is setting up terrific dislocations in nature."

The Pattern of Animal Communities, published in 1966, emerged from years of surveying species, populations, communities and habitats in the Wytham Woods not far from Oxford. In this book, his primary intent was to describe and classify the diverse habitats available to terrestrial animals, and most of the chapters of the book are given to specific habitats for specialized kinds of organisms. Though not generally considered a theoretical ecologist, his early thinking did help to shape the field. In this book, late in his career, he summarized that thinking in a chapter titled "The Whole Pattern," in which he presents a set of fifteen "new concepts of the structure of natural systems," which he stated as a "series of propositions," though some reviewers labeled them "principles" of ecology.

Always the pragmatist, Elton devoted considerable time to the practical, applied aspects of ecology. Nowhere is this better demonstrated than in the work he turned to early in World War II. One of his original purposes in establishing the Bureau of Animal Populations was to better understand the role of disease in the fluctuations of animal numbers. At the beginning of the war, he turned the research focus of the Bureau to the control of rodent pests, especially to help in controlling human disease and to contribute toward the reduction of crop losses to rodents.

He was an early conservationist, stating in the preface to his 1927 text that "ecology is a branch of zoology which is perhaps more able to offer immediate practical help to mankind than any of the others [particularly important] in the present rather parous state of civilisation." Elton strongly advocated the preservation of biological diversity, and pressed hard for the prevention of extinctions; this is what he emphasizes in his chapter on "The Reasons for Conservation" in the *Invasions* book. But he also expanded his conception of conservation to mean looking for some "general basis for understanding what it is best to do" and "looking for some wise principle of co-existence between man and nature, even if it has to be a modified kind of man and a modified kind of **nature**." He even took the unusual step (unusual for professional ecologists in his time and still unusual today) of going into the broadcast booth to popularize the importance of ecology in helping to achieve those goals though environmental management as applied ecology.

Elton's service to ecology as a learned discipline was enormous. In the early twentieth century, ecology was still in its formative years, so Elton's ideas and contributions came at a critical time. He took the infant field of animal ecology to maturity, building it to a status equal that of the more established plant ecology. His research Bureau at Oxford fostered innovative research and survey methods, and provided early intellectual nurture and professional development to ecologists who went on to become major contributors to the field, one example being the American ecologist **Eugene Odum**. As its first editor, Elton was "in a very real sense the creator" of the *Journal of Animal Ecology*, serving in the position for almost twenty years. He was one of the founders of the British Ecological Society. His books and ideas continue to influence ecologists today.

[*Gerald L. Young*]

FURTHER READING

Crowcroft, P. *Elton's Ecologists: A History of the Bureau of Animal Population*. Chicago: University of Chicago Press, 1991.

Elton, C. S. *Animal Ecology*. London: Sidgwick & Jackson, 1927.

———. *The Ecology of Invasions by Animals and Plants*. London: Methuen, 1958.

———. *The Pattern of Animal Communities*. London: Methuen, 1966.

———. *Voles, Mice and Lemmings: Problems in Population Dynamics*. Oxford: The Clarendon Press, 1942.

Hardy, A. "Charles Elton's Influence in Ecology," *The Journal of Animal Ecology* 37, no. 1, (February 1968): 1-8

Emergency Planning and Community Right-to-Know Act (1986)

The Emergency Planning and Community Right-to-Know Act (EPCRA), also known as Title III, is a statute enacted by Congress in 1986 as a part of the **Superfund Amendments and Reauthorization Act (SARA)**. It was enacted in response to public concerns raised by the accidental release of poisonous gas from a Union Carbide plant in **Bhopal, India** which killed over 2,000 people.

EPCRA has two distinct yet complementary sets of provisions. First, it requires communities to establish plans for dealing with emergencies created by chemical leaks or spills and defines the general structure these plans must assume. Second, it extends to communities the same kind of right-to-know provisions which were guaranteed to employees earlier in the 1980s. Overall, EPCRA is an important step away from crisis-by-crisis environmental enforcement toward a proactive or preventative approach. This proactive approach depends on government monitoring of potential environmental hazards, which is being accomplished by using computerized files of data submitted by businesses.

Under the provisions of EPCRA, the governors of every state were required to establish a State Emergency Response Commission by 1988. Each state commission was required in turn to establish various emergency planning districts and to appoint a local emergency planning committee for each. Each committee was required to prepare plans for potential chemical emergencies in their communities, which includes the identities of facilities, the procedures to be followed in the event of a chemical release, and the identities of community emergency coordinators as well as a facility coordinator from each business subject to EPCRA.

A facility is subject to EPCRA if it has a substance in a quantity equal to or greater than the threshold planning quantity specified on a list of about 400 extremely hazardous substances published by the **Environmental Protection Agency**. Also, after public notice and comment either the state governor or the State Emergency Response Commission may designate facilities to be covered outside of these guidelines. Each covered facility is required to provide facility notification information to the state commission and to designate a facility coordinator to work with the local planning committee.

EPCRA requires these facilities to report immediately any accidental releases of **hazardous material** to the Community Coordinator of its local emergency committee. There are two classifications for such hazardous substances. The substance must be either on the EPA's extremely hazardous substance list, or defined under the **Comprehensive Environmental Response Compensation and Liability Act** (CERCLA). In addition to the initial emergency notice, follow-up notices and information are required.

EPCRA's second major set of provisions is designed to establish and implement a community right-to-know program. Information about the presence of chemicals at facilities within the community is collected from businesses and made available to public officials and the general public. Businesses must submit two sets of annual reports: the Hazardous Chemical Inventory and **Toxic Chemicals Release Inventories** (TRIs), also known as Chemical Release Forms.

For the Hazardous Chemical Inventory, each facility in the community must prepare or obtain a Material Safety Data Sheet for each chemical on its premises meeting the threshold quantity. This information is then submitted to the Local Emergency Planning Committee, the local fire department, and the State Emergency Response Commission. These data sheets are identical to those required under the **Occupational Safety and Health Act**'s worker right-to-know provisions. For each chemical reported in the Hazardous Chemical Inventory, a Chemical Inventory Report must be filed each year.

The second set of annual reports required as a part of the community right-to-know program is the Toxic Release Inventory (TRI), which must be filed annually. Releases reported on this form include even those made legally with permits issued by the EPA and its state counterparts. Releases made by the facility into air, land, and water during the preceding twelve months are summarized in this inventory. The form must be filed by companies having ten or more employees if that company manufactures, stores, imports, or otherwise uses designated toxic chemicals at or above threshold levels.

The information submitted pursuant to both the emergency planning and the right-to-know provisions of EPCRA is available to the general public through the Local Emergency Planning Committees. In addition, health professionals may obtain access to specific chemical identities even if that information is claimed by the business to be a trade secret in order to treat exposed individuals or protect potentially exposed individuals.

During the late 1980s, the EPA and its state counterparts emphasized public awareness and education about the requirements of EPCRA, rather than enforcement. But Congress has provided stiff penalties for noncompliance, and these agencies have now begun to implement their enforcement tools. Civil penalties of up to $25,000 per day for a first violation and up to $75,000 per day for a second may be assessed against a business failing to comply with reporting requirements, and citizens have the right to sue companies that fail to report. Further, enforcement by the government may include criminal prosecution and imprisonment.

In June of 1996, in response to community pressure, the U.S. Congress took up its first major vote on Community Right to Know since 1986. In the 1996 vote, the House of Representatives removed provisions from an EPA budget appropriation which would have made substantial cuts in funds allocated to compiling of Toxics Release Inventories (TRI). In addition, Congress passed an EPA proposal that added seven additional industries to the number of industries which must report under TRI, thus bringing the total number of industries required to report to twenty-seven. Those twenty-seven include more than 31,000 facilities across the United States. These Congressional votes are viewed by environmentalists as victories for right to know. Looking ahead, EPCRA may be further strengthened through provisions included in The Children's Environmental Protection and Right to Know Act of 1997 which was introduced to Congress in May of 1997 by Rep. Henry Waxman (D) and Rep. Jim Saxton (Republican).

Studies have revealed that EPCRA has had far-reaching effects on companies and that industrial practices and attitudes toward chemical risk management are changing. Some firms have implemented new **waste reduction** programs or adapted previous programs. Others have reduced the potential for accidental releases of hazardous chemicals by developing safety audit procedures, reducing their chemical inventories, and using less hazardous chemicals in their operations.

As information included in reports such as the annual Toxics Release Inventory has been disseminated throughout the community, businesses have found they must be concerned with risk communication. Various industry groups throughout the United States have begun making the information required by EPCRA readily available and helping citizens to interpret that information. For example, the Chemical Manufacturers Association has conducted workshops for its members on communicating EPCRA information to the community and on how to communicate about risk in general. Similar seminars are now made available to businesses and their employees through trade associations, universities, and other providers of continuing education. *See also* Chemical spills; Environmental monitoring; Environmental Monitoring and Assessment Program; Hazardous

Materials Transportation Act; Toxic substance; Toxic Substances Control Act; Toxics use reduction legislation

[*Paulette L. Stenzel*]

FURTHER READING

Emergency Planning and Community Right-to-Know Act of 1986, 42 U.S.C. §11001-11050 (1986).

Stenzel, P. L. "Small Business and the Emergency Planning and Community Right-to-Know Act." *Michigan Bar Journal* (February 1990): 181-183.

Stenzel, P. L. "Toxics Use Reduction Legislation: An Important 'Next Step' After Right to Know." *Utah Law Review* 76 (1991): 707-747.

Emission

Release of material into the environment either by natural or human-caused processes. This term is used especially in describing **air pollution** for volatile or suspended contaminants that result from processes such as burning fuel in an engine. Definitions of **pollution** are complicated by the fact that many of the materials that damage or degrade our atmosphere have both human and natural origins. **Volcano**es emit ash, acid mists, hydrogen sulfide, and other toxic gases. Natural forest fires release **smoke**, soot, carcinogenic **hydrocarbons**, **dioxin**s, and other toxic chemicals as well as large amounts of **carbon dioxide**. Do these emissions constitute pollution when they originate from human sources but not if released by natural processes? Is it reasonable to restrict human emissions if there are already very large natural sources of those same materials in the environment? An important consideration in answering these questions lies in the regenerative capacity of the environment to remove or neutralize contaminants. If we overload that capacity, a marginal additional emission may be important. Similarly, if there are thresholds for response, an incremental addition to ambient levels may be very important.

Emission standards

Federal, state, and local stack and **automobile** exhaust emission limits that regulate the quantity, rate, or concentration of **emission**s. Emission standards can also regulate the opacity of **plume**s of smoke and dust from point and area emission sources. They can also assess the type and quality of fuel and the way the fuel is burned, hence the type of technology used. With the exception of plume opacity, such standards are normally applied to the specific type of source for a given pollutant. Federal standards include New Source Performance Standards (NSPS) and **National Emission Standards for Hazardous Air Pollutants (NESHAPS)**. Emission standards may include prohibitory rules that restrict existing and new source emission to specific emission concentration levels, mass emission rates, plume opacity, and emissions relative to process throughput emission rates. They may also require the most practical or best available technology in case of new emission in pristine areas.

New sources and modifications to existing sources can be subject to new source permitting procedures which require technology-forcing standards such as **Best Available Control Technology** and **Lowest Achievable Emission Rate (LAER)**. However, these standards are designed to consider the changing technological and economic feasibility of ever-more stringent emission controls. As a result, such requirements are not stable and are determined through a process involving discretionary judgements of appropriateness by the governing air pollution authority. *See also* Point source

Emissions trading

See **Trade in pollution permits**

Emphysema

Emphysema is an abnormal, permanent enlargement of the airways responsible for gas-exchange in the lungs. Primary emphysema is commonly linked to a genetic deficiency of the enzyme α_1-antitrypsin which is a major component of α_1-globulin, a plasma protein. Under normal conditions α_1-antitrypsin inhibits the activity of many proteolytic **enzyme**s which breakdown proteins. This results in the increased likelihood of developing emphysema as a result of proteolysis (breakdown) of the lung tissues.

Emphysema begins with destruction of the alveolar septa. This results in "air hunger" characterized by labored or difficult breathing, sometimes accompanied by pain. Although emphysema is genetically linked to deficiency in certain enzymes, the onset and severity of asthmatic symptoms has been definitively linked to irritants and pollutants in the **environment**. A significantly greater proportion of the individuals manifesting emphysemic symptoms is observed in smokers, populations clustered around industrial complexes, and **coal** miners. *See also* Asthma; Cigarette smoke; Respiratory diseases

Endangered species

An "endangered species" under United States law (the **Endangered Species Act (1973)**) is a creature "in danger of **extinction** throughout all or a significant portion of its range." A "threatened" species is one that is likely to become endangered in the foreseeable future.

For most people, the endangered species problem involves the plight of such well-known animals as eagles, **tigers, whales, chimpanzees, elephants, wolves**, and **whooping crane**s. However, literally millions of lesser-known or unknown **species** are endangered or becoming so,

and the loss of these life forms could have even more profound effects on humans than that of large mammals with whom we more readily identify and sympathize.

The Global 2000 Report states that "between half a million and 2 million species—15 to 20 percent of all species on earth—could be extinguished by the year 2000. . . . Extinction of species on this scale is without precedent in human history." Most experts on species extinction, such as **Edward O. Wilson** of Harvard and Norman Myers, estimate current and projected *annual* extinctions at anywhere from 15,000 to 50,000 species, or 50 to 150 *per day*, mainly invertebrates such as insects in **tropical rain forest**s. At this rate, 5 to 10 percent of the world's species, perhaps more, could be lost in the next decade and a similar percentage in coming decades.

The single most important common threat to **wildlife** worldwide is the loss of **habitat**, particularly the destruction of biologically-rich tropical rain forests. Additional factors have included commercial exploitation, the introduction of non-native species, **pollution**, hunting, and trapping. Thus, we are rapidly losing a most precious heritage, the diversity of living species that inhabit the earth. Within one generation, we are witnessing the threatened extinction of between one fifth and one half of all species on the planet.

Species of wildlife are becoming extinct at a rate that defies comprehension and threatens our own future. These losses are depriving this generation and future ones of much of the world's beauty and diversity, as well as irreplaceable sources of food, drugs, medicines, and natural processes that are or could prove extremely valuable, or even necessary, to the well-being of our society.

Today's rate of extinction exceeds that of all of the **mass extinction** in geologic history, including the disappearance of the dinosaurs 65 million years ago. It is impossible to know how many species of plants and animals we are actually losing, or even how many species exist, since many have never been "discovered" or identified. What we do know is that we are rapidly extirpating from the face of the earth countless unique life forms that will never again exist.

Most of these species extinctions will occur—and are occurring—in tropical rain forests, which are the richest biological areas on earth and are being cut down at a rate of one or two acres *a second*. Although tropical forests cover only about five to seven percent of the world's land surface, they are thought to contain over half of the species on earth.

There are more bird species in one Peruvian preserve than in the entire United States. There are more species of fish in one Brazilian river than in all the rivers of the United States. And a single square mile in lowland Peru or Amazonian Ecuador or Brazil may contain over 1500 species of butterflies, more than twice as many as are found in all of the United States and Canada. Half an acre of Peruvian rain forest may contain over 40,000 species of insects.

Eric Eckholm in *Disappearing Species: The Social Challenge* notes that when a plant species is wiped out, some 10 to 30 dependent species can also be jeopardized, such as insects and even other plants. An example of the complex relationship that has evolved between many tropical species is the 40 different kinds of fig trees native to Central America, each of which has a specific insect pollinator. Other insects, including pollinators for other plants, depend on certain of these fig trees for food.

Thus, the extinction of one species can set off a chain reaction, the ultimate effects of which cannot be foreseen. As Eckholm puts it, "Crushed by the march of civilization, one species can take many others with it, and the ecological repercussion and arrangements that follow may well endanger people." The loss of so many unrecorded, unstudied species will deprive the world not only of beautiful and interesting life forms, but also much-needed sources of medicines, drugs, and food that could be of critical value to humanity. Every day, we could be losing plants that could provide cures for **cancer** or **AIDS** or could become food staples as important as rice, wheat, or corn. We will simply never know the value or importance of the untold thousands of species vanishing each year.

As of the end of 1992, the **U.S. Department of the Interior**'s list of endangered and threatened species included 905 animals (mammals, birds, reptiles, amphibians, fish, snails, clams, crustaceans, insects, and arachnids), of which 379 arc found in the United States, and 373 plants, of which 370 are native to America.

Under the Endangered Species Act, the Department of the Interior is given general responsibility for listing and protecting endangered wildlife, except for marine species (such as whales and seals), which are the responsibilities of the Commerce Department.

In addition, the United States is subject to the provisions of the **Convention on International Trade in Endangered Species of Wild Flora and Fauna (CITES)**, which regulates global commerce in **rare species**. But in many cases, the government has not been enthusiastic about administering and enforcing the laws and regulations protecting endangered wildlife. Conservationists have for years criticized the Interior Department for its slowness and even refusal to list hundreds of endangered species that, without government protection, were becoming extinct. Indeed, the Department admits that some three dozen species have become extinct while undergoing review for listing.

In December 1992, the department settled a lawsuit brought by animal protection groups by agreeing to expedite the listing process for some 1300 species and to take a more comprehensive "multispecies, **ecosystem** approach" to protecting wildlife and their habitat. Moreover, the new Secretary of the Interior, Bruce Babbitt, is expected to make additional improvements in the Department's endangered species program. In October 1992, at the national conference of the **Humane Society of the United States** held in Boulder, Colorado, Babbitt in his keynote address lauded the Endangered Species Act as "an extraordinary achievement," emphasized the importance of preserving endangered species and biological diversity, and noted: "The extinction of a species is a permanent loss for the entire world. It is millions of years of growth and development put out forever."

But the Department is still resisting listing species that clearly need protection. In March, 1997, for example, a

federal judge ordered the Fish and Wildlife Service to reconsider its 1995 decision refusing to list the lynx as "endangered," which it first proposed to do in 1982. The Service's own biologists had warned that the large cats were nearing extinction, and that only a few hundred remained in a few areas in the lower 48 states. *See also* Biodiversity

[*Lewis G. Regenstein*]

FURTHER READING

"Endangered and Threatened Wildlife and Plants." U. S. Department of the Interior. *Federal Register* (29 August 1992).

Mitchell, G. J. *World on Fire: Saving an Endangered Earth.* New York: Charles Scribner's Sons, 1991.

Myers, N. *The Sinking Ark: A New Look at Disappearing Species.* Oxford: Pergamon Press, 1979.

———. *A Wealth of Wild Species: Storehouse for Human Welfare.* Boulder: Westview Press, 1983.

Porritt, J. *Save the Earth.* Atlanta: Turner Publishing, 1991.

Raven, P. H. "Endangered Realm." In *The Emerald Realm.* Washington, DC: National Geographic Society, 1990.

Wilson, E. O., ed. *Biodiversity.* Washington, DC: National Academy Press, 1988.

Endangered Species Act (1973)

The Endangered Species Act (ESA) is a law designed to save **species** from **extinction**. What began as an informal effort to protect several hundred North American vertebrate species in the 1960s has expanded into a program that could involve hundreds of thousands of plant and animal species throughout the world. As of November 1990, 1,117 species were listed as endangered or threatened, 596 in the United States and 521 in other countries. The law has become increasingly controversial as it has been viewed by commercial interests as a major impediment to economic development. This issue recently came to a head in the Pacific Northwest, where the **northern spotted owl** has been listed as threatened. This action has had significant affects on the regional forest products industry. The ESA was due to be re-authorized in 1992, but this was postponed due to that year's election. When the Act is considered, it will be hotly contested by environmentalists seeking to strengthen it and development interests seeking to weaken it.

Government action to protect **endangered species** began in 1964, with the formation of the Committee on Rare and Endangered Wildlife Species within the Bureau of Sport Fisheries and Wildlife [now the **Fish and Wildlife Service (FWS)**] in the **U.S. Department of the Interior**. In 1966, this committee issued a list of 83 native species (all vertebrates) that it considered endangered. Two years later, the first act designed to protect species in danger of extinction, the Endangered Species Preservation Act of 1966, was passed. The Secretary of the Interior was to publish a list, after consulting the states, of native vertebrates that were endangered. This law directed federal agencies to protect endangered species when it was "practicable and consistent with the primary purposes" of these agencies. The taking of listed endangered species was prohibited only within the

national wildlife refuge system; that is, species could be killed almost anywhere in the United States. Finally, the law authorized the acquisition of **critical habitat** for these endangered species.

In 1969, the Endangered Species Conservation Act was passed, which included several significant amendments to the 1966 Act. Species could now be listed if they were threatened with worldwide extinction. This substantially broadened the scope of species to be covered, but it also limited the listing of specific populations that might be endangered in some parts of the United States but not in danger elsewhere (e.g., **grizzly bears**, **bald eagle**s, timber **wolves**, all of which flourish in Canada and Alaska). The 1969 law stated that mollusks and crustaceans could now be included on the list, further broadening of the scope of the law. Finally, trade in illegally taken endangered species was prohibited. This substantially increased the protection offered such species, compared to the 1966 law.

The Endangered Species Act of 1973 built upon and strengthened the previous laws. The impetus for the law was a call by President Nixon in his state of the union message for further protection of endangered species and the concern in Congress that the previous acts were not working well enough. The goal of the ESA was to protect all endangered species through the use of "all methods and procedures necessary to bring any endangered or threatened species to the point at which the measures provided pursuant to [the] Act are no longer necessary." In other words, the goal was to bring endangered species to full recovery. This goal, like others included in environmental legislation at the time, was unrealistic. The ESA also expanded the number of species that could be considered for listing to all animals (except those considered **pests**) and plants. It stipulated that the listing of such species should be based on the best scientific data available. Additionally, it included a provision that allowed groups or individuals to petition the government to list or de-list a species. If the petition contained reasonable support, the agency had to respond to it.

The law created two levels of concern: endangered and threatened. An endangered species was "in danger of extinction throughout all or a significant portion of its range." A threatened species was "likely to become an endangered species within the foreseeable future throughout all or a significant portion of its range." Also, the species did not have to face worldwide extinction before it could be listed. No taking of any kind was allowed for endangered species; limited taking could be allowed for threatened species. Thus, the distinction between "endangered" and "threatened" species allowed for some flexibility in the program.

The 1973 Act divided jurisdiction of the program between the FWS and the National Marine Fisheries Service (NMFS), an agency of the **National Oceanic and Atmospheric Administration** in the Department of Commerce. The NMFS would have responsibility for species that were primarily marine; responsibility for marine mammals (**whales**, **dolphins**, etc.) was shared by the two agencies. The law also provided for the establishment of cooperative agreements between the federal government and the states on endan-

gered species protection. This has not proved very successful due to a lack of funds to entice the states to participate and due to frequent conflict between the states (favoring development and hunting) and the FWS.

The most controversial aspect of the Act was Section 7, which required that no action by a federal agency, such as the destruction of critical habitat, jeopardize any endangered species. So, before undertaking, funding, or granting a permit for a project, federal agencies had to consult with the FWS as to the effect the action might have on endangered species. This provision proved to have enormous consequences, as many federal developments could be halted due to their affect on endangered species. The most famous and controversial application of this provision involved the **snail darter** and **Tellico Dam** in Tennessee. The **Tennessee Valley Authority** (TVA) was building the nearly completed dam when the snail darter was listed as endangered. Its only known **habitat** would be destroyed if the dam was completed. The TVA challenged the FWS evidence, but the TVA was itself soon challenged in the courts by environmentalists. In a case that was appealed through the Supreme Court, *TVA v. Hill*, the courts ruled that the ESA was clear: no federal action could take place that would jeopardize an endangered species. The dam could not be completed.

In response to the conflicts that followed the passage of the ESA, especially the swelling estimates of the number of endangered species and the snail darter-Tellico Dam issue, the 1978 re-authorization of the ESA included heated debate and a few significant changes in the law. Perhaps the most important change was the creation of the Endangered Species Committee, sometimes referred to as the "God Committee." Created in response to the snail darter controversy and the *TVA v. Hill* decision, this committee could approve federal projects that were blocked due to their harmful effects on endangered species. If an agency's actions were blocked due to an endangered species, they could appeal to this committee for an exemption from the ESA. The committee, which consists of three cabinet secretaries, the administrators of the EPA and NOAA, the chair of the Council of Economic Advisors, and the governor from the state in which the project is located, weigh the advantages and disadvantages of the project and then make a decision as to the appeal. Ironically, the committee heard the appeal for Tellico Dam and rejected it. The committee has only been used three times, and only once, regarding the northern spotted owl and 1,700 acres (689 ha) of land in Oregon, has it approved an appeal. Nonetheless, the creation of the "God Committee" demonstrated that values beyond species survival had to be weighed into the endangered species equation.

Additionally, the 1978 amendments mandated: increased public participation and hearings when species were proposed for listing; a five-year review of all species on the list (to determine if any had improved to the point that they could be removed from the list); a requirement that the critical habitat of a species must be specified at the time the species is listed and that an economic assessment of the critical habitat designation must be done; the mandatory development of a recovery plan for each listed species; and a time limit between when a species was proposed for listing and when the final rule listing the species must be issued. These amendments were designed to do two things: to provide a loophole for projects that might be halted by the ESA and to speed up the listing process. Despite this latter goal, the many new requirements included in the amendments led to a further slowing of the listing process. It should also be noted that these amendments passed with overwhelming majorities in both the House and the Senate; there was still strong support for protecting endangered species, at least in the abstract, in Congress.

The 1982 re-authorization of the ESA did not lead to significant changes in the Act. The law was to have been re-authorized again in 1985, but opposition in the Senate prevented re-authorization until 1988. This demonstrated the growing uneasiness in Congress to the economic repercussions of the ESA. In addition to re-authorizing spending to implement the ESA through 1992, the 1988 amendments also increased the procedural requirements for recovery plans. This further underscored the tension between the desire for public participation at all stages of ESA implementation and the need for the government to move quickly to protect endangered species. Overall, the implementation of the ESA has not been successful. The law has suffered from two main problems: poor administrative capacity and fragmentation. The FWS has suffered from its lack of stature within the bureaucracy, its conflicting institutional mission, a severe lack of funds and personnel, and limited public support. Species assigned to the NMFS have fared even worse, as the agency has shown little interest in the ESA. Fragmentation is demonstrated with the division of responsibilities between the FWS and NMFS, the conflict with other federal agencies due to Section 7, and the federal-state conflicts over jurisdictional responsibility.

[*Christopher McGrory Klyza*]

FURTHER READING

Egan, T. "Strongest U. S. Environmental Law May Become Endangered Species." *New York Times* (26 May 1992): A1.

Harrington, W., and A. C. Fisher. "Endangered Species." In *Current Issues in Natural Resource Policy*, edited by P. R. Portney. Baltimore: Johns Hopkins University Press, 1982.

Kohm, K. A., ed. *Balancing on the Brink of Extinction: The Endangered Species Act and Lessons for the Future.* Washington, DC: Island Press, 1990.

Tobin, R. *The Expendable Future: U. S. Politics and the Protection of Biological Diversity.* Durham, NC: Duke University Press, 1990.

Endemic species

Endemic species are plants and animals that exist only in one geographic region. **Species** can be endemic to large or small areas of the earth: some are endemic to a particular continent, some to part of a continent, and others to a single island. Usually an area that contains endemic species is isolated in some way, so that species have difficulty spreading to other areas, or it has unusual environmental characteristics to which endemic species are uniquely adapted. Endemism, or the occurrence of endemic animals and plants, is more common in some regions than in others. In isolated **environment**s such as the **Hawaiian Islands**, Australia, and the southern tip of Africa, as many as 90 percent of naturally-occurring species are endemic. In less isolated regions, including Europe and much of North America, the percentage of endemic species can be very small.

Biologists who study endemism do not only consider species, the narrowest classification of living things; they also look at higher level classifications of genus, family, and order. These hierarchical classifications are nested so that, in most cases, an order of plants or animals contains a number of families, each of these families includes several genera (plural of "genus"), and each genus has a number of species. These levels of classification are known as "taxonomic" levels.

Species is the narrowest taxonomic classification, with each species closely adapted to its particular environment. Therefore species are often endemic to small areas and local environmental conditions. Genera, a broader class, are usually endemic to larger regions. Families and orders more often spread across continents. As an example, the order Rodentia, or rodents, occurs throughout the world. Within this order, the family Heteromyidae occurs only in western North America and the northern edge of South America. One member of this family, the genus *Dipodomys*, or kangaroo rats, is restricted to several western states and part of Mexico. Finally, the species *Dipodomys ingens*, occurs only in a small portion of the California coast. Most often endemism is considered on the lowest taxonomic levels of genus and species.

Animals and plants can become endemic in two general ways. Some evolve in a particular place, adapting to the local environment and continuing to live within the confines of that environment. This type of endemism is known as "autochthonous," or native to the place where it is found. An "allochthonous" endemic species, by contrast, originated somewhere else but has lost most of its earlier geographic range. A familiar autochthonous endemic species is the Australian koala, which evolved in its current environment and continues to occur nowhere else. A well-known example of allochthonous endemism is the California coast **redwood** (*Sequoia sempervirens*), which millions of years ago ranged across North America and Eurasia, but today exists only in isolated patches near the coast of northern California. Another simpler term for allochthonous endemics is "relict," meaning something that is left behind.

In addition to geographic relicts, plants or animals that have greatly restricted ranges today, there are what is known as "taxonomic relicts." These are species or genera that are sole survivors of once-diverse families or orders. **Elephants** are taxonomic relicts: millions of years ago the family Elephantidae had 25 different species (including woolly mammoths) in 5 genera. Today only two species remain, one living in Africa (*Loxodonta africana*) and the other in Asia (*Elephas maximus*). Horses are another familiar species whose family once had many more branches. Ten million years ago

North America alone had at least 10 genera of horses. Today only a few Eurasian and African species remain, including the **zebra** and the ass. Common horses, all members of the species *Equus caballus*, returned to the New World only with the arrival of Spanish conquistadors.

Taxonomic relics are often simultaneously geographic relics. The ginkgo tree, for example was one of many related species that ranged across Asia 100 million years ago. Today the family Ginkgoales contains only one genus, *Ginkgo*, with a single species, *Ginkgo biloba*, that occurs naturally in only a small portion of eastern China. Similarly the coelacanth, a rare fish found only in deep waters of the Indian Ocean near Madagascar, is the sole remnant of a large and widespread group that flourished hundreds of millions of years ago.

Where living things become relict endemics, some sort of environmental change is usually involved. The redwood, the elephant, the ginkgo, and the coelacanth all originated in the Mesozoic era, 245 to 65 million years ago, when the earth was much warmer and wetter than it is today. All of these species managed to survive catastrophic environmental change that occurred at the end of the Cretaceous period, changes that eliminated dinosaurs and many other terrestrial and aquatic animals and plants. The end of the Cretaceous was only one of many periods of dramatic change; more recently 2 million years of cold **ice age**s and warmer interglacial periods in the Pleistocene substantially altered the distribution of the world's plants and animals. Species that survive such events to become relicts do so by adapting to new conditions or by retreating to isolated refuges where habitable environmental conditions remain.

When endemics evolve in place, isolation is a contributing factor. A species or genus that finds itself on a remote island can evolve to take advantage of local food sources or environmental conditions, or its characteristics may simply drift away from those of related species because of a lack of contact and interbreeding. Darwin's Galapagos finches, for instance, are isolated on small islands, and on each island a unique species of finch has evolved. Each finch is now endemic to the island on which it evolved. Expanses of water isolated these evolving finch species, but other sharp environmental gradients can contribute to endemism, as well. The humid southern tip of Africa, an area known as the Cape region, has one of the richest plant communities in the world. A full 90 percent of the Cape's 18,500 plant species occur nowhere else. Separated from similar **habitat** for millions of years by an expanse of dry **grasslands** and **desert**, local families and genera have divided and specialized to exploit unique local **niche**s. Endemic speciation, or the evolution of locally unique species, has also been important in Australia, where 32 percent of genera and 75 percent of species are endemic. Because of its long isolation, Australia even has family-level endemism, with 40 families and sub-families found only on Australia and a few nearby islands.

Especially high rates of endemism are found on long-isolated islands, such as St. Helena, New Caledonia, and the Hawaiian chain. St. Helena, a volcanic island near the middle of the Atlantic, has only 60 native plant species, but 50 of these exist nowhere else. Because of the island's distance from any other landmass, few plants have managed to reach or colonize St. Helena. Speciation among those that have reached the remote island has since increased the number of local species. Similarly Hawaii and its neighboring volcanic islands, colonized millions of years ago by a relatively small number of plants and animals, now has a wealth of locally-evolved species, genera, and sub-families. Today's 1,200 to 1,300 native Hawaiian plants derive from about 270 successful colonists; 300 to 400 arthropods that survived the journey to these remote islands have produced over 6,000 descendent species today. Ninety-five percent of the archipelago's native species are endemic, including all ground birds. New Caledonia, an island midway between Australia and Fiji, consists partly of continental rock, suggesting that at one time the island was attached to a larger land mass and its resident species had contact with those of the mainland. Nevertheless, because of long isolation 95 percent of native animals and plants are endemic to New Caledonia.

Ancient, deep lakes are like islands because they can retain a stable and isolated habitat for millions of years. Siberia's **Lake Baikal** and East Africa's Lake Tanganyika are two notable examples. Lake Tanganyika occupies a portion of the African Rift Valley, 0.9 miles (1.5 km) deep and perhaps 6 million years old. Fifty percent of the lake's snail species are endemic, and most of its fish are only distantly related to the fish of nearby Lake Nyasa. Siberia's Lake Baikal, another rift valley lake, is 25 million years old and One mile (1.6 km) deep. Eighty-four percent of the lake's 2,700 plants and animals are endemic, including the nerpa, the world's only freshwater seal.

Because endemic animals and plants by definition have limited geographic ranges, they can be especially vulnerable to human invasion and habitat destruction. Island species are especially vulnerable because islands commonly lack large predators, and many island endemics evolved without defenses against predation. Cats, dogs, and other carnivores introduced by sailors have decimated many island endemics. The **flora** and **fauna** of Hawaii, exceptionally rich before Polynesians arrived with pigs, rats, and agriculture, were severely depleted because their range was limited and they had nowhere to retreat as human settlement advanced. **Tropical rain forest**s, with extraordinary species diversity and high rates of endemism, are also vulnerable to human invasion. Many of the species eliminated daily in Amazonian rain forests are locally endemic, so that their entire range can be eliminated in a short time. *See also* Adaptation; Biodiversity; Biogeography; Climate; Ecology; Endangered species; Introduced species; Rare species; Relict species

[*Mary Ann Cunningham*]

FURTHER READING

Berry, E. W. "The Ancestors of the Sequoias." *Natural History* 20 (1920): 153-55.

Brown, J. H., and A. C. Gibson *Biogeography*. St. Louis: Mosby, 1983.

Cox, G. W. *Conservation Biology*. Dubuque, IA: William C. Brown, 1993.

Kirch, P. "The Impact of the Prehistoric Polynesians on the Hawaiian Ecosystem." *Pacific Science* 36 (1982): 1-14.

Nitecki, M. W., ed. *Extinctions*. Chicago: University of Chicago Press, 1984.

Energy and the environment

Energy is a prime factor in environmental quality. Extraction, processing, shipping, and combustion of **coal**, oil, and **natural gas** are the largest sources of air pollutants, thermal and chemical **pollution** of surface waters, accumulation of mine tailings and toxic ash, and land degradation caused by surface mining in the United States.

On the other hand, a cheap, inexhaustible source of energy would allow us people to eliminate or repair much of the environmental damage done already and to improve the quality of the **environment** in many ways. Often, the main barrier to reclaiming degraded land, cleaning up polluted water, destroying wastes, restoring damaged **ecosystem**s, or remedying most other environmental problems is that solutions are expensive—and much of that expense is energy costs. Given a clean, sustainable, environmentally benign energy source, people could create a true utopia and extend its benefits to everyone.

Our ability to use external energy to do useful work is one of the main characteristics that distinguishes humans from other animals. Clearly, technological advances based on this ability have made our lives much more comfortable and convenient than that of our early ancestors. They have also allowed us to make bigger mistakes, faster than ever before. A large part of our current environmental crisis is that our ability to modify our environment has outpaced our capacity to use energy and technology wisely.

In the United States, **fossil fuels** supply about eighty-five percent of the commercial energy. This situation cannot continue for very long because the supplies of these fuels are limited and their environmental effects are unacceptable. Americans now get more than half of their oil from foreign sources at great economic and political costs. At current rates of use, known, economically extractable world supplies of oil and natural gas will probably last only a century or so. Reserves of coal are much larger, but coal is the dirtiest of all fuels. Its contribution of **greenhouse gases** that cause global warming are reason enough to curtail our coal use. In addition, coal burning is the largest single source in the United States of **sulfur dioxide** and **nitrogen oxides** (which cause respiratory health problems, ecosystem damage, and acid precipitation). Paradoxically, coal-burning power plants also release **radioactivity**, since radioactive minerals such as **uranium** and thorium are often present in low concentrations in coal deposits.

Nuclear power was once thought to be an attractive alternative to fossil fuels. Billed as "the clean energy alternative" and as an energy source "too cheap to bother metering," nuclear power was promoted in the 1960s as the energy source for the future. The disastrous consequences of accidents in nuclear plants, such as the explosion and fire at **Chernobyl** in the Ukraine in 1986, problems with releases of radioactive materials in mining and processing of fuels, and the inability to find a safe, acceptable permanent storage of nuclear waste have made nuclear power seem much less attractive in recent years. Between seventy and ninety percent of the citizens of most European and North American countries now regard nuclear power as unacceptable.

The United States Government once projected that 1,500 nuclear plants would be built. In 1992, only 107 plants were in operation and no new construction has been undertaken since 1975. Many of these aging plants are now reaching the end of their useful life. There will be enormous costs and technical difficulties in dismantling them and disposing of the radioactive debris. Some reactor designs are inherently safer than those now in operation, but public confidence in nuclear power technology is at such a low level that it seems unlikely that it will never supply much energy. Damming rivers to create hydroelectric power from spinning water turbines has the attraction of providing a low-cost, renewable, air pollution-free energy source. Only a few locations remain in the United States, however, where large hydroelectric projects are feasible. Many more sites are available in Canada, Brazil, India, and other countries, but the social and ecological effects of building large **dams**, flooding valuable river valleys, and eliminating free-flowing rivers are such that opposition is mounting to this energy source.

An example of the ecological and human damage done by large hydroelectric projects is seen in the **James Bay** region of Eastern Quebec. A series of huge dams and artificial lakes have flooded thousands of square miles of forest. Migration routes of caribou are disrupted, the habitat for game on which **indigenous people** depended is destroyed, and decaying vegetation has acidified waters, releasing **mercury** from the bedrock and raising mercury concentrations in fish to toxic levels. The hunting and gathering way of life of local Cree and Inuit people has probably been destroyed forever. This kind of tragedy has been repeated many times around the world by ill-conceived hydro projects.

There are several sustainable, environmentally benign energy sources that should be developed. Among these are wind power, **biomass** (burning renewable energy crops such as fast-growing trees or shrubs), small-scale hydropower (low head or run-of-the- river turbines), passive-solar space heating, active-solar water heaters, photovoltaic energy (direct conversion of sunlight to electricity), and ocean tidal or **wave power**. There may be unwanted environmental consequences of some of these sources as well, but they seem much better in aggregate than current energy sources. A big disadvantage is that most of these **alternative energy sources** are diffuse and not always available when or where we want to use energy.

We need ways to store and ship energy generated from these sources. There have been many suggestions that a breakthrough in battery technology could be on the horizon. Other possibilities include converting biomass into **methane** or **methanol** fuels or using electricity to generate **hydrogen** gas through electrolysis of water. These fuels would be easily storable, transportable, and used with current technology without great alterations of existing systems. It is estimated that some combination of these sustainable energy sources could supply all of American energy needs by utilizing only a small fraction (perhaps less than one percent) of United States land area. If means are available to move this energy efficiently, these energy farms could be in remote locations with little other value.

Clearly, the best way to protect the environment from damage associated with energy production is to use energy more efficiently. Many experts estimate that people could enjoy the same comfort and convenience but use only half as much energy if they practiced energy conservation using currently available technology. This would not require great sacrifices economically or in one's lifestyle. *See also* Acid rain; Air pollution; Greenhouse effect; Photovoltaic cell; Solar energy; Thermal pollution; Wind energy

[*William P. Cunningham*]

FURTHER READING

Davis, G. R. *Energy for Planet Earth*. New York: W. H. Freeman, 1991.

Häfele, W. "Energy from Nuclear Power." *Scientific American* 263 (September 1990): 136-42+.

Lenssen, N. "Providing Energy in Developing Countries." *State of the World 1993*. New York: Norton, 1993.

Weinberg, C. J., and R. H. Williams. "Energy from the Sun." *Scientific American* 263 (September 1990): 146-55.

Energy conservation

Energy conservation was a concept largely unfamiliar to America—and to much of the rest of the world—prior to 1973. Certainly some thinkers prior to that date thought about, wrote about, and advocated a more judicious use of the world's energy supplies. But in a practical sense, it seemed that the world's supply of **coal**, oil, and **natural gas** was virtually unlimited.

In 1973, however, the **Organization of Petroleum Exporting Countries** (OPEC) placed an arbitrary limit on the amount of petroleum that non-producing nations could buy from them. Although the OPEC embargo lasted only a short time, the nations of the world were suddenly forced to consider the possibility that they might have to survive on a reduced and ultimately finite supply of the **fossil fuels**.

In the United States, the OPEC embargo set off a flurry of administrative and legislative activity, designed to ensure a dependable supply of energy for the nation's further needs. Out of this activity came acts such as the Energy Policy and Conservation Act of 1976, the Energy Conservation and Production Act of 1976, and the National Energy Act of 1978.

An important feature of the nation's (and the world's) new outlook on energy was the realization of how much energy is wasted in transportation, residential and commercial buildings, and industry. When energy supplies appeared to be without limit, waste was a matter of small concern. However, when energy shortages began to be a possibility, conservation of energy sources assumed a high priority.

Energy conservation is certainly one of the most attainable goals the federal government can set for the United States. Almost every way we use energy results in enormous waste. Only about 20 percent of the energy content of **gasoline**, for example, is actually put to productive work in an **automobile**. Each time we make use of electricity, we produce waste when coal is burned to heat water to drive a turbine to operate a generator to make electricity. No wonder more than ninety percent of the energy generated in the electrical process is wasted.

Fortunately, a vast array of conservation techniques are available in each of the major categories of energy use: transportation, residential and commercial buildings, and industry. In the area of transportation, conservation efforts focus on the nation's use of the private automobile for most personal travel. Certainly, the private automobile is an enormously wasteful method for moving people from one place to another. It is hardly surprising, therefore, that conservationists have long argued for the development of alternative means of transportation: bicycles, motorcycles, mopeds, carpools and van-pools, dial-a-rides, and various forms of **mass transit**. The amount of energy needed to move a single individual on the average is about one-third on a bus what it is in a private car. One need only compare the relative energy cost per passenger for eight people travelling in a commuter van-pool to the cost for a single individual in her private automobile to see the advantages of some form of mass transit.

For a number of reasons, however, mass transit systems in the United States are not very popular. While the number of new cars sold continues to rise year after year, investment in and use of heavy and light rail systems, trolley systems, subways and various types of pools remain modest.

Many authorities believe that the best hope for energy conservation in the field of transportation is to make private automobiles more efficient or to increase the tax on their use. Some experts argue that technology already exists for the construction of 100-mile-per-gallon (42.5 km/liter) automobiles if industry will make use of that technology. They also argue for additional research on electric cars as an energy-saving and pollution-reducing alternative to internal **combustion** vehicles.

Increasing the cost of using private automobiles has also been explored. One approach is to raise the tax on gasoline to a point where commuters begin to consider mass transit as an economical alternative. Increased parking fees and more aggressive traffic enforcement have also been tried. Such approaches often fail—or are never attempted—because public officials are reluctant to anger voters.

Other methods that have been suggested for increasing **energy efficiency** in automobiles include the design and construction of smaller, lighter cars, extending the useful life of a car, improving the design of cars and tires, and encouraging the design of more efficient cars through federal grants or tax credits.

The concept of energy-efficient buildings is relatively new. Until recently, architects, contractors, and owners gave little thought to reducing the costs of heating and cooling a building. A dramatic example of this philosophy is New York City's World Trade Center, which uses as much electricity as a city of 100,000 people. None of the windows in the 110-story building can be opened, so no amount of natural heating or cooling is possible. As originally designed, the building's automatic heating and cooling system functions in exactly the same way whether the building is full or empty.

A number of techniques are well known and could be used, however, to conserve energy in buildings as large as the World Trade Center or as small as a two-room cottage. A thorough insulation of floors, walls, and ceilings, for example, can save up to 80 percent of the cost of heating and cooling a building.

In addition, buildings can be designed and constructed to take advantage of natural heating and cooling factors in the environment. A home in Canada, for example, should be oriented with windows oriented toward the south so as to take advantage of the sun's heating rays. A home in Mexico might have quite a different orientation.

One of the most extreme examples of environmental-friendly buildings are those that have been constructed at least partially underground. The earthen walls of these buildings provide a natural cooling effect in the summer and provide excellent insulation during the winter.

The kind, number, and placement of trees around a building can also contribute to energy efficiency. Trees that lose their leaves in the winter will allow sunlight to heat a building during the coldest months, but will shield the building from the sun during the hot summer months.

Energy can also be conserved by modifying appliances used within a building. Prior to 1973, consumers became enamored with all kinds of electrical devices, from electric toothbrushes to electric shoe-shine machines to trash compactors. As convenient as these appliances may be, they are energy wasteful and do not always meet a basic human need.

Even items as simple as light bulbs can become a factor in energy conservation programs. Fluorescent light bulbs use at least 75 percent less energy than do incandescent bulbs, and they often last twenty times longer. Although many commercial buildings now use fluorescent lighting exclusively, it still tends to be relatively less popular in private homes.

As the largest single user of energy in American society, industry is a prime candidate for conservation measures. Always sensitive to possible money-saving changes, industry has begun to develop and implement energy savings devices and procedures. One such idea is **cogeneration**, the use of waste heat from an industrial process for use in the generation of electricity.

Another approach is the expanded use of **recycling** by industry. In many cases, re-using a material requires less energy than producing it from raw materials. Finally, researchers are continually testing new designs for equipment that will allow that equipment to operate on less energy.

Governments and utilities have two primary methods by which they can encourage energy conservation. One approach is to penalize individuals and companies that use too much energy. For example, an industry that uses large amounts of electricity might be charged at a higher rate per kilowatt hour than one that uses less electricity, a policy just the opposite of that now in practice in most places.

A more positive approach is to encourage energy conservation by techniques such as tax credits. Those who insulate their homes might, for example, be given cash bonuses by the local utility or a tax deduction by state or federal government.

In recent years, another side of energy conservation has come to the fore, its environmental advantages. Obviously, the less coal, oil, and natural gas that humans use, the fewer pollutants are released into the environment. Thus, a practice that is energy-wise, conservation, can also provide environmental benefits. Those concerned with global warming and climate change have been especially active in this area. They point out that reducing our use of fossil fuels will both reduce our consumption of energy and our release of **carbon dioxide** to the atmosphere. We can take a step toward heading off climate change, they point out, by taking the wise step of wasting less energy.

Energy conservation does not yet appear to have won the heart of most Americans. The general public concern about energy waste engendered by the 1973 OPEC **oil embargo** eventually dissolved into complacency. To be sure, some of the sensitivity to energy conservation created by that event has not been lost. Many people have switched to more energy-efficient forms of transportation, think more carefully about leaving house lights on all night, and take energy efficiency into consideration when buying major appliances.

But some of the more aggressive efforts to conserve energy have become stalled. Higher taxes on gasoline, for example, still are certain to raise an enormous uproar among the populace. And energy-saving construction steps that might well be mandated by law still remain optional, and frequently ignored.

In an era of apparently renewed confidence in an endless supply of fossil fuels, many people are no longer convinced that energy conservation is very important or have the will to act on their suspicion that it is. And governments, reflecting the will of the people, do not take leadership action to change that trend.

[*David E. Newton*]

FURTHER READING

Fardo, S. *Energy Conservation Guidebook*. Englewood Cliffs, NJ: Prentice Hall, 1993.

Reisner, M. "The Rise and Fall and Rise of Energy Conservation." *Amicus Journal* 9 (Spring 1987): 22-31.

Energy crops

See **Biomass**

Energy efficiency

The utilization of energy for human purposes is a defining characteristic of industrial society. The conversion of energy from one form to another and the efficient production of mechanical work for heat energy has been studied and improved for centuries. The science of thermodynamics deals with the relationship between heat and work and is based on two fundamental laws of nature, the first and second laws of thermodynamics. The utilization of energy and the conservation of critical, nonrenewable energy resources are controlled by these laws and the technological improvements in the design of energy systems.

The First Law of Thermodynamics states the principle of conservation of energy: energy can be neither created nor destroyed by ordinary chemical or physical means, but it can be converted from one form to another. Stated another way, *in a closed system, the total amount of energy is constant.* An interesting example of energy conversion is the incandescent light bulb. In the incandescent light bulb, electrical energy is used to heat a wire (the bulb filament) until it is hot enough to glow. The bulb works satisfactorily except that the great majority (95 percent) of the electrical energy supplied to the bulb is converted to heat rather than light. The incandescent bulb is not very efficient as a source of light. In contrast, a fluorescent bulb uses electrical energy to excite atoms in a gas, causing them to give off light in the process at least four times more efficiently than the incandescent bulb. Both light sources, however, conform to the First Law in that no energy is lost and the total amount of heat and light energy produced is equal to the amount of electrical energy flowing to the bulb.

The Second Law of Thermodynamics states that whenever heat is used to do work, some heat is lost to the surrounding environment. The complete conversion of heat into work is not possible. This is not the result of inefficient engineering design or implementation but, rather, a fundamental and theoretical thermodynamic limitation. The maximum, theoretically possible efficiency for converting heat into work depends solely on the operating temperatures of the heat engine and is given by the equations: $E = 1 - T_2/T_1$. T_1 is the absolute temperature at which heat energy is supplied and T_2 is the absolute temperature at which heat energy is exhausted.

The maximum possible thermodynamic efficiency of a four-cycle internal **combustion** engine is about 54 percent; for a diesel engine, the limit is about 56 percent; and for a steam engine, the limit is about 32 percent. The actual efficiency of real engines, which suffer from mechanical inefficiencies and parasitic losses (eg. friction, drag, etc.) is significantly lower than these levels. Although thermodynamic principles limit maximum efficiency, substantial improvements in energy utilization can be obtained through further development of existing equipment such as **power plants**, refrigerators, and **automobile**s and the development of new energy sources such as solar and geothermal.

Experts have estimated the efficiency of other common energy systems. The most efficient of these appear to be electric power generating plants (33 percent efficient) and steel plants (23 percent efficient). Among the least efficient systems are those for heating water (1.5-3 percent), for heating homes and buildings (2.5-9 percent), and refrigeration and air-conditioning systems (4-5 percent). It has been estimated that about 85 percent of the energy available in the United States is lost due to inefficiency.

The predominance of low efficiency systems reflects the fact that such systems were invented and developed when energy costs were low and there was little customer demand for energy efficiency. It made more sense then to build appliances that were inexpensive rather than efficient because the cost to operate them was so low. Since the 1973 **oil embargo** by the **Organization of Petroleum Exporting Countries (OPEC)**, that philosophy has been carefully re-examined. Experts began to point out that more expensive appliances could be designed and built if they were also more efficient. The additional cost to the manufacturer, industry and homeowner could usually be recovered within a few years because of the savings in fuel costs.

The concept of energy efficiency suggests a new way of looking at energy systems and that is the examination of the total lifetime energy use and cost of the system. Consider the common light bulb. The total cost of using a light bulb includes both its initial price and the cost of operating it throughout its lifetime. When energy was cheap, this second factor was small. There was little motivation to make a bulb that was more efficient when the life-cycle savings for its operation was minimal.

But as the cost of energy rises, that argument no longer holds true. An inefficient light bulb costs more and more to operate as the cost of electricity rises. Eventually, it makes sense to invent and produce more efficient light bulbs. Even if these bulbs cost more to buy, they pay back that cost in long-term operating savings.

Thus, consumers might balk at spending $25 for a fluorescent light bulb unless they knew that the bulb would last ten times as long as an incandescent bulb that costs $3.75. Similar arguments can and have been used to justify the higher initial cost of energy-saving refrigerators, solar-heating systems, household insulation, improved internal combustion engines and other energy-efficient systems and appliances.

Governmental agencies, utilities, and industries are gradually beginning to appreciate the importance of increasing energy efficiency. The 1990 amendments to the **Clear Air Act** encourage industries and utilities to adopt more efficient equipment and procedures. Certain leaders in the energy field, such as Pacific Gas and Electric and Southern California Edison have already implemented significant energy efficiency programs. Pacific Gas and Electric, for example, expects to meet three-quarters of its new demand through the year 2000 with efficiency and conservation procedures.

[*David E. Newton and Richard A. Jeryan*]

FURTHER READING

Council on Environmental Quality. *Environmental Quality*, 21st annual report. Washington, DC: U. S. Government Printing Office, 1990.

Miller, G. T., Jr. *Energy and Environment: The Four Energy Crises.* 2nd edition. Belmont, CA: Wadsworth Publishing Company, 1980.

Sears, F. W. and M. W. Zemansky. *University Physics.* 2nd edition. Reading, MA: Addison-Wesley Publishing, 1957.

Energy flow

Understanding energy flow is vital to many environmental issues. One can describe the way **ecosystem**s function by saying that matter cycles and energy flows. This is based on the laws of conservation of matter and energy and the second **law of thermodynamics**, or the law of energy degradation.

Energy flow is strictly one way, such as from higher to lower or from hotter to colder. Objects cool only by loss of heat. All cooling units, such as refrigerators and air conditioners, are based on this principle: they are essentially heat pumps, absorbing heat in one place and expelling it to another.

This heat flow is explained by the laws of radiation, as seen in fire and the color wheel. All objects emit radiation, or heat loss, but the hotter the object the greater the amount of radiation, and the shorter and more energetic the wavelength. As energy intensities rise and wavelengths shorten, the radiation changes from infrared to red, then orange, yellow, green, blue, violet, and ultraviolet. A blue flame, for example, is desired for gas appliances. A well-developed wood fire is normally yellow, but as the fire dies out and cools, the color gradually changes to orange, then red, then black. Black coals may still be very hot, giving off invisible, infrared radiation. These varying wavelengths are the main differences seen in the electromagnetic spectrum.

All chemical reactions and **radioactivity** emit heat as a by-product. Because this heat radiates out from the source, the basis of the second law of thermodynamics, one can never achieve 100 percent **energy efficiency**. There will always be a heat-loss tax. One can slow down the rate of heat loss through insulating devices, but never stop it. As the insulators absorb heat, their temperatures rise and they in turn lose heat.

There are three main applications of energy flow to environmental concerns. First, only 10 percent of the food passed on up the **food chain/web** is retained as body mass; 90 percent flows to the **atmosphere** as heat. In terms of caloric efficiency, more calories are obtained by eating plant food than meat. Since fats are more likely to be part of the 10 percent retained as body mass, **pesticide**s dissolved in fat are subject to **bioaccumulation** and **biomagnification**. This explains the high levels of **DDT** in birds of prey like the **peregrine falcon** (*Falco peregrinus*) and the **brown pelican** (*Pelecanus occidentalis*).

Second, the percentage of waste heat is an indicator of energy efficiency. In light bulbs, 5 percent produces light and 95 percent heat, just the opposite of the highly efficient fire fly. Electrical generation from **fossil fuels** or **nuclear power** produces vast amounts of waste heat.

Third, control of heat flow is a key to comfortable indoor air and solving global warming. Well-insulated buildings retard heat flow, reducing energy use. Atmospheric **greenhouse gases**, such as **anthropogenic carbon dioxide** and **methane**, retard heat flow to space, which theoretically should cause global temperatures to rise. Poli-

cies that reduce these greenhouse gases allow a more natural flow of heat back to space. *See also* Greenhouse effect

[*Nathan H. Meleen*]

FURTHER READING

"Energy." *National Geographic* 159 (February 1981): 2-23.

Fowler, J. M. *Energy and the Environment.* 2nd ed. New York: McGraw-Hill, 1984.

Miller, G. T., Jr. *Energy and Environment: the Four Energy Crises.* 2nd ed. Belmont, CA: Wadsworth, 1980.

U. S. Department of Agriculture. *Cutting Energy Costs: 1980 Yearbook of Agriculture.* Washington, DC: U. S. Government Printing Office, 1980.

Energy Information Administration
See **U. S. Department of Energy**

Energy path, hard vs. soft

What will energy use patterns in the year 2100 look like? Such long-term predictions are difficult, risky, and perhaps impossible. Could an American citizen in 1860 have predicted what the pattern of today's energy use would be like?

Yet, there are reasons to believe that some dramatic changes in the ways we use energy may be in store over the next century. Most importantly, the world's supplies of non-renewable energy—especially, **coal**, oil, and **natural gas**—continue to decrease. Critics have been warning for a least two decades that time was running out for the **fossil fuels** and that we could not count on using them as prolifically as we had in the past.

For at least two decades, experts have debated the best way to structure our energy use patterns in the future. The two most common themes have been described (originally by physicist **Amory Lovins**) as the "hard path" and the "soft path."

Proponents of the hard path argue essentially that we should continue to operate in the future as we have in the past, except more efficiently. They point out that predictions from the 1960s and 1970s that our oil supplies would be depleted by the end of the century have been proved wrong. If anything, our reserves of fossil fuels may actually have increased as economic incentives have encouraged further exploration.

Our energy future, the hard-pathers say, should focus on further incentives to develop conventional energy sources such as fossil fuels and **nuclear power**. Such incentives might include tax breaks and subsidies for coal, **uranium** and **petroleum** companies. When our supplies of fossil fuels do begin to be depleted, our emphasis should shift to a greater reliance on nuclear power.

An important feature of the hard energy path is the development of huge, centralized coal-fired and nuclear-powered plants for the generation of electricity. One characteristic of most hard energy proposals, in fact, is the emphasis on very large, expensive, centralized systems. For example, one would normally think of solar energy as a part of the soft energy path. But one proposal developed by the National Aeronautics and Space Administration (NASA) calls for a gigantic solar power station to be orbited around the earth. The station could then transmit power via microwaves to centrally-located transmission stations at various points in the Earth's surface.

Those who favor a soft energy path have a completely different scenario in mind. Fossil fuels and nuclear power must diminish as sources of energy as soon as possible, they say. In their place, alternative sources of power such as hydropower, **geothermal energy**, **wind energy**, and **photovoltaic cell**s must be developed.

In addition, the soft-pathers say, we should encourage conservation to extend coal, oil, and natural gas supplies as long as possible. Also since electricity is one of the most wasteful of all forms of energy, its use should be curtailed.

Most importantly, soft-path proponents maintain energy systems of the future should be designed for small-scale use. The development of more efficient solar cells, for example, would make it possible for individual facilities to generate a significant portion of the energy they need.

Underlying the debate between hard- and soft-pathers is a fundamental question as to how society should operate. On the one hand are those who favor the control of resources in the hands of a relatively small number of large corporations. On the other hand are those who prefer to have that control decentralized to individual communities, neighborhoods, and families. The choice made between these two competing philosophies will probably determine which energy path the United States and the world will ultimately follow. *See also* Alternative energy sources; Alternative fuels; Energy and the environment

[*David E. Newton*]

FURTHER READING

Lovins, A. *Soft Energy Paths.* San Francisco: Friends of the Earth, 1977.

———. "World Energy Strategies, Parts 1 and 2." *Bulletin of the Atomic Scientists* (March 1973): 29–35.

Miller, G. T., Jr. *Energy and Environment: The Four Energy Crises.* 2nd ed. Belmont, CA: Wadsworth 1980.

Energy policy

Energy policies are the actions governments take to affect the demand for energy as well as the supply of it. These actions include the ways in which governments cope with energy supply disruptions and their efforts to influence energy consumption and economic growth.

The energy policies of the United States government have often worked at cross purposes, both stimulating and suppressing demand. Taxes are perhaps the most important kind of energy policy, and **energy taxes** are much lower in the U. S. than in other countries. This is partially responsible for the fact that energy consumption per capita is higher than elsewhere, and there is less incentive to invest in **conservation** or alternative technologies. Following the 1973 Arab **oil embargo**, the federal government instituted price controls which kept energy prices lower than they would otherwise have been, thereby stimulating consumption. Yet the government also instituted policies at the same time, such as fuel-economy standards for automobiles, which were designed to increase conservation and lower energy use. Thus, policies in the period after the embargo were contradictory: what one set of policies encouraged, the other discouraged.

The United States government has a long history of different types of interference in energy markets. The Natural Gas Act of 1938 gave the **Federal Power Commission** the right to control prices and limit new pipelines from entering the market. In 1954 The Supreme Court extended price controls to field production. Before 1970, the Texas Railroad Commission effectively controlled oil output (in the United States) through prorationing regulations that provided multiple owners with the rights to underground pools. The federal government provided tax breaks in the form of intangible drilling expenses and gave the oil companies a depletion allowance. A program was also in place from 1959 to 1973 which limited oil imports and protected domestic producers from cheap foreign oil. The ostensible purpose of this policy was maintaining national security, but it contributed to the depletion of national reserves.

After the oil embargo, Congress passed the Emergency Petroleum Allocation Act giving the federal government the right to allocate fuel in a time of shortage. In 1974 President Gerald Ford announced Project Independence which was designed to eliminate dependence on foreign imports. Congress passed the Federal Non-Nuclear Research and Development Act in 1974 to focus government efforts on non-nuclear research. Finally, in 1977 Congress approved the cabinet-level creation of the **U. S. Department of Energy** (DOE) which had a series of direct and indirect policy approaches at its disposal, designed to encourage and coerce both the energy industry as well as the commercial and residential sectors of the country to make changes. After Ronald Reagan became president, many DOE programs were abolished, though DOE continued to exist, and the net impact has probably been to increase economic uncertainty.

Energy policy issues have always been very political in nature. Different segments of the energy industry have often been differently affected by policy changes, and various groups have long proposed divergent solutions. The energy crisis, however, intensified these conflicts. Advocates of strong government action called for policies which would alter consumption habits, reducing dependence on foreign oil and the nation's vulnerability to an oil embargo. They have been opposed by proponents of free markets, some of whom considered the government itself responsible for the crisis. Few issues were subject to such intensive scrutiny and fundamental conflicts over values as energy policies were during this period. Interest groups representing causes from **energy conservation** to **nuclear power** mobilized. Business interests also expanded their lobbying efforts.

An influential advocate of the period was **Amory Lovins**, who helped create the renewable energy movement.

His book, *Soft Energy Paths: Toward A Durable Peace* (1977), argued that energy problems existed because large corporations and government bureaucracies had imposed expensive centralized technologies like **nuclear power** on society. Lovins argued that the solution was in small scale, dispersed, technologies. He believed that the "hard path" imposed by corporations and the government led to an authoritarian, militaristic society while the "soft path" of small-scale dispersed technologies would result in a diverse, peaceful, self-reliant society.

Because **coal** was so abundant, many in the 1970s considered it a solution to American dependence on foreign oil, but this expectation has proved to be mistaken. During the 1960s, the industry had been controlled by an alliance between management and the union, but this alliance disintegrated by the time of the energy crisis, and wildcat strikes hurt productivity. Productivity also declined because of the need to address safety problems following passage of the 1969 Coal Mine Health and Safety Act. Environmental issues also hurt the industry following passage of the **National Environmental Policy Act** of 1969, the **Clean Air Act** of 1970, the **Clean Water Act** of 1972, and the 1977 **Surface Mining Control and Reclamation Act**. Worker productivity in the mines dropped sharply from 19 tons per worker day to 14 tons, and this decreased the advantage coal had over other fuels. The 1974 Energy Supply and Environmental Coordination Act and the 1978 Fuel Use Act, which required utilities to switch to coal, had little effect on how coal was used because so few new plants were being built.

Other energy-consuming nations responded to the energy crises of 1973-74 and 1979-80 with policies that were different from the United States. Japan and France, although via different routes, made substantial progress in decreasing their dependence on Mideast oil. Great Britain was the only major industrialized nation to become completely self-sufficient in energy production, but this fact did not greatly aid its ailing economy. When energy prices declined and then stabilized in the 1980s, many consuming nations eliminated the conservation incentives they had put in place.

Japan is the most heavily petroleum-dependent industrialized nation. To pay for a high level of energy and raw material imports, Japan must export the goods which it produces. When energy prices increased after 1973, it was forced to expand exports. The rate of economic growth in Japan began to decline. Annual growth in GNP averaged nearly 10 percent from 1963-1973, and from 1973-1983 it was just under 4 percent, although the association between economic growth and energy consumption has weakened.

The Energy Rationalization Law of 1979 was the basis for Japan's energy conservation efforts, providing for the financing of conservation projects and a system of tax incentives. It has been estimated that over 5 percent of total Japanese national investment in 1980 was for energy-saving equipment. In the cement, steel, and chemical industries over 60 percent of total investment was for energy conservation, Japanese society shifted from **petroleum** to a reliance on

other forms of energy including nuclear power and **liquefied natural gas**.

In France, energy resources at the time of the oil embargo were extremely limited. It possessed some natural gas, coal, and hydropower, but together these sources constituted only 0.7 percent of the world's total energy production. By 1973, French dependence on foreign energy had grown to 76.2 percent: oil made up 67 percent of the total energy used in France, up from 25 percent in 1960.

France had long been aware of its dependence on foreign energy and had taken steps to overcome it. Political instability in the Mideast and North Africa had led the government to take a leading role in the development of civilian nuclear power after World War II. In 1945 Charles de Gaulle set up the French Atomic Energy Commission to develop military and peaceful uses for nuclear power. The nuclear program proceeded at a very slow pace until the 1973 embargo, after which there was rapid growth in France's reliance on nuclear power. By 1990, more than 50 reactors had been constructed and over 70 percent of France's energy came from nuclear power. France now exports electricity to nearly all its neighbors, and its rates are about the lowest in Europe. Starting in 1976 the French government also subsidized 3,100 conservation projects at a cost of more than 8.4 billion francs, and these subsidies were particularly effective in encouraging energy conservation.

Concerned about oil supplies during World War I, the British government had taken a majority interest in British Petroleum and tried to play a leading role in the search for new oil. After the World War II, the government nationalized the coal, gas, and electricity industries, creating, for ideological reasons as well as for postwar reconstruction, the National Coal Board, British Gas Corporation, and Central Electricity Generating Board. After the discovery of oil reserves in the 1970s in the North Sea, the government established the British National Oil Company. This government corporation produced about 7 percent of North Sea oil and ultimately handled about 60 percent of the oil produced there.

All the energy sectors in the United Kingdom were thus either partially or completely nationalized. Government relations with the nationalized industries often were difficult, because the two sides had different interests. The government intervened to pursue macroeconomic objectives such as price restraint, and it attempted to stimulate investment at times of unemployment. The electric and gas industries had substantial operating profits and they could finance their capital requirements from their revenues, but profits in the coal industry were poor, the work force was unionized, and opposition to the closure of uneconomic mines was great. Decision-making was highly politicized in this nationalized industry, and the government had difficulty addressing the problems there. It was estimated that 90 percent of mining losses came from 30 of the 190 pits in Great Britain, but only since 1984-85 has there been rapid mine closure and enhanced productivity. New power-plant construction was also poorly managed, and comparable coal-fired power stations cost twice as much in Great Britain as in France or Italy.

The Conservative Party proposed that the nationalized energy industries be privatized. However, with the exception of coal, these energy industries had natural monopoly characteristics: economies of scale and the need to prevent duplicate investment in fixed infrastructure. The Conservative Party called for regulation after privatization to deal with the natural monopoly characteristics of these industries, and it took many steps toward privatization. In only one area, however, did it carry its program to completion, abolishing the British National Oil Company and transferring its assets to private companies. *See also* Alternative energy sources; Corporate Average Fuel Efficiency Standards; Economic growth and the environment; Electric utilities; Energy and the environment; Energy efficiency; Energy path, hard vs. soft

[*Alfred A. Marcus*]

FURTHER READING

Marcus, A. A. *Controversial Issues in Energy Policy*. Phoenix, AZ: Sage Press, 1992.

Energy recovery

A fundamental fact about energy use in modern society is that huge quantities are lost or wasted in almost every field and application. For example, the series of processes by which nuclear energy is used to heat a home with electricity results in a loss of about 85 percent of all the energy originally stored in the **uranium** used in the nuclear reactor. Industry, utilities, and individuals could use energy far more efficiently if they could find ways to recover and reuse the energy that is being lost or wasted.

One such approach is **cogeneration**, the use of waste heat for some useful purpose. For example, a factory might be redesigned so that the steam from its operations could be used to run a turbine and generate electricity. The electricity could then be used elsewhere in the factory or sold to power companies. Cogeneration in industry can result in savings of between 10 and 40 percent of energy that would otherwise be wasted.

Cogeneration can work in the opposite direction also. Hot water produced in a utility plant can be sold to industries that can use it for various processes. Proposals have been made to use the wasted heat from electricity plants to grow flowers and vegetables in greenhouses, to heat water for commercial fish and shell-fish farms, and to maintain warehouses at constant temperatures. The total **energy efficiency** resulting from this sharing is much greater than it would be if the utility's water was simply discarded.

Another possible method of recovering energy is by generating or capturing **natural gas** from **biomass**. For example, as organic materials decay naturally in a **landfill**, one of the products released is **methane**, the primary component of natural gas. Collecting methane from a landfill is a relatively simple procedure. Vertical holes are drilled into the landfill and porous pipes are sunk into the holes. Methane diffuses into the pipes and is drawn off by pumps. The recovery system at the Fresh Kills landfill on Staten Island, New York, for example, produces enough methane to heat 10,000 homes.

Biomass can also be treated in a variety of ways to produce methane and other combustible materials. Sewage, for example, can be subjected to **anaerobic digestion**, the primary product of which is methane. Pyrolysis is a process in which organic wastes are heated to high temperatures in the absence of oxygen. The products of this reaction are solid, liquid, and gaseous **hydrocarbons** whose composition is similar to those of **petroleum** and natural gas. Perhaps the most known example of this approach is the manufacture of **methanol** from biomass. When mixed with gasoline, a new fuel, **gasohol**, is obtained.

Energy can also be recovered from biomass simply by **combustion**. The waste materials left after sugar is extracted from sugar cane, known as *bagasse*, have long been used as a fuel for the boilers in which the sugar extraction occurs. The burning of **garbage** has also been used as an energy source in a wide variety of applications such as the heating of homes in Sweden, the generation of electricity to run streetcars and subways in Milan, Italy, and the operation of a desalination plant in Hempstead, Long Island.

The recovery of energy that would otherwise be lost or wasted has a secondary benefit. In many cases, that wasted energy might cause pollution of the **environment**. For example, the wasted heat from an electric power plant may result in **thermal pollution** of a nearby waterway. Or the escape of methane into the **atmosphere** from a landfill could contribute to **air pollution**. Capture and recovery of the waste energy not only increases the efficiency with which energy is used, but may also reduce some pollution problems.

[*David E. Newton*]

FURTHER READING

Franke, R. G., and D. N. Franke. *Man and the Changing Environment*. New York: Holt, Rinehart and Winston, 1975.

Moran, J. M., M. D. Morgan, and J. H. Wiersma. *Introduction to Environmental Science*. 2nd ed. New York: W. H. Freeman, 1986.

Energy Reorganization Act (1973)

Passed in 1974 during the Ford Administration, this act created the **Energy Research and Development Administration** (ERDA) and **Nuclear Regulatory Commission** (NRC). The purpose of the act was to begin an extensive non-nuclear federal research program, separating the regulation of the **nuclear power** from research functions. Regulation was carried out by the NRC, while nuclear power research was carried out by the ERDA. The passage of the 1974 Energy Reorganization Act ended the existence of the **Atomic Energy Commission**, which had been the main instrument to implement nuclear policy. In 1977 ERDA incorporated into the newly created **U.S. Department of Energy**. *See also* Alternative energy sources; Energy policy

Energy Research and Development Administration

This agency was created in 1974 from the non-regulatory parts of the **Atomic Energy Commission** (AEC), and it existed until 1977, when it was incorporated into the **U.S. Department of Energy**. In its short life span, the Energy Research and Development Administration (ERDA) started to diversify U.S. energy research outside of **nuclear power**. Large-scale demonstration projects were begun in numerous areas. These included projects to convert **coal** and **solid waste**s into liquid and gaseous fuels; experiments on methods to extract and process **oil shale** and tar sands, as well as an effort to develop a viable breeder reactor that would ensure a virtually inexhaustible source of **uranium** for electricity. The agency also supported research on **solar energy** for space heating, industrial process heat, and electricity. In the short time available, basic problems could not be solved, and the achievements of many of the demonstration projects were disappointing. Nevertheless, many important advances were made in commercializing cost-effective technologies for energy **conservation**, such as energy-efficient lighting systems, improved heat pumps, and better heating systems. The agency also conducted successful research in environmental, safety, and health areas.

Energy taxes

The main energy tax levied in the United States is the one on **petroleum**, though the U. S. tax is half of the amount levied in other major industrialized nations. As a result, **gasoline** prices in the United States are much lower than elsewhere, and both environmentalists and others have argued that this encourages energy consumption and **environmental degradation** and causes national and international security problems.

In 1993, the House passed a **Btu** tax while the Senate passed a more modest tax on transportation fuels. A Btu tax would restrict the burning of **coal** and other **fossil fuels** and proponents maintain that this would be both environmentally and economically beneficial. Every barrel of oil and every ton of coal that is burned adds **greenhouse gases** to the **atmosphere**, increasing the likelihood that **future generations** will face a global climatic calamity. United States dependence on foreign oil, much of it from potentially unstable nations like Iraq, now approaches 50 percent. A Btu tax would create incentives for **energy conservation**, and it would help stimulate the search for alternatives to oil. It would also help reduce the burgeoning trade deficit, of which foreign petroleum and petroleum-based products now constitute nearly 40 percent.

President Bill Clinton has urged Americans to support higher energy taxes because of the considerable effect they could have on the federal budget deficit. For instance, if the government immediately raised gasoline prices to levels commonly found in other industrial nations (about $4.15 a gallon), the budget deficit would almost be eliminated. It is estimated that every penny increase in gasoline taxes, yields a billion dollars in revenue for the federal treasury, and in January 1993 the budget deficit was estimated to be about $300 billion.

Of course, to raise gasoline taxes immediately to these levels is utterly impractical, as the effects on the economy would be catastrophic. It would devastate the economics of rural and western states. Inflation across the country would soar and job losses would skyrocket. Supporters of increasing energy taxes agree that the increases must be gradual and predictable, so people can adjust. Many believe they should take place over a 15 year period, after which energy prices in the United States would be roughly equivalent to those in other industrial nations.

Many economists emphasize that the positive effects of higher energy taxes will be felt only if there are no increases in government spending. It is, they believe, ultimately a question of how Americans want to be taxed. Do they want wages, profits, and savings to be taxed, as they are now, or their use of energy? In the former case, the government is taxing a desirable activity which should be encouraged for the sake of job creation and economic expansion. In the latter case, it is taxing undesirable activity which should be discouraged for the sake of protecting the **environment** and preserving national security. *See also* Energy policy; Environmental economics

[*Alfred A. Marcus*]

FURTHER READING

Marcus, A. A. *Controversial Issues in Energy Policy*. Phoenix, AZ: Sage Press, 1992.

Eniwetok Atoll
See **Bikini Atoll**

Enteric bacteria

Enteric bacteria are defined as bacteria which reside in the intestines of animals. Members of the Enterobacteriaceae family, enteric bacteria are important because some of them symbiotically aid the digestion of their hosts, while other *pathogenic* species cause disease or death in their host organism. The pathogenic members of this family include species from the genera *Escherichia*, *Salmonella*, *Shigella*, *Klebsiella*, and *Yersinia*. All of these **pathogen**s are closely associated with fecal contamination of foods and water. In North America, the reported incidence of salmonellosis outweighs the occurrence of all of the other reportable diseases by other enteric bacteria combined.

Most infections from enteric pathogens require large numbers of organisms to be ingested by immunocompetent adults, with the exception of *Shigella*. Symptoms include gastrointestinal distress and diarrhea. The enteric bacteria related to *Escherichia coli* are known as the *coliform* bacteria. Coliform bacteria are used as indicators of pathogenic enteric bacteria in drinking and recreational waters. *See also* Sewage treatment

Entrainment
See **Air Pollution**

Environment

When people say "I am concerned about the environment," what do they mean? What does the use of the definite article mean in such a statement? Is there such a thing as "the" environment?

Environment is derived from the French words *environ* or *environner*, meaning "around," "round about," "to surround," "to encompass"; these in turn originated from the Old French *virer* and *viron* (together with the prefix *en*), which mean "a circle, around, the country around, or circuit." Etymologists frequently conclude that, in English usage at least, *environment* is the total of the things or circumstances around an organism—including humans—though *environs* is limited to the "surrounding neighborhood of a specific place, the neighborhood or vicinity."

Even a brief etymological encounter with the word environment provokes two persuasive suggestions for possible structuring of a contemporary definition. First, the word environment is identified with a totality, the everything that encompasses each and all of us, and this association is established enough to be not lightly dismissed. The very notion of "environment," as Anatol Rapoport indicated, suggest the partitioning of a "portion of the world into regions, an inside and an outside." The environment is the outside. Second, the word's origin in the phrase "to environ" indicates a process derivative, one that alludes to some sort of action or interaction, at the very least inferring that the encompassing is active, in some sense reciprocal, that the environment, whatever its nature, is not simply an inert phenomenon to be impacted without response or without affecting the organism in return. Environment must be a relative word, because it always refers to something "environed" or enclosed.

Ecology as a discipline is focused on studying the interactions between an organism of some kind and its environment. So ecologists must be concerned with what H. L. Mason and J. H. Langenheim described as a "key concept in the structure of ecological knowledge," but a concept with which ecologists continue to have problems of confusion between ideas and reality—the concept of environment. Mason and Langenheim's article "Language Analysis and the Concept Environment" continues to be the definitive statement on the use of the word environment in experimental ecology.

The results of Mason and Langenheim's analysis were essentially four-fold: 1) they limited environmental phenomena "in the universal sense" to only those phenomena that have an operational relation with any organism: other phenomena present that do not enter a reaction system are excluded, or dismissed as not "environmental phenomena"; 2) they restricted the word environment itself to mean "the class composed of the sum of those phenomena that enter a reaction system of the organism or otherwise directly impinge upon it" so that physical exchange or impingement becomes the clue to a new and limited definition; 3) they specifically note that their definition does not allude to the larger meaning implicit in the etymology of the word; and 4) they designate their limited concept as *operational environment* but state that when the word environment is used with qualification, then it still refers to the operational construct, establishing that "'environment' per se is synonymous with 'operational environment'."

This definition does allow a prescribed and limited conception of environment and might work for experimental ecology but is much too limited for general usage. Environmental phenomena of relevance to the aforementioned concern for "the" environment must incorporate a multitude of things other than those that physically impinge on each human being. And it is much more interactive and overlapping than a restricted definition would have people believe. To better understand contemporary human interrelationships with the world around them, environment must be an incorporative, holistic term and concept.

Thinking about the environment in the comprehensive sense—with the implication that *everything* is the environment with each entity connected to each of a multitude of others—makes environment what David Currie in a book of case studies and material on **pollution** described "as not a modest concept." But, such scope and complexity, difficult as they are to resolve, intensify rather than eliminate the very real need for a kind of transcendence. The assumption seems valid that human consciousness regarding environment needs to be raised, not restricted. Humans need increasingly to comprehend and care about what happens in far away places and to people they do not know but that do affect them, that do impact even their localized environments, that do impinge on their individual well-being. And they need to incorporate the reciprocal idea that their actions impact people and environments outside the immediate in place and time: in the world today, environmental impacts transcend the local. Thus it is necessary that human awareness of those impacts also be transcendent.

It is uncertain that confining the definition of environment to operationally narrow physical impingement could advance this goal. One suspects instead that it would significantly retard it, a retardation that contemporary human societies can ill afford. Internalization of a larger environment, including an understanding of common usages of the word, might on the other hand aid people in caring about, and assuming responsibility for, what happens to that environment and to the organisms in it.

An operational definition can help people find the mechanisms to deal with problems immediate and local, but can, if they are not careful, limit them to an unacceptable mechanistic and unfeeling approach to problems in the environment-at-large.

Acceptance of either end of the spectrum—a limited operational definition or an incorporative holistic definition—as the only definition creates more confusion than clarification. Both are needed. Outside the laboratory, however, in study of the interactional, interdependent world of contemporary humankind, the holistic definition must have a place. A sense of the comprehensive "out there," of the totality of world and people as a functionally significant, interacting unit should be seeping into the consciousness of every person.

Carefully chosen qualifiers can help deal with the complexity: "natural" or "built" or "perceptual" all specify aspects of human surroundings more descriptive and less incorporative than "environment" used alone, without adjectives. Other noun can also pick up some of the meanings of environment, though none are direct synonyms: **habitat**, milieu, mis en scence, ecumene all designate specified and limited aspects of the human environment, but none except "environment" are incorporative of the whole complexity of human surroundings.

An understanding of environment must not be limited to an abstract concept that relates to daily life only in terms of whether to recycle cans or walk to work. The environment is the base for all life, the source of all goods. Poor people in underdeveloped nations know this; their day-to-day survival depends on what happens in their local environments. Whether it rains or does not, whether commercial seiners move into local fishing grounds or leave them alone, and whether local forest products are lost to the cause of world timber production affect these people more directly. What they, like so many other humans around the world, may not also recognize, is that "environment" now extends far beyond the bounds of the local: environment is the intimate enclosure of the individual or a local human population *and* the global domain of the human species.

The Brundtland report **Our Common Future** recognized this with a healthy, modern definition: "The environment does not exist as a sphere separate from human actions, ambitions, and needs, and attempts to defend it in isolation from human concerns have given the word 'environment' a connotation of naivety in some political circles." The report goes on to note that "the 'environment' is where we all live . . . and 'development' is what we all do in attempting to improve our lot within that abode. The two are inseparable."

Each human being lives in a different environment than any other human because every single one screens their surroundings through their own individual experience and perceptions. Yet all human beings live in the same environment, an external reality that all share, draw sustenance from, and excrete into. So understanding environment becomes a dialectic, a resolution and synthesis of individual characteristics and shared conditions. Solving environmental problems depends on the intelligence exhibited in that resolution.

[*Gerald L. Young*]

FURTHER READING

Bates, M. *The Human Environment.* Berkeley: University of California, School of Forestry, 1962.

Dubos, R. "Environment." *Dictionary of the History of Ideas*, edited by P. P. Wiener. New York: Charles Scribner's Sons, 1973.

Mason, H. L., and J. H. Langenheim. "Language Analysis and the Concept Environment." *Ecology* 38 (April 1957): 325–340.

Patten, B. C. "Systems Approach to the Concept of Environment." *Ohio Journal of Science* 78 (July 1978): 206–222.

Young, G. L. "Environment: Term and Concept in the Social Sciences." *Social Science Information* 25 (March 1986): 83–124.

Environment Canada

Environment Canada is the agency with overall responsibility for the development and implementation of policies related to environmental protection, monitoring, and research within the government of Canada. Parts of this mandate are shared with other federal agencies, including those responsible for agriculture, forestry, fisheries, and **nonrenewable resources** such as minerals. Environment Canada also works with the **environment**-related agencies of Canada's ten provincial and two territorial governments through such groups as the Canadian Council of Ministers of the Environment.

The head of Environment Canada is a minister of the federal cabinet, who is "responsible for policies and actions to preserve and enhance the quality of the environment for the benefit of present and future generations of Canadians."

In 1990, following a lengthy and extensive consultation process organized by Environment Canada, the Government of Canada released its *Canada's Green Plan for a Healthy Environment*, which details the broader goals, as well as many specific objectives, to be pursued towards achieving a state of ecologically sustainable economic development in Canada. The first and most general of the national objectives under the *Green Plan* is to "secure for current and future generations a safe and healthy environment, and a sound and prosperous economy."

The *Green Plan* is intended to set a broad environmental framework for all government activities and objectives, including the development of policies. The government of Canada has specifically committed to working toward the following priority objectives: (1) clean air, water, and land; (2) **sustainable development** of **renewable resources**; (3) protection of special places and **species**; (4) preserving the integrity of northern Canada; (5) global environmental security; (6) environmentally responsible decision making at all levels of society; and (7) minimizing the effects of environmental emergencies. Environment Canada will play the lead role in implementing the vision of the *Green Plan* and in coordinating the activities of the various agencies of the government of Canada.

In order to be able to integrate the dual challenges of a new environmental agenda (set by the expectations of Canadians in general and the federal government in particular) and the need to continue to deliver traditional programs, Environment Canada is moving from a three-program to a one-program administrative structure. Under that single program, six activities are coordinated: (1) the Atmospheric Environment Service activity, through which information is provided and research conducted on weather, **climate**, oceanic conditions, and **air quality**; (2) the Conservation and Protection Service activity, which focuses on special species and places, global environmental integrity, the integrity of Canadian **ecosystem**s, environmental emergencies, and ecological and economic interdependence; (3) the Canadian Parks Service activity, concentrating on the ecological and cultural integrity of special places, as well as on environmental and cultural citizenship; (4) the Corporate Environmental Affairs activity, dealing with environmentally responsible decision making and ecosystem-science leadership; (5) the State of the Environment Reporting activity, through which credible and comprehensive environmental information, linked with socio-economic considerations, is provided to Canadians; and (6) the Administration activity, covering corporate management and services. *See also* Environment; Future generations.

[Bill Freedman]

FURTHER READING

Canada's Green Plan for a Healthy Environment. Ottawa: Government of Canada, 1990.

Environment Canada. *Annual Report, 1988-1990.* Ottawa: Government of Canada, 1990.

Environmental accounting

A system of national or business accounting where such environmental assets as air, water, and land are not considered to be free and abundant resources but instead are considered to be scarce economic assets. Any environmental damage caused by the production process must be treated as an economic expense and entered on the balance sheet accordingly. It is important to include in this framework the full environmental cost occurring over the full life cycle of a product, including not only the environmental costs incurred in the production process, but also the environmental costs resulting from use, **recycling** and disposal of products. This is also known as the cradle-to-grave approach. *See also* Ecological economics

Environmental aesthetics

In his journal, **Henry David Thoreau** asked in 1859 "In what book is this world and its beauty described? Who has plotted the steps toward the discovery of beauty?" Almost a 100 years later, in his book *The Sand County Almanac*, ecologist **Aldo Leopold** addressed Thoreau's question by advocating what he called a "**conservation** esthetic" as the door to appreciating the richness of the natural world, and a resulting conservation ethic.

Leopold suggested that increased ecological awareness would more finely tune people's perception of the world around them. The word aesthetics is, after all, derived from the Greek word *aisthesis*, literally "perception by the senses." Leopold claimed that perception, "like all real treasures of the

mind, can be split into infinitely small fractions without losing its quality," a necessity if we are to revive our appreciation of the richness and diversity of the world that surrounds us. Instead, he thought that most recreationists are like "motorized ants who swarm the continents before learning to see [their] own back yard," so that recreational development becomes "a job not of building roads into lovely country, but of building receptivity into the still unlovely human mind."

Despite the fact that Thoreau and Leopold are both widely read by environmentalists and others, aesthetics has remained largely the domain of philosophy, and environmental aesthetics until recently a neglected domain in general. In philosophy, aesthetics has developed quite narrowly as an esoteric subdiscipline focused on theories of the arts, but a philosophy exclusive of **nature** and **environment**. An environmental philosophy has emerged in recent years, but this has developed mainly from the ethics tradition in philosophy and has, for some reason, neglected the aesthetic tradition (though Sepänmaa, and some other philosophers, have tried to encourage an environmental aesthetics at the intersection of traditions: on the environment as an aesthetic object and on environmental aesthetics as the philosophy of environmental criticism). While extensive literature has emerged on environmental ethics, the gap left by philosophy for environmental aesthetics has been filled by writers in a number of disciplines, notably psychology and geography, especially through empirical research on perception. Yi Fu Tuan's pioneering works (e.g., *Topophilia*, in 1974) broadened the study of aesthetics, transcended his own discipline of geography, and continue to shape the debate today about the content and concepts appropriate to an environmental aesthetic.

In classical aesthetics, sight and hearing are considered the primary senses since they are most immediately involved in the contemplation and appreciation of art and music. Arguably, the other three senses—touch, smell, and taste—must also be brought to bear for a true sensing of all the arts. Certainly, all five of the basic senses are central to an environmental aesthetic, an aesthetic sense, as Berleant notes, of all "the continuities that join integrated human persons with their natural and cultural condition." To achieve this, Berleant suggests, requires what he calls "an integrated sensorium," a "recognition of synaesthesia," i.e., a "fusion of the sense modalities." He claims that "perception is not passive but an active, reciprocal engagement with environment"; environmental aesthetics is what Berleant calls "an aesthetics of engagement."

Aesthetic engagement with environment involves not only the five senses, but the individual, behavioral and personal history of each person, as well as the cultural context and continuity in which that person has developed. An environmental aesthetic is "always contextual, mediated by the [long and complex] variety of conditions and influences that shape all [human] experience." An environmental aesthetic is also contingent on place. A sense of place, or a developed, knowledgeable understanding of the place in which one lives, is central to a well-developed environmental aesthetic. This can lead to greater engagement with place, and more involvement with local planning and land-use decisions, among other issues.

An understanding of environmental aesthetics cannot be attained without some notion of how the word and concept 'environment' itself is defined. Before recent publications on environmental aesthetics, most writers on the subject focused on the beauty of nature, for example as experienced in the national parks of the United States. As a more formal environmental aesthetics has emerged, the definition of environment (and environmental beauty) has enlarged. Sepänmaa, for example, defines "environmental aesthetics [as] the aesthetics of the real world" and includes in this "all of the observer's external world: the natural environment, the cultural environment, and the constructed environment."

Berleant also claims that "the idea of an aesthetic environment is a new concept that enlarges the meaning of environment." But he considers environment not only as everything "out there," but as "everything that there is; it is all-inclusive, a total, integrated, continuous process." This conception is hard to grasp but "nonetheless soberly realistic, for it recognizes that ultimately everything affects everything else, that humans along with all other things inhabit a single intraconnected realm." Berleant's conception of environment "does not differentiate between the human and the natural and...interprets everything as part of a single, continuous whole." He advocates "the largest idea of environment [which] is the natural process as people live it, however they live it. Environment is nature experienced, nature lived." An environmental aesthetic then, depends on education in **human ecology**, on more complete understanding of how people connect with other people, and of how they interact with a wide range of environments, local to global.

Better understanding is both a result of, and a cause of, more engagement with place and surroundings. The resulting connections and commitment have ramifications for the design and planning of the built environment, and for exploiting and managing the natural environment. Aesthetics, in this ecological, integrated sense, can contribute to cost-benefit decisions about how we use the environments in which we live, including city and regional planning, and in design at all levels, from individual artifact to our grasp of the global realities of the contemporary world.

Berleant argues that environmental perception becomes an aesthetic only through a complete understanding of the totality. Though that is not possible for any one person, an appreciation of the richness and diversity of the earth's natural and human domain is necessary to achieve such an aesthetic. An environmental aesthetic then is necessarily complex, but it can also provide simple commandments for everyday life: as Thoreau suggested, "to affect the quality of the day, that is the highest of arts."

[*Gerald L. Young*]

FURTHER READING

Bartuska, T. J., and G.L. Young. "Aesthetics and Ecology: Notes on the Circle and the Sphere." *Journal of Aesthetic Education* 9 (1975): 78-91.

Berleant, A. *The Aesthetics of Environment*. Philadelphia, PA: Temple University Press, 1992.

Kemal, S., and I. Gaskell, eds. *Landscape, Natural Beauty and the Arts.* Cambridge, UK: Cambridge University Press, 1993.

Nasar, J.L., ed. *Environmental Aesthetics: Theory, Research, and Applications.* New York: Cambridge University Press, 1988.

Sepänmaa, Y. *The Beauty of Environment: A General Model for Environmental Aesthetics*. Helsinki, Finland: Suomalainen Tiedeakatemia, 1986.

Environmental auditing

The environmental auditing movement gained momentum in the early 1980s as companies beset by new liabilities associated with Superfund and old **hazardous waste** sites wanted to insure that their operations were adhering to federal and local policies and company procedures. Most audits were initiated to avoid legal conflicts, and many companies brought in outside consultants to do the audits. The audits served many useful functions, including increasing management and employee awareness of environmental issues and initiating data collection and central monitoring of matters previously not watched as carefully. In many companies environmental auditing played a useful role in organizing information about the environment. It paved the way for the **pollution** prevention movement which had a great impact on company environmental management in the late 1980s when some companies started to view all of their pollution problems comprehensively and not in isolation from one another.

Environmental chemistry

Environmental chemistry refers to the occurrence, movements, and transformations of chemicals in the **environment**. Environmental chemistry deals with naturally occurring chemicals such as metals, other elements, organic chemicals, and biochemicals that are the products of biological metabolism. Environmental chemistry also deals with synthetic chemicals that have been manufactured by humans and dispersed into the environment, such as **pesticide**s, **polychlorinated biphenyls (PCBs)**, **dioxins**, furans, and many others.

The occurrence of chemicals refers to their presence and quantities in various compartments of the environment and **ecosystem**s. For example, in a terrestrial ecosystem such as a forest, the most important compartments to consider are the mineral **soil**, water and air present in spaces within the soil, the above-ground **atmosphere**, dead **biomass** within the soil and lying on the ground as logs and other organic debris, and living organisms, the most abundant of which are trees. Each of these components of the forest ecosystem contains a wide variety of chemicals in some concentration, and in some amount. Chemicals move between all of these compartments, as fluxes that represent elements of nutrient and mineral cycles.

The movements of chemicals within and among compartments often involve a complex of transformations among potential molecular states. There may also be changes in physical states, such as evaporation of liquids, or crystallization of dissolved substances. The transformations of chemicals among molecular states can be illustrated by reference to the environmental cycling of sulfur. Sulfur (S) is commonly emitted to the atmosphere as the gases sulfur dioxide (SO_2) or hydrogen sulfide (H_2S), which are transformed by photochemical reactions into the negatively-charged ion, sulfate (SO_4^{-2}). The sulfate may eventually be deposited with precipitation to a terrestrial ecosystem, where it may be absorbed along with soil water by tree roots, and later used to synthesize biochemicals such as proteins and amino acids. Eventually, the plant may die and its biomass deposited to the soil surface as litter. Microorganisms can then metabolize the organic matter as a source of energy and nutrients, eventually releasing simple inorganic compounds of sulfur such as sulfate or hydrogen sulfide into the environment. Alternatively, the plant biomass may be harvested by humans and used as a fuel, with the organic sulfur being oxidized during **combustion** and emitted to the atmosphere as **sulfur dioxide**. Organic and mineral forms of sulfur also occur in **fossil fuels** such as **petroleum** and **coal**, and the combustion of those materials also results in an **emission** of sulfur dioxide to the atmosphere.

Contamination and Pollution

Contamination and **pollution** both refer to the presence of chemicals in the environment, but it is useful to distinguish between these two conditions. Contamination refers to the presence of one or more chemicals in concentrations higher than normally occurs in the ambient environment, but not high enough to cause biological or ecological damages. In contrast, pollution occurs when chemicals occur in the environment in concentrations high enough to cause damages to organisms. Pollution results in toxicity and ecological changes, but contamination does not cause those damages.

Chemicals that are commonly involved in pollution include the gases sulfur dioxide and ozone, diverse kinds of pesticides, elements such as **arsenic, copper, mercury, nickel**, and selenium, and some naturally occurring biochemicals. In addition, large concentrations of nutrients such as phosphate and nitrate can cause eutrophication, a type of pollution associated with excessive ecological productivity. Although any of these chemicals can cause pollution in certain situations, they most commonly occur in concentrations too small to cause toxicity or other ecological damages.

Modern analytical chemistry has become extremely sophisticated, and this allows trace contamination of potentially toxic chemicals to be measured at levels that are much smaller than what is required to cause demonstrable physiological or ecological damages.

Environmental Chemistry of The Atmosphere

Nitrogen gas (N_2) comprises about 79% of the mass of Earth's **atmosphere**, while 20% is oxygen (O_2), 0.9% argon (Ar), 0.035% **carbon dioxide** (CO_2), and the remainder composed of a variety of trace gases. The atmosphere also contains variable concentrations of water vapor, which can range from 0.01% in frigid arctic air to 5% in humid tropical air.

The atmosphere also can contain high concentrations of gases, vapors, or particulates that are potentially harmful to people, other animals, or vegetation, or that cause damages to buildings, art, or other materials. The most important gaseous air pollutants (listed alphabetically) are ammonia (NH_3), **carbon monoxide** (CO), fluoride (F, usually occurring HF), nitric oxide and nitrogen dioxide (NO and NO_2, together known as oxides of nitrogen, or NO_x), **ozone** (O_3), **peroxyacetyl nitrate** (PAN), and **sulfur dioxide** (SO_2).

Vapors of elemental mercury and **hydrocarbons** can also be air pollutants. Particulates with tiny diameters (less than 1µm) can also be important, including dusts containing such toxic elements as arsenic, copper, lead, nickel, and vanadium, organic aerosols that are emitted as smoke during combustions (including toxins known as polycyclic aromatic hydrocarbons), and non-reactive minerals such as silicates.

Some so-called "trace toxics" also occur in the atmosphere in extremely small concentrations. The trace toxics include persistent organochlorine chemicals such as the pesticides **DDT** and dieldrin, **polychlorinated biphenyls (PCBs)**, and the dioxin, TCDD. Other, less persistent pesticides may also be air pollutants close to places where they are used.

Environmental Chemistry of Water

Earth's surface waters vary enormously in their concentrations of dissolved and suspended chemicals. Other than the water, the chemistry of oceanic water is dominated by sodium chloride (NaCl), which has a typical concentration of about 3.5% or 35 g/L. Also important are sulfate (2.7 g/L), magnesium (1.3 g/L), and potassium and calcium (both 0.4 g/L). Some saline lakes can have much larger concentrations of dissolved ions, such as Great Salt Lake in Utah, which contains more than 20% salts.

Fresh waters are much more dilute in ions, although the concentrations are variable among waterbodies. The most important cations in typical fresh waters are calcium (Ca^{2+}), magnesium (Mg^{2+}), sodium (Na^+), ammonium (NH_4^+), and hydrogen ion (H^+; this is only present in acidic waters, otherwise hydroxy ion or OH^- occurs). The most important anions are bicarbonate (HCO_3^-) sulfate (SO_4^{2+}), chloride (Cl^-), and nitrate (NO_3^-). Some fresh waters have high concentrations of dissolved organic compounds, known as humic substances, which can stain the water a tea-like color. Typical concentrations of major ions in fresh water are: calcium 15 mg/L, sulfate 11 mg/L, chloride 7 mg/L, silica 7 mg/L, sodium 6 mg/L, magnesium 4 mg/L, and potassium 3 mg/L.

The water of clean precipitation is considerably more dilute than that of surface waters such as lakes. For example, precipitation at a remote place in Nova Scotia contained 1.6 mg/L of sulfate, 1.3 mg/L chloride, 0.8 mg/L sodium, 0.7 mg/L nitrate, 0.13 mg/L calcium, 0.08 mg/L ammonium, 0.08 mg/L magnesium, and 0.08 mg/L potassium. Because that site is about 31 mi (50 km) from the Atlantic Ocean, its precipitation is influenced by sodium and chloride originating with sea spray. In comparison, a more central location in North America had a sodium concentration of 0.09 mg/L and chloride 0.15 mg/L.

Pollution of surface waters is most often associated with the dumping of human or industrial **sewage**, nutrient inputs from agriculture, **acidification** caused by acidic precipitation or by acid-mine drainage, and industrial inputs of toxic chemicals. Eutrophication is caused when nutrient inputs cause large increases in aquatic productivity, especially in fresh waters and shallow marine waters into which sewage is dumped or that receive **runoff** containing agricultural fertilizers. In general, marine ecosystems become eutrophic when they are fertilized with nitrate, and freshwater systems with phosphate. Only 35-100 µg/L or more of phosphate is enough to significantly increase the productivity of most shallow lakes, compared with the background concentration of about 10 µg/L or less.

Freshwater ecosystems can become acidified by receiving drainage from bogs, by the deposition of acidifying substances from the atmosphere (such as acidic rain), and by acid-mine drainage. Atmospheric depositions have caused a widespread acidification of surface waters in eastern North America, Scandinavia, and other places. Surface waters acidified by atmospheric depositions commonly develop pHs of about 4.5 -5.5. Tens of thousands of lake and running-water ecosystems have been damaged in this way. Acidification has many biological consequences, including toxicity caused to many species of plants and animals, including fish.

Some industries emit metals to the environment, and these may pollute fresh and marine waters. For instance, lakes near large smelters at **Sudbury, Ontario**, have been polluted by sulfuric acid, copper, nickel, and other metals, which in some cases occur in concentrations large enough to cause toxicity to aquatic plants and animals.

Mercury contamination of fish is also a significant problem in many aquatic environments. This phenomenon is significant in almost all large fish and sharks, which accumulate mercury progressively during their lives and commonly have residues in their flesh that exceed 0.5 ppm (this is the criterion set by the World Health Organization for the maximum concentration of mercury in fish intended for human consumption). It is likely, however, that the oceanic mercury is natural in origin, and not associated with human activities. Many fresh-water fish also develop high concentrations of mercury in their flesh, also commonly exceeding the 0.5 ppm criterion. This phenomenon has been demonstrated in many remote lakes. The source of mercury may be mostly natural, or it may originate with industrial sources whose emissions are transported over a long distance in the atmosphere before they are deposited to the surface. Severe mercury pollution has also occurred near certain factories, such as chlor-alkali plants and pulp mills. The most famous example occurred at Minamata, Japan, where industrial discharges led to the pollution of marine organisms, and then resulted in the poisoning of fish-eating animals and people.

Environmental Chemistry of Soil and Rocks

The most abundant elements in typical **soil**s and rocks are oxygen (47%), silicon (28%), aluminum (8%), and iron (3-4%). Virtually all of the other stable elements are also present in soil and rocks, and all of these can occur in a great variety of molecular forms and minerals. Under certain circumstances, some of these chemicals can occur in relatively high concentrations, sometimes causing ecological damages.

This can occur naturally, as in the case of soils influenced by so-called serpentine minerals, which can contain hundreds to thousands of ppm of nickel. In addition, industrial emissions of metals from smelters have caused severe pollution. Soils near Sudbury, for example, can contain nickel and copper concentrations up to 5,000 ppm each. Even urban environments can be severely contaminated by certain metals. Soils collected near urban factories for recycling old automobile batteries can contain lead in concentrations in the percent range, while the edges of roads can contain thousands of ppm of lead emitted through the use of leaded **gasoline**.

Trace Toxics

Some chemicals occur in minute concentrations in water and other components of the environment, yet still manage to cause significant damages. These chemicals are sometimes referred to as trace toxics. The best examples are the numerous compounds known as halogenated hydrocarbons, particularly **chlorinated hydrocarbons** such as the insecticides DDT, DDD, and dieldrin, the dielectric fluids PCBs, and the chlorinated dioxin, TCDD. These chemicals are not easily degraded by either **ultraviolet radiation** or by metabolic reactions, so they are persistent in the environment. In addition, chlorinated hydrocarbons are virtually insoluble in water, but are highly soluble in lipids such as fats and oils. Because most lipids in ecosystems occur within the bodies of organisms, chlorinated hydrocarbons have a marked tendency to bioaccumulate (i.e., to occur preferentially in organisms rather than in the non-living environment). This, coupled with the persistence of these chemicals, results in their strong tendency to **food-chain/web** accumulate or biomagnify (i.e., to occur in their largest concentrations in top predators).

Fish-eating birds are examples of top predators that have been poisoned by exposure to chlorinated hydrocarbons in the environment. Some examples of species that have been affected by this type of ecotoxicity include the **peregrine falcon** (*Falco peregrinus*), **bald eagle** (*Haliaeetus leucocephalus*), osprey (*Pandion haliaetus*), **brown pelican** (*Pelecanus occidentalis*), double-crested cormorant (*Phalacrocorax auritus*), and western grebe (*Aechmophorus occidentalis*). Concentrations of chlorinated hydrocarbons in the water of aquatic habitats of these birds is generally less than 1 µg/L (part per billion, or ppb), and less than 1 ng/L (part per trillion, or ppt) in the case of TCDD. However, some of the chlorinated hydrocarbons can biomagnify to tens to hundreds of mg/kg (ppm) in the fatty tissues of fish-eating birds. This can cause severe toxicity, characterized by reproductive failures, and even the deaths of adult birds, both of which can cause populations to collapse.

Other trace toxics also cause ecological damages. For example, although it is only moderately persistent in aquatic environments, the insecticide carbofuran can accumulate in acidic standing water in recently treated fields. If geese, ducks, or other birds or mammals utilize those temporary aquatic habitats, they can be killed by the carbofuran residues.

Large numbers of wildlife have been killed this way in North America.

Petroleum

Water pollution can also result from the occurrence of hydrocarbons in large concentrations, especially after spills of crude oil or its refined products. Oil pollution can result from accidental spills of **petroleum** from wrecked tankers, offshore drilling platforms, broken pipelines, and from spills during warfare, as occurred during the **Gulf War** of 1991. Other important sources of oil pollution include operational discharges from tankers disposing oily bilge waters, and chronic releases from oil refineries and urban **runoff**.

The concentration of natural hydrocarbons in seawater is about 1 ppb, mostly due to releases from **phytoplankton** and bacteria. Beneath a slick of petroleum spilled at sea, however, the concentration of dissolved hydrocarbons can exceed several ppm, enough to cause toxicity to some organisms. There are also finely suspended droplets of petroleum in water beneath slicks, as a result of wave action on the floating oil. The slick and the sub-surface emulsion of oil-in-water are highly damaging to organisms that become coated with these substances.

[*Bill Freedman*]

FURTHER READING

Freedman, B. *Environmental Ecology*, 2nd ed. San Diego: Academic Press, 1995.

Hemond, H.F., and E.J. Fechner. *Chemical Fate and Transport in the Environment*. San Diego: Academic Press, 1994.

Manahan, S. *Environmental Chemistry*, 6th ed. Boca Raton, FL: Lewis Publishers, 1994.

Environmental Defense Fund (New York, New York)

The Environmental Defense Fund (EDF) is a **public interest group** founded in 1967 and concerned primarily with the protection of the **environment** and the concomitant improvement of public health. Originally a group of Long Island scientists organized to oppose local spraying of the pesticide **DDT**, EDF is still staffed by scientists as well as lawyers and economists but has expanded its interests over the years to include **air quality**, energy, **solid waste**, **water resources**, agriculture, **wildlife**, **habitat**s, and international environmental issues. EDF presently has a membership of approximately 200,000, an annual budget of $18 million, and a staff of 120 working out of six regional offices.

EDF seeks to protect the environment by initiating legal action in environment-related matters and also conducts public service and educational campaigns. It publishes the *EDF Letter*, a bimonthly newsletter detailing the organization's activities, as well as occasional books, reports, and monographs. EDF also conducts and encourages research relevant to environmental issues and promotes administrative, legislative, and corporate actions and policies in defense of the environment.

EDF's strategies and orientation have changed somewhat over the years from the early days when the group's motto was "Sue the bastards!" At about the time that Frederic D. Krupp became its executive director in 1984, EDF began to view environmental problems more in view of economic needs. As Krupp put it, the practical effectiveness of the environmental movement in the future would depend on its realization that behind environmental problems "there are nearly always legitimate social needs—and that long-term solutions lie in finding alternative ways to meet those underlying needs."

With this in mind, Krupp proposed a "third stage of **environmentalism**" which combined direct opposition to environmentally harmful practices with proposals for realistic, economically-viable alternatives. This strategy was first applied successfully to large-scale power production in California, where utilities were planning a massive expansion of generating capacity. EDF demonstrated that this expansion was largely unnecessary (thereby saving the utilities and their customers a considerable amount of money while also protecting the environment) by showing that the use of existing and well-established technology could greatly reduce the need for new capacity without affecting the utility's customers. EDF also showed that it was economically effective to buy power generated from renewable energy resources, including **wind energy**.

More recently, EDF worked with the McDonalds Corporation on a task force to reduce the fast food giant's estimated two million pound-per-day effusion of waste. One of the most widely publicized results of these efforts was that McDonald's was convinced to stop packaging its hamburgers in polystyrene containers. Combined with other strategies, McDonald's estimates that the task force's recommendations will eventually reduce its waste flow by 75 percent.

EDF continues to search for ways to harness economic forces in ways that destroy incentives to degrade the environment. This approach has made EDF one of the most respected and heeded environmental groups among United States corporations. EDF virtually ghost-wrote the Bush Administration's Acid Rain Bill, which makes considerable use of market-oriented strategies such as the issuing of tradable **emission**s permits. These permits allow for a set amount of **pollution** per firm based on ceilings set for entire industries. Companies can buy, sell, and trade these permits, thus providing them with a profit motive to reduce harmful emissions. Contact: Environmental Defense Fund, 257 Park Avenue South, New York, NY 10010.

[*Lawrence J. Biskowski*]

Environmental degradation

Degradation is the act or process of reducing something in value or worth. Environmental degradation, therefore, is the de-valuing of and damage to the environment by natural or **anthropogenic** causes. The loss of **biodiversity, habitat**

destruction, depletion of energy or mineral sources, and exhaustion of **groundwater aquifer**s are all examples of environmental degradation.

Presently there are four major areas of global concern due to environmental degradation: marine environment, **ozone layer**, **smog** and **air pollution**, and the vanishing **rain forest**. Pollution, at some level, is found throughout the world's oceans, which cover two-thirds of the planet's surface. Marine debris, farm **runoff**, industrial waste, sewage, dredge material, stormwater runoff, and atmospheric deposition all contribute to **marine pollution**. The level of degradation varies from region to region, but its effects are seen in such remote places as **Antarctica** and the Bering Sea.

Issues of **waste management** and disposal have had a large degrading impact on these areas. There are major national and international efforts to control pollution from shipping (including **oil spills** and general pollution due to ship ballast) and direct ocean or **estuary** discharges. Clean up has been started in some areas with some initial success.

Another major problem facing the world is the depletion of the ozone layer, which is linked to the use of a group of chemicals called **chlorofluorcarbons** (CFCs). These chemicals are widely used by industry as refrigerants and in polystyrene products. Once released into the air they rise to the **stratosphere** and eat away at the ozone layer. This layer is important because it protects us from harmful **ultraviolet radiation**, which is the chief cause of skin **cancer**. The United States has led worldwide efforts to eliminate the use of CFCs by the year 2000.

Smog in urban areas and **air quality** in general have become crucial issues in the last few decades. **Acid rain**, which occurs when sulfur dioxide and nitrogen oxide—as **emission**s from **power plants** and industries—change in the atmosphere to form harmful compounds that fall to earth in rain, fog, and snow. Acid rain damages lakes and streams as well as buildings and monuments. Air **visibility** is curtailed and the health of humans as well as plants and trees can be affected.

Automobile emissions of **nitrogen oxides**, **carbon monoxide**, and **volatile organic compounds**— although much reduced in the United States—also contribute to smog and acid rain. Carbon monoxide continues to be a problem in cities such as Los Angeles where there is heavy automobile congestion.

The vanishing rain forest is also of major global concern. The degradation of the rain forest—with its extensive logging, **deforestation**, and massive destruction of habitat—has threatened the survival of many species of plants and animals as well as disrupting climate and weather patterns locally and globally. Although **tropical rain forest**s cover only about five to seven percent of the world's land surface, they contain about one-half to two-thirds of all species of plants and animals, some which have never been studied for their medicinal or food properties.

The problem of environmental degradation has been addressed by various environmental organizations throughout the world. Environmentalists are no longer solely concerned with the local region and efforts to stop or at least slow

down environmental degradation has taken on a global significance.

[*James L. Anderson*]

FURTHER READING

The Global Ecology Handbook: What You Can Do About the Environmental Crisis. Boston: Beacon Press, 1990.

Our Common Future. World Commission on Environmental Development. New York: Oxford University Press, 1987.

Preserving Our Future Today. U.S. Environmental Protection Agency. Washington, DC: U.S. Government Printing Office, 1991.

Silver, C. S., and R. S. Defries. *One Earth, One Future: Our Changing Global Environment.* Washington, DC: National Academy Press, 1990.

Triedjell, S. T. "Soil and Vegetative Systems." In *Contemporary Problems in Geography.* Oxford: Clarendon Press, 1988.

Weiner, J. *The Next One Hundred Years: Shaping the Fate of Our Living Earth.* New York: Bantam, 1990.

Environmental dispute resolution

Environmental Dispute Resolution (EDR) or Alternative Dispute Resolution (ADR), as it is more generally known, is an out-of-court alternative to litigation to resolve disputes between parties. Although ADR can be used with virtually any legal dispute, it is often used to resolve environmental disputes. There are several types of ADR, ranging from the least formal to the most formal process: (a) negotiation, (b) mediation, (c) adjudication, (d) arbitration, (e) minitrial, and (f) summary jury trial.

Negotiation: Negotiation is the simplest and most often practiced form of ADR. The parties do not enter the judicial system, but rather settlements are reached in an informal setting and then reduced to written terms.

Mediation: Mediation is an extension of the direct negotiation process. The term is loosely used and is often confused with arbitration or informal processes in general. Mediation is a process in which a neutral third-party intervenes to help disputants reach a voluntary settlement. The mediator has no authority to force the parties to reach an agreement.

Mediation is often the most appropriate technique for environmental disputes because the parties often have no prior negotiating relationship and, because there are often many technical and scientific uncertainties, the assistance of a qualified professional is helpful.

Mediation is also used with varying success in environmental policy-making, standard setting, determination of development choices, and the enforcement of environmental standards. Many states explicitly recognize mediation as the primary method for initially dealing with environmental disputes, and mediation procedures are written into federal environmental policy, specifically in the regulations dealing with the **Comprehensive Environmental Response, Compensation and Liability Act** (CERCLA) and the **Resource Conservation and Recovery Act** (RCRA).

Mediation is not appropriate, however, with all environmental disputes because some **environmental law**s were designed to encourage a slower examination of issues that impact society.

Adjudication: Adjudication is sometimes referred to as "private judging." It is an ADR process in which the parties give their evidence and arguments to a neutral third-party who then renders an objective, binding decision. It is a voluntary procedure and private unless one party seeks judicial enforcement or review after the decision is made. The parties must agree on the adjudication and procedural rules for the process and each side is contractually bound for the length of the proceeding.

The advantage of adjudication is that a law- and/or environment-trained third party renders an objective decision based on the presented facts and legal arguments. The parties set their own rules so an adjudicator is not bound to legal principles of any particular jurisdiction. Private organizations provide adjudication services for fees but they can be expensive.

Arbitration: Arbitration is a process whereby a private judge, or arbitrator, hears the arguments of the parties and renders a judgment. The process works much like a court except that the parties choose the arbitrator and the substantive law he or she should apply. The arbitrator also has much more latitude in creating remedies which are fair to both parties. People often confuse the responsibilities of arbitrators and mediators. Arbitrators are passive functionaries who determine right or wrong; mediators are active functionaries who attempt to move the parties to reconciliation and agreement, regardless of who is right or wrong.

Parties cannot be forced into arbitration unless the contract in question includes an arbitration clause or the parties consented to enter into arbitration after the dispute developed. Since arbitration is a contractual remedy, the arbitrator can consider only those disputes and remedies which the parties agreed to submit to arbitration.

Minitrial: A minitrial is a private process in which parties agree to voluntarily reach a negotiated settlement. They present their cases in summary form before a panel of designated representatives of each party. The panel offers non-binding conclusions on the probable outcome of the case, were it to be litigated. The parties may then use the results to assist with negotiation and settlement.

Summary Jury Trial: A summary jury trial is similar to a minitrial except that the evidence is presented to a non-expert, impartial jury, rather than a panel chosen by the parties, which subsequently prepares non-binding conclusions on each of the issues in dispute. Parties may then use the assessment of the jury's "verdict" to help with negotiation and settlement.

[*Kevin Wolf*]

FURTHER READING

Kubasek, N., and G. Silverman, "Environmental Mediation." *American Business Law Journal* 26 (Fall 1988): 533-555.

Loew, W. R., and A. M. Ramirex. "Resolving Environmental Disputes with ADR." *The Practical Real Estate Lawyer* 8 (May 1992): 15-23.

Environmental economics

Environmental economics is a relatively new field, but its roots go back to the end of the nineteenth century when economists first discussed the problem of **externality**. Economic transactions have external effects which are not captured by the price system. Prime examples of these externalities are **air pollution** and **water pollution**. The absence of a price for nature's capacity to absorb wastes has an obvious solution in economic theory. Economists advocate the use of surrogate prices in the form of pollution taxes and discharge fees. The non-priced aspect of the transaction then has a price, which sends a signal to the producers to economize on the use of the resource.

In addition to the theory of externalities, economists have recognized that certain goods, such as those provided by **nature**, are common property. Lacking a discrete owner, they are likely to be over-utilized. Ultimately, they will be depleted. Few will be left for **future generations**, unless common property goods like the air and water are protected.

Besides pollution taxes and discharge fees, economists have explored the use of marketable **emission** permits as a means of rectifying the market imperfection caused by **pollution**. Rather than establishing a unit charge for pollution, government would issue permits equivalent to an agreed-upon environmental standard. Holders of the permits would have the right to sell them to the highest bidder. The advantage of this system, wherein a market for pollution rights has been established, is that it achieves environmental quality standards. Under a charge system, trial-and-error tinkering would be necessary to achieve the standards.

Besides discharge fees and markets for pollution rights, economists have advocated the use of **cost-benefit analysis** in environmental decision making. Since control costs are much easier to measure than pollution benefits, economists have concentrated on how best to estimate the benefits of a clean environment. They have relied on two primary means of doing so. First, they have inferred from the actual decisions people make in the marketplace what value they place on a clean and healthy environment. Second, they have directly asked people to make trade-off choices. The inference method might rely on residential property values, decomposing the price of a house into individual attributes including **air quality**, or it might rely on the wage premium risky jobs enjoy. Despite many advances, the problem of valuing environmental benefits continues to be controversial with special difficulties surrounding the issues of quantifying the value of a human life, recreational benefits, and ecological benefits including **species** and **habitat** survival.

For instance, the question of how much a life is worth is repellent and absurd since human worth cannot be truly captured in monetary terms. Nonetheless it is important to determine the benefits for cost-benefit purposes. The costs of reducing pollution often are immediate and apparent, while the benefits are far-off and hard to determine. So, it is important to try to gauge what these benefits might be worth.

Economists call for a more rational ordering of risks. The funds for risk reduction are not limitless, and the costs keep mounting. Estimates are that, by the year 2000, three percent of GNP will go for environmental clean-up alone. Risks should be viewed in a detached and analytical way. Polls suggest that Americans worry most about such dangers as **oil spills**, **acid rain**, **pesticide**s, **nuclear power**, and **hazardous waste**s, but scientific **risk assessment**s show that these are only low or medium-level dangers. The greater hazards come from **radon**, **lead**, indoor air pollution, and fumes from **chemicals** such as **benzene** and formaldehyde. Radon, the odorless gas that naturally seeps up from the ground and is found in people's homes, causes as many as 20,000 lung **cancer** deaths per year, while hazardous waste dumps cause at most 500 cancer deaths. Yet the **Environmental Protection Agency (EPA)** spends over $6 billion a year to clean up hazardous waste sites while its spends only $100 million a year for radon protection. To test a home for radon costs about $25, and to clean it up if it is found contaminated costs $1,000. To make the entire national housing stock free from radon would cost a few billion dollars. In contrast, projected spending for cleaning up hazardous waste sites is likely to exceed $500 billion despite the fact that only about 11 percent of such sites pose a measurable risk to human health.

Greater rationality would mean that less attention would be paid to some risks and more attention to others. For instance, scientific risk assessment suggests that sizable new investments will be needed to address the dangers of **ozone layer depletion** and greenhouse warming. Ozone depletion is likely to result in 100,000 more cases of skin cancer by the year 2050. Global warming has the potential to cause massive catastrophe.

For businesses, risk assessment provides a way to allocate costs efficiently. They are increasingly using it as a management tool. To avoid another accident like **Bhopal, India**, Union Carbide has set up a system by which it rates its plants "safe," "made safer," or "shut down." Environmentalists, on the other hand, generally see risk assessment as a tactic of powerful interests used to prevent regulation of known dangers or permit building of facilities where there will be known fatalities. Even if the chances of someone contracting cancer and dying is only one in a million, still someone will perish, which the studies by **risk assessors** indeed document. Among particularly vulnerable groups of the population (allergy sufferers exposed to benzene for example) the risks are likely to be much greater, perhaps as great as one fatality for every 100 persons. Environmentalists conclude that the way economists present their findings is too conservative. By treating everyone alike, they overlook the real danger to particularly vulnerable people. Risk assessment should not be used as an excuse for inaction.

Environmentalists have also criticized environmental economics for its emphasis on economic growth without considering the unintended side-effects. Economists need to supplement estimates of the economic costs and benefits of growth with estimates of the effects of that growth that cannot be measured in economic terms. Many environmentalists also believe that the burden of proof should rest with new technologies, in that they should not be allowed

simply because they advance material progress. In affluent societies especially, economic expansion is not necessary.

Growth is promoted for many reasons to restore the balance of payments, to make the nation more competitive, to create jobs, to reduce the deficit, to provide for the old and sick, and to lessen poverty. The public is encouraged to focus on statistics on productivity, balance of payments, and growth, while ignoring the obvious costs. Environmental groups, on the other hand, have argued for a **steady-state economy** in which population and per capita resource consumption stabilize. It is an economy with a constant number of people and goods, maintained at the lowest feasible flows of matter and energy. Human services would play a large role in a steady-state economy because they do not require much energy or material throughput and yet contribute to economic growth. Environmental clean-up and energy conservation also would contribute, since they add to economic growth while also having a positive effect on the environment.

Growth can continue, according to environmentalists, but only if the forms of growth are carefully chosen. Free time, in addition, would have to be a larger component of an environmentally-acceptable future economy. Free time removes people from potentially harmful production. It also provides them with the time needed to implement alternative production processes and techniques, including organic gardening, **recycling**, public transportation, and home and appliance maintenance for the purposes of energy conservation.

Another requirement of an environmentally acceptable economy is that people accept a *new frugality*, a concept that also has been labeled *joyous austerity*, *voluntary simplicity*, and *conspicuous frugality*.

Economists represent the environment's interaction with the economy as a materials balance model. The production sector, which consists of mines and factories, extracts materials from nature and processes them into goods and services. Transportation and distribution networks move and store the finished products before they reach the point of consumption. The environment provides the material inputs needed to sustain economic activity and carries away the wastes generated by it. People have long recognized that nature is a source of material inputs to the economy, but they have been less aware that the environment plays an essential role as a receptacle for society's unwanted by-products. Some wastes are recovered by recycling, but most are absorbed by the environment. They are dumped in **landfill**s, treated in incinerators, and disposed of as ash. They end up in the air, water, or **soil**.

The ultimate limits to economic growth do not come only from the availability of raw materials from nature. Nature's limited capacities to absorb wastes also set a limit on the economy's ability to produce. Energy plays a role in this process. It helps make food, forest products, **chemicals**, **petroleum** products, metals, and structural materials such as stone, steel, and cement. It supports materials processing by providing electricity, heating, and cooling services. It aids in transportation and distribution. According to the law of the conservation of energy, the material inputs and energy that enter the economy cannot be destroyed. Rather they change form, finding their way back to nature in a disorganized state as unwanted and perhaps dangerous by-products.

Environmentalists use the laws of physics (the notion of entropy) to show how society systematically dissipates low entropy, highly concentrated forms of energy by converting it to high entropy, little concentrated waste that cannot be used again except at very high cost. They project current resource use and **environmental degradation** into the future to demonstrate that civilization is running out of critical resources. They believe that the earth is in great danger, with a catastrophe possible as early as the late twentieth century. The earth cannot tolerate additional contaminants. Human intervention in the form of technological innovation and capital investment complemented by substantial human ingenuity and creativity is insufficient to prevent this outcome unless drastic steps are taken soon. Nearly every economic benefit has an environmental cost, and the sum total of the costs in an affluent society often exceed the benefits. The notion of **carrying capacity** is used to show that the earth has a limited ability to tolerate the disposal of contaminants and the depletion of resources.

Economists counter these claims by arguing that limits to growth can be overcome by human ingenuity, that benefits afforded by environmental protection have a cost, and that government programs to clean up the environment are as likely to fail as the market forces that produce pollution. The traditional economic view is that production is a function of labor and capital and, in theory, that resources are not necessary since labor and/or capital are infinitely substitutable for resources. Impending resource scarcity results in price increases which lead to technological substitution of capital, labor, or other resources for those that are in scarce supply. Price increases also create pressures for efficiency-in-use, leading to reduced consumption. Thus, resource scarcity is reflected in the price of a given commodity. As resources become scarce, their prices rise accordingly. Increases in price induce substitution and technological innovation.

People turn to less scarce resources that fulfill the same basic technological and economic needs provided by the resources no longer available in large quantities. To a large extent, the energy crises of the 1970s (the 1973 price shock induced by the Arab **oil embargo** and 1979 price shock following the Iranian Revolution) were alleviated by these very processes: higher prices leading to the discovery of additional supply and to conservation. By 1985, energy prices in real terms were lower than they were in 1973.

Humans respond to signals about scarcity and degradation. Extrapolating past consumption patterns into the future without considering the human response is likely to be a futile exercise, economists argue. As far back as the end of the eighteenth century, thinkers such as **Thomas Malthus** have made predictions about the limits to growth, but the lesson of modern history is one of technological innovation and substitution in response to price and other societal signals, not one of calamity brought about by resource exhaustion. In general, the prices of **natural resources** have been declining despite increased production and demand. Prices have fallen because of discoveries of new resources and because of innovations in the extraction and refinement process. *See also* Greenhouse effect; Trade in pollution permits; Tragedy of the Commons

[*Alfred A. Marcus*]

FURTHER READING

Cropper, M. L., and W. E. Oates. "Environmental Economics." *Journal of Economic Literature* (June 1992): 675-740.

Ekins, P., M. Hillman, and R. Hutchinson. *The Gaia Atlas of Green Economics*. New York: Doubleday, 1992.

Kneese, A., R. Ayres, and R. D'Arge. *Economics and the Environment: A Materials Balance Approach*. Washington, DC: Resources for the Future, 1970.

Marcus, A. A. *Business and Society: Ethics, Government, and the World Economy*. Homewood, IL: Irwin Publishing, 1993.

Environmental education

Environmental education is fast emerging as one of the most important disciplines in the United States and in the world. Merging the ideas and philosophy of **environmentalism** with the structure of formal education systems, it strives to increase awareness of environmental problems as well as to foster the skills and strategies for solving those problems. Environmental issues have traditionally fallen to the state, federal, and international policymakers, scientists, academics, and legal scholars. Environmental education (often referred to simply as "EE") shifts the focus to the general population. In other words, it seeks to empower *individuals* with an understanding of environmental problems and the skills to solve them.

Background

The first seeds of environmental education were planted roughly a century ago and are found in the works of such writers as **George Perkins Marsh**, **John Muir**, **Henry David Thoreau**, and **Aldo Leopold**. Their writings served to bring the country's attention to the depletion of **natural resources** and the often detrimental impact of humans on the **environment**. In the early 1900s, three related fields of study arose that eventually merged to form the present-day environmental education.

Nature education expanded the teaching of biology, botany, and other natural sciences out into the natural world, where students learned through direct observation. **Conservation** education took root in the 1930s, as the importance of long-range, "wise use" management of resources intensified. Numerous state and federal agencies were created to tend **public land**s, and citizen organizations began forming in earnest to protect a favored animal, park, river, or other resource. Both governmental and citizen entities included an educational component to spread their message to the general public. Many states required their schools to adopt conservation education as part of their curriculum. Teacher training programs were developed to meet the increasing demand.

The Conservation Education Association formed to consolidate these efforts and help solidify citizen support for natural resource management goals. The third pillar of modern EE is outdoor education, which refers more to the method of teaching than to the subject taught. The idea is to hold classrooms outdoors; the topics are not restricted to environmental issues but includes art, music, and other subjects.

With the burgeoning of industrial output and natural resource depletion following World War II, people began to glimpse the potential environmental disasters looming ahead. The environmental movement exploded upon the public agenda in the late 1960s and early 1970s, and the public reacted emotionally and vigorously to isolated environmental crises and events. Yet it soon became clear that the solution would involve nothing short of fundamental changes in values, lifestyles, and individual behavior, and that would mean a comprehensive educational approach.

In August 1970, the newly-created **Council on Environmental Quality** called for a thorough discussion of the role of education with respect to the environment. Two months later, Congress passed the Environmental Education Act, which called for EE programs to be incorporated in all public school curricula. Although the act received little funding in the following years, it energized EE proponents and prompted many states to adopt EE plans for their schools. In 1971, the National Association for Environmental Education formed, as did myriad of state and regional groups.

Definition

What EE means depends on one's perspective. Some see it as a teaching method or philosophy to be applied to all subjects, woven into the teaching of political science, history, economics, and so forth. Others see it as a distinct discipline, something to be taught on its own. As defined by federal statute, it is the "education process dealing with people's relationships and their natural and manmade surroundings, and includes the relation of population, **pollution**, resource allocation and depletion, conservation, transportation, technology and urban and rural planning to the total human environment."

One of the early leaders of the movement is William Stapp, a former professor at the University of Michigan's School of Natural Resources and the Environment. His three-pronged definition has formed the basis for much subsequent thought: "Environmental education is aimed at producing a citizenry that is *knowledgeable* concerning the biophysical environment and its associated problems, *aware* of how to help solve these problems, and *motivated* to work toward their solution."

Many environmental educators believe that programs covering kindergarten through 12th grade are necessary to successfully instill an **environmental ethic** in students and a comprehensive understanding of environmental issues so that they are prepared to deal with environmental problems in the real world. Further, an emphasis is placed on problem-solving, action, and informed behavioral changes. In its broadest sense, EE is not confined to public schools but

includes efforts by governments, interest groups, universities, and news media to raise awareness. Each citizen should understand the environmental issues of his or her own community: land-use planning, traffic congestion, economic development plans, **pesticide** use, **water pollution** and **air pollution**, and so on.

International level

Concurrently with the emergence of EE in this country, other nations began pushing for a comprehensive approach to environmental problems within their own borders and on a global scale. In 1972, at the **United Nations Conference on the Human Environment** in Stockholm, the need for an international EE effort was clearly recognized and emphasized. Three years later, an International Environmental Education Workshop was held in Belgrade, from which emerged an eloquent, urgent mandate for the drastic reordering of national and international development policies. The "Belgrade Charter" called for an end to the military arms race and a new global ethic in which "no nation should grow or develop at the expense of another nation." It called for the eradication of poverty, hunger, illiteracy, pollution, exploitation, and domination. Central to this impassioned plea for a better world was the need for environmental education of the world's youth. That same year, the UN approved a $2 million budget to facilitate the research, coordination, and development of an international EE program among dozens of nations.

Effectiveness

There has been criticism over the last 15 years that EE too often fails to educate students and makes little difference in their behavior concerning the environment. Researchers and environmental educators have formulated a basic framework for how to improve EE: 1) Reinforce individuals for positive environmental behavior over an extended period of time. 2) Provide students with positive, informal experiences outdoors to enhance their "environmental sensitivity." 3) Focus instruction on the concepts of "ownership" and "empowerment." The first concept means that the learner has some personal interest or investment in the environmental issues being discussed. Perhaps the student can relate more readily to concepts of **solid waste** disposal if there is a **landfill** in the neighborhood. Empowerment gives learners the sense that they can make changes and help resolve environmental problems. 4) Design an exercise in which students thoroughly investigate an environmental issue and then develop a plan for citizen action to address the issue, complete with an analysis of the social, cultural, and ecological consequences of the action.

Despite the efforts of environmental educators, the movement has a long way to go. The scope and number of critical environmental problems facing the world today far outweigh the successes of EE. Further, most countries still do not have a comprehensive EE program that prepares them, as future citizens, to make ecologically sound choices and to participate in cleaning up and caring for the environment. Lastly, educators, including the media, are largely focused on explaining the problems but fall short on explaining or offering possible solutions. The notion of "empowerment" is often absent.

Recent developments and successes in the United States

Project WILD, based in Boulder, Colorado, is a K-12 supplementary conservation and environmental education program emphasizing **wildlife** protection, sponsored by fish and wildlife agencies and environmental educators. The project sets up workshops in which teachers learn about wildlife issues. They in turn teach children and help students understand how they can act responsibly on behalf of wildlife and the environment. The program, begun in 1983, has grown tremendously in terms of the number of educators reached and the monetary support from states, which, combined, are spending about $3.6 million annually.

The Global Rivers Environmental Education Network (GREEN), begun just a few years ago at the University of Michigan under the guidance of William Stapp, has likewise been enormously successful, perhaps more so. Teachers all over the world take their students down to their local river and show them how to monitor **water quality**, analyze **watershed** usage, and identify socioeconomic sources of river degradation. Lastly, and most importantly, the students then present their findings and recommendations to the local officials. These students also exchange information with other GREEN students around the world via computers.

Another promising development is the National Consortium for Environmental Education and Training (NCEET), also based at the University of Michigan. The partnership of academic institutions, non-profit organizations, and corporations, NCEET was established in 1992 with a three-year, $4.8 million grant from the **Environmental Protection Agency (EPA)**. Its main purpose is to dramatically improve the effectiveness of environmental education in the United States. The program has attacked its mission from several angles: to function as a national clearinghouse for K-12 teachers, to make available top-quality EE materials for teachers, to conduct research on effective approaches to EE, to survey and assess the EE needs of all 50 states, to establish a computer network for teachers needing access to information and resources, and to develop a teacher training manual for conducting EE workshops around the country.

[*Cathryn McCue*]

FURTHER READING

"The Belgrade Charter." *Connect: Unesco-UNEP Environmental Education Newsletter* 1 (January 1976).

Gerston, R. *Just Open the Door: A Complete Guide to Experiencing Environmental Education.* Danville, IL: Interstate Printers and Publishers, 1983.

Hungerford, H. R., and T. L. Volk. "Changing Learner Behavior Through Environmental Education." *Journal of Environmental Education* 21 (Spring 1990): 8-21.

Swan, M. "Forerunners of Environmental Education." In *What Makes Education Environmental?*, edited by N. McInnis and D. Albrect. Louisville, KY: Data Courier and Environmental Educators, 1975.

Environmental enforcement

Environmental enforcement is the set of actions that a government takes to achieve full implementation of environmental requirements (compliance) within the regulated community and to correct or halt situations or activities that endanger the **environment** or public health. Experience with environmental programs has shown that enforcement is essential to compliance because many people and institutions will not comply with a law unless there are clear consequences for noncompliance. Enforcement by the government usually includes inspections to determine the compliance status of the regulated community and to detect violations; negotiations with individuals or facility managers who are out of compliance to develop mutually agreeable schedules and approaches for achievement of compliance; legal action when necessary to compel compliance and to impose some consequences for violation of the law or for posing a threat to public health and the environment; and compliance promotion, such as educational programs, technical assistance, and subsidies, to encourage voluntary compliance.

Nongovernmental groups may become involved in enforcement by detecting noncompliance, negotiating with violators, and commenting on governmental enforcement actions. They may also, if the law allows, take legal actions against a violator for noncompliance or against the government for not enforcing environmental requirements. The banking and insurance industries may be indirectly involved with enforcement by requiring assurance of compliance with environmental requirements before they issue a loan or an insurance policy to a facility. Strong social sanctions for noncompliance with environmental requirements can also be effective to ensure compliance. For example, the public may choose to boycott a product if they believe the manufacturer is harming the environment.

Environmental enforcement is based on environmental laws. An environmental law provides the vision, scope, and authority for environmental protection and restoration. Some environmental laws contain requirements while others specify a structure and criteria for establishing requirements, which are then developed separately. Requirements may be general, in which they apply to a group of facilities, or facility-specific.

Examples of environmental enforcement programs include those that govern the ambient environment, performance, technology, work practices, dissemination of information and product or use bans.

Ambient standards (media quality standard) are goals for the quality of the ambient environment (that is, air and water quality). Ambient standards are usually written in units of concentration, and they are used to plan the levels of emissions that can be accommodated from individual sources while still meeting an area-wide goal. Ambient standards can also be used as triggers, i.e., when a standard is exceeded, monitoring or enforcement efforts are increased. Enforcement of these standards involves relating an ambient measurement to emissions or activities at a specific facility, which can be difficult.

Performance standards, widely used for regulations, permits, and monitoring requirements, limit the amount or rate of particular chemicals or discharges that a facility can release into the environment in a given period of time. These standards allow sources to choose which technologies they will use to meet the standards. Performance standards are often based on output that can be achieved by using the best available control technology. Some standards allow a source with multiple emissions to vary its emissions from each stack as long as the total sum of emissions does not exceed the permitted total. Compliance with emission standards is accomplished by sampling and monitoring, which in some cases may be difficult and/or expensive.

Technology standards require the regulated community to use a particular type of technology (i.e., "best available technology") to control and/or monitor emissions. Technology standards are effective if the equipment specified is known to perform well under the range of conditions experienced by the source. Compliance is measured by whether the equipment is installed and operating properly. However, proper operation over a long period of time is more difficult to monitor. The use of technology standards can inhibit technological innovation.

Practice standards require or prohibit work activities that may have environmental impacts (e.g., prohibition of carrying hazardous liquids in uncovered containers). Regulators can easily inspect for compliance and take action against noncomplying sources, but ongoing compliance is not easy to ensure.

Dissemination of information and product or use bans are also governed by environmental enforcement programs. Information standards require a source of potential pollution (e.g., a manufacturer or facility involved in generating, transporting, storing, treating, and disposing of **hazardous wastes**) to develop and submit information to the government. For example, a source generating **pollution** may be required to monitor, maintain records, and report on the level of pollution generated and whether or not the source exceeds performance standards. Information requirements are also used when a potential pollution source is a product such as a new chemical or pesticide. The manufacturer may be required to test and report on the potential of the product to cause harm if released into the environment. Finally, product or use bans are used to prohibit a product (i.e., ban the manufacture, sale, and/or use of a product) or they may prohibit particular uses of a product.

An effective **environmental law** should include the authority or power necessary for its own enforcement. An effective authority should govern implementation of environmental requirements, inspection, and monitoring of facilities, and legal sanctions for noncompliance. One type of authority that is used is guidance for the implementation of environmental laws by issuance of regulations, permits, licenses, and/or guidance policies. Regulations establish, in greater detail than is specified by law, general requirements that must be met by the regulated community. Some regulations are directly enforced while others provide criteria and procedures for developing facility-specific requirements util-

izing permits and licenses to provide the basis of enforcement. Permits are used to control activities related to construction or operation of facilities that generate pollutants. Requirements in permits are based on specific criteria established in laws, regulations, and/or guidance. General permits specify what a class of facilities is required to do, while a facility-specific permit specifies requirements for a particular facility, often taking into account the conditions there. Licenses are permits to manufacture, test, sell, and/or distribute a product that may pose an environmental or public health risk if improperly used. Licenses may be general or facility-specific. Written guidance and policies, which are prepared by the regulator, are used to interpret and implement requirements to ensure consistency and fairness. Guidance may be necessary because not all applications of requirements can be anticipated, or when regulation is achieved by the use of facility-specific permits or licenses.

Authority is also required to provide for inspection and monitoring of facilities, with legal sanctions for noncompliance. Requirements may either be waived or prepared for facility-specific conditions. The authority will inspect regulated facilities and gain access to their records and equipment to determine if they are in compliance.

Authority is necessary to ensure that the regulated community monitors its own compliance, maintains records of its compliance activities and status, reports this information periodically to the enforcement program, and provides information during inspections.

An effective law should also include the authority to take legal action against noncomplying facilities, imposing a range of monetary penalties and other sanctions on facilities that violate the law, as well as criminal sanctions on those facilities or individuals who deliberately violate the law (e.g., facilities that knowingly falsify data). Also, power should be granted to correct situations that pose an immediate and substantial threat to public health and/or the environment.

The range and types of environmental enforcement response mechanisms available depend on the number and types of authorities provided to the enforcement program by environmental and related laws. Enforcement mechanisms may be designed to return violators to compliance, impose a sanction, or remove the economic benefits of noncompliance. Enforcement may require that specific actions be taken to test, monitor, or provide information. Enforcement may also correct environmental damages and modify internal company management problems.

Enforcement response mechanisms include informal responses such as phone calls, site visits and inspections, warning letters, and notices of violations, which are more formal than warning letters. They provide the facility manager with a description of the violation, what should be done to correct it, and by what date. Informal responses do not penalize but can lead to more severe responses if ignored. The more formal enforcement mechanisms are backed by law and are accompanied by procedural requirements to protect the rights of the individual. Authority to use formal enforcement mechanisms for a specific situation must be provided in the applicable environmental law. Civil administrative orders are legal, independently enforceable orders issued directly by enforcement program officials that define the violation, provide evidence of the violation, and require the recipient to correct the violation within a specified time period. If the recipient violates the order, program managers can take further legal action using additional orders or the court system to force compliance with the order.

Further legal action includes the use of field citations, which are administrative orders issued by inspectors in the field. They require the violator to correct a clear-cut violation and pay a small monetary fine. Field citations are used to handle more routine types of violations that do not pose a major threat to the environment. Legal action may also lead to civil judicial enforcement actions, which are formal lawsuits before the courts. These actions are used to require action to reduce immediate threats to public health or the environment, to enforce administrative orders that have been violated, and to make final decisions regarding orders that have been appealed. Finally, a criminal judicial response is used when a person or facility has knowingly and willfully violated the law or has committed a violation for which society has chosen to impose the most serious legal sanctions available. This response involves criminal sanction, which may include monetary penalties and imprisonment. The criminal response is the most difficult type of enforcement, requiring intensive investigation and case development, but it can also create a significant deterrence.

Environmental enforcement must include processes to balance the rights of individuals with the government's need to act quickly. A notice of violation should be issued before any action is taken so that the finding of violation can be contested, or so that the violation can be corrected before further government action. Appeals should be allowed at several stages in the enforcement process so that the finding of violation, the required remedial action, or the severity of the proposed sanction can be reviewed. There should also be dispute resolution processes for negotiations between program officials and the violator, which may include face-to-face discussions, presentations before a judge or hearing examiner, or use of third party mediators, arbitrators, or facilitators.

[*Judith Sims*]

FURTHER READING

Wasserman, C. E. *Principles of Environmental Enforcement.* Washington, D.C.: U.S. Environmental Protection Agency, 1992.

Environmental engineering

The development of environmental engineering as a discipline is a reflection of the modern need to maintain public health by providing safe drinking water and sanitation, and by treating and disposing of sewage, **municipal solid waste** and **pollution**. Originally, sanitary engineering, a limited subdiscipline of civil engineering, performed some of these functions. But with the growth of concern for protecting the **environment** and the passage of laws regulating disposal of wastes, environmental engineering has grown into a discrete discipline encompassing a wide range of activities including: "proper disposal or **recycling** of **wastewater** and **solid waste**s, adequate drainage of urban and rural areas for proper sanitation, control of water, soil and atmospheric pollution and the social and environmental impact of these solutions." Education for environmental engineers requires that they be "well informed concerning engineering problems in the field of public health, such as control of insect-borne diseases, the elimination of industrial health hazards, and the provision of adequate sanitation in urban, rural and recreational areas, and the effect of technological advance on the environment." More broadly environmental engineering is defined by W. E. Gilbertson as "that branch of engineering which is concerned with the application of scientific principles to (1) the protection of human populations from the effects of adverse environmental factors, (2) the protection of environments, both local and global, from the potentially deleterious effects of human activities, and (3) the improvement of environmental quality of man's health and well-being."

The American Academy of Environmental Engineers (AAEE) has defined environmental engineering as "the application of engineering principles to the management of the environment for the protection of human health; for the protection of nature's beneficial **ecosystem**s and for environment-related enhancement of the quality of human life."

Degree-granting institutions in the United States do not necessarily consider environmental engineering as a separate discipline. A report by the U. S. Engineering Manpower Commission found that only 192 baccalaureate environmental engineering degrees were granted in 1988; however C. Robert Baillod estimates that at least 10 percent of the 8,800 annual graduates from baccalaureate civil engineering programs are educated to function as environmental engineers. If similar estimates are made for chemical, mechanical, geological and other engineers who function as environmental engineers, 1,000 to 2,000 graduates are entering the profession each year. Data collected by Baillod indicate that the supply of environmental engineers will satisfy half the demand for 2,000 to 5,000 new environmental engineering graduates per year for the next decade.

From 1970 to 1985, an increasing number of environmental statutes passed at the federal and state level in the United States while parallel legislation was being established internationally to regulate and control environmental pollution. In the United States, the establishment of the **Comprehensive Environmental Response, Compensation and Liability Act (CERCLA)**—known as *Superfund* for short—has provided the impetus for significant activity in remediation as well as providing industries and municipalities with incentives (such as liability for environmental damage) to clean up and avoid pollution. In order to comply with environmental laws and also to maintain good business practice, corporations are including impacts on the environment in planning for their process engineering. A serious potential for fines or costly liability suits exists if the design of processes is not carefully conducted with environmental safeguards.

In addition to employment by the private sector, state and federal governments also employ environmental engineers. The primary function of environmental engineers in government is research and development for implementation of regulations and their enforcement. At the federal level, agencies such as the **Environmental Protection Agency (EPA)**, as well as the Departments of Commerce, Energy, Interior and Agriculture, employ environmental engineers.

Environmental engineering is proving crucial in addressing an array of environmental needs. Techniques recently conceived by environmental engineers include:

(1) The development of an oil-absorbing, floating sponge-like material as a re-usable first response material for remediating **oil spills** on open bodies of water.

(2) Design and operation of a plant to process electrolytic plating wastes collected from a large urban area to **reuse** the metals and detoxify the cyanide as a means of avoiding the discharges of these wastes into the sewer system.

(3) Development of a process for reusing the **lead**, zinc, and **cadmium** which would otherwise be lost as a fume in the remelting of automotive scrap to form steel products.

(4) Use of naturally-occurring bacterial agents in cleanup of underground **aquifer**s contaminated by prior discharges of creosote, a substance used to preserve wood products.

(5) Development of processes for removal of and destruction of **PCB**s and other hazardous organic agents from spills into **soil**.

(6) Development of sensing techniques which enable tracing of pollution to **point source**s and the determination of the degree of pollution which has occurred for application of legal remedies.

(7) Development of process design and control instrumentation in nuclear reactors to prevent, contain and avoid nuclear releases.

(8) Design and development of **feedlot**s for animals in which the waste products are made into reusable agricultural products.

(9) Development of sterilization, **incineration** and gas cleanup systems for treatment of hospital wastes.

(10) Certification of properties to verify the absence of factors which would make new owners liable to environmental litigation (for example, absence of **asbestos**, absence of underground storage tanks for **hazardous material**)s.

(11) Redesign of existing chemical plants to recycle or eliminate **waste stream**s.

(12) Development of processes for recycling wastes (for example, processes for de-inking and reuse of newsprint or reuse of **plastics**).

These wide-ranging examples are typical of the solutions which are being developed by a new generation of technically-trained individuals. In an increasingly populated and industrialized world, environmental engineers will continue to play a pivotal role in devising technologies needed to minimize the impact of humans on the earth's resources.

[*Malcolm T. Hepworth*]

FURTHER READING

American Academy of Environmental Engineers. AAEE Bylaws. Annapolis, Maryland: 1990.

Baillod, C. Robert, *et al.* "Development of Environmental Engineering Baccalaureate Programs and Degrees." A Position Paper for Discussion at the Sixth Conference on Environmental Engineering Education, Oregon State University, August 18-20, 1991.

Cartledge, B., ed. *Monitoring the Environment.* New York: Oxford University Press, 1992.

Corbitt, Robert A.: *Standard Handbook of Environmental Engineering.* New York: McGraw-Hill, 1989.

Crucil, C. "Environmentally Sound Buildings Now Within Reach." *Alternatives* 19 (January-February 1993): 9-10.

Gilbertson, W. E. "Environmental Quality Goals and Challenges." *Proceedings of the Third National Environmental Engineering Education Conference* edited by P. W. Purdon. American Academy of Environmental Engineers and the Association of Environmental Engineering Professors, Drexel University, 1973.

Jacobsen, J., ed. *Human Impact on the Environment: Ancient Roots, Current Challenges.* Boulder, CO: Westview Press, 1992.

Environmental estrogens

The United States **Environmental Protection Agency (EPA)** defines an "environmental endocrine disruptor"—the term the Agency uses for environmental estrogens—as "an exogenous agent that interferes with the synthesis, secretion, transport, binding, action, or elimination of natural hormones in the body that are responsible for the maintenance of **homeostasis**, reproduction, development, and/or behavior." Dr. Theo Colborn, a zoologist and senior scientist with the **World Wildlife Fund**, and the person most credited with raising national awareness of the issue, describes these chemicals as "hand-me-down poisons" that are passed from mothers to offspring and may be linked to a wide range of adverse effects, including low sperm counts, infertility, genital deformities, breast and prostate **cancer**, neurological disorders in children such as hyperactivity and attention deficits, and developmental and reproductive disorders in wildlife. Colborn discusses these effects in her 1996 book, *Our Stolen Future*—co-authored with Dianne Dumanoski and John Peterson Myers—which asks: "Are we threatening our fertility, intelligence, and survival?" Some other names used for the same class of chemicals are hormone disruptors, estrogen mimics, endocrine disrupting chemicals, and endocrine modulators.

While EPA takes the position that it is "aware of and concerned" about data indicating that exposure to environmental endocrine disruptors may cause adverse impacts on human health and the environment, the Agency at present does not consider endocrine disruption to be "an adverse endpoint *per se*." Rather, it is "a mode or mechanism of action potentially leading to other outcomes"—such as the health effects Colborn described drawing from extensive research of numerous scientists—but, in EPA's view, the link to human health effects remains an unproven hypothesis. For Colborn and a significant number of other scientists, however, enough is known to support prompt and far-reaching action to reduce exposures from these chemicals and myriad products that are manufactured using them. Foods, plastic packaging, and pesticides are among the sources of exposure Colborn raises concerns about in her book.

Ultimately, the environmental estrogens issue is about whether these chemicals are present in the environment at high enough levels to disrupt the normal functioning of wildlife and human endocrine systems and thereby cause harmful effects. The endocrine system is one of at least three important regulatory systems in humans and other animals (the nervous and immune systems are the other two) and includes such endocrine glands as the pituitary, thyroid, pancreas, adrenal, and the male and female gonads, or testes and ovaries. These glands secrete hormones into the bloodstream where they travel in very small concentrations and bind to specific sites called "cell receptors" in target tissues and organs. The hormones affect development, reproduction, and other bodily functions. The term "endocrine disruptors" includes not only estrogens but also antiandrogens and other agents that act on the endocrine system.

The question of whether environmental endocrine disruptors may be causing effects in humans has arisen over the past decade based on a growing body of evidence about effects in wildlife exposed to **dichlorodiphenyltrichlorethane (DDT)**, **polychlorinated biphenyls (PCBs)**, and other chemicals. For instance, field studies have proven that tributyltin (TBT), which is used as an antifouling paint on ships, can cause "imposex" in female snails, which are now commonly found with male genitalia, including a penis and vas deferens, the sperm-transporting tube. TBT has also been shown to cause decreased egg production by the periwinkle (*Littorina littorea*). As early as 1985, concerns arose among scientists and the public in the United Kingdom over the effects of synthetic estrogens from birth control pills entering rivers, a concern that was heightened when anglers reported catching fish with both male and female characteristics. Other studies have found **Great Lakes** salmon to invariably have thyroids that were abnormal in appearance, even when there were no overt goiters. Herring gulls (*Larus argentatus*) throughout the Great Lakes have also been found with enlarged thyroids. In the case of the salmon and gulls, no agent has been determined to be causing these effects. But other studies have linked DDT exposure in the Great Lakes to eggshell thinning and breakage among **bald eagles** and other birds. In Lake Apopka, Florida, male alligators (*Alligator mississippiensis*) exposed to a mixture of dicofol, DDT, and dichlorodiphenyldichloroethylene (DDE) have been "demasculinized," with phalluses one-half to one-fourth the normal size. Red-eared turtles (*Trachemys scripta*) in the lake have also been demasculinized. One 1988 study reported that

4 of 15 female black bears (*Ursus americanus*) and 1 of 4 female brown bears (*Ursus arctos*) had, to varying degrees, male sex organs. These and nearly 300 other peer-reviewed studies have led EPA—in conjunction with the multi-agency White House Committee on Environment and Natural Resources—to develop a "framework for planning" and an extensive research agenda to answer questions about the effects of endocrine disruptors. The goal is to better understand the potential effects of such chemicals on human beings before implementing regulatory actions.

The federal research agenda has been evolving through a series of workshops. As early as 1979, the **National Institute of Environmental Health Sciences (NIEHS)**, based in Research Triangle Park, North Carolina, held an "Estrogens in the Environment" conference to evaluate the chemical properties and diverse structures among environmental estrogens. NIEHS held a second conference in 1985 that addressed numerous potential toxicological and biological effects from exposure to these chemicals. NIEHS's third conference, held in 1994, focused on detrimental effects in wildlife. At an April 1995 EPA-sponsored workshop on "Research Needs for the Risk Assessment of Health and Environmental Effects of Endocrine Disruptors," a number of critical research questions were discussed: What do we know about the carcinogenic effects of endocrine-disrupting agents in humans and wildlife? What are the research needs in this area, including the highest priority research needs? Similar questions were discussed for reproductive effects, neurological effects, immunological effects, and a variety of risk assessment issues. Drawing on the preceding conferences and workshops, in February 1997 EPA issued a *Special Report on Environmental Endocrine Disruption: An Effects Assessment and Analysis* that recommended key research needs to better understand how environmental endocrine disruptors may be causing the variety of specific effects in human beings and **wildlife** hypothesized by some scientists. For instance, male reproductive research should include tests that evaluate both the quantity and quality of sperm produced. Furthermore, when testing the endocrine-disrupting potential of chemicals, it is important to test for both estrogenic and antiandrogenic activity because new data suggest that it is possible the latter—antiandrogenic activity—not estrogenic activity, is causing male reproductive effects. In the area of ecological research, EPA's special report highlighted the need for research on such issues as what chemicals or class of chemicals can be considered genuine endocrine disruptors and what dose is needed to cause an effect.

Even before environmental estrogens received a place on the federal environmental agenda as a priority concern, Colborn and other scientists first met in July 1991 in Racine, Wisconsin, to discuss their misgivings about the prevalence of estrogenic chemicals in the environment. From that meeting came the landmark "Wingspread Consensus Statement" of 21 leading researchers. The statement asserted that the scientists were certain that a large number of human-made chemicals that have been released into the environment, as well as a few natural ones, "have the potential to disrupt the endocrine system of animals, including humans," and that many wildlife populations are already affected by these chemicals. Furthermore, the scientists expressed certainty that the effects may be entirely different in the embryo, fetus, or perinatal organisms than in the adult; that effects are more often manifested in offspring than in exposed parents; that the timing of exposure in the developing organism is crucial; and that, while embryonic development is the critical exposure period, "obvious manifestations may not occur until maturity." Besides these and other "certain" conclusions, the scientists estimated with confidence that "some of the developmental impairments reported in humans today are seen in adult offspring of parents exposed to synthetic hormone disruptors (agonists and antagonists) released in the environment" and that "unless the environmental load of synthetic hormone disruptors is abated and controlled, large scale dysfunction at the population level is possible." The Wingspread Statement included numerous other consensus views on what models predict and the judgment of the group on the need for much greater research and a comprehensive inventory of these chemicals.

The Food Quality Protection Act of 1996 (FQPA) and the Safe Drinking Water Act Amendments of 1996 require EPA to develop a screening program to determine whether **pesticide**s or other substances cause effects in humans similar to effects produced by naturally occurring estrogens and other endocrine effects. The FQPA requires pesticide registrants to test their products for such effects and submit reports, and it requires that registrations be suspended if registrants fail to comply. Besides the EPA screening program, the United Nations Environment Programme is pursuing a multinational effort to manage "persistent organic pollutants," including DDT and PCBs, which, though banned in the United States, are still used elsewhere and can persist in the environment and be transported long-distance. In February 1997, Illinois became the first state to issue a strategy for endocrine disruptors that requires every Illinois EPA program to assess its current activities affecting these chemicals and to begin monitoring a list of known, probable, and suspected chemicals in case further action is needed in the future.

[*David Clarke*]

FURTHER READING

Colborn, T., D. Dumanoski, and J. P. Myers. *Our Stolen Future*. New York: Penguin Books, 1996.

"Estrogens in the Environment," *Environmental Health Perspectives Supplements* 3, supplement 7. North Carolina: Research Triangle Park, 1995.

National Science and Technology Council. Committee on Environment and Natural Resources. *The Health and Ecological Effects of Endocrine Disrupting Chemicals, A Framework for Planning*. Washington, D.C., 1996.

U.S. Environmental Protection Agency. *Special Report on Environmental Endocrine Disruption: An Effects Assessment and Analysis*. (EPA/630/R-96/012). Washington, D.C.: GPO, 1997.

Environmental ethics

Ethics is a branch of philosophy that deals with morals and values. Environmental ethics refers to the moral relationships between humans and the natural world. It addresses such questions as, do humans have obligations or responsibilities toward the natural world, and if so, how are those responsibilities balanced against human needs and interests? Are some interests more important than others?

Efforts to answer such ethical questions have led to the development of a number of schools of ethical thought. One of these is **utilitarianism**, a philosophy associated with the English eccentric Jeremy Bentham and later modified by his godson John Stuart Mill. In its most basic terms, utilitarianism holds that an action is morally right if it produces the greatest good for the greatest number of people. The early environmentalist **Gifford Pinchot** was inspired by utilitarian principles and applied them to **conservation**. Pinchot proposed that the purpose of conservation is to protect **natural resources** to produce "the greatest good for the greatest number for the longest time." Although utilitarianism is a simple, practical approach to human moral dilemmas, it can also be used to justify reprehensible actions. For example, in the nineteenth century many white Americans believed that the extermination of native peoples and the appropriation of their land was the right thing to do. However, most would now conclude that the good derived by white Americans from these actions does not justify the genocide and displacement of native peoples.

The tenets of utilitarian philosophy are presented in terms of human values and benefits, a clearly **anthropocentric** world view. Many philosophers argue that only humans are capable of acting morally and of accepting responsibility for their actions. Not all humans, however, have this capacity to be moral agents. Children, the mentally ill, and others are not regarded as moral agents, but, rather, as moral subjects. However, they still have rights of their own—rights that moral agents have an obligation to respect. In this context, moral agents have **intrinsic value** independent of the beliefs or interests of others.

Although humans have long recognized the value of non-living objects, such as machines, minerals, or rivers, the value of these objects is seen in terms of money, aesthetics, cultural significance, etc. The important distinction is that these objects are useful or inspiring to some person—they are not ends in themselves but are means to some other end. Philosophers term this instrumental value, since these objects are the instruments for the satisfaction of some other moral agent. This philosophy has also been applied to living things, such as domestic animals. These animals have often been treated as simply the means to some humanly-desired end without any inherent rights or value of their own.

Aldo Leopold, in his famous essay on environmental ethics, pointed out that not all humans have been considered to have inherent worth and intrinsic rights. As examples he points to children, women, foreigners, and **indigenous peoples**—all of whom were once regarded as less than full persons; as objects or the property of an owner who could do with them whatever he wished. Most civilized societies now recognize that all humans have intrinsic rights, and, in fact, these intrinsic rights have also been extended to include such entities as corporations, municipalities, and nations.

Many environmental philosophers argue that we must also extend recognition of inherent worth to all other components of the natural world, both living and non-living. In their opinion, our anthropocentric view, which considers components of the natural world to be valuable only as the means to some human end, is the primary cause of **environmental degradation**. As an alternative, they propose a biocentric view which gives inherent value to all the natural world regardless of its potential for human use.

Paul Taylor outlines four basic tenets of biocentrism in his book, *Respect for Nature*. These are: 1) Humans are members of earth's living community in the same way and on the same terms as all other living things; 2) Humans and other species are interdependent; 3) Each organism is a unique individual pursuing its own good in its own way; 4) Humans are not inherently superior to other living things. These tenets underlie the philosophy developed by Norwegian **Arne Naess** known as **deep ecology**.

From this biocentric philosophy Paul Taylor developed three principles of ethical conduct: 1) Do not harm any natural entity that has a good of its own; 2) Do not try to manipulate, control, modify, manage or interfere with the normal functioning of natural **ecosystem**s, **biotic communities**, or individual wild organisms; 3) Do not deceive or mislead any animal capable of being deceived or misled. These principles led Professor Taylor to call for an end to hunting, fishing and trapping, to espouse **vegetarianism**, and to seek the exclusion of human activities from **wilderness** areas. However, Professor Taylor did not extend intrinsic rights to non-living natural objects, and he assigned only limited rights to plants and domestic animals. Others argue that all natural objects, living or not, have rights.

Regardless of the appeal that certain environmental philosophies may have in the abstract, it is clear that humans must make use of the natural world if they are to survive. They must eat other organisms and compete with them for all the essentials of life. Humans seek to control or eliminate harmful plants or animals. How is this intervention in the natural world justified? Stewardship is a principle that philosophers use the justify such interference. Stewardship holds that humans have a unique responsibility to care for domestic plants and animals and all other components of the natural world. In this view, humans, their knowledge, and the products of their intellect are an essential part of the natural world, neither external to it nor superfluous. Stewardship calls for humans to respect and cooperate with nature to achieve the greatest good. Because of their superior intellect, humans can improve the world and make it a better place, but only if they see themselves as an integral part of it.

Ethical dilemmas arise when two different courses of action each have valid ethical underpinnings. A classic ethical dilemma occurs when any course of action taken will cause harm, either to oneself or to others. Another sort of dilemma arises when two parties have equally valid, but incompatible, ethical interests. To resolve such competing ethical claims Paul Taylor suggests five guidelines: 1) it is usually permissible for moral agents to defend themselves; 2) basic interests, those interests necessary for survival, take precedence over other interests; 3) when basic interests are in conflict, the least amount of harm should be done to all parties involved; 4) whenever possible, the disadvantages resulting from competing claims should be borne equally by all parties; 5) the greater the harm done to a moral agent, the great is the compensation required.

Ecofeminists do not find that utilitarianism, biocentrism or stewardship provide adequate direction to solve environmental problems or to guide moral actions. In their view, these philosophies come out of a patriarchal system based on domination—of women, children, minorities and **nature**. As an alternative, ecofeminists suggest a pluralistic, relationship-oriented approach to human interactions with the **environment**. **Ecofeminism** is concerned with nurturing, reciprocity, and connectedness, rather than with rights, responsibilities, and ownership. It challenges humans to see themselves as related to others and to nature. Out of these connections, then, will flow ethical interactions among individuals and with the natural world. *See also* Animal rights; Bioregionalism; Callicott, J. Baird; Ecojustice; Environmental racism; Environmentalism; Future generations; Humanism; Intergenerational justice; Land stewardship; Rolston, Holmes; Speciesism

[*Christine B. Jeryan*]

FURTHER READING

Devall, B., and G. Sessions. *Deep Ecology.* Layton, UT: Gibbs M. Smith, 1985.

Odell, R. *Environmental Awakening: The New Revolution to Protect the Earth.* Cambridge, MA: Ballinger, 1980.

Olson, S. *Reflections From the North Country.* New York: Knopf, 1980.

Plant, J. *Healing the Wounds: The Promise of Ecofeminism.* Santa Cruz, CA: New Society Publishers, 1989.

Rolston, H. *Environmental Ethics.* Philadelphia, Temple University Press, 1988.

Taylor, P. *Respect for Nature.* Princeton, NJ: Princeton University Press, 1986.

Environmental health

Environmental health is concerned with the medical effects of chemicals, pathogenic (disease-causing) organisms, or physical factors in our environment. Because our environment affects nearly every aspect of our lives in some way or other, environmental health is related to virtually every branch of medical science. The special focus of this discipline, however, tends to be health effects of polluted air and water, contaminated food, and toxic or hazardous materials in our **environment**. Concerns about these issues makes environmental health one of the most compelling reasons to be interested in environmental science.

For a majority of humans, the most immediate environmental health threat has always been pathogenic organisms. Improved sanitation, nutrition, and modern medicine in the industrialized countries have reduced or eliminated many of the communicable diseases that once threatened us. But for people in the less developed countries where nearly 80% of the world's population lives, bacteria, viruses, fungi, parasites, worms, flukes, and other infectious agents remain major causes of illness and death. Hundreds of millions of people suffer from major diseases such as malaria, gastrointestinal infections (diarrhea, dysentery, cholera), tuberculosis, influenza, and pneumonia spread through the air, water, or food. Many of these terrible diseases could be eliminated or greatly reduced by a cleaner environment, inexpensive dietary supplements, and better medical care.

For the billion or so richest people in the world—including most of the population of the United States and Canada—diseases related to lifestyle or longevity tend to be much greater threats than more conventional environmental concerns such as dirty water or polluted air. Heart attacks, strokes, **cancer**, depression and hypertension, traffic accidents, trauma, and **AIDS** lead as causes of sickness and death in wealthy countries. These diseases are becoming increasingly common in the developing world as people live longer, exercise less, eat a richer diet, and use more drugs, tobacco, and alcohol. Epidemiologists predict that by the middle of the next century, these diseases of affluence will be leading causes of sickness and death everywhere.

Although a relatively minor cause of illness compared to the factors above, toxic or hazardous synthetic chemicals in the environment are becoming an increasing source of concern as industry uses more and more exotic materials to manufacture the goods we all purchase. There are many of these compounds to worry about. Somewhere around five million different chemical substances are known, about 100,000 are used in commercial quantities, and about 10,000 new ones are discovered or invented each year. Few of these materials have been thoroughly tested for toxicity. Furthermore, the process of predicting what our chances of exposure and potential harm might be from those re-leased into the environment remains highly controversial. Toxins are poisonous, which means that they react specifically with cellular components or interfere with unique physiological processes. A particular chemical may be toxic to one organism but not another, or dangerous in one type of exposure but not others. Because of this specificity, they may be harmful even in very dilute concentrations. Ricin, for instance, is a protein found in castor beans and one of the most toxic materials known. Three hundred picograms (trillionths of a gram) injected intravenously is enough to kill an average mouse. A single molecule can kill an individual cell. If humans were as sensitive as mice, a few teaspoons of this compound, divided evenly and distributed uniformly could kill everyone in the world. By the way, this points out that not all toxins are produced by industry. Many natural products are highly toxic.

Toxins that have chronic (long-lasting) or irreversible effects are of special concern. Among some important examples are neurotoxins (attack nerve cells), mutagens (cause genetic damage), teratogens (result in birth defects), and carcinogens (cause cancer). Many **pesticide**s and **metals** such as **mercury**, **lead**, and chromium are neurotoxins. Loss of even a few critical neurons can be highly noticeable or may even be lethal making this category of great importance. Chemicals or physical factors such as radiation that damage genetic material can harm not only cells produced in the

exposed individual, but also the offspring of those individuals as well.

Among the most dread characteristics of all these chronic environmental health threats are that the initial exposure may be so small or have results so unnoticeable that the victim doesn't even know that anything has happened until years later. Furthermore the results may be catastrophic and irreversible once they do appear. These are among our worst fears and are powerful reasons that we are so apprehensive about environmental contaminants. There may be no exposure—no matter how small—of some chemicals that is absolutely safe. Because of these fears, we often demand absolute protection from some of the most dread contaminants. Unfortunately, this may not be possible. There may be no way to insure that we are never exposed to any amount of some hazards. It may be that our only recourse is to ask how we can reduce our exposure or mitigate the consequences of that exposure.

In spite of the foregoing discussion of the dangers of chronic effects from minute exposures to certain materials or factors, not all pollutants are equally dangerous nor is every exposure an unacceptable risk. Our fear of unknown and unfamiliar industrial chemicals can lead to hysterical demands for zero exposure to risks. The fact is that life is risky. Furthermore, some materials are extremely toxic while others are only moderately or even slightly so.

This is expressed in the adage of the German physician, Paracelsus, who said in 1540 that "The dose makes the poison." It has become a basic principle of toxicology that nearly everything is toxic at some concentration but most materials have some lower level at which they present an insignificant risk. Sodium chloride (table salt), for instance, is essential for human life in small doses. If you were forced to eat a kilogram all at once, however, it would make you very sick. A similar amount injected all at once into your blood stream would be lethal.

How a material is delivered—at what rate, through which route of entry, in what form—is often as important as what the material is. The movement, distribution, and fate of materials in the environment are important aspects of environmental health. Solubility is one of the most important characteristics in deter- mining how, when, and where a material will travel through the environment and into our bodies. Chemicals that are water soluble move more rapidly and extensively but also are easier to wash off, excrete, or eliminate. Oil or fat soluble chemicals may not move through the environment as easily as water-soluble materials but may penetrate very efficiently through the skin and into tissues and organs. They also may be more likely to be concentrated and stored permanently in fat deposits in the body.

The most common route of entry into the body for many materials is through ingestion and absorption in the gastrointestinal (GI) tract. The GI tract, along with the urinary system are the main routes of excretion of dangerous materials. Not surprisingly, those cells and tissues most intimately and continuously in contact with dangerous materials are among the ones most likely to be damaged. Ulcers, infections, lesions, or tumors of the mouth, esophagus, stomach, intestine, colon, kidney, bladder, and associated glands are among the most common manifestations of environmental toxins. Other common routes of entry for toxins are through the respiratory system and the skin. These also are important routes for excreting or discharging unwanted materials.

Some of our most convincing evidence about the toxicity of particular chemicals on humans has come from experiments in which volunteers (students, convicts, or others) were deliberately given measured levels under controlled conditions. Because it is now considered unethical to experiment on living humans, we are forced to depend on proxy experiments using computer models, tissue cultures, or laboratory animals. These proxy tests are difficult to interpret. We can't be sure that experimental methods can be extrapolated to how real living humans would react. The most commonly used laboratory animals in toxicity tests are rodents like rats and mice. However, different species can react very differently to the same compound. Of some 200 chemicals shown to be carcinogenic in either rats or mice, for instance, about half caused cancer in one species but not the other. How should we interpret these results? Should we assume that we are as sensitive as the most susceptible animal, as resistant as the least sensitive, or somewhere in between?

It is especially difficult to determine responses to very low levels of particular chemicals, especially when they are not highly toxic. The effects of random events, chance, and unknown complicating factors become troublesome, often resulting in a high level of uncertainty in predicting risk. The case of the sweetener saccharin is a good example of the complexities and uncertainties in risk assessment. Studies in the 1970s suggested a link between saccharin and bladder cancer in male rats. Critics pointed out that humans would have to drink 800 cans of soft drink per day to get a dose equivalent to that given to the rats. Furthermore, they argued, most people are not merely large rats.

The **Food and Drug Administration** uses a range of estimates of the probable toxicity of saccharine in humans. At current rates of consumption, the lower estimate predicts that only one person in the United states will get cancer every 1,000 years from saccharine. That is clearly inconsequential considering the advantages of reduced weight, fewer cases of diabetes, and other benefits from this sugar substitute. The upper estimate, however, suggests that 3,640 people will die each year from this same exposure. That is most certainly a risk worth worrying about.

An emerging environmental health concern with a similarly high level of uncertainty but potentially dire consequences is the disruption of endocrine hormone functions by synthetic chemicals. About ten years ago, wildlife biologists began to report puzzling evidence of reproductive failures and abnormal development in certain wild animal populations. Alligators in a lake in central Florida, for instance, were reported to have a 90% decline in egg hatching and juvenile survival along with feminization of adult males including abnormally small penises and lack of sperm production. Similar reproductive problems and developmental defects were reported for trout in the Great Lakes, seagulls in

California, panthers in Florida, and a number of other species. Even humans may be effected if reports of global reduction of sperm counts and increases of hormone-dependent cancers prove to be true.

Both laboratory and field studies point to a possible role of synthetic chemicals in these problems. More than 50 chemicals, if present in high enough concentrations, are now known to mimic or disrupt the signals conveyed by naturally occurring endocrine hormones that control almost every aspect of development, behavior, immune functions, and metabolism. Among these chemicals are **dioxin**, **polychlorinated biphenyl**, and several persistent pesticides. This new field of research promises to be of great concern in the next few years because it combines dread factors of great emotional power such as undetectable exposure, threat to future generations, unknown or delayed consequences, and involuntary or inequitable distribution of risk.

In spite of the seriousness of the concerns expressed above, the **Environmental Protection Agency** warns that we need to take a balanced view of environmental health. The risks associated with allowable levels of certain organic solvents in drinking water or some pesticides in food are thought to carry a risk of less than one cancer in a million people in a lifetime. Many people are outraged about being exposed to this risk, yet they cheerfully accept risks thousands of times as higher from activities they enjoy such as smoking, driving a car, or eating an unhealthy diet. According to the EPA, the most important things we as individuals can do to improve our health are to reduce smoking, drive safely, eat a balanced diet, exercise reasonably, lower stress in our lives, avoid dangerous jobs, lower indoor pollutants, practice safe sex, avoid sun exposure, and prevent household accidents. Many of these factors over which we have control are much more risky than the unknown, uncontrollable, environmental hazards we fear so much.

[*William P. Cunningham*]

FURTHER READING

Foster, H.D. *Health, Disease and the Environment*. Boca Raton, FL: CRC Press, 1992.

Hall, J.V., et al. "Valuing the Health Benefits of Clean Air." *Science* 255 (14 February 1991): 812-17.

Moeller, D.W. *Environmental Health*. Cambridge: Harvard University Press, 1992.

Morgan, M.T. *Environmental Health*. Madison: Brown & Benchmark, 1993.

Environmental history

Much of human history has been a struggle for food, shelter, and survival in the face of **nature**'s harshness. Three major events or turning points have been the use of fire, the development of agriculture, and the invention of tools and machines. Each of these advances has brought benefits to humans but often at the cost of **environmental degradation**. Agriculture, for instance, increased food supplies but also caused soil erosion, population explosions, and support of sedentary living and urban life. It was the Industrial

Revolution that gave humankind the greater power to conquer and devastate our environment. Jacob Bronowski called it an energy revolution, with power as the prime goal. As he noted, it is an ongoing revolution, with the fate of literally billions of people hanging on the outcome.

The Industrial Revolution, with its initial dependence on the steam engine, iron works, and heavy use of coal, made possible our modern lifestyle with its high consumption of energy and material resources. With it, however, has come devastating levels of air, water, land, and chemical **pollution**. In essence, environmental history is the story of the growing recognition of our negative impact upon nature and the corresponding public interest in correcting these abuses. Cunningham and Saigo (1997) describe four stages of **conservation** history and environmental activism: 1) pragmatic resource conservation; 2) moral and aesthetic resource preservation; 3) growing concern over the impact of pollution on health and **ecosystem**s; and 4) global environmental citizenship.

Environmental history, like all history, is very much a study of key individuals and events. Included here are **Thomas Robert Malthus, George Perkins Marsh, Theodore Roosevelt,** and **Rachel Carson**. Writing at the end of the eighteenth century, Malthus was the first to develop a coherent theory of population, arguing that growth in food supply could not keep up with the much larger growth in population. Of cruel necessity, population growth would inevitably be limited by famine, pestilence, disease, or war. Modern supporters are labeled "neoMalthusians" and include notable spokespersons **Paul Erlich** and **Lester Brown**.

In his 1864 book *Man in Nature*, George Perkins Marsh was the first to attack the American myth of superabundance and inexhaustible resources. Citing many examples from Mediterranean lands and the United States, he described the devastating impact of land abuse through deforestation and soil erosion. Lewis Mumford called this book "the fountainhead of the conservation movement," and Stewart Udall described it as the beginning of land wisdom in this country. Marsh's work led to forest preservation and influenced President Theodore Roosevelt and his chief forester, **Gifford Pinchot**.

Effective forest and wildlife protection began during Theodore Roosevelt's presidency whose term of office (1901-09) has been called "The Golden Age of Conservation." His administration established the first **wildlife refuge**s and **national forest**s.

At this time key differences emerged between proponents of conservation and preservation. Pinchot's policies were utilitarian, emphasizing the wise use of resources. By contrast, preservationists led by **John Muir** argued for leaving nature untouched. A key battle was fought over the **Hetch Hetchy Reservoir** in **Yosemite National Park**, a proposed water supply for San Francisco, California. Although Muir lost, the **Sierra Club** (founded in 1882) gained national prominence. Similar battles are now being waged over petroleum extraction in Alaska's **Arctic National Wildlife Refuge** and mining permits on federal lands, including wilderness areas.

Rachel Carson gained widespread fame through her battle against the indiscriminate use of pesticides. Her 1962 book *Silent Spring* has been hailed as the "fountainhead of the modern environmental movement." It has been translated into over 20 languages and is still a best seller. She argued against pesticide abuse and for the right of common citizens to be safe from pesticides in their own homes. Though vigorously opposed by the chemical industry, her views were vindicated by her overpowering reliance on scientific evidence, some given surreptitiously by government scientists. In effect, *Silent Spring* was the opening salvo in the battle of ecologists against chemists. Much of the current mistrust of chemicals stems from her work.

Several historical events are relevant to environmental history. The closing of the American frontier at the end of the nineteenth century gave political strength to the Theodore Roosevelt presidency. The 1908 White House Conference on Conservation, organized and chaired by Gifford Pinchot, is perhaps the most prestigious and influential meeting ever held in the United States.

During the 1930s, the drought in the American Dust Bowl awakened the country to the soil erosion concerns first voiced by Marsh. The establishment of the Soil Conservation Service in 1935 was a direct response to this national tragedy.

In 1955, an international symposium entitled "Man's Role in Changing the Face of the Earth" was held at Princeton University. An impressive assemblage of scholars led by geographer Carl Ortwin Sauer, zoologist Marston O. Bates, and urban planner Lewis Mumford documented the history of human impact on the earth, the processes of human alteration of the environment, and the prospects for future habitability.

The Apollo moon voyages, especially *Apollo 8* in December 1968 and the dramatic photos taken of Earth from space, awakened the world to the concept of "spaceship earth." It was as though the entire human community gave one collective gasp at the small size and fragile beauty of this one planet we call home.

The two energy price shocks of the 1970s spawned by the 1973 Arab-Israeli War and the 1979 Iranian Islamic Revolution fundamentally altered American energy habits. Our salvation came in part from our horrific waste. Simple energy conservation measures and more fuel-efficient automobiles, predominantly of foreign manufacture, produced enough savings to cause a mid-1980s crash in petroleum prices. Nonetheless, many efficiencies begun during the 1970s remain.

The Montreal Accord of 1988 is notable for being the first international agreement to phase out a damaging chemical, **chlorofluorocarbons (CFCs)**. This was a direct response to evidence from satellite data over Antarctica that chlorine-based compounds were destroying the stratospheric **ozone** shield, which provides vital protection against damaging ultraviolet radiation.

Key accidents and corresponding media coverage of environmental concerns have powerfully influenced public opinion. Common themes during the 1960s and 1970s included the "death of Lake Erie," the ravages of strip mining for coal, the confirmation of automobile exhaust as a key source of photochemical smog, destruction of the ozone layer, and the threat of global warming. The ten-hour Annenberg CPB project, *Race to Save the Planet*, is now common fare in environmental science telecourses.

Media coverage of specific accidents or sites has had some of the greatest impact on public awareness of environmental problems. Oil spills have provided especially vivid and troubling images. The wreck of the **Torrey Canyon** in 1967 off southern England was the first involving a supertanker, and a harbinger of even larger disasters to come, such as the **Exxon Valdez** spill in Alaska. The blowout of an oil well in California's Santa Barbara Channel played nightly on network television news programs. Scenes of oil-covered birds and muddy shorelines were powerful images in the battle for environmental awareness and commitment.

The **Cuyahoga River** in Cleveland was so polluted with petroleum waste that it actually caught fire twice. Love Canal, a forgotten chemical waste dump in Niagara Falls, New York, became the inspiration for passage of the Superfund Act, a tax on chemical companies to pay for cleanup of abandoned hazardous waste sites. It was also personal vindication for **Lois Marie Gibbs**, leader of the **Love Canal** Homeowners Association.

One air pollution episode in New York City was blamed for the deaths of about 300 people. In response to another in Birmingham, Alabama, a federal judge ordered the temporary shutdown of local steel mills.

The loudest alarms raised against the growing use of nuclear power in the U.S. were sounded by the combination of the 1979 near-meltdown at **Three Mile Island Nuclear Reactor** in Pennsylvania and the subsequent (1986) **Chernobyl Nuclear Power Station** disaster in the Ukraine.

Media coverage and growing public awareness of pollution problems, has led to widespread support for corrective legislation. A large body of such legislation was passed between 1968 and 1980. Especially notable were the **National Environmental Policy Act**, which created the **Environmental Protection Agency**, clean air and water acts, **Superfund**, and the **Surface Mining Control and Reclamation Act**. The latter required miners to reshape the land to near its original contour and to replace topsoil, both essential keys to the long-term recovery of the land.

Earlier noteworthy legislation includes the establishment in 1872 of Yellowstone as the world's first national park; establishment of national wildlife refuges, forests, and parks, and the agencies to oversee them; and the creation of the **Soil Conservation Service**. The **Wilderness Act** of 1964 sought to set aside government land for nondestructive uses only.

Much has been accomplished, and environmental issues now command widespread public attention. A list of books, journals, environmental organizations, and relevant government agencies now fills six pages of small print in one popular environmental textbook. Nonetheless, important challenges lie ahead in the pursuit of a quality environment that will tax environmental organizations, government policymakers, and voters.

Some key issues for the future can be grouped into the following four categories. 1) Rapidly increasing costs as control standards reach higher and higher levels. The inexpensive and easy solutions have mostly been tried. Solving the air pollution problems within the Los Angeles basin is a prime example of this challenge. 2) Control of phosphates and nitrates in our waterways will require increasing commitment to tertiary (or chemical) sewage treatment plants. We may also find it necessary to reroute all urban runoff through such plants. 3) Solutions to the global warming problem, if supported by ongoing scientific research, will require alternative energy strategies, especially as large, newly emerging economies of China, India, Brazil, and other countries seek a growing share of the total energy pie. 4) There is a growing conservative trend and related hostility to environmental concerns among our younger population. Consequently, the need for meaningful environmental education and dialogue will only continue to increase.

[*Nathan H. Meleen*]

FURTHER READING

The American Experience. "Rachel Carson's *Silent Spring*." Boston: Public Broadcasting System, 1993.

Cunningham, W. P., and B. W. Saigo. *Environmental Science: A Global Concern*. 4th ed. Dubuque, IA: Wm. C. Brown, 1997.

Marsh, G. P. *Man and Nature, or Physical Geography as Modified by Human Action*. 1864. Reprint, Cambridge, MA: Harvard University Press, 1965.

Miller, G. T. Jr. *Living in the Environment*. 9th ed. Belmont, CA: Wadsworth, 1996.

Thomas, W. L. Jr., ed. *Man's Role in Changing the Face of the Earth*. Chicago: University of Chicago Press, 1956.

Environmental impact assessment

A written analysis or process that describes and details the probable and possible effects of planned industrial or civil project activities on the **ecosystem**, resources, and environment. The **National Environmental Policy Act (NEPA)** first promulgated guidelines for environmental impact assessments with the intention that the **environment** receive proper emphasis among social, economic, and political priorities in governmental decision-making. This act required environmental impact assessments for major federal actions affecting the environment. Many states now have similar requirements for state and private activities. Such written assessments are called **Environmental Impact Statement**s or EISs.

EISs range from brief statements to extremely detailed multi-volume reports that require many years of data collection and analysis. In general, the environmental impact assessment process requires consideration and evaluation of the proposed project, its impacts, alternatives to the project, and mitigating strategies designed to reduce the severity of adverse effects. The assessments are completed by multidisciplinary teams in government agencies and consulting firms. The experience of the United States **Army Corps of Engineers** in detailing the impacts of projects such as **dams** and waterways is particularly noteworthy, as the Corps has developed comprehensive methodologies to assess impacts of such major and complex projects. These include evaluation of direct environmental impacts as well as social and economic ramifications.

The content of the assessments generally follows guidelines in the National Environmental Policy Act. Assessments usually include the following sections:

(1) Background information describing the affected population and the environmental setting, including archaeological and historical features, public utilities, cultural and social values, **topography**, **hydrology**, geology and **soil**, climatology, **natural resources**, and terrestrial and aquatic communities;

(2) Description of the proposed action detailing its purpose, location, time frame, and relationship to other projects;

(3) The environmental impacts of proposed action on natural resources, ecological systems, population density, distribution and growth rate, **land use**, and human health. These impacts should be described in detail and include primary and secondary impacts, beneficial and adverse impacts, short and long term effects, the rate of recovery, and importantly, measures to reduce or eliminate adverse effects;

(4) Adverse impacts that cannot be avoided are described in detail, including a description of their magnitude and implications;

(5) Alternatives to the project are described and evaluated. These must include the "no action" alternative. A comparative analysis of alternatives permits the assessment of environmental benefits, risks, financial benefits and costs, and overall effectiveness;

(6) The reason for selecting the proposed action is justified as a balance between risks, impacts, costs, and other factors relevant to the project;

(7) The relationship between short and long term uses and maintenance is described, with the intent of detailing short and long term gains and losses;

(8) Reversible and irreversible impacts;

(9) Public participation in the process is described;

(10) Finally, the EIS includes a discussion of problems and issues raised by interested parties, such as specific federal, state, or local agencies, citizens, and activists.

The environmental impact assessment process provides a wealth of detailed technical information. It has been effective in stopping, altering, or improving some projects. However, serious questions have been raised about the adequacy and fairness of the process. For example, assessments may be too narrow or may not have sufficient depth. The alternatives considered may reflect the judgment of decision-makers who specify objectives, the study design, and the alternatives considered. Difficult and important questions exist regarding the balance of environmental, economic, and other interests. Finally, these issues often take place in a politicized and highly-charged atmosphere that may not be amenable to negotiation. Despite these and other limitations, environmental impact assessments help to provide a system-

atic approach to sharing information that can improve public decision-making. *See also* Risk assessment

[*Stuart Batterman*]

FURTHER READING

The National Environmental Policy Act of 1969, as Amended, P.L. 91-140 (1 January 1970), amended P.L. 94-83 (9 August 1975).

Rau, J., and D. G. Wooten, eds. *Environmental Impact Analysis Handbook.* New York, McGraw-Hill, 1980.

Environmental Impact Statement

The **National Environmental Policy Act (1969)** made all federal agencies responsible for analyzing any activity of theirs "significantly affecting the quality of the human environment." Environmental Impact Statements (EIS) are the assessments stipulated by this act, and these reports are required for all large projects initiated, financed, or permitted by the federal government. In addition to examining the damage a particular project might have on the environment, federal agencies are also expected to review ways of minimizing or alleviating these adverse effects—a review which can include consideration of the environmental benefits of abandoning the project altogether. The agency compiling an EIS is required to hold public hearings; it is also required to submit a draft to public review, and it is forbidden from proceeding until it releases a final version of the statement.

The NEPA has been called "the first comprehensive commitment of any modern state toward the responsible custody of its environment," and the EIS is considered one of the most important mechanisms for its enforcement. It is often difficult to identify environmental damages with remedies that can be pursued in court, but the filing of an EIS and the standards the document must meet are clear and definite requirements for which federal agencies can be held accountable. These requirements have allowed environmental groups to focus legal challenges on the adequacy of the report, contesting the way an EIS was prepared or identifying environmental effects that were not taken into account. The expense and the delays involved in defending against these challenges have often given these groups powerful leverage for convincing a company or an agency to change or omit particular elements of a project. Many environmental organizations have taken advantage of these opportunities; between 1974 and 1983, over 100 such suits were filed every year.

Although litigation over impact statements can have a decisive influence on a wide range of decisions in government and business, the legal status of these reports and the legal force of the NEPA itself are not as strong as many environmentalists believe they should be. The act does not require agencies to limit or prevent the potential environmental damage identified in an EIS. The Supreme Court upheld this interpretation in 1989, deciding that agencies are "not constrained by NEPA from deciding that other values outweigh the environmental costs." The government, in other words, is required only to identify and evaluate the adverse impacts of proposed projects; it is not required, at least by NEPA, to do anything about them. Environmentalists have long argued that environmental protection needs a stronger legal grounding than this act provides; some such as **Lynton Caldwell**, who was originally involved in the drafting of the NEPA, maintain that only a constitutional amendment will serve this purpose.

In addition to the controversies over what should be included in these reports and what should be done about the information, there have also been a number of debates over who is required to file them. Environmental groups have filed suit in the Pacific Northwest alleging that the government should require logging companies to file impact statements. And many people have observed that an EIS is not actually required of all government agencies; the **U. S. Department of Agriculture**, for instance, is not required to file such reports on its commodity support programs.

Impact statements have been opposed by business and industrial groups since they were first introduced. An EIS can be extremely costly to compile, and the process of filing and defending them can take years. Businesses can be left in limbo over projects in which they have already invested large amounts of money, and the uncertainties of the process itself have often stopped development before it has begun. In the debate about these statements, many advocates for business interests have pointed out that environmental regulation accounts for 23 percent of the 400 billion dollars the federal government spends on regulation each year. They argue that impact statements restrict the ability of the United States to compete in international markets by forcing American businesses to spend money on compliance that could be invested in research or capital improvements. Many people believe that impact statements seriously delay many aspects of economic growth, and business leaders have questioned the priorities of many environmental groups, who seem to value **conservation** over social benefits such as high-levels of employment.

In July of 1993, a judge in a federal district court ruled that the North American Free Trade Agreement (NAFTA) could not be submitted to Congress for approval until the Clinton Administration had filed an EIS on the treaty. The controversy over whether an EIS should be required for NAFTA is a good example of the battle between those who want to extend the range of the EIS and those who want to limit it, as well as the practical problems with positions held by both sides.

Environmentalists fear the consequences of free trade in North America, particularly free trade with Mexico. They believe that most industries would not take any precautions about the environment unless they were forced to observe them. Environmental protection in Mexico, when it exists, is corrupt and inefficient; if NAFTA is approved by Congress, many believe that businesses in the United States will move south of the border to escape environmental regulations. This could have devastating consequences for the environment in Mexico, as well as an adverse impact on the United States economy. It is also possible that an extensive economic downturn, if perceived to be the result of such relocations, could affect the future of environmental regulation in this country as the United States begins to compete with Mexico over the incentives it can offer industry.

Opponents of the decision to require an EIS for NAFTA insist that such a document would be almost impossible to compile. The statement would have to be enormously complex; it would have to consider a range of economic as well as environmental factors, projecting the course of economic development in Mexico before predicting the impact on the environment. Extending the range of impact statements and the NEPA would cause the same expensive delays for this treaty that these statutes have caused for projects within the United States, and critics have focused mainly on the effect such an extension would have on our international competitiveness. They argue that this decision, if upheld, could have broad ramifications for American foreign policy. An EIS could be required for every treaty the government signs with another country, including negotiations over fishing rights, arms control treaties, and other trade agreements. Foreign policy decisions could then be subject to extensive litigation over the adequacy of the EIS filed by the appropriate agency. Many environmentalists would view this as a positive development, but others believe it could prevent us from assuming a leadership role in international affairs.

Carol Browner, the new chief administrator of the **Environmental Protection Agency (EPA)**, has announced that her agency is determined to reduce some of the difficulties of complying with environmental regulations. She is especially concerned with increasing efficiency and limiting the delays and uncertainties for business. But whatever changes she is able to make, the process of compiling an EIS will never seem cost effective to business, at least in the short term, and the controversy over these statements will continue. *See also* Economic growth and the environment; Environmental auditing; Environmental economics; Environmental impact assessment; Environmental Monitoring and Assessment Program; Environmental policy; Life-cycle assessment; Risk analysis; Sustainable development

[*Douglas Smith*]

FURTHER READING

Burck, C. "Surprise Judgement on NAFTA." *Fortune* 128 (26 July 1993): 12.

Davies, J. "Suit Threatens Washington State Industry." *Journal of Commerce* 390 (21 October 1991): 9A.

Dentzer, S. "Hasta la Vista in Court, Baby." *U.S. News and World Report* 115 (12 July 1993): 47.

Ember, L. "EPA's Browner to Take Holistic Approach to Environmental Protection." *Chemical and Engineering News* 71 (1 March 1993): 19.

Gregory, R., R. Keeney, and D. von Wintervelt. "Adapting the Environmental Impact Statement Process to Inform Decisionmakers." *Journal of Policy Analysis and Management* (Winter 1992): 58.

Environmental labeling

See **Blue Angel; Ecomark; Green Cross; Green Seal**

Environmental law

Environmental law has been defined as the law of planetary housekeeping. It is concerned with protecting the planet and its people from activities that upset the earth and its life-sustaining capabilities, and it is aimed at controlling or regulating human activity toward that end.

Until the 1960s, most environmental legal issues in the United States involved efforts to protect and conserve **natural resources**, such as forests and water. Public debate focused on who had the right to develop and manage those resources. In the succeeding decades, lawyers, legislators and environmental activists increasingly turned their attention to the growing and pervasive problem of **pollution**. In both instances, environmental law—a term not coined until 1969—evolved mostly from a grassroots movement that forced Congress to pass sweeping legislation, much of which contained provisions for citizen suits. As a result, the courts were thrust into a new era of judicial review of the administrative processes and of scientific uncertainty.

Initially, environmental law formed around the principles of common law, which is law created by courts and judges that rests upon a foundation of judicial precedents. However, environmental law soon moved into the arena of administrative and legislative law, which encompasses most of today's environmental law. The following discussion looks at both areas of law, reviews some of the basic issues involved in environmental law, and outlines some landmark cases.

Generally speaking, common law is based on the notion that one party has done harm to another, in legal terms called a *tort*. There are three broad types of torts, all of which have been applied in environmental law with varying degrees of success. Trespass is the physical invasion of one's property, which has been interpreted to include situations such as **air pollution**, **runoff** of liquid wastes, or contamination of **groundwater**.

Closely associated with trespass are the torts of private and public nuisance. *Private nuisance* is interference with the use of one's property. Environmental examples include **noise pollution**, **odor**s and other air pollution, and **water pollution**. The operation of a **hazardous waste** site fits the bill for private nuisance, where the threat of personal discomfort or disease interferes with the enjoyment of one's home. A *public nuisance* adversely affects the safety or health of the public or causes substantial annoyance or inconvenience to the public. In these situations, the courts tend to balance the plaintiff's interest against the social and economic need for the defendant's activity.

Lastly, *negligence* involves the defendant's conduct. To prove negligence it must be shown that the defendant was obligated to exercise *due care*, that the defendant breached that duty, that the plaintiff suffered actual loss or damages, and that there is a reasonable connection between the defendant's conduct and the plaintiff's injury.

These common law remedies have not been very effective in protecting the overall quality of our environment. The lawsuits and resulting decisions were fragmented and site specific as opposed to issue oriented. Further, they rely heavily on a level of hard scientific evidence that is elusive in environmental issues. For instance, a trespass action must be based on a somehow visible or tangible invasion, which is difficult if not impossible to prove in pollution cases. Common law presents other barriers to action. Plaintiffs must prove actual physical injury (so-called "aesthetic injuries" don't count) and a causal relationship to the plaintiff's activity, which again, is a difficult task in environmental issues.

In the early 1970s, environmental groups, aided by the media, focused public attention on the broad scope of the environmental crisis, and Congress reacted. It passed a host of comprehensive laws, including amendments to the **Clean Air Act** (CAA), the **Endangered Species Act** (ESA), the **National Environmental Policy Act** (NEPA), the **Resource Conservation and Recovery Act** (RCRA), the **Toxic Substances Control Act** (TSCA), and others. These laws, or statutes, are implemented by federal agencies, who gain their authority through "organic acts" passed by Congress or by executive order.

As environmental problems grew more complicated, legislators and judges increasingly deferred to the agencies' expertise on issues such as the health risk from airborne lead, the threshold at which a species should be considered endangered, or the engineering aspects of a hazardous waste incinerator. Environmental and legal activists then shifted their focus toward administrative law—challenging agency discretion and procedure as opposed to specific regulations—in order to be heard. Hence, most environmental law today falls into the administrative category.

Most environmental statutes provide for administrative appeals by which interest groups may challenge agency decisions through the agency hierarchy. If no solution is reached, the federal Administrative Procedures Act provides that any person aggrieved by an agency decision is entitled to judicial review.

The court must first grant the plaintiff "standing," the right to be a party to legal action against an agency. Under this doctrine, plaintiffs must show they have been injured or harmed in some way. The court must then decide the level of judicial review based on one of three issues—interpretation of applicable statutes, factual basis of agency action, and agency procedure—and apply a different level of scrutiny in each instance.

Generally, courts are faced with five basic questions when reviewing agency action: Is the action or decision constitutional? Did the agency exceed its statutory authority or jurisdiction? Did if follow legal procedure? Is the decision supported by substantial evidence in the record? Is the decision arbitrary or capricious? Depending on the answers, the court may uphold the decision, modify it, remand or send it back to the agency to redo or reverse it.

By far the most important statute that cracked open the administrative process to judicial review is NEPA. Passed in 1969, the law requires all agencies to prepare an **Environmental Impact Statement** (EIS) for all major federal actions, including construction projects and issuing permits. Environmental groups have used this law repeatedly to force agencies to consider the environmental consequences of their actions, attacking various procedural aspects of EIS preparation. For example, they often claim that a given agency failed to consider alternative actions to the proposed one, which might reduce environmental impact.

In filing a lawsuit, plaintiffs might seek an injunction against a certain action, say, to stop an industry from dumping toxic waste into a river, or stop work on a public project such as a dam or a timber sale that they claim causes environmental damage. They might seek compensatory damages to make up for a loss of property or for health costs, for instance, and punitive damages, money awards above and beyond repayment of actual losses.

Boomer v. Atlantic Cement Co. (1970) is a classic common law nuisance case. The neighbors of a large cement plant claimed they had incurred property damage from dirt, **smoke** and vibrations. They sued for compensatory damages and to enjoin or stop the polluting activities, which would have meant shutting down the plant, a mainstay of the local economy. The New York court rejected a long-standing practice and denied the injunction. Further, in an unusual move, the court ordered the company to pay the plaintiffs for present *and* future economic loss to their properties. A dissenting judge said the rule was a virtual license for the company to continue the nuisance so long as it paid for it.

Sierra Club v. Morton (1972) opened the way for environmental groups to act on behalf of the public interest, and of nature, in the courtroom. The **Sierra Club** challenged the U.S. **Forest Service**'s approval of Walt Disney Enterprises' plan to build a $35 million complex of motels, restaurants, swimming pools and ski facilities that would accommodate up to 14,000 visitors daily in Mineral King Valley, a remote, relatively undeveloped national game refuge in the Sierra Nevada Mountains of California. The case posed the now-famous question: Do trees have standing? The Supreme Court held that the Sierra Club was not "injured in fact" by the development and therefore did not have standing. The Sierra Club reworded its petition, gained standing and stopped the development.

Citizens to Preserve Overton Park v. Volpe (1971) established the so-called "hard look" test to which agencies must adhere even during informal rule making. It opened the way for more intense judicial review of the administrative record to determine if an agency had made a "clear error of judgment." The plaintiffs, local residents and conservationists, sued to stop the U.S. Department of Transportation from approving a six-lane interstate through a public park in Memphis, Tennessee. The court found that Secretary Volpe had not carefully reviewed the facts on record before making his decision and had not examined possible alternative routes around the park. The case was sent back to the agency, and the road was never built.

Tennessee Valley Authority v. Hill (1978) was the first major test of the Endangered Species Act and gained the tiny **snail darter** fish fame throughout the land. The Supreme Court authorized an injunction against completion of a multi-million dollar dam in Tennessee because it threatened the snail darter, an **endangered species**. The court balanced the act against the money that had already been spent

and ruled that Congress's intent in protecting endangered species was paramount.

Just v. Marinette County (1972) involved **wetlands**, the public trust doctrine and private property rights. The plaintiffs claimed that the county's ordinance against filling in wetlands on their land was unconstitutional, and that the restrictions amounted to taking their property without compensation. The county argued it was exercising its normal police powers to protect the health, safety and welfare of citizens by protecting its water resources through zoning measures. The Wisconsin appellate court ruled in favor of the defendant, holding that the highest and best use of land does not always equate to monetary value, but includes the natural value. The opinion reads, ". . . we think it is not an unreasonable exercise of that [police] power to prevent harm to public rights by limiting the use of private property to its natural uses."

Although some progress was made in curbing **environmental degradation** through environmental law in the 1970s, environmental legislation has been significantly weakened by the Supreme Court in the 1980s.

[*Cathryn McCue*]

FURTHER READING

Anderson, F., D. R. Mandelker, and A. D. Tarlock. *Environmental Protection: Law and Policy.* New York: Little, Brown, 1984.

Findley, R., and D. Farber. *Environmental Law in a Nutshell.* St. Paul, MN: West Publishing Co., 1988.

Plater, Z., R. Abrams, and W. Goldfarb. *Environmental Law and Policy: Nature, Law and Society.* St. Paul, MN: West Publishing Co., 1992.

Environmental Law Institute (Washington, D.C.)

Environmental Law Institute (ELI) is an independent research and education center involved in developing **environmental law**s and policies at both national and international levels. The institute was founded in 1969 by the Public Law Education Institute and the Conservation Foundation to conduct and promote research on environmental law. In the ensuing years it has maintained a strong and effective presence in forums ranging from colleges courses to law conferences. For example, ELI has organized instructional courses at universities for both federal and non-governmental agencies. In addition, it has sponsored conferences in conjunction with such bodies as the American Bar Association, the American Law Institute, and the Smithsonian Institute.

Within the field of environmental law, ELI provides a range of educational programs and services. In 1991, for instance, the institute helped develop an environmental law course for practicing judges in the New England area. Through funding and endowments, the institute has since managed to expand this particular judicial education program into other regions. A similar program enables ELI to offer training courses to federal judges currently serving in district, circuit, and even bankruptcy courts.

ELI also offers various workshops to the general public. In New Jersey, the institute provided a course designed to guide citizens through the state's environmental laws and thus enable them to better develop **pollution**-prevention programs in their communities. Broader right-to-know guidance has since been provided—in collaboration with the **World Wildlife Fund**—at the international level.

ELI's endeavors at the federal level include various interactions with the **Environmental Protection Agency (EPA)**. The two groups worked together to develop the National Wetlands Protection Hotline, which answers public inquiries on **wetlands** protection and regulation, and to assess the dangers of exposure to various pollutants.

Since its inception, ELI has evolved into a formidable force in the field of environmental law. In 1991, for example, it drafted a statute to address the continuing problem of **lead** poisoning in children. The institute has also worked—in conjunction with federal and private groups, including scientists, bankers, and even realtors—to address health problems attributable to **radon** gas.

ELI has compiled and produced several publications. Among the leading ELI books are *Law of Environmental Protection*, a two-volume handbook (updated annually) on **pollution control** law, and *Practical Guide to Environmental Management*, a resource book on worker health and safety. In addition, ELI has worked with the EPA in producing *Environmental Investments: The Cost of a Clean Environment*. The institute's principal periodical is *Environmental Law Reporter*, which provides analysis and coverage of topics ranging from courtroom decisions to regulation developments. ELI also publishes *Environmental Forum*—a policy journal intended primarily for individuals in environmental law, policy, and management—and *National Wetlands Newsletter*, which reports on ensuing developments—legal, scientific, regulatory—related to wetlands management. Contact: Environmental Law Institute, 1616 P Street, NW, Suite 200, Washington, DC 20036. Internet: http://www.eli.org/.

[*Les Stone*]

Environmental mediation and arbitration
See **Environmental dispute resolution**

Environmental monitoring

Environmental monitoring detects changes in the health of an **ecosystem** and indicates whether conditions are improving, stable, or deteriorating. This quality, too large to gauge as a whole, is assessed by measuring indicators, which represent more complex characteristics. The concentration of **sulfur dioxide**, for example, is an indicator that reflects the presence of other air pollutants. The abundance of a predator indicates the health of the larger environment. Other indicators include **metabolism**, population, community, and land-

scape. All changes are compared to an ideal, pristine ecosystem. The SER (stressor-exposure-response) model, a simple but widely used tool in environmental monitoring, classifies indicators as one of three related types:

(1) Stressors, which are agents of change associated with physical, chemical, or biological constraints on environmental processes and integrity. Many stressors are caused by humans, such as **air pollution**, the use of **pesticide**s and other **toxic substance**s, or **habitat** change caused by forest clearing. Stressors can also be natural processes, such as **wildfire**, **hurricane**s, **volcano**es, and **climate** change.

(2) Exposure indicators, which link a stressor's intensity at any point in time to the cumulative dose received. Concentrations or accumulations of toxic substances are exposure indicators; so are **clear-cutting** and urbanization.

(3) Response indicators, which shows how organisms, communities, processes, or ecosystems react when exposed to a stressor. These include changes in physiology, productivity, or **mortality**, as well as changes in **species** diversity within communities and in rates of **nutrient** cycling.

The SER model is useful because it links ecological change with exposure to **environmental stress**. Its effectiveness is limited, however. The model is a simple one, so it cannot be used for complex environmental situations. Even with smaller-scale problems, the connections between stressor, exposure, and response are not understood in many cases, and additional research is required.

Environmental monitoring programs are usually one of two types, extensive or intensive. Extensive monitoring occurs at permanent, widely spaced locations, sometimes using remote-sensing techniques. It provides an overview of changes in the ecological character of the landscape, often detecting regional trends. It measures the effects of human activities like farming, forestry, mining, and urbanization. Information from extensive monitoring is often collected by the government to determine such variables as water and **air quality**, to calculate allowable forest harvests, set bag limits for hunting and fishing, and establish the production of agricultural commodities.

Extensive monitoring usually measures stressors (such as **emission**s) or exposure indicators (concentration of pollutants in the air). Response indicators, if measured at all in these programs, almost always have some economic importance (damage to forest or agricultural crops). Distinct species or ecological processes do not have economic value and are not usually assessed in extensive-monitoring programs, even though these are the most relevant indicators of ecological integrity.

Intensive monitoring is used for detailed studies of structural and functional **ecology**. Unlike extensive monitoring, a relatively small number of sites provide information on stressors such as climate change and **acid rain**. Intensive monitoring is also used to conduct experiments in which stressors are manipulated and the responses studied, for example by acidifying or fertilizing lakes, or by conducting forestry over an entire watershed. This research, aimed at understanding the dynamics of ecosystems, helps develop ecological models that distinguish between natural and **anthropogenic** change.

Support for ecological monitoring of either kind has been weak, although more countries are beginning programs and establishing networks between monitoring sites. The United States has founded the Long-Term Ecological Research (LTER) network to study extensive ecosystem function, but little effort is directed toward understanding environmental change. The **Environmental Monitoring and Assessment Program** (EMAP) of the **Environmental Protection Agency (EPA)** studies intensive environmental change, but its activities are not integrated with LTER. In comparison, an ecological-monitoring network being designed by the government of Canada to study changes in the environment will integrate both extensive and intensive monitoring.

Communication between the two types of monitoring is important. Intensive information provides a deeper understanding of the meaning of extensive-monitoring indicators. For example, it is much easier to measure decreases in surface-water **pH** and alkalinity caused by acid rain than to monitor resulting changes in fish or other biological variables. These criteria can, however, be measured at intensive-monitoring sites, and their relationships to pH and alkalinity used to predict effects on fish and other **fauna** at extensive sites where only pH and alkalinity are monitored.

The ultimate goal of environmental monitoring is to measure, anticipate, and prevent the deterioration of ecological integrity. Healthy ecosystems are necessary for healthy societies and sustainable economic systems. Environmental monitoring programs can accomplish these goals, but they are expensive and require a substantial commitment by government. Much has yet to be accomplished.

[*Bill Freedman and Cynthia Staicer*]

FURTHER READING

Franklin, J. F., C. S. Bledsoe, and J. T. Callahan. "Contributions of the Long-term Ecological Research Program." *Bioscience* 40 (1990): 509-524.

Freedman, B., C. Staicer, and N. Shackell. *A Framework for a National Ecological-Monitoring Program for Canada*. Ottawa: Environment Canada, 1992.

Odum, E. P. "Trends Expected in Stressed Ecosystems." *Bioscience* 35 (1985): 419-422.

Schindler, D. W. "Experimental Perturbations of Whole Lakes as Tests of Hypotheses Concerning Ecosystem Structure and Function." *Oikos* 57 (1990): 25-41.

Environmental Monitoring and Assessment Program

The Environmental Monitoring and Assessment Program (EMAP), established in 1990, is a federal project designed to create a continually updated survey of ecological resources in the United States. This comprehensive list monitors and links resource data from several U.S. agencies, including the **National Oceanic and Atmospheric Administration**, the **Fish and Wildlife Service**, the **U.S. Department of Agriculture**, and the **Environmental Protection Agency (EPA)**.

Research from the program is intended to illustrate changes in specific **ecosystem**s in the U.S. and to determine if those changes could have resulted from "human-induced stress."

Environmental policy

Strictly, an environmental policy can be defined as a government's chosen course of action or plan to address issues such as **pollution**, **wildlife** protection, **land use**, energy production and use, waste generation and waste disposal. In reality, the way a particular government handles environmental problems is most often *not* a result of a conscious choice from a set of alternatives. More broadly, then, we may characterize a government's environmental policy by examining the overall orientation of its responses to environmental challenges as they occur, or by defining its policy as the sum of plans for, and reactions to, environmental issues made by any number of different arms of government.

A society's environmental policy will be shaped by the actions of its leaders in relation to the five following questions:

(1) Should government intervene in the regulation of the environment or leave resolution of environmental problems to the legal system or the market?

(2) If government intervention is desirable, at what level should that intervention take place? In the United States, for example, how should responsibility for resolution of environmental problems be divided between and among federal, state and local governments and who should have *primary* responsibility?

(3) If government intervenes at some level, how much protection should it give? How safe should the people be and what are the economic trade-offs necessary to ensure that level of safety?

(4) Once environmental standards have been set, what are the methods to attain them? How does the system control the sources of environmental destruction so that the environmental goals are met?

(5) Finally, how does the system monitor the environment for compliance to standards and how does it punish those who violate them?

Policy in the United States

The United States has no single, overarching environmental policy and its response to environmental issues—subject to conflicting political, corporate and public influence, economic limitation and scientific uncertainty—is rarely monolithic. American environmental policies are an amalgamation of Congressional, state and local laws, regulations and rules formulated by agencies to implement those laws, judicial decisions rendered when those rules are challenged in court, programs undertaken by private businesses and industry, as well as trends in public concerns.

In Congress, many environmental policies were originally formed by what are commonly known as "iron triangles." These involve three groups of actors who form a powerful coalition: the Congressional committee with jurisdiction over the issue; the relevant federal agency handling the problem; and the interest group representing the particular regulated industry. For example, the key actors in forming policy on **clear-cutting** in the **national forest**s are the House subcommittee on Forests, Family Farms and Energy, the U.S. **Forest Service** (USFS), and the National Forest Products Association, which represents many industries dependent on timber.

For more than a century, conservation and environmental groups worked at the fringes of the traditional "iron triangle." Increasingly, however, these **public interest group**s—which derived their financial support and sense of mission from an increasing number of citizen members—began gaining more influence. Scientists, whose studies and research today play a pivotal role in decision-making, also began to emerge as major players.

The Watershed Years

Catalyzed by vocal, energetic activists and organizations, the emergence of an "environmental movement" in the late 1960s prompted the government to grant environmental protection a greater priority and visibility. 1970, the year of the first celebration of **Earth Day**, saw the federal government's landmark passage of the **Clean Air Act** and the **National Environmental Policy Act**, as well as Richard Nixon's creation of an **Environmental Protection Agency (EPA)** which was given the control of many environmental policies previously administered by other agencies. In addition, some of the most serious problems such as **DDT** and **mercury** contamination began to be addressed between 1969 and 1972. Yet, environmental policies in the 1970s developed largely in an adversarial setting pitting environmental groups on one side and the traditional iron triangles on the other.

The first policies that came out of this era were designed to clean up visible pollution—clouds of industrial soot and dust, **detergent**-filled streams and so forth—and employed "end-of-pipe" solutions to target **point source**s, such as **wastewater** discharge pipes, smokestacks, and other easily identifiable emitters.

An initial optimism generated by improvements in air and **water quality** was dashed by a series of frightening environmental episodes at **Times Beach, Missouri, Three Mile Island, Love Canal, New York** and other locations. Such incidents (as well as memory of the devastation caused by the recently-banned DDT) shifted the focus of public concern to specific toxic agents. By the early 1980s, a fearful public led by environmentalists had steered governmental policy toward tight regulation of individual, invisible toxic substances—**dioxin, PCB**s and others—by backing measures limiting **emission**s to within a few **parts per million**. Without an overall governmental framework for action, the result has been a multitude of regulations and laws that address specific problems in specific regions that sometimes conflict and often fail to protect the environment in a comprehensive manner. "It's been reactionary, and so we've lost the integration of thought and disciplines that is essential in environmental policy making," says **Carol Browner**, administrator of the U.S. EPA.

One example of policy-making gone awry is the 1980 **Comprehensive Environmental Response, Compensation and Liability Act (CERCLA)**, or *Superfund* toxic waste program. The law grew as much out of the public's perception and fear of toxic waste as it did from crude scientific knowledge of actual health risks. Roughly $2 billion dollars a year has been spent cleaning up a handful of the nation's worst toxic sites to near pristine condition. EPA officials now believe the money could have been better spent cleaning up *more* sites, although to a somewhat lesser degree.

Current Trends in Environmental Policy

Today, governmental bodies and public interest groups are drawing back from "micro management" of individual chemicals, individual species and individual industries to focus more on the interconnections of environmental systems and problems. This new orientation has been shaped by several (sometimes conflicting) forces, including:

(1) industrial and public resistance to tight regulations fostered by fears that such laws impact employment and economic prosperity; (2) financial limitations that prevent government from carrying out tasks related to specific contaminants, such as cleaning up waste sites or closely monitoring toxic discharges; (3) a perception that large-scale, global problems such as the greenhouse effect, **ozone layer depletion, habitat** destruction and the like should receive priority; (4) the emergence of a "preventative" orientation on the part of citizen groups that attempts to link economic prosperity with environmental goals. This approach emphasizes **recycling**, efficiency, and environmental technology and stresses the prevention of problems rather than their remediation after they reach a critical stage. This strategy also marks an attempt by some citizen organizations to a more conciliatory stance with industry and government.

This new era of environmental policy is underscored by the election of Bill Clinton and **Albert Gore**, who made the environment a cornerstone of their campaign. In all likelihood, the Clinton administration will transform the EPA into the cabinet-level position of Department of the Environment, giving the agency more stature and power. The EPA, the USFS and other federal environmental agencies have announced a new "ecosystem" approach to resource management and **pollution control**. In a bold first move, Congressional Democratic leaders are simultaneously reviewing four major environmental statutes (the **Resource Conservation and Recovery Act** [RCRA], Clean Water Act [CWA], **Endangered Species Act** [ESA] and Superfund) in the hopes of integrating the policies into a comprehensive program. *See also* Pollution Prevention Act

[*Cathryn McCue, Kevin Wolf and Jeffrey Muhr*]

FURTHER READING

Browner, Carol, Administrator of U.S. Environmental Protection Agency, comments during a press conference in Ann Arbor, MI, March 23, 1993.

Environmental and Energy Study Institute. *Special Report.* 14 Oct. 1992.

Lave, Lester B. *The Strategy of Social Regulation.* Washington, DC: Brookings Institution, 1981.

Logan, Robert, Wendy Gibbons and Stacy Kingsbury. *Environmental Issues for the '90s: A Handbook for Journalists.* Washington DC: The Media Institute, 1992.

Portney, Paul R., ed. *Public Policies for Environmental Protection.* Washington, DC: Resources for the Future, 1991.

Schneider, Keith. "What Price Clean Up?" *New York Times,* 21-26 March 1993.

Smith, Fred. "A Fresh Look at Environmental Policy." *SEJ Journal* 3 (Winter 1993).

Wolf, Charles, Jr. *Markets or Government.* Cambridge, Massachusetts: MIT Press, 1988.

World Resources Institute. *1992 Environmental Almanac.* Boston: Houghton Mifflin Co., 1992.

Environmental Protection Agency (EPA)

The United States Environmental Protection Agency (EPA) was created on December 2, 1970. It was formed during a landmark year for environmental concerns, having been preceded by the passing of the **National Environmental Policy Act** in January and the first **Earth Day** celebrations in April. Unlike most agencies of the federal government, the EPA was not created by an act of Congress but by an executive order of President Richard Nixon. It was created to consolidate the environmental activities of the federal government into one agency.

At the time the EPA was formed, at least fifteen programs in five different government departments and agencies were handling environmental policy issues. These were all transferred to the EPA. **Air pollution control**, solid **waste management**, radiation control, and the drinking water program were transferred from the U.S. Department of Health, Education and Welfare (currently known as the **U.S. Department of Health and Human Services**). The **water pollution** control and **pesticide**s research programs were acquired from the **U.S. Department of the Interior**. Registration and regulation of pesticides was transferred from the **U.S. Department of Agriculture**, and the responsibility for setting tolerance levels for pesticides in food was acquired from the **Food and Drug Administration**. The EPA also took over responsibility for setting some environmental radiation protection standards from the **Atomic Energy Commission** and assumed some of the duties of the Federal Radiation Council. Some environmental programs were not transferred to the EPA, instead the EPA works with other agencies on particular environmental problems. For example, the United States Coast Guard and the EPA work together on flood control, shoreline protection, and **dredging** and filling activities.

Today, the EPA's main office is in Washington, D.C., and there are ten EPA regional offices and field laboratories. The main office develops national environmental policy and programs, oversees the regional offices and laboratories, requests an annual budget from Congress, and conducts research. The regional offices implement the national policies, oversee environmental programs delegated to the states,

and review **Environmental Impact Statement**s for federal actions. The field laboratories conduct research, which are used to develop policies and provide analytical support for monitoring, enforcement, and permit programs.

The administrator of the EPA is appointed by the president and approved by the Senate. The same procedure is used to appoint a deputy administrator, who assists the administrator; nine assistant administrators, who oversee programs and support functions; an inspector general, responsible for investigating environmental crimes; and a general counsel, who provides legal support. There are four program offices in the EPA: Solid Waste and Emergency Response; Pesticides and Toxic Substances; Air and Radiation; and Water. These programs work in tandem with functional offices such as Research and Development and Enforcement.

All of the offices and programs of the EPA are directed by five main objectives, referred to as "core functions." These core functions help define the agency's mission and bring a common thread to all agency activities. The core functions are:

1) Pollution Prevention—taking measures to prevent **pollution** from being created rather than just cleaning up what's already been released. Also known as source reduction.
2) Risk Assessment and Risk Reduction—identifying problems that pose the greatest risk to human health and the environment and taking measures to reduce those risks.
3) Science, Research and Technology—conducting research that will help in developing environmental policies and promoting innovative technologies to solve environmental problems.
4) Regulatory Development—developing requirements such as operating procedures for facilities and standards for **emission**s of pollutants.
5) Enforcement—assuring compliance with established regulations.
6) **Environmental Education**—developing educational materials, serving as an information clearinghouse, and providing grant assistance to local educational institutions.

In March 1997, EPA Administrator Carol M. Browner announced three new offices created to oversee key EPA policy priorities: Office of Children's Health and Protection; Office of Reinvention (to implement "Reinventing Environmental Regulation"); and Center for Environmental Information and Statistics.

Many of EPA's programs are established by legislation enacted by Congress. For example, many of the activities carried out by the Office of Solid Waste and Emergency Response originated in the **Resource Conservation and Recovery Act (RCRA)**. It is through such legislation that the EPA obtains authority to develop regulations and enforce them. Environmental regulations drafted by the agency are subject to an intensive review process before they are finalized. This process includes approval by the president's Office of Management and Budget and input from other govern-

Organizational chart of the Environmental Protection Agency.

ment agencies, private businesses and organizations, and the general public. Since most state governments in the United States have their own environmental protection departments, the EPA delegates the implementation and enforcement of some federal programs to the states.

[*Teresa C. Donkin*]

FURTHER READING

Environmental Management. Washington, DC: U. S. Environmental Protection Agency, October 1991.

Keating, B., and D. Russell. "Inside the EPA: Yesterday and Today...Still Hazy After All These Years." *E Magazine* 3 (August 1992): 30-37.

Environmental racism

The term environmental racism was coined in a 1987 study conducted by the United Church of Christ that examined the location of **hazardous waste** dumps and found an "insidious form of racism." Concern had surfaced five years before, when opposition to a **polychlorinated biphenyl (PCB) landfill** prompted Congress to examine the location of hazardous waste sites in the Southeast, the **Environmental Protection Agency (EPA)**'s Region IV. They found that three of the four facilities in the area were in communities primarily inhabited by people of color. Subsequent studies, such as Ben Goldman's *The Truth about Where You Live*, have

contended that exposure to environmental risks is significantly greater for racial and ethnic minorities than for nonminority populations. However, an EPA study contends that there is not enough data to draw such broad conclusions.

The *National Law Journal* found that official response to environmental problems may be racially biased. According to their study, penalties for environmental crimes were higher in white communities. They also found that the EPA takes 20 percent longer to place a hazardous waste site in a minority community on the Superfund's **National Priorities List** (NPL). And, once assigned to the NPL, these clean ups are more likely to be delayed.

Advocates also contend that environmentalists and regulators have tried to solve environmental problems without regard for the social impact of the solutions. For example, the Los Angeles Air Quality Management District wanted to require businesses to set up programs that would discourage their employees from driving to work. As initially conceived, employers could have simply charged fees for parking spaces without helping workers set up car pools. The Labor-Community Strategy Center, a local activist group, pointed out that this would have disproportionately affected people who could not afford to pay for parking spaces. As a compromise, regulators will now review employers' plans and only approve those that mitigate the any unequal effects on poor and minority populations.

In response to the concern that traditional **environmentalism** does not recognize the social and economic components of environmental problems and solutions, a national movement for "environmental and economic justice" has spread across the country. Groups like the Southwest Network for Environmental and Economic Justice attempt to frame the **environment** as part of the fight against racism and other inequalities.

In addition, the federal government has begun to address the debate over environmental racism. In 1992, the EPA established an Environmental Equity office. In addition, several bills that advocate environmental justice have been introduced. *See also* Comprehensive Environmental Response, Compensation, and Liability Act (CERCLA); Environmental economics; Environmental law; Hazardous waste siting; South

[*Alair MacLean*]

FURTHER READING

Alston, D., ed. *We Speak for Ourselves: Social Justice, Race and Environment.* Washington, DC: The Panos Institute, 1990.

Goldman, B. A. *The Truth About Where You Live: An Atlas for Action on Toxins and Mortality.* New York: Times Books, 1991.

Lee, C. *Toxic Wastes and Race in the United States: A National Report on the Racial and Socio-Economic Characteristics of Communities with Hazardous Waste Sites.* New York: United Church of Christ, Commission for Racial Justice, 1987.

Russell, D. "Environmental Racism." *Amicus Journal* 11 (Spring 1989): 22-32.

U. S. Environmental Protection Agency. *Environmental Equity: Reducing Risk for All Communities: Report to the Administrator from the EPA Environmental Equity Workgroup.* Washington, DC: U. S. Government Printing Office, 1992.

U. S. General Accounting Office. *Siting of Hazardous Waste Landfills and Their Correlation with Racial and Economic Status of Surrounding Communities.* Washington, DC: U. S. Government Printing Office, 1983.

Environmental refugees

The term environmental refugee was coined in the late 1980s by the **United Nations Environment Programme** and refers to people who are forced to leave their community of origin because the land can no longer support them. Environmental factors such as **soil** erosion, drought, or floods, which are often coupled with poor socioeconomic conditions, are the cause of this loss of stability and security. Many environmental influences may cause such a displacement and include the deterioration of agricultural land, natural or "unnatural" disasters, climate change, the destruction resulting from war, and environmental scarcity.

Environmental scarcity can be supply induced, demand induced, or structural. Supply induced scarcity refers to the depletion of agricultural resources, as in the erosion of cropland or overgrazing. Demand induced scarcity occurs when consumption of a resource increases or when population growth occurs, as is occurring in countries such as Philippines, Kenya, and Costa Rica. Structural scarcity results from the unequal social distribution of a resource within a community. The causes of environmental scarcity can occur simultaneously and in combination with each other, as seen in South Africa during the years of apartheid. Approximately 60% of the cropland in South Africa is marked by low organic

content, and half of the country receives less than 19.5 in (500 mm) of annual precipitation. When these factors were coupled with the rapid soil erosion, overcrowding, and unequal social distribution of resources experienced at this time, environmental scarcity resulted. Other environmental influences such as climate change and natural disasters can greatly compound the problems related to scarcity. Those countries which are especially vulnerable to these other influences are those which are already experiencing the precursors to scarcity, for example, highly populated countries such as Egypt and Bangladesh. On Haiti, per capita grain production is half of what it was only 40 years ago and residents only get about 80% of their minimum nutritional needs. Environmental problems place an added burden on a situation that is already under pressure. When this combination occurs in societies without strong social ties or political and economic stability, many times the people within the population have no choice but to relocate.

Environmental refugees tend to come from rural areas and developing countries—those most vulnerable to the influences of scarcity, climate change, and natural disasters. According to the **Centers for Disease Control and Prevention**, since the early 1960s most emergencies involving refugees have taken place in these less developed countries where resources are inadequate to support the population during times of need. In 1995, CDC directed 45 relief missions to developing countries such as Angola, Bosnia, Haiti, and Sierra Leone.

The number of displaced people is rising worldwide. Of these, the number forced to migrate because of economic and environmental conditions is growing more rapidly than refugees from political strife. According to Dr. Norman Myers at the University of Oxford, there are 25 million environmental refugees today, compared with 20 million officially recognized refugees migrating due to political, religious, or ethical problems. Myers has predicted that by the year 2010, this number could rise to 50 million. The number of migrants seeking environmental refuge is grossly underestimated because many do not actually cross borders but are forced to wander within their own country. The number of these internally displaced persons was estimated to be 25 million in 1995. As global warming causes major **climate** changes, these numbers could increase even more. Climate change alone may displace 150 million more people by the middle of the next century. Not only would a global climate change increase the number of refugees, it could have a negative impact on agricultural production which would seriously limit the amount of food surpluses available to help displaced people.

Although approximately three out of every five refugees are fleeing from environmental hardships, this group of refugees is not legally recognized. According to the 1951 Convention on the Status of Refugees as modified by the 1967 Protocol, a legal refugee is a person who escapes a country and cannot re-enter due to fear of persecution for reasons of race, religion, nationality, social affiliation, or political opinion. This definition requires both the element of persecution as well as cross-border migration. Because of these two requirements, states are not legally compelled to recognize environmental refugees; as mentioned above, many of these refugees never leave their own country, and it is unreasonable to expect them to prove fear of persecution. Environmental refugees are often forced to enter a country illegally since they cannot be granted protection or asylum. Many of the Mexican immigrants who enter the United States are escaping the sterile, unproductive land they have been living on. Over 60% of the land in Mexico is degraded, with soil erosion contributing to over 494,000 acres (200,000 ha) more land being rendered unproductive every year. Many of the people considered to be economic migrants are actually environmental refugees. Those that are recognized as political refugees often must live in overcrowded refugee camps which are no more prepared to sustain the population than the land they are escaping from. Two thousand Somali refugees forced to live in such camps on the border of Kenya were displaced once more when flooding in 1994 ended a long drought but destroyed relief food. Many environmental refugees never resettle and must live the rest of their lives migrating from place to place, looking for land that can sustain them.

Researchers are currently working on ways to predict where the next large migrations will come from and how to prevent them from occurring. Predictive models are extremely difficult to produce because of the interaction between the socioeconomic status of the people and the environmental influences on the land. Stuart Liederman, an environmental scientist at the University of New Hampshire, is developing a model which will predict which areas are at risk of producing environmental refugees. This model is a mathematical formula which could be used with any population. One side of the equation combines the rate of environmental decay, the amount of time over which this deterioration will take place, and the susceptibility of the people and the environment. The other side of the equation combines the restoration rate, the time it would take to reestablish the environment, and the potential for recovery of the people and the land. These predictions will allow for preventive measures to be taken, for preparations to be made for future refugees, and for restoring the devastated homelands of past migrants. Creation of a working model may also help convince policymakers that those escaping unlivable environmental conditions need to be legally recognized as refugees.

Until environmental refugees are granted legal status, there will be no protection or compensation granted these individuals. The most effective way to deal with the growing number of displaced persons is to concentrate on the reasons they are being forced to leave their homelands. The increasing number of people forced to leave their homeland due to ecological strife is an indicator of environmental quality. Environmental protection is necessary to prevent the situation in many countries from getting worse. In the meantime, measures must be taken to accommodate the needs of these refugees, and the environment must be recognized as a legitimate source of conflict for individuals seeking protection in other lands.

[*Jennifer L. McGrath*]

FURTHER READING

Centers for Disease Control. *Famine Affected, Refugee, and Displaced Populations: Recommendations For Public Health Issues.* MMWR 1992; 41 (No RR-13).

Fell, N. "Outcasts from Eden." *New Scientist Magazine* 151, no. 2045 (August 1996): 24-7.

Homer-Dixon, T.F. "Environmental Change and Economic Decline in Developing Countries." *International Studies Notes* 16, no. 1 (Winter 1991): 18.

Jacobson, J.L. *Environmental Refugees: A Yardstick of Habitability.* Worldwatch Institute, 1988.

Lindahl-Kiessling, K., and H. Landberg, eds. *Population, Economic Development, and the Environment.* New York: Oxford University Press, 1994.

Myers, N. "Environmental Refugees in a Globally Warmed World." *BioScience* 43, no. 11 (December 1993): 752-61.

Tickell, C. "Environmental Refugees: The Human Impact of Global Environmental Change." *Greenhouse Glasnost: The Crisis of Global Warming.* Ed. T. Minger. New York: Ecco Press, 1990.

Environmental resources

An environmental resource is any material, service, or information from the environment that is valuable to society. This can refer to anything that people find useful in their environs, or surroundings. Food from plants and animals, wood for cooking, heating, and building, metals, **coal**, and oil are all environmental resources. Clean land, air, and water are environmental resources, as are the abilities of land, air, and water to absorb society's waste products. Heat from the sun, transportation and **recreation** in lakes, rivers, and oceans, a beautiful view, or the discovery of a new **species** are all environmental resources.

The environment provides a vast array of materials and services that people use to live. Often these resources have competing uses and values. A piece of land, for instance, could be used as a farm, a park, a parking lot, or a housing development. It could be mined or used as a garbage dump. The topic of environmental resources, then, raises the question, what do people find valuable in their environment, and how do people choose to use the resources that their environment provides?

Some resources are renewable, or infinite, and some are non-renewable, or finite. **Renewable resources** like energy from the sun are plentiful and will be available for a long time. Finite resources, like oil and coal, are non-renewable because once they are extracted from the earth and burned they cannot be used again. These resources are in limited supply and need to be used carefully. Many resources are becoming more and more limited, especially as population and industrial growth place increasing pressure on the environment. Before the Industrial Revolution, for example, people relied on their own strength and their animals for work and transportation. The invention of the steam engine in the 1850s radically altered peoples' ability to do work and to consume energy. Today we have transformed our environment with machines, cars, and **power plants** and in the process we have burnt extraordinary amounts of coal, oil, and **natural gas**. Some predict that world coal deposits will last another two hundred years, while oil and natural gas reserves will last another one hundred years at current rates of consumption. This rate of use is clearly not sustainable. The terms finite and infinite are important because they indicate how much of a given resource is available, and how fast people can use that resource without limiting future supplies.

Some resources that were once taken for granted are now becoming more valuable. One of these resources is the environment's ability to absorb the waste that people produce. In Jakarta, Indonesia, people living in very close quarters in small shanties along numerous tidal canals use their only water supply for bathing, washing clothes, drinking water, fishing, and as a toilet. It is common to see people bathing just down stream from other people who are defecating directly into the river. This scene illustrates a central problem in environmental resource management. These people have only one water source and many needs in order to live. The demands that they place on these resources seriously affect the health and quality of life for all the people, but all of the needs must be met in some way. Thoughtful management of these environmental resources, like building latrines, could alleviate some of the strain on the river and improve other uses of the same resource. People all over the world have taken for granted the valuable resources of air, land, and **water quality** so that many rivers are undrinkable and unswimable because they contain raw sewage, chemical **fertilizer**s, and industrial wastes. As people make decisions about what they will take from their environment, they also must be conscious of what they intend to put back into that environment.

Resource economics was established during a time in human history when environmental resources were thought to be limitless and without value until they were harvested and brought to market. From this viewpoint, the world is big enough that when one resource is exhausted another resource can be found to take its place. Land is valuable according to what can be taken from it in order to make a profit. This kind of management leads to enormous short term gains and is responsible for the speed and efficiency of economic growth throughout the world. One the other hand, this view overlooks longer term profits and the reality that the world is an increasingly small, interconnected, and fragile system. People can no longer assume that they can find fresh new supplies when they use up what they have. Very few places on earth remain untouched and unexploited.

The world's remaining forests, if managed with care, could supply all of society's needs for timber and still remain relatively healthy and intact. Forest resources can be renewable, since forests grow quickly enough to replace themselves if used in moderation. Unfortunately, in many places forests are being destroyed at an alarming rate. In Costa Rica, Central America, twenty-five percent of the remaining forest land has disappeared since 1970. These forests have been cleared to harvest tropical hardwoods, to create farmland and pasture for animals, and to forage wood for cooking and heating. In a country struggling for economic growth, these are all important needs, but they do not always make long term economic sense. Farmers who graze cattle in **tropical rain forest**s or who clear trees off of steep hillsides destroy

their land in a matter of years with the idea that this is the fastest way to make money. In the same way, loggers harvest trees for immediate sale, even though many of these trees take hundreds of years to replenish themselves. In fact, the price for tropical hardwoods has gone up four-fold since 1970. The trees cut and sold in 1970 represent a huge economic loss to the Costa Rican economy, since they were sold for a fraction of their present value. Often, the **soil** on this land quickly erodes downhill into streams and rivers, clogging the rivers with **sediment** and killing fish and other **wildlife**. This has the added drawback of damaging hydroelectric and **irrigation** dams and hurting the fishing industry.

Despite these tragic losses, Costa Rica is a model in Central America and in the world for finding alternative uses for its **natural resources**. Costa Rica has set aside one fifth of its total land area for nature preserves and **national park** lands. These beautiful and varied parks are valuable for several reasons. First, they help to protect and preserve a huge diversity of tropical **species**, many undiscovered and unstudied. Second, they protect a great deal of vegetation that is important in producing oxygen, stabilizing atmospheric chemistry, and preventing global climate change. Third, the natural beauty of these parks attracts many international tourists. Tourism is one of Costa Rica's major industries, providing much needed economic development. People from around the world appreciate the beauty and the wonder—the intangible values—of these resources. Local people who would have been hired one time to cut down a forest can now be hired for a lifetime to work as park rangers and guides. Some would also argue that these nature preserves have value in themselves without reference to human needs, simply because they are filled with beautiful living birds, insects, plants, and animals.

Much of the dialogue in environmental resource management is about the need to balance the needs for economic growth and prosperity with needs for sustainable resource use. In a limited, finite world, there is a need to close the gap between the rates of consumption and rates of supply. The debate over how to assign value to different environmental resources is a lively one because the way that people think about their environment directly affects how they interact with the world.

[*John Cunningham*]

Further Reading

Ahmad, Y., et al. *Environmental Accounting and Sustainable Development: A UNEP World Bank Symposium.* Washington, DC: World Bank, 1989.

Repetto, R. "Accounting for Environmental Assets." *Scientific American* 266 (June 1992): 94-8+.

Environmental restoration
See **Restoration ecology**

Environmental risk analysis
See **Risk analysis**

Environmental science

Environmental science is often confused with other fields of related interest, especially **ecology**, environmental studies, **environmental education**, and **environmental engineering**. Renewed interest in environmental issues in the late 1960s and early 1970s, gave rise to numerous programs at many universities in the United States and other countries, most under two rubrics: environmental science or environmental studies. The former focused, as might be expected, on scientific questions and issues of environmental interest; the latter were often courses, with the emphasis on questions of **environmental ethics**, aesthetics, literature, etc.

These new academic units marked the first formal appearance of environmental science on most campuses, at least by that label. But environmental science is essentially the application of scientific methods and principles to the study of environmental questions, so it has probably been around in some form as long as science itself. Air and **water quality** research, for example, have been carried on in many universities for many decades: that research is environmental science.

By whatever label and in whatever unit, environmental science is not constrained within any one discipline; it is a comprehensive field. A considerable amount of environmental research is accomplished in specific departments such as chemistry, physics, civil engineering, or the various biology disciplines. Much of this work is confined to a single field, with no interdisciplinary perspective. These programs graduate scientists who build on their specific training to continue work on environmental problems, sometimes in a specific department, sometimes in an interdisciplinary environmental science program.

Many new academic units are interdisciplinary, their members and graduates specifically designated as environmental scientists. Most have been trained in a specific discipline, but they may have degrees from almost any scientific background. In these units, the degrees granted—from B.S. to Ph.D.—are in Environmental Science, not in a specific discipline.

Environmental science is not ecology, though that discipline may be included. Ecologists are interested in the interactions between some kind of organism and its surroundings. Most ecological research and training does not focus on environmental problems except as those problems impact the organism of interest. Environmental scientists may or may not include organisms in their field of view: they mostly focus on the environmental problem, which may be purely physical in **nature**. For example, **acid deposition** can be studied as a problem of **emission**s and characteristics of the **atmosphere** without necessarily examining its impact on organisms. An alternate focus might be on the **acidification** of lakes and the resulting implications for resident fish. Both studies require expertise from more than one traditional discipline; they are studies in environmental science. *See also* Air quality; Environment; Environmental ethics; Nature; Water quality

[*Gerald L. Young*]

FURTHER READING

Cunningham, W. P. *Environmental Science: A Global Concern.* Dubuque, IA: William C. Brown, 1992.

Henry, J. G., and G. W. Heinke. *Environmental Science and Engineering.* Englewood Cliffs, NJ: Prentice-Hall, 1989.

Jorgensen, S. E., and I. Johnson. *Principles of Environmental Science and Technology.* 2nd ed. Amsterdam, NY: Elsevier, 1989.

Environmental stress

In the ecological context, environmental stress can be considered any environmental influence that causes a discernible ecological change, especially in terms of a constraint on **ecosystem** development. Stressing agents (or stressors) can be exogenous to the ecosystem, as in the cases of long-range transported acidifying substances, toxic gases, or **pesticide**s. Stress can also cause change as a result of an accentuation of some pre-existing site factor beyond a threshold for biological tolerance, for example thermal loading, **nutrient** availability, wind, or temperature extremes.

Often implicit within the notion of environmental stress, particularly from the perspective of ecosystem managers, is a judgement about the quality of the ecological change. That is, from the human perspective, whether the effect is "good" or "bad."

Environmental stressors can be divided into several, not necessarily exclusive, classes of causal agencies:

(1) "Physical stress" refers to episodic events (or disturbance) associated with intense but usually brief loadings of kinetic energy, perhaps caused by a windstorm, volcanic eruption, tidal wave, or an explosion.

(2) **Wildfire** is another episodic stress, usually causing a mass **mortality** of ecosystem dominants such as trees or shrubs and a rapid **combustion** of much of the **biomass** of the ecosystem.

(3) **Pollution** occurs when certain **chemicals** are bioavailable in a sufficiently large amount to cause toxicity. Toxic stressors include gaseous air pollutants such as **sulfur dioxide** and **ozone**, metals such as **lead** and **mercury**, residues of **pesticide**s, and even nutrients that may be beneficial at small rates of supply but damaging at higher rates of loading.

(4) Nutrient impoverishment implies an inadequate availability of physiologically essential chemicals, which imposes an oligotrophic constraint upon ecosystem development.

(5) Thermal stress occurs when heat energy is released into an ecosystem, perhaps by aquatic discharges of low-grade heat from **power plant**s and other industrial sources.

(6) Exploitative stress refers to the selective removal of particular **species** or size classes. Exploitation by humans includes the harvesting of forests or wild animals, but it can also involve natural herbivory and predation, as with infestations of defoliating insects such as locusts, spruce budworm, or **gypsy moth**, or

irruptions of predators such as crown-of-thorns starfish.

(7) *Climatic stress* is associated with an insufficient or excessive regime of moisture, solar radiation, or temperature. These can act over the shorter term as weather, or over the longer term as **climate**.

Within most of these contexts, stress can be exerted either chronically or episodically. For example, the toxic gas sulfur dioxide can be present in a chronically elevated concentration in an urbanized region with a large number of **point sources** of **emission**. Alternatively, where the emission of sulfur dioxide is dominated by a single, large point source such as a **smelter** or power plant, the toxic stress associated with this gas occurs as relatively short-term events of **fumigation**.

Environmental stress can be caused by natural agencies as well as resulting directly or indirectly from the activities of humans. For example, sulfur dioxide can be emitted from smelters, power plants, and homes, but it can also be emitted in large quantities by **volcano**es. Similarly, climate change has always occurred naturally, but it may also be forced by human activities that result in emissions of **carbon dioxide**, **methane**, and nitrous oxide into the **atmosphere**.

Over most of Earth's history, natural stressors have been the dominant constraints on ecological development. Increasingly, however, the direct and indirect consequences of human activities are becoming dominant environmental stressors. This is caused by both the increasing human population and by the progressively increasing intensification of the per-capita effect of humans on the **environment**.

[*Bill Freedman*]

FURTHER READING

Freedman, B. "Environmental Stress and the Management of Ecological Reserves." In *Science and the Management of Protected Areas*, edited by J. H. M. Willison, et al. Amsterdam: Elsevier, 1992.

Grime, J. P. *Plant Strategies and Vegetation Processes.* New York: Wiley, 1979.

Environmental Stress Index (ZPG)

Environmental Stress Index (ZPG) is a survey to determine the quality of life in American cities. Zero Population Growth, Inc. based in Washington D.C., conducted this "Urban Stress Test" in the late 1980s. One hundred ninety-two cities were selected throughout the United States. The population-linked survey was based on eleven criteria: Population change; Population density; Education; Violent crime; Community economics; Individual economics (percent below federal poverty level and per capita income); Births (percent of teenage births and infant **mortality**); **Air quality** (meeting **Environmental Protection Agency (EPA)** standards); **Hazardous waste** (number of EPA-designated hazardous waste sites); Water (quality and supply); Sewage (model cities provide better than secondary treatment of their **wastewater**).

Cites were ranked one to six with number one being best. The cities with the lower scores were called model cities.

The cities with the higher scores were called the stressed cities. Among the model cities were Abilene, Texas, with an index of 1.6; Roanoke, Virginia, 1.6; Berkeley, California, 2.0; Colorado Springs, Colorado, 2.0; and Peoria, Illinois, 2.0.

Among America's worst cities were Phoenix, Arizona, 5; Houston, Texas, 4.5; Los Angeles, 4.3; Honolulu, Hawaii, 4.3; and Baltimore, Maryland, 4.3.

Environmental Working Group (Washington D.C.)

The Environmental Working Group is a public interest research group that monitors public agencies and public policies on topics relating to environmental and social justice. EWG publicizes its findings in research reports that emphasize both national and local implications of federal laws and activities. These research reports are based on analysis of public databases, often obtained through the Freedom of Information Act. In operation since 1993, EWG is a nonprofit organization funded by grants from private foundations. EWG is based in Washington, D.C., and is associated with the Tides Center of San Francisco. The organization performs its research both independently and in collaboration with other public interest research groups such as the **Sierra Club** and the Surface Transportation Policy Project (a nonprofit coalition focusing on social and environmental quality in transportation policy).

EWG specializes in analyzing large computer databases maintained by government agencies, such as the Toxic Release Inventory database maintained by the **Environmental Protection Agency** to record spills of toxic chemicals into the air or water, or the Regulatory Analysis Management System, maintained by the **Army Corps of Engineers** for internal tracking of permits granted for filling and draining **wetlands**. Because many of these data sources are capable of exposing actions or policies embarrassing to public agencies, EWG has often obtained data by using the Freedom of Information Act, which legally enforces public release of data belonging to the public domain. Many of the databases researched by EWG have never been thoroughly analyzed before, even by the agency collecting the data. EWG is unusual in working with primary data—going directly to the original database—rather than basing its research on secondary sources, anecdotal information, or interviews.

Research findings are published both in print and electronically on the Worldwide Web. Electronic publishing allows immediate and inexpensive distribution of reports that concern issues of current interest. EWG is a prolific source of information, producing extensive, detailed reports, often at a rate of more than one a month. Among the environmental topics on which the EWG has reported are drinking water quality, wetland protection and destruction, and the impacts of agricultural **pesticide**s on both farm workers and consumers. Social justice and policy issues that EWG has researched include campaign finance reform, inequalities and inefficiency in farm subsidy programs, and threats to public health and the environment from medical waste. For each general topic, EWG usually publishes a series of articles ranging from the nature and impacts of a federal law to what individuals can do about the current problem. Also included with research reports are state-by-state and county summaries of statistics, which provide details of local implications of the general policy issues.

[*Mary Ann Cunningham*]

FURTHER READING

Cook, K. A., and A. Art. *City Slickers: Farm Subsidy Recipients in America's Big Cities*. Washington, D.C.: Environmental Working Group, 1995.

Environmental Working Group. *Dishonorable Discharge: Toxic Pollution of America's Waters*. Washington, D.C.: Environmental Working Group, 1996.

———. *Comments on the Proposed Reissuance of the U.S. Army Corps of Engineers' Nationwide Permits, 1996*. Worldwide Web site: http://www.ewg.org/pub/home/reports/nwp/nwp_contents .html

———. *About the Environmental Working Group, 1995*. Worldwide Web site: http://www.ewg.org/pub/home/about/about.html

Environmentalism

Environmentalism is the ethical and political perspective that places the health, harmony, and integrity of the natural **environment** at the center of human attention and concern. From this perspective human beings are viewed as *part of* **nature** rather than as overseers. Therefore to care for the environment is to care about human beings since we cannot live without the survival of the natural **habitat**.

Although there are many different views within the very broad and inclusive environmentalist perspective, several common features can be discerned. The first is environmentalism's emphasis on the interdependence of life and the conditions that make life possible. Human beings, like other animals, need clean air to breathe, clean water to drink, and nutritious food to eat. Without these necessities, life would be impossible. Environmentalism views these conditions as being both basic and interconnected. For example, fish contaminated with **polychlorinated biphenyl (PCB)**, **mercury**, and other **toxic substance**s are not only hazardous to humans but to bears, eagles, gulls, and other predators. Likewise, mighty **whales** depend on tiny **plankton**, cows on corn, koala bears on eucalyptus leaves, bees on flowers, and flowers on bees and birds, and so on through all species and **ecosystem**s. All animals, human and nonhuman alike, are interdependent participants in the cycle of birth, life, death, decay, and rebirth.

A second emphasis of environmentalism is on the sanctity of life—not only human life but all life, from the tiniest microorganism to the largest whale. Since the fate of our species is inextricably tied with theirs and since life requires certain conditions to sustain it, environmentalists contend that we have an obligation to respect and care for the conditions that nurture and sustain life in its many forms.

While environmentalists agree on some issues, there are also a number of disagreements about the purposes of environmentalism and about how to best achieve those ends. Some environmentalists emphasize the desirability of conserving **natural resources for recreation**, sightseeing,

hunting, and other human activities, both for present and **future generations**. Such a utilitarian view has been sharply criticized by **Arne Naess** and other proponents of **deep ecology** who claim that the natural environment has its own **intrinsic value** apart from any aesthetic, recreational, or other value assigned to it by human beings. Bears, for example, have their own intrinsic value or worth, quite apart from that assigned to their existence via **shadow pricing** or other mechanism by bear-watchers, hunters, or other human beings.

Environmentalists also differ on how best to conserve, reserve, and protect the natural environment. Some groups, such as the **Sierra Club** and the **Nature Conservancy**, favor gradual, low-key legislative and educational efforts to inform and influence policy makers and the general public about environmental issues. Other more radical environmental groups, such as the **Sea Shepherd Conservation Society** and **Earth First!**, favor carrying out direct action by employing the tactics of ecotage (ecological sabotage), or **monkey-wrenching**, to stop **strip mining**, logging, **drift net** fishing, and other activities that they deem dangerous to animals and ecosystems. Within this environmental spectrum are many other groups, including the **World Wildlife Fund**, **Greenpeace**, **Earth Island Institute**, **Clean Water Action**, and other organizations which use various techniques to inform, educate, and influence public opinion regarding environmental issues and to lobby policy makers.

Despite these and other differences over means and ends, environmentalists agree that the natural environment, whether valued instrumentally or intrinsically, is valuable and worth preserving for present and future generations.

[*Terence Ball*]

FURTHER READING

Chase, S., ed. *Defending the Earth: A Dialogue Between Murray Bookchin and Dave Foreman*. Boston: South End Press, 1991.

Devall, B., and G. Sessions. *Deep Ecology: Living as if Nature Mattered*. Layton, UT: Gibbs M. Smith, 1985.

Eckersley, R. *Environmentalism and Political Theory*. Albany, NY: State University of New York Press, 1992.

Naess, A. *Ecology, Community and Lifestyle*. New York: Cambridge University Press, 1989.

Worster, D. *Nature's Economy: A History of Ecological Ideas*. New York: Cambridge University Press, 1977.

Environmentally responsible investing

Environmentally responsible investing is one component of a larger phenomenon known as *socially responsible investing*. The idea is that investors should use their money to support industries whose operations accord with the investors' personal ethics. This concept is not a new one. In the early part of the century, Methodists, Presbyterians, and Baptists shunned companies that promoted sinful activities such as smoking, drinking, and gambling. More recently, many investors chose to protest apartheid by divesting from companies with operations in South Africa. Investors today might arrange their investment portfolios to reflect companies' commitment to affirmative action, human rights, **animal rights**, the **environment**, or any other issues the investors believe to be important.

The purpose of environmentally responsible investing is to encourage companies to improve their environmental records. The recent emergence and growth of mutual funds identifying themselves as environmentally oriented funds indicates that environmentally responsible investing is a popular investment area for the 1990s. In 1990, around $1 billion were invested in environmentally oriented mutual funds. The naming of these funds can be misleading, however. Some funds have been developed for the purpose of being environmentally responsible; others have been developed for the purpose of reaping the profits anticipated to occur in the environmental services sector as environmentalists in the marketplace and environmental regulations encourage the purchasing of **green products** and technology. These funds are not necessarily environmentally responsible; some companies in the environmental clean-up industry, for example, have less than perfect environmental records.

As the idea of environmentally responsible investing is still new, a generally accepted set of criteria for identifying environmentally responsible companies has not yet emerged. The fact is that everyone pollutes to some extent. The question is where to draw the line between acceptable and unacceptable behavior toward the environment.

When grading a company in terms of its behavior toward the environment, one could use an absolute standard. For example, one could exclude all companies that have violated any **Environmental Protection Agency (EPA)** standards. The problem with such a standard is that some companies that have very good overall environmental records have sometimes failed to meet certain EPA standards. Alternatively, a company could be graded on its efforts to solve environmental problems. Some investors prefer to divest of all companies in heavily polluting industries, such as oil and chemical companies; others might prefer to use a relative approach and examine the environmental records of companies within industry groups. By directly comparing oil companies with other oil companies, for example, one can identify the particular companies committed to improving the environment.

For consistency, some investors might choose to divest from all companies that supply or buy from an environmentally irresponsible company. It then becomes an arbitrary decision as to where this process stops. If taken to an extreme, the approach rejects holding United States treasury securities, since public funds are used to support the military, one of the world's largest polluters and a heavy user of nonrenewable energy.

A potential new indicator for identifying environmentally responsible companies has been developed by the Coalition for Environmentally Responsible Economies (CERES); it is a code called the **Valdez Principles**. The principles are the environmental equivalent of the Sullivan Principles, a code of conduct for American companies operating in South Africa. The Valdez Principles commit companies to strive to achieve sustainable use of **natural resources** and the reduction and safe disposal of waste. By signing the principles, companies commit themselves to continually improving their behavior toward the environment over time. So far, however, few companies have signed the code, possibly because it requires companies to appoint environmentalists to their boards of directors.

As there is no generally accepted set of criteria for identifying environmentally responsible companies, investors interested in such an investment strategy must be careful about accepting "environmentally responsible" labels. Investors must determine their own set of screening criteria based on their own personal beliefs about what is appropriate behavior with respect to the environment.

[*Barbara J. Kanninen*]

FURTHER READING

Brill, J. A., and A. Reder. *Investing From the Heart.* New York: Crown, 1992.

Harrington, J. C. *Investing With Your Conscience.* New York: Wiley, 1992.

McMurdy, D. "Green Is the Color of Money [Environmental Investing in Canada]." *Maclean's* 104 (16 December 1991): 49-50.

Rauber, P. "The Stockbroker's Smile [Environmental Sector Funds]." *Sierra* 75 (July-August 1990): 18-21.

Enzyme

Enzymes are catalysts, compounds (a protein) that speed up the rate at which chemical reactions occur within living organisms without undergoing any permanent change themselves. They are crucial to life since, without them, the vast majority of biochemical reactions would occur too slowly for organisms to survive.

In general, enzymes catalyze two quite different kinds of reactions. The first type of reaction includes those by which simple compounds are combined with each other to make new tissue from which plants and animals are made. For example, the most common enzyme in nature is probably carboxydismutase, the enzyme in green plants that couples **carbon dioxide** with an acceptor molecule in one step of the photosynthesis process by which carbohydrates are produced.

Enzymes also catalyze reactions by which more complex compounds are broken down to provide the energy needed by organisms. The principal digestive enzyme in the human mouth, for example, is ptyalin (also known as a - amylase), which begins the digestion of starch.

Enzymes have both beneficial and harmful effects in the environment. On the one hand, environmental hazards such as **heavy metals**, **pesticide**s, and radiation often exert their effects on an organism by disabling one or more of its critical enzymes. As an example, arsenic is poisonous to animals because it forms a compound with the enzyme glutathione. The enzyme is disabled and prevented from carrying out its normal function, the maintenance of healthy red blood cells.

On the other hand, uses are now being found for enzymes in cleaning up the environment. For example, the Novo Nordisk company has discovered that adding an enzyme known as Pulpzyme® can vastly reduce the amount of chlorine needed to bleach wood pulp in the manufacture of paper. Since chlorine is a serious environmental contaminant, this technique may represent a significant improvement on present pulp and paper manufacturing techniques.

[*David E. Newton*]

Ephemeral species

Ephemeral species are plants and animals whose lifespan lasts only a few weeks or months. The most common types of ephemeral **species** are **desert** annuals, plants whose seeds remain dormant for months or years but which quickly germinate, grow, and flower when rain does fall. In such cases the amount and frequency of rainfall determine entirely how frequently ephemerals appear and how long they last. Tiny, usually microscopic, insects and other invertebrate animals often appear with these desert annals, feeding on briefly available plants, quickly reproducing, and dying in a few weeks or less. Ephemeral ponds, short-duration desert rain pools, are especially noted for supporting ephemeral species. Here small insects and even amphibians have ephemeral lives. The spadefoot toad (*Scaphiopus multiplicatus*), for example, matures and breeds in as little as eight days after a rain, feeding on short-lived brine shrimp, which in turn consume algae and plants that live as long as water or **soil** moisture lasts. Eggs, or sometimes the larvae of these animals, then remain in the soil until the next moisture event.

Ephemerals play an important role in many plant communities. In some very dry deserts, as in North Africa, ephemeral annuals comprise the majority of living species—although this rich **flora** can remain hidden for years at a time. Often widespread and abundant after a rain, these plants provide an essential food source for desert animals, including domestic livestock. Because water is usually unavailable in such environments, many desert perennials also behave like ephemeral plants, lying dormant and looking dead for months or years but suddenly growing and setting seed after a rare rain fall.

The frequency of desert ephemeral recurrence depends upon moisture availability. In the Sonoran Desert of California and Arizona, annual precipitation allows ephemeral plants to reappear almost every year. In the drier deserts of Egypt, where rain may not fall for a decade or more, dormant seeds must survive for a much longer time before germination. In addition, seeds have highly sensitive germination triggers. Some annuals that require at least one inch (two to three cm) of precipitation in order to complete their life cycle will not germinate when only one centimeter has fallen. In such a case seed coatings may be sensitive to soil **salinity**, which decreases as more rainfall seeps into the ground. Annually-recurring ephemerals often respond to temperature, as well. In the Sonoran Desert some rain falls in both summer and winter. Completely different summer and winter floral communities appear in response. Such **adaptation** to different temporal **niche**s probably helps decrease **competition** for space and moisture and increase each species' odds of success.

Although they are less conspicuous, ephemeral species also occur outside of desert environments. Short-duration food supplies or habitable conditions in some marine environments lead to ephemeral species growth. Ephemerals successfully exploit such unstable environments as **volcano**es and steep slopes prone to slippage. More common are spring ephemerals in temperate deciduous forests. For a few weeks between snow melt and closure of the overstory canopy, quick-growing ground plants, including small lilies and violets, sprout and take advantage of available sunshine. Flowering and setting seed before they are shaded out by larger vegetation, these ephemerals disappear by mid-summer. Some persist in the form of underground root systems, but others are true ephemerals, with only seeds remaining until the next spring. *See also* Adaptation; Food chain/web; Opportunistic organism

[*Mary Ann Cunningham*]

FURTHER READING

Hughes, J. "Effects of Removal of Co-Occurring Species on Distribution and Abundance of *Erythronium americanum* (Liliaceae), a Spring Ephemeral." *American Journal of Botany* 79 (1990): 1329-39.

Went, F. W. "The Ecology of Desert Plants." *Scientific American* 192 (1955): 68-75.

Whitford, W. G. *Pattern and Process in Desert Ecosystems*. Albuquerque: University of New Mexico Press, 1986.

Zahran, M. A., and A. J. Willis. *The Vegetation of Egypt*. London: Chapman and Hall, 1992.

Epidemiology

Epidemiology, the study of epidemics, is sometimes called the medical aspect of **ecology** because it is the study of diseases in animal populations, including humans. The epidemiologist is concerned with the interactions of organisms and their environments as related to the presence of disease. Environmental factors of disease include geographical features, **climate**, and concentration of **pathogen**s in **soil** and water. Epidemiology determines the numbers of individuals affected by a disease, the environmental circumstances under which the disease may occur, the causative agents, and the transmission of disease.

Epidemiology is commonly thought to be limited to the study of infectious diseases, but that is only one aspect of the medical specialty. The epidemiology of the environment and lifestyles has been studied since Hippocrates's time. More recently, scientists have broadened the world-wide scope of epidemiology to studies of violence, of heart disease due to lifestyle choices, and to the spread of disease because of **environmental degradation**.

Epidemiologists at the Epidemic Intelligence Service (EIS) of the **Centers for Disease Control and Prevention** have played important roles in landmark epidemiologic investigations. Those include the identification in 1955 of a lot of poliovirus vaccine, supposedly dead, that was contaminated with live polio virus; an investigation of the definitive epidemic of Legionnaires' disease in 1976; identification of tampons as a risk factor for toxic-shock syndrome; and investigation of the first cluster of cases that came to be called acquired immunodeficiency syndrome (**AIDS**). EIS officers are increasingly involved in the investigation of non-infectious disease problems, including the risk of injury associated with all-terrain vehicles and cluster deaths related to flour contaminated with parathion.

The epidemiological classification of disease deals with the incidence, distribution, and control of disorders of a population. Using the example of typhoid, a disease spread through contaminated food and water, scientists first must establish that the disease observed is truly caused by *Salmonella typhosa*, the typhoid organism. Investigators then must know the number of cases, whether the cases were scattered over the course of a year or occurred within a short period, and the geographic distribution. It is critical that the precise locations of the diseased patients be established. In a hypothetical case, two widely separated locations within a city might be found to have clusters of cases of typhoid arising simultaneously. It might be found that each of these clusters revolved around a family unit, suggesting that personal relationships might be important. Further investigation might disclose that all of the infected persons had dined at one time or at short intervals in a specific home, and that the person who had prepared the meal had visited a rural area, suffered a mild attack of the disease, and now was spreading it to family and friends by unknowing contamination of food.

One very real epidemic of cholera in the West African nation of Guinea-Bissau was tracked by CDC researchers using maps, interviews, and old-fashioned footwork door-to-door through the country. An investigator eventually tracked the source of the cholera outbreak to contaminated shellfish.

Epidemic diseases result from an ecological imbalance of some kind. Ecological imbalance, and hence, epidemic disease may be either naturally caused or induced by man. A breakdown in sanitation in a city, for example, offers conditions favorable for an increase in the rodent population, with the possibility that diseases may be introduced into and spread among the human population. In this case, an epidemic would result as much from an alteration in the environment as from the presence of a causative agent. For example, an increase in the number of epidemics of viral encephalitis, a brain disease, in man has resulted from the ecological imbalance of mosquitoes and wild birds caused by man's exploitation of lowland for farming. Driven from their natural **habitat** of reeds and rushes, the wild birds, important natural hosts for the **virus** that causes the disease, are forced to feed near farms; mosquitoes transmit the virus from birds to cattle to man.

Lyme disease, which was tracked by epidemiologists from man to deer to the ticks which infest deer, is directly related to environmental changes. The lyme disease spirochete probably has been infecting ticks for a long time; museum specimens of ticks collected on Long Island in the 1940s were found to be infected. Since then, tick populations in the Northeast have increased dramatically, triggering the epidemic.

There are more ticks because many of the forests that had been felled in the Northeast have returned to forestland. Deer populations in those areas have exploded, close to concentrated human populations, as have the numbers of *Ixodes dammini* ticks which feed on deer. The deer do not become ill, but when a tick bite infects a human host, the result can be a devastating disease, including crippling arthritis and memory loss.

Disease detectives, as epidemiologists are called, are taking on new illnesses like heart disease and **cancer**, diseases that develop over a lifetime. In 1948, epidemiologists enrolled 5,000 people in Framingham, Massachusetts, for a study on heart disease. Every two years the subjects have undergone physicals and answered survey questions. Epidemiologists began to understand what factors put people at risk, such as high blood pressure, elevated cholesterol levels, smoking, and lack of exercise.

CDC epidemiologists are now tracking the pattern of violence, traditionally a matter for police. If a pattern is found, then young people who are at risk can be taught to stop arguments before they escalate to violence, or public health workers can recognize behaviors that lead to spouse abuse, or the warning signs of teenage suicide, for example.

In the 1980s, classic epidemiology discovered that a puzzling array of illnesses was linked, and it came to be known as AIDS. Epidemiologists traced the disease to sexual contact, then to contaminated blood supplies, then proved the AIDS virus could cross the placental barrier, infecting babies born to HIV-infected mothers.

The AIDS virus, called human immunodeficiency virus, may have existed for centuries in African monkeys and apes. Perhaps 40 years ago, this virus crossed from monkey to man, although researchers do not know how or why. African chimpanzees can be infected with HIV, but they don't develop the disease, suggesting that chimps have developed protective immunity. Eventually AIDS, over centuries, probably will develop into a less deadly disease in humans. But before then, researchers fear that new, more deadly, diseases will evolve.

As human communities change and create new ways for diseases to spread, viruses and bacteria constantly evolve as well. Rapidly increasing human populations prove a fertile breeding ground for microbes, and as the planet becomes more crowded, the distances that separate communities become smaller.

Epidemiology has become one of the important sciences in the study of nutritional and biotic diseases around the world. The United Nations supports, in part, a World Health Organization investigation of nutritional diseases.

Epidemiologists have also been called upon in times of natural emergencies. When **Mount St. Helens** erupted on May 18, 1980, CDC epidemiologists were asked to assist in an epidemiologic evaluation. The agency funded and assisted in a series of studies on the health effects of dust exposure, occupational exposure, and mental health effects of the volcanic eruption.

In 1990, CDC epidemiologists began research for the Department of Energy to study people who have been exposed to radiation. A major task of the study is to quantify exposures based on historical reconstructions of **emissions** from nuclear plant operations. Epidemiologists have undertaken a major thyroid disease study for those people exposed to radioactive iodine as a result of living near the **Hanford Nuclear Reservation** in Richland, Washington, during the 1940s and 1950s.

[*Linda Rehkopf*]

FURTHER READING

Friedman, G. D. *Primer of Epidemiology.* 3rd ed. New York: McGraw-Hill, 1987.

Goldsmith, J. R., ed. *Environmental Epidemiology: Epidemiological Investigations of Community Environmental Problems.* St. Louis, MO: CRC Press, 1986.

Kopfler, F. C., and G. Craun, eds. *Environmental Epidemiology. Chelsea, MI: Lewis, 1986.*

Erodible

Susceptible to **erosion** or the movement of **soil** or earth particles due to the primary forces of wind, moving water, ice and gravity. Tillage implements may also move soil particles, but this transport is usually not considered erosion.

Erosion

Erosion is the wearing away of the land surface by running water, wind, ice, or other geologic agents, including such processes as gravitational creep.

The term geologic erosion refers to the normal, natural erosion caused by geological processes acting over long periods of time, undisturbed by humans. Accelerated erosion is a more rapid erosion process influenced by human, or sometimes animal, activities. Accelerated erosion in North America has only been recorded for the past few centuries, and in research studies, postsettlement erosion rates were found to be eight to 350 times higher than presettlement erosion rates.

Soil erosion has been both accelerated and controlled by humans since recorded history. In Asia, the Pacific, Africa, and South America, complex terracing and other erosion control systems on **arable land** go back thousands of years. Soil erosion and the resultant decreased food supply have been linked to the decline of historic, particularly Mediterranean, civilizations, though the exact relationship with the decline of governments such as the Roman Empire is not clear.

A number of terms have been used to describe different types of erosion, including gully erosion, rill erosion, interrill erosion, sheet erosion, splash erosion, saltation, surface creep, suspension, and siltation. In gully erosion, water accumulates in narrow channels and, over short periods, removes the soil

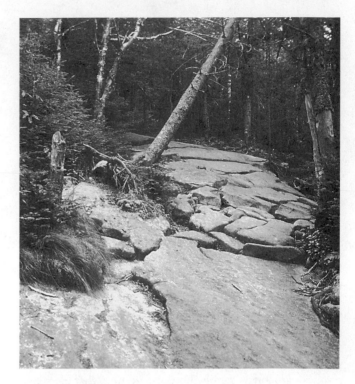

Soil erosion on a trail in the Adirondack Mountains.

from this narrow area to considerable depths, ranging from 1.5 feet (0.5 m) to as much as 82 to 98 feet (25 to 30 m).

Rill erosion refers to a process in which numerous small channels of only a few inches in depth are formed, usually occurring on recently cultivated soils. Interrill erosion is the removal of a fairly uniform layer of soil on a multitude of relatively small areas by rainfall splash and film flow.

Usually interpreted to include rill and interril erosion, sheet erosion is the removal of soil from the land surface by rainfall and surface **runoff**. Splash erosion, the detachment and airborne movement of small soil particles, is caused by the impact of raindrops on the soil.

Saltation is the bouncing or jumping action of soil and mineral particles caused by wind, water, or gravity. Saltation occurs when soil particles 0.1 to 0.5 mm in diameter are blown to a height of less than 6 inches (15 cm) above the soil surface for relatively short distances. The process includes gravel or stones effected by the energy of flowing water, as well as any soil or mineral particle movement downslope due to gravity.

Surface creep, which usually requires extended observation to be perceptible, is the rolling of dislodged particles 0.5 to 1.0 mm in diameter by wind along the soil surface. Suspension occurs when soil particles less than 0.1 mm diameter are blown through the air for relatively long distances, usually at a height of less than 6 inches (15cm) above the soil surface. In siltation, decreased water speed causes deposits water-borne **sediment**s, or silt, to build up in stream channels, lakes, **reservoir**s, or **flood plain**s.

In the water erosion process, the eroded sediment is often higher (enriched) in organic matter, **nitrogen, phosphorus**, and potassium than in the bulk soil from which it came. The amount of enrichment may be related to the soil, amount of erosion, the time of sampling within a storm, and other factors. Likewise, during a wind erosion event, the eroded particles are often higher in clay, organic matter, and plant **nutrient**s. Frequently, in the Great Plains, the surface soil becomes increasingly more sandy over time as wind erosion continues.

Erosion estimates using the Universal Soil Loss Equation (USLE) and the Wind Erosion Equation (WEE) estimate erosion on a point basis expressed in mass per unit area. If aggregated for a large area (e.g. state or nation), very large numbers are generated and have been used to give misleading conclusions. The estimates of USLE and WEE indicate only the soil moved from a point. They do not indicate how far the sediment moved or where it was deposited. In cultivated fields, the sediment may be deposited in other parts of the field with different crop cover or in areas where the land slope is less. It may also be deposited in **riparian land** along stream channels or in flood plains.

Only a small fraction of the water-eroded sediment leaves the immediate area. For example, in a study of five river **watershed**s in Minnesota, it was estimated that from less than 1 to 27 percent of the eroded material entered stream channels, depending on the soil and topographic conditions. The deposition of wind-eroded sediment is not well quantified, but much of the sediment is probably deposited in nearby areas more protected from the wind by vegetative cover, stream valleys, road ditches, woodlands, or farmsteads.

While a number of national and regional erosion estimates for the United States have been made since the 1920s, the methodologies of estimation and interpretations have been different, making accurate time comparisons impossible. The most extensive surveys have been made since the Soil, Water and Related Resources Act was passed in 1977. In these surveys a large number of points were randomly selected, data assembled for the points, and the Universal Soil Loss Equation (USLE) or the Wind Erosion Equation (WEE) used to estimate erosion amounts. While these equations were the best available at the time, their results are only estimations, and subject to interpretation. Considerable research on improved methods of estimation is underway by the **U.S. Department of Agriculture**.

In the cornbelt of the United States, water erosion may cause a 1.7 to 7.8 percent drop in soil productivity over the next one hundred years, as compared to current levels, depending on the **topography** and soils of the area. The U.S.D.A. results, based on estimated erosion amounts for 1977, only included sheet erosion, not losses of plant nutrients. Though the figures may be low for this reason, other surveys have produced similar estimates.

In addition to depleting farmlands, eroded sediment causes off-site damages that, according to one study, may exceed on-site loss. The sediment may end up in a domestic water supply, clog stream channels, even degrade **wetlands**, wildlife **habitat**s, and entire **ecosystem**s. *See also* Environmental degradation; Gillied land; Soil eluviation; Soil organic matter; Soil texture

[*William E. Larson*]

FURTHER READING

Brown, L. R., and E. Wolf. "Soil Erosion: Quiet Crisis in the World Economy." *Worldwatch Paper #60.* Washington DC: Worldwatch Institute, 1984.

Paddock, J. N., and C. Bly. *Soil and Survival: Land Stewardship and the Future of American Agriculture.* San Francisco: Sierra Club Books, 1987.

Resource Conservation Glossary. 3rd ed. Ankeny, IA: Soil Conservation Society of America, 1982.

Steinhart, P. "The Edge Gets Thinner." *Audubon* 85 (November 1983): 94-106+.

Estuary

Estuaries represent one of the most biologically productive aquatic **ecosystem**s on earth. An estuary is a coastal body of water where chemical and physical conditions modulate in an intermediate range between the freshwater rivers that feed into them and the salt water of the ocean beyond them. It is the point of mixture for these two very different aquatic ecosystems. The freshwater of the rivers mix with the salt water pushed by the incoming tides to provide a **brackish** water **habitat** ideally suited to a tremendous diversity of coastal marine life.

Estuaries are nursery grounds for the developing young of commercially important fish and shellfish. The young of any **species** are less tolerant of physical extremes in their **environment** than adults. Many species of marine life cannot tolerate the concentrations of salt in ocean water as they develop from egg to subadult, and by providing a mixture of fresh and salt water, estuaries give these larval life forms a more moderate environment in which to grow. Because of this, the adults often move directly into estuaries to spawn.

Estuaries are extremely rich in **nutrient**s, and this is another reason for the great diversity of organisms in these ecosystems. The flow of freshwater and the periodic **flooding** of surrounding marshlands provides an influx of nutrients, as does the daily surges of tidal fluctuations. Constant physical movement in this environment keeps valuable nutrient resources available to all levels within the **food chain/ web**.

Coastal estuaries also provide a major filtration system for waterborne pollutants. This natural **water treatment** facility helps maintain and protect **water quality**, and studies have shown that one acre of tidal estuary can be the equivalent of a $75,000 waste treatment plant. When its value for **recreation** and seafood production are included in this estimate, a single acre of estuary has been valued at $83,000. An acre of farmland in America's Corn Belt, for comparison, has a top value of $1,200 and an annual income through crop production of $600.

Throughout the ages man has settled near bodies of water and utilized the bounty they provide, and the economic value of estuaries, as well as the fact that they are a coastal habitat, has made them vulnerable to exploitation. **Chesapeake Bay** on the Atlantic coast is the largest estuary in the United States, draining six states and the District of Columbia. It is the largest producer of oysters in the country; it is the single largest producer of blue crabs in the world, and 90 percent of the striped bass found on the East Coast hatch there. It one of the most productive estuaries in the world, yet its productivity has declined in recent decades due to a huge increase in the number of people in the region. Between the 1940s and the 1990s, the population jumped from about three and a half million to over 15 million, bringing with it an increase in **pollution** and **overfishing** of the bay. **Sewage treatment** plants contribute large amounts of phosphates, while agricultural, urban, and suburban **discharge**s deposit nitrates, which in turn contribute to **algal bloom**s and oxygen depletion. **Pesticide**s and industrial toxics also contribute to the bay's problems. Since the early 1980s concerted efforts to clean up the Chesapeake Bay and restore its seafood productivity have been undertaken by state and federal agencies. Progress has been made but there is still much to be done, both to restore this vital ecosystem and to insure prolonged cooperation between government agencies, industry, and the general populace. *See also* Agricultural pollution; Aquatic chemistry; Commercial fishing; Dissolved oxygen; Nitrates and nitrites; Nitrogen cycle; Restoration ecology

[*Eugene C. Beckham*]

FURTHER READING

Baretta, J. W., and P. Ruardij, eds. Tidal Flat Estuaries. New York: Springer-Verlag, 1988.

Horton, T. "Chesapeake Bay: Hanging in the Balance." *National Geographic* 183 (1993): 2-35.

McLusky, D. *The Estuarine Ecosystem.* New York: Chapman & Hall, 1989.

Ethanol

Ethanol is an organic compound with the chemical formula C_2H_5OH. Its common names include ethyl alcohol and grain alcohol. The latter term reflects one method by which the compound can be produced: the distillation of corn, sugar cane, wheat and other grains. Ethanol is the primary component in many alcoholic drinks such as beer, wine, vodka, gin and whiskey. Many scientists believe that ethanol can and should be more widely used in automotive fuels. When mixed in a one to nine ratio with **gasoline**, it is sold as **gasohol**. The reduced costs of producing gasohol have only recently made it a viable economic alternative to other automotive fuels. *See also* Alternative fuels

Eurasian milfoil (*Myriophyllum spicatum*)

Eurasian milfoil is a feathery-looking underwater plant that has become a major nuisance in waterways in the United States. Introduced into the country over 70 years ago as an ornamental tank plant by the aquarium industry, it has since spread to the East Coast from Vermont to Florida and grows as far west as Wisconsin and Texas. It is also found in California. It is particularly abundant in the **Chesapeake Bay**, the Potomac River, and in some Tennessee Valley **reservoir**s.

Eurasian milfoil is able to tolerate a wide range of **salinity** in water and grows well in inland fresh waters as well as in **brackish** coastal waters. The branched stems grow from one to ten feet (3 m) in length and are upright when young, becoming horizontal as they get older. Although most of the plant is underwater, the tips of the stems often project out at the surface. Where the water is hard, the stems may get stiffened by calcification. The leaves are arranged in whorls of four around the branches with 12-16 pairs of leaflets per leaf. As with other milfoils, the red flowers of Eurasian milfoil are small and inconspicuous. As fragments of the plant break off, they disperse quickly through an area, with each fragment capable of putting out roots and developing into a new plant. Due to its extremely dense growth, Eurasian milfoil has become a nuisance that often impedes the passage of boats and vessels along navigable waterways. It can cause considerable damage to underwater equipment and lead to losses of time and money in the maintenance and operation of shipping lanes. It also interferes with recreational water uses such as fishing, swimming, and diving. In the **prairie** lakes of North Dakota, the woody seeds of this plant are eaten by some waterfowl such as ducks. However, this plant appears to have little **wildlife** value, although it may provide some cover to fishlife.

Aquatic weed control experts recommend that vessels that have passed through growths of Eurasian milfoil be examined and plant fragments removed. They also advocate the physical removal of plant growths from shorelines and other areas with a high potential for dispersal. Additionally, chemical agents are also often used to control the weed. Some of the commonly used **herbicide**s include **2,4-D** and Diquat. These are usually diluted with water and applied at the rate of one to two gallons per acre. The application of herbicides to control aquatic weed growth is regulated by environmental agencies due to the potential of harm to non-target organisms. Application times are restricted by season and duration of exposure and depend on the kind of herbicide used, its mode of action, and its impacts on the other biota in the aquatic system. *See also* Aquatic chemistry; Commercial fishing

[*Usha Vedagiri*]

FURTHER READING

Gunner, H. B. *Microbiological Control of Eurasian Watermilfoil.* Washington, DC: U. S. Army Engineer Waterways Experiment Station, 1983.

Hotchkiss, N. *Common Marsh Underwater and Floating-Leaved Plants of the United States and Canada.* Mineola, NY: Dover Publications, 1972.

Schmidt, J. C. *How to Identify and Control Water Weeds and Algae.* Milwaukee, WI: Applied Biochemists, Inc., 1987.

European Economic Community (EEC)

An economic and political community of 12 European states that sets agreed-upon tariffs, has internal free trade, and in certain cases negotiates political agreements as a single body. The European Economic Community (EEC) protects collective economic interests by forming a large negotiating body with financial power equal to that of other world economic powers, notably the United States and Japan. Established in 1957 by the Treaty of Rome, the EEC's original seven signatories were France, West Germany, the Netherlands, Belgium, Luxembourg, and Italy. Another six states joined the association by 1982: Denmark, the Republic of Ireland, the United Kingdom, Greece, Spain, and Portugal. EEC headquarters are in Brussels, Belgium, with the Court of Justice located in Luxembourg and the Parliament in Strasbourg, France.

European Greens
See **Green politics**

Eutectic

Refers to a type of solar heating system which makes use of phase changes in a chemical storage medium. At its melting point, any chemical compound must absorb a quantity of heat in order to change phase from solid to liquid, and at its boiling point, it must absorb an additional quantity of heat to change to a gas. Conversely, a compound *releases* a quantity of heat when condensing or freezing. Therefore, a chemical warmed by **solar energy** through a phase change releases far more energy when it cools than, for example, water heated from a cool liquid to a warm liquid state. For this reason, solar heating systems that employ phase-changing chemicals can store more energy in a compact space than a water-based system.

Eutrophication
See **Cultural eutrophication**

Evapotranspiration

Evapotranspiration is a key part of the **hydrologic cycle**. Some water evaporates directly from **soil**s and water bodies, but much is returned to the atmosphere by transpiration (a word combining transport and evaporation) from plants via openings in the leaves called stomata. Within the same climates, forests and lakes yield about the same amount of water vapor. The amount of evapotranspiration is dependent on energy inputs of heat, wind, humidity, and the amount of stored soil water. In climate studies this term is used to indicate levels of surplus or deficit in water budgets. Aridity may be defined as an excess of potential evapotranspiration over actual precipitation, while in humid regions the amount of **runoff** correlates well with the surplus of precipitation over evapotranspiration.

Everglades

Described as a vast, shallow sawgrass (*Cladium effusum*) marsh with tree islands, wet **prairie**s, and aquatic sloughs, the Everglades historically covered most of southeastern Florida, prior to massive drainage and **reclamation** projects launched at the turn of the century. The glades constitute the southern end of the Kissimmee Lake Okeechobee Everglades system, which encompasses most of south and central Florida below Orlando. Originally, the Everglades covered an area approximately 40 miles (64 km) wide and 100 miles (161 km) long—2.5 million acres—but large segments have been isolated by canals and levees. Today, intensive agriculture in the north and rapid urban development in the east are among the Everglades' various land uses.

Two general habitat regions can be demarcated in the Everglades. The first includes three **water conservation** areas, basins created to preserve portions of the glades and provide multiple uses, such as **water supply**. This region is located in the northern Everglades and contains most of the intact natural marsh. The second is the southern habitat, which includes the Everglades National Park and the southern third of the three water conservation areas. The park has been designated a World Heritage Site of international ecological significance, and the Everglades as a whole are one of the outstanding freshwater **ecosystem**s in the United States.

Topographically flat, elevations in the Everglades are generally less than 20 feet (6.1 m). The ground slopes north to south at an average gradient of 0.15 feet per mile, with the highest elevations in the north and the lowest in the south. The **climate** is generally subtropical, with long, hot, humid, and wet summers from May to October followed by mild, dry winters from November to April. During the wet season severe storms can result in lengthy periods of **flooding**, while during the dry season cool, sometimes freezing temperatures can be accompanied by thunderstorms, tornadoes, and heavy rainfall.

Before the Everglades were drained, large areas of the system were inundated each year as Lake Okeechobee overflowed its southern rim. The "River of Grass" flowed south and was in constant flux through **evapotranspiration**, rainfall, and water movement into and out of the Everglades' **aquifer**. The water discharged into the tidewaters of south Biscayne Bay, Florida Bay, and Ten Thousand Islands.

In the early 1880s, Philadelphia industrialist Hamilton Disston began draining the Everglades under a contract with Florida trustees. Disston, whose work ceased in 1889, built a substantial number of canals, mainly in the upper waters of the Kissimmee River, and constructed a canal between Lake Okeechobee and the Calooshatchee River to provide an outlet to the Gulf of Mexico. The Miami River was channelized beginning in 1903, and other canals—the Snapper Creek Canal, the Cutler Canal, and the Coral Gables Waterway—were opened to help drain the Everglades. **Water table**s in south Florida fell five to six feet (1.5 ot 1.8 m) below 1900 levels, causing stress to **wetlands** systems and losses of peat up to six feet (1.8 m) in depth.

A swampy area in the Everglades.

Full-scale drainage and reclamation occurred under Governor W. S. Jennings (1901-1905) and Governor Napoleon Bonaparte Broward (1905-1909). In 1907, the Everglades Drainage District was created and built six major canals over 400 miles long before it suffered financial collapse in 1928. These canals enabled agriculture to flourish within the region. In the late 1920s, when settlers realized better water control and flood protection were needed, low muck levees were built along Lake Okeechobee's southwest shore, eliminating the lake's overflow south to the Everglades. But hurricanes in 1926 and 1928 breached the levees, destroying property and killing 2,100 people. As a result, the Lake Okeechobee Flood Control District was established in 1929, and over the following fifteen years the United States **Army Corps of Engineers** constructed and enlarged flood control canals.

It was only in the mid-1950s, with the development and implementation of the Central and Southern Florida Project for Flood Control & Other Purposes (C&SF Project), that water control took priority over uncontrolled drainage of the Everglades. The project, completed by 1962, was to provide flood protection, water supply, and environmental benefits over a 16,000 square-mile (41,440 sq-km) area. It consists of 1,500 miles (2,415 km) of canals and levees, 125 major water control structures, 18 major pumping stations, 13 boat locks, and several hundred smaller structures.

Interspersed throughout the Everglades is a series of **habitat**s, each dominated by a few or in some cases a single plant **species**. Seasonal wetlands and upland pine forests, which once dominated the historic border of the system, have come under the heaviest pressure from urban and agricultural development. In the system's southern part, freshwater wet-lands are superseded by muhly grass (*Muhlenbergia filipes*), prairies, upland pine and tropical hardwood forests, and mangrove forests that are influenced by the tides.

Attached algae, also known as periphyton, are an important component of the Everglades **food web**, providing both organic food matter and habitat for various grazing invertebrates and forage fish that are eaten by wading birds, reptiles, and sport fish. These algae include calcareous and filamentous blue-green algae (*Scytonema hoffmani, Schizothrix calcicola*) and hard water diatoms (*Mastogloia smithii v. lacustris*).

Sawgrass (*Cladium jamaicense*) constitutes one of the main plants occurring throughout the Everglades, being found in 65 to 70 percent of the remaining freshwater marsh. In the north, the sawgrass grows in deep **peat soils** and is both dense and tall, reaching up to ten feet (3 m) in height. In the south, it grows in low-nutrient marl soils and is less dense and shorter, averaging two and a half to five feet (0.75 to 1.5 m). Sawgrass is adapted to survive both flooding and burning. Stands of pure sawgrass as well as mixed communities are found in the Everglades. The mixed communities can include maidencane (*Panicum hemitomon*) arrowhead (*Sagittaria lancifolia*), water hyssop (*Bacopa caroliniana*), and spikerush (*Eleocharis cellulosa*).

Wet prairies, which together with aquatic sloughs provide habitat during the rainy season for a wide variety of aquatic invertebrates and forage fish, are another important habitat of the Everglades system. They are seasonally inundated wetland communities that require certain standing water for six to ten months. Once common, today more than 1,500 square miles (3,885 sq km) of these prairies have been drained or destroyed.

The lowest elevations of the Everglades are ponds and sloughs, which have deeper water and longer inundation periods. They occur throughout the system, and in some cases can be formed by **alligator**s in peat soils. Among the types of emergent vegetation commonly found in these areas are white water lily (*Nymphaea odorata*), floating heart (*Nymphoides aquatica*), and spatterdock (*Nuphar luteum*). Common submerged species include bladderwort (*Utricularia*) and the periphyton mat community. Ponds and sloughs serve as important feeding areas and habitat for Everglades **wildlife**.

At the highest elevations are found communities of isolated trees surrounded by marsh called tree islands. These provide nesting and roosting sites for colonial birds and habitat for deer and other terrestrial animals during high-water periods. Typical dominant species constituting tree islands are red bay (*Persa borbonia*), swamp bay (*Magnolia virginiana*), dahoon holly (*Ilex cassine*), pond apple (*Annona glabra*), and wax myrtle (*Myrica cerifera*). Beneath the canopy grows a dense shrub layer of cocoplum (*Chrysobalanus icacao*), buttonbush (*Cephalanthus accidentalis*), leather leaf fern (*Acrostichum danaeifolium*), royal fern (*Osmunda regalis*), cinnamon fern (*O. cinnamonea*), chain fern (*Anchistea virginica*), bracken fern (*Pteridium aquilinium*), and lizards tail (*Saururus cernuus*).

In addition to the indigenous plants of the Everglades, numerous exotic and nuisance species have been brought into Florida and have now spread in the wild. Some threaten to invade and displace indigenous species. Brazilian pepper (*Schinus terebinthifolius*), Australian pine (*Casuarina equisetifolia*), and melaleuca (*Melaleuca quinquenervia*) are three of the most serious **exotic species** that have gained a foothold and are displacing native plants.

The Florida Game and Fresh Water Fish Commission has identified 25 threatened or **endangered species** with the Everglades. Mammals include the **Florida panther** (*Felis concolor coryi*), mangrove fox squirrel (*Sciurus niger avicennia*), and black bear (*Ursus americanus floridanus*). Birds include the wood stork (*Mycteria americana*), snail kite (*Rostrhamus sociabilis*), and the red-cockaded woodpecker (*Picoides borealis*). Endangered or threatened reptiles and amphibians include the gopher tortoise (*Gopherus polyphemus*), the eastern indigo snake (*Drymarchon corais couperi*), and the loggerhead **sea turtle** (*Caretta caretta*).

The alligator (*Alligator mississippiensis*) was once endangered due to excessive alligator hide hunting. In 1972, the state made alligator product sales illegal. Protection allowed the species to recover, and it is now widely distributed in wetlands throughout the state. It is still listed as threatened by the federal government, but in 1988 Florida instituted an annual alligator harvest.

Faced with pressures on Everglades habitats and the species within them, as well as the need for water management within the rapidly developing state, in 1987 the Florida legislature passed the Surface Water Improvement and Management Act (1987). The law requires the state's five water management districts to identify areas needing preservation or restoration. The Everglades Protection Area was identified as a priority for preservation and improvement planning. Within the state's protection plan, excess nutrients, in large part from agriculture, have been targeted as a major problem that causes natural periphyton to be replaced by species more tolerant of **pollution**. In turn, sawgrass and wet prairie communities are overrun by other species, impairing the Everglades' ability to serve as habitat and forage for higher **trophic level** species.

[*David Clarke*]

FURTHER READING

Douglas, M. S. *The Everglades: River of Grass.* New York: H. Wolff, 1947.

Johnson, R. "New Life for the 'River of Grass.'" *American Forests* 98 (July-August 1992): 38-43.

Stover, D. "Engineering the Everglades." *Popular Science* 241 (July 1992): 46-51.

Evolution

Evolution is an all-pervading concept in modern science applied to physical as well as biological processes. The phrase *theory of evolution*, however, is most commonly associated with organic evolution, the origin and evolution of the enormous diversity of life on this planet.

The idea of organic evolution arose from attempts to explain the immense diversity of living organisms and dates from the dawn of culture. Attempts to formulate a naturalistic explanation of the phenomena of evolution in one form or another had been proposed, and by the end of the eighteenth century a number of naturalists from Carolus Linnaeus (1707-1778) to Jean-Baptiste Lamarck (1744-1829) had questioned the prevailing doctrine of fixity of **species**. Lamarck came the closest to proposing a complete theory of evolution, but for several reasons his theory fell short and was not widely accepted.

Two English naturalists conceived the first truly complete theory of evolution. In a most remarkable coincidence, working quite independently, **Charles Darwin** and Alfred Russell Wallace (1823-1913) arrived at essentially the same thesis, and their ideas were initially publicized jointly in 1858. However, it is to Charles Darwin that the recognition of the founder of modern evolution is attributed. His continued efforts toward a detailed development of the evidence and the explication of a complete, convincing theory of organic evolution resulted in the publication in 1859 of his book *On the Origin of Species by Natural Selection*. With the publication of this volume, widely regarded as one of the most influential books ever written, regardless of subject matter, the science of biology would never be the same.

Darwin was the first evolutionist whose theories carried conviction to a majority of his contemporaries. He set forth a formidable mass of supporting evidence in the form of direct observations from nature, coupled with a comprehensive and convincing synthesis of current knowledge. Most significantly, he proposed a rational, plausible instrumentality for evolutionary change: natural selection.

The theory Darwin presented is remarkably simple and rational. In brief, the theoretical framework of evolution presented by Darwin contained three basic elements. First is the existence of variation in natural populations. In nature there are no individuals who are exactly alike, therefore natural populations always consist of members who all differ from one another to some degree. Many of these differences are heritable and are passed on from generation to generation. Second, some of these varieties are better adapted to their environment than others. Third, the reproductive potential of populations is unlimited. All populations have the capacity to overproduce, but populations in nature are limited by high **mortality**. Thus, if all offspring cannot survive each generation, the better-adapted members have a greater probability of surviving each generation than those less adapted.

Thomas Henry Huxley (1825-1895), when first presented with Darwin's views, was supposed to have exclaimed: "How extremely stupid not to have thought of that." This apocryphal statement expresses succinctly the immediate intelligibility of this momentous discovery.

Darwin's theory as presented was incomplete, as he was keenly aware, but the essential parts were adequate at the time to demonstrate that the material causes of evolution are possible and can be investigated scientifically.

One of the most critical difficulties with Darwin's theory was the inability to explain the source of hereditary variations observed in populations and, in particular, the source of hereditary innovations which, through the agency of natural selection, could eventually bring about the transformation of a species. The lack of existing knowledge of the mechanism of heredity in the mid-1800s precluded a scientifically sound solution to this problem.

The re-discovery in 1900 of Gregor Mendel's experiments demonstrating the underlying process of inheritance did not at first provide a solution to the problem facing Darwinian evolutionary theory. In fact, in one of the most extraordinary paradoxes in the history of science, during the first decades of Mendelian genetics, a temporary decline occurred in the support of Darwinian selectionism. This was primarily because of the direction and level of research as much as the lack of knowledge in further details of the underlying mechanisms of inheritance.

It was not until the publication of Theodosius Dobzhansky's *Genetics and the Origin of Species* (1937) that the modern synthetic theory of evolution began to take form, renewing confidence in selectionism and the Darwinian theory. In his book, Dobzhansky, for the first time, integrated the newly developed mathematical models of population genetics with the fats of chromosomal theory and **mutation** together with observations of variation in natural populations.

Dobzhansky also stimulated a series of books by several major evolutionists which provided the impetus and direction of research over the next decade, resulting in a reformulation of Darwin's theory. This became known as the *synthetic theory of evolution*. Synthetic is used here to indicate that there has been a convergence and synthesis of knowledge from many disciplines of biology and chemistry.

The birth of molecular genetics in 1950 and the enormous expansion of knowledge in this area have affected the further development and refinement of the synthetic theory markedly. But it has not altered the fundamental nature of the theory. Darwin's initial concept in this expanded, modernized form has taken on such stature as to be generally considered as the most encompassing theory in biology. To the majority of biologists, the synthetic theory of evolution is a grand theory that forms the core of modern biology. It also provides the theoretical foundation upon which most all other theories find support and comprehension. Or, as the distinguished evolutionary biologist Dobzhansky so succinctly put it: "Nothing in life makes sense except in the light of evolution."

If the three main elements of the Darwinian theory were to be restated in terms of the modern synthetic theory, they would be as follows. First, genetic systems governing heredity in each organism are composed of genes and chromosomes which are discrete but tightly interacting units of different levels of complexity. The genes, their organized associations in chromosomes, and whole sets of chromosomes, have a large degree of stability as units. But these units are shuffled and combined in various ways by sexual processes of reproduction in most organisms. The result of this process, called *recombination*, maintains a considerable amount of variation in any population in nature without introducing any new hereditary factors. Genetic experimentation, is, in fact, occurring all the time in natural populations. Each genera-

tion, as a result of recombination, is made up of members who carry different hereditary combinations drawn from the common pool of the population. Each member generation in turn interacts within the same environmental matrix which, in effect, "tests" the fitness of these hereditary combinations. The sole source of hereditary innovation from within the population, other than recombination, would come from mutation affecting individual genes, chromosomes or sets of chromosomes, which are then fed into the process of recombination.

Second, populations of similar animals—members of the same species—usually interbreed among themselves making up a common pool of genes. The **gene pool**s of established populations in nature tend to remain at equilibrium from generation to generation. An abundance of evidence has established the fact, as Darwin and others before him had observed, that populations have greater reproductive capacity than they can sustain in nature.

Third, change, over time, in the makeup of the gene pool, may occur by one of four known processes: mutation, fluctuation in gene frequencies—known as "sampling errors," or "genetic drift," which is generally effective only in small, isolated populations—introduction of genes from other populations, and differential reproduction.

The first three of these processes do not produce adaptive trends. These are essentially random in their effects, usually nonadaptive and only rarely and coincidentally produce adaptation. Of the four processes, differential reproduction results in adaptive trends. Differential reproduction describes the consistent production of more offspring, on an average, by individuals with certain genetic characteristics than those without those characteristics. This is the modern understanding of natural selection, with emphasis upon success in reproduction. The Darwinian and Neo-Darwinian concepts, on the other hand, placed greater emphasis upon "survival of the fittest" in terms of mortality and survival. Natural selection, in the Darwinian sense, was non-random and produced trends that were adaptive. Differential reproduction produces the same result. In what may appear to be a paradox, differential selection also acts in stabilizing the gene pool by reducing the reproductive success of those members whose hereditary variation result in non-adaptive traits.

As Darwin first recognized, the link between variability or constancy of the **environment** and evolutionary change or stability is provided by natural selection. The interaction between organisms and their environment will inevitably affect the genetic composition of each new generation. As a result of differential selection, the most fit individuals, in terms of reproductive capacity, contribute the largest proportion of genes or alleles to the next generation. The direction in which natural selection guides the population depends upon both the nature of environmental change or stability and the content of the gene pool of the population.

From the very beginning, evolutionists have recognized the significance of the environment/evolution linkage. This linkage always involves the interactions of a great many individuals both within populations of a single species (intraspecific) and among members of different species (interspecific linkage). These are inextricably linked with changes in the physical environment.

Dobzhansky estimated that the world may contain four to five million different kinds of organisms, each exploiting in various ways a large number of habitats. The complexity of **ecosystem**s is based upon thousands of different ways of exploiting the same habitats in which each species is adapted to its specifically defined niche within the total habitat. The diversity of these population-environment interactions is responsible for the fact that natural selection can be conservative—(normalizing selection)—and can promote constancy in the gene pool. It directs continuous change (directional selection), or promotes diversification into new species (diversifying selection).

Recent trends in research have been of special significance in understanding the dynamics of these processes. They have greatly increased the body of information related to the ecological dimension of population biology. These studies have developed methods of analysis and sophisticated models which have made major advances in the study and understanding of the nature of the selective forces that direct evolutionary change. It is increasingly clear that a reciprocal imperative exists between ecological and environmental studies to further our understanding of the role of evolutionary and counterrevolutionary processes affecting stability in biological systems over time. The urgency of the need for an expanded synthesis of ecological and evolutionary studies is driven by the accelerating and expanding counterrevolutionary changes in the world environment resulting from human actions.

Evolutionary processes are tremendously more complex in detail than this brief outline suggests. This spare outline, however, should be sufficient to show that here is a mechanism, involving materials and processes known beyond doubt to occur in nature, capable of shaping and changing species in response to the continuously dynamic universe in which they exist.

[*Donald A. Villeneuve*]

FURTHER READING

Dobzhansky, T., et al. *Evolution.* San Francisco: W. H. Freeman, 1977.

Simpson, G. G. *The Meaning of Evolution.* New Haven, CT: Yale University Press, 1967.

Existence value

See **Debt for nature swap**

Exotic species

A plant or animal **species** introduced to a region or a continent, often unintentionally, through human **migration** or trade. Some exotic species, including most tropical fish, birds, and house plants brought to colder **climate**s, can

survive only under continuous care. Others prove extremely adaptable and thrive in their new environments—often becoming a serious threat to the survival of native species. Species useful to man, such as horses, goats, pigs, edible plants including wheat, and oats are often introduced intentionally. But accidental introductions (including the Mediterranean fruit fly, the Japanese beetle, Africanized "killer" bees, Norwegian rats, cockroaches, disease causing **virus**es) are equally common. The Federal Government's Office of Technology Assessment has estimated that more than 2,000 plant species from around the world currently live and thrive in the United States, and that 15 of these have caused more than $500 million worth of damage. Economic costs associated with exotic species include agricultural losses; damage to infrastructure, as when aquatic plants clog water intakes; and the costs of attempts to restore native species overrun by introduced species.

Exotic species are most are most noticeable when they adapt readily to their new environment and compete successfully with native species. Often these plant and animals are extremely sucessful becuase, unlike their native neighbors, they have no natural pests, parasites, diseases, or predators. For example, purple loosestrife (Lythrum salicaria) is a showy wetland plant with tall pruple flowers that was provaly imported to North America as a garden ornamental. In its native northern Europe, where resident beetles are adapted to feed on its roots and leaves, loosestrife may appear only occasionally and temporarily in distrubed sites. When loosestrife arrived in America, the beetles, along with other pests nd diseases, were left behind. Loosestrife has proven to be extremely adaptable and has become an aggressive weed acrosss much of the American East and Midwest, often taking over an entire wetland and choking out other plants, eliminating many wetland habitat benefits.

In addition to the advantage of having gew predators, exotic plants and animals that are recognized as weeds or nuisance species may have lifestyle or ecological characteristecs that make them especially competitive. They may be hardy, adaptable to diverse havitat conditions, and thrive on a variety of food sources. They may reproduce rapidly, generating large numbers of seeds or young that spread out quickly into new range. If they are aggressive colonizers and accustomed to living in marginal habitat, introduced species can drive resident natives from nesting sites and food sources, especially around the disturbed environments of human settlement. This competitiveness has been a serious problem with English sparrows and starlings, which may drive sparrows, swallows, and other birds from their nests or kill their young. Exotic plants are noticed as a nuisance when they crowd, shade, or out-propagate their competitors. In some cases, introduced species force natives to retreat by destroying feeding or breeding habitats. Because of these advantages, exotic species can be extraordinarily effective colonists, spreading quickly and eliminating competition as they go.

The list of species introduced to the Americas from Europe and Asia is immense. Some notable examples are kudzu (*Pueraria lobata*), the **zebra mussel** (*Dreissena polymorpha*), **Africanized bees** (*Apis mellifera scutellata*), and **Eurasian milfoil** (*Myriophyllum spicatum*). Kudzu, a cultivated legume in Japan, was brought to the southern United States for ground cover and **erosion** control. Fast growing and tenacious, kudzu quickly overwhelms houses, tangles in electric lines, and chokes out native vegetation. Africanized "killer" bees were accidentally released by a Brazilian beekeeper in 1957. These aggressive insects have no more venom than standard honey bees (also an Old World import), but they attack more quickly and in great numbers. Breeding with resident bees and sometimes travelling with cargo shipments, Africanized bees have spread at a rate of up to 200 miles (321.8 km) a year and now threaten to invade lucrative fruit orchards and domestic hives in Texas and California. The zebra mussel, introduced to the **Great Lakes** in about 1985, presumably in ballast water dumped by ships arriving from Europe, colonizes any hard surface, including docks, industrial water intake pipes, and the shells of native bivalves. Each bean-sized female zebra mussel can produce 50,000 larvae in a single year. Growing in masses with up to 70,000 individuals per square foot, these mussels clog pipes, suffocate native clams, and destroy breeding grounds for other aquatic animals. The region's economy now suffers as well as its environment: area industries spend hundreds of millions of dollars annually unclogging pipes and equipment.

Eurasian milfoil is a common aquarium plant that can propagate by seeds or cuttings. A tiny section of stem and leaves introduced by a recreational boat or trailer can grow into great mats, colonizing an entire lake. When these mats of vegetation have consumed all available **nutrient**s, they die and rot, robbing fish and other aquatic animals of oxygen.

Exotic species have brought similar disasters to every continent, but some of the most tragic cases have occurred on isolated islands where resident species have lost their defensive strategies. Ground-breeding birds on Pacific islands have been devastated by rats, cats, dogs, and mongooses introduced by eighteenth-century sailors. Rare flowers in Hawaii suffer from grazing goats and rooting pigs, both of which have established wild populations. Grazing sheep threaten delicate plants on weather-beaten North Atlantic islands, while rats, cats, and dogs endanger northern seabird breeding colonies.

Human populations have always carried plants and animals as they migrated from one continent to another, but few notice the effects of these introductions. Many seem benign, useful, or even pleasing to have around. When an exotic plant or animal threatens human livelihoods or economic activity, as do kudzu, zebra mussels, and "killer" bees, humans begin to seek ways to control their spread. Control efforts may include introducing natural predators and parasites from the home range of the exotic plant or animal. For example, beetles that naturally prey on purple loosestrife have been experimentally introduced in American loosestrife populations. This deliberate introduction requires a great deal of care, research, and monitoring, however, to ensure that a still worse problem does not result. Such solutions, and the time and money to develop them, are usually elusive, so in most cases effective control methods remain unavailable. *See also*

Adaptation; Hawaiian Islands; Introduced species; Opportunistic organism; Pest; Predator-prey interactions

[*Mary Ann Cunningham*]

FURTHER READING

Barrett, S. C. H. "Waterweed Invasions." *Scientific American* 261 (October 1989): 90-7.

Cunningham, W. *Understanding Our Environment: An Introduction.* Dubuque, IA: William C. Brown, 1993.

Rendall, Jay. " Invasive Species". J.F. Bell Museum of Natural History, *Imprint* vol. 7 no. 4: 1-8, 1990.

Walker, T. "Dreissena Disaster—Scientists Battle an Invasion of Zebra Mussels." *Science News* 139 (4 May 1991): 282-84.

Experimental Lakes Area

The Experimental Lakes Area (ELA) in northwestern Ontario is in a remote landscape characterized by Precambrian bedrock, northern mixed-species forests, and oligotrophic lakes, bodies of water deficient in plant **nutrient**s. The Canadian Department of Fisheries and Oceans began developing a field-research facility at ELA in the 1960s, and the area has become the focus of a large number of investigations by D. W. Schindler and others into chemical and biological conditions in these lakes.

Of the limnological investigations conducted at ELA, the best known is a series of whole-lake experiments designed to investigate the ecological effects of perturbation by a variety of **environmental stress** factors, including eutrophication, **acidification**, metals, radionuclides, and **flooding** during the development of **reservoir**s.

The integrated, whole-lake projects at ELA were initially designed to study the causes and ecological consequences of eutrophication. In one long-term experiment, Lake 227 was fertilized with phosphate and **nitrate** . This experiment was designed to test whether **carbon** could limit algal growth during eutrophication, so none was added. Lake 227 responded with a large increase in primary productivity by drawing on the **atmosphere** for carbon, but it was not possible to determine which of the two added nutrients, phosphate or nitrate, had acted as the primary limiting factor.

Observations from experiments at other lakes in ELA, however, clearly indicated that phosphate is the primary limiting nutrient in these oligotrophic water bodies. Lake 304 was fertilized for two years with **phosphorus, nitrogen**, and carbon, and it became eutrophic. It recovered its oligotrophic condition again when the phosphorus fertilization was stopped, even though nitrogen and carbon fertilization were continued. Lake 226, an hourglass-shaped lake, was partitioned with a vinyl curtain into two basins, one of which was fertilized with carbon and nitrogen, and the other with phosphorus, carbon, and nitrogen. Only the latter treatment caused an **algal bloom**. Lake 302 received an injection of all three nutrients directly into its hypolimnion during the summer. Because the lake was thermally stratified at that time, the hypolimnetic nutrients were not available to fertilize plant growth in the epilimnetic euphotic zone, and no algal bloom resulted. Nitrogen additions to Lake 227 were reduced in 1975 and eliminated in 1990. The lake continued with high levels of productivity by fixing nitrogen from the atmosphere.

Research of this sort was instrumental in confirming conclusively the identification of phosphorus as the most generally limiting nutrient to eutrophication of freshwaters. This knowledge allowed the development of **waste management** systems which reduced eutrophication as an environmental problem by reducing the phosphorus concentration in **detergents**, removing phosphorus from sewage, and diverting sewage from lakes.

Another well known ELA project was important in gaining a deeper understanding of the ecological consequences of the acidification of lakes. Sulfuric acid was added to Lake 223, and its acidity was increased progressively, from an initial **pH** near 6.5 to pH 5.0-5.1 after six years. Sulfate and hydrogen ions were also added to the lake in increasing concentrations during this time. Other chemical changes were caused indirectly by acidification: manganese increased by 980 percent, zinc by 550 percent, and **aluminum** by 155 percent.

As the acidity of Lake 223 increased, the **phytoplankton** shifted from a community dominated by golden-brown algae to one dominated by chlorophytes and dinoflagellates. Species diversity declined somewhat, but productivity was not adversely affected. A mat of the green alga *Mougeotia* sp. developed near the shore after the pH dropped below 5.6. Because of reduced predation, the density of cladoceran **zooplankton** was larger by 66 percent at pH 5.4 than at pH 6.6, and copepods were 93 percent more abundant. The nocturnal zooplankton predator *Mysis relicta*, however, was an important extinction. The crayfish *Orconectes virilis* declined because of reproductive failure, inhibition of carapace hardening, and effects of a parasite. The most acid-sensitive fish was the fathead minnow (*Pimephales promelas*), which declined precipitously when the lake pH reached 5.6.

The first of many year-class failures of lake trout (*Salvelinus namaycush*) occurred at pH 5.4, and failure of white sucker (*Catastomus commersoni*) occurred at pH 5.1. One minnow, the pearl dace (*Semotilus margarita*), increased markedly in abundance but then declined when pH reached 5.1. Adult lake trout and white sucker were still abundant, though emaciated, at pH 5.0-5.5, but in the absence of successful reproduction they would have become extinct. Overall, the Lake 223 experiment indicated a general sensitivity of many organisms to the acidification of lake water. However, within the limits of physiological tolerance, the tests showed that there can be a replacement of acid-sensitive species by relatively tolerant ones.

In a similarly designed experiment in Lake 302, nitric acid was shown to be nearly as effective as sulfuric acid in acidifying lakes, thereby alerting the international community to the need to control atmospheric **emission**s of gaseous nitrogen compounds. *See also* Acid rain; Algicide; Aquatic chemistry; C:N ratio; Cultural eutrophication; Water pollution

[*Bill Freedman*]

FURTHER READING

Freedman, B. *Environmental Ecology*. San Diego: Academic Press, 1989.

Schindler, D. W. "The Coupling of Elemental Cycles by Organisms: Evidence from Whole-Lake Chemical Perturbations." In *Chemical Processes in Lakes*, edited by W. Stumm. New York: Wiley, 1985.

Schindler, D. W., et al. "Long-Term Ecosystem Stress: The Effects of Years of Experimental Acidification of a Small Lake." *Science* 228 (21 June 1985): 1395-1401.

Exponential growth

The distinction between arithmetic and exponential growth is crucial to an understanding of the nature of growth. Arithmetic growth takes place when a constant amount is being added, as when a child puts a dollar a week in a piggybank. Although the total amount increases, the amount being added remains the same. Exponential growth, on the other hand, is characterized by a constant or even accelerating rate of growth.

At a constant rate of increase, measured in percentages, the amounts added grow themselves. Growth is then usually measured in doubling times because these remain constant while the amounts added increase. When the annual rate of increase is 1 percent, the doubling time will be 70 years. From this fact, a simple formula to calculate doubling times given a rate of increase can be derived: dividing 70 by the percentage rate will yield the number of years it takes to double the original amount.

A savings account with, say, a fixed annual interest rate of 5 percent furnishes a convenient example. If the original deposit is $1000, then the growth over the first year is $50. Over the second year, growth will be $52.50. In 14 years, there will be $2000 in the account (70 divided by 5 equals 14). In the first period of 14 years, then, total growth will be $1000, but in the second period of 14 years total growth will be $2000, and so on. During the tenth 14-year period, $512,000 is added, and at the end of that period the total amount in the account will be $1,024,000. As this example illustrates, growth will be relatively slow initially, but it will start speeding up dramatically over time. When growth takes place at an accelerating rate of increase, doubling times of course will become shorter and shorter.

The notion of exponential growth is of particular interest in **population biology** because all populations of organisms have the capacity to undergo exponential growth. The biotic potential or maximum rate of reproduction for all living organisms is very high, that is to say that all species theoretically have the capacity to reproduce themselves many, many times over during their lifetimes. In actuality, only a few of the offspring of most species survive, due to reproductive failure, limited availability of space and food, diseases, predation, and other mishaps. A few species, such as the lemming, go through cycles of exponential **population growth** resulting in severe overpopulation. A catastrophic **dieback** follows, during which the population is reduced enormously, readying it for the next cycle of growth and dieback. Interacting species will experience related fluctuations in population levels. By and large, however, populations are held stable by environmental resistance, unless an environmental disturbance takes place.

Climatological changes and other natural phenomena may cause such **habitat** disturbances, but more usually they result from human activity. **Pollution**, **predator control**, and the introduction of foreign species into habitats that lack competitor or predator species are a few examples among many of human activities that may cause declines in some populations and exponential growth in others.

An altogether different case of exponential population growth is that of humans themselves. The human population has grown at an accelerating rate, starting at a low average rate of 0.002 percent per year early in its history and reaching a record level of 2.06 percent in 1970. Since then the rate of increase has dropped below 2 percent, but human population growth is still alarming and many scientists predict that humans are headed for a catastrophic dieback.

[*Marijke Rijsberman*]

FURTHER READING

Cunningham, W., and B. W. Saigo. "Dynamics of Population Growth." In *Environmental Science: A Global Concern*. Dubuque, IA: Wm. C. Brown Publishers, 1990.

Miller, G. T. "Human Population Growth." In *Living in the Environment*. Belmont, CA: Wadsworth Publishing, 1990.

External costs

See **Internalizing costs**

Externality

Most economists argue that markets ordinarily are the superior means for fulfilling human wants. In a market, deals are ideally struck between consenting adults only when the parties feel they are likely to benefit. Society as a whole is thought to gain from the aggregation of individual deals that take place. The wealth of a society grows by means of what is called the hidden hand of free market mechanisms, which offers spontaneous coordination with a minimum of coercion and explicit central direction. However, the market system is complicated by so-called externalities, which are effects of private market activity not captured in the price system.

Economics distinguishes between positive and negative externalities. A positive externality exists when producers cannot appropriate all the benefits of their activities. An example would be research and development, which yields benefits to society that the producer cannot capture, such as employment in subsidiary industries. **Environmental degradation**, on the other hand, is a negative externality, or an imposition on society as a whole of costs arising from specific market activities. Historically, the United States have encouraged individuals and corporate entities to make use of **natural resources** on **public land**s, such as water, timber, and even the land itself, in order to speed development of the

country. Many undesirable by-products of the manufacturing process, in the form of exhaust gases or toxic waste, for instance, were simply released into the **environment** at no cost to the manufacturer. The agricultural revolution brought new farming techniques that relied heavily on **fertilizer**s, **pesticide**s, and **irrigation**, all of which affect the environment. **Automobile** owners did not pay for the **air pollution** caused by their cars. Virtually all human activity has associated externalities in the environmental arena, which do not necessarily present themselves as costs to participants in these activities. Over time, however, the consequences have become unmistakable in the form of a serious depletion of **renewable resources** and in **pollution** of the air, water, and **soil**. All citizens suffer from such environmental degradation, though not all have benefited to the same degree from the activities that caused them.

In economic analysis, externalities are closely associated with common property and the notion of **free riders**. Many natural resources have no discrete owner and are therefore particularly vulnerable to abuse. The phenomenon of degradation of common property is known as the **Tragedy of the Commons**. The costs to society are understood as costs to nonconsenting third parties, whose interests in the environment have been violated by a particular market activity. The consenting parties inflict damage without compensating third parties because without clear property rights there is no entity that stands up for the rights of a violated environment and its collective owners.

Nature's owners are a collectivity which is hard to organize. They are a large and diverse group that cannot easily pursue remedies in the legal system. In attempting to gain compensation for damage and force polluters to pay for their actions in the future the collectivity suffers from the free rider problem. Although everyone has a stake in ensuring, for example, good **air quality**, individuals will tend to leave it to others to incur the cost of pursuing legal redress. It is not sufficiently in the interest of most members of the group to sue because each has only a small amount to gain. Thus, government intervention is called for to protect the interests of the collectivity, which otherwise would be harmed.

The government has several options in dealing with externalities such as pollution. It may opt for regulation and set standards of what are considered acceptable levels of pollution. It may require reduced **lead** levels in **gasoline** and require automakers to manufacture cars with greater fuel economy and reduced **emission**s, for instance. If manufacturers or social entities such as cities exceed the standards set for them, they will be penalized. With this approach, many polluters have a direct incentive to limit their most harmful activities and develop less environmentally costly technologies. So far, this system has not proved to be very effective. In practice, it has been difficult (or not politically expedient) to enforce the standards and to collect the fines. Supreme Court decisions since the early 1980s have reinterpreted some of the laws to make standards much less stringent. Many companies have found it cheaper to pay the fines than to invest in reducing pollution. Or they evade fines by declaring bankruptcy and reorganizing as a new company.

Economists tend to favor pollution taxes and discharge fees. Since external costs do not enter the calculations a producer makes, the producer manufactures more of the good than is socially beneficial. When polluters have to absorb the costs themselves, to internalize them, they have an incentive to reduce production to acceptable levels or to develop alternative technologies. A relatively new idea has been to give out marketable pollution permits. Under this system, the government sets the maximum levels of pollution it will tolerate and leaves it to the market system to decide who will use the permits. The costs of past pollution (in the form of permanent environmental damage or costly clean-ups) will still be borne disproportionately by society as a whole. The government generally tries to make responsible parties pay for clean-ups, but in many cases it is impossible to determine who the culprit was and in others the parties responsible for the pollution no longer exist.

A special case is posed by externalities that make themselves felt across national boundaries, as is the case with **acid rain**, **ozone layer depletion**, and the pollution of rivers that run through more than one country. Countries that suffer from environmental degradation caused in other countries receive none of the benefits and often do not have the leverage to modify the polluting behavior. International **conservation** efforts must rely on agreements specific countries may or may not follow and on the mediation of the United Nations. *See also* Internalizing cost; Trade in pollution permits

[*Alfred A. Marcus and Marijke Rijsberman*]

FURTHER READING

Mann, D., and H. Ingram. "Policy Issues in the Natural Environment." In *Public Policy and the Natural Environment*, edited by H. Ingram and R. K. Goodwin. Greenwich, CT: JAI Press, 1985.

Marcus, A. A. *Business and Society: Ethics, Government, and the World Economy*. Homewood, IL:. Irwin Press, 1993.

Extinction

Extinction is the complete disappearance of a **species**, when all of its members have died or been killed. As a part of natural selection, the extinction of species has been on-going throughout the earth's history. However, with modern human strains on the **environment**, plants, animals, and invertebrates are becoming extinct at an unprecedented rate of thousands of species per year, especially in **tropical rain forest**s. Many thousands more are threatened and endangered.

Scientists have determined that **mass extinction**s have occurred periodically in prehistory, coming about every 50 million years or so. The greatest of these came at the end of the Permian period, some 250 million years ago, when up to 96 percent of all species on earth may have died off. Dinosaurs and many ocean species disappeared during a well-documented mass extinction at the end of the Cretaceous period (about 65 million years ago). It is estimated that of the billions of species that have lived on earth during the last 3.5 billion years, 99.9 percent are now extinct.

It is thought that most prehistoric extinctions occurred because of climatological changes, loss of food sources, destruction of **habitat**, massive volcanic eruptions, or asteroids or meteors striking the earth. Extinctions, however, have never been as rapid and massive as they have been in the modern era. During the last two centuries, more than 75 species of mammals and over 50 species of birds have been lost, along with countless other species that had not yet been identified. James Fisher has estimated that since 1600, including species and subspecies, the world has lost at least 100 types of mammals and 258 kinds of birds.

The first extinction in recorded history was the European lion, which disappeared around 80 AD. In 1534, seamen first began slaughtering the great auk, a large, flightless bird once found on rocky North Atlantic islands, for food and oil. The last two known auks were killed in 1844 by an Icelandic fisherman motivated by rewards offered by scientists and museum collectors for specimens. Humans have also caused the extinction of many species of marine mammals. Steller's sea cow, once found on the Aleutian Islands off Alaska, disappeared by 1768. The sea mink, once abundant along the coast and islands of Maine, was hunted for its fur until about 1880, when none could be found. The Caribbean monk seal, hunted by sailors and fishermen, has not been found since 1962.

The early European settlers of America succeeded in wiping out several species, including the Carolina parakeet and the **passenger pigeon**. The pigeon was one of most plentiful birds in the world's history, and accounts from the early 1800s describe flocks of the birds blackening the sky for days at a time as they passed overhead. By the 1860s and 1870s tens of millions of them were being killed every year. As a result of this **overhunting**, the last passenger pigeon, Martha, died in the Cincinnati Zoo in 1914. The pioneers who settled the West were equally destructive, causing the disappearance of sixteen separate types of **grizzly bear**, six of **wolves**, one type of fox, and one cougar. Since the Pilgrims arrived in North America in 1620, over 500 types of native American animals and plants have disappeared.

In the last decade of the twentieth century, the rate of species loss is unprecedented and accelerating. In 1980, the ***Global 2000 Report*** to the President, prepared by the President's Council on Environmental Quality and the U.S. Department of State, projected that "between half a million and two million species—15 to 20 percent of all species on earth—could be extinguished by the year 2000." Most of these species extinctions will occur—and are occurring—in tropical rain forests, the richest biological areas on earth. Rain forests are being cut down at a rate of one to two acres per second.

In 1984, **wildlife** expert Norman Myers estimated that the world was then probably losing about 400 species of plants and animals a year, just over one a day. By 1990, he projected, the annual loss might rise to 10,000, and to 50,000 by the turn of the century. In 1988, Harvard professor and biologist **Edward O. Wilson** estimated the current annual rate of extinction at up to 17,500 species, including many unknown rain forest plants and animals that have never been studied or even seen, by humans. Botanist Peter Raven, director of the Missouri Botanical Garden, calculated that by the year 2000, ten percent of the world's species could disappear, and a total of one-quarter could be gone by 2010. A 1989 study by the **World Resources Institute** projected an annual loss of 15,000 to 50,000 species, or 50 to 150 species a day, and warns that "if current trends continue, roughly 5 to 10 percent of the world's species will be lost per decade over the next quarter century." The study further pointed out that humans have accelerated the extinction rate to 100 to 1,000 times its natural level.

While it is impossible to predict the magnitude of these losses or the impact they will have on the earth and its **future generations**, it is clear that the results will be profound, possibly catastrophic. In his book, *Disappearing Species: The Social Challenge*, Eric Eckholm of the **Worldwatch Institute** observed that humans, in their ignorance, have changed the natural course of **evolution** with current mass-extinction rates. "Should this biological massacre take place, evolution will no doubt continue, but in a grossly distorted manner. Such a multitude of species losses would constitute a basic and irreversible alteration in the nature of the **biosphere** even before we understand its workings..."

Eckholm further notes that when a plant species is wiped out, some 10 to 30 dependent species, such as insects and even other plants, can also be jeopardized. An example of the complex relationship that has evolved between many tropical species is the 40 different kinds of fig trees native to Central America, each of which has a specific insect pollinator. Other insects, including pollinators of other plants, depend on these trees for food. Thus, the extinction of one species can set off a chain reaction, the ultimate effects of which cannot be foreseen.

Although scientists know that human life will be harmed by these losses, the weight of the impact is unclear. As the Council on Environmental Quality states in its book *The Global Environment and Basic Human Needs*, over the next decade or two, "unique **ecosystem**s populated by thousands of unrecorded plant and animal species face rapid destruction - irreversible genetic losses that will profoundly alter the course of evolution." This report also cautions that species extinction entails the loss of many useful products. Perhaps the greatest industrial, agricultural and medical costs of species reduction will stem from future opportunities unknowingly lost. Only about five per cent of the world's plant species have yet been screened for pharmacologically active ingredients. Ninety per cent of the food that humans eat comes from just twelve crops, but scores of thousands of plants are edible, and some will undoubtedly prove useful in meeting human food needs. *See also* Biodiversity; Climate; Dodo; Endangered species

[*Lewis G. Regenstein*]

Further Reading

Etheredge, N. *The Miner's Canary: A Paleontologist Unravels the Mysteries of Extinction.* Englewood Cliffs, NJ: Prentice-Hall, 1991.

Raup, D. M. *Extinction: Bad Genes or Bad Luck?* New York: Norton, 1991.

Tudge, C. *Last Animals at the Zoo: How Mass Extinction Can Be Stopped.* Washington, DC: Island Press, 1992.

Exxon Valdez

On 24 March 1989 the 987-foot super tanker *Exxon Valdez* outbound from Port Valdez, Alaska, with a full load of oil from Alaska's Prudhoe Bay passed on the wrong side of a lighted channel marker guarding a shallow stretch of **Prince William Sound**. The momentum of the large ship carried it onto Bligh Reef and opened a 6 x 20 ft hole in the ship's hull. Through this hole poured 265,000 barrels (42 million liters) of crude oil, approximately 22 percent of the ship's 1.2 million barrel (190 million liters) cargo, making it the largest oil spill in the history of the United States.

The oil spill resulting from the *Exxon Valdez* accident created a 1,776 square miles (4,600 sq km) spill and coated 3,167 miles (5,100 km) of shore along pristine Prince William Sound with oil and tar. An estimated 100,000 to 600,000 birds, 5,500 **sea otter**s, 30 seals, and 22 **whales** were killed. These figures are undoubtedly an underestimate of the animals killed by the oil because many of the carcasses probably sank or washed out to sea before they could be collected. Most of the birds died from hypothermia due to the loss of insulation caused by oil-soaked feathers. Many predatory birds, such as **bald eagle**s, died as a result of ingesting contaminated fish and birds. Many of the otters also died from hypothermia, but oil proved to be more toxic to marine mammals than previously suspected, as many of the dead mammals had lung damage due to oil fumes. Fortunately, most fish were not adversely affected by the oil. While the 1989 **salmon** harvest was interrupted by the spill and subsequent clean up, a record 43 million salmon were caught in Prince William Sound the following year.

Response to the oil spill was slow and generally ineffective. The Alyeska Oil Spill Team responsible for cleaning up **oil spills** in the region took more than 24 hours to respond, despite previous assurances that they could mount a response in three hours. Much of the oil containment equipment was missing, broken, or barely operable. By the time oil containment and recovery equipment were in place, 42 million liters of oil had already spread over a large area. Ultimately, less than 10 percent of this oil was recovered, the remainder dispersing into the air, water, and **sediment** of Prince William Sound and adjacent sounds and fjords. Exxon spent $2.2 billion to clean up the oil. Much of this money employed 10,000 people to clean up oil-fouled beaches; yet after the first year, only three percent of the soiled beaches had been cleaned. Nature was the most effective cleaner of beaches; winter storms removed the majority of both surface and buried oil from the beaches. By the following winter, less than 6 miles (10 km) of shoreline was considered seriously fouled. By the time all the legal fees and claims are settled, the total cost of the oil spill will probably exceed $4 billion.

The Captain of the *Exxon Valdez* was exonerated of all charges, despite his confession that he had been drinking while on duty. The oil spilled by the *Exxon Valdez* represents

Crude oil swirls on the surface of the water as the *Exxon Valdez* sits at anchor near Naked Island, Alaska, awaiting repairs to its hull after hitting Bligh Reef on 24 March 1989. Containment booms can be seen attached to the ship.

only about 5 percent of all the oil spilled during the exploration and transportation of oil in 1989.

[*William G. Ambrose and Paul E. Renaud*]

FURTHER READING

Davidson, A. *In the Wake of the Exxon Valdez: The Devastating Impact of the Alaska Oil Spill.* San Francisco: Sierra Club Books, 1990.

Exxon Valdez Oil Spill: A Management Analysis. Washington, DC: Center for Marine Conservation, 1989.

Keeble, J. *Out of the Channel: The Exxon Valdez Oil Spill in Prince William Sound.* New York: Harper Collins, 1991.

Raloff, J. "Valdez Spill Leaves Lasting Oil Impacts." *Science News* 143 (13 February 1993): 102-103.

Steiner, R. "Probing an Oil-Stained Legacy." *National Wildlife* 31 (April-May 1993): 4-11.

F

Falcon

See **Peregrine falcon**

Fallout

See **Radioactive fallout**

Family planning

The population of the world is unknown but believed to have surpassed 5 billion in the late 1980s; it continues in its unrelenting growth especially in developing countries. World-wide **famine** has been postponed thanks to modern agricultural procedures, known as the Green Revolution, which have greatly increased grain production. Nevertheless, with limited land and resources that can be devoted to food production—and increasing numbers of humans who need both space and food—there appears to be a significant risk of catastrophe by overpopulation. Because of this, there is increased interest in family planning. Family planning in this context means birth control to limit family size.

The subject of "family planning" is not limited to birth control but includes procedures designed to overcome difficulties in becoming pregnant. About 15 percent of couples are unable to conceive children after a year of sexual activity without using birth control. Many couples feel an intense desire and need to conceive children. Aid to these couples is thus a reasonable part of family planning. However, for most discussions of family planning, the emphasis is on limitation of family size, not augmentation.

Birth control procedures have evolved rapidly in this century. Further, utilization of existing procedures is changing with different age groups and different populations. Thus any account of birth control is likely to become rapidly obsolete. An example of the changing technology includes oral contraception with pills containing hormones. Birth control pills have been marketed in the United States since the 1960s. Since that time there have been many formulations with significant reductions in dosage. In 1988, there was much greater acceptance of pills by American women under the age of 24 than by women over 35 years of age. The intrauterine device (IUD) was much more popular in Sweden

than in the United States whereas sterilization was more common in the United States than in Sweden. Continuing change should be expected well into the twenty-first century.

A very common form of birth control is the condom, which is a thin rubber sheath worn by men during sexual intercourse. They are generally readily accessible, cheap, and convenient for those individuals who may not have sexual relations regularly. Sperm cannot penetrate the thin (0.3-0.8 mm thick) latex. Neither the human immunodeficiency virus (HIV) associated with **AIDS** nor the other pathogenic agents of sexually transmitted diseases (STDs) are able to penetrate the latex barrier. Some individuals are opposed to treating healthy bodies with drugs (hormones) for birth control, and for these individuals, condoms have a special appeal. Natural "skin" (lamb's intestine) condoms are still available for individuals who may be allergic to latex, but this product provides less protection to HIV and other STDs.

The reported failure rate of condoms is high and is most likely due to improper use. Yet during the Great Depression in the 1930s—when pills and other contemporary birth control procedures were not available—it is thought that the proper use of condoms caused the birth rate in the United States to plummet. Some find another drawback of condoms to be that condoms reduce sexual pleasure. There is no reliable evidence that this is true, but if one wishes to argue the point, one could contend that the alleged reduction only prolongs sexual pleasure.

Spermicides—surface active agents which inactivate sperm and STD pathogens—can be placed in the vagina in jellies, foam, and suppositories. Condoms used in conjunction with spermicides have a failure rate lower than either method used alone and may provide added protection against some infectious agents.

The vaginal diaphragm, like the condom, is another form of barrier. The diaphragm was in use in World War I and was still used by about one third of couples by the time of World War II. However, because of the efficacy and ease of use of oral contraceptives, and perhaps because of the protection against disease by condoms, the use of vaginal diaphragms is down. The diaphragm, which must be fitted by a physician, is designed to prevent sperm access to the cervix and upper reproductive tract. It is used in conjunction with spermicides. Other similar barriers include the cervical cap and the contraceptive sponge. The cervical cap is smaller than the diaphragm and fits only around that portion of the uterus that protrudes into the vagina. The contraceptive sponge, which contains a spermicide, is inserted into the vagina prior to sexual intercourse and retained for several hours afterwards to insure that no living sperm remain. An interesting statistic is that women who do not use barrier methods have twice the rate of cervical **cancer** as those who do.

Intrauterine devices (IUDs) were popular during the 1960s and 1970s in the United States, but their use today has dwindled. However in China, a nation which is rapidly attending to its population problems, about 60 million women use IUDs. The failure rate of IUDs in less developed countries is reported to be less than that with the pill. The devices may be plastic, copper, or stainless steel. The plastic versions may be impregnated with barium sulfate to permit visualization by **X-ray** and also may slowly release hormones such as progesterone. Ovulation continues with IUD use. Efficacy probably results from a changed uterine environment which kills sperm.

Oral contraception is by means of the "pill." Pills contain an estrogen and a progestational agent, and current dosage is very low compared with several decades ago. The combination of these two agents is taken daily for three weeks followed by one week with neither hormone. Frequently a drug-free pill is taken for the last week to maintain the pill-taking habit and thus enhance the efficacy of the regimen. The estrogenic component prevents follicle maturation, and the progestational component prevents ovulation. Pill-taking women who have multiple sexual partners may wish to consider the addition of a barrier method to minimize risk for STDs. The reliability of the pill reduces the need for abortion or surgical sterilization. There may be other salutary health effects which include less endometrial and ovarian cancer as well as fewer uterine fibroids. Use of oral contraceptives in women over the age of 35 who also smoke is thought to increase the risk of heart and vascular disease.

Contraceptive hormones can be administered by routes other than oral. Subdermal implants of progestin-containing tubules have been available since 1990 in the United States. In this device familiarly known as Norplant, six tubules are surgically placed on the inside of the upper arm, and the hormone diffuses through the wall of the tubules to provide long term contraceptive activity. Another form of progestin-only contraception is by intramuscular injection which must be repeated every three months.

Fears engendered by IUD litigation are thought to have increased the reliance of many American women on surgical sterilization (tubal occlusion). Whatever the reason, more American women rely on the procedure than do their European counterparts. Tubal occlusion involves the mechanical disruption of the oviduct, the tube that leads from the ovary to the uterus, and prevents sperm from reaching the egg. Inasmuch as the fatality rate for the procedure is lower than that of childbirth, surgical sterilization is now the safest method of birth control. Tubal occlusion is far more common now that it was in the 1960s because of the lower cost and reduced surgical stress. Use of the laparoscope and very small incisions into the abdomen have allowed the procedure to be completed during an office visit.

Male sterilization, another method, involves severing the vas deferens, the tube that carries sperm from the testes to the penis. Sperm comprise only a small portion of the ejaculate volume, and thus ejaculation is little changed after vasectomy. The male hormone is produced by the testes and production of that hormone continues as does erection and orgasm.

Most abortions would be unnecessary if proper birth control measures were followed. That of course is not always the case. Legal abortion has become one of the leading surgical procedures in the United States. Morbidity and **mortality** associated with pregnancy have been reduced more with legal abortion than with any other event since the introduction of antibiotics to fight puerperal fever.

Other methods of birth control are used by individuals who do not wish to use mechanical barriers, devices, or drugs (hormones). One of the oldest of these methods is withdrawal (*coitus interruptus*), in which the penis is removed from the vagina just before ejaculation. Withdrawal must be exquisitely timed, is probably frustrating to both partners, is not thought to be reliable, and provides no protection against HIV and other STD infections. Another barrier-and-drug-free procedure is natural family planning (also known as the rhythm method). Abstinence of sexual intercourse is scheduled for a period of time before and after ovulation. Ovulation is calculated by temperature change, careful record keeping of menstruation (the calendar method), or by vaginal mucous inspection. Natural family planning has appeal for individuals who wish to limit their exposure to drugs, but it provides no protection against HIV and other STDs.

The population of the world increases by about 140,000,000 every year, while the world is unable to sustain its new residents adequately. That increase signals the need for family planning education and the continued development of ever more efficient birth control methods. *See also* Population Council; Population growth; Population Institute

[*Robert G. McKinnell*]

FURTHER READING

Sitruk-Ware, R., and C. W. Bardin. *Contraception*. New York: Marcel Dekker, 1992.

Speroff, L., and P. D. Darney. *A Clinical Guide for Contraception*. Baltimore, MD: Williams & Wilkins, 1992.

Famine

Famine is widespread hunger and starvation. A region struck with famine experiences acute shortages of food, massive loss of lives, social disruption, and economic chaos. Images of starving mothers and children with emaciated eyes and swollen bellies during recent crises in Ethiopia and Somalia have brought international attention to the problem of famine. Other well-known famines include the great Irish potato famines of the 1850s that drove millions of immigrants to America, and a Russian famine during Stalin's agricultural revolution that killed twenty million people in the 1930s. The worst recorded famine in recent history occurred in China between 1958 and 1961, when twenty-three to thirty million people died as a result of the failed agricultural program, "the great leap forward."

Even though we may think of these tragedies as single, isolated events, famine and chronic hunger continue to be serious problems. Between eighteen and twenty million people, three-quarters of them children, die each year of starvation or diseases caused by malnourishment. How can this be? Environmental problems like overpopulation, scarce resources, and natural disasters affect people's ability to produce food. Political and economic problems like unequal distribution of wealth, delayed or insufficient action by local governments, and imbalanced trade relationships between countries affect people's ability to buy food when they cannot produce it.

Perhaps the most common explanation for famine is overpopulation. The world's population, now more than five billion people, grows by 250,000 people every day. It seems impossible that the natural world could support such rapid growth. Indeed, the pressures of rapid growth have had a devastating impact on the environment in many places. Land that once fed one family must now feed 10 families and resulting over-use harms the quality of the land. The world's **desert**s are rapidly expanding as people destroy fragile **topsoil** by poor farming techniques, clearing vegetation, and **overgrazing**.

Although the demands of **population growth** and industrialization are straining our **environment**, we have yet to exceed the limits of growth. Since the 1800s some have predicted that humans, like rabbits living without predators, would foolishly reproduce far beyond the **carrying capacity** of their environment and then die in masses from lack of food. This argument assumes that the supply of food will remain the same as populations grow, but as populations have grown, people have learned to grow more food. World food production increased two-and-a-half times between 1950 and 1980. Alter World War II, agriculture specialists caused a "green revolution," developing new crops and farming techniques that radically increased food production per acre. Farmers began to use special hybrid crop strains, chemical **fertilizer**s, **pesticide**s, and advanced **irrigation** systems. Today, there is more than enough food available to feed everyone. In fact, the United States government spends billions of dollars every year to store excess grain and to keep farmers from farming portions of their land.

Many famines occur in the aftermath of natural disasters like floods and droughts. In times of **drought**, crops cannot grow because they do not have enough water. In times of flood, excess water washes out fields, destroying crops and disrupting farm activity. These disasters have several effects. First, damaged crops cause food shortages, making nutrients difficult to find and making any food available too expensive for many people. Second, reduced food production means less work for those who rely on temporary farm work for their income. Famines usually affect only the poorest five to ten percent of a country's population. They are most vulnerable because during a crisis wages for the poorest workers go down as food prices go up.

Famine is a problem of distribution as well as production. Environmental, economic, and political factors together determine the supply and distribution of food in a country. Starvation occurs when people lose their ability to obtain food by growing it or by buying it. Often, poor decisions and organizations aggravate environmental factors to cause human suffering. In Bangladesh, floods during the summer of 1974 interfered with rice transplantation, the planting of small rice seedlings in their rice patties. Although the crop was only partly damaged, speculators hoarded rice, and fears of a shortage drove prices beyond the reach of the poorest in Bangladesh. At the same time, disruption of the planting meant lost work for the same people. Even though there was plenty of rice from the previous year's harvest, deaths from starvation rose as the price of rice went up. In December of 1974, when the damaged rice crop was harvested, the country found that its crop had been only partly ruined. Starvation resulted not from a shortage of rice, but from price speculation. The famine could have been avoided completely if the government had responded more quickly, acting to stabilize the rice market and to provide relief for famine victims.

In other cases, governments have acted to avoid famine. The Indian state of Maharahtra offset affects of a severe drought in 1972 by hiring the poorest people to work on public projects like roads and wells. This provided a service for the country and at the same time diverted a catastrophe by providing an income for the most vulnerable citizens to compete with the rest of the population for a limited food supply. At the same time, the countries of Mali, Niger, Chad, and Senegal experienced severe famine, even though the average amount of food per person in these countries was the same as in Maharahtra. The difference, it would seem, lies in the actions and intentions of the governments. The Indian government provides a powerful example. Although India lags behind many countries in economic development, education, and health care, the Indians have managed to avert serious famine since 1943, four years before they gained independence from the British.

Responsibility for hunger and famine rests also with the international community. Countries and peoples of the world are increasingly interconnected, continuously exchanging goods and services. We are more and more dependent on one another for success and for survival. The world economic and political order dramatically favors the wealthiest industrialized countries, in Europe and North America. Following patterns established during colonial expansion, **Third World** nations often produce raw materials, unfinished goods, and basic commodities like bananas and coffee that they sell to the **First World** at low prices. The First World nations then manufacture and refine these products and sell back information and technology, like machinery and computers for a very high price. As a result, the wealthiest nations amass capital and resources, and enjoy very high standards of living, while the poorest nations retain huge national debts and struggle to remain stable economically and politically. The word's poorest countries, then, are left vulnerable to all of the conditions which cause famine, economic hardship, political instability, overpopulation, and over-taxed resources.

Furthermore, large colonial powers often left behind unjust political and social hierarchies that are very good at extracting resources and sending them north, but not as good at promoting social justice and human welfare. Many Third World countries are dominated by a small ruling class who own most of the land, control industry, and run the government. Since the poorest people, who suffer most in famines, have little power to influence government policies and manage the countries economy, their needs are often unheard and unmet. A government that rules without democratic support of its people has less incentive to protect those who would suffer in times of famine. In addition, the poorest often do not benefit from the industry and agriculture that does exist in a developing country. Large corporate farms often force small subsistence farmers off of their land. These farmers must then work for day wages, producing food for export, while local people go without adequate nutrition.

Economic and social arrangements, as well as environmental conditions, are central to the problems of hunger and starvation. Famine is much less likely to occur in countries that are concerned with issues of social justice. In the same way, famine is much less likely to occur in a world that is concerned with issues of social justice. Environmental pressures of population growth and human use of **natural resources** will continue to be issues of great concern. Natural disasters like droughts and floods will continue to occur. The best response to the problem of famine lies in working to better manage environmental resources and crisis situations and to change political and economic structures that cause people to go without food.

[*John Cunningham*]

FURTHER READING
Lappe, F. M. *World Hunger: Twelve Myths* New York: Grove Press, 1986.
Sen, A. "Economics of Life and Death." *Scientific American* 268 (May 1993): 40-47.

Farming

See **Agricultural revolution; Conservation tillage; Dryland farming; Feedlots; Organic gardening and farming; Shifting cultivation; Slash and burn agriculture; Strip-farming; Sustainable agriculture**

Fauna

All animal life that lives in a particular geographic area during a particular time in history. The type of fauna to be found in any particular region is determined by factors such as plant life, physical environment, topographic barriers, and evolutionary history. Zoologists sometimes divide the earth into six regions inhabited by distinct faunas: Ethiopian (Africa south of the Sahara, Madagascar, Arabia), Neotropical (South and Central America, part of Mexico, the West Indies), Australian (Australia, New Zealand, New Guinea), Oriental (Asia south of the Himalaya Mountains, India, Sri Lanka, Malay Peninsula, southern China, Borneo, Sumatra, Java, the Philippines), Palearctic (Europe, Asia north of the Himalaya Mountains, Afghanistan, Iran, North Africa), and Nearctic (North America as far south as southern Mexico).

Fecundity

Fecundity comes from the Latin word *fecundus*, meaning fruitful, rich, or abundant. It is the rate at which individual organisms in the population produce offspring. Although the term can apply to plants, it is typically restricted to animals.

There are two aspects of reproduction: 1) fertility, referring to the physiological ability to breed, and 2) fecundity, referring to the ecological ability to produce offspring. Thus, higher fecundity is dependent on advantageous conditions in the environment that favor reproduction (e.g., abundant food, space, water and mates; limited predation, parasitism, and competition). The intrinsic rate of increase (denoted as "r") equals the birth rate minus the death rate. It is a population characteristic that takes into account that not all individuals have equal birth rates and death rates. It therefore refers to the reproductive capacity in the population made up of individual organisms. Fecundity, on the other hand, is an individual characteristic. It can be further subdivided into *potential* and *realized* fecundity. For example, deer can potentially produce four or more fawns per year, but they typically give birth to only one or two per year. In good years with ample food, they often have only two fawns.

Animals in **nature** are limited by environmental conditions that control their life history characteristics such as birth, survivorship, and death. A graph of the number of offspring per female per age class (e.g., year) is a fecundity curve. This can then be used to interpret the individuals of a certain age class who contribute more to the **population growth** than others. In other words, certain age classes have a greater reproductive output than others. **Wildlife** managers often use this type of information in deciding which individuals in a population can be hunted verses those that should be protected so they can reproduce.

As the number of animals increase, competition for food may become more intense and, therefore, growth and reproduction may decrease. The result is an example of density-dependent fecundity. Fecundity in predators typically increases with an increase in the prey population. Conversely, fecundity in prey **species** typically increases when predation pressure is low.

Some scientists have found that fecundity is inversely related to the amount of parental care given to the young. In other words, small organisms such as insects and fish which typically invest less time and energy into caring for the young usually have higher fecundity. Larger organisms such as birds and mammals which expend a lot of energy on caring for the young through building of nests, feeding, protecting, and caring have lower fecundity rates.

[*John Korstad*]

FURTHER READING

Colinvaux, P. A. *Ecology*. New York: Wiley, 1986.

Krebs, C. J. *Ecology: The Experimental Analysis of Distribution and Abundance*. 3rd ed. New York: Harper and Row, 1985.

Ricklefs, R. E. *Ecology*. 3rd ed. New York: W. H. Freeman, 1990.

Smith, R. E. *Ecology and Field Biology*. 4th ed. New York: Harper and Row, 1990.

Federal Energy Regulatory Commission

The Federal Energy Regulatory Commission (FERC) is an independent, five-member commission within the **U.S. Department of Energy**. The Commission was created in October 1977 as a part of the Federal government's mammoth effort to restructure and reorganize its energy program. The Commission was assigned many of the functions earlier assigned to the **Federal Power Commission** (FPC).

The Federal Power Commission had existed since 1920 when it was created to license and regulate hydroelectric **power plants** situated on interstate streams and rivers. Over the next half century, the Power Commission was assigned more and more responsibility for the management of United States energy reserves. In the Public Utilities Holding Company Act of 1935, for example, Congress gave to the Commission responsibility for setting rates for the wholesale pricing of electricity shipped across state lines. FPC's mission was expanded even further in the 1935 Natural Gas Act. That act gave the Commission the task of regulating the nation's **natural gas** pipelines and setting rates for the sale of natural gas.

Regulating energy prices in the pre-1970s era was a very different problem than it is in the 1990s. That era was one of abundant, inexpensive energy. Producers, consumers and regulators consistently dealt with a surplus of energy. There was more energy of almost any kind than could be consumed. That situation began to change in the early 1970s, especially after the **oil embargo** instituted by the **Organization of Petroleum Exporting Countries** in 1973. The resulting energy crisis caused the United States government to re-think carefully its policies and practices regarding energy production and use.

One of the studies that came out of that re-analysis was the 1974 Federal Energy Regulation Study Team report. The team found a number of problems in the way energy was managed in the United States. They reported that large gaps existed in some areas of regulation, with no agency responsible, while other areas were characterized by overlaps, with two, three, or more agencies all having some responsibility for a single area. The team also found that regulatory agencies were more oriented to the past than to current problems or future prospects, worked with incomplete or inaccurate date, and employed procedures that were too lengthy and drawn out.

As one part of the Department of Energy Organization Act of 1977, then, the FPC was abolished and replaced by the Federal Energy Regulatory Commission. The Commission is now responsible for setting rates and charges for the transportation and sale of natural gas and for the transmission and sale of electricity. It continues the FPC's old responsibility for the licensing of hydroelectric plants.

In addition, the Commission has also been assigned responsibility for establishing the rates for the transportation of oil by pipelines as well as determining the value of the pipe lines themselves. Overall, the Commission now controls the pricing of 60 percent of all the natural gas and 30 percent of all the electricity in the United States.

Ordinary citizens sometimes do not realize the power and influence of independent commissions like the FERC. But they can have significant impact on federal policy and practice. As one writer has said, "While Energy Secretaries come and go, and Congress can do little more than hold hearings, the five-member FERC is making national energy policy by itself." *See also* Electric utilities; Energy policy; Petroleum

[*David E. Newton*]

Federal Insecticide, Fungicide and Rodenticide Act (1972)

The **Environmental Protection Agency** (EPA) is the primary regulatory agency of **pesticide**s. The EPA's authority on pesticides is given in the Congressionally-enacted Federal Insecticide, Fungicide and Rodenticide Act (FIFRA)—a comprehensive regulatory program for pesticides and **herbicide**s enacted in 1972 and amended nearly 50 times over the years. The goal of FIFRA is to regulate the use of pesticides through registration.

Section 3 of FIFRA mandates that the EPA must first determine that the product "will perform its intended function without unreasonable adverse effects on the **environment**" before it is registered. The Act defines adverse effects as "any unreasonable effects on man or the environment, taking into account the economic, social and environmental costs and benefits of using any pesticide." To further this objective, Congress placed a number of regulatory tools at the disposal of the EPA. Congress also made clear that the public was not to bear the risk of uncertainty concerning the safety of a pesticide. To grant registration, the EPA must conclude that the food production benefits of a pesticide outweigh any risks.

To make the cost-benefit determination required to register a pesticide as usable, manufacturers must submit to EPA detailed tests on the chemical's health and environmental effects. The burden rests on the manufacturer to provide the data needed to support registration for use on a particular crop. The pesticide manufacturer is required to submit certain health and safety data to establish that the use of the pesticide will not generally cause unreasonable adverse effects. Data required include disclosure of the substance's chemical and toxicological properties, likely distribution in the environment, and possible effects on **wildlife**, plants, and other elements in the environment.

FIFRA is a licensing law. Pesticides may enter commerce only after they are approved or "registered following an evaluation against statutory risk/benefit standards." The Administrator may take action to terminate any approval whenever it appears, on the basis of new information or a re-evaluation of information, that the pesticide no longer meets the statutory standard. These decisions are made on a use-by-use basis since the risks and benefits of a pesticide vary from one use to another.

FIFRA is also a control law. Special precautions and instructions may be imposed. For example, pesticide applicators may be required to wear protective clothing, or the use of certain pesticides may be restricted to trained and certified applicators. Instructions, warnings, and prohibitions are incorporated into product labels, and these labels may not be altered or removed.

FIFRA embodies the philosophy that those who would benefit by government approval of a pesticide product should bear the burden of proof that their product will not pose unreasonable risks. This burden of proof applies both when initial marketing approval is sought and in any proceeding initiated by the Administrator to interrupt or terminate registration through suspension or cancellation. Of course, while putting the burden on industry, the assumption is that industry will be honest in its research and reports.

Licensing decisions are usually based on tests furnished by an applicant for registration. The tests are performed by the petitioning company in accordance with testing guidelines prescribed by the EPA. Current requirements for the testing of pesticides for major use can be met only through the expenditure of several millions of dollars and up to four years of laboratory and field testing.

However, major changes in test standards, advances in testing methodology, and the heightened awareness of the potential chronic health effects of long-term, low-level exposure to **chemicals** which have come into the marketplace within the past several decades have brought the need to update EPA mandates. Thus, Congress directed that the EPA reevaluate its licensing decisions through a process of re-registration. That means if the government once approved a certain product for domestic use, it does not mean the EPA can be confident today that its use can continue.

The EPA has the power to suspend or cancel products. Cancellation means the product in question is no longer considered safe. It must be taken off the commercial market and is no longer available for use. Suspension means the product in question is not to be sold or used under certain conditions or in certain places. This may be a temporary decision, usually dependent on further studies.

There may be certain products that, in the opinion of the administrator, may be harmful. But no action is taken if and when the action is incompatible with administration priorities. That is because the EPA administrator is responsible to the directives and priorities of the President and the executive branch. Thus, some regulatory decisions are political.

There is a statutory way to avoid the re-registration process. It is called Section 18. Section 18 under FIFRA allows for the use of unregistered pesticides in certain emergency situations. It provides that "the Administrator may, at his discretion, exempt any Federal or State agency from any

provisions of this subchapter if he determines that emergency conditions exist which requires such exemption. The Administrator, in determining whether or not such emergency conditions exist, shall consult with the Secretary of Agriculture and the Governor of any state concerned if they request such determination."

From 1978 to 1983, the General Accounting Office (GAO) and the House Subcommittee on Department Operations, Research and Foreign Agriculture of the Committee on Agriculture (DORFA Subcommittee) thoroughly examined the EPA's implementation of Section 18. Under the auspices of Chair George E. Brown, Jr., (D-CA) the DORFA Subcommittee held a series of hearings which revealed numerous abuses in EPA's administration of Section 18. A report was issued in 1982 and reprinted as part of the Committee's 1983 Hearings.

The Subcommittee found that "the rapid increase in the number and volume of pesticides applied under Section 18 was clearly the most pronounced trend in the EPA's pesticide regulatory program." According to the Subcommittee report, "a primary cause of the increase in the number of Section 18 exemptions derived from the difficulty the Agency had in registering chemicals under Section 3 of FIFRA in a timely manner." The DORFA committee stated:

> Regulatory actions involving suspect human **carcinogen**s which meet or exceed the statute's "unreasonable adverse effects" criterion for chronic toxicity often become stalled in the Section 3 review process for several years. The risk assessment procedures required by States requesting Section 18 actions, and by EPA in approving them, are generally less strict. For example, a relatively new insecticide, first widely used in 1977, was granted some 140 Section 18 emergency exemptions and over 300 (Section 24c) Special Local Needs registrations in the next four years while the Agency debated the significance to man of positive evidence of oncogenicity in laboratory animals.

The EPA's practices changed little over the next eight years. In the spring of 1990, the Subcommittee on Environment of the House Science, Space and Technology Committee (Chair: James H. Scheuer, D-NY) investigated the EPA's procedures under Section 18 of FIFRA and found if anything, the problem had gotten worse. The report states: "Since 1973, more than 4,000 emergency exemptions have been granted for the use of pesticides on crops for which there is no registration." A large number of these emergency exemptions have been repeatedly granted for the same uses for anywhere from fourteen, to ten, to eight, to five years. The House Subcommittee also found that the EPA required less stringent testing procedures for pesticides under the exemption, which put companies that follow the normal procedure at a disadvantage. The Subcommittee concluded that the large numbers of emergency exemptions arose from "the EPA's failure to implement its own regulations."

The Subcommittee identified "emergencies" as "routine predicted outbreaks and foreign competition" and "a company's need to gain market access for use of a pesticide on a new crop, although the company often never intends to submit adequate data to register the chemical for use."

As for the re-registration requirement, the Subcommittee observed:

The EPA's reliance on Section 18 may be related to the Agency's difficulty in re-registering older chemical substances. Often, Section 18 requests are made for the use of older chemicals on crops for which they are not registered. These older chemicals receive repetitive exemptions for use despite the fact that many of these substances may have difficulty obtaining re-registration since they have been identified as potentially carcinogenic. Thus, by liberally and repetitively granting exemptions to potentially carcinogenic substances, little incentive is provided to encourage companies to invest in the development of newer, safer pesticides or alternative agricultural practices.

The report concluded, "...Allowing these exemptions year after year in predictable situations provides 'back-door' pre-registration market access to potentially dangerous chemicals." *See also* Environmental law; Integrated pest management; National Coalition Against the Misuse of Pesticides; Pesticide Action Network; Risk analysis

[*Liane Clorfene Casten*]

FURTHER READING

"EPA Data Is Flawed, Says GAO." *Chemical Marketing Reporter* 243 (11 January 1993): 7+.

Rodgers, W. H., Jr. *Environmental Law: Pesticides and Toxic Substances.* 3 vols. St. Paul, MN: West, 1988.

"Controlling the Risk in Biotech." *Technology Review* 92 (July 1989): 62-9.

U. S. Environmental Protection Agency. *Federal Insecticide, Fungicide, and Rodenticide Act: Compliance-Enforcement Guidance Manual.* Rockville, MD: Government Institutes, 1984.

Federal Land Policy and Management Act (1976)

The Federal Land Policy and Management Act (FLPMA), passed in 1976, is the statutory grounding for the **Bureau of Land Management** (BLM), giving the agency authority and direction for the management of its lands. The initiative leading to the passage of FLPMA can be traced to the BLM itself. The agency was concerned about its insecure status—it was formed by executive reorganization rather than by a congressional act, it lacked a clear mandate for land management, and it was uncertain of the federal government's plans to retain the lands it managed. This final point can be traced to the **Taylor Grazing Act**, which included a clause that these public lands would be managed for grazing "pending final disposal." The BLM wanted a law that would address each of these issues, so that the agency could undertake long-range, multiple use planning like their colleagues in the **Forest Service**.

Agency officials drafted the first "organic act" in 1961, but two laws passed in 1964 served to really get the legislative process moving. The Public Land Law Review Commission (PLLRC) Act established a commission to examine the body of public land laws and make recommendations as to how to proceed in this policy area. The Classification and Multiple Use Act instructed the BLM to inventory its lands and classify them for disposal or retention. This would be the first inventory of these lands and resources, and suggested that at least some of these lands would be retained in federal ownership.

The PLLRC issued its report in 1970. In the following years, Congress began to consider three general types of bills in response to the PLLRC report. The administration and the BLM supported a BLM organic act without additional major reforms of other **public land** laws. The second approach provided the BLM with an organic act, but also made significant revisions in the Mining Law of 1872 and included environmental safeguards for BLM activities. This variety of bill was supported by environmentalists. The final type of bill provided a general framework for more detailed legislation in the future. This general framework tended to support commodity production, and was favored by livestock, mining, and timber interests.

In 1973, a bill of the second variety, introduced by Henry Jackson of Washington, passed the Senate. A similar bill died in the House, though, when it was denied a rule, and hence a trip to the floor, by the Rules Committee. Jackson re-introduced a bill that was nearly identical to the bill previously passed, and the Senate passed this bill in February 1976. In the House, things did not move as quickly. The main House bill, drafted by four western members of the Interior and Insular Affairs Committee, included significant provisions dealing with grazing—most importantly, a provision to adopt a statutory grazing fee formula based upon beef prices and private forage cost. This bill had the support of commodity interests, but was opposed by the administration and environmental groups. The bill passed the full House by fourteen votes in July 1976.

The major differences that needed to be addressed in the conference committee included law enforcement, the grazing provisions, mining law provisions, wild horses and burros, unintentional trespass, and the California Desert Conservation Area. By late September, four main differences remained, three involving grazing, and one dealing with mining. For a period it appeared that the bill might die in committee, but final compromises on the grazing and mining issues were made and a bill emerged out of conference. The bill was signed into law in October 1976 by President Gerald Ford.

As passed, FLPMA dealt with four general issue areas: 1) the organic act sections, giving the BLM authority and direction for managing the lands under its control; 2) grazing policy; 3) preservation policy; and 4) mining policy. The act begins by stating that these lands will remain in public ownership: "The Congress declares that it is the policy of the United States that ... the public lands be retained in public ownership." This represented the true, final closing of the public domain; the federal government would retain the vast majority of these lands. To underscore this point, FLPMA repealed hundreds of laws dealing with the public lands that were no longer relevant. The BLM, under the authority of the Secretary of the Interior, was authorized to manage these lands for multiple use and **sustained yield** and was required to develop **land use** plans and resource inventories for the lands based on long-range planning. A director of the BLM was to be appointed by the President, subject to confirmation by the Senate.

FLPMA limited the withdrawal authority of the Secretary, often used to close lands to mineral development or to protect them for other environmental reasons, by repealing many of the sources of this authority and limiting its uses in other cases. The act allowed for the sale of public lands under a set of guidelines. In a section of the law that received much attention, the BLM was authorized to enforce the law on the lands it managed. The agency was directed to cooperate with local law enforcement agencies as much as possible in this task. It was these agencies, and citizens who lived near BLM lands, who were skeptical of this new BLM enforcement power. Other important provisions of the law allowed for the capture, removal, and relocation of wild horses and burros from BLM lands and authorized the Secretary of the Interior to grant rights-of-way across these lands for most pipelines and electrical transmission lines.

The controversial grazing fee formula in the House bill, favored by the livestock industry, was dropped in the conference committee. In its place, FLPMA froze grazing fees at the 1976 level for one year and directed the Secretaries of Agriculture and the Interior to undertake a comprehensive study of the grazing fee issue so that an equitable fee could be determined. This report was completed in 1977, and Congress established a statutory fee formula in 1978. That formula was only binding until 1985, though, and since that time Congress has debated the grazing fee issue numerous times, but the issue remains unsettled.

FLPMA also provided that grazing permits be for ten year periods, and that at least two year notice be given before permits were cancelled (except in an emergency). At the end of the ten year lease, if the lands are to remain in grazing, the current permittee has the first priority on renewing the lease to those lands. This virtually guarantees a rancher the use of certain public lands as long as they are to be used for grazing. The permittee is also to receive compensation for private improvements on public lands if the permit is cancelled. These provisions, advocated by livestock interests, further demonstrated their belief, and the belief of their supporters in Congress, that these grazing permits were a type of property right. Grazing advisory boards, originally started after the Taylor Grazing Act but terminated in the early 1970s, were resurrected. These boards consist of local grazing permittees in the area, and advise the BLM on the use of range improvement funds and on allotment management plans.

Important provisions regarding the preservation of BLM lands were also included in FLPMA. BLM lands were not covered in the **Wilderness Act** of 1964, and FLPMA dealt with this omission by directing that these lands be reviewed for potential **wilderness** designation, and that recommendations be made by the agency of which lands should be designated as wilderness. These designations would then be acted upon by Congress. This process is well underway. As has been the case with additions to the National Wilderness Preservation System on **national forest** lands since RARE II, BLM wilderness designation is being considered on a state-by-state basis. Thus far, a comprehensive wilderness designation law has only been passed for Arizona and California. Recent controversy has centered over the designation of wilderness in Utah.

FLPMA established a special California Desert Conservation Area, and directed the BLM to study this area and develop a long-range plan for its management. In 1994, after eight years of consideration, Congress passed the California Desert Protection Act. Senator Dianne Feinstein of California played the major role in guiding the legislation to passage, including overcoming an opposition-led filibuster against the act in October. The act, which included a number of compromises with desert users, established two new national parks and a new national preserve as well as designating approximately 7.5 million acres of California desert as wilderness (in the two parks, the preserve, and nearly seventy new wilderness areas). The new national parks were created by enlarging and upgrading the existing Death Valley and Joshua Tree National Monuments. The Mojave National Preserve was originally to be a third national park in the desert, but its status was reduced to a national preserve to allow continued hunting, a compromise that helped gain further support for the bill. This law protected more wilderness than any law since the 1980 Alaska Lands Act. The following year, however, there was a move to alter these provisions. As part of the 1996 fiscal year Interior Appropriations bill, Congress directed that the BLM—not the National Park Service—manage the new Mojave National Preserve. According to Republican supporters, the BLM would allow for more use of the land. President Clinton vetoed this appropriations bill in December 1995, in part due to this change in California Desert management. When the final Interior Appropriations Act was passed in April 1996, it included a provision requiring the Park Service to manage the Mojave under the less restrictive BLM standards, but it also allowed the President to waive this provision. Clinton signed the bill, and then immediately waived the provision, so the Mojave is being managed by the National Park Service under its own standards.

FLPMA required that all mining claims, based on the 1872 Mining Law, be recorded with the BLM within three years. Claims not recorded were presumed abandoned. In the past, such claims only had to be recorded at the county courthouse in the county in which the claim was located. This allowed for increased knowledge about the number and location of such claims. The law also included amendments to the **Mineral Leasing Act** of 1920, increasing the share of the revenues from such leases that went to the states, allowing the states to spend these funds on any public facilities needed (rather than just roads and schools), and reducing the amount of revenues going to the fund to reclaim these mineral funds.

The implementation of FLPMA has been problematic. One consequence of the act, and the planning and management that it has required, was the stimulation of western hostility to the BLM and the existence of so much federal lands. According to a number of analysts, FLPMA was largely responsible for starting the **Sagebrush Rebellion**, the movement to have federal lands transferred to the states. The foremost implementation problems have been due to the poor bureaucratic capacity of the BLM: the lack of adequate funding, the lack of an adequate number of employees, poor standing within the **U.S. Department of the Interior** and presidential administrations, and its history of subservience to grazing and mining interests.

[*Christopher McGrory Klyza*]

FURTHER READING

Dana, S. T., and S. K. Fairfax. *Forest and Range Policy.* 2nd ed. New York: McGraw-Hill, 1980.

"Fragile California Desert Bill Blooms Late in Session." Congressional Quarterly Almanac, vol. 50: 227-231, 1994.

"Public Land Management." *Congressional Quarterly Almanac* 32 (1976): 182-188.

Senzel, I. "Genesis of a Law, Part 1." *American Forests* (January 1978): 30-32+.

———. "Genesis of a Law, Part 2." *American Forests* (February 1978): 32-39.

Federal Power Administrations
See **U. S. Department of Energy**

Federal Power Commission

The Federal Power Commission was established June 23, 1930, under the authority of the Federal Water Power Act, which was passed on March 3, 1921. The commission was terminated on August 4, 1977, and its functions were transferred to the Federal Energy Regulatory Commission under the umbrella of the **U.S. Department of Energy**.

The most important function of the commission during its 57-year existence was the licensing of water-power projects. It also reviewed plans for water-development programs submitted by major federal construction agencies for conformance with the interests of public good. In addition, the commission retained responsibility for interstate regulation of **electric utilities** and the siting of hydroelectric power plants as well as their operation. It also set rates and charges for the transportation and sale of **natural gas** and electricity. The five members of the commission were appointed by the president with approval of the Senate; three of the members were the Secretaries of the Interior, Agriculture, and War (later designated as U.S. Department of the Army). The commission retained its status as an independent regulatory agency for decision making, which is considered necessary for national security purposes.

Feedlot runoff

Feedlots are containment areas used to raise large numbers of animals to an optimum weight within the shortest time span possible. Most feedlots are open air, and are thereby subject to variable weather conditions. A substantial portion of the feed is not converted into meat, and is excreted, thus degrading the air, ground, and surface **water quality**. The issues of odor and **water pollution** from such facilities center on the traditional attitudes of producers that farming has always produced odors, and manure is a **fertilizer**, not a waste from a commercial undertaking.

Animal excrement is indeed rich in **nutrient**s, particularly **nitrogen**, **phosphorus**, and potassium. A single 1,300-lb (590 kg) steer will excrete about 150 lb (68 kg) of nitrogen; 50 lb (23 kg) of phosphorus; and 100 lb (45 kg) of potassium in the course of a year. That is almost as much nutrient as would be required to grow one acre of corn, which needs 185 lb (84 kg) of nitrogen; 80 lb (36 kg) of phosphorus; and 215 lb (98 lb) of potassium. Unfortunately, manure is costly to transport, difficult to apply, and its nutrient quality is inconsistent. Artificial fertilizers, on the other hand, offer ease of application and storage and proven quality and plant growth.

Legislative and regulatory action have increased with encroachment of urban population and centers of high sensitivity, such as shopping malls and recreation facilities. Since odor is difficult to measure, control of these facilities is being achieved on the grounds that they must not pose a "nuisance," a principle that is being sustained by the courts.

Odor is influenced by feed, number and species of animal, lot surface and manure removal frequency, wind, humidity, and moisture. These factors, individually and collectively, influence the type of **decomposition** that will occur. Typically, it is an **anaerobic** process which produces a sharp pungent odor of ammonia, the nauseating odor of rotten eggs from hydrogen sulfide, and the smell of decaying cabbage or onions from methyl mercaptan.

Odorous compounds seldom reach concentrations that are dangerous to the public. However, levels can become dangerously elevated with reduced ventilation in winter months or during pit cleaning. It is this latter activity, in conjunction with disposal onto the surface of the land, that is most frequently the cause of complaints. Members of the public respond to feedlot odors depending on their individual sensitivity, previous experience, and disposition. It can curtail outdoor activities and require windows to be closed, which means the additional use of air purifiers or air-conditioning systems.

Surface water contamination is the problem most frequently attributed to open feedlot and manure spreading activities. It is due to the dissolving, eroding action of rain striking the manured-covered surface. Duration and intensity of rainfall dictates the concentration of contaminants that will flow into surface waters. Their dilution or retention in ponds, rivers, and streams depends on area **hydrology** (dry or wet conditions) and **topography** (rolling or steeply graded landscape). Such factors also influence conditions in those parts of the continent where precipitation is mainly in the form of snow. Large snow drifts form around wind breaks, and in the early spring, substantial volumes of snowmelt are generated.

Odor and water pollution control techniques include simple operational changes, such as increasing the frequency of removing manure, scarifying the surface to promote **aerobic** conditions, and applying disinfectants and feed-digestion supplements. Other control measures require construction of additional structures or the installation of equipment at feedlots. These measures include installing water spargelines, adding impervious surfaces, drains, pits and roofs, and installing extraction fans. *See also* Animal waste; Odor control

[*George M. Fell*]

FURTHER READING

Larson, R. E. *Feedlot and Ranch Equipment for Beef Cattle.* Washington, DC: U. S. Government Printing Office, 1976.

Peters, J. A. *Source Assessment: Beef Cattle Feedlots.* Research Triangle Park, NC: U. S. Environmental Protection Agency, 1977.

Feedlots

A feedlot is an open space where animals are fattened before slaughter. Beef cattle usually arrive at the feedlot directly from the ranch or farm where they were raised, while poultry and pigs often remain in an automated feedlot from birth until death. Feed (often grains, alfalfa, and molasses) is provided to the animals so they do not have to forage for their food. This feeding regimen promotes the production of higher quality meat more rapidly. There are no standard parameters for the number of animals per acre in a feedlot, but the density of animals is usually very high. Some feedlots can contain 100,000 cows and steers. **Animal rights** groups actively campaign against confining animals in feedlots, a practice they consider inhumane, wasteful, and highly polluting.

Feedlots were first introduced in California in the 1940s, but many are now found in the Midwest, closer to grain supplies. Feedlot operations are highly mechanized and large numbers of animals can be handled with relatively low labor input. About half of the beef produced in the United States is feedlot-raised.

Feedlots are a significant **nonpoint source** of the **pollution** flowing into surface waters and **groundwater** in the United States. At least half a billion tons of **animal waste** are produced in feedlots each year. Since this waste is concentrated in the feedlot rather than scattered over grazing lands, it overwhelms the **soil**'s ability to absorb and **buffer** it and creates nitrate-rich, bacteria-laden **runoff** to pollute streams, rivers, and lakes. Dissolved pollutants can also migrate down through the soil into **aquifer**s, leading to groundwater pollution over wide areas. To protect surface waters, most states require that **feedlot runoff** be collected. However, protection of groundwater has proved to be a more

difficult problem, and successful regulatory and technological controls have not yet been developed.

[*Christine B. Jeryan*]

FURTHER READING

Kerr, R. S. *Livestock Feedlot Runoff Control By Vegetative Filters.* Ada, OK: U. S. Environmental Protection Agency, 1979.

Larson, R. E. *Feedlot and Ranch Equipment for Beef Cattle.* Washington, DC: U. S. Government Printing Office, 1976.

Peters, J. A. *Source Assessment: Beef Cattle Feedlots.* Research Triangle Park, NC: U. S. Environmental Protection Agency, 1977.

Fens
See **Wetlands**

Ferret
See **Black-footed ferret**

Fertility
See **Biological fertility**

Fertilizer

Any substance that is applied to land to encourage plant growth and produce higher crop yield. Fertilizers may be made from organic material—such as recycled waste, animal manure, **compost**, etc.—or chemically manufactured. Most fertilizers contain varying amounts of **nitrogen**, **phosphorus**, and potassium, inorganic **nutrient**s that plants need to grow.

Since the 1950s crop production worldwide has increased dramatically because of the use of fertilizers. In combination with the use of **pesticide**s and insecticides, fertilizers have vastly improved the quality and yield of such crops as corn, rice, wheat, and cotton. However overuse and improper use of fertilizers have also damaged the **environment** and affected the health of humans, animals, and plants.

In the United States, it is estimated that as much as 25 percent of fertilizer is carried away as **runoff**. Fertilizer runoff has contaminated **groundwater** and polluted bodies of water near and around farmlands. High and unsafe nitrate concentrations in drinking water have been reported in countries that practice intense farming, including the United States. Accumulation of nitrogen and phosphorus in waterways from chemical fertilizers has also contributed to the eutrophication of lakes and ponds. Ammonia, released from the decay of fertilizers, causes minor irritation to the respiratory system.

While very few advocate the complete eradication of chemical fertilizers, many environmentalists and scientists urge more efficient ways of using them. For example, some farmers use up to 40 percent more fertilizer than they need. Frugal applications—in small doses and on an as-needed-basis on specific crops—helps reduce fertilizer waste and runoff. The use of organic fertilizers, including **animal waste**, crop residues, or grass clippings, is also encouraged as an alternative to chemical fertilizers. *See also* Cultural eutrophication; Recycling; Sustainable agriculture; Trace element/micronutrient

Fibrosis

A medical term that refers to the excessive growth of fibrous tissue in some part of the body. Many types of fibroses are known, including a number that affect the respiratory system. A number of these respiratory fibroses, including such conditions as **black lung disease**, silicosis, **asbestosis**, berylliosis, and byssinosis, are caused by environmental factors. A fibrosis develops when a person inhales very tiny solid particles or liquid droplets over many years or decades. Part of the body's reaction to these foreign particles is to enmesh them in fibrous tissue. The disease name usually suggests the agent that causes the disease. Silicosis, for example, is caused by the inhalation of silica, tiny sand-like particles. Occupational sources of silicosis include rock mining, quarrying, stone cutting, and sandblasting. Berylliosis is caused by the inhalation of beryllium particles over a period of time, and byssinosis (from byssos, the Greek word for flax) is found among textile workers who inhale flax, cotton or hemp fibers.

Field capacity

Field capacity refers to the amount of water that can be held in the **soil** after all the gravitational water has drained away. Sandy soils will have less water held at field capacity than clay soils. The more water a soil can hold at field capacity the more water is available for plants.

Filters

Primarily devices for removing particles from **aerosol**s. Filters utilize a variety of microscopic forms and a variety of mechanisms to accomplish this. Most common are fibrous filters, in which the fibers are of cellulose (paper filters), but almost any fibrous material, including glass fiber, wool, **asbestos**, and finely spun polymers, has been used. Microscopically, these fibers collect fine particles because fine particles vibrate around their average position due to collision with air molecules (Brownian motion). These vibrations are likely to cause them to collide with the fibers as they pass through the filter. Larger particles are removed because, as the air stream carrying them passes through the filter, some of the particles are intercepted as they pass close to the fibers and touch them. Other particles are in air streams that would cause them to miss the fibers, but when the air stream bends to go around the fibers the momentum, of the particles is too

much to let them remain with the stream, so that they are "centrifuged out" onto the fibers (impaction). By electrophoresis, still other particles may be attracted to the fibers by electric charges of opposite sign on the particles and on the fibers. Finally, particles may simply be larger than the space between fibers, and be sifted out of the air in a process called sieving.

Filters are also formed by a process in which polymers such as cellulose esters are made into a film out of a solution in an organic solvent containing water. As the solvent evaporates, a point is reached at which the water separates out as microscopic droplets, in which the polymer is not soluble. The final result is a film of polymer full of microscopic holes where the water droplets once were. Such filters can have pore sizes from a small fraction of a micrometer to a few micrometers. (One micrometer equals 0.00004 in.) These are called membrane filters.

Another form of membrane filter is formed from the polymer called polycarbonate. A thin film of this material is fastened to a surface of **uranium** metal and placed in a nuclear reactor for a time. In the reactor, the uranium undergoes **nuclear fission**, and gives off particles called fission fragments, atoms of the elements formed when the uranium atoms split. Every place that an atom from the fissioning uranium passes through the film is disturbed on a molecular scale. After removal from the reactor, if the polymer sheet is soaked in alkali, the disturbed material is dissolved. The amount of material dissolved is controlled by the temperature of the solution and the amount of time the film is treated. Since the fission fragments are very energetic, they travel in straight lines, and so the holes left after the alkali treatment are very straight and round. Again, pore sizes can be from a small fraction of a micrometer to a few micrometers. These filters are known by their trade name, *Nuclepore.*

In both types of membrane filters, the small pore size increases the role of sieving in particle removal. Because of their very simple structure, Nuclepore filters have been much studied to understand **filtration** mechanisms, since they are far easier to represent mathematically than a random arrangement of fibers.

It was mentioned above that small particles are collected because of their Brownian motion, while larger particles are removed by interception, impaction, and sieving. Under many conditions, a particle of intermediate size may pass through, too large for Brownian diffusion, and too small for impaction, interception, or sieving. Hence many filters may show a penetration maximum for particles of a few tenths of a micrometer. For this reason, standard methods of filter testing specify that the aerosol test for determining the efficiency of filters should contain particles in that size range. This phenomenon has also been used to select relatively uniform particles of that size out of mixtures of many sizes.

In circumstances where filter strength is of paramount importance, such as in industrial filters where a large air flow must pass through a relatively small filter area, filters of woven cloth are used, made of materials ranging from cotton to glass fiber and asbestos, these last for use when very hot gases must be filtered. The woven fabric itself is not a particularly good filter, but it retains enough particles to form a particle cake on the surface, and that soon becomes the filter. When the cake becomes thick enough to slow airflow to an unacceptable degree, the air flow is interrupted briefly, and the filters are shaken to dislodge the filter cake, which falls into bins at the bottom of the filters. Then filtration is resumed, allowing the cloth filters to be used for months before being replaced. A familiar domestic example is the bag of a home vacuum cleaner. Cement plants and some electric **power plants** use dozens of cloth bags up to several feet in diameter and more than ten feet (three meters) in length to remove particles from their waste gases.

Otherwise poor filters can be made efficient by making them thick. A glass tube can be partially plugged with a wad of cotton or glass fiber, then nearly filled with crystals of sugar or naphthalene and used as a filter; this is advantageous since sugar can be dissolved in water, or naphthalene will sublime away if gently heated, leaving behind the collected particles. *See also* Baghouse; Electrostatic precipitation; Odor control; Particulate

[*James P. Lodge, Jr.*]

Filtration

A common technique for separating substances in two physical states. For example, a mixture of solid and liquid can be separated into its components by passing the mixture through a **filter** paper. Filtration has many environmental applications. In water purification systems, impure water is often passed through a charcoal filter to remove the solid and gaseous contaminants that give water a disagreeable odor, color, or taste. Trickling filters are used to remove **solid waste**s in **sewage treatment** plants. Solid and liquid contaminants in waste industrial gases can be removed by passing them through a filter prior to discharge in a smokestack.

Fire

See **Prescribed burn; Wildfire**

Fire ants

Two distinct species of fire ants (genus *Solenopsis*) from South America have been introduced into the United States this century. The South American black fire ant was first introduced into the United States in 1918. Its close relative, the red fire ant, was introduced in 1940, probably escaping from a South American freighter docked in Mobile, Alabama. Both species became established in the southeastern

United States, spreading into nine states from Texas across to Florida and up into the Carolinas. It is estimated that they have infested over 150 million acres (61 million ha).

Successful **introduced species** are often more aggressive than their native counterparts, and this is definitely true of fire ants. They are very small, averaging 0.2 in (5 mm) in length, but their aggressive, swarming behavior makes them a threat to livestock and pets as well as humans. These industrious, social insects build their nests in the ground—the location is easily detected by the elevated earthen mounds created from their excavations. The mounds are 18-36 in (46-91 cm) in diameter and may be up to 36 in (91 cm) high, although mounds are generally 6-10 in (15-25 cm) high. Each nest contains as many as 25,000 workers, and there may be over 100 nests on an acre of land.

If the nest is disturbed, fire ants swarm out of the mound by the thousands and attack with swift ferocity. As with other aspects of ant behavior, a chemical alarm pheromone is released that triggers the sudden onslaught. Each ant in the swarm uses its powerful jaws to bite and latch onto whatever disturbed the nest, while using the stinger on the tip of its abdomen to sting the victim repeatedly. The intruder may receive thousands of stings within a few seconds.

The toxin produced by the fire ant is extremely potent, and it immediately causes an intense burning pain that may continue for several minutes. After the pain subsides, the site of each sting develops a small bump which expands and becomes a tiny, fluid-filled blister. Each blister flattens out several hours later and fills with pus. These swollen pustules may persist for several days before they are absorbed and replaced by scar tissue. Fire ants obviously pose a problem for humans. Some people may become sensitized to fire ant venom, have a generalized systematic reaction, and go into anaphylactic shock. Fire-ant induced deaths have been reported. Because these **species** prefer open, grassy yards or fields, pets and livestock may fall prey to fire ant attacks as well.

Early attempts to eradicate this pest involved the use of several different generalized **pesticide**s, as well as the widespread use of **gasoline** either to burn the nest and its inhabitants or to kill the ants with strong toxic vapors. A more recent approach involves the use of specialized crystalline pesticides which are spread on or around the nest mound. The workers collect them and take them deep into the nest, where they are fed to the queen and other members of the colony, killing the inhabitants from within. As effective as some of these methods are, fire ants are probably too numerous and well established to be eradicated in North America. *See also* Gypsy moth; Zebra mussel

[*Eugene C. Beckham*]

FURTHER READING

Conniff, R. "You Never Know What the Fire Ant Is Going to Do Next." *Smithsonian* 21 (July 1990): 48-55.

Holldobler, B. *The Ants*. Cambridge: Harvard University Press, 1990.

Lockhead, C. "Fire Ants Are Nipping at Our Heels." *Insight* 5 (8 May 1989): 20-22.

Revkin, A. C. "March of the Fire Ants." *Discover* 10 (March 1989): 70-76.

First World

The world's more wealthy, politically powerful, and industrially developed countries are unofficially, but commonly, designated as the First World. The term differentiates the powerful, capitalist states of Western Europe and North America and Japan from the (formerly) communist states (**Second World**) and from the nonaligned, developing countries (**Third World**) in world systems theory. In common usage, First World refers mainly to a level of economic strength. The level of industrial development of the First World, characterized by an extensive infrastructure, mechanized production, efficient and fast transport networks, and pervasive use of high technology, consumes huge amounts of **natural resources** and requires an educated and skilled work force. However, such a system is usually highly profitable. Often depending upon raw materials imported from poorer countries (wood, metal ores, **petroleum**, food, and so on), First World countries efficiently produce goods that less developed countries desire but cannot produce themselves, including computers, airplanes, optical equipment, and military hardware. Generally, high domestic and international demand for such specialized goods keeps First World countries wealthy, allowing them to maintain a high standard of material consumption, education, and health care for their citizens.

Fish and Wildlife Service

The United States Fish & Wildlife Service based in Washington, D.C., is charged with conserving, protecting, and enhancing fish, **wildlife**, and their **habitat**s for the benefit of the American people. As a division of the **U.S. Department of the Interior**, the Service's primary responsibilities are for the protection of migratory birds, **endangered species**, freshwater and anadromous (saltwater **species** that spawn in freshwater rivers and streams) fisheries, and certain marine mammals.

In addition to its Washington, D.C., headquarters, the Service maintains seven regional offices and a number of field units. Those include **national wildlife refuge**s, national fish hatcheries, research laboratories, and a nationwide network of law enforcement agents.

The Service manages 450 refuges that provide habitats for migratory birds, endangered species, and other wildlife. It sets migratory bird hunting regulations, and leads an effort to protect and restore endangered and threatened animals and plants in the United States and other countries.

Service scientists assess the effects of contaminants on wildlife and habitats. Its geographers and cartographers work with other scientists to map **wetlands** and carry out programs to slow wetland loss, or preserve and enhance these habitats. Restoring fisheries that have been depleted by **overfishing**, **pollution**, or other habitat damage is a major program of the Service. Efforts are underway to help four important **species**: lake trout in the upper **Great Lakes**; striped bass in both the **Chesapeake Bay** and Gulf Coast;

Atlantic **salmon** in New England; and salmonid species of the Pacific Northwest.

Fish and Wildlife biologists working with scientists from other federal and state agencies, universities, and private organizations develop recovery plans for endangered and threatened species. Among its successes are the American **alligator**, no longer considered endangered in some areas, and a steadily increasing **bald eagle** population.

Internationally, the Service cooperates with forty wildlife research and **wildlife management** programs, and provide technical assistance to many other countries. Its 200 special agents and inspectors help enforce wildlife laws and treaty obligations. They investigate cases ranging from individual migratory bird hunting violations to large-scale poaching and commercial trade in protected wildlife.

It its "Vision for the Future" statement, the Fish and Wildlife Service states its mission to "provide leadership to achieving a national net gain of fish and wildlife and the natural systems which support them." Into the twenty-first century, this vision statement calls for new **conservation** compacts with all citizens to increase the value of the United States wildlife holdings in number and **biodiversity**, and to provide increased opportunities for the public to use, associate with, learn about and enjoy America's wildlife wealth. Internet: http://www.fws.gov:80/. *See also* Critical habitat; Migration; National Wildlife Federation; Overhunting; Wildlife refuge; Wildlife rehabilitation

[*Linda Rehkopf*]

FURTHER READING

U. S. Fish and Wildlife Service. "Vision for the Future." Washington, DC: U. S. Government Printing Office, 1991.

Fish farming
See **Blue revolution**

Fish kills

Fishing has long been a major provider of food and livelihood to people throughout the world. In the United States, 50 million people enjoy fishing as an outdoor **recreation**—38 million in fresh water and 12 million in salt water. Combined, they spend over $315 million annually on this sport. It is no surprise, then, that public attitude towards factors that influence fishing is strong.

The **Environmental Protection Agency (EPA)** is charged with overseeing the quality of the nation's waterways. In 1977 they received information on 503 separate incidents in which 16.5 million fish were killed. In 1974, a record 47 million fish were killed in the Black River near Essex, Maryland, by a **discharge** from a sewage plant.

Fish kills can result from natural as well as human causes. Natural causes include sudden changes in temperature, oxygen depletion, toxic gases, epidemics of **virus**es and bacteria, infestations of **parasites**, toxic **algal bloom**s, lightning, **fungi**, and other similar factors. Human influences that lead to fish kills include **acid rain**, sewage **effluent**, and toxic spills.

In a ten-year study of the causes of 409 documented fish kills totaling 3.6 million fish in the state of Missouri, S. M. Czarnezki determined the percentage contributions as: 26 percent municipal-related (sewage effluent), 17 percent from agricultural activities, 11 percent from industrial operations, 8 percent by transportation accidents, 7 percent each by oxygen depletions, non-industrial operations, and mining, 4 percent by disease, 3 percent by "other" factors, and 10 percent as undetermined.

Fish kills may occur quite rapidly, even within minutes of a major toxic spill. Usually, however, the process takes days or even months, especially in natural causes. Experienced fishery biologists usually need a wide variety of physical, chemical, and biological tests of the **habitat** and fish to determine the exact causative agent or agents. The investigative procedure is often complex and may require a lot of time.

Species of fish vary in their susceptibility to the different factors that contribute to **die-off**s. Some species are sensitive to almost any disturbance, while other fish are tolerant of changes. As discussed below, predatory fish at the top of the **food chain/web** are typically the first fish affected by toxic substances that accumulate slowly in the water.

The most common contributor to fish kills by natural causes is oxygen depletion, which occurs when the amount of oxygen utilized by respiration, **decomposition**, and other processes exceeds oxygen input from the **atmosphere** and **photosynthesis**. Oxygen is more soluble in cold than warm water. Summer fish kills occur when lakes are thermally stratified. If the lake is eutrophic (highly productive), dead plant and animal matter that settles to the bottom undergoes decomposition, utilizing oxygen. Under windless conditions, more oxygen will be used than is gained, and animals like fish and **zooplankton** often die from suffocation.

Winter fish kills can also occur. Algae can photosynthesize even when the lake is covered with ice because sunlight can penetrate through the ice. However, if heavy snowfall accumulates on top of the ice, light may not reach the underlying water, and the phytoplankton die and sink to the bottom. Decomposers and respiring organisms again use up the remaining oxygen and the animals eventually die. When the ice melts in the spring, dead fish are found floating on the surface. This is a fairly common occurrence in many lakes in Michigan, Wisconsin, Minnesota, and surrounding states. For example, dead alewives (*Alosa pseudoharengus*) often wash up on the southwestern shore of Lake Michigan near Chicago during spring thaws following harsh winters.

In summer and winter, artificial **aeration** can help prevent fish kills. The addition of oxygen through aeration and mixing is one of the easiest and cheapest methods of dealing with low oxygen levels. In intensive aquaculture ponds, massive fish deaths from oxygen depletion are a constant threat. Oxygen sensors are often installed to detect low oxygen levels and trigger the release of pure oxygen gas from nearby cylinders.

Natural fish kills can also result from the release of toxic gases. In 1986, 1,700 villagers living on the shore of Lake Nyos, Cameroon, mysteriously died. A group of scientists sent to investigate determined that they died of asphyxiation. Evidently a **landslide** caused the trapped **carbon dioxide**-rich bottom waters to rapidly rise to the surface much like a popped champagne bottle. The poisonous gas killed everyone in its downwind path. Fish in the upper oxygenated waters of the lake were also killed as the carbon dioxide passed through.

Hydrogen sulfide (H_2S), a foul-smelling gas naturally produced in the oxygen-deficient **sediment**s of eutrophic lakes, can also cause fish deaths. Even in oxygenated waters, high H_2S levels can cause a condition in fish called "brown blood." The brown color of the blood is caused by the formation of sulfhemoglobin, which inhibits the blood's oxygen-carrying capacity. Some fish survive, but sensitive fish such as trout usually die.

Fish kills can also result from toxic algal blooms. Some bluegreen algae in lakes and dinoflagellates in the ocean release toxins that can kill fish and other vertebrates, including humans. For example, dense blooms of bluegreen algae such as *Anabaena*, *Aphanizomenon*, and *Microcystis* have caused fish kills in many farm ponds during the summer. Fish die not only from the toxins but also from asphyxiation resulting from decomposition of the mass of algae that also die due to lack of sunlight in the densely-populated lake water. In marine waters, toxic dinoflagellate blooms called **red tide**s are notorious for causing massive fish kills. For example, blooms of *Gymnodinium* or *Gonyaulax* periodically kill fish along the East and Gulf Coasts of the United States. Die-offs of **salmon** in aquaculture pens along the southwestern shoreline of Norway have been blamed on these organisms. Millions of dollars can be lost if the fish are not moved to clear waters. Saxitoxin, the toxic chemical produced by *Gonyaulax*, is 50 times more lethal than strychnine or curare.

Pathogens and parasites can also contribute to fish kills. Usually the effect is more secondary than direct. Fish weakened by parasites or infections of bacteria or viruses usually are unable to adapt to and survive changes in water temperature and chemistry. Under stressful conditions of over-crowding and malnourishment, gizzard shad often die from minor infestations of the normally harmless bacterium *Aeromonas hydrophila*. In the same way, fungal infections such as *Ichthyophonus hoferia* can contribute to fish kills. Most fresh water aquarium keepers are familiar with the threat of "ick" for their fish. The telltale white spots under the epithelium of the fins, body, and gills are caused by the protozoan parasite *Ichthyophthirius multifiliis*.

Changes in **pH** of lakes resulting from acid rain are a modern example of how humans can cause fish kills. Atmospheric pollutants such as nitrogen dioxide and sulfur dioxide released from automobiles and industries mix with water vapor and cause the rainwater to be more acid than normal (< pH 6.5). Non-protected lakes downwind that receive this rainfall increase in acidity, and sensitive fish eventually die.

Most of the once-productive trout streams and lakes in the southern half of Norway are now devoid of these prized fish. Sweden has combatted this problem by adding enormous quantities of lime to their affected lakes in the hope of neutralizing the acid's effects.

Sewage treatment plants add varying amounts of treated **effluent** to streams and lakes. Sometimes during heavy rainfall raw sewage escapes the treatment process and pollutes the aquatic environment. The greater the organic matter that comprises the effluent, the more decomposition occurs, resulting in oxygen usage. Scientists call this the biological or **biochemical oxygen demand (BOD)**, the quantity of oxygen required by bacteria to oxidize the organic waste aerobically to carbon dioxide and water. It is measured by placing a sample of the **wastewater** in a glass-stoppered bottle for five days at 71 degrees Fahrenheit (20 degrees Celsius) and determining the amount of oxygen consumed during this time. Domestic sewage typically has a BOD of about 200 milligrams per liter, or 200 **parts per million** (ppm); rates for industrial waste may reach several thousand milligrams per liter. Reports of fish kills in industrialized countries have greatly increased in recent years. Sewage effluent not only kills fish; it can also create a barrier to fish migrating upstream because of the low oxygen levels. For example, coho salmon will not pass through water with oxygen levels below 5 ppm. Oxygen depletion is often more detrimental to fish than thermal shock.

Toxic **chemical spills**, whether via sewage treatment plants or other sources, are the major cause of fish kills. Sudden discharges of large quantities of highly **toxic substance**s usually cause massive death of most aquatic life. If they enter the **ecosystem** at sublethal levels over a long time, the effects are more subtle. Large predatory or omnivorous fish are typically the first ones affected. This is because toxic chemicals like methyl **mercury**, **DDT**, PCBs, and other organic pollutants have an affinity for fatty tissue and progressively accumulate in organisms up the food chain. This is called the principle of **biomagnification**. Unfortunately for human consumers, these fish do not usually die right away, so people who eat a lot of tainted fish become sick and possibly die. Such is the case for **Minamata disease**, named for the first documented connection between the death of fishermen and methyl mercury contamination. *See also* Acid mine drainage; Aquatic chemistry; Bioaccumulation; Plankton; Runoff; Water pollution; Water quality

[*John Korstad*]

FURTHER READING

Czarnezki, J. M. *A Summary of Fish Kill Investigations in Missouri, 1970-1979*. Columbia, MO: Missouri Dept. of Conservation, 1983.

Ehrlich, P. R., A. H. Ehrlich, and J. P. Holdren. *Ecoscience: Population, Resources, Environment*. San Francisco: W. H. Freeman, 1977.

Goldman, C. R., and A. J. Horne. *Limnology*. New York: McGraw-Hill, 1983.

Hill, D. M. "Fish Kill Investigation Procedures." In *Fisheries Techniques*, edited by L. A. Nielson and D. L. Johnson. Bethesda, MD: American Fisheries Society, 1983.

Keup, L. E. "How to 'Read' a Fish Kill." *Water and Sewage Works* 12 (1974): 48-51.

Meyer, F. P., and L. A. Barclay, eds. *Field Manual for the Investigation of Fish Kills*. Washington, DC: U. S. Fish and Wildlife Service, 1990.

Moyle, P. B., and J. J. Cech, Jr. *Fishes: An Introduction to Ichthyology*. 2nd ed. New York: Prentice-Hall, 1988.

Fish nets

See **Drift nets; Gill nets**

Fisheries and Oceans Canada

The Department of Fisheries and Oceans (DFO) in Canada was created by the Department of Fisheries and Oceans Act on April 2, 1979. This act formed a separate government department from the Fisheries and Marine Service of the former Department of Fisheries and the Environment. The new department was needed, in part, because of increased interest in the management of Canada's oceanic resources, and also because of the mandate resulting from the unilateral declaration of the 200-nautical-mile Exclusive Economic Zones in 1977.

At its inception, the DFO assumed responsibility for seacoast and inland fisheries, fishing and recreational vessel harbors, hydrography and ocean science, and the coordination of policy and programs for Canada's oceans. Four main organizational units were created: Atlantic Fisheries, Pacific and Freshwater Fisheries, Economic Development and Marketing, and Ocean and Aquatic Science. Among the activities included in the department's original mandate were: comprehensive husbandry of fish stocks and protection of **habitat**; "best use" of fish stocks for optimal socioeconomic benefits; adequate hydrographic surveys; the acquisition of sufficient knowledge for defense, transportation, energy development and fisheries, with provision of such information to users; and continued development and maintenance of a national system of harbors.

Since its inception, the department's mandate has changed in minor ways, to include new terminology such as "sustainability" and to include Canada's "ecological interests." Recently, attention has been given to support those who make their living or benefit from the sea. This constituency includes the public first, but the DFO also directs its efforts toward commercial fishers, fish plant workers, importers, aquaculturists, recreational fishers, native fishers, and the ocean manufacturing and service sectors. There are now six DFO divisions: Science, Atlantic Fisheries, Pacific Fisheries, Inspection Services, International, and Corporate Policy and Support administered through six regional offices.

A primary focus of DFO's current work is the failing cod and groundfish stocks in the Atlantic; the department has commissioned two major inquiries in recent years to investigate those problems. In addition, the DFO has increased regulation of foreign fleets, and works to manage straddling stocks in the Atlantic Exclusive Economic Zone through the North Atlantic Fisheries Organization, the Pacific **drift nets** fisheries, recreational fishing and aquaculture development. In 1992, management problems in the major fisheries arose on both the Pacific and Atlantic coasts. American fisheries managers reneged on quotas established through the Pacific Salmon Treaty, northern cod stocks in Newfoundland virtually failed, and the Aboriginal Fishing Strategy was adopted as part of a land claim settlement on the Pacific coast.

There are several major problems associated with ocean resource and **environment** management in Canada—problems that the DFO has neither the resources, the legislative infrastructure, nor the political will to address. One result of this has been the steady decline of commercial fish stocks, highlighted by the virtual collapse of Atlantic cod (*Gadus callarias*), which is Canada's, and perhaps, the Atlantic's most historically significant fishery. A second result has been an increased need to secure international agreements with Canada's ocean neighbors. A third result of social significance is the perception that fisheries have been used in a political sense in cases of regional economic incentives and land claims settlements. *See also* Commercial fishing; Department of Fisheries and Oceans (DFO), Canada

[*David A. Duffus*]

Fishing

See **Commercial fishing; Drift nets; Gill nets**

Flocculation

See **Water treatment**

Flooding

Technically, flooding occurs when the water level in any stream, river, bay or lake rises above bank full. Bays may flood as the result of a **tsunami** or tidal wave induced by an earthquake or volcanic eruption; or as a result of a tidal storm surge caused by a **hurricane** or tropical storm moving inland. Streams, rivers and lakes may be flooded by high amounts of surface **runoff** resulting from widespread precipitation or rapid snow melt. On a smaller scale, flash floods due to extremely heavy precipitation occurring over a short period of time can flood streams, creeks and low lying areas in a matter of a few hours. Thus, there are various temporal and spatial scales of flooding. Historical evidence suggests that flooding causes greater loss of life and property than any other natural disaster. The magnitude, seasonality, frequency, velocity, and load are all properties of flooding which are studied by meteorologists, climatologists and hydrologists.

Spring and winter floods occur with some frequency primarily in the mid-latitude regions of the earth, and particularly where continental **climate** is the norm. Five climatic features contribute to the spring and winter flooding potential of any individual year or region: 1) heavy winter snow cover; 2) saturated **soil**s or soils at least near their field capacity for storing water; 3) rapid melting of the winter's snow pack; 4) frozen soil conditions which limit **infiltration**; and 5) somewhat heavy rains, usually from large scale cyclonic storms. Any combination of three of these five climatic features usually leads to some type of flooding. This type of flooding can cause hundreds of millions of dollars in property damage, but it can usually be predicted well in advance, allowing for evacuation and other protective action to be taken (sandbagging, for instance). In some situations flood control measures such as stream or channel diversions, **dams**, and levees can greatly reduce the risk of flooding. This is more often done in floodplain areas with histories of very damaging floods. In addition, **land use** regulations, encroachment statutes and building codes are often intended to protect the public from the risk of flooding.

Flash flooding is generally caused by violent weather, such as severe thunderstorms and hurricanes. This type of flooding more frequently occurs during the warm season when convective thunderstorms develop more frequently. Rainfall intensity is so great that the **carrying capacity** of streams and channels is rapidly exceeded, usually within hours, resulting in sometimes life-threatening flooding. It is estimated that the average death toll in the United States exceeds 200 per year as a result of flash flooding. Many government weather services provide the public with flash flood watches and warnings to prevent loss of life. Many flash floods occur as the result of afternoon and evening thundershowers which produce rainfall intensities ranging from a few tenths of an inch per hour to several inches per hour. In some highly developed urban areas, the risk of flash flooding has increased over time as the native vegetation and soils have been replaced by buildings and pavement which produce much higher amounts of surface runoff. In addition, the increased usage of parks and recreational facilities which lie along stream and river channels has exposed the public to greater risk. *See also* Urban runoff

[*Mark W. Seeley*]

FURTHER READING

Battan, L. J. *Weather In Your Life*. San Francisco: W. H. Freeman, 1983.
Critchfield, H. J. *General Climatology*. 4th ed. Englewood Cliffs, NJ: Prentice-Hall, 1983.

Floodplain

An area that has been built up by stream deposition, generally represented by the main drainage channel of a **watershed**, is called a floodplain. This area, usually relatively flat with respect to the surrounding landscape, is subject to periodic **flooding**, with

return periods ranging from one year to 100 years. Floodplains vary widely in size, depending on the area of the drainage basin with which they are associated. The soils in floodplains are often dark and fertile, representing material lost the to erosive forces of heavy precipitation and **runoff**. These soils are often farmed, though subject to the risk of periodic crop losses due to flooding. In some areas, floodplains are protected by flood control measures such as **reservoirs**

and levees and are used for farming or residential development. In other areas, land-use regulations, encroachment statutes and local building codes often prevent development on floodplains.

Flora

All forms of plant life that live in a particular geographic region at a particular time in history. A number of factors determine the flora in any particular area, including temperature, sunlight, **soil**, water, and evolutionary history. The flora in any given area is a major factor in determining the type of **fauna** found in the area. Scientists have divided the earth's surface into a number of regions inhabited by distinct flora. Among these regions are the African-Indian **desert**, western African **rain forest**, Pacific North American region, Arctic and Sub-arctic region, and the Amazon.

Florida panther (*Felis concolor coryi*)

The Florida panther, a subspecies of the mountain lion, is a member of the cat family, Felidae, and is severely threatened with **extinction**. Listed as endangered, the Florida panther population currently numbers between 30 and 50 individuals. Its former range probably extended from western Louisiana and Arkansas eastward through Mississippi, Alabama, Georgia, and southwestern South Carolina to the southern tip of Florida. Today the Florida panther's range extends over a nine county area of south Florida, mostly south of Lake Okeechobee; however, the sparse population has been fragmented into four main areas of suitable **habitat**. The preferred habitat for this large cat is subtropical forests comprised of dense stands of trees, vines, and shrubs, typically in low, swampy areas.

Several factors have contributed to the decline of the Florida panther. Historically the most significant factors have been habitat loss and persecution by humans. **Land use** patterns have altered the **environment** throughout the former range of the Florida panther.

With shifts to cattle ranching and agriculture, lands were drained and developed, and with the altered vegetation patterns came a change in the prey base for this top carnivore. The main prey item of the Florida panther is white-tailed deer (*Odocoileus virginianus*). Formerly, the spring and summer rains kept the area wet, and then, as it dried out, fires would renew the grassy meadows at the forest edges, creating an ideal habitat for the deer. With development and increased deer hunting by humans, the panther's prey base declined and so did the number of panthers. Prior to the 1950s, Florida had a bounty on Florida panthers because the animal was considered a "threat" to humans and livestock. During the 1950s, state law protected the dwindling popula-

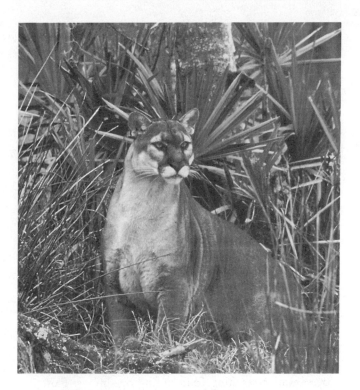

Florida panther.

tion of panthers. In 1967 the Florida panther was listed by the U. S. **Fish and Wildlife Service** as an **endangered species**.

Land development is still moving southward in Florida. With the annual influx of new residents, fruit orchards being moved south due to recent freezes, and continued draining and clearing of land, panther habitat continues to be destroyed. The Florida panther is forced into areas that are not good habitat for white-tailed deer, and the panthers are catching armadillos and raccoons for food. The panthers then become underweight and anemic due to poor nutrition.

Development contributes to the Florida panther's decline in other ways, too. Its range is currently split in half by the east-west highway known as Alligator Alley. During peak seasons, over 30,000 vehicles traverse this stretch of highway daily, and, since 1980, nine panthers have been killed by cars, the largest single cause of death for these cats in recent decades.

Biology is also working against the Florida panther. Because of the extremely small population size, **inbreeding** of panthers has yielded increased reproductive failures, due to deformed or infertile sperm. The spread of feline distemper virus also is a concern to **wildlife** biologists. All these factors have led officials to develop a recovery plan that includes a captive breeding program using a small number of injured animals, as well as a mark and recapture program, using radio collars, to inoculate against disease and track young panthers with hopes of saving this valuable part of the biota of south Florida's **Everglades** ecosystem. *See also* Captive propagation and reintroduction

[*Eugene C. Beckham*]

FURTHER READING

Belden, R. "The Florida Panther." In *Audubon Wildlife Report 1988/1989.* San Diego: Academic Press, 1988.

Miller, S. D., and D. D. Everett, eds. *Cats of the World: Biology, Conservation, and Management.* Washington, DC: National Wildlife Federation, 1986.

Flotation

An operation in which submerged materials are floated, by means of air bubbles, to the surface of a water and removed. Bubbles are generated through a system called dissolved air flotation (DAF), which is capable of producing clouds of very fine, very small bubbles. A large number of small-sized bubbles is generally most efficient for removing material from water.

This process is commonly used in **wastewater** treatment and by industries, but not in **water treatment**. For example, the mining industry uses flotation to concentrate fine ore particles, and flotation has been used to concentrate **uranium** from sea water. It is commonly used to thicken the **sludge**s and to remove grease and oil at wastewater treatment plants. The textile industry often uses flotation to treat process waters resulting from dyeing operations. Flotation might also be used to remove surfactants. Materials that are denser than water or that dissolve well in water are poor candidates for flotation. Flotation should not be confused with foam separation, a process in which surfactants are added to create a foam that affects the removal or concentration of some other material.

Flue gas

The exhaust gas vented from **combustion**, a chemical reaction, or other physical process, which passes through a duct into the **atmosphere**. Exhaust air is usually captured by an enclosure and brought into the exhaust duct through induced or forced ventilation. Induced ventilation is created by lowering the pressure in the duct using fans at the end of the duct. Forced ventilation occurs when exhaust air is forced into the duct using high pressure inlet air. Flues are valuable because they not only direct polluted air to a **pollution control** device, but also keep the air pollutant concentrations high. High concentrations can be important if the air pollutant removal process is concentration dependent. *See also* Air pollution control

Flue-gas scrubbing

Flue-gas scrubbing is a process for removing oxides of sulfur and nitrogen from the waste gases emitted by various industrial processes. Since the oxides of sulfur and nitrogen have been implicated in a number of health and environmental problems, controlling them is an important issue. The basic principle of scrubbing is that **flue gas**es are forced through a system of baffles within a smokestack. The baffles contain some chemical or **chemicals** that remove pollutants from these gases.

A number of scrubbing processes are available, all of which depend on the reaction between the oxide and some other chemical to produce a harmless compound that can then be removed from the smokestack. For example, currently the most common scrubbing reaction involves the reaction between **sulfur dioxide** and lime. In the first step of this process, limestone is heated to produce lime. The lime then reacts with sulfur dioxide in flue gases to form calcium sulfite, which can be removed with **electrostatic precipitation**.

Many other scrubbing reactions have been investigated. For example, magnesium oxide can be used in place of calcium oxide in the scrubber. The advantage of this reaction is that the magnesium sulfite that is formed decomposes readily when heated. The magnesium oxide that is regenerated can then be reused in the scrubber while the sulfur dioxide can be used to make sulfuric acid. In yet another process, a mixture of sodium citrate and citric acid is used in the scrubber. When sulfur dioxide is absorbed by the mixture, a reaction occurs in which elemental sulfur is precipitated out.

Although the limestone/lime process is by far the most popular scrubbing reaction, it has one serious disadvantage. The end product, calcium sulfite, is a solid that must be disposed of in some way. **Solid waste** disposal is already a serious problem in many areas, so adding to that problem is not desirable. For that reason, reactions such as those involving magnesium oxide, sodium citrate and citric acid have been carefully studied. The products of these reactions, sulfuric acid and elemental sulfur, are valuable raw materials that can be sold and used. In spite of that fact, the limestone/lime scrubbing process, or some variation of it, remains the most popular method of extracting sulfur dioxide from flue gases today.

Scrubbing to remove **nitrogen oxides** is much less effective. In principle, reactions like those used with sulfur dioxide are possible. For example, experiments have been conducted in which ammonia or **ozone** is used in the scrubber to react with and remove oxides of nitrogen. But such methods have had relatively little success and are rarely used by industry.

Flue gas scrubbing has long met with resistance from utilities and industries. For one thing, they are not convinced that oxides of sulfur and nitrogen are as dangerous as environmentalists sometimes claim. In addition, they argue that the cost of installing **scrubbers** is often too great to justify their use. *See also* Air pollution control; Dry alkali injection; Stack emissions

[*David E. Newton*]

FURTHER READING

American Chemical Society. *Cleaning Our Environment: A Chemical Perspective.* 2nd edition. Washington, DC: American Chemical Society, 1978.

Bretz, E. A. "Efficient Scrubbing Begins With Proper Lime Prep, Handling." *Electrical World* 205 (March 1991): 21-22.

"New Choices in FGD Systems Offer More Than Technology." *Electrical World* 204 (November 1990): 46-47.

"Scrubbers, Low-Sulfur Coal, of Plant Retirements?" *Electrical World* 204 (June 1990): 18.

Fluidized bed combustion

Of all **fossil fuels**, **coal** exists in the largest amount. In fact, the world's coal resources appear to be sufficient to meet our energy needs for many hundreds of years. One aim of energy technology, therefore, is to find more efficient ways to make use of these coal reserves. One efficiency procedure that has been under investigation for at least two decades is known as fluidized bed combustion.

In a fluidized bed boiler, granulated coal and limestone are fed simultaneously onto a moving grate. A stream of air from below the grate lifts coal particles so that they are actually suspended in air when they begin to burn. The flow of air, small size of the coal particles, and exposure of the particles on all sides contribute to an increased rate of **combustion**. Heat produced by burning the coal is then used to boil water, run a turbine, and drive a generator, as in a conventional power plant.

The fluidized bed process has much to recommend it from an environmental standpoint. Sulfur and **nitrogen oxides** react with limestone added to the boiler along with the coal. The product of this reaction, primarily calcium sulfite and calcium sulfate, can be removed from the bottom of the boiler. However, disposing of large quantities of this waste product represents one of the drawbacks of the fluidized bed system.

Fly ash is also reduced in the fluidized bed process. As coal burns in the boiler, particles of fly ash tend to adhere to each other, forming larger particles that eventually settle out at the bottom of the boiler. Conventional methods of removal in the stack, such as **electrostatic precipitation**, can further increase efficiency with which particles are removed.

Incomplete combustion of coal is common in the fluidized bed process. However, **carbon monoxide** and hydrogen sulfide formed in this way are further oxidized in the space above the moving grate. The products of this further oxidation are then removed by the limestone (which reacts with **sulfur dioxide**) or allowed to escape harmlessly in to the air (in the case of the **carbon dioxide**). After being used as a scavenger in the process, the limestone, calcium sulfite, and calcium sulfate can be treated to release sulfur dioxide and regenerate the original limestone. The limestone can then be re-used and the sulfur dioxide employed to make sulfuric acid.

A further advantage of the fluidized bed process is that it operates at a lower temperature than does a conventional power plant. Thus, the temperature of cooling water ejected from the plant is lower, and the amount of **thermal pollution** of nearby waterways correspondingly lessened.

Writers in the 1970s expressed high hopes for the future of fluidized bed combustion systems, but those hopes had still not been realized by the early 1990s. The cost of such systems is still at least double that of a conventional plant. They are also only marginally more efficient than a conventional plant. Still, their environmental assets are obvious.

Fluidized bed combustion. Fuel is lifted by a stream of air from underneath the bed. Fuel efficiency is good and sulfur dioxide and nitrogen oxide emissions are lower than with conventional boilers.

They should reduce the amount of sulfur dioxide emitted by up to 90 percent and the amount of nitrogen oxides by more than 60 percent. *See also* Air pollution control; Stack emissions

[*David E. Newton*]

FURTHER READING

Balzhiser, R. E., and K. E. Yeager. "Fluidized Bed Combustion." *Scientific American* 257 (September 1987): 100-107.

Electric Power Research Institute. *Atmospheric Fluidized Bed Combustion Development.* Palo Alto, CA: EPRI, 1982.

Government Institutes, Inc. Staff, eds. *Evaluating the Fluidized Bed Combustion Option, 1988.* Rockville, MD: Government Institutes, 1988.

Marshall, A. R. *Reduced NOx Emissions and Other Phenomena in Fluidized Bed Combustion.* Lanham: UNIPUB, 1992.

Fly ash

The fine ash from **combustion** processes that becomes dispersed in the air. To the casual observer it might appear as **smoke**, and indeed it is often found mixed with smoke. Fly ash arises because fuels contain a small fraction of incombustible matter. In a fuel like **coal**, ash has a rock-like siliceous composition, but the high temperatures at which it is formed often means that metals such as iron are incorporated into the ash particles, which take on the appearance of small, colored, glassy spheres. **Petroleum** produces less ash, but it is often associated with a range of oxides such as vanadium (in the case of fuel oils) and, more noticeably, hollow spheres of **carbon**. In traditional furnaces, much ash remained on the grate, but modern furnaces produce such fine ash that it is carried away in the hot exhaust gas.

Early power stations dispersed so much fine fly ash throughout the nearby environment that they were soon forced to adopt early pollution abatement techniques. They adopted "cyclones" in which centrifugal force removes the particles by causing the waste gas stream to flow on a curved or vortical course. This technique is effective down to particle sizes of about 10 μm, but smaller particles are not removed well by **cyclone collector**s and here **electrostatic precipitation** process often proves more successful, coping with a size range 30-0.1 μm. In electrostatic precipitators the particles are given a negative charge and then attracted to a positive electrode where they are collected and removed. Cloth or paper filters and spraying water through the exhaust gases can be useful in removing fly ash.

Fly ash is a nuisance at high concentrations because it accumulates as grit on the surfaces of buildings, clothes, cars, and outdoor furnishings. It is a highly visible and very annoying aspect of industrial **air pollution**. The deposition of fly ash increases cleaning costs incurred by people who live near poorly controlled combustion sources. Fly ash also has health impacts because the finer particles can penetrate into the human lung. If the deposits are especially heavy, fly ash can also inhibit plant growth.

Each year millions of tons of fly ash are produced from coal-powered furnaces, most of which are dumped in waste tips. Care needs to be taken that toxic metals and alkalis are not leached from these disposal sites into watercourses. Fly ash may be used as a low grade cement in road building because it contains a large amount of calcium oxide but generally, the demand is rather low.

[*Peter Brimblecombe*]

FURTHER READING

Sellers, B. H. *Pollution of Our Atmosphere.* Bristol: Adam Hilger, 1984.

Flyway

The route taken by migratory birds and waterfowl when they travel between their breeding grounds and their winter homes. Flyways often follow geographic features such as mountain ranges, rivers, or other bodies of water. Protecting flyways is one of the many responsibilities of **wildlife** managers. Draining of **wetlands**, residential and commercial development, and **overhunting** are some of the factors that threaten flyway sites visited by birds for food and rest during **migration**. In most cases, international agreements are needed to guarantee protection along the entire length of a flyway. In the United States, flyway protection is financed to a large extent by funds produced through the Migratory Bird Hunting Stamp Act passed by the U.S. Congress in 1934.

Food additives

Food additives are substances added to food as flavorants, nutrients, preservatives, emulsifiers, or colorants. In addition, foods may contain residues of chemicals used during the production of plant or animal crops, including **pesticide**s, antibiotics, and growth hormones. The use of most food additives is clearly beneficial because it results in improved public health and prevention of spoilage, which enhances the food supply. Nevertheless, there is controversy about the use of many common additives and over the presence of contaminants in food. This is partly because some people are hypersensitive and suffer allergic reactions if they are exposed to certain of these chemicals. In addition, some people believe that low levels of chronic toxicity and diseases may be caused in the larger population by exposure to some of these substances. Although there is no compelling scientific evidence that this is indeed the case, the possibility of chronic damage caused by food additives and chemical residues is an important social and scientific issue.

The use of food additives in the United States is closely regulated by the government agencies responsible for health, consumer safety, and agriculture. This is also the case of other developed countries in Europe, Canada, and elsewhere. Chemicals cannot be used as additives in those countries unless regulators are convinced that they have been demonstrated to be toxicologically safe, with a wide margin of security. In addition, chemicals added to commercially prepared foods must be listed on the packaging so that consumers can know what is present in the foodstuffs that they choose to eat. Because of the intrinsic nature of low-level, toxicological risks, especially those associated with diseases that may take a long time to develop, scientists are never able to demonstrate that trace exposures to any chemical are absolutely safe—there is always a level of risk, however small. Because some people object to these potential, low-level, often involuntary risks, a certain degree of controversy will always be associated with the use of food additives. This is also true of the closely related topic of residues of pesticides, antibiotics, and growth hormones in foods.

Flavorants

Certain chemicals are added to foods to enhance their flavor. This is particularly true of commercially processed or prepared foods, such as canned vegetables and frozen foods and meals. One of the most commonly added flavorants is table salt (or sodium chloride), a critical nutrient for humans and other animals. In large amounts, however, sodium chloride can predispose people to developing high blood pressure, a factor that is important in strokes and other circulatory and heart diseases.

Table sugar (or sucrose), manufactured from sugar cane or sugar beets, and fructose, or fruit sugar, are commonly used to sweeten prepared foods. Such foods include sugar candies, chocolate products, artificial drinks, sweetened fruit juices, peanut butter, jams, ketchup, and most commercial breads. Sugars are easily assimilated from foods and are a useful form of metabolic energy. In large amounts, however, sugars can lead to weight gain, tooth decay, and hypoglycemia and diabetes in genetically predisposed people. Artificial sweeteners such as saccharine, aspartame, and sodium cyclamate avoid the nutritional problems associated with eating too much sugar. These nonsugar sweeteners may have their own problems, however, and some people consider them to be a low-level health hazard.

Monosodium glutamate (or MSG) is commonly used as a flavor enhancer, particularly in processed meats, prepared soups, and oriental foods. Some people are relatively sensitive to this chemical, developing headaches and other symptoms that are sometimes referred to as "Chinese food syndrome." Other flavorants used in processed foods include many kinds of spices, herbs, vanilla, mustard, nuts, peanuts, and wine. Some people are extremely allergic to even minute exposures to peanuts or nuts in food and can rapidly develop a condition known as anaphylactic shock, which is life-threatening unless quickly treated with medicine. This is one of the reasons why any foods containing peanuts or nuts as a flavoring ingredient must be clearly labeled as such.

Many flavorants are natural in origin. Increasingly, however, synthetic flavorants are being discovered and used. For example, vanilla used to be extracted from a particular species of tropical orchid and was therefore a rather expensive flavorant. However, a synthetic vanilla flavorant can now be manufactured from wood-pulp lignins, and this has made this pleasant flavor much more readily available than it used to be.

Nutrients

Many foods are fortified with minerals, vitamins, and other micronutrients. One such example is table salt, which has iodine added (as potassium iodide) to help prevent goiter in the general population. Goiter used to be relatively common but is now rare, in part because of the widespread use of iodized salt.

Other foods that are commonly fortified with minerals and vitamins include milk and margarine (with vitamins A and D), flour (with thiamine, riboflavin, niacin, iron), and some commercial breads and breakfast cereals (with various vitamins and minerals, particularly in some commercial cereal preparations). Micronutrient additives in these and other commercial foods are carefully formulated to help contribute to a balanced diet in their consumers. Nevertheless, some people believe that it is somehow un-natural and un-healthy to consume foods that have been adulterated in this manner, and they prefer to eat "natural" foods that do not have any vitamins or minerals added to them.

Preservatives

Preservatives are substances added to foods to prevent spoilage caused by bacteria, fungi, yeasts, insects, or other biological agents. Spoilage can lead to a decrease in the nutritional quality of foods, to the growth of food-poisoning microorganisms such as the botulism bacterium, or to the production of deadly chemicals, such as aflatoxin, that can be produced in stored grains and seeds (such as peanuts) by species of fungi.

Salt has long been used to preserve meat and fish, either added directly to the surface or by immersing the food in a briny solution. Nitrates and nitrites (such as sodium nitrate, or saltpetre) are also used to preserve meats, especially cured foods such as sausages, salamis, and hams. These chemicals are especially useful in inhibiting the growth of *Clostridium botulinum*, the bacterium that causes deadly botulism. Vinegar and wood smoke are used for similar purposes. **Sulfur dioxide**, sodium sulfite, and benzoic acid are often used as preservatives in fruit products, such beverages as wine and beer, and in ketchup, pickles, and spice preparations.

Anti-oxidants are chemicals added to certain foods to prevent a deterioration in their quality or flavor, occurring due to the exposure of fats and oils to atmospheric oxygen. Examples of commonly used antioxidants are ascorbic acid (or vitamin C), butylated hydroxyanisole (or BHA), butylated hydroxytoluene (or BHT), gallates, and ethoxyquin.

Stabilizers and Emulsifiers

Stabilizers and emulsifiers are added to prepared foods to maintain suspensions of fats or oils in water matrices (or vice versa), or to prevent the caking of ingredients during storage or preparation. One example of an emulsifying additive is glyceryl monostearate, often added to stored starch products to maintain their texture. Alginates are compounds added to commercial ice cream, salad dressing, and other foods to stabilize emulsions of oil- or fat-in-water during storage.

Colorants

Some prepared foods have colors added to "improve" their aesthetic qualities and thereby to make them more attractive to consumers. This practice is especially common in the preparation of confectionaries such as candies, chocolate bars, ice creams, and similar products, and in fancy cakes and pastries. Similarly, products such as ketchup and strawberry preserves have red dyes added to enhance their color, relishes and tinned peas have green colors added, and dark breads may contain brown colorants. Most margarines have yellow colors added, to make them appear more similar to butter. Artificial drinks and drink-mixes contain food colorants appropriate to their flavor—cherry and raspberry contain red dyes, and so forth.

Various chemicals are used as food colorants, some of them being extracted from plants (for example, yellow and orange carotenes), while many others are synthetic chemicals derived from coal tars and other organic substances. The acute toxicity (i.e., short-term poisoning) and chronic toxicity (i.e., longer-term damage associated with diseases, **cancer**s, and developmental abnormalities) of these colorants are stringently tested on animals in the laboratory, and the substances must be demonstrated to be safe before they are allowed to be used as food additives. Still, some people object to having these chemicals in their food, and choose to consume products that are not adulterated with colorants.

Residues of Pesticides, Antibiotics, and Growth Hormones

Insecticides, fungicides, herbicides, and other **pesticide**s are routinely used in modern, industrial agriculture. Some of these chemicals are persistent, because they do not quickly break down in the **environment** to simpler substances, and/or they do not readily wash off produce. The chemicals in such cases are called residues, and it is not unusual for them to be present on or in foodstuffs in low concentrations. The permissible residue levels allowed in foodstuffs intended for human consumption are closely regulated by government. However, not all foods can be properly inspected, so it is common for people to be routinely exposed to small concentrations of these chemicals in their diet.

In addition, most animals cultivated in intensive agricultural systems, such as feedlots and factory farms, are routinely treated with antibiotics in their feed. This is done to prevent outbreaks of communicable diseases under densely crowded conditions. Antibiotic use is especially common during the raising of chickens, turkeys, pigs, and cows. Small residues of these chemicals remain in the meat, eggs, milk, or other products of these animals, and are ingested by human consumers. Also, growth hormones are given to beef and dairy cows to increase their productivity. Small residues of these chemicals also occur in products eaten by consumers.

Strictly speaking, residues of pesticides, antibiotics, and growth hormones are not additives because they are not added directly to foodstuffs. Nevertheless, these chemicals are present in foods eaten by people, and many consumers find this to be objectionable. So-called organic foods are cultivated without the use of synthetic pesticides, antibiotics, or growth hormones, and many people prefer to eat these foods instead of the much more abundantly available foodstuffs that are typically sold in commercial outlets. (Note that the term "organic foods" is somewhat of a misnomer, because all foods are organic in nature. The phrase "organic" in this sense is used to refer to foods containing additives and/or residues, etc.)

Irradiation of Food

Irradiation is a new technology that can be used to prevent spoilage of foods by sterilizing most or all of the microorganisms and insects that they may contain. This process utilizes gamma radiation, and it is not known to cause any chemical or physical changes in foodstuffs, other than the intended benefit of killing organisms that can cause spoilage. Although this process displaces some of the uses of preservative chemicals as food additives, irradiation itself is somewhat controversial. Even though there is no scientific evidence that food irradiation poses tangible risks to consumers, some people object to the use of this technology and prefer not to consume foodstuffs processed in this manner.

[*Bill Freedman*]

FURTHER READING

British Nutrition Foundation. *Why Additives? The Safety of Foods.* London: Forbes, 1977.

Etherton, T.D. "The Impact Of Biotechnology On Animal Agriculture And The Consumer." *Nutrition Today* 29, no. 4 (1994): 12-18.

Freed, D.L.J. *Health Hazards of Milk.* London: Bailliere Tindall, 1984.

Marcus, A.I. *Cancer from Beef: DES, Federal Food Regulation, and Consumer Confidence.* Baltimore, MD.: Johns Hopkins University Press, 1994.

Miller, M. *Danger! Additives at Work: A Report on Food Additives, Their Use and Control.* London: London Food Commission, 1985.

Safety and Nutritional Adequacy of Irradiated Food. Geneva, Switzerland: World Health Organization, 1994.

Food chain/web

Food chains and food webs are methods of describing an **ecosystem** by describing how energy flows from one **species** to another.

First proposed by the English zoologist Charles Elton in 1927, food chains and food webs describe the successive transfer of energy from plants to the animals that eat them, and to the animals that eat those animals, and so on. A food chain is a model for this process which assumes that the transfer of energy within the community is relatively simple. A food chain in a **grassland** ecosystem, for example, might be: Insects eat grass, and mice eat insects, and fox eat mice. But such an outline is not exactly accurate, and many more species of plants and animals are actually involved in the transfer of energy. Rodents often feed on both plants and insects, and some animals, such as predatory birds, feed on several kinds of rodents. This more complex description of the way energy flows through an ecosystem is called a food web. Food webs can be thought of as interconnected or intersecting food chains.

The components of food chains and food webs are producers, consumers, and decomposers. Plants and chemosynthetic bacteria are producers. They are also called primary producers or **autotroph**s ("self-nourishing") because they produce organic compounds from inorganic **chemicals** and outside sources of energy. The groups that eat these plants are called primary consumers or herbivores. They have adaptations that allow them to live on a purely vegetative diet which is high in cellulose. They usually have teeth modified for chewing and grinding; ruminants such as deer and cattle have well-developed stomachs, and lagomorphs such as rabbits have caeca which aid their digestion. Animals that eat herbivores are called secondary consumers or primary carnivores, and predators that eat these animals are called tertiary consumers. Decomposers are the final link in the energy flow. They feed on dead organic matter, releasing **nutrient**s back into the ecosystem. Animals that eat dead plant and animal matter are called scavengers, and plants that do the same are known as saprophytes.

The components of food chains and food webs exist at different stages in the transfer of energy through an ecosystem. The position of every group of organisms obtaining their food in the same manner is known as a **trophic level**. The term comes from a Greek word meaning "nursing," and the implication is that each stage nourishes the next. The first tropic level consists of autotrophs, the second herbivores, the third primary carnivores. At the final trophic level exists what is often called the "top predator." Organisms in the same trophic level are not necessarily connected taxonomically; they are connected ecologically, by the fact they obtain their energy in the same way. Their trophic level is determined by how many steps it is above the primary producer level. Most organisms occupy only one trophic level; however some may occupy two. Insectivorous plants like the venus flytrap are

In an ecosystem, food chains become interconnected to form food webs.

both primary producers and carnivores. Horseflies are another example: the females bite and draw blood, while the males are strictly herbivores.

In 1942, Raymond Lindeman published a paper entitled "The Tropic-Dynamic Aspect of Ecology." Although a young man and only recently graduated from Yale University, he revolutionized ecological thinking by describing ecosystems in the terminology of energy transformation. He used data from his studies of Cedar Bog Lake in Minnesota to construct the first energy budget for an entire ecosystem. He measured harvestable net production at three trophic levels, primary producer, herbivore, and carnivore. He did this by measuring gross production minus growth, reproduction, **respiration**, and excretion. He was able to calculate the assimilation efficiency at each tropic level, and the efficiency of energy transfers between each level. Lindeman's calculations are still widely regarded today, and his conclusions are usually generalized by saying that the ecological efficiency of energy transfers between trophic levels averages about 10 percent.

Lindeman's calculations and some basic laws about physics reveal important truths about food chains, food webs, and ecosystems in general. The First Law of Thermodynamics states that energy cannot be created or destroyed; energy input must equal energy output. The Second Law of Thermodynamics states that all physical processes proceed in such a way that the availability of the energy involved decreases. In other words, no transfer of energy is completely efficient.

Using the generalized 10 percent figure from Lindeman's study, a hypothetical ecosystem with 1,000 kcal of energy available (net production) at the primary-producer level would mean that only 100 kcal would be available to the herbivores at the second trophic level, 10 kcal to the primary carnivores at the third level, and 1 kcal to the secondary carnivores at the fourth level. Thus, no matter how much energy is assimilated by the autotrophs at the first level of an ecosystem, the eventual number of trophic levels is limited by the laws which govern the transfer of energy. The number of links in most natural food chains is four.

The relationships between trophic levels has sometimes been compared to a pyramid, with a broad base which narrows to an apex. Trophic levels represent successively narrowing sections of the pyramid. These pyramids can be described in terms of the number of organisms at each trophic level. This was first proposed by Charles Elton, who observed that the number of plants usually exceeded the number of herbivores, which in turn exceeded the number of primary carnivores, and so on. Pyramids of number can be inverted, particularly at the base; an example of this would be the thousands of insects which might feed on a single tree. The pyramid-like relationship between trophic levels can also be expressed in terms of the accumulated weight of all living matter, known as **biomass**. Although upper-level consumers tend to be large, the population of organisms at lower trophic levels are usually much higher, resulting in a larger combined biomass. Pyramids of biomass are not normally inverted, though they can be under certain conditions. In aquatic ecosystems, the biomass of the primary producers may be less than that of the primary consumers because of the rate at which they are being consumed; **phytoplankton** can be eaten so rapidly that the biomass of **zooplankton** and other herbivores are greater at any particular time. The relationship between trophic levels can also described in terms of energy, but pyramids of energy cannot be inverted. There will always be more energy at the bottom than there is at the top.

Humans are the top consumer in many ecosystems, and they exert strong and sometimes damaging pressures on food chains. For example, **overfishing** or **overhunting** can cause a large drop in the number of animals, resulting in changes in the food-web interrelationships. On the other hand, overprotection of some animals like deer or moose can be just as damaging. Another harmful influence is that of **biomagnification**. Toxic chemicals such as **mercury** and **DDT** released into the **environment** tend to become more concentrated as they travel up the food chain. Some ecologists have proposed that the stability of ecosystems is associated with the complexity of the internal structure of the food web and that ecosystems with a greater number of interconnections are more stable. Although more studies must be done to test this hypothesis, we do know that food chains in constant environments tend to have a greater number of species and more trophic links, whereas food chains in unstable environments have fewer species and trophic links.

[*John Korstad and Douglas Smith*]

FURTHER READING

Hairston, N. G., F. E. Smith, and L. B. Slobodkin. "Community Structure, Population Control, and Competition." *American Naturalist* 94 (1960): 421-25.

Krebs, C. J. *Ecology: The Experimental Analysis of Distribution and Abundance.* 3rd ed. New York: Harper & Row, 1985.

Lindeman, R. L. "The Trophic-Dynamic Aspect of Ecology." *Ecology* 23 (1942): 399-418.

Food and Drug Administration

Founded in 1927, the Food and Drug Administration (FDA) is an agency of the Untied States **Public Health Service**. One of the nation's oldest consumer protection agencies, the FDA is charged with enforcing the Federal Food, Drug, and Cosmetics Act, and other related public health laws. The agency assesses risks to the public posed by foods, drugs, and cosmetics, as well as medical devices, blood, and medications such as insulin which are made from living organisms. It also tests food samples for contaminants, sets labeling standards, and monitors the public health effects of drugs given to animals raised for food.

To carry out its mandate of consumer protection, the FDA employs 1,100 investigators and inspectors and 2,100 scientists who collect domestic and imported product samples for examination by FDA scientists. The FDA has the power to remove from the market those foods, drugs, chemi-

cals, or medical devices it finds unsafe. The FDA often seeks voluntary recall of the product by manufacturers, but the agency can also stop sales and destroy products through court action. About 3,000 products a year are found to be unfit for consumers and are withdrawn from the marketplace based on FDA action. Also, about 30,000 import shipments each year are detained at the port of entry on FDA orders.

FDA scientists analyze samples of products to detect contamination, or review test results submitted by companies seeking agency approval for drugs, vaccines, food additives, dyes, and medical devices. The FDA also operates the National Center for Toxicological Research at Jefferson, Arkansas, which conducts research to investigate the biological effects of widely used chemicals. The Agency's Engineering and Analytical Center at Winchester, Massachusetts, tests medical devices, radiation-emitting products, and radioactive drugs. The Bureau of Radiological Health was formed in 1971 to protect against unnecessary human exposure to radiation from electronic products such as microwave ovens.

The FDA is one of several federal organizations that oversees the safety of **biotechnology**, such as the industrial use of microorganisms to processes waste and water products.

In 1996, when the FDA declared that cigarettes and smokeless tobacco are nicotine-delivery devices, it took responsibility for regulating those products under the authority of the Federal Food, Drug, and Cosmetics Act. With regard to these products, the FDA has issued federal mandates concerning sales to minors, sales from vending machines, and advertising campaigns.

Internet: http://www.fda.gov/. *See also* Center for Science in the Public Interest; Genetic engineering; Radiation exposure

[*Linda Rehkopf*]

FURTHER READING

Gibbons, A. "Can David Kessler Revive the FDA?" *Science* 252 (12 April 1991): 200-3.

Iglehart, J. K. "The Food and Drug Administration and Its Problems." *New England Journal of Medicine* 325 (18 July 1991): 217-20.

Food policy

Through a variety of agricultural, economic, and regulatory programs which support or direct policies related to the production and distribution of food, the United States government has a large influence on how agriculture business is conducted. The government's major impact on agriculture is the setting of prices and mandates regarding how land can be used by farmers that participate in government programs. These policies can also have a large impact on the adoption or use of alternative practices and technologies that may be more efficient and sustainable in the world marketplace.

In the past, farm commodity programs have had a large influence in the past on the kinds and amounts of crops grown as well as on the choice of management practices used to grow them. Prices under government commodity programs have often been above world market prices which meant that many farmers felt compelled to preserve or build their farm commodity program base acres, since acreage determines program eligibility and future income. These programs strongly influenced land-use decisions on about two-thirds of the harvested cropland in the United States.

Price and income support programs for major commodities also influence growers not in the programs. For example, pork producers are not a part of a government program, and in the past they have paid higher feed prices because of high price supports on production of feed grains. At other times, particularly after the Food Security Act of 1985, they benefited from policies resulting in lower food costs. So as the government changes policy in one area, there can be widespread indirect impacts in other areas. For example, the federal dairy termination program, which ran from 1985-87 was designed to reduce overproduction of milk. Those farmers who sold their milk cows and decided to produce hay for local cash markets caused a steep decline in the prices received by other established hay producers.

Federal policy evolved as a patchwork of individual programs, each created to address individual problems. There was not a coherent strategy to direct programs toward a common set of goals. Many programs such as **soil conservation** and export programs have had conflicting objectives, but attempts have now been made in the most current farm legislation to address some of these problems.

Government food policy has produced a wide variety of results. The policy has not only affected commodity prices and the level of output, but it has also shaped technological change, encouraged uneconomical capital investments in machinery and facilities, inflated the value of land, subsidized crop production practices that have led to resource degradation (such as **soil erosion** and surface and groundwater pollution), expanded the interstate highway system, financed **irrigation** projects, and promoted farm commodity exports. Together with other economic forces, government policy has had a far-reaching structural influence on agriculture, much of it unintended and unanticipated.

Federal commodity programs were put into place beginning in the 1930s, primarily with the Agriculture Adjustment Act of 1938. The purpose of these programs born out of the Depression was primarily to protect crop prices and farmer income which has been done by a number of programs over the years. A variety of methods have been used including setting prices, making direct payments to farmers, and subsidizing exports. However, by the mid-1980s and early 1990s, an increasing number of people felt that these programs impeded movement toward alternative types of agriculture, to the detriment of family farms and society in general.

Two components in particular were highlighted as being problems: base acre requirements and cross-compliance. All crop price and income support programs relied on the concept of an acreage base planted with a given commodity that would produce a predictable yield. Most of this acreage was planted to maximize benefits and was based on a five-year average. A farmer knew that if he/she reduced their

acres for a given crop, they would not only lose the current year's benefits, but would also lose future benefits.

Cross-compliance was instituted in the Food Security Act of 1985. It was designed to control government payments and production by attaching financial penalties to the expansion of program crop base acres. It served as an effective financial barrier to diversification of crops by stipulating that to receive any benefits from an established crop acreage base, the farmer must not exceed his or her acreage base for any other program crop. This had a profound impact on farmers and crop growers since about 70% of the United States' cropland acres were enrolled in the programs.

In addition to citing these problem areas, critics of food policy programs argued that many farmers faced economic penalties for adopting beneficial practices such as crop rotation or strip cropping, practices that in general reduce soil erosion and improve environmental quality. The economic incentives built into commodity programs, for example, encouraged heavier use of **fertilizer**, **pesticide**s, and irrigation. These programs also encouraged surplus production, subsidized inefficient use of inputs, and they resulted in increased government expenditures. Critics argued that the rules associated with these programs discouraged farmers from pursuing alternative practices or crops, or technologies that might have proved more effective in the long term or that were more environmentally friendly.

Critics also contend that much of the research conducted over the past 40 years has responded to the needs of farmers operating under a set of economic and policy incentives that encouraged high yields without regard to the long-term environmental impacts. As recently as the late 1980s and early 1990s, several **U.S. Department of Agriculture** research and education programs have been instituted to determine whether current levels of production can be maintained with reduced levels of fertilizers and pesticides, to examine more intensive management practices, to increase understanding of biological principles, and to improve profitability per unit of production with less government support. As the impacts of the alternative production systems on the environment are evaluated, it will be important to have policies in place that will allow the farmer to easily adopt those practices that increase efficiency and reduce impacts. In the most current farm bill (passed in 1996) there are provisions that change these commodity programs. Labeled the "right to farm provisions," these allow farmers to make decisions on what they grow and establish a phased seven-year reduction in price supports. Critics have said that, rather than helping the family farm, this will simply cause a continued erosion in the number of family farms. The final results of this policy shift will become apparent over the next decade.

Food quality and safety are major concerns addressed as a part of federal policy. Programs addressing these concerns are primarily designed to prevent health risks and acute illnesses from chemical and microbial contaminants in food. Supporters say that this has provided the country with the safest food supply in the world. However, critics contend that a number of regulations do not enhance quality or safety and put farmers that use or would adopt alternative agricultural practices at a disadvantage. Several examples can be cited. Critics of government food policy point out that until recently, meat grading standards awarded producers of fatty beef which has been linked to the increased likelihood of heart disease.

The use of pesticides provides another example. The Environmental Protection Agency establishes pesticide residual tolerance levels in food which are monitored for compliance. For some types of risk, **cancer** in particular, there is a great deal of uncertainty, and critics point out which cosmetic standards that increase prices for fruits and vegetables may encourage higher risks of disease among consumers. Also, certain poultry slaughter practices can result in microbiological contamination. Of particular concern is salmonella food poisoning which has become widespread.

Government food policy heavily influences on-farm decision making. In some cases one part of the policy has negative or unintended consequences for another policy or segment of farmers. As we look to the future, the struggle will be to continue to provide a coherent, coordinated policy. The recent changes in policy will need to be evaluated from the standpoint of sustainability and environmental impacts.

[*James L. Anderson*]

FURTHER READING

Alternative Agriculture. Board on Agriculture, National Research Council., Washington, D.C.: National Academy Press, 1989.

Agriculture and the Environment. The 1991 Yearbook of Agriculture. U.S. Government Printing Office. Washington, D.C.

Food waste

Waste food from residences, grocery stores, and food services accounts for nearly seven percent of the **municipal solid waste** stream. The per capita amount of food waste in municipal solid waste has been declining since 1960 due to increased use of **garbage** disposals and increased consumption of processed foods. Food waste ground in garbage disposals goes into sewer systems and thus ends up in **wastewater**. Waste generated by the food processing industry is considered to be industrial waste, and is not included in municipal solid waste estimates.

Waste from the food processing industry includes: vegetables and fruits unsuitable for canning or freezing; vegetable, fruit and meat trimmings; and pomace from juice manufacturing. Vegetable and fruit processing waste is sometimes used as animal feed and waste from meat and seafood processing can be composted. Liquid waste from juice manufacturing can be applied to cropland as a **soil** amendment. Much of the waste generated by all types of food processing is wastewater due to such processes as washing, peeling, blanching, and cooling. Some food industries recycle wastewaters back into their processes, but there is potential for more of this wastewater to be reused.

Grocery stores generate food waste in the form of lettuce trimmings, excess foliage, unmarketable produce, and meat trimmings. Waste from grocery stores located in rural areas is often used as hog or cattle feed, whereas grocery waste in urban areas is usually ground in garbage disposals. There is potential for more urban grocery store waste to be either used on farms or composted, but lack of storage space, odor, and pest problems prevent most of this waste from being recycled.

Restaurants and institutional cafeterias are the major sources of food service industry waste. In addition to food preparation wastes, they also generate large amounts of cooking oil and grease waste, post-consumer waste (uneaten food), and surplus waste. In some areas small amounts of surplus waste is utilized by feeding programs, but most waste generated by food services goes to **landfill**s or into garbage disposals.

Most food waste is generated by sources other than households. However, a greater percentage of household food waste is disposed of because there is a higher rate of **recycling** of industrial and commercial food waste. Only a very small segment of households compost or otherwise recycle their food wastes.

[*Teresa C. Donkin*]

FURTHER READING

U. S. Environmental Protection Agency. Solid Waste and Emergency Response. *Characterization of Municipal Solid Waste in the United States: 1992 Update (Executive Summary).* Washington, DC: U. S. Government Printing Office, July 1992.

U. S. Environmental Protection Agency. Solid Waste and Emergency Response. *Characterization of Municipal Solid Waste in the United States: 1990 Update.* Washington, DC: U. S. Government Printing Office, June 1990.

Youde, J., and B. Prenguber. "Classifying the Food Waste Stream." *Biocycle* 32 (October 1991): 70-71.

Foreman, Dave (1947? -)

American radical environmentalist

Dave Foreman is a self-described radical environmentalist, Co-founder of **Earth First!**, and a leading defender of "**monkey-wrenching**" as a direct-action tactic to slow or stop **strip mining**, clear-cut logging of old-growth forests, the damming of wild rivers, and other environmentally destructive practices.

The son of a United States Air Force employee, Foreman traveled widely while growing up. In college he chaired the conservative Young Americans for Freedom and worked in the 1964 presidential election campaign of Senator Barry Goldwater. In the 1970s Foreman was a conservative Republican and moderate environmentalist who worked for the **Wilderness Society** in Washington, D.C. He came to believe that the petrochemical, logging, and mining interests were "extremists" in their pursuit of profit, and that government agencies—the **Forest Service**, the **Bureau of Land Management**, the **U.S. Department of Agriculture**, and others—were "gutless" and unwilling or unable to stand up to wealthy and powerful interests intent upon profiting from the destruction of American **wilderness**. Well-meaning moderate organizations like the **Sierra Club**, **Friends of the Earth**, and the Wilderness Society were, with few exceptions, powerless to prevent the continuing destruction. What was needed, Foreman reasoned, was an immoderate and unrespectable band of radical environmentalists like those depicted in **Edward Abbey**'s novel *The Monkey Wrench Gang* (1975) to take direct action against anyone who would destroy the wilderness in the name of "development." With several like-minded friends, Foreman founded Earth First!, whose motto is "No compromise in defense of Mother Earth."

From the beginning, Earth First! was unlike any other radical group. It did not issue manifestoes or publish position papers; it had "no officers, no bylaws or constitution, no incorporation, no tax status; just a collection of women and men committed to the Earth." Earth First!, Foreman wrote, "would be big enough to contain street poets and cowboy bar bouncers, agnostics and pagans, vegetarians and raw steak eaters, pacifists and those who think that turning the other cheek is a good way to get a sore face." Its weapons would include "monkey-wrenching," civil disobedience, music, "media stunts [to hold] the villains up to ridicule," and self-deprecating humor: "Radicals frequently verge toward a righteous seriousness. But we felt that if we couldn't laugh at ourselves we would be merely another bunch of dangerous fanatics who should be locked up (like the oil companies). Not only does humor preserve individual and group sanity, it retards hubris, a major cause of environmental rape, and it is also an effective weapon." But besides humor, Foreman called for "fire, passion, courage, and emotionalism.... We [environmentalists] have been too reasonable, too calm, too understanding. It's time to get angry, to cry, to let rage flow at what the human cancer is doing to Mother Earth."

In 1987 Foreman published *Ecodefense: A Field Guide to Monkeywrenching*, in which he described in detail the tools and techniques of environmental sabotage or monkey-wrenching. These techniques included "spiking" old-growth **redwoods** and Douglas firs to prevent loggers from felling them; "munching" logging roads with nails; sabotaging bulldozers and other earth-moving equipment; pulling up surveyors' stakes; and toppling high-voltage power lines. These tactics, Foreman said, were aimed at property, not at people. But critics quickly charged that loggers' lives and jobs were endangered by tree-spiking and other techniques that could turn deadly. Moderate or mainstream environmental organizations joined in condemning the confrontational tactics favored by Foreman and Earth First!

In his autobiography *Confessions of an Eco-Warrior* (1991) Foreman defends monkey-wrenching as an unfortunate tactical necessity that has achieved its primary purpose of attracting the attention of the American people and the media to the destruction of the nation's remaining wilderness. It also attracted the attention of the FBI, whose agents arrested Foreman at his home in 1989 for allegedly financing and encouraging *ecoteurs* (ecological saboteurs) to topple high-voltage power poles. Foreman was put on trial to face felony charges, which he denied. The charges were questioned when it was disclosed that an FBI informant had infiltrated Earth First! with the intention of framing Foreman and discrediting the organization. In a plea bargain,

Foreman pleaded guilty to a lesser charge and received a suspended sentence.

Foreman left Earth First! to found and direct The Wildlands Project in Tucson, Arizona. He continues to lecture and write about the protection of the wilderness.

[*Terence Ball*]

FURTHER READING

Foreman, D. *Confessions of an Eco-Warrior*. New York: Harmony Books, 1991.

———, and B. Haywood. *Ecodefense: A Guide to Monkeywrenching*. Tucson, AZ: Ned Ludd Books, 1985.

———. "Earth First!" In *Ideals and Ideologies: A Reader*, edited by T. Ball and R. Dagger. New York: Harper-Collins, 1991.

List, P. C., ed. *Radical Environmentalism: Philosophy and Tactics*. Belmont, CA: Wadsworth, 1993.

Manes, C. *Green Rage: Radical Environmentalism and the Unmaking of Civilization*. Boston: Little, Brown, 1990.

Scarce, R. *Eco-Warriors: Understanding the Radical Environmental Movement*. Chicago: Noble Press, 1990.

Forest and Rangeland Renewable Resources Planning Act (1974)

The Forest and Rangeland Renewable Resources Planning Act (RPA) was passed in response to the growing tension between the timber industry and environmentalists in the late 1960s and the early 1970s. These tensions can be traced to increased controversy over and restrictions on timber harvesting on the **national forest**s, due especially to **wilderness** designations and study areas and **clear-cutting**. These environmental restrictions, coupled with a dramatic increase in the price of timber in 1969, made Congress receptive to timber industry demands for a steadier supply of timber. Numerous bills addressing timber supply were introduced and debated in Congress, but none passed due to strong environmental pressure. A task force appointed by President Richard Nixon, the President's Panel on Timber and the Environment, delivered its recommendations in 1973, but these were geared toward dramatically increased harvests from the national forests, and hence were also unacceptable to environmentalists.

One aspect of the various proposals that proved to be acceptable to all interested parties—the timber industry, environmentalists, and the **Forest Service**—was increased long-range resource planning. Senator Hubert Humphrey of Minnesota drafted a bill creating such a program and helped guide it to passage in Congress. RPA planning is based on a two-stage process, with a document accompanying each stage. The first stage is called the *Assessment*, which is an inventory of the nation's forest and range resources (public and private). The second stage, which is based on the *Assessment*, is referred to as the *Program*. Based on the completed inventory, the Forest Service provides a plan for the use and development of the available resources. The *Assessment* is to be done every ten years. A *Program* based on the *Assessment* will be completed every five years. This planning was to be done by interdisciplinary teams and to incorporate widespread public involvement.

The RPA was quite popular with the Forest Service since the plans generated through the process gave the agency a solid foundation to base its budget requests on, increasing the likelihood of increased funding. This has proved to be successful, as the Forest Service budget increased dramatically in 1977, and the agency has fared much better than other resource agencies in the 1980s and 1990s.

The RPA was amended by the **National Forest Management Act** of 1976. Based on this law, in addition to the broad national planning mandated in the 1974 law, an *Assessment* and *Program* was required for each unit of the national forest system. This has allowed the Forest Service to use the plans to help shield itself from criticism. Since these plans address all uses of the forests, and make budget recommendations for these uses, if Congress does not fund these recommendations, the Forest Service can point to Congress as the culprit. However, the plans have also been more visible targets for interest group criticism.

Overall, the RPA has met with mixed results. The Forest Service has received increased funds and the planning process has been expanded to each national forest unit, but planning at such a scale is a difficult task. The act has also led to increased controversy and to increased bureaucracy. Perhaps most importantly, planning cannot solve a problem based on conflicting values, commodity use versus forest preservation, which is at the heart of **forest management** policy. *See also* Old-growth forest

[*Christopher McGrory Klyza*]

FURTHER READING

Clary, D. A. *Timber and the Forest Service.* Lawrence: University Press of Kansas, 1986.

Dana, S. T., and S. K. Fairfax. *Forest and Range Policy.* 2nd ed. New York: McGraw-Hill, 1980.

Stairs, G. R., and T. E. Hamilton, eds. *The RPA Process: Moving Along the Learning Curve.* Durham, NC: Center for Resource and Environmental Policy Research, Duke University.

Forest decline

In recent decades there have been observations of widespread declines in vigor and **dieback** of mature forests in many parts of the world. In many cases, **pollution** may be a factor contributing to forest decline, for example in regions where air quality is poor because of acidic deposition or contamination with **ozone**, **sulfur dioxide**, **nitrogen** compounds, or metals. However, forest decline also occurs in some places where the air is not polluted, and in these cases it has been suggested that the phenomenon is natural.

Forest decline is characterized by a progressive, often rapid deterioration in the vigor of trees of one or several **species**, sometimes resulting in mass mortality (or dieback) within stands over a large area. Decline often selectively affects mature individuals, and is thought to be triggered by a particular stress or a combination of stressors, such as severe weather, **nutrient** deficiency, **toxic substance**s in **soil**, and **air pollution**. According to this scenario, excessively stressed trees suffer a large decline in vigor. In this weakened condition, trees are relatively vulnerable to lethal attack by insects and microbial **pathogen**s. Such secondary agents may not be so harmful to vigorous individuals, but they can cause the death of severely stressed trees.

The preceding is only a hypothetical etiology of forest dieback. It is important to realize that although the occurrence and characteristics of forest decline can be well documented, the primary environmental variable(s) that triggers the decline disease are not usually known. As a result, the etiology of the decline syndrome is often attributed to a vague but unsubstantiated combination of biotic and abiotic factors.

The symptoms of decline differ among tree species. Frequently observed effects include: (1) decreased productivity; (2) chlorosis, abnormal size or shape, and premature abscission of foliage; (3) a progressive death of branches that begins at the extremities and often causes a "stag-headed" appearance; (4) root dieback; (5) an increased frequency of secondary attack by fungal pathogens and defoliating or wood-boring insects; and (6) ultimately mortality, often as a stand-level dieback.

One of the best-known cases of an apparently natural forest decline, unrelated to human activities, is the widespread dieback of birches that occurred throughout the northeastern United States and eastern Canada from the 1930s to the 1950s. The most susceptible species were yellow (*Betula alleghaniensis*) and paper birch (*B. papyrifera*), which were affected over a vast area, often with extensive mortality. For example, in 1951 at the time of peak dieback in Maine, an estimated 67 percent of the birch trees had been killed. In spite of considerable research effort, a single primary cause has not been determined for birch dieback. It is known that a heavy mortality of fine roots usually preceded deterioration of the above-ground tree, but the environmental cause(s) of this effect are unknown, although deeply frozen soils caused by a sparse winter snow cover are suspected as being important. No biological agent was identified as a primary predisposing factor, although fungal pathogens and insects were observed to secondarily attack weakened trees and cause their death.

Another apparently natural forest decline is that of ohia (*Metrosideros polymorpha*), an **endemic species** of tree usually occurring in monospecific stands, that dominates the native forest of **Hawaiian Islands**. There are anecdotal accounts of events of widespread mortality of ohia extending back at least a century, but the phenomenon is probably more ancient than this. The most recent widespread decline began in the late 1960s and resulted in about 200 square miles (50,000 hectares) of forest with symptoms of ohia decline in a 1982 survey of 308 square miles (76,900 hectares). In most declining stands only the canopy individuals were affected. Understory saplings and seedlings were not in decline, and in fact were released from competitive stresses by dieback of the overstory.

An hypothesis to explain the cause of ohia decline has been advanced by D. Mueller-Dombois and co-workers, who believe that the stand-level dieback is caused by the phenomenon of "cohort senescence." This is a stage of the life history of ohia characterized by a simultaneously decreasing vigor in many individuals, occurring in old-growth stands. The development of senescence in individuals is governed by genetic factors, but the timing of its onset can be influenced by environmental stresses. The decline-susceptible, over mature, life history stage follows a more vigorous, younger, mature stage in an even-aged stand of individuals of the same generation (i.e., a cohort) that had initially established following a severe disturbance. In Hawaii, lava flows, events of deposition of volcanic ash, and hurricanes are natural disturbances that initiate succession. Sites disturbed in this way are colonized by a cohort of ohia individuals, which produce an even-aged stand. If there is no intervening catastrophic disturbance, the stand matures, then becomes senescent and enters a decline and dieback phase. The original stand is then replaced by another ohia forest comprised of an advance regeneration of individuals released from the understory. Therefore, according to the cohort senescence theory, the ohia dieback should be considered to be a characteristic of the natural population dynamics of the species.

Other forest declines are occurring in areas where the air is contaminated by various potentially toxic **chemicals**, and these cases might be triggered by air pollution. In North America, prominent declines have occurred in ponderosa pine (*Pinus ponderosa*), red spruce (*Picea rubens*) and sugar maple (*Acer saccharum*). In western Europe, Norway spruce (*Picea abies*) and beech (*Fagus sylvatica*) have been severely affected.

The primary cause of the decline of ponderosa pine in stands along the western slopes of the mountains of southern California is believed to be the toxic effects of **ozone**. Ponderosa pine is susceptible to the effects of this gas at the concentrations that are commonly encountered in the declining stands, and the symptomalogy of damage is fairly clear.

In the other cases of decline noted above that are putatively related to air pollution, the evidence so far is less convincing. The recent forest damage in Europe has been described as a "new" decline syndrome that may in some way be triggered by stresses associated with air pollution. Although the symptoms appear to be similar, the "new" decline is believed to be different from diebacks that are known to have occurred historically and are believed to have been natural. The modern decline syndrome was first noted in fir (*Abies alba*) in Germany in the early 1970s. In the early 1980s a larger-scale decline was apparent in Norway spruce, the most commercially-important species of tree in the region, and in the mid 1980s decline became apparent in beech and oak (*Quercus* spp.).

Decline of this type has been observed in countries throughout Europe, extending at least to western Russia. The decline has been most intensively studied in Germany, which has many severely damaged stands, although a widespread dieback has not yet occurred. Decline symptoms are variable in the German stands, but in general: (1) mature stands older than about 60 years tend to be more severely affected; (2) dominant individuals are relatively vulnerable; and (3) individuals located at or near the edge of the stand are

more-severely affected, suggesting that a shielding effect may protect trees in the interior. Interestingly, epiphytic **lichens** often flourish in badly damaged stands, probably because of a greater availability of light and other resources caused by the diminished cover of tree foliage. In some respects this is a paradoxical observation, since lichens are usually hypersensitive to air pollution, especially toxic gases.

From the information that is available, it appears that the "new" forest decline in Europe is triggered by a variable combination of environmental stresses. The weakened trees then decline rapidly, and may die as a result of attack by secondary agents such as fungal disease or insect attack. Suggestions of the primary inducing factor include gaseous air pollutants, **acidification**, toxic metals in soil, nutrient imbalance, and a natural climatic effect, in particular **drought**. However, there is not yet a consensus as to which of these interacting factors is the primary trigger that induces forest decline in Europe, and it is possible that no single stress will prove to be the primary cause. In fact, there may be several "different" declines occurring simultaneously in different areas.

The declines of red spruce and sugar maple in eastern North America involve species that are long-lived and shade-tolerant, but shallow-rooted and susceptible to drought. The modern epidemic of decline in sugar maple began in the late 1970s and early 1980s, and has been most prominent in Quebec, Ontario, New York, and parts of New England. During the late 1980s and early 1990s, the decline appeared to reverse, and most stands became more healthy. The symptoms are similar to those described for an earlier dieback, and include abnormal coloration, size, shape, and premature abscission of foliage, death of branches from the top of the tree downward, reduced productivity, and death of trees. There is a frequent association with the pathogenic fungus *Armillaria mellea*, but this is believed to be a secondary agent that only attacks weakened trees. Many declining stands had recently been severely defoliated by the forest tent caterpillar (*Malacosoma disstria*), and many stands were tapped each spring for sap to produce maple sugar. Because the declining maple stands are located in a region subject to a high rate of atmospheric deposition of acidifying substances, this has been suggested as a possible predisposing factor, along with soil acidification and mobilization of available **aluminum**. Natural causes associated with **climate**, especially drought, have also been suggested. However, little is known about the modern sugar maple decline, apart from the fact that it occurred extensively; no conclusive statements can yet be made about its causal factor(s).

The stand-level dieback of red spruce has been most frequent in high-elevation sites of the northeastern United States, especially in upstate New York, New England, and the mid- and southern-Appalachian states. These sites are variously subject to acidic precipitation (mean annual **pH** about 4.0-4.1), to very acidic fog water (pH as low as 3.2-3.5), to large depositions of sulfur and nitrogen from the atmosphere, and to stresses from metal toxicity in acidic soil.

Declines of red spruce are anecdotally known from the 1870s and 1880s in the same general area where the modern decline is occurring. Up to one-half of the mature red spruce in the Adirondacks of New York was lost during that early episode of dieback, and there was also extensive damage in New England. As with the European forest decline, the "old" and "new" episodes appear to have similar symptoms, and it is possible that both occurrences are examples of the same kind of disease.

The hypotheses suggested to explain the initiation of the modern decline of red spruce are similar to those proposed for European forest decline. They include acidic deposition, soil acidification, aluminum toxicity, drought, winter injury exacerbated by insufficient hardiness due to nitrogen fertilization, **heavy metals** in soil, nutrient imbalance, and gaseous air pollution. Climate change, in particular a long term warming that has occurred subsequent to the end of the Little Ice Age in the early 1800s, may also be important.

At present, not enough is known about the etiology of the forest declines in Europe and eastern North America to allow an understanding of possible role(s) of air pollution and of natural environmental factors. This does not necessarily mean that air pollution is not involved. Rather, it suggests that more information is required before any conclusive statements can be made regarding the causes and effects of the phenomenon of forest decline. *See also* Forest management

[*Bill Freedman*]

FURTHER READING

Barnard, J. E. "Changes in Forest Health and Productivity in the United States and Canada." In *Acidic Deposition: State of Science and Technology*. Vol. 3, *Terrestrial, Materials, Health, and Visibility Effects*. Washington DC: U. S. Government Printing Office, 1990.

Freedman, B. *Environmental Ecology*. San Diego: Academic Press, 1989.

Mueller-Dombois, D. "Natural Dieback in Forests." *Bioscience* 37 (1987): 575-583.

Forest management

The question of how we should use forest resources goes beyond the science of growing and harvesting trees; forest management must solve the problems of balancing economic, aesthetic, and biological value to entire **ecosystem**s. The earliest forest managers in North America were native peoples, who harvested trees for building and burned forests to make room for grazing animals. But many native populations were wiped out by European diseases soon after Europeans arrived. By the mid-nineteenth century, it became apparent to many Americans that **overharvesting** of timber along with wasteful practices, such as uncontrolled burning of logging waste, was denuding forests and threatening future ecological and economic stability. The **Forest Service** (established in 1905) began studying ways to preserve forest resources for their economic as well as aesthetic, recreational, and **wilderness** value.

From the 1600s to 1820s, 370 million acres (150 million ha) of forests—about 34 percent of the U.S. total— were cleared, leaving about 730 million acres (296 million ha)

today. Only 10 to 15 percent of the forests have never been cut. Many previously harvested areas, however, have been replanted and the annual growth now exceeds harvest overall. But the nature of the forests has been altered, many believe for the worse. If logging of **old-growth forest**s were to continue at the rate maintained during the 1980s, all remaining unprotected stands would be gone by 2015. Some 33,000 timber-related jobs could also be lost during that time, not just from environmental protection but also from overharvesting, increased mechanization, and increasing reliance on foreign processing of whole logs cut from private lands. Recent federal and court decisions, most notably to protect the **northern spotted owl** in the United States, have slowed the pace of old-growth harvesting and for now has put more old forests under protection. But the questions of how to use forest resources is still under fierce debate.

For decades, **clear-cutting** of tracts has been the standard forestry management practice. Favored by timber companies, clear-cutting takes virtually all material from a tract. But clear-cutting has come under increasing criticism from environmentalists, who point out that the practice replaces mixed-age, biologically diverse forests with single-age, single or few **species** plantings. Clear-cutting also relies heavily on roads to haul out timber, causing root damage, **topsoil erosion**, and **siltation** of streams. Industry standards such as "best management practices (BMPs)" prevent most erosion and siltation by keeping roads away from stream beds. But BMPs only address **water quality**. Clear-cutting also removes small trees, snags, boles, and woody debris that are important to invertebrates and **fungi**.

Rather than focusing on what is removed from a forest, sustainable forest management focuses on what is left behind. In sustainable forestry, tracts are never clear-cut: instead, individual trees are selected and removed to maintain diversity and health of the remaining ecosystem. Such methods avoid artificial replanting, **herbicide**s, insecticides, and **fertilizer**s. However, much debate remains on which trees and how many are chosen for harvesting under sustainable forestry.

In a new management style known most commonly as new forestry, 85 to 90 percent of trees on a site are harvested, and the land is left alone for decades to recover. Proponents say this method would cut down on erosion and increase diversity left behind on a tract, especially where one or two species dominate. The Forest Service and some Northwest states are studying new forestry, but environmentalists say too little is known about its effects on old-growth stands to use the practice. Timber companies say more and larger tracts would have to be harvested under new forestry to meet demand.

Those who make their living from America's forests, and those who place value on the biological ecosystems they support, must resolve the debate on how to best preserve our forests. One-third of forest resources now come from Forest Service lands, and the debate is an increasingly public one, involving interests ranging from the **Sierra Club** and sporting clubs to the **Environmental Protection Agency (EPA)**, the Agriculture Department (and its largest agency, the Forest Service), and timber companies and their employees.

The future of our forests depends on balancing real short-term needs with the high price of long-term forest health.

[*L. Carol Ritchie*]

FURTHER READING

Franklin, K. "Timber! The Forest Disservice." *The New Republic* 200 (2 January 1989): 12-14.

Gillis, A. M. "The New Forestry: An Ecosystem Approach to Land Management." *BioScience* 40 (September 1990): 558-62.

Lansky, M. *Beyond the Beauty Strip: Saving What's Left of Our Forests.* Gardiner, ME: Tilbury House Publishers, 1992.

McLean, H. E. "Paying the Price for Old Growth." *American Forests* 97 (September-October 1991): 22-25.

Steen, H. K. "Americans and Their Forests: A Love-Hate Story." *American Forests* 98 (September-October 1992): 18-20.

Forest Service

The **national forest** system in the United States must be considered one of the great success stories of the **conservation** movement. This remains true despite the continual controversies that seem to accompany administration of national forest lands by the United States Forest Service.

The roots of the Forest Service began with the appointment in 1876 of Franklin B. Hough as a "forestry agent" in the **U.S. Department of Agriculture** to gather information about the nation's forests. Ten years later, Bernhard E. Fernow was appointed chief of a fledgling Division of Forestry. Part way through Fernow's tenure, Congress passed the Forest Reserve Act of 1891, which authorized the president to withdraw lands from the public domain to establish federal forest reserves. The public lands were to be administered, however, by the General Land Office in the **U.S. Department of the Interior**.

Gifford Pinchot succeeded Fernow in 1899 and was Chief Forester when President **Theodore Roosevelt** approved the transfer of 63 million acres (25 million ha) of forest reserves into the Department of Agriculture in 1905. That same year, the name of the Bureau of Forestry was changed to the United States Forest Service. Two years later, the reserves were redesignated national forests.

The Forest Service today is organized into four administrative levels: the office of the Chief Forester in Washington, D.C.; nine regional offices; 155 national forests; and 637 ranger districts. The Forest Service also administers twenty national **grasslands**. In addition, a research function is served by a forest products laboratory in Madison, Wisconsin, and eight other field research stations.

These lands are used for a wide variety of purposes and given official statutory status with the passage of the **Multiple Use-Sustained Yield Act** of 1960. That act officially listed five uses—timber, water, range, **wildlife**, and **recreation**—to be administered on national forest lands. **Wilderness** was later included. Forest Service now administers more than 34 million acres (14 million ha) in 387 units of the wilderness preservation system.

Despite a professionally trained staff and a sustained spirit of public service, Forest Service administration and management of national forest lands has been controversial from the beginning. The agency has experienced repeated attempts to transfer it to the Department of the Interior (or once to a new Department of Natural Resources); its authority to regulate grazing and timber use, including attempts to transfer national forest lands into private hands, has been frequently challenged and some of the Service's management policies have been the center of conflict. These policies have included **clear-cutting** and "subsidized" logging, various recreation uses, preservation of the **northern spotted owl**, and the cutting of **old-growth forest**s in the Pacific Northwest.

[*Gerald L. Young*]

FURTHER READING

Clary, D. A. *Timber and the Forest Service.* Lawrence: University Press of Kansas, 1986.

O'Toole, R. *Reforming the Forest Service.* Washington, DC: Island Press, 1988.

Steen, H. K. *The United States Forest Service: A History.* Seattle: University of Washington Press, 1976.

———. *The Origins of the National Forests.* Durham, NC: Forest History Society, 1992.

Forestry Canada

Forestry Canada is a federal government agency with a responsibility to conduct research and analyze information related to the sustainable use of the Canadian forest resource. Because of the importance of the forest industries to the Canadian economy, Forestry Canada is a department with its own minister in the federal cabinet.

In Canada, provincial and territorial governments have the responsibility for establishing allowable forest harvests and establishing criteria for acceptable management plans for provincial-crown land, which comprises the bulk of the economic forest resource of the nation. Forestry Canada integrates with relevant departments of the provinces and territories through the Canadian Council of Forest Ministers.

Forestry Canada operates six forest research centers in the regions of Canada, as well as two research institutes: the Petawawa National Forestry Institute at Chalk River, Ontario, and the Forest Pest Management Institute at Sault Ste. Marie, Ontario. Collectively, these institutions and their staff comprise the major force in forestry-related research in Canada.

The Government of Canada has committed to the practice of ecologically sustainable forestry, and Forestry Canada works with other levels of government, industry, educational institutions, and the public towards this end.

Research programs within Forestry Canada are diverse, and include activities related to tree anatomy, physiology, and productivity, techniques of **biomass** and stand inventory, determination of site quality, and research of forest harvesting practices, management practices aimed at increasing productivity and economic value, and forest **pest** management.

Forestry Canada also supports much of the **forest management** and research conducted within each of the provinces and territories, through joint federal-provincial Forest Development Agreements. Forestry Canada also supports much of the forestry research conducted at Canadian universities through research contracts and joint-awards programs with other government agencies and industry.

An important initiative, begun in 1992, is the Model Forest Program under Canada's *Green Plan*. The intent of this program is to provide substantial support for innovative forest management and research, conducted by integrated teams of partners involving industry, all levels of government, universities, non-government organizations, woodlot owners, and other groups and citizenry. A major criterion for success in the intense competition for funds towards a model forest is that the consortium of proponents demonstrate a vision of ecologically sustainable forest management, and a likely capability of achieving that result. *See also* Environment Canada; Forest decline

[*Bill Freedman*]

FURTHER READING

The State of Canada's Forests, 1991. Second Report to Parliament. Ottawa: Forestry Canada, 1992.

Forests

See **Coniferous forest; Deciduous forest; Hubbard Brook Experimental Forest; National forest; Old-growth forest; Rain forest; Taiga; Temperate rain forest; Tropical rainforest**

Fossey, Dian (1932-1985)

American primatologist

Dian Fossey is remembered by her fellow scientists as the world's foremost authority on mountain gorillas. But to the millions of wildlife conservationists who came to know Fossey through her articles and book, she will always be remembered as a martyr. Throughout the nearly 20 years she spent studying mountain gorillas in central Africa, the American primatologist tenaciously fought the poachers and bounty hunters who threatened to wipe out the endangered primates. She was brutally murdered at her research center in 1985 by what many believe was a vengeful poacher.

Fossey's dream of living in the wilds of Africa dates back to her lonely childhood in San Francisco. She was born

Dian Fossey photographing mountain gorillas in Zaire.

in 1932, the only child of George, an insurance agent, and Kitty, a fashion model, (Kidd) Fossey. The Fosseys divorced when Dian was 6 years old. A year later, Kitty married a wealthy building contractor named Richard Price. Price was a strict disciplinarian who showed little affection for his stepdaughter. Although Fossey loved animals, she was allowed to have only a goldfish. When it died, she cried for a week.

Fossey began her college education at the University of California at Davis in the preveterinary medicine program. She excelled in writing and botany, she failed chemistry and physics. After two years, she transferred to San Jose State University, where she earned a bachelor of arts degree in occupational therapy in 1954. While in college, Fossey became a prize-winning equestrian. Her love of horses in 1955 drew her from California to Kentucky, where she directed the occupational therapy department at the Kosair Crippled Children's Hospital in Louisville.

Fossey's interest in Africa's gorillas was aroused through primatologist George Schaller's 1963 book, *The Mountain Gorilla: Ecology and Behavior.* Through Schaller's book, Fossey became acquainted with the largest and rarest of three subspecies of gorillas, *Gorilla gorilla beringei.* She learned that these giant apes make their home in the mountainous forests of Rwanda, Zaire and Uganda. Males grow up to 6 ft (1.8 m) tall and weigh 400 lbs (182 kg) or more. Their arms span up to 8 ft (2.4 m). The smaller females weigh about 200 lbs (91 kg).

Schaller's book inspired Fossey to travel to Africa to see the mountain gorillas in their homeland. Against her family's advice, she took out a three-year bank loan for $8,000 to finance the seven-week safari. While in Africa,

Fossey met the celebrated paleoanthropologist **Louis Leakey**, who had encouraged **Jane Goodall** in her research of chimpanzees in Tanzania. Leakey was impressed by Fossey's plans to visit the mountain gorillas.

Those plans were nearly destroyed when she shattered her ankle on a fossil dig with Leakey. But just two weeks later, she hobbled on a walking stick up a mountain in the Congo (now Democratic Republic of the Congo) to her first encounter with the great apes. The sight of six gorillas set the course for her future. "I left Kabara (gorilla site) with reluctance but with never a doubt that I would, somehow, return to learn more about the gorillas of the misted mountains," Fossey wrote in her book, *Gorillas in the Mist*.

Her opportunity came three years later, when Leakey was visiting Louisville on a lecture tour. Fossey urged him to hire her to study the mountain gorillas. He agreed, if she would first undergo a preemptive appendectomy. Six weeks later, he told her the operation was unnecessary; he had only been testing her resolve. But it was too late. Fossey had already had her appendix removed.

The L.S.B. Leakey and the Wilkie Brothers foundations funded her research, along with the National Geographic Society. Fossey began her career in Africa with a brief visit to Jane Goodall in Tanzania to learn the best methods for studying primates and collecting data.

She set up camp early in 1967 at the Kabara meadow in Zaire's Parc National des Virungas, where Schaller had conducted his pioneering research on mountain gorillas a few years earlier. The site was ideal for Fossey's research. Because Zaire's park system protected them against human intrusion, the gorillas showed little fear of Fossey's presence. Unfortunately, civil war in Zaire forced Fossey to abandon the site six months after she arrived.

She established her permanent research site September 24, 1967, on the slopes of the Virunga Mountains in the tiny country of Rwanda. She called it the Karisoke Research Centre, named after the neighboring Karisimbi and Visoke mountains in the Parc National des Volcans. Although Karisoke was just five miles from the first site, Fossey found a marked difference in Rwanda's gorillas. They had been harassed so often by poachers and cattle grazers that they initially rejected all her attempts to make contact.

Theoretically, the great apes were protected from such intrusion within the park. But the government of the impoverished, densely populated country failed to enforce the park rules. Native Batusi herdsmen used the park to trap antelope and buffalo, sometimes inadvertently snaring a gorilla. Most trapped gorillas escaped, but not without seriously mutilated limbs that sometimes led to gangrene and death. Poachers who caught gorillas could earn up to $200,000 for one by selling the skeleton to a university and the hands to tourists. From the start, Fossey's mission was to protect the endangered gorillas from extinction--indirectly, by researching and writing about them, and directly, by destroying traps and chastising poachers.

Fossey focused her studies on some 51 gorillas in four family groups. Each group was dominated by a sexually mature silverback, named for the characteristic gray hair on its back. Younger, bachelor males served as guards for the silverback's harem and their juvenile offspring.

When Fossey began observing the reclusive gorillas, she followed the advice of earlier scientists by concealing herself and watching from a distance. But she soon realized that the only way she would be able to observe their behavior as closely as she wanted was by "habituating" the gorillas to her presence. She did so by mimicking their sounds and behavior. She learned to imitate their belches that signal contentment, their barks of curiosity and a dozen other sounds. To convince them she was their kind, Fossey pretended to munch on the foliage that made up their diet. Her tactics worked. One day early in 1970, Fossey made history when a gorilla she called Peanuts reached out and touched her hand. Fossey called it her most rewarding moment with the gorillas.

She endeared laymen to Peanuts and the other gorillas she studied through her articles in National Geographic magazine. The apes became almost human through her descriptions of their nurturing and playing. Her early articles dispelled the myth that gorillas are vicious. In her 1971 *National Geographic* article she described the giant beasts as ranking among "the gentlest animals, and the shiest." In later articles, Fossey acknowledged a dark side to the gorillas. Six of 38 infants born during a 13-year-period were victims of infanticide. She speculated the practice was a silverback's means of perpetuating his own lineage by killing another male's offspring so he could mate with the victim's mother.

Three years into her study, Fossey realized she would need a doctoral degree to continue receiving support for Karisoke. She temporarily left Africa to enroll at Cambridge University, where she earned her Ph.D. in zoology in 1974. In 1977, Fossey suffered a tragedy that would permanently alter her mission at Karisoke. Digit, a young male she had grown to love, was slaughtered by poachers. Walter Cronkite focused national attention on the gorillas' plight when he reported Digit's death on the CBS Evening News. Interest in gorilla conservation surged. Fossey took advantage of that interest by establishing the Digit Fund, a non-profit organization to raise money for anti-poaching patrols and equipment.

But the money wasn't enough to save the gorillas from poachers. Six months later, a silverback and his mate from one of Fossey's study groups were shot and killed defending their three-year-old son, who had been shot in the shoulder. The juvenile later died from his wounds. It was rumored that the gorilla deaths caused Fossey to suffer a nervous breakdown, although she denied it. What is clear is that the deaths prompted her to step up her fight against the Batusi poachers by terrorizing them and raiding their villages. "She did everything short of murdering those poachers," Mary Smith, senior assistant editor at National Geographic, told contributor Cynthia Washam in an interview. A serious calcium deficiency that causes bones to snap and teeth to rot forced Fossey to leave Africa in 1980. She spent her three-year sojourn as a visiting associate professor at Cornell University. Fossey completed her book, *Gorillas in the Mist*, during her stint at Cornell. It was published in 1983. Although some scientists criticized the book for its abundance of anecdotes and lack of scientific discussion, lay readers and reviewers received it warmly.

When Fossey returned to Karisoke in 1983, her scientific research was virtually abandoned. Funding had run dry. She was operating Karisoke with her own savings. "In the end, she became more of an animal activist than a scientist," Smith said. "Science kind of went out the window."

On Dec. 27, 1985, Fossey, 54, was found murdered in her bedroom at Karisoke, her skull split diagonally from her forehead to the corner of her mouth. Her murder remains a mystery that has prompted much speculation. Rwandan authorities jointly charged American research assistant Wayne McGuire, who discovered Fossey's body, and Emmanuel Rwelekana, a Rwandan tracker Fossey had fired several months earlier. McGuire maintains his innocence. At the urging of U.S. authorities, he left Rwanda before the charges against him were made public. He was convicted in absentia and sentenced to die before a firing squad if he ever returns to Rwanda.

Farley Mowat, the Canadian author of Fossey's biography, *Woman in the Mists,* believes McGuire was a scapegoat. He had no motive for killing her, Mowat wrote, and the evidence against him appeared contrived. Rwelekana's story will never be known. He was found dead after apparently hanging himself a few weeks after he was charged with the murder. Smith, and others, believe Fossey's death came at the hands of a vengeful poacher. "I feel she was killed by a poacher," Smith said. "It definitely wasn't any mysterious plot."

Fossey's final resting place is at Karisoke, surrounded by the remains of Digit and more than a dozen other gorillas she had buried. Her legacy lives on in the Virungas, as her followers have taken up her battle to protect the endangered mountain gorillas. The Dian Fossey Gorilla Fund, formerly the Digit Fund, finances scientific research at Karisoke and employs camp staff, trackers and anti-poaching patrols.

The Rwanda government, which for years had ignored Fossey's pleas to protect its mountain gorillas, on September 27, 1990, recognized her scientific achievement with the Ordre (sic) National des Grandes Lacs, the highest award it has ever given a foreigner. Gorillas in Rwanda are still threatened by cattle ranchers and hunters squeezing in on their habitat. According to the Colorado-based Dian Fossey Gorilla Fund, by the early 1990s, fewer than 650 mountain gorillas remained in Rwanda, Zaire, and Uganda. The Virunga Mountains is home to about 320 of them. Smith is among those convinced that the number would be much smaller if not for Fossey's 18 years of dedication to save the great apes. "Her conservation efforts stand above everything else (she accomplished at Karisoke)," Smith said. "She single-handedly saved the mountain gorillas."

[*Cynthia Washam*]

FURTHER READING

Brower, Montgomery, "The Strange Death of Dian Fossey," *People,* February 17, 1986, p. 46-54.

Fossey, D. *Gorillas in the Mist.* Houghton Mifflin Company, 1983.

Hayes, H.T.P., *The Dark Romance of Dian Fossey.* Simon and Schuster, 1990.

Mowat, Farley, *Woman in the Mists.* Warner Books, 1987.

Schoumatoff, Alex, *African Madness.* Alfred A. Knopf, 1988.

Fossil fuels

In early societies, wood or other biological fuels were the main energy source. Today in many non-industrial societies, they continue to be used widely. Biological fuels may be seen as part of a solar economy where energy is extracted from the sun in a way that makes them renewable. However industrialization requires energy sources at much higher density and these have generally been met through the use of fossil fuels such as **coal**, gas, or oil. In the twentieth century a number of other options such as nuclear or higher density renewable energy sources (wind power, hydro-electric power, etc.) have also been available. Nevertheless fossil fuels represent the principal source of energy for most of the industrialized world.

Fossil fuels are types of sedimentary organic materials, often loosely called bitumens, with asphalt, a solid, and **petroleum**, the liquid form. More correctly bitumens are sedimentary organic materials that are soluble in **carbon** disulfide. It is this that distinguishes asphalt from coal, which is an organic material largely insoluble in carbon disulfide.

Petroleum can probably be produced from any kind of organism, but the fact that these sedimentary deposits are more frequent in marine **sediment**s has suggested that oils arise from the fats and proteins in material deposited on the sea floor. These fats would be stable enough to survive the initial decay and burial but sufficiently reactive to undergo conversion to petroleum **hydrocarbons** at low temperature. Petroleum consists largely of paraffins or simple alkanes, with smaller amounts of napthenes. There are traces of aromatic compounds such as **benzene** present at the percent level in most crude oils. **Natural gas** is an abundant fossil fuel that consists largely of **methane** and ethane, although traces of higher alkanes are present. In the past, natural gas was regarded very much as a waste product of the petroleum industry and was simply burnt or flared off. Increasingly it is being seen as the favored fuel.

Coal, unlike petroleum, contains only a little **hydrogen**. Fossil evidence shows that coal is mostly derived from the burial of terrestrial vegetation with its high proportion of lignin and cellulose.

Most sediments contain some organic matter, and this can rise to many percent in shales. Here the organic matter can consist of both coals and bitumens. This organic material, often called sapropel, can be distilled to yield petroleum. **Oil shale**s containing the sapropel kerogen are very good sources of petroleum. Shales are considered to have formed where organic matter was deposited along with fine grain sediments, perhaps in fjords, where restricted circulation keeps the oxygen concentrations low enough to prevent decay of the organic material.

Fossil fuels are mined or pumped from geological **reservoir**s where they have been stored for long periods of time. The more viscous fuels, such as heavy oils, can be quite difficult to extract and refine, which has meant that the latter half of the twentieth century has seen lighter oils being favored. However, in recent decades natural gas has been popular because it is easy to pipe and has a somewhat less damaging impact on the **environment**. These fossil fuel reserves, although large, are limited and non-renewable. The total recoverable light to medium oil reserves are estimated at about 1.6 trillion barrels, of which about a third has already been used. Natural gas reserves are estimated at the equivalent of 1.9 trillion barrels of oil and about a sixth has already been used. Heavy oil and bitumen amount to about 0.6 and 0.34 trillion barrels, most of which has remained unutilized. The gas and lighter oil reserves lie predominantly in the eastern hemisphere, which accounts for the enormous petroleum industries of the Middle East. The heavier oil and bitumen reserves lie mostly in the western hemisphere. These are more costly to use and have been for the most part untapped. Of the 7.6-trillion ton coal reserve, only 2.5 percent has been used. Almost two thirds of the available coal is shared between China, the former Soviet Union, and the United States.

Petroleum is not burnt in its crude form but must be refined, which is essentially a distillation process that splits the fuel into batches of different volatility. The lighter fuels are used in **automobile**s, with heavier fuels used as diesel and fuel oils. Modern refining can use chemical techniques in addition to distillation to help make up for changing demands in terms of fuel type and volatility.

The **combustion** of fuels represents an important source of air pollutants. Although the combustion process itself can lead to the production of pollutants such as carbon or **nitrogen oxides**, it has often been the trace impurities in fossil fuels that have been the greatest source of **air pollution**. Natural gas is a much favored fuel because it has only traces of impurities such as hydrogen sulfide. Many of these impurities are removed from the gas by relatively simple scrubbing techniques, before it is distributed. Oil is refined, so although it contains more impurities than natural gas, these become redistributed in the refining process. Sulfur compounds tend to be found only in trace amounts in the light automotive fuels. Thus automobiles are only a minor source of **sulfur dioxide** in the atmosphere. Diesel oil can have as much as a percent of sulfur, and heavier fuel oils can have even more, so in some situations these can represent important sources of sulfur dioxide in the **atmosphere**. Oils also dissolve metals from the rocks in which they are present. Some of the organic compounds in oil have a high affinity for metals, most notably **nickel** and vanadium. Such metals can reach high concentration in oils, and refining will mean that most become concentrated in the heavier fuel oils. Combustion of fuel oil will yield ashes that contain substantial fractions of the trace metals present in the original oil. This means that an element like vanadium is a useful marker of fuel oil combustion.

Coal is often seen as the most polluting fuel because low grade coals can contain large quantities of ash, sulfur, and **chlorine**. However, it should be emphasized that the quanti-

ty of impurities in coal can vary widely, depending on where it is mined. The sulfur present in coal is found both as iron pyrites (inorganic) and bound up with organic matter. The nitrogen in coal is almost all organic nitrogen. Coal users are often careful to choose a fuel that meets their requirements in terms of the amount of ash, **smoke** or pollution risk it imposes. High rank coals such as **anthracite** have a high carbon content. They are mined in locations such as Pennsylvania and South Wales and contain little volatile matter and burn almost smokelessly. Much of the world's coal reserve is bituminous, which means that it contains about 20 to 25 percent volatile matter.

The fuel industry is often seen as responsible for pollutants and environmental risks that go beyond those produced by the combustion of its products. Mining and extraction processes result in spoil heaps, huge holes in open cast mining, and the potential for slumping of land (conventional mining). Petroleum refineries are large sources of hydrocarbons, although not usually the largest anthropogenic source of **volatile organic compound**s in the atmosphere. Refineries also release sulfur, carbon, and nitrogen oxides from the fuel that they burn. Liquid natural gas and **oil spills** are experienced both in the refining and transport of petroleum.

Being a solid, coal presents somewhat less risk when being transported, although wind-blown coal dust can cause localized problems. Coal is sometimes converted to coke or other refined products such as Coalite, a smokeless coal. These derivatives are less polluting, although much concern has been expressed about the pollution damage that occurs near the factories that manufacture them. Despite this, the conversion of coal to less polluting synthetic solid, and liquid and gaseous fuels would appear to offer much opportunity for the future.

One of the principal concerns about the current reliance on fossil fuels relates not so much to their limited supply, but more to the fact that combustion releases such large amounts of **carbon dioxide**. Our use of fossil fuels over the last century has increased the concentration of carbon dioxide in the atmosphere. Already there is mounting evidence that this has increased the temperature of the earth through an enhanced **greenhouse effect**.

[*Peter Brimblecombe*]

FURTHER READING

Campbell, I. M. *Energy and the Atmosphere*. New York: Wiley, 1986.

Fossil water

Water that occurs in an **aquifer** or **zone of saturation** protected or isolated from the current **hydrologic cycle**. This water, because it is old, does not have the levels of **chemicals** or contaminants used in of our industrialized society, and its unblemished nature often makes it prized drinking water. In other cases, however, these aquifers are so isolated and the original condition of the water is so high in inorganic salts that scientists have suggested using them for waste disposal or containment areas. *See also* Drinking-water supply; Groundwater; Hazardous waste siting; Water quality

Four Corners

The Hopi believe that the Four Corners—where Colorado, Utah, New Mexico and Arizona meet—is the center of the universe and holds all life on Earth in balance. It also has some of the largest deposits of **coal, uranium**, and **oil shale** in the world. According to the National Academy of Sciences the Four Corners is a "national sacrifice area." This ancestral home of the Hopi and Dineh (Navajo) people is the center of the most intense energy development in the United States. Traditional grazing and farm land are being swallowed up by uranium mines, coal mines, and **power plants**.

The Four Corners, sometimes referred to as the "joint-use area," is comprised of 1.8 million acres (729,000 ha) of high **desert** plateau where Navajo sheep herders have grazed their flocks on idle Hopi land for generations. In 1972 Congress passed Public Law (PL) 93-531, which established the Navajo/Hopi Relocation Commission who had the power to enforce livestock reduction and the removal of over 10,000 traditional Navajo and Hopi, the largest forced relocation within the United States since the Japanese internment during World War II. Elders of both Nations issued a joint statement that officially opposed the relocation:

> The traditional Hopi and Dineh (Navajo) realize that the so-called dispute is used as a disguise to remove both people from the JUA (joint use area), and for non-Indians to develop the land and mineral resources.... Both the Hopi and Dineh agree that their ancestors lived in harmony, sharing land and prayers for more than four hundred years ... and cooperation between us will remain unchanged.

The traditional Navajo and Hopi leaders have been replaced by Bureau of Indian Affairs (BIA) tribal councils. These councils, in association with the **U.S. Department of the Interior**, Peabody Coal, the Mormon Church, attorneys and public relation firms, created what is commonly known as the "Hopi-Navajo land dispute" to divide the joint-use area, so that the area could be opened up for energy development.

In 1964, 223 Southwest utility companies formed a consortium known as the Western Energy and Supply Transmission Associates (WEST) which includes water and power authorities on the West Coast as well as Four Corners area utility companies. WEST drafted plans for massive coal **surface mining** operations and six coal-fired, electricity-generating plants on Navajo and Hopi land. By 1966 John S. Boyden, attorney for the Bureau of Indian Affairs Hopi Tribal Council, secured lease arrangements with Peabody Coal to surface mine 58,000 acres (23,490 ha) of Hopi land

and contracted WEST to build the power plants. This was done despite objections by the traditional Hopi leaders and the self-sufficient Navajo shepherds. Later that same year Kennecott Copper, owned in part by the Mormon Church, bought Peabody Coal. Peabody supplies the Four Corners' power plant with coal. The plant burned 5 million tons of coal a year which is the equivalent of ten tons per minute. It emits over 300 tons of **fly ash** and other particles into the San Juan River Valley every day. Since 1968 the coal mining operations and the power plant have extracted over 60 million gallons (227 million liters) of water a year from the Black Mesa **water table**, which has caused extreme **desertification** of the area, causing the ground in some areas to sink by up to 12 feet (3.6 m).

The worst nuclear accident in American history occurred at Church Rock, New Mexico, on July 26, 1979, when a Kerr-McGee uranium **tailings pond** spilled over into the Rio Puerco. The spill contaminated drinking water from Church Rock to the Colorado River, over 200 miles (322 km) to the west. The mill tailings dam broke—two months prior to the break cracks in the dam structure were detected yet repairs were never made—and discharged over 100 million gallons (379 million liters) of highly radioactive water directly into the Rio Puerco River. The main source of potable water for over 1,700 Navahoes was contaminated. When Kerr-McGee abandoned the Shiprock site in 1980 they left behind 71 acres (29 ha) of "raw" uranium tailings, which retained 85 percent of the original radioactivity of the ore at the mining site. The tailings were at the edge of the San Juan River and have since contaminated communities located downstream.

What is the future of the Four Corners area, with its 100 plus uranium mines, uranium mills, five power plants, depleted **watershed** and radioactive contamination? One "solution" offered by the United States government is to zone the land into uranium mining and milling districts so as to forbid human habitation.

[*Debra Glidden*]

FURTHER READING

Garrity, M. "The U.S. Colonial Empire Is As Close As the Nearest Reservation." In *Trilateralism: The Trilateral Commission and Elite Planning For World Management.* Boston: South End Press, 1980.

Kammer, J. *The Second Long Walk: The Navajo-Hopi Land Dispute.* Albuquerque, NM: University of New Mexico Press, 1980.

Moskowitz, M. *Everybody's Business.* New York: Harper and Row, 1980.

Scudder, T., et al. *Expected Impacts of Compulsory Relocation on Navajos, with Special Emphasis on Relocation from the Former Joint Use Area Required by Public Law 93-531.* Binghamton, NY: Institute for Development of Anthropology, 1979.

Tso, H., and L. Shields. "Navajo Mining Operations: Early Hazards and Recent Interventions." *New Mexico Journal of Science* 20 (June 1980): 13.

Francis of Assisi, St. (1181/82-1226)

Italian saint

Born the son of a cloth merchant in the Umbrian region of Italy, Giovanni Francesco Bernardone became St. Francis of

Assisi, one of the most inspirational figures in Christian history. As a youth, Francis was entranced by the French troubadours, but then planned a military career. While serving in a war between Assisi and Perugia in 1202, he was captured and imprisoned for a year. He intended to return to combat when he was released, but a series of visions and incidents, such as an encounter with a leper, led him in a different direction.

This direction was toward Jesus. Francis was so taken with the love and suffering of Jesus that he set out to live a life of prayer, preaching, and poverty. Although he was not a priest, he began preaching to the townspeople of Assisi and soon attracted a group of disciples, which Pope Innocent III recognized in 1211, or 1212, as the Franciscan order. The order grew quickly, but Francis never intended to found and control a large and complicated organization. His idea of the Christian life led elsewhere, including a fruitless attempt to end the Crusades peacefully. In 1224 he undertook a 40-day fast at Mount Alverna, from which he emerged bearing stigmata—wounds resembling those Jesus suffered on the cross. He died in 1226 and was canonized in 1228.

Francis's unconventional life has made him attractive to many who have questioned the direction of their own societies. In recent years his rejection of warfare and material goods has brought him the title of "the hippie saint"; Leonardo Boff has seen him as a foreshadowing of liberation theology. **Lynn White** has proposed him as "a patron saint for ecologists."

There is no doubt that Francis loved **nature**. In his "Canticle of the Creatures," he praises God for the gifts, among others, of "Brother Sun," "Sister Moon," and "Mother Earth, Who nourishes and watches us. . . ." But this is not to say that Francis was a pantheist or nature worshipper. He loved nature not as a whole, but as the assembly of God's creations. As G. K. Chesterton remarked, Francis "did not want to see the wood for the trees. He wanted to see each tree as a separate and almost a sacred thing, being a child of God and therefore a brother or sister of man."

For White, Francis was "the greatest radical in Christian history since Christ" because he departed from the traditional Christian view in which humanity stands over and against the rest of nature—a view, White charges, that is largely responsible for current ecological crises. Against this view, Francis "tried to substitute the idea of the equality of all creatures, including man, for the idea of man's limitless rule of creation." *See also* Ecology; Environmental ethics; Environmentalism

[*Richard K. Dagger*]

FURTHER READING

Boff, L. *St. Francis: A Model for Human Liberation,* translated by J. W. Diercksmeier. New York: Crossroad, 1982.

Chesterton, G. K. *St. Francis of Assisi.* New York: Doubleday Image Books, 1990.

Cunningham, L., ed. *Brother Francis.* New York: Harper & Row, 1972.

White, L., Jr. "The Historical Roots of Our Ecological Crisis." *Science* 155 (10 March 1967): 1203-7.

Free riders

A free rider, in the broad sense of the term, is anyone who enjoys a benefit provided, probably unwittingly, by others. In the narrow sense, a free rider is someone who receives the benefits of a cooperative venture without contributing to the provision of those benefits. A person who does not participate in a cooperative effort to reduce **air pollution** by driving less, for instance, will still breathe cleaner air—and thus be a free rider—if the effort succeeds.

In this sense, free riders are a major concern of the theory of collective action. As developed by economists and social theorists, this theory rests on a distinction between private and public (or collective) goods. A public good differs from a private good because it is indivisible and nonrival. A public good, such as clean air or national defense, is indivisible because it cannot be divided among people the way food or money can. It is nonrival because one person's enjoyment of the good does not diminish anyone else's enjoyment of it. Smith and Jones may be rivals in their desire to win a prize, but they cannot be rivals in their desire to breathe clean air, for Smith's breathing clean air will not deprive Jones of an equal chance to do the same.

Problems arise when a public good requires the cooperation of many people, as in a campaign to reduce **pollution** or conserve resources. In such cases, individuals have little reason to cooperate, especially when cooperation is burdensome. After all, one person's contribution—using less **gasoline** or electricity, for example—will make no real difference to the success or failure of the campaign, but it will be a hardship for that person. So the rational course of action is to try to be a free rider who enjoys the benefits of the cooperative effort without bearing its burdens. If everybody tries to be a free rider, however, no one will cooperate and the public good will not be provided. If people are to prevent this from happening, some way of providing selective or individual incentives must be found, either by rewarding people for cooperating or punishing them for failing to cooperate.

The free rider problem posed by public goods helps to illuminate many social and political difficulties, not the least of which are environmental concerns. It may explain why voluntary campaigns to reduce driving and to cut energy use so often fail, for example. As formulated in **Garrett Hardin's Tragedy of the Commons**, moreover, collective action theory accounts for the tendency to use common resources—grazing land, fishing banks, perhaps the earth itself—beyond their **carrying capacity**. The solution, as Hardin puts it, is "mutual coercion, mutually agreed upon" to prevent the overuse and destruction of vital resources. Without such action, the desire to ride free may lead to irreparable ecological damage. *See also* Conservation; Economic growth and the environment; Environmental education; Environmental law; Green taxes; Recycling; Waste reduction

[*Richard K. Dagger*]

FURTHER READING

Hardin, G. "The Tragedy of the Commons." *Science* 162 (13 December 1968): 1243-48.

Hardin, R. *Collective Action*. Baltimore, MD: Johns Hopkins University Press, 1982.

Olson, M. *The Logic of Collective Action*. New York: Schocken Books, 1971.

Freon

The generic name for several **chlorofluorocarbons** (CFCs) widely used in refrigerators and air conditioners, including the systems in houses and cars. Freon—comprised of **chlorine**, fluorine, and **carbon** atoms—is a non-toxic gas at room temperature. It is environmentally significant because it is extremely long-lived in the atmosphere, with a typical residence time of 70 years. This long life-span permits CFCs to disperse, ultimately reaching the stratosphere 19 miles (30 kilometers) above the earth's surface. Here, high energy photons in sunlight break down freon, and chlorine atoms liberated during this process participate in other chemical reactions that consume **ozone**. The final result is to decrease the stratospheric ozone layer that shields the earth from damaging **ultraviolet radiation**. Under the 1987 **Montreal Protocol**, 31 industrialized countries agreed to phase out CFC freon production. Freon substitutes use bromine atoms to replace the chlorine atoms, providing a substitute refrigeration compound that appears less damaging, although considerably more expensive and less energy efficient.

Fresh water ecology

The study of fresh water **habitat**s is called **limnology**, coming from the Greek word *limnos*, meaning "pool, lake, or swamp." Fresh water habitats are normally divided into two groups: the study of standing bodies of water such as lakes and ponds (called lentic **ecosystem**s) and the study of rivers, streams, and other moving sources of water (called lotic ecosystems). Another important area that should be included is fresh water **wetlands**.

The historical roots of limnology go back to F. A. Forel, who studied Lake Geneva, Switzerland, in the late 1800s and E. A. Birge and C. Juday, who studied lakes in Wisconsin in the early 1900s. More recently, the modern "father" of limnology can arguably be attributed to G. Evelyn Hutchinson, who died in 1991 after teaching at Yale University for more than 40 years. Among his prolific writings are four treatises on limnology which offer the most detailed descriptions of lakes that have been published.

Fresh water ecology is an intriguing field because of the great diversity of aquatic habitats. For example, lakes can be formed in different ways: volcanic origin such as Crater Lake, Oregon; tectonic (earth movement) origin like **Lake Tahoe** in California/Nevada and **Lake Baikal** in Siberia; glacially-derived lakes like the **Great Lakes** or smaller kettle hole or cirque lakes; oxbow lakes which form as rivers change their meandering paths; and human-created reservoirs. Aquatic

habitats are strongly influenced by the surrounding **watershed**, and lakes in the same geographic area tend to be of the same origin and have similar water quality.

Lakes are characteristically non-homogeneous. Physical, chemical, and biological factors contribute to both horizontal and vertical zonations. For example, light penetration creates an upper photic (lighted) zone and a deeper aphotic (unlit) zone. **Phytoplankton** (microscopic algae such as diatoms, desmids, and filamentous algae) inhabit the photic zone and produce oxygen through **photosynthesis**. This creates an upper productive area called the trophogenic (productive) zone. The deeper area where respiration prevails is called the tropholytic (unproductive) zone. **Zooplankton** (microscopic invertebrates such as cladocerans, copepods, and rotifers) and nekton (free-swimming animals such as fish) inhabit both of these zones. The boundary area where oxygen produced from photosynthesis equals that consumed through respiration is called the compensation depth. Nearshore areas where light penetrates to the bottom and aquatic macrophytes such as cattails and bulrushes grow, are called the littoral zone. This is typically the most productive area, and it is more pronounced in ponds than in lakes. Open water areas are called the limnetic zone, where most plankton inhabit. Some species of zooplankton are found more concentrated in deeper waters during the day and in greater numbers in the upper waters during the night. One explanation for this vertical migration is that these zooplankton, often large and sometimes pigmented, are avoiding visually-feeding planktivorous fish. These zooplankton are thus able to feed on phytoplankton in the trophogenic zone during periods of darkness, and then swim to deeper waters during daylight hours. Phytoplankton are also adapted for existence in the limnetic zone. Some species are quite small in size (less than 20 microns in diameter and called nannoplankton), allowing them to be competitive at nutrient uptake due to their high surface-to-volume ratio. Other groups form large colonies, often with spines, lessening the negative impacts of herbivory and sinking. Blue-green algae produce oils that help them float on or near the water's surface. Some are able to fix atmospheric **nitrogen** (called nitrogen fixation), giving them a competitive advantage in low-nitrogen conditions. Other species of blue-greens produce toxic chemicals, making them inedible to herbivores. There have even been reports of cattle deaths following ingestion of water with dense growths of these algae.

Lakes can be isothermal (uniform temperature from top to bottom) during some times of the year, but during the summer months they are typically thermally stratified with an upper, warm layer called the epilimnion (upper lake), and a colder, deeper layer called the hypolimnion (lower lake). These zones are separated by the metalimnion, which is determined by the depths with a temperature change of more than 1°C per meter depth, called the thermocline. The summer temperature stratification creates a density gradient that effectively prevents mixing between zones.

Wind is another physical factor that influences aquatic habitats, particularly in lakes with broad surface areas exposed to the main direction of the wind, called fetch. Strong winds can produce internal standing waves called seiches that create a rocking motion in the water once the wind dies down. Other types of wind-generated water movements include Ekman spirals and Langmuir cells. Deep or chemically-stratified lakes that never completely mix are called meromictic. Lakes in tropical regions that mix several times a year are called polymictic. In regions with severe winters resulting in ice covering the surface of the lake, mixing normally occurs only during the spring and fall when the water is isothermal. These lakes are called dimictic, and the mixing process is called overturn. People living downwind of these lakes often notice a rotten egg smell caused by the release of hydrogen sulfide. This gas is a product of benthic (bottom-dwelling) bacteria that inhabit the anaerobic muds of productive lakes (discussed below in more detail).

Lakes that receive a low-nutrient input remain fairly unproductive, and are called oligotrophic (low nourished). These lakes typically have low concentrations of phytoplankton, with diatoms being the main representative. Moderately productive lakes are called mesotrophic. Eutrophic (well nourished) lakes receive more nutrient input and are therefore more productive. They are typically shallower than oligotrophic lakes and have more accumulated bottom sediments that often experience summer anoxia. These lakes have an abundance of algae, particularly blue-greens (Cynaobacteria) which are often considered nuisance algae because they float on the surface and out-compete the other algae for nutrients and light.

Most lakes naturally age and become more productive over time; however, large, deep lakes may remain oligotrophic. The maturing process is called eutrophication and it is regulated by the input of nutrients which are needed by the algae for growth. Definitive limnological studies done in the 1970s concluded that phosphorus is the key limiting nutrient in most lakes. Thus, the accelerated input of this chemical into streams, rivers, and eventually lakes by excess fertilization, **sewage** input (both human and animal), and erosion is called **cultural eutrophication**. Much debate and research has been spent on how to slow down or control this process. One interesting management tool is called biomanipulation, in which piscivorous (fish-eating) fish are added to lakes to consume planktivorous (plankton-eating) fish. Because the planktivores are visual feeders on the largest prey, this allows higher numbers of large zooplankton to thrive in the water, which consume more phytoplankton, particularly non-toxic blue-green algae. A more practical approach to controlling cultural eutrophication is by limiting the nutrient loading into our bodies of water. Although this isn't easy, we must consider ways of limiting excessive uses of fertilizers, both at home and on farms, as well as more effectively regulating the release of treated sewage into rivers and lakes, particularly those which are vulnerable to eutrophication. Another lake management tool is to aerate the bottom (hypolimnetic) water so that it remains oxygenated. This keeps iron in the oxidized state (Fe^{+3}), which chemically binds with phosphate (PO_4) and prevents it from being available for algal uptake. Lakes that have anoxic bottom water keep iron in the reduced state (Fe^{+2}), and

phosphate is released from the sediment into the water. Fall and spring turnover then returns this limiting nutrient to the photic zone, promoting high algal growth. When these organisms eventually die and sink to the bottom, decomposers use up more oxygen, and we get a "snow ball" effect. Thus, productive lakes can become more eutrophic with time, and may eventually develop into hypertrophic (overly productive) systems.

Lotic ecosystems differ from lakes and ponds in that currents are more of a factor and primary production inputs are generally external (allochthonous) instead of internal (autochthonous). Thus, a river or stream is considered a heterotrophic ecosystem along most of its length. Gradients in physical and chemical parameters also tend to be more horizontal than vertical in running water habitats and organisms living in lotic ecosystems are specially adapted for surviving in these conditions. For example, trout require higher amounts of dissolved oxygen, and are primarily found in relatively cold, fast-moving water with low nutrient input. Carp are able to tolerate warmer, slower, more productive bodies of running water. Darters are fish that quickly dart back and forth behind rocks in the bottom of fast-moving streams and rivers as they feed on aquatic insects. Many of these insects are shredders and **detritivores** on the organic material like leaves that enter the water. Other groups specialize by scraping algae and bacteria off rocks in the water.

Recently, ecologists have begun to take a greater interest in studying fresh water wetlands. These areas are defined as being inundated or saturated by surface or ground water for most of the year, and therefore having characteristic wetland vegetation. Although some people consider these areas a nuisance and prefer them being drained, ecologists realize that they are valuable habitats for migrating water fowl. They also serve as major "adsorptive" areas for nutrients, which are particularly useful around sewage **lagoon**s. We must therefore take greater care in preserving these habitats.

[John Korstad]

FURTHER READING

Horne, A. J., and C. R. Goldman. *Limnology*. New York: McGraw Hill, 1994.

Hutchinson, G.E. *A Treatise on Limnology*. vol. 1: *Geography, Physics, Chemistry*; vol. 2: *Introduction to Lake Biology and Limnoplankton*; vol. 3: *Limnological Botany*; vol. 4: *The Zoobenthos*. New York: Wiley; 1957, 1967, 1975, 1993.

Smith, R.L. *Ecology and Field Biology*, 4th ed. New York: Harper Collins, 1996.

Wetzel, R. *Limnology*, 2nd ed. Philadelphia: Saunders, 1983.

Friends of the Earth (Washington, D.C.)

Friends of the Earth (FOE) is a public interest environmental group committed to the **conservation**, restoration, and rational use of the **environment**. Founded by **David Brower** and other militant environmentalists in San Francisco in 1969, FOE works on the local, national, and international levels to prevent and reverse **environmental degradation**, and to promote the wise use of **natural resources**.

In the United States, FOE has a membership of 50,000, a staff of 40, and an annual budget of $3.4 million. Its particular areas of interest include **ozone layer depletion**, greenhouse effect, toxic chemical safety, **coal** mining, coastal and ocean **pollution**, the destruction of tropical forests, **groundwater** contamination, corporate accountability, and **nuclear weapons** production. In addition to its efforts to influence policy and increase public awareness of environmental issues, FOE's ongoing activities include the operation of the Take Back the Coast Project and the administration of the Oceanic Society. Over the years, FOE has published numerous books and reports on various topics of concern to environmentalists.

FOE was originally organized to operate internationally and now has national organizations in some 47 countries. In several of these, most notably the United Kingdom, FOE is considered to be the best-known and most effective **public interest group** concerned with environmental issues.

The organization has changed its strategies considerably over the years, and not without considerable controversy within its own ranks. Under Brower's leadership, FOE's tactics were media-oriented and often confrontational, sometimes taking the form of direct political protests, boycotts, sit-ins, marches, and demonstrations. Taking a **holistic approach** to the environment, the group argued that fundamental social change was required for lasting solutions to many environmental problems.

FOE eventually moved away from confrontational tactics and towards a new emphasis on lobbying and legislation, which helped provoke the departure of Brower and some of the group's more radical members. FOE began downplaying several of its more controversial stances (for example, on the control of nuclear weapons) and moved its headquarters from San Francisco to Washington, D.C. More recent controversies have concerned FOE's endorsement of so-called **green products** and its acceptance of corporate financial contributions.

FOE remains committed, however, to most of its original goals, even if it has foresworn its earlier illegal and disruptive tactics. Relying more on the technical competence of its staff and the technical rationality of its arguments than on idealism, FOE has been highly successful in influencing legislation and in creating networks of environmental, consumer, and human rights organizations worldwide. Its publications and educational campaigns have been quite effective in raising public consciousness of many of the issues with which FOE is concerned. Contact: Friends of the Earth, 218 D Street, SE, Washington, DC 20003; or Friends of the Earth International, P.O. Box 19199, 1000 GD Amsterdam, The Netherlands. Internet: http://www.essential.org/FOE/FOE.html.

[*Lawrence J. Biskowski*]

Frogs

Frogs are small amphibians of the order anura. The anuran group has nearly 2,700 species throughout the world and includes both frogs and toads. The etymology of the word *anura* means "without a tail," and the term applies to most adult frogs. The anura are distinguished from tailed amphibians (urodeles) such as salamanders because the latter retain a tail as an adult. The amphibian class contains another little known group of worm-like creatures of the tropics known as caecilians.

The northern leopard frog, *Rana pipiens*, is known to most children, to people who love the outdoors, and to scientists. It occurs in much of the northern and eastern part of the United States. Much of which follows is descriptive of the northern leopard frog. However, with many more than two thousand species occurring worldwide in a diversity of environmental conditions, the anura display a bewildering array of anatomical and behavioral variation—much more than can be covered here.

Leopard frogs mate in the early spring and their egg masses may be seen in transient ponds where frogs are common. Early embryonic development occurs within the jelly membranes of the eggs after which hatching occurs releasing small swimming tadpoles. The tadpoles feed on plants through much of the spring and early summer. Metamorphosis occurs during the same summer. Metamorphosis is the process whereby the aquatic and vegetarian larvae lose their gills and become terrestrial, insect-eating, air-breathing frogs. Metamorphosis is indeed complex and involves not only the loss of the tail and the development of limbs, but also a major reorganization of the gut, from the long intestine of a vegetarian to the short gut of a carnivore. Metamorphosis obviously profoundly affects respiration as the animal loses it gills (contained in a gill chamber similar in function to that of a fish) and air-breathing lungs become functional. Metamorphosis not only affects anatomy, but it also affects behavior. Tadpoles have a near pastoral existence as they peacefully graze on aquatic plant life. After metamorphosis, they become aggressive terrestrial predators who seek and devour insects during the warm months.

Many students first encounter chordate anatomy with the dissection of an adult frog. Physiologists have used frogs for the study of muscle contraction and the circulation of blood in capillaries that can readily be seen in the webbing between the toes of a frog. Embryologists long have used the animal because of its abundance of eggs. A mature female may release 3,000 or more eggs during spawning. Compare that abundance of eggs with the 10-20 of a superovulated mouse and it becomes obvious why *R. pipiens* has been the vertebrate organism of choice for experimental embryologists for several generations. Not only are the eggs abundant, but they are much larger than mouse eggs and therefore, experimentation and manipulation are easier with frog than with mouse eggs. Recently, many biologists have found that the South African clawed toad (or frog as it is sometimes called), *Xenopus laevis*, is a useful substitute for *R. pipiens*. *Xenopus* is

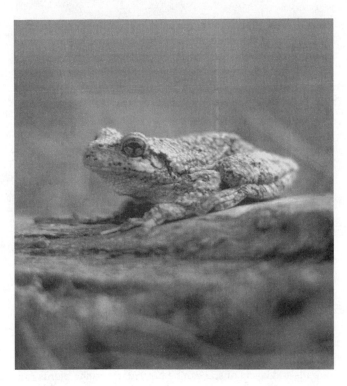

A lesser gray treefrog, one of the most widely distributed of the 13 species in North America.

useful because it can be reared to metamorphosis easily and it can be bred at any season.

Frogs and Biomedical Research

Many biological discoveries have been made or enhanced by using frogs. The role of sperm in development was studied in the late 1700s in frogs. Amphibians in general, including frogs, have significantly more **deoxyribose nucleic acid (DNA)** per cell than do other chordates. Thus, their chromosomes are large and easy to see with the microscope. Induced ovulation by pituitary injection was developed during the early 1930s. Endocrinologists studied the role of the hormone thyroxine in frog development as long ago as 1912. The role of viruses in animal and human **cancer** is receiving renewed interest—the first herpesvirus known to cause a cancer was the frog cancer herpesvirus, known since the 1930s, which causes a kidney cell carcinoma. Cloning was much in the news in 1997 because of the remarkable lamb, Dolly, produced in Scotland. Students of cloning know, of course, that the first vertebrate cloned was *Rana pipiens* and the successful cloning experiment was published by Thomas King and Robert Briggs in 1952. There is a long history of biomedical research. Experiments with frogs have contributed greatly to that history.

Several years ago, some students were on a field trip with their teacher at a pond near the Minnesota community of Henderson (south of Minneapolis and St. Paul). These students discovered a number of frogs with abnormal limbs. Their teacher, Cindy Reinitz, and the students contacted the Minnesota Pollution Control Agency and it was not long before biologists from that state agency and from the University of Minnesota confirmed the presence of many abnormal

frogs at that site. Word of these anomalous frogs spread and soon other sites with abnormal frogs were reported and confirmed. By late 1996, many sites in many Minnesota counties were reported to have abnormal frogs.

A historical perspective is needed to evaluate the significance of anatomical aberrations. It should be emphasized that just as calves with six legs (or other anatomical abnormalities) have been seen at county fairs since the Middle Ages or earlier, so too, have abnormal frogs been reported from time to time. An article in the *Philosophical Transactions of the Royal Society of London* published in 1740 describes a grossly abnormal frog. Other old reports are found in the scientific literature of many countries. What seems to be different in the Minnesota case of frog abnormalities, is the abundance of sites in many counties with abnormal frogs and the high prevalence of frogs with abnormalities at the various sites. Reasonable people seek to understand why abnormal frogs were found in Minnesota. The sought for cause was made more urgent when abnormal animals were reported in a number of other states, in Canada, and in Japan. Many of the abnormal frogs were found in agricultural areas. However, they have been reported from **nature** preserves as well.

Perhaps a reason for concern is that toxic **xenobiotic** chemicals are metabolized in much the same way in frogs as they are in humans. All animals are exposed to a diversity of toxic or potentially **toxic substance**s. Many of these chemicals would be retained in the body causing havoc were it were not for liver enzymes which increase the solubility of the substances by metabolically adding oxygen, or hydroxyl groups, and otherwise changing the molecular structure of the compound. The metabolically changed substances can then be excreted. Obviously, Minnesota frogs in 1996 were not competent to manage whatever it was that was causing the abnormalities. Because of the similarity of metabolic capabilities of liver enzymes in both frogs and humans, there is concern that whatever caused frog abnormalities could cause human abnormalities also if human exposure should occur.

Identification of a toxic insult would be greatly facilitated if it could be ascertained at what stage in the life cycle of the frog exposure occurs. Adult frogs forage in fields and meadows during the summer and early autumn. Many fields are treated with chemicals and one could postulate that exposure to a toxic substance could occur to adult frogs at that time. Frogs leave the meadows to gather around the margins of lakes and rivers with the onset of cold weather. They enter the cold water to remain there until the following spring. **Runoff** from agricultural areas accumulates in lakes and rivers. If the toxic material is water soluble and if it accumulates in water, hibernating adult frogs could be exposed during the winter months. With the beginning of hibernation, adult frogs already have mature gametes that will be used during the following spring. Do eggs and sperm become damaged by the water of overwintering lakes? After overwintering, the northern leopard frog and other anurans leave the lakes to breed at ephemeral ponds. The ponds are produced by snow melt from the preceding winter and spring rains. Tadpoles produced by already-damaged eggs and sperm could result in the abnormal larvae and juvenile adults found in or near the ponds, or exposure of larvae to toxic substances in the pond water while they develop could produce the abnormal animals that have been reported.

At the present time, it is not known where exposure occurs or at what stage it occurs. A tantalizing early observation was made by Dr. David Hoppe of the University of Minnesota Morris during the 1996 collection season. He studied a small Minnesota lake that was the breeding site for six species of anurans. The prevalence of abnormalities was directly related to the length of time that larvae remained in the water. The mink frog, *Rana septentrionalis*, has overwintering tadpoles that do not undergo metamorphosis until the second year. The mink frog larvae thus spent more time in the water than the other five species of anurans observed by Dr. Hoppe and the mink frogs were the most profoundly affected. They had many bizarre anatomical abnormalities. A species which developed more rapidly than the mink frogs and emerged as juveniles early in the first year, *Rana pipiens*, were less abnormal than the mink frog but significantly more abnormal than the other four species. The other four species developed much more rapidly, left the water much sooner, and had few abnormalities. The seminal study of Hoppe points to an aquatic **teratogen**. It is this sort of inspired biological analysis that may provide a solution to the perplexing problem of abnormal frogs.

[*Robert G. McKinnell*]

FURTHER READING

Behler, J.L., and F.W. King. *National Audubon Society Field Guide to North American Reptiles & Amphibians*. New York: Alfred A. Knopf, Inc., 1997.

Carlson, D.L., L.A. Rollins-Smith, and R.G. McKinnell. "The Lucké Herpesvirus Genome: Its Presence in Neoplastic and Normal Kidney Tissue," *Journal of Comparative Pathology* 110 (1995): 349–355.

Cheh, A.M., A.B. Hooper, J. Skochdopole, C.A. Henke, and R.G. McKinnell. "A Comparison of the Ability of Frog and Rat S-9 to Activate Promutagens in the Ames Test," *Environmental Mutagenesis* 2 (1980): 487–508.

DiBerardino, M.A. *Genomic Potential of Differentiated Cells*. New York: Columbia University Press, 1997.

Duellman, W.E., and L. Trueb. *Biology of Amphibians*. New York: McGraw-Hill Book Company, 1986.

Gilbert, S.F. *Development Biology*, 5th ed. Sunderland, MA: Sinauer Associates, Inc., 1997.

Stebbins, R.C., and N.W. Cohen. *A Natural History of Amphibians*. Princeton, N.J.: Princeton University Press, 1995.

Frontier economy

An economy similar to that which was prevalent at the "frontier" of European settlement in North America in the eighteenth and nineteenth centuries. A frontier economy is characterized by relative **scarcities** (and high prices) of capital equipment and skilled labor, and by a relative abundance (and low prices) of **natural resources**. Because of these factors, producers will look to utilize natural resources

instead of capital and skilled labor whenever possible. For example, a sawmill might use a blade that creates large amounts of wood waste since the cost of extra logs is less than the cost of a better blade. The long-term environmental effects of high natural resource use and **pollution** from wastes are ignored since they seem insignificant compared to the vastness of the natural resource base.

A frontier economy is sometimes contrasted with a spaceship economy, in which resources are seen as strictly limited and need to be endlessly recycled from waste products.

Frost heaving

The lifting of earth by **soil** water as it freezes. Freezing water expands by approximately nine percent and exerts a pressure of about fifteen tons per square inch. Although this pressure and accompanying expansion are exerted equally in all directions, movement takes place in the direction of least resistance, namely upward. As a result, buried rocks, varying from pebbles to boulders, can be raised to the ground surface; small mounds and layers of soil can be heaved up; young plants can be ripped from the earth or torn apart below ground; and pavement and foundations can be cracked and lifted. Newly planted tree seedlings, grass, and agricultural crops are particularly vulnerable to being lifted by acicular ice crystals during early fall and late spring frosts. Extreme cases in cold **climate**s at high latitudes or high elevation at mid-latitudes result in characteristic patterned ground.

Fuel cells

Fuel cells are sometimes compared to batteries because, like batteries, they have two electrodes, an anode and a cathode, posts through which an electrical current flows into and out of the cell. But fuel cells are fundamentally different electrical devices from batteries since the latter simply store electrical energy, while the former are a source of electrical energy.

The fuel cell concept was invented in 1839 by the British physicist Sir William Grove. A practical, working model of the concept was not developed until a century later, however. In a fuel cell, chemical energy is converted directly into electrical energy by means of an oxidation-reduction reaction. The earliest fuel cells carried out this energy conversion by means of the reaction in which **hydrogen** gas and oxygen gas react to form water. In this chemical change, each hydrogen atom loses one electron to an oxygen atom. The exchange of electrons, from hydrogen to oxygen, is what constitutes an oxidation-reduction reaction.

A fuel cell is a device that establishes a pathway through which electrons lost by hydrogen atoms must flow before they reach oxygen atoms. The cell typically consists of four basic parts: an anode, a cathode, an electrolyte, and an external circuit.

In the simplest fuel cell, hydrogen gas is pumped into one side of the fuel cell where it passes into a hollow, porous anode. At the anode, hydrogen atoms lose an electron to hydroxide ions present in the electrolyte. The source of the hydroxide is a water solution of potassium hydroxide. The electrons released in this reaction travel up the anode, out of the fuel cell, and into the external circuit. The external circuit is a wire that carries the flow of electrons (an electric current) to some device such as a light bulb where it can be used.

Meanwhile, a second reaction is taking place at the opposite pole of the fuel cell. Oxygen gas is pumped into this side of the fuel cell where it passes into the hollow, porous cathode. Oxygen atoms pick up electrons from the cathode and react with water in the electrolyte to regenerate hydroxide **ion**s.

As a result of the two chemical changes taking place at the two poles of the fuel cell, electrons are removed from hydroxide ions at the anode, passed through the external circuit where they can be used to do work, returned to the cell through the cathode, and then returned to water molecules in the electrolyte. Meanwhile, oxygen and hydrogen are used up in the production of water. A fuel cell such as the one described here should have a voltage of 1.23 volts and a theoretical efficiency (based on the heat of combustion of water) of 83 percent. The actual voltage of a typical hydrogen/oxygen fuel cell normally falls in the range of 0.6 to 1.1 volts depending on the conditions under which it operates.

Fuel cells have many advantages as energy sources. In the first place, they are significantly more efficient than energy sources such as nuclear or fossil-fueled **power plants**. In addition, a fuel cell is technically simple in construction and is light-weight. Also, the product of the fuel cell reaction—water—is, of course, harmless to humans and the rest of the environment. Finally, both hydrogen and oxygen, the raw materials used in a fuel cell, are abundant. They can both be obtained from water, the most common single compound on the planet.

Still, until recently, electricity produced from fuel cells was more expensive than that obtained from other sources, and they have been used in only specialized situations. One of these is in spacecraft, where their light weight is an important advantage. The fuel cell used on an 11-day Apollo moon flight, for example, weighed 500 pounds (227 kg), while a conventional generator would have weighed several tons. In addition, the water produced in the cell has been purified and then used for drinking in space vehicles.

A great many variations on the simple hydrogen/oxygen fuel cell have been investigated. As a first step, any fuel that contains hydrogen can be used, in theory, at the anode, while any oxidizing agent can be used at the cathode. Elemental hydrogen and oxygen are only the simplest, most fundamental examples of each.

Among the hydrogen-containing compounds explored as possible fuels are hydrazine, **methanol**, ammonia, and a variety of **hydrocarbons**. The order in which these fuels are listed here corresponds to the efficiency with which they react in a fuel cell, with hydrazine being most reactive (after hydrogen itself) and the hydrocarbons being least reactive.

Each of these potential alternatives has serious disadvantages. Hydrazine, for example, is expensive to manufacture and dangerous to work with.

In addition to oxygen, liquid oxidants such as hydrogen peroxide and nitric acid have also been studied as possible cathode reactants. Again, neither compound works as efficiently as oxygen itself, and each presents problems of its own as a working fluid in a fuel cell.

The details of fuel cell construction often differ depending on the specific use of the cell. Cells used in spacecraft, for example, use cathodes made of nickel oxide or gold and anodes made of a platinum alloy. The hydrogen and oxygen used in such cells are supplied in liquid form that must be maintained at high pressure and very low temperature.

Fuel cells can also operate with an acidic electrolyte such as phosphoric or a fluorinated sulfuric acid. The chemical reactions that occur in such a cell are different from those described for the alkaline (potassium hydroxide) cell described above. Fuel cells of the acidic type are more commonly used in industrial applications. They operate at a higher temperature than alkaline cells, with slightly less efficiency.

Another type of fuel cell makes use of a molten salt instead of a water solution as the electrolyte. In a typical cell of this kind, hydrogen is supplied at the anode of the cell, **carbon dioxide** is supplied at the cathode, and molten potassium carbonate is used as the electrolyte. In such a cell, the fundamental process is the same as in an aqueous electrolyte cell. Electrons are released at the anode. The electrons then travel through the external circuit where they can do work. They return to the cell through the cathode where they make the cathodic reaction possible.

Yet a third type of fuel cell is now being explored, one that makes use of state-of-the-art and sometimes exotic solid-state technology. This is the high-temperature solid ionic cell. In one design of this cell, the anode is made of nickel metal combined with zirconium oxide while the cathode is composed of a lanthanum-manganese alloy doped with strontium. The electrolyte in the cell is a mixed oxide of yttrium and zirconium. The fuel provided to the cell is carbon monoxide or hydrogen, either of which is oxidized by the oxygen in ordinary air. A series of these cells are connected to each other by connections made of lanthanum chromite doped with magnesium metal.

The solid ionic cell is particularly attractive to **electric utilities** and other industries because it contains no liquid, as other types of fuel cells do. The presence of such liquids creates problems in the handling and maintenance of conventional fuel cells that are not experienced with the all-solid cell.

Some experts are enthusiastic about the future role of fuel cells in the world's energy equation. If costs can be reduced, their high efficiency should make them attractive alternatives to fossil-fuel- and nuclear-generated electricity.

For that reason, still more variations in the fuel cell are being explored. One of the most intriguing of these future possibilities is a cell no more than 1-2 millimeters in diameter. These cells have the advantage of greater electrode surface area on which oxidation and reduction occur than do conventional cells. The distance that electrons have to travel in such cells is also much shorter, resulting in their having a greater power output per unit volume than do conventional cells. The technology for constructing and maintaining such small cells is not, however, fully developed.

[*David E. Newton*]

FURTHER READING

Dorf, R. D. *The Energy Factbook.* New York: McGraw-Hill, 1981.

Joesten, M. D., et al. *World of Chemistry.* Philadelphia: Saunders College Publishing, 1991.

Fuel switching

Fuel switching is the substitution of one energy source for another in order to meet requirements for heat, power, and/or electrical generation. Generally, this term refers to the practices of some industries that can substitute among **natural gas**, electricity, **coal**, and LPG within 30 days without modifying their fuel-consuming equipment and that can resume the same level of production following the change. The **U.S. Department of Energy** estimates that among manufacturers in 1991, 2.8 quadrillion Btus of energy consumption could be switched from a total consumption of about 20.3 quadrillion Btus, representing about 14%. Price is the primary reason for fuel switching; however, additional factors may include environmental regulations, agreements with energy or fuel suppliers, and equipment capabilities.

Fugitive emissions

Contaminants that enter the air without going through a smokestack and, thus, are often not subject to control by conventional **emission** control equipment or techniques. Most fugitive emissions are caused by activities involving the production of dust, such as soil **erosion** and **strip mining**, or building demolition, or the use of volatile compounds. In a steel-making complex, for example, there are several identifiable smokestacks from which emissions come, but there are also numerous sources of fugitive emissions, which escape into the air as a result of processes such as producing coke, for which there is no identifiable smokestack. The control of fugitive emissions is generally much more complicated and costly than the control of smokestack emissions for which known add-on technologies to the smokestack have been developed. **Baghouse**s and other costly mechanisms typically are needed to control fugitive emissions.

Fumigation

Most commonly, fumigation refers to the process of disinfecting a material or an area by using some type of toxic material in gaseous form. The term has a more specialized meaning in environmental science, where it refers to the process by which pollutants are mixed in the atmosphere. Under certain conditions, emitted pollutants rise above a stable layer of air near the ground. These pollutants remain aloft until convective currents develop, often in the morning, at which time the cooler pollutants "trade places" with air at ground level as it is warmed by the sun and rises. The resulting damage to ecosystems from the pollutants is most obvious around metal smelters.

Fund for Animals (New York, New York)

Founded in 1967 by author and humorist **Cleveland Amory**, the Fund is one of the most activist of the national animal protection groups. Formed "to speak for those who can't," it has led sometimes militant campaigns against sport hunting, trapping, and wearing furs, as well as the killing of whales, seals, bears, and other creatures. Amory, in particular, has campaigned tirelessly against these activities on television and radio, and in lectures, articles, and books.

In the early 1970s, the Fund worked effectively to rally public opinion in favor of passage of the **Marine Mammal Protection Act**, which was signed into law in October 1972. This act provides strong protection to **whales**, **seals and sea lions**, **dolphins**, **sea otter**s, polar bears, and other ocean mammals. In 1978, the Fund bought a British trawler and renamed it *Sea Shepherd*. Under the direction of its captain, Paul Watson, they used the ship to interfere with the baby seal kill on the ice floes off Canada. Activists sprayed some 1,000 baby harp seals with a harmless dye that destroyed the commercial value of their white coats as fur, and the ensuing publicity helped generate worldwide to the seal kill and a ban on imports into Europe. In 1979, *Sea Shepherd* hunted down and rammed *Sierra*, an outlaw whaling vessel that was illegally killing protected and **endangered species** of whales. After *Sea Shepherd* was seized by Portuguese authorities, Watson and his crew scuttled the ship to prevent it from being given to the owners of *Sierra* for use as a whaler.

Also in 1979, the Fund used helicopters to airlift from the Grand Canyon almost 600 wild burros that were scheduled to be shot by the **National Park Service**. The airlift was so successful, and generated so much favorable publicity, that it led to similar rescues of feral animals on **public land**s that the government wanted removed to prevent damage to vegetation. Burros were also airlifted by the Fund from Death Valley National Monument, as were some 3,000 wild goats on San Clemente Island, off the coast of California, scheduled to be shot by the United States Navy.

Many of the wild horses, burros, goats, and other animals rescued by the Fund end up, at least temporarily before adoption, at Black Beauty Ranch, its 600-acre (243-ha) sanctuary near Arlington, Texas. The ranch has provided a home for abused race and show horses, a non-performing elephant, and "Nim," the famous signing chimpanzee who was saved from a medical laboratory.

Legal action initiated by the Fund has resulted in the addition of almost 200 **species** to the **U.S. Department of**

the Interior's list of threatened and endangered species, including the **grizzly bear**, the Mexican wolf, the Asian elephant, and several species of kangaroos. The Fund is also active on the grassroots level, working on measures to restrict hunting and trapping. A recent example is the passage of an initiative in Colorado in November 1992 banning the use of dogs and bait to hunt bears, and halting the spring bear hunt, when mothers are still nursing their cubs. Contact: The Fund for Animals, 200 West 57th Street, New York, NY 10019. Internet: http://envirolink.org/arrs/fund/home.html.

[*Lewis G. Regenstein*]

Fungi

Fungi are one of the five Phyla of organisms. Fungi are broadly characterized by cells that possess nuclei and rigid cell walls but lack chlorophyll. Fungal spores germinate and grow slender tube-like structures called *hyphae*, separated by cell walls called *septae*. The vegetative **biomass** of most fungi in **nature** consists of masses of hyphae, or *mycelia*. Most **species** of fungi inhabit **soil**, where they are active in the **decomposition** of organic matter. The biologically most complex fungi periodically form spore-producing fruiting structures, known as mushrooms. Some fungi occur in close associations, known as **mycorrhizae**, with the roots of many species of vascular plants. The plant benefits mostly through an enhancement of **nutrient** uptake, while the fungus benefits through access to metabolites. Certain fungi are also partners in the **symbioses** with algae known as **lichens**. *See also* Fungicide

Fungicide

A fungus is a tiny plant-like organism that obtains its nourishment from dead or living organic matter. Some examples of fungi include mushrooms, toadstools, smuts, molds, rusts, and mildew.

Fungi have long been recognized as a serious threat to natural plants and human crops. They attack food both while it is growing and also after it has been harvested and placed into storage. One of the great agricultural disasters of the second half of the twentieth century was caused by a fungus. In 1970, the fungus that causes southern corn-leaf blight swept through the southern and midwestern United States and destroyed about 15 percent of the nation's corn crop. Potato blight, wheat rust, wheat smut, and grape mildew are other important disasters caused by fungi.

Chestnut blight is another example of the devastation that can be caused by fungi. Until 1900, chestnut trees were common in many parts of the United States. In 1904, however, chestnut trees from Asia were imported and planted in parts of New York. The imported trees carried with them a fungus that attacked and killed the native chestnut trees. Over a period of five decades, the native trees were all but totally eliminated from the eastern part of the country.

It is hardly surprising that humans began looking for fungicides—substances that will kill or control the growth of fungi—early on in history. The first of these fungicides was a naturally occurring substance, sulfur. One of the most effective of all fungicides, Bordeaux mixture was invented in 1885. Bordeaux mixture is a combination of two inorganic compounds, copper sulfate and lime.

With the growth of the chemical industry during the twentieth century, a number of synthetic fungicides have been invented; these include ferbam, ziram, captan, naban, dithiocarbonate, quinone, and 8-hydroxyquinoline.

For a period of time, compounds of **mercury** and **cadmium** were very popular as fungicides. Until quite recently, for example, the compound methylmercury was widely used by farmers in the United States who used it to protect growing plants and to treat stored grains.

During the 1970s, however, evidence began to accumulate about a number of adverse effects of mercury- and cadmium-based fungicides. The most serious effects were observed among birds and small animals who were exposed to sprays and dusting or who ate treated grain. A few dramatic incidents of methylmercury poisoning among humans, however, were also recorded. The best known of these was the 1953 disaster at Minamata Bay, Japan.

At first, scientists were mystified by an epidemic that spread through the Minamata Bay area between 1953 and 1961. Some unknown factor caused serious nervous disorders among residents of the region. Some sufferers lost the ability to walk, others developed mental disorders, and still others were permanently disabled. Eventually researchers traced the cause of these problems to methylmercury in fish eaten by residents of the area. For the first time, the terrible effects of the compound had been confirmed.

As a result of the problems with mercury and cadmium compounds, scientists have tried to develop less toxic substitutes for the more dangerous fungicides. Dinocap, binapacryl, and benomyl are three examples of such compounds.

Another approach has been to use **integrated pest management** and to develop plants that are resistant to fungi. The latter approach was used with great success during the corn blight disaster of 1970. Researchers worked quickly to develop strains of corn that were resistant to the corn-leaf blight fungus and by 1971 had provided farmers with seeds of the new strain. *See also* Minamata disease

[*David E. Newton*]

FURTHER READING

Chemistry and the Food System. A Study by the Committee on Chemistry and Public Affairs. Washington, DC: American Chemical Society, 1980.

Fletcher, W. W. *The Pest War*. New York: Wiley, 1974.

Selinger, B. *Chemistry in the Marketplace*. 4th ed. Sydney: Harcourt Brace Jovanovich, 1989.

Future generations

According to demographers, a generation is an age-cohort of people born, living, and dying within a few years of each other. Human generations are roughly defined categories, and the demarcations are not as distinct as they are in many other **species**. As the Scottish philosopher David Hume (1711-1776) noted in the eighteenth century, generations of human beings are not like generations of butterflies, who come into existence, lay their eggs, and die at about the same time, with the next generation hatching thereafter. But distinctions can still be made, and future generations are all age-cohorts of human beings who have not yet been born.

The concept of future generations is central to **environmental ethics** and **environmental policy**, because the health and well-being—indeed the very existence—of human beings depends on how people living today care for the natural **environment**.

Proper stewardship of the environment affects not only the health and well-being of people in the future but their character and identity. In *The Economy of the Earth*, Mark Sagoff compares environmental damage to the loss of our rich cultural heritage. The loss of all our art and literature would deprive future generations of the benefits we have enjoyed and render them nearly illiterate. By the same token, if we destroyed all our wildernesses and dammed all our rivers, allowing **environmental degradation** to proceed at the same pace, we would do more than deprive people of the pleasures we have known. We would make them into what Sagoff calls "environmental illiterates," or "yahoos" who would neither know nor wish to experience the beauties and pleasures of the natural world. "A pack of yahoos," says Sagoff, "will like a junkyard environment" because they will have known nothing better.

The concept of future generations emphasizes both our ethical and aesthetic obligations to our environment. In relations between existing and future generations, however, the present generation holds all the power. While we can affect them, they can do nothing to affect us. Though, as some environmental philosophies have argued, our moral code is in large degree based on reciprocity, the relationship between generations cannot be reciprocal. Adages such as "like for like," and "an eye for an eye," can apply only among contemporaries. Since an adequate environmental ethic would require that moral consideration be extended to include future people, views of justice based on the norm of reciprocity may be inadequate.

A good deal of discussion has gone into what an alternative environmental ethic might look like and on what it might be based. But perhaps the important point to note is that the treatment of generations yet unborn has now become a lively topic of philosophical discussion and political debate. *See also* Environmental education; Environmentalism; Intergenerational justice

[*Terence Ball*]

FURTHER READING

Barry, B., and R. I. Sikora, eds. *Obligations to Future Generations*. Philadelphia: Temple University Press, 1978.

Fishkin, J., and P. Laslett, eds. *Justice Between Age Groups and Generations*. New Haven, CT: Yale University Press, 1992.

Partridge, E., ed. *Responsibilities to Future Generations*. Buffalo, NY: Prometheus Books, 1981.

Sagoff, M. *The Economy of the Earth: Philosophy, Law and the Environment*. Cambridge and New York: Cambridge University Press, 1988.

G

Gaia hypothesis

The Gaia hypothesis was only recently developed by British biochemist **James Lovelock**, but it incorporates two older ideas. First, the idea implicit in the ancient Greek term *Gaia*, that the earth is the mother of all life, the source of sustenance for all living beings, including humans. Second, the idea that life on earth and many of earth's physical characteristics have coevolved, changing each other reciprocally as the generations and centuries pass.

Lovelock's theory contradicts conventional wisdom, which holds "that life adapted to the planetary conditions as it and they evolved their separate ways." The Gaia hypothesis is a startling break with tradition for many, although ecologists have been teaching the **coevolution** of organisms and **habitat** for at least several decades, albeit more often on a local than a global scale.

The hypothesis also states that Gaia will persevere no matter what humans do. This is undoubtedly true, but the question remains: in what form, and with how much diversity? If humans don't change the nature and scale of some of their activities, the earth could change in ways that people may find undesirable—loss of **biodiversity**, more "weed" **species**, increased **desertification**, etc.

Many people, including Lovelock, take the Gaia hypothesis a step further and call the earth itself a living being, a long-discredited organismic analogy. Recently a respected **environmental science** textbook defined the Gaia hypothesis as a "proposal that Earth is alive and can be considered a system that operates and changes by feedbacks of information between its living and nonliving components." Similar sentences can be found quite commonly, even in the scholarly literature, but upon closer examination they are not persuasive. A furnace operates via a positive and negative feedback system—does that imply it is alive? Of course not. The important message in Lovelock's hypothesis is that the health of the earth and the health of its inhabitants are inextricably intertwined. *See also* Balance of nature; Biological community; Biotic community; Ecology; Ecosystem; Environment; Environmentalism; Evolution; Nature; Sustainable biosphere

[*Gerald L. Young*]

FURTHER READING

Joseph, L. E. *Gaia: The Growth of an Idea*. New York: St. Martin's Press, 1990.

Lovelock, J. E. *Gaia: A New Look at Life on Earth*. Oxford: Oxford University Press, 1979.

———. *The Ages of Gaia: A Biography of Our Living Earth*. New York: Norton, 1988.

Lyman, F. "What Gaia Hath Wrought: The Story of a Scientific Controversy." *Technology Review* 92 (July 1989): 54-61.

Schneider, S. H., and P. J. Boston, eds. *Scientists on Gaia*. Cambridge: MIT Press, 1991.

Galápagos Islands

Within the theory of **evolution**, the concept of adaptive radiation (evolutionary development of several **species** from a single parental stock) has had as its prime example, a group of birds known as Darwin's finches. **Charles Darwin** discovered and collected specimens of these birds from the Galápagos Islands in 1835 on his five-year voyage around the world aboard the HMS *Beagle*. His cumulative experiences, copious notes, and vast collections ultimately led to the publication of his monumental work, *On the Origin of Species*, in 1859. The Galápagos Islands and their unique assemblage of plants and animals were an instrumental part of the development of Darwin's evolutionary theory.

The Galápagos Islands are located at 90° W longitude and 0° latitude (the equator), about 600 miles (965 km) west Ecuador. These islands are volcanic in origin and are about 10 million years old. The original colonization of the Galápagos Islands occurred by chance transport over the ocean as indicated by the gaps in the **flora** and **fauna** of this archipelago compared to the mainland. Of the hundreds of species of birds along the northwestern South American coast, only seven species colonized the Galápagos Islands. These evolved into 57 resident species, 26 of which are endemic to the islands, through adaptive radiation. The only native land mammals are a rat and a **bat**. The land reptiles include iguanas, a single species each of snake, lizard, and gecko, and the Galápagos giant tortoise (*Geochelone elephantopus*). No amphibians and few insects or mollusks are found in the Galápagos. The flora has large gaps as well—no conifers or palms have colonized these islands. Many of the open **niche**s have been filled by the colonizing groups. The

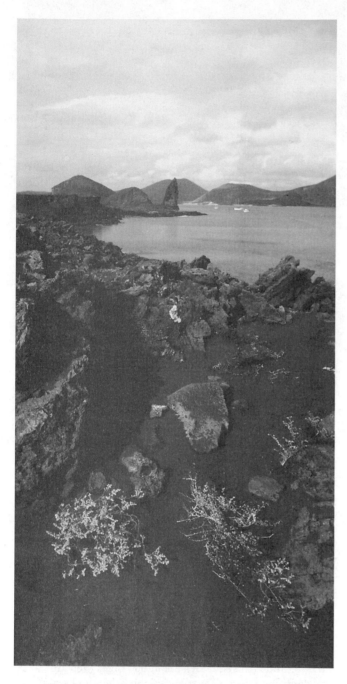

Coastline in the Galápagos Islands.

under the bark of trees, having filled the niche of the woodpecker. Darwin's finches are named in honor of their discoverer, but they are not referred to as Galápagos finches because there is one of their numbers that has colonized Cocos Island, located 425 miles (684 km) north-northeast of the Galápagos.

Because of the Galápagos Islands' unique **ecology**, scenic beauty and tropical **climate**, they have become a mecca for tourists and some settlement. These human activities have introduced a host ofenvironmental problems, including **introduced species** of goats, pigs, rats, dogs, and cats, many of which become feral and damage or destroy nesting bird colonies by preying on the adults, young, or eggs. Several races of giant tortoise have been extirpated or are severely threatened with **extinction**, primarily due to exploitation for food by humans, destruction of their food resources by goats, or predation of their hatchlings by feral animals. Most of the 13 recognized races of tortoise have populations numbering only in the hundreds. Three races are tenuously maintaining populations in the thousands, one race has not been seen since 1906, but it is thought to have disappeared due to natural causes, another race has a population of about 25 individuals, and the Abingdon Island tortoise is represented today by only one individual, "Lonesome George," a captive male at the Charles Darwin Biological Station. For most of these tortoises to survive, an active capture or extermination program of the feral animals will have to continue. One other potential threat to the Galápagos Islands is tourism. Thousands of tourists visit these islands each year and their numbers can exceed the limit deemed sustainable by the Ecuadoran government. These tourists have had, and will continue to have, an impact on the fragile **habitat**s of the Galápagos. *See also* Endemic species; Ecotourism

[*Eugene C. Beckham*]

FURTHER READING

The Conservation Biology of Tortoises, edited by I. R. Swingland, M. W. Klemens, and the Durrell Institute of Conservation and Ecology. Occasional Papers of the IUCN Species Survival Commission No. 5. Gland, Switzerland: IUCN—The World Conservation Union, 1989.

Harris, M. *A Field Guide to the Birds of the Galápagos*. London: Collins, 1982.

Root, P., and M. McCormick. *Galápagos Islands*. New York: Macmillan, 1989.

Steadman, D. W., and S. Zousmer. *Galápagos: Discovery on Darwin's Islands*. Washington, DC: Smithsonian Institution Press, 1988.

tortoises and iguanas are large and have filled niches normally occupied by mammalian herbivores. Several plants, such as the prickly pear cactus, have attained large size and occupy the ecological position of tall trees.

The most widely known and often used example of adaptive radiation is Darwin's finches, a group of 14 fourteen species of birds that arose from a single ancestor in the Galápagos Islands. These birds have specialized on different islands or into niches normally filled by other groups of birds. Some are strictly seed eaters, while others have evolved more warbler-like bills and eat insects, still others eat flowers, fruit, and/or nectar, and others find insects for their diet by digging

Game animal

Birds and mammals commonly hunted for sport. The major groups include upland game birds (quail, pheasant, and partridge), waterfowl (ducks and geese), and big game (deer, antelope, and bears). Game animals are protected to varying degrees throughout most of the world, and hunting levels are regulated through the licensing of hunters as well as by seasons and bag limits. In the United States, state **wildlife** agencies assume primary responsibility for enforcing hunting regulations, particularly for resident or non-migratory **species**. The **Fish and Wildlife Service** shares responsibility with state agencies for regulating harvests of migratory game animals, principally waterfowl.

Game preserves

Game preserves (also known as game reserves, or **wildlife refuge**s) are a type of protected area in which **hunting** of certain species of animals is not allowed, although other kinds of resource harvesting may be permitted. Game preserves are usually established to conserve populations of larger game species of mammals or waterfowl. The protection from hunting allows the hunted species to maintain relatively large populations within the sanctuary. However, animals may be legally hunted when they move outside of the reserve during their seasonal migrations or when searching for additional habitat.

Game preserves help to ensure that populations of hunted species do not become depleted through excessive harvesting throughout their range. This conservation allows the species to be exploited in a sustainable fashion over the larger landscape.

Although hunting is not allowed, other types of resource extraction may be permitted in game reserves, such as timber harvesting, livestock grazing, some types of cultivated agriculture, mining, and exploration and extraction of **fossil fuels**. However, these land-uses are managed to ensure that the habitat of game species is not excessively damaged. Some game preserves are managed as true ecological reserves, where no extraction of natural resources is allowed. However, low-intensity types of land-use may be permitted in these more comprehensively protected areas, particularly non-consumptive recreation such as hiking and wildlife viewing.

Game Preserves as a Tool in Conservation

The term "**conservation**" refers to the wise (i.e. sustainable) use of **natural resources**. Conservation is particularly relevant to the use of **renewable resources**, which are capable of regenerating after a portion has been harvested. Hunted species of animals are one type of renewable resource, as are timber, flowing water, and the ability of land to support the growth of agricultural crops. These renewable resources have the potential to be harvested forever, as long as the rate of exploitation is equal to or less than the rate of regeneration. However, potentially renewable resources can also be harvested at a rate exceeding their regeneration. This is known as over-exploitation, a practice that causes the stock of the resource to decline and may even result in its irretrievable collapse.

Wildlife managers can use game preserves to help conserve populations of hunted species. Other methods of conservation of game animals include: (1) regulation of the time of year when hunting can occur; (2) setting of "bag limits" that restrict the maximum number of animals that any hunter can harvest; (3) limiting the total number of animals that can be harvested in a particular area, and; (4) restricting the hunt to certain elements of the population. Wildlife managers can also manipulate the habitat of game species so that larger, more productive populations can be sustained, for example by increasing the availability of food, water, shelter, or other necessary elements of **habitat**. In addition, **wildlife** managers may cull the populations of natural predators to increase the numbers of game animals available to be hunted by people.

Some or all of these practices, including the establishment of game preserves, may be used as components of an integrated game management system. Such systems may be designed and implemented by government agencies that are responsible for managing game populations over relatively large areas such as counties, states, provinces, or entire countries.

Conservation is intended to benefit humans in their interactions with other species and ecosystems, which are utilized as valuable natural resources. When defined in this way, conservation is very different from the preservation of indigenous species and ecosystems for their ecocentric and biocentric values, which are considered important regardless of any usefulness to humans or their economic activities.

Examples of Game Preserves

The first **national wildlife refuge** in the United States was established by President **Theodore Roosevelt** in 1903. This was a breeding site for **brown pelicans** (*Pelecanus occidentalis*) and other birds in Florida. The U.S. national system of wildlife refuges now totals some 437 sites covering 91.4 million acres (37 million ha); an additional 79 million acres (32 million ha) of habitat are protected in national parks and monuments. The largest single wildlife reserve is the Alaska Maritime Wildlife Refuge, which covers 3.5 million acres (1.4 million ha); in fact, about 85% of the national area of wildlife refuges is in Alaska. Most of the national wildlife refuges protect migratory, breeding, and wintering habitats for waterfowl, but others are important for large mammals and other species. Some wildlife refuges have been established to protect critical habitat of **endangered species**, such as the Aransas Wildlife Refuge in coastal Texas, which is the primary wintering grounds of the **whooping crane** (*Grus americana*). Since 1934, sales of *Migratory Bird Hunting Stamps*, or "duck stamps," have been critical to providing funds for the acquisition and management of federal wildlife refuges in the United States.

Although hunting is not permitted in many National wildlife refuges, in 1988, closely regulated hunting was permitted in 60% of the refuges, and fishing was allowed in 50%. In addition, some other resource-related activities are allowed in some refuges. Depending on the site, it may be possible to harvest timber, graze livestock, engage in other kinds of agriculture, or explore for or mine metals or fossil fuels. The various components of the multiple-use plans of particular national wildlife refuges are determined by the Secretary of the Interior. Any of these economically important activities may cause damage to wildlife habitats, and this has resulted in intense controversy between economic interests and some environmental groups. Environmental organizations such as the **Sierra Club**, **Ducks Unlimited**, and the

Audubon Society have lobbied federal legislators to further restrict exploration and extraction in national wildlife refuges, but business interests demand greater access to valuable resources within national wildlife refuges.

Many states and provinces also establish game preserves as a component of wildlife-management programs on their lands. For example, many jurisdictions in eastern North America have set up game preserves for management of populations of white-tailed deer (*Odocoileus virginianus*), a widely hunted species. Game preserves are also used to conserve populations of mule deer (*Odocoileus hemionus*) and elk (*Cervus canadensis*) in more western regions of North America.

Some other types of protected areas, such as state, provincial, and national parks are also effective as wildlife preserves. These protected areas are not primarily established for the conservation of natural resources— rather, they are intended to preserve natural ecosystems and wild places for their intrinsic value. Nevertheless, relatively large and productive populations of hunted species often build up within parks and other large ecological reserves, and the surplus animals are commonly hunted in the surrounding areas. In addition, many protected areas are established by non-governmental organizations, such as the **Nature Conservancy**, which has preserved more than 16 million acres (6.5 million ha) of natural habitat throughout the United States.

Yellowstone National Park is one of the most famous protected areas in North America. Hunting is not allowed in Yellowstone, and this has allowed the build-up of relatively large populations of various species of big-game mammals, such as white-tailed deer, elk, **bison** (*Bison bison*), and **grizzly bear** (*Ursus arctos*). Because of the large populations in the park, the overall abundance of game species on the greater landscape is also larger. This means that a relatively high intensity of hunting can be supported. This is considered important because it provides local people with meat and subsistence as well as economic opportunities through guiding and the marketing of equipment, accommodations, food, fuel, and other necessities to non-local hunters.

By providing a game-preserve function for the larger landscape, wildlife refuges and other kinds of protected areas help to ensure that hunting can be managed to allow populations of exploited species to be sustained, while providing opportunities for people to engage in subsistence and economic activities.

[*Bill Freedman*]

FURTHER READING

Freedman, B. *Environmental Ecology*, 2nd ed. San Diego, CA: Academic Press, 1995.

Miller, G.T. *Resource Conservation and Management*. Belmont, CA: Wadsworth Publishing Co., 1990.

Owen, O.S., and D.D. Chiras. *Natural Resource Conservation. Management for a Sustainable Future*. Englewood Cliffs, NJ: Prentice Hall, 1995.

Robinson, W.L. and E.G. Bolen. *Wildlife Ecology and Management*, 3rd ed. New York: MacMillan Publishing Co., 1995.

Gamma ray

High energy forms of electromagnetic radiation with very short wavelengths. Gamma rays are emitted by cosmic sources or by radioactive decay of atomic nuclei which occurs during nuclear reactions or the detonation of **nuclear weapons**. Gamma rays are the most penetrating of all forms of nuclear radiation. They travel about 100 times deeper into human tissue than **beta particle**s and 10,000 times deeper than **alpha particle**s. Gamma rays cause chemical changes in cells through which they pass. These changes can result in the cells' death or the loss of their ability to function properly. Organisms exposed to gamma rays may suffer illness, genetic damage, or death. Cosmic gamma rays do not usually pose a danger to life because they are absorbed as they travel through the **atmosphere**. *See also* Ionizing radiation; Radiation exposure; Radioactive fallout

Gandhi, Mohandas Karamchand (1869-1948)

Indian nationalist and spiritual leader

Mohandas Karamchand Gandhi led the movement that freed India from colonial occupation by the British. His leadership was based not only on his political vision but also on his moral, economic, and personal philosophies. Gandhi's beliefs have influenced many political movements throughout the world, including the civil rights movement in the United States, but their relevance to the modern environmental movement has not been widely recognized or understood until recently.

In developing the principles that would enable the Indian people to form a united independence movement, one of Gandhi's chief concerns was preparing the groundwork for an economy that would allow India to be both self-sustaining and egalitarian. He did not believe that an independent economy in India could be based on the Western model; he considered a consumer economy of unlimited growth impossible in his country because of the huge population base and the high level of poverty. He argued instead for the development of an economy based on the careful use of indigenous **natural resources**. His was a philosophy of **conservation**, and he advocated a lifestyle based on limited consumption, **sustainable agriculture**, and the utilization of labor resources instead of imported technological development.

Gandhi's plans for India's future were firmly rooted both in moral principles and in a practical recognition of its economic strengths and weaknesses. He believed that the key to an independent national economy and a national sense of identity was not only indigenous resources but indigenous products and industries. Gandhi made a point of wearing only homespun, undyed cotton clothing that had been handwoven on cottage looms. He anticipated that the practice of wearing homespun cotton cloth would create an industry for a product that had a ready market, for cotton was a resource that was both indigenous and renewable. He recognized that India's major economic strength was its vast labor pool, and the low level of technology needed for this product would encourage the development of an industry that was highly decentralized. It could provide employment without encouraging mass migration from rural to urban areas, thus stabilizing rural economies and national demography. The use of cotton textiles would also prevent dependence on expensive synthetic fabrics that had to be imported from Western nations, consuming scarce foreign exchange. He also believed that synthetic textiles were not suited to India's **climate**, and that they created an undesirable distinction between the upper classes that could afford them and the vast majority that could not.

The essence of his economic planning was a philosophical commitment to living a simple lifestyle based on need. He believed it was immoral to kill animals for food and advocated **vegetarianism**; advocated walking and other simple forms of transportation contending that India could not afford a car for every individual; and advocated the integration of ethical, political, and economic principles into individual lifestyles. Although many of his political tactics, particularly his strategy of civil disobedience, have been widely embraced in many countries, his economic philosophies have had a diminishing influence in a modern, independent India, which has been pursuing sophisticated technologies and a place in the global economy. But to some, his work seems increasingly relevant to a world with limited resources and a rapidly growing population.

[*Usha Vedagiri and Douglas Smith*]

FURTHER READING

Fischer, L. *The Life of Mahatma Gandhi.* New York: Harper, 1950.
Mehta, V. *Mahatma Gandhi and His Apostles.* New York: Viking, 1977.

Garbage

In 1990, the United States generated 195 million tons of **municipal solid waste**, compared with 151 million tons in 1980, according to **Environmental Protection Agency (EPA)** estimates. On average, each person generated 4.3 pounds (2.04 kg) of such waste per day in 1990, and the EPA expects that amount to increase by the year 2000. That waste includes cans, bottles, newspapers, paper and plastic packages, uneaten food, broken furniture and appliances, old tires, lawn clippings, and other refuse. This waste can be placed in **landfill**s, incinerated, recycled, or in some cases composted.

Landfilling—waste disposed of on land in a series of layers that are compacted and covered, usually with **soil**—is the main method of **waste management** in this country, accounting for about 130 million tons in 1990. But old landfills are being closed and new ones are hard to site because of community opposition. Landfills once were open dumps, causing unsanitary conditions, **methane** explosions, and releases of hazardous **chemicals** into **groundwater** and air. Old dumps make up 22 percent of the sites on the Superfund National Priorities List. Today, landfills must have liners, gas collection systems, and other controls man-

dated under Subtitle D of the **Resource Conservation and Recovery Act (RCRA)**.

Incineration has been popular among solid waste managers because it helps to destroy bacteria and toxic chemicals and to reduce the volume of waste. But public opposition, based on fears that toxic metals and other chemical **emission**s will be released from incinerators, has made the siting of new facilities extremely difficult. In the past, garbage burning was done in open fields, in dumps, or in backyard drums, but the **Clean Air Act** (1970) banned open burning, leading to new types of incinerators, most of which are designed to generate energy.

Recycling, which consists of collecting materials from waste streams, preparing them for market, and using those materials to manufacture new products, is catching national attention as a desirable waste management method. As of March 1993, 39 states and the District of Columbia had some type of statewide recycling law aimed at promoting greater recycling of glass, paper, metals, **plastics**, and other materials. Used oil, household batteries, and lead-acid automotive batteries are recyclable waste items of particular concern because of their toxic constituents.

Composting is a waste management approach that relies on heat and microorganisms—mostly bacteria and **fungi**—to decompose yard wastes and food scraps, turning them into a **nutrient**-rich mix called **humus** or compost. This mix can be used as **fertilizer**. However, as with landfills and incinerators, **composting** facilities have been difficult to site because of community opposition, in part because of the disagreeable smell generated by some composting practices.

Recently, waste managers have shown interest in source reduction, reducing either the amount of garbage generated in the first place or the toxic ingredients of garbage. Reusable blankets instead of throw-away cardboard packaging for protecting furniture is one example of source reduction. Businesses are regarded as a prime target for source reduction, such as implementing double-sided photocopying to save paper, because the approach offers potentially large cost savings to companies.

[*David Clarke*]

FURTHER READING

Blumberg, L., and R. Gottlieb. *War on Waste: Can America Win Its Battle With Garbage?* Washington, DC: Island Press, 1989.
Underwood, J., A. Hershkowitz, and M. de Kadt. *Garbage—Practices, Problems, Remedies.* New York: INFORM, 1988.
U. S. Office of Technology Assessment. *Facing America's Trash: What Next For Municipal Solid Waste?* Washington, DC: U. S. Government Printing Office, 1989.

Garbage Project

The Garbage Project was founded in 1973, shortly after the first **Earth Day**, by **William Rathje**, professor of anthropology, and fellow archaeologists at the University of Arizona. The objective was to apply the techniques and tools of their science to the study of modern civilization by analyzing its **garbage**.

Using sample analysis and assessing biodegradation, they also hoped to increase their understanding of resource depletion and environmental and **landfill**-related problems. Because it requires sunlight, moisture, and oxygen, as well as organic material and bacteria, little biodegradation actually takes place in landfills, resulting in perfectly preserved heads of lettuce, 40-year-old hot dogs, and completely legible 50-year-old newspapers.

In *Rubbish: The Archaeology of Garbage*, published in 1992, Rathje and *Atlantic Monthly* managing editor Cullen Murphy discuss some of the data gleaned from the project. For example, the accumulation of refuse has raised the City of New York 6-30 ft (1.8-9 m) since its founding. Also, the largest proportion—40%—of landfilled garbage is paper, followed by the leftovers from building construction and demolition. In fact, newspapers alone make up about 13% of the total volume of trash.

Just as interesting as what they found was what they did not find. Contrary to much of public opinion, fast-food packaging made up only one-third of 1% of the total volume of trash landfilled between 1980 and 1989, while expanded polystyrene foam accounted for no more than 1%. Even disposable diapers averaged out at only 1% by weight of the total **solid waste** contents (1.4% by volume). Of all the garbage examined, plastics constituted from 20-24%. Surveys of several national landfills revealed that organic materials made up 40-52% of the total volume of waste.

The Garbage Project also debunked the idea that the U.S. is running out of space for landfills. While it is true that many landfills have been shut down, it is also true that many of those were quite small to begin with and that they now pose fewer environmental hazards. It is estimated that one landfill 120 ft (35.4 m) deep and measuring 44 mi² (71 km²) would adequately handle the needs of the entire nation for the next 100 years (assuming current levels of waste production).

In "A Perverse Law of Garbage" (*Garbage*, Dec/Jan 1993:22), Rathje extrapolated from "Parkinson's Law" to define his Parkinson's Law of Garbage: "Garbage expands so as to fill the receptacles available for its containment." As evidence he cites a Garbage Project study of the recent mechanization of garbage pick-up in some larger cities and the ensuing effects. As users were provided with increasingly larger receptacles (in order to accommodate the mechanized trucks), they continued to fill them up. Rathje attributes this to the newfound convenience of disposing of that which previously had been consigned to the basement or second-hand store, and concludes that the move to automation may be counterproductive to any attempt to reduce garbage and increase **recycling**.

[*Ellen Link*]

FURTHER READING

"Anatomy of a Garbage Heap." *Newsletter of the Southwest Recycling Committee* 1, no. 5 (12 Sept. 1995). World Wide Web: http://www.swmed.edu/home_pages/facultystaff/may/Recycling/v01

Contemporary Authors 143 (1994): 357. Detroit: Gale Research.

Lilienfeld, R. M. "Six Enviro-Myths: Recycling is the Key." *New York Times* (21 Jan 1995): 23(L).

Rathje, W. L. "A Perverse Law of Garbage." *Garbage* 4, no. 6 (Dec/Jan 93): 22.

Rathje, W. L., and C. Murphy. *Rubbish!: The Archaeology of Garbage*. New York: Harper Collins, 1992.

Garbology

The study of **garbage**, through either archaeological excavation of **landfill**s or analysis of fresh garbage, to determine what the composition of **municipal solid waste** says about the society that generated it. The term is associated with the Garbage Project of the University of Arizona (Tucson), co-directed by William Rathje and Wilson Hughes, which began studying trash in 1973 and excavating landfills in 1987. They found that little degradation occurs in landfills; New York newspapers from 1949 and an ear of corn discarded in 1971 were found intact. Unexpectedly, the project also found that **plastics** make up less than one percent of the total volume of landfills.

Gardens

> *See* **Botanical garden; Organic gardening and farming**

Gasohol

Gasohol is a term used for the mixture of 10 percent ethyl alcohol (also called ethanol or grain alcohol) with **gasoline**. Ethanol raises the octane rating of lead-free **automobile** fuel and significantly decreases the **carbon monoxide** released from tailpipes. It has also been promoted as a means of reducing corn surpluses; as recently as 1989, 840 million gallons of ethanol were produced from corn for fuel. However, ethanol also raises the vapor pressure of gasoline, and it has been reported to increase the release of "evaporative" volatile **hydrocarbons** from the fuel system and oxides of **nitrogen** from the exhaust. These substances are components of urban **smog**, and thus the role of ethanol in reducing **pollution** is controversial.

Gasoline

Crude oil in its natural state has very few practical uses. However, when it is separated into its component parts by the process of fractionation, or refining, those parts have an almost unlimited number of applications.

In the first sixty years after the process of **petroleum** refining was invented, the most important fraction produced was kerosene, widely used as a home heating product. The petroleum fraction slightly lighter than kerosene — gasoline — was regarded as a waste product and discarded. Not until the 1920s, when the **automobile** became popular in the United States, did manufacturers find any significant use for gasoline. From then on, however, the importance of gasoline has increased with automobile use.

The term gasoline refers to a complex mixture of liquid **hydrocarbons** that condense in a fractionating tower at temperatures between 100° and 400°F (40° and 205°C). The hydrocarbons in this mixture are primarily single- and double-bonded compounds containing five to twelve **carbon** atoms.

Gasoline that comes directly from a refining tower, known as naphtha or "straight-run" gasoline, was an adequate fuel for the earliest motor vehicles. But as improvements in internal **combustion** engines were made, problems began to arise. The most serious problem was "knocking."

If a fuel burns too rapidly in an internal combustion engine, it generates a shock wave that makes a "knocking" or "pinging" sound. The shock wave will, over time, also cause damage to the engine. The hydrocarbons that make up straight-run gasolines proved to burn too rapidly for automotive engines developed after 1920.

Early in the development of automotive fuels, engineers adopted a standard for the amount of knocking caused by a fuel and, hence, for the fuel's efficiency. That standard was known as "octane number." To establish a fuel's octane number, it is compared with a very poor fuel (n-heptane), assigned an octane number of zero, and a very good fuel (isooctane), assigned an octane number of 100. The octane number of straight-run gasoline is anywhere from fifty to seventy.

As engineers made more improvements in automotive engines after the 1920s, chemists tried to keep pace by developing better fuels. One approach they used was to subject straight-run gasoline (as well as other crude oil fractions) to various treatments that changed the shape of hydrocarbon molecules in the gasoline mixture. One such method, called cracking, involves the heating of straight-run gasoline or another petroleum fraction to high temperatures. The process results in a better fuel from newly-formed hydrocarbon molecules.

Another method for improving the quality of gasoline is catalytic reforming. In this case, the cracking reaction takes place over a catalyst such as **copper**, platinum, rhodium, or other "noble" metal, or a form of clay known as zeolite. Again, hydrocarbon molecules formed in the fraction are better fuels than straight-run gasoline. Gasoline produced by catalytic cracking or reforming has an octane number of at least eighty.

A very different approach to improving gasoline quality is the use of additives, **chemicals** added to gasoline to improve the fuel's efficiency. Automotive engineers learned more than fifty years ago that adding as little as two grams of **tetraethyl lead**, the best-known additive, to one gallon of gasoline raises its octane number by as much as ten points.

Until the 1970s, most gasolines contained tetraethyl lead. Then, concerns began to grow about the release of **lead** to the **environment** during the combustion of gasoline. Lead concentrations in urban air had reached a level five to

ten times that of rural air. Residents of countries with few automobiles, such as Nepal, had only one-fifth the lead in their bodies as did residents of nations such as the United States, with many automotive vehicles.

The toxic effects of lead on the human body have been known for centuries, and risks posed by leaded gasoline became a major concern. In addition, leaded gasoline became a problem because it damaged a car's **catalytic converter**, which reduced air pollutants in exhaust.

Finally, in 1973, the **Environmental Protection Agency (EPA)** acted on the problem and set a time-scale for the gradual elimination of leaded fuels. According to this schedule, the amount of lead was to be reduced from 2 to 3 grams per gallon (the 1973 average) to 0.5 grams per gallon by 1979. Ultimately, the additive was to be totally eliminated from all gasoline.

The elimination of leaded fuels has been made possible by the invention of new and safer additives. One of the most popular is methyl-t-butyl ether (MTBE). By 1988 MTBE had become so popular that it was among the forty most widely produced chemicals in the United States.

Yet another approach to improving fuel efficiency is the mixing of gasoline and ethyl or **methanol**. This product, known as **gasohol**, has the advantage of high octane rating, lower cost, and reduced **emission** of pollutants, compared to normal gasoline. *See also* Air pollution; Alternative fuels

[*David E. Newton*]

FURTHER READING

Joesten, M. D., et al. *World of Chemistry*. Philadelphia: Saunders, 1991.

Lapedes, D. N., ed. *McGraw-Hill Encyclopedia of Energy*. New York: McGraw-Hill, 1976.

"MBTE Growth Limited Despite Lead Phasedown in Gasoline." *Chemical & Engineering News* (July 15, 1985): 12.

Williams, R. "On the Octane Trail." *Technology Illustrated* (May 1983): 52-53.

Gasoline tax

Gasoline taxes include federal, state, county and municipal taxes imposed on **gasoline** motor vehicle fuel. In the United States, most of the federal tax is used to fund maintenance and improvements in such transportation infrastructures as interstate highways. In 1993, the federal excise tax on gasoline increased from 14.1 cents per gallon to 18.4 cents per gallon. State excise taxes range from 7.5 cents in Georgia to 33 cents in Connecticut. The weighted national average state tax is 22 cents per gallon. Local taxes range from none to 33 cents in New York, and the national average is about 2 cents. Thus, the U.S. national average gasoline tax is 42.5 cents per gallon ($0.11 per liter). In the U.S., about one billion dollars in annual revenues are raised per penny of the gasoline tax.

In some countries (including the U.S.), diesel fuels are taxed and priced less than gasoline. Previously, commercial vehicles were the largest consumers of diesel, and lower taxes avoided undue impacts on trucking and commerce. Recently, many motorists have purchased diesel-fueled vehicles to benefit from their lower operating costs (including lower taxes).

Gasoline taxes have been collected for many decades. Federal taxes were imposed in the 1940s at 1.5 cents per gallon, increased to 4 cents in the 1960s, 9 cents in the mid 1980s, 14 cents in 1991, and 18.4 cents in 1993. Over this time, gasoline prices increased from about 20 cents per gallon to 120.5 cents in 1995. (1995 figures from the American Petroleum Institute). Thus, the average national gasoline tax (42.5 cents per gallon) constitutes 35% of the average national retail price. At present, the tax is greater than the cost of manufacturing, distributing, and marketing (37.1 cents per gallon), and somewhat greater than the cost of crude oil (41 cents per gallon; note however, that the price of crude is quite volatile). Since the 1980s, the share of the retail price paid as tax has increased, and gasoline taxes are the largest single component in the retail price of gasoline.

Gasoline taxes have been criticized as regressive and thus inequitable, i.e., lower income individuals pay a greater share of their income as tax than higher income individuals. Also, the tax as a share of the pump price has been increasing. Finally, gasoline taxes are very visible, marked clearly at each pump. However, it should be noted that the general trend of the real price of gasoline (adjusted for inflation and including taxes) has been declining for many decades. Also, automobile efficiency (mileage) has been improving and thus the fuel requirements and cost-per-mile-traveled have declined. These factors can be viewed as largely or completely offsetting the impact of gasoline taxes. For example, Congress attempted in May 1996 to rollback the 4.3 cents tax increase of 1993. The impact of this repeal for a family of four who drive 12,000 miles a year at 20 miles per gallon is a savings of $26, which in the House debates was compared to the cost of a family dinner at McDonald's.

In most other countries, gasoline prices are far higher ($4.00 per gallon), and taxes constitute 50-80% of the pump price. In addition to funding governments, high gasoline taxes form part of a strategy to encourage the use of public transportation, reduce pollution, conserve energy, and improve national security (since most gasoline is imported). Some individuals in the U.S. have called for a gradual phase-in of a 50 cent per gallon federal gasoline tax. While this increase would keep the gasoline tax below international norms, political considerations make such increases unlikely.

[*Stuart Batterman*]

Gastropods

Gastropods are invertebrate animals that make up the largest class in the phylum Mollusca. Examples of common gastropods include all varieties of snails, abalone, limpets, and land and sea slugs. There are over 35,000 existing species, as well an additional 15,000 separate fossil species. Gastropods first appeared in the fossil record during the early Cambrian period, approximately 550 million years ago.

This diverse group of animals is characterized by a soft body, made up of three main parts: the head, foot, and visceral mass. The head contains a mouth and often sensing tentacles. The lower portion of the body makes up the foot, which allows slow creeping along rocks and other solid surfaces. The visceral mass is the main part of the body, containing most of the internal organs. In addition to these body parts, gastropods possess a mantle, or fold which secretes a hard, calcium carbonate shell. The single, asymmetrical shell of a gastropod is most often spiral shaped, however, it can be flattened or cone-like. This shell is an important source of protection. Predators have a difficult time accessing the soft flesh inside, especially if there are sharp points on the outside, as there are on the shells of some of the more ornate gastropods. There are also some gastropods, such as slugs and sea hares, that do not have shells or have greatly reduced shells. Some of the shelless types that live in the ocean (i.e. nudibranchs or sea slugs) are able to use stinging cells from prey that they have consumed as a means of protection.

In addition to a spiraling of their shells, the soft bodies of most gastropods undergo 180 degrees of twisting, or torsion, during early development, when one side of the visceral mass grows faster than the other. This characteristic distinguishes gastropods from other molluscs. Torsion results in a U-shaped digestive tract, with the anal opening slightly behind the head. The torsion of the soft body and the spiraling of the shell are thought to be unrelated evolutionary events.

Gastropods have evolved to live in a wide variety of habitats. The great majority are marine, living in the world's oceans. Numerous species live in fresh water, while others live entirely on land. Of those that live in water, most are found on the bottom, attached to rocks or other surfaces. There are even a few species of gastropods without shells, including sea butterflies, that are capable of swimming. Living in different habitats has resulted in a wide variety of structural adaptations within the class Gastropoda. For example, those gastropods that live in water use gills to obtain the oxygen necessary for respiration, while their terrestrial relatives have evolved lungs to breathe.

Gastropods are important links in food webs in the habitats in which they live, employing a wide variety of feeding strategies. For example, most gastropods move a rasping row of teeth on a tongue like organ called a radula back and forth to scrape microscopic algae off rocks or the surface of plants. Because the teeth on the radula gradually wear away, new teeth are continuously secreted. Other gastropods have evolved a specialized radula for drilling through shells of animals to get at their soft flesh. For example, the oyster drill, a small east coast gastropod, bores a small hole in the shell of neighboring molluscs such as oysters and clams so that it can consume the soft flesh. In addition, some terrestrial gastropods such as snails use their radula to cut through pieces of leaves for food.

Gastropods are eaten by numerous animals, including various types of fish, birds, and mammals. They are also eaten by humans throughout the world. Abalone, muscular shelled gastropods that cling to rocks, are consumed on the west coast of the United States and in Asia. Fritters and chowder are made from the large, snail-like queen conch on many Caribbean islands. Escargot (snails in a garlicky butter sauce) are a European delicacy.

[*Max Strieb*]

FURTHER READING

Barnes, R. D. *Invertebrate Zoology*, 5th ed. Philadelphia: Saunders College Publishing, 1987.

Gene bank

The term gene bank refers to any system by which the genetic composition of some population is identified and stored. Many different kinds of gene banks have been established for many different purposes. Perhaps the most numerous gene banks are those that consist of plant seeds, known as germ banks.

The primary purpose for establishing a gene bank is to preserve examples of threatened or **endangered species**. Each year, untold numbers of plant and animal **species** become extinct because of natural processes and more commonly, as the result of human activities. Once those species become extinct, their **gene pool**s are lost forever.

Scientists want to retain those gene pools for a number of reasons. For example, agriculture has been undergoing a dramatic revolution in many parts of the world over the past half century. Scientists have been making available to farmers plants that grow larger, yield more fruit, are more disease-resistant, and have other desirable characteristics. These plants have been produced by agricultural research in the United States and other nations. Such plants are very attractive to farmers, and they are also important to governments as a way of meeting the food needs of growing populations, especially in **Third World** countries.

When farmers switch to these new plants, however, they often abandon older, more traditional crops that may then become extinct. Although the traditional plants may be less productive, they have other desirable characteristics. They may, for example, be able to survive **drought**s or other extreme environmental conditions that new plants cannot.

Placing seeds from traditional plants in a gene bank allows them to be preserved. At some later time, scientists may want to study these plants further and perhaps identify the genes that are responsible for various desirable properties of the plants. The **U.S. Department of Agriculture (USDA)** has long maintained a **seed bank** of plants native to the United States. About 200,000 varieties of seeds are stored at the USDA's Station at Fort Collins, Colorado, and another 100,000 varieties are kept at other locations around the country.

Efforts are now underway to establish gene banks for animals, too. Such banks consist of small colonies of the animals themselves. Animal gene banks are desirable as a way of maintaining species whose natural population is very low. Sometimes the purpose of the bank is simply to maintain the species to prevent its becoming extinct. In other cases, species are being preserved because they were once used as farm animals although they have since been replaced by more productive modern hybrid species. The Fayoumi chicken native to Egypt, for example, has now been abandoned by farmers in favor of imported species. The Fayoumi, without some form of protection, is likely to become extinct. Nonetheless, it may well have some characteristics (genes) that are worth preserving. In 1992, the United Nations **Food and Agriculture Organization** launched a five-year, $15-million program to develop a gene bank for endangered animals such as the Fayoumi chicken.

In recent years, another type of gene bank has become possible. In this kind of gene bank, the actual base sequence of important genes in the human body will be determined, collected, and catalogued. This effort, begun in 1990, is a part of the Human Genome Project effort to map all human genes. *See also* Agricultural revolution; Extinction; Genetic engineering; Population growth

[*David E. Newton*]

FURTHER READING

Anderson, C. "Genetic Resources: A Gene Library That Goes 'Moo'." *Nature* 355 (30 January 1992): 382.

Crawford, M. "USDA Bows to Rifkin Call for Review of Seed Bank." *Science* 230 (6 December 1985): 1146-1147.

Roberts, L. "DOE to Map Expressed Genes." *Science* 250 (16 November 1990): 913.

Gene pool

The term gene pool refers to the sum total of all the genetic information stored within any given population. A gene is a specific portion of a **DNA (deoxyribose nucleic acid)** molecule, so a gene pool is the sum total of all of the DNA contained within a population of individuals.

The concept of gene pool is important in ecological studies because it reveals changes that may or may not be taking place within a population. In a population living in an ideal **environment** for its needs, the gene pool is likely to undergo little or no change. If individuals are able to obtain all the food, water, energy, and other resources they need, they experience relatively little stress and there is no pressure to select one or another characteristic.

Changes do occur in gene frequency because of natural factors in the environment. For example, natural **radiation exposure** causes changes in DNA molecules that are revealed as genetic changes. These natural **mutation**s are one of the factors that make possible continuous changes in the genetic constitution of a population that, in turn, allows for **evolution** to occur.

Natural populations seldom live in ideal situations, however, and so they experience various kinds of stress that lead to changes in the gene pool. A classical example of this kind of change was reported by **J. B. S. Haldane** in 1937. Haldane found that a population of moths gradually became darker in color over time as the trees on which they lived also became darker because of **pollution** from factories. Moths in the population who carried genes for darker color were better able to survive and reproduce than were their lighter-colored cousins, so the composition of the gene pool changed to relieve stress.

Humans have the ability to make conscious changes in gene pools that no other **species** has. Sometimes we make those changes in the gene pools of plants or animals to serve our own needs for food or other resource. Hybridization of plants to produce populations that have some desirable quality such as resistance to disease, shorter growing season, or better-tasting fruit. The modern science of **genetic engineering** is perhaps the most specific and deliberate way of changing in gene pools today.

Humans can also change the gene pool of their own species. For example, individuals with various genetic disorders were at one time doomed to death. Our inability to treat diabetes, sickle-cell anemia, phenylketonuria, and other hereditary conditions meant that the frequency of the genes causing those disorders in the human gene pool was kept under control by natural forces.

Today, many of those same disorders can be treated by medical or genetic techniques. That results in positive benefit for the individuals who are cured, but raises questions about the quality of the human gene pool overall. Instead of having many of those deleterious genes being lost naturally by an individual's death, they are now retained as part of the gene pool. This fact has at times raised questions about the best way in which medical science should deal with genetic disorders. *See also* Agricultural revolution; Birth defects; Extinction; Gene bank; Population growth

[*David E. Newton*]

FURTHER READING

Patt, D. I., and G. R. Patt. *An Introduction to Modern Genetics*. Reading, MA: Addison-Wesley, 1976.

Genetic engineering

Genetic engineering is the manipulation of the hereditary material of organisms at the molecular level. The hereditary material of most cells is found in the chromosomes, and it is made of **DNA** (deoxyribose nucleic acid). The total DNA of an organism is referred to as its genome. Structurally, the DNA molecule is a double helix, formed from two complementary strands of nucleotides twisted around one another. Biochemically, nucleotides are chains of repeating molecular units comprising a sugar, a base, and phosphoric acid. There are four bases—adenine, thymine, guanine, and cytosine—which pair up in the double helix of DNA, forming complementary base pairs. The sequence of nucleotide base pairs on the DNA molecule that encodes genetic information is called the genetic code. Genes are specific sequences of these nucleotides which code for a particular character. They comprise only 2 percent of the human genome; the remaining 98 percent does not code any proteins and its function is unknown.

Genetic engineering relies on recombinant DNA technology to manipulate genes. Methods are now available for rapidly sequencing the nucleotides of pieces of DNA, as well as for identifying particular genes of interest, and for isolating individual genes from complex genomes. Isolated genes from one organism can be joined to the DNA of a different organism, forming a recombined, or chimeric, DNA molecule. The recombinant DNA strand is usually inserted into a living cell where it is duplicated (cloned) when the host cell divides. These procedures alter the genetic constitution of the host individual, producing a transgenic organism. Recombinant DNA research therefore bypasses the sexual or asexual processes that normally restrict the transfer of genes between entirely different **species**.

The biochemical tools used by genetic engineers or molecular biologists include a series of **enzyme**s which can "cut and paste" genes. Enzymes are used to cut a piece of DNA, insert into it a new piece of DNA from another organism, and then seal the joint.

One important group of these are restriction enzymes, of which well over 500 are known. Most restriction enzymes are endonucleases—enzymes that break the double helix of DNA within the molecule, rather than attacking the ends of the helix. Every restriction enzyme is given a specific name to identify it uniquely. The first three letters, in italics, indicate the biological source of the enzyme, the first letter being the initial of the genus, the second and third letters being the first two letters of the species name. Thus restriction enzymes from *Escherichia coli* are called *Eco*, those from *Haemophilus influenzae* are *Hin*, from *Diplococcus pneumoniae* comes *Dpn*, and so on.

The genetic engineer can use a restriction enzyme to locate and cut almost any sequence of bases. Cuts can be made anywhere along the DNA, dividing it into many small fragments or a few longer ones. The results are repeatable: cuts made by the same enzyme on a given sort of DNA will always be the same. Some enzymes recognize sequences as long as six or seven bases; these are used for opening a circular strand of DNA at just one point. Other enzymes have a smaller recognition site, three or four bases long; these produce small fragments that can then be used to determine the sequence of bases along the DNA.

The cut that each enzyme makes varies from enzyme to enzyme. Some, like *Hin* dII, make a clean cut straight across the double helix which leaves DNA fragments with ends that are flush. Other enzymes (*Eco* RI) make a staggered break, which leaves single strands with protruding cohesive ends ("sticky ends") that are complementary in base sequence. Following breakage, and under the right conditions, the complementary bases from different sources can be rejoined to form recombinant DNA.

Another important biochemical tool used by genetic engineers is DNA polymerase, an enzyme that normally catalyses the growth of a nucleic acid chain. DNA polymerase is used by genetic engineers to seal the gaps between the two sets of fragments in newly-joined chimera molecules of recombinant DNA. DNA polymerase is also used to label DNA fragments, for DNA polymerase labels practically every base, allowing minute quantities of DNA to be studied in detail. If a piece of **RNA** (ribonucleic acid) of the target

DNA injected into a mouse embryo.

gene is the starting point, then the enzyme reverse transcriptase is used to produce a strand of complementary DNA (cDNA).

Genetic engineers usually need large numbers of genetically-identical copies of the DNA fragment of interest. One way of doing this is to insert the gene into a suitable gene carrier, called a cloning vector. Common cloning vectors are bacterial plasmids or **virus**es such as the bacteriophage lambda, which are small circles of DNA found in bacterial cells independently of the main DNA molecule. When the cloning vectors divide, they replicate both themselves and the foreign DNA segment linked to it.

In the plasmid insertion method, restriction enzymes are used to cleave the plasmid double helix so that a stretch of DNA (previously cleaved with the same enzyme) can be inserted into the plasmid. As a result, the "sticky ends" of the plasmid DNA and the foreign DNA are complementary and base-pair when mixed together. The fragments held together by base pairing are permanently joined by DNA ligase. The host bacterium, with its 20-30 minute reproductive cycle, is like a manufacturing plant. With repeated doublings of its offspring on a controlled culture medium, millions of clones of the purified DNA fragments can be produced overnight.

Similarly, if viruses (bacteriophages) are used as cloning vectors, the gene of interest is inserted into the phage DNA, and the virus is allowed to enter the host bacterial cell where it multiplies. A single parental lambda phage particle containing recombinant DNA can multiply to several hun-

dred progeny particles inside the bacterial cell (*E. coli*) within roughly 20 minutes. Cosmids are another type of viral cloning vehicle that attaches foreign DNA to the packaging sites of a virus and thus introduces the foreign DNA into an infective viral particle. Cosmids allow researchers to insert very long stretches of DNA into host cells where cell multiplication amplifies the amount of DNA available. Large artificial chromosomes of yeast (called megaYACs) are also used as cloning vehicles, since they can store even larger pieces of DNA, 35 times more than can be stored conventionally in bacteria.

The polymerase chain reaction (PCR) technique is an important new development in the field of genetic engineering, since it allows the mass production of short segments of DNA directly, and offers the advantage of bypassing the several steps involved in using bacterial and viruses as cloning vectors.

DNA fragments can be introduced into mammalian cells, but a different method must be used. Here, genes packed in solid calcium phosphate are placed next to a cell membrane which surrounds the fragment and transfers it to the cytoplasm. The gene is delivered to the nucleus during mitosis (when the nuclear membrane has disappeared) and the DNA fragments are incorporated into daughter nuclei, then into daughter cells. A mouse containing human **cancer** genes (the onchomouse) was patented in 1988.

The potential benefits of recombinant DNA research are enormous. **Biotechnology** uses bacterial "factories" to mass-produce enzymes and hormones from instructions encoded in human genes incorporated into bacterial DNA. Insulin (formerly extracted from pig livers), growth hormone (formerly from the pituitary glands of human cadavers), and interferon (formerly from human cadavers) are now produced in this way. Gene manipulation is also increasing the understanding and treatment of inherited human conditions, such as Huntington's disease.

Genetic engineering has produced transgenic food crops modified for disease resistance, as well as for greater yields, longer freshness, and for enhanced **nitrogen** uptake. Recombinant DNA technologies are also the basis of DNA fingerprinting methods. Genetic engineering is now being used to uncover the nucleic acid sequence of entire chromosomes, of the entire genome of simple species, and soon, the entire human genome. *See also* Gene bank; Gene pool

[*Neil Cumberlidge*]

FURTHER READING

Cherfas, J. *Man Made Life: An Overview of the Science and Technology and Commerce of Genetic Engineering.* New York: Pantheon Books, 1982.

Coghlan, A. "Engineering the Therapies of Tomorrow." *New Scientist* 137 (24 April 1993): 26-31.

Kahn, P. "Genome on the Production Line." *New Scientist* 137 (24 April 1993): 32-36.

Miller, S. K. "To Catch a Killer Gene." *New Scientist* 137 (24 April 1993): 37-40.

Verma, I. M. "Gene Therapy." *Scientific American* 263 (November 1990): 68-84.

Watson, J. D, J. Tooze, and D. T. Kurtz. *Recombinant DNA: A Short Course.* San Francisco: W. H. Freeman, 1983.

Wheale, P. R., and R. M. McNally. *Genetic Engineering: Catastrophe or Utopia?* New York: St. Martin's Press, 1988.

Genetic resistance (or genetic tolerance)

Genetic resistance (or genetic tolerance) refers to the ability of certain organisms to endure environmental conditions that are extremely stressful or lethal to non-adapted individuals of the same species. Such tolerance has a genetic basis, and it evolves at the population level in response to intense selection pressures.

Genetic resistance occurs when genetically variable populations contain some individuals that are relatively tolerant of an exposure to some environmental factor, such as the presence of a high concentration of a specific chemical. If the tolerance is genetically based (i.e., due to specific information embodied in the **DNA** of the organism's chromosomes), some or all of the offspring of these individuals will also be tolerant. Under conditions in which the chemical occurs in concentrations high enough to cause toxicity to non-tolerant individuals, the resistant ones will be relatively successful. As time passes their offspring will become increasingly more prominent in the population. Acquiring genetic resistance is an evolutionary process, involving increased tolerance within a population, for which there is a genetic basis, and occurring in response to selection for resistance to the effects of a toxic

chemical. Some of the best examples of genetic resistance involve the tolerance of certain bacteria to antibiotics and of certain pests to pesticides.

Resistance to Antibiotics

Antibiotics are chemicals used to treat bacterial infections of humans and domestic animals. Examples of commonly used antibiotics include various kinds of penicillins, streptomycins, and tetracyclines, all of which are metabolic byproducts created by certain microorganisms, especially fungi. There are also many synthetic antibiotics.

Antibiotics are extremely toxic to non-resistant strains of bacteria, and this has been very beneficial in the control of bacterial infections and diseases. However, if even a tiny fraction of a bacterial population has a genetically based tolerance to a specific antibiotic, evolution will quickly result in the development of a population that is resistant to that chemical. Bacterial resistance to antibiotics was first demonstrated for penicillin, but the phenomenon is now quite widespread. This is an important medical problem because some serious **pathogen**s are now resistant to virtually all of the available antibiotics, which means that infections by these bacteria can be extremely difficult to control. Bacterial resistance has recently become the cause of infections by some virulent strains of *Staphylococcus* and other potentially deadly bacteria. Some biologists believe that this problem has been made worse by the failure of many people to finish their course of prescribed antibiotic treatments, which can allow tolerant bacteria to survive and flourish. Also possibly important has been the routine use of antibiotics to prevent diseases in livestock kept under crowded conditions in industrial farming. The small residues of antibiotics in meat, eggs, and milk may be resulting in low-level selection for resistant bacteria in exposed populations of humans and domestic animals.

Resistance to Pesticides

The insecticide **dichlorodiphenyl-trichloroethane (DDT)** was the first **pesticide** to which insect pests developed resistance. This occurred because the exposure of insect populations to toxic DDT results in intense selection for resistant genotypes. Tolerant populations can evolve because genetically resistant individuals are not killed by the pesticide and therefore survive to reproduce. Almost 500 species of insects and mites have populations that are known to be resistant to at least one insecticide. There are also more than 100 examples of fungicide-resistant plant pathogens and about 50 herbicide-resistant weeds. Insecticide resistance is most frequent among species of flies and their relatives (order Diptera), including more than 50 resistant species of malaria-carrying *Anopheles* mosquitoes. In fact, the progressive evolution of insecticide resistance by *Anopheles* has been an important factor in the recent resurgence of malaria in countries with warm climates. In addition, the protozoan *Plasmodium*, which actually causes malaria, has become resistant to some of the drugs that used to effectively control it.

Crop geneticists have recently managed to breed varieties of some plant species that are resistant to glyphosate, a commonly used agricultural herbicide that is effective against a wide range of weeds, including both monocots and dicots.

The development of glyphosate-tolerant varieties of such crops as rapeseed means that this effective herbicide can be used to control difficult weeds in planted fields without causing damage to the crop.

[*Bill Freedman*]

FURTHER READING

Freedman, B. *Environmental Ecology*, 2nd ed. San Diego, CA: Academic Press, 1995.

Hayes, W.C., and E.R. Laws (eds.) *Handbook of Pesticide Toxicology*. San Diego, CA: Academic Press, 1991.

National Research Council (NRC). *Pesticide Resistance*. NRC, Washington, D.C.: National Academy Press, 1986.

Raven, P.H., and G.B. Johnson. *Biology*, 3rd ed. St. Louis, MO.: Mosby Year Book, 1992.

Genetically engineered organism

The modern science of genetics began in the mid-nineteenth century with the work of Gregor Mendel, but the nature of the gene itself was not understood until James Watson and Francis Crick announced their findings in 1953. According to the Watson and Crick model, genetic information is stored in molecules of **DNA (deoxyribose nucleic acid)** by means of certain patterns of **nitrogen** base that occur in such molecules. Each set of three such nitrogen bases were codes, they said, for some particular amino acid, and a long series of nitrogen bases were codes for a long series of amino acids or a protein.

Deciphering the genetic code and discovering how it is used in cells has taken many years of work since that of Watson and Crick. The basic features of that process, however, are now well understood. The first step involves the construction of a **RNA (ribonucleic acid)** molecule in the nucleus of a cell, using the code stored in DNA as a template. The RNA molecule then migrates out of the nucleus to a ribosome in the cell cytoplasm. At the ribosome, the sequence of nitrogen bases stored in RNA act as a map that determines the sequence of amino acids to be used in constructing a new protein.

This knowledge is of critical importance to biologists because of the primary role played by proteins in an organism. In addition to acting as the major building materials of which cells are made, proteins have a number of other crucial functions. All hormones and **enzyme**s, for example, are proteins, and therefore nearly all of the chemical reactions that occur within an organisms are mediated by one protein or another.

Our current understanding of the structure and function of DNA makes it at least theoretically possible to alter the biological characteristics of an organism. By changing the kind of **nitrogen** bases in a DNA molecule, or their sequence, or both, a scientist can change the genetic instructions stored in a cell and thus change the kind of protein produced by the cell.

One of the most obvious applications of this knowledge is in the treatment of genetic disorders. A large majority of genetic disorders occur because an organism is unable to manufacture correctly a particular protein molecule. An example is Lesch-Nyhan syndrome. It is a condition characterized by self-mutilation, mental retardation, and cerebral palsy which arises because a person's body is unable to manufacture an enzyme known as hypoxanthine guanine phosphoribosyl transferase (HPRT).

The general principles of the techniques required to make such changes are now well understood. The technique is referred to as **genetic engineering** or genetic surgery because it involves changes in an organism's gene structure. When used to treat a particular disorder in humans, the procedure is also called human gene therapy. Developing specific experimental techniques for carrying out genetic engineering has proved to be an imposing challenge, yet impressive strides have been made. A common procedure is known as recombinant DNA (rDNA) technology.

The first step in an rDNA procedure is to collect a piece of DNA that carries a desired set of instructions. For a genetic surgery procedure for a person with Lesch-Nyhan syndrome, a researcher would need a piece of DNA that codes for the production of HPRT. That DNA could be removed from the healthy DNA of a person who does not have Lesch-Nyhan syndrome, or the researcher might be able to manufacture it by chemical means in the laboratory.

One of the fundamental tools used in rDNA technology is a closed circular piece of DNA found in bacteria called a plasmid. Plasmids are the vehicle or vector that scientists use for transferring new pieces of DNA into cells. The next step in an rDNA procedure, then, would be to insert the correct DNA into the plasmid vector. Cutting open the plasmid can be accomplished using certain types of enzymes that recognize specific base sequences in a DNA molecule. When these enzymes, called restriction enzymes, encounter the recognized sequence in a DNA molecule, they cleave the molecule. After the plasmid DNA has been cleaved and the correct DNA mixed with it, a second type of enzyme is added. This kind of enzyme inserts the correct DNA into the plasmid and closes it up. The process is known as gene splicing.

In the final step, the altered plasmid vector is introduced into the cell where it is expected to function. In the case of a Lesch-Nyhan patient, the plasmid would be introduced into the cells where it would start producing HPRT from instructions in the correct DNA. Many technical problems remain with rDNA technology, and this last step has caused some of the greatest obstacles. It has proven very difficult to make introduced DNA function. Even when the plasmid vector with its new DNA gets into a cell, it may never actually begin to function.

Any organism whose cells contain DNA altered by this or some other technique is called a genetically engineered organism. The first human patient with a genetic disorder who is treated by human gene therapy will be a genetically engineered organism. The use of genetic engineering on human subjects has gone forward very slowly for a number of reasons. One reason is that humans are very complex organisms. Another reason is that changing the genetic make-up of a human involves more ethical questions and more difficult questions than does the genetic engineering of bacteria, mice, or cows.

Most of the existing examples of genetically engineered organisms, therefore, involve plants, non-human animals, or microorganisms. One of the earliest success stories in genetic engineering involved the altering of DNA in microorganisms to make them capable of producing chemicals they do not normally produce. Recombinant DNA technology can be used, for instance, to insert the DNA segment or gene that codes for insulin production into bacteria. When these bacteria are allowed to grow and reproduce in large fermentation tanks, they produce insulin. The list of chemicals produced by this mechanism now includes somatostatin, alpha interferon, tissue plasminogen activator (tPA), Factor VIII, erythroprotein, and human growth hormone, and this list continues to grow each year. *See also* Biotechnology; Chemicals; Gene bank; Gene pool

[*David E. Newton*]

FURTHER READING

Hoffman, C. A. "Ecological Risks of Genetic Engineering of Crop Plants." *BioScience* 40 (June 1990): 434-437.

Kessler, D. A., et al. "The Safety of Foods Developed by Biotechnology." *Science* 256 (26 June 1992): 1747-1749+.

Kieffer, G. H. *Biotechnology, Genetic Engineering, and Society.* Reston, VA: National Association of Biology Teachers, 1987.

Mellon, M. *Biotechnology and the Environment.* Washington, DC: National Biotechnology Policy Center of the National Wildlife Federation, 1988.

Pimentel, D., et al. "Benefits and Risks of Genetic Engineering in Agriculture." *BioScience* 39 (October 1989): 606-614.

Weintraub, P. "The Coming of the High-Tech Harvest." *Audubon* 94 (July-August 1992): 92-4+.

Wheale, P. R., and R. M. McNally. *Genetic Engineering: Catastrophe or Utopia?* New York: St. Martin's Press, 1988.

Geodegradable

The term geodegradable refers to a material that could degrade in the **environment** over a geologic time period. While **biodegradable** generally refers to items that may degrade within our lifetime, geodegradable material does not decompose readily and may take hundreds or thousands of years. **Radioactive waste**, for example, is degraded only over thousands of years. The glass formed as an end result of a **hazardous waste** treatment technology known as "in situ vitrification," is considered geodegradable only after a million years. *See also* Half-life; Hazardous waste site remediation; Hazardous waste siting; Waste management

Geological Survey

The United States Geological Survey (USGS) is the federal agency responsible for surveying and publishing maps of topography (giving landscape relief and elevation), geology, and **natural resources**—including minerals, fuels, and water. The USGS, part of the **U. S. Department of the Interior**, was formed in 1879 as the United States began systematically to explore its newly expanded western territories. Today it has an annual budget of about $700 million, which is devoted to primary research, resource assessment and monitoring, map production, and providing information to the public and to other government agencies.

The United States Geological Survey, now based in Reston, Virginia, originated in a series of survey expeditions sent to explore and map western territories and rivers after the Civil War. Four principal surveys were authorized between 1867 and 1872: Clarence King's exploration of the fortieth parallel, Ferdinand Hayden's survey of the Rocky Mountain territories, **John Wesley Powell**'s journey down the **Colorado River** and through the Rocky Mountains, and George Wheeler's survey of the 100th meridian. Twelve years later, in 1879, these four ongoing survey projects were combined to create a single agency, the United States Geological Survey. The USGS' first director was Clarence King. In 1881 his post was taken by John Wesley Powell, whose name is most strongly associated with the early Survey. It was Powell who initiated the USGS topographic mapping program, a project that today continues to produce the most comprehensive map series available of the United States and associated territories.

In addition to topographic mapping, the USGS began detailed surveys and mapping of mineral resources in the 1880s. Mineral exploration led to mapping geologic formations and structures and a gradual reconstruction of geologic history in the United States. Research and mapping of glacial history and fossil records naturally followed from mineral explorations, so that the USGS became the primary body in the United States involved in geologic field research and laboratory research in experimental geophysics and geochemistry. During World Wars I and II, the USGS' role in identifying and mapping tactical and strategic resources increased. Water and fuel resources (**coal**, oil, **natural gas**, and finally **uranium**) were now as important as **copper**, gold, and mineral ores, so the Survey took on responsibility for assessing these resources as well as topographic and geologic mapping.

Today the USGS is one of the world's largest earth science research agencies and the United States' most important map publisher. The Survey conducts and sponsors extensive laboratory and field research in geology, **hydrology**, oceanography, and cartography. The agency's three divisions, Water Resources, Geology, and National Mapping, are responsible for basic research. They also publish, in the form of maps and periodic written reports, information on the nation's topography, geology, fuel and mineral resources, and other aspects of earth sciences and natural resources. Most of the United States' hydrologic records and research, including streamflow rates, **aquifer** volumes, and water quality, are produced by the USGS. In addition, the USGS publishes information on natural hazards, including earthquakes, **volcano**es, **landslide**s, floods, and **drought**s. The Survey is the primary body responsible for providing basic earth science information to other government agencies, as well as to the public. In addition, the USGS undertakes or assists research and mapping in other countries whose geologic survey systems are not yet well developed.

[*Mary Ann Cunningham*]

FURTHER READING

U. S. Geological Survey. *Maps for America*. Reston, VA: U. S. Government Printing Office, 1981.

USGS Yearbook: Fiscal Year 1985. Washington, DC: U. S. Government Printing Office, 1985.

Geosphere

The solid portion of the Earth. It is also known as the lithosphere. From a technical standpoint, the geosphere includes inner parts of the Earth virtually inaccessible to human study, the inner and outer core and mantle, as well as the outermost crust. For the most part, however, environmental scientists are primarily interested in the relatively thin outer layer of the crust on which plants and animals live, in the ores and minerals that occur within the crust, and in the changes that take place in the crust as a result of **erosion** and mountain-building.

Geothermal energy

Geothermal energy is obtained from hot rocks beneath the earth's surface. The planet's core, which may generate temperatures as high as 8,000°F (4,500°C), heats its interior, whose temperature increases, on an average, by about 1°C (2°F) for every 18 meters (60 feet) nearer the core. Some heat is also generated in the mantle and crust as a result of the **radioactive decay** of **uranium** and other elements.

In some parts of the earth, rocks in excess of 100°C (212°F) are found only a few miles beneath the surface. Water that comes into contact with the rock will be heated above its boiling point. Under some conditions, the water becomes super-heated, that is, is prevented from boiling even though its temperature is greater than 100°C. Regions of this kind are known as wet steam fields. In other situations the water is able to boil normally, producing steam. These regions are known as dry steam fields.

Humans have long been aware of geothermal energy. Geysers and fumaroles are obvious indications of water heated by underground rock. The Maoris of New Zealand, for example, have traditionally used hot water from geysers to cook their food. Natural hot spring baths and spas are a common feature of many cultures where geothermal energy is readily available.

The first geothermal well was apparently opened accidentally by a drilling crew in Hungary in 1867. Eventually, hot water from such **wells** was used to heat homes in some parts of Budapest. Geothermal heat is still an important energy source in some parts of the world. More than 99 percent of the buildings in Reykjavik, the capital of Iceland, are heated with geothermal energy.

The most important application of geothermal energy today is in the generation of electricity. In general, hot steam or super-heated water is pumped to the planet surface where it is used to drive a turbine. Cool water leaving the generator is then pumped back underground. Some water is lost by evaporation during this process, so the energy that comes from geothermal wells is actually non-renewable. However, most zones of heated water and steam are large enough to allow a geothermal mine to operate for a few hundred years.

A dry steam well is the easiest and least expensive geothermal well to drill. A pipe carries steam directly from the heated underground rock to a turbine. As steam drives the turbine, the turbine drives an electrical generator. The spent steam is then passed through a condenser where much of it is converted to water and returned to the earth.

Dry steam fields are relatively uncommon. One, near Larderello, Italy, has been used to produce electricity since 1904. The geysers and fumaroles in the region are said to have inspired Dante's *Inferno*. The Larderello plant is a major source of electricity for Italy's electric railway system. Other major dry steam fields are located near Matsukawa, Japan, and at Geysers, California. The first electrical generating plant at the Geysers was installed in 1960. It and companion plants now provide about 5 percent of all the electricity produced in California.

Wet steam fields are more common, but the cost of using them as sources of geothermal energy is greater. The temperature of the water in a wet steam field may be anywhere from 360° to 660°F (180° to 250°C). When a pipe is sunk into such a reserve, some water immediately begins to boil, changing into very hot steam. The remaining water is carried out of the reserve with the steam.

At the surface, a separator is used to remove the steam from the hot water. The steam is used to drive a turbine and a generator, as in a dry steam well, before being condensed to a liquid. The water is then mixed with the hot water (now also cooled) before being returned to the earth.

The largest existing geothermal well using wet steam is in Wairakei, New Zealand. Other plants have been built in Russia, Japan, and Mexico. In the United States, pilot plants have been constructed in California and New Mexico. The technology used in these plants is not yet adequate, however, to allow them to compete economically with fossil-fueled **power plants**.

Hot water (in contrast to steam) from underground reserves can also be used to generate electricity. Plants of this type make use of a binary (two-step) process. Hot water is piped from underground into a heat exchanger at the surface. The heat exchanger contains some low-boiling point liquid (the "working fluid"), such as a freon or isobutane. Heat from the hot water causes the working fluid to evaporate. The vapor then produced is used to drive the turbine and generator. The hot water is further cooled and then returned to the rock **reservoir** from which it came.

In addition to dry and wet steam fields, a third kind of geothermal reserve exists: pressurized hot water fields located deep under the ocean floors. These reserves contain **natural gas** mixed with very hot water. Some experts believed that these geopressurized zones are potentially rich energy sources although no technology currently exists for tapping them.

Another technique for the capture of geothermal energy makes use of a process known as hydrofracturing. In hydrofracturing, water is pumped from the surface into a layer of heated dry rock at pressures of about 7,000 pounds per square inch (500 kilograms per square centimeter). The pressurized water creates cracks over a large area in the rock layer. Then, some material such as sand or plastic beads is also injected into the cracked rock. This material is used to help keep the cracks open.

Subsequently, additional cold water can be pumped into the layer of hot rock, where it is heated just as natural **groundwater** is heated in a wet or dry steam field. The heated water is then pumped back out of the earth and into a turbine-generator system. After cooling, the water can be re-injected into the ground for another cycle. Since water is continually re-used in this process and the earth's heat is essentially infinite, the hydrofracturing system can be regarded as a renewable source of energy.

Considerable enthusiasm was expressed for the hydrofracturing approach during the 1970s and a few experimental plants were constructed. But, as oil prices dropped and interest in **alternative energy sources** decreased in the 1980s, these experiments were terminated.

Geothermal energy clearly has some important advantages as a power source. The raw material — heated water and steam — is free and readily available, albeit in only certain limited areas. The technology for extracting hot water and steam is well developed from **petroleum**-drilling experiences, and its cost is relatively modest. Geothermal mining, in addition, produces almost no **air pollution** and seems to have little effect on the land where it occurs.

On the other hand, geothermal mining does have its disadvantages. One is that it can be achieved in only limited parts of the world. Another is that it results in the release of gases, such as **hydrogen** sulfide, **sulfur dioxide**, and ammonia, that have offensive odors and are mildly irritating. Some environmentalists also object that geothermal mining is visually offensive, especially in some areas that are otherwise aesthetically attractive. Pollution of water by **runoff** from a geothermal well and the large volume of cooling water needed in such plant are also cited as disadvantages.

At their most optimistic, proponents of geothermal energy claim that up to 15 percent of the United States' power needs can be met from this source. Lagging interest and research in this area over the past decade have made this goal unreachable. Today, no more than 0.1 percent of the nation's electricity comes from geothermal sources. Only in California is geothermal energy a significant power source. As an example, GeoProducts Corporation, of Moraga, California, has constructed a $60 million geothermal plant near Lassen National Park that generates 30 **megawatt**s of power.

Until the government and the general public becomes more concerned about the potential of various types of alternative energy sources, however, geothermal is likely to remain a minor energy source in the country as a whole. *See*

also Alternative fuels; Fossil fuels; Renewable resources; Water pollution

[*David E. Newton*]

FURTHER READING

Fishman, D. J. "Hot Rocks." *Discover* 12 (July 1991): 22-23.

Moran, J. M., M. D. Morgan, and J. H. Wiersma. *Environmental Science.* Dubuque, IA: W. C. Brown, 1993.

National Academy of Sciences. *Geothermal Energy Technology.* Washington, DC: National Academy Press, 1988.

Rickard, G. *Geothermal Energy.* Milwaukee, WI: Gareth Stevens, 1991.

U. S. Department of Energy. *Geothermal Energy and Our Environment.* Washington, DC: U. S. Government Printing Office, 1980.

Giant panda (*Ailuropoda melanoleuca*)

Today, the giant panda is one the best known and most popular large mammals among the general public. Although its existence was known long ago, having been mentioned in a 2,500-year-old Chinese geography text, Europeans did not learn of its existence until its discovery by a French missionary in 1869. The first living giant panda did not reach the Western Hemisphere until 1937. The giant panda, variously classified with the true bears or, often, in a family of its own, once ranged throughout much of China and Burma, but is now restricted to a series of 12 **wildlife** reserves totalling just over 2,200 square miles (569,799 ha) in three central and western Chinese provinces. The giant panda population has been decimated over the past 2,000 years by hunting and **habitat** destruction. Giant pandas are one of the rarest mammals in the world, with current estimates of their population size ranging from 500 to 1,000 individuals. Today human pressure on giant panda populations has diminished, although **poaching** continues. Giant pandas are protected by tradition and sentiment, as well as by law in the Chinese mountain forest reserves. Despite this progress, however, **IUCN—The World Conservation Union** and the U. S. **Fish and Wildlife Service** consider the giant panda to be endangered. Some of this **species**' unique **niche** requirements and habits do seem to put them in jeopardy.

The anatomy of the giant panda indicates that it is a carnivore, however, its diet consists almost entirely of bamboo, whose cellulose cannot be digested by the panda. Since the giant panda obtains so little **nutrient** value from the bamboo, it must eat enormous quantities of the plant each day, about 35 lbs (16 kg) of leaves and stems, in order to satisfy its energy requirements. Whenever possible, it feeds solely on the young succulent shoots of bamboo, which, being mostly water, requires it to eat almost 90 lbs (41 kg) per day. This translates into 10-12 hours per day that pandas spend eating. Giant pandas have been known to supplement their diet with other plants such as horsetail and pine bark, and they will even eat small animals, such as rodents, if they can catch them, but well over 95 percent of their diet consists of the bamboo plant.

Bamboo normally grows by sprouting new shoots from underground rootstocks. At intervals from 40 to 100 years, the bamboo plants blossom, produce seeds, then die. New bamboo then grows from the seed. In some regions it may take up to six years for new plants to grow from seed and produce enough food for the giant panda. Undoubtedly this has produced large shifts in panda population size over the centuries. Within the last quarter century, two bamboo flowerings have caused the starvation of nearly 200 giant pandas, a significant portion of the modern population. Although the wildlife reserves contain sufficient bamboo, much of the vast bamboo forests of the past have been destroyed for agriculture, leaving no alternative areas to move to should bamboo blossoming occur in their current range.

Low **fecundity** and limited success in captive breeding programs in **zoo**s does not bode well for replenishing any significant losses in the wild population. For the time being, the giant panda population appears stable, a positive sign for one of the world's scarcest and most popular animals. *See also* Captive propagation and reintroduction; Endangered species; Rare species

[*Eugene C. Beckham*]

FURTHER READING

Drew, L. "Are We Loving the Panda to Death?" *National Wildlife* 27 (1989): 14-17.

Nowak, R. M., ed. *Walker's Mammals of the World.* 5th ed. Baltimore: Johns Hopkins University Press, 1991.

Schaller, G. B. "Pandas in the Wild." *National Geographic* 160 (1981): 735-49.

———, et al. *The Giant Pandas of Wolong.* Chicago: University of Chicago Press, 1985.

Giardia

Giardia is the genus (and common) name of a protozoan **parasite** in the phylum Sarcomastigophora. It was first described in 1681 by Antoni van Leeuwenhoek (called "The Father of Microbiology"), who discovered it in his own stool. The most common species is *Giardia intestinalis* (also called *lamblia*), which is a fairly common parasite found in humans. The disease it causes is called giardiasis.

The trophozoite (feeding) stage is easily recognized by its pear-shaped, bilaterally-symmetrical form with two internal nuclei and four pairs of external flagella; the thin-walled cyst (infective) stage is oval. Both stages are found in the upper part of the small intestine in the mucosal lining. The anterior region of the ventral surface of the troph stage is modified into a sucking disc used to attach to the host's abdominal epithelial tissue. Each troph attaches to one epithelial cell. In extreme cases, nearly every cell will be covered, causing severe symptoms. Infection usually occurs through drinking contaminated water. Homosexual practices also favor transmission. Symptoms include diarrhea, flatu-

Giardia.

lence (gas), abdominal cramps, fatigue, weight loss, anorexia, and/or nausea and may last for more than five days. Diagnosis is usually done by detecting cysts or trophs of this parasite in fecal specimens.

Giardia has a worldwide distribution. It is more common in warm, tropical regions than in cold regions. Hosts include frogs, cats, dogs, beaver, muskrat, horses, and humans. Children as well as adults can be affected, although it is more common in children. It is highly contagious. Normal infection rate in the United States ranges from 1.5-20 percent. In one case involving scuba divers from the New York City police and fire fighters, 22-55 percent were found to be infected, presumably after they accidentally drank contaminated water in the local rivers while diving. In another case, an epidemic of giardiasis occurred in Aspen, Colorado, in 1965 during the popular ski season and 120 people were infected. Higher infection rates are common in some areas of the world, including Iran and countries in Sub-Saharan Africa.

Giardia can typically withstand sophisticated forms of **sewage treatment**, including **filtration** and **chlorination**. It is therefore hard to eradicate and may potentially increase in polluted lakes and rivers. For this reason, health officials should make concerted efforts to prevent contaminated feces from infected animals (including humans) from entering lakes used for drinking water.

The most effective treatment for giardiasis is the drug Atabrine (quinacrine hydrochloride). Adult dosage is 0.1 g taken after meals three times each day. Side effects are rare and minimal. *See also* Cholera; Coliform bacteria

[*John Korstad*]

FURTHER READING

Markell, E. K., M. Voge, and D. T. John. *Medical Parasitology.* 7th ed. Philadelphia: W. B. Saunders, 1992.

Schmidt, G. D., and L. S. Roberts. *Foundations of Parasitology.* 4th ed. St. Louis: Times Mirror/Mosby, 1989.

U. S. Department of Health and Human Services. *Health Information for International Travel.* Washington, DC: U. S. Government Printing Office, 1991.

Gibbons

Gibbons (genus *Hylobates*, meaning "dweller in the trees") are the smallest members of the ape family which also includes **gorillas**, **chimpanzees**, and **orangutan**s. They spend most of their lives at the tops of trees in the jungle, eating leaves and fruit. They are extremely agile, swinging with their long arms on branches to move from tree to tree. They have no tails and are often seen walking upright on tree branches. Gibbons are known for their loud calls and songs, which they use to announce their territory and warn away others. They are devoted parents, raising usually one or two offspring at a time and showing extraordinary affection in caring for them. Conservationists and animal protectionists who have worked with gibbons describe them as extremely intelligent, sensitive, and affectionate.

Gibbons have long been hunted for food, for medical research, and for sale as pets and zoo specimens. A common method of collecting them is to shoot the mother and capture the nursing or clinging infant, if it is still alive. The mortality rate in collecting and transporting gibbons to areas where they can be sold is extremely high, and this coupled with the destruction of their jungle **habitat** has resulted in severe depletion of their numbers.

Gibbons are found in southeast Asia, China, and India, and nine **species** are recognized. All nine species are considered endangered by the **U.S. Department of the Interior** and are listed in the most endangered category of the **Convention on International Trade in Endangered Species of Wild Fauna and Flora (CITES)**. **IUCN—The World Conservation Union** considers three species of gibbon to be endangered and two species to be vulnerable. Despite the ban on international trade in gibbons conferred by listing in Appendix I of CITES, illegal trade in gibbons, particularly babies, continues on a wide scale in markets throughout Asia. *See also* Endangered species; Pet trade

[*Lewis G. Regenstein*]

FURTHER READING

Benirschke, K. *Primates: The Road to Self-Sustaining Populations*. New York: Springer-Verlag, 1986.

Preuschoft, H., et al. *The Lesser Apes: Evolutionary and Behavioral Biology*. Edinburgh: Edinburgh University Press, 1984.

Gibbs, Lois (1951-)

American environmentalist and community organizer

An activist dedicated to protecting communities from **hazardous waste**s, Lois Gibbs began her political career as a housewife and homeowner near the **Love Canal, New York**. She was born in Buffalo on June 25, 1951, the daughter of a bricklayer and a full-time homemaker. Gibbs was twenty-one and a mother when she and her husband bought their house near a buried dump containing **hazardous material**s from industry and the military, including wastes from the research and manufacture of chemical weapons.

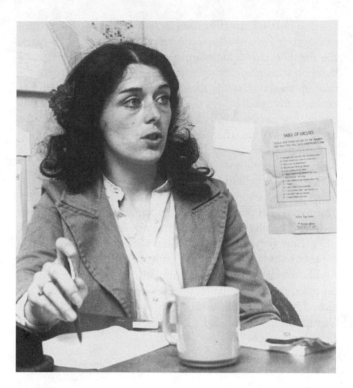

Lois Gibbs at her desk during her fight to win permanent relocation for the families living at Love Canal.

From the time the first articles about Love Canal began appearing in newspapers in 1978, Gibbs has petitioned for state and federal assistance. She began when she discovered the school her son was attending had been built directly on top of the buried canal. Her son had developed epilepsy and there were many similar, unexplained disorders among other children at the school, yet the superintendent was refusing to transfer anyone. The New York State Health Department then held a series of public meetings in which officials appeared more committed to minimizing the community perception of the problem than to solving the problem itself. The governor made promises he was unable to keep, and Gibbs herself was flown to Washington to appear at the White House for what she later decided was little more than political grandstanding. In the book she wrote about her experience, *Love Canal: My Story*, Gibbs describes her frustration and her increasing disillusionment with government, as the threats to the health of both adults and children in the community became more obvious and as it became clearer that no one would be able to move because no one could sell their homes.

While state and federal agencies delayed, the media took an increasing interest in their plight, and Gibbs became more involved in political action. To force federal action, Gibbs and a crowd of supporters took two officers from the **Environmental Protection Agency (EPA)** hostage. A group of heavily armed FBI agents occupied the building across the street and gave her seven minutes before they stormed the offices of the Homeowners' Association, where the men were being held. With less than two minutes left in the countdown, Gibbs appeared outside and released the hostages in front of a national television audience. By the middle of the next week, the EPA had announced that the Federal Disaster Assistance Administration would fund immediate evacuation for everyone in the area.

But the families who left the Love Canal area still could not sell their homes, and Gibbs fought to force the federal government to purchase them and underwrite low-interest loans. After she accused President Jimmy Carter of inaction on a national talk show, in the midst of an approaching election, he agreed to purchase the homes. But he refused to meet with her to discuss the loans. Carter signed the appropriations bill in a televised ceremony at the Democratic National Convention in New York City, and Gibbs simply walked onstage in the middle of it and repeated her request for mortgage assistance. The president could do nothing but promise his political support, and the assistance she had been asking for was soon provided.

Gibbs was divorced soon after her family left the Love Canal area. She moved to Washington D.C. with her two children and founded the **Citizen's Clearinghouse for Hazardous Wastes** in 1981. Its purpose is to assist communities in fighting toxic waste problems, particularly plans for toxic waste dumping sites, and the organization has worked with over 7,000 neighborhood and community groups. Gibbs has also published *Dying from Dioxin, A Citizen's Guide to Reclaiming Our Health and Rebuilding Democracy.* She has appeared on many television and radio shows and has been featured in hundreds of newspaper and magazine articles. She has also been the subject of several documentaries and television movies. She often speaks at conferences and seminars and has been honored with numerous awards, including the prestigious Goldman Environmental Prize in 1991. Because of Gibbs' activist work, no commercial sites for hazardous wastes have been opened in the United States since 1978.

[*Lewis G. Regenstein and Douglas Smith*]

FURTHER READING

Gibbs, L. *Love Canal: My Story.* Albany: State University of New York Press, 1982.

Wallace, A. *Eco-Heroes.* San Francisco: Mercury House, 1993.

Gill nets

Gill nets are panels of diamond-shaped mesh netting used for catching fish. When fish attempt to swim through the net their gill covers get caught and they cannot back out. Depending on the **target species**, different mesh sizes are available for use. The top line of the net has a series of floats attached for buoyancy, and the bottom line has lead weights to hold the net vertically in the water column.

Gill nets have been in use for many years. They became popular in commercial fisheries in the nineteenth century, evolving from cotton twine netting to the more modern nylon twine netting and monofilament nylon netting. As with many other aspects of **commercial fishing**, the use of gill nets has developed from minor utilization to a major environmental issue. Coupled with **overfishing**, the use of gill nets has caused serious concern throughout the world.

Because gill nets are so efficient at catching fish, they are just as efficient at catching many non-target species, including other fishes, **sea turtles**, sea mammals, and sea birds. Gill nets have been used extensively in the commercial fishery for **salmon** and capelin (*Mallotus villosus*). **Dolphins**, seals, and **sea otters** (*Enhydra lutris*) get tangled in the nets, as do diving sea birds such as murres, guillemots, auklets, and puffins that rely on capelin as a mainstay in their diet. Sea turtles are also entangled and drown.

The problem has gotten worse over the last decade with the introduction and extensive use, primarily by foreign fishing fleets, of **drift nets**. Described as "the most indiscriminate killing device used at sea," drift nets are monofilament gill nets up to 40 miles in length. Left at sea for several days and then hauled on board a fishing vessel, these drift nets contain vast numbers of dead marine life, besides the target species, that are simply discarded over the side of the boat. The outrage expressed regarding these "curtains of death" led to a United Nations resolution banning their use in commercial fisheries after the end of 1992. Commercial fishermen who use other types of nets for catching fish, such as the purse seines used in the tuna fishing industry and the bag trawls used in the shrimping industry, have modified their nets and fishing techniques to attempt to eliminate the killing of dolphins and sea turtles, respectively. Unfortunately, such modifications of gill nets are nearly impossible due to the nets' design and the way these nets are used. *See also* Turtle excluder device

[*Eugene C. Beckham*]

FURTHER READING

Norris, K. "Dolphins in Crisis." *National Geographic* 182 (1992): 2-35.

Glaciation

The covering of the earth's surface with glacial ice. The term also includes the alteration of the surface of the earth by glacial **erosion** or deposition. Due to the passage of time, ice erosion can be almost unidentifiable; the weathering of hard rock surfaces often eliminates minor scratches and other evidence of such glacial activities as the carving of deep valleys. The evidence of deposition, known as depositional imprints, can vary. It may consist of specialized features a few meters above the surrounding terrain, or it may consist of ground materials several meters in thickness covering wide areas of the landscape.

Only 10 percent of the earth's surface is currently covered with glacial ice, but it is estimated that 30 percent had been covered with glacial ice at some time. During the last major glacial period, most of Europe and more than half of the North American continent were covered with ice. The glacial ice of modern day is much thinner than it was in the **ice age**, and the majority of it (85 percent) is found in **Antarctica**. About 11 percent of the remaining glacial ice is in Greenland, and the rest is scattered in high altitudes throughout the world.

Moisture and cold temperatures are the two main factors for the formation of glacial ice. Glacial ice in Antarctica is the result of relatively small quantities of snow deposition and low loss of ice because of the cold **climate**. In the middle and low latitudes where the loss of ice, known as ablation, is higher, snowfall tends to be much higher and the glaciers are able overcome ablation by generating large amounts of ice. These types of systems tend to be more active than the glaciers in Antarctica, and the most active of these are often located at high altitudes and in the path of prevailing winds carrying marine moisture.

The **topography** of the earth has been shaped by glaciation. Hills have been reduced in height and valleys created or filled in the movement of glacial ice. *Moraine* is a French term used to describe the ridges and earthen dikes formed near the edges of regional glaciers. Ground moraine is material that accumulates beneath a glacier and has low-relief characteristics, and end moraine is material that builds up along the extremities of a glacier in a ridge-like appearance.

In England, early researchers found stones that were not common to the local ground rock and decided they must have "drifted" there, carried by icebergs on water. Though geology has changed since that time, the term remains and all deposits made by glacial ice are usually identified as drift. These glacial deposits, also known as till, are highly varied in composition. They can be a fine grained deposit, or very coarse with rather large stones present, or a combination of both.

Rock and other **soil**-like debris are often crushed and ground into very small particles, and they are commonly found as **sediment** in waters flowing from a glacial mass. This material is called glacial flour, and it is carried downstream to form another kind of glacial deposit. During certain cold, dry periods of the year winds can pick up portions of this deposit and scatter it for miles. Many of the different soils in the American "Corn Belt" originated in this way, and they have become some of the more important agricultural soils in the world.

[*Royce Lambert*]

FURTHER READING

Flint, R. F. *Glacial and Pleistocene Geology*. New York: Wiley, 1972.

Glen Avon, California

See **Stringfellow**

Glen Canyon Dam

Until 1963, Glen Canyon was one of the most beautiful stretches of natural scenery in the American West. The canyon had been cut over thousands of years as the **Colo-**

rado River flowed over sandstone that once formed the floor of an ancient sea. The colorful walls of Glen Canyon were often compared to those of the Grand Canyon, only about 50 miles (80 km) downstream.

Humans have long seen more than beauty in the canyon, however. They have envisioned the potential value of a water **reservoir** that could be created by damming the Colorado. In a region where water can be as valuable as gold, plans for the construction of a giant **irrigation** project with water from a Glen Canyon **dam** go back to at least 1850.

Flood control was a second argument for the construction of such a dam. Like most western rivers, the Colorado is wild and unpredictable. When fed by melting snows and rain in the spring, its natural flow can exceed 300,000 cubic feet (8,400 cu m) per second. At the end of a hot dry summer, flow can fall to less than one percent of that value. The river's water temperature can also fluctuate widely, by more than 36°F (20°C) in a year. A dam in Glen Canyon held the promise of moderating this variability.

By the early 1900s, yet a third argument for building the dam was proposed—the generation of hydroelectric power. Both the technology and the demand were reaching the point that power generated at the dam could be supplied to Phoenix, Los Angeles, San Diego, and other growing urban areas in the Far West.

Some objections were raised in the 1950s when construction of a Glen Canyon Dam was proposed, and environmentalists fought to protect this unique natural area. The 1950s and early 1960s were not, however, an era of high environmental sensitivity, and plans for the dam eventually were approved by the U. S. Congress. Construction of the dam, just south of the Utah-Arizona border, was completed in 1963 and the new lake it created, Lake Powell, began to develop. Seventeen years later, the lake was full holding a maximum of 27 million acre-feet of water.

The environmental changes brought about by the dam are remarkable. The river itself has changed from a muddy brown color to a clear crystal blue as the **sediment**s it carries are deposited behind the dam in Lake Powell. **Erosion** of river banks downstream from the dam has lessened considerably as spring floods are brought under control. Natural beaches and sandbars, once built up by deposited sediment, are washed away. River temperatures have stabilized at an annual average of about 50°F (10°C). These physical changes have brought about changes in **flora** and **fauna** also. Four species of fish native to the Colorado have become extinct, but at least ten **species** of birds are now thriving where they barely survived before. The **biotic community** below the dam is significantly different from what it was before construction.

During the 1980s, questions about the dam's operation began to grow. A number of observers were especially concerned about the fluctuations in flow through the dam, a pattern determined by electrical needs in distant cities. During peak periods of electrical demand, operators increase the flow of water though the dam to a maximum of 30,000 cubic feet (840 cu m) per second. At periods of low demand, that flow may be reduced to 1,000 cubic feet (28 cu m) per second.

As a result of these variations, the river below the dam can change by as much as 13 ft (4 m) in height in a single 24-hour period. This variation can severely damage riverbanks and can have unsettling effects on **wildlife** in the area as, for example, fish are stranded on the shore or swept away from spawning grounds. River-rafting is also severely affected by changing river levels as rafters can never be sure from day to day what water conditions they may encounter.

Operation of the Glen Canyon Dam is made more complex by the fact that control is divided up among at least three different agencies in the **U. S. Department of the Interior**, the **Bureau of Reclamation**, the **Fish and Wildlife Service**, and the **National Park Service**, all with somewhat different missions. In 1982, a comprehensive re-analysis of the Glen Canyon area was initiated. A series of environmental studies called the Glen Canyon Environmental Studies were designed and carried out over much of the following decade. In addition, Interior Secretary Manuel Lujan announced in 1989 that an **environmental impact statement** on the downstream effects of the dam would be conducted.

The purpose of the environmental impact statement was to find out if other options were available for operating the dam that would minimize harmful effects on the environment, recreational opportunities, and Native American activities while still allowing the dam to produce sufficient levels of hydroelectric power. The effects studied included water, sediment, fish, vegetation, wildlife and habitat, endangered and other special-status species, cultural resources, air quality, recreation, hydropower, and non-use value (i.e., general appreciation of natural resources).

Nine different operating options for the dam were considered. These options fell into three general categories: unrestricted fluctuating flows (two alternative modes); restricted fluctuating flows (four modes); and steady flows (three modes).

The final choice made was one that involves "periodic high, steady releases of short duration" that reduce the dam's performance significantly below its previous operating level. The criterion for this decision was the protection and enhancement of downstream resources while continuing to permit a certain level of flexibility in the dam's operation.

A later series of experiments was designed to see what could be done to restore certain downstream resources that have been destroyed or damaged by the dam's operation. Between March 26 and April 2, 1996, the U.S. Bureau of Reclamation released unusually large amounts of water from the dam. The intent was to reproduce the large scale flooding on the Colorado River that had normally occurred every spring before the dam was built.

The primary focus of this project was to see if downstream sandbars could be restored by the flooding. The sandbars have traditionally been used as campsites and have been a major mechanism for the removal of silt from backwater channels used by native fish. Depending on the final results of this study, the Bureau will determine what changes, if any, should be taken in adjusting flow patterns over the dam to provide for maximum environmental benefit down-stream along with power output. *See also* ; Riparian land; Wild river

[*David E. Newton*]

FURTHER READING

Elfring, C. "Conflict in the Grand Canyon." *BioScience* (November 1990): 709-711.

Udall, J. R. "A Wild, Swinging River." *Sierra* (May 1990): 22-26.

Global Environment Monitoring System

A data-gathering project administered by the **United Nations Environment Programme**. The Global Environment Monitoring System (GEMS) is one aspect of the modern understanding that environmental problems ranging from the **greenhouse effect** and **ozone layer depletion** to the preservation of **biodiversity** are international in scope. The system was inaugurated in 1975, and it monitors weather and **climate** changes around the world, as well as variations in **soil**s, the health of plant and animal **species**, and the environmental impact of human activities.

GEMS was not intended to replace any existing systems; it was designed to coordinate the collection of data on the **environment**, encouraging other systems to supply information it believed was being omitted. In addition to coordinating the gathering of this information, the system also publishes it in an uniform and accessible fashion, where it can be used and evaluated by environmentalists and policy makers.

GEMS operates 25 information networks in over 142 countries. These networks monitor **air pollution**, including the release of **greenhouse gases** and changes in the ozone layer, and **air quality** in various urban center; they also gather information on **water quality** and food contamination in cooperation with the World Health Organization and the Food and Agriculture Organization of the United Nations.

Global Forum (New York, New York)

The Global Forum of Spiritual and Parliamentary Leaders on Human Survival is a worldwide organization of scientists, leaders of world religions, and parliamentarians who are attempting to change environmental and developmental values in their countries. Members include local, national, and international leaders in the arts, business, community action, education, faith, government, media, and youth sectors.

Historically, lawmakers and spiritual leaders have differed in their views toward stewardship of the earth. A conference held in Oxford, England, in 1988, and attended by 200 spiritual and legislative leaders brought these groups together with scientists to discuss solutions to worldwide environmental problems. Speakers included the Dalai Lama, Mother Teresa, and the Archbishop of Canterbury, who conferred with experts such as Carl Sagan, Kenyan environmentalist Wangari Maathai, and **Gaia hypothesis** scientist **James Lovelock**. As a result of the Oxford conference, the Soviet Union invited the Global Forum to convene an international meeting on critical survival issues. The Moscow conference, called the Global Forum on Environment and Development, took place in January 1990. Over 1,000 spiritual and parliamentary leaders, scientists, artists, journalists, businessmen, and young people from eighty-three countries attended the Moscow Forum. One initiative of the Moscow Forum was a joint commitment by scientists and religious leaders to preserve and cherish the earth.

The Global Forum tries not to duplicate the activities of other environmental groups but works to relate global issues to local **environment**s. For example, participants at the first U.S.-based Global Forum conference in Atlanta in May 1992, learned about the local effects of global problems such as **tropical rain forest** destruction, global warming, and **waste management**. The Global Forum has initiated seminars worldwide on ethical implications of the environmental crisis. Artists learn about the role of the arts in communicating global survival issues. Business leaders promote **sustainable development** at the highest levels of business and industry. Young people petition their schools to include curriculum on environmental issues as required subjects. Contact: Global Forum, 304 East 45th St., 4th Floor, New York, NY 10017.

[*Linda Rehkopf*]

Global Releaf (Washington, D.C.)

Global Releaf, an international citizen action and education program, was initiated in 1988 by the 115-year-old **American Forestry Association** in response to the worldwide concern over global warming and the **greenhouse effect**. Campaigning under the slogan "Plant a tree, cool the globe," its over 112,000 members began the effort to reforest the earth one tree at a time.

In 1990, Global Releaf began Global Releaf Forest, an effort to restore damaged **habitat** on public lands through tree plantings Global Releaf Fund is its urban counterpart. Using each one-dollar donation to plant one tree resulted in the planting of more than four million trees on 70 sites in 33 states. By involving local citizens and resource experts in each project, the program ensures that the right species are planted in the right place at the right time. Results include the protection of endangered and threatened animals, restoration of native species, and improvement of recreational opportunities.

Funding for the program has come largely from government agencies, corporations, and non-profit organizations. Chevrolet-Geo celebrated the planting of its millionth tree in October 1996. The Texaco/Global Releaf Urban Tree Initiative, utilizing more than 6,000 Texaco volunteers, has helped local groups plant more than 18,000 large trees and invested over $2.5 million in projects in twelve cities.

Outfitter Eddie Bauer began an "Add a Dollar, Plant a Tree" program to fund eight Global Releaf Forest sites in the U.S. and Canada, planting close to 350,000 trees.

The Global Releaf Fund also helps finance urban and rural reforestation on foreign soil in projects undertaken with its international partners. Engine manufacturer, Briggs & Stratton, for example, has made possible tree plantings both in the United States and in Ecuador, England, Germany, Poland, Romania, Slovakia, South Africa, and Ukraine, while Costa Rica, Gambia, and the Philippines have benefitted from picture-frame manufacturer Larsen-Juhl.

Unfortunately, not enough funding exists to grant all the requests; in 1996, only 40% of the proposed projects received financial backing. Forced to pick and choose, the review board favors those projects which aim to protect endangered and threatened species. Burned forests and natural disaster areas—like the Francis Marion National Forest in South Carolina, devastated by 1989's Hurricane Hugo—are also high on the priority list, as are streamside woodlands and **landfill**s.

Looking to the future, Global Releaf 2000 was launched in 1996 with the aim of encouraging the planting of 20 million trees, increasing the canopy in select cities by 20%, and expanding the program to include private lands and sanitary landfills. A 20-city survey done in 1985 by American Forests showed that four trees die for every one planted in U.S. cities and that the average city tree lives only 32 years (just seven years, downtown). With these facts in mind, Global Releaf asks that communities plant twice as many trees as are lost in the next decade. Contact: Global Releaf 2000, P.O. Box 2000, Washington, D.C. 20013; phone: 800-873-5323 or 202-667-3300; World Wide Web, http://www.amfor.org.

[*Ellen Link*]

FURTHER READING

"Global Releaf 2000." *American Forests* 103, no. 4 (Autumn 1996): 30.

"A Helping Hand for Damaged Land." *American Forests* 102, no. 3 (Summer 1996): 33-35.

"Planting One for the Millennium." *American Forests* 102, no. 3 (Summer 1996): 13-15.

Sobel K. L., S. Orrick, and R. Honig. *Environmental Profiles: A Global Guide to Projects and People.* New York: Garland, 1993.

Global Tomorrow Coalition (Washington, D.C.)

The Global Tomorrow Coalition (GTC) is a group of approximately 125 nongovernmental organizations, business and schools, and 600 individuals united to safeguard the against further damage and deterioration. Established in 1981, the GTC principally concentrates its efforts on public awareness. The group promotes broader public understanding of a range of global problems and issues, including **population growth**, resource consumption, alternative agricultural and energy technologies, and **sustainable development**.

The GTC is active internationally, serving as an intermediary between U.S. nongovernmental groups and those of less developed countries. It also works with the United Nations and the U.S. Congress to bring about changes in current **environmental policy**. Through its members the coalition amasses a wide range of materials, including research studies, policy analysis, and technological data. GTC acts as a clearinghouse, making these materials available through its Global Issues Resource Centers. In addition, GTC helped to develop and manages the International Network for Environmental Policy, a computer network and database available worldwide to government agencies, businesses, nongovernmental organizations, and universities.

GTC provides a significant range of educational materials. In 1990 the coalition produced *The Global Ecology Handbook*, a general-interest publication offering information on global environmental problems. The handbook integrates analysis of these issues with examples of their effects on individuals throughout the world. Solutions currently in place or under consideration are also described.

GTC has also developed a global issues education set, a six-unit curriculum for elementary and secondary students. Emphasizing simulations, group discussions, hands-on activities, and role-playing, the six units explore **tropical rain forest**s, population, **biodiversity**, sustainable development, marine and coastal resources, and global awareness.

Among GTC's other projects is a series of video discussion guides for use with PBS's ten-part *Race to Save the Planet* (1990). The GTC tapes, called *The Community Discussion Guide*, summarize the various episodes and propose additional topics for group discussion and analysis. GTC has also produced *The Race to Save the Planet Environmental Education Activity Guide* for use in high school classrooms.

GTC membership is open to both organizations and individuals. Only organizations may join as participating members. Participating members vote in annual elections of officers and board members and provide policy advice. Individuals and organizations not choosing participating-member status may join as affiliate members. Contact: Global Tomorrow Coalition, 1325 G Street, NW, Washington, DC 20005. Internet: http://eco-web.com:80/register/00890.html.

[*Les Stone*]

The Global 2000 Report

Released in July 1980, this landmark study warned of grave consequences for humanity if changes were not made in **environmental policy** around the globe. Prepared over a three year period by the President's **Council on Environmental Quality** (CEQ) in cooperation with the U.S.

Department of State and other federal agencies, this was the first comprehensive and integrated report by the United States or any other government projecting long-term environmental, resource, and population trends. It was the subject of extensive publicity, attention, and debate, influencing political leaders and policy makers the world over.

In announcing release of the report, CEQ warned that "U.S. Government projections show that unless the nations of the world act quickly and decisively to change current policies, life for most of the world's people will be more difficult and more precarious in the year 2000."

Specifically, the study states that "If present trends continue, the world in 2000 will be more crowded, more polluted, less stable ecologically, and more vulnerable to disruption than the world we live in now...For hundreds of millions of the desperately poor, the outlook for food and other necessities of life will be no better. For many, it will be worse."

Among the report's findings and conclusions were the following:

(1) The world will add almost 100 million people a year to its population, which will grow from 4.5 billion in 1980 to 6 billion in 2000;

(2) Billions of tons and millions of acres of cropland are being lost each year to **erosion** and development, and **desertification** is claiming an area the size of Maine each year;

(3) The planet's genetic resource base is being severely depleted, and between 500,000 and 2 million plant and animal **species**—15 to 20 percent of all species on the earth—could be extinguished by the year 2000;

(4) Periodic and severe water shortages will be accompanied by a doubling of the demand for water from 1971 levels; increased burning of **coal** and other **fossil fuels** will cause **acid rain**-induced damage to lakes, crops, forests, and buildings, and could lead to catastrophic **climate** change (global warming) "that could have highly disruptive effects on world agriculture."

(5) Depletion of the stratospheric **ozone** layer by industrial **chemicals** (**chlorofluorocarbons**) could cause serious damage to food crops and human health.

The report noted the ongoing worldwide efforts to protect and replant forests, conserve energy, promote **family planning** and birth control programs, prevent **soil** erosion and desertification, and find alternatives to the present reliance on toxic **pesticide**s and non-renewable, polluting energy sources such as **petroleum** and coal. But the study emphasized that "Encouraging as these developments are, they are far from adequate to meet the global challenges projected in this study. Vigorous, determined new initiatives are needed if worsening poverty and human suffering, **environmental degradation**, and international tension and conflicts are to be prevented."

Some skeptics criticized the report's pessimistic tone and dire warnings as exaggerated and overblown, and its recommendations later were largely ignored by the Reagan and Bush administrations. However, it is now apparent that its major points were not only well founded but may turn out to be far too conservative, rather than radical and alarmist. *See also* Drought; Deforestation; Energy conservation; Environmental policy; Gene pool; Greenhouse effect; Ozone layer depletion; Pollution control; Population growth; Sustainable agriculture; Water allocation

[*Lewis G. Regenstein*]

FURTHER READING

Council on Environmental Quality. *The Global 2000 Report to the President.* 3 vols. Washington DC: Government Printing Office, 1980.

Global warming
See **Greenhouse effect**

GOBI
See **Child survival revolution**

Goiter

Generally refers to any abnormal enlargement of the thyroid gland. The most common type of goiter, the simple goiter, is caused by a deficiency of iodine in the diet. In an attempt to compensate for this deficiency, the thyroid gland enlarges and may become the size of a large softball in the neck. The general availability of table salt to which potassium iodide has been added ("iodized" salt) has greatly reduced the incidence of simple goiter in many parts of the world. A more serious form of goiter, toxic goiter, is associated with hyperthyroidism. The etiology of this condition is not well understood. A third form of goiter occurs primarily in women and is believed to be caused by changes in hormone production.

Goodall, Jane (1934-)
English ethologist

Jane Goodall is known worldwide for her studies of the chimpanzees of the Gombe Stream Reserve in Tanzania, Africa. She is well respected within the scientific community for her ground-breaking field studies and is credited with the first recorded observation of chimps eating meat and using and making tools. Because of Goodall's discoveries, scientists have been forced to redefine the characteristics once considered as solely human traits. Goodall is now leading efforts to ensure that animals are treated humanely both in their wild habitats and in captivity.

Jane Goodall

Goodall was born in London, England, on April 3, 1934, to Mortimer Herbert Goodall, a businessperson and motor-racing enthusiast, and the former Margaret Myfanwe Joseph, who wrote novels under the name Vanne Morris Goodall. Along with her sister, Judy, Goodall was reared in London and Bournemouth, England. Her fascination with animal behavior began in early childhood. In her leisure time, she observed native birds and animals, making extensive notes and sketches, and read widely in the literature of zoology and ethology. From an early age, she dreamed of traveling to Africa to observe exotic animals in their natural habitats.

Goodall attended the Uplands private school, receiving her school certificate in 1950 and a higher certificate in 1952. At age eighteen she left school and found employment as a secretary at Oxford University. In her spare time, she worked at a London-based documentary film company to finance a long-anticipated trip to Africa. At the invitation of a childhood friend, she visited South Kinangop, Kenya. Through other friends, she soon met the famed anthropologist **Louis Leakey**, then curator of the Coryndon Museum in Nairobi. Leakey hired her as a secretary and invited her to participate in an anthropological dig at the now famous Olduvai Gorge, a site rich in fossilized prehistoric remains of early ancestors of humans. In addition, Goodall was sent to study the vervet monkey, which lives on an island in Lake Victoria.

Leakey believed that a long-term study of the behavior of higher primates would yield important evolutionary information. He had a particular interest in the chimpanzee, the second most intelligent primate. Few studies of chimpanzees had been successful; either the size of the safari frightened the chimps, producing unnatural behaviors, or the observers spent too little time in the field to gain comprehensive knowledge. Leakey believed that Goodall had the proper temperament to endure long-term isolation in the wild. At his prompting, she agreed to attempt such a study. Many experts objected to Leakey's selection of Goodall because she had no formal scientific education and lacked even a general college degree.

While Leakey searched for financial support for the proposed Gombe Reserve project, Goodall returned to England to work on an animal documentary for Granada Television. On July 16, 1960, accompanied by her mother and an African cook, she returned to Africa and established a camp on the shore of Lake Tanganyika in the Gombe Stream Reserve. Her first attempts to observe closely a group of chimpanzees failed; she could get no nearer than five hundred yards before the chimps fled. After finding another suitable group of chimpanzees to follow, she established a nonthreatening pattern of observation, appearing at the same time every morning on the high ground near a feeding area along the Kakaombe Stream valley. The chimpanzees soon tolerated her presence and, within a year, allowed her to move as close as 30 ft (9 m) to their feeding area. After two years of seeing her every day, they showed no fear and often came to her in search of bananas.

Goodall used her newfound acceptance to establish what she termed the "banana club," a daily systematic feeding method she used to gain trust and to obtain a more thorough understanding of everyday chimpanzee behavior. Using this method, she became closely acquainted with more than half of the reserve's one hundred or more chimpanzees. She imitated their behaviors, spent time in the trees, and ate their foods. By remaining in almost constant contact with the chimps, she discovered a number of previously unobserved behaviors. She noted that chimps have a complex social system, complete with ritualized behaviors and primitive but discernible communication methods, including a primitive "language" system containing more than twenty individual sounds. She is credited with making the first recorded observations of chimpanzees eating meat and using and making tools. Tool making was previously thought to be an exclusively human trait, used, until her discovery, to distinguish man from animal. She also noted that chimpanzees throw stones as weapons, use touch and embraces to comfort one another, and develop long-term familial bonds. The male plays no active role in family life but is part of the group's social stratification. The chimpanzee "caste" system places the dominant males at the top. The lower castes often act obsequiously in their presence, trying to ingratiate themselves to avoid possible harm. The male's rank is often related to the intensity of his entrance performance at feedings and other gatherings.

Ethologists had long believed that chimps were exclusively vegetarian. Goodall witnessed chimps stalking, killing, and eating large insects, birds, and some bigger animals, including baby baboons and bushbacks (small antelopes). On one occasion, she recorded acts of cannibalism. In another instance, she observed chimps inserting blades of grass or leaves into termite hills to lure worker or soldier termites onto the blade. Sometimes, in true toolmaker fashion, they modified the grass to achieve a better fit. Then they used the grass as a long-handled spoon to eat the termites.

In 1962 Baron Hugo van Lawick, a Dutch wildlife photographer, was sent to Africa by the National Geographic Society to film Goodall at work. The assignment ran longer than anticipated; Goodall and van Lawick were married on March 28, 1964. Their European honeymoon marked one of the rare occasions on which Goodall was absent from Gombe Stream. Her other trips abroad were necessary to fulfill residency requirements at Cambridge University, where she received a Ph.D. in ethology in 1965, becoming only the eighth person in the university's long history who was allowed to pursue a Ph.D. without first earning a baccalaureate degree. Her doctoral thesis, "Behavior of the Free-Ranging Chimpanzee," detailed her first five years of study at the Gombe Reserve.

Van Lawick's film, *Miss Goodall and the Wild Chimpanzees*, was first broadcast on American television on December 22, 1965. The film introduced the shy, attractive, unimposing yet determined Goodall to a wide audience. Goodall, van Lawick (along with their son, Hugo, born in 1967), and the chimpanzees soon became a staple of American and British public television. Through these programs, Goodall challenged scientists to redefine the long-held "differences" between humans and other primates.

Goodall's fieldwork led to the publication of numerous articles and five major books. She was known and respected first in scientific circles and, through the media, became a minor celebrity. *In the Shadow of Man,* her first major text, appeared in 1971. The book, essentially a field study of chimpanzees, effectively bridged the gap between scientific treatise and popular entertainment. Her vivid prose brought the chimps to life, although her tendency to attribute human behaviors and names to chimpanzees struck some critics being as manipulative. Her writings reveal an animal world of social drama, comedy, and tragedy where distinct and varied personalities interact and sometimes clash.

From 1970 to 1975 Goodall held a visiting professorship in psychiatry at Stanford University. In 1973 she was appointed honorary visiting professor of Zoology at the University of Dar es Salaam in Tanzania, a position she still holds. Her marriage to van Lawick over, she wed Derek Bryceson, a former member of Parliament, in 1973. He has since died. Until recently, Goodall's life has revolved around Gombe Stream. But after attending a 1986 conference in Chicago that focused on the ethical treatment of chimpanzees, she began directing her energies more toward educating the public about the wild chimpanzee's endangered habitat and about the unethical treatment of chimpanzees that are used for scientific research.

To preserve the wild chimpanzee's environment, Goodall encourages African nations to develop nature-friendly tourism programs, a measure that makes wildlife into a profitable resource. She actively works with business and local governments to promote ecological responsibility. Her efforts on behalf of captive chimpanzees have taken her around the world on a number of lecture tours. She outlined her position strongly in her 1990 book *Through a Window*: "The more we learn of the true nature of non-human animals, especially those with complex brains and corresponding complex social behaviour, the more ethical concerns are raised regarding their use in the service of man-whether this be in entertainment, as 'pets,' for food, in research laboratories or any of the other uses to which we subject them. This concern is sharpened when the usage in question leads to intense physical or mental suffering-as is so often true with regard to vivisection."

Goodall's stance is that scientists must try harder to find alternatives to the use of animals in research. She has openly declared her opposition to militant animal rights groups who engage in violent or destructive demonstrations. Extremists on both sides of the issue, she believes, polarize thinking and make constructive dialogue nearly impossible. While she is reluctantly resigned to the continuation of animal research, she feels that young scientists must be educated to treat animals more compassionately. "By and large," she has written, "students are taught that it is ethically acceptable to perpetrate, in the name of science, what, from the point of view of animals, would certainly qualify as torture."

Goodall's efforts to educate people about the ethical treatment of animals extends to young children as well. Her 1989 book, *The Chimpanzee Family Book*, was written specifically for children, to convey a new, more humane view of wildlife. The book received the 1989 Unicef/Unesco Children's Book-of-the-Year award, and Goodall used the prize money to have the text translated into Swahili. It has been distributed throughout Tanzania, Uganda, and Burundi to educate children who live in or near areas populated by chimpanzees. A French version has also been distributed in Burundi and Congo.

In recognition of her achievements, Goodall has received numerous honors and awards, including the Gold Medal of Conservation from the San Diego Zoological Society in 1974, the J. Paul Getty Wildlife Conservation Prize in 1984, the Schweitzer Medal of the Animal Welfare Institute in 1987, the National Geographic Society Centennial Award in 1988, and the Kyoto Prize in Basic Sciences in 1990. Many of Goodall's endeavors are conducted under the auspices of the Jane Goodall Institute for Wildlife Research, Education, and Conservation, a nonprofit organization located in Ridgefield, Connecticut.

[*Tom Crawford*]

FURTHER READING

Goodall, J. *Jane Goodall's Animal World: Chimpanzees*, Macmillan, 1989.

—*Through a Window: My Thirty Years with the Chimpanzees of Gombe*, Houghton, 1990.

Green, T. *The Restless Spirit: Profiles in Adventure*. Walker, 1970.

Montgomery, S. *Walking with the Great Apes: Jane Goodall, Dian Fossey, Birute Galdikas*. Houghton Mifflin, 1991.

Smith, W. "The Wildlife of Jane Goodall," *USAir*, February, 1991, pp. 42-7.

Gore, Albert, Jr. (1948-)

Vice President of the United States and environmentalist

A former United States Senator from Tennessee and current Vice President of the United States, Gore is a leading environmentalist and the author of *Earth in the Balance* (1992).

Albert Gore, Jr. was born and raised in Washington, D.C., where his father was a well-known and widely respected Representative and later Senator from Tennessee. Young Albert attended St. Alban's Episcopal School for Boys, where he excelled both academically and athletically. He later went to Harvard College, earning a B.A. in Government. After graduation he enlisted in the U.S. Army, serving as a reporter in Viet Nam in a war he was opposed to. After completing his tour of duty, in 1974 Gore entered the Law School at Vanderbilt University. Following in his father's footsteps, Gore ran for Congress, was elected, and served five terms before running for and winning a Senate seat in 1984. He served in the Senate until 1992, when then-governor and Democratic presidential candidate Bill Clinton selected him as his Vice Presidential running-mate. After winning the 1992 election Vice President Gore became the Clinton Administration's chief environmental advisor. He was also largely responsible for President Clinton's selection of Carol Browner as head of the Environmental Protection Agency (EPA) and Bruce Babbit as Secretary of the Interior.

A self-described "raging moderate," Gore has for more than two decades championed environmental causes and drafted and sponsored environmental legislation in the Senate. He was one of two U.S. Senators to attend and take an active part in the 1992 U.N. sponsored Rio Summit on the environment and, since assuming the Vice-Presidency in 1993, he has taken a leading role in shaping the Clinton Administration's environmental agenda. As Vice President, Gore's ability to shape that agenda has so far been somewhat limited. At the close of Clinton's first term, most environmental organizations rated his administration's record on environmental matters as mixed, at best. Whether Vice President Gore will be the Democratic nominee for President in the year 2000, whether he will be elected — and what difference to the natural environment a Gore Administration might make —remains to be seen.

It is probably fair to say that Gore's greatest contribution to the environmental movement to date has been as an author. With a wealth of statistical and scientific evidence, Gore's book, *Earth in the Balance* makes the case that careless "development" and "growth" have damaged the natural environment; but better policies and regulations will supply incentives for more environmentally responsible actions by individuals and corporations. For example, a "carbon tax" could provide financial incentives for developing new, nonpolluting energy sources such as solar and wind power. Corporations could also be given tax credits for using these new sources. By structuring a system of incentives that favors the protection and restoration of the natural environment, government at the local, national, and (through the United

Albert Gore, Jr.

Nations) international levels can restore the balance between satisfying human needs and protecting the earth's environment.

But restoring this balance, Gore maintains, requires more than public policy and legislation; it requires changes in basic beliefs and attitudes toward **nature** and all living creatures. More specifically, environmental protection and restoration requires a willingness on the part of individuals to accept responsibility for their actions (or inaction). At the individual level, environmental protection means living, working, eating, and recreating responsibly, with an eye to one's effects on the natural and social environment, now and in the future in which our children and their children will survive.

[*Terence Ball*]

FURTHER READING

Gore, A., Jr. *Earth in the Balance*. Boston: Houghton Mifflin, 1992; Penguin paperback edition, 1993, with a new preface by the author.

Gorillas

Gorillas inhabit the forests of Central Africa and are the largest and most powerful of all primates. Adult males stand 6 ft (1.8 m) upright (an unnatural position for a gorilla) and weigh up to 450 lbs (200 kg), while females are much smaller. Gorillas live to about 44 years and mature males (those usually over 13 years), or silverbacks, are marked by a band of silver-gray hair on their backs.

Gorillas live in small family groups of several females and their young, led by a dominant silverback male. The females comprise a harem for the silverback, who holds the sole mating rights in the troop. Like humans, female gorillas produce one infant after a gestation period of nine months. The large size and great strength of the silverback are advantages in competing with other males for leadership of the group and in defending the group against outside threats.

During the day these ground-living apes move slowly through the forest, selecting **species** of leaves, fruit, and stems from the surrounding vegetation. Their home range is about 9-14 square miles (25-40 sq km). At night the family group sleeps in trees, resting on platform nests that they make from branches; silverbacks usually sleep at the foot of the tree.

Gorillas belong to the family Pongidae (which includes **chimpanzees**, **orangutan**s (*Pongo pygmaeus*), and **gibbons**). Together with chimpanzees, gorillas are the animal species most closely related to man. Like most megavertebrates, gorilla numbers are declining rapidly and only 50,000 remain in the wild. There are three subspecies, the western lowland gorilla (*G. g. gorilla*), the eastern lowland gorilla (*G. g. graueri*), and the mountain gorilla (*G. g. beringei*). The rusty-gray western lowland gorillas are found in Nigeria, Cameroon, Equatorial Guinea, Gabon, Congo, Angola, Central African Republic, and Zaire (now Democratic Republic of the Congo [DRC]). The black-haired Eastern lowland gorillas are found in eastern DRC. **Deforestation** and hunting now threaten lowland gorillas throughout their range.

The mountain gorilla has been intensely studied in the field, notably by George Schaller and Dian Fossey, upon whose life the film *Gorillas in the Mist* is based. This endangered subspecies is found in the misty mountains of eastern DRC, Rwanda, and Uganda at altitudes of up to 9000 ft (3,000 m) and in the Impenetrable Forest in southwest Uganda. Field research has shown these powerful primates to be intelligent, peaceful and shy, and of little danger to humans.

Other than humans, gorillas have no real predators, although leopards will occasionally take young apes. Hunting, **poaching** (a mountain gorilla is worth $150,000), and **habitat** loss are causing gorilla populations to decline. The shrinking forest refuge of these great apes is being progressively felled in order to accommodate the ever-expanding human population. Mountain gorillas are somewhat safeguarded in the Virunga Volcanoes National Park in Rwanda. Their protection is funded by strictly controlled small-group gorilla-viewing tourist experiences that exist alongside long-term field research programs. Recent population estimates are 44,000 western lowland gorillas, 3000-5000 eastern lowlands gorillas, and 320 mountain gorillas.

[*Neil Cumberlidge*]

FURTHER READING

Dixson, A. F. *The Natural History of the Gorilla*. New York: Columbia University Press, 1981.

Fossey, D. *Gorillas in the Mist*. Boston: Houghton Mifflin, 1983.

Schaller, G. B. *The Mountain Gorilla: Ecology and Behavior*. Chicago: University of Chicago Press, 1988.

———. *The Year of the Gorilla*. Chicago: University of Chicago Press, 1988.

Grand Canyon

See **Colorado River; Glen Canyon Dam; Kaibab Plateau**

Grand Staircase - Escalante National Monument

The Grand Staircase - Escalante National Monument, encompassing 1.7 million acres (700,000 ha) of public lands on the Colorado Plateau in south-central Utah, was created on September 18, 1996, by presidential proclamation under authority of the Antiquities Act of 1906 (34 Stat. 225, 16 U.S.C. 431). The **U.S. Department of the Interior** had first recommended the creation of the Escalante National Monument along the Colorado and Green Rivers in 1936. In 1937, Capitol Reef National Monument was established in the area northeast of the Escalante Canyons along the upper portion of Waterpocket Fold. In 1941, the **National Park Service** studied the basin in conjunction with a comprehensive study of water resources in the **Colorado River** Basin. The study, published in 1946, identified the Aquarius Plateau/Escalante River Basin as "a little known, but potentially important recreation area." The area was recognized as a strategic link between the **national park**s in southwestern Utah and the canyon country of southeastern Utah.

A national monument is the designation given to a particular area to protect "historic landmarks, historic and prehistoric structures, and objects of historic or scientific interest that are situated upon the lands owned or controlled by the government of the United States." President **Theodore Roosevelt** exercised this authority to ensure protection for the Grand Canyon. More than 100 national monuments have been established by Presidents over the past 90 years, including Zion, Bryce Canyon, Glacier Bay, Death Valley, and Grand Teton. The Grand Staircase - Escalante National Monument was dedicated from the Grand Canyon National Park in Arizona, and no elected official from Utah was at the ceremony because of the controversy in Utah about the monuments designation.

The Grand Staircase - Escalante National Monument was created to preserve geological, paleontological, archaeological, biological, and historical features of the area. Geological features include clearly exposed stratigraphy and structures. The sedimentary rock layers are relatively undeformed and unobscured by vegetation, providing a view to understanding of the processes of the formation of the Earth. A wide variety of geological formations in colors such as red, pink, orange, and purple have been exposed by millennia of **erosion**. The monument contains significant portions of a vast geological stairway, which was named the Grand Staircase by the geologist Clarence Dutton. This stairway rises 5,500 ft (1,678 m) to the rim of Bryce Canyon in an unbroken sequence of cliffs and plateaus. The monument also includes the canyon country of the upper Paria Canyon system, major components of the White and Vermillion Cliffs and associat-

ed benches, and the Kaiparowits Plateau. The Kaiparowits Plateau includes about 1,600 mi² (2, 574 km²) of sedimentary rock and consists of south-to-north ascending plateaus or benches, deeply cut by steep-walled canyons. Naturally burning underground coal seams have changed the tops of the Burning Hills to brick-red. A major landmark, the East Kaibab Monocline, or Cockscomb, is aligned with the Paunsaugant, Sevier, and Hurricane Faults, which may indicate that it may also be a fault at depth. The Circle Cliffs, which features intensively colored red, orange, and purple mounds and ledges at the base of the Wingate Sandstone Cliffs, are one of the most distinctive landscapes of the Colorado Plateau. Inclusion of part of the Waterpocket Fold completes the protection of this geologic feature, which was begun with the establishment of the Capitol Reef National Monument in 1936. There are many arches and natural bridges within the monument boundaries, including the 130-ft (39.4-m) high Escalante Natural Bridge, with a 100-ft (30.3-m) span and the Grosvenor Arch, a double arch. The upper Escalante Canyons, in the northeastern part of the monument, include several major arches and bridges and geological features in narrow, serpentine canyons, where erosion has exposed sandstone and shale deposits in colors of red, maroon, brown, tan, gray, and white.

Paleontological features include petrified wood, such as large unbroken logs more than 30 ft (9 m) in length. The stratigraphy of the Kaiparowits Plateau provides one of the best and most continuous records of the paleontology of the late Cretaceous Era. Fossils of marine and brackish water mollusks, turtles, **crocodiles**, lizards, dinosaurs, fishes, and mammals (including a marsupial primitive mammal) have been recovered from the Dakota, Tropic Shale, and Wahweap Formations and the Tibbett Canyon, Smoky Hollow, and John Henry members of the Straight Cliffs Formation.

Archeological inventories show extensive use of places within the monument by Native American cultures. Recorded sites include rock art panels, occupation sites, rock shelters, campsites, and granaries.

Historical evidence indicates that the monument was occupied by both Kayenta and Fremont agricultural cultures for a period of several hundred years centered around 1100 AÞ.ÚÐÞ.. The area has been used by modern tribal groups, including the Southern Paiute and the Navajo. In 1872, an expedition of **John Wesley Powell** did initial mapping and scientific field work in the area. The expedition discovered the Escalante River, naming it in honor of the Friar Silvester Valez de Escalante expedition of 1776. The Escalante River Canyons have been a major barrier to east-west travel in the region in historic times. The river is presently bridged only at its upper end. Early Mormon pioneers left many historic objects, including trails, inscriptions, ghost towns such as the Old Paria townsite (built in 1874 and abandoned in 1890), rock houses, cowboy camps, and they built the Hole-in-the-Rock Trail in 1879-1880 as part of their colonization activities. Sixty miles (96.6 km) of the Hole-in-the-Rock Trail are within the monument, as well as Dance Hall Rock, used by Mormon pioneers for meetings and dances, and now a National Historic Site.

As a biological resource, the Grand Staircase - Escalante National Monument spans five life zones, from low-lying desert to coniferous forest. Remoteness, limited travel corridors, and low visitation have helped to preserve the ecological features, such as areas of relict vegetation, many of which have existed since the Pleistocene. Pinon-juniper communities containing trees up to 1,400 years old and relict sagebrush-grass park vegetation can be found on No Man's Mesa, Little No Man's Mesa, and Four Mile Bench Old Tree Area. These relict areas can be used to establish a baseline against which to measure changes in community dynamics and biogeochemical cycles in areas impacted by human activity. The monument contains an abundance of unique isolated communities such as hanging gardens and canyon bottom communities, with riparian plants and their pollinators; tinajas, which contain tadpoles, fairy and clam shrimp, amphibians, and snails; saline seeps, with plants and animals adapted to highly saline conditions; dunal pockets, with species adapted to shifting sands; rock crevice communities, consisting of slow-growing species that can thrive in extremely infertile sites; and cryptobiotic crusts, which stabilize the highly erodible desert soils and provide nutrients for plants. The wildlife of the monument is characterized by a diversity of species, where both northern and southern habitat species intermingle. Mountain lions, bears, and desert bighorn sheep, as well as over 200 species of birds, including bald eagles and peregrine falcons, can be found within the monument. The wildlife concentrates around the Paria and Escalante Rivers and other riparian areas.

The Secretary of the Interior, through the **Bureau of Land Management** (BLM), which in the past has been responsible for the public lands included within the monument area, will manage the monument. This is the first national monument that will be managed by the BLM. The BLM will develop a management plan to address measures necessary to protect the scientific and historic features within the monument by three years after the date of establishment of the monument. The BLM will consult with state and local governments, other federal agencies, and tribal governments to prepare the land use plan.

The boundaries of the Grand Staircase - Escalante National Monument were drawn to exclude as much private land as possible, as well as the towns of Escalante, Boulder, Kanab, and Tropic. The national monument designation applies only to Federal land and not to the approximately 9,000 acres (3,644 ha) of private land remaining within the boundaries of the monument. Private landowners continue to have existing rights of access to their property. The landowners may participate in land exchanges with the BLM to trade land within the monument for land of equal value outside the area. The State of Utah owns about 180,000 acres (73,800 ha) of isolated, 640-acre (262 ha) sections of school lands within the boundaries of monument. The State will be allowed to exchange these isolated school lands for federal lands of equal value outside the monument boundaries. All federal lands were withdrawn from sale or leasing under the public land laws upon designation as a national monument. The designation also prohibited the issuance of any new

mineral leases in the area, including new claims made under the Mining Law of 1872. Existing uses under federal or state laws, such as **hunting**, camping, travel, hiking, backpacking, and other recreational activities, as well as grazing permits, continue under current policies and rules. The proclamation did not reserve water or make any federal water rights claims. As part of the management plan, the BLM will evaluate the extent to which water is necessary for the care and management of objects of the monument and the extent to which further action may be necessary under federal or state law to ensure availability of water.

[*Judith Sims*]

FURTHER READING

Bureau of Land Management. *List of Historic and Scientific Objects of Interest: Grand Staircase - Escalante National Monument*. Salt Lake City, UT: Bureau of Land Management, 1997.

———. *Questions and Answers on the Grand Staircase - Escalante National Monument*. Salt Lake City, UT: Bureau of Land Management, 1997.

Clinton, W. J. *Establishment of the Grand Staircase - Escalante National Monument: A Proclamation*. Washington, D.C.: The White House, 1996.

Grasslands

Grasslands are environments in which herbaceous **species**, especially grasses, make up the dominant vegetation. Natural grasslands, commonly called **prairie**, pampas, shrub steppe, palouse, and many other regional names, occur in regions where rainfall is sufficient for grasses and forbs but too sparse or too seasonal to support tree growth. Such conditions occur at both temperate and tropical latitudes around the world. In addition, thousands of years of human activity—clearing pastures and fields, burning, or harvesting trees for materials or fuel—have extended and maintained large expanses of the world's grasslands beyond the natural limits dictated by **climate**. Precipitation in temperate grasslands (those lying between about 25 and 65 degrees latitude) usually ranges from approximately 10 to 30 inches (25 to 75 cm) per year. At tropical and subtropical latitudes, annual grassland precipitation is generally between 24 and 59 inches (60 and 150 cm). Besides its relatively low volume, precipitation on natural grasslands is usually seasonal and often unreliable. Grasslands in **monsoon** regions of Asia can receive 90 percent of their annual rainfall in a few weeks; the remainder of the year is dry. North American prairies receive most of their moisture in spring, from snow melt and early rains that are followed by dry, intensely hot summer months. Frequently windy conditions further evaporate available moisture.

Grasses (family Gramineae) can make up 90 percent of grassland **biomass**. Long-lived root masses of perennial bunch grasses and sod-forming grasses can both endure **drought** and allow asexual reproduction when conditions make reproduction by seed difficult. These characteristics make grasses especially well suited to the dry and variable conditions typical of grasslands. However, a wide variety of grass-like plants (especially sedges, Cyperaceae) and leafy, flowering forbs contribute to species richness in grassland **flora**. Small shrubs are also scattered in most grasslands, and **fungi**, mosses, and **lichens** are common in and near the **soil**. The height of grasses and forbs varies greatly, with grasses of more humid regions standing 7 feet (2 m) or more, while **arid** land grasses may be less than one-half meter tall. Wetter grasslands may also contain scattered trees, especially in low spots or along stream channels. As a rule, however, trees do not thrive in grasslands because the soil is moist only at intervals and only near the surface. Deeper tree roots have little access to water, unless they grow deep enough to reach **groundwater**.

Like the plant community, grassland animal communities are very diverse. Most visible are large herbivores—from American **bison** and elk to Asian camels and horses to African kudus and wildebeests. Carnivores, especially **wolves**, large cats, and bears, historically preyed on herds of these herbivores. Because these carnivores also threatened domestic herbivores that accompany people onto grasslands, they have been hunted, trapped, and poisoned. Now most wolves, bears, and large cats have disappeared from the world's grasslands. Smaller species compose the great wealth of grassland **fauna**. A rich variety of birds breed in and around ponds and streams. Rodents perform essential roles in spreading seeds and turning over soil. Reptiles, amphibians, insects, snails, worms, and many other less visible animals occupy important **niche**s in grassland **ecosystem**s.

Grassland soils develop over centuries or millennia along with regional vegetation and according to local climate conditions. Tropical grassland soils, like tropical forest soils, are highly leached by heavy rainfall and have moderate to poor **nutrient** and contents. In temperate grasslands, however, generally light precipitation lets nutrients accumulate in thick, organic upper layers of the soil. Lacking the acidic leaf or pine needle litter of forests, these soils tend to be basic and fertile. Such conditions historically supported the rich growth of grasses on which grassland herbivores fed. They can likewise support rich grazing and crop lands for agricultural communities. Either through crops or domestic herbivores, humans have long relied on grasslands and their fertile, loamy soils for the majority of their food.

Along a moisture gradient, the margins of grasslands gradually merge with moister **savanna**s and woodlands or with drier, **desert** conditions. As grasslands reach into higher latitudes or altitudes and the climate becomes to cold for grasses to flourish, grasslands grade into **tundra**, which is dominated by mosses, sedges, willows, and other cold-tolerant plants.

[*Mary Ann Cunningham*]

FURTHER READING

Coupland, R. T., ed. *Grassland Ecosystems of the World: Analysis of Grasslands and Their Uses.* London: Cambridge University Press, 1979.

Cushman, R. C., and S. R. Jones. *The Shortgrass Prairie.* Boulder, CO: Pruett Publishing Co., 1988.

Great Lakes

The advance and retreat of glaciers over millions of years scraped and scoured the Great Lakes basins until they attained their present form about 10,000 years ago. Forming the largest system of inland lakes in the world, the Great Lakes have a surface area of 94,200 square miles (244,000 km²) and a volume of more than 28 trillion cubic yards (22,000 km³) of water, 20 percent of the world's surface freshwater.

Lake Superior, with more than 31,660 square miles (82,000 km²) of water, has the largest surface area of freshwater on earth. Lake Huron, the world's fifth largest lake, is at the same elevation and about the same size as Lake Michigan, the world's sixth largest lake. The two are joined by the narrow, deep Straits of Mackinac. Their accumulated waters empty into the St. Clair River which flows into the 460 square mile (1190 km²) Lake St. Clair. The water continues its flow into the Detroit River before entering **Lake Erie**, the eleventh largest lake in the world. It is the oldest, shallowest, busiest, and most eutrophic of the Great Lakes. The waterway continues on into the Niagara River, then to the famous Niagara Falls, where the water descends a total of 325 ft (99 m) before it empties into the last Great Lake, Ontario. The fourteenth largest lake on earth, Lake Ontario is the smallest in surface area but the second deepest of the Great Lakes. It discharges into the St. Lawrence River, which flows into the Atlantic Ocean at the Gulf of St. Lawrence.

The first European explorers discovered a great variety of native fish. Approximately 153 **species** were eventually identified before human interference disrupted the **ecosystem**, first by **overfishing**, and then by lumbering and industrial development. As many species of fish have disappeared, about twenty new species have been introduced. Some, such as the Pacific salmonids, carp, and smelt, were introduced intentionally. Others, such as the sea lamprey, alewife, and **zebra mussel**, gained access through the Erie and Welland Canals or by release with the ballast water of vessels transporting other cargo.

Today, lake trout, burbot, and whitefish are the principal catches of a once extraordinarily rich fisheries enterprise. Despite the decline in the quality and numbers of suitable fish, sport and **commercial fishing** are still vital Great Lakes industries. The sport fishery consists primarily of coho, chinook **salmon**, steelhead trout, walleye, and perch. They now attract about five million anglers annually with a regional economic benefit of about $2 billion.

Besides directly water-related activities, presently, one-fifth of the industry and commerce of the United States is located in the Great Lakes catchment basin because of the availability of abundant cheap and clean freshwater and accessible, efficient water transportation among the lakes and to the oceans. As a consequence, **pollution** has taken some obvious as well as more subtle forms. Using the lakes as a cheap sewage disposal site for shoreline city populations began in the early seventeenth and eighteenth centuries and continued until the early 1970s. To improve the quality of the

Great Lakes, the first efforts concentrated on preventing or removing conventional pollutants such as phosphates, suspended solids, and **nitrogen**.

More deadly toxic contaminants often are not visible and so initially attracted less attention. Over the past fifty years municipal and industrial wastes so polluted the waters, especially the lower Great Lakes, that, beginning in the middle 1960s **organochloride**s were identified as serious contaminants. Fish were collecting, through **bioaccumulation**, relatively large concentrations of agricultural **pesticide**s such as **DDT** and dieldrin as well as the industrial chemical **polychlorinated biphenyl (PCB)** in their tissues. These were passed into the human **food chain/web**. By 1980 more than 400 organic and heavy metals contaminants had been found in fish, and fishermen were warned to limit their consumption. The effects of pollutants are seen primarily at the tops of food chains and are usually discovered through changes in population levels of predator species. Organochlorines and methylated **mercury**, for example, bioaccumulate to levels that may cause reproductive failures in fish-eating birds and animals such as cormorants, eagles, and mink.

Between 1969 and 1972 legislation was enacted in several states bordering the Great Lakes basin to restrict or ban the use of dieldrin, DDT, PCBs, mercury and other toxic **chemicals**. After **point source** discharges were regulated, lake trout and chub, especially in Lake Michigan, showed dramatic declines in these contaminants. By 1978-79, however, the fish contaminant declines were only slight; or the levels remained relatively constant, reflecting airborne inputs as well as the remobilization of contaminants from the **sediment**.

This problem is likely to continue because the turnover rates of the Great Lakes are very slow; and mercury, PCBs and the pesticides DDT, dieldrin and chlordane are very resistant to degradation in the **environment**. Also, these compounds continue to enter the Great Lakes ecosystem from highly diffuse **nonpoint source**s such as airborne deposition, agricultural and urban **runoff**, remobilization from the sediments, **leaching** from municipal and industrial **landfill**s, municipal and industrial discharges, and illegal dumping. *See also* Agricultural chemicals; Agricultural pollution; Great Lakes Water Quality Agreement; Heavy metals and heavy metal poisoning; Industrial waste treatment; Methylation; Water pollution

[*Frank M. D'Itri*]

FURTHER READING

Ashworth, W. *The Late, Great Lakes: An Environmental History*. New York: Knopf, 1986.

Great Lakes, Great Legacy. Washington, DC: Conservation Foundation, 1989.

Hough, J. L. *Geology of the Great Lakes*. Urbana, IL: University of Illinois Press, 1958.

Sixth Biennial Report on Great Lakes Water Quality. Windsor, Ont.: International Joint Commission, 1992.

Weller, P. *Fresh Water Seas: Saving the Great Lakes, Between the Lines*. Toronto, Canada: Publishers, 1990.

Great Lakes Water Quality Agreement (1978)

The Great Lakes Water Quality Agreement of 1978 amended and strengthened the International Great Lakes Water Quality Agreement between Canada and the United States, which was signed in 1972. The original agreement established a framework for research, clean-up, and **pollution control** based on goals determined by the two nations. The existing **International Joint Commission**, in cooperation with the newly-created International Great Lakes Water Quality Board, was to oversee the implementation of the agreement. Chief goals of the agreement were to reduce the amount of **phosphorus** being dumped into the lakes by 50 percent, to require all municipal **sewage treatment** plants to be at the secondary level (removing nutrients such as phosphorous and **nitrogen**), and to control toxic **water pollution**.

The impetus for action in 1972, and again in 1978, was the decreasing **water quality** in the **Great Lakes**. Two incidents best symbolized this to the nation. First, the massive algal blooms in Lake Erie, due to **eutrophication**, led many commentators to declare that the lake was dead. And second, when the **Cuyahoga River** in Cleveland caught fire in 1969, it provided a clear visual message to the rest of the country about the state of **pollution** in the Great Lakes. Perhaps not as visible, but just as serious, the Great Lakes were also suffering from toxic **chemical** pollution, which was a problem for water use, and also for sports and recreational fishing. Limits, and in some cases, bans, were placed on how much fish from the lakes could be consumed.

The 1978 Agreement substantially strengthened the 1972 accord. The new agreement focused especially on toxic pollutants and phosphorous, the chief **nutrient** responsible for eutrophication in the Great Lakes. A stricter definition of a **toxic substance** was included, as well as specific water quality objectives for certain heavy metals, **polychlorinated biphenyl (PCB)**, and **pesticide**s, and a list of hundreds of hazardous and potentially **hazardous material**s. Phosphorous entering the lakes would be reduced further in certain lakes, primarily by improved **municipal solid waste** plants. Additional sections of the agreement dealt with pollution resulting from airborne toxins, **dredging**, shipping, and **nonpoint source** pollution. A contingency plan between the two nations to respond to spills or other severe pollution episodes was also to be created. The Agreement is an Executive Agreement with no force of law in either Canada or the United States. Rather, each nation must depend on existing laws to meet these joint goals.

The Great Lakes Critical Programs Act, passed in 1990, was designed to increase the efforts of the **Environmental Protection Agency (EPA)** and the states in cleaning up the Great Lakes. Evaluations of the 1978 Agreement indicated that neither the EPA nor the states had been putting sufficient effort into the implementation of the necessary programs.

By the middle 1990's, significant progress had been made on reducing phosphorous pollution and improving municipal sewage treatment by building new plants and improving existing plants. Phosphorous loadings were below 1978 target loads for Superior, Huron, and Michigan, and at or near target loads for Erie and Ontario. Hence, this aspect of the water quality agreement has largely been achieved. There has also been significant improvement on point source pollution of toxic chemicals such as PCBs. Toxic substances in the lakes remain a major problem due to air pollution, runoff (non-point source pollution), and releases from already contaminated sediments. For instance, the source of over 75% of the PCBs entering Lake Superior and 95% of the lead entering the Great Lakes is air pollution. In 1995, Canada and the United States agreed to develop a coordinated binational strategy to virtually eliminate persistent toxic substances from the Great Lakes Basin. That same year, the EPA launched the Great Lakes Water Quality Initiative as a framework for achieving that goal. *See also* Agricultural runoff; Chemical spills; Heavy metals and heavy metal poisoning; Oil spills

[*Christopher McGory Klyza*]

FURTHER READING

Ashworth, W. *The Late, Great Lakes.* New York: Knopf, 1986.

Council on Environmental Quality. *Environmental Quality: 21st Annual Report.* Washington DC: U. S. Government Printing Office, 1990.

"U. S., Canada Reach Pollution Pact." *New York Times* (1 June 1978): B6.

Great Smoky Mountains

The Great Smoky Mountains (GSM) National Park covers approximately 543,400 acres (220,000 hectares) of western North Carolina and southeastern Tennessee, making the park the single largest **wilderness** area in the eastern United States. The mountains received their name from the Cherokee for the smoke-like clouds which frequently shroud their peaks and the grey-green haze of the wooded slopes. In early fall, this grey-green haze becomes a blaze of autumnal colors. The GSM are known for their large stands of some of the world's best remaining examples of temperate deciduous forest, and for their "balds" or treeless mountain tops. The park's size, scenic beauty, and geographical proximity to large population centers are features that contribute to attracting more visitors annually than any other national park (including the somewhat better-known **Yellowstone**, **Yosemite**, and Grand Canyon National Parks).

The GSM are situated in what had been one of the least accessible areas of the eastern United States. Natural barriers contributed to relatively low levels of development and exploitation through the eighteenth and nineteenth centuries. GSM National Park was authorized in 1926. Land purchase (funded in part by a five million dollar donation from foundations associated with the Rockefeller family) began in 1930 and was established through an act of Congress in June of 1934. The Park was formally dedicated by President Franklin D. Roosevelt in 1940. In 1976, the Park was recognized as a biosphere reserve, and in 1983 the GSM were selected as a World Heritage Site.

The GSM contain several of the highest mountain peaks in the United States east of the Mississippi River. The Park's Mt. Guyot, Mt. Chapman, and Mt. Leconte all tower over 6,000 ft (1,830 m). At 6,643 ft (2,025 m), Clingman's Dome, on the Tennessee side, is the highest point in the Park, as well as the crest of the Appalachian Trail. This peak was named after General Thomas L. Clingman, a soldier and scientist who, while exploring the area with Arnold Guyot in the late nineteenth century, was the first to measure the summit's elevation.

Among the oldest mountains in the world, the GSM also contain some of the oldest rock strata in the eastern United States. Sheetlike layers of slate (a fine-grained rock originally formed from mud sediment) create jagged outcrops of spectacularly-angled rock, glinting in areas where mica deposits (a sparkling mineral formed when slate is heated) show through to the surface. The slate that makes up much of the jagged central ridge line tells the story of how the mountains were formed by repeated elevations rather than by one single geological event. The bedrock ranges in age from about 600 million-1 billion years and exhibits a range of different characteristics owing to metamorphoses caused by the heat and violence of geological shifts.

More than 148,200 acres (60,000 ha) of GSM National Park are pristine or primitive. Early in the summer, the characteristic "balds" of the GSM (clear, treeless patches on the summits) are brightened by rhododendron blooms around their peripheries. Several varieties of spruce, buckeye, birch, hemlock, dogwood are also common. The abundant sunshine and frequent rain of the region help support over 1,500 species of flowering plants, including eight species of trillium, thirty-two species of violets, and twenty-nine species of orchids. During the last ice age, the highlands were a refuge for northern plant species displaced by the continental ice sheet. Remnants of some of these species, including red spruce and Fraser fir, can still be found at the higher elevations but virtually nowhere else at this latitude. The Park contains the largest virgin forests of red spruce and balsam fir, and the finest virgin hardwood forests left in the United States. Indeed, the slopes of the GSM may support more virgin timber than the rest of the eastern United States combined. In the fall, when the green chlorophyll in deciduous leaves begins to break down, these forests put on a spectacular show of color. Fall colors generally peak between October 15-25, when up and down the mountains may be seen the brilliant reds of maples, golden yellow of beech, and the deeper hues of oaks and more southerly species. But Park visitation also peaks at this time, and those visitors who use the main roads through the Park frequently find themselves in bumper-to-bumper traffic jams with other nature-lovers.

Despite the huge annual invasion of tourists and hikers, GSM National Park nevertheless still supports abundant wildlife. Wild hogs, white-tailed deer, turkey, groundhogs, and ruffed grouse are among the species that can be seen and/or heard in the back country. Black bear have done particularly well under the protection and management of the **National Park Service**, to the extent that they have become habituated to the presence of humans and frequent rest-stops, campsites, and picnic areas. Campers, hikers, and even day trippers in vehicles need to be knowledgeable about bear behavior and about food storage and **garbage** disposal procedures which help to minimize unwanted attention from the bears.

Several species of trout are found in abundance in the cool and clear mountain streams. Estimating conservatively, about 250 species of birds may be seen in the Park at various times during the year, 165 of these species being resident. The avian population includes twenty varieties of warbler, thirty of finch, and twenty of geese and ducks. The higher elevations provide habitat for ravens and hawks, as well as occasional **peregrine falcons** and eagles.

GSM National Park also contains approximately 72 mi (116 km) of the Appalachian Trail, which runs along the crest of the Appalachians all the way from Mt. Katahdin, a granite monolith in Maine, south to Springer Mountain in Georgia. In the Park, the Appalachian Trail runs from the Pigeon River to the Little Tennessee River, and here can be found the highest, roughest, and some of the most scenic segments of the entire route. Over 900 mi (1,450 km) of other trails provide hikers and horseback riders with access to dozens of waterfalls, mountain meadows, and scenic, grassy balds.

[*Lawrence J. Biskowski*]

Green advertising and marketing

In the last decade growing consumer interest in environmental issues has significantly impacted how advertisers market their products and companies. The evidence regarding this greater concern for the environmental impact of commercial goods has been documented by several marketing groups. A 1989 survey by Michael Peters consultants found that 53 percent of the Americans asked had refused to buy a product in that year because of the effect of the product or package on the **environment**; 75 percent indicated that they would purchase a product with **biodegradable** or **recyclable** packaging even if it meant spending more money. In 1990 an Abt Associates study of American consumers showed that 90 percent of those interviewed were willing to pay more for environmentally-friendly products. For many years, German, Scandinavian, and Dutch consumers had shown a willingness to buy phosphate-free **detergents** and other so-called environmentally-friendly products. Indeed, a German business was saved from bankruptcy by offering a washing machine that consumed less water, detergent, and energy than its rivals. In England, *The Green Consumer Guide*, by John Elkington and Julia Hailes, was a best-seller for four weeks after its publication. Generally, the most environmentally-concerned consumers were well-to-do with the most discretionary income and the highest educational level. In short, they were trend-setters that advertising and marketing people could not ignore.

Marketers began to commonly use the terms "environmentally friendly," "safe for the environment," "re-cycled," "degradable," "biodegradable," "compostable," and "recyclable." Cause-related marketing also became popular as companies promised to support moderate environmental organizations such as **World Wildlife Fund**. While the advertising practices of many companies went uncontested by environmental groups, concerns arose regarding the claims of certain companies. For example, the Mobil Oil Corporation was sued for misleading advertising after claiming that its **plastic** Hefty garbage bags were recyclable. After suffering much embarrassment, British Petroleum was forced to withdraw its claim that its new brand of unleaded **gasoline** caused no **pollution**. Reacting to these and similar findings, ten state Attorney Generals issued a report in 1990 calling for greater accountability in "green" marketing. The **Environmental Protection Agency (EPA)** and the Federal Trade Commission also devised standards to evaluate the claims made by advertisers.

Often, the issue has been whether one product is really better for the environment than another. For instance, phosphate-free detergents created a controversy when they were introduced in France. Some companies claimed that they were no more environmentally benign than detergents that had phosphates. Rhone-Poulenc, the French producer of the detergents with phosphates, ran ads of dead fish apparently killed by the substances in the detergents which did not have phosphates. Proctor & Gamble launched a campaign which claimed that **disposable diapers** actually had less negative environmental impacts than reusable diapers. They pointed to the detergents, hot water, and energy used in washing cloth diapers, the energy needed to bring them to consumers, and the **pesticide**s that were in the cotton out of which they were made.

Life-cycle assessments came into vogue as companies argued about the relative environmental merits of various products. Assessments exam the total environmental impact of using the product and how it rates—environmentally—to other similar products. Migros, the large Swiss retailer, has developed an "eco-balance" or life-cycle program to analyze the impact of its packaging in terms of the resources used and how they are disposed of.

Green labeling programs exist in Germany (**Blue Angel**), Canada (Environmental Choice), and Japan (**Ecomark**). They are run by the governments of these countries, but the United States government has not been willing to give this kind of endorsement to commercial products. Instead, various environmental groups have seals of approval which they have applied to selected goods that pass their tests of environmental acceptability. *See also* Environmentalism; Green packaging; Green products; Recycling

[*Alfred A. Marcus*]

FURTHER READING

Cairncross, F. *Costing the Earth*. Boston: Harvard Business School Press, 1992.

Elkington, J., and J. Hailes. *The Green Consumer Guide*. London: Gollancz, 1988.

Green consumerism

See **Green advertising and marketing; Green packaging; Green products**

Green belt/greenway

A green belt is an area of land that usually surrounds a town or city, and is kept open by government restrictions on further development. Often it comprises both public and private land.

Green belts provide both recreational areas and landscape, but their main purpose is to contain cities, diverting future growth, and preventing cities and towns from merging.

It grew out of Sir Ebenezer Howard's "Garden City" approach to town planning, which aimed to provide natural areas for residents of cities. Garden cities were surrounded by countryside; city expansion was only to take place by developing new garden cities on the other side of the green belt. The result would be clusters of cities grouped around a central city. Several garden cities (e.g., Welwyn in England) were built in Britain.

In the 1920s, London's government called for study of an "agricultural belt," although the farming function was considered incidental. Its key purpose was to act as a barrier to growth. Ultimately, these were to serve as open spaces. Sir Raymond Unwin proposed a "green girdle" of spaces easily accessible to towns and cities. This plan led to the 1938 Green Belt Act, and about 38,000 acres (15,580 ha) were purchased. After World War II, green belts were again proposed as a means to limit development. A green belt about 5 mi deep (8 km) separated the inner city and the suburbs from the outer countryside. Land was both purchased and controlled through zoning compensation and by purchasing development rights. Typically, farming was allowed, but housing was not. By 1959, 840 mi^2 (2175 km^2) had been secured. The green belt was not considered completely successful, as it did not halt London's growth, and residents' use of the lands was not high, as they were not easily accessible.

Other difficulties, according to William H. Whyte, author of *The Last Landscape,* were the time and expense of controlling land and maintaining it, arbitrary placement of the green belt areas (not following natural boundaries) and lack of function attached to the land.

Green belts today emphasize the landscape and recreational values of open areas. Containment is negative and it does not work, a conclusion the Japanese came to in 1965 when they abandoned a proposed London-type green belt to contain Tokyo.

The green belt concept came to the United States much later, and many would say that it grew into the *greenways* concept, which have the specific purpose of providing open space and recreational areas. In the United States, the term is often used interchangeably with the term greenway, although the meaning is somewhat different.

Greenways, according to Jennifer Howard, author of *Greenways: A Citizen's Guide,* are linear corridors of land and water and the natural, cultural, and recreational resources they link together. They help conserve a variety of resources and create recreational opportunities.

Greenways were inspired both by green belts and by the work of landscape architect **Frederick Law Olmstead**, who, in the late 1800s, designed a number of urban park systems he called "parkways." One of his most notable is the Emerald Necklace, a string of park areas around Boston.

They may take the form of a riverfront walkway, a bicycle path, an urban walking trail connecting historic sites and neighborhood parks, a wildlife migration corridor, among others. Greenways are typically categorized as river greenways, paths and trails, cultural and historic greenways, **wildlife** corridors. They are typically comprising both public and private lands, and can include trails, riverways, habitat and resource conservation areas, notable natural features, scenic roads, historic structures, vacant urban lands, forestland, and farm fields—basically any resource that is significant to a community. Greenways help make these resources accessible to residents without need for a car. Four categories of land and water resources can be incorporated into a greenway system: resource-conservation areas, parks and open spaces, cultural and historic resources, and the corridors of land and water which connect these other elements together.

In the last 20 years, the greenway concept has increased in recognition and popularity. Today, hundreds are underway. In 1987, The President's Commission on Americans Outdoors focused national attention on greenways, and recommended their establishment "to link together the rural and urban spaces in the American landscape."

In Massachusetts, several greenways exist. The Connecticut River Greenway State Park in Massachusetts comprises about 3,500 acres (14,350 ha) of land owned or controlled by the Department of Environmental Management along a 70-mi (113-km) stretch of the Connecticut River. Much of the land is in private ownership and includes farms and woodlots.

The Massachusetts Bay Circuit encircles the entire Boston Metropolitan area; within Boston, the Emerald Necklace, a string of parkways, was planned by Frederick Law Olmsted. Other notable green belts exist in Portland, Oregon; Vienna; and Tokyo.

[*Carol Steinfeld*]

FURTHER READING

Howard, J., *Creating Greenways: A Citizen's Guide.* The Department of Environmental Management, 1997.

Whyte, W. H. *The Last Landscape.* New York: Doubleday & Company, 1968.

Green Cross

Long used by several organizations, the Green Cross has become a symbol of environmental awareness and responsibility.

A religiously oriented group officially called the American Association of the Green Cross is based in Colorado Springs, Colorado, and describes itself as "a new Christian environmental organization whose purpose is to address the ethical and moral issues underlying ecological issues, and to mobilize volunteers in service to Creation." The group's motto is "serving and keeping Creation," and it encourages such activities as "the development of every church as a Creation-awareness center, education about Christian responsibility for the earth, local action to address ecological issues." The group also promotes tree planting, urban gardening, **habitat** restoration, resource **conservation**, and **waste reduction**. It is associated with the North American Conference on Christianity and Ecology, and it plans to establish a network of chapters in churches, schools, youth groups, and colleges.

The International Green Cross and Green Crescent is a new environmental group formed in April 1993 and headed by former Soviet President Mikhail S. Gorbachev. Hoping to do for the **environment** what the Red Cross and Red Crescent have done for disaster relief, the International Green Cross will work to coordinate environmental efforts on a global scale. Mr. Gorbachev has said that he accepted leadership of the group because "I am convinced that saving the environment is the number one priority for all countries." Sponsors of the organization include an array of distinguished world political and spiritual leaders, including India's Mother Teresa and Javier Perez de Cuellar, the former Secretary General of the United Nations.

The Green Cross Certification Company is the former name of a non-profit group that awarded certifications to manufacturers whose products met certain limited environmental standards. The certification program is now administered by Scientific Certification Systems, Inc. (SCS), a private, for-profit laboratory that charges manufacturers a fee to research products and to verify their performance and claims. SCS says that it is "committed to developing programs that motivate private industry to work toward an environmentally sustainable future" by "conducting independent, unbiased evaluations of products and product claims, and recognizing products achieving exceptional environmental performance goals." The SCS Environmental Report Card summarizes the environmental performance of a product, including the amount of "environmental burden" associated with the product and its packaging.

SCS emphasizes that it does not approve products as "green" or environmentally acceptable, but rather verifies the environmental claims that companies make for their products and analyses their environmental impact. SCS tries to evaluate a product's life cycle program, the impact it has from manufacture to disposal. Factors considered usually include the toxic waste generated and the energy used in production, the recycled content of the product, and its recyclability or biodegradability upon disposal. Different product categories have varying standards of acceptability depending on the state of technology for the above factors for the particular product or industry. *See also* Environmental consumers; Environmental ethics; Green advertising and marketing; Green products; Nongovernmental organization

[*Lewis G. Regenstein*]

Green packaging

Packaging is the largest form of domestic **garbage**. In 1988 it amounted to 43 percent of **solid waste** as measured by weight in the United States. Significant waste prevention implies reductions in packaging. There simply is not enough room in **landfills** or incinerators for all the excess packaging the industry produces. Between 1970 and 1988, the volume of **municipal solid waste** which had to be disposed of in landfills and incinerators rose by 14 percent.

People value products not only for their content but also for the packaging. It gives products a better feel and a more attractive appearance and suggests less of a risk of contamination. It prolongs the life of the product and allows people to make fewer trips to the supermarket.

Nonetheless, the German parliament in 1990 passed a strict new law on the **recycling** of packaging. Retailers are responsible for taking away the outer packaging before they offer a product for sale, or else they must provide a place where customers can deposit the package before taking it home for use. Stores are also required to post signs telling customers that they can remove the packaging on the spot and leave it for the retailer to dispose. All packages will carry green dots signifying that the manufacturer has paid a fee which guarantees that the package can be recycled. The German government hopes to achieve 50 percent recycling of all packaging by 1995.

For purely economic reasons most packages are becoming lighter. **Aluminum** cans, for instance, are 45 percent lighter today than they once were. Shrink wrap film and a plastic base are increasingly taking the place of corrugated boxes. Some companies are trying to eliminate packaging entirely. Outer boxes were once thought to be absolutely essential for the sale of toothpaste, but the giant Swiss retailer, Migros, discovered that consumers ultimately became accustomed to unboxed tubes and that sales did not suffer as a result. McDonald's and other fast food restaurants in the United States have stopped using polystyrene boxes to package their sandwiches, turning instead to paper wraps. Other innovations in packaging are also occurring. For instance, Procter & Gamble is no longer using metal-based inks for printing on packages. *See also* Container deposit legislation; Green advertising and marketing; Waste reduction

[*Alfred A. Marcus*]

FURTHER READING

Cairncross, F. *Costing the Earth*. Boston: Harvard Business School Press, 1992.

Green plans

Green plans are comprehensive environmental strategies that are intended to improve environmental quality and make rapid progress towards sustainability. (In its use here, the word "green" is non-political and non-ideological, and merely refers to a context of environmental protection and sustainable development.) Green plans are characterized by a longer-term view, while being thorough in their consideration and integration of environmental issues. Green plans also take account of economic realities, while consistently ensuring an appropriate degree of protection of environmental quality and natural ecological values (such as the needs of **endangered species** and rare **ecosystem**s).

Green plans represent an extremely important tool for the longer-term protection of environmental quality, conservation of natural resources and ecological values, and achievement of a sustainable economic system. Green plans do this by proposing sustainable alternatives to the many kinds of modern activities that are causing damages to the environment and biosphere. Green plans attempt to integrate the economic, scientific, and political interests of society to develop a strategy that can achieve a sustainable prosperity for present and future generations of humans and their economic systems, while also supporting other species and natural ecosystems.

Green plans are designed to replace more conventional methods for protecting the environment. These conventional methods include the following:

(1) *Sectoral structures of government and administration.* This type of structure can be a problem because there is often a lack of integration among sectors, even though there may be important environmental linkages. For example, environmental management by government typically involves separate agencies responsible for **air pollution**, **water pollution**, forestry, agriculture, fisheries, metal resources, fossil-fuel resources, industrial development, human health, **biodiversity** (i.e., the conservation of indigenous species and ecosystems), and other environment-related mandates. Because the responsibilities of these agencies are not well integrated, they often work at cross-purposes. For instance, agencies responsible for managing harvests of timber may not take adequate consideration of the interests of agencies concerned with **pollution**, endangered species, or rare ecosystems (such as old-growth forests). This commonly results in environmental and ecological damages being caused by timber harvesting, with attendant controversies.

(2) *Single-issue policies.* Single-issue policies may result from the actions of special-interest groups, which are seeking to advance their particular environmental, ideological, or socio-economic agendas. This can, however, result in poor integration among issues, and divisive political and social controversies that can impair the development of policies that would achieve balanced levels of environmental protection. Single-issue policies often result in regulation through short-term objectives and standards that focus on individual issues, such as the concentrations of particular chemicals, or the abundances of certain species. This can result in actions that focus on compliance with narrow regulatory criteria, rather than the more comprehensive, longer-term environmental goals that are pursued by green plans.

Green plans can be implemented by agencies of government at all levels (that is, federal, state or provincial, county, and city or town), and by companies of any size. Green plans can be designed by any of these organizations, but this is done in close consultation with the public, non-

governmental organizations, and environmental specialists. In fact, multi-sectoral and multi-organizational discussions are one of the most important aspects of green plans. This process allows a broad degree of understanding to be reached among the spectrum of interest groups, allowing green plans to bridge political and ideological differences concerning environmental issues.

Green plans have already been implemented by the national governments of Canada, the Netherlands, New Zealand, and Singapore. Green plans are also being developed or seriously considered by the national governments of Austria, Denmark, Germany, Norway, Sweden, and the United Kingdom, and by the European Community as a whole. In addition, many state and provincial governments, municipalities, and companies in some of those countries have implemented green plans. Non-governmental environmental organizations are also advocating that green plans be designed by federal and state governments and companies in the United States. Unfortunately, significant actions in this regard have not yet been undertaken in that country. It is likely, however, that green plans will also be developed in the United States, once their benefits become more broadly recognized.

[*Bill Freedman*]

FURTHER READING

Green Plan Center. "*A Green Plan Primer.*" Website, http://www.rri.org/gparchive/gp-primer.html (May 1997).

Johnson, H. D. *Green Plans. Greenprint for Sustainability*. Lincoln, NB: University of Nebraska Press, 1995.

Green politics

Green Politics is a relatively recent political movement that places a concern for nature and its myriad species at the top of its agenda. New social and political movements arise in response to crises that are perceived to be both long-term and systemic. The crisis out of which the broadly based Green movement has emerged is the environmental crisis, which is actually a series of interconnected crises caused by **population growth**, air and water **pollution**, the destruction of the tropical and temperate **rain forest**s, the rapid extinction of entire **species** of plants and animals, the **greenhouse effect**, **acid rain**, **ozone layer depletion**, and other now familiar instances of **environmental degradation**. Many are by-products of technological innovations, such as the internal combustion engine. But the causes of these environmental crises are not only technological but are also broadly cultural and political. They stem from beliefs and attitudes that place human beings above or apart from **nature**. Despite their differences, the major mainstream political perspectives—liberalism, socialism, and conservatism—are alike in viewing nature as either a hostile force to be conquered or a resource base to be exploited for human purposes. All, in short, share an anthropocentric, or human-centered, bias.

Against these views, the modern environmental or Green movement counterpoises its own perspective. Many **Greens** prefer not to call their perspective a political ideology, but an environmental ethic. Earlier ecological thinkers, such as **Aldo Leopold**, spoke of a "land ethic." Others, such as Christopher stone, speak of an ethic with the earth itself at its center, while still others, such as Hans Jonas, speak of an emerging "planetary ethic." Despite differences of accent and emphasis, however, all are alike in several important respects. An environmental or Ecological ethics, they say, would include several key features. First, such an ethic would emphasize the web of interconnections and mutual dependence within which we and other species live. From the this recognition of interconnectedness a second feature follows: a respect for all life, however humble humans may believe it to be, because the fate of our species is tied in with theirs. And since life requires certain conditions to sustain it, the third feature follows: we have an obligation to respect and care for the conditions that nurture and sustain life in its myriad forms. Since nature nourishes her creatures within a complex web of interconnected conditions, to damage one part of this life-sustaining web is to damage the others, and to endanger the existence of the creatures that depend upon it.

Green thinkers hold that the enormous power that humans have over nature imposes on our species a special responsibility for restraining our reach and using our power wisely and well. Greens point out that the fate of the earth and all its creatures now depends, to an unprecedented degree, on human decisions and actions. For not only do we depend on nature, but nature depends on our care and restraint and forbearance. Humans have the nuclear means to destroy in mere minutes the earth's inhabitants and the **ecosystem**s that sustain them. From this emerges a fourth feature of a "green" political perspective: Greens must oppose militarism and work for peace.

But the earth is in danger not only from global thermo-nuclear war but from the slower destruction of the natural **environment**. Such destruction is a consequence not only of large-scale policies but of small-scale, everyday acts. And each of us bears full responsibility for our actions and also, since we live in a democracy, some share of responsibility for cumulative effects and collective outcomes. Each of us has, or can have, a hand in making the laws under which we live. It is for this reason that Greens give equal emphasis to our collective and individual responsibility for protecting the environment that protects us. The fifth feature of the Green political perspective, then, is to emphasize the importance of informed and active democratic citizenship at the grass-roots level. Hence the Green adage, "Think globally and act locally."

On this much most Greens agree. But there are also a number of unresolved differences of approach, emphasis, and political strategy. The internal ideological spectrum ranges from "light green" conservationists to "dark green" radicals, and includes assorted anarchist beliefs, **deep ecology**, **ecofeminism**, **social ecology**, **bioregionalism**, New Age Gaia worship, and other groupings, each differing in various ways form the others. Among these are differences regarding the basic beliefs underlying and motivating the green movement. Some New Age Greens envision an environmental ethic grounded in spiritual or religious values. We should, they say, look upon the earth as a benevolent and kindly deity—the goddess *Gaia* (from the Greek word for "earth")—to be worshiped in reverence and awe. In this way we can liberate ourselves from the restrictive rationalism that characterizes modern science. Other Greens disapprove of such a spiritual or religious orientation, contending that such beliefs are politically pernicious and inimical to the rational scientific thinking required to diagnose and solve environmental problems.

Other differences have to do with the political strategies and tactics to be employed by the environmental movement. Some say that Greens should take an active part in electoral politics, perhaps even following the lead of Greens in Germany and organizing a Green Party. Aware of the formidable obstacles facing minority third parties, most have favored other strategies, such as working within existing mainstream parties (especially the Democratic Party in the United States), or hiring lobbyists to influence legislation. Still other Greens favor working outside of traditional interest group politics, believing the earth and its inhabitants hardly constitute a special interest. Others, such as social ecologists, tend to favor local, grass-roots campaigns which involve neighbors, friends, and fellow citizens in efforts to protect the environment. Some social ecologists are anarchists who see the state and its pro-business and pro-growth policies as the problem, rather than the solution, and seek its eventual replacement by a decentralized system of communes and cooperatives. Greens of the "bioregionalist" persuasion add that such social and political organization ought to be based on biological or natural, rather than artificial or political, boundaries and regions.

Although all Greens agree on the importance of informing and educating the public, they disagree as to how this might best be done. Some groups, such as **Greenpeace**, favor dramatic direct action calculated to make headlines and capture public attention. Even more militant groups, such as the **Sea Shepherd Society** and **Earth First!**, have advocated **monkey-wrenching** as a morally justifiable means of publicizing and protesting practices destructive of the natural environment.

Such militant tactics are decried by moderate or mainstream groups, which tend to favor subtle, low-key efforts to influence legislation and inform the public on environmental matters. The **Sierra Club**, for example, lobbies Congress and state legislatures to pass environmental legislation. It also publishes books and produces films and videos about a wide variety of environmental issues. Similar strategies are followed by other groups, such as the Environmental Defense Fund. Another group, the **Nature Conservancy**, solicits funds to buy land for nature preserves.

Differences over strategy and tactics are, however, differences about means and not necessarily about basic assumptions and ends. Despite their political differences, Greens are alike in assuming that all things are connected—**ecology** is, after all, the study of interconnections—and they agree that complex ecosystems and the myriad life-forms they sustain are valuable and worthy of protection by political and other means. *See also* Abbey, Edward; Bioregional Project; Bookchin, Murray; Brower, David Ross; Environmental attitudes/values; Environmental Defense Fund; Foreman, Dave; Green advertising and marketing; Green products; Sea Shepherd Society; Sierra Club

[*Terence Ball*]

FURTHER READING

Bahro, R. *Building the Green Movement.* London: G.R.P., 1978.

Biehl, J. *Rethinking Ecofeminist Politics.* Boston: South End Press, 1991.

Bookchin, M. *The Modern Crisis.* Philadelphia: New Society Publishers, 1986.

Capra, F., and C. Spritnak. *Green Politics.* New York: Dutton, 1984.

Foreman, D. *Confessions of an Eco-Warrior.* New York: Harmony Books, 1991.

Leopold, A. *The Sand County Almanac.* New York: Oxford University Press, 1948.

Jonas, H. *The Imperative of Responsibility.* Chicago: University of Chicago Press, 1984.

Manes, C. *Green Rage: Radical Environmentalism and the Unmaking of Civilization.* Boston: Little Brown, 1990.

Milbrath, L. W. *Envisioning a Sustainable Society.* Albany: State University of New York Press, 1989.

Paehlke, R. *Environmentalism and the Future of Progressive Politics.* New Haven, CT: Yale University Press, 1989.

Porritt, J. *Seeing Green: The Politics of Ecology Explained.* Oxford: Basil Blackwell, 1984.

Seed, J., et al. *Thinking Like a Mountain.* Philadelphia: New Society Publishers, 1988.

Worster, D. *Nature's Economy: A History of Ecological Ideas.* Cambridge: Cambridge University Press, 1977.

Green products

Some companies have thrived by marketing product lines as environmentally correct or "green." A prime example is Body Shop, a cosmetics company that is strongly and explicitly pro-**environment** with regard to its products. It strives, for instance, to develop products made with substances derived from threatened **tropical rain forest**s so that they can be preserved.

The American ice cream manufacturer, Ben and Jerry's, has adopted a similar approach to using rain forest products in what it sells. **Mercury**- and **cadmium**-free batteries have been marketed by Varta, a German company. Ecover, a small Belgian company, made major sales gains when it began to market a line of phosphate-free **detergents**. Wal-Mart is another company that provides its customers with green products. Loblaw, a Canadian grocery chain, has introduced a "green-line" of environmentally-friendly products and has sold more than twice the amount than it had initially projected. Seventh Generation, a mail-order company based in California, has successfully marketed its own line of recycled toilet paper, **biodegradable** soaps and cleansers, and phosphate-free laundry and dishwashing detergent.

Many factors comprise a green product. The product has to be made with the fewest raw materials and produced with the least amount of contaminants released into the environment and with the smallest effect on human health.

Consideration must also be given to how consumers will use the product and how they will dispose of it when they are finished. To reduce its waste potential, a product must often last a significant amount of time or be reusable or recyclable.

As consumers become more aware of environmental issues, they will likely look to producers and governments to provide more products that will permit them to maintain a life-style that is less harmful to the environment. Therefore, the very nature of products will have to change. They will have to be lighter, smaller, and more durable so that they can consume fewer resources in their production and use and take up less space when they are disposed of.

Ultimately, a real revolution in the use of green products would mean replacing or substantially modifying virtually the capital stock of society—appliances, **automobile**s, housing, highways, etc.—with a different type of product. In contrast to old **smoke**stack industries, new technologies and emerging industries—such as telecommunications, computers, and information—should be able to offer products that are less environmentally harmful. They should be able to produce many new types of green products and modify existing products so that they are less damaging to the environment. See also Green packaging

[*Alfred A. Marcus*]

FURTHER READING

Buchholz, R., A. Marcus, and J. Post. *Managing Environmental Issues.* Englewood Cliffs, NJ: Prentice-Hall, 1992.

Cairncross, F. *Costing the Earth.* Boston: Harvard Business School Press, 1992.

Green revolution

See **Agricultural revolution; Borlaug, Norman Ernest; Consultative Group on International Agricultural Research**

Green Seal (Palo Alto, California)

An independent, non-profit group that encourages the production and sale of consumer products that are environmentally responsible, Green Seal allows the use of its certification mark on products that meet its strict environmental standards. The mark has a green check over a blue globe.

A growing number of people are becoming aware that consumer demand for certain products causes great harm to the **environment** and provides an economic incentive for activities that damage the planet. Some examples are products that contain **chemicals** such as **chlorofluorocarbons (CFCs)**, which deplete the earth's protective **ozone** layer; mahogany and other kinds of wood from rapidly-disappear-

Green Seal symbol.

ing **tropical rain forest**s; fur coats made from rare and **endangered species**; tuna caught using techniques that kill **dolphins**; and products that waste energy or water, are over-packaged, cannot be recycled, or are harmful when disposed of.

By avoiding these products and buying those that do not cause harm to **wildlife** or degrade the environment, consumers can encourage corporations to make and sell goods that are environmentally responsible. With the public's growing commitment to protecting the environment, store shelves are now full of products that claim to be earth friendly, environmentally friendly, recycled, **biodegradable**, natural, organic, or are labeled in such a way as to take advantage of **green advertising and marketing**.

The Green Seal certification mark helps consumers choose those products that actually are less harmful to the planet and are not simply marketed in a clever way. Green Seal uses the highly respected Underwriters Laboratory (UL) for most of its product testing and certification. Through its certification process and its educational activities, Green Seal encourages people to think about how they can help protect the environment in their everyday activities and their daily lives.

Green Seal points out that its research shows that four out of five consumers are more likely to buy a product with its certification mark when choosing between similar products. A Gallup survey found that the Green Seal certification would have more impact on consumers than would government guidelines. Thus, consumers, guided by Green Seal, have the opportunity to influence the actions of major corporations and their impact on the environment through their purchasing decisions.

Green Seal is headed by Norman L. Dean, a long-time environmental researcher and attorney who serves as its President and Chief Executive Officer. Its Chairman of the Board is **Denis Hayes**, the well-known environmentalist and **solar energy** advocate who organized the 1970 and 1990 **Earth Day** celebrations. Contact: Green Seal, P.O. Box 1694, Palo Alto, CA 94302.

[*Lewis G. Regenstein*]

Green taxes

The search for alternatives to command and control legislation and enforcement of **environmental policy** led a 1988 bipartisan Congressional study group (Project 88) to call for the use of market forces, including taxes, to protect the **environment**. Project 88's advocacy of these "green" taxes and other economic incentives for reducing **pollution** is actually an old idea. Charles Schultze, chairman of the Council of Economic Advisers under President Jimmy Carter, maintained in the 1976 Godkin Lectures at Harvard University (later published as a book titled *The Public Use of the Private Interest*) that detailed laws and bureaucratic requirements were a costly and ineffective way to control pollution. Instead, reliance should be placed on taxes and subsidies that would make private interests more congruent with public goals.

The economists' argument, as made by Project 88, Schultze, and others, is that the harm pollution causes to health, property, and aesthetics is not paid for by business. Industries have no reason to consider this harm in their production decisions. By taxing pollution the government would make polluters pay for the damage they inflect. External production costs would be incorporated into ordinary production decisions. This would correct a market defect and the market would become more efficient. Green taxes would not lower environmental standards; they would provide more protection at the same level of expenditure, or the same protection with less money.

The current regulatory system is expensive and inefficient. The amount of litigation is high, and relations between business and government suffer. The uniform standards that are currently imposed often do not make sense, because different companies have different removal costs depending on their production process and many other factors. For example, a study in the St. Louis area found that removing a ton of **particulate** matter from a paper factory cost $4, removing the same material from a brewery cost $600.

Industries that can easily reduce pollution should be encouraged to go beyond the standard and not stop at mere compliance. Businesses for whom pollution reduction is a great burden should be able to pay a fine equivalent to the damage caused. To impose the same requirements on all businesses regardless of cost seems arbitrary. Moreover, current regulations do not allow any pollution-reducing experiments. Companies should be allowed to choose the lowest-cost method whether it means treating wastes, modifying production processes, substituting less-polluting raw materials, or making other innovations. By shifting away from uniform standards, pollution-control costs can be cut in half. An equivalent **air quality** can be achieved at 10 percent of existing costs, according to one study.

Why have governments been so slow to use green taxes? Taxes have never been popular, with legislators or their constituents. No interest group supported them either. Businesses preferred court delays and reliance on lobbyists, who knew how to work the system, to the certainty of taxes. Environmentalists argued that pollution had to be eliminated and that companies should not be given the right to pollute for a fee. Bureaucrats, moreover, were comfortable with the existing system. Pollution-tax proposals from Presidents Lyndon Johnson and Richard Nixon were almost immediately dismissed.

Now there is new interest and support from the **Environmental Protection Agency** (EPA), the **Environmental Defense Fund** and other environmental organizations, General Motors, and Vice President **Albert Gore, Jr.**. Green taxes are also being considered for **solid waste** and **hazardous waste** disposal and **recycling**. An estimated $100-per-ton charge on **carbon dioxide** emissions would yield $120 billion for the Federal Treasury. If phased in over ten years, such a tax also would reduce CO_2 **emission**s by 8-36 percent by the year 2000. The levy would also stimulate economic growth since it reduces market inefficiencies and discourages undesirable activities (as opposed to distortionary taxes like corporate profit and income taxes that suppress productive behavior). Moreover, a **carbon** tax would not necessarily place a burden on low-income households since the negative environmental effects of rich households in terms of major indicators such as air and **water pollution**, **pesticide** and energy use, and **garbage** and other wastes is more than twice that of poor households.

Another option, a **gasoline** tax increase of 50 cents per gallon would reduce gas consumption by 10-15 percent, reduce oil imports by 500,000 barrels per day, and generate $40 billion in revenue. Many economists feel that this tax conserves more fuel than a higher fuel-efficiency standard. *See also* Corporate Average Fuel Efficiency Standards; Environmental economics; Externality; Internalizing costs; Pollution control; Pollution control costs and benefits

[*Alfred A. Marcus*]

FURTHER READING

Stavins, R. N., ed. *Project 88—Harnessing Market Forces to Protect the Environment.* A Public Policy Study Sponsored by Senator Timothy E. Wirth and Senator John Heinz. Washington, DC: U. S. Government Printing Office, 1988.

————, and B. W. Whitehead. 1992. "Dealing With Pollution: Market-Based Incentives for Environmental Protection." *Environment* 34 (September 1992): 7-42.

Greenhouse effect

The greenhouse effect is a natural phenomenon that traps radiation within the earth's atmosphere. Natural greenhouse gases include water vapor, carbon dioxide, nitrous oxide, methane and ozone, all essential to support life. The enhanced greenhouse effect, the direct result of human activities, increases concentrations of these gases in the atmosphere, and leads to **pollution** of the lower **atmosphere** and contributes to global warming. These gases let in sunlight but tend to insulate Earth against the loss of heat, as do the glass walls of a greenhouse. A higher concentration of the greenhouse gases means a warmer climate. For example, the twentieth century has been one degree warmer on worldwide

average than the nineteenth century — warming at a rate twenty times faster than average.

Carbon dioxide (CO_2) is considered the predominant greenhouse gas and has the greatest impact on global heat. From April 1958, when monthly measurements of CO_2 from atop the Mauna Loa volcano began, through June 1991, the CO_2 concentration in **parts per million** went from 316 ppm to almost 360 ppm. The peak concentration is due to the destruction of **tropical rain forest**s and the burning of **fossil fuels**, which accounts for half of the greenhouse gases added to the atmosphere. CO_2 is dumped into the atmosphere at a much faster rate than it can be withdrawn or absorbed by the oceans or living things in the **biosphere**; since 1765, its presence in the atmosphere has increased by 27 percent. CO_2 buildup in the next few decades to centuries could be one of the principal controlling factors of the near-future climate.

Methane, another greenhouse gas, is produced when oxygen is not freely available and bacteria have access to organic matter, such as in swamps, bogs, rice paddies and moist **soil**s. Methane also is produced in the guts of termites and cows, in **garbage** dumps, **landfill**s, emissions from coal mining, natural gas production and distribution, and changing land use. Methane concentrations have increased over 100 percent since 1765.

Nitrous oxide concentrations have increased in recent years due to fertilizer use and chemical production, such as in the manufacture of nylon. Nitrous oxide is also dispersed during fossil fuel combustion, biomass burning and changing land use.

CFCs (**chlorofluorocarbons**), also implicated in **ozone layer depletion**, act as greenhouse gases. While useful and widely used as refrigerants, their total effect is significant because compared to a molecule of carbon dioxide, each molecule of CFC absorbs much more radiation, thereby trapping heat in the atmosphere.

Other greenhouse gases are ground-level **ozone** (sunlight reacting with **automobile emission**s). and water vapor. Water vapor represents about two percent of total atmospheric composition, and is the most abundant greenhouse gas. With methane and carbon dioxide, it plays an important role in regulating the temperature of the planet through the production of clouds.

Rain forest destruction also contributes to global warming. When the canopy of leaves is removed through **clearcutting** or burning, the sudden warming of the forest floor releases methane and CO_2, in a kind of biochemical burning. The massive increase in the number of dead tree trunks and branches leads to a population explosion of termites, which themselves produce methane. Dead trees can no longer store CO_2 or convert it to oxygen.

Two factors which appear to mitigate the effect of enhanced greenhouse gases are aerosols and dust. Aerosols, minute solid particles, are finely dispersed in the atmosphere and have become an influence on the greenhouse effect. Aerosols are produced by combustion, but they also come from natural sources, primarily volcanoes. By blocking light, aerosols and dust can offset warming from greenhouse gasses.

The greenhouse effect.

For example, a significant cooling trend in the spring and summer of 1992 seemed to correlate with the eruption of Mount Pinatubo in the Philippines. The fall and winter of 1992 were fairly mild on worldwide average. As all the particulate matter from the Mt. Pinatubo eruption settled out of the atmosphere, the surface cooling effects abated and the global warming trend resumed.

Anthropogenic (human-caused) greenhouse gases now appear responsible for increasing the global average temperature. According to current projections, global temperatures may rise as much as 2-3° C above the pre-industrial temperatures by the year 2100. To place this change in perspective, the temperature rise that brought the planet out of the most recent ice age was only about 3-4° C.

The top six warmest years of average global recorded temperatures were 1995, 1990, 1991, 1994, 1988 and 1983, years that saw devastating fires in Yellowstone National Park, flooding in Bangladesh, record number of hurricanes and tornados, and a deadly heat wave and drought in the southeastern United States. It is probable, based on computer models, that a resumption in warming will accompany changes in regional weather. A 40-year trend of increased precipitation in Europe and decreased precipitation in the African Sahel (Ethiopia, the Sudan, Somalia) may be an early consequence of global warming due to the greenhouse effect. Longer and more frequent heat waves would result in public health threats as well as inconveniences such as road buckling, electrical brownouts, or blackouts.

Precipitation is likely to increase regionally because as the temperature increases, more evaporation takes place, leading to more precipitation. The average precipitation event is likely to be heavier: wetter **monsoon**s in coastal subtropics; more frequent and heavier winter snows at high altitudes and high latitudes; an earlier snowmelt, and a wetter spring.

Increases in rain- or snowfall are not expected to offset the effects of higher temperatures on soil, however. Higher temperatures are expected to dry the soil in North America and southern Europe, among other places, by boosting the rates of evaporation and transpiration through plants. More favorable agricultural conditions in high latitudes could move the center of agriculture farther north into Canada and Siberia and out of the U.S.

Other consequences of global warming from the enhanced greenhouse effect include the reduction of sea ice, coastal sea level rises of several feet per century, more frequent and powerful hurricanes, and more frequent and severe forest fires. In the United States, the frequency of tornadoes is near or above record levels for the years 1990-1994.

The rise of sea level is the most easily predicted consequence. The one-degree increase in temperature over the past century contributed to a four to eight-inch (10-20 cm) rise in mean sea level. This could lead to severe and frequent storm damage, flooding and disappearance of wetlands and lowlands, coastal erosion, loss of beaches and low islands, wildlife extinctions, and increased salinity of rivers, bays and aquifers. However, because the global atmosphere operates as a complex system, it is difficult, even with today's sophisticated computer models, to predict the exact nature of the changes we are likely to cause with increased greenhouse gases. Scientists have predicted that low-lying areas and islands, including the Seychelles, the Maldives, the Marshall Islands, and large areas of Bangladesh, Egypt, Florida, Louisiana, and North Carolina will disappear over the next few decades.

The earth's natural atmospheric cleanser — rain — may wash excess greenhouse gases out of the atmosphere. But until rates of greenhouse gases slow their rapid increases or actually begin to decrease, the planet will get warmer. In response to climate projections, the United Nations Framework Convention on Climate Change (UNFCC), adopted and signed by 162 countries in 1992 at the Rio Earth Summit, sets country-by=country standards to reduce the emissions of greenhouse gases, particularly carbon dioxide. It was agreed that these emissions should be returned to 1990 levels by the year 2000 in many nations through the establishment of national programs, international information exchange, joint implementation and the promotion of sustainable development in devcloping nations.

Policy-makers in the United States, including Vice President **Albert Gore, Jr.**, propose stricter requirements for more fuel-efficient cars, "**environment** taxes" that penalize heavy polluters and help pay for cleansing the atmosphere, and trading technological advances for rain forest protection in **Third World** countries. However, because global warming often is made a political ping-pong ball, changes in political administrations worldwide can extend to policy makers and climate researchers, who depend on government assistance for research.

The greatest controversy over slowing the rate of greenhouse gases injected into the atmosphere seems to be how to do it. Some scientists advocate increased use of nuclear power to reduce dependence on fossil fuels, but that carries its own controversies. Nuclear power plants are so energy-intensive just to build, the trade-off is negligible. Conservation and a switch from a dependence on fossil fuels to dependence on renewable resources such as wind and solar energy, slows the rate of increase of carbon dioxide emissions into the atmosphere. *See also* Environmental economics; Environmental policy; Global Tomorrow Coalition; *The Global 2000 Report*

[*Linda Rehkopf*]

FURTHER READING

Abrahamson, D. E., ed. *The Challenge of Global Warming.* Covelo, CA: Island Press, 1989.

Bates, A. X. *Climate in Crisis.* Summertown, TN: The Book Publishing Co., 1990.

Changing by Begrees: Steps to Reduce Greenhouse Gases. U.S. Congress, Office of Technology Asessment, 1991.

Edgerton, L. T. *The Rising Tide.* Washington, DC: Island Press (The Natural Resources Defense Council), 1991.

Houghton, R. A., and G. M. Woodwell. "Global Climatic Change." *Scientific American* 260 (1989): 36-44.

Houghton, J.T. and L.G. Meira Filho, ed. Climate Change 1995: The Science of Climate Change. Contribution of Working Group I to the Second Assessment Report of the Intergovernmental Panel on Climate Change. Cambridge University Press, 1996.

Indices of Climate for the United States. Bulletin of the American Meteorological Society, vol.77, no. 2. (February 1996): 279-292.

Phillips, Ed. *Crisis in the Atmosphere.* Phoenix, AZ: D.B. Clark & Co., 1990.

Revkin, A. *Global Warming: Understanding the Forecast.* New York: Abbeville Press, 1992.

Schneider, S. H. *Global Warming: Are We Entering the Greenhouse Century?* New York: Random House, 1989.

Greenhouse gases

Greenhouse gases are gases in the **atmosphere** that absorb and re-emit energy from the sun. They are believed to cause the global climatic changes known as the **greenhouse effect**.

The earth's **climate** depends on a wide variety of gases, vapors, and aerosols, and many of these contribute to global warming. **Carbon dioxide** is the most abundant; the atmosphere contains about 700 billion tons of this gas, and the oceans contain about fifty times this amount. Water vapor also contributes to global warming, and other important greenhouse gases include **ozone**, **methane**, nitrous oxide, and **chlorofluorocarbons**. Halogenated gases and a variety of volatile organic **hydrocarbons** are also important trace gases. Volatile compounds can absorb solar and infrared radiation directly; they can also affect the photochemistry of ozone, increasing the transmission of heat and thus indirectly affecting the climate. While not gases, small long-lived ambient particles, such as particulate and sulfate, may affect solar and infrared radiation.

Greenhouse gases have both natural and human sources. Most of the gases, except for cholorofluorocarbons, are emitted by natural sources. Forests emit greenhouse gases, as well as **soil**s, agricultural fields, **wetlands**, and oceans. Industrial **emission**s of greenhouses gases consist largely of carbon dioxide; these arise from burning **fossil fuels** such as **coal**, oil, and **natural gas**.

Increases in the concentrations of carbon dioxide and methane in the atmosphere during this century have been attributed in part to rapid increases in the utilization of fossil fuels. Efforts to reduce greenhouse gases have focused on limiting and controlling the burning of these fuels. There have been programs to encourage the utilization of other sources of energy such as **nuclear power**, or **alternative energy sources** such as **solar energy** or hydropower. Technologies for controlling fossil fuel emissions and sequestering ambient carbon dioxide have also been developed, and researchers have emphasized the importance of improving energy efficiency and energy **conservation**. *See also* Air pollution; Air pollution control; Flue gas; Pollution control

[*Stuart Batterman and Douglas Smith*]

FURTHER READING

Dickinson, R. E., R. J. Cicerone. "Future Global Warming from Atmospheric Trace Gases." *Nature* 319 (1986): 109-115.

Hansen, J., A. Lacis, and M. Prather. "Greenhouse Effect of Chlorofluorocarbons and Other Trace Gases." *Journal of Geophysical Research* 94 (1989): 16417-21.

Greenpeace (Washington, D.C.)

Founded in 1971, Greenpeace is an international environmental organization dedicated to protecting the global **environment** through non-violent direct action, public education, and legislative lobbying. With a worldwide membership of over four million (approximately 1.8 million in Greenpeace USA), Greenpeace operates offices in some thirty countries and maintains a scientific base in **Antarctica**.

Having mounted successful campaigns on a wide variety of environmental issues, Greenpeace is perhaps best known for its direct and often confrontational crusades against nuclear testing and commercial **whaling**. The group has also garnered wide publicity for protesting various environmental abuses by hanging enormous banners from **smoke**stacks, buildings, bridges, and the scaffolding used in the renovation of the Statue of Liberty.

Greenpeace is presently active in four broadly defined environmental issue areas—Atmosphere and Energy; Ocean Ecology and Forests; Toxics; and Disarmament. In the area of **Atmosphere** and Energy, Greenpeace works to eliminate widespread dependence upon **fossil fuels** and lobbies for laws and policies encouraging **energy efficiency** and renewable energy sources. The group is also working to halt the spread of **nuclear power** and the dumping of **radioactive waste** as well as to ban **ozone**-depleting **chemicals** such as **chlorofluorocarbons** (CFCs).

With regard to Ocean **Ecology** and Forests, Greenpeace seeks to protect both **habitat**s and threatened **species**, including **whales**, harp seals, **dolphins**, **sea turtles**, **elephants**, and birds of prey. It works to discourage **overfishing** and other wasteful fishing practices, particularly the killing of dolphins in tuna nets. Greenpeace was instrumental in protecting Antarctica by persuading twenty-three nations to sign an accord banning all mining in Antarctica for at least fifty years. Supporting the principle of **biodiversity**, the group also works to protect tropical and temperate forests around the world.

In the area of Toxics, Greenpeace is especially concerned with stopping the use of unneeded **chlorine** in the bleaching of paper and with preventing the dumping of **hazardous waste** in **Third World** nations. Particularly concerned in recent years with **dioxin, polychlorinated biphenyl (PCB)**, CFCs, and **pesticide**s, the group regularly investigates, publicizes, and lobbies against chemical **pollution**. Greenpeace also conducts research on the effects of **toxic substance**s on human beings and the environment and encourages **recycling** as a means of reducing pollution.

Also concerned with Disarmament issues, Greenpeace conducts research into the effects of warfare on human beings and the environment and advocates the global elimination of

The Greenpeace ship, *Rainbow Warrior,* sailing up the St. George's Channel off the west coast of England (1989).

nuclear weapons. More immediately, the group also urges the cessation of all nuclear and chemical weapons testing and is trying to persuade the major powers to agree to a global ban on naval nuclear propulsion.

In an effort to avoid compromising its goals and activities, Greenpeace does not seek corporate or government funding. Nor does it become directly involved in the electoral process in any of the nations in which it is active. Greenpeace's frequently confrontational tactics have on occasion provoked angry responses from various governmental authorities, including the bombing and sinking of Greenpeace's flagship vessel *Rainbow Warrior* by agents of the French government in 1985. The *Rainbow Warrior* had been in New Zealand preparing to protest French nuclear testing in the South Pacific when it was sabotaged. More recently (October, 1992) one of Greenpeace's ships was seized by the Russian coast guard while investigating Russian nuclear waste dumping in Arctic waters. Contact: Greenpeace International, Keizersgracht 176, 1016 DW Amsterdam, The Netherlands. Greenpeace USA, 1436 U Street, NW, Washington, DC 20009. Internet: http://www.greenpeace.org/.

[*Lawrence J. Biskowski*]

Greens

The name given to those who engage in **green politics**. The term originated in Germany, where members of the environmentally-oriented Green Party were quickly dubbed *die Grünen*, or "the Greens." In the United States, greens refers not to a particular political party, but to any individual or group making environmental issues the central focus and main political concern. Thus the term covers a wide array of political perspectives and organizations, ranging from moderate or mainstream "light green" groups such as the **Sierra Club** and **Greenpeace** to more militant or "dark green" movements and direct-action organizations such as the **Sea Shepherd Conservation Society** and **Earth First!**, as well as **ecofeminists**, bioregionalists, social ecologists, and deep ecologists. Greens in the United States are divided over many issues. Some, for example, are in favor of organizing as interest groups to lobby for environmental legislation, while others reject politics in favor of a more spiritual orientation. Some greens (for example, social ecologists and ecofeminists) see their cause as connected to questions of social justice—the elimination of exploitation, militarism, racism, sexism, and so on—while others (deep ecologists, for instance) seek to separate their cause from such humanistic concerns, favoring a biocentric instead of an anthropocentric orientation. Despite such differences, however, all greens agree that the preservation and protection of the natural environment is a top priority and a precondition for every other human endeavor. *See also* Environmental ethics; Environmentalism

Grizzly bear (*Ursus arctos*)

The grizzly bear, a member of the family Ursidae, is the most widely distributed of all bear **species**. Although reduced from prehistoric times, its range today extends from Scandinavia to eastern Siberia, Syria to the Himalayan Mountains, and, in North America, from Alaska and northwest Canada into the northwestern portion of the lower 48 states. Even though the Russian, Alaskan, and Canadian populations remain fairly large, the grizzly bear population in the northwestern continental United States represents only about one percent of its former size of less than 200 years ago. Grizzly bears occupy a variety of **habitat**s, but in North America they seem to prefer open areas including **tundra**, meadows, and coastlines. Before the arrival of Europeans on the continent, grizzlies were common on the Great Plains. Now they are found primarily in **wilderness** forests with open areas of moist meadows or **grasslands**.

Female grizzly bears vary in size from 200-450 lbs (91-204 kg), whereas the much larger males can weigh up to 800 lbs (363 kg). The largest individuals—from the coast of southern Alaska—weigh up to 1,720 lbs (780 kg). Grizzly bears measure from 6.5-9 ft (2-2.75 m) tall when standing erect. To maintain these tremendous body sizes, grizzly bears must eat large amounts of food daily. They are omnivorous and are highly selective feeders. During the six or seven months spent outside their den, grizzly bears will consume up to 35 lbs (16 kg) of food, chiefly vegetation, per day. They are particularly fond of tender, succulent vegetation, tubers, and berries, but also supplement their diet with insect grubs,

small rodents, carrion, **salmon**, trout, young deer, and livestock, when the opportunity presents itself. In Alaska, along the McNeil River in particular, when the salmon are migrating upstream to spawn in July and August, it is not unusual to see congregations of dozens of grizzly bears, along the riverbank or in the river, catching and eating these large fish.

Grizzly bears breed during May or June, but implantation of the fertilized egg is delayed until late fall when the female retreats to her den in a self-made or natural cave, or a hollow tree. Two or three young are born in January, February, or March, and are small (less than 1 lb/0.45 kg) and helpless. They remain in the den for three or four months before emerging, and stay with their mother for one and a half to four years. The age at which a female first reproduces, litter size, and years between litters are determined by nutrition, which induces females to establish foraging territories which exclude other females. These territories range from less than 10 square miles (2,590 ha) to nearly 75 square miles (19,425 ha). Males tend to have larger ranges extending up to 400 square miles (103,600 ha) and incorporate the territories of several females. Young females, however, often stay within the range of their mother for some time after leaving her care, and one case was reported of three generations of female grizzly bears living within the same range.

Grizzly bear populations have been decimated over much of their original range. Habitat destruction and hunting are the primary factors involved in their decline. The North American population, particularly in the lower 48 states, has been extremely hard hit. Grizzly bears numbered near 100,000 in the lower 48 states as little as 180 years ago, but, today, fewer than 1,000 remain on less than two percent of their original range. This population has been further fragmented into seven small, isolated populations in Washington, Idaho, Montana, Wyoming, and Colorado. This decline and fragmentation makes their potential for survival tenuous. The U. S. **Fish and Wildlife Service** considers the grizzly bear to be threatened in the lower 48 states.

A revised grizzly bear recovery plan was drafted in 1992. Because it does not ensure habitat protection and maintains isolated populations, most experts believe it will do little to protect this declining species in the lower 48 states. Habitat loss due to timbering, road building, and development in this region is still a major problem and will continue to impact these threatened populations of bears. *See also* Endangered species

[*Eugene C. Beckham*]

FURTHER READING

Craighead, F. J., Jr. *Track of the Grizzly*. San Francisco: Sierra Club Books, 1979.

"New Grizzly Bear Recovery Plan: Bad News for Bears." *Wild Forever* [Newsletter of the Collaborative Grizzly Bear Project] (1993).

Nowak, R. M., ed. *Walker's Mammals of the World* 5th ed. Baltimore: Johns Hopkins University Press, 1991.

U. S. Fish and Wildlife Service. "The Grizzly Bear Recovery Plan." Washington, DC: U. S. Fish and Wildlife Service, 1982.

Groundwater

Groundwater occupies the void space in a geological strata. It is one element in the continuous process of moisture circulation on earth, termed the **hydrologic cycle**.

Almost all groundwater originates as surface water. Some portion of rain hitting the earth runs off into streams and lakes, and another portion soaks into the **soil**, where it is available for use by plants and subject to evaporation back into the **atmosphere**. The third portion soaks below the root zone and continues moving downward until it enters the groundwater. Precipitation is the major source of groundwater. Other sources include the movement of water from lakes or streams and contributions from such activities as excess **irrigation** and seepage from canals. Water has also been purposely applied to increase the available supply of groundwater. Water-bearing formations called **aquifer**s act as **reservoir**s for storage and conduits for transmission back to the surface.

The occurrence of groundwater is usually discussed by distinguishing between a **zone of saturation** and a zone of **aeration**. In the zone of saturation the pores are entirely filled with water, while the zone of aeration has pores that are at least partially filled by air. Suspended water does occur in this zone. This water is called vadose, and the zone of aeration is also known as the **vadose zone**. In the zone of aeration, water moves downward due to gravity, but in the zone of saturation it moves in a direction determined by the relative heights of water at different locations.

Water that occurs in the zone of saturation is termed groundwater. This zone can be thought of as a natural storage area of reservoir whose capacity is the total volume of the pores of openings in rocks.

An important exception to the distinction between these zones is the presence of ancient sea water in some sedimentary formations. The pore spaces of materials that have accumulated on an ocean floor, which has then been raised through later geological processes, can sometimes contain salt water. This is called connate water.

Formations or strata within the saturated zone from which water can be obtained are called aquifers. Aquifers must yield water through wells or springs at a rate that can serve as a practical source of water supply. To be considered an aquifer the geological formation must contain pores or open spaces filled with water, and the openings must be large enough to permit water to move through them at a measurable rate. Both the size of pores and the total pore volume depends on the type of material. Individual pores in fine-grained materials such as clay, for example, can be extremely small, but the total volume is large. Conversely, in coarse material such as sand, individual pores may be quite large but total volume is less. The rate of movement from fine-grained materials, such as clay, will be slow due to the small pore size, and it may not yield sufficient water to wells to be considered an aquifer. However, the sand is considered an aquifer even though they yield a smaller volume of water because, they will yield water to a well.

The water table is not stationary but moves up or down depending on surface condition such as excess precipitation, **drought**, or heavy use. Formations where the top of the saturated zone or water table define the upper limit of the aquifer are called unconfined aquifers. The hydraulic pressure at any level with an aquifer is equal to the depth from the water table, and there is a type known as a water-table aquifer, where a well drilled produces a static water level which stands at the same level as the water table.

A local zone of saturation occurring in an aerated zone separated from the main water table is called a perched water table. These most often occur when there is an impervious strata or significant particle-size change in the zone of aeration which causes the water to accumulate. A confined aquifer is found between impermeable layers. Because of the confining upper layer, the water in the aquifer exists within the pores at pressures greater than the atmosphere. This is termed an artesian condition and gives rise to an **artesian well**.

Groundwater has always been an important resource, and it will become more so in the future as the need for good quality water increases due to urbanization and agricultural production. It has recently been estimated that 50 percent of the drinking water in the United States comes from groundwater; 75 percent of the nation's cities obtain all or part of their supplies from groundwater, and rural areas are 95 percent dependent upon it. For these reasons, it is widely believed that every precaution should be taken to protect groundwater purity. Once contaminated, groundwater is difficult, expensive, and sometimes impossible to clean up. The most prevalent sources of contamination are waste disposal, the storage, transportation and handling of commercial materials, mining operations, and **nonpoint source**s such as agricultural activities. *See also*: Agricultural pollution; Aquifer restoration; Contaminated soil; Drinking water supply; Safe Drinking Water Act; Water quality; Water table draw-down

[*James L. Anderson*]

FURTHER READING

Collins, A. G., and A. I. Johnson, eds. *Ground-Water Contamination: Field Methods*. Philadelphia: American Society for Testing and Materials, 1988.

Davis, S. N., and R. J. M. DeWiest. *Hydrogeology*. New York: Wiley, 1966.

Fairchild, D. M. *Ground Water Quality and Agricultural Practices*. Chelsea, MI: Lewis, 1988.

Freeze, R. A., and J. A. Cherry *Ground Water*. Englewood Cliffs, NJ: Prentice-Hall, 1979.

Ground Water and Wells. St. Paul: Edward E. Johnson, 1966.

Groundwater monitoring

Monitoring **groundwater** quality and **aquifer** conditions can detect contamination before it becomes a problem. The appropriate type of monitoring and the design of the system depends upon **hydrology**, **pollution** sources, and the population density and **climate** of the region. There are four basic types of groundwater monitoring systems: ambient monitoring, source monitoring, enforcement monitoring, and research monitoring.

Ambient monitoring involves collection of background **water quality** data for specific aquifers as a way to detect and evaluate changes in water quality. Source monitoring is performed in an area surrounding a specific, actual, or potential source of contamination such as a **landfill** or spill site. Enforcement monitoring systems are installed at the direction of regulatory agencies to determine or confirm the origin and concentration gradients of contaminants relative to regulatory compliance. Research monitoring wells are installed for detection and assessment of cause and effect relationships between groundwater quality and specific **land use** activities. *See also* Aquifer restoration; Contaminated soil; Drinking-water supply; Hazardous waste siting; Leaching; Water quality standards

Groundwater pollution

When contaminants in **groundwater** exceed the levels deemed safe for the use of a specific aquifer use the groundwater is considered polluted. There are three major sources of groundwater **pollution**. These include natural sources, waste disposal activities, and spills, leaks, and **nonpoint source** activities such as agricultural management practices.

All groundwater naturally contains some dissolved salts or minerals. These salts and minerals may be leached from the **soil** and from the aquifer materials themselves and can result in water that poses problems for human consumption, is considered polluted, or does not meet the **secondary standards** for water quality. Natural minerals or salts that may result in polluted ground water include chloride, nitrate, **fluoride**, iron and sulfate.

There are currently no feasible methods for the large-scale disposal of waste that do not have the potential for serious pollution of the **environment**, and there are a number of waste-disposal practices the specifically threaten groundwater. These include activities which range from separate **sewage treatment** systems for individual residences, used by 30 percent of the population in the United States, to the storage and disposal of industrial wastes. Many of the problems posed by industrial waste arise from the use of surface storage facilities that rely on evaporation for disposal. These facilities are also known as discharge ponds, and there are other types in which waste is treated to standards suitable for discharge to surface water. But in the use of both facilities the potential exists for the movement of contaminants into groundwater. Many of the numerous sanitary **landfill**s in the country are in the same situation. Water moving down and away from these sites into groundwater **aquifer**s carries with it a variety of **chemicals** leached from the material deposited in the landfills. The liquid that moves out of landfills is called leachate.

Agricultural practices also contribute to groundwater pollution, and there have been increases in nitrate concentrations and low-level concentrations of **pesticide**s. For control of groundwater pollution, one of the most important agricultural practices is the management of **nitrogen** from all sources—**fertilizer**, nitrogen fixing plants, and **organic waste**. Once nitrogen is in the nitrate form it is subject to **leaching**, so it is important that the amount applied not exceed the crops' ability to use it. At the same time crops need adequate nitrogen to obtain high yields, and a good balance must be maintained. Low-level pesticide contamination occurs in areas where aquifers are sensitive to surface activity, particularly areas of shallow aquifers beneath rapidly permeable soils, and regions of "karst" topography where deep and wide range pollution can occur due to fractures in the bedrock.

Except in cases of **deep-well injection** waste or substances contained in sanitary landfills, most contaminants move from the land surface to aquifers. The water generally moves through an unsaturated zone, in which biological and chemical processes may act to degrade or change the contaminant. Plant uptake can also act to reduce some of the pollution. Once in the aquifer, how the contaminant moves with the water will depend the solubility of the compound, and the speed of contamination will depend on how fast water moves through the aquifer. Chemical and biological degradation of contaminants can occur in the aquifer, but usually at a slower rate than it does on the surface due to lower temperatures, less available oxygen, and reduced biological activity. In addition aquifer contaminants exist in lower concentrations, diluted by the large water volume. Most pollution remains relatively localized in aquifers, since movement of the contaminants usually occurs in **plume**s that have definite boundaries and do not mix with the rest of the water. This does provide an advantage for isolation and treatment.

The types of chemicals that pollute groundwater are as varied as their sources. They range from such simple inorganic materials as nitrate from fertilizers, **septic tank**s, and feedlots, chloride from high salt, and heavy metals such as chromium from metal plating processes, to very complex organic chemicals used in manufacturing and household cleaners.

One of the main criteria in judging risk is public health. Acute effects from immediate exposure to a concentrated product is often well documented, but little written evidence exists to link physiological effects with long-term chronic exposure. About all that is available are epidemiological data that suggest possible effects, but are by no means conclusive. Environmental effects are even less well understood, but some have suggested that the best way to determine the potential danger is to look at how long a substance persists. Those that remain the longest are most likely to pose long-term risks.

The most efficient way to protect groundwater is to limit activities in recharge areas. For confined aquifers it may be possible to control activities that can result in pollution, but this is extremely difficult for unconfined aquifers which are essentially open systems and subject to effects from any

Sources of groundwater pollution.

land activity. In areas of potential salt-water intrusion excess pumping can be regulated, and this can also be done where water is being used for irrigation faster than the recharge rate, so that the water is becoming saline. Another important activity for the protection of groundwater is the proper sealing of all wells that are not currently being used.

Classification of aquifers according to their predominant use is another management tool now employed in a number of states. This establishes water-quality goals and standards for each aquifer, and means that aquifers can be regulated according to their major use. This protects the most valuable aquifers, but leaves the problem of predicting future needs. Once an aquifer is contaminated, it is very expensive if not impossible to restore, and this management tool may have serious drawbacks in the future.

In rural areas of the United States, 95 percent of the population draws their drinking water from the groundwater supply. With a growing population, continued industrialization, and increasing agricultural reliance on the use of chemicals, many believe it is now more important than ever to protect groundwater. Contamination problems have been encountered in every state, but prevention is far more efficient and effective than restoration after damage has been done. Prevention can be achieved through regional planning and enforcement of state and federal regulations. *See also* Agricultural pollution; Aquifer restoration; Contaminated soil; Drinking-water supply; Feedlot runoff; Groundwater monitoring; Hazardous waste site remediation; Hazardous

waste siting; Heavy metals and heavy metal poisoning; Waste management; Water quality; Water quality standards; Water treatment

[*James L. Anderson*]

FURTHER READING

Freeze, R. A., and J. A. Cherry. *Ground Water*. Englewood Cliffs, NJ: Prentice-Hall, 1979.

Hallberg, G. R. "From Hoes to Herbicides: Agriculture and Groundwater Quality." *Journal of Soil and Water Conservation* (Nov-Dec 1986): 358-59.

Pye, V. I., R. Patrick, and J. Quarles. *Ground Water Contamination in the United States*. Philadelphia: University of Pennsylvania Press, 1983.

Growth curve

A graph in which the number of organisms in a population is plotted against time. Such curves are amazingly similar for populations of almost all organisms from bacteria to human beings and are considered characteristic of populations.

Growth curves typically have a sigmoid or S-shaped curve. When a few individuals enter a previously unoccupied area, growth is at first slow during the positive acceleration phase. The growth then becomes rapid and increases exponentially, called the logarithmic phase. The growth rate eventually slows down as environmental resistance gradually increases; this phase is called the negative acceleration phase.

It finally reaches an equilibrium or saturation level. The final stage of the growth curve is termed the **carrying capacity** of the **environment**.

A good example of a **species**' growth curve is demonstrated by the sheep population in Tasmania. Sheep were introduced into Tasmania in 1800. Careful records of their numbers were kept, and by 1850 the sheep population had reached 1.7 million. The population remained more or less constant at this carrying capacity for nearly a century.

The figures used to plot a growth curve—time and the total number in the population—vary from one species to another, but the shape of the growth curve is similar for all populations. Once a population has become established in a certain region and has reached the equilibrium level, the numbers of individuals will vary from year to year depending on various environmental factors. Comparing these variations for different species living in the same region is helpful to scientists who manage **wildlife** areas or who track factors that affect populations.

For example, a study of the population variations of the snowshoe hare and the lynx (*Lynx canadensis*) in Canada is a classic example of species interaction and interdependence. The peak of the hare population comes about a year before the peak of the lynx population. Since the lynx feeds on the hare, it is obvious that the lynx cycle is related to the hare cycle. This leads to a decline in the population of hares and secondarily to a decline in the lynx population. This permits the plants to recover from the overharvesting by the hares, and the cycle can begin again.

Growth curves are just one of the characteristics of populations. Other characteristics that are a function of the whole group and not of the individual members include population density, birth rate, death rate, age distribution, biotic potential, and rate of dispersion. *See also* Population growth

[*Linda Rehkopf*]

Growth, exponential
See **Exponential growth**

Growth limiting factors

There are a number of essential conditions which all organisms, both plants and animals, require to grow. These are known as growth factors. Plants, for example, require sunlight, water, and **carbon dioxide** in order to perform **photosynthesis**. They require **nutrient**s such as **nitrogen**, **phosphorus**, and various **trace element**s in order to form tissues. The **environment** in which the plant is growing does not contain a unlimited supply of these growth factors. When one or more of them is present in levels or concentrations low enough to constrain the growth of the plant, it is known as a growth limiting factor. The rate or magnitude of the growth of any organism is controlled by the growth factor that is available in the lowest quantities. This concept is analogous to the saying that a chain is only as strong as its weakest link.

These factors limit **population growth**. If they did not exist, a population could increase exponentially, limited only by its own intrinsic lifespan. Growth limiting factors are essential to the traditional concept of **carrying capacity**, which rests on the assumption that the available resources limit the population that can be sustained in that area. Advances in technology have enabled people to increase the carrying capacity in certain areas by manipulating the growth limiting factors. Perhaps the best example of this is the use of **fertilizer**s on farmland.

In the field of population **ecology**, identifying growth limiting factors is part of establishing the constraints and pressures on populations and predicting growth in various conditions. Algal growth in New York Harbor provides an example of the importance of identifying growth limiting factors. In New York Harbor, several billion gallons of untreated **wastewater** are released daily, bringing enormous quantities of nutrients and **suspended solid**s into the water. Algae in the harbor take advantage of the nutrient loads and grow more than they would under nutrient-poor conditions. At the same time, however, the suspended solids and **silt**s brought into harbor cause the water to become very turbid, limiting the amount of sunlight that penetrates it. Sunlight is rarely a growth limiting factor for algae; nutrients are usually what limits their growth, but in this case nutrients are in excess supply. This means that if **pollution control** in the harbor ever results in control of the turbidity in the water, there will probably be a sharp increase in the growth of algae.

Consideration of growth limiting factors is also very important in the field of **conservation** biology and **habitat** protection. If the goal is to protect a bird such as the heron, which may feed on fish from a lake and nest in upland trees nearby, limiting factors must be taken into account not only for the growth of the individual but also for the population. Conservation efforts must not be directed only toward ensuring there are enough fish in the lake. Enough trees must also be left uncut and undisturbed for nesting in order to address all of the growth requirements for the population. Regardless of how abundant the fish are, the number of herons will only grow to the extent allowed by the number of available nesting sites.

Environmentalists use growth limiting factors to distinguish between undisturbed **ecosystem**s and unstable or stressed systems. In an ecosystem that has been distressed or disturbed, the nature of growth limiting factors changes, and these changes are often human-induced, as they are in New York Harbor. Though the change in circumstances may not always appear negative in impact, it still represents a shift away from the original balance, and it may have effects on other **species** or lead to subtle long-term changes in the system. Any cleanup or management strategy must use these new growth limiting factors to identify the nature of the imbalance that has occurred and develop a procedure to restore the system to its original condition.

Growth limiting factors are extensively used in the field of **bioremediation**, in which microbes are used to clean up environmental contaminants by breakdown and **decomposition**. **Oil spills** are a good example. Bacteria that can break down and degrade oils are naturally present in small quantities in **soil**, but under normal conditions their growth is limited by both the availability of essential nutrients and the availability of oil. In the event of an oil spill on land, the only growth limiting factor for these bacteria is nutrients. Bioremediation scientists can add nitrogen and phosphorus to the soil in these circumstances to stimulate growth, which increases degradation of the oil. Techniques such as these, which use naturally occurring bacterial populations to control contamination, are still in development; they are most useful when the contaminants are present in high concentrations and confined to a limited area. *See also* Algal bloom; Decline spiral; Ecological productivity; Exponential growth; Food chain/web; Restoration ecology

[*Usha Vedagiri and Douglas Smith*]

FURTHER READING

Mayer, G. *Ecological Stress and the New York Bight: Science and Management.* Columbia, SC: Estuarine Research Federation, 1982.

Smith, R.L. *Ecology and Field Biology.* New York: Harper and Row Publishers, 1980.

Growth, logistic
See **Logistic growth**

Growth, population
See **Population growth**

Guano

Manure created by flying animals that is deposited in a central location because of nesting habits. Guano can occur in caves from **bats** or in nesting grounds where large populations of birds congregate. Guano was frequently used as a source of **nitrogen** fertilizer prior to the time when nitrogen **fertilizer** was commercially manufactured from **natural gas**. *See also* Animal waste

Gulf War Syndrome

Approximately 697,000 U.S. service members were deployed to the Persian Gulf from January to March 1991 as part of a multinational effort to stop Iraq's attack against Kuwait. And while the war itself was short, a long battle has been taking place ever since by veterans, the government and scientists to determine what has caused "Gulf War Syndrome," a mysterious collection of symptoms reported by as many as 70,000 U.S. men and women who served in the war. They are joined by British veterans in their health complaints, and in smaller numbers by Canadians, Czechs and Slovaks.

Gulf War Syndrome is a complex array of symptoms, including chronic fatigue, rashes, headaches, diarrhea, sleep disorders, joint and muscle pain, digestive problems, memory loss, difficulty concentrating, and depression. A small percentage of veterans have had babies born with twisted limbs, congestive heart failure and missing organs. The veterans blamed these abnormalities on their service in the Gulf. The U.S. **Environmental Protection Agency** has also found high rates for brain and nervous system cancers among these veterans, up to 7-14 times higher than among the general population, depending on the age group. Considering that most soldiers and veterans are younger and in better physical shape than the general population, researchers find such figures more than surprising.

Collectively, these ailments suggest that neurological processes may have been altered, or immune systems damaged. While no single cause has been identified, various analyses of the Gulf War experience point to low-level exposure of chemical weapons, combined with other environmental and medical factors, as key contributors to the health problems triggered years after exposure.

The war was unique in the levels of physical and emotional stresses created for those who served, as well as for their families. A significant portion of troops were from the reserves, rather than active enlistees. Deployment occurred at unprecedented speed. Most troops were given multiple vaccinations that singularly do not have adverse effects; their combined effects were not tested before distribution. Detectors often signaled the presence of chemical weapons during the conflict, but were mostly ignored as inaccurate. The soldiers worked long hours in extreme temperatures, lived in crowded and unsanitary conditions where **pesticide**s were used indiscriminately to rid areas of flies, snakes, spiders, and scorpions, and breathed and had dermal exposures to chemicals from the continuous oil fires—burning trash, feces, fuels, and solvents. Blazing sun, blowing sand and biting sandflies further increased the discomfort and stress of military life in the desert. Exposures to the various fumes often exceeded federal standards and World Health Organization health guidelines; these alone could have caused "permanent impairment," according to a 1994 National Institutes of Health report.

The U.S. military now admits it was inadequately prepared for chemical and biological warfare, which it knew Iraq had previously used. Three of four reserve units, for example, didn't have protective gear. The drug pyridostigmine bromide (PB, 3-dimethylaminocarbonyloxy-N-methylpyridium bromide) was given to almost 400,000 troops before and during the Gulf War to combat the effects of nerve gas, even though it is approved by the **Food and Drug Administration** (FDA) only for treatment of the neurological disorder myasthenia gravis. The FDA agreed on the condition that commanders inform troops what they were taking and what the potential side effects were. One survey, however, found that 63 of 73 veterans who had taken the drug did not receive such information. Records were not kept on who took which drugs or vaccines, as required by FDA and Defense Department guidelines.

While the Defense Department and other government agencies have spent more than $80 million to try to identify the cause of veterans' ailments, a privately funded team of toxicologists and epidemiologists may have discovered an explanation for at least some problems experienced by Gulf War veterans. Researchers treated chickens in 1996 with nonlethal doses of three chemicals veterans were exposed to: DEET (N,N-diethyl-m-toluamide) and chlorpyrifos (O,O-diethyl O-3,5,6-trichloropyridinyl phosphorothioate), used topically or sprayed on uniforms as insecticides, and the anti-nerve gas drug pyridostigmine bromide. They found that simultaneous exposure to two or more of the insecticides and drugs damaged the chickens' nervous system, even though none of the chemicals caused problems by itself. The range of symptoms the chickens developed is similar to those the veterans describe. A similar study by the Defense Department found that the chemicals were more toxic to rats when given together than individually. Follow up studies are underway to determine if this also holds for humans.

The researchers hypothesize that multiple chemicals overwhelmed the animals' ability to neutralize them. The enzyme butyrylcholinesterase, which circulates in the blood, breaks down a variety of nitrogen-containing organic compounds, including the three substances tested. But the anti-nerve gas drug, in particular, can monopolize the enzyme, preventing it from dealing with the insecticides. Those chemicals could then sneak into the brain, and cause damage they would not produce on their own.

Many veterans believe that, while the drugs and pesticides may have played a role in their ailments, so have chemical weapons. Troops could have been subjected to much more low-level exposure of chemical weapons than previously believed, either directly or via air plumes, because 75% of Iraq's chemical weapons production capability, along with 21 chemical weapons storage sites, were destroyed by allied air raids.

In addition, U.S. battalions blew up an Iraqi arms dump soon after the war was over, before many troops had left the Gulf. Khamisiyah, an enormous ammunition storage site, covered 20 mi² (50 km²) with 100 ammunition bunkers and other storage facilities. Two large explosions were set off, one on March 4 and a second on March 10, 1991. Smaller demolition operations continued in the area through most of April 1991.

While the site was not believed to have contained chemical weapons at the time, the Defense Department admitted in June 1996 that the complex had included nerve and mustard gases. The Central Intelligence Agency also admitted in April 1997 that it knew in 1986 that thousands of mustard gas weapons had been stored at the Khamisiyah depot, but the agency failed to include it on a list of suspected sites provided to the Defense Department before the 1991 war, which led troops to assume it was safe to blow it up.

Weather data shows that upper-level winds in the gulf were blowing in a southerly direction during and after the bombing. Thus, vapors carried by these winds could have contaminated troops hundreds of miles away. A 1974 report, *Delayed Toxic Effects of Chemical Warfare Agents*, found that chemicals weapons plant workers suffer as many chronic symptoms as those now suffered by Gulf War veterans, including neurological, gastrointestinal and heart problems, loss of memory and a greater risk of cancer; exposure to these chemicals may also create birth effects in children. A 1995 study by a British medical researcher found many of the same symptoms in Third World people exposed to **organophosphate** insecticides, like DEET used in the Gulf War, which are diluted versions of chemical weapons.

While British, Canadian and Slovak veterans have reported similar ailments, albeit in smaller numbers, no French veterans have complained of such illnesses, despite extensive publicity. This is also providing valuable clues to the U.S. veterans' maladies, in several ways. For example, the French did not use many of the vaccines that the British and Americans used, including pyridostigmine bromide. French camps were not sprayed with insecticides as a preventive measure, rather only when needed to control pest populations. When they did spray, they did not use organophosphates. Finally, the French were nowhere near the Khamisiyah munitions depot when the destruction occurred.

In February 1997, a series of study results established the most definitive links between Gulf War syndrome and chemicals to date. The research identifies six "syndromes," or clusters of like symptoms in discrete groups of veterans, and associates each with distinct events during the war. Troops who reported exposure to chemical weapons, for example, are likely to suffer from confusion, balance problems, impotence and depression. Other sets of symptoms correspond to the use of insect repellants and anti-nerve gas drugs. While not conclusive, these findings will likely spur further research into the effects of low-level exposure to certain chemicals.

Such research was advocated by the presidential advisory committee, a 12-member panel of veterans, scientists, and health care and policy experts established in 1995. The committee held 18 public meetings between August 1995 and November 1996 to investigate the nature of Gulf War veterans' illnesses, health effects of Gulf War risk factors, and the government's response to Gulf War illnesses. While the committee's final report in January 1997 concluded that no single, clinically recognizable disease can be attributed to Gulf War service, it recommended additional research on the long-term health effects of low-level exposures to chemical weapons, on the synergistic effects of pyridostigmine bromide with other Gulf War risk factors, and on the body's physical response to stress.

While the debate continues, the Veterans Affairs and the Defense Departments are providing free medical help to any veteran who believes he or she is suffering from Gulf War Syndrome. In January 1997, President Clinton proposed new regulations that would extend the time available to veterans to prove their disabilities are related to Gulf War service from two to ten years, through the year 2001. He also initiated a

Gully erosion in Australia.

presidential review to ensure that in any future deployments the health of service men and women and their families is better protected.

Definitive answers as to the causes and treatments for veterans' ailments may be years away. What is clear is that the complex biological, chemical, physical and psychological stresses of the Persian Gulf War appear to have produced a variety of complex adverse health effects. No single disease or syndrome is apparent, but rather multiple illnesses with overlapping symptoms and causes. If what had been considered acceptable trace levels of chemical agents in the war environment are found to be harmful, the U.S. military will have to revamp the way it protects its forces against even those tiny amounts. Tragically, that would mean that not only did "friendly fire" account for nearly 25% of the 146 U.S. deaths, but also that allied actions were responsible for the war's most persistent and haunting pain.

[*Sally Cole-Misch*]

FURTHER READING

Abou-Donia, M.B., et. al. "Increased Neurotoxicity Following Concurrent Exposure to Pyridostigmine Bromide, DEET and Chlorpyrifos." *Fundamental and Applied Toxicology* 34, no. 190 (1996): 201-222.

Barry, J., and R. Watson. "Scent of War." *Newsweek* 127, no. 14 (September 30, 1996): 38-39.

——. "A Gulf War Cover-up?" *Newsweek* 127, no. 20 (November 11, 1996): 48-49.

Cary, P., and M. Tharp. "The Gulf War's Grave Aura." *U.S. News & World Report* 121, no. 2, (July 8, 1996): 38-39.

Cowley, G., and M. Hager. "Poisoned in the Gulf?" *Newsweek* 127, no. 18 (April 29, 1996): 74.

"Darkness at Noon." *The Economist* 342, no. 7999 (January 1, 1997): 71-74.

National Institutes of Health Technology Assessment Workshop Panel. "The Persian Gulf Experience and Health." *Journal of the American Medial Association* 272, no. 5 (August 3, 1994): 391-395.

Pennisi, E. "Chemicals Behind Gulf War Syndrome." *Science* 272, no. 5261 (April 26, 1996): 479-480.

Shenon, P. "CIA Says It Knew of Iraq Chemicals." *Detroit Free Press*, April 10, 1997: 1-3A.

Thompson, M. "The Silent Treatment." *Time* 148, no. 28 (December 23, 1996): 33-37.

Waldman, A. "Credibility Gulf." *The Washington Monthly* 28, no. 12 (December 1996): 28-35.

Gullied land

Areas where all diagnostic **soil** horizons have been removed by flowing water, resulting in a network of V-shaped or U-shaped channels. Generally, gullies are so deep that extensive reshaping is necessary for most uses. They cannot be crossed with normal farm machinery. While gullied land can occur on any land, they are often most prevalent on loess, sandy, or other soils with low cohesion. *See also* Erosion; Soil profile; Soil texture

Gypsy moth females laying eggs.

Gypsy moth (*Portheria dispar*)

The gypsy moth, a native of Europe and parts of Asia, has been causing both ecological and economic damage in the eastern United States and Canada since its introduction in New England in the 1860s.

Harvard entomologists brought live specimens of the insect to Cambridge, Massachusetts for experimentation with silk production. Several individual specimens escaped and became an established population over the next twenty years. The destructive abilities of the gypsy moth became readily apparent to Boston area residents, who watched large stands of forest be destroyed by their larvae. From the initial infestation in eastern Massachusetts, the gypsy moth spread throughout the northeastern United States and southeastern Canada. In just over a hundred years, it has spread to the southern half of Maine, to Virginia and West Virginia, and west through Pennsylvania to the northeast corner of Ohio, as well as west through southern Ontario to Michigan. The **U. S. Department of Agriculture** reports that virtually all areas that have experienced an invasion of gypsy moths continue to have extremely high levels of infestation.

Gypsy moths have a voracious appetite for leaves, and the primary environmental problem caused by them is the destruction of huge areas of forest. Gypsy moth caterpillars defoliate a number of **species** of broadleaf trees including birches, larch, and aspen, but prefer the leaves of several species of oaks, though they have also been found to eat some evergreen needles. One caterpillar can consume up to one square foot of leaves per day. In 1989 Michigan reported over a quarter of a million acres defoliated by these insects, and Pennsylvania has more recently documented over one and a half million acres of forested land damaged by gypsy moths. The sheer number of gypsy moth caterpillars produced in one generation can create other problems as well. Some areas become so heavily infested that the insects have covered houses and yards, causing psychological difficulties as well as physical.

There are few natural predators of the gypsy moth in North America, and none that can keep its population under control. Attempts have been made since the 1940s to control the insect with **pesticide**s, including **DDT**, but these efforts have usually resulted in further contaminating of the **environment** without controlling the moths or their caterpillars. Numerous attempts have also been made to introduce species from outside the region to combat it, and almost one hundred different natural enemies of the gypsy moth have been introduced into the northeast United States. Most of these have met at best, with limited success. Recent progress has been made in experiments with a Japanese fungus which attacks and kills gypsy moth. The fungus enters the body of the caterpillar through its pores and begins to destroy the insect from the inside out. It is apparently non-lethal to all other species in the infested areas, and its use has met with limited success in parts of Rhode Island and upstate New York. It remains unknown however, whether it will control the gypsy moth, or at least stem the dramatic population increases and severe infestations commonplace in the 1980s. *See also* Deforestation; Fire ants; Introduced species; Zebra mussel

[*Eugene C. Beckham*]

FURTHER READING

Ford, P. "At War With the Gypsy Moth." *Country Journal* 17 (May-June 1990): 44-49.

Gibbons, A. "Asian Gypsy Moth Jumps Ships to United States." *Science* 255 (31 January 1992): 526.

Pond, D., and W. Boyd. "Gypsy on the Move." *American Forests* 98 (March-April 1992): 21-25.

H

Haagen-Smit, Arie Jan (1900-1977)

Dutch atmospheric chemist

The discoverer of the causes of **photochemical smog**, Haagen-Smit was one of the founders of atmospheric chemistry, but first made significant contributions to the chemistry of essential oils.

Haagen-Smit was born in Utrecht, Holland, in 1900, and graduated from the University of Utrecht. He became head assistant in organic chemistry there and later, served as a lecturer until 1936. He came to the United States as a lecturer in biological chemistry at Harvard, then became associate professor at the California Institute of Technology in Pasadena. He retired as Professor of Biochemistry in 1971, having served as executive officer of the department of biochemistry and director of the plant environment laboratory. Haagen-Smit also contributed to the development of techniques for decreasing **nitrogen oxide** formation during **combustion** in electric **power plants** and autos, and to studies of damage to plants by **air pollution**.

While early workers on the haze and eye irritation that developed in Los Angeles, California, tried to treat it as identical with the smog (smoke + fog) then prevalent in London, England, Haagen-Smit knew at once it was different. In his reading, Haagen-Smit had encountered a 1930s Swiss patent on a process for introducing random oxygen functions into **hydrocarbons** by mixing the hydrocarbons with **nitrogen dioxide** and exposing the mixture to ultraviolet light. He thought this mixture would smell much more like a smoggy day in Los Angeles than would some sort of mixture containing **sulfur dioxide**, a major component of London smog. He followed the procedure and found his supposition was correct. Simple analysis showed the mixture now contained **ozone**, organic peroxides, and several other compounds. These findings showed that the sources of the problems of Los Angeles were **petroleum** refineries, **petrochemical** industries, and ubiquitous **automobile** exhaust.

Haagen-Smit was immediately attacked by critics, who set up laboratories and developed instruments to prove him wrong. Instead the research proved him right, except in minor details.

Haagen-Smit had a long and distinguished career. In addition to his work on the chemistry of essential flower oils and famous findings on smog, he also contributed to the chemistry of plant hormones and plant alkaloids and the chemistry of microorganisms. He was a founding editor of the *International Journal of Air Pollution*, now known as *Atmospheric Environment*, one of the leading air pollution research journals. Though he found the work uncongenial, he stayed with it for the first year, then retired to the editorial board, where he served until 1976.

Once it was obvious that he had correctly identified the cause of the Los Angeles smog, he was showered with honors. These included membership in the National Academy of Science, receipt of the Los Angeles County Clean Air Award, the Chambers Award of the Air Pollution Control Association (now the **Air and Waste Management Association**), the Hodgkins Medal of the Smithsonian Institution, and the National Medal of Science. In his native Netherlands he was made a Laureate of Labor by the Netherlands Chemical Society, and Knight of the Order of Orange Nassau. *See also* Atmosphere; Automotive emissions; Greenhouse effect; Los Angeles Basin

[*James P. Lodge, Jr.*]

FURTHER READING

Lodge, J. P. "Obituary: A. J. Haagen-Smit," *Nature* 267 (1977): 565-566.

Habitat

Refers to the type of **environment** in which an organism or **species** occurs, as defined by its physical properties (e.g., rainfall, temperature, topographic position, **soil texture**, soil moisture) and its chemical properties (e.g., soil acidity, concentrations of **nutrient**s and toxins, oxidation reduction status). Some authors include broad biological characteristics in their definitions, for instance forest versus **prairie** habitats, referring to the different types of environments occupied by trees and grasses. Within a given habitat there may be different micro-habitats, for example the hummocks and hollows on bogs or the different soil horizons in forests.

Habitat fragmentation

Inseparable from such issues as **biodiversity** and **endangered species** protection, **habitat** fragmentation results from human settlement, agriculture, forestry, and other activities that create a mosaic of patchy habitats amidst cities, roads, farms, houses, clearcut forests, and other disturbances of human activity. Habitat fragmentation is an area of great scientific uncertainty in **conservation biology** because the structure of **ecosystem**s takes several hundreds to thousands of years to develop, and therefore the complete consequences of subdividing natural **environment**s into fragments may be unknown for several human generations. Biologists disagree on how much the subdividing of habitats, and the associated subdividing of native populations, influences the susceptibility of species to extinction. Habitat simply means the place where a plant or animal species naturally lives and grows, and ecologists and biologists study these places as interacting communities of both living organisms and "abiotic" or non-living environmental factors such as temperature, moisture, light, topography, and **soil** chemistry.

In the past, the larger types of habitats in which organisms thrive—deciduous and coniferous forests, rain forests, grasslands, oceans, rivers, marshes, the unique Florida Everglades ecosystem—were exploited for timber, grazing, farming, development, and the like without regard for the impacts of these activities on the species within the habitats. But, with the growing awareness of the need to preserve species and the natural systems they depend on, both for human self-preservation and for ethical reasons, ecologists have focused increasingly on the goal of ecosystem "sustainability," or managing ecosystems for future generations. With this goal in mind, scientists and others have become deeply concerned about the extinction of numerous species in the face of a habitat loss and fragmentation as human populations and settlements expand. The issue of habitat fragmentation can be examined from the perspective of two major impacts—the reduction of the original habitat's total size, and the creation of "edge effects" along the perimeter of fragmented habitats.

Fragmentation reduces the area of formerly continuous habitat areas, replacing continuous forests with patches or "islands" of habitat too small to fully support the plant and animal populations of the original contiguous habitat. By some estimates, a 75% reduction in habitat eliminates one-fourth to one-third of the species sharing the habitat, while a 90% reduction eliminates half the original species. Fragmentation and its impacts on species is occurring globally. As of the early 1990s, some 40% of the Earth's land area had been converted to cropland and pasture at the expense of forests and grasslands. This is true even though a massive tree-planting program in China resulted in greater afforestation than **deforestation** in the 1980s in the Asia and the Pacific, and even though forests are returning along the East Coast of the United States. A comprehensive assessment of the world's forests has not been conducted because such conditions as "naturalness" and "degradation" are hard to observe and quantify regionally and globally, though fragmentation is recognized as a major threat to tropical and temperate forests. Next to severe disturbances of forests, such as their reduction to shrublike formations, fragmentation represents the second commonest form of forest degradation, representing approximately 12% of total forest change worldwide. Some scientists believe that the total loss of pristine habitat, and the reduced density of native plants and animals associated with habitat fragmentation, potentially affects these organisms more than any other single factor.

Reducing the area of the original habitat has a number of adverse effects on native plants and animals. Native fauna, faced with roads, farms, and other human development, may be cut off from food, mates, or new territory. They can be killed while crossing roads, as happened, for instance, to 50 Florida black bears (*Ursus americanus floridanus*) in 1994. These black bears, which once numbered more than 12,000 and roamed through the region of southern Georgia, Alabama, and Florida, even to the Florida Keys, now number fewer than 1,500. Although isolated bear populations require 500,000-1 million acres to ensure their long-term survival, this size habitat is only found in the Apalachicola National Forest region. Most remaining bears survive in scattered, isolated populations, reduced to less than 20% of their historic range. Many birds also require resources that are spread out over a large home range. For instance, a single pair of breeding ivory-billed woodpeckers (*Campephilus principalis*) requires 2.5-3.0 mi^2 (6.5-7.6 km^2) of continuous bottomland forest. A single European goshawk (*Accipiter gentilis*) requires 12-20 mi^2 (30-50 km^2) for its home range. Some species require two or more habitat types, and are therefore susceptible to local extinction due to habitat fragmentation. During the breeding season, for example, the blue-grey gnatcatcher (*Polioptila caerulea*) goes from deciduous woodland to chaparral, and if it cannot readily find one of these two habitat types, it can easily become locally extinct. Habitat fragmentation is considered a severe threat to the survival of Asian tigers (*Panthera tigris*), one of the world's most threatened carnivores. On the Indian subcontinent, South East Asia, and the Russian Far East, remaining tigers must compete with people for limited habitat and resources. The isolation that habitat fragmentation imposes on formerly interacting populations of animals can also reduce their genetic diversity by creating barriers to migration, thereby reducing the ability of plants and animals to adapt to changes by moving away from one area and potentially creating inbreeding that magnifies harmful genetic mutations.

Human fragmentation of landscapes can directly contribute to the extinction of species within isolated habitat areas by creating favorable conditions for species that are highly adaptive to changing conditions. Populations of such highly adaptive species can grow rapidly in landscapes dominated by human alterations, harming species that rely exclusively on remaining patches of interior habitat that previously were buffered by surrounding natural habitat. For example, populations of the brown-headed cowbird (*Molothrus ater*) have increased substantially since the North American landscape has been altered. The cowbird, a nest parasite, replaces the eggs of other species with its own, thereby having other species unknowingly incubate its own eggs and raise its young. As a result, forest-dwelling songbird populations have suffered declines. One study of birds in western Australia's wheatbelt found that as a result of fragmentation 41% of the native birds had decreased in range and abundance since the 1900s. Although some birds benefitted, far more were adversely affected. Typically, animal species that benefit from habitat fragmentation are those able to adapt to various habitat conditions, including such fauna as raccoons, opossums, crows, cowbirds, and deer, and such flora as the box elder, tulip tree, cherry, and exotic weeds. Other species, such as black bear, tigers, various songbirds, salamanders, and herbs such as trillium and ginseng that are adapted to specific habitat conditions do not benefit from fragmented landscapes. Loss of any species from a community can have secondary effects throughout the ecosystem. If, for example, a top predator is lost because habitat fragmentation reduces the area it needs to survive, the populations of small omnivores can increase and begin to prey on songbird eggs and hatchlings, thereby reducing their populations. Conservation biologists caution, however, that with regard to specific ecosystems few absolutes can be asserted, leaving room for argument about the effects of specific landscape alterations.

Tropical species are often more susceptible than temperate species to local extinction as a result of habitat fragmentation because they populate their habitats less densely, are less widely distributed, and are often less able to disperse outside their habitats. Tropical species also have complex mutual relationships, such as those between plant-pollinator or plant-seed disperser, and the extinction of one species in the relationships leads to the extinction of the other. For instance, the Australian cassowary (*Casuarius casuarius*) requires large contiguous **rain forest** areas, in which it wanders seeking plants that fruit episodically. In this way, the cassowary disperses large seeds by digesting them. Thus, if the cassowary's habitat is fragmented and it becomes extinct, so will the fruiting plants that depend on them.

Besides reducing their habitat and limiting species' ability to find food or mates, habitat fragmentation produces "edge" effects, or the effects on patchy habitats of interfacing with other types of habitats and the species they support. Edge areas, in which habitat changes are abrupt rather than gradual, often create positive conditions for plants and animals that do not require the protection of the original habitat to thrive, but negative conditions for native species, as seen with the cowbird and other species. Edge effects can include changes in microclimates as a result of structural changes in the environment—for instance, more sunlight penetrating into a woodland. Edges can cause habitats to undergo major changes in vegetation as exotic species from agricultural and urban settings invade the habitat remnant, and trees are exposed to increased wind, causing more trees to fall.

With the increasing recognition of the need to preserve habitat suited to the needs of individual species, a number of national and international programs have been initiated by such organizations as the **World Resources Institute**, the World Conservation Union, the **United Nations Environ-**ment Programme, and **Defenders of Wildlife**. In the United States, a growing trend in conservation to protect endangered species is for state and local governments to develop habitat conservation plans focused not on single species but on habitat regions or corridors in which many species may survive.

[*David Clarke*]

FURTHER READING

Noss, R. F., and R. L. Peters, *Endangered Ecosystems, A Status Report on America's Vanishing Habitat and Wildlife*. Washington, D.C.: Defenders of Wildlife, 1995.

National Research Council, *Science and the Endangered Species Act*. Washington, D.C.: National Academy Press, 1995.

Snape III, W. J., ed. *Biodiversity and the Law*. Washington, D.C.: Island Press, 1996.

World Resources Institute (WRI), The World Conservation Union (IUCN), United Nations Environment Programme (UNEP), *Global Biodiversity Strategy*. U.S.A.: copyright WRI, IUCN, UNEP, 1992.

Haeckel, Ernst (1834-1919)

German naturalist

Ernst Haeckel was born in Potsdam, Germany. As a young boy he was interested in **nature**, particularly botany, and kept a private herbarium, where he noticed that plants varied more than the conventional teachings of his day advocated. Despite these natural interests, he studied medicine—at his father's insistence—at Würzburg, Vienna, and Berlin between 1852 and 1858. After receiving his license he practiced medicine for a few years, but his desire to study *pure science* won over, and he enrolled at the University of Jena to study zoology. Following completion of his dissertation, he served as professor of zoology at the university from 1862 to 1909. The remainder of his adult life was devoted to science.

Haeckel was considered a liberal non-conformist of his day. He was a staunch supporter of **Charles Darwin**, one of his contemporaries. Haeckel was a prolific researcher and writer. He was the first scientist to draw a "family tree" of animal life, depicting the proposed relationships between various animal groups. Many of his original drawings are still used in current textbooks. One of his books, *The Riddle of the Universe* (1899), exposited many of his theories on **evolution**. Prominent among these was his theory of recapitulation, which explained his views on evolutionary vestiges in related animals. This theory, known as the *Biogenic Law*, stated that "ontogeny recapitulates phylogeny"—the development of the individual (ontogeny) repeats the history of the race (phylogeny). In other words, he argued that when an embryo develops, it passes through the various evolutionary stages that reflect its evolutionary ancestry. Although this theory was widely prevalent in biology for many years, scientists today consider it inaccurate or only partially correct. Some even argue that Haeckel falsified his diagrams to prove his theory.

In **environmental science**, Haeckel is perhaps best known for coining the term **ecology** in 1869, which he defined as "the body of knowledge concerning the economy

Ernst Haeckel.

of nature—the investigation of the total relationship of the animal both to its organic and its inorganic **environment** including, above all, its friendly and inimical relations with those animals and plants with which it directly or indirectly comes into contact—in a word, ecology is the study of all those complex interrelations referred to by Darwin as the conditions for the struggle for existence."

[*John Korstad*]

FURTHER READING

Gasman, D. *The Scientific Origins of National Socialism: Social Darwinism in Ernst Haeckel and the German Monist League.* New York: American Elsevier, 1971.

Hitching, F. *The Neck of the Giraffe: Darwin, Evolution, and the New Biology.* Chula Vista, CA: Mentor, 1982.

Smith, R. E. *Ecology and Field Biology.* 4th ed. New York: Harper and Row, 1990.

Half-life

A term primarily used to describe the physical half-life, how **radioactive decay** processes cause unstable atoms to be transformed into another element, but can also refer to the biological half-life of substances that are not radioactive.

Specifically, the physical half-life is the time required for half of a given initial quantity to disappear (or be converted into something else). This description is useful because radioactive decay proceeds in such a way that a fixed percentage of the atoms present are transmuted during a given period of time (a second, a minute, a day, a year). This means that many atoms are removed from the population when the total number present is high, but the number removed per unit of time decreases quickly as the total number falls.

For all practical purposes, the number of radioactive atoms in a population never reaches zero because decay affects only a fraction of the number present. Some infinitesimal number will still be present even after an infinite number of half-lives because with each time period half of what was present before decays and is lost from the sample. Therefore, determining the point at which half of the original number disappears (the half-life) is usually the most accurate way of describing this process. *See also* Radioactivity

Hanford Nuclear Reservation (near Richland, Washington)

The Hanford Engineering Works was conceived in June 1942 under the direction of Major General Leslie R. Groves to produce **plutonium** and other nuclear materials for use in the development of **nuclear weapons**. By December 1942, a decision was reached to proceed with plant construction with two plants to be located at the Clinton Engineering Works in Tennessee and a third at the Hanford Engineering Works in Washington, located in the southeastern portion of the state between the Yakima Range and the Columbia River, approximately 15 miles (24 km) northwest of Pasco, Washington. During World War II, 17,000 people operated in complete secrecy with few knowing the nature of the operation. The reservation occupies approximately 560 square miles of **desert** with the Columbia river flowing through its northern region. Hanford was initially operated by the Pacific Northwest Laboratories, which was at one time owned by General Electric Corporation, then by the Batelle Memorial Institute, and currently by Westinghouse Electric Corporation. Originally the controlling government agency was the **Atomic Energy Commission**; however, control was transferred to the **U.S. Department of Energy** (DOE) when this agency was created.

Over the period from 1943 to 1963, nine plutonium-production reactors were built at Hanford, with the last reactor running from 1971 to 1988. The plutonium fuel was processed on site at a Plutonium and **Uranium** Extraction Plant (PUREX) which is currently idle. In the processing of plutonium, a substantial quantity of **radioactive waste** is produced; at Hanford, it amounts to 60 percent by volume of the nation's **high-level radioactive waste** from weapons production. Extraction of 2.2 lbs (1 kg) of plutonium at the PUREX plant produced over 340 gallons (1,289 l) of liquid high-level radioactive wastes, 55,000 gallons (208,450 l) of low-to-intermediate level radioactive wastes and over 2.5 million gallons (9.5 million l) of cooling waters. The magnitude of the problem can be viewed in terms of the 220,000 pounds (100,000 kg) of plutonium which the United States has produced for military use. The high-level radioactive waste from the PUREX operation is contained in approximately 175 tanks for underground storage. The low-to-intermediate-level radioactive wastes were put into trenches which are similar to **septic-tank** drainage fields. In 1958 a General Electric memo notes that **strontium 90** was being dumped in concentrations thousands or tens-of-thousands of times higher than allowable limits for public access. By May of 1958 workers found radioactive rabbit and coyote dung scattered over 2,000 acres (800 ha). Animals had been using the radioactive **chemicals** as a salt lick. Currently, as reported by the Government Accounting Office, there are 1700 waste sites at Hanford with the underground tanks having leaked at least 750,000 gallons (2.9 million l) into the surrounding **soil**. This same Office reports that 268 million curies of radioactive remains in the double shell tanks.

In the height of the Cold War years, the management of Hanford was under severe pressure to maintain production, and flows to the underground storage tanks represented occasional bottle-necks to production. As a result, when blockages in the lines to the tanks occurred, some high-level radioactive wastes were diverted from the relatively safe underground storage to surface trenches. About 100 million gallons (379 million l) of high-level wastes are estimated to have been improperly disposed of in this manner. In addition, the **Environmental Protection Agency (EPA)** is aware of about 200 billion gallons (758 billion l) of **low-level radioactive waste**s which have been disposed of in a series of ponds and trenches at the Hanford site. These wastes contain **cesium 137**, technetium 99, plutonium 239 and 240, strontium 90, and cobalt 60. So much low-level waste was dumped that the **groundwater** under the reservation was observed to rise by as much as 75 feet (23 m). A underground **plume** of radioactive tritium is entering the Columbia River on the eastern border of the reservation; earlier assessments had estimated that contaminated groundwater would not reach the Columbia River for more than 50 years. The Department of Energy estimates that at least 30 years will be required for the clean up.

The underground storage tanks have recently been a matter of public concern since the Department of Energy gave public information in 1990 indicating that some of the tanks are in danger of exploding and might potentially leak their contents into the **atmosphere**. This situation arose when Hanford managers added ferrocyanide and sodium titanate to some of the tanks in order to precipitate some of the liquid cesium 137 and strontium 90. An undesired side-effect of this practice is the formation of **hydrogen** gas in these large underground storage tanks which requires careful venting. Unfortunately, in one of the tanks, the contents have formed a *viscous slurry*, which covers the liquids and traps the hydrogen. Periodically, as seen by a remote video camera, the entire contents tend to "burp," causing the hydrogen content to rise to about 35 percent of the total gases. This hydrogen is sufficient to cause an explosion if ignited. Hanford officials say, however, that for a disaster to occur, there would either have to be an ignition source, or the internal temperature would have to rise significantly, and even if an explosion were to occur, the tanks are strong enough not to rupture in their present condition.

Even though the Hanford site is an area which causes considerable concern to environmentalists, it does represent a location where innovative approaches to the clean-up and immobilization of radioactive wastes is taking place. For instance, one program at Hanford is the study of *in situ vitrification*, a process in which electrodes are buried in a contaminated soil in a circular zone to a depth of about 20 feet (6 m). By passing electrical current through the soil, melting occurs and fuses the radioactive constituents into the soil. The gases which are produced must be collected and treated. An Environmental and Molecular Sciences Laboratory is currently being built with funding from the Department of Energy which will house a wide range of experimental programs aimed at solving pollution problems. *See also* Radioactive pollution; Radioactive waste management

[*Malcolm T. Hepworth*]

FURTHER READING

D'Antonio, M. *Atomic Harvest: Hanford and the Lethal Toll of America's Nuclear Arsenal.* New York: Crown, 1993.

Gerber, M. S. *On the Home Front: The Cold War Legacy of the Hanford Nuclear Site.* Lincoln, NB: University of Nebraska Press, 1992.

Russell, D. "In the Shadow of the Bomb." *Amicus Journal* 12 (Fall 1990): 18-31.

Shulman, Seth. "Operation Restore Earth: The U. S. Military Gets Ready to Clean Up After the Cold Ware." *E Magazine* 4 (March-April 1993): 36-43.

———. *The Threat At Home: Confronting the Toxic Legacy of the U. S. Military.* Boston: Beacon Press, 1992.

Hardin, Garrett (1915-)

American environmentalist and writer

Trained as a biologist (University of Chicago undergraduate degree; Ph.D. from Stanford in 1942 in microbial ecology), Garrett Hardin spent most of his career at the University of California at Santa Barbara, where his title was Professor of Human Ecology. He was born in Dallas, Texas, and grew up in various places in the Midwest, spending summers on his grandparents' farm in Missouri.

Very few biologists, short of **Charles Darwin**, have generated the levels of controversy that Hardin's thinking and writing have. The controversies, which continue today, center on two metaphors of human-ecological relationships; "the tragedy of the commons" and "the life-boat ethic."

Hardin is widely credited with inventing the idea of the tragedy of the commons, but his work was long preceded by an ancient rhyme about the tragedy that results from stealing the commons from the goose. He did popularize the idea, though, and it made him a force to reckon with in population studies. Seldom is an academic author so identified with one article (though his thoughts on life-boat ethics have since become almost equal in identification and impact). The idea is very simple: resources held in common will be exploited by individuals for personal gain in disregard of public impacts; individual profit belongs to individual exploiters while they bear the brunt of only part of the impacts. Much of the controversy centers on Hardin's solutions to the tragedy: first, that private property owners "recognize their responsibility to care for" the land, thus lending at least implicit support to privatization efforts and second, the paradoxical idea that since exercise of individual freedom leads to ruin, such freedom cannot be tolerated, thus we must turn to "mutual coercion mutually agreed upon." As Hardin noted, "if everyone would restrain himself, all would be well; but it takes only one less than everyone to ruin a system of voluntary restraint. In a crowded world of less than perfect human beings, mutual ruin is inevitable if there are no controls. This is the tragedy of the commons." Hardin has since expanded on his thesis, answering his critics by incorporating the differences between an open access system and an closed one. But the debate continues.

His other widely debated metaphor was of a lifeboat (standing for a nation's land and resources) occupied by rich people in an ocean of poor people (who have fallen out of their own, inadequate lifeboats). If the rich boat is close to its margin of safety, what should its occupants do about the poor people in the ocean? Or in the other boats? If the occupants let in even a few more people, the boat may be swamped, thus creating an ethical dilemma for the rich occupants. How do these occupants of the already full lifeboat justify taking in additional people if it guarantees the collapse for all? Ever since, Hardin has been accused of social Darwinism, of racism, of ignoring the possibility that "the poverty of the poor may be caused in part by the affluence of the rich," and of isolationism (since he argued that "for the foreseeable future survival demands that we govern our actions by the ethics of a [sovereign] lifeboat" rather than "space-ship" ethics that [arguably] try to care for all equitably).

What Hardin was trying to do in both of these cases was to look unemotionally at population growth and resource use, employing the rationale and language of a scientist viewing human populations in an objective, evolutionary perspective. Biologists know that "natural" populations that overuse their resources, that exceed the carrying capacity of their range, are then adjusted—in numbers or in resource use levels—also naturally and often brutally (from the perspective of many people). The problems remain that the division between the rich and the poor in the world is widening, and that many resources and ecosystems on earth are being stressed, though how close to the breaking point no one really knows. Also, nation-states are arbitrary divisions, and perhaps—in a corollary to the space-ship metaphor—the ultimate lifeboat is the Earth and all the inhabitants must exist in it together.

Hardin retired as a professor emeritus of human ecology, a rare title that reflects his attempts to fold the human species into the evolutionary ecology perspective developed in biology. Ultimately what he tried to get across was what he called an *ecolate* view: *ecolacy* asks the question "and then what?" The basic insight of the ecolate citizen is that the world is a complex of systems so intricately interconnected that we can seldom be very confident that a proposed intervention in this system of systems will produce the consequences we want." Hardin's views are rich and varied— the themes presented here are only two of many—but he still summarizes the human condition by what he labels "the ecolate predicament": that all human interventions are doomed to failure if a population exceeds its carrying capacity, wheth-

er of a region or of the world. Doing so "will bring everyone down to a level of poverty."

[*Gerald L. Young*]

FURTHER READING

Bajema, C. J. "Garrett James Hardin: Ecologist, Educator, Ethicist, and Environmentalist," *Population and Environment* 12, no. 3, (Spring 1991): 193-212.

Hardin, G. "Living on a Lifeboat," *BioScience* 24, no. 10, (October 1974): 561-568.

———. *Living Within Limits: Ecology, Economics, and Population Taboos*. New York: Oxford University Press, 1993: 339.

———. "The Tragedy of the Commons," *Science* 162, (13 December 1968): 1243-1248.

Hawaiian Islands

The Hawaiian Islands are made up of a chain of ancient volcanic islands that have formed at irregular intervals over the last ten million years. There are over 100 islands in the chain, eight of which are considered major. Of the eight major islands, Kauai is the oldest, and the island of Hawaii is the youngest, having formed within the past million years. This vast discrepancy in age has contributed to the tremendous **biodiversity** that has evolved there. The other factor responsible for Hawaii's great **species** diversity is the island chain's remoteness. The nearest continent is 2,400 miles (3,862 km) away, thus limiting the total colonization that could, or has, taken place. The niches available to these colonizing species are very diverse due to geophysical events. For example, on the island of Kauai, the average annual rainfall on the windward side of Mount Waialeale is 460 inches (1,169 cm), whereas on its leeward side, it is only 19 inches (48 cm). The temperature on the islands ranges from 75-90°F (24-32°C) for 300 days each year. The lowest temperature ever recorded in Hawaii was 54°F (12°C). Thus with its tropical climate and unique biotic communities, it is easy to understand why Hawaii has been considered a paradise. But now this paradise is threatened by serious environmental problems caused by humans.

The impact of humans has been felt in the Hawaiian Islands since their first arrival, but perhaps never more so than today. In the last quarter century tourism has replaced sugar cane and pineapple as the islands' main revenue source. Over six million tourists visit Hawaii each year spend $11 million a day. With tourism comes development that often destroys natural **habitat**s and strains existing **natural resources**. Hawaii has more than 60 golf courses, with plans to develop at least 100 more. This would destroy thousands of acres of natural vegetation, require the use of millions of gallons of freshwater for **irrigation**, and necessitate the use of tons of chemical **fertilizer**s and **pesticide**s in their maintenance. The increased number of tourists, many of whom visit the islands to enjoy its natural beauty, are often destroying the very thing they are there to see. Along the shore of Hanauma Bay, just south of Honolulu, over 90 percent of the **coral reef** is dead, primarily because people have trampled it in their desire to see and experience this unique piece of **nature**.

Much of Hawaii's **fauna** and **flora** are unique. Over 10,000 species are native to the Hawaiian Islands, having evolved and filled specialized niches there through the process of adaptive radiation from the relatively few original colonizing species. Examples are found in virtually every group of plants and animals in Hawaii. The avian adaptive radiation in the Hawaiian Islands surpasses even the best-known example, Darwin's finches of the **Galapagos Islands**. From as few as 15 colonizing species evolved 90 native species of birds in the Hawaiian archipelago. Included in this number are the Hawaiian honeycreepers of the family Drepanididae. This endemic family of birds arose from a single ancestral species, which gave rise to 23 species, including 24 subspecies, of honeycreepers spread throughout the main islands. **Niche** availability and reproductive isolation contributed greatly to the spectacular diversity of forms that evolved. These birds developed adaptations such as finch-like bills for crushing seeds, parrot-like bills for foraging on larvae in wood, long decurved bills for taking nectar and insects from specialized flowers, and small forcep-like bills for capturing insects.

Introductions of vast numbers of alien species is taking its toll on native Hawaiian species, a process that began when the first humans settled the islands over 1,500 years ago. Many native species of birds had experienced drastic population declines by the time Europeans first encountered the islands over 200 years ago. Since then at least 23 species of Hawaii's native birdlife have become extinct, and currently over 30 additional avian species are threatened with **extinction**. Through the process of primary ecological **succession**, one new species became established in the Hawaiian Islands every 70,000 years. Introductions of alien species are taking place a million times faster, and are thus eliminating native species at an unprecedented rate. Recent estimates indicate that there are over 8,000 introduced species of plants and animals throughout the Hawaiian Island chain. The original Polynesian settlers brought with them pigs, dogs, chickens, and rats, along with a variety of plants they had cultivated for fiber, food, and medicine. With the Europeans came cattle, horses, sheep, cats, and additional rodents. The mongoose was introduced purposefully to control the rat populations; however, they presented more of a threat to ground-nesting birds. The introduction of rabbits caused the loss of vast quantities of vegetation and ultimately the extinction of three bird species on Laysan Island. Over 150 species of birds, including escaped cage birds, have been introduced to the islands. However, most of these have not established breeding populations.

Although Hawaii represents only 0.2 percent of the United States's land base, almost 75 percent of the total extinctions of birds and plants of the nation have occurred in this state. Hawaii's endemic flora are disappearing rapidly. Introduced mammalian browsers are decimating the native plantlife, which never needed to evolve defense mechanisms against such predators, and other introduced animals are destroying populations of native pollinators. Habitat destruction and opportunistic non-native vegetation are also working against the endemic Hawaiian plant species. Organizations such as the Hawaii Plant Conservation Center are working to preserve the state's floral diversity by collecting and propagating as many of the rare and **endangered species** as possible. Their greenhouses now contain over 2,000 plants representing almost two thirds of Hawaii's native species, and their goal is to propagate 400 of the state's most endangered plants.

Introduced plant and animal species and their assault on native species are by no means the only environmental problems facing the Hawaiian Islands. Because Hawaii's population is growing at a higher rate than the national average, and in part due to its isolation, it is facing many environmental problems on a grander scale and at a more rapid rate than its sister states on the mainland. Energy is one of the primary problems. Much of Hawaii's electricity is produced by burning imported oil, which is extremely expensive. Because of limited reserve capabilities with regard to electrical generation, Hawaii faces the potential for blackouts.

Planners have been, over the past several decades, looking at the feasibility of tapping into Hawaii's seemingly vast geothermal energy resources. Hawaii has the most active **volcano** in the world, Kilauea, whose underground network of geothermal reserves is the largest in the state. The proposed Hawaii Geothermal Deep Water Cable project would supply the energy for a 500-**megawatt** power plant, the electrical power of which would be transmitted from the island of Hawaii to Oahu by three undersea cables. This would, of, course, be of economic and environmental benefit by reducing dependence on oil reserves. Opponents of this geothermal power plant point to several problems. They are concerned with the potential for the release of **toxic substance**s, such as **hydrogen** sulfide, **lead**, **mercury**, and chromium, into the **environment** from well-heads. They also have voiced negative opinions concerning construction of a geothermal plant so near the lava flows and fissures of Hawaii's two active volcanoes. An alternately proposed site would have the facility located in Hawaii's last major inholding of lowland **tropical rain forest**. To avoid economic disaster from escalating prices for imported oil and the problem of frequent blackouts, Hawaii must reach some compromise on geothermal energy and/or research the potential for getting its electricity from one or more of wind, wave, or **solar energy**.

Hawaii is also faced with environmental problems of another sort—natural disasters. Volcanoes not only provide the potential for geothermal energy, they also have the potential for massive destruction. Over the past 200 years, Hawaii's two active volcanoes, Kilauea and Mauna Loa, have covered nearly 200,000 acres of land with lava, and geologists expect them to remain active for centuries to come. Severe **hurricane**s and tidal waves also hold the potential for vast destruction, not only of human property and lives, but of natural areas and the **wildlife** it holds. Many of the **endemic species** of Hawaii are threatened or endangered, and their populations are often so low that a single storm could wipe out most or all of its numbers.

There are efforts to reverse the environmental destruction in the Hawaiian Islands. Several organizations comprised of native Hawaiians are working to stem the destruction and loss of the **wilderness** paradise discovered by their ancestors.

[*Eugene C. Beckham*]

FURTHER READING

Pratt, D., P. Brunner, and D. Berret. *The Birds of Hawaii and the Tropical Pacific.* Princeton, NJ: Princeton University Press, 1987.

Scott, J., and J. Sincock. "Hawaiian Birds." *Audubon Wildlife Report 1985.* New York: National Audubon Society, 1985.

Shallenberger, R., ed. *Hawaii's Birds.* 3rd ed. Honolulu: Hawaii Audubon Society, 1981.

Stewart, F., ed. *A World Between Waves: Writings on Hawaii's Rich Natural History.* Washington, DC: Island Press, 1992.

White, D. "Plants in a Precarious State." *National Wildlife* 31 (May 1993): 30-35.

Hayes, Denis (1944-)

American environmentalist and Earth Day organizer

As executive director of the first **Earth Day** in April 1970, Hayes helped launch the modern movement of **environmentalism**, and has promoted the use of **solar energy** and other **renewable resources**. A native of Camas, Washington, Hayes acquired his appreciation of **nature** exploring and enjoying the mountains, lakes, and beaches of the Pacific Northwest. At age 19, he dropped out of Clark College in Vancouver, Washington, and spent the next three years traveling the world. He installed church pews in Honolulu, taught swimming and modeled in Tokyo, and hitchhiked through Africa.

After returning to the United States, Hayes enrolled at Stanford as a history major, was elected student body president, and became active in the anti-Viet Nam War movement, occupying laboratories that researched military projects. After graduating from Stanford, he went to Harvard Law School, but dropped out in 1970 to help organize the first Earth Day. During the Carter administration, Hayes headed the federal Solar Energy Research Institute. He left after the agency's $120 million budget was cut by the Reagan administration. From 1983-92, after completing his law degree at Stanford, he served there as an adjunct professor of engineering.

In 1990, as the international chairman of Earth Day on its twentieth anniversary, Hayes helped to organize participation by over 200 million people in 141 countries. This event generated extraordinary publicity for and concern about global environmental problems. In 1992, Hayes was named president of the Seattle-based Bullitt Foundation, which works to protect the **environment** of the Pacific Northwest and to help disadvantaged children. He also serves as chairman of the board of **Green Seal**, a group that endorses consumer products meeting strict environmental standards and co-chairs the group promoting the "**Valdez Principles**" of corporate responsibility.

Denis Hayes.

Hayes has received awards and honors from many groups, including the **Humane Society of the United States**, the Interfaith Center for Corporate responsibility, the **National Wildlife Federation**, and the **Sierra Club**. In 1990, *Life* magazine named him one of the eighteen Americans most likely to have an impact on the twenty-first century.

Hayes has written over 100 papers and articles, and his book on solar energy, *Rays of Hope: The Transition to a Post-Petroleum World,* has been published in six languages. He has long advocated increased development of solar and other renewable energy sources, which he believes could provide most of the nation's energy supply within a few years.

In 1990, Hayes wrote that "Time is running out. We have at most ten years to embark on some undertakings if we are to avoid crossing some dire environmental thresholds. Individually, each of us can do only a little. Together, we can save the world." *See also* Alternative energy sources; Environmental education; *Exxon Valdez*; Solar Research, Development, Demonstration Act

[*Lewis G. Regenstein*]

FURTHER READING

Hayes, D. "Earth Day 1990: Threshold of the Green Decade." *Natural History* 99 (April 1990): 55-60.

_ "The Green Decade." *Amicus Journal* 12 (Spring 1990): 10-21.

_ *Rays of Hope: The Transition to a Post-Petroleum World.* New York: Norton, 1977.

Reed, S. "Twenty Years After He Mobilized Earth Day, Denis Hayes Is Still Racing to Save Our Planet." *People Weekly* 33 (2 April 1990): 96-99.

Chemical	Source	Health Effects
Pesticides		
DDT	Insecticides	Cancer, damages liver, embryo, bird eggs
BHC	Insecticides	Cancer, embryo damage
Petrochemicals		
Benzene	Solvents, pharmaceuticals and detergent production	Headaches, nausea, loss of muscle coordination, leukemia, linked to damage of bone marrow
Vinyl chloride	Plastics production	Lung and liver cancer, depresses central nervous system, suspected embryotoxin
Other Organic Chemicals		
Dioxin	Herbicides, waste incineration	Cancer, birth defects, skin disease
PCBs	Electronics, hydraulic fluid, fluorescent lights	Skin damage, possible gastro-intestinal damage, possibly cancer-causing
Heavy Metals		
Lead	Paint, gasoline	Neurotoxic, causes headaches, irritability, mental impairment in children brain, liver, and kidney damage
Cadmium	Zinc processing, batteries, fertilizer processing	Cancer in animals, damage to liver and kidneys

Health effects of hazardous substances.

Ridenour, J. M., et al. "Global Prescription: Leading Conservationists Look to the Future and Speak Their Minds." *National Parks* 64 (March-April 1990): 16-18.

Hazardous chemicals

See **Hazardous material; Hazardous waste**

Hazardous material

Any agent that presents a risk to life-forms or the **environment** can be considered a hazardous material. This is a very broad term which encompasses pure compounds and mixtures, raw materials and other naturally occurring substances, as well as industrial products and wastes. Depending on the nature and the length of exposure, virtually all substances can have toxic effects, ranging from headaches and dizziness to **cancer**. The challenge facing any legislation is not only to devise regulations for the safe handling of hazardous materials but also to define the term itself.

The legislation that offers the most detailed and comprehensive definition of hazardous materials is the **Resource Conservation and Recovery Act (RCRA)**, enacted in 1976. RCRA classifies a waste mixture or compound as hazardous if it fails what is called a *characteristic test* or appears on one of a few lists. The lists of **hazardous waste**s include those from specific and nonspecific sources and those which are acutely hazardous and generally hazardous. There are four characteristic tests: ignitability, reactivity, corrosivity, and extraction-procedure toxicity.

A waste fails the ignitable test if it is a liquid with flash point below 140 degrees Fahrenheit (60 degrees Celsius); or a solid that, under standard temperature and pressure, causes fire through friction, absorbing moisture, or spontaneous changes and burns vigorously and persistently; or a compressed gas defined by the Department of Transportation (DOT) as an oxidizer or as being ignitable. Spent solvents, paint removers, epoxy resins, and waste inks are often classified as hazardous under this definition.

A waste fails the corrosivity test if it is aqueous and has a **pH** of either 2 or less or 12.5 or more, or if it is a liquid that corrodes steel at a rate equal to or more than 0.25 inches (6.35 millimeters) per year. Examples of corrosive wastes include various **acids and bases** such as nitric acid, ammonium hydroxide, perchloric acid, sulfuric acid, and sodium hydroxide, though a waste will not be classified as hazardous in this test if these acids and bases are neutralized or present at low levels.

Reactivity is related to one of the following criteria: If the material is unstable, with the potential for violent reactions with water, or generates toxic fumes; if it has cyanide and sulfide content; if it can be easily detonated; or is defined by DOT as a Class A or B explosive. Compounds commonly causing wastes to fall into this category are chromic acid, hypochlorites, picric acid, nitroglycerin, dinitrophenol, and organic peroxides.

Extraction-Procedure toxicity is determined through the extraction of **solid waste**, in a procedure referred to as the *Toxicity Characteristic Leaching Procedure* (TCLP). Liquid waste can also fail this test, although a liquid containing less than 0.5 percent solids after **filtration** does not need to undergo it. Such a liquid can be directly analyzed for contaminants. In the TCLP, solids are extracted in a mildly acidic medium (pH 5.0) for 18 hours using a tumbling apparatus, and the resulting liquid extract is then analyzed for contaminants. The waste is deemed to be hazardous if the level of a contaminant detected in this extraction procedure exceeds a given level. If liquid extracts contain **arsenic** at a concentration greater than 5.0 mg/L, for example, the waste is classified as hazardous. Different methods are recommended by the **Environmental Protection Agency (EPA)** for measuring the contaminants in each class.

The Resource Conservation and Recovery Act (1976) and the Hazardous and Solid Waste Amendments added to it in 1984 were intended to protect **groundwater**, surface water, and land from improper management of solid wastes. The act and the amendments defined the responsibilities of industries and others who generate and transport hazardous waste. They also set standards for land disposal facilities and underground storage tanks, as well as standards for proper management of hazardous materials from "cradle to grave."

The **Toxic Substances Control Act (1976)** is another important piece of legislation concerning hazardous materials. It was intended to regulate the introduction and use of new, potentially hazardous substances. The bill requires industry to test extensively **chemicals** that may be harmful, and it requires industries to provide the EPA with information about the production, use, and health effects of any new substances or mixtures before they are manufactured.

The **Comprehensive Environmental Response, Compensation and Liabilities Act (CERCLA) (1980)** and the **Superfund Amendments and Reauthorization Act (SARA) (1986)** set policy for situations in which hazardous materials have been mismanaged in the past. These legislations have established a system for ranking sites that need remediation, called the Hazard Ranking System, as well as a procedure for raising funds to support these efforts. The bills also impose schedules for site investigations, feasibility studies, and remedial action.

The definition of hazardous materials remains a difficult and complex issue. There are changes in public perceptions about certain materials, such as **asbestos** or **lead**, and there are scientific contributions which result in the addition or deletion of various chemicals or compounds from lists of hazardous materials. The definition is therefore dynamic, but changes are made within a regulatory framework designed to protect both life and the environment.

[*Gregory D. Boardman*]

FURTHER READING

Corbitt, R. A. *Standard Handbook of Environmental Engineering.* New York: McGraw-Hill, 1990.

Freeman, H. M. *Standard Handbook of Hazardous Waste Treatment and Disposal.* New York: McGraw-Hill, 1989.

Martin, E. J., and J. H. Johnson. *Hazardous Waste Management Engineering.* New York: Van Nostrand Reinhold, 1987.

Sax, N. I. *Dangerous Properties of Industrial Materials.* 6th ed. New York: Van Nostrand Reinhold, 1984.

Wagner, T. P. *Hazardous Waste Identification and Classification Manual.* New York: Van Nostrand Reinhold, 1990.

Wentz, C. A. *Hazardous Waste Management.* New York: McGraw-Hill, 1989.

Hazardous materials, solidification of

See **Solidification of hazardous materials**

Hazardous materials, storage and transport

See **Storage and transport of hazardous materials**

Hazardous Materials Transportation Act (1975)

The Hazardous Materials Transportation Act, enacted in 1975 as part of a law dealing with transportation safety, strengthened the 1970 Hazardous Materials Transportation Control Act. The impetus for this act was increased illegal, or midnight, dumping; increasing spills; and poor enforcement. Illegal dumping increased in the 1970s as many **landfills** began to refuse to take **hazardous waste**, thus dramatically increasing the costs of disposal. The illegal dumping took place in vacant lots, along highways, or actually on the highways. In the congressional debate on the act, the U. S. Department of Transportation (DOT), which administers the law, estimated that 75 percent of all hazardous waste shipments violated the existing regulations. This poor enforcement was due to a lack of inspection personnel, fragmented jurisdiction, and lack of coordination among the Coast Guard, the Federal Aviation Administration, the Federal Highway Administration, and the Federal Railroad Administration.

The law establishes minimum standards of regulation for the transport of **hazardous material**s by air, ship, rail, and motor vehicle. The DOT regulates the packing, labeling, handling, vehicle routing, and manufacture of packing and transport containers for hazardous materials transportation. The hazardous materials and wastes covered by the law, based on DOT regulations, are those on the **Resource Conservation and Recovery Act (RCRA)** list and certain substances designated by the **Environmental Protection Agency** under the authority of Superfund. All hazardous waste transporters must register as such with the proper state and federal agencies; they must use the RCRA uniform manifest system to track the pick-up and delivery of all shipments; they must only deliver to permitted hazardous waste facilities; they must notify the proper agencies of any accidents; they must clean up any discharges that occur during the transportation process. The law also provides a significant role for the states, though there are provisions in the act to prevent overly strict state and local regulations of hazardous waste transport. The Hazardous Materials Transportation Act includes numerous information requirements, also designed to increase public safety. Each vehicle carrying hazardous materials must display a sign identifying the hazard class of the cargo, and emergency response information has been required since 1990. Each shipment must also be accompanied by its RCRA hazardous waste manifest.

The manifest system is part of the RCRA "cradle-to-grave" approach to regulating hazardous materials. The system is supposed to prevent illegal dumping, since hazardous waste transporters could not accept hazardous waste without a manifest, and, similarly, hazardous waste treatment and disposal facilities could not accept waste from transporters without a manifest. Since all hazardous materials could be traced and accounted for through such manifests, illegal dumping should stop. Nevertheless, it is unclear how much effect the manifest system has had on illegal dumping since such dumping is still less costly than proper disposal.

In 1990, the Hazardous Materials Transportation Uniform Safety Act was passed, the first major amendments to the 1975 Act. Poor enforcement of the existing law was the stimulus for action. The law focused on better enforcement by increasing the number of inspectors, increasing the civil and criminal penalties for violation of the regulations, and helping states better respond to accidents involving hazardous materials. *See also* Chemical spills; Comprehensive Environmental Response, Compensation and Liability Act (CERLA) (1980); Hazardous waste siting; Solidification of hazardous material; Storage and transport of hazardous materials

[*Christopher McGrory Klyza*]

FURTHER READING

Dower, R. C. "Hazardous Wastes." *Public Policies for Environmental Protection*, edited by P. R. Portney. Washington, DC: Resources for the Future, 1990.

"Hazardous Materials Law Strengthened." *Congressional Quarterly Almanac* 46 (1990): 380-82.

Mazmanian, D., and D. Morell. *Beyond Superfailure: America's Toxics Policy for the 1990s*. Denver, CO: Westview Press, 1992.

Hazardous Substances Act (1960)

This law was one of Congress's first forays into consumer protection, and it helped to pave the way for the explosion in consumer protection legislation that began in the mid-1960s. The Hazardous Substances Labeling Act was passed in 1960 (the word "Labeling" was deleted by the 1966 amendments the act). The law authorized the Secretary of the Department of Health, Education, and Welfare (HEW) to require warning labels for household substances that were deemed hazardous. These substances were categorized as: toxic, corrosive, irritant, strong sensitizer, flammable or combustible, pressure generating, or radioactive. The law does not cover **pesticides** (which are regulated by the **Federal Insecticide, Fungicide, and Rodenticide Act**); food, drugs, or cosmetics (which are covered by the Federal Food, Drug, and Cosmetics Act); radioactive materials related to **nuclear power**; fuels for cooking, heating, or refrigeration; or **tobacco** products.

A product is defined to be hazardous if it might lead to personal injury or substantial illness, especially if there is a reasonable danger that a child might ingest the substance. When the HEW Secretary declares a substance to be hazardous, a label is required. The label must include a description of the chief hazard and first aid instructions, along with handling and storage instructions. If its chief hazard is flammable, corrosive, or toxic, it must say DANGER on the label; other hazardous substances require either CAUTION or WARNING. In addition, all labels must include the statement "Keep out of the reach of children."

Major amendments to the act, the Child Protection Act, were passed in 1966. These amendments, largely in response to the message on consumer issues by President Lyndon Johnson, expanded federal control over hazardous substances. The **Food and Drug Administration** (FDA), which administered the law, could now ban substances (after formal hearings) that were deemed too hazardous, even if they had a warning label, if "the degree or nature of the hazard involved in the presence or use of such substance in households is such that the objective of the protection the public health and safety can be adequately served" only by such a ban. The amendments also extended the scope of the law to pay greater attention to toys and children's articles. This meant the government could require a warning on all household items, rather than just packaged items.

The Child Protection and Toy Safety Act of 1969 further amended the Hazardous Substances Act. Toys could be declared hazardous if they presented electrical, mechanical, or thermal dangers. Also, substances that were hazardous to children, including toys, could be banned automatically. As the titles of these amendments suggest, the Hazardous Substances Act became the primary vehicle to protect children from dangerous substances and toys. Administration of the act has been shifted to the Consumer Product Safety Commission. If the Commission finds a "substantial risk of injury," children's clothes, furniture, and toys can be pulled from the market immediately. *See also* Environmental law; Hazardous material; Hazardous Materials Transportation Act; Hazardous waste; Hazardous waste siting; Radioactive waste; Radioactivity

[*Christopher McGrory Klyza*]

FURTHER READING

"Child Protection." *Congressional Quarterly Almanac* 22 (1966): 325-7.

"Toy Safety," *Congressional Quarterly Almanac* 25 (1969): 248-50.

Hazardous waste

Of the thousands of millions of tons of waste generated in the United States annually, approximately 60 million tons are classified as hazardous. Hazardous waste is legally defined by the **Resource Conservation and Recovery Act (RCRA)** of 1976. The RCRA defines hazardous waste as any waste or combination of wastes, which because of its quantity, concentration, or physical, chemical, or infectious characteristics may: A) cause, or significantly contribute to, an increase in **mortality** or an increase in serious irreversible or incapacitating illness; or, B) pose a substantial present or potential hazard to human health or the **environment** when improperly treated, stored, transported, disposed of, or otherwise managed.

In the Code of Federal Regulations, the **Environmental Protection Agency (EPA)** specifies that a **solid waste** is hazardous if it meets any of four conditions: 1) It exhibits ignitability, corrosivity, reactivity, or EP toxicity; 2) has been listed as a hazardous waste; 3) is a mixture containing a listed hazardous waste and a nonhazardous waste, unless the mixture is specifically excluded or no longer exhibits any of the four characteristics of hazardous waste; 4) is not specifically excluded from regulation as a hazardous waste.

The EPA established two criteria for selecting the characteristics given above. The first criterion is that the characteristic is capable of being defined in terms of physical, chemical, or other properties. The second criterion is that the properties defining the characteristic must be measurable by standardized and available test procedures. For example under the term ignitability (Hazard code label "I"), any one of four criteria can be met: 1) A liquid with a flash point less than 60°F (16°C); 2) If not a liquid, then it is capable under standard temperature and pressure of causing fire through friction, absorption of moisture, or spontaneous chemical changes, and when ignited, burns so vigorously and persistently that it creates a hazard; 3) It may be an ignitable compressed gas; 4) It is an oxidizer.

Similarly under the characteristics of corrosivity, reactivity, and toxicity, there are specifically defined requirements which are spelled out in the Code of Federal Register (CFR). Further examples are given below:

Corrosivity (Hazard code "C") has either of the following properties: an aqueous waste with a **pH** equal to or less than 2.0 or greater than 12.5; or a liquid which will corrode carbon steel at a rate greater than 0.250 inches per year.

Reactivity (Hazard code "R") has at least one of the following properties: a substance which is normally unstable and undergoes violent physical and/or chemical change without being detonated; a substance which reacts violently with water (for example, sodium metal); a substance which forms a potentially explosive mixture when mixed with water; a substance which can generate harmful gases, vapors, or fumes when mixed with water; a cyanide- or sulfide-bearing waste which can generate harmful gases, vapors, or fumes when exposed to pH conditions between 2 and 12.5; a waste which, when subjected to a strong initiating source or when heated in confinement, will detonate and/or generate an explosive reaction; a substance which is readily capable of detonation at standard temperature and pressure.

Toxicity (Hazard code "E") has the properties such that an aqueous extract contains contamination in excess of that allowed (e. g. **arsenic** >5 mg/l; barium 0.100 mg/l; **cadmium** >1 mg/l; chromium >5 mg/l; **lead** >5 mg/l). Additional codes under toxicity include an "acute hazardous waste" with code "H": a substance which has been found to be fatal to humans in low doses or has been found to be fatal in corresponding human concentrations in laboratory animals. Toxic waste (hazard code "T") designates wastes which have been found through laboratory studies to be a **carcinogen**, **mutagen**, or **teratogen** for humans or other life forms.

Certain wastes are specifically excluded from classification as hazardous wastes under RCRA, including domestic sewage, irrigation return flows, household waste, and nuclear waste. The latter is controlled via other legislation. The impetus for this effort at legislation and classification comes from several notable cases such as **Love Canal, New York**; **Bhopal, India**; **Stringfellow Acid Pits (Glen Avon, California)**; and **Seveso, Italy**; which have brought media and public attention to the need for identification and classification of dangerous substances, their effects on health and the environment, and the importance of having knowledge about the potential risk associated with various wastes.

A notable feature of the legislation is its attempt at defining terms so that professionals in the field and government officials will share the same vocabulary. For example, the difference between "toxic" and "hazardous" has been established; the former denotes the capacity of a substance to produce injury and the latter denotes the *probability* that injury will result from the use of (or contact with) a substance.

The RCRA legislation on hazardous waste is targeted toward larger generators of hazardous waste rather than small operations. The small generator is one who generates less than 2,205 lb (1000 kg) per month; accumulates less than 2,205 lb (1000 kg); produces wastes which contain no more than 2.2 lb (1 kg) of acutely hazardous waste; has containers no larger than 5.3 gal (20 liters) or contained in liners less than 22 lb (10 kg) of weight of acutely hazardous waste; has no greater than 220 lb (100 kg) of residue or **soil** contaminated from a spill, etc. The purpose of this exclusion is to enable the system of regulations to concentrate on the most egregious and sizeable of the entities that contribute to hazardous waste and thus provide the public with the maximum protection within the resources of the regulatory and legal systems.

[*Malcolm T. Hepworth*]

FURTHER READING

Dawson, G. W., and B. W. Mercer. *Hazardous Waste Management*. New York: Wiley, 1986.

Dominguez, G. S., and K. G. Bartlett. *Hazardous Waste Management.* Vol. 1, *The Law of Toxics and Toxic Substances.* Boca Raton, FL: CRC Press, 1986.

Hazardous Waste Management: A Guide to the Regulations. Washington, DC: U. S. Environmental Protection Agency, 1980.

Wentz, C. A. *Hazardous Waste Management.* New York: McGraw-Hill, 1989.

Hazardous waste site remediation

The overall objective in remediating hazardous waste sites is the protection of human health and the **environment** by reducing risk. There are three primary approaches which can be used in site remediation to achieve acceptable levels of risk:

1) the **hazardous waste** at a site can be contained to preclude additional migration and exposure;
2) the hazardous constituents can be removed from the site to make them more amenable to subsequent ex situ treatment, whether in the form of detoxification or destruction; or
3) the hazardous waste can be treated in situ (in place) to destroy or otherwise detoxify the hazardous constituents.

Each of these approaches has positive and negative ramifications. Combinations of the three principal approaches may be used to address the various problems at a site. There is a growing menu of technologies available to implement each of these remedial approaches. Given the complexity of many of the sites, it is not uncommon to have treatment trains with a sequential implementation of various in situ and/or ex situ technologies to remediate a site.

Hazardous waste site remediation usually addresses **soil**s and **groundwater**. However, it can also include wastes, surface water, **sediment**, **sludge**s, bedrock, buildings, and other man-made items. The hazardous constituents may be organic, inorganic and, occasionally, radioactive. They may be elemental **ion**ic, dissolved, sorbed, liquid, gaseous, vaporous, solid, or any combination of these.

Hazardous waste sites may be identified, evaluated, and if necessary, remediated by their owners on a voluntary basis to reduce environmental and health effects or to limit prospective liability. However, in the United States, there are two far-reaching federal laws which may mandate entry into the remediation process: the **Comprehensive Environmental Response, Compensation, and Liability Act** (CERCLA, also called the Superfund law), and the **Resource Conservation and Recovery Act** (RCRA). In addition, many of the states have their own programs concerning abandoned and uncontrolled sites, and there are other laws that involve hazardous site remediation, such as the clean-up of **polychlorinated biphenyl** (PCB) under the auspices of the federal **Toxic Substances Control Act** (TSCA).

Potential sites may be identified by their owners, by regulatory agencies, or by the public in some cases. Site evaluation is usually a complicated and lengthy process. In the federal Superfund program, sites at which there has been a release of one or more hazardous substances that might result in a present or potential future threat to human health and/or the environment are first evaluated by a Preliminary Assessment/Site Inspection (PA/SI). The data collected at this stage is evaluated, and a recommendation for further action may be formulated. The Hazard Ranking System (HRS) of the U. S. **Environmental Protection Agency** (EPA) may be employed to score the site with respect to the potential hazards it may pose and to see if it is worthy of inclusion on the **National Priorities List** (NPL) of sites most deserving the attention of resources.

Regardless of the HRS score or NPL status, the EPA may require the parties responsible for the release (including the present property owner) to conduct a further assessment, in the form of the two-phase Remedial Investigation/Feasibility Study (RI/FS). The objective of the RI is to determine the nature and extent of contamination at and near the site. The RI data is next considered in a baseline **risk assessment**. The risk assessment evaluates the potential threats to human health and the environment in the absence of any remedial action, considering both present and future conditions. Both exposure and toxicity are considered at this stage.

The baseline risk assessment may support a decision of no action at a site. If remedial actions are warranted, the second phase of the RI/FS, an engineering Feasibility Study, is performed to allow for educated selection of an appropriate remedy. The final alternatives are evaluated on the basis of nine criteria in the federal Superfund program. The EPA selects the remedial action it deems to be most appropriate and describes it and the process which led to its selection in the Record of Decision (ROD). Public comments are solicited on the proposed clean-up plan before the ROD is issued. There are also other public comment opportunities during the RI/FS process. Once the ROD is issued, the project moves to the Remedial Design/Remedial Action (RD/RA) phase unless there is a decision of no action. Upon design approval, construction commences. Then, after construction is complete, long-term operation, maintenance, and monitoring activities begin.

For Superfund sites, the EPA may allow one or more of the responsible parties to conduct the RI/FS and RD/RA under its oversight. If possibly responsible parties are not willing to participate or are unable to be involved for technical, legal, or financial reasons, the EPA may choose to conduct the project with government funding and then later seek to recover costs in lawsuits against the parties. Other types of site remediation programs often replicate or approximate the approaches described above. Some states, such as Massachusetts, have very definite programs, while others are less structured.

Containment is one of the available treatment options. There are several reasons for using containment techniques. A primary reason is difficulty in excavating the waste or treating the hazardous constituents in place. This may be caused by construction and other man-made objects located over and in the site. Excavation could also result in uncontrollable releases at concentrations potentially detrimental to the surrounding area. At many sites, the low levels of risks posed, in conjunction with the relative costs of treatment technologies, may result in the selection of a containment remedy.

One means of site containment is the use of an impermeable cap to reduce rainfall infiltration and to prevent exposure of the waste through **erosion**. Another means of containment is the use of cut-off walls to restrict or direct the movement of groundwater. In situ solidification can also be used to limit the mobility of contaminants. Selection among alternatives is very site specific and reflects such things as the site **hydrogeology**, the chemical and physical nature of the contamination, proposed **land use**, and so on. Of course, the resultant risk must be acceptable.

As with any in situ approach, there is less control and knowledge of the performance and behavior of the technology than is possible with off-site treatment. Since the use of containment techniques leaves the waste in place, it usually results in long-term monitoring programs to determine if the remediation remains effective. If a containment remedy were to fail, the site could require implementation of another type of technology.

The ex situ treatment of hazardous waste provides the most control over the process and permits the most detailed assessments of its efficacy. Ex situ treatment technologies offer the biggest selection of options, but include an additional risk factor during transport. Examples of treatment options include **incineration**; innovative thermal destruction, such as infrared incineration; **bioremediation**; stabilization/solidification; soil washing; chemical extraction; chemical destruction; and thermal desorption. Another approach to categorizing the technologies available for hazardous waste site remediation is based upon their respective levels of demonstration. There are existing technologies, which are fully demonstrated and in routine commercial use. Performance and cost information is available. Examples of existing technologies include **slurry** walls, caps, incineration, and conventional solidification/stabilization.

The next level of technology is innovative and has grown rapidly as the number of sites requiring remediation grew. Innovative technologies are characterized by limited availability of cost and performance data. More site-specific testing is required before an innovative technology can be considered ready for use at a site. Examples of innovative technologies are vacuum extraction, bioremediation, soil washing/flushing, chemical extraction, chemical destruction, and thermal desorption. Vapor extraction and in situ bioremediation are expected to be the next innovative technologies to reach "existing" status as a result of the growing base of cost and performance information generated by their use at many hazardous waste sites.

The last category is that of emerging technologies. These technologies are at a very early stage of development and therefore require additional laboratory and pilot scale testing to demonstrate their technical viability. No cost or performance information is available. An example of an emerging technology is electrokinetic treatment of soils for metals removal.

Groundwater contaminated by hazardous materials is a widespread concern. Most hazardous waste site remediations use a pump and treat approach as a first step. Once the groundwater has been brought to the surface, various treatment alternatives exist, depending upon the constituents present. In situ air sparging of the groundwater using pipes, wells, or curtains is also being developed for removal of volatile constituents. The vapor is either treated above ground with technologies for off-gas **emission**s, or biologically in the unsaturated or **vadose zone** above the **aquifer**. While this approach eliminates the costs and difficulties in treating the relatively large volumes of water (with relatively low contaminant concentrations) generated during pump-and-treat, it does not necessarily speed up remediation.

Contaminated bedrock frequently serves as a source of groundwater or soil recontamination. Constituents with densities greater than water enter the bedrock at fractures, joints or bedding planes. From these locations, the contamination tends to diffuse in all directions. After many years of accumulation, bedrock contamination may account for the majority of the contamination at a site. Currently, little can be done to remediate contaminated bedrock. Specially designed vapor stripping applications have been proposed when the constituents of concern are volatile. Efforts are on-going in developing means to enhance the fractures of the bedrock and thereby promote removal. In all cases, the ultimate remediation will be driven by the diffusion of contaminants back out of the rock, a very slow process.

The remediation of buildings contaminated with hazardous waste offers several alternatives. Given the cost of disposal of hazardous wastes, the limited disposal space available, and the volume of demolition debris, it is beneficial to determine the extent of contamination of construction materials. This contamination can then be removed through traditional engineering approaches, such as scraping or sand blasting. It is then only this reduced volume of material that requires treatment or disposal as hazardous waste. The remaining building can be reoccupied or disposed of as nonhazardous waste. *See also* Hazardous material; Hazardous waste siting; Solidification of hazardous materials; Vapor recovery system

[*Ann N. Clarke and Jeffrey L. Pintenich*]

FURTHER READING

U. S. Environmental Protection Agency. *Technology Screening Guide for Treatment of CERCLA Soils and Sludges.* Washington, DC: U. S. Government Printing Office, 1988.

U. S. Environmental Protection Agency. Office of Emergency and Remedial Response. *Guidance for Conducting Remedial Investigations and Feasibility Studies Under CERCLA.* Washington, DC: U. S. Government Printing Office, 1988.

U. S. Environmental Protection Agency. Office of Emergency and Remedial Response. *Guidance on Remedial Actions for Contaminated Groundwater at Superfund Sites.* Washington, DC: U. S. Government Printing Office, 1988.

U. S. Environmental Protection Agency. Office of Emergency and Remedial Response. *Handbook: Remedial Action at Waste Disposal Sites.* Washington, DC: U. S. Government Printing Office, 1985.

U. S. Environmental Protection Agency. Office of Environmental Engineering. *Guide for Treatment Technologies for Hazardous Waste at Superfund Sites.* Washington, DC: U. S. Government Printing Office, 1989.

U. S. Environmental Protection Agency. Office of Solid Waste and Emergency Response. *Innovative Treatment Technologies*. Washington, DC: U. S. Government Printing Office, 1991.

U. S. Environmental Protection Agency. Risk Reduction Engineering Laboratory. *Handbook on In Situ Treatment of Hazardous Waste: Contaminated Soils*. Washington, DC: U. S. Government Printing Office, 1990.

Hazardous waste siting

Regardless of the specific technologies to be employed, there are many technical and nontechnical considerations to be addressed before **hazardous waste** can be treated or disposed of at a given location. The specific nature and relative importance of these considerations to the successful siting reflect the chemodynamic behavior (i.e., transport and fate of the waste and/or treated residuals in the **environment** after **emission**) as well as the specifics of the location and associated, proximate areas. Examples of these considerations are: the nature of the **soil** and hydrogeological features such as depth to and quality of **groundwater**; quality, use, and proximity of surface waters; and **ambient air** quality and meteorological conditions; and nearby critical environmental areas (**wetlands**, preserves, etc.), if any. Other considerations include surrounding **land use**; proximity of residences and other potentially sensitive receptors such as schools, hospitals, parks, etc.; availability of utilities; and the capacity and quality of the roadway system. It is also critical to develop and obtain the timely approval of all appropriate local, state, and federal permits. Associated with these permits is the required documentation of financial viability as established by escrowed closure funds, site insurance, etc. Site-specific standard operating procedures as well as contingency plans for use in emergencies are also required. Additionally, there needs to be baseline and ongoing monitoring plans developed and implemented to determine if there are any releases to or general degradation of the environment. One should also anticipate public hearings before permits are granted. Several states in the United States have specific regulations which restrict the siting of hazardous waste management facilities.

Haze

An **aerosol** in the **atmosphere** of sufficient concentration and extent to decrease **visibility** significantly when the relative humidity is below saturation is known as haze. Haze may contain dry particles or droplets or a mixture of both, depending on the precise value of the humidity. In the use of the word, there is a connotation of some degree of permanence. For example, a dust storm is not a haze, but the coarse particles may settle rapidly and leave a haze behind once the velocity drops.

Human activity is responsible for many hazes. Enhanced **emission** of **sulfur dioxide** results in the formation of aerosols of sulfuric acid. In the presence of ammonia, which is excreted by most higher animals including humans, such emissions result in aerosols of ammonium sulfate and bisulfate. Organic hazes are part of **photochemical smog**, such as the **smog** often associated with Los Angeles, and they consist primarily of polyfunctional, highly oxygenated compounds with at least five **carbon** atoms. Such hazes can also form if air with an enhanced **nitrogen oxide** content meets air containing the natural terpenes emitted by vegetation.

All hazes, however, are not products of human activity. Natural hazes can result from forest fires, dust storms, and the natural processes that convert gaseous contaminants into particles for subsequent removal by precipitation or deposition to the surface or to vegetation. Still other hazes are of mixed origin, as noted above, and an event such as a dust storm can be enhanced by human-caused devegetation of **soil**.

Though it may contain particles injurious to health, haze is not of itself a health hazard. It can have a significant economic impact, however, when tourists cannot see scenic views, or if it becomes sufficiently dense to inhibit aircraft operations. *See also* Air pollution; Air quality; Air quality criteria; Los Angeles Basin; Mexico City, Mexico

[*James P. Lodge, Jr.*]

FURTHER READING

Husar, R. B. *Trends in Seasonal Haziness and Sulfur Emissions Over the Eastern United States*. Research Triangle Park, NC: U. S. Environmental Protection Agency, 1989.

Husar, R. B., and W. E. Wilson. "Haze and Sulfur Emission Trends in the Eastern United States." *Environmental Science and Technology* 27 (January 1993): 12-16.

Malm, W. C. "Characteristics and Origins of Haze in the Continental United States." *Earth-Science Reviews* 33 (August 1992): 1-36.

Raloff, J. "Haze May Confound Effects of Ozone Loss." *Science News* 141 (4 January 1992): 5.

Heavy metals and heavy metal poisoning

Heavy metals are generally defined as environmentally stable elements of high specific gravity and atomic weight. They have such characteristics as luster, ductility, malleability, and high electric and thermal conductivity. Whether based on their physical or chemical properties, the distinction between heavy metals and non-metals is not sharp. For example, **arsenic**, germanium, selenium, tellurium, and antimony possess chemical properties of both metals and non-metals. Defined as metalloids, they are often loosely classified as heavy metals. The category "heavy metal" is, therefore, somewhat arbitrary and highly non-specific because it can refer to approximately 80 of the 103 elements in the periodic table. The term **"trace element"** is commonly used to describe substances which cannot be precisely defined but most frequently occur in the environment in concentrations of a few **parts per million (ppm)** or less. Only a relatively small number of heavy metals such as **cadmium**, **copper**, iron, cobalt, zinc, **mercury**, vanadium, **lead**, **nickel**, chromium, manganese, molybdenum, silver, and tin as well as the metalloids arsenic and selenium are associated with environmental, plant, animal, or human health problems.

While the chemical forms of heavy metals can be changed, they are not subject to chemical/biological destruction. Therefore, after release into the **environment** they are persistent contaminants. Natural processes such as bedrock and **soil** weathering, wind and water **erosion**, volcanic activity, sea salt spray, and forest fires release heavy metals into the environment. While the origins of **anthropogenic** releases of heavy metals are lost in antiquity, they probably began as our prehistoric ancestors learned to recover metals such as gold, silver, copper, and tin from their ores and to produce bronze. The modern age of heavy metal **pollution** has its beginning with the Industrial Revolution. The rapid development of industry, intensive agriculture, transportation, and urbanization over the past 150 years, however, has been the precursor of today's environmental contamination problems. Anthropogenic utilization has also increased heavy metal distribution by removing the substances from localized ore deposits and transporting them to other parts of the environment. Heavy metal by-products result from many activities including: ore extraction and smelting, **fossil fuel** combustion, dumping and **landfill**ing of industrial wastes, exhausts from leaded **gasoline**s, steel, iron, cement and **fertilizer** production, refuse and wood **combustion**. Heavy metal cycling has also increased through activities such as farming, **deforestation**, construction, **dredging** of harbors, and the disposal of municipal **sludge**s and industrial wastes on land.

Thus, anthropogenic processes, especially combustion, have substantially supplemented the natural atmospheric **emission**s of selected heavy metals/metalloids such as selenium, mercury, arsenic, and antimony. They can be transported as gases or adsorbed on particles. Other metals such as cadmium, lead, and zinc are transported atmospherically only as particles. In either state heavy metals may travel long distances before being deposited on land or water.

The heavy metal contamination of soils is a far more serious problem than either air or **water pollution** because heavy metals are usually tightly bound by the organic components in the surface layers of the soil and may, depending on conditions, persist for centuries or millennia. Consequently, the soil is an important geochemical sink which accumulates heavy metals rapidly and usually depletes them very slowly by **leaching** into **groundwater** aquifers or bioaccumulating into plants. However, heavy metals can also be very rapidly translocated through the environment by **erosion** of the soil particles to which they are adsorbed or bound and redeposited elsewhere on the land or washed into rivers, lakes, or oceans to the **sediment**.

The cycling, bioavailability, toxicity, transport, and fate of heavy metals are markedly influenced by their physico-chemical forms in water, sediments, and soils. Whenever a heavy metal containing **ion** or compound is introduced into an aquatic environment, it is subjected to a wide variety of physical, chemical, and biological processes. These include: hydrolysis, chelation, complexation, redox, biomethylation, precipitation and **adsorption** reactions. Often heavy metals experience a change in the chemical form or speciation as a result of these processes and so their distribution, bioavailability, and other interactions in the environment are also affected.

The interactions of heavy metals in aquatic systems are complicated because of the possible changes due to many dissolved and **particulate** components and non-equilibrium conditions. For example, the speciation of heavy metals is controlled not only by their chemical properties but also by environmental variables such as: 1) **pH**; 2) redox potential; 3) **dissolved oxygen**; 4) ionic strength; 5) temperature; 6) **salinity**; 7) alkalinity; 8) hardness; 9) concentration and nature of inorganic ligands such as carbonate, bicarbonate, sulfate, sulfides, chlorides; 10) concentration and nature of dissolved organic chelating agents such as organic acids, humic materials, peptides, and polyamino-carboxylates; 11) the concentration and nature of particulate matter with surface sites available for heavy metal binding; and 12) biological activity.

In addition, various **species** of bacteria can oxidize arsenate or reduce arsenate to arsenite, or oxidize ferrous iron to ferric iron, or convert mercuric ion to elemental **mercury** or the reverse. Various **enzyme** systems in living organisms can biomethylate a number of heavy metals. While it had been known for at least 60 years that arsenic and selenium could be biomethylated, microorganisms capable of converting inorganic mercury into monomethyl and dimethylmercury in lake sediments were not discovered until 1967. Since then, numerous heavy metals such as lead, tin, cobalt, antimony, platinum, gold, tellurium, thallium, and palladium have been shown to be biomethylated by bacteria and **fungi** in the environment.

As environmental factors change the chemical reactivities and speciation of heavy metals, they influence not only the mobilization, transport, and bioavailability, but also the toxicity of heavy metal ions toward biota in both freshwater and marine **ecosystem**s. The factors affecting the toxicity and **bioaccumulation** of heavy metals by aquatic organisms include: 1) the chemical characteristics of the ion; 2) solution conditions which affect the chemical form (speciation) of the ion; 3) the nature of the response such as acute toxicity, bioaccumulation, various types of chronic effects, etc.; 4) the nature and condition of the aquatic animal such as age or life stage, species, or trophic level in the **food chain**. The extent to which most of the methylated metals are bioaccumulated and/or biomagnified is limited by the chemical and biological conditions and how readily the methylated metal is metabolized by an organism. At present, only methylmercury seems to be sufficiently stable to bioaccumulate to levels that can cause adverse effects in aquatic organisms. All other methylated metal ions are produced in very small concentrations and are degraded naturally faster than they are bioaccumulated. Therefore, they do not biomagnify in the food chain.

The largest proportion of heavy metals in water is associated with suspended particles, which are ultimately deposited in the bottom sediments where concentrations are orders of magnitude higher than those in the overlying or interstitial waters. The heavy metals associated with suspended particulates or bottom sediments are complex mixtures of: 1) weathering and erosion residues such as iron and aluminum oxyhydroxides, clays and other aluminosilicates; 2) methylated and non-methylated forms in organic matter such as living organisms, bacteria and algae, detritus and **humus**; 3) inorganic hydrous oxides and hydroxides, phosphates and silicates; and 4) diagenetically produced iron and manganese oxyhydroxides in the upper layer of sediments and sulfides in the deeper, anoxic layers.

In anoxic waters the precipitation of sulfides may control the heavy metal concentrations in sediments while in oxic waters adsorption, absorption, surface precipitation and coprecipitation are usually the mechanisms by which heavy metals are removed from the water column. Moreover, physical, chemical and microbiological processes in the sediments often increase the concentrations of heavy metals in the pore waters which are released to overlying waters by diffusion or as the result of consolidation and bioturbation. Transport by living organisms does not represent a significant mechanism for local movement of heavy metals. However, accumulation by aquatic plants and animals can lead to important biological responses. Even low environmental levels of some heavy metals may produce subtle and chronic effects in animal populations.

Despite these adverse effects, at very low levels, some metals have essential physiological roles as micronutrients. Heavy metals such as chromium, manganese, iron, cobalt, molybdenum, nickel, vanadium, copper, and selenium are required in small amounts to perform important biochemical functions in plant and animal systems. In higher concentrations they can be toxic, but usually some biological regulatory mechanism is available by means of which animals can speed up their excretion or retard their uptake of excessive quantities.

In contrast, non-essential heavy metals are primarily of concern in terrestrial and aquatic systems because they are toxic and persist in living systems. Metal ions commonly bond with sulfhydryl and carboxylic acid groups in amino acids, which are components of proteins (enzymes) or polypeptides. This increases their bioaccumulation and inhibits excretion. For example, heavy metals such as lead, cadmium, and mercury bind strongly with -SH and -SCH$_3$ groups in cysteine and methionine and so inhibit the metabolism of the bound enzymes. In addition, other heavy metals may replace an essential element, decreasing its availability and causing symptoms of deficiency.

Uptake, translocation, and accumulation of potentially toxic heavy metals in plants differ widely depending on soil type, pH, redox potential, moisture, and organic content. Public health officials closely regulate the quantities and effects of heavy metals that move through the agricultural food chain to be consumed by human beings. While heavy metals such as zinc, copper, nickel, lead, arsenic, and cadmium are translocated from the soil to plants and then into the animal food chain, the concentrations in plants are usually very low and generally not considered to be an environmental problem. However, plants grown on soils either naturally enriched or highly contaminated with some heavy metals can bioaccumulate levels high enough to cause toxic effects in the animals or human beings that consume them.

Contamination of soils due to land disposal of sewage and industrial **effluent**s and sludges may pose the most significant long term problem. While cadmium and lead are the greatest hazard, other elements such as copper, molybdenum, nickel, and zinc can also accumulate in plants grown on sludge-treated land. High concentrations can, under certain conditions, cause adverse effects in animals and human beings that consume the plants. For example, when soil contains high concentrations of molybdenum and selenium, they can be translocated into edible plant tissue in sufficient quantities to produce toxic effects in ruminant animals. Consequently, the U. S. **Environmental Protection Agency** has issued regulations which prohibit and/or tightly regulate the disposal of contaminated municipal and industrial sludges on land to prevent heavy metals, especially cadmium, from entering the food supply in toxic amounts. However, presently, the most serious known human toxicity is not through bioaccumulation from crops but from mercury in fish, lead in gasoline, paints and water pipes, and other metals derived from occupational or accidental exposure. *See also* Aquatic chemistry; Ashio, Japan; Atmospheric pollutants; Biomagnification; Biological methylation; Contaminated soil; Ducktown, Tennessee; Hazardous material; Heavy metals precipitation; Itai-Itai disease; Methylmercury seed dressings; Minamata disease; Smelters; Sudbury, Ontario; Xenobiotic

[*Frank M. D'Itri*]

FURTHER READING

Craig, P. J. "Metal Cycles and Biological Methylation." *The Handbook of Environmental Chemistry*. Volume 1, Part A, edited by O. H. Hutzinger. Berlin: Springer Verlag, 1980.

Förstner, U., and G. T. W. Wittmann. *Metal Pollution in the Aquatic Environment*. 2nd ed. Berlin: Springer Verlag, 1981.

Kramer, J. R., and H. E. Allen, eds. *Metal Speciation: Theory, Analysis and Application*. Chelsea, MI: Lewis, 1988.

Heavy metals precipitation

The principle technology to remove metals pollutants from wastewater is by chemical precipitation. Chemical precipitation includes two secondary removal mechanisms, **coprecipitation** and **adsorption**. Precipitation processes are characterized by the solubility of the metal to be removed. They are generally designed to precipitate trace metals to their solubility limits and obtain additional removal by coprecipitation and adsorption during the precipitation reaction.

There are many different treatment variables that affect these processes. They include the optimum **pH**, the type of chemical treatments used, and the number of treatment stages, as well as the temperature and volume of **wastewater**, and the chemical specifications of the pollutants to be removed. Each of these variables directly influences treatment objectives and costs. Treatability studies must be performed to optimize the relevant variables, so that goals are met and costs minimized.

In theory, the precipitation process has two steps, nucleation followed by particle growth. Nucleation is represented by the appearance of very small particle seeds which are generally composed of 10-100 molecules. Particle growth involves the addition of more atoms or molecules into this particle structure. The rate and extent of this process is dependent upon the temperature and chemical characteristics of the wastewater, such as the concentration of metal initially present and other ionic species present, which can compete with or form soluble complexes with the target metal species.

Heavy metals are present in many industrial wastewaters. Examples of such metals are **cadmium**, **copper**, **lead**, **mercury**, **nickel**, and zinc. In general, these metals can be complexed to insoluble species by adding sulfide, hydroxide, and carbonate **ion**s to a solution. For example, the precipitation of copper (Cu) hydroxide is accomplished by adjusting the pH of the water to above 8, using precipitant **chemicals** such as lime ($Ca(OH)_2$) or sodium hydroxide (N_aOH). Precipitation of metallic carbonate and sulfide species can be accomplished by the addition of calcium carbonate or sodium sulfide. The removal of coprecipitive metals during precipitation of the soluble metals is aided by the presence of solid ferric oxide, which acts as an adsorbent during the precipitation reaction. For example, hydroxide precipitation of ferric chloride can be used as the source of ferric oxide for coprecipitation and adsorption reactions. Precipitation, coprecipitation, and adsorption reactions generate **suspended solid**s which must be separated from the wastewater. Flocculation and clarification are again employed to assist in solids separation. The treatment is an important variable which must be optimized to effect the maximum metal removal possible.

Determining the optimal pH range to facilitate the maximum precipitation of metal is a difficult task. It is typically accomplished by laboratory studies, such as by-jar tests rather than theoretical calculations. Often the actual **wastestream** behaves differently, and the theoretical metal solubilities and corresponding optimal pH ranges can vary considerably from theoretical values. *See also* Heavy metals and heavy metal poisoning; Industrial waste treatment; Itai-itai disease; Minamata disease; Sludge; Waste management

[*James W. Patterson*]

FURTHER READING

Nemerow, N. L., and A. Dasgupta. *Industrial and Hazardous Waste Treatment.* New York: Van Nostrand Reinhold, 1991.

Heilbroner, Robert L. (1919 -)

American economist and author

An economist by profession, Robert Heilbroner is the author of a number of books and articles that put economic theories and developments into historical perspective and relate them

Robert L. Heilbroner.

to contemporary social and political problems. He is especially noteworthy for his gloomy speculations on the future of a world confronted by the environmental limits to economic growth.

Born in New York City in 1919, Heilbroner received a bachelor's degree from Harvard University in 1940 and a Bronze Star for his service in World War II. In 1963 he earned a Ph.D. in economics from the New School for Social Research in New York, and in 1972, became the Norman Thomas Professor of Economics there. His books include *The Worldly Philosophers* (1955), *The Making of Economic Society* (1962), *Marxism: For and Against* (1980), and *The Nature and Logic of Capitalism* (1985). He has also served on the editorial board of the socialist journal *Dissent*.

In 1974, Heilbroner published *An Inquiry into the Human Prospect*, in which he argues that three "external challenges" confront humanity: the population explosion, the threat of war, and "the danger . . . of encroaching on the environment beyond its ability to support the demands made on it." Each of these problems, he maintains, arises from the development of scientific technology, which has increased human life span, multiplied weapons of destruction, and encouraged industrial production that consumes **natural resources** and pollutes the **environment**. Heilbroner believes that these challenges confront all economies, and that meeting them will require more than adjustments in economic systems. Societies will have to muster the will to make sacrifices.

Heilbroner goes on to argue that persuading people to make these sacrifices may not be possible. Those living in one part of the world are not likely to give up what they have for the sake of those in another part, and people living now are not likely to make sacrifices for **future generations**. His reluctant conclusion is that coercion is likely to take the place of persuasion. Authoritarian governments may well supplant democracies because "the passage through the gantlet ahead may be possible only under governments capable of rallying obedience far more effectively than would be possible in a democratic setting. If the issue for mankind is survival, such governments may be unavoidable, even necessary."

Heilbroner wrote *An Inquiry into the Human Prospect* in 1972 and 1973, but his position had not changed by the end of the decade. In a revised edition written in 1979, he continued to insist upon the environmental limits to economic growth: "the industrialized capitalist and socialist worlds can probably continue along their present growth paths" for about twenty-five years, at which point "we must expect . . . a general recognition that the possibilities for expansion are limited, and that social and economic life must be maintained within fixed . . . material boundaries." Heilbroner has published a number of books, including *21st Century Capitalism* and *Visions of the Future*. He also received the New York Council for the Humanities Scholar of the Year award in 1994. *See also* Carrying capacity; Economic growth and the environment; Environmental economics; Hardin, Garrett; Population growth

[*Richard K. Dagger*]

FURTHER READING

Heilbroner, Robert L. *An Inquiry into the Human Prospect*. Rev. ed. New York: Norton, 1980.

———. *The Making of an Economic Society*. 6th ed. Englewood Cliffs, NJ: Prentice-Hall, 1980.

———. *The Nature and Logic of Capitalism*. New York: Norton, 1985.

———. *Twenty-First Century Capitalism*. Don Mills, Ont.: Anansi, 1992.

———. *The Worldly Philosophers: The Lives, Times and Ideas of the Great Economic Thinkers*. 6th ed. New York: Simon & Schuster, 1986.

Straub, D., ed. *Contemporary Authors: New Revision Series*. Vol. 21. Detroit, MI: Gale Research, 1987.

Hells Canyon

Hells Canyon is a stretch of canyon on the Snake River between Idaho and Oregon. This canyon, deeper than the Grand Canyon and formed in ancient basalt flows, contains some of the United States' wildest rapids and has provided extensive **recreation**al and scenic boating since the 1920s. The narrow canyon has also provided outstanding dam sites. Hells Canyon became the subject of nationwide controversy between 1967 and 1975, when environmentalists challenged hydroelectric developers over the last stretch of free-flowing water in the Snake River from the border of Wyoming to the Pacific.

Historically Hells Canyon, over 100 miles (161 km) long, filled with rapids, and averaging 6,500 feet (1,983 m) deep, presented a major obstacle to travelers and explorers crossing the mountains and deserts of southern Idaho and eastern Oregon. Nez Percé, Paiute, Cayuse, and other Native American groups of the region had long used the area as a mild wintering ground with good grazing land for their horses. European settlers came for the modest timber and with cattle and sheep to graze. As early as the 1920s travelers were arriving in this scenic area for recreational purposes, with the first river runners navigating the canyon's rapids in 1928. By the end of the Depression the **Federal Power Commission** was urging regional utility companies to tap the river's hydroelectric potential, and in 1958 the first dam was built in the canyon.

Falling from the mountains in southern **Yellowstone National Park** through Idaho, and into the Columbia River, the Snake River drops over 7,000 vertical feet (2,135 m) in 1,000 miles (1,609 km) of river. This drop and the narrow gorges the river has carved presented excellent dam opportunities, and by the end of the 1960s there were 18 major dams along the river's course. By that time the river was also attracting great numbers of whitewater rafters and kayakers, as well as hikers and campers in the adjacent **national forest**s. When a proposal was developed to dam the last free-running section of the canyon, protesters brought a suit to the United States Supreme Court. In 1967, Justice William O. Douglas led the majority in a decision directing the utilities to consider alternatives to the proposed dam.

Hells Canyon became a national environmental issue. Several members of Congress flew to Oregon to raft the river. The **Sierra Club** and other groups lobbied vigorously. Finally, in 1975 President Gerald Ford signed a bill declaring the remaining stretch of the canyon a National Scenic Waterway, creating a 650,000-acre (260,000 ha) Hells Canyon National Recreation Area, and adding 193,000 acres (77,200 ha) of the area to the National Wilderness Preservation System. *See also* Wild and Scenic Rivers Act; Wild river

[*Mary Ann Cunningham*]

FURTHER READING

Collins, R. O., and R. Nash. *The Big Drops*. San Francisco: Sierra Club Books, 1978.

Hells Canyon Recreation Area. "Hells Canyon." Washington, DC: U. S. Government Printing Office, 1988.

Henderson, Hazel (1933-)

Anglo-American environmental activist

Hazel Henderson is an environmental activist and futurist who has called for an end to current "unsustainable industrial modes" and urges redress for the "unequal access to resources which is now so dangerous, both ecologically and socially."

Born in Clevedon, England, Henderson immigrated to the United States after finishing high school; she became a naturalized citizen in 1962. After working for several years as a freelance journalist, she married Carter F. Henderson, former London bureau chief of the *Wall Street Journal* in 1957. Her activism began when she became concerned about **air quality** in New York City, where she was living. To raise public awareness, she convinced the FCC and television networks to broadcast the **air pollution index** with the

weather report. She persuaded an advertising agency to donate their services to her cause and teamed up with a New York City councilman to co-found Citizens for Clean Air. Her endeavors were rewarded in 1967, when she was commended as Citizen of the Year by the New York Medical Society.

Henderson's career as an advocate for social and environmental reform took flight from there. She argued passionately against the spread of industrialism, which she called "pathological" and decried the use of an economic yardstick to measure quality of life. Indeed, she termed economics "merely politics in disguise" and even "a form of brain damage." Henderson believed that society should be measured by less tangible means, such as political participation, literacy, education, and health. "Per-capita income," she felt, is "a very weak indicator of human well-being."

She became convinced that traditional industrial development wrought little but "ecological devastation, social unrest, and downright hunger. . . . I think of development, instead, . . . as investing in **ecosystem**s, their restoration and management."

Even the fundamental idea of labor should, Henderson argued,

> "be replaced by the concept of 'Good Work'—which challenges individuals to grow and develop their faculties; to overcome their ego-centeredness by joining with others in common tasks; to bring forth those goods and services needed for a becoming existence; and to do all this with an ethical concern for the interdependence of all life forms. . . ."

To advance her theories, Henderson published two books, *Creative Alternative Futures: The End of Economics* (1978) and *The Politics of the Solar Age: Alternatives to Economics* (1981), contributed to several periodicals, and lectured at colleges and universities. In 1972 she co-founded the Princeton Center for Alternative Futures, of which she is still a director. She is a member of the board of directors for **Worldwatch Institute** and the Council for Economic Priorities, among other organizations. In 1982 she was appointed a Horace Allbright Professor at the University of California at Berkeley.

[*Amy Strumolo*]

FURTHER READING

Henderson, H. "The Legacy of E.F. Schumacher." *Environment* 20 (May 1978): 30-36.

Holden, C. "Hazel Henderson: Nudging Society Off Its Macho Trip." *Science* 190 (28 November 1975): 863-64.

Telephone Interview with Hazel Henderson. *Whole Earth Review* (Winter 1988): 58-59.

Herbicide

Herbicides are chemical **pesticide**s that are used to manage vegetation. Usually, herbicides are used to reduce the abundance of weedy plants, so as to release desired crop plants from competition. This is the context of most herbicide use

in agriculture, forestry, and for lawn management. Sometimes herbicides are not used to protect crops, but to reduce the quantity or height of vegetation, for example along highways and transmission corridors. The reliance on herbicides to achieve these ends has increased greatly in recent decades, and the practice of chemical weed control appears to have become an entrenched component of the modern technological culture of humans, especially in agro**ecosystem**s.

The total use of pesticides in the United States in the mid-1980s was 957 million pounds per year (434 million kilograms/year), used over 592,000 square miles (148 million hectares). Herbicides were most widely used, accounting for 68 percent of the total quantity [646 million pounds per year (293 million kilograms/year)], and applied to 82 percent of the treated land [484,000 square miles per year (121 million hectares/year)]. Note that especially in agriculture, the same land area can be treated numerous times each year with various pesticides.

A wide range of chemicals is used as herbicides, including:

(1) chlorophenoxy acids, especially **2,4-D** and **2,4,5-T**, which have an auxin-like growth-regulating property and are selective against broadleaved angiosperm plants;
(2) triazines such as **atrazine**, simazine, and hexazinone;
(3) chloroaliphatics such as dalapon and trichloroacetate;
(4) the phosphonoalkyl chemical, glyphosate, and
(5) inorganics such as various arsenicals, cyanates, and chlorates.

A "weed" is usually considered to be any plant that interferes with the productivity of a desired crop plant or some other human purpose, even though in other contexts weed **species** may have positive ecological and economic values. Weeds exert this effect by competing with the crop for light, water, and **nutrient**s. Studies in Illinois demonstrated an average reduction of yield of corn or maize (*Zea mays*) of 81 percent in unweeded plots, while a 51 percent reduction was reported in Minnesota. Weeds also reduce the yield of small grains, such as wheat (*Triticum aestivum*) and barley (*Hordeum vulgare*), by 25 to 50 percent.

Because there are several herbicides that are toxic to dicotyledonous weeds but not grasses, herbicides are used most intensively used in grain crops of the Gramineae. For example, in North America almost all of the area of maize cultivation is treated with herbicides. In part this is due to the widespread use of no-tillage cultivation, a system that reduces **erosion** and saves fuel. Since an important purpose of plowing is to reduce the abundance of weeds, the no-tillage system would be impracticable if not accompanied by herbicide use. The most important herbicides used in maize cultivation are atrazine, propachlor, alachlor, 2,4-D, and butylate. Most of the area planted to other agricultural grasses such as wheat, rice (*Oryza sativa*), and barley is also treated with herbicide, mostly with the phenoxy herbicides 2,4-D or MCPA.

The intended ecological effect of any pesticide application is to control a **pest** species, usually by reducing its abundance to below some economically acceptable threshold. In a few situations, this objective can be attained without important nontarget damage. For example, a judicious spot-application of a herbicide can allow a selective kill of large lawn weeds in a way that minimizes exposure to nontarget plants and animals.

Of course, most situations where herbicides are used are more complex and less well-controlled than this. Whenever a herbicide is broadcast-sprayed over a field or forest, a wide variety of on-site, nontarget organisms is affected, and sprayed herbicide also drifts from the target area. These cause ecotoxicological effects directly, through toxicity to nontarget organisms and ecosystems, and indirectly, by changing **habitat** or the abundance of food species of **wildlife**. These effects can be illustrated by the use of herbicides in forestry, with glyphosate used as an example.

The most frequent use of herbicides in forestry is for the release of small coniferous plants from the effects of competition with economically undesirable weeds. Usually the silvicultural use of herbicides occurs within the context of an intensive harvesting-and-management system, which may include **clear-cutting**, scarification, planting seedlings of a single desired species, spacing, and other practices.

Glyphosate is a commonly used herbicide in forestry and agriculture. The typical spray rate in silviculture is about 1-2.2 kg active ingredient/ha, and the typical projection is for one to two treatments per forest rotation of forty to one hundred years.

Immediately after an aerial application in forestry, glyphosate residues are about six times higher than litter on the forest floor, which is physically shielded from spray by overtopping foliage. The persistence of glyphosate residues is relatively short, with typical half-lives of two to four weeks in foliage and the forest floor, and up to eight weeks in **soil**. The disappearance of residues from foliage is mostly due to translocation and wash-off, but in the forest floor and soil glyphosate is immobile (and unavailable for root uptake or **leaching**) because of binding to organic matter and clay, and residue disappearance is due to microbial oxidation. Residues in oversprayed waterbodies tend to be small and short-lived. For example, two hours after a deliberate overspray on Vancouver Island, Canada, residues of glyphosate in stream water rose to high levels, then rapidly dissipated through flushing to only trace amounts ninety-four hours later.

Because glyphosate is soluble in water, there is no propensity for **bioaccumulation** in organisms in preference to the inorganic **environment**, or to occur in larger concentrations at higher levels of the **food chain/web**. This is in marked contrast to some other pesticides such as **DDT**, which is soluble in organic solvents but not in water, so it has a strong tendency to bioaccumulate into the fatty tissues of organisms.

As a plant poison, glyphosate acts by inhibiting the pathway by which four essential amino acids are synthesized. Only plants and some microorganisms have this metabolic pathway; animals obtain these amino acids from food. Consequently, glyphosate has a relatively small acute toxicity to animals, and there are large margins of toxicological safety in comparison with environmental exposures that are realistically expected during operational silvicultural sprays.

Acute toxicity of chemicals to mammals is often indexed by the oral dose required to kill 50 percent of a test population, usually of rats (i.e., rat LD_{50}). The LD_{50} value for pure glyphosate is 5,600 mg/kg, and its silvicultural formulation has a value of 5,400 mg/kg. Compare these to LD_{50}s for some chemicals which many humans ingest voluntarily: nicotine 50 mg/kg, caffeine 366, acetylsalicylic acid (ASA) 1,700, sodium chloride 3,750, and **ethanol** 13,000. The documented risks of longer-term, chronic exposures of mammals to glyphosate are also small, especially considering the doses that might be received during an operational treatment in forestry.

Considering the relatively small acute and chronic toxicities of glyphosate to animals, it is unlikely that wildlife inhabiting sprayed clearcuts would be directly affected by a silvicultural application. However, glyphosate causes large habitat changes through species-specific effects on plant productivity, and by changing habitat structure. Therefore, wildlife such as birds and mammals could be secondarily affected through changes in vegetation and the abundance of their arthropod foods. These indirect effects of herbicide spraying are within the context of **ecotoxicology**. Indirect effects can affect the abundance and reproductive success of terrestrial and aquatic wild life on a sprayed site, irrespective of a lack of direct, toxic effects.

Studies of the effects of habitat changes caused by glyphosate spraying have found relatively small effects on the abundance and species composition of wildlife. Much larger effects on wildlife are associated with other forestry practices, such as clear-cutting and the broadcast spraying of insecticides. For example, in a study of clearcuts sprayed with glyphosate in Nova Scotia, Canada, only small changes in avian abundance and species composition could be attributed to the herbicide treatment. However, such studies of bird abundance are conducted by enumerating territories, and the results cannot be interpreted in terms of reproductive success. Regrettably, there are not yet any studies of the reproductive success of birds breeding on clearcuts recently treated with a herbicide. This is an important deficiency in terms of understanding the ecological effects of herbicide spraying in forestry.

An important controversy related to herbicides focused on the military use of herbicides during the Viet Nam war. During this conflict, the United States Air Force broadcast-sprayed herbicides to deprive their enemy of food production and forest cover. More than 5,600 square miles (1.4 million hectares) were sprayed at least once, about 1/7 the area of South Viet Nam. More than 55 million pounds (25 million kilograms) of 2,4-D, 43 million pounds (21 million kilograms) of 2,4,5-T, and 3.3 million pounds (1.5 million kilograms) of picloram were used in this military program. The most frequently used herbicide was a 50:50 formulation of 2,4,5-T and 2,4-D known as **Agent Orange**. The rate of application was relatively large, averaging about 10 times the application rate for silvicultural purposes. About 86 percent of spray missions were targeted against forests, and the remainder against cropland.

As was the military intention, these spray missions caused great ecological damage. Opponents of the practice labelled it "**ecocide**," i.e., the intentional use of anti-environmental actions as a military tactic. The broader ecological effects included severe damage to mangrove and tropical forests, and a great loss of wildlife habitat.

In addition, the Agent Orange used in Viet Nam was contaminated by the **dioxin** isomer known as TCDD, an incidental by-product of the manufacturing process of 2,4,5-T. Using post-Viet Nam manufacturing technology, the contamination by TCDD in 2,4,5-T solutions can be kept to a concentration well below the maximum of 0.1 parts per million (ppm) set by the United States **Environmental Protection Agency (EPA)**. However, the 2,4,5-T used in Viet Nam was grossly contaminated with TCDD, with a concentration as large as 45 ppm occurring in Agent Orange, and an average of about 2.0 ppm. Perhaps 243 to 375 pounds (110-170 kilograms) of TCDD was sprayed with herbicides onto Viet Nam. TCDD is well known as being extremely toxic, and it can cause **birth defects** and miscarriage in laboratory mammals, although as is often the case, toxicity to humans is less well understood. There has been great controversy about the effects on soldiers and civilians exposed to TCDD in Viet Nam, but epidemiological studies have been equivocal about the damages. It seems likely that the effects of TCDD added little to human mortality or to the direct ecological effects of the herbicides that were sprayed in Viet Nam.

A preferable approach to pesticide use is **integrated pest management** (IPM). In the context of IPM, pest control is achieved by employing an array of complementary approaches, including:

(1) use of natural predators, **parasites**, and other biological controls;

(2) use of pest-resistant varieties of crops;

(3) environmental modifications to reduce optimality of pest habitat;

(4) careful monitoring of pest abundance; and

(5) a judicious use of pesticides, when necessary as a component of the IPM strategy.

A successful IPM program can greatly reduce, but not necessarily eliminate, the reliance on pesticides.

With specific relevance to herbicides, more research into organic systems and into procedures that are pest-specific are required for the development of IPM systems. Examples of pest-specific practices are the biological control of certain introduced weeds, for example:

(1) St. John's wort (*Hypericum perforatum*) is a serious weed of pastures of the United States Southwest because it is toxic to cattle, but it was controlled by the introduction in 1943 of two herbivorous leaf beetles; and

(2) the prickly pear cactus (*Opuntia* spp.) became a serious weed of Australian rangelands after it was introduced as an ornamental plant, but it has been controlled by release of the moth *Cactoblastis cactorum*, whose larvae feed on the cactus.

Unfortunately, effective IPM systems have not yet been developed for most weed problems for which herbicides

are now used. Until there are alternative, pest-specific methods to achieve an economically acceptable degree of control of weeds in agriculture and forestry, herbicides will continue to be used for that purpose. *See also* Agricultural chemicals

[*Bill Freedman*]

FURTHER READING

Freedman, B. *Environmental Ecology.* San Diego, CA: Academic Press, 1989.

_. "Controversy Over the Use of Herbicides in Forestry, With Particular Reference to Glyphosate Usage." *Environmental Carcinogenesis Reviews* C8 (1991): 277-286.

McEwen, F. L., and G. R. Stephenson. *The Use and Significance of Pesticides in the Environment.* New York: Wiley, 1979.

Pimentel, D., et al. "Environmental and Economic Effects of Reducing Pesticide Use." *Bioscience* 41 (1991): 402-409.

Heritage Conservation and Recreation Service

The Heritage Conservation and Recreation Service (HCRS) was created in 1978 as an agency of the **U. S. Department of the Interior** (Secretarial Executive Order 3017) to administer the National Heritage Program initiative of President Carter. The new agency was an outgrowth of and successor to the former Bureau of Outdoor Recreation. The HCRS resulted from the consolidation of some 30 laws, executive orders, and interagency agreements that provided federal funds to states, cities, and local community organizations to acquire, maintain, and develop historic, natural and **recreation** sites. HCRS focused on the identification and protection of the nation's significant natural, cultural and recreational resources. It classified and established registers for heritage resources, formulated policies and programs for their preservation, and coordinated federal, state and local resource and recreation policies and actions. In February 1981 HCRS was abolished as an agency and its responsibilities were transferred to the **National Park Service**.

Hetch Hetchy Reservoir

The Hetch Hetchy Reservoir, located on the Tuolumne River in **Yosemite National Park**, was built to provide water and hydroelectric power to San Francisco. Its creation in the early 1900s led to one of the first conflicts between preservationists and those favoring utilitarian use of **natural resources**. The controversy spanned the presidencies of Roosevelt, Taft, and Wilson.

A prolonged conflict between San Francisco and its only water utility, Spring Valley Water Company, drove the city to search for an independent water supply. After surveying several possibilities, the city decided to build a **dam** and **reservoir** in the Hetch Hetchy Valley because the river there could supply the most abundant and purest water. This option was also the least expensive, since the city planned to use the dam to generate hydroelectric power. It would also provide an abundant supply of **irrigation** water for area farmers and the **recreation** potential of a new lake.

The city applied to the **U.S. Department of the Interior** in 1901 for permission to construct the dam, but the request was not approved until 1908. The department then turned the issue over to Congress to work out an exchange of land between the federal government and the city. Congressional debate spanned several years and produced a number of bills. Part of the controversy involved the Right of Way Act of 1901, which gave Congress power to grant rights of way through government lands; some claimed this was designed specifically for the Hetch Hetchy project.

Opponents of the project likened the valley to Yosemite on a smaller scale. They wanted to preserve its high cliff walls, waterfalls, and diverse plant **species**. One of the most well-known opponents, **John Muir**, described the Hetch Hetchy Valley as "a grand landscape garden, one of Nature's rarest and most precious mountain temples." Campers and mountain climbers fought to save the campgrounds and trails that would be flooded.

As the argument ensued, often played out in newspapers and other public forums, overwhelming national opinion appeared to favor the preservation of the valley. Despite this public support, a close vote in Congress led to the passage of the Raker Act, allowing the O'Shaughnessy Dam and Hetch Hetchy Reservoir to be constructed. President Woodrow Wilson signed the bill into law on December 19, 1913.

The Hetch Hetchy Reservoir was completed in 1923 and still supplies water and electric power to San Francisco. In 1987, Secretary of the Interior Donald Hodel created a brief controversy when he suggested tearing down O'Shaughnessy Dam. *See also* Economic growth and the environment; Environmental law; Environmental policy

[*Teresa C. Donkin*]

FURTHER READING

Jones, Holway R. *John Muir and the Sierra Club: The Battle for Yosemite.* San Francisco: Sierra Club, 1965.

Nash, Roderick. "Conservation as Anxiety." In *The American Environment: Readings in the History of Conservation.* 2nd ed. Reading, Mass: Addison-Wesley Publishing Company, 1976.

Heterotroph

A heterotroph is an organism that derives its nutritional **carbon** and energy by oxidizing (i.e., decomposing) organic materials. The higher animals, **fungi**, actinomycetes, and most bacteria are heterotrophs. These are the biological consumers that eventually decompose most of the organic matter on the earth. The **decomposition** products then are available for chemical or biological **recycling**. *See also* Biogeochemical cycles; Oxidation reduction reactions

High-grading (mining, forestry)

The practice of high-grading can be traced back to the early days of the California gold rush, when miners would sneak into claims belonging to others and steal the most valuable pieces of ore. The practice of high-grading remains essentially unchanged today. An individual or corporation will enter an area and selectively mine or harvest only the most valuable specimens, before moving on to a new area. High-grading is most prevalent in the mining and timber industries. It is not uncommon to walk into a forest, particularly an **old-growth forest**, and find the oldest and finest specimens marked for harvesting. *See also* Forest management; Strip mining

High-level radioactive waste

High-level radioactive waste consists primarily of the by-products of **nuclear power** plants and defense activities. Such wastes are highly radioactive and often decay very slowly. They may release dangerous levels of radiation for hundreds or thousands of years. Most high-level radioactive wastes have to be handled by remote control by workers who are protected by heavy shielding. They present, therefore, a serious health and environmental hazard. No entirely satisfactory method for disposing of high-level wastes has as yet been devised. Currently, the best approach seems to involve immobilizing the wastes in a glass-like material and then burying them deep underground. *See also* Low-level radioactive waste; Radioactive decay; Radioactive pollution; Radioactive waste management; Radioactivity

High-solids reactor

Solid waste disposal is a serious problem in the United States and other developed countries. Solid waste can constitute valuable raw materials for commercial and industrial operations, however, and one of the challenges facing scientists is to develop an economically efficient method for utilizing it.

Although the concept of bacterial waste conversion is simple, achieving an efficient method for putting the technique into practice is difficult. The main problem is that efficiency of conversion requires increasing the ratio of solids to water in the mixture, and this makes mixing more difficult mechanically. The high-solids reactor was designed by scientists at the Solar Energy Research Institute (SERI) to solve this problem. It consists of a cylindrical tube on a horizontal axis, and an agitator shaft running through the middle of it, which contains a number of Teflon-coated paddles oriented at 90 degrees to each other. The pilot reactors operated by SERI had a capacity of 2.6 gallons (10 liters).

SERI scientists modeled the high solids reactor after similar devices used in the **plastics** industry to mix highly viscous materials. With the reactor, they have been able to process materials with 30 to 35 percent solids content, while existing reactors normally handle wastes with five to eight percent solid content. With higher solid content, SERI reactors have achieved a yield of **methane** five to eight times greater than that obtained from conventional mixers. Researchers hope to be able to process wastes with solid content ranging anywhere from zero to 100 percent. They believe that they can eventually achieve 80 percent efficiency in converting **biomass** to methane.

The most obvious application of the high-solids reactor is the processing of **municipal solid waste**s. Initial tests were carried out with **sludge** obtained from **sewage treatment** plants in Denver, Los Angeles, and Chicago. In all cases, conversion of solids in the sludge to methane was successful, and other applications of the reactor are also being considered. For example, it can be used to leach out **uranium** from mine wastes: **anaerobic** bacteria in the reactor will reduce uranium in the wastes and the uranium will then be absorbed on the bacteria or on **ion exchange** resins. The use of the reactor to clean **contaminated soil** is also being considered in the hope is that this will provide a desirable alternative to current processes for cleaning soil, which create large volumes of contaminated water. *See also* Biomass fuel; Solid waste incineration; Solid waste recycling and recovery; Solid waste volume reduction; Waste management

[*David E. Newton*]

FURTHER READING

"High Solids Reactor May Reduce Capital Costs," *Bioprocessing Technology* (June 1990).

"SERI Looking for Partners for Solar-Powered High Solids Reactor," *Waste Treatment Technology News* (October 1990).

High-voltage power lines

See **Electromagnetic fields**

High-yield crops

See **Borlaug, Norman Ernest; Consultative Group on International Agricultural Research**

Hiroshima, Japan

Hiroshima is a beautiful modern city located near the southwestern tip of the main Japanese island of Honshu. It had been a military center with the headquarters of the Japanese southern army and a military depot prior to the end of World War II. The city is now a manufacturing center with a major university and medical school. It is most profoundly remembered because it was the first city to be exposed to the devastation of an atomic bomb.

At 8:15 A.M. on the morning of August 6, 1945, a single B29 bomber flying in from Tinian Island in the

Marinas released the bomb at 2,000 ft (606.6 m) above the city. The target was a "T"-shaped bridge near the city center. The only surviving building in the city center after the atomic bomb blast was a domed cement building at ground zero, just a few yards from the bridge. An experimental bomb developed by the Manhattan Project had been exploded at Alamagardo, New Mexico, only a few weeks earlier. The Alamagardo bomb had the explosive force of 15,000 tons of TNT. The Hiroshima **uranium**-235 bomb, with the explosive power of 20,000 tons of TNT, was even more powerful than the New Mexico bomb. The immediate effect of the bomb was to destroy by blast, winds, and fire an area of 4.4 mi^2 (7 km^2). Two-thirds of the city was destroyed. A portion of Hiroshima was protected from the blast by hills, and this is all that remains of the old city. Destruction of human lives was caused immediately by the blast force of the bomb or by burns or **radiation sickness** later. Seventy-five thousand people were killed or were fatally wounded; there was an equal number of wounded survivors. **Nagasaki,** to the south and west of Hiroshima, was bombed on August 9, 1945, with much loss of life. The bombing of these two cities brought World War II to a close. The lessons that Hiroshima (and Nagasaki) teach are the horrors of war with its random killing of civilian men, women, and children. That is the major lesson—war is horrible with its destruction of innocent lives.

The why of Hiroshima should be taken in the context of the battle for Okinawa which occurred only weeks before. America forces suffered 12,000 dead with 36,000 wounded in the battle for that small island 350 mi (563.5 km) from the mainland of Japan. The Japanese were reported to have lost 100,000 men. The determination of the Japanese to defend their homeland was well known, and it was estimated that the invasion of Japan would cost no less than 500,000 American lives. Japanese casualties were expected to be larger. It was the military judgment of the American President that a swift termination of the war would save more lives than it would cost: both American and Japanese. Whether this rationale for the atomic bombing of Hiroshima was correct, i.e., whether more people would have died if Japan was invaded, will never be known. However, it certainly is a fact that the war came to a swift end after the bombing of the two cities.

The second lesson to be learned from Hiroshima is that **radiation exposure** is hazardous to human health and radiation damage results in radiation sickness and increased **cancer** risk. It had been known since the development of **x ray**s at the turn of the century that radiation has the potential to cause cancer. However, the thousands of survivors at Hiroshima and Nagasaki were to become the largest group ever studied for radiation damage. The Atomic Bomb Casualty Commission, now referred to as the Radiation Effects Research Foundation (RERF), was established to monitor the health effects of radiation exposure and has studied these survivors since the end of World War II. The RERF has reported a 10-15 times excess of all types of **leukemia** among the survivors compared with populations not exposed to the bomb. The leukemia excess peaked 4-7 years after exposure but still persists among the survivors. All

The Japanese city of Hiroshima after the atomic bomb was dropped on it.

forms of cancer tended to develop more frequently in heavily irradiated individuals, especially children under the age of ten at the time of exposure. Thyroid cancer was also increased in these children survivors of the bomb.

War is destructive to human life. The particular kind of destruction at Hiroshima, due to an atomic bomb, continues to be relentlessly destructive. The city of Hiroshima is known as a Peace City.

[*Robert G. McKinnell*]

Holistic approach

First formulated by Jan Smuts, holism has been traditionally defined as a philosophical theory that states that the determining factors in **nature** are wholes which are irreducible to the sum of their parts and that the **evolution** of the universe is the record of the activity and making of such wholes. More generally, it is the concept that wholes cannot be analyzed into parts or reduced to discrete elements without unexplainable residuals. Holism may also be defined by what it is not: it is not synonymous with organicism; holism does not require an entity to be alive or even a part of living processes. And neither is holism confined to spiritual mysticism, unaccessible to scientific methods or study.

The holistic approach in **ecology** and **environmental science** derives from the idea proposed by Harrison

Brown that "a precondition for solving [complex] problems is a realization that all of them are interlocked, with the result that they cannot be solved piecemeal." For some scholars holism is the rationale for the very existence of ecology. As David Gates notes, "the very definition of the discipline of ecology implies a holistic study."

The holistic approach has been successfully applied to environmental management. The United States Forest Service, for example, has implemented a multi-level approach to management that takes into account the complexity of forest **ecosystem**s, rather than the traditional focus on isolated incidents or problems.

Some people believe that a holistic approach to nature and the world will counter the effects of "reductionism"—excessive individualism, atomization, mechanistic worldview, objectivism, materialism, and anthropocentrism. Advocates of holism claim that its emphasis on connectivity, community, processes, networks, participation, synthesis, systems, and emergent properties will undo the "ills" of reductionism. Others warn that a balance between reductionism and holism is necessary. American ecologist Eugene Odum mandated that "ecology must combine holism with reductionism if applications are to benefit society." Parts and wholes, at the macro- and micro-level, must be understood. The basic lesson of a combined and complementary parts-whole approach is that every entity is both part *and* whole—an idea reenforced by Arthur Koestler's concept of a *holon*. A holon is any entity that is both a part of a larger system and itself a

521

system made up of parts. It is essential to recognize that holism can include the study of *any* whole, the entirety of any individual in all its ramifications, without implying any organic analogy other than organisms themselves. A holistic approach alone, especially in its extreme form, is unrealistic, condemning scholars to an unproductive wallowing in an unmanageable complexity. Holism and reductionism are both needed for accessing and understanding an increasingly complex world. *See also* Environmental ethics

[*Gerald L. Young*]

FURTHER READING

Bowen, W. "Reductions and Holism." In *Thinking About Nature: An Investigation of Nature, Value and Ecology.* Athens: University of Georgia Press, 1988.

Johnson, L. E. "Holism." In *A Morally Deep World: An Essay on Moral Significance and Environmental Ethics.* Cambridge: Cambridge University Press, 1991.

Krippner, S. "The Holistic Paradigm." *World Futures* 30 (1991): 133-40.

Marietta, D. E., Jr. "Environmental Holism and Individuals." *Environmental Ethics* 10 (Fall 1988): 251-58.

McCarty, D. C. "The Philosophy of Logical Wholism." *Synthese* 87 (April 1991): 51-123.

Savory, A. *Holistic Resource Management.* Covelo, CA: Island Press, 1988.

Van Steenbergen, B. "Potential Influence of the Holistic Paradigm on the Social Sciences." *Futures* 22 (December 1990): 1071-83.

Homeostasis

Humans, all other organisms, and even ecological systems, live in an **environment** of constant change. The persistently shifting, modulating, and changing milieu would not permit survival, if it were not for the capacity of biological systems to respond to this constant flux by maintaining a relatively stable internal environment. An example taken from mammalian biology is temperature which appears to be "*fixed*" at approximately 98.6°F (37°C). While humans can be exposed to extreme summer heat, and arctic mammals survive intense cold, body temperature remains constant within vary narrow limits. Homeostasis is the sum total of all the biological responses that provide internal equilibrium and assure the maintenance of conditions for survival.

The human **species** has a greater variety of living conditions than any other organism. The ability of humans to live and reproduce in such diverse circumstances is due to a combination of homeostatic mechanisms coupled with cultural (behavioral) responses.

The scientific concept of homeostasis emerged from two scientists: Claude Bernard (1813-1878), a French physiologist, and Walter Bradford Cannon (1871-1945), an American physician. Bernard contrasted the external environment which surrounds an organism and the internal environment of that organism. He was, of course, aware that the external environment fluctuated considerably in contrast to the internal environment which remained remarkably constant. He is credited with the enunciation of the constancy of the internal environment ("*La fixité du milieu intérieur* . .

.") in 1859. Bernard believed that the survival of an organism depended upon this constancy, and he observed it not only in temperature control but in the regulation of all of the systems that he studied. The concept of the stable "*milieu intérieur*" has been accepted and extended to the many organ systems of all higher vertebrates. This precise control of the internal environment is effected through hormones, the autonomic nervous system, endocrines, etc.

The term "homeostasis," derived from the Greek *homoios* meaning similar and *stasis* meaning to stand, suggests an internal environment which remains relatively similar or the same through time. The term was devised by Cannon in 1929 and used many times subsequently. Cannon noted that, in addition to temperature, there were complex controls involving many organ systems that maintained the internal stability within narrow limits. When those limited are exceeded, there is a reaction in the opposite direction that brings the condition back to normal, and the reactions returning the system to normal is referred to as negative feedback. Both Bernard and Cannon were concerned with human physiology. Nevertheless, the concept of homeostasis is applied to all levels of biological organization from the molecular level to ecological systems, including the entire **biosphere**. Engineers design self-controlling machines known as servomechanisms with feedback control by means of a sensing device, an amplifier which controls a servomotor which in turn runs the operation of the device. Examples of such devices are the thermostats which control furnace heat in a home or the more complicated automatic pilots of aircraft. While the human-made servomechanisms have similarities to biological homeostasis, they are not considered here.

As indicated above, temperature is closely regulated in humans and other homeotherms (birds and mammals). The human skin has thermal receptors sensitive to heat or cold. If cold is encountered, the receptors notify an area of the brain known as the hypothalamus via a nerve impulse. The hypothalamus has both a heat-promoting center and a heat-losing center, and, with cold, it is the former which is stimulated. Thyroid-releasing hormone, produced in the hypothalamus, causes the anterior pituitary to release thyroid stimulating hormone which, in turn, causes the thyroid gland to increase production of thyroxine which results in increased metabolism and therefore heat. Sympathetic nerves from the hypothalamus stimulate the adrenal medulla to secrete epinephrine and norepinephrine into the blood which also increases body metabolism and heat. Increased muscle activity will generate heat and that activity can be either voluntary (stamping the feet for instance) or involuntary (shivering). Since heat is dissipated via body surface blood vessels, the nervous system causes surface vasoconstriction to decrease that heat loss. Further, the small quantity of blood that does reach the surface of the body, where it is chilled, is reheated by countercurrent heat exchange resulting from blood vessels containing cold blood from the limbs running adjacent to blood vessels from the body core which contain warm blood. The chilled blood is prewarmed prior to returning to the body core. A little noted response to chilling is the voluntary reaching for a jacket or coat to minimize heat loss.

The body responds with opposite results when excessive heat is encountered. The individual tends to shed unnecessary clothing, and activity is reduced to minimize metabolism. Vasodilation of superficial blood vessels allows for radiation of heat. Sweat is produced, which by evaporation reduces body heat. It is clear that the maintenance of body temperature is closely controlled by a complex of homeostasis mechanisms.

Each step in temperature regulation is controlled by negative feedback. As indicated above, with exposure to cold the hypothalamus, through a series of steps, induces the synthesis and release of thyroxine by the thyroid gland. What was not indicated above was the fact that elevated levels of thyroxine control the level of activity of the thyroid by negative feedback inhibition of thyroid stimulating hormone. An appropriate level of thyroid hormone is thus maintained. In contrast, with inadequate thyroxine, more thyroid stimulating hormone is produced. Negative feedback controls assure that any particular step in homeostasis does not deviate too much from the normal.

Historically, biologists have been particularly impressed with mammalian and human homeostasis. Lower vertebrates have received less attention. However, while internal physiology may vary more in a frog than in a human, there are mechanisms which assure the survival of frogs. For instance, when the ambient temperature drops significantly in the autumn in northern latitudes, leopard frogs move into lakes or rivers which do not freeze. Moving into lakes and rivers is a behavioral response to a change in the external environment which results in internal temperature stability. The metabolism and structure of the frog is inadequate to protect the frog from freezing, but the specific heat of the water is such that freezing does not occur except at the surface of the overwintering lake or river. Even though life at the bottom of a lake with an ice cover moves at a slower pace than during the warm summer months, a functioning circulatory system is essential for survival. In general, frog blood (not unlike crankcase oil prior to the era of multiviscosity oil) increases in viscosity with as temperature decreases. Frog blood, however, decreases in viscosity with the prolonged autumnal and winter cold temperatures, thus assuring adequate circulation during the long nights under an ice cover. This is another control mechanism that assures the survival of frogs by maintaining a relatively stable internal environment during the harsh winter. With a return of a warm external environment, northern leopard frogs leave cold water to warm up under the spring sun. Warm temperature causes frog blood viscosity to increase to summer levels. It may be that the behavioral and physiological changes do not prevent oscillations that would be unsuitable for warm blooded animals but, in the frog, the fluctuations do not interfere with survival, and in biology, that is all that is essential.

There is homeostasis in ecological systems. Populations of animals in complex systems fluctuate in numbers, but the variations in numbers are generally between limits. For example, predators survive in adequate numbers as long as prey are available. If predators become too great in number, the population of prey will diminish. With fewer prey, the numbers of predators plummet through negative feedback thus permitting recovery of the preyed upon species. The situation becomes much more complex when other food sources are available to the predator.

Many organisms encounter a negative feedback on growth rate with crowding. This density dependent population control has been studied in larval frogs, as well as many other organisms, where excretory products seem to specifically inhibit the crowded species but not other organisms in the same environment. Even with adequate food, high density culture of laboratory mice results in negative feedback on reproductive potential with abnormal gonad development and delayed sexual maturity. Density independent factors affecting populations are important in population control but would not be considered homeostasis. Drought is such a factor, and its effects can be contrasted with crowding. Populations of tadpoles will drop catastrophically when breeding ponds dry. Instead of fluctuating between limits (with controls), all individuals are affected the same (i.e., they die). The area must be repopulated with immigrants at a subsequent time, and the migration can be considered a population homeostatic control. The inward migration results in maintenance of population within the geographic area and aids in the survival of the species.

[*Robert G. McKinnell*]

FURTHER READING

Hardy, R. N. *Homeostasis.* London: Edward Arnold, Ltd., 1976.

Langley, L. L. *Homeostasis.* New York: Reinhold Publishing Co., 1965.

Tortora, G. J., and N. P. Anagnostakos. *Principles of Anatomy and Physiology.* 5th ed. New York: Harper and Row, 1987.

Homestead Act (1862)

The Homestead Act was signed into law in 1862. It was a legislative offer on a vast scale of free homesteads on unappropriated **public land**s. Any citizen (or alien who filed a declaration of intent to become a citizen) who had reached the age of 21 and was the head of a family could acquire title to a stretch of public land of up to 160 acres (65 ha) after living on it and farming it for five years. The only payment required was administrative fees. The settler could also obtain the land without the requirement of residence and cultivation for five years, against payment of $1.25 per acre. With the advent of machinery to mechanize farm labor, 160-acre tracts soon became uneconomical to operate, and Congress modified the original act to allow acquisition of larger tracts. The Homestead Act is still in effect, but good unappropriated land is scarce. Only Alaska still offers opportunities for homesteaders.

The Homestead Act was designed to speed development of the United States and to achieve an equitable distribution of wealth. Poor settlers, who lacked the capital to buy land, were now able to start their own farms. Indeed, the

Homesteaders in Nebraska.

act contributed greatly to the growth and development of the country, particularly in the period between the Civil War and World War I, and it did much to speed settlement west of the Mississippi River. In all, well over a quarter of a billion acres of land has been distributed under the Homestead Act and its amendments. However, only a small percentage of land granted under the act between 1862 and 1900 was in fact acquired by homesteaders. According to estimates, only at most one of every six acres and possibly only one in nine acres passed into the hands of family farmers.

The railroad companies and land speculators obtained the bulk of the land, sometimes through gross fraud using dummy entrants. Moreover, the railroads often managed to get the best land while the homesteaders, ignorant of farming conditions on the Plains, often ended up with tracts least suitable to farming. Speculators frequently encouraged settlement on land that was too dry or had no sources of water for domestic use. When the homesteads failed, many settlers sold the land to speculators.

The environmental consequences of the Homestead Act were many and serious. The act facilitated railroad development, often in excess of transportation needs. In many instances, competing companies built lines to connect the same cities. Railroad development contributed significantly to the destruction of **bison** herds, which in turn led to the destruction of the way of life of the Plains Indians. Cultivation of the Plains caused wholesale destruction of the vast **prairie**s, so that whole ecological systems virtually

disappeared. Overfarming of semi-**arid** lands led to another environmental disaster, whose consequences were fully experienced only in the 1930s. The great **Dust Bowl**, with its terrifying dust storms, made huge areas of the country unlivable.

The Homestead Act was based on the notion that land held no value unless it was cultivated. It has now become clear that reckless cultivation can be self-destructive. In many cases, unfortunately, the damage can no longer be undone.

[*William E. Larson and Marijke Rijsberman*]

FURTHER READING

Shimkin, M. N. "Homesteading on the Republican River." *Journal of the West* 26 (October 1987): 58-66.

Horizon

Layers in the **soil** develop because of the additions, losses, translocations, and transformations that take place as the soil ages. The soil layers occur as a result of water percolating through the soil and leaching substances downward. The layers are parallel to the soil surface and are called horizons. Horizons will vary from the surface to the **subsoil** and from one soil to the next because of the different intensities of the above processes. Soils are classified into different groups based on the characteristics of the horizons.

Hospital Wastes
See **Medical Wastes**

Hubbard Brook Experimental Forest

The Hubbard Brook Experimental Forest is located in West Thornton, New Hampshire. It is an experimental area established in 1955 within the White Mountains National Forest in New Hamphire's central plateau and is administered by the U.S. **Forest Service**. Hubbard Brook was the site of many important ecological studies beginning in the 1960s which established the extent of **nutrient** losses when all the trees in a **watershed** are cut.

Hubbard Brook is a north temperate watershed covered with a mature forest, and it is still accumulating biomass. In one early study, vegetation cut in a section of Hubbard Brook was left to decay while nutrient losses were monitored in the **runoff**. Total **nitrogen** losses in the first year were twice the amount cycled in the system during a normal year. With the rise of nitrate in the runoff, concentrations of calcium, magnesium, sodium, and potassium rose. These increases caused eutrophication and **pollution** of the streams fed by this watershed. Once the higher plants had been destroyed, the **soil** was unable to retain nutrients.

Early evidence from the studies indicated that total losses in the **ecosystem** due to the **clear-cutting** were a large number of the total inventory of **species**. The site's ability to support complex living systems was reduced. The lost nutrients could accumulate again, but erosion of primary minerals would limit the number of plants and animals sustained in the area.

Another study at the Hubbard Brook site investigated the effects of forest cutting and **herbicide** treatment on nutrients in the forest. All of the vegetation in one of Hubbard Brook's seven watersheds was cut and then the area was treated with the herbicides. At the time the conclusions were startling: **deforestation** resulted in much larger run-offs into the streams. The **pH** of the drainage stream went from 5.1 to 4.3, along with a change in temperature and electrical conductivity of the stream water. A combination of higher nutrient concentration, higher water temperature, and greater solar radiation due to the loss of forest cover produced an **algal bloom**, the first sign of eutrophication. This signaled that a change in the ecosystem of the watershed had occurred. It was ultimately demonstrated at Hubbard Brook that the use of herbicides on a cut area resulted in their transfer to the outgoing water.

Hubbard Brook Experimental Forest continues to be an active research facility for foresters and biologists. Most current research focuses on **water quality** and nutrient

exchange. The Forest Service also maintians an acid rain monitoring station, and conducts research on **old-growth forests**. The results from various studies done at Hubbard Brook have shown that mature forest ecosystems have a greater ability to trap and store nutrients for recycling within the ecosystem. In addition, mature forests offer a higher degrees of **biodiversity** than do forests that are clear-cut. *See also* Aquatic chemistry; Cultural eutrophication; Decline spiral; Experimental Lakes Area; Nitrogen cyle

[*Linda Rehkopf*]

FURTHER READING

Bormann, F. H. *Pattern and Process in a Forested Ecosystem: Disturbance Development and the Steady State Based on the Hubbard Brook Ecosystem Study.* New York: Springer-Verlag, 1991.

Botkin, D. B. *Forest Dynamics: An Ecological Model.* New York: Oxford University Press, 1993.

Miller, G. "Window Into a Water Shed." *American Forests* 95 (May-June 1989): 58-61.

Hudson River

Starting at Lake Tear of the Clouds, a two-acre (0.8 ha) pond in New York's **Adirondack Mountains**, the Hudson River runs 315 miles (507 km) to the Battery on Manhattan Island's southern tip, where it meets the Atlantic Ocean. Although polluted and extensively dammed for hydroelectric power, the river still contains a wealth of aquatic **species**, including massive sea sturgeon (*Acipenser oxyrhynchus*) and short-nosed sturgeon (*A. brevirostrum*).

The upper Hudson is fast-flowing trout stream, but below the Adirondack Forest Preserve, **pollution** from municipal sources, paper companies, and industries degrades the water. Stretches of the upper Hudson contain so-called warm water fish, including northern pike (*Esox lucius*), chain pickerel (*E. niger*), smallmouth bass (*Micropterus dolomieui*), and largemouth bass (*M. salmoides*). These latter two fish swam into the Hudson through the **Lake Erie** and Lake Champlain canals, which were completed in the early nineteenth century.

The Catskill Mountains dominate the mid-Hudson region, which is rich in fish and **wildlife**, though dairy farming, a source of **runoff** pollution, is strong in the region. American shad (*Alosa sapidissima*), historically the Hudson's most important commercial fish, spawn on the river flats between Kingston and Coxsackie. Marshes in this region support snapping turtles (*Chelydra serpentina*) and, in the winter, muskrat (*Ondatra zibethicus*) and mink (*Mustela vison*). Water chestnuts (*Trapa natans*) grow luxuriantly in this section of the river.

Deep and partly bordered by mountains, the lower Hudson resembles a fiord. The unusually deep lower river makes it suitable for navigation by ocean-going vessels for 150 miles (241 km) upriver to Albany. Because the river's surface elevation does not drop between Albany and Manhattan, the tidal effects of the ocean are felt all the way upriver to the Federal Lock and Dam above Albany. These powerful tides make long stretches of the lower Hudson saline or **brackish**, with saltwater penetrating as high as 60 miles (97 km) upstream from the Battery.

The Hudson contains a great variety of botanical species. Over a dozen oaks thrive along its banks, including red oaks (*Quercus rubra*), black oaks (*Q. velutina*), pin oaks (*Q. palustris*), and rock chestnut (*Q. prinus*). Numerous other trees also abound, from mountain laurel (*Kalmia latifolia*) and red pine (*Pinus resinosa*) to flowering dogwood (*Cornus florida*), together with a wide variety of small herbaceous plants.

The Hudson River is comparatively short. More than 80 American rivers are longer than it, but it plays a major role in New York's economy and **ecology**. Pollution threats to the river have been caused by the **discharge** of industrial and municipal waste, as well as **pesticide**s washed off the land by rain. From 1930 to 1975, one chemical company on the river manufactured approximately 1.4 billion pounds of **polychlorinated biphenyl**s (PCBs), and an estimated 10 million pounds a year entered the **environment**. In recent decades, **chlorinated hydrocarbons**, dieldrin, endrin, **DDT**, and other pollutants have been linked to the decline in populations of the once common Jefferson salamander (*Ambystoma jeffersonianum*), fish hawk (*Pandion haliaetus*), and **bald eagle** (*Haliaeetus leucocephalus*). *See also* Agricultural pollution; Dams; Estuary; Feedlot runoff; Fertilizer runoff; Industrial waste treatment; Sewage treatment; Wastewater

[*David Clarke*]

FURTHER READING

Boyle, R. H. *The Hudson River, A Natural and Unnatural History.* New York: Norton, 1979.

Peirce, N. R., and J. Hagstrom. *The Book of America, Inside the Fifty States Today.* New York: Norton, 1983.

Human ecology

Human ecology may be defined as the branch of knowledge concerned with relationships between human beings and their **environment**s. Among the disciplines contributing seminal work in this field are sociology, anthropology, geography, economics, psychology, political science, philosophy, and the arts. Applied human ecology emerges in engineering, planning, architecture, landscape architecture, **conservation**, and public health. Human ecology, then, is an interdisciplinary study which applies the principles and concepts of **ecology** to human problems and the human condition. The notion of interaction—between human beings and the environment and between human beings—is fundamental to human ecology, as it is to biological ecology.

Human ecology as an academic inquiry has disciplinary roots extending back as far as the 1920s. However, much work in the decades prior to the 1970s was narrowly drawn and was often carried out by a few individuals whose intellectual legacy remained isolated from the mainstream of their disciplines. The work done in sociology offers an exception to the latter (but not the former) rule; sociological human ecology is traced to the Chicago school and the intellectual lineage of Robert Ezra Park, his student Roderick D. Mackenzie, and Mackenzie's student Amos Hawley. Through the influence of these men and their school, human ecology, for a time, was narrowly identified with a sociological analysis of spatial patterns in urban settings (although broader questions were sometimes contemplated).

Comprehensive treatment of human ecology is first found in the work of Gerald L. Young, who pioneered the study of human ecology as an interdisciplinary field and as a conceptual framework. Young's definitive framework is founded upon four central themes. The first of these is interaction, and the other three are developed from it: levels of organization, functionalism (part-whole relationships), and holism. These four basic concepts form the foundation for a series of field derivatives (**niche**, community, and **ecosystem**) and consequent notions (institutions, proxemics, alienation, ethics, world community, and stress/capacitance). Young's emphasis on linkages and process set his approach apart from other synthetic attempts in human ecology, which were largely cumbersome classificatory schemata. These were subject to harsh criticism because they tended to embrace virtually all knowledge, resolve themselves into superficial lists and mnemonic "building blocks," and had little applicability to real-world problems.

Generally, comprehensive treatment of human ecology is more advanced in Europe than it is in the United States. A comprehensive approach to human ecology as an interdisciplinary field and conceptual framework gathered momentum in several independent centers during the 1970s and 1980s. Among these have been several college and university programs and research centers, including those at the University of Göteborg, Sweden, and, in the United States, at Rutgers University and the University of California at Davis. Interdisciplinary programs at the undergraduate level were first offered in 1972 by the College of the Atlantic (Maine) and The Evergreen State College (Washington). The Commonwealth Human Ecology Council in the United Kingdom, the International Union of Anthropological and Ethnological Sciences' Commission on Human Ecology, the Centre for Human Ecology at the University of Edinburgh, the Institute for Human Ecology in California, and professional societies and organizations in Europe and the United States have been other centers of development for the field.

Dr. Thomas Dietz, President of the Society for Human Ecology, defined some of the priority research problems which human ecology addresses in recent testimony before the U.S. House of Representatives Subcommittee on Environment and the National Academy of Sciences Committee on Environmental Research. Among these, Dietz listed global change, values, post-hoc evaluation, and science and conflict in **environmental policy**. Other human ecologists would include in the list such items as commons problems, **carrying capacity**, **sustainable development**, human health, ecological economics, problems of resource use and distribution, and family systems. Problems of epistemology or cognition such as environmental perception, consciousness, or paradigm change also receive attention.

Our Common Future, the report of the United Nation's World Commission on Environment and Development of 1987, has stimulated a new phase in the development of human ecology. A host of new programs, plans, conferences and agendas have been put forth, primarily to address phenomena of global change and the challenge of sustainable development. These include the *Sustainable Biosphere Initiative* published by the Ecological Society of America in 1991 and extended internationally; the United Nations Conference on Environment and Development; the proposed new United States National Institutes for the Environment; the **Man and the Biosphere Program**'s Human-Dominated Systems Program; the report of the National Research Council Committee on Human Dimensions of Global Change and the associated National Science Foundation's Human Dimensions of Global Change Program; and green plans published by the governments of Canada, Norway, the Netherlands, the United Kingdom, and Austria. All of these programs call for an integrated, interdisciplinary approach to complex problems of human-environmental relationships. The next challenge for human ecology will be to digest and steer these new efforts and to identify the perspectives and tools they supply.

[*Jeremy Pratt*]

FURTHER READING

Jungen, B. "Integration of Knowledge in Human Ecology." In *Human Ecology: A Gathering of Perspectives*, edited by R. J. Borden, et al., Selected papers from the First International Conference of the Society for Human Ecology, 1986.

Young, G. L. *Human Ecology As An Interdisciplinary Concept: A Critical Inquiry. Advances in Ecological Research* 8 (1974): 1-105.

———. *Origins of Human Ecology.* Stroudsberg, PA: Hutchinson & Ross, 1983.

———. *Conceptual Framework For An Interdisciplinary Human Ecology. Acta Oecologiae Hominis* 1 (1989): 1-136.

Humane Society of the United States (Washington, D.C.)

The largest animal protection organization in the United States, Humane Society of the United States (HSUS) works to preserve **wildlife** and **wilderness**, save **endangered species**, and promote humane treatment of all animals. Formed in 1954, HSUS specializes in education, cruelty investigations and prosecutions, wildlife and **nature** preservation, environmental protection, federal and state legislative activities, and other actions designed to protect animal welfare and the **environment**.

Major projects undertaken by HSUS in recent years have included campaigns to stop the killing of **whales**, **dolphins**, **elephants**, bears, and **wolves**; to help reduce the number of animals used in medical research and to improve the conditions under which they are used; to oppose the use of fur by the fashion industry; and to address the problem of pet overpopulation.

The group has worked extensively to ban the use of tuna caught in a way that kills dolphins, largely eliminating the sale of such products in the United States and western Europe. It has tried to stop international airlines from transporting exotic birds into the United States. Other high priority projects have included banning the international trade in elephant ivory, especially imports into the United States, and securing and maintaining a general worldwide moratorium on commercial **whaling**.

HSUS companion animals section works on a variety of issues affecting dogs, cats, birds, horses, and other animals commonly kept as pets, striving to promote responsible pet ownership, particularly the spaying and neutering of dogs and cats to reduce the tremendous overpopulation of these animals. HSUS works closely with local shelters and humane societies across the country, providing information, training, evaluation, and consultation.

Several national and international environmental and animal protection groups are affiliated and work closely with HSUS. Humane Society International works abroad to fulfill HSUS's mission and to institute reform and educational programs that will benefit animals. EarthKind, a global environmental protection group that emphasizes wildlife protection and humane treatment of animals, has been active in Russia, India, Thailand, Sri Lanka, the United Kingdom, Romania, and elsewhere, working to preserve forests, **wetlands**, **wild river**s, natural **ecosystem**s, and endangered wildlife.

The National Association for Humane and Environmental Education is the youth education division of HSUS, developing and producing periodicals and teaching materials designed to instill humane values in students and young people, including *KIND (Kids in Nature's Defense) News*, a newspaper for elementary school children, and *KIND TEACHER*, an 80-page annual full of worksheets and activities for use by teachers.

The Center for Respect of Life and the Environment works with academic institutions, scholars, religious leaders and organizations, arts groups, and others to foster an ethic of respect and compassion towards all creatures and the natural environment. Its quarterly publication, *Earth Ethics*, examines such issues as earth education, sustainable communities, ecological economics, and other values affecting our relationship with the natural world. The Interfaith Council for the Protection of Animals and Nature promotes **conservation** and education mainly within the religious community, attempting to make religious leaders, groups, and individuals more aware of our moral and spiritual obligations to preserve the planet and its myriad life forms.

HSUS has been quite active, hard-hitting, and effective in promoting its animal protection programs, such as leading the fight against the fur industry. It accomplishes its goals through education, lobbying, grassroots organizing, and other traditional, legal means of influencing public opinion and government policies.

With over 3.5 million members or "constituents" and an annual budget of over $35 million, HSUS is considered the largest and one of the most influential animal protection groups in the United States and, perhaps, the world. Contact: Humane Society of the United States, 2100 L Street NW, Washington, D.C. 20037. Internet: http://www.hsus.org/.

[*Lewis G. Regenstein*]

Humanism

A perspective or doctrine that focuses primarily on the interests, capacities, and achievements of human beings. This focus on human concerns has led some to conclude that human beings have rightful dominion over the earth and that their interests and well-being are paramount and take precedence over all other considerations. *Religious humanism*, for instance, generally holds that God made human beings in His own image and put them in charge of His creation. *Secular humanism* views human beings as the source of all value or worth. Some environmentally-minded critics, such as **Lynn White**, Jr., and David Ehrenfeld claim that much environmental destruction can be traced to "the arrogance of humanism."

Human-powered vehicles

Finding easy modes of transportation seems to be a basic human need, but finding easy *and clean* modes is becoming imperative in the late twentieth century. Traffic congestion, overconsumption of **fossil fuels** and **air pollution** are all direct results of automotive lifestyles around the world. The logical alternative is human-powered vehicles (HPVs), perhaps best exemplified in the bicycle, the most basic HPV. New high-tech developments in HPVs are not yet ready for mass production, nor are they able to compete with cars. Pedal-propelled HPVs in the air, on land, or under the sea are still in the expensive, design-and-race-for-a-prize category. But the challenge of human-powered transport has inspired a lot of inventive thinking, both amateur and professional.

Bicycles and rickshaws comprise the most basic HPVs. Of these two vehicles, bicycles are clearly the most popular, and production of these HPVs has surpassed production of **automobile**s in recent years. The number of bicycles in use throughout the world is roughly double that of cars; China alone contains 270 million bicycles, or one third of the total bicycles worldwide. Indeed the bicycle has overtaken the automobile as the preferred mode of transportation in many nations. There are many reasons for the popularity of the bike: it fulfills both recreational and functional needs, it is an economical alternative to automobiles, and it does not contribute to the problems facing the **environment**.

Although the bicycle provides a healthy and scenic form of **recreation**, people also find it useful in basic transportation. In the Netherlands, bicycle transportation accounts for 30 percent of work trips and 60 percent of school trips. One-third of commuting to work in Denmark is by bicycle. In China, the vast majority of all trips there are made via bicycle.

A surge in bicycle production occurred in 1973, when in conjunction with rising oil costs, production doubled to 52 million per year. Soaring fuel prices in the 1970s inspired people to find inexpensive, economical alternatives to cars, and many turned to bicycles. Besides being efficient transportation, bikes are simply cheaper to purchase and to maintain than cars. There is no need to pay for parking or tolls, no expensive upkeep, and no high fuel costs.

The lack of fuel costs associated with bicycles leads to another benefit: bicycles do not harm the environment. Cars consume fossil fuels and in so doing release more than two-thirds of the United States' **smog**-producing **chemicals**. They are furthermore considered responsible for many other environmental ailments: depletion of the **ozone** layer through release of **chlorofluorocarbons** from automobile air conditioning units; cause of **cancer** through toxic **emission**s; and consumption of the world's limited fuel resources. With human energy as their only requirement, bicycles have none of these liabilities.

Nevertheless, in many cases—such as long trips or travelling in inclement weather—cars are the preferred form of transportation. Bicycles are not the optimal choice in many situations. Thus engineers and designers seek to improve on the bicycle and make machines suitable for transport under many different conditions. They are striving to produce new human-powered vehicles—HPVs that maximize air and sea currents, that have reasonable interior ergonomics, and that can be inexpensively produced. Several machines designed to fit this criteria exist.

As for developments in human-powered aircraft, success is judged on distance and speed, which depend on the strength of the pedaller and the lightness of the craft. The current world record holder is Greek Olympic cyclist Kanellos Kanellopoulos who flew *Daedalus 88*. *Daedalus 88* was created by engineer John Langford and a team of MIT engineers and funded by American corporations. Kanellopoulos flew *Daedalus 88* for 3 hours and 54 minutes across the Aegean Sea between Crete and Santorini, a distance of 74 miles (119 km), in April 1988. The craft averaged 18.5 mph (29 kph) and flew 15 feet (4.6 m) above the water. Upon arrival at Santorini, however, the sun began to heat up the black sands and generate erratic shore winds and *Daedalus 88* plunged into the sea. It was a few yards short of its goal, and the tailboom of the 70-lb (32-kg) vehicle was snapped by the wind. But to cheering crowds on the beach, Kanellopoulos rose from the sea with a victory sign and strode to shore.

In the creation of a human-powered helicopter, students at California Polytechnic State University have been working on perfecting one since 1981. In 1989 they achieved liftoff with Greg McNeil, a member of the United States National Cycling Team, pedalling an astounding 1.0 hp. The

Zzipper

Vector single

Avatar 2000

Schöndorf all—weather vehicle

Innovative bicycle designs.

graphite epoxy, wood, and Mylar craft, *Da Vinci III*, rose 7 in (17.7 cm) for 6.8 seconds. But rules for the $10,000 Sikorsky prize, sponsored by the American Helicopter Society, stipulate that the winning craft must rise nearly 10 ft, or 3 m, and stay aloft one minute.

On land, recumbent vehicles, or recumbents, are wheeled vehicles in which the driver pedals in a semi-recumbent position, contained within a windowed enclosure. The world record was set in 1989 by American Fred Markham at the Michigan International Speedway in an HPV named *Goldrush*. Markham pedalled more than 72 kph (about 44 mph).

Unfortunately, the realities of road travel cast a long shadow over recumbent HPVs. Crews discovered that they tended to be unstable in crosswinds, distracted other drivers and pedestrians, and lacked the speed to correct course safely in the face of oncoming cars and trucks.

In the sea, being able to maneuver at your own pace and be in control of your vehicle—as well as being able to beat a fast retreat undersea—are the problems faced by HPV submersible engineers. Human-powered subs are not a new idea. The Revolutionary War created a need for a bubble sub that was to plant an explosive in the belly of a British ship in New York Harbor. (The naval officer, breathing one-half hour's worth of air, failed in his night mission, but survived).

The special design problems of modern two-person HP-subs involve controlling buoyancy and ballast, pitch and yaw (nose up/down/sideways), reducing drag, increasing thrust, and positioning the pedaller and the propulsor in the flooded cockpit (called "wet") in ways that maximize air intake from scuba tanks and muscle power from arms and legs.

Depending on the design, the humans in HP-subs lie prone, foot to head or side by side, or sit, using their feet to pedal and their hands to control the rudder through the underwater currents. Studies by the United States Navy Experimental Dive Unit indicate that a well-trained athlete can sustain 0.5 hp for 10 minutes underwater.

On the surface of the water, fin-propelled water-craft—lightweight inflatables that are powered by humans kicking with fins—are ideal for fishermen whom maneuverability, not speed, is the goal. Paddling with the legs, which does not disturb fish, leaves the hands free to cast. In most designs, the fisherman sits on a platform between tubes, his feet in the water. Controllability is another matter, however: in open windy water, the craft is at the mercy of the elements in its current design state. Top speed is about 50 yards (46 m) in three minutes.

Finally, over the surface of the water, the first human-powered hydrofoil, *Flying Fish*, with national track sprinter Bobby Livingston, broke a world record in September 1989 when it traveled 100 meters over Lake Adrian, Michigan, at 16.1 knots (18.5 mph). A vehicle that pedalled like a bicycle, resembled a model airplane with a two-blade propeller and a 6-ft (1.8-m) carbon graphite wing, *Flying Fish* sped across the surface of the lake on two pontoons.

[*Stephanie Ocko and Andrea Gacki*]

FURTHER READING

Banks, R. "Sub Story." *National Geographic World* (July 1992): 8-11.

Blumenthal, T. "Outer Limits." *Bicycling* (December 1989): 36.

Britton, P. "Muscle Subs." *Popular Science* (June 1989): 126-129.

———. "Technology Race Beneath the Waves." *Popular Science* (June 1991): 48-54.

Horgan, J. "Heli-Hopper: Human-powered Helicopter Gets Off the Ground." *Scientific American* 262 (March 1990): 34.

Kyle, C. R. "Limits of Leg Power." *Bicycling* (October 1990): 100-101.

Langley, J. "Those Flying Men and Their Magnificent Machines." *Bicycling* (April 1992): 74-76.

Lowe, M. "Bicycle Production Outpaces Autos." In *Vital Signs 1992: The Trends That Are Shaping Our Future,* edited by L. R. Brown, C, Flavin, and H. Hane. New York: Norton, 1992.

"Man-Powered Helicopter Makes First Flight." *Aviation Week and Space Technology* (December 1989): 115.

Martin, S. "Cycle City 2000." *Bicycling* (March 1992): 130-131.

Humus

Humus is essentially decomposed organic matter in **soil**. Humus can vary in color but is often dark brown. Besides containing valuable **nutrient**s, there are many other benefits of humus: it stabilizes soil mineral particles into aggregates, improves pore space relationships and aids in air and water movement, aids in water holding capacity, and influences the absorption of **hydrogen ion**s as a **pH** regulator.

Hunting and trapping

Wild animals are a potentially renewable **natural resource**. This means that they can be harvested in a sustainable fashion, as long as then birth rate is greater than the rate of exploitation by humans. In the sense meant here, "harvesting" refers to the killing of wild animals as a source of meat, fur, antlers, or other useful products, or as an outdoor sport. The harvesting can involve trapping, or hunting using guns, bows-and-arrows, or other weapons. (Fishing is also a kind of hunting, but it is not dealt with here). From the ecological perspective, it is critical that the exploitation is undertaken in a sustainable fashion; otherwise, serious damages are caused to the resource and to **ecosystem**s more generally.

Unfortunately, there have been numerous examples in which wild animals have been harvested at grossly unsustainable rates, which caused their populations to decline severely. In a few cases this caused species to become extinct—they no longer occur anywhere on Earth. For example, commercial hunting in North America resulted in the extinctions of the great auk (*Pinguinnis impennis*), passenger pigeon (*Ectopistes migratorius*), and Steller's sea cow (*Hydrodamalis stelleri*). Unsustainable commercial hunting also brought other species to the brink of extinction, including the Eskimo curlew (*Numenius borealis*), northern right whale (*Eubalaena glacialis*), northern fur seal (*Callorhinus ursinus*), grey whale (*Eschrichtius robustus*), and American **bison** or buffalo (*Bison bison*).

Fortunately, these and many other examples of over-exploitation of wild animals by humans are regrettable cases from the past. Today, the exploitation of wild animals in North America is undertaken with a view to the longer-term **conservation** of their stocks, that is, an attempt is made to manage the harvesting in a sustainable fashion. This means that trapping and hunting are much more closely regulated than they used to be.

If harvests of wild animals are to be undertaken in a sustainable manner, it is critical that harvest levels are determined using the best available understanding of population-level productivity and stock sizes. It is also essential that harvest quotas are respected by trappers and hunters and that illegal exploitation (or **poaching**) does not compromise what might otherwise be a sustainable activity. The challenge of modern wildlife management is to ensure that good conservation science is sensibly integrated with effective monitoring and management of the rates of exploitation.

Ethics of Trapping and Hunting

From the strictly ecological perspective, sustainable trapping and hunting of wild animals is no more objectionable than the prudent harvesting of timber or agricultural crops. However, people have widely divergent attitudes about the killing of wild (or domestic) animals for meat, sport, or profit. At one end of the ethical spectrum are people who see no problem with the killing wild animals as a source of meat or cash. At the other extreme are individuals with a profound respect for the rights of all animals, and who believe that killing any sentient creature is ethically wrong. Many of these latter people are animal-rights activists, and some of them are involved in organizations that undertake high-profile protests and other forms of advocacy to prevent or restrict trapping and hunting. In essence, these people object to the lethal exploitation of wild animals, even under closely regulated conditions that would not deplete their populations. Most people, of course, have attitudes that are intermediate to those just described.

Trapping

The fur trade was one a very important commercial activity during the initial phase of the colonization of North America by Europeans. During those times, as now, furs were a valuable commodity that could be obtained from nature and could be sold at a great profit in urban markets. In fact, the quest for furs was the most important reason for much of the early exploration of the interior of North America, as fur traders penetrated all of the continent's great rivers seeking new sources of pelts and profit. Most fur-bearing animals are harvested by a form of hunting known as trapping.

Until recently, most trapping involved leg-hold traps, a relatively crude method that results in many animals enduring cruel and lingering deaths. Fortunately, other, more humane alternatives now exist in which most trapped animals are killed quickly and do not suffer unnecessarily. In large part, the movement towards more merciful trapping methods has occurred in response to effective, high-profile lobbying by organizations that oppose trapping, and the trapping industry has responded by developing and using more humane methods of killing wild furbearers.

Various species of furbearers are trapped in North America, particularly in relatively remote, wild areas, such as the northern and montane forests of the continental United States, Alaska, and Canada. Among the most valuable fur-bearing species are beaver (*Castor canadensis*), muskrat (*Ondatra zibethicus*), mink (*Mustela vison*), river otter (*Enhydra lutris*), bobcat (*Lynx rufus*), lynx (*Lynx canadensis*), red fox (*Vulpes vulpes*), wolf (*Canis lupus*), and coyote (*Canis latrans*). The hides of other species are also valuable, such as black bear (*Ursus americanus*), white-tailed deer (*Odocoileus virginianus*), and moose (*Alces alces*), but these species are not hunted primarily for their pelage.

Some species of seals are hunted for their fur, although this is largely done by shooting, clubbing, or netting, rather than by trapping. The best examples of this are the harp seal (*Phoca groenlandica*) of the northwestern Atlantic Ocean and the northern fur seal (*Callorhinus ursinus*) of the Bering Sea. Many seal pups are killed by commercial hunters in the spring when their coats are still white and soft. This harvest has been highly controversial and is the subject of intense opposition from animal rights groups.

Game Mammals

Hunting is a popular sport in North America, enjoyed by about 16 million people each year, most of them men. In 1991, hunting contributed more than $12 billion to the U.S. economy, about half of which was spent by big-game hunters.

Various species of terrestrial animals are hunted in large numbers. This is mostly done by stalking the animals and shooting them with rifles, although shotguns and bow-and-arrow are sometimes used. Some hunting is done for subsistence purposes, that is, the meat of the animals is used to feed the family or friends of the hunters. Subsistence hunting is especially important in remote areas and for aboriginal hunters. Commercial or market hunts also used to be common, but these are no longer legal in North America (except under exceptional circumstances) because they have generally proven to be unsustainable. However, illegal, semi-commercial hunting (or poaching) still takes place in many remote areas where game animals are relatively abundant and where there are local markets for wild meat.

In addition, many people hunt as a sport, that is, for the excitement and accomplishment of tracking and killing wild animals. In such cases, using the meat of the hunted animals may be only a secondary consideration, and in fact the hunter may only seek to retain the head, antlers, or horns of the prey as a trophy (although the meat may be kept by the hunter's guide). Big-game hunting is an economically important activity in North America, with large amounts of money being spent on the equipment, guides, and transportation necessary to undertake this sport.

The most commonly hunted big-game mammal in North America is the white-tailed deer. Other frequently hunted ungulates include the mule deer (*Odocoileus hemionus*), moose, elk or wapiti (*Cervus canadensis*), caribou (*Rangifer tarandus*), and pronghorn antelope (*Antilocapra americana*). Black bear and grizzly bear (*Ursus arctos*) are also hunted, as are bighorn sheep (*Ovis canadensis*) and mountain goat (*Oreamnos americanus*). Commonly hunted small-game species include various species of rabbits and hares, such as the cottontail rabbit (*Sylvilagus floridanus*), snowshoe hare (*Lepus americanus*), and jackrabbit (*Lepus californicus*), as well as the grey or black squirrel (*Sciurus carolinensis*) and woodchuck (*Marmota monax*). Wild boar (*Sus scrofa*) are also hunted in some regions—these are feral animals descended from escaped domestic pigs.

Game birds

Various larger species of birds are hunted in North America for their meat and for sport. So-called upland game birds are hunted in terrestrial habitats and include ruffed grouse (*Bonasa umbellus*), willow ptarmigan (*Lagopus lagopus*), bobwhite quail (*Colinus virginianus*), wild turkey (*Meleagris gallopava*), mourning dove (*Zanaidura macroura*), and woodcock (*Philohela minor*). Several introduced species of upland gamebirds are also commonly hunted, particularly ring-necked pheasant (*Phasianus colchicus*) and Hungarian or grey partridge (*Perdix perdix*).

Much larger numbers of waterfowl are hunted in North America, including millions of ducks and geese. The most commonly harvested species of waterfowl are mallard (*Anas platyrhynchos*), wood duck (*Aix sponsa*), Canada goose (*Branta canadensis*), and snow and blue goose (*Chen hyperborea*), but another 35 or so species in the duck family are also hunted. Other hunted waterfowl include coots (*Fulica americana*) and moorhens (*Gallinula chloropus*).

[*Bill Freedman*]

FURTHER READING

Robinson, W.L., and E.G. Bolen. *Wildlife Ecology and Management*, 3rd ed. New York: Macmillan, 1996.

Freedman, B. *Environmental Ecology*, 2nd ed. San Diego: Academic Press, 1995.

Halls, L.K., ed. *White-tailed Deer: Ecology and Management*. Harrisburg: Stackpole Books, 1984.

Novak, M., et al. *Wild Furbearer Management and Conservation in North America*. North Bay: Ontario Trappers Association, 1987.

Phillips, P.C. *The Fur Trade* (2 vols.). Norman: University of Oklahoma, 1961.

Hurricane

Hurricanes, called typhoons or tropical cyclones in the Far East, are intense cyclonic storms which form over warm tropical waters, and generally remain active and strong only while over the oceans. Their intensity is marked by a distinct spiraling pattern of clouds, very low atmospheric pressure at the center, and extremely strong winds blowing at speeds greater than 74 mph (120 kph) within the inner rings of clouds. Typically when hurricanes strike land and move inland, they immediately start to disintegrate, though before they do they bring widespread destruction of property and loss of life. The radius of such a storm can be 100 miles (160 km) or greater. Thunderstorms, hail, and tornados frequently are imbedded in hurricanes.

Hurricanes occur in every tropical ocean except the South Atlantic, and with greater frequency from August through October than any other time of year. The center of a hurricane is called the eye. It is an area of relative calm, few clouds and higher temperatures, and represents the center of the low pressure pattern. Hurricanes usually move from east to west near the tropics, but when they migrate poleward to the mid-latitudes they can get caught up in the general west to east flow pattern found in that region of the earth. *See also* Tornado and cyclone

Hydrocarbons

Any compound composed of elemental **carbon** and **hydrogen**, hydrocarbons may also contain **chlorine**, oxygen, **nitrogen**, and other atoms. Hydrocarbons are classified according to the arrangement of carbon atoms and the types of chemical bonds. The major classes include *aromatic* or carbon ring compounds, *alkanes* (also called aliphatic or paraffin) compounds with straight or branched chains and single bonds, and *alkenes* and *alkynes* with double and triple bonds, respectively. Most hydrocarbon fuels are a mixture of many compounds. **Gasoline**, for example, includes several hundred hydrocarbon compounds, including paraffins, olefins, and aromatic compounds, and consequently exhibits a host of possible environmental effects. All of the **fossil fuels**, including crude oils and **petroleum**, as well as many other compounds important to industries, are hydrocarbons. Hydrocarbons are environmentally important for several reasons. First, hydrocarbons give off **greenhouse gases**, especially **carbon dioxide**, when burned and are important contributers to smog. In addition, many aromatic hydrocarbons and hydrocarbons containing halogens are toxic or **carcinogen**ic.

Hydrochlorofluorocarbons

The term hydrochlorofluorocarbon (HCFC) refers to halogenated **hydrocarbons** that contain **chlorine** and/or fluorine in place of some hydrogen atoms in the molecule. They are chemical cousins of the **chlorofluorocarbons** (CFCs), but differ from them in that they have less chlorine. A special subgroup of the HCFCs is the hydrofluorocarbons (HFCs), which contain no chlorine at all.

A total of 53 HCFCs and HFCs are possible. Some examples of these families with their identifying product numbers are shown below.

The HCFCs and HFCs have become commercially and environmentally important since the 1980s. Their growing significance has resulted from increasing concerns about the damage being done to stratospheric **ozone** by CFCs.

Significant production of the CFCs began in the late 1930s. At first, they were used almost exclusively as refrigerants.

CHF_3	HFC-23
$CHCl_2CF_3$	HCFC-123
CH_2FCClF_2	HCFC-133b
CH_3CHClF	HCFC-151a

Gradually other applications—especially as propellants and blowing agents—were developed. By 1970, the production of CFCs was growing by more than 10 percent per year, with a worldwide production of well over 662 million pounds (300 million kilograms) of one family member alone, CFC-11.

Environmental studies began to show, however, that CFCs decompose in the upper **atmosphere**. Chlorine atoms produced in this reaction attack ozone molecules (O_3), converting them to normal oxygen (O_2). Since stratospheric ozone provides protection for humans against solar **ultraviolet radiation**, this finding was a source of great concern. By 1987, 31 nations had signed the Montreal Protocol, agreeing to cut back significantly on their production of CFCs.

The question became how nations were to find substitutes for the CFCs. The problem was especially severe in developing nations where CFCs are widely used in refrigeration and air-conditioning systems. Countries like China and India refused to take part in the CFC-reduction plan unless developed nations helped them switch over to an equally satisfactory substitute.

Scientists soon learned that HCFCs were a more benign alternative to the CFCs. They discovered that compounds with less chlorine than the amount present in traditional CFCs were less stable and often decomposed before they reached the **stratosphere**. By mid 1992, the United States **Environmental Protection Agency (EPA)** had selected 11 **chemicals** that they considered to be possible replacements for CFCs. Nine of those compounds are HFCs and two are HCFCs.

The HCFC-HFC solution is not totally satisfactory, however. Computer models have shown that nearly all of the proposed substitutes will have at least some slight effect on the ozone layer and the **greenhouse effect**. In fact, the British government considered banning one possible substitute for CFCs, HCFC-22, almost as soon as the compound was developed. In addition, one of the most promising candidates, HCFC-123, was found to be carcinogenic in rats.

Finally, the cost of replacing CFCs with HCFCs and HFCs is expected to be high. One consulting firm, Metroeconomica, has estimated that CFC substitutes may be six to fifteen times as expensive as CFCs themselves. It predicted that developed nations would have to pay $995 million by the year 2000 to help developing nations convert from CFCs to safer chemicals. *See also* Aerosol; Air pollution; Air pollution control; Air quality; Carcinogen; Ozone layer depletion; Pollution; Pollution control

[*David E. Newton*]

FURTHER READING

Johnson, J. "CFC Substitutes Will Still Add to Global Warming," *New Scientist* 126 (14 April 1990): 20.

MacKenzie, D. "Cheaper Alternatives for CFCs," *New Scientist* 126 (30 June 1990): 39-40.

Pool, R. "Red Flag on CFC Substitute," *Nature* 352 (11 July 1991): 352.

Stone, R. "Ozone Depletion: Warm Reception for Substitute Coolant." *Science* 256 (3 April 1992): 22.

Hydrogen

The lightest of all chemical elements, hydrogen has a density about one-fourteenth that of air. It has a number of special chemical and physical properties. For example, hydrogen has the second lowest boiling and freezing points of all elements. The combustion of hydrogen produces large quantities of heat, with water as the only waste product. From an environmental standpoint, this fact makes hydrogen a highly desirable fuel. Many scientists foresee the day when hydrogen will replace **fossil fuels** as our most important source of energy.

Hydrogeology

Sometimes called **groundwater** hydrology or geohydrology, this branch of **hydrology** is concerned with the relationship of subsurface water and geologic materials. Of primary interest is the saturated zone of subsurface water, called groundwater, which occurs in rock formations and in unconsolidated materials such as sands and gravels. Groundwater is studied in terms of its occurrence, amount, flow, and quality. Historically, much of the work in hydrogeology centered on finding sources of groundwater to supply water for drinking, **irrigation**, and municipal uses. More recently, groundwater contamination by **pesticide**s, chemical **fertilizer**s, toxic wastes, and **petroleum** and **chemical spills** have become new areas of concern for hydrogeologists.

Hydrologic cycle

The natural circulation of water on earth is called the hydrologic cycle. Water cycles from bodies of water, via evaporation to the **atmosphere**, and eventually returns to the oceans as precipitation, **runoff** from streams and rivers, and **groundwater** flow. Water molecules are transformed from liquid to vapor and back to liquid within this cycle. On land, water evaporates from the **soil** or is taken up by plant roots and eventually transpired into the atmosphere through plant leaves; the sum of evaporation and transpiration is called **evapotranspiration**.

Water is recycled continuously. The molecules of water in a glass used to quench your thirst today, at some point in time may have dissolved minerals deep in the earth as groundwater flow, fallen as rain in a tropical typhoon, been transpired by a tropical plant, been temporarily stored in a mountain glacier, or quenched the thirst of people thousands of years ago.

The hydrologic cycle has no real beginning or end but is a circulation of water that is sustained by **solar energy** and influenced by the force of gravity. Because the supply of water on earth is fixed, there is no net gain or loss of water over time. On an average annual basis, global evaporation must equal global precipitation. Likewise, for any body of land or water, changes in storage must equal the total inflow minus the total outflow of water. This is the hydrologic or water balance.

At any point in time, water on earth is either in active circulation or in storage. Water is stored in icecaps, soil, groundwater, the oceans, and other bodies of water. Much of this water is only temporarily stored. The residence time of water storage in the atmosphere is several days and is only about 0.04 percent of the total freshwater on earth. For rivers and streams, residence time is weeks; for lakes and reservoirs, several years; for groundwater, hundreds to thousands of years; for oceans, thousands of years; and for icecaps, tens of thousands of years. As the driving force of the hydrologic cycle, solar radiation provides the energy necessary to evaporate water from the earth's surface, almost three-quarters of which is covered by water. Nearly 86 percent of global precipitation originates from ocean evaporation. Energy consumed by the conversion of liquid water to vapor cools the temperature of the evaporating surface. This same energy, the latent heat of vaporization, is released when water vapor changes back to liquid. In this way, the hydrologic cycle globally redistributes heat energy as well as water.

Once in the atmosphere, water moves in response to weather circulation patterns and is transported often great distances from where it was evaporated. In this way, the hydrologic cycle governs the distribution of precipitation and hence, the availability of fresh water over the earth's surface. About 10 percent of atmospheric water falls as precipitation each day and is simultaneously replaced by evaporation. This 10 percent is unevenly distributed over the earth's surface and, to a large extent, determines the types of **ecosystem**s that exist at any location on earth and likewise governs much of the human activity that occurs on the land.

The earliest civilizations on earth settled in close proximity to fresh water. Subsequently, and for centuries, humans have been striving to correct, or cope with, this uneven distribution of water. Historically, we have extracted stored water or developed new storages in areas of excess, or during periods of excess precipitation, so that water could be available where and when it is most needed.

Understanding processes of the hydrologic cycle can help us develop solutions to water problems. For example, we know that precipitation occurs unevenly over the earth's surface because of many complex factors that trigger precipitation. For precipitation to occur, moisture must be available and the atmosphere must become cooled to the **dew point**, the temperature at which air becomes saturated with water vapor. This cooling of the atmosphere occurs along storm fronts or in areas where moist air masses move into mountain

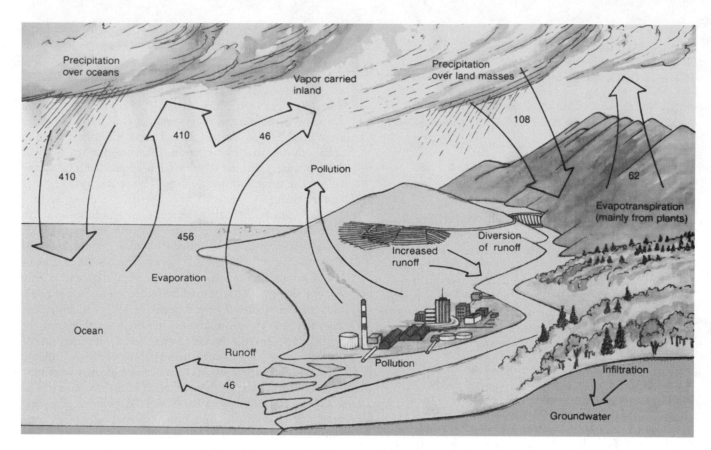

The hydrologic or water cycle.

ranges and are pushed up into colder air. However, atmospheric particles must be present for the moisture to condense upon, and water droplets must coalesce until they are large enough to fall to earth under the influence of gravity.

Recognizing the factors that cause precipitation has resulted in efforts to create conditions favorable for precipitation over land surfaces via cloud seeding. Limited success has been achieved by seeding clouds with particles, thus promoting the condensation-coalescence process. Precipitation has not always increased with cloud seeding and questions of whether cloud seeding limits precipitation in other downwind areas is of both economic and environmental concern.

Parts of the world have abundant moisture in the atmosphere, but it occurs as fog because the mechanisms needed to transform this moisture into precipitation do not exist. In dry coastal areas, for example, some areas have no measurable precipitation for years, but fog is prevalent. By placing huge sheets of **plastic** mesh along coastal areas, fog is intercepted, condenses on the sheets, and provides sufficient drinking water to supply small villages.

Total rainfall alone does not necessarily indicate water abundance or scarcity. The magnitude of evapotranspiration compared to precipitation determines to some extent whether water is abundant or in short supply. On a continent basis, evapotranspiration represents from 56 to 80 percent of annual precipitation. For individual **watershed**s within continents, these percentages are more extreme and point to the importance of evapotranspiration in the hydrologic cycle.

Weather circulation patterns responsible for water shortages in some parts of the world are also responsible for excessive precipitation, floods, and related catastrophes in other parts of the world. Precipitation that falls on land, but that is not stored, evaporated or transpired, becomes excess water. This excess water eventually reaches groundwater, streams, lakes, or the ocean by surface and subsurface flow. If the soil surface is impervious or compacted, water flows over the land surface and reaches stream channels quickly. When surface flow exceeds a channel's capacity, flash **flooding** is the result. Excessive precipitation can saturate soils and cause flooding no matter what the pathway of flow. For example, in 1988 catastrophic flooding and mudslides in Thailand caused over 500 fatalities or missing persons, nearly 700 people were injured, 4,952 homes were lost, and 221 roads and 69 bridges were destroyed. A three-day rainfall of over nearly 40 inches (1,000 millimeters) caused hillslopes to become saturated. The effects of heavy rainfall were exacerbated by the removal of natural forest cover and conversion to rubber plantations and agricultural crops.

Although floods and mudslides occur naturally, many of the pathways of water flow that contribute to such occurrences can be influenced by human activity. Any time vegetative cover is severely reduced and soil exposed to direct rainfall, surface water flow and soil **erosion** can degrade watershed systems and their aquatic ecosystems.

The implications of global warming or **greenhouse effect**s on the hydrologic cycle raise several questions. The possible changes in frequency and occurrence of **drought**s and floods are of major concern, particularly given projections of **population growth**. Global warming can result in some areas becoming drier while others may experience higher precipitation. Globally, increased temperature will increase evaporation from oceans and ultimately result in more precipitation. The pattern of precipitation changes over the earth's surface, however, cannot be predicted at the present time.

The hydrologic cycle influences **nutrient** cycling of ecosystems, processes of soil erosion and transport of **sediment**, and the transport of pollutants. Water is an excellent liquid solvent; minerals, salts, and nutrients become dissolved and transported by water flow. The hydrologic cycle is an important driving mechanism of nutrient cycling. As a transporting agent, water moves minerals and nutrients to plant roots. As plants die and decay, water leaches out nutrients and carries them downstream. The physical action of rainfall on soil surfaces and the forces of running water can seriously erode soils and transport sediments downstream. Any minerals, nutrients, and pollutants within the soil are likewise transported by water flow into groundwater, streams, lakes, or estuaries.

Atmospheric moisture transports and deposits atmospheric pollutants, including those responsible for **acid rain**. Sulfur and **nitrogen oxides** are added to the atmosphere by the burning of **fossil fuels**. Being an excellent solvent, water in the atmosphere forms acidic compounds that become transported via the atmosphere and deposited great distances from their original site. Atmospheric pollutants and acid rain have damaged freshwater lakes in the Scandinavian countries and terrestrial vegetation in eastern Europe. In 1983, such pollution caused an estimated $1.2 billion loss of forests in the former West Germany alone. Once pollutants enter the atmosphere and become subject to the hydrologic cycle, problems of acid rain have little chance for resolution. However, programs that reduce atmospheric **emission**s in the first place provide some hope.

An improved understanding of the hydrologic cycle is needed to better manage **water resources** and our **environment**. Opportunities exist to improve our global environment, but better knowledge of human impacts on the hydrologic cycle is needed to avoid unwanted environmental effects. *See also* Estuary; Leaching

[*Kenneth N. Brooks*]

FURTHER READING

Lee, R. *Forest Hydrology*. New York: Columbia University Press, 1980.

Nash, N. C. "Chilean Engineers Find Water for Desert by Harvesting Fog in Nets," *New York Times* (14 July 1992): B5.

Opportunities in the Hydrologic Sciences. Committee on Opportunities in the Hydrologic Sciences, Water Sciences Technology Board. National Research Council. Washington, DC: National Academy Press, 1991.

Postel, S. "Air Pollution, Acid Rain, and the Future of Forests." *Worldwatch Paper 58*. Washington, DC: Worldwatch Institute, 1984.

Rao, Y. S. "Flash Floods in Southern Thailand." *Tiger Paper* 15 (1988): 1-2. Regional Office for Asia and the Pacific (RAPA), Food and Agricultural Organization of the United Nations. Bangkok.

Van der Leeden, F., F. L. Troise, and D. K. Todd. *The Water Encyclopedia*. 2nd ed. Chelsea, MI: Lewis Publishers, 1990.

Hydrology

The science and study of water, including its physical and chemical properties and its occurrence on earth. Most commonly, hydrology encompasses the study of the amount, distribution, circulation, timing, and quality of water. It includes the study of rainfall, snow accumulation and melt, water movement over and through the **soil**, the flow of water in saturated, underground geologic materials (**groundwater**), the flow of water in channels (called streamflow), evaporation and transpiration, and the physical, chemical and biological characteristics of water. Solving problems concerned with water excesses, **flooding**, water shortages, and **water pollution** are in the domain of hydrologists. With increasing concern about water pollution and its effects on humans and on aquatic **ecosystem**s, the practice of hydrology has expanded into the study and management of chemical and biological characteristics of water.

Hydropower

See **Aswan High Dam, Egypt; Dams (environmental effects); Glen Canyon Dam; James Bay hydropower project; Low-head hydropower; Tellico Dam; Tennessee Valley Authority; Three Gorges Dam (China)**

Hydroponics

Hydroponics is the practice of growing plants in water as opposed to soil. It comes from the Greek *hydro* ("water") and *ponos* ("labor"), implying "water working." The essential macro- and micro- (trace) nutrients needed by the plants are supplied in the water.

Hydroponic methods have been used for more than 2,000 years, dating back to the Hanging Gardens of Babylon. More recently, it has been used by plant physiologists to discover which nutrients are essential for plant growth. Unlike **soil**, where nutrient levels are unknown and variable, precise amounts and kinds of minerals can be added to deionized water, and removed individually, to find out their role in plant growth and development. During World War II hydroponics was used to grow vegetable crops by U.S. troops stationed on some Pacific islands.

Today, hydroponics is becoming a more popular alternative to conventional agriculture in locations with low or inaccessible sources of water or where land available for farming is scarce. For example, islands and desert areas like the American Southwest and the Middle East are prime regions for hydroponics. Plants are typically grown in greenhouses to prevent water loss. Even in temperate areas where fresh water is readily available, hydroponics can be used to grow crops in greenhouses during the winter months.

Two methods are traditionally used in hydroponics. The original technique is the water method, where plants are supported from a wire mesh or similar framework so that the roots hang into troughs which receive continuous supplies of nutrients. A recent modification is a nutrient-film technique (NFT), also called the nutrient-flow method, where the trough is lined with plastic. Water flows continuously over the roots, decreasing the stagnant boundary layer surrounding each root, and thus enhances nutrient uptake. This provides a versatile, lightweight, and inexpensive system. In the second method, plants are supported in a growing medium such as sterile sand, gravel, crushed volcanic rock, vermiculite, perlite, sawdust, peatmoss, or rice hulls. The nutrient solution is supplied from overhead or underneath holding tanks either continuously or semi-continuously using a drip method. The nutrient solution is usually not reused.

On some Caribbean Islands like St. Croix, hydroponics is being used in conjunction with intensive fish farms (e.g., tilapia) which use recirculated water (a practice is more recently known as aquaponics). This is a "win-win" situation because the nitrogenous wastes, which are toxic to the fish, are passed through large greenhouses with hydroponically-grown plants like lettuce. The plants remove the nutrients and the water is returned to the fish tanks. There is a sensitive balance between stocking density of fish and lettuce production. Too high a ratio of lettuce plants to fish results in lower lettuce production due to nutrient limitation. Too low a ratio also results in low vegetable production, but this time as a result of the buildup of toxic chemicals. The optimum yield came from a ratio of 1.9 lettuce plants to 1 fish. One pound (0.45 kg) of feed per day was appropriate to feed 33 lbs (15 kg) of tilapia fingerlings, which sustained 189 lettuce plants and produced nearly 3,300 heads of lettuce annually. When integrated systems (fish-hydroponic recirculating units) are compared to separate production systems, the results clearly favor the former. The combined costs and chemical requirements of the separate production systems was nearly two to three times greater than that of the recirculating system to produce the same amount of lettuce and fish. However, there are some drawbacks that must be considered—disease outbreaks in plants and/or fish; the need to critically maintain proper nutrient (especially trace element), plant, and fish levels; uncertainties in fish and market prices; and the need for highly-skilled labor. The integrated method can be adapted to grow other types of vegetables like strawberries, ornamental plants like roses, and other types of animals such as shellfish. Some teachers have even incorporated this technique into their classrooms to illustrate ecological as well as botanical and culture principles.

Some proponents of hydroponic gardening make fairly optimistic claims and state that a sophisticated unit is no more expensive than an equivalent parcel of farmed land. They also argue that hydroponic units (commonly called "hydroponicums") require less attention than terrestrial agriculture. Some examples of different types of "successful" hydroponicums are: a person in the desert area of southern California has used the NFT system for over 18 years and grows his plants void of substate in water contained in open cement troughs that cover 3 acres (7.5 ha); a hydroponicum in Orlando, Florida, utilizes the Japanese system of planting seedlings on styrofoam boards that float on the surface of a nutrient bath which is constantly aerated; an outfit in Queens, New York, uses the Israeli Ein-Gedi system which allows plant roots to hang free inside a tube which is sprayed regularly with a nutrient solution, yielding 150,000 lbs (68,000 kg) of tomatoes, 100,000 lbs (45,500 kg) of cucumbers, and one million heads of lettuce per acre (0.4 ha) each year; and finally, a farmer in Blooming Prairie, Minnesota, uses the NFT system in a greenhouse to grow Bibb and leafy lettuce year-round so he can sell his produce to area hospitals, some supermarkets, and a few produce warehouses.

Most people involved in hydroponics agree that the main disadvantage is the high cost for labor, lighting, water, and energy. Root fungal infections can also be easily spread. Advantages include the ability to grow crops in arid regions or where land is at a premium; more controlled conditions, such as the ability to grow plants indoors, and thus minimize pests and weeds; greater planting densities; and constant supply of nutrients. Hydroponic gardening is becoming more popular for home gardeners. It may also be a viable option to growing crops in some developing countries. Overall, the future looks bright for hydroponics.

[*John Korstad*]

FURTHER READING

Nicol, E. "Hydroponics and Aquaculture in the High School Classroom." *The American Biology Teacher* 52 (1990): 182-4.

Rakocy, J. E. "Hydroponic Lettuce Production in a Recirculating Fish Culture System." *Island Perspectives* 3 (1988-89): 5-10.

Resh, H.M. *Hydroponic Food Production: A Definitive Guidebook for the Advanced Home Gardener and Commercial Hydroponci Grower*, 5th ed. Santa Barbara: Woodbridge Press (1995).

Saffell, H.L. *How to Start on a Shoestring and Make a Profit with Hydroponics.* Franklin, TN: Mayhill Press (1994).

Hypolimnion

See **Great Lakes**

I

Ice age

Ice age usually refers to the Pleistocene epoch, the most recent occurrence of continental **glaciation**. Beginning several million years ago in **Antarctica**, it is marked by at least four major advances and retreats (excluding Antarctica). Ice ages occur during times when more snow falls during the winter than is lost by melting, evaporation, and loss of ice chunks in water during the summer. Alternating glacial and interglacial stages are best explained by a combination of earth's orbital cycles and changes in carbon dioxide levels. These cycles operate on time scales of tens of millennia. By contrast, global warming projections involve decades, a far more imminent concern for humankind.

Ice age refugia

The series of **ice age**s that occurred between 2.4 million and 10,000 years ago had a dramatic effect on the **climate** and the life forms in the tropics. During each glacial period the tropics became both cooler and drier, turning some areas of **tropical rain forest** into dry seasonal forest or **savanna**. For reasons associated with local **topography**, geography, and climate, some areas of forest escaped the dry periods, and acted as refuges (refugia) for forest biota. During subsequent interglacials, when humid conditions returned to the tropics, the forests expanded and were repopulated by plants and animals from the **species**-rich refugia.

Ice age refugia today correspond to present day areas of tropical forest that typically receive a high rainfall and often contain unusually large numbers of species, including a high proportion of endemic species. These species-rich refugia are surrounded by relatively species-poor areas of forest. Refugia are also centers of distribution for obligate forest species (such as the **gorilla**) with a present day narrow and disjunct distribution best explained by invoking past episodes of **deforestation** and reforestation. The location and extent of the forest refugia have been mapped in both Africa and South America. In the African rain forests there are three main centers of species richness and endemism recognized for mammals, birds, reptiles, amphibians, butterflies, freshwater crabs, and flowering plants. These centers are in Upper Guinea, Cameroon, and Gabon, and the eastern rim of the Zaire basin. In the **Amazon Basin** more than twenty refugia have been identified for different groups of animals and plants in Peru, Columbia, Venezuela, and Brazil.

The precise effect of the ice ages on **biodiversity** in tropical rain forests is currently a matter of debate. Some have argued that the repeated fluctuations between humid and **arid** phases created opportunities for the rapid **evolution** of certain forest organisms. Others have argued the opposite — that the climatic fluctuations resulted in a net loss of species diversity through an increase in the **extinction** rate. It has also been suggested that refugia owe their species richness not to past climate changes but to other underlying causes such as a favorable local climate, or **soil**.

The discovery of centers of high biodiversity and endemism within the tropical rain forest **biome** has profound implications for **conservation** biology. A "refuge rationale" has been proposed by conservationists, whereby ice age refugia are given high priority for preservation, since this would save the largest number of species, (including many unnamed, threatened, and **endangered species**), from extinction.

Since refugia survived the past dry-climate phases, they have traditionally supplied the plants and animals for the restocking of the new-growth forests when wet conditions returned. Modern deforestation patterns, however, do not take into account forest history or biodiversity, and both forest refugia and more recent forests are being destroyed equally. For the first time in millions of years, future tropical forests which survive the present mass deforestation episode could have no species-rich centers from which they can be restocked. *See also* Biotic community; Deciduous forest; Desertification; Ecosystem; Environment; Mass extinction

[Neil Cumberlidge]

FURTHER READING

"Biological Diversification in the Tropics." *Proceedings of the Fifth International Symposium of the Association for Tropical Biology, at Caracas, Venezuela, February 8-13, 1979*, edited by Ghillean T. Prance. New York: Columbia University Press, 1982.

Collins, Mark, ed. *The Last Rain Forests*. London: Mitchell Beazley Publishers, 1990.

Kingdon, Jonathan. *Island Africa: The Evolution of Africa's Rare Animals and Plants*. Princeton, NJ: Princeton University Press, 1989.

Sayer, Jeffrey A., et al., eds. *The Conservation Atlas of Tropical Forests*. New York: Simon and Schuster, 1992.

Whitmore, T. C. *An Introduction to Tropical Rain Forests.* Oxford, England: Clarenden Press, 1990.

Wilson, E. O., ed. *Biodiversity.* Washington D.C.: National Academy Press, 1988.

Impervious material

As used in **hydrology**, this term refers to rock and **soil** material that occurs at the earth's surface or within the subsurface which does not permit water to enter or move through them in any perceptible amounts. These materials normally have small-sized pores or have pores that have become clogged (sealed) which severely restrict water entry and movement. At the ground surface, rock outcrops, road surfaces, or soil surfaces that have been severely compacted would be considered impervious. These areas shed rainfall easily, causing overland flow or surface **runoff** which pick up and transport soil particles and cause excessive soil **erosion**. Soils or geologic strata beneath the earth's surface are considered impervious, or impermeable, if the size of the pores is small and/or if the pores are not connected.

Improvement cutting

Removal of crooked, forked, or diseased trees from a forest in which tree diameters are 5 in (13 cm) or larger. In forests where trees are smaller, the same process is called cleaning or weeding. Both have the objective of improving **species** composition, stem quality and/or growth rate of the forest. Straight, healthy, vigorous trees of the desired species are favored. By discriminating against certain tree species and eliminating trees with cavities or insect problems, improvement cuts can reduce the variety of **habitat**s and thereby diminish **biodiversity**. An improvement cut is the initial step to prepare a neglected or unmanaged stand for future harvest. *See also* Clear-cutting; Forest management; Selection cutting

In situ mining
See **Bureau of Mines**

Inbreeding

Inbreeding occurs when closely related individuals mate with one another. Inbreeding may happen in a small population or due to other isolating factors; the consequence is that little new genetic information is added to the **gene pool**. Thus recessive, deleterious alleles become more plentiful and evident in the population. Manifestations of inbreeding are known as *inbreeding depression*. A general loss of fitness often results and may cause high infant mortality, and lower birth weights, **fecundity**, and longevity. Inbreeding depression is a major concern when attempting to protect small populations from **extinction**.

Incineration

As a method of **waste management**, incineration refers to the burning of waste. It helps reduce the volume of **landfill** material and can render **toxic substance**s non-hazardous, provided certain strict guidelines are followed. There are two basic types of incineration: municipal and **hazardous waste** incineration.

Municipal Waste Incineration

The process of incineration involves the combination of organic compounds in **solid waste**s with oxygen at high temperature to convert them to ash and gaseous products. A municipal incinerator consists of a series of unit operations which include a loading area under slightly negative pressure to avoid the escape of odors, a refuse bin which is loaded by a grappling bucket, a charging hopper leading to an inclined feeder and a furnace of varying type—usually of a horizontal burning grate type—a **combustion** chamber equipped with a bottom ash and clinker discharge, followed by a gas flue system to an expansion chamber. If byproduct stream is to be produced either for heating or power generation purposes, then the downstream flue system includes heat exchanger tubing as well. After the heat has been exchanged, the **flue gas** proceeds to a series of gas cleanup systems which neutralizes the acid gases (**sulfur dioxide** and hydrochloric acid, the latter resulting from burning chlorinated plastic products), followed by gas **scrubbers** and then solid/gas separation systems such as **baghouse**s before dischargement to **tall stacks**. The stack system contains a variety of sensing and control devices to enable the furnace to operate at maximum efficiency consistent with minimal **particulate** emissions. A continuous log of monitoring systems is also required for compliance with county and state environmental quality regulations.

There are several products from a municipal incinerator system: items which are removed before combustion such as large metal pieces; grate or bottom ash (which is usually water-sprayed after removal from the furnace for safe storage); fly (or top ash) which is removed from the flue system generally mixed with products from the acid neutralization process; and finally the flue gases which are expelled to the **environment**. If the system is operating optimally, the flue gases will meet **emission** requirements, and the **heavy metals** from the wastes will be concentrated in the **fly ash**. (Typically these heavy metals, which originate from volatile metallic constituents, are **lead** and **arsenic**.) The fly ash typically is then stored in a suitable landfill to avoid future

Diagram of a municipal incinerator.

problems of **leaching** of heavy metals. Some municipal systems blend the bottom ash with the top ash in the plant in order to reduce the level of heavy metals by dilution. This practice is undesirable from an ultimate environmental viewpoint.

There are many advantages and disadvantages to municipal waste incineration. Some of the advantages are as follows: 1) The waste volume is reduced to a small fraction of the original. 2) Reduction is rapid and does not require semi-infinite **residence time**s in a landfill. 3) For a large metropolitan area, waste can be incinerated on site, minimizing transportation costs. 4) The ash residue is generally sterile, although it may require special disposal methods. 5) By use of gas clean-up equipment, **discharge**s of flue gases to the environment can meet stringent requirements and be readily monitored. 6) Incinerators are much more compact than landfills and can have minimal odor and vermin problems if properly designed. 7) Some of the costs of operation can be reduced by heat-recovery techniques such as the sale of steam to municipalities or electrical energy generation.

There are disadvantages to municipal waste incineration as well. For example: 1) Generally the capital cost is high and is escalating as **emission standards** change. 2) Permitting requirements are becoming increasingly more difficult to obtain. 3) Supplemental fuel may be required to burn municipal wastes, especially if **yard waste** is not removed prior to collection. 4) Certain items such as **mercury**-containing batteries can produce emissions of mercury which the gas

cleanup system may not be designed to remove. 5) Continuous skilled operation and close maintenance of process control is required, especially since stack monitoring equipment reports any failure of the equipment which could result in mandated shut down. 6) Certain materials are not burnable and must be removed at the source. 7) Traffic to and from the incinerator can be a problem unless timing and routing are carefully managed. 8) The incinerator, like a landfill, also has a limited life, although its lifetime can be increased by capital expenditures. 9) Incinerators also require landfills for the ash. The ash usually contains heavy metals and must be placed in a specially-designed landfill to avoid leaching.

Hazardous Waste Incineration

For the incineration of hazardous waste, a greater degree of control, higher temperatures, and a more rigorous monitoring system are required. An incinerator burning hazardous waste must be designed, constructed, and maintained to meet **Resource Conservation and Recovery Act (RCRA)** standards. An incinerator burning hazardous waste must achieve a destruction and removal efficiency of at least 99.99 percent for each principal organic hazardous constituent. For certain listed constituents such as **polychlorinated biphenyl (PCB)**, mass air emissions from an incinerator are required to be greater than 99.9999 percent. The **Toxic Substances Control Act** requires certain standards for the incineration of PCBs. For example, the flow of PCB to the incinerator must stop automatically whenever the combustion temperature drops below the specified value; there must be continuous monitoring of the stack for a list of emissions; scrubbers must be used for hydrochloric acid control; among others.

Recently **medical waste**s have been treated by steam sterilization, followed by incineration with treatment of the flue gases with activated **carbon** for maximum absorption of organic constituents. The latter system is being installed at the Mayo Clinic in Rochester, Minnesota, as a model medical disposal system. *See also* Fugitive emissions; Solid waste incineration; Solid waste volume reduction; Stack emissions

[*Malcolm T. Hepworth*]

FURTHER READING

Brunner, C. R. *Handbook of Incineration Systems.* New York: McGraw-Hill, 1991.

Edwards, B. H., et al. *Emerging Technologies for the Control of Hazardous Wastes.* Park Ridge, NJ: Noyes Data Corporation, 1983.

Hickman, H. L., Jr., et al. *Thermal Conversion Systems for Municipal Solid Waste.* Park Ridge, NJ: Noyes Publications, 1984.

Vesilind, R. A., and Rimer, A. E. *Unit Operations in Resource Recovery Engineering.* Englewood Cliffs, NJ: Prentice-Hall, 1981.

Wentz, C. A. *Hazardous Waste Management.* New York: McGraw-Hill, 1989.

Incineration, solid waste
See **Solid waste incineration**

Indicator organism

Indicator organisms, sometimes called **bioindicator**s, are plant or animal **species** known to be either particularly tolerant or particularly sensitive to **pollution**. The health of an organism can often be associated with a specific type or intensity of pollution, and its presence can then be used to indicate polluted conditions relative to unimpacted conditions.

Tubificid worms are an example of organisms that can indicate pollution. Tubificid worms live in the bottom **sediment**s of streams and lakes, and they are highly tolerant of sewage. In a river polluted by **wastewater discharge** from a **sewage treatment** plant, it is common to see a large increase in the numbers of tubificid worms in stream sediments immediately downstream. Upstream of the discharge, the numbers of tubificid worms are often much lower or almost absent, reflecting cleaner conditions. The number of tubificid worms also decreases downstream, as the discharge is diluted.

Pollution-intolerant organisms can also be used to indicate polluted conditions. The larvae of mayflies live in stream sediments and are known to be particularly sensitive to pollution. In a river receiving wastewater discharge, mayflies will show the opposite pattern of tubificid worms. The mayfly larvae are normally present in large numbers above the discharge point; they decrease or disappear at the discharge point and reappear further downstream as the effects of the discharge are diluted.

Similar examples of indicator organisms can be found among plants, fish, and other biological groups. Giant reedgrass (*Phragmites australis*) is a common marsh plant that is typically indicative of disturbed conditions in **wetlands**. Among fish, disturbed conditions may be indicated by the disappearance of sensitive species like trout which require clear, cold waters to thrive.

The usefulness of indicator organisms is limited. While their presence or absence provides a reliable general picture of polluted conditions, they are often little help in identifying the exact sources of pollution. In the sediments of New York Harbor, for example, pollution-tolerant insect larvae are overwhelmingly dominant. However, it is impossible to attribute the large larval populations to just one of the sources of pollution there, which include ship traffic, sewage and industrial discharge, and **storm runoff**. As more is learned about the physiology and life history of indicator organisms and their individual responses to different types of pollution, it may be possible to draw more specific conclusions. *See also* Algal bloom; Nitrogen cycle; Water pollution

[*Usha Vedagiri*]

FURTHER READING

Browder, J. A., ed. *Aquatic Organisms As Indicators of Environmental Pollution.* Bethesda, MD: American Water Resources Association, 1988.

Connell, D. W., and G. J. Miller. *Chemistry and Ecotoxicology of Pollution.* New York: Wiley-Interscience, 1984.

Indigenous peoples

Cultural or ethnic groups living in an area where their culture developed or where their people have existed for many generations. Most of the world's indigenous peoples live in remote forests, mountains, **desert**s, or arctic **tundra**, where modern technology, trade, and cultural influence are slow to penetrate. Many had much larger territories historically but have retreated to, or been forced into, small, remote areas by the advance of more powerful groups. Indigenous groups, also sometimes known as native or tribal peoples, are usually recognized in comparison to a country's dominant cultural group. In the United States the dominant, non-indigenous cultural groups speak English, has historic roots in Europe, and maintain strong economic, technological, and communication ties with Europe, Asia, and other parts of the world. Indigenous groups in the United States, on the other hand, include scores of groups, from the southern Seminole and Cherokee to the Inuit and Yupik peoples of the Arctic coast. These groups speak hundreds of different languages or dialects, some of which have been on this continent for thousands of years. Their traditional economies were based mainly on small-scale subsistence gathering, hunting, fishing, and farming. Many indigenous peoples around the world continue to engage in these ancient economic practices.

It is often difficult to distinguish who is and who is not indigenous. European-Americans and Asian-Americans are usually not considered indigenous even if they have been here for many generations. This is because their cultural roots connect to other regions. On the other hand, a German residing in Germany is also not usually spoken of as indigenous, even though by any strict definition she or he *is* indigenous. This is because the term is customarily reserved to denote economic or political minorities—groups that are relatively powerless within the countries where they live.

Historically, indigenous peoples have suffered great losses in both population and territory to the spread of larger, more technologically advanced groups, especially (but not only) Europeans. Hundreds of indigenous cultures have disappeared entirely just in the past century. In recent decades, however, indigenous groups have begun to receive greater international recognition, and they have begun to learn effective means to defend their lands and interests—including attracting international media attention and suing their own governments in court. The main reason for this increased attention and success may be that scientists and economic development organizations have recently become interested in biological diversity and in the loss of world **rain forest**s. The survival of indigenous peoples, of the world's forests, and of the world's gene pools are now understood to be deeply interdependent. Indigenous peoples, who know and depend on some of the world's most endangered and biologically diverse **ecosystem**s, are increasingly looked on as a unique source of information, and their subsistence economies are beginning to look like admirable alternatives to large-scale logging, mining, and conversion of jungles to monocrop agriculture.

There are probably between 4,000 and 5,000 different indigenous groups in the world; they can be found on every continent (except **Antarctica**) and in nearly every country. The total population of indigenous peoples amounts to between 200 million and 600 million (depending upon how groups are identified and their populations counted) out of a world population just over 5.5 billion. Some groups number in the millions; others comprise only a few dozen people. Despite their world-wide distribution, indigenous groups are especially concentrated in a number of "cultural diversity hot spots," including Indonesia, India, Papua New Guinea, Australia, Mexico, Brazil, Zaire, Cameroon, and Nigeria. Each of these countries has scores, or even hundreds, of different language groups. Neighboring valleys in Papua New Guinea often contain distinct cultural groups with unrelated languages and religions. These regions are also recognized for their unusual biological diversity. Both indigenous cultures and rare **species** survive best in areas where modern technology does not easily penetrate. Advanced technological economies involved in international trade consume tremendous amounts of land, wood, water, and minerals. Indigenous groups tend to rely on intact ecosystems and on a tremendous variety of plant and animal species. Because their numbers are relatively small and their technology simple, they usually do little long-lasting damage to their **environment** despite their dependence on the resources around them. The remote areas where indigenous peoples and their natural environment survive, however, are also the richest remaining reserves of natural resources in most countries. Frequently state governments claim all tim-

ber, mineral, water, and land rights in areas traditionally occupied by tribal groups. In Indonesia, Malaysia, Burma (Myanmar), China, Brazil, Zaire, Cameroon, and many other important cultural diversity regions, timber and mining concessions are frequently sold to large or international companies that can quickly and efficiently destroy an ecological area and its people. Usually native peoples, because they lack political and economic clout, have no recourse to losing their homes. Generally they are relocated, attempts are made to integrate them into mainstream culture, and they join laboring classes in the general economy.

Indigenous rights have begun to strengthen in recent years. As long as international media attention continues to give them the attention they need—especially in the form of international economic and political pressure on state governments—and as long as indigenous leaders are able to continue developing their own defense strategies and legal tactics, the survival rate of indigenous peoples and their environments may improve significantly.

[*Mary Ann Cunningham*]

FURTHER READING

Durning, A. T. *Guardians of the Land: Indigenous Peoples and the Health of the Earth. Worldwatch Paper* 112. Washington, DC: Worldwatch Institute, 1992.

Redford, K. H., and C. Padoch. *Conservation of Neotropical Forests: Working from Traditional Resources Use.* New York: Columbia University Press, 1992.

Indoor air quality

An assessment of air quality in buildings and homes based on physical and chemical monitoring of contaminants, physiological measurements, and/or psychosocial perceptions. Factors contributing to the quality of indoor air include lighting, ergonomics, thermal comfort, **tobacco smoke**, noise, ventilation, and psychosocial or work-organizational factors such as employee stress and satisfaction. "**Sick building syndrome**" (SBS) and "building-related illness" (BRI) are responses to indoor air pollution commonly described by office workers. Most symptoms are nonspecific; they progressively worsen during the week, occur more frequently in the afternoon, and disappear on the weekend.

Poor indoor air quality (IAQ) in industrial settings such as factories, coal mines, and foundries has long been recognized as a health risk to workers and has been regulated by the **U.S. Occupational Safety and Health Administration (OSHA)**. The contaminant levels in industrial settings can be hundreds or thousands of times higher than the levels found in homes and offices. Nonetheless, indoor air quality in homes and offices has become an environmental priority in many countries, and federal IAQ legislation has been introduced in the U.S. Congress for the past several years. However, none has yet passed, and currently the U.S. **Environmental Protection Agency (EPA)** has no enforcement authority in this area.

Importance of IAQ

The prominence of IAQ issues has risen in part due to well-publicized incidents involving outbreaks of Legion-

Chloroform
Source: Chlorine-treated water in hot showers
Possible threat: Cancer

Para-dichlorobenzene
Source: Air fresheners, mothball crystals
Threat: Cancer

Tetrachloroethylene
Source: Dry-cleaning-fluid fumes on clothes
Threat: Nerve disorders, damage to liver and kidneys, possible cancer

1,1,1-Trichloroethane
Source: Aerosol sprays
Threat: Dizziness, irregular breathing

Formaldehyde
Source: Furniture stuffing, paneling, particle board, foam insulation
Threat: Irritation of eyes, throat, skin, and lungs; nausea; dizziness

Nitrogen Oxides
Source: Unvented gas stoves and kerosene heaters, wood stoves
Threat: Irritated lungs, children's colds, headaches

Benzo-a-pyrene
Source: Tobacco smoke, wood stoves
Threat: Lung cancer

Styrene
Source: Carpets, plastic products
Threat: Kidney and liver damage

Asbestos
Source: Pipe insulation, vinyl ceiling and floor tiles
Threat: Lung disease, lung cancer

Tobacco Smoke
Source: Cigarettes
Threat: Lung cancer, respiratory ailments, heart diseases

Carbon Monoxide
Sources: Faulty furnaces, unvented gas stoves and kerosene heaters, wood stoves
Threat: Headaches, drowsiness, irregular heartbeat

Methylene Chloride
Source: Paint strippers and thinners
Threat: Nerve disorders, diabetes

Radon-222
Source: Radioactive soil and rock surrounding foundation, water supply
Threat: Lung cancer

Some major indoor air pollutants.

naires' disease, Pontiac fever, sick building syndrome, multiple chemical sensitivity, and **asbestos** mitigation in public buildings such as schools. Legionnaire's disease, for example, caused twenty-nine deaths in 1976 in a Philadelphia hotel due to infestation of the building's air conditioning system by a bacterium called *Legionella pneumophila*. This microbe affects the gastrointestinal tract, kidneys, and central nervous system. It also causes the non-fatal Pontiac fever.

IAQ is important to the general public for several reasons. First, individuals typically spend the vast majority of their time—80 or 90 percent—indoors. Second, an emphasis on energy conservation measures, such as reducing air exchange rates in ventilation systems and using more energy efficient but synthetic materials, has increased levels of air contaminants in offices and homes. New "tight" buildings have few cracks and openings so minimal fresh air enters such buildings. Low ventilation and exchange rates can increase indoor levels of **carbon monoxide**, **nitrogen oxides**, **ozone**, **volatile organic compound**s, bioaerosols, and **pesticide**s and maintain high levels of second-hand tobacco smoke generated inside the building. Thus, many contaminants are found indoors at levels that greatly exceed outdoor levels. Third, an increasing number of synthetic chemicals—found in building materials, furnishing, cleaning and hygiene products—are used indoors. Fourth, studies show that exposure to indoor contaminants such as **radon**, asbestos, and tobacco smoke pose significant health risks. Fifth, poor IAQ is thought to adversely affect children's development

and lower productivity in the adult population. Demands for indoor air quality investigations of "sick" and problem buildings have increased rapidly in recent years, and a large fraction of buildings are known or suspected to have IAQ problems.

Indoor Contaminants

Indoor air contains many contaminants at varying but generally low concentration levels. Common contaminants include radon and radon progeny from the entry of soil gas and groundwater and from concrete and other mineral-based building materials; tobacco smoke from cigarette and pipe smoking; formaldehyde from polyurethane foam insulation and building materials; volatile organic compounds (VOCs) emitted from binders and resins in carpets, furniture, or building materials, as well as VOCs used in dry cleaning processes and as propellants and constituents of personal use and cleaning products, like hair sprays and polishes; pesticides and insecticides; carbon monoxide, nitrogen oxides, and other combustion productions from gas stoves, appliances, and vehicles; asbestos from high temperature insulation; and biological contaminants including **virus**es, bacteria, molds, pollen, dust mites, and indoor and outdoor biota. Many or most of these contaminants are present at low levels in all indoor environments.

The quality of indoor air can change rapidly in time and from room to room. There are many diverse sources that emit various physical and chemical forms of contaminants.

Some releases are slow and continuous, such as out-gassing associated with building and furniture materials, while others are nearly instantaneous, like the use of cleaners and **aerosol**s. Many building surfaces demonstrate significant interactions with contaminants in the form of sorption-desorption processes. Building-specific variation in air exchange rates, mixing, filtration, building and furniture surfaces, and other factors alter dispersion mechanisms and contaminant lifetimes. Most buildings employ filters that can remove particles and aerosols. Filtration systems do not effectively remove very small particles and have no effect on gases, vapors, and odors. Ventilation and air exchange units designed into the heating and cooling systems of buildings are designed to diminish levels of these contaminants by dilution. In most buildings, however, ventilation systems are turned off at night after working hours, leading to an increase in contaminants through the night. Though operation and maintenance issues are estimated to cause the bulk of indoor air quality problems, deficiencies in the design of the heating, ventilating and air conditioning (HVAC) system can cause problems as well. For example, locating a building's fresh air intake near a truck loading dock will bring diesel fumes and other noxious contaminants into the building.

Health Impacts

Exposures to indoor contaminants can cause a variety of health problems. Depending on the pollutant and exposure, health problems related to indoor air quality may include non-malignant respiratory effects, including mucous membrane irritation, allergic reactions, and **asthma**; cardiovascular effects; infectious diseases such as Legionnaires' disease; immunologic diseases such as hypersensitivity pneumonitis; skin irritations; malignancies; neuropsychiatric effects; and other non-specific systemic effects such as lethargy, headache, and nausea. In addition indoor air contaminants such as radon, formaldehyde, asbestos, and other chemicals are suspected or known carcinogens. There is also growing concern over the possible effects of low level exposures on suppressing reproductive and growth capabilities and impacting the immune, endocrine, and nervous systems.

Solving IAQ Problems

Acute indoor air quality problems can be greatly eliminated by identifying, evaluating, and controlling the sources of contaminants. IAQ control strategies include the use of higher ventilation and air exchange rates, the use of lower emission and more benign constituents in building and consumer products (including product use restriction regulations), air cleaning and filtering, and improved building practices in new construction. Radon may be reduced by inexpensive subslab ventilation systems. New buildings could implement a day of "bake-out," which heats the building to temperatures over 90°F (32°C) to drive out volatile organic compounds. Filters to remove ozone, organic compounds, and sulfur gases may be used to condition incoming and recirculated air. Copy machines and other emission sources should have special ventilation systems. Building designers, operators, contractors, maintenance personnel, and occupants are recognizing that healthy buildings result from combined and continued efforts to control emission sources, provide adequate ventilation and air cleaning, and good maintenance of building systems. Efforts toward this direction will greatly enhance indoor air quality.

[*Stuart Batterman*]

FURTHER READING

Godish, T. *Indoor Air Pollution Control*. Chelsea, MI: Lewis, 1989.

Kay, J. G., et al. *Indoor Air Pollution: Radon, Bioaerosols and VOCs*. Chelsea, MI: Lewis, 1991.

Kreiss, K. "The Epidemiology of Building-Related Complaints and Illnesses." *Occupational Medicine: State of the Art Reviews* 4 (1989): 575-92.

Samet, J. M., and J. D. Spengler. *Indoor Air Pollution: A Health Perspective*. Baltimore: Johns Hopkins University Press, 1991.

Industrial waste treatment

Many different types of solid, liquid, and gaseous wastes are discharged by industries. Most industrial waste is recycled, treated and discharged, or placed in a landfill. There is no one means of managing industrial wastes because the nature of the wastes varies widely from one industry to another. One company might generate a waste that can be treated readily and discharged to the environment (direct discharge) or to a sewer in which case final treatment might be accomplished at a publicly owned treatment works (POTW). Treatment at the company before discharge to a sewer is referred to as pretreatment. Another company might generate a waste which is regarded as hazardous and therefore requires special management procedures related to storage, transportation and final disposal.

The pertinent legislation governing to what extent wastewaters need to be treated before discharge is the 1972 Clean Water Act (CWA). Major amendments to the CWA were passed in 1977 and 1987. The Environmental Protection Agency (EPA) was also charged with the responsibility of regulating the priority pollutants under the CWA. The CWA specifies that toxic and nonconventional pollutants are to be treated with the Best Available Technology (BAT). Gaseous pollutants are regulated under the Clean Air Act (CAA), promulgated in 1970 and amended in 1977 and 1990. An important part of the CAA consists of measures to attain and maintain National Ambient Air Quality Standards (NAAQS). Hazardous air pollutant (HAP) emissions are to be controlled through Maximum Achievable Control Technology (MACT) which can include process changes, material substitutions and/or air pollution control equipment. The "cradle to grave" management of hazardous wastes is to be performed in accordance with the Resource Conservation and Recovery Act (RCRA) of 1976 and the Hazardous and Solid Waste Amendments (HSWA) of 1984.

In 1990, the United States, through the Pollution Prevention Act, adopted a program designed to reduce the volume and toxicity of waste discharges. Pollution prevention (P2) strategies might involve changing process equipment or chemistry, developing new processes, eliminating products, minimizing wastes, recycling water or chemicals, trading wastes with another company, etc. In 1991, the EPA instituted the 33/50 program which was to result in an overall 33% reduction of 17 high priority pollutants by 1992 and a 50% reduction of the pollutants by 1995. Both goals were surpassed. Not only has this program been successful, but it sets an important precedence because the participating companies volunteered. Additionally, P2 efforts have led industries to rigorously think through product life cycles. A Life Cycle Analysis (LCA) starts with consideration for acquiring raw materials, moves through the stages related to processing, assembly, service and reuse, and ends with retirement/disposal. The LCA therefore reveals to industry the costs and problems versus the benefits for every stage in the life of a product.

In designing a waste management program for an industry, one must think first in terms of P2 opportunities, identify and characterize the various solid, liquid and gaseous waste streams, consider relevant legislation, and then design an appropriate waste management system. Treatment systems that rely on physical (e.g., settling, floatation, screening, sorption, membrane technologies, air stripping) and chemical (e.g., coagulation, precipitation, chemical oxidation and reduction, pH adjustment) operations are referred to as physicochemical, whereas systems in which microbes are cultured to metabolize waste constituents are known as biological processes (e.g., activated sludge, trickling filters, biotowers, aerated lagoons, anaerobic digestion, aerobic digestion, composting). Oftentimes, both physicochemical and biological systems are used to treat solid and liquid waste streams. Biological systems might be used to treat certain gas streams, but most waste gas streams are treated physicochemically (e.g., cyclones, electrostatic precipitators, scrubbers, bag filters, thermal methods). Solids and the sludges or residuals that result from treating the liquid and gaseous waste streams are also treated by means of physical, chemical, and biological methods.

In many cases, the systems used to treat wastes from domestic sources are also used to treat industrial wastes. For example, municipal wastewaters often consist of both domestic and industrial waste. The local POTW therefore may be treating both types of wastes. To avoid potential problems caused by the input of industrial wastes, municipalities commonly have pretreatment programs which require that industrial wastes discharged to the sewer meet certain standards. The standards generally include limits for various toxic agents such as metals, organic matter measured in terms of biochemical oxygen demand (bod) or chemical oxygen demand, nutrients such as nitrogen and phosphorus, pH and other contaminants that are recognized as having the potential to impact on the performance of the POTW. At the other end of the spectrum, there are wastes that need to be segregated and managed separately in special systems. For example, an industry might generate a hazardous waste that needs to be placed in barrels and transported to an EPA approved treatment, storage or disposal facility (TSDF).

Thus, it is not possible to simply use one train of treatment operations for all industrial waste streams, but an effective, generic strategy has been developed in recent years for considering the waste management options available to an industry. The basis for the strategy is to look for P2 opportunities and to consider the life cycle of a product. An awareness of waste stream characteristics and the potential benefits of stream segregation is then melded with the knowledge of regulatory compliance issues and treatment system capabilities/performance to minimize environmental risks and costs.

[*Gregory D. Boardman*]

FURTHER READING

Freeman, H. M. *Industrial Pollution Prevention Handbook*. New York: McGraw-Hill, Inc., 1995.

Haas, C. N. and Vamos, R. J. *Hazardous and Industrial Waste Treatment*. Englewod Cliffs: Prentice Hall, Inc., 1995.

LaGrega, M. D., Buckingham, P. L., and Evans, J. C. *Hazardous Waste Management*. New York: McGraw-Hill, Inc., 1994.

Metcalf and Eddy, Inc. *Wastewater Engineering Treatment, Disposal and Reuse*. Revised by G. Tchobanoglous and F. Burton. New York: McGraw-Hill, Inc., 1991.

Nemerow, N. L. and Dasgupta, A. *Industrial and Hazardous Waste Treatment*. New York: Van Nostrand Reinhold, 1991.

Peavy, H. S., Rowe, D. R., and Tchobanoglous, G. *Environmental Engineering*. New York: McGraw-Hill Book Company, 1985.

Tchobanoglous, G., Theisen, H., and Vigil, S. A. *Integrated Solid Waste Management Engineering Principles and Management Issues*. New York: McGraw-Hill, Inc., 1993

Inertia

See **Resistance**

Infiltration

In **hydrology**, infiltration refers to the maximum rate at which a **soil** can absorb precipitation. This is based on the initial moisture content of the soil or on the portion of precipitation that enters the soil. In soil science, the term refers to the process by which water enters the soil, generally by downward flow through all or part of the soil surface. The rate of entry relative to the amount of water being supplied by precipitation or other sources determines how much water enters the root zone and how much runs off the surface. *See also* Groundwater; Soil profile; Water table

INFORM (New York, New York)

INFORM was founded in 1973 by environmental research specialist Joanna Underwood and two colleagues. Seriously concerned about **air pollution**, the three scientists decided to establish an organization that would identify practical ways to protect the **environment** and public health. Since then, their concerns have widened to include **hazardous waste**, solid **waste management**, **water pollution**, and land, energy, and **water conservation**. The group's primary purpose is "to examine business practices which harm our air, water, and land resources" and pinpoint "specific ways in which practices can be improved."

INFORM's research is recognized throughout the United States as instrumental in shaping environmental policies and programs. Legislators, conservation groups and business leaders use INFORM's authority as an acknowledged basis for research and conferences. Source reduction has become one of INFORM's most important projects. A decrease in the amount and/or toxicity of waste entering the **waste stream**, source reduction includes any activity by an individual, business, or government that lessens the amount of **solid waste**—or **garbage**—that would otherwise have to be recycled or incinerated. Source reduction does not include **recycling, municipal solid waste composting**, household hazardous waste collection, or beverage container deposit and return systems.

The first priority in source reduction strategies is elimination; the second, **reuse**. Public education is a crucial part of INFORM's program. To this end INFORM has published *Making Less Garbage: A Planning Guide for Communities*. This book details ways to achieve source reduction including buying reusable, as opposed to disposable, items; buying in bulk; and maintaining and repairing products to extend their lives.

INFORM's outreach program goes well beyond its source reduction project. The staff of over 25 full-time scientists and researchers and 12 volunteers and interns makes presentations at national and international conferences and local workshops. INFORM representatives have also given briefings and testimony at Congressional hearings and produced television and radio advertisements to increase public awareness on environmental issues. The organization also publishes a quarterly newsletter, *INFORM Reports*. Contact: INFORM, 381 Park Avenue South, New York, NY 10016.

[*Cathy M. Falk*]

INFOTERRA (U.N. Environment Programme)

INFOTERRA has its international headquarters in Kenya and is a global information network operated by the Earthwatch program of the **United Nations Environment Programme (UNEP)**.

Under INFOTERRA, participating nations designate institutions to be national focal points, such as the **Environmental Protection Agency (EPA)** in the United States. Each national institution chosen as a focal point, prepares a list of its national environmental experts and selects what it considers the best sources for inclusion in INFOTERRA's international directory of experts.

INFOTERRA initially used its directory only to refer questioners to the nearest appropriate experts, but the organization has evolved into a central information agency. It consults sources, answers public queries for information, and analyzes the replies. INFOTERRA is used by governments, industries, and researchers in 139 countries. Contact:

INFOTERRA, UNEP Regional Office for North America, 2 United Nations Plaza, New York, NY 10017.

[*Linda Rehkopf*]

Injection well

Injection wells are used to dispose waste into the subsurface zone. These wastes can include brine from oil and gas wells, liquid hazardous wastes, agricultural and urban **runoff**, municipal sewage, and return water from air-conditioning. Recharge wells can also be used for injecting fluids to enhance oil recovery, injecting treated water for artificial aquifer recharge, or enhancing a pump-and-treat system. If the wells are poorly designed or constructed, or if the local geology is not sufficiently studied, injected liquids can enter an aquifer and cause **groundwater** contamination. Injection wells are regulated under the Underground Injection Control Program of the **Safe Drinking Water Act** . *See also* Aquifer restoration; Deep-well injection; Drinking-water supply; Groundwater monitoring; Groundwater pollution; Water table

Inoculate

To inoculate involves the introduction of microorganisms into a new **environment**. Originally the term referred to the insertion of a bud or shoot of one plant into the stem or trunk of another to develop new strains or hybrids. These hybrid plants would be resistant to botanic disease or they would allow greater harvests or range of climates. With the advent of vaccines to prevent human and animal disease, the term inoculate has come to represent injection of a serum to prevent, cure, or make immune from disease.

Inoculation is of prime importance in that the introduction of specific microorganism **species** into specific macroorganisms may establish a symbiotic relationships where each organism benefits. For example, the introduction of **mycorrhiza** fungus to plants improves the plants' ability to absorb **nutrient**s from the **soil**. *See also* Symbiosis

Insecticide
See **Pesticide**

Integrated pest management

Integrated pest management (IPM) is a newer science that aims to give the best possible **pest** control while minimizing damage to human health or the environment. IPM means either using fewer **chemicals** more effectively or finding ways, both new and old, that substitute for **pesticide** use.

Technically, IPM is the selection, integration and implementation of pest control based on predicted economic, ecological and sociological consequences. IPM seeks maximum use of naturally occurring pest controls, including weather, disease agents, predators and **parasites**. In addition, IPM utilizes various biological, physical, and chemical control and **habitat** modification techniques. Artificial controls are imposed only as required to keep a pest from surpassing intolerable population levels which are predetermined from assessments of the pest damage potential and the ecological, sociological, and economic costs of the control measures. Farmers have come to understand that the presence of a pest species does not necessarily justify action for its control. In fact, tolerable infestations may be actually desirable, providing food for important beneficial insects. Why this change in farming practices?

The introduction of synthetic organic pesticides such as the insecticide **DDT**, and the herbicide **2,4-D** (half the formula in **Agent Orange**) after World War II began a new era in pest control. These products were followed by hundreds of synthetic organic **fungicide**s, nematicides, rodenticides and other chemical controls. These chemical materials were initially very effective and very cheap. Synthetic chemicals eventually became the primary means of pest control in productive agricultural regions, providing season-long crop protection against insects and weeds. They were used in addition to **fertilizer**s and other treatments.

The success of modern pesticides led to widespread acceptance and reliance upon them, particularly in this country. Of all the chemical pesticides applied worldwide in agriculture, forests, industry and households, one-third to one-half were used in the United States. **Herbicide**s have been used increasingly to replace hand labor and machine cultivation for control of weeds in crops, in forests, on the rights-of-way of highways, utility lines, railroads and in cities. Agriculture consumes perhaps 65 percent of the total quantity of synthetic organic pesticides used in the United States each year. In addition, chemical companies export an increasingly larger amount to **Third World** countries. Pesticides banned in the United States such as DDT, EDB and **chlordane**, are exported to countries where they are applied to crops imported by the United States for consumption.

For more than a decade, problems with pesticides have become increasingly apparent. Significant groups of pests have evolved with genetic resistance to pesticides. The increase in resistance among insect pests has been exponential, following extensive use of chemicals in the last forty years. Ticks, insects and spider mites (nearly 400 species) are now especially resistant, and the creation of new insecticides to combat the problem is not keeping pace with the emergence of new strains of resistant insect pests. Despite the advances in modern chemical control and the dramatic increase in chemical pesticides used on U.S. cropland, annual crop losses from all pests appear to have remained constant or to have increased. Losses caused by weeds have declined slightly, but those caused by insects have nearly doubled. The price of synthetic organic pesticides has increased significantly in recent years, placing a heavy financial burden on those who use large quantities of the materials. As farmers and growers across the United States realize the limitations and human health consequences of using artificial chemical pesticides,

interest in the alternative approach of integrated pest management grows.

Integrated pest management aims at management rather than eradication of pest species. Since potentially harmful species will continue to exist at tolerable levels of abundance, the philosophy now is to manage rather than eradicate the pests. The **ecosystem** is the management unit. (Every crop is in itself a complex ecological system.) Spraying pesticides too often, at the wrong time, or on the wrong part of the crop may destroy the pests' natural enemies ordinarily present in the ecosystem. Knowledge of the actions, reactions, and interactions of the components of the ecosystems is requisite to effective IPM programs. With this knowledge, the ecosystem is manipulated in order to hold pests at tolerable levels while avoiding disruptions of the system.

The use of natural controls is maximized. IPM emphasizes the fullest practical utilization of the existing regulating and limiting factors in the form of parasites, predators, and weather, which check the pests' **population growth**. IPM users understand that control procedures may produce unexpected and undesirable consequences, however. It takes time to change over and determination to keep up the commitment until the desired results are achieved.

An interdisciplinary systems approach is essential. Effective IPM is an integral part of the overall management of a farm, a business or a forest. For example, timing plays an important role. Certain pests are most prevalent at particular times of the year. By altering the date on which a crop is planted, serious pest damage can be avoided. Some farmers simultaneously plant and harvest, since the procedure prevents the pests from migrating to neighboring fields after the harvest. Others may plant several different crops in the same field, thereby reducing the number of pests. The variety of crops harbor greater numbers of natural enemies and make it more difficult for the pests to locate and colonize their host plants. In Thailand and China, farmers flood their fields for several weeks before planting to destroy pests. Other farmers turn the soil, so that pests are brought to the surface and die in the sun's heat.

The development of specific IPM program depends on the pest complex, resources to be protected, economic values, and availability of personnel. It also depends upon adequate funding for research and to train farmers. Some of the techniques are complex, and expert advice is needed. However, while it is difficult to establish absolute guidelines, there are general guidelines that can apply to the management of any pest group.

Growers must analyze the "pest" status of each of the reputedly injurious organisms and establish economic thresholds for the "real" pests. The economic threshold is, in fact, the population level, and is defined as the density of a pest population below which the cost of applying control measures exceeds the losses caused by the pest. Economic threshold values are based on assessments of the pest damage potential and the ecological, sociological, and economic costs associated with control measures. A given crop, forest area, backyard, building, or recreational area may be infested with dozens of potentially harmful species at any one time. For each situation, however, there are rarely more than a few pest species whose populations expand to intolerable levels at regular and fairly predictable intervals. Key pests recur regularly at population densities exceeding economic threshold levels and are the focal point for IPM programs.

Farmers must also devise schemes for lowering equilibrium positions of key pests. A key pest will vary in severity from year to year, but its average density, known as the equilibrium position, usually exceeds its economic threshold. IPM efforts manipulate the environment in order to reduce a pest's equilibrium position to a permanent level below the economic threshold. This reduction can be achieved by deliberate introduction and establishment of natural enemies (parasites, predators, and diseases) in areas where they did not previously occur. Natural enemies may already occur in the crop in small numbers or can be introduced from elsewhere. Certain microorganisms, when eaten by a pest, will kill it.

Newer chemicals show promise as alternatives to synthetic chemical pesticides. These include insect attractant chemicals, weed and insect disease agents and insect growth regulators or hormones. A pathogen such as ***Bacillus thuringiensis*** (BT), has proven commercially successful. Since certain crops have an inbuilt resistance to pests, pest-resistant or pest-free varieties of seed, crop plants, ornamental plants, orchard trees, and forest trees can be used. Growers can also modify the pest environment to increase the effectiveness of the pest's biological control agents, to destroy its breeding, feeding, or shelter habitat or otherwise render it harmless. This includes crop rotation, destruction of crop harvest residues and soil tillage, and selective burning or mechanical removal of undesirable plant species and pruning, especially for forest pests.

While nearly permanent control of key insect and plant disease pests of agricultural crops has been achieved, emergencies will occur, and all IPM advocates acknowledge this. During those times, measures should be applied that create the least ecological destruction. Growers are urged to utilize the best combination of the three basic IPM components: natural enemies, resistant varieties and environmental modification. However, there may be a time when pesticides may be the only recourse. In that case, it is important to coordinate the proper pesticide, the dosage and the timing in order to minimize the hazards to nontarget organisms and the surrounding ecosystems.

Pest management techniques have been known for many years and were used widely before World War II. They were deemphasized by insect and weed control scientists and by corporate pressures as the synthetic chemicals became commercially available after the war. Now there is a renewed interest in the early control techniques and in new chemistry.

Reports detailing the success of IPM are emerging at a rapid rate as thousands of farmers yearly join the ranks of those who choose to eliminate chemical pesticides. Sustainable agricultural practice increases the richness of the soil by replenishing the soil's reserves of fertility. IPM does not produce secondary problems such as pest resistance or resurgence. It also diminishes soil erosion, increases crop yields

and saves money over the long haul. Organic foods are reported to have better cooking quality, better flavor and greater longevity in the storage bins. And with less **pesticide residue**, our food is clearly more healthy to eat. *See also* Sustainable agriculture

[*Liane Clorfene Casten*]

FURTHER READING

Baker, R. R., and P. Dunn. *New Directions in Biological Control: Alternatives for Supressing Agricultural Pests and Diseases.* New York: Wiley, 1990.

Bottrell, D. G., and R. F. Smith. "Integrated Pest Management." *Environmental Science & Technology* 16 (May 1982): 282A-288A.

Burn, A. J., et al. *Integrated Pest Management.* New York: Academic Press, 1988.

DeBach, P., and D. Rosen. *Biological Control By Natural Enemies.* 2nd ed. Cambridge, MA: Cambridge University Press, 1991.

Pimentel, D. *The Pesticide Question: Environment, Economics and Ethics.* New York: Chapman & Hall, 1992.

Interest group
See **Public interest groups**

Intergenerational justice

One of the key features of an environmental ethic or perspective is its concern for the health and well-being of **future generations**. Questions about the rights of future people and the responsibilities of those presently living are central to **environment**al theory and practice and are often asked and analyzed under the term *intergenerational justice*. Most traditional accounts or theories of justice have focused on relations between contemporaries: What distribution of scarce goods is fairest or optimally just? Should such goods be distributed on the basis of merit or need? These and other questions have been asked by thinkers from Aristotle through John Rawls. Recently, however, some philosophers have begun to ask about just distributions over time and across generations.

The subject of intergenerational justice is a key concern for environmentally-minded thinkers for at least two reasons. First, human beings now living have the power to permanently alter or destroy the planet (or portions thereof) in ways that will affect the health, happiness, and well-being of people living long after we are all dead. One need only think, for example, of the **radioactive waste**s generated by **nuclear power** plants which will be intensely "hot" and dangerous for many thousands of years. No one yet knows how to safely store such material for a hundred, much less many thousands, of years. Considered from an intergenerational perspective then, it would be unfair—that is, unjust—for the present generation to enjoy the benefits of nuclear power, passing on to distant posterity the burdens and dangers caused by our (in)action.

Second, we not only have the power to affect future generations, but we *know* that we have it. And with such knowledge comes the moral responsibility to act in ways that will prevent harm to future people. For example, since we know about the health effects of radiation on human beings, our having that knowledge imposes upon us a moral obligation not to needlessly expose anyone—now or in the indefinite future—to the harms or hazards of radioactive wastes. Many other examples of intergenerational harm or hazard exist: global warming, **topsoil erosion**, disappearing **tropical rain forest**s, depletion and/or pollution of **aquifer**s, among others. But whatever the example, the point of the intergenerational view is the same: the moral duty to treat people justly or fairly applies not only to people now living, but to those who will live long after we are gone. To the extent that our actions produce consequences that may prove harmful to people who have not harmed (and in the nature of the case cannot harm) us is, by any standard, unjust. And yet it seems quite clear that we in the present generation are in many respects acting unjustly toward distant posterity. This is true not only for harms or hazards bequeathed to future people, but the point applies also to deprivations of various kinds.

Consider, for example, the present generation's profligate use of **fossil fuels**. Reserves of oil and **natural gas** are both finite and nonreplaceable; once burned (or turned into **plastic** or some other **petroleum**-based material), a gallon of oil is gone forever; every drop or barrel used now is therefore unavailable for future people. As **Wendell Berry** observed, the claim that fossil fuel energy is *cheap* rests on a simplistic and morally doubtful assumption about the *rights* of the present generation:

> We were able to consider [fossil fuel energy] "cheap" only by a kind of moral simplicity: the assumption that we had a "right" to as much of it as we could use. This was a "right" made solely by might. Because fossil fuels, however abundant they once were, were nevertheless limited in quantity and not renewable, they obviously did not "belong" to one generation more than another. We ignored the claims of posterity simply because we could, the living being stronger than the unborn, and so worked the "miracle" of industrial progress by the theft of energy from (among others) our children.

And that, Berry adds, "is the real foundation of our progress and our affluence. The reason that we are a rich nation is not that we have earned so much wealth — you cannot, by any honest means, earn or deserve so much. The reason is simply that we have learned, and become willing, to market and use up in our own time the birthright and livelihood of posterity."

These and other considerations have led some environmentally-minded philosophers to argue for limits on present-day consumption, so as to save a fair share of scarce resources for future generations. John Rawls, for instance, constructs a *just savings principle* according to which members of each generation may consume no more than their fair share of scarce resources. The main difficulty in arriving at and applying any such principle lies in determining what counts as fair share. As the number of generations taken into account increases, the share available to any single generation then becomes smaller; and as the number of generations

approaches infinity, any one generation's share approaches zero.

Other objections have been raised against the idea of intergenerational justice. These objections can be divided into two groups, which we can call conceptual and technological. One conceptual criticism is that the very idea of intergenerational justice is itself incoherent. The idea of justice is tied with that of reciprocity or exchange; but relations of reciprocity can exist only between contemporaries; therefore the concept of justice is inapplicable to relations between existing people and distant posterity. Future people are in no position to reciprocate; therefore people now living cannot be morally obligated to do anything for them. Another conceptual objection to the idea of intergenerational justice is concerned with rights. Briefly, the objection runs as follows: future people do not (yet) exist; only actually existing people have rights, including the right to be treated justly; therefore future people do not have rights which we in the present have a moral obligation to respect and protect. Critics of this view counter that it not only rests on a too-restrictive conception of rights and justice, but that it also paves the way for grievous intergenerational injustices.

Several arguments can be constructed to counter the claim that justice rests on reciprocity (and therefore applies only to relations between contemporaries) and the claim that future people do not have rights, including the right to be treated justly by their predecessors. Regarding reciprocity: since we acknowledge in ethics and recognize in law that it is possible to treat an infant or a mentally disabled or severely retarded person justly or unjustly, even though they are in no position to reciprocate, it follows that the idea of justice is not necessarily connected with reciprocity. Regarding the claim that future people cannot be said to have rights that require our recognition and respect: one of the more ingenious arguments against this view consists of modifying John Rawls's imaginary *veil of ignorance*. Rawls argues that principles of justice must not be partisan or favor particular people but must be blind and impartial. To ensure impartiality in arriving at principles of justice, Rawls invites us to imagine an original position in which rational people are placed behind a veil of ignorance wherein they are unaware of their age, race, sex, social class, economic status, etc. Unaware of their own particular position in society, rational people would arrive at and agree upon impartial and universal principles of justice. To ensure that such impartiality extends across generations, one need only *thicken* the veil by adding the proviso that the choosers be unaware of the generation to which they belong. Rational people would not accept or agree to principles under which predecessors could harm or disadvantage successors.

Some critics of intergenerational justice argue in technological terms. They contend that existing people need not restrict their consumption of scarce or nonrenewable resources in order to save some portion for future generations. For, they argue, substitutes for these resources will be discovered or devised through technological innovations and inventions. For example, as fossil fuels become scarcer and more expensive, new fuels—gasohol or fusion-derived nuclear fuel—will replace them. Thus we need never worry about depleting any particular resource because every resource can be replaced by a substitute that is as cheap, clean, and accessible as the resource it replaces. Likewise, we need not worry about generating nuclear wastes that we do not yet know how to store safely. Some solution is bound to be devised sometime in the future.

Environmentally-minded critics of this technological line of argument claim that it amounts to little more than wishful thinking. Like Charles Dickens's fictional character Mr. Micawber, those who place their faith in technological solutions to all environmental problems optimistically expect that "something will turn up." Just as Mr. Micawber's faith was misplaced, so too, these critics contend, is the optimism of those who expect technology to solve all problems, present and future. Of course such solutions may be found, but that is a gamble and not a guarantee. To wager with the health and well-being of future people is, environmentalists argue, immoral.

There are of course many other issues and concerns raised in connection with intergenerational justice. Discussions among and disagreements between philosophers, economists, environmentalists, and others are by no means purely abstract and academic. How these matters are resolved will have a profound effect on the fate of future generations.

[*Terence Ball*]

FURTHER READING

Auerbach, B.E. *Unto the Thousandth Generation: Conceptualizing Intergenerational Justice.* New York: Peter Lang, 1995.

Ball, T. *Transforming Political Discourse.* Oxford, England: Blackwell, 1988.

Barry, B., and R. I. Sikora, eds. *Obligations to Future Generations.* Philadelphia: Temple University Press, 1978.

Barry, B. *Theories of Justice.* Berkeley: University of California Press, 1988.

Berry, W. *The Gift of Good Land.* San Francisco: North Point Press, 1981.

De-Shalit, A. *Why Posterity Matters: Environmental Policies and Future Generations.* London and New York: Routledge, 1995.

Fishkin, J. And P. Laslett (eds.). *Justice Between Age Groups and Generations.* New Haven, CT: Yale University Press, 1991.

MacLean, D., and P. G. Brown, eds. *Energy and the Future.* Totawa, NJ: Rowman & Littlefield, 1983.

Partridge, E., ed. *Responsibilities to Future Generations.* Buffalo, NY: Prometheus Books, 1981.

Rawls, J. *A Theory of Justice.* Cambridge: Harvard University Press, 1971.

Wenz, P. S. *Environmental Justice.* Albany: State University of New York Press, 1988.

Intergovernmental Panel on Climate Change

The Intergovernmental Panel on Climate Change (IPCC) was established in 1988 as a joint project of the **United Nations Environment Programme** and the World Meteorological Organization. The primary mission of the IPCC is to gather, assess, and disseminate scientific information about **climate** change with a view to informing international and national policy formation. The IPCC has become the highest-profile and best-regarded international agency concerned with the climatic consequences of massive emissions of "**greenhouse gases**" such as **carbon dioxide** and methane as a byproduct of the **combustion** of **fossil fuels**. It is, nevertheless, an organization that has been and continues to be at the center of a great deal of controversy.

The IPCC was established partly in response to Nobel Laureate **Mario Molina**'s 1985 documentation of chemical processes which occur when human-made chemicals deplete the Earth's atmospheric **ozone** shield. Ozone depletion is likely to cause increased levels of **ultraviolet radiation** to reach the Earth's surface, producing a host of health, agricultural, and environmental problems. Molina's work helped to persuade most of the industrialized nations to ban **chlorofluorocarbons** and several other ozone-depleting chemicals. It also established a context in which national and international authorities began to pay serious attention to the global environmental consequences of atmospheric changes resulting from industrialization and ongoing reliance on fossil fuels.

Continuing to operate under the auspices of the United Nations, the IPCC is organized into three sections or working groups with specific substantive assignments, an IPCC Secretariat, and an IPCC Bureau, presently chaired by Professor Bert Bolin of Sweden. The first working group gathers data and analyzes the functioning of the climate system with special attention to the detection of potential changes resulting from human activity. The second group's assignment is to assess the various potential impacts of climate change. It also is charged with exploring strategies for the reduction of greenhouse gas emissions. The third group focuses specifically on the evaluation of the economic implications of climate change. These include direct and indirect economic consequences of global warming, particularly for agriculture and human habitation. The costs associated with climate change are then weighed against the costs of reducing emissions via cost-benefit analysis and various economic modeling techniques.

The IPCC has published its major findings in "Full Assessment" Reports issued in 1990 and 1995. The Tenth Session of the IPCC (Nairobi, 1994) directed that future full assessments should be prepared approximately every five years. Supplemental reports are also published from time to time, as was a special report on the radiative forcing of climate (1994). A series of technical reports have also been published or planned, the latest being "Technologies, Policies, and Measures for Mitigating Climate Change" (December, 1996).

The IPCC has drawn a great deal of criticism virtually from its inception. A great deal of money is at stake in policy decisions which might seek to limit greenhouse gas emissions, and much of the criticism directed at the IPCC tends to come from lobbying and research groups funded in large part by industries that either produce or use large quantities of fossil fuels. Thus, a lobbying group sponsored by energy, transportation, and manufacturing interests called the Global Climate Coalition attacked parts of the 1995 report as unscientific. At the core of the controversy was Chapter Eight of the report, "Detection of Climate Change and Attribution of Causes." Although the IPCC was careful to hedge its conclusions in various ways, acknowledging difficulties in measurement, disagreements over methodologies for interpreting data, and general uncertainty about the conclusivity of its findings, it nevertheless suggested a connection between greenhouse gas emissions and global warming. Not satisfied with such caveats, the Global Climate Coalition charged that the IPCC's conclusions had been presented as far less debatable than they actually were. This cast a cloud of uncertainty over the report, at least for some policymakers.

In the summer of 1996, however, results of new studies of the upper atmosphere were published which provided a great deal of indirect support for the IPCC's conclusions. Investigators found significant evidence of cooling in the upper atmosphere and warming in the lower atmosphere, with this effect being especially pronounced in the southern hemisphere. These findings precisely confirmed the predictions of global warming models such as those employed by the IPCC.

Perhaps emboldened by this confirmation, but still facing a great deal of political opposition, the IPCC released its most unequivocal statement yet about global warming and its causes in November 1996. The IPCC declared that "the balance of evidence suggests that there is a discernible human influence on global climate." The statement made clear that a preponderance of evidence and a majority of scientific experts indicated that observable climate change was a result of human activity. The IPCC urged that all nations limit their use of fossil fuels and develop more energy-efficient technologies.

These conclusions and recommendations provoked considerable criticism from less-developed countries. Leaders of the less-industrialized areas of the world tend to view potential restrictions on the use of fossil fuels as a further and unfair hindrance of its efforts to catch up with the United States and Western Europe in industry, transportation, economic infrastructure, and standards of living. The industrialized nations, they point out, were allowed to develop without any such restrictions and now account for the vast majority of the world's energy consumption and greenhouse gas emissions. These industrialized nations therefore should bear the brunt of any efforts to protect the global climate, substantially exempting the developing world from restrictions on or increased liability for the use of fossil fuels.

The IPCC's conclusions and recommendations have also drawn strong opposition from industry groups in the United States, such as the American Petroleum Institute, and conservative Republican politicians. These critics charge that the IPCC's supposed new evidence is only fashionable but warmed-over theory, and that no one has yet proven conclusively that climate change is indeed related to human influence. In view of the likely massive economic impact of any aggressive program aimed at the reduction of emissions, there is no warrant for following the IPCC's dangerous and ill-considered advice. In the words of Representative Dana Rohrbacher, global warming is "assumed at best to be unproven and at worst to be liberal clap-trap, trendy but soon to go out of style in our Newt Congress." Under Republican leadership, Congress has slashed funds for **Environmental Pro-**

tection Agency and **U.S. Department of Energy** programs concerned with global warming and its causes.

Whatever the merits of the underlying argument, these cuts create a certain foreign relations problem for the Clinton Administration. They may make it impossible for the United States to honor former President Bush's 1992 pledge (at the Rio de Janeiro **Earth Summit**) to reduce the country's emission of carbon dioxide and methane to 1990 levels by the year 2000. Indeed, owing in part to low oil prices and a strong domestic economy, the United States is consuming more energy and emitting more greenhouse gases than ever before.

The IPCC has started preliminary planning for its third "full assessment" report, which is due to be published in 2000. These preparations include the drafting of discussion papers, the formation of task groups, and the formulation of goals and guidelines. Related activities will include the organization of workshops and the publication of technical papers, special reports, and a white paper. A special "Task Group of Experts" has been formed to strengthen analytical methodology (and make conclusions more difficult to assail) by encouraging increased cooperation between the organization's economic modelers and scientists measuring and estimating environmental impacts. This group has also been charged with responsibility for making data available and accessible, and for planning follow-up studies.

The four special reports are to be published between 1997 and 1999 and will focus on the following topics: "Regional Impacts of Climate Change," "Global Atmospheric Effects of Aviation," "Methodological Issues in Technology Transfer," and "Emissions Scenarios." Other planned activities will be organized around topics of "Modeling and Assessment," "Mitigation and Adaptation Cost Assessment," "Risk Management Techniques," and "Modeling Stabilization of Greenhouse Gas Concentrations." Contact via e-mail: ipccweb@usgcrp.gov

[Lawrence J. Biskowski]

FURTHER READING

"API girds for Clinton greenhouse tax battle," *Oil and Gas Journal* 94/47 (18 November 1996): 24-5.

"Controversy erupts over climate report," *Science News* 150/1 (6 July 1996): 15.

Kerr, R.A. "Sky-high Findings Drop New Hints of Greenhouse Warming," *Science* 273/5271 (5 July 1996): 34.

Kriz, M. "Global Warming: Proof and Politics," *National Journal* 27/49 (9 December 1995): 3062.

Internal costs

See **Internalizing costs**

Internalizing costs

Private market activities create so-called externalities. An example of a negative **externality** is **air pollution**. It occurs when a producer does not bear all the costs of an activity in which he or she engages. Since external costs do not enter into the calculations producers make, they will make few attempts to limit or eliminate **pollution** and other forms of **environmental degradation**.

Negative externalities are a type of market defect all economists believe is appropriate to try to correct. Milton Friedman refers to such externalities as "neighborhood effects," (although it must be kept in mind that some forms of pollution have an all but local effect). The classic neighborhood effect is pollution. The premise of a free market is that when two people voluntarily make a deal, they both benefit. If society gives everyone the right to make deals, society as a whole will benefit. It becomes richer from the aggregation of the many mutually beneficial deals that are made. However, what happens if in making mutually beneficial deals there is a waste product that the parties release into the **environment** and that society must either suffer from or clean up? The two parties to the deal are better off, but society as a whole has to pay the costs. Friedman points out that individual members of a society cannot appropriately charge the responsible parties for external costs or find other means of redress.

Friedman's answer to this dilemma is simple: society, through government, must charge the responsible parties the costs of the clean-up. Whatever damage they generate must be internalized in the price of the transaction. Polluters can be forced to internalize environmental costs through pollution taxes and discharge fees, a method generally favored by economists. When such taxes are imposed, the market defect (the price of pollution which is not counted in the transaction) is corrected. The market price then reflects the true social costs of the deal, and the parties have to adjust accordingly. They will have an incentive to decrease harmful activities and develop less environmentally damaging technology. The drawback of such a system is that society will not have direct control over pollution levels, although it will receive monetary compensation for any losses it sustains. However, if the government imposed a tax or charge on the polluting parties, it would have to place a monetary value on the damage. In practice, this is difficult to do. How much for a human life lost to pollution? How much for a vista destroyed? How much for a plant or animal **species** brought to **extinction**? Finally, the idea that pollution is all right as long as the polluter pays for it is unacceptable to many people.

In fact, the government has tried to control activities with associated externalities through regulation, rather than by supplementing the price system. It has set standards for specific industries and other social entities. The standards are designed to limit environmental degradation to acceptable levels and are enforced through the **Environmental Protection Agency (EPA)**. They prohibit some harmful activities, limit others, and prescribe alternative behaviors. When market actors do not adhere to these standards they are subject to penalties. In theory, potential polluters are given incentives to reduce and treat their waste, manufacture less harmful products, develop alternative technologies, and so on. In practice, the system has not worked as well as it was hoped in the 1960s and 1970s, when much of the environmental legislation presently in force was enacted. Enforcement has been fraught with political and legal difficulties. Extensions on deadlines are given to cities for not meeting clean air standards and to the **automobile** industry for not meeting standards on fuel economy of new cars, for instance. It has been difficult to collect fines from industries found to have been in violation. Many cases are tied up in the courts through a lengthy appeals process. Some companies simply declare bankruptcy to evade fines. Others continue polluting because they find it cheaper to pay fines than to develop alternative production processes.

Alternative strategies presently under debate include setting up a trade in pollution permits. The government would not levy a tax on pollution but would issue a number of permits that altogether set a maximum acceptable pollution level. Buyers of permits can either use them to cover their own polluting activities or resell them to the highest bidder. Polluters will be forced to internalize the environmental costs of their activities so that they will have an incentive to reduce pollution. The price of pollution will then be determined by the market. The disadvantage of this system is that the government will have no control over where pollution takes place. It is thinkable that certain regions will have high concentrations of industries using the permits, which may result in local pollution levels that are unacceptably high. Whether marketable pollution permits address present pollution problems more satisfactorily than does regulation alone has yet to be seen. *See also* Environmental economics

[*Alfred A. Marcus and Marijke Rijsberman*]

FURTHER READING

Friedman, M. *Capitalism and Freedom.* Chicago, IL: University of Chicago Press, 1962.

Marcus, A. *Business and Society: Ethics, Government, and the World Economy.* Homewood, IL: Irwin Press, 1993.

International Atomic Energy Agency (UNESCO)

The first decade of research on **nuclear weapons** and nuclear reactors was characterized by extreme secrecy, and the few nations that had the technology carefully guarded their information. In 1954, however, that philosophy changed, and the United States, in particular, became eager to help other nations use nuclear energy for peaceful purposes. A program called "Atoms for Peace" brought foreign students to the United States for the study of nuclear sciences and provided enriched **uranium** to countries wanting to build their own reactors, encouraging interest in nuclear energy throughout much of the world.

But this program created a problem. It increased the potential diversion of nuclear information and nuclear materials for the construction of weapons, and the threat of nuclear proliferation grew. The United Nations created the

International Atomic Energy Agency (IAEA) in 1957 to address this problem. The agency had two primary objectives: to encourage and assist with the development of peaceful applications of **nuclear power** throughout the world and to prevent the diversion of nuclear materials to weapons research and development.

The first decade of IAEA's existence was not marked by much success. In fact, the United States was so dissatisfied with the agency's work that it began signing bilateral non-proliferation treaties with a number of countries. Finally, the 1970 nuclear non-proliferation treaty more clearly designated the IAEA's responsibilities for the monitoring of nuclear material.

Today the agency is an active division of the United Nations Educational, Scientific, and Cultural Organization (UNESCO), and its headquarters are in Vienna. The IAEA operates with a staff of more than 800 professional workers, about 1,200 general service workers, and a budget of about $150 million. To accomplish its goal of extending and improving the peaceful use of nuclear energy, IAEA conducts regional and national workshops, seminars, training courses, and committee meetings. It publishes guidebooks and manuals on related topics and maintains the International Nuclear Information System, a bibliographic database on nuclear literature that includes more than 1.2 million records. The database is made available on magnetic tape to its 42-member states.

The IAEA also carries out a rigorous program of inspection. In 1987, for example, it made 2,133 inspections at 631 nuclear installations in 52 non-nuclear weapon nations and four nuclear weapon nations. In a typical year, IAEA activities include conducting safety reviews in a number of different countries, assisting in dealing with accidents at nuclear power plants, providing advice to nations interested in building their own nuclear facilities, advising countries on methods for dealing with **radioactive waste**s, teaching nations how to use radiation to preserve foods, helping universities introduce nuclear science into their curricula, and sponsoring research on the broader applications of nuclear science. The agency is located at: International Atomic Energy Agency, Vienna International Centre, Wagramerstrasse 5, Postfach 100, A-1400 Vienna, Austria. *See also* Atomic Energy Commission; Nuclear Regulatory Commission; Radioactive waste management; Radioactivity

[*David E. Newton*]

International Convention for the Regulation of Whaling (1946)

The International Whaling Commission (IWC) was established in 1949 following the inaugural International Convention for the Regulation of Whaling, which took place in Washington, D.C., in 1946. Many nations have membership in the IWC, which primarily sets quotas for **whales**. The purpose of these quotas is twofold: they are intended to protect the whale **species** from **extinction** while allowing a limited **whaling** industry. In recent times, however, the IWC has come under attack. The vast majority of nations in the Commission have come to oppose whaling of any kind and object to the IWC's practice of establishing quotas. Furthermore, some nations—principally Iceland, Japan, and Norway—wish to protect their traditional whaling industries and are against the quotas set by the IWC. With two such divergent factions opposing the IWC, its future is as doubtful as that of the whales.

Since its inception, the Commission has had difficulty implementing its regulations and gaining approval for its recommendations. In the meantime whale populations have continued to dwindle. In its original design, the IWC consisted of two sub-committees, one scientific and the other technical. Any recommendation that the scientific committee put forth was subject to the politicized technical committee before final approval. The technical committee evaluated the recommendation and changed it if it was not politically or economically viable; essentially, the scientific committee's recommendations have often been rendered powerless. Furthermore, any nation that has decided an IWC recommendation was not in its best interest could have dismissed it by simply registering an objection. In the 1970s this gridlock and inaction attracted public scrutiny; people objected to the IWC's failure to protect the world's whales. Thus in 1972 the **United Nations Conference on the Human Environment** voted overwhelmingly to stop commercial whaling.

Nevertheless, the IWC retained some control over the whaling industry. In 1974 the Commission attempted to bring scientific research to management strategies in its "New Management Procedure." The IWC assessed whale populations with finer resolution, scrutinizing each species to see if it could be hunted and not die out. It classified whales as either "initial management stocks" (harvestable), "sustained management stocks" (harvestable), or "protection stocks" (unharvestable). While these classifications were necessary for effective management, much was unknown about whale population **ecology**, and quota estimates contained high levels of uncertainty.

Since the 1970s, public pressure has caused many nations in the IWC to oppose whale hunting of any kind. At first, one or two nations proposed a whaling moratorium each year. Both pro- and anti-whaling countries began to encourage new IWC members to vote for their respective positions, thus dividing the Commission. In 1982, the IWC enacted a limited moratorium on commercial whaling, to be in effect from 1986 until 1992. During that time it would thoroughly assess whale stocks and afterward allow whaling to resume for selected species and areas. Norway and Japan, however, attained special permits for whaling for scientific research: they continued to catch approximately 400 whales per year, and the meat was sold to restaurants. Then in 1992—the year when whaling was supposed to have resumed—many nations voted to extend the moratorium. Iceland, Norway, and Japan objected strongly to what they saw as an infringement on their traditional industries and eating customs. Iceland subsequently left the IWC, and

Japan and Norway have threatened to follow. These countries intend to resume their whaling programs. Members of the IWC are torn between accommodating these nations in some way and protecting the whales, and amid such controversy it is unlikely that the Commission can continue in its present mission.

Although the IWC has not been able to marshall its scientific advances or enforce its own regulations in managing whaling, it is broadening its original mission. The Commission may begin to govern the hunting of small cetaceans such as **dolphins** and porpoises, which are believed to suffer from **overhunting**.

[*David A. Duffus and Andrea Gacki*]

FURTHER READING

Burton, R. *The Life and Death of Whales*. London: Andre Deutsch Ltd., 1980.

Holt, S. J. "Let's All Go Whaling." *The Ecologist* 15 (1985): 113-124.

Kellog, R. *The International Whaling Commission*. International Technical Conference on Conservation of Living Resources of the Sea. New York: United Nations Publications, 1955.

Pollack, A. "Commission to Save Whales Endangered, Too." *The New York Times* (18 May 1993): B8.

International Council for Bird Preservation (Washington, D.C.)

"From research...to action. From birds...to people." So reads the cover of the International Council for Bird Preservation's (ICBP) annual report. This statement perfectly describes the beliefs of ICBP, a group founded in 1922 by well-known American and European bird enthusiasts for the **conservation** of birds and their **habitat**s.

Under the leadership of Christopher Imboden, the council works to protect endangered birds worldwide and to promote public awareness of their ecological importance. ICBP has grown from humble beginnings in England to a federation of over 300 member organizations representing approximately 10 million people in 110 countries. This includes developing tropical countries where few, if any, conservation movements existed prior to ICBP. There is also a worldwide network of enthusiastic volunteers.

ICBP is a key group in international efforts to protect bird **migration** routes, and also works to educate the public about **endangered species** and their ecological importance. The ICBP gathers and disseminates information about birds, maintaining a computerized data bank from which it generates reports. It conducts periodic symposiums on bird-related issues, runs the World Bird Club, maintains a Conservation Fund, runs special campaigns when opportunities such as the Migratory Bird Campaign present themselves, and develops and carries out priority projects in their Conservation Programme.

The ICBP Conservation Programme has undertaken many projects on behalf of endangered birds. In 1975, ICBP began a captive breeding program for the pink pigeon (*Nesoenas mayeri*), a native of the island of Mauritius in the Indian Ocean, because the total population of this species had dwindled to less than 20 birds. As a result of these efforts, well over 100 of the birds were successfully raised in captivity. Later, several pairs were released at Mauritius' Botanic Gardens of Pamplemousses. ICBP has focused on other seriously endangered birds as well, most recently the imperial parrot (*Amazona imperialis*). In an attempt to protect its threatened habitat, ICBP has helped buy a forest reserve in Dominica, where only 60 of the parrots still survive. With the help of local citizens and educational facilities, ICBP hopes that their efforts to save the imperial parrot will be as successful as their work with pink pigeons.

Another important ICBP project is the group's work to save the red-tailed parrot (*Amazona brasiliensis*) of southeastern Brazil. This project involves support of an extensive plan to convert an entire nearby island into a refuge for the parrots, which exist in only a very few isolated parts of Brazil. ICBP has also focused on islands in other conservation projects. The council purchased Cousin Island (famous for its numerous seabirds), in an effort to save the Seychelles brush warbler (*Acrocephalus sechellensis*). Native only to Cousin Island, this entire brush warbler species numbered only 30 individuals before ICBP bought their island. Today, there are more than 300 bush warblers, and ICBP continues to be actively involved in helping to breed more.

ICBP's publications are many and varied. Quarterly, it issues *Bird Conservation International*, *U.S. Birdwatch*, and *World Birdwatch* newsletter; annually, the group produces the *ICBP Bulletin*; and periodically, it issues *Bustard Studies*. It also publishes the well-respected series *Bird Red Data Books*, and such monographs as *Important Bird Areas in Europe* and *Key Forests for Threatened Birds in Africa*. ICBP produces numerous technical publications and study reports, and, occasionally, Conservation Red Alert pamphlets on severely threatened birds. Contact: International Council for Bird Preservation, 1250 24th Street NW, Washington, DC, 20037

[*Cathy M. Falk*]

International Geosphere-Biosphere Programme (U.N. Environmental Programme)

Research scientists from all countries have always interacted with each other closely. But in recent decades, a new type of internationalism has begun to evolve, in which scientists from all over the world work together on very large projects concerning our planet.

An example is research on global change. A number of scientists have come to believe that human activities, such as use of **fossil fuels** and **deforestation** of **tropical rain forest**s, may be altering the earth's **climate**. To test that hypothesis, a huge amount of meteorological data must be collected from around the world, and no single institution can possibly obtain and analyze it all.

A major effort to organize research on important, worldwide scientific questions such as climate change was begun in the early 1980s. Largely through the efforts of scientists from two United States organizations, the National Aeronautics and Space Administration (NASA) and the National Research Council, a proposal was developed for the creation of an International Geosphere-Biosphere Programme (IGBP). The purpose of the IGBP was to help scientists from around the world focus on major issues about which there was still too little information. Activity funding comes from national governments, scientific societies, and private organizations.

IGBP was not designed to be a new organization, with new staff, new researchers, and new funding problems. Instead, it was conceived of as a coordinating program that would call on existing organizations to attack certain problems. The proposal was submitted in September 1986 to the General Assembly of the International Council of Scientific Unions (ICSU), where it received enthusiastic support.

Within two years, more than twenty nations agreed to cooperate with IGBP, forming national committees to work with the international office. A small office, administered by Harvard oceanographer James McCarthy, was installed at the Royal Swedish Academy of Sciences in Stockholm.

IGBP has moved forward rapidly. It identified existing programs that fit the Programme's goals and developed new research efforts. Because many global processes are gradual, a number of IGBP projects are designed with time frames of ten to twenty years.

By the early 1990s, IGBP had defined a number of projects, including the Joint Global Ocean Flux Study, the Land-Ocean Interactions in the Coastal Zone study, the Biospheric Aspects of the Hydrological Cycle research, Past Global Changes, Global Analysis, Interpretation and Modeling, and Global Change System for Analysis, Research and Training. *See also* Biosphere; Greenhouse effect; Hydrologic cycle; Nongovernmental organization; Ozone layer depletion

[*David E. Newton*]

FURTHER READING

Edelson, E. "Laying the Foundation." *Mosaic* (Fall/Winter 1988): 4-11.

Kupchella, C. E. *Environmental Science: Living within the System of Nature.* Boston: Allyn and Bacon, Inc., 1986.

Perry, J. S. "International Institutions for the Global Environment." *MTS Journal* (Fall 1991): 27-8.

International Institute for Sustainable Development (Winnipeg, MB, Canada)

The International Institute for Sustainable Development (IISD) is a nonprofit organization that serves as an informa-

tion and resources clearinghouse for policy makers promoting **sustainable development**. IISD aims to promote sustainable development in decision making worldwide by assisting with policy analysis, providing information about practices, measuring sustainability, and building partnerships to further sustainability goals. It serves businesses, governments, communities, and individuals in both developing and industrialized nations. IISD's stated aim is to "create networks designed to move sustainable development from concept to practice." Founded in 1990 and based in Winnipeg, Canada, IISD is funded by foundations, governmental organizations, private sector sources, and revenue from publications and products.

IISD works in seven program areas. The Business Strategies program focuses on improving competitiveness, creating jobs, and protecting the environment through sustainability. Projects include several publications and the EarthEnterprise program, which offers entrepreneurial and employment strategies. IISD's Trade and Sustainable Development program works on building positive relationships between trade, the **environment**, and development. It examines how to make international accords, such as those made by the World Trade Organization, compatible with the goals of sustainable development. The Community Adaptation and Sustainable Livelihoods program identifies adaptive strategies for drylands in Africa and India, and it examines the influences of policies and new technology on local ways of life. The Great Plains program works with community, farm, government, and industry groups to assist communities in the Great Plains region of North America with sustainable development. It focuses on government policies in agriculture, such as the Western Grain Transportation Act, as well as loss of transportation subsidies, the **North American Free Trade Agreement (NAFTA)**, **soil** salination and loss of **wetlands**, job loss, and technological advances. Measurement and Indicators aims to set measurable goals and progress indicators for sustainable development. As part of this, IISD offers information about the successful uses of taxes and subsidies to encourage sustainability worldwide. Common Security focuses on initiatives of peace and consensus-building.

IISD's Information and Communications program offers several publications and Internet sites featuring information on sustainable development issues, terms, events, and media coverage. This includes *Earth Negotiations Bulletin*, which provides on-line coverage of major environmental and development negotiations (especially United Nations conferences), and IISDnet, with information about sustainable development worldwide. IISD also publishes more than 50 books, monographs, and discussion papers, including *Sourcebook on Sustainable Development*, which lists organizations, databases, conferences, and other resources. IISD produces five journals that include *Developing Ideas*, published bimonthly both in print and electronically, and featuring articles on sustainable development terms, issues, resources, and recent media coverage. *Earth Negotiations Bulletin* reports on conferences and negotiations meetings, especially United Nations conferences. IISD's Internet journal, */linkages/*

journal, is a bimonthly electronic multi-media subscription magazine focusing on global negotiations. Its reporting service, Sustainable Developments, reports on environmental and development negotiations for meetings and symposia via the Internet. IISD also operates IISDnet (http://iisd1.iisd.ca/), an Internet information site featuring research, new trends, global activities, contacts, information on IISD's activities and projects, including United Nations negotiations on environment and development, corporate environmental reporting, and information on trade issues.

IISD is the umbrella organization for Earth Council, an international nongovernmental organization (NGO) created in 1992 as a result of the **United Nations Earth Summit**. The organization creates measurements for achieving sustainable development and assesses practices and economic measures for their effects on sustainable development. Earth Council coordinated the Rio+5 Forum in Rio de Janeiro in March 1997, which assessed progress towards sustainable development since the Earth Summit in 1992. IISD has produced two publications, *Trade and Sustainable Development* and *Guidelines for the Practical Assessment of Progress Toward Sustainable Development*.

IISD has an international board of directors. Contact: 161 Portage Ave. E., 6th Fl., Winnipeg, MB, Canada R3B 0Y4; telephone: (204)958-770; fax: (204)958-7710; e-mail: reception@iisdpost.iisd.ca. Web page: http://www.iisd.ca/.

[*Carol Steinfeld*]

International Joint Commission (Washington, D.C.)

The International Joint Commission (IJC) is a permanent, independent organization of the United States and Canada formed to resolve trans-boundary ecological concerns. Founded in 1912 as a result of provisions under the Boundary Waters Treaty of 1909, the IJC was patterned after an earlier organization, the Joint Commission, which was formed by the United States and Britain.

The IJC consists of six commissioners, with three appointed by the President of the United States, and three by the Governor-in-Council of Canada, plus support personnel. The commissioners and their organizations generally operate freed from direct influence or instruction from their national governments. The IJC is frequently cited as an excellent model for international dispute resolution because of its history of successfully and objectively dealing with **natural resources** and environmental disputes between friendly countries.

The major activities of the IJC have dealt with apportioning, developing, conserving, and protecting the binational **water resources** of the United States and Canada. Some other issues, including transboundary **air pollution**, have also been addressed by the Commission.

The power of the IJC comes from its authority to initiate scientific and socio-economic investigations, conduct quasi-judicial enquiries, and arbitrate disputes.

Of special concern to the IJC have been issues related to the **Great Lakes**. Since the early 1970s, IJC activities have been substantially guided by provisions under the 1972 and 1978 **Great Lakes Water Quality Agreement** plus updated protocols. For example, it is widely acknowledged, and well documented, that environmental quality and **ecosystem** health have been substantially degraded in the Great Lakes. In 1985, the Water Quality Board of the IJC recommended that states and provinces with Great Lakes boundaries make a collective commitment to address this communal problem, especially with respect to **pollution**. These governments agreed to develop and implement remedial action plans (RAPs) towards the restoration of **environmental health** within their political jurisdictions. Forty-three areas of concern have been identified on the basis of environmental pollution, and each of these will be the focus of a remedial action plan.

An important aspect of the design and intent of the overall program, and of the individual RAPs, will be developing a process of integrated ecosystem management. Ecosystem management involves systematic, comprehensive approaches toward the restoration and protection of environmental quality. The ecosystem approach involves consideration of interrelationships among land, air, and water, as well as those between the inorganic environment and the biota, including humans. The ecosystem approach would replace the separate, more linear approaches that have traditionally been used to manage environmental problems. These conventional attempts have included directed programs to deal with particular resources such as fisheries, migratory birds, **land use**, or **point source**s and area sources of toxic emissions. Although these non-integrated methods have been useful, they have been limited because they have failed to account for important interrelationships among environmental management programs, and among components of the ecosystem. Contact: International Joint Commission, 1250 23rd Street NW, Ste. 100, Washington, DC 20440

[*Bill Freedman*]

International Primate Protection League (Summerville, South Carolina)

Founded in 1974 by Shirley McGreal, International Primate Protection League (IPPL) is a global **conservation** organization that works to protect nonhuman primates, especially monkeys and apes (**chimpanzees**, **orangutan**s, **gibbons**, and **gorillas**).

IPPL has 30,000 members, branches in the United Kingdom, Germany, and Australia, and field representatives in some 32 countries. Its advisory board consists of scientists, conservationists, and experts on primates, including the world-renowned primatologist Jane Goodall, whose famous studies and books are considered the authoritative texts on chimpanzees. Her studies have also heightened public interest and sympathy for chimpanzees and other nonhuman primates.

IPPL runs a sanctuary and rehabilitation center at its Summerville, S.C. headquarters, which houses two dozen gibbons and other abandoned, injured, or traumatized primates who are refugees from medical laboratories or abusive pet owners. IPPL concentrates on investigating and fighting the multi-million dollar commercial trafficking in primates for medical laboratories, the **pet trade**, and zoos, much of which is illegal trade and smuggling of **endangered species** protected by international law. IPPL is considered the most active and effective group working to stem the cruel and often lethal trade in primates.

IPPL's work has helped to save the lives of literally tens of thousands of monkeys and apes, many of which are threatened or endangered species. For example, the group was instrumental in persuading the governments of India and Thailand to ban or restrict the export of monkeys, which were being shipped by the thousands to research laboratories and pet stores across the world.

The trade in primates is especially cruel and wasteful, since a common way of capturing them is by shooting the mother, which then enables poachers to capture the infant. And many captured monkeys and apes die enroute to their destinations, often being transported in sacks, crates, or hidden in other devices.

IPPL often undertakes actions and projects that are dangerous and require a good deal of skill. Its investigations have recently led to the conviction of a Miami, Florida, animal dealer for conspiring to help smuggle six baby orangutans captured in the jungles of Borneo. The endangered orangutan is protected by the **Convention on International Trade in Endangered Species of Fauna and Flora (CITES)**, as well as by the United States **Endangered Species Act**. In retaliation, the dealer unsuccessfully sued McGreal, as did a multi-national corporation she once criticized for its plan to capture chimpanzees and use them for hepatitis research in Sierra Leone.

IPPL publishes *IPPL News* several times a year and sends out periodic letters alerting members of events and issues that affect primates. Contact: International Primate Protection League, P.O. Box 766, Summerville, SC 29484. Internet: http://www.sims.net/organizations/ippl/ippl.html.

[*Lewis G. Regenstein*]

International Register of Potentially Toxic Chemicals (U. N. Environment Programme)

The International Register of Potentially Toxic Chemicals is published by the **United Nations Environment Programme (UNEP)**. Part of UNEP's three-pronged Earthwatch program, the register is an international inventory of **chemicals** that threaten the **environment**. Along with the **Global Environment Monitoring System** and **INFOTERRA**, the register monitors and measures environmental problems worldwide. Information from the register is routinely shared with agencies in developing countries. **Third World** countries have long been the toxic dumping grounds for the world, and they still use many chemicals that have been banned elsewhere. Environmental groups regularly send information from the register to toxic chemical users in developing countries as part of their effort to stop the export of toxic **pollution**. *See also* Bhopal, India; Emergency Planning and Community Right-to-Know-Act; Hazardous waste siting; International trade in toxic waste

International Society for Environmental Ethics (College Park, Maryland)

The International Society for Environmental Ethics (ISEE) is an organization that seeks to educate people about the environmental ethics and philosophy concerning nature. An environmental ethic is the philosophy that humans have a moral duty to sustain the natural **environment** and attempts to answer how humans should treat other species (plant and animal), use Earth's **natural resources**, and place value on the aesthetic experiences of **nature**.

The society is an auxiliary organization of the American Philosophical Association, with about 700 members in over 20 countries. Many of ISEE's current members are philosophers, teachers, or environmentalists. The ISEE officers include president Mark Sagoff (Institute for Philosophy and Public Policy, University of Maryland) and **John Baird Callicott**, vice president, (professor of philosophy at the University of North Texas). Two other key members are editors of the ISEE newsletter, Jack Weir and **Holmes Rolston, III**. (Professor of Philosophy, Colorado State University). All have contributed to the ongoing ISEE Master Environmental Ethics Bibliography.

ISEE publishes a quarterly newsletter available to members in print form and maintains an Internet site of back issues. Of special note is the ISEE Bibliography, an ongoing project that contains over 5,000 records from journals such as *Environmental Ethics, Environmental Values*, and the *Journal of Agricultural and Environmental Ethics*.

Another work in progress, the ISEE Syllabus Project, continues to be developed by Callicott and Robert Hood, doctoral candidate at Bowling Green State University. They maintain a database of course offerings in environmental philosophy and ethics, based on information from two-year community colleges and four-year state universities, private institutions, and master's- and doctorate-granting universities. ISEE supports the enviroethics program which has spurred many Internet discussion groups and is constantly expanding into new areas of communication. Most of ISEE materials are available on the Internet (http://

www.cep.unt.edu/ISEE.html) as well as in print and diskette formats. Contact: Institute for Philosophy and Public Policy, University of Maryland, College Park, MD 20742.

[*Nicole Beatty*]

International trade in toxic waste

Just as VCRs, cars, and laundry soap are traded across borders, so too is the waste that accompanies their production. In the United States alone, industrial production accounts for at least 500 million lbs (230 million kg) of **hazardous waste** a year. The industries of other developed nations also produce waste. While some of it is disposed within national borders, a portion is sent to other countries where costs are cheaper and regulations less stringent than in the waste's country of origin.

Unlike consumer products, internationally traded hazardous waste has begun to meet local opposition. In some recent high-profile cases, barges filled with waste have traveled the world looking for final resting places. In at least one case, a ship may have dumped about ten tons of toxic municipal incinerator ash in the ocean after being turned away from dozens of ports. In recent years national and international bodies have begun to voice official opposition to this dangerous trade through bans and regulations.

The international trade in toxic wastes is, at bottom, waste disposal with a foreign-relations twist. Typically a manufacturing facility generates waste during the production process. The facility manager pays a waste-hauling firm to dispose of the waste. If the **landfill**s in the country of origin cost too much, or if there are no landfills that will take the waste, the disposal firm will find a cheaper option, perhaps a landfill in another country. In the United States, the shipper must then notify the **Environmental Protection Agency (EPA)**, which then notifies the State Department. After ascertaining that the destination country will indeed accept the waste, American regulators approve the sale.

Disposing of the waste overseas in a landfill is only the most obvious example of this international trade. Waste haulers also sell their cargo as raw materials for **recycling**. For example, used **lead**-acid batteries discarded by American consumers are sent to Brazil where factory workers extract and resmelt the lead. Though the lead-acid alone would classify as hazardous, whole batteries do not. Waste haulers can ship these batteries overseas without notification to Mexico, Japan, and Canada, among other countries. In other cases, waste haulers sell products, like **DDT**, that have been banned in one country to buyers in another country that has no ban. Whatever the strategy for disposal, waste haulers are most commonly small, independent operators who provide a service to waste producers in industrialized countries.

These haulers bring waste to other countries to take advantage of cheaper disposal options and less stringent regulatory climates. Some countries forbid the disposal of the certain kinds of waste. Countries without such prohibitions will import more waste. Cheap landfills depend on cheap labor and land. Countries with an abundance of both can become attractive destinations. Entrepreneurs or government officials in countries, like Haiti, or regions within countries, such as Wales, that lack a strong manufacturing base, view waste disposal as a viable, inexpensive business. Inhabitants may view it as the best way to make money and create jobs. Simply by storing hazardous waste, the country of Guinea-Bissau could have made $120 million, more money than its annual budget.

Though the **less developed countries (LDC)** predictably receive large amounts of toxic waste, the bulk of the international trade occurs between industrialized nations. Canada and the United Kingdom in particular import large volumes of toxic waste. Canada imports almost 85 percent of the waste sent abroad by American firms, approximately 150,000 lbs (70,000 kg) per year. The bulk of the waste ends up at an incinerator in Ontario or a landfill in Quebec. Because Canada's disposal regulations are less strict than United States laws, the operators of the landfill and incinerator can charge lower fees than similar disposal sites in the United States.

A waste hauler's life becomes complicated when the receiving country's government or local activists discover that the waste may endanger health and the **environment**. Local regulators may step in and forbid the sale. This happened many times in the case of the *Khian Sea*, a ship that had contracted to dispose of Philadelphia's incinerator ash. The ship was turned away from Haiti, from Guinea-Bissau, from Panama, and from Sri Lanka. For two years, beginning in 1986, the ship carried the toxic ash from port to port looking for a home for its cargo before finally mysteriously losing the ash somewhere in the Indian Ocean.

This early resistance to toxic-waste dumping has since led to the negotiation of international treaties forbidding or regulating the trade in toxic waste. In 1989, the African, Caribbean, and Pacific countries (ACP) and the countries belonging to the **European Economic Community** (EEC) negotiated the Lome IV Convention, which bans shipments of nuclear and hazardous waste from the EEC to the ACP countries. ACP countries further agreed not to import such waste from non-EEC countries. Environmentalists have encouraged the EEC to broaden its commitment to limiting waste trade.

In the same year, under the auspices of the **United Nations Environment Programme** (UNEP), the Basel Convention on the Control of Transboundary Movements of Hazardous Wastes and Their Disposal was negotiated. This requires shippers to obtain government permission from the destination country before sending waste to foreign landfills or incinerators. Critics contend that Basel merely formalizes the trade.

In 1991, the nations of the Organization of African Unity negotiated another treaty restricting the international waste trade. The Bamako Convention on the Ban of the Import into Africa and the Control of Transboundary Movement and Management of Hazardous Wastes within Africa criminalized the import of all hazardous waste. Bamako further forbade waste traders from importing to Africa materials that had been banned in one country to a country that has no such ban. Bamako also radically redefined the assessment of what constitutes a health hazard. Under the treaty, all **chemicals** are considered hazardous until proven otherwise.

These international strategies find their echoes in national law. Less developed countries have tended to follow the Lome and Bamako examples. At least eighty-three African, Latin-Caribbean, and Asian-Pacific countries have banned hazardous waste imports. And the United States, in a policy similar to the Basel Convention, requires hazardous waste shipments to be authorized by the importing country's government.

The efforts to restrict toxic waste trade reflect, in part, a desire to curb environmental inequity. When waste flows from a richer country to a poorer country or region, the inhabitants living near the incinerator, landfill, or **recycling** facility are exposed to the dangers of toxic compounds. For example, tests of workers in the Brazilian lead resmelting operation found blood-lead levels several times the United States standard. Lead was also found in the water supply of a nearby farm after five cows died. The loose regulations that keep prices low and attract waste haulers mean that there are fewer safeguards for local health and the environment. For example, leachate from unlined landfills can contaminate local **groundwater**. Jobs in the disposal industry tend to be lower paying than jobs in manufacturing. The inhabitants of the receiving country receive the wastes of industrialization without the benefits.

Stopping the waste trade is a way to force manufacturers to change production processes. As long as cheap disposal options exist, there is little incentive to change. A waste-trade ban makes hazardous waste expensive to discard, and will force business to search for ways to reduce this cost.

Companies that want to reduce their hazardous waste may opt for source reduction, which limits the hazardous components in the production process. This can both reduce production costs and increase output. A Monsanto facility in Ohio saved more than $3 million dollars a year while eliminating more than 17 million lbs (8 million kg) of waste. According to officials at the plant, average yield increased by 8 percent. Measures forced by a lack of disposal options can therefore benefit the corporate bottom line, while reducing risks to health and the environment. *See also* Environmental law; Environmental policy; Groundwater pollution; Hazardous waste siting; Incineration; Industrial waste treatment; Leaching; Ocean dumping; Radioactive waste; Radioactive waste management; Smelter; Solid waste; Solid waste incineration; Solid waste recycling and recovery; Solid waste volume reduction; Storage and transport of hazardous materials; Toxic substance; Waste management; Waste reduction

[*Alair MacLean*]

FURTHER READING

Chepesiuk, R. "From Ash to Cash: The International Trade in Toxic Waste." *E Magazine* 2 (July-August 1991): 30-37.

Dorfman, M., W. Muir, and C. Miller. *Environmental Dividends: Cutting More Chemical Waste.* New York: INFORM, 1992.

Moyers, B. D. *Global Dumping Ground: The International Traffic in Hazardous Waste.* Cabin John, MD: Seven Locks Press, 1990.

Vallette, J., and H. Spalding. *The International Trade in Wastes: A Greenpeace Inventory.* Washington, DC: Greenpeace, 1990.

International Union for the Conservation of Nature and Natural Resources
See IUCN—The World Conservation Union

International Whaling Commission
See International Convention for the Regulation of Whaling

International Wildlife Coalition

The International Wildlife Coalition (IWC) was established by a small group of individuals who came from a variety of environmental and **animal rights** organizations in 1984. Like many NGOs (nongovernmental organizations) that arose in the 1970s and 1980s their initial work involved the protection of whales. The IWC raised money for whale **conservation** programs on endangered Atlantic humpback whale populations. This was one of the first species where researchers identified individual animals through tail photographs. Using this technique the IWC developed what is now a common tool, a whale adoption program based on individual animals with human names.

From that basis, the fledgling group established itself in an advocacy role with three principles in their mandate: to prevent cruelty to wildlife, to prevent killing of **wildlife**, and to prevent destruction of wildlife **habitat**. In light of those principles, the IWC can be characterized as an extended animal rights organization. They maintain the "prevention of cruelty" aspect common to humane societies, perhaps the oldest progenitor of animal rights groups. In standing by an ethic of preventing killing, they stand with animal rights groups, but by protecting habitat they take a more significant step by acting in a broad way to achieve their initial two principles.

The program thus works at both ends of the spectrum, undertaking wildlife rehabilitation and other programs dealing with the individual animals, as well as lobbying and promoting letter writing campaigns to improve wildlife legislation. For example, they have used their Brazilian office to create pressure to combat the international trade in exotic pets, and their Canadian office to oppose the harp seal hunt and the deterioration of Canada's impending endangered species legislation. Their United States-based operation has built a reputation in the research field working with government agencies to ensure that whale-watching on the eastern seaboard does not harm the whales. Offices in the United Kingdom are a focus for the IWC concern over the European

Community policies, such as lifting their ban on importing fur from animals killed in leg hold traps.

It has become evident that the diversity within the varied groups that constitute the environmental community is a positive force, however, most conservation NGOs do not cross the gulf between animal rights and habitat conservation. A clear distinction exists between single animal approaches and broader conservation ideals, as they appeal to different protection strategies, and potentially different donors. Although the emotional appeal of releasing porpoises from fishing nets alive outranks backroom lobbying for changes in fishing regulations, the lobbying efforts protect more porpoises. The IWC may be deemed more successful by exploiting a range of targets, or less so than a dedicated advocacy group applying all its focus to one issue. They can point to a growth from a modest 3,000 supporters in the beginning, to over 100,000 people supporting the International Wildlife Coalition today. Contact: World Wide Web— http://www.webcom.com/iwcwww/wurld_wild_web/welcome.html.

[*David Duffus*]

Intrinsic value

Saying that an object has intrinsic value means that, even though it has no specific use, market, or monetary value, it nevertheless can be valuable in and of itself and for its own sake. The **Northern spotted owl** (*Strix occidentalis caurina*) for example, has no instrumental or market value; it is not a means to any human end, nor is it sold or traded in any market. But, environmentalists argue, utility and price are not the only measures of worth. Indeed, they say, some of the things humans value most—truth, love, respect—are not for sale at any price, and to try to put a price on them would only tend to cheapen them. Such things have "intrinsic value."

Similarly, environmentalists say, the natural **environment** and its myriad life-forms are valuable in their own right. Wilderness, for instance, has intrinsic value and is worthy of protecting for its own sake. To say that something has intrinsic value is not necessarily to deny that it may also have instrumental value for humans and non-human animals alike. Deer, for example, have intrinsic value; but they also have instrumental value as a food source for wolves and other predator species. *See also* Shadow pricing

Introduced species

Introduced **species** (also called invasive species) are those that have been released by humans into an area to which they are not native. These releases can occur accidently, from places such as the cargo holds of ships. They can also occur intentionally, and species have been introduced for a range of ornamental and recreational uses, as well as for agricultural, medicinal, and pest control purposes.

Introduced species can have dramatically unpredictable effects on the **environment** and native species. Such effects can include overabundance of the introduced species, competitive displacement, and disease-caused **mortality** of the native species. Numerous examples of adverse consequences associated with the accidental release of species or the long term effects of deliberately introduced species exist in the United States and around the world. Introduced species can be beneficial as long as they are carefully regulated. Almost all the major varieties of grain and vegetables used in the United States originated in other parts of the world. This includes corn, rice, wheat, tomatoes, and potatoes.

The kudzu vine, which is native to Japan, was deliberately introduced into the southern United States for **erosion** control and to shade and feed livestock. It is, however, an extremely aggressive and fast-growing species, and it can form continuous blankets of foliage that cover forested hillsides, resulting in malformed and dead trees. Other species introduced as ornamentals have spread into the wild, displacing or outcompeting native species. Several varieties of cultivated roses, such as the multiflora rose, are serious pests and nuisance shrubs in field and pastures. The **purple loosestrife**, with its beautiful purple flowers, was originally brought from Europe as a garden ornamental. It has spread rapidly in freshwater **wetlands** in the northern United States, displacing other plants such as cattails. This is viewed with concern by ecologists and **wildlife** biologists since the food value of loosestrife is minimal, while the roots and starchy tubes of cattails are an important food source to muskrats. Common ragweed was accidently introduced to North America, and it is now a major health irritant for many people.

Introduced species are sometimes so successful because human activity has changed the conditions of a particular environment. The Pine Barrens of southern New Jersey form an **ecosystem** that is naturally acidic and low in **nutrient**s. Bogs in this area support a number of slow-growing plant species that are adapted to these conditions, including peat moss, sundews, and pitcher plants. But **urban runoff**, which contain **fertilizer**s, and **wastewater effluent**, which is high in both **nitrogen** and **phosphorus**, have enriched the bogs; the waters there have become less acidic and shown a gradual elevation in the concentration of nutrients. These changes in **aquatic chemistry** have resulted in changes in plant species, and the acidophilus mosses and herbs are being replaced by fast-growing plants that are not native to the Pine Barrens.

Zebra mussels were transported by accident from Europe to the United States, and they are causing severe problems in the **Great Lakes**. They proliferate at a prodigious rate, crowding out native species and clogging industrial and municipal water-intake pipes. Many ecologists fear that shipping traffic will transport the zebra mussel to harbors all over the country. Scattered observations of this tiny crustacean have already been made in the lower **Hudson River** in New York.

Although introduced species are usually regarded with concern, they can occasionally be used to some benefit. The **water hyacinth** is an aquatic plant of tropical origin that has become a serious clogging nuisance in lakes, streams, and waterways in the southern United States. Numerous methods of physical and chemical removal have been attempted to eradicate or control it, but research has also established that the plant can improve **water quality**. The water hyacinth has proved useful in the withdrawal of nutrients from sewage and other wastewater. Many constructed wetlands, polishing ponds, and waste lagoons in waste treatment plants now take advantage of this fact by routing wastewater through floating beds of water hyacinth.

The reintroduction of native species is extremely difficult, and it is an endeavor that has had low rates of success. Efforts by the **Fish and Wildlife Service** to reintroduce the endangered **whooping crane** into native **habitat** in the southwestern United States were initially unsuccessful because of the fragility of the eggs, as well as the poor parenting skills of birds raised in captivity. The service then devised a strategy of allowing the more common sandhill crane to incubate the eggs of captive whooping cranes in **wilderness** nests, and the fledglings were then taught survival skills by their surrogate parents. Such projects, however, are extremely time and labor intensive; they are also costly and difficult to implement for large numbers of most species.

Due to the difficulties and expense required to protect native species and to eradicate introduced species, there are not many international laws and policies that seek to prevent these problems before they begin. Thus customs agents at ports and airports routinely check luggage and cargo for live plant and animal materials to prevent the accidental or deliberate transport of non-native species. Quarantine policies are also designed to reduce the probability of spreading introduced species, particularly diseases, from one country to another.

There are similar concerns about **genetically engineered organism**s, and many have argued that their creation and release could have the same devastating environmental consequences as some introduced species. For this reason, the use of bioengineered organisms is highly regulated; both the **Food and Drug Administration** and the **Environmental Protection Agency (EPA)** impose strict controls on the field testing of bioengineered products, as well as on their cultivation and use.

Conservation policies for the protection of native species are now focused on habitats and ecosystems rather than single species. It is easier to prevent the encroachment of introduced species by protecting an entire ecosystem from disturbance, and this is increasingly well recognized both inside and outside the **conservation** community. *See also* Bioremediation; Endangered species; Fire ants; Gypsy moth; Rabbits in Australia; Wildlife management

[*Usha Vedagiri and Douglas Smith*]

FURTHER READING

Common Weeds of the United States. United States Department of Agriculture. New York: Dover Publications, 1971.

Forman, R. T. T., ed. *Pine Barrens: Ecology and Landscape.* New York: Academic Press, 1979.

Inversion
See **Atmospheric inversion**

Iodine 131

A radioactive **isotope** of the element iodine. During the 1950s and early 1960s, iodine-131 was considered a major health hazard to humans. Along with **cesium-137** and **strontium-90**, it was one of the three most abundant isotopes found in the fallout from the atmospheric testing of **nuclear weapons**. These three isotopes settled to the earth's surface and were ingested by cows, ultimately affecting humans by way of dairy products. In the human body, iodine-131, like all forms of that element, tends to concentrate in the thyroid, where it may cause **cancer** and other health disorders. The **Chernobyl** nuclear reactor explosion is known to have released large quantities of iodine-131 into the atmosphere. *See also* Radioactivity

Ion

Forms of ordinary chemical elements that have gained or lost electrons from their orbit around the atomic nucleus and, thus, have become electrically charged. Positive ions (those that have lost electrons) are called *cations* because when charged electrodes are placed in a solution containing ions the positive ions migrate to the cathode (negative electrode). Negative ions (those that have gained extra electrons) are called *anions* because they migrate toward the anode (positive electrode). Environmentally important cations include the **hydrogen** ion (H^+) and dissolved metals. Important anions include the hydroxyl ion (OH^-) as well as many of the dissolved ions of nonmetallic elements. *See also* Ion exchange; Ionizing radiation

Ion exchange

The process of replacing one ion that is attached to a charged surface with another. A very important type of ion exchange is the exchange of cations bound to **soil** particles. Soil **clay minerals** and organic matter both have negative surface charges that bind cations. In a fertile soil the predominant exchangeable cations are Ca^{2+}, Mg^{2+} and K^+. In acid soils Al^{3+} and H^+ are also important exchangeable ions. When materials containing cations are added to soil, cations **leaching** through the soil are retarded by cation exchange.

Ionizing radiation

High-energy radiation with penetrating competence such as **X-ray**s and **gamma ray**s which induces ionization in living material. Molecules are bound together with covalent bonds, and generally an even number of electrons binds the atoms together. However, high-energy penetrating radiation can fragment molecules resulting in atoms with unpaired electrons known as "free radicals." The ionized "free radicals" are exceptionally reactive, and their interaction with the macromolecules (**DNA, RNA,** and proteins) of living cells can, with high dosage, lead to cell death. Cell damage (or death) is a function of penetration ability, the kind of cell exposed, the length of exposure, and the total dose of ionizing radiation. Cells that are mitotically active and have a high oxygen content are most vulnerable to ionizing radiation. *See also* Radiation exposure; Radiation sickness; Radioactivity

Iron minerals

The oxides and hydroxides of ferric iron (Fe(III)) are very important minerals in many **soil**s, and are important **suspended solid**s in some fresh water systems. Important oxides and hydroxides of iron include goethite, hematite, lepidocrocite, and ferrihydrite.

These minerals tend to be very finely divided and can be found in the clay-sized fraction of soils, and like other clay-sized minerals, are important adsorbers of ions. At high **pH** they adsorb hydroxide (OH^-) ions, creating negatively charged surfaces that contribute to cation exchange surfaces. At low pH they adsorb hydrogen (H^+) ions creating anion exchange surfaces. In the pH range between 8 and 9 the surfaces have little or no charge. Iron hydroxide and oxide surfaces strongly adsorb some environmentally important anions, such as phosphate, arsenate and selanite, and cations like **copper, lead**, manganese and chromium. These ions are not exchangeable, and in **environment**s where iron oxides and hydroxides are abundant, surface **adsorption** can control the mobility of these strongly adsorbed ions.

The hydroxides and oxides of iron are found in the greatest abundance in older highly weathered landscapes. These minerals are very insoluble and during soil weathering they form from the iron that is released from the structure of the soil-forming minerals. Thus, iron oxide and hydroxide minerals tend to be most abundant in old landscapes that have not been affected by **glaciation**, and in landscapes where the rainfall is high and the rate of soil mineral weathering is high. These minerals give the characteristic red (hematite or ferrihydrite) or yellow-brown (goethite) colors to soils that are common in the tropics and subtropics. *See also* Arsenic; Erosion; Ion exchange; Phosphorus; Soil profile; Soil texture

Irradiation of food

Despite raging controversy and concerns about safety issues, irradiation is used in the United States and abroad to preserve food. Irradiation of food has three main uses: extension of shelf life, destruction of bacteria, and elimination of insects. The **Food and Drug Administration** (FDA) has approved the use of irradiation for spices, fruits, vegetables,

nuts, teas, wheat flour, pork, and poultry. In the United States all irradiated food must be clearly labeled with the radura symbol and the package must read "Treated With Radiation."

Irradiation technology involves exposing food to an array of **gamma ray**s from radioactive cobalt or cesium, **X-ray**s or electronic beams. The amount of radiation absorbed by the product from the **ionizing radiation** used during processing is measured in units called RADs (radiant energy absorbed). One hundred RADs is one gray. Food is typically treated with four to eight kilograys. Many people fear that irradiation will make the food radioactive, but this is not the case. The process is similar to luggage going through an airport scanner: the rays pass through the luggage but the luggage never comes into direct contact with radioactive material. Thus food is not contaminated and at the low energy levels used, there is very little chance of secondary activation of elements in the irradiated material.

The irradiation process itself is relatively simple. Food enters a lead-lined chamber by means of a conveyor belt. Cobalt-60 rods, which look like pencils, are sealed in stainless steel tubes. The food is irradiated in the chamber with gamma rays for forty-five minutes to an hour; the temperature of the food rises only two or three degrees during the process. Changes in the taste, texture, and color of the food are minimal since there is very little fluctuation in temperature.

When food products are irradiated a radiolytic product (RP) is created. First, the energy from gamma rays displaces electrons in the food. Displacement of electrons slows cell division and kills bacteria and pests. This displacement also produces free radicals, which are unstable chemical compounds. The free radicals react with other molecules to form stable molecules—RPs. RPs such as **carbon dioxide** also occur when food is processed in traditional ways such as canning or cooking. However, about ten percent of the RPs found in irradiated food are unique to the irradiation process and little is known about the effects that they may have on human health. Food irradiation, however, destroys many of the bacteria and organisms that can cause food-borne illnesses like salmonella, botulism, and many other forms of food poisoning.

Fruit must be certified free of insects and pests before it can be imported into the United States. Treating fruit and produce with irradiation can eliminate the need for chemical fumigation after harvesting. The shelf life is extended by the reduction and elimination of organisms that cause spoilage. It also slows cell division, thus delaying the ripening process, and in some types of produce irradiation extends the shelf life for up to a week. Advocates of irradiation claim that it is a safe alternative to the use of fumigants several of which have been banned in the United States.

Nevertheless, irradiation removes some of the nutrients from foods, particularly vitamins A, C, E, and the B-complex vitamins. Advocates of irradiation claim that this is a moot point since cooking can destroy these same nutrients. Research suggests that cooking an irradiated food compounds the problem of loss of nutrients.

Even if irradiation is 100 percent safe and beneficial there are numerous environmental concerns. Many opponents of irradiation cite the proliferation of radioactive material and the environmental hazards. The mining and on-site processing of radioactive materials are devastating to regional **ecosystem**s. There are safety hazards associated with the transportation of radioactive material, production of **isotope**s, and disposal. *See also* Radiation exposure; Radioactivity

[*Debra Glidden*]

FURTHER READING

Castleman, M. "Radiant Grub." *Sierra* 78 (May-June 1993): 27-8.

"Food Irradiation: Harmful or Helpful?" *Mayo Clinic Health Letter* 8 (May 1992): 1.

"Food Irradiation: The Controversy Heats Up." *Tufts University Diet and Nutrition Letter* 10 (March 1992): 4.

Gibbs, G. *Food That Would Last Forever: Understanding the Danger of Food Irradiation.* Wayne, NJ: Avery Publishing Group, 1993.

"Irradiation: Is it Safe?" *Mayo Clinic Nutrition Letter* 2 (July 1989): 6.

Papizan, R. "Food Irradiation: A Hot Issue." *Harvard Health Letter* 17 (August 1992): 1.

Irrigation

Irrigation is the method of supplying water to land to support plant growth. This technology has had a powerful role in the history of civilization. In **arid** regions sunshine is plentiful and **soil** is usually fertile, so irrigation supplies the critical factor needed for plant growth. Yields have been high, but not without costs. Historic problems include **salinization** and **water logging**; contemporary difficulties include immense costs, spread of water-borne diseases, and degraded aquatic **environment**s.

One geographer described California's Sierra Nevada as the "mother nurse of the San Joaquin Valley." Its heavy winter snowpack provides abundant and extended **runoff** for the rich valley soils below. Numerous irrigation districts, formed to build diversion and storage **dams**, supply water through gravity-fed canals. The snow melt is low in **nutrient**s, so salinization problems are minimal. Wealth from the lush fruit orchards has enriched the state.

By contrast, the **Colorado River**, like the Nile, flows mainly through arid lands. Deeply incised in places, the river is also limited for irrigation by the high salt content of **desert** tributaries. Still, demand for water exceeds supply. Water crossing the border into Mexico is so saline that the federal government has built a **desalinization** plant at Yuma, Arizona. Colorado River water is imperative to the Imperial Valley, which specializes in winter produce in the rich, delta soils. To reduce salinization problems, one-fifth of the water used must be drained off into the growing Salton Sea.

Salinization and water logging have long plagued the Tigris, Euphrates, and Indus River **flood plain**s. Once fertile areas of Iraq and Pakistan are covered with salt crystals. Half of the irrigated land in our western states is threatened by salt buildup.

Some of the worst problems are degraded aquatic environments. The **Aswan High Dam** in Egypt has greatly amplified surface evaporation, reduced **nutrient**s to the land and to fisheries in the delta, and has contributed to the spread of **schistosomiasis** via water snails in irrigation ditches. Diversion of drainage away from the **Aral Sea** for cotton irrigation has severely lowered the shoreline, and threatens this water body with ecological disaster.

Spray irrigation in the High Plains is lowering the **Ogallala Aquifer**'s **water table**, raising pumping costs. Kesterson Marsh in the San Joaquin Valley has become a hazard to **wildlife** because of selenium poisoning from irrigation drainage. The federal **Bureau of Reclamation** has invested huge sums in dams and **reservoir**s in western states. Some question the wisdom of such investments, given the past century of farm surpluses, and argue that water users are not paying the true cost.

Irrigation still offers great potential, but only if used with wisdom and understanding. New technologies may yet contribute to the world's ever-increasing need for food. *See also* Climate; Commercial fishing; Reclamation

[*Nathan H. Meleen*]

FURTHER READING

Huffman, R. E. *Irrigation Development and Public Water Policy.* New York: Ronald Press, 1953.

Powell, J. W. "The Reclamation Idea." In *American Environmentalism: Readings in Conservation History.* 3rd ed., edited by R. F. Nash. New York: McGraw-Hill, 1990.

U.S. Department of Agriculture. *Water: 1955 Yearbook of Agriculture.* Washington, DC: U. S. Government Printing Office, 1955.

Wittfogel, K. A. "The Hydraulic Civilizations." In *Man's Role in Changing the Face of the Earth*, edited by W. L. Thomas, Jr. Chicago: University of Chicago Press, 1956.

Zimmerman, J. D. *Irrigation.* New York: Wiley, 1966.

ISO 14000: International Environmental Management Standards

ISO 14000 refers to a series of environmental management standards that were adopted by the International Organization for Standardization (ISO) in 1996 and are beginning to be implemented by businesses across the world. Any person or organization interested in the **environment** and in the goal of improving environmental performance of businesses should be interested in ISO 14000. Such interested parties include businesses themselves, their legal representatives, environmental organizations and their members, government officials, and others.

What is the ISO and What Are ISO Standards?

The International Organization for Standardization (ISO) is a private (nongovernmental) worldwide organization whose purpose is to promote uniform standards in international trade. Its members are elected representatives from national standards organizations in 111 countries. The ISO covers all fields involving promoting goods, services, or products and where a Member Body suggests that standardization is desirable, with the exception of electrical and electronic engineering, which are covered by a different organization called the International Electrotechnical Commission (IEC). However, the ISO and the IEC work closely together.

Since the ISO began operations in 1947, its Central Secretariat has been located in Geneva, Switzerland. Between 1951 (when it published its first standard) and 1997, the ISO issued over 8,800 standards. Standards are documents containing technical specifications, rules, guidelines, and definitions to ensure equipment, products, and services perform as specified.

Among the best known standards published by the ISO are those that comprise the ISO 9000 series, which was developed between 1979-1986, and published in 1987. Because ISO 9000 is a forerunner to ISO 14000, it is important to understand the basic structure and function of ISO 9000. The ISO 9000 series is a set of standards for quality management and quality assurance. The standards apply to processes and systems that produce products; they do not apply to the products themselves. Further, the standards provide a general framework for any industry; they are not industry-specific. A company that has become registered under ISO 9000 has demonstrated that it has a documented system for quality that is in place and consistently applied. ISO 9000 standards apply to all kinds of companies whether large or small, in services or manufacturing.

The latest major set of standards published by the ISO is the ISO 14000 series. The impetus for that series came from the United Nations Conference on the Environment and Development (UNCED), which was held in Rio De Janeiro in 1992 and attended by representatives of over one hundred nations. One of the documents resulting from that conference was the *Global Environmental Initiative*, which prompted the ISO to develop its ISO 14000 series of international environmental standards. The ISO's goal is to insure that businesses adopt common internal procedures for environmental controls including, but not limited to, audits. It is important to note that the standards are process standards, not performance standards. The goal is to ensure that businesses are in compliance with their own national and local applicable **environmental law**s and regulations. The initial standards in the series include numbers 14001, 14004, and 14010-14012; all of them adopted by the ISO in 1996.

Provisions of ISO 14000 Series Standards

ISO 14000 sets up criteria pursuant to which a company may become registered or certified as to its environmental management practices.

Central to the process of registration pursuant to ISO 14000 is a company's Environmental Management System (EMS). The EMS is a set of procedures for assessing compliance with environmental laws and company procedures for environmental protection, identifying and resolving with problems, and engaging the company's workforce in a commitment to improved environmental performance by the company.

ISO 14001 series can be divided into two groups: guidance documents and specification documents. The series sets out standards against which a company's EMS will be evaluated. For example, it must include an accurate summary of the legal standards with which the company must comply, such as permit stipulations, and relevant provisions of statutes and regulations, and even provisions of administrative or court-certified consent judgments. To become certified, the EMS must: (1) include an **environmental policy**; (2) establish plans to meet environmental goals and comply with legal requirements; (3) provide for implementation of the policy and operation under it including training for personnel, communication, and document control; (4) set up monitoring and measurement devices and an audit procedure to insure continuing improvement; and (5) provide for management review. The EMS must be certified by a registrar who has been qualified under ISO 13012, a standard that predates the ISO 14000 series.

The ISO 14004 series is a guidance document that gives advice that may be followed but is not required. It includes five principles each of which corresponds to one of the five areas of ISO 14001 listed above.

ISO 14010, 14011, and 14012 are auditing standards. For example, 14010 covers general principles of environmental auditing, and 14011 provides guidelines for auditing of an Environmental Management System (EMS). ISO 14012 provides guidelines for establishing qualifications for environmental auditors, whether those auditors are internal or external.

Plans for Additional Standards within the ISO 14000 Series Standards

The ISO is considering proposals for standards on training and certifying independent auditors (called registrars) who will certify that ISO 14000-certified business have established and adhere to stringent internal systems to monitor and improve their own environmental protection actions. Later the ISO may also establish standards for assessing a company's environmental performance. Standards may be adopted to for use of eco-labeling and **life cycle assessment** of goods involved in international trade.

Benefits and Consequences of ISO 14000 Series Standards

A company contemplating obtaining ISO 14000 registration must evaluate its potential advantages as well as its costs to the company.

ISO 14000 certification may bring various rewards to companies. For example, many firms are hoping that, in return for obtaining ISO 14000 certification (and the actions required to do so), regulatory agencies such as the U.S. **Environmental Protection Agency (EPA)** will give them more favorable treatment. For example, leniency might be shown in less stringent filing or monitoring requirements or even less severe sanctions for past or present violations of environmental statutes and regulations.

Further, compliance may be merely for good public relations, leading consumers to view the certified company as a good corporate citizen that works to protect the environment. There is public pressure on companies to demonstrate their environmental stewardship and accountability; obtaining ISO 14000 certification is one way to do so.

The costs to the company will depend on the scope of the Environmental Management System (EMS). For example, the EMS might be international, national, or limited to individual plants operated by the company. That decision will affect the costs of the environmental audit considerably. National and international systems may prove to be costly.

On the other hand, a company may realize cost savings. For example, an insurance company may give reduced rates on insurance to cover accidental pollution releases to a company that has a proven environmental management system in place. Internally, by implementing an EMS, a company may realize cost savings as a result of waste reduction, use of less fewer toxic chemicals, less energy use, and **recycling**.

A major legal concern raised by lawyers studying the ISO 14000 standards relates to the question of confidentiality. There are serious questions as to whether a governmental regulatory agency can require disclosure of information discovered during a self-audit by a company. The use of a third-party auditor during preparation of the EMS process may weaken a company's argument that information discovered is privileged.

ISO 14000 has potential consequences with respect to international law as well as international trade. ISO 14000 is intended to promote a series of universally accepted EMS practices and lead to consistency in environmental standards between and among trading partners. Some developing countries such as Mexico are reviewing ISO 14000 standards and considering incorporating their provisions within their own environmental laws and regulations. On the other hand, some developing countries have suggested that environmental standards created by ISO 14000 may constitute non-tariff barriers to trade in that costs of ISO 14000 registration may be prohibitively high for small- to medium-size companies.

Companies that have implemented ISO 9000 have learned to view their companies' operations through a "quality of management" lens and implementation of ISO 14000 may lead to use of "environmental quality" lens. ISO 14000 has the potential to lead to two kinds of cultural changes. First, within the corporation, it has the potential to lead to consideration of environmental issues throughout the company and its business decisions ranging from hiring of employees to marketing. Second, ISO 14000 has the potential to become part of a global culture as the public comes to view ISO 14000 certification as a benchmark connoting good environmental stewardship by a company.

[*Paulette L. Stenzel*]

FURTHER READING

Kass, S.L. "The Lawyer's Role in Implementing ISO 14000," *Natural Resources & Environment* 3, no. 5 (Spring 1997).

Tibor, T., and I. Feldman. *ISO 14000: A Guide to the New Environmental Management Standards*. Irwin Publishing Company, 1996.

von Zharen, W.M. *ISO 14000: Understanding the Environmental Standards*. Government Institutes, 1996.

Isotope

Different forms of atoms of the same element. Atoms consist of a nucleus, containing positively-charged particles (protons) and neutral particles (neutrons), surrounded by negatively-charged particles (electrons). Isotopes of an element differ only in the number of neutrons in the nucleus and hence in atomic weight. The nuclei of some isotopes are unstable and undergo radioactive decay. An element can have several stable and radioactive isotopes, but most elements have only two or three isotopes that are of any importance. Also, for most elements the radioactive isotopes are only of concern in material exposed to certain types of radiation sources. **Carbon** has three important isotopes with atomic weights of 12, 13, and 14. C-12 is stable and represents 98.9 percent of natural carbon. C-13 is also stable and represents 1.1 percent of natural carbon. C-14 represents an insignificant fraction of naturally-occurring carbon, but it is radioactive and important because its radioactive decay is valuable in the dating of fossils and ancient artifacts. It is also useful in tracing the reactions of carbon compounds in research. *See also* Nuclear fission; Nuclear power; Radioactivity; Radiocarbon dating

Itai-itai disease

The symptoms of Itai-Itai disease were first observed in 1913 and characterized between 1947 and 1955; it was 1968, however, before the Japanese Ministry of Health and Welfare officially declared that the disease was caused by chronic **cadmium** poisoning in conjunction with other factors such as the stresses of pregnancy and lactation, aging, and dietary deficiencies of vitamin D and calcium. The name arose from the cries of pain, "itai-itai" (ouch-ouch) by the most seriously stricken victims, older Japanese farm women. Although men, young women, and children were also exposed, 95 percent of the victims were post-menopausal women over fifty years of age. They usually had given birth to several children and had lived more than thirty years within two miles (three kilometers) of the lower stream of the Jinzu River near Toyama.

The disease started with symptoms similar to rheumatism, neuralgia, or neuritis. Then came bone lesions, osteomalacia, and osteoporosis, along with renal disfunction and proteinuria. As it escalated, pain in the pelvic region caused the victims to walk with a duck-like gait. Next, they were incapable of rising from their beds because even a slight strain caused bone fractures. The suffering could last many years before it finally ended with death. Overall, an estimated 199 victims have been identified, of which 162 had died by December 1992.

The number of victims increased during and after World War II as production expanded at the Kamioka Mine owned by the Mitsui Mining and Smelting Company. As 3,000 tons of zinc-lead ore per day were mined and smelted, cadmium was discharged in the **wastewater**. Downstream, farmers withdrew the fine particles of flotation **tailings** in the Jinzu River along with water for drinking and crop **irrigation**. As rice plants were damaged near the irrigation inlets, farmers dug small **sedimentation** pools that were ineffective against the nearly invisible poison.

Both the numbers of Itai-Itai disease patients and the damage to the rice crops rapidly decreased after the mining company built a large **settling basin** to purify the wastewater in 1955. However, even after the discharge into the Jinzu River was halted, the cadmium already in the rice paddy soils was augmented by airborne exhausts. Mining operations in several other Japanese prefectures also produced cadmium-contaminating rice, but afflicted individuals were not certified as Itai-Itai patients. That designation was applied only to those who lived in the Jinzu River area.

In 1972 the survivors and their families became the first **pollution** victims in Japan to win a lawsuit against a major company. They won because in 1939 Article 109 of the Mining Act had imposed strict liability upon mining facilities for damages caused by their activities. The plaintiffs had only to prove that cadmium discharged from the mine caused their disease, not that the company was negligent. As epidemiological proof of causation sufficed as legal proof in this case, it set a precedent for other pollution litigation as well.

Despite legal success and compensation, the problem of contaminated rice continues. In 1969 the government initially set a maximum allowable standard of 0.4 **parts per million** (ppm) cadmium in unpolished rice. However, because much of the contaminated farmland produced grain in excess of that level, in 1970 under the Foodstuffs Hygiene Law this was raised to 1 ppm cadmium for unpolished rice and 0.9 ppm cadmium for polished rice. To restore contaminated farmland, Japanese authorities instituted a program in which, each year, the most highly **contaminated soil**s in a small area are exchanged for uncontaminated soils. Less contaminated soils are rehabilitated through the addition of lime, phosphate, and a cadmium sequestering agent, EDTA.

As of 1990 about 10,720 acres (4,340 hectares), or 66.7 percent of the approximately 16,080 acres (6,510 hectares) of the most highly cadmium contaminated farmland had been restored. In the remaining contaminated areas where farm families continue to eat homegrown rice, the symptoms are alleviated by treatment with massive doses of vitamins B1, B12, D, calcium, and various hormones. New methods have also been devised to cause the cadmium to be excreted more rapidly. In addition, the high costs of compensation and restoration are leading to the conclusion that prevention is not only better but cheaper. This is perhaps the most encouraging factor of all. *See also* Bioaccumulation; Environmental law; Heavy metals and heavy metal poisoning; Mine spoil waste; Smelter; Water pollution

[*Frank M. D'Itri*]

FURTHER READING

Kobayashi, J. "Pollution by Cadmium and the Itai-Itai Disease in Japan." In *Toxicity of Heavy Metals in the Environment, Part 1*, edited by F. W. Oehme. New York: Marcel Dekker, 1978.

Kogawa, K. "Itai-Itai Disease and Follow-Up Studies." In *Cadmium in the Environment, Part II*, edited by J. O. Nriagu. New York: Wiley, 1981.

Tsuchiya, K., ed. *Cadmium Studies in Japan: A Review*. Tokyo, Japan, and Amsterdam, Netherlands: Kodansha and Elsevier/North-Holland Biomedical Press, 1978.

IUCN—The World Conservation Union (Gland, Switzerland)

Founded in 1948 as the International Union for the Conservation of Nature and Natural Resources (IUCN), IUCN works with governments, conservation organizations, and industry groups to conserve **wildlife** and approach the world's environmental problems using "sound scientific insight and the best available information." Its membership, currently over 650, comes from 120 countries and includes 56 sovereign states, as well as government agencies and **nongovernmental organizations**. IUCN exists to serve its members, representing their views and providing them with the support necessary to achieve their goals. Above all, IUCN works with its members "to achieve development that is sustainable and that provides a lasting improvement in the quality of life for people all over the world." IUCN's three basic **conservation** objectives are: (1) to secure the conservation of **nature**, and especially of biological diversity, as an essential foundation for the future; (2) to ensure that where the earth's **natural resources** are used this is done in a wise, equitable, and sustainable way; (3) to guide the development of human communities toward ways of life that are both of good quality and in enduring harmony with other components of the **biosphere**.

IUCN is one of the few organizations to include both governmental agencies and nongovernmental organizations. It is in a unique position to provide a neutral forum where these organizations can meet, exchange ideas, and build partnerships to carry out conservation projects. IUCN is also unusual in that it both develops environmental policies and then implements them through the projects it sponsors. Because the IUCN works closely with, and its membership includes, many government scientists and officials, the organization often takes a conservative, pro-management, as opposed to a "preservationist," approach to wildlife issues. It may encourage or endorse limited hunting and commercial exploitation of wildlife if it believes this can be carried out on a sustainable basis.

IUCN maintains a global network of over 5,000 scientists and wildlife professionals who are organized into six standing commissions that deal with various aspects of the union's work. There are commissions on Ecology, Education, Environmental Planning, Environmental Law, National Parks and Protected Areas, and Species Survival. These commissions create action plans, develop policies, advise on projects and programs, and contribute to IUCN publications, all on an unpaid, voluntary basis.

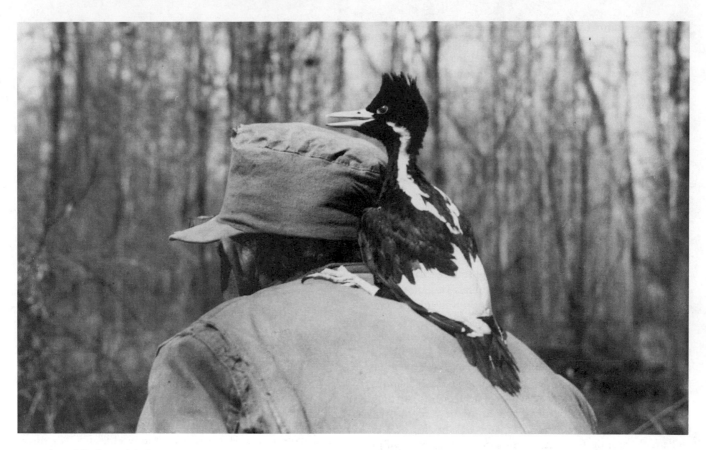

Ivory-billed woodpecker.

IUCN publishes an authoritative series of "Red Data Books," describing the status of rare and endangered wildlife. Each volume provides information on the population, distribution, **habitat** and **ecology**, threats, and protective measures in effect for listed **species**. The "Red Data Books" concept was originated in the mid-1960s by the famous British conservationist Sir Peter Scott, and the series now includes a variety of publication on regions and species. The *1990 IUCN Red List of Threatened Animals*, compiled from data supplied by The World Conservation Monitoring Center in Cambridge, England, lists more than 5,000 threatened taxa, including 698 mammals, 1,047 birds, 171 reptiles, 63 amphibians, 762 fishes, and 2,250 invertebrates. Other titles in the series of "Red Data Books" include *Dolphins, Porpoises, and Whales of the World*; *Lemurs of Madagascar and the Comoros*; *Threatened Primates of Africa*; *Threatened Swallowtail Butterflies of the World*; *Threatened Birds of the Americas*; and books on plants and other species of wildlife, including a series of conservation action plans for threatened species.

Other notable IUCN works include *World Conservation Strategy: Living Resources Conservation for Sustainable Development* and its successor document *Caring for the Earth—A Strategy for Sustainable Living*; and the *United Nations List of Parks and Protected Areas*. IUCN also publishes books and papers on regional conservation, habitat preservation, **environmental law** and policy, ocean ecology and management, and conservation and development strategies. Contact: IUCN—The World Conservation Union, Rue

Mauverney 28, CH-1196 Gland, Switzerland. Internet: http://w3.iprolink.ch/iucnlib/themes/themes.html. *See also* Biodiversity; Endangered species

[*Lewis G. Regenstein*]

Ivory-billed woodpecker (*Campephilus principalis*)

The ivory-billed woodpecker is one of the rarest birds in the world and is considered by most authorities to be extinct in the United States. The sole remaining individuals are of a Cuban race which was last seen in 1987 or 1988. Although occasional sightings of the ivory-billed woodpecker in the United States have been reported, no firm evidence of their existence has been presented since the 1960s.

The ivory-colored bills of these birds were prized as decorations by native Americans, but impact on the population by this group was probably negligible. The real decline was caused before the turn of the century by the timber industry, which cut the majority of the ivory-billed woodpecker's prime **habitat**. Ivory-billed woodpeckers required large tracts of land in the bottomland cypress, oak, and black gum forests of the Southeast. This **species** was the largest woodpecker in North America, and they preferred the largest of these trees, the same one targeted by timber companies as the most profitable to harvest.

The territory for breeding pairs of ivory-billed woodpeckers consists of about three square miles of undisturbed, swampy forest, and there was little prime habitat left for them after 1900, for most of these areas had been heavily timbered. By the 1930s, one of the only virgin cypress swamps left was the Singer Tract in Louisiana, and a team of ornithologists descended on it to locate, study, and record some of the last ivory-bills in existence. They found the birds and were able to film and photograph them, as well as make the only sound recordings of them in existence. Despite the efforts of conservationists to preserve this great stand of cypress, the Singer Tract was logged out in 1948 for soybean cultivation. One of the giant cypress trees that was felled contained the nest and eggs of an ivory-billed woodpecker.

Few sightings of these woodpeckers were made in the 1940s, and none exist for the 1950s. But in the early 1960s ivory-bills were reported seen in South Carolina, Texas, and Louisiana. Intense searches, however, left scientists with little hope by the end of that decade, as only six birds were reported to exist. Subsequent decades have yielded a few individual sightings in the United States, but none have been confirmed.

In 1985 and 1986, there was a search for the Cuban race of the ivory-billed woodpecker. The first expedition yielded no birds, but trees were found that had apparently been worked by the birds. The second expedition found at least one pair of ivory-bills. Most of the land formerly occupied by the Cuban race was cut over for sugar cane plantations by the 1920s, and surveys in 1956 indicated that this population had declined to about a dozen birds. The last reported sightings of the species occurred in the Sierra de Moa area of Cuba. They are still considered to exist, but the health of any remaining individuals must be in question, given the inbreeding that must occur with such a low population level and the fact that so little suitable habitat remains. *See also* Deforestation; Endangered species; Extinction; International Council for Bird Preservation; Wildlife management

[*Eugene C. Beckham*]

FURTHER READING

Collar, N. J., et al. *Threatened Birds of the Americas: The ICBP/IUCN Red Data Book.* Washington, DC: Smithsonian Institution Press, 1992.

Ehrlich, P. R., D. S. Dobkin, and D. Wheye. *The Birder's Handbook.* New York: Simon & Schuster, 1988.

Ehrlich, P. R., D. S. Dobkin, and D. Wheye. *Birds in Jeopardy: The Imperiled and Extinct Birds of the United States and Canada, Including Hawaii and Puerto Rico.* Stanford: Stanford University Press, 1992.

Izaak Walton League (Arlington, Virginia)

In 1922, 54 sportsmen and sportswomen—all concerned with the apparent destruction of American fishing water-ways—established the Izaak Walton League of America (IWLA). They looked upon Izaak Walton, a seventeenth-century English fisherman and author of *The Compleat Angler*, as inspiration in protecting the waters of America. The Izaak Walton League has since widened its focus: as a major force in the American **conservation** movement, IWLA now pledges in its slogan "to defend the nation's **soil**, air, woods, water, and **wildlife**."

When sportsmen and sportswomen formed IWLA approximately 70 years ago, they worried that American industry would ruin fishing streams. Raw sewage, soil **erosion**, and rampant pollution threatened water and wildlife. Initially the League concentrated on preserving lakes, streams, and rivers. In 1927, at the request of President Calvin Coolidge, IWLA organized the first national **water pollution** inventory. Izaak Walton League members (called "Ikes") subsequently helped pass the first national water pollution control act in the 1940s. In 1969 IWLA instituted the Save Our Streams program, and this group mobilized forces to pass the groundbreaking **Clean Water Act** of 1972. The League did not only concentrate on the preservation of American waters, however. From its 1926 campaign to protect the black bass, to the purchase of a helicopter in 1987 to help game law officers protect waterfowl from poachers in the Gulf of Mexico, IWLA has also been instrumental in the preservation of wildlife. In addition, the League has fought to protect **public land**s such as the National Elk Refuge in Wyoming, the **Everglades** National Park, and the Isle Royale National Park.

IWLA currently sponsors several **environmental** programs designed to conserve **natural resources** and educate the public. The aforementioned Save Our Streams (SOS) program is a grassroots organization designed to monitor **water quality** in streams and rivers. Through 200 chapters nationwide, SOS promotes "stream rehabilitation" through stream adoption kits and water pollution law training. Another program, Wetlands Watch, allows local groups to purchase, adopt, and protect nearby **wetlands**. Similarly, the Izaak Walton League Endowment buys land to save it from unwanted development. IWLA's Uncle Ike Youth Education program aims to educate children and convince them of the necessity of preserving the environment. A last major program from the League is its internationally acclaimed Outdoor Ethics program. Outdoor Ethics works to stop **poaching** and other illegal and unsportsmanlike outdoor activities by educating hunters, anglers, and others.

The League also sponsors and operates regional conservation efforts. Its Midwest Office, based in Minnesota, concentrates on preservation of the Upper Mississippi River region. The Chesapeake Bay Program is a major regional focus. Almost 25 percent of the "Ikes" live in the region of this estuary, and public education, awards, and local conservation projects help protect **Chesapeake Bay**. In addition the Soil Conservation Program focuses on combating soil erosion and **groundwater** pollution, and the Public Lands

Restoration Task Force works out of its headquarters in Portland, Oregon, to strike a balance between forests and the desire for their natural resources in the West.

IWLA makes its causes known through a variety of publications. *Splash*, a product of SOS, enlightens the public as to how to protect streams in America. *Outdoor Ethics*, a newsletter from the program of the same name, educates recreationists to responsible practices of hunting, boating, and other outdoor activities. The League also publishes a membership magazine, *Outdoor America*, and the *League Leader*, a vehicle of information for IWLA's 2,000 chapter and division officers. IWLA has also produced the longest-running weekly environmental program on television. Entitled *Make Peace with Nature*, the program has aired on PBS for almost 20 years and presents stories of environmental interest.

Having expanded its scope from water to the general environment, IWLA has become a vital force in the national conservation movement. Through its many and varied programs, the League continues to promote constructive and active involvement in environmental problems. Contact: Izaak Walton League of America, 1401 Wilson Boulevard, Level B, Arlington, VA 22209. Internet: http://www.iwla.org:80/.

[*Andrea Gacki*]

J

Jackson, Wes (1936-)

American environmentalist

Wes Jackson is a plant geneticist, writer, and co-founder, with his wife Dana Jackson, of the **Land Institute** in Salina, Kansas. He is one of the leading critics of conventional agricultural practices, which in his view are depleting **topsoil**, reducing genetic diversity, and destroying small family farms and rural communities. Jackson is also critical of the culture that provides the pretext and the context within which this destruction occurs and is justified as "necessary," "efficient," and "economical." He contrasts a culture or mind-set that emphasizes humanity's mastery or dominion over **nature** with an alternative vision that takes "nature as the measure" of human activity. The former viewpoint can produce temporary triumphs but not long-lasting or sustainable livelihood; only the latter holds out the hope that humans can live with nature, on nature's terms.

Jackson was born in 1936 in Topeka, Kansas, the son of a farmer. Young and restless, Jackson held various jobs—welder, farm hand, ranch hand, teacher—before devoting his time to the study of agricultural practices in the United States and abroad. He attended Kansas Wesleyan University, the University of Kansas, and North Carolina State University, where he earned his doctorate in plant genetics in 1967.

According to Jackson, agriculture as we know it is unnatural, artificial, and, by geological time-scales, of relatively recent origin. It requires plowing, which leads to loss of topsoil, which in turn reduces and finally destroys fertility. Large-scale "industrial" agriculture also requires large investments, complex and expensive machinery, **fertilizer**s, **pesticide**s and **herbicide**s, and leads to a loss of genetic diversity, to **soil erosion** and **compaction**, and other negative consequences. It is also predicated on the planting and harvesting of annual crops — corn, wheat, soybeans — that leaves fields uncovered for long periods and thus leaves precious topsoil unprotected and vulnerable to erosion by wind and water. For every bushel of corn harvested, a bushel of topsoil is lost. Jackson estimates that America has lost between one-third and one-half of its topsoil since the arrival of the first European settlers.

At the Land Institute, Jackson and his associates are attempting to re-think and revise agricultural practices so as to "make nature the measure" and enable farmers to "meet the expectations of the land," rather than the other way

around. In particular, they are returning to, and attempting to learn from, the native **prairie** plants and the **ecosystem**s that sustain them. They are also exploring the feasibility of alternative farming methods that might minimize or even eliminate entirely the planting and harvesting of annual crops, favoring instead the use of perennials that protect and bind topsoil.

Jackson's emphasis is not exclusively scientific or technical. Like his long-time friend **Wendell Berry**, Jackson emphasizes the *culture* in agriculture. Why humans grow food is not at all mysterious or problematic: we must eat in order to live. But how we choose to plant, grow, harvest, distribute, and consume food is clearly a cultural and moral matter having to do with our attitudes and beliefs. Our contemporary consumer culture is out of kilter, Jackson contends, in various ways. For one, the economic emphasis on minimizing costs and maximizing yields ignores longer-term environmental costs that come with the depletion of topsoil, the diminution of genetic diversity, and the depopulation of rural communities. For another, most Americans have lost (and many have never had) a sense of connectedness with the land and the natural environment; Jackson contends that they are unaware of the mysteries and wonder of birth, death and rebirth, and of cycles and seasons, that are mainstays of a meaningful human life. To restore this sense of mystery and meaning requires what Jackson calls *homecoming* and "the resettlement of America," and "becoming native to this place." More Americans need to return to the land, to repopulate rural communities, and to re-learn the wealth of skills that we have lost or forgotten or never acquired. Such skills are more than matters of method or technique, they also have to do with ways of relating to nature and to each other.

Wes Jackson has been called, by critics and admirers alike, a radical and a visionary. Both labels appear to apply. For Jackson's vision is indeed radical, in the original sense of the term (from the Latin *radix*, or root). It is a vision not only of "new roots for agriculture" but of new and deeper roots for human relationships and communities that, like protected prairie topsoil, will not easily erode.

[*Terence Ball*]

FURTHER READING

Berry, W. "New Roots for Agricultural Research." In *The Gift of Good Land*. San Francisco: North Point Press, 1981.

Eisenberg, E. "Back to Eden." *The Atlantic* (October 1989): 57-89.

————. *New Roots for Agriculture*. San Francisco: Friends of the Earth, 1980.

————, W. Berry, and B. Coleman, eds. *Meeting the Expectations of the Land*. San Francisco: North Point Press, 1984.

————. *Becoming Native to this Place*. Lexington, KY: University Press of Kentucky, 1994.

Jackson, Wes. *Altars of Unhewn Stone*. San Francisco: North Point Press, 1987.

James Bay hydropower project

James Bay forms the southern tip of the much larger Hudson Bay in Quebec, Canada. To the east lies the Quebec-Labrador peninsula, an undeveloped area with vast expanses of pristine wilderness. The region is similar to Siberia, covered in tundra and sparse forests of black spruce and other evergreens. It is home to roughly 100 species of birds, twenty species of fish and dozens of mammals, including muskrat, lynx, black bear, red fox, and the world's largest herd of caribou. The area has also been home to the Cree and other Native Indian tribes for centuries. Seven rivers drain the wet, rocky region, the largest being La Grande.

In the 1970s, the government-owned Hydro-Quebec electric utility began to divert these rivers, **flooding** 3,861 square miles (10,000 km²) of land. They built a series of **reservoir**s, **dams** and dikes on La Grande that generate 10,300 megawatts of power for homes and businesses in Quebec, New York, and New England. With its $16 billion price tag, the project is one of the world's largest energy projects. When completed in 1995, the complex will pump out a total of 15,000 megawatts. A second phase of the project will add two more hydroelectric complexes, supplying another 12,000 megawatts of power—the equivalent of more than thirty-five nuclear **power plants**.

But the project has many opponents. The Crees and other Inuit tribes have joined forces with American environmentalists to protest the project. Its environmental impact has had scant analysis; in fact, damage has been severe. Ten thousand caribou drowned in 1984, while crossing one of the newly-dammed rivers on their migration route. When the utility flooded land, it destroyed **habitat** for countless plants and animals. The graves of Cree Indians, who for millennia, had hunted, traveled, and lived along the rivers, were inundated. The project has also altered the ecology of the James and Hudson bays, disrupting spawning cycles, **nutrient** systems, and other important maritime resources. Naturally-occurring **mercury** in rocks and **soil** is released as the land is flooded and accumulates as it passes through the **food chain/web** from microscopic organisms to fish to humans. A majority of the native people in some villages where fish are a main part of the diet now show symptoms of mercury poisoning.

Despite these problems, Hydro-Quebec is pursuing the project, partly because of Quebec's long-standing struggle for independence from Canada. The power is sold to corporate customers, providing income for the province and attracting industry to Quebec.

In 1992, New York canceled a $13 billion contract with Hydro-Quebec for 1,000 megawatts. This seemed a certain end to phase II of the project. However, the New York Power Authority now has an 800-megawatt purchase agreement with the utility.

The Cree and environmentalists, joined by New York congressmen, have taken their fight to court. On Earth Day 1993, they filed suit against New York Power Authority in United States District Court in New York, challenging the legality of the agreement, which will go into effect in 1999. Their claim is based on the United States Constitution and the 1916 Migratory Bird Treaty with Canada. *See also* Environmental law; Hetch Hetchy Reservoir; Nuclear energy

[*Cathryn McCue*]

FURTHER READING

McCutcheon, S. *Electric Rivers: The Story of the James Bay Project*. Montreal: Black Rose Books, 1991.

Picard, A. "James Bay II." *Amicus Journal* 12 (Fall 1990): 10-16.

Japanese logging

In recent decades the timber industry has intensified efforts to harvest logs from tropical, temperate, and boreal forests worldwide to meet an increasing demand for wood and wood products. Japanese companies have been particularly active in logging and in importing timber from around the world. Because of wasteful and destructive logging practices that have often resulted from the efforts to maximize financial gains of companies involved with this trade, those interested in reducing **deforestation** have raised many concerns about Japan's logging industry.

The world's forests, especially tropical **rain forest**s, are rich in species of all kinds, including plants, insects, birds, reptiles, and mammals. Many of these species exist only in very limited areas where conditions are suitable for their existence. These endangered forest dwellers contain unique and irreplaceable genetic material that might contribute to the betterment of domestic plants and animals. The forests could yield medically useful **cancer**-controlling drugs, for example, or antibiotics. Healthy intact forests stabilize watersheds by absorbing rainfall and retarding runoff to streams and rivers. Mat roots help to control **soil** erosion, preventing siltation of waterways and damage to reefs, fisheries, and spawning grounds.

The United Nations Food and Agriculture Organization reports tropical deforestation rates of 42 million acres (over 17 million ha) per year. One half of the Earth's primary tropical forest area has vanished, and half of the remaining forest has been degraded. While Brazil contains about a third of the world's remaining tropical rain forest, southeast Asia is now the major supplier of tropical woods. Burma, Thailand, Laos, Vietnam, Kampuchea, Malaysia, Indonesia, Borneo, New Guinea, and the Philippines contain 20% of the world's remaining tropical forests. With current rates of deforestation, it is estimated that almost all of Southeast Asia's primary forests will be gone by the year 2010. While a number of countries make use of rain forest wood, Japan is the number one importer of tropical timber. Japan's imports account for about 30% of the world trade in tropical lumber.

Japan also imports large amounts of timber from temperate and boreal forests in Canada, Russia, and the United States. These three countries contain most of the remaining boreal forests, and they supply more than half of the world's industrial wood. As demand for timber continues to climb, hitherto undisturbed virgin forests are increasingly being used. To speed harvesting, logging roads are built to provide access, and heavy equipment is brought in to hasten work. In the process, soils are compacted, making plant regrowth difficult or impossible. Although these practices are not limited to one country, Japanese firms have been cited by environmentalists as particularly insensitive to the environmental impacts of logging activities.

The globe's forests are sometimes referred to as the 'lungs of the planet,' exchanging **carbon dioxide** for oxygen. Critics claim that the wood harvesting industry is destroying this vital natural resource, and in the process this industry is endangering the planet's ability to nurture and sustain life. Certainly, widespread destruction of the world's forests is a serious concern. Large Japanese companies, or companies affiliated with Japanese firms, have logged old growth forests in several parts of the globe to supply timber to the Japanese forest products industry. **Clear-cutting** of trees over large areas in tropical rain forests has made preservation of the original flora and fauna impossible. Many species are becoming extinct. Replanting may in time restore the trees, but it will not restore the array of organisms that were present in the original forest.

Large scale logging activities have had a largely negative impact on local economies in exporting regions when whole logs are shipped to Japan for further processing. Developed countries such as the United States and Canada, that in the past both harvested timber and processed it into lumber and other products, have lost jobs to Japanese industry. Living in tropical forests, the indigenous cultures that may have thrived in harmony with their forest homelands for eons are displaced and destroyed. Provision has not been made for the survival of local flora and fauna dependent on the trees, and provision for forest re-establishment may be inadequate. As resentment has grown in impacted areas, and among environmentalists, efforts have emerged to limit or stop large-scale timber harvesting and exporting.

Although concern has been voiced over all large-scale logging operations, special concern has been raised over harvesting of tropical timber from previously undisturbed primary forest areas. Tropical rain forests are especially unique and valuable natural resources for many reasons, including the high species density and variety within their borders. It is feared that exploitation of these unique ecosystems will result in the extinction of many potentially valuable species of plants and animals that exist nowhere else. Many of these forms of life have not yet been named, scientifically studied, and characterized. With their disappearance may

also go an opportunity to use them to benefit humanity. Also, over harvesting of tropical rainforests has a negative effect on weather patterns, especially by reducing rainfall in particular areas.

Japan is a major importer of tropical timber from Malaysia, New Guinea, and the Solomon Islands. The number of imported logs has declined in recent years, but this has been matched by an increase in imported tropical plywood manufactured in Indonesia and Malaysia, and the total amount of timber removed has remained fairly constant. An environmentalist group called the Rainforest Action Network (RAN) has issued an alarm concerning recent expansion of logging activity by firms affiliated with Japanese importers. The RAN alleges that:

> "After laying waste to the rain forests of Asia and the Pacific islands, giant Malaysian logging companies are setting their sights on the Amazon. This past year, some of Southeast Asia's biggest forestry conglomerates have moved into Brazil, and are buying controlling interests in area logging companies, and purchasing rights to cut down vast rain forest territories for as little as $3 U.S. dollars per acre. In the last few months of 1996 these companies quadrupled their South American interests, and now threaten 15% of the Amazon with immediate logging. According to *The Wall Street Journal*, up to 30 million acres (12.3 million ha) are at stake. Major players include the WTK Group, Samling, Mingo, and Rimbunan Hijau."

The RAN claims that "the same timber companies in Sarawak, Malaysia, worked with such rapacious speed that they devastated the region's forest within a decade, displacing traditional peoples and leaving the landscape marred with silted rivers and eroded soil."

One large Japanese firm, the Mitsubishi Corporation, has been targeted for criticism and boycott by the RAN, as one of the world's largest importers of timber. The boycott is an effort to encourage environmentally sensitive consumers to stop buying a wide variety of products marketed by companies affiliated with the huge conglomerate, including automobiles, cameras, beer, cellular phones, and consumer electronics equipment. Through its subsidiaries, Mitsubishi has logged or imported timber from the Philippines, Malaysia, Papua New Guinea, Bolivia, Indonesia, Brazil, Chile, Canada (British Columbia and Alberta), Siberia, and the United States (Alaska, Oregon, Washington, and Texas). The RAN charges that "Mitsubishi Corporation is one of the most voracious destroyers of the world's rain forests. Its timber purchases have laid waste to forests in the Philippines, Malaysia, Papua New Guinea, Indonesia, Brazil, Bolivia, Australia, New Zealand, Siberia, Canada, and even the United States." The Mitsubishi Corporation itself does not sell consumer products, but it consists of 190 interlinked companies and hundreds of associated firms that do market to consumers. Together this conglomerate forms one of the world's largest industrial and financial powers. The Mitsubishi umbrella includes Mitsubishi Bank, Mitsubishi Heavy Industries, Mitsubishi Electronics, Mitsubishi Motors, and other major components. To force Mitsubishi and other corporations involved with timber harvesting to operate in a more environmentally responsible way and to end "their destructive logging and trading practices," the international boycott was organized in 1990 by the World Rainforest Movement (tropical forests) and the Taiga Rescue Network (boreal forests).

The Mitsubishi Corporation has countered criticism by launching a program "to promote the regeneration of rain forests...in Malaysia that plants seedlings and monitors their development. One tract planted in 1991 is expected to reach a completely natural state within 10-15 years." In 1990, the corporation formed an Environmental Affairs Department, one of the first of its kind in Japan, reporting to top management, to draft environmental guidelines, and coordinate corporate environmental activities. In the words of the Mitsubishi Corporation Chairman, "A business cannot continue to exist without the trust and respect of society for its environmental performance." Mitsubishi Corporation reports that they have launched a program to support experimental reforestation projects in Malaysia, Brazil, and Chile. In Malaysia, the company is working with a local agricultural university, under the guidance of a professor from Japan, where about 300,000 seedlings were planted on a barren site in 1991. Within five years, the trees were over 33 feet (10 m) in height and the corporation claimed that they were "well on the way to establishing techniques for regenerating tropical forest on burnt or barren land using indigenous species."

Similar projects are underway in Brazil and Chile. The company is also conducting research on sustainable management of the Amazon rain forests. In Canada, Mitsubishi Corporation has participated in a pulp project called Al-Pac to start a mill "which will supply customers in North America, Europe, and Asia," meeting "the strictest environmental standards by employing advanced, environmentally safe technology. In forest management, Al-Pac harvests only around 0.25% of its total area annually and all harvested areas will be reforested."

[*Douglas C. Pratt*]

FURTHER READING

Marshall, G. "The Political Economy of the Logging: The Barnett Inquiry into Corruption in the Papua New Guinea Timber Industry," *The Ecologist* 20, no. 5 (1990).

Marx, M.J. "The Mitsubishi Campaign: First Year Report." Rainforest Action Network, San Francisco, 1993.

Mitsubishi Corporation Annual Report 1996. Mitsubishi Corporation, Tokyo, 1996.

Neff, R., and W. J. Holstein. "Mitsubishi is on the Move," *Business Week.* United States: McGraw Hill Inc., September 24, 1990.

Wakker, E. "Mitsubishi's Unsustainable Timber Trade: Sarawak," *Restoration of Tropical Forest Ecosystems.* L. and M. Lohmann, eds. Netherlands: Kluwer Academic Publishers, 1993.

World Rainforest Report XII, no. 4 (October-December, 1995). San Francisco: Rainforest Action Network.

K

Kapirowitz Plateau

The Kapirowitz Plateau, a **wildlife refuge** on the northern rim of the Grand Canyon, has come to symbolize **wildlife management** gone awry, a classic case of misguided human intervention intended to help wildlife that ended up damaging the animals and the **environment**. The Kapirowitz is located on the Colorado River in northwestern Arizona, and is bounded by steep cliffs dropping down to the Kanab Canyon to the west, and the Grand and Marble canyons to the south and southeast. Because of its inaccessibility, according to naturalist James B. Trefethen, the Plateau was considered a "biological island," and its deer population "evolved in almost complete genetic isolation."

The lush grass meadows of the Kapirowitz Plateau supported a resident population of 3,000 mule deer (*Odocoileus hemionus*), which were known and renowned for their massive size and the huge antlers of the old bucks. Before the advent of Europeans, Paiute and Navajo Indians hunted on the Kapirowitz in the fall, stocking up on meat and skins for the winter. In the early 1900s, in an effort to protect and enhance the magnificent deer population of the Kapirowitz, the federal government prohibited all killing of deer, and even eliminated the predator population in the area. As a result, the deer population exploded, causing massive overbrowsing, starvation, and a drastic decline in the health and population of the herd.

In 1893, when the Kapirowitz and surrounding lands were designated the Grand Canyon National Forest Reserve, hundreds of thousands of sheep, cattle, and horses were grazing on the Plateau, resulting in **overgrazing**, **erosion**, and large-scale damage to the land. On November 28, 1906, President **Theodore Roosevelt** established the million-acre (400,000 ha) Grand Canyon National Game Preserve, which provided complete protection of the Kapirowitz's deer population. By then, however, overgrazing by livestock had destroyed much of the native vegetation and changed the Kapirowitz considerably for the worse. Continued pasturing of over 16,000 horses and cattle degraded the Kapirowitz even further.

The **Forest Service** carried out President Roosevelt's directive to emphasize "the propagation and breeding" of the mule deer by not only banning hunting, but also natural predators as well. From 1906-1931, federal agents poisoned, shot, or trapped 4,889 coyotes, 781 mountain lions, 554 bobcats, and 20 **wolves**. Without predators to remove the old, the sick, the unwary, and other biologically unfit animals, and keep the size of the herd in check, the deer herd began to grow out of control, and to lose those qualities that made its members such unique and magnificent animals. After 1906, the deer population doubled within ten breeding seasons, and by 1918 (two years later), it doubled again. By 1923, the herd had mushroomed to at least 30,000 deer, and perhaps as many as 100,000 according to some estimates.

Unable to support the overpopulation of deer, range grasses and land greatly deteriorated, and by 1925, 10,000-15,000 deer were reported to have died from starvation and malnutrition. Finally, after relocation efforts mostly failed to move a significant number of deer off of the Kapirowitz, hunting was reinstated, and livestock grazing was strictly controlled. By 1931, hunting, disease, and starvation had reduced the herd to under 20,000. The range grasses and other vegetation returned, and the Kapirowitz began to recover. In 1975 James Trefethen wrote, "the Kapirowitz today again produces some of the largest and heaviest antlered mule deer in North America."

In the fields of wildlife management and biology, the lessons of the Kapirowitz Plateau are often cited (as in the writings of naturalist **Aldo Leopold**) to demonstrate the valuable role of predators in maintaining the **balance of nature** (such as between herbivores and the plants they consume) and survival of the fittest. The experience of the Kapirowitz shows that in the absence of natural predators, prey populations (especially ungulates) tend to increase beyond the **carrying capacity** of the land, and eventually the results are overpopulation and malnutrition. *See also* Predator control; Predator-prey interactions

[*Lewis G. Regenstein*]

FURTHER READING

Leopold, A. *A Sand County Almanac*. New York: Oxford University Press, 1949.

Rasmussen, D. I. "Biotic Communities of the Kapirowitz Plateau," *Ecological Monographs* 3 (1941): 229-275.

Trefethen, J. B. *An American Crusade for Wildlife*. New York: Winchester Press, 1975.

Kepone

Kepone ($C_{10}Cl_{10}O$) is an organochlorine **pesticide** that was manufactured by the Allied Chemical Corporation in Virginia from the late 1940s to the 1970s. Kepone was responsible for human health problems and extensive contamination of the James River and its **estuary** in the **Chesapeake Bay**. It is a milestone in the development of a public environmental consciousness, and its history is considered by many to be a classic example of negligent corporate behavior and inadequate oversight by state and federal agencies.

Kepone is an insecticide and **fungicide** that is closely related to other chlorinated pesticides such as **DDT** and aldrin. As with all such pesticides, Kepone causes lethal damage to the nervous systems of its target organisms. A poorly water-soluble substance, it can be absorbed through the skin, and it bioaccumulates in fatty tissues from which it is later released into the bloodstream. It is also a contact poison; when inhaled, absorbed, or ingested by humans, it can damage the central nervous system as well as the liver and kidneys. It can also lead to neurological symptoms such as tremors, muscle spasms, sterility, and **cancer**. Although the manufacture and use of Kepone is now banned by the **Environmental Protection Agency (EPA)**, organochlorines have long half-lives, and these compounds, along with their residues and degradation products, can persist in the **environment** over many decades.

Allied Chemical first opened a plant to manufacture **nitrogen**-based **fertilizer**s in 1928 in the town of Hopewell, on the banks of the James River in Virginia. This plant began producing Kepone in 1949. Commercial production was subsequently begun, although a battery of toxicity tests indicated that Kepone was both toxic and carcinogenic and that it caused damage to the functioning of the nervous, muscular, and reproductive systems in fish, birds, and mammals. It was patented by Allied in 1952 and registered with federal agencies in 1957. The demand for the pesticide grew after 1958, and Allied expanded production by entering into a variety of subcontracting agreements with a number of smaller companies, including the Life Science Products Company.

In 1970, a series of new environmental regulations came into effect which should have changed the way wastes from the manufacture of Kepone were discharged. The Refuse Act Permit Program and the National Pollutant Discharge Elimination Program (NPDES) of the **Clean Water Act** required all dischargers of **effluent**s into United States waters to register their **discharge**s and obtain permits from federal agencies. At the time these regulations went into effect, Allied Chemical had three pipes discharging Kepone and plastic wastes into the Gravelly Run, a tributary of the James River, about 75 miles (120 km) north of Chesapeake Bay.

A regional **sewage treatment** plant which would accept industrial wastes was then under construction but not scheduled for completion until 1975. Rather than installing expensive pollution control equipment for the interim period, Allied chose to delay. They adopted a strategy of misinformation, reporting the releases as temporary and unmonitored discharges, and they did not disclose the presence of untreated Kepone and other process wastes in the effluents. The Life Science Products Company also avoided the new federal permit requirements by discharging their wastes directly into the local Hopewell sewer system. These discharges caused problems with the functioning of the biological treatment systems at the sewage plant; the company was required to reduce concentrations of Kepone in sewage, but it continued its discharges at high concentrations, violating these standards with the apparent knowledge of plant treatment officials.

During this same period, an employee of Life Science Products visited a local Hopewell physician, complaining of tremors, weight loss, and general aches and pains. The physician discovered impaired liver and nervous functions, and a blood test revealed an astronomically high level of Kepone—7.5 **parts per million**. Federal and state officials were contacted, and the epidemiologist for the state of Virginia toured the manufacturing facility at Life Science Products. This official reported that "Kepone was everywhere in the plant," and that workers wore no protective equipment and were "virtually swimming in the stuff." Another investigation discovered 75 cases of Kepone poisoning among the workers; some members of their families were also found to have elevated concentrations of the chemical in their blood. Further investigations revealed that the environment around the plant was also heavily contaminated. The **soil** contained 10,000 to 20,000 ppm of Kepone. **Sediment**s in the James River, as well as local **landfill**s and trenches around the Allied facilities were just as badly contaminated. Government agencies were forced to close 100 mi (161 km) of the James River and its tributaries to commercial and recreational fishing and shellfishing.

In the middle of 1975, Life Science Products finally closed its manufacturing facility. It has been estimated that since 1966, it and Allied together produced 3.2 million pounds of Kepone and were responsible for releasing 100,000 to 200,000 pounds into the environment. In 1976, the Northern District of Virginia filed criminal charges against Allied, Life Science Products, the city of Hopewell, and six individuals on 1,097 counts relating to the production and disposal of Kepone. The indictments were based on violations of the permit regulations, unlawful discharge into the sewer systems, and conspiracy related to that discharge.

The case went to trial without a jury. The corporations and the individuals named in the charges negotiated lighter fines and sentences by entering pleas of "no contest." Allied ultimately paid a fine of 13.3 million dollars, although their annual sales reach three billion dollars. Life Science Products was fined four million dollars, which it could not pay due to lack of assets. Company officers were fined 25,000 dollars each, and the town of Hopewell was fined 10,000 dollars. No one was sentenced to a jail term. Civil suits brought against Allied and the other defendants' resulted in a settlement of 5.25 million dollars to pay for cleanup expenses and to repair the damage that had been done to the sewage treatment

Breeding populations of American coots were affected by selenium poisoning at Kesterson National Wildlife Refuge.

plant. Allied paid another three million dollars to settle civil suits brought by workers for damage to their health.

Environmentalists and many others considered the results of legal action against the manufacturers of Kepone unsatisfactory. Some have argued that these results are typical of environmental litigation. It is difficult to establish criminal intent beyond a reasonable doubt in such cases, and even when guilt is determined, sentencing is relatively light. Corporations are rarely fined in amounts that affect their financial strength, and individual officers are almost never sent to jail. Corporate fines are generally passed along as costs to the consumer, and public bodies are treated even more lightly, since it is recognized that the fines levied on public agencies are paid by taxpayers.

Today, the James River has been reopened to fishing for those **species** that are not prone to the **bioaccumulation** of Kepone. Nevertheless, sediments in the river and its estuary contain large amounts of deposited Kepone which is released during periods of turbulence. Scientists have published studies which document that Kepone is still moving through the **food chain/web** and the **ecosystem** in this area, and Kepone toxicity has been demonstrated in a variety of invertebrate test species. There are still deposits of Kepone in the local sewer pipes in Hopewell; these continue to release the chemical, endangering treatment plant operations and polluting receiving waters.

[*Usha Vedagiri and Douglas Smith*]

FURTHER READING

Goldfarb, W. *Kepone: A Case Study*. New Brunswick, NJ: Rutgers University, 1977.

Sax, N. I. *Dangerous Properties of Industrial Materials*. 6th ed. New York: Van Nostrand Reinhold, 1984.

Kesterson National Wildlife Refuge

One of a dwindling number of freshwater marshes in California's San Joaquin Valley, Kesterson National Wildlife Refuge achieved national notoriety in 1983 when refuge managers discovered that agricultural **runoff** was poisoning the area's birds. Among other elements and **agricultural chemicals** reaching toxic concentrations in the **wetlands**, the naturally occurring element selenium was identified as the cause of falling fertility and severe **birth defects** in the refuge's breeding populations of stilts, grebes, shovellers, coots, and other aquatic birds. Selenium, lead, boron, chromium, molybdenum, and numerous other contaminants were accumulating in refuge waters because the refuge had become an evaporation pond for tainted water draining from the region's fields.

The **soil**s of the **arid** San Joaquin valley are the source of Kesterson's problems. The flat valley floor is composed of ancient sea bed **sediment**s that contain high levels of **trace elements**, heavy metals, and salts. But with generous applications of water, this sun-baked soil provides an excellent medium for food production. Perforated pipes buried in the fields drain away excess water—and with it dissolved salts and trace elements—after flood irrigation. An extensive system of underground piping, known as tile drainage, carries **wastewater** into a network of canals that lead to Kesterson Refuge, an artificial basin constructed by the **Bureau of Reclamation** to store irrigation runoff from central California's heavily-watered agriculture. Originally a final drainage canal from Kesterson to San Francisco Bay was planned, but because an outfall point was never agreed upon, contaminated drainage water remained trapped in Kesterson's 12 shallow ponds. In small doses, selenium and other trace elements are not harmful and can even be dietary necessities. But steady evaporation in the refuge gradually concentrated these contaminants to dangerous levels.

Wetlands in California's San Joaquin valley were once numerous, supporting huge populations of breeding and migrating birds. In the past half century drainage and the development of agricultural fields have nearly depleted the area's marshes. The new ponds and cattail marshes at Kesterson presented a rare opportunity to extend breeding **habitat**, and the area was declared a **national wildlife refuge** in 1972, one year after the basins were constructed. Eleven years later, in the spring of 1983, observers discovered that a shocking 60 percent of Kesterson's nestlings were grotesquely deformed. High concentrations of selenium were found in their tissues, an inheritance from parent birds who ate algae, plants, and insects—all tainted with selenium—in the marsh.

Following extensive public outcry the local water management district agreed to try to protect the birds. Alternate drainage routes were established, and by 1987 much of the most contaminated drainage had been diverted from the **wildlife refuge**. The California Water Resource Control Board ordered the Bureau of Reclamation to drain the ponds and clean out contaminated sediments, at a cost of well over $50 million. However, these contaminants, especially in such large volumes and high concentrations, are difficult to contain, and similar problems could quickly emerge again. Furthermore, these problems are widespread. Selenium poisoning from irrigation runoff has been discovered in least nine other national **wildlife** refuges, all in the arid west, since it appeared at Kesterson. Researchers continue to work on affordable and effective responses to such contamination in wetlands, an increasingly rare habitat in this country. *See also* Agricultural pollution; Bioaccumulation; Biological fertility; Biomagnification; Food chain/web; Groundwater pollution; Heavy metals precipitation; Water pollution

[*Mary Ann Cunningham*]

FURTHER READING

Claus, K. E. "Kesterson: An Unsolvable Problem?" *Environment* 89 (1987): 4-5.

Harris, T. "The Kesterson Syndrome." *Amicus Journal* 11 (Fall 1989): 4-9.

———. *Death in the Marsh.* Washington, DC: Island Press, 1991.

Marshal, E. "Selenium in Western Wildlife Refuges." *Science* 231 (1986): 111-12.

Tanji, K., A. Läuchli, and J. Meyer. "Selenium in the San Joaquin Valley." *Environment* 88 (1986): 6-11.

Keystone species

Keystone species have a major influence on the structure of their ecological community. The profound influence of keystone species occurs because of their position and activity within the **food chain/web**. In the sense meant here, a "major influence" means that removal of a keystone species would result in a large change in the abundance, and even the local extirpation, of one or more species in the community. This would fundamentally change the structure of the overall community in terms of species composition, productivity, and other characteristics. Such changes would have substantial effects on all of the species that are present, and could allow new species to invade the community.

The original use of the word "keystone" was in architecture. An architectural keystone is a wedge-shaped stone that is strategically located at the summit of an arch. The keystone serves to lock all other elements of the arch together, and it thereby gives the entire structure mechanical integrity. Keystone species play an analogous role in giving structure to the "architecture" of their ecological community.

The concept of keystone species was first applied to the role of certain predators (i.e., keystone predators) in their community. More recently, however, the term has been extended to refer to other so-called "strong interactors." This has been particularly true of keystone herbivores that have a relatively great influence on the species composition and relative abundance of plants in their community.

Keystone species directly exert their influence on the populations of species that they feed upon, but they also have indirect effects on species lower in the food web. Consider, for example, a hypothetical case of a keystone predator that regulates the population of a herbivore. This effect will also, of course, indirectly influence the abundance of plant species that the herbivore feeds upon. Moreover, by affecting the competitive relationships among the various species of plants in the community, the abundance of plants that the herbivore does not eat will also be indirectly affected by the keystone predator. Although keystone species exert their greatest influence on species with which they are most closely linked through feeding relationships, their influences can ramify throughout the food web.

Ecologists have documented the presence of keystone species in many types of communities. The phenomenon does not, however, appear to be universal, in that keystone species have not been identified in many ecosystems.

Predators as Keystone Species

The term "keystone species" was originally used by the American ecologist Robert Paine to refer to the critical influence of certain predators. His original usage of the concept was in reference to rocky intertidal communities of western North America, in which the predatory starfish *Pisaster ochraceous* prevents the mussel *Mytilus californianus* from monopolizing the available space on rocky habitats and thereby eliminating other, less-competitive herbivores and even seaweeds from the community. By feeding on mussels, which are the dominant competitor among the herbivores in the community, the starfish prevents these shellfish from achieving the dominance that would otherwise be possible. This permits the development of a community that is much richer in species than would occur in the absence of the predatory starfish. Paine demonstrated the keystone role of the starfish by conducting experiments in which the predator was excluded from small areas using cages. When this was done, the mussels quickly became strongly dominant in the community and eliminated virtually all other species of herbivores. Paine also showed that once mussels reached a certain size they were safe from predation by the starfish. This prevented the predator from eliminating the mussel from the community.

Sea otters (*Enhydra lutris*) of the west coast of North America are another example of a keystone predator. This species feeds heavily on sea urchins when these invertebrates are available. By greatly reducing the abundance of sea urchins, the sea otters prevent these herbivores from over-grazing kelps and other seaweeds in subtidal habitats. Therefore, when sea otters are abundant, urchins are not, and this allows luxurious kelp "forests" to develop. In the absence of otters, the high urchin populations can keep the kelp populations low, and the habitat then may develop as a rocky "barren ground." Because sea otters were trapped very intensively for their fur during the eighteenth and nineteenth centuries, they were extirpated over much of their natural range. In fact, the species had been considered extinct until the 1930s, when small populations were "discovered" off the coast of California and in the Aleutian Islands of Alaska. Thanks to effective protection from **trapping**, and deliberate re-introductions to some areas, populations of sea otters have now recovered over much of their original range. This has resulted in a natural depletion of urchin populations, and a widespread increase in the area of kelp forests.

Herbivores as Keystone Species

Some herbivorous animals have also been demonstrated to have a strong influence on the structure and productivity of their ecological community. One such example is the spruce budworm (*Choristoneura fumiferana*), a moth that occasionally irrupts in abundance and becomes an important pest of conifer forests in the northeastern United States and eastern Canada. The habitat of spruce budworm is mature forests dominated by balsam fir (*Abies balsamea*), white spruce (*Picea glauca*), and red spruce (*P. rubens*). This native species of moth is always present in at least small populations, but it sometimes reaches very high populations, which are known as irruptions. When budworm populations are high, many species of forest birds and small mammals occur in relatively large populations that subsist by feeding heavily on larvae of the moth. However, during irruptions of budworm most of the fir and spruce foliage is eaten by the abundant larvae, and after this happens for several years many of the trees die. Because of damages caused to mature trees in the forest the budworm epidemic collapses, and then a successional recovery begins. The plant communities of early succession contain many species of plants that are uncommon in mature conifer forests. Eventually, however, another ma-

tures, conifer forest redevelops, and the cycle is primed for the occurrence of another irruption of the budworm. Clearly, spruce budworm is a good example of a keystone herbivore, because it has such a great influence on the populations of plant species in its habitat, and also on the many animal species that are predators of the budworm.

Another example of a keystone herbivore concerns snow geese (*Chen caerulescens*) in salt marshes of western Hudson Bay. In the absence of grazing by flocks of snow geese this ecosystem would become extensively dominated by several competitively superior species, such as the salt-marsh grass *Puccinellia phryganodes* and the sedge *Carex subspathacea*. However, vigorous feeding by the geese creates bare patches of up to several square meters in area, which can then be colonized by other species of plants. The patchy disturbance regime associated with goose grazing results in the development of a relatively complex community, which supports more species of plants than would otherwise be possible. In addition, by manuring the community with their droppings, the geese help to maintain higher rates of plant productivity than might otherwise occur. In recent years, however, large populations of snow goose have caused severe damages to the salt-marsh habitat by over-grazing. This has resulted in the development of salt-marsh "barrens" in some places, which may take years to recover.

Plants as Keystone Species

Some ecologists have also extended the idea of keystone species to refer to plant species that are extremely influential in their community. For example, sugar maple (*Acer saccharum*) is a competitively superior species that often strongly dominates stands of forest in eastern North America. Under these conditions most of the community-level productivity is contributed by sugar-maple trees. In addition, most of the seedlings and saplings are of sugar maple. This is because few seedlings of other species of trees are able to tolerate the stressful conditions beneath a closed sugar-maple canopy.

Other ecologists prefer to not use the idea of keystone species to refer to plants that, because of their competitive abilities, are strongly dominant in their community. Instead, these are sometimes referred to as "foundationstone species." This term reflects the facts that strongly dominant plants contribute the great bulk of the biomass and productivity of their community, and that they support almost all herbivores, predators, and **detritivores** that are present.

[Bill Freedman]

FURTHER READING

Begon, M., J.L. Harper, and C.R. Townsend, *Ecology. Individuals, Populations and Communities*, 3rd ed. London: Blackwell Sci. Pub., 1996.

Krebs, C.J. *Ecology. The Experimental Analysis of Distribution and Abundance*. San Francisco: Harper and Row, 1985.

Paine, R.T. "Intertidal community structure: Experimental studies of the relationship between a dominant competitor and its principal predator," *Oecologia* 15 (1974): 93-120.

Ricklefs, R.E. *Ecology*. New York: W.H. Freeman and Co., 1990.

Killer bees

See **Africanized bees**

Kirtland's warbler (*Dendroica kirtlandii*)

Kirtland's warbler is an **endangered species** and one of the rarest members of the North American wood warbler family. Its entire breeding range is limited to a seven-county area of north-central Michigan. The restricted distribution of the Kirtland's warbler and its specific **niche** requirements have probably contributed to low population levels throughout its existence, but human activity has had a large impact on their numbers over the past hundred years.

The first specimen of Kirtland's warbler was taken by Samuel Cabot in October 1841, and brought on ship in the West Indies during an expedition to the Yucatan. But this specimen went unnoticed until 1865, long after the species had been formally described. Charles Pease is credited with discovering Kirtland's warbler. He collected a specimen on May 13, 1851 near Cleveland, Ohio, and gave it to his father-in-law, Dr. Jared P. Kirtland, a renowned naturalist. Kirtland sent the specimen to his friend, ornithologist Spencer Fullerton Baird, who described the new species the following year and named it in honor of the naturalist.

The wintering grounds of Kirtland's warbler is the Bahamas, a fact which was well established by the turn of the century, but its nesting grounds went undiscovered until 1903, when Norman Wood found the first nest in Oscoda County, Michigan. Every nest found since then has been within a sixty mile radius of this spot.

In 1951 the first exhaustive census of singing males was undertaken in an effort to establish the range of Kirtland's warblers as well as its population level. Assuming that numbers of males and females are approximately equal and that a singing male is defending an active nesting site, the total of 432 in this census indicated a population of 864 birds. Ten years later another census counted 502 singing males, indicating the population was over 1,000 birds. In 1971, annual counts began, but this revealed that the population had dropped to about 400 birds, based on 201 singing males. The number of males counted in censuses since 1971 have fluctuated between 167 in 1974 and 1987 and 392 males in 1992.

The first problem facing this endangered species centers on its specialized nesting and **habitat** requirements. The Kirtland's warbler nests on the ground, and its reproductive success is tied closely to its selection of young jack pine trees as nesting sites. When the jack pines are 5-20 ft (1.5-6 m) tall, at an age of 8-20 years, their lower branches are at ground level and provide the cover this warbler needs. The life cycle of the pine, however, is dependent on forest fires, as the intense heat is needed to open the cones for seed release. The advent of fire protection in **forest management** reduced the production of the number of young trees the warblers needed and the population suffered. Once this relationship was fully understood, jack pine stands were managed for Kirtland's warbler, as well as commercial harvest, by instituting controlled burns on a 50 year rotational basis.

The second problem is the population pressures brought to bear by a nest **parasite**, the brown-headed cowbird, which lays its eggs in the nests of other songbirds. Originally a bird of open plains, it did not threaten Kirtland's warbler until Michigan was heavily deforested, thus providing it with appropriate habitat. Once established in the warbler's range, it has increasingly pressured the Kirtland's population. Cowbird chicks hatch earlier than other birds and they compete successfully with the other nestlings for nourishment. Efforts to trap and destroy this nest parasite in the warbler's range have resulted in improved reproductive success for Kirtland's warbler. *See also* Deforestation; Endangered Species Act; International Council on Bird Preservation; Rare species; Wildlife management

[*Eugene C. Beckham*]

FURTHER READING

Ehrlich, P. R., D. S. Dobkin, and D. Wheye. *Birds in Jeopardy: The Imperiled and Extinct Birds of the United States and Canada, Including Hawaii and Puerto Rico.* Stanford: Stanford University Press, 1992.

Weinrich, J. A. "Status of Kirtland's Warbler, 1988." *Jack-Pine Warbler* 67 (1989): 69-72.

Krakatoa

The explosion of this triad of volcanoes on August 27, 1883, the culmination of a three-month eruptive phase, astonished the world because of its global impact. Perhaps one of the most influential factors, however, was its timing. It happened during a time of major growth in science, technology, and communications, and the world received current news accompanied by the correspondents' personal observations. The explosion was heard some 3,000 miles away, on the Island of Rodriguez in the Indian Ocean. The glow of sunsets was so vivid three months later that fire engines were called out in New York City and nearby towns.

Krakatoa (or Krakatau), located in the Sunda Strait between Java and Sumatra, is part of the Indonesian volcanic system, which was formed by the subduction of the Indian Ocean plate under the Asian plate. A similar explosion occurred in A.D. 416, and another major eruption was recorded in 1680. Now a new volcano is growing out of the caldera, likely building toward some future cataclysm.

This immense natural event, perhaps twice as powerful as the largest **hydrogen** bomb, had an extraordinary impact on the solid earth, the oceans, and the **atmosphere**, and demonstrated their interdependence. It also made possible the creation of a **wildlife refuge** and **tropical rain forest** preserve on the Ujung Kulon Peninsula of southwestern Java.

Studies revealed that this caldera, like Crater Lake, Oregon, resulted from Krakatoa's collapse into the now empty magma chamber. The explosion produced a 131-ft (40-m) high tsunami, or tidal wave, which carried a steamship nearly two m (3.2 km) inland, and caused most of the fatalities resulting from the eruption. Tidal gauges as far away as San Francisco Bay and the English Channel recorded fluctuations.

The explosion provided substantial benefits to the young science of **meteorology**. Every barometer on earth recorded the blast wave as it raced towards its antipodal position in Columbia, and then reverberated back and forth in six more recorded waves. The distribution of ash in the **stratosphere** gave the first solid evidence of rapidly flowing westerly winds, as debris encircled the equator over the next thirteen days. Global temperatures were lowered about 0.9°F (0.5°C), and did not return to normal until five years later.

An ironic development is that the Ujung Kulon Peninsula was never resettled after the tsunami killed most of the people. Without Krakatoa's explosion, the population would have most likely grown significantly and much of the **habitat** there would likely have been altered by agriculture. Instead, the area is now a **national park** that supports a variety of **species**, including the Javan rhino, one of earth's rarest and most **endangered species**. This park has provided a laboratory for scientists to study **nature**'s healing process after such devastation. *See also* Mount Pinatubo, Philippines; Mount Saint Helens, Washington; Volcano

[*Nathan H. Meleen*]

FURTHER READING

Ball, R. "The Explosion of Krakatoa," *National Geographic* 13 (June 1902): 200-203.

Nardo, D. *Krakatoa*. World Disasters Series. San Diego: Lucent Books, 1990.

Plage, D., and M. Plage. "Return of Java's Wildlife," *National Geographic* 167 (June 1985): 750-71.

Simkin, T., and R. Fiske. *Krakatau 1883: The Volcanic Eruption and Its Effects*. Washington, DC: Smithsonian Books, 1983.

Krill

Marine crustaceans in the order Euphausiacea. Krill are **zooplankton**, and most feed on microalgae by filtering them from the water. In high latitudes, krill may account for a large proportion of the total zooplankton. Krill often occur in large swarms and in a few **species** these swarms may reach several hundred square meters in size with densities over 60,000 individuals per square meter. This swarming behavior makes them valuable food sources for many species of **whales** and seabirds. Humans have also begun to harvest krill for use as a dietary protein supplement.

Krutch, Joseph Wood (1893-1970)

American literary critic and naturalist

Through much of his career, Krutch was a teacher of criticism at Columbia University and a drama critic for *The Nation*. But then respiratory problems led him to early retirement in the desert near Tucson, Arizona. He loved the desert and there turned to biology and geology, which he applied to maintain a consistent, major theme found in all of

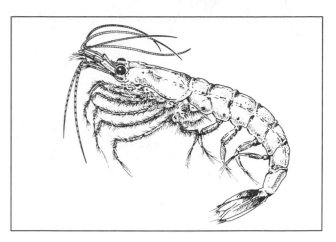

Krill.

his writings, that of the relation of humans and the universe. Krutch subsequently became an accomplished naturalist.

Readers can find the theme of man and universe in Krutch's early work, for example *The Modern Temper* (1929), and in his later writings on human-human and human-nature relationships, including natural history—what **Rene Jules Dubos** described as "the social philosopher protesting against the follies committed in the name of technological progress, and the humanist searching for permanent values in man's relationship to nature." Assuming a pessimistic stance in his early writings, Krutch despaired about lost connections, arguing that for humans to reconnect, they must conceive of themselves, nature, "and the universe in a significant reciprocal relationship."

Krutch's later writings repudiated much of his earlier despair. He argued against the dehumanizing and alienating forces of modern society and advocated systematically reassembling—by reconnecting to nature—"a world man can live in." In *The Voice of the Desert* (1954), for instance, he claimed that "we must be part not only of the human community, but of the whole community." In such books as *The Twelve Seasons* (1949) and *The Great Chain of Life* (1956), he demonstrated that humans "are a part of Nature...whatever we discover about her we are discovering also about ourselves." This view was based on a solid anti-deterministic approach that opposed mechanistic and behavioristic theories of **evolution** and biology.

His view of modern technology as out of control was epitomized in the **automobile**. Driving fast prevented people from reflecting or thinking or doing anything except controlling the monster: "I'm afraid this is the metaphor of our society as a whole," he commented. Krutch also disliked the proliferation of suburbs, which he labeled "affluent slums." He argued in *Human Nature and the Human Condition* (1959) that "modern man should be concerned with achieving the good life, not with raising the [material] standard of living."

An editorial ran in *The New York Times* a week after Krutch's death: today's younger generation, it read, "unfamiliar with Joseph Wood Krutch but concerned about the environment and contemptuous of materialism," should "turn to a reading of his books with delight to themselves and profit to the world."

[*Gerald L. Young*]

FURTHER READING

Gorman, J. "Joseph Wood Krutch: A Cactus Walden." *MELUS: The Journal of the Society for the Study of the Multi-Ethnic Literature of the United States* 11 (Winter 1984): 93-101.

Holtz, W. "Homage to Joseph Wood Krutch: Tragedy and the Ecological Imperative." *The American Scholar* 43 (Spring 1974): 267-279.

Krutch, J. W. *The Desert Year*. New York: Viking, 1951.

Lehman, A. L. "Joseph Wood Krutch: A Selected Bibliography of Primary Sources." *Bulletin of Bibliography* 41 (June 1984): 74-80.

Margolis, J. D. *Joseph Wood Krutch: A Writer's Life*. Knoxville, TN: The University of Tennessee Press, 1980.

Pavich, P. N. *Joseph Wood Krutch*. Western Writers Series, no. 89. Boise, ID: Boise State University, 1989.

Kudzu

Pueraria lobata or kudzu, also jokingly referred to as "foot-a-night" and "the vine that ate the South," is a highly aggressive and persistent semi-woody vine introduced to the United States in the late nineteenth century. It has since become a symbol of the problems possible for native **ecosystem**s caused by the introduction of **exotic species**. Kudzu's best known characteristic is its extraordinary capacity for rapid growth, managing as much as 12 in (30.5 cm) a day and 60-100 ft (18-30 m) a season under ideal conditions. When young, kudzu has thin, flexible, downy stems that grow outward as well as upward, eventually covering virtually everything in its path with a thick mat of leaves and tendrils. This lateral growth creates the dramatic effect, common in southeastern states such as Georgia, of telephone poles, buildings, neglected vehicles, and whole areas of woodland being enshrouded in blankets of kudzu. Kudzu's tendency towards aggressive and overwhelming colonization has many detrimental effects, killing stands of trees by robbing them of sunlight and pulling down or shorting out utility cables. Where stem nodes touch the ground, new roots develop which can extend 10 ft (3 m) or more underground and eventually weigh several hundred pounds. In the nearly ideal climate of the Southeast, the prolific vine easily overwhelms virtually all native competitors and also infests cropland and yards.

A member of the pea family, kudzu is itself native to China and Japan. Introduced to the United States at the Japanese garden pavilion during the 1876 Philadelphia Centennial Exhibition, kudzu's broad leaves and richly fragrant reddish-purple blooms made it seem highly desirable as an ornamental plant in American gardens. It now ranges along the eastern seaboard from Florida to Pennsylvania, and westward to Texas. Although hardy, kudzu does not tolerate cold weather and prefers acidic, well-drained **soil**s and bright sunlight. It rarely flowers or sets seed in the northern part of its range and loses its leaves at first frost.

For centuries, the Japanese have cultivated kudzu for its edible roots, medicinal qualities, and fibrous leaves and stems, which are suitable for paper production. After its initial introduction as an ornamental, kudzu also was touted as a forage crop and as a cure for **erosion** in the United States. Kudzu is nutritionally comparable to alfalfa, and its tremendous durability and speed of growth were thought to outweigh the disadvantages caused for cutting and baling by its rope-like vines. But its effectiveness as a ground cover, particularly on steeply-sloped terrain, is responsible for kudzu's spectacular spread. By the 1930s, the United States **Soil Conservation Service** was enthusiastically advocating kudzu as a remedy for erosion, subsidizing farmers as well as highway departments and railroads, with as much as $8 an acre to use kudzu for soil retention. The Depression-era Civilian Conservation Corps also facilitated the spread of kudzu, planting millions of seedlings as part of an extensive erosion control project.

Kudzu also has had its unofficial champions, the best known of whom is Channing Cope of Covington, Georgia. As a journalist for Atlanta newspapers and popular radio broadcaster, Cope frequently extolled the virtues of kudzu, dubbing it the "miracle vine" and declaring that it had replaced cotton as "King" of the South. The spread of the vine was precipitous. In the early 1950s, the federal government began to question the wisdom of its support for kudzu. By 1953, the Department of Agriculture stopped recommending the use of kudzu for either fodder or ground cover. In 1982, kudzu was officially declared a weed.

Funding is now directed more at finding ways to eradicate kudzu or at least to contain its spread. Continuous over-grazing by livestock will eventually eradicate a field of kudzu, as will repeated applications of defoliant herbicides. Even so, stubborn patches may take five or more years to be completely removed. **Controlled burning** is usually ineffective and attempting to dig up the massive root system is generally an exercise in futility, but kudzu can be kept off lawns and fences (as an ongoing project) by repeated mowing and enthusiastic pruning.

A variety of new uses are being found for kudzu, and some very old uses are being rediscovered. Kudzu root can be processed into flour and baked into breads and cakes; as a starchy sweetener, it also may be used to flavor soft drinks. Medical researchers investigating the scientific bases of traditional herbal remedies have suggested that isoflavones found in kudzu root may significantly reduce craving for alcohol in alcoholics. Eventually, derivatives of kudzu may also prove to be useful for treatment of high blood pressure. Methane and gasohol have been successfully produced from kudzu, and kudzu's stems may prove to be an economically viable source of fiber for paper production and other purposes. The prolific vine has also become something of a humorous cultural icon, with regional picture postcards throughout the south portraying spectacular and only somewhat exaggerated images of kudzu's explosive growth. Fairs, festivals, restaurants, bars, rock groups, and road races have all borrowed their name and drawn some measure of inspiration from kudzu, poems have been written about it, and kudzu cookbooks and guides to kudzu crafts are readily available in bookstores.

[*Lawrence J. Biskowski*]

FURTHER READING

Dolby, V. "Kudzu Grows Beyond Erosion Control to Help Control Alcoholism," *Better Nutrition* 58, no. 11 (November 1996): 32.

Hipps, C. "Kudzu," *Horticulture* 72, no. 6 (June 1994): 36-9.

Tenenbaum, D. "Weeds from Hell," *Technology Review* 99, no. 6 (August 1996): 32-40.

Kwashiorkor

One of many severe protein energy malnutrition disorders that are a widespread problem among children in developing countries. The word's origin is in Ghana, where it means a deposed child, or a child that is no longer suckled. The disease usually affects infants between one and four years of age who have been weaned from breast milk to a high starch, low protein diet. The disease is characterized by lethargy, apathy, or irritability. Over time the individual will experience retarded growth processes both physically and mentally. Approximately 25 percent of children suffer from recurrent relapses of kwashiorkor, interfering with their normal growth.

Kwashiorkor results in amino acid deficiencies which inhibit protein synthesis in all tissues. The lack of sufficient plasma proteins, specifically albumin, results in systemic pressure changes, ultimately causing generalized edema. The liver swells with stored fat because there are no hepatic proteins being produced for digestion of fats. Kwashiorkor additionally results in reduced bone density and impaired renal function. If treated early on in its development the disease can be reversed with proper dietary therapy and treatment of associated infections. If the condition is not reversed in its early stages, prognosis is poor and physical and mental growth will be severely retarded. *See also* Sahel; Third World

L

Lagoon

A lagoon is a shallow body of water separated from a larger, open body of water. It is typically associated with the ocean, such as coastal lagoons and **coral reef** lagoons. It can also be used to describe shallow areas of liquid waste material as in **sewage** lagoons. Oceanic lagoons can be formed in several ways. Coastal lagoons are typically found along coastlines where there are sand bars or **barrier island**s that separate the open ocean from the near shore body of water. Coral reef lagoons can form in two ways. The first type is found in barrier reefs such as those in **Australia** and Belize, where there is a body of water (lagoon) which is separated from the open ocean by the reef formed many miles off shore. Another type of lagoon is that formed in the center of atolls, which are circular or horse-shoe shaped bodies of water in the middle of partially sunken volcanic islands with coral reefs growing around their periphery. Some of these atoll lagoons are more than 30 mi (50 km) across and have breath-taking visibility, thus providing superb sites for SCUBA diving.

Lake Baikal, Russia

The **Great Lakes** are a prominent feature of the North American landscape, but Russia holds the distinction of having the "World's Great Lake." Called the "Pearl of Siberia" or the "Sacred Sea" by locals, Lake Baikal is the world's deepest and largest lake by volume. It has a surface area of 12,162 square miles (31,500 sq km), a maximum depth of 5,370 ft (1,637 m), or slightly more than 1 mile, an average depth of 2,428 ft (740 m), and a volume of 30,061 cu yd (23,000 cu m). It thus contains more water than the combined volume of all of the Great Lakes—20 percent of the world's fresh water (and 80 percent of the fresh water of the former Soviet Union).

Lake Baikal is located in Russia in south-central Siberia near the northern border of Mongolia. Scientists estimate that the lake was formed 25 million years ago by tectonic (earthquake) displacement, creating a crescent-shaped, steep-walled basin 395 miles (635 km) long by 50 miles (80 km) wide and nearly 5.6 miles (9 km) deep. In contrast, the Great Lakes were formed by glacial scouring a mere 10,000 years ago.

Although **sedimentation** has filled in 80 percent of the basin over the years, the lake is believed to be widening and deepening ever so slightly with time because of recurring crustal movements. The area surrounding Lake Baikal is underridden by at least three crustal plates, causing frequent earthquakes. Fortunately, most are too weak to feel.

Like similarly ancient Lake Tanganyika in Africa, the waters of Lake Baikal host a great number of unique **species**. Of the 1200 known animal and 600 known plant species, more than 80 percent are endemic to this lake. These include many species of fish, shrimp, and the world's only fresh water sponges and seals. Called *nerpa* or *nerpy* by the natives, these seals (*Phoca sibirica*) are silvery-gray in color and can grow to 5 ft (1.5 m) long and weigh up to 286 lbs (130 kg). Their diet consists almost exclusively of a strange-looking relict fish called *golomyanka* (*Comephorus baicalensis*), rendered translucent by its fat-filled body. Unlike other fish, they lack scales and swim bladders and give birth to live larvae rather than eggs. The seal population is estimated at 60,000. Commercial hunters are permitted to kill 6,000 each year.

Although the waters of Lake Baikal are pristine by the standards of other large lakes, increased **pollution** threatens its future. Towns along its shores and along the stretches of the Selenga River, the major tributary flowing into Baikal, add human and industrial wastes, some of which is non-**biodegradable** and some highly toxic. A hydroelectric dam on the Angara River, the lake's only outlet, raised the water level and placed spawning areas of some fish below the optimum depth. Most controversial to the people who depend on this lake for their livelihood and pleasure, however, was the construction of a large cellulose plant at the southern end near the city of Baikalsk in 1957. Built originally to manufacture high-quality aircraft tires (ironically, synthetic tires proved superior), today it produces clothing from bleached cellulose and employs 3,500 people. Uncharacteristic public outcry over the years has resulted in the addition of advanced **sewage treatment** facilities to the plant. Although some people would like to see it shut down, the local (and national) economy has taken precedence.

In 1987 the Soviet government passed legislation protecting Lake Baikal from further destruction. Logging was prohibited anywhere close to the shoreline and nature reserves and **national park**s were designated. However, with the recent political turmoil and crippling financial situation in the former Soviet Union, these changes have not

A view of the Strait of Olkhon, on the west coast of Lake Baikal, Russia. Olkhon Island appears on the horizon.

been enforced and the lake continues to receive pollutants. Much more needs to be done to assure the future of this magnificent lake. *See also* Endemic species

[*John Korstad*]

FURTHER READING

Belt, D. "Russia's Lake Baikal, the World's Great Lake." *National Geographic* 181 (June 1992): 2-39.

Feshbach, M., and A. Friendly, Jr. *Ecocide in the USSR*. New York: Basic Books, 1992.

Matthiessen, P. *Baikal: Sacred Sea of Siberia*. San Francisco: Sierra Club Books, 1992.

Lake Erie

Lake Erie is the most productive of the **Great Lakes**. Located along the southern fringe of the Precambrian Shield of North America, Lake Erie has been ecologically degraded by a variety of **anthropogenic** stressors including **nutrient** loading; extensive **deforestation** of its **watershed** that caused severe **siltation** and other effects; vigorous **commercial fishing**; and **pollution** by toxic **chemicals**.

The watershed of Lake Erie is much more agricultural and urban in character than are those of the other Great

Lakes. Consequently, the dominant sources of **phosphorus** (the most important nutrient causing eutrophication) to Lake Erie are agricultural **runoff** and municipal **point sources**. The total input of phosphorus to Lake Erie (standardized to watershed area) is about 1.3 times larger than to Lake Ontario and more than five times larger than to the other Great Lakes.

Because of its large loading rates and concentrations of nutrients, Lake Erie is more productive and has a larger standing crop of **phytoplankton**, fish, and other biota than the other Great Lakes. During the late 1960s and early 1970s, the eutrophic western basin of Lake Erie had a summer-chlorophyll concentration averaging twice as large as in Lake Ontario and 11 times larger than in oligotrophic Lake Superior. However, since that time the eutrophication of Lake Erie has been alleviated somewhat, in direct response to decreased phosphorus inputs with sewage and **detergents**. A consequence of the eutrophic state of Lake Erie was the development of anoxia (lack of oxygen) in its deeper waters during summer **stratification**. In the summer of 1953, this condition caused a collapse of the population of benthic mayfly larvae (*Hexagenia* spp.), a phenomenon that was interpreted in the popular press as the "death" of Lake Erie.

Large changes have also taken place in the fish community of Lake Erie, mostly because of its fishery, the damming of streams required for spawning by anadromous fishes (fish that ascend rivers or streams to spawn), and **sedimentation** of shallow-water **habitat** by **silt** eroded from deforested parts of the watershed. Lake Erie has always had the most productive fishery on the Great Lakes, with fish landings that typically exceed the combined totals of all the other Great Lakes. The peak years of commercial fishery in Lake Erie were in 1935 and 1956 (62 million lb/28 million kg), while the minima were in 1929 and 1941 (24 million lb/11 million kg). Overall, the total catch by the commercial fishery has been remarkably stable over time, despite large changes in **species**, effort, eutrophication, toxic pollution, and other changes in habitat.

The historical pattern of development of the Lake Erie fishery was characterized by an initial exploitation of the most desirable and valuable species. As the populations of these species collapsed because of unsustainable fishing pressure, coupled with habitat deterioration, the fishery diverted to a progression of less-desirable species. The initial fishery focused on lake white fish (*Coregonus clupeaformis*), lake trout (*Salvelinus namaycush*), and lake herring (*Leucichthys artedi*), all of which rapidly declined to scarcity or **extinction**. The next target was "second-choice" species, such as blue pike (*Stizostedion vitreum glaucum*) and walleye (*S. v. vitreum*), which are now extinct or rare. Today's fishery is dominated by species of much smaller economic value, such as yellow perch (*Perca flavescens*), rainbow smelt (*Osmerus mordax*), and carp (*Cyprinus carpio*). *See also* Cultural eutrophication; Water pollution

[*Bill Freedman*]

FURTHER READING

Ashworth, W. *The Late, Great Lakes: An Environmental History.* New York: Knopf, 1986.

Freedman, B. *Environmental Ecology.* San Diego: Academic Press, 1989.

Regier, H. A., and W. L. Hartman. "Lake Erie's Fish Community: 150 Years of Cultural Stresses." *Science* 180 (1973): 1248-55.

Lake Tahoe

A beautiful lake 6,200 feet (1,891 m) high in the Sierra Nevada, straddling the California-Nevada state line, Lake Tahoe is a jewel to both **nature**-lovers and developers. It is the tenth deepest lake in the world, with a maximum depth of 1,600 feet (488 m) and a volume of 61 cubic miles (156 cubic km). Tahoe and Crater Lake are the only two large alpine lakes remaining in the country. Visitors have expressed their awe of the lake's beauty since it was discovered by General John Frémont in 1844. Mark Twain, for example, wrote that it was "the fairest sight the whole Earth affords."

The arrival of Europeans in the Tahoe area was quickly followed by environmental devastation. Between 1870 and 1900, forests around the lake were heavily logged to provide timber for the mine shafts of the Comstock Lode. While this logging dramatically altered the area's appearance for years, the natural **environment** eventually recovered and no long-term damage to the lake can now be detected.

The same can not be said for a later assault on the lake's environment. Shortly after World War II, people began moving into the area to take advantage of the region's natural wonders—the lake itself and superb snow skiing—as well as the young casino business on the Nevada side of the lake. Lakeside population grew from about 20,000 in 1960 to more than 50,000 today, with an estimated tourist population of another 12 million each year.

By the late 1960s, changes were already observable in the lake. Early records showed that the lake was once clear enough to allow visibility to a depth of about 130 feet (40 m). By the late 1960s, that figure had dropped to about 100 feet (30 m), and today, it is closer to 80 feet (25 m).

The reason for this change is that Tahoe is now undergoing eutrophication at a fairly rapid rate. Algal growth is being encouraged by sewage and **fertilizer** produced by human activities. Natural **pollution control**s, such as trees and plants, have largely been removed to make room for residential and commercial development. The lack of significant flow into and out of the lake also contributes to a favorable environment for algal growth.

Efforts to protect the pristine beauty of Lake Tahoe go back at least to 1912. Three efforts were made during that decade to have the lake declared a **national park**, but all failed. By 1958, concerned conservationists had formed the Lake Tahoe Area Council to "promote the preservation and long-range development of the Lake Tahoe basin." The Council was followed by other organizations with similar objectives, the League to Save Lake Tahoe among them.

An important step in resolving the conflict between preservationists and developers occurred in 1969 with the creation of the Tahoe Regional Planning Agency (TRPA). The agency was the first and only **land use** commission with authority in more than one state. It consisted of fourteen members, seven appointed by each of the governors of the two states involved, California and Nevada. For more than a decade, the agency attempted to write a land-use plan that would be acceptable to both sides of the dispute. The conflict became more complex when the California Attorney General, John Van de Kamp, filed suit in 1985 to prevent TRPA from granting any further permits for development. Developers were outraged but lost all of their court appeals.

By 1990, the two opposing sides had begun to reach compromise on a number of issues. Preservationists have agreed to some modest growth, 300 new homes in environmentally resilient areas, for example. Developers have agreed to protect the most environmentally sensitive parts of the area and to repair of some damaged **ecosystem**s. *See also* Algal bloom; Cultural eutrophication; Environmental degradation; Fish kills; Sierra Club; Water pollution

[*David E. Newton*]

FURTHER READING

Goldman, C. R. "Lake Tahoe: Preserving a Fragile Ecosystem." *Environment* 31 (September 1989): 6-11+.

Stuller, J. "Battle-Weary Lake Tahoe Combatants Try Compromise." *Audubon* 89 (May 1987): 44-67.

Lake Washington

One of the great messages to come out of the environmental movement of the 1960s and 1970s is that, while humans can cause **pollution**, they can also clean it up. Few success stories illustrate this point as clearly as that of Lake Washington. Lake Washington lies along the state of Washington's west coastline, near the city of Seattle. It is 24 mi (39 km) from north to south and its width varies from 2-4 mi (3-6 km).

For the first half of this century, Lake Washington was clear and pristine, a beautiful example of the Northwest's spectacular natural scenery. Its shores were occupied by extensive wooded areas and a few small towns with populations of no more than 10,000. The lake's purity was not threatened by Seattle, which dumped most of its wastes into Elliot Bay, an arm of Puget Sound. This situation changed rapidly during and after World War II. In 1940, the spectacular Lake Washington Bridge was built across the lake, joining its two facing shores with each other and with Seattle. Population along the lake began to boom, reaching more than 50,000 by 1950.

The consequence of these changes for the lake are easy to imagine. Many of the growing communities dumped their raw sewage directly into the lake or, at best, passed their wastes though only preliminary treatment stages. By one estimate, 20 million gallons (76 million liters) of wastes were being dumped into the lake each day. On average these wastes still contained about half of their pollutants when they reached the lake. In less than a decade, the effect of these practices on lake **water quality** were easy to observe. Water clarity was reduced from at least 15 ft (4.6 m) to 2.5 ft (0.8 m) and levels of **dissolved oxygen** were so low that some **species** of fish disappeared. In 1956, W. T. Edmonson, a zoologist and pollution authority, and two colleagues reported their studies of the lake. They found that eutrophication of the lake was taking place very rapidly as a result of the dumping of domestic wastes into its water.

Solving this problem was especially difficult because **water pollution** is a regional issue over which each individual community had relatively little control. The solution appeared to be the creation of a new governmental body that would encompass all of the Lake Washington communities, including Seattle. In 1958, a ballot measure establishing such an agency, known as Metro, was passed in Seattle but defeated in its suburbs. Six months later, the Metro concept was redefined to include the issue of sewage disposal only. This time it passed in all communities.

Metro's approach to the Lake Washington problem was to construct a network of sewer lines and **sewage treatment** plants that directed all sewage away from the lake and delivered it instead to Puget Sound. The lake's pollution problems were solved within a few years. By 1975 the lake was back to normal, water clarity returned to 15 feet and levels of potassium and **nitrogen** in the lake decreased by more than 60 percent. Lake Washington's biological oxygen demand (BOD), a critical measure of water purity, decreased by 90 percent and fish species that had disappeared were once again found in the lake. *See also* Aquatic chemistry; Cultural eutrophication; Waste management; Water quality standards

[*David E. Newton*]

FURTHER READING

Edmonson, W. T. "Lake Washington." In *Environmental Quality and Water Development*, edited by C. R. Goodman, et al. San Francisco: W. H. Freeman, 1973.

___ *The Uses of Ecology: Lake Washington and Beyond.* Seattle: University of Washington Press, 1991.

Lakes

See **Experimental Lakes Area; Great Lakes; Lake Baikal; Lake Erie; Lake Tahoe; Lake Washington; Mono Lake; National lakeshore**

Land degradation

See **Desertification**

Land ethic

Land ethic refers to an approach to issues of **land use** that emphasizes **conservation** and respect for our natural **environment**. Rejecting the belief that all **natural resources** should be available for unchecked human exploitation, a land ethic advocates land use without undue disturbances of the complex, delicately balanced ecological systems of which humans are a part. Land ethic, **environmental ethics**, and ecological ethics are sometimes used interchangeably.

Discussions of land ethic, especially in the United States, usually begin with a reference of some kind to **Aldo Leopold**. Many participants in the debate over land and resource use admire Leopold's prescient and pioneering quest and date the beginnings of a land ethic to his *A Sand County Almanac*, published in 1949. However, Leopold's earliest formulation of his position may be found in "A Conservation Ethic," a benchmark essay on ethics published in 1933.

Even recognizing Leopold's remarkable early contribution, it is still necessary to place his pioneer work in a larger context. Land ethic is not a radically new invention of the twentieth century but has many ancient and modern antecedents in the Western philosophical tradition. The Greek philosopher Plato, for example, wrote that morality is "the effective harmony of the whole"—not a bad statement of an ecological ethic. Reckless exploitation has at times been justified as enjoying divine sanction in the Judeo-Christian tradition (man was made master of the creation, authorized to do with it as he saw fit). However, most Christian thought through the ages has interpreted the proper human role as one of careful husbandry of resources that do not, in fact, belong to humans. In the nineteenth century, the Huxleys, Thomas and Julian, worked on relating **evolution** and ethics. The mathematician and philosopher Bertrand Russell wrote that "man is not a solitary animal, and so long as social life survives, self-realization cannot be the supreme principle of ethics." **Albert Schweitzer** became famous—at about the same time that Leopold formulated a land ethic—for teaching reverence for life, and not just human life. Many nonwestern traditions also emphasize harmony and a respect for all living things. Such a context implies that a land ethic cannot easily be separated from age-old thinking on ethics in general. *See also* Land stewardship

[*Gerald L. Young and Marijke Rijsberman*]

FURTHER READING

Bormann, F. H., and S. R. Kellert, eds. *Ecology, Economics, Ethics: The Broken Circle.* New Haven, CT: Yale University Press, 1991.

Kealey, D. A. *Revisioning Environmental Ethics.* Albany: State University of New York Press, 1989.

Leopold, A. *A Sand County Almanac.* New York: Oxford University Press, 1949.

Nash, R. F. *The Rights of Nature: A History of Environmental Ethics.* Madison: University of Wisconsin Press, 1989.

Rolston, H. *Environmental Ethics.* Philadelphia: Temple University Press, 1988.

Turner, F. "A New Ecological Ethics." In *Rebirth of Value.* Albany: State University of New York Press, 1991.

Land Institute (Salina, Kansas)

Founded in 1976 by Wes and Dana Jackson, the Land Institute is both an independent agricultural research station and a school devoted to exploring and developing alternative agricultural practices. Located on the Smoky Hill River near Salina, Kansas, the Institute attempts—in **Wes Jackson**'s words—to "make **nature** the measure" of human activities so that humans "meet the expectations of the land," rather than abusing the land for human needs. This requires a radical rethinking of traditional and modern farming methods. The aim of the Land Institute is to find "new roots for agriculture" by reexamining its traditional assumptions.

In traditional tillage farming, furrows are dug into the **topsoil** and seeds planted. This leaves precious topsoil exposed to **erosion** by wind and water. Topsoil loss can be minimized but not eliminated by **contour plowing**, the use of windbreaks, and other means. Although critical of traditional tillage agriculture, Jackson is even more critical of the methods and machinery of modern industrial agriculture, which in effect trades topsoil for high crop yields (roughly one bushel of topsoil is lost for every bushel of corn harvested). It also relies on plant **monoculture**s—genetically uniform strains of corn, wheat, soybeans, and other crops. These crops are especially susceptible to disease and insect infestations and require extensive use of **pesticide**s and **herbicide**s which, in turn, kill useful creatures (for example, worms and birds), pollute streams and **groundwater**, and produce other destructive side effects. Although spectacularly successful in the short run, such an agriculture is both nonsustainable and self-defeating. Its supposed strengths—its productivity, its efficiency, its economies of scale—are also

its weaknesses. Short-term gains in production do not, Jackson argues, justify the longer term depletion of topsoil, the diminution of genetic diversity, and such social side-effects as the disappearance of small family farms and the abandonment of rural communities.

If these trends are to be questioned—much less slowed or reversed—a practical, productive, and feasible alternative agriculture must be developed. To develop such a workable alternative is the aim of the Land Institute. The Jacksons and their associates are attempting to devise an alternative vision of agricultural possibilities. This begins with the important but oft-neglected truism that agriculture is not self-contained but is intertwined with and dependent on nature. The Institute explores the feasibility of alternative farming methods that might minimize or even eliminate the planting and harvesting of annual crops, turning instead to "herbaceous perennial seed-producing polycultures" that protect and bind topsoil. Food grains would be grown in pasture-like fields and intermingled with other plants that would replenish lost **nitrogen** and other **nutrient**s, without relying on chemical **fertilizer**s. Covered by a rooted living net of diverse plant life, the soil would at no time be exposed to erosion and would be aerated and rejuvenated by natural means. And the farmer, in symbiotic partnership, would take nature as the measure of his methods and results.

The experiments at the Land Institute are intended to make this vision into a workable reality. It is as yet too early to tell exactly what these continuing experiments might yield. But the re-visioning of agriculture has already begun and continues at the Land Institute. Contact: The Land Institute, 2440 E. Water Well Road, Salina, KS 67401. Internet: *See also* Agroecology; Berry, Wendell; Conservation tillage; Land Stewardship Project; Sustainable agriculture

[*Terence Ball*]

Land reform

Land reform is a social and political restructuring of the agricultural systems through redistribution of land. Successful land reform policies take into account the political, social, and economic structure of the area.

In agrarian societies, large landowners typically control the wealth and the distribution of food. Land reform policies in such societies allocate land to small landowners, to farm workers who own no land, to collective farm operations, or to state farm organizations. The exact nature of the allocation depends on the motivation of those initiating the changes. In areas where absentee ownership of farmland is common, land reform has become a popular method for returning the land to local ownership. Land reforms generally favor the family-farm concept, rather than absentee landholding.

Land reform is often undertaken as a means of achieving greater social equality, but it can also increase agricultural productivity and benefit the **environment**. A tenant farmer may have a more emotional and protective relation to the land he works, and he may be more likely to make agricultural decisions that benefit the **ecosystem**. Such a farmer might, for instance, opt for natural pest control. An absentee owner often does not have the same interest in **land stewardship**.

Land reform does have negative connotations and is often associated with the state collective farms under communism. Most proponents of land reform, however, do not consider these collective farms good examples, and they argue that successful land reform balances the factors of production so that the full agricultural capabilities of the land can be realized. Reforms should always be designed to increase the efficiency and economic viability of farming.

Land reform is usually more successful if it is enacted with agrarian reforms, which may include the use of agricultural extension agents, agricultural cooperatives, favorable labor legislation, and increased public services for farmers, such as health care and education. Without these measures land reform usually falls short of redistributing wealth and power, or fails to maintain or increase production. *See also* Agricultural pollution; Sustainable agriculture; Sustainable development

[*Linda Rehkopf*]

FURTHER READING

Mengisteab, K. *Ethiopia: Failure of Land Reform and Agricultural Crisis.* Westport, CT: Greenwood Publishing Group, 1990.

Perney, L. "Unquiet on the Brazilian Front." *Audubon* 94 (January-February 1992): 26-9.

Land stewardship

Little has been written explicitly on the subject of land stewardship. Much of the literature that does exist is limited to a biblical or theological treatment of stewardship. However, literature on the related ideas of sustainability and the **land ethic** has expanded dramatically in recent years, and these concepts are at the heart of land stewardship.

Webster's and the *Oxford English Dictionary* both define "steward" as an official in charge of a household, church, estate, or governmental unit, or one who makes social arrangements for various kinds of events; a manager or administrator. Similarly, stewardship is defined as doing the job of a steward or, in ecclesiastical terms, as "the responsible use of resources," meaning especially money, time and talents, "in the service of God."

Intrinsic in those restricted definitions is the idea of responsible caretakers, of persons who take good care of the resources in their charge, including **natural resources**. "Caretaking" universally includes caring for the material resources on which people depend, and by extension, the land or **environment** from which those resources are extracted. Any concept of steward or stewardship must include the notion of ensuring the essentials of life, all of which derive from the land.

While there are few works written specifically on land stewardship, the concept is embedded implicitly and explicitly in the writings of many articulate environmentalists. For example, **Wendell Berry**, a poet and essayist, is one of the foremost contemporary spokespersons for stewardship of the land. In his books, *Farming: A Handbook* (1970), *The Unsettling of America* (1977), *The Gift of Good Land* (1981), and *Home Economics* (1987), Berry shares his wisdom on caring for the land and the necessity of stewardship. He finds a mandate for good stewardship in religious traditions, including Judaism and Christianity: "The divine mandate to use the world justly and charitably, then, defines every person's moral predicament as that of a steward." Berry, however, does not leave stewardship to divine intervention. He describes stewardship as "hopeless and meaningless unless it involves long-term courage, perseverance, devotion, and skill" on the part of individuals, and not just farmers. He suggests that when we lost the skill to use the land properly, we lost stewardship.

However, Berry does not limit his notion of stewardship to a biblical or religious one. He lays down seven rules of land stewardship—rules of "living right." These are:

(1) using the land will lead to ruin of the land unless it "is properly cared for";

(2) if people do not know the land intimately, they cannot care for it properly;

(3) motivation to care for the land cannot be provided by "general principles or by incentives that are merely economic";

(4) motivation to care for the land, to live with it, stems from an interest in that land that "is direct, dependable, and permanent";

(5) motivation to care for the land stems from an expectation that people will spend their entire lives on the land, and even more so if they expect their children and grandchildren to also spend their entire lives on that same land;

(6) the ability to live carefully on the land is limited; owning too much acreage, for example, decreases the quality of attention needed to care for the land;

(7) a nation will destroy its land and therefore itself if it does not foster rural households and communities that maintain people on the land as outlined in the first six rules.

Stewardship implies at the very least, then, an attempt to reconnect to a piece of land. Reconnecting means getting to know that land as intimately as possible. This does not necessarily imply ownership, though enlightened ownership is at the heart of land stewardship. People who own land have some control of it, and effective stewardship requires control, if only in the sense of enough power to prevent abuse. But, ownership obviously does not guarantee stewardship—great and widespread abuses of land are perpetrated by owners. Absentee ownership, for example, often means a lack of connection, a lack of knowledge, and a lack of caring. And public ownership too often means non-ownership, leading to the **"Tragedy of the Commons."** Land ownership patterns are critical to stewardship, but no one type of ownership guarantees good stewardship.

Berry argues that true land stewardship usually begins with one small piece of land, used or controlled or owned by an individual who lives on that land. Stewardship, however, extends beyond any one particular piece of land. It implies knowledge, and caring for, the entire system of which that land is a part, a knowledge of a land's context as well as its content. It also requires understanding the connections between land owners or land users and the larger communities of which they are a part. This means that stewardship depends on interconnected systems of **ecology** and economics, of politics and science, of sociology and planning. The web of life that exists interdependent with a piece of land mandates attention to a complex matrix of connections. Stewardship means keeping the web intact and functional, or at least doing so on enough land over a long-enough period of time to sustain the populations dependent on that land.

Berry and many other critics of contemporary land-use patterns and policies claim that little attention is being paid to maintaining the complex communities on which sustenance, human and otherwise, depends. Until holistic, ecological knowledge becomes more of a basis for economic and political decision-making, they assert, stewardship of the critical land-base will not become the norm. *See also* Environmental ethics; Holistic approach; Land use; Sustainable agriculture; Sustainable biosphere; Sustainable development

[*Gerald L. Young*]

FURTHER READING

Byron, W. J. *Toward Stewardship: An Interim Ethic of Poverty, Power and Pollution.* New York: Paulist Press, 1975.

Jouvenel, B. de. "The Stewardship of the Earth." In *The Fitness of Man's Environment.* New York: Harper & Row, 1968.

Paddock, J., N. Paddock, and C. Bly. *Soil and Survival: Land Stewardship and the Future of American Agriculture.* San Francisco: Sierra Club Books, 1986.

Land Stewardship Project (Marine, Minnesota)

The Land Stewardship Project (LSP) is a nonprofit organization based in Minnesota and committed to promoting an ethic of environmental and agricultural stewardship. The group believes that the natural **environment** is not an exploitable resource but a gift given to each generation for safekeeping. To preserve and pass on this gift to **future generations**, for the LSP, is both a moral and a practical imperative.

Founded in 1982, the LSP is an alliance of farmers and city-dwellers dedicated both to preserving the small family farm and practicing **sustainable agriculture**. Like **Wendell Berry** and **Wes Jackson** (with whom they are affiliated), the LSP is critical of conventional agricultural practices that emphasize plant **monoculture**s, large acreage, intensive tillage, extensive use of **herbicide**s and **pesticide**s, and the economies of scale that these practices make possible. The group believes that agriculture conducted on such an industrial scale is bound to be destructive not only of the natural environment but of family farms and rural communities as well. The LSP accordingly advocates the sort of smaller scale agriculture that, in Berry's words, "depletes neither **soil**, nor people, nor communities."

The LSP sponsors legislative initiatives to save farmland and **wildlife** habitat, to limit **urban sprawl** and

protect family farms, and to promote sustainable agricultural practices. It supports educational and outreach programs to inform farmers, consumers, and citizens about agricultural and environmental issues. The LSP also publishes a quarterly *Land Stewardship Letter* and distributes video tapes about sustainable agriculture and other environmental concerns. Contact: Land Stewardship Project, 14758 Ostlund Trail North, Marine, MN 55047. Internet: http://www.centers.agri.umn.edu:80/misa/lsphp.html. *See also* Agroecology; Environmental ethics; Land Institute; Land stewardship

[*Terence Ball*]

Land trusts

A land trust is a private, legally incorporated, nonprofit organization that works with property owners to protect open land through direct, voluntary land transactions. Land trusts come in many varieties, but their intent is consistent. Land trusts are developed for the purpose of holding land against a development plan until the public interest can be ascertained and served. Some land trusts hold land open until public entities can purchase it. Some land trusts purchase land and manage it for the common good. In some cases land trusts buy development rights to preserve the land area for future generations while leaving the current use in the hands of private interests with written documentation as to how the land can be used. This same technique can be used to adjust land use so that some part of a parcel is preserved while another part of the same parcel can be developed, all based on land sensitivity.

There is a hierarchy of land trusts. Some trusts protect areas as small as neighborhoods, forming to address one land use issue after which they disband. More often, land trusts are local in nature but have a global perspective with regard to their goals for future land protection. The big national trusts are names that we all recognize such as the Conservation Fund, the **Nature Conservancy**, the **American Farmland Trust**, and the Trust for Public Land. The Land Trust Alliance coordinates the activities of many land trusts. Currently, there are over 1,000 local and regional land trusts in the United States. Some of these trusts form as a direct response to citizen concerns about the loss of open space. Most land trusts evolve out of citizen's concerns over the future of their state, town, and neighborhood. Many are preceded by failures on the part of local governments to respond to stewardship mandates by the voters.

Land trusts work because they are built by concerned citizens and funded by private donations with the express purpose of securing the sustainability of an acceptable quality of life. Also, land trusts are effective because they purchase land (or development rights) from local people for local needs. Transactions are often carried out over a kitchen table with neighbors discussing priorities. In some cases the trust's board of directors might be engaged in helping a citizen to draw up a will leaving farmland or potential recreation land to the community. This home rule concept is the backbone of the land trust movement. Additionally, land trusts gain strength from public/private partnerships that emerge as a result of shared objectives with government agencies. If the work of the land trust is successful, part of the outcome is an enhanced ability to cooperate with local government agencies. Agencies learn to trust the land trust staff and begin to rely on the special expertise that grows within a land trust organization. In some cases the land trust gains both opportunities and resources as a result of its partnership with governmental agencies. This public/private partnership benefits citizens as projects come together and land use options are retained for current and future generations.

Flexibility is an important and essential quality of a land trust which enables it to be creative. Land trusts can have revolving accounts, or lines of credit, from banks that allow them to move quickly to acquire land. Compensation to land owners who agree to work with the trust may come in the form of extended land use for the ex-owner, land trades, tax compensation, and other compensation packages. Often some mix of protection and compensation packages will be created that a government agency simply does not have the ability to implement. A land trust's flexibility is its most important attribute. Where a land trust can negotiate land acquisition based on a discussion among the board members, a governmental agency would go through months or even years of red tape before an offer to buy up land for the public domain could be made. This quality of land trusts is one reason why many government agencies have built relationships with land trusts in order to protect land that the agency deems sensitive and important.

There are some limiting factors constraining what land trusts can do. For the more localized trusts, limited volunteer staff and extremely limited budgets cause fund raising to become a time-consuming activity. Staff turnover can be frequent so that a knowledge base is difficult to maintain. In some circumstances influential volunteers can capture a land trust organization and follow their own agenda rather than letting the agenda be set by affected stakeholders.

Training is needed for those committed to working within the legal structure of land trusts. The national Trust for Public Lands has set up training opportunities to better prepare local land trust staff for the complex negotiations that are needed to protect public lands. Staff that work with local citizenry to protect local needs must be aware of the costs and benefits of land preservation mechanisms. Lease purchase agreements, limited partnerships, and fee simple transactions all require knowledge of real estate law. Operating within enterprise zones and working with economic development corporations requires knowledge of state and federal programs that provide money for projects on the urban fringe. In some cases urban renewal work reveals open space within the urban core that can be preserved for community gardens or parks if that land can be secured using HUD funds or other government financing mechanisms. A relatively new source of funding for land acquisition is mitigation funds. These funds are usually generated as a result of settlements with industry or government agencies as compensation for negative land impacts. Distinguishing among financing mechanisms requires specialized knowledge that land trust staff

need to have available within their ranks in order to move quickly to preserve open space and enhance the quality of life for urban dwellers. On the other hand some land trusts in rural areas are interested in conserving farmlands using preserves that allow farmers to continue to farm while protecting the rural character of the countryside. Like their urban counterparts, these farmland preserve programs are complex, and if they are to be effective the trust needs to employ its solid knowledge of economic trends and resources.

The work that land trusts do is varied. In some cases a land trust incorporates as a result of a local threat, such as a pipeline or railway coming through an area. In some cases a trust forms to counter an undesirable land use such as a **landfill** or a low level **radioactive waste** storage facility. In other instances, a land trust comes together to take advantage of a unique opportunity, such as a family wanting to sell some pristine forest close to town or an industry deciding to relocate leaving a lovely waterfront location with promise as a riverfront recreation area. It is rare that a land trust forms without a focused need. However, after the initial project is completed, its success breeds self-confidence in those who worked on the project and new opportunities or challenges may sustain the goals of the fledgling organization.

There are many examples of land trusts and the few highlighted here may help to enhance understanding of the value of land trust activities and to offer guidance to local groups wanting to preserve land. One outstanding example of land trust activity is the Rails to Trails program in Michigan. Under this program, abandoned railroad right of ways are preserved to create **green belts** for recreation use through agreements with the railroad companies. The Trust for Public Lands (TPL) has assisted many local land trusts to implement a wide variety of land acquisition projects. One such complex agreement took place in Tucson, Arizona. In this case, the Tucson city government wanted to acquire seven parcels of land that totaled 40 acres (164 ha). For financial reasons the city was not able to acquire the land. At that point the Trust for Public Land was asked to become a private nonprofit partner and to work with the city to acquire the land. TPL used its creative expertise to help each of the landowners make mutually beneficial arrangements with the city so that a large urban park could become a reality. In some cases the TPL offered a life tenancy to the current owners in exchange for a reduced land price. In another case they offered a five year tenancy and a job as caretaker, in exchange for a reduced purchase price. As the community worked on the future of the park, another land owner who owned a contiguous parcel stepped forward with an offer to sell. Each of these transactions was successful because the land trust was flexible, considerate of the land owners and up front about the goals of their work, and responsive to their public partner, the city government.

Our current land trust effort in the United States has affected the way we protect our sensitive lands, reclaim damaged lands, and respond to local needs. Land trusts conserve land, guide future planning, educate local citizens and government agencies to a new way of doing business, and do it all with a minimum amount of confrontation and legal interaction. These private, non-profit organizations have stepped in and filled a niche in the environmental **conservation** movement started in the 1970s and have gotten results through a system of cooperative and well-informed action.

[*Cynthia Fridgen*]

FURTHER READING

Diamond, H.L., and P.F. Noonan, *Land Use in America: The Report of the Sustainable Use of Land Project.* Lincoln Institute of Land Policy, Washington, D.C.: Island Press, 1996.

Endicott, E., ed. *Land Conservation Through Public/Private Partnerships.* Lincoln Institute of Land Policy, Washington D.C.: Island Press, 1993.

Platt, R.H. *Land Use and Society: Geography, Law, and Public Policy.* Washington D.C.: Island Press, 1996.

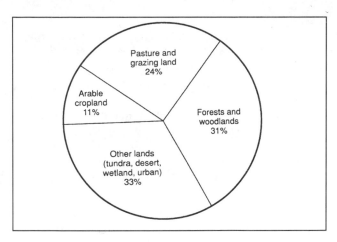

World land use.

Land use

Land is any part of the earth's surface that can be owned as property. Land comprises a particular segment of the earth's crust and can be defined in specific terms. The location of the land is extremely important in determining land use and land value.

Land is limited in supply, and, as our population increases, we have less land to support each person. Land nurtures the plants and animals that provide our food and shelter. It is the **watershed** or **reservoir** for our water supply. Land provides the minerals we use, the space on which we build our homes, and the site of many recreational activities. Land is also the depository for much of the waste created by modern society. The growth of human population only provides a partial explanation for the increased pressure on land resources. Economic development and a rise in the standard of living have brought about more demands for the products of the land. This demand now threatens to erode the land resource.

We are terrestrial in our activities and as our needs have diversified, so has land use. Conflicts among the competing land uses have created the need for land-use planning. Previous generations have used and misused the land as though the supply was inexhaustible. Today, goals and decisions about land use must take into account and link information from the physical and biological sciences with the current social values and political realities.

Land characteristics and ownership provide a basis for the many uses of land. Some land uses are classified as irreversible, for example, when the application of a particular land use changes the original character of the land to such a extent that reversal to its former use is impracticable. Reversible land uses do not change the **soil** cover or landform, and the land manager has many options when overseeing reversible land uses.

A framework for land-use planning requires the recognition that plans, policies, and programs must consider physical and biological, economical, and institutional factors. The physical framework of land focuses on the inanimate resources of soil, rocks and geological features, water, air, sunlight, and **climate**. The biological framework involves living things such as plants and animals. A key feature of the physical and biological framework is the need to maintain healthy ecological relationships. The land can support many human activities, but there are limits. Once the resources are brought to these limits, they can be destroyed and replacing them will be difficult.

The economic framework for land use requires that operators of land be provided sufficient returns to cover the cost of production. Surpluses of returns above costs must be realized by those who make the production decisions and by those who bear the production costs. The economic framework provides the incentive to use the land in a way that is economically feasible. The institutional framework requires that programs and plans be acceptable within the working rules of society. Plans must also have the support of current governments. A basic concept of land use is the *right of land*—who has the right to decide the use of a given tract of land. Legal decisions have provided the framework for land resource protection.

Attitudes play an important role in influencing land use decisions, and changes in attitudes will often bring changes in our institutional framework. Recent trends in land use in the United States show that substantial areas have shifted to urban and transportation uses, state and **national parks**, and **wildlife refuge**s since 1950. The use of land has become one of our most serious environmental concerns. Today's land use decisions will determine the quality of our future lifestyles and environment. The land use planning process is one of the most complex and least understood domestic concerns facing the nation. Additional changes in the institutional framework governing land use are necessary to allow society to protect the most limited resource on the planet—the land we live on. *See also* Economic growth and the environment; Intergenerational justice; Land stewardship; Land-use control; Sustainable development

[*Terence H. Cooper*]

FURTHER READING

Beaty, M. T. *Planning the Uses and Management of Land.* Series in Agronomy, no. 21. Madison, WI: American Standards Association, 1979.

Davis, K. P. *Land Use.* New York: McGraw-Hill, 1976.

Fabos, J. G. *Land-Use Planning: From Global to Local Challenge.* New York: Chapman and Hall, 1985.

McHarg, I. L. *Design With Nature.* Garden City, NY: Doubleday, 1971.

Land-use control

Land-use control is a relatively new concept. For most of human history, it was assumed that people could do whatever they wished with their own property. However, societies have usually recognized that the way an individual uses private property can sometimes have harmful affects on neighbors.

Land-use planning has reached a new level of sophistication in developed countries over the last century. One of the first restrictions on **land use** in the United States, for example, was a 1916 New York City law limiting the size of skyscrapers because of the shadows they might cast on adjacent property. Within a decade, the federal government began to act aggressively on land control measures. It passed the **Mineral Leasing Act** of 1920 in an attempt to control the exploitation of oil, **natural gas**, phosphate and potash. It adopted the Standard State Zoning Act of 1922 and the Standard City Planning Enabling Act of 1928 to promote the concept of zoning at state and local levels. Since the 1920s, every state and most cities have adopted zoning laws modeled on these two federal acts.

Often detailed, exhaustive, and complex zoning regulations now control the way land is used in nearly every governmental unit. They specify, for example, whether land can be used for single-dwelling construction, multiple-dwelling construction, farming, industrial (heavy or light) development, commercial use, **recreation** or some other purpose. Requests to use land for purposes other than that for which it is zoned requires a variance or conditional use permit, a process that is often long, tedious, and confrontational.

Many types of land require special types of zoning. For example, coastal areas are environmentally vulnerable to storms, high tides, **flooding**, and strong winds. The federal government passed laws in 1972 and 1980, the National **Coastal Zone Management Act**s, to help states deal with the special problem of protecting coastal areas. Although initially slow to make use of these laws, states are becoming more aggressive about restricting the kinds of construction permitted along seashore areas.

Areas with special scenic, historic, or recreational value have long been protected in the United States. The nation's first **national park**, **Yellowstone National Park**, was created in 1872. Not until 44 years later, however, was the **National Park Service** created to administer Yellowstone and other parks established since 1872. Today, the National Park Service and other governmental agencies are responsible

for a wide variety of national areas such as forests, wild and scenic rivers, historic monuments, trails, battlefields, memorials, seashores and lakeshores, parkways, recreational areas, and other areas of special value.

Land-use control does not necessarily restrict usage. Individuals and organizations can be encouraged to use land in certain desirable ways. An enterprise zone, for example, is a specifically designated area in which certain types of business activities are encouraged. The tax rate might be reduced for businesses locating in the area or the government might relax certain regulations there.

Successful land-use control can result in new towns or planned communities, designed and built from the ground up to meet certain pre-determined land-use objectives. One of the most famous examples of a planned community is Brasilia, the capital of Brazil. The site for a new capital—an undeveloped region of the country—was selected and a totally new city was built in the 1950s. The federal government moved to the new city in 1960, and it now has a population of more than 1.5 million. *See also* Bureau of Land Management; Riparian rights

[*David E. Newton*]

FURTHER READING

Kupchella, C. E. *Environmental Science: Living within the System of Nature.* 3rd ed. Boston: Allyn and Bacon, 1993.

Moran, J. M., M. D. Morgan, and J. H. Wiersma. *Environmental Science.* Dubuque, IA: W. C. Brown, 1993.

Newton, D. E. *Land Use, A - Z.* Hillside, NJ: Enslow Press, 1991.

Landfill

Surface water, oceans and landfills are traditionally the main repositories for society's solid and **hazardous waste**. Landfills are located in excavated areas such as sand and gravel pits or in valleys that are near waste generators. They have been cited as sources of surface and **groundwater** contamination and are believed to pose a significant health risk to humans, domestic animals and **wildlife**. Despite these adverse effects and the attendant publicity, landfills are likely to remain a major waste disposal option for the immediate future.

Among the reasons that landfills remain a popular alternative are their simplicity and versatility. For example, they are not sensitive to the shape, size or weight of a particular waste material. Since they are constructed of **soil**, they are rarely affected by the chemical composition of a particular waste component or by any collective incompatibility of co-mingled wastes. By comparison, **composting** and **incineration** require uniformity in the form and chemical properties of the waste for efficient operation. Landfills also have been a relatively inexpensive disposal option, but this situation is rapidly changing. Shipping costs, rising land prices, and new landfill construction and maintenance requirements contribute to increasing costs. For example, in Philadelphia the cost to dispose of a ton of **solid waste** went from $20 in 1980 to $100 in 1987.

About 80 percent of the solid waste generated in the United States still is dumped in landfills. In a sanitary landfill, refuse is compacted each day and covered with a layer of dirt. This procedure minimizes odor and litter, and discourages insect and rodent populations that may spread disease. Although this method does help control some of the **pollution** generated by the landfill, the fill dirt also occupies up to 20 percent of the landfill space, reducing its waste-holding capacity. Sanitary landfills traditionally have not been enclosed in a waterproof lining to prevent **leaching** of **chemicals** into groundwater, and many cases of **groundwater pollution** have been traced to landfills.

Historically landfills were placed in a particular location more for convenience of access than for any environmental or geological reason. Now more care is taken in the siting of new landfills. For example, sites located on faulted or highly permeable rock are passed over in favor of sites with a less-permeable foundation. Rivers, lakes, floodplains, and groundwater recharge zones are also avoided. It is believed that the care taken in the initial siting of a landfill will reduce the necessity for future clean-up and site rehabilitation. Due to these and other factors, it is becoming increasingly difficult to find suitable locations for new landfills. Easily accessible open space is becoming scarce and many communities are unwilling to accept the siting of a landfill within their boundaries. Many major cities have already exhausted their landfill capacity and must export their trash, at significant expense, to other communities or even to other states and countries.

Although a number of significant environmental issues are associated with the disposal of solid waste in landfills, the disposal of hazardous waste in landfills raises even greater environmental concerns. A number of urban areas contain hazardous waste landfills. **Love Canal** is, perhaps, the most notorious example of the hazards associated with these landfills. This Niagara Falls, New York neighborhood was built over a dump containing 20,000 metric tons of toxic chemical waste. Increased levels of **cancer**, miscarriages, and **birth defects** among those living in Love Canal led to the eventual evacuation of many residents. The events at Love Canal were also a major impetus behind the passage of the **Comprehensive Environmental Response, Compensation and Liability Act** in 1980, designed to clean up such sites. The U. S. **Environmental Protection Agency** estimates that there may be as many as 2,000 hazardous waste disposal sites in this country that pose a significant threat to human health or the environment.

Love Canal is only one example of the environmental consequences that can result from disposing of hazardous waste in landfills. However, techniques now exist to create secure landfills that are an acceptable disposal option for hazardous waste in many cases. The bottom and sides of a secure landfill contain a cushion of recompacted clay that is flexible and resistant to cracking if the ground shifts. This clay layer is impermeable to groundwater and safely contains the waste. A layer of gravel containing a grid of perforated drain pipes is laid over the clay. These pipes collect any seepage that escapes from the waste stored in the landfill.

A secure landfill.

Over the gravel bed a thick polyethylene liner is positioned. A layer of soil or sand covers and cushions this plastic liner, and the wastes, packed in drums, are placed on top of this layer.

When the secure landfill reaches capacity it is capped by a cover of clay, plastic and soil, much like the bottom layers. Vegetation in planted to stabilized the surface and make the site more attractive. Sump pumps collect any fluids that filter through the landfill either from rain water or from waste leakage. This liquid is purified before it is released. Monitoring wells around the site ensure that the groundwater does not become contaminated. In some areas where the **water table** is particularly high, above-ground storage may be constructed using similar techniques. Although such facilities are more conspicuous, they have the advantage of being easier to monitor for leakage.

Although technical solutions have been found to many of the problems associated with secure landfills, several nontechnical issues remain. One of these issues concerns the transportation of hazardous waste to the site. Some states do not allow hazardous waste to be shipped across their territory because they are worried about the possibility of accidental spills. If hazardous waste disposal is concentrated in only a few sites, then a few major transportation routes will carry large volumes of this material. Citizen opposition to hazardous waste landfills is another issue. Given the past record of corporate and governmental irresponsibility in dealing with hazardous waste, it is not surprising that community residents greet proposals for new landfills with the **NIMBY** (Not In My BackYard) response. However, the waste must go somewhere. These and other issues must be resolved if secure landfills are to be a viable long-term solution to hazardous waste disposal. *See also* Groundwater monitoring; International trade in toxic waste; Storage and transportation of hazardous materials

[*George M. Fell and Christine B. Jeryan*]

FURTHER READING

Bagchi, A. *Design, Construction and Monitoring of Sanitary Landfill.* New York: Wiley, 1990.

"Experimental Landfills Offer Safe Disposal Options." *Journal of Environmental Health* 51 (March-April 1989): 217-18.

Loupe, D. E. "To Rot or Not; Landfill Designers Argue the Benefits of Burying Garbage Wet vs. Dry." *Science News* 138 (6 October 1990): 218-19+.

Neal, H. A. *Solid Waste Management and the Environment: The Mounting Garbage and Trash Crisis.* Englewood Cliffs, NJ: Prentice-Hall, 1987.

Noble, G. *Siting Landfills and Other LULUs.* Lancaster, PA: Technomic Publishing, 1992.

Requirements for Hazardous Waste Landfill Design, Construction and Closure. Cincinnati, OH: U. S. Environmental Protection Agency, 1989.

Wingerter, E. J., et al. "Are Landfills and Incinerators Part of the Answer? Three Viewpoints." *EPA Journal* 15 (March-April 1989): 22-6.

Landscape ecology

Landscape ecology is an interdisciplinary field that emerged from several intellectual traditions in Europe and North America. An identifiable landscape **ecology** started in central Europe in the 1960s and in North America in the late 1970s and early 1980s. It became more visible with the establishment, in 1982, of the International Association of Landscape Ecology, with the publication of a major text in the field, *Landscape Ecology*, by Richard Forman and Michel Godron in 1984, and with the publication of the first issue of the association's journal, *Landscape Ecology* in 1987.

The phrase 'landscape ecology' was first used in 1939 by the German geographer, Carl Troll. He suggested that the "concept of landscape ecology is born from a marriage of two scientific outlooks, the one geographical (landscape), the other biological (ecology)." Troll coined the term landscape ecology to denote "the analysis of a physico-biological complex of interrelations, which govern the different area units of a region." He believed that "landscape ecology...must not be confined to the large scale analysis of natural regions. Ecological factors are also involved in problems of population, society, rural settlement, land use, transport, etc."

Landscape has long been a unit of analysis and a conceptual centerpiece of geography, with scholars such as Carl Sauer and J.B. Jackson adept at "reading the landscape," including both the natural landscape of landforms and vegetation, and the cultural landscape as marked by human actions and as perceived by human minds.

Zev Naveh has been working on his own version of landscape ecology in Israel since the early 1970s. Like Troll, Naveh includes humans in his conception, in fact enlarges landscape ecology to a global human ecosystem science, sort of a "bio-cybernetic systems approach to the landscape and the study of its use by [humans]." He sees landscape ecology first as a holistic approach to biosystems theory, the centerpiece being "recognition of the total human ecosystem as the highest level of integration," and, second, as playing a central role in cultural evolution and as a "basis for interdisciplinary, task-oriented, environmental education."

Landscape architecture is also to some extent landscape ecology, since landscape architects design complete vistas, from their beginnings and at various scales. This concern with designing and creating complete landscapes from bare ground can certainly be considered ecological, as it includes creating or adapting local land forms, planting appropriate vegetation, and designing and building various kinds of 'furniture' and other artifacts on site. The British Landscape Institute and the British Ecological Society held a joint meeting in 1983, recognizing "that the time for ecology to be harnessed for the service of landscape design has arrived." The meeting produced the twenty-fourth symposium of the British Ecological Society titled *Ecology and Design in Landscape.*

Landscape planning can also to some degree be considered landscape ecology, especially in the ecological approach to landscape planning developed by **Ian McHarg** and his students and colleagues, and the LANDEP, or Landscape Ecological Planning, approach designed by Ladislav Miklos and Milan Ruzicka. Both of these ecological planning approaches are complex syntheses of spatial patterns, ecological processes, and human needs and wants.

Building on all of these traditions, yet slowly finding its own identity, landscape ecology is considered by some as a sub-domain of biological ecology and by others as a discipline in its own right. In Europe, landscape ecology continues to be an extension of the geographical tradition which is preoccupied with human-landscape interactions. In North America, landscape ecology has emerged as a branch of biological ecology, more concerned with landscapes as clusters of interrelated natural **ecosystem**s. The European form of landscape ecology is applied to land and resource **conservation**, while in North America it focuses on fundamental questions of spatial pattern and exchange. Both traditions can address major environmental problems, especially the extinction of species and the maintenance of biological diversity.

The term landscape, despite the varied traditions and emerging disciplines described above, remains somewhat indeterminate, depending on the criteria set by individual researchers to establish boundaries. Some consensus exists on its general definition in the new landscape ecology, as described in the composite form attempted here: a terrestrial landscape is miles- or kilometers-wide in area; contains a cluster of interacting ecosystems repeated in somewhat similar form; and is a heterogeneous mosaic of interconnected land forms, vegetation types, and land uses. As Risser and his colleagues emphasize, this interdisciplinary area focuses explicitly on spatial patterns: "Specifically, landscape ecology considers the development and dynamics of spatial hetereogeneity, spatial and temporal interactions and exchanges across heterogeneous landscapes, influences of spatial heterogeneity on biotic and abiotic processes, and management of spatial heterogeneity." Instead of trying to identify homogeneous ecosystems, landscape ecology focuses particularly on the heterogeneous patches and mosaics created by human disruption of natural systems, by the intermixing of cultural and natural landscape patterns. The real rationale for a landscape ecology perhaps should be this acknowledgment of the heterogeneity of contemporary landscape patterns, and the need to deal with the patchwork mosaics and intricate matrices that result from long-term human disturbance, modification, and utilization of natural systems.

Typical questions asked by landscape ecologists include these formulated by Risser and his colleagues: "What formative processes, both historical and present, are responsible for the existing pattern in a landscape?" "How are fluxes of organisms, of material, and of energy related to landscape heterogeneity?" "How does landscape heterogeneity affect the spread of disturbances?" While the first question is similar to ones long asked in geography, the other two are questions traditional to ecology, but distinguished here by the focus on heterogeneity.

Richard Forman, a prominent figure in the evolving field of landscape ecology, thinks the field has matured enough for general principles to have emerged; not ecological laws as such, but principles backed by enough evidence and examples to be true for 95% of landscape analyses. His 12 principles are organized by four categories: landscapes and regions; patches and corridors; mosaics; and applications. The principles outline expected or desirable spatial patterns and relationships, and how those patterns and relationships affect system functions and flows, organismic movements and extinctions, resource protection, and optimal environmental conditions. Forman claims the principles "should be applicable for any environmental or societal land-use objective," and that they are useful in more effectively "growing wood, protecting species, locating houses, protecting **soil**, enhancing game, protecting water resources, providing recreation, locating roads, and creating sustainable environments."

Perhaps Andre Corboz provided the best description when he wrote of "the land as palimpsest:" landscape ecology recognizes that humans have written large on the land, and that behind the current writing visible to the eye, there is earlier writing as well, which also tells us about the patterns we see. Landscape ecology also deals with gaps in the text and tries to write a more complete accounting of the landscapes in which we live and on which we all depend.

[*Gerald L. Young*]

FURTHER READING

Forman, R.T.T. "Some General Principles of Landscape and Regional Ecology," *Landscape Ecology* (June 1995): 133-142.

Forman, R.T.T., and M.G. *Landscape Ecology*. New York: Wiley, 1986.

Golley, F.B. "Introducing Landscape Ecology." *Landscape Ecology* 1, no. 1 (1987): 1-3.

Naveh, Z. "Landscape Ecology as an Emerging Branch of Human Ecosystem Science," *Advances in Ecological Research* 12 (1982): 189-237.

Risser, P.G., J.R. Karr, and R.T.T. Forman. *Landscape Ecology: Directions and Approaches*. Champaign, IL: Illinois Natural History Survey, 1983.

Tjallingii, S.P., and A.A. de Veer, eds. *Perspectives in Landscape Ecology: Contributions to Research, Planning and Management of Our Environment*. Wageningen, The Netherlands: Pudoc, 1982. (Proceedings of the International Congress Organized by the Netherlands Society for Landscape Ecology, Veldhoven, The Netherlands, 6-11 April, 1981).

Troll, C. *Landscape Ecology*. Delft, The Netherlands: The ITC-UNESCO Centre for Integrated Surveys, 1966.

Zonneveld, I.S., and R.T.T. Forman, eds. *Changing Landscapes: An Ecological Perspective*. New York: Springer-Verlag, 1990.

Landslide

A general term for the discrete downslope movement of rock and **soil** masses under gravitational influence along a failure zone. The term "landslide" can refer to the resulting land form, as well as to the process of movement. Many types of landslides occur, and they are classified by several schemes, according to a variety of criteria. Landslides are categorized most commonly on basis of geometric form, but also by size, shape, rate of movement, and water content or fluidity. Translational, or planar, failures, such as debris avalanches and earth flows, slide along a fairly straight failure surface which runs approximately parallel to the ground surface. Rotational failures, such as rotational slumps, slide along a spoon shaped failure surface, leaving a hummocky appearance on the landscape. Rotational slumps commonly transform into earthflows as they continue down slope. Landslides are usually triggered by heavy rain or melting snow, but major earthquakes can also cause landslides.

Latency

Latency refers to the period of time it takes for a disease to manifest itself within the human body. It is the state of seeming inactivity that occurs between the instant of stimulation or initiating event and the beginning of response. The latency period differs dramatically for each stimulation and as a result, each disease has its unique time period before symptoms occur.

When **pathogen**s gain entry into a potential host, the body may fail to maintain adequate immunity and thus permits progressive viral or bacterial multiplication. This time lapse is also known as the incubation period. Each disease has definite, characteristic limits for a given host. During the incubation period, dissemination of the pathogen takes place and leads to the inoculation of a preferred or target organ. Proliferation of the pathogen, either in a target organ or throughout the body, then creates an infectious disease.

Botulism, tetanus, gonorrhea, diphtheria, staphylococcal and streptococcal disease, pneumonia, and tuberculosis are among the diseases that take varied periods of time before the symptoms are evident. In the case of the childhood diseases—measles, mumps, and chicken pox—the incubation period is 14-21 days.

In the case of **cancer**, the latency period for a small group of transformed cells to result in a tumor large enough to be detected is usually 10-20 years. One theory postulates that every cancer begins with a single cell or small group of cells. The cells are transformed and begin to divide. Twenty years of cell division ultimately results in a detectible tumor. It is theorized that very low doses of a **carcinogen** could be sufficient to transform one cell into a cancerous tumor.

In the case of **AIDS**, an eight- to eleven-year latency period passes before the symptoms appear in adults. The length of this latency period depends upon the strength of the person's immune system. If a person suspects he or she has been infected, early blood tests showing HIV antibodies or antigens can indicate the infection within three months of the stimulation. The three-month period before the appearance of HIV antibodies or antigens is called the "window period."

In many cases, doctors may fail to diagnose the disease at first, since AIDS symptoms are so general they may be confused with the symptoms of other, similar diseases. Childhood AIDS symptoms appear more quickly since young children have immune systems that are less fully developed.

[*Liane Clorfene Casten*]

LD₅₀

LD_{50} is the dose of a chemical that is lethal to 50 percent of a test population. It is therefore a measure of a particular median response which, in this case, is death. The term is most frequently used to characterize the response of animals such as rats and mice in acute toxicity tests. The term is generally not used in connection with aquatic or inhalation toxicity tests. It is difficult, if not impossible, to determine the dosage of an animal in such tests; results are most commonly represented in terms of lethal concentrations (LC), which refer to the concentration of the substance in the air or water surrounding an animal.

In LD testing, dosages are generally administered by means of injection, food, water, or forced feeding. Injections are used when an animal is to receive only one or a few dosages. Greater numbers of injections would disturb the animal and perhaps generate some false-positive types of responses. Food or water may serve as a good medium for administering a chemical, but the amount of food or water wasted must be carefully noted. Developing a healthy diet for an animal which is compatible with the chemical to be tested can be as much art as science. The chemical may interact with the foods and become more or less toxic, or it may be objectionable to the animal due to taste or odor. Rats are often used in toxicity tests because they do not have the ability to vomit. The investigator therefore has the option of gavage, a way to force-feed rats with a stomach tube or other device when a chemical smells or tastes bad.

Toxicity and LD_{50} are inversely proportional, which means that high toxicity is indicated by a low LD_{50} and vice versa. LD_{50} is a particular type of effective dose (ED) for 50 percent of a population (ED_{50}). The midpoint (or effect on half of the population) is generally used because some individuals in a population may be highly resistant to a particular toxicant, making the dosage at which all individuals respond a misleading data point. Effects other than death, such as headaches or dizziness, might be examined in some tests, so EDs would be reported instead of LDs. One might also wish to report the response of some other percent of the test population, such as the 20 percent response (LD_{20} or ED_{20}) or 80 percent response (LD_{80} or ED_{80}).

The LD is expressed in terms of the mass of test chemical per unit mass of the test animals. In this way, dose is normalized so that the results of tests can be analyzed consistently and perhaps extrapolated to predict the response of animals that are heavier or lighter. Extrapolation of such data is always questionable, especially when extrapolating from animal response to human response, but the system appears to be serving us well. However, it is important to note that sometimes better dose-response relations and extrapolations can be derived through normalizing dosages based on surface area or the weight of target organs. *See also* Bioassay; Dose response; Ecotoxicology; Hazardous material; Toxic substance

[*Gregory D. Boardman*]

FURTHER READING

Doull, J., C. D. Klaassen, and M. O. Amdur. *Toxicology: The Basic Science of Poisons.* 2nd ed. New York: Macmillan, 1980.

Hodgson, E., R. B. Mailman, and J. E. Chambers. *Dictionary of Toxicology.* New York: Van Nostrand Reinhold, 1988.

Lu, F. C. *Basic Toxicology Fundamentals, Target Organs, and Risk Assessment.* Washington, DC: Hemisphere, 1985.

Rand, G. M., and S. R. Petrocelli. *Fundamentals of Aquatic Toxicology Methods and Applications.* Washington, DC: Hemisphere, 1985.

Leachate

See **Contaminated soils; Landfill**

Leaching

The process by which soluble substances are dissolved out of a material. When rain falls on farmlands, for example, it dissolves weatherable minerals, **pesticide**s, and **fertilizer**s as it soaks into the ground. If enough water is added to the **soil** to fill all the pores, then water carrying these dissolved materials moves to the **groundwater**—the soil becomes leached. In soil chemistry, leaching refers to the process by which nutrients in the upper layers of soil are dissolved out and carried into lower layers, where they can be a valuable **nutrient** for plant roots. Leaching also has a number of environmental applications. For example, toxic chemicals and radioactive materials stored in sealed containers underground may leach out if the containers break open over time. *See also* Landfill; Leaking underground storage tank

Lead

One of the oldest metals known to humans, lead compounds were used by Egyptians to glaze pottery as far back as 7000 B.C. The toxic effects of lead also have been known for many centuries. In fact, the Romans limited the amount of time slaves could work in lead mines because of the element's harmful effects. Some consequences of lead poisoning are anemia, headaches, convulsions, and damage to the kidneys and central nervous system. The widespread use of lead in plumbing, **gasoline**, and lead-acid batteries, for example, has made it a serious **environmental health** problem. Bans on the use of lead in motor fuels and paints attempt to deal with this problem. *See also* Heavy metals and heavy metal poisoning; Lead shot

Lead management

Lead, a naturally occurring bluish-gray metal, is extensively used throughout the world in the manufacture of storage batteries, chemicals including paint and **gasoline**, and various metal products including sheet lead, solder, pipes, and ammunition. Due to its widespread use, large amounts of lead exist in the **environment**, and substantial quantities of lead continue to be deposited into air, land, and water. Lead is a poison that has many adverse effects, and children are especially susceptible. At present, the production, use and disposal of lead are regulated with demonstrably effective results. However, because of its previous widespread use and persistence in the environment, lead exposure is a pervasive problem that affects many populations. Effective management of lead requires an understanding of its effects, blood action levels, sources of exposure, and policy responses, topics reviewed in that order.

Effects of Lead

Lead is a strong toxicant that adversely affects many systems in the body. Severe lead exposures can cause brain and kidney damage to adults and children, coma, convulsions and death. Lower levels, e.g., lead concentrations in blood (PbB) below 50 µg/dL, may impair hemoglobin synthesis, alter the central and peripheral nervous systems, cause hypertension, affect male and female reproductive systems, and damage the developing fetus. These effects depend on the level and duration of exposure and on the distribution and kinetics of lead in the body. Most lead is deposited in bone, and some of this stored lead may be released long after exposure due to a serious illness, pregnancy, or other physiological event. Lead has not been shown to cause **cancer** in humans, however, tumors have developed in rats and mice given large doses of lead and thus several United States agencies consider lead acetate and lead phosphate as human carcinogens.

Children are particularly susceptible to lead poisoning. PbB levels as low as 10 µg/dL are associated with decreased intelligence and slowed neurological development. Low PbB levels also have been associated with deficits in growth, vitamin metabolism, and effects on hearing. The neurological effects of lead on children are profound and are likely persistent. Unfortunately, childhood exposures to chronic but low lead levels may not produce clinical symptoms, and many cases go undiagnosed and untreated. In recent years, the number of children with elevated blood lead levels has declined substantially. For example, the average PbB level has decreased from over 15 µg/dL in the 1970s to about 5 µg/dL in the 1990s. As described later, these decreases can be attributed to the reduction or elimination of lead in gasoline,

food can and plumbing solder, and residential paint. Still, childhood lead poisoning remains the most widespread and preventable childhood health problem associated with environmental exposures, and childhood lead exposure remains a public health concern since blood levels approach or exceed levels believed to cause effects. Though widely perceived as a problem of inner city minority children, lead poisoning affects children from all areas and from all socioeconomic groups.

The definition of a PbB level that defines a level of concern for lead in children continues to be an important issue in the US. The childhood PbB concentration of concern has been steadily lowered by the Centers for Disease Control (CDC) from 40 µg/dL in 1970 to 10 µg/dL in 1991. The **Environmental Protection Agency** lowered the level of concern to 10 µg/dL ("10-15 and possibly lower") in 1986, and the **Agency for Toxic Substance Disease Registry** (ATSDR) also identified 10 µg/dL in its 1988 Report to Congress on childhood lead poisoning.

In the workplace, the medical removal PbB concentration is 50 µg/dL for three consecutive checks and 60 µg/dL for any single check. Blood level monitoring is triggered by an air lead concentration above 30 µg/m^3. A worker is permitted to return to work when his blood lead level falls below 40 µg/dL. In 1991, the **National Institute for Occupational Safety and Health** (NIOSH) set a goal of eliminating occupational exposures that result in workers having PbB levels greater than 25 µg/dL.

Exposure and Sources

Lead is a persistent and ubiquitous pollutant. Since it is an elemental pollutant, it does not dissipate, biodegrade, or decay. Thus, the total amount of lead pollutants resulting from human activity increases over time, no matter how little additional lead is added to the environment. Lead is a multimedia pollutant, i.e., many sources contribute to the overall problem, and exposures from air, water, **soil**, dust and food pathways may be important.

For children, an important source of lead exposure is from swallowing nonfood items, an activity known as pica (an abnormal eating habit e.g., chips of lead-containing paint) most prevalent in 2 and 3 year-olds. Children who put toys or other items in their mouths may also swallow lead if lead-containing dust and dirt are on these items. Touching dust and dirt containing lead is commonplace, but relatively little lead passes through the skin. The most important source of high level lead exposure in the United States is household dust derived from deteriorated lead-based paint. Numerous homes contain lead-based paint and continue to be occupied by families with small children, including 21 million pre-1940 homes and rental units which, over time, are rented to different families. Thus, a single house with deteriorated lead-based paint can be the source of exposure for many children.

In addition to lead-based paint in houses, other important sources of lead exposure include (1) contaminated soil and dust from deteriorated paints originally applied to buildings, bridges and water tanks; (2) drinking water into which lead has leached from lead, bronze or brass pipes, fixtures (including lead-soldered pipe joints) in houses, schools, and public buildings; (3) occupational exposures in smelting and refining industries, steel welding and cutting operations, battery manufacturing plants, gasoline stations, and radiator repair shops; (4) airborne lead from smelters and other point sources of air pollution, including vehicles burning leaded fuels; (5) hazardous waste sites which contaminate soil and water; (6) food cans made with lead-containing solder and pottery made with lead-containing glaze; and (7) food consumption if crops are grown using fertilizers that contain sewage sludge or if much lead-containing dust is deposited onto crops. In the atmosphere, the use of leaded gasoline has been the single largest source of lead (90%) since the 1920s, although the use of leaded fuel has been greatly curtailed and gasoline contributions are now greatly reduced (35%). As discussed below, leaded fuel and many other sources have been greatly reduced in the US, although drinking water and other sources remain important in some areas. A number of other countries, however, continue to use leaded fuel and other lead-containing products.

Government Responses

Many agencies are concerned with lead management. Lead agencies in the United States include the Environmental Protection Agency, the Centers for Disease Control, the **U.S. Department of Health and Human Services**, the Department of Housing and Urban Development, the **Food and Drug Administration**, the Consumer Product Safety Commission, the National Institute for Occupational Safety and Health, and the **Occupational Safety and Health Administration**. These agencies have taken many actions to reduce lead exposures, several of which have been very successful. General types of actions include: (1) restrictions or bans on the use of many products containing lead where risks from these products are high and where substitutes products are available, e.g., interior paints, gasoline fuels, and solder; (2) recycling and safer ultimate disposal strategies for products where risks are lower, or for which technically and economically feasible substitutes are not available, e.g., lead-acid automotive batteries, lead-containing wastes, pigments and used oil; (3) **emission** controls for lead smelters, primary metal industries, and other industrial point sources, including the use of the best practicable control technology (BPCT) for new lead smelting and processing facilities and reasonable available control technologies (RACT) for existing facilities, and; (4) education and abatement programs where exposure is based on past uses of lead.

The current goals of the Environmental Protection Agency (EPA) strategy are to reduce lead exposures to the fullest extent practicable, to significantly reduce the incidence of PbB levels above 10 µg/dL in children, and to reduce lead exposures that are anticipated to pose risks to children, the general public, or the environment. Several specific actions of this and other agencies are discussed below.

The Residential Lead-based Paint Hazard Reduction Act of 1992 (Title X) provides the framework to reduce hazards from lead-based paint exposure, primarily in hous-

ing. It establishes a national infrastructure of trained workers, training programs and proficient laboratories, and a public education program to reduce hazards from lead exposure in paint in the nation's housing stock. Earlier, to help protect small children who might swallow chips of paint, the Consumer Product Safety Commission (CPSC) restricted the amount of lead in most paints to 0.06% by weight. CDC further suggests that inside and outside paint used in buildings where people live be tested for lead. If the level of lead is high, the paint should be removed and replaced with a paint that contains an allowable level of lead. CPSC published a consumer safety alert/brochure on lead paint in the home in 1990, and has evaluated lead test kits for safety, efficacy, and consumer-friendliness. These kits are potential screening devices that may be used by the consumer to detect lead in paint and other materials. Title X also requires EPA to promulgate regulations that ensure personnel engaged in abatement activities are trained, to certify training programs, to establish standards for abatement activities, to promulgate model state programs, to establish a laboratory accreditation program, to establish a information clearinghouse, and to disclose lead hazards at property transfer.

The Department of Housing and Urban Development (HUD) has begun activities that include updating regulations dealing with lead-based paint regulations in HUD programs and federal property; providing support for local screening programs; increasing public education; supporting research to reduce the cost and improve the reliability of testing and abatement; increasing state and local support; and providing more money to support abatement in low and moderate income households. HUD estimated that the total cost of testing and abatement in high-priority hazard homes will be $8 to 10 billion annually over ten years, although costs could be substantially lowered by integrating abatement with other renovation activities.

CPSC, EPA, and states are required by the Lead Contamination Control Act of 1988 to test drinking water in schools for lead and to remove lead if levels are too high. Drinking water coolers must also be lead-free and any that contain lead must be removed. EPA regulations limit lead in drinking water to 0.015 mg/L.

To manage environmental exposures resulting from inhalation, EPA regulations limit lead to 0.1 and 0.05 g/gal (0.38 and 0.19 g/L) in leaded and unleaded gasoline, respectively. Also, the National Ambient Air Quality Standards set a maximum lead concentrations of 1.5 µg/m³ using a 3 month average, although typical levels are far lower, 0.1 or 0.2 µg/m³.

To identify and mitigate sources of lead in the diet, the Food and Drug Administration (FDA) has undertaken efforts that include voluntary discontinuation of lead solder in food cans by the domestic food industry, and elimination of lead in glazing on ceramic ware. Regulatory measures are being introduced for wine, dietary supplements, crystal ware, food additives and bottled water.

For workers in lead-using industries, the Occupational Safety and Health Administration (OSHA) has established environmental and biological standards that include maximum air and blood levels. This monitoring must be conducted by the employer, and elevated PbB levels may require the removal of an individual from the work place (levels discussed previously). The Permissible Exposure Level (PEL) limits air concentrations of lead to 50 μg/m³, and, if 30 μg/m³ is exceeded, employers must implement a program that includes medical surveillance, exposure monitoring, training, regulated areas, respiratory protection, protective work clothing and equipment, housekeeping, hygiene facilities and practices, signs and labels, and record keeping. In the construction industry, the PEL is 200 μg/m³. The National Institute for Occupational Safety and Health (NIOSH) recommends that workers not be exposed to levels of more than 100 μg/m³ for up to 10 hours, and NIOSH has issued a health alert to construction workers regarding possible adverse health effects from long-term and low-level exposure. NIOSH has also published alerts and recommendations for preventing lead poisoning during blasting, sanding, cutting, burning or welding of bridges and other steel structures coated with lead paint.

Finally, lead screening for children has recently increased. The CDC recommends that screening (testing) for lead poisoning be included in health care programs for children under 72 months of age, especially those under 36 months of age. For a community with a significant number of children having PbB levels between 10-14 μg/dL, community-wide lead poisoning prevention activities should be initiated. For individual children with PbB levels between 15-19 μg/dL, nutritional and educational interventions are recommended. PbB levels exceeding 20 μg/dL should trigger investigations of the affected individual's environment and medical evaluations. The highest levels, above 45 μg/dL, require both medical and environmental interventions, including chelation therapy. CDC also conducts studies to determine the impact of interventions on children's blood lead levels.

These regulatory activities have resulted in significant reductions in average levels of lead exposure. Nevertheless, lead management remains an important public health problem.

[*Stuart Batterman*]

Lead shot

The small pellets that are fired by shotguns while hunting waterfowl or upland fowl, or while skeet shooting. Most lead shots miss their target and are dissipated into the environment. Because the shot is within the particle-size range that is favored by medium-sized birds as grit, it is often ingested and retained in the gizzard to aid in the mechanical abrasion of plant seeds, the first step in avian digestion. However, the shot also abrades during this process, releasing toxic **lead** which can poison the bird. It has been estimated that as much as 2-3 percent of the North American waterfowl population, or several million birds, may die from shot-caused lead poisoning each year. This problem will decrease in intensity,

however, because lead shot is now being substantially replaced by steel shot in North America. *See also* Heavy metals and heavy metal poisoning

League of Conservation Voters (Washington, D.C.)

In 1970 Marion Edey, a House committee staffer, founded the League of Conservation Voters (LCV) as the nonpartisan political action arm of the United States' environmental movement. LCV works to establish a pro-environment—or "green"—majority in Congress and to elect environmentally conscious candidates throughout the country. Through campaign donations, volunteers, and endorsements, pro-environment advertisements, and annual publications such as the *National Environmental Scorecard*, the League raises voter awareness of the environmental positions of candidates and elected officials.

Technically it has no formal membership, but the League's supporters—who make donations and purchase its publications—number 100,000. The board of directors is comprised of 24 important environmentalists associated with such organizations as the **Sierra Club**, the **Environmental Defense Fund**, and **Friends of the Earth**. Because these organizations would endanger their charitable tax status if they participated directly in the electoral process, environmentalists developed the League. Since 1970 LCV has influenced many elections.

From its first effort in 1970—wherein LCV successfully prevented Rep. Wayne Aspinall of Colorado from obtaining a democratic nomination—the League has grown to be a significant force in American politics. In the 1989-90 elections LCV supported 120 pro-environment candidates and spent approximately $250,000 on their campaigns. In 1990 the League developed new endorsement tactics. First it invented the term "greenscam" to identify candidates who only appear green. Next LCV produced two generic television advertisements for candidates. One advertisement, entitled "Greenscam," attacked the aforementioned candidates; the other, entitled "Decisions," was an award-winning, positive advertisement in support of pro-environment candidates. By the 1992 campaign the League had attained an unprecedented degree of influence in the electoral process. That year LCV raised and donated $600,000 and supported 169 candidates in a variety of ways.

In endorsing a candidate the League no longer simply contributes money to a campaign. It provides "in-kind" assistance—for example, it places a trained field organizer on a staff, creates radio and television advertisements, or develops grassroots outreach programs and campaign literature. In addition to supporting specific candidates, LCV holds all elected officials accountable for their track records on environmental issues. The League's annual publication *National Environmental Scorecard* lists the voting records of House and Senate members on environmental legislation. Likewise, the

Presidential Scorecard identifies the positions that presidential candidates have taken. Through these publications and direct endorsement strategies, the League continues to apply pressure in the political process and elicit support for the **environment**. Contact: League of Conservation Voters, 1707 L Street, NW, Suite 550, Washington, DC 20036. Internet: http://www.lcv.org/. *See also* Green politics; Greens

[*Andrea Gacki*]

Leakey, Louis (1903-1972)

African-born English paleontologist and anthropologist

A pioneer in the field of paleoanthropology--the study of early humans and prehumans through both their fossilized remains and the cultural artifacts (mostly stone tools) they left behind—Louis Leakey helped change the prevailing view of humankind's origins. Along with other paleoanthropologists, he sought clues to, among other mysteries, how and when modern humans and apes split off from a common ancestor, and the identification of the point at which a creature appeared on the earth who can accurately be given the designation "human."

Louis Seymour Bazett Leakey was born on August 7, 1903, in Kabete, Kenya. His parents, Mary Bazett (d. 1948) and Harry Leakey (1868-1940) were Church of England missionaries at the Church Missionary Society, Kabete, Kenya. Louis spent his childhood in the mission, where he learned the Kikuyu language and customs (he later compiled a Kikuyu grammar book). As a child, while pursuing his interest in ornithology—the study of birds—he often found stone tools washed out of the soil by the heavy rains, which Leakey believed were of prehistoric origin. Stone tools were primary evidence of the presence of humans at a particular site, as toolmaking was believed at the time to be practiced only by humans and was, along with an erect posture, one of the chief characteristics used to differentiate humans from nonhumans. Scientists at the time, however, did not consider East Africa a likely site for finding evidence of early humans; the discovery of *Pithecanthropus* in Java in 1894 (the so-called Java Man, now considered to be an example of *Homo erectus*) had led scientists to assume that Asia was the continent from which human forms had spread.

Shortly after the end of World War I, Leakey was sent to a public school in Weymouth, England, and later attended St. John's College, Cambridge. Suffering from severe headaches resulting from a sports injury, he took a year off from his studies and joined a fossil-hunting expedition to Tanganyika (now Tanzania). This experience, combined with his studies in anthropology at Cambridge (culminating in a degree in 1926), led Leakey to devote his time to the search for the origins of humanity, which he believed would be found in Africa. Anatomist and anthropologist Raymond A. Dart's discovery of early human remains in South Africa was the first concrete evidence that this view was correct. Leakey's next expedition was to northwest Kenya, near Lakes Nakuru and Naivasha, where he uncovered materials from the Late Stone Age; at Kariandusi he discovered a 200,000-year-old hand ax.

In 1928 Leakey married Henrietta Wilfrida Avern, with whom he had two children: Priscilla, born in 1930, and Colin, born in 1933; the couple was divorced in the mid-1930s. In 1931 Leakey made his first trip to Olduvai Gorge—a 350-mi (564-km) ravine in Tanzania—the site that was to be his richest source of human remains. He had been discouraged from excavating at Olduvai by Hans Reck, a German paleontologist who had fruitlessly sought evidence of prehistoric humans there. Leakey's first discoveries at that site consisted of both animal fossils, important in the attempts to date the particular stratum (or layer of earth) in which they were found, and, significantly, flint tools. These tools, dated to approximately one million years ago, were conclusive evidence of the presence of hominids—a family of erect primate mammals that use only two feet for locomotion—in Africa at that early date; it was not until 1959, however, that the first fossilized hominid remains were found there.

In 1932, near Lake Victoria, Leakey found remains of *Homo sapiens* (modern man), the so-called Kanjera skulls (dated to 100,000 years ago) and Kanam jaw (dated to 500,000 years ago); Leakey's claims for the antiquity of this jaw made it a controversial find among other paleontologists, and Leakey hoped he would find other, independent, evidence for the existence of *Homo sapiens* from an even earlier period—the Lower Pleistocene.

In the mid-1930s, a short time after his divorce from Wilfrida, Leakey married his second wife, Mary Douglas Nicol; she was to make some of the most significant discoveries of Leakey's team's research. The couple eventually had three children: Philip, Jonathan, and **Richard E. Leakey**. During the 1930s, Leakey also became interested in the study of the Paleolithic period in Britain, both regarding human remains and geology, and he and **Mary Leakey** carried out excavations at Clacton in southeast England.

Until the end of the 1930s, Leakey concentrated on the discovery of stone tools as evidence of human habitation; after this period he devoted more time to the unearthing of human and prehuman fossils. His expeditions to Rusinga Island, at the mouth of the Kavirondo Gulf in Kenya, during the 1930s and early 1940s produced a large number of finds, especially of remains of Miocene apes. One of these apes, which Leakey named *Proconsul africanus,* had a jaw lacking in the so-called simian shelf that normally characterized the jaws of apes; this was evidence that *Proconsul* represented a stage in the progression from ancient apes to humans. In 1948 Mary Leakey found a nearly complete *Proconsul* skull, the first fossil ape skull ever unearthed; this was followed by the unearthing of several more *Proconsul* remains.

Louis Leakey began his first regular excavations at Olduvai Gorge in 1952; however, the Mau Mau (an anti-white secret society) uprising in Kenya in the early 1950s disrupted his paleontological work and induced him to write *Mau Mau and the Kikuyu*, in an effort to explain the rebellion from the perspective of a European with an insider's knowledge of the Kikuyu. A second work, *Defeating Mau Mau*, followed in 1954.

During the late 1950s, the Leakeys continued their work at Olduvai. In 1959, while Louis was recuperating from an illness, Mary Leakey found substantial fragments of a hominid skull that resembled the robust australopithecines—African hominids possessing small brains and near-human dentition—found in South Africa earlier in the century. Louis Leakey, who quickly reported the find to the journal *Nature*, suggested that this represented a new genus, which he named *Zinjanthropus boisei*, the genus name meaning "East African man," and the species name commemorating Charles Boise, one of Leakey's benefactors. This species, now called *Australopithecus boisei*, was later believed by Leakey to have been an evolutionary dead end, existing contemporaneously with *Homo* rather than representing an earlier developmental stage.

In 1961, at Fort Ternan, Leakey's team located fragments of a jaw that Leakey believed were from a hitherto unknown genus and species of ape, one he designated as *Kenyapithecus wickeri*, and which he believed was a link between ancient apes and humans, dating from fourteen million years ago; it therefore represented the earliest hominid. In 1967, however, an older skull, one that had been found two decades earlier on Rusinga Island and which Leakey had originally given the name *Ramapithecus africanus*, was found to have hominid-like lower dentition; he renamed it *Kenyapithecus africanus*, and Leakey believed it was an even earlier hominid than *Kenyapithecus wickeri*. Leakey's theories about the place of these Lower Miocene fossil apes in human evolution have been among his most widely disputed.

During the early 1960s, a member of Leakey's team found fragments of the hand, foot, and leg bones of two individuals, in a site near where *Zinjanthropus* had been found, but in a slightly lower and, apparently, slightly older layer. These bones appeared to be of a creature more like modern humans than *Zinjanthropus*, possibly a species of *Homo* that lived at approximately the same time, with a larger brain and the ability to walk fully upright. As a result of the newly developed potassium-argon dating method, it was discovered that the bed from which these bones had come was 1.75 million years old. The bones were, apparently, the evidence for which Leakey had been searching for years: skeletal remains of *Homo* from the Lower Pleistocene. Leakey designated the creature whose remains these were as *Homo habilis* ("man with ability"), a creature who walked upright and had dentition resembling that of modern humans, hands capable of toolmaking, and a large cranial capacity. Leakey saw this hominid as a direct ancestor of *Homo erectus* and modern humans. Not unexpectedly, Leakey was attacked by other scholars, as this identification of the fragments moved the origins of the genus *Homo* back substantially further in time. Some scholars felt that the new remains were those of australopithecines, if relatively advanced ones, rather than very early examples of *Homo*.

Health problems during the 1960s curtailed Leakey's field work; it was at this time that his Centre for Prehistory and Paleontology in Nairobi became the springboard for the careers of such paleontologists as **Jane Goodall** and **Dian Fossey** in the study of nonhuman primates. A request came

in 1964 from the Israeli government for assistance with the technical as well as the fundraising aspects involved in the excavation of an early Pleistocene site at Ubeidiya. This produced evidence of human habitation dating back 700,000 years, the earliest such find outside Africa.

During the 1960s, others, including Mary Leakey and the Leakeys' son Richard, made significant finds in East Africa; Leakey turned his attention to the investigation of a problem that had intrigued him since his college days: the determination of when humans had reached the North American continent. Concentrating his investigation in the Calico Hills in the Mojave Desert, California, he sought evidence in the form of stone tools of the presence of early humans, as he had done in East Africa. The discovery of some pieces of chalcedony (translucent quartz) that resembled manufactured tools in sediment dated from 50,000 to 100,000 years old stirred an immediate controversy; at that time, scientists believed that humans had settled in North America approximately 20,000 years ago. Many archaeologists, including Mary Leakey, criticized Leakey's California methodology—and his interpretations of the finds—as scientifically unsound, but Leakey, still charismatic and persuasive, was successful in obtaining funding from the National Geographic Society and, later, several other sources. Human remains were not found in conjunction with the supposed stone tools, and many scientists have not accepted these "artifacts" as anything other than rocks.

Shortly before Louis Leakey's death, Richard Leakey showed his father a skull he had recently found near Lake Rudolf (now Lake Turkana) in Kenya. This skull, removed from a deposit dated to 2.9 million years ago, had a cranial capacity of approximately 800 cubic centimeters, putting it within the range of *Homo* and apparently vindicating Leakey's long-held belief in the extreme antiquity of that genus; it also appeared to substantiate Leakey's interpretation of the Kanam jaw. Leakey died of a heart attack in early October, 1972, in London.

Some scientists have questioned Leakey's interpretations of his discoveries. Other scholars have pointed out that two of the most important finds associated with him were actually made by Mary Leakey, but became widely known when they were interpreted and publicized by him; Leakey had even encouraged criticism through his tendency to publicize his somewhat sensationalistic theories before they had been sufficiently tested. Critics have cited both his tendency toward hyperbole and his penchant for claiming that his finds were the "oldest," the "first," the "most significant"; in a 1965 *National Geographic* article, for example, Melvin M. Payne pointed out that Leakey, at a Washington, D.C., press conference, claimed that his discovery of *Homo habilis* had made all previous scholarship on early humans obsolete. Leakey has also been criticized for his eagerness to create new genera and species for new finds, rather than trying to fit them into existing categories. Leakey, however, recognized the value of publicity for the fundraising efforts necessary for his expeditions. He was known as an ambitious man, with a penchant for stubbornly adhering to his interpretations, and he used the force of his personality to communicate his various finds and the subsequent theories he devised to scholars and the general public.

Leakey's response to criticism was that scientists have trouble divesting themselves of their own theories in the light of new evidence. "Theories on prehistory and early man constantly change as new evidence comes to light," Leakey remarked, as quoted by Payne in *National Geographic*. "A single find such as *Homo habilis* can upset long-held—and reluctantly discarded—concepts. A paucity of human fossil material and the necessity for filling in blank spaces extending through hundreds of thousands of years all contribute to a divergence of interpretations. But this is all we have to work with; we must make the best of it within the limited range of our present knowledge and experience." Much of the controversy derives from the lack of consensus among scientists about what defines "human"; to what extent are toolmaking, dentition, cranial capacity, and an upright posture defining characteristics, as Leakey asserted?

Louis Leakey's significance revolves around the ways in which he changed views of early human development. He pushed back the date when the first humans appeared to a time earlier than had been believed on the basis of previous research. He showed that human evolution began in Africa rather than Asia, as had been maintained. In addition, he created research facilities in Africa and stimulated explorations in related fields, such as primatology (the study of primates). His work is notable as well for the sheer number of finds—not only of the remains of apes and humans, but also of the plant and animal species that comprised the ecosystems in which they lived. These finds of Leakey and his team filled numerous gaps in scientific knowledge of the evolution of human forms. They provided clues to the links between prehuman, apelike primates, and early humans, and demonstrated that human evolution may have followed more than one parallel path, one of which led to modern humans, rather than a single line, as earlier scientists had maintained.

[*Michael Sims*]

FURTHER READING

Cole, S. *Leakey's Luck: The Life of Louis Seymour Bazett Leakey, 1903-1972*. Harcourt, 1975.

Isaac, G., and E.R. McCown, eds., *Human Origins: Louis Leakey and the East African Evidence*. Benjamin-Cummings, 1976.

Johanson, D.C., and M.A. Edey. *Lucy: The Beginnings of Humankind*. Simon & Schuster, 1981.

Leakey, M. *Disclosing the Past*. Doubleday, 1984.

Leakey, R. *One Life: An Autobiography*. Salem House, 1984.

Malatesta, A., and R. Friedland, *The White Kikuyu: Louis S. B. Leakey*. McGraw-Hill, 1978.

Leakey, Mary (1913-)

English paleontologist and anthropologist

For many years Mary Leakey lived in the shadow of her husband, **Louis Leakey**, whose reputation, coupled with the prejudices of the time, led him to be credited with some of

Mary Leakey

his wife's discoveries in the field of early human archaeology. Yet she has established a substantial reputation in her own right and has come to be recognized as one of the most important paleoanthropologists of the twentieth century. It was Mary Leakey who was responsible for some of the most important discoveries made by Louis Leakey's team. Although her close association with Louis Leakey's work on Paleolithic sites at Olduvai Gorge—a 350-mile (564-km) ravine in Tanzania—has led to her being considered a specialist in that particular area and period, she has in fact worked on excavations dating from as early as the Miocene Age (an era dating to approximately 18 million years ago) to those as recent as the Iron Age of a few thousand years ago.

Mary Leakey was born Mary Douglas Nicol on February 6, 1913, in London. Her mother was Cecilia Frere, the great-granddaughter of John Frere, who had discovered prehistoric stone tools at Hoxne, Suffolk, England, in 1797. Her father was Erskine Nicol, a painter who himself was the son of an artist, and who had a deep interest in Egyptian archaeology. When Mary was a child, her family made frequent trips to southwestern France, where her father took her to see the Upper Paleolithic cave paintings. She and her father became friends with Elie Peyrony, the curator of the local museum, and there she was exposed to the vast collection of flint tools dating from that period of human prehistory. She was also allowed to accompany Peyrony on his excavations, though the archaeological work was not conducted in what would now be considered a scientific way—artifacts were removed from the site without careful study of the place in the earth where each had been found, obscuring valuable data that could be used in dating the artifact and analyzing its context. On a later trip, in 1925, she was taken to Paleolithic caves by the Abbe Lemozi of France, parish priest of Cabrerets, who had written papers on cave art. After her father's death in 1926, Mary Nicol was taken to Stonehenge and Avebury in England, where she began to learn about the archaeological activity in that country and, after meeting the archaeologist Dorothy Liddell, to realize the possibility of archaeology as a career for a woman.

By 1930 Mary Nicol had undertaken coursework in geology and archaeology at the University of London and had participated in a few excavations in order to obtain field experience. One of her lecturers, R.E.M. Wheeler, offered her the opportunity to join his party excavating St. Albans, England, the ancient Roman site of Verulamium; although she only remained at that site for a few days, finding the work there poorly organized, she began her career in earnest shortly thereafter, excavating Neolithic (early Stone Age) sites in Henbury, Devon, where she worked between 1930 and 1934. Her main area of expertise was stone tools, and she was exceptionally skilled at making drawings of them. During the 1930s Mary met Louis Leakey, who was to become her husband. Leakey was by this time well known because of his finds of early human remains in East Africa; it was at Mary and Louis's first meeting that he asked her to help him with the illustrations for his 1934 book, *Adam's Ancestors: An Up-to-Date Outline of What Is Known about the Origin of Man.*

In 1934 Mary Nicol and Louis Leakey worked at an excavation in Clacton, England, where the skull of a hominid— a family of erect primate mammals that use only two feet for locomotion—had recently been found and where Louis was investigating Paleolithic geology as well as fauna and human remains. The excavation led to Mary Leakey's first publication, a 1937 report in the *Proceedings of the Prehistoric Society.*

By this time, Louis Leakey had decided that Mary should join him on his next expedition to Olduvai Gorge in Tanganyika (now Tanzania), which he believed to be the most promising site for discovering early Paleolithic human remains. On the journey to Olduvai, Mary stopped briefly in South Africa, where she spent a few weeks with an archaeological team and learned more about the scientific approach to excavation, studying each find *in situ*—paying close attention to the details of the geological and faunal material surrounding each artifact. This knowledge was to assist her in her later work at Olduvai and elsewhere.

At Olduvai, among her earliest discoveries were fragments of a human skull; these were some of the first such remains found at the site, and it would be twenty years before any others would be found there. Mary Nicol and Louis Leakey returned to England. Leakey's divorce from his first wife was made final in the mid-1930s, and he and Mary Nicol were then married; the couple returned to Kenya in January of 1937. Over the next few years, the Leakeys excavated Neolithic and Iron Age sites at Hyrax Hill, Njoro River Cave, and the Naivasha Railway Rock Shelter, which yielded a large number of human remains and artifacts.

During World War II, the Leakeys began to excavate at Olorgasailie, southwest of Nairobi, but because of the complicated geology of that site, the dating of material found there was difficult. It did prove to be a rich source of material, however; in 1942 Mary Leakey uncovered hundreds, possibly thousands, of hand axes there. Her first major discovery in the field of prehuman fossils was that of most of the skull of a *Proconsul africanus* on Rusinga Island, in Lake Victoria, Kenya, in 1948. *Proconsul* was believed by some paleontologists to be a common ancestor of apes and humans, an animal whose descendants developed into two branches on the evolutionary tree: the *Pongidae* (great apes) and the *Hominidae* (who eventually evolved into true humans). *Proconsul* lived during the Miocene Age, approximately 18 million years ago. This was the first time a fossil ape skull had ever been found—only a small number have been found since—and the Leakeys hoped that this would be the ancestral hominid that paleontologists had sought for decades. The absence of a "simian shelf," a reinforcement of the jaw found in modern apes, is one of the features of *Proconsul* that led the Leakeys to infer that this was a direct ancestor of modern humans. *Proconsul* is now generally believed to be a species of *Dryopithecus*, closer to apes than to humans.

Many of the finds at Olduvai were primitive stone hand axes, evidence of human habitation; it was not known, however, who had made them. Mary's concentration had been on the discovery of such tools, while Louis's goal had been to learn who had made them, in the hope that the date for the appearance of toolmaking hominids could be moved back to an earlier point. In 1959 Mary unearthed part of the jaw of an early hominid she designated *Zinjanthropus* (meaning "East African Man") and whom she referred to as "Dear Boy"; the early hominid is now considered to be a species of *Australopithecus*— apparently related to the two kinds of australopithecine found in South Africa, *Australopithecus africanus* and *Australopithecus robustus*— and given the species designation *boisei* in honor of Louis Leakey's sponsor Charles Boise. By means of potassium-argon dating, recently developed, it was determined that the fragment was 1.75 million years old, and this realization pushed back the date for the appearance of hominids in Africa. Despite the importance of this find, however, Louis Leakey was slightly disappointed, as he had hoped that the excavations would unearth not another australopithecine, but an example of *Homo* living at that early date. He was seeking evidence for his theory that more than one hominid form lived at Olduvai at the same time; these forms were the australopithecines, who eventually died out, and some early form of *Homo*, which survived— owing to toolmaking ability and larger cranial capacity—to evolve into *Homo erectus* and, eventually, the modern human. Leakey hoped that Mary Leakey's find would prove that *Homo* existed at that early level of Olduvai. The discovery he awaited did not come until the early 1960s, with the identification of a skull found by their son Jonathan Leakey that Louis designated as *Homo habilis* ("man with ability"). He believed this to be the true early human responsible for making the tools found at the site.

In her autobiography, *Disclosing the Past*, released in 1984, Mary Leakey reveals that her professional and personal relationship with Louis Leakey had begun to deteriorate by

1968. As she increasingly began to lead the Olduvai research on her own, and as she developed a reputation in her own right through her numerous publications of research results, she believes that her husband began to feel threatened. Louis Leakey had been spending a vast amount of his time in fundraising and administrative matters, while Mary was able to concentrate on field work. As Louis began to seek recognition in new areas, most notably in excavations seeking evidence of early humans in California, Mary stepped up her work at Olduvai, and the breach between them widened. She became critical of his interpretations of his California finds, viewing them as evidence of a decline in his scientific rigor. During these years at Olduvai, Mary made numerous new discoveries, including the first *Homo erectus* pelvis to be found. Mary Leakey continued her work after Louis Leakey's death in 1972. From 1975 she concentrated on Laetoli, Tanzania, which was a site earlier than the oldest beds at Olduvai. She knew that the lava above the Laetoli beds was dated to 2.4 million years ago, and the beds themselves were therefore even older; in contrast, the oldest beds at Olduvai were two million years old. Potassium-argon dating has since shown the upper beds at Laetoli to be approximately 3.5 million years old. In 1978 members of her team found two trails of hominid footprints in volcanic ash dated to approximately 3.5 million years ago; the form of the footprints gave evidence that these hominids walked upright, thus moving the date for the development of an upright posture back significantly earlier than previously believed. Mary Leakey considers these footprints to be among the most significant finds with which she has been associated.

In the late 1960s Mary Leakey received an honorary doctorate from the University of the Witwatersrand in South Africa, an honor she accepted only after university officials had spoken out against apartheid. Among her other honorary degrees are a D.S.Sc. from Yale University and a D.Sc. from the University of Chicago. She received an honorary D.Litt. from Oxford University in 1981. She has also received the Gold Medal of the Society of Women Geographers.

Louis Leakey was sometimes faulted for being too quick to interpret the finds of his team and for his propensity for developing sensationalistic, publicity-attracting theories. In recent years Mary Leakey has been critical of the conclusions reached by her husband—as well as by some others—but she has not added her own interpretations to the mix. Instead, she has always been more concerned with the act of discovery itself; she has written that it is more important for her to continue the task of uncovering early human remains to provide the pieces of the puzzle than it is to speculate and develop her own interpretations. Her legacy lies in the vast amount of material she and her team have unearthed; she leaves it to future scholars to deduce its meaning.

[*Michael Sims*]

FURTHER READING

Cole, S. *Leakey's Luck: The Life of Louis Seymour Bazett Leakey, 1903-1972.* Harcourt, 1975.

Isaac, G., and E.R. McCown, eds. *Human Origins: Louis Leakey and the East African Evidence.* Benjamin-Cummings, 1976.

Johanson, D.C., and M.A. Edey, *Lucy: The Beginnings of Humankind.* Simon & Schuster, 1981.

Leakey, L. *By the Evidence: Memoirs, 1932-1951.* Harcourt, 1974.

Leakey, R. *One Life: An Autobiography.* Salem House, 1984.

Malatesta, A., and R. Friedland, *The White Kikuyu: Louis S. B. Leakey.* McGraw-Hill, 1978.

Moore, R.E., *Man, Time, and Fossils: The Story of Evolution.* Knopf, 1961.

Reader, J. *Missing Links.* Little, Brown, 1981.

Leakey, Richard E. (1944-)

African-born English paleontologist and anthropologist

The son of paleoanthropologists **Mary Leakey** and **Louis Leakey**, Richard Erskine Frere Leakey was born on December 19, 1944, in Nairobi, Kenya. Continuing the work of his parents, Leakey has pushed the date for the appearance of the first true humans back even further than they had, to nearly three million years ago. This represents nearly a doubling of the previous estimates. Leakey also has found more evidence to support his father's still controversial theory that there were at least two parallel branches of human evolution, of which only one was successful. The abundance of human fossils uncovered by Richard Leakey's team has provided an enormous number of clues as to how the various fossil remains fit into the puzzle of human evolution. The team's finds have also helped to answer, if only speculatively, some basic questions: When did modern human's ancestors split off from the ancient apes? On what continent did this take place? At what point did they develop the characteristics now considered as defining human attributes? What is the relationship among and the chronology of the various genera and species of the fossil remains that have been found?

While accompanying his parents on an excavation at Kanjera near Lake Victoria at the age of six, Richard Leakey made his first discovery of fossilized animal remains, part of an extinct variety of giant pig. Richard Leakey, however, was determined not to "ride upon his parents' shoulders," as Mary Leakey wrote in her autobiography, *Disclosing the Past*. Several years later, as a young teenager in the early 1960s, Richard demonstrated a talent for trapping wildlife, which prompted him to drop out of high school to lead photographic safaris in Kenya. His paleontological career began in 1963, when he led a team of paleontologists to a fossil-bearing area near Lake Natron in Tanganyika (now Tanzania), a site that was later dated to approximately 1.4 million years ago. A member of the team discovered the jaw of an early hominid—a member of the family of erect primate mammals that use only two feet for locomotion—called an *Australopithecus boisei* (then named *Zinjanthropus*).) This was the first discovery of a complete *Australopithecus* lower jaw and the only *Australopithecus* skull fragment found since Mary Leakey's landmark discovery in 1959. Jaws provide essential clues about the nature of a hominid, both in terms of its structural similarity to other species and, if teeth are present, its diet. Richard Leakey spent the next few years occupied with more

Richard Leakey.

excavations, the most important result of which was the discovery of a nearly complete fossil elephant.

In 1964 Richard married Margaret Cropper, who had been a member of his father's team at Olduvai the year before. It was at this time that he became associated with his father's Centre for Prehistory and Paleontology in Nairobi. In 1968, at the age of twenty-three, he became administrative director of the National Museum of Kenya.

While his parents had mined with great success the fossil-rich Olduvai Gorge, Richard Leakey concentrated his efforts in northern Kenya and southern Ethiopia. In 1967 he served as the leader of an expedition to the Omo Delta area of southern Ethiopia, a trip financed by the National Geographic Society. In a site dated to approximately 150,000 years ago, members of his team located portions of two fossilized human skulls believed to be from examples of *Homo sapiens*, or modern humans. While the prevailing view at the time was that *Homo sapiens* emerged around 60,000 years ago, these skulls were dated at 130,000 years old.

While on an airplane trip, Richard Leakey flew over the eastern portion of Lake Rudolf (now Lake Turkana) on the Ethiopia-Kenya border, and he noticed from the air what appeared to be ancient lake sediments, a kind of terrain that he felt looked promising as an excavation site. He used his next National Geographic Society grant to explore this area. The region was Koobi Fora, a site that was to become Richard Leakey's most important area for excavation. At Koobi Fora his team uncovered more than four hundred hominid fossils and an abundance of stone tools, such tools being a primary indication of the presence of early humans. Subsequent excavations near the Omo River in Kenya, from 1968, unearthed more examples of early humans, the first

found being another *Australopithecus* lower jaw fragment. At the area of Koobi Fora known as the KBS tuff (tuff being volcanic ash; KBS standing for the Kay Behrensmeyer Site, after a member of the team) stone tools were found. Preliminary dating of the site placed the area at 2.6 million years ago; subsequent tests over the following few years determined the now generally accepted age of 1.89 million years.

In July of 1969, Richard Leakey came across a virtually complete *Australopithecus boisei* skull—lacking only the teeth and lower jaw—lying in a river bed. A few days later a member of the team located another hominid skull nearby, comprising the back and base of the cranium. The following year brought the discovery of many more fossil hominid remains, at the rate of nearly two per week. Among the most important finds was the first hominid femur to be found in Kenya, which was soon followed by several more. It was at about this time that Leakey obtained a divorce from his first wife, and in October of 1970, he married Meave Gillian Epps, who had been on the 1969 expedition.

In 1972, Richard Leakey's team uncovered a skull that appeared to be similar to the one identified by his father and called *Homo habilis* ("man with ability"). This was the early human that Louis Leakey maintained had achieved the toolmaking skills that precipitated the development of a larger brain capacity and led to the development of the modern human—*Homo sapiens*. This skull was more complete and apparently somewhat older than the one Louis Leakey had found and was thus the earliest example of the species *Homo* yet discovered. They labeled the new skull, which was found below the KBS tuff, "Skull 1470," and this proved to among Richard Leakey's most significant discoveries. The fragments consisted of small pieces of all sides of the cranium, and, unusually, the facial bones, enough to permit a reasonably complete reconstruction. Larger than the skulls found in 1969 and 1970, this example had approximately twice the cranial capacity of *Australopithecus* and more than half that of a modern human—nearly 800 cubic centimeters. At the time, Leakey believed the fragments to be 2.9 million years old (although a more recent dating of the site would place them at less than 2 million years old). Basing his theory in part on these data, Leakey developed the view that these early hominids may have lived as early as 2.5 or even 3.5 million years ago and gave evidence to the theory that *Homo habilis* was not a descendant of the australopithecines, but a contemporary.

By the late 1960s, relations between Richard Leakey and his father had become strained, partly because of real or imagined competition within the administrative structure of the Centre for Prehistory, and partly because of some divergences in methodology and interpretation. Shortly before Louis Leakey's death, however, the discovery of Skull 1470 by Richard Leakey's team allowed Richard to present his father with apparent corroboration of one of his central theories.

Richard Leakey did not make his theories of human evolution public until 1974. At this time, scientists were still grappling with Louis Leakey's interpretation of his findings that there had been at least two parallel lines of human evolution, only one of which led to modern humans. After Louis Leakey's death, Richard Leakey reported that, based on new finds, he believed that hominids diversified between 3 and 3.5 million years ago. Various lines of australopithecines and *Homo* coexisted, with only one line, *Homo,* surviving. The australopithecines and *Homo* shared a common ancestor; *Australopithecus* was not ancestral to *Homo*. As did his father, Leakey believes that *Homo* developed in Africa, and it was *Homo erectus* who, approximately 1.5 million years ago, developed the technological capacity to begin the spread of humans beyond their African origins. In Richard Leakey's scheme, *Homo habilis* developed into *Homo erectus*, who in turn developed into *Homo sapiens,* the present-day human.

As new finds are made, new questions arise. Are newly discovered variants proof of a plurality of species, or do they give evidence of greater variety within the species that have already been identified? To what extent is sexual dimorphism responsible for the apparent differences in the fossils? In some scientific circles, the discovery of fossil remains at Hadar in Ethiopia by archaeologist Donald Carl Johanson and others, along with the more recent revised dating of Skull 1470, cast some doubt on Leakey's theory in general and on his interpretation of *Homo habilis* in particular. Johanson believed that the fossils he found at Hadar and the fossils Mary Leakey found at Laetoli in Tanzania, and which she classified as *Homo habilis*, were actually all australopithecines; he termed them *Australopithecus afarensis* and claimed that this species is the common ancestor of both the later australopithecines and *Homo* . Richard Leakey has rejected this argument, contending that the australopithecines were not ancestral to *Homo* and that an earlier common ancestor would be found, possibly among the fossils found by Mary Leakey at Laetoli.

The year 1975 brought another significant find by Leakey's team at Koobi Fora: the team found what was apparently the skull of a *Homo erectus*, according to Louis Leakey's theory a descendent of *Homo habilis* and probably dating to 1.5 million years ago. This skull, labeled "3733," represents the earliest known evidence for *Homo erectus* in Africa.

Richard Leakey began to suffer from health problems during the 1970s, and in 1979 he was diagnosed with a serious kidney malfunction. Later that year he underwent a kidney transplant operation, his younger brother Philip being the donor. During his recuperation Richard completed his autobiography, *One Life*, which was released in 1984, and following his recovery, he renewed his search for the origins of the human species. The summer of 1984 brought another major discovery: the so-called Turkana boy, a nearly complete skeleton of a *Homo erectus*, missing little but the hands and feet, and offering, for the first time, the opportunity to view many bones of this species. It was shortly after the unearthing of Turkana boy—whose skeletal remains indicate that he was a twelve-year-old youngster who stood approximately five-and-a-half feet tall—that the puzzle of human evolution became even more complicated. The discovery of a new skull, called the Black Skull, with an *Australopithecus boisei* face but a cranium that was quite apelike, introduced

yet another complication, possibly a fourth branch in the evolutionary tree.

[*Michael Sims*]

FURTHER READING

Leakey, M. *Disclosing the Past: An Autobiography* . Doubleday, 1984.

Leakey, R., and R. Lewin *Origins Reconsidered: In Search of What Makes Us Human.* Doubleday, 1992.

Reader, J. *Missing Links*. Little, Brown, 1981.

Leaking underground storage tank

Leaking underground storage tanks (LUST) that hold **toxic substance**s have come under new regulatory scrutiny in the United States because of the health and environmental hazards posed by the materials that can leak from them. These storage tanks typically hold **petroleum** products and other toxic **chemicals** beneath gas stations and other petroleum facilities. An estimated 63,000 of the nation's underground storage tanks have been shown to leak contaminants into the environment or are considered to have the potential to leak at any time. One reason for the instability of underground storage tanks is their construction. Only five percent of underground storage tanks are made of corrosion-protected steel, while 84 percent are made of bare steel, which corrodes easily. Another 11 percent of underground storage tanks are made of fiberglass.

Hazardous materials seeping from some of the nation's six million LUSTs can contaminate **aquifer**s, the water-bearing rock units that supply much of the earth's drinking water. An aquifer, once contaminated, can be ruined as a source of fresh water. In particular, **benzene** has been found to be a contaminant of **groundwater** as a result of leaks from underground **gasoline** storage tanks. Benzene and other **volatile organic compound**s have been detected in bottled water despite manufacturers' claims of purity.

According to the **Environmental Protection Agency (EPA)**, more than 30 states reported groundwater contamination from petroleum products leaking from underground storage tanks. States also reported water contamination from **radioactive waste** leaching from storage containment facilities. Other reported **pollution** problems include leaking hazardous substances that are corrosive, explosive, readily flammable, or chemically reactive. While **water pollution** may be the most visible consequence of leaks from underground storage tanks, fires and explosions are dangerous and sometimes real possibilities in some areas.

The EPA is charged with exploring, developing, and disseminating technologies and funding mechanisms for cleanup. The primary job itself, however, is left to state and local governments. Actual cleanup is sometimes funded by the Leaking Underground Storage Tank trust fund established by Congress in 1986. Under the **Superfund Amendment and Reauthorization Act**, owners and operators of underground storage tanks are required to take corrective action to prevent leakage. *See also* Comprehensive Environmental Response, Compensation and Liability Act;

Groundwater monitoring; Groundwater pollution; Storage and transport of hazardous materials; Toxic Substances Control Act

[*Linda Rehkopf*]

FURTHER READING

Breen, B. "A Mountain and a Mission." *Garbage* 4 (May-June 1992): 52-57.

Epstein, L., and K. Stein. *Leaking Underground Storage Tanks—Citizen Action: An Ounce of Prevention.* New York: Environmental Information Exchange (Environmental Defense Fund), 1990.

Hoffman, R. D. R. "Stopping the Peril of Leaking Tanks." *Popular Science* 238 (March 1991): 77-80.

Leopold, Aldo (1887-1948)

American ecologist and writer

Leopold was a noted forester, game manager, conservationist, college professor, and ecologist. Yet he is known worldwide for *A Sand County Almanac*, a little book considered an important, influential work to **conservation** movement of the twentieth century. In it, Leopold established the **land ethic**, guidelines for respecting the land and preserving its integrity.

Leopold grew up in Iowa, in a house overlooking the Mississippi River, where he learned hunting from his father and an appreciation of **nature** from his mother. He received a master's degree in forestry from Yale and spent his formative professional years working for the United States **Forest Service** in the American Southwest.

In the Southwest, Leopold began slowly to consider preservation as a supplement to **Gifford Pinchot**'s "conservation as wise use—greatest good for the greatest number" land management philosophy that he learned at Yale and in the Forest Service. He began to formulate arguments for the preservation of **wilderness** and the **sustainable development** of wild game. Formerly a hunter who encouraged the elimination of predators to save the "good" animals for hunters, Leopold became a conservationist who remembered with sadness the "dying fire" in the eyes of a wolf he had killed. In the *Journal of Forestry*, he began to speculate that perhaps Pinchot's principle of highest use itself demanded "that representative portions of some forests be preserved as wilderness."

Leopold must be recognized as one of a handful of originators of the wilderness idea in American conservation history. He was instrumental in the founding of the **Wilderness Society** in 1935, which he described in the first issue of *Living Wilderness* as "one of the focal points of a new attitude—an intelligent humility toward man's place in nature." In a 1941 issue of that same journal, he asserted that wilderness also has critical practical uses "as a base-datum of normality, a picture of how healthy land maintains itself," and that wilderness was needed as a living "land laboratory."

This thinking led to the first large area designated as wilderness in the United States. In 1924, some 574,000 acres (232,000 ha) of the Gila National Forest in New Mexico was

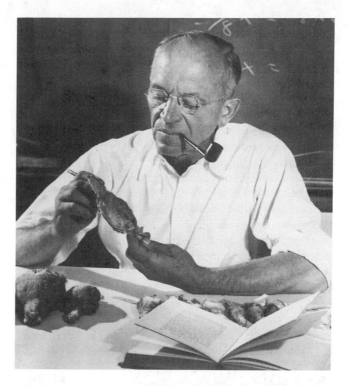

Aldo Leopold examining a gray partridge.

officially named a wilderness area. Four years before, the much smaller Trappers Lake valley in Colorado was the first area designated "to be kept roadless and undeveloped."

Aldo Leopold is also widely acknowledged as the founder of **wildlife management** in the United States. His classic text on the subject, *Game Management* (1933), is still in print and widely read. Leopold tried to write a general management framework, drawing upon and synthesizing **species** monographs and local manuals. "Details apply to game alone, but the principles are of general import to all fields of conservation," he wrote. He wanted to coordinate "science and use" in his book and felt strongly that land managers could either try to apply such principles, or be reduced to "hunting rabbits." Here can be found early uses of concepts still central to conservation and management, such as limiting factor, **niche**, saturation point, and **carrying capacity**. Leopold later became the first professor of game management in the United States at the University of Wisconsin.

Leopold's *A Sand County Almanac*, published in 1949, a year after his death, is often described as "the bible of the environmental movement" of the second half of the twentieth century. The *Almanac* is a beautifully written source of solid ecological concepts such as trophic linkages and **biological community**. The book extends basic ecological concepts, forming radical ideas to reformulate human thinking and behavior. It exhibits an ecological conscience, a conservation aesthetic, and a land ethic. He advocated his concept of ecological conscience to fill in a perceived gap in conservation education: "Obligations have no meaning without conscience, and the problem we face is the extension of the social conscience from people to land."

Lesser known is his attention to the aesthetics of land: according to the *Almanac*, an acceptable land aesthetic emerges only from learned and sensitive perception of the connections and needs of natural communities. The last words in the *Almanac* are that a true conservation aesthetic is developed "not of building roads into lovely country, but of building receptivity into the still unlovely human mind."

Leopold derived his now famous land ethic from an ecological conception of community. All ethics, he maintained, "rest upon a single premise: that the individual is a member of a community of interdependent parts." He argued that "the land ethic simply enlarges the boundaries of the community to include **soil**s, waters, plants, and animals, or collectively: the land." Perhaps the most widely quoted statement from the book argues that "a thing is right when it tends to preserve the integrity, stability, and beauty of the **biotic community**. It is wrong when it tends otherwise."

Leopold's land ethic was first proposed in the *Journal of Forestry* article in 1933 and later expanded in the *Almanac*. It is a plea to care for land and its biological complex, instead of considering it a commodity. As Wallace tegner noted, Leopold's ideas were heretical in 1949, and to some people still are. "They smack of socialism and the public good," he wrote. "They impose limits and restraints. They are anti-Progress. They dampen American initiative. They fly in the face of the faith that land is a commodity, the very foundation stone of American opportunity." As a result, Stegner and others do not think Leopold's ethic had much influence on public thought, though the book has been widely read. Leopold recognized this. "The case for a land ethic would appear hopeless but for the minority which is in obvious revolt against these 'modern' trends," he commented. Nevertheless, the land ethic is alive and still flourishing, in an ever-growing minority. Even Stegner argued that "Leopold's land ethic is not a fact but [an on-going] task." Leopold did not shrink from that task, being actively involved in many conservation associations, teaching management principles and the land ethic to his classes, bringing up all five of his children to become conservationists, and applying his beliefs directly to his own land, a parcel of "logged, fire-swept, overgrazed, barren" land in Sauk County, Wisconsin. As his work has become more recognized and more influential, many labels have been applied to Leopold by contemporary writers. He is a "prophet" and "intellectual touchstone" to Roderick Nash a "founding genius" to **J. Baird Callicott** "an American Isaiah" to Stegner the "Moses of the new conservation impulse" to Donald Fleming. In a sense, he may have been all of these, but more than anything else, Leopold was an applied ecologist who tried to put into practice the principles he learned from the land. *See also* Environmental education; Environmental ethics; Land stewardship; Land use; Land-use control; National forest; Trophic level; Wildlife

[*Gerald R. Young*]

FURTHER READING

Callicott, J. B., ed. *Companion to A Sand County Almanac: Interpretive and Critical Essays.* Madison: University of Wisconsin Press, 1987.

Flader, S. L., and J. B. Callicott, eds. *The River of the Mother of God and Other Essays by Aldo Leopold.* Madison: University of Wisconsin Press, 1991.

Fritzell, P. A. "A Sand County Almanac and The Conflicts of Ecological Conscience." In *Nature Writing and America: Essays Upon a Cultural Type.* Ames: Iowa State University Press, 1990.

Leopold, A. *Game Management.* New York: Charles Scribner's Sons, 1933.

———. *A Sand County Almanac.* New York: Oxford University Press, 1949.

Meine, C. *Aldo Leopold: His Life and Work.* Madison: University of Wisconsin Press, 1988.

Oelschlaeger, M. "Aldo Leopold and the Age of Ecology." In *The Idea of Wilderness: From Prehistory to the Age of Ecology.* New Haven, CT: Yale University Press, 1991.

Strong, D. H. "Aldo Leopold." In *Dreamers and Defenders: American Conservationists.* Lincoln: University of Nebraska Press, 1988.

Less developed countries (LDC)

Less developed countries have lower levels of economic prosperity, health care, and education than most other countries. Development or improvement in economic and social conditions encompasses various aspects of general welfare, including infant survival, expected life span, nutrition, literacy rates, employment, and access to material goods. Less developed countries (LDCs) are identified by their relatively poor ratings in these categories. In addition, most LDCs are marked by high **population growth**, rapidly expanding cities, low levels of technological development, and weak economies dominated by agriculture and the export of **natural resources**. Because of their limited economic and technological development, LDCs tend to have relatively little international political power compared to **more developed countries** (MDC) such as Japan, the United States, and Germany.

A variety of standard measures, or development indices, are used to assess development stages. These indices are generalized statistical measures of quality of life for individuals in a society. Multiple indices are usually considered more accurate than a single number such as Gross National Product, because such figures tend to give imprecise and simplistic impressions of conditions in a country. One of the most important of the multiple indices is the infant **mortality** rate. Because children under five years old are highly susceptible to common diseases, especially when they are malnourished, infant mortality is a key to assessing both nutrition and access to health care. Expected life span, the average age adults are able to reach, is used as a measure of adult health. Daily calorie and protein intake per person are collective measures that reflect the ability of individuals to grow and function effectively. Literacy rates, especially among women, who are normally the last to receive an education, indicate access to schools and preparation for technologically advanced employment.

Fertility rates are a measure of the number of children produced per family or per woman in a population and are regarded as an important measure of the confidence parents have in their childrens' survival. High birth rates are associated with unstable social conditions because a country with a rapidly growing population often cannot provide its citizens with food, water, sanitation, housing space, jobs, and other basic needs. Rapidly growing populations also tend to undergo rapid urbanization. People move to cities in search of jobs and educational opportunities, but in poor countries the cost of providing basic infrastructure in an expanding city can be debilitating. As most countries develop, they pass from a stage of high birth rates to one of low birth rates, as child survival becomes more certain and a family's investment in educating and providing for each child increases.

Most LDCs were colonies under foreign control during the past 200 years. Colonial powers tended to undermine social organization, local economies, and natural resource bases, and many recently independent states are still recovering from this legacy. Thus, much of Africa, which provided a wealth of natural resources to Europe between the seventeenth and twentieth centuries, now lacks the effective and equitable social organization necessary for continuing development. Similarly, much of Central America (colonized by Spain in the fifteenth century) and portions of South and Southeast Asia (colonized by England, France, the Netherlands, and others) remain less developed despite their wealth of natural resources. The development processes necessary to improve standards of living in LDCs may involve more natural resource extraction, but usually the most important steps involve carefully choosing the goods to be produced, decreasing corruption among government and business leaders, and easing the social unrest and conflicts that prevent development from proceeding. All of these are extraordinarily difficult to do, but they are essential for countries trying to escape from poverty. *See also* Child survival revolution; Debt for nature swap; Economic growth and the environment; Indigenous peoples; Shanty towns; South; Sustainable development; Third World; Third World pollution; Tropical rain forest; World Bank

[*Muthena Naseri*]

FURTHER READING

Gill, S., and D. Law. *The Global Political Economy.* Baltimore: Johns Hopkins University Press, 1991.

World Bank. *World Development Report: Development and the Environment.* Oxford, England: Oxford University Press, 1992.

Leukemia

Leukemia is a disease of the blood-forming organs. Primary tumors are found in the bone marrow and lymphoid tissues, specifically the liver, spleen, and lymph nodes. The characteristic common to all types of leukemia is the uncontrolled proliferation of leukocytes (white blood cells) in the blood stream. This results in a lack of normal bone marrow growth, and bone marrow is replaced by immature and undifferentiated leukocytes or "blast cells." These immature and undifferentiated cells then migrate to various organs in the body, resulting in the pathogenesis of normal organ development and processing.

Leukemia occurs with varying frequencies at different ages, but it is most frequent among the elderly who experience 27,000 cases a year in the United States to 2,200 cases a year for younger people. Acute lymphoblastic leukemia, most common in children, is responsible for two-thirds of all cases. Acute nonlymphoblastic leukemia and chronic lymphocytic leukemia are most common among adults they are responsible for 8,000 and 9,600 cases a year respectively. The geographical sites of highest concentration are the United States, Canada, Sweden, and New Zealand. While there is clear evidence that some leukemias are linked to genetic traits, the origins of this disease in most cases is mysterious. It seems clear, however, that environmental exposure to radiation, **toxic substance**s, and other risk factors play an important role in many leukemias. *See also* Cancer; Carcinogen; Radiation exposure; Radiation sickness

Lichens

Lichens are composed of **fungi** and algae. Varying in color from pale whitish green to brilliant red and orange, lichens usually grow attached to rocks and tree trunks and appear as thin, crusty coatings as networks of small, branched strands or as flattened, leaf-like forms. Some common lichens are reindeer moss and the red "British soldiers." There are approximately 20,000 known lichen **species**. Because they often grow under cold, dry, inhospitable conditions, they're usually the first plants to colonize barren rock surfaces.

The fungus and the alga form a symbiotic relationship within the lichen. The fungus forms the body of the lichen, called the thallus. The thallus attaches itself to the surface of a rock or tree trunk, and the fungal cells take up water and **nutrient**s from the **environment**. The algal cells grow inside the fungal cells and perform **photosynthesis**, as do other plant cells, to form carbohydrates.

Lichens are essential in providing food for other organisms, breaking down rocks, and initiating **soil** building. They are also important indicators and monitors of **air pollution** effects. Since lichens grow attached to rock and tree surfaces, they are fully exposed to airborne pollutants, and chemical analysis of lichen tissues can be used to measure the quantity of pollutants in a particular area. For example, **sulfur dioxide**, a common **emission** from **power plants**, is a major air pollutant. Many studies show that as the concentrations of sulfur dioxide in the air increase, the number of lichen species decreases. The disappearance of lichens from an area may be indicative of other, widespread biological impacts.

Sometimes, lichens are the first organisms to transfer contaminants to the **food chain**. Lichens are abundant through vast regions of the arctic **tundra** and form the main food source for caribou (*Rangifer tarandus*) in winter. The caribou are hunted and eaten by northern Alaskan Eskimos in spring and early summer. When the effects of **radioactive fallout** from weapons-testing in the arctic tundra were studied, it was discovered that lichens absorbed virtually all of the radionuclides that were deposited on them. **Strontium-90** and **cesium-137** were two of the major radionuclide contaminants. As caribou grazed on the lichens, these radionuclides were absorbed into the caribou' tissues. At the end of the winter, caribou flesh contained three to six times as much cesium-137 as it did in the fall. When the caribou flesh was consumed by the Eskimos, the radionuclides were transferred to them as well. *See also* Indicator organism; Symbiosis

[*Usha Vedagiri*]

FURTHER READING

Connell, D. W., and G. J. Miller. *Chemistry and Ecotoxicology of Pollution.* New York: Wiley, 1984.

Smith, R. L. *Ecology and Field Biology.* New York: Harper and Row, 1980.

Weier, T. E., et al. *Botany: An Introduction to Plant Biology.* New York: Wiley, 1982.

Life cycle assessment

Life cycle assessment (or LCA) refers to a relatively new process in industrial **ecology** by which the products, processes, and facilities used to manufacture specific products are each examined for their environmental impacts. A balance sheet is prepared for each product that considers: the use of materials; the consumption of energy; the **recycling**, re-use, and/or disposal of non-used materials and energy (in a less-enlightened context, these are referred to as "wastes"); and the recycling or re-use of products after their commercial life has passed. By taking a comprehensive, integrated look at all of these aspects of the manufacturing and use of products, life cycle assessment finds ways to increase efficiency, to re-use, reduce, and recycle materials, and to lessen the overall environmental impacts of the process.

Lignite
See **Coal**

Limits to Growth (1972) and *Beyond the Limits* (1992)

Published at the height of the oil crisis in the 1970s, the *Limits to Growth* study is credited with lifting environmental concerns to an international and global level. Its fundamental conclusion is that if rapid growth continues unabated in the five key areas of population, food production, industrialization, **pollution**, and consumption of nonrenewable **natural resources**, the planet will reach the limits of growth within one hundred years. The most probable result will be a "rather sudden and uncontrollable decline in both population and industrial capacity."

The study grew out of an April 1968 meeting of 30 scientists, educators, economists, humanists, industrialists, and national and international civil servants who had been brought together by Dr. Aurelio Peccei, an Italian industrial manager and economist. Peccei and the others met at the Accademia dei Lincei in Rome to discuss the "present and future predicament of man," and from their meeting came

the **Club of Rome**. Early meetings of the club resulted in a decision to initiate the Project on the Predicament of Mankind, intended to examine the array of problems facing all nations. Those problems ranged from poverty amidst plenty and **environmental degradation** to the rejection of traditional values and various economic disturbances.

In the summer of 1970, Phase One of the project took shape during a series of meetings in Bern, Switzerland and Cambridge, Massachusetts. At a two-week meeting in Cambridge, Professor Jay Forrester of the Massachusetts Institute of Technology (MIT) presented a global model for analyzing the interacting components of world problems. Professor Dennis Meadows led an international team in examining the five basic components, mentioned above, that determine growth on this planet and its ultimate limits. The team's research culminated in the 1972 publication of the study, which touched off intense controversy and further research.

Underlying the study's dramatic conclusions is the central concept of **exponential growth**, which occurs when a quantity increases by a constant percentage of the whole in a constant time period. "For instance, a colony of yeast cells in which each cell divides into two cells every ten minutes is growing exponentially," the study explains. The model used to capture the dynamic quality of exponential growth is a System Dynamics model, developed over a 30-year period at MIT, which recognizes that structure of any system determines its behavior as much as any individual parts of the system. The components of a system are described as "circular, interlocking, sometimes time-delayed." Using this model (called World3), the study ran scenarios—what-if analyses—to reach its view of how the world will evolve if present trends persist.

"Dynamic modeling theory indicates that any exponentially growing quantity is somehow involved with a positive feedback loop," the study points out. "In a positive feedback loop a chain of cause-and-effect relationships closes on itself, so that increasing any one element in the loop will start a sequence of changes that will result in the originally changed element being increased even more."

In the case of world **population growth**, the births per year act as a positive feedback loop. For instance, in 1650, world population was half a billion and was growing at a rate of 0.3 percent a year. In 1970, world population was 3.6 billion and was growing at a rate of 2.1 percent a year. Both the population and the rate of population growth have been increasing exponentially. But in addition to births per year, the dynamic system of population growth includes a negative feedback loop: deaths per year. Positive feedback loops create runaway growth, while negative feedback loops regulate growth and hold a system in a stable state. For instance, a thermostat will regulate temperature when a room reaches a certain temperature, the thermostat shuts off the system until the temperature decreases enough to restart the system. With population growth, both the birth and death rates were relatively high and irregular before the Industrial Revolution. But with the spread of medicines and longer life expectancies, the death rate has slowed while the birth rate has risen. Given these trends, the study predicted a worldwide jump in population of seven billion over 30 years.

This same dynamic of positive and negative feedback loops applies to the other components of the world system. The growth in world industrial capital, with the positive input of investment, creates rising industrial output, such as houses, **automobile**s, textiles, consumer goods, and other products. On the negative feedback side, depreciation, or the capital discarded each year, draws down the level of industrial capital. This feedback is "exactly analogous to the death rate loop in the population system," the study notes. And, as with world population, the positive feedback loop is "strongly dominant," creating steady growth in worldwide industrial capital and the use of raw materials needed to create products.

This system in which exponential growth is occurring, with positive feedback loops outstripping negative ones, will push the world to the limits of exponential growth. The study asks what will be needed to sustain world economic and population growth until and beyond the year 2000 and concludes that two main categories of ingredients can be defined. First, there are physical necessities that support all physiological and industrial activity: food, raw materials, fossil and nuclear fuels, and the ecological systems of the planet that absorb waste and recycle important chemical substances. **Arable land**, fresh water, metals, forests, and oceans are needed to obtain those necessities. Second, there are social necessities needed to sustain growth, including peace, social stability, education, employment, and steady technological progress.

Even assuming that the best possible social conditions exist for the promotion of growth, the earth is finite and therefore continued exponential growth will reach the limits of each physical necessity. For instance, about 1 acre (0.4 ha) of arable land is needed to grow enough food per person. With that need for arable land, even if all the world's arable land were cultivated, current population growth rates will still create a "desperate land shortage before the year 2000," the study concludes. The availability of fresh water is another crucial limiting factor, the study points out. "There is an upper limit to the fresh water **runoff** from the land areas of the earth each year, and there is also an exponentially increasing demand for that water."

This same analysis is applied to **nonrenewable resources**, such as metals, **coal**, iron, and other necessities for industrial growth. World demand is rising steadily and at some point demand for each nonrenewable resource will exceed supply, even with **recycling** of these materials. For instance, the study predicts that even if 100 percent recycling of chromium from 1970 onward were possible, demand would exceed supply in 235 years. Similarly, while it is not known how much pollution the world can take before vital natural processes are disrupted, the study cautions that the danger of reaching those limits is especially great because there is usually a long delay between the time a pollutant is released and the time it begins to negatively affect the **environment**.

While the study foretells worldwide collapse if exponential growth trends continue, it also argues that the neces-

sary steps to avert disaster are known and are well within human capabilities. Current knowledge and resources could guide the world to a sustainable equilibrium society provided that a realistic, long-term goal and the will to achieve that goal are pursued.

The sequel to the 1972 study, *Beyond the Limits*, was not sponsored by the Club of Rome, but it is written by three of the original authors. While the basic analytical framework remains the same in the later work—drawing upon the concepts of exponential growth and feedback loops to describe the world system—its conclusions are more severe. No longer does the world only face a potential of "overshooting" its limits. "Human use of many essential resources and generation of many kinds of pollutants have already surpassed rates that are physically sustainable," according to the 1992 study. "Without significant reductions in material and energy flows, there will be in the coming decades an uncontrolled decline in per capita food output, energy use, and industrial output."

However, like its predecessor, the later study sounds a note of hope, arguing that decline is not inevitable. To avoid disaster requires comprehensive reforms in policies and practices that perpetuate growth in material consumption and population. It also requires a rapid, drastic jump in the efficiency with which we use materials and energy.

Both the earlier and the later study were received with great controversy. For instance, economists and industrialists charged that the earlier study ignored the fact that technological innovation could stretch the limits to growth through greater efficiency and diminishing pollution levels. When the sequel was published, some critics charged that the World3 model could have been refined to include more realistic distinctions between nations and regions, rather than looking at all trends on a world scale. For instance, different continents, rich and poor nations, **North**, **South**, and East, various regions—all are different, but those differences are ignored in the model, thereby making it unrealistic even though modeling techniques have evolved significantly since World3 was first developed. *See also* Sustainable development

[*David Clarke*]

FURTHER READING

Meadows, D., et al. *The Limits to Growth: A Report for The Club of Rome's Project on the Predicament of Mankind.* New York: Universe Books, 1972.

Meadows, D., D. L. Meadows, and J. Randers. *Beyond the Limits: Confronting Global Collapse, Envisioning a Sustainable Future.* Post Mills, VT: Chelsea Green, 1992.

Limnology

Derived from the Greek word *limne*, meaning marsh or pond, the term limnology was first used in reference to lakes by F. A. Forel in 1892 in a paper titled "Le Léman: Monographie Limnology," a study of what we now call Lake

Liquid metal fast breeder reactor.

Geneva in Switzerland. Limnology, also known as aquatic **ecology**, refers to the study of fresh water communities within continental boundaries. It can be subdivided into the study of lentic (standing water **habitat**s such as lakes, ponds, bogs, swamps, and marshes) and lotic (running water habitats such as rivers, streams, and brooks) **environment**s. Collectively, limnologists study the morphological, physical, chemical, and biological aspects of these habitats.

Liquid metal fast breeder reactor

The liquid metal fast breeder reactor (LMFBR) is a nuclear reactor that has been modified to increase the efficiency at which non-fissionable uranium-238 is converted to fissionable plutonium-239, which can be used as fuel in the production of **nuclear power**. The reactor uses "fast" rather than "slow" **neutron**s to strike a uranium-238 nucleus, resulting in the formation of plutonium-239. In a second modification, it uses a liquid metal, usually sodium, rather than neutron-absorbing water as a more efficient coolant. Since the reactor produces new fuel as it operates, it is called a breeder reactor.

The main appeal of breeder reactors is that they provide an alternative way of obtaining fissionable materials. The supply of natural **uranium** in the earth's crust is fairly large, but it will not last forever. Plutonium-239 from breeder reactors might become the major fuel used in reactors built a few hundred or thousand years from now.

However, the potential of LMFBRs has not as yet been realized. One serious problem involves the use of liquid sodium as coolant. Sodium is a highly corrosive metal and in an LMFBR it is converted into a radioactive form, sodium-24. Accidental release of the coolant from such a plant could, therefore, constitute a serious environmental hazard. In addition, **plutonium** itself is difficult to work with. It is one of the most **toxic substance**s known to humans, and its **half-life** of 24,000 years means that its release presents long-term environmental problems.

Small-scale pilot LMFBR reactors have been tested in the United States, Saudi Arabia, Great Britain, and Germany since 1966, and all have turned out to be far more expensive than had been anticipated. The major United States research program based at Clinch, Tennessee, began in 1970. By 1983, the United States Congress refused to continue funding the project due to its slow and unsatisfactory progress. *See also* Nuclear fission; Nuclear Regulatory Commission; Radioactivity; Radioactive waste management

[*David E. Newton*]

FURTHER READING

Enger, E. D., et al. *Environmental Science: The Study of Relationships.* 3rd ed. Dubuque, IA: William C. Brown, 1989.

Miller, G. T., Jr. *Energy and Environment: The Four Energy Crises.* 2nd ed. Belmont, CA: Wadsworth, 1980.

Mitchell, W., III, and S. E. Turner. *Breeder Reactors.* Washington, DC: U. S. Atomic Energy Commission, 1971.

Liquified natural gas

Natural gas is a highly desirable fuel in many respects. It burns with the release of a large amount of energy, producing almost entirely **carbon dioxide** and water as waste products. Except for possible **greenhouse effect**s of carbon dioxide, these compounds produce virtually no environmental hazard. Transporting natural gas through transcontinental pipelines is inexpensive and efficient where **topography** allows the laying of pipes. Oceanic shipping is difficult, however, because of the flammability of the gas and the high volumes involved. The most common way of dealing with these problems is to condense the gas first and then transport it in the form of liquified natural gas (LNG). But LNG must be maintained at temperatures of about -260°F (-160°C) and protected from leaks and flames during loading and unloading. *See also* Fossil fuels

Lithology

The study of rocks, their description and classification, emphasizing macroscopic physical characteristics, including grain size, mineral composition, and color. Lithology and its related field, petrography (the description and systematic classification of rocks), are subdisciplines of petrology, which also considers microscopic and chemical properties of minerals and rocks as well as their origin and decay.

Littoral zone

In marine systems, littoral zone is synonymous with intertidal zone and refers to the area on marine shores that is periodically exposed to air during low tide. The freshwater littoral zone is that area near the shore characterized by submerged, floating, or emergent vegetation. The width of a particular littoral zone may vary from several miles to a few feet. These areas typically support an abundance of organisms and are important feeding and nursery areas for fishes, crustaceans, and birds. The distribution and abundance of individual **species** in the littoral zone is dependent on predation and **competition** as well as tolerance of physical factors. *See also* Neritic zone; Pelagic zone

Loading

The term loading has a wide variety of specialized meanings in various fields of science. In general, all refer to the addition of something to a system, just as loading a truck means filling it with objects. In the science of acoustics, for example, loading refers to the process of adding materials to a speaker in order to improve its acoustical qualities. In **environmental science**, loading is used to describe the contribution made to any system by some component. One might analyze, for example, how an increase in **chlorofluorocarbon** (CFC) loading in the **stratosphere** might affect the concentration of **ozone** there.

Logistic growth

Assuming the rate of immigration is the same as emigration, population size increases when births exceed deaths. As population size increases, population density increases, and the supply of limited available resources per organism decreases. There is thus less food and less space available for each individual. As food, water, and space decline, fewer births or more deaths may occur, and this imbalance continues until the number of births are equal to the number of deaths at a population size that can be sustained by the available resources. This equilibrium level is called the **carrying capacity** for that **environment**.

A temporary and rapid increase in population may be due to a period of optimum growth conditions including physical and biological factors. Such an increase may push a population beyond the environmental carrying capacity. This sudden burst will be followed by a decline, and the population will maintain a steady fluctuation around the carrying capacity. Other population controls, such as predators and weather extremes (**drought**, frost, and floods), keep populations below the carrying capacity. Some environmentalists believe that the human population has exceeded the earth's carrying capacity.

Logistic growth, then, refers to growth rates that are regulated by internal and external factors that establish an equilibrium with environmental resources. The sigmoid (idealized S-shaped) curve illustrates this logistic growth where environmental factors limit **population growth**. In this model, a low-density population begins to grow slowly, then goes through an exponential or geometric phase, and then levels off at the environmental carrying capacity. *See also* Exponential growth; Growth limiting factors; Sustainable development; Zero population growth

[*Muthena Naseri*]

London Dumping Convention
See **Convention on the Prevention of Marine Pollution by Dumping of Waste and Other Matter**

Lopez, Barry (1945-)

American environmental writer

Barry Lopez has often called his own nonfiction writing natural history, and he is often categorized as a **nature** writer. This partially describes his work, but limiting him to that category is misleading, partly because his work transcends the kinds of subjects implicit in that classification. He could as well, for example, be called a travel writer, though that label also does not completely describe his work. He has in addition published a number of unusual works of fiction, and even has one children's book (on *Crow and Weasel*) to his credit.

Barry Lopez was born in Port Chester, New York, but he spent several early childhood years in rural southern California and, at the age of ten, returned to the East to grow up in New York City. He earned a BA degree from the University of Notre Dame, followed by an MAT from the University of Oregon in 1968. His initial goal was to teach, but in the late 1960s he set out to become a professional writer and since 1970 has earned his living writing (as well as by lecturing and giving readings).

Lopez's nonfiction writing transcends the category of natural history because his real topic, as Rueckert suggests, is the search for human relationships with nature, relationships that are "dignified and honorable." Natural history as a category of literature implies a focus on primeval nature undisturbed by human activity, or at least on nature as it exists in its own right rather than as humans relate to it. He is a practitioner of what some have called "the new naturalism—a search for the human as mirrored in nature." Lopez's focus then is **human ecology**, the interactions of human beings with the world around them, especially the natural world. Even his most 'natural' book of natural history, *Of Wolves and Men*, is not just about the natural history of wolves but about how that species' existence or 'being' in the wild is affected by human perceptions and actions, and it is as well about the image of the wolf in human minds.

His fiction works can be called unusual, partly because they are often presented as brief notes or sketches, and partly because they are frequently blended into and combined with legends, factual observations of nature, and personal meditations. Everything Lopez writes, however, is in the form of a story, whether fiction, natural history, folklore, or travel writing. His story-telling makes all of his writing enjoyable to read, easy to access and ingest, and often memorable.

Lopez as a story teller, occupies the spaces between truth-teller and mystic, between natural scientist and folklorist. He has written of wolves and humans, and then of people with blue skins who could not speak and, apparently, subsisted only on clean air. He writes of the land in reality and the land in our imaginations, frequently in the same text. His writings on natural history provide the reader with great detail about the places in the world he describes, but his fiction can force the shock of recognition of places in the mind.

Barry Lopez is in part a naturalist, in the best sense of that word. He is also something of an anthropologist. He is a student of folklore and mythology. He travels widely, but he studies his own home place and local environment intently. And, of course, he is a writer.

[*Gerald L. Young*]

FURTHER READING

Lopez, B. *Arctic Dreams: Imagination and Desire in a Northern Landscape.* New York: Scribner, 1986.

———. *Crossing Open Ground.* New York: Scribner, 1988.

———. *Desert Notes; Reflections in the Eye of a Raven.* Kansas City, KS: Sheed, Andrews & McMeel.

Paul, S. "Barry Lopez," *Hewing to Experience: Essays and Reviews on Recent American Poetry and Poetics, Nature and Culture.* Iowa City: University of Iowa Press, 1989.

Rueckert, W.H. "Barry Lopez and the Search for a Dignified and Honorable Relationship With Nature," *Earthly Words: Essays on Contemporary American Nature and Environmental Writers*, ed. J. Cooley. Ann Arbor: University of Michigan Press, 1994.

Los Angeles Basin

The second most populous city in the United States, Los Angeles has perhaps the most fascinating environmental history of any urban area in the country. The Los Angeles Basin, into which more than eighty communities of Los Angeles County are crowded, is a trough-shaped region bounded on three sides by the Santa Monica, Santa Susana, San Gabriel, San Bernadino, and Santa Ana Mountains. On its fourth side, the county looks out over the Pacific Ocean.

The earliest settlers arrived in the Basin in 1769 when Spaniard Gaspar de Portolá and his expedition set up camp along what is now known as the Los Angeles River. The site was eventually given the name El Pueblo de la Reyna de Los Angeles (the Town of the Queen of the Angels).

For the first century of its history, Los Angeles grew very slowly. Its population in 1835 was only 1,250. By the end of the century, however, the first signs of a new trend appeared. In response to the promises of sunshine, warm weather, and "easy living," immigrants from the East Coast began to arrive in the Basin. Its population more than quadrupled between 1880 and 1890, from 11,183 to 50,395.

The rush was on, and it has scarcely abated today. The metropolitan population grew from 102,000 in 1900 to 1,238,000 in 1930 to 3,997,000 to 1950 to 8,345,000 in 1970.

The **pollution** facing Los Angeles results from a complex mix of natural factors and intense **population growth**. The first reports of Los Angeles's famous **photochemical smog** go back to 1542. The "many smokes" described by Juan Cabrillo in that year were not the same as today's smog, but they occurred because of geographic and climatic conditions that are responsible for modern environmental problems.

The Los Angeles Basin has one of the highest probabilities of experiencing thermal inversions of any area in the United States. An inversion is an atmospheric condition in which a layer of cold air becomes trapped beneath a layer of warm air. That situation is just the reverse of the most normal atmospheric condition in which a warm layer near the ground is covered by a cooler layer above it. In this situation, the warm air has a tendency to rise, and the cool air has a tendency to sink. As a result, natural mixing occurs. In a thermal inversion, the denser cool air remains near the ground while the less dense air above it tends to stay there.

Smoke and other pollutants released into a thermal inversion are unable to rise upward and tend to be trapped in the cool lower layer. Furthermore, horizontal movements of air that might clear out pollution in other areas are blocked by the mountains surrounding the county. The lingering haze of the "many smokes" described by Cabrillo could have been nothing more than the smoke from campfires trapped by inversions that must have existed even in 1542.

As population and industrial growth occurred in Los Angeles during the second half of the twentieth century, the amount of pollutants trapped in thermal inversions also grew. By the 1960s, Los Angeles had become a classic example of how modern cities were being choked by their own wastes.

The geographic location of the Los Angeles Basin contributes another factor to Los Angeles's special environmental problems. Sunlight warms the Basin for most of the year and attracts visitors and new residents. **Solar energy** fuels reactions between components of Los Angeles's polluted air, producing chemicals even more toxic than those from which they came. The complex mixture of noxious compounds produced in Los Angeles has been given the name *smog*, reflecting the combination of human (*smoke*) and natural factors (*fog*) that make it possible.

As Los Angeles grew in area and population, conditions which guaranteed a continuation of smog increased. The city and surrounding environs eventually grew to cover 400 square miles (1,036 square kilometers), a widespread community held together by freeways and cars. A major oil company bought the city's public transit system, then closed it down, ensuring the wide use of **automobile** transportation. Thus, gases produced by the **combustion** of **gasoline** added to the city's increasing pollution levels. By the 1970s, smog was detectable on more than 250 days out of the year.

Los Angeles and the State of California have been battling air pollution for over twenty years. The state now has the most severe **emission standards** of any state in the nation. And the city has begun to develop mass transit systems once again. For an area that has long depended on the automobile, however, most such actions can do little more than hold the status quo.

Another of Los Angeles's population-induced problems is its enormous demand for water. As early as 1900, it was apparent that the Basin's meager water resources would be inadequate to meet the needs of the growing urban area. The city turned its sights on the Owens Valley, 200 miles (322 kilometers) to the northeast in the Sierra Nevada. After a lengthy dispute, the city won the right to tap the **water resources** of this distant valley. A 200-mile aqueduct, the Los Angeles Aqueduct, was completed in 1913.

This development did not satisfy the area's growing need for water, however, and in the 1930s, a second canal was built. This canal, the **Colorado River** Aqueduct, carries water from the Colorado River to Los Angeles over a distance of 444 miles (714 kilometers). Even this addition proved to be inadequate, however, and the search for additional water sources has gone on almost without stop. In fact, one of the great on-going debates in California is between legislators from Northern California, where the state's major water resources are located, and their counterparts from Southern California, where the majority of the state's people live. Since the latter contingent is larger in number, it has won many of the battles so far over distribution of the state's water resources.

Of course, Los Angeles has also experienced many of the same problems as urban areas in other parts of the world, regardless of its special geographical character. For example, the Basin was at one time a lush agricultural area, with some of the best **soil** and growing conditions found anywhere. From 1910 to 1950, Los Angeles County was the wealthiest agricultural region in the nation. But as urbanization progressed, more and more farmland was sacrificed for commercial and residential development. During the 1950s, an average of 3,000 acres (1,215 hectares) of farmland per day was taken out of production and converted to residential, commercial, industrial, or transportation use.

One of the mixed blessings faced by residents of the Los Angeles Basin is the existence of large oil reserves in the area. On the one hand, the oil and **natural gas** contained in these reserves is a valuable natural resource. On the other hand, the presence of working oil wells in the middle of a modern metropolitan area creates certain problems. One is aesthetic, as busy pumps in the midst of barren or scraggly land contrasts with sleek new glass and steel buildings.

Another problem is that of land **subsidence**. As oil and gas are removed from underground, land above it begins to sink. This phenomenon was first observed as early as 1937. Over the next two decades, subsidence had reached 16 feet (5 meters) at the center of the Wilmington oil fields. Horizontal shifting of up to nine feet (2.74 meters) was also recorded.

Estimates of subsidence of up to 45 feet (14 meters) spurred the county to begin remedial measures in the 1950s. These measures included the construction of levees to prevent seawater from flowing into the subsided area and the repressurizing of oil zones with water injection. These measures have been largely successful, at least to the present time, in halting the subsidence of the oil field.

As if population growth itself were not enough, the Basin poses its own set of natural challenges to the community. For example, the area has a typical Mediterranean climate with long, dry, hot summers, and short winters with little rain. Summers are also the occasion of Santa Ana winds, severe windstorms in which hot air sweeps down out of the mountains and across the Basin. Urban and forest fires that originate during a Santa Ana wind not uncommonly go out of control causing enormous devastation to both human communities and the natural environment.

The Los Angeles Basin also sits within a short distance of one of the most famous fault systems in the world, the San Andreas Fault. Other minor faults spread out around Los Angeles on every side. Earthquakes are common in the Basin, and the most powerful earthquake in Southern California history struck Los Angeles in 1857. Sixty miles (97 kilometers) from the quake's epicenter, the tiny community of Los

Weeds grow around boarded up homes in Love Canal, New York (1980).

Angeles lost the military base at Fort Tejon although only two lives were lost in the disaster. Like San Franciscans, residents of the Los Angeles Basin live not wondering if another earthquake will occur, but only when The Big One will hit. *See also* Air quality; Atmospheric inversion; Environmental Protection Agency (EPA); Mass transit; Oil drilling

[*David E. Newton*]

FURTHER READING

Hundley, N., Jr. *The Great Thirst: Californians and Water, 1770s-1990s.* Berkeley: University of California Press, 1992.

Poland, J. F., and G. H. Davis, "Land Subsidence Due to Withdrawal of Fluids." In *Man's Impact on Environment,* edited by T. R. Detwyler. New York: McGraw-Hill Book Company, 1971.

Love Canal, New York

Probably the most infamous of the nation's **hazardous waste** sites, the Love Canal neighborhood of Niagara Falls, New York, was largely evacuated of its residents in 1980 after testing revealed high levels of toxic **chemicals** and genetic damage.

Between 1942 and 1953, the Olin Corporation and the Hooker Chemical Corporation buried over 20,000 tons of deadly chemical waste in the canal, much of which is known to be capable of causing **cancer**, **birth defects**, miscarriages, and other health disorders. In 1953, Hooker deeded the land to the local board of education but did not clearly warn of the deadly nature of the chemicals buried there, even when homes and playgrounds were built in the area.

The seriousness of the situation became apparent in 1976, when years of unusually heavy rains raised the **water table** and flooded basements. As a result, houses began to reek of chemicals, and children and pets experienced chemical burns on their feet. Plants, trees, gardens, and even some pets died.

Soon neighborhood residents began to experience an extraordinarily high number of illnesses, including cancer, miscarriages, and deformities in infants. Alarmed by the situation, and frustrated by inaction on the part of local, state, and federal governments, a 27-year-old housewife named **Lois Gibbs** began to organize her neighbors. In 1978 they formed the Love Canal Homeowners Association and began a two-year fight to have the government relocate them into another area.

In August 1978 the New York State Health Commissioner recommended that pregnant women and young children be evacuated from the area, and subsequent studies documented the extraordinarily high rate of birth defects, miscarriages, genetic damage and other health affects. In 1979, for example, of 17 pregnant women in the neighborhood, only two gave birth to normal children. Four had miscarriages, two suffered stillbirths, and nine had babies with defects.

Eventually, the state of New York declared the area "a grave and imminent peril" to human health. Several hundred families were moved out of the area, and the others were advised to leave. The school was closed and barbed wire placed around it. In October 1980 President Jimmy Carter declared Love Canal a national disaster area.

In the end, some 60 families decided to remain in their homes, rejecting the government's offer to buy their properties. The cost for the cleanup of the area has been estimated at $250 million. Ironically, twelve years after the neighborhood was abandoned, the state of New York approved plans to allow families to move back to the area, and homes were allowed to be sold.

Love Canal is not the only hazardous waste site in the country that has become a threat to humans—only the best known. Indeed, the United States **Environmental Protection Agency** has estimated that up to 2,000 hazardous waste disposal sites in the United States may pose "significant risks to human health or the **environment**," and has called the toxic waste problem "one of the most serious problems the nation has ever faced." *See also* Contaminated soil; Hazardous waste site remediation; Hazardous waste siting; Leaching; Storage and transport of hazardous material; Stringfellow Acid Pits; Toxic substance

[*Lewis G. Regenstein*]

FURTHER READING

Brown, M. H. "Love Canal Revisited." *Amicus Journal* 10 (Summer 1988): 37-44.

———. "A Toxic Ghost Town: Ten Years Later, Scientists Are Still Assessing the Damage From Love Canal." *The Atlantic* 263 (July 1989): 23-26.

Gibbs, Lois. *Love Canal: My Story.* Albany: State University of New York Press, 1982.

Kadlecek, M. "Love Canal—10 Years Later." *Conservationist* 43 (November-December 1988): 40-43.

Regenstein, L. G. *How to Survive in America the Poisoned.* Washington, DC: Acropolis Books, 1982.

Lovelock, Sir James Ephraim (1919-)

British chemist

Sir James Lovelock is the framer of the **Gaia hypothesis** and developer of, among many other devices, the electron capture gas chromatographic detector. The highly selective nature and great sensitivity of this detector made possible not only the identification of **chlorofluorocarbons** in the **atmosphere**, but led to the measurement of many **pesticide**s, thus providing the raw data that underlie **Rachel Carson**'s *Silent Spring*.

Sir James Lovelock was born in Letchworth Garden City, earned his degree in chemistry from Manchester University, and took a Ph.D. in medicine from the London School of Hygiene and Tropical Medicine. His early studies in medical topics included work at Harvard University Medi-

Sir James E. Lovelock at his home in Cornwall with the device he invented to measure chlorofluorocarbons in the atmosphere.

cal School and Yale University. He spent three years as a professor of chemistry at Baylor University College of Medicine in Houston, Texas. It was from that position that his work with the Jet Propulsion Laboratory for NASA began.

The Gaia hypothesis, Sir James Lovelock's most significant contribution to date, grew out of the work of Sir James Lovelock and his colleagues at the lab. While attempting to design experiments for life detection on Mars, Sir James Lovelock, Dian Hitchcock, and later Lynn Margulis, posed the question, "If I were a Martian, how would I go about detecting life on Earth?" Looking in this way, the team soon realized that our atmosphere is a clear sign of life and it is totally impossible as a product of strictly chemical equilibria. One consequence of viewing life on this or another world as a single homeostatic organism is that energy will be found concentrated in certain locations rather than spread evenly, frequently, or even predominantly, as chemical energy. Thus, against all probability, the earth has an atmosphere containing about 21 percent free oxygen and has had about this much for millions of years. Sir James Lovelock bestowed on this superorganism comprising the whole of the **biosphere** the name "Gaia," one spelling of the name of the Greek earth-goddess, at the suggestion of a neighbor, William Golding, author of *Lord of the Flies*.

Sir James Lovelock's hypothesis was initially attacked as requiring the whole of life on earth to have purpose, and hence in some sense, common intelligence. Sir James Lovelock then developed a computer model called "Daisyworld" in which the presence of black and white daisies controlled the global temperature of the planet to a nearly constant value despite a major increase in the heat output of its sun. The concept that the biosphere keeps the **environment** constant has been attacked as sanctioning **environmental degradation**, and accusers took a cynical view of Sir James Lovelock's service to the British **petrochemical** industry. However, the hypothesis has served the environmental community well in suggesting many ideas for further studies, virtually all of which have given results predicted by the hypothesis.

Since 1964, Sir James Lovelock has operated a private consulting practice, first out of his home in Bowerchalke, near Salisbury, England, and later from a home near Launceston, Cornwall. He has authored over 200 scientific papers, covering research that ranged from techniques for freezing and successfully reviving hamsters to global systems science, which he has proposed to call geophysiology. Sir James Lovelock has been honored by his peers worldwide with numerous awards and honorary degrees, including Fellow of the Royal Society. He was also named a Commander of the British Empire by Queen Elizabeth in 1990. *See also* Chromatography; Environmental science; Homeostasis

[*James P. Lodge, Jr.*]

FURTHER READING

Joseph, L. E. *Gaia: The Growth of an Idea*. New York: St. Martin's Press, 1990.

Lovelock, J. *The Ages of Gaia, A Biography of Our Living Earth*. New York: Norton, 1988.

———. *Gaia, a New Look at Life on Earth*. Oxford: Oxford University Press, 1979.

———, and M. Allaby. *The Greening of Mars*. New York: St. Martin's Press, 1984.

Lovins, Amory B. (1947 -)

American physicist and energy conservationist

Amory Lovins is a physicist specializing in environmentally safe and sustainable energy sources. Born in 1947 in Washington, D.C., Lovins attended Harvard and Oxford universities. He has had a distinguished career as an educator and scientist. After resigning his academic post at Oxford in 1971, Lovins became the British representative of **Friends of the Earth**. He has been Regents' Lecturer at the University of California at Berkeley and has served as a consultant to the United Nations and other international and environmental organizations. Lovins is a leading critic of hard energy paths and an outspoken proponent of soft alternatives.

According to Lovins, an energy path is "hard" if the route from source to use is complex and circuitous requires extensive, expensive, and highly complex technological means and centralized power to produce, transmit, and store the energy produces toxic wastes or other unwanted side effects has hazardous social uses or implications and tends over time to harden even more, as other options are foreclosed or precluded as the populace becomes ever more dependent on energy from a particular source. A hard energy path can be seen in the case of **fossil fuel** energy. Once readily abundant

Amory Lovins.

and cheap, **petroleum** fueled the internal combustion engines and other machines on which humans have come to depend, but as that energy source becomes scarcer, oil companies must go farther afield to find it, potentially causing more environmental damage. As oil supplies run low and become more expensive, the temptation is to sustain the level of energy use by turning to another, and even harder, energy path—nuclear energy.

With its complex technology, its hazards, its long-lived and highly toxic wastes, its myriad military uses, and the possibility of its falling into the hands of dictators or terrorists, **nuclear power** is perhaps the hardest energy path. No less important are the social and political implications of this hard path: **radioactive waste**s will have to be stored somewhere nuclear power plants and **plutonium** transport routes must be guarded we must make trade-offs between the ease, convenience, and affluence of people presently living and the health and well-being of **future generations** and so on. A hard energy path is also one that, once taken, forecloses other options because, among other considerations, the initial investment and costs of entry are so high as to render the decision, once made, nearly irreversible. The longer term economic and social costs of taking the hard path, Lovins argues, are astronomically high and incalculable.

Soft energy paths, by contrast, are shorter, more direct, less complex, cheaper (at least over the long run), are inexhaustible and renewable, have few if any unwanted side-effects, have minimal military uses, and are compatible with decentralized local forms of community control and decision-making. The old windmill on the family farm offers an early example of such a soft energy source newer versions of the windmill, adapted to the generation of electricity, supply a more modern example. Other soft technologies include **solar energy**, **biomass** furnaces burning peat, dung or wood chips, and **methane** from the rotting of vegetable matter, manure, and other cheap, plentiful, and readily available organic material.

Much of Lovins's work has dealt with the technical and economic aspects, as well as the very different social impacts and implications, of these two competing energy paths. In 1989 Lovins and his wife Hunter won the Onassis Foundation's first Delphi Prize for their "essential contribution towards finding alternative solutions to energy problems." *See also* Biomass fuel; Composting; Energy and the environment; Energy path, hard vs. soft; Wind energy

[*Terence Ball*]

FURTHER READING

Louma, J. R. "Generate 'Nega-Watts' Says Fossil Fuel Foe." *New York Times* (2 April 1993): B5, B8.

Lovins, A. B. *Soft Energy Paths.* San Francisco: Friends of the Earth, 1977.

———, and L. H. Lovins. *Energy Unbound: Your Invitation to Energy Abundance.* San Francisco: Sierra Club Books, 1986.

Nash, H., ed. *The Energy Controversy: Amory B. Lovins and His Critics.* San Francisco: Friends of the Earth, 1979.

Lowest Achievable Emission Rate

Governments have explored a number of mechanisms for reducing the amount of pollutants released to the air by factories, **power plant**s, and other stationary sources. One mechanism is to require that a new or modified installation releases no more pollutants than determined by some law or regulation determining the lowest level of pollutants that can be maintained by existing technological means. These limits are known as the Lowest Achievable Emission Rate (LAER). The **Clean Air Act** of 1970 required, for example, that any new source in an area where minimum **air pollution** standards were not being met had to conform to the LAER standard. *See also* Air quality; Best Available Control Technology (BAT); Emission standards

Low-head hydropower

The term hydropower often suggests giant **dams** capable of transmitting tens of thousands of cubic feet of water per minute. Such dams are responsible for only about six percent of all the electricity produced in the United States today.

Hydropower facilities do not have to be massive buildings. At one time in the United States—and still, in many places around the world—electrical power is generated at low-head facilities, dams where the vertical drop through which water passes is a relatively short distance and/or where water flow is relatively modest. Indeed, the first commercial hydroelectric facility in the world consisted of a waterwheel on the Fox River in Appleton, Wisconsin. The facility, opened in 1882, generated enough electricity to operate lighting systems at two paper mills and one private residence.

Electrical demand grew rapidly in the United States during the early twentieth century, and hydropower supplied much of that demand. By the 1930s, nearly 40 percent of the electricity used in this country was produced by hydroelectric facilities. In some Northeastern states, hydropower accounted for 55-85 percent of the electricity produced.

A number of social, economic, political, and technical changes soon began to alter that pattern. Perhaps most important was the vastly increased efficiency of **power plants** operated by **fossil fuels**. The fraction of electrical power from such plants rose to more than 80 percent by the 1970s.

In addition, the United States began to move from a decentralized energy system in which many local energy companies met the needs of local communities, to large, centralized utilities that served many counties or states. In the 1920s, more than 6,500 electric power companies existed in the nation. As the government recognized power companies as monopolies, that number began to drop rapidly. Companies that owned a handful of low-head dams on one or more rivers could no longer compete with their giant cousins that operated huge plants powered by oil, **natural gas**, or **coal**.

As a result, hundreds of small hydroelectric plants around the nation were closed down. According to one study, over 770 low-head hydroelectric plants were abandoned between 1940 and 1980. In some states, the loss of low-head generating capacity was especially striking. Between 1950 and 1973, Consumers Power Company, one of Michigan's two electric utilities, sold off 44 hydroelectric plants.

Some experts believe that low-head hydropower should receive more attention today. Social and technical factors still prevent low-head power from seriously competing with other forms of energy on a national scale. But it may meet the needs of local communities in special circumstances. For example, a project has been undertaken to rehabilitate four low-head dams on the Boardman River in northwestern Michigan. The new facility is expected to increase the electrical energy available to nearby Traverse City and adjoining areas by about 20 percent.

Low-head hydropower appears to have a more promising future in less-developed parts of the world. For example, China has more than 76,000 low-head dams that generate a total of 9,500 **megawatt**s of power. An estimated 50 percent of rural townships depend on such plants to meet their electrical needs. Low-head hydropower is also of increasing importance in nations with fossil-fueled plants and growing electricity needs. Among the fastest growing of these are Peru, India, the Philippines, Costa Rica, Thailand, and Guatemala. *See also* Alternative energy sources; Electric utilities; Wave power

[*David E. Newton*]

FURTHER READING

Kakela, P., G, Chilson, and W. Patric. "Low-Head Hydropower for Local Use." *Environment* (January-February 1984): 31-38.

Lapedes, D. N., ed. *McGraw-Hill Encyclopedia of Energy.* New York: McGraw-Hill, 1976.

Low-input agriculture

See **Sustainable agriculture**

Low-level radioactive waste

Low-level radioactive waste consists of materials used in a variety of medical, industrial, commercial, and research applications. They tend to release a low level of radiation that dissipates in a relatively short period of time. Although care must be taken in handling such materials, they pose little health or environmental risk. Among the most common low level radioactive materials are rags, papers, protective clothing, and filters. Such materials are often stored temporarily in sealed containers at their use site. They are then disposed of by burial at one of three federal sites: Barnwell, South Carolina; Beatty, Nevada; or Hanford, Washington. *See also* Hanford Nuclear Reservation; High-level radioactive waste; Radioactive waste; Radioactivity

LUST

See **Leaking underground storage tank**

Lysimeter

A device for 1) measuring **percolation** and **leaching** losses from a column of **soil** under controlled conditions, or 2) for measuring gains (precipitation, **irrigation**, and condensation) and losses (**evapotranspiration**) by a column of soil. Many kinds of lysimeters exist: weighing lysimeters record the weight changes of a block of soil; non-weighing lysimeters enclose a block of soil so that losses or gains in the soil must occur through the surface; suction lysimeters are devises for removing water and dissolved **chemicals** from locations within the soil.

M

Mad cow disease

Mad cow disease, a relatively newly discovered malady, was first identified in Britain in the mid-1980s, after some farmers' cows began to tremble, stumble, and eventually die. It was later determined that a variation of this fatal neurological disease could be passed on to humans.

It is still not known to what extent the population of England and perhaps other countries is at risk from consumption of contaminated meat and animal by-products. The significance of the Mad cow problem lies in its as yet unquantifiable potential to not only damage Britain's $7.5 billion beef industry, but also to endanger millions of people with the threat of a fatal brain disease.

The disease, formally known as Bovine Spongiform Encephalopathy (BSE), was first detected in England in 1986, initially by farmers who noticed that their cows' behavior had changed. As the disease progressed, the cows began to shake and fall, became unable to walk or even stand, and eventually died or had to be killed. What stood out in the autopsies of infected animals were the holes and lesions in the brains, which have been described as resembling a sponge or Swiss cheese.

This was the first clue that BSE was a type of untreatable, fatal brain diseases called transmissible spongiform encephalopathies (TSEs). These include a very rare human malady known as Creutzfeldt-Jakob Disease (CJD), which normally strikes just one person in a million, usually the elderly and middle-aged.

As the epidemic of BSE progressed, the number of British cows so diagnosed began doubling almost yearly, growing from some 7,000 cases in 1989, to 14,000 in 1990, to over 25,000 in 1991. Concomitantly, the incidence of CJD in Britain was also increasing, almost doubling between 1990 and 1994, and reaching 55 cases by the latter year. In response to the problem and growing public concerns over it, the government's main strategy was to issue reassurances. But it did undertake two significant measures to try to safeguard public health. In July, 1988, it ostensibly banned meat and bone meal from cow feed, but failed to strictly enforce the action. In November, 1989, it passed a law supposedly removing from the public food supply those bovine body parts considered to be the most highly infective: the brain, spinal cord, spleen, tonsils, intestines, and thymus. A 1995 government report revealed that half of the time, the law was not being adhered to by slaughterhouses. Thus, livestock—and the public—continued to be potentially exposed to BSE.

As the disease continued to spread, so did public fears that it might be transmissible to humans, and could represent a serious threat to human health. But the British government, particularly the Ministry of Agriculture, Fisheries, and Food (MAFF), anxious to protect the multibillion dollar cattle industry, insisted that there was no danger to humans.

But all this changed on March 20, 1996. On that date, in an embarrassing reversal, the government officially admitted that there could be a link between BSE and the unusual incidence of CJD among young people. At the time, 15 people had been newly diagnosed with CJD. Shocking the nation and making headlines around the world, the Minister of Health Stephen Dorrell announced to the House of Commons that consumption of contaminated beef was "the most likely explanation" for the outbreak of a new variant CJD in ten people under the age of 42, including several teenagers. Four dairy farmers, including some with infected herds, had also contracted CJD, as had a Frenchman who died in January 1996.

British authorities estimated that some 163,000 British cows had contracted BSE. But other researchers, using the same database, put the figure at over 900,000, with 729,000 of them having been consumed by humans. In addition, an unknown number had been exported to Europe, traditionally a large market for British cattle and beef. Many non-meat products may also have been contaminated. Gelatin, made from ligaments, bones, skin, and hooves, is found in ice cream, lipstick, candy, and mayonnaise; keratin, made from hooves, horns, nails, and hair, occurs in shampoo; fat and tallow are used in candles, cosmetics, deodorants, soap, margarine, detergent, lubricants, and **pesticide**s; and protein meal is made into medical and pharmaceutical products, fertilizer, and food additives. Bone meal, made from dead cows, and used as fertilizer on roses and other flowers and plants, is handled and often inhaled by gardeners.

In reaction to the government announcement, sales of beef dropped by 70%; cattle markets were deserted; and even hamburger chains stopped serving British beef. Prime Minister Major called the temporary reaction "hysteria" and blamed the press and opposition politicians for fanning it.

On March 25, 1996, the European Union banned the import of British beef, which had since 1990 been excluded from the United States and 14 other countries. Shortly afterwards, in an attempt to have the European ban lifted, Britain announced that it would slaughter all of its 1.2 million cows over the age of 30 months (an age before which cows do not show symptoms of BSE), and began the arduous task of killing and incinerating 22,000 cows a week. The government later agreed to slaughter an additional 100,000 cows considered most at risk from BSE.

A prime suspect in causing BSE is a by-product derived from the rendering process, in which the unusable parts of slaughtered animals are boiled down or "cooked" at high temperatures to make animal feed and other products. One such product, called meat and bone meal (MBM), is made from the ground-up, cooked remains of slaughtered livestock—cows, sheep, chicken, and hogs—and made into nuggets of animal feed. Some of the cows and sheep used in this process were infected with fatal brain disease. (Although MBM was ostensibly banned as cattle feed in 1988, spinal cords continued to be used.)

It is theorized that sheep could have played a major role in initially infecting cows with BSE. For over 200 years, British sheep have been contracting scrapie, another TSE that results in progressive degeneration of the brain. Scrapie causes the sheep to tremble and itch, and to "scrape" or rub up against fences, walls, and trees to relieve the sensation. The disease, first diagnosed in British sheep in 1732, may have recently jumped the species barrier when cows ate animal feed that contained brain and spinal cord tissue from diseased sheep.

Scrapie and perhaps these other spongiform brain diseases are believed to be caused not by a virus (as originally thought) but rather by a form of infectious protein-like particles called prions, which are extremely tenacious, surviving long periods of high intensity cooking and heating. They are, in effect, a new form of contagion. The first real insights into the origins of these diseases were gathered in the 1950s by Dr. D. Carleton Gajdusek, who was awarded the 1976 Nobel Prize in Medicine for his work. His research on the fatal degenerative disease "kuru" among the cannibals of Papua, New Guinea, which resulted in the now-familiar brain lesions and cavities, revealed that the malady was caused by consuming or handling the brains of relatives who had just died.

In the United States, Department of Agriculture officials say that the risk of Mad cow and other related diseases is believed to be small, but cannot be ruled out. No Mad cow disease has been detected in the United States, and no cattle or processed beef is known to have been imported from Britain since 1989. However, several hundred mink in Idaho and Wisconsin have died from an ailment similar to BSE, and many of them ate meat from diseased "downer" cows, those that fall and cannot get up. Some experts believe that Mad cow disease can occur spontaneously, without apparent exposure to the disease, in one or two cows out of a million every year. This would amount to an estimated 150-250 cases annually among the United States cow population of some 150 million. Moreover, American feed processors render the carcasses of some 100,000 downer cows every year,

thus utilizing for animal feed cows that are possibly seriously and neurologically diseased.

In June 1997, the federal **Food and Drug Administration** (FDA) announced a partial ban on using in cattle feed remains from dead sheep, cattle, and other animals that chew their cud. But the ruling exempts from the ban some animal protein, as well as feed for poultry, pigs, and pets. In March of that year, a coalition of consumer groups, veterinarians, and federal meat inspectors had urged the FDA to include pork in the animal feed ban, citing evidence that pigs can develop a form of TSE, and that some may already have done so. The coalition had recommended that the United States adopt a ban similar to England's, where protein from all mammals is excluded from animal feed, and some criticized the FDA's action as "totally inadequate in protecting consumers and public health."

The outlook for mad cow disease is uncertain. Since tens of millions of people in Britain may have been exposed to the infectious agent that causes BSE, plus an unknown number in other countries, some observers fear that a latent epidemic of serious proportions could be in the offing. (There is also concern that some of the four million Americans alone now diagnosed with Alzheimer's disease may actually be suffering from CJD.) There are others who feel that a general removal of most infected cows and animal brain tissue from the food supply has prevented a human health disaster. But since the incubation period for CJD is thought to be 7-40 years, it will be some time before it is known how many people are already infected, and the extent of the problem becomes apparent.

[*Lewis G. Regenstein*]

FURTHER READING

Blakeslee, S. "Fear of Disease Prompts New Look at Rendering," *The New York Times*, 11 March 1997.

Lanchester, J. "A New Kind of Contagion," *The New Yorker*, 2 December 1996.

Rhodes, R. *Deadly Feasts*. New York: Simon & Schuster, 1997.

Madagascar

Described as a crown jewel among earth's **ecosystem**s, this 1,000-mi long (1,610-km) island-continent is a microcosm of **Third World** ecological problems. It abounds with unique **species** which are being threatened by the exploding human population. Many scientists consider Madagascar the world's foremost **conservation** priority. Since 1984 united efforts have sought to slow the island's deterioration, hopefully providing a model for treating other problem areas.

Madagascar is the world's fourth largest island, with a **rain forest** climate in the east, **deciduous forest** in the west, and thorn scrub in the south. Its Malagasy people are descended from African and Indonesian seafarers who arrived about 1,500 years ago. Most farm the land using ecologically devastating **slash and burn agriculture** which has turned Madagascar into the most severely eroded land on earth. It has been described as an island with the shape, color, and fertility of a brick; second growth forest does not do well.

Having been separated from Africa for 160 million years, this unique land was sufficiently isolated during the last 40 million years to become a laboratory of **evolution**. There are 160,000 unique species, mostly in the rapidly disappearing eastern rain forests. These include 65 percent of its plants, half of its birds, and all of its reptiles and mammals. Sixty percent of the earth's chameleons live here. Lemurs, displaced elsewhere by monkeys, have evolved into 26 species. Whereas Africa has only one species of baobab tree, Madagascar has six, and one is termite resistant. The thorn scrub abounds with potentially useful poisons evolved for plant defense. One species of periwinkle provides a substance effective in the treatment of childhood (lymphocytic) leukemia.

Humans have been responsible for the loss of 93 percent of tropical forest and two-thirds of rain forest. Four-fifths of the land is now barren as the result of **habitat** destruction set in motion by the exploding human population (3.2 percent growth per year). Although **nature** reserves date from 1927, few Malagasy have ever experienced their island's biological wonders; urbanites disdain the bush, and peasants are driven by hunger. If they can see Madagascar's rich ecosystems first hand, it may engender respect which, in turn, may encourage understanding and protection.

The people are awakening to their loss and the impact this may have on all Madagascar's inhabitants. Pride in their island's unique **biodiversity** is growing. The **World Bank** has provided $90 million to develop and implement a 15-year Environmental Action Plan. One private preserve in the south is doing well and many other possibilities exist for the development of **ecotourism**. If **population growth** can be controlled, and high yield farming replaces slash and burn agriculture, there is yet hope for preserving the diversity and uniqueness of Madagascar. *See also* Deforestation; Erosion; Tropical rain forest

[*Nathan H. Meleen*]

FURTHER READING

Attenborough, D. *Bridge to the Past: Animals and People of Madagascar.* New York: Harper, 1962.

Harcourt, C. and J. Thornback. *Lemurs of Madagascar and the Comoros: The IUCN Red Data Book.* Gland, Switzerland: IUCN, 1990.

Jenkins, M. D. *Madagascar: An Environmental Profile.* Gland, Switzerland: IUCN, 1987.

Jolly, A. "Madagascar: A World Apart." *National Geographic* 171 (February 1987): 148-83.

Magnetic separation

An on-going problem of environmental significance is **solid waste** disposal. As the land needed to simply throw out solid wastes becomes less available, **recycling** becomes a greater priority in **waste management** programs. One step in recycling is the magnetic separation of ferrous (iron-containing) materials. In a typical recycling process, wastes are first shredded into small pieces and then separated into organic and inorganic fractions. The inorganic fraction is then passed through a magnetic separator where ferrous materials are extracted. These materials can then be purified and reused as scrap iron. *See also* Iron minerals; Resource recovery

Malaria

Malaria is a disease that affects hundreds of millions of people worldwide. In the developing world malaria contributes to a high infant mortality rate and a heavy loss of work time. Malaria is caused by the single-celled protozoan parasite, *Plasmodium*. The disease follows two main courses: tertian (three day) malaria and quartan (four day) malaria. *Plasmodium vivax* causes benign tertian malaria with a low mortality (5 percent), while *Plasmodium falciparum* causes malignant tertian malaria with a high mortality (25 percent) due to interference with the blood supply to the brain (cerebral malaria). Quartan malaria is rarely fatal.

Plasmodium is transmitted from one human host to another by female mosquitoes of the genus *Anopheles*. Thousands of **parasites** in the salivary glands of the mosquito are injected into the human host when the mosquito takes blood. The parasites (in the sporozoite stage) are carried to the host's liver where they undergo massive multiplication into the next stage (cryptozoites). The parasites are then released into the blood stream, where they invade red blood cells and undergo additional division. This division ruptures the red blood cells and releases the next stage (the merozoites), which invade and destroy other red blood cells. This red blood cell destruction phase is intense but short-lived. The merozoites finally develop into the next stage (gametocytes) which are ingested by the biting mosquito.

The pattern of chills and fever characteristic of malaria is caused by the massive destruction of the red blood cells by the merozoites and the accompanying release of parasitic waste products. The attacks subside as the immune response of the human host slows the further development of the parasites in the blood. People who are repeatedly infected gradually develop a limited immunity. Relapses of malaria long after the original infection can occur from parasites that have remained in the liver, since treatment with drugs kills only the parasites in the blood cells and not in the liver. Malaria can be prevented or cured by a wide variety of drugs (quinine, chloroquine, paludrine, proguanil, or pyrimethamine). However, resistant strains of the common species of *Plasmodium* mean that some prophylactic drugs (chloroquine and pyrimethamine) are no longer totally effective.

Malaria is controlled either by preventing contact between humans and mosquitoes or by eliminating the mosquito vector. Outdoors, individuals may protect themselves from mosquito bites by wearing protective clothing, applying mosquito repellents to the skin, or by burning mosquito coils that produce smoke containing insecticidal pyrethrins. Inside houses, mosquito-proof screens and nets keep the vectors out, while insecticides (**DDT**) applied inside the house kill those that enter. The aquatic stages of the mosquito can be destroyed by eliminating temporary breeding pools, by spraying ponds with synthetic insecticides, or by applying a layer of oil to the surface waters. Biological control includes introducing fish (*Gambusia*) that feed on mosquito larvae into small ponds. Organized campaigns to eradicate malaria are usually successful, but the disease is sure to return unless the measures are vigilantly maintained. *See also* Epidemiology; Pesticide

[*Neil Cumberlidge*]

FURTHER READING

Bullock, W. L. *People, Parasites, and Pestilence: An Introduction to the Natural History of Infectious Disease.* Minneapolis: Burgess Publishing Company, 1982.

Knell, A. J., ed. *Malaria: A Publication of the Tropical Programme of the Wellcome Trust.* New York: Oxford University Press, 1991.

Markell, E. K., M. Voge, and D. T. John. *Medical Parasitology.* 7th ed. Philadelphia: Saunders, 1992.

Phillips, R. S. *Malaria.* Institute of Biology's Studies in Biology, No. 152. London: E. Arnold, 1983.

Malignant tumors

See **Cancer**

Malthus, Thomas Robert (1766-1834)

English economist

Malthus' name has come to represent a pessimistic philosophy labeled *neo-Malthusian* that sees population explosion as one of the world's most serious problems. Malthus was the first to put in writing a consistent theory of population. His *Essay on the Principle of Population* first appeared in 1798, with numerous later editions.

Thomas Robert Malthus was born in Surrey on February 17, 1766. He graduated from Cambridge University and served as a clergyman until 1805 when he became a professor of history and political economy in the college of the East India Company. He held this post until his death. Malthus' population theory is based on the fact that **population growth** occurs by multiplication, similar to compound interest (2, 4, 8, 16, 32), while the food supply increases arithmetically (2, 4, 6, 8, 10). Because of this, Malthus believed that population growth must ultimately overwhelm the food supply unless or until checked by rising death rates from famine, pestilence, disease, or war. Though later tempering his harshest conclusions, Malthus' main emphasis was always on the simple relationships among life, death, and the means of subsistence.

Malthus' theory describes what is now called biotic potential, and his work profoundly influenced both **Charles Darwin** and Alfred Wallace in their theories of **evolution**. Darwin wrote: "In October 1838...I happened to read for amusement 'Malthus on Population,' and being well prepared to appreciate the struggle for existence...it at once

struck me that under these circumstances favourable variations would tend to be preserved, and unfavourable ones to be destroyed. The result of this would be the formation of new **species**. Here then I had at last got a theory by which to work."

Malthus' motivation came from his opposition to ideas expressed by such eighteenth century philosophers as the Marquis de Condorcet. He believed that the law of population presented an insurmountable barrier to the idea that science and human reason could create a world of plenty and a happier social system. His contemporary relevance comes from what is often described by the phrase, the Malthusian dilemma, which essentially states that aid to poor or starving people will only result in increased numbers, leading to greater poverty and death. By the term *neo-Malthusian*, Malthus' name is now firmly linked to proponents of population control by all feasible means. Malthus himself would have opposed this, since he viewed birth control devices as a form of vice.

Few scientists seem to have actually read Malthus. His views are much less harsh and far more optimistic than commonly thought. Believing that class differences would always exist, he yet expressed the hope that the percentages "may be so altered as greatly to improve the harmony and beauty of the whole." And, referring to the formidable obstacles represented by his ideas, he challenged us to not "give up the improvement of human society in despair. The partial good which seems to be attainable is worthy of all our exertions...." *See also* Third World; Zero population growth

[*Nathan H. Meleen*]

FURTHER READING

McCleary, G. F. *The Malthusian Population Theory.* London: Faber & Faber, 1953.

Sauvy, A. *Fertility and Survival: Population Problems from Malthus to Mao-Tsetung.* New York: Criterion Books, 1961.

Young, L. B. *Population in Perspective.* New York: Oxford University Press, 1968.

Man and the Biosphere Program

The Man and the Biosphere (MAB) program is a global system of **biosphere reserve**s begun in 1986 and organized by the United Nations Educational, Social, and Cultural Organization (UNESCO). MAB reserves are designed to conserve natural **ecosystem**s and **biodiversity** and to incorporate the sustainable use of natural ecosystems by humans in their operation. The intention is that local human needs will be met in ways compatible with resource **conservation**. Furthermore, if local people benefit from tourism and the harvesting of surplus **wildlife**, they will be more supportive of programs to preserve **wilderness** and protect wildlife.

MAB reserves differ from traditional reserves in a number of ways. Instead of a single boundary separating nature inside from people outside, MAB reserves are zoned into concentric rings consisting of a core area, a buffer zone, and a transition zone. The core area is strictly managed for wildlife and all human activities are prohibited, except for restricted scientific activity such as ecosystem monitoring. Surrounding the core area is the buffer zone, where non-destructive forms of research, education and tourism are permitted, as well as some human settlements. Sustainable light resource extraction such as rubber tapping, collection of nuts, or selective logging is permitted in this area. Pre-existing settlements of **indigenous peoples** are also allowed. The transition zone is the outermost area, and here increased human settlements, traditional land use by native peoples, experimental research involving ecosystem manipulations, major restoration efforts, and tourism are allowed.

The MAB reserves have been chosen to represent the world's major types of regional ecosystems. Ecologists have identified some fourteen types of **biome**s and 193 types of ecosystems around the world and about two-thirds of these ecosystem types are represented so far in the 276 biosphere reserves now established in 72 countries. MAB reserves are not necessarily pristine wilderness. Many include ecosystems that have been modified or exploited by humans, such as **rangelands**, subsistence farmlands, or areas used for hunting and fishing. The concept of biosphere reserves has also been extended to include coastal and marine ecosystems, although in this case the use of core, buffer, and transition areas is inappropriate.

The establishment of a global network of biosphere reserves still faces a number of problems. Many of the MAB reserves are located in debt-burdened developing nations, because many of these countries lie in the biologically rich tropical regions. Such countries often cannot afford to set aside large tracts of land, and they desperately need the short-term cash promised by the immediate exploitation of their lands. One response to this problem is the **debt for nature swap**s in which a conservation organization buys the debt of a nation at a discount rate from banks in exchange for that nation's commitment to establish and protect a nature reserve.

Many reserves are effectively small, isolated islands of natural ecosystems surrounded entirely by developed land. The protected organisms in such islands are liable to suffer genetic **erosion**, and many have argued that a single large reserve would suffer less genetic erosion than several smaller reserves which cumulatively protect the same amount of land. It has also been suggested that reserves sited as close to each other as possible and corridors that allow movement between them, would increase the **habitat** and **gene pool** available to most **species**. *See also* Ecotourism; National wildlife refuge; Restoration ecology; Sustainable development; Wildlife management; Wildlife refuge

[*Neil Cumberlidge*]

FURTHER READING

Batisse, M. "Developing and Focusing the Biosphere Reserve Concept. *Nature and Resources* 22 (1986): 1-10.

Gregg, W. P., and S. L. Krugman, eds. *Proceedings of the Symposium on Biosphere Reserves*. Atlanta, GA: U. S. National Park Service, 1989.

Office of Technology Assessment. *Technologies to Maintain Biological Diversity*. Philadelphia: Lippincott, 1988.

Manatees

A relative of the elephant, manatees are totally aquatic, herbivorous mammals of the family Trichechidae. This group arose 15 to 20 million years ago during the Miocene period, a time which also favored the development of a tremendous diversity of aquatic plants along the coast of South America. Manatees are adapted to both marine and freshwater **habitat**s and are divided into three distinct **species**: the Amazonian manatee (*Trichechus inunguis*), restricted to the freshwaters of the Amazon River; the West African manatee (*Trichechus senegalensis*), found in the coastal waters from Senegal to Angola; and the West Indian manatee (*Trichechus manatus*), ranging from the northern South American coast through the Caribbean to the southeastern coastal waters of the United States. Two other species, the dugong (*Dugong dugon*) and Steller's sea cow (*Hydrodamalis gigas*), along with the manatees, make up the order Sirenia. Steller's sea cow is now extinct, having been exterminated by man in the mid-1700s for food.

Manatees are unique among aquatic mammals because of their herbivorous diet. Manatees are non-ruminants, therefore, unlike cows and sheep, they do not have a chambered stomach. They do have, however, extremely long intestines (up to 150 feet/46 m) that contain a paired blind sac where bacterial digestion of cellulose takes place. Other unique traits of the manatee include horizontal replacement of molar teeth and the presence of only six cervical, or neck, vertebrae, instead of seven as in all other mammals. The intestinal sac and tooth replacement are adaptations designed to counteract the defenses evolved by the plants that the manatees eat. Several plant species contain tannins, oxalates, and nitrates, which are toxic, but which may be detoxified in the manatee's intestine. Other plant species contain silica spicules, which, due to their abrasiveness, wear down the manatee's teeth, necessitating the need for tooth replacement. The life span of manatees is long, greater than 30 years, but their reproductive rate is low, with females giving birth to one calf every two years. Because of this the potential for increasing the population is low, thus leaving the population vulnerable to environmental problems.

Competition for food is not a problem. In contrast to terrestrial herbivores, which have a complex division of food resources and competition for the high-energy level land plants, manatees have limited competition from **sea turtles**. This is minimized by different feeding strategies employed within the two groups. Sea turtles eat blades of seagrasses at greater depths than manatees feed, and manatees tend to eat not only the blades, but also the rhizomes of these plants, which contain more energy for the warm-blooded mammals.

Because manatees are docile creatures and a source of food, they have been exploited by man to the point of **extinction**. Also because manatees are slow moving, a more recent threat is taking its toll on these shallow-swimming animals. Power boat propellers have struck hundreds of manatees in recent years. This has resulted in death, permanent injury, or scarring to others. **Conservation** efforts and public awareness have helped reduce some of these problems

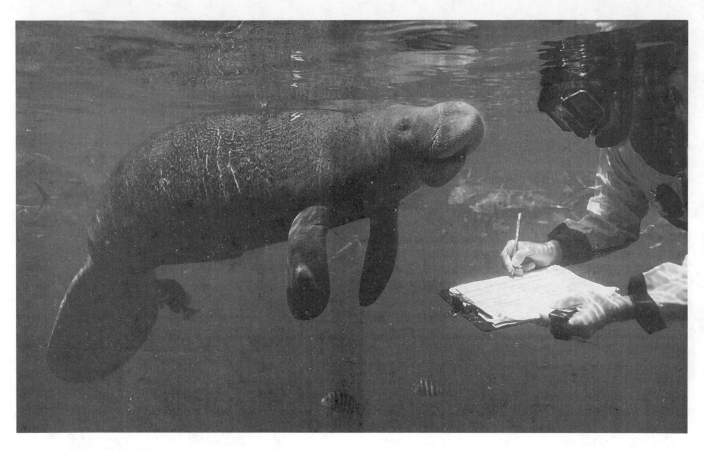

Manatee with a researcher, Homosossa Springs, Florida.

but much more will have to be done to prevent the extirpation of the manatees, the animals thought to have inspired the legend of the mermaid.

[*Eugene C. Beckham*]

FURTHER READING

O'Shea, T. J., et al. "An Analysis of Manatee Mortality Patterns in Florida, 1976-1981." *Journal of Wildlife Management* 49 (1985): 1-11.

Ridgway, S. H., and R. Harrison, eds. *Handbook of Marine Mammals.* Vol. 3, *The Sirenians and Baleen Whales.* London: Academic Press, 1985.

Mangrove swamp

Mangrove swamps or forests are the tropical equivalent of temperate salt marshes. They grow in protected coastal embayments in tropical and subtropical areas around the world, and some scientists estimate that 60-75 percent of all tropical shores are populated by mangroves.

The term "mangrove" refers to individual trees or shrubs that are angiosperms (flowering plants) and belong to more than 80 **species** within 12 genera and five families. Though unrelated taxonomically, they share some common characteristics. Mangroves only grow in areas with minimal wave action, high **salinity**, and low **soil** oxygen. All of the trees have shallow roots, form pure stands, and have adapted to the harsh **environment** in which they grow. The man-

grove swamp or forest community as a whole is called a mangal.

Mangroves typically grow in a sequence of zones from seaward to landward. This zonation is most highly pronounced in the Indo-Pacific regions, where 30-40 species of mangroves grow. Starting from the shore-line and moving inland, the sequence of genera there is *Avicennia* followed by *Rhizophora, Bruguiera,* and finally *Ceriops.* In the Caribbean, including Florida, only three species of trees normally grow: red mangroves (*Rhizophora mangle*) represent the pioneer species growing on the water's edge, black mangroves (*Avicennia germinans*) are next, and white mangroves (*Laguncularia racemosa*) grow mostly inland. In addition, buttonwood (*Conocarpus erectus*) often grows between the white mangroves and the terrestrial vegetation.

Mangrove trees have made special **adaptation**s to live in this environment. Red mangroves form stilt-like prop roots that allow them to grow at the shoreline in water up to several feet deep. Like cacti, they have thick succulent leaves which store water and help prevent loss of moisture. They also produce seeds which germinate directly on the tree, then drop into the water, growing into a long, thin seedling known as a "sea pencil." These seedlings are denser at one end and thus float with the heavier hydrophilic (water-loving) end down. When the seedlings reach shore, they take root and grow. One acre of red mangroves can produce three tons of seeds per year, and the seeds can survive floating on the ocean for more than 12 months. Black mangroves produce straw-

Mangrove creek in the Everglades National Park.

like roots called pneumatophores which protrude out of the **sediment**, thus enabling them to take oxygen out of the air instead of the **anaerobic** sediments. Both white and black mangroves have salt glands at the base of their leaves which help in the regulation of osmotic pressure.

Mangrove swamps are important to humans for several reasons. They provide water-resistant wood used in construction, charcoal, medicines, and dyes. The mass of prop roots at the shoreline also provides an important habitat for a rich assortment of organisms, such as snails, barnacles, oysters, crabs, periwinkles, jellyfish, tunicates, and many species of fish. One group of these fish, called mud skippers (*Periophthalmus*), have large bulging eyes, seem to skip over the mud, and crawl up on the prop roots to catch insects and crabs. Birds such as egrets and herons feed in these productive waters and nest in the tree branches. Prop roots tend to trap sediment and can thus form new land with young mangroves. Scientists reported a growth rate of 656 feet (200 m) per year in one area near Java. These coastal forests can be helpful buffer zones to strong storms.

Despite their importance, mangrove swamps are fragile **ecosystem**s whose ecological importance is commonly unrecognized. They are being adversely affected worldwide by increased **pollution**, use of **herbicide**s, filling, **dredging**, channelizing, and logging. *See also* Marine pollution; Wetlands

[John Korstad]

FURTHER READING

Castro, P., and M.E. Huber. *Marine Biology*. St. Louis: Mosby, 1992.

Lugo, A.E., and S.C. Snedaker. "The Ecology of Mangroves." *Annual Review of Ecology and Systematics* 5 (1974): 39-64.

Nybakken, J.W. *Marine Biology: An Ecological Approach*. 2d ed. New York: Harper & Row, 1988.

Rützler, K., and C. Feller. "Mangrove Swamp Communities." *Oceanus* 30 (1988): 16-24.

Smith, R.E. *Ecology and Field Biology*. 4th ed. New York: Harper & Row, 1990.

Tomlinson, P.B. *The Botany of Mangroves*. Cambridge: Cambridge University Press, 1986.

Manure

See **Animal waste**

Manville Corporation

See **Asbestos**

Marasmus

A severe deficiency of all **nutrient**s, categorized along with other protein energy malnutrition disorders. Marasmus, which means "to waste" can occur at any age but is most commonly found in neonates (children under one year old). Starvation resulting from marasmus is a result of protein and carbohydrate deficiencies. In developing countries and impoverished populations, early weaning from breast feeding and over dilution of commercial formulas places neonates at high risk for getting marasmus.

Because of the deficiency in intake of all dietary nutrients, metabolic processes—especially liver functions—are preserved, while growth is severely retarded. Caloric intake is too low to support metabolic activity such as protein synthesis or storage of fat. If the condition is prolonged, muscle tissue wasting will result. Fat wasting and anemia are common and severe. Severe vitamin A deficiency commonly results in blindness, although if caught early, this process can be reversed. Death will occur in 40 percent of children left untreated.

Marine ecology and biodiversity

Understanding the nature of ocean life and the patterns of its diversity represents a difficult challenge. Not only are there technical difficulties involved with studying life under water (high pressure, need for oxygen tanks, lack of light), there is an urgency to develop a greater understanding of marine life as links between ocean processes and the larger patterns of terrestrial life become more well known. Our current understanding of oceanic life is based on three principal concepts: size, complexity, and spatial distribution.

Our knowledge about the size of the ocean's domain is grounded in three great discoveries of the past few centuries. When Magellan first circumnavigated the earth he inadvertently found that the oceans were a continuous water body, rather than a series of discrete bodies of water. Some time later, the encompassing nature of the world oceans was further clarified by the discovery that the oceans were a chemically uniform aqueous system. All of the principal ions (sodium, chloride, and sulfate) exist in the same concentrations. The third discovery, still underway, is that the ocean is composed of comparatively immense ecological systems. Thus in most ways the oceans are a unified system which is the first defining characteristic of the marine **environment**.

There is, however, a dichotomy between the integral nature of the ocean and the external forces played upon it. Mechanical, thermodynamic, chemical, and biological forces create variation through such things as differential heating, Coriolis force, wind, dissolved gases, salinity differences, and evaporation. The actions in turn set controls in motion which move toward physical equilibrium through feedback mechanisms. Those physical changes then interact with biological systems in nonlinear ways, that is, out of synchronization with the external stimuli and become quite difficult to predict. Thus, we have the second broad characteristic of the oceans, complexity.

The third major aspect of ocean life is that life itself is sparse in terms of the overall volume of the oceans, but locally productive systems can create immense populations and/or

sites with exceptionally high species diversity. Life is arranged in active layers dictated by nutrients and light in the horizontal planes, and by vertical current (downwelling and upwelling) in the vertical planes. Life decreases through the depth zones from the epipelagic zone in the initial 328 ft (100 m) of the water column to the bottom layers of water, and then jumps again at the benthic layer at the water-substrate interface. Life also decreases from the littoral zones along the world's shorelines to the open ocean, interrupted by certain areas with special life supporting systems, like floating sargasso weed beds.

In the past twenty years the focus of **conservation** has shifted to include not only individual species or habitats, but to a phenomenon called biological diversity, or **biodiversity** for short. Biological diversity encompasses from three to four levels. Genetic diversity is the level of genotypic differences within all the individuals that constitute a population of organisms; species diversity refers to the number of species in an area; and community diversity to the number of different community types in a landscape. The highest level, landscape diversity has not frequently been applied in aqueous environments and will not be discussed here.

Commonly, species diversity is interpreted as biological diversity, and since few marine groups, except marine mammals, have had very much genetic work done, and community functions are only well known from a few systems, it is the taxonomic interpretation of diversity that is most commonly discussed (e.g., species or higher taxonomic levels such as families and classes, orders and phyla). Of all the species that we know, roughly 16% are from the seas. General diversity patterns in the sea are similar to those on land, there are more smaller than larger species, and there are more tropical species than temperate or polar species. There are centers of diversity for specific taxa, and the structure of communities and **ecosystem**s is based on particular patterns of energy availability. For example, **estuary** systems are productive due to importation of **nitrogen** from the land, **coral reef**s are also productive, but use scarce nutrients efficiently by specially adapted filter feeding mechanisms. Abyssal communities, on the other hand, depend on their entire energy supply from detritus fall from upper levels in the ocean. Perhaps the most specifically adapted of all life forms are the hydrothermal vent communities that employ chemosynthesis rather than **photosynthesis** for primary production. Water temperature, salinity, and pressure create differing ecosystems in ways that are distinctly different from terrestrial systems. In addition, the boundaries between systems may be dynamic, and are certainly more difficult to detect than on land.

Most marine biodiversity occurs at higher taxonomic levels, while the land holds more species, most of them are arthropods. Most of the phyla (32 of 33) that we now know are either marine, or both marine and non-marine, while only one is exclusively non-marine. Thus most of the major life plans exist in the sea.

We are now learning that the number of species in the ocean is probably underestimated as we discover more cryptic species, very similar organisms that are actually distinct, many of which have been discovered on the deep ocean floor. This is one of the important diversity issues in the marine environment. Originally, the depths were cast as biological deserts, however, that view may have been promoted by a lack of samples, the small size of many benthic invertebrates, and the low density of benthic populations in the deep sea beds.

Improved sampling since the 1960s changed that view to one of the ocean floor as a highly species diverse environment. The deep sea is characterized by a few individuals in each of many species; rarity dominates. Whereas, in shallow water benthic environments, there are large, dense populations dominated by a few species. At least three theoretical explanations for this pattern have been made. The stability-time hypothesis suggests that ocean bottoms have been very stable environments over long periods of time. This condition causes very finely tuned adaptations to narrow niches, and results in many closely related species. The disturbance or "cropper" hypothesis suggests that intense predation of limited food sources prevents populations from reaching high levels and because the food source is dominated by detrital rain, generalist feeders abound and compete for the same food, which results in only small differences between species. A third hypothesis is that the area of the deep sea bed is so large it supports many species, following from generalizations made by the species area relationship concept used in island biogeography theory. The picture of species number and relative rarity is still not clearly understood.

In general, some aspects of marine biology are well studied. Rocky intertidal life has been the subject of major ecological research and yielded important theoretical advances. Similarly, coral reefs are the subject of many studies of life history adaptation and evolutionary biology and ecology. Physiology and morphology research has used many marine animals as examples of organisms' functions under extreme conditions. This new found knowledge is timely. Up until now we have considered the oceans as an inexhaustible source of food and a sink for our wastes, yet we now realize they are neither. Relative to the land, the sea is in good ecological condition, but to prevent major ecological problems in the marine environment we need to increase human knowledge rapidly and manage our behavior toward the oceans very conservatively, which is a difficult task under the conditions where the ocean is treated as a common resource.

[*David Duffus*]

Marine Mammals Protection Act (MMPA) (1972)

The Marine Mammals Protection Act (MMPA) was initially passed by Congress in 1972 and is the most comprehensive federal law aimed at the protection of marine mammals. The MMPA prohibits the taking (i.e., harassing, hunting, capturing, or killing, or attempting to harass, hunt, capture, or kill) on the high seas of any marine mammal by persons or vessels subject to the jurisdiction of the United States. It also prohibits the taking of marine mammals in waters or on land subject to United States jurisdiction and the importation into

the United States of marine mammals, parts thereof, or products made from such animals. The MMPA provides that civil and criminal penalties apply to illegal takings.

The MMPA specifically charges the National Marine Fisheries Service (NMFS) with responsibility for the protection and conservation of marine mammals. The NMFS is given statutory authority to grant or deny permits to take **whales**, **dolphins**, and other mammals from the oceans.

The original legislation established "a moratorium on the taking of marine mammals and marine mammal products...during which time no permit may be issued for the taking of any marine mammal and no marine mammal may be imported into the United States." Four types of exceptions allowed for limited numbers of marine mammals to be taken: (1) animals taken for scientific review and public display, after a specified review process; (2) marine mammals taken incidentally to commercial fishing operations prior to October 21, 1974; (3) animals taken by Native Americans and Inuit Eskimos for subsistence or for the production of traditional crafts or tools; and (4) animals taken under a temporary exemption granted to persons who could demonstrate economic hardship as a result of MMPA (this exemption was to last for no more than a year and was to be eliminated in 1974). MMPA also sought specifically to reduce the number of marine mammals killed in purse-seine or **drift net** operations by the commercial tuna industry.

The language used in the legislation is particularly notable in that it makes clear that the MMPA is intended to protect marine mammals and their supporting **ecosystem**, rather than to maintain or increase commercial harvests:

> [T]he primary objective in management should be to maintain the health and stability of the marine ecosystem. Whenever consistent with this primary objective, it should be the goal to obtain an optimum sustainable population keeping in mind the optimum carrying capacity of the **habitat**.

All regulations governing the taking of marine mammals must take these considerations into account. Permits require a full public hearing process with the opportunity for judicial review for both the applicant and any person opposed to the permit. No permits may be issued for the taking or importation of a pregnant or nursing female, for taking in an inhumane manner, or for taking animals on the **endangered species** list.

Subsidiary legislation and several court decisions have modified, upheld, and extended the original MMPA: *Globe Fur Dyeing Corporation v. United States* upheld the constitutionality of the statutory prohibition of the killing of marine mammals less than eight months of age or while still nursing.

In *Committee for Humane Legislation v. Richardson*, the District of Columbia Court of Appeals ruled that the NMFS had violated MMPA by permitting tuna fishermen to use the purse-seine or drift net method for catching yellowfin tuna, which resulted in the drowning of hundreds of thousands of porpoises.

Under the influence of the Reagan Administration, MMPA was amended in 1981 specifically to allow this type of fishing, provided that the fishermen employed "the best marine mammal safety techniques and equipment that are economically and technologically practicable." The Secretaries of Commerce and the Interior were empowered to authorize the taking of small numbers of marine mammals, provided that the species or population stocks of the animals involved were not already depleted and that either Secretary found that the total of such taking would have a negligible impact.

The 1984 reauthorization of MMPA continued the tuna industry's general permit to kill incidentally up to 20,500 porpoises per year, but provided special protection for two threatened species. The new legislation also required that yellowfin tuna could only be imported from countries that have rules at least as protective of porpoises as those of the United States.

In *Jones v. Gordon* (1985), a federal district court in Alaska ruled in effect that the **National Environmental Policy Act** provided regulations which were applicable to the MMPA permitting procedure. Significantly, this decision made an **environmental impact statement** mandatory prior to the granting of a permit.

Presumably owing to the educational, organizing, and lobbying efforts of environmental groups and the resulting public outcry, the MMPA was amended in 1988 to provide a three-year suspension of the "incidental take" permits, so that more ecologically responsible standards could be developed. Subsequently, Congress decided to prohibit the drift netting method as of the 1990 season.

[*Lawrence J. Biskowski*]

FURTHER READING

Dolgin, E. L., and T. G. P. Guilbert, eds. *Federal Environmental Law*. St. Paul, MN: West Publishing Co., 1974.

Freedman, W. *Federal Statutes on Environmental Protection*. New York: Quorum Books, 1987.

Hofman, J. "The Marine Mammals Protection Act: A First of Its Kind Anywhere." *Oceanus* 32 (Spring 1989): 7-16.

Marine pollution

Marine pollution is a major threat to any organism living in or depending upon the ocean. Human impact on coastal and open ocean **habitat**s comes in many forms: **nutrient** loading from agricultural **runoff** and sewage discharges, toxic chemical inputs from industry and agriculture, **petroleum** spills, and inert **solid waste**s. While there has been some recognition of the destruction of marine systems from **pollution**, regulations are often weak or are not enforced. Recent efforts have lead to slow recovery of some coastal areas, but many of the detrimental practices continue and some systems may never recover.

Nutrient loading is perhaps the most well-studied form of pollution, and its biological consequences have been observed and documented. **Algal bloom**s, including **red tide**s, have been attributed to elevated nutrient levels in coastal systems. These blooms, through their **respiration** and **decomposition**, can deplete the levels of **dissolved oxygen** in the waters to almost zero, killing **zooplankton**, fish, and shellfish. These nutrients often come from runoff of agricultural **fertilizer**s, the use of which has increased sevenfold since 1950. It is estimated that approximately 25 percent of the 46.8 million metric tons of fertilizer used in the United States annually enters rivers and coastal waters.

Another source of nutrients is the discharge of sewage. The United States and England are the only countries that dump **sludge** into the oceans, averaging 17 million metric tons annually between them. Throughout the world, however, raw sewage is released into rivers and coastal habitats by many countries, leading to algal blooms and increased **biochemical oxygen demand**. BOD, the rate at which oxygen disappears from a sample of water, increases dramatically with loading of organic material such as sewage, and results in the lowering of dissolved oxygen levels. The wastes of domesticated animals may also have a major impact in some systems. A single cow produces approximately 31 lb (14 kg) of waste per day, the equivalent of ten people. When discharged into rivers or coastal waters, wastes produced by large herds or feedlots may have substantial effects.

Boston Harbor is considered to be one of the most polluted harbors in the United States. Since Europeans settled in the Boston area, domestic wastes have been discharged directly into the harbor. As Boston's population grew, so did the dumping, a problem exacerbated by the growth of industry in the late nineteenth and early twentieth centuries. Fish and shellfish in the harbor contain toxic levels of **polychlorinated biphenyl (PCB)** and heavy metals, BOD levels are astronomical, and dissolved oxygen levels are low. In 1984, the Massachusetts Water Resources Authority (MWRA) was formed and has managed to improve **water quality** of the harbor slightly. Recommendations of the MWRA have been hard to enact, however. **Sewage treatment** modifications have been met with **Environmental Protection Agency (EPA)** and State objections, shelving the project while courts decide the fate of environmental quality in Boston Harbor.

Toxic substances are introduced into the marine environment from various sources, some of which may be hundreds of kilometers away. Heavy metals, **pesticide**s, and **acid rain** threaten not only coastal and estuarine systems, but also life in the open ocean. Heavy metals occur in many forms, some of which are soluble in seawater. These soluble compounds may not be the forms in which they were originally released into the environment, often making their sources difficult to determine. Many heavy metals are released in industrial **effluent**s, especially from chemical plants, **smelter**s, and mining runoff. These compounds may affect humans directly through contact, or indirectly, from the consumption of fish and shellfish, where metals often accumulate in tissues.

Between the late 1930s and the mid-1950s, a Japanese chemical company manufacturing acetaldehyde discharged **mercury** into Minamata Bay, where it formed a soluble compound that accumulated in fish. It was not until 50 people died of **Minamata disease** and hundreds were left with debilitating nervous disorders from eating poisoned fish that environmental studies were initiated. Finally, in 1969, the plant was closed. Other metals, such as zinc, **cadmium**, **copper**, and silver, are commonly discharged into marine systems by industry. Not only are these metals toxic by themselves, but synergistic effects compound their toxicity.

Acid precipitation is rain, snow, or fog that has a lower **pH** than normal and is caused by inputs of nitric and sulfuric acid into the **atmosphere** from manufacturing and the burning of **fossil fuels**, as in **automobile**s. These causes may be far from the area of impact since prevailing winds can carry pollutants considerable distances. The ocean has a high **buffer** capacity, that is, the ability to neutralize many of the acid inputs. Therefore, most of the severe effects of acid rain are observed in freshwater lakes and rivers. Some estuaries, however, may also be seriously impacted, as has been observed in the upper **Chesapeake Bay**. The pH of a river feeding the Bay dropped from 6.3 to 5.8 between 1972 and 1978. Juvenile and spawning striped bass may not be able to tolerate such high acidity. Precipitation of nitrogen-based acid also increases nutrient loading in aquatic systems.

Toxic organic compounds, especially pesticides and a family of chemicals known as PCBs, have been shown to have serious effects on marine systems. Runoff has introduced considerable amounts of PCBs, **DDT**, and many other synthetic organic compounds into coastal areas. These compounds may persist for many years. In 1976, Congress banned the manufacture of PCBs, but they are still found today as coolants in older transformers and buried in **sedi-ment**s. It is estimated that 1 percent of PCBs used have reached the ocean. In 1987- 1988, 700 bottlenose **dolphins** washed up on the U.S. Atlantic coast and some were found to have elevated levels of PCBs and DDE (a form of DDT). Biologists claim that these compounds inhibited the dolphins' immune systems, making them vulnerable to infections. In 1975, workers at a chemical plant on the Chesapeake were poisoned when the insecticide **Kepone** was leaked or dumped into the bay. The Kepone spread downstream where it poisoned fish and shellfish.

One of the most publicized sources of marine pollution is that caused by petroleum products. While large **oil spills** can devastate a local area, equally important is the discharge of crude oil while cleaning bilges and emptying tanks at sea. Over the past decade, an average of approximately 32 million gallons (120 million l) of oil have been spilled annually. The Gulf of Mexico has recorded the most spills, while spills in the Persian Gulf average 2 million gallons (7 million l) per year. Since tanker ports and refineries are, by necessity, located on the coast, these sensitive areas receive considerable damage from the spills. The damage to marine life is staggering. Seabirds are killed by the hundreds of thousands annually, their oil-matted plumage making flight impossible and exposing them to hypothermia. Oil-soaked fur of marine mammals loses its water repellency, also leading to death by hypothermia. Ingestion of oil by fishes, birds, and mammals also may result in death.

Hundreds of tons of inert solid wastes are dumped into the oceans from ships annually. Of these, **plastics** and polystyrene (styrofoam) are deadly to marine life. Often

floating for hundreds of miles and lasting for many years, plastics are frequently mistaken for food by fishes, turtles, and mammals, and proceed to either interfere with subsequent feeding or strangle the consumer. It has been estimated that plastics and discarded fishing gear, such as monofilament line and discarded nets, kill one million seabirds and 150,000 marine mammals each year.

Beginning with the Refuse Act of 1899 and the Water Pollution Act of 1948, there have been efforts to remedy the polluted oceans. Not until 1972, however, was legislation drafted that was powerful enough, and sufficient monies appropriated, to effect any change. With the Federal Water Pollution Act, or **Clean Water Act**, improvement of water quality in the United States began. By 1985, five of the goals of the 1972 Act were reached, and since then, the Clean Water Act has been rewritten to reflect increasing national concerns.

Pollution of the world's oceans had become so pervasive that an international convention was convened in 1973 to establish laws governing the discharge of all wastes into the ocean. The International Convention for the Prevention of Pollution from Ships (1978), commonly known as MARPOL, and subsequent annexes to the convention, covers all garbage discharged by ships at sea beyond three miles from shore. While it is too soon to tell, adherence to the MARPOL agreement should significantly reduce the amount of solid wastes polluting the world's oceans.

Boston Harbor, the Chesapeake Bay, and the **Mediterranean Sea** are the most publicized examples of marine pollution. However, the problem is widespread. Many estuaries in Southeast Asia, many coastal areas in Japan, and the waters off Rio de Janeiro are also areas where historical and current use of the waters as dumping grounds has left them in disastrous conditions. The Golden Horn **estuary** around Istanbul, Turkey, has been declared dead, containing no living organisms and posing a threat to surrounding waters at the eastern end of the Mediterranean.

Since humans have been living along the coasts and using the seas as waste dumping grounds for thousands of years, these areas are the most heavily impacted. What makes matters worse is that coastal waters are vital spawning and nursery grounds for most of the commercially harvested fish and shellfish in marine systems. Destruction of these areas has significant nutritional and economic repercussions. Examples of the world-wide destruction of marine habitats due to pollution are numerous, but, with increased international efforts to limit inputs and rehabilitate damaged areas, improvements in the health of marine systems may be seen. *See also* Bioaccumulation; Estuary; Food chain/web; Heavy metals and heavy metal poisoning

[*William G. Ambrose, Jr. and Paul E. Renaud*]

FURTHER READING

Clark, R. B. *Marine Pollution.* New York: Oxford University Press, 1989.

Dolin, E. J. "Boston's Murky Political Waters." *Environment* 34 (1992): 6-33.

Nybakken, J. W. *Marine Biology: An Ecological Approach.* 2nd ed. New York: Harper and Row, 1988.

Marine Protection, Research and Sanctuaries Act (1972)

The Marine Protection, Research and Sanctuaries Act of 1972 is a comprehensive law designed to deal with ocean resources. The law has three main sections: first, it regulates **ocean dumping**; second, it authorizes **marine pollution** research; third, it establishes the marine sanctuary program. These sanctuaries can be established to protect areas of significant **conservation**, cultural, ecological, educational, esthetic, historical, or recreational values. A fourth component to the law, added in 1990, establishes regional marine research programs.

The law established a permit process administered by the **Environmental Protection Agency** to regulate all ocean dumping, with the exception of **dredging** materials, which require a permit from the **Army Corps of Engineers**. The act mandated that ocean dumping of sewage **sludge** and industrial waste end by 1981, but this deadline was missed. The **Ocean Dumping Ban Act** of 1988 amended the 1972 law, establishing a deadline of December 31, 1991, for the end of ocean dumping of sewage sludge. A system of escalating fees and fines was incorporated into the act to help reach the deadline. The law also immediately prohibits the dumping of **medical waste** in the ocean

The marine sanctuaries can be designated in coastal waters or in the **Great Lakes**. Thus far, thirteen National Marine Sanctuaries have been designated: Channel Islands (off the coast of California), Cordell Bank (California), Fagatele Bay (American Samoa), Florida Keys (Florida), Flower Garden Banks (Louisiana/Texas), Gray's Reef (Georgia), Gulf of the Farallones (California), Humpback Whale (Hawaii), Key Largo (Florida), Looe Key (Florida), Monitor (North Carolina), Monterey Bay (California), and Sellwagen Bank (Massachusetts). Numerous additional sites are being studied for designation. The sanctuaries range in size from the one-quarter sq. mi. Fagatele Bay to the 5,312 square miles at Monterey Bay (larger than Connecticut).

Designation is usually made by the Secretary of Commerce, after consultation with other agencies and the affected states' governments. State waters can be included in a sanctuary if the state agrees.

In the 1980s Congress and environmental groups were concerned with the slow pace of sanctuary designation. Congress acted to expedite the designation process, and in 1990 by-passed the usual process completely to designate the Florida Keys Marine Sanctuary, largely in response to a number of ship groundings in the area.

The Sanctuaries and Reserves Division of the **National Oceanic and Atmospheric Administration (NOAA)**, in the Department of Commerce, is responsible for the administration of these sanctuaries. Management of the sanctuaries is based on a multiple use approach: the significant resources within the sanctuaries are to be protected, but uses such as diving and sport and **commercial fishing** may also continue in most cases if such uses do not harm the significant resources. Regulations as to what is allowed and not allowed are established for each particular sanctuary, depending on what resources are present and being protected. Offshore gas and **oil drilling**, for example, is not allowed in sanctuaries, but shipping (including oil tankers) often is. In addition to protection and use, the sanctuaries are also sites for research and marine education.

Administration of the sanctuaries is difficult due to budgetary constraints: in 1993 the entire program received $7 million. *See also* Environmental education; Environmental science; Recreation

[*Christopher McGrory Klyza*]

FURTHER READING

James, A. "Watery Keep." *Outside* (January 1993): 19-20.

National Oceanic and Atmospheric Administration. *National Marine Sanctuary Program.* Washington, DC: U. S. Government Printing Office, 1990.

"Ocean Pollution Controlled." *Congressional Quarterly Almanac* 44 (1988): 160-61.

Marsh
See **Wetlands**

Marsh, George Perkins (1801-1882)
American diplomat and author

A long-time diplomat, Marsh served twenty-one years as ambassador to Italy and a shorter term in Turkey. He was a skilled lawyer, a Congressman from Vermont, a many-times-failed businessman, a learned scholar, and master of numerous languages. He was also author of *Man and Nature: Physical Geography as Modified by Human Action*, a book that **Gifford Pinchot** called "epoch-making" and that Lewis Mumford, in *The Brown Decades*, described as "the fountainhead of the **conservation** movement." **Rene Jules Dubos** described Marsh himself as "the first American prophet of **ecology**" and not a few have ascribed to him the actual founding of the science.

Marsh was born and grew up in Woodstock, Vermont, or as he put it, he was "born in the woods." As a young person, poor eyesight turned him from avid book-worm to student of **nature**, and created his lifelong attitude: "the power most important to cultivate and, at the same time, hardest to acquire, is that of seeing what is before [you]." What he saw, especially in the over-grazed, deforested lands of Italy and Turkey, is what inspired the writing of *Man and Nature*.

The emphasis in Marsh's book is on human beings as agents of change, too often change that is detrimental to nature. "Man is everywhere a disturbing agent. Wherever he plants his foot, the harmonies of nature are turned to discords," he wrote. He went on to emphasize that "not a sod has been turned, not a mattock struck into the ground, without leaving its enduring record of the human toils and aspirations that accompany the act." The consequence of this change, Marsh wrote, is that "the earth is fast becoming an unfit home" for its human inhabitants.

Nevertheless, Marsh was also an early humanist, believing that human dominion over nature could be used constructively: he saw the purpose of his book as not only tracing human ravages of nature, but as also suggesting "the possibility and the importance of the restoration of disturbed harmonies and the material improvements of waste and exhausted regions." His writings and activities spurred others into action.

His reaction to **deforestation** directly influenced the United States Congress to establish a federal forest commission and, eventually, to the reserves now part of the vast system of **national forest**s in the United States. While ambassador to Italy, he wrote a report on **irrigation** for the U.S. Commissioner of Agriculture that led to the formation of the **Bureau of Reclamation** in 1902. His claim that it is "desirable that some large and easily accessible region of American **soil** should remain as far as possible in its primitive condition" influenced **wilderness** advocates such as **John Muir** and **Aldo Leopold** and was an early clarion call for the setting aside of pristine wildlands.

Though not a trained scientist nor a particularly skilled writer, Marsh sensed early the destructive capability and impact of human activities. He assessed those impacts with great clarity and did much to establish a base for intelligent restorative actions. *See also* Forest Service; Overgrazing; Wildlife management

[*Gerald L. Young*]

FURTHER READING

Curtis, J., W. Curtis, and F. Lieberman. *The World of George Perkins Marsh: America's First Conservationist and Environmentalist.* Woodstock, VT: The Countryman Press, 1982.

Gade, D. W. "The Growing Recognition of George Perkins Marsh." *The Geographical Review* 73 (July 1983): 341–344.

Strong, D. H. "The Forerunners: Thoreau, Olmsted, Marsh." In *Dreamers and Defenders: American Conservationists.* Lincoln: University of Nebraska Press, 1988.

Marshall Islands
See **Bikini Atoll**

Marshall, Robert (1901-1939)
Wilderness advocate

Bob Marshall was the son of a prominent New York lawyer who helped insert the phrase "forever wild" into the state constitution, a key to preserving the forests of the Adirondack region. His experiences in the **Adirondack Mountains** as a youth, at his family's summer place, and the early habit of taking long walks, gave early shape to his preoccupation with the importance of wilderness. Marshall worked diligently for the protection of wilderness in the United

States for aesthetic reasons and for the psychological health of the American people by counteracting the "drabness" and "horrible banality" of modern civilization.

Marshall earned a forestry degree from Syracuse University, a Masters of Forestry from Harvard, and ultimately a doctorate in plant physiology from Johns Hopkins. He first worked for the United States Forest Service at an experimental station in Missoula, Montana, before leaving to continue his education in graduate school. His experience in Montana exposed him to "the working man's" view of forestry, views that conditioned his later opinions on social reform.

The death of his father left him financially independent, but Marshall returned to the **Forest Service** in 1932 and 1933 to work on the National Plan for American Forestry. He later left to become director of forestry for the Office of Indian Affairs and then returned as chief of the Division of Recreation and Lands. In his Indian Affairs position, he worked for a greater role by Native Americans in the management of the forests on their reservations. As head of the Forest Service Division of Recreation and Lands, he became one of the twentieth century's best known voices in support of protection of **wilderness** areas in **national forest**s. His last achievement may have been the adoption in 1939 of the Regulation U1, governing wilderness areas and Regulation U2 governing wild areas (the two known together as the U Regulations). The Regulations were signed by Agriculture Secretary, Henry Wallace, as a Forest Service policy to endorse the recommendations developed by Marshall (and others on a committee) in an effort to protect these areas from development, including—and especially—road building (but also, logging, building, etc.), and to give such areas more permanence by requiring public notice and a waiting period before any alterations.

Bob Marshall's travels to Alaska in the late twenties and thirties resulted in detailed mapping of parts of the Brooks Range. This led in part to their preservation as wilderness and to a better understanding of tree growth at timberline in the Arctic.

Two books were written based on his travels to Alaska. The first, *Arctic Village* (1933), based on a year's residence in the Arctic village of Wiseman, earned him wide recognition, both critically and popularly, and was almost an ethnographic study of life among both the Eskimo and the white settlers in the wilderness back country of northern Alaska. The second, *Arctic Wilderness*, published in 1956 (well after his death), was more in line with his well-deserved reputation as a scholar and activist with vast knowledge of wilderness conditions.

Bob Marshall contributed also as one of the founders and financial supporters of the **Wilderness Society**. The Wilderness Society was a culmination of his call for "an organization of spirited people who will fight for the freedom of the wilderness." The Society helped to implement his dream of wilderness preservation through its decisive role in the eventual passage of the **Wilderness Act**, though that did not take place until more than two decades after Marshall's death. The Bob Marshall Wilderness system in Montana was later named in his honor.

[*Gerald L. Young*]

FURTHER READING

Glover, J.M. *A Wilderness Original: The Life of Bob Marshall*. Seattle, WA: The Mountaineers, 1986.

Jackson, D.D. "Just Plain Bob Was the Best Friend Wilderness Ever Had," *Smithsonian* 25, no. 5, (August 1994): 92-100.

Marshall, R. *The People's Forests*. New York: H. Smith and R. Haas, 1933.

Marshall, R. "The Problem of the Wilderness," *Scientific Monthly*, 30, (February 1930), 141-148.

Marshall, R. "The Universe of the Wilderness is Vanishing," *The Living Wilderness*, 35, no. 114, (Summer 1971): 8-14.

Nash, R. "The Strenuous Life of Bob Marshall," *Forest History*, 10, no. 3, (October 1966): 18-25.

Mass burn

Mass burn refers to the **incineration** of unsorted municipal waste in a Municipal Waste Combustor (MWC) or other incinerator designated to burn only waste from municipalities. This **waste management** method avoids the expensive and unpleasant task of sorting through the garbage for unburnable materials. All waste received at the facility is shredded into small pieces and fed into the incinerator. Steam produced in the incinerator's boiler can be used to generate electricity or to heat nearby buildings. The residual ash and unburnable materials, representing about 10-20 percent of the original volume of waste, are taken to a **landfill** for disposal. Mass burn incineration also has several drawbacks. Since the waste is unsorted, it often generates more polluting **emission**s than sorted waste, and it is more likely to corrode burner grates and chimneys. The residual ash and unburned materials may be toxic and require special treatment.

The **Environmental Protection Agency (EPA)** establishes standards for the burning of municipal waste. A MWC is designed so that it cannot burn continuously 24 hours a day. Waste cannot be fed to the unit nor can ash be removed while **combustion** is occurring. As a result, burning occurs in batches or spurts. A large MWC plant has a capacity greater than 250 tons per day. A very large MWC plant has a capacity of about 1,100 tons per day.

Municipal solid waste includes household, commercial or retail, and institutional waste. Household waste includes material discarded by single and multiple residential dwellings, hotels, motels, and other similar permanent or temporary housing establishments. Commercial or retail waste includes material discarded by stores, offices, restaurants, warehouses, and nonmanufacturing activities at industrial facilities. Institutional waste includes material discarded by schools, hospitals, and nonmanufacturing activities at prisons, government facilities, and other similar establishments.

Household, commercial or retail, and institutional wastes do not include sewage, wood pallets, construction and demolition wastes, industrial process or manufacturing wastes, or motor vehicles (including motor vehicle parts or vehicle fluff). Municipal solid waste also does not include solely segregated **medical waste**s. However, any mixture of segregated medical wastes and other wastes which contains more than 30 percent medical waste discards is considered to be acceptable as municipal solid waste.

The *Code of Federal Regulations* (CFR) specifically defines a Municipal Waste Combustor (MWC) unit as any device that combusts solid, liquid or gasified municipal solid waste including but not limited to field-erected incinerators (with or without heat recovery), modular incinerators (starved air or excess air), boilers (steam generating units), furnaces (whether suspension-fired, grate-fired, mass-fired or fluidized bed-fired), and gasification/combustion units. This does not include combustion units, engines or other devices that combust landfill gases collected by landfill gas collection systems.

According to the CFR, terms connected with a MWC must be clearly defined. MWC acid gases are defined as all acid gases emitted in the exhaust gases from MWC units including **sulfur dioxide** and hydrogen chloride gases. MWC organics are defined as organic compounds emitted in the exhaust gases from MWC units including total tetra- (4) through octa- (8) chlorinated di-benzo-p-dioxins and dibenzofurans. This class of chlorinated chemicals (where **chlorine** gas binds with certain organic matter, especially **carbon** atoms) includes **dioxin** or TCDD.

EPA also identifies some of following as potential discharges from a MWC: hydrogen chloride, sulfur dioxide, **refuse-derived fuel** (RDF), **nitrogen oxides**, and **carbon monoxide**. The amounts of these emissions discharged are closely monitored. EPA sets allowable standards and compliance schedules for each emission. These standards are legally enforceable regulations.

EPA also sets standards for facility operations. These standards include guidelines for monitoring, for handling ash, for reporting and recordkeeping, for operating the MWC unit within acceptable standards, for maintaining proper combustion air supply levels, and for start-up, shut-down and malfunction of the unit. Compliance and performance testing guidelines are also included in the CFR. These standards and guidelines apply to MWCs constructed, modified, or reconstructed after December 20, 1989. The Code pertaining to MWC is updated periodically. The latest update was issued in February 1991.

However, there are many older MWC units that still burn municipal wastes. These are not as technologically sophisticated or as rigorously monitored as are the newer incinerators. Emissions tests are not as stringent or comprehensive for these older units. They are listed as Sub Part E under the 1971 Code (amended in 1974). These MWC units were constructed, modified, or reconstructed before December 20, 1989 and burn up to 50 tons per day. *See also* Fly ash; Hazardous waste; Scrubbers; Solid waste; Solid waste incineration

[*Liane Clorfene Casten*]

FURTHER READING

Clarke, M. J. *Burning Garbage in the U. S.: Practice vs. State of the Art*. New York: INFORM, 1991.

Denison, R. *Recycling and Incineration: Evaluating the Choices*. Covelo, CA: Island Press, 1990.

Griffin, R. D. "Garbage Crisis." *CQ Researcher* 2 (20 March 1992): 243-248.

"So Much Smoke? Incineration." *The Economist* 326 (13 February 1993): A26-27.

Mass extinction

Periodically, every fifty to one hundred million years or so, the earth has experienced mass **extinction**s, the relatively rapid, large-scale disappearance of many if not most living creatures. The world may be experiencing this phenomenon now at a far more rapid pace than ever before.

Of the five largest mass extinctions, the oldest occurred during the lower Ordovician period some 435 million years ago, when approximately one-quarter of all ocean families, and half of ocean genera, disappeared. (Creatures living in the sea are often used to measure the severity of mass extinctions, because the fossil record of marine **sediment**s is more complete than that for terrestrial animals.) Among the creatures lost during this time were many types of trilobites, cephalopods, and crinoids, all of which are thought to have died out in shallow tropical waters because of sudden changes in ocean levels.

During the late Devonian period, about 357 million years ago, over a fifth of marine families and more than half of marine genera gradually died out over what may have been a ten-million-year interval. **Climate** and sea-level changes apparently doomed many types of corals, trilobites, fish, and brachiopods.

The most severe mass extinction of all took place at the end of the Permian period 250 million years ago. This destroyed as much as 96 percent of all plant and animal **species**, probably over an interval of at least a million years. Over half of all ocean families were wiped out, as were up to 80 percent of the marine genera. This was fatal for the remaining trilobites and most land species. But the "great dying," as the event is called, also created ecological **niche**s for future life forms, including the dinosaurs.

In the Permian extinctions the suspected but unproven cause is a massive and extremely violent volcanic eruption in Siberia, which catapulted huge quantities of sunlight-blocking dust and **aerosol** droplets into the **atmosphere**. This, in turn, cooled the climate abruptly, expanding the polar icecaps, shrinking the oceans, and causing a new **ice age**. The rapid fluctuations in sea levels decimated the marine creatures of this period. To make matters worse, volcanic explosions could also have turned sulfate minerals into sulfuric acid and **sulfur dioxide** gas, which would have produced a ruinous rain of acidic precipitation. Over a 600,000 year period, these eruptions spewed a flood of molten basalt that created rock formations 870 miles (1400 km) in diameter next to **Lake Baikal**, an area called the Siberian Traps.

Another mass extinction occurred about 198 million years ago, during the late Triassic period, when a quarter of marine families and half or more of marine genera disappeared. Cephalopods, gastropods, bivalves, brachiopods, and reptiles, were destroyed, as were the conodonts, the fish from which vertebrates may have descended.

The most recent and best known mass extinction occurred a mere 65 million years ago, at the end of the Cretaceous period. It brought about the end of many creatures, including the dinosaurs and ammonites (shellfish). Sixteen percent of marine families and up to 46 percent of marine genera were lost at this time.

Scientists are still debating the causes of this catastrophic event. It could have coincided with (and may have been caused or accelerated by) a massive volcanic eruption and lava flood in what is now India, where it created a rock formation called the Deccan Traps. Some scientists suggest that a catastrophic climate change and a drastic cooling of the atmosphere made survival impossible for the dinosaurs, since they had no fur, feathers, or hibernating dens to shield them from the cold, nor could they migrate to a warmer climate. Other experts believe that the explosion of a nearby star cooled the atmosphere and emitted deadly radiation for thousands of years. Or perhaps herbivorous dinosaurs starved because they could not adapt to the new types of vegetation that developed. Their extinction would have killed off the carnivorous dinosaurs that preyed on the plant-eaters. Maybe the dinosaurs could not compete for food with the newly-emerging mammals, which ultimately replaced them as the dominant creatures on the planet.

In truth, much is unknown about the causes of the past mass extinctions. A theory with the weight of some evidence behind it raises the possibility that one or more comets or asteroids may have hit the earth, flinging billions of tons of dust and other debris — or ice crystals, if the object impacted in the oceans — into the atmosphere. By blocking out the sunlight for several months, and plunging the earth into darkness, the collision could have lowered temperatures below freezing, killing off the dinosaurs and the plants on which they fed. This hypothesis is based in part on the 1979 discovery, by Dr. Walter Alvarez of the University of California at Berkeley, of the unusual presence of the precious metal iridium in sediments from the time of the dinosaurs' extinction. Iridium, which belongs to the platinum family of elements, is much more plentiful in meteorites than planetary rocks, but it is also frequently found in strata from volcanic eruptions. Other scientists contend that virtually all mass extinctions could have been caused by volcanic eruptions and the huge floods of basalt resulting from such explosions. Evidence supports both theories. University of Chicago paleobiologist Dr. David M. Raup may have put it best when he wrote, "The disturbing reality is that for none of the thousands of well-documented extinctions in the geologic past do we have a solid explanation of why the extinction occurred."

Mass extinctions are not just a phenomenon of ancient geologic history; the last few thousand years have witnessed several such events, albeit on a far smaller geographic scale than those previously discussed. For example, the extinction of the giant animals of North America appears to have coincided with the arrival of humans on the continent, with the changing climate at the end of the last ice age also

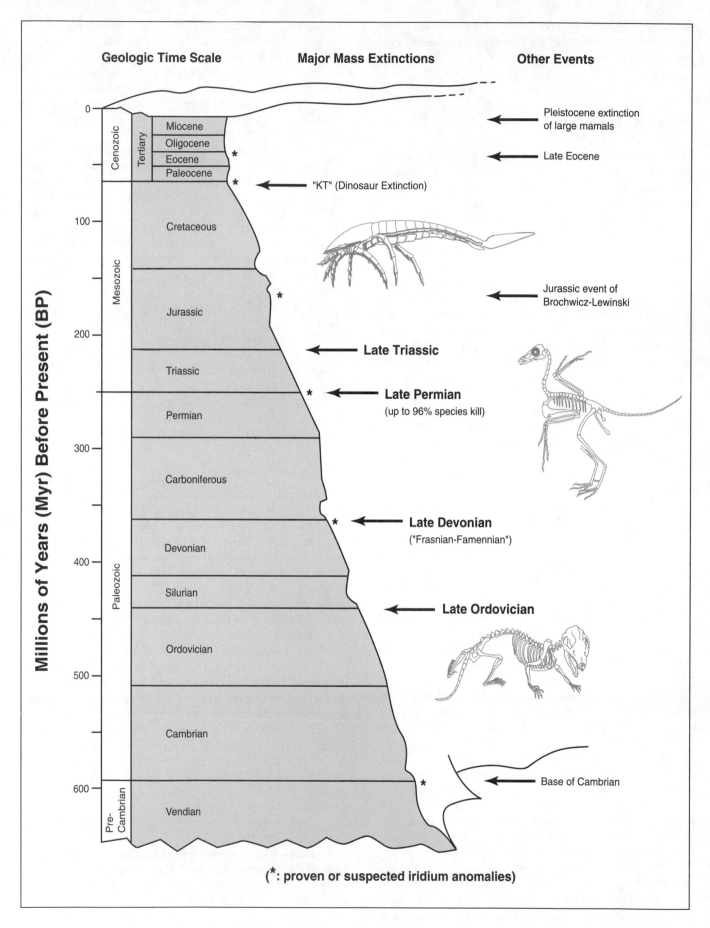

Geologic Time Scale

Cenozoic	Tertiary	Miocene
		Oligocene
		Eocene
		Paleocene

Mesozoic — Cretaceous, Jurassic, Triassic

Paleozoic — Permian, Carboniferous, Devonian, Silurian, Ordovician, Cambrian

Pre-Cambrian — Vendian

Millions of Years (Myr) Before Present (BP)

0 — 100 — 200 — 300 — 400 — 500 — 600

Major Mass Extinctions

* *

* "KT" (Dinosaur Extinction)

*

Late Triassic

* **Late Permian**
(up to 96% species kill)

* **Late Devonian**
("Frasnian-Famennian")

Late Ordovician

*

Other Events

Pleistocene extinction of large mamals

Late Eocene

Jurassic event of Brochwicz-Lewinski

Base of Cambrian

(*: proven or suspected iridium anomalies)

Timeline showing the five major mass extinction events of the past 600 million years. The most severe mass extinction took place at the end of the Permian period about 250 million years ago, when up to 96 percent of all plant and animal species on earth disappeared.

a possible factor. Crossing the Bering land bridge linking Siberia and Alaska about 12,000 years ago, primitive tribespeople, possibly from Siberia, found a population of large mammals, including giant beavers, **bison**, camels, mammoths, mastodons, and even lions in North America. These prehistoric hunters, moving south from Alaska towards South America, may have wiped out most of these species within 1,000 years.

Fossil remains of these Pleistocene mammals, some with spear points imbedded in them, reveal such creatures as the elephant-like mastodon; the huge-tusked, shaggy red-haired mammoth; a giant beaver weighing over 400 pounds (181 kg); the fabled saber toothed "tiger"; a seven-foot (2.1 m) wide, long-necked camel; 20-foot (6 m) long ground sloths; a bison seven feet (2.1 m) high at the hump, with a six foot (1.8 m) spread between its horns; and huge wolves, lions, bears, and horses.

As the twenty-first century approaches, the earth faces another threat of mass extinctions which may occur over a few years or decades, instead of thousands or millions of years. Particularly endangered are those species that are less well known, and in many cases not yet identified by science. Many of these are plants, animals, and invertebrates found in **tropical rain forest**s, which are rapidly being cut and destroyed.

For example, the 1980 **_Global 2000 Report_** to the President, compiled by the President's **Council on Environmental Quality** and the State Department, with the help of other federal agencies, projected that "...between half a million and two million species—15 to 20 percent of all species on earth—could be extinguished by the year 2000." And a report issued by the **World Resources Institute** in 1989 predicted that "between 1990 and 2020, species extinctions caused primarily by tropical **deforestation** may eliminate somewhere between 5 and 15 percent of the world's species...This would amount to a potential loss of 15,000 to 50,000 species per year, or 50 to 150 species per day." In 1988, Harvard biologist **Edward O. Wilson** put the annual rate of species extinction at up to 17,500.

Many of these lost species may be potential sources of food or medicines, and may perform essential ecological functions critical to sustaining life on the planet. It is impossible to predict precisely what the effects of these modern mass extinctions will be, but the ecological disruptions that will inevitably occur could have drastic consequences for human welfare and survival. *See also* Acid rain; Biodiversity; Endangered species; Food chain/web; Greenhouse effect; Ice age refugia; Radioactivity; Radiocarbon dating; Rare species; Volcano

[*Lewis G. Regenstein*]

FURTHER READING

Donovan, S. K., ed. *Mass Extinctions: Processes and Evidence.* New York: Columbia University Press, 1991.

Hecht, J. "Global Catastrophes and Mass Extinctions." *Analog: Science Fiction-Science Fact* 111 (May 1991): 78-89.

Tudge, C. *Last Animals at the Zoo: How Mass Extinction Can Be Stopped.* Covelo, CA: Island Press, 1992.

Mass spectrometry

A technique of **elemental analysis** first developed by Sir Francis Aston in the early twentieth century. In a mass spectrometer, a sample is first vaporized and then converted to positively charged **ion**s. These ions are accelerated to a high speed and then passed through a magnetic field. Since ions of different weight are bent by different amounts in the magnetic field, elements can be identified on the basis of how far they are bent in the field. Mass spectrometry is a very sensitive analytical technique that permits the detection of trace amounts of a substance, such as the amount of **ozone** in a sample of air. *See also* Measurement and sensing

Mass transit

Mass transit systems transport large numbers of people simultaneously in single vehicles. Examples of mass transit systems include buses, ferries, rapid rail, light rail, commuter rail and intercity rail systems. Although popular before the age of the **automobile**, mass transit systems have become marginal transportation modes in many cities in the United States. Recently however, as the negative impacts of automobile use have become of greater public concern, a renewed interest in encouraging mass transit has emerged. The Intermodal Surface Transportation Efficiency Act (ISTEA) of 1991 explicitly allocated funds toward improving mass transit systems.

Transportation congestion is worsening in the United States. In addition to the opportunity costs of time associated with traffic congestion, there are environmental costs associated with automobile use: **emission** of **greenhouse gases**, **air pollution**, **noise pollution**, and increased suburban sprawl and **land use**. Other social costs include increased probability of traffic accidents, increased occurrence of stress-related disorders, and increased social severance. Yet in most cities, people seem to be unwilling to use alternative modes of transportation, such as public transit, carpooling, or bicycling, which might impose lower environmental and time costs on society. Nationally, the automobile occupancy rate during commute hours was 1.1 in 1990. Trends indicate the situation will worsen over time.

The social costs associated with automobile use, including environmental **pollution**, congestion, accidents and public health effects, are known in the economics literature as "externalities." These are costs associated with automobile use that are not borne directly by the individuals making the decisions to use their automobiles. Although everyone experiences the negative effects of air pollution, and all drivers experience the negative effects of congestion, each individual driver only experiences a fraction of the total social cost produced when he or she drives. When a driver makes the decision about whether or not to drive an automobile, the full costs of driving are not taken into account. The result is that too many commuters choose to drive, and the social costs far outweigh the private benefits associated with the existing level of driving.

The solution from an economic standpoint is to force drivers to "internalize the externalities" or bear the full cost of their driving. This can be done through policy tools such as congestion pricing or gasoline taxes, both of which discourage driving. An alternative solution to the inefficiency is to encourage more use of mass transit by making mass transit less costly to commuters. Many people believe driving is more safe, comfortable, and convenient than mass transit. In order to compete with automobile use, mass transit must either be less expensive than automobiles or more attractive in amenities.

A commonly-held misconception about mass transit is that it must pay for itself. Mass transit is a public good that benefits all commuters, including those who use mass transit and those driving who enjoy less-congested roads and less-polluted communities. Because benefits are received by both users and non-users, it makes sense for the public sector to be subsidizing mass transit. In fact, because the external benefits of mass transit are difficult to quantify, it is unclear how much subsidization of mass transit is optimal. More subsidization creates lower transit fares and a more convenient system which encourages more riders; both riders and non-riders benefit from this.

In order to be an effective solution to the transportation problem, mass transit should satisfy several criteria. It should be cost-effective and less polluting per passenger mile than automobile use. Its public benefits should outweigh the public costs of operating the system. Investment in mass transit is only worthwhile if it will cause a significant number of people to switch to transit from using automobiles. National statistics show the number of vehicle occupants moving closer to one over time, demonstrating the high value the general public seems to place on driving their cars. Alternative modes such as mass transit must be competitive with automobiles in order to cause a decrease in automobile usage and a subsequent improvement in the **environment**.

Mass transit systems have significant environmental benefits, including substantial reductions in greenhouse gases, energy consumption and traffic congestion, provided enough commuters switch to using it. A fully occupied train can remove 100 cars from the road during rush hour, a bus forty, and a vanpool thirteen. Associated energy savings can be around 40 to 60 percent, and cleaner fuels can reduce emissions even further. Mass transit systems in different ways. Park and ride systems for example, are much less environmentally friendly than transit-only options. During the first few miles of an automobile trip, emissions and fuel use are very high, due to the cold start. In a ten-mile trip for example, 90 percent of emissions are produced in the first few miles. Although they offer fewer environmental benefits than full transit systems, they still decrease traffic congestion and accidents.

Not every city in the United States is suited for mass transit systems. Large cities such as New York City and Washington, D.C. have the density of people and businesses necessary to make the systems viable, and mass transit systems are heavily used. Many cities have grown in a sprawling manner, due mainly to the dominance of the automobile, so that the density of the population makes good

mass transit infeasible. On the other hand, if a good mass transit system were in place, one could envision the development of business and residential hubs around the transit system which would eventually increase population density and ridership. An addition to the above-mentioned benefits of mass transit, the revitalization of downtowns, many of which have deteriorated with the growth of the suburbs, might occur as development adapts to improved mass transit systems.

Future technological developments might improve the attractiveness of mass transit relative to automobile use. Intelligent Vehicle Highway Systems (IVHS) refer to the application of advanced technologies, especially communications technologies, to improve the efficiency of the nation's surface transportation system. Potential outcomes of this endeavor include the creation and implementation of "smart cars," "smart transit," and "smart streets."

A great deal of IVHS is devoted to improving the efficiency of automobile transportation. IVHS might offer traffic signal timing and smart car technology which would reduce congestion and traffic accidents. These technologies will make automobile use more convenient and safe than before, encouraging more automobile travel. On the other hand, IVHS offers the possibility of implementing a congestion pricing system where automobile users pay a fee when using certain roads at congested times. This cost would make transit more competitive relative to automobiles during heavy commute hours.

Certain components of IVHS might improve convenience to make mass transit more competitive with automobiles. A component of IVHS is the development of communications systems controlling traffic patterns and flows on streets and highways. These systems can be used in conjunction with HOV (high-occupancy vehicle) lanes to make transit systems more competitive in travel time. Also, computerized fare-collection devices speed transit boarding, a time-consuming aspect of present transit travel. These technologies make transit and ridesharing more convenient and attractive to commuters, increasing transit use relative to individual vehicle use.

IVHS could encourage or discourage mass transit use. For planning purposes, it is important to consider the implications of the different components of IVHS to the future of mass transit systems. The benefits associated with increased mass transit use are generally public as opposed to private. Yet, the individual decision about which transportation mode to use is a private decision. Increasing mass transit use requires the development of attractive, competitive mass transit systems that are a convenient, safe, and comfortable option to automobile travel. Improved mass transit in these ways should pay off in terms of an improved environment and quality of life. *See also* Environmental economics; Externality; Urban sprawl

[*Barbara J. Kanninen*]

FURTHER READING

Brown, Lester R. ed. *The World Watch Reader on Global Environmental Issues.* New York: W.W. Norton & Co., 1991.

Gordon, Deborah. *Steering a New Course: Transportation, Energy, and the Environment.* Washington, D.C.: Island Press, 1991.

Small, Kenneth A. *Urban Transportation Economics.* Chur, Switzerland: Harwood Academic Publishers, 1992.

Material Safety Data Sheets

The use of a Material Safety Data Sheet (MSDS), as mandated by the **Occupational Health and Safety Administration** (OSHA), is an integral part of hazard communication and "**right-to-know**" in the work place. An MSDS for a chemical substance is designed to provide both workers and emergency personnel with procedures for handling or working with that substance. An MSDS provides information concerning safe handling procedures, first aid measures, and procedures to be taken when the substance is accidentally spilled or released. MSDSs are provided by the manufacturer and supplier of chemicals and should be available to all employees at all times. MSDSs for many substances are available on the Internet. Many MSDSs are complete, accurate, and informative, while others, especially for those chemicals a manufacturer considers to be proprietary, may be missing key pieces of information. An MSDS must contain (written in English) the information described below.

An MSDS contains information on ingredients and their physical and chemical characteristics. Except for trade secrets, the MSDS gives the specific chemical name, chemical formula, and common names for the ingredients that have been determined by OSHA to be hazardous chemicals (i.e., any chemical that is defined as a physical or health hazard). If the substance is a mixture that has been tested as a whole to determine its hazardous properties, the chemical and common names of the ingredients that contribute to those known hazards and the common names for the mixture are listed.

If the substance is a mixture that has not been tested as a whole, the chemical and common names are listed for all ingredients that are determined to be health hazards and that comprise 1% or more of the mixture; identified as carcinogens and present at 0.1% or more; or determined to present a physical hazard when present in the mixture.

The MSDS also gives information about physical and chemical characteristics that indicate what a material or mixture is like and how it behaves, including boiling point, vapor pressure, vapor density, water solubility, specific gravity, evaporation rate, and reactivity with water and other substances.

An MSDS also contains information describing hazards, precautions, control measures, and emergency procedures. It describes physical hazards such as combustibility, flammability, and explosiveness, and it identifies health hazards, which include acute and chronic hazards that result from exposure, as well as whether the substance is listed as a confirmed or potential carcinogen. In addition, the MSDS gives the applicable precautions for safe handling and use, including steps to be followed if material is spilled or released; waste disposal methods for spilled substances, which must follow federal, state, and local regulations; precautions to be taken in handling and storage; personal protective equipment that are required; signs and symptoms of exposure; and description of routes of entry into the human body during normal usage or a foreseeable emergency. The MSDS describes the applicable control measures such as special fire fighting procedures and extinguishing media and emergency first aid procedures.

Finally, MSDSs describe exposure limits and give information about responsible parties. The document lists the OSHA Permissible Exposure Limit (PEL), the American Conference of Governmental Industrial Hygienists (ACGIH) Threshold Limit Value (TLV), and any other recommended exposure limits that might apply. The MSDS includes the date of preparation or latest revision, with the name of the person responsible for preparing the MSDS being optional. It also lists the name, address, and telephone number of the manufacturer, importer or other responsible party.

[*Judith L. Sims*]

Materials balance approach

A materials (or mass) balance approach for contaminants of public health and/or environmental concern is used to determine the presence, fate and transport of contaminants in the **environment**. The materials balance approach, a fundamental principle of science, engineering, and industrial research and **risk analysis**, is familiar to professionals trained in the physical or life sciences and engineering. The use of a materials balance approach provides a technique to describe the environment as it is today and as it might be under conditions resulting from remedial actions or from changes in the way society produces, uses, and disposes of **chemicals** of environmental concern. It also provides a rational and fundamental basis for asking specific questions and for obtaining specific information, which is necessary for determining fate and transport of contaminants, selecting and evaluating remedial treatment options, and monitoring treatment effectiveness.

The determination or construction of a materials balance is dependent on **conservation** of materials. Material is not created nor is it destroyed by ordinary processes, but it is transformed. When applied to chemicals of environmental concern, conservation of materials requires that a chemical entering a specific environment must be transformed, held in, or transported out of the environment. The amount of a chemical that leaves any process, environmental compartment, or area must be exactly balanced by the amount that enters minus net accumulation within the process or compartment boundaries. This materials balance can be stated as a simple equation:

Change in mass in a volume = Mass entering a volume − Mass leaving a volume

The control volume (compartment) for analysis, the shape of the volume, and the identification of input and output flows as well as the processes acting within the control volume all must be chosen carefully in order for the materials balance to provide useful information for the assessment of environmental impacts and the control of environmental effects.

The steps involved in determining a materials balance of contamination in an environment include:

(1) Where is the contamination, in what form(s) does it exist and in what concentrations is it present?

(2) Where is the contamination going under the influence of natural geochemical and geobiological processes (that is, what are key pathways of transport and fate; what are the processes that affect mobility and degradation of contaminants)?

(3) Based on the answers to questions 1 and 2, how can the contamination be contained, destroyed, or immobilized in the specific phases in which it is found? Through time, as natural and remedial processes act upon specific contaminants, additional determination of the materials balance is required to assess the fate and transport of the contaminants or their transformation products and to develop further treatment or containment methodologies.

(4) Based on the answers to questions 1 and 2, what environmental phases should be monitored through time to assess the fate and transport of the contamination and effectiveness of treatment or containment under both natural and remedial processes?

Data to answer questions 1 and 2 may be obtained from three categories: (1) direct data from administrative records regarding the type and quantity of contamination, as well as where it entered the environment; (2) direct data from chemical measurements; and (3) indirect data from modelling and simulations of natural processes.

Types of direct data may include an assessment of the presence of contaminants in all environmental compartments present in a specific environment, which may include the air phase, aqueous and non-aqueous liquid phases, and solid phases. Contaminants may be transformed partially or completely in the **respiration** process to obtain energy to synthesize new microbial cells, so an estimate of mineralization (for example, by measuring oxygen utilization or **carbon dioxide** production in **aerobic** systems) may also provide important information.

A determination of the accuracy of a materials balance assessment is indicated by a good agreement between direct and indirect measurements, suggesting that the control volume was well-bounded and the processes acting within the volume were well-defined. The study of the materials balance approach involves both art and science, but if well-implemented, can provide an understanding of the environment of concern. *See also* Biogeochemical cycles; Risk assessment; Waste management

[Judith Sims]

FURTHER READING

Ayres, R. U., F. C. McMichael, and S. R. Rod. "Measuring Toxic Chemicals in the Environment: A Materials Balance Approach." In: *Toxic Chemicals, Health, and the Environment*, edited by L. B. Lave and A. C. Upton. Baltimore, MD: Johns Hopkins University Press, 1987.

Sims, R. C. "Soil Remediation Techniques at Uncontrolled Hazardous Waste Sites: A Critical Review." *Journal of the Air & Waste Management Association* 40 (1990): 703-732.

Maximum permissible concentration

In radiology, the maximum permissible concentration refers to the recommended upper limit for the dose which may be safely received during a specific period by a person exposed to **ionizing radiation**. It is also sometimes called permissible dose. *See also* LD_{50}; Threshold dose

Maximum social welfare
See **Pareto optimality**

McHarg, Ian (1920-)
American design ecologist

Clydebank, Scotland, where Ian McHarg was born and raised (and where he received education through high school) produced one of America's best known design ecologists. Before his first move to the United States, McHarg had attended two colleges in Scotland and spent eight years in the British army, including active battle service in World War II. He entered the army as an enlisted man, after four years attended Officer Training School, and was demobilized in 1946 at the rank of major.

That same year, McHarg entered Harvard University to study landscape architecture, from which he graduated with a bachelor's degree in landscape architecture 1949 and a master's in the same subject, one year later. He returned to Scotland for a short while and then earned another Harvard degree, a master's, in city planning (1951). For a short time, he returned to Scotland, serving as a planning officer in the country's Department of Health and teaching a course in landscape architecture at Edinburgh College of Art and then at Glasgow College of Art. His career in the United States began in 1954 when he accepted an appointment as an assistant professor of landscape architecture and city planning at the University of Pennsylvania, where a year later he was instrumental in creating the Department of Landscape Architecture. Though an active designer, planner, and consultant, and though now retired from teaching, he is still most closely associated by many with his work at the university.

While many practitioners still consider landscape architecture a traditional design field that creates back yards for the well-to-do, McHarg is widely credited with a revolution in the field. At the university, he taught landscape architecture and planning from an interdisciplinary, ecological perspective, bringing in ecologists, geologists, anthropologists, and even lawyers to participate in team-taught courses. From the university, his students have emerged to foment McHarg's ecological revolution in university design and planning departments, in planning agencies, and in design firms across the country.

As an active designer and planner outside the university McHarg put his ecological ideas into practice in such places as Hazleton, Pennsylvania, Medford, New Jersey, Amelia Island, Florida, Teheran, Iran, and Taroko, Taiwan. What one person can plan and build in a lifetime is limited, so it is McHarg's ideas (and the students, readers, and practitioners instilled with those ideas) that will remain significant far into the future.

The best known distillation and presentation of those ideas is in his *Design With Nature*, published in 1969 and reissued in a twenty-fifth anniversary edition in 1992. Lewis Mumford, in his preface to the first edition, best describes McHarg's accomplishment:

"McHarg's emphasis is not on either design or nature by itself, but upon the preposition *with*, which implies human cooperation and biological partnership. He seeks, not arbitrarily to impose design, but to use to the fullest the potentialities—and with them, necessarily, the restrictive conditions—that nature offers. So, too, in embracing nature, he knows that man's own mind, which is part of nature, has something precious to add that is not to be found at such a high point of development in raw nature untouched by man." Later, Mumford exclaims "here are the foundations for a civilization."

In *Design With Nature*, McHarg tried, and to a large degree succeeded, to direct planning away from its socioeconomic preoccupation toward an in-depth consideration of **environment**; to help integrate the physical and life sciences into an applied environmental science; to explore the role of values in planning, and to present a theory and method of planning as a way to understand and channel human adaptations to the environment.

McHarg's ideas have changed both landscape architecture and planning, but perhaps the latter more so. In planning, the human ecological philosophy he developed and advocates—in *Design With Nature* (and in numerous articles)—and the very practical method of comprehensive data collection and utilization he worked out in many years of classes and design projects, are today employed worldwide, including integrated applications in new GIS systems. Known by many as the father of ecological planning, McHarg moved from a limited environmental determinism to a contemporary interdisciplinary approach that defines planning as interactive, as applied **human ecology**.

[*Gerald L. Young*]

FURTHER READING

Landecker, H. "Ian McHarg: In Search of an Arbiter," *Profiles in Landscape Architecture*. Washington, D.C.: American Society of Landscape Architects, 1992.

McHarg, I.L. *A Quest for Life: An Autobiography*. New York: John Wiley & Sons, 1996.

———. *Design With Nature, 25th Anniversary Edition*. New York: John Wiley & Sons, 1992.

———. "Human Ecological Planning at Pennsylvania," *Landscape Planning* 8 (1981): 109-120.

Miller, E. L., and S. Pardal. The *Classic McHarg: An Interview*. Lisbon, Portugal: CESUR, Technical University of Lisbon, 1992.

McKibben, Bill (1960-)

American environmentalist and writer

William E. "Bill" McKibben is an American **nature** writer who was born in Palo Alto, California. He graduated from Harvard University in 1982 and was a staff writer and editor at *The New Yorker* until 1987 when he began his free-lance career. He now lives with his wife in the **Adirondack Mountains** in New York, and this region figures prominently in his writings.

In *The End of Nature*, McKibben's first book, he argues that the **greenhouse effect** is not only part of humanity's destruction of the **environment**, but a symptom of Man's alienation from the natural world. He calls for an end to practices that contribute to the greenhouse effect, such as burning **fossil fuels**. Such practices, he writes, "will lead us, if not straight to hell, then straight to a place with a similar temperature."

Some critics dismiss McKibben's arguments as "too absolute," and "more a slogan and hyperbole than scientific insight." Environmentalists, however, praise the book, calling it the "*Silent Spring* of the '90s"—a reference to the book by **Rachel Carson** which in 1962 awakened the nation to the indiscriminate use of **pesticide**s. However, McKibben's lament over the "end of nature" is a personal account of how human activity has changed not just the industrialized centers of the world, but his own backyard.

McKibbon's second book, *The Age of Missing Information* (1993), is a study of the seduction of television. On one day he videotaped every show on every cable channel available in his area, more than 1,000 hours of television, and then watched it all. To contrast that experience, he spent a day camping in the woods near his Adirondack home. "This book is about the results of that experiment—about the information that each day imparted," he says. Talking about this book, McKibben says, "Television...is a very private experience, with an almost constant message of 'you are the most important, this Bud's for you.' And if you are at the center of the world, it's hard to live environmentally aware."

McKibben has also edited *Birch Browsings: A John Burroughs Reader* (1992). **John Burroughs**, a nature writer whose career spanned 60 years beginning in 1865, is credited with establishing the nature essay as a literary genre. Many environmentalists are returning to the writings of such early nature writers as Burroughs, **John Muir**, and **Aldo Leopold** to study their ideas about **land stewardship**.

[*Linda Rehkopf*]

FURTHER READING

Magill, Frank N., ed. *Magill's Literary Annual*. Vol. 1. Pasadena: Salem Press, 1990.

McKibben, Bill. *The Age of Missing Information*. New York: Plume, 1993.

———. *Birch Browsings: A John Burroughs Reader*. New York: Penguin Books, 1992.

———. *The End of Nature.* New York: Random House, 1989.

Trosky, Susan M., ed. *Contemporary Authors.* Vol. 130. Detroit: Gale Research, 1990.

Measurement and sensing

A fundamental premise of all scientific research is that scientists can make measurements, expressed in precise mathematical terms, of conditions and events. Indeed, some argue that a field of study can only be called a science to the extent that the data being collected can be mathematically measured. These criteria apply to **environmental science** as they do to other physical and biological sciences.

Measurements serve a number of functions in environmental studies. One is to provide baseline information about certain aspects of the **environment**. A source of concern to scientists and non-scientists alike is the change that appears to be taking place in the earth's **ozone** layer. Mounting evidence appears to suggest that, as a result of human activities, the concentration of ozone in the **stratosphere** seems to be decreasing. That finding is significant because the ozone layer acts as a shield against potentially harmful **ultraviolet radiation** from the sun.

But how do scientists know that changes are taking place in the ozone layer? Such a conclusion can be drawn only if information exists regarding the "normal" concentrations of ozone in the stratosphere. One purpose of measurements, therefore, is to accumulate a huge volume of information regarding the "normal" condition of the environment.

A second purpose of measuring is to determine how some aspect of the environment may be changing, often as a result of human activities. Our concern about the ozone layer, for example, arises out of readings taken by high-flying aircraft over a period of more than a decade. Those readings show consistent changes (decreases) from the level that is regarded as natural or normal. These levels are not fluctuating, that is, decreasing and regaining normalcy. Rather, there is a trend toward decreased ozone levels.

Dozens of techniques are available for measuring environmental characteristics. Many of these techniques are not unique to environmental science. For example, the use of thermometers to record temperatures is vitally important in many environmental studies. But temperature-taking is not a specialized procedure used by environmental scientists. The measurement of **radioactivity** is another example. Geiger counters are used to determine the level of radiation in environmental studies just as they are in scientific research, medical applications, industrial processes and other situations.

Over the years, a number of techniques have been developed for measuring specific environmental characteristics. Many of these techniques can be classified according to their use in the measurement of **air quality** or **water quality**.

An example of the former is the high-volume sampler (HVS) used in measuring **particulate**s in the **atmosphere**. An HVS is essentially a modified vacuum cleaner that sucks air into a hose and forces it through a filter paper. The difference in the weight of the paper before and after it has trapped the particulate matter is used to determine the weight of the particulates. Since the total volume of air passing through the HVS can be easily measured, the systems provides of measure of particulates in mass per volume.

Techniques for measuring various components of a gas are also becoming more sophisticated. At one time, for example, the determination of ozone levels was made simply by suspending a piece of natural rubber of known size and weight in the air. Since ozone causes rubber to crack, the speed at which cracking occurred was taken as a measure of ozone levels in the air.

As with most other gases, ozone is now measured by chemical means. A sample of gas is passed through some device, often a "bubbler," that contains a compound that will react with the gas being tested. The concentration of that gas can be measured, then, by determining the amount of chemical change that takes place in the measuring device.

For example, a reaction with which many high school students are familiar can be used to determine the level of **sulfur dioxide** in the air. Sulfur dioxide reacts with **lead** dioxide (PbO_2) to form a characteristic black precipitate of lead sulfate.

$$SO_2 + PbO_2 \rightarrow PbSO_4$$

If lead dioxide is added to a bubbler through which a sample of gas is passed, the amount of darkening in the device (due to the formation of lead sulfate) is a measure of the concentration of sulfur dioxide in the gas.

Many environmental measurements now make use of sophisticated chemical techniques. One example is infrared spectrometry. The term *spectrometry* refers to the measurement of energy absorbed or emitted by various compounds. All molecules are held together by electrons that vibrate with characteristic frequencies. If energy is added to those molecules, they will absorb frequencies of energy that match their characteristic frequencies, but no others. Each kind of molecule can be identified, therefore, by a "map" of the frequencies that it does and does not absorb.

Infrared spectrometry is the most common form of the technique used because most molecules vibrate with frequencies in the infrared region. Techniques such as infrared spectrometry are valuable because they can detect concentrations of a material at much lower levels than can most chemical systems.

The increasing sophistication of measuring techniques does not mean that all simple procedures have been abandoned. For example, one method for measuring the level of **air pollution** requires no more than good eyesight and a reference card. The reference card contains the Ringelmann scale, a set of six squares that range from pure white to pure black. Each square contains an amount of hatching that corresponds to completely pure air (pure white, no hatching) to badly polluted air (totally black). The four intermediary squares contain increasingly more hatching, constituting equivalents of 20 percent, 40 percent, 60 percent and 80 percent "blackness."

For comparison, opacity (darkening) of air can also be determined by electronic means more precisely. A photometer, for example, is a device that records the amount of light transmitted by a sample of air. The light is converted to an electric current that can be read on a meter. In some industrial and **power plants**, a photometer is attached to the smokestack to obtain a continuous record of the opacity of the gases being emitted.

The two most common types of air quality measurements are those for **ambient air** quality and **emission**s. Ambient air refers to the outdoor air that surrounds us. Ambient air quality measurements provide information on the possible accumulation of harmful compounds such as **carbon monoxide**, sulfur dioxide, **nitrogen oxides**, and **hydrocarbons**.

Emission measurements reveal the level of such compounds being released from a power plant, a factory, or some other source. In many cases, emissions can be studied by simply drilling a hole in a smokestack, extracting a small sample of exhaust gases, and studying their composition by methods described above.

Many biological, chemical, and physical methods are available for measuring water quality. The presence of **pathogen**s in a sample of water can be determined, for example, by standard bacteriological techniques in which a water sample is allowed to incubate for some period of time and the number of bacteria produced counted visually or electronically.

At one time, most water tests were fairly straightforward chemical tests. The concentration of **nitrogen** in a water sample, for example, can be determined by a standard procedure known as the Kjeldahl test and the amount of chlorination by precipitation with a silver salt. Today, most water tests can be conducted by more sophisticated instrumental techniques. A photometer can be used to compare an unknown water sample with a known standard to determine the concentration of nitrogen, **phosphorus**, **chlorine**, or some other component.

One of the most basic measurements of water quality is that of oxygen demand. The more polluted a water sample is, the more organic matter it is likely to contain. The more organic matter, the greater the amount of oxygen the sample will require to decompose the organic material.

Traditionally, the method for determining this characteristic was **biochemical oxygen demand (BOD)**, a test in which a sample of water is studied over a five-day period. To overcome the lengthy time required to conduct this test, modifications such as total organic carbon (TOC) have been developed.

Specialized measuring techniques are sometimes required for particular types of environmental studies. Determining the amount of **noise pollution** in an area, for example, requires the use of a sound level meter, a device consisting of a microphone, amplifier, frequency-measuring circuit, and read-out screen.

One consequence of the improved technology now available for making measurements is that smaller and smaller concentrations of a substance can be detected. Chemical means can routinely detect the presence of a substance to the level of one part in a thousand or one **part per million**

(ppm). The most advanced technologies today have stretched that sensitivity to levels of one **part per billion** (ppb) and even one **part per trillion** (ppt).

The efficiency of these measuring devices poses some new issues for environmentalists. What does it mean, for example, to learn that a **toxic substance** exists in the **soil** at a level of one ppb if we know the material is harmful only in much higher concentrations? Does any level of exposure to the substance pose a hazard, or can we safely ignore such a minuscule quantity of the substance?

A field of measurement of increasing importance in environmental studies is remote sensing. The term refers to any method by which an object or an area is studied at some great distance. Most commonly today, the term is used to describe surveys of the earth's surface by satellites orbiting around it.

Remote sensing procedures depend on the fact that various types of materials absorb and reflect solar energy in different ways. Instruments in satellites that can measure these differences can, therefore, detect variations in land and ocean surfaces.

Remote sensing uses three parts of the electromagnetic spectrum: the visible, infrared, and microwave regions. Perhaps the most common form of remote sensing is that which uses photography. Photographic equipment has now been developed to the point where objects of no more than a few yards apart can be distinguished from outer space.

Since some objects and features emit radiation in electromagnetic regions other than the visual, infrared, and microwave techniques are also used. The images obtained from any one of these methods can be further improved by computer enhancement of the original photographs.

Remote sensing has now been used for a number of environmental applications. Some examples include the locating of possible mineral reserves, the tracing of water drainage patterns, the determination of soil moisture, the tracing of plant diseases, the calculation of snow and ice masses, and the measurement of biological productivity in the oceans. *See also* Drinking-water supply; Emission standards; Greenhouse gases; National Ambient Air Quality Standards; Ozone layer depletion; Radiocarbon dating; Water pollution

[*David E. Newton*]

FURTHER READING

McGraw-Hill Encyclopedia of Science & Technology. 7th ed. New York: McGraw-Hill, 1992.

Vesilind, P. A., J. J. Peirce, and R. Weiner. *Environmental Engineering*, 2nd ed. Boston: Butterworths, 1988.

Medical waste

Medical waste is a subcategory of **hazardous waste** that is attracting increasing concern. The **Environmental Protection Agency (EPA)** lists the following categories of medical waste: cultures and stocks; pathological wastes which includes body parts; blood and blood products; used "sharps"

such as needles and scalpels; **animal waste** or animal corpses which have been inoculated with infectious substances in medical research; isolation wastes, which come from people with highly contagious diseases; and unused, discarded "sharps."

Ten to fifteen percent of medical waste is considered infectious, although guidelines on just what is infectious medical waste vary from state to state. As a result, state and federal guidelines on disposal of these wastes are a hodgepodge of confusing laws and regulations. And the guidelines that do exist usually exempt generators of 50 pounds (23 kg) or less per month from any regulatory action.

The need to address medical waste began soon after such items as syringes, IV bags, and scalpels were observed washing up on ocean beaches in the summer of 1988. Congress directed the EPA to gather data on their sources, associated health hazards, and current procedures and regulations for management and disposal and to evaluate the health hazards associated with transporting them, incinerating them, burying them in a **landfill**, and disposing of them in a sanitary sewer system.

A two-year, voluntary program enacted by Congress, the Medical Waste Tracking Act of 1988, was instituted in response to public concern over the treatment of medical waste. The Act created a "cradle-to-grave" tracking system based on detailed shipping records, similar to the program in place for hazardous waste. The pilot program has now expired, the EPA data has been sent to Washington administrators, and any action on the findings of the EPA's study is in limbo. It is doubtful that the EPA report on medical waste will ever be submitted to Congress or find its way into the *Federal Register* because many of the states that participated in the program went on to pass strict medical-**waste management** guidelines of their own. All the states participating at least revised their municipal **solid waste** guidelines to include the category of medical waste, whether or not management practices were included.

Another complicating factor in the regulation of medical waste is that at least four different federal agencies are involved with medical-waste issues: the EPA, the **Occupational Safety and Health Administration (OSHA)**, the **Centers for Disease Control (CDC)**, and the **Agency for Toxic Substances and Disease Registry**.

The EPA's study reported that 3.2 million tons of medical waste was produced in the United States each year. Not surprisingly, hospitals, long-term health care facilities, and physician's offices are the major producers of medical wastes, which account for about 0.3 percent by weight of all **municipal solid waste**. The EPA found out that current practices of management and disposal range from handling the waste as nonhazardous municipal solid waste to strict segregation, packaging, labeling, and tracking from the generator to the disposal site, the so-called "cradle-to-grave" management.

Health care workers are required by federal law to segregate medical waste in special containers; if the waste is transported for treatment, it must be labeled with the generator's name and carry a biological hazard symbol. But facilities that produce less than 50 pounds (23 kg) of medical waste per month are exempt from most requirements. Home and small generator medical wastes fall through the cracks. Insulin-dependent diabetics, for instance, typically dispose of used syringes in their household trash or flush them down the toilet. In some northeastern cities, New York City for example, antiquated sewage systems pour material into rivers and oceans during heavy rainfalls. Depending on tides and currents, syringes can end up on beaches, which is what New York and New Jersey coastlines experienced in 1988 and 1989.

A growing source of medical waste that is not regulated is that generated by home health-care providers. As a result of new patient-care strategies and rising medical costs, more long-term illnesses are being treated at home. That means that medical waste is being disposed of in ordinary household trash. Medical clinics and intravenous drug users are also suspected of contributing to unsafe dumping of medical wastes. Even U.S. Navy vessels contributed to beach medical waste.

The need to address the problem evolved long before wastes washed up on northeastern beaches, however. Over the last 10 years, and partly in response to the **AIDS** and hepatitis epidemics, the use of disposable health care products has contributed to the increased volume of medical waste. Cost-containment measures have increased the use of plastic disposables in health care settings. From syringes to bedpans, health care aids are increasingly thrown away.

Common treatment techniques of medical waste include steam sterilization and **incineration**, although some waste is discarded into sewage systems. During autoclaving, the waste is exposed to steam at a temperature of 250°F (121°C) for at least 45 minutes. Autoclaving fails to reduce the volume of waste that must be landfilled, and is only preferred in areas where there is no appropriate incineration equipment. Proper incineration efficiently destroys all categories of infectious wastes, effectively kills live and dormant forms of pathogenic organisms, and alters the waste volume.

About 60 percent of medical waste is treated on site at hospital facilities. After treatment, ash residues or sterilized and disinfected materials must be transported to commercial treatment facilities or taken directly to landfills. Other options for medical waste treatment include compaction, microwaving, and mechanical or chemical disinfection, which could be less costly and alleviate concerns about **emission**s from incinerators.

According to the congressional Office of Technology Assessment (OTA), air emissions of **dioxin** and heavy metals from hospital incinerators average 10 to 100 times more per gram of waste burned than emissions from well-controlled municipal waste incinerators. And while waste generators are generally required to track with manifests the route their wastes take to reach disposal, strict requirements do not exist for on-site treatment facilities.

Some industry watchers, environmentalists, and policy makers are advocating a medical waste disposal program similar to some in Europe. Virtually all medical wastes in Switzerland and Germany, for example, go to regional incineration facilities. Stringent air-quality regulations in these countries make it impractical for hospitals to do on-site incineration, but the regional facilities made advanced **air pollution** control devices cost-effective. In Munich, operators dump the resulting ash in specially lined landfills. Hospitals in Canada are turning away from disposable supplies in favor of products that can be cleaned and reused.

For a regional system to work, however, medical waste must be safely transported. In the U.S., there are no federal statutes governing the transport of medical refuse. Refrigerated trucks legally can and do carry food after transporting medical wastes.

A proposal to manage home users of syringes and medicines that end up in municipal solid waste landfills would include a pharmacy "swap" system. In Switzerland and Germany, for example, pharmacies accept old medicines for appropriate disposal, then send the medicine to regional incineration outlets. A deposit-and-return system on syringes has been advocated in this country to insure the safe disposal of syringes.

[*Linda Rehkopf*]

FURTHER READING

Carlile, J. "Finding Disposal Options for Medical Waste." *American City and County* (November 1989): 66.

Groves, L. "Hospitals Re-Think Disposables." *Alternatives* (January-February 1993): 13.

Hershkowitz, A. "Without a Trace: Handling Medical Waste Safely." *Technology Review* (August-September 1990): 35.

"Managing Medical Waste." *The Futurist* (September-October 1991): 49.

Moeller, D. W. *Environmental Health.* Cambridge: Harvard University Press, 1992.

"Tracking Seaside Medical Wastes." *Science News* (16 September 1989): 191.

Mediterranean Sea

For centuries, the Mediterranean Sea has been the focal point of western civilization. It is an area rich in history and has played critical roles in the development of shipping and trade, as a resource for feeding growing populations, and as an aid to the spread and mingling of races and cultures.

The Mediterranean began to form about 250 million years ago when the Eurasian and African continental plates began moving toward each other, pinching off the Tethys Sea, an extensive shallow sea that separated Europe and much of Asia from Africa and India. It now has only two outlets, the Straits of Gibraltar and the Bosporus, a narrow strait between the Mediterranean and Black Seas. While the central basin of the Mediterranean reaches depths of several thousand yards, there is a sill under the Straits of Gibraltar that is only 1,970 feet (600 m) below the surface. Through this passageway flows surface water from the Atlantic Ocean.

Since the Mediterranean is situated in one of the world's **arid** belts, the inputs from precipitation and rivers is far less than the water lost through evaporation. If the

straight at Gibraltar were to close due to further plate movements, the Mediterranean would dry up. In fact, data from the Deep Sea Drilling Project, seismic surveys, and fossil analysis have found evidence of salt deposits, ancient river valleys, and fresh water animals, all suggesting that this has occurred at least once. Since the African and Eurasian plates are moving together, this will probably happen again.

Humans can do nothing about this impending geological disaster. There are, however, events that people can influence. Domestic sewage, industrial **discharge**, agricultural **runoff**, and **oil spills** are seriously threatening the Mediterranean, fouling its once clear waters, altering its chemical cycling, and killing its organisms. Along its northern coastline are some of the most heavily industrialized nations in the world, whose industries are destroying nearshore nursery **habitat**s, damaging fisheries. **Dams** on inflowing rivers reduce the **sediment** inputs, making coastal **erosion** a major problem. Shipping, once the hallmark of Mediterranean civilization, releases every manner of waste into the Sea, including oil. Annually, 6 million barrels of oil end up in the Mediterranean. The limited water circulation patterns of the Mediterranean compound this problem as pollutants accumulate.

Today seafood contamination and eye, skin, and intestinal diseases are frequently experienced by coastal residents. Marine mammal and **sea turtle** populations are threatened by habitat loss and **nondegradable pollutant**s dumped into the waters. Sea grass (*Posidonia oceanica*), which provides food and habitat for some 400 **species** of algae and thousands of species of fish and invertebrates, is disappearing. **Nutrient** enrichment of the Mediterranean results in large **plankton** blooms which, combined with destructive fishing practices, contribute to the demise of the sea grass beds.

These problems have been recognized, and efforts are being made to reverse the declining health of the Mediterranean. Early efforts included the 1910 construction of one of the first institutions for study of the seas, the Musée Oceanographique by Prince Albert I of Monaco. Since then, the conflicts between the political and religious ideologies of the 18 nations surrounding the Mediterranean have been major hurdles in completing cleanup plans. In 1976, the *Mediterranean Action Plan* was signed by 13 of the nations. A major component of this agreement was the Blue Plan, a study of future effects of increasing coastal populations. Other efforts include the Genoa Declaration in 1985 and the Nicosia Charter in 1990. The latter commits resources of the community, the **World Bank**, the European Investment Bank, and the **United Nations Environment Programme** to achieve a Mediterranean environment compatible with **sustainable development** by 2025. Hopefully, these efforts can reverse the decline of this natural wonder. *See also* Algal bloom; Biofouling; Commercial fishing; Environmental degradation; Ocean dumping; Water pollution

[*William G. Ambrose and Paul E. Renaud*]

FURTHER READING

Batisse, M. "Probing the Future of the Mediterranean Basin." *Environment* 32 (1990): 4-15.

Heezen, B. C., and C. D. Hollister. *Faces of the Deep.* London: Oxford University Press, 1971.

Thurman, H. V. *Essentials of Oceanography.* Columbus, OH: Merrill, 1983.

Megawatt (MW)

A megawatt is a unit of power equivalent to one million watts (10^6 watts), or one thousand kilowatts. As a unit of power, a megawatt expresses the rate at which energy is produced. A megawatt is equivalent to one million joules per second. A megawatt is a fairly large unit of power and is used, therefore, when discussing the size of a **power plant**, a nation's total energy-generating capacity, or some other such large statistic. For example, the total electrical energy generating capacity for the state of California in 1988 was 45,900 megawatts. *See also* Energy and the environment; Energy efficiency

Mendes, Chico (1944-1988)

Brazilian union leader and environmental activist

Francisco Alvo Mendes Filho, known as Chico Mendes, was a defender of the **tropical rain forest**s and a champion of the concept of sustainable harvest as a means of saving and protecting that threatened **ecosystem**. As president of the local Rural Workers Union, representing rubber tappers in his native Brazil, Mendes became too powerful and politically influential for ranchers who wanted to turn the **rain forest** into grazing land for their cattle. The struggle between them ended in 1988, when Mendes was assassinated.

Chico Mendes was born in 1944 in Acre Province of Brazil, along the upper reaches of the Amazon River not far from the border with Peru and Bolivia. Following his father, he was a *seringueiro*, a rubber tapper. He farmed a small clearing, but relied on the sale of rubber from several hundred native rubber trees in the rain forest itself to provide income for him and his family. Mendes inherited the land and the trees from his father who had begun tapping them in the 1930s. Two long v-shaped cuts made with care in the bark of each rubber tree would yield one or two cups of the milky latex sap each week, which could then be dried to make natural rubber.

Mendes would also collect other natural forest products, such as fruits and Brazil nuts, to supplement his income. There are approximately 100,000 other rubber tappers living throughout the rain forest, and this is what they do as well. It is sustainable harvest which does not destroy the forest and provides a substantial income. On average, logging yields a one-time profit of $1,290 per acre; if the land is converted to cattle pasture, it yields an income of about $61 per acre per year. The sustainable yield of forest products, on the other hand, provides an income of $2,762 per acre per year.

Land speculators and large cattle ranching concerns are more interested in the short-term profits they can realize

Chico Mendes.

by cutting down the forest, selling the timber, and converting the land for cattle grazing. Ranching requires huge tracts of land, and satellite images indicate that in 1988 alone about 30 million acres of forest was destroyed for this industry. Low land prices, low tax rates, and direct subsidies to ranchers further encourage this practice. The Brazilian government had further aided ranching by building and maintaining roads into the forest, which are then used to ship cattle to market.

Chico Mendes fought to end this destruction of the tropical rain forest. He made many political inroads, gaining influence with the Interior Ministry as well as the public. His main adversary was Darli Alves da Silva, a cattle rancher who had begun acquiring forest land in Acre through strong-arm tactics and he vowed that Mendes would not live out 1988. Mendes had helped establish several forest reserves that year, thus all but ending forest clearing in Acre.

Mendes, his wife, and two policemen assigned to guard him were playing cards at his home on the night of December 22, 1988. Mendes stepped outside for a moment and was killed by a shotgun blast to the chest from a waiting assassin. The local police claimed no clues or suspects in the case, but local and international protests forced the Brazilian government to enter the investigation. Evidence led them to the ranch of Darli da Silva. In the summer of 1989 indictments for murder were handed down to Darli da Silva, his son Darci Pereia da Silva, and Jerdeir Pereia, one of da Silva's ranch hands. Testimony indicated that Darli ordered the murder and that Darci supervised as Jerdeir carried out the plot. There is evidence that other prominent ranchers may have been involved in the plot, and they are currently under investigation. *See also* Deforestation; Rainforest Action Network; Slash and burn agriculture; Sustainable agriculture; Sustainable development; Sustained yield

[*Eugene C. Beckham*]

FURTHER READING

Dwyer, A. *Into the Amazon: The Struggle for the Rain Forest.* San Francisco: Sierra Club Books, 1990.

Revkin, A. *The Burning Season: The Murder of Chico Mendes and the Fight for the Amazon Rain Forest.* New York: Houghton Mifflin, 1991.

Willrich, M. "Murder in Acre." *Amicus Journal* 11 (Spring 1989): 10-13.

Mercury

Mercury is a naturally occurring element in minerals, rocks, **soil**, water, air, plants, and animals. The predominant forms in the **atmosphere**, water, and **aerobic** soils and **sediment**s are elemental and mercuric mercury; while cinnabar is commonly found in mineralized ore deposits and **anaerobic** soils and sediments. Mercury is present throughout the atmosphere because of its relatively high vapor pressure. It vaporizes from the earth's surface and is transported in a global cycle, sometimes for hundreds of kilometers, before being deposited again with **particulate**s, rain, or snow. The background concentrations in rocks and soils typically range between 20 and 100 µg Hg/kg with a worldwide average of about 50 µg Hg/kg. Natural background concentrations in the uncontaminated atmosphere are in the order of between 1 and 10 ng/m^3 increasing to between 50 and 1,000,000 ng/m^3 or more over mineralized areas. Mercury is transported to aquatic **ecosystem**s via surface **runoff** and atmospheric deposition. Airborne concentrations associated with **anthropogenic** activities such as **coal** burning, smelting, industry, and **incineration** range between 100 and 100,000 ng/m^3.

The annual worldwide production from cinnabar was about 11,500 metric tons in 1990. The element can be divided into two major categories, organic and inorganic. Inorganic mercury includes the elemental (Hg^0) silvery liquid metal (mp, 38°C; bp, 357°C) as well as mercurous ion (Hg^+), mercuric ion (Hg^{++}), and their compounds. Organic mercury includes chemical compounds which contain **carbon** atoms that are covalently bound to a mercury atom, such as methylmercury (CH_3-Hg^+).

During the latter half of the twentieth century, inorganic mercury was used extensively to produce caustic soda and **chlorine** as well as to manufacture batteries, switches, street lamps, and fluorescent lamps. Gold mining, dental amalgams, pharmaceuticals, and other consumer items also consume inorganic mercury. Organic mercury applications have mostly been eliminated in agricultural **fungicide**s, slimicides in paper pulp production, bacteriostats in water based paints, and industrial catalysts.

Over the centuries the symptoms of inorganic mercury poisoning were well documented by the exposure of miners and industrial workers as mercury accumulated in their brains, kidneys, and livers. Loose teeth, tremors, and psychopathological symptoms were common at low exposure, but removal from the source would often enable the victims to recover. However, the effects of organic alkyl mercurials, such as methylmercury, were more severe. With a **half-life** in the human body of about seventy days, continued exposure elevates the levels. It also crosses the blood/brain and placental barriers, attacking the central nervous system and inducing teratogenic changes in the fetus. The neurological symptoms include: loss of coordination in walking; slurred speech; constriction of the field of vision; loss of sensation, especially in the fingers, toes, and lips; and loss of hearing. Severe poisoning can cause coma, blindness, and death.

The concentrations of mercury in the ocean and uncontaminated freshwater are generally believed to be less than 300 and 200 ng/l respectively. However, new ultra clean analytical techniques indicate that the actual concentrations may be three to five fold lower. In contaminated aquatic systems concentrations as high as 5 µg Hg/l have been reported. In the water column, mercury readily adsorbs onto organic particulates, metal oxides, and clays. Then they settle into the sediments. Historically, depending on their location, the natural background concentrations of mercury in sediments have ranged between 10 and 200 µg/kg. However, most aquatic systems have received some mercury contamination, and the rate has increased during the past century. Among sites that have been measured, the total concentrations have usually been from five to ten times greater than background and ranged from less than 0.5 mg Hg/kg (dry weight) in remote areas to 2010 mg Hg/kg (dry weight) in Minamata Bay, Japan.

In the aquatic ecosystem inorganic mercury is converted to methylmercury by both biotic and abiotic processes. It is then released, and aquatic organisms bioaccumulate it easily and metabolize and excrete it very poorly. The biological half-life in fish may be as long as one to three years. Exposed organisms at each level of the food chain bioconcentrate methylmercury and pass it on to animals at the higher **trophic level**s.

Depending on the **species** of fish and the type and amount of mercury being released from the sediments, it may be magnified biologically from 1,000 and 100,000 times or more. While background levels of total mercury in freshwater and marine fishes from unpolluted waters typically range from less than 0.1 to about 0.2 mg Hg/kg, higher concentrations are found in some pelagic top predator ocean fishes such as tuna and shark, sometimes exceeding 1:5 mg/kg. Conversely, fish from contaminated waters typically contain levels between 0.5 and 5.0 mg Hg/kg and up to 35 to 50 mg Hg/kg in highly contaminated areas.

Several standards have been developed to protect the public's health from the threat of mercury poisoning. The maximum permissible concentration allowed by the United States **Environmental Protection Agency (EPA)** under its drinking water standards is 2 µg Hg/l. The United States **Food and Drug Administration** guideline for mercury in seafood is 1 mg Hg/kg freshweight; however, some states, such as Michigan, adhere to a more restrictive guideline of 0.5 mg Hg/kg freshweight. The Food and Agriculture

Organization of the United Nations (FAO), on the other hand, recommends a provisional tolerable intake (PTI) of 0.3 mg mercury per week for a person weighing 154 lb (70 kg), of which no more than 0.2 should be in the methylated form. *See also* Biological methylation; Birth defects; Food chain/web; Minamata disease; Teratogen; Water pollution; Xenobiotic

[*Frank M. D'Itri*]

FURTHER READING

D'Itri, F. M., et al. *An Assessment of Mercury in the Environment.* Washington, DC: National Academy of Sciences, 1978.

D'Itri, F. M. "Mercury Contamination: What We Have Learned Since Minamata." *Environmental Monitoring and Assessment* 19 (1991): 165-82.

Metabolism

The sum total of biochemical reactions occurring in living organisms by which energy is made available to the organism. Metabolism consists of *catabolism*, the chemical breakdown of large molecules into their smaller molecular components (e.g., from proteins to amino acids), and *anabolism*, the reconstruction or chemical synthesis of large molecules. In physiology, metabolism also describes regulated sequences of chemical reactions (physiological pathways), such as protein metabolism or urea metabolism. In **ecology**, the metabolism of lakes or ponds is the sum of the chemical reactions taking place between the inhabitants and the **environment**.

Metals, as contaminants

Metals, objects made from metal, and chemical compounds containing metal are pervasive in the home, workplace, and **environment**. Although metals play an essential role in modern human society, there are many instances where they occur as unneeded and harmful contaminants. Heavy metals such as **mercury**, **cadmium**, **lead**, **uranium**, chromium, manganese, **nickel**, thallium, and bismuth are all industrially useful, but they are also potentially harmful at high concentrations in the environment or when found in food or drinking water. Environmental contamination with heavy metals can result from many activities including mining, large-scale combustion of **coal** in heating or power plants, mineral and metal processing, and use of fungicides and **pesticide**s.

The metal mercury (Hg), a useful component of many products including thermometers, pesticides, drugs, paints, and batteries, is unusual in that it is a liquid at ordinary temperatures. It forms a variety of useful salts and organic compounds. Misuse of products containing mercury can lead to serious health problems. Disorders caused by mercury depend on the form of mercury ingested and the method of exposure. Ingestion of mercury salts can lead to kidney damage and death. Exposure to mercury vapor can lead to inhalation or absorption through the skin. Brain function is affected, and loss of memory, depression, anxiety, and other personality changes may result. Ingestion of organic mercury compounds used in pesticides can result in permanent neurological damage. One very serious mercury pollution incident occurred in the 1950s at Minamata Bay, Japan, where releases of mercury in effluent from a manufacturing plant were ingested by fish. People eating the fish developed serious, and in some cases fatal, neurological maladies. Infants and children were particularly vulnerable to this "**Minimata disease**."

Lead (Pb) has been used for many purposes for thousands of years. However, toxicity has been largely unnoticed or ignored until recent decades. Lead uptake by the body is quite slow, but its rate of excretion is even slower. Thus in cases of long term exposure, lead levels in the body gradually increase. There are many sources of contamination. Lead water pipes were once used to carry domestic water. Until recently, lead-containing solder was use to join **copper** piping in homes. Lead contamination of drinking water resulted, and symptoms of lead toxicity were noted in those who used the water. Until recently, white lead pigment was widely used in house paint. Deteriorating and chipping paint poisoned occupants, particularly children, who accidentally ingested or inhaled dust and fragments. Symptoms of lead toxicity can be both chronic and acute. Weakness, loss of appetite, anemia, vomiting, and convulsions have all been reported. Lead causes lesions in the central nervous system and serious long-term damage.

Cadmium (Cd) is useful both as an element and in compounds. The element is a lustrous silvery metal that is usually associated in nature with zinc. It is used to plate steel, copper, brass, and other alloys and serves to retard corrosion. Cadmium oxide is used in nickel-cadmium storage batteries and as a pigment in paints and inks. Although metallic cadmium is not dangerous under ordinary conditions, cadmium ions, produced when the metal is attacked by mineral acids, are very toxic. Toxicity symptoms resemble those of mercury.

Uranium (U) with an atomic number of 92, is one of the heaviest of all elements. Once thought to be rare, it is now known to be widely distributed in the Earth's crust. Its concentration in sea water exceeds those of mercury and cadmium and is at about the same level as copper and lead. Interest in uranium and its use expanded dramatically with the development of atomic power and **nuclear weapons**. Environmental and health concerns have centered on the radioactive nature of uranium, but chemical toxicity is also a potential problem. Uranium contamination surrounding mining and mill tailings in southwestern United States has been a major concern for Native Americans living nearby.

Each of the heavy metals has its own specific toxic effects on human health and the environment. Before this fact was generally realized, mining, smelting and manufacturing activities often resulted in appalling instances of environmental contamination. While greater concern has resulted in improvement, serious problems remain in instances where proper control has not been practiced.

[*Douglas C. Pratt*]

FURTHER READING

Baselt, R.C. *Disposition of Toxic Drugs and Chemicals in Man*, 3rd ed. Chicago: Year Book Medical Publishers, 1989.

Eichstaedt, P.H. *If You Poison Us: Uranium and Native Americans*. Santa Fe, N.M.: Red Crane Books, 1994.

Friberg, L., et al., eds. *Handbook on the Toxicology of Metals*, 2nd edition. Amsterdam, New York: Elsevier, 1986.

Meteorology

Meteorology is derived from the Greek words *meteora* meaning things in the air or things above, and *logy* meaning science or discourse. It is a branch of physics concerned with the study and theory of atmospheric phenomena and is frequently equated to atmospheric science. One of the earliest references to this branch of physics is Aristotle's *Meteorologica* written around 340 B.C.

In the modern context meteorology is founded upon the basic physical principles and laws governing the energy and mass exchanges within the earth's **atmosphere** and involves the study of short term variations of atmospheric properties (temperature, moisture, wind) and interactions with the earth's surface. The ability to predict and explain short term changes in the atmosphere from observations and numerical models (using the laws of physics) is an important dimension of meteorology as well. Thus the words meteorologist and forecaster are often used interchangeably to describe someone who can predict the weather.

Meteorologists are trained in observations, instrumentation, data processing, and modeling techniques for the purpose of analyzing and predicting trajectories of major weather systems, including their associated temperature, precipitation, wind, and sky conditions. Modern methods include the use of automated surface observation systems, radar, satellites, radiosondes, wind profilers, and high resolution computer models (sometimes called global circulation models) to estimate temporal and spatial variability. *See also* Acid rain; Climate; Cloud chemistry; Hydrologic cycle; Photochemical smog

Methane

An organic compound with the chemical formula CH_4, methane occurs naturally in air at a concentration of about 0.0002 percent. It is produced in processes such as the **anaerobic** decay of organic matter, the growth of certain types of plants, and the belching of cattle. Methane is the major component of **natural gas**, making up about 85 percent of that fuel. Environmental scientists are increasingly concerned about methane as a possible greenhouse gas. Like **carbon dioxide**, methane traps heat reflected from the earth and, therefore, may contribute to global warming. Increases in agricultural and dairying activities have resulted in an increase in methane production, possibly contributing to **climate** change. *See also* Greenhouse effect; Greenhouse gases

Methane digester

Methane digesters are systems that use anaerobes to produce **methane** through fermentation. Methane is a main constituent of **natural gas** and can be readily substituted for that **nonrenewable resource**.

The anaerobes used in methane digesters are methanogenes, bacteria belonging to the genera *Methanobacterium*; *Methanosarcina*; and *Methanoccus*. They can be found in the gastrointestinal tracts of animals such as cows and other ruminants, as well as in **soil**, water, and sewage. In **septic tank**s, bacteria liquefy some of the organic matter; which releases energy for the bacteria and by products such as methane and **carbon dioxide**.

Methane digesters are also known as biogass digesters and organic digesters. The central portion is an airtight drum, called a digester unit, which contains the methanogenes. Raw material is place into the drum, and the unit is kept at a constant temperature of about 95°F (35°C). Some of the methane produced by the digester heats the water. Outlets on the digester unit take away the various products of the system. Liquid and solid **fertilizer**s are collected to be used for crops and other plants. Methane is stored in a tank, from which it can be drawn off for fuel for a variety of purposes. Carbon dioxide and hydrogen sulfide can be filtered out of the methane and put under pressure for use in turning turbines.

Common household **organic waste**s can be put into a digester, and the methane produced can be used to make electricity. It can also be used for cooking, illumination, heating, and **automobile** fuel. One system at the University of Maine produced over $8,000 worth of power a year in the early 1990s; the digester also produced a **sludge** that could be used as a nutritious and relatively odorless plant fertilizer. Some sludges, however can contain high level of metals if the original material is unsorted municipal waste.

Methane is a clean and nontoxic automobile fuel, and it produces no pollutants when burned. It has an octane number of 130. Italy has used it as a motor fuel for over 40 years, and Modesto, California, has a small fleet of methane-powered cars. Because of its cleanliness, it extends the life of engines as well as making starting easier.

The organic matter this system converts into other uses would otherwise have decomposed in a **landfill**, **leaching** into the surrounding **environment** and contaminating **groundwater** supplies. In a digester, it becomes a useful resource. *See also* Alternative energy sources; Alternative fuels; Anaerobic digestion; Bioremediation; Groundwater pollution

[*Nikola Vrtis*]

FURTHER READING

Trans, W. B. "Just Plug It Into That Cherry Tomato Over There." *Sierra*. 75 (May-June 1990): 20-21.

Methanol

Methanol is an organic compound with the chemical form CH_3OH. It is also known as methyl alcohol or wood alcohol. Like most alcohols, methanol is very toxic. Its ingestion can cause severe nerve damage leading to blindness, insanity, and death. Methanol can be prepared through destructive distillation of **coal**, wood and wood products, **garbage**, sewage **sludge**, and other forms of **biomass**. It is an excellent automotive fuel and has long been used to power racing cars. Existing methods of production are still too expensive, however, to make it an economically viable alternative to **gasoline** in the general market. *See also* Alternative fuels; Fuel-switching

Methylation

A chemical reaction in which the methyl radical ($-CH_3$) is added to some substance. The most common mechanism by which methylation occurs in the **environment** is biological methylation, which involves the action of living organisms. Bacteria in oxygen-poor **soil**s, for example, can convert metallic mercury to an organic compound, methyl **mercury**. Similar reactions occur with other metals, including **arsenic**, selenium, tin, and **lead**. These reactions are significant because they convert non-soluble metals of low toxicity into soluble forms with high toxicity. Light can also induce methylation. Photomethylation has occurred in the laboratory, but its relative importance in environmental systems is not yet well understood.

Methylmercury seed dressings

Seed dressings were devised to prevent diseases caused by a wide variety of seed-borne plant-pathogenic **fungi**, to protect the germinating seeds against secondary infections, and to increase crop yields. Various **chemicals**, including several heavy metals, have been used as **fungicide**s to treat seeds since the end of the nineteenth century. The effectiveness of these fungicides was greatly increased when aryl organomercurials were introduced around 1914. They had a wider spectrum of fungicidal activity than nonmercurial formulations and were used extensively until the mid-1980s to control fungus diseases through their application as seed dressings on many grains, vegetables, and nuts, as well as to protect fruit trees, rice, turf grasses, and golf courses. However, with the introduction of the more effective alkyl **mercury** compounds in the 1930s, especially methyl mercury and ethyl mercury, severe poisoning incidents followed. In developing countries hundreds of people died or became incapacitated due to either the consumption of grains treated with alkylmercury compounds or meat from animals that had eaten such treated seeds.

Poisonings from eating alkylmercury-treated grains occurred on several occasions in various parts of Iraq. Destitute, illiterate rural families either did not understand the words or poison symbols on the bags of grain or did not believe government warnings that it was unsafe to eat. In some instances the families fed some of the grain to chickens and swine first. When they did not observe poisoning symptoms in the livestock and poultry after a few days, the farmers became convinced that the warnings were false and the grain was safe to eat. However, depending on the amount of methyl mercury consumed, there is a latency period of weeks or months between exposure and the development of poisoning symptoms.

When the seed grain was ground into flour, baked into bread, and consumed by the rural victims, both sexes and all ages were affected. The ingested quantities of methylmercury ranged from small amounts that produced no overt effects to lethal doses. Fetuses suffered the most damage. Among the rest of the population, the severity of the neurological and psychiatric symptoms was almost directly proportional to the amount of bread consumed. In cities where bread was produced from government-inspected flour mills, not a single case of poisoning was reported.

The first documented incident occurred in Iraq in 1956. Of the two hundred persons afflicted, seventy died. In 1960 an estimated 1000 persons were affected in a similar incident and over 200 died. During the 1960s other smaller but similar episodes of alkylmercury poisoning occurred on a more limited scale in West Pakistan, Guatemala, Ghana, and in other countries such as Mexico and the United States. The total death toll in these countries was 42 with approximately 197 individuals less seriously affected.

But the most serious outbreak of poisoning from eating methyl mercury-poisoned bread occurred in Iraq early in 1972. In October and November of 1971 a total of about 73,000 tons of high-yield Mexipac wheat seed grain and 22,000 tons of barley seed grain, all treated with alkyl mercury fungicide, had been distributed by cooperatives to farmers for planting throughout the country. Some of this grain, as before, was used to prepare homemade bread. The Iraqi government estimated that the treated grain was distributed to no more than five percent of the rural population, about 200,000 people. Most of the fatalities occurred within three months after the end of the exposure, although a few long-term illnesses resulted in fatalities as well.

By March 1973, up to 40,000 persons, residents of every province, were unofficially estimated to have been poisoned. The total number of casualties will never be known precisely because hospitals were quickly overloaded, and many victims did not have access to them. In addition, most of the poisonings occurred in rural areas, and many were not reported to authorities. The government officially acknowledged that 6,530 persons were hospitalized and 459 died. These figures were not confirmed because news reporters were denied entry to the country and the movements of foreigners were restricted. However, tourists reported that large numbers of Iraqis suffered brain damage, blindness, and paralysis. Since then, with the exception of a few follow-up scientific reports published between 1985 and 1989, hardly any new information relative to the long term health effects on the thousands of victims has been published or released by

Polluted air over Mexico City.

the Iraqi government although this was the largest such tragedy of this kind. Because of the highly toxic nature of the alkyl mercurials, as well as the severity of the accidents caused by misuse of the treated seeds, they were banned in 1970 in the United States and many other countries. *See also* Agricultural chemicals; Birth defects; Heavy metals and heavy metal poisoning; Minamata disease; Plant pathology; Teratogen; Xenobiotic

[*Frank M. D'Itri*]

FURTHER READING

Bakir, F., et al. "Methylmercury Poisoning in Iraq." *Science* 181 (1973): 230-241.

"Conference on Intoxication Due to Alkyl Mercury-Treated Seed." *World Health Organization* 53 (Suppl.) (1976): 138.

D'Itri, P. A., and F. M. D'Itri. *Mercury Contamination: A Human Tragedy.* New York: Wiley-Interscience, 1977.

Greenwood, M. R. "Methylmercury Poisoning in Iraq: An Epidemiological Study of the 1971-72 Outbreak." *Journal of Applied Toxicology* 5 (1985): 148-159.

Mexico City, Mexico

Founded in the fourteenth century, Mexico City has been a center for three great civilizations: the Aztecs, the Spanish, and the modern-day Mexicans. But in addition to an imposing political background, its geographical location has assured the city a fascinating ecological and environmental history. Mexico City lies in a basin 7,350 feet (2,240 m) high. It is surrounded by mountain ranges on all sides, and the presence of the extinct **volcano**es Ixtacihuatl and Popocatepetl to the east are a reminder that the city lies on an active earthquake fault.

Most of Mexico City's environmental problems are caused by a combination of its geographical location and growing population. In 1900, the population was estimated at 350,000; the rest of the century has seen nothing but rapid growth. Population has leapt from 1,029,000 in 1930 to 4,871,000 by 1960, and then to 12,000,000 in the mid-1970s, and then 15,000,000 by 1981. According to some estimates, Mexico City will have more than 32 million inhabitants by the year 2000, making it the most populous urban area in the world.

The amount of **pollution** produced by a city of this size would be difficult to control in even the most favorable geographic circumstances. But the basin in which Mexico City is built traps the **ozone**, **nitrogen oxides**, sulfur, and **particulate**s that are released each day. Soft **coal**, wood, and low-grade **gasoline** and oil are burned widely throughout the city, contributing greatly to this problem. In addition, prevailing winds from the northeast carry dust particles into the city from rural areas, further degrading **air quality**. The city has gone from having one of the most perfect natural settings and ideal **climate**s in the world to being the most heavily polluted. Pollution levels can rise so high that schools are occasionally forced to close so students can remain indoors and not breathe the polluted air. Entrepreneurs have even set up booths on city streets where people can pay to breath oxygen from tanks.

Lying near the boundary of the Pacific and North American geological plates, Mexico City has long been at risk for major earthquakes, a risk which has been greatly increased by the city's history. When the Aztecs first settled the area, it was largely covered by an enormous lake, Lake Tenochititlán, which either was filled in or dried out as the city began to grow. Today, Mexico City sits on a soft **subsoil** that is highly unstable. Some parts it are actually sinking into the old lake bed, while the whole area rides out each earthquake like a boat on an unsettled ocean.

The geographical instability of the area has been worsened by the fact that residents traditionally obtain their water from **wells**. As the population grows, more water is removed and **subsidence** increases. In some parts of the old city, buildings have actually sunk more than six feet (2 m) below street level. Since measurements were first made in 1891, subsidence in some areas has exceeded 26 feet (8 m), and it measures at least 13 feet (4 m) in nearly all parts of the city. *See also* Air pollution control; Air quality criteria; Los Angeles Basin; Nitrogen cycle; Population growth; Sulfur cycle; Sulfur dioxide

[*David E. Newton*]

FURTHER READING

"Line Up to Breathe." *BioScience* (September 1991): 591.

Poland, J. F., and G. H. Davis, "Land Subsidence Due to Withdrawal of Fluids." In *Man's Impact on the Environment*, edited by T. R. Detwyler. New York: McGraw-Hill, 1971.

"School Days and Lethal Haze." *Environment* 30 (March 1988): 23.

Microbes (microorganisms)

Microbes, also known as microorganisms, are defined solely on the basis of their size—they are too small to be seen by the naked eye. Microorganisms can only be viewed if they are magnified in size, using an optical or electron microscope.

Apart from their size, the major groups of microorganisms have little affinity in terms of their evolutionary history and systematics. Included among the microorganisms are viruses, bacteria, blue-green bacteria, some algae, some fungi, yeasts, and protozoans.

Viruses

Although viruses are commonly considered to be microorganisms, they are actually "pseudo-organisms" because they do not display all of the characteristics of life. Viruses consist only of bits of **nucleic acid** (either **deoxyribonucleic acid (DNA)**, or **ribonucleic acid (RNA)**) surrounded by a protein capsule (called a capsid). Viruses are not capable of independent reproduction, and they cannot perform other important metabolic functions. To reproduce and grow viruses must invade and parasitize the living cells of other organisms, and appropriate the metabolic capabilities of their host.

It is probable that all living cells are infected by viruses of various sorts, and in some cases serious diseases are caused. Viral diseases of humans include colds, flu, and more deadly ailments such as smallpox, yellow fever, rabies, herpes, polio, and human immunodeficiency syndrome (HIV, also known as **AIDS**). Some viral diseases can be controlled by vaccination, a practice that involves infecting hosts with killed but intact virus bodies. These are non-virulent but nevertheless cause the host to develop resistance to pathogenic forms of the strain. Vaccination made it possible to achieve the eradication of smallpox, a disease that had long been a scourge of humans.

Bacteria and Blue-green Bacteria

Bacteria and blue-green bacteria are in the kingdom of life known as Monera. Most species in this group are bacteria; these have rigid or semi-rigid cell walls, propagate by binary division of the cell, and do not display mitosis during cell division. Blue-green bacteria or cyanobacteria (sometimes incorrectly referred to as blue-green algae) utilize chlorophyll dispersed within their cytoplasm as a pigment for capturing light energy during **photosynthesis**. The genetic material of monerans is organized as a single strand of DNA, and it is not contained within a membrane-bounded organelle called a nucleus, so these microorganisms are referred to as being prokaryotic. (All of the other kingdoms have a nucleus within their cells, and are known as eukaryotic.) In addition, prokaryotes do not display meiosis or mitosis, their reproduction is by asexual cellular division, and they do not have organelles such as chloroplasts, mitochondria, or flagella. Prokaryotes were the first organisms to evolve, about 3.5 million years ago. It was not until 2 million years later that the first eukaryotes evolved.

About 4,800 species of bacteria have been named, but microbiologists believe that there are many additional species that have not yet been discovered. Bacteria are capable of exploiting an astonishing range of ecological and metabolic opportunities. Some species can only function in the presence of oxygen, and others only under anaerobic conditions, although some species are able to opportunistically switch between these metabolic types. Some bacteria can tolerate very extreme environments, surviving in hot springs at temperatures as hot as 172°F (78°C), while other species have been found active in the frigid conditions that occur as deep as 436 yd (400 m) in glaciers.

Most free-living bacteria are heterotrophic, and among the diversity of bacterial species are some that are capable of metabolizing virtually any organic substances as a source of nutrition. Other species of bacteria are photosynthetic (including blue-green bacteria), capable of capturing sunlight and using it to reduce **carbon dioxide** and water into simple sugars, which are used as a source of energy in more complex biochemical syntheses. Other bacteria are chemosynthetic, coupling their biosynthetic abilities to energy released during the oxidation of certain inorganic compounds, as when pyritic sulfur or sulfide are oxidized to sulfate.

Many species of bacteria are not free-living, and instead live in a mutualistic symbiosis with more complex organisms, such as plants or invertebrate or vertebrate animals. For example, numerous species of bacteria live as a microbial community within the rumen of cows and sheep, while others live in the gut of humans and other primates. These gut bacteria help with the digestion of complex organic foods, and they also synthesize vitamins and micronutrients that are useful to their host. Other bacteria in the genus *Rhizobium* live in a mutualism with the roots of peas, clovers, and other leguminous plants, fixing atmospheric dinitrogen gas (N_2) into ammonia (NH_3), which after conversion to ammonium (NH_4), it becomes a source of **nitrogen** that plants can utilize as a nutrient.

Many bacteria are parasites of other organisms, and some cause important diseases. Significant diseases of humans caused by bacteria include various kinds of infections, bacterial pneumonia, cholera, diphtheria, gastric ulcers, gonorrhea, Legionnaire's disease, leprosy, scarlet fever, syphilis, tetanus, tooth decay, tuberculosis, whooping cough, most types of food poisoning, and the "flesh-eating disease," which is caused by a virulent strain of *Streptococcus*. Bacteria also cause diseases of other species, and this is sometimes used to the advantage of humans. For example, *Bacillus thuringiensis* is a pathogen of many species of moths, butterflies, and blackflies, and strains of this bacterium have been used as a biological insecticide against certain insect pests in agriculture and forestry.

Microscopic Protists

The kingdom Protista consists of a wide range of simple eukaryotic organisms, including numerous unicellular and multicellular species. Microbial protists include protozoans, foraminifera, slime molds, single-celled algae, and multicellular algae. (Some other multicellular algae are not microscopic—the largest seaweeds, known as kelps, can grow fronds longer than 11 yd [10 m]!) Eukaryotic organisms have their genetic material organized within a membrane-bounded nucleus, containing paired chromosomes of DNA. Protists have flagellated spores, and mitochondria and plastids are often, but not always, present.

Recent systematic treatments have divided the kingdom Protista into about 14 phyla, consisting of about 40,000 named species. Many of these phyla, however, differ enormously from the others in basic elements of their biology. It is likely that additional systematic research of this extremely diverse group will result in the Protista being divided into several kingdoms.

Several phyla of protists are photosynthetic, and these are collectively known as algae. Most species in the following groups are microscopic: diatoms (phylum Bacillariophyta), green algae (Chlorophyta), dinoflagellates (Dinoflagellata), euglenoids (Euglenophyta), and red algae (Rhodophyta). The brown algae and kelps (Phaeophyta) are macroscopic, as are some colonial species in several of the other groups. Algae are important primary producers in marine and freshwater **ecosystem**s. Uncommon phenomena known as "**red tide**s" are natural blooms of certain species of marine dinoflagellates that produce toxic biochemicals.

Other phyla of microbial protists have a heterotrophic nutrition. Protozoans are single-celled microorganisms, gener-ally considered to be microscopic animals. Protozoans reproduce by binary fission, and are often motile, usually using cilia or flagella for propulsion. Some protozoans are colonial. Protozoans are abundant in most aquatic environments.

Other heterotrophic protists include the ciliates (Ciliophora), forams (Foraminifera), amoebae (Rhizopoda), and unicellular flagellates (Zoomastigina). Forams are unicellular microorganisms that form a "shell" of calcium carbonate. Chalk is a mineral that is formed from the remains of forams that have accumulated over geologically long periods of time. (The white cliffs of Dover, England, consist of the fossil remains of innumerable forams).

Some species of protists cause diseases of humans, such as *Plasmodium*, a unicellular blood parasite that causes malaria and is spread to people and other vertebrate animals by mosquitoes. Some species of amoebae are parasites of animals, causing amoebic dysentery in humans. Hiker's diarrhea (or beaver fever) is a water-borne disease caused by the ciliate *Giardia*, which is the reason why even the cleanest-looking natural waters should be boiled or otherwise disinfected before drinking.

Microscopic Fungi

The kingdom Fungi consists of single-celled microorganisms known as yeasts, plus the fungi, which are multicelled, filamentous in their growth form, and reproduce by budding or by cellular fission. All yeasts and fungi are heterotrophic, excreting enzymes that digest complex organic materials, allowing simple organic compounds to be ingested.

A few species of yeasts are economically important because they have the ability to ferment sugars under anaerobic (O_2-deficient) conditions, yielding gaseous CO_2 and ethyl alcohol (or ethanol). The CO_2 produced during fermentation can be utilized to raise bread dough prior to baking, while the alcohol can be used by brewers to produce beer, wine, and other intoxicating beverages.

Microorganisms are characterized only by their microscopic size. Otherwise they comprise a wide range of diverse but not necessarily related groups of organisms. As a larger group, microorganisms are extremely important as primary producers in ecosystems, as agents of decay of dead organisms and **recycling** of the nutrients contained in their **biomass**, and as **parasites** and diseases of humans and other species.

[*Bill Freedman*]

FURTHER READING

Atlas, R.M., and R. Bartha. *Microbial Ecology*. Menlo Park, CA: Benjamin/Cummings, 1987

Raven, P.H,. and G.B. Johnson. *Biology*, 3rd ed, St. Louis, MO: Mosby Year Book, 1992.

Starr, C., and R. Taggart. *Biology. The Unity and Diversity of Life*. Belmont, CA: Wadsworth Pub. Co., 1992.

Microclimate

In general, **climate** conditions near the ground are called microclimates. More specifically, microclimate refers to the climate characteristics of highly localized areas, ranging from the area around an individual plant to a field of crops or a small forested area. The horizontal area considered may be less than one square meter or up to several thousands of square meters. The vertical extent may range from a few centimeters involving the still layers of air within a plant canopy, for instance, to 100 meters or more, when the **atmosphere** surrounding a forested area is studied.

Microclimates are governed to a large extent by the interactions of surface features with the overlying atmosphere, and their characteristics may differ markedly from those of the surrounding large-scale climate. Microclimates exhibit great ranges in environmental conditions depending on the moisture and radiation properties of the surface. They typically show large diurnal temperature ranges and are highly influenced by slope, aspect, and elevation. Most plants and animals are adapted to highly specific microclimatic conditions.

Micronutrient

See **Trace element/micronutrient**

Migration

Although some scientists define animal migration as any animal movement, this definition becomes cumbersome because it does not distinguish between small-scale daily movements, annual migrations, and irrupting dispersions. Mobile animals tend to move frequently, and migration should be distinct from emigration (directional one-way movement) and dispersal (non-directional one-way movement), and it should refer primarily to regular round trip movement that happens at least once in the life span of the organism. Migration is a spatial behavior pattern that allows animals to locate themselves in the most favorable portions of their **habitat** for as long as necessary. Such favorable conditions may vary according to season or life history, but in both cases it is related to adaptive fitness. This allows the organism to take in **nutrient**s in excess of energy expenditures and to successfully reproduce.

Generally animal migration can be divided into two areas of study: the behavioral aspects, which concentrates on "how" migration happens; and the ecological aspects, which addresses "why" migrations takes place. The ecological questions also concern **evolution**, for spatial behavior is an evolved compromise between differing requirements of an organism's life. Most migratory behavior depends on food abundance. In most habitats productivity varies with the seasons, and thus energy availability also varies at all upper levels of food chains. Migration must often accommodate several energy and reproductive requirements. As a result migration patterns tend to be complicated with subsections of migrants taking slightly differing paths at various times to serve different needs.

Many species of North American waterfowl use several breeding areas, from the northern **prairie**s to the Arctic coast, and travel along several major flyways to wintering areas that range from the southern prairies to the **estuaries** of northern South America. Within that framework, males desert the hens during nesting season and make shorter migrations to molting areas, afterward meeting with the females and newly fledged young during the fall migration. In either of those sites, requirements for habitat differ in terms of water-cover ratios, water permanence, and food preferences.

The altitudinal migration of mountain sheep (*Ovis canadensis*) in the Rocky Mountains brings them into more productive habitats during the summer in the alpine meadows and into the mountain forest during the winter. Thus, food intake requirements are accommodated and, simultaneously, the sheep take advantage of the **microclimate** of the forested area during the winter to supplement energy losses from body temperature maintenance.

Migration can also be a response to particular breeding site requirements, mate location, and a combination of several forces acting together. The longest mammal migration, that of the California gray whale (*Eschrichtius robustus*), places the breeding-ready adults and newly impregnated females in the productive shallows of the Bering and Chukchi Seas, the non-breeding animals in the more patchy feeding grounds of the northeast Pacific Coast, and the calving females in the warm shallow lagoons of the Baja Peninsula.

[*David A. Duffus*]

FURTHER READING

Clark, C. W. "Moving With the Heard (Hydrophonic Monitoring of Migratory Bowhead Whales)." *Natural History* (March 1991): 38-42.

Dybas, C. L. "Secret Creatures of the Night; When the Moon is New and Darkness Falls, American Eels Begin Their Eerie Autumn Migration." *National Wildlife* 28 (October-November 1990): 18-23.

Hansson, L. "The Lemming Phenomenon: Or Why the Legendary Mass Migrations of Rodents Are Restricted to the Extreme North." *Natural History* (December 1989): 38-43.

"Recent Developments in the Study of Animal Migration." [Symposium on Recent Developments in the Study of Animal Migration.] *American Zoologist* 31 (1991): 151-276.

Wallace, D. R. "Avian Nations: The Patterns and Problems of Migrating Birds." *Wilderness* 54 (Fall 1990): 42-9+.

Milankovitch weather cycles

According to the theory of the Milankovitch weather cycles, **ice age**s are cyclical, caused by changes in the earth's orbit. The theory was developed by Serbian geophysicist Milutin Milankovitch (1879-1958) in the 1930s, and it postulates that the amount of available sunlight in the northern hemisphere is affected by the earth's orientation in space. Because the earth is a globe in motion, sunlight strikes the earth differently depending on the following factors: The eccentricity of its orbit, which returns to the same point every 100,000 years; the tilt of the axis of its rotation, a 41,000-year cycle; and the precession of the equinoxes, a 23,000-year cycle. Milankovitch proposed that decreased sunlight prevents ice and snow from melting in the summer in the northern latitudes. This, in turn, cools the **atmosphere**, because ice reflects 90 percent of solar radiation back into space, and over a long period of time, the ice accumulates and moves south.

The theory has gone through its own cycles of acceptance and rejection. The first problem for proponents of the theory was to prove the occurrence of glacial-interglacial patterns during the Pleistocene era, the epoch preceding ours. It was also necessary to date the onset of each ice age in order to calculate the date of the next one. During the last fifty years, data collection improvements in astronomy and geology, especially in satellites and deep-sea **sediment** coring, have challenged and refined the theory. Supported first by astronomical and geological data, the theory encountered opposition in the 1950s when scientists used the newly-developed Carbon-14 method to date warm-era fossils in supposed ice-age deposits. But examination of fossilized microscopic sea creatures on the ocean bed, known as foraminifera, revealed two types, the larger of which flourished when the ocean was warm. In 1955, geologist Cesare Emiliani refined dating techniques of the foraminifera retrieved by deep-sea coring. He isolated oxygen isotopes. Oxygen 16, a lighter **isotope**, evaporates more quickly and becomes trapped in ice, while oxygen 18, which thrives in warm waters, was absorbed by the shells of the foraminifera. From the evidence of theses oxygen isotopes, Emiliani was able to reconstruct glacial-interglacial periods for 300,000 years. His date agreed with Milankovitch's orbital dates.

In 1971 John Imbrie of Brown University created Project CLIMAP, which coordinated all of the data relevant to Milankovitch's cycles. From this data, scientists were able to develop a "rosetta stone" for Pleistocene glacial-interglacial dates. In the 1980s, Project SPECMAP brought together all of the deep-sea core data. It was from this data that scientists predicted the next ice age was imminent.

But critics have argued that the Milankovitch orbital theory does not take into account the concept of chaos as well as the climatic influence of the heat transfer between the atmosphere and the ocean. In 1992, United States **Geological Survey** hydrogeologist Isaac Winograd challenged the Milankovitch theory when a scuba team with a submersible drill retrieved a 14-inch (36-cm) core of calcite in a water-filled fault called Devils Hole in Nevada. The ice age dates for this core of calcite differed from the Milankovitch dates, and this suggested to Winograd that ice ages were tied less to orbital cycles than to an interaction of heat and moisture between the atmosphere, the ocean, and ice sheets. Imbrie and many others defended Milankovitch against these findings. They stood on their mountain of ocean-sediment core data, and they argued that the calcite core from Devils Hole reflected local rather than global changes.

Another problem for the Milankovitch theory is identifying the effects of human activity on the **environment**. The current interglacial period began 10,000 years ago, and according to Imbrie, it might become a "super interglacial" period due to the burning of **fossil fuels** and the subsequent **greenhouse effect**. Imbrie has argued that the natural cooling cycle which began 7,000 years ago will be postponed

until the excess **carbon dioxide** is exhausted in 2,000 years. Then, after another 1,000 years, serious cooling will set in, expected to last for 23,000 years. *See also* Climate; Glaciation; Ice age refugia; Ozone layer depletion; Radiocarbon dating

[*Stephanie Ocko*]

FURTHER READING

Berger, A., et al. *Milankovitch and Climate.* Proceedings of the NATO Advanced Research Workshop on Milankovitch and Climate. Dordrecht: D. Reidel Publishing, 1982.

Imbrie, J. and K. P. Imbrie. *Ice Ages: Solving the Mystery.* Short Hills, NJ: Enslow, 1979.

Kerr, R. A. "Milankovitch Climate Cycles Through the Ages." *Science* 235 (27 February 1987): 973-4.

Winograd, I. J., et al. "Continuous 500,000-Year Climate Record from Vein Calcite in Devils Hole, Nevada." *Science* 258 (9 October 1992): 255-260.

Milfoil
See **Eurasian milfoil**

Minamata disease

The town of Minamata, near the southern tip of Japan's Kyushu Island, gave its name to one of the most notorious examples of environmental contamination known. Minamata disease is really alkylmercury poisoning, caused by eating food such as fish or grain contaminated with **mercury** or its derivatives. At Minamata people were poisoned when they ate large quantities of methylmercury-contaminated fish. Often the victims were the poorest members of society, who could not afford to stop eating the cheap fish known to be affected by **effluent** discharged from the local chemical company. The first victims were reported in 1956; before that, cats were seen moving strangely, sometimes flinging themselves into the sea, and birds were observed flying awkwardly or even falling out of the sky.

The Chisso Company, a leading chemical manufacturer, produced acetaldehyde by passing acetylene gas across an inorganic mercury catalyst, leaving methylmercury as a by-product. The company was a major local employer and the only significant major source of industrial waste discharged into Minamata Bay. There, methylmercury in the water biomagnified to high levels in fish and shellfish consumed by the local inhabitants. Methylmercury concentrates in specific regions of the central nervous system and readily crosses the blood/brain barrier as well as the placental barrier. It is a human **teratogen** which causes brain damage during prenatal exposures, resulting in congenital or fetal Minamata disease. The compound has a **half-life** of about 70 days in the human body, and the damage is generally irreversible. Although company officials knew that similar symptoms could be induced in cats by feeding them fish taken from the

A mother from Minamata, Japan, bathes her daughter who suffers from Minamata disease. The daughter's brain damage and birth defects are due to alkylmercury poisoning from mercury-contaminated seafood that her mother ate while pregnant.

bay, Chisso was not blamed by the Japanese government for the disaster until 1968. Despite the evidence, it was difficult to be certified as a Minamata disease victim. Those affected were not compensated until after another epidemic occurred at Niigata, Japan, in 1965. That one was caused by methylmercury waste discharged from the Showa Denko Corporation Kanose factory into the Agano River. The company also manufactured acetaldehyde using the same process as Chisso.

Nearly four decades after Minamata disease was identified, the full range of its neurological symptoms is still not known, nor have the total number of sufferers been determined. While some children were born with contorted bodies and severe retardation, in milder cases the victims may be moderately retarded or exhibit only sensory disturbances. Even as the symptoms advance in adult patients, it is often difficult to determine whether they are the result of long-term poisoning, delayed effects of residual methylmercury, aging, or other complications. Therefore, even thirty years later, as of December 31, 1992, only 2,945 individuals were officially certified as Minamata Disease victims and 1,343 of them had died. Another 13,761 had been denied certification and the fate of 2,430 was still pending.

Lawsuits dragged on for more than twenty-five years, and victims seeking compensation tried confrontation tactics like an encampment that lasted a year and a half in front of Chisso's main headquarters in Tokyo. **Reclamation** of the

environment has been even slower. The Chisso Company installed waste treatment equipment in 1966 and stopped making acetaldehyde in 1968. By then 400 to 600 tons of mercury and 60,000 tons of **sludge** had been dumped into the shallow Minamata Bay. Mercury levels in fish remained elevated. **Dredging** scheduled to begin in 1975 did not get underway until 1982. Since then, mercury levels in ten **species** of fish have dropped; but as of March 1993, they were still two or three times higher than what the government deems acceptable. Consequently, fishermen have lost their livelihood and health and gained a social stigma. The Chisso company's fortunes also declined and were further strained by lawsuits that mandated restitution. *See also* Agricultural chemicals; Biomagnification; Birth defects; Environmental law; Food chain/web; Heavy metals and heavy metal poisoning; Marine pollution; Methylmercury seed dressings; Water pollution; Xenobiotic

[*Frank M. D'Itri*]

FURTHER READING

D'Itri, F. M. "Mercury Contamination—What We Have Learned Since Minamata." *Environmental Monitoring and Assessment* 19 (1991): 165-182.

Harada, M. "Methyl Mercury Poisoning Due to Environmental Contamination (Minamata Disease)." In *Toxicity of Heavy Metals in the Environment, Part 1*, edited by F. W. Oehme. New York: Marcel Dekker, 1978.

Ui, J. "Minamata Disease." In *Industrial Pollution in Japan*, edited by J. Ui. Tokyo, Japan: United Nations University Press, 1992.

Mine drainage

See **Acid mine drainage**

Mine spoil waste

Most human extractions of earth materials, such as clay for pottery or **coal** for power generation, produce some waste. The raw materials are rarely pure, so unwanted detritus is discarded, usually close to the extraction site. Over the last two centuries, exponential industrial growth has resulted in huge increases in the production of mine spoil waste. The management of this waste has become an increasingly important issue.

New technologies allow the mining of ever lower grades of ore, with mounting waste as a byproduct. Early mining actually wasted ore, since only the richest veins were extracted. However, less waste was generated by this high grade ore. Now operations tend to remove varying grades of ore *en mass*, yielding a higher return, but multiplying the waste produced. Where concentrations are high, it has even been profitable to rework older **tailings**.

Surface mining accounts for most mining waste, but underground work also contributes. Metallic ores, sand, gravel, and building stone, including aggregate for concrete, are usually extracted from open pit mines. **Strip mining** is effective where resources lie in sedimentary layers, and is particularly used for coal, phosphate, and gypsum. Much of the waste from strip mining comes from **overburden** removal. **Dredging** is used to extract sand and heavy placer deposits such as gold and tin; it reinjects large amounts of fluvial **sediment** into the flowing water. Hydraulic mining with high pressure hoses is common in gold fields; devastating effects are still visible in the foothills of California's Sierra Nevada Mountains, more than a century later.

Environmental impacts of mining include the creation of new landforms, severe **ecosystem** disruption, and the formation of dangerous **chemicals**. The scale of operation varies enormously, but some projects are immense. The holes and mountains of overburden created may become useful as chat for railroad beds, sub-base material for roads, or recreational lakes. But, severe environmental problems are a more common result. Ecosystem disruption stems mainly from loss of **topsoil**, rich in organisms and **nutrient**s; sterile landscapes with high sediment runoff are a common outcome.

The most serious problem resulting from mine wastes is acid drainage and **leaching** of hazardous substances. When these wastes are moved from a reducing environment (oxygen deficient) to an oxidizing environment, sulfuric acids are formed by the oxidation of the sulfides in metallic ores or the sulfur that commonly accompanies coal deposits. These acids may flow into surface waters or may leach hazardous metals from the waste. The best solution is to minimize exposure to oxygen, usually by burial.

Mining presents the dilemma of short term gains versus long term losses, especially of land suitable for agriculture or forestry. The goal of sustainability makes **reclama-**tion of mine spoil wastes imperative. *See also* Acid mine drainage; Erosion; Hazardous material; Sustainable development; Waste management

[*Nathan H. Meleen*]

FURTHER READING

Caudill, H. M. *Night Comes to the Cumberlands*. Boston: Atlantic-Little Brown, 1963.

Meleen, N. H. "Mining Wastes and Reclamation." In *Magill's Survey of Science: Earth Science Series*, edited by Frank N. Magill. Pasadena, CA: Salem Press, 1990.

U.S. Department of the Interior. *Surface Mining and Our Environment*. Washington, DC: U.S. Government Printing Office, 1967.

Mineral Leasing Act (1920)

The Mineral Leasing Act of 1920 regulates the exploitation of fuel and **fertilizer** minerals on the **public land**s. The act resulted from the perceived failure of existing federal laws dealing with **coal** and oil resources. Coal lands had been managed under an 1873 law, allowing the coal to be mined for either $10 or $20 per ton on tracts of 160 or 320 acres (64.8 or 129.6 ha). These acreage limitations led to abuse of the law, and in 1906 over 65 million acres (26.3 million ha) of land were withdrawn from coverage under of the coal lands law. These lands were then reclassified according to whether they contained coal or not, and the price for lands containing coal was increased. The withdrawal and reclassification process slowed development and led many to argue for a new approach. The fate of these coal lands was soon tied to the fate of oil lands.

Oil resources were being managed based on the Mining Law of 1870 and the Oil Placer Act of 1897. Neither law, however, sufficiently recognized the difference between **petroleum** and other minerals this in turn resulted in major problems in the exploitation of petroleum. These problems included overproduction, market instability, claim jumping, and national security concerns. In 1909, President William Howard Taft withdrew over three million acres of public land from oil development in California and Wyoming, thereby initiating a policy debate over how to manage petroleum resources on the public lands.

The first leasing bill, supported by the Taft administration, was introduced in Congress in 1913, but because it was so controversial in the western states, the Mineral Leasing Act was not passed until 1920. The law, which applies to deposits of coal, oil, gas, **oil shale**, phosphate, potash, sodium, and sulfur on the public lands, has two main features: federal regulatory authority and conditional access to the public lands. Controversy centered on the oil provisions of the Act. These gave the Secretary of the Interior the authority to issue permits for prospecting on land that was not known to have any oil. If oil were discovered, the prospector acquired lease rights for 20 years and paid a royalty fee of five percent. For proven oil-producing lands, tracts were offered under a system of competitive bidding based on royalty payments. The minimum area covered was 640 acres

(259.2 ha), and the minimum royalty accepted was 12.5 percent. These royalties were to be divided among the Reclamation Fund (for western water projects), the states in which the land is located (for education and roads), and the federal government.

Amendments to the act have done away with prospecting permits, increased the size of tracts that can be leased, and changed the bidding procedures for leases. Most lands that are not known to contain oil are leased through a lottery conducted by the **U. S. Department of the Interior**. For known oil lands, a competitive bidding procedure is used. In addition to the bid fee, a 12.5 percent royalty and an annual rental fee of $2.00 per acre is also required.

The Mineral Leasing Act was a significant departure from past mining policy, based on the Mining Law of 1872, which granted free access to the public lands, the potential for inexpensive purchase of mineral lands, and included no royalty payments to the government.

[*Christopher McGrory Klyza*]

FURTHER READING

Hays, S. P. *Conservation and the Gospel of Efficiency: The Progressive Conservation Movement, 1890-1920.* New York: Atheneum, 1975.

Mayer, C. J., and G. A. Riley. *Public Domain, Private Dominion: A History of Public Mineral Policy in America.* San Francisco: Sierra Club Books, 1985.

Swenson, R. W. "Legal Aspects of Mineral Resources Exploitation." In *History of Public Land Law Development*, by Paul W. Gates. Washington, DC: U. S. Government Printing Office, 1968.

Minerals, strategic
See **Strategic minerals**

Minimum-tillage agriculture
See **Conservation tillage**

Mining
See **Acid mine drainage; Ashio, Japan; Ducktown, Tennessee; Itai-Itai disease; Mine spoil waste; Placer mining; Silver Bay, Minnesota; Strip mining; Sudbury, Ontario; Surface mining**

Mining, undersea

Practically all of the mineral and energy resources found on land are present under the sea. Development, however, is limited by extraction costs that increase with depth of water, by the relative abundance of resources on land, and by political questions involving ownership of deep ocean resources.

Worth $80 billion, the most valuable undersea commodity is oil and **natural gas**, representing 90% of the resources obtained from the seafloor. Continental-margin deposits comprise about one-third of the world's estimated oil and gas reserves. Large deposits have been found on the continental shelves in the Gulf of Mexico, the Persian Gulf, the North Sea, and off the coasts of northern **Australia**, southern California, and the Arctic Ocean. Other sites are promising, and many other continental shelves remain relatively unexplored. The harsh conditions found in the North Sea have fostered huge investments in colossal offshore rigs. Extraction costs on the continental shelves are several times higher than on land, and projected costs in the Arctic Ocean are several times higher again. Such fields are profitable only because of their high flow rates and reserves. Oil exploration continues to push the limits of profitable extraction into deeper and deeper waters. One commercially promising well in the Gulf of Mexico was drilled in waters well over 1 mi (1.6 km).

Nearshore resources are much more likely to be mined than distant ones. Sand and gravel predominate in volume. Though in great demand for use in concrete and as fill material and beach sand, their low value restricts usage to local areas.

Delta sediments are often mined for valuable deposits washed from the land, including gold, platinum, tin, diamonds, iron, and **uranium**. Japan, an island country with limited land resources, is especially eager to exploit such deposits; **coal** beds are also being mined.

Phosphorite is the source rock for phosphate, a key **fertilizer**. Phosphorite deposits occur where **upwelling** brings dissolved phosphate to the surface, where, in turn, rising temperature and pH cause them to precipitate out. Their value comes from their high grade, since they are not diluted by land-derived sediments.

Manganese nodules were first discovered on the deep-ocean floor during the 1873-76 voyage of the British ship, *Challenger.* Although rich in valuable ferroalloys used in steelmaking, these potato-like ores have yet to be mined commercially. The deposits are immense, but the technology for profitable mining does not currently exist.

Another tantalizing resource is the sulfide ores precipitated out of ocean water around hydrothermal vents in deep-ocean rift systems. Commercial extraction is being attempted in the Red Sea, and experimental vehicles have been built for use in the deep ocean, but technological and economic limitations hinder commercial development.

Economic considerations are one of the greatest limitations to the growth of undersea mining, along with uncertain environmental impact. Only highly profitable ventures, as in oil and gas extraction, or readily accessible, near-shore, bulk resources, such as sand and gravel, are currently feasible. Undersea mining appears to hold great potential resources for the future, when supplies and extraction costs of land-based resources tip the scales in its favor.

Political considerations, especially questions of ownership and the sharing of profits, are also key factors here, with developing countries clamoring for their share. During the 1970s, the United Nations strove for a treaty to regulate deep-ocean exploitation. The 1982 Law of the Sea Treaty claimed manganese nodules as the heritage of all humankind, to be regulated by the United Nations' seabed authority and with profits to be shared. The United States chose not to sign the treaty, and has joined with other developed countries in a provisional understanding to award exploitation licenses.

These political and environmental issues are insignificant, so long as the economic realities favor resources on land. It will be beneficial if the time spent waiting for development of undersea mining creates the opportunity for more productive international discussions and agreements.

[*Nathan Meleen*]

FURTHER READING

Duxbury, A.C., and A.B. Duxbury. *An Introduction to the World's Oceans*, 3rd ed. Dubuque, IA: Wm. C. Brown Publishers, 1991.

Ingmanson, D.E., and W.J. Wallace. *Oceanograph*, 5th ed. Belmont, CA: Wadsworth Publishing, 1995.

Mirex

An organic compound that was manufactured for use as an insecticide against imported **fire ants** and, secondarily, as a fire retardant for **plastics**, rubber, paint, paper, and electrical products. It has a molecular weight of 545.59 and consists of twelve **chlorine** atoms attached to a ten **carbon** cage. Its full name is dodecachloro-octahydro-1,3,4-metheno-1H-cyclobuta[c,d]pentalene. The United States **Environmental Protection Agency (EPA)** has classified it as a **carcinogen**. Mirex can be degraded to the toxic **pesticide Kepone** in the **environment**. Due to **discharge**s from manufacturing facilities in the state of New York, it is found in the water, **sediment**s, and biota of Lake Ontario at levels of concern. *See also* Cancer; Great Lakes; Toxic substance

Mitsui Mining and Smelting Company
See Itai-Itai disease

Mixing zones

Most **wastewater** treatment plants and industrial facilities discharge their **effluent** into the nearest available body of surface water such as a stream or river. The mixing zone is the localized area in the receiving stream within which the mixing, dispersal, or dissipation of the effluent can be detected. For example, cooling water **discharge**s from **power plants** typically create a mixing zone in the receiving stream where the temperature is higher than the ambient background temperature of the stream waters. Environmental regulations usually require that the mixing zone be limited in size and not create a nuisance or hazardous conditions.

Modeling (computer applications)

Computer modeling is a mathematical tool used to analyze complicated systems or to predict events such as floods, **climate** changes, or population changes. Computer models are applied in many disciplines, from engineering (predicting the strength of a bridge or dam) to economics (predicting inflation rates) to **ecology** (describing a **food chain/web** or projecting the survival chances of an **endangered species**). A model may consist of a few simple calculations on a spreadsheet, or it may involve millions of calculations on hundreds of thousands of input parameters, as in the case of general circulation models used to describe and predict climate conditions. Both simple and complex models involve quantifying input variables and the relationships between them, in order to produce numeric output that can describe or predict some real world phenomenon or condition. Models are often criticized because they can generalize real-world phenomena unrealistically, or because any errors in initial assumptions are expanded as assumptions are added and multiplied together. However, modeling remains a common tool because it is often the only available method to find answers to important research questions.

Models let researchers "experiment" with systems that do not allow manipulative experimentation. You cannot actually build a power plant just to test its effect on a population, and you cannot deliberately change the temperature of the **atmosphere** in order to see what happens to plant populations and sea levels. Instead a model can be used to predict probable outcomes of known conditions. Different variables can also be easily introduced in a model, for example, on the computer a programmer can easily add pollution control equipment to the power plant and observe its effect on lung disease rates in the surrounding population, or a modeler can easily reduce worldwide **carbon dioxide** emissions and calculate the impact on atmospheric temperatures.

Computer models have many applications. Some aid in assessing or visualizing a phenomenon. Three-dimensional geological models are used to help visualize or approximate the volume and dimensions of an aquifer, an oil reserve, or a magma chamber beneath a volcano. A simple **ecosystem** model can help identify general relationships between populations and resources, by letting the modeler adjust variables and see which arrangements most closely approximate observed data. Other models are used to predict the outcome of known conditions: a demographic model representing known rates of population growth, reproduction, and death can reasonably predict a country's population a century from now. Still other models are used to test "what if" questions. A pollution dispersion model showing how much **pollution** could spread from a power plant to a town can be used to test different scenarios: What if there were a northwest wind for an entire week? What if the power plant needed to double its energy production? What if the town expanded in the direction of the power plant? Models used to describe or visualize a system are known as descriptive models. Models that project or predict the results of input conditions are known as predictive models.

Anything that approximates or simulates a real-world phenomenon could be considered a model. A plaster replica of a landform, a diagram drawn on paper to describe links in a food web, or a verbal description of a storm could be considered models, because each of these describes or simulates a real phenomenon. Computer models approximate phenomena in the real world by performing calculations on input variables. These calculations produce numeric output that predicts the outcome of the variables in the model. For example, a wolf population model might multiply the number of breeding adults (A) by the average number of pups per litter (P) to produce the expected number of young wolves in a year (N): $A \times P = N$.

This is a very simple, and not very realistic, mathematical model. A computer model can produce a more realistic representation of a wolf population, by incorporating more variables, by using randomized variables, by performing more complicated mathematical functions, and by repeating calculations many times in order to produce a statistically significant number of "experiments."

Models can be composed of variables, parameters, and constants. A variable is any factor that is changeable. The number of breeding adults in a wolf population might change from year to year, as might the number of pups per adult. Parameters are sometimes distinguished from variables as input factors that are unlikely to change: the number of litters in a wolf pack is unlikely to be more than one per year, or the month in which pups are born might reasonably be expected not to change from one year to the next. Constants are input factors that are assumed to be unchanging. In a model of a dam's structure and strength, the force of gravity on the water behind the dam would be a constant. In addition, randomized (stochastic), values can also be used to introduce an element of chance into the model. For example, in a simulation of population change in wolves a realistic birth rate may be somewhere between 4–9 pups per breeding female per year. A computer model can randomly select a number between 4–9, for this variable each time the model is run. In addition there might be a 70% chance that each pup would survive its first year. This stochastic variable could be added to increase the precision of the model's prediction of population at the end of the year. As the computer processes the model it arbitrarily picks a value for the stochastic variable. Stochastic variables can improve a model by making it better represent real events that are somewhat random, or at least unpredictable.

Deterministic and Stochastic Models

A deterministic model produces a single answer for each set of variables; that is, the input variables determine the outcome. Different results can be produced only by entering different values for the input variables. Deterministic models are useful where the values of input variables are reliably known. For example, if an engineer knows with reasonable certainty the strength of a concrete dam and the force applied by a full reservoir, a deterministic model should be used to calculate the water level that would cause the dam to break.

A stochastic model, in contrast, includes an element of randomness, so that there will probably be a different result each time the model is run. For example, a population model might include a slightly randomized birth rate, or a reservoir model might include a randomized variable for rainfall, which in fact varies unpredictably from year to year. An advantage of using a stochastic (random) variable is that it helps the model approximate the fluctuations that can occur in a real system: there is no way to predict the actual number of pups a wolf pack will have each year, but it is possible to predict with some precision the minimum and maximum number that is likely. Running a stochastic model repeatedly can produce a statistically significant sample of experimental results. Statistical analysis can be used to assess the probability of various outcomes, such as a 25% probability that a wolf population will rise over the next 100 years.

Development of Modeling

Although mathematical models and analog models (physical structures such as clay models of landforms or river basins) have been used in environmental problem solving for a long time, the growth of modern computer modeling began in the 1960s with the development of computers. One of the first publicized computer models was a climate model that calculated climate conditions based on three input parameters: temperature, air pressure, and wind speed. Since then models have been used to predict weather, stream discharge, soil erosion, population growth, pollution impacts, and many other occurrences. The ability to use a computer greatly increased the complexity of models that could be developed, and the widespread availability of computers increased the number of people developing models for a growing number of purposes. Models are used in environmental monitoring and management, physics, engineering, **hydrology**, economics, demographics, and many other fields. One reason modeling developed more or less simultaneously in many disciplines is that the techniques of programming a computer to simulate real-world variables are highly portable: the structure of a model used to interpret water flow might be modified and applied to magma movement in the earth or to nutrient flows through a landscape. Modeling is now a widespread technique that is used to help explain how natural systems function and to inform public policy concerning the environment, the economy, and many other issues.

Sensitivity Analysis, Calibration, and Validation

Once a model is developed it is usually tested against observed events or data to indicate how reliable it is or where its weaknesses lie. One of the first tests usually run is sensitivity analysis. A model's outcome may be more sensitive to changes in one variable or process than another: in a beach erosion model, for example, the predicted erosion rate is likely to be influenced more by wave energy than by sand particle size, even though both factors need to be considered. It is essential to know to which factors the model is most sensitive, because error in estimating those factors could introduce significant error into the results. Sensitivity analysis involves adjusting variables or processes and then running the model to see which factors cause the greatest variability in outcomes.

Once the input variables and relationships in a model are established, the model can be calibrated, or tuned, to make it better represent reality. Calibration usually entails adjusting different parameters in order to produce a result similar to some observed results in the real world. Calibrating a model for forest growth, for example, might involve running the model repeatedly with different growth rates until the model approximates observed historic growth rates and densities.

Validation is like calibration, in that it involves comparing a model's results to observed data. The objective of validation, though, is to demonstrate that the model is reliable. The assumption of model validation is that if the model predicts the correct results in a known situation, then it will probably predict correctly in an unknown, experimental situation.

General Circulation Models

A type of model that has received much attention since the mid-1980s is the general circulation model, or GCM. This is a class of highly complex models designed to predict with reasonable accuracy the behavior of the earth's atmosphere (climate) or oceans. GCMs have been used to predict worldwide global warming as a result of increased concentrations of carbon dioxide in the atmosphere. GCMs are complex because they simulate the behavior of the atmosphere and the oceans, which have complex three-dimensional movements or flows of air masses or water. Predicting how changes in heat input at one location impacts temperatures and flow rates at another location requires thousands of calculations performed on many inter-related variables at thousands of points in space. Because GCMs must keep track of so many variables and so many points in space, they are usually run on supercomputers that can perform (billions) of calculations per second.

The appropriate complexity of a model depends on its intended use. A model designed to describe ocean circulation over space and time to produce realistic results on which to base public policy might incorporate many variables. A model built to test very general relationships between variables, in order to stimulate a researcher's insight into a small aspect of ecosystem functions, may more appropriately be quite simple, with only a few input parameters and equations.

[*Mary Ann Cunningham*]

FURTHER READING

Gordon, S.I. *Computer Models in Environmental Planning.* New York: Van Nostrand Reinhold, 1985.

Hardisty, J., D.M. Taylor, and S.E. Metcalfe. *Computerised Environmental Modelling.* New York: Wiley, 1993.

Starfield, A.M., K.A. Smith, and A.L. Bleloch. *Model It: Problem Solving for the Computer Age.* New York: McGraw-Hill, 1990.

Molina, Mario (1943-)

Mexican-American chemist

Mario Molina was born on March 19, 1943 in Mexico. He received his bachelor's degree from the National Autono-

mous University of Mexico in 1965 and his Ph.D. in physical chemistry from the University of California at Berkeley in 1972. After teaching for a year at the National Autonomous University, he returned to Berkeley as a research associate for one year.

In 1973, Molina joined the research laboratory of **F. Sherwood Rowland** at the University of California at Irvine. Molina was looking for a topic on which he could do his post-doctoral research with Rowland, and Rowland was ready with a suggestion because he had just come from a scientific meeting where he became interested in the possible effects of an important commercial chemical, trichlorofluoromethane, also known as chlorofluorocarbon-11, or CFC-11. The compound was a member of a widely-successful group of **chemicals**, called **freon**s, produced by Dow Chemical Company.

In particular, the question that interested Rowland was what effects, if any, this compound would have on atmospheric gases. CFC-11 was rapidly becoming very popular as a propellant in hair sprays, spray paints, and other **aerosol** products. By 1974, more than $2 billion of CFC-11 and related **chlorofluorocarbons** were being used each year.

Rowland and Molina developed a theory about the fate of CFC molecules released in the **troposphere**, the layer of the **atmosphere** in which we live. They predicted that those molecules would rise into the **stratosphere**, the layer of air above the troposphere. There, they said, **solar energy** would cause CFC molecules to decompose, releasing free **chlorine** atoms.

If that were to happen, they hypothesized, the free chlorine would be likely to attack **ozone** molecules, converting them to ordinary oxygen. The chlorine oxide formed in that reaction might then react with single oxygen atoms, to form more oxygen and regenerate the original chlorine.

Two important conclusions can be drawn from this series of reactions. First, a single atom of chlorine would be capable of destroying many (Rowland and Molina predicted about 100,000) molecules of ozone. Second, since ozone in the stratosphere absorbs **ultraviolet radiation**, this process would result in more ultraviolet radiation reaching the Earth's surface and causing an increase of skin **cancer** among humans.

When Rowland and Molina first proposed this theory, no measurements had ever been made of chlorine in the stratosphere. By 1979, they had carried out the first of those measurements and obtained results that closely matched their predictions. An important new environmental problem, **ozone layer depletion**, had been identified.

Molina held positions as a research associate, assistant professor, and associate professor at the University of California at Irvine. In 1983, he left Irvine to become Senior Research Scientist at the Jet Propulsion Laboratory at the California Institute of Technology in Pasadena. Molina was awarded the American Chemical Society's Esselen Award in 1987 and the Society of Hispanic Engineers Award in 1983. *See also* Atmospheric inversion; Greenhouse effect; Greenhouse gases; Tropopause

[*David E. Newton*]

FURTHER READING

Rowland, F. S. "Atmospheric Chemistry: Causes and Effects." *MTS Journal* (Fall 1991): 12-18.

———, and M. J. Molina. "Chlorofluoromethanes in the Environment." *Review of Geophysical Space Research* (January 1975): 1-35.

Molluscicide

See **Pesticide**

Monkey-wrenching

Also called *ecotage* (ecological sabotage), monkey-wrenching refers to techniques used by some radical environmentalists to stop or slow the machinery used in logging, **strip mining**, and other sorts of environmentally destructive activities. The term was popularized by **Edward Abbey**'s novel, *The Monkey Wrench Gang* (1975) and the concept was developed by **Dave Foreman** in *Ecodefense: A Field Guide to Monkeywrenching* (1987). The techniques of monkey-wrenching include "spiking" old-growth trees to prevent loggers from cutting them down, "munching" logging roads with nails to puncture the tires of logging vehicles, pulling up surveyors' stakes, putting sand or grinding compound in the gas tanks or oil intakes (or oatmeal or Minute Rice in the radiators) of bulldozers and logging trucks, and other forms of disruption or destruction.

Mono Lake, California

Clear, cold water tumbles from snowcapped peaks and alpine fields at 13,000 feet (4,000 m) down the precipitous eastern escarpment of California's Sierra Nevada. The water feeds semi-**arid**, sagebrush–covered Mono Basin and, at the basin's heart, majestic Mono Lake. This is a salt lake with an area of 60 square miles (155 km²) at an elevation of 6,400 feet (2,000 m), and mountain waters have flowed to it for at least the past half million years, making it one of the oldest lakes in North America.

Mono Basin lies in the **rain shadow** of the Sierra Nevada; shielded from moist Pacific air masses to the west, it has a semi-arid **climate**. Being surrounded by higher ground, it also has no natural outlet. Over the millennia, the major water loss from Mono Lake has been by evaporation, a process that removes pure water and leaves dissolved salts behind, and the water in the lake has become alkaline as a result and two and a half times saltier than sea water.

The salty, alkaline lake water excludes fish, but it does provide ideal conditions for several life forms that normally are uncommon to inland waters. Algae blooms in abundance during winter, sometimes turning the lake water pea–soup green, and it provides summer sustenance to a profusion of brine flies and tiny brine shrimp. Brine flies and brine shrimp make Mono Lake a summer haven for hundreds of thousands of nesting and migratory birds. The lake's islands provide safe

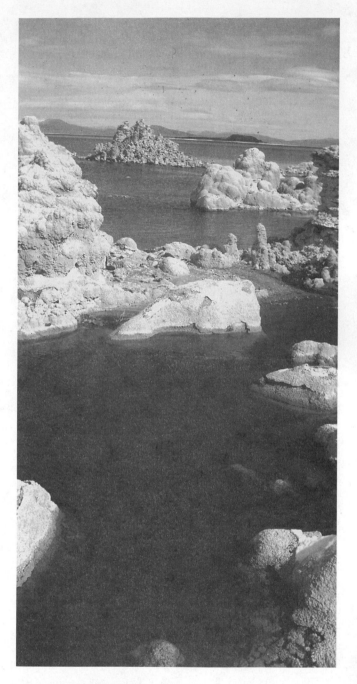

Mono Lake, California.

nesting for tens of thousands of California gulls and snowy plovers. Nearly 90 percent of the state's population of California gulls, which live mainly along the Pacific coast, are hatched on these islands. More than 70 **species** of migratory birds use Mono Lake—most notably, several hundred thousand eared grebes which stop over during their fall **migration**, and more than 100,000 phalaropes which come from South America for the summer.

Mono Lake's **aquatic chemistry**, combined with its unusual geologic and topographic **environment**, has given rise to the lake's signature feature: tufa towers. Tufa is a type of limestone which consists of calcium carbonate that forms around fresh water springs emanating from the lake bottom. Calcium carried by the spring water combines with carbonate in the alkaline lake to form soft rock masses that slowly grow into underwater pinnacles. These towers were almost entirely covered by water until recently; they were first exposed when the lake level started dropping in the early 1940s, because the growing city of Los Angeles had begun intercepting fresh water from streams feeding the lake and diverting it south to the city in a 250–mile (400 km) long aqueduct.

By the mid-1980s, Mono Basin supplied nearly 20 percent of the water used by Los Angeles, and the lake level had dropped more than forty feet (12 m). As the water level dropped, the lake's **salinity** increased and shoreline **habitat** for brine flies decreased. Tufa formations became more exposed, dust storms grew more frequent and severe, and predators occasionally found access to island nesting sites. Meanwhile, California created the Mono Lake Tufa State Reserve, and the United States Congress established the Mono Basin National Forest Scenic Area.

Ultimately, the demand for water by Los Angeles clashed with the demands of environmental groups, who sought to maintain Mono Lake's ecological integrity and the fish habitat of streams feeding the lake. Lawsuits have been fought in state and federal courts, and in 1989 California's State Supreme Court ordered the Los Angeles Department of Water and Power (LADWP) to reduce the amount of water it was diverting from the lake. In 1993, the State Water Resources Control Board recommended that the diversion be cut again, this time by half. LADWP has disagreed, arguing that Los Angeles needs the water and that the reduction is neither ecologically necessary nor economically wise.

The war over eastern Sierra water began at the turn of the twentieth century, when Los Angeles acquired rights to water previously used by farmers and ranchers in the Owens Valley, just south of Mono Lake. By mid–century the battleground had spread north to Mono Basin, and the war promises to continue well into the next century. *See also* Drinking-water supply; Hydrologic cycle; Los Angeles Basin; National forest; Water allocation; Water resources; Water rights

[*Ronald D. Taskey*]

FURTHER READING

Lane, P. H., and A. Rossmann. "Owens Valley Groundwater Conflict." In *Deepest Valley*, edited by Genny Smith. Los Altos, CA: William Kaufmann, 1978.

Patten, D. T. *The Mono Basin Ecosystem*. Washington, DC: National Academy Press, 1987.

Monoculture

The agricultural practice of planting only one or two crops over large areas. In the United States, corn and soybean are the only crops grown on most farms in the central Midwest, while on the Great Plains wheat is almost exclusively grown. Although it minimizes farmers' investments in large, expensive implements, the practice exposes crops to the risk of

The Indian subcontinent experiences monsoons each summer. Warming air rises over the plains of central India in summer, creating a low-pressure cell that draws in warm, moisture-laden air from the ocean. The moist air rises over the Western Ghats or the Himalayas and cools, resulting in heavy monsoon rains.

being wiped out by a single predator. This happened with the Irish potato blight of the 1840s and the corn leaf blight of 1970 in the United States, which destroyed millions of acres of corn. Ecologists warn against monoculture's oversimplification of the **food chain/web**, arguing that complex webs are more stable.

Monsoon

Monsoon (from Arabic, *mausim*, season) technically means a reversal of winds, that point between the dry and the wet seasons in tropical and subtropical India, Southeast Asia, and parts of Africa and Australia, when seasonal winds change their direction. When the land heats up, the hot air rises, causing a low pressure zone that sucks in moisture-filled cooler ocean air, creating clouds and producing rain. In winter, the opposite happens: warm air over the ocean rises and makes a low pressure zone that draws the cooler air off the land.

Although monsoon winds have always been watched by traders and sailors in the Eastern Hemisphere, their arrival is critical to millions of people who depend on agriculture. Cultural and religious customs, especially in India and southeast Asia, are tied to the monsoon rains that bring a season of fertility after a long hot and sterile dry period.

Coastal radar and satellites aid in weather prediction, but the climatological components of monsoons are complex. Tied to the heat and moisture exchange between land and oceans, their effect can be altered by changes in the circulation of hemispheric winds at the equator, as well as by precessional changes in the orbit of the earth.

Environmental changes such as **deforestation** or soil **erosion** can invite severe **flooding**, as in Bangladesh during the 1980s. Scientists believe a rise in sea surface temperature in the Atlantic Ocean, possibly related to the **greenhouse effect**, prevented the monsoon rain from reaching the African **Sahel** and contributed to recent **drought**s. This ocean temperature rise may also be tied to the **El Niño** event in the Pacific Ocean.

Any fluctuations in monsoon rain patterns can cause disease and death, along with millions of dollars in damage. If the rains are delayed, or never come, or fall too heavily in the beginning or at the end of the growing season, disastrous results often follow. *See also* Climate; Cloud chemistry; Meteorology

Montreal Protocol on Substances That Deplete the Ozone Layer (1987)

An historical agreement made in 1987 by members of the United Nations to phase out substances that are harmful to the earth's **ozone** layer. The ozone layer protects life on earth by blocking out the sun's harmful **ultraviolet radiation**. Since the 1970s scientists have documented the depletion of the ozone by **chlorofluorocarbons** (CFCs), commonly used for refrigeration and as solvents and **aerosol** propellants. Alarmed by this growing global trend, scientists and policymakers urged a decrease in the use and production of CFCs as well as other ozone-damaging **chemicals**. Ratifying the 1987 Montreal Protocol was a difficult process, however, with the European Community, the former Soviet Union, and Japan reluctant to pose strict controls on chemicals reduction. United States, Canada, Norway, Sweden, among others, favored stronger control and negotiated with these nations to cut back and eventually phase out completely ozone-depleting substances.

An amendment of the Montreal Protocol was made in 1990 by 93 nations, including China and India, who had not previously participated, to eliminate the use of CFCs, **carbon** tetrachloride, and halon gases by the year 2000 and eliminate the production of methyl chloroform by 2005. Some countries, like the United States, have accelerated the schedule to 1995. This 1990 amendment also established the "Montreal Protocol Multilateral Fund" to help developing countries become less dependent on ozone-depleting chemicals.

In November 1992 delegates from all over the world met again in Copenhagen, Denmark, to further revise the Montreal Protocol and accelerate the phase-out of ozone-damaging substances and regulate three additional chemicals. Some of the new provisions are as follows:

1) phase out production of CFCs and carbon tetrachloride by 1996;
2) ban halons by 1994;
3) end production of methyl chloroform by 1996;
4) control the use of **hydrochloroflurocarbons** (HCFCs) and eliminate them by 2030;
5) increase funding for the Multilateral Fund (between $340 million to $500 million by 1996).

As of December 1992, 92 nations have ratified the Montreal Protocol. However, while countries have volunteered to control ozone-damaging chemicals, individual companies can still produce the banned chemicals for "essential uses and for servicing certain existing equipment." The Alliance for Responsible CFC Policy in Arlington, Vermont, praised the concession for balancing environmental and economic concerns. Others, such as members of the **Friends of the Earth**, decry the provision as a "big loophole" that undermines the initiative of the Montreal Protocol. *See also* Ozone layer depletion

[*Kyung-Sun Lim*]

FURTHER READING

Benedick, R.E. "Ozone Diplomacy." *Issues in Science and Technology* 6 (Fall 1989): 43-50.

"Ozone-Protection Treaty Strengthened." *Science News* 142 (12 December 1992): 415.

More developed country (MDC)

This term and **less developed countries (LDC)** are terms coined by economists to classify the world's 183 countries on the basis of economic development (average annual per capita income and gross national product). The 33 countries (including the United States, Canada, Japan, Australia, New Zealand and all the western European countries) in the MDC group are wealthy and industrially-developed. They tend to have temperate **climate**s and fertile **soil**s. About 23 percent of the world's population live in MDCs, but they consume about 80 percent of its mineral and energy resources. In contrast the LDCs are poorer and less industrially-developed. They tend to be located in the Southern Hemisphere where the climate is less favorable and soils are generally less fertile. Though the boundaries are purposely vague, this dichotomy is useful for contrasting the economic and social welfare of the richer and poorer countries and in critical environmental categories involving mainly demographic, economic, and social statistics. *See also* Environmental economics; First World; Third World

[*Nathan H. Meleen*]

FURTHER READING

Ehrlich, P. R., and A. H. Ehrlich. "Growing, Growing, Gone (Rich Nations Must Recognize Their Responsibility to Aid Overpopulated Third World)." *Sierra* 75 (March-April 1990): 36-40.

Preston, S. H. "Population Growth and Economic Development." *Environment* (March 1986): 6-9+.

Mortality

A measure of the death rate in a biological population, usually presented in terms of the number of deaths per hundred or per thousand. If there are 100 mice at the beginning of the year and fifteen of them die by the end of the year, the group's mortality rate is fifteen per 100 individuals (the initial population), or 15 percent. In ecological and demographic studies of populations mortality is an important measurement, along with birth rates (natality), immigration, and emigration, used to assess changes in population size over time. In human populations mortality rates are often figured for specific age and gender groups, or for other population categories including race, income level, occupation, and so on. This way group mortality rates can be compared and risks for each subgroup can be evaluated. *See also* Evolution; Extinction; Population growth; Zero population growth

Mount Pinatubo, Philippines

Mount Pinatubo in the Philippines erupted on June 15, 1991. When the 5,770-foot (1760 m) mountain shot **sulfur dioxide** 25 miles (40 km) into the **atmosphere**, the cloud mixed with water vapor and circled the globe in 21 days, temporarily offsetting the effects of global warming. Satellite images taken of the area after the eruption showed a dustlike smudge in the **stratosphere**. The sulfur dioxide cloud deflected 2 percent of the earth's incoming sunlight and lowered temperatures on worldwide average. Although the effects on global temperatures were significant, they are thought to be temporary. These light sulfur dioxides are expected to remain in the stratosphere for years and contribute to damage to the **ozone** layer.

The Philippine islands originated as **volcano**es built up from the ocean floor. Most volcanoes erupt along plate edges where ocean floors plunge under continents and melting rock rises to the surface as magma. The earth's crust pulls apart, creating gaps where the magma can rise. The island of Luzon, where Mount Pinatubo is located, has thirteen active volcanoes. The pattern of volcanoes around the rim of the Pacific Ocean is called the Ring of Fire.

Mount Pinatubo sits in the center of a three-mile (5-km) wide *caldera*, a depression from an earlier eruption that made the volcano collapse in on itself. A new cone formed over time, and geothermal vents gave a clue that the volcano was active. Before the 1991 eruption, Mount Pinatubo last erupted 600 years ago. In April 1991 steam eruptions, earthquakes, increasing sulfur dioxide emissions, and rapid growth of a lava dome all indicated a powerful impending blast. Minor explosions began on the mountain on June 12, 1991.

This major eruption occurred in a country with an already shaky economy, and the human effects are likely to be significant for a long period of time. A total of 42,000 homes and 100,000 acres (40,500 ha) of crops were destroyed. Nine hundred people died and 200,000 were relocated, with 20,000 people remaining in tent cities. More than 500 of those have died from disease and exposure. The country suffered over $1 billion in economic losses. Nevertheless, many lives were saved as a consequence of scientists' predictions of the eruption.

The destruction from Mount Pinatubo came mostly from lahars, rushs of cementlike mud, formed when heavy rains loosened the tons of ash dumped on the mountain's sides. These lahars can bury towns and roads and virtually anything else in the way. Also deadly were the pyroclastic flows, killer clouds of hot gases, pumice, and ash that traveled up to 80 miles (130 km) per hour across the countryside, up to 11 miles (18 km) away from the volcano. *See also* Geothermal energy; Greenhouse effect; Ozone layer depletion; Plate tectonics

[*Linda Rehkopf*]

FURTHER READING

Berreby, D. "Acid-Flecked Candy-Colored Sunscreen." *Discover* 13 (January 1992): 44-46.

Brasseur, G. "Mount Pinatubo Aerosols, Chlorofluorocarbons, and Ozone Depletion." *Science* 257 (28 August 1992): 1239-42.

Grove, N. "Volcanoes: Crucibles of Creation." *National Geographic* 182 (December 1992): 5-41.

Kerr, R. A. "Pinatubo Global Cooling on Target." *Science* 259 (29 January 1993): 594.

Monastersky, R. "Pinatubo Deepens the Antarctic Ozone Hole." *Science News* 142 (24 October 1992): 278-79.

Mount St. Helens, Washington

On May 18, 1980, Mount St. Helens exploded with a force comparable to 500 Hiroshima-sized atom bombs. David Johnston, a United States **Geological Survey** (USGS) geologist based at a monitoring station six miles (9.7 km) away announced the eruption with his final words, "Vancouver, Vancouver, this is it." Dramatic photograph's provided the public with an awesome display of nature's power.

Mount St. Helens, in southwestern Washington near Portland, Oregon, is part of the Cascade Range, a chain of subduction **volcano**es running from northern California through Washington. The Mount St. Helens eruption was instrumental in the expansion of the USGS Volcano Hazards Program. Research at the new Cascades Volcano Observatory in Vancouver, Washington, has strengthened basic understanding of volcanic processes and the ability to predict eruptions. Highly relevant ecological studies have corrected previous errors and misconceptions, leading to a new theory about **nature**'s ability to recover after such events.

Research has heightened public awareness of the inherent instability of high, snow-covered volcanoes, where even small eruptions can almost instantaneously melt large volumes of snow. A relatively small 1985 eruption at Nevado del Ruiz in central Colombia killed more than 23,000 people. The Mount St. Helens blast and subsequent collapse generated a 0.7 cubic mile (2.8 km³) mud flow which raced 22

Mount St. Helens erupting with Mt. Hood in the background.

miles (35 km) at speeds as high as 157 mph (253 kph). This caused massive problems, even halting traffic on the Columbia River. These flows may also create unstable **dams**, which may burst years after the intial eruption.

In addition to its awesome power and destructive force, the Mount St. Helens eruption has provided rich material for research. Conductivity studies have located a large rotating block under Mounts Rainier, Adams, and St. Helens, the friction from which is a likely source of eruptions. Geologic mapping and historical research, coupled with field studies of current volcanism, have corrected misconceptions and given clues to hazard frequency. Studies of nature's recovery efforts have produced surprises, notably the early arrival in the eruption zone of predatory insects; elk grazing in open, reforested areas; and the explosive growth of uncommon, dangerous bacteria due to the high temperatures generated by the eruption. *Biological legacy* has emerged as the unifying theory describing nature's recovery capabilities, an idea with direct applications to forestry practices and **reclamation** of human-disturbed land. Nature's mess provides valuable nutrients and nurseries; furthermore, old growth areas within managed **ecosystem**s nurture the recovery of **biodiversity**.

Mount St. Helens has provided a unique laboratory for study of volcano hazards and nature's ability to recover from the devastation caused by volcanic eruptions. *See also* Mount Pinatubo, Philippines; Reclamation; Topography

[*Nathan H. Meleen*]

FURTHER READING

Bilderback, D. E., ed. *Mount St. Helens, 1980: Botanical Consequences of the Explosive Eruptions.* Berkeley: University of California Press, 1987.

Decker, R., and B. Decker. "Eruption of Mount St. Helens." *Scientific American* 244 (March 1981): 68-80.

Tilling, R. I., L. J. Topinka, and D. A. Swanson. *Eruptions of Mount St. Helens: Past, Present, and Future.* USGS General Interest Publication. Washington, DC: U. S. Government Printing Office, 1990.

Wright, T. L., and T. C. Pierson. *Living With Volcanoes: The USGS Volcano Hazards Program.* USGS Circular 1073. Washington, DC: U. S. Government Printing Office, 1992.

Muir, John (1838-1914)

American naturalist and writer

John Muir is considered one of the towering giants of the **conservation**/environmental movement in the United States. Anyone seriously interested in natural history, conservation, **wilderness** preservation, or the **national park**s in this country should be aware of John Muir's work. He was a spirited, joyous naturalist, a serious student of glaciers, an influential advocate of wilderness preservation, and the acknowledged founder of the national park idea.

Born in Dunbar, Scotland, Muir emigrated with his family to the United States in 1849 when he was eleven years

John Muir and his dog.

old. He spent his youth working on a farm in the Wisconsin wilderness, trying to please his father, who was a deeply religious man. The wilderness, his religious background, and the hard labor influenced his thinking the rest of his life.

Muir's father believed the Bible to be the only book necessary for a young person, but Muir managed to educate himself and to spend several years at the University of Wisconsin (where he chose his own curriculum and so left without a degree). After school, he worked at various jobs, generally quite successfully, until a factory accident temporarily blinded him. He vowed that if his sight returned, he would leave the factory and see as much of the world as possible. After about a month, his sight did return and he left for various jaunts in the wilderness, including a famous 1000-mile walk through the country to the Gulf of Mexico, an account recorded in *A Thousand Mile Walk to the Gulf* (1916).

His eventual goal was to reach South America and wander through the Amazonian tropical **rain forest**s. He reached Cuba, but a bout with fever (carried over from the humid lowlands of Florida) turned him instead toward the drier West, especially California and the Yosemite Valley, about which he had seen a brochure and which he determined to see for himself. "Seeing for himself" also became a life-time habit, and he eventually traveled over much of the world. As he had planned, he did make it up the Amazon, in 1911, at the age of 73.

Arriving in California in 1868, he made his way to Yosemite and spent several years studying its landforms, **wildlife**, and waterways, earning his living by herding sheep, working in a sawmill, and other odd jobs. As Edward Hoagland noted, Muir "lived to hike," a mode of transportation that involved him intimately in the landscape. He

traveled light, and alone, often with little more than some dry bread in a sack, tea in a pocket, a few matches and a tin cup, and perhaps a plant press.

Through his travels in Yosemite, he became convinced that the spectacular land forms of Yosemite had been carved by glaciers or, as he put it, "nature chose for a tool...the tender snow-flowers noiselessly falling through unnumbered centuries." His belief in glacial origins placed him in conflict with the established scientific ideas of the time, especially those held by the California state geologist. But Muir eventually prevailed, his ideas vindicated when he found the first known glacier in the Sierra range. The results of his years of intense glacial investigations are available in *Studies in the Sierra* (1950). Current views have verified his theories, changing only the number of glacial events and emphasizing the role of water in cutting the canyons. Muir also made five trips to Alaska to study glaciers there, one of which is named for him.

His glacial studies were the principle contributions Muir made as an original scientist, most of his life being devoted to travel, writing, and conservation activism. Even as early as 1868, Muir was concerned with the effects sheepherding had on plant life and **soil erosion**.

Muir's travels were interrupted for a time when, in early 1880, he married Louise Strentzel, the daughter of a fruit rancher in the Alhambra valley. Muir helped run the ranch, first rented and then bought some of the acreage, applying his inventiveness and hard work to fruit growing. Reportedly, he was a good businessman, prospering after only a decade to ensure a measure of financial independence. He then sold part of the ranch and leased the rest, which allowed him time with his daughters, to return to his beloved wilderness, and to write and actively promote his wilderness ideas. Muir's intimate acquaintance with the Yosemite area and the Sierra Nevada exposed him not only to the depredations of sheep but also to the rapid felling of giant old Sequoias, cut up for shingles and grape stakes. Muir's response: "As well sell the rain clouds, and the snow, and the river, to be cut up and carried away...." In 1889, he escorted the editor of *Century* magazine to Yosemite and showed him the negative impacts of sheep, which he called "hoofed locusts." A series of articles in that magazine alerted the public to the destruction of the land, and they eventually pressured Congress to establish the Yosemite area a national park in 1890.

An earlier attempt to rally interest in the plight of the western forests—a suggestion for a government commission to survey the forests and recommend conservation measures—was also realized with the appointment of such a commission in 1896. Charles Sargent, the chair of the commission, invited Muir to participate and, on the basis of the Sargent Commission's recommendation, President Grover Cleveland created thirteen forest preserves, setting aside 21 million acres. Negative reaction from commercial interests, however, nullified most of these gains. Muir responded by writing two articles on forest reserves and parks in *Harper's Weekly* and *Atlantic Monthly* in 1897. These articles helped to rally public support and in 1898, the annulments were reversed by Congress.

Muir influenced the public and extended his influence by friendships and correspondence with some of the most powerful people of his time. A number of the successes of the early conservation movement, for example, can be attributed to his influence on such figures as **Theodore Roosevelt**. After a three-day camping trip with Muir under the Big Trees in 1903, Roosevelt added many millions more acres to the **national forest** system, as well as national monuments and national parks and created what became the **national wildlife refuge** system.

Known for his many successes, Muir was much saddened by his one big loss: the damming of Hetch Hetchy valley in **Yosemite National Park** as a reservoir to supply water to San Francisco. Muir's public image was damaged by the excessive vehemence of his attacks upon the citizens of San Francisco, whom he denounced as "satanic," and following the Hetch Hetchy incident, Muir retired to his ranch to edit his journals for publication.

Muir never considered himself much of a writer and begrudged the time it took away from his beloved mountains and forests. Most of his books were published late in life, after the turn of the century. His writings are still widely read today by students, scholars, activists, and philosophers. In the opinion of most observers, the primary importance of Muir's writings lies not in their literary quality but in the fact that they persuaded a large number of Americans to regard scenic wilderness areas as irreplaceable **natural resources** which must be protected and preserved. *See also* Glaciation; Hetch Hetchy Reservoir; Overgrazing

[*Gerald L. Young*]

FURTHER READING

Browning, P., ed. *John Muir in His Own Words: A Book of Quotations.* Lafayette, CA: Great West Books, 1988.

Cohen, M. P. *The Pathless Way: John Muir and the American Wilderness.* Madison: University of Wisconsin Press, 1984.

Fox, S. *John Muir and His Legacy: The American Conservation Movement.* Madison: University of Wisconsin Press, 1985.

Hoagland, E. "In Praise of John Muir." *Anteus* No. 52 (Spring 1984): 170-83.

Turner, F. *Rediscovering America: John Muir in His Time and Ours.* New York: Viking Penguin, 1985.

Wadden, K. A. "John Muir and the Community of Nature." *The Pacific Historian* 19 (Summer-Fall 1985): 94-102.

Mulch

Material applied to the surface of a **soil** to protect the soil or to improve the **environment** of the soil's surface. Mulch can be made from many different kinds of organic or inorganic materials like stones, bark, compost, leaves, wood chips, and manure. The benefits of using mulch include the following: protection of soil from **erosion**, evaporation reduction, increased water infiltration, reduction in weed seed germination, increased seed germination, and reduction of **compaction** of soil. *See also* Animal waste; Composting; Fertilizer; Soil organic matter; Soil texture; Topsoil

Multiple chemical sensitivity

Regarded by skeptics as a manifestation of "technophobia" and "chemophobia," multiple chemical sensitivity is a highly controversial disorder associated with low levels of environmental chemicals in general and volatile organic chemicals in particular. Sufferers experience fatigue, malaise, headache, dizziness, lack of concentration, and loss of memory, and are often so disabled that they cannot live or work except in completely chemical-free environments. Critics argue that this condition should not receive clinical recognition as a disease, insisting that the condition has no uniform cause or consistent, measurable features. Advocates for sufferers say it is a chronic condition marked by heightened sensitivity to even slight chemical exposures; and that multiple symptoms occur in multiple organ systems, usually caused by large "triggering" exposures such as to new carpeting that emits chemicals.

Multiple Use-Sustained Yield Act (1960)

On June 12, 1960, Congress passed the Multiple Use-Sustained Yield Act, designed to prevent the obliteration of **national forest**s by logging and water **reclamation** projects. This law officially mandated the management of national forests to "best meet the needs of the American people." The forests were to be used not primarily for economic gain, but for a balanced combination of "outdoor **recreation**, range, timber, **watershed**, and **wildlife** and fish purposes."

The Multiple Use Act emerged from a strong history of diverse uses of the federal reserves. Early settlers assumed access to and free use of **public land**s. The text of the Sundry Civil Act of 1897 mandated that no public forest reservation was to be established except to improve and protect forests and water flow. The act also provided for free use of timber and stone and of all reservation waters by miners and residents. The Act of February 28, 1899, strengthened use policy by providing for recreational use of the reserves.

When the reserves were transferred from the General Land Office to the Bureau of Forestry, the Secretary of Agriculture signed a letter (actually written by **Gifford Pinchot**) dictating formal forest policy: "all the resources of the forest reserves are for use . . . you will see to it that the water, wood, and forage of the reserves are conserved and wisely used." The first and subsequent editions of the *Use Book*—an extensive guide to management and use of national forest lands—stated concisely that the aim of **Forest Service** policy was that "the timber, water, pasture, mineral and other resources of the forest reserves are for the use of the people."

The first use of the term "multiple use" appears to be in two Forest Service reports of 1933. That year's chief's report reaffirmed that the "principle to govern the use of land . . . is multiple-purpose use." The "National Plan for American Forestry" (the Copeland Report) emphasized that "the peculiar and highly important multiple use characteristics of forest land [involve] five major uses—timber production, watershed protection, recreation, production of forage, and **conservation** of wildlife."

Multiple use has always been controversial. Some critics argued that multiple uses meant that the Forest Service was losing sight of its original protective function: a 1927 article in the *Outlook* claimed that "the Forest Service will have to be called from its enthusiasm for entertaining visitors to the original but more somber work of forestry." Many similar statements can be identified. A writer in the *Journal of Forestry* in 1946 went so far as to propose separating all the lands in each use class, consolidating each type into a separate bureau under one cabinet officer. The **Sierra Club** proposed a vast land exchange in 1959, hoping to move scenic areas out of the Forest Service and into the **U.S. Department of the Interior**.

Critics have argued, and feel that subsequent policy and events on the ground bear them out, that the Multiple Use Act did not reduce confusion because it did not eliminate water and timber as priority uses. Proponents of the act feel that it did give statutory authority to all uses as equal to timber and did give the other four uses more stature and visibility. *See also* Bureau of Land Management; Commercial fishing; Public Lands Council

[*Gerald L. Young*]

FURTHER READING

Bowes, M. D., and J. V. Krutilla. *Multiple-Use Management: The Economics of Public Forestlands.* Washington, DC: Resources for the Future, 1989.

Frederick, K. D., and R. A. Sedjo, eds. *America's Renewable Resources: Historical Trends and Current Challenges.* Washington, DC: Resources for the Future, 1991.

Steen, H. K. "Multiple Use: The Greatest Good of the Greatest Number" and "Multiple Use Tested: An Environmental Epilogue." In *The United States Forest Service: A History.* Seattle, WA: University of Washington Press, 1976.

Municipal solid waste

Americans generate about 160 million tons of municipal solid waste (MSW) per year not counting construction debris. That's enough **garbage** to fill a convoy of trash trucks reaching half way from the earth to the moon. That much garbage equals about 1,300 pounds (590 kg) of waste per year for every person in the United States, or about 25 pounds (11.5 kg) per person per week. The **Environmental Protection Agency (EPA)** tells us that every year Americans throw away 60 billion cans, 28 million bottles, 4 million tons of plastic, 40 million tons of paper, 100 million tires, and 3 million cars. If growth in disposal rates continue, Americans may generate nearly 2,000 million tons of MSW by the year 2000.

Municipal solid waste is waste generated by households, commercial businesses, institutions, light industry and agricultural enterprises and nontoxic wastes from hospitals and laboratories. Municipal waste is composed of (in order of volume contribution) paper/packaging, **yard waste**, **food waste**, magazines/newspapers, **plastics**, glass, wood/fabric, **disposable diapers**, and other contributions such as tires, appliances, and nontoxic home maintenance supplies. In addition to this relatively benign list, there is other municipal waste that ends up in a **landfill** inappropriately—e.g., leftover paint, crankcase oil, batteries, and parts of some appliances such as capacitors in refrigerators and air conditioners. In some cases sewage **sludge** from the local **wastewater** treatment facility ends up in the landfill with other municipal solid waste. It is these inappropriate wastes that cause concern in the minds of local officials as they ponder the siting of landfills.

Since municipal waste is a non-homogeneous stream of materials, its impact is unpredictable. Although only about two percent of the municipal waste stream is toxic, even that small amount has the potential of contaminating large amounts of **groundwater** if the leachate from landfills reach the **aquifer**. In addition, landfills situated near a lake or a stream can leak laterally and contaminate surface water. In spite of the fact that the engineering of landfills has become much more sophisticated in the last 10 years, there is still sincere concern about the impact of municipal waste on ground and surface water.

Several methods for managing municipal solid waste have been designed and implemented over the last 20 years. In the United States, 80 percent or more of the municipal solid waste ends up in landfills, about 10 percent is incinerated, and about 11 percent is recycled. Waste-to-energy **incineration** is an option aimed at reducing the volume of municipal waste and producing an ongoing supply of energy for nearby markets. The complication of this treatment method is the ash residue and its disposal as well as air pollution. Probably the most desirable management technique for MSW is **recycling**.

Recycling captures the embodied energy in the products to be discarded. The conversion of the **waste stream** into a second or third generation of usable products is far superior to simple volume destruction or land burial. Unfortunately, recycling requires behavioral change on the part of the waste generator and behavioral and infrastructure change on the part of industry in order to create markets for post consumer materials. Individuals must learn to clean and separate household garbage and make it ready for recycling. Industry must make the investment to change manufacturing processes to accommodate a heterogeneous "raw" material.

Even more desirable than recycling is source reduction and **reuse** of household products and industrial and business supplies. Buying durable and re-usable products reduces the volume of the MSW stream. Packaging that can be reused after the product has been used is another way of shrinking municipal solid waste volume. In some European countries like Germany, manufacturers are required to take back all their packaging materials.

The cost of MSW disposal has increased dramatically over the last 10 years. Part of this cost is due to the pressure being put on fewer and fewer landfills as older landfills close. Many metropolitan areas of the United States have exhausted their landfill capacity and are transporting waste into rural areas. Unfortunately, in rural areas the volume of MSW is not sufficient for landfill companies to make the investment and build state-of-the-art landfills. Furthermore there is increasing concern that many towns and cities are dumping their MSW in areas where people have less political power or need the revenue from **tipping fee**s. Consequently the management of waste has become a social issue as well as an environmental concern.

Currently there are approximately 3,500 licensed landfills operating in the United States. Tipping fees have increased as have transport fees. States are transporting MSW hundreds of miles to other states because they can't build landfills due to citizen opposition. The **NIMBY** (Not In My Backyard) syndrome makes it difficult to create more landfills. **Waste management** companies are offering extensive incentive packages to local communities in order to get approval for landfill siting. Yet, almost without exception, local citizens attempt to block the construction of landfills.

Municipal solid waste is a renewable resource. We will always have new supplies of it. Even though many citizens are beginning to turn to nondisposable items and there is a real effort to launch recycling programs nationwide, we are still faced with an increasing volume of municipal waste. It is a complex problem that will require behavioral change on the part of individuals, a commitment on the part of local city planners, and an investment on the part of industry in order to recycle the waste stream. *See also* Medical waste

[*Cynthia Fridgen*]

FURTHER READING

Blumberg, L., and R. Gottlieb. *War on Waste: Can America Win Its Battle with Garbage?* Washington, DC: Island Press, 1989.

Rathje, W., and C. Cullen. *Rubbish! The Archaelogy of Garbage.* New York: Harper-Collins Publishers, 1992.

The Solid Waste Dilemma: An Agenda for Action. Washington, DC: Environmental Protection Agency, 1989.

Municipal solid waste composting

Municipal Solid Waste (MSW) composting is a rapidly growing method of **solid waste** management in the United States. MSW includes the residential, commercial, and institutional solid waste generated within a community. MSW composting is the process by which the organic, **biodegradable** portion of MSW is microbiologically degraded under **aerobic** conditions.

During the process of degradation, bacteria are used to decompose and break down the organic matter into water and **carbon dioxide**, which produces large amounts of heat and water vapor in the process. Given sufficient oxygen and optimum temperatures, the **composting** process achieves a high degree of volume reduction and also generates a stable end product called compost that can be used for mulching, **soil** amendment, and soil enhancement. As a form of solid waste management, MSW composting reduces the amount of waste that would otherwise end up in **landfill**s.

Although composting has been practiced by humans for centuries, the concept of composting mixed solid waste as a form of large-scale solid waste management is still in an early stage of development in the United States. MSW generally consists of a mixture of organic compostable materials such as food waste and paper and inert, nonbiodegradable materials such as **plastics** and glass. The introduction of non-compostable materials may pose problems in materials handling during the composting process and also hinder the formation of a uniform, homogeneous compost. Therefore, in order to practice MSW composting as a form of **waste management**, the composting system must be designed to remove the non-compostable materials either by presorting and screening or by sifting and removal at the end of the process.

The three most common methods of MSW composting are closed in-vessel, windrow, and static aerated pile composting. The method of choice depends on the volume of waste to be composted and the availability of space for composting. In the closed in-vessel method, the MSW is physically contained within large drums or cylinders and all necessary aeration and agitation is supplied to the vessel. In windrows, the MSW is heaped in long rows of material approximately four to seven feet high. Air and ventilation are supplied by physically turning over the piles with mechanical windrow turners. In static aerated compost piles, the MSW piles are not physically agitated, rather air is supplied and excess heat is removed by a system of sensors and pipes within the pile. In all cases, the goal is to ensure a steady, optimum rate of composting by providing adequate oxygen and ventilation to remove excess heat and water so that microbiological action is not impaired. When there is insufficient air supply, microbial action is unable to fully decompose the waste and the piles become **anaerobic** and unpleasant odors and putrefaction may result. Strong neighborhood complaints against odors is the single most common reason for the failure and shutdown of composting plants.

In the United States, numerous, small-scale, pilot projects have demonstrated the feasibility of MSW composting for townships and municipalities. However, there are relatively few operations that successfully carry out MSW composting on a large, commercial scale. The operational large-scale facilities are located mainly in Florida and Minnesota, two states that have traditionally shown interest in innovative waste management options. *See also* Aerobic sludge digestion; Solid waste incineration; Solid waste recycling and recovery; Waste reduction

[*Usha Vedagiri*]

FURTHER READING

Goldstein, N., and R. Steuteville. "Solid Waste Composting in the United States." *Biocycle* 33 (1992): 44-52.

Mutagen

Any agent, chemical or physical, that has the potential for inducing permanent change to the genetic material of an organism by altering its **DNA**. The alteration may be either a point **mutation** (nucleotide substitution, insertion, or deletion) or a chromosome aberration (translocation, inversion, or altered chromosome complement). There are long lists of chemical mutagens which include such diverse agents as formaldehyde, mustard gas, triethylenemelamine, **vinyl chloride**, aflatoxin B, **benzo(a)pyrene**, and acridine orange. Chemical mutagens may be direct acting, or they may have to be converted by metabolic activity to the ultimate mutagen. Physical mutagens include (but are not limited to) **X-ray**s and **ultraviolet radiation**. *See also* Agent Orange; Birth defects; Chemicals; Gene pool; Genetic engineering; Love Canal, New York

Mutation

A mutation is a change in the **DNA** of an organism, which is genetically transmitted, and may give rise to a heritable variation. **Mutagen**s, substances that have the competence to produce a mutation, may be subject to chromosomal changes such as deletions, translocations, or inversions. Mutations may also be more subtle, resulting in changes of only one or a few nucleotides in the sequence of DNA. These more subtle mutations are called as "point mutations," and it is these that most people refer to when discussing mutation.

Ordinarily, mutation is thought of as a genetic change that results in alterations in a subsequent generation. Germinal tissue, which gives rise to spermatozoa and ova, is the tissue in which such mutations occur. However, mutations can arise in many cell types in addition to the germ line, and these changes to non-germinal DNA are referred to as somatic mutations. Although somatic mutations are not passed to subsequent generations, they are not less important than germinal mutations. **Ionizing radiation** and certain **chemicals** can have mutagenic effects on somatic cells which often result in **cancer**.

Mutations may be either spontaneous or induced. The term spontaneous is perhaps misleading; even these mutations have a physical basis in cosmic rays, natural background radiation, or simply kinetic effects of molecular motion. Induced mutations ensue from known exposure to a diversity of chemicals and certain ionizing radiations.

DNA is composed of a linear array of nucleotides, which are translocated through **RNA** into protein. The genetic code consists of consecutive nucleotide triplets which correspond to particular amino acids, and it may be altered by substitution, insertion, or deletion of individual nucleotides. Substitution of a nucleotide in some cases can be inconsequential, since the substituted nucleotide may specify an amino acid which does not affect the function of the protein. On the other hand, substitution of one nucleotide for another one can result in a protein gene product with a changed amino acid sequence that has a major biological effect. An example of such a single nucleotide substitution is sickle cell hemoglobin, which differs from normal hemoglobin by a single amino acid. The substitution of a valine for a glutamic

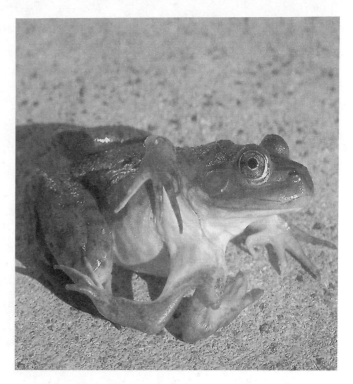

A six-legged green frog, the result of a genetic mutation.

acid in the mutant hemoglobin molecule results in sickle cell disease, which is characterized by chronic hemolytic anemia.

The insertion or deletion of a single nucleotide pair results in what is known as a frameshift mutation; this is because the mutation changes the sequence of molecules beyond the point at which it occurs, causing them to be read in different groups of three. Consequently, there is a miscoding of the nucleotides into their gene product. Such proteins are usually shortened in length and no longer functional. *See also* Birth defects; Carcinogen; Gene pool; Genetic engineering; Genetically engineered organism

[*Robert G. McKinnell*]

FURTHER READING

Mutagenic Effects of Environmental Contaminants. New York: Academic Press, 1972.

Mycorrhiza

Refers to a close, symbiotic relationship between a fungus and the roots of a higher plant. Mycorrhiza (from the Greek *myketos* meaning fungus and *rhiza* meaning root) are common among trees in temperate and tropical forests. There are generally two forms—ectomycorrhiza, where the fungus forms a sheath around the plant roots, and endomycorrhiza, where the fungus penetrates into the cells of the plant roots. In both cases, the fungus acts as extended roots for the plant and therefore increase its total surface area. This allows for greater adsorption of water and **nutrient**s vital to growth. Mycorrhiza even allow plants to utilize nutrients bound up in silicate minerals and phosphate-containing rocks that are normally unavailable to plant roots. They also can stimulate the plants to produce **chemicals** that hinder invading **pathogen**s in the **soil**. In addition to the physical support, the mycorrhiza obtain carbohydrates from the higher, photosynthetic plant. This obligate relationship between **fungi** and plant roots is especially important in nutrient-impoverished soils. In fact, many trees will not grow without mycorrhiza. *See also* Symbiosis; Temperate rain forest; Tropical rain forest

Mycotoxin

Mycotoxins are toxic biochemical substances produced by **fungi**. They are produced on grains, fishmeal, peanuts, and many other substances, including all kinds of decaying vegetation. Mycotoxins are produced by several **species** of fungi—especially *Aspergillus*, *Penicillium*, and *Fusarium*—under appropriate environmental conditions of temperature, moisture, and oxygen on crops in the field or in storage bins. In recent years, research on this subject has indicated considerable specialization in mycotoxin production by fungi. For example, aflatoxins B_1, B_2, G_1, and G_2 are relatively similar mycotoxins produced by the fungus *Aspergillus flavus* under conditions of temperatures ranging from 80-100°F (27-38°C) and 18-20 percent moisture in the grain. Aflatoxins are among the most potent **carcinogen**s among naturally occurring products. Head scab on wheat in the field is produced by the fungus *Fusarium graminearum* which produces a mycotoxin known as DON (*deoxynivalenol*), also known as Vomitoxin.

N

Nader, Ralph (1934-)

American consumer advocate

Born in Connecticut, Nader is the son of Lebanese immigrants who emphasized citizenship and industrial democracy and stressed the importance of justice rather than power. Nader earned his bachelor's degree in government and economics from Princeton University in 1955 and his law degree from Harvard University in 1958, having served as editor of the prestigious *Harvard Law Record*. Nader reads some fifteen publications daily and speaks several languages, including Arabic, Chinese, and Russian.

Nader published his first article, "American Cars: Designed for Death," as editor of the *Harvard Law Record*. Later, as a free-lance writer, he published similar safety-related pieces such as "Menace of Atomic Energy" (1977); "Who's Poisoning America?" (1981); and *The Big Boys*, which he co-authored with William Taylor in 1986. Perhaps his most influential work is *Unsafe at Any Speed* (1965). In the book Nader condemns U.S. automakers for valuing style over safety in developing their products and specifically targets General Motors and its Chevrolet Corvair. The controversy that *Unsafe at Any Speed* generated led to passage of the Traffic and Motor Vehicle Safety Act of 1966, which gave the government the right to enact and regulate safety standards for all **automobile**s sold in the United States.

Nader has championed a wide variety of causes. He worked for passage of the Wholesome Meat Act (1967), which set federal inspection standards for slaughterhouses and processing plants, and he worked to ensure passage of the Freedom of Information Act (1974). He played a key role in the establishment of the **Occupational Safety and Health Administration (OSHA)**, as well as the Consumer Product Safety Commission. One of his most important victories was the establishment of the **Environmental Protection Agency (EPA)** in 1970, during the Nixon administration. A 1971 Harris poll placed Nader as the sixth most popular figure in the nation, and he is still known as the most important consumer advocate in the country.

To assist him in his far-reaching investigative efforts, Nader created a watchdog team, known as "Nader's Raiders." This group of lawyers was the core of what became the Center for Study of Responsive Law (CSRL), which has been Nader's headquarters since 1968. A network of public interest organizations have branched off from CSRL, which include **U.S. Public Interest Research Group**, Public Citizen, Health Research Group, Critical Mass Energy Project, and Congress Watch. Other groups have been established by Nader's associates, and though not run by Nader himself, they follow the same ideals as CSRL and work toward similar goals. Among these groups are: the **Clean Water Action Project**, the Center for Auto Safety, and the **Center for Science in the Public Interest**.

Nader was at the height of his influence during the 1970s, and since then he has been less in the public eye. The Reagan years saw a loosening of the regulations for which he had fought, and Nader himself suffered many personal setbacks, including the death of his brother and his own neurological illness. In 1987, Nader vigorously campaigned for Proposition 103 in California, which would roll back automobile insurance rates. The bill passed and exit polls showed that Nader's efforts had made the difference. While he has changed his methods somewhat, using celebrities to emphasize the importance of automobile air bags, for example, his mission remains the same. He believes that there has been a takeover of democratic institutions by corporate interests and a need for more political competition is surfacing. So, Nader accepted the Greens 1996 presidential nomination with the hope of broadening the agenda and building up the Green party as a more formidable force in next presidential race.

[*Kimberley A. Peterson*]

FURTHER READING

Dennis, D. L. "The Resurrection of Ralph Nader." *Fortune* (22 May 1989): 106+.

Harbrecht, D. A. "The Second Coming of Ralph Nader." *Business Week* (6 March 1989): 28.

Naess, Arne (1912-)

Norwegian philosopher and naturalist

Arne Naess is a noted mountaineer and philosopher and the founder of the **deep ecology** movement. He was born to Ragnar and Christine Naess in Oslo, Norway, on January 27, 1912, the youngest of five children. Naess was an introspective child, and he displayed an early interest in logic and philosophy. After undergraduate work at the Sorbonne in

Paris, he did graduate work at the University of Vienna, the University of California—Berkeley, and the University of Oslo. While in Vienna, his interests in logic, language, and methodology drew him to the Vienna Circle of logical empiricism. He was awarded the Ph.D. in philosophy from the University of Oslo in 1938.

A year later, in 1939, Naess was made full professor of philosophy at the same university. He promptly reorganized Norwegian higher education, making the history of ideas a prerequisite for all academic specializations and encouraging greater conceptual sophistication and tolerance. From the beginning, Naess was interested in empirical semantics, that is, how ordinary persons use words to communicate. In *"Truth" as Conceived by Those Who Are Not Professional Philosophers* (1939), he was one of the first to use statistical methods and questionnaires to survey philosophical beliefs. Shortly after his appointment at the university, the Germans occupied Norway. Naess resisted any changes in academic routine, insisting that education be separate from politics. The increasing brutality of the Quisling regime, however, impelled him to join the resistance movement. While in the resistance he helped avert the shipment of thousands of university students to concentration camps. Immediately after the war, he confronted Nazi atrocities by mediating conversations between the families of torture victims and their pro-Nazi Norwegian victimizers.

In the post-War period, Naess's academic interests and accomplishments were many and varied. He continued his work on language and communication in *Interpretation and Preciseness* (1953) and *Communication and Argument* (1966), concluding that communication is not based on a precise and shared language. Rather we understand words, sentences, and intentions by interpreting their meaning. Language is thus a double-edged sword. Communication is often difficult and requires successive interpretations. Even so, the ambiguity of language allows for a tremendous flexibility in verbal meaning and content. Because of his work in communication and his resistance to the Nazis, Naess was selected by the United Nations Educational, Scientific and Cultural Organization [UNESCO] in 1949 to explore the meanings of democracy. This project resulted in *Democracy, Ideology and Objectivity* (1956). In 1958, he founded the journal *Inquiry*, serving as its editor until 1976. The magazine explores the relations of philosophy, science, and society, especially as they reflect normative assumptions and implications. He also published on diverse topics, including Gandhian nonviolence, the philosophies of science, and the Dutch philosopher Baruch Spinoza (1632-1677). These works include *Gandhi and the Nuclear Age* (1965), *Skepticism* (1968), *Four Modern Philosophers: Carnap, Wittgenstein, Heidegger, Sartre* (1968), *The Pluralist and Possibilist Aspect of the Scientific Enterprise* (1972), and *Freedom, Emotion and Self-Subsistence: The Structure of a Central Part of Spinoza's "Ethic"* (1972).

Naess began examining humanity's relationship with **nature** during the early 1970s. The genesis of this interest is best understood in the context of Norway's environment, culture, and politics. Nature, not humanity, dominates the landscape of Norway. The nation has the lowest population density in Europe, and over ninety percent of the land is undeveloped. As a consequence, the interior of Norway is relatively wild and diverse, a mixture of mountains, glaciers, fjords, forests, **tundra**, and small human settlements. Moreover, Norwegian culture deeply values nature; environmental themes are common in Norwegian literature, and the majority of Norwegians share a passion for outdoor activities and **recreation**. This passion is known as *friluftsliv*, meaning "open air life." Friluftsliv is widely touted as one means of reconnecting with the natural world. Norwegian environmental politics has been wracked by a succession of ecological and resource conflicts. These conflicts involve **predator control**, recreation areas, **national park**s, industrial **pollution**, **dams** and hydroelectric power, nuclear energy, North Sea oil, and economic development. During the 1960s Naess became deeply involved in environmental activism. Indeed, his participation in protests lead to his arrest for nonviolent civil disobedience. He even wrote a manual to help environmental and community activists participate in nonviolent resistance. Growing up, Naess was deeply moved by his experiences in the wild places of Norway. He became an avid mountaineer, leading several ascents of the Tirich Mir (25,300 feet [7700 m]) in the Hindu Kush range. In 1937, he built a small cabin near the final assent to the summit of Hallingskarvet, a mountain approximately 111 miles (180 km) northeast of Oslo. He named it *Tvergastein*, meaning "across the stones."

Since his retirement, Naess has published widely on environmental topics. His main contributions are in ecophilosophy, **environmental policy**, and **conservation** biology. The insight and controversy surrounding these writings have propelled him to the forefront of **environmental ethics** and politics.

Naess regards philosophy as "wisdom in action." He notes that many policy decisions are "made in a state of philosophical stupor" wherein narrow and short-term goals are all that is considered or recommended. Lucid thinking and clear communication help widen and lengthen the options available at any point in time. Naess describes this work as a labor in "ecophilosophy," that is, an inquiry where philosophy is used to study the natural world and humanity's relationship to it. Recalling the ambiguity of language and communication, he distinguishes ecophilosophy from **ecosophy**—a personal philosophy whose conceptions guide one's conduct toward nature and human beings. While important elements of our ecosophies may be shared, we each proceed from assumptions, norms, and hypotheses that vary in substance and/or interpretation. Of central importance to Naess's exploration of ecophilosophy are norms and beliefs about what one should or ought to do based on what is prudent or ethical. Norms play a leading role in any ecophilosophy. While science may explain nature and human ecology, it is norms that justify and motivate our actions in the natural world. Along with the concept of norms, Naess stresses the importance of depth. By depth, Naess means reflecting deeply on our concepts, emotions and experiences of nature, as well as digging to the cultural, personal, and

The aftermath from the atom bomb that was dropped on Nagasaki during World War II.

social roots of our environmental problems. Thinking deeply means taking a broad and incisive look at our values, lifestyles, and community life. In so doing, we discover if our way of life is consistent with our most deeply felt norms.

An ecophilosophy which deeply investigates and clarifies its norms is called a "deep ecological philosophy." A social movement that incorporates this process, shares significant norms, and seeks deep personal and social change is termed "deep ecology movement." Naess coined the term "deep ecology" in 1973, intending to highlight the importance of norms and social change in environmental decision-making. He also coined the term "shallow ecology" to describe what he considered short-term technological solutions to environmental concerns. Naess's own ecophilosophy is called "Ecosophy T." The "T" symbolizes Tvergastein. Ecosophy T stresses a number of themes, including the **intrinsic value** of nature, the importance of cultural and natural diversity, and the norm of self-realization for persons, cultures, and non-human life-forms. Naess offers his ecosophy as a tentative template, encouraging others to construct their own ecosophies.

Deep ecology is therefore a rubric representing many philosophies and practices, each differing in significant ways. Naess encourages this diversity, recognizing that many mutually acceptable interpretations of deep ecology are possible. On the whole, therefore, Naess is philosophically and environmentally non-dogmatic. He avoids rigid dichotomies pitting individual versus social accounts, liberal versus radical

solutions, or **wilderness** versus justice concerns. To paraphrase Naess, "the frontier is long and there are many places to stand." Some may focus their thoughts and efforts on nature, others on society, still others on culture. According to Naess, these are legitimate and necessary foci and should be encouraged as separate endeavors and joint undertakings.

[*William S. Lynn*]

FURTHER READING

Naess, A. "The Shallow and the Deep, Long-Range Ecology Movements." *Inquiry* 16 (1973): 95-100.

————. "Intrinsic Value: Will the Defenders of Nature Please Rise?" In *Conservation Biology: The Science of Scarcity and Diversity*, edited by M. E. Soule. Sunderland, MA: Sinauer Associates, 1986.

————. *Ecology, Community and Lifestyle: Outline of an Ecosophy*. Cambridge, UK: Cambridge University Press, 1989.

Reed, P., and D. Rothenberg, eds. *Wisdom in the Open Air: The Norwegian Roots of Deep Ecology*. Minneapolis, MN: University of Minnesota Press, 1993.

Rothenberg, D. *Is It Painful to Think? Conversations with Arne Naess.* Minneapolis, MN: University of Minnesota Press, 1993.

Nagasaki, Japan

Nagasaki is a harbor city located at the southwestern tip of Japan. It is Japan's oldest open port. Traders from the western world started arriving in the mid-sixteenth century. It became a major shipbuilding center by the twentieth century.

It was the second city to be devastated by an atomic bomb which was dropped on August 9, 1945, just 3 days after the bomb that destroyed **Hiroshima**. The bomb that was dropped at Nagasaki resulted in 35,000-40,000 men, women, and children killed with an equal number injured. Like Hiroshima, most of the city was destroyed. The Nagasaki survivors of the atomic bomb have an increased risk for **radiation**-induced **cancer** and are part of a continuing study by the Atomic Bomb Casualty Commission which is now known as the Radiation Effects Research Foundation (RERF). The city was rebuilt after the end of World War II and is now a tourist attraction.

[*Robert G. McKinnell*]

National Air Toxics Information Clearinghouse

The National Air Toxics Information Clearinghouse (NATIC) is a program administered by the **Environmental Protection Agency (EPA)**. This information network was developed by the EPA to provide state and federal **air pollution control** experts with **air pollution** data. The computerized data base is headquartered in North Carolina, but air pollution control officers nationwide are able to access the data.

NATIC is a "one-stop shop" for **emission**s data for state enforcement officers, according to the EPA. Included on the network is information on air toxics programs, **ambient air** quality standards, **pollution research**, non-health related impact of air pollution, permits, emissions inventories, and ambient air quality monitoring programs.

National Ambient Air Quality Standard (NAAQS)

The key to national **air pollution** control policy since the passage of the **Clean Air Act** amendments of 1970 are the National Ambient Air Quality Standards (NAAQSs). Under this law, the **Environmental Protection Agency (EPA)** had to establish NAAQSs for six of the most common air pollutants, sometimes referred to as **criteria pollutant**s, by April 1971. Included are **carbon monoxide, lead** (added in 1977), **nitrogen oxides, ozone, particulate** matter, and **sulfur dioxide. Hydrocarbons** originally appeared on the list of pollutants, but were removed in 1978 since they were adequately regulated through the ozone standard. The provisions of the law allow the EPA to identify additional substances as pollutants and add them to the list.

For each of these pollutants, primary and secondary standards are set. The primary standards are designed to protect human health. Secondary standards are to protect crops, forests, and buildings if the primary standards are not capable of doing so; a secondary standard presently exists only for sulfur dioxide. These standards apply uniformly throughout the country, in each of 247 **Air Quality Control Region**s. All parts of the country were required to meet the NAAQSs by 1975, but this deadline was extended, in some cases, to the year 2010. The states monitor **air pollution**, enforce the standards, and can implement stricter standards than the NAAQSs if they desire.

The primary standards must be established at levels that would "provide an adequate margin of safety ... to protect the public ... from any known or anticipated adverse effects associated with such air pollutant[s] in the **ambient air**." This phrase was based on the belief that there is a threshold effect of **pollution**: pollution levels below the threshold are safe, levels above are unsafe. Although such an approach to setting the standards reflected scientific knowledge at the time, more recent research suggests that such a threshold probably does not exist. That is, pollution at any level is unsafe. The NAAQSs are also to be established without consideration of how much it will cost to achieve them; they are to be based on the **Best Available Control Technology (BAT)**. The secondary standards are to "protect the public welfare from any known or anticipated adverse effects."

The NAAQSs are established based on the EPA's "criteria documents," which summarize the effect on human health caused by each pollutant, based on current scientific knowledge. The standards are usually expressed in parts of pollutant per million parts of air and vary in the duration of time a pollutant can be allowed into the environment, so that only a limited amount of contaminant may be emitted per hour, week, or year, for example. The 1977 Clean Air Act amendments require the EPA to submit criteria documents to the Clean Air Scientific Advisory Committee and the EPA's Science Advisory Board for review. Several revisions of the criteria documents are usually required. Although standards should be based on scientific evidence, politics often become involved as environmentalists and public health advocates battle industrial powers in setting standards.

The six criteria pollutants come from a variety of sources and have a variety of health effects. Carbon monoxide is a gas produced by the incomplete **combustion** of **fossil fuels**. It can lead to damage of the cardiovascular, nervous, and pulmonary systems, and can also cause problems with short-term attention span and sensory abilities.

Lead, a heavy metal, has been traced to many health effects, mainly brain damage leading to learning disabilities and retardation in children. Most of the lead found in the air came from **gasoline** fumes until a 1973 court case, *Natural Resources Defense Council v. EPA*, prompted its inclusion as a criteria pollutant. Lead levels in gasoline are now monitored.

Nitrogen oxide is formed primarily by fossil fuel combustion. It not only contributes to **acid rain** and the formation of ground-level ozone, but it has been linked to respiratory illness.

Ground-level ozone is produced by a combination of hydrocarbons and nitrogen oxides in the presence of sunlight, and heat. It is the prime component of **photochemical smog**, which can cause respiratory problems in humans, reduce crop yields, and cause forest damage. In 1979, the first revision of an original NAAQS slightly relaxed the photo-chemical oxidant standard and renamed it the ozone standard. Experts are currently debating whether this standard is low enough, and in 1991 the American Lung Association sued the EPA for failure to review the ozone NAAQS in light of new evidence.

Particulate matter is composed of small pieces of solid and liquid matter, including soot, dust, and organic matter. It reduces visibility and can cause eye and throat irritation, respiratory ailments, and **cancer**. Through 1987, total suspended particulates were the basis of the NAAQS. In 1987, the standard was revised and based on particulate matter with an aerodynamic diameter of 10 micrometers or less (PM-10), which was identified as the main health risk.

Sulfur dioxide is a gas produced primarily by coal-burning utilities and other fossil fuel combustion. It is the chief cause of acid rain and can also cause respiratory problems.

To achieve the NAAQSs for these six pollutants, the Clean Air Act incorporated three strategies. First, the federal government would establish **New Source Performance Standard**s (NSPSs) for stationary sources such as factories and **power plants**; they would also establish **emission standards** for mobile sources. Finally, the states would develop State Implementation Plans (SIPs) to address existing sources of air pollution. If the federal government determined that an SIP was not adequate to assure that the state would meet the NAAQSs, it could impose federal controls to meet them. According to the EPA, the SIPs must be designed to bring sub-standard air quality regions up to the NAAQSs, or to make sure any area already meeting the requirements continued to do so. The SIPs should prevent increased air pollution in areas of noncompliance, either by preventing significant expansions of existing industries or the opening of new plants. In order to allow economic development and growth in such non-attainment areas while still working to reduce air pollution, the 1977 amendments to the Clean Air Act required that new sources of pollution in non-attainment areas must control emissions to the **lowest achievable emission rate** (LAER) for that type of source and pollution and demonstrate that the new pollution would be offset by new emission reductions from existing sources in the area, reductions that went beyond existing permits and compliance plans. So, new sources were allowed, but only if the additional pollution were offset by reductions at existing sources.

Between 1978 and 1987, data collected nationally at 84 to 1,726 sites (varying for each pollutant) indicate that annual average concentrations of total suspended particulates fell by 21 percent, sulfur dioxide levels fell by 35 percent, carbon monoxide levels fell by 32 percent, lead levels fell by 88 percent, nitrogen dioxide levels fell by 12 percent, and ozone levels fell by 9 percent. With the exception of ozone, the average concentrations are below the NAAQSs. It is unclear how these reductions have improved human health conditions, but illnesses due to chronic lead exposure are down. Ozone probably causes the most health problems in affected areas, since the NAAQS for it is most often exceeded. Due to other complex factors, though, it is unclear how much of a problem it is.

Though the Clean Air Act allows one violation per year for each of the one-hour, eight-hour, and twenty-four hour NAAQSs for each pollutant, most urban areas, called non-attainment areas, violate standards much more often. For example, in Los Angeles the ozone standard was exceeded an average of 123 times annually in 1983, 1984, and 1985. As of 1989, 341 counties had ozone non-attainment, 317 had particulate non-attainment, 123 had carbon monoxide non-attainment, sixty-seven had sulfur dioxide non-attainment, and four had nitrogen dioxide non-attainment. A total of 529 counties had not met standards on at least one criteria pollutant.

The 1990 amendments to the Clean Air Act dealt with the problem of such non-attainment areas. Six categories of ozone non-attainment were established, ranging from marginal to extreme, and two categories for both carbon monoxide and particulate matter were established. Deadlines to achieve the NAAQSs were extended from three to twenty years. Increased restrictions were required in non-attainment areas; existing controls were tightened and smaller sources were made subject to regulation. Also, annual reduction goals were mandated. Areas considered to have made inadequate progress toward reaching attainment are subjected to stringent regulations on new plants and limited use of federal highway funds. *See also* Air pollution control; Air pollution index; Air quality criteria; Heavy metals and heavy metal poisoning; Nonpoint source; Point source

[*Christopher McGrory Klyza*]

FURTHER READING

Bryner, G. C. *Blue Skies, Green Politics: The Clean Air Act of 1990.* Washington, DC: CQ Press, 1993.

Melnick, R. S. *Regulation and the Courts: The Case of the Clean Air Act.* Washington, DC: Brookings Institution, 1983.

Portney, P. R. "Air Pollution Policy." In *Public Policies for Environmental Protection*, edited by P. R. Portney. Washington, DC: Resources for the Future, 1990.

National Audubon Society (New York, New York)

The National Audubon Society (NAS) is one of the largest and oldest **conservation** organizations in the world. Founded in New York City in February 1886, its original purpose was to protect American birds from destruction for the millinery trade. Many **species** of birds were being killed and sold as adornments to women's hat and bonnets, as well as other clothing. The first preservation battle taken on by the NAS was the snowy egret—a white, wading marshland bird—whose long plumes were in high demand. The group was instrumental in securing passage of the New York Bird Law in 1886, an act for the preservation of the state's avifauna.

The NAS was named after **John James Audubon**, the nineteenth-century artist and naturalist. Audubon was not a conservationist; he often killed dozens of birds to get a single individual that was right for his paintings. But he had published his life-sized renderings of all the birds in North America in 1850, and his name was the one most closely associated with birds when the society was founded.

The protection of **wildlife** and **habitat**s continues to be the primary focus of the NSA. Since their founding, much of their conservation work has been accomplished through education. Their *Audubon* magazine is perhaps their most important educational tool. They also publish *American Birds*, which records many of the field observations reported to the society from around the country.

One of the most important observations published in *American Birds* is the data recorded on Christmas Bird Counts, an annual winter bird census maintained by NAS since 1900. During a three-week period from December to early January, teams of observers count and record every different species of bird observed within a 24-hour period in a designated circle, 15 miles (24 km) in diameter. The count circles remain constant from year to year which allows for comparison of data collected. The first circle was Central Park in New York City; the number of circles have grown from one to over 1600 in recent years. Thousands of people participate in this annual event.

Additional educational and conservation programs have proven successful for NAS over the years, including a **nature** club for children and a series of **ecology** camps for the field study of different **ecosystem**s in North America. The society has also produced nature films and nationally televised programs on environmental issues facing the world today. The NAS also addresses these issues through lobbying on a national level in Washington, DC, and on regional and local levels by members of the several hundred local Audubon Societies, clubs, and state coalitions nationwide. With a half million environmentally-conscious members, the National Audubon Society continues to make a difference in the battle to conserve the natural world and the wildlife in it. Contact: National Audubon Society, 950 Third Ave., New York, NY 10022. Internet: http://www.audubon.org/.

[*Eugene C. Beckham*]

National Biological Service
See **Biological Resources Division**

National Coalition Against the Misuse of Pesticides (Washington, D.C.)

Founded in 1981, the National Coalition Against the Misuse of Pesticides (NCAMP) is a non-profit, grassroots network of groups and individuals concerned with the dangers of **pesticide**s. Members of NCAMP include individuals, such as "victims" of pesticides, physicians, attorneys, farmers and farmworkers, gardeners, and former chemical company scientists, as well as health, farm, consumer, and church groups. All want to limit pesticide use through NCAMP, which publishes information on pesticide hazards and alternatives, monitors and influences legislation on pesticide issues, and provides seed grants and encouragement to local groups and efforts.

Administered by a fifteen-member board of directors and a small full-time staff, including one toxicologist and one ecologist, NCAMP is now the most prominent organization dealing with the pesticide issue. It was established on the premise that much is unknown about the toxic effects of pesticides and the extent of public exposure to them. Because such information is not immediately forthcoming, members of NCAMP believe the only available way of reducing both known and unknown risks is by limiting or eliminating pesticides. The organization takes a dual-pronged approach to accomplish this. First NCAMP draws public attention to the risks of conventional pest management; second it promotes the least-toxic alternatives to current pesticide practices.

An important part of NCAMP's overall program is the Center for Community Pesticide and Alternatives Information. The Center is a clearinghouse of information, providing a 2,000-volume library about pest control, chemicals, and pesticides. To concerned individuals it sells inexpensive brochures and booklets, which cover topics such as alternatives to controlling specific pests and chemicals; the risks of pesticides in schools, to food, and in reproduction; and developments in the **Federal Insecticide, Fungicide and Rodenticide Act (FIFRA)**, the national law governing pesticide use and registration in the United States. Through the Center NCAMP also publishes *Pesticides and You* (*PAY*) five times a year. It is a newsletter sent to approximately 4,500 people, including NCAMP members, subscribers, and members of Congress. The Center also provides direct assistance to individuals through access to NCAMP's staff ecologist and toxicologist.

In 1991 NCAMP also established the Local Environmental Control Project after the Supreme Court decision affirming local communities' rights to regulate pesticide use. Although NCAMP supported bestowing local control over pesticide use, it needed a new program to counteract the subsequent mobilization of the pesticide industry to reverse the Supreme Court decision. The Local Environmental Control Project campaigns first to preserve the right accorded by the Supreme Court decision and second to encourage communities to take advantage of this right.

NCAMP marked its tenth anniversary in 1991 with a forum entitled "A Decade of Determination: A Future of Change." It included workshops on **wildlife** and **groundwater** protection, **cancer** risk assessment, and the implications of GATT and free trade agreements. NCAMP has also established the annual National Pesticide Forum. Through such conferences, its aid to victims and groups, and its many publications, NCAMP above all encourages local action to limit pesticides and change the methods of controlling pests. Contact: National Coalition Against the Misuse of Pesticides, 701 E Street SE, Washington, D.C. 20003. Internet: http://www.csn.net/ncamp/.

[*Andrea Gacki*]

National Emission Standards for Hazardous Air Pollutants

Emission standards for hazardous air pollutants that were not covered by the **National Ambient Air Quality Standard** were provided for under Section 112 of the **Clean Air Act** of 1970. This section directed the **Environmental Protection Agency (EPA)** to issue a list of hazardous pollutants that were to be regulated. However, the 1970 Clean Air Act provisions to deal with hazardous pollutants proved to be ineffective. Although more than 300 **toxic substance**s are known to be emitted into the air, between 1970 and 1990 **emission standards** were established for only eight substances: **asbestos**, **benzene**, beryllium, coke oven emissions, inorganic **arsenic**, **mercury**, radionuclides, and **vinyl chloride**. The EPA knew that over sixty other airborne toxins were known to cause **cancer**, **birth defects**, or neurological disease, but these were still unregulated. The Section 112 regulatory process was expensive and conservative. It required the EPA to gather enough evidence to demonstrate that the air toxin was hazardous before it could act, but often there was a lack of scientific information on the health effects of these toxins. There was also a strong potential for legal challenges by industry.

Inventories begun in 1987 indicated that over 2 billion pounds of toxic chemicals were released into the air annually, from 1987 through 1989. Furthermore, more toxic chemicals were released into the air than into any other medium during these three years. Environmentalists and their supporters in Congress argued that the 1970 program had failed. The air toxins problem was a major **air pollution** problem, yet it was not being adequately addressed by Section 112. Hence, an improved air toxins program became a central component in the efforts to amend the Clean Air Act.

One of the major initiatives in the 1990 Clean Air Act was the provisions to deal with hazardous air pollutants. Title III of the law required the thousands of sources of air toxins in the country to use specific technologies to control hazardous air pollutants (HAPs). The act listed 189 chemicals that are considered HAPs, thereby taking that power from the EPA, though a mechanism is provided to add more HAPs to the regulatory program. All major stationary sources, regardless of age, location, or size, are required to meet emission standards for each HAP established by the EPA by 2000. Major sources of HAPs (those emitting at least 10 tons of one pollutant or 25 tons of a combination of pollutants, per year) are required to apply "maximum achievable control technology" (MACT) and will be required to receive emission permits. An incentive-based provision of the 1990 Clean Air

Act ensured that sources that voluntarily and permanently achieve HAP reductions of 90 percent (from 1987 levels) may postpone instillation of MACT for up to six years.

Under the new law, the EPA must focus on those HAPs and sources that are deemed the most dangerous. By 1995, the EPA is to have devised a strategy to control all sources of HAPs in urban areas. Over a nine-year period, the agency is to identify the thirty HAPs that are the greatest threat to human health, and to identify the sources generating 90 percent of these emissions. The EPA is also to devise a strategy to reduce HAP-related cancer risk by 75 percent. It is estimated that these new provisions will reduce hazardous air pollutants from industrial sources by 75 to 90 percent.

[*Christopher McGrory Klyza*]

FURTHER READING

Bryner, G. C. *Blue Skies, Green Politics: The Clean Air Act of 1990.* Washington, DC: CQ Press, 1993.

Mazmanian, D. and D. Morell. *Beyond Superfailure: America's Toxics Policy for the 1990s.* Boulder, CO: Westview Press, 1992.

Portney, P. R. "Toxic Substance Policy and the Protection of Human Health." In *Current Issues in U. S. Environmental Policy,* edited by P. R. Portney. Washington, DC: Resources for the Future, 1978.

Rosenbaum, W. A. *Environmental Politics and Policy.* 2nd ed. Washington, DC: CQ Press, 1991.

National Environmental Policy Act (1969)

The National Environmental Policy Act (NEPA) of 1969 was signed into law on January 1, 1970, launching a decade marked by passage of key environmental legislation and increased awareness of environmental problems. The act established the first comprehensive national policies and goals for the protection, maintenance, and use of the **environment**. The act also established the **Council on Environmental Quality (CEQ)** to oversee NEPA and advise the president on environmental issues.

Title I of NEPA declares that the federal government will use all practicable means and measures to create and maintain conditions under which people and **nature** can exist in productive harmony, while fulfilling the social and economic requirements of the American people. Included in this declaration are goals to attain the widest range of beneficial uses of the environment without undesirable consequences and to preserve culturally and aesthetically important features of the landscape. The declaration also commits each generation of Americans to stewardship of the environment for **future generations**.

To achieve the national environmental goals, the act directs all federal agencies to evaluate the impacts of major federal actions upon the environment. Before taking an action, each federal agency must prepare a statement describing (1) the environmental impact of the proposed action, (2)

adverse environmental effects that cannot be avoided, (3) alternatives to the proposal, (4) short-term versus long-term impacts, and (5) any irreversible effects on resources that would result if the action were implemented. The act requires any federal, state, or local agency with jurisdiction over the impacted environment to take part in the decision-making process. The general public also is given opportunities to take part in the NEPA process through hearings and meetings, or by submitting written comments to agencies involved in a project.

Title II of NEPA created the CEQ, as part of the Executive Office of the President, to oversee implementation of NEPA and assist the president in preparing an annual environmental quality report. The CEQ existed until February 1993, when President Clinton abolished the council and established the White House Office on Environmental Policy, with broader powers to coordinate national environmental policy. The CEQ issued regulations in 1978 which implement NEPA and are binding on all federal agencies. The regulations (40 CFR Parts 1500-1508) cover procedures and administration of NEPA, including preparation of environmental assessments and **environmental impact statement**s. Many federal agencies have established their own NEPA regulations, following CEQ regulations, but customized for the particular activities of the agencies. In addition, 11 states have passed state environmental policy acts, sometimes called "little NEPAs."

Federal agencies must incorporate the NEPA review process early in project planning. A complete environmental analysis can be very complex, involving potential effects on physical, chemical, biological and social factors of the proposed project and its alternatives. Various systematic methods have been developed to deal with the complexity of environmental analysis. There are three levels at which an action may be evaluated, depending on how large an impact it will have on the environment.

The first level is categorical exclusion which allows an undertaking to be exempt from detailed evaluation if it meets previously determined criteria designated as having no significant environmental impact. Some federal agencies have lists of actions which have been thus categorically excluded from evaluation under NEPA.

When an action cannot be excluded under the first level of analysis, the agency involved may prepare an environmental assessment to determine if the action will have a significant environment effect. An environmental assessment is a brief statement of the impacts of the action and alternatives. If the assessment determines there will not be significant environmental consequences, the agency issues a finding of no significant impact (FONSI). The finding may describe measures that will be taken to reduce potential impacts. An agency can skip the second level if it anticipates in advance that there will be significant impacts.

An action moves to the third level of analysis, an environmental impact statement (EIS), if the environmental assessment determines there will be significant environmental impacts. An EIS is a detailed evaluation of the action and alternatives, and it is used to make decisions on how to proceed with the action. An agency preparing an EIS must release a draft statement for comment and review by other agencies, local governments, and the general public. A final statement is released with modifications based on the results of the public review of the draft statement. When more than one agency is involved in an action, a lead agency is designated to coordinate the environmental analysis. An agency also may be called upon to cooperate in an environmental analysis if it has expertise in an area of concern. The CEQ regulations describe a process for settling disagreements which arise between agencies involved in an environmental analysis.

In addition to having to prepare their own environmental assessments and environmental impact statements, the **Environmental Protection Agency (EPA)** is involved in all NEPA review processes of other federal agencies, as mandated by Section 309 of the **Clean Air Act**. Section 309 was added to the Clean Air Act in 1970, after NEPA was passed and the EPA formed, with the purpose of ensuring independent reviews of all federal actions impacting the environment. As a result, the EPA reviews and comments on all federal environmental impact statements in draft and final form, on proposed environmental regulations and legislation, and on other proposed federal projects the EPA considers to have significant environmental impacts. The EPA's procedures for carrying out the Section 309 requirements are contained in the publication "Policies and Procedures for the Review of Federal Actions Impacting the Environment" (revised 1984). The EPA is also responsible for many of the administrative aspects of the EIS filing process. The NEPA review process includes an evaluation of a project's compliance with other environmental laws such as the Clean Air Act. Federal agencies often integrate NEPA reviews with review requirements of other environmental laws to expedite decision-making and reduce costs and effort.

NEPA requires that previously unquantified environmental amenities be given consideration in decision-making along with more technical considerations. That means that the environmental analysis can be a subjective process, guided by the values of the particular players in any given project. The act does not define what constitutes a major action or what is considered a significant effect on the environment. Some agencies have developed their own guidelines for what types of actions are considered major. Examples of major actions include construction projects such as highway expansion and creek channelization. However, major actions do not always involve construction. For example, legislative changes which may affect the environment may come under NEPA review. When an action will be controversial or clearly violate a pre-set environmental standard, it also may be categorized as a major action with significant impacts. Actions which will have less measurable effects, such as disrupting scenic beauty, must be categorized more subjectively. The courts are frequently used to settle disputes about whether actions require compliance with NEPA.

Although NEPA is targeted to federal agencies, its implementation has resulted in closer scrutiny of major environmental actions other than those sponsored by the government. Environmental analyses also are required for private developments which need federal **pollution control** permits such as water **discharge**s, air **emission**s, waste disposal, and **wetlands** filling. *See also* Environmental impact assessment

[*Teresa C. Donkin*]

FURTHER READING

Caldwell, L. K. "20 Years With NEPA Indicates the Need." *Environment* 31 (December 1989): 6-15.

Facts about the National Environmental Policy Act. Washington, DC: U. S. Environmental Protection Agency, September 1989.

Fogelman, V. M. *Guide to the National Environmental Policy Act: Interpretations, Applications and Compliance.* Westport, CT: Greenwood, 1990.

Parenteau, P. A. "NEPA at Twenty: Great Disappointment or Whopping Success?" *Audubon* 92 (March 1990): 104-07.

National Environmental Satellite, Data and Information Service

See **National Oceanic and Atmospheric Administration**

National forest

A national forest is forest land owned and administered by a national government. Mandates designating national forest ownership, administration and the distribution of benefits vary greatly around the world. Some nations (e.g. Canada) retain little or no national forest, delegating **public land** ownership to regional provinces or communities. Other nations (e.g. Albania and other formerly Communist States) retain all public forests as national forests. In many former colonies, national forest administration is patterned after that of the colonizing nation, and lands now comprising national forests were appropriated from **indigenous peoples**. In all cases, the term national forest refers to a type of *state* (i.e. government) property and must not be confused with forests that are owned as *common* property (i.e. private forest owned by a group) or *private* property. The precepts of modern national forests originated in early eighteenth century France and Germany where feudal lords set aside forests to preserve hunting grounds. National forest administration stems from this tradition of managing the forests for the direct benefit of central government authorities.

As in several nations in Southeast Asia, national forests in Indonesia comprise the vast majority of national territory, and colonial-style legal and organizational structures continue to dominate management. Forests are centrally administered by the State Forest Corporation with provinces given some authority over harvesting and marketing. Shared government and private party forestry successions are common. Indonesia derives a substantial portion of national income from timber production and has been charged with excluding the concerns of indigenous peoples from management decision.

In 1957 the government of Nepal nationalized all forested land, the majority of which was previously managed as community common property. This act resulted in the breakdown of community management systems and accelerated **deforestation** and forest degradation. The Forest Act of 1992 seeks to reverse these trends and divides national forests into five classes: community forests (managed by community user groups); leasehold forests (leased to private entities for timber production); government managed forests (retained by government for national purposes); protection forests (managed by government for environmental protection); and religious forests.

In the United States the term national forest refers to specific federal land units that are administered by the U.S. Department of Agriculture Forest Service (USDAFS). The USDAFS currently administers 156 national forests entailing 223 million acres and covering about one-tenth of the nation's land area. Establishment of these forests beginning in 1903 was largely a response to growing public fears of timber famine, **wildfire**s, **flooding**, depleted **wildlife** populations, and damage to the beauty of the national landscape. National forest management is governed by federal law and edicts from the executive branch of government. The USDAFS is currently mandated to: 1) manage forests for multiple uses (wood, water, **recreation**, wildlife, and **wilderness** in perpetuity); 2) protect the **habitat**s of **endangered species**; 3) impartially serve the public interest in choosing between management alternatives. National forests have been the focus of great conflict since the 1960s when the environmental movement began challenging USDAFS actions. Recent legislation, and numerous federal court decisions, have resulted in greater integration of public opinion into the USDAFS decision-making process.

[*T. Anderson White*]

FURTHER READING

Bromley, D. W. "Property Relations and Economic Development: The Other Land Reform." *World Development* 17 (1989): 867-77.

Gericke, K. L., J. Sullivan, and J. D. Wellman. "Public Participation in National Forest Planning: Perspectives, Procedures and Costs." *Journal of Forestry* 90 (1992): 35-38.

Pardo, R. "Back to the Future: Nepal's New Forestry Legislation." *Journal of Forestry* 91 (1993): 22-26.

Peluso, N. L. *Rich Forests, Poor People: Resource Control and Resistance in Java.* Berkeley: University of California Press, 1992.

Poffenberger, M., ed. *Keepers of the Forest: Land Management Alternatives in Southeast Asia.* West Hartford, CT: Kumarian Press, 1990.

National Forest Management Act (1976)

The National Forest Management Act (NFMA), passed in 1976, is the law that established the guidelines for the management of **national forest**s. The act replaced the Organic Act of 1897, which had supplied such guidelines for the previous seventy-nine years. The impetus for this new bill was a court case related to **clear-cutting** on the

Monongahela National Forest in West Virginia. Such clear-cutting had begun on this forest in the 1960s, and many environmental and **recreation** groups opposed it. When the **Forest Service** continued this management technique, the **Izaak Walton League** filed suit against the agency, claiming that clear-cutting violated the Organic Act on three counts: that only mature timber was to be harvested, that all timber cut had to be marked and designated, and that all timber cut had to be removed from the forest. The Court ruled in favor of the Izaak Walton League; clear-cutting did violate the Organic Act on each of these counts (*Izaak Walton League v. Butz*, (1973)). The judge issued an injunction against any cutting in West Virginia that violated the Organic Act. The Forest Service appealed, but lost, and the injunction was spread throughout the Fourth Circuit of the Court of Appeals (*Izaak Walton League v. Butz* (1975)). Injunctions based on similar cases were soon issued in Alaska and Texas. With timber harvesting on the national forests in chaos, the Forest Service and timber industry turned to Congress for new management authority.

Congressional action came quickly due to these court decisions. The debate centered around bills introduced by Senator Hubert Humphrey of Minnesota, more favorable to industry, and by Senator Jennings Randolph of West Virginia, supported by environmentalists. The final act was based primarily on the Humphrey bill. The act basically gave legislative approval to how the Forest Service had been managing the national forests. It granted the agency a great deal of administrative discretion to manage the forests based on the general philosophy of multiple use and **sustained yield**.

Five of the most contentious issues regarding national forest management were discussed in the law, but the fundamental issues were left unresolved. Clear-cutting is recognized as a legitimate management technique, and the Forest Service was given qualified discretion to determine when and how this approach would be used. **Species** diversity is to be considered in **forest management**, but the specifics are left to agency discretion. The Forest Service is directed to identify marginal lands and, based on agency discretion, to move away from timber management on these lands. Trees should be cut at a mature age when possible, but rotation age can be lessened if the agency deems it necessary. Finally, timber is to be harvested based on nondeclining even flow, which is a very conservative approach to sustained yield. Forest Service management decisions on these decisions have continued to stir debate. The NFMA also substantially amended the interdisciplinary national forest planning provisions of the Resources Planning Act of 1974. *See also* Biodiversity; Deforestation; Forest decline; Environmental law; Sustainable development

[*Christopher McGrory Klyza*]

FURTHER READING

Clary, D. A. *Timber and the Forest Service.* Lawrence, KS: University Press of Kansas, 1986.

Dana, S. T., and S. K. Fairfax. *Forest and Range Policy.* 2nd ed. New York: McGraw-Hill, 1980.

National Institute for the Environment

The National Institute for the Environment (NIE) is a proposed federal agency conceived in 1989 by a group of scientists, environmentalists, and policy analysts who were concerned that our nation's decision makers did not have adequate scientific information to make suitable environmental policies. They were also concerned that the existing federal environmental research and development activities were spread over many uncoordinated agencies, each with different missions and interests therefore preventing an integrated effort to resolve environmental problems. Led by Dr. Stephen Hubbell of Princeton University and Dr. Henry Howe of the University of Illinois, Chicago, the group developed a proposal to establish the NIE. This initiative to create the NIE is currently promoted by the Committee for the National Institute for the Environment.

Formed in the late 1980s, the CNIE is a national nonprofit organization comprising 15 board members and over 9,000 scientists, educators, business leaders, state and local government officials, environmental advocates, and other interested individuals from around the country whose goal is to work with the United States Congress to establish the National Institute for the Environment (NIE). The CNIE is exploring different alternatives for establishing NIE as part of the federal government, the most favored of which is to set up NIE as an independent agency. Also under consideration are making NIE an agency within a new Department of the Environment or creating a single agency that merges existing environmental programs from several federal agencies.

The goal of the NIE is to have an independent, nonregulatory, federal institute similar to the National Institutes of Health that focuses on environmental problems. The NIE would promote better communication between scientists and policy makers to help balance social, economic, and environmental goals. The NIE would concentrate activities in four integrated areas: identification and assessment of current knowledge of environmental problems of national interest through a Center for Environmental Assessment; the funding of peer-reviewed, interdisciplinary research to increase scientific understanding of these environmental problems through three research divisions; development of an electronic, on-line library (the National Library for the Environment) to disseminate environmental information; and support of education and training of scientists and other professionals interested in working on environmental issues. The NIE would be led by a President-appointed Board of Governors representing federal and nonfederal scientists, state and local government, environmental organizations, citizen groups, academia, and industry.

Within the NIE, a Center for Environmental Assessment would be established to perform evaluations on the current state of knowledge of particular environmental issues. Assessments would include a review of existing scientific information on an identified environmental problem, an assessment of policy decisions made based on existing information, and the identification of additional research needed to fill information gaps to improve the scientific basis for policy development.

The centerpiece of the NIE would be the research it would sponsor. Experts in the natural sciences, engineering, economics, and the social sciences would work cooperatively on complex environmental topics that could potentially require long-term investigations. Research funded by NIE would be administered by three directors: a Director of Environmental Resources, a Director of Environmental Systems, and a Director of Environmental Sustainability. The Director of Environmental Resources would develop research programs to inventory natural resources, monitor and predict change to environmental systems, and develop tools for improved environmental assessment. The Director of Environmental Systems would focus on creating a research program to improve understanding of the functioning of environmental systems and human impact on these systems. For example, possible research programs could include an evaluation of the ecological and social effects of global **climate** change and research to distinguish between natural **ecosystem** variation and environmental change due to human activities. The director of Environmental Sustainability would concentrate on issues related to maintaining environmental health while utilizing resources in such a way to ensure their availability and viability in the future.

A key component of the NIE would be to provide information to decision makers, researchers, environmental managers, educators and other professionals, and the public at large. An electronic, on-line National Library for the Environment would be developed. The Committee for the National Institute for the Environment is in the process of establishing a prototype that can be accessed electronically. The prototype library will include research reports from the Congressional Research Service, an environmental encyclopedia, and peer-reviewed and nonpeer-reviewed research articles.

The NIE would support higher education training (i.e., education above the high school level) through research grants, fellowships, teacher training, and grants to develop environmental programs at colleges and universities. The NIE would also maintain a small in-house Center for Integrative Studies on the Environment that would invite visiting scholars to work with a core of scientific staff to evaluate emerging environmental issues on which NIE and other federal agencies need to focus.

The NIE proposal is endorsed by over 150 colleges and universities, scientific, professional, environmental, and business organizations, and state and local governments. Legislation to create the NIE was first introduced in 1989. The legislation was reintroduced in the 103rd Congress and again more recently in 1995 during the 104th Congress by Representative Jim Saxton (R-NJ). The bill was co-sponsored by numerous Democratic and Republican members of Congress. The bill was referred to the House Committee on Science where in 1997 it awaited consideration by the Subcommittee on Energy and the Environment.

[*Marci L. Bortman*]

FURTHER READING

Benedick, R. "NIE: its Time Has Come," *Chemistry and Industry* (1996): 64.

Committee for the National Institute for the Environment. *Executive Summary, A Proposal for a National Institute for the Environment.* From Internet: http://www.cnie.org/summary.html, 1997.

Committee for the National Institute for the Environment. *Outline of Legislation to Establish the NIE.* From Internet: http://www.cnie.org/billsum. html, 1997.

National Institute of Environmental Health Sciences (Research Triangle Park, North Carolina)

The National Institute of Environmental Health Sciences (NIEHS) is one of twenty-four components of the National Institutes of Health (NIH), which is part of the U.S. Department of Health and Human Services (DHHS). The mission of NIEHS is to conduct research on environment-related diseases. The focus of research is on understanding how environmental factors, individual susceptibility, and age interrelate to cause human illness and on the development of methods to reduce these illnesses. NIEHS achieves its mission through biomedical research programs, prevention and intervention activities, and communication strategies that include training, education, technology transfer, and community outreach.

NIEHS was established as the Division of Environmental Health Sciences within NIH in 1966. In 1967, the Research Triangle Foundation in North Carolina presented the U.S. Surgeon General with 509 acres in the Research Triangle Park to serve as a site for NIEHS. In 1969, the Division of Environmental Health Sciences was raised to Institute status.

Research is conducted through both on-site resources and an extramural science program. The Division of Extramural Research and Training (DERT) supports a network of university-based **environmental health** science centers and also provides research and training grants and contracts for research and development. Through DERT, NIEHS supported the research of Dr. **Mario J. Molina** of the Massachusetts Institute of Technology (MIT), who was a co-recipient of the 1995 Nobel Prize in Chemistry for work showing the loss of the Earth's protective **ozone** shield.

The purpose of the Division of Intramural Research (DIR) is to provide research to address the environmental components of many different diseases. Dr. Martin Rodbell, an NIEHS scientist in DIR, was a co-recipient of the Nobel Prize in Medicine for discoveries about the communication system that regulates cellular activity. DIR is organized into programs for Environmental Biology, Environmental Diseases and Medicine, and Environmental Toxicology. The program for Environmental Biology includes the work of three laboratories. The Laboratory of Molecular Genetics studies the basic mechanisms of the mutational process, fundamental mechanisms of genomic stability, and the impact of environmental agents on the genetic apparatus. The Laboratory of Signal Induction studies the effects of environmental agents on physiological processes, and the Laboratory of Structural Biology studies environmentally associated diseases resulting from perturbations in biological.

The second DIR program, for Environmental Diseases and Medicine, includes three branches: Epidemiology, Biostatistics, and Comparative Medicine. The Epidemiology Branch studies the impacts of environmental toxicants on human health and reproduction using sensitive health endpoints, susceptible sub-groups, and highly exposed populations; four laboratories support this research. The Laboratory of Reproductive and Developmental Toxicology develops an understanding of the basic mechanisms underlying normal and abnormal development and reproduction. The Laboratory of Pulmonary Pathobiology studies the respiratory tract system biology at the cellular, biochemical, and molecular level in order to develop an understanding of **pathogen**ic mechanisms involved in the onset of diseases of the airways. The Laboratory of Molecular Carcinogenesis studies the mechanisms of environmental carcinogenesis by identifying the target genes in the process and by defining how chemicals act on these genes to influence **cancer** development. The Laboratory of Environmental Carcinogenesis and Mutagenesis focuses on chemical, physical, and environmental causes of cancer and uses transgenic and computer models to distinguish carcinogens and the mechanisms by which they act.

The second branch of the program for Environmental Diseases and Medicine, Biostatistics, conducts research in biomathematics and population genetics and in design and analysis of laboratory animal toxicology and carcinogenicity studies to develop methodology for epidemiological and clinical studies, and to provide statistical and computational support to NIEHS scientists. The third branch, Comparative Medicine, provides services and collaborative support to NIEHS scientists in the areas of animal facilities management, animal procurement, health surveillance and disease diagnosis, clinical veterinary services, rodent breeding, technical and surgical assistance, and quality assurance support.

The third DIR program, that for Environmental Toxicology, uses the research conducted at three laboratories. Laboratory of Computational Biology and Risk Analysis conducts and coordinates research into the development and use of mechanistic data and models for characterizing and quantifying human health risks associated with exposure to environmental agents. It maintains a research program in computer-based mathematical modeling, ranging from modeling cellular and molecular levels to whole animals and focusing on describing and evaluating chemical structures, biological response mechanisms, and their perturbations by potentially hazardous environmental agents. It also develops and uses cellular and molecular markers to investigate the link between environmental exposures and toxicity. It provides approaches for the evaluation of human susceptibility factors that affect toxic environmental effects.

Two other laboratories aid DIR's Environmental Toxicology program. The Laboratory of Toxicology conducts studies to characterize chemical toxic effects, including immune, reproductive, genetic, respiratory, and nervous system toxicities. It studies interactions of chemicals and metabolites with subcellular macromolecules, and it develops methods for characterizing toxicity of chemicals and other agents. The Laboratory of Pharmacology and Chemistry studies the exposure and disposition of environmental chemicals; it studies the enzyme systems involved in the metabolism of environmental chemicals and drugs; and, it studies the mechanisms responsible for the toxic effects of **xenobiotic**s and their metabolites, including photochemical and free radical mechanisms. The lab utilizes alternative model systems from comparative and marine biology to study the pharmacology and toxicology of chemicals and drugs, and it provides chemical support for NIEHS scientists, including the assessment of chemical purity, stability, and biotransformation.

NIEHS sponsors research on the effects of environmental impacts in several areas. Some research topics include birth and developmental defects and sterility; women's health issues, including breast cancer susceptibility and osteoporosis; and Alzheimer's and other neurologic disorders. NIEHS sponsors research on hazards to the poor due to likely exposure to **lead** paint, hazardous chemicals at work, **air** and **water pollution**, and **hazardous waste** sites in their communities; some researchers focus on agricultural **pollution**, including natural materials (e.g., grain dust) and agricultural chemicals, while other researchers study signal error, i.e., whether environmental chemicals can mimic hormonal growth factors and contribute to the development of cancer or reproductive disorders. Still other research investigates animal alternatives, to reduce the number of animals used in research, to refine the design of experiments to obtain more information at lower cost, and to replace animals with microbial and tissue cultures. Some research identifies biomarkers to measure the uptake and exposure to environmental toxins.

NIEHS is the headquarters for the National Toxicology Program (NTP), an interagency program within DHHS. The NTP was established in 1978 to coordinate toxicology research and testing activities within the Department of Health and Human Services, to provide information about potentially toxic chemicals to regulatory and research agencies, and to strengthen the scientific basis of toxicology. The NTP coordinates toxicology activities of NIEHS, the **National Institute for Occupational Safety** and Health of the **Centers for Disease Control** (NIOSH/CDC), and the National Center for Toxicological Research of the **Food and Drug Administration** (NCTR/FDA). The director of NIEHS is also the director of the NTP. Primary research support within NIEHS for NTP is in the Environmental Toxicology Program.

The Superfund Basic Research Program (SBRP), in coordination with the U.S. **Environmental Protection Agency** (U.S. EPA), is also administered by NIEHS. The **Superfund Amendments and Reauthorization Act** (SARA) of 1986 established a university-based program of basic research within NIEHS. The SBRP receives funding from the U.S. EPA through an interagency agreement using Superfund Trust monies. The funding is used to study human health effects of hazardous substances in the **environment**, especially those found at uncontrolled, leaking waste disposal sites. The primary objectives of SBRP are to find methods, through basic research, to reduce the amount and toxicity of hazardous substances and to prevent adverse human health effects. The SARA legislation specifically mandates that the basic research program administered by NIEHS focus on: methods and technologies to detect hazardous substances in the environment; development of advanced techniques for the detection, assessment, and evaluation of the effects on human health of hazardous substances; basic biological, chemical, and physical methods to reduce the amount and toxicity of hazardous substances.

In support of these mandates, NIEHS supports projects in the areas of engineering, ecological, and hydrogeological research in conjunction with biomedically related components, thus encouraging collaborative efforts among researchers. Specific research areas included in the SBRP include health effects, exposure/risk assessment, ecology, fate and transport, **remediation**, **bioremediation**, analytical chemistry, biomarkers, epidemiology, **metals**, and waste site characterization.

NIEHS was also given responsibility for initiating a training grants program under SARA. The major objective of the NIEHS Worker Education and Training Program, initiated in 1987, is to prevent work-related harm by assisting the training of workers to know how to protect themselves and their communities from exposure to hazardous materials during hazardous waste operations, hazardous materials transportation, environmental restoration of **nuclear weapons** facilities, or chemical emergency response. Through this program, non-profit organizations with a demonstrated record of providing occupational safety and health education develop safety and health curriculum for workers involved in handling hazardous waste or in responding to emergency releases of hazardous materials. Information concerning this program is disseminated through the National Clearinghouse for Worker Safety and Health Training.

The SBRP, through an Interagency Agreement, provides additional training by support of the NIOSH Hazardous Substance Continuing Education Program (HST), initiated in 1988 for hazardous substance professionals, and the NIOSH Hazardous Substance Academic Training Program (HSAT), a graduate academic program initiated in 1993 allowing occupational safety and health professionals to specialize in the study of hazardous substances.

In coordination with the Department of Energy, NIEHS is overseeing the implementation of the Electric and Magnetic Fields (EMF) Research and Public Information Dissemination (RAPID) program, established by the 1992 Energy Policy Act. The EMF RAPID program is a five-year federally coordinated effort to conduct research on potential effects on biological systems of exposure to 60 Hz electric and magnetic fields produced by the generation, transmission, and use of electric energy and to evaluate developing technologies for characterizing and mitigating these fields. The program also involves collection, compilation, publication, and dissemination of information to the public concerning possible human effects of electric and magnetic fields; types and extent of human exposure to electrical and magnetic

fields in various occupational and residential settings; technologies to measure and characterize electric and magnetic fields; and methods to assess and manage exposure to electric and magnetic fields.

The NIEHS Clearinghouse is an information service staffed with scientists who respond to questions concerning environmental health issues. Information on research is also provided through an NIEHS-sponsored journal, *Environmental Health Perspectives*. Contact: NIEHS, P.O. Box 1233, Research Triangle Park, NC 27709.

[*Judith Sims*]

National Institute for Urban Wildlife (Columbia, Maryland)

Since its founding in 1973 as the Urban Wildlife Research Center, this organization has promoted the preservation of **wildlife** in urban settings. In 1983, it became the National Institute for Urban Wildlife and continues to provide support to individuals and organizations involved in maintaining a place for wildlife in the expanding American cities and suburbs. The institute conducts research exploring the relationship between humans and wildlife in urban areas, publicizes methods of urban **wildlife management**, and raises public awareness of the value of wildlife in city settings. Its activities are divided into four programs: research, urban **conservation** education, technical services, and urban wildlife sanctuaries.

The research program provides specific information on the interplay between urban dwellers and wildlife. Developers, engineers, government agencies, industry, planners, students, and the general public use the research conducted by the institute. Some of the studies published by the institute have included *Planning for Wildlife in Cities and Suburbs*; *Urban Wetlands for Stormwater Control and Wildlife Enhancement*; *Planning for Urban Fishing and Waterfront Recreation*; *Highway-Wildlife Relationships: A State-of-the-Art Report*; and *An Annotated Bibliography on Planning and Management for Urban-Suburban Wildlife*.

Through its educational arm, the institute publishes numerous documents on the major issues of wildlife to professional environmentalists as well as to the general public. Among these publications is the quarterly *Urban Wildlife News*, the official publication of the organization. In addition to the newsletter, the institute publishes other resources such as the *Urban Wildlife Manager's Notebook*, the *Wildlife Habitat Conservation Teacher's PAC* series, and *A Guide to Urban Wildlife Management*.

Technical services are provided by the institute to urban planners, developers, land managers, state and federal non-game programs, and homeowners. Among the information and services offered are environmental assessments and impact statements, open space planning and management, recreational planning, experimental design, urban **wetlands** enhancement, data analysis, literature research, and expert testimony.

The urban wildlife sanctuaries program is designed to create a network of certified sanctuaries on public and private land across the United States. Landowners who dedicate their land to wildlife preservation and are certified by the institute receive support from the institute's wildlife biologists.

The institute's 1,000 members include organizations and individuals who are concerned with the preservation of wildlife in urban settings. Although there is no official volunteer program offered through the institute, guidance is available to members working in grassroots organizations. Contact: National Institute for Urban Wildlife, 10921 Trotting Ridge Way, Columbia, MD 21044.

[*Linda M. Ross*]

National Institute of Occupational Safety and Health (NIOSH)

The National Institute of Occupational Safety and Health (NIOSH) is a research institute created by the **Occupational Safety and Health Act** of 1970, and since 1973 it has been a division of the **Centers for Disease Control (CDC)**. The purpose of NIOSH is to gather data documenting incidences of occupational disease, exposure, and injury in the United States. After gathering and evaluating data, the agency develops "Criteria Documents" for specific hazards; in some cases the **Occupational Safety and Health Administration (OSHA)** has used these documents as the basis for specific legal standards to be followed by industry. NIOSH has developed databases which are available to other federal agencies, as well as state governments, academic researchers, industry, and private citizens. The organization also conducts seminars for those in the field of occupational safety and health, as well as for industry, labor, and other government agencies. NIOSH prepares various publications for sale to the public, and it provides a telephone hotline in its Cincinnati, Ohio office to answer inquiries.

In April of 1996, NIOSH and the Occupational Safety and Health Administration (OSH) commemorated their 25th anniversary in an event that was jointly sponsored by those two agencies and by the Smithsonian Institute. CDC Director David Satcher stated, "Thanks in large measure to NIOSH's efforts, the Nation has made dramatic advancements in recognizing that safe and healthful workplaces are an integral part of good public health, and that the tools we use to curb infectious diseases also work against occupational diseases - knowledge, timely intervention, and prevention." *See also* Agency for Toxic Substances and Disease Registry; Public Health Service; U.S. Department of Health and Human Services

National lakeshore

National lakeshores are part of a system of United States coastlines administered by the **National Park Service** and preserved for their scenic, recreational, and **habitat** resources. The national lakeshore system is an extension of the **national seashore**s system established in the 1930s to preserve the nation's dwindling patches of publicly-owned coastline on the Atlantic, Pacific, and Gulf coasts. Since before 1930 the movement to preserve both seashores and lakeshores has been a conservationist response to the rapid privatization of coastlines by industrial interests and private home owners. In 1992 the United States had four designated National Lakeshores: Indiana Dunes on the southern tip of Lake Michigan, Sleeping Bear Dunes on Lake Michigan's eastern shore, and the Apostle Islands and Pictured Rocks, both on Lake Superior's southern shore.

Attention focused on disappearing **Great Lakes** shorelines, sometimes called the United States' "fourth coastline," as midwestern development pressures increased after World War II. During the 1950s lakeshore industrial sites became especially valuable with the impending opening of the **St. Lawrence Seaway**. The seaway, giving landlocked lake ports access to Atlantic trade from Europe and Asia, promised to boost midwestern industry considerably. Facing this threat to remaining wild lands, the National Park Service conducted a survey in 1957-58, attempting to identify and catalog the Great Lakes' remaining natural shoreline. The survey produced a list of 66 sites qualified for preservation as natural, scenic, or recreational areas. Of these, five sites were submitted to Congress in the spring of 1959.

The Indiana Dunes site was a spearhead for the movement to designate national lakeshores. Of all the proposed preserves, this one was immediately threatened in the 1950s and 1960s by northern Indiana's expanding steel industries. Residents of neighboring Gary were eager for jobs and industrial development, but conservationists and politicians of nearby Chicago argued that most of the lake was already developed and lobbied intensely for preservation. The Indiana Dunes provided a rare patch of undeveloped acreage that residents of nearby cities valued for **recreation**. Equally important, the dunes and their intradunal ponds, **grasslands**, and mixed **deciduous forest**s provided habitat for animals and migratory birds, most of whose former range already held the industrial complexes of Gary and Chicago. In addition, the dunes harbored patches of relict boreal habitat left over from the last **ice age**. After years of debate, the Indiana Dunes and Great Sleeping Bear Dunes National Lakeshores were established in 1966, with the remaining two lakeshores designated four years later.

The other three national lakeshores are less threatened by industrial development than Indiana Dunes, but they preserve important scenic and historic resources. Sleeping Bear Dunes contains some of Michigan's sandy pine forests as well as **arid** land forbs, grasses, and sedges that are rare in the rest of the Midwest. Two prized aspects of this national lakeshore are its spectacular bluffs and active dunes, some standing hundreds of feet high along the edge of Lake Michigan.

Wisconsin's Apostle Islands, a chain of 22 glacier-scarred, rocky islands, bear evidence of perhaps 12,000 years of human habitation and activity. However most of the historic relics date from the nineteenth century, when loggers, miners, and sailors left their mark. In this area the coniferous

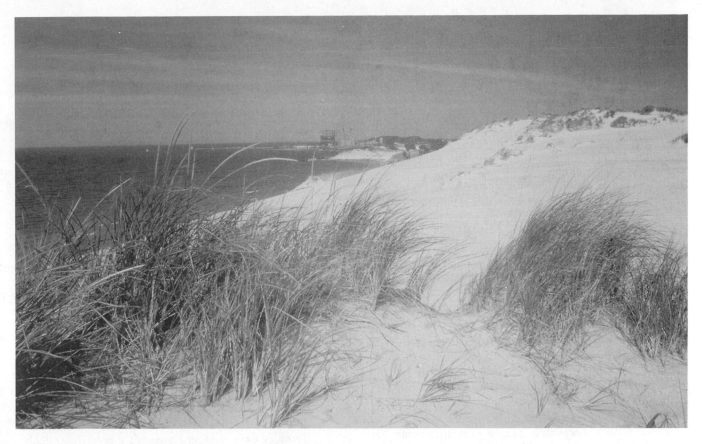

Indiana Dunes National Lakeshore.

boreal forest of Canada meets the deciduous Midwestern forests, producing an unusual mixture of sugar maple, hemlock, white cedar, and black spruce forests. Nearly 20 **species** of orchids find refuge in these islands. Pictured Rocks National Lakeshore preserves extensive historic navigation relics, including sunken ships, along with its scenic and recreational resources. *See also* Coniferous forest; Conservation; Ecosystem; Glaciation; National Parks and Conservation Association; Privatization movement; Wilderness

[*Mary Ann Cunningham*]

FURTHER READING

Bowles, M. L., et al. "Endangered Plant Inventory and Monitoring Strategies at Indiana Dunes National Lakeshore." *Natural Areas Journal* 6 (1986): 18-26.

Cockrell, R. *A Signature of Time and Eternity: The Administrative History of Indiana Dunes National Lakeshore, Indiana*. Omaha, NE: U.S. National Park Service, Midwest Regional Office, 1988.

Herbert, R. D., D. A. Wilcox, and N. B. Pavlovic. "Vegetation Patterns in and among Pannes (Calcerious Intradunal Ponds) at the Indiana Dunes National Lakeshore, Indiana." *American Midland Naturalist* 116 (1986): 276-81.

National Marine Fisheries Service
See **National Oceanic and Atmospheric Administration**

National Mining and Minerals Act (1970)

The Mining and Minerals Policy Act of 1970 was the first of a series of efforts by the United States Congress to address the seeming lack of a coordinated and comprehensive federal minerals policy. The act directed the Secretary of the Interior to follow a policy that encouraged the private mining sector in four ways: to develop a financially viable and stable domestic mining sector, to develop domestic mineral sources in an orderly manner, to conduct research to further "wise and efficient use" of these minerals, and to develop methods of mineral extraction and processing that would be as environmentally benign as possible. Given the broad and vague nature of these directives, it is difficult to determine what, if any, effect the law has had. For example, the **U.S. Department of the Interior**'s report on the bill found that it did not provide the department any new authority. There was one clear directive included in the law: the Secretary of the Interior was to report to Congress annually on the mining industry and to make any legislative recommendations to help the industry at that time.

Two additional general mining policy laws were passed within fifteen years of the Mining and Minerals Policy Act. The National Materials and Minerals Policy, Research and Development Act was passed in 1980. Like the 1970 Act, this law was an effort to develop a coordinated national minerals policy. But, like its predecessor, this law also had little effect due to its lack of specifics. The 1984 National Critical Materials Act underscored the concern among some in Congress that the United States had become vulnerable, due to foreign dependence, in the supply of such strategic defense and high technology minerals as cobalt and platinum group metals. This law was also filled with vague generalities, though it did create a three-person National Critical Materials Council and charged this Council with overseeing minerals policy. As with the prior two acts, the 1984 law has seemingly had little effect.

The growing concern for mineral policy in the 1970s and 1980s can be traced to three sources: administrative law and capacity, environmental concerns, and national security concerns. The federal government had little control over mining policy. On federal lands, mining policy had been essentially privatized by the 1872 Mining Law. Individuals or private firms could stake claims on **public land**s and remove the minerals; the government received no royalties and issued no permits. The mining policy regime was also fragmented. Three agencies had major roles in mining policy: the **Bureau of Land Management**, the **Bureau of Mines**, and the United States **Geological Survey**. Throughout the 1970s and 1980s, concern for the **environment** grew in the country, and a significant concern of environmentalists was mining operations, which often generated large amounts of **pollution** and had significant effects on the land. Hence, environmentalists successfully sought to restrict mining in certain areas and regulate the mining that continued. Partially in response to the reduced access and increased regulation, the mining industry and its supporters began to focus on the United States's foreign dependence on **strategic minerals**. They argued that more lands should be open to mining, and regulations should be relaxed. Despite the passage of these three laws, though, no significant change in federal mining policy has occurred. *See also* Environmental law; Environmental policy; Natural resources

[*Christopher McGrory Klyza*]

FURTHER READING

Leshy, J. D. *The Mining Law: A Study in Perpetual Motion.* Washington, DC: Resources for the Future, 1987.

National Ocean Service
See **National Oceanic and Atmospheric Administration**

National Oceanic and Atmospheric Administration (NOAA)

The National Oceanic and Atmospheric Administration (NOAA) is a multi-faceted agency of the United States government that concerns itself with a variety of challenges, from making five-day weather forecasts to protecting **sea turtles**. Under the U.S. Department of Commerce, NOAA is unusual because it functions not only as a service agency, providing weather reports, for example, but also as a regulatory and research agency. Many of its regulatory functions appear to overlap with those of the **Environmental Protection Agency (EPA)**, and much of its research parallels that of National Aeronautics and Space Administration (NASA). NOAA's National Ocean Service, for example, assessed the damage to the Alaskan coast and **wildlife** from the disastrous **oil spill** of the *Exxon Valdez*; NOAA also monitors the rate and speed of the earth's rotation.

Created in 1807 by President Thomas Jefferson as the National Ocean Service, its first duty was to survey the coasts to set up shipping lanes for trade routes in the United States. Later, its function as an air and sea chart-making agency, when known as the U.S. Coast and Geodetic Survey, was in high demand, especially during World Wars I and II.

In 1970, when the National Oceanic and Atmospheric Administration was instituted, it settled into five major service branches and a NOAA Corps. The Corps, called "the seventh and smallest uniformed service," consists of about 400 men and women trained to perform diverse duties, such as fly into the eye of a **hurricane** and make descents in ocean submersibles to do deep ocean research.

NOAA's five branches are as follows:

1) National Weather Service (NWS): For a long time, NOAA was the U.S. Weather Bureau. NWS has provided daily weather forecasts for several decades by gathering data from manned weather forecast offices around the country. To perfect its capability, to increase accuracy, and to lengthen predictions for severe weather, NOAA is implementing a long-term program to modernize the National Weather Service by installing 1,000 automatic sensors in all the states. Already the Hydrometeorological Information Center can issue spring flood warnings from river forecast centers well in advance of their occurrence. Nexrad ("Next generation radar"), a new Doppler radar that can pick up severe weather 125 miles (201 km) away, predicts tornadoes with a 19-minute lead time, giving residents more time to find shelter.

2) The Office of Oceanic and Atmospheric Research collects data from polar-orbiting and geostationary satellites. These not only provide televised weather pictures, but also monitor elements of **climate** change (such as **greenhouse gases** in the **stratosphere**). At NOAA's Environmental Research Labs, studies of the **ozone** layer are additionally being conducted jointly with NASA; NOAA and Japan have also joined forces to study the thermal vents 20,000 feet (6096 m) down in the Marianna Trench under the Pacific Ocean. NOAA funds university research through the National Sea Grant College Program and the National Undersea Research Program.

3) The National Environmental Satellite, Data and Information Service (NESDIS), one of the world's largest banks of information on earth geophysics, solar activity, geomagnetic variations, and paleoclimates,

stores data collected from NOAA's satellites and environmental research labs.

4) The National Ocean Service still makes coastal charts for trade ships as well as for weekend sailors. But now it also assesses ocean and coastal **pollution**, protects **wetlands**, and is charged with creating and maintaining sanctuaries for various sea creatures including **whales** and living **coral reefs**.

5) The National Marine Fisheries Service (NMFS) manages fisheries by overseeing coastal fish-breeding **habitat**s, restoring **endangered species**, collecting abandoned **drift nets**, and trying to save turtles, **dolphins**, and whales that swallow sunken plastic balloons or get caught in plastic six-pack circles. The NMFS instituted the use of **Turtle Excluder Device**s (TEDs) on shrimp nets to keep turtles from being strangled.

NOAA also operates a rescue satellite, known as COSPAS-SARSAT (Satellite-Aided Search and Rescue). Stranded fishermen and sailors, whose boats are equipped with an Emergency Position Indicating Radio Beacon (EPIRB), send a signal to the satellite that relays it to a ground station which responds by sending a rescue vessel within hours of the initial signal.

Because NOAA is unusual in its functions as a regulatory, research, and service agency, it is often an easy target for budget-cutting. Underfunded during most of the 1980s and always dependent on Congressional funding, NOAA is currently struggling to streamline its duties in the face of rapid climate change and increased **marine pollution**.

NOAA publishes educational booklets, charts, and maps. Its NESDIS center at Boulder, Colorado, provides information to the interested public. Contact: Office of Public Affairs, NOAA, U.S. Dept. of Commerce, Room 6013, Washington, D.C. 20230. Internet: http://www.noaa.gov/.

[*Stephanie Ocko*]

FURTHER READING

Kerr, R. A. "NOAA Revived for the Green Decade." *Science* 248 (8 June 1990): 1177-79.

National Implementation Plan for the Modernization and Restructuring of the National Weather Service. Washington, DC: U. S. Department of Commerce, 1992.

Toward a New National Weather Service. Second Report. Washington, DC: National Research Council, 1992.

National park

National parks are areas that have been legally set apart by national governments because they have cultural or **natural resources** which are deemed significant for the particular country. National parks are typically large areas that are mostly undisturbed by human occupation or exploitation. They are characterized by spectacular scenery, abundant **wildlife**, unique geologic features, or interesting cultural or historic sites.

National parks are managed to eliminate or minimize human disturbances, while allowing human visitation for recreational, educational, cultural, or inspirational purposes. Activities consistent with typical national park management include hiking, camping, picnicking, wildlife observation, and photography. Fishing is usually allowed, but hunting is often prohibited. In the United States, national parks are distinguished from **national forest**s and other federal lands because timber harvesting, cattle grazing, and mining are, with a few exceptions, not permitted in national parks, whereas they are permitted on most other federal lands.

The United States was the first country to establish national parks. The Yosemite Grant of 1864 was the first act that formally set aside land by the federal government for "public use, resort and recreation." Twenty square miles (52 sq km) of land in the Yosemite valley and four square miles (10 sq km) of giant sequoia were put under the care of the State of California to be held "inalienable for all time." In 1872, President Ulysses S. Grant signed into law the establishment of **Yellowstone National Park**. Yellowstone differed from Yosemite in that it was to be managed and controlled by the federal government, not the state, and therefore has received the honor of being considered the first national park. Years later, Yosemite was turned over to the federal government for federal management also. Since 1916, national parks in the United States have been administered by the **National Park Service** an agency in the **U.S. Department of the Interior**.

The concept of national parks has caught on all over the world and continues to spread. Between the years 1972 and 1982 the number of national parks in the world increased by 47 percent and the area encompassed in the parks increased 82 percent. Today over 1000 national parks can be found worldwide in more than 120 countries.

Many national parks in both developed and developing countries are facing threats, however. The most commonly reported threats are illegal removal of wildlife, destruction of vegetation, and increased **erosion**. Often there is a lack of personnel to deal with these threats. Management problems also arise because demand for use of park resources is increasing. Many of these uses are conflicting, and virtually all would have significant impacts on the resources that characterize the parks.

Although parks consist of natural resources, they are conceived, established, maintained, and often threatened by humans. It is necessary for a society to derive benefits from the parks to maintain public support for them. In light of the need for public support, merely putting a fence around the park and keeping people out is likely to fail in the long term. Paradoxically then, some development and use is necessary for **conservation** of the resources. Deciding on the appropriate amounts and kind of uses compatible with the resources is the key to successful park management.

During the summer of 1962 the first World Conference on National Parks was held in Seattle, Washington. This historic conference and subsequent ones have given people of many nations a forum to discuss threats facing their parks and strategies for meeting the demand for conflicting

Grand Canyon National Park in Arizona.

uses. Only through such international dialogue and continued diligence will these treasures we call national parks be saved for **future generations**.

[*Ted T. Cable*]

FURTHER READING

Machlis, G. E., and D. L. Tichnell. *The State of the World's Parks.* Boulder, CO: Westview Press, 1985.

Runte, A. *National Parks and American Experience.* 2nd ed. Lincoln: University of Nebraska Press, 1987.

National Park Service

The National Park Service, an agency in the **U.S. Department of the Interior**, was established by the National Park Service Act of 1916 making it the first such agency in the world. Its mission as stated in the Act is: "to conserve the scenery and the natural and historic objects and the wild life therein and to provide for the enjoyment of the same in such a manner and by such means as will leave them unimpaired for the enjoyment of **future generations**."

The mission has not changed over the years but the ambiguous wording of the act has sparked much debate over what the primary use of a **national park** should be. Some people feel the parks should be commercially developed in order to best "provide for the enjoyment" of the resources, whereas others think the highest priority should be preserving the resources in an "unimpaired" state for future generations. These conflicting views have existed ever since the agency was established, and the debate will likely continue. The dual mandate of providing enjoyment from the resources and leaving them unchanged has been called the "preservation/use paradox." Striking the balance between use and preservation is still at the forefront of current national park policy issues.

National parks existed in the United States prior to the establishment of the National Park Service. The Yosemite Grant of 1864 was the first act that formally set aside land by the federal government for "public use, resort and **recreation**." Twenty square miles (5180 ha) of land in the Yosemite valley and four square miles (1036 ha) of giant sequoia were put under the care of the State of California by President Abraham Lincoln. This land was to be held "inalienable for all time." In 1872, President Ulysses S. Grant signed into law the establishment of **Yellowstone National Park**. Yellowstone differed from Yosemite in that it was to be managed and controlled by the federal government, not the state, and therefore has received the honor of being considered the first national park. Years later, Yosemite was also turned over to the federal government for management.

Originally no money had been set aside for the protection and care of the national parks. The parks suffered from illegal timber harvesting, grazing, **poaching**, and vandalism.

The U.S. Cavalry was sent in to protect the lands and did so until 1916 when the National Park Service was formed.

Horace Albright was named Assistant for Parks in 1913 by the Secretary of Interior Franklin Lane. Albright, in turn, recruited self-made millionaire and **nature** lover Stephen Mather to help him establish an agency to manage the parks. All the parks thus far had been created through separate acts of Congress with no unified guidelines to manage and control them. Bills to form an agency to oversee the parks had been introduced to Congress, but none had yet passed. Through the intensive lobbying efforts of Albright, Mather, and others, the National Park Service was formed in 1916. Upon its creation the National Park Service took over the management of fourteen national parks and twenty-one national monuments. Mather was the named the agency's first Director and Albright became his assistant. Later Albright would become the second Director of the National Park Service.

Albright and Mather believed that if the park system was to successfully defend itself from attacks by individuals with utilitarian philosophies (i.e., those believing timber cutting, grazing, and mining should be allowed on federal lands) it would have to have a strong base of public support. They emphasized a tourism effort to "See America First" and embarked on a policy of development and expansion to include tennis courts, golf courses, and swimming pools. As the **automobile** became popular they encouraged visitation by car and tried to make the parks easily accessible. Through their efforts park use soared.

Although public support was strong, lands still had to be deemed worthless for agriculture or economic development to be set aside as parks by Congress. Therefore, parks typically were high altitude with steep rocky terrain. Also, because they were still being justified and preserved as tourist destinations, only those areas of spectacular scenery were included within the park boundaries. This has resulted in many management problems, as today park managers attempt to look after park resources that are a part of **ecosystem**s which extend beyond the park boundaries.

The number of visitors to the parks increased so greatly that by the 1920s the limited facilities could no longer keep up with the growing demand. Overcrowding and **pollution** were becoming problems. Conservationists complained that tourism was given priority over preservation and that the parks were being degraded. Lodges and other amenities continued to be added to the parks to handle the increased visitation.

Until the establishment of **Everglades** National Park in 1934, all of the national parks had been designated from land that was already under federal government control. Everglades was the first park taken from annexed private land. It was also the first park that was not preserved for its spectacular scenery. Rather it was primarily established to preserve its fragile ecosystem, especially its colorful and conspicuous **wildlife**. Shortly thereafter, Great Smoky Mountain and Shenandoah National Parks were established. These were developed from private lands that were purchased using donations from private citizens, including John D. Rockefeller.

With the growing environmental awareness of the 1970s increased public scrutiny was focused on the balance between providing an enjoyable experience for visitors while preserving the park resources. The National Park Service looked for ways to accommodate the increasing numbers of visitors while minimizing the impacts to the **environment**. For example, to cut down on pollution and congestion, shuttle buses now take visitors into Yosemite, Grand Canyon and Denali national parks. The National Park Service continues to seek creative ways to simultaneously achieve their dual missions of use and preservation.

The National Park Service administers 355 sites covering 80 million acres in forty-nine states. Fifty of these sites are national parks, sometimes referred to as the "crown jewels" of the United States. The largest of the parks is Wrangell-St. Elias covering 13.2 million acres in Alaska. In 1989 use at National Park Service facilities was measured at 114 million visitor days. The most visited national park is Great Smoky Mountain National Park.

In addition to the national parks, the National Park Service also administers seventy-nine National Monuments, sixty-nine National Historic Sites, and twenty-nine National Historic Parks. They manage sites in twenty-two different categories including wild and scenic rivers, seashores, lakeshores, scenic trails, parkways, preserves and even the White House. Each of the sites are placed into one of these categories based on such attributes as size, level of development, and significance. They are managed under policies appropriate for that type of site. For example, a national preserve is typically set aside to protect a particular resource. Hunting, fishing, mining, or extraction of fuels can be allowed on the preserve so long as it does not threaten the specific resource being preserved.

Each year millions of people from around the world come to the National Parks to recreate, to learn, and to be inspired in these wondrous places. Truly, the National Park Service is the caretaker of America's "crown jewels." *See also* Conservation; Ecotourism; National lakeshore; National seashore; Utilitarianism; Wild river; Yosemite National Park

[*Ted T. Cable*]

FURTHER READING

Ibrahim, H., and K. A. Cordes. *Outdoor Recreation.* Dubuque, IA: WCB Communications, 1993.

Runte, A. *National Parks and American Experience.* 2nd ed. Lincoln: University of Nebraska Press, 1987.

National Parks and Conservation Association (Washington, D.C.)

The National Parks Conservation Association (NPCA) was founded in 1919 for the defense, promotion, and improvement of the United States' **national park** system and the education of the general public regarding national parks.

Throughout its history, the NPCA has worked toward a three-fold goal: to save the parks from exploitation, **pollution**, and degradation of their **natural resources**; to facilitate easy access to the national parks for all Americans; and to preserve the great variety of **wildlife** found within the boundaries of the parks.

With a membership of 280,000—including both individuals and organizations—the NPCA boasts considerable political influence and is particularly effective in organizing ground swell support. Members are kept informed of political, environmental, and other issues through *National Parks*, the official NPCA publication. The magazine also contains articles of interest on state parks, international public lands, and matters of general environmental importance.

For more than seventy years, the NPCA has helped increase the holdings of the National Park System by lobbying for the expansion of existing grounds and for the establishment of new parks. Through the National Park Trust Fund, the NPCA has acquired and donated land to the National Park System. It has labored to protect national parks from overdevelopment and encroaching urban sprawl and has participated in studies to analyze and minimize the impact of visitor traffic.

Other support programs sponsored by the NPCA include fund raisers such as the March for Parks program, independent studies of resource management in national parks, and efforts to protect and revitalize populations of wild animals within the parks. Working in conjunction with other conservation groups, the NPCA has dealt with such wide ranging environmental issues as **air pollution**, **acid rain**, **water pollution**, **endangered species**, and damage to costal areas.

Through its bi-monthly magazine, *National Parks*, the NPCA helps coordinate grassroots activities such as the Park Watchers Program, a network of concerned local parties who keep track of potential threats to the Park System, and the Contact System which alerts members to make their views known to public officials on issues concerning the environment. Services to its members include special tours of national parks, general information about environmental issues and their impact on the Park System, and periodic legislative updates and action alerts.

A second bi-monthly publication, *Exchanges*, is directed to those who participate in NPCA volunteer programs. These volunteers serve in a variety of capacities, including public relations, trip coordination, event planning, and fundraising.

The NPCA also has significant political influence, supporting such proposals as the American Heritage Trust Act, which would "protect our historic and natural heritage" with funding provided by royalties from offshore **oil drilling**. Internships are offered by the NPCA to college students and graduates who want to work in the legislative process. Contact: The National Parks and Conservation Association, 1015 Thirty-first Street, NW, Washington, DC 20007. Internet: http://www.npca.org/wwwhome.html#top.

[*Linda M. Ross*]

National Priorities List

The National Priorities List is a list compiled by the **Environmental Protection Agency (EPA)** as a part of the "Superfund" program under the **Comprehensive Environmental Response, Compensation and Liability Act (CERCLA)**. Superfund legislation requires the EPA to annually identify **hazardous waste** sites throughout the United States. After preliminary assessment, the EPA selects from this initial list those sites whose conditions are considered serious enough to place them on the National Priorities List (NPL). After more in-depth testing and studies, a site is placed on the NPL in an order ranking the most seriously contaminated sites at the top of the list. Sites selected for clean up under the Superfund Program come from the top of that list. Thus, it often takes years between the time a site is placed on the list and when cleanup begins. As of June 1996, there were 1,227 sites listed on the NPL, 1,073 of which are categorized under the "General Superfund Section" and 154 of which are in the "Federal Facilities Section." Those under the General Section are evaluated and cleaned up by the EPA while clean up of sites listed under the "Federal Facilities Section" are evaluated and cleaned up by other Federal agencies. *See also* Hazardous waste site remediation; Hazardous waste siting; Superfund Amendments and Reauthorization Act

National Recycling Coalition (Washington, D.C.)

Founded in 1978, the National Recycling Coalition (NRC) is a non-profit organization comprised of concerned individuals and environmental, labor, and business organizations who wish to promote the recovery and reuse of materials and energy. Believing that **recycling** is vital to the nation's well-being, NRC encourages collection, the development of more processing venues, and the purchase and promotion of recycled materials.

Originally formed by a small group of recycling professionals to convince others that recycling provides many benefits to America's economy, NRC has since grown to 3,000 members. They participate in several different projects, including the Peer Match Program—in which NRC gives technical advice and direct assistance in recycling—and technical councils such as the Rural Recycling Council and the Minority Council. The most prominent of these councils is the Recycling Advisory Council (RAC)

The Coalition established the RAC in 1989 to build consensus on recycling issues. Partially funded by the U.S. **Environmental Protection Agency (EPA)**, the mission of the RAC is to "examine the current status of recycling in the United States with the aim of recommending consensus public policies and private initiatives to increase recycling, consistent with the protection of public health and the environment." The NRC Board of Directors selects members of the RAC from among high-ranking environmental and public interest groups, recycling professionals, and business and industry. The RAC examines information on a specific recycling topic and then issues recommendations; both public and private organizations recognize the standards the RAC sets. Some topics about which the Council has made decisions include the definition of recycling; solid **waste management** costs; and policies and initiatives to promote the recycling of paper and **plastics**.

The most recent campaign of the NRC has been the "Buy Recycled Business Alliance." Twenty-five major American businesses in cooperation with NRC have agreed to increase the number of their products and packages made with recycled materials. In conjunction with the Alliance, NRC launched the "Buy Recycled" campaign. Aimed at consumers, it promotes a market for recycled products by encouraging the patronage of companies that sell such products. NRC maintains that first, one must request and buy recycled products, then one must ask governments and businesses to buy recycled material, and third, one should help develop a lasting system for procuring recyclable material.

NRC sponsors an annual conference, the National Recycling Congress and Exposition. Regarded as the nation's most significant recycling event, this membership meeting exhibits the latest innovations in recycling and allows networking within the recycling industry. NRC also publishes a quarterly newsletter and the *National Policy on Recycling and Policy Resolutions*, thereby keeping members and the concerned public abreast of recycling matters. Contact: National Recycling Coalition, 1101 30th Street, NW, Suite 305, Washington, DC 20007.

[*Andrea Gacki*]

National Research Council (Washington, D.C.)

The National Research Council (NRC) was organized by the National Academy of Sciences (NAS) in 1916 to connect the broad community of science and technology with the goals of the NAS, i.e., advancing the state of knowledge and advising the federal government. The NRC has become the principal agency of both the NAS and the National Academy of Engineering (NAE) in providing services to the government, the public, and the scientific and engineering communities. The NRC is administered by both Academies and the Institute of Medicine.

During the early years of World War I, there was concern about the lack of American preparedness if the United States should enter the war. The NAS had been active during the Civil War and for some years after the end of the war, but had become inactive during the latter part of the nineteenth century and into the first decade of the twentieth century. In 1915, George Ellery Hale, an astrophysicist and member of the NAS since 1902, advocated to the NAS president the offering of the services of the NAS to the U.S. Government in case of entry in the war. In April of 1916, Hale introduced a resolution to the NAS, which passed unanimously, that stated:

"That the President of the Academy be requested to inform the President of the United States that in the event of a break in diplomatic relations with any other country the academy desires to place itself at the disposal of the Government for any service within its scope."

President Woodrow Wilson agreed to the proposal, and a Committee for the Organization of the Scientific Resources of the Country for National Service was appointed. Members of the committee included some of the leading scientists of the time: physicist Robert A. Millikan, biologist Edwin G. Conklin, medical laboratory director Simon Flexner, and physical chemist Arthur A. Noyes. In June of 1916 the committee called for:

"A National Research Council, the purpose of which shall be to bring into cooperation government, educational, industrial, and other research organizations with the object of encouraging the investigation of natural phenomena, and increased use of scientific research in the development of American industries, the employment of scientific methods in strengthening the national defense, and such other applications of science as will promote the national security and welfare."

The plan was approved by the NAS and by President Wilson. The NRC was organized in September, 1916, with Hale as the first chairman. Members represented the government, various branches of the military, universities, and private research laboratories. Members were grouped into Divisions, which were organized according to disciplines or functions. Smaller units within the Divisions worked on specific projects and studies.

Although organized to meet a specific emergency, the NRC, due to its valuable wartime service, was made a permanent organization by an executive order of President Wilson in 1918.

Presently, the activities of the NRC are supervised by Major Program Units. The Major Program Units may conduct projects on the their own, but more frequently supervise projects organized under numerous subsidiary standing boards and committees. These boards and committees, which provide independent advice to the government, are comprising experts who serve without compensation. They provide draft reports on issues of concern and subject the draft reports to rigorous review before release to ensure quality and integrity. The composition and balance of the study committees are carefully monitored to avoid potential conflict of interest and bias. Major Program Units include: Policy Division; Center for Sciences, Mathematics, and Engineering Education, Commission on Behavioral and Social Sciences and Education; Commission on Engineering and Technical Systems; Commission on Geosciences, Environment, and Resources; Commission on Life Sciences; Commission on Physical Sciences, Mathematics, and Applications; Office of International Affairs, Office of Scientific and Engineering Personnel; Board on Agriculture; and Transportation Research Board.

The NRC also provides library services to the staffs and committee members of the NAS, NAE, and the Institute of Medicine as well as to the NRC.

To prepare the government and other involved in the development and implementation of public policies involving science and technology for the challenges of the twenty-first century, the NRC Governing Board has recently prepared a series of reports under the title of *Preparing for the 21st Century* that address the issues of science and engineering research, technology, education, social policy, the environment, and health care. Contact: National Research Council, 2101 Constitution Ave., Washington, D.C. 20418.

[*Judith Sims*]

FURTHER READING

National Research Council. *The Organization of the National Research Council.* Washington, D.C.: National Research Council, 1996.

National seashore

The **National Park Service**, under the **U.S. Department of the Interior**, manages ten tracts of coastal land known as national seashores. Over 435 miles (700 km) of Atlantic, Gulf, and Pacific coastline, including over 592,800 acres (240,000 hectares) of beaches, dunes, sea cliffs, maritime forests, fresh ponds, marshes, and **estuaries** comprise the National Seashore System.

Protection of the sensitive natural **habitat**s is only one of the objectives of the National Seashores System that the Park Service has established. These areas are also lightly developed for recreational purposes, including roads, administrative buildings, and some commercial businesses. In fact, until recently it was stipulated that public access must be provided to these areas. A third objective is to combat coastal **erosion**, as beaches and dunes are important as buffers to coastal storms.

The need to preserve coastal areas in their natural states was recognized as long ago as 1934, when the Park Service surveyed the Gulf and Atlantic coasts and identified 12 areas deserving of federal protection. The first of these to be authorized was Cape Hatteras National Seashore, a narrow strip of **barrier island** on the North Carolina outer banks. Acquiring the land, however, remained a problem until after World War II, when the Mellon Foundation matched state contributions and purchased the first of what is now over 100 miles (160 km) of beaches, dunes, marsh, and maritime forest.

In 1961, Cape Cod National Seashore in Massachusetts was the second area to be so designated. Protecting beach and dune areas of biological and geologically significance, this site was acquired with legislation that set the standard for future Park Service acquisitions. The "Cape Cod Formula" is the model for current regulation and purchase of private improved lands by the Park Service.

Five more sites were authorized between 1962 and 1966, including Fire Island on Long Island, New York, and Point Reyes National Seashore, the only national seashore on the west coast. Assateague Island, on the eastern shore of Maryland and Virginia, was deemed too developed to become a protected area but a nor'easter storm in March 1962 destroyed or seriously damaged nearly all of the development. By 1965, about 31 miles (50 km) of shoreline were purchased and became part of the National Seashore System.

In the 1970s, the final three national seashores were authorized. Gulf Islands is a non-continuous collection of estuarine, barrier island, and marsh habitats in Mississippi and Florida. It also includes an historic Spanish fort. Cumberland Island, Georgia, is the most "natural" of the ten national sea shores and is completely undeveloped with the only access being a public ferry from the mainland. The other National Seashores are Padre Island, in Texas; Cape Lookout, in North Carolina; and the newest national seashore, Florida's Cape Canaveral.

The National Historic Preservation Act (passed in 1966), the **Coastal Zone Management Act** (1972), and the National Seashore Act (1976) have been written to ensure that not all natural coastal areas fall to development. Public recognition and subsequent congressional action have saved these few areas that are important as fish and shellfish spawning and nursery areas, bird and **sea turtle** nesting grounds, and refuges for threatened vegetation and **wildlife**. *See also* Wetlands

[*William G. Ambrose, Jr.*]

FURTHER READING

Kaufman, W., and O. Pilkey, Jr. *The Beaches Are Moving: The Drowning of America's Shoreline.* Durham, NC: Duke University Press, 1983.

Mackintosh, B. *The National Historic Preservation Act and the National Park Service: A History.* Washington, DC: U. S. Dept. of the Interior, 1986.

Sutton, A., and M. Sutton. *Wilderness Areas of North America.* New York: Funk and Wagnalls, 1974.

National Weather Service

See **National Oceanic and Atmospheric Administration**

National Wildlife Federation (Washington, D.C.)

With over five million members or supporters, the National Wildlife Federation (NWF) is the country's largest and one of its most influential **conservation** organizations. The NWF has worked since 1936 to "promote wise use of the nation's wildlife and **natural resources**," and their primary goal is "to educate citizens about the need for sustainable use and proper management of our natural resources."

NWF sponsors National Wildlife Week, held during Earth Action Month, and it distributes over 600,000 education kits to more than 20 million elementary school students. NWF also operates the Institute for Wildlife Research, which concentrates on such creatures as bears, wild cats, and birds of prey. Their Backyard Wildlife Habitat Program distributes information and encourages homeowners to set up their own refuges for wild animals by providing food, water, and shelter, and by planting or preserving trees and shrubs and building backyard ponds. The program has certified more than 6,000 backyard **habitat**s nationwide, and the group maintains a model backyard habitat at Laurel Ridge Conservation Center in Vienna, Virginia.

The National Wildlife Federation also sponsors a variety of **nature**-oriented meetings and programs. These include workshops and training sessions for grassroots leaders, children's wildlife camps and Teen Adventure Programs at facilities in North Carolina and Colorado, and NatureQuest, a leadership training program for young people. The organization also offers conservation internships, allowing young people to work with their professional staff; outdoor vacations for adults and families; symposiums and lectures on urban wildlife and gardening at the Laurel Ridge Conservation Center; and the National Conservation Achievement Awards, recognizing outstanding work in the field. Other NWF activities include co-presenting the PBS series "Conserving America," producing a biweekly column called "The Backyard Naturalist," which appears in 7,000 publications nationwide, and publishing books on **wildlife** for adults and children.

NWF's magazines have a combined circulation of 1.7 million, and include the bimonthly publications *National Wildlife* and *International Wildlife* for adults, *Ranger Rick* for elementary school children, and *Your Big Backyard* for preschoolers. NWF also publishes *The Conservation Directory*, a comprehensive listing of about 2,000 regional, national, and international conservation groups, agencies, and officials, and *NatureScope*, a science and nature school activity series used by over 30,000 teachers of elementary and middle school students.

Each year, NWF issues its Environmental Quality Index, assessing the status of air, water, wildlife, and other natural resources, as well as the quality of life in America. It also coordinates a nationwide **bald eagle** count each year and distributes millions of its famous wildlife stamps. NWF has been involved in a wide range of political campaigns. They have challenged government **strip mining** and timber cutting programs, worked to upgrade the **Environmental Protection Agency (EPA)** to cabinet-level status, helped strengthen enforcement of the **Safe Drinking Water Act**, and created the Corporate Conservation Council to encourage dialogue with industry on conservation issues.

The National Wildlife Federation differs from many other conservation groups in that the organization, and especially its state affiliates, strongly advocates hunting and trapping, emphasizing consumptive management of wildlife over pure preservation and protection. This has, at times, placed NWF at odds with other conservation groups, particularly during the 1979-80 fight over the Alaska lands legislation. In this battle, the federation strongly opposed protectionist bills supported by the general conservation community and fought instead for legislation supported by oil and gas interests, as well as hunting supporters. However, under the recent leadership of Jay D. Hair, the NWF has become somewhat less anti-preservationist (although most of its affiliates remain in that mold). The group is now considered a stronger advocate for environmental causes,

even some controversial causes it would not have supported in earlier years. Contact: National Wildlife Federation, 1400 Sixteenth Street, NW, Washington, DC 20036-2266.

[*Lewis G. Regenstein*]

National wildlife refuge

The United States began establishing **wildlife refuge**s under **Theodore Roosevelt**. In 1903 he declared Pelican Island in Florida a refuge for the **brown pelican**, protecting a **species** that was close to **extinction**. In 1906 Congress closed all refuges to hunting, and in 1908, it established the National **Bison** Range refuge in Montana to protect that **endangered species**.

The refuge system continued to expand later in the century, with a primary emphasis on migratory waterfowl. In 1929 Congress passed the Migratory Bird Convention Act, followed by the Migratory Bird Hunting Stamp Act of 1934, which provided funding for waterfowl reserves. **Wetlands** now make up roughly 75 percent of the national wildlife refuges and serve as linked management units along the major waterfowl **flyway**s.

The second focus in the expansion of the refuge system has been the need to protect endangered and rare species. Several acts have been passed for this purpose, going as far back as the Migratory Bird Treaty Act of 1918, but most recently the **Endangered Species Act** of 1973. For example, the **whooping crane** is protected by a series of national wildlife refuges in Texas, Oklahoma, and Kansas which are linked to wildlife management areas in Kansas and Nebraska, and these are linked to a national wildlife area in Saskatchewan and their primary breeding grounds in a Canadian **national park**.

A third recent focus has been on the addition of high-latitude **wilderness** in Alaska. In 1980 Congress passed the **Alaska National Interest Conservation Lands Act** which added roughly 54 million acres (22 million ha) of Alaskan land to the national wildlife refuge system.

The refuge system now consists of slightly over 400 refuges, which encompass 99 million acres (40 million ha) of land in parcels ranging from 2.5 acres (1 ha) to 17 million acres (7 million ha) in size. It is administered by the U.S. **Fish and Wildlife Service**, which was consolidated under the **U.S. Department of the Interior** in 1940. As it is officially written, the mandate is to provide, preserve, restore, and manage a national network of land and water for the benefit of society. The wording of the mandate has resulted in an open policy approach, and NWRs have been used for a variety of activities, some of which seem to many incompatible with the ideal of a refuge. For example, a consequence of having financial support from the sale of duck stamps has been the opening of refuges to waterfowl hunting. Other activities, such as **fertilizer runoff** and other **agricultural pollution** have seriously impacted the ecological integrity of several reserves in the western United States, including **Kesterson National Wildlife Refuge** in California's San Joaquin Valley.

Perhaps the most significant test of the government's ability to maintain the ecological integrity of the refuge system came over the fight to open the **Arctic National Wildlife Refuge** for oil exploration. This is the second largest reserve in the system, and perhaps the most spectacular in terms of wilderness values. Although the proposal had the support of two successive Presidents, Congress rejected it. Critics argued that it was inconsistent to maintain that oil production would benefit the country when it was earmarked for export. And the disaster caused by the **Exxon Valdez** made oil companies' claims of environmental sensitivity seem to lack credibility.

The general challenges now facing the refuge system arise both from pressure to develop in order to accommodate increased visitor demand and the vague criteria defined in the National Wildlife Refuge Administration Act of 1966 for multiple use. *See also* Forest Service; Migration; National Park Service; Oil drilling; Pinchot, Gifford; Wilderness Study Area; Wildlife management

[*David A. Duffus*]

FURTHER READING

Doherty, J. "Refuges on the Rocks." *Audubon* 85 (July 1983): 4, 6, 74-117.

Reed, N. P., and D. Drabelle. *The United States Fish and Wildlife Service.* Boulder, CO: Westview Press, 1984.

"The Wildlife Refuges (National Wildlife Refuge System)." *Wilderness* 47 (Fall 1983): 2-38.

Natural gas

Naturally occurring gas that primarily contains **methane**, CH_4. A **fossil fuel** like **coal** and **petroleum**, it is the hottest and cleanest burning of these fuels and is increasingly touted as a substitute for petroleum. It is, however, an explosion hazard in coal mines and an unwanted byproduct of **anaerobic** digestion in **landfill**s. It is most commonly found with petroleum or at depths which vaporize oil. Use is hampered by transportation difficulties and risks, and thus it is limited to pipelines and compression tanks. Huge quantities exist as unconventional sources, including coal gasification and conversion to **methanol**. *See also* Liquified natural gas

Natural radiation
   See **Background radiation**

Natural resource accounting
   See **Environmental accounting**

Natural resources

Natural resources, unlike man-made resources, exist independently of human labor. Natural resources can be viewed as an endowment or a gift to humankind. These resources are, however, not unlimited and must be used with care. Some natural resources are called "fund resources" because they can be exhausted through use, like the burning of **fossil fuels**. Other fund resources such as metals can be dissipated or wasted if they are discarded instead of being reused or recycled. Some natural resources can be used up like fund resources, but they can renew themselves if they're not completely destroyed. Examples of the latter would include the **soil**, forests, and fisheries.

Because of **population growth** and a rising standard of living, the demand for natural resources is steadily increasing. For example, the rising demand for minerals, if continued, will deplete the known and expected reserves within the coming decades.

The world's industrialized nations are consuming nonrenewable resources at an accelerating pace, with the United States ranking first on a per capita basis. With only 5 percent of the global population, Americans consumes 30 percent of the world's resources. Because of their tremendous demand for goods, Americans have also created more waste than is generated by any other country. The environment in the United States has been degraded with an ever-increasing volume and variety of contaminants. In particular, a complex of synthetic **chemicals** with a vast potential for harmful effects on human health has been created. The long-term effects of a low dosage of many of these chemicals in our environment will not be known for decades. The three most important causes for global environmental problems today are population growth, excessive resource consumption, and high levels of **pollution**. All of these threaten the natural resource base.

[*Terence H. Cooper*]

FURTHER READING

Craig, J. R. *Resources of the Earth.* Englewood Cliffs, NJ: Prentice-Hall, 1988.

Meadows, D. H., et al. *The Limits to Growth.* New York: Universe Books, 1972.

Simmons, I. G. *Earth, Air, and Water: Resources and Environment in the Late 20th Century.* London: Edward Arnold, 1991.

World Resources, 1990-91: A Report. New York: Oxford University Press, 1990.

Natural Resources Defense Council (New York, New York)

Founded in 1970, the Natural Resources Defense Council (NRDC) is a major national environmental organization active in most areas of concern to environmentalists and conservationists. It boasts a membership of 170,000 and an annual budget in excess of $17 million dollars. These resources are employed in the organization's quest for "a world in which human beings live in harmony with our **environment**." NRDC seeks a sustainable society and believes that economic growth can continue only if it does not destroy the **natural resources** that fuel it. NRDC's stated goals include access to pure air and water and safe food for every human being. NRDC's philosophy is based increasingly on a belief in the inherent sanctity of the natural environment.

Generally regarded as an influential and highly effective mainstream environmental organization, many of NRDC's successes have come from its expertise in lobbying governmental officials, helping to draft **environmental law**s, and working with public utility officials to reduce wasteful and environmentally destructive practices. NRDC has also made considerable use of the judicial system in defense of environmental causes and retains on its staff some of the nation's top environmental lawyers.

Among its many notable achievements, NRDC has been instrumental in setting national standards for building and appliance efficiency. It has collaborated with over a dozen states and Canadian provinces on the reform of **electric utilities** and helped the Soviet Union design an electrical planning program in the late 1980s. NRDC has helped protect dozens of **national forest**s from abusive logging practices, including forests in the Greater Yellowstone **ecosystem** and **old-growth forest**s in the Sierra Nevada. In addition, NRDC led the fight for the national phase-out of **lead** from **gasoline** and lobbied intensively for passage of the 1990 **Clean Air Act**. It has been a sponsor of the Nuclear Non-Proliferation Act and helped prove that an underground nuclear test ban treaty could be verified.

The NRDC is currently active in six broad program areas—Air and Energy, Water and Coastal, Land, International and Nuclear, Public Health, and Urban. Its ongoing projects are numerous and include the continuing protection of the **Arctic National Wildlife Refuge** and California coastal areas from **oil drilling**. NRDC continues to monitor the policies and practices of the **Environmental Protection Agency (EPA)** and has convinced the EPA to strengthen its rules regarding the reporting of releases of **toxic substance**s into the environment. It is lobbying the government to designate new funds for the protection of **endangered species**, to include environmental standards and controls in the North American Free Trade Agreement, to close loopholes in proposed rules for controlling **acid rain**, and to strengthen automobile **pollution** standards, as well as on many other environmental issues. Internationally, NRDC seeks the eventual elimination of **nuclear weapons**, the protection of **habitat** and ecosystems in developing countries, and the worldwide phaseout of **chlorofluorocarbons**. It promotes alternative agricultural techniques to reduce the use of **pesticide**s, the strengthening of regulations governing the disposal of waste in **landfill**s, and the testing and treatment of poor children for lead poisoning. NRDC is urging states and municipalities to stop the **ocean dumping** of sewage **sludge** and encouraging **mass transit** programs as an alternative to automobiles and new highways. Contact: Natural Resources Defense Council, 40 West 20th Street, New York, NY 10011. Internet: http://www.nrdc.org/.

[*Lawrence J. Biskowski*]

Natural selection
See **Evolution**

Nature

The word nature stems from the Latin *natura*, whose meaning ranges from "birth" to "the order of things." In English, nature comprises all plants, animals, and **ecosystem**s, as well as the biological and nonbiological materials and processes of our planet. This range of meaning narrows if we consider the use of the word *natural*. Something is natural if it is not artificial, if it pertains to or comes from the natural world. When we speak of bears, mountains, or **evolution** and say, "they are natural," we mean they are neither human nor created by humans. Thus the concept of nature is often restricted to beings, things, or processes which are not human in origin.

Conceptual and empirical inquiries into nature loosely center on eight questions. The first question is a scientific one, which simply asks what constitutes nature: What are its essential properties and how shall we classify them? The second seeks purpose in nature, asking whether the earth is a designed home for humankind or an accident of cosmic history. A third question explores the effect of the natural **environment** on human physiology, psychology and culture, examining whether nature determines who we are or constrains what we can do. A fourth examines the metaphors used to understand nature: Is nature an organism subject to death or a machine of fungible parts? The fifth question studies how nature changes: Is it dynamic, changing as a result of internal processes, or static, changing in response to external human disturbances? A sixth surveys how people have transformed the natural world, and the seventh queries whether human beings and their societies are part of or separate from nature. The final question investigates whether nature has a structure of intrinsic moral values: Does nature have values or a good of its own, and if so, should human beings respect these values or promote this good?

We lack unambiguous answers to these questions, though the questions are important in themselves, for they help us clarify our assumptions about nature. Humans, for example, have emerged from the evolutionary processes of nature. Thus our thoughts and actions are certainly natural, yet our societies and technologies are unique in the natural world, and the scope of our impact on nature is without precedent in other **species**. It seems that while we are part of nature biologically, we are separate from the rest of nature in our social and technological characteristics, and to declare humanity natural or non-natural is unhelpful. The best alternative may be to accept the ambiguity of our relationship to nature, conceiving of humankind as relatively natural and non-natural depending on the time, place, and activity. *See also* Bioregionalism; Deep ecology; Ecosophy; Environmental attitudes/values; Environmental ethics; Environmentalism; Humanism; Speciesism

[*William S. Lynn*]

FURTHER READING

Collingwood, R. G. *The Idea of Nature.* Oxford, UK: Oxford University Press, 1945.

Glacken, C. J. *Traces on the Rhodian Shore: Nature and Culture in Western Thought From Ancient Times to the End of the Eighteenth Century.* Berkeley: University of California Press, 1967.

Lyon, T. J., ed. *This Incomparable Lande: A Book of American Nature Writing.* New York: Houghton Mifflin, 1989.

Lyon, T. J., and P. Stine, eds. *On Nature's Terms.* College Station, TX: Texas A & M University Press, 1992.

Nash, R. F. *The Rights of Nature.* Madison: University of Wisconsin, 1989.

Williams, R. "Nature." In *Keywords: A Vocabulary of Culture and Society.* New York: Oxford University Press, 1985.

Nature Conservancy (Arlington, Virginia)

The Nature Conservancy is America's fourth-largest environmental organization, with 600,000 members and a budget of $156 million. It owns over 1,000 **nature** preserves—5.5 million acres (2.2 million ha) in the United States, Canada, and the Caribbean—valued at nearly $400 million. It is dedicated to protecting nature and its animal inhabitants by preserving their **habitat**s.

The organization was incorporated in 1951 by American Dick Pough, who had been inspired by the British government's nature preserves of the same name. Unlike the English version, Pough's organization was funded privately. The Conservancy's early years were difficult financially, but Pough eventually secured two major endowments that made the society solvent: a $100,000 donation from Mrs. DeWitt Wallace, co-owner of *Readers Digest,* and a $55-million bequest from Minnesota Mining heiress Katharine Ordway. Most of the latter money went for land purchases. Subsequent purchases have acquired millions of acres, although some tracts are later traded or sold to the government, individuals, or other environmental organizations.

In addition to its own preserves, the Conservancy works with state and international governments to manage over 100 million acres (40.5 million ha) around the world. One example of this administration is the **debt for nature swap**s that have been contracted in Central America. These allow the Conservancy, in conjunction with the Department of Defense, to conduct ecological inventories and supervise over 25 million acres (10 million ha). Other projects, such as Parks in Peril, have given the Conservancy charge of over 91 million acres (37 million ha) in Latin America and the Caribbean. In the United States, a partnership with **Ducks Unlimited** restored riparian forests and **wetlands** in several states. A three-year program, the Rivers of the Rockies, spent $5 million to preserve 20 sites along Colorado rivers and tributaries. Similar projects are underway in other states as well. The group cooperates with federal land and **wildlife** agencies, as well as other environmental associations, and is instrumental in helping to identify land of critical environmental interest.

In addition, the Conservancy identifies and protects animal life, especially the "rarest of the rare," those **species** most in need of preservation. The organization maintains its Heritage database at its headquarters in Arlington, Virginia, in which **endangered species** are ranked by status both globally and within each state. Contact: Nature Conservancy, 1815 N. Lynn Street, Arlington, VA 22209. Internet: http://www.tnc.org/.

[*Nathan H. Meleen and Amy Strumolo*]

Nature reserve
See **Biosphere reserve**

Nearing, Scott (1883-1983)
American conservationist

A prolific and iconoclastic writer, a socialist, and a conservationist, Scott Nearing—along with his wife Helen—is now considered the "great-grandparent" of the back-to-the-land movement. Nearing was born August 6, 1883, in Morris Run, Pennsylvania. He is the author of nearly fifty books and thousands of pamphlets and articles, some of which have become classics of modern **environmentalism**.

Originally a law student at the University of Pennsylvania, Nearing received his B.S. from that university in 1905 and a Ph.D. in economics in 1909. He was the secretary of the Pennsylvania Child Labor Commission from 1905 to 1907. He taught economics at the Wharton School, at Swarthmore College, and at the University of Toledo in Toledo, Ohio. In 1915, he was dismissed from his position at the Wharton School for his politics, particularly his position on child labor. A pacifist, he was arrested during World War I and charged with obstructing recruitment for the armed forces. He was a Socialist candidate for United States Congress in 1919. His socialism, his pacifism, and his politics in general made it increasingly difficult for him to find and maintain teaching positions after 1917, and he supported himself for the rest of his life by writing, lecturing, and farming.

In 1932, Nearing and his wife bought a small, dilapidated farm in Vermont, hoping, in their words, "to live sanely and simply in a troubled world." They restored the land and removed or rebuilt the buildings there. They farmed organically and without machinery, feeding themselves from their garden, and making and selling maple sugar. They wrote about their experiences in *The Maple Sugar Book* (1950) and *Living the Good Life* (1954). Their small farm became a mecca for people seeking both to simplify their lives and to live in harmony with **nature**, as well as each other.

In his 1972 autobiography, *The Making of a Radical,* Nearing wrote that the attempt "to live simply and inexpensively in an affluent society dedicated to extravagance and waste" was the most difficult project he had ever undertaken, but also the most physically and spiritually rewarding. He defined the good life he was striving towards as life stripped to its essentials—a life devoted to labor and learning, to doing no harm to humans or animals, and to respecting the land. As he wrote in his autobiography, he tried to live by three basic principles: "To learn the truth, to teach the truth, and to help build the truth into the life of the community."

Confronted by the growth of the recreational industry in Vermont during the 1950s, particularly the construction of a ski resort near them, the Nearings sold their property and moved their farm to Harborside, Maine, where Scott Nearing died on August 24, 1983, just over two weeks after his one-hundredth birthday.

Reviled as a radical for most of his life, Nearing's critique of the wastefulness of modern consumer society, his emphasis on smallness, self-reliance, and the restoration of ravaged land, as well as his **vegetarianism**, have struck a responsive chord in many Americans since the late 1960s. He is considered by some as the representative of twentieth century American counterculture, and he has inspired activists throughout the environmental movement, from the editors of *The Whole Earth Catalog* and the founders of the first **Earth Day** to proponents of appropriate technology. He was made an honorary professor emeritus of economics at the Wharton School in 1973. *See also* Bioregionalism; Conservation; Environmental ethics; Organic gardening and farming; Thoreau, Henry David

[*Terence Ball*]

FURTHER READING

Nearing, S. *The Making of a Radical: A Political Autobiography.* New York: Harper and Row, 1972.

————, and H. Nearing. *Living the Good Life: How to Live Sanely and Simply in a Troubled World.* Reissued with an introduction by Paul Goodman. New York: Schocken Books, 1970.

————, and H. Nearing. *The Maple Sugar Book.* New York: Schocken Books, 1971.

Nematicide

See **Pesticide**

Neoplasm

Neoplasm results in the formation of both benign and, more particularly, malignant tumors or **cancer**s. A neoplasm is a mass of new cells, which proliferate without control and serve no useful function. This lack of control is particularly marked in malignant tumors (cancer). The difference between a benign tumor and a malignant one is that the former remains at its site of origin while the latter acquires the ability to escape from its original location, migrate to another place, and invade and colonize other tissues and organs. This results in the death of the surrounding cells as the neoplasm grows rapidly.

Neotropical migrants

Birds that migrate each year between the American tropics and higher latitudes, especially in North America, are known as neotropical migrants. So called because they migrate from the tropics of the "new world" (the Western hemisphere), neotropical migrants are a topic of concern because many species have been declining in recent years, and because they are vulnerable to **habitat** destruction and other hazards in both winter and summer ranges. One survey of 62 forest-dwelling migrant bird species found that 44 declined significantly from 1978-1987. Migrants' dependence on nesting and feeding habitat in multiple regions, usually in different countries, makes **conservation** difficult, since habitat protection often requires cooperation between multiple countries. In addition, it is often unclear whose fault it is when populations fall. Most of the outcry over neotropical migrants has been raised in the United States and Canada, where summer bird populations have thinned noticeably in recent decades. Conservationists in northern latitudes tend to attribute bird disappearances to the destruction of tropical forests and other winter habitat. In response, governments in Mexico, Central America, and South America argue that loss of suitable summer nesting habitat, as well as summer feeding and shelter requirements, are responsible for the decline of migratory birds.

About 250 species of birds breed in North America and winter in the south. In the southern and western United States 50-60% of breeding birds are migrants, a number that rises to 80% in southern Canada and to 90% in the Canadian sub-arctic. Among the familiar migrants are species of orioles, hummingbirds, sandpipers and other wading birds, herons and bitterns, flycatchers, swallows, and almost all warblers. Half of these winter in Mexico, the Bahamas, and the Greater Antilles islands. Some 30 species winter as far south as the western Amazon Basin and the foothills of the Andes Mountains, where forest clearance poses a significant threat. Species most vulnerable to habitat loss may be those that require large areas of continuous habitat, especially the small woodland birds, and aquatic birds whose wetland habitats are being drained, filled, or contaminated in both summer and winter ranges.

In addition to habitat loss, neotropical migrants suffer from agricultural **pesticide**s, which poison both food sources and the birds themselves. The use of pesticides, including such persistent chemicals as **dichlorodiphenyltrichloroethane (DDT)**, has risen in Latin America during the same period that logging has decimated forest habitat. Furthermore, some ecologists argue that migrants are especially vulnerable in their winter habitat because winter ranges tend to be geographically more restricted than summer ranges. Sometimes an entire population winters in just a few islands, swamps, or bays. Any habitat damage, pesticide use, or predation could impact a large part of the population if the birds concentrate in a small area.

Population declines are by no means limited to loss of wintering grounds. An estimated 40% of North America's eastern **deciduous forest**s, the primary breeding grounds of many migrants, have either been cleared or fragmented. Habitat fragmentation is the term used to describe breaking up a patch of habitat into small, dispersed units, or dissecting a patch of habitat with roads or suburban developments. This problem is especially severe on the outskirts of urban areas, where suburbs continue to cut into the surrounding countryside. For reasons not fully understood, neotropical migrants appear to be more susceptible to habitat fragmentation than short-distance migrants or species that remain in residence year round. Hazards of fragmentation include nesting failure due to predation (often by raccoons, snakes, crows, or jays), nesting failure due to competition with human-adapted species such as starlings and English sparrows, and mortality due to domestic house cats. (An Australian study of house cat predation estimated that 500,000 cats in the state of Victoria had killed 13 million small birds and mammals, including 67 different native bird species.) In addition to hazards in their summer and winter ranges, threats along **migration** routes can impact migratory bird populations. Loss of stop-over **wetlands**, forests, and **grasslands** can reduce food sources and protective cover along migration routes. Sometimes birds are even forced to find alternative migration paths.

European-African migrants suffer similar fates and risks to those of American migrants. In addition to wetland drainage, habitat fragmentation, and increased pesticide use, Europeans and Africans also continue to hunt their migratory birds, a hazard that probably impacts American migrants but that is little documented here. It is estimated that in Italy alone, some 50 million songbirds are killed each year as epicurean delicacies. **Hunting** is also practiced in Spain and France, as well as in African countries where people truly may be short of food.

One of the principal sources of data on bird population changes is the North American Breeding Bird Survey, an annual survey conducted by volunteers who traverse a total of 3,000 established transects each year and report the number of breeding birds observed. While this record is by no means complete, it provides the best available approximation of general trends. Not all birds are disappearing. Some have even increased slightly, as a consequence of reduced exposure to DDT, a pesticide outlawed in the United States because it poisons birds, and because of habitat restoration efforts. However the BBS has documented significant and troubling declines in dozens of species.

Declines in migrant bird populations alarm many people because birds are often seen as indicators of more general ecosystem health. Birds are highly visible and their disappearance is noticeable, but they may indicate the simultaneous declines of insects, amphibians, fish, and other less visible groups using the same habitat areas.

[*Mary Ann Cunningham*]

FURTHER READING

Friesen, L., P.F. Eagles, and R.J. Mackay. "Effects of Residential Development on Forest-Dwelling Neotropical Migrant Songbirds," *Conservation Biology* 9, no.6 (1995): 1408-14.

Keast, A. "The Nearctic-Neotropical Bird Migration System," *Israel Journal of Zoology* 4, no. 1, (1995): 455-70.

Maurer, R.A., and S.G. Heywood. "Geographic Range Fragmentation and Abundance in Neotropical Migratory Birds," *Conservation Biology* 7, no. 3 (1993): 501-09.

Terbogh, J. *Where Have All the Birds Gone?* Princeton, N.J.: Princeton University Press, 1989.

Youth, H. "Flying Into Trouble," *Worldwatch* 7 (1994): 110-17.

Neritic zone

The portion of the marine **ecosystem** that overlies the world's continental shelves. This subdivision of the **pelagic zone** includes some of the ocean's most productive water. This productivity supports a **food chain** culminating in an abundance of commercially important fish and shellfish and is largely a consequence of abundant sunlight and **nutrient**s. In the shallow water of the neritic zone, the entire water column may receive sufficient sunlight for **photosynthesis**. Nutrients are delivered to the area by terrestrial runoff and through resuspension from the bottom by waves and currents. Runoff and dumping of waste also deliver pollutants to the neritic zone, and this area is consequently among the ocean's most polluted.

Neurotoxin

Neurotoxins are a special class of metabolic poisons that attack nerve cells. Disruption of the nervous system as a result of exposure to neurotoxins is usually quick and destructive. Neurotoxins are categorized according to the nature of their impact on the nervous system. Anesthetics (ether, chloroform, halothane), **chlorinated hydrocarbons** (**DDT**, Dieldrin, Aldrin), and **heavy metals** (**lead**, **mercury**) disrupt the **ion** transport across cell membranes essential for nerve action. Common **pesticide**s, including carbamates such as Sevin, Zeneb and Maneb and the **organophosphate**s such as Malathion and Parathion, inhibit acetylcholinesterase, an enzyme that regulates nerve signal transmission between nerve cells and the organs and tissues they innervate.

Environmental exposure to neurotoxins can occur through a variety of mechanisms. These include improper use, improper storage or disposal, occupational use, and accidental spills during distribution or application. Since the identification and ramifications of all neurotoxins are not fully known, there is risk of exposure associated with this lack of knowledge.

Cell damage associated with the introduction of neurotoxins occurs through direct contact with the chemical or a loss of oxygen to the cell. This results in damage to cellular components, especially in those required for the synthesis of protein and other cell components.

The symptoms associated with pesticide poisoning include eye and skin irritation, miosis, blurred vision, headache, anorexia, nausea, vomiting, increased sweating, increased salivation, diarrhea, abdominal pain, slight bradycardia, ataxia, muscle weakness and twitching, and generalized weakness of respiratory muscles. Symptoms associated with poisoning of the central nervous system include giddiness, anxiety, insomnia, drowsiness, difficulty concentrating, poor recall, confusion, slurred speech, convulsions, coma with the absence of reflexes, depression of respiratory and circulatory centers, and fall in blood pressure.

The link between environmental neurotoxin exposure and neuromuscular and brain dysfunction has recently been identified. Physiological symptoms of Alzheimer's disease, amyotrophic lateral sclerosis (ALS, or Lou Gehrig's disease), and lathyrism have been identified in populations exposed to substances containing known neurotoxins. For example studies have shown that heroin addicts who used synthetic heroin contaminated with methylphenyltetrahydropyridine developed a condition which manifests symptoms identical to those associated with Parkinson disease. On the island of Guam, the natives who incorporate the seeds of the false sago plant (*Cycas circinalis*) into their diet develop a condition very similar to ALS. The development of this condition has been associated with the specific nonprotein amino acid, B methylamino-1-alanine, present in the seeds.

[*Brian R. Barthel*]

FURTHER READING

Agency for Toxic Substances and Disease Registry, Annual Report 1989 and 1990. Atlanta, GA: U.S. Department of Health and Human Services.

Aldrich, T., and J. Griffith. *Environmental Epidemiology.* New York: Van Nostrand Reinhold, 1993.

Griffith, J., R.C. Duncan, and J. Konefal. "Pesticide Poisonings Reported By Florida Citrus Field Workers." *Environmental Science and Health* 6 (1985): 701-27.

Neutron

A subatomic particle with a mass of a proton and no electric charge. It is found in the nuclei of all atoms except **hydrogen**-1. A free neutron is unstable and decays to form a proton and an electron with a half life of 22 minutes. Because they have no electric charge, neutrons easily penetrate matter, including human tissue. They constitute, therefore, a serious health hazard. When a neutron strikes certain nuclei, such as that of **uranium**-235, it fissions those nuclei, producing additional neutrons in the process. The **chain reaction** thus initiated is the basis for **nuclear weapons** and **nuclear power**. *See also* Nuclear fission; Radioactivity

Nevada Test Site (Mercury, Nevada)

The Nevada Test Site (NTS) is one of two locations (the South Pacific being the other) at which the United States has conducted the majority of its **nuclear weapons** tests. The site was chosen for weapons testing in December 1950 by President Harry S. Truman and originally named the Nevada Proving Ground. The first test of a nuclear weapon was carried out at the site in January 1951 when a B-50 bomber dropped a bomb for the first of five tests in "Operation Ranger."

The Nevada Test Site is located 65 miles (105 km) northwest of Las Vegas. It occupies 1,350 square miles (3,497 km²), an area slightly larger than the state of Rhode Island. Nellis Air Force Base and the Tonopath Test Range surround the site on three sides.

Over 11,000 people are employed by NTS, 5,000 of whom work on the site itself. The site's annual budget is about $1 billion, 81 percent of which goes for weapons testing and 19 percent of which is spent on the development of a **radioactive waste** storage facility at nearby **Yucca Mountain**.

The first nuclear tests at the site were conducted over an area known as Frenchman Flat. Between 1951 and 1962, a total of fourteen atmospheric tests were carried out in this area to determine the effect of nuclear explosions on structures and military targets. Ten underground tests were also conducted at Frenchman Flat between 1965 and 1971.

Since 1971, most underground tests at the site have been conducted in the area known as Yucca Flat. These tests are usually carried out in wells 10 feet (3 m) in diameter and 600 feet (182 m) to one mile (1.6 km) in depth. On an average, about twelve tests per year are carried out at NTS.

Some individuals have long been concerned about possible environmental effects of the testing carried out a NTS. During the period of atmospheric testing, those effects (**radioactive fallout**, for example) were relatively easy to observe. But the environmental consequences of underground testing have been more difficult to determine.

One such consequence is the production of earthquakes, an event observed in 1968 when a test code-named "Faultless" produced a fault with a vertical displacement of 15 feet (5 m). Such events are rare, however, and of less concern than the release of radioactive materials into **groundwater** and the escape of radioactive gases through venting from the test well.

In 1989, the Office of Technology Assessment (OTA) of the United States Congress carried out a study of the possible environmental effects from underground testing. OTA concluded that the risks to humans from underground testing at NTS are very low indeed. It found that, in the first place, there is essentially no possibility that any release of radioactive material could go undetected. OTA also calculated that the total mount of radiation a person would have received by standing at the NTS boundary for every underground test conducted at the site so far would be about equal to 1/1000 of a single chest x ray or equivalent to 32 minutes more of exposure to natural **background radiation** in a person's lifetime. *See also* Groundwater pollution; Hazardous waste; Nuclear fission; Radiation exposure; Radioactive decay; Radioactivity

[*David E. Newton*]

FURTHER READING

"Press Releases Don't Tell All." *Bulletin of the Atomic Scientists* 46 (January-February 1990): 4-5.

"New Bomb Factory to Open Soon at Test Site." *Bulletin of the Atomic Scientists* 46 (April 1990): 56.

Office of Technology Assessment. *The Containment of Underground Nuclear Explosions*. OTA-ISC-414. Washington, D.C.: U.S. Government Printing Office, 1989.

Slonit, R. "In the State of Nevada." *Sierra* (September-October 1991): 90-101.

New Madrid, Missouri

Those who think that earthquakes are strictly a California phenomenon might be amazed to learn that the most powerful earthquake in recorded American history occurred in the middle of the country near New Madrid (pronounced MAD-rid), Missouri. Between December 16, 1811, and February 7, 1812, about 2,000 tremors shook southeastern Missouri and adjacent parts of Arkansas, Illinois, and Tennessee. The largest of these earthquakes is thought to have had a magnitude of 8.8 on the Richter scale, making it one of the most massive ever recorded.

Witnesses reported shocks so violent that trees 6 feet (2 meters) thick were snapped like matchsticks. More than 150,00 acres (60,000 ha) of forest were flattened. Fissures several yards wide and many miles long split the earth. Geysers of dry sand or muddy water spouted into the air. A trough 150 miles (242 km) long, 40 miles (64 km) wide, and up to 30 feet (19 m) deep formed along the fault line. The town of New Madrid sank about 12 feet (4 m). The Mississippi River reversed its course and flowed north rather than south past New Madrid for several hours. Many people feared that it was the end of the world.

One of the most bizarre effects of the tremors was **soil** liquefaction. Soil with high water content was converted instantly to liquid mud. Buildings tipped over, hills slid into the valleys, and animals sank as if caught in quicksand. Land surrounding a hamlet called Little Prairie suddenly became a soupy swamp. Residents had to wade for miles through hip-deep mud to reach solid ground. The swamp was not drained for nearly a century.

Some villages were flattened by the earthquake, while others were flooded when the river filled in subsided areas. The tremors rang bells in Washington, D.C., and shook residents out of bed in Cincinnati, Ohio. Since the country was sparsely populated in 1812, however, few people were killed.

The situation is much different now, of course. The damage from an earthquake of that magnitude would be calamitous. Much of Memphis, Tennessee, only about 100 miles (160 km) from New Madrid, is built on landfill similar to that in the Mission District of San Francisco where so much damage occurred in the earthquake of 1990. St. Louis had only 2,000 residents in 1812; nearly a half million live there now. Scores of smaller cities and towns lie along the fault line and transcontinental highways and pipelines cross the area. Few residents have been aware of earthquake dangers or how to protect themselves. Midwestern buildings generally are not designed to survive tremors.

Anxiety about earthquakes in the Midwest was aroused in 1990 when climatologist Iben Browning predicted a 50-50 chance of an earthquake 7.0 or higher on or around December 3, in or near New Madrid. Browning based his prediction on calculations of planetary motion and gravitational forces. Many geologists were quick to dismiss these techniques, pointing out that seismic and geochemical analyses predict earthquakes much more accurately than the methods he used. Although there were no large earth quakes along the New Madrid fault in 1990, the probability of a major tremor there remains high.

While the general time and place of some earthquakes have been predicted with remarkable success, mystery and uncertainty still abound concerning when and where "the next big one" will occur. Will it be in California? Will it be in the Midwest? Or will it be somewhere entirely unexpected? Meanwhile, residents of New Madrid are planning emergency exit routes and stocking up on camping gear and survival supplies.

[*William P. Cunningham*]

FURTHER READING

Finkbeiner, A. "California's Revenge: Someday a Major Earthquake Will Ravage the United States—in the East." *Discover* 11 (September 1990): 78-82, 84-5.

Johnson, A. C., and L. R. Kanter. "Earthquakes in Stable Continental Crust." *Scientific American* 262 (March 1990): 68-75.

New Source Performance Standard

The **Clean Air Act**s of 1963 and 1967 gave to the **Environmental Protection Agency (EPA)** the authority to establish **emission standards** for new and modified stationary sources. These standards are called new source performance standards (NSPS) and are determined by the best **emission** control technology available, the energy needed to use the technology, and its overall cost. An example of an NSPS is the standard set for plants that make Portland cement. Such plants are allowed to release no more than 0.30 pounds of emissions for each ton of raw materials used and to produce an emission with no more than 20 percent opacity.

New York Bight

A bight is a coastal embayment usually formed by a curved shoreline. The New York Bight forms part of the Middle Atlantic Bight, which runs along the east coast of the United States. The dimensions of the New York Bight are roughly square, encompassing an area that extends out from the New York-New Jersey shore to the eastern limit of Long Island and down to the southern tip of New Jersey. The apex of the bight, as it is known, is the northwestern corner, which includes the **Hudson River** estuary, the Passaic and Hackensack River estuaries, Newark Bay, Arthur Kill, Upper Bay, Lower Bay, and Raritan Bay.

The New York Bight contains a valuable and diverse **ecosystem**. The waters of the bight vary from relatively fresh near the shore to **brackish** and salty as one moves eastward, and the range of salinity, along with the islands and shore areas present within the area, have created a diversity of environmental conditions and **habitat**s, which include marshes, woods, and beaches, as well as highly developed urban areas. The portion of the bight near the shore lies directly in the path of one of the major transcontinental migratory pathways for birds, the North Atlantic **flyway**.

The New York Bight has a history of extremely intensive use by humans, especially at the apex, and here environmental impacts have been most severe. Beginning with the settlement of New York City in the 1600s, the bight area has supported one of the world's busiest harbors and largest cities. It receives more than two billion gallons per day of domestic sewage and industrial **wastewater**. Millions of gallons of **nonpoint source** runoff also pours into the bight during storms, and regulated **ocean dumping** of dredge spoils also occurs.

Numerous studies have shown that the **sediment**s of the bight, particularly at the apex, have been contaminated. Levels of **heavy metals** such as **lead**, **cadmium** and **copper** in the sediments of the apex are of special concern because they far exceed current guidelines on acceptable concentrations. Similarly, organic pollutants such as **polychlorinated biphenyls (PCBs)** from transformer oil and **polycyclic aromatic hydrocarbons (PAHs)** degraded from **petroleum** compounds are also in the sediments at levels high enough to be of concern. Additionally, the sewage brings enormous quantities of **nitrogen** and **phosphorus** into the bight which promotes excessive growth of algae.

The continual polluting of the bight since the early days of settlement has progressively reduced its capacity as a food source for the surrounding communities. The oyster and shellfishing industry that thrived in the early 1800s began declining in the 1870s, and government advisories currently prohibit shellfishing in the waters of the bight due to the high concentrations of contaminants that have accumulated in shellfish. Fishing is highly regulated throughout the area, and health advisories have been issued for consumption of fish caught in the bight. The bottom-dwelling worms and insect larvae in the sediments of the apex consist almost entirely of **species** that are extremely tolerant of **pollution**; sensitive species are absent and **biodiversity** is low.

There are, however, some reasons to be optimistic. The areas within the bight closest to the open ocean are much cleaner than the highly degraded apex. In these less-impacted areas, the bottom-dwelling communities have higher species diversity and include species that prefer unimpacted conditions. Since the 1970s, enforcement of the **Clean Water Act** has helped greatly in reducing the quantities of untreated wastewater entering the bight. Some fish species that had been almost eliminated from the area have returned, and today striped bass again swim up the Hudson River to spawn. *See also* Algal bloom; Environmental stress; Marine pollution; Pollution control; Sewage treatment; Storm runoff

[*Usha Vedagiri*]

FURTHER READING

Meyer, G. *Ecological Stress and the New York Bight.* Crownsville, MD: Estuarine Research Federation, 1982.

New York-New Jersey Harbor Estuary Program. *Toxics Characterization Report.* Washington, DC: U. S. Environmental Protection Agency, 1992.

Payton, B. M. "Ocean Dumping in the New York Bight." *Environment* 27 (1985): 26.

NGO

See **Nongovernmental organization**

Niche

The term niche is used in **ecology** with a variety of distinct meanings. It may refer to a spatial unit or to a function unit. One definition focuses on niche as a role claimed exclusively by a **species** through **competition**. The word is also used to refer to "utilization distribution" or the frequency with which populations use resources. Still, niche is well enough established in ecology that Stephen Jay Gould can label it as "the fundamental concept" in the discipline, "an expression of the location and function of a species in a habitat." Niche is used to address such questions as what determines the species diversity of a biological community, how similar organisms coexist in an area, how species divide up the resources of an **environment**, and how species within a community affect each other over time.

Niche has not been applied very satisfactorily in the ecological study of humans. Anthropologists have used it perhaps most successfully in the study of how small pre-industrial tribal groups adapt to local conditions. Sociologists have not been very successful with niche, subdividing the human species by occupations or roles, creating false analogies that do not come very close to the way niche is used in biology. More recently, sociologists have extended niche to help explain organizational behavior, though again distorting it as an ecological concept.

Some attempts were made to build on the vernacular sense of niche as in "he found his niche," a measure of how individual human beings attain multidimensional "fit" with their surroundings. But this usage was again criticized as too much of a distortion of the original meaning of niche in biology. The word and related concepts remain common, however, and are widely understood in vernacular usage to describe how individual human beings make their way in the world.

The niche concept has not been much employed by environmental scientists, though it might be helpful in attempts to understand the relationships between humans and their environments, for instance. Efforts to formulate niche or a synonym of some sort for use in the study of such relationships will probably continue. The best use of niche might be in its utility as an indicator of the richness and diversity of **habitat**, serving in this way as an indicator of the general health of the environment.

[*Gerald L. Young*]

FURTHER READING

Broussard, C. A., and G. L. Young. "A Reorientation of Niche Theory in Human Ecology: Toward a Better Explanation of the Complex Linkages between Individual and Society." *Sociological Perspectives* 29 (April 1986): 259-283.

Colinvaux, P. A. "Towards a Theory of History: Fitness, Niche, and Clutch of *Homo Sapiens*." *Coevolution Quarterly* 41 (Spring 1984): 94-107.

Mark, J., G. M. Chapman, and T. Gibson. "Bioeconomics and the Theory of Niches." *Futures* 17 (December 1985): 632-51.

Schoener, T. W. "The Ecological Niche." In *Ecological Concepts*, edited by J. M. Cherrett. Oxford, England: Blackwell Scientific Publications, 1989.

Nickel

Nickel is a heavy metal, and it can be an important toxic chemical in the environment. Natural **pollution** by nickel is associated with **soil**s that have a significant presence of a mineral known as serpentine. Serpentine-laced soils are toxic to nonadapted plants, and although the most significant toxic stressor is a large concentration of nickel, sometimes the presence of cobalt and/or chromium, along with high **pH** and an impoverished supply of **nutrient**s also create a toxic environment. Serpentine sites often have a specialized **flora** dominated by nickel-tolerant **species**, many of which are endemic to such sites. Nickel pollution can occur through human influence as well—most often in the vicinity of nickel **smelter**s or refineries. The best-known example of a nickel-polluted environment occurs around the town of **Sudbury, Ontario**, where smelting has been practiced for a century. *See also* Heavy metals and heavy metal poisoning

Nickel mining
See **Sudbury, Ontario**

NIMBY (Not In My Backyard)

NIMBY is an acronym for "Not In My Backyard" and is often heard in discussions of **waste management**. While every community needs a site for waste disposal, frequently no one wants it near his or her home. In the early part of this century, in fact, up until the early 1970s, the town dump was a smelly, rodent-infested place that caught fire on occasion. Loose debris from these facilities would also blow onto adjacent property. Citizens were justified in their aversion to **landfill**s because **hazardous waste** and **chemicals** were often dumped into landfills, which contaminated **groundwater** and surface water. After the passage of the **Resource Conservation and Recovery Act (RCRA)** in 1976, many of these facilities were closed and dumps converted into sanitary landfills that required daily cover, fencing, leachate collection systems, and other design elements

that made them much better neighbors. Still, many citizens refused to have landfills close to their homes.

In addition to landfills, citizens are also concerned about having other waste management facilities near them. Large open air **composting** facilities are not popular because of the odor they produce. A materials **recycling** facility (MRF) is not always a desirable neighbor because of the noise it generate.

Despite assurances by experts of the improvements and safety of modern waste management facilities, communities continue to be wary of them. In order to overcome the NIMBY attitude, professionals in the waste management field must collaborate with communities so that citizens gain understanding and ownership of **solid waste** management problems. The problem of waste is generated at the community level so the solution must be generated at the community level. With sensible planning and patience there may be less NIMBY-mentality in the future.

[*Cynthia Fridgen*]

FURTHER READING

Brion, D. J. *Essential Industry and the NIMBY Phenomenon: A Problem of Distributive Justice.* Westport, CT: Greenwood, 1991.

Guerra, S. "NIMBY, NIMTOF, and Solid Waste Facility Siting." *Public Management* 73 (October 1991): 11-15.

Piller, C. *The Fail-Safe Society: Community Defiance and the End of American Technological Optimism.* New York: Basic Books, 1991.

Shields, P. "Overcoming the NIMBY Syndrome." *American City and County* 105 (May 1990): 54.

Nitrates and nitrites

Nitrates and nitrites are families of chemical compounds containing atoms of **nitrogen** and oxygen. Occurring naturally, nitrates and nitrites are critical to the continuation of life on the earth, since they are one of the main sources from which plants obtain the element nitrogen. This element is required for the production of amino acids which, in turn, are used in the manufacture of proteins in both plants and animals.

One of the great transformations of agriculture over the past century has been the expanded use of synthetic chemical **fertilizer**s. Ammonium nitrate is one of the most important of these fertilizers. In recent years, this compound has ranked in the top fifteen among synthetic **chemicals** produced in the United States.

The increased use of nitrates as fertilizer has led to some serious environmental problems. All nitrates are soluble, so whatever amount is not taken up by plants in a field is washed away into **groundwater** and, eventually, into rivers, streams, ponds, and lakes. In these bodies of water, the nitrates become sources of food for algae and other plant life, resulting in the formation of **algal bloom**s. Such blooms are usually the first step in the eutrophication of a pond or lake. As a result of eutrophication, a pond or lake slowly evolves into a marsh or swamp, then into a bog, and finally into a meadow.

Nitrates and nitrites present a second, quite different kind of environmental issue. These compounds have long been used in the preservation of red meats. They are attractive to industry not only because they protect meat from spoiling, but also because they give meat the bright red color that consumers expect.

The use of nitrates and nitrites in meats has been the subject of controversy, however, for at least twenty years. Some critics argue that the compounds are not really effective as preservatives. They claim that preservation is really effected by the table salt that is usually used along with nitrates and nitrites. Furthermore, some scientists believe that nitrates and nitrites may themselves be **carcinogen**s or may be converted in the body to a class of compounds known as the nitrosamines, compounds that are known to be carcinogens.

In the 1970s, the **Food and Drug Administration** (FDA) responded to these concerns by dramatically cutting back on the quantity of nitrates and nitrites that could be added to foods. By 1981, however, a thorough study of the issue by the National Academy of Sciences showed that nitrates and nitrites are only a minor source of nitrosamine compared to smoking, drinking water, cosmetics, and industrial chemicals. Based on this study, the FDA finally decided in January 1983 that nitrates and nitrites are safe to use in foods. *See also* Agricultural revolution; Cancer; Cigarette smoke; Denitrification; Drinking-water supply; Fertilizer runoff; Nitrification; Nitrogen cycle; Nitrogen waste

[*David E. Newton*]

FURTHER READING

Canter, L. W. *Nitrates in Ground Water*. Chelsea, MI: Lewis, 1992.

Cassens, R. G. *Nitrate-Cured Meat: A Food Safety Issue in Perspective*. Trumbull, CT: Food and Nutrition Press, 1990.

"Clearest Lake Clouding Up." *Environment* 30 (January-February 1988): 22-3.

Raloff, J. "New Acid Rain Threat Identified." *Science News* 133 (30 April 1988): 276.

Selinger, B. *Chemistry in the Marketplace*. 4th ed. Sydney, Australia: Harcourt Brace Jovanovich, 1989.

Nitrification

A biological process involving the conversion of **nitrogen**-containing organic compounds into **nitrates and nitrites**. It is accomplished by two groups of chemo-synthetic bacteria that utilize the energy produced. The first step involves the oxidation of ammonia to nitrite, and is accomplished by *Nitrosomas* in the soil and *Nitrosoccus* in the marine environment. The second step involves the oxidation of nitrites into nitrates, releasing 18 kcal of energy. It is accomplished by *Nitrobacter* in the soil and *Nitrococcus* in salt water. Nitrification is an integral part of the **nitrogen cycle**, and is usually considered a beneficial process, since it converts organic nitrogen compounds into nitrates which can be absorbed by green plants. The reverse process of nitrification, occurring in oxygen-deprived environments, is called **denitrification** and is accomplished by other species of bacteria.

Nitrites

See **Nitrates and nitrites**

Nitrogen

Comprising about 78 percent of the earth's **atmosphere**, nitrogen (N_2) has an atomic number of seven and an atomic weight of 14. It has a much lower solubility in water than in air—there is approximately 200 times more nitrogen in the atmosphere than in the ocean. The main source of gaseous nitrogen is volcanic eruptions; the major nitrogen sinks are synthesis of nitrate in electrical storms and biological nitrogen fixation. All organisms need nitrogen. It forms part of the chlorophyll molecule in plants, it forms the nitrogen base in **DNA** and **RNA**, and it is an essential part of all amino acids, the building blocks of proteins. Nitrogen is needed in large amounts for **respiration**, growth, and reproduction. **Nitrogen oxides** (NO_x), produced mainly by motor vehicles and internal combustion engines, are one of the main contributors to **acid rain**. They react with water molecules in the atmosphere to form nitric acid. *See also* Nitrates and nitrites; Nitrogen cycle

Nitrogen cycle

Nitrogen is a macronutrient essential to all living organisms. It is an integral component of amino acids which are the building blocks of proteins; it forms part of the nitrogenous bases common to **DNA** and **RNA**; it helps make up ATP, and it is a major component of the chlorophyll molecule in plants. In essence, life as we know it cannot exist without nitrogen.

Although nitrogen is readily abundant as a gas (it comprises 79 percent of atmospheric gases by volume), most organisms cannot use it in this state. It must be converted to a chemically usable form such as ammonia (NH_3) or **nitrate** (NO_3) for most plants, and amino acids for all animals. The processes involved in the conversion of nitrogen to its various forms comprise the nitrogen cycle. Of all the **nutrient** cycles, this is considered the most complex and least well understood scientifically. The processes that make up the nitrogen cycle include nitrogen fixation, ammonification, **nitrification**, and **denitrification**.

Nitrogen fixation refers to the conversion of atmospheric nitrogen gas (N_2) to ammonia (NH_3) or nitrate (NO_3). The latter is formed when lightning or sometimes cosmic radiation causes oxygen and nitrogen to react in the **atmosphere**. Farmers are usually delighted when electrical storms move through their areas because it supplies "free" nitrogen to their crops, thus saving money on **fertilizer**. Ammonia is produced from N_2 by a special group of microbes in a process called biological fixation, which accounts for about 90 percent of all fixed N_2 each year worldwide. This process is accomplished by a relatively small number of species of bacteria and blue-green algae, or blue-green bacteria. The most well known of these nitrogen-fixing

The nitrogen cycle.

organisms are the bacteria in the genus *Rhizobium* which are associated with the root nodules of legumes. The legumes attract these bacteria by secreting a chemical into the soil that stimulates the bacteria to multiply and enter the root hair tips. The resultant swellings contain millions of bacteria and are called root nodules, and here, near the **soil**'s surface, they actively convert atmospheric N_2 to NH_3, which is taken up by the plant. This is an example of a symbiotic relationship, where both organisms benefit. The bacteria benefit from the physical location in which to grow, and they also utilize sugars supplied by the plant photosynthate to reduce the N_2 to NH_3. The legumes, in turn, benefit from the NH_3 produced. The energetic cost for this nutrient is quite high, however, and legumes typically take their nitrogen directly from the soil rather than from their bacteria when the soil is fertilized.

Although nitrogen fixation by legume bacteria is the major source of biological fixation, other species of bacteria are also involved in this process. Some are associated with non-legume plants such as toyon (*Ceanothus*), silverberry (*Elaeagnus*), water fern (*Azolla*), and alder (*Alnus*). With the exception of the water fern, these plants are typically pioneer **species** growing in low-nitrogen soil. Other nitrogen-fixing bacteria live as free-living species in the soil. These include microbes in the genera *Azotobacter* and *Clostridium*, which live in aerobic and anaerobic **sediment**s, respectively.

Blue-green algae are the other major group of living organisms which fix atmospheric N_2. They include approximately forty species in such genera as *Aphanizomenon*, *Anabaena*, *Calothrix*, *Gloeotrichia*, and *Nostoc*. They inhabit both soil and freshwater and can tolerate adverse and even extreme conditions. For example, some species grow in hot springs where the water is 212°F (100°C), whereas other species inhabit glaciers where the temperature is 32°F (0°C).

The characteristic bluish-green coloration is a telltale sign of their presence. Some blue-green algae are found as pioneer species invading barren soil devoid of nutrients, particularly nitrogen, either as solitary individuals or associated with other organisms such as **lichens**. Flooded rice fields are another prime location for nitrogen-fixing blue-green algae.

Perhaps the most common **environment**s where blue-green algae are found are lakes and ponds, particularly when the body of water is eutrophic—containing high concentrations of nutrients, especially **phosphorus**. Algae can reach bloom proportions during the warm summer months and are often considered a nuisance because they float on the surface, forming dense scum. The resultant odor following decomposition is usually pungent, and fish such as catfish often acquire an off-flavor taste from ingesting these algae.

The next major component of the nitrogen cycle is ammonification. It involves the breakdown of organic matter (in this case amino acids) by decomposer organisms to NH_3, yielding energy. It is therefore the reverse reaction of amino acid synthesis. Dead plant and animal tissues and waste materials are broken down to amino acids and eventually NH_3 by the saprophagous bacteria and **fungi** in both soil and water.

Nitrification is a biological process where NH_3 is oxidized in two steps, first to NO_3 and next to nitrate (NO2). It is accomplished by two genera of bacteria, *Nitrosomonas* and *Nitrobacter* in the soil, and *Nitrosococcus* and *Nitrococcus* in salt water. Since nitrification is an oxidation reaction, it requires oxygenated environments.

Dentrification is the reverse reaction of nitrification and occurs under **anaerobic** conditions. It involves the breakdown of nitrates and nitrites into gaseous N_2 by microorganisms and fungi. Bacteria in the genus *Pseudomonas* (e.g., *P. dentrificans*) reduce NO_3 in the soil.

The cycling of nitrogen in an **ecosystem** is obviously complex. In aquatic ecosystems, nitrogen can enter the food chain through various sources, primarily surface **runoff** into lakes or rivers, mixing of nutrient-rich bottom waters (normally only during spring and fall turnovers in north temperate lakes), and biological fixation of atmospheric nitrogen by blue-green algae. **Phytoplankton** (microscopic algae) then rapidly take up the available nitrogen in the form of NH_3 or NO_3 and assimilate it into their tissues, primarily as amino acids. Some nitrogen is released by leakage through cell membranes. Herbivorous zooplankton that ingest these algae convert their amino acids into different amino acids and excrete the rest. Carnivorous or omnivorous zooplankton and fish that eat the herbivores do the same. Excretion (usually as NH_3 and urea) is thus a valuable nutrient recycling mechanism in aquatic ecosystems. Different species of phytoplankton actively compete for these nutrients when they are limited. Decomposing bacteria in the lake, particularly in the top layer of the bottom sediments, play an important role in the breakdown of dead organic matter which sinks to the bottom. The cycle is thus complete.

The cycling of nitrogen in marine ecosystems is similar to that in lakes, except that nitrogen lost to the sediments in the deep open water areas is essentially lost. Recycling only occurs in the nearshore regions, usually through a process called **upwelling**. Another difference is that marine phytoplankton prefer to take up nitrogen in the form of NH_3 rather than NO_3.

In terrestrial ecosystems, NH_3 and NO_3 in the soil is taken up by plants and assimilated into amino acids. As in aquatic habitats, the nitrogen is passed through the **food chain/web** from plants to herbivores to carnivores, which manufacture new amino acids. Upon death, decomposers begin the breakdown process, converting the organic nitrogen to inorganic NH_3. Bacteria are the main decomposers of animal matter and fungi are the main group that break down plants. Shelf and bracket fungi, for example, grow rapidly on fallen trees in forests. The action of termites, bark beetles, and other insects that inhabit these trees greatly speed up the process of **decomposition**.

There are three major differences between nitrogen cycling in aquatic versus terrestrial ecosystems. First, the nitrogen reserves are usually much greater in terrestrial habitats because nutrients contained in the soil remain accessible, whereas nitrogen released in water and not taken up by phytoplankton sinks to the bottom where it can be lost or held for a long time. Secondly, nutrient recycling by herbivores is normally a more significant process in aquatic ecosystems. Thirdly, terrestrial plants prefer to take up nitrogen as NO_3 and aquatic plants prefer NH_3.

Forces in nature normally operate in a balance, and gains are offset by losses. So it is with the nitrogen cycle in freshwater and terrestrial ecosystems. Losses of nitrogen by detritrification, runoff, sedimentation, and other releases equal gains by fixation and other sources.

Humans, however, have an influence on the nitrogen cycle that can greatly change normal pathways. Fertilizers used in excess on residential lawns and agricultural fields add tremendous amounts of nitrogen (typically as urea or ammonium nitrate) to the target area. Some of the nitrogen is taken up by the vegetation, but most washes away as surface runoff, entering streams, ponds, lakes, and the ocean. This contributes to the accelerated eutrophication of these bodies of water. For example, periodic unexplained blooms of toxic dinoflagellates off the coast of southern Norway have been blamed on excess nutrients, particularly nitrogen, added to the ocean by the **fertilizer runoff** from agricultural fields in southern Sweden and northern Denmark. These algae have caused massive dieoffs of salmon in the mariculture pens popular along the coast, resulting in millions of dollars of damage. Similar circumstances have contributed to blooms of other species of dinoflagellates, creating what are known as **red tide**s. When filter-feeding shellfish ingest these algae, they become toxic, both to other fishes and humans. Paralytic shellfish poisoning may result within thirty minutes, leading to impairment of normal nerve conduction, difficulty in breathing, and possible death. Saxotoxin, the toxin produced by the dinoflagellate *Gonyaulax*, is fifty times more lethal than strychnine and curare.

Other forms of human intrusion into the nitrogen cycle include harvesting crops, logging, sewage, **animal wastes**, and exhaust from **automobiles** and factories. Harvesting crops and logging remove nitrogen from the system. The other processes are **point sources** of excess nitrogen. Autos and factories produce nitrous oxides (NO_x) such as nitrogen dioxide (NO_2), a major air pollutant. NO_2 contributes to the formation of **smog**, often irritating eyes and leading to breathing difficulty. It also reacts with water vapor in the atmosphere to form weak nitric acid (HNO_3), one of the major components of **acid rain**. *See also* Agricultural pollution; Air pollution; Aquatic weed control; Marine pollution; Nitrogen waste; Soil fertility; Urban runoff

[*John Korstad*]

FURTHER READING

Brill, W. J. "Biological Nitrogen Fixation." *Scientific American* 236 (1977): 68-81.

Delwiche, C. C. "The Nitrogen Cycle." *Scientific American* 223 (1970): 136-46.

Ehrlich, P. R., A. H. Ehrlich, and J. P. Holdren. *Ecoscience: Population, Resources, Environment.* New York: W. H. Freeman, 1977.

Ricklefs, R. E. *Ecology.* 3rd ed. New York: W. H. Freeman, 1990.

Smith, R. E. *Ecology and Field Biology.* 4th ed. New York: Harper and Row, 1990.

Nitrogen oxides

Five oxides of nitrogen are known: N_2O, NO, N_2O_3, NO_2, and N_2O_5. Environmental scientists usually refer to only two of these, nitric oxide and nitrogen dioxide, when they use the term nitrogen oxides. The term may also be used, however, for any other combination of the five compounds. Nitric oxide and nitrogen dioxide are produced during the **combustion** of **fossil fuels** in **automobiles**, jet aircraft, industrial processes, and electrical power production. The gases have a number of deleterious effects on human health, including irritation of the eyes, skin, respiratory tract, and lungs; chronic and acute bronchitis; and heart and lung damage. *See also* Ozone; Smog

Nitrogen scrubbing
See **Raprenox**

Nitrogen waste

Nitrogen waste is a component of sewage that comes primarily from human excreta and **detergents** but also from **fertilizer**s and such industrial processes as steel-making. Nitrogen waste consists primarily of **nitrates and nitrites** as well as compounds of ammonia. Because they tend to clog waterways and encourage algae growth, nitrogen wastes are undesirable. They present a problem for **wastewater** treatment since they are not removed by either primary or secondary treatment steps. Their removal at the tertiary stage can be achieved only by specialized procedures. Another approach is to use wastewater on farmlands. This use removes about 50 percent of nitrogen wastes from water by turning it into **nutrient**s for the **soil**. *See also* Sewage treatment

Nitrous oxide

Nitrous oxide (N_2O), also called di-nitrogen monoxide, is one of several gaseous oxides of **nitrogen**. It is sometimes referred to as laughing gas, because when inhaled it causes a feeling of intoxication, mild hysteria, and sometimes laughter. The gas is colorless and has a faint odor and slightly sweet taste. It can lessen the sensation of pain and is used as an anesthetic in dentistry and in minor surgery of short duration. For more complex surgery, it is combined with other anesthetics to produce a deeper and longer-lasting state of anesthesia. Nitrous oxide also is commonly used as a **propellant** for pressurized food products, and sometimes is used in race cars to boost the power of high performance engines. It is one of the few gases capable of supporting combustion. In this process, it transfers its oxygen to the material being combusted and is converted to molecular nitrogen (N_2).

Nitrous oxide is an important component of the Earth's upper **atmosphere** at heights above 30 mi (45 km). It is one of the **greenhouse gases**, together with **carbon dioxide**, **methane**, and **ozone**, that allow radiation from the Sun to reach the Earth's surface but prevent the infrared or heat component of sunlight from re-irradiating into space. This leads to the so-called **greenhouse effect**, and results in warmer temperatures at the Earth's surface. Greenhouse warming is important in creating surface temperatures suitable for life, but recent studies have shown that the levels of some greenhouse gases are increasing at rates that are a cause for concern. Human-made gases, such as **chlorofluorocarbons**, are also contributing to the greenhouse effect. An increase in the Earth's ability to trap infrared radiation can be expected to result in global **climate** change with wide-ranging consequences.

Concern over greenhouse gases has centered on reports of increasing concentrations of atmospheric carbon dioxide (CO_2). Two factors thought to be responsible are the widespread use of **fossil fuels** (which add CO_2 to the atmosphere) and the rapid destruction of tropical **rain forest**s which remove CO_2). The levels of other greenhouse gases may also be changing. Studies indicate that atmospheric levels of nitrous oxide may also be increasing as a result of human activity. Nitrous oxide is produced in nature by microorganisms acting on nitrogen-containing compounds in the soil. Increased use of nitrogen **fertilizer** in lawns, gardens, and agricultural fields may stimulate microbial production of nitrous oxide. Manure and municipal sludge, applied as **soil** enhancers and fertilizers, and burning fossil fuels also may contribute to an increase.

Nitrous oxide production in soils is greatly influenced by soil temperature, moisture level, organic content, soil type, pH, and oxygen availability. In agricultural soil, rates of fertilizer application, fertilizer type, tillage practices, crop type, and irrigation all influence nitrous oxide production. High soil temperature, moisture, and organic content tend to enhance production, whereas tilling of the soil tends to lower it. The relative importance of each of these factors has not been determined, and further study is needed to develop recommendations to limit harmful nitrous oxide emissions from soils.

[*Douglas C. Pratt*]

FURTHER READING

Inventory 1990. St. Paul, MN: Minnesota Pollution Control Agency, 1995.

Minnesota Pollution Control Agency, Air Quality Division. *Minnesota Greenhouse Gas*

Smith, S.C. "N_2O Laughing Gas: Has the NHRA Been Looking the Other Way after Allegations That Pro Stock Champions Got There with the Help of Nitrous Oxide?" *Car and Driver* 41, no. B (February 1996): 105.

Umarov, M. "Biotic Sources of Nitrous Oxide (N_2O) in the Context of Global Budgets of Nitrous Oxide," *Soils and the Greenhouse Effect*, A. Bowman, ed. Chicester, U.K.: John Wiley and Sons, 1990.

U.S. Department of Energy. *Emissions of Greenhouse Gases in the United States, 1985–1990*. DOE/EIA-0573. Washington, D.C.: GPO, 1993.

U.S. Environmental Protection Agency. *State Workbook: Methodologies for Estimating Greenhouse Gas Emissions*. EPA-230-B-92-002, Washington, D.C.: GPO, 1992.

Noise pollution

Every year since 1973, the U.S. Department of Housing and Urban Development has conducted a survey to find out what city residents dislike about their environment. And every year the same factor has been named most objectionable. It is not crime, **pollution**, or congestion; it is noise—something that affects every one of us every day.

We have known for a long time that prolonged exposure to noises, such as loud music or the roar of machinery, can result in hearing loss. Evidence now suggests that noise-related stress also causes a wide range of psychological and physiological problems ranging from irritability to heart disease. An increasing number of people are affected by noise in their environment. By age forty, nearly everyone in America has suffered hearing deterioration in the higher frequencies. An estimated ten percent of Americans (24 million people) suffer serious hearing loss, and the lives of another 80 million people are significantly disrupted by noise.

What is noise? There are many definitions, some technical and some philosophical. What is music to your ears might be noise to someone else. Simply defined, noise pollution is any unwanted sound or any sound that interferes with hearing, causes stress, or disrupts our lives. Sound is measured either in dynes, watts, or decibels. Note that decibels (db) are logarithmic; that is, a 10 db increase represents a doubling of sound energy.

Noises come from many sources. Traffic is generally the most omnipresent noise in the city. Cars, trucks, and buses create a roar that permeates nearly everywhere. Around airports, jets thunder overhead, stopping conversation, rattling dishes, some times even cracking walls. Jackhammers rattle in the streets; sirens pierce the air; motorcycles, lawn-mowers, snowblowers, and chain saws create an infernal din; and music from radios, TVs, and loudspeakers fills the air everywhere.

We detect sound by means of a set of sensory cells in the inner ear. These cells have tiny projections (called microvilli and kinocilia) on their surface. As sound waves pass through the fluid-filled chamber within which these cells are suspended, the microvilli rub against a flexible membrane lying on top of them. Bending of fibers inside the microvilli sets off a mechanico-chemical process that results in a nerve signal being sent through the auditory nerve to the brain where the signal is analyzed and interpreted.

The sensitivity and discrimination of our hearing is remark able. Normally, humans can hear sounds from about 16 cycles per second (hz) to 20,000 hz. A young child whose hearing has not yet been damaged by excess noise can hear the whine of a mosquito's wings at the window when less than one quadrillionth of a watt per cm² is reaching the eardrum.

The sensory cell's microvilli are flexible and resilient, but only up to a point. They can bend and then spring back up, but they die if they are smashed down too hard or too often. Prolonged exposure to sounds above about 90 decibels can flatten some of the microvilli permanently and their function will be lost. By age thirty, most Americans have lost 5 db of sensitivity and cannot hear anything above 16,000 Hertz (Hz); by age sixty-five, the sensitivity reduction is 40 db for most people, and all sounds above 8,000 Hz are lost. By contrast, in the Sudan, where the **environment** is very quiet, even seventy-year-olds have no significant hearing loss.

Extremely loud sounds—above 130 db, the level of a loud rock band or music heard through earphones at a high setting—actually can rip out the sensory microvilli, causing aberrant nerve signals that the brain interprets as a high-pitched whine or whistle. Many people experience ringing ears after exposure to very loud noises. Coffee, aspirin, certain antibiotics, and fever also can cause ringing sensations, but they usually are temporary.

A persistent ringing is called tinnitus. It has been estimated that 94 percent of the people in the United States suffer some degree of tinnitus. For most people, the ringing is noticeable only in a very quiet environment, and we rarely are in a place that is quiet enough to hear it. About 35 out of 1,000 people have tinnitus severely enough to interfere with their lives. Sometimes the ringing becomes so loud that it is unendurable, like shrieking brakes on a subway train. Unfortunately, there is not yet a treatment for this distressing disorder. One of the first charges to the **Environmental Protection Agency (EPA)** when it was founded in 1970 was to study noise pollution and to recommend ways to reduce the noise in our environment. Standards have since been promulgated for noise reduction in automobiles, trucks, buses, motorcycles, mopeds, refrigeration units, power lawn-mowers, construction equipment, and airplanes. The EPA is considering ordering that warnings be placed on power tools, radios, chain saws, and other household equipment. The **Occupational Safety and Health Administration**

(OSHA) also has set standards for noise in the workplace that have considerably reduced noise-related hearing losses.

Noise is still all around us, however. In many cases, the most dangerous noise is that to which we voluntarily subject ourselves. Perhaps if people understood the dangers of noise and the permanence of hearing loss, we would have a quieter environment.

[*William P. Cunningham*]

FURTHER READING

Bronzaft, A. "Noise Annoys." *E Magazine* 4 (March-April 1993): 16-20.

Chatwal, G. R., ed. *Environmental Noise Pollution and Its Control.* Columbia: South Asia Books, 1989.

Energy and Environment 1990: Transportation-Induced Noise and Air Pollution. Washington, DC: Transportation Research Board, 1990.

OECD Staff. *Fighting Noise in the Nineteen Nineties.* Washington, DC: Organization for Economic Cooperation and Development, 1991.

O'Brien, B. "Quest for Quiet." *Sierra* 77 (July-August 1992): 41-2.

Nonattainment area

Any locality found to be in violation of one or more **National Ambient Air Quality Standard**s set by the **Environmental Protection Agency (EPA)** under the provisions of the **Clean Air Act**. However, a nonattainment area for one standard may be an **attainment area** for a different standard. The seven **criteria pollutant**s for which standards were established in 1970 under the Clean Air Act are **carbon monoxide**, **lead**, **nitrogen** dioxide, **ozone** (a key ingredient in **smog**), **particulate** matter, **sulfur dioxide**, and **hydrocarbons**. Violation of National Ambient Air Quality Standards for one of the seven criteria pollutants can have a variety of consequences for an area, including restrictions on permits for new stationary sources of **pollution** (or significant modifications to existing ones), mandatory institution of vehicle **emission**s inspection programs, or loss of federal funding (including funding unrelated to pollution problems). *See also* Automobile emissions

Noncriteria pollutant

Pollutants for which specific standards or criteria have not been established. Although some air pollutants are known to be toxic or hazardous, they are released in relatively small quantities or in locations where individual regulation is not required. Others are not yet regulated because data is insufficient to set definite criteria for acceptable ambient levels or control methods. Political and economic interests have also blocked regulatory action. The **Clean Air Act** Amendments of 1990 required the **Environmental Protection Agency (EPA)** to establish **emission standards** for some 189 toxic air pollutants and 250 source categories, thus changing many noncriteria pollutants to criteria ones. *See also* Criteria pollutant

Nondegradable pollutant

A pollutant that is not broken down by natural processes. Some nondegradable pollutants, like the **heavy metals**, create problems because they are toxic and persistent in the **environment**. Others, like synthetic **plastics**, are a problem because of their sheer volume. One way of dealing with nondegradable pollutants is to reduce the quantity released into the environment either by **recycling** them for reuse before they are disposed of, or by curtailing their production. A second method is to find ways of making them degradable. Scientists have been able to develop new types of bacteria, for example, that do not exist in **nature**, but that will degrade plastics. *See also* Decomposition; Pollution

Nongame wildlife

Terrestrial and semi-aquatic vertebrates not normally hunted for sport. The majority of wild vertebrates are contained in this group. In the United States **wildlife** agencies are funded largely by hunting license fees and by excise taxes on arms and ammunition used for hunting, and they have had to develop other revenue sources for nongame wildlife. The most common method is the state income-tax checkoff, by which citizens may donate portions of their tax returns to nongame wildlife programs. A limited amount of federal aid for such programs has recently been made available to state wildlife agencies through the Nongame Wildlife Act of 1980. *See also* Game animal

Nongovernmental organization (NGO)

A nongovernmental organization is any group outside of government whose purpose is the protection of the **environment**. The term encompasses a broad range of indigenous groups, private charities, advisory committees, and professional organizations; it includes mainstream environmental groups such as the **Sierra Club** and **Defenders of Wildlife**, and more radical groups such as **Greenpeace** and **Earth First!**

In the United States, NGOs have played a pivotal role in the creation of **environmental policy**, directing lobbying efforts and mobilizing the kind of popular support which have made such changes possible. They have been involved in the protection of many **endangered species** and threatened **habitat**s, including the **northern spotted owl** and the **old-growth forest**s in the Pacific Northwest. Organizations such as **Earthwatch**, **Earth Island Institute**, and **Sea Shepherd Conservation Society** raised international awareness about the environmental dangers of using **drift nets** in the **commercial fishing** industry. Their campaign

included drift-net monitoring, public education, and direct action, and their efforts led to an international ban on this method. NGOs are extensively involved in the current debate about the future of environmental protection and issues such as **sustainable development** and **zero population growth**.

The number of NGOs worldwide is estimated at over 12,000. They have grown rapidly in number and influence during the last 20 years. In 1972, NGOs had little representation at the **United Nations Conference on the Human Environment** in Stockholm, which was called by industrialized nations primarily to discuss **air pollution**. But these groups had become a much more significant international presence by 1992, and over 9,000 NGOs sent delegates to the Earth Summit in Rio de Janeiro, Brazil. The political pressure NGOs were able to bring to bear had an important, if indirect, effect on the long and complicated preparations for the summit. During the summit itself, NGOs organized a "shadow assembly" or Global Forum in a park near Guanabara Bay, where they monitored official negotiations and held conferences of their own. *See also* Animal rights; Bioregionalism; Environmental education; Environmental ethics; Environmental monitoring; Environmentalism; Green politics; Greens; United Nations Earth Summit

[*Douglas Smith*]

Nonpoint source

A diffuse, scattered source of **pollution**. Nonpoint sources have no fixed location where they discharge pollutants into the air or water as do chimneys, outfall pipes, or other **point source**s. Nonpoint sources include runoff from agricultural fields, **feedlots**, lawns, golf courses, construction sites, streets, and parking lots, as well as emissions from quarrying operations, forest fires, and the evaporation of volatile substances from small businesses such as dry cleaners. Unlike pollutants discharged by **point source**s, nonpoint pollution is difficult to monitor, regulate, and control. Also, it frequently occurs episodically rather than predictably. Where treatment plants have been installed to control discharge from point sources, nonpoint sources can be responsible for most of the pollution found in bodies of water. As much as 90 percent of the pollution load in a body of water may come from nonpoint sources. *See also* Water pollution

Nonrenewable resources

Any naturally occurring, finite resources that diminish with use, such as oil and **coal**. In terms of the human timescale, a nonrenewable resource cannot be renewed once it has been consumed. Most nonrenewable resources can only be renewed over geologic time, if at all. All the **fossil fuels** and mineral resources fall into this category. **Renewable resources** occur naturally and cannot be used up, such as

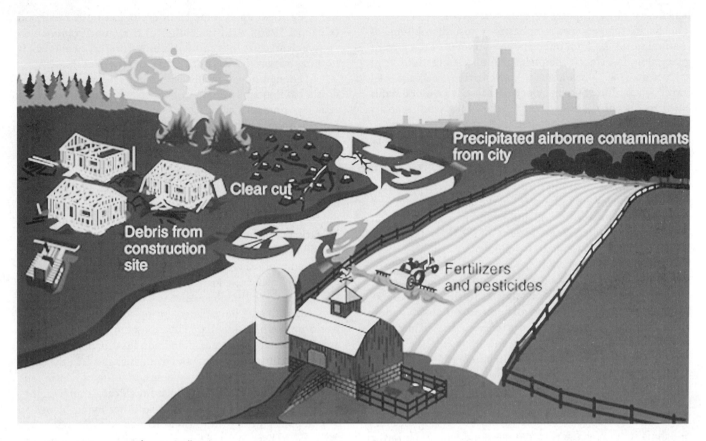

Nonpoint sources of water pollution.

solar energy or **wave power**. As resource depletion has become more common, the process of **recycling** has somewhat reduced reliance on virgin nonrenewable resources.

Non-Western environmental ethics

Ordinary people are powerfully motivated to do things that can be justified in terms of their religious beliefs. Therefore, distilling environmental ethics from the world's living religions is extremely important for global **conservation**. Christianity is a world religion, but so are Islam and Buddhism. Other major religious traditions, such as Hinduism and Confucianism, while more regionally restricted, nevertheless claim millions of devotees. The well-documented effort of Jewish and Christian conservationists to formulate the Judeo-Christian Stewardship Environmental Ethic in biblical terms suggests an important new line of inquiry: How can effective conservation ethics be formulated in terms of other sacred texts? In *Earth's Insights: A Multicultural Survey of Ecological Wisdom*, a comprehensive survey is offered, but to provide even a synopsis of that study would be impossible in this entry. However, a few abstracts of traditional non-Western conservation ethics may be suggestive.

Muslims believe that Islam was founded in the seventh century A.D., by Allah (God) communicating to humanity through the Arabian prophet, Mohammed, who regarded himself to be in the same prophetic tradition as Moses and Jesus. Therefore, since the Hebrew Bible and the New Testament are earlier divine revelations underlying distinctly Muslim belief, the basic Islamic worldview has much in common with the basic Judeo-Christian worldview. In particular, Islam teaches that human beings have a privileged place in **nature**, and, going further in this regard than Judaism and Christianity, that indeed, all other natural beings were created to serve humanity. Hence, there has been a strong tendency among Muslims to take a purely instrumental approach to the human-nature relationship. As to the conservation of **biodiversity**, the Arabian oryx was hunted nearly to extinction by oil-rich sheikhs armed with military assault rifles in the cradle of Islam. But callous indifference to the rest of creation in the Islamic world is no longer sanctioned religiously.

Islam does not distinguish between religious and secular law. Hence, new conservation regulations in Islamic states must be grounded in the Koran, Mohammed's book of divine revelations. In the early 1980s, a group of Saudi scholars scoured the Koran for environmentally relevant passages and drafted *The Islamic Principles for the Conservation of the Natural Environment*. While reaffirming "a relationship of utilization, development, and subjugation for man's benefit and the fulfillment of his interests," this landmark document also clearly articulates an Islamic version of stewardship: "he [man] is only a manager of the earth and not a proprietor, a beneficiary not a disposer or ordainer: (Kadr, et al, 1983). The Saudi scholars also emphasize a just distribution of "natural resources," not only among members of the present generation, but among members of future generations. And as Norton (1991) has argued, conservation goals are well served when future human beings are accorded a moral status equal to that of those currently living. The Saudi scholars have found passages in the Koran that are vaguely ecological. For example, God "produced therein all kinds of things in due balance" (Kadr, et al, 1983).

Ralph Waldo Emerson and **Henry David Thoreau**, thinkers at the fountainhead of North American conservation philosophy, were influenced by the subtle philosophical doctrines of Hinduism, a major religion in India. Hindu thought also inspired **Arne Naess**'s (1989) contemporary "Deep Ecology" conservation philosophy. Hindus believe that at the core of all phenomena there is only one Reality or Being. God, in other words, is not a supreme Being among other lesser and subordinate beings, as in the Judeo-Christian-Islamic tradition. Rather, all beings are a manifestation of the one essential Being, called *Brahman*. And all plurality, all difference, is illusory or at best only apparent.

Such a view would not seem to be a promising point of departure for the conservation of biological diversity, since the actual existence of diversity, biological or otherwise, seems to be denied. Yet in the Hindu concept of *Brahman*, Naess (1989) finds an analogue to the way ecological relationships unite organisms into a systemic whole. However that may be, Hinduism, unambiguously invites human beings to identify with other forms of life, for all life-forms share the same essence. Believing that one's own inner self, *atman*, is identical, as an expression of *Brahman*, with the selves of all other creatures leads to compassion for them. The suffering of one life-form is the suffering of all others; to harm other beings is to harm oneself. As a matter of fact, this way of thinking has inspired and helped motivate one of the most persistent and successful conservation movements in the world, the Chipko movement, which has managed to rescue many of India's Himalayan forests from commercial exploitation (Guha 1989b; Shiva 1989).

Jainism is a religion with a relatively few adherents, but a religion of great influence in India. Jains believe that every living thing is inhabited by an immaterial soul, no less pure and immortal than the human soul. Bad deeds in past lives, however, have crusted these souls over with *karma*-matter. *Ahimsa* (noninjury of all living things) and asceticism (eschewing all forms of physical pleasure) are parallel paths that will eventually free the soul from future rebirth in the material realm. Hence, Jains take great care to avoid harming other forms of life and to resist the fleeting pleasure of material consumption. Extreme practitioners refuse to eat any but leftover food prepared for others, and carefully strain their water to avoid ingesting any waterborne organisms—not for the sake of their own health, but to avoid inadvertently killing other living beings. Less extreme practitioners are strict vegetarians and own few material possessions. The Jains are bidding for global leadership in environmental ethics. Their low-on-the-**food-chain** and low-level-of-consumption

lifestyle is held up as a model of ecological right livelihood (Chappel 1986). And the author of the *Jain Declaration on Nature* claims that the central Jain moral precept of ahimsa "is nothing but **environmentalism**" (Singhvi, n.d.).

Though now virtually extinct in its native India, Buddhism has flourished for many hundreds of years elsewhere in Asia. Its founder, Siddhartha Gautama, first followed the path of meditation to experience the oneness of Atman-Brahman, and then the path of extreme asceticism in order to free his soul from his body—all to little effect. Then he realized that his frustration, including his spiritual frustration, was the result of desire. Not by obtaining what one desires—which only leads one to desire something more—but by stilling desire itself can one achieve enlightenment and liberation. Further, desire distorts one's perceptions, exaggerating the importance of some things and diminishing the importance of others. When one overcomes desire, one can appreciate each thing for what it is.

When the Buddha realized all this, he was filled with a sense of joy, and he radiated loving-kindness toward the world around him. He shared his enlightenment with others, and formulated a code of moral conduct for his followers. Many Buddhists believe that all living beings are in the same predicament: we are driven by desire to a life of continuous frustration. And all can be liberated if all can attain enlightenment. Thus Buddhists can regard other living beings as companions on the path to Buddhahood and *nirvana*.

Buddhists, no less than Jains and Christians, are assuming a leadership role in the global conservation movement. Perhaps most notably, the Dalai Lama of Tibet is the foremost conservationist among world religious leaders. In 1985, the Buddhist Perception of Nature Project was launched to extract and collate the many environmentally relevant passages from Buddhist scriptures and secondary literature. Thus, the relevance of Buddhism to contemporary conservation concerns could be demonstrated and the level of conservation consciousness and conscience in Buddhist monasteries, schools, colleges, and other institutions could be raised (Davies 1987). Bodhi (1987) provides a succinct summary of Buddhist environmental ethics: "With its philosophic insight into the interconnectedness and thoroughgoing interdependence of all conditioned things, with its thesis that happiness is to be found through the restraint of desire, with its goal of enlightenment through renunciation and contemplation and its ethic on non-injury and boundless loving-kindness for all beings, Buddhism provides all the essential elements for a relationship to the natural world characterized by respect, care, and compassion."

One-fourth of the world's population is Chinese. Fortunately, traditional Chinese thought provides excellent conceptual resources for a conservation ethic. The Chinese word *tao* means way or road. The Taoists believe that there is a *Tao*, a Way, of **Nature**. That is, natural processes occur not only in an orderly but also in a harmonious fashion. Human beings can discern the *Tao*, the natural well-orchestrated flow of things. And human activities can either be well adapted to the tao, or they can oppose it. In the former case, human goals are accomplished with ease and grace and without disturbing the natural environment; but in the latter, they are accomplished, if at all, with difficulty and at the price of considerable disruption of neighboring social and natural systems. Capital-intensive Western technology, such as nuclear power plants and industrial agricultural, is very "unTaoist" in esprit and motif.

Modern conservationists find in Taoism an ancient analogue of today's countermovement toward appropriate technology and **sustainable development**. The great Mississippi Valley flood of 1993 is a case in point. The river system was not managed in accordance with the *Tao*. Thus, levees and flood walls only exacerbated the big flood when it finally came. Better to have located cities and towns outside the flood plain and allowed the mighty Mississippi River occasionally to overflow. The rich alluvial soils in the river's floodplains could be farmed in dryer year, but no permanent structures should be located there. That way, the floodwaters could periodically spread over the land, enriching the soil and replenishing **wetlands** for **wildlife**, and the human dwellings on higher ground could remain safe and secure. Perhaps the officers of the **U.S. Army Corps of Engineers** should study Taoism. We can hope that their counterparts in China will abandon newfangled Maoism for old-fashioned Taoism before going ahead with their plans to contain, rather than cooperate with, the Yangtze River.

The other ancient Chinese religious worldview is Confucianism. To most people, Asian and Western alike, Confucianism connotes conservativism, adherence to rigid customs and social forms, filial piety, and resignation to feudal inequality. Hence, it seems to hold little promise as an intellectual soil in which to cultivate a conservation ethic. Ames (1992), however, contradicts the received view: "There is a common ground shared by the teachings of classical Confucianism and Taoism...Both express a 'this-worldly' concern for the concrete details of immediate experience rather than...grand abstractions and ideals. Both acknowledge the uniqueness, importance, and primacy of particular persons and their contributions to the world, while at the same time expressing the ecological interrelatedness and interdependence of this person with his context."

From a Confucian point of view, a person is not a separate immortal soul temporarily residing in a physical body; a person is, rather, the unique center of a network of relationships. Since his or her identity is constituted by these relationships, the destruction of one's social and environmental context is equivalent to self-destruction. Biocide, in other words, is tantamount to suicide.

In the West, since individuals are not ordinarily conceived to be robustly related to and dependent upon their context—not only for their existence but for their very identity—then it is possible to imagine that they can remain themselves and be "better off" at the expense of both their social and natural environments. But from a Confucian point of view, it is expanded from its classic social to its current environmental connotation, Confucianism offers a very firm foundation upon which to build a contemporary Chinese conservation ethic.

[*J. Baird Callicott*]

FURTHER READING

Ames, R.T. "Taoist ethics" in L. Becker, ed., *Encyclopedia of Ethics*. New York: Garland Press, 1992.

Bodhi, B. "Foreword," in *Buddhist Perspectives on the Ecocrisis*. Kandy, Sri Lanka: Buddhist Publication Society.

Callicott, J.B. *Earth's Insights: A Multicultural Survey of Ecological Wisdom*. Berkeley, CA: University of California Press, 1994.

Chappel, C. "Contemporary Jaina and Hindu Responses to the Ecological Crisis." Paper presented at the 1990 meeting of the College Theological Society, Loyola University, New Orleans, 1990.

Davies, S. *Tree of Life: Buddhism and Protection of Nature*. Hong Kong: Buddhist Perception of Nature Project, 1987.

Kadr, A., et al. *Islamic Principles for the Conservation of the Natural Environment*. Gland, Switzerland: International Union for the Conservation of Nature and Natural Resources, 1983.

Naess, A. *Ecology, Community, and Lifestyle*. Cambridge, MA: Cambridge University Press, 1989.

Norton, B.G. *Toward Unity among Environmentalists*. New York: Oxford University Press, 1991.

Shiva, V. *Staying Alive: Women, Ecology, and Development*. London: Zed Books, 1989.

No-observable-adverse-effect-level (NOAEL)

The NOAEL is the lowest "dose" or exposure level to a non-**cancer**-causing chemical at which no increase in adverse effects is seen in test animals compared with animals in a control group. First, a NOAEL is determined. For instance, it is established that no adverse effects are seen in test animals after they have been exposed to a set amount, such as an ounce per day for a year, whereas a higher exposure causes adverse effects. Then this level is divided by one or more uncertainty factors to establish an acceptable human exposure level. Regulatory agencies typically use a factor of 10, 100, or 1,000 to account for the uncertainty arising from the fact that the NOAEL is based on an animal study but is being extrapolated to set a "safe" level of exposure for human beings.

North

Often the term "North" refers to the countries located in the northern hemisphere of the globe. Scholars who are concerned with worldwide problems such as global **climate** change, sometimes tend to think of the planet as consisting of two halves, the North and the South. The North, or northern hemisphere, is a region where only about one-fifth of the Earth's population lives, but where four-fifths of its goods and services are consumed. Environmental issues of interest to the North are those related to high technology, high consumption, and high energy use. These are areas of relatively less concern to those who live in the South. Although the North/South dichotomy may be simplistic, it highlights differences in the way peoples of various nation view global environmental problems.

North American Association for Environmental Education (Troy, Ohio)

The North American Association for Environmental Education, founded in 1971, is a nonprofit network for professionals and students working in the field of **environmental education**. It claims to be the world's largest association of environmental educators, with members in the United States and more than 55 countries. The organization's stated mission is to "go beyond consciousness-raising about these issues. [It] must prepare people to think together about the difficult decisions they have to make concerning environmental stewardship, and to work together to improve and try to solve environmental problems." It advocates a cooperative and nonconfrontational approach to environmental education.

NAAEE conducts an annual conference and produces publications, including a member newsletter, the *Environmental Communicator*, and a *Directory of Environmental Educators*. It also operates a Skills Bank and numerous programs. Several of these programs focus on community-based activities. The VINE (Volunteer-led Investigations of Neighborhood Ecology) Network promotes programs using volunteers to lead children in explorations of the **ecology** of their urban neighborhoods. The Urban Leadership Collaboratives Program aims to develop collaborative environmental education programs in cities. The Environmental Issues Forums (EIF) Program assists students and adults in working with controversial environmental issues in their communities and nationally.

Other NAAEE programs have a wider focus. The NAAEE Training and Professional Development Institute offers workshops and training events on such topics as fundraising and long-range planning, as well as courses for educators from developing countries in cooperation with United States Assistance for International Development (USAID) and the Smithsonian Institute. The Environmental Education and Training Partnership (EETAP), under a U.S. **Environmental Protection Agency** grant, coordinates a consortium of 18 environmental education organizations that promote training. The NAAEE Policy Institute aims to develop standards for environmental education. Additional NAAEE activities include writing reports to the United States Congress on environmental education issues, reviewing proposals submitted for funding under the National Environmental Education Act of 1990, and testifying to support environmental education legislation and innovative programs. Internationally, the organization has helped to establish environmental education centers in Moscow and Kiev and a program in Thailand, and has assisted with developing educational materials in Sri Lanka.

NAAEE maintains four member sections that represent different contexts of environmental education and conduct individual activities: Conservation Education Section, Elementary and Secondary Education Section, Environmental Studies Section, and Nonformal Section (for members working outside of formal school settings).

In 1996, the Conservation Education Association was incorporated into NAAEE. Contact: NAAEE, P.O. Box 400, Troy, OH 45373. Website: www.nceet.snve.umich.edu/naaee.html.

[*Carol Steinfeld*]

North American Free Trade Agreement (NAFTA)

The North American Free Trade Agreement (NAFTA) is an international trade agreement among the United States, Canada, and Mexico, which became effective on January 1, 1994. Pursuant to NAFTA most tariffs among the three countries are being phased out over a period of fifteen years. In addition, the agreement liberalizes rules regulating investment by United States and Canadian firms in Mexico. NAFTA includes side agreements on environment, labor, and dealing with import surges. Controversy surrounding the adoption of NAFTA by the United States in 1993 included issues related to trade, employment, immigration, labor law, and environmental protection. And, several years after its effective date, observers continue to debate the wisdom of the agreement.

While NAFTA's adoption was being debated, environmentalists were divided in response to whether or not we are environmentally better off with NAFTA. Thus, its adoption was opposed by some environmental groups and supported by others. Major groups opposing it included the **Sierra Club**, **Greenpeace**, the **United States Public Interest Research Group** (U.S. PIRG), Citizen's Action, Public Citizen: the Clean Water Fund, and the Student Environmental Action Coalition. However, it was supported by a coalition of major environmental organizations including the **National Wildlife Federation**, the **World Wildlife Fund**, the **National Audubon Society**, the Environmental Defense Council, the **Natural Resources Defense Council**, **Conservation International**, and **Defenders of Wildlife**, and the **Nature Conservancy**. Such division among environmentalists with respect to NAFTA and its consequences for the **environment** continues through the present day.

NAFTA's Provisions

NAFTA is first and overall a trade agreement. Thus, the majority of the provisions within its over 1,200 pages focus on elimination of barriers to trade. Over a period of fifteen years, beginning on January 1, 1994, tariffs on over 9,000 products traded among the United States, Mexico, and Canada are being phased out. In addition, other "non-tariff" barriers to trade are being eased or eliminated.

Elimination of Tariffs

Tariffs on approximately 4,500 products traded among the NAFTA parties were eliminated on January 1, 1994, and by 1999 tariffs will remain on only about 3,000 products. The remainder will be phased out by the year 2009.

The period during which tariffs are phased out gives producers time to adjust gradually to competition from products of other NAFTA countries. Those products for which tariffs are being phased out gradually are labeled "sensitive products" and include many farm commodities. For example, to protect Mexican producers, corn and dry beans are being protected through a "phase out" period for tariffs. U.S. producers are being protected with respect to sugar, asparagus, orange juice concentrate, and melons.

The automobile industry is another area for which NAFTA includes special provisions. NAFTA sets out formulas requiring a certain minimum percentage of content from North America (the three NAFTA parties) for an automobile to qualify for duty-free treatment. By 2002, automobiles must contain 62.5% North American content to qualify for such treatment.

The fact that Mexico agreed to abolish tariffs in certain sectors of the economy is important to U.S. investors. For example, telecommunications in Mexico are underdeveloped, and that country has a poor quality telephone system. By 1998, Mexico will have phased out all tariffs on telecommunications service and equipment.

Removal of Non-Tariff Barriers to Trade

NAFTA removes certain barriers to trade which are not in the form of tariffs. For example, NAFTA allows financial service providers of a NAFTA country to establish banking, insurance, securities operations, and other types of financial services in another NAFTA country. NAFTA also provides U.S. and Canadian firms with greater access to Mexico's energy markets. Under NAFTA, U.S. and Canadian firms can sell products to PEMEX, Mexico's federally owned **petroleum** company. In addition, Mexico has opened operation of self-generation, cogeneration, and independent power plants in Mexico to investment by U.S. or Canadian firms.

Transportation is being facilitated, also. Since 1995, U.S., Mexican, and Canadian firms have been allowed to establish cross-border routes.

NAFTA does not create a common market for movement of labor, but it does provide for temporary entry of business people from one NAFTA country into another. The four different categories for such movement of workers include business visitors in marketing, sales and related activities, traders and investors, specified kinds of intracompany transfers, and specified professionals meeting educational or special knowledge requirements.

Dispute Resolution

Administration of NAFTA is handled by a Commission of cabinet-level officers each of whom has been appointed by one of the NAFTA countries. The Commission includes a Secretary, who is the chief administrator.

The process for resolution of disputes under NAFTA is cumbersome and time-consuming. When a dispute arises with respect to a NAFTA country's rights under the agreement, a consultation can be requested. If the consultation does not resolve the dispute, the Commission will seek to resolve the dispute through alternative dispute resolution procedures. If those are unsuccessful, the complaining country can request the establishment of a five member arbitration panel which will recommend solutions, monitor results, and, if necessary, impose sanctions.

NAFTA's Side Agreements

In areas involving labor law and environmental protection, NAFTA's provisions are limited.

Labor Side Agreement

The North American Agreement on Labor Cooperation, also known as the "Side Agreement on Labor" or "Labor Side Agreement," was negotiated in response to concerns that NAFTA itself did little to protect workers in Mexico, the U.S., and Canada. In the Labor Side Agreement, the three countries articulate their desire to improve labor conditions and encourage compliance with labor laws. Each party agrees to enforce its own labor laws, but new laws protecting workers are not established. The Agreement establishes a multiple step process for dealing with instances in which a NAFTA country has exhibited a "consistent pattern of ... failure to effectively enforce its own occupational safety and health, child labor, or minimum wage labor standards." If the three NAFTA parties cannot agree to a resolution, then a committee of experts can be convened to assist in resolving the dispute.

Environmental Side Agreement

The North American Agreement on Environmental Cooperation, also known as the "Environmental Side Agreement," was adopted along with the Labor Side Agreement and was negotiated in response to concerns that the body of NAFTA did little to protect the environment. In the Environmental Side Agreement, the three parties articulate their desire to promote environmental concerns without harming the economy, and promote open public discussion of environmental issues. As in the Labor Side Agreement with respect to labor laws, each party agrees to enforce its own environmental laws, but no new environmental laws are made. The agreement establishes a Commission for Environmental Cooperation that includes a Secretariat and a Council, which is charged with implementing the side agreement.

The Environmental Side Agreement allows a **nongovernmental organization** (such as an environmental group) or a private citizen to file a complaint with the Commission asserting that a NAFTA country "has shown a persistent pattern of failure to effectively enforce its environmental laws." Thus, such groups and individuals can serve as watchdogs for the Commission.

The Environmental Side Agreement allows a NAFTA country to request a consultation with a second NAFTA country regarding that second country's persistent pattern of failure to enforce its environmental laws. If a resolution is not reached as a result of the consultation, a party can request that the Council meet. If the Council is unable to resolve the dispute, it can convene an arbitration panel, which will study the dispute and issue a report. After the parties submit comments, the report is made final. The parties are given an opportunity to reach their own action plan, but, if there is no such agreement, the panel can be reconvened to establish a plan. If an imposed fine is not paid, as under the Labor Side Agreement, NAFTA benefits can be suspended.

Environmental Consequences of NAFTA

Environmentalists share many concerns with respect to NAFTA, three of which will be introduced here. First, environmentalists fear NAFTA represents a threat to U.S. sovereignty because U.S. environmental laws may be challenged under NAFTA. For example, it is feared that the U.S. will not be allowed to refuse entry of goods produced in Mexico even if those goods are produced using production methods that do not meet U.S. environmental, health, or food safety standards. This is based on U.S. experience under the General Agreement on Tariffs and Trade (GATT) when a GATT panel declared that a U.S. embargo on Mexican tuna caught using methods violating the U.S. **Marine Mammal Protection Act** was illegal. The GATT panel held that products must be treated equally regardless of how they are produced.

Second, environmentalists label Mexico as a "**pollution** haven" for U.S. businesses seeking less-stringent enforcement of environmental laws than that which occurs in the United States. Concerns about environmental degradation in Mexico due to increased industrialization do seem to be valid. Environmentalists, business leaders, and government officials from the three NAFTA countries agree that environmental contamination had reached serious proportions in northern Mexico in the decades preceding the 1994 effective date of NAFTA. Such contamination continues to spread as Mexico becomes more heavily industrialized under NAFTA.

On paper, Mexico has environmental laws which parallel many, but not all, of the federal environmental laws of the United States. Mexico's 1988 Código Ecológico, known in English as the "General Ecology Law," is a comprehensive statute addressing pollution, resource conservation, and environmental enforcement. Often, however, Mexico's environmental laws are not enforced. This lack of enforcement can be attributed to a variety of reasons. For one thing, the statutes are relatively new, dating only from 1988, and regulations have not been made to supplement the laws. Also, Mexico is a country in which people distrust the legal system and where there are widespread violations of law in various areas (not limited to environmental laws.) Noncompliance with law is accepted and expected in many areas in Mexico. As a developing country which states that it is striving to implement open, democratic systems of government, this is a significant hurdle to be overcome throughout Mexican society.

Third, Mexico is a debt-ridden country which continues to struggle with periodic financial crises. Thus, even if Mexico's leaders were convinced that there should be vigorous enforcement of environmental laws and regulations, Mexico lacks money for such enforcement. In connection with its lack of capital, Mexico lacks technology and it lacks

infrastructure such as water treatment plants, sewage systems, and waste disposal facilities. For example, as of mid-1997, in the entire country of Mexico, there was only one facility licensed for disposal of hazardous wastes. Lacking a place to dispose of toxics and knowing the low probability of being cited by government officials for violations, most companies and individuals continue to dump hazardous wastes into Mexico's waters and air and onto its land. Mexico's citizens do not want to live with the contamination any more than we do in the U.S. However, they feel that they are less empowered to "do something about it" than we are as U.S. citizens.

Looking Ahead

NAFTA represents a significant turning point in international law, because it recognizes explicitly that trade policy and environmental policy are inextricably linked. Through its Environmental Side Agreement, it establishes mechanisms for dealing with citizens' concerns and for dealing with that party or country that systematically fails to enforce its own environmental laws. However, NAFTA's environmental provisions provide only a foundation upon which citizens and governments of the U.S., Mexico, and Canada must build if the environment of North America is to be protected from the often detrimental effects of expanded trade.

[Paulette L. Stenzel]

FURTHER READING

Bello, J.H., A.F. Holmer, and J.J. Norton, eds. *NAFTA: a New Frontier in International Trade and Investment in the Americas*, published by American Bar Association Section of International Law & Practice, 1994.

Hufbauer, G.C., and J.J. Schott, *NAFTA: An Assessment.* (rev. ed.). The Institute for International Economics, 1993.

Moran, R.T., and J. Abbott, *NAFTA: Managing the Cultural Differences.* Gulf Publishing Company, 1994.

Stenzel, P.L. "Can NAFTA's Environmental Provisions Promote Sustainable Development?" 59 *Albany Law Review* 59 (1995): 423-480.

North American Water And Power Alliance

Numerous schemes were suggested in the 1960s to accomplish large-scale water transfers between major basins in North America, and one of the best known is the North American Water and Power Alliance (NAWAPA). The plan was devised by the Ralph M. Parson Company of Los Angeles "to divert 36 trillion trillion gallons of water (per year) from the Yukon River in Alaska (through the Great Bear and Great Slave Lakes) southward to 33 states, seven Canadian provinces and northern Mexico."

The proposed NAWAPA system would bring water in immense quantities from western Canada and Alaska through the plains and **desert** states all the way down to the Rio Grande **watershed** and into the Northern Sonora and Chihuahua provinces of Mexico. The Rocky Mountain

Trench, Peace River, Great Slave Lake, Lesser Slave Lake, North Saskatchewan River, Columbia River, Lake Winnipeg, **Hudson River**, James Bay, and numerous tributaries are part of the proposed NAWAPA feeder system designed to channel water from Canada to Mexico.

A second feeder system in the plan would channel large quantities of water into the western portion of Lake Superior. This influx of water would wash the pollutants dumped into the **Great Lakes** out into the Atlantic Ocean. It would also boost the capacity of the area for generating hydroelectricity.

The NAWAPA plan was also designed to develop hydroelectric plants within northern Quebec and Ontario which would produce power that would be diverted to the United States. The **James Bay hydropower project** in Quebec was completed in the early 1970s. It flooded an area 4,250 square miles (11,000 km²), and 90 percent of its power goes directly into the Northeastern United States and Ohio. The James Bay II Project in Ontario will eventually incorporate over eighty **dams**, divert three major rivers, and flood traditional Cree land. The majority of its hydroelectric output will also go to the United States.

Proponents of inter-basin transfers tend to focus on the impending water shortages in the western and southwestern United States. In the Great Plains, the **Ogallala Aquifer** is rapidly being depleted. The Black Mesa **water table** is almost exhausted, due to the excessive quantities of water used in mining operations, and California has been consistently unable to meet the needs of both its industries and its population. Supporters of NAWAPA have long argued that this plan is the only way the nation can solve these problems. On February 22, 1965, *Newsweek* hailed the NAWAPA plan as "the greatest, the most colossal, stupendous, supersplendificent public works project in history."

NAWAPA was described as "a monstrous concept—a diabolical thesis" by a former chairperson of the **International Joint Commission**. Much of the opposition to the plan in the 1960s was nationalist rather than environmental in character: The plans were viewed as an attempt to appropriate Canadian resources. Today, many people are asking whether it is necessary or even right to re-engineer hydrologically the **ecosystem**s of North America in order to meet the water needs of the United States. Environmentalists point out that entire ecosystems in many western states have already been disrupted by various water projects. They argue that it is time to investigate other methods, such as **conservation**, which would bring water consumption to levels sustainable by the watersheds of the plains and deserts. *See also* Alternative energy sources; Aquifer; Drinking-water supply; Irrigation; Pollution control; Water resources; Water table draw-down; Watershed management

[*Debra Glidden*]

FURTHER READING

Canadian Council of Resource Ministers. *Water Diversion Proposals of North America*. Ottawa: Canadian Council of Resource Ministers, 1968.

Higgins, J. "Hydro-Quebec and Native People." *Cultural Survival Quarterly* 11 (1987).

Reisner, M. *Cadillac Desert: The American West and Its Disappearing Water*. New York: Viking Press, 1986.

Royal Society of Canada. *Water Resources of Canada*. Ottawa: Royal Society of Canada, 1968.

Welsh, F. *How to Create a Water Crisis*. Boulder, CO: Johnson Publishing, 1985.

Northern spotted owl (*Strix occidentalis caurina*)

The northern spotted owl (*Strix occidentalis caurina*) is one of the three subspecies of the spotted owl (*Strix occidentalis*). Adults are brown, irregularly spotted with white or light brown spots. The face is round with dark brown eyes and a dull yellow colored bill. They are 16-19 inches (41-48 cm) long and have wing spans of about 42 inches (107 cm). The average weight of a male is 1.2 pounds (544 g), whereas the average female weighs 1.4 pounds (635 g).

This subspecies of the spotted owl is found only in the southwestern portion of British Columbia, western Washington, western Oregon, and the western coastal region of California south to the San Francisco Bay. Occasionally the bird can be found on the eastern slopes of the Cascade Mountains in Washington and Oregon. It is estimated that there are about 4,000-6,000 individuals of this subspecies.

The other two subspecies of spotted owl are the California spotted owl (*S. o. occidentalis*) found in the coastal ranges and western slopes of the Sierra Nevada mountains from Tehama to San Diego counties, and the Mexican spotted owl (*S. o. lucida*) found from northern Arizona, southeastern Utah, southwestern Colorado, south through western Texas to central Mexico.

It is thought that spotted owls mate for life and are monogamous. Breeding does not occur until the birds are two to three years of age. The typical clutch size is two, but sometimes as many as four eggs are laid in March or early April. The incubation period is 28-32 days. The female performs the task of incubating the eggs while the male bird brings food to the newly-hatched young. The owlets leave the nest for the first time around 32-36 days old. Without fully mature wings, the young are not yet able to fly well and must often climb back to the nest using their talons and beak. Juvenile survivorship may be only 11 percent.

Spotted owls hunt by sitting quietly on elevated perches and diving down swiftly on their prey. They forage during the night and spend most of the day roosting. Mammals make up over 90 percent of the spotted owl's diet. The most important prey **species** is the northern flying squirrel (*Glaucomys sabrinus*) which makes up about 50 percent of the owl's diet. Woodrats and hares also are important. In all, 30 species of mammals, 23 species of birds, two reptile species, and even some invertebrates have been found in the diets of spotted owls.

Northern spotted owls live almost exclusively in very old **coniferous forest**s. They are found in virgin stands of Douglas fir, western hemlock, grand fir, red fir, and areas of

Northern spotted owl

redwoods that are at least 200 years old. They favor areas that have an old-growth overstory with layers of second-growth understory beneath. The overstory is the preferred nesting site and the owls tend to build their nests in trees that have broken tops or cavities, or on stick platforms. In one study, 64 percent of the nests were in cavities, and the remainder were on stick platforms or other debris on tree limbs. All of the nests in this study were in conifers, all but two of which were living.

Little is known about what features of a stand are critical for spotted owls. The large trees that have nest sites may be important, particularly those producing a multi-layered canopy in which the owls can find a benign **microclimate**. A thick canopy may be critical in sheltering juvenile owls from avian predators, whereas the understory may be important in providing a cool place for the birds to roost during the warm summer months.

Because of this subspecies' dependence on old-growth coniferous forests and because it feeds at the top **trophic level** in the old-growth forest **food chain/web**, it is considered an "indicator species." Indicator species are used by ecologists to measure the health of the **ecosystem**. If the indicator species is endangered, then it is likely that scores of other species in the ecosystem are just as endangered.

The owls are nonmigratory, with dispersal of young being the only regularly observed movement out of established home ranges. The home range size of spotted owls varies from an average of 4,200 acres (1,700 ha) in Washington to about 2,000 acres (800 ha) in California. In 1987, a team of scientists recommended that in order to be reasonably sure of the species' survival that **habitat** for 1,500 pairs

be set aside. This would necessitate preserving 4-5 million acres (1.5 to 2 million ha) of **old-growth forest**s—most of what remains.

Unfortunately for these owls, old-growth forests are a scarce habitat which is commercially valuable for timber. Because of the demand for old-growth timber these birds have been the center of controversy between timber interests and environmentalists. The declining numbers of owls alarm preservationists who want old-growth forests set aside to protect the owls, while the loggers feel it is in the public's best interest to continue to cut the economically valuable old-growth timber. Timber companies claim that 12,000 jobs will be lost along with about $300 million annually if felling is restricted.

It has been argued that since old-growth forests are being destroyed, these jobs and revenue will be lost eventually anyway. It has also been argued that the U. S. **Forest Service**, which manages most of the remaining old-growth forests, subsidizes the timber industry by building expensive access roads and selling the timber at artificially low prices. Environmentalists suggest that the social costs associated with not cutting old growth could be mitigated by redirecting these monies to retraining programs and income supplements.

In 1990, the northern spotted owl was designated by the U. S. **Fish and Wildlife Service** as a "threatened species." This requires that the owl's habitat be protected from logging. Although the decision to list the spotted owl as "threatened" did not affect existing logging contracts, timber companies are trying to avoid compliance with the decision. Specifically, they are trying to persuade the President and Congress to revise the **Endangered Species Act** to allow consideration of economic impacts or to make a specific exception for some or all of the spotted owl's habitat. Currently, under certain circumstances, economic factors can take precedence over biological criteria in deciding whether it is necessary to comply with habitat protection measures. In these cases a special seven-person interdisciplinary committee can assess the economic impacts of protecting the habitat and circumvent the Endangered Species Act if they believe it is warranted. President Bush's Secretary of Interior Manuel Lujan convened the committee to consider allowing logging in spotted owl habitat on some **Bureau of Land Management** lands.

A team of scientists appointed by the federal government to study the situation recommended that the annual harvest on old-growth forests be reduced by 47 percent. However, President George Bush rejected this recommendation and instead proposed that harvest be reduced by 21 percent. This angered both the environmentalists and the timber industry and the two sides became deadlocked. In the meantime, spotted owl policy is being determined by federal judges rather than biologists. For example, it was a court order that forced the U. S. Fish and Wildlife Service to identify 11.6 million acres (4.7 million ha) as **critical habitat**. In 1991, a federal judge issued an injunction stopping all new timber sales in areas where the spotted owls live on **national forest** land. The judge also mandated that the Forest Service produce a conservation plan and **Environ-**

mental Impact Statement by March 1992. This controversy continued into the presidency of Bill Clinton who convened a Forest Summit in Portland, Oregon on April 2, 1993 to gather information from loggers and environmentalists. Following the summit President Clinton asked his cabinet to devise a balanced solution to the old-growth forest dilemma within 60 days.

Ultimately the fate of the northern spotted owl will be decided in the court rooms and halls of government, where environmentalists and timber interests continue to battle. It is important to realize that the dispute is not merely over one species of owl. The spotted owl is just one of many species dependent on old-growth forests, and may not be in the greatest danger of **extinction**. As an indicator of the prosperity of old-growth ecosystems in the Pacific Northwest, though, its survival means continued health for the entire **biological community**. *See also* American Forestry Association; Deforestation; Earth First!; Environmental economics; Environmental law; Forest and Rangeland Renewable Resources Planning Act (1974); Forest decline; Forest management; Indicator organism; Multiple Use-Sustained Yield Act (1960); National Forest Management Act (1976); Sierra Club; Wildlife management

[*Ted T. Cable*]

FURTHER READING

Casey, C. "The Bird of Contention." *American Forests* 97 (1991): 28-68.

Hunter, M. L., Jr. *Wildlife, Forests, and Forestry*. Englewood Cliffs, NJ: Prentice-Hall, 1990.

Johnsgard, P. A. *North American Owls*. Washington, DC: Smithsonian Institution Press, 1988.

Not In My Backyard
See **NIMBY**

Nuclear accidents
See **Chelyabinsk, Russia; Chernobyl Nuclear Power Station; Radioactive pollution; Three Mile Island Nuclear Reactor; Windscale Advanced Gas Cooled Reactor**

Nuclear fission

When a **neutron** strikes the nucleus of certain **isotope**s, the nucleus breaks apart into two roughly equal parts in a process known as nuclear fission. The two parts into which the

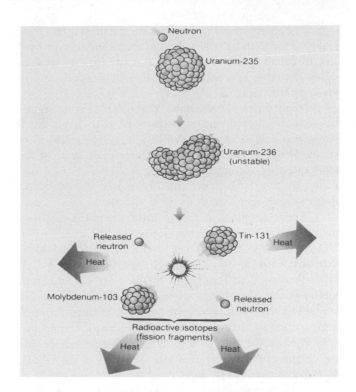

The process of nuclear fission as carried out in the core of a nuclear reactor. A neutron strikes the unstable isotope Uranium-235. This isotope absorbs the neutron and splits or fissions into tin-131 and molybdenum-103. Two or three neutrons are released per fission event and continue the chain reaction. The reaction product has a total mass slightly less than the starting material with the residual mass converted into energy (primarily heat).

nucleus splits are called fission products. In addition to fission products, one or more neutrons is also produced. The fission process also results in the release of large amounts of energy.

The release of neutrons during fission makes possible a **chain reaction**. That is, the particle needed to initiate a fission reaction—the neutron—is also produced as a result of the reaction. Each neutron produced in a fission reaction has the potential for initiating one other fission reaction. Since the average number of neutrons released in any one fission reaction is about 2.3, the rate of fission in a block of material increases rapidly.

A chain reaction will occur in a block of fissionable material as long as neutrons (1) do not escape from the block and (2) are not captured by nonfissionable materials in the block. Two steps in making fission commercially possible, then, are (1) obtaining a block of fissionable material large enough to sustain a chain reaction—the critical size—and (2) increasing the ratio of fissionable to nonfissionable material in the block—enriching the material.

Atomic bombs, developed in the 1940s, obtain all of their energy from fission reactions while hydrogen bombs use fission reactions to trigger **nuclear fusion**. A long-term environmental problem accompanying the use of these weapons is their release of radioactive fission products during detonation.

The energy available from fission reactions is far greater, pound for pound, than can be obtained from the **combustion** of **fossil fuels**. This fact has made fission reactions highly desirable as a source of energy in weapons and in power production.

Many experts in the post-World War II years argued for a massive investment in **nuclear power** plants. Such plants were touted as safe, reliable, nonpolluting sources of energy. When operating properly, they release none of the pollutants that accompany power generation in fossil fuel plants. By the 1970s, more than a hundred nuclear power plants were in operation in the United States.

Then, questions began to arise about the safety of nuclear power plants. These concerns reached a peak when the cooling water system failed at the **Three Mile Island Nuclear Reactor** at Harrisburg, Pennsylvania, in March 1979. That accident resulted in at least a temporary halt in nuclear power plant construction in the United States. No new plants have been authorized since that time. A much more serious accident occurred at **Chernobyl**, Ukraine, in 1986 when one of four reactors on the site exploded, spreading a cloud of radioactive material over parts of the USSR, Poland, and northern Europe.

Perhaps the most serious environmental concern about fission reactions relates to fission products. The longer a fission reaction continues, the more fission products accumulate. These fission products are all radioactive, some with short half lives, other with longer half lives. The former can be stored in isolation for a few years until their radioactivity has reduced to a safe level. The latter, however, may remain hazardous for hundreds or thousands of years. As of the early 1990s, no completely satisfactory method for storing these nuclear wastes had been developed. *See also* Nuclear fusion; Nuclear weapons; Radiation exposure; Radioactive pollution; Radioactive waste; Radioactive waste management; Radioactivity

[*David E. Newton*]

FURTHER READING

Fowler, J. M. *Energy-Environment Source Book.* Washington, DC: National Science Teachers Association, 1975.

Inglis, D. R. *Nuclear Energy: Its Physics and Social Challenge.* Reading, MA; Addison-Wesley, 1973.

Joesten, M. D., et al. *World of Chemistry.* Philadelphia: Saunders, 1991.

Nuclear fusion

The process by which stars produce energy has always been of great interest to scientists. Not only would the answer to that puzzle be of value to astronomers, but it might also suggest a method by which energy could be generated for human use on earth.

In 1938, German-American physicist Hans Bethe suggested a method by which solar energy might be pro-

Nuclear power plants are a peacetime application of energy initiated through nuclear fission.

duced. According to Bethe's hypothesis, four **hydrogen** atoms come together and fuse—join together—to produce a helium atom. In the process, very large amounts of energy are released.

This process is not a simple one, but one that requires a series of changes. In the first step, two hydrogen atoms fuse to form an atom of deuterium, or "heavy" hydrogen. In later steps, hydrogen atoms are regenerated, providing the materials needed to start the process over again. Like **nuclear fission**, then, nuclear fusion is a **chain reaction**.

Since Bethe's original research, scientists have discovered other fusion reactions. One of these was used in the first practical demonstration of fusion on earth, the "hydrogen" bomb. It involved the fusion of two hydrogen **isotope**s, deuterium and tritium.

Nuclear fusion reactions pose a difficult problem. Fusing isotopes of hydrogen requires that two particles with like electrical charges be forced together. Overcoming the electrical repulsion of these two particles requires the initial input into a fusion reaction of very large amounts of energy. In practice, this means heating the materials to be fused to very high temperatures, a few tens of millions of degrees Celsius. Because of these very high temperatures, fusion reactions are also known as thermonuclear reactions.

Temperatures of a few millions of degrees Celsius are common in the center of stars, so nuclear fusion can easily be imagined there. On earth, the easiest way to obtain such temperatures is to explode a fission (atomic) bomb. That explosion momentarily produces temperatures of a few tens of millions of degrees Celsius. A fusion weapon such as a hydrogen bomb consists, therefore, of nothing other than a fission bomb surrounded by a mass of hydrogen isotopes.

As with nuclear fission, there is a strong motivation to find ways of controlling nuclear fusion reactions so that they can be used for the production of power. This research, however, has been hampered by some extremely difficult technical challenges. Obviously, no ordinary construction material can withstand the temperatures of the hot, gaseous-like material, or plasma, involved in a fusion reaction. Efforts have been aimed, therefore, at finding ways of containing the reaction with a magnetic field. The tokamak reactor, originally developed by Russian scientists, appears to be one of the most promising methods of solving this problem.

Research on controlled fusion has been a slow, but continuous, progress. Some researchers are confident that a solution is close at hand. Others doubt the possibility of bringing nuclear fusion under human control. All agree, however, that successful completion of this research could provide humans with perhaps the "final solution" to their energy needs.

[*David E. Newton*]

FURTHER READING

Hippenheimer, T. A. *The Man-Made Sun: The Quest for Fusion Power.* Boston: Little Brown, 1984.

Inglis, D. R. *Nuclear Energy: Its Physics and Social Challenge.* Reading, MA; Addison-Wesley, 1973.

Lidsky, L. M. "The Trouble With Fusion." *Technology Review* (1984): 52-6.

Rafelski, J., and S. E. Jones. "Cold Nuclear Fusion." *Scientific American* 257 (1987): 84-9.

Nuclear power

When nuclear reactions were first discovered in the 1930s, many scientists doubted they would ever have any practical application. But the successful initiation of the first controlled reaction at the University of Chicago in 1942 put these doubts to rest.

In the first controlled nuclear reaction, scientists discovered a source of energy greater than anyone had previously imagined possible. They discovered that the nuclei of certain **isotope**s of **uranium** could be split. The reaction occurred when the nuclei of certain isotopes of uranium were struck and split by neutrons. This is now known as **nuclear fission**, and the fission reaction results in the formation of three types of products: energy, **neutron**s, and smaller nuclei about half the size of the original uranium nucleus.

Neutrons are actually produced in a fission reaction, and this fact is critical for energy production. The release of neutrons in a fission reaction means that the particles needed to initiate fission are also a product of the reaction. Once initiated in block of uranium, fission occurs over and over again, in a **chain reaction**. Calculations done during these early discoveries showed that the amount of energy released in each fission reaction is many times greater than that released during a conventional chemical explosion.

These elements of nuclear fission were used in the development of the atomic bomb. After the dropping of this bomb brought World War II to an end, scientists began researching the possibility of harnessing nuclear energy for other applications, primarily the generation of electricity. In developing the first nuclear weapons, scientists only needed to find a way to initiate nuclear fission—there was no need to control it once it had begun. In developing the peacetime application of nuclear power, however, the primary challenge was to develop a mechanism for keeping the reaction under control once it had begun so the energy released could be managed and used. This is the principal purpose of nuclear **power plants**, controlling and converting the energy produced by nuclear reactions.

There are many types of nuclear power plants, but all plants have a reactor core and every core has three elements. Fuel rods are the first of these elements; these are long, narrow, cylindrical tubes that hold small pellets of some fissionable material. At present only two such materials are in practical use, uranium-235 and **plutonium**-239. The uranium used for nuclear fission is known as enriched uranium, because it is actually a mixture of uranium-235 with uranium-238. Uranium-238 does not fission and the necessary chain reaction will not occur if the fraction of uranium-235 is not at least three percent.

The second component of the reactor core is a moderator. Only slow-moving neutrons are capable of initiating a nuclear fission reaction, but the neutrons produced as a result of nuclear fission are fast moving. These neutrons are too fast moving to initiate other reactions, and moderators are used to slow down the neutrons. Two of the most common moderators are graphite (pure **carbon**) and water.

The third component of the reactor core is the control rods. In operating a nuclear power plant safely and efficiently, it is of utmost importance to have exactly the right amount of neutrons in the reactor core. If there are too few, the chain reaction comes to an end and energy ceases to be produced. If there are too many, fission occurs too quickly, too much energy is released all at once, and the rate of reaction increases until it can no longer be controlled or contained. Control rods can monitor the number of neutrons in the core because they are made of material that has a strong tendency to absorb neutrons. **Cadmium** and boron are materials that are both commonly used. The rods are mounted on pulleys allowing them to be raised or lowered into the reactor core. When the rods are fully inserted, most of the neutrons in the core are absorbed and relatively few are available to initiate a chain reaction. As the rods are withdrawn from the core, more and more neutrons are available to initiate fission reactions. The reactions reach a point where the number of neutrons produced in the core is almost exactly equal to the number being used to start fission reactions, and it is then that a controlled chain reaction can occur.

The heat energy produced in a reactor core is used to boil water and make steam, which is then used to operate a turbine and generate electricity. The various types of nuclear power plants differ primarily in the way in which heat from the core is used to do this. The most direct approach is to surround the core with a huge tank of water, some of which can be boiled directly by heat from the core. One problem with boiling-water reactors is that the steam produced can be contaminated with radioactive materials. Special precautions must be taken with these reactors to prevent contaminated steam from being released into the **environment**. A second type of nuclear reactor makes use of a heat exchanger. Water around the reactor core is heated and pumped to a heat exchange unit, where this water is used to boil water in an external system. The steam produced in this exchange is then used to operate the turbine and generator.

There is also a type of nuclear reactor known as a breeder reactor because it not only produces energy but also generates more fuel in the form of plutonium-239. In conventional reactors, water is used as a coolant as well as a moderator, but in breeder reactors the coolant used is sodium. Neutrons have to be moving quickly to produce plutonium, not slowly and sodium does not moderate their speed as much as water does.

Although nuclear power plants could never explode like an atomic bomb, because the necessary quantity of uranium-235 is never present in the reactor core, they do pose a number of well-known safety hazards. The scientists and engineers involved in the development of nuclear power tried to anticipate the dangers these reactions posed and developed safety measures. Thus, control rods were developed to prevent the fission reactions from generating too much heat. The reactor and its cooling system are always enclosed in a containment shell made of thick sheets of steel to prevent the escape of radioactive materials. The nuclear power plants these scientists and engineers designed are highly complex facilities, with back-up systems for increased safety which are themselves supported by other back-up systems. But the components of these systems age, and people make mistakes; safety measures do not always function the way there were designed.

On December 2, 1957, the first nuclear power plant opened in Shippingport, Pennsylvania, and to many the nuclear age seemed to have begun. Over the next two decades, more than 50 plants were put into operation, and dozens more were ordered. But safety problems plagued the industry. An experimental reactor in Idaho Falls, Idaho, had already experienced a partial meltdown as a result of operator error in 1955. In October of 1957, just months before the Shippingport plant came on line, a production reactor near Liverpool, England, caught fire, releasing radiation over Great Britain and northern Europe.

The most critical event in the history of nuclear power in the United States was the accident at the **Three Mile Island Nuclear Reactor** near Harrisburg, Pennsylvania. In March of 1979, fission in the reactor core went out of control, generating huge amounts of heat, and a meltdown resulted. Fuel rods and the control rods were melted; the cooling water was turned to steam and the containment structure itself was threatened. No new plants have been ordered in the United States since this accident, and 65 plants on order at that time were cancelled. The explosion at the Chernobyl reactor near Kiev, Ukraine, dealt a second blow to the industry.

Even without these accidents, another problem with nuclear power would remain. This is the problem of **radioactive waste**s. About a third of the 10 million fuel pellets used in any reactor core must be removed each year because they have been so contaminated with fission by-products that they no longer function efficiently. These highly radioactive pellets must be disposed of in a safe fashion, but fifty years after the first controlled reaction, no method has yet been discovered for doing this. Today, these wastes are most commonly stored on a temporary basis at or near the power plant itself. Many people have argued that further development of nuclear power should not even be considered until better methods for **radioactive waste management** have been developed.

The role nuclear power will play in energy production throughout the world is uncertain. But the current absence of nuclear power plant development in the United States should not be taken as indicative of future trends, as well as trends in the rest of world. France, for example, obtains more than half of its electricity from nuclear power, despite the safety problems. And many believe that nuclear power should be an important part of energy production in the United States as well. Proponents of nuclear power argue that its dangers have been greatly exaggerated in this country. The risks, they argue, must be compared with the health and environmental hazards of other fuels, particularly **fossil fuels**.

For some, hope for the future of nuclear power rests with the development of **nuclear fusion**. A nuclear power plant based on a fusion reaction would amount to a controlled version of a hydrogen bomb, just as conventional nuclear plants are equivalent to a controlled version of an atomic bomb. But the problem of managing the reaction is far more difficult with fusion than it is with fission, and scientists have been working on this issue unsuccessfully for more than 40 years. Some believe that a fusion power plant can become a reality in the next century, but many now doubt that such a plant will ever be feasible.

[*David E. Newton*]

FURTHER READING

Ahearne, J. F. "Nuclear Power after Chernobyl." *Science* (8 May 1987): 673-79.

Dresser, P. D., ed. *Nuclear Power Plants Worldwide.* Detroit, MI: Gale Research, 1993.

Gofman, J., and A. R. Tamplin. *Poisoned Power: The Case against Nuclear Power before and after Three Mile Island.* Emmaus, PA: Rodale Press, 1979.

Haggin, J. "New Era of Inherently Safe Nuclear Reactor Technology." *Chemical & Engineering News* (11 August 1986): 18-22.

Jagger, J. *The Nuclear Lion: What Every Citizen Should Know about Nuclear Power and Nuclear War.* New York: Plenum, 1991.

League of Women Voters. *A Nuclear Power Primer: Issues for Citizens.* Washington, DC: League of Women Voters, 1982.

Lester, R. K. "Rethinking Nuclear Power." *Scientific American* 254 (March 1986): 31-9.

Weinburg, A. M. *Continuing the Nuclear Dialogue.* La Grange Park, IL: American Nuclear Society, 1985.

Nuclear Regulatory Commission (NRC)

The development of **nuclear weapons** during World War II raised a number of difficult nonmilitary questions for the United States. Most scientists and many politicians realized that the technology used in weapons research had the potential for use in a variety of peacetime applications. In fact, research on techniques for controlling **nuclear fission** for the production of electricity was well under way before the end of the war.

An intense Congressional debate over the regulation commercial **nuclear power** resulted in the creation in 1946 of the **Atomic Energy Commission (AEC)**. The AEC had two major functions: to support and promote the development of nuclear power in the United States and to monitor and regulate the applications of nuclear power.

Some critics pointed out early on that these two functions were inherently in conflict. How could the AEC act as a vigorous protector of the public safety, they asked, if it also had to encourage industry growth? The validity of that argument did not become totally obvious for nearly two decades. It was not until the early 1970s that the suppression of information about safety hazards from existing plants by the AEC became public knowledge.

The release of this information prompted Congress and the President to rethink the government's role in nuclear power issues. The result of that process was the **Energy Reorganization Act** of 1973 and Executive Order 11834 of January 15, 1975. These two actions established two new governmental agencies, the Nuclear Regulatory Commission (NRC) and the **Energy Research and Development Agency (ERDA)**. NRC was assigned all of AEC's old regulatory responsibilities, while ERDA assumed its energy development functions.

The mission of the Nuclear Regulatory Commission is to ensure that the civilian uses of nuclear materials and facilities are conducted in a manner consistent with public health and safety, environmental quality, national security, and anti-trust laws. The single most important task of the commission is to regulate the use of nuclear energy in the generation of electric power.

In order to carry out this mission, the commission has a number of specific functions. It is responsible for inspecting and licensing every aspect of nuclear **power plant** construction and operation, from initial plans through actual construction and operation to disposal of **radioactive waste** materials. The commission also contracts for research on issues involving the commercial use of nuclear power and holds public hearings on any topics involving the use of nuclear power. An important ongoing NRC effort is to establish safety standards for nuclear **radiation exposure**.

A fair amount of criticism is still directed at the Nuclear Regulatory Commission. Critics feel that the NRC has not been an effective watchdog for the public in the area of nuclear safety. For example, the investigation of the 1979 **Three Mile Island Nuclear Reactor** accident found that the commission was either unaware of existing safety problems at the plant or failed to inform the public adequately about these problems. *See also* Nuclear fission; Nuclear winter; Price-Anderson Act (1957); Radiation sickness

[*David E. Newton*]

Nuclear test ban

The Comprehensive Test Ban Treaty (CTBT), which prohibits all nuclear explosions either for military or "peaceful" purposes, was adopted by the United Nations General Assembly in September 1996. Although disputes remain in some countries over the ratification of the treaty, the adoption of the text by the General Assembly marks the culmination of several decades of intermittent negotiation aimed at the worldwide prohibition of nuclear explosions within the United Nations nuclear nonproliferation framework. The CTBT aims at preventing the development and proliferation of **nuclear weapons** and is viewed by the United Nations as an important step toward eventual nuclear disarmament.

President Dwight D. Eisenhower first suggested a ban on atmospheric testing in 1955, but it was not until August 1963, in the aftermath of the 1962 superpower showdown over the stationing of nuclear-capable missiles in Cuba, that the United States and the U.S.S.R. agreed to a Partial Test Ban Treaty (PTBT). This agreement banned all atmospheric tests of nuclear weapons, but allowed both parties to set off explosions in the more frequently-used underground tests. With both superpowers concerned about issues of sovereignty and espionage, the PTBT limited procedures for verification of compliance to what were called "national technical means," which consisted mainly of satellite, communications, and long-distance seismic monitoring. While the PTBT's overall impact on arms control is generally thought to have been negligible, it did serve to prevent a great deal of **pollution** of the **atmosphere** and the Earth's surface by **plutonium** and other radioactive substances.

In 1974, the PTBT was supplemented by the signing of a Threshold Test Ban Treaty (TTBT) that limited the explosive yield of underground nuclear tests. Initially, the TTBT also relied on national technical means for verification. But in 1990, the original protocol was replaced with a new agreement on verification means that allowed for on-site inspections and in-country seismic monitoring.

Fourteen years after the adoption of the PTBT, the United States, U.S.S.R., and United Kingdom convened trilateral talks aimed at achieving a comprehensive test ban. Some limited progress was made toward resolving several points of disagreement, but in general the parties achieved few tangible results in these negotiations. This lack of success combined with a general toughening of United States policy towards the U.S.S.R. after the 1980 elections to all but end discussion of a test ban treaty.

Against the wishes of both the United States and the United Kingdom, a series of amendments was suggested in January 1991, under the authority of the existing treaties' revision procedures. A conference of the nuclear powers was convened to consider the proposed amendments. These negotiations were inconclusive, but they did signal considerable international interest in a comprehensive ban. Political momentum toward this end was given a boost in 1992, when Russia, France, and the United States declared a nine-month moratorium on all testing. In doing so, the United States reversed official doctrine introduced in the 1980s, which held that testing via explosions was a necessary component of national security. The radical geopolitical changes associated with the disintegration of the U.S.S.R. also played a role in changing the climate of negotiations. As a result, the 1994 Conference on Disarmament created a committee with a mandate to establish a framework for a comprehensive ban. By extending its own moratorium on nuclear tests, the Clinton Administration signaled its willingness to sign the resulting CTBT, giving the final process of negotiation an important boost.

Technological and political developments, however, are already raising new issues for arms control experts and negotiators. Advances in communications and surveillance technology aid the verification of compliance. But advances in nuclear physics and weapons technology, such as the advent of so-called micro-nukes and hydronuclear tests with greatly reduced yields, make the very definition of nuclear testing problematic. Several countries, especially India and Pakistan, have expressed strong misgivings about the CTBT. Although the United States strongly supports the treaty on an official level, substantial and deep-rooted opposition to the CTBT persists, including some notable critics among those charged with oversight of its huge nuclear arsenal. Opponents of the treaty argue that limited testing is necessary for checking the safety and reliability of existing nuclear warheads and for maintaining the credibility of the nuclear deterrent.

[*Lawrence J. Biskowski*]

Nuclear waste

See **Radioactive waste**

Nuclear weapons

There are two types of nuclear weapons, each of which utilizes a different nuclear reaction: **nuclear fission** and **nuclear fusion**. The bomb developed by the Manhattan Project and dropped on Japan during World War II were fission weapons, also known as atomic bombs. **Hydrogen** bombs are fusion weapons, and these were first developed and produced during the early 1950s.

In fission weapons, the explosive energy is derived from nuclear fission, in which large atomic nuclei are split into two roughly equal parts. Every time a nucleus divides, it releases a large amount of energy. Each fission reaction also produces one or more **neutron**s, the subatomic particles that are needed to initiate a fission reaction. Thus, once a fission reaction has been started in a few nuclei, it rapidly spreads to other nuclei around it, creating a **chain reaction**. The two

nuclei most commonly used for this type of nuclear reaction are **uranium**-235 and **plutonium**-239.

The necessary fission reaction will not occur if an atomic bomb carries any single piece of fissionable material that is more than a few kilograms. The bomb can contain more than one piece of this size, but it seldom contains more than three or four. Thus there is a limit to the size of a fission weapon, as well as the energy it can release. Nuclear weapons and the force of their blasts are measured in kilotons, each of which is equivalent to a thousand tons of TNT. Fission weapons are limited to 20 or 30 kilotons.

Fusion weapons derive their explosive power from a reaction which is the opposite of fission. In fusion, two small nuclei combine or fuse, releasing large amounts of energy in the process. The materials needed to initiate another fusion reaction are produced as a byproduct, and fusion, like fission, is a cyclic reaction.

In contrast to fission weapons, a hydrogen bomb can be of almost any size. Such a bomb consists of a fission bomb at the core, surrounded by a mass of hydrogen **isotope**s used in the fusion reactions. No limit to the mass of hydrogen that can be used exists, and there is thus no theoretical limit to the size of fusion weapons. The practical limit is simply the necessity of transporting it to a target; the bomb cannot be so large that a rocket or an airplane is unable to carry it effectively.

Both fission and fusion weapons are often classified as strategic or tactical. Strategic weapons are long-range weapons intended primarily for attack on enemy land. Tactical weapons are designed for use on the battlefield, and their destructive power is adjusted for their shorter range.

Nuclear weapons cause destruction in a number of different ways. They create temperatures upon explosion that are, at least initially, millions of degrees hot. Some of their first effects are heat effects, and materials are often incinerated on contact. The heat from the blast also causes rapid expansion of air, resulting in very high winds that can blow over buildings and other structures. A weapon blast also releases high levels of radiation, such as neutrons, **X-ray**s, and **gamma ray**s. Humans and other animals close to the center of the blast suffer illness and death from **radiation exposure**. The set of symptoms associated with such exposure is known as **radiation sickness**. Many individuals who survive radiation sickness eventually develop **cancer** and their offspring frequently suffer genetic damage. Finally, a weapon's blast releases huge amounts of radioactive materials. Some of these materials settle out of the **atmosphere** almost immediately, creating widespread contamination. Others remain in the atmosphere for weeks or months, resulting in long-term **radioactive fallout**.

Because of their destructive power, the nations of the world have been trying for many years to reach agreements on limiting the manufacture and possession of nuclear weapons. In 1963, the United States and the former Soviet Union agreed to a Limited Nuclear Test Ban Treaty that banned explosions in the atmosphere, outer space, and underwater. The 1974 Threshold Test Ban Treaty restricts the underground testing of nuclear weapons by the United States and the former Soviet Union to yields no greater than 150 kilotons. Some observers hope that the nations of the world may eventually be able to agree on a total ban of all nuclear weapons.

[*David E. Newton and Douglas Smith*]

FURTHER READING

Ahearne, J. F. "Nuclear Power after Chernobyl." *Science* (8 May 1987): 673-79.

Dresser, P. D., ed. *Nuclear Power Plants Worldwide*. Detroit, MI: Gale Research, 1993.

Gofman, J., and A. R. Tamplin. *Poisoned Power: The Case against Nuclear Power before and after Three Mile Island*. Emmaus, PA: Rodale Press, 1979.

Haggin, J. "New Era of Inherently Safe Nuclear Reactor Technology." *Chemical & Engineering News* (11 August 1986): 18-22.

Jagger, J. *The Nuclear Lion: What Every Citizen Should Know about Nuclear Power and Nuclear War*. New York: Plenum, 1991.

League of Women Voters. *A Nuclear Power Primer: Issues for Citizens*. Washington, DC: League of Women Voters, 1982.

Lester, R. K. "Rethinking Nuclear Power." *Scientific American* 254 (March 1986): 31-39.

Weinburg, A. M. *Continuing the Nuclear Dialogue*. La Grange Park, IL: American Nuclear Society, 1985.

Nuclear weapons testing
See **Bikini Atoll; Nevada Test Site**

Nuclear winter

Many of the horrible consequences of a global nuclear conflict have been well known for nearly half a century. Though much research has been conducted in this area, there is still much to be learned. The early 1980s saw the discovery of another potential catastrophic effect of nuclear war: a nuclear winter.

Some scientists believe that the **smoke** produced as a result of a nuclear conflict would reduce the transmission of sunlight to the Earth's surface over a significant portion of the planet. According to the theory, this reduction in sunlight would then cause a cooling on land surfaces of anywhere from 18°F to 65°F (10° to 35°C). Interior parts of a continent would experience greater cooling than would coastal regions. Some parts of the planet that now experience a temperate **climate** might be plunged into winter-like conditions that could continue for months or years.

Since it was first proposed in 1982, the nuclear winter hypothesis has been subjected to severe scrutiny. The United States National Academy of Sciences, the United States Office of Science and Technology Policy, the World Meteorological Organization, the International Council of Scientific Unions, and the Scientific Committee on Problems of the Environment, as well as dozens of individual scientists, have analyzed the potential for a nuclear winter and the problems that it might engender. These studies have not resolved the many issues surrounding a possible nuclear winter effect, but they have clarified a number of factors involved in that effect.

First, the fundamental logic behind a possible nuclear winter effect has been considerably strengthened. Experts estimate that about 9,000 teragrams (9,000 billion grams) of finished lumber exist in the world. A large portion of that is found in urban areas that are likely to be the focus of a nuclear attack. By one estimate, anywhere from 25 to 75 percent of the wood in an urban area would be ignited in a nuclear attack.

A second resource vulnerable to nuclear attack is the world's **petroleum** reserves. Most experts agree that oil refineries, oil storage centers, and other concentrations of oil deposits would be likely targets in a nuclear attack. These materials would also serve as fuel in a widespread fire storm.

The main product of concern in the combustion of wood, petroleum, and other materials (**plastics**, tar, asphalt, vegetation, etc.) would be sooty smoke. This smoke would decrease solar radiation by as much as 50 percent. In addition, it would not easily be washed out of the **atmosphere** by rain, snow and other forms of precipitation. Computer models have also shown that soot in the atmosphere may be more stable than first imagined.

Studies also suggest that a nuclear winter effect could have serious consequences for the **ozone** layer. One effect would be the dislocation of the ozone layer over the Northern Hemisphere towards the Southern Hemisphere. Another effect would involve actual destruction of the ozone layer by nitrogen oxide molecules carried aloft by smoke.

Scientists have studied a number of natural phenomena with nuclear winter-like effects. Volcanic eruptions, massive forest fires, natural dust clouds, urban fires, and extensive wild fires all produce massive amounts of smoke similar to what would be expected in a nuclear conflict. For example, massive wildfires in China during May of 1987 were found to reduce daytime temperatures in Alaska by 4°F to 12°F (2°C to 6°C) in ensuing months. Possible climatic effects from the enormous oil well fires during the **Persian Gulf War**, as well as recent volcanic eruptions, are also being studied. One scientist studying this phenomenon has said, however, that "severe environmental anomalies—possible leading to more human casualties globally than the direct effects of nuclear war—would be not just a remote possibility, but a likely outcome." *See also* Lovelock, James H.; Natural resources; Nitrogen oxides; Nuclear power; Nuclear weapons; Particulate; Volcano

[*David E. Newton*]

FURTHER READING

Baum, R. "Climate Changes Focus of Research on Effects of Nuclear War." *Chemical & Engineering News* (19 December 1983): 16-17.

Overbye, D. "Prophet of the Cold and Dark." *Discover* 6 (January 1985): 24-32.

Raloff, J. "Beyond Armageddon." *Science News* (12 November 1983): 314-17.

———. "Nuclear Winter: Shutting Down the Farm?" *Science News* (14 September 1985): 171-73.

Revkin, A. C. "Hard Facts about Nuclear Winter." *Science Digest* (March 1985): 62-8+.

Turco, R. P., et al. "Climate and Smoke: An Appraisal of Nuclear Winter." *Science* (12 January 1990): 166-75.

Nucleic acid

Nucleic acids are macromolecules composed of polymerized nucleotides. Nucleotides, in turn, are structured of phosphoric acid, pentose sugars, and organic bases. Deoxyribonucleic acid (**DNA**) most commonly exists as a double stranded helix. The genetic information of some **virus**es, bacteria, and all higher organisms is encoded in DNA, and the physical basis of heredity of these organisms is dependent upon the molecular structure of DNA.

DNA is transcribed into single stranded ribonucleic acid (**RNA**), which is then translated into protein. The conversion of the genetic information of a species into the fabric of that organism involves several kinds of RNA, *viz.*, messenger RNA (mRNA), transfer RNAs (tRNA), and ribosomal RNAs (rRNA). The genetic material of some viruses is RNA.

Nutrient

All plants and animals require certain **chemicals** for growth and survival. These chemicals are called biogenic salts or nutrients (from the Latin word *nutrio* meaning to feed, rear, or nourish). They can be categorized as those needed in large amounts called macronutrients, and those needed in minute amounts called micronutrients or **trace element**s. Macronutrients include **nitrogen** (an essential building block of chlorophyll and protein), **phosphorus** (used to make **DNA** and ATP), calcium (a component of cell walls and bones), sulfur (a component of amino acids), and magnesium (a component of bones and chlorophyll). Micronutrients, although needed only in trace amounts, are still essential for survival. Examples include cobalt (used in the synthesis of vitamin B_{12}), iron (essential for **photosynthesis** and blood respiratory pigment), and sodium (used in the maintenance of proper acid-based balance called osmoregulation, nerve transmission, and several other functions). Some micronutrients, such as copper and zinc, can be harmful in large amounts. The borderline between necessary and excessive is often narrow and varies among species.

Oak Ridge, Tennessee

Along with towns such as Los Alamos, New Mexico, and the area around the Savannah River in Georgia, Oak Ridge is central to the history of the development of **nuclear weapons** in the United States. It has also come to represent many of the environmental consequences of nuclear research and weapons production.

Oak Ridge was a small, sleepy town when it was selected as a research site in the 1940s for the development of the atomic bomb. Amidst an atmosphere of intense secrecy, the government built the Oak Ridge National Laboratories within a period of months and assembled a force of 75,000 scientists. These physicists, engineers, and others worked under extreme security to design various components of the hydrogen bomb. Their research was carried out under the auspices of the Manhattan Project, though the tasks were compartmentalized and few scientists are though to have been aware of the larger significance of their work.

After the end of World War II, the laboratories at Oak Ridge were used for the research activities and weapons production of the Cold War. Although the area did experience decreases in the number of highly trained personnel, the research center remained an important part of the government's network of national laboratories. During this period, the **U.S. Department of Energy** (DOE) took over the management of the Oak Ridge laboratories and subcontracted administrative operations to such private corporations as Union Carbide and the Martin Marietta Corporation. Peacetime activities also included major research and educational initiatives developed in association with the local university.

Because of the urgency and secrecy under which military research was conducted at Oak Ridge, little attention was paid to the health impacts of **radiation** or the safe disposal of **hazardous waste**. Starting in 1951, the research facilities were responsible for storing 2.7 million gallons (10.2 million liters) of concentrated acids and **radioactive waste**s in open ponds. 76,000 rusting barrels and drums containing mixed radioactive wastes remain on the site. Millions of cubic yards of toxic and radioactive waste were also buried in the ground with no containment precautions. 2.4 million pounds (1 million kg) of **mercury** and an unknown amount of **uranium** are estimated to have been released into the ambient environment through the air, water and **soil** pathways. The DOE has spent $1.5 billion evaluating the level of contamination and planning remediation and treatment activities, and that figure is expected to grow exponentially. Cleanup programs are now the focus of much of the research done by the nuclear scientists at Oak Ridge.

Vegetation and **wildlife** (water fleas, frogs and deer) around the laboratories have set off high readings of radioactivity in Geiger counters. Radionuclides such as strontium, tritium and **plutonium** have been traced in surface waters 40 miles (64 km) downstream of the plant. However, few published studies exist on human health effects from hazardous waste disposal in the area. Studies that examined short term **cancer** rates in the male worker population found no correlation between cancer risk and worker **radiation exposure**; these studies also noted that Oak Ridge employees were actually 20 percent less likely to die from cancer as the rest of the country—a fact which may be due to the quality of their medical care. Yet studies that followed the health patterns of workers over a period of 40 years documented that cancer risk did indeed increase by 5 percent with each rem of increasing radiation exposure. These studies also found that white male workers at the laboratories had a 63 percent higher leukemia death rate than the national average.

In 1977 large amounts of employee health records were deliberately destroyed at the Oak Ridge National Laboratories, and the DOE has attempted to influence the interpretation and publication of health studies on the effects of radiation exposure. These facts raise troubling questions for many about the level of knowledge at the research center of the effects of low-level radiation. Both the laboratories and the town itself are considered case studies of the environmental problems that can be caused by large federal facilities operating under the protection of national security.

[*Usha Vedagiri and Douglas Smith*]

FURTHER READING

"Low-Level Radiation: Higher Long-Term Risk?" *Science News* 139 (23 March 1991): 181.

Thompson, D. "Living Happily Near a Nuclear Trash Heap." *Time* 139 (11 May 1992): 53-54.

Occupational Safety and Health Act (1970)

The Occupational Safety and Health Act (1970) was intended to reduce the incidence of personal injuries, illness, and deaths as a result of employment. It requires employers to provide each of their employees with a workplace that is free from recognized hazards, which may cause death or serious physical harm. The act directed the creation of the **Occupational Safety and Health Administration (OSHA)** within the U. S. Department of Labor. This agency is responsible for developing and promulgating safety and health standards, issuing regulations, conducting inspections, and issuing citations as well as proposing fines for violations. *See also* Right-to-act legislation

Occupational Safety and Health Administration (OSHA)

The Occupational Safety and Health Administration (OSHA) was established pursuant to the **Occupational Safety and Health Act** (1970). Within the Department of Labor, OSHA has the responsibility for occupational safety and health activities pursuant to the Act which covers virtually every employer in the country except all types of mines which are regulated separately under the Mine Safety and Health Act (1977). The Occupational Safety and Health Administration develops and promulgates standards, develops and issues regulations, conducts inspections to insure compliance, and issues citations and proposes penalties. In the case of a disagreement over the results of safety and health inspections performed by OSHA, employers have the right of appeal to the Occupational Safety and Health Review Commission, which works to ensure the timely and fair resolution of these cases.

Ocean dumping

Ocean dumping is defined as "the transport of wastes at sea for the purpose of dumping." The discharge of sewage and other **effluent**s from a pipeline or the discharge of waste generated by ships is not considered ocean *dumping*, but ocean *discharge*. Wastes have been dumped into the ocean for thousands of years. Fish and fish processing wastes, rubbish, industrial wastes, sewage **sludge**, dredged material, **radioactive waste**, pharmaceutical wastes, drilling fluids, munitions, coal wastes, cryolite, ocean incineration wastes, and wastes from ocean mining have all been dumped at sea.

Ocean dumping has been used as a method for municipal waste disposal in the United States for about 80 years, and even longer for dredged material. Millions of metric tons of sewage sludge, industrial waste, and dredged material are dumped worldwide primarily by developed countries. Ocean dumping has historically been more economically attractive, when compared with other land-based waste management options.

The 1972 **Convention on the Prevention of Marine Pollution by Dumping of Waste and Other Matter**, commonly called the London Dumping Convention, came into force in 1975 to control ocean dumping activities. The framework of the London Dumping Convention includes a *black list* of materials that may not be dumped at sea under any circumstances, a *grey list* of materials considered less harmful that may be dumped after a special permit is obtained, and criteria that countries must consider before issuing an ocean dumping permit. These criteria require the consideration of the effects dumping activities can have on marine life, amenities, and other uses of the ocean, and encompass factors related to disposal operations, waste characteristics, attributes of the site, and availability of land-based alternatives. The International Maritime Organization is responsible for administrative activities related to the London Dumping Convention, and it ensures cooperation among the countries participating in the Convention. As of 1990, 65 countries had ratified the Convention.

The law to regulate ocean dumping in the United States, the **Marine Protection, Research, and Sanctuaries Act** of 1972 has been revised by the United States Congress and the judicial system in the years since its enactment. In 1974, Congress amended this Act to conform with the London Dumping Convention. In 1977, the Act was amended to incorporate a ban by 1982 on ocean dumping of wastes that may unreasonably degrade the marine environment. As a result of this ban, approximately 150 permittees dumping sewage sludge and industrial waste stopped ocean dumping of these materials. However, the United States federal district court overturned this ban in 1981 allowing New York City and neighboring municipalities in New York and New Jersey to continue ocean dumping. In 1988, the **Ocean Dumping Ban Act** was passed to prohibit ocean dumping of all sewage sludge and industrial waste by 1992.

At the time of this 1988 amendment to the 1972 law, approximately eight million wet metric tons of sewage sludge and 160,000 wet metric tons of industrial waste were dumped annually at a site located off the coast of southern New Jersey. Approximately 30,000 metric tons of hydrochloric acid waste was dumped at a site in the **New York Bight**. The United Kingdom and the North Sea countries also intend to end ocean dumping of sewage sludge eventually. In 1990, the countries participating in the London Dumping Convention agreed to terminate all industrial ocean dumping by the end of 1995. Currently, there are approximately 50 permits issued worldwide for ocean dumping of sewage sludge and 150 permits for industrial waste. There are some 380 permits for dredged materials and about 50 permits for other matter such as **low-level radioactive waste**s and at-sea incineration of **chlorinated hydrocarbons**. While the volume of sewage sludge and industrial waste dumped at sea is decreasing, ocean dumping of dredged material is increasing.

Physical properties of wastes, such as density, and its chemical composition affect the dispersal, and settling of the wastes dumped at sea. Many contaminants such as metals found in trace amounts in natural materials are enriched in wastes by orders of magnitude. After material is dumped at

A ship dumping jarosite waste into the ocean off the Australia coast.

sea, there is usually initial, rapid dispersion of the waste. For example, some wastes are dumped from a moving vessel, with dilution rates of 1,000 to 100,000 from the ship's wake. As the wake subsides, naturally occurring turbulence and currents further disperse wastes eventually to nondetectable background levels in water in a matter of hours to days, depending on the type of wastes and physical oceanic processes. Dilution is greater if the material is released slower and in smaller amounts, with dispersal rates decreasing over time. Wastes, such as dredged material, that are much denser than the surrounding seawater sink rapidly. Less dense waste sinks more slowly, depending on the type of waste and physical processes of the dumpsite. As sinking waste particles reach seawater of equal density, they begin to spread horizontally, with individual particles slowly settling to the sea bottom. The accumulation of the waste on the sea floor varies with the location and characteristics of the dumpsite. Quiescent waters with little tidal and wave action in enclosed shallow environments have more waste accumulate on the bottom in the general vicinity of the dumpsite. Wastes dumped in more open, well-mixed ocean waters are transported away from the dumpsite by currents and can disperse over a very large area, as much as several hundred square kilometers.

The physical and chemical properties of wastes change after the material has been dumped into the ocean. As wastes mix with seawater, acid-base neutralization, dissolution or precipitation of waste solids, particle adsorption and desorption, volatilization at the sea surface, and changes in the oxidation state may occur. For example, when acid-iron waste is dumped at sea, the buffering capacity of seawater rapidly neutralizes the waste. Hydrous iron oxide precipitates are formed as the iron reacts with seawater and changes from a dissolved to a solid form.

The fraction of the waste that settles to the bottom is further changed as it undergoes geochemical and biological processes. Some of the elements of the waste may be mobilized in organic-rich **sediment**; however, if sulfide ions are present, metals in waste may be immobilized by precipitation of metal sulfides. Organisms living on the sea floor may ingest waste particles, or mix waste deeper in the sediment by burrowing activities. Microorganisms decompose **organic waste**, potentially **recycling** elements from the waste before it becomes part of the sea floor sediments. Generally sediment-related processes will act on waste particles over a longer time scale than hydrologic processes in the water column.

The effects of dumping on the ocean are difficult to measure and depend on complex interactions of factors including type, quantity, and physical and chemical properties of the wastes; method and rate of dumping; toxicity to the **biotic community**; and numerous site-specific characteristics, such as water depth, currents (turbulence), water column density structure, and sediment type. Many studies have found that the effects of ocean dumping on the water column are usually temporary and that the ocean floor receives the most impact. Impacts from dumping dredged material are usually limited to the dumpsite. Burial of some benthic organisms (organisms living at or near the sea floor) may occur; however, burrowing organisms may be able to move vertically through the deposited material and fishes typically leave the area. Seagrasses, coral reefs, and oyster beds may never recover after dredged material is dumped on them. There also can be topographic changes to the sea floor. The mud dumpsite in the New York Bight Apex, which is approximately 7 miles (11 km) from the coast of New Jersey and has been used for disposal of dredged material for over 90 years, is reaching capacity and threatens to become a hazard to navigation. Release of **cadmium**, methyl **mercury**, chlorinated and **polycyclic aromatic hydrocarbons**, and other toxicants from dumping dredged material may impact marine organisms; however, it is difficult to measure the amount of impact and potential **bioaccumulation** of these contaminants from dumping activities.

Studies of copepods (small marine crustaceans) within the plume of a fresh dump of industrial waste found reduced respiration, feeding, and egg production among these organisms. However, such responses appear to occur only within the plume of the dumped material. One change measured from pharmaceutical wastes dumped off the coast of Puerto Rico from 1973 until 1981 was the complete replacement of bacteria normally found in the area with other bacterial species including human **pathogen**s. There were also shifts in the composition and size of the **phytoplankton** community. Both water column and sediment effects on marine organisms have been found to occur from sewage sludge dumping. The deposition of particles from sludge dumping alter the physical and chemical nature of sediments, producing changes in species composition of benthic (ocean bottom) communities. Like dredged material, sewage sludge may be contaminated with high levels of metals, halogenated **hydrocarbons**, **petroleum** hydrocarbons, nutrients, and pathogens. High levels of fecal **coliform bacteria**, an indicator of pathogens, have led to the closing of shellfish beds in the vicinity of sludge dumpsites.

The cessation of sewage sludge dumping at the 12-mile (19-km) dumpsite in the New York Bight Apex in 1987 provided an opportunity for marine scientists to study the recovery of the area. For the past five years, the National Marine Fisheries Service (NMFS) has been studying the response of the marine system to the removal of sludge dumping activities at the dumpsite. Some of the findings have included: oxygen consumption rates have declined to background levels; surface sediment metal levels have decreased; numbers of crustaceans, mollusks, and other species have increased; and incidence of finrot, cysts, and lymphocystis in fish have been reduced. These studies may be extended to the 106-mile (171-km) deep water dumpsite, where ocean dumping of sewage sludge ended in June 1992. *See also* Dredging

[*Marci L. Bortman*]

FURTHER READING

Duedall, I. W., et al., eds. *Wastes in the Ocean.* Vol. 1, *Industrial and Sewage Wastes in the Ocean.* New York: Wiley, 1983.

Graham, F. "Facing the Tragedy of Trash in Our Oceans." *Audubon* 93 (July-August 1991): 12.

Marshall, E. "A Scramble for Data on Actic Radioactive Dumping." *Science* 257 (31 July 1992): 608-09.

Norton, M. G., and M. A. Champ. "The Influence of Site-Specific Characteristics on the Effects of Sewage Sludge Dumping." In *Oceanic Processes in Marine Pollution.* Vol. 4, *Scientific Monitoring Strategies for Ocean Waste Disposal,* edited by D. W. Hood, A. Schoener, and P. Kilho Park. Malabar, FL: Robert E. Krieger, 1989.

Studholme, A. L., M. C. Ingham, and A. Pacheco, eds. *Response of the Habitat and Biota of the Inner New York Bight to Abatement of Sewage Sludge Dumping, Third Annual Progress Report, 1989.* NOAA Technical Memorandum NMFS-F/NEC-82. Washington, DC: U. S. Government Printing Office, 1991.

Swanson, R. L., and G. F. Mayer. "Ocean Dumping of Municipal and Industrial Wastes in the United States." In *Oceanic Processes in Marine Pollution,* Vol. 3, *Marine Waste Management: Science and Policy,* edited by M. A. Champ and P. Kilho Park. Malabar, FL: Robert E. Krieger, 1989.

U. S. Army Corps of Engineers. *Managing Dredged Material, Evaluation of Disposal Alternatives in the New York-New Jersey Metropolitan Region,* Washington, DC: U. S. Government Printing Office, 1989.

U. S. Congress, Office of Technology Assessment. *Wastes in Marine Environments,* Washington, DC: U. S. Government Printing Office, 1987.

Ocean dumping act

See **Marine protection; Research and Sanctuaries Act**

Ocean Dumping Ban Act (1988)

The Ocean Dumping Ban Act of 1988 (Public Law 100-688) marked an end to almost a century of sewage **sludge** and industrial waste dumping into the ocean. The law was enacted amid negative publicity about beach closures from high levels of **pathogen**s and floatable debris washing up along New York and New Jersey beaches and strong public sentiment that ending **ocean dumping** may improve coastal **water quality**. The Ban Act prohibits sewage sludge and industrial wastes from being dumped at sea after December 31, 1991. This law is an amendment to the **Marine Protection, Research, and Sanctuaries Act** of 1972 (Public Law 92-532), which regulates the dumping of wastes into ocean waters. These laws do not cover wastes that are discharged from outfall pipes such as from **sewage treatment** plants or industrial facilities or that are generated by vessels.

The Ocean Dumping Ban Act was not the first attempt to prohibit dumping of sewage sludge and industrial wastes at sea. An earlier ban was developed by the U. S. **Environmental Protection Agency (EPA)** and later passed by the U.S. Congress (Public Law 95-153) in 1977, amending the 1972 act. This 1977 law prohibits ocean dumping that "may unreasonably degrade the marine environment" by December 31, 1981. Approximately 150 entities dumping sewage sludge and industrial waste sought alternative disposal options. However, New York City, and eight municipalities in New York and New Jersey filed a lawsuit against the

EPA objecting to the order to end their ocean dumping practices. A Federal district court granted judgment in their favor, allowing them to continue ocean dumping under a court order. The court held that the EPA must balance, on a case-by-case basis, all relevant statutory criteria with the economics of ocean dumping against land-based alternatives. After 1981, the New York and New Jersey entities were the only dumpers of sewage sludge, and there were only two companies dumping industrial waste at sea.

In anticipation of the 1988 Ocean Dumping Ban Act, one of the two industries stopped its dumping activities in 1987. The remaining industry, which was dumping hydrochloric acid waste, also ceased its activities before the 1988 Ban Act became law. The entities from New Jersey and New York continued to dump a total of approximately eight million wet metric tonnes of sewage sludge (half from New York City) annually into the ocean.

From 1924 to 1987, sludge dumpers used a site approximately 12 miles (19 km) off the coasts of New Jersey and New York. The EPA, working with the **National Oceanic and Atmospheric Administration** (NOAA), determined that ecological impacts such as shellfish bed closures, elevated levels of metals in sediments, and introduction of human pathogens into the marine environment were attributed entirely or in part to sludge dumping at the 12 mile site. As a result the EPA decided to phase out the use of this site by December 31, 1987. The sewage sludge dumpers were required to move their activities farther offshore to the 106-mile (171-km) deep water dumpsite, located at the edge of the continental shelf off southern New Jersey. Industries had used this dumpsite from 1961 to 1987.

The Ocean Dumping Ban Act prohibits all dumping of sewage sludge and industrial waste into the ocean, without exception. The law also prohibits any new dumpers, and required existing dumpers to obtain new permits that included plans to phase-out sewage sludge dumping at sea. The Ban Act also established ocean dumping fees and civil fines for any dumpers that continue their activities after the mandated end date. The fines were included in the law in part because legislators assumed that some sludge dumpers would not be able to meet the December 31, 1991 deadline. The law required fees of $100 per dry ton of sewage sludge or industrial waste in 1989, $150 per dry ton in 1990, and $200 per dry ton in 1991. After the 1991 deadline penalties rose to $600 per ton for any sludge dumped, and increased incrementally in each subsequent year. Those ocean dumpers that continue beyond December 31, 1991 are allowed to use a portion of their penalties for developing and implementing alternative sewage sludge management strategies. While the amount of the penalty increased each year after 1991, the amount that could be devoted to developing land-based disposal alternatives decreased.

As part of the law, the EPA, in cooperation with NOAA, is responsible for implementing an environmental monitoring plan at the 12-mile site, the 106-mile site, and surrounding areas potentially influenced by dumping activities to determine the effects of dumping on living marine resources. The Ban Act also includes provisions not directly

associated with dumping of sewage sludge or industrial waste at sea. Massachusetts Bay-MA, Barataria Terrebonne Estuary Complex-LA, Indian River Lagoon-FL, and Peconic Bay-NY were named as priority areas for consideration to the National Estuary Program by EPA. The law also includes a prohibition on the disposal of **medical waste** at sea by public vessels. Finally, the Ban Act requires vessels transporting **solid waste** over the New York Harbor to the Staten Island **Landfill** to use nets to secure the waste to minimize the amount that may spill overboard.

The New Jersey dumpers ceased ocean dumping by March 1991. The two New York counties stopped ocean dumping by December 1991 and New York City, the last entity to dump sewage sludge into the ocean, stopped zn June 1992. Landfilling is currently used as an alternative to ocean dumping and other sewage sludge management strategies are under consideration including **incineration** (after the sludge is dewatered), **composting**, land application, and pelletization. *See also* Convention on the Prevention of Marine Pollution by Dumping of Waste and Other Matter

[*Marci L. Bortman*]

FURTHER READING

"Ocean Dumping Ban Advances." *Journal of the Water Pollution Control Federation* 60 (August 1988): 1320+.

Kitsos, T. R., and J. M. Bondareff. "Congress and Waste Disposal at Sea." *Oceanus* 33 (Summer 1990): 23-28.

Millemann, B. "Wretched Refuse Off Our Shores." *Sierra* 74 (January-February 1989): 26-28.

Weis, J. S. "Ocean Dumping Revisited." *BioScience* 38 (December 1988): 749.

Ocean farming

Although oceans cover about 70% of the Earth's surface, most food is produced on land areas through agriculture and animal husbandry. This is because 90% of the ocean is unproductive. The productive areas are near shore, such as continental shelfs, upwellings, **coral reef**s, mangrove swamps (also known as mangal communities), and estuaries. The primary reason why these near shore areas are more productive than the open ocean is because of the supply of nutrients which are needed for plant (primarily **phytoplankton**) productivity, which fuels the **food chain/web**.

A worldwide plateau in harvesting of natural fish catch was reached in about 1989, so commercial and sport fisheries in the oceans cannot be increased unless something is changed. One possibility is to enhance production through fertilization of the water. Another, more practical, possibility is through **aquaculture**. As wild harvests decrease and per capita seafood consumption increases, aquaculture should have an important role. For example, the U.S. imports 60% of its seafood, which contributes to its trade imbalance. Aquaculture can help by providing jobs as well as food products for domestic consumption and for export.

Aquaculture done in seawater is known as mariculture. Fish and shellfish are grown in improved conditions to produce more and better food in environments with lower predation and disease. There are several forms of aquaculture: intensive, extensive, and open ocean. In extensive aquaculture, relatively little control is exerted by the mariculturist. These typically occur near shore where organisms are grown in several different ways: floating cages or pens; cordoned-off bodies of water which can be fertilized for enhanced production; or racks and other structures (to grow shellfish). For example, oyster farmers in the Chesapeake Bay place clean substrates in selected areas of the bottom mud each summer to collect young oyster larvae (called "spat") as they settle down from the **plankton**. These young oysters attach and grow on the substrates, which are periodically transferred to new locations to prevent them from being covered with mud and silt. After several years, the oysters are large enough to be marketed. Other culture methods for bivalves such as oysters and clams utilize the stake method, which involves the use of bamboo or other poles driven into the sediment and placed approximately 6 ft (2 m) apart. Nylon ropes hanging from floats can also be used to collect larvae. Following growout, the shellfish are collected and sold on the market. Farmers in the Philippines are able to produce nearly 1.5 tons per acre (0.60 tons per ha) of mussels and 1.7 tons per acre (0.70 tons per ha) of oysters annually. These techniques all have relatively low cost and maintenance. Sometimes there are problems with pollution from domestic and industrial waste, and periodic blooms of toxic dinoflagellates (a type of phytoplankton), which create **red tide**s. Red tides can be unhealthy and even lethal to humans.

Intensive mariculture systems involve the production of large quantities of marine animals in relatively small areas. They are relatively expensive to build and maintain, so typically only highly-valued species are used, such as lobsters, shrimp, halibut, and certain other fish. Intensive systems can sometimes be located in tanks on land, using either pumped salt water from the nearby ocean or recirculated artificial seawater if the system is located farther away from the ocean. Typically, however, nearshore or offshore floating tanks or pens are used. The organisms are raised from eggs to market size in these controlled environments. Salmon have been raised in sea pens (netted cages) for over 20 years along the Pacific coast of the United States and Canada and along the Atlantic coasts of France, Scotland, and the Scandinavian countries, especially Norway. This process typically involves the growth of salmon from fertilized eggs through the fry stage in indoor fresh water hatcheries. This is followed by the transfer of parr (the stage after the fry in which the fish develop vertical lines along their sides) to outdoor tanks or cages in salt water. The fish are fed either commercial pellets or "trash" fish such as herring, capelin, menhaden, and anchovies. The feeding process can be quite labor-intensive, and thus translates into one of the highest expenses for the salmon farmer. After one to two years, the salmon go through a process called smoltification, which involves a physiological change that allows them to live in salt water. The smolt are then transferred to salt water cages for another one to two

years until they reach a market size of about 4-12 lbs (2-5 kg). Rainbow and sea trouts are handled in a similar way, although they are usually larger when moved into sea pens. As with the extensive method, problems can arise through **pollution** and red tides.

Most mariculture industries use both near shore and offshore cages for raising the fish. The near shore cages are necessary for raising young fish, but the offshore cages are better for raising fish to maturity because of enhanced growing conditions (cleaner water and lower mortality). Improvements are still needed, such as methods to remove dead fish, make grading (sorting) of fish possible, make harvesting easier and feeding possible (particularly during adverse weather), and make fouling removal easier. It will also be helpful to construct 24-hour living accommodations on some of the larger offshore units.

A third form of mariculture is known as ocean ranching, or "enhancement aquaculture." This can be compared to cattle ranching on land. For example, salmon are raised in hatcheries until they reach the smolt stage, and are then released at a particular point along the shore where they swim away until they reach reproductive maturity. Like other anadromous fish, they return to that same area several years later, where they are recaptured, processed, and sold on the market. Salmon are ideal fish for this because they are "self-herding." However, normal returns range from only 1-20%, depending upon the water quality of the return environment and the release size of the fish. For example, Coho salmon fry that were around 0.5 oz (14 g) showed a 1-2% return while those twice this size had a 7-8% return rate. Recent research has shown that released salmon can be imprinted to return to salt water sites, which has the added advantages of lower cost (due to not needing more expensive property located along streams that enter the ocean), and better meat quality (which declines when salmon swim from salt to fresh water). The Sea Run, Inc. salmon company of Kennebunkport, Maine, rears Pacific pink and chum salmon from eggs to fingerlings in a hatchery located near the discharge of an oil-fired power plant. The water has a characteristic temperature and smell which attracts the salmon back to the same area each year. They have also experimented with the release of morpholine and phenyethyl alcohol (synthetic organic compounds) to the water to aid in imprinting.

Similar ocean ranching techniques have been used in other countries. For example, in Japan the natural catch of Red Sea bream has declined for the last 24 years (more than a 51% decrease) due to over-exploitation, so these fish have been raised in tanks and cages since 1962. Other species commonly raised in Japan include salmon, flounder, mackerel, bluefin tuna, shrimp, scallops, and abalone. Many of these species have a high consumer demand and thus are highly priced. Abalone can also be grown to a small size of approximately 1 in (3 cm) and used to re-seed areas where the natural population has declined. They can then be harvested as adults about three to five years later. However, recapture rates are typically low (only 0.5-10%).

Ocean farming or ranching is becoming popular worldwide. In Equador, Mazatlan Yellowtail fish are grown to commercial size (2.7 lbs; 1.2 kg) in six months with a 90% survival rate. Other species raised in this country include flounder, snook, red drum, and Pacific pompano. In Australia, oysters are commonly raised via sea ranching. Scallops and salmon are now raised in Canada. Mussels, oysters, clams, bream, turbot, and salmon are common mariculture species in Spain, where the warm water allows these species to be grown to market size in a shorter time.

Recent work has been done on algal turf mariculture around some Caribbean islands in natural, unfertilized waters. Test plots have shown that they can raise up to 25 million tons (23 million metric tonnes) of dry algae per year without harming the natural ecosystem. This product can then be used for direct human ingestion or as food to raise marine invertebrates (such as West Indian spider crabs, conchs, and whelks) as well as some herbivorous fish. This would be particularly helpful because conch are now an **endangered species** through over-harvesting in this area.

Ocean ranching, along with other forms of aquaculture, is an exciting field that should be in greater demand in the future. Our progeny may depend on it more for global food production to feed the increasing human population.

[*John Korstad*]

FURTHER READING

Adey, W.H. "Food Production in Low-Nutrient Seas." BioScience 37 (1987): 340-8.

Landau, M. *Introduction to Aquaculture*. New York: Wiley, 1992.

Reinertsen, H., L.A. Dahle, L. Jo/rgensen, and K. Tvinnereim. *Fish Farming Technology*. Proceedings of the First International Conference on Fish Farming Technology, Trondheim, Norway, August 9-12, 1993. Brookfield, VT: Balkema Publishers, 1993.

Shelty, H.P.C., and G.P. Satyanarayana Rao. "Aquaculture in India." World Aquaculture 27 (1996): 20-24.

Ocean outfalls

Pipelines extending into coastal and ocean waters that are used by various industries and municipal **wastewater** treatment facilities to discharge treated **effluent**. Some may be simple pipes serving as conveyances from land-based facilities; others include diffusers that help to rapidly dilute effluent or risers that ensure effluent is discharged at a certain height above the ocean floor. The conveyances may extend more than three miles (5 km) offshore, beyond coastal waters into open ocean. Offshore oil and gas exploration, development, and production rigs also possess ocean outfalls. **Discharge**s from these pipes must be permitted under the **Clean Water Act** national pollutant discharge elimination system. *See also* Sewage treatment

Ocean pollution
See **Marine pollution; Ocean dumping**

Ocean thermal energy conversion

For many years, scientists have been aware of one enormous **reservoir** of energy on the earth's surface: the oceans. As sunlight falls on the oceans, its energy is absorbed by seawater. The oceans are in one sense, therefore, a huge "storage tank" for **solar energy**. The practical problem is finding a way to extract that energy and make it available for human use.

The mechanism suggested for capturing heat stored in the ocean depends on a thermal gradient always present in seawater. Upper levels of the ocean may be as much as 36°F (20°C) warmer than regions 0.6 mile (1 km) deeper. The technology of ocean thermal energy conversion (OTEC) takes advantage of this temperature gradient.

An OTEC plant would consist of a very large floating platform with pipes at least 100 feet (30 m) in diameter reaching to a depth of up to 0.6 mile (1 km). The "working fluid" in such a plant would be ammonia, propane, or some other liquid with a low boiling point.

Warm surface waters would be pumped into upper levels of the plant, causing the working fluid to evaporate. As the fluid evaporates, it will also exert increased pressure. That pressure can be used to drive a turbine that, in turn, generates electricity. The electricity could be carried to shore along large cables or used directly on the OTEC plant to desalinize water, electrolyze water, or produce other chemical changes.

In the second stage of operation, cold water from deeper levels of the ocean would be brought to the surface and used to cool the working fluid. Once liquified, the working fluid would be ready for a second turn of the generating cycle.

OTEC plants are attractive **alterative energy sources** in regions near the equator, where surface temperatures may reach 77°F (25°C) or more. These parts of the ocean are often adjacent to **less developed countries**, where energy needs are growing.

Wherever they are located, OTEC plants have a number of advantages. For one thing, oceans cover nearly 70 percent of the planet's surface so that the raw material OTEC plants need—seawater—is readily available. The original energy source—sunlight—is also plentiful and free. Such plants are also environmentally attractive since they produce no **pollution** and cause no disruption of land resources. Planners suggest that a by-product of OTEC plants might be **nutrient**s brought up from deeper ocean levels and used to feed "farms" of fish or shellfish.

Unfortunately, many disadvantages exist also. The most important is the enormous cost of building and maintaining the mammoth structures needed for an OTEC plant. Also, the temperature differential available under even the best of conditions means that an OTEC plant will not be more than about 3 percent efficient.

Currently, the disadvantages of OTEC plants are so great that none has even been built. Research continues in a number of countries, but some experts believe that the low efficiency of OTEC means that this technology will never be able to compete economically with other alternative sources

The Open Cycle Ocean Thermal Electric Generator requires a water temperature differential of at least 20°C (36°F) to produce both fresh water and electricity.

of energy. *See also* Desalinization; Energy efficiency; Power plant; Thermal stratification (water)

[*David E. Newton*]

FURTHER READING

Fisher, A. "Energy from the Sea." *Popular Science* (June 1975): 78-83.

Haggin, J. "Ocean Thermal Energy Conversion Experiment Slated for Hawaii." *Chemical & Engineering News* (10 February 1986): 24-26.

Penney, T. R., and D. Bharathan, "Power from the Sea." *Scientific American* 256 (January 1987): 86-92.

Walters, S. "Power in the Year 2001, Part 2—Thermal Sea Power." *Mechanical Engineering* (October 1971): 21-25.

Whitmore, W. "OTEC: Electricity from the Ocean." *Technology Review* (October 1978): 58-63.

Octane rating

Octane rating is a method for describing antiknock properties of **gasoline**. Knocking is a pinging sound produced by internal combustion engines when fuel ignites prematurely during the engine's compression cycle. Because knocking can damage an engine and rob it of power, gasoline formulations have been developed to minimize the problem. Gasolines containing relatively large amounts of straight-chain **hydrocarbons** (such as n-heptane) have an increased tendency to knock, whereas those containing branched-chain forms (such as isooctane) burn more smoothly. In addition to isooctane, other compounds also reduce engine knocking. By using an index called octane number, it is possible to compare the antiknock properties of gasoline mixtures. A higher octane number indicates that a mixture has the equivalent antiknock properties of a gasoline containing a higher percentage of isooctane.

Although gasoline used as automotive fuel is now "deleaded," gasoline used as aviation fuel still contains tetraethyl **lead** as an octane enhancer and antiknock agent.

Odén, Svante

Swedish agricultural scientist

One of the great environmental issues of the 1970s and 1980s was the problem of acid precipitation. Research studies suggested that rain, snow, and other forms of precipitation in certain parts of the world had become increasingly acidic over the preceding century. The southern parts of Scandinavia and England, the Northeastern United States, and Eastern Canada were four regions in which the phenomenon was particularly noticeable.

Evidence began to accumulate that the increasing level of acidity might be associated with environmental damage, such as the death of trees and aquatic life. Scientists began to ask how extensive this damage might be and what sources of acid precipitation could be identified.

If any single person could be credited with raising international awareness of this problem, it would probably be the Swedish agricultural scientist Svante Odén. Odén was certainly not the first person to recognize the existence, effects, or origins of acid precipitation. That honor belongs to an English chemist, **Robert Angus Smith**. As early as 1852, Smith hypothesized a connection between **air pollution** in Manchester and the high acidity of rains falling in the area. He first used the term **acid rain** in a book he published in 1872.

Smith's research held relatively little interest to most scientists, however. Those who did study acid rain approached their work with little concern about the environment and did so, as one of them later said, "with no environmental consciousness," but simply because "it was an interesting situation."

Odén's attitude was quite different. He had been asked by the Swedish government to prepare a report on his hypothesis that acid rain falling on Swedish land and lakes had its origins hundreds or thousands of miles away. In preparing his report, he came to the conclusion that acid rain might be responsible for widespread **fish kills** then being reported by Swedish fishermen. Odén was shocked by this discovery because, as he later said, it was the "first real indication that acid precipitation had an impact on the biosystem."

Odén's method of dealing with his discoveries was unorthodox. In most cases, a researcher sends the report of his or her work to a scientific journal, which has the report reviewed by other scientists in the same field. If the research is judged to have been well done, the report is published.

In this instance, however, Odén sent his report to a Stockholm newspaper, *Dagens Nyheter*, where it was published on October 24, 1967. Odén's decision undoubtedly disturbed some scientists, but it did have the effect of bringing the issue of acid rain to the attention of the general public.

A year later, Odén published a more formal report of his research, "The Acidification of Air and Precipitation, and Its Consequences," in the *Ecology Committee Bulletin*. The article was later translated into English. Odén carried his message about acid precipitation to the United States in person in 1971, when he presented a series of 14 lectures on the topic at various institutions across the country. In his presentations, he argued that acid rain was an international phenomenon that, in Europe, originated especially in England and Germany and was spreading over thousands of miles to other parts of the continent, especially Scandinavia. His work also laid the foundation for Sweden's case study for the United Nations Conference on the Human Environment

"Air Pollution Across National Boundaries" presented at Stockholm in 1972. He further suggested that a number of environmental effects, such as the death of trees and fish and damage to buildings, could be traced to acid precipitation. Odén's passionate commitment to publicizing his findings about acid precipitation was certainly a critical factor in awakening the world's awareness to the potential problems of this environmental danger.

[*David E. Newton*]

FURTHER READING

Boyle, R. H., and R. A. Boyle. *Acid Rain*. New York: Nick Lyons Books, 1983.

Cowling, E. B. "Acid Precipitation in Historical Perspective." *Environmental Science and Technology* 16 (1982): 110A-123A.

Luoma, J. *Troubled Skies, Troubled Waters*. New York: Viking Press, 1984.

Park, C. *Acid Rain: Rhetoric and Reality*. London: Methuen, 1987.

Odor control

Refuse-handlers and many industries release unpleasant odors into the air which can travel for miles. Odors inside factories can also make it difficult for people to work, and pollutants can impart a strong odor to water.

Odors can be released from **chemicals**, chemical reactions, fires, or rotting material. The air carries odor-producing gas molecules, and they are detected by breathing or sniffing. The molecules stimulate receptor cells in the nose, which in turn send nerve impulses to the brain where they are processed into information about the odor.

Research is being performed to quantify and characterize odors. Tests such as sniff chromatography, **emission** rate measurement, and hedonics are being used in an effort to develop a better definition of what offensive odors are.

Scientists have found that the perception of odors is highly subjective. What one person might not like, another person might not be able to smell at all, and what people define as an offensive odor depends on age and sex, as well as other characteristics.

One method of controlling unpleasant smells is deodorizers. Deodorizers either disguise offensive odors with an agreeable smell or destroy them. Some deodorizers do this by chemically changing odor-producing particles while others merely remove them from the air. Disinfectants, such as formaldehyde, can kill bacteria, **fungi** or molds that create odors. Odors can also be removed through ventilation systems. The air can be "scrubbed" by forcing it through liquid or through filters containing such materials as charcoal, methods which trap and remove odor-producing particles from the air. Factories can also employ a process known as "re-odorization," which works on the principle that there are seven basic odor types: camphoraceous, mint, floral, musky, ethereal, putrid, and pungent. The process is based on the theory that different combinations of these odor types produce different smells, and re-odorization releases chemicals into the air to combine with the regular factory odors and generate a more pleasant smell.

Aeration is one method of removing objectionable odors from water. The surface of the water is mixed with air and the oxygen oxidizes various materials that would otherwise turn the water foul. Aeration can be accomplished by running the water over steps or spraying the water through nozzles. Trickling the water over trays of coke also helps eliminate offensive odors, and adding activated charcoal can have the same effect.

Even though science has shown that the perception of odors is subjective, many people are offended by them. It is often considered a quality-of-life issue, and politicians have been strongly influenced by their constituencies. Nuisance regulations have been passed in many states and municipalities, and though they often vary, their attempts to distinguish between acceptable and unacceptable odors are often vague and difficult to apply. Proving that odors interfere with the quality of life is not only subjective but nearly impossible. Refuse-handlers and factories are perhaps the most adversely affected; they often receive heavy fines for odors, although there is no proven method for eliminating them. Many believe a more concrete system of regulations is needed, but science has not been able to provide the basis on which to build one. *See also* Noise pollution; Pollution control

[*Nikola Vrtis*]

FURTHER READING

Bowker, P. G. *Odor and Corrosion Control in Sanitary Sewerage Systems and Treatment Plants.* New York: Hemisphere, 1989.

Hesketh, H. E. *Odor Control Including Hazardous-Toxic Odors.* Lancaster, PA: Technomic, 1988.

Hunt, P., and K. Hauck. "Raising a Stink Over Composting Odors." *American City and County* 105 (December 1990): 64-65.

Kreis, R. D. *Control of Animal Production Odors: The State-of-the-Art.* Ada, OK: U. S. Environmental Protection Agency, 1978.

Odum, Eugene P. (1913-)

American ecologist

Eugene P. Odum has been called "the ecologist's ecologist," meaning that he has been of special significance to his colleagues in the development of the discipline, and in

formulating its content, outlines, and boundaries. He helped lay the foundations for what might be called the "modern" study of **ecology** in the 1940s and 1950s by redirecting the field to studies based on energetics, on the relatively new **ecosystem** concept, and on functional as well as structural analyses of living communities. From early in his career, he has worked to define general principles in ecology. His colleagues and associates have recognized him by electing him president of the **Ecological Society of America**, through election to the National Academy of Sciences, and through the awarding of prestigious prizes, including the Tyler Award in 1977 and the Crafoord Prize in 1987.

Odum was born in Lake Sunapee, New Hampshire, to an academic family. His father, Howard W. Odum, was a well-known sociologist, remembered today especially for his work on regionalism. His brother, Howard T. Odum, is a well-known systems ecologist. Eugene Odum received his bachelor's and master's degrees in biology from the University of North Carolina, and his Ph.D. in ecology and ornithology from the University of Illinois in 1939. He spent brief stints as an instructor at Western Reserve University and as a research biologist at the Edmund Niles Huck Preserve in New York. In 1940, he accepted a teaching position at the University of Georgia, spent the next four decades there, and since his retirement in 1984, has been an emeritus professor. During his tenure in Georgia, the university has become a world center for the study of ecology, through various departments but also through the Institute of Ecology, which he helped initiate and of which he was the long-time director.

Odum's best-known work is his "landmark" general text, *Fundamentals of Ecology*, first published in 1953, with a third edition published in 1971. This text dominated the market for two decades and is still a book to consult, including an extensive and still useful reference list. Odum revised the third edition "in light of the increasing importance of the subject in human affairs." That edition is organized into three parts: basic ecological principles and concepts, emphasizing energy and ecosystems; "the habitat approach," which discusses freshwater, marine, estuarine, and terrestrial ecology; and applications and technology, which includes chapters on resources, pollution and **environmental health**, radiation ecology, remote sensing, and microbial ecology. Since Odum is a well-known radiation ecologist, that chapter especially is still timely.

Odum's early work was on birds, an interest threaded into his publications for many years. His research focused for several years on various aspects of radiation ecology. He turned early to an emphasis on energetics and on ecosystem studies, becoming almost as well known for systems ecology as his younger brother. A lot of his work has been on productivity in estuaries and marshes. And he is known for his work on old fields in the southern United States. That research has, in many instances, been applied to problems in environmental management, and to issues of human impact and reciprocity.

In recent years, a considerable amount of his energy has been devoted to human interactions with and impacts on environmental systems. That last interest has turned Odum into something of a philosopher, resulting in the publication of several papers on values and ethics. One influence of his thinking that will be debated for a long time is his repeated attempts to outline ecology as an integrative discipline, and to locate ecologists as scientists interested in every level of integration, from micro to macro. That work has led him several times, with mixed success, to move away from the classical reductionist approach in science and to try an outline for a holistic approach in ecology.

[*Gerald L. Young*]

FURTHER READING

Odum, E. P. *Ecology: A Bridge Between Science and Society*. Sunderland, MA: Sinauer Associates, 1996.

———. "The Emergence of Ecology as a New Integrative Discipline," *Science*, 195, no. 4284, (March 25, 1977).

———. *Fundamentals of Ecology*, 3rd ed. Philadelphia, PA: W.B. Saunders Company, 1971.

———. "Great Ideas in Ecology for the 1990s," *BioScience* 42, no. 7, (July 1992): 542-545.

Office of Civilian Radioactive Waste Management (OCRWM)

Humans have been using nuclear materials for nearly forty years. Nuclear reactors and **nuclear weapons** account for the largest volume of these materials, while industrial, medical, and research applications account for smaller volumes. One of the largest single problems involved with the use of nuclear materials is the volume of wastes resulting from these applications. By one estimate, 8,000 to 9,000 metric tons (8,816-9,918 tons) of **high-level radioactive waste**s alone are produced in the United States every year. It is something of a surprise, therefore, to learn that as late as 1982, the United States had no plan for disposing of the **radioactive waste**s produced by its commercial, industrial, research, and defense operations.

In that year, the United States Congress passed the Nuclear Waste Policy Act establishing national policy for the disposal of radioactive waste. Responsibility for the implementation of this policy was assigned to the **U.S. Department of Energy** through the Office of Civilian Radioactive Waste Management (OCRWM). OCRWM manages federal programs for recommending, constructing, and operating repositories for the disposal of high-level radioactive wastes and spent nuclear fuel. It is also responsible for arranging for the interim storage of spent nuclear fuel and for research, development, and demonstration of techniques for the disposal of high-level radioactive waste and spent nuclear fuel.

In addition, OCRWM oversees the Nuclear Waste Fund, also established by the 1982 act. The fund was established to enable the federal government to recover all costs of developing a disposal system and of disposing of high-level waste and spent nuclear fuel. It is paid for by companies that produce **nuclear power**, power consumers, and those involved in the use of nuclear materials for defense purposes.

OCRWM has published a number of short pamphlets dealing with the problem of waste disposal. They cover topics such as "Nuclear Waste Disposal," "What Will a Nuclear Waste Repository Look Like?" "What Is Spent Nuclear Fuel?" "Can Nuclear Waste Be Transported Safely?" and "How Much High-Level Nuclear Waste Is There?"

OCRWM experienced a number of setbacks in the first decade of its existence. No state was willing to allow the construction of a high-level nuclear waste repository within its borders. The technology for immobilizing wastes seemed still too primitive to guarantee that wastes would not escape in to the **environment**.

Eventually, however, OCRWM announced that it had chosen a site under **Yucca Mountain** in southeastern Nevada. The site lies on the boundaries of the **Nevada Test Site** and Nellis Air Force Base. It is near the town of Beatty, 100 miles (161 km) northwest of Las Vegas. The site has been studied since 1977 and should be ready to receive wastes early in the twenty-first century. Some residents of Nevada are unhappy with the choice of Yucca Mountain as a nuclear waste repository, however, and continue to fight OCRWM's decision. *See also* Environmental law; Hazardous waste site remediation; Low-level radioactive waste; Nuclear fission; Radiation exposure; Uranium

[*David E. Newton*]

Office of Energy Research
See **U. S. Department of Energy**

Office of Management and Budget

The Office of Management and Budget (OMB), established in 1939 within the office of the President, determines both how much money will be spent by the federal government and what kinds of regulations will be adopted to implement all environmental and other legislated programs.

According to the 1946 Administrative Procedures Act, regulations "interpret, implement or prescribe law or policy." Draft regulations must be publicized, and agencies must incorporate public comments into the final regulations. Executive Orders 12291 and 12498, issued in 1981 and 1984, respectively, gave the Office of Information and Regulatory Affairs (OIRA), a division of OMB, the authority to review and approve all regulations and paperwork drafted by the **Environmental Protection Agency**, as well as all other federal agencies. *See also* Regulatory review

Office of Oceanic and Atmospheric Research

See **National Oceanic and Atmospheric Administration**

Office of Surface Mining, Reclamation and Enforcement

In 1977 the Office of Surface Mining, Reclamation and Enforcement (OSM) was created to police **coal** extraction within the United States and to enforce the federal **Surface Mining Control and Reclamation Act** (SMRCA). Under the auspices of OSM, citizens are empowered to enforce reclamation of surface mines, as well as deep mines, that have damaged surface features.

The government, industry, or a combination of both is required to pay all expenses, including legal fees, when citizens bring successful administrative or judicial complaints for noncompliance under the SMRCA. The reclamation of abandoned mines is funded by a tax on coal. To fund the reclamation of new mines OSC requires performance bonds that must cover the cost of reclamation should the operator not complete the process.

The majority of mining states have been granted "primacy" by OSM, which means that the individual states are authorized to handle reclamation enforcement, with OSM stepping in only when states fail to enforce the SMRCA. There are almost 30,000 known violations that remain uncorrected, yet OSM issues less than 25 citations a year. The majority of citations issued are disposed of by vacating the citation or by making arrangements with the company.

OSM predicts that by the year 2,000 between five and ten percent of all coal mines abandoned prior to 1977 will be reclaimed, using coal tax money generated by the SMRCA. There are 24,000 operations including surface mines, deep mines, refuse piles and prep plants that come under the act, (including those that went into operation after 1977); about 17,000 of these have been reclaimed. Many of these reclaimed sites are merely grass planted over **desert**, incapable of supporting any form of **wildlife**. The reclamation plans developed for many surface mining sites designate the post mining land use to be pastureland, but due to the remoteness and inaccessibility, many reclaimed sites sit idle devoid of all wildlife.

Environmentalists and other opponents of the mining industry charge that coal industries and OSM personnel are the same group. It is interesting to note that Harry Snyder, the current director of OSM, was a former lobbyist for CSX railroad and is a heavy investor in coal. According to many critics the coal industry has become adept at manipulating the OSM and SMCRA for its own purposes. The OSM is currently trying to push through legislation that would eliminate the SMRCA's attorney fee provisions. The agency is also in the process of throwing out numerous other SMCRA regulations that are burdensome to the coal industry, including one that bans deep mining from national parks and wildlife refuges.

[*Debra Glidden*]

FURTHER READING

Brown, F. "The Miner's Watchdog Doesn't Bite." *Sierra* 34 (September-October 1986): 28-31.

"Coal Mining: Profit Reclamation." *The Economist* 319 (6 April 1991): A24-26.

Sherwood, T. "Strip Search". *Common Cause Magazine* 15 (May-June 1989): 8-10.

Off-road vehicles

Off-road vehicles (ORVs) include motorcycles, dirt bikes, bicycles, and all-terrain vehicles (ATVs) that can be ridden or driven in areas where there are no paved roads. While the use of off-road vehicles has gained in popularity, conservationists and landowners have prompted some legislatures to restrict their use because of the damage the vehicles do to the environment.

A popular sport in desert areas, mountain passes, and riverbeds, owners and drivers of off-road vehicles defend their right to ride wherever they like. But environmentalists claim that the vehicles scar the land, kill **wildlife**, destroy vegetation, and cause noise, safety and **pollution** problems. The knobby tires of mountain bicycles contribute to **erosion** in delicate desert areas and along the sides of steep mountain trails. Motorized off-road vehicles are more devastating to local **ecology** as landowners across the country are finding.

A rider maneuvers his Honda three-wheeler over sand dunes.

In Missouri's Black River, off-roaders typically discard beer cans, used baby diapers, and empty motor-oil cans. Usually clear, the Black River in places run as green as a sewage ditch when algae are stirred up by the commotion of off-road vehicles. Some drivers drain their crankcases into the river. Inevitably, the oil and gas from motorized vehicles seeps into the river **ecosystem**. A bill passed by the Missouri legislature in April 1988 restricted the vehicles to areas of the river where landowners gave permission. Since much of the area is not posted, however, the law failed to halt a good deal of the use of off-road vehicles in the river.

At the Chincoteague Wildlife Refuge in Virginia, an environmental assessment of the effects of off-road vehicles and foot traffic found the effects devastating to some **species**, particularly the threatened piping plover. The assessment recommended that the area be closed to the vehicles and to all recreation during the nesting season, concluding that the nesting site is subject to damage not only from off-road vehicles, but also from the human intrusion accompanying the use of these vehicles.

In California, about 500,000 acres of public land are open to use by off-road vehicles, and California conservationists have fought since the late 1980s to ban the sport in state parks. Off-roaders, however, waged their own battle. Editorials in magazines for off-road vehicles users urged readers to ignore posted property, sue for the right to use the land, and "pound on politicians [sic] desks."

In another magazine article, devoted to off-roading Colorado's mountain passes, riders were urged to pack their own water during trips. "What with extensive backpacking, dirt bikes and widespread use of 4x4s, the high country now sees so much use and so many people that indigenous water is no longer fit for human consumption," the article writer states. Apparently, the writer failed to notice the irony.

More than 30 states now have enacted legislation that regulates the sale and use of off-road vehicles, especially motorized ones. The legislation was more a reaction to the safety problems inherent in three-wheel vehicles than to the detrimental ecological effects of the vehicles in pristine areas. The Consumer Product Safety Commission listed almost 1,000 deaths related to the use of ATVs from 1982 to 1988, and hundreds of product liability suits have been brought against manufacturers.

[*Linda Rehkopf*]

FURTHER READING

Holmes, H. "Hawaii Survive-o." *Garbage* 4 (October-November 1992): 24.

Jackson, J. P. "On the Trail of ORVs." *American Forests* 99 (January-February 1993): 20.

Kerner, I. "Wheels in the Wilderness." *Progressive* 54 (July 1990): 13.

Opre, T. "Off-Road Alternatives." *Outdoor Life* 191 (March 1993): 17-18+.

Offshore drilling
See **Oil drilling**

Ogallala Aquifer

The Ogallala Aquifer is an extensive underground reservoir that supplies water to most of the irrigated agriculture in the central United States. Discovered early in the nineteenth century, this aquifer—also known as the High Plains regional aquifer—became a major economic resource in the 1960s and 1970s when advanced pumping technology made large-scale irrigation possible. In 1980 this aquifer supported 170,000 **wells** and provided one third of all irrigation water pumped in the United States. In the last several decades, Ogallala-irrigated agriculture has redefined the landscape of the central United States by fostering economic expansion, population growth, and the development of large-scale agribusiness in an arid region.

The High Plains regional aquifer underlies eight states, including most of Nebraska and portions of South Dakota, Wyoming, Colorado, Kansas, Oklahoma, Texas, and New

The Ogallala, or High Plains, Aquifer.

Mexico. Covering an area of 175,000 square miles (453,250 sq km), the aquifer runs 800 miles (1,288 km) from north to south, and stretches 200 miles (322 km) at its widest point. Nebraska holds by far the greatest amount of water, with 400-1200 feet (130-400 m) of saturated thickness, while much of the aquifer's southern extent averages less than 100 feet (30 m) thick. Geologically, this aquifer comprises a number of porous, unconsolidated sand, silt, and clay formations that were deposited by wind and water from the Rocky Mountains. The most important of these formations is the Ogallala formation, which makes up seventy-seven percent of the regional aquifer. The aquifer's total drainable water is about 3.25 billion acre feet.

Large volume use of **groundwater** became possible with the invention of powerful pumps and center-pivot irrigation in the late 1950s. The center pivot sprays water from a rotating arm long enough to water a quarter section (160-acre) field. This irrigation technique is responsible for the characteristic circular pattern visible from the air in most agricultural landscapes in the western United States. Although installation is extremely expensive, center pivots and powerful pumps enable farmers to produce great amounts of corn, wheat, sorghum, and cotton where low rainfall had once made most agriculture impossible.

High-volume pumping has also reduced the amount of available groundwater. Most water in the High Plains aquifer is "**fossil water**," which has been stored underground for thousands or millions of years. New water enters the aquifer extremely slowly. In most of the Ogallala region, pumping exceeds recharge rates, a process known as water mining, and the net volume is steadily decreasing. Region-wide, less than 0.5 percent of the water pumped each year is replaced by infiltration of rainwater. At current rates of pumping, the resource should be 80 percent depleted by about 2020.

As saturation levels in the aquifer fall, consequences on the surface are clearly visible. Many streams and rivers, dependent on groundwater for base flow, run dry. The state of Kansas alone has lost more than 700 miles (1,126 km) of rivers that once flowed year round. Center pivot irrigation, requiring a well that can pump 750 gallons (2,839 liters) per minute, is beginning to disappear in Texas and New Mexico, where the aquifer can no longer provide this volume. **Groundwater pollution** is becoming more concentrated as more agricultural chemicals seep into a shrinking reservoir of Ogallala water. Many high plains towns, formerly rich with pure, clean groundwater, now have tap water that is considered unhealthy for children and pregnant women. As the Ogallala runs dry, the region's demographics are also changing. Many farmers assumed heavy debt burdens in the 1970s when they installed center pivots. Drying wells and falling production have led to farm foreclosures and the depopulation of small, rural towns. Regional populations that swelled with irrigated agriculture are beginning to shrink again. Land ownership, formerly held by independent families and ranchers, is increasingly in the hands of banks, insurance companies, and corporations, which provide little support to local communities.

[*Mary Ann Cunningham*]

FURTHER READING

Aucoin, J. *Water in Nebraska—Use, Politics, Policies.* Lincoln: University of Nebraska Press, 1984.

Kromm, D. E., and S. E. White. *Groundwater Exploitation in the High Plains.* Lawrence: University Press of Kansas, 1992.

Oil

See **Petroleum**

Oil drilling

Petroleum occurs naturally in the earth in porous rock, found anywhere from thousands of meters underground all the way to the earth's surface. The porous layer of rock normally lies between two nonporous layers, so oil does not flow out of its **reservoir**. In most cases water and/or **natural gas** occur along with petroleum in the rock. Oil can be extracted from the rock by sinking a pipe into the earth until it penetrates the saturated porous rock. In most cases, oil will then begin to flow of its own accord out of the rock and into the pipe.

The upward flow of oil can be caused by a number of different factors. In some cases, the porous layer of rock is covered by a hollow cap filled with natural gas. Pressure of the gas forces petroleum out of the rock into the pipe. In some cases, gas pressure will be so great as to force oil out of a new well in a fountain-like effect known as a "gusher."

In other cases, the pressure of water also present in the saturated rock pushes oil towards and into the pipe. In still other instances, gases dissolved in petroleum exert pressure on it, forcing it up the pipe.

The ease with which oil flows through a rock layer and into a well depends on a number of factors. In addition to water and gas pressure, viscosity of the oil determines how easily it will move through rock. Even under the most favorable conditions, no more than about 30 percent of the oil in a rock layer can be extracted by any of the natural methods described above.

The term *primary recovery* is used to describe the natural flow of oil by any of the means described above. By adding a pump to the well—*secondary recovery*—an additional quantity of oil can be removed. Even after primary and secondary recovery, however, 40 to 80 percent of the oil may still remain in a reservoir. All or most of that oil can be recovered by a variety of techniques described as *tertiary recovery*.

All forms of tertiary recovery involve the injection of some kind of fluid into the oil-bearing stratum. A long pipe is stuck into the ground parallel to the oil-recovery pipe. Into the second pipe is injected a mixture of **carbon dioxide** in water, steam, or some combination of water and chemicals. In any one of these cases, the injected material diffuses through the oil-bearing rock, pushing the petroleum out and up into the recovery pipe.

Yet another tertiary recovery approach is to set fire to the oil remaining in one part of the stratum. The heat thus generated reduces the viscosity of the unburned oil remaining in the stratum, allowing it to flow more easily into the recovery pipe. Any form of tertiary recovery is relatively expensive and is not used, therefore, until the price of oil justifies this approach. The same can be said for off-shore drilling.

Organic materials washed into the oceans from rivers often settle on the sloping underwater area known as the continental shelf. In this oxygen-free environment, those materials often decay to produce petroleum and natural gas. In recent decades, oil companies have found it profitable to locate and drill for oil in these off-shore reserves.

The technique for drilling from off-shore **wells** is generally the same as that used on land. The major difference is that before drilling may begin a stable platform on the water's surface for the drilling rig and ancillary equipment must be constructed. The drilling platform must be protected from high winds, waves, and serious storms. In addition, special safeguards must be taken to protect pipes from breaking and releasing oil into the environment. *See also* Oil Pollution Act (1990); Oil spills

[*David E. Newton*]

FURTHER READING

Carey, J. "Hot Science in Cold Lands." *National Wildlife* 29 (April-May 1991): 4-13.

Freudenburg, W. R. *Oil in Troubled Waters: Perceptions, Politics, and the Battle Over Offshore Drilling.* Albany: State University of New York Press, 1994.

Holing, D. *Coastal Alert: Ecosystems, Energy, and Offshore Oil Drilling.* Covelo, CA: Island Press, 1990.

"Oil and Gas Drilling Threatens Grizzlies." *National Parks* 67 (May-June 1993): 13-14.

Petulla, J. M. *American Environmental History.* 2nd ed. San Francisco: Boyd & Fraser, 1988.

Oil embargo

The year of 1973 marks one of the most important turning points in the history of the twentieth century. Prior to 1973, the world had become accustomed to a plentiful supply of inexpensive **fossil fuels**: **coal**, **petroleum**, and **natural gas**. Developed nations had built economies that depended not just on these fossil fuels, but also on their relatively low cost. Patterns of urban growth in the United States, to take just one example, reflected the fact that the average person could easily afford to drive her **automobile** many miles a day. The average price of a barrel of oil in 1973, for example, was $2.70 and the average cost of **gasoline** at the pump about 35¢ a gallon.

A number of factors combined in 1973, however, to change this picture dramatically. The most obvious of those factors was a decision made by the Arab members of the **Organization of Petroleum Exporting Countries** (OPEC) to cut back on its export of petroleum to many nations of the world. The reason given for this decision was the support given by the United States to Israel during the 18-day war with Syria and Egypt. The action, taken on October 18, 1973, reduced the direct flow of oil from the Arab states to the United States to zero.

OPEC had been established in 1960 by a Venezuelan oil man Juan Perez Alfonso. An extremely conservative businessman who rode a bicycle and read by candlelight to save energy, Perez Alfonso saw OPEC as an organization that could encourage energy **conservation** throughout the world.

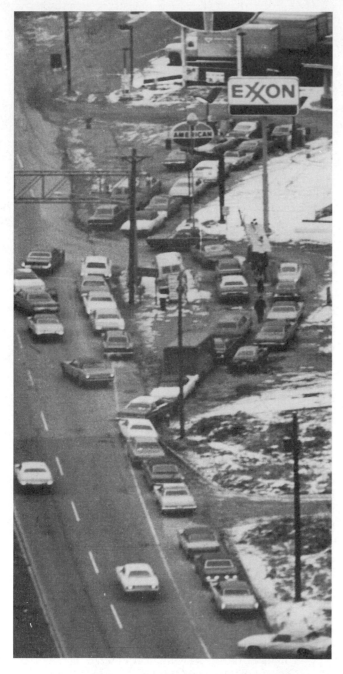

Cars line up for gasoline along Route 4 in Fort Lee, New Jersey, in 1974.

His objectives were certainly achieved in some places as a result of the 1973 embargo. Americans, along with citizens of other developed nations, found themselves waiting in long lines to buy gasoline, turning their thermostats down to 60°, and learning how to live with less energy in general.

The embargo also had a devastating effect on national economies. In the United States, inflation climbed to more than 10 percent a year, an enormous trade deficit developed, and interest rates climbed to the high teens. Elsewhere, a global recession began.

By the time the embargo ended in March 1974, oil prices had climbed to nearly $12 a barrel, an increase of 330 percent. Gasoline prices had also begun to climb, reaching 57¢ a gallon by 1975, 86¢ a gallon by 1979, and $1.19 a gallon by 1980.

The embargo caused developed nations to rethink their dependence on fossil fuels. Research on **alternative energy sources** such as wind, tides, geothermal, and **solar energy** suddenly attained a new importance. The United States government responded to the new era of expensive energy by formulating an entirely new energy policy expressed in such legislation as the Energy Policy and Conservation Act of 1976, the Energy Conservation and Production Act of 1976, the **Energy Reorganization Act** of 1974, and the National Energy Act of 1978.

Interestingly enough, the OPEC embargo had impacts that were relatively little known and discussed at the time. For example, the United States was importing only about 7 percent of its oil from Arab nations in 1973. Yet, almost as soon as the embargo was announced, prices at the gasoline pump began to rise. Such a fast response is, at first, difficult to understand since "old," cheap oil was still on its way from the Middle East and was still being processed, shipped and stored by petroleum companies.

The embargo must also be understood, therefore, as an opportunity for which oil companies had been looking to increase their prices and profits. In the years preceding the embargo, these companies had been feeling increased pressures from domestic environmental groups to cut back on drilling in sensitive areas. They were also losing business to small, independent competitors.

The embargo afforded the companies an opportunity to turn this situation around and once more increase profitability, which they did. In the one year following the embargo, for example, the seven largest oil companies reported profits from 40 to 85 percent. Two years after the embargo, one of these companies (Exxon) became the nation's richest corporation, with revenues of $45.1 billion.

Neither have the long term effects of the embargo been what observers in 1973 might have expected. In 1990 the United States imports a larger percentage of its oil from Arab OPEC members than it did in 1973. And the enthusiasm for alternative energy sources of the 1970s has largely diminished. *See also* Alternative fuels; Energy conservation; Geothermal energy; Wave power; Wind energy

[*David E. Newton*]

FURTHER READING

Commoner, Barry. *The Politics of Energy.* New York: Knopf, 1979.

Silber, D., ed. *The Arab Oil Embargo: Ten Years Later.* Washington, DC: Americans for Energy Independence, 1984.

Oil pipeline

See **Trans-Alaska pipeline**

Oil Pollution Act (1990)

President George Bush signed the Oil Pollution Act (OPA) of 1990 on August 18 in the wake of the environmental and anti-big-business outcry that followed the wreck of the oil tanker ***Exxon Valdez*** in March 1989. Before the crash, Congress had spent 15 years debating the need to improve U.S. laws regulating oil tankers. It was not until the *Valdez* spewed more than 10 million gallons of crude oil into **Prince William Sound** off Alaska was Congress able to agree on the inadequacy of those laws. Weak penalties, unrealistic and confused cleanup plans, and the allowance for little or no federal money to assist the cleanups combined to make these laws ineffective.

The OPA set up a comprehensive federal liability system for all **oil spills**, established a federal trust fund to help pay for cleanups, strengthened civil and criminal penalties against oil companies and tanker contractors involved in spills, and required companies to have spill contingency and readiness plans in place before they can operate. The primary goal, the OPA's authors agreed, was to prevent further spills.

Under the OPA, oil tankers and facilities must have plans in place that detail how they would respond to their own worst-case spills and describe personnel training, equipment testing, and response strategies. The plans must be reviewed by the **Environmental Protection Agency (EPA)** and the Coast Guard and be approved by the President before they can operate. The OPA further requires all new tankers to be built with double hulls to provide an additional layer of protection in collisions. This provision silenced a long-standing debate, between proponents of the requirement and opponents of double-hulls. The opponents of these hulls argued that when the outer hull is punctured, water can enter the space between the hulls and make the vessel less stable. Some smaller tankers and ships that unload at deepwater ports are exempted from OPA requirements, but all other single-hulled vessels be must be phased out by January 1, 2010.

Spillers were previously liable only for the cleanup costs incurred by the federal government. The OPA expands liability to include costs and damages incurred by local governments, agencies, and private parties. This provision came too late, however, for the small Alaskan town of Valdez—which was overwhelmed by cleanup workers and the press—to collect for its damages. Also available to finance cleanups is the newly created Federal Oil Spill Liability Trust Fund, funded principally by a five-cent per-barrel tax on oil, to be used to pay for cleanups when the spiller is either unidentifiable, not liable, or a foreign company. Even with a $1 billion per-incident cap, this fund would not have covered Exxon's obligations for the *Valdez* spill. However, it is likely to be enough to cover cleanup for most spills, which are much smaller. The OPA does not preempt state laws regarding oil spill cleanups. As is the case with many other **environmental law**s, states are free to enact their own regulations that are stricter than the federal act.

The preservation of state power, the expansion of liability, the increase in penalties, and increased federal authority to carry out cleanups represents an anti-oil industry bias and is a victory for environmentalists, but many feel the law should go further to deter shippers from spilling oil. Oil companies, for their part, have threatened to stop shipping through U. S. ports unless their liability is lessened. But after the protracted debate and difficult compromises that resulted in the OPA, most feel the issues won't be re-opened—at least not unless a spill that matches the *Exxon Valdez* in drama and damage can prove or disprove the OPA's effectiveness.

[*L. Carol Ritchie*]

FURTHER READING

Wilkinson, C. M., L. Pittman, and R. F. Dye. "Slick Work: An Analysis of the Oil Pollution Act of 1990." *Journal of Energy, Natural Resources and Environmental Law* 12 (1992).

Oil shale

The term oil shale is technically incorrect in that the rock to which it refers, marlstone, is neither oil nor shale. Instead, it is a material that contains an organic substance known as *kerogene*. When heated to a temperature of 900°F (480°C) or more, kerogene decomposes, forming a **petroleum**-like liquid and a combustible gas. Huge amounts of high-grade oil shale exist in the western United States. By some estimates, these reserves could meet the nation's fuel needs for about a century. Although the technology for tapping these reserves already exists, it is still too expensive to compete with conventional **fossil fuels** or other sources of energy now in use. *See also* Alternative fuels

Oil spills

These environmental disasters are a tragic byproduct of an energy-dependent world. Giant supertankers and offshore oil wells are a constant threat to coastlines. Even so, the mind-boggling environmental terrorism unleashed by Iraq during the 1991 **Persian Gulf War** far surpasses all other petroleum-related catastrophes.

Oil spills on land and inland waterways are relatively confined and are easier to stop and to clean up; also, they are usually far smaller. By contrast, oceanic spills are nearly impossible to handle because of rapid dispersal and thinning, evaporation of up to half the **petroleum**, and hindrances from storms.

Much oil in the sea comes from the use of ocean water as ballast for returning oil tankers; when pumped out near loading facilities some of the oil escapes. However, increasingly effective techniques are being developed to reduce this source, now up to 95 percent effective, and the relatively dispersed nature of such oil makes it far less threatening than concentrated spills.

The 1956 Arab-Israeli conflict exposed Europe's vulnerability to petroleum supplies routed through the Suez Canal. As a consequence, supertankers large enough to

Workers clean up an oil-fouled California beach.

operate profitably while sailing around Africa were developed. By the 1960s, the term supertanker was being used to describe ships of over 100,000 tons. Tanker size increased dramatically, with feasibility studies indicating success for a 500,000-ton tanker, and design studies prepared for 1,000,000-ton tankers. The *Braer*, which shipwrecked in 1993, was a 600,000-ton tanker. Only the slowdown in demand following the 1973 and 1979 price shocks has limited the production of these behemoths. Actually, if stringent safety measures were followed, including double-hulled design and aircraft-type redundant systems, and managed routes followed, the risk to the **environment** could be substantially reduced.

Unfortunately, the record since the 1967 wreck of the **Torrey Canyon** and the 1969 blowout of a well in the Santa Barbara channel has included a number of catastrophic spills. These include the groundings of **Amoco Cadiz** off Brittany, France, in 1978; the **Exxon Valdez** in **Prince William Sound** near Valdez, Alaska, in 1989; and the above-mentioned *Braer* off the south coast of the Shetland Islands, Scotland. Other spills include the 1979 blowout of Ixtoc I in the Gulf of Mexico and incidents related to military actions in the Persian Gulf.

The *Torrey Canyon* struck granite rocks off the southwest coast of England, an accident related to pressure on the captain to make port during a narrow window of high tide and with a malfunctioning steering wheel. Much was learned from this disaster: the harsh impact of the accident on the intertidal zone, the remarkable ability of storms and other natural sources to repair the damage, the ineffectiveness of cleanup operations both offshore and onshore, and the terrible toll on seabirds. The latter suffered especially from oil ingested in efforts to clean their feathers and from hypothermia induced by the loss of waterproofing and insulating capabilities of their down.

A number of important lessons from the *Torrey Canyon* are still relevant today. **Detergents** used to clean the beaches exacted a high toll on grazers. The use of straw to absorb oil coming ashore, though labor intensive, was highly effective since straw retains 10-30 times its weight in oil. Dispersing agents applied quickly offshore were effective in countering the formation of mousse, a difficult-to-handle oily threat; the tiny oil droplets created by the dispersants are more readily evaporated or consumed by microbes.

The Santa Barbara oil spill is notable for its massive press coverage, especially on the evening news, at a time when legislation which created the **Environmental Protection Agency** was under consideration. This blowout through a weak, upper-layer geologic structure was ultimately abated by draining the **reservoir** through relief **wells**.

The *Amoco Cadiz* lost its steering and foundered on rocks during a period of extremely stormy weather and rough seas off Brittany, the same general region of France where *Torrey Canyon* oil came ashore. Though nearly twice the size of the *Torrey Canyon* spill, high wave energy rapidly dispersed the oil and provided ideal conditions for biodegradation.

Ixtoc I, a runaway well in the Gulf of Mexico, gushed more than one million gallons per day for several months. The damage was mitigated by the distance offshore, which allowed time for the aromatic (benzene-based) fractions to evaporate; the oil that did come ashore landed mainly along the sparsely populated Mexican coastline.

The *Exxon Valdez* grounding generated the largest human effort at cleaning up a maritime spill. Exxon Company spent well over $1 billion, yet in retrospect, some researchers think it would have been better to let nature do much of the work, such as coastline washing by winter storms. This accident halted efforts to open up the **Arctic National Wildlife Refuge** to **oil drilling**.

This spill is being carefully studied, since it was the first major spill in the Arctic environment. One encouraging note has been the apparent success of fertilized microbes to clean up some beaches. On the other hand, **sea otter**s (*Enhydra lutris*), who depend on insulating fur for warmth rather than subcutaneous fat as do seals, died from hypothermia much like the seabirds killed in the *Torrey Canyon* disaster. In retrospect, given the experience with supertanker spills, it might be best to clean up and disperse as much as possible, inject microorganisms and **fertilizer** into the intertidal zone, and leave the rest to the resilience of nature.

None of the previously described tragedies can compare with the environmental terrorism unleashed by Iraq during the 1991 war. An estimated six billion barrels of oil were released into the Persian Gulf through a combination of damage to a storage tank during the battle for Al Khalfji, the release of oil at the Sea Island loading area, and the deliberate dumping of oil from at least five tankers. The spill could have been much worse but for the efforts of four Kuwaiti oil field workers who anticipated the sabotage. Under cover of darkness they closed a valve on the 48-inch (122-cm) pipeline from the tank farm to the loading docks, relabeling the valve as open.

Equally monstrous was the blowing up of wells prior to the land invasion. Fortunately, much of the oil either burned off, which also produced numerous environmental and health problems, or pooled in desert depressions. One such pool measured one mile (1.6 km) long and three feet (91 cm) deep. Capping efforts started slowly, owing to bureaucratic procedures, booby-trapped well-head areas, and the need to clear unexploded ordnance. Major problems here included the enormous well-head pressures and the difficulty of obtaining water for cooling the fires. As contracts were resolved, more teams were sent, equipment began to flow, and the pace of successful cappings rose to six a day. It was an international effort, led by five teams from the United States; 41 of the 732 wells on fire were handled by a Kuwaiti team. As each team worked, their experience helped them on the next well, and their success rate increased. The job was finished in eight months, not the two years predicted by Red Adair. Controlling the damage cost Kuwait over $2 billion, and the country lost three percent of its reserves.

Fortunately, the predictions of global catastrophe and climate change did not occur. However, the evaporation of large petroleum lakes continued to release deadly chemicals into the atmosphere. The Persian Gulf will remain an important laboratory for years to come, especially for tropical environments. Because of its shallow depth and flat shoreline, these waters abound with sea grass and algae, shrimp and finfish; large, intertidal areas support migratory fowl.

There are, nevertheless, some heartening stories. Relatively primitive techniques still recovered up to 30,000 barrels per day from Gulf waters. A number of cormorants were salvaged through a combination of rehydration therapy, careful washing with household detergents, and use of the drug Inderal to reduce the stress response of these highly sensitive birds by depressing their heart rate. By contrast, however, grebes tended to swallow the oily sand on their feathers, which formed a lethal stone in their gizzard.

With all the improved techniques, maritime oil spills still present formidable challenges. Unquestionably, the best course is prevention. *See also* Oil Pollution Act (1990)

[*Nathan H. Meleen*]

FURTHER READING

Browne, M. W., et al. "War and the Environment." *Audubon* 93 (September-October 1991): 88-96+.

Canby, T. Y. "After the Storm (the Persian Gulf)." *National Geographic* 180 (August 1991): 2-35.

Davidson, A. *In the Wake of the Exxon Valdez*. San Francisco: Sierra Club Books, 1990.

Easton, R. *Black Tide: The Santa Barbara Oil Spill and Its Consequences*. New York: Delacorte Press, 1972.

Hodgson, B. "Alaska's Big Spill: Can the Wilderness Heal?" *National Geographic* 177 (January 1990): 2-43.

Jackson, J. B. C., et al. "Ecological Effects of a Major Oil Spill on Panamanian Coastal Marine Communities." *Science* 243 (6 January 1989): 37-44.

National Academy of Sciences. *Oil in the Sea*. Washington, DC: National Academy Press, 1985.

Office of Technology Assessment. *Coping With Oiled Environments*. Washington, DC: U. S. Government Printing Office, 1989.

Oil-recycle toilet

See **Toilets**

Old-growth forest

The trees stand tall and thick of girth. The air about them is cool and moist. The **soil** is rich and matted by a thick organic blanket. People marvel at the forest, imbibing its grandeur, coveting its timber. In another area, across the mountains, perhaps, the trees stand stooped and scraggly. The air about them is parched. The soil is coarse, barren, and hardened to the elements. People pass by the forest, ignoring its dignity, rejecting its worth.

These images reflect extremes in old–growth forests. The first is the compelling one: it exemplifies the common perception of a **ecosystem** at the center of a bitter environmental controversy. The second depicts an equally valid

Old-growth Douglas fir forest, Pacific Northwest.

old–growth forest, but it is one whose fate few people care to debate.

The controversy over old-growth forests is the result of **competition** for what has become a scarce natural resource—large, old trees that can be either harvested to produce high value lumber products or preserved as notable relics as a forest proceeds through its stages of ecological **succession**. This competition is a classic environmental struggle, impelled by radically different perceptions of value and conflicting goals of consumptive and nonconsumptive use.

What is an old–growth forest? Before the modern debates, the definition seemed simple. Old–growth was a

mature virgin forest; it consisted of giant old trees, many past their prime, which towered over a shady, multilayered understory and a thick, fermenting forest floor. In contrast to second–growth timber, the stand never had been harvested. It was something that existed in the West, having long since been cut in the East.

In the mid- to late-1980s several professional and governmental organizations, including the Society of American Foresters, the U.S. **Forest Service**, and California's State Board of Forestry, began efforts to define formally "old–growth forest" and the related term "ancient forest" for ecological and regulatory purposes. The task was complicated by the great diversity in forest types, as well as by different views of the purpose and use of the definition. For example, 60 years of age might be considered old for one type, whereas 200 or 1,000 years might be more accurate for other types. Moreover, forest attributes other than age are more important for the wellbeing of certain **species** which are dependent on forests commonly considered old growth, such as the **northern spotted owl** and marbled murrelet. Nonetheless, some common attributes and criteria were developed.

Old–growth forests are now defined as those in a late seral stage of ecological succession, based on their composition, structure, and function. Composition is the representation of plant species—trees, shrubs, forbs, and grasses—that comprise the forest. Often, in referring to an old–growth stand foresters limit composition to the tree species present). Structure includes the concentration, age, size, and arrangement of living plants, standing dead trees (called "snags"), fallen logs, forest-floor litter, and stream debris. Function refers to the forest's broad ecological roles, such as **habitat** for terrestrial and aquatic organisms, a repository for genetic material, a component in the hydrologic and biogeochemical cycles, and a climatic buffer. Each of these factors vary and must be defined and evaluated for each forest type in the various physiographic regions, while accounting for differences in disturbance history, such as **wildfire**s, landslides, hurricanes, and human activities. The problem of specifically defining and determining use of these lands is exceedingly complex, especially for managers of multiple–use **public land**s who often are squeezed between the opposing pressures of commercial interests, such as the timber industry, and environmental preservation groups. The modern controversy centers primarily around forests in the northwest of United States and Canada—forests consisting of virgin redwoods, Douglas firs, and mixed conifers.

As an example of old–growth characteristics, the Douglas–fir forests are characterized by large, old, live trees, many more than 150 feet (46 m) tall, 4 ft (1.2 m) in diameter, and 200 years old. Interspersed among the trees are snags of various sizes—skeletons of trees long dead, now home to birds, small climbing mammals, and insects. Below the giants are one or more layers of understory—subdominant and lower growing trees of the same or perhaps different species, and beneath them are shrubs, either in a thick tangle providing dense cover and blocking passage or separated and allowing easy passage. The trees are not all healthy and vigorous. Some are malformed, with broken tops or multiple trunks, and infected by fungal rots whose conks protrude through the bark. Eventually, these will fall, joining others that fell decades or centuries ago, making a criss–cross pattern of rotting logs on the forest floor. In places, high in the trees, neighboring crowns touch all around, permanently shading the ground; elsewhere, gaps in the canopy allow sunlight to reach the forest floor.

Proponents of harvesting mature trees in old–growth forests assert that the forests cannot be preserved, that they have reached the **carrying capacity** of the site and the stage of decadence and declining productivity that ultimately will result in loss of the forests as well as their high commercial value which supports local lumber–based economies. They feel that society would be better served by converting these aged, slow-growing ecosystems to healthy, productive, managed forests. Management proponents also argue that adequate old–growth forests are permanently protected in designated **wilderness**es and national and state parks. Moreover, they point out that even though most old–growth forests are on public land, many forests are privately owned, and that land owners not only pay taxes on the forests, but they also have made an investment from which they are entitled a reasonable profit. If the forests are to be preserved, land owners and others suffering loss from the preservation should be reimbursed.

Proponents of saving the large old trees and their environments claim that the forests are dynamic, that although the largest, oldest trees will die and rot, they also will be returned to earth to support new growth, foster biological diversity, and preserve genetic linkages. Moreover, protection of the forests will help ensure survival of dependent species, some of which are threatened or endangered. Defenders claim that the trees will not be wasted; they simply will have alternative value. They believe that their cause is one of moral as well as biological imperative. More than 90 percent of America's old–growth forests have been logged, depriving **future generations** of the scientific, social, and psychic benefits of these forests. As a vestige of North American heritage, the remaining forests, they believe, should be manipulated only insofar as necessary to protect their integrity and minimize threats of natural fire or disease from spreading to surrounding lands. *See also* American Forestry Association; Endangered species; National forest; National Forest Management Act; Restoration ecology

[*Ronald D. Taskey*]

FURTHER READING

Arrandale, T. *The Battle for Natural Resources.* Washington, DC: Congressional Quarterly, Inc., 1983.

Kaufmann, M. R., W. H. Moir, and R. L. Bassett. *Old–Growth Forests in the Southwest and Rocky Mountain Regions.* Proceedings of a Workshop. Washington, DC: U. S. Forest Service, Rocky Mountain Forest and Range Experiment Station, 1992.

Spies, T. A., and J. F. Franklin. "The Structure of Natural Young, Mature, and Old–Growth Douglas–Fir Forests in Oregon and Washington." In *Wildlife and Vegetation of Unmanaged Douglas-Fir Forests,* edited by L. F. Ruggiero, et al. Washington, DC: U. S. Forest Service, Pacific Northwest Forest and Range Experiment Station, 1991.

Olmsted, Frederick Law Sr. (1822-1903)

American landscape designer

The famous landscape designer of Central Park (on which he collaborated with the architect Calvert Vaux), Frederick Law Olmsted Sr. is widely known for that accomplishment alone. Considering the impact of the park on city life in New York, and on other designs around the world, that would be accomplishment enough. But Olmsted other achievements are so overshadowed by the Central Park project, that he is still not as well known in environmental circles as he should be.

Many people don't know, or are confused by, the fact that there were two Frederick Law Olmsteds: father and son, FLO Sr., and FLO Jr. Both of them were landscape architects, and FLO Jr. followed directly in his father's footsteps, assuming "leadership of the country's largest and most prestigious landscape architecture firm" after his father's death.

Olmsted Sr., was born in "the rural environs" of Hartford, Connecticut, the oldest son of a well-to-do merchant, from an old New England family. He was educated in a series of boarding schools in the rural Connecticut area where he grew up. More unorthodox educational benefits accrued from his apprenticeships as civil engineer and farmer along with his stint as a ship's cabin boy on a trip to China.

Reportedly, Olmsted's firm laid out some 1,000 parks in 200 cities. He also designed university campuses (U.C. Berkeley, Harvard, Amherst, Yale, etc.), cemeteries, hospital grounds (including the grounds for the hospital where he died, unhappy—even while suffering a terminal illness—that his plans for the hospital had not been followed carefully enough). A source of unhappiness in general was the fact that many of his plans were modified in ways he did not agree with (e.g., Stanford University), or even suppressed, as happened with his plan for **Yosemite National Park**.

The crown jewel of Olmsted's creativity is, of course, Central Park in New York City. As Bill Vogt describes it: "the entire area was man-made, literally from the ground up. It sprang from an 843-acre eyesore of stinking quagmire, rubbish heaps, rocky outcroppings, and squatters shacks." An army of workers created a lake, shoveled in enormous quantities of top **soil** to create natural-appearing meadows, and planted whole forests to screen the park from the city. Charles McLaughlin, the editor of Olmsted's papers, claimed that one of the reasons Olmsted was virtually forgotten for so long was that his designs have an "always been there" quality, resulting in landscapes that today "in their maturity...appear so 'natural' that one thinks of them as something not put there by artifice but merely preserved by happenstance." What Olmsted and Vaux created stands today as an oasis and respite from what Olmsted described as the city's "constantly repeated right angles, straight lines, and flat surfaces."

Among Olmsted's lesser known accomplishments were both his role in the Commission to establish Yosemite Park (a task undertaken in 1864, long before **John Muir** first saw Yosemite Valley) and preserve Niagara Falls, a movement which resulted in creation of the Niagara Falls State Reservation in 1888. He also was a prominent participant in the campaign to preserve the Adirondack region in upstate New York.

Even less well known are his writings not directly associated with landscape architecture or ecological design. Olmsted was quite an accomplished travel writer, producing still readable books like a *Saddle-trip on the Southwestern Frontier of Texas*, or his first book titled *Walks and Talks of an American Farmer in England*. Olmsted's travels in the South were as a roving journalist for the *New York [Daily] Times*; he was an acute observer and his travel books on the south were also commentaries on the institution of slavery (that he believed "to be both economically ruinous and morally indefensible.") Books from this period included *The Cotton Kingdom: A Traveler's Observations on Cotton and Slavery in the American Slave States*, *A Journey in the Seaboard Slave States*, and *Slavery and the South, 1852-1857*. He was also a founder of the liberal journal of commentary, *The Nation*. He never dissociated his design work from its social context (believing, in his words, that his works should have "a manifest civilizing effect"), and his biggest disappointments occurred when he was not allowed to incorporate his ideas on social change into his various designs.

[*Gerald L. Young*]

FURTHER READING

Beveridge, C. E., and P. Rocheleau. *Frederick Law Olmsted: Designing the American Landscape*. New York: Rizzoli, 1995.

Fein, A. *Frederick Law Olmsted and the American Environmental Tradition*. New York: George Braziller, 1972.

Hall, L. *Olmsted's America*. Boston: Little, Brown, 1995.

Kalfus, M. *Frederick Law Olmsted: The Passion of a Public Artist*. New York: New York University Press, 1990.

Olmsted, F. L. *The Papers of Frederick Law Olmsted*, edited by C. C. McLaughlin. Baltimore, MD: The Johns Hopkins University Press, 1977.

White, D. F. "Frederick Law Olmsted, Placemaker," *Two Centuries of American Planning*, edited by Daniel Schaffer. Baltimore: The Johns Hopkins University Press, 1988.

Onchocerciasis
See **River blindness**

Open system

The relationship between any system and its surrounding **environment** can be described in one of three ways. In an isolated system, neither matter nor energy is exchanged with its environment. In a closed system, energy, but not matter, is exchanged. In an open system, both matter and energy are exchanged between the system and its surrounding environment. Any **ecosystem** is an example of an open system. Energy can enter the system in the form of sunlight, for example, and leave in the form of heat. Matter can enter the system in many ways. Rain falls upon it and leaves by

evaporation or streamflow, or animals migrate into the system and leave in the form of decay products.

Opportunistic organism

Opportunistic organisms commonly refer to animals and plants that tolerate variable environmental conditions and food sources. Some opportunistic species can thrive on almost any available **nutrient** source: omnivorous rats, bears, and raccoons are all opportunistic feeders. Many opportunists flourish under varied environmental conditions: the common house sparrow (*Passer domesticus*) can survive both in the warm, humid **climate** of Florida and in the cold, dry conditions of a Midwestern winter. Aquatic opportunists, often aggressive fish **species**, fast-spreading **plankton**, and water plants, frequently tolerate fluctuations in water **salinity** as well as temperature.

A secondary use of the term "opportunistic" signifies species that can quickly take advantage of favorable conditions when they arise. Such species can postpone reproduction, or even remain dormant, until appropriate temperatures, moisture availability, or food sources make growth and reproduction possible. Some springtime-breeding lizards in Australian **desert**s, for example, can spend months or years in a juvenile form, but when temperatures are right and a rare rainfall makes food available, no matter what time of year, they quickly mature and produce young while water is still available. More familiar opportunists are **virus**es and bacteria that reside in the human body. Often such organisms will remain undetected with a healthy host for a long time. But when the host's immune system becomes weak, resident viruses and bacteria seize an opportunity to grow and spread. Thus people suffering from malnutrition, exhaustion, or a prolonged illness are especially vulnerable to common opportunistic diseases such as the common cold or pneumonia.

Adaptable and prolific reproductive strategies usually characterize opportunistic organisms. While some plants can reproduced only when pollinated by a specific, rare insect and many animals can breed only in certain conditions and at a precise time of year, opportunistic species often reproduce at any time of year or under almost any conditions. House mice (*Mus musculus*) are extremely opportunistic breeders: they can produce sizeable litters at any time of year. Opportunistic feeding aids their ability to breed year round; these mice can nourish their young with almost any available vegetable matter, fresh or dry.

The common dandelion (*Taraxacum officinale*) is also an opportunistic breeder. Producing thousands of seeds per plant from early spring through late fall, the dandelion can reproduce despite **competition** from fast-growing grass, under heavy applications of chemical **herbicide**s, and even with the violent weekly disturbance of a lawn mower. Once mature, dandelion seeds disperse rapidly and effectively, riding on the wind or on the fur of passing rodents. The common housefly (*Musca domestica*) is also an opportunistic feeder and reproducer—it can both feed and lay eggs on almost any organic material as long as it is fairly warm and moist.

Because of their adaptability, opportunistic organisms commonly tolerate severe environmental disturbances. Fire, floods, **drought**, and **pollution** disturb or even eliminate plants and animals that require stable conditions and have specialized nutrient sources. Fireweed (*Epilobium angustifolium*), an opportunist that readily takes advantage of bare ground and open sunlight, spreads quickly after land is cleared by fire or by human disturbance. Because they tolerate, or even thrive, in disturbed **environment**s, many opportunists flourish around human settlements, actively expanding their ranges as human activity disrupts the **habitat** of more sensitive animals and plants. Opportunists are especially visible where chemical pollutants contaminate habitat. In such conditions overall species diversity usually declines, but the population of certain opportunistic species may increase as competition from more sensitive or specialized species is eliminated.

Because they are tolerant, prolific, and hardy, many opportunistic organisms, including the house fly, the house mouse, and the dandelion, are considered **pest**s. Where they occur naturally and have natural limits to their spread, however, opportunists play important environmental roles. By quickly colonizing bare ground, fireweed and opportunistic grasses help prevent **erosion**. Cottonwood trees (*Populus spp.*), highly opportunistic propagators, are among the few trees able to spread into **arid** regions, providing shade and nesting places along stream channels in deserts and dry plains. Some opportunists that are highly tolerant of pollution are now considered indicators of otherwise undetected **chemical spills**. In such hard-to-observe environments as the sea floor, sudden population explosions among certain bottom-dwelling marine mollusks, plankton, and other invertebrates have been used to identify **petrochemical** spills around drilling platforms and shipping lanes. *See also* Adaptation; Contaminated soil; Environmental stress; Flooding; Growth limiting factors; Indicator organism; Parasites; Resilience; Scavenger; Symbiosis

[*Mary Ann Cunningham*]

FURTHER READING

Alexander, S. P. "Oasis Under the Ice." *International Wildlife* 18 (November-December 1988): 32-7.

Arcieri, D. T. "The Undesirable Alien—The House Sparrow." *The Conservationist* 46 (1992): 24-25.

Bradshaw, S. D., H. S. Giron, and F. J. Bradshaw. "Patterns of Breeding in Two Species of Agamid Lizards in the Arid Subtropical Pilbara Region of Western Australia." *General and Comparative Endocrinology* 82 (1991): 407-24.

Foster, H. D. *Health, Disease and the Environment.* Boca Raton, FL: CRC Press, 1992.

Moreno, J. M., and W. C. Oechel. "Fire Intensity Effects on Germination of Shrubs and Herbs in Southern California Chaparral." *Ecology* 72 (1991): 1993-2004.

Shafir, A. "Dynamics of a Fish Ectoparasite Population: Opportunistic Parasitism in *Argulus japonicus.*" *Crustaceana* 62 (1992): 50-64.

Orangutan (*Pongo pygmaeus*)

The orangutan, one of the Old World great apes, has its population restricted to the **rain forest**s of the Indonesian islands of Sumatra and Borneo. The Orangutan is the largest living arboreal mammal, and it spends most of the daylight hours moving slowly and deliberately through the forest canopy in search of food. Sixty percent of their diet consists of fruit, and the remainder is composed of young leaves and shoots, tree bark, mineral-rich **soil**, and insects. Orangutans are long-lived, with many individuals reaching between fifty and sixty years of age in the wild. These large, chestnut-colored, long-haired apes are facing possible **extinction** from two different causes: **habitat** destruction and the wild animal trade.

The rain forest **ecosystem** on the islands of Sumatra and Borneo is rapidly disappearing. Sumatra loses 370 square miles (960 km²) of forest a year, or about 1.6 percent, faster than any other Indonesian island. The rest of central Indonesia, of which Borneo comprises a major part, loses about 2,700 square miles (7,000 km²) per year. Some experts believe this estimate is too low, and they argue it could be closer to 4,600 square miles (12,000 km²) per year. Another devastating blow was dealt Borneo's rain forests just over a decade ago, when more than 15,400 square miles (40,000 km²) of the island's tropical forest was destroyed by **drought** and fire between 1982 and 1983. The fire was set by farmers who claimed to be unaware of the risks involved in burning off vegetation in a drought stricken area. Even though Indonesia still has over 400,000 square miles (1,000,000 km²) of rain forest habitat remaining, the rate of loss threatens the continued existence of the wild orangutan population, which is now estimated at about 25,000 individuals.

Both the Indonesian government and the **Convention on International Trade in Endangered Species of Wild Fauna and Flora** (CITES) have banned international trade of orangutans, yet their population continues to be threatened by the black market. In order to meet the demand for these apes as pets around the world, poachers kill the mother orangutan to secure the young ones, and the mortality rate of these orphans is extremely high, with less than 20 percent of those smuggled ever arriving alive at their final destination. This high mortality rate is directly due to stress, both emotional and physiological, on the young orangutans. The transportation scheme involved in smuggling these animals out of Indonesia to major trade centers throughout the world is intricate and time-consuming, and the way in which they are concealed for shipping is inhumane. These are two more reasons why only one out of five or six orangutan babies will survive the ordeal.

Some hope for the species rests in a global effort to manage a captive propagation program in zoos. A potentially self-sustaining captive population of more than 850 orangutans has been established. An elaborate system of networking and recording of all legally held individuals may also aid in the recognition and recapture of smuggled animals. Researchers have also developed methods of determining whether smuggled orangutans are of Bornean or Sumatran origin, thus providing a means of maintaining genetic integrity for those that can be bred in captivity or relocated. *See also* Captive propogation and reintroduction ; Chimpanzees; Deforestation; Endangered species; Gibbons; Pet trade; Tropical rain forest; Wildlife management

[*Eugene C. Beckham*]

FURTHER READING

Collins, M. *The Last Rain Forests: A World Conservation Atlas.* New York: Oxford University Press, 1990.

Speart, J. "Orang Odyssey." *Wildlife Conservation* 95 (1992): 18-25.

Oregon silverspot butterfly.

Order of magnitude

A mathematical term used loosely to indicate tenfold differences between values. This concept is crucial to interpreting logarithmic scales such as **pH** or earthquake magnitude, where each number differs by a factor of 10, and two numbers differ by a factor of 100 (10 times 10). For example, a pH of 4 is 100 times as acidic as a pH of 6 because they differ by two orders of magnitude. Scientists often generalize with this term; for example "our ability to measure pollutants has improved by several orders of magnitude" means that whereas before we were able to measure **parts per million (ppm)**, we can now measure **parts per billion (ppb)**.

Oregon silverspot butterfly (*Speyeria zerene hippolyta*)

The Oregon silverspot butterfly is a medium-sized butterfly, predominantly orange and brown with black veins and spots on its hindwings and bright silver spots on its forewings. The length of its forewings is about 1.1 in (2.9 cm). The female is usually slightly larger than the male. This butterfly is listed as threatened by the U. S. **Fish and Wildlife Service**.

Inhabiting a very restricted range, the Oregon silverspot occurs only in salt spray meadows along the Pacific coast in Oregon and Washington. This **habitat** is characterized by heavy rainfall, fog, and mild temperatures. The most critical feature of this habitat, however, is the presence of the western blue violet (*Viola adunca*), the host plant of the butterfly's larva. For two months each spring, larval Oregon silverspots feed on violet leaves before entering the pupa stage of development. This butterfly was historically present at 17 locations along the coasts of Oregon and Washington, but now only five populations in Oregon are known to exist with certainty. Two other populations, one in Washington and one in Oregon, are believed to be close to extirpation.

Housing developments and recreational uses of the coast that destroy or degrade butterfly habitat are the major threats to this subspecies's survival. Natural fire patterns in its meadow habitat have been suppressed, allowing non-native vegetation to mix with native plants and changing the habitat's character. An area of Lane County, Oregon with a

healthy population of Oregon silverspots has been designated **critical habitat** for this subspecies. Expansion of the population of western blue violets in this area will be encouraged by control of saplings and other invading plants. Transplantation of western blue violets to other sites with suitable meadow habitat may also be attempted. Although the Oregon silverspot butterfly is not in immediate danger of **extinction**, its specific habitat requirements and the vulnerability of that habitat to degradation and destruction, makes intervention necessary to ensure the long-term survival of this subspecies. *See also* Endangered species

[*Christine B. Jeryan*]

FURTHER READING

Howe, W. H. *The Butterflies of North America.* Garden City, NY: Doubleday, 1975.

The Oregon Silverspot Butterfly Recovery Plan. Portland, OR: U. S. Fish and Wildlife Service, 1982.

Organic fertilizer
See **Organic gardening and farming**

Organic gardening and farming

Agriculture has changed dramatically since the end of World War II. As a result of new technologies, mechanization, increased chemical use, specialization, and government policies, food and fiber productivity has soared. While some of these changes have led to positive effects, there have been significant costs: **topsoil** depletion, **groundwater** contamination, harmful **pesticide residue**, the decline of family farms, and increasing costs of production. To counterbalance these costs, there is a growing movement to grow plants organically.

On a local level, suburban homeowners and city dwellers are finding ways to plant their own food for personal consumption in plots that are not sprayed with **chemicals** or treated with synthetic **fertilizer**s. City dwellers may team up to work a collective, organic garden on a vacant lot. Home-owners have the option to create **mulch** piles—a mixture of leaves and organic materials, vegetable leavings, egg shells, coffee grounds, etc.—that eventually become a rich **soil**, thanks to the breakdown of these elements by tiny organisms. This enriched soil becomes a fertile, clean foundation for a bountiful garden. The inevitable weeds that grow can be picked by hand.

On a larger level, emerging as an answer to some of these farming problems is a movement called "**sustainable agriculture**." Sustainability rests on the principle that we must meet the needs of the present without compromising the ability of future generations to meet their own needs.

Organic farming is part of this movement. Most significantly, organic foods are grown without synthetic fertilizers, pesticides, or **herbicide**s. Organic farming and gardening is the result of the belief that the best food crops come from soil that is nurtured rather than treated. Organic farmers take great care to give the soil nutrients to keep it healthy, just as a person works to keep his or her body healthy with certain nutrients. Thus, organic farmers prefer to provide those essential soil builders in natural ways: using cover crops instead of chemical fertilizers, releasing predator insects rather than spraying pests with pesticides and hand weeding rather than applying herbicides.

Organic production practices involve a variety of farming applications. Specific strategies must take into account **topography**, soil characteristics, **climate**, **pest**s, local availability of inputs, and the individual grower's goals. Despite the site-specific and individual nature of this approach, several general principles can be applied to help growers select appropriate management practices. Growers must:

1. Select **species** and varieties of crops that are well suited to the site and to the conditions of the farm.
2. Diversify the crops, including livestock and cultural practices, to enhance the biological and economic stability of the farm.
3. Manage the soil to enhance and protect its quality.

Making the transition to sustainable agriculture is a process. For farmers, the transition normally requires a series of small, realistic steps. For example in California, where there has been a water shortage, steps are being taken to develop **drought**-resistant farming systems, even in normal years. Farmers are encouraged to improve **water conservation** and storage measures, provide incentives for selecting specific crops that are drought-tolerant, reduce the volume of **irrigation** systems, and manage crops to reduce water loss.

In order to stop soil **erosion**, farmers are encouraged to reduce or eliminate tillage, manage irrigation to reduce **runoff**, and keep the soil covered with plants or mulch.

Farmers are also encouraged to diversify, since diversified farms are usually more economically and ecologically resilient. By growing a diversity of crops, farmers spread economic risk and the crops are less susceptible to the infestation of certain predators that feed off one crop. Diver-

sity can buffer a farm biologically. For example, in annual cropping systems, crop rotation can be used to suppress weeds, **pathogen**s, and insect pests.

Cover crops can have a stabilizing effect on the agro-ecosystem. Cover crops hold soil and nutrients in place, conserve soil moisture with mowed or standing dead mulches, and increase the water infiltration rate and soil water holding capacity. Cover crops in orchards and vineyards can buffer the system against pest infestations by increasing beneficial arthropod populations and can therefore reduce the need for chemicals. Using a variety of cover crops is also important in order to protect against the failure of a particular species to grow and to attract and sustain a wide range of beneficial arthropods.

Optimum diversity may be obtained by integrating both crops and livestock in the same farming operation. This was the common practice for centuries until the mid-1900s, when technology, government policy, and economics compelled farms to become more specialized. Mixed crop and livestock operations have several advantages. First, growing row crops only on more level land and pasture or forages on steeper slopes will reduce soil erosion. Second, pasture and forage crops in rotation enhance soil quality and reduce erosion; livestock manure in turn contributes to soil fertility. Third, livestock can buffer the negative impacts of low rainfall periods by consuming crop residue that in "plant only" systems would have been considered failures. Finally, feeding and marketing are more flexible in animal production systems. This can help cushion farmers against trade and price fluctuations and, in conjunction with cropping operations, make more efficient farm labor.

Animal production practices are also sustainable or organic. In the midwestern and northeastern United States, many farmers are integrating crop and animal systems, either on dairy farms or with range cattle, sheep, and hog operations. Many of the principles outlined in the crop production section apply to both groups. The actual management practices will, of course, be quite different.

Animal health is crucial, since unhealthy stock waste feed and require additional labor. A herd health program is critical to sustainable livestock production. Animal nutrition is another major issue. While most feed may come from other enterprises on the ranch, some purchased feed is usually imported. If the animals feed from the outside, this feed should be as free of chemicals as possible.

A major goal of organic farming is a healthy soil. Healthy soil will produce healthy crops and plants that have optimum vigor and less susceptibility to pests. In organic or sustainable systems, the soil is viewed as a fragile and living medium that must be protected and nurtured to ensure its long-term productivity and stability. Fertilizers and other inputs may be needed, but they are minimized as the farmer relies on natural, renewable, and on-farm inputs.

While many crops have key pests that attack even the healthiest of plants, proper soil, water, and **nutrient** management can help prevent some pest problems brought on by crop stress or nutrient imbalance. Additionally, crop management systems that impair soil quality often result in greater inputs of water, nutrients, pesticides, and/or energy for tillage to maintain yields.

Sustainable approaches are those that are the least toxic and least energy intensive and yet maintain productivity and profitability. Farmers are encouraged to use preventive strategies and other alternatives before using chemical inputs from any source. However, there may be situations where the use of synthetic chemicals would be more "sustainable" than a strictly nonchemical approach or an approach using toxic "organic" chemicals. For example, one grape grower in California switched from tillage to a few applications of a broad spectrum contact herbicide in his vine row. This approach may use less energy and may compact the soil less than numerous passes with a cultivator or mower.

Coalitions have been created to address the growing organic movement concerns on a local, regional, and national level. The Organic Food Production Association of North America is the trade and marketing arm of the organic industry in the United States and Canada. The Farm Bill of 1990—Organic Foods Production Act—addressed the growing organic farming movement. Title 21 of the bill is the section that will be dealing with the regulations regarding organic certification. The **U.S. Department of Agriculture**, with the guidance of an advisory committee or National Organic Standards Board, is in the process of establishing the federal regulations that will standardize the rules for the entire organic industry in the United States, from growing and manufacturing to distribution. Presently, the organic movement includes growers, retailers, distributors, traders, urban and individual consumers, processors, and various nonprofit organizations nationwide.

Until the regulations are in place, the standards established by individual states vary, or in some states do not exist at all. The 1990 law requires that organic farmers wait for three years before they are officially certified—to ensure most of the chemicals have been eliminated. With proper documentation, on-site inspectors are then able to certify the farm. Organic groups admit that no organic program can claim absolutely it is residue free. The issue here is a process—of farming and producing product in as chemically free and healthy an **environment** as is possible.

The international community is joining the organic movement. Europe—the European Common Market—Australia, Argentina, and many countries in South America are establishing their own organic standards and have joined together under the organization called International Federation of Organic Agricultural Movements.

In addition to the upcoming United States federal standardization of organic farming, more policies are needed to promote simultaneously environmental health and economic profitability.

For example, commodity and price support programs could be restructured to allow farmers to realize the full benefits of the productivity gains made possible through alternative practices. Tax and credit policies could be modified to encourage a diverse and decentralized system of family farms rather than corporate concentration and absentee ownership. Government and land grant university research could be modified to emphasize the development of sustainable alternatives. Congress can become more rigorous in preventing the application of certain pesticides, especially those that have been shown to be carcinogenic. Marketing orders and cosmetic standards (i.e. color and uniformity of product, etc.) could be amended to encourage reduced pesticide use.

Consumers play a key role. Through their purchases, they send strong messages to producers, retailers, and others in the system about what they think is important. Food cost and nutritional quality have always influenced consumer choices. The challenge now is to find strategies that broaden consumer perspectives so that environmental quality and resource use are also considered in shopping decisions. Coalitions organized around improving the food system are one specific method of systemizing growing and delivery for the producers, retailers, and consumers.

"Clean" meat, vegetables, fruits, beans, and grains are available, as are products such as organically grown cotton. As consumer demands increase, growers will respond. *See also* Biodiversity; Monoculture

[*Liane Clorfene Casten*]

FURTHER READING

Conford, P., ed. *Organic Tradition: An Anthology of Writings on Organic Farming, 1900-1950.* Cincinnati, OH: Seven Hills Book Distributors, 1991.

Dudley, N. *G is for EcoGarden: An A to Z Guide to a More Organically Healthy Garden.* New York: Avon, 1992.

Erickson, J. *Gardening for a Greener Planet: A Chemical-Free Approach.* Blue Ridge Summit, PA: TAB Books, 1992.

Krueger, S. "Green Acres: Farmers Are Hoping Chemical-Free Crops Will Help Get Them Out of the Red (includes an article on the Chemical Fertilizer Act)." *Nature Canada* 21 (Spring 1992): 42-48.

National Research Council. *Alternative Agriculture.* Washington, DC: National Academy Press, 1989.

Rodale, R. *Regenerative Farming Systems.* Emmaus, PA: Rodale Press, 1985.

Organic waste

Organic wastes contain materials which originated from living organisms. There are many types of organic wastes and they can be found in municipal **solid waste**, industrial solid waste, agricultural waste, and **wastewater**s. Organic wastes are often disposed of with other wastes in **landfill**s or incinerators, but since they are biodegradable, some organic wastes are suitable for **composting** and land application.

Organic materials found in municipal solid waste include food, paper, wood, sewage sludge, and yard waste. Because of recent shortages in landfill capacity, the number of municipal composting sites for yard wastes is increasing across the country, as is the number of citizens who compost yard wastes in their backyards. On a more limited basis, some mixed municipal waste composting is also taking place. In these systems, attempts to remove inorganic materials are made prior to composting.

Some of the organic materials in municipal solid waste are separated before disposal for purposes other than composting. For example, paper and cardboard are commonly removed for **recycling**. Food waste from restaurants and grocery stores is typically disposed of through garbage disposals, therefore, it becomes a component of wastewater and sewage sludge.

A large percentage of sewage sludge is landfilled and incinerated, but it is increasingly being applied to land as a fertilizer. Sewage sludge may be used as an agricultural **fertilizer** or as an aid in reclaiming land devastated by **strip mining**, **deforestation**, and over-application of inorganic fertilizers. It may also be applied to land solely as a means of disposal, without the intention of improving the **soil**.

The organic fraction of industrial waste covers a wide spectrum including most of the components of municipal organic waste, as well as countless other materials. A few examples of industrial organic wastes are papermill sludge, meat processing waste, brewery wastes, and textile mill fibers. Since a large variety and volume of industrial organic wastes are generated, there is a lot of potential to recycle and compost these materials. Waste managers are continually experimenting with different "recipes" for composting industrial organic wastes into soil conditioners and soil amendments. Some treated industrial wastewaters and **sludge**s contain large amounts of organic materials and they too can be used as soil fertilizers and amendments.

Production of biogas is another use of organic waste. Biogas is used as an alternative energy source in some third world countries. It is produced in digester units by the anaerobic decomposition of organic wastes such as manures and crop residues. Beneficial byproducts of biogas production include sludges that can be used to fertilize and improve soil, and the inactivation of pathogens in the waste. In addition, there is ongoing research on using organic wastes in developing countries: (1) in fish farming; (2) to produce algae for human and animal consumption, fertilizer, and other uses; and (3) to produce aquatic macrophytes for animal feed supplements.

[*Teresa C. Donkin*]

FURTHER READING

Logsdon, G. "Composting Industrial Waste Solves Disposal Problems." *Biocycle* 29 (May-June 1988): 48-51.

Polprasert, C. *Organic Waste Recycling*. New York: Wiley, 1989.

Organization of Petroleum Exporting Countries (OPEC)

Established in 1960 by Iran, Iraq, Kuwait, and Venezuela, the Organization of Petroleum Exporting Countries (OPEC) was created to control the price of oil by controlling the volume of production. Modelled on the Texas Railroad Commission in the United States, the group was also intended to make other decisions about **petroleum** policy and to provide technical and economic support to its members. Indonesia, Libya, Qatar, and Abu Dhabi have been admitted

since 1960, and it is now estimated that the nations in OPEC control nearly two-thirds of the world's oil reserves.

In October 1973, members of OPEC met at their headquarters in Vienna and voted to raise oil prices by 70 percent. OPEC is dominated by oil-producing countries from the Middle East, and this decision was designed to retaliate against Western support of Israel during its war with Egypt. At a conference in Tehran, Iran, in December of that same year, OPEC countries raised oil prices an additional 130 percent, and they enacted an embargo on shipments to the United States and the Netherlands. The Iranian revolution in 1979 further restricted the world supply of oil, intensifying the effects of OPEC policies; between 1973 and 1980, the price of a barrel of oil rose from three dollars to thirty-five dollars.

The steep rise in oil prices had a disruptive effect in the United States, which is the largest oil importer in the world. It had an ever greater economic impact on industrialized countries such as Japan, which have little or no petroleum reserves of their own. But the economies in **less developed countries (LDC)** were the hardest hit; the rising price of oil decreased their purchasing power, increasing their trade deficit as well as their level of debt. There was a rapid transfer of wealth to oil-producing countries during this period, with the annual income of OPEC countries increasing 22.5 billion dollars in 1973 to 275 billion dollars in 1980.

The organization was not, however, able to maintain its influence over the international oil market in the 1980s, and prices dropped to as low as ten dollars a barrel during this decade. World oil consumption reached a peak in 1979, at a high of 66 million barrels a day, and then dropped sharply in the years that followed. Many Western countries were encouraging **conservation**; they had also invested in other sources of energy, most notably **nuclear power**. Oil exploration had resulted in discoveries in Alaska and the North Sea; Mexico and Soviet Union, oil-exporting countries that were not members of OPEC, had also become an increasingly important part of the international petroleum trade. As their power over the price of oil became more diffused, consensus within OPEC became more difficult, and these internal divisions were made worse by political conflicts within the Middle East, particularly the war between Iran and Iraq.

From an environmental perspective, the most important effect of the oil price shocks of the 1970s may have been how it changed world patterns of energy consumption. Though the increase in prices forced many countries to use **coal** and nuclear power despite the damage they can do to the environment, economic pressures also stimulated research into many **alternative energy sources**, such as **solar energy**, **wind energy**, and hydroelectric power. The sudden decrease in oil prices in the last decade has limited the sense of urgency as well as the funding for many of these research projects, and some environmentalists have suggested that higher oil prices might be better for the environment and the global economy over the long term. *See also* Oil embargo

[*Douglas Smith*]

Organochloride

Usually refers to organochlorine **pesticide**s, although it could also refer to any chlorinated organic compound. The organochlorine pesticides can be classified by their molecular structures. The cyclopentadiene pesticides are aliphatic, cyclic structures made from Diels-Alder reactions of pentachlorocyclopentadiene, and include **chlordane**, nonachlor, heptachlor, heptachlor epoxide, dieldrin, aldrin, endrin, **mirex**, and **kepone**. Other subclasses of organochlorine pesticides are the **DDT** family and the hexachlorocyclohexane isomers. All of these pesticides have low solubilities and volatilities and are resistant to breakdown processes in the **environment**. Their toxicities and environmental persistence have led to their restriction or suspension for most uses in the United States. *See also* Organophosphate

Organochlorine pesticide

See **Organochloride**

Organophosphate

Refers to classes of organic compounds that are often used in insecticides. Many of the organophosphate **pesticide**s were developed over the last 30 years to replace organochlorine insecticides. They generally have the highest solubilities and shortest half-lives of the common classes of pesticides, but tend to have higher acute toxicities. Organophosphates act by disrupting the central nervous system, specifically by blocking the action of the **enzyme** acetylcholinesterase, which controls nerve impulse transmission. Organophosphates can impact human health at moderate levels of exposure, causing disorientation, numbness, and tremors. Acute exposures can cause blindness and death. Well-known organophosphate pesticides include parathion, malathion, **diazinon**, and phosdrin. *See also* Cholinesterase inhibitor; Organochloride

Organophosphate pesticide

See **Organophosphate**

Orr, David W. (1944-)

American environmental writer

In recent years, an effort has been undertaken to make every citizen numerate, that is, able to use mathematics at a level that is minimally functional in modern society. David Orr, and writers and thinkers of kindred mind, believe that for citizens to be minimally functional in the complex, interdependent world of the twenty-first century, they must go beyond literacy in language and beyond numeracy and attain also a certain level of ecological literacy.

David Orr is best known for his 1992 book titled *Ecological Literacy* and for his brief editorial essays in the journal *Conservation Biology*, written from his position as education editor for that journal. Born in Des Moines, Iowa, and raised in New Wilmington, Pennsylvania, he holds degrees from Westminster College (BA), Michigan State University (MA), and the University of Pennsylvania (Ph.D. in International Relations). He was a professor of political science before becoming Professor and Chair of the Environmental Studies Program at Oberlin College in Ohio. He is well-known for his criticism of the **environmental degradation** brought about by the free market system, his critique of the American educational system, and his activist attempts to change both systems toward more ecologically sustainable behavior.

Though the free market system seems to be in the ascendancy today, Orr believes that capitalism "is failing because it produces too much and shares too little." He especially laments conservatives in the capitalist system who do not understand the history and meaning of what conservative means. He claims that a genuine conservatism would be conservation oriented and not intent, for example, on perpetual economic growth that "has become the most radicalizing force for change in the modern world."

Much of this failure in the western system he traces to an ecological crisis that "represents, in large measure, a failure of education." He faults every level of education in general for not teaching students how to learn, while in school and throughout life, and for failing to define knowledge adequately for postmodern life. Too many disciplines do not consider the interrelations between people and the earth on which they live. This failure, Orr claims, can "ultimately...be traced to our schools and to our proudest universities."

Much of Orr's work focuses on changing universities, to eliminate what he considers the nationwide campus emphasis on "fast knowledge," or "ignorant knowledge" that is "cut off from its ecological and social context." He laments the over-professionalization of the professorate, researchers who churn out fast knowledge and create students (and citizens) who are "knowledge technicians instead of broadly thoughtful, liberally educated persons." He relates narrowness and self-interest to "the problem of ecological denial," in which people cannot think in the long term or about the "large and messy questions" associated with environmental issues.

Orr believes that campus buildings even teach negative lessons: "the design, construction, and operation of academic buildings can be a liberal education in a microcosm that includes virtually every discipline in the catalog." Thus, he has undertaken what is proving to be a life-long campaign to change campuses to educational laboratories for ecological systems and environmental sustainability.

[*Gerald L. Young*]

FURTHER READING

Orr, D.W. *Ecological Literacy: Education and the Transition to a Postmodern World.* Albany, N.Y.: State University of New York Press, 1992.

———. *Earth in Mind: On Education, Environment, and the Human Prospect.* Washington, D.C.: Island Press, 1994.

Osborn, Henry Fairfield (1887-1969)

American naturalist

Born in Princeton, New Jersey, Osborn was the son of a renowned paleontologist who was also president of the American Museum of Natural History. Osborn graduated from Princeton in 1909 and attended Cambridge University in England. He then held a variety of jobs, working in freight and railroad yards and serving as a soldier in World War I. He finally took a position at a bank dealing in Wall Street investments.

Throughout his life, Osborn had accompanied his father on paleontological expeditions. As these trips continued into his adulthood, Osborn realized that his true vocation lay not finance but in natural science. In 1935 he accepted a position as secretary of the New York Zoological Society, an organization devoted to the "instruction and recreation of the people of New York." He was named president of the Society five years later and remained in office until 1968. As president, he actively pursued the creation of the Marine Aquarium at Coney Island, New Jersey, as well as improvements to the Bronx Zoological Park.

Osborn recognized the crucial need for an organization that would foster the preservation of **endangered species** and their **habitat**s. With this purpose in mind, he founded in 1947 the Conservation Foundation (CF), an adjunct of the New York Zoological Society. CF was absorbed in 1990 by the **World Wildlife Fund** which still works for the conservation of endangered **wildlife** and natural areas.

Osborn used his knowledge of nature and his positions within these organizations to influence policy in Washington. He served on the Conservation Advisory Committee of the **U.S. Department of the Interior** as well as on the Planning Committee of the Economic and Social Council of the United Nations.

Like **William Vogt** and later **Paul R. Ehrlich**, Osborn often expressed concern about **population growth** and available **natural resources**. He fully realized the serious ramifications of environmental and ecological neglect and understood the steps needed to conserve existing resources and develop improved methods of distribution.

He published two highly successful books, *Our Plundered Planet* (1948) and *The Limits of the Earth* (1953), each of which outlined the importance of conservationist ideals and the perils of a population explosion.

Osborn was an active member of the **Save-the-Redwoods League, International Council for Bird Preservation**, and other related organizations. He died in New York City in 1968 at the age of 82. *See also* Economic growth and the environment; Family planning; Population

Institute; Shumacher, E. F.; Sustainable agriculture; Sustainable development; Zero population growth

[*Kimberley A. Peterson*]

FURTHER READING

Osborn, Henry Fairfield. *Cope: Master Naturalist.* Salem, NH: Ayer, 1978.

———. *Major Papers on Early Primates, Compiled From the Publications of the American Museum of Natural History.* New York: AMS Press, 1980.

———. *Naturalist in the Bahamas: October 12, 1861–June 25, 1891.* New York: AMS Press, 1910.

———. *Origin and Evolution of Life: On the Theory of Action, Reaction and Interaction of Energy.* Salem, NH: Ayer, 1980.

Osmosis

Taken from the Greek word *osmos* (meaning a thrusting, an impulse, or a pushing), osmosis is the diffusion of water (the major biological solvent) through a selectively permeable membrane from a region of higher concentration of water to a region of lower concentration of water. In other words, water is diffused through a semipermeable membrane: 1) from a region of lower solute (the substance that is dissolved, in this case by water) concentration to a higher solute concentration; and 2) from a hypertonic (more solute, less solvent) solution to a hypotonic (less solute, more solvent) solution. Thus, osmosis is the process cells use to equalize dilution on both sides of their membranes. Fresh water fish are hypertonic compared to their aquatic medium and thus must actively excrete the water that diffuses into their cells. Conversely, salt water fish are hypotonic compared to the ocean and must actively conserve water and therefore excrete concentrated urine.

Otter

See **Sea otter**

Our Common Future (Brundtland Report)

In late 1983 **Gro Harlem Brundtland**, the former Prime Minister of Norway, was asked by the Secretary-General of the United Nations to establish and chair the World Commission on Environment and Development, a special, independent commission convened to formulate "a global agenda for change."

The Secretary-General's request emerged from growing concern in the General Assembly about a number of issues, including: long-term **sustainable development**;

co-operation between developed and developing nations; more effective international management of environmental concerns; the differing international perceptions of long-term environmental issues; and strategies for protecting and enhancing the **environment**.

The commission worked for three years and produced what is commonly known as "The Brundtland Report." Published in book form in 1987 as *Our Common Future*, the report addresses what it identifies as "common concerns," such as a threatened future, sustainable development, and the role of the international community. The report also examines "common challenges," including **population growth**, food security, **biodiversity**, and energy choices, as well as how to make industry more efficient. Finally, the report lists "common endeavours," such as managing the commons, maintaining peace and security while not suspending development or degrading the environment, and changing institutional and legal structures. A chapter on each one of these concerns, challenges, and endeavors is included in the book.

Two years after publication of the report, Brundtland summarized its findings in a speech to the National Academy of Sciences in the United States. The reports's core concepts, she explained, were "that development must be sustainable, and the environment and world economy are totally, permanently intertwined." She went on to assert that these concepts "transcend nationality, culture, ideology, and race." She summarized by repeating the report's urgent warning: "Present trends cannot continue. They must be reversed."

The Brundtland Report issued a multitude of recommendations to help attain sustainable development and to address the problems posed by a global economy that is intertwined with the environment. The report recommends ways to deal with the debt crisis in developing nations, and insists on linking poverty and environmental deterioration: "A world in which poverty is endemic will always be prone to ecological and other catastrophes." The report also argues that security issues should be defined in environmental rather than military terms.

The members of the commission felt that a vast array of institutional changes were necessary if progress was to be made, and the report addresses these issues. It declares that the problems confronting the world are all tied together, "yet most of the institutions facing those challenges tend to be independent, fragmented, working to relatively narrow mandates with closed decision processes." Much of the work done by the commission focused on policy issues such as long-term, multifaceted population policies and ways to create effective incentive systems to encourage production, especially of food crops. Recommendations also include methods for a successful transition from **fossil fuels** to "low-energy" paths based on renewable resources.

The report repeatedly notes the differences between developed and developing nations in terms of energy use, environmental degradation, and urban growth, but it also emphasizes that "specific measures must be located in a wider context of effective [international] cooperation, if the problems are to be solved." The report always brings the problems back to people, to the importance of meeting basic human needs and the necessity of decreasing the disparities between developed and developing countries: "All nations will have a role to play in changing trends, and in righting an international economic system that increases rather than decreases inequality, that increases rather than decreases numbers of poor and hungry."

The report is not merely a grim listing of "ever increasing environmental decay, poverty, and hardship in an ever more polluted world among ever decreasing resources." Surprising to some, it is also a documentation of "the possibilities for a new era of economic growth," an on-going era of sustainable, non-destructive growth. *See also* Economic growth and the environment; Environmental economics; Environmental monitoring; Environmental policy; Environmental stress; Green politics; International Geosphere-Biosphere Programme; United Nations Earth Summit; United Nations Environment Programme; World Bank

[*Gerald L. Young*]

FURTHER READING

Silver, C. S., and R. S. DeFries. *One Earth One Future: Our Changing Global Environment*. Washington, DC: National Academy Press, 1990.

World Commission on Environment and Development. *Our Common Future*. New York: Oxford University Press, 1987.

Overburden

Refers to the rock and **soil** above a desired economic resource, such as **coal** or an ore body. It is normally associated with **surface mining**, in contrast to underground mining where **tailings** are a more common byproduct. The depth of overburden is a critical economic factor when assessing the feasibility of mining. Unless the **topsoil** is stored for later **reclamation**, overburden removal usually destroys this crucial resource, greatly magnifying the task of natural or cultural revegetation. In North America, overburden removal requires blasting through hard caprock, which leave landscapes resembling fields of glacial debris. *See also* Mine spoil waste

Overfishing

With the tremendous increase in the human population since the industrial revolution, there has been an ever increasing use and, often, exploitation of many of the world's natural resources. The demand for fish and shellfish has exemplified this misuse of natural resources. Paralleling the changes in agriculture, the fisheries industry has progressed from a small-scale, subsistence operation to a highly mechanized, ultra-efficient means of securing huge quantities of fish and shellfish to satisfy the burgeoning market demand. These industrialized commercial fisheries have allowed fishermen to easily work the far offshore waters, and more efficient refrigeration has allowed greater travel time, thus allowing for longer excursions.

Overfishing results in the removal of a substantial portion of a species' population so that there are too few individuals left to reproduce and bring the population back to the level it was the year before. Overfishing has a tremendous negative impact on nontarget species as well. More than half, and occasionally as much as 90%, of a catch may be discarded, and this can adversely affect the **environment** by altering predator-prey ratios and adding excess organic waste through the dumping of nearly 30 million tons of dead or dying fish and shellfish overboard annually. Overfishing has also negatively impacted diving seabird, **sea turtle**, and **dolphin** populations since these animals often get trapped and killed in fishing nets. It is estimated that 44,000 albatrosses are killed each year by Japanese tuna fishermen, and that, over the years, tuna purse seine nets in the Eastern Tropical Pacific have caused the death of millions of dolphins.

The offshore waters are not regulated as are the coastal waters of our continents, therefore several populations of commercially important species have been overfished. Often, fishermen simply try to catch as many fish as possible (as fast as possible), because they believe that any fish left in the water will be caught by someone else. The codfish industry of the Atlantic coast of Canada and the United States had been a productive fishery since the time of the early settlers, hundreds of years ago. But with the introduction, in 1954, of a new kind of highly industrialized fishing vessel, the factory trawler, conditions changed for the cod population. In 1968, exceeding the normal catch for the region by over 500,000 tons, 810,000 tons of cod were taken off Labrador and the Grand Banks off Newfoundland. In the decade to follow, the cod population declined to the point that the number of spawning codfish off Newfoundland in 1977 showed a 94% decrease from the number in 1962. Another species to show population decline due to overfishing is the American shad, often referred to as the poor man's salmon. Harvested by Native Americans and the early colonists, the shad fishery was supplying one of the most commercially valuable fish to the region surrounding the Chesapeake Bay during the 1800's. Overfishing, combined with an increase in pollution and the disruption of spawning runs by the damming of rivers, took a fishery with an annual harvest of nearly 18 million pounds at the turn of the century to less than 2 million pounds in the 1970s.

Lack of regulations is not the only reason fishermen are going farther offshore. Many populations have been overfished in coastal waters, but fish and shellfish populations have declined in these waters due to near-shore pollution as well. Decreased water quality has had an impact on the population numbers and also on the quality of the fish itself, therefore creating a demand for fish and shellfish from distant, presumably cleaner, waters. Being driven farther offshore to make their catches, commercial fishermen may often overfish a population to bring in more revenues to offset their huge debt incurred on their equipment, crew, and ever increasing fuel costs.

During the 1980s, when a New Orleans chef popularized "blackened redfish" and the dish was in demand across the country, the Gulf of Mexico population of "redfish," actually the Red drum, was nearly decimated by overfishing. Because of its unpopularity as a food and game fish, the Red drum was not regulated as are the more important commercial fish and shellfish species of this region. Therefore, when orders for the fish started coming in from across the nation, commercial fishermen began catching them in record numbers. There were cases in which great numbers of dead redfish were washing up on the shores of the Gulf states because fishermen had caught too many to process on their vessels and dumped the excess overboard. In just a couple of years the Red drum population crashed in the Gulf of Mexico, prompting the fish and game officials in all of the Gulf states to halt commercial fishing for redfish. (A recovery program, however, is meeting with success.) This problem could have been avoided had the original dish been named "blackened fish" or had the nation's seafood markets and restaurants known that the flavor in "blackened redfish" is in the seasonings and not in the fish itself, thus relying on local fisheries and the redfish of the Gulf of Mexico.

One means of offsetting overfishing by commercial fishing fleets, and reducing fuel use as well, is aquaculture, the cultivation and harvesting of fish and shellfish under controlled conditions. With pressures on fish populations from overfishing, increased pollution problems, and a dying industry strapped with higher costs of fuel and equipment, "fish farming" may offer a true alternative to greatly reduced quantities and inferior quality seafood in the future. *See also* Commercial fishing

[*Eugene C. Beckham*]

FURTHER READING

Bricklemyer, E., S. Iudicello, and H. Hartmann. "Discarded Catch in U.S. Commercial Marine Fisheries." *Audubon Wildlife Report.* San Diego: Academic Press, 1990-91.

Kunzig, Robert. 1995. Twilight of the Cod. *Discover* magazine, Apr. 1995, pp 44-49, 52-57, 60.

U. S. Fish and Wildlife Service. Internet article: American Shad, Life History, Decline,

Lawren, B. "Net Loss." *National Wildlife* 30 (1992): 46-53.

Overgrazing

Overgrazing is one of the most critical environmental problems facing the western United States. **Rangelands** have been mismanaged for over a hundred years, mainly due to cattle grazing. In addition to consuming vegetation, cattle alter the **ecosystem** of rangeland by tramping, urination, defecation, and trashing. Degradation due to heavy livestock grazing continues to occur in many diverse and fragile ecosystems, including **savanna**, **desert**, meadow, and alpine communities.

Riparian lands, highly vegetated, narrow strips of land bordering rivers or other natural watercourses, make up only two percent of rangelands, but have the most diverse populations of vegetation and **wildlife**. Overgrazing has had a devastating effect on these areas. Cattle eat the seedlings of young trees, which has led to the elimination of some **species**, and this has reduced the species of birds in these areas and disrupted migratory patterns. Lack of new tree growth in riparian areas has also resulted in the drying up of stream beds and the loss of **habitat** for fish and amphibians. It has contributed to the problem of soil **erosion**, **desertification** and the **greenhouse effect**. Other rangeland ecosystems are facing similar disruption.

The **Bureau of Land Management** (BLM) part of the **U. S. Department of the Interior** is the largest landholder in the United States. They are responsible for 334 million acres of land which fall under multiple-use mandates. The BLM leases much of this **public land** to individuals for grazing purposes, charging ranchers approximately $1.35 per month to graze one cow and a calf. It has been estimated that the fair market value for such forage is $6.65, and the agency has come under attack for leasing grazing rights at extremely low rates. It has also been criticized for allowing abusive land management practices. Critics claim that those who utilize these public lands try to maximize profits by putting excessive numbers of livestock on the range, and they argue that almost half of the range areas in the United States are in dire need of **conservation**.

Environmentalists argue that it is possible to eliminate overgrazing and manage rangelands in a way that both preserves ecosystems and meets the needs of ranchers. They advocate above all the reduction of herds. They also suggest that cattle should not be allowed to roam at will and should be rotated among various pastures, so that all rangeland areas can receive back-to-back spring and summer rest.

Perhaps the main obstacle in conservation of rangelands is the lack of knowledge regarding their diverse ecosystems. Rangelands are regions where natural revegetation tends to be slow. Artificial attempts to introduce and establish plant growth have been frustrated by the fact that development is a long-term process in these environments as well as by other factors. Knowledge of the dynamics of **competition**, reaction, and stabilization of species is minimal. For over a century, rangers have tried to eliminate sagebrush, planting wheatgrass in its place. The solution has been short-lived because sagebrush usually prevails over wheatgrass in the natural succession of plants. To further compound the problem, overgrazing has depleted the perennial grasses that compete with sagebrush, and the plant has become even more prolific. A better understanding of the dynamic relationship between plants, animals, microorganisms, soil, and the **climate** is necessary to reestablish rangeland areas. *See also* Agricultural pollution; Agricultural Stabilization and Conservation Services; Agroecology; Feedlot runoff; Feedlots; Land use; Sagebrush Rebellion; Taylor Grazing Act (1934)

[*Debra Glidden*]

FURTHER READING

Heitschmidt, R. K., ed. *Grazing Management: An Ecological Perspective.* Portland, OR: Timber Press, 1991.

Senft, R., et al. "Large Herbivore Foraging and Ecological Hierarchies; Landscape Ecology Can Enhance Traditional Foraging Theory." *Bioscience* 37 (December 1987): 789-95.

Spedding, C. R. W. *Grassland Ecology.* London: Oxford University Press, 1971.

Strickland, R. "Taking the Bull by the Horns: Conservationists Have Been Wrangling Politely With Land Managers For Years—But Have Failed to Halt Overgrazing Throughout the West." *Sierra* 75 (September-October 1990): 46-48.

Overhunting

Overhunting is any hunting activity that has an adverse impact on the total continuing population of a **species**. With the tremendous increase in the human population since the industrial revolution, there has been an ever increasing use and, often, exploitation of many of the world's **natural resources**. The demand for fish and shellfish has exemplified this misuse of natural resources. The amount of hunting pressure that a species can tolerate depends on its productivity, and it may change seasonally and annually because of **drought**, **habitat** alteration, **pollution**, or other mortality factors. Hunting which is well-regulated can be sustained, and sportsmen in countries with regulated hunting are quick to point out that they are not responsible for the endangerment or **extinction** of any species.

In unregulated situations, however, overhunting does occur, and it has endangered **wildlife**, even driving some species to extinction. The great auk (*Alca impennis*), a large, flightless, penguin-like bird of the North Atlantic coasts, was so easy to catch that sailors could kill hundreds in a few minutes, and by 1844 they had become extinct. Even the world's most abundant bird, the **passenger pigeon** (*Ectopistes migratorius*), was driven to extinction by overhunting. In the 1800s there were 3 to 5 billion passenger pigeons, about one-fourth of all North American land birds, and enormous flocks of them would darken the sky for days as they flew overhead. One colony in Wisconsin covered 850 square miles (220,149 ha) and included 135 million adult birds. Commercial hunting sent train loads of these birds to markets, including 15 million birds from a single colony in Michigan, and eliminated the species in the early 1900s.

There are several cases where overhunting has nearly exterminated a species. In 1850 there were 60 million American **bison** (*Bison bison*) on the Great Plains of the United States, and within 40 years, overhunting had reduced the wild population to 150 individuals. At the turn of the century, snowy egrets (*Leucophoyx thula*) were almost wiped out by hunters who the sold the feathers to be made into fashionable women's hats. Many species of **whales** were also driven to the brink of extinction by whalers.

Many species continue to be overhunted today. Although protected by law, African **rhinoceroses** are endangered by poachers who sell the horns to Yemen and China. In Yemen the horns are used to make dagger handles for wealthy businessmen, and in China they are made into an aphrodisiac and fever-reducing drug which is reportedly useless. Likewise, **elephants** are being slaughtered for their ivory tusks. There were 4.5 million elephants in 1970, and by 1990, only 610,000.

Many large cat species are also threatened by overhunting, because the economic incentive to poach these animals far outweighs the risks of being caught and fined. For example, a Bengal **tiger** (*Panthera tigris tigris*) fur coat sells for $100,000; an ocelot (*Felis pardalis*) skin sells for $40,000;

a snow leopard (*Panthera uncia*) skin sells for $14,000; and tiger meat sells for $629 per pound ($286/kg).

Even when appropriate hunting regulations do exist, there are often not enough rangers or conservation officers to enforce them. As species become more scarce, the demand increases on the black market, inflating the price, and the economic incentive for **poaching** only becomes greater. Unless appropriate laws are enacted and enforced other species will become extinct from overhunting. *See also* Conservation; Convention on International Trade in Endangered Species of Fauna and Flora; Defenders of Wildlife; Endangered species; Endangered Species Act; Fish and Wildlife Service; IUCN—The World Conservation Union; Wildlife management; Wildlife rehabilitation

[*Ted T. Cable*]

FURTHER READING

Jackson, P. "They've Shot Miro." *International Wildlife* 22 (November-December 1992): 38-43.

Ofcansky, T. P. *Paradise Lost: A History of Game Preservation in East Africa.* Morgantown: West Virginia University Press, 1993.

Owens, D., and M. Owens. *Eye of the Elephant: Life and Death in an African Wilderness.* New York: Houghton Mifflin, 1992.

Owl

See **Northern spotted owl**

Oxidation reduction reactions

An oxidation-reduction or redox reaction is transformation involving electron transfer. It consists of a half reaction in which a substance loses an electron or electrons (oxidation) and another half reaction in which a substance gains an electron or electrons (reduction).

The substance that gains electrons is the **oxidizing agent**, while the substance that gives up electrons is the reducing agent. Adding the two half equations algebraically and eliminating the free electrons gives the complete oxidation-reduction equation. This equation, however, is not an assurance that the reaction will proceed spontaneously as written. One way to know the direction of the reaction is to determine the value of the standard free energy change, ΔG^0, and then to calculate the free energy change, ΔG, for the complete redox reaction. If the resulting value of ΔG is negative, the reaction will proceed spontaneously as written. If ΔG is positive, the reaction can proceed spontaneously in the opposite direction. If ΔG is zero, the reaction is in equilibrium.

Simple redox reactions occur with the direct transfer of electrons from the reducing agent to the oxidizing agent. An example is the reaction between **hydrogen** (H_2) and **chlorine** (Cl_2) to form hydrogen chloride. In this reaction, hydrogen, the reducing agent, donates two electrons to chlorine which is the oxidizing agent. Because it gains electrons, the oxidizing agent changes in valence and be-

comes more negative or less positive. In the given example, the valence of chlorine changes from 0 to -1. The reducing agent, on the other hand, loses electrons and hence becomes more positive. Thus hydrogen, being the reducing agent in the given example, changes in valences from 0 to +1.

Some common applications of redox reactions in **wastewater** treatment are the detoxification of cyanide and the precipitation of chromium. Highly toxic cyanide is converted to nontoxic cyanate and finally to **carbon dioxide** and **nitrogen** gas by the action of strong oxidizing agents, such as chlorine gas or sodium hypochlorite. In removing hexavalent chromium, the objective is to reduce it to trivalent chromium, which is less toxic and can be precipitated out in the form of hydroxide. Hexavalent chromium is reduced by sodium bisulfite or ferrous sulfate in an acid medium. Lime can then be applied to precipitate out the trivalent chromium as chromium hydroxide, which collects as a chemical **sludge** upon settling.

In biochemical redox reactions, however, the electrons go through a series of transfers before reaching the terminal acceptor, which is oxygen in **aerobic** systems. Examples of these electron carriers are NAD (nicotinamide adenine dinucleotide), NADP (nicotinamide adenine dinucleotide phosphate), and flavoproteins. In **anaerobic** systems, other materials such as nitrates, sulfates, and carbon dioxide may become the electron acceptor, as in the process of **denitrification** in which nitrate (NO_3) is reductively degraded to molecular nitrogen (N_2). In either case, organic or inorganic matter, which serves as food for the microorganisms, is the substance oxidized. A simplified stoichiometry of the complete aerobic biochemical oxidation of glucose, for example, produces six moles of carbon dioxide and six moles of water with the release of 686 kilocalories per mole. *See also* Corrosion and material degradation; Electron acceptor and donor; Industrial waste treatment; Sewage treatment; Waste management

[*James W. Patterson*]

FURTHER READING

Eckenfelder, W. W., Jr. *Industrial Water Pollution Control.* New York: McGraw-Hill, 1989.

Snoeyink, V. L., and D. Jenkins. *Water Chemistry.* New York: Wiley, 1980.

Oxidizing agent

Any substance that donates oxygen or that gains electrons in a chemical reaction. Perhaps the most common example of an oxidizing agent is the element oxygen itself. When a substance burns, rusts, or decays, that substance combines with oxygen in the air around it. Oxidizing agents can have both beneficial and harmful environmental effects. **Chlorine** gas is used as an oxidizing agent to kill bacteria in the purification of water. **Ozone** damages plant and animal cells by oxidizing them.

Oxygen, dissolved

See **Dissolved oxygen**

Ozonation

The process which takes advantage of the oxidizing properties of **ozone** is known as ozonation. Ozone can be used in a variety of applications including the treatment of drinking water, bottled water, beverages, **wastewater**, industrial wastes, air pollutants, swimming pool water, and cooling tower water. In addition, there are a number of proprietary processes that use ozone, ranging from carpet cleaning to the making of gourmet ice cubes. Ozonation consists of four fundamental tasks: drying and cleaning the oxygen-containing feed-gas; generating ozone in a silent corona discharge generator; bringing the ozone into contact with the material being treated; and finally destroying remaining ozone prior to releasing the waste gas to the atmosphere. All ozonation processes require ozone generation and contacting, but not all applications require feed-gas preparation and off-gas treatment.

Ozone can be generated by three processes: electrical discharge, **photochemical reaction** with **ultraviolet radiation**, and electrolytic reactions. The latter two methods produce very low concentrations of ozone, limiting their application. Electrical discharge generators are currently the most economical choice for producing large quantities of ozone. Feed-gas must contain oxygen and be free of contaminants such as particles, **hydrocarbons**, and water vapor. For optimum production of ozone, the feed-gas should have a **dew point** of at least -37°F (-40°C) and preferably -73°F (-60°C). Small ozonation systems can use air which is dried before entering the ozone generator. Larger systems may find pure oxygen is economically viable. The temperature of the feed-gas and the generator is one of the most important parameters affecting the production of ozone. High temperatures reduce the concentration of ozone and greatly decrease the life of ozone in the gas phase. The recycling of ozone process gases increases the concentration of **nitrogen**, which leads to decreases in ozone production, and, in the presence of water vapor, to the production of corrosive nitric acid.

Contacting ozone with the material to be treated is complicated by several factors: ozone is reactive and disappears, so it must be generated at the site where it is used, and the waste ozone in the exhaust gas is toxic. When choosing ozone contacting devices for an aquatic system, two types of reactions must be taken into account. In mass-transfer limited reactions ozone is being consumed faster than it can be transferred to solution. In reaction rate limited reactions ozone is in surplus in solution but the material being oxidized is rate limiting, so that ozone is wasted. Bubble-diffuser systems are commonly used in water treatment because they are good compromises for satisfying the need to control both mass-transfer and rate limited reactions. However, in some aquatic applications in-line dissolution and contacting may be the optimum technique for ozonating the water in question.

Exhaust gas or off-gas requires treatment to remove traces of ozone remaining in the gas after contacting. Thermal destruction is one of the most commonly used methods for removing ozone from the waste gas. Other methods for destroying ozone include catalytic destruction, activated carbon **adsorption**, and zeolites. *See also* Industrial waste treatment; Water treatment

[*Gordon R. Finch*]

FURTHER READING

Langlais, B., D. A. Reckhow, and D. R. Brink, eds. *Ozone in Water Treatment: Application and Engineering.* Chelsea, MI: Lewis Publishers, 1991.

Rice, R. G., and A. Netzer, eds. *Handbook of Ozone Technology and Applications.* Volume 1. Ann Arbor, MI: Ann Arbor Science Publishers, 1982.

Rice, R. G., and A. Netzer, eds. *Handbook of Ozone Technology and Applications.* Volume 2. Boston, MA: Butterworth Publishers, 1984.

Ozone

Ozone is a toxic, colorless gas (but can be blue when in high concentration) with a characteristic acrid odor. A variant of normal oxygen, it had three oxygen atoms per molecule rather than the usual two. Ozone strongly absorbs **ultraviolet radiation** at wavelengths of 220 through 290 nm with peak absorption at 260.4 nm. Ozone will also absorb infrared radiation at wavelengths in the range 9-10 µm. Ozone occurs naturally in the ozonosphere (ozone layer), which surrounds the earth, protecting living organisms at the earth's surface from ultraviolet radiation. The ozonosphere is located in the stratosphere from 6 to 31 miles (10 to 50 km) above the earth's surface, with the highest concentration between 7.5 and 12 miles (12 and 20 km). The concentration of ozone in the ozonosphere is 1 molecule per 100,000 molecules, or if the gas were at standard temperature and pressure, the ozone layer would be 0.12 inch (3 mm) thick. However, the ozone layer absorbs about 90 percent of incident ultraviolet radiation.

Ozone in the **stratosphere** results from a chemical equilibrium between oxygen, ozone, and ultraviolet radiation. Ultraviolet radiation is absorbed by oxygen and produces ozone. Simultaneously, ozone absorbs ultraviolet radiation and decomposes to oxygen and other products. **Ozone layer depletion** occurs as a result of complex reactions in the atmosphere between organic compounds that react with ozone faster than the ozone is replenished. Compounds of most concern include the byproducts of ultraviolet degradation of **chlorofluorocarbons** (CFCs), chlorine and fluorine.

Ozone is also a secondary air pollutant at the surface of the earth as a result of complex chemical reactions between sunshine and primary pollutants, such as **hydrocarbons** and oxides of **nitrogen**. Ozone can also be generated in the presence of oxygen from equipment that gives off intense light, electrical sparks, or creates intense static electricity, such as photocopiers and laser printers. Human olfactory senses are very sensitive to ozone, being able to detect ozone odor at concentrations between 0.02 and 0.05 **parts per million**. Toxic symptoms for humans from exposure to ozone include headaches and drying of the throat and respiratory tracts. Ozone is highly toxic to many plant species and destroys or degrades many building materials, such as paint, rubber, and some plastics. The total losses in the United States each year due to ozone damage to crops, livestock, buildings, natural systems, and human health is estimated to be in the tens of billions of dollars. The threshold limit value (TLV) for **air quality** standards is 0.1 ppm or 0.2 mg O_3 per m^3 of air.

Industrial uses of ozone include chemical manufacturing and air, water, and waste treatment. Industrial quantities of ozone are typically generated from air or pure oxygen by means of silent corona discharge. Ozone is used in water treatment as a disinfectant to kill **pathogen**ic microorganisms or for oxidation of organic and inorganic compounds. Combinations of ozone and hydrogen peroxide or ultraviolet radiation in water can generate powerful oxidants useful in breaking down complex synthetic organic compounds. In **wastewater** treatment, ozone can be used to disinfect **effluent**s, or decrease their color and odor. In some industrial applications, ozone can be used to enhance biodegradation of complex organic molecules. Industrial cooling tower treatment with ozone prevents transmission of airborne pathogenic organisms and can reduce odor. *See also* Biodegradable; Ozonation

[*Gordon R. Finch*]

FURTHER READING

Horváth, M., L. Bilitzky, and J. Hüttner. *Ozone*. Amsterdam: Elsevier, 1985.

Kaufman, D. G., and C. M. Franz. *Biosphere 2000: Protecting Our Global Environment*. New York: HarperCollins College Publishers, 1993.

Ozone layer depletion

Ozone, a form of oxygen consisting of three atoms of oxygen instead of two, is considered an air pollutant when found at ground levels and is a major component of **smog**. It is formed by the reaction of various air pollutants in the presence of sunlight. Ozone is also used commercially as a bleaching agent and to purify municipal water supplies. Since ozone is toxic, the gas is harmful to health when generated near the earth's surface. Because of its high rate of breakdown, such ozone never reaches the upper atmosphere.

But the ozone that shields the earth from the sun's radiation is found in the **stratosphere**, a layer of the upper atmosphere found 9-30 miles (15-50 kilometers) above ground. This ozone layer is maintained as follows: the action of ultraviolet light breaks O_2 molecules into atoms of ele-

mental oxygen (O). The elemental oxygen then attaches to other O_2 molecules to form O_3. When it absorbs ultraviolet radiation that would otherwise reach the earth, ozone is, in turn, broken down into O_2 + O. The elemental oxygen generated then finds another O_2 molecule to become O_3 once again.

In 1974, chemists **F. Sherwood Rowland** and **Mario J. Molina** realized that **chlorine** from **chlorofluorocarbon** (CFC) molecules was capable of breaking down ozone in the stratosphere. In time, evidence began accumulate that the ozone layer was indeed being broken apart by these industrial chemicals, and to a lesser extent by **nitrogen oxide** emissions from jet airplanes as well as hydrogen chloride **emission**s from large volcanic eruptions.

When released into the environment, CFCs slowly rise into the upper atmosphere, where they are broken apart by solar radiation. This releases chlorine atoms that act as *catalysts*, breaking up molecules of ozone by stripping away one of their oxygen atoms. The chlorine atoms, unaltered by the reaction, are each capable of destroying ozone molecules repeatedly. Without a sufficient quantity of ozone to block its way, ultraviolet radiation from the sun passes through the upper atmosphere and reaches the surface of the earth.

When damage to the ozone layer first became apparent in 1974, propellants in aerosol spray cans were a major source of CFC **emission**s, and CFC aerosols were banned in the United States in 1978. However, CFCs have since remained in widespread use in thermal insulation, as cooling agents in refrigerators and air conditioners, as cleaning solvents, and as foaming agents in plastics, resulting in continued and accelerating depletion of stratospheric ozone.

The Antarctic Ozone Hole

The most dramatic evidence of the destruction of the ozone layer has occurred over Antarctica, where a massive "hole" in the ozone layer appears each winter and spring, apparently exacerbated by the area's unique and violent climatological conditions. The destruction of ozone molecules begins during the long, completely dark, and extremely cold Antarctic winter, when swirling winds and ice clouds begin to form in the lower stratosphere. This ice reacts with chlorine compounds in the stratosphere (such as hydrogen chloride and chlorine nitrate) that come from the breakdown of CFCs, creating molecules of chlorine.

When spring returns in August and September, a seasonal vortex—a rotating air mass—causes the ozone to mix with certain chemicals in the presence of sunlight. This helps break down the chlorine molecules into chlorine atoms, which, in turn, react with and break up the molecules of ozone. A single chlorine, bromine, or nitrogen molecule can break up literally thousands of ozone molecules.

During December, the ozone-depleted air can move out of the Antarctic area, as happened in 1987, when levels of ozone over southern Australia and New Zealand sank by 10 percent over a three week period, causing as much as a 20 percent increase in ultraviolet radiation reaching the earth. This may have been responsible for a reported increase in skin cancers and damage to some food crops.

The ozone layer in the earth's upper atmosphere helps make life on the planet possible by shielding it from 95-99 percent of the sun's potentially deadly ultraviolet radiation.

The seasonal hole in the ozone layer over Antarctica has been monitored by scientists at the National Aeronautics and Space Administration's (NASA) Goddard Space Flight Center outside Washington, D.C. NASA's NIMBUS-7 satellite first discovered drastically reduced ozone levels over the Southern Hemisphere in 1985, and measurements are also being conducted with instruments on aircraft and balloons. Some of the data that has been gathered is alarming.

In October 1987, ozone levels within the Antarctic ozone hole were found to be 45 percent below normal, and similar reductions occurred in October 1989. A 1988 study revealed that since 1969, ozone levels had declined by 2 percent worldwide, and by as much as 3 percent or more over highly populated areas of North America, Europe, South America, Australia and New Zealand.

In September 1992, the NIMBUS-7 satellite found that the depleted ozone area over the southern polar region had grown 15 percent from the previous year, to a size three times bigger than the area of the United States, and was 80 percent thinner than usual. The ozone hole over Antarctica was measured at approximately 8.9 million square miles (23 million square kilometers), as compared to its usual size of 6.5 million square miles (17 square kilometers). The contiguous 48 states is, by comparison, about 3 million square miles (7.8 million square kilometers), and all of North America covers 9.4 million square miles (24.3 million square kilometers).

Researchers attributed the increased thinning not only to industrial chemicals but also to the 1991 volcanic eruptions of Mount Pinatubo in the Philippines and Mount Hudson in Chile, which emitted large amounts of **sulfur dioxide** into the atmosphere.

Dangers Of Ultraviolet Radiation

The major consequence of the thinning of the ozone layer is the penetration of more solar radiation, especially Ultraviolet-B (UV-B) rays, the most dangerous type, which can be extremely damaging to plants, wildlife, and human health. Because UV-B can penetrate the ocean's surface, it is potentially harmful to marine life forms and indeed to the entire chain of life in the seas as well.

UV-B can kill and affect the reproduction of fish, larvae, and other plants and animals, especially those found in shallow waters, including **phytoplankton**, which forms the basis of the oceanic **food chain/web**. The National Science Foundation reported in February 1992 that its research ship, on a six week Antarctic cruise, found that the production of phytoplankton decreases at least 6-12 percent during the period of greatest ozone layer depletion, and that the destructive effects of UV radiation could extend to depths of 90 feet (27 m).

A decrease in phytoplankton would affect all other creatures higher on the food chain and dependent on them, including **zooplankton**, microscopic ocean creatures that feed on phytoplankton and are also an essential part of the ocean food chain. And marine phytoplankton are the main food source for **krill**, tiny Antarctic shrimp that are the major food source for fish, squid, penguins, seals, **whales**, and other creatures in the Southern Hemisphere.

Moreover, phytoplankton are responsible for absorbing, through **photosynthesis**, great amounts of **carbon dioxide** (CO_2) and releasing oxygen. It is not known how a depletion of phytoplankton would affect the planet's supply of life-giving oxygen, but more CO_2 in the atmosphere would exacerbate the critical problem of global warming, the so-called **greenhouse effect**.

There are numerous reports, largely unconfirmed, of animals in the southern polar region being harmed by ultraviolet radiation. Rumors abound in Chile, for example, of pets, livestock, sheep, rabbits, and other wildlife getting cataracts, suffering reproductive irregularities, or even being blinded by solar radiation. Many residents of Chile and Antarctica believe these stories, and wear sunglasses, protective clothing, and sun-blocking lotion in the summer, or even stay indoors much of the day when the sun is out. If the ozone layer's thinning continues to spread, the lifestyles of people across the globe could be similarly disrupted for generations to come.

Particularly frightening have been incidents reported to have taken place in Punta Arenas, Chile's southernmost city, at the tip of Patagonia. After several days of record low levels of ozone were recorded in October 1992, people reported severe burns from short exposure to sunlight. Sheep and cattle became blind, and some starved because they could not find food. Trees wilted and died, and melanoma-type skin cancers seem to have increased dramatically. Similar stories have been reported from other areas of the southern hemisphere. And malignant melanoma, once a rare disorder, is now the fastest rising cancer in the world.

Ozone Thinning Spreads

Indeed, ozone layer depletion is spreading at an alarming rate. In the 1980s, scientists discovered that an ozone hole was also appearing over the Arctic region in the late winter months, and concern was expressed that similar thinning might begin to occur over, and threaten, heavily populated areas of the globe. These fears were confirmed in April 1991, when the **Environmental Protection Agency (EPA)** announced that satellite measurements had recorded an ominous decrease in atmospheric ozone, amounting to an average of 5 percent over the mid-latitudes (including the United States), almost double the loss previously thought to be occurring.

The data showed that ozone levels measured in the late fall, winter, and early spring over large areas of the United States, Europe, and the mid-latitudes of the Northern and Southern Hemisphere had dropped by 4-6 percent over the last decade—twice the amount estimated in earlier years. The greatest area of ozone thinning in the United States was found north of a line stretching from Philadelphia to Denver to Reno, Nevada. One of the most alarming aspects of the new findings was that the ozone depletion was continuing into April and May, a time when people spend more time outside, and crops are beginning to sprout, making both more vulnerable to ultraviolet radiation.

The new findings led the EPA to project that over the next 50 years, thinning of the ozone layer could cause Americans to suffer some 12 million cases of skin cancer, 200,000 of which would be fatal. Several years earlier, the agency had calculated that over the next century, there could be an additional 155 million cases of skin cancers and 3.2 million deaths if the ozone layer continued to thin at the then current rate. Another EPA projection made in the 1980s was that the increase in radiation could cause Americans to suffer 40 million cases of skin cancer and 800,000 deaths in the following 88 years, plus some 12 million eye cataracts.

No one can say how accurate such varying projections will turn out to be, but evidence of ozone layer thinning is well-documented. In October 1991, additional data of spreading ozone layer destruction were made public. Dr. Robert Watson, a NASA scientist who co-chairs an 80-member panel of scientists from 80 countries, called the situation "extremely serious," saying that "we now see a significant decrease of ozone both in the Northern and Southern Hemispheres, not only in winter but in spring and summer, the time when people sunbathe, putting them at risk for skin cancer, and the time when we grow crops."

In February 1992, a team of NASA scientists announced that they had found record high levels of ozone-depleting chlorine over the Northern Hemisphere. This could, in turn, lead to an ozone "hole" similar to the one that appears over Antarctica developing over populated areas of the United States, Canada, and England. The areas over which increased levels of chlorine monoxide were found extended as far south as New England, France, Britain, and Scandinavia.

Action To Protect The Ozone Layer

As evidence of the critical threats posed by ozone layer depletion has increased, the world community has begun to take steps to address the problem. In 1987, the United States and 22 other nations signed the **Montreal Protocol**, agreeing, by the year 2000, to cut CFC production in half, and to phase out two ozone-destroying gases, Halon 1301 and Halon 1211. Halons are man-made bromine compounds used mainly in fire extinguishers, and can destroy ozone at a rate 10 to 40 times more rapidly than CFCs. Fortunately, these restrictions appear to already be having an impact. In 1992, it was found that the rate at which these two Halon gases were accumulating in the atmosphere had fallen significantly since 1987. The rate of increase of levels of Halon 1301 was about 8 percent a year from 1989 to 1992, about half of the average annual rate of growth over previous years. Similarly, Halon 1211 was increasing at only 3 percent annually, much less than the previous growth of 15 percent a year.

Since the Montreal Protocol, other international treaties have been signed limiting the production and use of ozone-destroying chemicals. When alarming new evidence on the destruction of stratospheric ozone became available in 1988, the world's industrialized nations convened a series of conferences to plan remedial action. In March 1989, the 12-member **European Economic Community** (EEC) announced plans to end the use of CFCs by the turn of the century, and the United States agreed to join in the ban. A week later, 123 nations met in London to discuss ways to speed the CFC phase-out. The industrial nations agreed to cut their own domestic CFC production in half, while continuing to allow exports of CFCs, in order to accommodate third world nations.

Ironically, the large industrial nations, which have created the CFC problem, are now much more willing to take effective action to ban the compounds than are many developing nations, such as India and China. The latter nations resist restrictions on CFCs on the grounds that the chemicals are necessary for their own economic development.

After the meeting in London, leaders and representatives from 24 countries met in an environmental summit at The Hague, and agreed that the United Nations' authority to protect the world's ozone layer should be strengthened.

In May 1989, members of the EEC and 81 other nations that had signed the 1987 Montreal Protocol decided at a meeting in Helsinki to try to achieve a total phase-out of CFCs by the year 2000, as well as phase-outs as soon as possible of other ozone-damaging chemicals like carbon tetrachloride, halons, and methyl chloroform. In London in June 1990, most of the Montreal Protocol's signatory nations formally adopted a deadline of the year 2000 for industrial nations to phase out the major ozone-destroying chemicals, with 2010 being the goal for developing countries.

Finally, in November 1992, 87 nations meeting in Copenhagen decided to strengthen the action agreed to under the Montreal Protocol and move up the phase-out deadline from 2000 to January 1, 1996 for CFCs, and to January 1, 1994 for halons. A timetable was also agreed to for eliminating **hydrochlorofluorocarbons** (HCFCs) by the year 2030. HCFCs are being used as substitutes for CFCs even though they also deplete ozone, albeit on a far lesser scale than CFCs. The conference failed to ban the production of the **pesticide** methyl bromide, which may account for 15 percent of ozone depletion by the year 2000, but did freeze production at 1991 levels.

Environmentalists were disappointed that stronger action was not taken to protect the ozone layer. But Environmental Protection Agency (EPA) Administrator **William K. Reilly**, who headed the U.S. delegation, estimated that the reductions agreed to could, by the year 2075, prevent a million cases of cancer and 20,000 deaths.

Although the restrictions apply to developed nations, which produce most of the ozone-damaging chemicals, it was also agreed to consider moving up a phase-out of such compounds by developing nations from 2010 to 1995. A month after the Copenhagen conference, the nations of the European Community agreed to push bans on the use of CFCs and carbon tetrachloride to 1995 and to cut CFC emissions by 85 percent by the end of 1993.

The private sector has also taken action to reduce CFC production. The world's largest manufacturer of the chemicals, DuPont Chemical Company, announced in 1988 that it was working on a variety of substitutes for CFCs, would phase out production of them by 1996, and would partially replace them with HCFCs. Environmentalists charge that DuPont has been moving too slowly to eliminate production of these chemicals.

There are many ways that individuals can help reduce the release of CFCs into the atmosphere, mainly by avoiding products that contain or are made from CFCs, and by recycling CFCs whenever possible. Although CFCs have not generally been used in spray cans in the United States since 1978, they are still used in many consumer and industrial products, such as styrofoam. Other products manufactured using CFCs include solvents and cleaning liquids used on electrical equipment, polystyrene foam products, and fire extinguishers that use halons.

Refrigerants in cars and home air conditioning units contain CFCs and must be poured into closed containers to be cleaned or recycled, or they will evaporate into the atmosphere. Using foam insulation to seal homes also releases CFCs. Many alternatives to foam insulation exist, such as cellulose fiber, gypsum, fiberboard, and fiberglass.

Unfortunately, whatever steps are taken in the next few years, the problem of ozone layer depletion will continue even after the release of ozone-destroying chemicals is limited or halted. It takes six to eight years for some of these compounds to reach the upper atmosphere, and once there, they will destroy ozone for another 20-25 years. Thus, even if all emissions of destructive chemicals were stopped, compounds already released would continue to damage the ozone layer for another quarter century.

Understanding Ozone Depletion

As detailed collection of data about interactions in the stratosphere progresses, the observational support for the ozone depletion theory continues to grow more compelling. Yet atmospheric scientists are beginning to realize that their understanding of the upper atmosphere is still quite crude. While certain key reactions which maintain and destroy ozone are theoretically and observationally supported, scientists will have to comprehend the interaction of dozens, if not hundreds, of reactions between natural and artificial species of hydrogen, nitrogen, bromine, chlorine and oxygen before a complete picture of ozone-layer dynamics emerges. The recent eruption of Mt. Pinatubo, for example, made scientists aware that *heterogenous processes*—those reactions which require cloud surfaces to take place—may play a far greater role in causing ozone depletion than originally believed. Such reactions had previously been observed taking place only at the Earth's poles, where stratospheric clouds form during the long winter darkness, but it is now thought that sulfur aerosols ejected by Pinatubo may be serving as a catalyst to speed ozone depletion at nonpolar latitudes.

Ironically, ozone-depleting reactions are best understood around the thinly inhabited polar regions, where stable and isolated conditions over the winter allow scientists to understand stratospheric changes most easily. In contrast, at the temperate latitudes where constantly moving air masses undergo no seasonal isolation, it is difficult to determine whether a fluctuation in a given chemical's density is a result of local reactions or atmospheric turbulence. In 1995, the Nobel Prize for Chemistry was awarded to F. Sherwood

Roland, Mario Molina and Paul Crutzen for their work on the formation and destruction of the ozone layer. It is hoped that increasingly detailed measurements using a new generation of equipment (such as NASA's *Perseus* remote-control aircraft) will begin to shed more light on the processes occurring away from the poles. Joe Waters of NASA's Jet Propulsion Laboratory summarizes the urgent task: "We must be able to lay out the catalytic cycles that are destroying ozone at all altitudes all over the globe—from its production region in the tropics to the higher latitudes and the polar regions." *See also* Photochemical reaction

[*Lewis G. Regenstein*]

FURTHER READING

Benedick, R. E. *Ozone Diplomacy: New Directions in Safeguarding the Planet.* Washington, DC: World Wildlife Fund, 1991.

Clark, S. L. *Protecting the Ozone Layer: What You Can Do.* New York: Environmental Information Exchange, 1988.

Lyman, F. "As the Ozone Thins, the Plot Thickens." *Amicus Journal* 13 (Summer 1991): 20-28, 30.

Monastersky, R. "Ozone Layer Shows Record Thinning." *Science News* 143 (24 April 1993): 260.

State of the World 1993. Washington, DC: Worldwatch Institute, 1993.

Zurer, P. S. "Ozone Depletion's Recurring Surprises Challenge Atmospheric Scientists." *Chemical and Engineering News* (24 May 1993): 8-18.

P

PAH

See **Polycyclic aromatic hydrocarbons**

Paleoecology/paleolimnology

Paleoecology, the scientific study of ancient environments and the interrelationships of their plants and animals, and paleolimnology, the scientific study of evidence of ancient inland waterways, including lakes, ponds, freshwater marshes, and streams, were both established at the end of the nineteenth century. The roots of both disciplines can be traced to early nineteenth-century botanical and chemical studies, and later, geological studies of the consolidated sediments of ancient lake beds, in which their organisms and **environment**s were examined in relationship to both the lakes and the surrounding uplands.

By the early 1920s, limnologists began to collect sediment cores from lakes and to interpret stratigraphic data from plant and animal fossils as a record of a lake's history. This provided clues to how lakes had changed over time as a result of either natural events or human activities. Data collected from lakes and **wetlands** provide baselines to compare the impacts of a activities such as land clearance, drainage, **water pollution**, and **air pollution**. They can also be used to assess the rate of recovery from the activities once they have ended.

Lake and wetland sediments contain detailed archeological records of how the overlying **ecosystem**s have been affected over time. It is in many ways equivalent to archeological reconstruction of past civilizations by examining their stratified remains. Lake sediments and wetland **peat** deposits form a selective trap for a variety of plant and animal remains and elements such as **carbon, phosphorus**, sulfur, iron, and manganese that are stored at varying concentrations depending on the activities that were occurring at the time the sediment layer was formed. Changes in this profile record not only the history of the lake or peatland but also what happened in the surrounding **watershed**. Initially, limnologists collected core samples from lakes and interpreted them on the basis of plant and animal fossils. The limnologists observed that in some lakes there were thin laminated sediments. These were shown to result from an annual deposition cycle which involves summer deposition of

calcium carbonate and deposition of organic matter during the rest of the year. These alternating light and dark layers represent a yearly cycle. Using these bands, or laminae, scientists can count back in time and date individual strata of sediment cores.

Studying plant and animal microfossil remains (such as pollen, diatom shells, and remains of **zooplankton** bodies) in the sediment cores and knowing the environments in which these organisms occur today allow a limnologist to reconstruct historical conditions in a lake as well as in its drainage basin. Such wetland studies were limited, however, until the development of radioisotope dating methods in the 1950s and 1960s. Today radioisotopes such as carbon-14 and lead-210 can be used to date the time a sediment was deposited.

Other methods limnologists use include the pollen, which indicates what types of land vegetation were present. They also examine plant and animal fossil remains, including cell fragments and molecules such as plant pigments, all of which provide clues about vegetation and aquatic life. Limnologists also search for organic pollutants and certain trace elements, whose presence indicates the result of human activities.

Analysis of the layers in sediment cores from lakes and wetlands has provided information about regional variations in past climatic conditions and watershed vegetation patterns which indicates the causes of environmental change. Studies on recently deposited lake sediments have provided evidence for the timing and causes of lake pollution, including the effects of excess nutrients on lake ecology and information about atmospheric transport of various pollutants.

These techniques have also been applied to address basic plant ecology questions regarding plant succession, on which there are two major schools of thought. The first is the community concept which has three basic attributes: vegetation occurs in recognizable and characteristic communities; community change through time occurs because of the vegetation; and the changes occur in a sequence that leads to a mature stable climax ecosystem. The community explanation can be contrasted with the continuum concept. Here, the distribution of vegetation is determined by the environment. Since each plant species adapts differently, no two occupy the exact same location. Additionally, the observed replacement sequence is influenced by the chance occurrence of viable seeds that allows a certain plant to grow on the site. This results in a continuum of overlapping sets of species. In this scenario although ecosystems change, it is not directed toward a particular climax community.

One of the areas where these two concepts directly collide is in the study of wetlands and peatlands. The classical community view of succession is that wetlands are a transitional stage in the progression from shallow lake to terrestrial forested climax community. This view requires that lakes gradually fill in as organic material from dying plants accumulates and minerals are carried down from upslope into the water. At first change is slow, but it accelerates when the lake becomes shallow enough to support rooted aquatic plants. When the water becomes even more shallow, it supports the development of a peat mat, allowing trees and shrubs to grow which further modifies the site by not only adding organic matter but also by drying the site through **evapotranspiration**. According to the community version, in the final stages a climax forest occupies the site. This sequence implies that most of the change is caused by plants and not external environmental changes.

Paleoecological analyses of peat beds have provided information refuting the validity of the community concept's explanation. Fossil records including analysis of pollen in northern peat lands provide two generalizations: in some sites the present vegetation has existed for several thousand years and climatic change and glaciation had a large impact on plant species and distribution. Generally, bogs expanded during warm, wet periods and contracted during cool, drier periods although the influence of local topographic and drainage conditions often mask climatic shifts.

While this evidence supports the continuum assumptions that other environmental factors overwhelm the vegetation effects, there is evidence within the bogs that says that vegetation can have a large impact on the character of the landscape. In particular, this is evidenced by the patterned landscape of these peatlands as the water flow is changed due to the vegetation. It seems that in the wetlands or bogs themselves there can be changes in vegetation that occur over time as a result of succession. However, these changes do not necessarily point toward a terrestrial climax. In fact, pollen profiles indicate that a bog, not some type of terrestrial forest, is the endpoint. These studies confirmed conclusions from a classical study on the Lake Aggassiz Plain (Minnesota and south-central Canada) that indicates most of the peatlands developed during a moist climate about 4,000 years ago when surface water levels rose about 12 ft (4 m). This implies that while there may be changes within the peatlands, they are stable, so the central concepts of succession in this case are not supported.

Examples of the findings and results of some significant types of paleolimnological studies show how they are useful in evaluating changes and as indicators of potential problems due to human activities. The Red Lake peatland in northwestern Minnesota has been used as a study site to document the occurrence of **acid rain** and global warming. Based on past changes in the type of vegetation and changes in **pH**, future impacts on the bog surface can be evaluated. If **acid deposition** were to lower the pH of the bog signifi-

cantly, different types of mosses would be evident. Likewise, if global warming were to lower the water tables' moss types, characteristics of drier conditions would occur.

Using sediment cores from lakes and observing the changes in flora, fauna, and chemistry allows the evaluation of impacts of human settlement on lakes in the upper Midwest of the United States. A lake studied in northern Minnesota on the iron range shows these changes. There was a distinct increase in hematite (iron) grains in the sediments as mining began and a decrease as it declined. Settlement was also marked by a rise in the concentration or ragweed pollen which reflects the replacement of the forests with agricultural fields. There were also changes in the type of diatom shells reflecting the nutrient enrichment of the lake due to the discharge of sewage directly to the lake. By analyzing the pH preferences of individual species of diatoms and algae the past pH conditions in a lake can be determined. Using the results of these studies it has been demonstrated that lakes in the **Adirondack Mountains** were not naturally acidic. Current monitoring suggests that these lakes that were acidified due to acid rain have not yet responded reductions in the amount of sulfate deposition.

[*James L. Anderson*]

FURTHER READING

Freshwater Ecosystems: Revitalizing Educational Programs in Limnology. Washington, D.C.: National Academy Press, 1996.

Mitsch, W.J., and J.G. Gosselink. *Wetlands.* New York: Van Nostrand Reinhold, 1993.

Panda

See **Giant panda**

Panther

See **Florida panther**

Paper mills

See **Pulp and paper mills**

Parasites

Organisms that live in or upon the body of a host organism and are metabolically dependent on the host for completion of their life cycle. Parasites may be plants, animals, **virus**es, bacteria, or **fungi**. Parasites feed either on their host directly or upon its surplus fluids. Some parasites, known as endoparasites, live inside their host, while ectoparasites live on the outside of their host. Organisms in which parasites reach maturity are called definitive hosts, and hosts harboring parasite stages are called intermediate hosts. Organisms which spread parasite stages between hosts are known as vectors. Full-time, or obligatory, parasites have an absolute dependence on their hosts. Examples of this type are viruses, which can only live and multiply inside living cells, and tapeworms, which can only live and multiply inside other **species**. Part-time, or facultative, parasites, such as wood ticks, have parasitic and free-living stages in their life cycle and are only temporary residents of their hosts.

The effects of parasites on their hosts depend on the health of the host, as well as the severity of the infestation. In diseased, old, or poorly-fed individuals, parasite infestations can be fatal, but parasites do not typically kill their hosts, though they can slow growth and cause weight loss. Some plant parasites do kill their host and then live on its decomposing remains, and certain species of hymenopteran insect are parasitoids, whose larva feeds within the living body of the host, eventually killing it. Some parasites, such as *Sacculina*, castrate their host by infecting its reproductive organs. Cuckoos are brood parasites, and they lay their eggs in the nest of another bird species, evicting the eggs that were there and leaving the young cuckoos to be raised by the parents of the host species.

In community **ecology**, parasites are often grouped together with predators, since both feed directly upon other organisms, either harming them or killing them. Ecologically, small disease-causing organisms (viruses, bacteria, protozoans) are regarded as microparasites, while larger parasites (flatworms, roundworms, lice, fleas, ticks, rusts, mistletoe) are macroparasites. Together with predators and diseases, parasites are one of the natural components of environmental resistance which serves to limit **population growth**. Microparasites that are transmitted directly between infected hosts, such as rabies or distemper, target herd animals with a high host density and can significantly reduce population levels. Macroparasites that employ one or more intermediate hosts, such as flukes, tapeworms, or roundworms, have highly effective transmission stages but usually have only a limited effect on the population of the host.

Parasites can play a larger role in altered **ecosystem**s. In the eastern United States parasitic infections have held populations of cottontail rabbits well below the carrying capacity of the **habitat**. Parasitic insects have been used to control populations of the olive scale insect, a serious pest of olive trees in California. Accidentally introduced parasites have negatively impacted populations of commercial species by altering the balance of the ecosystem. For example, a protozoan parasite infecting California oysters was introduced to French oyster beds, wiping out the native European oysters and seriously damaging **commercial fishing** there. *See also* Population biology; Predator-prey interactions

[*Neil Cumberlidge*]

FURTHER READING

Bullock, W. L. *People, Parasites, and Pestilence: An Introduction to the Natural History of Infectious Disease.* Minnesota: Burgess Publishing Company, 1982.

Crew, W., and D. R. W. Haddock. *Parasites and Human Disease.* London: Edward Arnold, 1985.

Despommier, D. D., and J. W. Karapelou. *Parasite Life Cycles.* New York: Springer-Verlag, 1987.

Noble, E. R., and G. A. Noble. *Parasitology: The Biology of Animal Parasites.* 6th ed. Philadelphia: Lea & Febiger, 1989.

Schmidt, G. D., and L. S. Roberts. *Foundations of Parasitology.* 4th ed. St. Louis: Times Mirror/Mosby College Pub., 1989.

Smith, R. L. *Elements of Ecology.* 3rd ed. New York: Harper Collins, 1991.

Pareto optimality (Maximum social welfare)

Usually, one thinks of efficiency as not being wasteful or getting the most out of the resources one has available. Economists offer the Pareto optimum—"a situation where no one can be better off without making someone worse off." Derived from the work of the Italian economist and sociologist Vilfredo Pareto, whose late nineteenth-century writings on political economy inspired much thinking about what made an economy efficient, Pareto optimality has come to mean making at least one person better off without making anyone else worse off. For an economy, it means that the allocation of resources is optimal if no other allocation exists wherein a person is better off and everyone is at least as well off. Economic theory holds that these conditions are met if consumers maximize utility, producers maximize profits, competition prevails, and information is adequate for the making of rational decisions. A free market unconstrained by government involvement, it is assumed, will achieve Pareto optimality by an invisible hand, that is, automatically, provided that production and consumption decisions do not entail substantial environmental disamenities. Imperfect market conditions, which include environmental disamenities on a large scale, challenge the assumptions of Pareto optimality and call for remedial measures such as **pollution** taxes or **emission** rights to restore market efficiency. *See also* Externalities

Parrots and parakeets

These intelligent, brightly colored, affectionate birds are found mainly in warm, tropical regions and have long been popular as pets, in large part because many of them can learn to talk. But capture of wild parrots for the **pet trade**, along with the destruction of forests, have decimated populations of these birds, and many **species** are now threatened with **extinction**.

About half of the approximately 315 species of parrots in the world are native to Central and South America. Members of the parrot order (Psittaciformes) include the macaws of Central and South America, which are the largest parrots, with bright feathers; cockatoos of Australia with white feathers and crests on their heads; lorikeets of Australia with orange-red bills and brightly-colored feathers; cockatiels, which are small, long-tailed, crested parrots also from Australia; and parakeets, which are small, natural acrobats, usually with green feathers. Parakeets include lovebirds from Africa and budgies from Australia. Budgies are the most common type of pet parakeet, and they can be trained to say many words. Most parakeets sold as pets are bred for that purpose, thus their trade does not usually threaten wild populations.

Part of the attraction of parrots is their high intelligence, but this can make them unsuitable pets. The birds are often loud and they demand a great deal of attention, and many people who buy parrots give them up because of the frustrations of owning one of these complex birds. In addition, parrots often carry a disease called *psittacosis* which can be transmitted to humans and commercially raised poultry. For this reason, parrots must be examined by officials from the **U.S. Department of Agriculture** (USDA) before entering the United States, and hundreds of thousands of parrots have been destroyed to prevent the spread of psittacosis.

The large scale capture of parrots for the legal and illegal pet trade has been a major factor in the depletion of these beautiful birds. The world trade in wild birds has been estimated at over seven million annually, and the United States is the world's largest consumer of exotic birds. Over 1.4 million wild birds were imported into this country during 1988-1990, and half of these were parrots and other birds supposedly protected under the **Convention on International Trade in Endangered Species of Wild Fauna and Flora** (CITES). The mortality rate for birds transported in international trade is massive. For every wild bird that makes it to the pet store, at least as many as five may have died on the way, and USDA statistics show that 79,192 birds perished in transit to the United States from 1985-1990, and 258,451 died while in quarantine or because they were refused entry due to Newcastle disease. In 1991 one airline shipment alone included 10,000 dead birds. Moreover, the shock of capture and caging the birds before shipment may cause even greater mortality rates.

As a species becomes rare or endangered, it often becomes more valuable and sought-after, and some parrots have been sold for $10,000 or more. In October 1992, shortly before being named Secretary of the Interior, former Arizona governor Bruce Babbitt addressed the annual meeting of the **Humane Society of the United States**. Expressing dismay at "the looming extinction of tropical parrots and macaws in South America," he described their exploitation in the following terms: "These birds are captured for buyers in the United States who will pay up to $30,000 for a hyacinth macaw. You can stand on docks outside Manaus, Brazil, and other towns in the Amazon and see confiscated crates with blue and yellow macaws, their feet taped, their beaks wired, stacked up like cordwood in boxes. They have a fatality rate of 50 percent by the time they're smuggled into Miami."

Some progress has been made in restricting the international trade in parrots. By the end of 1992 over 100 airlines had agreed to forbid the carrying of wild birds. The Wild Bird Conservation Act, signed into law on October 27, 1992, bans trade immediately for several severely exploited bird species and, within a year of passage, outlaws commerce in all parrots and other birds protected under CITES. The act requires exploiters to prove that a species can withstand removal from the wild. Conservation groups, such as the Humane Society of the United States and the Animal Welfare Institute, have worked for years to secure passage of this legislation.

Nevertheless, the persistence of smuggling as well as the legal trade in some species of these birds will continue to threaten wild populations. This is especially true when the trees in which parrots nest are cut down to provide collectors access to chicks in the nest. As of early 1993, fifteen parrot species, ten parakeet species and three macaw species were listed as **endangered species** by the **U.S. Department of the Interior**, and all species of parrots, parakeets, macaws, lories, and cockatoos are listed in the most endangered categories of CITES. **IUCN—The World Conservation Union** includes 79 members of the parrot order in its 1990 list of threatened animals.

One parrot is already extinct. The beautiful orange, yellow, and green Carolina parakeet (*Conuropsis carolinensis*) once ranged in large numbers from Florida to New York and Illinois, but the demand for its feathers by the millinery trade was so great that the species was hunted into extinction between 1904 and 1920. Conservationists fear that several other species of the parrot family may soon join the Carolina parakeet on the list of extinct birds. *See also* Endangered Species Act; Overhunting; Poaching; Rare species; Wildlife management

[*Lewis G. Regenstein*]

FURTHER READING

Beissinger, S. R., and E. H. Bucher. "Can Parrots Be Conserved Through Sustainable Harvesting?" *BioScience* 42 (March 1992): 164-73.

————, eds. *New World Parrots in Crisis: Solutions From Conservation Biology.* Washington, DC: Smithsonian Institution Press, 1991.

Defreitas, M. "Feathering a Nest in the Windwards." (Saving the Santa Lucian parrot) *Americas* 43 (March-April 1991): 40-45.

Particulate

An adjective describing anything that consists of, or relates to, particles. The term was formerly used in laboratory slang to stand for "particulate matter," but this use has nearly disappeared since its repudiation by the **Environmental Protection Agency (EPA)**. The term particulate matter, which often means the particle content of a given volume of air, is used as a more inclusive variant of "particles."

Typical atmospheric particulate matter may comprise three populations of particles according to size. The smallest of these is found only near sources, since the particles rapidly aggregate to larger sizes. The upper size limit for these particles is near 0.1 micrometer (1 micrometer = 1 μm = 0.001 mm). Number concentrations can be quite high. This population is referred to as the nuclei mode of particles. The next larger size class, which begins at a diameter of about 0.1 μm and extends to about 2.0 μm, is called the accumulation mode, since once in the air it tends to remain for days; number concentrations have become low enough that agglomeration is slow, and settling velocities are very small. The sum of the nuclei mode and the accumulation mode is called the fine particles. These are characteristically formed by condensation from the gas phase, or by agglomeration of particles formed from the gas phase. The final particle population in air is called the coarse mode, or simply the coarse particles. These are of any size larger than about 2 μm (about 1/10,000 inch), and are formed by mechanical grinding of larger masses of matter. Coarse particles are usually particles of local **soil** or rocks.

Parts per billion (ppb)

A means of expressing minute concentrations, often of an element, compound, or particle that contaminates **soil**, water, air, or blood. The expression may be on either a mass or a volume basis, or a combination of the two, such as micrograms of a chemical per kilogram of soil, or micrograms of chemical per liter of water. In the United States, one billion equals 1×10^9. **Dioxin**, a contaminant associated with the **herbicide** 2,4,5-T and implicated in the formation of **birth defects**, can cause concern at concentrations measured in ppb.

Parts per million (ppm)

A means of expressing small concentrations, usually of an element, compound, contaminant, or particle in water or a mixed medium such as **soil** and normally on a mass basis. Units that are equivalent to ppm include micrograms per gram, milligrams per kilogram, and milligrams per liter. One ppm times 10,000 equals one part per hundred or one percent. The **nutrient phosphorus** and the contaminant **lead** found in soil are commonly measured in ppm.

Parts per trillion (ppt)

A means of expressing extremely minute concentrations of substances in water or air. In the United States, the concentration is the number of units of the substance found in 1×10^{12} units of water or air; an equivalent unit is nanograms per kilogram. Detection of concentrations this low, which was not possible until the late twentieth century, is limited to only a few types of chemical compounds. For example, one gram of sulfur hexafluoride, used as a tracer in studies of ocean mixing, can be detected in a cubic kilometer of sea water, a concentration of 1,000 parts per trillion.

Passenger pigeon (*Ectopistes migratorius*)

The passenger pigeon, perhaps the world's most abundant bird **species** at one time, became extinct due directly to human activity. In the mid-1800s passenger pigeons travelled in flocks of astounding numbers. Alexander Wilson, the father of American ornithology, noted a flock he estimated to contain two billion birds. The artist and naturalist **John James Audubon** once observed a flock over a three-day

Passenger pigeon

period and estimated the birds were flying overhead at a rate of 300 million per hour.

The species became extinct within a span of 50 years, several factors having led to its rapid demise. The passenger pigeon was considered an agricultural pest, thus providing ample reason to kill large numbers of the birds. It was also in demand as food, largely due to the fact that nesting flocks were easily accessible. Young squabs were easy prey for hunters who knocked them from their nests or forced them out by setting fires below them. Adults were also killed in huge numbers. They were baited with alcohol-soaked grain or with captive pigeons set up as decoys, then trapped and shot. A common practice of the day was to use the live pigeons as targets in shooting galleries. In 1878, near Petoskey, Michigan, a professional market hunter earned $60,000 by killing over three million passenger pigeons near their nesting grounds. Once killed, many of the birds were packed in barrels and shipped to cities where they were sold in markets and restaurants. The demand was particularly high on the East Coast where forest clearing and hunting had already eradicated the species from the area.

By the 1880s commercial hunting of passenger pigeons was no longer profitable, because the population had been depleted to only several thousand birds. Michigan provided their last stronghold, but that population became extinct in 1889. The remaining small flocks of birds were so spread out and isolated that their numbers were too low to be maintained. The disruption of the population in the 1860s and 1870s had been so severe that breeding success was permanently reduced. At one time the sheer numbers of passenger pigeons in a flock was enough to discourage potential predators. Once the population was split into small, isolated remnants, however, natural predation also contributed to the species' rapid decline.

The last individual passenger pigeon was a female named Martha, which died in the Cincinnati Zoo in 1914. It is now on display at the National Museum of Natural History in Washington, D. C. *See also* Endangered species; Extinction; Overhunting; Rare species

[*Eugene C. Beckham*]

FURTHER READING

Schorger, A. W. *Passenger Pigeon: Its Natural History and Extinction.* Norman, OK: University of Oklahoma Press, 1973.

Wilcove, D. "In Memory of Martha and Her Kind." *Audubon* 91 (September 1989): 52-55.

Worsnop, R. L. "Evolving Attitudes." *CQ Researcher* 2 (24 January 1992): 58-60.

Passive solar design

Looking into the sky on a sunny day, the notion that humans could have an "energy crisis" seems absurd. Each day, the earth receives 1.78×10^{14} kilowatts of energy, more than 10,000 times the amount needed by the whole world this year. All that is required is a way to collect and harness the energy of sunlight.

Humans have explored systems for the capture of **solar energy** for centuries. The Roman architect Vitruvius described a plan in the first century B.C. for building a bathhouse heated by sunlight. He explained that the building should "look toward the winter sunset" because that would make the bathhouse warmer in the late afternoon. More recently, water heaters operated by solar energy were built and widely sold in the early 1990s, especially in California and Florida.

Most historical examples illustrate the principles of passive solar heating, namely constructing a building so that it can take advantage of normal sunlight without the use of elaborate or expensive accessory equipment. A home built on this principle, for example, has as much window space as possible facing toward the south, with few or no windows on other sides of the house. Sunlight enters the south-facing window and is converted to heat, which is then trapped inside the house. To reduce loss of heat produced in this way, the window panes are double- or triple-glazed, that is, consist of two or three panes separated by air pockets. The rest of the house is also as thoroughly insulated as possible. In some cases, a house can be built directly into a south-facing hill so that the earth itself acts as insulation for the north-, east-, and west-facing walls.

Adjustments can also be made to take account of changing sun angles throughout the year. In the winter, when the sun is low in the sky, solar heat is needed most. In the summer, when the sun is high in the sky, heating is less important. An overhang of some kind over the south-facing window can provide the correct amount of sunlight at various times of the year. Changing seasonal temperatures can also be managed by installing insulating screens on the south-facing window. When the screens are open, they allow solar energy to come in. When they are closed (as at night), they keep heat inside the building.

The primary drawback to the use of solar energy is its variability. Often the energy supply and the energy requirements are out of balance for weeks or months depending on season, amount of cloud cover, latitude, etc. Thus, there is frequently the need for storage of energy for later use. Several technologically-simple methods for storing solar energy are commonly used in passive solar design. A large water tank on top of the house, for example, provides one way to store this energy. Sunlight warms the water during the day and the water can then be pumped into the house at night as a heat source. A heat sink such as a dark-colored masonry wall or concrete floor near the south facing windows can also enhance a passive solar system by absorbing heat during the day and slowly radiating it into the room during the night. A Trombe wall may also be installed. This masonry wall, 6-18 inches (15-46 cm) thick with gaps at the top and bottom, faces the sun. The space in front of the wall is enclosed by glass. Air between the glass and the masonry wall is heated by the sun, rises and passes into the room behind the wall through the upper gap. Cooler air is drawn from the room into the space through the lower gap. The masonry wall also acts as a heat sink.

[*David E. Newton*]

FURTHER READING

Anderson, B. *Passive Solar Energy: The Homeowner's Guide to Natural Heating and Cooling.* Amherst, MA: Brick House Publishing, 1993.

Balcomb, J. D. *Passive Solar Buildings.* Cambridge: MIT Press, 1992.

Mazria, E. *The Passive Solar Energy Book: A Complete Guide to Passive Solar Home, Greenhouse, and Building Design.* Emmaus, PA: Rodale Press, 1979.

Passmore, John A. (1914 -)

Australian philosopher

As a philosopher, John Passmore has defended Western civilization against the charge that such societies "can solve their ecological problems only if they abandon the analytical, critical approach which has been their peculiar glory and go in search of a new ethics, a new metaphysics, a new religion." We do indeed face daunting ecological crises, Passmore states, but the best hope for solving them lies in "a more general adherence to a perfectly familiar ethic."

Born in Manly, New South Wales, Australia, on September 9, 1914, Passmore earned his B.A. and M.A. degrees from the University of Sydney, where he taught philosophy from 1935 to 1949. He then served on the faculties of Otago University in New Zealand and the Australian National University, holding the chair of philosophy at the latter from 1959 to 1979. The best known of his many publications are *Hume's Intentions* (1952), *A Hundred Years of Philosophy* (1957), *The Perfectibility of Man* (1970), and *Man's Responsibility for Nature* (1974).

Part of Passmore's argument in *Man's Responsibility for Nature* is that people in the West, like people everywhere, cannot simply adopt a new and unfamiliar way of thinking: one must begin where one is at. He also insists that Western civilization encompasses more than one way of thinking. He argues that "central Stoic-Christian traditions are not favourable to the solution of [the West's] ecological problems . . ." but that these "are not the only Western traditions and their influence is steadily declining." More favorable are traditions such as Jewish thought and, especially, modern science. These are hospitable to two attitudes—a sense of stewardship and a sense of cooperation with **nature**—that are incompatible with the Stoic-Christian traditions, "which deny that man's relationships with nature are governed by any moral principles and assign to nature the very minimum of independent life."

As a champion of stewardship and cooperation with nature, Passmore sharply disagrees with those who see civilization as an enemy of nature or a blight upon it. On the contrary, Passmore sees in civilization "man's great memorials—his science, his philosophy, his technology, his architecture, his countryside . . . all of them founded upon his attempt to understand and subdue nature." He considers the transformation of the natural **environment** necessary and, when done with care, desirable. For there is "no good ground . . . for objecting to transforming as such; it can make the world more fruitful, more diversified, and more beautiful."

Passmore's case for a more responsible attitude toward nature rests, finally, on a rejection of mysticism that includes a rejection of religion and the concept of the sacred: "To take our ecological crises seriously . . . is to recognize, first, man's utter dependence on nature, but secondly, nature's vulnerability to human depredations—the fragility, that is, of both man and nature, for all their notable powers of recuperation. And this means that neither man nor nature is sacred or quasi-divine." *See also* Environmental ethics; Environmentalism

[*Richard K. Dagger*]

FURTHER READING

Evory, A., ed. *Contemporary Authors: New Revision Series 6* Detroit, MI: Gale Research Co., 1982.

Passmore, J. *Hume's Intentions.* 3rd ed. London: Duckworth, 1980.

———. *A Hundred Years of Philosophy.* Rev. ed. New York: Basic Books, 1966.

———. *Man's Responsibility for Nature: Ecological Problems and Western Traditions.* London: Duckworth, 1974.

———. *The Perfectibility of Man.* New York: Scribner Sons, 1970.

Pathogen

A pathogen is an agent that causes disease. Pathology is the scientific study of human disease. One could argue that anything that causes disease is therefore by definition a "pathogen." Sunlight is the environmental agent that (with excessive exposure) induces the potentially fatal skin cancer known as melanoma. Ordinarily, however, most people do not consider sunlight to be a pathogen. An unbalanced diet may result in nutritional deficiencies which can lead to diseases such as pellagra (caused by a niacin deficiency) and scurvy (caused by inadequate vitamin C in the diet). Nevertheless, the *failure* to consume a balanced diet is not considered to be a pathogen. Generally, most students of disease refer to biological agents when they use the term pathogen. Such agents, which include **virus**es, bacteria, **fungi**, protozoa, and worms, cause a tremendous diversity of diseases.

Viruses, while considered biological agents, are not cellular organisms and accordingly, are not living in the usual sense. They are tiny particles consisting of either **DNA** or **RNA** as the genetic material and a protein coat, and they are incapable of **metabolism** outside of a living cell. Pathogenic viruses cause diseases of the respiratory system such as colds, laryngitis, croup, and influenza. Skin eruptions such as measles, rubella, chicken pox, and foot-and-mouth disease are viral in origin. The long list of viral diseases include insect-borne Western equine encephalitis and yellow fever. Recently, some human **cancer**s have been thought to be associated with viruses, perhaps because animal cancers such as the Lucké renal carcinoma and mouse mammary carcinoma are known to be caused by viruses. One such human cancer is Burkitt's lymphoma, a childhood malignancy occurring primarily in Africa, which is associated with a herpes virus. **AIDS** results from infection with HIV and is a pandemic viral disease.

Bacteria are true cells but their genetic material, DNA, is not packaged in a nucleus as in all higher forms of life. Not all bacteria are pathogens, but many well-known diseases are caused by bacterial infections. Tuberculosis, cholera, plague, gonorrhea, syphilis, rheumatic fever, typhus, and typhoid fever are some of the very serious diseases caused by pathogenic bacteria.

Probably 100 million cases of **malaria** occur each year primarily in Africa, Asia, and Central and South America. Malaria is caused by four **species** of the protozoan *Plasmodium*. *Amebiasis* and *giardiasis* are parasitic protozoa infections. Protozoa are single-celled animals. Thrush (*candidiasis*) is a common infection of mucous membranes with a yeast-like fungus. Valley fever (*coccidioidomycosis*) is a fungal infection generally limited to the lungs. Athlete's foot is a common skin infection caused by a fungus.

Worms that infect humans are a significant health problem in those parts of the world where there is inadequate public health protection. Examples of helminth infections are the beef and pork tapeworms. The consumption of inadequately cooked pork can result in trichinosis, which is a roundworm (nematode) infection of human muscle. Trematode flukes cause an extraordinarily important infection in Asia and Africa called **schistosomiasis** with hundreds of millions of individuals infected. Perhaps the most common parasitic helminth infection in the United States is *enterobiasis* known as pinworm or seatworm infection, which is a common condition of children with improper personal hygiene.

Many diseases caused by microbial pathogens can be treated with a diversity of antibiotics and other drugs. However, viral pathogens remain intractably difficult to manage with drugs.

[*Robert G. McKinnell*]

Patrick, Ruth (1907-)

American botanist and limnologist

Emphasizing the vital importance of environmental cleanup and **conservation**, Ruth Patrick has spent a lifetime facilitating cooperation among the scientific and political communities to find solutions to biospheric **pollution**. Her aggressive endeavors in freshwater research, including work on diatoms and the biodynamic cycles of rivers, have made much progress toward rectifying damage done by pollutants.

Her enthusiasm and concern for the **biosphere** began at an early age in her hometown of Kansas City, where, as a child, she conducted many expeditions through the countryside surrounding her family home. Collecting specimen materials and identifying them set the course for Patrick's future. She was fascinated by the microscopic world that could be found even in the smallest drop of water.

Patrick continued to foster her interests in science as she grew older. She attended Coker College in Hartsville, South Carolina, and earned a bachelor's degree in botany there in 1929. She then attended the University of Virginia where she earned a doctoral degree in 1934. Throughout her career, Patrick has been awarded honorary degrees from many institutions, including Princeton University and Wake Forest University. In 1975, she received the prestigious John and Alice Tyler Ecology Award (through Pepperdine University); the award amount of $150,000 is the largest amount granted for a scientific award.

Patrick was a key force in the founding of **limnology**, the scientific study of the biological, physical, and chemical conditions of freshwater. By conducting further studies, she also became widely known as an expert on diatoms, the basic food substance of freshwater organisms, and she later developed the diatometer. The diatometer is used to measure the levels of diatoms in freshwater, a measurement which is used in evaluating the pollution levels and general health of freshwater bodies. During the late 1960s and early 1970s, she acted as a consultant in both the private sector and in government, and her vast knowledge and influence enabled her to play an active role in the development of **environmental policy**. She worked with the **U.S. Department of the Interior** and served on numerous committees, including the Hazardous Waste Advisory Committee of the **Environmental Protection Agency (EPA)** and the Science Advisory Council of the **World Wildlife Federation**. She has often been called the "**Ralph Nader** of **water pollution**," and she has a wide reputation as a dauntless watchdog. Patrick has conducted most of her work through her offices at the Academy of Natural Sciences in Philadelphia, where she has been on staff since the late 1930s. She was the first female board chairperson at the academy.

Patrick also maintains membership in such organizations as the National Academy of Sciences, the National Academy of Engineering, the American Academy of Arts and Sciences, the International Limnological Society, the American Society of Limnology and Oceanography, and the American Society of Naturalists. She has been bestowed dozens of awards from schools, institutions, and organizations, and she has written four books, including *Diatoms of the United States* (with C. W. Reimer). She was also presented with a 1996 National Medal of Science by President Clinton for her work in pioneering the field of limnology. *See also* Aquatic chemistry; Ecology; Environmental monitoring;

Hydrologic cycle; Pollution control; Water quality; Water quality standards

[*Kimberley A. Peterson*]

FURTHER READING

Kunreuther, H., and Ruth Patrick. "Managing the Risks of Hazardous Waste." *Environment* 33 (April 1991): 12-21.

Patrick, Ruth. *Diatoms of the United States, Exclusive of Alaska and Hawaii.* Philadelphia: University of Pennsylvania Press, 1966.

———. *Groundwater Contamination in the United States.* Philadelphia: University of Pennsylvania Press, 1987.

———. *Surface Water Quality: Have the Laws Been Successful?* Princeton, NJ: Princeton University Press, 1992.

PBB
See **Polybrominated biphenyl**

PCB
See **Polychlorinated biphenyl**

PCP
See **Pentachlorophenol**

Peat soils

A **soil** that is derived completely from the decomposing remains of plants. Plants that commonly form peat include reeds, sedges, sphagnum moss, and grasses. The plant remains do not decompose but continue to accumulate because the wet and/or cool **environment** in which they occur is not conducive to **aerobic** decomposition. Vegetable crops are often grown on peat soils. Peat can also be harvested for use in horticulture or as a fuel for heating and cooking. *See also* Peatlands

Peatlands

Expansive areas of **peat soils** are referred to as peatlands. These areas are often located in what were once lakes or oceans. The clay deposits from the former lake provide an impermeable layer so that water accumulates. Plants growing in this wet **environment** will not be able to decompose because of a lack of oxygen. Accumulations of plants will continue to increase the thickness of the peat deposit until a soil formed entirely of peat is created. These deposits can be 40 feet (12 m) or more thick. Extensive peatlands occur in Minnesota, Wisconsin, Michigan, New England, Russia, England, and Scandinavian countries.

Pedology

The scientific study of **soil** as a natural body, without emphasizing the practical uses or ecological significance of the soil. Pedology includes soil formation and morphology, its basic physical and chemical properties, its distribution, and the erosional processes affecting it without direct regard to plants or animals. Pedology provides the foundation for the study of soil as a medium of biological activity, called **edaphology**, and for the study of soil necessary in construction and drainage projects.

Pelagic zone

The entire water column in marine **ecosystem**s, regardless of depth. Plants and algae in the pelagic zone directly or indirectly support most of the ocean's animal life. Because plant growth is confined to the shallow depths of the pelagic zone reached by light (epipelagic zone, 0-650 ft/0-200 m), much of the biological activity in the pelagic zone is concentrated in near-surface waters. The pelagic zone is further subdivided by depth into the mesopelagic zone (650-3,280 ft/200-1000 m), bathypelagic zone (3,280-13,125 ft/1000-4000 m) and abyssopelagic zone (greater than 13,125 ft/4000 m), each zone inhabited by a distinctive **fauna**. These deeper fauna are nourished largely by organic matter (e.g. dead **plankton**, fecal material) settling from surface waters. *See also* Littoral zone; Neritic zone; Photic zone; Phytoplankton; Zooplankton

Pelican

See **Brown pelican**

Pentachlorophenol (PCP)

One of the most widely manufactured **chemicals** in the world, PCP is used extensively as a wood preservative for telephone poles, fences, and indoor or outdoor construction materials. It has also been used for slime control in the pulp and paper manufacturing process, for weed control, termite control, and as a paint preservative. Technical grade PCP contains trace amounts of less-chlorinated phenols and

certain chlorinated **dioxin**s and furans. Concerns over its toxicity have curtailed the use of PCP in the United States to treat materials that humans or animals will have contact with. Readily absorbed through skin and also volatile, it is acutely toxic from dermal exposure or inhalation.

People for the Ethical Treatment of Animals (Washington, D.C.)

Founded in 1980 by Alex Pacheco and Ingrid Newkirk, People for the Ethical Treatment of Animals (PETA) is a nonprofit charitable organization dedicated to protecting and promoting **animal rights**. These rights are not, of course, civil or religious, but rather, the right to live lives free from human-caused pain or predation. To this end, PETA has mounted campaigns against the use of animals in painful and frequently fatal medical experiments, as well as in the testing of cosmetics and other products. They have also campaigned against the trapping of fur-bearing animals, so-called "factory farming," such as confining cattle in crowded feedlots, and the cruel use of animals in rodeos, carnivals and circuses. Through its newsletter, *PETA News*, and its "Factsheets," PETA publicizes these and other abuses and encourages readers to take action. Members write to the offending organizations, organize boycotts of their products or services, and contact their political representatives in support of proposed or pending legislation regarding the treatment of animals.

Drawing many of its ideas and much of its inspiration from philosophers such as **Tom Regan** and **Peter Singer**, PETA is attempting (in Singer's words) to "expand the circle" of creatures considered worthy of respect and protection. Although other forms of discrimination, such as racism and sexism, have been widely discredited (if not yet eliminated), another form of discrimination has barely begun to be recognized. **Speciesism** is the view that one particular species, *Homo sapiens*, is superior to all other **species** and that therefore humans have the unquestionable and unlimited right to use or to kill those other species for food, fur, leather, labor, or amusement. Such speciesist beliefs and attitudes are deeply rooted in our culture, Regan and Singer argue, and challenging them is often very difficult.

Animal rights advocates have been accused of putting the interests of animals above or at least on a par with those of human beings. Many critics of PETA quote, out of context, Ingrid Newkirk's statement that "a rat is a pig is a dog is a boy," thereby purporting to prove that PETA and other animal rights organizations equate the rights and interests of human and nonhuman animals. This statement of Newkirk's was actually intended to show that humans, like animals, are sentient beings because they have a central nervous system and are therefore able to feel pleasure and pain. "When it comes to having a central nervous system and the ability to feel pain, hunger, and thirst," said Newkirk, "a rat is a pig is a dog is a boy." More elaborate and extended versions of the

About 50 members of People for the Ethical Treatment of Animals and several dogs protest against a furrier in Atlanta, Georgia. The protestors wore red shirts to symbolize the blood spilled to make fur garments.

argument about sentience can be found in Peter Singer's *Animal Liberation* (1990) and in Tom Regan's *The Case for Animal Rights* (1983). But PETA's primary aim is not to engage in philosophical disputation but to participate in political, economic, and educational campaigns on behalf of creatures who cannot defend themselves against humanly caused pain and predation. Contact: People for the Ethical Treatment of Animals, P.O. Box 42516, Washington, DC 20015-0516. Internet: http://www.envirolink.org/arrs/peta/.

[*Terence Ball*]

Peptides

A chemical compound consisting of two or more amino acids joined to each other through a bond between the **nitrogen** atom of one amino acid to an oxygen atom of its neighbor. A more precise term describes the number of amino acid units involved. A dipeptide or tripeptide consists of two or three amino acid units respectively. A few oligopeptides (about ten amino acid units) are of physiological importance. The antibiotics bacitracin, gramicidin S, and tyrocidin A are examples of oligopeptides. The largest polypeptides contain dozens or hundreds of amino acid units and are better known as proteins. The bond between peptide units is especially

sensitive to attack by various types of corrosive poisons such as strong **acids and bases**.

Percolation

The movement of water through **soil** and the unsaturated zone into and through the pores of materials in the **zone of saturation**. **Groundwater** is recharged by this movement of water through the unsaturated zone. From a soil science perspective, percolation refers to the drainage of initially wetted areas of soil and movement of water beyond the rooting zone of plants toward the **water table**. Sanitarians commonly use percolation, however, in reference to results of the common soil test, known as the Perk test, which evaluates the rate at which soils accept water. The rate water moves into the soil is referred to as percolation. *See also* Aquifer; Aquifer restoration; Drinking water supply; Recharge zone; Vadose zone; Water table draw-down

Peregrine falcon (*Falco peregrinus*)

The peregrine falcon, a bird of prey in the family Falconidae, is one of the most wide-ranging birds in the world with populations in both the Eastern and Western Hemispheres.

Peregrine falcon on ledge, downtown Detroit, Michigan.

However, with extensive **pesticide** use, particularly **DDT**, beginning in the 1940s, many populations of these birds were decimated. In the United States by the 1960s, the peregrine falcon was completely extirpated from the eastern half of the country because DDT and related compounds, which are amplified in the **food chain/web**, caused the birds' eggshells to become thin and fragile. This led to reproductive failures, as eggs were crushed in the nest during incubation. Prior to the DDT-induced losses, there were about 400 breeding pairs of peregrine falcons in the eastern United States. In the early 1970s there were over 300 active nests in the western states, but within a single decade that number dropped to 200. In 1978 there were no breeding pairs of peregrine falcons in the eastern United States. In 1984, due to reintroduction efforts, there were 27 nesting pairs, and in 1985, 38 nesting pairs were present in the East with at least 16 pairs fledging young. Also in 1985, 260 young, captive-raised peregrine falcons were released into the wild, 125 in the eastern states, and 135 in the west. By 1986, 43 pairs were nesting, and 25 of those pairs fledged 53 young. By 1991, over 100 breeding pairs were found in the East, and 400 pairs were found in the west.

The recovery success of the peregrine falcon is due largely to the efforts of two groups, the Peregrine Fund based at Cornell University in Ithaca, New York, and the **Canadian Wildlife Service** at Camp Wainwright in Alberta. Much of their research centered on captive breeding for release in the wild and finding ways to induce the falcons to

nest and raise young in their former range. With great patience, and limited early success, the projects paid off.

The restoration projects also yielded much valuable information as well as innovative approaches to reestablishing peregrine falcon populations. For captive breeding, falcons trapped as nestlings stood a much better chance of reproducing in captivity than when trapped as flying immatures or adults. Since **habitat** destruction and human encroachment limit potential nesting sites—which typically are cliff ledges—researchers found that a potential, and ultimately successful, alternative nest site was the window ledge of tall, city buildings. These locations mimic their natural nest sites, and these "Duck hawks," as they were once called, had a readily available prey in their new urban **ecosystem**. Peregrine falcons immediately began killing Rock Doves for food, which some saw as a service to the cities, since these "pigeons" tended to be regarded as a "nuisance" **species**.

Since it began in the 1970s, this captive breeding and release program has become well established, with over 3,000 captive-bred peregrine falcons released over the past two decades. *See also* Captive propagation and reintroduction

[*Eugene C. Beckham*]

FURTHER READING

Cade, T. J. *The Falcons of the World*. Ithaca, NY: Cornell University Press, 1982.

Ehrlich, P., D. Dobkin, and D. Wheye. *Birds in Jeopardy.* Stanford, CA: Stanford University Press, 1992.

Ratcliffe, D. A. *The Peregrine Falcon.* Vermillion, SD: Buteo Books, 1980.

Temple, S., ed. *Endangered Birds: Management Techniques for Preserving Threatened Species.* Madison: University of Wisconsin Press, 1977.

Permaculture

Permaculture is an approach to land management that creates high-yielding, low-energy, self-perpetuating systems by which the functions of animals, plants, humans, and Earth are integrated to maximize their value and create sustainable human **habitat**s. Permaculture brings together disciplines relating to food, shelter, energy, water, **waste management**, economics, and social sciences. It aims to maximize a site's productivity, while maintaining **ecosystem**s and restoring damaged land to a healthy, life-promoting state. Bill Mollison has written five books on this topic: *Introduction to Permaculture, Permaculture: A Designer's Manual, Permaculture One; Permaculture Two;* and *Permaculture: A Practical Guide for a Sustainable Future.* Several permaculture organizations and model projects exist around the world.

The term was first coined in 1972 by Bill Mollison of Tasmania, **Australia**, by merging the terms, "permanent" and "agriculture." Although originally developed for small subsistence farms, the practice has expanded to apply to gardens and urban settings. Some consider it a lifestyle as much as a design approach.

Permaculture principles focus on designs for small-scale intensive systems that are labor-efficient and use biological resources instead of **fossil fuels**. These designs stress ecological connections and closed energy and material loops. The core of permaculture is integrating working relationships and connections between all things. Each component in a system performs multiple functions, and each function is supported by many elements. Key to efficient permaculture design is observing and replicating natural ecosystems. Designers maximize diversity with polycultures, stress efficient energy planning for houses and settlements, and use and accelerate natural plant succession. The philosophy behind permaculture is one of working with rather than against nature, looking at systems in all of their functions, and using systems for multiple purposes. It is a method of agriculture that aims to endure without constant human inputs and does not deplete the land.

According to Mollison, permaculture has several distinct characteristics. It makes the most of small landscapes, using intensive practices. Ideally, nothing is wasted, and everything is arranged so that the least amount of effort is exerted and the highest yield from the systems is gained. Systems are designed that use and complement the natural systems that are present. For example, storm water is controlled with planted swales (marshy depressions), not concrete drains. The design harvests the natural flows of energy through the landscape (such as sunlight, rain, and plant and animal behaviors). Diversity is promoted in plant species, varieties, yield, microclimate, and habitat. Permaculture maintains that, in a monoculture, a single species cannot make full use of all of the available energy and nutrients. Wild or seldom-selected animal and plant species are used. Each element performs many functions in the system. For example, a fruit tree provides not only a crop, but also wind shelter, a trellis, **soil** conditioning, and shade and roosting for birds. The long-term evolution of the land is recognized, and those changes are incorporated in planning. All activities involving the land—agriculture, animal husbandry, extant forest management, animal cropping, and landform engineering—are integrated. Difficult landscapes (rocky, marshy, marginal, or steep) not typically suited to other systems are utilized. Permaculture involves long-term and evolving land-use planning, using diverse flora and fauna in various ways at different times, recognizing that different species use different nutrients and resources.

Permaculture systems typically feature: passive energy systems and minimal external energy needs; on site climate control; planned future developments; on-site provision for food self-sufficiency; safe on-site disposal of wastes; low-maintenance structures and grounds; assured and conserved water supply; and control and direction of fire, cold, excess heat, and wind factors.

Permaculture originated as a strategy for designing systems for "permanent" or perennial agriculture, by creating agroforestry systems using tree crops, shrubs, vines and, herbaceous plants in highly productive symbiotic assemblages. The practice was originally oriented to subsistence farms in Tasmania, which typically were small and on poor land. It was then extended to include other landscapes, urban settings, and climates worldwide, and has even been applied to other systems such as houses and factories.

Permaculture as a Life Philosophy

Some consider permaculture a life philosophy. In this context, permaculture emphasizes putting oneself into a symbiotic relationship with Earth and one's community. Permaculture is oriented to place, with reliance on native plants and a close awareness of the ecosystem. It revolves around self-reliance, growing food and building attractive energy-efficient structures from local materials. Designing a permaculture landscape begins with assessing a site's native features (such as soil structure, microclimates, cycles of decay, and existing flora and fauna), in order to take advantage of existing resources. This assessment also helps·in selecting and adapting technologies to the site. These technologies might include methods of composting, gardening, irrigating, or generating electricity. Multifunctional living systems abound in a typical permaculture design.

Examples of Permaculture Practices and Approaches

Animals are raised for their value as producers of food, skins, and manure, and as pollinators, heat sources, gas producers, earth tillers, and pest controller. For example, rabbits raised in a rabbit hutch are fed kitchen scraps. Their droppings fall into worm bins (vermiculture) as fodder for worms, and the resulting worm castings are used to fertilize gardens. In the winter, the rabbits are harvested for their meat and fur. As another example, movable chicken hutch can be used to place chickens in gardens where they effectively till and fertilize the soil.

Particular varieties of trees are chosen for their fuel, forage, material (for fences, structures and shelters), heat reflector and windbreak values, as well as for crop diversification. When they are young, the trees may act as hedgerows, then grow to serve as a fuel source. Plants provide many services for other plants. They act as trellises, for other screen and shade them, provide nutrients, cross-fertilize them (as happens with varieties of plums and nuts), help to repel pests, prevent erosion, and provide spare parts (grafts) for other plants. Fruit trees and vines are planted strategically around a house to provide shade. In a home's front yard, attractive gardens feature high-yielding food, medicinal and culinary plants where they are easily accessed. Some crops are planted for their self-propagating patterns, such as leeks, onions, potatoes, and garlic.

Water harvesting is an essential function in a permaculture landscape, and is supported by as many components as possible. Filtration of water for animals may be provided with shells and water plants. Water pathways are traced, and systems are created for collecting it. Swales may direct rain water and run-off to fruit trees. **Run-off** water from culverts may be directed to ponds where water plants and fish are raised, and where it can be used for irrigation and firefighting. Water can be collected from roofs. Composting toilets and septic systems with planted leaching beds can be employed.

Insects and crops are used to aerate the soil. Mulching, growing green crops, composting, and strategic planting are employed to build soil health. Permaculture grows forests and shrubs to protect the soil, and uses plows that do not turn the soil. Food crops, such as corn and legumes, are chosen for their low-maintenance qualities and their ability to fix **nitrogen** in the soil.

Permaculture emphasizes reactive homes, sheltered from cold winds with windbreak planting. Such homes are oriented on an east-west axis facing the sun, usually with a greenhouse, and are well-sealed. They should use few resources not found on site. Shelters can be built into the earth, with living turf roofs. Sometimes, living trees and plants are used to create shelters.

Permaculture offers an environmental design practice for making better use of resources in a variety of growing settings. What started as a method for cultivating desert land has grown into a system that integrates living systems, fostering greater consciousness of ecosystems and helping to ensure economic and ecological sustainability for its practitioners. Contact: Permaculture Resources, 56 Farmersville Rd., Califon, N.J. 07830; phone: 800-832-6285.

[*Carol Steinfeld*]

FURTHER READING

Barnes, L. "The Permaculture Connections," *Southeastern Permaculture Network News*

Mollison, B. *Permaculture: A Designer's Manual, Permaculture One,* and *Permaculture Two.* Australia: Tagari, 1979.

Permafrost

Permafrost is any ground, either of rock or **soil**, which is perennially frozen. Continuous permafrost refers to areas which have a continuous layer of permafrost. Discontinuous permafrost occurs in patches. It is believed that continuous permafrost covers approximately 4 percent of the Earth's surface and can be as deep as 3,281 feet (1,000 m), though normally it is much less. Permafrost tends to occur when the mean annual air temperature is less than the freezing point of water. Permafrost regions are characterized by a seasonal thawing and freezing of a surface layer known as the active layer which is typically 3 to 10 feet (1 to 3 m) thick.

Permanent retrievable storage

Permanent retrievable storage is a method for handling highly toxic **hazardous waste**s on a long-term basis. At one time, it was widely believed that the best way of dealing with such wastes was to seal them in containers and either bury them underground or dump them into the oceans. However, these containers tended to leak, releasing these highly dangerous materials into the **environment**.

The current method is to store such wastes in a quasi-permanent manner in salt domes, rock caverns, or secure buildings. This is done in the expectation that scientists will eventually find effective and efficient methods for converting these wastes into less hazardous states, in which they can then be disposed of by conventional means. One chemical for which permanent retrievable storage has been used so far is the group of compounds known as **polychlorinated biphenyl (PCB)**s.

Permanent retrievable storage has its disadvantages. Hazardous wastes so stored must be continuously guarded and monitored in order to detect breaks in containers or leakage into the surrounding environment. In comparison with other disposal methods now available for highly toxic materials, however, permanent retrievable storage is still the preferred alternative means of disposal. *See also* Hazardous waste site remediation; Hazardous waste siting; NIMBY; Toxic use reduction legislation

[*David E. Newton*]

FURTHER READING

Flynn, J., et al. "Time to Rethink Nuclear Waste Storage." *Issues in Science and Technology* 8 (Summer 1992): 42-46.

Kliewer, G. "The 10,000-Year Warning." *The Futurist* 26 (September-October 1992): 17-19.

Makhijani, A. *High-Level Dollars, Low-Level Sense: A Critique of Present Policy for the Management of Long-Lived Radioactive Wastes and Discussion of an Alternative Approach.* New York: Apex Press, 1992.

Schumacher, A. *A Guide to Hazardous Materials Management.* New York: Quorum Books, 1988.

Permeable

In **soil** science, permeable is a qualitative description for the ease with which water or some other fluid can pass through soil. Permeability in this context is a function not only of the total pore volume but also of the size and distribution of the pores. In geology, particularly with reference to **groundwater**, permeability is the ability of water to move through any water-bearing formation, rock, or unconsolidated material. This condition can be measured in the laboratory by measuring the volume of water that flows through a sample over a certain period of time. *See also* Aquifer; Recharge zone; Soil profile; Vadose zone; Zone of saturation

Peroxyacetyl nitrate (PAN)

The best known member of a class of photochemical **oxidizing agents** known as the peroxyacyl nitrates. The peroxyacyl nitrates are formed when **ozone** reacts with **hydrocarbons** such as those found in unburned **petroleum**. They are commonly found in **photochemical smog**. The peroyxacyl nitrates attack plants, causing spotting and discoloration of leaves, destruction of flowers, reduction in fruit production and seed formation, and death of the plant. They also cause red, itchy, runny eyes and irritated throats in humans. Cardiac and respiratory conditions, such as **emphysema** and chronic **bronchitis**, may result from long-term exposure to the peroxyacyl nitrates. *See also* Air pollution; Los Angeles Basin

Persian Gulf War

The Persian Gulf War in 1991 had a variety of environmental consequences for the Middle East. The most devastating of these effects were from the **oil spills** and oil fires deliberately committed by the Iraqi army. There were extensive press coverage of these events at the time, and the United States accused the Iraqis of "environmental terrorism." These accusations were seen by some as propaganda effort, and there was almost certainly some political motivation to both how the damage was estimated and how it was characterized during the war. But it is clear now that the note of outrage often struck by the Allies was not out of place. The devastation, though not as extensive as originally supposed, was still substantial.

The Iraqis began discharging oil into the Persian Gulf from the Sea Island Terminal and other supertanker terminals off the coast of Kuwait on January 23, 1991. Allied bombers tried to limit the damage by striking at pipelines carrying oil to these locations, but the flow continued throughout the war. Estimates of the size of the spill have varied widely and the controversy still continues, with a number of diplomatic and political pressures preventing many government agencies from committing themselves to specific figures. But it now seems likely that this was the worst oil spill in history, probably 20 times larger than the *Exxon Valdez*

spill in **Prince William Sound, Alaska**, and twice the size of the 1979 spill from the blowout of Ixtoc I well in the Gulf of Mexico.

Whatever the actual size of the spill, it occurred in an area that was already one of the most polluted in the world. Oil spills and oil dumping are common in the Persian Gulf; it has been estimated that as many as two million barrels of oil are spilled in these waters every year. Some ecologists believe that the **ecosystem** in the area has a certain amount of resistance to the effects of **pollution**. Other scientists have maintained that the high level of **salinity** in the Gulf will prevent the oil from having many long-term effects and that the warm water will increase the speed at which the oil degrades. But the Gulf has a slow circulation system and large areas are very shallow; many scientists and environmentalists have predicted that it will be many years before the water can clear itself.

The spill killed thousands of birds within months after it began, and it had an immediate and drastic effect on **commercial fishing** in the region. Oil soaked miles of coastline; **coral reef**s and **wetlands** were damaged, and the seagrass beds of the Gulf were considered particularly vulnerable. **Mangrove swamp**s, migrant birds, and **endangered species** such as green turtles and the dugong, or sea cow, are still threatened by the effects of the spill. The Saudi Arabian government has protected the water they draw from the Gulf for **desalinization**, but little has been done to limit or alleviate the environmental damage. This has been the result, at least in part, of a shortage of resources during and after the war, as well as obstacles such as floating mines and shallow waters which restricted access for boats carrying cleanup equipment.

At the end of the war, the retreating Iraqi army set over 600 Kuwaiti oil wells on fire. When the last burning well was extinguished on November 6, 1991, these fires had been spewing oil **smoke** into the atmosphere for months, creating a cloud which spread over the countries around the Gulf and into parts of Asia. It was thought at the time that the cloud of oil smoke would rise high enough to cause global climatic changes. Carl Sagan and other scientists, who had first proposed the possibility of a **nuclear winter** as one of the consequences of a nuclear war, believed that rain patterns in Asia and parts of Europe would be affected by the oil fires, and they predicted failed harvests and widespread starvation as a result. Though there was some localized cooling in the Middle East, these kinds of global predictions did not occur, but the smoke from the fire has still been an environmental disaster for the region. **Air quality** levels have caused extensive health problems, and **acid rain** and acid deposition have damaged millions of acres of forests in Iran.

The oil fires and oil spills were not the only environmental consequences of the Persian Gulf War. The movement of troops and military machinery, especially tanks, damaged the fragile **desert soil**s and increased wind **erosion**. Wells sabotaged by the Iraqis released large amounts of oil that was never ignited, and lakes of oil as large as half a mile wide formed in the desert. These lakes continue to pose a hazard for animals and birds, and tests have shown that the oil is seeping deeper into the ground, causing long-term contamination and perhaps, eventually, **leaching** into the Gulf. *See also* Gulf War Syndrome

[*Douglas Smith*]

FURTHER READING

Peck, L. "The Spoils of War." *The Amicus Journal* 3 (Spring 1991): 6-9.

Zimmer, C. "Ecowar." *Discover* 13 (January 1992): 37-39.

Persistent compound

A persistent compound is slow to degrade in the **environment**, which often results in its accumulation and deleterious effects on human and **environmental health** if the compound is toxic. Toxic metals such as **lead** and **cadmium**, **organochloride**s such as **polychlorinated biphenyl**s (PCBs), and **polycyclic aromatic hydrocarbons** (PAHs) are persistent compounds.

Persistent molecules are termed recalcitrant if they fail to degrade, metabolize, or mineralize at significant rates. Their compounds can be transported through the environment over long periods of time and over long distances, resulting in long-term exposure and possible changes in organisms and **ecosystem**s. However, organisms and ecosystems may adapt to the compounds, and deleterious effects may weaken or even disappear.

Compounds may be persistent for several reasons. A compound can be persistent due to its chemical structure. For example, in a molecule, the number and arrangement of **chlorine** ions or hydroxyl groups can make a compound recalcitrant. It can also persist due to unfavorable environmental conditions such as **pH**, temperature, ionic strength, potential for **oxidation reduction reactions**, unavailability of **nutrient**s, and absence of organisms that can degrade the compound.

The period of persistence can be expressed as the time required for half of the compound to be lost, the **half-life**. It is also often expressed as the time for detectable levels of the compound to disappear entirely. Compounds are classified for environmental persistence in the following categories:(1) Not degradable, compound half-life of several centuries; (2) Strong persistence, compound half-life of several years; (3) Medium persistence, compound half-life of several months; and (4) Low persistence, compound half-life less than several months.

Non-degradable compounds include metals and many **radioisotope**s, while semi-degradable compounds (of medium to strong persistence) include PAHs and chlorinated compounds. Compounds with low persistence include most organic compounds based on **nitrogen**, sulfur, and **phosphorus**.

In general, the greater the persistence of a compound, the more it will accumulate in the environment and the **food chain/web**. Non-degradable and strongly persistent compounds will accumulate in the environment and/or organisms. For example, because of **bioaccumulation** through the food chain, dieldrin can reduce populations of birds of prey. Compounds with intermediate persistence may or may not accumulate, while non-persistent pollutants generally do not accumulate. However, even compounds with low persistence can have long-term deleterious effects on the environment. **2,4-D** and **2,4,5-T** can cause defoliation, which may result in soil **erosion** and long-term effects on the ecosystem.

Chemical properties of a compound can be used to assess persistence in the environment. Important properties include: (1) rate of biodegradation (both **aerobic** and **anaerobic**); (2) rate of hydrolysis; (3) rate of oxidation or reduction; and (4) rate of photolysis in air, **soil**, and water. In addition, the effects of key parameters, such as temperature, concentration, and pH, on the rate constants and the identity and persistence of transformation products should also be investigated. However, measured values for these properties for many persistent compounds are not available, since there are thousands of **chemicals**, and the time and resources required to measure the desired properties for all the chemicals is unrealistic. In addition, the data that are available are often of variable quality.

Persistence of a compound in the environment is dependent on many interacting environmental and compound-specific factors, which makes understanding the causes of persistence of a specific compound complex and in many cases incomplete. *See also* Chronic effects; Heavy metals and heavy metal poisoning; Toxic substance

[*Judith Sims*]

FURTHER READING

Ayres, R. U., F. C. McMichael, and S. R. Rod. "Measuring Toxic Chemicals in the Environment: A Materials Balance Approach." In *Toxic Chemicals, Health, and the Environment*, edited by L. B. Lave and A. C. Upton. Baltimore, MD: Johns Hopkins University Press, 1987.

Govers, H., J. H. F. Hegeman, and H. Aiking. "Long-Term Environmental and Health Effects of PMPs." In *Persistent Pollutants: Economics and Policy*, edited by H. Opschoor and D. Pearce. Dordrecht, Netherlands: Kluwer Academic Publishers, 1991.

Lyman, W. J. "Estimation of Physical Properties." In *Environmental Exposure from Chemicals*, edited by W. B. Neely and G. E. Blau. Vol. I. Boca Raton, FL: CRC Press, 1985.

Pest

A pest is any organism that humans consider destructive or unwanted. Whether or not an organism is considered a pest can vary with time, geographical location, and individual attitude. For example, some people like pigeons, while others regard them as pests. Some pests are merely an inconvenience. In the United States, mosquitoes are thought of as pests because they are an annoyance, not because they are dangerous. The most dangerous pests are those that carry disease or destroy crops. One direct way of controlling pests is by poisoning them with toxic chemicals (**pesticide**s). A more environmentally sensitive approach is to find natural predators that can be used against them (biological controls). *See also Bacillus thuringiensis*; Integrated pest management; Population biology

Pesticide

Pesticides are **chemicals** that are used to kill insects, weeds, and other organisms to protect humans, crops, and livestock. There have been many substantial benefits of the use of pesticides. The most important of these have been: (1) an increased production of food and fibre because of the protection of crop plants from **pathogen**s, **competition** from weeds, defoliation by insects, and parasitism by nematodes; (2) the prevention of spoilage of harvested, stored foods; and (3) the prevention of debilitating illnesses and the saving of human lives by the control of certain diseases.

Unfortunately, the considerable benefits of the use of pesticides are partly offset by some serious environmental damages. There have been rare but spectacular incidents of toxicity to humans, as occurred in 1984 at **Bhopal, India**, where more than 2,800 people were killed and more than 20,000 seriously injured by a large **emission** of poisonous methyl isocyanate vapor, a chemical used in the production of an agricultural insecticide.

A more pervasive problem is the widespread environmental contamination by persistent pesticides, including the presence of chemical residues in **wildlife**, in well water, in produce, and even in humans. Ecological damages have included the poisoning of wildlife and the disruption of ecological processes such as productivity and **nutrient** cycling. Many of the worst cases of environmental damage were associated with the use of relatively persistent chemicals such as **DDT**. Most modern pesticide use involves less-persistent chemicals.

Pesticides can be classified according to their intended **pest** target: (1) **fungicide**s protect crop plants and animals from fungal pathogens; (2) **herbicide**s kill weedy plants, decreasing the competition for desired crop plants; (3) insecticides kill insect defoliators and vectors of deadly human diseases such as **malaria**, yellow fever, plague, and typhus; (4) acaricides kill mites, which are pests in agriculture, and ticks, which can carry encephalitis of humans and domestic animals; (5) molluscicides destroy snails and slugs, which can be pests of agriculture or, in waterbodies, the vector of human diseases such as **schistosomiasis**; (6) nematicides kill nematodes, which can be **parasites** of the roots of crop plants; (7) rodenticides control rats, mice, gophers, and other rodent pests of human habitation and agriculture; (8) avicides kill birds, which can depredate agricultural fields; and (9) antibiotics treat bacterial infections of humans and domestic animals.

The most important use-categories of pesticides are in human health, agriculture, and forestry:

Human Health

In various parts of the world, **species** of insects and ticks play a critical role as vectors in the transmission of disease-causing pathogens of humans. The most important of these diseases and their vectors are: (1) malaria, caused by the protozoan *Plasmodium* and spread to humans by an *Anopheles*-mosquito vector; (2) yellow fever and related viral diseases such as encephalitis, also spread by mosquitoes; (3) trypanosomiasis or sleeping sickness, caused by the protozo-

ans *Trypanosoma* spp. and spread by the tsetse fly *Glossina* spp.; (4) plague or black death, caused by the bacterium *Pasteurella pestis* and transmitted to people by the flea *Xenopsylla cheops*, a parasite of rats; and (5) typhoid fever, caused by the bacterium *Rickettsia prowazeki* and transmitted to humans by the body louse *Pediculus humanus*.

The incidence of all of these diseases can be reduced by the judicious use of pesticides to control the abundance of their vectors. For example, there are many cases where the local abundance of mosquito vectors has been reduced by the application of insecticide to their aquatic breeding **habitat**, or by the application of a persistent insecticide to walls and ceilings of houses, which serve as a resting place for these insects. The use of insecticides to reduce the abundance of the mosquito vectors of malaria has been especially successful, although in many areas this disease is now re-emerging because of the **evolution** of tolerance by mosquitoes to insecticides.

Agriculture

Modern, technological agriculture employs pesticides for the control of weeds, arthropods, and plant diseases, all of which cause large losses of crops. In agriculture, arthropod pests are regarded as competitors with humans for a common food resource. Sometimes, defoliation can result in a total loss of the economically harvestable agricultural yield, as in the case of acute infestations of locusts. More commonly, defoliation causes a reduction in crop yields. In some cases, insects may cause only trivial damage in terms of the quantity of **biomass** that they consume, but by causing cosmetic damage they can greatly reduce the economic value of the crop. For example, codling moth (*Carpocapsa pomonella*) larvae do not consume much of the apple that they infest, but they cause great esthetic damage by their presence and can render produce unsalable.

In agriculture, weeds are considered to be any plants that interfere with the productivity of crop plants by competing for light, water, and nutrients. To reduce the effects of weeds on agricultural productivity, fields may be sprayed with a herbicide that is toxic to the weeds but not to the crop plant. Because there are several herbicides that are toxic to dicotyledonous weeds but not to members of the grass family, fields of maize, wheat, barley, rice, and other grass-crops are often treated with those herbicides to reduce weed populations.

There are also many diseases of agricultural plants that can be controlled by the use of pesticides. Examples of important fungal diseases of crop plants that can be managed with appropriate fungicides include: (1) late blight of potato, (2) apple scab, and (3) *Pythium*-caused seed-rot, damping-off, and root-rot of many agricultural species.

Forestry

In forestry, the most important uses of pesticides are for the control of defoliation by epidemic insects and the reduction of weeds. If left uncontrolled, these pest problems could result in large decreases in the yield of merchantable timber. In the case of some insect infestations, particularly spruce budworm (*Choristoneura fumiferana*) and **gypsy moth** (*Lymantria dispar*), repeated **defoliation** can cause the death of trees over a large area of forest. Most herbicide use in

Type	Examples	Characteristics	Type	Examples	Characteristics
Insecticides			Plant products and synthetic analogs	Nicotine, rotenone, pyrethrum, allethrin, decamethrin, resmethrin, fenvalerate, permethrin, tetramethrin	Natural botanical products and synthetic analogs, fast acting, broad insecticide action, low toxicity to mammals, expensive
Inorganic chemicals	Mercury, lead, arsenic, copper sulfate	Highly toxic to many organisms, persistent, bioaccumulates			
Organochlorines	DDT, methoxychlor, heptachlor, HCH, pentachloraphenol, chlordane, toxaphene, aldrin, endrin, dieldrin, lindane	Mostly neurotoxins, cheap, persistent, fast acting, easy to apply, broad spectrum, bioaccumulates, biomagnifies	*Fungicides*	Captan, maneb, zeneb, dinocap, folpet, pentachlorphenol, methyl bromide, carbon bisulfide, chlorothalonil (Bravo)	Most prevent fungal spore germination and stop plant diseases; among most widely used pesticides in United States.
Organophosphates	Parathion, malathion, diazinon, dichlorvos, phosdrin, disulfoton, TEPP, DDVP	More soluble, extremely toxic nerve poisons, fast acting, quickly degraded, toxic to many organisms, very dangerous to farm workers	*Fumigants*	Ethylene dibromide, dibromochloro-propane, carbon tetrachloride, carbon disulfide, methyl bromide	Used to kill nematodes, fungi, insects, and other pests in soil, grain, fruits; highly toxic, cause nerve damage, sterility, cancer, birth defects
Carbamates and urethanes	Carbaryl (Sevin), aldicarb, carbofuran, methomyl, Temik, mancozeb	Quickly degraded, do not bioaccumulate, toxic to broad spectrum of organisms, fast acting, very toxic to honey bees	*Herbicides*	2,4 D; 2,4,5 T; paraquat, dinoseb, diaquat, atrazine, Silvex, linuron	Block photosynthesis, act as hormones to disrupt plant growth and development, or kill soil micro-organisms essential for plant growth
Formamidines	Amitraz, chlordimeform (Fundal and Galecron)	Neurotoxins specific for certain stages of insect development, act synergistically with other insecticides			
Microbes	*Bacillus thuringensis*	Kills caterpillars			
	Bacillus popilliae	Kills beetles			
	Viral diseases	Attack a variety of moths and caterpillars			

Pesticides.

forestry is for the release of desired conifer species from the effects of competition with angiosperm herbs and shrubs. In most places, the quantity of pesticide used in forestry is much smaller than that used in agriculture.

Pesticides can also be classified according to their similarity of chemical structure. The most important of these are:

(1) Inorganic pesticides, including compounds of **arsenic**, **copper**, **lead**, and **mercury**. Some prominent inorganic pesticides include Bordeaux mixture, a complex pesticide with several copper-based active ingredients, used as a fungicide for fruit and vegetable crops; and various arsenicals used as non-selective herbicides and soil sterilants and sometimes as insecticides.

(2) Organic pesticides, which are a chemically diverse group of chemicals. Some are produced naturally by certain plants, but the great majority of organic pesticides have been synthesized by chemists. Some prominent classes of organic pesticides are:

(a) Natural organic pesticides extracted from plants. Important insecticides are the alkaloid nicotine and other nicotinoids, largely extracted from tobacco (*Nicotiana tabacum*) and often applied as the salt nicotine sulfate. Another insecticide is pyrethrum, a complex of chemicals extracted from the daisy-like *Chrysanthemum cinerariaefolium*.

(b) Synthetic organo-metallic fungicides such as the organomercurials, including methylmercury.

(c) Phenols used as fungicides in the preservation of wood, for example, **pentachlorophenol**.

(d) **Chlorinated hydrocarbons**, especially the insecticides DDT, DDD, and methoxychlor.

(e) Organophosphorus pesticides are a diverse group of chemicals, most of which are used as insecticides, acaricides, or nematicides. The **organophosphate**s generally have a high acute toxicity to arthropods but a short persistence in the environment. Some of the insecticides are highly toxic to non-target organisms such as fish, birds, and mammals. Some prominent examples are the insecticides parathion, fenitrothion, malathion, and phosphamidon. Glyphosate, an important herbicide, is not very toxic to animals.

(f) Carbamate pesticides generally have a high acute toxicity to arthropods but a moderate environmental persistence. Important examples are carbaryl, aminocarb, and carbofuran.

(g) Triazine herbicides, for example, simazine, **atrazine**, and hexazinone, are mostly used in corn **monoculture**.

(3) Biological pesticides are bacteria, **fungi**, or **virus**es that are toxic to pests. One of the most widely used biological insecticide is a preparation manufactured from spores of the bacterium *Bacillus thuringiensis*, or B.t. Because this insecticide has a relatively specific activity against leaf-eating lepidopteran pests and a few other insects such as blackflies and mosquitoes, its non-target effects are small.

The intended ecological effect of a pesticide application is to control a pest species, usually by reducing its abundance to an economically acceptable level. In a few situations, this objective can be attained without important non-target damage. However, whenever a pesticide is broadcast-sprayed over a field or forest, a wide variety of on-site, non-target organisms are affected. In addition, some of the sprayed pesticide invariably drifts away from the intended site of deposition, and it deposits onto non-target organisms and **ecosystem**s. The ecological importance of any damage caused to non-target, pesticide-sensitive organisms partly depends on their role in maintaining the integrity of their ecosystem. From human perspective, however, the importance of a non-target pesticide effect is also influenced by specific economic and esthetic considerations.

Some of the best known examples of ecological damage caused by pesticide use concern effects of DDT and other chlorinated **hydrocarbons** on predatory birds, marine mammals, and other wildlife. These chemicals accumulate to large concentrations in predatory birds, affecting their reproduction and sometimes killing adults. There have been high-profile, local and/or regional collapses of populations of **peregrine falcon** (*Falco peregrinus*), **bald eagle** (*Haliaeetus leucocephalus*), and other raptors, along with **brown pelican** (*Pelecanus occidentalis*), western grebe (*Aechmorphorus occidentalis*), and other waterbirds. It was the detrimental effects on birds and other wildlife, coupled with the discovery of a pervasive presence of various chlorinated hydrocarbons in human tissues, that led to the banning of DDT in most industrialized countries in the early 1970s. These same chemicals are, however, still manufactured and used in some tropical countries.

Some of the pesticides that replaced DDT and its relatives also cause damage to wildlife. For example, the commonly used agricultural insecticide carbofuran has killed thousands of waterfowl and other birds that feed in treated fields. Similarly, broadcast-spraying of the insecticides phosphamidon and fenitrothion to kill spruce budworm in infested forests in New Brunswick, Canada, has killed untold numbers of birds of many species.

These and other environmental effects of pesticide use are highly regrettable consequences of the broadcast-spraying of these toxic chemicals in order to cope with pest management problems. So far, similarly effective alternatives to most uses of pesticides have not been discovered, although this is a vigorously active field of research. Researchers are in the process of discovering pest-specific methods of control that cause little non-target damage and in developing methods of **integrated pest management**. So far, however, not all pest problems can be dealt with in these ways, and there will be continued reliance on pesticides to prevent human and domestic-animal diseases and to protect agricultural and forestry crops from weeds, diseases, and depredations caused by economically important pests. *See also* Agent Orange; Agricultural chemicals; Agricultural pollution; Algicide; Chlordane; Cholinesterase inhibitor; Diazinon; Environmental health; Federal Insecticide, Fungicide and Rodenticide Act (1947); Kepone; Methylmercury seed dressings; National Coalition Against the Misuse of Pesticides; Organochloride; Persistent compound; Pesticide Action Network; Pesticide residue; 2,4-D; 2,4,5-T

[*Bill Freedman*]

FURTHER READING

Baker, S., and C. Wilkinson, eds. *The Effect of Pesticides on Human Health*. Princeton, NJ: Princeton Scientific Publishing, 1990.

Freedman, B. *Environmental Ecology*. San Diego: Academic Press, 1989.

Hayes, W. J., and E. R. Laws, eds. *Handbook of Pesticide Toxicology*. San Diego: Academic Press, 1991.

McEwen, F. L., and G. R. Stephenson. *The Use and Significance of Pesticides in the Environment*. New York: Wiley, 1979.

Pesticide Action Network (North American Regional Center, San Francisco, California)

The Pesticide Action Network is an international coalition of more than 300 **nongovernmental organization**s (NGOs) that works to stop both **pesticide** misuse and the proliferation of pesticide use worldwide. The Pesticide Action Network North America Regional Center (PANNA) is the North American member.

The Pesticide Action Network serves as a clearinghouse to disseminate information to pesticide action groups and individuals in this country and abroad. It promotes research on and implementation of alternatives to pesticide use in agriculture, such as **integrated pest management** programs. With a library of 6,000 books, reports, articles, slides and other materials, it sponsors a pesticide issues referral and information service.

Formerly called the Pesticide Education Action Project, which was founded in 1982, PANNA conducts the Dirty Dozen Campaign to "replace the most notorious pesticides with sustainable, ecologically sound alternatives." Various materials published by PANNA include brochures, pamphlets and books on U.S. pesticide problems and on global pesticide use. It publishes a quarterly newsletter, *Global Pesticide Campaigner*, and a bimonthly publication, *PANNA Outlook*.

The organization also publishes a number of books dealing with pesticides and pest control including *Problem Pesticides, Pesticide Problems: A Citizen's Action Guide to the UN Food and Agriculture Organization's (FAO) International Code of Conduct on the Distribution and Use of Pesticides; FAO Code: Missing Ingredients*; and *Breaking the Pesticide Habit: Alternatives to 12 Hazardous Pesticides*. While PANNA is not a membership organization for individuals outside of the member NGOs, it does offer subscriptions to its quarterly newsletter. Contact: Pesticide Action Network, North American Regional Center, 965 Mission Street, No. 514, San Francisco, CA 94103. Internet: http://www.panna.org/panna/.

[*Linda Rehkopf*]

Pesticide residue

Chemical substances—**pesticide**s and **herbicide**s—that are used as weed and insect control on crops and animal feed always leave some kind of residue either on the surface or within the crop itself after treatment. The amounts of residue vary, but they do remain on the crop when ready for harvest and consumption.

While these **chemicals** are generally registered for use on food crops, it does not necessarily mean they are "safe." As part of its program to regulate the use of pesticides, **Environmental Protection Agency (EPA)** sets "tolerances" which are the maximum amount of pesticides that may remain in or on food and animal feed. Tolerances are set at levels that are supposed to ensure that the public (including infants and children) is protected from unreasonable health risks posed by eating foods that have been treated.

Tolerances are initially calculated by measuring the amount of pesticide that remains in or on a crop after it is treated with the pesticide at the proposed maximum allowable level. The EPA then calculates the possible risk posed by that proposed tolerance to determine if it is acceptable.

In calculating risk, the EPA estimates exposure based on the "theoretical maximum residue concentration" (TMRC) normally assuming three factors: that all of the crop is treated, that residues on the crop are all at the maximum level, and that all consumers eat a certain fixed percent of the commodity in their diet. This exposure calculation is then compared to an "allowable daily intake" (ADI) and calculated on the basis of the pesticide's inherent toxicity.

The ADI represents the level of exposure in animal tests at which there appears to be no significant toxicological effects. If the residue level for that crop—the TMRC—exceeds the allowable daily intake, then the tolerance will not be granted as the residue level of the pesticide on that crop is presumed unsafe. On the other hand, if the residue level is lower than the ADI, then the tolerance would normally be approved. Exposure rates are based on assumptions regarding the amount of treated commodities that an "average" adult person, weighing 132 pounds (60 kg), eating an "average" diet would consume.

To set tolerances that are protective of human health, the needs information about the anticipated amount of pesticide residues found on food, the toxic effects of these residues, and estimates of the types and amounts of foods that make up our diet. The burden of proof is on the manufacturer—which has a vested interest in getting EPA approval. A pesticide manufacturer begins the tolerance-setting process by proposing a tolerance level, which is based on field trials reflecting the maximum residue that may occur as a result of the proposed use of the pesticide. The petitioner must provide food residue and toxicity studies to show that the proposed tolerance would not pose an unreasonable health risk.

The Federal Food, Drug, and Cosmetic Act (FFDCA) requires that the manufacturer of any substances apply to the EPA for a tolerance or maximum residue level to be allowed in or on food. Because of the way pesticide residues are defined and incorporated into the food additive provisions of the FFDCA, there are actually several kinds of tolerances, each subject to different decisional criteria. A given pesticide can thus have many tolerances, both for use on different crops and for any one crop. For example, for each crop for which it is registered, a pesticide may need a raw tolerance, a food additive tolerance, and an animal feed tolerance, each of which will be subject to particular decisional criteria.

The EPA sets tolerances on the basis of data the manufacturer is required to submit on the nature, level, and toxicity of a substance's residue. According to the EPA, one requirement is for the product chemistry data, which is information about the content of the pesticide products, including the concentration of the ingredients and any impurities. The EPA also requires information about how plants and animals metabolize (break down) pesticides to which they are exposed and whether residues of the metabolized pesticides are detectable in food or feed. Any products of pesticide **metabolism**, or "metabolites," that may be significantly toxic are considered along with the pesticide itself in setting tolerances.

The EPA also requires field experiments for pesticides and their metabolites for each crop or crop group for which a tolerance is requested. This includes each type of raw food derived from the crop. Manufacturers must also provide information on residues found in many processed foods (such as raisins), and in animal products if animals are exposed to pesticides directly through their feed.

A pesticide's potential for causing adverse health effects, such as **cancer**, **birth defects**, and other reproductive disorders, and adverse effects on the nervous system or other organs, is identified through a battery of tests. Tests are conducted for both short-term or "acute" toxicity and long-term or "chronic" toxicity. In several series of tests, laboratory animals are exposed to different doses of a pesticide and EPA scientists evaluate the tests to find the highest level of exposure that did not cause any effect. This level is called the "No Observed Effect Level" or NOEL.

Then, according to the EPA, the next step in the process is to estimate the amount of the pesticide to which the public may be exposed through the food supply. The EPA uses the Dietary Risk Evaluation System (DRES) to estimate the amount of the pesticide in the daily diet, which is based upon a national food consumption survey conducted by the **U.S. Department of Agriculture**. The USDA survey provides information about the diets of the overall American population and any number of subgroups, including several different ethnic groups, regional populations, and age groups such as infants and children.

Finally, for non-cancer risks, the EPA compares the estimated amount of pesticide in the daily diet to the Reference Dose. If the DRES analysis indicates that the dose consumed in the diet by the general public or key subgroups exceeds the Reference Dose, then generally the EPA will not approve the tolerance. For potential **carcinogen**s, the EPA ordinarily will not approve the tolerance if the dietary analysis indicates that exposure will cause more than a negligible risk of cancer.

There have been serious problems in carrying out the law. Although the law requires a thorough tolerance review for chemical pesticides prior to registration for health and environmental impacts, the majority of pesticides currently on the market and in use today were registered before modern testing requirements were established. "Thus," according to a 1987 report published by the National Research Council Board on Agriculture, "many older pesticides do not have an adequate data base, as judged by current standards, particularly data about potential chronic health effects."

The 1972 amendments to the **Federal Insecticide, Fungicide and Rodenticide Act (FIFRA)** required a review—or registration—of all then-registered products according to contemporary standards. Originally, the EPA was to complete the review of all registered products within three years, but this process broke down completely. In 1978, amendments were added to FIFRA that authorized the EPA to group together individual substances by active ingredients for an initial "generic" review of similar chemicals in order to identify data gaps and assessment needs. The amendments mandate that after this generic review, the EPA is to establish as "registration standard" for the active ingredient basis. Then, the EPA must wait for additional data in order to establish specific requirements for each substance's specific use on differing crops. (The EPA does not specifically address inert ingredients, although inert ingredients have been found to be just as potentially toxic as the active ingredients.)

The 1988 amendments extended the deadline for re-registration until 1997. To date, however, the EPA only has complete residue data on less than 25 percent of pesticides used on foods, and less than ten products, as yet, have been registered. Thus, the backlog of substances awaiting re-registration is on the order of some 16,000 to 20,000 compounds, including, according to the General Accounting Office, over 650 active ingredients. As a consequence, most of these untested chemicals temporarily retain their registration status under the former testing requirements.

Once tested in accordance with contemporary standards, many of the older pesticides are likely to be identified as carcinogenic. In fact, the National Academy of Sciences estimates that 25-33 percent of the pesticides to undergo re-registration procedures are likely to be found to be oncogenic. An oncogen causes tumors in laboratory animals and is considered potentially cancerous to humans. In general, such older pesticides, registered prior to 1972, have not been tested adequately for oncogenicity. For a substance to be used on a new crop, however, current data must be submitted in order to obtain a tolerance.

One way pesticide companies are able to completely skirt EPA regulations is to send pesticides that are suspended or banned in the United States to **Third World** countries. At least 25 percent of American pesticide exports are products that are banned, heavily restricted or have never been registered for use in the United States. Hazardous pesticide exports are a major source of **pollution** in Third World countries where lack of regulation, illiteracy, and repressive working conditions can turn even a "safe" pesticide into a deadly weapon for the field workers. These pesticides are returned to the United States, unexamined, as residues in the imported food American consumers eat.

[*Liane Clorfene Casten*]

FURTHER READING

Briggs, S. A. *Basic Guide to Pesticides: Their Characteristics and Hazards.* Washington, DC: Hemisphere, 1992.

Dinham, B. *Pesticide Hazard: Global Health and Environmental Audit.* Highlands, NJ: Humanities Press International, 1993.

Raloff, J., and D. Pendick. "Pesticides in Produce May Threaten Kids." *Science News* 144 (3 July 1993): 4-5.

Somerville, L. *Pesticide Effects on Terrestrial Wildlife.* London: Taylor and Francis, 1990.

Pet trade

Pets are part of human cultures all around the world. We keep animals to admire their beauty or to enjoy their companionship or devotion. The pet trade is big business throughout the world but with its positive aspects, there are distinct negative ones as well. As with any commodity, economics dictates that the rarer an item is, the more valuable it becomes in the market place. Many **rare species** thus become quite valuable to wealthy collectors, who are willing to pay exorbitant prices to black market dealers for certain **species**—even though they are protected by international treaties and laws.

Because these illegal pets must be smuggled into the market arenas, concealment almost always requires physical abuse of the animals. This may be in the form of constrictive bindings, overcrowded or confined spaces, exposure to extreme heat, or lack of oxygen due to these restrictions. Such treatment results in the death of many individuals during transit, with **mortality** that often approaches 80 to 90 percent. Therefore, collectors and smugglers must overcollect specimens in order to ensure the delivery of a sufficient quantity to realize a profit. Two groups, monkeys and parrots, have been the recipients of the bulk of this treatment. Due to their popularity as pets, there is a lucrative business in their illegal trade, and because the rarer species bring a higher price, these practices further threaten **extinction** of certain species.

This problem extends beyond the black market trade in birds and mammals. Other animal groups, as well as the legal pet trade, are also involved. Exotic reptiles, snakes and lizards in particular, are a target group. Legitimate pet dealers get involved in this problem when they, often unknowingly, purchase pets that were illegally caught or smuggled.

The aquarium trade has also faced illegal collecting. Over-collecting and poor handling of specimens during shipment have been problems in the freshwater segment of this business, but recent years have produced rampant abuses in the marine aquarium trade. Advances in technology over the past twenty years have made marine aquaria more accessible to the general public, and the sheer beauty of the brilliant, often neon-like, colors of many of the **coral reef** fish has fascinated a new breed of aquarists.

The main problems here still include the removal of large numbers of specimens of localized populations of rare or low density species and their illegal trade. Now, new and profound problems exist in the capture of these marine creatures: the total destruction of their **habitat** and the killing of unwanted, non-commercial species. Although legitimate collecting of marine fish is done with nets, it is estimated that during the 1980s about 80 percent of specimens for the marine aquarium trade were collected by using poison. Since most of the target species use coral reefs as hiding places, collectors use a squeeze bottle filled with sodium cyanide to force the fish out into the open water. The stunned, gasping fish are thus more easily caught, but the section of coral reef sprayed with poison, and the animals that did not escape, are now dead. Lingering effects of the poison and abusive shipping practices lead to mortality rates of 60 to 80 percent for these pets.

Public awareness and some governmental regulations have eased some of the abuses of these animals, but the illegal pet trade is still a profitable business. As long as people are willing to purchase rare species, the illegal pet trade will threaten the very species the collectors hold in high esteem. *See also* Endangered Species Act; Overhunting; Parrots and parakeets; Poaching; Wildlife management

[*Eugene C. Beckham*]

FURTHER READING

Bergman, C. "The Bust!" *Audubon* 93 (1991): 66-77.

Derr, M. "Raiders of the Reef." *Audubon* 94 (1992): 48-56.

Forshaw, J., and W. Cooper. *Parrots of the World*. Melbourne, Australia: Lansdowne Press, 1973.

McLarney, W. "Still a Dark Side to the Aquarium Trade." *International Wildlife* 18 (1988): 46-51.

Speart, J. "What's Wildlife Worth?" *Wildlife Conservation* 95 (1992): 44-47.

Peterson, Roger Tory (1908-1996)

American ornithologist

A small book, tucked away in innumerable back-packs and car pockets, ever ready to hand for perhaps the majority of birders in the United States, is quite likely to be Roger Tory Peterson's *A Field Guide to the Birds*, first published in 1934, revised and reissued several times, and still a must-have for many bird-watchers, serious or otherwise. In 1941 it was joined by a companion volume, *A Field Guide to Western Birds*. Together, the two guides (the first rejected by four publishers before Houghton Mifflin finally accepted it) have sold on the order of seven million copies by 1997. The critic William Zinser suggested that Peterson's *Field Guide* was "the single most revolutionary development in American birding." He was the first to introduce simplified, comparative drawings and to point out key field marks (distinguishing characteristics) that help identification in the field. Later critics judged Peterson harshly for his last revision of the *Guide* as "not knowing much about contemporary identification skills." But the revolutionary importance of the *Guides* lies in the number of people they have "turned on" to birds and to birding; they still sell, and are still used by birders at every level.

The man who has been called the modern successor to **John James Audubon** was born in Jamestown, New York, of a Swedish immigrant father and a German immigrant mother. Reportedly a loner, a boy considered strange by other children, Peterson came out of his shell when one of his teachers started a Junior Audubon Club. Birds became a passion for the eleven-year old, and he sought a job as a newspaper delivery boy so that he could buy a camera to photograph birds. Some seven decades later, he was still making pictures of birds. The prescient caption under his photograph in his high school yearbook read "Woods! Birds! Flowers! Here are the makings of a great naturalist."

Peterson studied art rather than ornithology, and he considered himself first a painter, then a writer, and only third a naturalist. Yet such was his reputation and standing among people interested in natural history that the *New York Times* could announce his death as that of "the best-known ornithologist of the twentieth century." Because his work reached so many people, because it helped them become involved in knowing more about the world around them, and because it inspired them to actually get out in the field and get involved, Peterson might even deserve *Sports Afield's* label of "the twentieth century's most influential naturalist." Academically trained or not, he spent his lifetime doing ornithology, i.e., studying birds, and in getting other people to join in that passion. His guides provided clear access to bird identification, even for the most rank amateur. Along with his many awards for art, he was also honored as a Fellow in the American Association for the Advancement of Science, and was bestowed with the Linné gold medal of the Royal Swedish Academy of Sciences.

After art school, he taught at a boys' school in Massachusetts. The success of the first field guide allowed him to return to New York to a position as an educational specialist and art editor for *Audubon Magazine*. He remained associated with the **National Audubon Society** for the rest of his professional life, serving in various capacities as artist, writer, secretary, and two different terms as director.

His passion for nature centered on birds, certainly, but he also was enthusiastic for all of the natural world, worked on many fronts to protect its diversity, and became an advocate for and teacher about managing the **environment** wisely. For example, he and his wife shared a love of flowers, and created and maintained butterfly gardens; one of his best known field guides is for wildflowers. All told, he published almost fifty books, including his edition of *Audubon's Birds of America*, and wrote many articles on birds as well as on other topics in conservation and management of gardens and wildlands.

As stated in a *New York Times* editorial, Peterson did indeed become "a great naturalist and more. He was one of the pioneers in teaching twentieth-century Americans to walk more gently on their land."

[*Gerald L. Young*]

FURTHER READING

Devlin, J. C., and G. Naismith. *The World of Roger Tory Peterson: an Authorized Biography.* New York: New York Times Books, 1977.

Peterson, R. T., and R. Hoglund, eds. *Roger Tory Peterson; Art and Photography from the World's Foremost Birder.* New York: Rizzoli, 1994.

Petrochemical

Petroleum is probably best known as a source for many important fuels, such as **gasoline**, kerosene, acetylene, and **natural gas**. However, many of the organic compounds that make up the complex mixture known as petroleum have another use. They are raw materials used in the production of a host synthetic products. These **chemicals** are known as petrochemicals. To a large extent, these petrochemicals are **hydrocarbons**. Some of these petrochemicals and the products into which they are made include ethylene (**plastics**, synthetic fibers, and anti-freeze), **benzene** (synthetic rubber, latex paints and paper coatings), propylene (drugs and **detergents**), and phenol (adhesives, perfumes, flavorings, and **pesticide**s). *See also* Fossil fuels; Synthetic fuels; Volatile organic compound

Petroleum

Petroleum is a complex mixture of solid, liquid, and gaseous **hydrocarbons** normally found a few miles beneath the earth's surface. It, along with **coal** and **natural gas**, is one of the **fossil fuels**. That name comes from the most common scientific theory that these three materials were formed

between 10 and 20 million years ago as a product of the decay of plants and animals. Petroleum is sometimes called crude oil or, simply, oil, although some authorities give slightly different means to these terms.

Most commonly, petroleum and natural gas occur together under dome-shaped layers of rock. When **wells** are drilled into such domes, gas pressure forces petroleum up into the well, producing the "gushers" that are typical of successful new wells.

Petroleum has been known to and used by humans for thousands of years. Collecting the liquid that seeped to the surface, the Egyptians, Babylonians, and Native American Indians used petroleum for waterproofing, embalming, caulking ships, warpaint, and medicine. The first successful oil well in the United States was drilled in 1859 by "Colonel" Edwin Drake.

The number and variety of compounds found in petroleum are large, and its composition varies significantly from location to location. Petroleum from Pennsylvania tends to have a high proportion of aliphatic (open-chain) **hydrocarbons**, those from the West contain more aromatic (**benzene**-based) hydrocarbons, and those from the Midwest contain a more even mix of the two.

The most common impurities (non-hydrocarbon compounds) in petroleum are compounds of sulfur and **nitrogen**. The percentage of sulfur in a sample of petroleum determines its status as "sweet" (low-sulfur) or "sour" (high-sulfur) crude oil. The emphasis on sulfur derives from the fact that one of the most undesirable products of the **combustion** of petroleum is **sulfur dioxide**. Oil with low sulfur is, therefore, more desirable than that with high sulfur.

The complex mix of compounds that make up petroleum results in its having relatively few important uses in its natural state. It becomes an important product only when some method is used to separate the native liquid into its component parts. The fractional distillation of petroleum results in the production of portions known as petroleum ether, **gasoline**, kerosene, heating oil, lubricating oil, and a semi-solid residue that includes paraffin, pitch, and tar. Each of these fractions can then be utilized directly or subdivided even further.

Few naturally occurring materials have as many environmental effects as does petroleum. During its removal from the earth, it may escape from wells and contaminate **groundwater**. The combustion of some of its most important components, gasoline, kerosene and fuel oil results in the release of **carbon dioxide**, **carbon monoxide**, **carbon**, sulfur dioxide, and **nitrogen oxides**, all compounds that contribute to **air pollution**, global warming, or other environmental problems.

In recent decades, petroleum has found another major use: in the production of **petrochemical**s. The compounds found in oil are now important starting materials in the manufacturing of a nearly limitless number of synthetic products. The manufacture, use and disposal of these petrochemical products contributes to additional environmental problems such as **hazardous waste** disposal and **solid waste** accumulation. *See also* Alternative fuels;

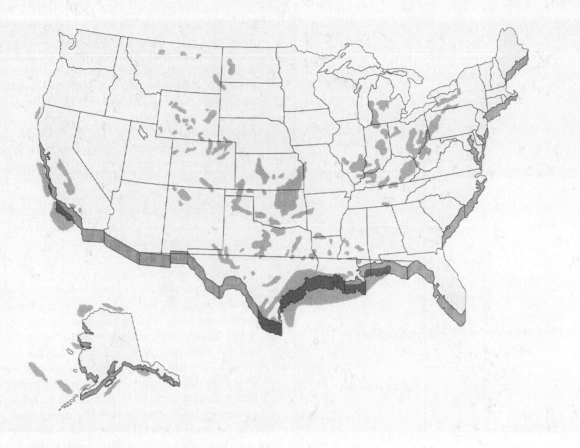

Natural gas and oil deposits in the United States.

Decomposition; Emission standards; Greenhouse effect; Groundwater pollution; Oil drilling; Oil spills

[*David E. Newton*]

FURTHER READING

Fesharaki, F., and R. Reed, eds. *The Petroleum Market in the 1990s.* Boulder, CO: Westview Press, 1989.

Flavin, C. "World Oil: Coping With the Dangers of Success." *Worldwatch Paper #66.* Washington, DC: Worldwatch Institute, 1985.

Kupchella, C. E. *Environmental Science: Living within the System of Nature.* 3rd ed. Boston: Allyn and Bacon, 1993.

Metzger, N. "Getting More Oil." In *Energy and the Way We Live*, by M. Kranzberg and T. A. Hall. San Francisco: Boyd & Fraser, 1980.

Petroleum Exploration: Continuing Need. Washington, DC: American Petroleum Institute, 1986.

Petulla, J. M. *American Environmental History.* 2nd ed. San Francisco: Boyd & Fraser, 1988.

pH

A measure of the acidity or alkalinity of a solution based on its **hydrogen** ion (H^+) concentration. The pH of a solution is the negative logarithm (base 10) of its H^+ concentration. Since the scale is logarithmic, there is a tenfold difference in hydrogen ion concentration for each pH unit. The pH scale ranges from 0 to 14 with 7 indicating neutrality ((H^+) = (OH^-)). Values above 7 indicate progressively greater alkalinity, while values below 7 indicate progressively increasing acidity. *See also* Acid and base; Buffer

Phosphates

Phosphorus is essential to the growth of biological organisms, including both their metabolic and photosynthetic processes. **Phosphorus** occurs naturally in bodies of water mainly in the form of phosphate (i.e., a compound of phosphorus and oxygen). Addition of phosphates through the activities of humans can accelerate the eutrophication process of nutrient enrichment that results in accelerated ecological aging of lakes and streams. Phosphorus, especially in inland waters, is often the nutrient that limits growth of aquatic plants. Thus when it is added to a body of water, it may result in increased plant growth that gradually fills in the lake. Critical levels of phosphorus in water, above which eutrophication is likely to be triggered, are approximately 0.03 mg/l of dissolved phosphorus and 0.1 mg/l of total phosphorus. The discharge of raw or treated **wastewater**, agricultural drainage, or certain industrial wastes that contain phosphates to a surface water body may result in a highly eutrophic state, in which the growth of photosynthetic aquatic micro- and macroorganisms are stimulated to nuisance levels. Aquatic plants and mats of algal scum may cover the surface of the water. As these algal mats and aquatic

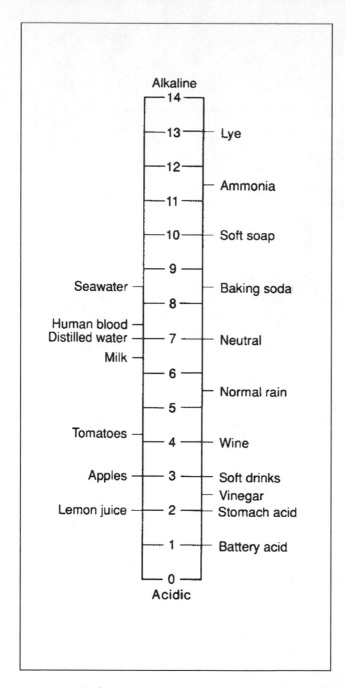

Alkaline
— 14 —
— 13 — Lye
— 12 —
— 11 — Ammonia
— 10 — Soft soap
— 9 —
Seawater — 8 — Baking soda
Human blood
Distilled water — 7 — Neutral
Milk —
— 6 —
— Normal rain
— 5 —
Tomatoes — 4 — Wine
Apples — 3 — Soft drinks
— Vinegar
Lemon juice — 2 — Stomach acid
— 1 — Battery acid
— 0 —
Acidic

pH scale of acidity and alkalinity.

plants die, they sink to the bottom, where their **decomposition** by **microorganisms** uses most of the oxygen dissolved in the water. The decrease in oxygen severely inhibits the growth of many aquatic organisms, especially more desirable fish (e.g., recreational catch fish such as trout) and in extreme cases may lead to massive fish kills. Excessive input of phosphorus can change clear, oxygen-rich, good-tasting water into cloudy, oxygen-poor, foul smelling, and possibly toxic water. Therefore, control of the amount of phosphates entering surface waters from domestic and industrial waste discharges, natural **runoff**, and **erosion** may be required to prevent eutrophication.

Rocks may contain phosphates; those with calcium phosphate upon heat treatment with sulfuric acid serve as a source of **fertilizer**s. Phosphates, in addition to those found in fertilizers, are also present in such consumer products as detergent, baking powders, toothpastes, cured meats, evaporated milk, soft drinks, processed cheeses, pharmaceuticals, and water softeners. Phosphates are classified as orthophosphates (PO_4^{-3}, HPO_4^{-2}, $H_2PO_4^-$, and H_3PO_4); condensed phosphates, or polyphosphates, which are molecules with two or more phosphorus atoms, oxygen atoms and in some cases, hydrogen atoms, combined in a complex molecule; and organically-bound phosphates.

Orthophosphates in an aqueous solution can be used for biological metabolism without further breakdown. Orthophosphates applied to agricultural or residential cultivated land as fertilizers may be carried into surface waters with storm runoff and melting snow.

Polyphosphates can be added to water when it is used for laundering or cleaning, for polyphosphates are present as builders of some commercial cleaning preparations for the public health sector. Massive **algal bloom**s in lakes and floating foam on rivers aroused alarm in the U.S. in the 1970s. After it was shown that phosphates from detergents were a key factor, legislation banning the use of phosphates in home laundry detergents was passed in many areas. Phosphate legislation usually includes exemptions for products such as hard-surface cleaner and automatic dishwashing detergents used in the public health sector. Polyphosphates may also be added to water supplies during culinary water treatment and during treatment of boiler water. Polyphosphates slowly undergo hydrolysis in aqueous solutions and are converted to the orthophosphate forms.

Organic phosphates are formed primarily by biological processes. They enter sewage water through body wastes and food residues. They may also be formed from orthophosphates in biological treatment processes and by receiving water organisms. Like polyphosphates, they are biologically transformed back to orthophosphates.

One means of surface water protection from phosphorus addition in both domestic and industrial wastewaters is the use of phosphorus removal processes in wastewater treatment. Phosphates are typically present in raw wastewaters at concentrations near 10 mg/l as P. During wastewater treatment, about 10-30% of the phosphates in raw wastewater is utilized during secondary biological treatment for microbial cell synthesis and energy transport. Additional removal is required to achieve low effluent concentration levels from the wastewater treatment process. Effluent limits usually range from 0.1-2 mg/l as P, with many established at 1.0 mg/l. Removal processes for phosphates from wastewaters utilize incorporation into suspended solids and the subsequent removal of those solids. Phosphates can be incorporated into chemical precipitates that are insoluble or of low solubility or into biological solids, (e.g, microorganisms).

Chemical precipitation is accomplished by the addition of metal salts or lime, with polymers often used as flocculant aids. The precipitation of phosphates from wastewater can occur during different phases within the wastewater treatment process. Pre-precipitation, where the chemicals are added to raw wastewater in primary sedimentation facilities, removes the precipitated phosphates with the primary sludge. In co-precipitation, the chemicals are added during secondary treatment to the effluent from the primary sedimentation facilities; to the mixed liquor in the activated-sludge process; or to the effluent from a biological treatment process before secondary sedimentation. They are removed with the waste biological sludge. In post-precipitation, the chemicals are added to the effluent from secondary sedimentation facilities and are removed in separate sedimentation facilities or in effluent filters.

The most commonly used metal salts are ferric chloride and aluminum sulfate (alum), which combine with phosphate to form the precipitates aluminum phosphate and iron phosphate, with one mole of iron or aluminum precipitating one mole of phosphate. However, because of competing reactions and the effects of alkalinity, **pH**, trace elements, and ligands found in wastewater, appropriate dosages are established on the basis of bench-scale or full-scale testing. Less commonly used metal salts are ferrous sulfate and ferrous chloride, which are available as by-products of steel production operations. Because polyphosphates and organic phosphorus are less easily removed than orthophosphates, adding metal salts after secondary treatment, where organic phosphorus and polyphosphates are transformed into orthophosphates, usually results in the best control.

Lime ($CaOH)_2$) is used less frequently because of the larger amounts of sludge produced as compared with the use of metal salts. Also, operating and maintenance problems are associated with the handling, storage, and feeding of lime. As lime is added to water, it reacts with natural bicarbonate alkalinity to precipitate $CaCO_3$. As the pH of the wastewater increases beyond about 10, excess calcium ions react with phosphates to precipitate hydroxylapatite, $Ca_{10}(PO_4)_6(OH)_2$. The amount of lime required will be independent of the amount of phosphate present and will depend primarily on the alkalinity of the wastewater and the degree of phosphate removal required. The pH of the wastewater must be adjusted by recarbonation with **carbon dioxide** (CO_2) before subsequent treatment or disposal. Lime can be added to primary sedimentation tanks or following secondary treatment.

Biological phosphate removal is accomplished by sequencing and producing appropriate environmental conditions in a reactor system in which microorganisms absorb and store phosphorus. The *Acinetobacter* bacteria are one of the primary microorganisms responsible for phosphorus uptake. The sludge containing the microorganisms with the excess phosphorus can either be wasted or removed and treated in a side stream to release the excess phosphate, which can then be treated with chemical precipitation processes. Wasted sludge, if it has a relatively high phosphorus content (3-5%), may have fertilizer value.

In natural treatment systems for wastewater, which include managed land-farms, landscape **irrigation** sites, **groundwater** recharge sites, and constructed **wetlands**, phosphates are removed by sorption with clay minerals in the **soil** matrix and by chemical precipitation. Sorbed phosphates

are held tightly and are generally resistant to leaching until the soil sorptive capacity for phosphates becomes saturated. Chemical precipitation with calcium (in soils with neutral or alkaline pH) or with iron or aluminum (at acid pH) occurs at a slower rate than sorption, but is also an important removal mechanism. The degree of phosphorus removal in a natural treatment system depends on the degree of wastewater contact with the soil matrix.

Transport of phosphates into surface waters from nonpoint sources is controlled by practices that minimize soil erosion and runoff water. Phosphate losses from a watershed can be increased by a number of human activities, including timber harvest, intensive livestock grazing, soil tillage, and soil application of animal manures and phosphate-containing fertilizers. Since most soils, except for very sandy soils or soils with high levels of organic matter, retain phosphates through sorption and precipitation, techniques that prevent soil transport will also prevent transport of phosphates. Control of runoff water is required to prevent dissolved phosphates from entering rivers and lakes.

[Judith L. Sims]

FURTHER READING

Metcalf & Eddy. *Wastewater Engineering: Treatment, Disposal, and Reuse*, 3rd ed. New York: McGraw-Hill, 1991.

Phosphorus

An important chemical element, which has the atomic number 15 and atomic weight 30.9738. Phosphorus forms the basis of a large number of compounds, by far the most environmentally important of which are phosphates. All plants and animals need phosphates for growth and function, and in many natural waters the production of algae and higher plants is limited by the low natural levels of phosphorus. As the amount of available phosphorus in an aquatic environment increases, plant and algal growth can increase dramatically leading to eutrophication. In the past, one of the major contributors to phosphorus pollution was household **detergents** containing phosphates. These substances have now been banned from these products. Other contributors to phosphorus pollution are **sewage treatment** plants and runoff from cattle **feedlots**. (Animal feces contain significant amounts of phosphorus.) **Erosion** of farmland treated with phosphorus **fertilizer**s or animal manure also contributes to eutrophication and **water pollution**. *See also* Cultural eutrophication

Phosphorus removal

Phosphorus (usually in the form of phosphate, PO^{3-}_4) is a normal part of the **environment**. It occurs in the form of phosphate-containing rocks and as the excretory and decay products of plants and animals. Human contributions to the phosphorus cycle result primarily from the use of phosphorus-containing **detergents** and **fertilizers**.

The increased load of phosphorus in the environment as a result of human activities has been a matter of concern for more than four decades. The primary issue has been to what extent additional phosphorus has contributed to the eutrophication of lakes, ponds, and other bodies of water. Scientists have long recognized that increasing levels of phosphorus are associated with eutrophication. But the evidence for a direct cause and effect relationship is not entirely clear. Eutrophication is a complex process involving **nitrogen** and **carbon**, as well as phosphorus. The role of each **nutrient** and the interaction among them is still not entirely clear.

In any case, environmental engineers have long explored methods for the removal of phosphorus from **wastewater** in order to reduce possible eutrophication effects. Primary and secondary treatment techniques are relatively inefficient in removing phosphorus with only about ten percent extracted from raw wastewater in each step. Thus, special procedures during the tertiary treatment stage are needed to remove the remaining phosphorus.

Two methods are generally available: biological and chemical. Bacteria formed in the activated **sludge** produced during secondary treatment have an unusually high tendency to adsorb phosphorus. If these bacteria are used in a tertiary treatment stage, therefore, they are very efficient in removing phosphorus from **wastewater**. The sludge produced by this bacterial action is rich in phosphorus and can be separated from the wastewater leaving water with a concentration of phosphorus only about five percent that of its original level.

The more popular method of phosphorus removal is chemical. A compound is selected that will react with phosphate in wastewater, forming an insoluble product that can then be filtered off. The two most common substances used for this process are alum, aluminum sulfate $[Al_2(SO_4)_3]$ and lime, or calcium hydroxide $[Ca(OH)_2]$. An alum treatment works in two different ways. Some aluminum sulfate reacts directly with phosphate in the waste water to form insoluble aluminum phosphate. At the same time, the aluminum ion hydrolyzes in water to form a thick, gelatinous precipitate of aluminum hydroxide that carries phosphate with it as it settles out of solution.

The addition of lime to wastewater results in the formation of another insoluble product, calcium hydroxyapatite, which also settles out of solution.

By determining the concentration of phosphorus in wastewater, these chemical treatments can be used very precisely. Exactly enough alum or lime can be added to precipitate out the phosphate in the water. Such treatments are normally effective in removing about 95 percent of all phosphorus originally present in a sample of wastewater.

[*David E. Newton*]

FURTHER READING

Phosphorus Management Strategies Task Force. *Phosphorus Management for the Great Lakes.* Windsor, Ont.: International Joint Commission, 1980.

Retrofitting POTWs for Phosphorus Removal in the Chesapeake Bay Drainage Basin: A Handbook. Cincinnati, OH: U. S. Environmental Protection Agency, 1987.

Symposium on the Economy and Chemistry of Phosphorus. *Phosphorus in the Environment: Its Chemistry and Biochemistry.* New York: Elsevier, 1978.

Photic zone

The surface waters of an ocean or lake that receive sufficient solar radiation to support **photosynthesis**, (i.e. the growth of **vascular plant**s and **phytoplankton**). When sunlight falls on the surface of a lake or ocean, a large part of the light is reflected, scattered, or absorbed. Some light penetrates the water, but its intensity decreases quite rapidly with depth. The photic zone can be up to 328 ft (100 m) deep, and, typically, its limit is reached when the light intensity falls below one percent of the incident radiation.

Photochemical reaction

Photochemical reactions are driven by light or near-visible electromagnetic radiation. In general, incoming units of energy, known as photons, excite effected molecules, raising their energy to a point where they can undergo reactions that would normally be exceedingly difficult. The process is distinguished from thermal reactions, which take place with molecules in their normal energy states. Under sunlit conditions, photochemical processes can generate small amounts of extremely reactive molecules which initiate important chemical reaction sequences.

To initiate a photochemical reaction, two requirements need to be met. First, the photon must have enough energy to initiate the photochemical reaction in the molecule. Second, the compound must be colored, in order to be able to react with visible or near-visible photon radiation.

In environmental chemistry, photochemical reactions are of considerable importance to the trace chemistry of the **atmosphere**. The Los Angeles **photochemical smog** is an example of a system of photochemical reactions. Perhaps one of the most important reactions in this system is the photochemically driven conversion of **nitrogen dioxide**, a major component of **automobile** exhaust, to nitric oxide and an atom of oxygen, which usually occurs in pairs in the air. The oxygen atom subsequently attaches to an oxygen molecule to form the secondary pollutant, **ozone**. Photochemically initiated reactions are also responsible for generating the all important hydroxyl radical, a key intermediate in the trace chemistry of the lower atmosphere.

Photochemical reactions are also important in natural waters. Here they may be responsible for enhancing the reaction rate of organic compounds or changing the oxidation state of metallic **ion**s in solution. However, some of these compounds are not colored, and are unable to absorb light. In such cases reactions may be mediated by photosensitizers, compounds capable of being energized by absorbed light which then pass the energy onto other molecules. Seawater appears to contain natural photosensitizers, perhaps in the form of fulvic acid or chlorophyll derivatives. Photosensitizers activated by sunlight can react with organic compounds or dissolved oxygen to produce the reactive singlet-oxygen, which can react rapidly with many seawater compounds.

Photochemical reactions also occur in solids. Since solids often lack the transparency required for the light to penetrate the surface, reactions are usually limited to the surface, where incoming photons initiate reactions in the top-most molecules. There is also some evidence that, under extremely bright desert sunlight, traces of **nitrogen** and water absorbed on titanium and zinc oxides can be photochemically converted to ammonia. Such processes are no doubt also important on planetary surfaces. *See also* Air pollution; Air quality; Emission; Los Angeles Basin

[*Peter Brimblecombe*]

FURTHER READING

Findlayson-Pitts, B. J., and J. N. Pitts. *Atmospheric Chemistry*. New York: Wiley, 1986.

Photochemical smog

A form of **smog** that characterizes polluted **atmosphere**s where high concentrations of **nitrogen oxide**s and **volatile organic compounds**—often from gas-driven **automobile**s—mixed with sunlight promote a series of photochemical reactions that lead to the formation of **ozone** and a range of oxidized and nitrated organic compounds. The smog turns brownish in color and lowers visibility towards the middle of the day as sunlight becomes intense. The smog also causes eye irritation and a range of less distinct short- and long-term health effects. Photochemical smog, though typified by the atmosphere of the **Los Angeles Basin**, is increasingly found in cities all over the world where volatile fuels are used.

Photodegradable plastic

Plastics are clearly one of the great chemical inventions of all time. It would probably be impossible to list all the ways in which plastics are used in everyday life. Suffice to say that, in the early 1990s, more than 60 billion pounds (27 billion kg) of plastics were produced in the United States alone each year.

For their many advantages, plastics also create some serious environmental problems. About one third, 20 billion pounds (9 billion kg), of all plastics now produced are used for short-term purposes, such as shopping bags and wrapping material. These plastics are used once, briefly, and then discarded.

Current estimates are that plastic materials make up about 7 percent by weight and 18 percent by volume of all municipal wastes. Since most plastics do not degrade naturally, they will continue to be a part of the nation's (and the world's) **solid waste** problem for decades.

One solution to the accumulation of plastics is to do a better job of **recycling** them. Technical, economic, and social factors have limited the success of this approach so far, and no more than 1 percent of all discarded plastics are ever recycled. Another solution is to fabricate plastics in such a way that they will degrade. Addition of starch as a filler in plastics, for example, tends to make them more **biodegradable**, that is, degradable by naturally-occurring organisms.

Yet another approach is photodegradable plastics, plastics that will decompose when exposed to sunlight. The process of photodegradation is well understood by chemists. In general, when light strikes a molecule, it may initiate any number of reactions that result in the destruction of that molecule. For example, light may dislocate one or more electrons that make up a **chemical bond** in the molecule. When the bond is broken, the molecule is destroyed.

On a practical level, that means that light can cause certain materials to decompose. Among the plastics, aromatic-based polymers (those that have **benzene**-like ring structures) are particularly susceptible to photodegradation. Those that lack an aromatic structure are less susceptible to the effects of light. Polyethylene, polypropylene, **polyvinyl chloride**, polymethyl methacrylate, polyamides, and polystyrene—some of the most widely used plastics—fall into that latter category.

In addition to the type of plastic, the kind of light that falls on a material affects the rate of photodegradation. Ultraviolet (UV) light is more effective, in general, in degrading all plastics than are most other forms of light.

The chemist's task, then, is to find a mechanism for converting a substance that is normally non-photodegradable (like polystyrene) into a form that is decomposed by light. In principle, that challenge is rather easily met. Certain metallic **ion**s and organic groups are known to absorb visible light strongly. If these ions or groups are included in a plastic material, their absorption of light will contribute to the decay of the plastic.

Photodegradable plastics are not a new market item. Webster Industries, of Peabody, Massachusetts, has been making photodegradable plastic bags since 1978. And Mobil Chemical focused some of its advertising in 1990 on Hefty trash bags that were designed to photodegrade.

But critics raise a number of points about photodegradable (as well as biodegradable) plastic materials. For one thing, most plastics are disposed of in sanitary **landfill**s where they are rapidly covered with other materials. The critics question the good of having a photodegradable plastic that is not exposed to sunlight after it is discarded.

Questions have also been raised about the possible by-products of photodegradation. It is possible that the very additives used to make a plastic photodegradable may have toxic or other harmful environmental effects, critics say.

Finally, photodegradable plastics take so long to decay (typically two months to two years) that they will still pose a hazard to **wildlife** and contribute to solid waste volume. The "false promise" of photodegradability may, in fact, actually encourage the use of more plastics and add to the present problem, rather than helping to solve it. *See also* Decomposition; Green packaging; Green products; Ultraviolet radiation

[*David E. Newton*]

FURTHER READING

Denison, R. A., and J. Wirka. *Degradable Plastics: The Wrong Answer to the Right Question.* New York: Environmental Defense Fund, 1989.

Donnelly, J. "Degradable Plastics." *Garbage* 2 (May-June 1990): 42-47.

"The Problem with Plastics." *Horticulture* (August 1989): 18-19.

Thayer, A. M. "Degradable Plastics Generate Controversy in Solid Waste Issues." *Chemical & Engineering News* (25 June 1990): 7-14.

Photoperiod

The light phase in a cycle of alternating periods of light and dark. Changes in light-dark cycles, such as changes in day-length, are the most dependable external time cues (zeitgebers). The physiological response to the length of the day or night, known as photoperiodism, is mediated by an internal or biological clock that synchronizes daily activities with external light-dark cycles. Most **species** studied show a circadian or daily rhythm set to a 24-hour cycle. Organisms also show long-term photoperiodism where their seasonal activities, such as courtship, mating, reproduction, **migration**, flowering, and seed production, are coordinated with others in the population and within the community.

Photosynthesis

Photosynthesis is the process by which green plants capture sunlight and convert its kinetic energy into chemical energy by manufacturing complex sugar molecules or carbohydrates. The plants use **carbon dioxide** from the air and water as the source materials for photosynthesis. Both carbon dioxide and water store relatively small amounts of energy. The carbohydrates manufactured are rich in energy. Later, during the process of **respiration**, the plant breaks down these carbohydrates, and the energy that is then released is used to fuel the growth and **metabolism** of the plant. The photosynthetic process also releases oxygen along with the formation of the carbohydrates. The water (H_2O) that is used in the photosynthetic reaction contributes its **hydrogen** to the formation of the carbohydrate. The oxygen that is released comes from the remaining, unused portion of the water molecule. Therefore, water is just as essential a component as carbon dioxide to the photosynthetic process. The entire reaction is carried out with the help of green, light-sensitive pigments within the plant, known as chlorophylls.

Photosynthesis is vital to the earth in two ways. It is the process by which plant life is established, thereby providing food and supporting all the other consumers in the **food chain/web**. The release of oxygen also ensures a livable, breathable atmosphere for all other oxygen-dependent life forms. The maintenance of a stable balance between the processes of photosynthesis (which produces oxygen) and respiration (which consumes oxygen) is critical to the **environment**. For example, a large amount of organic matter goes into a lake receiving sewage. This organic matter will be used as a food source by bacteria which break it down by the process of respiration just as humans do. During the respira-

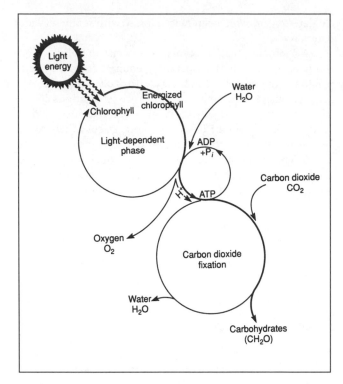

Photosynthesis.

tion process, the oxygen that is dissolved in the water is used up. If there is insufficient plant material in the lake to restore this used-up oxygen by photosynthesis, the total supply of dissolved oxygen in the waters of the lake may drop dangerously. Since fish are completely dependent on the dissolved oxygen for their breathing requirements, severe drops in the concentration of dissolved oxygen may kill the fish, leading to sudden, and sometimes massive, **fish kills**.

Another aspect of environmental **pollution** are the effects on the process of photosynthesis itself. A number of contaminants have been shown to affect plant growth and metabolism by inhibiting the plant's ability to photosynthesize. Frequently, as in the case of metals like **copper**, **lead** and **cadmium**, the mechanism of inhibition is due to the contaminant's effect on the chlorophyll pigment. Copper replaces the necessary magnesium in the chlorophyll molecule, and the copper-substituted chlorophyll cannot effectively capture light energy. Therefore, the effectiveness of the photosynthetic process is greatly diminished, which leads to a stunting of plant growth and a depletion of oxygen in the environment. The maintenance of a healthy level of photosynthesis is thus essential to the life of the planet, both on the global and the micro-environmental scales.

[Usha Vedagiri]

FURTHER READING

Connell, D. W., and G. J. Miller. *Chemistry and Ecotoxicology of Pollution.* New York: Wiley, 1984.

Weier, T. E., et al. *Botany: An Introduction to Plant Biology.* New York: Wiley, 1982.

Photovoltaic cell

Photovoltaics is the direct conversion of sunlight into electrical energy using solar cells. All energy on earth is received from the sun through its electromagnetic spectrum. At any one instant, the sun delivers 1,000 watts (kw) per square meter to the earth's surface. Most of this energy is absorbed as heat by the lithosphere (**soil**), hydrosphere (water), and **atmosphere** but **photovoltaic cell**s (PVC) are capable of converting it into a non-polluting, ecologically sound, and dependable source of electrical power. Although the photovoltaic effect was discovered 150 years ago, economically viable applications were not possible until the recent development of efficient semiconductor material and processing methods.

The physics of converting sunlight into electricity is simple. Most photovoltaic cells are a standard negative/positive type with attached leads. The negative terminal lead is soldered on the light sensitive side of the cell, and the positive lead is attached to the back side of the cell. When simply exposed to light, each cell produces about the same voltage between the two terminals. But if the cell is exposed to light when a load such as a discharged battery or an electric motor is connected between the two terminals, the voltage difference causes a flow of electrons. This current is caused by the formation of hole-electron pairs by the absorbed light photons, and the amount of current is dependent on the amount of absorbed light, which is dependent in turn on the incident light intensity and the surface area of the absorbing photovoltaic cell.

There are two main types of solar cells: thick-film cells with a thickness greater than 25 microns of crystalline silicon and thin-film cells with a thickness of less than 10 microns. Thin-film cells are made of various materials, including amorphous silicon and **copper** indium diselenide, and by combining several varieties of these in tandem, each with unique absorbing characteristics, the solar flux can be more efficiently utilized. Because these cells use less material, they are less costly to produce and will probably replace thick-film cells.

Both thick-film and thin-film cells are classified by the materials from which they are made—as crystalline (a wafer sliced from a large ingot), amorphous (The condensed gaseous form of a semi-conductor material such as silicon), and polycrystalline. Material combinations known as compound semiconductors have been investigated in the 1990s. These are cell materials whose active layers are comprised of various semiconductor materials, such as gallium arsenide, copper sulfide, and **cadmium** telluride.

To increase voltage, multiple cells are connected in a series by attaching the positive lead of one cell to the negative lead of another. The series most commonly used for both commercial and domestic applications is known as a module and usually consists of 36 cells. One or more modules can be connected directly to a load, such as a battery, a water pump, or an exhaust fan. A typical photovoltaic system consists of the modules, a storage battery, a charge and voltage regulator, and a suitable load. Some compact high performance mod-

The operation of a photovoltaic cell.

ules are designed to charge 12-volt batteries or directly power a 12-volt DC motor.

Photovoltaic modules may be installed on a standard ground mount or on a tracker. When installed on a standard ground mount, the modules can be adjusted from 15 to 65 degrees at 5 degree increments. Ground mounts can support two to eight modules. The tracker utilizes a variable thermal expansion of gas, due to the changing solar exposure, and actually follows the sun at approximately 15 degrees plus latitude valve. To maximize efficiency, several modules are mounted on a tracker supported by a single pole.

The net cost per kilowatt hour is the most important factor in the future of photovoltaic cell production and application. In industrialized countries, the economic viability of this form of **solar energy** is determined by their cost relative to competitive energy sources, particularly **fossil fuels** and **nuclear power**, and the environmental impact of each source. The world market price for solar cells in 1993 was four dollars a watt, based on rated output, and prices are expected to drop 50 percent by the end of the decade, when most photovoltaic cells will be manufactured with thin-film technology.

Decentralized single dwellings, cattle ranches and tree farms remote from electric power lines, and small villages with limited power demands are one of the three market segments where photovoltaic cells can be utilized competitively. The consumer and leisure market is another, and solar cells are already widely used in boats, motor homes, and camp sites, as well as in calculators and other electronics. The third market is in industrial applications such as offshore buoys, lighthouses, illuminated road signs, and railroad and traffic signals.

The market for photovoltaic cells is increasing at an overall annual rate of about 10 percent. Current worldwide demand is estimated at about 100 megawatts of electrical power, and predictions for the year 2000 estimate a demand of several times this size. Growth is the fastest in the remote market; rural consumer applications are increasing at an annual rate of approximately 35 percent. There are millions of people around the world who are not served by electric utilities due to their remote location and the high cost of electrical transmission. These populations generally depend on a 12-volt automobile battery powered by a generator for their electrical needs, which include water pumping, lighting, and radio and television reception. The initial cost of a photovoltaic kit offsets the cost of owning and operating a generator within three years. As the life span of a module is usually 15 years, this option is much more economical in many of these situations.

Prior to 1989, the largest manufacturer of photovoltaic cells was ARCO Solar, a division of Atlantic Richfield Oil Company. In 1989, Siemens Solar Industries (SSI), which already had a joint manufacturing enterprise in Munich, Germany, with ARCO, had purchased ARCO Solar. SSI has manufacturing plants in Camarillo, California, and Munich, Germany.

Converting sunlight into electricity with photovoltaic cells is a versatile and simple process. Unlike diesel or **gasoline** generators, all-weather modules have no moving parts to wear out or break down, and they produce electricity without contributing to **air pollution**. Solar cells do not produce any noise and they do not require alternating-current power lines, since photovoltaic electricity is direct current. Maintenance is minimal and requires little technical skill; systems are easy to expand and there are no expensive fuels to purchase on a continuous basis. Photovoltaic cells are a cheap and dependable source of power for a variety of uses. *See also* Alternative energy sources; Alternative fuels; Energy and the environment; Energy policy

[*Muthena Naseri and Douglas Smith*]

FURTHER READING

Edelson, E. "Solar Cell Update." *Popular Science* 240 (June 1992): 95-99.

Lasnier, F., and T. Ang. *Photovoltaic Engineering Handbook.* New York: American Institute of Physics, 1990.

Lewis, N. S. "More Efficient Solar Cells." *Nature* 345 (24 May 1990): 293-4.

Spinks, P. "Plug Into the Sun." *New Scientist* 127 (22 September 1990): 48-51.

Phytoplankton

Photosynthetic **plankton**, including microalgae, blue-green bacteria, and some true bacteria. These organisms are produced in surface waters of aquatic **ecosystem**s, to depths where light is able to penetrate. Sunlight is necessary since, like terrestrial plants, phytoplankton use solar radiation to convert **carbon dioxide** and water into organic molecules such as glucose. Phytoplankton form the base of nearly all aquatic **food chain/web**s, directly or indirectly supplying the energy needed by most aquatic protozoans and animals. Temperature, **nutrient** levels, light intensity, and consumers (grazers) are among the factors that influence phytoplankton community structure.

Phytoremediation

Phytoremediation combines the Greek word *phyton*, "plant," with the Latin word *remediare*, "to remedy," to describe a system whereby certain plants, working together with **soil** organisms, can transform contaminants into harmless and often, valuable, forms. This practice is increasingly used to remediate sites contaminated with heavy metals and toxic organic compounds.

Phytoremediation takes advantage of plants' nutrient utilization processes to take in water and nutrients through roots, transpire water through leaves, and act as a transformation system to metabolize organic compounds, such as oil and **pesticide**s. Or they may absorb and bioaccumulate toxic trace elements, such as the heavy **metals**, **lead**, **cadmium**, and selenium. In some cases, plants contain 1,000 times more metal than the soil in which they grow. Heavy metals are closely related to the elements plants use for growth. In many cases, the plants cannot tell the difference, according to Ilya Raskin, Professor of Plant Sciences in the Center for Agricultural Molecular Biology at Rutgers University.

Phytoremediation is an affordable technology that is most useful when contaminants are within the root zone of the plants (top 3-6 ft [1-2 m]). For sites with contamination spread over a large area, phytoremediation may be the only economically feasible technology. The process is relatively inexpensive because it uses the same equipment and supplies used in agriculture.

Soil microorganisms can degrade organic contaminants. This is called bioremediation and has been used for many years both as an in situ process and in land farming operations with soil removed from sites.

Ilya Raskin and his interdisciplinary team at Rutgers AgBiotech Center were first to demonstrate the utility of certain varieties of mustard plants in removing such metals as chromium, lead, cadmium, and zinc from contaminated soil. Related technology developed by Raskin's group used hydroponic plant cultures to remove toxic metals from aqueous waste streams.

Plants can accelerate bioremediation in surface soils by their ability to stimulate soil microorganisms through the release of nutrients from and the transport of oxygen to their roots. The zone of soil closely associated with the plant root, the rhizosphere, has much higher numbers of metabolically active microorganisms than unplanted soil. The rhizosphere is a zone of increased microbial activity and **biomass** at the root-soil interface that is under the interface of the plant roots. It is this symbiotic relationship between soil microbes that is responsible for the accelerated degradation of soil contaminants.

The interaction between plants and microbial communities in the rhizosphere is complex and has evolved to the mutual benefit of both organisms. Plants sustain large microbial populations in the rhizosphere by secreting substances such as carbohydrates and amino acids through root cells and by sloughing root epidermal cells. Also, root cells secrete mucigel, a gelatinous substance that is a lubricant for root penetration through the soil during growth. Using this supply of nutrients, soil microorganisms proliferate to form the plant rhizosphere.

In addition to this rhizosphere effect, plants themselves are able to passively take up a wide range of organic wastes from soil through their roots. One of the more important roles of soil microorganisms is the decomposition of organic residues with the release of plant nutrient elements such as **carbon**, **nitrogen**, potassium, phosphate, and sulfur. A significant amount of the **carbon dioxide** (CO_2) in the atmosphere is utilized for organic matter synthesis primarily through **photosynthesis**. This transformation of carbon dioxide and the subsequent sequestering of the carbon as root biomass contributes to balancing the effect of burning **fossil fuels** on global warming or cooling.

Compounds are frequently transformed in the plant tissue into less toxic forms or sequestered and concentrated so they can be removed (harvested) with the plant. For example, mustard greens were used to remove 45% of the excess lead from a yard in Boston, Massachusetts, to ensure the safety of children who play there. The sequestered lead was carefully removed and safely disposed of. Besides mustard greens, pumpkin vines were used to clean up an old Magic Marker factory site in Trenton, New Jersey. Hydroponically grown sunflowers were used to absorb radioactive metals near the **Chernobyl** nuclear site in the Ukraine and a uranium plant in Ohio. The mustard's hyper-accumulation results in much less material for disposal. The composting of plant material can be another highly efficient stage in the breakdown of contaminants removed from the soil.

When trees are used, such as poplars, the idea is to move as much water through them as possible, so that they take up as much of the contaminants as possible. Once the heavy metals are absorbed, they are sequestered in the trees' roots. Any organic compounds that are absorbed are metabolized.

Absorption of large amounts of nutrients by plants and only a small amount of plant toxins that might be harmful to them, is the key factor. Plants generally absorb large amounts of elements they need for growth and only small amounts of toxic elements that could harm them. Therefore, phytoremediation is a cost-effective alternative to conventional remediation methods. Cleaning the top 6 in (15 cm) of contaminated soil with phytoremediation costs an estimated $2,500-$15,000 per hectare (2.5 acres), compared to $7,500-$20,000 per hectare for on-site microbial remediation. If the soil is moved, the costs escalate, but phytoremediation costs are still far below those of traditional remediation methods, such as stripping the contaminants from the soil using physical, chemical, or thermal processes, according to Dr. Scott Cunningham, a scientist at Dupont Central Research for Environmental Biotechnology.

Plants are effective at remediating soils contaminated with organic chemical wastes, such as solvents, petrochemicals, wood preservatives, explosives, and pesticides. The conventional technology for soil clean-up is to remove the soil and isolate it in a **hazardous waste** landfill or incinerate it.

Phytoremediation, says Dr. Ray Hinchman, botanist and plant physiologist at Argonne National Laboratory, is "an *in situ* approach," not reliant on the transport of contaminated material to other sites. Organic contaminants are, in many cases, completely destroyed (converted to CO_2 and H_2O) rather than simply immobilized or stored.

Salt-tolerant plants, called halophytes, have reduced the salt levels in soils by 65% in only two years in one project involving brine-damaged land from run-off from oil and gas production in Oklahoma. After the salt was reduced, the halophytes died and native grasses, which failed to thrive when too much salt entered the soil, naturally returned, replacing the salt-converting plants.

The establishment of vegetation on a site also reduces soil erosion by wind and water, which helps to prevent the spread of contaminants and reduces exposure of humans and animals.

Classes of organic compounds that are more rapidly degraded in rhizosphere soil than in unplanted soil include: total **petroleum hydrocarbons**; polycyclic aromatic hydrocarbons; chlorinated pesticides (PCP, 2,4-D); other chlorinated compounds (PCBs, TCE); explosives (TNT, DNT); organophosphate insecticides (**diazanon** and parathion); and surfactants (detergents).

Some plants used for phytoremediation are: alfalfa, symbiotic with hydrocarbon-degrading bacteria; arabidopsis, carries a bacterial gene that transforms mercury into a gaseous state; bladder campion, accumulates zinc and copper; brassica juncea (Indian mustard greens), accumulates selenium, sulfur, lead, chromium, cadmium, nickel, zinc, and copper; buxaceae (boxwood), accumulates nickel; compositae family (symbiotic with arthrobacter bacteria), accumulates cesium and strontium; euphorbiaceae (succulent), accumulates nickel; ordinary tomato, accumulates lead, zinc, and copper; poplar, used in the absorption of the pesticide, **atrazine**; and thlaspi caerulescens (alpine pennycress), accumulates zinc and cadmium.

[*Carol Steinfeld*]

FURTHER READING

Elliott, L.F., Stevenson, F.J. "Soils for the Management of Wastes and Waste Waters." Madison, WI: Soil Science Society of America, 1977.

Anderson, G. and W. "Bioremediation, Environmental Science and Technology." *American Chemical Society*, Vol. 27, No. 13,, 1993.

Howe, P. "Plants doing the dirty work in cleanup of toxic waste," *Boston Globe* (10 March 1997.)

Phytotoxicity

Phytotoxicity refers to the damage to plants caused by exposure to some toxic stressor. Phytotoxicity can be evidenced by acute injury such as obviously damaged, necrotic tissues. Chronic phytotoxicity does not present such obvious symtoms and may result in such "hidden injuries" as a decrease in productivity or a change in growth form. Plants can be poisoned by naturally occurring toxins, such as **nickel** in serpentine-influenced **soils**. Humans also release phytotoxic chemicals into the **environment**. Such **emission**s occur when, for example, gascous and/or metal pollutants around **smelter**s damage vegetation. Deliberate use of phytotoxic **chemicals** includes the use of **herbicide**s in agriculture or forestry to decrease the abundance of unwanted plants or weeds.

Pinchot, Gifford (1865-1946)

American forester and conservationist

Pinchot was born in Simsbury, Connecticut, to a prosperous business and industrial family, part of whose wealth came from timber holdings in several states. The Pinchots, like other lumber investors of their day, practiced **clear-cutting** on forests to maximize their profits, shipped the logs to market, and with the returns, repeated the cycle. Young Gifford was pressured by his grandfather to enter the family business, but his father James was beginning to dislike the **deforestation** of his area, and he encouraged his son to pursue forestry.

Pinchot was educated at Exeter and then Yale, graduating in 1889. After graduation, his family supported further education at L'Ecole nationale forestiere in Nancy, France, where he studied silviculture, or forest **ecology**. It was in Nancy that he learned "*le coup d'oeil forestier*—the forester's eye, which sees what it looks at in the woods." In his 1947 book, *Breaking New Ground*, Pinchot noted that it was in France that he began to think of "the forest as a crop," that forests could sustain human use by a "fixed and annual supply of trees ready for the axe."

Returning to the United States in 1892, Pinchot engaged in "the first scientific forestry in America" on the Vanderbilt estate in North Carolina, hoping to prove that "trees could be cut and the forest preserved at one and the same time." Pinchot figured out how to sustain the forest while maintaining its yield, and thus its income. He called his first successful year "a balance on the side of practical forestry."

Pinchot then worked as a consulting forester in New York City, where he attracted increasing attention for his ideas. The National Academy of Science appointed him to the new National Forest Commission, organized by the **U.S. Department of the Interior**. On the Commission's recommendation, President Grover Cleveland added thirteen more forest reserves totaling 21 million acres (8.5 million ha). Pinchot, voicing a minority opinion on the Commission, saw the reserves as property for public use, not as a way to lock up the nation's **natural resources**.

In 1898 Pinchot became head of the **U.S. Department of Agriculture**'s Division of Forestry. The division did not operate the nation's forest reserves, which were then administered by the Department of the Interior's General Land Office. Pinchot lobbied hard to have the reserves transferred to his division, but his efforts were unsuccessful until William McKinley's assassination moved **Theodore Roosevelt** into the White House. Pinchot and Roosevelt together mustered enough support in Congress to approve the transfer to the renamed Bureau of Forestry in 1905, marking the beginning of the **national forest** system and what became the U.S. **Forest Service**.

Pinchot's long-time collaboration with Roosevelt was one of the benchmarks of the **conservation** movement, which culminated in the creation of what have been called the "midnight forests." These sixteen million acres of forest were set aside as reserves late in the night before a Congressional

Gifford Pinchot.

bill to limit the President's power to do so took effect. After Roosevelt left office, Pinchot's association with President William Howard Taft soured quickly, climaxing in a feud with Richard Ballinger, Taft's Secretary of the Interior and ending in 1910, when Pinchot was fired by the President.

Despite leaving before he had accomplished all that he wished, Pinchot left his mark on the Forest Service. Ironically, both are often criticized by modern environmentalists for their utilitarian policies. Yet this early conservationist was one of first to protect national forest lands from the industrial powers who sought to destroy them completely.

Pinchot still generates controversy today. Most writers trace the conflict between conservationists and preservationists to his falling-out with **John Muir** over the **Hetch-Hetchy Reservoir** in California. Pinchot, with his pragmatic approach, argued that the river valley served the greatest public good as a dependable source of water for the people of San Francisco. Muir maintained that Hetch Hetchy was sacred and too beautiful to flood. He also believed the dam would betray the **national park** ideal, since Hetch Hetchy was in **Yosemite National Park**.

As he grew older, Pinchot did become less utilitarian, creating what he called the "new conservationism," but even his "new" approach was an extension of his long-held conviction that the forests of the nation belonged first to the people, to be used by them wisely and in perpetuity. To Pinchot, conservation meant "the greatest good to the greatest number for the longest time." Pinchot's beliefs, which have been revived in recent years, make sense both ecologically and economically. He claimed that "the central thing for which Conservation stands is to make this country the best possible place to live in, both for us and our descendants."

Pinchot was active on many fronts of the struggle for conservation. The **Society of American Foresters**, a professional association and major force in resource management and conservation today was created in 1900, due in part to his efforts. He served two terms as Governor of Pennsylvania (1923-27; 1931-35), and his efforts to relieve the effects of the Great Depression led to the creation of emergency work camps there, providing a model for the Civilian Conservation Corps started by President Franklin Roosevelt.

Pinchot recognized that people *must* live off the resources of land where they live. In *The Fight for Conservation* (1910), he stated bluntly that "the first principle of conservation is development, the use of the natural resources now existing on the continent for the benefit of the people who live here now." But, he also recognized that use of resources could quickly turn into abuse of resources, especially by exploitation for the few. He believed that destruction of forest resources was detrimental to the **environment** and to the many who depended on it.

Pinchot's ideas and his national forests are still with us today. His concern with producing the greatest totality of **land use** produced the **wilderness** that is preserved but accessible and forest that is logged and renewed. Pinchot, a giant of the conservation and the environmental movements, leaves his legacy of a vast forest domain that belong to the American people. *See also* Environmental economics; Forest decline; ; Green politics; Greens

[*Gerald L. Young*]

FURTHER READING

McGeary, M. N. *Gifford Pinchot: Forester-Politician.* Princeton, NJ: Princeton University Press, 1960.

Miller, C. "The Greening of Gifford Pinchot." *Environmental History Review* 16 (Fall 1992): 1-20.

Nash, R. "Gifford Pinchot." In *From These Beginnings: A Biographical Approach to American History.* Vol. 2. 2nd ed. New York: Harper & Row, 1978.

Norton, B. G. "Moralists and Aggregators: The Case of Muir and Pinchot." In *Toward Unity Among Environmentalists.* New York: Oxford University Press, 1991.

Pinchot, G. *Breaking New Ground.* Covelo, CA: Island Press, 1947.

Watkins, T. H. "Father of the Forests." *American Heritage* 42 (February-March 1991): 86-98.

Placer mining

Placer deposits are collections of some mineral existing in discrete particles, mixed with sand, gravel, and other forms of eroded rock. Some of the minerals most commonly found in placer deposits are diamond, gold, platinum, magnetite, rutile, monazite, and cassiterite. These deposits are formed by the action of wind, water, and chemical changes on more massive beds of the mineral. Placer deposits can be classified according to the method by which they are produced. Some examples include stream placers, eolian placers (formed by the action of winds), beach placers, and moraine placers (formed by glacial action).

Placer deposits are important sources of some minerals that are more dense than the sand or gravel around them. For example, the gold in a placer deposit tends to settle out and accumulate in a stream as surrounding materials wash away.

With few exceptions, the mining of placer deposits is carried out by traditional surface (compared to underground) mining. Four general methods are in use. The oldest and perhaps most familiar to the general public is the hand method. Placerville, California, commemorates by its name the type of mining that was done during the Gold Rush of 1849. As the worker rocks his or her box or pans back and forth, clay and sand are washed away, and the heavier gold (or other minerals) settles to the bottom. This method is less used today since deposits with which it works best have been largely depleted.

Artificial streams of water are used in a second method of placer mining—hydraulic mining. In this process, intense streams of water are directed with large hoses at a placer deposit. The water washes away the overlying sand and clay, leaving behind the desired mineral.

A number of variations of this procedure exists. In some cases, a natural stream is diverted from its course and directed against a placer deposit. The action of the stream substitutes for that of a hose in the traditional hydraulic method. In another variation, a stream may be dammed rather than diverted. When the dam is broken, the penned-up water is released all at once with a force that can tear apart a placer deposit. This technique is known as "booming" a deposit and although it is no longer used in the United States, the method is used around the world.

An increasingly popular approach to placer mining makes use of familiar **surface mining** machinery used to extract **coal** and other minerals. This machinery is often very large and efficient. It removes **overburden**, extracts mineral-containing earths with streams of water and then separates and processes the extracted material by gravity methods.

A fourth method of mining is used with deposits underwater, as in a lake or along the seashore. In this process, a large machine somewhat similar to a surface mining excavator is placed on a barge. The machine then scoops materials off the lake, stream, or ocean bottom and carries them to a processing area on another part of the barge. This type of dredging machine might be thought of as a very large, mechanized version of the old prospector's gold pan and rocker box.

Placer mining poses two kinds of environmental problems. The first is one that is common to all types of surface mining, the disturbance of land. Federal law now requires that land disturbed by surface mining such as placer mining be restored to a condition that approximates its original state.

The extensive use of water during placer mining is a second source of concern. By its nature, placer mining produces huge flows of water that have become contaminated with mud, sand, and other **suspended solids**. As this water is dumped into natural waterways, these solids may damage aquatic plant and animal life and, as they settle out, create new navigational hazards. In the United States, the **Clean Water Act**s and other environmental laws carry provisions to reduce the potential harm posed by placer mining.

[*David E. Newton*]

FURTHER READING

"Mining Companies Urged to Provide for Wildlife Habitats." *Engineering and Mining Journal* 194 (April 1993): 16.

Pynn, L. "The Legacy of Klondike Gold: Strange Things Done to the Landscape by the Men and Women Who Moil for Gold." *Canadian Geographic* 112 (May-June 1992): 52-61.

Sinclair, J. *Quarrying, Opencast and Alluvial Mining.* New York: Elsevier, 1969.

Wuerthner, G. "Hard Rock and Heap Leach." *Wilderness* 55 (Summer 1992): 14-21.

Plankton

Organisms that live in the water column, drifting with the currents. Bacteria, **fungi**, algae, protozoans, invertebrates, and some vertebrates are represented, some organisms spending only parts of their lives (e.g. larval stages) as members of the plankton. Plankton is a relative term since many planktonic organisms possess some means by which they may control their horizontal and/or vertical positions. For example, organisms may possess paddle-like flagella for propulsion over short distances, or they may regulate their vertical distributions in the water column by producing oil droplets or gas bubbles. Plankton comprise a major item in aquatic **food chain/web**s. *See also* Phytoplankton; Zooplankton

Plant pathology

Plant pathology is the study of plant diseases. The most common causes of plant diseases are bacteria, **fungi**, algae, **virus**es, and roundworms. Plant diseases can drastically affect a country's economy. They may be responsible for the loss of up to ten percent of human crops each year. Plant pathology is also important in environmental studies. Many plants are especially sensitive to pollutants in the air and water. They can be used as "early warning systems" of **pollution** problems that may affect humans as well. For example, **ozone** at a concentration of only 0.005 parts per million produces noticeable changes in **tobacco** plants.

Plasma

The term plasma has two major definitions in science. In biology, it refers to the clear, straw-colored liquid portion of blood. In physics, it refers to a state of matter in which atoms are completely ionized. By this definition, a plasma consists entirely of separate positive and negative **ion**s. Plasmas of this kind exist only at high temperatures. The study of plasma is extremely important in research on **nuclear fusion**. One of the most difficult problems in that research is to find ways of physically containing a plasma in which fusion reactions are occurring.

Plastics

The term plastic refers to any material that can be shaped or molded. In this sense, ordinary clay or a soft wax is a plastic material. Perhaps more commonly, plastic has become the term used to describe a class of synthetic materials more accurately known in chemistry as polymers. Some common examples of plastics are the polyethylenes, polystyrenes, vinyl polymers, methyl methacrylates, and polyesters. These synthetic materials may or may not be "plastic" in the pliable sense.

Research on plastic-like materials began in the mid-nineteenth century. At first, this research made use of natural materials. Credit for discovery of the first synthetic plastic is often given to the American inventor, John Wesley Hyatt. In 1869, Hyatt was awarded a patent for the manufacture of a hard, tough material made out a natural cellulose. He called the product "celluloid."

It was not until 1907, however, that an entirely synthetic plastic was invented. In that year, the Belgian-American chemist Leo Baekeland discovered a new compound that was hard, water- and solvent-resistant and electrically non-conductive. He named the product Bakelite. Almost immediately, the new material was put to use in the manufacture of buttons, radio cases, telephone equipment, knife handles, counter tops, cameras, and dozens of other products.

Today, thousands of different plastics are known. Their importance is illustrated by the fact that of the 50 **chemicals** produced in the greatest volume in the United States, 24 are used in the production of polymers. Products that were unknown until the 1920s are now manufactured by the millions of tons each year in the United States.

Despite the bewildering variety of plastics now available, most can be classified in one of a small number of ways. First, all plastics can be categorized as thermoplastic or thermosetting. A thermoplastic polymer is one that, after being formed, can be re-heated and re-shaped. If you warm the handle of a toothbrush in a flame, for example, you can bend it into another shape. A thermosetting polymer is different, however, since, once formed, it can be re-heated, but not re-shaped.

Polymers can also be classified according to the chemical reaction by which they are formed. Addition polymers are formed when one kind of molecule reacts with a second molecule of the same kind. This type of reaction can occur only when the molecules involved contain a special grouping of atoms containing double or triple bonds.

As an example one molecule of ethylene can react with a second molecule of ethylene. This reaction can continue, with a third ethylene molecule adding to the product. In fact, this reaction can be repeated many times until a very large molecule, polyethylene, results.

The prefix *poly*- means "many" indicating that many molecules of ethylene were used in its production. In the formation of a polymer like polyethylene, "many" can be equal to a few hundred or few thousand ethylene molecules. The basic unit of which the polymer is made (ethylene, in this case) is called the monomer. The process by which monomers combine with each other many times is known as polymerization.

A second type of polymer, the condensation polymer, is formed when two different molecules combine with each other through the loss of some small molecule, most commonly, water. For example, Baekeland's original Bakelite is made by the reaction between a molecule of phenol and a molecule of formaldehyde. Phenol and formaldehyde fragments condense to make a new molecule (C_6H_5CHO) when water is removed. As with the formation of polyethylene, this reaction can repeat hundreds or thousands of times to make a very large molecule.

The names of polymers often reveal how they are made. For example, polyethylene is made by the polymerization of ethylene, polypropylene by the polymerization of propylene, and polyvinyl chloride by the polymerization of vinyl chloride. The names of other polymers give no hint as to the way they are formed. One would not guess, for example, that nylon is a condensation polymer of adipic acid and hexamethylene diamine or that Teflon is an addition polymer of tetrafluorethylene.

Listing all the uses to which plastics have been put is probably impossible. Such a list would include squeeze bottles, electrical insulation, film, indoor-outdoor carpeting, floor tile, garden hoses, pipes for plumbing, trash bags, fabrics, latex paints, adhesives, contact lenses, boat hulls, gaskets, non-stick pan coatings, insulation, dinnerware, and table tops.

Plastics technology has become highly sophisticated in the last few decades. Rarely is a simple polymer used by itself in a product. Instead, all types of additives are available for giving the polymer special properties. Ultraviolet stabilizers, as one example, are added to absorb ultraviolet light that would otherwise attack the polymer itself. Many polymers become stiff and brittle when exposed to ultraviolet light.

Plasticizers are compounds that make a polymer more flexible. Foaming agents are used to convert a polymer to the kind of foam used in insulation or cooler chests. Fillers are materials like clay, alumina, or carbon black that add properties such as color, flame resistance, hardness, or chemical resistance to a plastic.

Some of the most widely used additives are reinforcing agents. These are fibers made of **carbon**, boron, glass, or some other material that add strength to a plastic. Reinforced plastics find application in car bodies and boat hulls and in many kinds of sporting equipment such as football helmets, tennis rackets, and bicycle frames.

One of the most interesting new variations in polymer properties is the development of conducting polymers. Until 1970, the word plastic was nearly synonymous with electrical non-conductance. In fact, one important use of plastics has been as electrical insulation. In 1970, however, a Korean university student accidentally produced a form of polyacetylene that conducts electricity.

For a number of reasons, that discovery did not lead to a commercial product until 1975. Then, two researchers at the University of Pennsylvania discovered that adding a small amount of iodine to polyacetylene increases its conductivity a trillion times.

A number of technical problems remain, but the day of plastic batteries is no longer a part of the distant future. Indeed, scientists are now studying dozens of ways in which conduction plastics can be substituted for metals in a variety of applications.

For all their many advantages, plastics have long posed some difficult problems for the **environment**. Perhaps the most serious of those problems, is their stability. Since plastics have not occurred in nature for very long, microorganisms that can degrade them have not yet had an opportunity to evolve. Thus, plastic objects that are discarded may tend to remain in the environment for hundreds or thousands of years.

Sometimes, this problem translates into one of sheer volume. In 1988, for example 19.9 percent by volume of all municipal **solid waste**s consisted of plastic products. That translated into 14.4 million tons of waste products, third only to paper products and yard and food wastes. At other times, the stability of plastics is actually life-threatening to various organisms. Stories of aquatic birds who are strangled by plastic beer can holders are no longer news because they occur so often.

The presence of plastics can interfere with some of the methods suggested for dealing with solid wastes. For example, **incineration** has been recommended as a way of getting rid of wastes and producing energy at the same time. But the combustion of some types of plastics results in the release of toxic hydrochloric acid, hydrogen cyanide, and other hazardous gases.

Scientists are now moving forward in the search for ways of dealing with waste plastic materials. Some success has been achieved, for example in the development of **photodegradable plastics**, polymers that degrade when exposed to light. One problem with such materials is that they are often buried in **landfills** and are never exposed to sunlight.

Research also continues to progress on the **recycling** of plastics. A major problem here is that some kinds of polymers are more easily recycled than others, and separating one type from the other is often difficult to accomplish in everyday practice.

The use of plastics is also interconnected with the world's energy problems. In the first place, the manufacture of most plastics is energy intensive. It takes only 24 million Btu to make one ton of steel, but 49 million Btu to make one ton of polyvinyl chloride and 106 million Btu to make one ton of low-density polyethylene.

Perhaps even more important is the fact that **petroleum** provides the raw materials from which the great majority of plastics are made. Thus, as our supplies of petroleum dwindle, as they inevitable will, scientists will have to find new ways to produce plastics. While they will probably be able to meet that challenge, the change-over from an industry based on petroleum to one based on other raw materials is likely to be long, expensive, and disruptive.

[*David E. Newton*]

FURTHER READING

Denison, R. A., and J. Wirka. *Degradable Plastics: The Wrong Answer to the Right Question*. New York: Environmental Defense Fund, 1989.

Joesten, M. D., et al. *World of Chemistry*. Philadelphia: Saunders, 1991.

Selinger, B. *Chemistry in the Marketplace*. 4th ed. Sydney: Harcourt Brace Jovanovich, 1989.

Williams, A. L., H. D. Embree, and H. J. DeBey. *Introduction to Chemistry*. 3rd ed. Reading, MA: Addison-Wesley, 1981.

Plate tectonics

Anyone who looks carefully at a map of the Atlantic Ocean is likely to be struck by an interesting point. The eastern coastline of South America bears a striking similarity to the western coastline of Africa. Indeed, it looks almost as if the two continents could somehow fit together—provided, of course, one could find a way to slide the land masses across the ocean floor.

The match of coastlines was noticed by scholars almost as soon as good maps were first available in the late fifteenth century. In 1620, for example, the English philosopher Sir **Francis Bacon** commented on this fact and argued that the match was "no mere accidental occurrence."

One obvious explanation for the South America-Africa fit was that the two continents had once been connected and had somehow become separated in the past. A few early scientists tried to use the Biblical story of The Flood to show how that might have happened. But as Biblical explanations for natural phenomena began to lose credibility, this approach was discarded.

That made the concept of moving continents even more difficult to believe. The earth's crust was generally thought to be solid and immoveable. How could one or two whole continents somehow slide through such a material?

Yet, over time, more and more evidence began to accumulate, supporting the notion that South America and Africa might once have been joined to each other. Much of that early evidence came from the research of the German geographer, Alexander von Humboldt. Von Humboldt spent a number of years traveling through South America, Africa, and other parts of the world. In his journeys, he collected plant and animal specimens and studied geological and geographic patterns. He was struck by the many similarities he observed between South America and Africa, similarities that went far beyond an obvious geographic fit of continental coastlines.

For example, he observed that mountain ranges in Brazil that end at the sea appear to match other mountain ranges in Africa that began at the coastline. He noted similar patterns among mountain ranges in Europe and North America.

During the nineteenth century, similarities among **fauna** and **flora** on either side of the Atlantic were observed. Although **species** in eastern South America do differ to some extent from those in western Africa, their similarities are often striking. Before long, similarities across other oceanic gaps began to be noted. Plant and animal fossils found in India, for example, were often remarkably similar to those found in Australia.

Attempts to explain the many similarities in various continental properties were consistently stymied by the beliefs that the earth's crust was solid and immoveable. One way around this problem was the suggestion that mammoth land bridges existed between continents. These large bridges would have allowed the movement of plants and animals from one continent to another. But no evidence for such bridges could be found, and this idea eventually fell into disrepute.

By the mid-1850s, an important breakthrough in geological thought began to occur. A few geologists started to accept the hypothesis that the earth's crust is not as solid and immovable as it appears. In fact, they said, it may be that the earth's outer layer is actually floating (and, thus, is moveable) on the layer below it, the mantle.

Still, it was not until the early years of the twentieth century that a new theory of "floating continents" was seriously proposed. Then, in a period of less than four years, two distinct theories of this kind were suggested. The first was offered in a December 29, 1908, paper by the American geologist Frank B. Taylor. Taylor outlined a theory that described how the continents had slowly shifted over time with a "mighty creeping movement."

Taylor's paper met largely with indifference. Such was not the fate, however, of the ideas of a German astronomer and meteorologist, Alfred Wegener. While browsing through the University of Marburg library in the fall of 1911, Wegener was introduced to the problem of continental similarities. Almost immediately, he decided to devote his attention to this question and began a study that was to dominate the rest of his professional life and to revolutionize the field of geology.

By January 1912, Wegener had developed a theory to explain continental similarities. Such similarities cannot be explained by sunken land bridges, he said, but are the result of continents having moved slowly across the face of the planet. Three more years of research were needed before Wegener's theory was completed. In 1915, he published *The Origins of Continents and Oceans*, summarizing his ideas about continental similarities.

According to Wegener's theory, the continents were once part of one large land mass, which he called Pangaea. Eventually this land mass broke into two parts, two supercontinents, which he called Gondwanaland and Laurasia. Over millions of years, Gondwanaland broke apart into South America, Africa, India, Australia, and **Antarctica**, he suggested, while Laurasia separated into North America and Eurasia.

The basic problem Wegener faced was to explain how huge land masses like continents can flow. His answer was

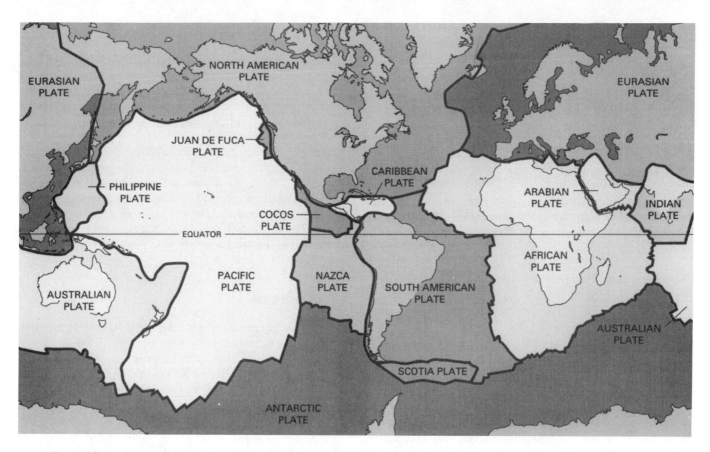

The world's tectonic plates.

that the materials of which the earth's crust is made are of two very different types. One, then call "sial," is relatively light, but strong. The other, then called "sima," can be compared to very thick tar. Continents are made of sial, he said, and sea floors of sima. The differences in these materials allows continents to "ride" very slowly across sea floors.

Wegener's theory was met with both rejection and hostility. Fellow scientists not only disagreed with his ideas, but also attacked him personally even for suggesting the ideas. The theory of continental drift did not totally disappear as a result of these attitudes, but it fell into disfavor for more than three decades.

Research dating to the mid-1930s revealed new features of the sea floor which made Wegener's theory more plausible. Scientists found sections of the ocean bottoms through which flows of hot lava were escaping from the mantle, somewhat like underwater **volcano**es. These discoveries provided a crucial clue in the development of plate tectonics, the modern theory of continental drift.

According to the theory of plate tectonics, the upper layer of the earth is made of a number of plates, large sections of crust, and the upper mantle. About ten major plates have been identified. The largest plate is the Pacific Plate, underlying the Pacific Ocean. The North and South American, Eurasian, African, Indian, Australian, Nazca, Arabian, Caribbean, and Antarctica are the other major plates.

Scientists believe that plates rest on an especially plastic portion of the mantle known as the "asthenosphere."

Hot magma from the asthenosphere seeps upward and escapes through the ocean floor by way of openings known as rifts. As the magma flows out of the rift, it pushes apart the plates adjoining the rift. The edge of the plate opposite the rift is ultimately forced downward, back into the asthenosphere. The region in which plate material moves down into the mantle is a trench.

Plates move at different speeds in different directions at different times. On an average, they travel 0.4 to 2 inches (1-5 cm) per year. To the extent that this theory is correct, a map of the earth's surface ten million years from now will look quite different from the way it does now.

The theory of plate tectonics explains a number of natural phenomena that had puzzled scientists for centuries. Earthquakes, for example, can often be explained as the sudden, rather than gradual, movement of two adjacent plates. One of the world's most famous earthquake zones, the San Andreas Fault, lies at the boundary of the Pacific and the North American plates. Volcanoes often accompany the movement of plates and earthquakes. The boundaries of the Pacific Plate, for example, define a region where volcanoes are very common, a region sometimes called the Ring of Fire.

Plate tectonics is now accepted as one of the fundamental theories of geology. Its success depends not only on the discovery of an adequate explanation for continental movement (sea-floor spreading, rifts, and trenches), but also on the discovery of more and more similarities between continents.

For example, modern geologists have re-examined Humboldt's ideas about the correlation of mountain ranges in South America and Africa. They have found that rock strata, or layers, in Brazil lie almost exactly where they should be expected if strata in Ghana are projected to the west. If the Atlantic Ocean could somehow be removed, the two strata could be made to coincide almost perfectly.

Some interesting data have come from studies of paleomagnetism also. Paleomagnetism refers to the orientation of iron crystals in very old rock. Since the earth's magnetic poles have shifted over time, so has the orientation of iron crystals in rock. Scientists have found that the orientation of iron crystals in one continent correspond very closely to those found in rocks of another continent thousands of miles away.

Fossils continue to be a crucial way of confirming continental drift. For example, scientists have learned that the fossil population of is much less like the fossil population of Africa (300 miles [483 km] to the west) than it is like the fossil population of India (3,000 miles/4,830 km to the northeast). This finding would make almost no sense at all unless one recognized that the theory of continental drift has Madagascar breaking off from India millions of years ago, not off Africa.

The flow of magma out of the asthenosphere often results in the formation of ores, regions that are rich in some mineral. For example, the high temperatures characteristic of a rift or a trench may be sufficient to cause the release of metals from their compounds. The flow of magma across rock may also result in a phenomenon known as contact metamorphism, a mechanism that also results in the formation of metals such as **lead** and silver. *See also* Biogeography; Endemic species; Evolution; Geosphere; Topography

[*David E. Newton*]

FURTHER READING

McGraw-Hill Encyclopedia of Science & Technology. 7th ed. New York: McGraw-Hill, 1992.

Miller, R., and the Editors of Time-Life Books. *Continents in Collision.* Alexandria, VA: Time-Life Books, 1983.

Moran, J. M., M. D. Morgan, and J. H. Wiersma. *Environmental Science.* Dubuque, IA: W. C. Brown, 1993.

Plow pan

A plow pan is a subsurface horizon or **soil** layer having a high bulk density and a lower total porosity than the soil directly above or below it as a result of pressure applied by normal tillage operations, such as plows, discs, and other tillage implements. Plow pans may also be called pressure pans, tillage pans, or traffic pans. Plow pans are not cemented by organic matter or **chemicals**. Plow pans are the result of pressure exerted by humans, whereas hard pans occur naturally. *See also* Soil compaction

Plume

A flowing, often somewhat conical, trail of **emission**s from a continuous **point source**, for example the plume of **smoke** from a chimney. As a plume spreads, its constituents are diluted into the surrounding medium. When plumes disperse in media with high turbulence, they can take on more complex shapes with loops and meanders. This somewhat chaotic nature has lead to probabilistic descriptions of the concentration of materials in plumes; for example, calculations concerning the downstream impact of pollutants released from pipes and chimneys will be couched in terms of average concentrations. Typically plumes are found in air or water, but plumes of trace contaminants may also be found in less-mobile media such as **soil**s.

Plutonium

A synthetically produced transuranium element. It does not exist in measurable amounts in the earth's crust. Glenn Seaborg and his colleagues at the University of California at Berkeley first prepared this element in 1940. Plutonium is by far the most important of all transuranium elements because one of its **isotope**s, plutonium-239, can be fissioned. Plutonium-239 is the only isotope other than **uranium**-235 that is readily available for use in **nuclear weapons** and nuclear reactors. Unfortunately plutonium is also one of the most toxic substances known to humans, making its commercial use a serious environmental hazard. With a **half-life** of 24,000 years, the isotope presents difficult disposal problems. *See also* Nuclear fission; Nuclear power

Poaching

Poaching is the stealing of game or fish from private property or from a place where shooting, trapping or fishing rights are reserved. Until the twentieth century, most poaching was subsistence hunting or fishing to augment scanty diets. Today, poaching is usually committed for sport or profit.

The **Fish and Wildlife Service** estimates that illegal trade in U.S. **wildlife** generates $200 million per year, a hefty slice of a $1.5 billion worldwide market. Big **game animal**s are shot as trophies, and animal parts such as bear gallbladders are sold for "medicinal" purposes—usually as tonics to enhance male virility. Poaching also attracts organized crime because wildlife crime sentences, if tendered, tend to be lenient and probation requirements are difficult to enforce.

Poaching has a long history in this country: spotlighting a deer at night or shooting a duck in the family pond for dinner have long been a part of rural life. Today, despite a 94 percent conviction rate for those caught, poachers feed a demand for wildlife on both domestic and global markets. They decapitate walruses for ivory tusks, net thousands of night-roosting robins for Cajun gumbo, and shoot anhingas nesting in the **Everglades** and raptors for decorative feathers. **Wolves** are

A poached rhinoceros with its horn removed.

tracked and shot from airplanes. Sturgeon and paddlefish are caught and killed for their caviar. Poaching poses a serious threat to wildlife because it kills off the biggest and best of a species' **gene pool**. A report by the Fish and Wildlife Service estimates that 3,600 threatened or **endangered species** receive little or no federal protection.

The **extinction** of the Labrador duck in the 1880s and the near extinction of a dozen other waterfowl **species** led to the U.S.-Canadian Migratory Bird Treaty Act of 1918. The enactment of kill limits and the ban on commercial market hunting helped populations of birds. The U.S. **Marine Mammal Protection Act** of 1972 makes it a crime for non-Native Americans to hunt or sell walruses, **sea otter**s, **seals and sea lions**, and polar bears. And the Lacey Act, passed in 1990, makes it a federal crime to transport illegally taken wildlife across state lines.

The sale of bear parts is legal in some states, creating a convenient outlet for poachers. Since merchandise such as bear meat, galls, and paws is difficult to track, the poachers are fairly safe. Uniform regulations in all 50 states would create a more difficult environment for poachers to operate in and might lead to a decrease in poaching, especially of bears.

As economic and political instability increased in many developing countries, so did poaching. A global demand for ivory caused wholesale slaughter of **elephants** and **rhinoceros**. As the big male elephants disappeared, poachers turned to females, the primary caretakers of the young. To help stop the carnage of elephant and rhinoceros for their

ivory, 105 nations party to the **Convention on International Trade in Endangered Species of Wild Fauna and Flora (CITES)** have agreed to ban the raw ivory trade. The ban has caused ivory prices to plummet to pre-1970s levels, making poaching much less attractive. In Zimbabwe, game wardens now also have orders to shoot on sight poachers who menace the rare black rhino. *See also* Grizzly bear

[*Linda Rehkopf*]

FURTHER READING

Chadwick, D. H. *Fate of the Elephant.* San Francisco: Sierra Club Books, 1992.

Hyman, R. "Check the Fine Print, Mate." *International Wildlife* 23 (January-February 1993): 22-5.

Manry, D., and U. Hirsch. "Cliff-hanger in Morocco." *International Wildlife* 23 (March-April 1993): 34-7.

Poten, C. J. "A Shameful Harvest." *National Geographic* 180 (September 1991): 106-132.

Point source

A localized, discrete, and fixed contaminant **emission** source, such as a smokestack or waste discharge pipe. Since point sources are usually easily identified, their discharges of **pollution** can be monitored readily. Point sources are distinguished from **nonpoint source**s and mobile (or vehicular)

Intensity of the
toxic stresses
decreases rapidly

Severe ecological
degradation
at point source

sources and historically were the first to receive emission controls. Some point sources release exceptionally large quantities of contaminants. For example, a smelter in **Sudbury, Ontario**, was for many years the largest single source of **sulfur dioxide** in North America, emitting several million tons of pollutants annually through a smokestack over 1,247 feet (380 m) tall.

Pollination

Pollination is the process of moving pollen grains, which contain male sex cells, from the anthers (the pollen-containing part of floral stamens, the male reproductive structure) of flowers to the stigma (the glandular female receptive portion) in the pistil (female reproductive organ). When a pollen grain lands on the female part of the flower, the male sex cell joins with the female sex cells in the flower in a process called fertilization to form a seed from which a new plant can grow. The anthers and stigma can be on the same flower (self-pollination) or on different flowers (cross-pollination), but must be of the same species. All higher plants, including flowers, herbs, bushes, grasses, conifers, and broad-leaved trees, use pollination for sexual reproduction.

Pollination can be accomplished by abiotic means such as wind and water. Many pollen grains are small (less than 0.05 mm, or 0.002 in). Thus wind can carry the pollen grains to other members of their species. Many plants, to ensure pollination, grow in dense stands and produce millions of pollen grains. Wind-pollinated plants generally have small, inconspicuous flowers that dangle in the wind (e.g., willow

catkins). Grasses have wispy plume-like flowers that catch grains floating in the air. Some water plants such as the hornwort have their pollen transferred by water currents.

Many plants use animals such as insects, birds, and bats to transport pollen grains. This process, referred to as biotic pollination, requires a relationship between the pollinator and the flower to be pollinated. Such a relationship is usually established by some kind of direct attractant, such as nectar, sweet-tasting pollen, odor, or visual attraction (e.g., brightly-colored flowers). There may also be an indirect attraction, such as when insects of prey visit flowers to catch other visiting pollinators.

Insects, including bees, beetles, flies, wasps, ants, butterflies, and moths, are common biotic pollinators. As an insect crawls in and out of flowers in its search for nectar or other food source, it receives a dusting of pollen grains from the anther, the male part. When the insect visits another flower, the pollen rubs off on the stigma, the female part. If the pollen is left on the same species of flower, a long tube grows from each pollen grain down the stalk (style) of the stigma and into the ovule at the base, which contains the female egg cells. The male cells from the pollen grains pass along the tubes to the female cells and fertilize them. Plants with trumpet-shaped flowers, such as petunias, have nectar at the bottom, so only insects with long tube-like tongues can act as their pollinators.

The best-known and best-adapted biotic pollinator is the bee. The bee is a relatively large insect with a large demand for food both for itself and for its carefully looked-after brood. It normally gets all of its food from flower blossoms. The bee has an ability to remember plant forms, which aids in its ability to find flowers. Social bees live together in a communal nest and often share foraging and nest activities. The amount of food carried into a hive by a honeybee has been estimated to be 100 times its own requirements. Social bees have developed communication systems that permit them to inform each other about the location and sources of food. These communication systems include odor paths, special buzz tones to alert other individuals, and dances that can indicate direction, distance to, and yield of a source of food. However, most of the world's 40,000 species of bees are solitary. The female bee mates and then constructs a nest underground or within woody stems containing many smooth-walled cells. The cells are filled with a mixture of nectar and pollen, which provides all the food required for larvae to complete their development into adult bees.

Biotic pollination may also be accomplished by such animals as birds and bats. For example, hummingbirds feeding from the hibiscus flower carry pollen on their beak and heads. Bats hover in front of flowers that open at night, licking nectar and covering their faces with pollen. Successful pollination, often mediated by animals but also accomplished abiotically, is extremely important for food production as well as maintenance of biological plant diversity. Pollination of plants is necessary for seed set, fruit yields, and reproduction of most food crops.

Many threats to animal pollinators and pollination processes have been identified. These include use of toxic chemicals, decline in pollinator populations, habitat loss, and migratory corridor fragmentation. Toxic chemicals can kill pollinators, and wild pollinators are often more vulnerable to insecticides and herbicides than domestic honeybees. Laws regulate and control the use of many pesticides during periods when pollinators are foraging, and use of toxic chemicals near pollinators' nesting sites should also be controlled. **Pesticide**s that are known to be less toxic to pollinators can be used to reduce stress on pollinator populations. Fewer pollinators will result in fewer plants. When factors such as the use of pesticides and **habitat fragmentation** reduce populations of pollinators, plants will have low reproductive success. Some endangered plant species may even become extinct. Appropriate pesticide spraying set-back distances should be based on on-site determinations made by pollination ecologists familiar with the plant and pollinator species involved.

Another threat to pollination processes is the decline in honeybee populations. Since 1990, U.S. beekeepers have lost one-fifth of their domestic managed honeybee colonies for reasons that include two kinds of mite infestations, diseases, spraying of pesticides, and several other factors. The *Varroa* mite is an external parasite that was identified in the United States in 1987 and affects bee colonies in thirty states. This mite lives and feeds on developing bee larvae so that when the bees hatch, they are small and deformed. *Varroa* mites can be controlled by placing medicated plastic strips inside hives to kill the mites. The bees walk on the strips and then carry the medicine on their feet to the larvae growing in the honeycomb. The tracheal mite infects the respiratory system of adult honeybees. These mites were found in the United States in 1984 and are now present in most states. These tracheal mites make bees weak and can kill an entire colony. To control the mites, an antibiotic powder, such as terramycin, is mixed into sugar and oil and is placed inside the bee hive.

Diseases and use of pesticides also take their toll on bee populations. There are several diseases that can kill bees; these include American foul brood, chalk brood, European foul brood, paralysis virus, sacbrood disease and kashmir virus. Some bacterial diseases can be treated by stirring antibiotics into feed sugar. Often, if a hive is badly infected, the hive is burned to prevent the infection of other hives. Also, the spraying of pesticides (e.g., by farmers for crop protection or by towns and communities for control of mosquitoes) when bees are foraging can result in their death. Some pesticides kill bees directly while they are in the crops, while others are carried back to the hives with the pollen, where they are stored in the honeycombs. The bees and larvae die when they eat the pollen, which can be at any time of year. Often the pesticide does not kill the entire colony, but makes the colony susceptible to mite infections or freezing in cold weather.

Several other factors have contributed to declining bee populations. Africanized bees, a type of highly defensive bee that is also known as the killer bee, became established in the United States in 1990, after years of northward migration from South America where they were first released. Beekeep-

ers often are forced to abandon their hives when Africanized bees move into an area. Also, bee populations that have been weakened by other factors are in danger of freezing in winter, due to an insufficient number of bees to provide necessary warmth; or an insufficient supply of food to convert to heat energy. Finally, loss of agricultural subsidies and price supports in the United States adversely affects the economics of managing bee colonies.

Habitat loss and the severing of migratory corridors also constitute threats to animal pollinators and pollination processes. Habitat fragmentation is the division of natural ecosystems into smaller areas due to land conversion for agriculture, forestry, and urbanization. As habitat areas become smaller and widely scattered, they may be insufficient to provide an adequate diversity of host plants and nectar sources that their pollinators require. Habitat fragmentation may also cause reduction in pollinator populations due to loss of nesting habitats. Ecologists need to monitor populations of pollinators and habitat fragmentation trends to determine possible causes of pollinator decline and to develop land use plans to protect pollinator populations such as maintenance of habitat set-asides or **greenbelts** near agricultural fields and timber areas.

The severing of migratory corridors can also disrupt pollination processes. Some pollinating animal species, such as nectarivorous bats, navigate through a variety of nectar-providing plants as they migrate from tropical to arid and temperate environments. A bat species may utilize a single type of flower in each local environment, but a series of plants are linked into a nectar corridor of successive flowering times along the bat's migration route. For example, a type of long-nosed bat flies a loop of 3,200 mi (5,152 km) to follow the sequential flowering of at least 16 flowering plants species, including tree morning glories, several century plants, and giant columnar cactus. Severing of migratory corridors by habitat and vegetation destruction or by spraying of toxic pesticides may adversely affect the success of the migration. For example, migratory monarch butterflies require critical habitats through their migratory cycle and can be affected if habitat is lost due to activities such as development. Monitoring of plant/pollinator changes in migratory corridors is required to develop appropriate protection strategies.

[*Judith L. Sims*]

FURTHER READING

Buchmann, S.L., and G.P. Nabhan. *Forgotten Pollinators.* Washington, D.C.: Island Press, 1996.

Faegri, K., and L. van der Pijl. *The Principles of Pollination Ecology*, 3rd ed (revised).

Oxford, England: Pergamon Press, 1979.

Meeuse, R.J.D. *The Story of Pollination.* New York: Ronald Press, 1961.

Pollution

Pollution can be defined as unwanted or detrimental changes in a natural system. Usually, pollution is associated with the presence of toxic **chemicals** in some large quantity, but pollution can also be caused by the presence of excess quantities of heat or by excessive fertilization with **nutrient**s.

Because pollution is judged on the basis of degradative changes, there is a strongly anthropocentric bias to its determination. In other words, humans decide whether pollution is occurring and how bad it is. Of course, this bias favors **species**, communities, and ecological processes that are especially desired or appreciated by humans. In fact, however, some other, *less-desirable* species, communities, and ecological processes may benefit from what we consider pollution.

An important aspect of the notion of pollution is that ecological change must actually be demonstrated. If some potentially polluting substance is present at a concentration or intensity that is less than the threshold required to cause a demonstrable ecological change, then the situation would be referred to as contamination, rather than pollution.

This aspect of pollution can be illustrated by reference to the stable elements, for example, **cadmium**, **copper**, **lead**, **mercury**, **nickel**, selenium, **uranium**, etc. All of these are consistently present in at least trace concentrations in the **environment**. Moreover, all of these elements are potentially toxic. However, they generally affect biota and therefore only cause pollution when they are present at water-soluble concentrations of more than about 0.01 to 1 parts per million (ppm).

Some other elements can be present in very large concentrations, for example, **aluminum** and iron, which are important constituents of rock and **soil**. Aluminum constitutes 8-10 percent of the earth's crust and iron 3-4 percent. However, almost all of the aluminum and iron present in minerals are insoluble in water and are therefore not readily assimilated by **biotic community** and cannot cause toxicity. In acidic environments, however, ionic forms of aluminum are solubilized, and these can cause toxicity in concentrations of less than one part per million. Therefore, the bio-availability of a chemical is an important determinant of whether its presence in some concentration will cause pollution.

Most instances of pollution result from the activities of humans. For example, **anthropogenic** pollution can be caused by:

(1) the **emission** of **sulfur dioxide** and metals from a **smelter**, causing toxicity to vegetation and acidifying surface waters and soil,

(2) the emission of waste heat from an electricity generating station into a river or lake, causing community change through thermal stress, or

(3) the discharge of nutrient-containing sewage wastes into a water body, causing eutrophication.

Most instances of anthropogenic pollution have natural analogues, that is, cases where pollution is not the result of human activities. For example, pollution can be caused by the emission of sulfur dioxide from **volcano**es, by the presence of toxic elements in certain types of soil, by thermal springs or vents, and by other natural phenomena. In many cases, natural pollution can cause an intensity of ecological damage that is as severe as anything caused by anthropogenic pollution. (This does not, of course, in any way justify anthropogenic pollution and its ecological effects.)

An interesting case of natural **air pollution** is the Smoking Hills, located in a remote and pristine **wilderness** in the Canadian Arctic, virtually uninfluenced by humans. However, at a number of places along the 18.63 miles (30 km) of seacoast, bituminous shales in sea cliffs have spontaneously ignited, causing a fumigation of the **tundra** with sulfur dioxide and other pollutants. The largest concentrations of sulfur dioxide (more than two parts per million) occur closest to the combustions. Further away from the sea cliffs the concentrations of sulfur dioxide decrease rapidly. The most-important chemical effects of the air pollution are **acidification** of soil and fresh water, which in turn causes a solubilization of toxic metals. Surface soils and pond waters commonly have **pH**s less than 3, compared with about pH 7 at non-fumigated places. The only reports of similarly acidic water are for volcanic lakes in Japan, in which natural pHs as acidic as 1 occur, and pH less than 2 in waters affected by drainage from coal mines.

At the Smoking Hills, toxicity by sulfur dioxide, acidity, and water-soluble metals has caused great damage to ecological communities. The most-intensively fumigated terrestrial sites have no vegetation, but further away a few pollution-tolerant species are present. About one kilometer away the toxic stresses are low enough that reference tundra is present. There are a few pollution-tolerant algae in the acidic ponds, with a depauperate community of six species occurring in the most-acidic (pH 1.8) pond in the area.

Other cases of natural pollution concern places where certain elements are present in toxic amounts. Surface mineralizations can have toxic metals present in large concentrations, for example copper at 10 percent in peat at a copper-rich spring in New Brunswick, or surface soil with three percent lead plus zinc on Baffin Island. Soils influenced by nickel-rich serpentine minerals have been well-studied by ecologists. The stress-adapted plants of serpentine **habitat**s form distinct communities, and some plants can have nickel concentrations larger than 10 percent in their tissues. Similarly, natural soils with large concentrations of selenium support plants that can hyperaccumulate this element to concentrations greater than one percent. These plants are poisonous to livestock, causing a toxic syndrome known as *blind staggers*.

Of course, there are many well-known cases where pollution is caused by anthropogenic emissions of chemicals. Some examples include:

(1) Emissions of sulfur dioxide and metals from smelters can cause damage to surrounding terrestrial and aquatic **ecosystem**s. The sulfur dioxide and metals are directly toxic. In addition, the deposition of sulfur dioxide can cause an extreme acidification of soil and water, which causes metals to be more bio-available, resulting in important, secondary toxicity. Because smelters are **point source**s of emission, the spatial pattern of chemical pollution and ecological damage displays an exponentially decreasing intensity with increasing distance from the source.

(2) The use of **pesticide**s in agriculture, forestry, and around homes can result in a non-target exposure of

birds and other **wildlife** to these chemicals. If the non-target biota are vulnerable to the pesticide, then ecological damage will result. For example, during the 1960s urban elm trees in the eastern United States were sprayed with large quantities of the insecticide **DDT**, in order to kill beetles that were responsible for the transmission of Dutch elm disease, an important **pathogen**. Because of the very large spray rates, many birds were killed, leading to reduced populations in some areas. (This was the "silent spring" that was referred to by **Rachel Carson** in her famous book by that title.) Birds and other non-target biota have also been killed by modern insecticide-spray programs in agriculture and in forestry.

(3) The deposition of acidifying substances from the atmosphere, mostly as acidic precipitation and the dry deposition of sulfur dioxide, can cause an acidification of surface waters. The acidity solubilizes metals, most notably aluminum, making them bio-available. The acidity in combination with the metals causes toxicity to the biota, resulting in large changes in ecological communities and processes. Fish, for example, are highly intolerant of acidic waters.

(4) **Oil spills** from tankers and pipelines can cause great ecological damage. When oil spilled at sea washes up onto coastlines, it destroys seaweeds, invertebrates, and fish, and their communities are changed for many years. Seabirds are very intolerant of oil and can die of hypothermia if even a small area of their feathers is coated by **petroleum**.

(5) Most of the **lead shot** fired by hunters and skeet shooters miss their target and are dispersed into the environment. Waterfowl and other avian wildlife actively ingest lead shot because it is similar in size and hardness to the grit that they ingest to aid in the mechanical abrasion of hard seeds in their gizzard. However, the lead shot is toxic to these birds, and each year millions of birds are killed by this source in North America.

Humans can also cause pollution by excessively fertilizing natural **ecosystem**s with nutrients. For example, freshwaters can be made eutrophic by fertilization with **phosphorus** in the form of phosphate. The most conspicuous symptoms of eutrophication are changes in species composition of the **phytoplankton** community and, especially, a large increase in algal **biomass**, known as a *bloom*. In shallow waterbodies there may also be a vigorous growth of vascular plants. These primary responses are usually accompanied by secondary changes at higher trophic levels, including arthropods, fish, and waterfowl, in response to greater food availability and other habitat changes. However, in the extreme cases of very eutrophic waters, the blooms of algae and other microorganisms can be noxious, producing toxic chemicals and causing periods of oxygen depletion that kill fish and other biota. Extremely eutrophic waterbodies are polluted because they often cannot support a fishery, cannot be used for drinking water, and have few recreational opportunities and poor esthetics.

Pollution, therefore, is associated with ecological degradation, caused by **environmental stress**es originating with natural phenomena or with human activities. The prevention and management of anthropogenic pollution is one of the greatest challenges facing modern society. *See also* Cultural eutrophication

[*Bill Freedman*]

FURTHER READING

Ehrlich, P. R., A. H. Ehrlich, and J. P. Holdren. *Ecoscience. Population, Resources, Environment.* San Francisco: W. H. Freeman & Co., 1977.

Freedman, Bill. *Environmental Ecology.* San Diego: Academic Press, 1989.

Speth, J. G. *Environmental Pollution: A Long-Term Perspective.* Washington, DC: World Resources Institute, 1988.

Pollution control

Pollution control is the process of reducing or eliminating the release of pollutants into the **environment**. It is regulated by various environmental agencies which establish pollutant **discharge** limits for air, water, and land.

Air pollution control strategies can be divided into two categories, the control of particulate **emissions** and the control of gaseous emissions. There are many kinds of equipment which can be used to reduce particulate emissions. Physical separation of the particulates from the air using settling chambers, **cyclone collector**s, impingers, **wet scrubbers**, electrostatic precipitators, and filtration devices, are all processes that are typically employed.

Settling chambers use gravity separation to reduce particulate emissions. The air stream is directed through a settling chamber, which is relatively long and has a large cross section, causing the velocity of the air stream to be greatly decreased and allowing sufficient time for the settling of solid particles.

A cyclone collector is a cylindrical device with a conical bottom which is used to create a tornado-like air stream. A centrifugal force is thus imparted to the particles, causing them to cling to the wall and roll downward, while the cleaner air stream exits through the top of the device.

An impinger is a device which uses the inertia of the air stream to impinge mists and dry particles on a solid surface. Mists are collected on the impinger plate as liquid forms and then drips off, while dry particles tend to build up or reenter the air stream. It is for this reason that liquid sprays are used to wash the impinger surface as well, to improve the collection efficiency.

Wet scrubbers control particulate emissions by wetting the particles in order to enhance their removal from the air stream. Wet scrubbers typically operate against the current by a water spray contacting with the gas flow. The particulate matter becomes entrained in the water droplets, and it is then separated from the gas stream. Wet scrubbers such as packed bed, venturi, or plate scrubbers utilize initial impaction, and cyclone scrubbers use a centrifugal force.

Electrostatic precipitators are devices which use an electrostatic field to induce a charge on dust particles and collect them on grounded electrodes. Electrostatic precipitators are usually operated dry, but wet systems are also used, mainly by providing a water mist to aid in the process of cleaning the particles off the collection plate.

One of the oldest and most efficient methods of particulate control, however, is filtration. The most commonly-used filtration device is known as a **baghouse** and consists of fabric bags through which the air stream is directed. Particles become trapped in the fiber mesh on the fabric bags, as well as the filter cake which is subsequently formed.

Gaseous emissions are controlled by similar devices and typically can be used in conjunction with particulate control options. Such devices include **scrubbers**, **adsorption** systems, condensers, flares, and incinerators.

Scrubbers utilize the phenomena of adsorption to remove gaseous pollutants from the air stream. There is a wide variety of scrubbers available for use, including spray towers, packed towers, and venturi scrubbers. A wide variety of solutions can be used in this process as absorbing agents. Lime, magnesium oxide, and sodium hydroxide are typically used.

Adsorption can also be used to control gaseous emissions. Activated **carbon** is commonly used as an adsorbent in configurations such as fixed bed and fluidized bed adsorbers.

Condensers operate in a manner so as to condense vapors by either increasing the pressure or decreasing the temperature of the gas stream. Surface condensers are usually of the shell-and-tube type, and contact condensers provide physical contact between the vapors, coolant, and condensate inside the unit.

Flaring and **incineration** take advantage of the combustibility of a gaseous pollutant. In general, excess air is added to these processes to drive the **combustion** reaction to completion, forming **carbon dioxide** and water.

Another means of controlling both particulate and gaseous air pollutant emission can be accomplished by modifying the process which generates these pollutants. For example, modifications to process equipment or raw materials can provide effective source reduction. Also, employing fuel cleaning methods such as desulfurization and increasing fuel-burning efficiency can lessen air emissions.

Water pollution control methods can be subdivided into physical, chemical, and biological treatment systems. Most treatment systems use combinations of any of these three technologies. Additionally, **water conservation** is a beneficial means to reduce the volume of **wastewater** generated.

Physical treatment systems are processes which rely on physical forces to aid in the removal of pollutants. Physical processes which find frequent use in water pollution control include screening, filtration, **sedimentation**, and flotation. Screening and filtration are similar methods which are used to separate coarse solids from water. Suspended particles are also removed from water with the use of sedimentation processes. Just as in air pollution control, sedimentation devices utilize gravity to remove the heavier particles from the water stream. The wide array of sedimentation basins in use

slow down the water velocity in the unit to allow time for the particles to drop to the bottom. Likewise, flotation uses differences in particle densities, which in this case are lower than water, to effect removal. Fine gas bubbles are often introduced to assist this process; they attach to the particulate matter, causing them to rise to the top of the unit where they are mechanically removed.

Chemical treatment systems in water pollution control are those processes which utilize chemical reactions to remove water pollutants or to form other, less toxic, compounds. Typical chemical treatment processes are chemical precipitation, adsorption, and disinfection reactions. Chemical precipitation processes utilize the addition of **chemicals** to the water in order to bring about the precipitation of dissolved solids. The solid is then removed by a physical process such as sedimentation or filtration. Chemical precipitation processes are often used for the removal of heavy metals and **phosphorus** from water streams. Adsorption processes are used to separate soluble substances from the water stream. Like air pollution adsorption processes, activated carbon is the most widely used adsorbent. Water may be passed through beds of granulated activated carbon (GAC), or powdered activated carbon (PAC) may be added in order to facilitate the removal of dissolved pollutants. Disinfection processes selectively destroy disease-causing organisms such as bacteria and **virus**es. Typical disinfection agents include **chlorine**, **ozone**, and **ultraviolet radiation**.

Biological water pollution control methods are those which utilize biological activity to remove pollutants from water streams. These methods are used for the control of biodegradable organic chemicals, as well as **nutrient**s such as **nitrogen** and phosphorus. In these systems, microorganisms consisting mainly of bacteria convert carbonaceous matter as well as cell tissue into gas. There are two main groups of microorganisms which are used in biological treatment, **aerobic** and **anaerobic** microorganisms. Each requires unique environmental conditions to do its job. Aerobic processes occur in the absence of oxygen. Both processes may be utilized whether the microorganisms exist in a suspension or are attached to a surface. These processes are termed suspended growth and fixed film processes, respectively.

Solid pollution control methods which are typically used include landfilling, **composting**, and incineration. Sanitary **landfill**s are operated by spreading the **solid waste** in compact layers which are separated by a thin layer of **soil**. Aerobic and anaerobic microorganisms help to break down the **biodegradable** substances in the landfill and produce carbon dioxide and **methane** gas which is typically venter to the surface. Landfills also generate a strong wastewater called leachate which must be collected and treated to avoid **groundwater** contamination.

Composting of solid wastes is the microbiological biodegradation of organic matter under either aerobic or anaerobic conditions. This process is most applicable for readily biodegradable solids such as sewage **sludge**, paper, food waste, and household garbage, including garden waste and organic matter. This process can be carried out in static pile, agitated beds, or a variety of reactors.

In an incineration process, solids are burned in large furnaces thereby reducing the volume of solid wastes which enter landfills, as well as reducing the possibility of groundwater contamination. Incineration residue can also be used for metal reclamation. These systems are typically supplemented with air pollution control devices. *See also* Air pollution index; Air quality criteria; Clean Air Act; Clean Water Act; Emission standards; Heavy metals and heavy metal poisoning; Industrial waste treatment; Primary standards; Secondary standards; Sewage treatment; Water quality standards

[*James W. Patterson*]

FURTHER READING

Advanced Emission Control for Power Plants. Paris: Organization for Economic Cooperation and Development, 1993.

Handbook of Air Pollution Technology. New York: Wiley, 1984.

Jorgensen, E. P., ed. *The Poisoned Well: New Strategies for Groundwater Protection.* Washington, DC: Island Press, 1989.

Kenworthy, L., and E. Schaeffer. *A Citizen's Guide to Promoting Toxic Waste Reduction.* New York: INFORM, 1990.

Wentz, C. A. *Hazardous Waste Management.* New York: McGraw-Hill, 1989.

Pollution control costs and benefits

There is a long-running debate over the costs of **pollution control** and the benefits to residents. A central part of this debate is the question of who should pay for pollution control—those who pollute or those who would benefit from decreased pollution.

In 1990, the **Environmental Protection Agency (EPA)** released the results of a nationwide study on the costs of pollution control. The study compared the costs from 1972 through the year 2000 for programs designed to control **air pollution**, **water pollution**, and **radioactive pollution**, as well as land, chemical, and multimedia pollution.

The EPA study found that total clean-up costs are still increasing, but they are doing so at a slower rate. The yearly rate of increase in total costs decreased from 14 percent of the gross national product to just around seven percent by the late 1980s. In 1972, the private sector bore 61.2 percent of all pollution control costs in the United States; local governments paid for 29 percent, states for 5.8 percent, and the EPA paid for 3.7 percent.

But by the 1980s, the percentage of pollution-control costs borne by state and local governments had dropped to 3.8 percent and 22.2 percent respectively, while the share borne by the EPA had risen to 7.9 percent and that of other federal agencies to 3.3 percent. Future projections indicate that there will be a rapid growth in the federal share, with declining contributions from all other sources.

From 1975 to 1987, total annual capital expenditures to clean up pollution were stable at about 25 billion to 30 billion dollars. From 1988 to 1992 the costs were expected to significantly higher, up to 46 billion dollars, due to the costs to clean up military and nuclear waste sites by the **U.S. Department of Energy** and the U.S. Department of

Defense. Between 1993 and 2000, the expenditures are expected to drop to roughly 39 billion dollars.

In reporting total expenditures, the EPA has claimed that the nation's pollution problems continue to diminish, but it has not been able to place a price on the benefit to individuals. According to the report: "Pollution controls have resulted in substantial and valuable national benefits in improved human health, recreational opportunities, visibility, and general environmental integrity. An ideal comparison of the costs and benefits of pollution control would require that these benefits be identified, quantified, and priced. This is an extremely difficult and data-intensive task and far beyond the scope of this analysis."

Some studies have determined the benefits of pollution control. A study conducted in Los Angeles identified and quantified the benefits of cleaning up the city's air. Conducted in 1989, the study estimated the cost to business for such a program at 13 billion dollars a year, but the benefits from reducing eye irritation and headaches alone could be as high as nine billion dollars annually. The study did not figure the benefits to the environment, or to those who suffer from disorders other than eye and head problems.

Many experts have argued that the cost of preventing or repairing environmental damage by industrial pollution must ultimately be met by the consumer. In Great Britain, for example, the cost of fitting gas-cleaning devices to 12 **coal**-fired electricity generating stations would exceed 2,000 million pounds in 1986. The price of electricity to the consumer would have increased about four percent. *See also* Clean Air Act; Clean Water Act; Comprehensive Environmental Response, Compensation and Liability Act; Los Angeles Basin; Superfund Amendments and Reauthorization Act

[*Linda Rehkopf*]

FURTHER READING

Carlin, A., P. F. Scodari, and D. H. Garner. "Environmental Investments: The Costs of Cleaning Up." *Environment* 34 (March 1992): 12-27.

"Emission Zero: Profits One." *Business Week* (30 December 1991): 86-93.

Krupnick, A. J., and P. R. Portney. "Controlling Urban Air Pollution: A Benefit-Cost Assessment." *Science* 252 (26 April 1991): 522-528.

Rapoport, R. "Sins of Emission." *California* 16 (September 1989): 201-228.

Pollution Prevention Act (1990)

The Pollution Prevention Act of 1990 is a piece of legislation intended to limit the creation of **pollution**. As part of the Omnibus Budget Reconciliation Act of 1990, the Pollution Prevention Act differed from previous legislation, which had generally treated pollution after it had been created. **Environmental Protection Agency (EPA)** administrator **William K. Reilly** strongly supported the act, believing that much hazardous or toxic pollution can be more effectively and economically controlled, and the **environment** protected more fully, if the pollution never occurs.

The impetus for this act lies in a 1986 EPA report to Congress entitled "Minimization of Hazardous Wastes." Based on this report, the agency began to take actions designed to reduce pollution. According to a subsequent report by the Office of Technology Assessment (OTA), however, the EPA needed to do more. The two reports identified four main approaches to prevent pollution: (1) manufacturing changes, (2) equipment changes, (3) product reformulations and substitutions, and (4) improved industrial housekeeping. By using such approaches, companies (and individuals) can both save money by reducing pollution control costs and have a cleaner environment because certain pollution will be prevented. The corporation 3M, for instance, has saved over $300 million since 1975 by reducing air, water, and **sludge** pollutants at the source. The OTA estimated that a ten percent reduction in **hazardous waste**s per year for five years could be achieved through source reduction. The reports also found that pollution prevention is primarily hindered not by a lack of technology but rather by a lack of knowledge and awareness due to institutional hurdles. The Pollution Prevention Act was designed to help overcome these hurdles through information collection, assistance in technology transfer, and financial assistance to state pollution prevention programs.

In addition to developing a general strategy to promote the reduction of pollution at its source, the act crated a new EPA office to administer the program. The major provisions of the law are as follows: a state grant program to aid states in establishing similar pollution prevention programs; EPA technical assistance for business; the development of a Source Reduction Clearinghouse, administered by the EPA and available for public use, to help in the collection and distribution of source reduction information; the establishment of an advisory committee on the issue; the creation of a training program on pollution prevention; and the creation of annual awards to businesses that achieve outstanding source reduction. Businesses using **toxic substance**s were required to meet special standards—to report on how many and the amount of toxic substances released into the environment, how much recycled, how they attempted to prevent the generation of toxic pollutants, and how they learned of source reduction techniques. Lastly, the EPA is to report biennially on the effectiveness of the new program and its components. The Act authorized $16 million each year for three years for the EPA to implement this program.

[*Christopher McGrory Klyza*]

FURTHER READING

"Budget Reconciliation Act Provisions." *Congressional Quarterly Almanac* 46 (1990): 141-163.

Environmental Quality: 21st Annual Report. Council on Environmental Quality. Washington, DC: Government Printing Office, 1990.

"Pollution Prevention Act of 1990." Senate Committee on Environment and Public Works, Senate Report 101-526, 1990, 101st Congress, 2d Session.

"Waste Reduction Act." House Committee on Energy and Commerce, House Report 101-555, 1990, 101st Congress, 2d Session.

Polybrominated biphenyls (PBBs)

A mixture of compounds having from one to ten bromine atoms attached to a biphenyl ring, analogous to **polychlorinated biphenyl (PCB)**s. Manufactured as fire retardants, PBBs were banned after a 1973 Michigan incident when pure product was accidently mixed with cattle feed and distributed throughout the state. PBBs were identified as the cause of weight loss, decreased milk production, and mortality in many dairy herds. Approximately 30,000 cattle, 1.5 million chickens, 1,500 sheep, 6,000 hogs, 18,000 pounds (8,100 kg) of cheese, 34,000 pounds (15,300 kg) of dried milk products, 5 million eggs, and 2,700 pounds (1,215 kg) of butter were eventually destroyed at an estimated cost of $1 million. Although human exposures have been well-documented, long term epidemiological studies have not shown widespread health effects.

Polychlorinated biphenyls (PCBs)

Mixture of compounds having from one to ten **chlorine** atoms attached to a biphenyl ring structure. There are 209 possible structures theoretically; the manufacturing process results in approximately 120 different structures. PCBs resist biological and heat degradation and were used in numerous applications, including dielectric fluids in capacitors and transformers, heat transfer fluids, hydraulic fluids, plasticizers, dedusting agents, adhesives, dye carriers in carbonless copy paper, and **pesticide** extenders. The United States manufactured PCBs from 1929 until 1977, when they were banned due to adverse environmental effects and ubiquitous occurrence. They **bioaccumulate** in organisms and can cause skin disorders, liver dysfunction, reproductive disorders, and tumor formation. They are one of the most abundant organochlorine contaminants found throughout the world. *See also* Organochloride

Polycyclic aromatic hydrocarbons (PAH)

Polycyclic aromatic hydrocarbons are a class of organic compounds having two or more fused **benzene** rings. While usually referring to compounds made of **carbon** and **hydrogen**, PAH also may include fused aromatic compounds containing **nitrogen**, sulfur, or cyclopentene rings. Some of the more common PAH include naphthalene (2 rings), anthracene (3 rings), phenanthrene (3 rings), pyrene (4 rings), chrysene (4 rings), fluoranthene (4 rings), **benzo(a)pyrene** (5 rings), benzo(e)pyrene (5 rings), perylene (5 rings), benzo(g,h,i)perylene (6 rings), and coronene (7 rings).

PAH are formed by a variety of human activities including incomplete **combustion** of **fossil fuels**, wood, and **tobacco**; the **incineration** of **garbage**; **coal gasification** and liquefaction processes; smelting operations; and coke, asphalt, and **petroleum** cracking; they are also formed naturally during forest fires and volcanic eruptions. Low molecular-weight PAH (those with four or fewer rings) are generally vapors while heavier molecules condense on submicron, breathable particles. It is estimated that more than 800 tons of PAH are emitted annually in the United States. PAH are found worldwide and are present in elevated concentrations in urban **aerosol**s, and in lake **sediment**s in industrialized countries. They also are found in developing countries due to **coal** and wood heating, open burning, coke production, and vehicle exhaust.

The association of PAH with small particles gives them atmospheric residence times of days to weeks, and allows them to be transported long distances. They are removed from the **atmosphere** by gravitational settling and are washed out during precipitation to the earth's surface, where they accumulate in **soil**s and surface waters. They also directly enter water in discharges, **runoff**, and **oil spills**. They associate with water particulates due to their low water solubility, and eventually accumulate in **sediment**s. They do not **bioaccumulate** in biota to any appreciable extent, as they are largely metabolized.

Many but not all PAH have carcinogenic and mutagenic activity; the most notorious is benzo(a)pyrene, which has been shown to be a potent **carcinogen**. Coal tar and soot were implicated in the elevated skin **cancer** incidence found in the refining, shale oil, and coal tar industries in the late nineteenth century. Subsequent research led to the isolation and identification of several carcinogens in the early part of this century, including benzo(a)pyrene. More recent research into the carcinogenicity of PAH has revealed that there is significant additional biological activity in urban aerosols and soot beyond that explained by known carcinogens such as benzo(a)pyrene. While benzo(a)pyrene must be activated metabolically, these other components have direct biological activity as demonstrated by the **Ames test**. They are polar compounds, thought to be mixtures of mono- and dinitro-PAH and hydroxy-nitro derivatives. **Tobacco** smoking exposes more humans to PAH than any other source.

[*Deborah L. Swackhammer*]

FURTHER READING

Dias, J. R. *Handbook of Polycyclic Aromatic Hydrocarbons*. New York: Elsevier, 1987.

Harvey, R. G. *Polycyclic Aromatic Hydrocarbons: Chemistry and Carcinogenicity*. New York: Cambridge University Press, 1991.

Polycyclic organic compounds

In organic chemistry, a cyclic compound is one whose molecules consist of three or more atoms joined in a closed ring. A polycyclic compound is one whose molecules contain two or more rings joined to each other. Environmentally, the most important polycyclic organic compounds are the **polycyclic aromatic hydrocarbons**, also known as polynuclear aromatic hydrocarbons (PAHs). Some examples of polycyclic organic compounds include naphthalene, anthracene, pyrene, and the benzopyrenes. A number of

polycyclic hydrocarbons pose hazards to human health. For example, **benzo(a)pyrene** from automobile exhaust and **tobacco** smoke is known to be a **carcinogen**. *See also* Cigarette smoke

Polynuclear aromatic hydrocarbons
See **Polycyclic aromatic hydrocarbons**

Polystyrene

Polystyrene is a lightweight transparent plastic derived from **petroleum** by-products and **natural gas**. It is widely used in the packaging industry, but most polystyrene is used to make durable goods such as television cabinets, appliances, and furniture. Polystyrene also has excellent insulating properties. As packaging, polystyrene is used both in foam and solid forms. Solid polystyrene is used in yogurt, sour cream, and cottage cheese containers, cutlery, clear clamshells used at salad bars, and video and audio cassette containers. As foam, polystyrene is used in cups, bowls, plates, trays, clamshell containers, meat trays, egg cartons, and packaging for electronics and other delicate items. Polystyrene foam is manufactured by processing solid polystyrene resin pellets with a gaseous expansion agent. In the past, about 30% of polystyrene foam products were made with **chlorofluorocarbons** (CFCs), which were identified as contributors to the deterioration of the ozone layer in the Earth's upper **atmosphere**. By 1990, manufacturers had phased out the use of CFCs as a polystyrene expansion agent. Some manufacturers switched to the use of **hydrochlorofluorocarbon**-22 (HCFC-22), which reduced **ozone layer depletion** potential by about 95% over CFCs. By 1994, as required by federal law, polystyrene foam manufacturers phased out the use of HCFC-22 and by 1997 were using alternative expansion agents, most commonly pentane gas. Pentane does not affect the ozone layer, but because it can contribute to **smog** formation some manufacturers recycle pentane emissions. **Carbon dioxide** (CO_2) is also used by manufacturers as a polystyrene expansion agent. CO_2 is nontoxic, nonflammable, does not contribute to smog, and has no atmospheric ozone depletion potential, but it has been implicated in global warming.

Polystyrene packaging accounts for about 1.2 % (by weight) of the total **solid waste** stream in the United States, and polystyrene makes up from about 2-10% of materials thrown away as litter. However, polystyrene can be recycled and used to make new polystyrene products such as wall insulation, packing filler, and cafeteria trays. Polystyrene has an energy content of 17,000 Btu/pound, about four times that of average municipal solid waste, and can be burned with other solid wastes in an incinerator that has appropriate **emission** controls to contain potentially toxic **combustion** products. Another potential environmental concern is the release of toxic metals such as **cadmium** and **lead** from combustion of inks used to tint the polystyrene. The polystyrene manufacturing industry is developing source reduction techniques, including improving resin properties to make stronger products with less material and making lighter-weight foam products.

Polystyrene is manufactured from styrene, which is a hazardous chemical. When styrene is heated to 392°F (198°C), it is converted into the polymer polystyrene. Health concerns have been raised about styrene residues remaining in polystyrene products, especially those that are used to contain food for consumption. Styrene is soluble in oil and in **ethanol**, substances commonly found in foods and alcoholic beverages. A U.S. EPA National Human Adipose Tissue Survey in 1986 identified styrene in 100% of the 46 human fat samples collected.

[*Judith Sims*]

FURTHER READING

Expansion Agents for Polystyrene Foam. Washington, D.C.: Polystyrene Packaging Council, 1997.

Polystyrene in the Solid Waste Stream. Washington, D.C.: Polystyrene Packaging Council, 1997.

Uses and Benefits of Polystyrene. Washington, D.C.: Polystyrene Packaging Council, 1997.

Polyvinyl chloride (PVC)

Polyvinyl chloride, also known as PVC, is a plastic produced by the polymerization of vinyl chloride. It is used with plasticizers to make packaging films, boots, garden hose, etc. Without plasticizers, PVC is used to make pipe, siding, shingles, window frames, toys, and other items. An attractive aspect of PVC for industry is its ability to withstand weathering and its resistance to **chemicals** and solvents. However, this attractive aspect is the major environmental concern for PVC and many other **plastics**. The great bulk of such plastic (about 98 percent) is neither reused nor recycled but occupies ever dwindling **landfill** space.

Population biology

Population biology is the study of the factors determining the size and distribution of a population, as well as the ways in which populations change over time. The discipline of population biology dates back to the 1960s, when researchers merged aspects of population **ecology** with aspects of population genetics. It employs a traditional empirical approach which consists of observation of the numbers of individuals in a population and the variation in those numbers over time and space, and the measurement of physical (abiotic) factors and the living (biotic) factors that may affect population numbers.

Given optimum conditions, the populations of most organisms grow at a constant rate of increase, doubling in size at regular intervals, which is known as **exponential growth**. Exponential **population growth** is explosive but it is usually opposed by factors that reduce numbers, such as disease, predation, or harsh **climate**s. The result is **logistic growth**, where the rapidly growing population slows and reaches a stable but dynamic equilibrium at or near the **carrying capacity** of the **environment**. The populations of some **species** such as migratory locusts show boom and bust cycles: in these cases explosive growth produces vast numbers of individuals that eventually overwhelm the carrying capacity and a catastrophic dieback follows.

The rate of growth of a population is the net result of the gains and losses from a number of intrinsic factors operating within the population. These include natality, **fecundity**, life span, longevity, **mortality**, and immigration and emigration. Patterns of survivorship and age structure created by these interacting factors show how a population is growing and indicate what general role a species plays in the **ecosystem**. Density-dependent biotic factors that decrease natality or increase mortality include the numbers of competitors both interspecific and intraspecific, as well as predators, prey, parasites, and other interactive species. Stress and overcrowding are other density-dependent biotic factors that limit population size through excessive intraspecific competition for limited resources.

The local distribution pattern of populations of most species is limited by physical factors such as temperature, moisture, light, **pH**, **soil** quality, and **salinity**. Within their areas of distribution, animals occur in varying densities (either scattered thinly or crowded) and in varying dispersal patterns (either spaced evenly or clumped into herds). Population density and dispersion are often studied together, and are important in ecology and management. Density is measured by direct visual count, and by trapping, collecting fecal pellets, using pelt records, monitoring vocalization frequencies, and so on. Life tables constructed from these data show precisely how a population is age-structured.

Population genetics recognizes two important attributes of a population—its gene frequencies and its total **gene pool**. Population size exerts some influence on the genetic composition of its members, since the number of sexually interbreeding individuals influences the transfer of genes within a population. It also affects the kinds of genotypes that are available, and the survival and reproductive capacity of individuals with certain genes. The application of the principles of population genetics is vital to the success of programs to improve the breeds of animals and plants for agricultural use, and for the captive breeding of **endangered species**. *See also* Captive propogation and reintroduction; Gene bank; Genetic engineering; Predator-prey interactions; Sustainable development; Wildlife management

[*Neil Cumberlidge*]

FURTHER READING

Begon, M., J. L. Harper, and C. R. Townsend. *Ecology: Individuals, Populations, and Communities.* 2nd Edition. Boston: Blackwell Scientific Publications, 1990.

Emmel, T. C. *Population Biology.* New York: Harper and Row, 1976.

Hendrick, P. W. *Population Biology: The Evolution and Ecology of Populations.* Boston: Jones and Bartlett, 1984.

Ricklefs, R. E. *The Economy of Nature*. 3rd ed. New York: W. H. Freeman, 1993.

Smith, R. L. *Elements of Ecology*. New York: HarperCollins, 1991.

Stiling, P. D. *Introductory Ecology*. Englewood Cliffs, NJ: Prentice Hall, 1992.

Population control
See **Family planning**

Population Council (New York, New York)

The Population Council was established in 1952 to find solutions to the world's population problems. Although based in New York, the Council is an international non-profit organization with regional offices in Bangkok, Cairo, Dakar, Mexico City, and Nairobi. In conducting research in health, social, and biomedical sciences, the Council has, among other accomplishments, broken ground in contraceptive devices, explored male fertility, and analyzed the social position of women and its concurrent effect on the population.

The Council seeks to use science and technology to provide relief to the population problems of developing countries. Governed by a board of twenty trustees from sixteen countries who meet twice a year, the Council has programs in fifty countries throughout Latin America, the Caribbean, Asia, and Africa. It receives funding from world governments, United Nations agencies, foundations, and individuals for its research and programs. The major programs and institutions of the Population Council are the Center for Biomedical Research, the Research Division, and the Programs Division.

The Center for Biomedical Research investigates new ways to regulate human fertility, primarily through development of new methods of contraception. For example the Center invented the Norplant levonorgestrel implant and a **copper**-bearing T-shaped intrauterine device (IUD). Both methods are for long-term protection and are reversible. New methods in development include a hormone-releasing IUD, Norplant II (with two implants instead of six), and contraceptive vaginal rings. Another idea in progress includes a vaginal contraceptive that provides protection from the human immunodeficiency virus (HIV). These methods are designed for women, but the Center for Biomedical Research also concentrates on controlling male fertility through research into male physiology. With particular interest in creating a contraceptive to block sperm production without dampening the male sex drive, the Center is working on a "nonsurgical" or "no-scalpel" vasectomy and male subdermal implants, akin to women's Norplant.

The Population Council does not restrict its research to the biomedical domain, however. Through its Research Division, it looks for solutions to population problems through social research. A small interdisciplinary group of demographers, economists, sociologists, and anthropologists make up the Research Division. Among notable studies is an ongoing project examining the consequences of high fertility in a family. For instance, early research indicates that in Maharashtra, India, the advantages associated with growing up in a small family exist for boys but not for girls. Apparently in many smaller families in India, girls have a proportionately heavier burden of labor. The Research Division also conducts many studies in China, where the state is heavily involved in regulating its population. Through research into **family planning** and fertility, child survival, and women's roles and status—a subject that has taken precedence in the Council's research since 1976—the Research Division provides theories that the Population Council puts to use in controlling worldwide population problems.

The Council applies the research conducted by the Center for Biomedical Research and the Research Division through its Programs Division. The Programs Division collaborates with governments, organizations, and scientific institutions of developing countries to formulate population policy. Many of the programs set forth by this division parallel studies being conducted by the Research Division. For example, the Programs Division conducts family planning and fertility counseling; works to insure reproductive health and child survival; and seeks to improve women's roles and status in developing countries. The contraceptive introduction program is also an important part of the Programs Division. The Council is attempting to achieve wide approval for and usage of the Norplant device and copper-bearing IUD by introducing it in developing countries.

In addition to its programs and research, the Council publishes two scholarly journals: *Population and Development Review* and *Studies in Family Planning*. Both contain studies of current ideas and theories in population control. The Population Council also sponsors outstanding scholars and scientists to further research into the technology needed to control the world's populations. Contact: Population Council, 1 Dag Hammarskjold Plaza, New York, NY 10017. Internet: http://popcouncil.org/.

[Andrea Gacki]

Population explosion
See **Population growth**

Population growth

A population is the number of individuals of a given **species**, usually within a specified **habitat** or area. Within the science of **ecology**, the study of population dynamics, or the ways in which the number of individuals in a community expands and contracts, makes up an important subfield known as **population biology**. While ecologists and **wildlife** biologists rely on understanding the nature of population change and the factors that influence population size, one of the main ways population studies have been used is in projecting the growth of the human population. Since the 1960s human population growth has been an issue of fierce theoretical debate. Many scientists and social planners predict that the human population, like animal populations frequently observed in nature, is growing at a perilous rate that will ultimately lead to a catastrophic die-off in which billions of people will perish. Other scholars and planners argue that current trends may not lead to disaster and that we may yet find a reasonable and stable population level. Both sides of the debate use ecological principles of population biology in predicting human population dynamics and their effect upon the conditions in which we may live in the future.

The extent of population growth is based on fertility, or the number of offspring that individuals of reproductive age successfully produce. In some animal and plant species (flies, dandelions) every individual produces a great number of offspring. These populations grow quickly, as long as nutrients and space are available. Other species (**elephants**, pandas) produce few offspring per reproductive adult; populations of these species usually grow slowly even when ample food and habitat are available. The maximum number of offspring an organism can produce under ideal conditions is known as the biotic potential of that organism. For instance, if an individual housefly can produce 120 young in her lifetime, and each of those successfully produces 120 young, and so on, the fly's biotic potential in one year (seven generations) is nearly six trillion flies. Clearly biotic potentials are rarely met: reproductive failures and life hazards usually prevent the majority of houseflies, like other species, from achieving their theoretical reproductive potential.

Populations increase through reproduction, but they do not increase infinitely because of environmental limitations, including disease, predation, **competition** for space and **nutrient**s, and nutrient shortages. These limits to population growth are collectively known as environmental resistance.

An important concept in environmental resistance is the idea of **carrying capacity**. Carrying capacity is the maximum number of individuals a habitat can support. In any finite system, there is a limited availability of food, water, nesting space, and other essentials, which limits that system's carrying capacity. When a population exceeds its environment's carrying capacity, shortages of nutrients or other necessities usually weaken individuals, reduce successful reproduction, and raise death rates from disease, until the population once again falls below its maximum size. A population that grows very quickly and exceeds its environment's carrying capacity is said to overshoot its environment's capacity. A catastrophic , when the population plummets to well below its maximum, usually follows an overshoot. In many cases populations undergo repeated overshoot-dieback cycles. Sometimes these cycles gradually decrease in severity until a stable population, in equilibrium with carrying capacity, is reached. In other cases, overshoot-dieback cycles go on continually, as in the well known case of lemmings. Prolific breeding among these small arctic rodents leads to a population explosion every four to six years. In overshoot years, depletion of the vegetation on which they feed causes widespread undernourishment, which results in starvation, weakness, and vulnerability to predators and disease. The lemming population collapses, only to begin rebuilding, gradually

approaching overshoot and another dieback. At the same time, related populations fluctuate in response to cycles in the lemming population: populations of owls and foxes surge when lemmings become plentiful and fall when lemmings are few. The grasses and forbs on which lemmings feed likewise prosper and diminish in response to the lemming population.

As a population grows, the number of breeding adults increases so that growth accelerates. Increase at a constant or accelerating rate of change is known as **exponential growth**. If each female lemming can produce four young females, and each of those produces another four, then the population is multiplied by four in each generation. After two generations there are 16 (or 2^4) lemmings; after three generations there are 64 (3^4); after four generations there are 256 (4^4) lemmings, if all survive. When environmental resistance (predation, nutrient limitations, and so on) causes a population to reach a stable level, without significant increases or decreases over time, population equilibrium is achieved. Generally we might consider stable (equilibrium) populations the more desirable situation because repeated diebacks involve extensive suffering and death.

These principles of population biology have strongly informed our understanding of human population changes. Over the centuries the world's human population has tended to expand to the maximum allowed by available food, water, and space. When humans exceeded their environment's carrying capacity, catastrophic diebacks (usually involving disease, **famine**, or war) sometimes resulted. However, in many cases, diebacks have been avoided through emigration, as in European migrations to the Americas, or through technological innovation, including such inventions as agriculture, **irrigation**, and mechanization, each of which effectively expanded environmental carrying capacities. For tens of thousands of years the human population climbed very gradually, until about the year 1000, when it began to grow exponentially. Where we once needed a thousand years (200 to 1200 A.D.) to double our population from 200 million to 400 million, at current rates of growth we would require only 40 years to double our population. Since the eighteenth century, population theorists have increasingly warned that our current pattern of growth is leading us toward a serious overshoot, perhaps one that will permanently damage our environment and result in a consequent dieback. The only course to avoid such a catastrophe, argue population theorists, is to stabilize our population somewhere below our environment's carrying capacity.

Popular awareness of population issues and agreement with the principle of population reduction have spread in recent years with the publication of such volumes as *The Population Bomb* by **Paul Ehrlich**, and ***The Limits to Growth*** by Donella Meadows and others. The current population debate, however has older roots, especially in the work of **Thomas Malthus**, an English cleric who in 1798 published *An Essay on the Principle of Population as It Affects the Future Improvement of Society*. Malthus argued that, while unchecked human population growth increases at an exponential rate, food supplies increase only arithmetically (a constant amount being added each year, instead of multiplying by a

Human population growth.

of resources, and social changes sometimes increase or decrease populations locally. Immigration and emigration tend to redistribute populations from one region to another, temporarily alleviating or exacerbating population excesses. Also unlike most animals, we have not historically been subject to a fixed environmental carrying capacity. The **agricultural revolution**, the industrial revolution and other innovations have expanded our environment's capacity to support humans. Some population theorists today, known as technological optimists, insist that, even as the human population continues to grow, our technological inventiveness will help us to feed and shelter the world's population. Even in the past 50 years, when the world's population has jumped from less than three billion to more than six billion, world food production has exceeded population growth. Technological optimists point to such historical evidence as support for their position.

Also unlike most animal populations, humans are, at least in principle, able to voluntarily limit reproductive rates. Most population theorists point to some sort of voluntary restraint as the most humane method of preventing a disastrous population overshoot. **Family planning** programs have been developed around the world in an effort to encourage voluntary population limits. Furthermore, human societies have been observed to go through a demographic transition as their economic and social stability has improved. A demographic transition is a period when (infant) mortality rates have decreased but people have not yet adjusted their reproductive behavior to improved life expectancies. After 20 to 30 years, people adjust, realizing that more children are surviving and that smaller families now have economic advantages. The birth rate then begins to fall. While families in poor countries often have five to ten children, the average family in developed countries has about two children.

Because of family planning programs and demographic transitions, birth rates around the world have fallen dramatically in just the last 20 years. Where the average number of children per woman was 6.1 in 1970, the average number in 1990 was only 3.4. This rate still exceeds the minimum replacement level (**zero population growth** level) of 2.1 children per woman, but if recent demographic trends continue the world's population will stabilize within the first decade of the twenty-first century.

No one knows exactly what the earth's carrying capacity is. Some warn that we have already surpassed our safe population size. Others argue that the earth can comfortably support far more people than it currently does. Many worry about what would happen to other species if the human population continues to expand. Most people agree that we would benefit from a decrease in population growth rates. How urgent the population question is and how best to curb growth rates are issues that continue to be hotly debated.

[*Mary Ann Cunningham*]

constant amount). The consequence of such a disparity in growth rates is starvation and death. The remedy is to reduce our reproductive rates, where possible by "moral restraint," but where necessary by force. Malthus' work has remained well-known principally because of its conclusion about social policy: because providing food and shelter to the poor only allows them to increase their rates of "breeding," assistance should be withheld. If the poorer classes should starve as a result, argued Malthus, at least greater rates of starvation at a later date would be avoided. This conclusion continues to be promoted today by neo-Malthusians, who protest the principle of aiding developing countries. Poorer countries, neo-Malthusians point out, have especially dangerous growth rates. If wealthy countries provide assistance today because they cannot bear to watch the suffering in poorer nations, they only make the situation worse. By giving aid, donor nations only postpone temporarily the greater suffering that will eventually result from artificially supported growth rates.

Naturally this conclusion is deeply offensive to developing nations and to those who sympathize with the plight of poorer countries. Malthusian conclusions are especially harsh in situations where military and economic repression, often supported by North American and European governments, have caused the poverty. Those who defend aid to developing countries argue that high reproductive rates often result from poverty, rather than vice versa. Where poor nutrition and health care make infant mortality rates high, parents choose to have many children, thus increasing the odds that at least some will survive to support them in their old age. Assistance to poor countries, and to poor areas within a single country, argue anti-Malthusians, helps to alleviate the poverty that necessitates high birth rates. When people become confident of their childrens' survival, then birth rates will drop and population equilibrium may be achieved.

There are some ways in which ecological principles of population dynamics do not necessarily fit the human population. Improving health care and increasing life expectancies have caused much of this century's population expansion. Wars, changes in prosperity, development and transportation

FURTHER READING

Cunningham, W. P. *Understanding Our Environment: an Introduction.* Dubuque, IA: Wm. C. Brown, 1993.

Ehrlich, P. R. *The Population Bomb.* New York: Ballantine Books, 1968.

Ehrlich, P. R., and A. H. Ehrlich. "The Population Explosion: Why Isn't Everyone As Scared As We Are?" *Amicus Journal* 12 (Winter 1990): 22-29.

Meadows, D. H., et al. *Limits to Growth*. New York: Universe Books, 1972.

Population Institute (Washington, D.C.)

Despite the fact they work with an annual budget of less than $2 million, the Population Institute, an information, education, and communication organization that spreads the word on population control, has been able to reach 150 countries, principally in the developing world. Based on the philosophy that overpopulation affects all social, economic, and political issues, the Institute's goal is to bring world population into balance with available environmental resources. To do this, the organization disseminates information via a World Population News Service which is picked up in developing countries in newspaper articles, editorial pieces, and radio and television broadcasts. In addition to making people aware of the perils of overpopulation, the Institute encourages birth control, without emphasizing any particular method.

Once a year the Institute funds an international journalism award, the Global Media Award in Population Reporting. The winner spends about one week touring a country with a successful population control program, visiting **family planning** clinics, and talking with government and private officials. Governmental leaders within the country usually present the award. The Institute benefits by keeping in contact not only with leaders and people at the grassroots level, but with local journalists.

Begun in 1969 by a Methodist minister with a strong conviction that overpopulation was a major cause of human misery, the Population Institute was one of the first groups organized specifically around population control. No longer connected to the Methodist church, the Institute is supported by grants from foundations, private individuals, and the sale of its bimonthly newsletter, *Popline*. In 1980 its domestic component split and formed the Center for Population Options, also headquartered in Washington, D.C.

If contraceptive use is a valid indicator, things are looking up for population control. Between 1970 and 1990, contraceptive use rose from 9 percent to 51 percent. If use can be increased to 72 percent by the year 2000, **World Bank** statistics predict that world population can be stabilized at 8.5-11 billion. Contact: The Population Institute, 107 2nd Street, NE, Washington, DC 20002. Internet: http://www.populationinstitute.org/.

[*Stephanie Ocko*]

Porter, Eliot Furness (1901-1990)

American photographer

Born in Winnetka, Illinois, Eliot Porter's fascination with **nature** (and birds in particular) was evident from a very early age. His father, an architect with a keen interest in Greek, Gothic, and Roman architecture and art, encouraged his son's insightful, artistic talents. Using the camera he received as a gift from his father, the young Porter began photographing primarily landscapes during the family's sojourns on islands off the coast of Maine. There he cultivated an enthusiasm and love for naturalist photography. He noted in the introduction of the classic book, *Birds of America*, "...the most satisfactory outlet for expressing my excitement over birds was the camera, rather than pencil or brush."

Porter began his undergraduate education at Harvard University in 1920. Casting aside his passion for photography, he pursued the more practical major of chemical engineering; he earned his bachelor's degree (cum laude) in 1924. He continued his education at Harvard's Medical School where he earned his doctor of medicine in 1929. Porter used his degrees to teach biochemistry and bacteriology at Harvard and Radcliffe College until 1939. In addition to his teaching, Porter was working through the Harvard Biology Department conducting numerous studies. By 1939, whatever attraction there had been to biochemistry diminished and Porter turned his energies back to photography.

Determined to transform bird photography from less-than-professional reportage to art, Porter became involved with the Eastman Kodak company. Porter was awarded Guggenheim Fellowships in 1941 and again in 1946 to finance experiments with Kodachrome photography—a new venture for Kodak. He believed that by using the new color film, the photographer could provide a more sensitive interpretation of the subject.

Finally achieving success with color film, Porter produced a number of bird photography publications, including a photo-essay pairing his photos with specific Thoreau excerpts. The book, *In Wildness Is the Preservation of the World*, was published by the Sierra Club. Porter produced subsequent books with the organization (*Baja California—The Geography of Hope* and *The Place No One Knew: Glen Canyon on the Colorado*), and later—until 1971—served on the Sierra Club's Board of Directors.

While Porter's photography took him to locations throughout the world (Greece, Iceland, Turkey, and the Galapagos Islands), his most brilliant work came from his travels in eleven of the United States. *Birds of America—A Personal Selection* was the result of his trip and became one of his best-known books. It combines rich, full-color photographs with anecdotal notes detailing his trials and tribulations in taking them. Porter's other publications include *Galapagos—The Flow of Wilderness*, *Antarctica*, and *Intimate Landscapes*.

Porter's one-man exhibits have appeared in some of the most influential art institutes and museums in the United States, among them: the George Eastman House, Museum of Modern Art, Metropolitan Museum of Art, and Stielglitz's An American Place. He maintained membership in several organizations including Advocates for the Arts, American Civil Liberties Union, American Ornithologists' Union, and the Audubon Society.

Porter died in November 1990 in New Mexico following a heart attack; he had also suffered from Lou Gehrig's disease.

[*Kimberley A. Peterson*]

FURTHER READING

"Eliot Porter: For More Than 50 Years, This Master of Color and Light Portrayed and Idealized the American Landscape." *Life* 14 (February 1991): 80-85.

Henry, G. "Eliot Porter." *ARTnews* 89 (Summer 1990): 178.

Porter, Eliot. *Eliot Porter's Southwest.* New York: Henry Holt, 1991.

———. *Nature's Chaos.* New York: Viking Penguin, 1990.

Positional goods

A concept coined by English economist Fred Hirsch (1931-1978) to describe goods or activities whose value depends on their exclusivity. For example, fame is considered a positional good since by definition only a few people can be famous and thus enjoy this "privilege." If everyone were famous, no one would be. Similarly, solitude on a mountain peak or in the **wilderness** would qualify as a positional good, since if one shared the peak or the wilderness with many other people, one could not experience solitude. Ironically, a positional good tends to diminish its own value because of the high demand it creates: as more people enjoy positional goods, they no longer become exclusive or valued. For instance, **automobile**s were once a positional good in America, but as more and more people began owning cars, they were no longer such a status symbol. A number of concerned environmentalists contend that access to wilderness areas should be restricted or limited to prevent the destruction of this *positional good.*

Posterity

See **Future generations**

Postmodernism and environmental ethics

Environmental ethics are a set of norms that a society accepts as a foundation for mediating and guiding their behavior towards the **environment**. In Western society, we have used our science, as well as other traditions (e.g. capitalist economics, humaneness, aesthetics), to form the foundation of our environmental behavior. We are in the midst of a search for new ethical foundations. Deep ecology has offered one possible route, Eastern religions have been another source for advancing our ethics, and yet none of these has proved palatable in our Western social systems.

Western science has guided the environmental interactions of our society which in turn has dominated global development processes, but this pattern has some definite shortcomings. While science has served to develop our understanding of nature and enhanced our knowledge of the ecological difficulties that we have created for ourselves, the system of which science is part has been very slow in responding to what many suggest is an ecological crisis. Sorting the science from the politics and the ethics of our society is not an easy task. Yet, science has been the target of criticism in the environmental arena because, while it has the power to expose the depth of our ecological crisis, it has done little in that regard. Critics point to that inaction as a negative structural attribute of how embedded science has become in our society.

An alternative proposed from within the humanist tradition in the social sciences suggests that science can only produce a false construction of nature. From this viewpoint science is tied to traditions that inevitably create an end product related to the position from which the observer views nature. Further it holds that all views of nature are constructed by humans who cannot step outside of ourselves to view the reality we think exists. Thus, no views are more or less closer to reality; they are all merely our creation. This alternative approach falls under the rubric of postmodernism and is elucidated through one of the principal methods in the postmodernist tool kit, deconstruction.

The deconstructionist approach of the postmodernist suggests that, even thought the views of all are equally worthy, an imbalance of power has been created by the dominant classes. The disempowered classes attempt to create a balance, a struggle which proceeds by dissecting everything down to its bare power relationships, so that having been revealed the wrong can be corrected. Deconstruction is a term that does not differ significantly from any other critical analytical method, but it pays particular homage to power and position, supposedly more conscientiously than other methods.

Nature "out there" then becomes a series of constructions made by humans with different positions within a continuum of power relations. Nature is the invention of humans in power and is constantly reinvented by people in those same positions. To the postmodernist, the present invention of **nature**, held by the current cadre of largely male, largely Caucasian scientists has given us a biased view of nature. The postmodernist wish is to level all points of view, so that life is seen as a struggle of words and nature becomes another, albeit large, "text" (a metatext). A rather curious outcome of this view of life is the idea that things in nature are doing what they do only because we think of them doing it. Furthermore, those who wish to protect nature may then become a force of oppression against those of other social orders who are struggling to gain power. Thus, a thinly disguised structuralist approach emerges. Power creates a framework within which the powerful struggle to remain empowered, and the remainder struggle to gain power. Environmental views supported by science are the handmaiden of the power elite and can only succeed in supporting the status quo.

While there is undoubtedly a cultural context in which nature is understood and in which science operates, this does not necessarily mean that context is equivalent to the content of nature. Even though reality may be seen as having been invented by words and the human shaping of sensory data, nevertheless there is much commonality across cultures regarding what we see in nature. The postmodernist view appears to be remote from the natural world, occupying an anthropocentric stronghold where humans are dominant. Interestingly, while humanists thus refer to a nature made by humans, scientists have since Darwin referred to humans as having been created by nature through natural selection.

The diametrically opposed view points under discussion here are not new; they merely reflect the range of opinions humans have always held about their relationship with nature. However, the postmodernist expression of human opinion about nature outlined above seems to be a position that is distinctly unhelpful, especially at this time in our existence. The heart of the environmental problems we currently experience has been blamed to a large degree on humanity's separation of itself from nature, and any proposal that maintains or widens that gap may exacerbate the problems. The postmodernist critique seems to ignore the power and influence that nature has on us, and instead uses an intricate semantics to describe the power we have over each other.

Most naturalists and ecologists are immediately struck by the apparent naiveté of a position that denies the creative strength in nature and the complex architecture of life provided by natural selection. A postmodern view is that our knowledge of distributions of organisms is a construct of the way we have studied distributions, and the whole idea of species is merely a human distinction. The notion of objective criteria devised by, critiqued by, and used by scientists is rendered unusable. The postmodern view renders the concept that ecological tolerance of the organisms, historical events, and climate create a relationship based on a combination of determinist relationships and stochastic events a mere artifact regardless of how many people agree to the concepts. This of course leads to a conclusion which provides little guidance for environmental ethics.

That does not mean that the entire postmodernist critique leads to the same less than useful conclusions. Rather, the very aspect of a critique that causes us to examine our position may be an important and valuable tool. We have relied heavily on science and found at the center of ecology some powerful, yet largely incorrect, metaphors firmly rooted in our conception of nature. The ideas of balance, succession, and homogeneity in nature have all fallen by the wayside in the past two decades. Those readjustments have given ecologists pause because they are strong examples of how viewpoint can influence our interpretation of nature, one that was originally thought to have been discovered by an objective science. Are there more misconceptions that we hold about ecology and environment that need to be examined? Clearly the possibility exists, and it serves us well to search for those by any and all reasonable methods. That postmodernism creates the notion that all human perspectives are inherently equal may create an obstacle to clear thinking about proposing a comprehensive ethic towards the environment. At this time we need to synthesize a more positive relationship

between nature and humanity to bring all of our cultures into an integrated understanding of nature. However, a revised ethical foundation for humanity's relationship with the environment may benefit from the tradition of critical thinking that various philosophical positions bring. An examination of biases linked to our present position.

[*David A. Duffus*]

Potable water
See **Drinking water supply**

Powell, John Wesley (1834-1902)
American explorer and scientist

John Wesley Powell—civil-war veteran, college professor, long-time head of the U.S. **Geological Survey**, member of the National Academy of Sciences, president of the American Association for the Advancement of Science, and instrumental in the establishment of the National Geographic Society, the Geological Society of America, the U.S. Geological Survey, the Bureau of Ethnology, and the **Bureau of Reclamation**—is best-known for two expeditions down the Green and **Colorado River**s.

Born in Mount Morris, New York, of English-born parents, Powell was discouraged from education by his father who believed that the ministry was the only purpose for which one needed to be educated. The younger Powell however, worked at a variety of jobs to support his attendance at numerous schools, but never completed a degree. His hard-won recognition as a scientist is based in large part on self-taught concepts and methods that he applied all his life and in everything he did.

Powell made significant contributions to **conservation** and **environmental science**. He was an early and ardent student of the culture of the fast-disappearing North American Indians tribes, and his work ultimately led to the creation of the Bureau of Ethnology, of which he was the first director. He served as the second Director of the United States Geological Survey (USGS) from 1881 to 1894, and as such he instigated extensive topographic mapping projects and geological studies, stimulated studies of **soil**s, **groundwater**, and rivers, and advocated work on flood control and **irrigation**. His Irrigation Survey led eventually to the creation of first the Reclamation Service and then the Bureau of Reclamation.

Powell was the author of the *Report on the Lands of the Arid Region of the United States*, published in 1878. Through this document, he became an early advocate of **land-use** planning. Powell was open to controlled development and suggested that "to a great extent, the redemption of...these lands will require extensive and comprehensive plans..." In

John Wesley Powell.

his role as director of the USGS, in his writings, his work on various commissions, and in public hearings, Powell advocated that the federal government assume a major role to insure an orderly and environmentally sound settlement of the **arid** lands of the West.

Wallace Stegner argues that Powell's ultimate importance derives from his impact as an agent of change, from setting in motion ideas and agencies that still benefit the country today. He also widens Powell's impact, asserting that Powell's ideas, through his friend and employee W. J. McGee, heavily influenced the whole conservation movement at the beginning of the twentieth century. Powell informed the American public of the grandeur and vulnerability of the arid lands and canyon lands of the West. The legacy of that heritage is the Grand Canyon still largely unspoiled as well as a better understanding of land use possibilities on arid and all lands.

[*Gerald L. Young*]

FURTHER READING

Murphy, D. *John Wesley Powell: Voyage of Discovery*. Las Vegas, NV: KC Publications, 1991.

Robinson, F. G. "A Useable Heroism: Wallace Stegner's *Beyond the Hundreth Meridian*." *South Dakota Review* 23 (1985): 58-69.

Stegner, W. *Beyond the Hundreth Meridian: John Wesley Powell and the Second Opening of the West*. New York: Penguin Books, 1992.

Power lines
See **Electromagnetic fields**

Power plants

The term *power plant* refers to any installation at which electrical energy is generated. Power plants can operate using any one of a number of fuels: oil, **coal**, nuclear material, or geothermal steam, for example. The general principle on which most power plants operate, however, is the same. In such a plant, a fuel such as coal or oil is burned. Heat from the burning fuel is used to boil water, converting it to steam. The hot steam is then used to operate a steam turbine.

A steam turbine is a very large machine whose core is a horizontal shaft of metal. Attached to the horizontal shaft are many fan-shaped blades. As hot steam is directed at the turbine, it strikes the blades and causes the horizontal shaft to rotate on its axis. The rotating shaft is, in turn, attached to the shaft of an electric generator. The pressure of hot steam on turbine blades, is therefore, ultimately converted into the generation of a electric current. One of the first steam turbines designed to be used for the generation of electricity was patented by Charles Parson in 1884. Twenty years later, entrepreneurs had already put such turbines to use for the generation of electricity for street lines, subways, train lines and individual appliances.

Most early power plants were fueled with coal. Coal was the best-know, most abundant **fossil fuel** at the time. It had several disadvantages, however. It was dirty to mine, transport, and work with. It also did not burn very cleanly. Areas around a coal-fired power plant were characterized by clouds of **smoke** belching from smokestacks and films of ash deposited on homes, cars, grass, and any other exposed surface.

By the 1920s interest in oil-fired power plants began to grow. The number of these plants remained relatively low, however, as long as coal was inexpensive. But, by the 1960s, there was a resurgence of interest in oil-fired plants, largely in response to increased awareness of the many harmful effects of coal **combustion** on the **environment**. One of the most troublesome effects of coal combustion is **acid rain**. Coal contains trace amounts of elements which produce acid-forming oxides when burned. The two most important of these elements are sulfur and **nitrogen**. During the combustion of coal, sulfur is oxidized to **sulfur dioxide** and nitrogen to nitric oxide. Both sulfur dioxide and **nitrogen oxide** undergo further changes in the **atmosphere**, forming sulfur trioxide and nitrogen dioxide. Finally, these two oxides combine with water in the atmosphere to produce sulfuric and nitric acids.

This series of chemical reactions in the atmosphere may take place over hundreds or thousands of miles. Oxides of sulfur and nitrogen that leave a power plant smokestack are then carried eastward by prevailing winds. It may be many days or weeks before these oxides are carried back to earth—now as acids—in rain, snow, or some other form of precipitation. During the 1960s and 1970s, many authorities became concerned about the possible effects of acid precipitation on the environment. They argued that the problem could be solved only at the source—the electric power-generating plant.

One approach to the reduction of pollutants from a power plant is the installation of equipment that will remove undesirable materials from waste gases. An **electrostatic precipitator** is one such device which removes **particulate**s. It attaches electrical charges to the particulates in waste gases and then applies an opposing electric field to a plate that attracts the particulates and removes them from the waste gas stream. **Scrubbers**, **filters**, and **cyclone collectors** also remove harmful pollutants from waste gases.

Another approach to acid rain and other power-plant-generated pollution problems is to switch fuel from coal to oil or **natural gas**. Although **petroleum** and natural gas also contain sulfur and nitrogen, the concentration of these elements is much less than it is in many forms of coal. As a result, a number of electrical utilities began to retrofit their generating plants in the 1960s and early 1970s to allow them to burn oil or natural gas rather than coal. This change-over is reflected in the increased use of petroleum by electrical utilities in the United States between 1965 and 1975. Consumption increased more than six-fold in that ten year period, from about 100 million barrels per year to more than 6,700 million barrels per year. Interestingly enough, the use of coal by utilities did not drop off during the same period, but continued to rise from about 200 million short tons to over 300 million short tons annually.

This pattern of fuel switching turned out to be short-lived, however. Although oil and natural gas are relatively clean fuels, they also appealed to utilities because of their relatively low cost. The **oil embargo** instituted by the **Organization of Petroleum Exporting Countries (OPEC)** in 1973 altered that part of the equation. Worldwide oil prices jumped from $1.36 per million Btu in 1973 to $2.23 per million Btu in 1975, an increase of 64 percent per million Btu in just two years. A decade later, the price of oil had more than doubled. And, the situation was even worse for natural gas. The cost of a million Btu of this resource skyrocketed from 36.7 cents in 1970 to 69.3 cents in 1975 to $2.23 in the mid-1980s.

Suddenly, the conversion of power plants from coal to oil and natural gas no longer seemed like such a wonderful idea. And the utilities industry began once more to focus on the fossil fuel in most plentiful supply—coal. Between 1975 and 1990, the fraction of power plants powered by oil and natural gas dropped from 12 percent to 4 percent for the former and from 24 percent to less than 10 percent for the latter. In the same period, the fraction of plants powered by coal rose from 46 percent to 57 percent.

Power plants using fossil fuels, of whatever kind, are not the world's final solution to the generation of electricity. In addition to the environmental problems they cause, there is a more fundamental limitation. The fossil fuels are a **nonrenewable resource**. The time will come—sooner or later—when coal, oil, and natural gas supplies will be depleted. Thus, research on alternatives to fossil-fuel-fired plants has gone on for many decades.

Thirty years ago, many people believed that **nuclear power** was the best solution to the world's need to produce large amounts of electricity. Indeed, the number of nuclear power plants in the United States grew from 6 in 1965 to 95 in 1985. By 1992, 421 nuclear plants were in commercial operation worldwide, supplying 17 percent of the world's electricity. But enthusiasm for nuclear power plants began to wane in the 1980s. One reason for this trend was the serious accidents at the **Three Mile Island Nuclear Power Plant** (Middletown, Pennsylvania) in 1979 and at the **Chernobyl Nuclear Power Station** (Chernobyl, Ukraine) in 1986. Another reason was the growing concern about disposal of the ever-increasing volume of dangerous **radioactive waste**s produced by a nuclear power plant. In any case, no new nuclear power plant has been ordered in the United States since the Three Mile Island accident and 65 plant orders have been canceled since that event. Forty-nine nuclear plants are now under construction in other parts of the world, but this number is only a quarter as many as were under construction a decade ago. Indeed, between 1990 and 1991, the total installed nuclear generating capacity worldwide declined for the first time since commercial nuclear power generation began. Given current economic and political conditions, a major revival of the nuclear power industry seems unlikely.

A nuclear power plant operates on much the same principle as does a fossil-fuel power plant. In a nuclear power plant, water is heated not by the combustion of a fuel like coal or oil, but by **nuclear fission** reactions that take place within the reactor core. Some scientists anticipate that another type of nuclear power plant—the fusion reactor—may provide a (if not *the*) long-term answer to the world's electrical power needs. In a fusion reactor, atoms of light elements are fused together to make heavier elements, releasing large amounts of energy in the process. **Nuclear fusion** is the process by which stars make their energy and is also the energy source in the **hydrogen** bomb. Research efforts to develop an economic and safe method of controlling fusion power have been underway for nearly 40 years. Although progress has been made, a full-scale commercial fusion power plant currently appears to be many decade in the future.

Other types of power plants also have been under investigation for many years. For example, it is possible to operate a steam turbine with hot gases that come directly from geothermal vents. In locations where geysers or other types of vents exist, geothermal power plants are an economical, safe and dependable alternative to fossil-fueled and nuclear power plants. In the early 1990s, for example Pacific Gas and Electric in northern California obtained about eight percent of its electrical power from geothermal plants.

Finally, power plants that do not use heat at all are possible. One of the oldest forms of power plant is, in fact, the hydroelectric power plant. In a hydroelectric power plant, the movement of water (as from a river) is directed again turbine blades, causing them to rotate. In 1970, 16 percent of all electric power in the United States came from hydropower although that portion has now fallen to less than eight percent.

Proposals for wind power generated-electricity, tidal power plants, and other **alterative energy sources** as substitutes for fossil fuels and nuclear power have been around for decades. During the 1960s and 1970s, governments aggressively encouraged research on these new technologies, offering both direct grants and tax breaks. Since 1980, however, the United States government has lost interest in alternative methods of power generation, preferring instead to encourage the growth and development of more traditional fuels, such as coal, oil and petroleum. *See also* Geothermal energy; Ocean thermal energy conversion; Solar energy; Tidal power; Wind energy

[*David E. Newton*]

FURTHER READING

Balzhiser, R. E., and K. E. Yeager. "Coal-fired Power Plants for the Future." *Scientific American* 257 (September 1987): 100-107.

Brown, L. R., et al. *Vital Signs, 1992.* New York: Norton, 1992.

McGraw-Hill Encyclopedia of Science & Technology. 7th ed. New York: McGraw-Hill, 1992.

Swain, H. "Power Plants Threaten Shenandoah's Air." *National Parks* 65 (March-April 1991): 14.

Prairie

An extensive temperate **grassland** with flat or rolling terrain and moderate to low precipitation. The term is most often applied to North American grasslands, which once extended from Alberta to Texas and from Illinois to Colorado, but similar grasslands exist around the world. Perennial bunchgrasses and forbes dominate prairie **flora**. In dry **climate** prairies, a lack of precipitation prohibits tree growth except in isolated patches, such as along stream banks. In wetter prairies, periodic fires are essential in preventing the incursion of trees and preserving open grasslands. Historically, huge herds of large mammals and scores of bird, rodent, and insect **species** composed native prairie **fauna**. During the nineteenth and twentieth centuries most of North America's native prairie habitat and its occupants disappeared in the face of agricultural settlement, cattle grazing, and fire suppression. Today the geographic extent of native prairie plants and animals is severely restricted, but pockets of remaining prairie are sometimes preserved for their ecological interest and genetic diversity.

While grasses make up the dominant vegetation type in all prairies, grass sizes and species vary from shortgrass prairies, usually less than 20 inches (50 cm) high, to tallgrass prairies, whose grasses can exceed 7 feet (2 m) in height. Following the gradual east-west decrease in precipitation rates on the Great Plains, eastern tallgrass prairies gradually gave way to midgrass and then shortgrass prairies in western states. On their margins, prairie grasslands extended into a mixed "parkland," or "**savanna**," with bushes and scattered trees such as oak and juniper. Characteristic prairie grasses are perennial bunchgrasses, which have deep, extensive root systems and up to a hundred shoots from a single plant. Bunchgrasses typically grow, sprout, and flower early in the summer when rainfall is plentiful in the prairies, and their deep root systems make the long-lived plants resistant to **drought**, hail, grazing, and fire. In addition to the dominant grasses, vast numbers of flowering annual and perennial

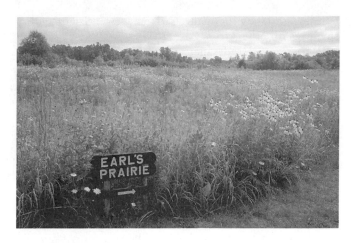

Earl prairie.

forbes—herbaceous flowering plants that are not grasses—add color to prairie landscapes.

Prairie plant species are well adapted to live with fire. Under natural conditions fires sweep across prairies every few years. Prairie fires burn intensely and quickly, fed by dry grass and prairie winds, but they burn mainly the dry stalks of previous years' growth. Below the fire's heat, the roots of prairie plants remain unharmed, and new stalks grow quickly, fertilized by ashes and unencumbered by accumulations of old litter. Before European settlement, many prairie fires were ignited by lightening, but some were started by Indians, who had an interest in maintaining good grazing land for **bison**, antelope, and other **game animal**s.

Well into the nineteenth century, prairie **habitat**s supported a tremendous variety of animal species. Vast herds of bison, pronghorn antelope, deer, and elk ranged the grasslands; smaller mammals from mice and prairie dogs to badgers and fox lived in or below the prairie grasses. Carnivores including grey **wolves**, coyotes, cougar, **grizzlies**, hawks, and owls fed on large and small herbivores. Shorebirds and migratory waterfowl thrived on millions of prairie pothole ponds and marshes. Most of these species saw their habitats severely diminished with the expansion of agricultural settlement and cattle grazing range. Prairie **soil**s, mainly mollisols, are rich and black with a thick, fertile organic layer composed of fine roots, microorganisms, and soil. Where water was available, this soil proved ideal for growing corn, wheat, soybeans, and other annual crops. Where water was scarce, nutritious bunchgrasses provided excellent grazing for cattle, which quickly replaced buffalo, elk, and antelope on the prairies in the middle of the nineteenth century.

Prairie habitat and animal species have also lost ground through fire suppression and **wetland** drainage. Farmers and ranchers have actively suppressed fires, allowing trees, exotic annuals, and other non-prairie species to become established. Widespread wetlands drainage has seriously diminished bird populations because of habitat loss. Especially in wetter northern and eastern regions, canals were cut into prairie wetlands, draining them to make arable fields. This practice continues today, even though it destroys scarce breeding grounds for many birds and essential migratory stopovers for others.

In recent decades increased attention has been given to preserving the few remaining patches of native prairie in North America. Public and private organizations now study and protect prairie grasslands and wetlands, but the long-term value of these efforts may be questionable because most remnant patches are small and widely separated. Whether genetic diversity can be maintained, and whether habitat for large or ranging animals can be reestablished under these conditions, is yet to be seen.

[*Mary Ann Cunningham*]

FURTHER READING

Cushman, R. C., and S. R. Jones *The Shortgrass Prairie*. Boulder, CO: Pruett Publishing Co., 1988.

Smith, R. L. *Ecology and Field Biology*. 3rd ed. New York: Harper and Row, 1980.

Whittaker, R. H. *Communities and Ecosystems*. 2d ed. New York: Macmillan, 1975.

Precycling

Precycling is source reduction and **reuse**. In most **waste management** planning the hierarchy is Reduce, Reuse, and Recycle. Reduction and reuse are the first lines of defense against increasing waste volume. Precycling are those actions that can be taken before **recycling** becomes an option. It is the decision on the part of a consumer to not purchase an unnecessary product or the decision to purchase a reusable as opposed to a disposable item. Precycling is using the china plates in the cupboard for a party instead of purchasing paper or plastic plates. It is also the decision to buy in bulk or to buy refillable containers and then purchasing the product in a bulk container that can refill a dispenser. Precycling is thinking ahead to the ultimate destination of the containers and packaging of products are bought and making the decision to reduce those that might end up in a **landfill**. In addition to individual decisions to reduce waste before it happens there is the decision on the part of industry to reuse **chemicals** and to buy from parts suppliers that take back packaging and reuse it. Precycling is stopping waste before it happens. *See also* Green packaging; Green products; Solid waste

Predator control

Predator control is a **wildlife management** policy specifically aimed at reducing populations of predatory **species** either to protect livestock or boost populations of **game animal**s. Coyotes, bobcats, grey and red **wolves**, bears, and mountain lions have been the most frequent targets. Historically, efforts were centered in government-run programs to hunt, trap, or poison predators, while bounties offered for

particular predatory species encouraged private citizens to do the same. Over time, however, it has become apparent that predator control is disruptive of **ecosystem**s and often inefficient.

Predator control is based on a lack of understanding of the complex interactive mechanisms by which natural **environment**s sustain themselves. Control efforts take the position that prey populations benefit when predators are removed. In the long term, however, removing predators is generally bad for the prey species and their ecosystems. The **conservation**ist **Aldo Leopold**, noticing the devastating effects of **overgrazing** by deer, realized as early as the 1920s that shooting wolves, although it led to an immediate increase in the deer population, ultimately posed a threat to the deer themselves as well as other **fauna** and **flora** in their environment. Another example can be found in the undesirable consequences of killing significant numbers of coyotes. Immediate benefits rebound not only to livestock but also to populations of rabbits and other rodents, which are normally controlled by predation. Since rabbits compete with livestock for the same **rangeland**, an explosion in the rabbit population simply means that the land can sustain fewer livestock animals.

In 1940, the **U.S. Department of the Interior** initiated a large-scale program against livestock predators, particularly aiming at the coyote and relying heavily on poisons. The poison most widely used in bait was sodium fluoroacetate, also called "compound 1080," which is highly persistent and wreaks havoc on many animals besides the coyote, including threatened and **endangered species**. Moreover, when a poisoned coyote dies, the carrion enters the **food chain/web**, with lethal effects primarily on **scavenger**s. Eagles, including the rare **bald eagle**, are particularly hard-hit by efforts to poison coyotes.

Rising environmental awareness has caused continuing controversy over predator control. By 1972, the government-appointed Committee on Predator Control concluded that the use of poisons had unacceptably harmful consequences. Government agencies discontinued the use of poisons, and poison was banned on **public land**s. Nevertheless, private citizens, mostly ranchers and hunters who feel that their interests have been sorely overlooked, have continued using poisons with little regard for the law. In the 1980s the government started taking a less progressive stance, and in 1985 the Reagan administration reinstituted the use of compound 1080 in "livestock collars." While nonpredatory species will not fall victim immediately, the poison still enters the food chain with every coyote killed.

In spite of aggressive methods, the fight against coyotes has mostly been unsuccessful. Even after decades of predator control, total annual losses are given in the hundreds of thousands of animals (mostly sheep and goats) by ranchers who claim they lose as much as 25 percent of their lambs to predators each year. Conservationists and supporters of **wildlife** say these numbers are inflated, but, even if they are accurate, the cost of lost livestock is significantly lower than the cost of the government's predator control programs. Conservation groups argue that it would be much cheaper to give up on predator control and reimburse ranchers for livestock lost to predation.

Besides killing predators, ranchers also have a number of other options when it comes to protecting their livestock. Sheep can be protected by letting it graze together with cattle or other animals too big for coyotes to handle. Llamas and donkeys have also been suggested for the purpose. Trained guard dogs are an effective deterrent to coyotes as well.

Although predator control can clearly have devastating consequences, it is by no means a thing of the past. Recently, Alaska began implementing a program to shoot 1000 wolves (out of a total population of 7000 wolves in the state). The program, which is to remove the wolves from a vast, centrally located stretch of **wilderness** over a period of five years, will have government agents tracking and shooting packs of wolves from the air. Private citizens are also allowed to shoot wolves. The object is to boost moose and caribou herds for hunting and tourist purposes. The view that the value of animal resources lies primarily in their usefulness to human beings still motivates many government policies and individual behaviors.

[*David A. Duffus and Marijke Rijsberman*]

FURTHER READING

Dasmann, R. *Environmental Conservation.* New York: Wiley, 1984.

Gilbert, F. F., and D. G. Dodds. *The Philosophy and Practice of Wildlife Management.* Malabar, FL: R. E. Kreiger, 1987.

Rolston, III, H. *Philosophy Gone Wild.* Buffalo, NY: Prometheus Books, 1989.

Wilson, E. O. *Biophilia.* Cambridge: Harvard University Press, 1984.

Predator-prey interactions

The relationship between predators and their prey within an **ecosystem** is often a quite complex array of offenses and defenses. Predation is the consumption of one living organism by another. Predators must have ways of finding, catching, and eating their prey (the offensive strategies), and prey organisms must have ways of avoiding or discouraging this activity (the defensive strategies). Predator-prey interactions are often simply thought of as one animal, a carnivore, catching and eating another animal, another carnivore or an herbivore. The interrelationships of predators and their prey is much more involved than this and encompasses all levels within an ecological **food chain/web**, from plant-herbivore systems to herbivore-carnivore systems to three-way interactions of interdependent plant-herbivore-carnivore systems.

Even though a plant may not be killed outright, removing leaves, stems, roots, bark, or the sap from plants will reduce its fitness and ultimately its ability to survive. The younger, more tender leaves and stems of a plant are typically consumed by herbivores. Because these are sites of active growth, the plants send stores of **nutrient**s from roots and other tissues to these developing regions. When they are eaten the plant is losing a disproportionate amount of nutrients that will be difficult to replenish. Severe defoliation results in a tremendous loss of vigor and the loss of the ability to photosynthesize and store energy reserves for the dormant season. Without this energy store available, the plants are more vulnerable to insect or disease attack the following year.

Plants have responded to herbivory in a variety of ways. Some plants have developed spines or thorns, whereas others have developed the ability to produce chemical products which deter herbivory by making the plant unpalatable, barely digestible, or toxic. Many herbivores have found ways to circumvent these defenses, however. Some insects are able to absorb or metabolically detoxify these **chemicals** from the plants. Other insects have learned to cut trenches in the leaves of plants before they eat them, which stops the flow of these chemical substances to the leaves. Other animals have developed digestive modifications, such as bacterial communities that break down cellulose, to enable them to ingest less nutritious, but more abundant, vegetation.

A classic example of predator-prey interactions in carnivores is the relationship of the lynx, snowshoe hare, and woody browse of northern coniferous forests. The hare feeds on buds and twigs of conifer, aspen, alder, and willow trees. Excessive browsing, as the hare population increases, decreases the subsequent year's growth, initiating a decline in the hare population. The lynx population follows that of the snowshoe hare, having greater reproductive success when more prey are available, then declining as hare populations drop. This relationship is cyclical and follows its course over a ten-year period.

The prey of carnivores, both herbivores and other carnivores, have developed a variety of defensive mechanisms to avoid being detected, caught, or eaten. Some employ chemicals, such as odorous secretions, stored toxic substances ingested from plants, or synthesized venom or poisons. Other animals have taken to hiding from predators through cryptic coloration, patterns, shapes, and postures. Mimicry, widespread in the animal kingdom, is a system whereby one animal, a palatable **species**, mimics an inedible species, and is thus avoided by the predator. Additional means of predator avoidance or discouragement involves the employment of armor coats or shells, the use of quills or spines, or living in groups. However, predators can benefit prey populations by removing sick or inferior individuals. Subtle, long-term interactions, in fact, can benefit both predator and prey as they co-evolve together into more highly adapted or finely-tuned forms. *See also* Evolution; Population biology

[*Eugene C. Beckham*]

FURTHER READING

Lawick, H. van. *Among Predators and Prey.* San Francisco: Sierra Club Books, 1986.

Predator-Prey Relationships: Perspectives and Approaches From the Study of Lower Vertebrates. Chicago: University of Chicago Press, 1986.

Predators and Predation: The Struggle for Life in the Animal World. New York: Facts on File, 1989.

Sunquist, F. "The Strange, Dangerous World of Folivory." *International Wildlife* 21 (1991): 4-11.

Taylor, R. J. *Predation.* New York: Chapman and Hall, 1984.

Prescribed burning

Intentional burning, usually in forests, **prairie**s, and **savanna**s, in order to maintain desired ecological conditions or prevent major **wildfires** that could result from accumulated dry, woody debris. Prescribed burning, also called controlled burning, has become a widely recognized component of modern **ecosystem management** in recent decades as ecologists and managers have recognized the role of fire in natural **ecosystem**s. In practice, though, prescribed burning is still used only on a small portion of public and private lands. In a forest, prescribed burning is usually aimed at removing accumulated fuel—fallen branches, pine needles, and other dry debris. In a prairie or savanna **environment**, prescribed burns may be used to prevent encroachment of trees, to reduce populations of nonnative grassland species, and to enhance the health of native grassland vegetation that is adapted to periodic fires.

The principle of prescribed burning is that fire is a normal component of ecosystems, and that frequent small fires can serve both to maintain species diversity and to prevent large, catastrophic wildfires. Under natural conditions wildfires, usually ignited by lightning, occur frequently in many forest and grassland **biome**s. Proponents of prescribed burning argue that these natural fires would usually be small and cool, occurring too frequently to allow excessive accumulation of fallen branches, dead grass, and other fuel. Frequent, low-intensity fires should do little damage either to mature trees or to the root systems of most plants. At the same time, by clearing away debris every few years, and by a natural fire regime should provide fresh ground, exposed to sunlight and freshly fertilized by ashes, to encourage new germination and plant growth.

Deliberate burning is also an age-old method of maintaining grazing lands in many parts of the world. Periodic forest burning to maintain pasturage and to clear farm plots has probably been practiced for millennia in Africa and South America. In North America, indigenous peoples used fire to maintain open forests and prairies that provide grazing for game animals such as deer and bison. In some areas, especially New England and the rural South, early European immigrants to the New World adopted Indian methods of burning. These practices differ from what is usually considered a prescribed burn, however, because they are often carried out without the planning and the careful fire control usually exercised in a controlled or prescribed burn. In most of North America, traditional burning practices have also disappeared as more and more forests have come under professional management for timber production.

The introduction of prescribed burning to professional land management strategies in the United States is often

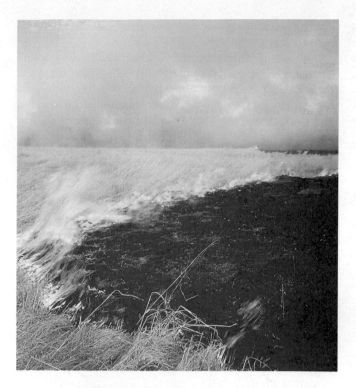

Prescribed burning of a prairie in South Dakota for land management purposes.

attributed to **Aldo Leopold**, who pointed out in 1924, while he was serving as a forester and firefighter in Arizona, that fire control programs were producing brush-choked forests susceptible to extreme wildfire. Leopold argued that decades of fire suppression had actually increased the probability of severe fires, and that forests were healthier when subject to regular, natural fires. Since Leopold began arguing for prescribed burning in the 1920s, ecosystem managers have widely recognized the ecological benefits of fire. The amount of prescribed burning carried out still remains modest, however. Between 1983-1994, prescribed burns were carried out on only about 0.1% of public lands in the United States each year, as compared to 0.3% burned annually by wildfires in the same interval.

Proponents of prescribed burning sometimes argue fire suppression techniques—bulldozed fire breaks, tree felling, air drops of chemical fire retardants, and other measures—cause more damage than the fires they are meant to control. In addition, these expensive, and dangerous, tactics may ultimately have little effect. Prescribed burn proponents argue that most large natural fires die out as a result of rainfall, cooler weather, or a lack of fuel, not because of the efforts of fire fighters. These opponents of standard military-style fire suppression programs propose that it would be more effective to use fire control budgets for planned burns than for impressive but useless shows of force against large forest fires. However events such as the **Yellowstone National Park** fires of 1988, a series of highly publicized fires that led to loud criticism from the media and politicians that Park officials were negligent in their duties to protect the park, demonstrate that the public is unlikely to settle for inactivity during a forest fire. During fires such as those in Yellowstone, the public is quick to criticize officials for doing nothing even if there is nothing to be done. Most of us would rather see a campaign to fight fires even if wastes money and causes serious damage to the forest.

Benefits of Prescribed Fires

Fire has many ecological benefits. By clearing patches of forest, fire allows tree seeds to germinate. The seedlings of many trees, including Douglas fir (*Pseudotsuga menziesii*) and white pine (*Pinus strobus*), both prized for timber, require the strong sunlight of an open patch in the forest to begin growing. Other species, such as jack pine (*Pinus banksiana*) require intense heat, such as that produced by a fire or extremely hot sun, to release the seeds from their resin-sealed cones. These trees are considered fire-adapted, because they reproduce best, or only, when seedlings can grow in the full sun and fresh ashes of recently burned patches of forest. Many prairie grasses and flowers are also fire adapted, thriving best when periodic fires remove dead stem litter and release stored nutrients to the **soil**.

Fire plays an important role in cleaning out damaged or diseased regions of a forest. Where **parasites**, fungus, or disease have damaged stands of trees, a fire can locally eliminate the pest population, reducing the risk of parasite or disease spread, at the same time as it removes standing dead trees and makes room for new seedlings to replace the damaged trees. Land managers in southern Alaska, faced with the worst spruce beetle outbreak ever in the United States, have recently begun to consider using prescribed fire to control beetles.

Undesirable species encroaching on **grasslands** and savannas can also be controlled with fire. Opportunistic trees and brush such as aspen, buckthorn, juniper and sumac, introduced European grasses, as well as nuisance species such as poison oak and poison ivy can all be set back by periodic burning. At the same time, prescribed burns can rejuvenate fire-adapted plant populations by clearing debris and releasing nutrients to the soil. In a burned area increased sunlight can extend the growing season, an important advantage in cold climates. In addition, periodic patchy burns help maintain habitat diversity by producing a mosaic of landscape types and different-aged tree stands. Because many animal species utilize a variety of environments for feeding and nesting, a mosaic landscape maintained by fire can benefit wildlife populations.

Methods

A prescribed burn is a fire set under conditions that should allow control of the fire. Usually this means identifying the limits of an area that should be burned and creating or identifying fire breaks that will prevent the uncontrolled spread of the fire once it has been lit. Often a backfire is used. A backfire is line of fire burned on the downwind edge of the area to be burned. The backfire is kept low and forced to burn upwind until it has created a swath of land clear of any combustible fuel. Flank fires, similarly, clear combustible materials from strips along the flanks of the burn area. The main fire, moving forward in a downwind direction, will die out due to a lack of fuel when it reaches the blacked zone created by the backfire. In addition to these precautions, prescribed burning usually requires selecting a day with high humidity and light winds, to keep the fire relatively low.

Ideally areas should be burned periodically in order to mimic the pattern of natural fires. Fire ecologists and managers usually attempt to burn areas with the frequency they estimate would occur in local ecosystems under natural conditions. In some areas natural fire frequency might be as often as every 2-3 years; elsewhere natural fires might normally occur as infrequently as every 10-20 years. Or managers may simply burn any areas in which debris has accumulated to dangerous levels.

Prescribed Natural Fires

Sometimes a prescribed burn policy means establishing a rule to let naturally ignited fires, usually started by lightning, burn themselves out. When rules establish that fires should be allowed to burn, fires that occur are referred to as prescribed natural fires. "Let-burn" policies are widely applied in **national park**s and forests in the United States. Seventy-five percent of **Yosemite National Park**, for example, is treated as a prescribed natural fire zone. In large part this is because it is more politically palatable to allow nature to take its course than it is to deliberately burn a park. In addition, it is less costly to let fires burn naturally than to maintain a burn crew, design burn plans and fire breaks, and carry out and monitor a regular program of prescribed burns. Usually a prescribed natural fire policy sets limits on the conditions and size of fires that will be allowed to burn, and any natural fires that do occur are closely monitored to ensure that they do not become too large or dangerous.

History of Prescribed Burning in the United States

Two factors influenced the development of prescribed burning in the United States. One was the observation that despite decades of fire suppression, the number and intensity of wildfires has actually increased since the advent of major fire suppression programs. One United States Forest Service study showed that total acreage burned, after declining from 1917 to 1955, increased steadily from the 1960s to the 1990s. The other factor was a transition in ecological theory toward understanding ecosystems as complex and dynamic, not static structures that should be maintained a single, undisturbed, optimal climax state. The shift in ecological theory developed partly from the observation that ecosystems maintained rigorously by managers were not necessarily healthier, than those that underwent periodic catastrophic events such as floods and fires. In fact, according to this theory, ecosystems may require periodic change and disruption in order to remain healthy.

The **Nature Conservancy**, which maintains scattered patches of native prairie, savanna, and other ecosystems, was one of the pioneers of prescribed burning. Since it conducted its first prescribed burn on a North Dakota prairie in the 1970s, the Nature Conservancy has expanded its prescribed burning program to a current level of over 40,000 acres (16,400 ha) of native habitat each year. The organization's objectives are controlling invasive plant species and maintaining the vigor of native fire-adapted plant communities.

Controversy over Prescribed Burns

Prescribed burning is controversial for several reasons. First, decades of education about fire suppression, both in the general public and among land management professionals, makes burning seem intuitively wrong to many people. Cultural icons such as Smokey Bear and Bambi, both fictional characters who suffered from forest fires, have symbolized the trauma and destruction of fires. The idea that fire might rejuvenate a forest is often harder to explain than the idea that fire destroys a forest. Second, people living near forests and grasslands fear that a controlled burn may escape and damage their property—an event that occurs rarely but is always a potential risk. Property owners are understandably nervous about the possibility of a fire escaping. On the other hand, prescribed burns have sometimes been used to protect property. A number of homes adjacent to the Wenatchee National Forest in Washington State were spared from the Tyee Creek fire of 1994 because previous burns had reduced fuel levels in the surrounding forest.

In addition to objections to fire danger, the smoke resulting from a prescribed fire is unpleasant and sometimes hazardous. There can be a real health risk for people with lung ailments or **asthma** if they are exposed to concentrated smoke. In addition, a deliberately set fire often violates air quality laws, making fires technically illegal in many populated areas. If the fire occurs near a road, visibility is also reduced, so that the road must often be closed while a burn is in progress. Although the smoke produced by a series of prescribed fires may be less than the smoke from a single large wildfire, prescribed fires are sensitive because the individual or group responsible for the fire is also liable for any damage or injury it causes.

Controversy over the use of prescribed burns has become especially serious in areas where human settlement is encroaching on natural areas. Where cities and suburbs spread into forested areas or reach the edges of preserves that are managed with fire, residents of new subdivisions usually object to the potential risks and inconvenience imposed by fire near their property. This problem is especially severe in the chaparral country of southern and central California. Chaparral is a fire-adapted ecosystem with highly combustible, dry vegetation that normally burns as every 30 years or so. As suburban development, with its high real estate values, moves into the chaparral, the economic and environmental costs of fire control have risen sharply. In wildlife and habitat preserves near metropolitan areas land managers have sometimes had to abandon successful fire management programs because of suburban sprawl.

[*Mary Ann Cunningham*]

FURTHER READING

Babbit, B. "To take up the torch," *American Forests* 101 (July/August 1995):17-18, 59.

de V. Booysen, P., and N. Tainton, eds. *Ecological effects of fire in South African ecosystems.* Ecological Studies vol. 48. New York: Springer-Verlag, 1995.

McLean, H. "Fighting fire with fire," *American Forests.* 101 (July/August 1995):13-16, 56-7.

Pyne, S.J. *Fire in America.* Princeton, N.J.: Princeton University Press, 1982.

United States Forest Service. *The Use of Fire in Forest Restoration.* USFS General Technical Report INT-GTR-341. Washington, D.C.: General Printing Office, 1996.

President's Council on Sustainable Development

An environmental advisory group created by President Bill Clinton in June 1993 to develop new approaches for combining environmental protection in the United States with economic development. The council is composed of 25 members drawn from government, industry, and environmental groups. One of the primary mandates of the President's Council on Sustainable Development is to develop plans for the U.S. to fulfill its role in the **biodiversity**, global warming, and other accords negotiated at the 1992 **United Nations Earth Summit**. *See also* Economic growth and the environment; Environmental policy; Greenhouse effect; Population growth; Sustainable development

Price-Anderson Act (1957)

The Price-Anderson Act, passed in 1957, limits the liability of civilian producers of **nuclear power** in the case of a catastrophic nuclear accident. In the case of such an accident, damages would be recovered from two sources: private insurance covering each plant and a common fund created by contributions from each nuclear **power plant**. This common fund would cover the difference in damages between the private insurance and the liability limit.

The act, named for its chief sponsors, Senator Clinton Anderson (NM) and Representative Melvin Price (IL), was passed to encourage private investment in nuclear power production. It was part of a general strategy to encourage and stimulate nuclear power production in the private sector. Without such liability limitations, the risk of nuclear power for utilities and manufacturers would be too great. Private insurance companies were not willing to underwrite the risks due to the uncertainty involved and the potential magnitude of damages.

The law requires the private operators to carry the maximum amount of private insurance available ($65 million in the late 1950s). The upper limit for liability was set at $560 million per accident for personal damages, with the common fund covering the difference (between $65 million and $560 million). Once the liability limit is reached this law protects the operator from further financial liability. In addition to setting liability limits, the law establishes a common fund for victims to draw on if the utility did not have the ability to pay damages up to the liability limit. In return for this limited liability, utilities had to accept sole responsibility for accidents; equipment manufacturers would not be liable for any damages.

The Price-Anderson Act serves as a subsidy to the nuclear power industry. If it were not for this liability limitation, it is unlikely that any private firms would have become involved in the production of nuclear power. As a further incentive to private industry, the federal government set the liability limits at a very low level. This was done despite a 1957 government estimate of the damages due to a catastrophic accident: 3,000 immediate deaths and $7 billion in property damage.

In 1977, the Carolina Environmental Study Group filed a lawsuit, claiming that the Price-Anderson Act was unconstitutional because it was a taking of private property without just compensation, a violation of the Fifth Amendment. If a nuclear accident did occur and compensation was limited, the argument went, a taking of private property had occurred and compensation was limited in advance. A federal district court ruled for the environmental group: the act was unconstitutional. In 1978, however, the Supreme Court overturned this ruling, maintaining the constitutionality of the Price-Anderson Act.

The 1988 amendments to the act increased the liability limit per accident from $720 million to $7.2 billion, with the utilities continuing to contribute to a common fund to help pay for any damages if a major accident did occur. The private insurance coverage was set at $160 million per plant, with the common fund to make up the over $7 billion difference. These liability limits will last through 2003. Despite this tremendous increase in liability limits, the nuclear power industry was pleased to retain any liability limit in the face of significant opposition. The amendments also protect **U.S. Department of Energy** nuclear contractors from damage claims and limit the liability for nuclear waste accidents to $7 billion. *See also* Environmental law; Environmental liability; Nuclear fission; Radioactive waste; Radioactivity; Three Mile Island Nuclear Reactor

[*Christopher McGrory Klyza*]

FURTHER READING

Kruschke, E. R., and B. M. Jackson. *Nuclear Energy Policy.* New York: ABC-Clio, 1990.

Jasper, J. M. *Nuclear Politics: Energy and the State in the United States, Sweden, and France.* Princeton: Princeton University Press, 1990.

Mazuzan, G. T., and J. S. Walker. *Controlling the Atom: The Beginnings of Nuclear Regulation 1946-1962.* Berkeley: University of California Press, 1985.

Primary pollutant

Primary pollutants cause **pollution** by their direct release into the **environment**. The substance released may already be present in some quantities, but it is considered a primary pollutant if the additional release brings the total quantity of the substance to pollution levels. For example, **carbon dioxide** is already naturally present in the **atmosphere**, but it becomes toxic when additional releases cause it to rise above its natural concentrations. The rise in levels of carbon dioxide is one contributing factor to the **greenhouse effect**.

The direct release into the atmosphere of a chemical that is not normally present in the air is also classified as a primary pollutant. **Hydrogen** fluoride, for example, is re-

leased from some **coal**-fired furnaces, but the compound is not usually present in unpolluted air.

A primary pollutant can be generated by many sources: **pesticide** dust sprayed intensively in agricultural areas, **emissions** from car and industrial exhausts, or dust kicked about from mining operations, to name a few. Some primary pollutants are composed of **particulate** matter that is not easily dispersed. **Smoke**, soot, dust, and liquid droplets released into the air either by the burning of fuel or other industrial or agricultural processes, are considered primary pollutants.

Primary pollutants also originate from natural sources. Volcanic ash, as well as grit and dust from volcanic explosions belong to this category. Salt dust blown inland by strong oceanic winds or gaseous pollution that originates from bogs, marshes, and other decomposing matter can also be classified as primary pollutants.

When two or more primary pollutants react in the atmosphere and cause additional atmospheric pollution, the result is called secondary pollution. **Nitrogen oxides**, for instance, can react with volatile organic compounds to from **smog**, a secondary pollutant. *See also* Air pollution; Air pollution index; Air quality criteria; National Ambient Air Quality Standard

[*Linda Rehkopf*]

FURTHER READING

Ney, R. E. *Where Did That Chemical Go? A Practical Guide to Chemical Fate and Transport in the Environment.* New York: Van Nostrand Reinhold, 1990.

Shinedecker, C. L. *Handbook of Environmental Contaminants: A Guide for Site Assessment.* Boca Raton, FL: Lewis, 1992.

Primary sewage treatment
See **Sewage treatment**

Primary standards

Primary standards are numerical limits of allowable air and water pollutants designed to protect human health but not necessarily other parts of the **environment**. Primary standards differ from **secondary standards**, which are those that protect against all adverse effects on the environment, such as those on animals and vegetation. While the term primary standards usually relates to **air pollution** or **air quality**, there are federal primary standards for the **drinking water supply**.

The **Clean Air Act** is the major piece of legislation that protects and enhances the nation's air quality. As part of the act, Congress required the **Environmental Protection Agency (EPA)** to establish **National Ambient Air Quality Standards (NAAQS)** for air pollutants, which were characterized by wide dispersal and **emission** from many sources.

The NAAQS, or primary air quality standards, define the level of air quality to be achieved and maintained nationwide for six **criteria pollutant**s: **sulfur dioxide, carbon monoxide, nitrogen oxides, ozone, particulate** matter, and **lead**. In general, these standards are not permitted to be exceeded more than once a year. In addition, the EPA is required to identify local hazardous air pollutants which could increase mortality or result in serious illnesses such as **cancer**, and establish national standards for them. Although hundreds of potentially hazardous air pollutants exist, only eight had been listed as of 1990: **mercury**, beryllium, **asbestos, vinyl chloride, benzene**, radioactive substances, coke oven emissions, and inorganic **arsenic**.

The Clean Air Act set a deadline of December 1987 for cities in the United States to meet federal primary standards. Some cities did meet the standards, increasing **automobile** emission inspections and instituting tighter regulations for incinerators, but some sixty cities could not comply. There has been a measurable increase in nitrogen oxide emissions in recent years, and more than 100 areas nationwide have exceeded standards at least part of the time for ozone and carbon monoxide levels. The EPA has estimated that 100 million people live in areas exceeding these standards. The most heavily-polluted areas of the **Los Angeles Basin**, Houston, and the New York corridor may take years to meet the air quality standards. Suggestions to hasten compliance have included plans to shut down industrial plants, ration gas, and restrict automobile use.

The 1990 Clean Air Act Amendments include provisions to tighten **pollution control** requirements in cities that have not attained the National Ambient Air Quality Standards. These provisions include, among others, requirements for stringent automobile **emission standards**. The new act also requires a 50 percent reduction in sulfur dioxide emissions, and it sets primary and secondary standards for dozens of **chemicals** that were not mentioned in the original act or amendments.

Primary standards are not consistent from country to country. For example, standards are defined for different average times, at varying numerical limits. In thirteen countries the sulfur dioxide standard ranges from 0.30 to 0.75 mg/m^3 for a 30-minute average, and from 0.05 to 0.38 mg/m^3 for a 24-hour average. Since **pollution** does not stay in once place, and since **acid rain** is often a source of controversy between bordering countries, the lack of international standards will continue to contribute to air pollution problems.

In the United States, concern about **water pollution** has resulted in higher standards for water cleanliness. These standards have been adopted by state and federal agencies, but the involvement of so many different agencies on different levels has contributed to a lack of agreement on some water standards.

The primary law to protect the integrity of the nation's water is the **Clean Water Act** (1972). The act requires the EPA to set **water quality** criteria based on the most recent scientific information. Under the Clean Water Act Reauthorization (1987), the EPA is required to publish revised water quality criteria, stress new programs to combat water pollution from toxics, and restrict waivers from national standards that had been easily obtained by discharges.

Criteria are not rules; they are a compilation of data about pollutants that can be used to formulate standards. Congress intended for the EPA to set the criteria and for the states to set the **water quality standards**. By 1990 the EPA had established criteria for 126 **priority pollutant**s. Of these, 109 dealt with primary standards and thirty-four with secondary standards. But although these criteria have been published, few states have actually established standards for toxic pollutants or have incorporated these standards into the regulation of toxic **discharge**.

Under the Safe Drinking Water Reauthorization Act (1986), the EPA is not only required to set standards for contaminants in drinking water, but it also must monitor public drinking water for unregulated contaminants and set deadlines for the issuance of new standards. By 1990, the EPA had set primary standards for drinking water that covered the inorganic chemicals arsenic, barium, **cadmium**, chromium, lead, mercury, nitrate, selenium, silver, and fluoride. Primary drinking water standards are measured in terms of maximum contaminant levels (MCLs), which are the maximum permissible level of a contaminant in water at the tap; they are health related and legally enforceable.

Organic chemicals regulated by primary standards for drinking water include the **pesticide**s Endrin, Lindane, Methoxychlor, and Toxaphene; the **herbicide**s 2,4-D and 2,4,5-T Silvex; and the organics benzene, carbon tetrachloride, p-dichlorobenzene, 1,2-dichlorobenzene, 1,2-dichloroethane, 1,1-dichloroethylene, 1,1,1-trichloroethane, trichloroethylene, vinyl chloride, and an organic compound referred to as total **trihalomethanes**. Microbiological standards for drinking water have been set for coliform bacterium such as *Escherichia coli*, which is present in sewage and which can cause gastroenteric infections, dysentery, hepatitis, and other diseases. Standards have also been set for turbidity, the murkiness of treated water which can interfere with disinfection processes. Radionuclides regulated by primary standards include **beta particle**s and photon activity, gross **alpha particle**s, and Radium-226 and -228.

As is the case with primary standards for air quality, an international comparison of primary standards for drinking water reveals a collection of confusing numbers. While the United States and Canada seem to agree on standards for organic compounds, this is where the similarity ends. As of 1990, the Canadian government had no primary drinking water standards for radionuclides other than radium, and it had not set primary standards for volatile organic chemicals such as benzene and vinyl chloride. By 1990, the **European Economic Community** had set primary drinking water standards only for total pesticides and trihalomethanes. The World Health Organization (WHO) has recommended primary standards only for the organics 2,4-D, methoxychlor, and trihalomethanes, beta and alpha radionuclides, and five of the eight volatile organic chemicals regulated in the United States.

In the United States, there is evidence that primary standards regarding air and water pollutants have had some impact on air and water quality. Some of the nation's surface waters have improved since the implementation of the Clean

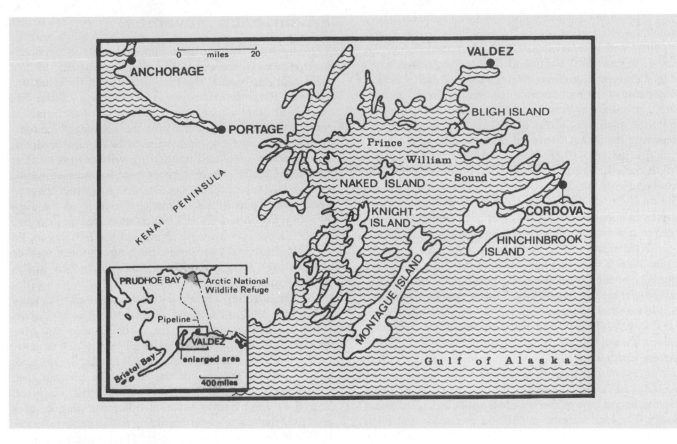

Prince William Sound, Alaska.

Water Act. **Coliform bacteria** counts and dissolved solids have been reduced, and **dissolved oxygen** levels have increased enough to permit the reestablishment of plants and animals that had died out in polluted waters.

Air quality standards have led to an overall 20 percent reduction in emissions of particulates, sulfur dioxide, and carbon monoxide during the 1980s. Los Angeles, which suffers as much or more than any American city from air pollution, has proposed an air quality plan that would surpass the EPA's standards, requiring lifestyle changes to help combat air pollution.

Implementing laws and regulations to enforce water and air standards that will protect the health of humans will be expensive: The yearly price tag just for implementation of the Clean Air Act of 1990 is estimated to be $25 billion. But many believe the savings in health costs and environmental damage to be incalculable. *See also* Air pollution index; Air Quality Control Region; Air quality criteria; Attainment area; Nitrates and nitrites; Nonattainment area; Radioactive waste; Safe Drinking Water Act; Sewage treatment; Toxic substance

[*Linda Rehkopf*]

FURTHER READING

Freeman, M. *Air and Water Pollution Regulation: Accomplishments and Economic Consequences.* Westport, CT: Greenwood Publishing Group, 1993.

Harte, John, et al. *Toxics A to Z.* Berkeley: University of California Press, 1991.

van der Leeden, F., et al. *The Water Encyclopedia.* Chelsea, MI: Lewis Publishers, 1990.

Prince William Sound, Alaska

British explorer Captain James Cook made the European discovery of Prince William Sound in 1778. Today, the 25,090-square-mile (65,000-square-kilometer) passage southeast of Anchorage, Alaska, is the focal point of an ongoing political and environmental issue: whether oil can be safely transported in extreme **climate**s without seriously threatening terrestrial and marine **habitat**s or the recreational, agricultural, and industrial interests of the region.

Prince William Sound is bordered on the north and west by the Chugach and Kenai mountain ranges, on the east by the Copper River, and by the Hinchinbrook Islands on the south. Ten percent of its area is open water, with depths ranging from 492-2,952 ft (149-895 m). The remainder consists of shallow coastal waters, shoals, and reefs. The combined 2,980 miles (4,800 km) of mainland and island shoreline are home to more than 200 **species** of birds, among them approximately 3,000 **bald eagle**s. Ten species of marine mammals, including sea lions, seals, **whales**, porpoises, and some 10,000 **sea otter**s thrive in its bountiful waters. The natural beauty of Prince William Sound is responsible for the area's healthy tourism industry.

The Sound is world-renowned for its **salmon** fishery. More than 300 streams are used by salmon for spawning and, combined with hatchery inputs, more than one billion fry are released annually into the Sound. The herring season brings in an additional 12 million dollars to the area each year. The inhabitants of the four communities on the Sound are supported primarily by fishing and its related industries. For economic reasons, residents of the area are concerned with preserving the Sound's **natural resources**.

In the mid-1970s, the Cordova Island fishermen fought the oil industry's plan to build an oil pipeline from Prudhoe Bay in northern Alaska to Prince William Sound. The decision was left to the United States Senate which, despite warnings from scientists and environmental groups, voted to approve the proposed pipeline route into the Sound.

Natural and man-induced disasters threaten the health of the Sound. The Alaskan coast makes up the western boundary of the North American continental plate and is, therefore, subject to considerable seismic activity. On March 24, 1964, an earthquake centered in the mountains surrounding Prince William Sound had substantial effects on the Sound. Twenty-five years later to the day, the oil tanker **Exxon Valdez** wrecked on the rocks of the Sound's Bligh Reef in waters less than 39 ft (12 m) deep. Approximately 265,000 barrels (42 million liters) of heavy crude oil leaked into the Sound, one of the worst **oil spills** in United States history. The local sea otter population was nearly destroyed; many pelagic and shore bird populations were also heavily impacted. Effects of the spill and subsequent clean-up efforts on shoreline and sea-floor communities are unknown, as are the long-term effects on Prince William Sound and adjacent habitats.

[*William G. Ambrose, Jr. and Paul E. Renaud*]

FURTHER READING

Dold, C. A., et al. "Just the Facts: Prince William Sound." *Audubon* 91 (1989): 80.

Heacox, K. "Sound of Silence." *Buzzworm* 5 (January-February 1993): 52.

Lethcoe, N., ed. *Prince William Sound Environmental Reader, 1989: Exxon Valdez Oil Spill.* Valdez, AK: Prince William Sound Books, 1989.

Steiner, R. "Probing an Oil-Stained Legacy." *National Wildlife* 31 (April-May 1993): 4-11.

Priority pollutant

Under the 1977 amendments to the **Clean Water Act**, the **Environmental Protection Agency** is required to compile a list of priority toxic pollutants and to establish toxic pollutant effluent standards. A list of 126 key water pollutants was produced by EPA in 1981, and is updated regularly, with the updates appearing in the *Code of Federal Regulations*. This list, consisting of metals and organic compounds and known as the Priority Toxic Pollutant list, also prescribes numerical **water quality standards** for each compound. State water quality programs must use these standards or develop their own standards of at least equal stringency.

Privatization movement

This movement, initiated and supported primarily by economists, peaked in the early 1980s. Public ownership of land was inefficient because the administration of the lands was removed from the incentives and discipline of the free market. The case for the transfer of these lands to the private sector was made most strongly for lands managed for commodities (e.g., grazing lands, mineral lands, timber lands), but some also advocated transferring **wilderness** lands to the private sector, where it, too, would be more efficiently managed. Many of the economists who supported the program were a part of a movement referred to as the New Resource Economics (NRE), which advocated an increased reliance on private property rights and the free market for managing **natural resources**. Such an approach meshed well with the Reagan Administration's philosophy of free market economics.

The privatization idea moved from theory to practice in February 1982 at a Cabinet Council on Economic Affairs meeting with the creation of the Asset Management Program. This program was designed to identify federal property for disposal, to develop legislation needed to dispose the land, and to oversee the sale of the land. The program was formalized by President Reagan in February 1982. The Fiscal Year (FY) 1983 budget proposal called for the sale of 5 percent of the nation's land (excluding Alaska), approximately 35 million acres, over five years. The revenues projected from the program were $17 billion from FY 1983 through FY 1987, the bulk of which was to come from sales of **Bureau of Land Management** (BLM) and **Forest Service** lands.

The BLM began to develop a program for land disposal, but in July 1983, Secretary of the Interior **James Watt** removed Interior Department lands from the Asset Management Program. He thought that the program was a mistake and was undermining the President's support in the West that had developed through the *good neighbor* program (which had defused the **Sagebrush Rebellion**).

In the summer of 1982, the Forest Service began to identify possible lands for disposal and announced that it would seek legislative authority to dispose the land. In March 1983, the agency announced that it would seek legislative authority to dispose of up to 6 million acres of land managed by the Forest Service (3.2 percent of the lands in the system). At this time, they indicated the specific amounts of land under consideration for disposal in each state, with high figures of 872,054 acres in Montana and 36 percent of its land in Ohio.

Opposition to the Asset Management Program was immediate and intense. The chief opponents were environmentalists, but they were also joined by the forestry profession and many western politicians. This already strong opposition to the program intensified once the specific areas for disposal were identified. In the face of this intense opposition, the Forest Service never presented legislation to Congress to allow the sale of these lands. The attempt to put privatization into practice was aborted by early 1984.

[*Christopher McGrory Klyza*]

FURTHER READING

Short, C. B. *Ronald Reagan and the Public Lands: America's Conservation Debate, 1979–1984*. College Station, TX: Texas A&M University Press, 1989.

Truluck, P. N., ed. *Private Rights and Public Lands*. Washington, DC: Heritage Foundation, 1983.

Propellants

Propellants are used to disperse **aerosol**s, powders and other materials in a wide variety of applications. Consumers are familiar with products such as cleaners, waxes, and spray paints that are packaged in "aerosol spray cans" that use propellants. In addition, many medical, commercial and industrial products use propellants. These products include adhesives; document preservation sprays; portable fire extinguishing equipment; insecticides; sterilants; animal repellants; medical devices such as anti-**asthma** inhalers and topical anesthetic applicators; lubricants, coatings and cleaning fluids used in the electrical, electronic, and aerospace industries; and blowing agents and mold release agents used in the production of foams, plastic and elastomeric materials. In many cases, the propellant pressurizes, atomizes and delivers the product as an aerosol spray. In other cases, the propellant itself is the sole or major "active ingredient" of the product, usually for solvent and/or cleaning applications.

Aerosol sprays and other dispersions made possible using propellants can form very small and uniform droplets with controllable properties. These characteristics are desirable or necessary in critical applications where a very thin layer or coating must be applied to a surface, e.g., as a lubricant coating in an aerospace application. Additionally, the small aerosols can be inhaled deeply into the lung and the droplet itself may evaporate quickly, depending on the product. Such characteristics help optimize the delivery of drugs using medical inhalers.

The ideal propellant should generate sufficient volume and pressure of vapor or gas for a particular application, should be safe to humans and the **environment**, inert with respect to reactions with other materials, miscible or highly soluble in the product, easy to handle, and inexpensive. Each chemical has its own physical and chemical properties that affect the selection of a propellant for a given product and application. Important properties are solvency, performance, cost, and environmental considerations. Many of these properties are well characterized. For example, the solvency of a propellant can be measured as its solubility in water or other chemicals. Performance properties include the amount and pressure of vapor generated from the liquid, measured as vapor pressure, the volume of vapor generated per mass or volume of the liquid, and the ratio of the volume of gas to the volume of liquid. Performance also includes the range of temperatures where the propellant will function adequately, measured as the boiling and freezing points of the propellant, and as the vapor generation rates at different temperatures. The flammability of the propellant is another often critical property, measured as the flammability limits in air and the flash point. Additional properties that may be important include the density of the liquid and gas, the critical tempera-

ture and pressure, the specific heat of gas and liquid, the heat of vaporization, the viscosity of the liquid propellant, the coefficient of liquid expansion, and the surface tension. Environmental characteristics of propellants include the toxicity (often measured as cancer causing potency), the **ozone** depleting potential, the greenhouse warming potential, and the reactivity (in terms of forming ground level ozone). It is the environmental considerations that have brought propellants forward in the last 20+ years as an national and international environmental issue.

Restrictions on the Use of Propellants

Prior to the late 1970s, aerosol propellants were frequently **chlorofluorocarbon (CFC)** propellants, and this use constituted over 50% of total U.S. CFC consumption. At the time, the most widely used CFCs were CFC-11 and CFC-12. (These chemicals were also used in refrigeration, foam blowing, and sterilization). Following concerns raised in 1974 regarding possible stratospheric ozone depletion resulting from CFCs, the U.S. **Environmental Protection Agency** (EPA) and the **Food and Drug Administration** (FDA) acted on March 17, 1978, to ban the use of CFCs as aerosol propellants in all but essential applications. This reduced aerosol use of CFCs by approximately 95% and achieved nearly a 50% reduction in the U.S. consumption of CFCs. This reduction was largely accomplished without economic penalty as consumers voluntarily responded to advertising for "ozone safe" substitutes. Also in the late 1970s, Canada and a few Nordic nations banned or restricted aerosol propellant uses, also resulting in a sharp drop in their total CFC use. Later in the 1980s, however, increases in other uses of CFCs, largely as solvents, offset the earlier decreases.

The 1978 ban specifically exempted certain products based on a determination of essentiality. Also excluded were products where the CFC itself was the active ingredient or sole ingredient in an aerosol or pressurized dispenser products, as this did not fit the ban's narrow definition of an "aerosol" propellant. These restrictions remained in effect until 1990. Title VI of the 1990 **Clean Air Act** Amendments (CAAA) included provisions relevant to use of ozone depleting chemicals used as propellants and expanded restrictions for propellants. EPA's response is the "Significant New Alternatives Policy" (SNAP) Program which includes the evaluation of alternatives to ozone-depleting substances, including an assessment of their **ozone layer depletion** potential, global warming potential, toxicity, flammability, and exposure potential (section 612 of the CAAA; 59 FR 13044).

In general, ozone-depleting substances are divided into two classes with different product bans (section 610 in the CAAA): Class I comprises CFCs, halons, carbon tetrachloride, methyl chloroform (MCF), hydrobromofluorocarbons and methyl bromide; and Class II comprises solely of **hydrochlorofluorocarbons (HCFCs)**. EPA is to prohibit the sale or distribution of certain "nonessential" products (as determined by Congress and EPA) that release class I substances, mandate the phaseout of class I and class II substances (sections 604 and 605), review substitutes (section

612), and prohibit the sale of certain nonessential products made with class I and class II substances (section 610). After its review, EPA issued regulations on January 15, 1993 (58 FR 4767) which banned CFC propellants in aerosols and other pressurized dispensers (and also in some other products such as flexible and packaging foam). Exceptions were made for a number of products, including certain medical devices; lubricants for pharmaceutical and tablet manufacture; gauze bandage adhesives and adhesive removers; topical anesthetic and vapocoolant products; lubricants, coatings and cleaning fluids for electrical and electronic equipment and aircraft maintenance that contain CFC-11, CFC-12 or CFC-113; release agents for molds used to produce plastic or elastomeric materials that contain CFC-11 or CFC-113; spinnerette lubricant/cleaning sprays used to produce synthetic fibers that contain CFC-114; CFCs used as halogen ion sources in plasma etching; document preservation sprays that contain CFC-113; and red pepper bear repellant sprays that contain CFC-113. However, these products are not exempted from the phase-out requirements for CFCs.

HCFCs can make excellent propellants, but their use has been limited due to their cost and restrictions regarding the class II ozone-depleting substances. In 1993, as a result of increased taxation and CFC phase-out, HCFCs were temporarily economically viable in applications where flammability is a concern and cheaper alternatives (**hydrocarbons**) could not be used. However, section 610(d) of the CAAA prohibits the sale or distribution of aerosol or foam products that contain or are manufactured with class II substances after January 1, 1994. Again, exceptions and exclusions from this ban have been made for "essential uses," i.e., if necessary due to flammability or worker safety issues and if the only available alternative is the use of a class I substance. On December 30, 1993, EPA published a final rule (58 FR 69637) which exempted medical devices, lubricants, coatings or cleaning fluids for electrical, electronic equipment, and aircraft maintenance, mold release agents used in the production of plastic and elastomeric materials and synthetic fibers, document preservation sprays containing HCFC-141b or HCFC-22, portable fire extinguishing equipment sold to commercial users, owners of boats, noncommercial aircraft, and wasp and hornet sprays for use near high-tension power lines. However, no other exceptions for class II propellants were made since substitutes are available.

Propellant Alternatives and Substitutes

Due to the restrictions on propellants use, a large number of propellant alternatives and substitutes have been investigated. Both EPA and industry have been active in this area.

Many products can be effectively packaged, distributed and used without employing a propellant. For example, some products are now sold for direct application as liquids or use manually operated finger and trigger pumps, two-compartment aerosol mechanism, mechanical pressure dispenser systems, and nonspray dispensers (e.g., solid stick dispensers). The elimination of propellants altogether can be viable option for some products and applications. In other cases,

however, this may not provide proper dispersal or accurate application of the product. Also, persons using manual pumps or sprays may become fatigued with the constant pumping motion and thus produce poor product performance. Because propellants are considered essential in a variety of uses, there remains a need to find propellants that are not environmentally damaging. Unfortunately, no propellant exists which has all favorable properties. For example, some CFC propellant substitutes, e.g., ammonia, butane and pentane, have problems with toxicity and flammability. There may be some essential applications for CFCs propellants for which no practical substitutes exist, and the use of CFC propellants in anti-asthma inhalers is a frequently cited example.

A variety of propellants are being considered or are being used as alternative propellants for class I and II controlled substances. Each alternative propellant has its own physical and chemical characteristics that influence its suitability for a given application. The primary substitutes for aerosol propellant uses of CFC-11, HCFC-22 and HCFC-142b are saturated hydrocarbons (C3-C6); dimethyl ether; compressed gases; and HFCs. A few EPA-approved alternative propellants are discussed below.

Of the hydrocarbons, butane, isobutane and propane may be used singly or in mixtures. All have low boiling points, are relatively nontoxic, inexpensive and readily available. (As with essentially any propellant, very high concentrations may result in asphyxiation because of the lack of oxygen.) However, these propellants are flammable and, for example, should not be used around electrical equipment if sparks could ignite the hydrocarbon propellant. To reduce product flammability, hydrocarbons can be used with water-based formulations. In the United States, nearly 50% of aerosol propellants were using hydrocarbon propellants prior to 1978, and nearly 90% in 1979 as a result of the CFC ban. Propane/butane propellants have been used since 1987 in the Scandinavian market.

Dimethyl ether (DME) is a medium pressure, flammable, liquefied propellant generally used in combination with other propellants. Its properties are similar to the hydrocarbons.

Compressed gases, including carbon dioxide, nitrogen, air, and nitrous oxide, are used in applications where a nonflammable propellant is necessary. These gases are inexpensive, readily available, nonflammable (although certain temperatures and pressures of nitrous oxide may create a moderate explosion risk), relatively nontoxic, and industrial practices for using these substitutes are well established. Since these gases are under significantly greater pressure than CFCs and HCFCs, containers holding these gases must be larger and bulkier, and safety precautions are necessary during filling operations. Often, modifications must be made to use compressed gases as they require new dispensing mechanisms and stronger containers due to the greater pressure; their low molecular weights restrict certain applications; high pressure compressed gases dispel material faster which may waste product; compressed gases cool upon expansion; and finally, they are not well suited for applications that require a fine and even dispersion. At present, about 7-9% of the aerosol products use compressed gases, and their use is expected to grow.

Hydrofluorocarbons (HFCs) such as HFC-134a, HFC-125 and HFC-152a are partially fluorinated hydrocarbons, developed relatively recently and currently priced significantly higher than HCFC-22. HFCs are less dense than HCFC-22, but can provide good performance in applications (but not products such as noise horns, which require a more dense gas). HFC-134a and HFC-125 are nonflammable and have very low toxicity. HFC-152a is slightly flammable. All three HFCs have zero ozone depletion potential, but are potential **greenhouse gases** although their atmospheric residence times are short. Additionally, these HFCs are chemically reactive and they contribute to the formation of tropospheric ozone. In ozone nonattainment areas, state and local controls on VOCs may restrict the use of these products. HFCs may be combined with flammable propellants to reduce the flammability of the mixtures. HFC-134a and HFC-227a are possible alternative propellants in medical applications (currently using CFC-12 and CFC-114). Approvals from both FDA and EPA are needed for these applications.

[Stuart Batterman]

Public health risk assessment

See **Risk assessment**

Public Health Service

The United States Public Health Service is the health component of the **U.S. Department of Health and Human Services**. It originated in 1798 with the organization of the Marine Hospital Service, out of concern for the health of the nation's seafarers who brought diseases back to this country. As immigrants came to America, they brought with them **cholera**, smallpox, and yellow fever; the Public Health Service was charged with protecting the nation from infectious diseases.

Today the Service helps city and state health departments with health problems. Its responsibilities include controlling infectious diseases, immunizing children, controlling sexually transmitted diseases, preventing the spread of tuberculosis, and operating a quarantine program.

The **Centers for Disease Control** in Atlanta, Georgia, is the Public Health Service agency responsible for promoting health and preventing disease. *See also* Agency for Toxic Substance and Disease Registry; Food and Drug Administration

Public interest group

Public interest groups may be defined as those groups pursuing goals the achievement of which ostensibly will provide benefits to the public at large, or at least to a broader population than the group's own membership. Thus, for example, if a public interest group concerned with **air quality** is successful in its various strategies and activities, the achieved benefit—cleaner air—is available to the public at large, not merely to the group's members. The competition of interest groups, each pursuing either its own good or its conception of the public good, has been an increasingly prominent feature of American politics in the latter half of the twentieth century.

There is no single, universally applicable definition or test of the public good, and thus there is often a great deal of disagreement about what happens to be in the public interest, with different public interest groups taking quite different positions on various issues. In any particular political controversy, moreover, there may be several quite different public interests at stake. For example, the question of whether to build a nuclear-powered generator plant may involve competing public interests in the protection of the **environment** from **radioactive waste** and other dangers, the maintenance of public safety, and the promotion of economic growth, among others.

Similarly, the question of who benefits from the activities of a public interest group can also be quite complicated. Some benefits that are generally available to the public may not be equally available or accessible to everyone. If **wilderness** preservation groups are successful, for example, in having land set aside in, say, Maine, that land is in principle available to potential recreational users from all over the country. But people from New England will find that benefit much more accessible than people from another region.

The membership, resources, and number of active public interest groups in the United States have all increased dramatically in the previous twenty-five years. There are now well over 2,500 national organizations promoting the public interest, as determined from almost every conceivable viewpoint, in a wide variety of issue areas. Over 40 million individual members support these groups with membership fees and other contributions totalling more than $4 billion every year. Many groups find additional support from various corporations, private foundations, and governmental agencies.

This growth in the public interest sector has been more than matched by, and partly was a response to, a similar explosion in the number and activities of organized interest groups and other politically active organizations pursuing benefits available only or primarily to their own members. Public interest groups often provide an effective counterweight to the activities of these more narrowly-oriented associations.

The growth of interest group politics has not been without its negative consequences. Some critics argue that every interest group, including "public interest groups," ultimately pursues relatively narrow goals important mainly to fairly limited constituencies. A politics based on the competition of these groups may be one in which well-organized narrow interests prevail over less well-organized broader interests. It may also produce decreased governmental performance and economic inefficiencies of various types. Public interest groups, moreover, seem to draw most of their support and membership from the middle and upper economic strata, whose interests and concerns are then disproportionately influential.

[*Lawrence J. Biskowski*]

FURTHER READING

Berry, J. M. *The Interest Group Society*. Boston: Little, Brown, 1984.

Cigler, A. J., and B. A. Loomis, eds. *Interest Group Politics*. Washington, DC: CQ Press, 1991.

McFarland, A. S. *Public Interest Lobbies*. Washington, DC: The American Enterprise Institute, 1976.

Schlozman, K. L., and J. T. Tierney. *Organized Interests and American Democracy*. New York: Harper and Row, 1986.

Public land

Public land refers to land owned by the government. Most frequently, it is used to refer to land owned and managed by the United States government, although it is sometimes used to refer to lands owned by state governments. The U.S. government owns 662 million acres, 29 percent of the land, in the country, the bulk of which is located in the western states, including Alaska. The lands are managed primarily by the **Bureau of Land Management**, the Department of Defense, the **Fish and Wildlife Service**, the **Forest Service**, and the **National Park Service**.

Public Lands Council (Washington, D.C.)

An important environmental debate is currently focused on the use of **public land**s by livestock owners, particularly owners of cattle and sheep. Historically, the federal government has sold leases and permits for grazing on public land to these individuals at very low prices, often a few cents per acre.

In recent years, many environmentalists have argued that cattle are responsible for the destruction of large tracts of **rangeland** in the western states. They believe the government should either greatly increase the rates they charge for the use of western lands or prohibit grazing entirely on large parts of it. In response, livestock owners have claimed that they practice good-land management techniques and that in many cases the land is in better condition than it was before they began using it.

The Public Lands Council (PLC) is one of the primary groups representing those who use public lands for grazing. It is a nonprofit corporation that represents approximately 31,000 individuals and groups who hold permits and leases allowing them to use federal lands in 14 western states for the grazing of livestock. Twenty-six state groups belong to the council, and in addition, the council coordinates the public lands policies of three other organizations, the National Cattlemen's Association, the American Sheep Industry Association, and the Association of National Grasslands.

The PLC also represents the interests of public land ranchers before the United States Congress. It lobbies and monitors Congress and various federal agencies responsible for grazing, water use, **wilderness**, **wildlife**, and other federal land management policies that are of concern to the livestock industry.

The council was founded in 1968 for the purpose of promoting principles of sound management of federal lands for grazing and other purposes. The council obtains its funds from dues collected by state organizations and by contributions from other organizations it represents. It has two classes of membership. General members are those who belong to a state organization that contributes to the PLC or those who make individual contributions. Voting members are elected by the general membership of each state, which may have a maximum of four voting members. Voting members meet at least once each year to establish PLC policy.

The PLC maintains a 500-volume library at its offices in Washington, D.C. It also publishes a quarterly newsletter, as well as news releases on specific issues, and regular columns in various western livestock publications. The council has also sponsored workshops and seminars on issues of importance to users of federal lands.

The American Lands and Resources Foundation has been established as an arm of the council for the purpose of receiving charitable and tax-deductible contributions to be used for the education of the general public about the benefits of using federal lands for livestock grazing. Contact: Public Lands Council, 1301 Pennsylvania Avenue, NW, Suite 300, Washington, DC 20004

[*David E. Newton*]

Public trust

The public trust doctrine is a legal doctrine dealing with the protection of certain uses and resources for public purposes, regardless of ownership. These uses or resources must be made available to the public, regardless of whether they are under public or private control. That is, they are held in trust for the public.

The modern public trust doctrine can be traced back at least as far as Roman civil law. It was further developed in English law as "things common to all." This public trust was applied mostly to navigation: the Crown possessed the ocean, the rivers, and the lands underlying these bodies of water (referred to as *jus publicum*). These were to be controlled in order to guarantee the public benefit of free navigation.

In the United States, the public trust doctrine is rooted in *Illinois Central Railroad Co. v. Illinois* (1892). In this case, the Supreme Court ruled that a grant held by the Illinois Central Railroad of the Chicago waterfront was void because it violated the state's public trust responsibilities to protect the rights of its citizens to navigate and fish in these waters. In making this decision, the court relied on English common law and served to underscore the existence of the public trust doctrine in the United States.

As a trustee, the government (federal or state) faces certain restrictions in protecting the public trust. These include using the trust property for common purpose and making it available for use by the public; not selling the trust property; and maintaining the trust property for particular types of uses. If any of these responsibilities are violated, the government can be sued by its citizens for neglecting its trust responsibilities.

With the rise of the environmental movement, the public trust doctrine has been applied with greater frequency and to a broader array of subjects. In addition to navigable waters, the doctrine has been applied to **wetlands**, state and **national park**s, and fossil beds. This expanded use of the doctrine has led to increased conflict. On the ground, there has been growing conflict over the limitations of private property. Landholders who find their actions limited argue that the public trust doctrine is a way to mask indirect takings and argue that they deserve just compensation in return for the restrictions. Among legal scholars, there is concern that the public trust doctrine is not firmly grounded in the law and simply reflects the opinions of judges in various cases. Proponents of the public trust doctrine, however, argue that it is a useful vehicle to temper unrestricted private property rights in the United States. Indeed, it has been argued that if public trust rights exist in private property, then no takings can occur since the regulation is merely recognizing the pre-existing limitation in the property.

[*Christopher McGrory Klyza*]

FURTHER READING

Brady, T. P. "'But Most of It Belongs to Those Yet to be Born:' The Public Trust Doctrine, NEPA, and the Stewardship Ethic." *Boston College Environmental Law Review* 17 (1990): 621-46.

Kagan, D. G. "Property Rights and the Public Trust: Opposing Lakeshore Funnel Development." *Boston College Environmental Law Review* 15 (1987): 105-34.

Plater, Z. J. B., R. H. Abrams, and W. Goldfarb, eds. *Environmental Law and Policy: Nature, Law, and Society.* New York: West Publishing, 1992.

Pulp and paper mills

Pulp and paper mills take wood and transform the raw product into paper. Hardwood logs (beech, birch, and maple) and softwoods (pine, spruce, and fir) are harvested from managed forestlands or purchased from local farms and timberlands across the world and are transported to mills for processing. Hardwoods are more dense, shorter fibered, and slower growing. Softwoods are less dense, longer fibered, and faster growing.

Today, the process is mainly done with high tech, sophisticated machinery. Wood products, which consist of lignin (30 percent), fiber (50 percent), and other materials—carbohydrates, proteins, fats, turpentine, resins, etc., (20 percent) are transformed into paper consisting of fiber, and additives—clay, titanium dioxide, calcium carbonate, water, rosin, alum, starches, gums, dyes, synthetic polymers, and pigments. Wood is about 50 percent cellulose fiber. The structure of paper is a tightly bonded web of cellulose fibers.

About 80 percent of a typical printing paper by weight is cellulose fiber. First in the process, the standard eight-foot (2.4-m) logs are debarked by tumbling them in a giant barking drum and then chipped by a machine that reduces them to half-inch chips. The chips are cooked, after being screened and steamed, in a digester using sodium bisulfite cooking liquor to remove most of the lignin, the sticky matter in a tree that bonds the cellulose fibers together. This is the pulping process.

Then the chips are washed, refined, and cleaned to separate the cellulose fibers and create the watery suspension called pulp. The pulp is bleached in a two-stage process with a number of possible chemicals. Those companies that choose to avoid **chlorine** bleach will use **hydrogen** peroxide and sodium hydrosulfite which yields a northern high-yield hardwood sulfite pulp. This pulp is blended with additional softwood kraft pulp after refining as part of the stock preparation process, which involves adding such materials as dyes, pigments, clay fillers, internal sizing, additional brighteners, and opacifiers.

Late in the process, the stock is further refined to adjust fiber length and drainage characteristics for good formation and bonding strength. The consistency of the stock is reduced by adding more water and the stock is cleaned again to remove foreign particles. The product is then pumped to the paper machine headbox.

From here, the dilute stock (99.5 percent water) flows out in a uniformly thin slice onto a Fourdrinier wire—an endless moving screen that drains water from the stock to form a self-supporting web of paper. The web moves off the wire into the press section which squeezes out more water between two press felts, then into the first drier section where more moisture is removed by evaporation as the paper web winds forward around an array of steam-heated drums. At the size press, a water-resistant surface sizing is added in an immersion bath.

From there the sheet enters a second drier section where the sheet is redried to the final desired moisture level before passing through the computer scanner. The scanner is part of a system for automatically monitoring and regulating basis weight and moisture. The paper enters the calendar stack, where massive steel polishing rolls give the sheet its final machine finish and bulking properties.

The web of paper is then wound up in a single long reel, which is cut and moved off the paper machine to a slitter/winder machine which slices the reel into rolls of the desired width and rewinds them onto the appropriate cores. The rolls are then conveyed to the finishing room where they are weighed, wrapped, labeled, and shipped.

In practice, all papers, even newsprint, are pulp blends, but they are placed in one of two categories for convenient description: groundwood and free sheet. And in practice, other pulp varieties enter into the picture. They may be reclaimed pulps such as de-inked or post-consumer waste; recycled pulps which included scraps, trim, and unprinted waste; cotton fiber pulps; synthetic fibers; and pulps from plants other than trees: bagasse, esparto, bamboo, hemp, water hyacinth; and banana, or rice. But the dominant raw material remains wood pulp. Paper makers choose and blend from the spectrum of pulps according to the demands on their grades for strength, cleanliness, brightness, opacity, printing, and converting requirements, aesthetics, and market price.

From cotton fiber-based sheets to the less expensive papers made from groundwood, to recycled grades manufactured with various percentages of wastepaper content, papermakers have consistently responded to the need of the marketplace. In today's increasingly environmentally conscious marketplace, papermakers are being called on to produce pulp that is environmentally friendly. Eliminating chlorine from the bleaching process is a major step in eliminating unwanted toxins. The changeover costs money and is the source of controversy here in the United States.

However, the chlorine-free trend has taken a firm hold in Europe. All of Sweden requires its printing and writing paper mills to be chlorine-free by the year 2010. France, Germany, and several other countries have several mills that are reported to be chlorine-free and the trend is moving across Canada.

While there are growing exceptions, most North American mills still use a chlorine bleaching process to create a bright, white pulp. Why the need to eliminate the chemical?

In the bleaching process, chlorine, chlorine dioxide, and other chlorine compounds create toxic byproducts. These byproducts consist of over 1,000 **chemicals**, some of which are the most toxic known to man. The list includes: **dioxin** and other organochlorines compounds such as **PCB**s, **DDT**, **chlordane**, aldrin, dieldrin, **toxaphene**, chloroform, heptachlor and furans. These are formed by the reaction of lignin in the pulp with chlorine or chlorine-based compounds used in the bleaching sequence of all kraft pulps.

These unwanted chemicals byproducts must be discharged and end up in the **effluent**. The effluent is released into our rivers, lakes and streams and is threatening the **groundwater** and our drinking water, as well as the **food chain** through fish and birds. Epidemic health effects among thirteen species of fish and **wildlife** near the top of the Great Lakes **food web** have been identified. Not only are these toxic chemicals causing **cancer** and birth deformities in humans and wildlife, but they are very persistent, building up in our waterways and eventually into our bodies.

Dioxin traces have been found in papers and even in coffee from chlorine-bleached coffee filters and milk from chlorine-bleached milk cartons, as well as in women's hygiene products. Most of the paper being sold in the United States today as "dioxin free" is actually "dioxin undetectable." That is because dioxin can be measured in parts per trillion or parts per quintillion, but beyond that level, there are no scientific measurements sophisticated enough. Or if measurable, the process becomes very expensive. (If exposed often enough, even these minuscule quantities build up in the **environment** and in humans.) To be truly dioxin free, the paper must be made from pulps that have been bleached without chlorine or chlorine-based compounds.

The newer trend is to eliminate chlorine from the bleaching process completely. Some North American mills

are turning to hydrogen peroxide, oxygen brightening, or **ozone** brightening. These compounds do not produce dioxin or other organochlorine compounds and are considered "environmentally-sound." The United States pulp and paper industry has sharply reduced its use of the chemical and plans to curtail use further during the next few years.

In part, this reduction can be traced to the increased sophistication of pulp and paper plants during the past decade. The cooking and bleaching operations have been fine-tuned. Wood chips are cooked more before they go to the bleach plant, so less bleaching is required. Also, in some plants, industry is trying chlorine dioxide as a substitute; it produces less dioxin, but still contains chlorine.

The result of these changes means an 80 percent reduction in the amount of dioxin associated with bleaching. Between 1988-1989, a total of 2.5 pounds (11.1 kg) of dioxin was produced. As of 1993, that number fell below 8 ounces (22.7 g) per year. Eight ounces sound like a small amount, but scientists measure dioxin in parts per million, billion, trillion and quintillion, so eight ounces is still too high.

A number of lawsuits have been filed by residents living near or downstream of dioxin-contaminated pulp mills because of the health threats. The more the plaintiffs win, the sooner will the use of chlorine be eliminated completely. It is estimated that the amount of chlorine used in pulp and paper bleaching will fall from 1.4 million tons in 1990 to 920,000 tons by 1995. The eventual goal is **zero discharge**.

[*Liane Clorfene Casten*]

FURTHER READING

Ferguson, K. *Environmental Solutions for the Pulp and Paper Industry*. San Francisco: Miller Freeman, 1991.

Jenish, D. "Cleaning Up a Chemical Soup." *Maclean's* 103 (29 January 1990): 32-4.

Purple loosestrife (*Lythrum salicaria*)

Purple loosestrife is an aggressive wetland plant **species** first introduced into the United States from Europe. It is a showy, attractive plant that grows up to 4 feet (1.2 m) in height with pink and purple flowers arranged on a spike, and it is common in shallow marshes and lakeshores all across the northern half of the United States.

Loosestrife is a perennial plant species that spreads rapidly because of the high quantity of seeds it produces (sometimes up to 300,000 seeds per plant) and the efficient dispersal of seeds by wind and water. The plant has a well-developed root system and is able to tolerate a variety of **soil** moisture conditions. This has made it an effective colonizer of disturbed ground as well as areas with fluctuating hydrological regimes. Because of its attractive flowers, it has also been planted as an ornamental species.

As a highly adaptive and tolerant plant, loosestrife is often able to outcompete native plant species in many **environments**, particularly in **wetlands** and disturbed areas. Other species often have difficulty surviving once it becomes

Purple loosestrife.

established, and loosestrife has low value as food and nesting **habitat**. For example, the cattail plants in many wetlands of New York state have been replaced by purple loosestrife. **Wildlife** experts prize cattails as plants whose roots and tubes are of high value as food source to small mammals and rodents, and the spread of loosestrife has led to a decline in the habitat values of these wetlands. So, in spite of its pleasing appearance, New York and a number of other states have embarked on purple loosestrife eradication programs.

The most commonly used chemical method for eradicating purple loosestrife is a **herbicide** known as Rodeo—a selective herbicide that kills only dicotyledonous or broadleaf plants. When a diluted solution of Rodeo is sprayed directly on mature leaves, it disrupts protein synthesis and causes plant death within two to seven days. Physical removal of the plants by mowing early in the growing season, prior to seed set, has also been effective in keeping areas free of loosestrife. *See also* Introduced species

[*Usha Vedagiri*]

FURTHER READING

Schmidt, J. C. *How to Identify and Control Water Weeds and Algae.* Milwaukee, WI: Applied Biochemists, 1987.

Thompson, D. Q. *Spread, Impact and Control of Purple Loosestrife (Lythrum salicaria) in North American Wetlands.* Washington, DC: U. S. Department of the Interior, 1987.

———. *Waterfowl Management Handbook. 13.4.11, Control of Purple Loosestrife.* Washington, DC: U. S. Fish and Wildlife Service, 1989.

R

Rabbits in Australia

Imported into Australia in the mid-nineteenth century, rabbits have overrun much of the country, causing extensive agricultural and environmental damage and demonstrating the dangers of introducing non-native **species** into an area. Before the first humans arrived in Australia, the only mammals living there were about 150 species of marsupials as well as **bats**, rats, mice, platypuses, and echidnas. The chief predator in Australia today is the dingo, a wild dog introduced about 40,000 years ago by Australia's first human settlers, the Aborigines. When the British settled Australia as a penal colony in the late 1700s, they brought a variety of pets and livestock with them, including rabbits.

The problems with rabbits began in 1859, when 12 pairs of European rabbits were released on a ranch. Since no significant numbers of natural predators were present in Australia, the rabbit population exploded within a few years. They overgrazed the grass used for sheep raising, and despite extensive efforts to reduce and control the population, by 1953 approximately 1.2 million square miles (3 million sq km) were inhabited by between several hundred million and over one billion rabbits.

The rabbits have caused considerable damage to Australia's environment, especially its native plants and wildlife. Their extensive burrows cause soil erosion, and they eat large quantities of grass and shoots of other plants, devastating native flora that birds, insects, and other creatures depend on for food and cover.

Repeated attempts have been made to exterminate the rabbits and limit their populations, often by fumigating and ripping up their burrows, or by using poison bait. The most effective effort undertaken involved the introduction of myxomatosis in the 1950s, a disease that is fatal to rabbits. But after an initial decline, the rabbit population began to recover, and much of Australia remained overrun by the animals.

Proponents of eradication say that the most promising new biological agent to control wild rabbits is know as RCV (rabbit calicivirus), which is thought to be a new disease, and has killed farmed rabbits in China and Europe. In its early stages, it kills over 90% of infected rabbits. In the laboratory, it has been shown to kill rabbits shortly after infection; and after 31 different native species were exposed to the virus, it

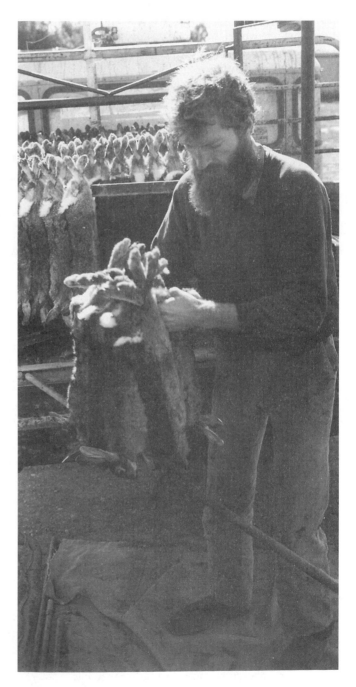

Chris Pert, rabbit hunter in Western Australia.

did not appear to be capable of infecting non-target animals. But the certainty of this is disputed by other scientists, who worry that release of the virus is "an uncontrollable and unpredictable" biological experiment; that it could eventually jump the species barrier, especially if it mutates into a different form; and that rabbits will eventually develop resistance to the virus, as they did to myxomatosis.

The elimination of rabbits might even have adverse consequences, such as removing an important food source from eagles and other predators who have come to depend on them. Wild dogs and cats, deprived of their normal prey, may turn to increased hunting of kangaroos and other marsupials. On the other hand, the number of feral canines and felines might decline with the demise of an easy and abundant food source, which would benefit marsupials. So, the ultimate impact of RCV is not entirely predictable.

But there is little danger of an immediate collapse of the rabbit population. The latest data estimate that the population has been reduced from about 200-300 million rabbits to 100 million.

The proliferation of rabbits in Australia has cost the government and ranchers billions of dollars. This situation remains a primary example of the harm that can result from the introduction of non-native species, no matter how seemingly harmless, into a foreign environment. *See also* Introduced species

[*Lewis G. Regenstein*]

FURTHER READING

Ecology of Biological Invasions. New York: Cambridge University Press, 1986.

Anderson, I., and Nowak, R., "Australia's Giant Lab," *New Scientist.*

Rachel Carson Council (Chevy Chase, Maryland)

The Rachel Carson Council focuses on the dangers of **pesticide**s and other toxic **chemicals** and their impact on human health, **wildlife**, and the **environment**. After the 1962 publication of her classic book on pesticides, *Silent Spring*, **Rachel Carson** was overwhelmed by the public interest it generated, including letters from many people asking for advice, guidance, and information. Shortly after her death in April 1964, colleagues and friends of Carson established an organization to keep the public informed on new developments in the field of chemical contamination. Originally called the Rachel Carson Trust for the Living Environment, it was incorporated in 1965 to work for **conservation** of **natural resources**, to increase knowledge about threats to the environment, and to serve as a clearinghouse of information for scientists, government officials, environmentalists, journalists, and the public.

The Council has long warned that many pesticides, regulated by the **Environmental Protection Agency (EPA)** and widely used by homeowners, farmers, and industry, are extremely harmful. Many of these chemicals can cause **cancer**, miscarriages, **birth defects**, genetic damage, and harm to the central nervous system in humans, as well as destroy wildlife and poison the environment and **food chain/web** for years to come.

Other, less acutely toxic chemicals that are commonly used, the organization points out, can cause "delayed neurotoxicity," a milder form of nerve damage that can show up in subtle behavior changes such as memory loss, fatigue, irritability, sleep disturbance, and altered brain wave patterns. Concerning termiticides used in schools, "children are especially vulnerable to this kind of poisoning," the Council observes, "and the implications for disturbing their ability to learn are especially serious."

Through its studies, publications, and information distribution, the Council has provided data strongly indicating that many pesticides now in widespread use should be banned or carefully restricted. The group has urged and petitioned the EPA to take such action on a variety of chemicals that represent serious potential dangers to the health and lives of millions of Americans and even to future generations.

The Council has also expressed strong concern about, and sponsored extensive research into, the link between exposure to toxic chemicals and the dramatic increase in recent years in cancer incidence and death rates. The group's publications and officials have warned that the presence of dozens of cancer-causing chemicals in our food, air, and water is constantly exposing us to deadly **carcinogen**s and is contributing to the mounting incidence of cancer, which eventually strikes almost one American in three, and kills over 500,000 Americans every year.

The Council publishes a wide variety of books, booklets, and brochures on pesticides and toxic chemicals and alternatives to their use. Its most recent comprehensive work, *Basic Guide to Pesticides: Their Characteristics and Hazards* (1992), describes and analyzes over 700 pesticides. Other publications discuss the least toxic methods of dealing with pests in the home, garden, and greenhouse; non-toxic gardening; ways to safely cure and prevent lawn diseases; and the dangers of poisons used to keep lawns green.

The Council's board of directors includes experts and leaders in the fields of environmental science, medicine, education, law, and consumer interest, and a board of consulting experts includes scientists from many fields. Contact: Rachel Carson Council, 8940 Jones Mill Road, Chevy Chase, MD 20815.

[*Lewis G. Regenstein*]

Radiation exposure

Radiation is defined as the emission of energy from an atom in the form of a wave or particle. Such energy is released as electromagnetic radiation or as **radioactivity**.

Electromagnetic radiation includes radio waves, infrared waves or heat, visible light, **ultraviolet radiation**, **X ray**s, **gamma ray**s and cosmic rays. Radioactivity, emitted when an atomic nucleus undergoes decay, usually takes the form of a particle such as an **alpha particle** or **beta particle**, though atomic decay can also release electromagnetic gamma rays.

While radiation in the form of heat, visible light and even ultraviolet light is essential to life, the word "radiation" is often used to refer only to those emissions which can damage or kill living things. Such harm is specifically attributed to radioactive particles as well as the electromagnetic rays with frequencies higher than visible light (ultraviolet, X rays, gamma rays). Harmful electromagnetic radiation is also known as **ionizing radiation** because it strips atoms of their electrons, leaving highly reactive ions called *free radicals* which can damage tissue or genetic material.

Effects of radiation

The effects of radiation depend upon the type of radiation absorbed, the amount or dose received, and the part of the body irradiated. While alpha and beta particles have only limited power to penetrate the body, gamma rays and X rays are far more potent. The damage potential of a radiation dose is expressed in *rems*, a quantity equal to the actual dose in *rads* (units per kg) multiplied by a quality factor, called Q, representing the potency of the radiation in living tissue. Over a lifetime, a person typically receives 7 to 14 rems from natural sources. Exposure to 5 to 75 rems causes few observable symptoms. Exposure to 75 to 200 rems leads to vomiting, fatigue, and loss of appetite. Exposure to 300 rems or more leads to severe changes in blood cells accompanied by hemorrhage. Such a dosage delivered to the whole body is lethal 50 percent of the time. An exposure of more than 600 rems causes loss of hair and loss of the body's ability to fight infection, and results in death. A dose of 10,000 rem will kill quickly through damage to the central nervous system.

The symptoms that follow exposure to a sufficient dose of radiation are often termed "radiation sickness" or "radiation burn." Bone marrow and lymphoid tissue cells, testes and ovaries, and embryonic tissue are most sensitive to radiation exposure. Since the lymphatic tissue manufactures white blood cells (WBCs), radiation sickness is almost always accompanied by a reduction in WBC production within 72 hours, and recovery from a radiation dose is first indicated by an increase in WBC production.

Any exposure to radiation increases the risk of **cancer**, **birth defects**, and genetic damage, as well as accelerating the aging process, and causing other health problems including impaired immunity. Among the chronic diseases suffered by those exposed to radiation are cancer, stroke, diabetes, hypertension, and cardiovascular and renal disease.

Sources of radiation

Some 82 percent of the average American's radiation exposure comes from natural sources. These sources include **radon** gas emissions from underground, cosmic rays from space, naturally occurring radioactive elements within our own bodies, and radioactive particles emitted from soil and

Radiation Sources	
Natural Sources	
Radon gas	55%
Inside body	11%
Rocks, soil, and groundwater	8%
Cosmic rays	8%
Artificial sources	
Medical X-rays	11%
Nuclear medicine	4%
Consumer products	3%
Miscellaneous*	<1%

*includes occupational exposure, nuclear fallout, and the production of nuclear materials for nuclear power and weapons

rocks. Man-made radiation, the other 18 percent, comes primarily from medical X rays and nuclear medicine, but is also emitted from some consumer products (such as smoke detectors and blue topaz jewelry), or originates in the production and testing of nuclear weapons and the manufacture of nuclear fuels (see table).

On the evidence of recent data, environmental scientists believe that radon, a radioactive gas, accounts for most of the radiation dose Americans receive. Released by the decay of **uranium** in the earth, radon can infiltrate a house through pores in block walls, cracks in basement walls or floors, or around pipes. The **Environmental Protection Agency** estimates that 8 million homes in the United States have potentially dangerous levels of radon, and calls radon "the largest environmental radiation health problem affecting Americans." Inhaled radon may contribute to 20,000 lung cancer deaths each year in the United States. The EPA now recommends that homeowners test their houses for radon gas and install a specialized ventilation system if excessive levels of gas are detected.

Though artificial sources of radiation contribute only a small fraction to overall radiation exposure, they remain a strong concern for two reasons. First, they are preventable or avoidable, unlike cosmic radiation, for example. Second, while the *average* individual may not receive a significant dose of radiation from artificial sources, geographic and occupational factors may mean dramatically higher doses of radiation for large numbers of people. For instance, many Americans have been exposed to radiation from nearly 600 nuclear tests conducted at the **Nevada Test Site**. From the early 1950s to the early 1960s, atmospheric blasts caused a lingering increase in radiation-related sickness downwind of the site, and increased the overall dose of radiation received by Americans by as much as seven percent. Once the tests were moved underground, that figure fell to less than 1 percent.

A February 1990 study of the **Windscale** plutonium processing plant in Britain clearly demonstrated the importance of the indirect effects of radiation exposure. The study correlated an abnormally high rate of **leukemia** among children in the area with male workers at the plant, who evidently passed a tendency to leukemia to their children even though they had been receiving radiation doses that were considered "acceptable."

Debate is currently raging over the possible impact of low-level radiation from electric power lines and appliances such as electric blankets, cellular phones, and television screens. A 1990 EPA study suggested that proximity to electric power lines and sources may be linked to leukemia and brain cancer. *See also* Chernobyl Nuclear Power Station; Electromagnetic fields; Hanford Nuclear Reservation

[*Linda Rehkopf and Jeffrey Muhr*]

FURTHER READING

Caufield, C. *Multiple Exposures.* Harper & Row, Publishers, New York, 1989.

Cobb, C. E., Jr. "Living With Radiation." *National Geographic* 175 (April 1989): 403-437.

Gould, J. M., and B. A. Goldman. *Deadly Deceit: Low-Level Radiation, High-Level Cover-Up.* New York: Four Walls Eight Windows, 1990.

Regenstein, L. G. *How to Survive in America the Poisoned.* Washington, DC: Acropolis Books, 1986.

Wagner, H. N., Jr., and L. E. Ketchum. *Living With Radiation: The Risk, the Promise.* Baltimore, MD: Johns Hopkins University Press, 1989.

Radiation sickness

Radiation sickness, also known as acute radiation syndrome or **ionizing radiation** injury, is illness resulting from human exposure to ionizing radiation. The radiation exposure may be from natural sources, such as radium, or from manmade sources, such as **X ray**s, nuclear reactors, or atomic bombs. Ionizing radiation penetrates cells of the body and ultimately causes damage to critically important molecules such as **nucleic acid**s and **enzyme**s. Immediate cell death may occur if the dose of ionizing radiation is sufficiently high; lower doses result in cell injury which may preclude cell replication. Tissues at greatest risk for radiation injury are those which have cells that are rapidly dividing. Blood forming cells, the lining to the gastrointestinal tract, skin, and hair forming cells are particularly vulnerable. Muscle, brain, liver, and other tissues, which have a low rate of cell division, are less so.

Epidemiological data on radiation sickness has been accumulated from the study of individual cases, as well as from the study of large numbers of afflicted individuals, such as the survivors of the atomic bombing of Hiroshima and Nagasaki and the 135,000 people evacuated from close proximity to the fire at the **Chernobyl Nuclear Power Station** in 1986.

In those who survive, radiation sickness may be characterized by four phases. The initial stage occurs immediately after exposure and is characterized by nausea, vomiting, weakness, and diarrhea. This is a period of short duration, typically one or two days. It is followed by a period of apparent recovery lasting for one to three weeks. No particular symptoms appear during this time. The third stage is characterized by fever, infection, vomiting, lesions in the mouth and pharynx, abscesses, bloody diarrhea, hemorrhages, weight loss, hair loss, bleeding ulcers, and petechiae, small hemorrhagic spots on the skin. During this phase, there is a loss of appetite, nausea, weakness and weight loss. These symptoms are due to the depletion of cells which would normally be rapidly dividing. Bone marrow depression occurs with reduced numbers of white blood cells, red blood cells, and blood platelets. Gut cells that are normally lost are not replaced and hair follicle cells are depressed resulting in hair loss. If death does not occur during this phase, a slow recovery follows. This is the fourth phase, but recovery is frequently accompanied by long-lasting or permanent disabilities including widespread scar tissue, cataracts, and blindness.

The toxic side effects of many **cancer** chemotherapeutic agents are similar to acute radiation sickness, because both radiation and chemotherapy primarily affect rapidly dividing cells. Little effective treatment can be administered in the event of casualties occurring in enormous numbers such as in war or a major nuclear power plant disaster. However, in individual cases such as in accidental laboratory or industrial exposure, some may be helped by isolation placement to prevent infection, transfusions for hemorrhage, and bone marrow transplantation. *See also* Epidemiology; Nuclear weapons; Nuclear winter; Radiation exposure; Radioactive pollution; Threshold dose

[*Robert G. McKinnell*]

FURTHER READING

Wald, N. "Radiation Injury." In *Cecil Textbook of Medicine*, edited by P. B. Beeson, et al. 15th ed. Philadelphia: Saunders, 1979.

Guskova, A. K., et al. "Acute Effects of Radiation Exposure Following the Chernobyl Accident." In *Treatment of Radiation Injuries*, edited by D. Browne et al. New York: Plenum Press, 1990.

Radioactive decay

Radioactive decay is the process by which an atomic nucleus undergoes a spontaneous change, emitting an **alpha particle** or **beta particle** and/or a **gamma ray**. Radioactive decay is a natural process that takes place in the air, water, and **soil** at all times. The decay of **isotope**s such as **uranium**-238, radium-226, **radon**-222, potassium-40, and carbon-14 produce radiation that poses an unavoidable and, probably, minimal hazard to human health. Scientists have also learned how to convert stable isotopes to radioactive forms. The radioactive decay of these isotopes has been added to the natural **background radiation** from naturally radioactive materials. *See also* Carbon; Radioactive fallout; Radioactivity

Radioactive fallout

In the 1930s, scientists found that bombarding **uranium** metal with **neutron**s caused the nuclei of uranium atoms to break apart, or fission. One significant feature of this reaction was that very large amounts of energy were released during

nuclear fission. The first practical application of this discovery was the **atomic bomb**, developed by scientists working in the United States in the early 1940s.

The atomic bomb takes advantage of the energy released during fission to bring about massive destruction of property and human life. However, every bomb blast is also accompanied by another event known as radioactive fallout. The term radioactive fallout refers to all radioactive dust and particles that fall to the earth after a nuclear explosion. This combination of dust and particles contains hundreds of **isotope**s formed when a uranium nucleus fissions. **Iodine-131** and yttrium-98 are only two of the many isotopes that are formed during an atomic bomb blast.

When these isotopes are formed, they come together as only very small particles. The force of the blast assures that large particles will not survive. In this form, the radioactive dust and particles may remain suspended in air for days, weeks, or months. Only when they have consolidated to form larger particles will they fall back to earth.

Once they have reached the earth, these particles face different fates. Some isotopes formed during fission have very short half-lives. They will decay rapidly and pose little or no environmental threat. Others have longer half-lives and may remain in the **environment** for many years.

The components of radioactive fallout that cause the greatest concern are those that can take some role in plant or animal **metabolism**. For example, the element strontium is chemically similar to the element calcium. Strontium can replace calcium in many biochemical reactions. That explains why the following scenario is so troubling.

Strontium-90 released during a fission bomb blast falls to the earth, coats grass, and is eaten by cows. The cows incorporate strontium-90 into their milk, just as they do calcium. When growing children drink that milk, the strontium-90 is used to build bones and teeth, just as calcium is. Once incorporated into bones and teeth, however, the radioactive strontium continues to emit harmful radiation for many years.

The dangers of radioactive fallout are one of the major reasons that the United States and the former Soviet Union were able to agree in 1963 on a limited ban of **nuclear weapons** testing. In that agreement, both nations promised to stop nuclear weapons testing in the atmosphere, under water, and in outer space. *See also* Half-life; Radioactive decay; Radioactivity

[*David E. Newton*]

FURTHER READING

Inglis, D. R. *Nuclear Energy: Its Physics and Social Challenge.* Reading, MA: Addison-Wesley, 1973.

Jagger, J. *The Nuclear Lion: What Every Citizen Should Know About Nuclear Power and Nuclear War.* New York: Plenum, 1991.

Radioactive pollution

Radioactive **pollution** can be defined as the release of radioactive substances or high-energy particles into the air, water, or earth as a result of human activity, either by accident or by design. The sources of such waste include: 1) **nuclear weapon** testing or detonation; 2) the *nuclear fuel cycle*, including the mining, separation, and production of nuclear materials for use in **nuclear power** plants or nuclear bombs; 3) accidental release of radioactive material from nuclear power plants. Sometimes natural sources of **radioactivity**, such as **radon** gas emitted from beneath the ground, are considered pollutants when they become a threat to human health.

Since even a small amount of **radiation exposure** can have serious (and cumulative) biological consequences, and since many radioactive wastes remain toxic for centuries, radioactive pollution is a serious environmental concern even though natural sources of radioactivity far exceed artificial ones at present.

The problem of radioactive pollution is compounded by the difficulty in assessing its effects. Radioactive waste may spread over a broad area quite rapidly and irregularly (from an abandoned dump into an **aquifer**, for example), and may not fully show its effects upon humans and organisms for decades in the form of cancer or other chronic diseases. For instance, radioactive **iodine-131**, while short-lived, may leave those who ingest it with long-term health problems. By the time a radioactive leak is revealed and a health survey is carried out, many of the individuals affected by the leak may have already moved from the area (or died without having been examined with the possible cause in mind). In addition, since most radioactive materials are under the jurisdiction of governmental agencies—usually in the secretive defense and military establishments—the dumping activities and accidental discharges that accompany nuclear materials production and bomb testing tend to remain concealed until governments are obligated to disclose them under public pressure.

Atmospheric pollution

Radioactive pollution that is spread through the earth's atmosphere is termed *fallout*. Such pollution was most common in the two decades following World War II, when the United States, the Soviet Union, and Great Britain conducted hundreds of nuclear weapons tests in the atmosphere. France and China did not begin testing nuclear weapons until the 1960s and continued atmospheric testing even after other nations had agreed to move their tests underground.

Three types of fallout result from nuclear detonations: local, tropospheric and stratospheric. Local fallout is quite intense but short-lived. Tropospheric fallout (in the lower atmosphere) is deposited at a later time and covers a larger area, depending on meteorological conditions. Stratospheric fallout, which releases extremely fine particles into the upper atmosphere, may continue for years after an explosion and attain a worldwide distribution.

The two best known examples illustrating the effect of fallout contamination are the bombing of Hiroshima and Nagasaki, Japan in 1945, and the **Chernobyl Nuclear Power Station** disaster in April 1986. Within five years of the American bombing of Japan, as many as 225,000 people had died as a result of long-term exposure to radiation from the bomb blast, chiefly in the form of fallout.

The disaster at the Chernobyl Nuclear Power Station in Ukraine on April 26, 1986 produced a staggering release of radioactivity. In ten days at least 36 million curies spewed across the world. The fallout contaminated approximately 1,000 square miles (2,590 sq km) of farmland and villages in the Soviet Union. Dangerous levels of radioactivity were reported in virtually every European country, and radioactive pollutants contaminated rainwater, pastures and food crops. Radiation alerts were posted in almost every country, children were kept indoors, and sales of milk, vegetables and meat were banned in some areas. In the Soviet Union alone, 135,000 people were evacuated from their homes. In addition to the hundreds killed at the time of the explosion, scientists predict the eventual Soviet death toll from the Chernobyl accident may reach 200,000; the estimated mortality in western Europe may approach 40,000.

Pollution on land and in water

The major sources of radioactive pollution on land and water include: 1) the nuclear fuel cycle—the extraction, separation and refinement of materials for use in nuclear weapons and nuclear power—and 2) the day-to-day operations of nuclear power plants.

At every stage in the production of nuclear fuels, contaminants are left behind. The mining of **uranium**, for example, produces highly radioactive *tailings* which can be blown into the air, contaminate soil, or leach into bodies of water. The magnitude of radioactive pollution caused by the nuclear fuel cycle, especially in the United States, Britain and the Soviet Union, has only recently been revealed. Through the years of the cold war, the extent of accidental discharges and intentional dumping carried out by government plants like Britain's **Windscale** and the United States' **Hanford Nuclear Reservation** remained largely unknown. Not until the late 1980s, for instance, was the legacy of flagrant pollution at Hanford exposed to public scrutiny. This legacy included the release of half a million curies of radioactive iodine into the air from 1944 to 1955, and the release of millions of curies of radioactive material into the Columbia River, Washington from 1944 through at least the 1960s. In 1956, 450,000 gallons (1.7 million liters) of high-level waste were accidently spilled on the Hanford grounds. Through the 1950s, additional millions of gallons of waste were dumped into the ground. Residents in the area and along the river were never notified about any of the radioactive discharges that took place at Hanford.

In 1988, the **U.S. Department of Energy** reported that radioactive wastes from Hanford were contaminating some underground water supplies; Hanford was shut down a year later. At present, a farm of deteriorating storage tanks at Hanford containing approximately 57 million gallons (216 million liters) of radioactive and toxic waste is being monitored for leaks. Officials are not even sure what chemicals lie in some of these tanks. Federal officials estimate that cleaning up Hanford and the U.S. government's other weapons facilities (at Fernald, Ohio, **Rocky Flats**, Colorado, **Savan-**

nah River, Georgia, and other locations) may cost over $200 billion.

Nuclear power plants also contribute to radioactive pollution. Spent nuclear fuel from these plants, a *high-level* waste, must be kept from human contact for hundreds or thousands of years, yet no completely reliable disposal method exists. At present, most high-level waste has simply been left in pools at power plant sites while the government seeks a location for permanent disposal. Most *low-level* waste (anything that is not spent fuel or transuranic waste) generated by nuclear power plants has been landfilled throughout the country. Three such landfill sites (Maxey Flats, Kentucky; West Valley, New York; and Sheffield, Illinois) have been shut down due to leakage of radioactive liquid into the ground.

Nuclear power plants also discharge wastes directly, as a result of malfunctions or intentional dumping. During the decade from 1979 to 1989, the **Nuclear Regulatory Commission** recorded 33,000 mishaps at power plants in the U.S., 1,000 of which it classified as "particularly significant." Though the vast majority of these incidents resulted in no release of radioactive material, some accidents, such as the **Three Mile Island** partial meltdown and the Chernobyl explosion, have caused significant discharges of radioactivity into the environment. A sampling of incidents:

1) the Vermont Yankee power plant, a power station with a poor safety record, was fined $30,000 for dumping 83,000 gallons (314,000 liters) of radioactive water into the Connecticut River in July 1976;

2) the accident at Three Mile Island, Pennsylvania in 1979 released 2.5 million curies of radioactive noble gases and a small quantity of radioactive iodine into the atmosphere;

3) In one of a series of 21 unreported leaks occurring up to March 1981, radioactive material from the Tsuruga nuclear power plant in Japan was dumped into Tsuruga Bay after warning alarms were shut off. Operators of the plant later admitted that they intentionally dumped wastes regularly;

4) In October 1982, heavy rains caused a flood at the Cofrentes nuclear power plant in Spain which released 154 gallons (580 liters) of radioactive waste;

5) In December 1985, a power failure at the Rancho Seco, California plant resulted in a release of a small quantity of radiation into the air. In 1989 the NRC fined the facility $100,000 for violating waste disposal regulations from 1983 to 1986;

6) At the Douglas Point, Canada, station in January 1986, it was discovered that **high-level radioactive** waste had been leaking from a spent-fuel "storage pond" at a rate of 60 liters per hour.

The health effects of radioactive leaks are still debated. While the harmful effects of Chernobyl are probably beyond question, analysis of the Three Mile Island incident has not detected a long-term increase in cancer or diseases as a result of the discharge there. Studies conducted in England, however, reveal increased rates of leukemia in areas surrounding the nuclear plants at Hinkley Point, Dounreay, and Windscale.

[*Linda Rehkopf and Jeffrey Muhr*]

FURTHER READING

Brill, A. Bertrand. *Low-Level Radiation Effects: A Fact Book.* New York: Society of Nuclear Medicine, 1985.

Caufield, Catherine. *Multiple Exposures.* New York: Harper & Row, Publishers, 1989.

Dresser, Peter D., ed. *Nuclear Power Plants Worldwide.* Detroit: Gale Research, 1993.

Goldsmith, E. et al. "Chernobyl: the End of Nuclear Power?" *The Economist* 16 (1986): 138-209.

Gore, Al. *Earth in the Balance.* New York: Houghton Mifflin, 1992.

Jagger, J. *The Nuclear Lion: What Every Citizen Should Know About Nuclear Power and Nuclear War.* New York: Plenum, 1991.

Jones, R. R., and R. Southwood, eds. *Radiation and Health.* New York: Wiley, 1987.

Regenstein, Lewis. *How to Survive in America the Poisoned.* Washington, DC: Acropolis Books Ltd., 1986.

Shulman, S. *The Threat at Home: Confronting the Toxic Legacy of the U.S. Military.* Boston: Beacon Press, 1992.

Radioactive waste

Radioactive waste is the "garbage" left as a result of the use of nuclear materials by human societies. Such waste can be categorized as low-level, intermediate-level, or high-level waste. The term *transuranic waste* is also used to describe materials consisting of elements heavier than **uranium** in the periodic table.

The term **low-level radioactive waste** usually refers to materials that contain a small amount of **radioactivity** dispersed in a large volume of material. Such materials are produced in a great variety of industrial, medical, and research procedures. A common practice is to store these materials in sealed containers until their level of radioactivity is very low and then to dispose of them by shallow burial or in other traditional **solid waste** disposal systems.

The assumption is that the level of radiation released by these wastes is too low to cause any harmful environmental effects. That assumption has been challenged by some scientists who believe that enough is not yet known about the long-term effects of radiation. They suggest that safer methods of disposal for such wastes need to be developed.

Intermediate-level wastes, as the name suggests, contain a higher level of radioactivity than low-level wastes, but a lower level than high-level wastes. These materials cannot be discharged directly into the **environment**. An important source of such wastes is the re-processing of nuclear fuels. At one time, large quantities of intermediate-level wastes were dumped into the deepest parts of the Atlantic Ocean. That practice has been discontinued and intermediate-level wastes are now being stored on land until a permanent disposal system is developed.

High-level radioactive wastes consist of materials that contain a large amount of radioactivity that will remain at dangerous levels for hundreds or even thousands of years. These materials pose the most difficult disposal problem of all since they must be completely isolated and stored for very long periods of time. The primary sources of high-level wastes are **nuclear power** plants and research and development of **nuclear weapons**.

A number of methods for the storage of high-level wastes have been suggested. Among these are burial in large chunks of concrete, encapsulation in glass or ceramic, projection of them inside rockets into outer space, and burial in the Antarctic ice sheet. Various countries around the world have developed a variety of methods for storing their high-level wastes. In Canada, such wastes have been stored in water-filled pools for more than 25 years. France, with one of the world's largest nuclear power establishments, has developed no permanent storage system but plans to build a large underground vault for its wastes by the early twenty-first century.

In the United States, Congress passed the Nuclear Waste Policy Act in 1982, outlining a complete program for the construction of a high-level waste repository in the early twenty-first century. In 1987, **Yucca Mountain**, Nevada, was selected as the location for that site. Current plans call for a huge vault 1000 feet (305 m) underground as the site for long-term, high-level waste storage at this location. *See also* Nuclear fission; Nuclear Regulatory Commission (NRC); Ocean dumping; Office of Civilian Radioactive Waste Management (OCRWM); Radioactive decay; Radioactive waste management

[*David E. Newton*]

FURTHER READING

Bartlett, D. L., and J. B. Steele. *Forevermore: Nuclear Waste in America.* New York: W. W. Norton, 1985.

Carter, L. J. *Nuclear Imperatives and Public Trust: Dealing With Radioactive Waste.* Baltimore, MD: Resources for the Future, 1987.

Hunt, C. B. "Disposal of Radioactive Wastes." *Bulletin of the Atomic Scientists* (April 1984): 44-46.

League of Women Voters. *The Nuclear Waste Primer.* Washington, DC: League of Women Voters, 1985.

Managing the Nation's Nuclear Waste. Washington, DC: Office of Civilian Radioactive Waste Management, March 1990.

Resnikoff, M. *Deadly Defense: Military Radioactive Landfills.* New York: Radioactive Waste Campaign, 1988.

Radioactive waste management

Radioactive waste materials are produced as by-products of research, **nuclear power** generation, and **nuclear weapons** manufacture. Radioactive waste is classified by the U.S. government into five groups: high-level, transuranic (chemical elements heavier than **uranium**), spent fuel, uranium mill tailings, and **low-level radioactive waste**.

The management and disposal of radioactive waste receives attention at all levels of state and local governments, but the regulations sometimes conflict or are confusing. The U.S. Congress passes relevant legislation, the **Environmental Protection Agency** (EPA) sets applicable environmental standards, and the **Nuclear Regulatory Commission** (NRC) develops regulations to implement the standards. For **high-level radioactive waste**, the **U.S. Department of Energy** (DOE) is responsible for the design, construction and operation of suitable disposal facilities. And courts have recently gotten into the act, ordering states to arrange to have necessary disposal facilities designed, constructed and operated for management of low-level wastes.

The principal federal laws related to the management and disposal of radioactive waste include the Atomic Energy Act (1954), the Uranium Mill Tailings Radiation Control Act (1978), the Low-Level Radioactive Waste Policy Act (1980), the Nuclear Waste Policy Act (1982), the Low-Level Radioactive Waste Policy Amendments Act (1985), and the Nuclear Waste Policy Amendments Act (1987). In addition, the Federal Facility Compliance Act (1992) forces the military to clean up its waste sites.

One of the more difficult aspects of the regulatory quagmire is the problem of dealing with waste, especially spent nuclear fuel and contaminated material such as worn-out reactor parts. Today, the official policy objective for nuclear waste is to dispose of it so that it will never do any appreciable damage to anyone, under any circumstances, for all time. However, for some radioactive waste, "for all time" is measured in thousands of years.

Although radioactive waste carries some hazard for many years, **radioactive decay** removes most of the hazard after a few hundred years. A well-designed waste storage system can be made safe for a long time, some scientists and policy-makers insist, provided that engineers ensure that **erosion**, **groundwater**, earthquakes and other unpredictable natural or human activities do not breach safety barriers.

Disposal methods for radioactive wastes have varied. Over the past 50 years, low-level wastes have been flushed down drains, dumped into the ocean, and tossed into **landfill**s. Uranium mill tailings have been mounded into small hills at sites throughout the western United States. Storage tanks and barrels at DOE sites hold millions of gallons of radioactive waste and toxic chemicals, the by-products of **plutonium** production for nuclear weapons.

Over 80 percent of the total volume of radioactive waste generated in the U. S. is considered low-level. There is now a shift away from the most common disposal method of shallow land burial. Because of public demand for disposal methods that provide the greatest safety and security, disposal methods now include above- and below-ground vaults and earth-mounded concrete bunkers.

However, the country's 17,000 laboratories, hospitals and nuclear power plants that produce low-level radioactive byproducts could become *de facto* disposal sites. The federal low-level radioactive waste policy enacted in 1980 was designed to remedy the inequity of shipping all the nation's low-level radioactive waste to three states (Illinois, Kentucky, and New York) which never agreed to serve as the nation's sole disposal facilities. Its intent was to require every

state to either build its own low-level repository or compact with other states to build regional facilities by 1986. The 1980 federal act was amended in 1985, when it became clear that the 1986 target would not be met, and the deadline was postponed to 1993. As of late 1992, however, few states had even determined sites for such facilities. And after 1996, the institutions generating low-level wastes will be held liable for all low-level wastes they produce.

The principal sources of high-level radioactive waste are nuclear power plants, and programs of the U. S. Department of Defense and DOE, especially those dealing with nuclear weapons. These wastes include spent fuel removed from nuclear plants, and fission products separated from military fuel that has been chemically processed to reclaim unused uranium and plutonium. In the U. S., commercial nuclear power plant fuel removed from those facilities is stored on-site until a geologic repository is completed. The expected completion date for the repository is 2010.

Typically, waste fuel is stored at the power station in a pressurized buffer storage tube for 28 days, then the fuel rod is broken down to component parts. Irradiated fuel elements then are stored for 80 days in a water-filled pond to allow for further decay. For the nonreusable radioactive waste that remains, about 2.5 percent, there is no totally safe method for disposal.

Radioactive waste from one of the first nuclear bomb plants is so volatile that the clean-up problems have stymied the experts. The plant at the DOE's **Hanford Nuclear Reservation** near Richland, Washington, is the nation's largest repository of nuclear waste. There, 177 tanks contain more than 57 million gallons of radioactive waste and toxic chemicals, byproducts of plutonium production for nuclear weapons. The DOE and Westinghouse Corporation (the contractor in charge of Hanford's clean-up) are still not sure exactly what mixture of **chemicals** and radioactive waste each tank contains, but a video taken inside one tank shows the liquid bubbling and roiling from chemical and nuclear reactions. Corrosive, highly radioactive liquids have eaten through Hanford's storage tanks and are being removed to computer-monitored, carbon-steel storage tanks. The clean-up at Hanford could cost as much as $57 billion. The only other country known to have had a waste problem as large as the one at Hanford is the former Soviet Union, where a nuclear waste dump exploded in the nuclear complex at **Chelyabinsk** in 1957, contaminating thousands of square miles of land.

As the military starts massive clean-up efforts, it has identified 17 nuclear facilities as among the worst of the more than 20,000 suspected toxic sites. For example, since the 1970s, about 77,000 barrels of low-level radioactive wastes have been stored at the **Oak Ridge, Tennessee** nuclear reservation. Today, some barrels are rusting and leaking radioactivity. Other identified radioactive waste sites include California's Lawrence Livermore National Laboratory and Sandia National Laboratory, Colorado's **Rocky Flats nuclear plant**, and New Mexico's Los Alamos National Laboratory. The **Savannah River nuclear plant** in South Carolina has been called especially dangerous. Both the

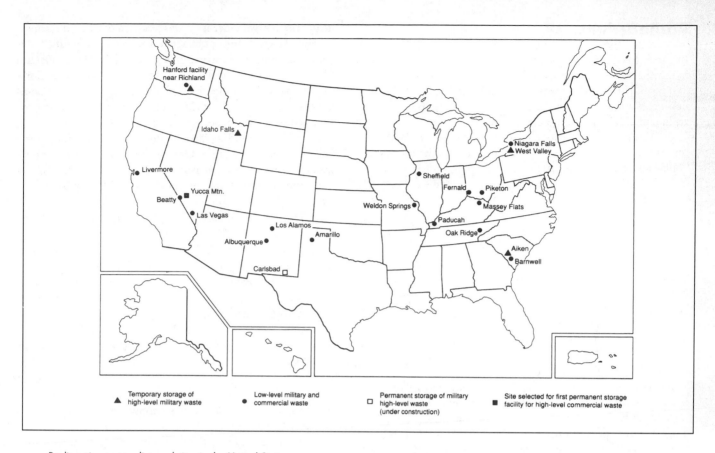

Radioactive waste disposal sites in the United States.

Savannah River site and the Hanford site pose the risk of the kind of massive nuclear waste explosion that occurred at Chelyabinsk.

One new technology in development for the treatment of hazardous and radioactive waste is *in situ vitrification* (ISV), which utilizes electricity to melt contaminated material in place. This technology was developed primarily to treat radioactive waste, but it also has applications to hazardous chemical wastes. The end-result glass formed by ISV is unaffected by extremes of temperature, is not biotoxic, should remain relatively stable for one million years, and passes government tests that measure the speed of contaminant leaching over time. The process permits treatment of mixtures of various wastes including organic, inorganic, and radioactive. The fact that it is not necessary to excavate the waste prior to treatment is seen as a major advantage of the technology, since excavation along with transportation increases health risks. The technology is currently being used in the U. S. at Superfund sites.

Incineration is also used for disposal of low-level radioactive waste, but incomplete **combustion** can produce **dioxin**s and other toxic ash and **aerosol**s. Although finding a site for ash disposal is difficult, the ash is considered a better form for burial than the original waste. It is biologically and structurally more stable, and many of the compounds it contains are insoluble. The residual waste produced by incineration also is less susceptible to **leaching** by rain and groundwater.

Although progress is slow and the situation is often chaotic in the United States, the state of radioactive waste management in much of the rest of the world is even less advanced. The situation is particularly acute in Eastern Europe and the former Soviet Union, since these countries have generated huge quantities of radioactive waste. In many cases the information-gathering necessary to plan clean-up efforts has not begun or is barely underway, and most, if not all, of the actual clean-up remains. *See also* Eastern European pollution; Ocean dumping; Radiation exposure; Radiation sickness; Radioactive pollution; Waste Isolation Pilot Plant; Yucca Mountain, Nevada

[*Linda Rehkopf*]

FURTHER READING

Deadly Defense: Military Radioactive Landfills. New York: Radioactive Waste Campaign, 1988.

Hammond, R. P. "Nuclear Wastes and Public Acceptance." *American Scientist* 67 (March-April 1979): 146-50.

Moeller, D. W. *Environmental Health.* Cambridge: Harvard University Press, 1992.

The Nuclear Waste Primer. Washington, DC: League of Women Voters, 1985.

Shulman, S. "Operation Restore Earth: Cleaning Up After the Cold War." *E Magazine* 4 (March-April 1993): 36-43.

Shulman, S. *The Threat at Home: Confronting the Toxic Legacy of the U. S. Military.* Boston: Beacon Press, 1992.

Radioactivity

In 1896, the French physicist Henri Becquerel accidentally found that an ore of **uranium**, pitchblende, emits an invisible form of radiation, somewhat similar to light. The phenomenon was soon given the name *radioactivity* and materials like pitchblende were called *radioactive*.

The radiation Becquerel discovered actually consists of three distinct parts, called alpha, beta and **gamma ray**s. Alpha and beta rays are made up of rapidly moving particles—helium nuclei in the case of alpha rays, and electrons in the case of beta rays. Gamma rays are a form of electromagnetic radiation with very short wavelengths.

Alpha rays have relatively low energies and can be stopped by a thin sheet of paper. They are not able to penetrate the human skin and, in most circumstances, pose a relatively low health risk. Beta rays are more energetic, penetrating a short distance into human tissue, but they can be stopped by a thin sheet of **aluminum**. Gamma rays are by far the most penetrating form of radiation, permeating wood, paper, plastic, tissue, water, and other low-density materials in the **environment**. They can be stopped, however, by sheets of **lead** a few inches thick.

Radioactivity is a normal and ubiquitous part of the environment. The most important sources of natural radioactivity are rocks containing radioactive **isotope**s of uranium, thorium, potassium, and other elements. The most common radioactive isotope in air is **carbon**-14, formed when **neutron**s from cosmic ray showers react with **nitrogen** in the **atmosphere**. Humans, other animals, and plants are constantly exposed to low-level radiation emitted from these isotopes, and they do suffer to some extent from that exposure. A certain number of human health problems—**cancer** and genetic disorders, for example—are attributed to damage caused by natural radioactivity.

In recent years, scientists have been investigating the special health problems related to one naturally occurring radioactive isotope, **radon**-226. This isotope is produced when uranium decays, and since uranium occurs widely in rocks, radon-226 is also a common constituent of the environment. Radon-226 is an alpha-emitter, and though the isotope does have a long **half-life** (1,620 years), the alpha particles are not energetic enough to penetrate the skin. The substance, however, is a health risk because it is a gas that can be directly inhaled. The alpha particles come into contact with lung tissue, and some scientists now believe that radon-226 may be responsible for a certain number of cases of lung cancer. The isotope can be a problem when homes are constructed on land containing an unusually high concentration of uranium. Radon-226 released by the uranium can escape into the basements of homes, spreading to the rest of a house. Studies by the **Environmental Protection Agency (EPA)** have found that as many as eight million houses in the United States have levels of radon-226 that exceed the **maximum permissible concentration** recommended by experts.

Though Becquerel had discovered radiation occurring naturally in the environment, scientists immediately began asking themselves whether it was possible to convert normally stable isotopes into radioactive forms. This question became the subject of intense investigation in the 1920s and 1930s, and was finally answered in 1934 when Irène Curie and Frèdèric Joliot bombarded the stable isotope **aluminum**-27 with alpha particles and produced **phosphorus**-30, a radioactive isotope. Since the Joliot-Curie experiment, scientists have found ways to manufacture hundreds of artificially radioactive isotopes. One of the most common methods is to bombard a stable isotope with gamma rays. In many cases, the product of this reaction is a radioactive isotope of the same element.

Highly specialized techniques have recently been devised to meet specific needs. Medical workers often use radioactive isotopes with short half-lives because they can be used for diagnostic purposes without remaining in a patient's body for long periods of time. But the isotope cannot have such a short half-life that it will all but totally decay between its point of manufacture and its point of use.

One solution to this problem is the so-called "molybdenum cow." The cow is no more then a shielded container of radioactive molybdenum-99. This isotope decays with a long half-life to produce technetium-99, whose half-life is only six hours. When medical workers require technetium-99 for some diagnostic procedure, they simply "milk" the molybdenum cow to get the short-lived isotope they need.

Artificially radioactive isotopes have been widely employed in industry, research, and medicine. Their value lies in the fact that the radiation they emit allows them to be tracked through settings in which they cannot be otherwise observed. For example, a physician might want to know if a patient's thyroid is functioning normally. In such a case, the patient drinks a solution containing radioactive iodine, which concentrates in the thyroid like stable iodine. The isotope's movement through the body can be detected by a Geiger counter or some other detecting device, and the speed as well as the extent to which the isotope is taken up by the thyroid is an indication of how the organ is functioning.

Artificially radioactive isotopes can pose a hazard to the environment. The materials in which they are wrapped, the tools with which they are handled, and the clothing worn by workers may all be contaminated by the isotopes. Even after they have been used and discarded, they may continue to be radioactive. Users must find ways of disposing of these wastes without allowing the release of dangerous radiation into the environment, a relatively manageable problem. Most materials discarded by industry, medical facilities, and researchers are **low-level radioactive waste**. The amount of radiation released decreases quite rapidly, and after isolation for just a few years, the materials can be disposed of safely with other non-radioactive wastes.

The same cannot be said for the **high-level radioactive waste** produced by **nuclear power** plants and defense research and production. Consisting of radioactive isotopes, such wastes are produced during fission reactions and release dangerously large amounts of radiation for hundreds or thousands of years.

Nuclear fission was discovered accidentally in the 1930s by scientists who were trying to produce artificial radioactive isotopes. In a number of cases, they found that the reactions they used did not result in the formation of new radioactive isotopes, but in the splitting of atomic nuclei, a process that came to be known as nuclear fission.

By the early 1940s, nuclear fission was recognized as an important new source of energy. That energy source was first put to use for destructive purposes, in the construction of **nuclear weapons**. Later, scientists found ways to control the release of energy from nuclear fission in nuclear reactors.

The most serious environmental problem associated with fission reactions is that their waste products are largely long-lived radioactive isotopes. Attempts have been made to isolate these wastes by burying them underground or sinking them in the ocean. All such methods have proved so far to be unsatisfactory, however, as containers break open and their contents leak into the environment.

The United States government has been working for more than four decades to find better methods for dealing with these wastes. In 1982, Congress passed a *Nuclear Waste Policy Act*, providing for the development of one or more permanent burial sites for high-level wastes. Political and environmental pressures have stalled the implementation of the act and a decade after its passage, the nation still has no method for the safe disposal of its most dangerous radioactive wastes. *See also* : Ecotoxicology; Hazardous waste; Nuclear fusion; Nuclear winter; Radiation exposure; Radiation sickness; Radioactive fallout; Radioactive pollution; Radioactive waste management

[*David E. Newton*]

FURTHER READING

Gofman, J. W. *Radiation and Human Health*. San Francisco: Sierra Club Books, 1981.

Inglis, D. R. *Nuclear Energy: Its Physics and Social Challenge*. Reading, MA: Addison-Wesley, 1973.

Jones, R. R., and R. Southwood, eds. *Radiation and Health*. New York: Wiley, 1987.

Wagner, H. N., and L. E. Ketchum. *Living With Radiation*,. Baltimore, MD: Johns Hopkins University Press, 1989.

Radiocarbon dating

Radiocarbon dating is a technique for determining the age of very old objects consisting of organic (**carbon**-based) materials, such as wood, paper, cloth, and bone. The technique is based on the fact that both stable and radioactive **isotope**s of carbon exist. These isotopes behave almost identically in biological, chemical, and physical processes.

Carbon-12, a stable isotope, makes up about 99 percent of all carbon found in nature. Radioactive carbon-14 is formed in the atmosphere when **neutron**s produced in cosmic ray showers react with **nitrogen** atoms.

Despite the fact that it makes up no more than .08 percent of the earth's crust, carbon is an exceedingly important element. It occurs in all living materials and is found in many important rocks and minerals, including limestone and marble, as well as in **carbon dioxide**. Carbon moves through the **atmosphere**, hydrosphere, lithosphere, and **biosphere** in a series of reactions known as the **carbon cycle**. Stable and radioactive isotopes of the element take part in identical reactions in the cycle. Thus, when green plants convert carbon dioxide to carbohydrates through the process of **photosynthesis**, they use both stable carbon-12 and radioactive carbon-14 in exactly the same way. Any living material consists, therefore, of a constant ration of carbon-14 to carbon-12.

In the mid-1940s, Willard F. Libby realized that this fact could be used to date organic material. As long as that material was alive, he pointed out, it should continue to take in both carbon-12 and carbon-14 in a constant ratio. At its death, the material would no longer incorporate carbon in any form into its structure. From that point on, the amount of stable carbon-12 would remain constant. The amount of carbon-14, however, would continuously decrease as it decayed by beta emission to form nitrogen. Over time, the ratio of carbon-14 to carbon-12 would grow smaller and smaller. That ratio would provide an indication of the length of time since the material had ceased being alive.

Radiocarbon dating has been used to estimate the age of a wide variety of objects ranging from charcoal taken from tombs to wood found in Egyptian and Roman ships. One of its most famous applications was in the dating of the Shroud of Turin. Some religious leaders had claimed that the Shroud was the burial cloth in which Jesus was wrapped after his crucifixion. If so, the material of which it was made would have to be nearly 2,000 years old. Radiocarbon dating of the material showed, however, that the cloth could not be more than about 700 years old.

Radiocarbon dating can be used for objects up to 30,000 years of age, but it is highly reliable only for objects less than 7,000 years old. These limits result from the fact that eventually carbon-14 has decayed to such an extent that it can no longer be detected well or, eventually, at all in a sample. For older specimens, radioisotopes with longer half-lives can be used for age determination. *See also* Half-life; Radioactive decay

[*David E. Newton*]

FURTHER READING

Taylor, R. E., et al, eds. *Radiocarbon Dating: An Archaeological Perspective*. Orlando, FL: Academic Press, 1987.

———. *Radiocarbon After Four Decades: An Interdisciplinary Perspective*. New York: Springer Verlag, 1992.

Radioisotope

The term radioisotope is shorthand for radioactive **isotope**. Isotopes are forms of an element whose atoms differ from each other in the number of **neutron**s contained in their nuclei and, hence, in their atomic masses. **Hydrogen**-1, hydrogen-2, and hydrogen-3 are all isotopes of each other.

Radioisotope	Half-life (Years)	Radiation Emitted
Americium-241	460	
Cesium-134	2.1	
Cesium-135	2,000,000	
Cesium-137	30	Beta and gamma
Curium-243	32	
Iodine-131	0.02	Beta and gamma
Krypton-85	10	Beta and gamma
Neptunium-239	2.4	
*Plutonium-239	24,000	Gamma and neutron
Radon-226	1,600	Alpha
Ruthenium-106	1	Beta and gamma
Strontium-90	28	Beta
Technetium-99	200,000	
*Thorium-230	76,000	
Tritium	13	Beta
*Uranium-235	713,000,000	Alpha and neutron
Xenon-133	0.01	
Zirconium-93	900,000	

*Used as fuel in nuclear reactions. All others are by-products.

Some radioisotopes associated with nuclear power.

Isotopes may be stable or radioactive. That is, they may exist essentially unchanged forever (stable), or they may spontaneously emit an **alpha particle** or **beta particle** and/or a **gamma ray**, changing in the process into a new substance. Hydrogen-1 and hydrogen-2 are stable isotopes, but hydrogen-3 is radioactive.

The first naturally occurring radioisotopes were discovered in the late 1890s. Scientists found that all isotopes of the heaviest elements—**uranium**, radium, **radon**, thorium, and protactinium, for example—are radioactive. This discovery raised the question as to whether stable isotopes of other elements could be converted to radioactive forms.

By the 1930s, the techniques for doing so were well established, and scientists routinely produced hundreds of radioisotopes that do not occur in nature. As an example, when the stable isotope **carbon**-12 is bombarded with neutrons, it may be converted to a radioactive cousin, carbon-13. This method can be used to manufacture radioisotopes of nearly every element.

Naturally occurring radioisotopes are responsible for the existence of **background radiation**. Background radiation consists of alpha and beta particles and gamma rays emitted by these isotopes. In addition to the heavy isotopes mentioned above, the most important contributors to background radiation are carbon-14 and potassium-40.

Synthetic radioisotopes have now become ubiquitous in human society. They occur commonly in every part of **nuclear power** plant operations. They are also used extensively in the health sciences, industry, and scientific research. A single example of their medical application is **cancer** therapy. Gamma rays emitted by the radioisotope cobalt-60 have been found to be very effective in treating some forms of

cancer. Other gamma-emitting radioisotopes can also be used in this procedure.

The potential for the release of radioisotopes to the **environment** is great. For example, **medical waste**s might very well contain radioisotopes that still emit measurable amounts of radiation. Stringent efforts are made, therefore, to isolate and store radioisotopes until their radiation has reached a safe level.

These efforts have two aspects. Some radioisotopes have short half-lives. The level of radiation they emit drops to less than one percent of the original amount in a matter of hours or days. These isotopes need only be stored in a safe place for a short time before they can be safely discarded with other **solid waste**s.

Other radioisotopes have half-lives of centuries or millennia. They will continue to emit harmful radiation for thousands of years. Safe disposal of such wastes may require burying them deep in the earth, a procedure that still has not been satisfactorily demonstrated. In spite of the potential environmental hazard posed by radioisotopes, they do not presently pose a serious threat to plants, animals, or humans. The best estimates place the level of radiation from artificial sources at less than five percent of that from natural sources. *See also* Half-life; Radioactive decay; Radioactive waste management; Radioactivity

[*David E. Newton*]

FURTHER READING

Baker, P., et al. *Radioisotopes in Industry.* Washington, DC: U. S. Atomic Energy Commission, 1965.

Corless, W. R., and R. L. Mead. *Power from Radioisotopes.* Washington, DC: U. S. Atomic Energy Commission, 1971.

Kisieleski, W. E., and R. Baserga. *Radioisotopes and Life Processes.* Washington, DC: U. S. Atomic Energy Commission, 1967.

Radiotracer

A radioactive **isotope** progressing through a biological or physical system can be followed by several tracking procedures. For example, **fertilizer** containing radioactive **phosphorus** can be added to **soil**. Plants grown in this soil then take up the radioactive phosphorus just as they do nonradioactive phosphorus. If one of these plants is placed on a photographic plate, radiation from the radioactive phosphorus exposes the plate. The plant "takes its own picture," showing where the phosphorus concentrates in the plant. Radiotracers are a highly desirable research technique as they do not require the destruction of an organism for its study.

Radon

Although it has received attention as an environmental hazard only recently, radon is a naturally occurring radioactive gas that is present at low concentrations everywhere in the **environment**. Colorless and odorless, radon is a decay product of radium; radium is a decay product of the radioac-

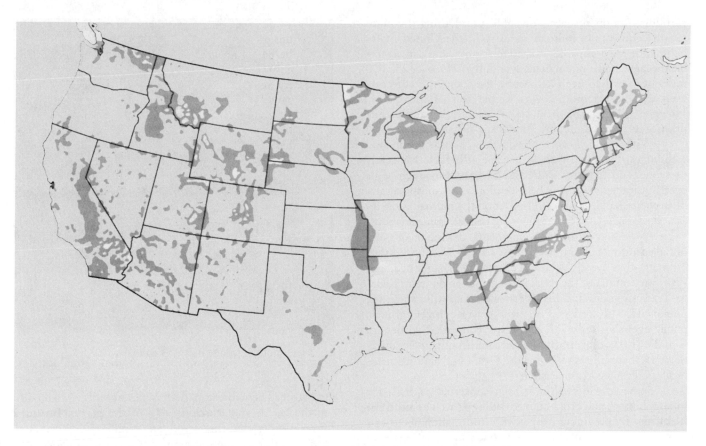

The shaded areas have potentially high levels of uranium in the soil and rocks. Radon levels may be high in these areas.

tive element **uranium**, which occurs naturally in the earth's crust. Radon continues to break down into products called radon progeny. Radon is measured in units called picocuries per liter (pCi/L), and it becomes a health concern when people are exposed to concentrations higher than normal background levels. Some geologic formations, such as the Reading Prong in New Jersey, are naturally very high in radon emissions.

During their normal decay process, radioactive elements emit several kinds of radiation, one of which is alpha radiation. The health effects of radon are associated with these **alpha particle**s. These particles are too heavy to travel far and they cannot penetrate the skin, but they can enter the body through the lungs during inhalation. Studies of miners exposed to high concentrations of radon have shown an increased risk of lung **cancer**, and this is the health effect most commonly associated with radon. Background levels are usually estimated at 1 pCi/L. It is estimated that a person exposed to this concentration for 18 hours a day for five years increases their risk of developing cancer to 1 in 1000. At radon levels of 200 pCi/L, the increased risk of lung cancer after five years of exposure at 18 hours per day rises to 60 in 1000. Because cancer is a disease that is slow to develop, it may take 5-50 years after exposure to radon to detect lung cancer. In the outdoor environment, radon gas and its decay products are usually too well-dispersed to accumulate to dangerous levels. It is indoors without proper ventilation, in places such as basements and ground floors, where radon can

seep from the soil and accumulate to dangerous concentrations. The most common methods of reducing radon buildup inside the home include installing blowers or simply opening windows. Plugging cracks and sealing floors that are in contact with soil also reduces the concentration. In the United States, environmental and public health agencies have instituted free programs to test for radon concentrations, and they also offer assistance and guidelines for remedying the problem. *See also* Radiation exposure; Radioactive decay; Radioactive pollution; Radioactivity

[*Usha Vedagiri*]

FURTHER READING

Brenner, D. J. *Radon: Risk and Remedy.* Salt Lake City, UT: W. H. Freeman, 1989.

Cohen, B. *Radon: A Homeowner's Guide to Detection and Control.* Mt. Vernon, NY: Consumer Report Books, 1988.

Kay, J. G., et al. *Indoor Air Pollution: Radon, Bioaerosols, and VOCs.* Chelsea, MI: Lewis, 1991.

Lafavore, M. *Radon: The Invisible Threat.* Emmaus, PA: Rodale Press, 1987.

Rails-to-Trails Conservancy (Washington, D.C.)

In 1985, the Rails-to-Trails Conservancy, a non-profit organization, was established to convert abandoned railroad corridors into open spaces for public use. During the nineteenth century, the railroad industry in the United States boomed as rail companies rushed to acquire land and assemble the largest rail system in the world. By 1916, over 250,000 miles of track had been laid across the country, connecting even the most remote towns to the rest of the nation. However, during the next few decades, the automobile drastically changed the way Americans live and travel.

With Henry Ford's introduction of mass production techniques, the **automobile** became affordable for nearly everyone, and industry shifted to trucking for much of its overland transportation. The invention and widespread use of airplanes had a significant impact on the railroad industry as well, and people began abandoning railroad transportation.

As a result of these developments, thousands of miles of rail corridors fell into disuse. Rails-to-Trails Conservancy estimates that over 3,000 miles of track are abandoned each year. Since much of the track is in the public domain, Rails-to-Trails strives to find uses for the land that will benefit the public. Thus Rails-to-Trails works with citizen groups, public agencies, railroads, and other concerned parties to, according to the organization, "build a transcontinental trailway network that will preserve for the future our nation's spectacular railroad corridor system."

Some of the rails have been converted to trails for hiking, biking, and cross-country skiing as well as **wildlife habitat**s. By providing people with information about upcoming abandonments, assisting public and private agencies in the effort to gain control of those lands, sponsoring short-term land purchases, and working with Congress and other federal and state agencies to simplify the acquisition of abandoned railways, Rails-to-Trails has mobilized a powerful grassroots movement across the country.

Rails-to-Trails also sponsors an annual conference and other special meetings and publishes materials related to railway **conservation**. Its quarterly newsletter, *Trailblazer*, is sent to members and keeps them aware of rails-to-trails issues. Many books and pamphlets are available through the group, as are studies such as *How to Get Involved with the Rails-to-Trails Movement* and *The Economic Benefits of Rails-to-Trails Conversions to Local Economies*. In addition, the Rails-to-Trails Conservancy provides legal support and advice to local groups seeking to convert rails to trails. Contact: Rails-to-Trails Conservancy, Suite 300, 1400 Sixteenth Street, NW, Washington, DC 20036. Internet: http://www.halcyon.com:80/fredwert/.

[Linda M. Ross]

Rain, acid

See **Acid rain**

Rain forest

The world's rain forests are biologically the richest **ecosystem**s on earth, containing an incredible variety of plant and

Temperate rainforest in Brazil.

animal life. These forests play an important role in maintaining the health and **biodiversity** of the planet. But rain forests throughout the world are rapidly being cut and destroyed, threatening the survival of millions of **species** of plants and animals and disrupting **climate** and weather patterns locally and globally. The rain forests of greatest current interest are **tropical rain forest**s, particularly those found in Central and South America, and the ancient **temperate rain forest**s along the northeastern coast of North America.

Tropical rain forests (TRFs) are amazingly rich and diverse biologically and may contain one-half to two-thirds of all species of plants and animals, though these forests cover only about 5-7 percent of the world's land surface. Tropical rain forests are found near the equatorial regions of Central and South America, Africa, Asia, and on Pacific Islands, with the largest remaining forest being the Amazon rain forest, which covers a third of South America.

TRFs remain warm, green, and humid throughout the year and receive at least 150 inches (381 cm) of rain a year, up to half of which may come from trees giving off water through the pores of their leaves in a process called **transpiration**. The tall, lush trees of the forest form a two- to three-layer closed canopy, allowing very little light to reach the ground. Although tropical forests are known for their lush, green vegetation, the **soil** stores very few nutrients. Dead and decomposing animals, trees, and leaves are quickly taken up by the forest organisms, and very little is absorbed into the ground.

In 1989 *World Resources Institute* predicted that "between 1990 and 2020, species **extinction**s caused primarily by tropical **deforestation** may eliminate somewhere between 5 and 15 percent of the world's species. . . . This would amount to a potential loss of 15,000 to 50,000 species per year, or 50 to 150 species per day." It is estimated that 30 million to 80 million species of insects alone may exist in TRFs, at least 97 percent of which have never been identified and "discovered."

Tropical forests also provide essential winter **habitat** for many birds that breed and spend the rest of the year in the United States. Some 250 species found in the United States and Canada spend the winter in the tropics, and their population levels are decreasing alarmingly due to forest depletion in Latin America.

Tropical rain forests have unique resources, many of which humans have as yet failed to utilize. Food, industrial products, and medicinal supplies are common examples in usage. Among the many fruits, nuts, and vegetables that we use on a regular basis and which originated in tropical forests are citrus fruits, coffee, yams, nuts, chocolate, peppers, and cola. A variety of oils, lubricants, resins, dyes, and steroids are also products of the forests. Natural rubber, the fourth biggest agricultural export of southeast Asian nations, brings in over $3 billion a year to the developing countries. The forests could also yield a sustainable supply of woods like teak, mahogany, bamboo, and others. Although only about one percent of known tropical plants have been studied for medicinal or pharmaceutical applications, these have produced some 25 to 40 percent of all prescription drugs used in the United States. Some 2,000 tropical plants now being studied have shown potential as **cancer**-fighting agents.

Scientists studying ways to commercially utilize these forests in a sustainable, non-destructive way have determined that two to three times more money could be made from the long-term collection of such products as nuts, rubber, medicines, and food, as from cutting the trees for logging or cattle ranching.

Perhaps the greatest value of tropical rain forests is the essential role they play in the earth's climate. By absorbing **carbon dioxide** and producing oxygen through **photosynthesis**, the forests help prevent global warming (the so-called **greenhouse effect**) and may be important in generating oxygen for the planet. The forests also help prevent **drought**s and **flooding**, soil **erosion** and stream **sedimentation**, and keep the **hydrologic cycle** going and streams and rivers flowing by absorbing rainfall and releasing moisture into the air.

Despite the worldwide outcry over deforestation, destruction is actually increasing. A 1990 study by the United Nations Food and Agriculture Organization found that tropical forests were disappearing at a rate exceeding 40 million acres (16.2 million ha) a year—an area the size of Washington state. This rate is almost twice that of the previous decade.

Timber companies in the United States and western Europe are responsible for most of this destruction, mainly for farming, cattle ranching, logging, and huge development projects. Japan, the world's largest hardwood importer, buys 40 percent of the timber produced, with the United States running second. Ironically, much of the destruction of forests worldwide has been paid for by American taxpayers through such government-funded international lending and develop-

ment agencies as the **World Bank**, the International Monetary Fund, and the Inter-American Development Bank, along with the United States Agency for International Development.

The demand from Americans, Europeans, and Latin Americans for beef has contributed heavily to the conversion of rain forest to pasture land. It is estimated that one-fourth of all tropical forests destroyed each year are cut and cleared for cattle ranching. Between 1950 and 1980, two-thirds of Central America's primary forests were cut, mostly to supply the United States with beef for fast food outlets and pet food.

In Brazil and other parts of the **Amazon Basin**, cattle ranchers, plantation owners, and small landowners often clear the forest by setting it on fire, causing an estimated 23 to 43 percent increase in **carbon** dioxide levels worldwide and spreading smoke over millions of square miles that has interfered with air travel and caused respiratory difficulties among people over a wide area.

Ironically, cleared forest that is turned into pasture land contains very poor quality soil and can only be ranched for a few years before the land becomes infertile and has to be abandoned. Eventually **desertification** sets in, causing the cattle rancher to move on to new areas of the forest.

While huge timber companies and multi-national corporations have justifiably received much of the blame for the destruction of TRFs, local people also play a major role. Populations of the **Third World** gather wood for heating and cooking, and the demand of their growing numbers has resulted in many deforested areas. The proliferation of coca farms, producing cocaine mainly for the American market, has also caused significant deforestation and **pollution**, as has gold prospecting in the Amazon.

The destruction of TRFs has already had devastating effects on the **indigenous peoples** in tropical regions. Entire tribes, societies, and cultures have been displaced by environmental damage caused or exacerbated by deforestation. Today in Brazil, only about 200,000 Indians remain, compared to a population of some six million 400 years ago. Sometimes they are killed outright when they come into contact with settlers, loggers, or prospectors, either by shooting or disease. And those who are not killed are often herded into miserable reservations or become landless peasants working for slave labor wages.

Today, less than five percent of the world's remaining TRFs have some type of protective status, and there is often little or no enforcement of prohibitions against logging, hunting, and other destructive activities.

The ancient rain forests of North America are also important ecosystems, composed in large part of trees that are hundreds and even thousands of years old. Temperate rain forests (or evergreen forests) are usually composed of conifers (needle-leafed, cone-bearing plants) or broadleaf evergreen trees. They thrive in cool coastal climates with mild winters and heavy rainfall and are found along the coasts of the Pacific Northwest area of North America, southern Chile, western New Zealand, and southeast Australia, as well as on the lower mountain slopes of western North America, Europe, and Asia.

The rain forest of the Pacific Northwest, the largest **coniferous forest** in the world, stretches over 112,000 square miles (290,000 km²) of coast from Alaska to northern California, and parts extend east into mountain valleys. The forests of the Pacific Northwest harbor several coniferous trees, including varieties of spruce, cedar, pine, Douglas fir, Hemlock, and Pacific yew. Broadleaf trees, such as Oregon oak, tanoak, and madrone, are also found there. **Redwoods** stretch to central California, and further south are the giant sequoias, the largest living organisms on earth, some of which are over 3,000 years old.

In some ways, the temperate rain forests of the Pacific Northwest may be the most biologically rich in the world. Although TRFs contain many more species, temperate rain forests have far more plant matter per acre and contain the tallest and oldest trees on earth. Over 210 species of fish and **wildlife** live in ancient forests, and one tree can support 100 different species of plants. One tree found in cool, moist forests is the slow-growing Pacific yew, whose bark and needles contain taxol, considered one of the most powerful anti-cancer drugs ever discovered. Taxol is used to treat several forms of cancer, including ovarian cancer.

Unfortunately, the **clear-cutting** of most of the ancient forests and their yew trees has caused a serious shortage of taxol for treatment and research purposes. Some are also unavailable for harvesting because they grow in forests protected as habitat for the endangered **northern spotted owl**. The logging of federal land under the jurisdiction of the **Bureau of Land Management** (BLM) and the U. S. **Forest Service** (USFS) is now eliminating some of the last and best habitats for the Pacific yew.

The remaining ancient forest, almost all of which is now on BLM and USFS land, is being cut at a rate of some 200,000 acres a year, as of 1992. At this rate it will be destroyed within less than two decades. The consequences of this destruction will include the disappearance of **rare species** dependent on this habitat, the **siltation** of waterways and erosion of soil, and the decimation of **salmon** populations, which provide the world's richest salmon fishery, worth billions of dollars annually.

Although the timber industry claims that logging maintains jobs in the Pacific Northwest, logging **national forest** often makes no economic sense. Because of the expense of building logging roads, surveying the area to be cut, and the low price it charges for trees, the USFS often loses money on its timber sales. As a result of such "deficit" or "below cost" timber sales between 1989 and 1992, the USFS lost an average of almost $300 million a year on selling timber in national forests.

Several private conservation groups, such as the **Wilderness Society** and the **Sierra Club**, are working to preserve the remaining ancient forests on BLM and USFS land through federal legislation, lawsuits, and other actions. In April 1993, President Bill Clinton attended a "timber summit" in Portland, Oregon, to discuss the ancient forests, **endangered species**, and timber jobs. But the cutting of old growth forests and "below cost" timber sales have continued much as before.

Two of the largest remaining temperate rain forests are Alaska's 16.9 million-acre Tongass National Forest and the Russian Taiga. Tongass is the last large, relatively undisturbed, temperate rain forest in the United States, stretching over 600 miles (966 km) of coast along the Alaska Panhandle. It has the highest concentration of **bald eagle**s and **grizzly bear**s anywhere on earth. In addition to reducing habitat for wildlife and salmon hatching, scenic areas are being destroyed, reducing tourism and **recreation** in the area.

The huge forests in the Russian Far East and Siberia are called the Taiga, and the Siberian portion is the world's largest forest. Comprising some two million square miles, the Taiga is much larger than the Brazilian Amazon and would cover the entirety of America's lower 48 states. With Russia becoming more market-oriented and in desperate need of hard currency, some have discussed selling logging rights to some of these forests to American, Japanese, and Korean logging companies.

Pressure from environmentalists and increasing public concern for rain forests has encouraged world leaders to consider more **environmental law**s. In June 1992, at the **United Nations Earth Summit** conference in Rio de Janeiro, Brazil, a set of voluntary principles to conserve the world's threatened forests were agreed upon. The document affirms the right of countries to economically exploit forests but states that this should be done "on a sustainable basis," recognizing the value of forests in absorbing carbon dioxide and slowing climate change. Initial hope that the agreement on principles might eventually be turned into a binding international convention has evaporated, and throughout the world, forests continue to be destroyed. Some of the last remaining untouched forests are being opened up to poaching, logging, and other exploitation, such as the one million acre virgin Ndoke rainforest of the northern Congo Republic, a wildlife paradise full of thousand-year-old trees, along with elephants, leopards, gorillas, and other endangered species. *See also* Compaction; Deciduous forest; Decomposition; Migration; Old-growth forest

[*Lewis G. Regenstein*]

FURTHER READING

Caufield, C. *In the Rainforest: Report From a Strange, Beautiful, Imperiled World.* Chicago: University of Chicago Press, 1986.

Mitchell, G. J. *World on Fire: Saving an Endangered Earth.* New York: Charles Scribner's Sons, 1991.

Myers, N. *The Sinking Ark: A New Look at Disappearing Species.* Oxford: Pergamon Press, 1979.

Porritt, J. *Save the Earth.* Atlanta, GA: Turner Publishing, 1991.

Raven, P. H. "The Cause and Impact of Deforestation." In *Earth 88: Changing Geographic Perspectives.* Washington, DC: National Geographic Society, 1988.

Repetto, R. *The Forest for the Trees? Government Policies and the Misuse of Resources.* Washington, DC: World Resources Institute, 1988.

Zuckerman, S. *Saving Our Ancient Forest.* Los Angeles: Living Planet Press, 1991.

Rain shadow

A region of relative dryness found on the downwind side of a mountain range or other upland area. As an air mass rises over the upwind side of a mountain range, pressure drops and temperature falls. This causes the relative humidity of the air mass to rise. Eventually the moisture in the air condenses and precipitation occurs. An air mass that is now cooler and drier passes over the top of the mountain range. As it descends on the downwind side of the range, it warms again and its relative humidity is further reduced. This reduction in relative humidity not only prevents further rainfall, but also causes the air mass to absorb moisture from other sources, drying the climate on the downwind side. The ultimate result is lush forest on the windward side of a mountain separated by the summit from an arid **environment** on the downwind side. Examples of rain shadows include the arid areas on the eastern sides of the mountain ranges of western North America, and the Atacama Desert in Chile on the downwind side of the Andes Mountains.

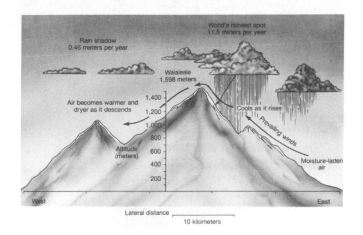

A rain shadow in Hawaii on the eastern side of Mount Waialeale.

Rainforest Action Network (San Francisco, California)

Rainforest Action Network (RAN), founded in 1985, is an activist group that works to protect **rain forest**s and their inhabitants worldwide. Its strategy includes imposing public pressure on those corporations, agencies, nations, and politicians whom the group believes are responsible for the destruction of the world's rain forests by organizing letter-writing campaigns and consumer boycotts. In addition to mobilizing consumer and environmental groups in the United States, RAN organizes and supports conservationists committed to rain forest protection around the world.

RAN's first direct action campaign was the boycott of Burger King. The fast-food restaurant chain was importing much of its beef from Central and South America, where large areas of forests have been turned into pastureland for cattle. RAN contends that "after sales dropped 12 percent during the boycott in 1987, Burger King canceled $35 million worth of beef contracts in Central America and announced that it had stopped importing rainforest beef. . . . The formation of Rainforest Action Groups (RAGs) that staged demonstrations and held letter-writing parties in U.S. cities helped make the boycott and other campaigns a success." RAN states that there are now over 150 RAGs in North America alone.

RAN also works with human rights groups around the world, attempting to protect and save the cultures of **indigenous peoples** dependent on rain forests. The group helps support ecologically sustainable ways to use the rain forest, such as rubber tapping and the harvesting of such foods as nuts and fruits.

RAN urges the public to avoid buying tropical wood, such as rosewood and mahogany, and plywood made from rain forest timber. The group also recommends that people not buy rain forest beef, which is often found in fast-food hamburgers and processed beef products.

RAN is strongly pushing its boycott of the Japanese conglomerate Mitsubishi, which makes televisions, VCRs, fax machines, and stereos. RAN points out that "Mitsubishi has big logging operations in Malaysia, Borneo, Philippines, Indonesia, Chile, Canada, and Brazil. . . . It is the world's number one importer of tropical timber." Other corporations that RAN has criticized for damaging rain forests include ARCO, Scott Paper, Coca-Cola, Texaco, and CONOCO, as well as such international agencies as the **World Bank** and the International Tropical Timber Organization (ITTO).

RAN operates an extensive media campaign targeted at companies and decision-makers who create policy on rain forests by running full-page advertisements in such major newspapers as *The New York Times* and the *Wall Street Journal*, RAN's publications include its quarterly *World Rainforest Report*; its monthly *Action Alerts*; *The Rainforest Action Guide*; and *The Rainforest Catalogue*, offering books, videos, bumper stickers, T-shirts, and other products promoting rain forest protection, as well as cosmetics and food made from rain forest plants.

Among the victories achieved by or with the help of RAN are the halting of a plan to cut down the one-million-acre La Mosquito Forest in Honduras—made famous by the movie *The Mosquito Coast*—which is essential to the cultures and livelihoods of some 35,000 indigenous people; forcing the World Bank to stop making loans to nations that destroy their rain forests; stopping **oil drilling** in the Ecuadorian Amazon by CONOC and Du Pont; preventing the opening of a major road to take timber out of the Amazon to the Pacific Coast; and persuading Coca-Cola to donate land in Belize for a **nature** preserve.

Nevertheless, the destruction of the world's rain forests continues on an enormous scale. As RAN's director Randall Hayes points out: "Over 50 percent of the world's **tropical rain forest**s are gone forever. Two-thirds of the southeast Asia forests have disappeared, mostly for hardwood shipped to Japan, Europe, and the U.S. And this destruction continues at a rate of 150 acres per minute, or a football field per second." Contact: Rainforest Action Network, 450 Sansome Street, San Francisco, CA 94111. Internet: http://www.ran.org/ran/.

[*Lewis G. Regenstein*]

Ramsar Convention

See **Convention on Wetlands of International Importance**

Rangelands

Concentrated in 16 western states, rangelands comprise 770 million acres and over one-third of the land base in the United States. Rangelands are vegetated predominately by shrubs, and they include **grasslands**, **tundra**, marsh, meadow, **savanna**, **desert**, and alpine communities. They are fragile **ecosystem**s that depend on a complex interaction of plant and animal **species** with limited resources, and many range areas have been severely damaged by **overgrazing**. Currently over 300 million acres within the United States alone are classified as being in need of **conservation** treatment and management. Effective range-management techniques include **soil conservation**, preservation of **wildlife habitat**, and protection of **watershed**s.

Raprenox (nitrogen scrubbing)

A recently-developed technique for removing **nitrogen oxides** from waste gases makes use of a common, nontoxic organic compound known as cyanuric acid, $C_3H_3N_3O_3$. When heated to temperatures of about 660°F (345°C), cyanuric acid decomposes to form isocyanic acid. The acid, in turn, reacts with oxides of **nitrogen** to form **carbon dioxide**, **carbon monoxide**, nitrogen, and water. The process has been given the name of *raprenox*, which comes from the expression *rap*id *r*emoval of *ni*trogen *ox*ides. In tests so far, the method has worked very well with internal **combustion** engines, removing up to 99 percent of all nitrogen oxides from exhaust gases. Its efficiency with gases released from smokestacks has not yet been determined. *See also* Scrubbers

Rare species

A **species** that is uncommon, few in number, or not abundant. A species can be rare and not necessarily be endangered or threatened, for example, an organism found only on an island or one that is naturally low in numbers because of a restricted range. Such species are, however, usually vulnerable to any exploitation, interference, or disturbance of their **habitat**s. Species may also be common in some areas but rare in others, such as at the edge of its natural range.

"Rare" is also a designation that the **IUCN—The World Conservation Union** gives to certain species "with small world populations that are not at present 'endangered' or 'vulnerable' but are at risk. These species are usually localized within restricted geographical areas or habitats or are thinly scattered over a more extensive range." Some American states have also employed this category in protective legislation.

Reactors

See **Arco, Idaho; Chernobyl Nuclear Power Station; High-solids reactor; Liquid metal fast breeder reactor; Nuclear power; Radioactive pollution; Three Mile Island Nuclear Reactor; Windscale (Sellafield) plutonium reactor**

Rathje, William (1945-)

American archeologist and "garbologist"

William Rathje is an archaeologist, professor of anthropology, and director of the Garbage Project at the University of Arizona. Calling himself a "garbologist," he and his associates analyze the composition and decomposition of rubbish in **landfills** as a way of understanding our own and other cultures. As he and co-author Cullen Murphy report in *Rubbish! The Archaeology of Garbage* (1992) many commonly held beliefs about **garbage** stored in landfills are quite mistaken. For example, it is widely believed that while styrofoam and other plastics do not decompose, materials such as newspapers and disposable baby diapers decompose fairly rapidly in landfills. But this, Rathje discovered, is not true. Deep within the landfill, the relative lack of oxygen, bacteria, and earthworms tends to preserve buried items. It is not uncommon to find newspapers that are still readable after fifty years. Having exposed this and other "myths of biodegration" we now need to re-think our views on rubbish and how best to dispose of it.

Besides being material, rubbish is also freighted with cultural meaning. Rathje regards garbage as a symbolically significant artifact. Just as tombs and temples tell us much about ancient people's practices and habits, garbage dumps and sanitary landfills tell us a great deal about the modern consumer society and its inhabitants. The layered contents of these sites supply significant evidence of the kind of character and culture that modern Americans have developed. The old saying "you are what you eat" should now be supplemented with "you are how you eat" and "you are what you throw away." The pervasive presence of plastic and styrofoam fast-food containers and disposable diapers bear mute testimony to the tempo of modern life and the premium that Americans now place on ease, speed, and convenience.

[*Terence Ball*]

FURTHER READING

Rathje, W., and C. Murphy, *Rubbish! The Archaeology of Garbage*. New York: HarperCollins, 1992.

Recharge zone

The area in which water enters an aquifer. In a recharge zone surface water or precipitation percolate through relatively porous, unconsolidated, or fractured materials, such as sand, moraine deposits, or cracked basalt, that lie over a water bearing, or aquifer, formation. In some cases recharge occurs where the water bearing formation itself encounters the ground surface and precipitation or surface water seeps directly into the aquifer. Recharge zones most often lie in topographically elevated areas where the **water table** lies at some depth. Aquifer recharge can also occur locally where streams or lakes, especially temporary ponds, are fed by precipitation and lie above an aquifer. Karst **sinkholes** also frequently serve as recharge conduits. A recharge zone can extend hundreds of square miles, or it can occupy only a small area, depending upon geology, rainfall, and surface **topography** over the aquifer. Recharge rates in an aquifer depend upon the amount of local precipitation, the ability of surface deposits to allow water to filter through, and the rate at which water moves through the aquifer. Water moves through the porous rock of an aquifer sometimes a few centimeters a day and sometimes, as in karst limestone regions, many kilometers in a day. Surface water can enter an aquifer only as fast as water within the aquifer moves away from the recharge zone.

Because recharge zones are the water intake for extensive underground **reservoir**s, they can easily be a source of **groundwater** contamination. Agricultural **pesticide**s and **fertilizer**s are especially common groundwater pollutants. Applied year after year and washed downward by rainfall and irrigation water, agricultural chemicals frequently percolate into aquifers and then spread through the local groundwater system. Equally serious are contaminants **leaching** from **solid waste** dumps. Rainwater percolating through household waste picks up dozens of different organic and inorganic compounds, and contamination appears to continue a long time: pollutants have recently been found leaching from waste dumps left by the Romans almost 2,000 years ago. Perhaps most serious are **petroleum** products, including **automobile** oil, which Americans dump or bury in their back yards at the rate of 240 million gallons (910 million liters) per year, or 4.5 million gallons (18 million liters) each week. On a more industrial scale, inadequately sealed toxic waste and radioactive materials contaminate extensive areas of groundwater when they are deposited near recharge zones. Because recharge occurs in a vast range of geologic conditions, all these contamination sources present real threats to groundwater quality. *See also* Hazardous waste; Radioactive waste

[*Mary Ann Cunningham*]

FURTHER READING

Fetter, C. W. *Applied Hydrology*. Columbus, OH: Charles E. Merrill, 1980.

Freeze, R. A., and J. A. Cherry. *Groundwater*. Englewood Cliffs, NJ: Prentice-Hall, 1979.

Reclamation

This term has been used environmentally in two distinct ways. The more historic use refers to making land productive for agriculture. The current usage refers mostly to the restoration of disturbed land to an ecologically stable condition.

The main application for agricultural purposes is the development of **irrigation**. That was the mission given in 1902 to the federal **Bureau of Reclamation** under the **U.S. Department of Agriculture**. This agency has built many dams and developed numerous water projects, mostly in the **arid** West. The term reclamation has also been used to describe the system of dikes and pumps in the Netherlands to allow farming of lands below sea level.

The main thrust of reclamation today is the restoration of land damaged by human activity, especially by **strip mining** for **coal**. Until 1977, strip-mined land was largely abused and neglected, with widely differing efforts by individuals and local governments to restore land while still allowing profitable mining. That year Congress passed the landmark legislation, the **Surface Mining Control and Reclamation Act**. It applies only to coal mining and restricts mining in prime western farmlands or where owners of surface rights object. The act requires mine operators to 1) demonstrate reclamation proficiency; 2) restore the shape of the land to the original contour and revegetate it if requested by the landowner; 3) minimize impacts on the local **watershed** and **groundwater** and prevent acid contamination; and 4) pay a fee on each ton of coal mined into a $4.1 billion fund to reclaim orphaned lands left by earlier mining.

From pioneer days the landowner was free to treat land however desired. As mining problems grew more rampant, the American public came to understand that derelict land not only degraded the local **environment** but also caused impacts downstream, a terrible legacy for their children. Even worse, in some states ownership of mineral rights took precedence over the surface rights, allowing mining regardless of the desires of those who lived there. As the clamor for reform grew, many states passed legislation but enforced it mainly through inadequate bonds, which the mining companies simply forfeited. Even after 1977, enforcement by the state mining office in Oklahoma was so poor that the federal government took over enforcement for a time.

Reclamation clearly adds to the cost of coal. For Appalachian coal this reaches 15 percent of the cost per **Btu** (British Thermal Unit). The 1977 act created a level playing field where all compete under the same rules. Costs easily involve $1,000 to $5,000 per acre, but this is small compared to royalties paid the landowner. In Germany, where coal seams are very thick and land values are at a premium because of heavy population pressure, great efforts are made to reclaim the land, even up to $10,000 per acre. In terms of productive farm, grazing, or timber lands, restoration after a one-time extraction of coal allows a return to **sustainable agriculture** or forestry.

Strip mining creates four landforms which the reclamation process must address: rows of spoil banks, final cut canyons, high walls adjacent to the final cut, and coal-haul roads. The first two are relatively easy, but the latter two require special treatment. Reshaping the land to the original contour and keeping the **soil** in place are major challenges in hilly terrain. Operators usually find it necessary to cut into the unmined hillside to make it grade into the mined land below. **Subsidence** of **overburden** could conceivably create a cliff face along the headwall if not adequately compacted. Coal-haul roads are very dense from the heavy vehicles traversing them. They must be ripped up and plowed for even minimal revegetation success or, less desirable, be buried under overburden.

Besides physically reshaping the land, for reclamation to succeed the essential needs of **erosion** control, **topsoil** replacement, and nurturing and protecting young vegetation until it can survive on its own must be met. These needs are interdependent. Vegetation is crucial for erosion control, especially as the slope gradient increases; however vegetation struggles without topsoil, critical **nutrients**, and protection from **wildlife** and livestock. One additional problem, **acid mine drainage**, is eliminated by good reclamation, as the oxidizing materials which produce the acid are buried.

The one most crucial element, and most expensive, is topsoil replacement. Original soils provide five major benefits: 1) a seedbed with the physical properties needed for survival; 2) a reservoir for needed nutrients; 3) a superior medium for water absorption and retention; 4) a source of native seeds and plants; and 5) an **ecosystem** where the decomposer and aerator-mixer organisms can thrive. The absence of even one of these categories often dooms reclamation efforts.

The more one studies this problem, the more important the topsoil becomes; truly it is one of the earth's most vital resources. Loose overburden is sometimes so coarse and lacking in nutrients that it can support little plant cover. A quick buildup of **biomass** is critical for erosion control, but without the topsoil to sustain both plant productivity and the microorganisms needed to decompose the dead biomass, any ground cover is soon lost, exposing the soil to increasingly higher erosion rates.

Some areas, such as flat lowlands, can revegetate with or without human aid. But for many lands, especially those with large fractures of rock and air voids, reclamation is practically an all or nothing venture, with little tolerance for halfway measures. Indeed, in conditions where most of the negative impacts are retained within the site, reclamation may easily worsen conditions by removing the barriers to **runoff** and **sediment**.

A case study from northeastern Oklahoma is relevant here. Operations included both area and contour strip mining and have been carried out through several periods of state and federal legislation. The only reclamation required between 1968 and 1971 was to level the tops of spoil banks with

a dozer. This had some benefit in lower, flat terrain, where surface materials were often fine-grained, a combination which, aided by plant growth, allowed more water and seed retention. However, this grading gave little improvement to hillside spoil banks. As with completely orphaned lands, much of the runoff and sediment production was retained on-site, even acid drainage from the base of exposed coal seams.

New state legislation passed in 1971 greatly worsened conditions. It required reshaping the land to a flat or rolling terrain, but without requiring topsoil replacement. The effect was to widen the area covered by somewhat sterile overburden, burying undisturbed topsoil below the mines and removing many of the barriers which had previously functioned as effective sediment traps. Sediment rates approached those measured at construction sites, up to 13 percent sediment by weight.

Mining begun in the 1980s was governed by the new federal act. Erosion berms surrounded the site, and topsoil was removed and stockpiled prior to mining. As soon as feasible after mining was completed, the slopes were regraded, the topsoil replaced, and grass planted and nurtured with the care of conscientious farmers. Managers found that curing the soil first by spreading it out prior to placement gave **aerobic** microorganisms a jump-start, with better revegetation performance as a result. State inspectors visited regularly to check on compliance.

Efforts to reclaim orphan lands, using funds collected under the 1977 act, did not fare so well. The same lack of topsoil as seen prior to 1977 plagued replanting efforts, even with heavy applications of **fertilizer**. Water retention in the rocky **subsoil** was likely a key problem.

Much of what is needed for effective reclamation is known. What has been missing has been the will to do it and the legal clout for enforcement. Key aspects of reclamation are erosion containment, reshaping the land, topsoil replacement to speed ecosystem recovery, and revegetation, with follow up and repair as needed for up to five years. Reclamation is an investment in the future, a gift to those who follow and an essential component of sustainable land use. *See also* Mine spoil waste; Restoration ecology

[*Nathan H. Meleen*]

FURTHER READING

Bradshaw, A. D., and M. J. Chadwick. *The Restoration of Land: The Ecology and Reclamation of Derelict and Degraded Land.* Berkeley: University of California Press, 1980.

Law, D. L. *Mined-Land Rehabilitation.* New York: Van Nostrand Reinhold, 1984.

Meleen, N. H. *Geomorphological Perspectives on Land Disturbance and Reclamation.* Oxford Polytechnic Discussion Papers in Geography, No. 22. Oxford, England: Oxford Polytechnic, 1986.

Narten, P. F., et al. *Reclamation of Mined Lands in the Western Coal Region.* U. S. Geological Survey Circular 872. Alexandria, VA: U. S. Geological Survey, 1983.

Powell, J. W. "The Reclamation Idea." In *American Environmentalism: Readings in Conservation History,* edited by R. F. Nash. 3rd ed. New York: McGraw-Hill, 1990.

Williams, R. D., and G. E. Schuman, eds. *Reclaiming Mine Soils and Overburden in the Western United States: Analytic Parameters and Procedures.* Ankeny, IA: Soil Conservation Society of America, 1987.

Recreation

The term recreation comes from the Latin word *recreatio*, referring to refreshment, restoration, or recovery. The modern notion of recreation is complex, and many definitions have been suggested to capture its meaning. In general, the term recreation carries the idea of purpose, usually restoration of the body, mind, or spirit. Modern definitions of recreation often include the following elements: 1) it is an activity rather than idleness or rest, 2) the choice of activity or involvement is voluntary, 3) recreation is prompted by internal motivation to achieve personal satisfaction, and 4) whether an activity is recreation is dependent on the individual's feelings or attitudes about the activity.

The terms "leisure" and "play" are often confused with recreation. Recreation is one kind of leisure, but only part of the expressive activity is leisure. Leisure may also include non-recreational pursuits such as religion, education, or community service. Although play and recreation overlap, play is not so much an activity as a form of behavior, characterized by make-believe, competition, or exploration. Moreover, whereas recreation is usually thought of as a purposeful and constructive activity, play may not be goal-oriented and in some cases may be negative and self-destructive.

The benefits of recreation include producing feelings of relaxation or excitement and enhancing self-reliance, mental health, and life-satisfaction. Societal benefits also result from recreation. Recreation can contribute to improved public health, increased community involvement, civic pride, and social unity. It may strengthen family structures, decrease crime, and enhance rehabilitation of individuals. Outdoor recreation promotes interest in protecting our environment and has played an important educational role. However, recreational activities have also damaged the environment. **Edward Abbey**, among others, have decried the tendency of *industrial tourism* to destroy wild areas and animal **habitat**s; for example, the damming of wild rivers to create lakes for boating and skiing and defacing mountain sides for ski runs and ski lifts.

Recreation is big business. It creates jobs and economic vitality. In 1984 American consumers spent $262 billion on recreation and leisure activities; $100 billion of which was spent on outdoor recreation. Much of these expenditures are for **wildlife**-related recreation. In 1985, adult Americans spent $55.7 billion on fishing, hunting, and nonconsumptive wildlife recreation such as bird-watching and wildlife photography.

Outdoor recreation also stimulates tourism. In 1984, Americans travelling in the United States generated business receipts of $225.1 billion and 4.7 million jobs. Foreign tourists to the United States spent an additional $100 billion.

More adults participate in walking for pleasure than any other recreational activity. Driving for pleasure, sightseeing, picnicking, and swimming are also among the top five recreational activities. Canoeing has been the fastest growing activity over the past 30 years. In 1985, 58.6 million people fished, 18.5 million hunted, and 160.9 million participated in nonconsumptive wildlife-associated recreation.

The United States has more than 778 million acres (315 million ha) of publicly owned recreation lands, more than any other nation. Over one-third of the contiguous United States is public recreation land; however, these lands are not evenly distributed. Most of these lands are in the sparsely populated western states. There are 8,373 acres (3,391 ha) of public recreation lands per 1,000 people in the West, whereas there is only 294 acres (119 ha) per 1000 people in the northeastern states. Almost 91 percent of the **public land**s area is administered by the federal government; 8 percent by states, 0.7 percent by counties, and 0.4 percent by municipalities. However, when number of sites, rather than acres, is considered, the recreation supply picture changes considerably. Almost 62 percent of all recreation sites are municipal, whereas only 1.6 percent of the sites are federal.

The private sector is also a major recreation supplier, particularly for certain activities. For example, there are more than 10,000 private campgrounds, 600 ski resorts, and 4,789 privately-owned golf courses in the United States.

Several important trends will affect the supply and demand of future recreation opportunities in the United States. Increasing populations, increasing ethnic diversity, the aging of the population, changes in leisure time, disposable income, and mobility will affect the demand for recreation. The loss of open spaces; **pollution** of our lakes, rivers, and coastlines; increasingly limited access to private lands; and increasing liability concerns will make the task of meeting future demand for recreation more difficult.

[*Ted T. Cable*]

FURTHER READING

Kelly, J. R. *Recreation Business.* New York: Wiley, 1985.

Kraus, R. *Recreation and Leisure in Modern Society.* 3rd ed. Dallas, TX: Scott, Foresman, 1984.

The Report of the President's Commission on Americans Outdoors, The Legacy, The Challenge. Washington, DC: Island Press, 1987.

U. S. Fish and Wildlife Service. *1985 National Survey of Fishing, Hunting, and Wildlife Associated Recreation.* Washington, DC: U. S. Government Printing Office, 1988.

Recyclables

Recyclables are products or materials that can be separated from the **waste stream** and used again in place of raw materials. Since colonial times, Americans have recycled a host of materials, ranging from corn husks used for mattress stuffing to old clothes used for quilts. Today, household recyclables include newspapers, mixed waste paper, glass, tin, **aluminum**, steel, **copper**, **plastics**, batteries, yard debris, wood, and used oil. Commercial recyclables include scrap metals, concrete, plastics, corrugated cardboard, and other

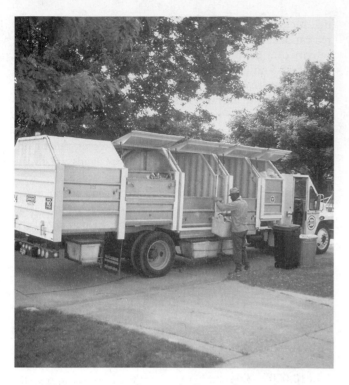

Many towns now have curbside recycling programs with trucks picking up recyclables on a weekly basis.

nonferrous scrap material. The list of recyclables will likely expand as technology meets a growing demand for more **recycling** in response to increased consumer awareness and waste disposal costs, dwindling **landfill** space, and more stringent **waste management** regulations. The **Environmental Protection Agency** has emphasized the importance of diverting recyclables from the waste stream by endorsing integrated waste management, in which municipal **solid waste** is managed according to a hierarchy of source reduction, recycling, **solid waste incineration**, and landfilling.

Programs to divert household recyclables from the waste stream are typically developed and implemented at the local or community level, while commercial recyclables are usually collected by private industry. Collection and preparation methods vary among recycling programs. Some communities have implemented curbside collection programs that require households to separate recyclables from their waste and sort them into segregated containers. Other curbside collection programs pick up recyclables separated from household waste but commingled together. Still other communities are responsible for picking out recyclables mixed in the waste stream. In some municipalities, recyclables are sorted and prepared for processing or the market at a Materials Recovery Facility (MRF). Most MRFs rely on workers to hand-sort recyclables, though some also use sorting equipment, including magnets for removing metals and blowers for sorting plastics. Plastics are also hand-sorted according to resins identified by a voluntary coding system consisting of a triangular arrow stamp with a number in the center and letters underneath that identify the seven major types of

plastic resins used in containers. Other equipment exists for size reduction (shredding or grinding), weighing, and baling recyclables.

Increasing both the type and quantity of recyclables are goals of many states. In 1988, the United States recycled approximately 10 percent of its municipal solid waste. Paper had the highest recovery rate of any recyclable; approximately 45 percent of all corrugated boxes were recovered for recycling. However, paper and paperboard are also the largest component of municipal solid waste by volume. An estimated 12 percent of glass was recovered from the waste stream. Approximately 7 percent of ferrous metals, by weight the largest category of municipal solid waste, were recovered for recycling. Plastics are a rapidly growing segment of the municipal solid waste stream, yet only 1 percent are recovered for recycling. Soft drink bottles and milk containers make up the largest component of plastic recyclables diverted from the waste stream. Another recyclable that is an increasing portion of the waste stream is aluminum. Almost 55 percent of aluminum beer and soft drink cans were recycled in 1988. Recyclables also exist in the form of durable goods, which are products that have a lifetime of over three years. These are usually bulky items, such as major appliances, which are not mixed with the rest of the waste stream. Ferrous metals can be recycled from refrigerators, washing machines, and other major appliances, known as "white goods."

Recyclables are commodities, and markets for these commodities fluctuate dramatically. The dynamic nature of markets is a key factor in whether a recyclable is actually recycled instead of being disposed in a landfill or combusted in an incinerator. Municipalities involved in recycling programs must deal with rapid shifts in the market for recyclables. For example, the demand for a particular recyclable may drop, reducing the price and forcing the municipality to pay for the material to be taken away for recycling or disposal. Consequently, recycling must compete with raw material markets, as well as waste disposal methods. *See also* Garbage; Green packaging; Municipal solid waste; Solid waste incineration; Waste reduction

[*Marci L. Bortman*]

FURTHER READING

Pollock, C. S. "Building a Market for Recyclables." *World Watch* 1 (May-June 1988): 12-18.

U.S. Environmental Protection Agency. *Characterization of Municipal Solid Waste in the United States: 1990 Update.* Washington, DC: U. S. Government Printing Office, 1990.

U.S. Office of Technology Assessment. 1989. *Facing America's Trash: What Next for Municipal Solid.* Washington, DC: U. S. Government Printing Office, 1989.

Recycling

Recycling waste is not a new idea. Throughout history, people have disposed **garbage** in myriad ways. They fed household garbage to domestic animals. Scavengers gleaned the **waste stream** for usable items that could be fixed, then sold or traded for other goods and services. Homemakers mended clothing, and children grew up in hand-me-downs. Durable goods were just that; goods that could be reused until their durability wore out. These practices were not due to a desire to reduce the waste stream, but rather a need to produce products from all available resources. Modern society has moved away from such straight-forward recycling practices, choosing instead to toss out the old and buy new goods. This throwaway society now faces a trash crisis.

The volume of **solid waste** generated in the United States has continued to increase, along with the cost of building **landfill**s and **incineration** facilities. Recycling some of this material into new uses saves existing landfill space, conserves energy and **natural resources**, reduces **pollution**, and saves tax money. Recycling can provide new jobs, create new industries, and contribute to the increase in the GNP. Instead of referring to what people discard every day as garbage, advocates of recycling emphasize the need to refer to waste products as Post Consumer Materials (PCMs) and consider them **renewable resources** for various manufacturing processes.

The challenge of collecting adequate volumes of recyclable materials in a form ready for manufacturing into new products is a formidable task. Unlike raw materials that are extracted from the earth or manufactured in a lab, PCMs are mixed materials, and are sometimes contaminated with toxic and non-toxic residue. PCMs must be cleaned and source-separated at the individual household and business level. Once the materials are made available at the point of generation, they must be collected and transported to a collection site, usually referred to as a Materials Recycling Facility (MRF). At this location, materials are processed to make transportation easier and increase their value. Glass is separated by color, **plastics** are pelletized, and paper is baled. Other materials may be cleaned and reduced in volume, depending on the equipment available. The exceptions to this rule are single materials collected and transported directly to the point of use, such as newspaper collected at a drop off site and transported to a local insulation manufacturer. The existence of an MRF enhances the recycling process because it allows large volumes of materials to be amassed at a single location, making marketing of PCMs more profitable. If manufacturers know that there are adequate volumes of high-quality raw material consistently available, they are more likely to agree to long-term purchasing contracts.

Manufacturers are being encouraged to retrofit, or retool, their manufacturing processes in order to use PCMs instead of raw materials. Many glass manufacturers now use cullet (cut glass) instead of silica and sand to make new glass containers, and some paper manufacturers have installed de-inking equipment in order to manufacture paper from used newsprint instead of wood pulp. Once the initial expense of equipment change has been absorbed, such changes can reduce costs. But these are long-term investments on the part of manufacturers, and they must be ensured that recycling is a long-term commitment on the part of consumers and communities.

Recycling begins with people, and the biggest challenge for recycling lies in educating and motivating the public upon whom successful **source separation** depends. Except in rare circumstances recycling is a voluntary act, so the attitudes, knowledge and feelings of the participants are the key to sustained recycling behavior. It has been found that people will change their behavior to protect the health of their families, the value of their property, and their own self-image, and recycling has often been justified in these terms. Once the rationale to begin recycling has been shared with community residents, a program for making recycling convenient and inexpensive must be institutionalized.

Curbside recycling is currently the most desirable recycling option, primarily because of its convenience. It is usually a commingled, or mixed, system. Residents clean and prepare glass, cans, paper, and plastic, before putting them together in a container and placing them at the curb. Most waste haulers pick up the **recyclables** on the same day as the rest of the waste, separating them into bins on the truck right at the curb. In more rural areas, where homes are too far apart, recycling often takes place at a drop off center. This is usually a tractor trailer with separate bins, which is hauled directly to an MRF when it is full and replaced by an empty trailer. Research has shown that the best system is one where curbside recycling is offered, but a drop-off site is also available as a backup in case residents miss their recycling day. In some communities there is a weekly or monthly drop-off. Trucks from different industries use a convenient parking lot and residents are encouraged to bring their recyclables to company representatives. Some communities also have buy-back centers where residents can sell PCMs to a broker who in turn sells the material to manufacturers.

In addition to residential recycling there is office or business recycling. Office paper recycling programs are usually set up so office workers separate the paper at their desks. The paper is taken regularly to a location where it is either baled or picked up loose and transported to a manufacturing plant. Offices that generate a large amount of white office paper can collect and market the paper directly to paper manufacturers. Smaller offices can cooperate with other businesses, contracting with paper manufacturers to pick up paper at a central location. Another example of business recycling is the recycling of corrugated cardboard by groceries and clothing stores. These businesses have been breaking down boxes and baling them on site for pickup by collection trucks. Dry cleaning establishments are currently taking back hangers and plastic bags from their customers for recycling. Businesses of many kinds have begun to realize that positive publicity can be achieved through their recycling efforts, and they have been increasingly inclined to participate.

One of the biggest challenges to recycling in the future is market development. For communities near to cities that have major manufacturers taking PCMs, marketing is not a problem. For smaller more rural communities, however, different strategies must be developed. In some cases a well run MRF that brokers recycled materials is adequate. In other cases, it may be necessary to search for local markets to utilize PCMs, such as the use of newspaper as animal bedding. Newspaper collected and processed within the community can be sold to local farmers at a lower cost less than straw or sawdust. Another approach is encouraging a niche industry to locate nearby, such as a small insulation contractor who is promised all the post-consumer newsprint from the community.

Ultimately, recycling will not be successful unless consumers buy products made from PCMs. Products made from these materials are becoming easier to find, and they are more clearly marked than in the past, though some green or earth-friendly product labeling has been controversial. Recycling advocates have argued that such labeling should not only say that the product is made from recycled material, it should also note what percentage of the material is post consumer waste, as opposed to manufacturing waste.

Many states are encouraging recycling through legislation. Some states have bills that require stores to take back beer and soft drink bottles and cans, giving consumers a refund. Certain states have banned all compostable materials from landfills in order to force **composting**. In some states, daily newspapers are required to use a certain percentage of recycled paper in order to publish. These and other legislative steps have enhanced the recycling movement nationwide. *See also* Container deposit legislation; Municipal solid waste; Solid waste recycling and recovery; Solid waste volume reduction; Transfer station; Waste management; Waste reduction

[*Cynthia Fridgen*]

FURTHER READING

BioCycle: Journal of Composting and Recycling. JG Press, 18 South Seventh Streer, Emmaus, PA 18049.

Carless, J. *Taking Out the Trash: A No-Nonsense Guide to Recycling.* Washington, DC: Island Press, 1992.

Coming Full Circle: Successful Recycling Today. New York: Environemental Defense Fund, 1988.

Pollock, C. *Mining Urban Wastes: The Potential for Recycling.* Worldwatch Institute Paper 76. Washington, DC: Worldwatch Institute, 1987.

Resource Recycling: North America's Recycling Journal. Box 10540, Portland, Oregon 97210-0540.

Recycling and recovery, solid waste

See **Solid waste recycling and recovery**

Red tide

Red tide is the common name for phenomenon created when toxic **algal bloom**s turn seawater red, killing marine life and making water unsuitable for human or animal use. Red tides are caused by several **species** of dinoflagellates and diatoms, microscopic unicellular **phytoplankton** that live in cold and warm seas. A red pigment, called peridinin, which collects light during **photosynthesis**, colors the water red when large numbers of the plankton populate an area.

Red tides are a danger because the toxins released by large numbers of these plankton can paralyze fish and bioaccumulate in the tissues of shellfish and filter-feeding mollusks. Predators of the shellfish, including humans, consume the toxins, causing paralysis and death.

Species of dinoflagellates that cause red tides generally belong to the "red tide genera," *Gymnodinium* and *Gonyaulax.* Though several are known to cause red tides, a single red tide is nearly always tied to a specific species. This may be the result of three factors. First, the conditions responsible for the bloom may also cause the red tide species to reproduce more rapidly than other phytoplankton, thus outcompeting them for available **nutrient**s. Second, the toxins excreted may prevent the growth of other species. Or, behavioral differences may give them competitive advantages.

Red tides have occurred periodically through recorded history in seas around the world. The Red Sea is thought to have been named for algal blooms back in biblical times. However, in recent decades red tides have been more frequent in areas where algal blooms have never been a problem.

The coast of Chile has reported red tides since the beginning of the nineteenth century, and the Peruvian coast has recorded red tides, which they named *aguajes,* since 1828. They appear more frequently in the summer months when the water becomes warmer, and they also seem to be associated with the **El Niño** current. Coastal up-welling events are also known to be essential for the occurrence of *Gonyaulax tamarensis* blooms in the Gulf of Maine.

Red tides have been plaguing the east and west coasts of Florida on a nearly annual basis since at least 1947. Blooms on the west Florida shelf are initiated by the Loop Current, an annual intrusion of oceanic waters into the Gulf of Mexico. Here, the toxic dinoflagellate *Gymnodinium breve* produces rather predictable blooms. The red tide is transported inshore by winds, tides, and other currents where it may be sustained if adequate nutrients are available.

In 1987 and 1988, red tide spread northward from the Gulf Coast of Florida as far as North Carolina, where it caused a loss of $25 million to the shellfish industry due to brevetoxin contamination. This was the first time that *G. breve* blooms were reported so far north, and it raises the question of whether blooms will occur annually in this region. Also during the 1987-88 blooms, 700 bottlenose **dolphins** washed ashore along the United States Atlantic coast. Red tides commonly occur along the northwest coast of British Columbia, Canada, and as far north as Alaska and along the Russian coast of the Bering Sea.

Researchers blame the recent spread of red tides and the occurrence of algal blooms, which ordinarily occur in harmless low concentrations, on the increasing amount of coastal **water pollution**. Sewage and agricultural **runoff** increase concentrations of nutrients, such as **nitrogen** and **phosphorus**, in coastal waters. This increase in nutrients may create favorable conditions for the growth of red tide organisms.

In April 1992, two fishermen suffered paralytic shellfish poisoning (PSP) within several minutes of eating a few butter clams from Kingcome Inlet, British Columbia. In August 1992, saxitoxin, another dinoflagellate toxin associated with PSP, was found in the digestive systems of dungeness crabs caught in Alaskan waters. On Prince Edward Island, Canada, in 1987, three people died and more than 100 others became ill from domoic acid-contaminated mussels. Some of those who became ill from this toxin developed amnesic shellfish poisoning, which still causes short-term memory loss.

It is difficult to accurately predict when and where red tides may occur, and how seriously they will contaminate shellfish. Monitoring levels of toxins in shellfish meat and population sizes of the dinoflagellates is important in preventing widespread poisoning of humans. Any detectable level of brevetoxin in 3.5 ounces (100 g) of shellfish meat is potentially harmful to humans. The **Food and Drug Administration** does not inspect shellfish growing areas regularly, but relies on state agencies to monitor toxin levels. In selected states, surveillance programs have been established that randomly examine shellfish that have been harvested and in natural shellfish beds. Florida is the only state that has a constant monitoring and research program for both shellfish poisoning and dinoflagellate blooms that cause poisoning. Monitoring for shellfish poisoning is costly, but the expense may increase if red tides become more frequent due to deteriorating coastal **water quality**. In April and May of 1996, 158 manatees in southwest Florida died from an unusual type of red tide. Which species will be affected next? *See also* Agricultural pollution; Bioaccumulation; Competition; Marine pollution; Sewage treatment

[*William G. Ambrose and Paul E. Renaud*]

FURTHER READING

Culotta, E. "Red Menace in the World's Oceans." *Science* 257 (1992): 1476-1477.

Konovalova, G. V. "Harmful Dinoflagellate Blooms Along the Eastern Coast of Kamchatka." *Harmful Algae News* 4 (1993): 2.

Taylor, D., and H. Seliger, eds. *Toxic Dinoflagellate Blooms.* Vol. 1. New York: Elsevier North Holland, 1979.

Taylor, F. J. R. "Artificial Respiration Saves Two From Fatal PSP in Canada." *Harmful Algae News* 3 (1992): 1.

Redwoods

There are three genera of redwood trees, each with a single **species**. The native range of the coast redwood (*Sequoia sempervirens*) is a narrow 450-mile (725-km) strip along the Pacific Ocean from central California to southern Oregon. The giant sequoia (*Sequoiadendron giganteum*) is restricted to about 75 groves scattered over a 260-mile (418-km) belt, nowhere more than 15 miles (24 km) wide, extending along the west slope of the Sierra Nevadas in central California. The third species, dawn redwood (*Metasequoia glyptostroboides*), was described first from a fossil and was presumed to be extinct. However, in 1946 live trees were discovered in a remote region of China. Since then, seeds have been brought to North America, and this species is now found in many communities as an ornamental planting. Unlike the coast redwoods and giant sequoias, dawn redwoods are deciduous.

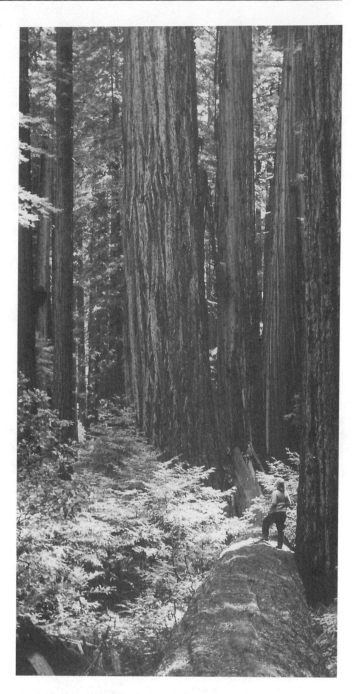

Coast redwoods.

Redwoods are named for the color of their heartwood and bark. The thick bark protects the trees from fires which occur naturally throughout their ranges. Their wood has a high tannin content which makes it resistant to **fungi** and insects, making redwood a particularly desirable building material. This demand for lumber was responsible for most of the destruction of the original redwood forests in North America. In 1918, the **Save-the-Redwoods League** was formed to save redwoods from destruction and to establish redwood parks. This organization has purchased and protected over 280,000 acres (113,400 ha) of redwood forests and was instrumental in the establishment of the Redwoods

National Park. The term *Sequoia* used in the generic names of these species, and in the common name giant sequoia, honors the Cherokee Chief Sequoyah who developed an alphabet for the Cherokee language.

Coast Redwoods

Coast redwoods are the tallest and one of the longest living tree species. Average mature trees are typically 200-240 feet (61-73 m) tall, although some trees exceed 360 feet (109 m). The world's tallest known tree is a coast redwood that stands 368 feet (112 m) tall on the banks of Redwood Creek in Redwood National Park. In some areas coast redwoods can live for more than 2,000 years. They are evergreen, with delicate foliage consisting of narrow needles one-half to three-quarters of an inch long, growing flat along their stems and forming a feathery spray.

Coast redwoods are prolific. Their cones are about an inch long and contain from 30-100 seeds. They produce seeds almost every year with maximum seed production occurring between the ages of 20-250 years old. They also have an advantage over other species in that new trees can sprout from the roots of damaged or fallen trees.

Unlike the other two species of redwoods, coastal redwoods cannot tolerate freezing temperatures. They thrive in areas below 2,000 feet (607 m), with summer fog, abundant winter rainfall, and moderate temperatures. Although coast redwoods are often found in mixed evergreen forest communities, they can form impressive pure stands, especially on flat, riparian areas with rich soils.

Giant Sequoia

The giant sequoia, although not as tall as the coast redwood, is a larger and more long-lived species. Giant sequoias can attain a diameter of 35 feet (10.6 m); whereas the largest Coast redwood has a 22-feet (6.7-m) diameter. The largest tree species by volume, giant sequoias the trees through which roads were built and rangers' residences hollowed out. The most massive specimen, the General Sherman tree, located in Sequoia National Park, has a bole volume of 52,500 cubic feet (1,575 m³).

The oldest giant sequoia is 3,600 years old, compared with 2,200 years old for the oldest coast redwood. This makes the giant sequoia the second oldest living thing on earth (the bristlecone pine is the most long-lived).

Giant sequoias can be found between elevations of 5,000 and 8,000 feet (1,517-2,427 m), growing best on mesic sites (such as bottomlands) with deep, well-drained sandy loam soil.s Unlike coast redwoods, mature trees of this species cannot sprout from the roots, stumps, or trunks of injured or fallen trees (young trees can produce stump sprouts subsequent to injury). It is paradoxical that one of the largest living organisms is produced by one of the smallest seeds. Three thousand seeds would weigh only an ounce. Typically, cones bearing fertile seeds are not produced until the tree is 150-200 years old. The cones are egg-shaped and 2.0-3.5 inches (5-9 cm) in length. Once cones develop they may continue to grow without releasing the seeds for another 20 years. A typical mature tree may produce 1,500 cones each year, and because they are not dropped annually, a tree may have 30,000 cones at one time, each with about 200 seeds.

Two species of animals, a wood-boring beetle (*Phymatodes nitidus*) and the chickaree or Douglas squirrel (*Tamiasciurus douglasii*), play important roles in dislodging the seed from the cones. Fire is also important in seed release as the heat dries the cones. Fire has the added advantage of also preparing a seed bed favorable for germination. The light seeds are well-adapted for wind dispersal, often travelling up to a quarter mile away from the source tree.

Like the other redwoods, the wood of the giant sequoia is extremely durable. Because of this durability and the ornate designs in the wood, this species was harvested extensively. One tree can produce up to 600,000 board feet of lumber, enough to fill 280 railroad freight cars or build 150 five-room houses. Unfortunately, because of the enormous size of the trees and the brittle nature of the wood, when a tree was felled, as much as half would be wasted because of splintering and splitting. Now that virtually all giant trees have been protected from logging, the greatest threats from humans are **soil compaction** around their bases and the elimination of fire which allows fuels to accumulate, thereby increasing the chances of deadly crown fires. Toppling over is the most common natural cause of death for mature giant sequoia trees. Weakening of the shallow roots and lower trunk by fire and decay, coupled with the tremendous weight of the trees, results in the tree falling over. Sometimes wind, heavy snows, undercutting by streams, or water-soaked soils contribute to the toppling. In its natural range this species is now valued primarily for its aesthetic appeal.

[*Ted T. Cable*]

FURTHER READING

Burns, R. M., and B. H. Honkala. *Silvics of North America.* Vol. 1. Conifers. Agricultural Handbook 654. Washington, DC: U. S. Dept. of Agriculture, 1990.

Dewitt, J. B. *California Redwood Parks and Preserves.* San Francisco: Save-the-Redwoods League, 1985.

Walker, L. C. *Trees: An Introduction to Trees and Forest Ecology for the Amateur Naturalist.* Englewood Cliffs, NJ: Prentice-Hall, 1984.

Refuse-derived fuels (RDF)

The concept of refuse-derived fuels (RDFs) is one that has the potential for solving two of the world's most troubling **environment**al problems—solid waste disposal and energy sources—at the same time. The term refuse-derived fuel refers to any method by which waste materials are converted into a form in which they can be burned as a source of energy.

In a world dominated by a throw-away ethic and swamped with essentially non-degradable materials, **solid waste**s continue to be a growing problem. In the United States in 1986, for example, every man, woman, and child produced an average of 3.6 pounds (1.6 kg) of waste each day.

Wastes are so-called because they tend to have no future use once they are discarded. Yet, by their very nature, most solid wastes are potentially valuable as fuels. A typical sample of municipal waste in the United States, for instance, may consist of about 30 to 40 percent paper, 5 percent textiles, 5 percent wood, and 20 to 30 percent organic material, all combustible materials. Metals, glass, **plastics**, sand, and other non-combustible materials constitute the remaining portion of a waste sample.

Clearly, such wastes would appear to have potential value as a fuel source. Yet, that potential has not, as yet, been extensively developed. In most countries, solid wastes are mainly disposed of in **landfills**. A small fraction is incinerated or used for other purposes. However, conversion of solid wastes to a useable fuel is still an experimental process.

The primary hindrance to the commercial development of RDFs so far is the economic cost of producing such fuels. Given that RDFs produced thus far have only about half the energy value of a typical sample of industrial **coal** and given the relatively low price of coal, there is little economic incentive for municipalities to build energy systems based on refuse-derived fuels.

Yet, many scientists see a positive future for refuse-derived fuels. As reserves are used up, they argue, the cost of **fossil fuels** such as coal will inevitably increase. In addition, RDFs tend to burn more cleanly and have a significant environmental advantage over coal and other fossil fuels. Research must continue, therefore, to develop more efficient and less expensive RDFs.

One of the fundamental problems in the development of refuse-derived fuels is obtaining the raw materials in a physical condition that will allow the extraction of combustible organic matter. The solid waste material in most landfills consists of a complex mixture of substances, some combustible and some not, some with commercial value and others without.

The first step in preparing wastes for the production of refuse-derived fuels is known as size reduction. In this step, wastes are shredded, chopped, sliced, pulverized, or otherwise treated in order to break them up into smaller pieces because methods for separating combustible from non-combustible materials may require that waste particles be small in size. Both magnetic separation and air classification will work only with small particles.

Size reduction serves a number of other functions also. For example, it breaks open plastic and glass bottles, releasing any contents that may still be in them. It also reduces the clumping and tangling that occurs with larger particles. Finally, when used as a fuel, particles of small size burn more efficiently than larger particles.

One indication of the importance of size reduction in the production of RDFs is the number of different machines that have been developed to accomplish this step. Bag breakers are used to tear open plastic bags and cardboard boxes. Chippers are machines that cut wood up into chips. Granulators are devices that have sharp knives on a rotating blade that cut materials against a stationary blade, somewhat similar to a pair of scissors. Flail mills are rotary machines that swing hammers around in a circle to smash materials. Ball and rod mills consist of cylindrical drums that hold balls or rods. When the drum spins, the balls or rods smash against the inside of the drum, crushing solid wastes also present in it.

Once waste materials have been reduced in size, the portion that is combustible must be removed from that which is not. Several different procedures can be used. A common process, for example, is to pass the solid wastes under a magnet. The magnet will extract all ferrous metals from the mixture.

Another technique is rotary screening, in which wastes are spun in a drum and sorted using screens that have openings of either 50 mm or 200 mm diameter. Sand, broken glass, dust, and other non-organic materials tend to be removed by this procedure.

A third process is known as air classification. When solid wastes are exposed to a blast of air, various components are separated from each other on the basis of their size, shape, density, and moisture content. A number of different kinds of air classifiers exist, and all are reasonably efficient in separating organic from inorganic material.

One type of air classifier is the horizontal model, in which size-reduced wastes are dropped into a horizontal stream of air. Various types of material are separated on the basis of the horizontal distance they travel from their point of origin. Vertical classifiers separate on a similar principle except particles are injected into a rising stream of air. The rotary classifier consists of an inclined cylindrical column into which wastes are injected and then separated by a rotating, rising column of air.

The organic matter that remains after size reduction and separation can be used as a fuel in about four distinct ways. First of all, it can be converted to other combustible forms through pyrolysis. Pyrolysis is a process in which organic materials are heated to high temperatures in an oxygen-free or oxygen-deficient atmosphere. The product of this reaction is a mixture of gaseous, liquid and solid compounds (the latter called *char*) that can, in turn, be used as fuels.

Two particularly valuable fuels, methane and ethanol (ethyl alcohol), can also be produced from organic wastes. Scientists have long known that methane is produced when anaerobic bacteria act on organic compounds found in solid wastes. They have been unsuccessful so far, however, in developing economically viable methods for using this principle on a commercial level.

Somewhat greater success has been obtained in the production of **ethanol** from wastes. This process separates cellulose-containing materials from other wastes and then hydrolyzes them in an acidic medium. Some experts had hoped that ethanol could be used as an additive to gasoline, producing a fuel that burns more cleanly and efficiently than pure **gasoline**. After an initial period in which the ethanol-gasoline mixture was sold as **gasohol**, the trend has been to replace the ethanol with the even more efficient **methanol**.

Some heating systems make use of the dried material produced as a result of size reduction and separation directly as a fuel. The Imperial Metal Industries (IMI) company in Birmingham, England, has operated such a plant since 1976. Solid wastes provided by the West Midlands County Council is delivered to the IMI plant where it is reduced in size, separated, dried, and then fed directly into furnaces, where it is burned. A similar plant operated by Commonwealth Edison and run on wastes from the city of Chicago was opened in 1978.

A convenient and popular method of handling RDFs is to process them as pellets or briquettes. Pellets are formed from wastes that have been size reduced, separated, and partially dried. The material is extruded through a dye or compacted into small nuggets in devices known as densifying machines. An important factor in the success of this method is keeping the wastes moist enough to stick together, but dry enough to burn efficiently.

Finally, some research has been done on the use of RDFs in experimental combustion systems, such as fluidized bed combustion. In this process, fuel is mixed with some material such as sand and suspended in a furnace by a stream of air. The second material makes thorough mixing of the fuel possible. The fuel is then burned in the air stream.

A considerable amount of research has been done on refuse-derived fuels. As of the early 1990s, however, only a few dozen commercial plants were in operation.

[*David E. Newton*]

FURTHER READING

Hasselriis, F. *Refuse-derived Fuel Processing.* Boston: Butterworth Publishers, 1984.

Norton, G. A., and A. D. Levine. "Cocombustion of Refuse-Derived Fuel and Coal: A Review of Selected Emissions." *Environmental Science and Technology* 23 (July 1989): 774-83.

Porteous, A. *Refuse Derived Fuels.* London: Applied Science Publishers, 1981.

Richards, K. "All Gas and Garbage." *New Scientist* 122 (3 June 1989): 38-41.

Vesilind, P. A., J. J. Peirce, and R. Weiner. *Environmental Engineering.* 2nd ed. Boston: Butterworth Publishers, 1988.

Regan, Tom [Thomas Howard] (1938 -)

American philosopher and animal rights activist

Regan is a well-known figure in the animal liberation movement. His *The Case for Animal Rights* (1983) is a systematic and scholarly defense of the controversial claim that animals have rights that humans are morally obligated to recognize and respect. Arguing against the views of earlier philosophers like René Descartes, who claimed that animals are machine-like and incapable of having mental states such as consciousness or feelings of pleasure or pain, Regan attempts to show that such a view is misguided, muddled, or incorrect.

Regan was born in Pittsburgh, Pennsylvania. He attended Thiel College and the University of Virginia, where he earned his doctorate in philosophy. Before publishing *The Case for Animal Rights*, Regan also edited *Animal Rights and Human Obligations* (1976) and *Matters of Life and Death* (1980). He is currently a professor of philosophy at North Carolina University.

Within the **animal rights** movement, Regan disagrees with certain philosophical arguments advanced in de-

fense of animal liberation by, most notably, the nineteenth-century English philosopher Jeremy Bentham and the twentieth-century Australian philosopher **Peter Singer**. Both Bentham and Singer are utilitarians who believe that morality requires the pleasures of all sentient creatures—human and nonhuman alike—be maximized and their pain minimized. From a utilitarian perspective, most discussions about rights are unnecessary. Regan disagrees, arguing that sentience—the ability to feel pleasure and pain—is an inadequate basis on which to build a case for animal rights and against such practices as meat-eating, factory farming, fur trapping, and the use of animals in laboratory experiments.

Regan views the case for animal rights as an integral part of a broader and more inclusive **environmental ethic**. He predicts and participates in the coming of a new kind of revolution—a revolution of gentility and concern—made not by a self-centered *me-generation* but by an emerging *thee generation* of caring and concerned people from every political party, religion, and socioeconomic class. Among the indications of this forthcoming revolution is the growing popularity of and financial support for the various groups and organizations that comprise the more broadly based environmental and animal rights movements. *See also* People for the Ethical Treatment of Animals

[*Terence Ball*]

FURTHER READING

Regan, Tom. *All That Dwell Therein: Essays on Animal Rights and Environmental Ethics.* Berkeley: University of California Press, 1982.

———. *The Case for Animal Rights.* Berkeley: University of California Press, 1983.

———. *The Thee Generation: Reflections on the Coming Revolution.* Philadelphia: Temple University Press, 1991.

Regulatory review

The regulatory review process allows the executive branch of the U. S. federal government to ensure that the regulations drafted by different agencies contribute to the administration's overall goals. In the past this process has emphasized a **cost-benefit analysis** that has tended to delay or halt the publication of environmental regulations.

Executive agencies carry out congressionally enacted laws by drafting and enforcing regulations. The **Environmental Protection Agency (EPA)** has responsibility for writing the regulations that implement environmental laws, like the **Clean Air Act** and the **Comprehensive Environmental Response, Compensation and Liability Act (Superfund)**. For example, when the **Resource Conservation and Recovery Act (RCRA)** called for states to protect **groundwater** from **landfill** leachate, the EPA drafted a regulation that included specifications for the kind of equipment that landfills should install to ensure that leachate would not leak.

Once drafted, before being published for public comment, all regulations are sent for review to the Office of Information and Regulatory Affairs (OIRA) within the **Office of Management and Budget (OMB)**. OIRA either approves, rejects, or asks for specific changes in the regulation. If a regulation is approved it can be published for public comment.

This centralization of the regulatory process was accomplished by Ronald Reagan's executive orders 12291 and 12498. Executive Order 12291, issued in 1981, established a cost-benefit review process. All federal agencies must weigh costs and benefits for each "major" regulation and submit these considerations to OIRA. (A "major" regulation costs more than $100 million or is otherwise deemed major by OIRA.) Agencies cannot publish proposed or final rules until OIRA has ensured that the benefits of a regulation outweigh the costs. Executive Order 12498, issued in 1984, requires agency heads to predict their regulatory actions for the following year. All regulations are then compiled into the *Regulatory Program*. Compiling this program allows OIRA to be involved in the early planning stages of all regulations.

In practice, this review process can delay the final publication of regulations for months or even years. For example, though the EPA had predicted publishing the landfill regulations required by RCRA in September 1990, the final rule was actually published a full year later. In drafting the final rule, the EPA had incorporated public comments submitted when the proposed rule was published in 1988. Commentators had objected to the loose definitions contained in the rule, so the EPA developed more stringent specifications. During review, OIRA staff complained that the landfill specifications were too costly with too little benefit.

Dozens of regulations required by the Clean Air Act Amendments were similarly delayed. Though the Bush Administration had provided the necessary impetus to pass the Amendments in 1990, it appeared that the Administration wanted to keep the law's requirements from becoming reality. This power to delay the publication of regulations mandated by law allows an administration to benefit politically from supporting strong environmental legislation and then gain strategically by watering down or postponing the legislation's implementation through regulatory review.

Though administrations and policy priorities change, the regulatory review process will most likely remain centralized in the Office of Information and Regulatory Affairs. This office allows the president to ensure that agencies implement legislation through regulations that reflect the central priorities of the administration.

[*Alair MacLean*]

FURTHER READING

Coleman, B. *Through the Corridors of Power: A Citizen's Guide to Federal Rulemaking.* Washington, DC: OMB Watch, 1987.

Gutfeld, R., and J. Bailey. "EPA Sets Rules For Pollution Curbs on State Landfills." *Wall Street Journal* (Sept. 12, 1991): A8.

Office of Management and Budget. *Regulatory Program of the United States Government: April 1, 1991–March 31, 1992.* Washington, DC: U.S. Government Printing Office, 1991.

Rehabilitation

Rehabilitation is a process which is being applied more frequently to the **environment**. It aims to reverse the deterioration of a **national resource**, even if it cannot be restored to its original state.

Attempts to rehabilitate deteriorated areas have a long history. In England, for example, gardener and architect Lancelot "Capability" Brown devoted his life to restoring vast stretches of the English countryside that had been dramatically modified by human activities.

Reforestation was one of the common forms of rehabilitation used by Brown, and this method continues to be used throughout the world. The demand for wood both as a building material and a source of fuel has resulted in the devastation of forests on every continent. Sometimes the objective of reforestation is to ensure a new supply of lumber for human needs, and in other cases the motivation is to protect the **environment** by reducing land **erosion**. Aesthetic concerns have also been the basis for reforestation programs. Recently, the role of trees in managing atmospheric **carbon dioxide** and global climate has created yet another motivation for the planting of trees.

Another activity in which rehabilitation has become important is **surface mining**. The process by which **coal** and other minerals are mined using this method results in massive disruption of the environment. For decades, the policy of mining companies was to abandon damaged land after all minerals had been removed. Increasing environmental awareness in the 1960s and 1970s led to a change in that policy, however. In 1977, the United States Congress passed the **Surface Mining Control and Reclamation Act (SMCRA)**, requiring companies to rehabilitate land damaged by these activities. The act worked well at first and mining companies began to take a more serious view of their responsibilities for restoring the land they had damaged, but by the mid-1980s that trend had been reversed to some extent. The Reagan and Bush administrations were both committed to reducing the regulatory pressure on American businesses, and tended to be less aggressive about the enforcement of environmental laws such as SMCRA.

Rehabilitation is also widely used in the area of human resources. For example, the spread of urban blight in American cities has led to an interest in the rehabilitation of public and private buildings. After World War II, many people moved out of central cities into the suburbs. Untold numbers of houses were abandoned and fell into disrepair. In the last decade, municipal, state, and federal governments have shown an interest in rehabilitating such dwellings and the areas where they are located. Many cities now have urban homesteading laws under which buildings in depressed areas are sold at low prices, and often with tax breaks, to buyers who agree to rehabilitate and live in them. *See also* Environmental degradation; Environmental engineering; Forest management; Greenhouse effect; Strip mining; Restoration ecology; Wildlife rehabilitation

[*David E. Newton*]

FURTHER READING

Moran, J. M., M. D. Morgan, and J. H. Wiersma. *Introduction to Environmental Science.* 2nd ed. New York: W. H. Freeman, 1986.

Newton, D. E. *Land Use, A - Z.* Hillside, NJ: Enslow Publishers, 1989.

Reilly, William K. (1940-)

American conservationist and Environmental Protection Agency administrator

Called the "first professional environmentalist" to head the EPA since its founding in 1970, Reilly came to the agency in 1989 with a background in law and urban planning. He had been appointed to President Richard Nixon's **Council on Environmental Quality** in 1970, and was named executive director of the Task Force on Land Use and Urban Growth two years later. In 1973, Reilly became president of the Conservation Foundation, a non-profit environmental research group based in Washington, D.C., which he is credited with transforming into a considerable force for environmental protection around the world. In 1985, the Conservation Foundation merged with the **World Wildlife Fund**; Reilly was named as president, and under his direction, membership grew to 600,000 with an annual budget of $35 million.

Reilly began to cautiously criticize White House environmental policy during Ronald Reagan's administration, objecting to the appointments of **James G. Watt**, and his successor William P. Clark, as secretary of the interior. He published articles and spoke publicly about **pollution, species** diversification, **rain forest** destruction, and **wetlands** loss.

After his confirmation as EPA administrator, Reilly laid out an agenda that was clearly different from his predecessor, **Lee Thomas**. Reilly promised "vigorous and aggressive enforcement of the **environmental law**s," a tough new **Clean Air Act**, and an international agreement to reduce **chlorofluorocarbons (CFCs)** in the **atmosphere**. Calling toxic waste cleanup a top priority, Reilly also promised action to decrease urban smog, remove dangerous chemicals from the market more quickly, encourage strict fuel efficiency standards, increase **recycling** efforts, protect wetlands, and encourage international cooperation on **global warming** and **ozone layer depletion**.

In March 1989, Reilly overruled a recommendation of a regional EPA director and suspended plans to build the Two Forks Dam on the South Platte River in Colorado. The decision relieved environmentalists who had feared construction of the dam would foul a prime trout stream, flood a scenic canyon, and disrupt **wildlife** migration patterns. That same year, Reilly criticized the federal government's response to the grounding of the ***Exxon Valdez*** and the **oil spill** in **Prince William Sound**, Alaska.

At Reilly's urging, President George Bush proposed major revisions of the Clean Air Act of 1970. The new act required public utilities to reduce **emission**s of **sulfur dioxide** by nearly half. It also contained measures that reduced emissions of toxic chemicals by industry and lowered the levels of urban smog.

William K. Reilly describing the Bush administration's clean air proposals in 1989.

Under Reilly's direction, the EPA also enacted a gradual ban on the production and importation of most products made of **asbestos**. He left the agency in 1992. *See also* Biodiversity; Comprehensive Environmental Response Compensation and Liability Act; Costle, Douglas; Energy efficiency; Environmental policy; Hazardous waste

[*Linda Rehkopf*]

FURTHER READING

Williams, T. "It's Lonely Being Green: In an Environmentally Unfriendly Administration, William K. Reilly and John Turner Have Stood Alone as Conservationists." *Audubon* 94 (September-October 1993): 52-6.

Relict species

A **species** surviving from an ancient time in isolated populations that represent the localized remains of a distribution which was originally much wider. These populations become isolated through disruptive geophysical events such as **glaciation**, or immigration to outlying islands, which is not followed by reunification of the fragmented populations. The origins and relationships of several relict species are well documented, and these include local Central American avian populations which are remnants of the North American avifauna left after the last glacial retreat. The origins of other relict species are unknown because all related species are extinct. This group includes lungfishes, rhynchocephalian reptiles (genus *Sphenodon*), and the duck-billed platypus

(*Ornithorhynchus anatinus*). *See also* California condor; Endangered species; Extinction; Rare Species

Religion and the environment

It is a little-known fact that all of the world's major faiths have, as integral parts of their laws and traditions, teachings requiring protection of the environment, respect for **nature** and **wildlife**, and kindness to animals. While such tenets are well-known in such eastern religions as Buddhism and Hinduism, there is also a largely-forgotten but remarkably strong tradition of such teachings in Christianity, Judaism, and Islam. All of these faiths recognize a doctrine of the Deity's love for the Creation, and for all of the living creatures of the world. The obligation of humans to respect and protect the natural environment and other life forms appears throughout the sacred writings of the prophets and leaders of the world's great religions.

These little known and seldom discussed tenets of "environmental theology" contained in the world's religions are even less-widely observed or practiced, but many theologians feel that they are more relevant today than ever. For at a time when the Earth faces a potentially fatal ecological crisis, they say, traditional religion shows us a way to preserve our planet and the interdependent life forms living on it. Efforts are under way by representatives of virtually all the major faiths to make people more aware of the strong **conservation** and humane teachings that are an integral part of the religions of most cultures around the globe. This movement holds tremendous potential to stimulate a spiritually-based ecological ethic throughout the world to improve and protect the natural environment and the welfare of humans who rely upon it.

The Bible's Ecological Message

The early founders and followers of monotheism were filled with a sense of wonder, delight, and awe by the greatness of God's creation. Indeed, nature and wildlife were sources of inspiration for many of the prophets of the Bible, and one cannot fully understand the teachings and symbolism of the scriptures without an appreciation for the natural environment that inspired so much of what appears there. The Bible contains a strong message of conservation, respect for nature, and kindness to animals. It is a reverence for life, for "God's Creation," over which humans were given stewardship responsibilities to care for and protect. The Bible clearly teaches that in despoiling nature, we are destroying the Lord's handiwork and violating our sacred trust as caretakers of the land over which we were given stewardship.

There is nothing in the Bible that would justify our modern day policies and programs that despoil the land, desecrate the environment, and destroy entire species of wildlife. Such actions clearly violate God's commands to humans to "replenish the Earth," conserve natural resources, and treat animals with kindness; our actions also suborn God's instructions to the animals to "be fruitful and multiply" and fill the Earth. For example, various laws requiring the protection of **natural resources** are found in the Mosaic

law, including passages mandating the preservation of fruit trees (Deuteronomy 20:19, Genesis 19:23-25); agricultural lands (Leviticus 25:2-4); and wildlife (Deuteronomy 22:6-7; Genesis 9). Numerous other biblical passages extol the wonders of nature (Psalms 19, 24, and 104), and teach kindness to animals, even including the Ten Commandments, which requires that farm animals be allowed to rest on the Sabbath.

Christianity: Jesus' Nature Teachings

The New Testament contains many references by Jesus and his disciples that teach people to protect nature and its life forms. Throughout the Sermon on the Mount, Jesus uses nature and pastoral imagery to illustrate his points and upholds the creatures of nature as worthy of being emulated. In stressing the lack of importance of material possessions such as fancy clothes, Jesus observes that "God so clothes the grass of the field" and cited wildflowers as possessing more beauty than any human garments ever could: "Consider the lilies of the field, how they grow; they toil not, neither do they spin. And yet I say unto you, that even Solomon in all his glory was not arrayed like one of these" (Matthew 6:28-30; Luke 12:27). In Luke (12:6) (and Matthew 10:29), Jesus stresses that even the lowliest of creatures is loved by God: "Are not five sparrows sold for two pennies? And not one of them is forgotten before God."

Judaism: a Tradition of Reverence for Nature

The teachings and laws of Judaism, going back thousands of years, strongly emphasize kindness to animals and respect for nature. Indeed, an entire code of laws relates to preventing "the suffering of living creatures." Also important are the concepts of "do not destroy" the elements of nature, and *tikkun olam*, "repairing the world." Jewish prayers, traditions, and literature contain countless stories and admonitions stressing the importance of the natural world and animals as manifestations of God's greatness and love for His creation.

Many examples of practices based on Judaism's respect for nature can be cited. Early Jewish law prevented **pollution** of waterways by mandating that **sewage** be buried in the ground, not dumped into rivers. In ancient Jerusalem, dung heaps and garbage piles were banned, and refuse could not be disposed of near water systems. The Israelites wisely protected their drinking water supply and avoided creating hazardous and unhealthy waste dumps, lessons our modern, polluted civilization would have done well to heed. The rabbis of old Jerusalem also dealt with the problem of **air pollution** from wheat chaff by requiring that threshing houses for grain be built no closer than 2 mi (3.2 km) from the city. In order to prevent foul odors, a similar ordinance existed for graves, carrion, and tanneries, with tanneries sometimes being required to be constructed on the edge of the city downwind from prevailing air currents. Wood from certain types of rare trees could not be burned at all, and the Talmud cautioned that lamps should be set to burn slowly so as not to use up too much naphtha. And the biblical injunction to allow land to lie fallow every seven years (Lev. 25:3-7), of course, permitted the **soil** to replenish itself.

In contrast to the Western religious tradition, the religions of the East have always recognized and stressed the importance of protecting natural resources and other living creatures.

Many other religions, including the Baha'is and those of Native Americans, Amazon Indian tribes, and other indigenous and tribal peoples, stress the sanctity of nature, and the need to conserve wildlife, forests, plants, water, fertile land, and other natural resources. Thus, we do not have to invent new religions in order to save our planet, but we do need to return to return to the roots of our old ones. *See also* Non-Western environmental ethics

[*Lewis G. Regenstein*]

FURTHER READING

Berry, T. *The Dream of the Earth.* San Francisco: Sierra Club Books, 1988.

Carson, R. *Silent Spring.* Cambridge, MA: Riverside Press, 1962.

Cobb, J. *Is It Too Late ? A Theology of Ecology.* Environmental Ethics Books, 1995.

Fox, M.W. *The Boundless Circle: Caring for Creatures and Creation.* Wheaton, IL: Quest Books, 1996.

Gore, A. *Earth in the Balance: Ecology and the Human Spirit.* New York: Houghton Mifflin, 1992.

Hoyt J. *Animals in Peril.* Garden City-Park, N.Y.: Avery, 1994.

Leopold, A. *A Sand County Almanac.* New York: Oxford University Press, 1949.

Regenstein, L.G. *Replenish the Earth: The Teachings of the World's Religions on Protecting Animals and Nature.* New York: Crossroads, 1991.

Wilson, E.O. *Biophilia.* Cambridge: Harvard University Press, 1984.

Remediation

The treatment of **hazardous waste**s in most industrialized countries is now controlled through regulations, policies, incentive programs, and voluntary efforts. However, until the 1980s, society was mostly ignorant of the harmful effects of less-structured management of hazardous wastes, which resulted in a myriad of contaminated sites and polluted **natural resources**. Even in the 1970s, when environmental legislation required disposal of hazardous wastes to **landfills**, waste piles, surface impoundments, or **deep-well injection** systems, contamination of **soil**s and **groundwater** continued, because these systems were often not secure and allowed contaminants to migrate to soils and groundwater. To meet the environmental and public health standards of the 1990s, these contaminated sites from past activities must be rehabilitated, or remediated, so they no longer pose a threat to the public or the **ecosystem**. Total costs for site **remediation** in the United States were estimated in 1992 to be between $370 billion-$1.7 trillion, depending on the requirements of remediation regulations.

The Superfund program for remediation of contaminated sites was created in 1980 by the **Comprehensive Environmental Response, Compensation, and Liability Act** (CERCLA) and was amended by the **Superfund Amendments and Reauthorization Act** (SARA) of 1984. The Superfund program is designed to provide an immediate response to emergency situations that pose an imminent hazards, known as *removal or emergency response-actions*, and to provide permanent remedies for environmental problems resulting from past practices (i.e., abandoned or inactive waste sites), know as *remedial-response actions*. Under the Superfund program, the remedial action process is implemented in structured stages: (1) Preliminary assessment; (2) Site inspection; (3) Listing on the National Priorities List (NPL), a rank ordering of sites representing the greatest threats; (4) Remedial investigation/ feasibility study (RI/FS); (5) U.S. **Environmental Protection Agency**'s Record of Decision (ROD); (6) Negotiation of a consent decree and remedial action plan between the U.S. Environmental Protection Agency and the responsible parties; and (7) Final design and construction.

In addition to the Superfund program, site remediation projects may be required for: the **Resource Conservation and Recovery Act** (RCRA) Corrective Action Program for operating treatment, storage, and disposal facilities; the underground storage tanks program established by RCRA; Federal Facility cleanup of sites operated primarily by the **U.S. Department of Energy** and the Department of Defense (regulated under both CERCLA and RCRA); and state-regulated, private, and voluntary programs. The cleanup of federal facilities is expected to be the most expensive, followed by the RCRA Corrective Action Program, and then Superfund. The costs of remediation are determined by the degree of remediation required. Superfund cleanup standards require that contaminated waters be remediated to concentrations at least as clean at the Maximum Contaminant Levels (MCLs) of the **Safe Drinking Water Act** and the water quality criteria of the **Clean Water Act**. Carcinogen risks from exposures to a Superfund site should be less than one excess **cancer** in a population of one million people. Some states require that remediation projects achieve background levels of contamination, i.e., restoring the site to an equivalent of its original condition.

Remedial techniques are divided into two basic types: on-site methods and removal methods. Most remedial techniques are used in combination (e.g., pump and treat systems) rather than singly. Generally remediation techniques that significantly reduce the volume, toxicity, or mobility of hazardous wastes are preferred for use. Off-site transport and disposal is usually the least favored option. On-site methods include containment, extraction, treatment, and destruction, while removal methods consist of excavation and **dredging**. Containment is used to contain liquid wastes or contaminated ground waters within a site; or to divert ground or surface waters away from the site. Containment is achieved by the construction of low-permeability or impermeable cutoff walls or diversions. On-site groundwater extraction is accomplished by pumping, which is usually followed by aboveground treatment (referred to as *pump and treat)*. Pumping is used to control water tables so as to contain or remove contaminated groundwater plumes or to prevent plume formation. Soil vapor extraction, by either passive or forced ventilation collection systems, is used to remove hazardous gases from the soil. Gases are collected in PVC perforated pipe wells or trenches and transported above ground to treatment or combustion units.

On-site treatment of hazardous wastes can be conducted above ground, following extraction or excavation, or below ground (*in situ*). Above ground treatment methods include the use of conventional environmental engineering unit processes. Below ground treatment can be nonbiological or biological. Non-biological *in situ* treatment involves the delivery of a treatment fluid through injection wells into the contaminated zone to achieve immobilization and/or detoxification of the contaminants. This treatment is accomplished by processes such as oxidation, reduction, neutralization, hydrolysis, precipitation, chelation, and stabilization/solidification. Biological *in situ* treatment (**bioremediation**) is accomplished by modifying site conditions to promote microbial degradation of organic compounds by naturally occurring microorganisms. Exogenous microorganisms that have been adapted to degrade specific compounds or classes of compounds are also sometimes pumped into ground water or applied to **contaminated soil**.

Finally, on-site destruction of organic hazardous wastes can be accomplished by the use of high-temperature incineration. Inorganic materials are not destroyed, so residues from the incineration process must be disposed of in a secure landfill. *In situ* vitrification (ISV), or thermal destruction, involves the heating of buried wastes to melting temperatures (by applying electric current to the soil) so that a chemically inert, stable glass block is produced. Nonvolatile materials are immobilized in the vitrified mass, and organic materials are pyrolyzed. Combustion off-gases are collected and treated.

Removal methods of remediation include extraction and dredging. Excavation of contaminated solid or semisolid hazardous wastes may be required if the wastes are not amenable to *in situ* treatment. Excavated materials may be treated and replaced or transported off-site. Dredging is used to remove contaminated sediments from streams, estuaries, or surface impoundments. Removal of well-consolidated sediments in shallow waters requires the use of a clamshell, dragline, or backhoe. Sediments with a high liquid content or that are located in deeper waters are removed by hydraulic dredging. Dredged materials are pumped or barged to treatment facilities.

Although not every remediation project has been a complete success, many Superfund sites have been cleaned up significantly. Procedures for remediation continue to be developed and refined. This remains a growth industry with a high potential to benefit the public good.

[*Judith L. Sims*]

FURTHER READING

Blackman, W.L., Jr. *Basic Hazardous Waste Management.* Boca Raton, FL: Lewis Publishers, 1993.

Freeman, H.M., ed. *Standard Handbook of Hazardous Waste Treatment and Disposal.* New York: McGraw-Hill, 1989.

Henry, J.G., and G. W. Heinke. *Environmental Science and Engineering,* 2nd ed. Upper Saddle River, N.J.: Prentice Hall, 1996.

Remote sensing
See **Measurement and sensing**

Renew America (Washington, D.C.)

Renew America serves as a clearinghouse for information on the **environment**. Renew America distributes reports, pamphlets, and books to educators, organizations, and the general public in an attempt to fulfill its primary goal of "renewing America's community spirit through environmental success." One of Renew America's major projects is the annual *Environmental Success Index*, a compilation of over 1,500 successful environmental programs throughout the United States. The index lists organizations involved in a variety of environmental issues, including **air pollution control**, drinking water and **groundwater** protection, hazardous and **solid waste** reduction and **recycling**, renewable energy, and forest protection and urban forestry. The purpose of the index is to disseminate information on organizations that can function as prototypes for other programs. Renew America also publishes an annual report entitled *State of the States*, which serves as a report card on **environmental policies** in all fifty states. *State of the States* is compiled in cooperation with over one hundred state and local environmental organizations.

In addition to disseminating published information, Renew America distributes the Renew America National Awards each year. The awards are the result of a national search conducted by the Renew America Advisory Council, which is composed of 28 environmental groups. Renew America also selects a recipient for the Robert Rodale Environmental Achievement Award. Rodale served as chair of Renew America and the Rodale Press and administered the **Rodale Institute**, a scientific and educational foundation focusing on food, health, and **natural resource** issues. The awards are presented at the Environmental Leadership Conference, which also features several environmentally-oriented workshops and panel discussions. Like the *Environmental Success Index*, the advisory council selects recipients from a broad range of environmental programs. Past winners have included a group that assists area residents in creating community food gardens; surfers who won a lawsuit under the federal **Clean Water Act**; an adopt-a-manatee program; and an asphalt recycling project.

Renew America also offers educational tools such as a community resource kit called *Sharing Success*, which features articles on ways to approach environmental problems and highlights special environmental groups. It was developed to meet the needs of local environmental groups and other interested activists who wanted to share successful approaches to environmental problems.

Renew America does not utilize volunteers or engage in grassroots projects itself but provides information on organizations that do. Members receive the *State of the States* report and a quarterly newsletter highlighting significant environmental issues. Board members include former congress member Claudine Schneider and actor Eddie Albert as well as officials from several prominent environmental organizations. Contact: Renew America, 1400 Sixteenth Street, NW, Suite 710, Washington, DC 20036.

[*Kristin Palm*]

Renewable Natural Resources Foundation (Bethesda, Maryland)

The Renewable Natural Resources Foundation (RNRF) was founded in 1972 to further education regarding **renewable resources** in the scientific and public sectors. According to the organization, it seeks to "promote the application of sound scientific practices in managing and conserving renewable **natural resources**; foster coordination and cooperation among professional, scientific, and educational organizations having leadership responsibilities for renewable resources; and develop a Renewable Natural Resources Center."

The Foundation is composed of organizations that are actively involved with renewable natural resources and related public policy, including the American Fisheries Society, the American Water Resources Association, the Association of American Geographers, **Resources for the Future**, the Soil and Water Conservation Society, the **Nature Conservancy**, and the Wildlife Society. Programs sponsored by the Foundation include conferences, workshops, summits of elected and appointed leaders of RNRF member organizations, the RNRF Round Table on Public Policy, publication of the *Renewable Resources Journal*, joint human resources development of member organizations, and annual awards to recognize outstanding contributions to the field of renewable resources.

In 1992, the RNRF organized the "Congress on Renewable Natural Resources: Critical Issues and Concepts for the Twenty-First Century." At the Congress, held in Vail, Colorado, 135 of America's leading scientists and resource professionals gathered to discuss critical natural resource issues that this nation will be facing as the twenty-first century approaches. According to the *Renewable Resources Journal*, the "synergy created by bringing together a diverse group—resource managers, policymakers, and physical, biological, and social scientists—resulted in scores of recommendations for innovative policies."

To foster the ongoing generation of this synergy, the Foundation has been constructing an office complex project in Bethesda, Maryland, since 1975. The Foundation's member organizations envision a workplace in which they can coordinate their efforts to achieve their common goals. Plans for the thirty-five acre site include lawns, formal landscaping, ponds, streams, and forest areas. As of 1992, two of the six planned office buildings had been constructed and county approval for the additional buildings had been secured. Contact: Renewable Natural Resources Foundation, 5430 Grosvenor Lane, Bethesda, MD 20814. Internet: http://www.crest.org/sustainable/renew_america/.

[*Linda Ross*]

Renewable resources

The earth's resources are commonly divided into perpetual, renewable, and nonrenewable resources. A perpetual resource is one that is not affected by human use, such as **solar energy** or **wind energy**. Renewable resources, on the other hand, are all organic and inorganic materials that are replenished by physical and **biogeochemical cycles**. Examples of organic renewable resources are all plant and animal **species** that people use for food, building materials, drugs, leisure, and so on. Examples of inorganic renewable resources are water and oxygen, which are replenished in the hydrological and oxygen cycles, respectively. Nonrenewable resources are those materials that are present in the earth in limited amounts (minerals) or are produced only over many, many millions of years (**fossil fuels**). Nonrenewable resources may be recyclable so that their usefulness to human beings can be extended, but often they are transformed during use into useless matter such as waste gas.

The classification of resources is not permanent. Some things may be resources at one time but not at others. Wind energy is an example. It was a widespread resource during the time of the windmills but was superseded by the steam engine and later the internal **combustion** engine. During the energy crisis of the 1970s, however, researchers once again turned their attention to wind as a potential resource. Similarly, certain plants and animals may be food resources to some people, while other people consider them inedible and useless.

More importantly, any renewable resource is only potentially renewable. Renewable resources can be depleted to the point where they can no longer reproduce themselves, as with any plant or animal species that is being used up faster than it is replenished. Renewable resources are sometimes called "flow resources," since their availability or sustainable yield actually depends on the rate of flow or the replacement rate instead of total volume.

Reckless use has already obliterated many renewable resources, and thousands of plant and animal species are threatened or endangered. The development of the American West in the nineteenth century provides a particularly flagrant example of heedless exploitation. Herds of **bison**, millions strong, roamed the Plains west of the Mississippi until the end of the Civil War. Then they disappeared in about 15 years at the hands of hunters and of travelers who shot them for sport from passing trains. Only small pockets of **prairie** still survive. Many plant and animal species that found a **habitat** there were swept away with the destruction of the prairies.

A renewable resource can be lost not only through depletion, but also through **pollution**. Both air and water are recycled constantly, but **air pollution** and **water pollution** can make them unsuitable for human use. Other causes of renewable resource loss include **urban sprawl**, overcultivation, overirrigation, **overhunting**, **overfishing**, **overgrazing**, **deforestation**, and the destruction of habitat through **predator control** and pest control. Despite **conservation** efforts, exploitation and indirect destruction of renewable resources still goes on on a large scale, since the immediate economic benefits often outweigh long-term costs in decision-making processes. The timber industry is currently capitalizing on the employment opportunities associated with continued logging on the West Coast. Such short-term interests may very well triumph over efforts to preserve remaining forests and other renewable resources.

[*Marijke Rijsberman*]

FURTHER READING

Cunningham, W., and B. W. Saigo. *Environmental Science: A Global Concern*. Dubuque, IA: William C. Brown, 1990.

Frederick, K. D., and R. A. Sedjo, eds. *America's Renewable Resources: Historical Trends and Current Challenges*. Washington, DC: Resources for the Future, 1991.

Reserve Mining Corporation

In 1947, the beginnings of one of the first classic cases of environmental conflict emerged when the Reserve Mining Corporation received permits to dump up to 67,000 tons per day of asbestos-like fiber tailings from its taconite mining operations in Silver Bay, Minnesota, into western Lake Superior. The Reserve case typifies the conflict that occurs when the complex problems of pollution, economics, politics, and law collide. After decades of investigation and lawsuits, the corporation stopped the dumping in spring 1980, but the change did not come easily for any of the participants.

Taconite is a low-grade iron ore, which can be crushed, concentrated, and pelletized to provide a good source of iron ore. Silver Bay, Minnesota, was created as a result of the mine's development by Reserve, and approximately 80% of the local labor force of 3,500 residents worked at the $350 million facility in 1980. The first permits were given to the company in 1947, on the condition that it would strictly comply with all provisions, including providing continued assurances that the discharges posed no harm to the lake or surrounding inhabitants. In 1956 and 1960, Reserve was allowed to increase its use of Lake Superior water, thus increasing its dumping of waste taconite tailings. This continued until the late 1960s, when two major signs emerged that the lake—and potentially local residents—were being harmed by the waste discharges.

The first sign was the obvious discoloration of the water on the northwest shores of Lake Superior. Up to 67,000 tons of tiny fibers resembling asbestos, a carcinogen, were dumped into the lake each day, turning the water into a green slime from Silver Bay to Duluth, Minnesota, and nearby Superior, Wisconsin. Second, several local citizens made the link between the company's discharge and possible harmful effects on humans when they read about a discovered connection between cancer and asbestos used to polish rice in Japan in the 1960s.

By June 1973, after completing several studies at the request of these local citizens, the U.S. Environmental Protection Agency concluded that the drinking water of Duluth and other northshore communities was contaminated with asbestos-like fibers, which might cause cancer. The Minnesota Pollution Control Agency followed with the finding that a suspected source of the fibers was the Reserve Mining Corporation discharge. Duluth and other affected communities installed filtration systems to prevent further contamination of local drinking water supplies, and convinced state and federal agencies to join citizen groups in legal action against the company.

In a series of subsequent court appearances, Reserve continually argued that the company would be forced to close its operations if Lake Superior discharges were stopped, presumably resulting in the demise of the town of Silver Bay as well. Five years of lawsuits seemingly ended on April 20, 1974, when federal District Judge Miles Lord completed a nine-month trial and ordered the plant to cease discharges of taconite tailings into the air and water within 24 hours. Less than 48 hours later, however, the plant was ordered reopened by three judges from the Eighth U.S. Circuit Court of Appeals. While concluding that the original permits issued to Reserve Mining were a "monumental environmental mistake," they allowed the company to remain open while it altered its production process to create alternative disposal methods. In June 1974, the governors of Minnesota and Wisconsin filed an appeal of this ruling to the Supreme Court, but were rebuffed when the court refused to reinstate Judge Lord's order. Justice William Douglas' written dissent to the court's ruling stated, "I am not aware of a constitutional principle that allows either private or public enterprises to despoil any part of the domain that belongs to all of the people. Our guiding principle should be Mr. Justice Holmes' dictum that our waterways, great and small, are treasures not garbage dumps or cesspools."

Six years later, Reserve Mining Company and its parent owners Armco and Republic Steel were fined more than one million dollars for their permit violations and intransigence in completing disposal upgrades. Reserve switched to onland disposal, via rail and pipeline, to a 6-mi^2 (9.7-km^2) basin 40 mi (64.4 km) inland, which kept tailings covered under ten feet of water to prevent fiber dust from escaping. The basin operated efficiently until a production cut resulted in more water and plant effluent being sent to the disposal basin than was used in the plant to concentrate the crushed taconite rock into iron ore. Reserve sought a permit in October 1985 from the Minnesota Pollution Control Agency to pump water out of the disposal basin to a filtration plant on the Beaver River, which flows into Lake Superior. After several arguments from environmental groups and others, the permit was eventually issued at a lowered level from 15 to 1 million fibers per liter. Operations ultimately closed in the summer of 1986, due to reduced demand for the taconite pellets.

The mine was purchased and reopened in 1990 by Cyprus Mining of Colorado, and operated at 30% of capacity. The one-million-fiber-per-liter limit has generally been met, and thus asbestos-like fibers continue to be discharged into Lake Superior, albeit at a drastically reduced rate from those discharged for decades directly into the largest freshwater lake in the world.

[*Sally Cole-Misch*]

FURTHER READING

Merritt, Grant. "The Reserve Mining Case: Promises, Promises," *Great Lakes Focus on Water Quality* 1, Issue 1 (Fall 1974): 1-3.

———. "The Reserve Mining Case—20 Years Later," *Focus on International Joint Commission Activities* 19, Issue 3 (November/December 1994): 1-4.

Rousmaniere, J., ed. *The Enduring Great Lakes, A Natural History Book.* New York: W.W. Norton & Company, 1979.

"Tailings' End," *Time*, March 31, 1980: 45.

Residence time

Residence time is the length of time that a substance, usually a **hazardous material**, can be detected in a given **environment**. For example, airborne pollutants are carried into the **atmosphere** by natural updrafts. The concentration and size of the **particulate**s and their residence time exerts varying degrees of influence on the solar radiation balance. Other examples include the period of time that oxidant concentrations such as PAN-type or **ozone** remain in the atmosphere, or the period of time that nuclear by-products are found in the atmosphere or in the **soil**. *See also* Hazardous waste siting; Radioactive waste

Reservoir

A reservoir is a body of water held by a **dam** on a river or stream, usually for use in **irrigation**, electricity generation, or urban consumption. By catching and holding floods in spring or in a rainy season, reservoirs also prevent **flooding** downstream. Most reservoirs fill a few miles of river basin, but large reservoirs on major rivers can cover thousands of square miles. Lake Nasser, located behind Egypt's **Aswan High Dam**, stretches 310 miles (500 km), with an average width of 6 miles (10 km). Utah's Lake Powell, on the **Colorado River**, fills almost 93 miles (150 km) of canyon.

Because of their size and their role in altering water flow in large **ecosystem**s, reservoirs have a great number of environmental effects, positive and negative. Reservoirs allow more settlement on flat, arable flood plains near the river's edge because the threat of flooding is greatly diminished. Water storage benefits farms and cities by allowing a gradual release of water through the year. Without a dam and reservoir, much of a river's annual discharge may pass in a few days of flooding, leaving the river low and muddy the rest of the year. Once a reservoir is built, water remains available for irrigation, domestic use, and industry even in the dry season.

At the same time, the negative effects of reservoirs abound. Foremost is the destruction of instream and stream side vegetation and **habitat** caused by flooding hundreds of miles of river basin behind reservoirs. Because reservoirs often stretch several miles across, as well as far upstream, they can drown habitat essential to aquatic and terrestrial plants, as well as extensive tracts of forest. Humans also frequently lose agricultural land and river-side cities to reservoir flooding. China's proposed **Three Gorges Dam** on the Chang Jiang (Yangtze River) will displace 1.4 million people when it is completed; India's Narmada Valley reservoir will flood the homes of 1.5 million people. In such cases the displaced populations must move elsewhere, clearing new land to reestablish towns and farms. Water loss from evaporation

and seepage can drastically decrease water volumes in a river, especially in hot or **arid** regions. Lakes Powell and Mead on the Colorado River annually lose 1.3 billion cubic yards (1 billion cubic m) of water through evaporation, water that both people and natural habitats downstream sorely need. Egypt's long and shallow Lake Nasser is even worse, losing as much as 20 billion cubic yards (15 billion cubic m) per year. Impounded water also seeps into the surrounding bedrock, especially in porous sandstone or limestone country. This further decreases river flow and sometimes causes slope instability in the reservoir's banks. A disastrous 1963 **landslide** in the waterlogged banks of Italy's Vaiont reservoir sloshed 192 million cubic yards (300 million cubic m) of water over the dam and down the river valley, killing almost 2,500 people in towns downstream. A further risk arises from the sheer weight of stored water, which can strain faults deep in the bedrock and occasionally cause earthquakes.

Sedimentation is another problem associated with reservoirs. Free flowing rivers usually carry a great deal of suspended **sediment**, but the still water of a reservoir allows these sediments to settle. As they accumulate in the reservoir, storage capacity decreases. The lake gradually becomes shallower and warmer, with an accompanying decrease in water quality. Even more important, sediment-free water downstream of the dam no longer adds sand and mud to river banks and deltas. **Erosion** of islands, banks, and deltas results, undermining bridges and walls as well as natural riverside habitat.

One of the losses felt most acutely by humans is that of scenic river valleys, gorges, and canyons. China's Three Gorges Dam will drown ancient cultural and historic relics to which travellers have made pilgrimages for centuries. In the United States, the loss of Utah's cathedral-like Glen Canyon and other beautiful or unusual environmental features are tragedies that many environmentalists still lament. *See also* Arable land; Environmental economics; Environmental policy; Riparian land; River basins

[*Mary Ann Cunningham*]

FURTHER READING

Driver, E. E., and W. O. Wunderlich, eds. *Environmental Effects of Hydraulic Engineering Works.* Proceedings of an International Symposium Held at Knoxville, Tennessee, Sept. 12-14, 1978. Knoxville: Tennessee Valley Authority, 1979.

Esteva, G., and M. S. Prakash. "Grassroots Resistance to Sustainable Development." *The Ecologist* 22 (1992): 45-51.

Freeze, R. A., and J. A. Cherry. *Groundwater.* Englewood Cliffs, NJ: Prentice-Hall, 1979.

Resilience

In ecology, resilience refers to the rate at which a community returns to some state of development after it has been displaced from that state. **Ecosystem**s comprised of communities with high inherent resilience are, over time, relatively stable in the face of **environmental stress**. These communities return to their original structure and functions, or similar ones, relatively quickly in response to a disturbance.

Of course, there are thresholds for resilience. If a perturbation is too intense, then the inherent resilience of the community may be exceeded, and the previous state of ecological development may not be rapidly reattained, if at all. Populations of **species** that are smaller in size, poor competitors, short-lived, with short generation times and the ability to spread quickly are relatively resilient. Those that are larger in size, competitive, longer-lived, with longer generation times and high investment in offspring have a higher threshold, or **resistance**, to a stress factor, but have less resilience, and regenerate more slowly. *See also* Biosphere; Biotic community

Resistance (inertia)

In ecology, resistance is the ability of a population or community to avoid displacement from some state of development as a result of an **environmental stress**. Populations or communities with inherently high resistance are relatively stable when challenged by such conditions. If the stress is greater than the population threshold, though, change must occur.

In general, **species** that are larger in size, relatively competitive, longer-lived, with longer generation times and high investment in offspring are relatively resistant to intensified stresses. When these species or their communities are overcome by environmental change, however, they have little **resilience** and tend to recover slowly.

In contrast, species that are smaller in size, short-lived, highly fecund, and with shorter generation times have little ability to resist the effects of perturbation. However, these species and their communities are resilient, and have the ability to quickly recover from disturbance. This assumes, of course, that the environmental change has not been too excessive, and that the **habitat** still remains suitable for their regeneration and growth. *See also* Biotic community; Ecosystem; Population biology

Resource Conservation and Recovery Act

The Resource Conservation and Recovery Act (RCRA), an amendment to the Solid Waste Disposal Act, was enacted in 1976 to address a problem of enormous magnitude—how to safely dispose of the huge volumes of municipal and industrial **solid waste** generated nationwide. It is a problem with roots that go back well before 1976.

There was a time when the amount of waste produced in the United States was small and its impact on the **environment** relatively minor. (A river could purify itself every 10 miles [16 km].) However, with the industrial revolution in the latter part of the nineteenth century, the country began to grow with unprecedented speed. New products were developed and consumers were offered an ever-expanding array of material goods.

This growth continued through the early twentieth century and took off after World War II when the nation's industrial base, strengthened by the war, turned its energies toward domestic production. The results of this growth were not all positive. With more goods came more waste, both hazardous and nonhazardous. In the late 1940s, the United States was generating roughly 500,000 metric tons of **hazardous waste** a year. In 1985, the **Environmental Protection Agency (EPA)** estimated that 275 million tons of hazardous waste were generated nationwide.

Waste management was slow in coming. Much of the waste produced made its way into the environment where it began to pose a serious threat to ecological systems and public health. In the mid-1970s, it became clear, to both Congress and the nation alike, that action had to be taken to ensure that solid wastes were managed properly. This realization began the process that resulted in the passage of RCRA. The goals set by RCRA were: to protect human health and the environment; to reduce waste and conserve energy and natural resources; to reduce or eliminate the generation of hazardous waste as expeditiously as possible.

To achieve these goals, four distinct yet interrelated programs exist under RCRA. The first program, under Subtitle D, encourages states to develop comprehensive plans to manage primarily nonhazardous solid waste, e.g. household waste. The second program, under Subtitle C, establishes a system for controlling hazardous waste from the time it is generated until its ultimate disposal—or from "cradle-to-grave." The third program, under Subtitle I, regulates certain underground storage tanks. It establishes performance standards for new tanks and requires leak detection, prevention and corrective action at underground tank sites. The newest program to be established is the **medical waste** program under Subtitle J. It establishes a demonstration program to track medical waste from generation to disposal.

Although RCRA created a framework for the proper management of hazardous and nonhazardous solid waste, it did not address the problems of hazardous waste encountered at inactive or abandoned sites or those resulting from spills that require emergency response. These problems are addressed by the **Comprehensive Environmental Response, Compensation and Liability Act (CERCLA)**, commonly called Superfund.

Today RCRA refers to the overall program resulting from the Solid Waste Disposal Act. The Solid Waste Disposal Act was enacted in 1965 for the primary purpose of improving solid waste disposal methods. It was amended in 1970 by the Resource Recovery Act and again in 1976 by RCRA. The changes embodied in RCRA remodeled our nation's solid waste management system and added provisions pertaining to hazardous waste management.

The Act continues to evolve as Congress amends it to reflect changing needs. It has been amended several times since 1976, most significantly on November 8, 1984. The 1984 amendments, called the Hazardous and Solid Waste Amendments (HSWA), expanded the scope and requirements of RCRA. Provisions resulting from the 1984 amendments are significant, since they tend to deal with the waste problems resulting from more complex technology.

The Act is a law that describes the kind of waste management program that Congress wants to establish. This description is in very broad terms—directing the EPA to develop and promulgate criteria for identifying the characteristics of hazardous waste. The Act also provides the Administrator of the EPA (or designated representative) with the authority necessary to carry out the intent of the Act—the authority to conduct inspections.

The Act includes a Congressional mandate for EPA to develop a comprehensive set of regulations. Regulations are legal mechanisms that define how a statute's broad policy directives are to be implemented. RCRA regulations have been developed by the EPA, covering a range of topics from guidelines for state solid waste plans to a framework for the hazardous waste permit program.

RCRA regulations are published according to an established process. When a regulation is proposed it is published in the *Federal Register*. It is usually first published as a proposed regulation, allowing the public to comment on it for a period of time—normally 30 to 60 days. Included with the proposed regulation is a discussion of the Agency's rationale for the regulatory approach and an explanation, or preamble, of the technical basis for the proposed regulation. Following the comment period, EPA evaluates public comments. In addressing the comments, the EPA usually revises the proposed regulation. The final regulation is published in the *Federal Register* ("promulgated"). Regulations are compiled annually and bound in the *Code of Federal Regulations* (CFR) according to a highly structured format. The codified RCRA regulations can be found in Title 40 of the CFLRL, Parts 240-280; regulations are often cited as 40 CAR.

Although the relationship between an Act and its regulations is the norm, the relationship between HSWA and its regulations differs. HSWA is unusual in that Congress placed explicit requirements in the statute in addition to instructing the EPA in general language to develop regulations. Many of these requirements are so specific that the EPA incorporated them directly into the regulations. HSWA is all the more significant because of the ambitious schedules that Congress established to implement the Act's provisions. Another unique aspect of HSWA is that it establishes "hammer" provisions—statutory requirements that go into effect automatically as regulations if EPA fails to issue these regulations by certain dates. EPA further clarifies its regulations through guidance documents and policy.

The EPA issues guidance documents primarily to elaborate and provide direction for implementing the regulations—essentially they explain how to do something. For example, the regulations in 40 CAR Part 270 detail what is required in a permit application for a hazardous management facility. The guidance for this part gives instructions on how to evaluate a permit application to see if everything is included. Guidance documents also provide the Agency's interpretations of the Act.

Policy statements, however, specify operating procedures that *should* be followed. They are a mechanism used by EPA program offices to outline the manner in which pieces of the RCRA program are to be carried out. In most cases, policy statements are addressed to staff working on implementation. Many guidance and policy documents have been developed to aid in implementing the RCRA Program. To find out what documents are available, the Office of Solid Waste's Directives System lists all RCRA-related policy guidance and memoranda and identifies where they can be obtained.

RCRA works as follows: Subtitle D of the Act encourages States to develop and implement solid waste management plans. These plans are intended to promote recycling of solid wastes and require closing or upgrading of all environmentally unsound dumps. Due to increasing volumes, solid waste management has become a key issue facing many localities and states. Recognizing this, Congress directed the EPA in HSWA to take an active role with the states in solving the difficult problem of solid waste management. The EPA has been in the process of revising the standards that apply to municipal solid waste landfills. Current with the revision of these standards, the EPA formed a task force to analyze solid waste source reduction and recycling options. The revised solid waste standards, together with the task force findings, form the basis for the EPA's development of strategies to better regulate municipal solid waste management.

Subtitle C establishes a program to manage hazardous wastes from "cradle-to-grave." The objective of the C program is to ensure that hazardous waste is handled in a manner that protects human health and the environment. To this end, there are Subtitle C regulations regarding the generation, transportation and treatment, storage, or disposal of hazardous wastes. In practical terms, this means regulating a large number of hazardous waste handlers. As of June, 1989, the EPA had on record more than 7,000 treatment, storage and disposal facilities; 17,000 transporters; and about 180,000 large and small quantity generators. By February, 1992, that number had increased substantially. (43,000 treatment, storage and disposal facilities, 19,700 transporters, 238,000 large and small quantity generators.)

The Subtitle C program has resulted in perhaps the most comprehensive regulations the EPA has ever developed. They first identify those solid wastes that are "hazardous" and then establish various administrative requirements for the three categories of hazardous waste handlers: generators, transporters and owners or operators of treatment, storage and disposal facilities (TSDFs). In addition, Subtitle C regulations set technical standards for the design and safe operation of TSDFs. These standards are designed to minimize the release of hazardous waste into the environment. Furthermore, the regulations for TSDFs serve as the basis for developing and using the permits required for each facility. Issuing permits is essential to making the Subtitle C regulatory program work, since it is through the permitting process that the EPA or a State actually applies the technical standards to facilities.

Subtitle I regulates petroleum products and hazardous substances (as defined under Superfund) stored in underground tanks. The objective of Subtitle I is to prevent leakage to **groundwater** from tanks and to clean up past releases. Under Subtitle I, the EPA developed performance standards for new tanks and regulations for leak detection, prevention, closure, financial responsibility, and corrective action at all underground tank sites. This program may be delegated to states.

Subtitle J was added by Congress when, in the summer of 1988, medical wastes washed up on Atlantic beaches, thus highlighting the inadequacy of medical waste management practices. Subtitle J instructed the EPA to develop a two-year demonstration program to track medical waste from generation to disposal in demonstration States. The demonstration program was completed in 1991 and Congress has yet to decide upon the merits of national medical waste regulation. At this point no Federal regulatory authority is administering regulations, but individual states are; some are setting up very stringent regulations on storage, packaging, transportation, and disposal.

Congress and the President set overall national direction for RCRA programs. The EPA's Office of Solid Waste and Emergency Response translates this direction into operating programs by developing regulations, guidelines and policy. the EPA then implements RCRA programs or delegates implementation to the states, providing them with technical and financial assistance.

Waste minimization or reduction is a major EPA goal. It is defined as any source reduction or recycling activity that results in either reduction of total volume of hazardous waste or reduction of toxicity of hazardous waste, or both, as long as that reduction is consistent with the general goal of minimizing present and future threats to human health and the environment. *See also* Waste reduction

[*Liane Clorfene Casten*]

FURTHER READING

Hazardous Waste Management Compliance Handbook. New York: Van Nostrand Reinhold, 1992.

RCRA Deskbook. Washington, DC: Environmental Law Institute, 1991.

U. S. Environmental Protection Agency. *RCRA Orientation Manual.* Washington, DC: U. S. Government Printing Office, 1990.

Resource recovery

Resource recovery is the process of recovering materials or energy from **solid waste** for **reuse**. The aim is to make the best use of the economic, environmental and social costs of these materials before they are permanently laid to rest in a **landfill**. The **Environmental Protection Agency (EPA)** and environmentalists have set up a hierarchy for resource recovery: reduce first, then reuse, recycle, incinerate with **energy recovery**, and landfill last. Following the hierarchy will cut solid waste and reduce resources consumed in production. Solid waste managers have turned to resource recovery in an effort to cut disposal costs, and the hierarchy has become not only an important guideline but a major inspiration for local **recycling** programs.

After the industrial revolution made a consumer society possible, **garbage** was considered a resource for a class of people who made their living sorting through open dumps, scavenging for usable items and recovering valuable scrap metals. Once public health concerns forced cities to institute

garbage collection and dump owners began to worry about liability for injuries, city dumps were for the most part closed to the public. Materials recovery continued in the commercial sector, however, with an entire industry growing up around the capturing of old refrigerators, junk cars, discarded clothing, and anything else that could be broken down into its raw materials and made into something else. That industry is still strong; it is represented by powerful trade associations, and accounts for three-quarters of all ocean-borne bulk cargo that leaves the Port of New York and New Jersey for foreign markets.

The Arab **oil embargo** of the 1970s focused attention on the fact that **natural resources** are limited and can be made unavailable, and environmentalists took up the cause of recycling. But only after a barge loaded with New York City garbage spent months stopping in port after port on the eastern seaboard because it was unable to find a landfill was the real problem recognized. There were too few places to put it. The places that did take garbage often leaked a toxic brew of leachate and were seldom subject to environmental requirements.

Environmental restrictions on waste disposal, however, began to change. The EPA required that landfills be lined with expensive materials; states began mandating complicated leachate collection systems to protect **groundwater**. Amendments to the **Clean Air Act** of 1990 changed the regulations for garbage incinerators and waste-to-energy plants, which capture the energy created from burning trash to run turbines or to heat and cool buildings. These facilities were now required to install **scrubbers** or other devices for cleaning **emission**s and to dispose of the ash in safe landfills. The result of all these changes was a dramatic increase in the cost of dumping; as the price shot up, municipal leaders took notice. Economics joined **environmentalism** to support recycling, and those charged with managing solid wastes began to look for ways to get the most out of their trash or avoid creating it altogether.

Reduction—cutting waste by using less material to begin with—is at the top of the resource recovery hierarchy because it eliminates entirely the need for disposal, while avoiding the environmental costs of using raw materials to make replacement goods. **Waste reduction**, or source reduction, requires a change in behavior that many say is unrealistic when both the culture and the economy in the United States is based on consumption. However, manufacturers have responded to consumer demands that products last longer and use fewer resources. The durability of the average passenger tire, for example, nearly doubled during the 1970s and 1980s. Makers of **disposable diapers** advertise the fact that they have reduced diaper size so that they take up less space in landfills.

Reuse also cuts the need for raw materials. Perhaps the best example is the reusable beverage bottles that were widely used until the second half of this century. Studies have shown that reusing a glass bottle takes less energy than making a new one or melting it down to make a new one.

Recycling has become a popular way to make new use of the resources in old products. In its purist and most efficient form, recycling means turning an old object into the same kind of new object—an old newspaper into a new one, an old plastic **detergent** jug into a new one. But new uses for certain materials are limited, and some laws prevent recycled plastic from coming into contact with food; in such cases old items can only be made into lesser products. Recycled plastic soda bottles, for example, can be used in carpeting, television sets, and plastic lumber. The act of recycling itself also uses energy and causes **pollution**. Materials must be shipped from drop-off site to the remanufacturer and then to producer before they can be returned to the retailer. Grinding plastic into pellets takes energy, and cleaning old newsprint produces by-products that can pollute water. Another drawback to recycling is the unstable price of materials, which has caused some solid waste managers to reevaluate local programs.

After **composting**, the resource recovery hierarchy lists **incineration** with energy recovery. As the last option before landfilling, incinerators or waste-to-energy plants only burn what cannot be recycled, and they can recover one-quarter to one-third of their operating costs by selling the energy, usually in the form of electricity or steam. But incineration also produces waste ash, which can contain toxic materials such as **lead** or **mercury**. Incinerator ash often meets EPA standards for **hazardous waste**s, but because it mainly comes from household garbage, it is considered non-hazardous no matter what is detected, although this may change in the future. Other **hazardous material**s escape out the stacks of incinerators in the form of **air pollution**, despite high-tech scrubbers and other **pollution control**s. Environmentalists also maintain that the resources used in making materials that are incinerated are lost, despite the energy that is produced when they burn. They claim that waste-to-energy proponents have adopted the term resource recovery for the process in an effort to mask its problems and put an updated face on an industry that once was unscientific and uncontrolled.

Last on the list is landfilling. Although the United States has potential landfill space to last centuries, much of it is socially or environmentally unsound. Even with extensive liner systems, landfills are expected to leak chemicals into groundwater. Most communities, moreover, are unwilling to have new landfills as neighbors, and citizens groups throughout the country have demonstrated an increasing ability to keep them out through sophisticated protests. Finding space for new landfills has become a nightmare for elected officials and public works managers.

Despite their need for solutions, the resource recovery hierarchy does not always prove practical for local officials who are usually faced with tight budgets and the restrictions of democratic politics. Many of the advantages of the methods at the top of the hierarchy, such as waste reduction or recycling, are distant in either time or geography for many municipalities. A city might be hundreds of miles from the nearest plant that recycles paper and from the forests that might benefit from an overall decrease in demand for trees, for instance. In such a case, recycling paper makes little sense on a small scale. Environmentalists believe that the solution is for manufacturers and solid waste managers to make

decisions together. Finding the most efficient use of resources derived from both virgin materials and recovered from wastes may have to be considered regionally or nationally to be fully realized. *See also* Container deposit legislation; Groundwater pollution; NIMBY; Plastics; Solid waste incineration; Solid waste volume reduction; Waste stream

[*L. Carol Richie*]

FURTHER READING

Brown, L. R., et al. *State of the World 1991.* New York: W.W. Norton, 1991.

Peterson, C. "What Does 'Waste Reduction' Mean?" *Waste Age* (January 1989).

Resource Recovery Report. 5313 18th Street, NW, Washington, DC 20015.

Schall, J. "Does the Hierarchy Make Sense?" *MSW Management* (January/February 1993).

Resources for the Future (Washington, D.C.)

In 1952 President Harry S. Truman's Materials Policy Commission, headed by William Paley of the Columbia Broadcasting System (CBS), released its final report. The commission had been asked to examine the status of the nation's material resources, such as fuels, metals, and minerals. It concluded that the country's material base was in quite good condition, but the report maintained that further research was necessary to insure the continued use of these resources. Paley established Resources for the Future (RFF) as a nonprofit corporation to carry out this research, especially the updating of resource statistics.

At the same time, the Ford Foundation had created a fund to support resource **conservation** issues and to organize a national conference on the issue. Paley allowed this fund to use the name and facilities of his new corporation, and RFF hosted the Mid-Century Conference on Resources for the Future in Washington, D.C. with Ford Foundation funding.

Perhaps the major result of the conference was organizational. The Ford Foundation decided that RFF should become the base of its resource research program as an independent foundation. These organizations began in 1954 with a five-year grant to RFF of $3.4 million "aimed primarily at the economics of the nation's resource base." This has been the goal of research at RFF ever since. Most of the staff and most of the visiting scholars, as well as most of the beneficiaries of their small grants program have been economists, analyzing the importance of material resources to the United States economy, and examining a wide range of intertwined economic, resource, conservation, and environmental issues.

Resources for the Future is now organized into two divisions, the Energy and Natural Resources Division, and the Quality of the Environment Division. There are also two centers, the National Center for Food and Agricultural Policy, and the Center for Risk Management. Well-known experts on resource and environmental issues such as Marion Clawson, Hans Landsberg, John Krutilla, and Allen Kneese are long-time staff members or "fellows" of RFF. The organization also supports resource and environmental research by non-staff scholars through visiting fellowships and its small grants program, and the range of these activities exceeds RFF's original mandate. RFF publishes an annual report and a quarterly journal called *Resources*. The annual report lists the year's publications by resident staff, making it a good reference source for up-to-date materials on a wide range of resource and environmental issues. *Resources* publishes short articles, mostly by staff members or visiting fellows, and a quarterly report entitled "Inside RFF."

A scan of these two documents on any given date reveals the range of RFF interests. A recent annual report included staff publications on energy on different aspects of agriculture and agricultural policy, on various aspects connecting economics and public **forest management**, on climatic change, on risk management, cost analysis, and regulations and regulatory activities affecting resources and the environment. Contact: Resources for the Future, 1616 P Street, NW, Washington, DC 20036. Internet: http://www.rff.org/.

[*Gerald L. Young*]

Respiration

The term respiration has two major definitions. On a cellular level, respiration is the chemical process by which food molecules are oxidized to release energy. In the process, **carbon dioxide** and water are also produced. Cellular respiration is, therefore, the reverse of **photosynthesis**, the process by which carbon dioxide and water are combined to form complex carbohydrate molecules. On an organismic level, respiration refers to the act of inhaling and exhaling. **Respiratory diseases** are among the most common of all environmental illnesses. Inhaling **particulate** matter in polluted air may result, for example, in various forms of pneumoconiosis.

Respiratory diseases

Respiratory diseases—diseases of the lungs and airways such as **asthma**, chronic **bronchitis**, **emphysema**, and lung **cancer**—have diverse causes. While cigarette smoking is the leading cause of most major respiratory diseases, air pollutants and workplace toxins can also contribute to respiratory illness.

The lungs are equipped with an elaborate defense system to repel toxins and invading organisms. Before air reaches the lungs, it passes through the nose, throat, and bronchi that are lined with mucus to trap irritants. Within the bronchi, smaller bronchial tubes and bronchioles are covered with cilia that sweep particles out. Lungs are far from vulnerable, however. The defenses can fail, leading to any number of respiratory diseases.

Cigarette smoking is the most important cause of Chronic Obstructive Pulmonary Disease (COPD), a name covering pulmonary emphysema and chronic bronchitis. These lung diseases damage the air passageways and interfere with the lung's ability to function. COPD is the fifth leading cause of death in the United States, and in a smoking, aging population, will probably not decline.

Chronic bronchitis is a persistent inflammation of the bronchial tubes. Mucus cells of the bronchial tree produce excess mucus, and the lungs may become permanently filled with fluid. Eventually, scar tissue from infection replaces the cilia, decreasing the lungs' efficiency. With each infection, mucus clogs the alveoli, or air sacs. Little or no gas exchange occurs, and the ventilation-blood flow imbalance reduces oxygen levels and raises **carbon dioxide** levels in the blood.

Chronic bronchitis usually accompanies the development of emphysema. The destruction of too many elastic fibers in the lungs' framework and air sac walls results in hyperinflated air sacs that impair the lungs' ability to recoil during expiration. Eventually, the alveoli merge into one large air sac, and the network of capillaries in the lungs is lost. This reduces gas exchange that occurs, and stale air is trapped in the lungs.

These two COPDs are not curable, but can be treated. Patients can prevent pulmonary infections and the inhalation of harmful substances, reduce airway obstruction, improve muscle conditioning and use supplemental oxygen.

Asthma is a disease characterized by a narrowing of the airways, episodic wheezing, tightness in the chest, shortness of breath, and coughing. There are various types of asthma, including exercise-induced asthma, occupational asthma triggered by irritants in the workplace, and asthmatic bronchitis. Trigger factors can include dust, odors, cold air, **sulfur dioxide** fumes, emotional stress, upper-respiratory infection, exertion, and airborne **allergen**s. Asthma is often preventable if trigger factors can be identified and eliminated.

Scientists are also turning their attention to health hazards posed by atmospheric acids and other air pollutants. One study at 79 southern Ontario hospitals showed a consistent association between the summer levels of atmospheric sulfates and **ozone** and hospital admissions for acute respiratory illnesses such as asthma, chronic bronchitis and emphysema.

This "acid air" forms when **emission**s of sulfur dioxide and **nitrogen oxides**, mostly from **coal**-burning **power plants** and motor vehicles, are transformed to sulfuric and nitric acids. Acid **aerosol** concentrations tend to be higher on hot summer days. The fine acid particles can penetrate the deepest, most delicate tissues of the lungs, inflame respiratory-tract tissue, depress pulmonary function, and constrict air passages. Health effects are more pronounced when acid aerosols are accompanied by ozone in the lower atmosphere. Together, ozone and acid aerosols produce changes in the lungs that inhibit their ability to clear themselves of toxins and other irritants.

High levels of air pollution may foster respiratory-disease symptoms in otherwise healthy individuals. One study indicates that **air pollution** in Los Angeles may begin to permanently "derange" an individual's lung cellular architecture by age 14. Another study has implicated wood-burning stoves, which foul the air with tiny **particulate**s that may cause or exacerbate outbreaks of respiratory illness-es. An environmental team studying respiratory problems at a Boston-area high school implicated the school's poorly designed ventilation system as the most likely cause of the students' high rate of respiratory illnesses.

Workplace-related respiratory diseases are on the increase. In 1990, the National Safety Council listed occupa-tional lung diseases as the leading work-related diseases in this country. The Chicago-based National Safe Workplace Institute recently concluded that 2 to 4 percent of pulmonary disease is related to working conditions. Diseases that top the list include **asbestosis**, lung cancer, silicosis, occupational asthma, and coal workers' pneumoconiosis, commonly known as **black lung disease**.

Asbestosis is a chronic fibrotic lung disease caused by the inhalation of inert dusts. This affliction has received widespread media coverage because the majority of its victims have been subjected to long-term exposure to asbestos. Asbestosis causes a scarring of lung tissue that can result in serious shortness of breath. Silicosis is a disease of the lungs caused by breathing in dust that contains silica. Black lung disease is a long-term lung disease caused by the settlement of coal dust on the lungs, eventually resulting in emphysema.

Insurance data indicates that people in certain high-risk occupations, including agriculture, construction, mining, and quarrying have three to four times the average death rate for all industries, mostly from respiratory diseases.

Residential homes are also vulnerable. **Chlorine** bleach and cleaning fluids, insecticides, wood-burning fireplaces, and gas stoves that produce nitrogen dioxide can be toxic to the lungs. The causes of the expected 170,000 new cases of lung cancer in 1993 include exposure to **cigarette smoke**, **ionizing radiation**, **heavy metals**, and industrial **car-cinogen**s. *See also* Air quality; Automobile emissions; Fibrosis; Respiration; Sick building syndrome; Smog; Smoke; Yokkaichi asthma

[*Linda Rehkopf*]

FURTHER READING

"Experts Finger Tight Building Syndrome." *Science News* 137 (9 June 1990): 365.

Fackelmann, K. "The High and Low of Respiratory Illness." *Science News* 137 (9 June 1990): 365.

Haas, F., et al. *The Chronic Bronchitis and Emphysema Handbook.* New York: Wiley Science Editions, 1990.

Moeller, D. W. *Environmental Health.* Cambridge, Mass.: Harvard University Press, 1992.

Raloff, J. "Air Pollution: A Respiratory Hue and Cry." *Science News* 139 (30 March 1991): 203.

Shepherd, S. L., et al. "Is Passive Smoking a Health Threat?" *Consumers Research Magazine* 74 (October 1991): 30-1.

Restoration ecology

Ecological restoration is an attempt to reset the ecological clock and return a damaged **ecosystem** to its predisturbance state—to turn a disused farm into a **prairie**, for example, or

to convert a parcel of low-lying acreage into a vigorous **wetland**. Precise replication of the predisturbance condi-tion is highly improbable because each ecosystem is the result of a sequence of climatic and biological events unrepeatable in precisely the same order and intensity as the original sequence. However, close approximations of the predisturbance condition are often possible, with differences from the origi-nal apparent only to professionals.

Within this limitation, restorationists strive to build ecosystems which, if not exactly like their original predeces-sors, possess the qualities of a healthy ecosystem. These properties include:

1) *sustainability*—the ability to perpetuate;
2) *invasibility*—the ability to resist invasion by alien or pest species;
3) *productivity*—the presence of healthy functions such as **photosynthesis**, **respiration**, plant and animal fecundity;
4) *nutrient retention*—the ability to generate nutrients such as **nitrogen** and store them in the ecosystem;
5) *biotic interactions*—a pattern of interaction between key species similar to the pattern found in undisturbed ecosystems, including relationships in the **food chain**.

Thus, merely re-creating the form of an ecosystem without attention to whether it is *functioning* as its predeces-sor did can lead to cosmetic or aesthetic improvement, but is not considered to be true ecological restoration.

Regrettably, the term *restoration* as used in the news media and by organizations responsible for ecological dam-age often refers to just such cosmetic activity—the clean up of oil, for instance, with the expectation that once a substan-tial amount of spilled oil has been removed then natural processes will restore the ecosystem to its former condition. The concept of restoration has also been abused by develop-ers who obtain desired wetlands for malls or residences on the condition that they will create equivalent or larger wetlands elsewhere, and then carry out substandard restoration efforts. In the words of William Burke, "too often, mall builders get away with paying the lowest bidder to plant some cattails in a mud patch."

Restoration ecology arose in the twentieth century as a response to the loss of **habitat** brought on by industrializa-tion, overpopulation and agricultural mismanagement. Pio-neering biologists such as **Aldo Leopold** began to advocate an approach to healing damaged ecosystems involving direct human intervention. Leopold helped to restore a prairie on the campus of the University of Wisconsin in 1932, and when he took a hoe to an abandoned farm owned by his family in Wisconsin, he helped introduce a land ethic summarized by Bill Jordan of the Society for Ecological Restoration: "what we could take apart an acre at a time, we can only put back one shovelful at a time."

Moreover, restoration ecology, more than just a kind of applied science that uses the insights of ecology to build ecosystems, is becoming an essential research technique with the capacity to test the accuracy of ecological theories through direct experience. For example, the role of fire in the mainte-nance of prairie ecosystems has come to be better understood through its application on restored tracts which were failing to thrive.

As habitat loss accelerates, restoration is taking on increasing importance as means of preserving habitat for threatened species, rekindling lost **biodiversity**, restoring mineral balance to eroded and infertile lands, improving **water quality** and preserving atmospheric gas balance. The task of restoration, seen as rather abstract in years past, is viewed with far more urgency today as the consequences of catastrophic destruction of habitat begin to be understood.

Though the specific stages of a restoration project depend entirely upon the initial state of the land and the desired end, a typical restoration project begins with certain steps which—while they appear crude—create the conditions necessary for natural processes to gain a foothold. On eroded and compacted soils, the first step is often to physically manipulate the damaged soil by tearing or furrowing to produce water retention and suitable microenvironments for plant seeds. It also might be necessary to lay **fertilizer** or organic mulch to provide initial replenishment of nutrients such as nitrogen and **phosphorus**.

Suitable plant seeds are introduced, usually key varieties called *matrix species*. *Nurse species*, which will create the conditions needed to hasten growth of other plants (a process called *facilitation*), may be introduced. Sometimes a sequence of species must be introduced in order. For example, on clay mining wastes, the best growth is obtained by planting annual grasses and legumes, then perennial grasses a year later.

Often animal colonization is left to nature, especially if the site under restoration is near other predisturbance sites, although suitable species could be introduced. Management of the site to monitor its progress (and to remove unwanted invading species) is usually carried out in succeeding months and years. If a restoration effort is successful, a site finally returns to its natural state and the need for further intervention decreases.

Ecological restoration requires contributions from a large number of academic disciplines, although the precise mixture will vary from one restoration project to another. The term *restoration ecology* is misleading in its implication that the activity is for ecologists only. All restoration projects require some degree of funding (unless carried out by volunteers), and large-scale projects (such as surface mine reclamation or restoration of a wetland, river, or lake) may require substantial funding. In addition, if the restored ecosystem is to be protected from further damage, societal understanding and support are necessary. As a consequence, disciplines that study societal values and identify those that are congruent with ecological values are extremely important for large-scale, long-term successful restoration efforts.

Equally important are the roles of climatologists, chemists, engineers (where restructuring is necessary), hydrologists, geologists, statisticians, forestry and wildlife specialists, geneticists, soils and sediment chemists, political scientists, attorneys, and a variety of other professions. Historians and anthropologists often have a crucial role because the manner in which systems were damaged over long time periods may be reconstructed with historic evidence, both in printed form and in cultural and biological artifacts and relics.

The role of private citizens in a restoration effort is often pivotal. Community leaders may provide funds toward carrying out restoration, while the work of local volunteers helps to connect the community with the organizations and institutions administering a project, as well as providing a project with a long-term focus months or years after the initial effort is complete. Moreover, the labor-intensive task of restoration seems to thrive when it is carried out by volunteers and concerned individuals working together with specialists.

Although the underlying theory in the field of restoration ecology is still in its infancy and the precise outcome of a project is almost always uncertain, restoration efforts virtually all result in improvement to damaged environments, and the condition of a restored system may be strikingly superior to the damaged condition. For example, the tidal Thames River in England had virtually no species at the time coronation ceremonies were held for Queen Elizabeth (during Eisenhower's tenure as President of the United States). However, many years after the restoration, Gameson and Wheeler reported over 100 species in the tidal area. All of this was done with technology available decades ago, and the result has been an economic asset as well as an aesthetic and ecologically pleasing one. In the United States, **Lake Washington** in the Pacific Northwest, the Kissimmee River in Florida, the Rio Blanco in Colorado, and the Hackensack River Meadowlands in the New York-northeastern New Jersey metropolitan area are among the numerous examples of successful ecological restoration following damage. Many of these efforts were citizen-initiated, and local residents feel a justifiable pride in their successful efforts.

Similar case histories, such as the Guanacaste dry forest in Costa Rica, show that citizens of developing countries with far less per capita income than in the United States can also have strong involvement in ecological restoration. In a time of environmental attrition, the restoration movement serves a key role in shaping the future by helping citizens develop a feeling of connection between themselves and their wild lands, while providing concrete improvements in ecological conditions.

[*John Cairns, Jr. and Jeffrey Muhr*]

FURTHER READING

Berger, J. J., ed. *Environmental Restoration: Science and Strategies for Restoring the Earth.* Covelo, CA: Island Press, 1989.

Bradshaw, A. D., and M. J. Chadwick. *The Restoration of Land.* Berkeley: University of California Press, 1980.

Burke, William K. "Return of the Native: The Art and Science of Environmental Restoration." *E Magazine*, July/August 1992.

Cairns, J., Jr. *Rehabilitating Damaged Ecosystems.* 2 vols. Boca Raton, FL: CRC Press, 1988.

Ehrlich, P. R., and A. H. Ehrlich. *Healing the Planet.* New York: Addison-Wesley, 1991.

Jordan, W. R., III, et al., eds. *Restoration Ecology: A Synthetic Approach to Ecological Research.* Cambridge: Cambridge University Press, 1990.

National Research Council. *Restoration of Aquatic Ecosystems: Science, Technology, and Public Policy.* Washington, DC: National Academy Press, 1991.

Retention time

Retention time refers to a time frame in which **chemicals** stay in a certain location. The term is sometimes used interchangeably with residence or renewal time, which in limnology (aquatic ecology) describes the length of time a water molecule or a chemical resides in a body of water. The residence time of water is called the hydraulic retention time. It may range from days to hundreds of years, depending on the volume of the lake and rates of inflow and outflow, and is often used in calculations of **nutrient** loading. Retention time can also refer to the length of time needed to detoxify harmful substances or to break down hazardous chemicals in pharmaceutical and **sewage treatment** plants; the length of time chemicals stay in a living organism; or the length of time needed to detect certain chemicals by instruments such as gas **chromatography**.

Reuse

Reuse, using a product more than once in its original form, is one of the preferred methods of **solid waste management** because it prevents materials from becoming part of the **waste stream**. It is a form of source reduction of waste.

Some products are specifically designed to be reusable while others are commonly reused as a matter of convenience. In the former instance, products such as canvas shopping bags and cloth napkins are meant to be used again and again, unlike their paper cousins. In the latter case, glass and plastic food containers are often reused for numerous household purposes, even though they are intended to be used only as food packaging.

Reuse of products is a basic component of diaper services and home bottled water delivery. Although neither of these services were originally created with waste reduction in mind, they do impact solid waste generation. A cotton diaper can be used 70 or more times, unlike a single-use disposable diaper. The three and five gallon bottles used by most bottled water services are picked up and taken back to the water plant for refilling, eliminating the need for consumers to buy individual gallon containers in supermarkets.

Deposit systems for beer and soft drink containers represent another form of product reuse. In these systems, consumers pay a nominal fee when they purchase beverages sold in specific types of containers. The fee is refunded when they return the empty containers to the retailer or other designated location. Virtually all beer and soft drinks used to be sold in returnable bottles. During the 1950s, the use of nonreturnable bottles and metal cans started to be more commonplace. By the mid-1980s, most beverages were packaged in nonreturnable bottles, cans or plastic containers.

Nine states currently have legislation requiring deposits on beverage containers. The deposits are meant to be incentives to consumers to return the bottles. Where such legislation exists, between 70 and 90 percent of the targeted containers are returned. Litter control rather than solid waste reduction is sometimes the purpose of beverage container deposit legislation. Reduction in litter has been documented to be as high as 80 percent, but the impact on solid waste disposal is more difficult to calculate since beverage containers account for a relatively small portion of the waste stream.

Another type of product reuse is resale of used clothing and household items through thrift stores and garage sales. Although calculating the impact of such practices on waste generation would be extremely difficult, there is no doubt that they result in some reduction in waste disposal. *See also* Recyclables; Recycling; Waste reduction

[*Teresa C. Donkin*]

FURTHER READING

Bohm, P. *Deposit–Refund Systems: Theory and Applications to Environmental, Conservation and Consumer Policy.* Baltimore: Johns Hopkins University Press, 1981.

Revegetation

See **Restoration ecology**

Rhinoceroses

Popularly called *rhinos*, rhinoceroses are heavily-built, thick-skinned herbivores with one or two horns on their snout and three toes on their feet. The family Rhinocerotidae includes five **species** found in Asia and Africa, all of which face **extinction**.

The two-ton, one-horned Great Indian rhinoceroses (*Rhinoceros unicornis*) are shy and inoffensive animals that seldom act aggressively. These rhinos were once abundant in Pakistan, northern India, Nepal, Bangladesh, and Bhutan. Today, there are about 2,000 Great Indian rhinos left in two game reserves in Assam, India, and in Nepal. The smaller one-horned Javan rhinoceros (*Rhinoceros sondaicus*) is the only species in which the females are hornless. Once ranging throughout southeast Asia, Javan rhinos are now on the verge of extinction, with only 65 living on reserves in Java and Vietnam.

The Sumatran rhinoceros (*Didermocerus sumatrensis*), the smallest of the rhino family, has two horns and a hairy hide. There are two subspecies—*D. s. sumatrensis* (found in Sumatra and Borneo) and *D. s. lasiotis* (found in Thailand, Malaysia, and Burma). Sumatran rhinos are found in hilly jungle terrain and once coexisted in southeast Asia with Javan rhinos. Now there are only 700 Sumatran rhinos left.

The two-horned, white, or square-lipped, rhinoceros (*Ceratotherium simum*) of the African **savanna** is the largest land mammal after the African elephant, standing 7 feet (2 meters) at the shoulder and weighing more than 3 tons. White rhinos have a wide upper lip for grazing. There are two subspecies—the northern white (*C. s. cottoni*) and the

Great Indian rhinoceros.

southern white (*C. s. simum*). Once common in the Sudan, Uganda, and Zaire, northern white rhinos are now extremely rare, with only 40 left (28 in Zaire, the rest in zoos). Southern African white rhinos are faring somewhat better (4,800) and are the world's most common rhino.

The smaller two-horned black rhinoceros (*Diceros bicornis*) has a pointed upper lip for feeding on leaves and twigs. Black rhinos can be aggressive but their poor eyesight makes for blundering charges. Black rhinos (which are actually dark brown) were once common throughout subsaharan Africa but are now found only in Kenya, Zimbabwe, Namibia, and South Africa. Today, there are only 3,000 black rhinos left in the wild, compared to 100,000 thirty years ago.

Widespread **poaching** has diminished rhino populations. The animals are slaughtered for their horns, which are made of hardened, compressed hair-like fibers. In Asia, the horn is prized for its supposed medicinal properties, and powdered horn brings $28,000 per kg. In Yemen, a dagger handle made of rhino horn can command up to $1,000. As a result, rhinos now survive only where there is strict protection from poachers. Captive breeding programs for endangered rhinos are hindered by the general lack of breeding success for most species in zoos and a painfully slow reproduction rate of only one calf every 3 to 5 years. The present world rhino population of about 10,600 is below half the estimated "safe" long-term survival number of 22,500.

[*Neil Cumberlidge*]

FURTHER READING

Cumming, D. H. M., R. F. Du Toit, and S. N. Stuart. *African Elephants and Rhinos: Status Survey and Conservation Action Plan.* Gland, Switzerland: IUCN-The World Conservation Union, 1990.

Khan, M. *Asian Rhinos: An Action Plan for Their Conservation.* Gland, Switzerland: IUCN-The World Conservation Union, 1989.

Penny, M. *Rhinos, Endangered Species.* New York: Facts on File, 1988.

Tudge, C. "Time to Save the Rhinoceroses." *New Scientist* 28 (September 1991): 30-5.

Richards, Ellen Henrietta Swallow (1842-1911)

American chemist

Ellen Swallow Richards was born in Ipswich, Massachusetts, and was a daughter of Peter and Fanny Swallow, who were school-teachers and part-time farmers. Ellen Swallow obtained a Baccalaureate (the equivalent of an undergraduate degree) from Vassar Female College, and in 1870 she became the first woman to be accepted as a student by the Massachusetts Institute of Technology (M.I.T.). Founded in Boston in 1865, MIT had rapidly become a highly regarded school of engineering and applied science. In 1873, she graduated as a Bachelor of Science in chemistry and in the same year received a Master of Arts degree from Vassar, based on a thesis involving examination of the vanadium content of an iron ore.

Ellen Swallow then spent several years studying towards a doctorate at MIT, but did not graduate, apparently because the faculty members of the department in which she was studying, all of whom were men, were unwilling to allow a woman to be the first-ever Doctor of Science graduate from their program. Ellen Swallow was undaunted by this and other forms of gender bias that were pervasive at the time. She went on to become a pioneer in the development of the new engineering field of public sanitation, and was a strong advocate of domestic science and home economics.

In 1875 Ellen Swallow married Robert Hallowell Richards, a professor of metallurgy and mining engineering at M.I.T. The couple shared a devotion to science and to each other, but had no children. Ellen Richards collaborated with her husband in his metallurgical and mining work, and her contributions in those fields were recognized later on, when she became the first woman to be elected to the American Institute of Mining and Metallurgical Engineers.

Ellen Richards understood that one of her major responsibilities was to foster the scientific education of American women. She was central in the establishment of a Women's Laboratory at M.I.T., as well as other facilities and programs that made important contributions towards allowing women to pursue careers in science. Some of her early research involved investigations of household and food chemistry and **food additives**. In 1882, she published *The Chemistry of Cooking and Cleaning*, and in 1885 *Food Materials and Their Adulterations*.

In 1884, Ellen Richards was appointed to a position in a new chemical laboratory at M.I.T. that specialized in the study of public sanitation. She held this position for 27 years until her death in 1911. One of her initial accomplishments was running the chemical laboratory responsible for the first survey of lakes and rivers in Massachusetts, an extensive study that became a classic in its field.

In 1890, M.I.T. established a ground-breaking program in sanitary engineering in which Ellen Richards taught the chemistry and analyses of water, **sewage**, and **atmosphere**. In collaboration with A.G. Woodman, in 1900 she published *Air, Water, and Food Chemistry for Colleges*, a textbook in support of the teaching of public sanitation. Her most important scientific contributions were in the field of water sanitation. She was, for example, an influential advocate of the **chlorination** of drinking water to kill **pathogen**ic bacteria. This practice was critical in lowering the high death rates that were being caused by drinking unsanitary water in most towns and cities of the time.

After about 1890, Ellen Richard's interests increasingly focused on what was to become known as the "home economics movement." This involved the study and teaching of nutrition, food preparation, household sanitation and hygiene, and related subjects, mostly in the public school system. The home economics movement can be likened to a domestic-science literacy program for the masses, and it became an important means by which urban women learned how to run economical and healthy households. Ellen Richards wrote numerous papers and several books in this subject area, including *Home Sanitation: A Manual for Housekeepers* in

1887, *Domestic Economy as a Factor in Public Education* in 1889, and *Euthenics: The Science of Controllable Environments* in 1912. Today Ellen Richards is considered a parent of home economics in the United States. For this contribution, she is indirectly responsible for many pervasive improvements in living conditions throughout America and in other countries where home economics has become a popular subject in school curricula.

[*Bill Freedman*]

FURTHER READING

James, E.T., J.W. James, and P.S. Boyer, eds. *Notable American Women. 1607-1950.* Cambridge, MA: Belknap Press, 1971.

Stern, M.B. "The First Woman Graduate of M.I.T.—Ellen H. Richards, Chemist," *We the Women: Career Firsts of Nineteenth Century America.* New York: Schulte Pub. Co., 1962.

Right-to-Act legislation

On September 3, 1991, 25 men and women perished in a fire in a chicken-processing plant in Hamlet, North Carolina. Workers were trapped inside the burning building because managers of the plant had illegally bolted emergency exits in order to prevent possible theft of chickens. The American public reacted with outrage to news of that fire, because it was recognized that the employees' deaths could have been prevented if **Occupational Safety and Health Administration (OSHA)** standards regarding access to fire exits had been enforced. As a result, labor representatives have called for new, more effective means for protecting Americans from the hazards of injury, illness, and death at their workplaces.

In North Carolina, the site of the 1991 poultry plant fire, Worker Right to Act (RTA) legislation has been enacted in an effort to meet those demands, and such legislation is being proposed in several other states. RTA legislation is designed to give workers some of the power they need to avoid or prevent exposure to workplace hazards such as those leading to the poultry plant fire and those associated with use of toxic **chemicals**. It is important to note that the goals of RTA legislation overlap with those of **Toxics Use Reduction (TUR) legislation**. TUR laws, which have been enacted in at least 26 states, require business facilities to reduce their use of toxic substances, thus protecting workers and other community residents.

Although North Carolina has adopted a number of RTA provisions through a series of separate statutes instead of in a comprehensive, single package, RTA laws are only in the proposal stage in most states in which they are being advocated. In New Jersey, a four-year campaign for adoption of Worker and Community RTA was unsuccessful. However, advocates of RTA in that state are optimistic that future efforts will be successful and that their experiences will benefit groups and individuals working for the enactment of RTA laws in other states. In Michigan, a comprehensive RTA bill was first considered in 1993 and has been reintroduced before the state legislature several times since then. Therefore, the bill proposed in Michigan is used here to illustrate the provisions of a comprehensive RTA statute. Second, some of North Carolina's RTA provisions are described to provide further examples of RTA mechanisms.

Michigan's Proposed RTA Law

A Worker RTA bill considered in Michigan in 1993 includes five sets of RTA protections. First, the bill mandates that worker-management committees be established at each worksite where the number of employees regularly exceeds ten. If there is a government-certified labor organization at the worksite, it will select the workers' representatives. If there is no certified labor organization, nonsupervisory employees will select their own representatives. The committee must: (1) inspect the site at least monthly for existing or potential safety, health, and environmental problems; (2) investigate accidents and exposures that have the potential to harm employees and the environment; and (3) conduct annual reviews. The committee's duties are cross-referenced to a proposed Toxics Use Reduction and Community Right to Act (TUR/CRTA) bill.

Second, the Michigan Worker RTA bill mandates that each employer develop and implement a worksite safety and health plan. Such plans must provide for periodic inspections of the worksite and require documentation of hazards and actions taken to correct them.

Third, there are provisions giving any employee or employee representative the right to request an inspection by the Michigan Department of Labor or the Michigan Department of Health if he or she believes that there is a violation of a standard and that that violation threatens physical harm to an employee. Before a representative of one of those agencies makes a determination as to imminent danger, an employee may choose not to perform an assigned task if the employee has a reasonable apprehension of death or serious injury and he or she reasonably believes that no less drastic alternative is available.

Fourth, the Michigan bill increases the authority of state inspectors regarding citations and penalties and authorizes employees to contest the failure of such inspectors to conduct inspections and issue citations. There are substantial penalties for willful or repeated violations of the Act. Fifth, an employer cannot discharge an employee or in any way discriminate against an employee or job applicant because he or she has filed a complaint under the Act or testified at a proceeding under the Act.

It is significant that the Michigan TUR bill, entitled the "Toxic Use Reduction and Community Right to Act Bill" (TUR/CRTR), also includes RTA provisions. A summary of some provisions of Michigan's TUR/CRTA bill illustrates the interrelationship between RTA and TUR laws. First, TUR/CRTA establishes a goal of a 50 percent reduction in toxics use and toxics waste generation over a period of five years, thus reducing workers' exposure to toxics. Second, companies and governmental bodies that must report information under the federal **Emergency Planning and Community Right to Know Act (EPCRA)** must conduct audits of toxics used and generated as waste, and they must prepare plans and set goals for reducing the amounts of those toxics at their facilities. Then, annual reports must be filed, documenting progress in reaching those goals. Third, communities are granted rights to monitor business facilities through "community environmental committees." This provision is cross-referenced to workers' rights to investigate hazards under the Worker RTA bill. Also, workers, through their committees established under Worker RTA, have the opportunity to review and provide input on the facility's TUR plan before it is completed. Fourth, there are provisions giving workers and community members the right to take companies to court to compel them to comply with the TUR/CRTA law.

North Carolina's RTA Statutes

North Carolina's RTA statutes include some of the same kinds of mechanisms in Michigan's Worker RTA bill, but, overall, they are not as comprehensive. For example, North Carolina requires workplace safety committees and the establishment of health and safety programs, but those requirements are imposed only on employers of eleven or more employees if those employers have a poor "experience rating" under workers' compensation laws. (A "1.5" rating or worse is the measure used.)

North Carolina's RTA statutes do include several provisions which are not in the Michigan bill. North Carolina has created a special emphasis inspection program to target employers with high rates of violations or high rates of illness, injury or death. Also, an interagency task force has been created to study and issue a report setting out a plan for reorganization of the occupational health and safety and fire safety networks within North Carolina.

Significance of RTA Laws

In Michigan, due to a change of leadership (a conservative Republican is currently governor), it does not appear that RTA legislation is likely to be adopted at the present. However, labor leaders and workers in Michigan and in other states continue to advocate adoption of RTA and are optimistic that it will be adopted as leaders and citizens become aware of the need for it and its benefits. RTA laws are designed to lead to better enforcement of existing OSHA standards. Under RTA, worker-management committees conduct inspections of a workplace on a regular basis instead of waiting for OSHA or its state counterpart to do so. Thus, management and workers, as a team, become the primary watchdogs for the work facility. A major reason for the lack of enforcement by OSHA and its state counterparts is their lack of funding for inspectors. Use of worker-management committees provides a means of protecting workers despite scarce government resources.

By mandating that employers prepare worksite safety and health plans and that employee representatives be included in that planning process, RTA laws are designed to prompt employers and their employees to take a proactive stance with respect to workplace hazards. Workers are included in planning because they are on the job day-to-day and are in a good position to identify hazards and to recommend safer ways of working.

An important feature of RTA laws is that protections are extended to non-unionized as well as unionized workers. This is significant in view of figures showing that as of 1993 union membership in the United States had shrunk to a five-decade low—16 percent of the work force.

Worker RTA also recognizes that even workers who know about on-the-job hazards often lack viable alternatives for safer ways to earn a living and support their families. RTA provides the worker with mechanisms for reporting hazards as well as the right to refuse to perform an assigned task because of a reasonable apprehension of death or serious injury. Also, anti-discrimination provisions encourage workers to exercise their rights under the RTA law.

Finally, the interrelationships between the goals and provisions of RTA and TUR statutes and the fact that such laws are being supported by a coalition of labor interests and environmentalists appear to signal a shift in public policy in this country. For decades U.S. laws have divided laws on health and safety regulatory authority according to site: OSHA in the workplace and the **Environmental Protection Agency (EPA)** outside the workplace. Also, existing laws have mandated different approaches to regulation of different media pursuant to separate laws such as the **Clean Air Act**, the **Clean Water Act**, and the Occupational Safety and Health Act. Supporters of RTA and TUR laws view workplace and environmental problems as interrelated parts of an integrated "whole." Therefore, the provisions of RTA and TUR have been drafted to reflect an holistic approach to regulation.

It remains to be seen whether legislators and citizens throughout the United States will be convinced that enactment of RTA laws is an appropriate way to deal with hazards faced by American citizens within and outside of their workplaces. It is clear, however, that, in view of proposals for OSHA reform being discussed by the U.S. Congress and the number of RTA statutes being presented before state legislatures, RTA concepts will be seriously examined and considered in the future.

[*Paulette L. Stenzel*]

FURTHER READING

Stenzel, P. L. "Right to Act: Advancing the Common Interests of Labor and Environmentalists", 57 *Albany Law Review* (1993): 1-40.

"Exits Blocked, 25 Die As Blaze Sweeps Plant." *Chicago Tribune*, Sept. 4, 1991.

Michigan Senate Bill 946 (1992).

Garland, S. B. "What a Way to Watch Out for Workers." *Business Week*, September 23, 1991.

Right-to-know

Many states and local governments, as well as the federal government, have passed legislation, referred to as right-to-know laws, that requires the release of information on the hazards associated with chemicals produced or used in a given facility. Most right-to-know laws address both community and employee access to information about potential hazards. Requirements of these laws usually include providing public access to information on **hazardous materials** present, conducting inventories or surveys, establish-

ing record-keeping and exposure reporting systems, and complying with labeling regulations. Notification of emergency releases of hazardous substances into the **environment** is also required under right-to-know laws, such as the Federal Emergency Planning and Community Right-to-Know Act of 1986 (EPCRA).

Rio Conference
See **United Nations Earth Summit**

Riparian land

Riparian land refers to terrain that is adjacent to rivers and streams and is subject to periodic or occasional **flooding**. The plant **species** that grow in riparian areas are adapted to tolerate conditions of periodically waterlogged **soil**s. Riparian lands are generally linear in shape and may occur as narrow strips of streambank vegetation in dry regions of the American Southwest or as large expanses of bottomland hardwood forests in the wetter Southeast. The **ecosystem**s of riparian areas are generally called riparian **wetlands**. In the western United States, riparian vegetation generally includes willows, cottonwoods, saltcedar, tamarisk, and mesquite, depending on the degree of dryness.

The riparian zone of bottomland hardwood forests can be differentiated into several zones based on the frequency of flooding and degree of wetness of the soils. Proceeding away from the channel of the river, the zones may be described as follows: intermittently exposed, semipermanently flooded, seasonally flooded, temporarily flooded, and intermittently flooded. The vegetation of each zone is adapted to survive and thrive under the conditions of flooding peculiar to that zone. Due to the irregularities in **topography** and the formation of streambank levees that are normal to any landscape, it is rare that these zones always occur in the same predictable sequence.

Intermittently exposed zones have standing water present throughout the year and the vegetation grows in saturated soil throughout the growing season. Bald cypress and water tupelo are typical trees of this zone and have adaptations such as stilt roots and **anaerobic** root **respiration** to cope with the permanently flooded conditions. Semipermanently flooded zones have standing water or saturated soils through most of the year, and flooding duration may last more than six to eight weeks of the growing season. Black willow and silver maple are abundant tree species of this zone. Seasonally flooded zones are areas where flooding is usually present for three to six weeks of the growing season. A number of hardwood tree species thrive in this zone, including green ash, American elm, sweetgum, and laurel oak. Temporarily flooded zones have saturated soils for one to three weeks of the growing season. For the rest of the year, the **water table** will be well below the soil surface. Many oaks, such as swamp chestnut oak and water oak, as well as hickories may be found here. Intermittently flooded zones are areas where soil saturation is rarely present and flooding occurs with no predictable frequency. This is an area that may actually be difficult to distinguish from the adjacent uplands. Many transitional and upland species such as eastern red cedar, beech, sassafras, and hop-hornbeam are common.

For all riparian wetlands in the field, these zones of moisture and vegetation gradients occur in an overlapping, intergrading fashion, and the plant species are distributed in varying degrees throughout the riparian zone. Riparian wetlands are valued for their specialized plantlife and **wildlife** values. They are recognized as interfaces where uplands and aquatic areas meet to form intermediate ecosystems that are themselves unique in their diversity, productivity, and function. They also provide significant economic benefits by minimizing flood and **erosion** damage.

[*Usha Vedagiri*]

FURTHER READING

Mitsch, W. J., and J. G. Gosselink. *Wetlands.* New York: Van Nostrand Reinhold, 1986.

Riparian rights

Riparian rights are the rights of persons who own **riparian land**—land bordering a river or other natural watercourse. A riparian right entitles the property owner to the use of both the shore and the bed as well as the water upon it. Such rights, however, may not be exercised to the detriment of others with similar rights to the same watercourse. As Sir William Blackstone observed in his *Commentaries on the Laws of England* (1765-69), "If a stream be unoccupied, I may erect a mill thereon, and detain the water; yet not so as to injure my neighbor's prior mill, or his meadow; for he hath by the first occupancy acquired a property in the current."

Riparian rights, or riparianism, is a legal doctrine used in the eastern United States to govern water claims. Riparian landowners have rights to the use of the water adjoining their property, but not to **groundwater** or artificial waterways such as canals. Riparian rights were once subject to the "natural flow doctrine," which held that the right-holder could use and divert the water adjoining his or her property at will unless this use diminished the quantity or quality of the natural flow to other right-holders. Since almost any use could be said to diminish the natural flow, this doctrine has given way to the "reasonable use" rule. David H. Getches explains the "reasonable use" rules in this way: "If there is insufficient water to satisfy the reasonable needs of all riparians, all must reduce usage of water in proportion to their rights, usually based on the amount of land they own."

In the **arid** western states, **water rights** are governed by the "prior appropriation" doctrine, under which rights are derived from the first use of water rather than ownership of riparian property. If someone bought land on a river and simply let it flow past, for instance, someone else could acquire a right to that water by putting it to use. The right remains in force, furthermore, unless the right-holder abandons the use of the water. Prior appropriation rights may

also be transferred, and some cities in Arizona and elsewhere in the arid Southwest have recently taken advantage of this option by buying large ranches with established water rights in order to secure water supplies for their residents.

California has given its name to a hybrid system, followed in several states, that combines features of the riparian and prior appropriation doctrines. Whatever the system, water rights are limited by the "reserved rights doctrine," intended to assure adequate water for Native American reservations and public lands. *See also* Irrigation; Water allocation; Water conservation; Water resources; Water table draw-down

[*Richard K. Dagger*]

FURTHER READING

Davis, C. *Riparian Water Law: A Functional Analysis.* Arlington, VA: National Water Commission, 1971.

Water Rights in the Fifty States and Territories. Denver, CO: American Water Works Association, 1990.

Waters and Water Rights. Charlottesville, VA: Michie, 1991.

Risk analysis

Risk is the chance that something undesirable will happen. Everyone faces personal risks daily; we all have a chance of being struck by a car or by lightning or of catching a cold. None of these are certain to happen today, but they all can and do happen occasionally, some more frequently than others. Even though all risk is unpleasant, the consequences of being struck by an **automobile** are much more serious than those of catching a cold. Most people would do more and pay more to avoid the risks they consider most serious. Thus, risk has two important components: (1) the consequences of an event and (2) its probability. In addition, while the threat of lightning has always been present, the possibility of being struck by a car emerged only in this century. Modern risks are constantly evolving.

Events that challenge the health of ecological systems are also becoming apparent. **Ecosystem**s have always faced the risk of severe damage from fire, **flooding**, and **volcano**es. More recently, however, population increases, especially in cities; global **climate** change; **deforestation**; **acid rain**; **pesticide**s; and sewage, garbage, and industrial waste disposal—have all threatened ecosystems.

Healthy ecosystems supply air, water, food, and raw materials that make life possible; they also process the wastes human societies produce. For these compelling reasons, we must protect them. In the United States, the **National Environmental Policy Act**, the **Toxic Substances Control Act**, the **Clean Water Act**, the **Federal Insecticide, Fungicide, and Rodenticide Act**, and other legislation has been passed by Congress to protect the **environment**.

Risk analysis can determine whether proposed actions will damage ecosystems. This screening process evaluates plans that might prove destructive, and allows people to make informed decisions about which would be most environmentally sound. Proposed utilities, roads, waste-disposal sites, factories, even new products can use risk analysis to address environmental concerns during planning stages, when changes are most easily made. The process also allows people to rank environmental problems and allocate attention, resources, and corrective efforts.

Risk analyses are made by both scholars and government decision makers. Scientists are interested in a thorough understanding of the way ecosystems function, but decision makers need quick and efficient tools for making choices.

Scholarly approaches take many forms: Synoptic surveys assess the characteristics of stressed and unstressed natural systems. Experiments determine how the whole or one part of an ecosystem (such as fish) will respond to stress. Extrapolations apply specific observations to other ecosystems, **chemicals**, or properties of interest by analyzing dose-response curves, establishing relationships between the molecular structure of a chemical and its likely environmental effects, or simulation of entire ecosystems on a computer. Using these tools, scientists can also measure change in ecosystems and translate the results for the general public.

A less precise method, often used by public officials and other nonscientists, is called ecosystem **risk assessment**. It uses available toxicological, ecological, geological, geographical, chemical, and sociological information to estimate possible damage. The process has three steps:

(1) The problem is identified. For example: could nutrient **runoff** from local agriculture affect **commercial fishing** on a nearby lake?

(2) Available scientific information is gathered to predict both the level of stress that could result and the likely ecosystem response. Where do the nutrients go and how are organisms exposed to them? How do increasing **nutrient** levels affect biological systems, especially fish?

(3) Risk is quantified by comparing exposure and effects data. If the predicted stress level is lower than those known to cause serious damage, risk is low. On the other hand, if the predicted stress is higher, risk is high.

Despite the reams of data available, there is never enough information about the possible effects of any stress. An assessment based squarely on facts is more reliable than one that uses scarce, preliminary information. Anyone charged with making decisions must weigh all options.

The possibility of an undesirable occurrence, the seriousness of the consequences, and the uncertainty involved in any prediction all factor into the estimate. Alternative actions and their risks and benefits must also be considered, and the consistency of the action balanced with other societal goals. An action's risks and benefits are often not distributed evenly in society. For example, people sharing the **water table** with a proposed **landfill** may shoulder more risk, while those who use many nonrecyclable consumer products may benefit disproportionately. Who benefits and who loses can also affect decisions.

Risk predictions are similar to weather forecasts—they are based on careful observation and are useful, but they are far from perfect. They indicate useful precautions—whether these involve carrying an umbrella or treating waste before it enters the water. They help us understand ecosystems and allow us to consider the environment before potentially harmful action is taken. If ecological risks are considered when decisions are being made, ecosystems on which people depend can be protected. *See also* Environmental policy; Environmental stress; Greenhouse effect; Industrial waste treatment; Sewage treatment; Solid waste

[*John Cairns, Jr. and B. R. Neiderlehner*]

FURTHER READING

Bartell, S. M., R. H. Gardner, and R. V. O'Neill. *Ecological Risk Estimation.* Chelsea, MI: Lewis Publishers, 1992.

Cairns, J., Jr., K. L. Dickson, and A. W. Maki, eds. *Estimating the Hazard of Chemical Substances to Aquatic Life, STP 657.* Philadelphia: American Society for Testing and Materials, 1978.

Ehrlich, P. R., and A. H. Ehrlich. *Healing the Planet: Strategies for Solving the Environmental Crisis.* New York: Addison-Wesley Publishing, 1992.

National Research Council. *Risk Assessment in the Federal Government: Managing the Process.* Washington, DC: National Academy Press, 1983.

Norton, S. B., et al. "A Framework for Ecological Risk Assessment at the EPA." *Environmental Toxicology and Chemistry* 11-12 (1992): 1663-672.

Risk assessment (public health)

Risk assessment refers to the process by which the short and long-term adverse consequences to individuals or groups in a particular area resulting from the use of specific technology, chemical substance, or natural hazard is determined. Generally, quantitative methods are used to predict the number of affected individuals, morbidity or mortality, or other outcome measures of adverse consequences. Many risk assessments have been completed over the last two decades to predict human and ecological impacts with the intent of aiding policy and regulatory decisions. Well-known examples of risk assessments include evaluating potential effects of **herbicide**s and insecticides, **nuclear power** plants, incinerators, **dams** (including dam failures), **automobile** pollution, **tobacco** smoking, and such natural catastrophes as **volcano**es, earthquakes, and hurricanes. Risk assessment studies often consider financial and economic factors as well.

Human Health Risk Assessments

Human health risk assessments for chemical substances that are suspected or known to have toxic or carcinogenic effects is one critical and especially controversial subset of risk assessments. These health risk assessments study small populations that have been exposed to the chemical in question. Health effects are then extrapolated to predict health impacts in large populations or to the general public who may be exposed to lower concentrations of the same chemical.

One mathematical formula that determines an individual's risk from chemical exposures is:

$$\text{Risk} = \frac{(emissions) \times (transport) \times}{(loss\ factor) \times (exposure\ period) \times} \\ (uptake) \times (toxicity\ factor).$$

For the case of a **hazardous waste** incinerator, **emission**s might be average smoke **stack emissions** of gas; the transport term represents dilution in the air from the stack to the community; the loss factor might represent chemical degradation of reactive contaminants as stack gases are transported in the **atmosphere**; the exposure period is the number of hours that the community is downwind of the incinerator; uptake is the amount of contaminants absorbed into the lung (a function of breathing rate and other factors); and toxicity is the chemical potency. Multiplying these factors indicates the probability of a specific adverse health impact caused by contaminants from the incinerator. In typical applications, such models give the incremental lifetime risk of **cancer** or other health hazards in the range of one in a million (equivalent to 0.000001). Cancers currently cause about one-third of deaths, thus, a one in a million probability represents a tiny increase in the total cancer incidence. However, calculated risks can vary over a large range—0.001 to 0.00000001.

While the same equation is used for all individuals, some assumptions regarding uptake and toxicity might be modified for certain individuals such as pregnant women, children, or individuals who are routinely exposed to the **chemicals**. In some cases, monitoring might be used to verify exposure levels. The equation illustrates the complexity of the risk assessment process.

Risk Assessment Process

The risk assessment/management procedure consists of five steps: (1) *Hazard assessment* seeks to identify causative agent(s). Simply put, is the substance toxic and are people exposed to it? The hazard assessment demonstrates the link between human actions and adverse effects. Often, hazard assessment involves a chain of events. For example, the release of **pesticide** may cause soil and ground **water pollution**. Drinking contaminated **groundwater** from the site or skin contact with contaminated **soil**s may therefore result in adverse health effects. (2) *Dose-response relationships* describe the toxicity of a chemical using models based on human studies (including clinical and epidemiologic approaches) and animal studies. Many studies have indicated a threshold or "no-effect" level, that is, an exposure level where no adverse effects are observed in test populations. Some health impacts may be reversible once the chemical is removed. In the case of potential **carcinogen**s, linear models are used almost exclusively. Risk or potency factors are usually set using animal data, such as experiments with mice exposed to varying levels of the chemical. With a linear dose-response model, a doubling of exposure would double the predicted risk. (3) *Exposure assessment* identifies the exposed population, detailing the level, duration, and frequency of exposure. Exposure *pathways* of the chemical include ingestion, inhalation, and dermal contact. Human and technological defenses against exposure must be considered. For example, respirators and other protective equipment reduce workplace exposures. In the case of prospective risk assessments for facilities that are not yet constructed—for example, a proposed hazardous waste incinerator—the exposure assessment uses mathematical models to predict emissions and distribution of contaminants around the site. Probably the largest effort in the risk assessment process is in estimating exposures. (4) *Risk characterization* determines the overall risk, preferably including quantification of uncertainty. In essence, the factors listed in the equation are multiplied for each chemical and for each affected population. To arrive at the total risk, risks from different exposure pathways and for different chemicals are added. Populations with the maximum risk are identified. To gauge their significance, results are compared to other environmental and societal risks. These four steps constitute the scientific component of risk assessment. (5) *Risk management* is the final decision-making step. It encompasses the administrative, political, and economic actions taken to decide if and how a particular societal risk is to be reduced to a certain level and at what cost. Risk management in the United States is often an adversarial process involving complicated and often conflicting testimony by expert witnesses. In recent years, a number of disputes have been resolved by mediation.

Risk Management and Risk Reduction

Options that result from the risk management step include performing no action, product labeling, and placing regulations and bans. Examples of product labeling include warning labels for consumer products, such as those on tobacco products and cigarette advertising, and Material Safety Data Sheets (MSDS) for chemicals in the workplace. Regulations might be used to set maximum permissible levels of chemicals in the air and water (e.g., air and water quality criteria is set by the U.S. **Environmental Protection Agency**). In the workplace, maximum exposures known as Threshold Limit Values (TLVs) have been set by the U.S. **Occupational Safety and Health Administration**. Such regulations have been established for hundreds of chemicals. Governments have banned the production of only a few materials, including **DDT** and **PCB**s, and product liability concerns have largely eliminated sales of some pesticides such as Paraquat and most uses of **asbestos**.

A variety of social and political factors influence the outcome of the risk assessment/management process. Options to reduce risk, like banning a particular pesticide that is a suspected carcinogen, may decrease productivity, profits, and jobs. Furthermore, agricultural losses due to insects or other pests if pesticide is banned might increase malnutrition and death in subsistence economies. In general, risk assessments are most useful when used in a relative or comparative fashion, weighing the benefits of alternative chemicals or agricultural practices to another. Risk management decisions must consider what degree of risk is acceptable, whether it is a voluntary or involuntary risk, and the public's perception of the risk. A risk level of one in a million is generally considered an acceptable lifetime risk by many federal and state regulatory agencies. This risk level is mathematically equivalent to a decreased life expectancy of 40 minutes for an individual with an average expected lifetime of 74 years. By comparison, the 40,000 traffic fatalities annually in the United States represent over a 1 percent lifetime chance of dying in a wreck—10,000 times higher than acceptable for a chemical hazard. The discrepancy between what an individual accepts for a chemical hazard in comparison to risks associated with personal choices like driving or smoking might indicate a need for more effective communication about risk management.

Risk assessments are often controversial. Scientific studies and conclusions about risk factors have been questioned. For example, animals are often used to determine dose-response and exposure relationships. Results from these studies are then applied to humans, sometimes without accounting for physiological differences. The scientific ability to accurately predict absolute risks is also poor. The accuracy of predictions might be no better than a factor of ten, thus 10 to 1,000 cancers or other health hazard might be experienced. The uncertainty might be even higher, a factor of 100, for example. Risks due to multiple factors are considered independent and additive. For instance, smoking and asbestos exposure together have been shown to greatly increase health risks than exposure to one factor alone. Conversely, multiple chemicals might inhibit or cancel risks. In nearly all cases, these factors cannot be modeled with our present knowledge. Finally, assessments often use a worst-case scenario, for example, the complete failure of a **pollution control** system, rather than a more modest but common failure like operator error.

Ecological Risk Assessment

Ecological risk assessments are similar to human health risk assessments but they estimate the severity and extent of ecological effects associated with an exposure to an **anthropogenic** agent or a perturbational change. Again, the risk estimate is stated in probability terms that reflect the degree of certainty. Ecological assessments tend to be more complex than human health assessments since a variety of dynamic ecological communities or systems may be involved, and these systems have important but often poorly understood interactions and feedback loops. In addition the current status and health of ecological systems must be defined by measurements and analysis before an assessment can begin. In some cases, animal **species** or **ecosystem**s may be more sensitive than humans. Contingency or hazard assessment resembles that made for human health but focuses on low probability events such as failure of dams, nuclear power plants, and industrial facilities that have the potential for significant public health and welfare damage. Finally, risk reduction approaches have been suggested that shift focus from end-of-pipe controls, for instance, pollution control equipment, to preventing **pollution** in the first place by minimizing waste and **recycling**.

[*Stuart Batterman*]

FURTHER READING

Chemical Risk: A Primer. Washington, DC: American Chemical Society, 1984.

Naugle, D. F., and T. K. Pierson. "A Framework for Risk Characterization of Environmental Pollutants." *Journal of the Air and Waste Management Association* 4 (1992): 1298-1307.

U.S. Environmental Protection Agency. *Integrated Risk Information System Background Document*. Washington, DC: U. S. Government Printing Office, 1991.

Risk assessors

Risk assessors endeavor to define a risk that will be realized under actual or anticipated conditions by establishing the "average truth" from numerous probabilities. Assessing risk based on conclusions drawn from an infinite number of integrations cannot be expressed in terms of "safe" or "nontoxic." Such expressions imply that a chemical or an event (e.g., accident) is without risk or harm, which may be misleading. Instead a chemical or an event is ranked as minor, moderate, or high to reflect the degree of risk that it represents within a given set of parameters. Such is the role of the risk assessor to calculate the effects of variables while classifying the uncertainties and presenting risk managers with a list of choices.

Comprehending the number of variables and uncertainties associated with an event can be explored in the following example. If one were to assess the number of deaths from **cancer** following a lifetime exposure to a chemical contained in drinking water, one must examine a diverse array of interlocking factors, such as the composition of the chemical, the chemical's observable effects on animals and/or **environment**, and whether the reported dose-exposure rates are applicable to humans. Likewise, if one were to examine the amount of chemical which can remain in the **soil** and not create **groundwater** contamination following a chemical spill, factors such as the following should be examined: the composition of the spilled chemical, its specific gravity, solubility, and viscosity; the soil's composition, **pH**, precipitation and infiltration rates; and hydrologic setting, the depth to the **water table** and its vertical and horizontal flow.

In addition to these factors, one must also take into account underlying uncertainties in data acquisition. For example, health databases and findings are typically derived from experimental or laboratory animal tests on a specific chemical or in connection with unrelated human studies. Therefore predictions from these studies may not be applicable to human subjects.

Sometimes lifestyle choices can also play a role in risk assessment. In addition to the chemical that a person is exposed to, other factors—such as smoking or exposure to another chemical substance—can have additive, accumulative, or antagonistic effects. Such anomalies require supplemental research, such as mathematical modeling.

Mathematical modeling mirrors the processes and interrelationships of real-life systems. The mathematical content of a model may extend to different equations or to simple look-up tables; its purpose is to reflect the required outcome of interest. For example, a health model frequently employed by the **Environmental Protection Agency (EPA)** is a Linearized Multistage Model because it yields the most conservative risk estimates when exposure occurs in very low doses. While ecological modeling is still in its infancy (because it involves outcomes at numerous levels from a single **species** to communities of organisms), models, nonetheless, provide valuable information to risk assessors.

[*George M. Fell*]

River basins

Recognition of the river as the dominant force in forming basins may be traced back to John Playfair in 1802. In contrast to the leading opinions, Playfair observed that rivers were proportional to valley size and tributaries were accordant, neither of which would be likely unless rivers had created the basins, rather than the other way around. Now known as Playfair's law, his observation has led to extensive efforts to quantify river basin characteristics.

In 1945, R. E. Horton developed the concept of stream order, and Arthur Strahler further elaborated on the subject. The smallest tributaries are labeled "1," and when two first order streams converge, they form a second order stream ("2"), and so forth. The ratio of lower order to higher order streams remains remarkably consistent throughout a given basin. Uniformity is the important factor in all of these because it demonstrates that drainage network characteristics are quantitatively consistent.

Renowned geomorphologist William Morris Davis, noted in *Water, Earth, and Man* (1969) that "the river is like the veins of a leaf; broadly viewed, it is like the entire leaf." There is, however, one critical difference. In the leaf, the flow of water and **nutrient**s is primarily from larger to smaller veins. However, in river basins all matter, good and bad, flows downstream. That is why when urban water systems use rivers, their intakes are located upstream and drainage outlets downstream. **Groundwater** pollution follows this same downward pathway, though at a far slower pace; it is one of our most serious problems.

The river basin, as part of the **hydrologic cycle**, is increasingly a technological and social system. For the United States, an estimated 10 percent of the national wealth is devoted to structures involving the movement of water, including **dams**, **irrigation** systems, water supply networks, and sewers, with increasingly sophisticated controls.

The importance of river basins is well illustrated by the **Tennessee Valley Authority** (TVA) project. Launched by the Roosevelt Administration in 1933, it was a massive economic and social effort aimed at the chronic problems of depleted **soil**s, rampant soil **erosion**, recurrent **flooding**, and economic desolation. Industrial demand for electricity has subsequently grown so large that hydroelectric power, the initial source, now supplies less than 20 percent of TVA demand. *See also* Environmental economics; Sewage treatment; Topography

[*Nathan H. Meleen*]

FURTHER READING

Chorley, R. J., ed. *Water, Earth, and Man: A Synthesis of Hydrology, Geomorphology, and Socio-economic Geography.* London: Methuen, 1969.

Gore, J. A., ed. *The Restoration of Rivers and Streams.* Boston: Butterworth, 1985.

Morisawa, M. *Streams: Their Dynamics and Morphology.* New York: McGraw-Hill, 1968.

Petulla, J. M. *American Environmental History: The Exploitation and Conservation of Natural Resources.* San Francisco: Boyd & Fraser, 1977.

River blindness

River blindness is a disease responsible for a high incidence of partial or total blindness in parts of tropical Africa and Central America. Also called *onchocerciasis*, the disease is caused by infection with *Onchocerca volvulus*, a thread-shaped round worm (a nematode), which is transmitted between people by the biting blackfly *Simulium*. The larvae of *Onchocerca* develop into the infective stage, called *L4*, inside the blackfly and are introduced into humans by the bite of an infected blackfly.

Adult *Onchocerca* (2.5 feet or 0.76 m in length) develop in the connective tissue under the skin of humans. The adult worms lie coiled within subcutaneous nodules several inches in diameter. The nodules are painless and cause little damage, but can be cosmetically unattractive; fortunately, they are easily removed by simple surgery. The more serious health problems associated with onchocerciasis are caused by the release of masses of early-stage larvae, known as *microfilaria*, into the host's connective tissue under the skin. The mobile larvae spread throughout the body, including the surface tissues of the eyes. It is the burrowing activities of these larvae that cause the symptoms associated with onchocerciasis—either severe *dermatitis* or blindness. Onchocerciasis can now be treated with drugs such as ivermectin, which kill the larvae, but the blindness is usually permanent.

Avoiding blackfly bites with protective clothing and skin repellents is not a practical control measure on a large scale. The major method of prevention of onchocerciasis in humans is the control of the blackfly intermediate hosts and vectors. The larvae and pupae of blackfly are strictly aquatic and are found only in fast-running water. In Kenya, the larval stages of *S. neavei* have been killed by releasing **DDT** into streams where the blackflies breed and evolve. However, the waterways must be treated frequently to prevent the reestablishment of blackfly populations, and there have been serious questions raised over the safety of DDT. In West Africa, *S. damnosum* is more difficult to control, since the adults can fly over considerable distances, and can easily reinfect cleared sites from up to 60 miles (97 km) away.

Onchocerciasis has long been socially debilitating in an 11-country area of West Africa where both the flies and **parasites** are abundant. Here, more than one-fifth of all males over the age of 30 may be blind, turning productive people into long-term dependents. The presence of the disease often results in the **migration** of people away from rivers to higher ground, which they then clear for cultivation. Clearing vegetation in Africa frequently results in soil **ero-**

A victim of river blindness is led through a sugar plantation in his village at Banfora, Burkina Faso (formerly Upper Volta).

sion and the formation of gullies that channel water during heavy rains. The moving water allows blackflies to breed, spreading the disease to the new area. The reappearance of river blindness results in still further human migration, until large areas of badly eroded land are left unpopulated and unproductive, and entire villages are abandoned. The disease has now been brought largely under control by a World Health Organization program begun in 1974, in which 63 million acres (25 million hectares) of land have been made safe for resettlement.

[*Neil Cumberlidge*]

FURTHER READING

Bullock, W. A. *People, Parasites, and Pestilence. An introduction to the Natural History of Infectious Disease.* Minnesota: Burgess Publishing Company, 1982.

Crosskey, R. W. *The Natural History of Blackflies.* New York: John Wiley and Sons, 1990.

Markell, E. K., M. Voge, and D. T. John. *Medical Parasitology.* 7th ed. Philadelphia: Saunders, 1992.

Rodger, F. C., ed. *Onchocerciasis in Zaire: a New Approach to the Problem of River Blindness.* New York: Pergamon Press, 1977.

Rivers

See **Amazon Basin; Colorado River; Cuyahoga River; Hudson River; River basins; Wild river**

RNA (ribonucleic acid)

RNA (ribonucleic acid) exists as a polymer constructed of four kinds of nucleotides. Ribonucleic acids are ordinarily involved in the conversion of genetic information from **DNA** into protein: information flows from the genetic material via RNA for the fabrication of an organism. Ribosomes are cytoplasmic particles structured of protein and ribosomal RNA (rRNA) and are the sites of protein synthesis. Messenger RNA (mRNA), transcribed from genomic DNA, translocates genetic information to the ribosomes. In addition, there are about 20 transfer RNAs (tRNA), which bind to specific amino acids and to particular regions of mRNA for the assembly of amino acids into proteins. The genetic material of some viruses is RNA. *See also* Nucleic acid

Road salt

See **Salt (road)**

Rocky Flats nuclear plant (near Denver, CO)

The production of **nuclear weapons** inherently poses serious risks to the **environment**. At any point in the production process, radioactive materials may escape into the surrounding air and water, and safe methods for the disposal of waste from the manufacturing process still have not been developed. The environmental risks posed by the production of nuclear weapons are illustrated by the history of the Rocky Flats Nuclear Munitions Plant, located 16 miles (26 km) northwest of Denver, Colorado.

Rocky Flats was built in 1952, following an extensive search for sites at which to build plants for the processing of **plutonium** metal, a critical raw material used in the production of nuclear weapons. Authorities wanted a location that was close enough to a large city to attract scientists, but far enough away to ensure the safety of city residents.

Another important factor in site selection was wind measurements. The government wanted to be sure that, in the event of an accident, radioactive gases would not be blown over heavily populated areas. The selection of Rocky Flats was justified on the basis of wind measurements made at Denver's Stapleton airport, showing that prevailing winds blow from the south in that area. Had the same studies been carried out at Rocky Flats itself, however, they would have shown that prevailing winds come from the northwest, and any release of radioactive gases would be carried not away from Denver but toward it.

Over the next four decades, this unfortunate mistake was to have serious consequences as spills, leaks, fires, and other accidents became routine at Rocky Flats. On September 11, 1957, for example, the filters on glove boxes caught fire and burned for 13 hours. These filters were used to prevent plutonium dust on used gloves from escaping into the outside air, but once the fire began this is exactly what happened. The release of plutonium was even accelerated when workers turned on exhaust fans to clear the plant of smoke. Smokestack monitors showed levels of plutonium 16,000 times greater than the maximum recommended level. Officials at Rocky Flats reportedly made no effort to notify local authorities or residents about the accidental release of the radioactive gases.

This incident reflects the contradiction between the commitment of the United States government to the development of nuclear weapons and its concern for protecting the health of its citizens, as well as the natural environment. In 1992, a government report on Rocky Flats accused the **Department of Energy** (DOE) of resisting efforts by the **Environmental Protection Agency (EPA)** and state environmental agencies to make nuclear weapons plants comply with environmental laws and regulations. DOE officials defended this policy by saying that Rocky Flats was the only site in the United States at which plutonium triggers for nuclear weapons were being produced.

The Rocky Flats plant was originally operated by Dow Chemical Company. In 1975, Rockwell International Corporation replaced Dow as manager of the plant. Over the next 14 years, Rockwell faced increasing criticism for its inattention to safety considerations both within the plant and in the surrounding area.

Rockwell's problems came to a head on a June morning in 1989, when a team of 75 FBI agents entered the plant and began searching the 6,550-acre (2,653-ha) complex for evidence of deliberate violations of environmental laws. As a result of the search, Rockwell was relieved of its contract at Rocky Flats and replaced by EG&G, Inc., an engineering firm based in Wellesley, Massachusetts. The ensuing investigation of safety violations lasted over two years and in March 1992 Rockwell plead guilty to 10 crimes, five of them felonies, involving intentional violations of environmental laws. The company agreed to pay $18.5 million in fines, the second largest fine for an environmental offense in United States history.

The fine did not, however, end the dispute over the safety record at Rocky Flats. Rockwell officials claimed that the Department of Energy was also at fault for the plant's poor environmental record. The company argued that the DOE had not only exempted them from environmental compliance but had even encouraged it to break environmental laws, especially **hazardous waste** laws. The federal grand jury that investigated the Rocky Flats case agreed with Rockwell. Not only was the DOE equally guilty, the grand jury decided, but the plant's new manager, EG&G, was continuing to violate environmental laws even as the case was being heard in Denver. Members of the jury were so angry about the way the case had been handled that they wrote President Bill Clinton, asking him to investigate the government's role at Rocky Flats.

Secretary of Energy James Watkins had closed Rocky Flats for repairs in November 1989 and it remained closed during the course of the investigation. Rocky Flat's problems appeared to be over in January 1992 when EG&G announced that, after spending $50 million in repairs, the plant was ready to re-open. Within a matter of days, however, Secretary Watkins ordered that weapons production at the plant permanently cease.

When Secretary Watkins made his decision to close Rocky Flats, the area faced two environmental challenges. In the first place, the site contained the largest stockpile of weapons grade plutonium in the United States, totaling more than 14 tons of the metal. The plutonium had been left in whatever form it occurred at the time of the plant shutdown, including water solutions, partially machined parts, and raw materials. The plutonium poses a threat because of its potential for starting fires, exposing workers to radiation, and threatening near-by communities in the event of an accident at the site.

In the second environmental challenge, buildings and facilities covering a 6,500 acre region had become seriously contaminated during the plant's 40-year lifetime. While a less serious short-term danger, this extensive contamination still poses a threat that could extend over centuries without some action to deal with it.

Agencies responsible for the future of Rocky Flats—primarily the EPA, the Colorado Department of Public Health and Environment, and the Defense Nuclear Facilities Safety Board—decided on a two-prong approach to the clean-up of Rocky Flats. The first step is to deal with the immediate threat of plutonium left behind on the site by finding safe ways of safely storing the material. This step involves activities such as draining tanks and pipes that have been used for plutonium-containing solutions; venting plutonium-containing waste drums and tanks of hydrogen gas that has built up within them; and re-packaging containers in which plutonium has been stored, making them safer for long-term storage. The cost of this operation in the site's first full year of clean-up was $573 million and employed an estimated 9,374 workers.

The second stage of the Rocky Flats clean-up operation will involve dealing with contamination that had developed on the site over its 40-year history. For this purpose, Rocky Flats was added to the National Priorities List for Superfund in 1989. Among the challenges to be solved in this clean-up are soil and groundwater that have been contaminated by the burial of nuclear materials, chemicals, spills, and other accidents. There are also tens of thousands of cubic yards of wastes produced while the plant was in operation that must now be shipped to some permanent storage area. The U.S. Department of Energy has estimated that the long-term phase of this clean-up could take 70 years and cost $23 billion. *See also* High-level radioactive waste; Nuclear fission; Nuclear fusion; Radiation exposure; Radiation sickness; Radioactive fallout; Radioactive pollution; Radioactive waste; Radioactivity; Savannah River nuclear plant

[*David E. Newton*]

FURTHER READING

Abas, B. "Rocky Flats: A Big Mistake from Day One." *Bulletin of the Atomic Scientists* 45 (December 1989): 19-24.

Pasternak, D. "A $200 Billion Scandal." *U.S. News & World Report* (14 December 1992): 34-37+.

Schneider, K. "U.S. Shares Blame in Abuses at A-Plant." *New York Times* (27 March 1992): A12.

"The Rocky Flats Cover-Up, Continued." *Harper's* (December 1992): 19-23.

Wald, M. L. "Rockwell To Plead Guilty and Pay Large Fine for Dumping Waste." *New York Times* (26 March 1992): A1.

———. "New Disclosures Over Bomb Plant." *New York Times* (22 November 1992): 23.

Rocky Mountain Arsenal, Colorado (RMA)

The Rocky Mountain Arsenal (RMA), a few miles northeast of Denver, was originally constructed and operated by the Chemical Corps of the United States Army. Beginning in 1942, the arsenal was the main site at which the Chemical Corps manufactured chemical weapons such as mustard gas, nerve gas, and phosgene. The Army eventually leased part of the 27 sq mi (70 sq km) plot of land to the Shell Oil Company which produced **DDT**, dieldrin, **chlordane**, parathion, aldrin, and other **pesticide**s at the site.

The presence of a chemical weapons plant has long been a source of concern for many Coloradans. In 1968, for example, a group of Denver-area residents complained that

nerve gas was being stored in an open pit directly beneath one of the flight paths into Denver's Stapleton International Airport.

Indeed, the Army was well aware of the hazard posed by its RMA products. In 1961, it found that wastes from manufacturing processes were seeping into the ground, contaminating **groundwater** and endangering crops in the area. The Army's solution was to institute a new method of waste disposal. In September 1961, engineers drilled a deep well 12,045 ft (3,654 m) into the earth. The lowest 75 ft (23 m) of the well was located in a highly fractured layer of rock. The Army's plan was to dump its chemical wastes into this deep well. The unexpressed principle seemed to be "out of sight, out of mind."

Fluids were first injected under pressure into the well on March 8, 1962, and pressure-injection continued over the next six months at the rate of 5.5 million gallons (21 million liters) per month. After a delay of about a year, wastes were once more injected at the rate of 2 million gallons (7.5 million liters) per month from August 1964 to February 1966. This practice was then terminated.

The reason for ending this method of waste disposal was the discovery that earthquakes had begun to occur in the Denver area at about the same time that the Army had started using its deep injection well. Seismologists found that the pattern of the earthquakes in the region between 1962 and 1966 closely matched the pattern of waste injection in the wells. When large volumes of wastes were injected into the well, many earthquakes occurred. When injection stopped, the number of earthquakes decreased. Scientists believe that the liquid wastes pumped into the injection well lubricated the joints between rock layers, making it easier for them to slide back and forth, creating earthquakes.

Earthquakes are hardly a new phenomenon for residents of Colorado. Situated high in the Rocky Mountains, they experience dozens each year although most are minor earthquakes. However, the suggestion that the Army's activity at RMA might be increasing the risk of earthquakes became a matter of great concern. The proximity of RMA to Denver raised the possibility of a major disaster in one of the West's largest metropolitan areas.

Faced with this possibility, the Army decided to stop using its injection well on February 20, 1966. Earthquakes continued to occur at an abnormally high rate, however, for at least another five years. Scientists hope that liquids in the well will eventually diffuse through the earth, reducing the risk of further major earthquakes.

In 1992 Congress announced plans to convert the arsenal to a wildlife refuge. The land around RMA had been so badly poisoned that humans essentially abandoned the area for many years. The absence of humans, however, made it possible for a number of **species** of **wildlife** to flourish.

On October 16, 1996, the U.S. Army announced its plans for the clean-up of the Rocky Mountain Arsenal. That plan dealt with three areas of environmental concern: water, structures, and soil. The Army declared its intent to continue its program of treating water supplies and groundwater on the site and to provide safe drinking water to neighboring off-site communities. It outlined plans to demolish all existing buildings for which no future use had been designated. These buildings along with all other contaminated materials were scheduled for disposal in new on-site capped landfills.

The most extensive clean-up efforts were to be focused on soil that had been contaminated by activities at the Arsenal. Any unexploded weapons were scheduled for removal and off-site detonation. Contaminated soils and other materials were to be buried in new waste landfills. These landfills were designed to consist of leak-proof barriers with 6 in (15 cm) concrete barrier caps and underground barrier walls to protect wildlife from their contents. Existing trenches and sewers are to be surrounded by barrier walls, covered with concrete barrier caps, and/or plugged with concrete caps, all to protect wildlife from their contents.

In addition to these physical plans, the Army announced plans for three other on-going activities at the Arsenal: (1) the discontinuation of any additional hazardous waste disposal activities at the Arsenal; (2) on-going medical monitoring at adjacent communities during the period of clean-up; and (3) monitoring and control of emissions and odors from the site during clean-up.

Clean-up activities at RMA are being directed by the U.S. Army under the supervision of the Environmental Protection Agency. The Shell Chemical Company is also participating in the study of environmental problems at RMA and in efforts to deal with those problems. Until the clean-up process has been completed, the former RMA site is being managed as a wildlife refuge by the U.S. Department of the Interior's Fish and Wildlife Service. At the conclusion of the process, the refuge will become a National Wildlife Refuge.

[*David E. Newton*]

FURTHER READING

Breen, B. "From Superfund Site to Wildlife Refuge." *Garbage* 4 (May-June 1992): 22.

Gascoyne, S. "From Toxic Site to Wildlife Refuge; If Approved an Ambitious Plan Would Transform a Former Chemical-Weapons Arsenal near Denver." *The Christian Science Monitor* (12 September 1991): 10.

Healy, J. H., et al. "The Denver Earthquakes." *Science* 161 (27 September 1968): 1301-10.

Rocky Mountain Institute (Old Snowmass, Colorado)

Founded by energy analysts Hunter and **Amory Lovins** in 1982, the Rocky Mountain Institute (RMI) is a nonprofit research and education center dedicated to the **conservation** of energy and other resources worldwide. According to literature published by the Institute, the Lovinses founded

RMI with the intention of fostering "the efficient and sustainable use of resources as a path to global security." RMI targets seven main areas for reform: energy, water, agriculture, transportation, economic renewal, green development, and global security.

RMI's energy and water programs attempt to promote energy efficiency and the use of **renewable resources**. The programs take an "end-use/least-cost" approach, promoting awareness of which activities require energy, how much and what types of energy those activities require, and the cheapest way that energy can be supplied. E Source, a subsidiary of the energy program, serves as a clearinghouse for technological information on energy efficiency.

The agriculture program at RMI focuses on several conservation-based methods, including low-input, organic and alternative-crop farming, efficient **irrigation**, local and direct marketing, and the raising of extra-lean and range beef. The program is closely linked to RMI's water project.

RMI's transportation program is based on the belief that "inefficient transportation systems shape and misshape our world." The project seeks an end to a transportation-based society and a start to one that is access-based, emphasizing superefficient vehicles and a decrease in the necessity to travel over mobility.

RMI's economic renewal program seeks to create lasting economic bases in rural areas. The project works on a grassroots level and has been tested in four towns. Through workshops and workbooks based on studies of several towns, RMI hopes to promote energy use based on sustainability in the future rather than industrialism in the present.

In the area of green development, RMI is involved in cost-effective innovative construction and energy planning for new towns. RMI has conducted efficiency studies for a new building and has acted as consultants on a prototype store for a major retailer as part of this project.

The global security program is more scholarship- and theory-oriented than RMI's other projects and is based on the concept that innovation in the other six areas—energy, water, agriculture, economic renewal, transportation, and green development—will lead to new ways of thinking with regards to global security. Through scholarly exchange and analysis of security practice around the world, the staff at RMI hope to help develop a post-Cold War, cooperative approach to global security that is less reliant on military strength.

RMI's technologically advanced, energy efficient facility that houses their headquarters features a semi-tropical bioshelter among other showcases of conservation innovations. The facility stands as a visible monument to RMI's commitment to conserving the world's resources.

Hunter and Amory Lovins have received several awards for their work with the Institute, including a Mitchell Prize in 1982, a Right Livelihood award in 1983, and the Onassis Foundation's first Delphi Prize in 1989. The Delphi Prize is considered one of the top two environmental awards in the world. Contact: Rocky Mountain Institute, 1739 Snowmass Creek Road, Old Snowmass, CO 81654-9199.

[*Kristin Palm*]

Rodale Institute (Emmaus, Pennsylvania)

The Rodale Institute developed out of the efforts begun by J. I. Rodale to promote **organic gardening and farming** in the 1930s. The notion of **recycling** organic matter back into the **soil** to yield healthier and more productive crops was not widely accepted at that time, so in 1942, Rodale began publishing *Organic Gardening and Farming* magazine.

From those simple beginnings, Rodale's mission grew to become a multi-faceted organization dedicated to "improving human health through regenerative farming and organic gardening." Today, the Rodale Institute supports and publishes research to further organic farming, facilitates farming networks, engages in international farming programs, and publishes numerous resources for gardeners and organic farmers.

The Rodale Institute Research Center is a 333-acre farm in Kutztown, Pennsylvania, where organic horticulture and **sustainable agriculture** techniques are tested. The Rodale staff focuses on farming projects that help enrich and protect the world's **natural resources**. Of particular importance to the institute's gardeners are the flower, fruit, vegetable, and herb gardens that are maintained at the Research Center. Practices that are employed in these gardens include the use of beneficial insects and cover crops to reduce reliance on chemical **pesticides**.

Another goal of the institute is to facilitate communication between farmers and urban dwellers. This is especially important as urban communities continue to expand into the countryside. The Rodale Institute sponsors programs to help these two seemingly competing groups work together for mutual benefit. For example, Rodale has initiated a community **composting** program whereby the grass cuttings and leaves from urban areas are collected and delivered to farms, where they are composted and used to enrich the soil. This program decreases the need for **landfill** space and provides soil-enriching organic matter to farmers. Rodale Institute also encourages mutual understanding between farmers and city dwellers by hosting such events as Field Days and GardenFest.

The Rodale Institute's networking program helps farmers link up with one another to share information on sustainable farming. These farms participate in Rodale Institute's research and often experiment with alternatives to conventional farming methods. Through the publication *The New Farm*, the cooperational farmers share their experiences and questions with many farmers across the country.

Rodale has recently established cooperative programs with several universities around the world to further their research. Among those universities are Pennsylvania State University, Cornell University, Michigan State University, University of Padova (Italy), Northeast Forestry University (China), South China Environmental Institute, Jiangsu Academy of Agricultural Sciences (China), and the Institute for Land Improvement and Grassland Farming (Poland).

Rodale Institute's programs extend to international farmers as well. With sights set on developing long-term, preventative measures against **famine** and poverty, the institute has established programs in Africa and South America. The African program is based in Senegal and brings together farmers, villages, government agencies, and other organizations to work toward famine prevention through **conservation** and soil quality improvement. In South America, Rodale works with Guatemalan farmers to encourage sustainable farming and help preserve the disappearing forest regions. This particular program combines modern knowledge with traditional Mayan farming techniques to produce high quality yields from healthy soil.

Perhaps to the non-farmer, Rodale is best known for its publications. In addition to *Organic Gardening* and *The New Farm* magazines, Rodale publishes a large selection of instructional books for farmers, gardeners, and others interested in organic farming. Contact: Rodale Institute, 222 Main Street, Emmaus, PA 18049.

[*Linda Ross*]

Rodenticide
See **Pesticide**

Rolston, Holmes (1932-)
American environmental and religious philosopher

Rolston has devoted his distinguished career to plausibly and meaningfully interpreting the natural world from a philosophical perspective and is regarded as one of the world's leading scholars on the philosophical, scientific, and religious conceptions of **nature**. His early work on values in nature, as well as his role as a founder of the influential academic journal *Environmental Ethics*, was critical not only in establishing but also in shaping and defining the modern field of environmental philosophy.

In his 1988 book *Environmental Ethics: Values in and Duties to the Natural World*, Rolston presented a philosophically sophisticated and defensible case for a value-centered ecological ethic, one which derives ethical conclusions from descriptive premises. Rolston clearly states that **intrinsic value**s objectively exist at the **species**, **biotic community**, and individual levels in nature and that these values impose on humans certain direct obligations to nonhuman entities, such as species and **ecosystem**s. These obligations are separate from and sometimes in conflict with those based on the instrumental value of nature, which may motivate humans to protect the **environment** for their own benefit.

Rolston is one of the most prolific writers and sought-after speakers in the field today. His work is unusually accessible to a wide audience, and he has pioneered the application of ethical theory to actual environmental problems by consulting with two dozen **conservation** and policy groups, including the United States Congress and a Presidential Commission.

Rolston came to prominence in this field in a roundabout way. Born in the Shenandoah Valley of Virginia, he

Holmes Rolston.

studied physics as an undergraduate at Davidson College before entering theological seminary. After completing his Ph.D. in theology and religious studies at the University of Edinburgh in Scotland, Rolston spent nearly a decade as a Presbyterian pastor in rural southwest Virginia. During this time, Rolston's love for and curiosity about nature and **wilderness** grew unabated. He fed his love of these things by learning the natural history of his surroundings in splendid detail and by becoming an activist on local environmental issues. In his search for a philosophy of nature to complement his biology, Rolston entered the philosophy program at the University of Pittsburgh, where he received a master's degree in philosophy of science in 1968. He then embarked on an academic career at Colorado State University, where he currently holds the prestigious position of University Distinguished Professor.

The major theoretical innovations of Rolston's work include the reconceptualization of ethical extensionism to accommodate intrinsic value at all levels of nature, a task for which the ordinary methods and vocabulary of traditional ethics proved inadequate. The result is a biologically-based account of natural values which is hierarchical but nonanthropocentric. He has thus established himself as the foremost proponent and defender of intrinsic natural value theory.

Rolston is often identified as the father of **environmental ethics** as a modern academic discipline. As such, he occupies a singular place of importance in modern philosophy. Rolston continues to integrate the practical and theoretical dimensions of his work, as he examines life to discover its meaning and expands the circle of moral significance to include all natural entities, processes, and systems. In addi-

tion to *Environmental Ethics*, Rolston has written several other critically acclaimed books, including *Philosophy Gone Wild*, *Science and Religion: A Critical Survey*, and *Conserving Natural Value*, and has contributed to dozen other books and professional and popular periodicals. Rolston is also an avid backpacker, accomplished field naturalist, and respected bryologist. *See also* Ecology; Environmental attitudes/values; Environmental education

[*Ann S. Causey*]

FURTHER READING

Rolston, Holmes. *Environmental Ethics: Duties to and Values in the Natural World.* Philadelphia: Temple University Press, 1988.

———. *Philosophy Gone Wild: Environmental Ethics.* Buffalo, NY: Prometheus Books, 1989.

———. *Science and Religion: A Critical Survey.* Philadelphia: Temple University Press, 1987.

———. "Values Deep in the Woods." *American Forests* 94 (May-June 1988): 33-7.

Roosevelt, Theodore (1858-1919)

American politician and conservationist

Historians often cite **conservation** of **natural resources** as Theodore Roosevelt's most enduring contribution to the country. As the nation's twenty-sixth President, Roosevelt was faced with critical conservation issues and made decisive moves to promote conservation, thus becoming the national leader most clearly associated with preservation of public land.

Roosevelt was born into a wealthy family in New York City, and early took an interest in the outdoors, partly to compensate for asthma and a frail constitution. He was an avid naturalist as a child, an early interest that lasted all his life and, as Paul R. Cutright documents in detail in his *Theodore Roosevelt: The Making of a Conservationist*, Roosevelt, was instrumental in creating a role model for conservationists. Certainly, much of his attention to conservation derived at least in part from his interest in the natural science that underlay those issues.

He was, for example, a life-long bird watcher and relished the fact that he could match **John Burroughs**'s prowess at identifing birds on a field walk with the naturalist-writer. Roosevelt's interest in the natural history of birds and other animals provided much of the motivation for two long and perilous trips taken after his presidency to South America and Africa, trips that compromised his health and may have shortened his life.

From a very young age, Roosevelt was also a politician. At the age of 23, he was elected to the New York State Assembly in 1881. Always contradictory, the young Roosevelt was conservative and pro-establishment but was also a reformer, anticorruption and anti-machine politics.

As governor of New York (1898-1900), Roosevelt defined and tried to act on conservation issues. In 1900, **Gifford Pinchot** helped Roosevelt formulate his message to

Theodore Roosevelt

the New York State Assembly about the need for **forest management**. The Governor also tried to outlaw the use of bird feathers for adornment. Historians claim that his actions so alarmed the Assembly that he was "manipulated" out of the governor's mansion into the Vice-Presidency, from there he became President after William McKinley's assassination.

Roosevelt's contribution to conservation can be divided into four categories: first, his role in setting aside and managing what are now called **national forest**s; second, his decisive initiation of a **national wildlife refuge** system; third, his impact on transforming the **arid** lands of the American West into irrigated farmland; and, fourth, his efforts to promote natural resources nation-wide.

Roosevelt is best known for his collaboration with Pinchot in appropriating public forest lands once controlled by private interests and "reserving" them for "our people unborn." Congress passed the Forest Reserve Act (authorizing the Presidents to create forest reserves from the public domain) in 1891, well before Roosevelt took office. The three Presidents immediately before him established forest reserves of some 50 million acres (20.3 million ha). Roosevelt publicized the value of forest reserves to the people; and reorganized management of the reserves, placing them under the Bureau of Forestry (later the Forest Service) in the Department of Agriculture. Increased the acreage in reserves—by 150 million acres (60.8 million ha), 16 million (6.5 million ha) of which were set aside almost overnight in a famous and successful action in 1907 by which he and Pinchot worked long hours to create the reserves before the President had to sign a congressional act with a rider limiting his powers to do so.

All of these actions remain controversial today. The Forest Service's timber management policies are still being criticized for catering to special interests, and not realizing Roosevelt's goal to preserve the forests for the people, not powerful private interests.

The story of Pelican Island illustrates perhaps better than any other incident in Roosevelt's administration his approach to conservation issues. Visited by naturalist friends alarmed at the decimation of birds on Florida's Pelican Island, Roosevelt asked if the law prevented him from declaring the island "a Federal Bird Reservation." Told that no such law existed, the President responded, "Very well, then I so declare it." During his tenure, Roosevelt created 50 additional wildlife refuges. His enthusiastic initiation of these preserves provided a base for the extensive national wildlife refuge system.

Roosevelt entered the Presidency with the idea that the western drylands could become productive through irrigation. He realized, however, that the scale of such projects prohibited private enterprise from undertaking the task. One of his first initiatives was to work with congressmen representing western states to pass the Reclamation Act of 1902. Sixteen projects were soon initiated in those states. Reclamation from Roosevelt's point of view—especially large dams—are considered a mixed blessing by many conservationists today.

Roosevelt, was a natural publicist and, along with Pinchot and **John Muir**, he provided an extraordinary legacy to the American people of a variety of lands and resources in public ownership. Roosevelt used the Presidency's "bully pulpit" effectively to arouse public interest in conservation issues. Harold Pinket argues that Roosevelt's main contribution to the conservation movement was "wielding his presidential prestige to craft a coalition of people with otherwise opposed perspectives on natural resources, from naturalists and civic leaders who favored preservation to utilitarian resource specialists and users." No accomplishment illustrates this better than the Governor's Conference of 1907. At this conference Roosevelt bought all the nation's governors and many other leaders together and, using his own enthusiasm for conservation, he ignited discussions, policies and actions that resonate still today at many levels of government.

Roosevelt's concern for conservation was reflected in his message to Congress, delivered two months after becoming President. It contained strong references to all the relevant issues of the time—preservation and use of forests, **soil** and water conservation, **wildlife** protection, **recreation**, and **reclamation** of **arid** lands. He is still recognized for his leadership on these areas.

In addition to his concern for conservation issues Roosevelt was a widely published author. Many readers can still be entertained by vivid accounts of hunting trips in the west or his life as a rancher in the Dakotas.

Most environmentalists pay strong tribute to Roosevelt's accomplishments as a conservationist and his contributions to the conservation movement. However, he is not universally admired. Some view Roosevelt as an elitist while other criticize what some consider his excessive slaughter as a hunter. Cutright defends Roosevelt, arguing "it was only after Roosevelt put the full force of his power as President behind the conservation program that it got off the ground." Theodore Roosevelt's energy and bluster, his cultivation of well-known naturalists and conservationists, his willingness to listen to and act on their advice, his political skills in getting policies enacted—all those endure in a lasting legacy of national forests, a national wildlife refuge system, a strengthened **national park** system, and increased and on-going awareness of the importance of protecting these for **future generations**. His words still ring true today, that "any nation which...lives only for the day, reaps without sowing, and consumes without husbanding, must expect the penalty of the prodigal." A very verbal leader, Roosevelt often had the last word: "For the people...must always include the people unborn as well as the people now alive, or the democratic ideal is not realized."

[*Gerald L. Young*]

FURTHER READING

Brooks, P. "A Naturalist in the White House." In *Speaking for Nature.* Boston: Houghton Mifflin, 1980.

Cutright, P. R. *Theodore Roosevelt: The Making of a Conservationist.* Champaign: University of Illinois Press, 1985.

Ponder, S. "Publicity in the Interest of the Public: Theodore Roosevelt's Conservation Crusade." *Presidential Studies Quarterly* 20 (Summer 1990): 547-555.

Roszak, Theodore (1933-)

American social critic

Perhaps most prominently associated with the counterculture movement in the 1960s, Roszak was born in 1933. He received his B.A. from the University of California at Los Angeles in 1955 and a Ph.D. from Princeton University in 1958. Roszak began his career as an instructor in history at Stanford University and is currently professor of history at California State University, Hayward. He received a Guggenheim fellowship in 1971.

Like his mentor Lewis Mumford, Roszak combines political and cultural criticism with a thoroughgoing critique of technology and technological society. Published in 1969, his first book was an effort to understand the counterculture movement. In *The Making of a Counterculture: Reflections on the Technocratic Society and its Youthful Opposition*, Roszak criticizes consumer society, the military-industrial complex it supports, the increasing concentration of populations in unclean, unsafe, and ungovernable cities, and the technocratic and bureaucratic mentality that views such dilemmas as essentially technical problems with technical or scientific solutions. Roszak is highly critical of this rationalist point-of-view and argues that modern society should attempt to recover and return to a sense of the sacred and mysterious dimensions of human life.

In 1972, Roszak published *Where the Wasteland Ends: Politics and Transcendence in Post-Industrial Society.* Here, he offers an outline of what he terms a "visionary commonwealth," an alternative society that would check or eliminate the destructive tendencies of modern technocratic civilization. The commonwealth he describes is decentralized and small in scale. Politics is participatory, technology is appropriate and intermediate, and there is widespread experimentation with different forms of social, economic, and political organization. Roszak believes that resettling populations into such small-scale, economically self-sufficient, and politically self-governing communities cannot happen quickly. However, he contends that such a shift will happen and he argues that it should happen, if humans are to live spiritually rich and meaningful lives. Roszak maintains that the possibilities for this utopia are present as "springs" within the technocratic wasteland, waiting to be discovered and used to transform this spiritual desert into a humanly habitable garden of earthly delights. It is he says, "more humanly beautiful to risk failure in searching for the hidden springs than to resign to the futurelessness of the wasteland."

Published in 1978, *Person/Planet* expands on Roszak's vision of the future of humanity and continues his critique of modern society. Roszak argues that industrial society is disintegrating in a way that, he maintains, is creative. Large, complex institutions, including government itself, are failing to attract the loyalty and allegiance they need to maintain their authority, and Roszak believes their disintegration will make his utopian commonwealth possible. For him, the needs of the individual and the needs of the planet are identical. Both flourish in an atmosphere of authenticity, diversity, and respect, and he argues that these are things that large industrial institutions, with their emphasis on uniformity, linearity, and wastefulness, can neither comprehend nor tolerate.

Roszak has been criticized for his romanticism and his utopianism. His attacks on science and rationalism, in particular, have been frequently condemned as vague and imprecise, and he has been accused of confusing the methodology of science with the failings of the people who employ it. However, many admire Roszak not only for his passionate prose but also for his vision of human possibilities, and his books are still frequently consulted for their images of people living reverently and responsibly in harmony with the earth. *See also* Bioregionalism; Environmental ethics; Environmentalism; Green politics

[*Terence Ball*]

FURTHER READING

Roszak, Theodore. *The Making of a Counterculture: Reflections on the Technocratic Society and its Youthful Opposition.* Garden City, NY: Doubleday, 1969.

———. *Person/Planet: The Creative Disintegration of Industrial Society.* Garden City, NY: Anchor Press/Doubleday, 1978.

———. *The Voice of the Earth.* New York: Simon & Schuster, 1992.

———. *Where the Wasteland Ends: Politics and Transcendence in Postindustrial Society.* New York: Doubleday, 1972.

Rowland, Frank Sherwood (1927-)

American chemist

Frank Sherwood "Sherry" Rowland was born in the central Ohio city of Delaware. After a brief period of service in the United States Navy, he attended Ohio Wesleyan University where he earned his bachelor's degree in chemistry in 1948. He balanced his semi-professional baseball career with his studies and continued his education in chemistry, earning master's and doctorate degrees at the University of Chicago in 1951 and 1952, respectively. Fresh out of school, Rowland pursued a career in education and research. He taught chemistry at Princeton University from 1952 to 1956 and the University of Kansas between 1963 and 1964.

Rowland has conducted research in many areas of the chemical and radiochemical fields. In 1971, for example, to calm an alarmed public, Rowland and a team of scientists investigated the seemingly high levels of **mercury** being found in tuna and swordfish. They tested the tissues of museum exhibit, century-old fish and found the levels of the dangerous substance were in about the same range as those recently pulled from the water, and therefore proved the fish were not a health threat. In addition to this type of testing, he completed work for such organizations as the International Atomic Energy Administration and the United States **Atomic Energy Commission**. Rowland is probably best known, however, for his work in atmospheric and chemical kinetics and especially his investigations of **chlorofluorocarbons (CFCs)**.

Inert and versatile compounds, CFCs were most often found in items like cooling devices and aerosol cans; CFCs are also found throughout the **atmosphere**. The inherent dangers of CFCs were unknown until Rowland teamed up with University of California associate **Mario J. Molina** in 1973 and found that certain atoms of those CFCs present in the atmosphere were combining with the **ozone**, causing rapid depletion of the protective ozone layer itself. Such destruction could result in drastic climatic changes, as well as increased atmospheric penetration by the sun's rays (causing a huge upswing of the occurrence of skin **cancer**).

Initially, Rowland's and Molina's theory was not readily accepted. In recent years however, the theory has come be accepted as an unpleasant fact; the importance of CFC elimination has been realized. Major industries are taking steps to address the CFC problem. Du Pont for example, a major developer and manufacturer of CFCs, has pledged to reduce its production of the compounds. Forty-seven nations have agreed to decrease their CFC production by 50 percent by the end of 1998.

Rowland is currently the chemistry department chairman at the University of California at Irvine, where he has been a faculty member since 1964. He maintains membership in numerous organizations, among them: the Ozone Commission of the International Association of Meteorological and Atmospheric Physics; Committee of Atmospheric Chemical and Global Pollution; and various committees of the United States National Academy of Science. *See also* Ozone layer depletion

[*Kimberley A. Peterson*]

FURTHER READING

Edelson, E. "The Man Who Knew Too Much." *Popular Science* 234 (January 1989): 60-65, 102.

Moreau, D. "Change Agents." *Changing Times* (January 1990): 99.

Rowland, F. S. "Chlorofluorocarbons and the Depletion of Stratospheric Ozone." *American Scientist* 77 (1989): 36-45.

Ruckleshaus, William (1934-)

Environmental Protection Agency administrator

Ruckleshaus is known as a lawyer, a loyal member of the Republican party, and a skilled administrator who has been able to work effectively with **environment**alists as well as industry representatives. His reputation also bespeaks his integrity in law enforcement and his ability to withstand pressure. However, Ruckleshaus is best known on the national level for his service as administrator of the **Environmental Protection Agency (EPA)** from 1970 to 1973 and again from 1983 to 1984.

Ruckleshaus was born on July 24, 1934 in Indianapolis, Indiana, into a renowned Republican family. He earned his bachelor of arts degree *cum laude* from Princeton University in 1957 and his law degree from Harvard University in 1960. His early career in the 1960s included the practice of law between 1960 and 1968 and service in the Indiana House of Representatives from 1967 to 1969. In 1969 he was appointed Assistant Attorney General for the United States by the newly elected President Richard Nixon. In 1970, President Nixon selected Ruckleshaus to become the first head of the recently created EPA. Under his direction, 15 environmental programs were brought together under the agency. Ruckleshaus left the EPA in 1973 to serve as acting director of the Federal Bureau of Investigation (FBI), and later that year, he was appointed Deputy Attorney General for the United States. In 1974 he resigned from that position rather than comply with President Richard Nixon's order to dismiss the special Watergate prosecutor.

From 1974 to 1976 he practiced law with the firm Ruckelshaus, Beveridge, Fairbanks and Diamond, in Washington, D.C. Ruckleshaus has been criticized for going through the "revolving door" of government. While at his law firm he was the legal representative of several companies that contested rules made by the EPA while he was its administrator. From 1975 to 1983 he was Senior Vice-President for Legal Affairs of the Weyerhaeuser Company, Tacoma, Washington, a large timber and wood products company.

Ruckleshaus was again called to head the Environmental Protection Agency in 1983. Early in 1983 the EPA came under criticism from the public and from Congress regarding allegations of mishandling of the federal Superfund program. Allegations included lax enforcement against polluters, mishandling of Superfund monies, manipulation of the Superfund for political purposes, and conflicts of interest involving ties between EPA officials and regulated businesses. The allegations and the ensuing investigation led to the resignation of twenty-one top EPA officials including its administrator, Anne Burford Gorsuch.

Upon Gorsuch's resignation in March 1993, President Ronald Reagan asked Ruckleshaus to serve as interim EPA administrator. He agreed to do so, serving until the appointment of his successor **Lee Thomas** in November of 1984. During this second period of service as the EPA's top administrator, Ruckleshaus used his experience, his skills as an administrator, and ability to work with industry and environmentalists to stabilize the EPA. He succeeded in quelling much of the criticism being leveled against the agency.

After leaving the EPA at the end of 1985, Ruckleshaus joined the firm Perkins Coie in Seattle, Washington. He has served on the boards of directors of several major corporations and on the board of advisors for the Wharton School of Business, University of Pennsylvania.

In 1989 he was named chairperson of Browning-Ferris Industries, Inc. (BFI) and, as of 1997, he continues to hold that position. BFI is the world's second largest waste management firm after WMX Technologies (Waste Management, Inc.) and owns and operates substantial hazardous and non-hazardous **waste**-disposal fascilities throughout the states. When Ruckleshaus took over as chairperson, BFI had been cited in various lawsuits related to its operations. BFI has been making steady progress since 1989 in obtaining required permits. Two major lawsuits against BFI were also settled under Ruckleshaus leadership in 1996. The U.S. Justice Department's antiturst division had alleged that BFI and WMX had used long-term contracts to keep competition out of certain states. Thus, over the past eight years, Ruckleshaus has been gaining substantial experience as the leader of a major waste disposal business.

In 1995, the Environmental Law Institiute (ELI) honored Ruckleshaus on the 25th anniversary of the U.S. EPA by presenting him with the 1995 ELI award. The ELI presents its award annually to a lifelong leader in environmental protection who represents the highest ideals of service.

For information about the ELI Award, contact Environmental Law Institute, 1616 9th Street NW, Ste. 200. Washington, DC 20036.

[*Paulette L. Stenzel*]

FURTHER READING

Ivey, M. "Can Bill Ruckelshaus Clean Up Browning-Ferris' Act?" *Business Week* (14 October 1991): 46.

King, Seth S. "Return of First E.P.A. Chief." *New York Times Biographical Service* (March 1983): 372.

"EPA: Ruckleshaus Bows Out." *Newsweek* (10 December 1984): 39.

"Government's Pollution Fighter." *New York Times* (12 April 1973): 22.

Simon, R. "Mr. Clean's New Mess." *Forbes* 146 (26 November 1990): 166-67.

Runoff

The amount of rainfall or snowmelt that either flows over the **soil** surface or that drains from the soil and enters a body of water, thereby leaving a **watershed**. This water is the excess amount of precipitation that is not held in the soil nor is it evaporated or transpired back to the **atmosphere**. Water that reaches deep **groundwater** and does not, therefore, directly flow into a surface body of water is usually not considered runoff. Runoff can follow many pathways on its journey to streams, rivers, lakes, and oceans. Water that primarily flows over the soil surface is surface runoff. It travels more quickly to bodies of water than water that flows through the soil, called subsurface flow. As a rule, the greater the proportion of surface to subsurface flow, the greater the chance of **flooding**. Likewise, the greater the amount of surface runoff, the greater the potential for soil **erosion**. *See also* Storm runoff

S

Safe Drinking Water Act (1974)

The Safe Drinking Water Act (SDWA, 1974) extended coverage of federal drinking water standards to all public water supplies. Previous standards, established by the United States Public Health Service beginning in 1914 and administered by the United States **Environmental Protection Agency (EPA)** since its creation in 1970, had legally applied only to water supplies serving interstate carriers (e.g., planes, ships, and rail cars engaged in interstate commerce), although many states and municipalities complied with them on a voluntary basis. Public water supplies were defined by the SDWA as publicly or privately owned community water supplies having at least fifteen connections or serving at least twenty-five year-round customers or non-community water supplies serving at least twenty-five non-residents for at least sixty days per year.

The SDWA required the EPA to promulgate primary drinking water regulations to protect public health and secondary drinking water regulations to protect aesthetic and economic qualities of the water. The EPA was granted authority to regulate: 1) contaminants which may affect health (e.g, trace levels of carcinogenic **chemicals** which may or may not have an impact on human health); 2) compounds which react during water treatment to form contaminants; 3) classes of compounds (if more convenient than regulating individual compounds); and 4) treatment techniques, when it is not feasible to regulate individual contaminants (e.g, disinfection is required in lieu of standards on individual disease-causing microorganisms).

Recognizing the right and the responsibility of the states to oversee the safety of their own drinking water supplies, the SDWA authorized the EPA to grant primacy to states willing to accept primary responsibility for administering their own drinking water program. To obtain primacy, a state must develop a drinking water program meeting minimum federal requirements and must establish and enforce primary regulations at least as stringent as those promulgated by EPA. States with primacy are encouraged to enforce the federal secondary drinking water regulations, but are not required to do so.

Other provisions of the SDWA authorized control of underground injection (e.g., waste disposal wells); required special protection of sole-source **aquifer**s (those providing the only source of drinking water in a given area); authorized

funds for research on drinking water treatment; required the EPA to conduct a rural water supply survey to investigate the quality of drinking water in rural areas; allocated funds to subsidize up to seventy-five percent of the cost of enlarging state drinking water programs; required utilities to publicly notify their customers when the primary regulations are violated; permitted citizens to file suit against the EPA or a state having primacy; and granted the EPA emergency powers to protect public health.

Dissatisfied with the slow pace at which new regulations were being promulgated by the EPA, which had in 1983 initiated a process to revise the primary and secondary standards, Congress amended the SDWA in 1986. The 1986 amendments required EPA: to set primary standards for nine contaminants within one year, forty more within two years, thirty-four more within three years, and twenty-five more by 1991; to specify criteria for **filtration** of surface water supplies and disinfection of **groundwater** supplies; to require large public water systems to monitor for the presence of certain unregulated contaminants; to establish programs to demonstrate how to protect sole-source aquifers; to require the states to develop well-head protection programs; and to issue, within eighteen months, rules regarding injection of waste below a water source.

The 1986 SDWA amendments also prohibited the use of **lead** solder, flux, and pipe; authorized the EPA to treat Indian tribes as states, making them eligible for primacy and grant assistance; required the EPA to conduct a survey of drinking water quality on Indian lands; authorized the EPA to initiate enforcement action if a state fails to take appropriate action within thirty days; and increased both civil and criminal penalties for failure to comply with the SDWA.

Since 1986 was a Congressional election year and every member of Congress wanted to go on record as having voted for safe drinking water, the amendments passed unanimously. The members of Congress also recognized that it would be unwise to raise taxes during an election year, so the 1986 amendments failed to provide federal funds to assist state programs in complying with the many new provisions of the SDWA. The average annual cost per state to comply with the SDWA by the year 1995 has been estimated to be nearly $500 million.

The cost of complying with the SDWA amendments poses a difficult problem for many states. Maintaining primacy will require a substantial increase in taxes, which is not likely to be popular with most voters; but giving up primacy will likely result in even higher taxes, since it is thought that the EPA will simply impose special tax assessments on utilities in states not having primacy. Of even greater concern to many state health department administrators is that federal legislation is dictating state funding priorities. The expenditure of such large sums of money on state drinking water programs, which have served the public extremely well throughout most of this century, may cause an overall decline in public health protection because less money will be available to address other (and perhaps more important) public health problems. Some states are negotiating with the EPA in an effort to reduce the cost of compliance or to delay implementation of certain provisions of the SDWA until adequate funding can be secured. *See also* Drinking water supply; Water quality; Water quality standards; Wells

[*Stephen J. Randtke*]

FURTHER READING

Calabrese, E. J., et al., eds. *Safe Drinking Water Act: Amendments, Regulations, Standards.* Chelsea, MI: Lewis, 1989.

Clean Water Deskbook. Rev. ed. Washington, DC: Environmental Law Institute, 1991.

Legislative History of the Safe Drinking Water Act Amendments, 1983-1992. Washington, DC: U. S. Government Printing Office, 1993.

Sagebrush Rebellion

A political movement in certain western states during the late 1970s, sparked by passage of the **Federal Land Policy and Management Act** in 1976. The federal government owns an average of 60 percent of the land in the twelve states that include the Rockies or lie west of them. Cattlemen, miners, loggers, developers, farmers, and others argued not only that federal ownership had an adverse impact on the economy of their states, but that it violated the principle of states' rights. This group demanded that the federal government transfer control over large amounts of this land to individual states, insisting on their right to make their own decisions about the management of both the land itself and the **natural resources**. The rebellion was defused after the election of Ronald Reagan in 1980. He appointed **James Watt**, who had been a leader of this movement, as Secretary of the Interior, and oversaw the institution of the so-called "good neighbor" policy for the management of federal lands. *See also* Wise use movement

Sahel

A 3,000-mile (5,000 km) band of semi-arid country extending across Africa south of the Sahara desert, the Sahel zone ("the shore" in Arabic) passes through Mauritania, Senegal, Mali, Burkina Faso, Niger, Chad, and the Cape Verde Islands. Similar semi-arid conditions prevail in Sudan, Ethiopia, and Somalia. These countries are among the poorest in the world. The low annual rainfall in this region is variable (4-20 in or 10-50 cm) and falls in a short, intense period in July and August. In some years the rains fail to develop, and **drought**s are a common occurrence. The uncertain rainfall of the Sahel makes it generally unfavorable for agriculture.

For centuries, the indigenous nomadic Tuareg people used the Sahel in a sustainable way, constantly moving herds of camels from one grazing area to the next; they practiced little agriculture. In the nineteenth and twentieth centuries, following European colonization, herds of water-dependent, non-native cattle were introduced, which were poorly suited to the **arid** conditions of the region. The above average rainfall of the 1950s and 1960s attracted large numbers of farmers and pastoralists into the Sahel, which placed new stresses on this fragile **ecosystem**. A series of droughts of the 1970s and 1980s in the Sahel resulted in episodes of large-scale starvation.

Studies of long-term climate patterns show that while droughts have been common in the Sahel for at least 2,500 years, the droughts of recent years have increased in frequency and duration. Records also show that the annual rainfall has decreased and that the sands of the Sahara have shifted some 60 miles (100 km) south into the region.

The causes of these changes have been linked to the expanding human settlement of the Sahel, with consequent increased demands on the area to produce more food and more firewood. These demands were met by increases in domestic animal herds and by more intensive agriculture. This in turn led to drastic reductions in vegetation cover. Land was cleared for farming and human settlements, vegetation was overgrazed, and large numbers of trees were cut for firewood. In this way, the natural vegetation of the Sahel (sparse, coarse grasses interspersed with thorn trees and shrubs) was dramatically altered and the ecosystem degraded.

Less vegetation cover meant more **soil erosion** and less groundwater recharge as heavy seasonal rainstorms hit exposed ground, carrying away valuable **topsoil** in flash floods. Less vegetation also meant more soil erosion from wind and rain, as there were fewer root systems to bind the soil together. In addition, fewer plants meant that less water was released into the air from their leaves to form rain-making clouds. The net result of these processes was the trend towards less annual rainfall, more soil erosion, and **desertification**. Other reasons for **famine** and desertification in the Sahel include political events (such as prolonged civil wars) and social changes (such as the breakdown of the old sustainable tribal systems of using the land).

[*Neil Cumberlidge*]

FURTHER READING

Brown, L. R., ed. *State of the World 1986.* New York: Norton, 1986.

Gorse, J. E., and D. R. Steeds. *Desertification in the Sahelian and Sudanian Zones of West Africa.* Washington, DC: World Bank, 1987.

Myers, N., ed. *The Gaia Atlas of Planet Management.* London: Pan Books, 1985.

Southwick, C. H. *Global Ecology.* Sunderland, MA: Sinauer, 1985.

St. Lawrence Seaway

The St. Lawrence Seaway is a series of canals, locks, and lakes giving ocean-going ships of the Atlantic access to the **Great Lakes** and dozens of inland ports, including Toronto, Cleveland, Chicago, and Duluth. A herculean engineering project built jointly by the Canadian and United States governments, the St. Lawrence Seaway has become an essential trade outlet for the Midwest. It has also become an inlet for exotic and often harmful aquatic plants and animals, from which the landlocked Great Lakes were historically protected. The seaway's canals and locks, completed in 1959 after decades of planning and five years of round-the-clock construction, bypass such drops as Niagara Falls and allow over 6,000 ships to sail in and out of the Great Lakes every year.

The initial impetus for canal construction came from the steel industries of Ohio and Pennsylvania. During the first half of this century these industries relied on rich ore supplies from the Mesabi iron range in northern Minnesota. The end of this source was in sight by the 1930s; mining engineers pointed to remote but rich iron deposits in Labrador as next alternative. Lacking a cheap transport method from Labrador to the Midwest, steel industry backers began lobbying for the St. Lawrence Seaway. Midwestern grain traders and manufacturers joined the effort, promoting the route as a public works and jobs project, an economic booster for inland states and provinces, and a symbol of joint United States and Canadian cooperation, power, nationalism, and progress.

Unfortunately the seaway and its heavy traffic have also brought modern problems to the Great Lakes. Aside from the **petroleum** and chemical leaks associated with active shipping routes, the seaway opened the Great Lakes to aggressive foreign animal and plant invaders. The world's largest freshwater **ecosystem**, the Great Lakes had been isolated from external invasion by steep waterfalls and sheer distance until the canals and locks opened. Since the 1960s an increasing number of Atlantic, European, and Asian species have spread through the lakes. Some arrive under their own power, but most appear to have entered with ocean-going ships. Until recently, ships arriving at Great Lakes ports commonly carried freshwater ballast picked up in Europe or Asia. When the ships reached their Great Lakes destinations they discharged their ballast and loaded grain, ore, automobiles, and other goods. A profusion of **plankton** and larvae riding in the ballast water thus entered a new **environment**; some of them thrived and spread with alarming speed.

One of the first **introduced species** to make its mark was the lamprey (*Petromyzon marinus*), an 18-inch long (45.7-cm), eel-shaped Atlantic **species** that attaches itself to the side of a fish with its circular, suction-like mouth. Once attached, the lamprey uses its rasping teeth to feed on the fish's living tissue, usually killing its host. After the lamprey's arrival in the 1960s, Lake Superior's commercial whitefish and trout fisheries collapsed. Between 1970 and 1980 Great Lakes trout and salmon populations plummeted by 90 percent. The region's $2 billion a year sport fishery nearly disappeared with **commercial fishing**. Since the

1970s innovative control methods, chiefly carefully-timed chemical spraying on spawning grounds, have reduced lamprey populations, and native game fish have shown some recovery.

However, many other invaders have reached the Great Lakes via the seaway. Tubenose gobies (*Proterorhinus marmoratus*), a bottom-dwelling fish from the Black Sea, compete for food and spawning grounds with native perch and sculpins. The prolific North European ruffes (*Gymnocephalus cernuus*, a small perch) and spiny water flea (*Bythotrephes cederstroemi*, a tiny crustacean) also compete with native fish, and having hard, sharp spines, both are difficult for other species to eat. Asian invaders include the Asiatic clam (*Corbicula fluminea*), which colonizes and blocks industrial water outlets.

Most threatening to the region's businesses and economies is the **zebra mussel** (*Dreissena polymorpha*). Originating in the Baltic region, this tiny, extraordinarily prolific bivalve colonizes and suffocates industrial water pipes, docks, hard lake-bottom surfaces, and even the shells of native clams. Ironically, the zebra mussel has also benefitted the lakes by raising public awareness of exotic invasions. Alarmed industries and states, faced with the enormous cost of cleaning and replacing zebra mussel-clogged pipes and screens, have begun supporting laws forcing incoming ships to dump their ballast at sea. Although reversals of exotic invasions are probably impossible, such remedial control measures may help limit damages. *See also* Biofouling; Exotic species; Introduced species; Parasites; Water pollution

[*Mary Ann Cunningham*]

FURTHER READING

Cunningham, W. *Understanding Our Environment: An Introduction.* Dubuque, IA: William C. Brown, 1994.

Mabec, C. *The Seaway Story.* New York: Macmillan Co., 1961.

Raloff, J. "From Tough Ruffe to Quagga: Intimidating Invaders Alter the Earth's Largest Freshwater Ecosystem." *Science News* 142 (25 July 1992): 56-8.

St. Lawrence Seaway: 1991 Navigation Season. Ottawa: Saint Lawrence Seaway Authority.

Sale, Kirkpatrick (1937-)

American environmental writer

Kirkpatrick Sale is an influential environmental writer whose work has focused on the threat that a growing, resource-hungry population poses to the **environment**.

Sale was born in Ithaca, New York. His father was an English professor at Cornell University who was considered something of a campus rebel. Sale attended Swarthmore College for one year before transferring to Cornell in 1955, where he majored in history and edited the student newspaper. By the time he graduated in 1958, writing had become more important to him than history and he decided to pursue a career in journalism.

Sale first worked as an editor for the *New Leader*, an important leftist journal. During the early 1960s, he spent time in Africa, which he believed would become the center of world attention, and then worked briefly at the *New York*

Times Magazine. By 1968, he had given up journalism and begun a career as a freelance writer. His first book, *SDS*, dealt with the radical Vietnam-era organization, Students for a Democratic Society. Working on the book, Sale later said, "radicalized me in a way beyond where I'd been." After *SDS* was published in 1972, Sale began work on *Power Shift*, an analysis of shifting political themes in America, published in 1975.

Power Shift was published at the height of the environmental movement in the United States. Like many, Sale had grown concerned about the future of a world in which an ethic of continuous progress and development required the continued consumption of **natural resources** at a terrifying rate. *In Human Scale* (1980) and *Dwellers in the Land* (1985), Sale focused on a concept that he defined as **bioregionalism**. He used the term to describe an ethic of living within the limitations of the environment. Society, he believed, must be a part of nature; human ends and means must accommodate nature, not the reverse.

The approaching quincentennial celebration of Columbus' arrival in the New World gave Sale the inspiration for his next book. For more than four years, he immersed himself in rereading source documents about the discoverer and his voyages. He began to think about the ways in which the transplantation of European culture and environmental ethics had transformed the New World and contributed to the modern environmental crisis. The result of this work was *Conquest of Paradise: Christopher Columbus and the Columbian Legacy.* One conclusion Sale reached in this book was that the very cultures destroyed by the European invasion, those of the Native Americans, had practiced many of the environmental concepts to which modern societies must return if the world is to survive.

Although Sale has expressed interest in writing novels, his early books have been devoted to activist topics because "the world is in such a mess, and it needs writing about." He continues: "I write my books to help save society and the planet."

[*David E. Newton*]

FURTHER READING

Baker, J. F. "Kirkpatrick Sale." *Publishers Weekly* (October 19, 1990): 41-42.

Sale, K. *The Conquest of Paradise.* New York: Knopf, 1990.

———. *Dwellers in the Land: The Bioregional Vision.* San Francisco: Sierra Club Books, 1983.

———. *Human Scale.* New York: Coward, McCann & Geoghegan, 1980.

Saline soil

Soils containing enough soluble salts to interfere with the ability of plants to take up water. The conventional measurement that determines the **salinity** of soil is a *deciSiemens meter*; soils are considered saline if the conductivity of their saturation extract solution exceeds 4 deciSiemens meter-1. This unit of measure closely approximates the ionic salt concentration, and it is relatively easy to evaluate. The most common salts are composed of mixtures of sodium, calcium, and magnesium with chlorides, sulfates, and bicarbonates. Other less soluble salts of calcium sulfate and calcium and magnesium carbonate may be present as well. The **pH** is commonly less than 8.5.

In saline soils, there is often what is known as a perched **water table**—water close to the surface of the land. This phenomenon can be caused by restricting layers of fine clay within the soil, or by the application of waters at a rate greater than the natural permeability of the ground. When the water table is so close to the top of the soil, water is often transmitted to the surface where evaporation occurs, leaving the **ion**s in the water to precipitate as salts. The resulting complex of salts can be seen on the surface of the soil as a white, crust-like layer.

The surface layers of a saline soil commonly have very good soil structure, and this is important to understand if the soil is to be reclaimed or leached of the high salt concentrations. This kind of structure has relatively large pores; water can flow quickly through them, which aids in carrying away salty water, thus making it easier to flush out the soil. Artificial drains can also be installed beneath the surface to provide an outlet for water trapped within the soil, and once these drains are in place, salt concentrations can be further reduced by the application of good quality water.

Excessive **irrigation** and the use of **fertilizer**s and animal wastes can all increase the salinity of soil. The yields of common crops and the level of agricultural production are severely reduced in areas where salts have been allowed to accumulate in the soil. **Salinization** can be so severe in some cases that only salt-tolerant crops can be grown. **Leaching** is often necessary to reduce the levels of salt and keep the soil suitable for crop production. But this process can remove other soluble components from the soil and carry them into the **waste stream**, polluting both **groundwater** and surface water. The **environmental degradation** from this form of **agricultural pollution** can be extensive, and a method needs to be developed for leaching saline soils without these consequences. If this problem cannot be solved, it will no longer be possible to use some saline soils for agriculture. As **population growth** continues and the global demand for food increases, another approach might be the development of more salt-tolerant plant **species**.

[*Royce Lambert and Douglas Smith*]

FURTHER READING

Brady, N. C. *The Nature and Properties of Soils.* 10th ed. New York: Macmillan, 1990.

Millar, R. W., and R. L. Danahue. *Soils: An Introduction to Soils and Plant Growth.* 6th ed. Englewood Cliffs, NJ: Prentice-Hall, 1990.

Salinity

A salt is a compound of a metal with a nonmetal other than **hydrogen** or oxygen. NaCl (sodium chloride) or table salt is the best-known example. The solubility of various salts in water at a standard temperature is highly variable. When salts are dissolved in water, the result is called a saline solution, and the salinity of the solution is measured by its ability to carry an electrical current. Salinity of water is one of the components of **water quality**. Salinity is also measured in **soil**. Soil can become salinized from water containing sufficient salts, from the natural degradation of soil minerals, or from materials added to the soil such as **fertilizer**. Large amounts of water may be required to leach the accumulated salts from the root zone and prevent reduced plant growth or plant desiccation. *See also* Soil profile; Water quality standards

Salinization

An increase in salt content, usually of agricultural **soil**s, **irrigation** water, or drinking water is called salinization. Salinization is a problem because most food crops, like the human body, require fresh (nonsaline) water to survive. Although a variety of natural processes and human activities serve to raise the salt contents of soil and water, irrigation is the most widespread cause of salinization. Almost any natural water source carries some salts; with repeated applications these salts accumulate in the soil of irrigated fields. In **arid** regions, streams, lakes, and even **aquifer**s can have high salt concentrations. Farmers forced to use such saline water sources for irrigation further jeopardize the fertility of their fields. In coastal areas, field salinization also results when seawater floods or seeps into crop lands. This occurs when falling water tables allow sea water to seep inland under ground, or where aquifer subsidence causes land to settle. Salinization also affects water sources, especially in arid regions where evaporation results in concentrated salt levels in rivers and lakes. Remedies for salinization include the selection of salt-tolerant crops and flood irrigation, which washes accumulated salts away from fields but deposits them elsewhere.

Most of the world's people rely on irrigated agriculture for food supplies. Regular applications of water, either from rivers, lakes, or underground aquifers, allow grain crops, vegetables, and fruits to grow even in dry regions. California's rich Central Valley is an outstanding example of irrigation-dependent agriculture. One of North America's primary gardens, the valley is naturally dry and sun baked. Canals carrying water from distant mountains allow strawberries, tomatoes, and lettuce to grow almost year round. The cost of this miraculous productivity is a gradual accumulation of salts, which irrigation water carries onto the valley's fields from ancient sea bed sediments in the surrounding mountains. Without heavy flooding and washing, Central Valley soils would become salty and infertile within a few years. Some of California's soils have become salty and infertile despite flooding. Similar situations are extremely widespread and have been known since humankind's earliest efforts in agriculture. The collapse of early civilizations in Mesopotamia and the Indus Valley resulted in large part from salt accumulation, caused by irrigation, which made food supplies unreliable.

Salts are a group of mineral compounds, composed chiefly of sodium, calcium, magnesium, potassium, sulfur, **chlorine**, and a number of other elements that occur naturally in rocks, clays, and soil. The most familiar salts are sodium chloride (table salt) and calcium sulfate (gypsum). These and other salts dissolve easily in water, so they are highly mobile. When plenty of water is available to dilute salt concentrations in water or wash away salt from soil, these naturally occurring compounds have little impact. Where salt-laden water accumulates and evaporates in basins or on fields, it leaves behind increasing concentrations of salts.

Most crop plants exposed to highly saline environments have difficulty taking up water and **nutrient**s. Healthy plants wilt, even when soil moisture is high. Leaves produced in saline conditions are small, which limits the photosynthetic process. Fruits, when fruiting is successful, are also small and few. Seed production is poor, and plants are weak. With increasing salinity, crop damage increases, until plants cannot grow at all. Water begins to have a negative effect on some crops when it contains 250-500 **parts per million (ppm)** salts; highly saline water, sometimes used for irrigation out of necessity, may contain 2,000 to 5,000 ppm or more. For comparison, sea water has salt concentrations upwards of 32,000 ppm. In soil, noticeable effects appear when salinity reaches 0.2 percent; soil with 0.7 percent salt is unsuitable for agriculture.

Another cause of soil salinization is **subsidence**. When water is pumped from underground aquifers, pore spaces within rocks and sediments collapse. The land then compacts, or subsides, often lowering several meters from its previous level. Sometimes this compaction brings the land surface close to the surface of remaining groundwater. Capillary action pulls this groundwater incrementally toward the surface, where it evaporates, leaving the salts it carried behind in the soil. Near coastlines such processes can be especially severe. Seawater often seeps below the land surface, especially when fresh-water aquifers have been depleted. When seawater, with especially high salt concentrations, rises to the surface it evaporates, leaving crystalline salt in the soil.

In such cases, the salinization of the aquifer itself is also a serious problem. Many near-shore aquifers are threatened today by seawater invasions. Usually seawater invasions occur when farms and cities have extracted a substantial amount of the aquifer's water volume. Water pressure falls in the fresh-water aquifer until it no longer equals pressure from adjacent sea water. Sea water then invades the porous aquifer formation, introducing salts to formerly fresh water supplies.

Rivers are also subject to salinization. Both cities and farms that use river water return their **wastewater** to the river after use. Urban storm sewers and **sewage treatment** plants often send poor quality water back to rivers; drainage canals carry intensely saline **runoff** from irrigated fields back to the rivers that provided the water in the first place. When **dams** block rivers, especially in dry regions, millions of cubic meters of water can evaporate from reservoirs, further intensifying in-stream salt concentrations.

The **Colorado River** is one familiar example out of many rivers suffering from artificial salinization. The Colorado, running from Colorado through Utah and Arizona, used to empty into the Sea of Cortez south of California's

Imperial Valley before human activities began consuming the river's entire discharge. Farms and cities in adjacent states consume the river's water, adding salts in wastewater returned to the river. In addition, the Colorado's two huge **reservoir**s, Lake Powell and Lake Mead, lie in one of the continent's hottest and driest regions and lose about 10 percent of the river's annual flow through evaporation each year. By the time it reaches the Mexican border, the river contains 850 ppm salts, too much for most urban or agricultural uses. Following a suit from Mexico, the United States government has built a $350 million **desalinization** plant to restore the river's water quality before it leaves Arizona. The Colorado's story is, unfortunately a common one. Similar situations abound on major and minor rivers from the Nile to the Indus to the Danube.

Salinization occurs on every occupied continent. The world's most severely affected regions are those with arid climates and long histories of human occupation or recent introductions of intense agricultural activity. North America's Great Plains, the southwestern states, California, and much of Mexico are experiencing salinization. Pakistan and northwestern India have seen losses in agricultural productivity, as have western China and inland Asian states from Mongolia and Kazakhstan to Afghanistan. Iran and Iraq both suffer from salinization, and salinization has become widespread in Africa. Egypt's Nile valley, long northern Africa's most bountiful bread basket, also has rising salt levels because of irrigation and subsidence. One of the world's most notorious case histories of salinization occurs around the **Aral Sea**, in southern Russia. This inland basin, historically saline because it lacks an outlet to the sea, is fed by two rivers running from northern Afghanistan. Since the 1950s, large portions of these rivers' annual discharge has been diverted for cotton production. Consequently, the Aral Sea is steadily drying and shrinking, leaving great wastes of salty, dried sea bottom. Dust storms crossing these new **desert**s carry salts to both cotton and food crops hundreds of kilometers away.

Avoiding salinization is difficult. Where farmers have a great deal of capital to invest, as in California's Central Valley and other major agricultural regions of the United States, irrigators install a network of perforated pipes, known as tiles, below their fields. They then flood the fields with copious amounts of water. Flooding washes excess salts through the soil and into the tiles, which carry the hypersaline water away from the fields. This is an expensive method that wastes water and produces a toxic brine that must be disposed of elsewhere. Usually this brine enters natural rivers or lakes, which are then contaminated unless their volume is sufficient to once again dilute salts to harmless levels. However this method does protect fields. More efficient irrigation systems, with pipes that drip water just near plant roots themselves may be an effective alternative that contaminates minimal volumes of water.

Water can also be purified after agricultural or urban use. Purification, usually by reverse **osmosis**, is an expensive but effective means of removing salts from rivers. The best way to prevent water salinization is to avoid dumping urban or irrigation wastes into rivers and lakes. Equally important is

avoiding evaporation by reconsidering large dam and reservoir developments. Unfortunately, most societies are reluctant to consider these options: reservoirs are widely viewed as essential to national development, and wastewater purification is an expensive process that usually benefits someone else downstream.

Perhaps the best way to deal with salinization is to find or develop crop plants that flourish under saline conditions. Governments, scientists, and farmers around the world are working hard to develop this alternative. Many wild plants, especially those native to deserts or sea coasts, are naturally adapted to grow in salty soil and water. Most food plants on which we now depend—wheat, rice, vegetables, fruits—originate in nondesert, nonsaline environments. When domestic food plants are crossed with salt-tolerant wild plants, however, salt-tolerant domestics can result. This process was used to breed tomatoes that can bear fruit when watered with 70 percent seawater. Other vegetables and grains, including rice, barley, millet, asparagus, melons, onions, and cabbage, have produced such useful crossbreeds.

Equally important are innovative uses of plants that are naturally salt tolerant. Some salt-adapted plants already occupy a place in our diet—beets, dates, quinoa (an Andean grain), and others. Furthermore, careful allocation of land could help preserve remaining salt-free acreage. Planting salt-tolerant fodder and fiber crops in soil that is already saline can preserve better land for more delicate food crops, thus reducing pressure on prime lands and extending soil viability. *See also* Salinization of soils

[*Mary Ann Cunningham*]

FURTHER READING

Frenkel, H., and A. Meiri, eds. *Soil Salinity: Two Decades of Research in Irrigated Agriculture.* New York: Van Nostrand Reinhold, 1985.

National Research Council. *Saline Agriculture.* Washington, DC: National Research Council, 1990.

Scabocs, I. *Salt-Affected Soils.* Boca Raton, FL: CRC Press, 1989.

Shainberg, I., and J. Shalhevet. *Soil Salinity Under Irrigation.* Berlin: Springer-Verlag, 1984.

Salinization of soils

Salinization of **soil** involves the processes of salt accumulation in the upper rooting zone so that many plants are inhibited or prohibited from normal growth. Salinization occurs primarily in the semi-arid and **arid** portions of the earth. Salinization is commonly thought to occur only in the hot climatic regions, but may be found in cooler to cold portions of the earth where precipitation is very limited. Where the annual precipitation exceeds about 20 inches (500 mm), there is usually adequate downward movement of salts through **leaching** to prohibit the development of **saline soil**. Occasionally salinization of soil will occur where there has been an inundation of land by sea water. Some areas of the world were once under sea water, but due to uplift the land is now many meters above sea level. These lands are common sources of "ancient salts" and may lead to the development of saline waters as these soils are slowly leached.

Natural sources of salts in soil are primarily from the **decomposition** of rocks and minerals through the processes of chemical weathering. With adequate amounts of moisture present, hydrolysis, hydration, solution, oxidation and carbonation cause the minerals to decompose and release the ionic constituents to form various salts. The more common cations are sodium, calcium and magnesium with lesser amounts of potassium and boron. The common anions are chloride and sulfate with lesser amounts of bicarbonate, carbonate and occasionally nitrate.

Inherent factors of the landscape may also lead to salinization of soils. One of the more common factors is the restriction of water drainage within the soil, often referred to as soil permeability. Soil becomes less **permeable** because of genetic or inherited layers within the **soil profile** that have relatively high amounts of clay. Because of the extremely small sizes of the clay particles, the natural pore size is also very small, frequently being less than 0.0001 mm average diameter. The natural tortuosity and small size combine to severely reduce the rate of water movement downward which tends to increase salt buildup.

In addition, because of the soil pore size, saline waters may be transported upward through the processes of capillary action. While the rate of upward movement of water may be relatively slow, the process can deliver saline water from several inches below the surface of the land and create a zone of highly saline soil at the surface of the earth.

Salinization of soils has also occurred in areas where **irrigation** waters have been applied to lands that have not been subject to long-term natural leaching by rainfall. In several cases the application of relatively good quality water to arid soils with poor internal drainage has caused the soil to develop a higher **water table** which in turn has permitted the salts within the soil to be carried to the surface by high evaporation demand. In other cases water of relatively high salt content has been applied to soils without proper drainage, resulting in the development of saline soils. As the water is evaporated from the soil or the plant surfaces, the salts are left to accumulate in the soil.

Because of the increasing demand for food and fiber, many marginal lands are being brought into agronomic production. Proper irrigation management and drainage decisions must be considered on a worldwide and long-term basis to avoid a deleterious influence on the ability to produce on these soils and to determine the appropriate environmental considerations for disposal of salts from salinized soils. *See also* Arable land; Nitrates and nitrates; Runoff; Soil conservation; Soil eluviation; Soil illuviation

[*Royce Lambert*]

FURTHER READING

Foth, H. D. *Fundamentals of Soil Science.* 7th ed. New York: Wiley, 1984.

Richards, L. A., ed. *Diagnosis and Improvement of Saline and Alkali Soils.* USDA Handbook 60. Washington, DC: U.S. Government Printing Office, 1964.

Singer, M. J., and D. N. Munns. *Soils: An Introduction.* 2nd ed. New York: Macmillan, 1991.

Salmon

Salmon is a popular fish for food and sport fishing. Five **species** of salmon live in the North Pacific Ocean: Pink, Sockeye, Coho, Chum, and Chinook. One species, the Atlantic salmon, lives in the North Atlantic Ocean. The Pacific Coast salmon populations are being threatened with extirpation from much, if not all, of their range.

At the heart of the salmons' range, and perhaps indicative of the heart of its problems, is the Columbia River basin. Covering parts of seven states and two Canadian provinces, the Columbia River system contains over 100 dams, 56 of which are major structures, including 19 major generators of hydroelectric power. These structures present an insurmountable obstacle for these migrating fishes. Adult salmon, after growing and maturing in the ocean, return to the freshwater stream of their origin as they swim upstream to spawn. The adults will die shortly after this culmination of their arduous journey, and, after hatching, the young salmon—called smolts—swim downstream to the ocean to continue this life cycle.

About three-fourths of all of the population declines of salmon are directly attributable to hydroelectric dams. The dams simply do not allow a majority of individuals to successfully complete their **migration**, and many salmon die as they swim, or are swept, directly into the turbines. Fish ladders, or artificial sloping waterfalls, intended as an aid for fish to bypass the dams, enable some salmon to continue their journey, but many do not find their way through. As they move downstream, the smolts are slowed or stopped by the **reservoir**s created by the dams. Here they are exposed to larger populations of predators than in their natural riverine **habitat**. They are exposed to a wide variety of **pathogen**s as well as a physical environment of warmer, slow moving waters, to which they are only moderately tolerant. Only 20 percent of the downstream migrants ever make it to the Pacific. Poor **water quality** in many stretches of the Columbia River may also take its toll on the young smolts.

Overfishing, both offshore and along the rivers, adds to the losses within the salmon populations. Fishery biologists have attempted to offset these losses of native stocks by releasing hatchery-raised fish. The heartiness of these released fish is doubtful, as research indicates that less than half of them ever make it to the first dam.

A positive outlook for these ecologically, as well as economically, important salmon populations will depend on changes in attitudes and behavior of man as well as changes in the physical environment for these fishes. More water is needed downstream to aid migration. This would mean less water for man's activities, most noticeably for **irrigation**. Placing stricter limits of fish harvests will put pressure on commercial and sport fishermen, as well as the Native Americans of the Pacific northwest, all of whom feel they have a right to harvest these fish. Less hydrogeneration of electricity and protective structures around the dams may reduce losses of salmon, but this will force economic pressures on all of the residents of the region.

Realizing the need for a more balanced management plan for the Columbia River basin, Congress passed the Northwest Power Act in 1980. This act addresses many of the above mentioned problems and provides a framework to meet long-term energy needs as well as plans to rebuild and re-establish the Pacific coast's salmon populations.

[*Eugene C. Beckham*]

FURTHER READING

Daniel, J. "Dance of Denial." *Sierra* 78 (March-April 1993): 64-73.

Endangered Species: Past Actions Taken to Assist Columbia River Salmon. Gaithersburg, MD: U.S. General Accounting Office, 1992.

Kerasote, T. "Can We Save Our Salmon?" *Sports Afield* 209 (March 1993): 23-25.

Stuebner, S. "Ed Chaney: He Speaks for Salmon." *National Wildlife* 30 (October-November 1992): 34-36.

Salt, Henry S. (1851-1939)

English writer and reformer

Although he is probably best known as the vegetarian author of *Animals' Rights Considered in Relation to Social Progress* (1892), Henry Salt was a man with many roles—teacher, biographer, literary critic, and energetic advocate of causes he grouped under the title of humanitarianism. These included pacifism and socialism as well as **vegetarianism**, antivivisectionism, and other attempts to promote the welfare of animals. Late in his life, Salt also advocated efforts to conserve the beauties of **nature**, especially wildflowers and mountain districts.

Salt was born in India in 1851, the son of a colonel in the Royal Bengal Artillery. When his parents separated a year later, Salt's mother moved to England, and he spent much of his childhood at the home of her well-to-do parents. Educated at Eton and Cambridge, he embarked on an apparently comfortable career when he returned to Eton as an assistant master. While teaching at Eton, however, Salt met some of the leading radicals and reformers of the day, including William Morris, John Ruskin, and George Bernard Shaw, with whom he formed a lasting friendship. During this period Salt became a vegetarian. He also read **Henry David Thoreau**'s *Walden*, which inspired Salt and his wife to leave Eton and move to a country cottage in 1885 to lead a simple, self-sufficient life. For Salt, the simple life was far from dull. He became a prolific writer, although his efforts brought little financial profit. In addition to *Animals' Rights*, his works include a biography of Thoreau, studies of Shelley and Tennyson, a translation of Virgil's *Aeneid*, and an autobiography, *Seventy Years Among Savages* (1921), in which he examined English life as if he were an anthropologist studying a primitive tribe. Another book, *A Plea for Vegetarianism*, came to the attention of **Mohandas Gandhi** when he was a student in London. Gandhi, who was raised a vegetarian, later wrote in his *Autobiography* that Salt's book

made him "a vegetarian by choice." Salt apparently met Gandhi in 1891, then corresponded with him in 1929 during Gandhi's nonviolent struggle for the independence of India—a struggle inspired, in part, by Thoreau's essay, "Civil Disobedience."

Perhaps the best statement of Salt's views is the address he wrote to be read at his funeral. Declaring himself "a rationalist, socialist, pacifist, and humanitarian," Salt disavowed any belief "in the present established religion," but acknowledged "a very firm religious faith" in "a Creed of Kinship:" "a belief that in years yet to come there will be a recognition of the brotherhood between man and man, nation and nation, human and sub-human, which will transform a state of semi-savagery...into one of civilization, when there will be no such barbarity as warfare, or the robbery of the poor by the rich, or the ill-usage of the lower animals by mankind." *See also* Animal rights; Conservation

[*Richard K. Dagger*]

FURTHER READING

Hendrick, G., and W. Hendrick, eds. *The Savour of Salt: A Henry Salt Anthology.* Fontwell, Sussex: Centaur Press, 1989.

Jolma, D. J. "Henry Salt and 100 Years of Animal Rights." *The Animals' Agenda* (November-December 1992): 30-2.

Salt marsh
See **Wetlands**

Salt (road)

While several **chemicals** are available for deicing winter roads, common salt (NaCl) is most frequently used. Approximately 20 billion pounds of salt are used each year in the United States for treating ice and snow on roads. Calcium chloride ($CaCl_2$), potassium chloride (KCl), and urea are also available but used in smaller quantities. Common salt is preferred because it is cheaper per pound and more effective. While the price per pound of salt is cheap, about 1.5 billion dollars is spent per year on the enormous quantity used, and its distribution and application.

Salt in its solid form does not melt ice. It first must go into solution to form a brine, and the brine effects a melting of ice and snow. Ordinarily, snow is packed on the road surface by vehicular traffic; known as the "hard-pack," it forms a bond with the underlying pavement that is frequently impossible to remove with snowplows. Salt melts through the hard-pack and breaks the ice-pavement bonding. Traffic breaks the loosened ice, and snowplows are then able to remove the broken ice and packed snow. Deicing facilitates traffic movement after a snow fall and it is thought to make winter driving safer.

But there are hidden costs in the use of salt. It corrodes steel, and it is estimated that about three billion dollars is spent annually to protect vehicles from rust with corrosion-resistant coatings. Some have added to this estimate the costs of frequent washings to save vehicles from rust. The expense of salt deicing does not stop, however, with motor vehicle protection and damage. The United States has about 500,000 bridges, of which an estimated 40 percent are currently considered deficient. Damage to bridges comes from a variety of causes, but many experts consider the most significant agent for premature deterioration is deicing salt. It is estimated that repair and protection to damaged bridges in the United States in the next decade will cost between one-half and two-thirds of a billion dollars. Salt damage is also causing bridges in Great Britain to deteriorate more rapidly than expected and is believed to be the principal cause of bridge damage with an anticipated cost of repair in the next decade of a half billion pounds.

Salt damages roadside vegetation, and it has been shown that waters downstream from a deiced highway contain significantly more (in one case 31 times as much) chloride than waters in the same rivers upstream. Well water can similarly become contaminated with salt, and both Massachusetts and Connecticut have large numbers of **wells** with a sodium content in excess of 20 mg per liter, which is considered to be the upper limit for individuals who must control sodium intake. One area of Massachusetts has quit using deicing salt because of concern for sodium in their drinking water.

It would be useful to develop a deicer that has less impact on the economy and the environment. One such alternative is calcium magnesium acetate (CME) which, while initially far more costly than salt, is believed to have less potential for damaging the **environment**. *See also* Automobile; Groundwater pollution; Salinity; Salinization

[*Robert G. McKinnell*]

FURTHER READING

Boice, L. P. "Environmental Management: CMA, An Alternative to Road Salt?" *Environment* 28 (1985): 45.

"Deicing Agents: A Primer." *Public Works* (July 1991): 50-51.

Dunker, K. F., and B. G. Rabbat. "Why America's Bridges Are Crumbling." *Scientific American* 268 (March 1993): 66-72.

"Highway Deicing: Comparing Salt and Calcium Magnesium Acetate." *TR News* 163 (November-December 1992): 17-19.

Reina, P. "Salt Breaks the Back of Motorway Bridges." *New Scientist* (29 April 1989): 30.

Salt water intrusion

Aquifers in coastal areas where fresh **groundwater** is discharged into bodies of salt water such as oceans are subject to salt water intrusion. Intrusion occurs when water usage lowers the level of freshwater contained in the aquifer. The

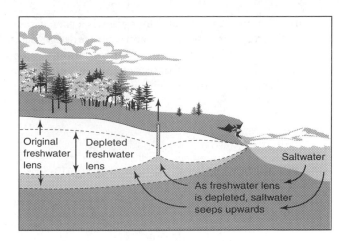

Saltwater intrusion into a coastal aquifer due to depletion of the freshwater in the aquifer.

natural gradient sloping down toward the ocean is changed, resulting in a decrease or reversal of the flow from the aquifer to the salt water body, which causes salt water to enter and penetrate inland. If salt water travels far enough inland well fields supplying freshwater can be ruined and the aquifer can become so contaminated that it may take years to remove the salt, even with fresh groundwater available to flush out the saline water.

Salt water intrusion can also develop where there is artificial access to salt water, such as sea level canals or drainage ditches. On the coastal perimeter of the United States there are a number of areas with such intrusion problems. There are five methods available to control intrusion: 1) the reduction or rearrangement of the pumping drawdown; 2) direct recharge; 3) the development of a pumping trough adjacent to the coast; 4) maintenance of a freshwater ridge above sea level along the coast; and 5) construction of artificial subsurface barriers.

Developing a pumping trough or maintaining a pressure ridge are methods that do not solve the basic problem: the overdraft or excessive withdrawal of water from the aquifer. Only when this problem is solved by reducing drawdown, or isolated by the subsurface barrier method, can the intrusion be stopped or reversed. In some areas, it is simply not economically feasible to control intrusion.

Oceanic islands, such as Hawaii, have unique problems with salt water intrusion. Most islands consist of sand, lava, coral, or limestone; they are relatively permeable, so freshwater is in contact with salt water on all sides. Because fresh water is supplied entirely by rainfall in these places, only a limited amount is available. A freshwater lens is formed by movement of the freshwater toward the coast. Depth to salt water at any location is a function of rainfall recharge, the size of the island, and permeability. Tidal and seasonal fluctuations may form a transition zone between freshwater and salt water.

The close proximity of salt water in oceanic islands can introduce saline water into fresh groundwater even without excessive overdraft. An island well pumping at a rate high enough to lower the **water table** disturbs the fresh-salt water equilibrium, and salt water then rises as a cone within the well. To avoid this condition, island wells are designed for minimum drawdown, and they skim freshwater from the top of the aquifer. In general, drawdowns of a few inches to a few feet provide plentiful water supplies.

[*James L. Anderson*]

FURTHER READING

Gorrie, P. "Water From the Ground." *Canadian Geographic* 112 (September-October 1992): 68-77.

Wagman, D. "Protecting Hidden Assets: Many American Cities and Counties Are Designing Groundwater Regulations to Protect Underground Aquifers." *American City and County* 105 (March 1990): 38-41.

Sand dune ecology

Dunes are mounds of sand that have been piled by the action of winds. The sand is usually composed of bits of minerals that have been eroded from rocks, picked up by water or winds, and then re-deposited somewhere else. Typically, the sand is deposited behind some object that is a barrier to the movement of air currents, which causes the windspeed to slow suddenly so that the load of sand particles can no longer be contained against the force of gravity, and it falls to the ground. If there is a suitable source of sand, dunes may deposit along the edges of oceans, large lakes, rivers, and even in inland locations.

The mineralogical composition of sand in dunes varies greatly from place to place. The most common minerals are quartzitic (this is a silica sand), but other minerals may also be mixed in, and they may dominate the composition of the sand in some places. The White Sands National Monument in New Mexico, for example, is characterized by a sand of gypsum (calcium sulfate). The grain size of sands varies depending on the strength of the winds that delivered the sand to the location where the dune has formed—the greater the typical windspeed, the larger the sand grains can be.

Once deposited to the surface, unconsolidated sand tends to be moved about and shifted by the winds. In fact, dunes tend to "migrate" in the direction of the prevailing winds, with sand being picked up at the windward side of the dune, and deposited on the leeward side. Because of the mechanical instability of their surface young dunes initially provide rather precarious **habitat**s for the establishment of vegetation. However, if plants do manage to establish a foothold on a dune, the progressive development of vegetation over time will help to stabilize the surface, allowing an ecosystem to develop through the process of succession.

Some of the most extensive dune systems in the world occur in deserts, including parts of the Sahara Desert of northern Africa, the Gobi Desert of eastern Asia, and the Great Western Desert of the United States and Mexico. Because of the aridity of those environments only a very limited amount of ecological development is possible. In places with a more moderate climate, however, sand dunes can be colonized by vegetation and succession can proceed to the development of tall, mixed-species forests. This type of succession is typical of many dune systems along the coasts of the oceans and many large lakes and rivers of North America.

Environmental Conditions

Sandy soils are generally free-draining, so that even in regions with abundant rainfall sand-dune habitats can be quite arid. The dry **soil** conditions are made worse by the frequently windy conditions in dune habitats, a factor that speeds the evaporation of water from plant foliage and the soil surface. Droughty conditions are especially important on the higher parts of dunes; in low places the water table may come to the surface, creating locally moist or wet conditions, which are sometimes referred to as dune slacks.

In addition, most sands contain few nutrients, so they provide rather infertile conditions for plant growth. Sandy soils are also lacking in organic matter, which prevents them from holding much water or nutrients for later uptake by plants. In fact, some sand-dune habitats can be referred to as ombrotrophic, or "fed from the clouds," which means that atmospheric deposition is the principal source of nutrient inputs in support of plant productivity. In addition, the low levels of calcium concentrations make sandy soils highly vulnerable to acidification, a condition that can be stressful to some species of plants.

Vegetation of Sand Dunes

The species of plants that grow on sand dunes vary depending on the climate, the stability of the dunes, soil chemistry, and **biogeography**. Dunes of the deserts of southern California, southwestern Arizona, and nearby Mexico are sparsely vegetated with a mixture of perennial grasses, such as *Pleuraphis rigida*, perennial herbs such as the sand sagebrush *Artemisia filifolia*, and species of shrubs, including ephedra (*Ephedra trifurca*), daleas (*Dalea* spp.), Colorado desert buckwheat (*Eriogonum deserticola*), and mesquite (*Propsis spp.*). During occasional rainy periods these sandy deserts can bloom prolifically with showy annual herbs, such as species of *Allionia*, *Boerhavia*, *Euphorbia*, *Oenothera*, and *Pectis*. Areas of gypsum-rich sand have other species that are specific to that soil type, including yucca (*Yucca elata*), ephedra (*Ephedra torreyana*), onion blanket (*Gaillardia multiceps*), and grasses such as *Bouteloua breviseta*.

In more humid climatic regimes of North America, younger sand-dune systems are initially colonized by species of dune-grasses, such as American beach grass (*Ammophila breviligulata*), sea oats (*Uniola paniculata*), sand rye (*Elymus mollis*), and beach grass (*Calamovilfa longifolia*). As the dunes stabilize, other species invade the community. These may form a **prairie** with interspersed shrub- and tree-dominated nuclei, which may eventually coalesce to form continuous forest (see the next section on dune succession). Some dune-rich areas of the east coast of the United States support forests of pines (*Pinus* spp.), oaks (*Quercus* spp.), and magnolia (*Magnolia virginiana*). Older dunes in the **Great Lakes** region tend to be covered by mixed stands of oaks, pines, and tulip-tree (*Liriodendron tulipifera*). The inland sand hills of

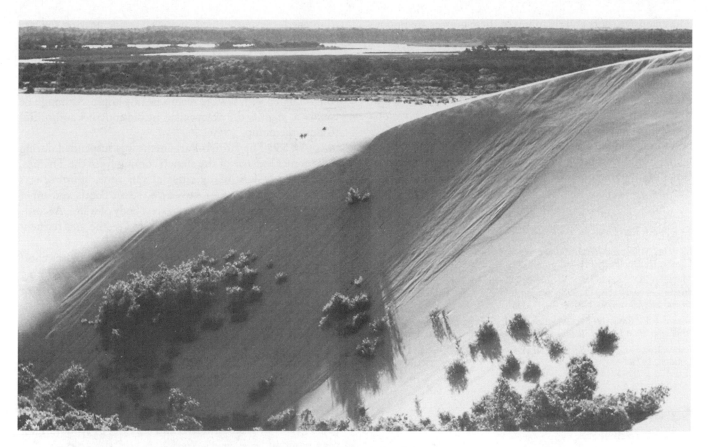

Moving sand dunes are slowly engulfing a forest in Nags Head, North Carolina.

northern Alberta are commonly occupied by stands of jack pine (*Pinus banksiana*).

Primary Succession on Sand Dunes

Succession on recently formed sand dunes is a type of primary succession. This is because the sandy substrate that is newly exposed for ecological development has no pre-existing biological capability to initiate the succession. Succession can not begin until microbes, plants, and animals have invaded the site from existing **ecosystem**s somewhere else. (Secondary succession occurs after a disturbance, but one that has allowed some of the original biota to survive, so they can play a prominent role in ecological recovery.)

Some classic studies of primary succession have involved sand-dune ecosystems. In North America, the most famous studies were conducted on systems of dune ridges at several places on Lake Michigan and Lake Huron. Dune ridges are actively developing in those places to this day. This occurs as sand is piled up onto the beach by wave action, to be moved inland by the prevailing on-shore winds and mostly deposited on the dune closest to the edge of the lake, on its leeward, or building side. This process of dune-building is an ancient phenomenon, and it has been actively occurring in the region since deglaciation, more than twelve thousand years ago.

The dune building is, however, superimposed upon another geological process—the slow rebounding in elevation of the regional ground surface, a phenomenon that is known as isostasy. This slow, uplifting process is still occurring in response to the long-ago melting of the continental glaciers that once covered virtually all of northern North America; when the glaciers were present, their enormous weight actually depressed crustal bedrocks beneath them into Earth's plastic mantle. The surface has been rebounding since deglaciation released the crust from the weight of the gigantic glaciers, at a fairly steady rate of about 1 yd (1 m) per century. Because of isostatic rebound, ancient shorelines of the Great Lakes are now higher in elevation than they used to be, and in some flatter areas well-defined dune systems formed on ancient shores can be found miles inland of the present shoreline of the lakes. These circumstances mean that dunes located further inland are older than dunes occurring closer to the modern lake shores. Because the ages of the various dunes can be dated, ecologists are able to study a series of dunes of various age and their associated communities. This so-called chronosequence technique allows the ecologists to reconstruct the basic elements of the successional process.

The first plants to colonize the embryonic dunes are annual and biennial plants of shoreline habitats, such as the American searocket (*Cakile edentula*), Russian thistle (*Salsola kali*), orache (*Atriplex patula*), and a small euphorb (*Eurphorbia polygonifolia*). Although buffeted by severe weather, these plants help in the initial stages of dune stabilization. The next invaders of the site are several species of dune grasses, particularly *Ammophila breviligulata* and *Calamovilfa longifolia*.

The extensive roots and rhizomes of these grasses are important in binding the sandy substrate, and in stabilizing the lakeward dune ridges and allowing them to grow larger. Once these grasses take hold, some other foredune plants can establish and begin to grow, including the beach pea (*Lathyrus maritimus*) and evening primrose (*Oenothera biennis*). With time, a tall grass prairie develops, dominated by various species of grasses and broad-leaved herbs. The prairie becomes invaded by shade-intolerant shrub and tree species, which form forest nuclei. Eventually a climax forest develops that is dominated by oaks, pines, and tulip-tree.

[*Bill Freedman*]

FURTHER READING

Barbour, M.G., and W.D. Billings. *North American Terrestrial Vegetation.* Cambridge University Press, Cambridge, U.K., 1988.

Morrison, R.G., and G.A. Yarranton. "Diversity, Richness, and Evenness during a Primary Sand Dune Succession at Grand Bend, Ontario," *Canadian Journal of Botany* 51 (1973): 2401-2411.

Olson, J.S. "Rates of Succession and Soil Changes on Southern Lake Michigan Sand Dunes," *Botanical Gazette* 119 (958): 125-170.

Ranwell, D.S. *Ecology of Salt Marshes and Sand Dunes.* Chapman and Hall, London, 1972.

Sanitary landfill
See **Landfill**

Sanitation

Sanitation can be defined as the measures, methods and activities that prevent the transmission of diseases and ensure public health. Specifically, "sanitation" refers to the hygienic principles and practices relating to the safe collection, removal and disposal of human excreta, refuse, and **wastewater**.

For a household, sanitation refers to the provision and ongoing operation and maintenance of a safe and easily accessible means of disposing of human excreta, garbage, and wastewater, and providing an effective barrier against excreta-related diseases.

The problems that result from inadequate sanitation can be illustrated by the following events in history:

1700 B.C.: Ahead of his time by a few thousand years, King Minos of Crete had running water in his bathrooms in his palace at Knossos. Although there is evidence of plumbing and sewerage systems at several ancient sites, including the cloaca maxima (or great sewer) of ancient Rome, their use did not become widespread until modern times.

1817: A major epidemic of **cholera** hit Calcutta, India, after a national festival. There is no record of exactly how many people were affected, but there were 10,000 fatalities among British troops alone. The epidemic then spread to other countries and arrived in the United States and Canada in 1832. The governor of New York quarantined the Canadian border in a vain attempt to stop the epidemic. When cholera reached New York City, people were so

frightened, they either fled or stayed inside, leaving the city streets deserted.

1854: A London physician, Dr. John Snow, demonstrated that cholera deaths in an area of the city could all be traced to a common public drinking water pump that was contaminated with sewage from a nearby house. Although he could not identify the exact cause, he did convince authorities to close the pump.

1859: The British Parliament was suspended during the summer because of the stench coming from the Thames. As was the case in many cities at this time, storm sewers carried a combination of **sewage**, street debris and other wastes, and storm water to the nearest body of water. According to one account, the river began to "seethe and ferment under a burning sun."

1892: The comma-shaped bacteria that causes cholera was identified by German scientist, Robert Loch, during an epidemic in Hamburg. His discovery proved the relationship between contaminated water and the disease.

1939: Sixty people died in an outbreak of typhoid fever at Manteno State Hospital in Illinois. The cause was traced to a sewer line passing too close to the hospital's water supply.

1940: A valve [that was] accidentally opened caused polluted water from the Genesee River to be pumped into the Rochester, New York, public water supply system. About 35,000 cases of gastroenteritis and six cases of typhoid fever were reported.

1955: Water containing a large amount of sewage was blamed for overwhelming a **water treatment** plant and causing an epidemic of hepatitis in Delhi, India. An estimated one million people were infected.

1961: A worldwide epidemic of cholera began in Indonesia and spread to eastern Asia and India by 1964; Russia, Iran, and Iraq by 1966; Africa by 1970; and Latin America by 1991.

1968: A four-year epidemic of dysentery began in Central America resulting in more than 500,000 cases and at least 20,000 deaths. Epidemic dysentery is currently a problem in many African nations.

1993: An outbreak of cryptosporidiosis in Milwaukee, Wisconsin, claimed 104 lives and infected more than 400,000 people, making it the largest recorded outbreak of waterborne disease in the United States.

The problem of sanitation in developed countries, who have the luxury of adequate financial and technical resources is more concerned with the consequences arising from inadequate commercial food preparation and the results of bacteria becoming resistant to disinfection techniques and antibiotics. Flush toilets and high quality drinking water supplies have all but eliminated cholera and epidemic diarrheal diseases. However, in many developing countries, such as the Pacific islands, inadequate sanitation is still the cause of life or death struggles.

In 1992, the South Pacific Regional Environment Programme (SPREP) and a Land-Based Pollutants Inventory stated that "[t]he disposal of solid and liquid wastes (particularly of human excrement and household garbage in urban areas), which have long plagued the Pacific, emerge now as perhaps the foremost regional environmental problem of the decade."

High levels of fecal coliform bacteria have been found in surface and coastal waters. The SPREP Land-Based Sources of Marine Pollution Inventory describes the Federated States of Micronesia's sewage pollution problems in striking terms: The prevalence of water-related diseases and water quality monitoring data indicate that the sewage pollutant loading to the environment is very high. A recent waste quality monitoring study (as part of a workshop) was unable to find a clean, uncontaminated site in the Kolonia, Pohnpei, area.

Many central wastewater treatment plants constructed with funds from United States **Environmental Protection Agency** in Pohnpei and in Chuuk States have failed due to lack of trained personnel and funding for maintenance.

In addition, septic systems used in some rural areas are said to be of poor design and construction, while pour-flush toilets and latrines—which frequently overflow in heavy rains—are more common. Over-the-water latrines are found in many coastal areas, as well.

In the Marshall Islands, signs of eutrophication—excess water plant growth due to too much nutrients—resulting from sewage disposal are evident next to settlements, particularly urban centers. According to a draft by the Marshall Islands NEMS, "one-gallon blooms occur along the coastline in Majuro and Ebeye, and are especially apparent on the **lagoon** side adjacent to households lacking toilet facilities." Stagnation of lagoon waters, reef degradation, and **fish kills** resulting from the low levels of oxygen have been well documented over the years. Additionally, **red tides** plague the lagoon waters adjacent to Majuro.

There is significant **groundwater pollution** in the Marshall Islands as well. The Marshall Island EPA estimates that more than 75% of the rural wells tested are contaminated with fecal coliform and other bacteria. Cholera, typhoid and various diarrheal disorders occur.

With very little industry present, most of these problems are blamed on domestic sewage, with the greatest contamination problems believed to be from pit latrines, septic tanks, and the complete lack of sanitation facilities for 60% of rural households. As is often the case, poor design and inappropriate placement of these systems are often identified as the cause of contamination problems. In fact, even the best of these systems in the most favorable **soil** conditions allow significant amounts of nutrients and pathogens into the surrounding environment, and the soil characteristics and high water table typically found on atolls significantly inhibit treatment. In addition, the lack of proper maintenance, due to a lack of equipment to pump out septic tanks, is likely to have degraded the performance of these systems even further.

Forty percent of the population in the Republic of Palau is served by a secondary sewage treatment plant in the state of Koror, which is generally thought to provide adequate treatment. However, the Koror State government has recently expressed concern over the possible contamination of Malakal Harbor, into which the plant discharges. Also, some low-lying areas served by the system experience periodic back-flows of sewage which run into mangrove areas, due to mechanical failures with pumps and electrical power outages. In other low-lying areas not covered by the sewer system, **septic tank**s and latrines are used, which also overflow, affecting marine **water quality**.

Rural areas primarily rely on latrines, causing localized marine contamination in some areas. Though there have been an increasing number of septic systems installed as part of a rural sanitation program funded by the United States, there is anecdotal evidence that they may not be very effective. Many of the septic tank leach fields may not be of adequate size. In addition, a number of the systems are not used at all, as some families prefer instead to use latrines since the actual toilets and enclosures are not provided with the septic tanks as part of the program.

Wastewater problems also result from agriculture. According to the EPA, pig waste is considered to be a more significant problem than human sewage in many areas.

Because sanitation has become a social responsibility, national, state and local governments have adopted regulations that, when followed, should provide adequate sanitation for the governed society. However, the very technologies and practices that were instituted to provide better health and sanitation now have been found to be contaminating ground and surface waters. For example, placing **chlorine** in drinking water and waste water to provide disinfection, has now been found to produce carcinogenic compounds called **trihalomethanes** and **dioxin**. Collecting sanitary waste and transporting them along with industrial waste to inadequate treatment plants costing billions of dollars has failed to provide adequate protection for public health and environmental security.

Increasingly, the solution seems to be found in methods and practices that borrow from the stable ecosystems model of waste management. That is, there are no wastes, only resources that need to be connected to the appropriate organism that requires the residuals from one organism as the nutritional requirement of another. New waterless composting toilets that destroy human fecal organisms while they produce fertilizer, are now the technology of choice in the developing world and have also found a growing niche in the developed world. Wash water, rather than being disposed of into ground and surface waters, is now being utilized for **irrigation**. The combination of these two ecologically engineered technologies provides economical sanitation, eliminates **pollution**, and creates valuable **fertilizer**s and plants, while reducing the use of potable water for irrigation and toilets.

Simple hand washing is now re-emerging as the most important measure in preventing disease transmission. Handwashing breaks the primary connection between surfaces contaminated with fecal organisms and the introduction of these **pathogen**s into the human body. The use of basic soap and water, not exotic disinfectants, when practiced before eating and after defecating may save more lives than all of the modern methodologies and technologies combined.

[*Carol Steinfeld*]

917

FURTHER READING

Fair, G., J. Geyer, and A. Okun, *Water and Wastewater Engineering* 1 (1992).

"Sanitation Problems in Micronesia," a report. Concord, MA: Sustainable Strategies, 1997.

Salvato, J. *Environmental Engineering and Sanitation*, 4th ed., 1992.

Savanna

A savanna is a dry grassland with scattered trees. Most ecologists agree that a characteristic savanna has an open or sparse canopy with 10 to 25 percent tree cover, a dominant ground cover of annual and perennial grasses, and less than 20 inches (50 cm) of rainfall per year. Greatly varied environments, from open **deciduous forest**s and parklands, to dry, thorny scrub, to nearly pure **grasslands**, can be considered savannas. At their margins these communities merge, more or less gradually, with drier **prairie**s or with denser, taller forests. Savannas occur at both tropical and temperate latitudes and on all continents except Antarctica. Most often savannas occupy relatively level, or sometimes rolling, terrain. Characteristic savanna **soil**s are dry, well-developed ultisols, oxisols, and alfisols, usually basic and sometimes lateritic. These soils develop under savannas' strongly seasonal rainfall regimes, with extended dry periods that can last up to 10 months. Under natural conditions an abundance of insect, bird, reptile, and mammal **species** populate the land.

Savanna shrubs and trees have leathery, sometimes thorny, and often small leaves that resist **drought**, heat, and intense sunshine normally found in this **environment**. Savanna grasses are likewise thin and tough, frequently growing in clumps, with seasonal stalks rising from longer-lived underground roots. Many of these plants have oily or resinous leaves that burn intensely and quickly in a fire. Extensive root systems allow most savanna plants to exploit moisture and nutrients in a large volume of soil. Most savanna trees stand less than 32 feet (10 m) tall; some have a wide spreading canopy while others have a narrower, more vertical shape. Characteristic trees of African and South American savannas include acacias and miombo (*Brachystegia* spp.). Australian savannas share the African baobab, but are dominated by eucalyptus species. Oaks characterize many European savannas, while in North America oaks, pines, and aspens are common savanna trees.

Because of their extensive and often nutritious grass cover, savannas support extensive populations of large herbivores. Giraffes, zebras, impalas, kudus, and other charismatic residents of African savannas are especially well-known. Savanna herbivores in other regions include North American **bison** and elk and Australian kangaroos and wallabies. Carnivores—lions, cheetahs, and jackals in Africa, tigers in Asia, wolves and pumas in the Americas—historically preyed upon these huge herds of grazers. Large running birds, such as the African ostrich and the Australian emu, inhabit savanna environments, as do a plethora of smaller animal species. In the past century or two many of the world's native savanna species, especially the large carnivores, have disappeared with the expansion of human settlement. Today ranchers and their livestock take the place of many native grazers and carnivores.

Savannas owe their existence to a great variety of convergent environmental conditions, including temperature and precipitation regimes, soil conditions, fire frequency, and **fauna**. Grazing and browsing activity can influence the balance of trees to grasses. Fires, common and useful for some savannas but rare and harmful in others, are an influential factor in these dry environments. Precipitation must be sufficient to allow some tree growth, but where rainfall is high some other factors, such as grazing, fire, or soil drainage needs to limit tree growth. Human activity also influences the occurrence of these lightly-treed grasslands. In some regions recent expansion of ranches, villages, or agriculture have visibly extended savanna conditions. Elsewhere centuries or millennia of human occupation make natural and anthropogenic conditions difficult to distinguish. Because savannas are well suited to human needs, people have occupied some savannas for tens of thousands of years. In such cases people appear to be an environmental factor, along with climate, soils, and grazing animals, that help savannas persist. *See also* Deforestation

[*Mary Ann Cunningham*]

FURTHER READING

Cole, M. M. *The Savannas: Biogeography and Geobotany.* London: Academic Press, 1986.

Danserreau, P. *Biogeography: An Ecological Perspective.* New York: Ronald Press Company, 1957.

de Laubenfels, D. J. *Mapping the World's Vegetation.* Syracuse, NY: Syracuse University Press, 1975.

White, R. O. *Grasslands of the Monsoon.* New York: Praeger, 1968.

Savannah River Site, South Carolina

From the 1950s to the 1990s, the manufacture of **nuclear weapons** was a high priority item in the United States. The nation depended heavily on an adequate supply of atomic and hydrogen bombs as its ultimate defense against enemy attack. As a result, the government had established 17 major plants in 12 states to produce the materials needed for nuclear weapons.

Five of these plants were built along the Savannah River near Aiken, South Carolina. The Savannah River Site (SRS) is about 20 miles (32 km) southeast of Augusta, Georgia, and 150 miles (242 km) upstream from the Atlantic Ocean. The five reactors sit on a 310-square-mile (803-sq-km) site that also holds 34 million gallons (129 million liters) of high-level radioactive wastes.

The SRS reactors were originally used to produce **plutonium** fuel used in nuclear weapons. In recent years, they have been converted to the production of tritium gas, an important component of fusion (hydrogen) bombs.

For more than a decade, environmentalists have been concerned about the safety of the SRS reactors. The reactors were aging; one of the original SRS reactors, for instance, had been closed in the late 1970s because of cracks in the reactor vessel.

The severity of safety issues became more obvious, however, in the late 1980s. In September 1987, the **U. S. Department of Energy (DOE)** released a memorandum summarizing 30 "incidents" that had occurred at SRS between 1975 and 1985. Among these were a number of unexplained power surges that nearly went out of control. In addition, the meltdown of a radioactive fuel element in November 1970 took 900 people three months to clean up.

E. I. du Pont de Nemours and Company, operator of the SRS facility, claimed that all "incidents" had been properly reported and that the reactors presented no serious risk to the area. Worried about maintaining a dependable supply of tritium, DOE officials accepted du Pont's explanation and allowed the site to continue operating.

In 1988, however, the problems at SRS began to snowball. By that time, two of the original five reactors had been shut down permanently and two, temporarily. Then, in August of 1988 an unexplained power surge caused officials to temporarily close down the fifth, "K," reactor. Investigations by federal officials found that the accident was a result of human errors. Operators were poorly trained and improperly supervised. In addition, they were working with inefficient, aging equipment that lacked adequate safety precautions.

Still concerned about its tritium supply, the DOE spent more than $1 billion to upgrade and repair the K reactor and to retrain staff at SRS. On December 13, 1991, Energy Secretary James D. Watkins announced that the reactor was to be re-started again, operating at 30 percent capacity.

During final tests prior to re-starting, however, 150 gallons (569 liters) of cooling water containing radioactive tritium leaked into the Savannah River. A South Carolina water utility company and two food processing companies in Savannah, Georgia, had to discontinue using river water in their operations.

The ill-fated reactor experienced yet another set-back only five months later. During another effort at re-starting the K reactor in May 1992, radioactive tritium once again escaped into the surrounding environment and, once again, start-up was postponed.

By the fall of 1992, changes in the balance of world power would cast additional doubt on the future of SRS. The Soviet Union had collapsed and neither Russia nor its former satellite states were regarded as an immediate threat to U.S. security, as former Soviet military might was now spread among a number of nations with urgent economic priorities. American president George Bush and Russian leader Boris Yeltsin had agreed to sharp cut-backs in the number of nuclear warheads held by both sides. In addition, experts determined that the existing supply of tritium would be sufficient for U.S. defense needs until at least 2012. Given all these considerations, it was no longer clear when, if ever, reactor K would once again go into operation. *See also* Radioactive pollution; Radioactive waste

[*David E. Newton*]

FURTHER READING

Applebome, P. "Anger Lingers After Leak at Atomic Site." *New York Times* (January 13, 1992): A7.

Schneider, K. "U. S. Dropping Plan to Build Reactor." *New York Times* (September 12, 1992): 5.

Sweet, W. "Severe Accident Scenarios at Issue in DOE Plan to Restart Reactor." *Physics Today* (November 1991): 78-81.

Wald, M. L. "How an Old Government Reactor Managed to Outlive the Cold War." *New York Times* (December 22, 1991): E2.

Save-the-Redwoods League (San Francisco, California)

The Save-the-Redwoods League was founded in 1918 to protect California's **redwood** forests for future generations to enjoy. Prominent individuals involved in the formation of the League included Stephen T. Mather, first Director of the **National Park Service**; Congressman William Kent, author of the bill creating the National Park Service; Newton Drury, Director of the National Park Service from 1940-1951; and John Merriam, paleontologist and later president of the Carnegie Institute. The impetus for forming the organization was a trip taken in 1917 by several of these men and others during which they witnessed widespread destruction of the forests by loggers. They were appalled to learn that not one tree was protected by either the state or the federal government. Upon their return, they wrote an article for *National Geographic* detailing the devastation. Shortly thereafter they formed the Save-the-Redwoods League. One of the League's first actions was to recommend to Congress that a Redwoods National Park be established.

The specific stated objectives of the organization are:

(1) "to rescue from destruction representative areas of our primeval forests,
(2) to cooperate with the California State Park Commission, the National Park Service, and other agencies, in establishing redwood parks, and other parks and reservations,
(3) to purchase redwood groves by private subscription,
(4) to foster and encourage a better and more general understanding of the value of the primeval redwood or sequoia and other forests of America as natural objects of extraordinary interest to present and future generations,
(5) to support reforestation and **conservation** of our forest areas."

This non-profit organization uses donations to purchase redwood lands from willing sellers at fair market value. All contributions, except those specified for research or reforestation, are used for land acquisition.

The League's members and donors have given more than $70 million in private contributions since the formation of the organization. These monies have been used to purchase and protect more than 280,000 acres of redwood park land. The establishment of the Redwoods National Park in 1968, and the park's subsequent expansion in 1978, represented milestones for the Save-the-Redwoods League which had fought for such a national park for 60 years.

Mere acquisition of the redwood groves does not ensure the long-term survival of the redwoods **ecosystem**. Based on almost 70 years of study by park planners and ecologists, a major goal of the Save-the-Redwoods League is to complete each of the existing redwoods parks as ecological units along logical **watershed** boundary lines. The acquisition of these watershed lands are necessary to act as a buffer around the groves to protect them from effects of adjacent logging and development. Contact: Save-the-Redwoods League, 114 Sansome Street, Room 605, San Francisco, CA 94104.

[*Ted T. Cable*]

Save the Whales (Washington, D.C.)

Save the Whales is a non-profit, grassroots organization that was founded and incorporated in 1977. It was conceived by 14-year-old Maris Sidenstecker II when she learned that **whales** were being cruelly slaughtered. She designed a T-shirt with a logo that read "Save The Whales" and designated the proceeds to help save whales. Her mother, Maris Sidenstecker I, helped co-found the organization and still serves as its executive director.

Unlike some environmental groups, **Greenpeace** for example, Save the Whales is involved in very few direct action protests and activities. Its primary focus is education. The group's educational staff is comprised of marine biologists, environmental educators and researchers. They speak to school groups, senior citizen organizations, clubs, and numerous other organizations. Save the Whales is opposed to commercial **whaling** and works to save all whale species from extinction. The group also sends a representative to the annual International Whaling Commission conference.

WOW!, Whales On Wheels, is an innovative program developed by Save the Whales. WOW! travels throughout California educating thousands of children and adults about marine mammals and their environment. WOW! features live presenters and incorporates audio and video into the program along with hands-on exhibits and marine mammal activity projects. In 1992 alone, Maris Sidenstecker II gave presentations to over 7,000 school children.

Save the Whales has also developed a regional Marine Mammal Beach Program for school aged children. It consists of an abbreviated WOW! lecture after which the participants assist in cleaning up a beach. Save the Whales has adopted Venice Beach in California and cleans it several times a year.

A five-minute educational video entitled "One Person Makes A Difference" has been produced by Save the Whales. It combines footage of the humpback whales, orcas and gray whales in the wild which is followed by shots of the slaughter

of pilot whales in the Faroe Islands. The video ends with brief interviews that advocate whale conservation and describe the ways in which one person can make a difference. Save the Whales is currently involved in raising funds to produce a 30-minute documentary film entitled "Barometers of The Ocean." This video will explore chemical pollution in the oceans and how it is affecting whale populations.

The organization also supports marine mammal research. It helps finance research on **seals and sea lions** in Puget Sound (Washington), and makes financial contributions to SCAMP (Southern California Migration Project) to support studies of gray whale migration. Save the Whales publishes a quarterly newsletter that is free with membership, and the organization currently has 2,000 members worldwide. Contact: Save the Whales, P.O. Box 3650, Washington, DC 20007.

[*Debra Glidden*]

Scarcity

As most commonly used, the term scarcity refers to a limited supply of some material. With the rise of environmental consciousness in the 1960s, scarcity of **natural resources** became an important issue. Critics saw that the United States and other developed nations were using natural resources at a frightening pace. How long, they asked, could non-renewable resources such as **coal**, oil, **natural gas**, and metals last at the rate they were being consumed?

A number of studies produced some frightening predictions. The world's oil reserves could be totally depleted in less than a century, according to some experts, and scarce metals such as silver, **mercury**, zinc, and cadmium might be used up even faster at then-current rates of use.

One of the most famous studies of this issue was that of the **Club of Rome**, conducted in the early 1970s. The Club of Rome was an international group of men and women from 25 nations concerned about the ultimate environmental impact of continued **population growth** and unlimited development. The Club commissioned a complex computer study of this issue to be conducted by a group of scholars at the Massachusetts Institute of Technology. The result of that study was the now famous book *The Limits to Growth*.

Limits presented a depressing view of the Earth's future if population and technological development were to continue at then-current rates. With regard to non-renewable resources such as metals and **fossil fuels**, the study concluded that the great majority of those resources would become "extremely costly 100 years from now." Unchecked population growth and development would, therefore, lead to widespread scarcity of many critical resources.

The *Limits* argument appears to make sense. There is only a specific limited supply of coal, oil, chromium, and other natural resources on Earth. As population grows and societies become more advanced technologically, those resources are used up more rapidly. A time must come, therefore, when the supply of those resources becomes more and more limited, that is, they become more and more scarce.

Yet, as with many environmental issues, the obvious reality is not necessarily true. The reason is that there is a second way to define scarcity, an economic definition. To an economist, a resource is scarce if people pay more money for it. Resources that are bought and sold cheaply are not scarce.

One measure of the *Limits* argument, then is to follow the price of various resources over time, to see if they are becoming more scarce in an economic sense. When that study is conducted, an interesting result is obtained. Supposedly "scarce" resources such as coal, oil, and various metals have actually become *less* costly since 1970 and must be considered, therefore, to be less scarce than they were two decades ago.

How this can happen has been explained by economist Julian Simon, a prominent critic of the *Limits* message. As the supply of a resource diminishes, Simon says, humans become more imaginative and more creative in finding and using the resource. For example, gold mines that were once regarded as exhausted have been re-opened because improved technology makes it possible to recover less concentrated reserves of the metal. Industries also become more efficient in the way they use resources, wasting less and making what they have go further.

In one sense, this debate is a long-term versus short-term argument. One can hardly argue that the Earth's supply of oil, for example, will last forever. However, given Simon's argument, that supply may last much longer than the authors of *Limits* could have imagined twenty years ago.

[*David E. Newton*]

FURTHER READING

Meadows, D. H., et al. *The Limits to Growth*. New York: Universe Books, 1972.

Ophuls, W., and A. S. Boyan, Jr. *Ecology and the Politics of Scarcity Revisited*. San Francisco: W. H. Freeman, 1992.

Simon, J. L. *The Ultimate Resource*. Princeton, NJ: Princeton University Press, 1981.

———, and H. Kahn, eds. *The Resourceful Earth*. Oxford: Basil Blackwell, 1984.

Scavenger

Any substance or organism that cleans a setting by removing dirt, decaying matter, or some other unwanted material. Vultures are typical biological scavengers because they feed on the carcasses of dead animals. Certain **chemicals** can act as scavengers in chemical reactions. Lithium and magnesium are used in the metal industry as scavengers since these metals react with and remove small amounts of oxygen and **nitrogen** from molten metals. Even rain and snow can be regarded as scavengers because they wash pollutants out of the atmosphere.

Schistosomiasis

Human blood fluke disease, also called schistosomiasis or bilharziasis, is a major parasitic disease affecting over 200 million people worldwide, mostly those in the tropics. Although sometimes fatal, schistosomiasis more commonly results in chronic ill-health and low energy levels. The disease is caused by small parasitic flatworms of the genus *Schistosoma*. Of the three species, two (*S. haematobium* and *S. mansoni*) are found in Africa and the Middle East, the third (*S. japonicum*) in the Orient. *Schistosoma haematobium* lives in the blood vessels of the urinary bladder and is responsible for over 100 million human cases of the disease a year. *Schistosoma mansoni* and *Schistosoma japonicum* reside in the intestine; the former species infect 75 million people a year and the latter 25 million.

Schistosomiasis is spread when infected people urinate or defecate into open waterways and introduce **parasite** eggs that hatch in the water. Each egg liberates a microscopic free-living larva called the *miracidium* which bores into the tissues of a water snail of the genus *Biomphalaria*, *Bulinus* or *Onchomelania*, the intermediate host. Inside the snail the parasite multiplies in sporocyst sacs to produce masses of larger, mobile, long-tailed larvae known as *cercariae*. The cercariae emerge from the snail into the water, actively seek out a human host, and bore deep into the skin. Larvae that reach the blood vessels are carried to the liver where they develop into adult egg-producing worms that settle in the vessels of the urinary bladder or intestine. Adult *Schistosoma* live entwined in mating couples inside the small veins of their host. Fertilized females release small eggs (0.2 mm long), at the rate of 3,500 per day, which are carried out of the body with the urine or the feces.

The symptoms of schistosomiasis correlate with the progress of the disease. Immediately after infection migrating cercariae cause itching skin. Subsequent establishment of larvae in the liver damages this organ. Later, egg release causes blood in the stool (dysentery), damage to the intestinal wall, or blood in the urine (hematuria), and damage to the urinary bladder.

Schistosomiasis is increasing in developing countries due in part to rapidly increasing human populations. In rural areas, attempts to increase food production that include more **irrigation** and more **dams** also increase the habitat for water snails. In urban areas the combination of crowding and lack of sanitation ensures that increasingly large numbers of people become exposed to the parasite.

Most control strategies for schistosomiasis target the snail hosts. One strategy kills snails directly by adding snail poisons (molluscicides) to the water. Another strategy either kills or removes vegetation upon which snails feed. Biological methods of snail control include the introduction of fish that feed on snails, of snails that kill schistosome snail hosts, of insect larvae that prey on snails, and of flukes that kill schistosomes inside the snail. Some countries, such as Egypt, have attempted to eliminate the parasite in humans through mass treatment with curative drugs including ambilar, niridazole, nicolifan, and praziquantel. Total eradication

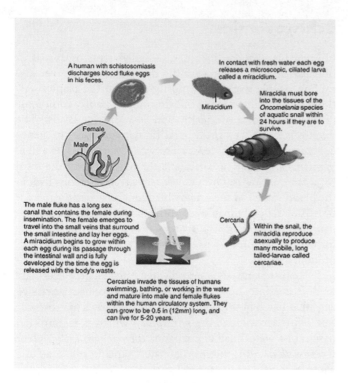

A human with schistosomiasis discharges blood fluke eggs in his feces.

In contact with fresh water each egg releases a microscopic, ciliated larva called a miracidium.

Miracidia must bore into the tissues of the *Oncomelania* species of aquatic snail within 24 hours if they are to survive.

Miracidium

Female

Male

The male fluke has a long sex canal that contains the female during insemination. The female emerges to travel into the small veins that surround the small intestine and lay her eggs. A miracidium begins to grow within each egg during its passage through the intestinal wall and is fully developed by the time the egg is released with the body's waste.

Cercaria

Within the snail, the miracidia reproduce asexually to produce many mobile, long tailed-larvae called cercariae.

Cercariae invade the tissues of humans swimming, bathing, or working in the water and mature into male and female flukes within the human circulatory system. They can grow to be 0.5 in (12mm) long, and can live for 5-20 years.

The life cycle of the blood fluke. This parasite causes the disease schistosomiasis in humans.

programs for schistosomiasis focus both on avoiding contact with the parasite through education, better sanitation, and on breaking its life cycle through snail control and human treatment.

[*Neil Cumberlidge*]

FURTHER READING

Basch, P. F. *Schistosomes: Development, Reproduction, and Host Relations.* New York: Oxford University Press, 1991.

Bullock, W. L. *People, Parasites, and Pestilence: An Introduction to the Natural History of Infectious Disease.* Minneapolis, MN: Burgess Publishing Company, 1982.

Malek, E. A. *Snail-Transmitted Parasitic Diseases.* Boca Raton, FL: CRC Press, 1980.

Markell, E. K., M. Voge, and D. T. John. *Medical Parasitology.* 7th ed. Philadelphia: Saunders, 1992.

Schumacher, Ernst Friedrich (1911-1977)

German-British economist

E. F. Schumacher combined his background in economics with an extensive background in theology to create a unique strategy for reforming the world's socioeconomic systems, and by the early 1970s he had risen nearly to folk hero status.

Schumacher was born in Bonn, Germany. He attended a number of educational institutions, including the universities of Bonn and Berlin, as well as Columbia University in the United States. He eventually received a diploma in economics from Oxford University, and emigrated to Eng-

land in 1937. During World War II, Schumacher was forced to work as a farm laborer in an internment camp. By 1946, however, he had become a naturalized British citizen, and in that same year he accepted a position with the British section of the Control Commission of West Germany. In 1953 he was appointed to Great Britain's National Coal Board as an economic advisor, and in 1963 he became director of statistics there. He stayed with the National Coal Board until 1970.

Schumacher recognized the contemporary indifference to the course of world development, as well as its implications. He began to seek alternative plans for **sustainable development**, and his interest in this issue led him to found the Intermediate Technology Development Group in 1966. Today, this organization continues to provide information and other assistance to **less developed countries**. Schumacher believed that in order to build a global community that would last, development could not exploit the **environment** and must take into account the sensitive links between the environment and human health. He promoted research in these areas during the 1970s as president of the Soil Association, an organization that advocates **organic farming** worldwide.

Schumacher also combined his studies of Buddhist and Roman Catholic theology into a philosophy of life. In his highly regarded book, *Small Is Beautiful: Economics as if People Mattered* (1973), he stresses the importance of self-reliance and promotes the virtues of working with nature rather than against it. He argues that continuous economic growth is more destructive than productive, maintaining that growth should be directly proportionate to human need. People in society, he continues, should apply the ideals of **conservation** (durable-goods production, **solar energy**, **recycling**) and appropriate technology in their lives whenever possible.

In his *A Guide For the Perplexed* (1977), published in 1977, Schumacher is even more philosophical. He attempts to provide personal rather than global guidance, encouraging self-awareness and urging individuals to embrace what he termed a "new age" ethic based on Judeo-Christian principles. He also wrote various pamphlets, including: *Clean Air and Future Energy*; *Think About Land*; and *Education for the Future*.

Schumacher died in 1977 while traveling in Switzerland from Lausanne to Zurich. *See also* Economic growth and the environment; Ehrlich, Paul; Family planning; Population growth; Population Institute; Sustainable agriculture; Zero population growth

[*Kimberley A. Peterson*]

FURTHER READING

Fraker, S., and G. C. Lubenow. "Mr. Small." *Newsweek* (28 March 1977): 18.

Schumacher, E. F. *A Guide for the Perplexed.* New York: Harper & Row, 1977.

———. *Small Is Beautiful: Economics As If People Mattered.* London: Blond and Briggs, 1973.

"Why It Is Important to Think Small." *International Management* (August 1977): 18-20.

Schweitzer, Albert (1875-1965)

French theologian, philosopher, physician, and musicologist

Albert Schweitzer was an individual of remarkable depth and diversity. He was born in the Upper Alsace region of what is now Germany. His parents, Louis (an Evangelical Lutheran pastor and musician) and Adele cultivated his inquisitive mind and passion for music. He developed a strong theological background and, under his father's tutelage, studied piano, eventually acting as substitute musician at the church.

As a young adult, Schweitzer pursued extensive studies in philosophy and theology at the University of Strasbourg, where he received doctorate degrees in both fields (1899 and 1900 respectively). He continued to further his interests in music. While on a fellowship in Paris (researching Kant), he also studied organ at the Sorbonne. He began a career as an organist in 1893 and was eventually renowned as expert in the area of organ construction and as one of the finest interpreters and scholars of Johann Sebastian Bach. His multitudinous published works include the respected *J. S. Bach: the Musician Poet* (1908).

In 1905, after years of pursuing various careers—including minister, musician, and teacher—he determined to dedicate his work to the benefit of others. In 1913 he and his wife, Helene, traveled to Lambarene in French Equatorial Africa (now Gabon), where they built a hospital on the Ogowe River. At the outbreak of World War I, they were allowed to continue working at the hospital for a time but were then sent to France as prisoners of war (both were German citizens). They were held in an internment camp until 1918. After their release, the Schweitzers remained in France and Albert returned to the pulpit. He also gave organ concerts and lectures. During this time in France he wrote "Philosophy of Civilization" (1923), an essay in which he described his philosophy of "reverence for life." Schweitzer felt that it was the responsibility of all people to "sacrifice a portion of their own lives for others." The Schweitzers returned to Africa in 1924, only to find their hospital overgrown with jungle vegetation. With the assistance of volunteers, the facility was rebuilt, using typical African villages as models.

Awarded the Nobel Peace Prize in 1952, Schweitzer used $33,000 of the Prize money to establish a leper colony near the hospital in Africa. It was not until late 1954 that he gave his Nobel lecture in Oslo. He took advantage of the opportunity to object to war as "a crime of inhumanity." Three more years passed before Schweitzer sent out an impassioned plea to the world in his "Declaration of Conscience," which he read over Oslo radio. He called for citizens to demand a ban of **nuclear weapons** testing by their governments. His words ignited a series of arms control talks among the superpowers that began in 1958 and, five years later, resulted in a limited but formal test-ban treaty.

Schweitzer received numerous awards and degrees. Among his long list of published works are *The Quest of the Historical Jesus* (1906), *The Mysticism of Paul the Apostle* (1931), *Out of My Life and Thought* (1933, autobiography), and *The Light Within Us* (1959).

Albert Schweitzer died at the age of 90 at Lambarene.

[*Kimberley A. Peterson*]

FURTHER READING

Bentley, J. *Albert Schweitzer: The Enigma*. New York: Harper Collins, 1992.

Miller, D. C. *Relevance of Albert Schweitzer at the Dawn of the Twenty-First Century*. Lanham: University Press of America, 1992.

Negri, M. "The Humanism of Albert Schweitzer." *Humanist* 53 (March-April 1993): 26-31.

Schweitzer, A. *Out of My Life and Thought*. New York: Henry Holt, 1990.

Scientists' Institute for Public Information (New York, New York)

Working to bridge a gap they perceive between scientists and the media, the Scientists' Institute for Public Information (SIPI) was established in 1963 to disseminate expert information on science and technology to journalists through a variety of means.

SIPI's best-known program is the Media Resource Service (MRS), which was founded in 1980. The MRS serves as a referral service for journalists seeking information from scientists, engineers, physicians, and policymakers. The MRS maintains a database listing more than 25,000 experts who are available for and willing to comment on a variety of topics. The service is free to any media outlet. The honorary chair of the MRS advisory committee is the highly regarded newscaster Walter Cronkite. The MRS is funded by such noteworthy news organizations as CBS Inc., the Scripps Howard Foundation, Time Warner, The Washington Post Company, the Associated Press, the National Broadcasting Company, and The New York Times Company Foundation.

In addition to the MRS, SIPI operates the Videotape Referral Service (VRS), another free resource service which aids broadcast journalists in finding videotapes to accompany science- and technology-related stories. The VRS also provides a list of videotapes for an annual SIPI conference called "TV News: The Cutting Edge," a meeting of scientists, television news directors, and science reporters. The VRS also publishes a monthly newsletter featuring topical listings of story ideas and a current catalogue of available videotapes on science-related issues.

An outgrowth of the MRS, SIPI also operates the International Hot Line in connection with its Global Change program. The hotline provides assistance to journalists worldwide by referring them to scientists and environmental experts. The Global Change program holds briefings to update the media on current international scientific and environmental issues as well.

SIPI also organizes roundtable discussions, seminars, and symposia for scientists and national journalists. These programs have focused on such issues as nuclear waste disposal, military technology and budget priorities, and human gene therapy. SIPI has also developed smaller-scale versions of these programs for state and regional press associations and journalism schools.

In addition, SIPI sponsors the Defense Writers Group. This group is made up of members of the Pentagon press corps who gather to discuss views with defense experts. In addition, SIPI publishes a newsletter addressing current issues in science policy and featuring reviews of media coverage of science and technology. Contact: Scientists' Institute for Public Information, 355 Lexington Avenue, New York, NY 10017.

[Kristin Palm]

Scrubbers

Scrubbers are air pollution control devices that help cleanse the emissions coming out of an incinerator's smoke stack. Hot exhaust gas comes out of the incinerator duct and scrubbers help to wash the **particulate** matter (dust) resulting from the combustion out of the gas. High efficiency scrubbers literally scrub the smoke by mixing dust particles and droplets of water (as fine as mist) together at a very high speed. Scrubbers force the dust to move like a bullet fired at high velocity into the water droplet. The process is similar to the way that rain washes the air.

Scrubbers can also be used as absorbers. Absorption dissolves material into a liquid, much as sugar is absorbed into coffee. From an air pollution standpoint, absorption is a useful method of reducing or eliminating the discharge of air contaminants into the atmosphere. The gaseous air contaminants most commonly controlled by absorption include **sulfur dioxide**, hydrogen sulfide, hydrogen chloride, **chlorine**, ammonia, **nitrogen oxides** and light **hydrocarbons**.

Gas absorption equipment is designed to provide thorough contact between the gas and liquid solvent in order to permit interphase diffusion and solution of the materials. This contact between gas and liquid can be accomplished by dispersing gas in liquid and visa versa. Scrubbers help wash out polluting chemicals from the exhaust gas by facilitating the mixture of liquid (solvent) and gas together.

A number of engineering designs serve to disperse liquid. These include a packed tower, a spray tower or spray chamber, venturi absorbers, and a bubble tray tower.

The most appropriate design for **incineration** facilities is the packed tower—a tower filled with one of many available packing materials. The packing material should provide a large surface area and, for good fluid flow, should be shaped to give large void space when packed. It should also be chemically inert and inexpensive. It must be designed so as to expose a large surface area and be made of materials, such as stainless steel, ceramic or certain forms of plastic.

Packing materials come in various manufactured shapes. They may look like a saddle, a thick tube, a many-faceted star, a scouring pad, or a cylinder with a number of holes carved in it. Packing may be dumped into the column at randomly or stacked in some kind of order. Randomly dumped packing has a higher gas pressure drop across the bed. The stacked packings have an advantage of lower pressure and higher possible liquid throughout, but the installation cost is much higher because they are packed by hand.

Rock and gravel have also been used as packing materials but are usually considered too heavy. They also have small surface areas, give poor fluid flow and at times are not chemically inert.

The liquid is introduced at the top of the tower and trickles down through to the bottom. Since the effectiveness of a packed tower depends on the availability of a large, exposed liquid film, poor liquid distribution that prevents a portion of the packing from being irrigated renders that portion of the tower ineffective. Poor distribution can result from improper introduction of the liquid at the top of the tower or using the wrong rate of liquid flow. The liquid rate must be sufficient to wet the packing but not flood the tower. A liquid rate of at least 800 pounds of liquid per hour per square foot of tower cross-section is typical.

While the liquid introduced at the top of the tower trickles down through the packing, the gas is introduced at the bottom and passes upward through the packing. This process results in the highest possible efficiency. Where the gas stream and solvent enter at the top of the column, there is initially a very high rate of absorption that constantly decreases until the gas and liquid exit in equilibrium.

Scrubbers are used in coal burning industries that generate electricity. They can be used in high sulfur coal emissions because high sulfur coal emits high levels of sulfur dioxide. Scrubbers are also utilized in industrial chemical manufacturing as an important operation in the production of a chemical compound. For example, one step in the manufacture of hydrochloric acid involves the absorption of hydrochloric acid gas in water. Scrubbers are used as a method of recovering valuable products from gas streams— as in **petroleum** production where natural **gasoline** is removed from gas streams by absorption in a special hydrocarbon oil. *See also* Air pollution; Flue-gas scrubbing; Tall stacks

[Liane Clorfene Casten]

FURTHER READING

"Fume Scrubbers Benefit Environment and Manufacturing." *Design News* 48 (24 August 1992): 28-9.

Schiffner, K. C. *Wet Scrubbers.* Chelsea, MI: Lewis, 1986.

"Scrubbing Emissions." *Environment* 31 (March 1989): 22.

Sea cow
See **Manatees**

Sea lion
See **Seals and sea lions**

Sea otter (*Enhydra lutris*)

The sea otter is found in coastal marine waters of the northeastern Pacific Ocean, ranging from California to as far north as the Aleutian Islands. Sea otters spend their entire lives in the ocean and even give birth while floating among the kelp beds. Their ability to use tools, often "favorite" rocks, to open clam shells and sea urchins is well-known and fascinating since few other animals are known to exhibit this behavior. Their playful, curious nature makes them the subjects of many **wildlife** photographers but also has aided in their demise. Many are injured or killed by ship propellers or in fishing nets.

Some sea otters are killed for their highly valued fur. Their thick hair traps air, insulating the otter from the cold water in which it lives. Before they were placed under international protection in 1924, 800,000 to 1 million sea otters were slaughtered for their pelts, eliminating them from large portions of their original range. Despite **poaching**, which remains a problem, they are slowly returning through relocation efforts and natural **migration**. Their proximity to human settlement, however, still poses a problem for their continued survival.

Pollution, especially from **oil spills**, is deadly to the sea otter. The insulating and water-repellant properties of their fur are inhibited when oil causes the fine hairs to stick together, and otters die from hypothermia. Ingestion of oil during grooming does extensive, often fatal, internal damage. In 1965, an oil spill near Great Sitkin Island, Alaska, reduced the island's otter population from six hundred to six. In 1989, the oil tanker **Exxon Valdez** spilled over 40 million liters (11 million gallons) of crude oil into **Prince William Sound, Alaska**, leading to the nearly complete elimination of the Sound's once thriving sea otter population. In California, fears that a similar incident could destroy the sea otter population there have led to relocation efforts.

Sea otters have few natural enemies, but they were extensively hunted by Aleuts and later by Europeans. Sea otters were hunted to **extinction** around several islands in Alaska, an event that led to studies on the importance of sea otters in maintaining marine communities. Attu Island, one of the islands that has lost its otter population, has high sea urchin populations that have, through their grazing, transformed a kelp forest into a "bare" hard ground of coralline and green algae. Few fish or abalone are present in these waters anymore. On nearby Amchitka Island, otters are present in densities of 20 to 30 per square kilometer and forage at depths up to 22 yards (20 m). In this area, few sea urchins persist and dense kelp forests harbor healthy fish and abalone populations. These in turn support higher-order predators such as **seals** and **bald eagle**s.

Effects of sea otter foraging have also been documented in soft-bottom communities, where they reduce densities of sea urchins and clams. In addition, disturbance of the bottom **sediment** leads to increased predation of small bivalves by sea stars. Otters' voracious appetite for invertebrates also brings them into conflict with people. Fishermen in northern California blame sea otters for the decline of the

A female sea otter eating squid.

abalone industry. Farther south, residents of Pismo Beach, an area noted for its clam industry, are exerting pressure to remove otters. Sea urchin and crab fishermen have also come into conflict with these competitors. It remains a challenge for fishermen, environmentalists, and regulators to arrive at a mutually agreeable management policy that will allow successful coexistence with sea otters.

[*William G. Ambrose, Jr. and Paul E. Renaud*]

FURTHER READING

Kvitek, R. G., et al. "Changes in the Alaskan Soft-Bottom Prey Communities Along a Gradient of Sea Otter Predation." *Ecology* 73 (1992): 413-28.

Nybakken, J. W. *Marine Biology: An Ecological Approach.* 2nd ed. New York: Harper and Row, 1988.

Raloff, J. "An Otter Tragedy." *Science News* 143 (1993): 200-02.

Simenstad, C. A., J. A. Estes, and K. W. Kenyon. "Aleuts, Sea Otters, and Alternate Stable State Communities." *Science* 200 (1978): 403-11.

Sumick, J. L. *An Introduction to the Biology of Marine Life.* 5th ed. Dubuque, IA: W. C. Brown, 1992.

Sea Shepherd Conservation Society (Santa Monica, California)

The Sea Shepherd Conservation Society was founded in 1977 by Paul Watson, one of the founding members of **Greenpeace**, as an aggressive direct action organization dedicated to the international **conservation** and protection of marine **wildlife** in general and marine mammals in particular. The society seeks to combat exploitative practices through education, confrontation, and the enforcement of existing laws, statutes, treaties, and regulations. It maintains offices in the United States, Great Britain, and Canada, and has an international membership of about 15,000.

Sea Shepherd regards itself virtually as a police force dedicated to ocean and marine life conservation. Most of its attention over the years has been devoted to the enforcement of the regulations of the International Whaling Commission (IWC), which makes policies for signatory states on **whaling** practices but does not itself have powers of enforcement. The stated objective of the society has been to harass, interfere with, and ultimately shut down all continuing illegal whaling activities.

Called a "samurai conservation organization" by the Japanese media, Sea Shepherd often walks a thin line between legal and illegal tactics. The society operates two research ships, the *Sea Shepherd* and the *Edward Abbey*, and has been known to ram illegal or pirate whaling ships and to sabotage **whale** processing operations. All crew members are trained in techniques of "creative non-violence": They are forbidden to carry weapons or explosives or to endanger human life and are enjoined to accept all moral responsibility and legal consequences for their actions.

Crew members also pledge never to compromise on the lives of the marine mammals they protect. The Society has documented on film illegal whaling operations in the former Soviet Union and presented this evidence to the IWC, despite being chased back to United States waters by a Soviet frigate and helicopter gunships. Moreover, members are not at all squeamish about the destruction of weapons, ships, and other property used in the slaughter of marine wildlife. In 1979, Sea Shepherd hunted down and rammed the pirate whaler *Sierra*, eventually putting it out of business. Publicity over the *Sierra* operation motivated the arrest of two other pirate whalers in South Africa. The next year Sea Shepherd was involved in the sinking of two Spanish whalers that had flagrantly exceeded whale quotas set by the IWC. In 1986, Sea Shepherd was involved in the sinking of two Icelandic whalers (half the Icelandic whaling fleet) in Reykjavik harbor and also managed to damage the nearby whale-processing plant. Seeking publicity, crew members demanded to be arrested for their actions, but Iceland refused to charge them. Indeed, Sea Shepherd claims that in all of its operations it has never caused nor suffered an injury, nor have any of its crew members been convicted in criminal proceedings.

Typically, Sea Shepherd invites members of the news media along to document and publicize the destructive and exploitative practices it opposes. Such documentary footage has been shown on major television networks in the United States, Britain, Canada, Australia, and Western Europe. This publicity played an important role in increasing public awareness of marine conservation issues and in mobilizing public opinion against the slaughter of marine mammals. Sea Shepherd helped to bring about the end of commercial **seal**-killing in Canada and in the Orkney Islands, Scotland.

Highly successful in its efforts against outlaw whalers, Sea Shepherd continues to conduct research on conservation and **pollution** issues and to monitor national and interna-

tional law on marine conservation issues. Its members are working to establish a wildlife sanctuary in the Orkney Islands. Its present campaign is focused primarily against **drift net** fishing in the North Pacific, in support of a United Nations call for a complete international ban on drift-net fishing. Contact: The Sea Shepherd Conservation Society, 1314 2nd St., Santa Monica, CA 90401. *See also* International Convention for the Regulation of Whaling

[*Lawrence J. Biskowski*]

Sea turtles

Sea turtle populations have dramatically declined in numbers over the past half century. Green sea turtles (*Chelonia mydas*), hawksbills (*Eretmochelys imbricata*), Kemp's Ridleys (*Lepidochelys kempii*), loggerheads (*Caretta caretta*), and leatherbacks (*Dermochelys coriacea*) have all had their numbers decimated by human activity. The decline has been caused by several factors, including the development of a highly industrialized fishery to meet the demand for seafood on a worldwide basis. The most economical fishing method involves pulling multiple nets underwater for extended periods of time, and any air-breathing animals, such as sea turtles, which get caught in the net are usually drowned before they are hoisted on board.

In the United States, this problem has led to the introduction of the **turtle excluder device (TED)**, which must be placed on each tow net used by commercial shrimpers and fishermen. These cage-like devices have a slanted section of bars which allow fish and shellfish into the net but deflect turtles. These highly controversial devices have been mandatory for less than a decade, but there are some indications that they are saving thousands of turtles per year.

As significant as the impact of commercial fishing may seem, it does little to sea turtle populations compared to losses incurred at the earliest stages of the turtles' life history. In the late 1940s, along an isolated beach near Tamaulipas, Mexico, an extremely dense assemblage of sea turtles were observed digging out nests and laying eggs at the beach. So many females were present that they were seen crawling over one another and digging out the nests of others in order to lay their own eggs. At this location alone, the sea turtle population was estimated in the millions. In the early 1960s, scientists realized that the turtles found at Tamaulipas were a distinct species, Kemp's Ridley, and that they nested nowhere else in the world; but by that time the population had declined to only a few hundred turtles.

Threats to the survival of newly hatched sea turtles have always been enormous; crows, gulls, and other predators attack them as they scurry seaward, and they are prey for waiting barracudas and jacks as they reach water. Other animals raid their nests for the eggs, and humans are among these nest predators, collecting the eggs for food. Sea turtles concentrate their numbers in small nesting locations such as Tamaulipas in order to greatly outnumber their natural

Loggerhead sea turtle returns to sea after laying eggs on a Florida beach.

predators, thus allowing for the survival of at least a few individuals to perpetuate the **species**. However, this congregating behavior has contributed to their demise, because it has made human predation easier and more profitable.

Adult turtles are harvested as a protein source in many **Third World** countries, and many turtles are also subjected to increasing levels of **marine pollution**. Both of these factors have contributed to the sharp decline in their population. Public awareness and **conservation** efforts may keep sea turtles from **extinction**, but it is not clear whether species will be capable of rebounding from the decimation that has already taken place. *See also* Endangered species; Endangered Species Act; Marine Protection, Research and Sanctuaries Act

[*Eugene C. Beckham*]

FURTHER READING

Bjorndal, K. A., ed. *Biology and Conservation of Sea Turtles.* Washington, D.C.: Smithsonian Institution Press, 1981.

Carr, Archie. *So Excellent a Fish: Tales of Sea Turtles.* New York: Scribners, 1984.

Ezell, C. "Turtle Recovery Could Take Many Decades." *Science News* 142 (22 August 1992): 118.

National Research Council. *Decline of the Sea Turtles: Causes and Prevention.* Washington, D.C.: National Academy Press, 1990.

Stolzenburg, W. "Requiem for the Ancient Mariner." *Sea Frontiers* 39 (March-April 1993): 16-18.

Seabed disposal

Over 70 percent of the earth's surface is covered by water. The coastal zone—the boundary between the ocean and land—is under the primary influence of humans, while the rest of the ocean remains fairly remote from human activity. This remoteness has in part led scientists and policy makers to examine the deep ocean, particularly the seabed, as a potential location for waste disposal.

Much of the deep ocean seabed consists of abyssal hills and vast plains that are geologically stable and have sparse numbers of bottom-dwelling organisms. These areas have been characterized as oozes, hundreds of meters thick, that are in effect "deserts" in the sea. Other attributes of the deep ocean seabed that have led scientists and policy makers to consider the sea bottom as a repository for waste include the immobility of the interstitial pore water within the **sediment**, and the tendency for **ion**s to adsorb or stick to the sediment, which limits movement of elements within the waste. Another important factor has been the lack of known commercial resources such as **hydrocarbons**, minerals, or fisheries.

The deep seabed has been studied as a potential disposal option specifically for the placement of **high-level radioactive waste**. Investigations on the feasibility of disposing **radioactive waste**s in the seabed were carried out for over a decade by a host of scientists from around the world. In 1976, the Organization for Economic Cooperation and Development (OECD) and the Nuclear Energy Agency coordinated research at the international level and formed the Seabed Working Group. Members of the group included Belgium, Canada, France, the Federal Republic of Germany, Italy, Japan, the Netherlands, Switzerland, United Kingdom, United States, and the Commission of European Communities. The Seabed Working Group focused its investigation on two sites in the Atlantic Ocean, Great Meteor East and the Southern Nares Abyssal Plain, and one site in the Pacific Ocean, known as E2. The Great Meteor East site lies between 30.5°N and 32.5°N, 23°W and 26°W, approximately 1,865 miles (3,000 km) southwest of Britain. The Southern Nares Abyssal Plain site lies between 22.58°N and 23.17°N, 63.25°W and 63.67°W, approximately 375 miles (600 km) north of Puerto Rico. Site E2 in the Pacific Ocean lies between 31.3°N and 32.67°N, 163.42°E and 165°E, and is approximately 1,240 miles (2,000 km) east of Japan.

This working group pursued a multidisciplinary approach to studying the deep-ocean sediments as a potential disposal option for high-level radioactive waste. High-level radioactive waste consists of spent nuclear fuel or by-products from the reprocessing of spent nuclear fuel. It also includes transuranic wastes, a byproduct of fuel assembly, weapons fabrications, and reprocessing operations, and **uranium** mill tailings, a byproduct of mining operations. **Low-level radioactive** waste is legally defined as all types of waste that do not fall into the high-level radioactive waste category. They are made up primarily of byproducts of nuclear reactor operations and products that have been in contact with the use of **radioisotope**s. Low-level radioactive wastes are characterized as having small amounts of **radioactivity** that do not usually require shielding or heat-removing equipment.

One proposal to dispose of high-level radioactive waste in the deep seabed involved the enclosure of the waste in an insoluble solid with metal sheathing or projectile-shaped canisters. When dropped overboard from a ship, the canisters would fall freely to the ocean bottom and bury themselves 33-44 yards (30-40 meters) into the soft sediments of the seabed. Other proposals recommend drilling holes in the seabed and mechanically inserting the canisters. After emplacement of the canisters, the holes would then be plugged with inert material.

The 1972 international **Convention on the Prevention of Marine Pollution by Dumping of Waste and Other Matter**, commonly called the London Dumping Convention, prohibits the disposal of high-level radioactive wastes. In the United States, the **Marine Protection, Research and Sanctuaries Act** of 1972 also bans the ocean disposal of high-level radioactive waste. However, Britain has recently considered using the continental shelf seabed for disposal of low- and intermediate-level radioactive waste. The European countries discontinued ocean dumping of low-level radioactive waste in 1982. In the United States, the ocean disposal of low-level radioactive waste ceased in the 1970s. Between 1951 and 1967, approximately 34,000 containers of low-level radioactive waste were dumped in the Atlantic Ocean by the United States.

Another important aspect in the debate about seabed disposal is the risk to humans, not only because of the potential for direct contact with wastes but also because of the possibility of accidents during transport to the disposal location and contamination of fishery resources. When comparing seabed disposal of high-level radioactive waste to land disposal, for example, the transportation risks may be higher because travel to a site at sea would likely be longer than travel to a location on land. Increased handling by personnel substantially increases the risk. Also, there is a statistically greater risk of accidents at sea than on land when transporting anything, especially radioactive wastes, although such an accident at sea would probably pose less risk to humans.

It is also a concern that the seabed environment may be more inhospitable than a land site to the metal canisters containing the radioactive waste, because corrosion of them is more rapid due to the salts in marine systems. In addition, it is uncertain how fast radionuclides will be transported away from the site. The heat associated with the decay of high-level radioactive waste may cause convection in the sediment pore waters, resulting in the possibility that the dissolved radioactive material will diffuse to the sediment-water interface. Predictions from calculations, however, indicate that convection may not be significant. According to laboratory experiments that simulate subseabed conditions, it would take roughly 1,000 years for radioactive waste buried at a depth of 33 yards (30 meters) to reach the sediment-water interface. Other technical considerations adding to the uncertainty of the ultimate fate of buried radioactive waste in the seabed involve possible **sorption** of the radionuclide cations to clay particles in the sediment, and possible uptake of radionuclides by bottom dwelling organisms.

The Seabed Working Group concluded from their investigation that seabed disposal of high-level radioactive waste is safe. Compared to land disposal sites, the predicted doses of possible radiation exposure are lower than published radiological assessments. However, there are political concerns over deep-ocean seabed disposal of wastes. Deep-ocean disposal sites would likely be in international waters.

Therefore, international agreements would have to be reached, which may be very difficult with countries without a **nuclear power** industry, particularly for disposal of radioactive waste. As of 1992, there were no plans by any countries to dispose high-level radioactive waste in the deep ocean seabed.

In 1991, the Woods Hole Oceanographic Institution held a workshop to discuss the research required to assess the potential of the abyssal ocean as an option for disposal of sewage **sludge**, incinerator ash, and other high volume benign wastes. The disposal technology considered at this workshop entailed employing an enclosed elevator from a ship to emplace the waste at or close to the seabed. One issue raised at the workshop was the need to investigate the incidence of benthic storms that may occur along the deep ocean seabed. These benthic storms, also called turbidity flows, are currents with high concentrations of sediment that can stir up the sea bottom, erode the seabed, and redistribute sediment further downstream. The consequences of benthic storms on waste disposed in the seabed in the deep sea are unknown, but they may disperse wastes to unwanted locations, and therefore warrant further study.

Woods Hole held a follow-up workshop in 1992. Included were a broader array of scientists and representatives from environmental organizations, and these two groups disagreed over the use of the ocean floor as a waste-disposal option. The researchers supported the consideration and study of the seabed and the ocean in general as sites for disposal of wastes. The environmentalists did not support ocean disposal of wastes. The environmentalists' view is consistent with the law passed in 1988, the **Ocean Dumping Ban Act**, which prohibits the dumping of sewage sludge and industrial waste in the marine environment. Any future ocean dumping activities of sewage sludge, industrial waste, radioactive materials, or other wastes would require a legislative amendment to the current ban. *See also* Convention on the Law of the Sea; Dredging; Hazardous waste siting; Marine pollution; Ocean dumping; Radioactive pollution

[*Marci L. Bortman*]

FURTHER READING

Chapman, N. A., and I. G. McKinley. *The Geological Disposal of Nuclear Waste.* New York: Wiley, 1987.

Freeman, T. J., ed. *Advances in Underwater Technology, Ocean Science and Offshore Engineering.* Vol. 18, *Disposal of Radioactive Waste in Seabed Sediments.* Boston: Graham & Trotman, 1989.

Krauskopf, K. B. *Radioactive Waste Disposal and Geology.* New York: Chapman and Hall, 1988.

Murray, R. L. *Understanding Radioactive Waste.* Judith A. Powell, ed. Columbus, OH: Battelle Press, 1989.

Spencer, D. W. "The Ocean and Waste Management." *Oceanus* 33 (Summer 1990): 7-23.

Seabrook Nuclear Reactor (Seabrook, New Hampshire)

Americans once looked to nuclear energy as the nation's great hope for power generation in the twenty-first century. Today, **nuclear power** plants are regarded with suspicion

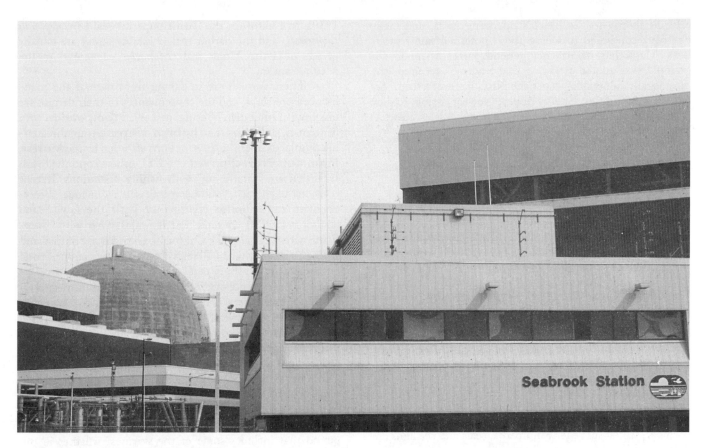

Seabrook Nuclear Reactor (Seabrook, New Hampshire).

and distrust, and new proposals to construct them are met with opposition. Perhaps the best transition in the perception of nuclear power is the debate that surrounded the construction of the Seabrook Nuclear Reactor in Seabrook, New Hampshire.

The plant was first proposed in 1969 by the Public Service Company of New Hampshire (PSC), an agency then responsible for providing 90 percent of all electrical power used in that state. The PSC planned to construct a pair of atomic reactors in marshlands near Seabrook in order to ensure an adequate supply of electricity in the future.

Residents were not enthusiastic about the plan. The marshlands and beaches around Seabrook have long been a source of pride to the community, and in March of 1976, the town voted to oppose the plant. Townspeople soon received a great deal of support. Seabrook is only a few miles north of the Massachusetts border, and residents and government officials from that state joined the opposition against the proposed plant. In addition, an umbrella organization of fifteen anti-nuclear groups called the Clamshell Alliance was formed to fight the PSC plan.

The next twelve years were characterized by almost non-stop confrontation between the PSC and its supporters and Clamshell Alliance and other groups opposed to the proposal. Hardly a month passed during the 1970s and 80s without news of another demonstration or the arrest of someone protesting construction. The issues became more complex as economic and technical considerations changed

during this time. The demand for electricity, for example, began to drop instead of increasing, as the PSC had predicted, and at least three other utilities that had agreed to work with PSC on construction of the plant withdrew from the program. The total cost of construction also continued to rise. When first designed, construction costs were estimated at $973 million for both reactors. Only one reactor was ever built, and by the time that it was finally licensed in 1990, total expenditures for it alone had reached nearly $6.5 billion.

The decision to build at Seabrook eventually proved to be a disaster financially and from a public relations stance for PSC. The company's economic woes peaked in 1979 when the courts ruled that PSC could not pass along additional construction costs at Seabrook to its customers. Over the next decade, the company fell into even more difficult financial straits, and on January 28, 1988, it filed for bankruptcy protection. The company promised that its action was not the end for the Seabrook reactor and maintained that the plant would eventually be licensed.

A little more than two years later, the **Nuclear Regulatory Commission (NRC)** granted a full-power operating license to the Seabrook plant. The decision was received enthusiastically by the utility companies in the New England Power Pool, who believed that Seabrook's additional capacity would reduce the number of power shortages experienced by consumers in the six-state region.

Private citizens and government officials were not as enthusiastic. Consumers faced the prospect of higher electrical bills to pay for Seabrook's operating costs, and many observers continued to worry about potential safety problems. Massachusetts attorney general, James Shannon, for example, was quoted as saying that Seabrook received "the most legally vulnerable license the NRC has ever issued." *See also* Electric utilities; Energy policy; Nuclear fission; Radioactive waste management; Three Mile Island Nuclear Reactor

[*David E. Newton*]

FURTHER READING

"Back from the Dead." *Forbes* (January 9, 1988): 134.

Dresser, P. D., ed. *Nuclear Power Plants Worldwide.* Detroit, MI: Gale Research, 1993.

Shulman, S. "More Woes for New England's Beleaguered Nuclear Power Plant." *Nature* (February 11, 1988): 72.

———. "Embattled Seabrook Wins License at Last." *Nature* (March 8, 1990): 96.

Wasserman, H. "Clamshell Alliance: Getting It Together." *Progressive* (September 1977): 14-18.

———. "Clamshell Reaction: Protest against Nuclear Power Plant at Seabrook, N.H. by Clamshell Alliance." *Nation* (June 18, 1977): 744-749.

———. "Nuclear War by the Sea." *Nation* (September 11, 1976): 203-205.

Seals and sea lions

Members of the suborder Pinnipedia, seals and sea lions are characterized by paddle-like flippers on a pair of limbs. Most pinnipeds are found in boreal or polar regions and are the most important predators in many high latitude areas, feeding primarily on fish and squid. Seals and sea lions catch their prey during extended dives of up to 25 minutes at depths of 2,625 feet (800 m) or more. Pinniped biologists are interested in the physiological changes these animals undergo during their dives. Known as mammalian dive response, a combination of reduced heart rate and a lowered core body temperature enables these warm-blooded animals to complete such dives.

Seals and sea lions must return to beaches and ice floes each year to give birth. Here they raise their pups in large congregations known as colonies. In some **species** the larger, more aggressive males will form polygamous mating groups, or harems, and claim and defend territories in these limited breeding areas. Males that do not get to mate form "bachelor male" groups in areas less suitable for weaning pups. Males of most species of pinnipeds do not mate before age four but may acquire harems when they attain large enough size and fighting experience. Some individual seals have been known to live as long as 46 years.

Because of the commercial value of their pelts, many species of seals and sea lions are threatened by hunting. One of the largest pinnipeds, the Stellar sea lion (*Eumetopias jubatus*) has been steadily decreasing in numbers. In three years, the new pup count at the Marmot Island Rookery, the largest known sea lion rookery in the world, has decreased from an average of 6,700 to only 2,910. The northern or Pribilof fur seal (*Callorhinus ursinus*) has been heavily exploited for its fur and has been in steady decline since the mid-

1950s. In California, the Guadeloupe fur seal (*Arctocephalus townsendi*) and the harbor seal (*Phoca vitulina*) are endangered, as is the Monk seal (*Monachus monachus*) in the Mediterranean.

These animals are in danger from natural and man-induced pressures, and the consequences of their demise are unknown. Other than hunting, perceived **competition** with fisherman, **pollution**, and **habitat** destruction are threatening pinnipeds. Despite the sanctions afforded by the **Marine Mammals Protection Act (1972)**, fishers continue to kill seals that are "interfering" with fishing operations. Recent revisions to the act require some vessels to include observers who can monitor compliance with the law. Some environmentalists contend that it is the fisher who "interferes" with the seals. The California Department of Fish and Game estimates that 2,000 seals die each year from accidental entanglement in fishing nets.

In the summer of 1988, 18,000 harbor seals washed up on European shores. They were discovered to be suffering from an acute viral infection, possibly due to an immune-system breakdown. Chemical pollutants, mainly **polychlorinated biphenyl (PCB)**, have been implicated in reduced immune function in marine mammals, and levels of PCBs have been constantly increasing in many coastal waters. A connection has also been made between mass seal **die-off**s and increasing temperature. Four of the six recorded mass mortalities have occurred in the past twelve years, a period that includes some of the warmest weather in the twentieth century. Other pollutants, such as **heavy metals**, may also affect seal health or reproductive ability. **Oil spills** also poison seal food sources and reduce the insulation ability of the seals' fur.

Finally, the reduction of habitat for feeding and reproduction has not been investigated thoroughly. Reputedly caused by reductions in prey-fish stocks due to **overfishing** and by development of coastal shorelines, this reduction may negatively affect pinniped populations.

[*William G. Ambrose, Jr. and Paul E. Renaud*]

FURTHER READING

Gentry, R. "Seals and Their Kin." *National Geographic* 171 (1987): 474-501.

Hersh, S. "Saga of North Sea Seals (Phocine Distemper Virus)." *Sea Frontiers* 36 (1990): 55.

Rosenberg, S. "Sea Lions of Monterrey." *Sea Frontiers* 35 (1989): 97-103.

Stirrup, M. "A Sea Lion Mystery." *Sea Frontiers* 36 (1990): 46-53.

Stolzenberg, W. "Seals Under Siege: A Heated Warning." *Science News* 138 (1990): 84.

Sumick, J. L. *An Introduction to the Biology of Marine Life.* 5th ed. Dubuque, IA: W. C. Brown, 1992.

Sears, Paul B. (1891-1990)
American ecologist and conservationist

Born in Bucyrus, Ohio, Paul Sears (1891-1990) obtained bachelor's degrees in zoology and economics, then earned a Ph.D. in botany from the University of Chicago. He spent most of his career as professor or head of various botany departments. In these positions, Sears researched changes in native flora as a result of human activities, conducted pioneering studies of fossil pollen, and studied the relationship between vegetation and climatic change. A respected and influential ecologist, he served as president of the Ecological Society of America (1948) and received the ESA's "Eminent Ecologist Award" in 1965. He spent the last ten years of his academic career as chair of the graduate program in **conservation** at Yale University and retired in 1960.

Sears was one of the few biological ecologists interested in **human ecology**, writing cogently and consistently in a field that he saw as a problem in synthesis. In his 1957 Condon Lecture at the University of Oregon, titled "The Ecology of Man," he mandated "serious attention to the ecology of man" and demanded "its skillful application to human affairs."

He considered **ecology** a "subversive subject," arguing that if it were taken seriously, it would "endanger the assumptions and practices accepted by modern societies, whatever their doctrinal commitments." But Sears was a optimist and believed that scientists would eventually agree because the nature of their work mandated that they have "confidence that the world hangs together."

As a conservationist, Sears believed that one of the basic lessons ecology teaches is that materials cycle and recycle through natural systems. Thus, he became a strong advocate of intensive **recycling** by human societies. He also taught that a return to greater use of human muscle power would be healthy for people because it would promote fitness and energy conservation, as well as an impact on the biosphere.

Sears was also one of the few prominent ecologists to successfully write for popular audiences. At least one of his popular books, *Deserts on the March*, first published in 1935, has become a minor American classic, reprinted in a fourth edition in 1980. The title provides an apt summary: in it, Sears documents the mistakes American farmers made in creating conditions that led to the disastrous **Dust Bowl**. This book had a major influence on the soil conservation movement in the United States.

Throughout his life, Sears believed that the best way to solve ecological problems was to teach every person about their own immediate **environment**: "Each of us can begin quite simply by learning to look about himself, wherever he may be." The touchstone of education, especially a scientific one, should be "the final ability to read and enjoy the landscape. While there is life there is hope, but only for the enlightened."

[*Gerald L. Young*]

FURTHER READING

Sears, P. B. *Deserts on the March*. 4th ed. Norman: University of Oklahoma Press, 1980.

———. "The Processes of Environmental Change by Man." In *Man's Role in Changing the Face of the Earth*, edited by W. L. Thomas, Jr. Chicago: The University of Chicago Press, 1956.

———. *Where There is Life: An Introduction to Ecology*. New York: Dell, 1970.

Seattle, Noah (1786-1866)

Duwamish chief

Noah Seattle (or See-athl) was a chief of the Duwamish or Suquamish tribe, one of the Salish group of the Northwest Coast of North America. Born in the Puget Sound area in 1786, Seattle lived there until his death on June 7, 1866. He was baptized a Roman Catholic about 1830 and is buried in the graveyard of the Port Madison Catholic Church. Ironically, Native Americans were banned by law from living in Seattle, Washington, the city named after him, one year after the chief's death.

By most accounts, Seattle was a great orator and a skilled diplomat. Although he never fought in a war against white people, he was a warrior with a reputation for daring raids on neighboring tribes. Seattle owned eight Native American slaves, but freed them after President Abraham Lincoln's Emancipation Proclamation. Hew was the first to sign the Port Elliott Treaty negotiations of 1855, which surrendered most Native American lands in the Puget Sound area for white settlement. He gave two short speeches on that occasion, which are preserved in the National Archives in Washington, D. C. Both speeches encouraged others to sign the agreement and to cooperate with the United States authorities.

Seattle has become famous in recent years as the author of one of the most widely quoted pieces of environmental literature in the world. Among some familiar passages are: "How can you buy or sell the sky, the warmth of the land? The earth is our mother. This we know, the earth does not belong to man. Man belongs to the earth. Whatever befalls the earth, befalls the sons of the earth. Man did not weave the web of life; he is merely a strand in it. Whatever he does to the web, he does to himself."

Generally called the speech, letter or lament of Chief Seattle, this text exists in many forms. It has been set to music, called the *Fifth Gospel* in religious services, and used to sell everything from toilet tissue to recyclable plastic bags. A version was used by artist Susan Jeffers in 1991 to accompany drawings in a best selling children's book called, *Brother Eagle, Sister Sky*. This piece is a poetic, moving, environmentally sensitive work that supports beliefs about the reverence of Native Americans for the earth. Unfortunately, there is no evidence that Chief Seattle ever said any of the wise words attributed to him.

Historian Rudolf Kaiser has traced the origins and myths surrounding the Chief Seattle text. The first report of what we now know as Seattle's speech appeared in an article by Dr. Henry A. Smith published in the *Seattle Sunday Star* on October 29, 1887, as part of a series of old pioneer reminiscences. Smith was recalling remarks made by the Chief in 1854 on the arrival of Governor Stevens to the territory. Although thirty-three years had passed since the event, Smith wrote that he clearly remembered the "grace and earnestness of the sable old orator."

As Smith reconstructed it, the speech was dark and gloomy, the farewell of a vanishing race. "Your God loves his people and hates mine...It matters but little where we pass the remainder of our days. They are not many...Some grim Nemesis of our race is on the redman's trail, and wherever he goes he will still hear the sure approaching footsteps of the fell destroyer." This version was mostly a justification for displacement of the native peoples by the pioneers. Smith remembered the Chief saying that the President's offer to buy Native American lands was generous "for we are no longer in need of a great country." This version has no mention of the web of life or other ecological concepts.

In 1969 Smith's stuffy Victorian prose was translated into modern English by poet William Arrowsmith. Two year later, Ted Perry wrote the script for a film called *Home* produced by the Southern Baptist Convention. He used some quotes from Arrowsmith's translation together with a great deal of imagery, symbolism, and sentiments of 1970s environmentalism. Perry is the source of ninety percent of what we now know as Seattle's speech. Over Perry's objections, the film's editors attributed the text to Chief Seattle to make it seem more authentic.

The piece has since assumed a life of its own. Some obvious inconsistencies exist, such as "hearing the lovely cry of the whippoorwill" or having "seen a thousand rotting buffaloes on the prairie, left by the white man who shot them from a passing train." Chief Seattle lived his whole life in the Puget Sound area and died thirteen years before the railroads reached the West Coast. He never heard a whippoorwill or saw a buffalo. Many people who use the speech are unperturbed by evidence that it is untrue. It so perfectly supports their view of Native Americans that they believe some Native American should have said these things even if Seattle did not.

This story is a good example of a myth that persists because it fits our preconceived views. In Chief Seattle, we seem to find an unsophisticated primitive who spoke in poetic, beautiful language and prophesied all the evils we now experience. Indigenous cultures probably contain much ecological wisdom that can be taught to others, but care must be taken not to blindly accept mythological texts such as this.

[*William P. Cunningham*]

FURTHER READING

Kaiser, R. "Chief Seattle's Speech(es): American Origins and European Reception—Almost a Detective Story." In *Indians in Europe*, edited by C. F. Feest. Gottingen, 1985.

Secchi disk

A simple instrument used to measure the transparency of surface water bodies such as lakes and reservoirs. A Secchi disk is a metal, plastic, or wooden disk that is 8-12 inches (20-30 centimeters) in diameter. It may be white or have alternating black and white quadrants. A long calibrated rope

Testing water clarity with a secchi disk.

is attached to the center of the disk. Researchers use the disk by lowering it into the water, usually from the shaded side of a boat, and measuring the depth at which it just disappears from sight. The disk is then lowered a little more and then raised until it reappears. The average of the depths at which the disk disappears and then reappears is known as the Secchi depth. The amount of **sediment**, algae, and other solids in the water affects clarity and depth of light penetration and thus, Secchi depth. Scientists use this measure of transparency as a simple indication of **water quality**, often by comparing Secchi depth measurements over a period of time to track changes in the clarity of a particular water body.

Second World

The former Soviet Union and those (formerly) communist states that were politically and economically allied with it are often informally called the Second World. The term developed after World War II to distinguish communist bloc states from powerful capitalist states (**First World**) and from smaller, nonaligned developing states (**Third World**). These terms developed as a part of theories that the world's countries together made up a single dynamic system in which these three sectors interacted. Although the term is often used to indicate countries and regions of intermediate economic strength, its proper meaning has to do with political economy, or the politics of communist-socialist economics. In recent years, with the shrinking role and then disintegration of the communist bloc, the term has become much less common than those of First and Third Worlds.

Secondary recovery technique

The term secondary recovery technique refers to any method for removing oil from a **reservoir** after all natural recovery methods have been exhausted. The term has slightly different meanings depending on the stage of recovery at which such methods are used.

The oil trapped in an underground reservoir is typically mixed with water, **natural gas**, and other gases. When a **well** is sunk into the reservoir, oil may flow up the well pipe to the earth's surface at a rate determined by the concentration of these other substances. If the gas pressure is high, for example, the oil may be pushed out in a fountain-like gusher.

Flow out of the reservoir continues under the influence of a number of natural factors, such as gravity, pressure of surrounding water, and gas pressure. Later, flow is continued by means of pumping. All such recovery approaches that depend primarily on natural forces are know as primary recovery techniques.

Primary recovery techniques normally remove no more than about thirty percent of the oil in a reservoir. **Petroleum** engineers have long realized that another fraction of the remaining oil can be forced out by fluid injection. The process of fluid injection involves the drilling of a second hole into the reservoir at some distance from the first hole through which oil is removed. Some gas or liquid is then pumped down into the second hole, increasing pressure on the oil remaining in the reservoir. The increased pressure forces more oil out of the reservoir and into the recovery pipe.

The single most common secondary recovery technique is water flooding. When water is pumped into the second well, it diffuses out into the oil reservoir and tends to displace oil from the particles to which it is absorbed. This process forces more of the residual oil up into the recovery pipe.

Water flooding was used as early as 1900, but did not become legal until 1921. A common practice was to drill a series of wells, some of which were still producing and others of which employed water injection. As the former became exhausted, they were converted to water injection wells and another group of producer wells were drilled. The process was repeated until all available oil was recovered from the field.

Recently, more sophisticated approaches to fluid injection have been developed from a reservoir. The two fluids that have been used most extensively in these approaches are liquid **hydrocarbons** and **carbon dioxide**. The principle behind liquid hydrocarbons is to find some material that will mix completely with oil and then push the oil-mixture that is formed out of the reservoir into the recovery pipe. A commonly used hydrocarbon for this process is liquified petroleum gas (LPG), which is completely miscible with oil.

Since LPG is fairly expensive, only a small volume is actually used. It is pumped down into the reservoir and followed by a "pusher gas." The pusher gas, often **methane**, is inexpensive and can be used in larger volume. The pusher gas forces LPG into the reservoir where it (the LPG) mixes with residual oil.

This system has worked well in the laboratory, but not so well in actual practice. The LPG has a tendency to get lost in the reservoir to an extent that it does not effectively remove very much residual oil.

The most effective fluid now available for injection appears to be **carbon dioxide**. A mixture of carbon dioxide and water is pumped down into the reservoir and followed by an injection of pure water that drives the carbon dioxide-water mixture through the reservoir. As carbon dioxide comes into contact with oil, it dissolves in the oil, causing it to expand and break loose from surrounding rock. The oil-carbon dioxide-water is then pumped out of the recovery pipe where the carbon dioxide is removed from the mixture and re-used in the next recovery pass.

The carbon dioxide process has been effective in removing oil after water flooding has already been used and only twenty-five percent of the oil in a reservoir still remains. In most cases, however, it is more efficiently used with reservoirs containing a larger fraction of residual oil.

Fluid injection is one type of secondary recovery technique. Another whole group of methods can also be used to extract the remaining oil from a reservoir. If these methods are employed after fluid injection has been tried, they are often referred to as tertiary recovery techniques. If they are used immediately after primary recovery, they are known as secondary recovery techniques. A whole set of recovery techniques can be called by different names, therefore, depending on the stage at which they are used. It is becoming more common today to refer to *any* method for removing the residual oil from a reservoir as an enhanced recovery technique.

Another technique for removing residual oil from a reservoir makes use of surfactants. A surfactant is a substance whose molecules are attracted to water at one end and oil at the other end. The most familiar surfactants are probably the soaps and **detergents** found in every home.

If surfactants are injected into an oil reservoir, they will form emulsions between the oil and water in the reservoir.

The oil is essentially washed off particles of rock in the reservoir the way grease is washed off a pan by a household detergent. The emulsion that is formed is then pushed through the reservoir and out the producer pipe by a flood of water pushed down the injection pipe.

The surfactant method works well in the laboratory, although it has been less successful in the field. Surfactants tend to adsorb on rock particles and get left behind as the water pushes forward. Methods for overcoming this problem are now being explored.

One of the fundamental problems with recovering residual oil in a reservoir is that oil droplets often have difficulty in squeezing through the small openings between adjacent rock particles. The use of surfactants is one way of helping the oil particles slip through those openings more easily. Another approach is to increase the temperature of the oil in the reservoir, thereby reducing its viscosity (tendency to flow). As it becomes less viscous, the oil can more easily force its way through pores in the reservoir.

One of the earliest applications of this principle, the steam soak method, was first used in Venezuela in 1959. In this method, steam is injected into one part of the reservoir and the producer pipe is closed off. After a few days, the pipe is reopened, and the loosened oil flows out. This process is repeated a few times before a change is made in the method and steam is piped in continuously while the producer pipe remains open.

Steam injection works especially well with heavy oils that are not easily displaced by other secondary recovery techniques. It is now used commercially in a number of fields, primarily in Venezuela and California.

A dramatic form of secondary recovery is *in situ* ("in place") combustion. The principle involved is fairly simple. A portion of the oil in the reservoir is set on fire. The heat from that fire then warms the remaining residual oil and reduces its viscosity, forcing it up the producer pipe.

In practice, the fire can sometimes be made to ignite spontaneously simply by pumping air down the injection well. In some cases, however, the oil must actually be ignited at the bottom of the well. The temperature produced in this process may reach 650°-1200°F (350°-650°C) and the region of burning oil may creep through the rock at a speed of one inch to one foot (three to thirty centimeters) per day. As the fire continues, air, and usually water, are continually pumped into the injection well to keep the combustion zone moving. Under the best of circumstances, *in situ* combustion has recovered up to half of all the oil remaining in a reservoir.

Research has demonstrated that each recovery method is suitable for particular kinds of reservoirs. Oil viscosity, rock porosity, depth of the reservoir, and amount of oil remaining in the reservoir are all factors in determining which method to use. To date, however, the only method that has proved to be practical in actual field situations is steam injection.

[*David E. Newton*]

FURTHER READING

Dickey, P. A. *Petroleum Development Geology.* 3rd ed. Tulsa, OK: PennWell Books, 1986.

Secondary sewage treatment
See **Sewage treatment**

Secondary standards

Pollution control levels that affect the welfare of plants, animals, buildings and materials. Secondary standards may relate to either **water quality** or **air pollution** under the control of either the **Safe Drinking Water Act** or the **Clean Air Act**. These so-called "welfare effects" are thought not to affect human health but primarily crops, livestock, vegetation and buildings. Secondary standards can refer to effects to which some monetary value could be ascribed, such as damage to materials, recreation, **natural resources**, community property, or aesthetics. **Primary standards**, on the other hand, refer to pollution levels that affect human health.

Second-hand smoke
See **Cigarette smoke**

Secure landfill
See **Landfill**

Sediment

A mixture of sand, **silt**, clay, and perhaps organic components. **Soil** eroded from one location and deposited in another is identified as sediment. The sedimentary fraction has the ability to carry not only the mineral (sand, silt, and clay) and organic (**humus**) components, but also other components that may be attached such as **nitrogen** compounds, **herbicide**s, and **pesticide**s. These riders are of high concern to those involved in environmental studies. Products applied to the soil in one location and beneficial to that system may be transported to other locations where the effect is detrimental to the **habitat** of other life forms. Care must be exercised 1) when applying supplementary items to the soil and 2) to develop systems that keep sediment from finding its way into the streams and water bodies.

Sedimentation

The deposition of material suspended in a liquid. Sedimentation is normally considered a function of water deposition of the finer **soil** separates of sand, **silt**, and clay, but it may also include organic debris. Sometimes this is referred to as the **siltation** process, although there may be other fractions of material present other than silt. The term can be applied to wind-transported **sediment**s as well. Sedimentation can be both harmful and beneficial. River and stream channels, reservoirs, and other water bodies may be degraded because of the deposition of sediment materials. Many of the most important food- and fiber-producing soils of the world have been developed from the deposition of fine particulates by both water and wind. In some cases, large topographic land forms are the result of long-term sedimentation processes.

Seed bank

A seed bank is the **reservoir** of viable seeds present in a plant community. Seed banks are evaluated by a variety of methods. For some **species**, it is possible to make careful, direct counts of viable seeds. In most cases, however, the surface substrate of the **ecosystem** must be collected and seeds encouraged to germinate by exposure to light, moisture, and warmth. The germinating seedlings are then counted and, where possible, identified to species.

In most cases, the majority of seeds is found in surface layers. For example, the organic-rich forest floor contains almost all of the forest's seed bank, with much smaller numbers of seeds present in the mineral **soil**.

The seeds of some plant species can be remarkably long-lived, extending the life of the seed bank. For example, in northeastern North America, the seeds of pin cherry (*Prunus pensylvanica*) and red raspberry (*Rubus idaeus*) can persist in the forest floor for perhaps a century or longer. This considerably exceeds the period of time that these ruderal species are present as mature, vegetative plants during the initial stages of post-disturbance forest **succession**. However, because these species maintain a more-or-less permanent presence on the site through their persistent seed bank, they are well placed to take advantage of temporary opportunities of resource availability that follow disturbance of the stand by **wildfire**, windstorm, or harvesting.

The seeds of many other plant species have only an ephemeral presence in the seed bank. In addition to some tropical species whose seeds are short-lived, many species in temperate and northern latitudes produce seeds that cannot survive exposure to more than one winter. This is a common trait in many grasses, asters, birches, and most conifers, including pines, spruces, and fir. Often these species produce seeds that disperse widely, and can dominate the short-lived seed banks during the autumn and springtime. Species with an ephemeral presence in the seed bank must produce large numbers of well-dispersed seeds each year or at least frequently, if they are to successfully colonize newly disturbed sites and persist on the landscape.

Although part of the plant community, seed banks are much less prominent than mature plants. In some situations, however, individual plants in the seed bank can numerically dominate the total-plant density of the community. For example, in some cultivated situations the persistent seed bank can commonly build up to tens of thousands of seeds per square meter and sometimes densities which exceed 75,000

seeds per square meter. Even natural communities can have seed banks in the low tens of thousands of seeds per square meter. However, these are much larger than the densities of mature plants in those ecosystems.

The seed bank of the plant community is of great ecological importance because it can profoundly influence the vigour and species composition of the vegetation that develops after disturbance.

[*Bill Freedman*]

FURTHER READING

Grime, P. *Plant Strategies and Vegetation Processes.* New York: Wiley, 1979.
Harper, J. L. *Population Biology of Plants.* San Diego: Academic Press, 1977.

Seed dressings
See **Methylmercury seed dressings**

Seepage

The process by which water gradually flows through the **soil**. Seepage is the cause of a variety of environmental problems. For example, **pesticide**s used on a farm may enter **groundwater** and be transported by seepage to a human water supply. In some cases, toxic or **radioactive waste**s stored in sealed tanks underground have gotten into water supplies by seepage after the tanks have rusted and broken apart. *See also* Water quality

Selection cutting

A harvesting method that removes mature trees individually or in small groups. The resulting gaps in the canopy allow understory trees to develop under the protection of the remaining overstory. Among all regeneration methods selection cuttings offer seedlings the most protection against sun and wind. They also protect against the **erosion** of **soil** and maintain aesthetic value in forests. On the negative side, selection logging can damage the remaining trees and requires highly skilled labor and more expense. Because most of the overstory remains, selection cutting favors shade-tolerant **species** and is not appropriate when the goal is growth of light-demanding species. *See also* Clear-cutting

Sellafield (U. K.)
See **Windscale Advanced Gas Cooled Reactor**

Sense of place

Every adult seems to remember a special place from their past: a place of refuge as a child; sites of family vacations; a grandparent's farm; somewhere shared with a loved one at a special time. Many people, though often with some embarrassment, will confess to a favorite place in the present where they can go to be alone, to gather with friends, or spend leisure time. Places we can identify with—and that feel special. A literature about that identification with place—that sense of place—has burgeoned in the last two decades of the twentieth century.

Yet, contemporary literature, both fictional and factual, is packed with documentation of alienation, rootlessness, displaced people, loss of connection to any particular place, loss of identity and character in suburb and city. In 1957, in *America as a Civilization*, Max Lerner documented the loss of community and the quest to regain it, claiming "this is what I call the problem of place in America, and unless it is somehow resolved, American life will become more jangled and fragmented than it is, and American personality will continue to be unquiet and unfulfilled." As the century ends, an increasing number of scholars, thinkers, and writers are advocating a reinhabitation of place, a reclamation of the spirit and sense of place as a solution to numerous contemporary problems, including **environmental degradation**, sustainability, and social alienation.

Sense of place as a phrase has at least two meanings. First, the particular characteristic of a place that makes it what it is. For example, though few people have visited **Antarctica**, most have some sense, an image in their mind's eye, of what that continent is like. That image may be realistic, or unrealistic, or may be dramatically simplified, but it will usually be based on physical characteristics that the place actually does have.

The second meaning is the particular sense that individuals have of places they know by experience; we all have a sense of many places that we have visited, but a sense of the same place is experienced in many ways by many different people. Even after a visit to Antarctica, for example, people will return with a variety of different views, depending on their reasons for being there, on how long they stayed, and on how much they know about the place. An explorer will carry one view, a natural scientist studying how organisms adapt to extreme environments will bring back a quite different view, and a tourist yet another viewpoint. Yi-Fu Tuan even claimed that "sense of place...implies a certain distance between self and place that allows the self to appreciate a place."

For many, a third meaning is the only one of consequence: that one can gain a sense of place only from being or becoming deeply involved with a place and by coming to know that one place and its inhabitants intimately. This is the meaning implicit in the claim that modern Americans must regain a sense of place to counteract their mobility and alienation from environment. The poet Gary Snyder refers to this when he claims that "there are many people on the planet now who are not 'inhabitants.' He teaches that spirit of place

is accessed only through knowledge gained by direct experience in a specific locale; "Know the plants" has become almost his mantra. When you really know the plants, you are beginning to get a sense of the place, a sense of what is possible and a sense of how to live there in harmony with the site and setting.

Interwoven with the concept of place is the sense of home. We all have a sense of many places (in the first two meanings of the phrase), but a feeling of home is always associated with a sense of that specific place where home is thought to be. Home can be a dwelling, a town, even a state or a nation (in the sense of 'homeland')—or all of these—but it always is a place, at one or several scales. Most of us live in some degree of intimacy with the place we call home; even if that is restricted to a dwelling, it is a place we know and are to some degree comfortable with. Beyond the dwelling, and even our identity with region and nation, to recognize what it means to say "the Earth is our home" might change the way we behave toward the world on which we live.

Scholars and students agree that sense of place in all three meanings is best developed by increasing one's knowledge of the locality in question. A full sense of the third meaning can only be developed by really getting to know one place well. That usually means living there, becoming engaged with the surroundings, getting involved with the community, making enough of a commitment of time to get beyond the surface. It takes real effort to get to know the plants (even in cities, to know what the trees and shrubs are in the parks and on the streets, and to know why those particular species are there rather than others), to know, in rural areas, what crops are planted and why, to know the climatic patterns and the reasons for those patterns. If such a sense of place could be enhanced and strengthened, this might change the way people use energy in their homes and cars, interact with other parts of the environment, and consider how connected each of us really is to the particular places where we live.

Some of the best American literature focuses on the complex relationships of an individual writer with a specific place. For example, **Henry David Thoreau**'s *On Walden Pond* trumpeted the personal significance and the transcendence of one small place. More recently, **Aldo Leopold**'s struggle to reclaim a ravaged farm in the sand counties of Wisconsin has become a metaphor for attempts to understand the importance to human lives of being immersed in the workings of a place of one's own. **Annie Dillard**'s mystical tome on Tinker Creek has, as a modern day Walden, helped many better understand the spirit of place. And, the "Refuge" Terry Tempest Williams found on the shores of the Great Salt Lake has generated empathy for the human condition and for the natural world with which it is so entwined.

If, says the poet **Wendell Berry**, you don't know where you are, you don't know who you are. People who have a better sense of who they are by knowing more about the places where they are, start paying attention to the impact those places have on their lives. Recognizing that place and identity are related, that place and well being cannot be disconnected, should lead to taking better care of those places.

[*Gerald L. Young*]

FURTHER READING

Cuba, L., and D.M. Hummon. "A Place to Call Home: Identification With Dwelling: Community, and Region," *The Sociological Quarterly* 34, no. 1 (Spring 1993): 111-131.

Swan, J. and R., eds. *Dialogues With the Living Earth: New Ideas on the Spirit of Place From Designers, Architects, and Innovators.* Wheaton, IL: Quest Books-Theosophical Publishing House, 1996.

Tall, D. *From Where We Stand: Recovering a Sense of Place.* Baltimore, MD: The Johns Hopkins University Press, 1993.

Septic tank

Nearly 20 million homes, which include almost 30 percent of the population of the United States, dispose of their **wastewater** through an on-site disposal system. The most commonly used type of system is the septic tank, which is an individual treatment system that uses the soil to treat small wastewater flows. The system is usually used in rural or large lot settings where centralized wastewater treatment is impractical. Septic tank systems are designed specifically for each site, using standardized design principles that are usually state-regulated. Septic tank systems commonly contain three components: the septic tank, a distribution box, and a drainfield, all of which are connected by conveyance lines.

The septic tank serves to separate solids from the liquids in the wastewater. All sources of wastewater, including those from sinks, baths, showers, washing machines, dishwashers, and **toilets**, are directed into the septic tank, since any of these waters can contain disease-causing microorganisms or environmental pollutants. The size of the septic tank varies depending on the number of bedrooms in the home, but an average tank holds 1,000 gallons (3,790 liters) of liquid. Wastewater in a septic tank is treated by **anaerobic** bacteria that digest organic materials, while encouraging the separation of solid materials from the wastewater. The solids accumulate and remain in the septic tank in the form of **sludge**, which collects at the bottom of the tank, and also in the form of scum, which floats on the top of the wastewater. Periodically (for example, every two or three years) the indigestible sludge and scum (referred to as septage) are removed from the tank by pumping and are disposed of in a septage disposal system (like a municipal **sewage treatment** system). Periodic pumping is designed to prevent the solids from leaking out of the septic tank in the wastewater effluent. The effluent from the septic tank is a cloudy liquid that still contains many pollutants (including **nitrogen** compounds, **suspended solid**s, and organic and inorganic materials) and microorganisms (including bacteria and **virus**es, some of which that may be potentially pathogenic), which require further treatment.

Treatment of the wastewater effluent from the septic tank is continued by transporting the wastewater by gravity to a **soil** absorption field through a connecting pipe. The absorption field is also referred to as the soil drainfield or the **nitrification** field. The absorption field consists of a series of underground perforated pipes covered with soil and turf, which may be connected in a closed loop system. The wastewater enters a constructed gravel bed (the trench) through perforations in the pipe, where it is stored before entering the underlying unsaturated soil. The wastewater is treated as it trickles into and through the soil by filtration and **adsorption** processes as well as by **aerobic** degradation processes before the wastewater enters the ground water. Filtration removes most of the suspended solids and may also remove microorganisms. Adsorption is the process by which pollutants and microorganisms are attracted to and held on the surfaces of soil particles, thus immobilizing them. Adsorption attracts such **nutrient**s such as **phosphorus** and some forms of nitrogen and is most effective when fine-textured soil is used as the adsorption medium. However, soils with a very fine texture, such as soils high in clay, may have too low permeability to allow much wastewater to pass through the soil. Microbial degradation results in the removal of many remaining nutrients and organic materials. If the volume and type of soil underlying a soil absorption system are adequate, most pollutants (with the exception of nitrate nitrogen) should be removed before the wastewater reaches the **groundwater**.

Although some difficulties can arise with septic systems, there are some simple practices that can prevent common problems. For example, groundwater **pollution** and surfacing of untreated or poorly filtered effluent from a septic tank system can be prevented by ensuring that excessive amounts of water are not allowed to enter or flood the drainfield. Reduced production of wastewater, or **water conservation**, is recommended to prevent system overload. Water from roof drains, basement sump pump drains, and other rain water or surface water drainage systems should be directed away from the absorption field. The functioning of the system can also be damaged by the addition of such materials as coffee grounds, wet-strength towels, disposable diapers, facial tissues, cigarette butts, and excessive amounts of grease, which can clog the inlet to the septic tank, or if carried out of the septic tank, may impede drainage of wastewater in the soil absorption field. The septic tank should be pumped more frequently if a garbage disposal is used.

Groundwater pollution can also be caused by the addition of hazardous **chemicals** to the septic tank system, which may be transported through the system to the ground water without removal or treatment in the system. Hazardous chemicals may be found in such commonly used products as **pesticide**s, solvents, latex paint, oven cleaners, dry cleaning fluids, motor oils, or degreasers.

Siting requirements for a soil absorption system depend on the amount of daily sewage flow and site conditions that affect the ability of the soil to absorb, treat, and dispose of septic tank effluent without creating a public health hazard or contamination of ground or surface waters. If a proposed site is located on a gently sloping surface that is not susceptible to flooding, and has at least six feet (1.8 m) of well-drained, permeable soil, with a low content of coarse fragments, only a minimum area is required for installation of the absorption drainfield. However, area requirements increase as slope increases and soil permeability, depth of suitable soil, and depth to groundwater decrease. However, at some sites, the soil type, depth, or site **topography** may not be suitable for the use of the conventional soil absorption drainfield, and modifications or additions to the conventional system may be required.

Siting requirements usually also include that sufficient area be reserved for installation of a repair system if the original system fails. This additional area should meet all requirements of the original soil absorption system and should be kept free of development and traffic. The disposal site should also be located at safe distances from ground water supply sources, lakes, streams, drain tile, and escarpments where seepage may occur, as well as set back from buildings and roads that may interfere with the proper operation of the system.

A common problem encountered in drainfields is excessive development of a clogging mat at the interface between the gravel bed in the absorption trench and the underlying soil due to the accumulation of organic materials and the growth of microorganisms. The development of a clogging mat is a natural process and at some sites, such as those with sandy soils, may be desirable to slow the movement of the water through the sandy materials to allow for treatment of the wastewater to occur. However, excessive development of a clogging mat may result in formation of anaerobic soil conditions, which are less conducive to degradation of the organic waste materials, as well as in surfacing of the effluent or backing up of the wastewaters into the residence.

At sites with limiting features or where problems with the excessive development of clogging mats occur, landowners may modify or enhance the conventional soil absorption drainfield to increase its performance. Examples of such alterations include:

(1) *Alternating drainfields.* The wastewater effluent from the septic tank is directed to two or more separate drainfields; a section of the drainfield receives effluent for six to twelve months and then is allowed to rest for a similar period of time. The clogging mat that forms at the soil/trench interface dries and is oxidized during this dormant period, thus increasing the expected life span of the section and restoring aerobic soil conditions.

(2) *Pressure distribution.* A pressure head is created within the distribution pipe system in the drainfield. This is usually achieved by using a dosing tank and a pump or a siphon and yields uniform distribution of the wastewater throughout the system. The pressure distribution system differs from a conventional system because approximately the same amount of effluent flows out of each hole in the distribution pipes, rather than a concentrated amount of effluent flowing by gravity into a few localized areas. The effluent is discharged periodically to the drainfield so that a dose/rest cycle is maintained, and in turn allows for the wastewater to be absorbed into the underlying soil before additional

effluent is added to the drainfield. The dose/rest cycle may also slow down the formation rate of the clogging mat that naturally occurs over time. Most commonly, landowners use these types of pressure distribution systems (which also employ vegetation to help evaporate liquids):

(a) low-pressure subsurface pipe distribution system, which consists of a network of small-diameter perforated plastic pipes buried in narrow, shallow trenches;

(b) mound system, in which wastewater is pumped to perforated plastic pipe that is placed in a vegetated sand mound constructed above the natural surface of the ground; and

(c) **evapotranspiration** bed, in which a vegetated sand bed is lined with plastic or other waterproof material.

A wide variety of onsite septic systems exist from which to select the most appropriate for a specific site. The primary criterion for selection of an appropriate system is the ability of the system to protect public health and to prevent **environmental degradation** at the specific site. *See also* Groundwater monitoring; Nitrates and nitrites; Wastewater treatment; Water pollution

[Judith Sims]

FURTHER READING

National Small Flows Clearinghouse. *So...Now You Own a Septic Tank.* Morgantown, WV: West Virginia University, 1990.

Northern Virginia Planning District Commission. *A Reference Guide for Homeowners: Your Septic System.* Morgantown, WV: West Virginia University, National Small Flows Clearinghouse, 1990.

Design Manual: Onsite Wastewater Treatment and Disposal Systems. Cincinnati, OH: U. S. Environmental Protection Agency, Municipal Environmental Research Laboratory, 1980.

Small Wastewater Systems: Alternative Systems for Small Communities and Rural Areas. Washington, DC: U. S. Environmental Protection Agency, Office of Water Program Operations, 1980.

Serengeti National Park

Serengeti National Park lies in northern Tanzania between Lake Victoria and the East African Rift Valley. It was established in 1929 (and expanded in 1940) to protect 5,600 square miles (14,500 sq. km) of the Serengeti plains **ecosystem**. This vast park spans an area twice the size of **Yellowstone National Park** and supports over 94 **species** of mammals, 400 species of birds, and includes the spectacular migration routes of the largest herds of grazing animals to be seen anywhere in the world.

Each year, migrating herds move clockwise around the Park, constantly seeking better feeding grounds. Changing water availability is the key factor in the annual **migration**s, which correlate closely with the local cycles of rainfall. At the right time of year, visitors to the Park can see hundreds of thousands of migrating herds of wildebeest (*Connochates taurinus*), running in winding lines several miles long. The

Zebras and wildebeests at Ngorongoro Crater, Serengeti National Park, Tanzania.

wildebeest are accompanied by herds of zebra (*Equus burchelli*) and Thomson's gazelle (*Gazella thomsoni*).

During the peak dry season (August to November), the grazers congregate in the Serengeti's northern extension, moving south east when the first storms appear in December. The greatest concentration of animals occurs in the short grass pastures of the eastern Serengeti from December to May when millions of the Park's migratory grazers assemble. They are accompanied by packs of nomadic predators such as lion (*Panthera leo*) and hyenas (*Crocuta crocuta*). As the dry season progresses (June and July) and the grazing gets worse, the massive herds move to the wooded **savanna**s of the western corridor of the Park. By mid-August, when this food supply is exhausted, the herds move back into the northern plains, crossing also into the adjacent Masai Mara National Reserve in Kenya.

The non-migrant inhabitants of the Serengeti plains include ostrich (*Struthio camelus*), impala (*Aepyceros melanious*), topi (*Damalicus korrigum*), buffalo (*Syncercus kaffer*), giraffe (*Giraffa camelopardalis*), Grant's gazelle (*Gazella granti*), leopard (*Panthera pardus*), cheetah (*Acinonyx jubatus*), hunting dogs (*Lycaeon pictus*), and jackals (*Canis adustus*).

The three principle species of migratory grazers—zebra, wildebeest, and Thomson's gazelle—do not compete directly for food, and it is common to find them grazing together. Zebras eat the upper parts of the grass shoots, exposing the softer leaf bases for the wildebeest. Grazing wildebeest in turn expose the herb layer beneath the grass,

which is eaten by gazelles. Balanced populations of grazers actively maintain the stability of **grassland** ecosystems: too little grazing will allow woody vegetation to grow, while too much grazing will turn grassland into **desert**.

Today, the Serengeti National Park is under pressure from the rapidly growing human population outside the Park. Domestic cattle herders and farmers operate inside Park boundaries, competing with the **wildlife** for food, water, and land, while well-armed poachers kill game for meat, horns, and tusks. Human ancestors (*Australopithecus robustus* and *Homo habilis*) once hunted game on the Serengeti plains, as evidenced by the finds of the **Louis** and **Mary Leakey** at Olduvai Gorge, which lies close to the Park's eastern entrance.

[*Neil Cumberlidge*]

FURTHER READING

Schaller, George B. *Golden Shadows, Flying Hooves.* Chicago: University of Chicago Press, 1970.

A Field Guide to the National Parks of East Africa. London: J. G. Williams, Collins, 1981.

Seveso, Italy

Accidents in which large quantities of dangerous **chemicals** are released into the environment are almost inevitable in the modern world. Toxic chemicals are produced in such large volumes today that it would be a surprise if such accidents were never to occur. One of the most infamous accidents of this kind occurred at Seveso, Italy, a town near Milan, on July 10, 1976.

The Swiss manufacturing firm of Hoffman-LaRoche operated a plant at Seveso for the production of hexachlorophene, a widely used disinfectant. One of the raw materials used in this process is 2,4,5-trichlorophenol (2,4,5-TCP). At one point in the operation, a vessel containing 2,4,5-TCP exploded, releasing the chemical into the atmosphere. A cloud 100 to 160 ft (30 to 50 m) high escaped from the plant and then drifted downwind. It eventually covered an area about 2,300 ft (700 m) wide and 1.2 miles (2 km) long.

Although 2,4,5-TCP is a skin irritant, it was not this chemical that caused concern. Instead, it was an impurity in 2,4,5-TCP, a compound called 2,3,7,8-tetrachlorodibenzo-p-dioxin, that caused alarm. This compound, one of a family known as **dioxin**s, is one the most toxic chemicals known to science. It occurs as a by-product in many manufacturing reactions in which 2,4,5-TCP is involved. Experts estimated that 7 to 35 pounds (3 to 16 kg) of dioxin were released into the atmosphere as a result of the Seveso explosion.

People living closest to the Hoffman-LaRoche plant were evacuated from their homes and the area was closed off. About 5,000 nearby residents were allowed to stay, but were prohibited from raising crops or farm animals.

Damage to plants and animals in the exposed area was severe. Thousands of farm animals died or had to be destroyed. More than 2.5 tons (225 kg) of contaminated soil were removed before planting could begin again. Short- and long-term effects on human health, however, were relatively modest. In the months following the accident, 176 individuals were found to have chloracne, an inflammation of the skin caused by chlorine-based chemicals. An additional 137 cases of the condition were found in a follow-up survey six months after the accident.

Other health problems were also detected in the human population. About eight percent of the exposed population had enlarged livers and a few residents showed signs of minor nerve damage. Some people claimed that exposed women had higher rates of miscarriage and of deformed children, but local authorities were unable to substantiate these claims. No human lives were lost in the accident.

[*David E. Newton*]

FURTHER READING

Harrison, R. M., ed. *Pollution: Causes, Effects, and Control.* Cambridge, Royal Society of Chemistry, 1990.

Walsh, J. "Seveso: The Questions Persist Where Dioxin Created a Wasteland." *Science* (9 September 1977): 1064-1067.

Whiteside, T. "Reporter at Large: TCDD Explosion at Icmesa Chemical Plant." *New Yorker* (25 July 1977): 41+.

———. "Reporter at Large: Dioxin Pollution of Seveso." *New Yorker* (4 September 1978): 34-36+.

Sewage treatment

Sewage is **wastewater** discharged from a home, business, or industry. Sewage is treated to remove or alter contaminants in order to minimize the impact of discharging wastewater into the **environment**. The operations and processes used in sewage treatment consist of physicochemical and biological systems.

The concerns of those involved in designing sewage treatment systems have changed over the years. Originally, the **biochemical oxygen demand** (BOD) and total **suspended solid**s (TSS) received most of the attention. This was primarily because excessive BOD and TSS levels could cause severe and readily apparent problems, such as oxygen deficits that led to odors and **fish kills**, and sludge deposits that suffocated benthic organisms. By removing BOD and TSS, other contaminants were also removed and other benefits were realized; so even today, some discharge permits contain only limits for BOD and TSS. However, many permits now contain limits on other contaminants as well, and these limits, as well as other requirements, are constantly changing.

Among the first contaminants to be added to the requirements for discharge permits were **nutrient**s. The most commonly regulated nutrients are **phosphorus** and **nitrogen**. Originally removing phosphorus and nitrogen could only be done through expensive, advanced methods. But scientists have recently discovered ways to accomplish enhanced removals of nutrients in conventional biological treatment plants with relatively minor operational and structural adjustments.

The most recently regulated pollutants are toxicants. There are regulations for specific toxic agents, and there are the generic-type regulations, which specify that the toxicity to certain test organisms should not exceed a certain level. For example, the wastewater discharged from a particular municipality may be restricted from killing more than 50 percent of the *Ceriodaphnia* in an aquatic toxicity test. The municipality would not need to determine what is causing the toxicity, just how to minimize its effects. Efforts to understand the causes of toxicity are referred to as toxicity reduction evaluations. The generic limit can therefore sometimes turn into a more specific standard, in the view of the municipality or industry, when the identity of a toxicant is determined; the general regulatory limit might remain, but treatment personnel are more cognizant of the role that a certain pollutant plays in overall, **effluent** toxicity.

The systems used to treat sewage can be divided into stages. The first stage is known as preliminary treatment. Preliminary treatment includes such operations as flow equalization, screening, comminution (or grinding), grease removal, flow measurement, and grit removal. Screenings and grit are taken to a **landfill**. Grease is directed to **sludge** handling facilities at the plant.

The next stage is primary treatment, which consists of gravity settling to remove suspended solids. Approximately 60 percent of the TSS in a domestic wastewater is removed during primary settling. Grease that floats to the surface of

Primary sewage treatment

Raw sewage
From sewer

Bar grate

Moving screen

Grit chamber

Effluent

To secondary
treatment

Sludge

To incineration, landfill,
or spread on cropland

Sludge drying bed

a.

Secondary treatment

From primary
treatment

Sludge inoculum   +   Effluent

Chlorine

Trickling bed
evaporation

Chlorination tank

Aeration tank
(activated sludge)

Air pump

Lagoon or marsh

To
river

b.

Schematic representation of a sewage treatment system.

the **sedimentation** tank is skimmed off and handled along with the sludge (known as primary sludge) collected from the bottom of the tank.

The next stage is secondary treatment, which is designed to remove soluble organics from the wastewater. Secondary treatment consists of a biological process and secondary settling. There are a number of biological processes. The most common is activated sludge, a process in which microbes, also known as **biomass**, are allowed to feed on organic matter in the wastewater. The make-up and dynamics of the biomass population is a function of how the activated sludge system is operated. There are many types of activated sludge systems that differ based on the time wastewater remains in the biological reactor and the time microbes remain there. They also differ depending on whether air or oxygen is introduced, how gas is introduced, and where wastewater enters the biological reactor, as well as the number of tanks and the mixing conditions.

There are also biological treatment systems in which the biomass is attached. Trickling filters and biological towers are examples of systems that contain biomass adsorbed to rocks plastic. Wastewater is sprayed over the top of the rocks or plastic and allowed to trickle down and over the attached biomass, which removes materials from the waste through sorption and biodegradation. A related type of attached-growth system is the rotating biological contactor, where biomass is attached to a series of thin, plastic wheels that rotate the biomass in and out of the wastewater.

It is important to note that each of the above biological systems is **aerobic**, meaning that oxygen is present for the microbes. **Anaerobic** biological systems are also available in both attached and suspended growth configurations. Examples of the attached and suspended growth systems are, respectively, anaerobic filters and upflow anaerobic sludge blanket units.

The end-products of aerobic and anaerobic processes are different. Under aerobic conditions, if completely oxidized, organic matter is transformed into products that are not hazardous. But an anaerobic process can produce **methane** (CH_4), which is explosive, and ammonia (NH_3) and hydrogen sulfide (H_2S), which are toxic. There are thus special design considerations associated with anaerobic systems, though methane can be recovered and used as a source of energy. Some materials are better degraded under anaerobic conditions than under aerobic conditions. In some cases, the combination of anaerobic and aerobic systems in a series provides better and more economical treatment than either system could alone. Many substances are not completely mineralized to the end-products mentioned above, and other types of intermediate metabolites can be considered in selecting a biological process.

Biomass generated during biological treatment is settled in secondary clarifiers. This settled biomass or secondary sludge is then piped to sludge-management systems or returned to the biological reactor in amounts needed to maintain the appropriate biomass level. The hydraulic detention time of secondary clarifiers is generally in the area of two hours.

As mentioned above, biological systems are designed on the basis of hydraulic residence time and sludge age. In a conventional activated-sludge system, sewage is retained in the reactor for about five to seven hours. Biomass, due to the recycling of sludge from the secondary clarifier, remains in the reactor, on average, for about ten days.

Disinfection follows secondary clarification in most treatment plants. Disinfection is normally accomplished with **chlorine**. Due to the potential environmental impact of chlorine, most plants now dechlorinate wastewater effluents before discharge.

Some facilities use another stage of treatment before disinfection. This stage is referred to as tertiary treatment or advanced treatment. Included among the more commonly used advanced systems are adsorption to activated **carbon**, filtration through sand and other media, **ion exchange**, various membrane processes, **nitrification-denitrification**, coagulation-flocculation, and fine screening.

The treatment systems used for municipal sewage can be different from the systems used by industry, for industrial wastes can pose special problems which require innovative applications of the technologies available. Additionally, industrial wastes are sometimes pretreated before being discharged to a sewer, as opposed to being totally treated for direct discharge to the environment. *See also* Aerobic sludge digestion; Anaerobic digestion; Bioremediation; Industrial waste treatment; Sludge treatment and disposal; Waste management

[*Gregory D. Boardman*]

FURTHER READING

Metcalf and Eddy, Inc. *Wastewater Engineering Treatment, Disposal, and Reuse*. Revised by G. Tchobanoglous and F. Burton. 3rd ed. New York: McGraw-Hill, 1991.

Peavy, H. S., Rowe, D. R., and Tchobanoglous, G. *Environmental Engineering*. New York: McGraw-Hill, 1985.

Viessman, W., and Hammer, M. J. *Water Supply and Pollution Control*. 4th ed. New York: Harper and Row, 1985.

Shadow pricing

A practice employed by some economists that involves putting a price on things that normally do not have a market value. For example, **pollution** degrades common property and the natural heritage of present and **future generations**, but because it is considered a "free" good, no one "pays" for it at the marketplace. Yet pollution has a cost even if the market fails to explicitly take into account this cost and assign it to responsible parties. Thus pollution is perceived by most economists as a defect that undermines otherwise efficient markets. To correct this defect, economists often advocate the use of some type of shadow pricing for pollution. Such prices are set by the "shadow" procedure of asking people what they would be willing to pay for breathing clean air, watching **whales** migrate, or preventing the **extinction** of a particular species of plant or animal. Hypothetical or shadow prices for these "commodities" can thereby be estimated. Some environmentalists and economists, however, criticize shadow pricing for falsely attempting to assign a monetary value to things that are invaluable precisely because they (like beauty, love, and respect) are not and cannot be bought, sold, or traded in markets. To assign a shadow price, these critics claim, is to make the mistake of assuming that nothing has **intrinsic value** and that the worth of everything can be measured and reduced to its utilitarian or instrumental value.

Shanty towns

The United Nations estimates that at least one billion people—twenty percent of the world's population—live in crowded, unsanitary slums of the central cities and in the vast shanty towns and squatter settlements that ring the outskirts of most **Third World** cities. Around 100 million people have no home at all. In Bombay, India, for example, it is thought that half a million people sleep on the streets, sidewalks, and traffic circles because they can find no other place to live. In São Paulo, Brazil, at least three million "street kids" who have run away from home or have been abandoned by their parents live however and wherever they can. This is surely a symptom of a tragic failure of social systems.

Slums are generally legal but otherwise inadequate multifamily tenements or rooming houses, either custom built for rent to poor people or converted from some other use. The *chals* of Bombay, for example, are high-rise tenements built in the 1950s to house immigrant workers. Never very safe or sturdy, these dingy, airless buildings are already crumbling and often collapse without warning. Eighty-four percent of the families in these tenements live in a single room; half of those families consist of six or more people. Typically they have less than 2.4 square yards (2 square meters) of floor space per person and only one or two beds for the whole family. They may share kitchen and bathroom facilities down the hall with fifty to seventy-five other people. Even more crowded are the rooming houses for mill workers, where up to twenty-five men sleep in a single room only seven meters square. Because of this overcrowding, household accidents are a common cause of injuries and deaths in cities of developing countries, especially to children. Charcoal braziers or kerosene stoves used in crowded homes are a routine source of fires and injuries. With no place to store dangerous materials beyond the reach of children, accidental poisonings and other mishaps are a constant hazard.

Shanty towns are created when people move onto undeveloped lands and build their own houses. Shacks are built of corrugated metal, discarded packing crates, brush, **plastic** sheets, or whatever building materials people can scavenge. Some shanty towns are simply illegal subdivisions where the landowner rents land without city approval. Others are spontaneous or popular settlements or squatter towns where people occupy land without the owner's permission. Sometimes this occupation involves thousands of people who

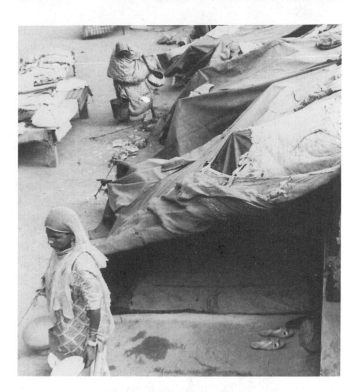

Living in tents on the streets of New Delhi, India.

move onto unused land in a highly organized, overnight land invasion, building huts and laying out streets, markets, and schools before authorities can evict them. In other cases, shanty towns gradually appear.

Called *barriads*, *barrios*, *favelas*, or *turgios* in Latin America, *bidonvillas* in Africa, or *bustees* in India, shanty towns surround every megacity of the developing world. They are not an exclusive feature of poor countries, however. Some 200,000 immigrants live in the *colonias* along the southern Rio Grande in Texas. Only two percent have access to adequate sanitation. Most live in conditions as poor as those of any city of a developing nation. Smaller enclaves of the poor and dispossessed can be found in most American cities.

The problem is magnified in **less developed countries**. Nouakchott, Mauritania, the fastest growing city in the world, consists almost entirely of squatter settlements and shanty towns. It has been called "the world's largest refugee camp." About eighty percent of the people in Addis Ababa, Ethiopia, and about seventy percent of those in Luanda, Angola, live in these squalid refugee camps. Two-thirds of the population of Calcutta live in shanty towns or squatter settlements and nearly half of the 19.4 million people in **Mexico City**, Mexico, live in uncontrolled, unauthorized shanty towns and squatter settlements. Many governments try to clean out illegal settlements by bulldozing the huts and sending riot police to drive out the settlers, but the people either move back or relocate to another shanty town elsewhere.

These popular but unauthorized settlements usually lack sewers, clean water supplies, electricity, and roads. Often the land on which they are built was not previously used because it is unsafe or unsuitable for habitation. In **Bhopal,**

India, and Mexico City, for example, squatter settlements were built next to deadly industrial sites. In such cities as Rio de Janiero, Brazil; La Paz, Bolivia; Guatemala City, Guatemala; and Caracas, Venezuela, they are perched on landslide-prone hills. In Bangkok, Thailand, thousands of people live in shacks built over a fetid tidal swamp. In Lima, Peru; Khartoum, Sudan; and Nouakchott, shanty towns have spread onto sandy deserts. In Manila in the Phillipines, 20,000 people live in huts built on towering mounds of **garbage** amidst burning industrial waste in city dumps.

Few developing countries can afford to build modern waste treatment systems for their rapidly growing cities, and the spontaneous settlements or shanty towns are the last to be served. The **World Bank** estimates that only thirty-five percent of urban residents in developing countries have satisfactory sanitation services. The situation is especially desperate in Latin America, where only two percent of urban sewage receives any treatment. In Egypt, Cairo's sewer system was built about 50 years ago to serve a population of two million people. It is now being overwhelmed by more than 11 million inhabitants. Only 217 of India's 3,119 towns and cities have even partial sewage systems and water treatment facilities. These systems serve less than sixteen percent of India's 200 million urban residents. In Colombia, the Bogota River, 125 mi. (200 km) downstream from Bogota's five million residents, still has an average fecal bacterial count of 7.3 million cells per liter, more than 7,000 times the safe drinking level and 3,500 times higher than the limit for swimming.

Some 400 million people, or about one-third of the population in developing world cities, do not have safe drinking water, according to the World Bank. Where people must buy water from merchants, it often costs 100 times as much as piped city water and may not be safe to drink after all. Many rivers and streams in Third World countries are little more than open sewers, and yet, they are all that poor people have for washing clothes, bathing, cooking, and, in the worst cases, for drinking. Diarrhea, dysentery, typhoid, and **cholera** are epidemic diseases in these countries, and infant **mortality** is tragically high.

A striking aspect of most shanty towns is the number of people selling goods and services of all types on the streets or from small stands in informal markets. Food vendors push carts through crowded streets; children dart between cars selling papers or cigarettes; curb-side mechanics make repairs using primitive tools and ingenuity. Nearly everything city residents need is available on the streets. These individual entrepreneurs are part of the informal economy: small-scale family businesses in temporary locations outside the control of normal regulatory agencies. In many developing countries, this informal sector accounts for sixty to eighty percent of the economy.

Governments often consider these independent businesses to be backward and embarrassing, a barrier to orderly development. It is difficult to collect taxes or to control these activities. In many cities, police drive food vendors, beggars, peddlers, and private taxis off the streets at the same time that they destroy shanties and squatter settlements.

Recent studies, however, have shown that this informal economy is a vital, dynamic force that is more often positive than negative. The sheer size and vigor of this sector means that it can no longer be ignored or neglected. The informal economy is often the only feasible source of new housing, jobs, food distribution, trash removal, transportation, or **recycling** for the city. Small businesses and individual entrepreneurs provide services that people can afford and that cities cannot or will not provide.

The businesses common to the informal sector are ideal in a rapidly changing world. They tend to be small, flexible, and labor intensive. They are highly competitive and dynamic, avoiding much of the corruption of developing nations' bureaucracies. Government leaders beginning to recognize that the informal sector should be encouraged rather than discouraged are making microloans and assisting communities with self-help projects. When people own their houses or businesses, they put more time, energy, and money into improving and upgrading them.

[*William P. Cunningham*]

FURTHER READING

Hardoy, J. E., and D. E. Satterthwaite. "Third World Cities and the Environment of Poverty." In *Global Possible*, edited by R. Repetto. Washington, DC: World Resources Institute, 1985.

Livermash, R. "Human Settlements." In *World Resources 1990-1991*. Washington, DC: World Resources Institute, 1990.

"The World's Urban Explosion." *Unesco Courier* (March 1985): 24-30.

Sheet erosion

See **Erosion**

Shepard, Paul (1925-1995)

Environmental theorist

A scientist, teacher, and environmental theorist, Shepard moved beyond the factual realm of biological science to expand upon the nature of human behavior and its roots in the natural world. He was a prolific writer who have had a profound influence on a variety of contemporary thinkers.

In his introduction to *The Subversive Science: Essays Toward an Ecology of Man*, edited with Daniel McKinley, Shepard discussed the reluctance of modern (as opposed to primitive) people to view humanity as one element of the whole of creation. Instead, humanity is wrongly seen as the singular focus or the intended culmination of creation, thereby denying the role played by all other life forms in the evolution of humankind. Shepard suggested this need to dominate has led to physical and mental separation from the whole, resulting in innumerable problems for humankind, among them **environmental degradation**. He believed that people should simultaneously appreciate the integrity of every being as well as the relatedness of all things, acquiring a world view that is inclusive and holistic rather than exclusive and superficially hierarchical: "Without losing our sense of a great human destiny and without intellectual surrender, we must affirm that the world is a being, a part of our own body."

Shepard continued to assess and emphasize the relationships between other living things and human development, particularly the role played by animals. In *The Others: How Animals Made Us Human*, he discusses the paradox of people who both love and kill or hunt animals, and contrasts them with those who would protect the "others" of the natural world from humans in the name of "animal rights": "In the perspective of the enormous history of life and the role of animals in human evolution for a million years, I feel only disconnected by the precept of untouchability...Great naturalists and primal peoples were motivated not by the ideal of untouchability but by a cautious willingness to consume and be consumed, both literally and in a mythic sense."

Shepard was born on July 12, 1925, in Kansas City, Missouri; his father was a horticulturist. During World War II he served in the U.S. Army from 1943-46, in the European theater. He received his B.A. from the University of Missouri (1949) and his M.S. in conservation (1952). His Ph.D. from Yale (1954) was based on an interdisciplinary study of **ecology**, landscape architecture, and art history. Shepard was a Fulbright senior research scholar in New Zealand in 1961, and later received both a Guggenheim fellowship to research the cultures of hunting-gathering peoples (1968-69) and a Rockefeller fellowship in the humanities (1979).

For 21 years Shepard taught concurrently at Pitzer College and Claremont Graduate School (both in Claremont, California), serving as the Avery Professor of Natural Philosophy and Human Ecology at Claremont from 1973 until his retirement in 1994. Earlier he had taught at other schools, including Knox College, Dartmouth College, and Smith College. He published numerous books, was a regular contributor to *Landscape* and *North American Review*, and also wrote for *BioScience, Perspectives in Biology and Medicine*, and *School Science and Mathematics*.

[*Ellen Link*]

FURTHER READING

Contemporary Authors. New rev. series, vol. 10. Detroit: Gale Research, 1983.

Oelschlaeger, M., ed. *The Company of Others: Essays in Celebration of Paul Shepard*. Durango, Co: Kivaki Press, 1995.

Pace, E. "Paul Shepard, Professor and Author, 71" (obituary). *New York Times*, July 22, 96: A15(L).

Shepard, Paul. *Environmental: Essays on the Planet as a Home*. Boston: Houghton, 1971.

——. *Man in the Landscape: A Historic View of the Esthetics of Nature*. New York: Knopf, 1967.

——. *Nature and Madness*. San Francisco: Sierra Club Books, 1982.

——, ed. *The Only World We've Got: A Paul Shepard Reader*. San Francisco: Sierra Club Books, 1996.

——. *The Others: How Animals Made Us Human*. Washington, D.C.: Island Press, 1996.

——. *The Tender Carnivore and the Sacred Game*. New York: Scribner, 1973.

——. *Thinking Animals: Animals and the Development of Human Intelligence*. New York: Viking Press, 1978.

Shepard, P., and D. McKinley, eds. *The Subversive Science: Essays Toward an Ecology of Man*. Boston: Houghton Mifflin, 1969.

Shepard, P., and B. Sanders. *The Sacred Paw: The Bear in Nature, Myth and Literature*. New York: Viking Press, 1983.

Shifting cultivation

Shifting cultivation refers to a practice whereby a tract of land is alternately used for crop production and then allowed to return to native vegetation for a period of years. Typically, the land is cleared of vegetation, crops are grown for two or three years, and then the land abandoned for a period of ten or more years. To facilitate land clearing prior to cultivation, the vegetation is cut and the debris burned. The practice is also called **slash-and-burn** agriculture or swidden agriculture.

Shifting cultivation is most common in the tropics where farming techniques are less technologically advanced. The **soil**s are usually low in plant **nutrient**s. For two or three years following land clearing, the nutrients brought to, or near, the soil surface by deep rooting trees, shrubs, and other plants support cultivated crops. With native management, the available nutrients are removed by the cultivated crops or leached so that after a few years the soil will support only minimal plant growth. It is then allowed to return to native vegetation which slowly concentrates the nutrients in the surface soil again. After a period of years the cycle repeats. **Erosion** is often severe on sloping land during the cultivated phase. On some soils, particularly in the tropics, the soil structure becomes massive and hard. *See also* Leaching; Soil compaction; Soil organic matter

[*William E. Larson*]

FURTHER READING

Monastersky, R. "Legacy of Fire: The Soil Strikes Back." *Science News* 133 (9 April 1988): 231.

Ramakrishnan, P. S. *Shifting Agriculture and Sustainable Development: An Interdisciplinary Study from North-Eastern India*. Park Ridge, NJ: Parthenon Publishing Group, 1992.

Vasey, D. E. *An Ecological History of Agriculture*. Ames: Iowa State University Press, 1992.

Sick Building Syndrome

Sick Building Syndrome (SBS) is a term applied to a building that makes its occupants sick because of indoor air pollutants. **Indoor air quality** (IAQ) problems fall into three categories: SBS, building-related illnesses, and multiple chemical sensitivity. Of the three, SBS accounts for 75 percent of all IAQ complaints.

Indoor air is a health hazard in 30 percent of all buildings, according to the World Health Organization. The **Environmental Protection Agency (EPA)** lists IAQ fourth among top environmental health threats. The problem of SBS is of increasing concern to employees and occupational health specialists, as well as landlords and corporations who fear the financial consequences of illnesses among tenants and employees. **Respiratory diseases** attributed to SBS account for about 150 million lost work days each year, $59 billion in indirect costs, and $15 billion in medical costs.

Sick building syndrome was first recognized in the 1970s around the time of the energy crisis and the move toward **conservation**. Because heating and air conditioning systems accounted for a major portion of energy consumption in the United States, buildings were sealed for **energy efficiency**. Occupants depend on mechanical systems rather than open windows for outside air and ventilation. A tight building, however, can seal in and create contaminants. Common complaints of SBS include headaches, fatigue, cough, sneezing, nausea, difficulty concentrating, bleary eyes, and nose and throat irritations. Symptoms are caused by a range of contaminants, including **volatile organic compound**s (VOC), which are **chemicals** that turn to gas at room temperature and are given off by paints, adhesives, caulking, vinyl, telephone cable, printed documents, furniture, and solvents. Most common VOCs are **benzene** and chloroform, both of which may be **carcinogen**s. Formaldehyde in building materials also is a culprit.

Biological agents such as **virus**es, bacteria, fungal spores, algae, pollen, mold, and dust mites add to the problems. These are produced by water-damaged carpet and furnishing or standing water in ventilation systems, humidifiers, and flush **toilets**.

Carbon dioxide levels increase as the number of people in a room increases, and too much can cause occupants to suffer hyperventilation, headaches, dizziness, shortness of breath, and drowsiness, as does **carbon monoxide** and the other toxins from **cigarette smoke**.

Schoolchildren are considered more vulnerable to SBS because schools typically have more people per room breathing the same stale air. Their size, childhood allergies, and **asthma**s add to their vulnerability.

Sick buildings can be treated by updating and cleaning ventilation systems regularly and using air cleaners and filtration devices. Also, plants spaced every 100 sq. ft. (9.3 m) in offices, homes, and schools have been shown to filter out pollutants in recycled air.

A simple survey of the indoor **environment** can detect many SBS problems. Check each room for an air source; if windows cannot be opened, every room should have a supply vent and exhaust vent. Clean the vents. Check to see if air is circulating by placing a strip of tissue at each vent opening. The tissue should blow out at a supply vent and blow in at an exhaust vent. Move partitions, file cabinets, and boxes away from vents. Supply and exhaust vents should be more than a few feet apart. Dead spaces where air stagnates and pollutants build up should be renovated. Move printing and copying machines away from people and give those machines adequate exhaust. Check that the ventilation system operates fully in every season and whenever people are in the building.

The EPA enforces tough laws on outdoor **air pollution**, but not for indoor air except for some smoking bans. Yet almost every pollutant, according to the EPA, is at higher levels indoors than out. Help in detecting and correcting sick building syndrome is available from the **National Institute of Occupational Safety and Health**, the federal agency responsible for conducting research and making recommendations for safe and healthy work standards. *See also* Occupational Safety and Health Administration (OSHA); Occupational Health and Safety Act

[*Linda Rehkopf*]

FURTHER READING

Kay, J. G., et al. *Indoor Air Pollution: Radon, Bioaerosols, and VOCs*. Chelsea, MI: Lewis, 1991.

Samet, J. M., and J. D. Spangler. *Indoor Air Pollution: A Health Perspective.* Baltimore, MD: Johns Hopkins University Press, 1991.

Soviero, M. M. "Can Your House Make You Sick?" *Popular Science* (July 1992): 80.

Sierra Club (San Francisco, California)

The Sierra Club is one of the nation's foremost conservation organizations and has worked for over 100 years to preserve "the wild places of the earth." Founded in 1892 by author and wilderness explorer **John Muir**, who helped lead the fight to establish **Yosemite National Park**, the group's first goal was to preserve the Sierra Nevada mountain chain. Since then, the club has worked to protect dozens of other national treasures.

The preserve of Mount Rainier was one of the Sierra Club's earliest achievements, and in 1899 Congress made that area into a **national park**. The group also helped to establish Glacier National Park in 1910. The Sierra Club supported the creation of the **National Park Service** in 1916, and in 1919 began a campaign to halt the indiscriminate cutting of **redwood** trees.

The club has helped secure many conservation victories in the twentieth century. They worked to create such national parks as Kings Canyon, Olympic, and Redwood, **national seashore**s such as Point Reyes in California and Padre Island in Texas, as well as the Jackson Hole National Monument. The club also campaigned to expand Sequoia and Grand Teton national parks. In the 1960s, the Sierra Club helped to secure such legislative victories as the **Wilderness Act** in 1964, the establishment of the National Wilderness Preservation System, and the expansion of the Land and Water Conservation Fund in 1968.

By 1970, the Sierra Club had 100,000 members, with chapters in every state, and the group took advantage of growing public support for the **environment** to accelerate progress towards conserving America's natural heritage. The **National Environmental Policy Act** was passed by Congress that year, and the **Environmental Protection Agency (EPA)** was created. Later, the club helped defeat a proposal to build a fleet of polluting Supersonic Transports, and they organized the Sierra Club Legal Defense Fund. In 1976, the club's lobbying efforts sped passage of the **Bureau of Land Management** (BLM) Organic Act, which increased governmental protection for an additional 459 million acres.

One of the most important victories for the Sierra Club came in 1980, when a year-long campaign culminated in passage of the **Alaska National Interest Conservation Act**, establishing 103 million acres as either national parks, monuments, refuges, or wilderness areas. Superfund legislation was also enacted to clean up the nation's abandoned toxic waste sites.

The decade of the 1980s, however, was a difficult one for conservationists. With **James Watt** as Secretary of Interior under President Ronald Reagan, and Ann Gorsuch Burford as EPA administrator, the Sierra Club was placed in a defensive position. The group focused mainly on preventing environmentally destructive projects and legislation—for example, blocking the MX missile complex in the Great Basin (1981), preventing weakening of the **Clean Air Act**, and stopping BLM from dropping 1.5 million acres from its wilderness inventory in 1983. Despite government interference, pressure from the public and from Congress helped the club continue its record of positive accomplishments, including the designation of 6.8 million acres of wilderness in 18 states (1984), new wilderness designations in Alabama, Oklahoma, and Washington, and the addition of 40 rivers to the National Wild and Scenic River System.

In 1990, after years of grassroots lobbying, a compromise Clean Air Act was reauthorized, strengthening safeguards against **acid rain** and air **pollution**. Current projects include protecting the last remaining ancient forests of the Pacific Northwest; preventing oil and gas drilling in the 1.5-million-acre Arctic National Wildlife Refuge in Alaska; securing wilderness and park areas in California, Colorado, Idaho, Montana, Nebraska, North Carolina, South Dakota, New Mexico, and Utah; and combatting global warming and the depletion of the world's protective **ozone** layer.

In 1991, the Sierra Club began its hundredth year of work to protect the environment. By 1992, it had grown to 600,000 members and had 58 chapters across the United States, with an annual budget of $38 million. Having become so large and influential, the Sierra Club is now considered one of the "big ten" American conservation organizations. An extensive professional staff is required to operate this complex organization, and members tend to have little influence over club policy at the national level. Some radical activists have criticized mainline organizations of this kind for being too conservative, too comfortable in their relationship to established powers, and too willing to compromise basic principles in order to maintain power and prestige. Supporters of the club argue that a spectrum of environmental organizations is desirable and that different organizations can play useful roles. Contact: Sierra Club, P.O. Box 7959, San Francisco, CA 94120-9943 *See also* Environmental ethics; Environmentalism; Green politics; Werbach, Adam

[*Lewis G. Regenstein*]

Silent Spring
See **Carson, Rachel Louise**

Silt

A **soil** separate consisting of particles of a certain equivalent diameter. The most commonly used size for silt is from 0.05 to 0.002 mm equivalent diameter. This is the size used by the Soil Science Society of America and the **U.S. Department of Agriculture**, but others recognize slightly different equivalent diameters. As compared to clay (less than 0.002 mm), the silt fraction is less reactive and has a low cation exchange capacity. Because of its size, which is intermediate between clay and sand, silt contributes to formation of desirable pore sizes, and the weathering of silt minerals provides available plant **nutrient**s. Wind-blown silt deposits are referred to as "loess." *See also* Soil conservation; Soil consistency; Soil profile

Siltation

The process or action of depositing **sediment**. Sediment is composed of solid material, mineral or organic, and can be of any texture. The material has been moved from its site of origin by the forces of air, water, gravity, or ice and has come to rest on the earth's surface. The term siltation does not imply the deposition of **silt** separates, although the sediment deposited from **erosion** of agricultural land is often high in silt because of the sorting action into soil separates during the erosion process.

Silver Bay, Minnesota

Silver Bay, on the Minnesota shore of Lake Superior, became the center of **pollution control** lawsuits in the 1970s when **cancer**-causing **asbestos**-type fibers, released into the lake by a Silver Bay factory, turned up in the drinking water of numerous Lake Superior cities. While pollution lawsuits have become common, Silver Bay was a landmark case in which a polluter was held liable for probable, but not proven, environmental health risks. Asbestos, a fibrous silicate mineral that occurs naturally in rock formations across the United States and Canada, entered Lake Superior in the waste material produced by Silver Bay's Reserve Mining Corporation. This company processed taconite, a low-grade form of iron ore, for shipment across the **Great Lakes** to steel-producing regions. Fibrous asbestos crystals removed from the purified ore composed a portion of the plant's waste **tailings**. These tailings were disposed of in the lake, an inexpensive and expedient disposal method. For almost twenty-five years the processing plant discharged wastes at a rate of 67,000 tons per day into the lake.

Generally clean, Lake Superior provides drinking water to most of its shoreline communities. However, water samples from Duluth, Minnesota, 50 miles (80.5 km) southwest of Silver Bay, showed trace amounts of asbestos-like fibers as early as 1939. While the term "asbestos" properly signifies a specific long, thin crystal shape that appears in many mineral types, both the long fibers and shorter ones, known as "asbestos-like" or "asbestiform," have been linked to cancer in humans.

Early incidences of asbestos-like fibers in drinking water probably resulted from nearby mining activities, but fiber concentrations suddenly increased in the late 1950s when **Reserve Mining** began its tailing discharge into the lake. By 1965 asbestiform fiber concentrations had climbed significantly, and municipal water samples in the 1970s were showing twice the acceptable levels defined by the federal **Occupational Safety and Health Administration (OSHA)**. Lawsuits filed against Reserve Mining charged that the company's activity endangered the lives of the region's residents.

Although industrial **discharge** often endangers communities, the Silver Bay case was a pivotal one because it was an early test of scientific uncertainty in cases of legal responsibility. Cancer that results from exposure to asbestos fibers appears decades after exposure, and in a large population an individual's probability of death may be relatively small. Asbestos concentrations in Lake Superior water also varied, depending largely upon weather patterns and city filtration systems. Finally, it was not entirely proven that the particular type of fibers released by Reserve Mining were as carcinogenic as similar fibers found elsewhere. In such circumstances it is difficult to place clear blame on the agency producing the pollutants. The 200,000 people living along the lake's western arm were clearly at some risk, but the question of how much risk must be proven to close company operations was difficult to answer. Furthermore, the Reserve plant employed nearly all the breadwinners from nearby towns. Plant closure essentially spelled death for Silver Bay.

In 1980 a federal judge ordered the plant closed until an on-land disposal site could be built. Reserve Mining did construct on-shore **tailings ponds**, which served the company for several years until economic losses finally closed the plant in the late 1980s.

[*Mary Ann Cunningham*]

FURTHER READING

Carter, L. J. "Pollution and Public Health: Taconite Case Poses Major Test." *Science* 186 (4 October 1974): 31-6.

Sigurdson, E. E. "Observations of Cancer Incidence Surveillance in Duluth, Minnesota." *Environmental Health Perspectives* 53 (1983): 61-7.

Singer, Peter (1946 -)

Australian philosopher and animal rights activist

Philosopher and leading advocate of the animal liberation movement, Singer was born in Melbourne, Australia. While teaching at Oxford University in England, Singer encountered a group of people who were vegetarians not because of any personal distaste for meat, but because they felt, as Singer later wrote, that "there was no way in which [maltreatment of animals by humans] could be justified ethically." Impressed by their argument, Singer soon joined their ranks. Out of his growing concern for the rights of animals came the book *Animal Liberation*, a study of the suffering we inflict upon animals in the name of scientific experimentation and food production. *Animal Liberation* caused a sensation when it was published in 1972 and soon became a major manifesto of the growing animal liberation movement in North America, Australia, England, and elsewhere.

As a utilitarian, Singer—like his nineteenth-century forebear and founder of **utilitarianism**, the English philosopher Jeremy Bentham—believes that morality requires that the total amount of happiness be maximized and pain minimized. Or, as the point is sometimes put, we are morally obligated to perform actions and promote policies and practices that produce "the greatest happiness of the greatest number." But, Singer says, the creatures to be counted within this number should include all sentient creatures, animals as well as humans.

To promote only the happiness of humans and to disregard the pains of animals Singer calls **speciesism**—the view that one **species**, *Homo sapiens*, is privileged above all others. Singer likens speciesism to sexism and racism. The idea that one sex or race is innately superior to another has been discredited. The next step, Singer believes, is to recognize that all sentient creatures—human and nonhuman alike—deserve moral recognition and respect. Just as we do not eat the flesh or use the skin of our fellow humans, so, Singer argues, should we not eat meat or wear fur from animals. Nor is it morally permissible for humans to kill animals, to confine them, or to subject them to lethal laboratory experiments.

Although Singer's conclusions are congruent with those of **Tom Regan** and other defenders of **animal rights**, the route by which he reaches them is quite different. As a utilitarian, Singer emphasizes sentience, or the ability to experience pleasure and pain. Regan, by contrast, emphasizes the **intrinsic value** or inherent moral worth of all living creatures. Despite their differences, both have come under attack from the fur industry, defenders of "factory farming," and advocates of animal experimentation. Singer remains a key figure at the center of this continuing storm. *See also* People for the Ethical Treatment of Animals; Vegetarianism

[*Terence Ball*]

FURTHER READING

Ball, T., and R. Dagger. "Liberation Ideologies." In *Political Ideologies and the Democratic Ideal*. New York: Harper-Collins, 1991.

Singer, P., and T. Regan, eds. *Animal Rights and Human Obligations*. Englewood Cliffs, NJ: Prentice-Hall, 1976.

Singer, P. *Practical Ethics*. New York: Cambridge University Press, 1979.

———. *Animal Liberation*. 2nd ed. New York: Random House, 1990.

Sinkholes

Sinkholes are one of the main landforms in karst topography, so named for the region in Yugoslavia where solution features such as caves, caverns, disappearing streams and hummocky terrain predominate. Karst features occur primarily in limestone but may also occur in dolomite, chert, or even gypsum (Alabaster Caverns in Oklahoma).

As the name implies, sinkholes are depressions formed by solution enlargement or the subsidence of a cavern roof. Subsidence may occur slowly, as the cavern roof is gradually weakened by solution, or rapidly as the roof collapses. Several of the latter occurrences have gained widespread coverage because of the size and amount of property damage involved.

An often-described sinkhole formed during May 1981 in Winter Park, Florida, swallowing a three-bedroom house, half a swimming pool, and six Porsches in a dealer's lot. The massive "December Giant" occurred near Montevallo, Alabama, and measured 400 ft (122 m) wide by 50 ft (15 m) deep. A nearby resident reported hearing a roaring noise and breaking timbers, as well as feeling earth tremors under his house.

Cenotes is the Spanish name for sinkholes. One sacred cenote at the Mayan city of Chichen Itza in Yucatan, Mexico, was known as "the Well of Sacrifice." Archaeologists postulate that, to appease the gods during a drought, human sacrifices were cast into the water 80 ft (24 m) below, followed by a showering of precious possessions from onlookers. Since most of the gold and silver objects from the New World were melted down, these sacrifices are now highly prized artifacts from pre-Columbian civilizations.

Although occurring naturally, sinkhole formation can be intensified by human activity. These sinkholes offer an easy pathway for injection of contaminated **runoff** and **sewage** from septic systems into the **groundwater**. Because karst landscapes have extensive underground channels, the polluted water often travels considerable distances with little filtration or chemical modification from the relatively inert limestone. Therefore, the most serious hazard posed by sinkholes is the access they provide for turbid, polluted surface waters. This allows bacteria to thrive, so testing of spring water that emerges within or below karst regions is vital.

Sinkholes also pose special problems for construction of highways, reservoirs, and other massive objects. Fluctuating water levels weaken the overlying rock when the water table is high, but remove support when water levels are low. Thornbury (1954) described the problems resulting from efforts by Bloomington, Indiana, to build a water supply reservoir on top of karst topography. Much valuable water escaped through channels in the limestone beneath the dam. This structure eventually was abandoned and a new **reservoir** constructed in a region composed of relatively impervious siltstone below the limestone.

Anthropogenic (human-caused) sinkholes form as a result of mine subsidence, often catastrophically. Collapsing mine tunnels within the 1,000-mi (1,600-km) labyrinth in the historic Tri-State Mines of Kansas, Missouri, and Oklahoma have created scenarios very similar to the Winter Park, Florida, example. Subsidence of the strata overlying underground coal mines is another rich source of these anthropogenic sinkholes.

[*Nathan H. Meleen*]

FURTHER READING

Coates, D.R., ed. *Environmental Geomorphology*. Binghampton, N.Y.: State University of New York, 1971.

"Into the Well of Sacrifice," *National Geographic Magazine* (October 1961): 540-561.

Keller, E.A. *Environmental Geology*, 4th ed. Columbus, OH: Charles E. Merrill Publishing Co., 1985.

Thornbury, W.D. *Principles of Geomorphology*. New York: John Wiley & Sons, 1954.

Site index

A means of evaluating a forest's potential to produce trees for timber. Site refers to a defined area, including all of its environmental features, that supports or is capable of supporting a stand of trees. Site index is an indicator used to predict timber yield based on the height of dominant and co-dominant trees in a stand at a given index age, usually 50 or 100 years. Normally, site index curves are prepared by graphically plotting projected tree height as a function of age. *See also* Forest management

Site remediation
See **Hazardous waste site remediation**

Skidding

A technique in forest harvesting by which logs or whole trees are dragged over the ground, as opposed to being lifted in the air, to a landing, where they are loaded on trucks for transport to a mill. The logs may be dragged by mechanical means, such as a crawler tractor or rubber-tired skidder, or by draft animals. Skidding normally disturbs the ground surface and forms "skid trails" which may be used once or reused in subsequent harvests. **Soil** in skid trails, especially on steep land, may channel water flow during rainfall and snow melt and be susceptible to **erosion**.

Slash

The waste material, consisting of limbs, branches, twigs, leaves, or needles, left after forest harvesting. Logging slash left on the ground can protect the **soil** from raindrop impacts and **erosion**, and it can decompose to make **humus** and recycle **nutrient**s. Unusually large amounts of slash, which may present a fire hazard or provide favorable **habitat** for harmful insects or disease organisms, usually must be reduced by burning or mechanical chopping.

Slash and burn agriculture

Also known as swidden cultivation or **shifting cultivation**, slash-and-burn agriculture is a primitive agricultural system in which sections of forest are repeatedly cleared, cultivated, and allowed to regenerate over a period of many years. This kind of cultivation was used in Europe during the Neolithic period, and it is still widely used by **indigenous peoples** and landless peasants in the **tropical rain forest**s of South America.

The plots used in slash-and-burn agriculture are small, typically 1-1.5 acres (0.4-0.6 hectare). They are also polycultural and polyvarietal; farmers plant more than one crop on them at a time, and each of these crops may be grown in several varieties. This helps control populations of agricultural pests. The cutting and burning involved in clearing the site releases **nutrient**s which the cultivated crops can utilize, and the fallow period, which usually lasts at least as long as 15 years, allows these nutrients to accumulate again. In addition to restoring fertility, re-growth protects the soil from **erosion**.

Families and other small groups practicing slash-and-burn agriculture generally clear one or two new plots a year, working a number of areas at various stages of cultivation at a time. These plots can be close to each other, even interconnected, or spread out at a distance through the forest, designed to take advantage of particularly fertile soils or to meet different needs of the group. As the nutrients are exhausted and productivity declines, the areas cleared for slash-and-burn agriculture are rarely simply abandoned; the fallow period begins gradually, and **species** such as fruit trees are still cultivated as the forest begins to reclaim the open spaces. The forest may contain originally cultivated species that still yield a harvest many years after the plot has been overgrown.

Although this system of agriculture was practiced for thousands of years with relatively modest effects on the **environment**, the pressures of a rapidly growing population in South America have made it considerably less benign. **Population growth** has greatly increased the number of peasants who do not own their own land; they have been forced to migrate into the **rain forest**s, where they subsist practicing slash-and-burn agriculture. In Brazil, the number of farmers employing this system of agriculture has increased by more than 15 percent a year since 1975. A recently released report by the United Nations Population Fund has emphasized the destruction this system can cause when practiced on such a large scale and identified it as a threat to species diversity. *See also* Agricultural revolution; Agricultural technology; Agroecology

[*Douglas Smith*]

Jungle in Guatemala is burned to clear land for raising corn and cattle.

Sludge

A suspension of solids in liquid, usually in the form of a liquid or a **slurry**. It is the residue that results from **wastewater** treatment operations, and typical concentrations range from 0.25 to 12 percent solids by weight. An estimated 8.5 million dry tons of municipal sludge is produced in the United States each year.

The volume of sludge produced is small compared with the volume of wastewater treated. The cost of sludge treatment, however, is estimated to be from 25 to 40 percent of the total cost of operating a wastewater-treatment plant. In the design of **sludge treatment and disposal** facilities, the term sludge refers to primary, biological, and chemical sludges, and excludes grit and screenings. Primary sludge results from primary **sedimentation**, while the sources of biological and chemical sludges are secondary biological and chemical settling and the processes used for thickening, digesting, conditioning, and dewatering the sludge from the primary and secondary settling operations.

Primary sludge is usually gray to dark gray in color and has a strong offensive odor. Fresh biological sludge—activated sludge, for example—is brownish and has a musty or earthy odor. Chemical sludge can vary in color depending on composition and may have objectionable odor. There are several sludge treatment options available. These operations and processes are principally intended for size reduction, grit removal, moisture removal, and stabilization of the organic matter in the sludge. Examples of these sludge processing methods are sludge grinding and cyclone degritter for the preliminary operations, chemical conditioning and heat treatment, centrifugation and vacuum filtration for dewatering operations, **aerobic** or **anaerobic digestion**, **composting** and **incineration** for sludge stabilization.

Other than its organic content, sewage sludge is known to contain some essential soil nutrients, such as **phosphorus** and **nitrogen**, that make it suitable for use as **fertilizer** or soil conditioner after further processing. Sludge may also be disposed of in **landfill**s. Landfilling and incineration, however, are strictly disposal methods and, unlike land application, do not recycle sludge.

Raw sludge contains potentially harmful **pathogen**s, heavy metals and toxic organics; it is regulated by the **Environmental Protection Agency (EPA)**. The EPA has recently proposed new regulations establishing management practices and other requirements for the disposal of sewage sludge. *See also* Aerobic sludge digestion; Contaminated soil; Industrial waste treatment; Sewage treatment; Waste management

[*James W. Patterson*]

FURTHER READING

Hasbach, A. C., ed. "Putting Sludge to Work." *Pollution Engineering* (December 1991).

Process Design Manual for Sludge Treatment and Disposal. Washington, DC: U. S. Environmental Protection Agency, 1979.

Sundstrom, D. W., and H. E. Klei. *Wastewater Treatment*. Englewood Cliffs, N.J.: Prentice-Hall, 1979.

Weber, W., Jr. *Physicochemical Processes for Water Quality Control*. New York: Wiley-Interscience, 1972.

Sludge digestion
See **Aerobic sludge digestion**

Sludge treatment and disposal

The proper treatment and disposal of **sludge** require knowledge of the origin of the solids to be handled, as well as their characteristics and quantities. The type of treatment employed and the method of operation determine the origin of sludge. In **sewage treatment** plants, sludge is produced by primary settling, which is used to remove readily settleable solids from raw **wastewater**. Biological sludges are produced by treatment processes such as activated sludge, trickling filter, and rotating biological contractors. Chemical sludges result from the use of **chemicals** to remove constituents through **precipitation**; examples of precipitates that are produced by this process include phosphate precipitates, carbonate precipitates, hydroxide precipitates, and polymer solids.

Sludge is characterized by the presence or absence of organic matter, **nutrient**s, **pathogen**s, metals and toxic organics. These characteristics are an important consideration for determining both the type of treatment to be used and the method of disposal after processing. According to the **Environmental Protection Agency (EPA)**, the typical

chemical compositions of untreated and digested primary sludge include solids, grease and fats, protein, **nitrogen**, **phosphorus**, potash, iron, silica, and **pH**.

Municipal sludge is a high-volume waste. Typical volumes for raw primary sludge range from 2,950 to 3,530 gallons per million gallons of wastewater treated. Volumes for trickling filter **humus** range from 530 to 750 gallons per million, while the volumes for activated sludge are much higher, from 14,600 to 19,400 gallons per million. It is possible to calculate the quantities of sludge theoretically, but the EPA recommends that treatment operations use pilot plant equipment to make these calculations whenever possible. In developing a treatment and disposal system, the EPA also recommends that large wastewater treatment plants adopt a methodical approach "to prevent cursory dismissal of options." For small plants, with a capacity of less than a million gallons a day, the task of determining an operating procedure is often shorter and less complex.

Sludge treatment and disposal generally include several unit processes and operations, which fall under the following classifications: thickening, stabilization, disinfection, conditioning, dewatering, drying, thermal reduction, miscellaneous processes, ultimate disposal or **reuse**.

Thickening is a volume-reducing process in which the sludge solids are concentrated to increase the efficiency of further treatment. It has recently been reported that sludge with 0.8 percent solids thickened to a content of 4 percent solids yields a five-fold decrease in sludge volume. Thickening methods commonly employed are gravity thickening, flotation thickening, and centrifuge.

Sludges are stabilized to eliminate offensive odors and reduce toxicity. A stable sludge has been defined as "one that can be disposed of without damage to the environment, and without creating nuisance conditions." In sludges, toxicity is characterized by high concentrations of metals and toxic organics, as well as by high oxygen demand, abnormally high or low pH levels, and unsafe levels of pathogenic microorganisms. There are a variety of technologies available for stabilizing toxic sludge; these include lime stabilization, heat treatment, and biological stabilization, which consists of **aerobic** or **anaerobic digestion** and **composting**.

Sludge that has been stabilized may also be disinfected in order to further reduce the level of pathogens. There are several methods of sludge disinfection: thermal treatment such as pasteurization, chemical treatment, and irradiation. This process is important for the reuse and application of sludge on land.

Dewatering is used to achieve further reductions in moisture content. It is a process designed to reduce moisture to the point where the sludge behaves like a solid; at the end of this process, the concentration of solids in sludge is often greater than 15 percent. Dewatering can include a number of unit operations: Sludge can be dried in drying beds or lagoons, filtered through a vacuum filter, a filter press, or a strainer, and separated in machines such as a solid-bowl centrifuge. It can be determined whether a sludge will settle in a centrifuge by testing it in a test-tube centrifuge, where the concentration of cake solids are determined as a function of centrifugal acceleration. The Capillary Suction Time (CST) and the specific resistance to filtration are important parameters for the filterability of sludge.

Sludge is conditioned to prepare it for other treatment processes; the purpose of sludge conditioning is to improve the effectiveness of dewater and thickening. The methods most commonly employed are the addition of organic materials such as polymers, or the addition of inorganic materials such as aluminum compounds. Heat treatment is also used; in this treatment, temperatures range from 356°-392°F (180°-200°C) for a period of 20-30 minutes.

After thickening and dewatering, further reduction of moisture is necessary if the sludge is going to be incinerated or processed into **fertilizer**. This is achieved by heat drying, which yields a product high in volatile solids with a moisture content of less than 10 percent. The types of driers include flash dryers, screw-conveyors, multiple-hearth systems, and rotary and atomized-spray towers.

Sludge combustion is a thermal process that involves total or partial oxidation of organic solids. Thermal processes include **incineration**, starved air combustion, co-disposal, and wet oxidation. These processes have a number of advantages. They can achieve maximum volume reduction; they can destroy toxic organic compounds, and they also produce heat energy which can be utilized. But sludge combustion cannot be considered an ultimate or long-term disposal option because of the residuals it produces, such ash and air **emission**s, which may have detrimental effects on the **environment**. **Landfill**s are another disposal option, but limitations on space as well as regulatory constraints restrict their long-term feasibility. Reuse is probably the best solution for the long-term management of sludge; the most feasible beneficial use option will probably be either land application, land reclamation, or raw material recovery. Examples include the conversion of sludge into commercial fertilizer, fuel, and building products.

Whatever the selected array of sludge treatment and disposal measures are, the main factors that influence the choice will always be cost-effectiveness, public health, and environmental protection. *See also* Activated sludge; Municipal solid waste composting; Solid waste; Waste management

[*James W. Patterson*]

FURTHER READING

Hasbach, A. C. "Putting Sludge to Work." *Pollution Engineering* (December 1991).

Process Design Manual for Sludge Treatment and Disposal. Washington, DC: U. S. Environmental Protection Agency, 1979.

Vesilind, P. A. *Treatment and Disposal of Wastewater Sludges*. Ann Arbor, MI: Ann Arbor Science Publishers, 1979.

Slurry

A thin mixture of water and fine, insoluble materials suitable for pumping as a liquid. Pipelines are the cheapest and most efficient means of moving materials long distances. In Arizona, the Black Mesa slurry pipeline carries eight tons of

powdered **coal** per minute to the electrical power plant near Page on Powell Reservoir. A much longer pipeline has been proposed for shipping subbituminous coal in Wyoming to Midwestern cities. Water supply is a crucial factor in these **arid** regions lying in the Rocky Mountain **rain shadow** zone.

Smelter

Smelters are industrial facilities that are used to treat metal ores or concentrates with heat, **carbon**, and oxygen in order to produce a crude-metal product, which is then sent to a refinery to manufacture pure metals.

In many cases, smelters process sulfide minerals, which yield gaseous **sulfur dioxide**, a significant waste product. Other smelters, including some that process iron ores, do not treat sulfide minerals. Similarly, secondary smelters used for **recycling** metal products, such as used **automobile** batteries, do not emit sulfur dioxide. However, all smelters emit metal **particulate**s to the **environment**, and unless this is prevented by **pollution control** devices, these **emission**s can cause substantial environmental damages.

The earliest large industrial smelting technique involved the oxidation of sulfide ores using roast beds, which were heaps of ore piled upon wood. The heaps were ignited in order to oxidize the sulfide-sulfur to sulfur dioxide, thereby increasing the concentration of desired metals in the residual product. The roast beds were allowed to smoulder for several months, after which the crude-metal product was collected for further processing at a refinery. The use of roast beds produced intense, ground-level **plume**s filled with sulfur dioxide, acidic mists, and metals, which could devastate local **ecosystem**s through direct toxicity and by causing **acidification**.

More modern smelters emit pollutants to the **atmosphere** through tall smokestacks. These can effectively disperse emissions, so that local air quality is enhanced, and damages are greatly reduced. However, the actual acreage of land affected by the contamination is enlarged because the tall smokestacks broadcast emissions over a greater distance and **acid rain** may be spread over a larger area as well.

Emissions of toxic chemicals can be reduced at the source. Metal-containing particulates can be controlled through the use of electrostatic precipitators or **baghouse**s. These devices can remove particulates from flue-gas streams, so that they can be recovered and refined into pure metals, instead of being emitted into the atmosphere. Electrostatic precipitators and baghouses can often achieve particle-removal efficiencies of 99 percent or better.

It is more difficult and expensive to reduce emissions of gases such as sulfur dioxide. Existing technologies usually rely on the reaction of sulfur dioxide with lime or limestone to produce a slurry of gypsum (calcium sulfate) that can be disposed into **landfill**s or sometimes manufactured into products such as wallboard. It is also possible to produce sulfuric acid by some flue-gas desulfurization processes. At best, removal efficiencies for sulfur dioxide are about 95 percent, and often considerably less.

The types of smelters that do not treat sulfide metals, such as iron ore smelters, logically do not emit sulfur dioxide. They do, however, spew metal particulates into the atmosphere. For example, a facility that has been operating for centuries at Gusum, Sweden, has caused a significant local pollution with copper and **lead**, the toxic effects of which have damaged vegetation. The surface organic matter of sites close to the Gusum facility has been polluted with as much as 2 percent each of zinc and copper. Secondary smelters also do not generally emit toxic gases, but they can be important sources of metal particulates. This has been especially well documented for secondary lead smelters, many of which are present in urban or suburban environments. The danger from these is that people can be affected by lead in their **environment**, in addition to long-lasting ecological effects. For example, lead concentrations in soil as large as less than 5 percent dry weight were found in the immediate vicinity of a battery smelter in Toronto, Ontario. In this case, people were living beside the smelter. Garden soils and vegetables, house dust, and human tissues were all significantly contaminated with lead in the vicinity of that smelter. Similar observations have been made around other lead-battery smelters, including many that are situated dangerously close to human habitation.

One of the best-known case studies of environmental damage caused by smelters concerns the effects of emissions from the metal processing plants around **Sudbury, Ontario**. This area has a long history as a mining community. For many years, roast beds were the primary metal-processing technology used at Sudbury. In fact, in its heyday, up to thirty roast beds were operating in Sudbury. Unforturnately, this process saturated the air and soil with sulfur dioxide, nickel, and copper. Local ecosystems were devastated by the direct toxicity of sulfur dioxide and, to a lesser extent, the metals. In addition, dry deposition of sulfur dioxide caused a severe acidification of lakes and soil. This caused much of the plant life to die, which in turn started soil **erosion**. Naked bedrock was exposed, and then blackened and pitted by reaction with the sulfurous plumes and acidic mists.

When the devastating consequences of the roast bed method became clear, the government prohibited their use. The processors turned to new technology in 1928 when they began construction of three smelters with tall stacks. Since these emitted pollutants high into the atmosphere, they showed substantial improvements in local air quality. However, the damage to vegetation continued; lakes and soils were still being acidified, and toxic contaminants were spread over an increasingly large area.

Over time, well-defined patterns of ecological damage developed around the Sudbury smelters. The problems that had occurred in the roast beds were being repeated on a large scale. The most devastated sites were close to the smelters, and had concentrations of nickel and copper in soil in the thousands of **parts per million**; they were very acidic with resulting **aluminum** toxicity, and frequently fumigated by sulfur dioxide. Such toxic sites were barren, or at most had

very little plant cover. The few plants that were present were usually specific ecotypes of a few widespread species that had evolved a tolerance to the toxic effects of nickel, copper, and acidity. Aquatic lake habitats close to the smelters were similarly affected. These waterbodies were acidified by the **dry deposition** of sulfur dioxide, and had large concentrations of soluble nickel, copper, aluminum, and other toxic metals. Of course, the plant and animal life of these lakes was highly impoverished and dominated by life forms that were specifically adapted to the toxic stresses associated with the metals and acidification.

It is well recognized that increased linear distance from the **point source** of toxic chemicals reduces deposition rates and toxic stress. Correspondingly, the pattern of environmental pollution and ecological damage around the Sudbury areas decreases more-or-less exponentially with increasing distance from the smelters. In general, it is difficult to demonstrate damages to terrestrial communities beyond 9 to 12 miles (15-20 km), although contamination with nickel and copper can be found at least 62 miles (100 km) away. In comparison, lakes that are deficient in plant life have little acid-neutralizing capacity and can be shown to have been damaged by the dry deposition of sulfur dioxide at least 25-30 miles (40-48 km) from Sudbury.

To improve regional air quality, the world's tallest smokestack, at 1,247 feet (380 m), was constructed at the largest of the Sudbury smelters. This "superstack" allowed for an even wider dispersion of smelter emissions. At the same time, a smelter was closed down, and steps were taken to reduce sulfur dioxide emissions by installing desulferization, or **flue-gas scrubbing**, equipment and by processing lower-sulfur ores. In aggregate, these actions resulted in a great improvement of **air quality** in the vicinity of Sudbury.

The improvement of air quality allowed vegetation to regenerate over large areas, with many existing species increasing in abundance and new **species** appearing in the progressively detoxifying **habitat**s. The revegetation has been actively encouraged by re-seeding and liming activities along roadways and other amenity areas where soil had not been eroded. Aquatic habitats have also considerably detoxified since 1972. Lakes near the superstack and the closed smelter have become less acidic, metal concentrations have decreased, and the plants and animals have increased **biomass**.

However, there is important controversy about contributions that the still-large emissions of sulfur dioxide from Sudbury may be making towards the regional acid rain problem. The superstack may actually exacerbate regional difficulties because of the wide dispersal of its emissions of sulfur dioxide. It is possible that height of the superstack may be decreased in order to increase the local dry deposition of emitted sulfur dioxide and reduce the long range dispersion of this acid-precursor gas.

The Sudbury scenario is by no means an unusual one. Many other smelters have substantially degraded their surrounding environment. The specifics of environmental pollution and ecological damage around particular smelters depend on the intensity of toxic stress and the types of ecological communities that are being affected. Nevertheless, broadly similar patterns of ecological change are observed around all point sources of toxic emissions, such as smelters.

In most modern smelters, a reduction of emissions at the source can eliminate the most significant of the ecological damages that have plagued older smelters. The latter were commissioned and operated under social and political climates that were much more tolerant of environmental damages than are generally considered to be acceptable today. *See also* Air pollutant transport; Electrostatic precipitation; Water pollution

[*Bill Freedman*]

FURTHER READING

Freedman, B. *Environmental Ecology.* San Diego: Academic Press, 1989.

———, and T. C. Hutchinson. "Sources of Metal and Elemental Contamination of Terrestrial Ecosystems." In *Metals in the Environment*, edited by N. W. Lepp. Vol. 2. London: Applied Science Publishers, 1981.

Nriagu, J., ed. *Environmental Impacts of Smelters.* New York: Wiley, 1984.

Smith, Robert Angus (1817-1884)

Scottish chemist

Smith has two claims to fame. Through his studies of **air pollution** he was, in 1852, the discoverer of **acid rain**, and his appointment as Queen Victoria's first inspector under the Alkali Acts Administration of 1863 made him the prototype of the scientific civil servant. He was one of the earlier scientists to study the chemistry of air and **water pollution** and among the first to see that such study was important in identifying and controlling environmental problems caused by industrial growth in urban centers. He was also interested in public health, disinfection, peat formation, and antiquarian subjects. Although his work has sometimes been dismissed as pedestrian, Smith's pioneering studies of the chemistry of atmospheric precipitation, published in 1872 in the book *Air and Rain*, were far ahead of their time and a major contribution to a new discipline that he called "chemical climatology."

[*Eville Gorham*]

FURTHER READING

Gorham, E. "Robert Angus Smith, F.R.S., and 'Chemical Climatology'." *Notes and Records of the Royal Society of London* 36 (1982): 267-72.

MacLeod, R.M. "The Alkali Acts Administration, 1863-84: The Emergence of the Civil Scientist." *Victorian Studies* 9 (1965): 85-112.

Smog

A term chosen by the Glasgow public health official Des Voeux at the beginning of the twentieth century to describe the smoky fogs that characterized **coal**-burning cities of the time. The word is formed by adding the words **smoke** and fog together and has persisted as a description of this type of urban **atmosphere**. It has more and more been used to describe **photochemical smog**, the haze that became a

characteristic of the **Los Angeles Basin** from the 1940s. "Smog" is even heard used to describe **air pollution** in general, even where there is no reduction in **visibility** at all. However, the term is most properly used to describe the two distinctive types of **pollution** that dominated the atmospheres of late nineteenth century London, England, known as winter smog, and twentieth century Los Angeles, called summer smog.

The city of London burned almost 20 million tons of coal annually by the end of the nineteenth century. Although industrialized, much coal was burned in domestic hearths, and the smoke and **sulfur dioxide** produced barely rose from the chimneys above the housetops. Only a few rather inaccurate measurements of the pollutant concentrations in the air were made in last century, although they hint at concentrations much higher than what we might expect in London today.

The smogs of nineteenth century London took the form of dense, vividly colored fogs. The smog was frequently so dense that people became lost and had to be lead home by linksmen. It is said that visibility became so restricted that fingers on an outstretched arm were invisible. The fog that rolled over window sills and into rooms became such an integral part of what we know as Victorian London that almost any Sherlock Holmes story mentions it.

With London's high humidity and incipient fog, smoke particles from coal-burning formed a nucleus for the condensation of vapor into large fog droplets. This water also serves as a site for chemical reactions, in particular the formation of sulfuric acid. Sulfur dioxide dissolved in fog droplets, perhaps aided by the presence of alkaline material such as ammonia or coal ash. Once in solution the sulfur was oxidized, a process often catalyzed by the presence of dissolved metallic ions such as **iron** and manganese. Dissolution and oxidation of sulfur dioxide gave rise to sulfuric acid droplets, and it was sulfuric acid that made the smog so damaging to the health of Londoners.

London's severe smogs occurred throughout the last decades of the nineteenth century. Detective writer Robert Barr even published *The Doom of London* at the turn of the century, which saw the entire population of London eliminated by an apocalyptic fog. Many residents of Victorian London recognized that the fogs increased death rates, but the most infamous incident occurred in 1952, when a slow-moving anti-cyclone stalled the air over the city. On the first morning the fog was thicker than many people could ever remember. By the afternoon people noticed the choking smell in the air and started experiencing discomfort. Those who walked about in the fog found their skin and clothing filthy after just a short time. At night the treatment of respiratory cases was running at twice its normal level. The situation continued for four days.

It was difficult to describe exactly what had happened, because primitive air pollution monitoring equipment could not cope with high and rapidly changing concentrations of pollutants, but it has been argued that for short periods the smoke and sulfur dioxide concentrations may have approached ten thousand micrograms per cubic meter. Today, in a

Smog over New York City.

relatively healthy city, the desired maximum is about a hundred micrograms per cubic meter in short-term exposures.

Normal death rates were exceeded by many thousands through the four-day period of the fog. Public feelings ran high, and the United Kingdom government, barraged with questions, set up an investigative committee. The Beaver Committee report eventually served as the basis for the UK Clean Air Act of 1956. This law was gradually adopted through many towns and cities of the UK and has been seen by many as a model piece of legislation. Although it is true that the classic London smog has gone, it is far from clear the extent to which this change came about through legislation rather than through broader social developments, such as the use of electricity in homes (although the act did encourage this).

Photochemical smog is sometimes called summer smog, because unlike the classical London type smog, it is more typical in summer at many localities, often because it requires long hours of sunshine to build up. When photochemical smogs were first noticed in Los Angeles, people believed them to be much the same as the smogs of London and Pittsburgh. Early attempts at control looked largely at local industry **emission**s. The **automobile** was eliminated as a likely cause because of low concentrations of sulfur in the fuel and the fact that only minute amounts of smoke were generated.

It was some time before the biochemist **Arie Jan Haagen-Smit** recognized that damage to crops in the Los

Angeles area arose not from familiar pollutants, but from a reaction that took place in the presence of **petroleum** vapors and sunlight. His observations focused unwelcome attention on the automobile as an important factor in the generation of summer smog.

The Los Angeles area proved an almost perfect place for generating smogs of this type. It had a large number of cars, long hours of sunshine, gentle sea breezes to back the pollutants up against the mountains, and high level **inversion**s preventing the pollutants from dispersing vertically.

Studies through the 1950s revealed that the smog was generated through a photolytic cycle. Sunlight split nitrogen dioxide into nitric oxide and atomic oxygen that could subsequently react and form **ozone**. This was the key pollutant that clearly distinguished the Los Angeles smogs from those found in London. Although the highly reactive ozone reacts rapidly with nitric oxide, converting it back into nitrogen dioxide, organic radicals produced from petroleum vapor react with nitric oxide very quickly. The nitrogen dioxide is again split by the sunlight, leading to the formation of more ozone. The cycle continues to build ozone concentrations to higher levels throughout the day.

The nitrogen oxide-ozone cycle is just one of many processes initiated in a smog of this kind. The photochemically active atmosphere contains a great number of reactive molecular fragments that lead to a range of complex organic compounds. Some of the hydrocarbon molecules of petroleum vapor are oxidized to aldehydes or ketones, such as acrolein or formaldehyde, which are irritants and suspected **carcinogen**s. Some oxygenated fragments of organic molecules react with the **nitrogen oxides** present in the atmosphere. The best-known product of these reactions is peroxyacetyl **nitrate**, often called PAN, one of a class of nitrated compounds causing eye irritation experienced in summer smogs.

The reactions that were recognized in the Los Angeles smog are now known to occur over wide areas of the industrialized world. The production of smog of this kind is not limited to urban or suburban areas, but may occur for many hundreds of miles to the lee of cities using large quantities of liquid fuel. The importance of **hydrocarbons** in sustaining the processes that generate photochemical smog has given rise to control policies that recognize the need to lower the emission of hydrocarbons into the atmosphere, and hence the emphasis of the use of **catalytic converter**s and low volatility fuels as part of **air pollution control** strategies. *See also* Alternative fuels; Environmental policy; Fossil fuels; Respiratory diseases

[*Peter Brimblecombe*]

FURTHER READING

Exhausting Our Future: An Eighty-Two City Study of Smog in the 80s. Washington, DC: U. S. Public Interest Research Group, 1989.

Findlayson-Pitts, B. J., and J. N. Pitts. *Atmospheric Chemistry.* New York: Wiley, 1986.

Smoke

Air pollutant, usually white, grey, or black in appearance, that arises from **combustion** processes. Benjamin Franklin recognized that smoke was the product of inefficient combustion and argued that one should "burn one's own smoke." Smoke generally forms when there is insufficient oxygen to oxidize all the vaporized fuel to **carbon dioxide**, so much remains as **carbon** or soot. Smoke is largely soot, although it also contains small amounts of **fly ash**. Although domestic smoke and poorly constructed chimneys had long been annoying to city dwellers, it was the development of the steam engine that drew particular attention to the need to get rid of unwanted smoke. The first half of the nineteenth century witnessed an awakening interest on the part of local administrators in Europe and North America to combat the smoke problem.

Smoke has long been recognized as more than just an aesthetic nuisance. It has been proven to have a broad range of effects on human health and well-being. Early laws were preoccupied with reducing black smoke, and various tests and "smoke shades" were created to test the color of smoke in the **atmosphere**. For example, the Ringelmann Chart showed a set of shades on a card, which was compared to the color of smoke in the atmosphere. Today it has been shown that the color of suspended smoke particles in cities have gradually changed as **coal** is used less frequently as an energy source. In many cities the principal soiling agent in the air is now diesel smoke. Diesel smoke blackens buildings and even gets inside

houses, and studies show that diesel smoke contains a range of **carcinogen**s.

While in many of the major cities smoke production has been reduced, coal, **peat**, and wood continue to be burnt in large quantities. In these locations, often in developing countries, smoke control represents considerable challenge as environmental agencies remain underfunded. *See also* Cigarette smoke; Smog; Tobacco

[*Peter Brimblecombe*]

FURTHER READING

Brimblecombe, P. *The Big Smoke.* London: Methuen, 1987.

Smoking

See **Cigarette smoke; Respiratory diseases; Tobacco**

Snail darter (*Percina tanasi*)

Most new **species** are discovered, then described in the scientific literature with little fanfare, and most are then known only to a relatively small group of specialists. This was not the case with the snail darter, a small member of the freshwater fish family of perches, *Percidae*. The snail darter's discovery cast it in the limelight of a highly controversial, environmental battle over the impoundment of the Little Tennessee River by the **Tellico Dam**. Because its discovery coincided with the enactment of the **Endangered Species Act**, its only known **habitat** was the free-flowing channel of the Little Tennessee River, and it was perceived as a means of successfully challenging the completion of this **Tennessee Valley Authority** project.

Two ichthyologists at the University of Tennessee, Drs. David Etnier and Robert Stiles, discovered the snail darter in the Little Tennessee River in August of 1973. After catching several specimens of these three-inch creatures, they returned to Knoxville to examine their find. By that fall, after careful comparison with other members of the genus, it was clear that they had found a new species of fish.

Because this darter was not known from any other location, Dr. Etnier submitted a status report on the species to the U. S. **Fish and Wildlife Service** the following year. The darter's existence was being threatened by the completion of the Tellico Dam, which would ultimately eliminate the free-flowing, clear, riverine habitat needed for its survival. The darter was recommended for listing as an **endangered species** in 1975, and in January 1976 its official scientific description was published. It was now the snail darter.

The notoriety this fish was beginning to receive did not go unnoticed by the TVA. They began transplanting snail

Snail darter.

darters to the Hiwassee River in 1975 and, by early 1976, had moved over 700 to the new location. All of this was done in secrecy, neither the Fish and Wildlife Service nor the appropriate Tennessee state agencies were notified. When the snail darter was designated an endangered species, the court battles began. Injunctions to halt completion of the Tellico Dam were granted and overturned all the way to the Supreme Court, where the justices ruled in favor of the snail darter. However, the High Court left an opening for the U. S. Congress to step in and exempt Tellico Dam from the Endangered Species Act. That is just what Congress did, and in January 1980 the gates closed and the **reservoir** behind Tellico Dam began to fill, thus sealing the fate of the Little Tennessee River and its darter population.

An additional population of snail darters has been discovered in the Hiwassee River, and this population seems to be thriving. Although still endangered, the snail darter, so named because of the principle component of its diet, continues its existence. The species' scientific name, *Percina tanasi*, is in reference to the ancient Cherokee Village and Native American burial ground of Tanasi, from which the state got its name, and which, now, lies at the bottom of Tellico's reservoir.

Snail darters live for an average of two years, with a maximum recorded longevity of four years. These darters reach sexual maturity at one year and migrate from their downstream, slackwater habitat to the sand and gravel shoals upstream, where they will eventually spawn. These clear, shallow shoal areas represent the habitat needed by the snail darters and their mollusk prey for survival.

[*Eugene C. Beckham*]

FURTHER READING

Etnier, D. "*Percina (Imostoma) tanasi*, A New Percid Fish From the Little Tennessee River, Tennessee." *Proceedings of the Biological Society of Washington* 88 (1976): 469-488.

Ono, R., J. Williams, and A. Wagner. *Vanishing Fishes of North America.* Washington, DC: Stone Wall Press, 1983.

Page, L. *Handbook of Darters.* Neptune City, NJ: TFH Publications, 1983.

Snow leopard

The snow leopard (*Uncia uncia*), also known as the ounce, or irbis, is a large cat that ranges over highland habitats in Central Asia. It occurs from Turkistan and northern Afghanistan in the western part of its range, through the Kashmir region of Pakistan and India, to southern Mongolia, extreme southwestern China, and Tibet. The snow leopard is sometimes referred to as *Panthera uncia*, which indicates affinity with other large cats, such as the tiger, African lion, and mountain lion, which are also named in the genus *Panthera*.

The snow leopard has an adult body length of 29-51 in (75-130 cm) and a tail of 27-39 in (70-100 cm). It stands 20-25 in (50-65 cm) at the shoulder, and has a body weight of 77-155 lb (35-70 kg). Its pelage is characterized by dense, long hair and a woolly underfur. The underbelly is whitish, while the upper parts of the animal are a creamy yellowish color, patterned by darker rings. Following a gestation period of about 93-103 days, snow leopards give birth in a rocky lair. Usually two cubs are born, but there can be as many as five. Cubs reach sexual maturity at an age of two years in captivity, but probably later in the wild. They have lived as long as 17-19 years in captivity, but the life span would be considerably less in the wild.

During the summer the snow leopard generally occurs in alpine **tundra** habitats, including meadows and rocky places above the forested tree line but below the snow line. During the summer snow leopards venture to 2,180 ft (6,000 m) and perhaps as high as 5,450 ft (15,000 m). During winter they occur as low as 545 ft (1,500 m), and in harsh winters they may occur in montane (or sub-alpine) forests. Because of the sparse populations of their natural prey species, snow leopards have large home ranges, typically amounting to several square miles. The ranges of adjacent animals can overlap to a substantial degree.

Snow leopards are solitary predators. They typically rest during the day and feed during the early morning or late afternoon on wild prey, such as ibex, sheep, musk deer, boar, hare, rabbit, pika, marmot, ptarmigan, and pheasant. Because of expanding human populations and agriculture within the range of snow leopards, they are increasingly feeding on domestic animals, such as goats, sheep, dogs, and chickens.

The global population of wild snow leopards may only be several thousand individuals. Another several hundred animals occur in zoos. Because of its small and decreasing populations the snow leopard is an **endangered species**. Although the snow leopard is officially protected throughout its range, it is nevertheless widely killed as a pest where it intersects with livestock-raising mountain people. It is also widely poached as a trophy and, more importantly, for its beautiful and valuable fur, which can be readily purchased in some rural marketplaces within the range of the species, even though its hunting is illegal. Most hunting of snow leopards is conducted using leg-hold traps or deep pits baited with a live goat or sheep.

[*Bill Freedman*]

FURTHER READING

Grzimek, B. ed. *Grzimek's Encyclopedia of Mammals.* London: McGraw Hill, 1990.

Nowak, R.M. *Walker's Mammals of the World,* 5th ed. Baltimore: Johns Hopkins University Press, 1991.

Snyder, Gary (1930-)

American poet

Snyder was born in San Francisco but grew up in the Northwest, learning about nature and life in cow pastures and second-growth forests. He earned his B.A. in anthropology at Reed College in Portland and spent some time at other universities, learning Asian languages and literatures. During the 1950s, Snyder became a part of the Beat Movement in San Francisco along with such noted figures as Jack Kerouac and Allen Ginsberg. While there he supported himself by working at a variety of odd jobs before leaving to study Zen Buddhism in Japan where he remained for nearly a decade.

Best known as a Pulitzer-prize-winning poet (for *Turtle Island,* 1974; *No Nature,* 1992), Snyder is also an elegant essayist whose collections include *The Practice of the Wild* (1990). Snyder is often described as *the* ecological poet, producing work that demonstrates a deep understanding of the subject. Through his poetry Snyder teaches **ecology**— as science, philosophy, and world view—to a wide audience.

Snyder's ecological principles center on eating and being eaten, house-keeping principles, the quest for community, identification with and fitting into locale and place, and understanding connective cycles, relationships and interdependence. He does not, for example, condemn hunting or taking life, but instead explains it as necessary and sacred: "there is no death that is not somebody's food, no life that is not somebody's death." But he urges his reader to treat the taking of life and the life ingested with respect. Because eating involves consuming other lives, Snyder believes, "eating is truly a sacrament." For Snyder, the primary ethical teaching of all times and places is "cause no unnecessary harm."

He declares that "there are many people on the planet now who are not 'inhabitants,'" meaning they do not identify with or know anything about the place in which they live. He emphasizes that "to know the spirit of a place is to realize that you are a part of a part and the whole is made of parts, each of which is whole. You start with the part you are whole in." He notes that "our relation to the natural world takes place in a *place,* and it must be grounded in information and experience"; basically, you "settle in and take responsibility and pay attention."

In *Myths & Texts,* Snyder notes that "As a poet I hold the most archaic values on earth. They go back to the upper Palaeolithic: the fertility of the soil, the magic of animals, the power-vision in solitude, the terrifying initiation and rebirth...the common work of the tribe." He is an activist who does not seek to return to an unclaimable past, but who tries to raise awareness of how humans are connected to each other, to other life-forms, and to the earth. *See also* Environmental ethics

[*Gerald L. Young*]

FURTHER READING

Halper, J., ed. *Gary Snyder: Dimensions of a Life.* San Francisco: Sierra Club Books, 1991.

Martin, J. "Speaking for the Green of the Leaf: Gary Snyder Writes Nature's Literature." *CEA Critic: An Official Journal of the College English Association* 54 (Fall 1991): 98-109.

Murphy, P. D. *Critical Essays on Gary Snyder.* Boston: G. K. Hall, 1990.

Paul, S. *In Search of the Primitive: Rereading David Antin, Jerome Rothenberg, and Gary Snyder.* Baton Rouge: Louisiana State University Press, 1986.

Snyder, G. *Myths & Texts.* New York: New Directions, 1978.

———. *No Nature.* New York: Pantheon Books, 1992.

———. *The Practice of the Wild.* San Francisco: North Point Press, 1990.

———. *Turtle Island.* New York: New Directions, 1974.

Social ecology

Social ecology has many definitions. It is used as a synonym for **human ecology**, especially in sociology; it is considered one form of ecological psychology; and it is the name chosen for the mix of approaches taught at the University of California, Irvine, as well as the radical revisionism of **Murray Bookchin**.

In her 1935 critique of the ecological approach in sociology, Milla Alihan clearly preferred the label "social ecology." In a book on urban society in the mid-forties, Gist and Halbert discussed the social ecology of the city, and Ruth Young examined the social ecology of a rural community in the journal *Rural Sociology* in the early 1970s. A bibliography for the Council for Planning Librarians went so far as to define social ecology as a "subfield of sociology that incorporates the influence of not only sociology but economics, biology, political science, and urban studies," and Mlinar and Teune, in their *Social Ecology of Change,* clearly considered it a part of sociology.

The Program in Social Ecology at the University of California, Irvine has been defined by Binder as "a new context for psychology," but it includes major subprograms in community psychology, urban and regional planning, environmental health, human ecology, criminal justice, and educational policy. He concluded by defining social ecology as the study of "the interaction of man with his environment in all of its ramifications." In a later article, Binder and others divided the ecological psychology into an ecological approach, an environmental approach, and social ecology itself, which they then enlarged into "a new departure in environmental studies" at Irvine.

Bookchin is equally ambitious, claiming to have "formulated a discipline unique to our age," and he defines social ecology as integrating "the study of human and natural **ecosystem**s through understanding the interrelationships of culture and **nature**. For Bookchin, social ecology "advances a critical, holistic world view and suggests that creative human enterprise can construct an alternative future:

reharmonizing people's relationship to the natural world by reharmonizing their relationship with each other." He goes on to claim that "this interdisciplinary approach draws on studies in the natural sciences, feminism, anthropology, and philosophy to provide a coherent critique of current anti-ecological trends and a reconstructive, communitarian, technical, and ethical approach to social life." Social ecology "not only provides a critique of the split between humanity and nature; it also poses the need to heal them." Bookchin established an Institute for Social Ecology in Plainfield, Vermont, which organizes conferences, publishes a journal, and offers in conjunction with Goddard College a graduate program leading to a Master of Arts degree in Social Ecology.

Social ecology, then, is defined in a variety of ways by different individuals. In general use, the term remains ambiguous. *See also* Bioregionalism; Ecology; Economic growth and the environment; Environmental economics; Environmental ethics; Environmentalism

[*Gerald L. Young*]

FURTHER READING

Alihan, M. A. *Social Ecology: A Critical Analysis.* New York: Cooper Square Publishers, 1964.

Bookchin, M. "What is Social Ecology?" In *The Modern Crisis.* Philadelphia, PA: New Society Publishers, 1986.

———. *The Philosophy of Social Ecology: Essays on Dialectical Naturalism.* Montreal: Black Rose Books, 1990.

Emery, R. E., and E. L. Trist. *Towards a Social Ecology: Contextual Appreciation of the Future in the Present.* New York: Plenum Publishing Corporation, 1973.

Society of American Foresters (Bethesda, Maryland)

Established in 1900 by **Gifford Pinchot**, considered to be America's first scientifically trained forester, the Society of American Foresters (SAF) is a scientific and educational organization representing the forestry profession in the United States. With a membership of over 18,700 in 1997, it is the largest professional society for foresters in the world. SAF's mission is to "...advance the science, education, technology, and practice of forestry; to enhance the competency of its members; to establish professional excellence; and to use the knowledge, skills, and **conservation** ethic of the profession to ensure the continued health and use of forest **ecosystem**s and the present and future availability of forest resources to benefit society." Although the focus of this organization is on forestry, the SAF addresses issues and concerns of a variety of natural resource professionals.

To be a professional member of SAF, one must hold a bachelor's or higher degree in forestry from an SAF-accredited or candidate institution, or hold a comparable degree in a closely related field of natural resources and have at least three years of forestry-related experience. There is a code of ethics for members that emphasizes stewardship of the land and that advocates land management that is consistent with ecologically sound principles. Members are expected to per-

form services consistent with their knowledge and skills, and for which they are qualified by education or experience.

The SAF provides an array of services for its members and for the forestry community as a whole, including the publication of the *Journal of Forestry*, the SAF's chief publication, three regional technical journals, a newsletter, and *Forest Science*, a quarterly research journal. Technical expertise is provided through the organization's 29 working groups that cover a broad range of subdisciplines and through supporting continuing education programs. The SAF accredits forestry programs in universities, ensuring that curricula meet standards considered to be needed by forestry graduates. It provides background and key testimony to natural resource policy makers on forestry issues, including timber harvesting methods, **forest management**, clean water legislation, and **wetlands**. For example, many of the recommendations of the SAF were incorporated into the Endangered Species Conservation and Management Act of 1995.

Environmental issues, particularly during the 1980s and 1990s, have stimulated a diversity of opinions and views about the profession of forestry and the role of the SAF. The spotted owl issue, the role of **clear-cutting** in forest management, the management and protection of old growth forests, and other forestry issues have been debated within the SAF just as they have been debated in society as a whole. Many views are represented by members of the SAF, including those with a forest products orientation and those promoting an ecosystems-based management approach that places high values on forest attributes such as **biodiversity**. Some members advocate the return to the basics of conservation, emphasizing both production and environmental protection. Clearly there is a broader view of the profession of forestry within SAF and perhaps a greater diversity of opinions than in the past. With this diversity, the SAF will continue to play a major role in how future forests are managed, particularly on public lands. Contact Society of American Foresters, 5400 Grosvenor Ln., Bethesda, MD 20814. Internet: http://www.safnet.org/saf/main.html.

[*Kenneth N. Brooks*]

Society for Conservation Biology (Seattle, Washington)

The idea of conservation biology as a scientific discipline with a specific application to society-at-large was brought to life in 1978 by organizers Michael Soule and Bruce Wilcox. They formalized their interest in a new **conservation** discipline at the first International Conference of Conservation Biology in San Diego. Between 1978 and 1985, the ideals of conservation biology survived through some growing pains, most importantly expanding from the idea of several single disciplines looking at a problem to a unified examination of a problem including the insights of many disciplines.

The core of that inter-disciplinary based approach formed a foundation from which, in 1985, the Society for

Conservation Biology was born. The Society is, in its own words,

> "... *an international professional organization dedicated to promoting the scientific study of the phenomena that affect the maintenance, loss, and restoration of biological diversity. The Society's membership is comprised of a wide range of people interested in the conservation and study of biological diversity; resource managers, educators, government and private conservation workers, and students.*"

What is unusual for a professional scientific group is that the Society was formed "to develop the scientific and technical means for the protection, maintenance, and restoration of life on this planet—its species, its ecological and evolutionary processes, and its particular and total environment." Thus, a mission is an inherent part of the Society mandate. That mission can be very broadly interpreted to include political, economic, and cultural ramifications, which are not commonly the arena for professional scientists.

To undertake the above mission the SCB promotes research, disseminates information, encourages communication and collaboration, educates, and recognizes outstanding contributions in the field. Part of that is done through a scientific journal, *Conservation Biology*, a newsletter, the development of local chapters, a Policy and Resolutions Committee, and the independent actions of the members.

The ideals noted above are based on the Society's official statements, but they undervalue the Society. It has grown to be a true meeting ground for scientists and non-scientists, and has maintained open and honest debate on vital topics, such as the roles of science and advocacy, that are touchstones for the new generation of conservation scientists. The message that comes through from the overall body of the Society's work is that careful science and compassion are not antithetical, rather they work together to promote nature in a natural way.

The journal *Conservation Biology* is the center of discussion and dissemination of thought for conservationists worldwide. Its overall quality, maintained by the highest editorial principles, has grown from a few articles in a quarterly issue to 300-400 page editions published six times per year. In each volume philosophical treatments are found alongside the latest molecular technique for recognizing levels of genetic variability.

The Society meets annually in a conference setting, complete with technical paper presentations, research posters, workshops, and a series of conservation awards. They occasionally meet in conjunction with other scientific groups and explore particular thematic topics in the Annual Meeting. Contact: SCB, University of Washington, P.O. Box 355320, Seattle, WA 98195-5320.

[*David Duffus*]

Sociobiology

A perennial debate about human nature, pitting the idea that behavior is culturally conditioned against the notion that human actions are innately controlled, was rekindled in 1975 when **Edward O. Wilson**'s *Sociobiology: The New Synthesis* introduced a new scientific discipline.

Sociobiology is defined by Wilson as "the systematic study of the biological basis of all social behavior" and can be described as a science that applies the principles of evolutionary biology to the social behavior of organisms, analyzing data from a number of disciplines, especially ethology (the biological study of behavior), **ecology**, and **evolution**. It employs two chief postulates. The first is the *interaction principle*, the idea that the action of any organism, including man, arises as a fusion of genotype and learning or experience. The second is the *fitness maximization* principle, the notion that all organisms will attempt to behave in a manner that passes copies of their genes to future generations.

Sociobiology provides several ways to understand the social behavior of an organism, including those acts termed "altruistic." First, social behaviors can be seen as the genetically conditioned attempts of an organism to save copies of its genes carried in others, especially close relatives. Such acts can also be viewed as a form of "genetic reciprocity" in which an organism helps another and the helped organism (or others) repays the help at some time in the future, thereby enhancing the fitness of each of the organisms involved. Finally, cooperative actions can be understood as the result of natural selection operating at the level of groups, in which "altruistic" groups pass their genes on more successfully than "selfish" groups.

In *Sociobiology*, Wilson, an entomologist specializing in the biology of ants, develops these concepts using the example of social insects. He shows how their cooperative and "altruistic" behaviors, never fully considered by traditional evolutionary biology, can be understood in terms of genetic fitness and natural selection. But the crucial aspect of Wilson's book is his assertion, within a single chapter, that such genetic theories can be applied to the social behavior of primates and man as well as to "lower" animals. Indeed, Wilson contends that scientists can shrink "the humanities and social sciences to specialized branches of biology" and predicts that to maintain the human species indefinitely, we will have to "drive toward total knowledge, right down to the levels of the neuron and gene," statements in which he seems to suggest that human beings can eventually be explained totally in "mechanistic terms."

Broadly, the premise of Wilson's argument finds its origins in the ideas of René Descartes and the mechanists of the eighteenth century such as Julien Offroy de La Mettrie, whose 1748 book, *L'homme-machine*, helped define the modern biological study of human beings. Wilson argues that if humans are indeed biological machines, then their actions in the realm of society should not be excluded from examination under biological principles, and dramatically defines his goal by stating that "when the same parameters and quantitative theory are used to analyze both termite colonies and troops of rhesus macaques, we will have a unified science of sociobiology."

Wilson's book, especially his statements in the final chapter, generated a storm of controversy. Some feared that a genetic approach to human behavior could be used by racists (and eugenicists) as a scientific base for their arguments of racial superiority, or that delving too deeply into human genetics might lead to manipulation of genes for undesirable purposes. Well-known evolutionary biologists such as Stephen Jay Gould and Richard Lewontin criticized Wilson for stepping over the line between science and speculation. Gould quite openly declares his unhappiness with the final chapter of *Sociobiology*, stating that it "is not about the range of potential human behavior or even an argument for the restriction of that range from a much larger total domain among all animals. It is, primarily, an extended speculation on the existence of genes for specific and variable traits in human behavior—including spite, aggression, xenophobia, conformity, homosexuality, and the characteristic behavior differences between men and women in Western society." Lewontin argues that sociobiology "is too theoretically impoverished to deal with real life," that "by its very nature, sociobiological theory is unable to cope with the extraordinary historical and cultural *contingency* of human behavior, nor with the diversity of individual behavior and its development in the course of individual life histories."

Feminists have also taken up the cudgel against sociobiology, asserting that it implicitly sanctions existing social behavior with a latent determinism. If, for example, repressive acts are defined as the result of direct genetic influence, the basis for their moral evaluation disappears.

Wilson has responded to his critics energetically and condemns those using sociobiological arguments to support societal evils by equating "what is" with "what should be." Wilson says: "The 'what is' in human nature is to a large extent the heritage of a Pleistocene hunter-gatherer existence. When any genetic bias is demonstrated, it cannot be used to justify a continuing practice in present and future societies. Since most of us live in a radically new environment of our own making, the pursuit of such a practice would be bad biology; and like all bad biology, it would lead to disaster. For example, the tendency under certain conditions to conduct warfare against competing groups might well be in our genes, having been advantageous to our Neolithic ancestors, but it could lead to global suicide now. To rear as many healthy children as possible was long the road to security; yet with the population of the world brimming over, it is now the way to environmental disaster." He goes on to suggest that "our primitive old genes will therefore have to carry the load of much more cultural change in the future" and, indeed, that our "genetic biases can be trespassed" by thinking and decision-making.

Sociobiology seems to have survived its vilification by critics. Indeed, Wilson's vigorous advocacy of a new synthesis between the social and biological sciences has helped bring into the open a debate about the relationship of biology and society that will probably bear a great deal of scientific fruit.

[*Gerald L. Young and Jeffrey Muhr*]

FURTHER READING

Lieberman, L., L.T. Reynolds, and D. Friedrich. "The Fitness of Human Sociobiology: The Future Utility of Four Concepts in Four Subdisciplines." *Social Biology* 39 (Spring-Summer 1992): 158-169.

Wilson, Edward O. *On Human Nature*. Cambridge, MA: Harvard University Press, 1978.

Wilson, Edward O. *Sociobiology: The New Synthesis*. Cambridge, MA: Harvard University Press, 1975.

Wolfe, Alan. "Social Theory and the Second Biological Revolution." *Social Research* 57 (Fall 1990): 615-648.

Soil

Soil is the unconsolidated mineral material on the immediate surface of the earth that serves as a natural medium for the growth of land plants. Soil is found on all surfaces except on steep, rugged mountain peaks and areas of perpetual ice and snow.

Soil is related to the earth much as the rind is related to an orange. But this rind of the earth is far less uniform than the rind of the orange. Soil is deep in some places and shallow in others. Soil can be red in Georgia and black in Iowa. It can be sand, loam, or clay. Soil is the link between the rock core of the earth and the living things on its surface. Soil is the foothold for the plants we grow and the foundation for the roads we travel and for the buildings we live in.

Soil consists of mineral and organic matter, air, and water. The proportions vary, but the major components remain the same. Minerals make up 50 percent of an ideal soil while air and water make up 25 percent each. Every soil occupies space. Soil extends down into the planet as well as over its surface. Soil has length, breadth, and depth. The concept that a soil occupies a segment of the earth is called the "soil body." A single soil in a soil body is referred to as a "pedon." The soil body is composed of many pedons and is thus called a "polypedon."

Every soil has a profile or a succession of layers (horizons) in a vertical section down into the non-soil zone referred to as the parent material. Parent materials can be soft rock, glacial drift, wind blown **sediment**s, or alluvial materials. The nature of the **soil profile** is important for determining a soil's potential for root growth, storage of water, and supply of plant nutrients.

Soil formation proceeds in steps and stages, none of which is distinct. It is impossible to determine where one step or stage in soil formation begins and another ends. The two major steps in the formation of soils are the accumulation of soil parent materials and the differentiation of horizons in the profile. Soil horizons develop due to the processes of additions, losses, translocations, and transformations. These processes act on the soil parent material to produce soil horizons. The intensity of any one process will vary from location to location due to five soil-forming factors:

(1) Soil forms from the parent material, and they can be rock, sand, glacial till, loess, alluvial sediments, or lacustrine clays.

(2) **Topography** is the position on the landscape where the parent material is located. Positions can be summits, sideslopes, and footslopes. **Erosion** and the depth

to the **water table** will influence soil formation as a result of topography.

(3) **Climate** acts on the parent material and determines the rate of rainfall and **evapotranspiration**, which influence the amount of **leaching** in the soil profile. The greater the leaching, the faster soil horizons develop.

(4) Biotic factors include vegetation and animals. Animals are important mixers of the soils and can destroy soil horizons. Vegetation influences soils by determining the amount of organic matter incorporated into the soils. Soils formed under prairie grasses will have a thick black surface layer, compared to soils formed under forests where the surface layer is thin with a light colored leached zone under it.

(5) Time refers to the number of years that the parent material has been acted on by climate and vegetation. The older a soil is, the greater the horizon development. Young soils will have very minimal horizon development. The age of a soil is thus dependent on its development and not on the total number of years. Therefore, developed soils in the Midwest may be 10,000 years old, while young soils in the valleys of California will also be 10,000 years old. Developed soils on high terraces in California can be as old as one million years.

Because the soil-forming factors vary from location to location, soils are different across the landscape. The ability to interpret where the soils will change has allowed soil scientists to make a map of these changes. The soil map is thus an interpretation of the soils that occur on a landscape. The soil map is published on a county-by-county basis and is called a **soil survey**. Soil surveys are very useful documents in planning **land use** according to the soil's potential.

Soil is an absolutely essential **natural resource** but one that is both limited and fragile. The soil is often overlooked when natural resources are listed. Throughout history the progress of civilizations have been marked by a trail of wind-blown or water-washed soils that resulted in barren lands. Continuing to use the soil without appropriate **soil conservation** management is very destructive to the environment. Protecting the quality of our nation's **topsoil** is largely within human control. To many soil scientists, saving our soil is much more important than saving oil, **coal**, or **natural gas** resources.

[*Terrence H. Cooper*]

FURTHER READING

Miller, R. W., and R. L. Donahue. *Soils: An Introduction to Soils and Plant Growth.* Englewood Cliffs, NJ: Prentice-Hall, 1990.

Stefferund, A., ed. *Soils: 1957 Yearbook of Agriculture.* Washington, DC: U. S. Government Printing Office, 1957.

Soil, buried

See **Buried soil**

Soil, contaminated

See **Contaminated soil**

Soil compaction

The forcing together of **soil** particles under pressure, usually by foot or vehicle traffic. Compaction decreases soil porosity and increases bulk density. The degree of compaction is determined by the amount of pressure applied and soil characteristics, including clay, water, and organic matter contents. Although compaction sometimes can be beneficial by improving seed and root contact with the soil and by increasing the soil's ability to hold water, most compaction is detrimental to plants and soil animals. It can destroy soil structure, decreasing water intake, **percolation**, gas exchange, and biological activity, while increasing water **run-off**, **erosion**, and resistance to root penetration. Soil compaction often is a serious problem in agricultural fields, forests, range lands, lawns, and golf courses. Conversely, soil compaction is necessary for most construction purposes.

Soil conservation

Soil conservation is the protection of **soil** against excessive loss of fertility by natural, chemical, or artificial means. It encompasses all management and **land-use** methods protecting soil against degradation, focusing on damage by **erosion** and **chemicals**. Soil conservation techniques can be divided into six categories, crop selection and rotation, **fertilizer** and lime application, **tilth**, residue management, contouring and strip cropping, and mechanical (e.g., terracing).

While the potential dangers of chemical degradation and soil erosion were recognized as early as the American Revolution, it was not until the early 1930s that soil **conservation** became a familiar term. The soil conservation movement was a result of the **drought**s during the 1930s, the effects of water erosion, the terrific dust storms created by wind erosion in the Great Plains, and by the urging of **Hugh Hammond Bennet**.

Dr. Bennet, a soil scientist from North Carolina, recognized the erosion damage to previously **arable land** in the Southeast, Midwest, and elsewhere in the 1920s and 1930s. In 1929, he published a bulletin entitled "Soil Erosion, A National Menace" and started a successful personal campaign to get federal support, beginning with a $160,000 appropriation by Congress to initiate a national study. In 1933, the **U.S. Department of the Interior** named Bennet as head of the Soil Erosion Service, which conducted soil erosion control demonstrations nationwide. In 1935, the **Soil Conservation Service**, led by Bennet, was established as a permanent agency of the **U.S. Department of Agriculture**.

Soil degradation problems addressed include **soil compaction**, **salinity** build-up, and excessive soil acidity. Because soil and water are so intimately related, the program also deals with **water conservation** and **water quality**. Under M.L. Wilson, then Assistant Secretary of Agriculture, the Soil Conservation Service established conservation districts guided by elected officials assisted by Soil Conservation Service personnel. Currently there are more than 3,000 districts in the United States.

Sharing the cost of conservation became federal policy with the passage of the Soil Conservation and Domestic Allotment Act of 1936. The act funded the shift of croplands to "soil-building" crops and established soil conservation practices on croplands and **grassland**s. The Great Plains Conservation Program, enacted by Congress in 1956, sought to shift some of the highly **erodible** land from cropland to grassland. The Water Bank and Experimental Rural Clean Waters Programs were an attempt to resolve disputes over drainage of "potholes" in the Midwest and Great Plains and demonstrate the influence of soil and water conservation practices on water quality.

As early as the 1930s, the federal government began to purchase "submarginal" lands outright. The Conservation Reserve segment of the Soil Bank (1956-1960) bought substandard farmland to conserve soil and alleviate surplus crop production. The current Conservation Reserve Program, authorized in a 1985 farm bill, paid farmers to convert land from cropland to grassland or trees under a long-term lease. Currently the "sodbuster," "swampbuster," and conservation compliance programs attempt to force farmers to comply with soil and water conservation programs to be eligible for other government programs, such as price supports.

The role of the Soil Conservation Service has changed over the years, but its central mission is still to provide technical information for good land use. Today the Soil Conservation Service is highly concerned with environmental problems, water quality, **wetland** preservation, and prime farm land protection, as well as urban concerns related to their mission. The soil conservation movement has spawned a number of professional societies, including the Soil and Water Conservation Society and the World Association of Soil and Water Conservation. *See also* Conservation tillage; Contour plowing; Dust Bowl; Environmental degradation; Soil organic matter; Strip-farming; Sustainable agriculture

[*William E. Larson*]

FURTHER READING

National Academy of Sciences. *Soil Conservation.* 2 vols. Washington, DC: National Academy Press, 1986.

Wilson, G. F., et al. *The Soul of the Soil: A Guide to Ecological Soil Management.* Quebec, Canada: Gaia Services, 1986.

Yudelman, M., et al. *New Vegetative Approaches to Soil and Water Conservation.* Washington, DC: World Wildlife Fund, 1990.

Soil Conservation Service

Soil erosion is an age-old problem, recorded in the Bible and many other documents of human civilizations. In the United States, Simms traces concern for soil **erosion**, and attempts to combat it, back to the very first European settlers. **U. S.** **Department of Agriculture** (USDA) bulletins on soil erosion date back at least to "Washed Soils: How to Prevent and Reclaim Them," dated 1894.

The contemporary Soil Conservation Service (SCS) was predated by the Bureau of Soils in the USDA, later called the Bureau of Chemistry and Soils. The catalyst for an action agency was **Hugh Hammond Bennett**, a soils scientist who went to work for the Bureau of Soils in 1903. From his urging, the USDA published the classic circular on "Soil Erosion, A National Menace," in 1928. Further pressure by Bennett resulted in the establishment of a temporary agency, the Soil Erosion Service, in the **U. S. Department of the Interior** in 1933, what Simms describes as "the first national action program of **soil conservation** anywhere in the world." Bennett was the agency's first director.

Hugh Bennett pushed his agenda hard, and his "primary tenet of soil conservation" can still be seen in the activities of the SCS today: "No single practice will suffice. A physical inventory of the land of the farm should be made, and each should be used in accordance with its adaptability and treated in accordance with its needs."

In 1935 President Franklin D. Roosevelt signed an executive order transferring the Soil Erosion Service to the USDA. The Department of Agriculture immediately consolidated all of its activities bearing on erosion control into the agency. Also in 1935 the Soil Conservation Act was passed and signed into law, establishing a permanent Soil Conservation Service in the USDA, with Hugh Bennett as the first Director.

Scanning lists of publications from the Soil Conservation Service shows work on a surprising range of contemporary **conservation** concerns. As one might expect, topping the list are numerous **soil survey**s of various counties in the United States: a soil survey of Esmeralda County, New York in 1991, one of the Asotin County area in Washington, and one of Crockett County, Tennessee. Less expected is a paper on **salinity** control in Colorado. Also included are status reports of various SCS programs: status of water quantity and **water quality** programs, and the situation regarding **wetlands** and riparian programs. The SCS also publishes a wide variety of maps, depicting, for example, major **watershed**s in Michigan, land resource regions and major land resource areas, and soil erosion in Colfax County, Nebraska.

The Service is beginning to provide appropriate databases for computer research, including a **pesticide**s properties database for environmental decision-making, state soil geographic databases, and a computer design for grassed waterways. The SCS provides local landowners a "how-to" video (1990) on "Better Land, Better Water." The United States still has severe erosion problems—Steiner notes that "only 3.23 percent of the cropland in the United States was considered adequately protected by the SCS in 1983." But, this and other conservation problems are not nearly as severe as they would be without Bennett's wisdom, foresight, and tenacity. He set the stage for 50 years of research and action by the national network of Soil Conservation Service offices and agents.

[*Gerald L. Young*]

FURTHER READING

Helms, D. "Conserving the Plains: The Soil Conservation Service in the Great Plains." *Agricultural History* 64 (Spring 1990): 58-73+.

Simms, D. H. *The Soil Conservation Service.* New York: Praeger, 1970.

Steiner, F. R. *Soil Conservation in the United States: Policy and Planning.* Baltimore: Johns Hopkins University Press, 1990.

Soil consistency

The manifestations of the forces of cohesion and adhesion acting within the **soil** at various water contents, as expressed by the relative ease with which a soil can be deformed or ruptured. Consistency states are described by terms such as friable, soft, hard, or very hard. These states are assessed by thumb and thumbnail penetrability and indentability, or more quantitatively, by Atterberg limits, which consist of liquid limit, plastic limit, and plasticity number. Atterberg limits are usually determined in the laboratory and are expressed numerically. *See also* Soil compaction; Soil conservation; Soil texture

Soil eluviation

When water moves through the **soil** it also moves small colloidal-sized materials. This movement or **leaching** of materials like clay, iron, or calcium carbonate is called eluviation. The area where the materials have been removed is the zone of eluviation and is called the E horizon. Zones of eluviation contain less **nutrient**s for plant growth. E horizons are often found in forested soils.

Soil illuviation

When water moves through the **soil** it moves small colloidal-sized particles with it. These particles of clay, iron, humus, and calcium carbonate will be deposited in zones below the surface or in the **subsoil**. The zones are called illuvial zones and the process is referred to as illuviation. Illuvial zones are most often referred to as B **horizon**s, and the subscript with the B designates the kind of material translocated (i.e., B_t = clay accumulation).

Soil liner

One of the requirements of modern sanitary **landfill**s is that a soil liner be placed on top of the existing **soil**. Liners are needed to prevent the penetration of landfill leachate into the soil. Without a liner leachate could move through the soil and contaminate the **groundwater**. Soil liners can be made of clay, **plastic**, rubber, blacktop, or concrete.

Soil loss tolerance

Soil loss tolerance is the maximum average annual **soil** removal by **erosion** that will allow continuous cropping and maintain soil productivity (T). It is occasionally defined as the maximum amount of soil erosion offset by the maximum amount of soil development while maintaining an equilibrium between soil losses and gains. T is usually expressed in terms of tons per acre or tons per ha. Because T values are difficult to quantify, they are usually inferred by human judgment rather than scientific analysis. In determining T values, the depth of the soil to consolidated material or depth to an unfavorable subsoil is considered. T values are an expression of concern for plant growth but may not adequately reflect environmental concerns.

Soil organic matter

Additions of plant debris to **soil**s will initiate the build up of organisms that will decompose the plant debris. After **decomposition** the organic material will be called organic matter or soil **humus**. This decomposed plant debris will be very small particles and will coat the sand, **silt**, and clay particles making up the mineral soil particles, thus making the soil black. The more organic matter accumulating in a soil, the darker the soil will become. Continued additions of organic matter are important to create a soft, tillable soil that is conducive to plant growth. Organic matter is important in soils because it will add **nutrient**s, store **nitrogen** and other positive cations, and create a stronger soil aggregate that will withstand the impact of raindrops and thus prevent water **erosion**.

Soil profile

The layers in the **soil** from the surface to the **subsoil**. The soil profile is the collection of soil **horizon**s. Soil profiles will vary from location to location because of the five soil-forming factors: **climate**, vegetation, **topography**, soil parent material, and the length of time the soil has been weathering. By looking at a soil's profile many interpretations can be made about **land use** and the suitability of the soil for a specific use.

Soil, saline

See **Saline soil**

Soil survey

A soil survey is a combination of field and laboratory activities intended to identify the basic physical and chemical properties of soils, establish the distribution of those **soil**s at

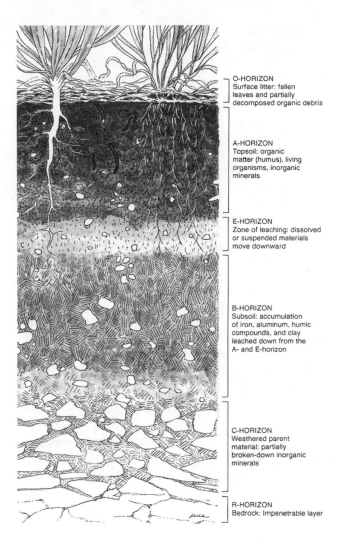

O-HORIZON
Surface litter: fallen leaves and partially decomposed organic debris

A-HORIZON
Topsoil: organic matter (humus), living organisms, inorganic minerals

E-HORIZON
Zone of leaching: dissolved or suspended materials move downward

B-HORIZON
Subsoil: accumulation of iron, aluminum, humic compounds, and clay leached down from the A- and E-horizon

C-HORIZON
Weathered parent material: partially broken-down inorganic minerals

R-HORIZON
Bedrock: Impenetrable layer

A soil profile showing the horizons in a soil in cross-section.

specific map scales, and interpret the information for a variety of uses.

There are two kinds of soil surveys, general purpose and specific use. General purpose surveys collect and display data on a wide range of soil properties which can be used to evaluate the suitability of the soil or area for a variety of purposes. Specific use soil surveys evaluate the suitability of the land for one specific use. Only physical and chemical data related to that particular use are collected, and map units are designed to convey that specific suitability.

A soil survey consists of three major activities: research, mapping, and interpretation. The research phase involves investigations that relate to the distribution and performance of soil; during the mapping phase, the land is actually walked and the soil distribution is noted on a map base which is reproducible. Interpretation involves the evaluation of the soil distribution and performance data to provide assessments of soil suitability for different kinds of **land use**.

During the research phase of the survey, soil scientists first establish which soil properties are important for that type of survey. They then establish field relationships be-

tween soil properties and landscape features, and they determine the types of soils to be mapped, preparing a map legend. In this phase, scientists also evaluate land productivity and recommend management practices as they relate to the mapping units proposed in the map legend.

Mapping is perhaps the most widely recognized phase of a soil survey. It is conducted by evaluating and delineating the soils in the field at a specified map intensity or scale. **Soil profile** observations are made at three levels of detail. Representative profiles are taken from soil pits, generally with laboratory corroboration of the observations made by soil scientists. Intermediate profiles are taken from soil pits, roadside excavations, pipelines or other chance exposures, and some sampling and description does occur at this level. Soil-type identifications are taken from auger holes or small pits, and only brief descriptions are made without laboratory confirmation.

With information gathered from sampling, as well as from the earlier research phase, soil scientists draw soil boundaries on an aerial photograph. These delineations or map units are systematically checked by field transects—straight-line traverses across the landscape with samples taken at specified intervals to confirm the map-unit composition.

Field research and the process of mapping produce a range of information that requires interpretation. Interpretations can include discussions of land use potential, management practices, avoidance of hazards, and economic evaluations of soil data. The interpretation of the information gained during a soil survey is based on crop yield estimates and soil response to specific management. Crop yields are estimated in the following ways: by comparison with data from experimental sites on identified soil types; by field experiments conducted within the survey area; from farm records, demonstration plots or other farm system studies; and by comparison of known crop requirements with the physical and chemical properties of soils. Soil response involves the evaluation of how the soils will respond to changes in use or management, such as **irrigation**, drainage, and land reclamation. Part of this evaluation includes an assessment of hazards that may result from changes such as **erosion** or **salinization**.

In general purpose surveys, which are the kind conducted in the United States, soils are mapped according to their properties on the hypothesis that soils which look and feel alike will behave the same, while those that do not will respond differently. A soil survey attempts to delineate areas that behave differently or will respond differently to some specified management, and the mapping units provide the basis for locating and predicting these differences. *See also* Contaminated soil; Soil conservation; Soil Conservation Service; Soil texture; U. S. Department of Agriculture

[*James L. Anderson*]

FURTHER READING

Dent, D., and A. Young. *Soil Survey and Land Evaluation.* Boston: Allen and Unwin, 1981.

Soil texture

The relative proportion of the mineral particles that make up a **soil** or the percent of sand, silt, and clay found in a soil. Texture is an important soil characteristic because it influences water infiltration, water storage, amount of aeration, ease of tilling the soil, ability to withstand a load, and soil fertility. Textural names are given to soil based on the percentage of sand, silt, and clay. For example, loam is a soil with equal proportions of sand, silt, and clay. It is best for growing most crops.

Soil and Water Conservation Society (Ankeny, Iowa)

Established in 1945, the Soil and Water Conservation Society (SWCS) is a nonprofit organization that advocates the "protection, enhancement and wise use of **soil**, water and related **natural resources**." The organization was formed during an era of public concern about soil erosion and water resource management following the dust bowl period of the 1930s in the United States. Improved farm tillage practices and an improved **conservation** ethic for land use were key objectives of the SWCS and became focal points for the organization. From its inception, the SWCS has been an advocate of soil conservation and improved use of soil and **water resources**, with its primary audience being professionals in agriculture.

In recent years, the SWCS has expanded its conservation focus to a broader natural resource perspective that goes beyond agriculture, although environmental issues associated with agriculture are still of significant interest. As a result, the SWCS membership is now made up of conservation professionals from many natural resource and agricultural disciplines. Individual and business membership in the SWCS exceeds 11,000, making it one of the largest multidisciplinary organizations for conservation professionals in the United States.

The SWCS actively promotes education, with the objective of a membership that can play leadership roles in dealing with environmental issues. Working groups within the SWCS develop policy statements on a wide range of environmental topics, including **water quality**, **wetlands**, **biodiversity**, **floodplain** management and **sustainable agriculture**. Through education programs and professional meetings, members of the society are challenged to set ethical standards that recognize the interdependence of people and their environment. Emphasis on sustainable land use practices and a sustainable **environment** have emerged as themes for its membership in the 1990s.

Educational programs have targeted policy makers and the general public alike. In 1995, the SWCS published a survey of 17,000 landowners who participated in the federal Conservation Reserve Program (CRP), which illustrated what farmers planned to do with their CRP land after their contracts expired. The intent was to inform policy makers about the environmental benefits of the CRP program and the consequences if this program was terminated. Other education programs focus on farmers, such as a White Paper on conservation tillage that stressed the environmental benefits of no-till farming. This had an important effect on farmers' attitudes toward no-till farming, assessing both the environmental benefits and costs of no-till farming.

Following the floods in the upper Mississippi River Valley in 1993, the SWCS supported Internet-linked communications with members about farm practices and their effects on the great flood. This program led to an 80% increase in farmer participation in the emergency Wetlands Reserve Program. The SWCS also played a key role in promoting conservation language and funding in the 1996 federal farm bill.

Continuing education programs on the latest developments in land and water management are carried out through workshops, field trips, conferences, and symposiums. The SWCS now sponsors a program for certifying professionals in soil erosion and sediment control. As part of its educational mission, the SWCS publishes the *Journal of Soil and Water Conservation*, a bimonthly publication that reports the results of new natural resource and agricultural research. Soil and Water Conservation Society, 7515 NE Ankeny Rd., Ankeny, IA 50021-9764. Internet: http://www.swcs.org/.

[*Kenneth N. Brooks*]

Solar cell

See **Photovoltaic cell**

Solar constant cycle

The solar constant is a measure of the amount of radiant energy reaching the earth's outer **atmosphere** from the sun. More precisely, it is equal to the rate at which solar radiation falls on a unit area of a plane surface at the top of the atmosphere and oriented at a perpendicular distance of 9.277×10^7 miles (1.496×10^8 kilometers) from the sun. That distance is the average (mean) distance between earth and sun during the course of a single year.

Measuring the solar constant has historically been a difficult challenge since there were few good methods for measuring energy levels at the top of the atmosphere. A solution to this problem was made possible in 1980 with the launching of the Solar Maximum (Solar Max) Mission spacecraft. After repair by the *Challenger* astronauts in 1984, Solar Max remained in orbit, taking measurements of solar phenomena until 1989. As a result of the data provided by Solar Max, the solar constant has now been determined to be 1.96 calories per square centimeter per minute, or 1,367 watts per meter. This result confirms the value of 2.0 calories per square centimeter per minute long used by scientists.

In addition to obtaining a good value for the solar constant, however, Solar Max made another interesting discovery. The solar constant is not, after all, really constant. It varies on a daily, weekly, monthly, and yearly basis, and

Soil texture depends on the relative proportions of sand, silt and clay in a soil, as represented in this diagram.

probably much longer. The variations in the solar constant are not large, averaging a few tenths of a percent.

Scientists have determined the cause of some variability in the solar constant and are hypothesizing others. For example, the presence of sun spots results in a decrease in the solar constant of a few tenths of a percent. Sunspots are regions on the Sun's surface where temperatures are significantly lower than surrounding areas. Since the sun presents a somewhat cooler face to the earth when sunspots are present, a decrease in the solar constant is not surprising.

Other surface features on the sun also affect the solar constant. Solar flares, for example, are outbursts or explosions of energy on the surface that may last for many weeks. Correlations have been made between the presence of solar flares and the solar constant over the twenty-seven-day period of the sun's rotation.

A longer-lasting effect is caused by the eleven-year sunspot cycle. As the number of sunspots increase during the cycle, so does the solar constant. For some unknown reason, this long-term effect is just the opposite of that observed for single sunspots.

Scientists believe that historical studies of the solar constant may provide some clues about changes in the earth's **climate**. The nineteenth-century British astronomer E. Walter Maunder pointed out that sunspots were essentially absent during the period 1645 to 1715, a period now called the Maunder minimum. The earth's climate experienced a dramatic change at about the same time, with temperatures

dropping to record lows. These changes are now known as the Little Ice Age. It seems possible that further study of the solar constant cycle may explain the connection between these two phenomena.

[*David E. Newton*]

FURTHER READING

Chorlton, Windsor, and the editors of Time-Life Books. *Ice Ages.* Alexandria, VA: Time-Life Books, 1983.

Hudson, Hugh S. "Solar Constant." In *McGraw–Hill Encyclopedia of Science & Technology.* 7th ed. New York: McGraw-Hill, 1992.

Solar detoxification

Solar energy is being investigated as a potential means to destroy environmental contaminants. In solar detoxification, photons in sunlight are used to break down contaminants into harmless or more easily treatable products. Solar detoxification is a "destructive" technology—it destroys contaminants as opposed to "transfer-of-phase" technologies such as activated carbon or air stripping, which are more commonly used to remove contaminants from the **environment**.

In a typical photocatalytic process, water or **soil** containing organic contaminants is exposed to sunlight in the presence of a catalyst such as titanium dioxide or humic and fulvic acids. The catalyst absorbs the high energy photons, and oxygen collects on the catalyst surface, resulting in the formation of reactive chemicals referred to as hydroxyl free-radicals and atomic oxygen (singlet oxygen). These reactive chemicals transform the organic contaminants into degradation products, such as **carbon dioxide** and water. Solar detoxification can be accomplished using natural sunlight or by using inside solar simulators or outside solar concentrators, both of which can concentrate light 20 times or more. The effectiveness of solar detoxification in both water and soil is affected by **sorption** of the toxic compounds on **sediment**s or soil and the depth of light penetration. Solar detoxification of volatilized toxic compounds may also occur naturally in the atmosphere.

For solar detoxification to be successfully accomplished, toxic chemicals should be converted to thermodynamically stable, non-toxic end products. For example, chlorinated compounds should be transformed to carbon dioxide, water, and hydrochloric acid through the general sequence:

$$\text{organic pollutants} \rightarrow \text{aldehydes}$$
$$\rightarrow \text{carboxylic acids} \rightarrow \text{carbon dioxide.}$$

Photocatalytic degradation such as this usually results in complete mineralization only after prolonged irradiation. If intermediates formed in the degradation pathway are non-toxic, however, the reaction does not have to be driven completely to carbon dioxide and water for acceptable detoxification to have occurred. In the solar detoxification of **pentachlorophenol (PCP)** and 2,4-dichlorophenol, for example, toxic intermediates were detected; however, with extended exposure to sunlight, the compounds were rendered completely nontoxic, as measured by respiration rate measurements in **activated sludge**.

Many applications of solar detoxification implemented at ambient temperatures have only 90 to 99 percent efficiency and do not completely mineralize the compounds. The rate of some photolytic reactions can be increased by raising the temperature of the reaction system, but the production of stable reaction intermediates (some of which may be toxic) is reduced. The changes in reaction rate have been attributed to a combination of a thermally induced increase in the photon-absorption rate, an increase in the quantum yield of the primary photoreaction, and the initiation of photoinduced radical-chain reactions.

Research conducted at the Solar Energy Research Institute (SERI), a laboratory funded by the **U.S. Department of Energy**, has demonstrated that **chlorinated hydrocarbons**, such as trichloroethylene (TCE), trichloroethane (TCA), and **vinyl chloride**, are vulnerable to photocatalytic treatment. Other toxic chemicals shown to be degraded by solar detoxification include a textile dye (Direct Red No. 79), pinkwater, a munitions production waste, and many types of **pesticide**s, including chlorinated cyclodiene insecticides, triazines, ureas, and dinitroaniline herbicides. In conjunction with **ozone** and hydrogen peroxide, both of which are strong oxidants, ultraviolet light has been shown to be effective in oxidizing some refractory chemicals such as methyl ethyl ketone, a degreaser, and

polychlorinated biphenyls (PCBs). *See also* Oxidizing agent

[Judith Sims]

FURTHER READING

Al-Ekabi, H., et al. "Advanced Technology for Water Purification by Heterogenous Photocatalysis." *International Journal of Environment and Pollution* 1, Nos. 1/2 (1991): 125-136.

Manilai, V.B., et al. "Photocatalytic Treatment of Toxic Organics in Wastewater: Toxicity of Photodegradation Products." *Water Research* 26, No. 8 (1992): 1035-1038.

Mill, T., and W. Mabey. "Photodegradation in Water." In *Environmental Exposure from Chemicals*, W.B. Neely and G.E. Blau, eds. CRC Press, Boca Raton, FL: 1985.

Solar Energy Research Institute, Development and Communications Office. *Solar Treatment of Contaminated Water.* SERI/SP-220-3517. Goldon, CO: Solar Heat Research Division, Solar Energy Research Institute, 1989.

Stephenson, F.A. "Chemical Oxidizers Treat Wastewater." *Environmental Protection* 3, No. 10 (1992): 23-27.

Solar energy

The sun is a powerful fusion reactor, where **hydrogen** atoms fuse to form helium and give off a tremendous amount of energy. The surface of the sun, also known as the photosphere, has a temperature of 6,000 K (10,000°F). The temperature at the core, the region of **nuclear fusion**, is 36,000,000°F. A ball of **coal** the size of the sun would burn up completely in 3,000 years, yet the sun has already been burning for three billion years and is expected to burn for another four billion. The power emitted by the sun is 3.9 x 10^{26} watts.

Only a very small fraction of the sun's radiant energy, or insolation, reaches the earth's **atmosphere**, and only about half of that reaches the surface of the earth. The other half is either reflected back into space by clouds and ice or is absorbed or scattered by molecules within the atmosphere. The sun's energy travels 93,000,000 miles to reach the earth's surface. It arrives about 8.5 minutes after leaving the photosphere in various forms of radiant energy with different wave lengths, known as the electromagnetic spectrum.

Solar radiation, also known as solar flux, is measured in Langlays per minute. One Langlay equals one calorie of radiant energy per square centimeter. One Langlay per minute equals 221 **British Thermal Unit (Btu)**s per square foot per hour. It is possible to appreciate the magnitude of the energy produced by the sun by comparing it to the total energy produced on earth each year by all sources. The annual energy output of the entire world is equivalent to the amount the sun produces in about five billionths of a second. Solar radiation over the United States each year is equal to 500 times its energy consumption.

The solar energy that reaches the surface of the earth and enters the biological cycle through **photosynthesis** is responsible for all forms of life, as well as all deposits of **fossil fuel**. All energy on earth comes from the sun, and it can be utilized directly or indirectly. Direct uses include passive solar

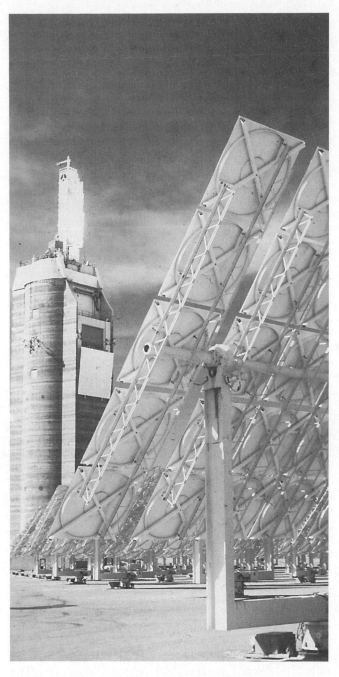

A solar furnace at Albuquerque, New Mexico.

wind and the effective surface areas of the blades, and the maximum extractable power is about 60 percent.

The use of the water wheel preceded windmills, and it may be the most ancient technology for utilizing solar energy. The sun causes water to evaporate, clouds form upon cooling, and the subsequent precipitation can be stored behind **dams**. This water is of high potential energy, and it is used to run water wheels or turbines. Modern turbines that run electric generators are approximately 90 percent efficient, and in 1993 hydroelectric energy produced about four percent of the primary energy used in the United States.

A passive solar heating system absorbs the radiation of the sun directly, without moving parts such as pumps. This kind of low temperature heat is used for space heating. Solar radiation may be collected by the use of south-facing windows in the northern hemisphere. Glass is transparent to visible light, allowing long-wave visible rays to enter, and it hinders the escape of long-wave heat, therefore raising the temperature of a building or a greenhouse.

A thermal mass such as rocks, brine, or a concrete floor stores the collected solar energy as heat and then releases it slowly when the surrounding temperature drops. In addition to collecting and storing solar energy as heat, passive systems must be designed to reduce both heat loss in cold weather and heat gain in hot weather. Reductions in heat transfer can be accomplished by heavy insulation, by the use of double glazed windows, and by the construction of an earth brim around the building. In hot summer weather, passive cooling can be provided by building extended overhangs or by planting deciduous trees. In dry areas such as in the southwestern United States or the Mediterranean, solar-driven fans or evaporative coolers can remove a great deal of interior heat. Examples of passive solar heating include roof-mounted, hot-water heaters, solarian glass walled rooms or patios, and earth-sheltered houses with windows facing south.

A simple and innovative technology in passive systems is a design based on the fact that at depth of 15 ft (5 m) the temperature of the earth remains at about 55° F (13° C) all year in a cold Northern climate and about 67° F (19° C) in warm Southern climate. By constructing air intake tubes at depths of 15 ft, the air can be either cooled or heated to reach the earth's temperature, proving an efficient air conditioning system.

Active solar systems differ from passive systems in that they include machinery such as pumps or electric fans, which lowers the net energy yield. The most common type of active systems are photovoltaic cells, which convert sunlight into direct current electricity. The thin cells are made from semiconductor material, mainly silicon, with small amounts of gallium arsenide or cadmium sulfide added so that the cell emits electrons when exposed to sunlight. Solar cells are connected in a series and framed on a rigid background. These modules are used to charge storage batteries aboard boats, operate lighthouses, and supply power for emergency telephones on highways. They are also used in remote areas not connected to a power supply grid for pumping water either for cattle or **irrigation**.

systems such as greenhouses and atriums, as well as windmills, hydropower, and the burning of **biomass**. Indirect uses of solar energy include **photovoltaic cell**s, in which semiconductor crystals convert sunlight into electrical power, and a process that produces methyl alcohol from plants.

Wind results from the uneven heating of the earth's atmosphere. About two percent of the solar energy which reaches the earth is used to move air masses, and at any one time the kinetic energy in the wind is equivalent to 20 times the current electricity use. Due to mechanical losses as well as other factors, windmills cannot extract all this power. The power produced by a windmill depends on the speed of the

Both passive and active solar systems can be installed without much technical knowledge. Neither produces **air pollution**, and both have a very low environmental impact. But a well-designed passive system is cheaper than active one and does not require as much operative maintenance. *See also* Alternative energy sources; Energy and the environment; Energy policy; Passive solar design

[*Muthena Naseri and Douglas Smith*]

FURTHER READING

Balcomb, J. D. *Passive Solar Building.* Cambridge: MIT Press, 1992.

Brown, L. R., et al. "A World Fit to Live In." *UNESCO Courier* (November 1991): 28-31.

Hedger, J. *Solar Energy—The Sleeping Giant: Basics of Solar Energy.* Deming: Akela West Publishers, 1993.

Peck, L. "Here Comes the Sun." *Amicus Journal* 12 (Spring 1990): 27-32.

Solar Energy Research, Development and Demonstration Act (1974)

Following the outbreak of the Arab-Israeli war in 1973, Arab oil-producing states imposed an embargo on oil exports to the United States. The embargo lasted from October 1973 to March 1974, and the long gas lines it caused highlighted the United States' dependence on foreign **petroleum**. Congress responded by enacting the Solar Energy Research, Development and Demonstration Act of 1974.

The act stated that it was henceforth the policy of the federal government to "pursue a vigorous and viable program of research and resource assessment of **solar energy** as a major source of energy for our national needs." The act's scope embraced all energy sources which are renewable by the sun—including solar thermal energy, photovoltaic energy, and energy derived from wind, sea thermal gradients, and **photosynthesis**. To achieve its goals, the act established two programs: the Solar Energy Coordination and Management Project and the Solar Energy Research Institute.

The Solar Energy Coordination and Management Project consisted of six members, five of whom were drawn from other federal agencies, including the National Science Foundation, the Department of Housing and Urban Development, the **Federal Power Commission**, NASA, and the **Atomic Energy Commission**. Congress intended that the project would coordinate national solar energy research, development, and demonstration projects, and would survey resources and technologies available for solar energy production. This information was to be placed in a Solar Energy Information Data Bank and made available to those involved in solar energy development.

Over the decade following the passage of the act in 1974, the United States government spent $4 billion on research in solar and other renewable energy technologies. During the same period, the government spent an additional $2 billion on tax incentives to promote these alternatives.

According to a **U.S. Department of Energy** report issued in 1985, these efforts displaced petroleum worth an estimated $36 billion.

Despite the promise of solar energy in the 1970s and the fear of reliance on foreign petroleum, spending on renewable energy sources in the United States declined dramatically during the 1980s. Several factors combined during that decade to weaken the federal government's commitment to solar power, including the availability of inexpensive petroleum and the skeptical attitudes of the Reagan and Bush administrations, which were distrustful of government-sponsored initiatives and concerned about government spending.

To carry out the research and development initiatives of the Solar Energy Coordination and Management Project, the act also established the Solar Energy Research Institute, located in Golden, Colorado. In 1991, the Solar Energy Research Institute was renamed the National Renewable Energy Laboratory and made a part of the national laboratory system. The laboratory continues to conduct research in the production of solar energy and energy from other renewable sources. In addition, the laboratory studies applications of solar energy. For example, it has worked on a project using solar energy to detoxify **soil** contaminated with **hazardous wastes**.

[*L. Carol Ritchie*]

FURTHER READING

"Federal R&D Funding for Solar Technologies." *Solar Industry Journal* (First Quarter 1992).

"Photovoltaics." *Solar Industry Journal* (First Quarter 1992).

Solar Energy Research, Development, and Demonstration Act of 1974, Pub. L. No. 93-473, 88 Stat. 1431 (1974), codified at 42 U.S.C. 5551, et seq. (1988).

Solid waste

Solid waste is composed of a broad array of materials discarded by households, businesses, industries, and agriculture. The United States generates more than 11 billion tons of solid waste each year. The waste is composed of 7.6 billion tons of industrial nonhazardous waste, 2 to 3 billion tons of oil and gas waste, over 1.4 billion tons of mining waste, and 195 million tons of **municipal solid waste**.

Not all solid waste is actually solid. Some semi-solid, liquid, and gaseous wastes are included in the definition of solid waste. The **Resource Conservation and Recovery Act (RCRA)** defines solid waste to include **garbage**, refuse, **sludge** from municipal **sewage treatment** plants, ash from solid waste incinerators, mining waste, waste from construction and demolition, and some **hazardous waste**s. Since the definition is so broad, it is worth considering what the act excludes from regulations concerning solid waste: untreated sewage, industrial **wastewater** regulated by the

Clean Water Act, irrigation return flows, nuclear materials and by-products, and hazardous wastes in large quantities.

RCRA defines and establishes regulatory authority for hazardous waste and solid waste. According to the act, some hazardous waste may be disposed of in solid waste facilities. These include hazardous wastes discarded from households, such as paint, cleaning solvents, and batteries, and small quantities of **hazardous material**s discarded by business and industry. Some states have their own definitions of solid waste which may vary somewhat from the federal definition. Federal oversight of solid-waste management is the responsibility of the **Environmental Protection Agency (EPA)**.

Facilities for the disposal of solid waste include municipal and industrial **landfill**s, industrial surface impoundments, and incinerators. Incinerators that recover energy as a by-product of waste **combustion** are called **resource recovery** or waste-to-energy facilities. Sewage sludge and agricultural waste may be applied to land surfaces as **fertilizer**s or **soil** conditioners. Other types of **waste management** practices include **composting**, most commonly of separated **organic waste**s, and **recycling**. Some solid waste ends up in illegal open dumps.

Three quarters of industrial nonhazardous waste comes from four industries: iron and steel manufacturers, **electric utilities**, companies making industrial inorganic chemicals, and firms producing **plastics** and resins. About one-third of industrial nonhazardous waste is managed on the site where it is generated, and the rest is transported to off-site municipal or industrial waste facilities. Although surveys conducted by some states are beginning to fill in the gaps, there is still not enough landfills and surface impoundments for industrial solid wastes. Available data suggests there is limited use of environmental controls at those facilities, but there is insufficient information to determine the extent of **pollution** they may have caused.

The materials in municipal solid waste (MSW) are discarded from residential, commercial, institutional, and industrial sources. The materials include plastics, paper, glass, metals, wood, food, and **yard waste**; the amount of each material is evaluated by weight or volume. The distinction between weight and volume is important when considering such factors as landfill capacity. For example, plastics account for only about eight percent of MSW by weight, but more than 21 percent by volume. Conversely, glass represents about seven percent of the weight and only two percent of the volume of MSW.

MSW has recently been the focus of much attention in the United States. Americans generated 4.3 pounds per day (ppd) of MSW in 1990, which was an increase from 4.0 ppd in 1980 and 2.7 ppd in 1960. The EPA has projected that waste generation will reach 4.5 ppd by 2000. This increase has been accompanied by tightening federal regulations concerning the use and construction of landfills. The expense of constructing new landfills to meet these regulations, as well as frequently strong public opposition to new sites for them, have sharply limited the number of disposal options available, and the result is what many consider to be a solid waste disposal crisis. The much publicized "garbage barge"

from Islip, New York, which roamed the oceans from port to port during 1987 looking for a place to unload, has become a symbol of this crisis.

The disposal of MSW is only the most visible aspect of the waste disposal crisis; there are increasingly limited disposal options for all the solid waste generated in America. In response to this crisis, the EPA introduced a waste management hierarchy in 1989. The hierarchy places source reduction and recycling above **incineration** and landfilling as the preferred options for managing solid waste.

Recycling diverts waste already created away from incinerators and landfills. Source reduction, in contrast, decreases the amount of waste created. It is considered the best waste management option, and the EPA defines it as reducing the quantity and toxicity of waste through the design, manufacture, and use of products. Source reduction measures include reducing packaging in products, reusing materials instead of throwing them away, and designing products to be long lasting. Individuals can practice waste reduction by the goods they choose to buy and how they use these products once they bring them home. Many businesses and industries have established procedures for waste reduction, and some have reduced waste toxicity by using less toxic materials in products and packaging. Source reduction can be part of an overall industrial pollution prevention and waste minimization strategy, including recapturing process wastes for **reuse** rather than disposal.

Some solid wastes are potentially threatening to the environment if thrown away but can be valuable resources if reused or recycled. Used motor oil is one example. It contains **heavy metals** and other hazardous substances that can contaminate **groundwater**, surface water, and soils. One gallon of used oil can contaminate one million gallons of water, but these problems can be avoided and energy saved, if used oil is rerefined into motor oil or reprocessed for use as industrial fuel. Much progress remains to be made in this area: of the 200 million gallons of used oil generated annually by people who change their own oil, only 10 percent is recycled.

Another solid waste with recycling potential are used tires, which take up a large amount of space in landfills and cause uneven settling. Tire stockpiles and open dumps can be breeding grounds for mosquitoes, and they are hazardous if ignited, emitting noxious fumes that are difficult to extinguish. Instead of being thrown away, tires can be shredded and recycled into objects such as hoses and door mats; they can also be mixed in road-paving materials or used as fuel in suitable facilities. Whole tires can be retreaded and reused on **automobile**s, or simply used for such purposes as artificial reef construction. Other solid wastes with potential for increased recycling include construction and demolition wastes (building materials), household appliances, and waste wood.

The EPA recommends implementation of this waste management hierarchy through integrated waste management. The agency has encouraged businesses and communities to develop systems where components in the hierarchy complement each other. For example, removing **recyclables** before burning waste for **energy recovery** not only provides all the benefits of recycling, but it reduces the amount of residual ash. Removing recyclable materials that are difficult to burn, such as glass, increases the **Btu** value of waste, thereby improving the efficiency of energy recovery.

Some state and local governments have chosen to conserve landfill space or reduce the toxicity of waste by instituting bans on the burial or burning of certain materials. The most commonly banned materials are automotive batteries, tires, motor oil, yard waste, and appliances. Where such bans exist, there is usually a complementary system in place for either recycling the banned materials or reusing them in some way. Programs such as these usually compost yard waste and institute separate collections for hazardous waste.

Perhaps because of the solid waste disposal crisis, there have been recent changes in solid waste management practices. About 67 percent of MSW was buried in landfills in 1990, down from 81 percent in 1980. At the same time use of incineration, with or without energy recovery, increased from 14 percent of MSW in 1986 to 16 percent in 1990. Recovery of materials for recycling and composting also increased, accounting for 17 percent in 1990, though it had only been three percent in 1988. *See also* Refuse-derived fuel; Sludge treatment and disposal; Solid waste incineration; Solid waste landfilling; Solid waste recycling and recovery; Solid waste volume reduction; Source separation

[*Teresa C. Donkin and Douglas Smith*]

FURTHER READING

Blumberg, L., and R. Grottleib. *War on Waste—Can America Win Its Battle With Garbage?* Covelo, CA: Island Press, 1988.

Glenn, J. "The State of Garbage in America." *Biocycle* (May 1992).

Neal, H. A., and J. R. Schubel. *Solid Waste Management and the Environment: The Mounting Garbage and Trash Crisis.* Englewood Cliffs, NJ: Prentice-Hall, 1987.

Robinson, W. D., ed. *The Solid Waste Handbook.* New York: Wiley, 1986.

Underwood, J. D., and A. Hershkowitz. *Facts About U. S. Garbage Management: Problems and Practices.* New York: INFORM, 1989.

U. S. Environmental Protection Agency. *Characterization of Municipal Solid Waste in the United States: 1992 Update (Executive Summary).* Washington, DC: U. S. Government Printing Office, July 1992.

U. S. Environmental Protection Agency. *Solid Waste Disposal in the United States.* Washington, DC: U. S. Government Printing Office, 1989.

Solid waste incineration

Incineration is the burning of waste in a specially designed **combustion** chamber. The idea of burning **garbage** is not new, but with the increase in knowledge about toxic **chemicals** known to be released during burning, and with the increase in the amount of garbage to be burned, incineration now is done under controlled conditions. It has become the method of choice of many **waste management** companies and municipalities.

According to the **Environmental Protection Agency (EPA)**, there are 135 operational waste combustion facilities in the United States. About 120 of them recover energy, and in all, the facilities process about 13 percent of the nation's 280 million tons of municipal solid waste produced each year.

There are several types of combustion facilities in operation. At incinerators, mixed trash goes in one end unsorted, and it is all burned together. The resulting ash is typically placed in a **landfill**. Incinerators in the United States process about 2.1 million tons of municipal **solid waste** per year.

At mass burn incinerators, also known as mass burn combustors, the heat generated from the burning material is turned into useable electricity. Mixed garbage burns in a special chamber where temperatures reach at least 2000° F (1093 °C). The byproducts are ash, which is landfilled, and combustion gases. As the hot gases rise from the burning waste, they heat water held in special tubes around the combustion chamber. The boiling water generates steam and or electricity. The gases are filtered for contaminants before being released into the air.

Modular combustion systems typically have two combustion chambers: one to burn mixed trash and another to heat gases. Energy is recovered with a heat recovery steam generator. Refuse-derived fuel combustors burn presorted waste and convert the resulting heat into energy. In all, incinerators in this country in 1992 typically consumed 80,100 tons (72,730 metric tons) of waste each day, and generated the annual equivalent of 16.4 million megawatts of usable power, equal to roughly 30 million barrels of oil.

One major problem with incineration is **air pollution**. Even when equipped with **scrubbers**, many substances, some of them toxic, are released into the atmosphere. In the United States, **emission**s from incinerators are among targets of the **Clean Air Act**, and research continues on ways to improve the efficiency of incinerators. For now, however, many environmentalists protest the use of incinerators.

Incinerators burning municipal solid waste produce the pollutants **carbon monoxide**, **sulfur dioxide**, and **particulate**s containing heavy metals. The generation of pollutants can be controlled by proper operation and by the proper use of air emission control devices, including dry scrubbers, electrostatic precipitators, fabric **filters**, and proper stack height.

Dry scrubbers wash particulate matter and gases from the air by passing them through a liquid. The scrubber removes acid gases by injecting a lime **slurry** into a reaction tower through which the gases flow. A salt powder is produced and collected along with the **fly ash**. The lime also causes small particles to stick together, forming larger particles that are more easily removed.

Electrostatic precipitators use high voltage to negatively charge dust particles, then the charged particulates are collected on positively charged plates. This device has been documented as removing 98 percent of particulates, including heavy metals; nearly 43 percent of all existing facilities use this method to control air pollution.

Fabric filters or **baghouse**s consist of hundreds of long fabric bags made of heat-resistant material suspended in an enclosed housing which filters particles from the gas stream. Fabric filters are able to trap fine, inhalable particles, up to 99 percent of the particulates in the gas flow coming out of the scrubber, including condensed toxic organic and heavy metal compounds. Stack height is an extra precaution taken to assure that any remaining pollutants will not reach the ground in a concentrated area.

Using the **Best Available Control Technology (BAT)**, the National Solid Wastes Management Association states more than 95 percent of gases and fly ash are captured and removed. However, such state-of-the-art facilities are more the exception than the rule. In a study of 15 mass burn and refuse-derived fuel plants of varying age, size, design, and control systems, the environmental research group IN-FORM found that only one of the 15 achieved the emission levels set by the group for six primary air pollutants (**dioxin**s and furans, particulates, carbon monoxide, sulfur dioxide, hydrogen chloride, and **nitrogen oxides**). Six plants did not meet any. Only two employed the safest ash management techniques. And the EPA is still trying to define standards for air emissions from municipal incinerators.

Ash is the solid material left over after combustion in the incinerator. It is composed of noncombustible inorganic materials that are present in cans, bottles, rocks and stones; and complex organic materials formed primarily from **carbon** atoms that escape combustion. Municipal solid waste ash also can contain **lead** and **cadmium** from such sources as old appliances and car batteries.

Bottom ash, the unburned and unburnable matter left over, comprises 75 to 90 percent of all ash produced in incineration. Fly ash is a powdery material suspended in the flue gas stream and is collected in the air pollution control equipment. Fly ash tends to have higher concentrations of certain metals and organic materials, and comprises 10 percent to 25 percent of total ash generated.

The greatest concern with ash is proper disposal and the potential for harmful substances to be released into the **groundwater**. Federal regulations governing ash are in transition because it is not known whether ash should be regulated as a hazardous or nonhazardous waste as specified in the **Resource Conservation and Recovery Act (RCRA)** of 1976.

EPA draft guidelines for handling ash include: ash containers and transport vehicles must be leak-tight; groundwater monitoring must be performed at disposal sites; and liners must be used at all ash disposal landfills.

While waste-to-energy plants can decrease the volume of solid waste by 60 to 90 percent and at the same time recover energy from discarded products, the cost of building such facilities is too high for most municipalities. The $400 million price tag for a large plant is prohibitive, even if the revenue from the sale of energy helps offset the cost. But without a strong market for produced energy, the plant may not be economically feasible for many areas.

The Public Utility Regulatory Policy Act (PURPA), enacted in 1979, helps to ensure that small power generators, including waste-to-energy facilities, will have a market for produced energy. PURPA requires utilities to purchase such energy from qualifying facilities at avoided costs, that is, the cost avoided by not generating the energy themselves. And

some waste-to-energy plants are developing markets themselves for steam produced. Some facilities supply steam to industrial plants or district heating systems.

Another concern over the use of incinerators to solve the garbage dilemma in the United States is that materials incinerated are resources lost—resources that must be recreated with a considerable effort, high expense, and potential environmental damage. From this point of view, incineration represents a failure of waste disposal policy. Waste disposal, many believe, requires an integrated approach that includes reduction, **recycling**, **composting**, and landfilling, along with incineration.

[*Linda Rehkopf*]

FURTHER READING

Clarke, M. *Improving Environmental Performance of MSW Incinerators.* New York: INFORM, 1988.

Denison, R. A., and J. Ruston, eds. *Recycling and Incineration: Evaluating the Choices.* New York: Environmental Defense Fund, 1990.

Environmental Review of Waste Incineration. Washington, DC: Institute for Local Self-Reliance, 1986.

To Burn or Not to Burn. New York: Environmental Defense Fund, 1985.

Solid waste landfilling

The **Resource Conservation and Recovery Act (RCRA)** defines **solid waste** as **garbage**, refuse, **sludge** from **sewage treatment** plants, ash from incinerators, mining waste, construction and demolition materials, and some hazardous waste in small quantities. Such waste can be disposed of in several ways: by **incineration**, **composting**, **recycling**, industrial surface impoundments, and **landfill**s. In some ways, disposing waste in landfills is easier than the other methods. For example, unlike for composting and incineration, the waste need not have a particular shape or contain certain chemical properties. Most often waste is compacted and dumped into excavated areas such as sand and gravel pits or in valleys. In sanitary landfills, waste is compacted each day and covered with a layer of dirt to decrease odor and discourage flies and other insects.

In 1990 each American generated 4.3 lbs (1.9 kg) of **municipal solid waste** a day. As people generate more and more waste, the supply of available landfill space is decreasing rapidly. The **NIMBY**—not in my backyard—attitude further prevents the construction of new landfills. With fewer landfills, the cost of disposing waste has increased dramatically. The kind of waste dumped into landfills is also important in terms of landfill capacity. For instance, **plastics** account for eight percent of municipal solid waste by weight, but more than 21 percent by volume. In an attempt to conserve land space, some cities have banned the burial of certain materials such as car batteries, used tires, motor oil, **yard waste**, and appliances.

In 1980, 81 percent of solid waste was buried in landfills; in 1990 it decreased to 67 percent. This decrease resulted, in part, from a concentrated effort by federal and local organizations to address the problems associated with landfills. Surface and **groundwater** contamination have been noted in areas near landfills. Because of these and other health-related problems associated with landfill use, the **Environmental Protection Agency (EPA)** has recommended source reduction, recycling, and incineration as the preferred **waste management** techniques over solid waste landfilling.

Solid waste management

See **Waste management**

Solid waste recycling and recovery

Recycling is the recovery and reuse of materials from wastes. **Solid waste** recycling refers to the reuse of manufactured goods from which resources such as steel, **copper**, or **plastics** can be recovered and reused. Recycling and recovery is only one phase of an integrated approach to solid **waste management** that also includes reducing the amount of waste produced, **composting**, incinerating, and landfilling.

Municipal solid waste (MSW) comes from household, commercial, institutional, and light industrial sources, and from some hospital and laboratory sources. The United States produces about 157.7 million tons (143.2 million metric tons) of MSW per year, almost four pounds (1.8 kilograms) per resident per day. By the year 2000, that figure is expected to grow to 192.7 million tons (175 million metric tons) per year. The percentages of MSW generated in this country include paper and paperboard, 41 percent; yard wastes, 17.9 percent; metals, 8.7 percent; glass, 8.2 percent; rubber, textiles, leather and wood, 8.1 percent; food wastes, 7.9 percent; plastics, 6.5 percent; and miscellaneous inorganic wastes, 1.6 percent.

Recycling is a significant way to keep large amounts of solid waste out of **landfill**s, conserve resources, and save energy. In 1991, Americans recycled about 14 percent of MSW, incinerated ten percent, and landfilled the other 76 percent. Recycling could realistically reduce the amount of MSW generated by about 25 percent.

The technology of recycling involves collection, separation, preparing the material to buyer's specifications, sale to markets, processing, and the eventual reuse of materials. Separation and collection is only the first step; if the material is not also processed and returned to commerce, then it is not being recycled. In many parts of the country, markets are not yet sufficiently developed to handle the growing supply of collected material.

Intermediate markets for recyclable materials include scrap dealers or brokers, who wait for favorable market conditions in which to sell their inventory. Final markets are facilities where recycled materials are converted to new products, the last phase in the recycling circle.

The materials recycled today include **aluminum**, paper, glass, plastics, iron and steel, scrap tires, and used oil. Aluminum, particularly cans, is a valuable commodity. By the late 1980s, over 50 percent of all aluminum cans were recycled. Recycling aluminum saves a tremendous amount of energy: it takes 95 percent less energy to produce an aluminum can from an existing one rather than from ore. Other aluminum products that are recycled include siding, gutters, door and window frames, and lawn furniture.

Over 30 percent of the paper and paperboard used in the U.S. is collected and utilized as either raw material to make recycled paper, or as an export to overseas markets. Recycled paper shows up in newsprint, roofing shingles, tar paper, and insulation. By 1991, recycled newspapers hit a record 6.6 million tons (6 million metric tons). Other recyclable paper products include old corrugated containers, mixed office waste, and high-grade waste paper. Contaminants must be removed from paper products before the remanufacture process can begin, however, such as food wastes, metal, glass, rubber, and other extraneous materials.

The market for crushed glass, or cullet, has increased. Recycled glass is used to make fiberglass and new glass containers. About 1.25 million tons (1.14 million metric tons) of glass is recycled annually in the United States.

Three types of plastic are successfully being recycled, the most common being PET (polyethylene terephthalate), or soft drink containers. Recycled PET is used for fiberfill in sleeping bags and ski jackets, carpet backing, automobile bumpers, bathtubs, floor tiles, and paintbrushes. HDPE plastic (high density polyethylene) is used for milk jugs and the bottoms of soft drink bottles. It can be recycled into trash cans and flower pots, among other items. Polystyrene foam is crushed into pellets and turned into plastic lumber for benches and walkways. Commingled plastics are recycled into fence posts and park benches.

Iron and steel are the most recycled materials used today. In 1987, 51 million tons were recycled, more than twice the amount of all other materials combined. The material is remelted and shaped into new products.

More than one billion discarded tires are stockpiled in the United States, but scrap tires can be shredded and used for asphalt-rubber or retreading; are incinerated for fuel; or used to construct artificial marine reefs.

Used oil is a valuable resource, and of the 1.2 billion gallons (4.5 billion liters) generated annually, two-thirds is recycled. The rest, about 400 million gallons (1.5 billion liters), is disposed of or dumped. About 57 percent of used oil is reprocessed for fuel, 26 percent is refined and turned into base stock for use as lubricating oil, and about 17 percent is recycled for other uses.

Composting is the aerobic biological **decomposition** of organic waste materials, usually lawn clippings. Composting is not an option for a major portion of the solid waste stream, but is an important component of the resource recovery program.

Recycling collection methods vary, but curbside collection is the most popular and has the highest participation rates. It is also the most expensive way for municipalities to collect recyclables in their communities. Collection centers do not yield as many recyclables because residents must do the sorting themselves, but centers offer the most affordable method of collection.

Precycling is an option that is gaining widespread recognition in this country. Basically, precycling refers to the consumer making environmentally sound choices at the point of purchase. It includes avoiding products with extra packaging, or products made to satisfy only short-term needs, such as disposable razors.

Resource recovery or materials recovery is the recycling of waste in an industrial setting. It does not involve recycling consumer waste or municipal solid waste, but includes reprocessed industrial material that, for whatever reason, is not able to be used as it was initially intended. Some consumer groups are pressing for government guidelines on labeling packaging or products "reprocessed" as opposed to "recycled."

While the **Environmental Protection Agency (EPA)** insists that no single alternative to the municipal solid waste problem should be relied upon, its generally accepted hierarchy of waste management alternatives is 1) source reduction and 2) reusing products. Waste that is not generated never enters the waste stream.

If recycling is to be used as a genuine MSW management alternative rather than a "feel good" way to conserve resources, then materials must be recovered and made into new products in large quantities. For some materials, however, an insufficient market exists, so communities must pay to have some recyclable materials taken away until a market is developed. Recycling programs depend on the will of the community to follow through, and in many areas, response is weak and enforcement lacking. However, dwindling landfill space in the 1990s may force communities to mandate recycling programs.

New EPA regulations scheduled for implementation by the end of 1993 are expected to seriously affect the number of operable landfills. The requirements include installing liners, collecting and treating liquids that leach, monitoring **groundwater** and surface water for harmful **chemicals**, and monitoring the escape of **methane** gas. These regulations will increase the number of corporate-run landfills, but the cost of building an maintaining a landfill that adheres to the regulations will top $125 million. The end cost to consumers to have trash hauled away may also force many **garbage** makers to become reducers, reusers, and recyclers.

[*Linda Rehkopf*]

FURTHER READING

Franklin, W. E., and M. A. Franklin. "Recycling." *The EPA Journal* (July-August 1992): 7.

Kharbanda, O. P., and E. A. Stallworthy. *Waste Management: Towards a Sustainable Society.* Westport, CT: Auburn House/Greenwood, 1990.

Robinson, W. D., ed. *The Solid Waste Handbook.* New York: Wiley, 1986.

Solid Waste Recycling: The Complete Resource Guide. Washington, DC: Bureau of National Affairs, 1990.

Solid waste volume reduction

Solid waste volume reduction can take place at several points in the **waste management** process. Solid waste volume reduction can take the form of as **precycling** or **reuse** behavior on the part of consumers. This behavior reduces **solid waste** at the source and prevents materials from ever entering the **waste stream**. Precycling on the part of consumers is the best initial activity to reduce the volume of solid waste. Reuse is also a measure that prevents or delays the migration of materials to the **landfill**. Once the decision is made that a product is no longer useful and needs to be discarded, there are several management techniques that can be used.

Recycling diverts large volumes of materials from the waste stream to a manufacturing process. Glass, **plastic**, paper, cardboard and other clean, source-separated materials are well-suited for use in the manufacture of new products. As markets become more readily available, the volume of materials that end up in landfills will be reduced even more. Such troublesome wastes as tires, appliances and construction debris are targets of serious recycling efforts since they are large-volume items, take up a lot of space in landfills, and do not provide good fuel for waste-to-energy facilities in their discarded state. Once **recyclables** have been separated from the waste stream, solid waste can be further reduced in volume through several methods.

Compaction of waste materials after **source separation** is useful for two reasons. Compaction prepares waste for efficient transport by truck, boat or rail car to landfills or other waste disposal facilities. Compacted waste takes up less space in a landfill, thereby extending the life of the landfill. In some cases, compacted waste can be stored for later disposal. It must be understood that the compaction of waste should only be done after all recyclables have been removed since this process contaminates post-consumer materials and makes it almost impossible to recover them for a manufacturing process.

Incineration has long been accepted as a waste volume reduction technique. The burning of solid waste can reduce the volume by 95 percent. In the early 1920s, incineration was used to reduce waste materials to what was thought of as a harmless ash. We now know that contaminants can become concentrated in the ash, qualifying it as a **hazardous waste**. It wasn't until the mid-1970s that waste-to-energy facilities using incineration were considered a viable option, as a consequence of the added benefit of energy supply. Most states now require that the residual ash from burning municipal solid waste be landfilled in a monofill. A monofill is a landfill compartment that can only be used for incinerator ash.

Composting is another volume reduction technique that can divert large volumes of waste material from the waste stream. Leaves, grass clippings and tree prunings can be reduced in volume through an active composting process both in the backyard and in municipal composting yards. Individual homeowners can compost in their back yards by using simple rounds of wire fencing placed in a shady, cool corner. The composting materials need to be managed through the addition of moisture, temperature monitoring, and frequent turning, until they become a rich **soil** for the garden. Municipal yards perform the same process on a much larger scale and then use the resulting soil in city parks or give it back to the homeowners for personal use. These solid waste volume reduction techniques for organics in the waste stream are simple and low cost and can be very effective.

Methods for encouraging solid waste volume reduction at the individual household level consist of various incentive programs. The most common technique is a system of volume-based user fees. With this method, homeowners are given free bags into which they can put anything that is designated by the city as a recyclable material. Distinctly different bags are sold at the local grocery store or city hall. These bags usually sell for somewhere between $2 and $5 a package and must be used for all materials destined for disposal. Homeowners who want to reduce their garbage disposal costs would try to reduce the number of purchased bags they need to use. They can do this through a concerted effort of solid waste volume reduction. Careful decisions at the supermarket to reduce packaging and single-use items, reuse of packaging and containers, careful source separation of recyclables, and composting of all organically based materials can reduce the volume of solid waste considerably and reduce the cost of garbage service. An even greater effort can be launched by dedicated individuals by taking used clothing to consignment shops or donating it to organizations for distribution to needy populations, taking clothes hangers back to cleaning establishments, and requesting that junk mail no longer be sent to their households. Of course, there is also the ongoing debate on using **disposable diapers**, which greatly add to the volume of the waste stream.

Businesses that contribute to the reduction of solid waste are those that have been set up to take back, repair, and reuse products and materials that would otherwise end up in the waste stream. Small appliance repair shops can recondition appliances and resell them. Businesses that repair wood pallets make a relatively new contribution to the effort to reduce the waste volume. Tires are being chipped for fuel in waste-to-energy incinerators, and are also being pulverized for use in soils for playing fields. All of these volume reduction techniques have a significant effect on how we live and how we do business. The goal of solid waste volume reduction is to view the waste stream as a resource to be "mined," leaving only those items behind that have truly outlived their usefulness. *See also* Solid waste incineration; Yard waste

[*Cynthia Fridgen*]

FURTHER READING

Blumberg, L., and R. Gottlieb. *War on Waste: Can America Win Its Battle With Garbage?* Covelo, CA: Island Press, 1989.

Kharbanda, O. P., and E. A. Stallworthy. *Waste Management: Toward a Sustainable Society.* Westport, CT: Auburn House/Greenwood, 1990.

Noyes, R., ed. *Pollution Prevention Technology Handbook.* Park Ridge, NJ: Noyes Press, 1993.

Porter, J. W., and J. Z. Cannon. "Waste Minimization: Challenge for American Industry." *Business Horizons* 35 (March-April 1992): 46-9.

Solidification of hazardous materials

Solidification refers to a process in which waste materials are bound in a solid mass, often a monolithic block. The waste may or may not react chemically with the agents used to create the solid. Solidification is generally discussed in conjunction with stabilization as a means of reducing the mobility of a pollutant. Actually, stabilization is a broad term which includes solidification, as well as other chemical processes that result in the transformation of a **toxic substance** to a less or non-toxic form.

Experts often speak of the technologies collectively as solidification and stabilization (S/S) methods. Chemical fixation, where chemical bonding transforms the toxicant to non-toxic form, and encapsulation, in which toxic materials are coated with an additive are processes referred to in discussions of S/S methods. There are currently about forty different vendors of S/S services in the United States, and though the details of some processes are privileged, many fundamental aspects are widely known and practiced by the companies.

S/S technologies try to decrease the solubility, the exposed surface area, and/or the toxicity of a **hazardous material**. While the methods also make wastes easier to handle, there are some disadvantages. Certain wastes are not good candidates for S/S. For example, a number of inorganic and organic substances interfere with the way that S/S additives will perform, resulting in weaker, less durable, more permeable solids or blocks. Another disadvantage is that S/S often double the volume and weight of a waste material, which may greatly affect transportation and final disposal costs (not considering potential costs associated with untreated materials contaminating the **environment**). S/S additives, such as encapsulators, are available which will not increase the weight and volume of the wastes so dramatically, but these additives tend to be more expensive and difficult to use.

Methods for S/S are characterized on the bases of binders, reaction type, and processing schemes. Binders may be inorganic or organic substances. Examples of inorganic binders which are often used in various combinations include cements; lime; pozzolans, which react with lime and moisture to form a cement, e.g. **fly ash**; and silicates. Among the organic types generally used are epoxies, polyesters, asphalt and polyolefins (e.g. polyethylene). Organic binders have also been mixed with inorganic types e.g., polyurethane and cement. The performance of a binder system for a given waste is evaluated on a case-by-case basis; however, much has been learned in recent years about the compatibility and performance of binders with certain wastes, which allows for some intelligent initial decisions related to binder selection and processing requirements.

Among the types of reactions used to characterize S/S are **sorption**, pozzolan, pozzolan-portland cement and thermoplastic microencapsulation. Sorption refers to the addition of a solid to sorb free liquid in a waste. Activated carbon, gypsum and clays have been used in this capacity. Pozzolan reactions typically involve adding fly ash, lime, and perhaps water to a waste. The mixture of fly ash, lime and water form a low-strength cement that physically traps contaminants. This system is very alkaline and therefore may not be compatible with certain wastes. For example, a waste containing high amounts of ammonium ions would pose a problem because under highly alkaline conditions the toxic gas, ammonia, would be released. Also, sodium borate, carbohydrates, oil, and grease are known to interfere with the process.

The pozzolan-portland cement process consists of adding a pozzolan, often fly ash, and a portland cement to a waste. It may be necessary to add water if enough is not present in the waste. The resulting product is a high-strength matrix that primarily entraps contaminants. The performance of the system can be enhanced through the use of silicates to prevent interference by metals, clays to absorb excessive liquids and certain **ion**s, surfactants to incorporate organic solvents, and a variety of sorbents that will hold on to toxicants as the solid matrix forms. Care is needed in selecting a sorbent because, for example, an acidic sorbent might dissolve a metal hydroxide, thereby increasing the mobility of the metal, or result in the release of toxic gases such as **hydrogen** sulfide or hydrogen cyanide. Borates, oil and grease can also interfere with this process.

Thermoplastic encapsulation is accomplished by blending a waste with materials such as melted asphalt, polyethylene, or wax. The technique is more difficult and costly than the other methods introduced above because specialized equipment and higher temperatures are required. At these higher temperatures it is possible that certain hazardous materials will violently react. Additionally, it is known that high **salt** levels, certain organic solvents and grease will interfere with the process.

There are basically four categories of processing schemes for S/S. For in-drum processing, S/S additives and waste are mixed and allowed to solidify in a drum. The drum and its contents are then disposed. In-plant processing is a second category which refers simply to performing S/S procedures at an established facility. The facility might have been designed by a company for their own wastes or as a S/S plant which serves a number of industries.

A third category is mobile-plant processing, in which S/S operations are moved from site to site. The fourth category is *in-situ* processing which involves adding S/S additives directly to a lagoon or **contaminated soil**.

As may be inferred from the above discussion, the goals of S/S operations are to remove free liquids from a waste, generate a solid matrix that will reliably contain hazardous materials, and/or create a waste that is no longer hazardous. The first goal is important because current regulations in the **Resource Conservation and Recovery Act (RCRA)** stipulate that free liquids are not to be disposed of in a **landfill**. The third goal is obviously important because disposing of a **hazardous waste**, called delisting, is much more costly and time-consuming than disposing of a regular waste.

Wastes are deemed to be hazardous on the bases of four characteristic tests and a series of listings. The tests are related to the ignitability, reactivity, corrosiveness and extraction procedure (EP) toxicity of the waste. It is possible that S/S procedures delist a waste in any of the four test characteristics. The processes may also chemically transform a substance listed as hazardous waste by the **Environmental Protection Agency (EPA)** into a non-hazardous chemical. However, S/S techniques generally delist a waste through effecting a change in the results of the EP toxicity test, related to the goal of proper containment. If a waste can be contained well, it may pass the extraction test.

The extraction procedure has changed somewhat in recent years. Originally, the solid waste to be tested was stirred in a weakly acidic solution overnight, and then the supernatant was tested for certain inorganic and organic agents. Recently, the test has been replaced by what is known as the Toxicity Characteristic Leaching Procedure (TCLP). Shortcomings of the original extraction procedure were recognized some years ago, as Congress directed the EPA to develop a more reliable, second generation test through the Hazardous and Solid Waste Amendments of 1984. Work on the TCLP test actually began in 1981. In the TCLP, a solid waste is again suspended in an acidic solution, but the method of contacting the liquid with the solid has been changed. The suspension is now placed in a container that revolves about a horizontal axis, tumbling solids amidst the extracting solution. The extraction is allowed to proceed for 18 hours, after which time the solution is filtered and tested for a variety of organic and inorganic substances. The number of compounds tested under the TCLP is greater than the number measured for the original EP test. Failing the TCLP test dictates that a waste is hazardous and must be managed as such. *See also* Hazardous Materials Transportation Act (1975); Storage and transport of hazardous materials

[*Gregory D. Boardman*]

FURTHER READING

"Background Document: Toxicity Characteristic Leaching Procedure." Report No. PB87-154886, Washington, DC: U. S. Environmental Protection Agency, 1986.

"Guide to the Disposal of Chemically Stabilized and Solidified Waste." Report No. SW-872, Washington, DC: U. S. Environmental Protection Agency, 1980.

Freeman, H. M. *Standard Handbook of Hazardous Waste Treatment and Disposal.* New York: McGraw-Hill, 1989.

Martin, E. J., and J. H. Johnson. *Hazardous Waste Management Engineering.* New York: Van Nostrand Reinhold, 1987.

Wentz, C. A. *Hazardous Waste Management.* New York: McGraw-Hill, 1989.

Sonic boom

When an object moves through a fluid, it displaces that fluid in the form of a shock wave. The path left by a speedboat in water is an example of a shock wave. A sonic boom is a special kind of shock wave produced when an object travels though air at a speed greater than the speed of sound [1,100 feet per second (335 m/sec) at sea level]. Supersonic aircraft, such as the *Concorde*, produce a sonic boom when they fly faster than the speed of sound. A number of adverse environmental effects have been attributed to sonic booms from supersonic airplanes. These include the breaking of windows and the frightening of animals and people.

Sorption

Term generally referring to either **adsorption** or absorption. Adsorption is the process by which one material attaches itself to the surface of a second material. Some air pollutants settle out and coat the outer surface of a building, for example. Absorption is the process by which one material soaks into a second material. Liquid air pollutants may actually soak into the surface of a building. The term sorption is most commonly used when the exact process involved, adsorption or absorption, is unknown. Various sorption methods are employed to reduce pollutants from contaminated air and water. *See also* Pollution control

Source reduction

See **Solid waste**

Source separation

Source separation is the segregation of different types of **solid waste** at the location where they are generated (a household or business). The number and types of categories into which wastes are divided usually depends on the collection system used and the final destination of the wastes. The most common reason for separating wastes at the source is for **recycling**. Recyclables that are segregated from other trash are usually cleaner and easier to process. Yard wastes are often separated so they may be composted or used as mulch. Some experimental municipal recycling projects also require homeowners to separate household compostibles, like food scraps, coffee grounds, bones, and **disposable diapers**. Some studies suggest that as much as 30 percent of household waste may be compostible; another 40 percent may be recyclable.

Separate collection of household trash, **recyclables**, and **yard waste** is gaining popularity in the United States. In some communities source separation is mandated, while in others it is voluntary. Many cities provide residents with recycling bins to be filled with recyclables and placed next to garbage cans on collection day. Source-separated yard waste is usually placed in **plastic** bags or bundled if it is bulky, like tree trimmings. In areas where curbside collection of recyclables and yard waste is not available, residents often take these source-separated wastes to drop-off centers, or sell recyclables to buy-back facilities. For source-separated recycling programs to be successful, citizen participation is essential. Incentives to increase participation, such as reduced trash collection charges for recyclers, are sometimes implemented.

Household recyclables that are source separated from trash can either be commingled (all recyclables mixed together in one container) or segregated into individual containers for each material (i.e., glass, newspaper, **aluminum**). Commingled recyclables are eventually separated manually, mechanically, or by some combination of both at transfer stations or materials recovery facilities. In some cases, commingled recyclables are manually separated at the curbside by the collection crew. Recyclables that residents have separated into individual containers are usually collected in trucks with compartments for each material. The collected materials are then processed further at materials-recovery facilities or other types of recycling plants.

Many businesses also separate their solid wastes. This can be as simple as placing recycling bins next to soda-vending machines in employee cafeterias or more complex separation systems on assembly lines. One of the most prevalent wastes from the commercial sector is corrugated cardboard (13 percent of **municipal solid waste** generated). Once it becomes contaminated by other wastes, it may not be suitable for recycling. Some businesses find it easier and more economical to separate and bale corrugated cardboard for recycling because this can reduce their waste-disposal costs.

Source-separation programs can reduce the undesirable effects of **landfill**s or incinerators. For instance, batteries and household **chemicals** can increase the toxicity of landfill leachate, air **emission**s from incinerators, and incinerator ash. In addition, some potentially noncombustible wastes, such as glass, can reduce the efficiency of incinerators. Reducing the volume of residual ash is another incentive for diverting wastes from incineration.

Recyclables and special wastes can be retrieved from the waste stream without source separation programs. Many communities find it more convenient or economical to separate wastes after collection. In these programs, recyclables and special wastes are manually or mechanically separated at transfer stations or materials-recovery facilities. Separating recyclables in this way may require more labor and higher energy costs, but it's more convenient for residents since it requires no extra effort beyond regular trash disposal procedures.

Source separation may be only one part of an overall community recycling program. These, in turn, are components of more comprehensive waste-management strategies. To reduce the environmental impact of waste disposal, the **Environmental Protection Agency (EPA)** encourages communities to develop strategies to decrease landfill use and lower the risks and inefficiencies of **incineration**. **Waste reduction** and recycling are considered to be the most environmentally beneficial methods to manage waste.

[*Teresa C. Donkin*]

FURTHER READING

U.S. Congress, Office of Technology Assessment. *Facing America's Trash: What Next for Municipal Solid Waste*. Washington, DC: U. S. Government Printing Office, October 1989.

U.S. Environmental Protection Agency, Solid Waste and Emergency Response. *Characterization of Municipal Solid Waste in the United States: 1990 Update.* Washington, DC: U. S. Government Printing Office, June 1990.

U.S. Environmental Protection Agency, Solid Waste and Emergency Response. *Decision-Makers Guide to Solid Waste Management.* Washington, DC: U. S. Government Printing Office, November 1989.

South

The **United Nations Earth Summit,** held in Rio de Janeiro in June of 1992, illuminated some major differences among the nations of the world, differences that are summarized in the terms North and South. The latter term, for example, refers to nations of the southern hemisphere—nations that have significantly different environmental concerns than do their northern neighbors. These concerns arise primarily from rapidly growing populations, low levels of technological and industrial development and, in general, difficult living conditions. An important conclusion drawn from the Rio conference is that the marked differences between North and South must somehow be reduced if global problems are to be solved.

Spaceship Earth

Spaceship Earth is a metaphor which suggests that the earth is a small, vulnerable craft in space.

Adlai Stevenson used the metaphor in his presidential campaign speeches during the 1950s, but it is not clear who originated it. Perhaps R. Buckminster Fuller was most responsible for popularizing it; he wrote a book entitled *Operating Manual for Spaceship Earth* and was described by one biographer as the ship's "pilot." Fuller was impressed by how negligible the craft was in the infinity of the universe, how fast it was flying, and how well it had been "designed" to support life.

Fuller took the metaphor further, noting that what interested him about the earth was "that it is a mechanical vehicle, just as is an automobile." He noted that people are quick to service their **automobile**s and keep them in running condition but that "we have not been seeing our Spaceship Earth as an integrally-designed machine which to be persistently successful must be comprehended and serviced in total." He did observe one difference between the spaceship and a car: there is no owner's manual for the earth. The lack of operating instructions was significant to Fuller because it has forced humans to use their intellect; but he also maintained that "designed into this Spaceship Earth's total wealth was a big safety factor" which allowed the support system to survive human ignorance until that intellect was sufficiently developed. It was Fuller's lifelong quest to persuade humans to use their intellect and become good pilots and mechanics for Spaceship Earth. He was an optimist, and believed that humans are all astronauts—"always have been, and so long as we exist, always will be"—and as such can learn the mechan-

ics of the system well enough to operate the vehicle satisfactorily.

Political scientist Barbara Ward borrowed the phrase from Fuller to claim that "planet earth, on its journey through infinity, has acquired the intimacy, the fellowship, and the vulnerability of a spaceship." She claimed this image to be "the most rational way of considering the whole human race today." Humans must begin to see humanity "as the ship's crew of a single spaceship on which all of us, with a remarkable combination of security and vulnerability, are making our pilgrimage through infinity." Ward used the metaphor to argue for the reality of global community: "This is how we have to think of ourselves. We are a ship's company on a small ship. Rational behavior is the condition of survival." The rational behavior she advocated was building the institutions, the laws, the habits, and the traditions needed to get along together in the world.

Nigel Calder appreciated the value of the spaceship metaphor and described it in more specific terms: "Whether its watchkeepers were microbes or dinosaurs, the Earth system of rocks, air, water and life worked like the life-support system of a manned spacecraft." He went on to suggest that "the gas and water tanks of Spaceship Earth are the air and the oceans" and that "the sun is the spaceship's main power supply." Calder used the metaphor as an introduction to a detailed consideration of what he describes as a new "Earth-system science," moving from there to a depiction of the globe as a total system.

Kenneth Boulding, an economist, has made essentially the same point, describing an inevitable transition from a "cowboy economy" where support systems are open with no linkage between inputs and outputs, to a "spaceman" economy where "the earth has become a single spaceship, without unlimited reservoirs of anything, either for extraction or for pollution, and in which, therefore, man must find his place in a cyclical ecological system which is capable of continuous reproduction of material form even though it cannot escape having inputs of energy."

The purpose of the spaceship metaphor is to persuade people that the earth has limits and that humans must respect those limits. It provides a modern, new-age image of a small, comprehensible system, which many people can understand. In that sense, the metaphor helps people understand their relationship to the environment by depicting a system, as Ward notes, that is small enough to be vulnerable and needs to be cared for if it is to sustain life.

But the image can also be delusive, even specious, with negative implications not generally recognized. A spaceship is an artifact, a structure of human creation. Some have argued that depicting the earth as such is seductive, but borders on the arrogant by implying, as Fuller seems to, that humans can completely "control" the operations of the earth. Furthermore, spaceships are commonly thought of as small and crowded, with a life-support system devoted exclusively to human inhabitants. Since humans are using more and more of the planet's resources for their own benefit, and the pressure of an increasing human population is extinguishing other life-forms, some environmentalists argue that the spaceship metaphor should be used with caution. *See also* Environmental ethics; Green politics

[*Gerald L. Young*]

FURTHER READING

Boulding, K. "The Economics of the Coming Spaceship Earth," and "Spaceship Earth Revisited." In *Valuing the Earth: Economics, Ecology and Ethics*. Cambridge, MA: The MIT Press, 1993.

Calder, N. *Spaceship Earth*. New York: Viking Penguin, 1991.

Fuller, R. B. *Operating Manual for Spaceship Earth*. New York: Simon and Schuster, 1969.

Ward, B. *Spaceship Earth*. New York: Columbia University Press, 1966.

Special use permit

An authorization from the appropriate governmental agency to another agency or to a private operator to use publicly-owned land for certain purposes. The Secretary of Agriculture and **Forest Service** issue permits for special uses not explicitly covered by timber, mining, or grazing laws or regulations on lands in the **national forest** system. Uses must be carefully controlled and be compatible with forest policy as well as with other uses. Commercial users pay a fair market fee to mine stone and gravel, operate ski areas, conduct sporting and planned recreation events, and construct rights-of-way, pipelines, power lines, and microwave stations. Other special uses include archeological explorations and leases for public buildings and summer homes.

Species

A species is a group of closely related, physically similar beings that can interbreed freely. In practice, the dividing lines between species or between species and subspecies are sometimes unclear.

In sorting out species, biologists search for easily recognized diagnostic characteristics. For example, it is easier to recognize a giraffe by its long neck than by its blood proteins. However, species differ from one another not just by conspicuous features. Members of a species share a common **gene pool** and have a common geographic range, **habitat**, and similar characteristics ranging from the biochemical and morphological to the behavioral.

In taxonomy, the hierarchy of biological classification, species is the category just below genus. The major groups in the classification hierarchy are kingdom, phylum (for animals) or division (plants), class, order, family, genus, species. Taxonomically, a species is designated in italics by the genus name followed by its specific name, as in *Felis domesticus*, or domestic cat. New species are named and existing species names are altered according to the International Rules of Botanical Nomenclature, the International Rules of Zoological Nomenclature, and the International Bacteriological Code of Nomenclature.

Isolating mechanisms prevent closely related species living in the same geographic area from mating with each other. These are called sympatric species, as opposed to allopatric species, which are closely related species living in different geographical areas. Sympatric species are very common. Bullfrogs, green frogs, wood frogs and pickerel frogs, all members of the genus *Rana*, may be found in or near the same pond. They are prevented from mating by reproductive isolating mechanisms.

Allopatric speciation allows new species to arise from one or more preexisting species, which is a long, slow process. Most allopatric species evolve when a small population becomes physically isolated from the main part of the species, and gene flow between them stops. Genetic differences spread and accumulate in the small, isolated group. This process is most likely to occur at the border of a species, where environmental conditions exceed the range of tolerance of members of the species and there is a barrier to the species' spread. The barrier could be a mountain range, a **desert**, forest, large body of water and so on.

Organisms that are part of a region's natural **flora** and **fauna** are called native or indigenous species. Those associated with the mature or **climax** form of community are called climax species. Fragments of a climax species that remain after a major disturbance, such as a forest fire, are referred to as **relic species**.

Nonnative organisms are called introduced or **exotic species**. They can wreak havoc when brought deliberately or by accident into a new area where they have no natural enemies or where they compete aggressively with other organisms in the environment. A classic example is the introduction of the **zebra mussel** into the **Great Lakes**, where it reproduces wildly and has clogged **water treatment** facilities. In south Florida, the Australian pine has overtaken many coastal areas: biologists are hoping that the destruction of many of the trees by Hurricane Andrew's winds will allow time to restore native plants.

All of the plants and animals found in a particular area, whether native or introduced, are called resident species. Where new species adapt well so that they do not need special help to perpetuate, they are said to be acclimatized or naturalized. Invader species are not original to a region but arrive after an area is disturbed, such as by fire or **overgrazing**. Native species that are the first to recolonize a disturbed area are called pioneer species. Several pioneer species quickly reappeared on and around Mount Saint Helens after the **volcano**'s 1980 eruption.

Species that are especially adapted to a highly variable, unpredictable, or transient environment are called opportunistic species. Within a particular area, dominant species are those that because of their number, coverage or size, strongly influence the conditions of other species in the area. For example, certain trees in **old-growth forest**s in the Pacific Northwest are vital to the success of other species in the area. Destruction of the forests by logging also causes the decline of other species, such as the spotted owl. In other areas, plants that are sought after by grazing animals are called ice cream species.

So-called indicator species, or **indicator organism**s, are watched for warning signs that their **ecosystem**s are ill.

The decline of migratory songbirds around the world is an indication that nesting and breeding grounds of the songbirds, particularly **rain forest**s, are in danger. Other indicator species are amphibians. Some scientists believe that the decline of many frog and toad populations is a result of environmental **pollution**. Since amphibians have highly permeable skins, they are particularly vulnerable to **environmental degradation** such as **pesticide** pollution. The depletion of the **ozone** layer which allows more **ultraviolet radiation** to penetrate the atmosphere has been blamed for the decline in other frog populations. Increased ultraviolet radiation is believed to be responsible for the destruction of frog eggs, which are deposited in shallow water. When the striped bass population in **Chesapeake Bay** declined in the 1975, it indicated pollution problems in the water. An indicator species also may be used to show the stage of development, or regeneration, of an ecosystem. For example, land use managers may watch plant species to assess the level of grazing use in **rangeland**.

If the survival of other species depends on the survival of a single species, that single species is called a **keystone species**. Where a species plays a role in more than one ecosystem, it is said to be a mobile link species.

A species population has a dimension in space, called a range, and a dimension in time. The population extends backwards in time, merging with other species populations much like the branches of a tree. The population has the potential to extend forward in time, but various factors may prevent the perpetuation of the species. When the continued existence of a species is in question, it is regarded as an **endangered species**. This causes great concern to conservationists, especially when the species is the only representative of its genus or family, as is the case with the **giant panda**. A species found in a very restricted geographic range is **endemic** or narrowly endemic, and is at special risk of becoming extinct. **Extinction** results from an imbalance between a species and the environment in which it is living.

Many species exist today in name only. On a 1991 United States **Fish and Wildlife Service** report on species, the following were removed from the endangered species list because they all became extinct since the 1980 report was issued: the Amistad Gambusia fish, the Tecopa pupfish, Sampson's pearly mussel, the blue pike, and the dusky seaside sparrow.

Species richness varies with the type of region, and it is especially diverse in areas of warm or wet places, such as tropical forests. Many biologists are concerned that the unprecedented destruction of tropical forests is forcing to extinction species that have not even been discovered. When a species is lost, it is lost forever, and with it the tremendous potential, especially in medicine, of that species' contributions to the world.

[*Linda Rehkopf*]

FURTHER READING

Villee, C., et. al. *General Zoology*. New York: Saunders College Publishing, 1984.

Species diversity
See **Biodiversity**

Speciesism

This term, popularized by author **Peter Singer** in his book *Animal Liberation* (1975), refers to a human attitude of superiority over other creatures and a tendency among humans to place the interests of their own **species** above all others. As Singer puts it, speciesism

> is as indefensible as the most blatant racism. There is no basis for elevating membership of one particular species into a morally crucial characteristic. From an ethical point of view, we all stand on an equal footing—whether we stand on two feet, or four, or none at all. That is the crux of the philosophy of the animal liberation movement. . . . Just as we have progressed beyond the blatantly racist ethic of the era of slavery and colonialism, so we must now progress beyond the speciesist ethic of the era of factory farming, seal hunting. . . and the destruction of **wilderness**.

Opposition to speciesism has become one of the foundations of the modern **animal rights** movement. *See also* Environmental ethics

Spectrometry, mass
See **Mass spectrometry**

Spoil

Normally used to describe **overburden** removed during **strip mining**. These operations leave long rows of intermixed rock and **soil**, commonly described as spoil banks. Often composed of loose shale and placed downhill from the final cut, they block outflow, forming lakes, and in level terrain store large amounts of **groundwater**. Prior to the 1977 enactment of the **Surface Mining Control and Reclamation Act**, these man-made landforms were often abandoned, creating a distinctive landscape. Efforts are now made to reclaim these aptly named "orphan" lands. However, unless properly done, **reclamation** may exacerbate **erosion**; in such cases they are best left undisturbed. Trees often lead the **succession**, perhaps hastening the day when effective reclamation might be feasible.

Spotted owl
See **Northern spotted owl**

Stability

The term stability refers to the tendency of an individual organism, a community, a population, or an **ecosystem** to maintain a more or less constant structure over relatively long periods of time. Stability does not suggest that changes do not occur, but that the net result of those changes is nearly zero. A healthy human body is an example of a stable system. Changes are constantly taking place in a body. Cells die and are replaced by new ones. Chemical compounds are manufactured in one part of the body and degraded in another part. But, in spite of these changes, the body tends to look very much the same from day to day, week to week, and month to month.

The same is true with groups of individuals. A **prairie** grassland may look the same from year to year, even though the individual plants that make up the community change. Many ecosystems exhibit mosaic stability. For instance, a forest with openings caused by windthrow or fire at different times regrows trees of the same **species**, so that the character of the forest remains unchanged.

Stability is threatened by various kinds of stress. For example, lack of food can threaten the stability of an individual person, and fire can endanger the stability of a **grassland** community. Both organisms and communities have a rather remarkable resilience to such threats, however, and are often able to return to their original structure. Given good food once again, a person can recover her or his health and structure, just as a grassland tends to regrow after a fire.

The biotic and abiotic elements of an ecosystem cause stress on each other which can threaten the stability of each. An unusually long dry spell, for example, can cause plants to die and endanger the **biotic community**'s stability. In turn, animals may multiply in number and physically degrade the soil and water in their **habitat**.

Because of the magnitude of the stress they place on other communities, humans are often the most serious threat to the stability of an ecosystem. An **old-growth forest** that has been clear-cut may, in theory, restore itself eventually to its original structure. But the time frame needed for such a restoration involves hundreds or thousands of years. For all practical purposes, therefore, the community of organisms in the region has ceased to exist as such.

One of the important mechanisms by which ecosystems maintain stability is negative feedback. Suppose, for example, that favorable weather conditions cause an unusually large growth of plants in a valley. Animals that live on those plants, then, will also increase in number and reproduce in greater quantity than in less abundant years. The increased population of animals will place a severe stress on the plant community if and when weather conditions return to normal. With decreased food supplies per individual organism, more animals will die off and the population will return to its previous size.

The factors that contribute to the stability of an ecosystem are not well understood. At one time, most scholars accepted the hypothesis that diversity was an important factor in maintaining stability. From a common sense perspective, it is reasonable to assume that the more organisms and more kinds of organisms in a system, the greater the distribution of stress and the more stable the system as a whole will be.

Some early experiments appeared to confirm this view, but those experiments were often conducted with artificial or only simplified systems. Ecologists are increasingly beginning to question the relationship between **biodiversity** and stability, at least partly because of examples from the real world. Some highly complex systems, such as **tropical rain forest**s, have been less successful in responding to external stress than have simpler systems, such as **tundra**.

The term stability has a more specialized meaning in atmospheric studies. There, it also refers to a condition in which vertical layers of air at different temperatures are in equilibrium with each other. *See also* Population biology

[*David E. Newton*]

FURTHER READING

Clapham, W. B., Jr. *Natural Ecosystems*. New York: The Macmillan Company, 1973.

Suthers, R. A., and R. A. Gallant. *Biology: The Behavioral View*. Lexington, MA: Xerox College Publishing, 1973.

Stack emissions

Stack **emission**s are those gases and solids that come out of the smoke stack after the **incineration** process. Incinerators can be designed to accept wastes of any physical form, including gases, liquids, solids, **sludge**s, and slurries. Incineration is primarily for the treatment of wastes that contain organic compounds. Wastes with a wide range of chemical and physical characteristics are considered suitable for burning. Most of these wastes are by-products of industrial manufacturing and chemical production processes or the result from the clean-up of contaminated sites.

There is a great deal of controversy about the content of incinerator stack emissions. The **Environmental Protection Agency (EPA)** supports incineration as a **waste management** tool and claims that these emissions are not dangerous. In an official publication, the EPA has stated:

Incinerator emission gases are composed primarily of two harmless inorganic compounds, **carbon dioxide** and water. The type and quantity of other compounds depends on the composition of the wastes, the completeness of the combustion process, and the **air pollution control** equipment with which the incinerator is equipped. These compounds include organic and inorganic compounds contained in the original waste and organic and inorganic compounds created during combustion.

Contrary to the EPA, many environmentalists believe that burning **hazardous waste**, even in "state-of-the-art" incinerators, releases far more **heavy metals**, unburned wastes, **dioxins**, and new **chemicals** formed during the incineration process (PICs)—than is healthy for the **environment** or humans. In a report published in 1990, *Playing with Fire*, **Greenpeace** disagrees strongly about the toxic materials emitted from incinerator stacks.

The report argues that metals are not destroyed during incineration; in fact, they are often released in forms that are far more dangerous than the original wastes. At least 19 metals have been identified in the air emissions of hazardous waste incinerators. An average-sized commercial incinerator burning hazardous waste with an average metals content emits these metals into the air at the rate of 204 pounds (92.6 kilograms) per year and deposits another 670,000 pounds (304,180 kilograms) of metals per year in its residual ashes and liquids, which must be properly disposed of in **landfill**s designed for that purpose.

The consequences to human health are significant. **Cancer**, **birth defects**, reproductive dysfunction, neurological damage, and other health effects are known to occur at very low exposures to many of the metals, organochlorines and other pollutants released by waste-burning facilities. Increased cancer rates, respiratory ailments, reproductive abnormalities, and other health effects have been noted among people living near some waste-burning facilities, according to scientific studies in other countries and surveys conducted by community groups and local physicians in the United States.

Hazardous waste incinerators in the United States are producing at least 324 million pounds (147 million kilograms) per year of ash residues. These ashes, which are buried in landfills, are contaminated by PICs, many of which are more toxic than the original waste. The ashes also contain increased concentrations of heavy metals, often in more leachable forms than in the original wastes.

Trial burns are used to determine an incinerator's destruction and removal efficiency (DRE). Under current federal regulations, an incinerator of general hazardous waste must, during the trial burn, demonstrate a DRE of 99.99 percent with just a few chemicals to be tested—perhaps one or two. Many environmentalists consider these standards unsatisfactory. In the unlikely event that this standard could be met at all times with all wastes burned throughout the lifetime of an incinerator, a hazardous waste incinerator of average size (70 million pounds per year,) (32 million kilograms per year) would still be emitting 7,000 pounds (3,178 kilograms) per year of unburned wastes. With corrections and accidents, emissions may be as high as 700,000 pounds (317,800 kilograms) per year. Environmentalists also argue that DRE addresses only the stack emissions of the few chemicals selected for the trial burn, and that it does not reflect other substances that are released. These include unburned chemicals other than those selected for the trial burn, heavy metals, or newly formed PICs. In addition, the present method for determining DREs does not account for the retention within the combustion system of the chemicals selected for the trial burn and their continued release for hours, or even days, after stack gas sampling has ceased. *See*

also Hazardous waste site remediation; Hazardous waste siting; Heavy metals precipitation; NIMBY (Not In My Backyard); Toxic use reduction legislation

[*Liane Clorfene Casten*]

FURTHER READING

Costner, P., and J. Thornton. "Playing With Fire: Hazardous Waste Incineration." A Greenpeace Report. 2nd ed. Washington, DC: Greenpeace, 1993.

Stakeholder analysis

Stakeholder analysis is an approach to making policy decisions, primarily in business, which is based on identifying and prioritizing the interests different groups have in an institution. A stakeholder analysis examines the stakes which shareholders, suppliers, customers, employees, or communities may have in a particular issue.

A stakeholder analysis is often used to develop generic strategies; these are meant to be broad descriptions of what the corporation stands for and how it intends to mediate between competing stakeholder concerns. Many firms have made public statements concerning these strategies. Hewlett-Packard has said that it is dedicated to the dignity and worth of its individual employees. Aetna Life and Casualty claims that tending to the broader needs of society is essential to fulfilling its economic role. Perhaps the most famous example of a stakeholder strategy is Johnson and Johnson's: "We believe our first responsibility is to the doctors, nurses and patients, to mothers and all others who use our products and services."

People both inside and outside the business world consider the stakeholder analysis an effective method for uniting business strategy with social responsibility. This approach can be used to provide a variety of business goals with an ethical basis, and it has played a role in developing the marketing of environmentally safe products, known as green marketing. While many environmentalists consider this kind of analysis a step in the right direction, some have argued that public statements of strategies can be misleading, and that companies can be more concerned with their image and their relationship with the media than they are with social responsibility. *See also* Green advertising and marketing

[*Alfred A. Marcus and Douglas Smith*]

FURTHER READING

Marcus, A. A. *Business and Society.* Homewood, IL: Irwin Press, 1992.

Steady-state economy

Steady-state economics is a branch of economic thinking which applies the perspectives of steady-state systems developed in thermodynamic physics to economic analysis. This direction in economics is largely associated with the work of Herman Daly, who has written the classic work in the field,

Steady-State Economics (1977). While its impact has been relatively minor within the discipline of economics itself, the concept of steady-state economics has gathered a significant audience among life scientists and within the larger environmental movement.

Steady-state economics is closely related to **sustainable development**, and many consider it as but one component of the larger issue of sustainability. The constraints imposed by the laws of physics determine, in Daly's terminology, the "ultimate means" or the "ultimate supply limit" beyond which no measure of human development can make better use of resources and energy. One of the fundamental criticisms of traditional economic thinking made by steady-state economics is founded on this concept of absolute limits: Standard economics implicitly assumes that it is always possible to cope with **population growth** and resource shortages by technical advances and the substitution of one resource for another. This is an assumption which steady-state economics views as not only wrong but dangerously misleading.

For Daly, the greater danger of this perspective is that it is ultimately a form of hubris, of acting as though we can surpass the limitations of the physical world and attain the freedom of the divine. This is the classic sin of pride, and Daly sees its corrective as the corresponding virtue of humility. Science, he claims, "sees man as a potentially infallible creator whose hope lies in his marvelous scientific creativity." He contrasts this with the view of steady-state economics, which "conceives of man as a fallen creature whose hope lies in the benevolence of his Creator not in the excellence of his own creations." In Daly's view, it is only when we are humble that we are able to see human life and the entire evolutionary process in which it is embedded as a gift bestowed upon us by God, not something we have made. For Daly, this gift of the evolution of life is a minimum definition of the "Ultimate End," whose preservation and further development must be the goal of all our actions. The "Ultimate End" is fostering the continuance of the evolutionary process, and the "ultimate means" is determined by the laws of physics; they both define boundaries only within which is it possible to have a steady-state economy and a sustainable society.

Daly offers three large-scale social institutions for the United States to help make a steady-state economy a reality. The first of these is a socially determined limit on the national population, with licenses issued to each person allocating exactly the number of births required to maintain **zero population growth** (approximately 2.1 births per female). These licenses could be purchased or otherwise transferred between individuals, so that those wishing no children could transfer their licenses to those wishing more than their allotment. The second institution would stabilize the stock of human artifacts and would maintain the resources needed to maintain and replace this stock at levels which do not exceed the physical limits of the **environment**. A set of marketable quotas for each resource would be the primary mechanism to attain this goal. The third institution would be a set of minimum and maximum limits on personal income and a maximum cap on personal wealth. The first two institutions

are designed to structure population and economic production within the fundamental thermodynamic limits or "ultimate means." The third is the extension into human society of the moral boundaries set by the goal of preserving and fostering life—in this case to ensure that all people in the steady-state economy have access to society's resources. *See also* Bioregionalism; Carrying capacity; Deep ecology; Family planning; Growth limiting factors; Sustainable agriculture

[*Eugene R. Wahl*]

FURTHER READING

Boulding, K. "The Economics of the Coming Spaceship Earth." In *Environmental Quality in a Growing Economy*, ed. by H. Jarrett. Baltimore, MD: Johns Hopkins University Press, 1966.

Daly, H. *Steady-State Economics*. 2nd ed. Washington, DC: Island Press, 1991.

Stegner, Wallace (1909-1993)

American writer

Wallace Stegner was an American novelist, historian, biographer, and teacher. Widely regarded as the dean of western writers, Stegner evoked a vivid sense of the western United States as a place and of the intimate relationship of the people with that place. Among his best known novels are *Big Rock Candy Mountain* (1943), *Angle of Repose* (1971), *The Spectator Bird* (1976), and *Crossing to Safety* (1987). His works of nonfiction include *Beyond the Hundredth Meridian* (1954), *Wolf Willow* (1963), *The Sound of Mountain Water* (1969), and *Where the Bluebird Sings to the Lemonade Springs: Living and Writing in the West* (1992).

Stegner was born on February 18, 1909, on a farm outside Lake Mills, Iowa, the second son of George and Hilda Paulson Stegner. His father, a restless and rootless risk-taker, moved the family to North Dakota, then to Washington state, and then to Saskatchewan, Montana, and Utah. His family was so poor that he was sent for a time to an orphanage. Stegner's early education was spotty, at best. He was an avid hunter and outdoorsman who enjoyed the company of Native Americans, cowboys, miners, Mormons, and others who eked out a precarious living in the west. In these hardscrabble early years Stegner met the people and endured the experiences that were later to reappear in fictional form in his novels and short stories.

At age sixteen, Stegner enrolled at the University of Utah, where he majored in English. In 1930 he began graduate work at the University of Iowa, where he earned a master's degree. Two years later he returned to the University of Utah, where he received his Ph.D. in 1935. He went on to teach at several universities, including Harvard, Wisconsin, and Stanford, where he founded the creative writing program that he directed until 1971. Among his students and the recipients of Stanford's Wallace Stegner Writing Fellowship were **Wendell Berry** and **Edward Abbey**. An ardent outdoorsman and conservationist, Stegner was active in the **Sierra Club** and fought successfully to save Echo Park from being dammed. In later years he said that his greatest regret was not having worked harder to prevent the damming of **Glen Canyon**.

Stegner was a pioneer in the environmental education of American citizens and their elected representatives. His new medium was the large coffee-table book featuring photographs of stunning seldom-seen places that were under threat from mining, logging, or development interests. Interspersed among pictures by photographers such as **Ansel Adams** were short essays by Stegner and others about the fragility and beauty of these wild places and the threats they faced. Published by the Sierra Club and distributed free to Senators and Congressmen, these books proved to be powerful weapons in the ongoing effort to protect the natural **environment** from the predations of developers.

Many of Stegner's works of fiction also deal with environmental themes and problems—the rush to develop the West, the desire to get rich by riding roughshod over fragile environments and **ecosystem**s, the wanton indifference to the peoples and the history of a place, and the ravages wrought by this onslaught. Arrayed against these forces are the quieter forces of history and memory, of respect for a region and its past, and the desire to preserve and pass these on to future generations.

Wallace Stegner died on April 12, 1993, from a heart attack resulting from a serious automobile accident two days earlier. In accordance with his wishes, his ashes were scattered on the western slope of Baker Hill in Vermont.

[*Terence Ball*]

FURTHER READING

Benson, J.J. *Wallace Stegner: His Life and Work*. New York: Viking Press, 1996.
Rankin, C.E., ed. *Wallace Stegner: Man and Writer*. Albuquerque: University of New Mexico Press, 1996.

Stochastic change

Any change that involves random behavior. The term stochastic is derived from the Greek *stokhiastikos*, meaning to guess at random. Stochastic changes obey the laws of probability. A familiar example of such a change is a series of card games. The way that cards fall in each hand is a random event, but well-known mathematical laws can describe the likelihood of various possibilities. For instance, if a traffic engineer wants to study traffic patterns at a busy downtown intersection, the engineer can use stochastic principles to analyze the traffic flow, since the movement of vehicles through that intersection is likely to occur at random. Some natural processes, such as genetic drift, also can best be characterized as the result of a series of stochastic changes.

Storage and transport of hazardous material

Hazardous materials consist of numerous types of explosive, corrosive, and poisonous substances. The materials might be used as a reactant in an industrial process, as an additive in water treatment (**acids and bases**, for example), or as a source of fuel or energy (**gasoline** and nuclear materials). These materials might also be produced, wasted, or contaminated and thus require management as a **hazardous waste**. In all cases, it is necessary to understand the characteristics of the chemical so that appropriate containers and labels for storage and transportation are used.

The U.S. Department of Transportation (DOT) and the **Environmental Protection Agency (EPA)** have issued regulation on how hazardous materials are to be stored, labeled, and transported. The DOT was actually the first to address these issues; the EPA simply adopted many of their regulations, and the agency continues to work closely with the DOT to minimize confusion, conflicts, and redundancy. The DOT was originally given authority to regulate the transportation of hazardous materials in 1966, but it was not until 1975 that the **Hazardous Materials Transportation Act** (HMTA) was passed, giving the DOT broad authority over all aspects of transporting hazardous materials. In 1980, the EPA adopted the DOT regulations, and the DOT amended their policies to make them more appropriate for hazardous wastes. The **Nuclear Regulatory Commission (NRC)** is also involved in overseeing the transportation of nuclear materials.

In 1976 the EPA promulgated the **Resource Conservation and Recovery Act (RCRA)** which dealt with many hazardous **waste management** issues, including storage and transportation. RCRA stipulated that the EPA was to adopt transportation regulations that were consistent with the HMTA, but hazardous waste storage and transportation posed some additional problems. For example, it was necessary to define the term "hazardous waste" and to develop a rigorous system to track the waste from generation ("cradle") to ultimate disposal ("grave"). The RCRA and later amendments (Hazardous and Solid Waste Amendments of 1984) distinguished between small and large quantity generators and established different regulations for them. Large quantity generators (LQG) are prohibited from storing hazardous wastes for more than 90 days. Small quantity generators (SQG) can store wastes for 180 or 270 days, depending upon how far they have to ship the wastes for disposal.

Transportation of hazardous wastes to disposal sites is carefully monitored; this is done by using a form known as a manifest. The manifest contains the name and EPA identification number of the generator, the transporter, and the treatment disposal facility (TSD facility). The manifest also provides a description of the waste and documents each step in the transportation network; generators that have TSD facilities on-site need not prepare a manifest.

The storage and transportation of hazardous materials is closely regulated. Despite these regulations, however, accidents do occur, and research is continuing in the development of better shipping and storage containers, more reliable means and routes for shipments, more accurate risk assessments, and improved systems for accident prevention and remediation of spills. *See also* Hazardous Substances Act; Hazardous waste siting; NIMBY (Not In My Backyard);

Toxic substance; Toxic Substances Control Act; Toxic use reduction legislation

[*Gregory D. Boardman*]

FURTHER READING

Freeman, H. M. *Standard Handbook of Hazardous Waste Treatment and Disposal.* New York: McGraw-Hill Book Company, 1989.

Martin, E. J., and J. H. Johnson. *Hazardous Waste Management Engineering.* New York: Van Nostrand Reinhold, 1987.

Wentz, C. A. *Hazardous Waste Management.* New York: McGraw-Hill, 1989.

Storm King Mountain, New York

One of the most important cases in environmental law involved the proposed construction in 1963 of a huge hydroelectric plant by Consolidated Edison on the shores of the **Hudson River** at the foot of Storm King Mountain. The plant was designed to generate electricity for New York City during its periods of peak demands. Objections to the planned construction were raised by the Scenic Hudson Preservation Conference, which claimed that the plant would seriously damage the area's natural beauty. After nearly a decade of hearings and court cases, Consolidated Edison received permission to build the plant. In the process, however, the right of citizen groups to argue the value of aesthetic considerations in such cases was affirmed. *See also* Electric utilities

Storm runoff

The amount of water that flows into streams and rivers soon after a rainfall, causing the stream to rise above its stable condition. Sometimes called stormflow, quickflow, or direct runoff, this flow of water occurs relatively quickly to channels and causes water levels to rise, peak, and then recede as the storm water drains from the **watershed** following the storm. Storm runoff is the sum of precipitation falling directly on the channel, overland flow, and subsurface flow. **Groundwater** generally takes a long period of time to contribute to streamflow and does not appreciably affect streamflow rise immediately after the storm; therefore, it is not considered a part of stormflow. When water levels rise above the banks of a stream or river, storm runoff is considered to cause a flood. In technical **hydrology** terms, stormflow is the portion of the hydrograph that is above base flow.

Storm sewer

Modern stormwater management consists of two components: the major drainage system comprising overland flow and retention facilities including ponds, playing fields, parking lots, underground **reservoir**s, and similar devices; and the minor drainage system consisting of storm sewers. The major system is designed to handle major regional storms which have an infrequent probability of occurrence. The minor system uses storm sewers to quickly drain the rainfall from yards, sidewalks, and streets after a rainfall event or during snow melt. Storm sewers are the single largest cost in servicing land for housing. Storm sewers typically discharge into surface waters such as creeks, rivers, or lakes without treatment. *See also* Storm runoff

Strategic minerals

American industry has a voracious appetite for minerals. The manufacture of a typical **automobile**, for example, requires not only such familiar metals as iron, **copper**, **lead**, and **aluminum**, but also such less-familiar metals as manganese, platinum, molybdenum, and vanadium. Fortunately, the United States has an abundant supply of many critical minerals. The country is essentially self-sufficient in major metals such as iron, copper, lead, and aluminum. In each case, we import less than a quarter of the metals used in industrial production.

But there are some minerals that do not occur naturally to any considerable extent in the United States. For example, the United States has essentially no reserves of columbium (niobium), strontium, manganese, tantalum, or cobalt metals or of sheet mica or bauxite ore. To the extent that these minerals are important in various industrial processes, they are regarded as critical or strategic minerals. Some examples of strategic minerals are tin, silver, cobalt, manganese, tungsten, zinc, titanium, platinum, chromium, bauxite, and diamonds. The United States has to import at least half of the amount of each of these minerals that it uses each year.

Insuring a constant and dependable supply of strategic minerals is a complex political problem. In some cases, the minerals we need can be obtained from friendly nations with whom we can negotiate relatively easily. Canada, for example, supplies a large part of the nickel, columbium, gallium, tantalum, cadmium, and cesium used by American industry. Nickel may be obtained from Norway, cobalt and antimony from Belgium, and fluorspar from Italy.

But other nations on which we depend tend to be less friendly, less dependable, or less stable. The south African nations of Zaire, Zambia, Zimbabwe, Botswana, and South Africa, for example, are major suppliers of strategic minerals such as chromium, gold, platinum, vanadium, manganese, and diamonds. When these nations experience political unrest, supplies of these minerals may be scarcer.

For well over a decade, the United States government has tried to protect American industry, especially defense industries, from the danger of running out of strategic minerals. The fear has been that political factors might result in the loss of certain minerals that are needed by industry, particularly those used in the manufacture of military hardware.

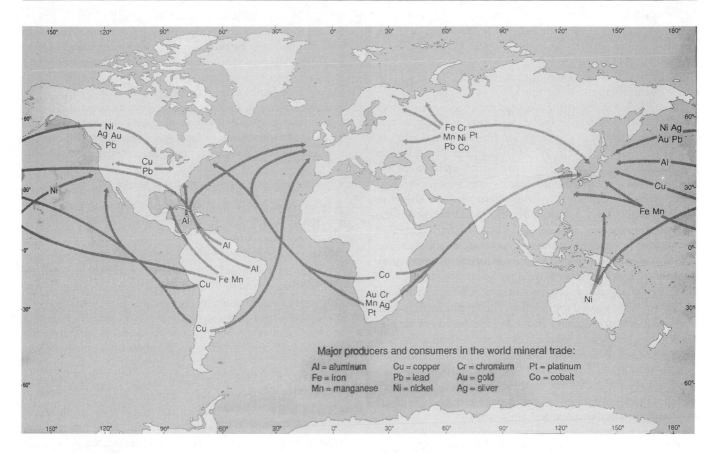

Global mineral trade.

In 1984, the United States Congress established the National Critical Materials Council to advise the President on issues involving strategic minerals. The Council monitors domestic and international needs and trends to insure that the nation will continue to have access to a dependable supply of strategic minerals.

A similar function is performed by the Defense Logistics Agency (DLA), a division of the Department of Defense. The DLA maintains and administers a stockpile of strategic minerals that are essential to all but especially to defense-related industries. Included in that stockpile in 1988 were about a dozen minerals, including 174,000 tons of tin valued at $1,316,000,000; 104,921,000 troy ounces of silver worth $640,000,000; 53,000,000 pounds of cobalt worth $398,000,000; 4,146,000 tons of manganese worth $665,000,000; and 466,000 troy ounces of platinum worth $261,000,000.

[*David E. Newton*]

FURTHER READING

Dorr, A. *Minerals—Foundations of Society.* Montgomery County, MD: League of Women Voters of Montgomery County Maryland, 1984.

Gordon, R. B., et al. *World Mineral Exploration: Trends and Issues.* Washington, DC: Resources for the Future, 1988.

Strategic Minerals: A Resource Crisis. Washington, DC: Council on Economics and National Security, 1981.

U. S. Bureau of Mines. *The Domestic Supply of Critical Minerals.* Washington, DC: U. S. Government Printing Office, 1983.

Stratification

The process by which a region is divided into relatively distinct, nearly horizontal, layers. Sedimentary rock often consists of various strata because the rock was laid at different times when different materials were being deposited. Lakes and oceans also consist of strata where plant and animal life may be very different depending on the temperature and amount of life available. The atmosphere is divided into strata that differ in density, temperature, chemical composition, and other factors. In the lower atmosphere, temporary stratification, such as temperature inversions, may occur, often resulting in severe **pollution** conditions.

Stratosphere

A layer of the **atmosphere** that lies between about 7 and 31 miles (11 and 50 km) above the earth's surface, bounded at the bottom by the **tropopause** and at the top by the stratopause. Scientists became aware of the presence of the stratosphere with observations of high level dust after the eruption of **Krakatoa** in 1883. However, the real discovery of the stratosphere had to await Teisserenc de Bort's work of 1900.

The stratosphere is characterized by temperatures that rise with height. As a result, the air is very stable, not mixing much vertically, and allowing distinct layers of air, or strata, to form. There are also persistent regular strong winds, of which the best known are the intense western winds during the winter called the polar night jet stream.

The air in the stratosphere has much the same composition as the lower atmosphere except for a higher proportion of **ozone**. Absorption of incoming **solar energy** by this ozone makes the upper parts of the stratosphere warm and sets up the characteristic temperature gradient. The relatively high ozone concentrations are maintained by **photochemical reaction**s. It has become clear in more recent years that other chemical reactions involving **nitrogen** and **chlorine** are also important in maintaining the ozone balance of the upper atmosphere. This balance can be easily disturbed through the input of additional **nitrogen oxides** and halogen compounds (from CFCs, or **chlorofluorocarbons**). Transfer of gases across the tropopause into the stratosphere is rather slow, but some gases, such as CFCs and nitrous oxide, are sufficiently long-lived in the troposphere to leak across into the stratosphere and cause **ozone layer depletion**. Large volcanic eruptions can have sufficient force to drive gases and particles into the stratosphere where they can also disturb the ozone balance. High flying aircraft represent another source of **pollution** in the stratosphere, but the lack of development of a supersonic passenger fleet has meant that this contribution has remained fairly small.

The stratosphere is extremely cold (about -112°F [-80°C] in places), so there is relatively little water. Nevertheless nacreous or mother-of-pearl clouds, although not frequently observed, have long been known. More recently there has been much interest in polar stratospheric clouds which had hitherto received little attention. Stratospheric cloud particles can be water-containing sulfuric acid droplets or solid nitric acid hydrates. Studies of the Antarctic ozone hole have revealed that these clouds are likely to play an important role in the depletion of ozone in the polar stratosphere. *See also* Acid rain; Cloud chemistry; Ozonation; Stratification; Volcano

[*Peter Brimblecombe*]

FURTHER READING

Chamberlain, J. W., and D. M. Hunten. *Theory of Planetary Atmospheres.* New York: Academic Press, 1987.

Stray voltage

See **Electromagnetic fields**

Stream channelization

The process of straightening or redirecting natural streams in an artificially modified or constructed stream bed. Channelization has been carried out for numerous reasons, most often to drain **wetlands**, direct water flow for agricultural use, and control **flooding**. While this process makes a stream more useful for human activities, it tends to interfere with natural river **habitat**s and to destabilize stream banks by destroying riparian vegetation. When annual flood patterns are disrupted, fertilizing **sediment** is no longer deposited on river banks and excessive sediment accumulation can occur downstream. Perhaps most importantly, wetland drainage and the removal of instream obstacles such as rocks, fallen trees, shallow backwaters, and sand bars eliminate feeding and reproductive habitats for fish, aquatic insects, and birds.

Stringfellow Acid Pits (Glen Avon, California)

Aerospace, electronics, and other high-technology businesses expanded rapidly in California during the 1950s, bringing **population growth** and rapid economic progress. These businesses also brought a huge volume of toxic wastes and the problem of safely disposing of them. A modern day reminder of those years is the Stringfellow Acid Pits located near the Riverside suburb of Glen Avon, 50 miles (80 km) east of Los Angeles.

The Acid Pits, also known as the Stringfellow Quarry Waste Pits, are located on a 20-acre (8-ha) site in Pyrite Canyon above Glen Avon. In the mid-1950s a number of high-tech companies began to dump their **hazardous waste**s into the canyon. No special precautions were taken in the dumping process; as one observer noted, the companies got rid of their wastes just as cave men did: "They dug a hole and dumped it in."

Over the next two decades, more than 34 million gallons (129 million l) of waste were disposed of in a series of pan-shaped **reservoir**s dug into the canyon floor. The wastes came from more than a dozen of the nation's most prominent companies, including McDonnell-Douglas, Montrose Chemical, General Electric, Hughes Aircraft, Sunkist Growers, Philco-Ford, Northrop, and Rockwell-International. The wastes consisted of a complex mixture of more than 200 hazardous **chemicals**. These included hydrochloric, sulfuric, and nitric acids; sodium hydroxide; trichlorethylene and methylene chloride; **polychlorinated biphenyls (PCBs)**; a variety of **pesticide**s; **volatile organic compounds (VOCs)**; and heavy metals, such as **lead**, **nickel**, **cadmium**, chromium, and manganese.

By 1972, residents of Glen Avon had begun to complain about health effects caused by the wastes in the Stringfellow Pits. They claimed that some chemicals were evaporating and polluting the town's air, while other chemicals were leaching out of the dump and contaminating the town's **drinking-water supply**. People attributed health problems to chemicals escaping from the dump; these problems ranged from nose bleeds, emotional distress, and insomnia to **cancer** and genetic defects. Medical studies were unable to confirm these complaints, but residents continued to insist that these problems did exist.

In November 1972, James Stringfellow, owner of the pits, announced that he was shutting them down. However, his decision did not solve the problem of what to do with the wastes still in the pit. Stringfellow claimed his company was without assets, and the state of California had to take over responsibility for maintaining the site.

The situation at Stringfellow continued to deteriorate under state management. During a March 1978 rainstorm, the pits became so badly flooded that officials doubted the ability of the existing **dams** to hold back more than 8 million gallons (30.3 million l) of wastes. To prevent a possible disaster, they released nearly a million gallons of liquid wastes into flood control channels running through Glen Avon. Children in nearby schools and neighborhoods, not knowing what the brown water contained, waded and played in the toxic wastes.

When the **Comprehensive Environmental Response, Compensation and Liability Act** (Superfund) was passed in 1980, the Stringfellow Pits were named the most polluted waste site in California. The pits became one of first targets for remediation by the **Environmental Protection Agency (EPA)**, but this effort collapsed in the wake of a scandal that rocked both the EPA and the Reagan administration in 1983. EPA administrators Rita Lavelle and Anne McGill Burford were found guilty of mishandling the Superfund program, and they were forced to resign from office along with 22 other officials.

During the early 1990s, citizens of Glen Avon finally began to experience some success in their battle to clean up the pits. The EPA had finally begun its remediation efforts in earnest, and residents won judgments of more then $34 million against Stringfellow and four companies that had used the site. In 1993 residents initiated the largest single civil suit over toxic wastes in history. The suit involved 4,000 plaintiffs from Glen Avon and 13 defendants, including the state of California, Riverside County, and a number of major companies. *See also* Contaminated soil; Groundwater pollution; Hazardous waste site remediation; Hazardous waste siting; Storage and transport of hazardous materials

[*David E. Newton*]

FURTHER READING

Brown, M. H. *Laying Waste: The Poisoning of America by Toxic Chemicals.* New York: Pantheon Books, 1980.

Gorman, T. "A Tainted Legacy: Toxic Dump Site in Riverside County Has Sparked the Nation's Largest Civil Suit." *Los Angeles Times* (10 January 1993): A3.

Madigan, N. "Largest-Ever Toxic-Waste Suit Opens in California." *New York Times* (5 February 1993): B16.

Mydans, S. "Settlements Reached on Toxic Dump in California." *New York Times* (24 December 1991): A11.

Strip-farming

In the United States, **soil conservation** first became an important political issue in the 1930s, when President Franklin D. Roosevelt led a campaign to study the loss of valuable **topsoil** because of **erosion**. It soon became clear that one source of the problem was the fact that farmers tended to plow and plant their fields according to property lines, which usually formed squares or rectangles. As a result, furrows often ran up and down the slope of a hill, forming a natural channel for the **runoff** of rain, and each new storm would wash away more fertile topsoil. This kind of erosion resulted not only in the loss of **soil**, but also in the **pollution** of nearby waterways.

The **Soil Conservation Service** was founded in 1935 as a division of the **U.S. Department of Agriculture**, and one of its goals was the development of farming techniques that would reduce the loss of soil. One such technique was strip-farming, also known as strip-cropping. Strip-farming involves the planting of crops in rows across the slope of the land at right angles to it rather than parallel to it. On gently sloping land, soil conservation can be achieved by plowing and planting in lines that simply follow along the slope of the land rather than cutting across it, a technique known as **contour plowing**. On very steep slopes, a more aggressive technique known as **terracing** is used. Strip-farming is a middle point between these two extremes, and it is used on land with intermediate slopes.

In strip-farming, two different kinds of crops are planted in alternate rows. One set of rows consists of crops in which individual plants can be relatively widely spaced, such as corn, soybeans, cotton, or sugar beets. The second set of rows contains plants that grow very close together, such as alfalfa, hay, wheat, or legumes. As a result of this system, water is channeled along the contour of the land, not down its slope. In addition, the closely-planted crops in one row protect the exposed soil in the more widely-spaced crops in the second row. Crops such as alfalfa also slow down the movement of water through the field, allowing it to be absorbed by the soil.

The precise design of a strip farm is determined by a number of factors, such as the length and steepness of the slope. The crops used in the strip, as well as the width of rows, can be adjusted to achieve minimal loss of soil. Under the most favorable conditions, soil erosion can be reduced by as much as 75 percent through the use of this technique. *See also* Agricultural pollution; Agricultural technology; Soil compaction; Soil loss tolerance

[*Lawrence H. Smith*]

FURTHER READING

Enger, E. D., et al. *Environmental Science: The Study of Relationships.* 2nd ed. Dubuque, Iowa: W. C. Brown, 1986.

Moran, J. M., M. D. Morgan, and J. H. Wiersma. *Introduction to Environmental Science.* 2nd ed. New York: W. H. Freeman, 1986.

Petulla, J. M. *American Environmental History.* San Francisco: Boyd & Fraser, 1977.

Strip mining

This technique is used for near-surface, relatively flat sedimentary mineral deposits. How deeply the mining can occur is essentially determined by the combination of technological capabilities and the economics involved. The latter includes the current value of the mineral, contractual arrangements with the landowner, and mining costs, including **reclamation**. Strip mining is used for mining phosphate **fertilizer** in Florida, North Carolina, and Idaho, and for obtaining gypsum (mainly for wallboard) in western states.

However, the most common association of strip mining is with **coal**. The examples of decimated land in Appalachia have motivated calls for prevention, or at least major efforts at reclamation. Strip mining for coal comprises well over half of the land that is strip-mined, which totaled less that 0.3 percent of land in the United States between 1930 and 1990. This is far less land than the amount lost to agriculture and urbanization. However, in agriculturally rich areas like Illinois and Indiana there is a growing concern over the one-time disruption of land for mineral extraction, compared to the long term use for food production.

Strip mining has occurred mainly in the Appalachian Mountains and adjacent areas, the Central Plains from Indiana and Illinois through Oklahoma, and new mines for subbituminous coal in North Dakota, Wyoming, and Montana. Important mining is also carried out on Hopi and Navajo lands, notably Black Mesa in northeastern Arizona.

Despite the small amount of land used in strip mining, the process radically alters landforms and **ecosystem**s where it is practiced. Depending on state laws, mining landscapes prior to 1977 were often left as is, dubbed "orphan lands." The 1977 act required the land to be restored as nearly as possible to the original condition. This is a nearly impossible task, especially when one considers the reconstruction the preexisting **soil** conditions and ecosystem. Even so, reclamation is a vital first step in the healing process. Generally the steeper the terrain the greater the impact on the landforms and river systems, and the more difficult the reclamation.

Detailed economic planning precedes any strip mining effort. Numerous cores are drilled to determine the depth, thickness, and quality of the coal, and to assess the difficulty of removing the **overburden**, which consists of **topsoil** and rock above the resource. If caprock is encountered, expensive and time-consuming blasting is required, a frequent occurrence in the United States. Economic analysis then determines the area and depth of profitable overburden removal. Finally, contracts must be negotiated with landowners; strip mines commonly end abruptly at property lines.

Two kinds of earth removal equipment are typically used: a front-loading bucket (the classic steam shovel), or a dragline bucket which pulls the material toward the operator. Power shovels and draglines built prior to World War II generally have bucket capacities of 30 to 50 cubic yards (23-38 yd³). Post-World-War-II equipment may have a capacity up to 200 cubic yards. A new development, encouraged by the 1977 reclamation law, is the combination of dozers and scrapers (belly loaders) more commonly seen on road-building or construction sites.

After the overburden is removed, mining begins. The process is conducted in rows, creating long ridges and valleys in the countryside that resemble a washboard. Coal extraction follows behind power shovels, leaving a flat, canyon-like

cut. Upon completion of a row, the shovel starts back in the opposite direction, placing the new overburden in the now-empty cut.

In hilly terrain, only a few cuts are all that is usually profitable because the depth of overburden increases rapidly into the hillside. Since the worst complications as a result of strip mining occur on hillsides, the environmental price for a limited amount of coal is very high. Hillside mining such as this is called "contour mining," in contrast to "area mining" on relatively flat terrain. In the latter, the number of rows are limited mostly by contractual arrangements. Consequently, the main difference between area and contour strip mining are the number of rows and the steepness of the terrain.

Both types of strip mining leave behind four basic land configurations: 1) spoil bank ridges; 2) a final-cut canyon often partially filled by a lake; 3) a high headwall marking the uphill end of the mining; and 4) coal-haul roads, usually at the base of the outermost spoil bank and through gaps in the spoil-bank rows left for this purpose. In some orphan lands, **wilderness**-like conditions prevail, where trees populate the spoil banks and aquatic ecosystems thrive in the final-cut lake. Left alone by man, these may afford a surprisingly rich **habitat** for **wildlife**, especially birds. Deer thrive in some North Dakota abandoned mines.

Reclamation of area mining is relatively simple compared to contour strip mining. Prior to mining, the topsoil is removed and stockpiled. The overburden from the initial cut may be used to fill in the final cut, and the top part of the headwall is sometimes cut down to grade into the spoil. The spoil banks are leveled and the topsoil replaced; fertilization and replanting, usually with grasses or trees for **erosion** control, and subsequent monitoring of revegetation efforts, complete the process. In large operations the leveling and replanting coincide with mining, which is the ideal since this rapidly rebuilds the vegetation cover.

Reclamation of contour mining presents far greater difficulties, primarily because of the slope angles encountered. Research in Great Britain revealed that even well-vegetated slopes were producing 50 to 200 times as much **sediment** as similar, undisturbed slopes. Furthermore, the greater slope angles allow much more of the sediment to reach the channel below, where it eventually flows into streams and rivers.

Another problem for orphan lands in hilly terrain is the ecological island left when hills are completely enclosed by high headwalls. This is not unlike the ecological islands created in the southwestern United States from **climate** changes and vertical zonation of vegetation. Though far more recent, ecologists hope these "orphan islands" will allow interesting case studies of genetic isolation.

The long-term effect of strip mining has been the subject of research in Kentucky, Indiana, and Oklahoma. For over a decade the United States **Geological Survey** studied Beaver Creek Basin, Kentucky, obtaining valuable data before and after contour mining. Their findings were published in a 1970 report authorized by C.R. Collier and others. As expected, mining left a degraded landscape, and resulted in much greater **runoff**, sediment production, and water quality problems. By contrast, area mining in Indiana trapped vast quantities of **groundwater** within the loosened soil, reducing peak discharges, extending base flow, and yielding water of acceptable quality.

In Oklahoma, a study conducted by Nathan Meleen dealt with a mix of both flat and hilly terrain. The findings were published as a doctoral dissertation in 1977 by Clark University. Area mining, Meleen found, produced far more benign impacts than did contour stripping. The worst conditions were encountered where contour mining was adjacent to streams below, especially around the end of ridges. The short distances and relatively steep gradients gave ideal conditions for sediment and acid drainage into the channels below. Summer runoff decreased while winter runoff increased. The huge holes left by these unreclaimed operations acted like **reservoir**s during the drier summer months, but in winter when wetter conditions prevailed, they yielded more outflow than before mining, because of altered infiltration rates.

Strangely enough, a 1971 Oklahoma law produced effects similar to what the Geological Survey found in Kentucky. The incomplete reclamation and lack of sediment retention or topsoil replacement created ideal erosion conditions, with rates approaching 13 percent sediment by weight. This focuses the crucial role of topsoil replacement and rapid revegetation as the preeminent needs in reclamation. Efforts to revegetate some orphan lands where topsoil replacement is impossible will only result in worse conditions, especially downstream. Given the fact that most impacts from area mining are retained onsite, and that orphan lands possess great potential for recreation, especially fishing and hiking, at least some should be left undisturbed. *See also* High-grading; Mine spoil waste; Surface mining

[*Nathan H. Meleen*]

FURTHER READING

Caudill, H. M. *Night Comes to the Cumberlands.* Boston: Atlantic-Little, Brown, 1963.

Collier, C. R., et al. "Influences of Strip Mining on the Hydrologic Environment of Parts of Beaver Creek Basin, Kentucky, 1955-66." USGS Professional Paper 427-C. Washington, DC: U. S. Government Printing Office, 1970.

Doyle, W. S. *Strip Mining of Coal: Environmental Solutions.* Park Ridge, NJ: Noyes Data Corp., 1976.

Landy, M. K. *The Politics of Environmental Reform: Controlling Kentucky Strip Mining.* Baltimore, MD: Johns Hopkins University Press, 1976.

U. S. Department of the Interior. "Surface Mining and Our Environment: A Special Report to the Nation." Washington, DC: U. S. Government Printing Office, 1967.

U. S. Environmental Protection Agency. "Erosion and Sediment Control: Surface Mining in the Eastern U. S.: Planning." Washington, DC: U. S. Government Printing Office, 1976.

Strontium 90

A radioactive **isotope** of strontium, produced during **nuclear fission**. The isotope was of great concern to environmental scientists during the period of atmospheric testing of **nuclear weapons**. Strontium 90 released in these tests fell

to the Earth's surface, adhered to grass and other green plants, and was eaten by cows and other animals. Since strontium is chemically similar to calcium, it follows the same metabolic pathways, ending up in an animal's milk. When a child drinks this milk, strontium 90 becomes incorporated into their bones and teeth. With a **half-life** of about 28 years, strontium 90 continues to emit radiation throughout the individual's lifetime.

Student Environmental Action Coalition (Chapel Hill, North Carolina)

Founded in 1990, the Student Environmental Action Coalition (SEAC) focuses on social justice and on environmental and political issues throughout the United States. The mission of SEAC is to unite youth that have exhibited leadership in their community and to create an environmental movement. It has 3,000 activists that build allegiances among local, regional, national, and international communities engaged in environmental struggles.

The unique aspect of SEAC membership is that there is not a national office that dictates an agenda to the local groups. Instead, local groups coordinate a National Council each year to run SEAC. The local groups are composed of schools or neighborhood clubs, with each choosing its own problem areas to focus on. Some topics that are frequently addressed include combating racism and sexism, and developing a sustainable living style.

Skills in each local group are developed at conferences held throughout the year. These conferences are led by students and consist of workshops on the strategies, lectures, and publicity for grassroots organizing. Educational resources used at the training are also sold through a clearinghouse or catalogues that contain information on both new and old activist groups.

SEAC publishes a monthly magazine, *Threshold*, that focuses on action alerts and organizational skills development. SEAC also updates their Internet page's online resource guide regularly to keep the local groups up to date on each other's activities. Contact: Student Environmental Action Coalition, P.O. Box 1168, Chapel Hill, NC 27514-1168.

[*Nicole Beatty*]

Subbituminous coal
See **Coal**

Subsidence

To subside is to sink or fall. Subsidence is commonly associated with the lowering of the earth's surface due to actions that have occurred below the surface. Sometimes this is a natural phenomenon, such as the solubilizing and removal of minerals by water. When the underground support system is removed in the process, the surface of the land sinks to a new level. This often leads to a special topographic form known as Karst **topography**. Human activities that lead to the extraction of ores, minerals, and **fossil fuels** often lead to a weakened mineral structural support and subsidence of the surface of the earth. In the **arid** portions of the earth, extraction of water from sub-surface **aquifer**s has led to subsidence of the earth's surface as well.

Subsoil

That portion of the **soil** that is below the surface. The subsoil is often referred to as the B **horizon**. Subsoils are generally lower in organic matter, lighter in color, denser, and often have a higher clay content than surface soils. Subsoils are generally not as productive as surface soils for plant growth. Thus, if surface soils are eroded, future productivity is reduced when the subsoil is used for crop production.

Succession

Succession is the gradual transformation or creation of a **biological community** as new **species** move into an area and modify local environmental conditions. Primary succession occurs when plant and animal species colonize a previously barren area, such as a new volcanic island, a sand dune, or recently glaciated ground. In these cases every living thing, from **soil** bacteria and **fungi** to larger plants and animals, must arrive from some adjacent **habitat**. Secondary succession is the development of communities in an area that has been disturbed by fire, hurricanes, field clearing, tree felling, or some other process that removes most plants and animals. Intermediate successional communities are known as "seral stages" or "seres."

As early successional species become established, they alter their **environment** and make it more habitable for later seral stages. Usually a disturbed or barren area has low soil **nutrient** levels, intense sunlight, and no protection from violent weather. Because precipitation quickly runs off the bare ground, little moisture is available for plant growth. Species that can survive under such harsh conditions have little competition, and they spread quickly. As they grow and thicken, these plants add organic matter to the soil, which aids moisture retention and helps soil bacteria to grow. As soil nutrients and moisture increase, larger shrubs and perennial plants can take root. The shade of these larger species weakens and eventually eliminates the original pioneering species, but it cools the local environment, further improving moisture availability and allowing species that demand relative environmental **stability**, such as woodland species, to begin moving in. Eventually, shade-tolerant species of plants will come to dominate the area that sun-loving plants had first colonized.

One of the most well-documented examples of primary succession occurred in 1883 when the **volcano** on the Indonesian island of **Krakatau** erupted, destroying most of the island and its life forms, and leaving a new island of bare volcanic rock and ash. Within a few years several species of grasses, ferns, and flowering shrubs had managed to arrive, carried by wind, water, or passing birds from islands 25 miles (40 km) or more distant. Just 40 years later, more than 300 plant species were growing, and in some areas over 30 centimeters of soil had developed: soil bacteria, insects, and decomposers had managed to reach the island and were turning fallen organic detritus into soil. Over the decades, the total number of species gradually stabilized, but the character of the community continued to change as incoming species replaced earlier arrivals. On Krakatau succession happened with unusual speed because the **climate** is warm and humid and because the fresh volcanic ash made a nutrient-rich soil.

Early successional species, those most able to quickly establish a foothold, are known as pioneer species. Usually pioneer species are opportunists, able to find nourishment and survive under a great variety of conditions, quick to grow, and able to produce a great number of seeds or offspring at once. Pioneer species have very effective means of dispersing seeds or young, and their seeds can often remain dormant in soil for some time, sprouting only after conditions become suitable. Dandelions are well-known pioneers because they can quickly produce a seed head with hundreds of seeds. Each tiny seed has a lightweight structure that allows the wind to carry it long distances. Dandelions are quick to invade a lawn because of this effective seed-dispersal tactic, because they can survive under sunny or shady conditions, and because they grow and reproduce quickly. In open sunshine, they are competitive enough to establish themselves despite the presence of a thick mat of turf grass.

Later successional species tend to be more shade tolerant, slower to grow and reproduce, and longer lived than pioneer species. Their larger seeds do not disperse as easily (compare the size of an acorn or walnut with that of a dandelion seed), and their seeds cannot remain dormant for very long before they lose viability. Seedlings of some late successional species, such as the Pacific Northwest hemlock, require shade to survive, and most require considerable moisture and soil nutrients.

We usually think of succession occurring after a catastrophic environmental disturbance, but in some cases the gradual environmental changes of succession proceed in the absence of disturbance. Two outstanding examples of this are bog succession and the invasion of **prairie**s by shrubs and trees.

In cool, moist, temperate climates, plant succession often turns ponds into forest through bog succession. Water-loving plants, mainly rush-like sedges and sphagnum moss, gradually creep out from the pond's edges. Often these plants form a floating mat of living and dead vegetation. Other plants—cranberries, Labrador tea, bog rosemary—become established on top of the mat. Organic detritus accumulates below the mat. Eventually the bog becomes firm enough to support black spruce, tamarack, and other tree species. As it fills in and dries, the former pond slowly becomes indistinguishable from the surrounding forest.

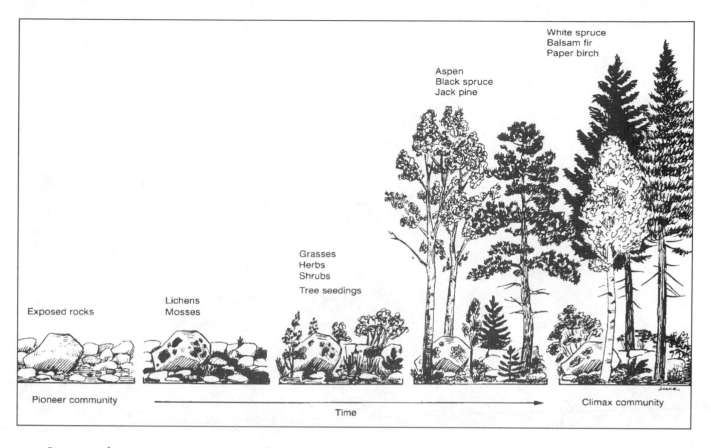

Five stages of primary succession on a terrestrial site.

Many **grasslands** persist only in the presence of occasional wildfires. During wet decades or when human activity prevents fires, woody species tend to creep in from the edges of a prairie. If sufficient moisture is available and if fires do not return, open grassland can give way to forest. Fire suppression has aided the advance of forests in this way across much of the United States, Canada, and Mexico. Grazing or browsing animals can also be important forces in maintaining biological communities. Adding or removing grazers can initiate successional processes.

Longer, slower disturbances than fire or field clearing can also initiate succession. Over the course of centuries, climate change can cause significant alteration in the character of **biome**s. Minor variations in rainfall or temperature ranges can alter community structure for decades or centuries. The end of the last glacial period about 10,000 years ago allowed tundra, then grasslands, then temperate forests to advance northward across North America. Even geologic activity, such as mountain building or changes in sea level, has caused succession. More recently, human introductions of species from one continent to another have caused significant restructuring of some biological communities.

Turnover from one community to another may occur in just a few years or decades, as it did on Krakatau. Stages in bog succession may take a hundred years or more. Often succession continues for centuries or millennia before a stable and relatively constant biological community emerges. This is especially likely in areas whose climate is moist and mild

enough to support the high species diversity of temperate or **tropical rain forest**s. However simpler **ecosystem**s such as arctic **tundra** may take centuries to recover from disturbance because low temperatures and short summers make growth rates almost universally slow.

Generally, successional processes are understood to lead ultimately to the emergence of a climax community, a group of species perfectly suited to a region's climate, soil types, and other environmental conditions. Climax communities are said to exist in equilibrium in their environments; where early successional species groups tend to facilitate the development of later stages, climax communities, sometimes called mature communities, tend to have self-perpetuating characteristics or mechanisms that help maintain local environmental conditions and help the community to persist. In the 1930s, F. E. Clements, one of the best-known plant ecologists in the United States, identified a list of just 14 climax communities that he claimed were the final result of succession for all the various sets of environmental conditions in the country.

More recent evaluations of climax communities, however, have concluded that climax forests are often a patchwork of stable and unstable areas. In an **old-growth forest** in the Pacific Northwest, hemlock and spruce may compose the local climax community, but every time a large tree falls it creates a sunny opening, making way for other seral species to grow for a time. Occasional fires disturb larger patches of forest, and succession starts again from the beginning in

The area around Sudbury, Ontario was deforested by emissions from nickel and copper smelting.

disturbed areas. The entire biome is more a shifting and changing mosaic than an uniform and unchanging forest. Often slight gradations in soil types, slope, exposure, and moisture cause a variety of stable communities to blend in an area. The term "polyclimax community" was developed to recognize the complexity of such assemblages.

In some cases, climax communities may be difficult to distinguish at all. For instance in a biome regularly disturbed by fire, "climax" species usually require fire to aid seed germination and eliminate competitors. Definitions here become somewhat blurred: Is a climax community one that exists without disturbance? Is fire a disturbance or a maintenance factor? Even if a very old forest community is considered, on a time scale of thousands of years, it may be difficult to determine whether what is observed today is really a permanent climax community or just a very longstanding seral stage. Despite these questions, the concept of an ultimate climax community is central to the idea of succession.

Usually climax communities are considered more diverse than intermediate communities. Because climax communities can remain stable for a long time, species can diversify and develop specialized **niche**s. This specialization can lead to the coexistence of a great number of species, as is the case in tropical rain forests, where thousands of species may share just a few hectares of forest. In some cases, however, intermediate seral stages actually have greater diversity because they contain elements of multiple communities at once. *See also* Biodiversity; Biological fertility; Climax

(ecological); Ecological productivity; Growth limiting factors; Introduced species; Restoration ecology

[*Linda Rehkopf*]

FURTHER READING

Brown, J. H., and A. C. Gibson. *Biogeography*. St. Louis, MO: Mosby, 1983.
Ricklefs, R. E. *Ecology*. 3rd ed. New York: W. H. Freeman and Co., 1990.

Sudbury, Ontario

The town of Sudbury, Ontario, has been the site of a large metal mining and processing industry since the latter part of the nineteenth century. The principal metals that have been sought from the Sudbury mines are **nickel** and **copper**. Because of Sudbury's long history of mining and processing, it has sustained significant ecological damage and has provided scientists and environmentalists with a clear case study of the results.

Mining and processing companies headquartered at Sudbury began by using a processing technique that oxidized sulfide ores using roast beds, or heaps of ore piled upon wood. The heaps were ignited and left to smoulder for several months, after which cooled metal concentrate was collected and shipped to a refinery for processing into pure metals. The side effect of roast beds was the intense, ground-level plumes of **sulfur dioxide** and metals, especially nickel and copper, they produced. The smoke devastated local **ecosystem**s through direct **phytotoxocity** and by causing **acidification** of **soil** and water. After the vegetative cover was killed, soils eroded from slopes and exposed naked granitic-gneissic bedrock, which became pitted and blackened from reaction with the roast-bed plumes.

After 1928, the use of roast beds was outlawed, and three **smelter**s with tall stacks were constructed. These emitted pollutants higher into the **atmosphere**, but some local vegetation damage was still caused, lakes were acidified, and toxic contaminants were spread over an increasingly larger area.

Over the decades, well-defined patterns of ecological damage developed around the Sudbury smelters. The most devastated sites occurred closest to the sources of **emission**. They had large concentrations of nickel, copper, and other metals, were very acidic with resulting toxicity from soluble **aluminum** ions, and were frequently subjected to toxic fumigations by sulfur dioxide. Such sites had very little or no plant cover, and the few species that were present were usually physiologically tolerant ecotypes of a few widespread **species**.

Ecological damage and environmental contamination decreased with increasing distance from the **point source** of emissions. Obvious damage to terrestrial ecosystems was difficult to detect beyond 10-12 miles (15-20 km), but contamination with nickel and copper could be observed much farther away. Oligotrophic lakes with clear water, low fertility, amd little buffering capacity, however, were acidified by the **dry deposition** of sulfur dioxide at least 25-31 miles (40-50 km) from Sudbury.

In 1972, a very tall, 1,247-foot (380-m) "superstack" was constructed at the largest of the Sudbury smelters. The superstack resulted in an even greater dispersion of smelter emissions. This, combined with closing of another smelter, and reduction of emissions by **flue gas** desulfurization and the processing of lower-sulfur ores, resulted in a substantial improvement of local **air quality**. Consequently, a notable increase in the cover and species richness of plant cover close to the Sudbury smelters has occurred, a process that has been actively encouraged by revegetation activities along roadways and other amenity areas where soil remained. Lakes close to the superstack and the closed smelter have also become less acidic, and their biota has responded accordingly. There is controversy, however, about the contributions that the still large emissions of sulfur dioxide may be making towards the regional **acid rain** problem. It is possible that height of the superstack will be decreased to reduce the longer-range transport of emitted sulfur dioxide. *See also* Air pollution; Contaminated soil; Water pollution

[Bill Freedman]

FURTHER READING

Freedman, B. *Environmental Ecology.* San Diego: Academic Press, 1989.

Nriagu, J., ed. *Environmental Impacts of Smelters.* New York: J. Wiley, 1984.

Sulfate particles

Sulfate particles are small sulfur-containing airborne particles with typical diameters of 0.3 micrometers. Most sulfate is a secondary pollutant, formed by the oxidation in the **atmosphere** of **sulfur dioxide** gas. Sulfur dioxide is emitted largely in **fossil fuel** combustion, particularly from power plants burning **coal**. A small fraction (generally well under 10%) of sulfur is emitted as primary sulfate at the **combustion** source. The use of coal-cleaning, scrubbers, and low sulfur coal have reduced sulfur dioxide emissions in the United States, and thus airborne sulfate concentrations have decreased.

In the atmosphere, sulfur dioxide (SO_2) emissions are slowly transformed to sulfate (SO_4) at a rate of 0.1-5% per hour, with the rate increased by higher temperatures, sunshine, and the presence of oxidants. Further reactions with water vapor may produce sulfuric acid (H_2SO_4), a corrosive acid which is injurious to **ecosystem**s and humans, and also ammonium sulfate ($(NH_4)_2SO_4$), which is particularly effective at impairing visibility. The atmospheric residence time for sulfate particles is long, 2-10 days, which permits transport on a regional or continental scale across hundreds or thousands of miles. Because sulfate particles are relatively soluble, precipitation effectively washes them out, resulting in **acid rain**. Of the various sizes of aerosols, sulfate particles are in the accumulation mode, and typically there might be about 10,000 particles per cm^3 in an urban area.

In addition to problems of acid rain and visibility degradation, sulfate particles can cause a number of health problems. Community epidemiological studies report associations of annual and multi-year average concentrations of PM_{10} (particulates), $PM_{2.5}$ (fine particulate), and sulfates with health effects that include premature mortality, increased respiratory symptoms and illness (e.g., **bronchitis** and cough in children), and reduced lung function. The risks associated with long-term exposures, although highly uncertain, appear to be larger than those associated with short-term exposures. Other analyses have shown statistically significant associations between sulfate and other particulate air pollutants with total and cardiopulmonary mortality. Additionally, animal studies suggest that concentrations approaching ambient levels of ammonium sulfate and nitrate can cause morphometric changes that could lead to a decrease in compliance or a "stiffening" of the lung.

Because of the long time and distance scales required for transformation, and because sulfate particles are small, which allows them to remain airborne for several days, sulfate concentrations tend to be uniformly distributed across broad regions. In the eastern United States, sulfate particles constitute half or more of fine fraction particle concentrations (also called $PM_{2.5}$, or that subset of airborne particles below 2.5 micrometer diameter). Thus, much of the sulfate in an urban area or airshed arises from distant or "regional" sources. If at high levels, this "background" component can pose a dilemma for air quality management, since emission reductions from local sources do not control the problem. Instead, transboundary agreements, such as the Canada-United

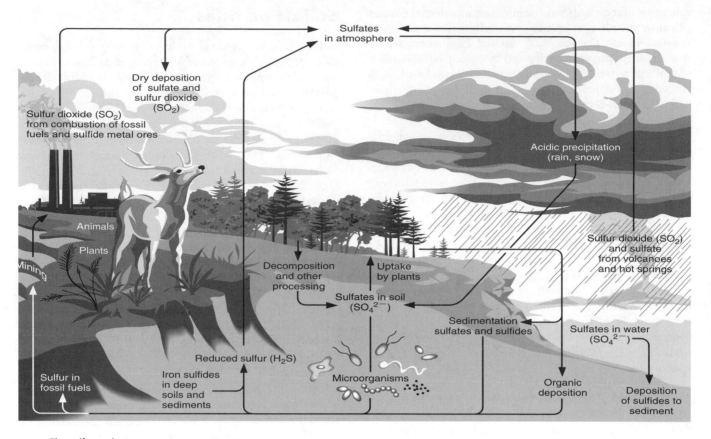

The sulfur cycle.

States Air Quality Agreement which was signed March 13, 1991, have been used recently to monitor and control emissions from distant sources that cause most of the emissions.

Governmental regulations in the United States do not directly address sulfate; however, the **National Ambient Air Quality Standards** do set limits on particulate concentrations (PM_{10}), and regulations on fine particulate ($PM_{2.5}$) have been proposed. In addition to these ambient standards, regulations limit emissions of sulfur dioxide at sources (in the New Source Performance Standards), and the degradation of existing air quality levels (Prevention of Significant Deterioration). In Europe, deposition of acidic compounds, largely from atmospheric sulfate, is controlled by setting critical loads that depend on the capacity of a region to withstand acid inputs without lake and **soil** acidification.

[*Stuart Batterman*]

Sulfur cycle

The series of chemical reactions by which sulfur moves through the earth's **atmosphere**, hydrosphere, lithosphere, and **biosphere**. Sulfur enters the atmosphere naturally from **volcano**es and hot springs and through the **anaerobic** decay of organisms. It exists in the atmosphere primarily as hydrogen sulfide and **sulfur dioxide**. After conversion to sulfates in the air, sulfur is carried to the earth's surface by

precipitation. There it is incorporated into plants and animals who return sulfur to the earth's crust when they die. Through their use of **fossil fuels**, humans have a large effect on the sulfur cycle, approximately tripling the amount of the element returned to the atmosphere.

Sulfur dioxide

One of the two common oxides of sulfur existing in the **atmosphere**, sulfur trioxide being the other. Sulfur dioxide is produced naturally in the atmosphere by the oxidation of hydrogen sulfide, a gas released from **volcano**es and hot springs. About 20 million metric tons of sulfur dioxide is released annually into the atmosphere by human activities, primarily during the **combustion** of **fossil fuels**. The amount of anthropogenic sulfur dioxide is roughly equal to that formed naturally from hydrogen sulfide. Sulfur dioxide reacts with water in clouds to form **acid rain**, causes damage in plants, and is responsible for a variety of respiratory problems in humans.

Superconductivity

In 1911, Dutch physicist Heike Kamerlingh-Onnes discovered that some materials, when cooled to very low temperatures—within a few degrees of absolute zero—become superconductive, losing all resistance to the flow of electric current. Potentially, that discovery had enormous practical significance since a large fraction of the electrical energy that flows through any appliance is wasted in overcoming resistance. Kamerlingh-Onnes's discovery remained a laboratory curiosity for over 70 years, however, because the low temperatures needed to produce superconductivity are difficult to achieve. Then, in 1985, scientists discovered a new class of compounds that become superconductive at much higher temperatures (about -170°C). The use of such materials in the manufacture of electrical equipment promises to greatly increase the efficiency of such equipment.

Superfund

See **Comprehensive Environmental Response, Compensation and Liability Act (CERCLA); Superfund Amendments and Reauthorization Act (SARA)**

Superfund Amendments and Reauthorization Act (SARA) (1986)

Commonly called *Superfund*, SARA is a program established to finance cleanup operations of abandoned **hazardous waste** dump sites in the United States. Initially authorized by Congress in 1980 as the **Comprehensive Environmental Response, Compensation, and Liability Act**, the Superfund is administered by the **Environmental Protection Agency** (EPA). The program was reauthorized in 1986 as the Superfund Amendment and Reauthorization Act (SARA), and several provisions were changed or clarified.

Superfund sites under the original legislation were virtually ignored during the early 1980s. Charges of mismanagement of the fund caused controversy and led to the resignations of key EPA officials. The EPA attempted to speed cleanup of contaminated sites, but progress was still too slow. When the program expired in September 1985, the cleanup of more than 200 sites was delayed for lack of funds. But concern about hazardous waste sites was sufficient to eventually facilitate reauthorization.

The Superfund was originally financed by a tax on receipt of hazardous waste, and by a tax on domestic refined or imported crude oil and **chemicals**. The SARA reauthorization increased funding from $1.6 billion to $8.5 billion over five years. It also authorized the use of contributions from potentially responsible parties. SARA declined to place the full financial burden of cleanup on oil and chemical companies, and funding now derives from a broad-based combination of business and public contributions.

SARA emphasizes the importance of remedial actions, specifically those that reduce the volume, toxicity, or mobility of hazardous substances, **pollutant**s and contaminants. Targets for long-term remedial actions are listed on the **National Priorities List** and updated annually.

More than 1,200 sites around the nation are on the priorities list, and these sites are considered the worst in the country. Factors used in the ranking system include the type quantity, and toxicity of the substance, as well as the number of people likely to be exposed, the pathways of exposure, and the vulnerability of the **groundwater** supply at the site. If a site poses immediate threats such as the risk of fire or explosion, the EPA may initiate short-term actions to remove those threats before actual cleanup begins.

By 1987, a national computerized registry had identified 25,000 potential Superfund sites, and close to 2,500 will probably be classified as such. Critics charge, however, that the number of hazardous waste sites nationwide that need attention is actually more than 28,000, and many states have developed their own programs to supplement the Superfund.

Under SARA guidelines, the **Agency for Toxic Substances and Disease Registry** performs health assessments at Superfund sites. This program, administered by the **Centers for Disease Control and Prevention**, also lists hazardous substances found on sites, prepares toxicological profiles, identifies gaps in research on health effects, and publishes findings. *See also* Chemical spills; Emergency Planning and Community Right-to-Know Act; Hazardous material; Hazardous Substances Act; Toxic Substances Control Act; Toxic substance; Toxic use reduction legislation

[*Linda Rehkopf*]

Further Reading

Church, T. W. *Cleaning Up the Mess: Implementation Strategies in the Superfund Program.* Washington, DC: Brookings Institute, 1993.

Fogelman, V. M. *Hazardous Waste Cleanup, Liability, and Litigation: A Comprehensive Guide to Superfund Law.* Westport, CT: Greenwood Publishing Group, 1992.

Surface mining

Surface mining techniques are used when a vein of **coal** or other substance lies so close to the surface that it can be mined with bulldozers, power shovels, and trucks instead of using deep shaft mines, explosive devices, or **coal gasification** techniques. Surface mining is especially useful when the rock contains so little of the ore being mined that conventional techniques, such as tunneling along veins, cannot be used. Surface mining removes the earth and rock that lies above the coal or mineral seam and places the **overburden** off to one side as **spoil**. The exposed ore is removed and preliminary processing is done on site or the ore is taken by truck to processing plants. After the mining operations are complete, the surface can be recontoured, restored, and reclaimed.

Surface mining already accounts for over 60 percent of the world's total mineral production, and the percentage is increasing substantially. Many factors contribute to the popularity of surface mining. The lead time for developing a surface mine averages four years, as opposed to eight years for underground mines. Productivity of workers at surface mines is three times greater than that of workers in underground mining operations. The capital cost for surface mine develop-

An open-pit copper mine.

ment is between 20 and 40 dollars per annual ton of salable coal, and the start-up expenses for underground mining operations are at least twice that, averaging around 80 dollars per annual ton.

The preliminary stages of mine development involve gathering detailed information about the potential mining site. Trenching and core drilling provide information on the coal seam as well as the overburden and the general geological composition of the site. Analysis of the drill core from the overburden is an important step in preventing environmental hazards. For example, when the shale between coal seams and the underlying strata is disturbed by mining, it can produce acid. If this instability in the strata is detected by analysis of the drill cores, acid **runoff** can be avoided by appropriate mine design. The data obtained from the preliminary drilling is plotted on topographic maps so that the relationship between seams of ore and the overlying terrain are clearly visible.

After test results and all other relevant data have been obtained, the information is entered into a computer system for analysis. Various mine designs and mining sequences are tested by the computer models and evaluated according to technical and economic criteria in order to determine the optimal mine design. Satellite imagery and aerial photographs are usually taken during the exploratory stages. These photographs serve as an excellent visual record of the actual environmental conditions prior to the mining operation, and they are frequently utilized during the **reclamation** process.

There are several types of surface mining, and these include area mining, contour mining, auger mining, and open-pit mining. Area mining is used predominantly in the midwest and western mountain states, where coal seams lie horizontally beneath the surface. Operations begin near the coal outcrop—the point where the ore lies closest to the surface. Large stripping shovels or draglines dig long parallel trenches; this removes the overburden, leaving the ore exposed. The overburden excavated from the trench is thrown into the previous trench, from which coal has already been extracted. The process is similar to a farmer plowing a field in furrows. Because of the steep slopes and rugged terrain frequently encountered in area mining operations, the ore is usually recovered by small equipment such as front end bucket loaders, bulldozers, and trucks.

Area mining is also practiced in Appalachia, where many of the coal seams lie under mountains or foothills. This type of area mining is commonly known as mountaintop removal. The mountains mined using this technique generally have long ridges with underlying deposits. A cut is made parallel to the ridge, and subsequent cuts are made parallel to the first; this results in the entire top of the mountain being leveled off and flattened out. When these areas are reclaimed, the most frequent designated uses are grazing lands or development sites.

Contour mining is used primarily at the point where the seam lies closest to the surface, on steep inclines such as in the Appalachian mountains. In these areas, coal usually lies in flat continuous beds, and the excavation continues along the side of the mountain. This produces a long narrow trench, with highwall extending along the trench—the contour line for horizontal coal seams. Recent federal regulations have outlawed many contour mining practices, such as leaving exposed highwall and spoil on the mountainside.

The auger process is used primarily in salvage operations. When it is no longer economically profitable to remove the overburden in the highwall, augering techniques are utilized to recover additional tonnage. The auger extracts coal by boring underneath the final highwall. Currently, auger mining only accounts for four percent of surface-mined coal production in the United States.

Open-pit mining is used primarily in western states, where coal seams are at least a hundred feet (30 m) thick. The thin overburden is removed and taken away from the site by truck, leaving the exposed coal seam. This type of mine operation is very similar to rock quarry operations.

The equipment used in surface mining ranges from bulldozers, front-end bucket loaders, scrapers, and trucks to gigantic power shovels, bucket-wheel excavators, and draglines. Over the past ten years, technological development has concentrated on mechanization and development of heavy-duty equipment. Due to economic factors, equipment manufacturers have focused on improving performance of existing equipment instead of developing new technologies. Since the recession of the 1980s, bucket capacity and the size of conventional machines have increased. Concentration of production technology has created mining systems that incorporate mining equipment with continuous transportation systems and integrated computers into all aspects of the industry.

Surface mining can have severe environmental effects. The process removes all vegetation, destroying microflora and microorganisms. The soil, **subsoil**, and strata are broken and removed. **Wildlife** is displaced, **air quality** suffers, and surface changes occur due to oxidation and topographic changes.

Hydrology associated with surface mining has a major effect on the environment. Removal of overburden may change the **groundwater** in numerous ways, including drainage of water from the area, altering the direction of **aquifer** flow, and lowering the **water table**s. It also creates channels that allow contaminated water to mingle with water of other aquifers. Acid water runoff from the mining operations can contaminate the area and other water sources. In addition to being highly acidic, the runoff from mining operations also contains many other trace elements that adversely affect the environment.

Federal regulations require that **topsoil** be redistributed after the mining is complete, but many people do not consider this requirement sufficient. When soil is removed, the soil structure breaks down and compacts, preventing normal organic matter from getting into the soil. Microorganisms are destroyed by the changes in the soil and the lack of organic components. The rate of **erosion** in mining areas is also greatly increased due to the lack of native vegetation.

The removal of vegetation and overburden at the mining site displaces all wildlife, and a large portion of it may be completely destroyed. Some forms of wildlife, such as birds and **game animal**s, may get out of the area safely, but those that hibernate or burrow usually die as a result of the mining. Ponds, streams and swamps are routinely drained before mining operations commence and all aquatic life in the region is destroyed.

In addition to the short-term environmental effects, surface mining also has long-term impact on the **flora** and **fauna** within the region of the mine. Salts, **heavy metal**s, acids, and other minerals exposed during removal of overburden suppress growth rate and productivity. Due to changes in soil composition, many native **species** of plants are unable to adjust. The loss of vegetation means a loss of feeding grounds, which in turn disrupts **migration** patterns. Displaced species encroach on neighboring **ecosystem**s which may cause overpopulation and disruption of adjacent **habitat**s. *See also* Surface Mining Control and Reclamation Act

[*Debra Glidden*]

FURTHER READING

Chironis, N. "With Dozers Bigger Is Better." *Coal Age* 91 (July 1986): 56.

Sanda, A. "Draglines Dominate Big Surface Mines." *Coal* 96 (July 1991): 30.

Schmidt, B. "GAO to Interior: Get Tough on Mining." *American Metal Market* 96 (21 December 1988): 2.

Singhal, R. K. "In Pit Crushing and Conveying Systems." *World Mining Equipment* 10 (January 1986): 24.

"Surface Mining Costs Decline in the Midwest." *Mining* 91 (May 1986): 10.

Surface Mining Control and Reclamation Act (1977)

This act set minimum federal standards for surface **coal** mining and **reclamation** of mining sites. The act requires that: (1) mine operators demonstrate reclamation capability; (2) previous uses must be restored and the land reshaped to its original contour, with **topsoil** replacement and replanting; (3) mining be prohibited on prime western agricultural land, with farmers and ranchers holding veto power; (4) the hydrologic environment must be protected, especially from acid drainage; and (5) a $4.1 billion fund be established to reclaim abandoned strip mines. States have enforcement responsibility, but the **U. S. Department of the Interior** steps in if they fail to act.

Surface-water quality
See **Water quality**

Survivorship

The term "survivorship" describes the likelihood that an organism will remain alive from one time period to the next. For example, the survivorship of human males in a given country to age 20 might be around 96.5 percent, while survivorship to age 70 might be 55 percent.

Age-specific **mortality** can be illustrated in the form of a *survivorship curve* that usually yields one of three patterns of survivorship: mortality concentrated at the end of the maximum life span; a constant probability of death for every age group; or high early mortality followed by high survival. Survivorship can also be depicted with a *life table* showing the number of survivors from a given starting population at specific intervals.

Suspended solid

Refers to a solid which is suspended in a liquid. Most treatment facilities for both municipal and industrial **wastewater**s must meet effluent standards for total suspended solids (TSS). A typical TSS limit for a secondary wastewater treatment plant is 20 mg/L. However, some industries may have permits that allow them to discharge much more; for example, 500 mg TSS/L. The test for TSS is commonly performed by filtering a known amount of water through a pre-weighed glass-fiber or 0.45 micron (μ) porosity filter. The filter with the solids is then dried in an oven (217°-221°F/103°-105°C) and weighed. The amount of dried solid matter on the filter per amount of water originally filtered is expressed in terms of mg/L. Solids which pass through the filter in the filtrate are referred to as dissolved solids. Settleable solids (i.e., those that settle in a standard test within 30 minutes) are a type of suspended solids, but not all suspended solids are settleable solids.

Sustainable agriculture

Because of concerns over **pesticide**s and nitrates in **groundwater**, **soil erosion**, **pesticide residue**s in food, pest resistance to pesticides, and the rising costs of purchased inputs needed for conventional agriculture, many farmers have begun to adopt alternative practices with the goals of reducing input costs, preserving the resource base, and protecting human health. This is being called "sustainable agriculture."

Many of the components of sustainable agriculture are derived from conventional agronomic practices and livestock husbandry. Sustainable systems more deliberately integrate and take advantage of naturally occurring beneficial interactions. Sustainable systems emphasize management; biological relationships, such as those between the pest and predator; and natural processes, such as **nitrogen** fixation instead of chemically intensive methods. The objective is to sustain and enhance, rather than reduce and simplify, the biological interactions on which production agriculture depends, thereby reducing the harmful off-farm effects of production practices.

Examples of practices and principles emphasized in sustainable agriculture systems include:

(1) Crop rotations that mitigate weed, disease, insect, and other pest problems; increase available soil nitrogen and reduce the need for purchased **fertilizer**s; and, in conjunction with **conservation** tillage practices, reduce soil erosion.

(2) **Integrated pest management** (IPM) that reduces the need for pesticides by crop rotations, scouting weather monitoring, use of resistant cultivars, timing of planting and biological pest controls.

(3) Soil and water conservation tillage practices that increase the amount of crop residues on the soil surface and reduce the number of times farmers have to till the soil.

(4) Animal production systems that emphasize disease prevention through health maintenance, thereby reducing the need for antibiotics.

Many farmers and people of rural communities are starting to explore the possibilities of systems of sustainable agriculture. The term systems is used because there is no one single way to farm sustainably. The possible ways are as numerous as farmers and potential farmers.

The first aspect of sustainable agriculture is the understanding that a respect for life, in its various forms, is not only desirable but necessary to human survival. A second aspect requires that the farming system not put life in jeopardy, its methods not deplete the soil or the water, or place farmers in situations where they themselves are depleted, either in numbers or in the quality of their lives.

Another aspect of sustainable agriculture recognizes that farming families are an essential part of a sustainable system. Farmers are the systems care-givers or stewards. As stewards they know their land better than anyone else and are equipped to shoulder the challenge of developing a sustainable system on that land. In a sustainable system farmers ideally will move toward less dependence on off-farm purchased inputs and more toward natural or organic materials. This is accomplished by gaining knowledge about the intricate biological and economic workings of the farm. Lastly, sustainable agricultural systems require the support of consumers as well; they can give support, for example, by selectively buying food raised in close proximity to a buyer's local market.

[*Terence H. Cooper*]

FURTHER READING

Alternative Agriculture. National Research Council Board on Agriculture. Washington, D.C.: National Academy Press, 1989.

Thesing, C. "What Is Sustainable Agriculture?" *The Land Stewardship Letter* 10 (1992): 13-14.

Sustainable architecture

Sustainable architecture refers to the practice of designing buildings which create living **environment**s that work to minimize human's use of resources. This is reflected both in a building's construction materials and methods and in its use of resources, such as in heating, cooling, power, water, and **wastewater** treatment.

The operating concept is that structures so designed "sustain" their users by providing healthy environments, improving the quality of life, and avoiding the production of waste, to preserve the long-term survivability of the human species.

Hunter and **Amory Lovins** of the Rocky Mountain Institute say the purpose of sustainable architecture is to "meet the needs of the present without compromising the ability of future generations to meet their own needs."

The term, however, is a broad one, and is used to describe a wide variety of aspects of building design and use.

For some, the term applies to designing buildings that produce as much energy as they consume. Another interpretation calls for a consciousness of the spiritual significance of a building's design, construction, and siting. Also, some maintain that integral to this approach is that buildings must foster the spiritual and physical well-being of their users.

One school of thought maintains that, in its highest form, sustainable architecture replicates a stable **ecosystem**. According to noted ecological engineer, David Del Porto, a building designed for sustainability is a balanced system where there are no wastes, because the outputs of one process become the inputs of another. Energy, matter, and information are cascaded through connected processes in cyclical pathways, which by virtue of their efficiency and interdependence, yield the matrix elements of environmental and economic security, high quality of life, and no waste. The constant input of the sun replenishes any energy lost in the process.

"Sustainability," as it relates to resources, became a widely used term with **Lester Brown**'s book, *Building a Sustainable Society,* and with the publishing of the **International Union on the Conservation of Nature**'s "World Conservation Strategy" in 1980.

Sustainability then came to describe a state whereby natural renewable resources are used in a manner that does not eliminate or degrade them or otherwise diminish their renewable usefulness for future generations, while maintaining effectively constant or non-declining stocks of natural resources such as soil, groundwater, and **biomass** (World Resources Institute).

Before "sustainable architecture," the term "solar architecture" was used to express the architectural approach to reducing the consumption of natural resources and fuels by capturing solar energy. This evolved into the current and broader concept of sustainable architecture, which expands the scope of issues involved to include water use, **climate** control, food production, air purification, **solid waste** reclamation, **wastewater** treatment, and overall energy efficiency. It also encompasses building materials, emphasizing the use of local materials, renewable resources and recycled materials, as well as the mental and physical comfort of the building's inhabitants. In addition, sustainable architecture calls for the siting and design of a building to harmonize with its surroundings.

The United Nations lists the following five principles of sustainable architecture:

1. *Healthful interior environment.* All possible measures are to be taken to ensure that materials and building systems do not emit toxic substances and gasses into the interior atmosphere. Additional measures are to be taken to clean and revitalize interior air with filtration and plantings.

2. *Resource efficiency.* All possible measures are to be taken to ensure that the building's use of energy and other resources is minimal. Cooling, heating, and lighting systems are to use methods and products that conserve or eliminate energy use. Water use and the production of wastewater are minimized.

3. *Ecologically benign materials.* All possible measures are to be taken to use building materials and products that minimize destruction of the global environment. Wood is to be selected based on non-destructive forestry practices. Other materials and products are to be considered based on the toxic waste output of production. Many practitioners cite an additional criterion: that the long-term environmental and societal costs to produce the building's materials must be considered and prove in keeping with sustainability goals.

4. *Environmental form.* All possible measures are to be taken to relate the form and plan of the design to the site, the region, and the climate. Measures are to be taken to "heal" and augment the ecology of the site. Accommodations are to be made for recycling and energy efficiency. Measures are to be taken to relate the form of building to a harmonious relationship between the inhabitants and nature.

5. *Good design.* All possible measures are to be taken to achieve an efficient, long-lasting and elegant relationship of area use, circulation, building form, mechanical systems and construction technology. Symbolic relationships with appropriate history, the Earth, and spiritual principles are to be searched for and expressed. Finished buildings shall be well built, easy to use, and beautiful.

Examples of sustainable architecture include: (1) The NMB Bank headquarters in Amsterdam, the Netherlands. Constructed in 1978, this approximately 150,000-ft^2 (45,500-m^2) complex is a meandering S-curve of ten buildings, each offering different orientations and views of gardens. Constructed of natural and low-polluting materials, the buildings feature organic design lines, indoor and outdoor gardens, passive solar elements, heat recovery, water features, and natural lighting and ventilation. Built for an estimated 5% more than a conventional office building, the NMB building's operating costs are only 30% of those of a conventional building; (2) The Solar Living Center in Hopland, California, employs both passive and photovoltaic solar elements, as well as ecological wastewater systems. The rice straw bale and cement building is constructed around a solar calendar.

Sustainable Architecture as a Movement

Some maintain that sustainability, as it relates to architecture, refers to a process and an attitude or viewpoint. Sustainability is "a process of responsible consumption, wherein waste is minimized, and buildings interact in balanced ways with natural environments and cycles, balancing the desires and activities of humankind within the integrity and carrying capacity of nature, and achieving a stable, long-term relationship within the limits of their local and global environment" (Rocky Mountain Institute).

However, sustainable architecture does not necessarily mean a reduction in material comfort. Sustainability represents a transition from a period of degradation of the natural environment (as represented by the industrial revolution and its associated unplanned and wasteful patterns of growth) to a more humane and natural environment. It is doing more with less.

Proponents of sustainable architecture occasionally debate the broader applications of the term. Some say that sustainable buildings should generate more energy over time (in the form of power, etc.) than was required to construct, fabricate their materials, operate, and maintain them. This is also referred to as "regenerative architecture," which John Tillman Lyle sums up in his book, *Regenerative Design for Sustainable Development* as "living on the interest yielded by natural resources rather than the capital." Others simply see it as an approach to making buildings less consumptive of natural resources.

Spiritual Aspects of Sustainable Architecture

A spiritual viewpoint is that sustainable architecture is "stewardship," a recognition and celebration of the human environment as a vital part of the larger universe and of humankind's role as caretakers of the earth. Viewed in this way, resources are regarded as sacred. Another perspective is that the creation of a building in the likeness of a living system is somewhat religious, as a divine entity creates a living order.

Although the term communicates slightly different meanings to various audiences, it nevertheless serves as a consciousness-raising focus for creating greater concern for the built environment and its long-term viability. Rather than representing a return to subsistence living, buildings designed for sustainability aim to improve the quality and standards of living. Sustainable architecture recognizes people as temporary stewards of their environments, working toward a respect for natural systems and a higher quality of life.

[*Carol Steinfeld*]

FURTHER READING

Barnett, D., and W. Browning. "A Primer on Sustainable Building," a report. Colorado: Rocky Mountain Institute, 1995.

Kremers, J. "Sustainable Architecture," *Architronic*, World Wide Web page: http://www.saed.kent.edu/Architronic/v4n3.03.homepage.html, December 1996.

Lyle, J. *Regenerative Design for Sustainable Development*. New York: John Wiley & Sons, Inc., 1994.

Nebel, B.J. *Environmental Science: The Way the World Works*, 3rd ed. New York: Prentice Hall, 1990.

Orr, D. W. *Ecological Literacy*. New York: State University of New York Press, 1992.

World Resources 1992-93: A Guide to the Global Environment. New York: Oxford University Press, 1992.

World Resources Institute. "Dimensions of Sustainable Development," a report. Washington, D.C.: WRI, 1990.

Sustainable biosphere

The **biosphere** is the region of the earth that supports life, and it includes all land, water, and the thin layer of air above the earth. A sustainable biosphere is one with the continuing ability to support life.

Some scientists have suggested that the oceans and atmosphere in the biosphere adjust to ensure the continuation of life—a theory known as the **Gaia Hypothesis**. **James Lovelock**, a British scientist first proposed it in the late 1970s. He argued that in the last 4,500 years of the earth's approximately five billion years of existence, humans have been placing increasingly greater stress on the biosphere. He called for a new awareness of the situation and insisted that changes in human behavior were necessary to maintain a biosphere capable of supporting life. Maintaining a sustainable biosphere involves the integrated management of land, water, and air.

The land management practices that many believe are necessary for sustaining the biosphere require **conservation** and planting techniques that control **soil erosion**. These techniques encourage farmers to use organic **fertilizer**s instead of synthesized ones. Recycled manure and composted plant materials can be used to put **nutrient**s back into the soil instead of increasing **pollution** in the **environment**. Crop rotation reduces crop loss to insects and it also increases **soil fertility**. Monitoring pest populations helps determine the best times as well as the best methods for eliminating them, and using **pesticide**s only when needed lowers pollution of soil and water and prevents insects from developing resistances.

China provides one model of good land management. Through techniques of **sustainable agriculture** which emphasize **organic farming**, China has meet (though not exceeded) the nutritional needs of most of its people. On Chinese farms, **methane digester**s recycle **animal waste**s, by-products, and general refuse; the gas produced from the digesters is in turn used as an energy source. Biological controls are also used to reduce the number of harmful insects and weeds. Crops are selected for their ability to grow in particular locations, and **strip-farming** and **terracing** help conserve the soil. Crops that put certain nutrients in the soil are planted in alternate rows with crops that deplete those nutrients. Forests, important for **watershed** and as a fuel source, are maintained. **Fish farming**, or aquaculture, is widely practiced, and the fish raised on these farms produce about ten times more animal protein than livestock raised on the same amount of land. In China, **agriculture** relies upon human labor rather than on more expensive and environmentally harmful machinery, which has the added advantage of keeping millions of people gainfully employed.

Another important aspect of land management is **biodiversity**. Each organism is specially suited for its **niche**, yet all are interconnected, each depending on others for nutrients, energy, the purification of wastes, and other needs. Plants provide food and oxygen for animals, sustain the hydrocycle, and protect the soil. Animals help pollinate plants and give off the **carbon dioxide** that plants need to generate energy. Microorganisms recycle wastes, which returns nutrients to the system. The activity of many of these organisms is directly useful to humans. Additionally, having a broad range of organisms means a broad source of genetic material from which to create new, as well as better, crops and livestock. However, a reduction in the number of species reduces biological diversity. Hunting can destroy **species**, as can eliminating **habitat**s by cutting down forests, draining **wetlands**, building cities and polluting excessively.

The water portion of the biosphere has two interconnected parts. Freshwater lakes and rivers account for about three percent of the earth's water while the oceans contain the other 97 percent. Oceans are important to the biosphere in a number of ways. They absorb some of the gases in the air, regulating its composition; they influence **climate** all over the earth, preventing drastic weather changes. Additionally, the ocean contains a myriad of plant and animal species, which provide food for humans and other organisms and aid in maintaining their environment.

However, according to many scientists, exploitation of the oceans must be curtailed to ensure that they remain viable. Too often species are harvested until they are destroyed, creating an imbalance in the ecosystem, and environmentalists have argued that fishing quotas that do not allow populations to be depleted faster than they can be replaced should be set and enforced. Rather than harvesting immature fish, the **commercial fishing** industry should release them, thus keeping the species population in equilibrium. Pressure must also be taken off individual species, and interactions in the ocean ecosystem should be examined. A strategy designed to consider these factors would benefit the whole ocean community as well as humans. Pollution of the ocean should also be reduced. Pollution can take the form of **garbage**, sewage, toxic wastes, and oil. In excess, these harm the organisms of the ocean, which in turn harms humans. Disposal of these substances should be controlled through, though not limited to, **sewage treatment**, discharge restrictions, and improved dispersal techniques.

Although freshwater is a renewable resource, care needs to be taken to keep it clean. Wise water management, which includes monitoring water supplies and **water quality**, can ensure that everyone's needs are met. Agriculture and commercial fishing require water, and manufacturing industries use water in many of their processes. Households consume water in cooking, cleaning, and drinking, among other activities. Without water, certain recreations, such as water skiing and swimming, would be impossible to enjoy. **Wildlife** and fish also need water to survive.

Pollutants reduce and damage the freshwater supply. Pollutants include **chemicals**, sewage, toxic waste, hot water, and many other organic and inorganic materials. Waste leaching from **landfill**s contaminates **groundwater**, and surface water is corrupted by wastes dumped into the water, by polluted groundwater flowing into the stream or lake, or by polluted rain. Like oceans, freshwater can break down small amounts of pollutants, but large amounts place great pressure on the system. Disposal of potential pollutants requires monitoring and treatment. A strategy needs to be designed which balances the demands of humans with the needs of the ecosystem, emphasizing conservation and pollution reduction.

As with land and water, the atmosphere has been adversely affected by pollution. Pollution in the air causes such phenomena as **smog, acid rain, atmospheric inversion**, and **ozone layer depletion**. Smog lowers the amount of oxygen in the air, which can cause health problems. Acid rain destroys plants, animals, and freshwater supplies. Atmospheric inversion exists when **air pollution** is unable to escape because a layer of warm air covers a layer of cooler air, trapping it close to the ground. Certain compounds, such as chlorofluoromethanes, thin the ozone layer by combining with **ozone** to split it apart. A thinner ozone layer provides less protection from the sun's **ultraviolet radiation**, which promotes skin **cancer** and reduces the productivity of some crops. Reducing or eliminating harmful **emissions** can also control air pollution.

Sustainable development is one approach to keeping the biosphere healthy. This method attempts to increase local food production without increasing the amount of land taken. It involves nature conservation and **environmental monitoring**, and it advocates encouraging and training local communities to participate in maintaining the environment. The goal is to balance human needs with environmental needs, and proponents of this view maintain that economic growth depends on **renewable resources**, which in turn depends on permanent damage to the environment being kept at a minimum.

The Ecological Society of America published the **Sustainable Biosphere Initiative** (SBI) in the early 1990s. This document was an attempt to define ecological priorities for the twenty-first century, and it is based on the realization that research in applied **ecology** is necessary for better management of the earth's resources and of the systems that support life. The SBI calls for basic ecological research and emphasizes the importance of education and policy and management decisions informed by such research.

The SBI sets out criteria for determining which research projects should be pursued, and it proposes three top research priorities: global change, biodiversity, and sustainable ecological systems. Global change research focuses on the causes and effects of various changes in all aspects of the biosphere (air, water, land). Biodiversity research focuses on both naturally occurring and human-caused changes in species. It also studies the consequences of those changes. Research on sustainable ecological systems exams the pressures placed on the biosphere, methods of correcting the damage and management of the environment to maintain life.

Creating a sustainable biosphere requires a cohesive policy for reducing consumption and seeking nonmaterial means of satisfaction. Many believe that such a cohesive policy would provide a much-needed focus for the many diverse environmental interests currently vying for public support.

[Nikola Vrtis]

FURTHER READING

"Biosphere Reserves." *Futurist* (May-June 1992): 31-32.

Lubchenco, J., et al. "The Sustainable Biosphere Initiative: An Ecological Research Agenda." *Ecology* 72 (1991): 371-412.

Myers, N., ed. *GAIA: An Atlas of Planet Management*. Garden City, NY: Anchor Press/Doubleday, 1984.

Risser, P.G., J. Lubchenco, and S.A. Levin. "Biological Research Priorities—A Sustainable Biosphere." *Bioscience* (October 1991): 625-627.

Sustainable development

Sustainable development is a term first introduced to the international community by ***Our Common Future***, the 1987 report of the World Commission on Environment and Development, which was chartered by the United Nations to examine the planet's critical social and environmental problems and to formulate realistic proposals to solve them in ways that ensure sustained human progress without depleting the resources of **future generations**. This Commission—which is chaired by **Gro Harlem Bruntdland**, Prime Minister of Norway, and is consequently often called the Bruntdland Commission—defined sustainable development as "meeting the needs of the present without compromising the ability of future generations to meet their own needs." The goal of sustainable development, according to the Commission, is to create a new era of economic growth as a way of eliminating poverty and extending to all people the opportunity to fulfill their aspirations for a better life.

Economic growth, in this view, is the only way to bring about a long-range transformation to more advanced and productive societies and to improve the lot of all people. As former President John F. Kennedy said: "A rising tide lifts all boats." But economic growth is not sufficient in itself to meet all essential needs. The Bruntdland Commission pointed out that we must make sure that the poor and powerless will get their fair share of the resources required to sustain that growth. The Commission stated that "an equitable distribution of benefits requires political systems that secure effective citizen participation in decision making and by greater democracy in international decision making."

The concept of "sustainable" growth of any sort is regarded as an oxymoron by some people because the availability of non-renewable resources and the capacity of the **biosphere** to absorb the effects of human activities are clearly limited and must impose limits to growth at some point. Nevertheless, supporters of sustainable development maintain that both technology and social organization can be managed and improved to meet essential needs within those limits.

To clarify this concept, a discussion of what is development and what is meant by "sustainable" is necessary. Development is a process by which something grows, matures, improves, or becomes enhanced or more fruitful. Organisms develop as they progress from a juvenile form to an adult. The plot in a novel develops as it becomes more complex, clearer, or more interesting. Human systems develop as they become more technologically, economically, or socially advanced and productive. In human history, social development usually means an improved standard of living or a more gratifying way of life.

Something is sustainable if it is permanent, enduring, or can be maintained for the long-term. Sustainable development, then, means improvements in human well-being that can be extended or prolonged over many generations rather than just a few years. The hope of sustainable development is that if its benefits are truly enduring, they may be extended to all humans rather than just the members of a privileged group.

Some development projects have been environmental, economic, and social disasters. Large-scale hydropower projects—for instance in the **James Bay** region of Quebec or the Brazilian Amazon—were supposed to be beneficial but displaced indigenous people, destroyed **wildlife**, and poisoned local **ecosystem**s with acids from decaying vegetation and heavy metals from flooded **soil**s released through **leaching**. Similarly, introduction of "miracle" crop varieties in Asia and huge grazing projects in Africa financed by international lending agencies crowded out wildlife, diminished the diversity of traditional crops, and destroyed markets for small-scale farmers.

Other development projects, however, work more closely with both nature and local social systems. Projects such as the Tagua Palm Nut project sponsored by **Conservation International** in South America encourage native people to gather natural products from the forest on a sustainable basis and to turn them into valuable products (in this case "vegetable ivory" buttons) that can be sold for good prices on the world market. Another exemplary local development project is the "microloan" financing pioneered by the *grameen* or village banks of Bangladesh. These loans, generally less than $100, allow poor people who usually would not have access to capital to buy farm tools, a spinning wheel, a three-wheeled pedicab, or some other means of supporting themselves. The banks are not concerned merely with finances, however; they also offer business management techniques, social organization, and education to ensure successful projects and loan repayment.

Still, critics of sustainable development argue that the term is self-contradictory because almost every form of development requires resource consumption. The limits and boundaries imposed by natural systems, they argue, must at some point make further growth unsustainable. Using ever-increasing amounts of goods and services to make human life more comfortable, pleasant, or agreeable must inevitably interfere with the survival of other species and eventually of humans themselves in a world of fixed resources.

Some types of development do not require material consumption, however. As the eminent economist John Stuart Mill wrote in 1857: "It is scarcely necessary to remark that a stationary condition of capital and population implies no stationary state of human improvement. There would be just as much scope as ever for all kinds of mental culture and moral and social progress; as much room for improving the art of living and much more likelihood of its being improved when minds cease to be engrossed by the art of getting on." In the rush to exploit nature and consume resources many have forgotten this sage advice.

Another criticism of sustainable development is that it may be merely a smokescreen to divert attention from the real problem of overconsumption. It tells us that we do not need to accept a lower throughput of material goods or reduce the craving for luxury, convenience, or power. Advocates of development often argue that the cornucopia of technology will provide everything we desire without sacrifice on our part. But the technological fixes, critics warn, are delusions that ignore looming ecological limits.

While it is probably true that traditional patterns of growth that require ever-increasing consumption of resources are unsustainable, development could be possible if it means: (a) finding more efficient and less environmentally stressful ways to provide goods and services; and (b) living with reduced levels of goods and services for those of us who are relatively rich so that more can be made available to the impoverished majority.

Many economists argue that the physical limits to growth are somewhat vague, not because the laws of physics are inaccurate, but because substituting one resource for another in producing goods and services allows a tremendous flexibility in the face of declining abundance of some resources. For example, the extremely rapid adoption of **petroleum** products as sources of energy and raw materials in the early twentieth century is a good case study of how quickly new discoveries and technical progress can change the resource picture.

From this perspective, the decline of known petroleum reserves and the effects of gases from the combustion of petroleum products on possible global warming—while serious problems—are also signals to humans to look for substitutes for these products, to explore for unknown reserves, and to develop more efficient and possibly altogether new ways of performing the tasks for which oil is now used. Teleconferencing, for instance, which allows people at widely distant places to consult without traveling to a common meeting site, is a good example of this principle. It is far more energy-efficient to transmit video and audio information than to move human bodies.

The issues of distributive justice or fairness between "developed" and "developing" societies—concerned with who should bear the burden of sustaining future development and how resources will be shared in development—raise many difficult questions. Similarly, the technical problems of finding new, efficient, non-destructive ways of providing goods and services require entirely new ways of doing things. The range of theoretical understanding, personal and group activity, and policy and politics encompassed by this project is so vast that it might be considered the first time humans have tried to grasp all their activities and the workings of nature in its entirety as one integrated, global system.

The first planet-wide meeting to address these global issues was the **United Nations Conference on the Human Environment** which took place in 1972. It was followed by the **United Nations Earth Summit** held in June, 1992, in Rio de Janeiro, Brazil. The scope of sustainability issues taken up at the Earth Summit is in itself remarkable. Agenda 21, a 900-page report drafted in preparation for the conference, included proposals for allocation of international aid to alleviate poverty and improve **environmental health**. Other recommendations included providing sanitation and clean water to everyone, reducing indoor **air pollution**, meeting basic healthcare needs for all, reducing soil **erosion** and degradation, introducing sustainable farming techniques, providing more resources for **family planning** and education (especially for young women), removing economic distortions and imbalances that damage the **environment**, protecting **habitat** and **biodiversity**, and developing non-carbon energy alternatives.

More heads of state (over one hundred) attended this meeting than any other in world history. Although many of the treaties and conventions passed at the Earth Summit are weaker than most environmentalists would have liked, this meeting is remarkable in the issues it raised and the discussions it initiated. It is regarded by many as a signal event in the history of humanity. And the concept of sustainable development is gaining a stronger following thanks to the conference. Since the Earth Summit—where the United States at first declined to participate in committees or sign several treaties—the country now has a 25-member **President's Council on Sustainable Development**. Perhaps the work begun in Rio de Janeiro will continue to have a lasting effect. *See also* Amazon basin; Greenhouse effect

[*Eugene R. Wahl and E. Shrdlu*]

FURTHER READING

Leonard, H. J., et al. *Environment and the Poor: Development Strategies for a Common Agenda.* New Brunswick: Transaction Books for the Overseas Development Council, 1989.

MacNeill, J., et al. *Beyond Interdependence: The Meshing of the World's Economy and the Earth's Ecology.* New York: Oxford University Press, 1991.

Ramphal, S. *Our Country, The Planet.* Covelo, CA: Island Press, 1992.

World Bank. *World Development Report: Development and the Environment.* New York: Oxford University Press, 1992.

World Commission on Environment and Development. *Our Common Future.* New York: Oxford University Press, 1987.

Sustainable forestry

Sustainability may be defined in terms of sustaining biophysical properties of the forest, in terms of sustaining a flow of goods and services from the forest, or a combination of the two. A combined definition follows: sustainable forests are able to provide goods and services to the present without impairing their capacity to be equally or more useful to **future generations**. The goods and services demanded of the forest include wood of specified quality; **habitat** for **wildlife**, fish, and invertebrates; recreational, aesthetic, and spiritual opportunities; sufficient water of appropriate quality; protection (e.g., against floods and **erosion**); and preservation of natural **ecosystem**s and their processes (i.e. allowing large forested landscapes to be affected only by natural dynamics); and the preservation of **species**.

To provide in perpetuity for future demands, the productivity, diversity, and function of the forest must be maintained and enhanced. A listing of key biophysical properties follows, along with examples of current threats to their maintenance: 1) **Soil** productivity (reduced by erosion and nutrient depletion from overharvesting). 2) **Biomass** (degraded in quantity and quality by overharvesting and destructive logging practices). 3) Climatic stability (possibly threatened by **emission** of **greenhouse gases**). 4) Atmospheric quality (lowered by **ozone** and **sulfur dioxide**). 5) Ground and surface waters (altered by **deforestation** or drainage). 6) Diversity of plants, animals, and ecosystems (reduced by deforestation, fragmentation, and replacement of complex natural forests with even-aged forests harvested at young ages).

Forest sustainability also depends on the maintenance and improvement of socio-economic factors. These include human talent and knowledge; infrastructure (e.g., roads); and political, social, and economic institutions (e.g., marketing systems, stable political systems, international cooperation, and peace). Also essential are technological developments which permit wiser use of the forest and substitute ways to meet human needs. Perhaps the major threat to forest sustainability arises from an ever-increasing population, especially in developing countries, combined with the ever-increasing material demands of the developed nations.

Forests have been managed as a renewable and sustainable resource by stable indigenous tribes for many generations. In recent years some governments have made efforts in this direction as well. Managing any forest for sustainability is a complex process. The spatial scale of sustainability is often global or regional, crossing land ownerships and political boundaries. The time horizons for sustainability exceeds many-fold those used for "long-term" planning by business or government.

Some people have even questioned the feasibility of sustainable forestry. Optimists believe technological innovation and changed value systems will enable us to achieve sustainability. Others feel demand will outstrip supply, leading to spiralling forest degradation, and they have called for conservative and careful management of existing forests.

[*Edward Sucoff*]

FURTHER READING

Kimmins, H. *Balancing Act*. UBI Press, 1992.

World Resources 1992-1993. World Resource Institute. New York: Oxford Press, 1992.

Swamp

See **Mangrove swamp; Wetlands**

Swordfish

The swordfish, *Xiphias gladius*, is classified in a family by itself, the Xiphiidae. This family is part of the Scombroidea, a sub-family of marine fishes that includes tuna and mackerel.

Tuna and mackerel are two of the fastest-swimming creatures in the ocean. Swordfish rival them, as well as mako sharks, with their ability to reach speeds approaching 60 miles per hour (96.5 kilometers per hour) in short bursts. Their streamlined form and powerful build account for their speed, as well as the fact that their torpedo-shaped body is scaleless and smooth, thus decreasing surface drag. Swordfish have a tall, sickle-shaped dorsal fin that cuts through the water like a knife, and their long pectoral fins, set low on their sides, are held tightly against their body while swimming. Swordfish lack pelvic fins, and they have reduced second dorsal and anal fins which are set far back on the body, adding to the streamlining. It has been suggested that their characteristic "sword"—a broad, flat, beak-like projection of the upper jaw—is the ultimate in streamlining. The shape of their bill is one of the characteristics that separates them from the true billfish, which include sailfish and marlin.

Swordfish live in temperate and tropical oceans and are particularly abundant between 30° and 45° north latitude. They are only found in colder waters during the summer months. Although fish in general are cold-blooded vertebrates, swordfish and many of their scombroid relatives are warm-blooded, at least during strenuous activity, when their blood will be several degrees higher than the surrounding waters. Another physiological adaptation is an increased surface area of the gills, which provides for additional oxygen transfer and thus allows swordfish to swim faster and longer than other **species** of comparable size.

Swordfish are valuable for both sport fishing and commercial fishing. The size of swordfish taken commercially is usually under 250 lb (114 kg), but some individuals have been caught that weigh over 1,000 lbs (455 kg). The seasonal migration of this species has meant that winter catches are limited, but long-lining in deep waters off the Atlantic coast of the United States has proven somewhat successful in that season.

Swordfish have only become popular as food over the past 50 years. Their overall commercial importance was reduced in the 1970s, however, when relatively high levels of **mercury** were discovered in their flesh. Because of this discovery, restrictions were placed on their sale in the United States, which had a negative effect on the fishery. Mercury contamination was thought to be solely the result of dramatic increase in industrial **pollution**, but recent studies have shown that high levels of mercury were present in museum specimens collected many years ago. Although still a critical environmental and health concern, industrial sources of mercury contamination have apparently only added to levels from natural sources. *See also* Blue revolution (fish farming); Salmon

[*Eugene C. Beckham*]

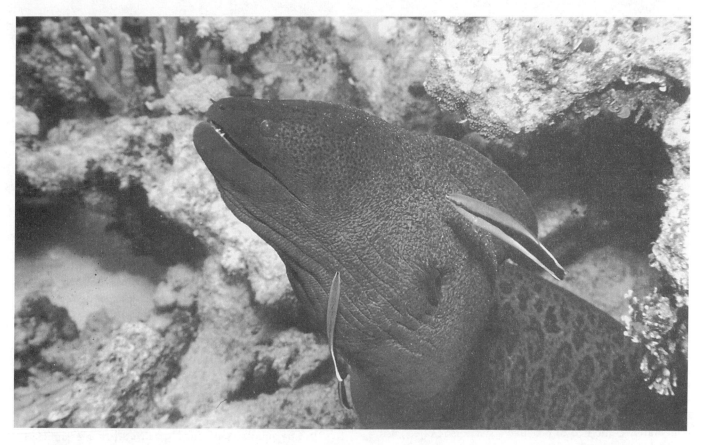

A Javan moray eel with cleaner wrasses on the Great Barrier Reef, Australia. This is an example of a symbiotic relationship.

FURTHER READING

Burton, R., C. Devaney, and T. Long. *The Living Sea: An Illustrated Encyclopedia of Marine Life*. New York: G. P. Putnam's Sons, 1974.

Hoese, H., and R. Moore. *Fishes of the Gulf of Mexico: Texas, Louisiana, and Adjacent Waters*. College Station: Texas A & M University Press, 1977.

McClane, A. *Field Guide to Saltwater Fishes of North America*. New York: Holt, Rinehart, & Winston, 1978.

Nelson, J. *Fishes of the World*. New York: Wiley, 1976.

Wheeler, A. *Fishes of the World: An Illustrated Dictionary*. New York: MacMillan, 1975.

Symbiosis

In the broad sense, symbiosis means simply "living together"—the union of two separately evolved organisms into a single functional unit regardless of the positive or negative influence on either **species**.

Symbiotic relationships fall into three categories. Mutualism describes the condition where both organisms benefit from the relationship, **commensalism** exists when one organism benefits and the other is unaffected, and parasitism describes a situation where one organism benefits while the other suffers. Symbionts may also be classified according to their mode of life. *Endosymbionts* carry out the relationship within the body of one species, the host. *Exosymbionts* are attached to the outside of the host in a variety of ways, or are unattached, seeking contact for specific

purposes or at particular times. Similarly, symbionts may either be host specific, co-evolved to one species in particular, or a generalist, able to make use of many potential partners. In either case, the relationship usually involves co-evolutionary levels of integration, where partners influence each other's fitness.

Symbiosis generally requires either behavioral or morphological **adaptation**. Morphological adaptation ranges from the development of special organs for attachment, color patterns that signal partners to chemical cues, and intercellular alterations to accommodate partners. Behavioral adaptations include a range of body postures and displays that indicate readiness to accommodate symbionts.

Symbiosis is fundamental to life. The various forms of relationships between species—principally symbiosis, **competition**, and predation—create the structure of **ecosystems** and produce co-evolutionary phenomena which shape species and communities. At the most fundamental level, the transition from non-nucleated prokaryotic cells to eukaryotic cells, which is the evolutionary link to multicellular organisms, is generally believed to be by symbiosis. In higher organisms, 90 percent of land plants use some sort of association between roots and mycorrhizal **fungi** to provide **nutrient** uptake from **soil**. Almost 6,000 species of fungi and about 300,000 land plants can form mycorrhizal associations. In the next step of most terrestrial **food chain** almost all herbivorous species of insects and mammals use symbionts in the gut to digest cellulose in plant cell walls and allow nutrient assimilation. Thus the energetics of life on earth, and certainly that of higher life forms, are, to a large degree, dependent on symbiotic relationships. *See also* Mycorrhiza; Parasites

[*David A. Duffus*]

FURTHER READING

Margulis, L., and R. Fester, eds. *Symbiosis As a Source of Evolutionary Innovation.* Cambridge, MA: MIT Press, 1991.

Synergism

Synergism is a term used by toxicologists to describe the phenomenon in which a combination of **chemicals** has a toxic effect greater than the sum of its parts.

Malathion and Delnav are two **organophosphate** insecticides that were tested separately for the number of fish deaths they would cause at certain concentrations. When the two chemicals were combined, however, their toxicity was significantly greater than the individual tests would have led scientists to expect. The toxicity of the mixture, in such cases, is greater than the total toxicity of the individual chemicals.

In the manufacture of **pesticide**s, toxic chemicals are deliberately combined to produce a synergistic effect, using an additive known as a "potentiator" or "synergist" to enhance the action of the basic active ingredient. *Piperonyl butoxide,* for example, is added to the insecticide *rotenone* to promote synergistic effects.

But the study of unintended synergistic effects is still in its early stages, and the majority of documented synergistic effects deal with toxicity to insects and fish. Laboratory studies on the effects of **copper** and **cadmium** on fish have established that synergistic interactions between multiple pollutants can have unanticipated effects. Both copper and cadmium are frequently released into the **environment** from a number of sources, without any precautions taken against possible synergistic impacts. Scientists speculate that there may be many similar occurrences of unpredicted and currently unknown synergistic toxicities operating in the environment.

Synergism has been cited as a reason to make environmental standards, such as the standards for **water quality,** more stringent. Current **water quality standards** for metals and organic compounds are derived from toxicological research on their individual effects on aquatic life. But pollutants discharged from a factory could meet all water quality standards and still harm aquatic life or humans because of synergistic interactions between compounds present in the **discharge** or in the receiving body of water. Many scientists have expressed reservations about current standards for individual chemicals and concern about the possible effects of synergism on the environment. But synergistic effects are difficult to isolate and prove under field conditions.

[*Usha Vedagiri*]

FURTHER READING

Connell, D. W., and G. J. Miller. *Chemistry and Ecotoxicology of Pollution.* New York: Wiley, 1984.

Rand, G. M., and S. R. Petrocelli. *Fundamentals of Aquatic Toxicology.* Bristol, PA: Hemisphere Publishing Corporation, 1985.

Synthetic fuels

Synthetic fuels are gaseous and liquid fuels produced synthetically, primarily from **coal** and **oil shale**. They are commonly referred to as *synfuels*.

The general principle behind coal-based synfuels is that coal can be converted to gaseous or liquid forms that are more easily transported and that burn more cleanly than coal itself. In either case, **hydrogen** is added to coal, converting some of the **carbon** it contains into **ozone**-depleting **hydrocarbons**. *Coal liquefaction* involves the conversion of solid coal to a petroleum-like liquid. The technology needed for this process is well known and has been used in special circumstances since the 1920s. During World War II, the Germans used this technology to produce gasoline from coal. In the Bergius process used in Germany, coal is reacted with hydrogen gas at high temperatures (about 890°F/475°C) and pressures (200 atmospheres). The product of this reaction is a mixture of liquid hydrocarbons that can be fractionated as is done with natural **petroleum**.

The processes of **coal gasification** are similar to those used for liquefaction. In one method, coal is first converted to coke (nearly pure carbon), which is then reacted with oxygen and steam. The products of this reaction are **carbon monoxide** and hydrogen, both combustible gases. The heat content of this gas is not high enough to justify transporting it great distances through pipelines, and it is used, therefore, only by industries that actually produce it.

A second type of gas produced from coal, synthetic natural gas (SNG), is chemically similar to natural gas. It has a relatively high heat content and can be economically transmitted through pipelines from source to use-site.

For all their appeal, liquid and gaseous coal products have many serious disadvantages. For one thing, they involve the conversion of an already valuable resource, coal, into new fuels with 30 to 40 percent less fuel content. Such a conversion can be justified only on environmental grounds or on the basis of other economic criteria.

In addition, coal liquefaction and gasification are water-intensive processes. In areas where they can be most logically carried out, such as the western states, sufficient supplies of water are often not available.

Another approach to the production of synfuels involves the use of oil shale or tar sands. These two materials are naturally occurring substances that contain petroleum-like oils trapped within a rocky (oil shale) or sandy (tar sand) base. The oils can be extracted by crushing and heating the raw material. Refining the oil obtained in this way results in the production of **gasoline**, kerosene, and other fractions similar to those collected from natural **petroleum**.

Yet a fifth form of synfuel is that obtained from **biomass**. For example, human and animal wastes can be converted into **methane** gas by the action of anaerobic bacteria in a digester. In some parts of the world, this technology is well advanced and widely used. China, India, and Korea all have tens of thousands of small digesters for use on farms and in private homes.

During the 1970s, the United States government encouraged the development of all five synfuel technologies. In 1980, the United States Congress created the United States Synthetic Fuels Corporation to distribute and manage $88 billion in grants to promote the development of synfuel technologies. The timing of this action could not have been worse, however. Within two years, the administration of President Ronald Reagan decided to place more emphasis on traditional fuels by deregulating the price of oil and natural gas and by extending tax breaks to oil companies. It also withdrew support from research on synfuels.

At the same time, worldwide prices for all **fossil fuels** dropped dramatically. There seemed to be no indication that synfuels would compete economically with fossil fuels in the foreseeable future. Unable to deal with all these setbacks, the United States Synthetic Fuels Corporation went out of business in 1992. *See also* Alternative fuels

[*David E. Newton*]

FURTHER READING

Douglas, J. "Quickening the Pace in Clean Coal Technology." *EPRI Journal* (January-February 1989): 4-15.

McGraw-Hill Encyclopedia of Science & Technology. 7th ed. New York: McGraw-Hill, 1992.

Moore, T. "How Advanced Options Stack Up." *EPRI Journal* (July-August 1987): 4-13.

Peterson, I. "Squeezing Oil Out of Stone." *Science News* 124 (3 December 1983): 362-364.

Shepard, M. "Coal Technologies for a New Age." *EPRI Journal* (January-February 1988): 5-17.

Systemic

Refers to a general condition of process or system, rather than a condition of one of the component pieces. For example, when a plant wilts in response to **drought**, the entire organism is responding to the effect of loss. Communities of plants and animals and their abiotic **environment** comprise an **ecosystem**. Whole ecosystems may respond to an event, such as changes in local **climate**, by undergoing a systemic change—for example, the composition and abundance of **species** may be altered, and the functional ecological processes of those organisms would be rearranged.

T

Taiga

Taiga is a generic term for a type of conifer-dominated boreal forest found in northern environments. The word was first used to describe dense forests of spruce (especially *Picea abies*) in northern Russia, and it has been extended to refer to boreal forests of similar structure in North America but dominated by other conifer **species** (especially *Picea mariana* and *Picea glauca*). Broad-leafed tree species are uncommon in taiga, although species of poplar (*Populus* spp.) and birch (*Betula* spp.) are present. Taiga environments are characterized by cool and short growing seasons. Plant roots can only exploit a superficial layer of seasonally thawed ground, the active layer, situated above permanently frozen substrate, or **permafrost**.

White spruce-willow taiga in Alaska.

Tailings

Tailings are produced when metallic ores are ground to a fine powder to free the metal-bearing mineral. Its maximum particle size of about two millimeters is small enough to retain water and support plant growth. Fine dust is one potential hazard, especially if trapped in the lungs of miners. The greatest revegetation difficulties come from metals in lethal concentrations and deficiencies of critical **nutrient**s, especially **nitrogen** and **phosphorus**. Some old tailings have remained barren for many years, with consequent high **erosion** rates. However, some metalophytes are able to survive on these wastes. Curiously, some plants have populations which can also survive on these tailings.

Tailings pond

Refers to the water stored on-site to wash ore and receive the waste **tailings** as a residue. This provides both a water supply and a **sediment** trap. Two serious **environment**al problems ensue. The water leaches out metals and other dangerous elements which were formerly trapped underground in a reducing (non-oxidizing) environment; acidic wastes amplify the **leaching**. And though usually stable, some **dams** have burst during flood stages, unleashing a torrent of toxic materials into the lower aquatic **ecosystem**s and posing a combined hazard of mudflow and **flooding**.

Takings

The term "takings" refers to the practice of taking, or otherwise restricting the use of, private property through the governmental power of eminent domain, environmental regulation, or other restrictions. The power of eminent domain—and the property owner's right to compensation—is stated in the Bill of Rights (Fifth Amendment to the U.S. Constitution): "nor shall private property be taken for public use, without just compensation." Likewise, the Fourteenth Amendment stipulates that no state may "deprive any person of life, liberty, or property, without due process of law; nor deny to any person within its jurisdiction the equal protection of the laws."

Critics of environmental regulation contend that government cannot constitutionally interfere with a property owner's freedom to do as he or she wishes with his or her own property, without compensating the owner. For example, a farmer who wishes to extend or improve his land by draining a swamp or other wetland cannot be forbidden to do so without adequate compensation. A rancher who is forbidden by law to shoot or trap wolves that threaten his cattle can claim compensation for livestock losses due to wolf predation.

To "take" or otherwise regulate or restrict the use of their property without full and fair compensation would constitute a violation of their constitutionally guaranteed rights under the Fifth and Fourteenth Amendments.

Many environmentalists maintain that the high cost of such compensation would mean the effective end of many environmental regulations regarding **wetlands**, woodlands, and other habitats on private property. They contend that the Constitution does not construe the concept of "takings" as broadly as their critics do. There have long been restrictions on what one may do to or with his or her property. There are, for example, restrictions on erecting billboards on private property along public highways. Automobile salvage yards can be required to erect walls to shut out the unsightly view. In neither case is the owner to be compensated for loss, cost, or inconvenience. In these instances the public interest in avoiding eyesores overrides the private interests of the property owners. So too, environmentalists contend, does the public interest in a clean, safe and sustainable natural environment empower the federal, state or local government to enact and enforce laws restricting what property owners may do with or to **wildlife** and the **habitat** that sustains them.

The legal and political battles over "takings" continues to be waged in the courts of law and public opinion. Some critics of environmental protection (most notably, libertarians associated with the Cato Institute) contend that the Constitution does not go far enough in guaranteeing the protection of private property rights and ought therefore to be further amended. Some environmentalists claim that the Constitution ought, on the contrary, to be amended to extend protection to animals, ecosystems, and future generations. It seems plausible to predict that these battles will be waged well into the twenty-first century.

[*Terence Ball*]

FURTHER READING

Epstein, R.A. *Takings: Private Property and the Power of Eminent Domain.* Cambridge, MA: Harvard University Press, 1985.

Tall stacks

The waste gases that escape from factories or **power plants** run on **fossil fuels** typically contain a variety of pollutants including **carbon monoxide**, **particulate**s, and **nitrogen oxides**, and sulfur. The first of these pollutants, carbon monoxide, tends to dispense rapidly once it is released to the **atmosphere** and seldom poses a serious threat to human health or the **environment**. The same cannot be said of the last three categories of pollutants, all of which pose a threat to the well-being of plants, humans, and other animals.

During the 1960s, humans became increasingly aware of the range of hazards, posed by pollutants escaping from smokestacks. One of the most common events of the time was for residents in the area immediately adjacent to a factory or plant to find their homes and cars covered with fine dust from time to time. They soon learned that the dust was **fly ash** released from the nearby smokestacks. Particulates (fine

particles of unburned **carbon**) also tend to settle out fairly rapidly and cover objects with a fine black powder.

It was clear that visible pollutants, such as fly ash and particulates, offered a hint that invisible pollutants, such as oxides of **nitrogen** and sulfur, were also accumulating in areas close to factories and power plants. As the health hazards of these pollutants became better known, efforts to bring them under control increased.

Certain technical methods of **air pollution control—electrostatic precipitation** and scrubbing, for example—were reasonably well known. However, many industries and utilities preferred not to make the significant financial investment needed to install these technologies. Instead, they proposed a simpler and less expensive solution: the construction of taller smokestacks.

The argument was that, with taller smokestacks, pollutants would be carried higher into the atmosphere. They would then have more time and space to disperse. Residents close to the plants and factories would be spared the fallout from the smokestacks. The "tall stack" solution met the requirements of the 1970 **Clean Air Act** as a "last-ditch alternative" to gas-cleaning technologies.

As a result, companies began building taller and taller smokestacks. The average stack height increased from about 200 feet (61 meters) in 1956 to over 500 feet (152 meters) in 1978. The tallest stack in the United States in 1956 was under 600 feet (182 meters) tall, but a decade later, some stacks were more than 1,000 feet (305 meters) high.

At first, this effort appeared to be a satisfactory way of dealing with air pollutants. The concentration of particulates and oxides of nitrogen and sulfur close to plants did, indeed, decrease after the installation of tall stacks.

But new problems soon began to appear, the most serious of which was acid deposition. The longer oxides of sulfur and nitrogen remain in the air, the more likely they are to be oxidized to other forms, sulfur trioxide and nitrogen dioxide. These oxides, in turn, have the tendency to react with water droplets in the atmosphere forming sulfuric and nitric acids, respectively. Eventually these acids fall back to earth as rain, snow, or some other form of precipitation. When they reach the ground, they then have the potential to damage plants, buildings, bridges, and other objects.

The mechanism by which stack gases are transported in the atmosphere is still not completely understood. Yet it is now clear that when they are emitted high enough into the atmosphere, they can be carried hundreds or thousands of miles away by prevailing winds. The very method that reduces the threat of air pollutants for communities near a factory or power plant, therefore, also increases the risk for communities farther away. *See also* Acid rain; Air quality; Criteria pollutant; Emission; Scrubbers; Smoke; Sulfur dioxide

[*David E. Newton*]

FURTHER READING

Harris, J. "How to Sell Smoke." *Forbes* 145 (11 June 1990): 204-5.

"New Clues to What An Incinerator Spews." *Science News* 140 (21 September 1991): 189.

"The Dirtiest Half-Dozen." *Time* 139 (8 June 1992): 31.

Target species

The object of a hunting, fishing, or collecting exercise; or an extermination effort aimed at destroying a particular organism. This term is often used to describe the intended victim of an application of **pesticide** or **herbicide**. Unfortunately, many non-target species can be affected by so-called targeted activities. For example, Pacific net fishermen target the yellowfin tuna, but also snare and kill non-target species such as **dolphins**. Pesticides applied to crops to kill insects (the target species), can enter the **food chain/web**, become biologically magnified, and kill non-target species such as fish-eating birds or birds of prey. *See also* Biomagnification

Taylor Grazing Act (1934)

This act established federal management policy on public grazing lands, the last major category of **public land**s to be actively managed by the government. The delay in its passage was due to a lack of interest (the lands were sometimes referred to as "the lands no one wanted") and due to competition between the Agriculture Department and the Interior Department over which department would administer the new program.

The purpose of the Taylor Grazing Act was to "stop injury to the public grazing lands ... to provide for their orderly use, improvement and development ... [and] to stabilize the livestock industry dependent on the public range...." To achieve these purposes, the Secretary of the Interior was authorized to establish grazing districts on the public domain lands. The lands within these established districts were to be classified for their potential use, with agricultural lands to remain open for homesteading. In 1934 and 1935, President Franklin D. Roosevelt issued Executive Orders that withdrew all remaining public lands for such classification, an action that essentially closed the public domain. The Secretary was authorized to develop any regulations necessary to administer these grazing districts, including the granting of leases for up to ten years, the charging of fees, the undertaking of range improvement projects, and the establishing of cooperative agreements with grazing land holders in the area.

Another important feature of the law called upon the Secretary of the Interior to cooperate with "local associations of stockmen" in the administration of the grazing districts, referred to by supporters of the law as "democracy on the range" or "home rule on the range." This was formalized in the creation of local advisory boards. The law created a Division of Grazing (renamed the Grazing Service in 1939) to administer the law, but for a number of reasons, the agency was ineffective. It became quite dependent on the local advisory boards and was often cited as an example of an agency captured by the interests it was supposed to be controlling. In 1946, the agency merged with the General Land Office to create the **Bureau of Land Management**.

Also included in the bill was the phrase "pending final disposal," which implied that these grazing lands would not necessarily be retained in federal ownership. This phrase was included because many thought the lands would eventually be transferred to the states or the private sector and because it lessened opposition to the law. The uncertainty introduced by this phrase made management of the grazing lands more difficult, and it was not eliminated until passage of the **Federal Land Policy and Management Act** in 1976.

The grazing fees charged to ranchers were initiated at a low level, based on a cost-of-administration approach rather than a market level approach. This has led to lower grazing fees on public lands than on private lands. Typically, three-fourths of the fees go to the local advisory boards and are used for range improvement projects.

[*Christopher McGrory Klyza*]

FURTHER READING

Dana, S. T., and S. K. Fairfax. *Forest and Range Policy*. 2nd ed. New York: McGraw-Hill, 1980.

Foss, P. O. *Politics and Grass*. Seattle: University of Washington Press, 1960.

Peffer, E. L. *The Closing of the Public Domain: Disposal and Reservation Policies, 1900-1950*. Stanford: Stanford University Press, 1951.

Technological risk assessment
See **Risk assessment**

Tellico Dam

In an effort to put people back to work during the Great Depression, several public works and **conservation** programs were set in motion. One of these, the **Tennessee Valley Authority** (TVA), was established in 1933 to protect the Tennessee River basin, its water, **soil**, forests, and **wildlife**. TVA initiated many projects to meet these agency goals, but also to provide employment to this impoverished area and to slow the emigration of the region's youth. Many of the projects completed and operated by TVA were **dams** and **reservoir**s along the Tennessee River and its tributaries. In 1936 one such project site was identified on the lower end of the Little Tennessee River. This proposal for Tellico Dam was reviewed, but it was abandoned because the cost was too high and the returns too low. The project was reconsidered in 1942, and plans were drawn up for its construction; however, World War II halted its development.

Two decades passed before the Tellico Dam project became active again. By this time, there was some opposition to the dam from local citizens, as well as from the Tennessee State Planning Commission. Opposition grew through the mid-1960s and congressional hearings were held to study the economic and environmental factors of this project. Supreme Court Justice William O. Douglas even visited the site to lend his support to the Eastern Band of the Cherokee Indian Nation, whose land would be inundated by Tellico's reservoir. Congress, however, approved the project in 1966 and authorized funds to begin construction the following year.

After construction started, opponents of Tellico Dam requested that TVA prepare an **Environmental Impact Statement** (EIS) to be in compliance with the **National Environmental Policy Act** of 1969. TVA refused because Tellico Dam was already authorized and under construction before the Act was passed. Local farmers and landowners, whose land would be affected by the reservoir, joined forces with conservation groups in 1971 and filed suit against TVA to halt the project because there was no impact statement. The court issued an injunction, and construction of Tellico Dam was halted until the EIS was submitted. TVA complied with the order and submitted the final EIS in 1973. That same year the **Endangered Species Act** was signed into law, and two ichthyologists from the University of Tennessee made a startling discovery in a group of fishes they collected from the Little Tennessee River.

They discovered a new **species** of fish, the **snail darter**, later scientifically described and named _Percina tanasi_. Its scientific name honors the ancient Cherokee village of Tanasi, a site that was threatened by Tellico Dam. The state of Tennessee also takes its name from this ancient village. The snail darter's common name refers to the small mollusks that comprise the bulk of its diet. In January 1975 the U. S. **Fish and Wildlife Service** was petitioned to list this new species as endangered. Foreseeing a potential problem, TVA transplanted snail darters into the nearby Hiwassee River without consulting with the Fish and Wildlife Service or the appropriate state agencies. Two more transplants of specimens in 1975 and 1976 brought the number of snail darters in the Hiwassee to over 700. Meanwhile, in October 1975, the snail darter was placed on the federal **endangered species** list, and the stretch of the Little Tennessee River above Tellico Dam was listed as **critical habitat**.

TVA worked feverishly to complete the project, in obvious violation of the Endangered Species Act, and also prepared for the ensuing court battles. A suit was filed for a permanent injunction on the project, but this was denied. An appeal was immediately made to the U. S. Court of Appeals, which overturned the decision and issued the injunction. TVA then appealed this decision to the Supreme Court, which, to the surprise of many, upheld the Court of Appeals ruling, but with a loophole. The Supreme Court left an opening for the U. S. Congress to come to the aid of Tellico Dam. In 1979 an amendment was attached to energy legislation to exempt Tellico Dam from all federal laws, including the Endangered Species Act. President Carter reluctantly, because of the amendment, signed the bill. In January 1980 the gates closed on Tellico Dam, **flooding** over 17,000 acres (6,885 ha) of valuable agricultural land, the homes of displaced landowners, the Cherokee's ancestral burial grounds at Tanasi, and the riverine **habitat** for the Little Tennessee River's snail darters.

Fortunately, Tellico Dam did not cause the **extinction** of the snail darter. During the 1980s, snail darter populations were found in several other rivers in Tennessee, Georgia, and Alabama, and the transplanted population in the Hiwassee River continues to thrive.

[_Eugene C. Beckham_]

FURTHER READING

Ono, R., J. Williams, and A. Wagner. _Vanishing Fishes of North America._ Washington, DC: Stone Wall Press, 1983.

Wheeler, W. B. _TVA and the Tellico Dam: 1936-1979: A Bureaucratic Crisis in Post-Industrial America._ Knoxville, TN: University of Tennessee Press, 1986.

Temperate rain forest

A temperate rain forest is an evergreen, broad-leaved or **coniferous forest** which generally occurs in a coastal **climate** with cool to warm summers, mild winters, and year-round moisture abundance, often as fog. Broad-leaved temperate forests are found in western Tasmania, southeastern Australia, New Zealand, Chile, southeastern China, southern Japan, and elsewhere. They often have close evolutionary ties to tropical and subtropical forests. Temperate conifer rain forests are more cold tolerant than broad-leaved rain forests and are rich in mosses while lacking tree ferns and vines. The original range of the temperate conifer rain forest included portions of Great Britain, Ireland, Norway and the Pacific Coast of North America. The Pacific Northwest (PNW) rain forest extends from Northern California to the Gulf of Alaska and is the most extensive temperate rain forest in the world. The eastern boundary of the PNW forest is sometimes set at the crest of the most western mountain range and sometimes extended further east to include all areas in the maritime climatic zone which have mild winters and only moderately dry summers. These forests are dominated by Douglas fir (_Pseudotsuga menziesii_), western hemlock (_Tsuga heterophylla_), sitka spruce (_Picea sitchensis_), western red cedar (_Thuja plicata_), coastal **redwoods** (_Sequoia sempervirens_), and associated hardwoods and conifers. In the absence of harvesting these forests are regenerated by small wind storms and very infrequent catastrophic disturbances.

The PNW forests are noteworthy in many ways. Of all the world's forests, they have the tallest trees, at 367 feet (112 m), and areas with the highest **biomass** (4,521 Mt per/ha). On better sites the dominant species typically live 400 to 1,250 years or more and reach 3-13 feet (1-4 m) in diameter and 164-328 feet (50-100 m) in height, depending on site and **species**.

The natural temperate rain forest is generally less biodiverse than its tropical counterpart, but still contains a rich **flora** and **fauna**, including several species that are unique to its **ecosystem**. Preservation of temperate rain forests is a global **conservation** issue. Humans have virtually eliminated them from Europe and left only isolated remnants in Asia, New Zealand, and Australia. In North America, sizeable areas of natural rain forest still exists, but those not specifically reserved are predicted to be harvested within 25 to 50 years.

The same pressures that previously converted most of the natural temperate rain forests to plantations and other **land use**s still threaten the remaining natural forests. There is the desire to harvest the massive trees and huge timber volumes before they are lost to insects or wind blow. There is also the desire to replace slow-growing natural forests with younger forests of fast-growing species. Those who favor preservation cite the connection between intact rain forests and high **salmon**/trout production. They note that the replacement forests, being simpler in structure and species composition, cannot offer the same biological diversity and ecosystem functioning. Also extolled are the aesthetic, spiritual, and scientific benefits inherent in a naturally functioning ecosystem containing ancient massive trees. *See also* Biodiversity; Clear-cutting; Deciduous forest; Deforestation; Forest Service; Tropical rain forest

[*Edward Sucoff and Klaus Puettmann*]

FURTHER READING

Adam, P. *Australian Rainforests*. Oxford: Clarendon Press, 1992.

Franklin, J. F. "Pacific Northwest Forests." In *North American Terrestrial Vegetation*, edited by M. G. Barbour and W. D. Billings. Cambridge: Cambridge University Press, 1988.

Tennessee Valley Authority

The idea for the Tennessee Valley Authority (TVA) emerged with the election of Franklin D. Roosevelt as President of the United States, and it became one of the major symbols of his "New Deal" policies designed to rescue the country from the social and economic problems of the Depression of the 1930s. TVA activities have included improved navigation, flood control, production of electricity (and its distribution to small towns and rural areas), **fertilizer** production, **soil** conservation and stabilization, reforestation, improved transportation facilities, and recreational sites.

The TVA was established when Roosevelt signed the Implementing Act in May of 1933. Within a few months of its passage, the Norris Dam and the town of Norris, Tennessee, were under construction, and the controversy began. Early opponents labeled it "socialistic" and un-American, contrary to the American ideal of private enterprise. The most enduring criticism has been that TVA is too single-minded in its emphasis on power production, especially after hydro-capacity was exhausted and the agency turned first to **coal** and then to **nuclear power** to fuel its **power plants**. TVA has most recently been criticized for being too concerned about profit-making and too little concerned about a project's environmental impacts, such as **air pollution** created by generating plants and effects on **endangered species**.

The Tennessee Valley Authority has, however, effected change in the intended region. Nearly all of the region's farms now have electricity, for example, compared to only 3 percent in 1933, and the area has been growing economically. It is now closer to the nation's norms for employment, income, purchasing power, and quality of life as measured by jobs, electrification, and recreational facilities. *See also* Dams; Deforestation; Energy and the environment; Environmental economics; Flooding

[*Gerald R. Young*]

FURTHER READING

Creese, W. L. *TVA's Public Planning: The Vision, The Reality*. Knoxville: University of Tennessee Press, 1990.

Hargrove, E. C., and P. K. Conkin, eds. *TVA: Fifty Years of Grass-Roots Bureaucracy*. Urbana: University of Illinois Press, 1983.

Neuse, S. M. "TVA at Age Fifty—Reflections and Retrospect." *Public Administration Review* 43 (November-December 1983): 491-9.

Nurick, A. J. *Participation in Organizational Change: The TVA Experiment*. New York: Praeger Publishers, 1985.

Teratogen

An environmental agent that can cause abnormalities in a developing organism resulting in either fetal death or congenital abnormality. The human fetus is separated from the mother by the placental barrier, but the barrier is imperfect and permits a number of chemical and infectious agents to pass to the fetus. Well known teratogens include (but are not limited to) alcohol, excess vitamin A and retinoic acid, the rubella **virus** and high levels of **ionizing radiation**. Perhaps the best known teratogenic agent is the drug thalidomide which induced severe limb abnormalities known as phocomelia, in children whose mothers took the drug. *See also* Birth defects; Environmental health; Mutagen

Terracing

A procedure to reduce the speed at which water is removed from the land. Water is directed to follow the gentler slopes of the terrace rather than the steeper natural slopes. Terracing is usually recommended only for intensively used, eroding cropland in areas of high-intensity rainfall. Terraces are costly to construct and require annual maintenance, but they are feasible where arable land is in short supply or where valuable crops can be grown. In order to become self-sufficient in food production, ancient civilizations in Peru often constructed terraces in very steep, mountainous areas. Today, in Nepal, people living in the foothills of the Himalayas use terraces in order to have enough land available for food production.

Territoriality

The attempt by an individual organism or group of organisms to control a specified area. The area or territory, once controlled, is usually bounded by some kind of marker (such as a scent or a fence). Control of territory usually means defense of that territory, primarily against other members of the same **species**. This defense, which may or may not be aggressive, typically involves threats, displays of superior features (e.g. size, color), or displays of fighting equipment (e.g. teeth, claws, antlers). Actual physical combat is relatively rare. A songbird establishes its territory by vigorous singing and will chase intruders away during the mating and nesting

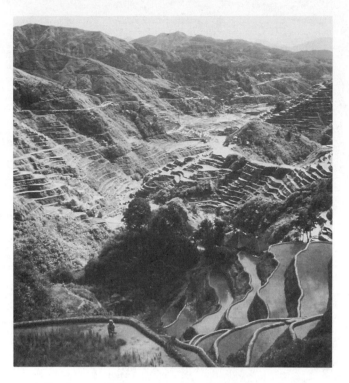

The famous Ifugao rice terraces 200 miles north of Manila, Philippines. These terraces cover about 100 square miles and rise to an altitude of 7,000 feet.

season. A leopard (*Panthera pardus*) marks the boundaries of its territory with urine and will defend this area from other leopards of the same sex. Territoriality is found in many organisms, probably including humans, and it serves several purposes. It may provide a good nesting or breeding site and a sufficient feeding or hunting area to support offspring. It may also protect a female from males other than her mate during the mating season.

Tertiary sewage treatment

See **Sewage treatment**

Tetraethyl lead

Tetraethyl **lead** is an organometallic compound with the chemical formula $(C_2H_5)_4Pb$. In 1922, automotive engineers found that the addition of a small amount of this compound to **gasoline** improves engine performance and reduces knocking. Knocking is a physical phenomenon that results when low-octane gasoline is burned in an internal **combustion** engine. Until 1975, tetraethyl lead was the most common additive used to reduce knocking in motor fuels. This additive presents an environmental hazard, however, since lead is expelled into the **environment** during operation of **auto-**

mobile engines using leaded fuels. Given the growing concern about the health effects of lead, the compound has now been banned for use in gasolines in the United States. *See also* Air pollution; Air pollution index; Emission; Gasohol

Thermal plume

Water used for cooling by **power plants** and factories is commonly returned to its original source at a temperature greater than its original temperature. This heated warm water leaves an outlet pipe in a stream-like flow known as a *thermal plume*. The water within the plume is significantly warmer than is the water immediately adjacent to it. Thermal plumes are environmentally important because the introduction of heated water into lakes or slow-moving rivers can have adverse effects on aquatic life. Warmer temperatures decrease the solubility of oxygen in water, thus lowering the amount of **dissolved oxygen** available to aquatic organisms. Warmer water also causes an increase in the **respiration** rates of these organisms, and they deplete the already-reduced supply of oxygen more quickly. Warmer water also makes aquatic organisms more susceptible to diseases, **parasites**, and **toxic substance**s. *See also* Thermal pollution

Thermal pollution

The **combustion** of **fossil fuels** always produces heat, sometimes as a primary, desired product, and sometimes as a secondary, less desired by-product. For example, families burn **coal**, oil, **natural gas**, or some other fuel to heat their homes. In such cases, the production of heat is the object of burning a fuel. Heat is also produced when fossil fuels are burned to generate electricity. In this case, heat is a by-product, not the main reason that fuels are burned.

Heat is produced in a number of other common processes. For example, electricity is also generated in **nuclear power** plants, where no combustion occurs. The decay of organic matter in **landfill**s also releases heat to the **atmosphere**.

It is clear, therefore, that a vast array of human activities result in the release of heat to the **environment**. As those activities increase in number and extent, so does the amount of heat released. In many cases, heat added to the environment begins to cause problems for plants, humans, or other animals. This effect is then known as *thermal pollution*.

One example of thermal pollution is the development of **urban heat island**s. An urban heat island consists of a dome of warm air over an urban area caused by the release of heat in the region. Since more human activity occurs in an urban area than in the surrounding rural areas, the atmosphere over the urban area becomes warmer than it is over the rural areas.

It is not uncommon for urban heat islands to produce measurable **climate** changes. For example, the levels of pollutants trapped in an urban heat island can reach 5 to 25 percent greater than the levels over rural areas. Fog and clouds may reach twice the level of comparable rural areas, wind speeds may be reduced by up to 30 percent, and temperatures may be 32.9°-35.6°F (0.5°-2°C) higher than in surrounding rural areas. Such differences may cause both personal discomfort and, in some cases, actual health problems for those living within an urban heat island.

The term thermal pollution has traditionally been used more often to refer to the heating of lakes, river, streams, and other bodies of water, usually by electric power generating plants or by factories. For example, a one **megawatt** nuclear **power plant** may require 1.3 billion gallons (five million m³) of cooling water each day. The water used in such a plant has its temperature increased by about 63°F (17°C) during the cooling process. For this reason, such plants are usually built very close to an abundant water supply such as a lake, a large river, or the ocean.

During its operation, the plant takes in cool water from its source, uses it to cool its operations, and then returns the water to its original source. The water is usually recycled through large cooling towers before being returned to the source, but its temperature is still likely to be significantly higher than it was originally. In many cases, an increase of only a degree or two may be "significantly higher" for organisms living in the water.

When heated water is released from a plant or factory, it does not readily mix with the cooler water around it. Instead, it forms a stream-like mass known as a **thermal plume** that spreads out from the outflow pipes. It is in this thermal plume that the most severe effects of thermal **pollution** are likely to occur. Only over an extended period of time does the plume gradually mix with surrounding water, producing a mass of homogenous temperature.

Heating the water in a lake or river can have both beneficial and harmful effects. Every **species** of plant and animal has a certain range that is best for its survival. Raising the temperature of water may cause the death of some organisms, but may improve the environment of other species. Pike, perch, walleye, and small mouth bass, for example, survive best in water with a temperature of about 84°F (29°C), while catfish, gar, shad, and other types of bass prefer water that is about 10°F (-12°C) warmer.

Spawning and egg development are also very sensitive to water temperature. Lake trout, walleye, Atlantic **salmon**, and northern pike require relatively low temperatures (about 48°F/9°C), while the eggs of perch and small mouth bass require a much higher temperature, around 68°F (20°C).

Clearly, changes in water temperature produced by a nuclear power plant, for example, is likely to change the mix of organisms in a waterway.

Of course, large increases in temperature can have disastrous effects on an aquatic environment. Few organisms could survive an accident in which large amounts of very warm water were suddenly dumped into a lake or river. This effect can be observed especially when a power plant first begins operation, when it shuts down for repairs, and when it restarts once more. In each case, a sudden change in water temperature can cause the death of many individuals and lead to a change in the make-up of an aquatic community. Sudden temperature changes of this kind produce an effect known as thermal shock. To avoid the worst effects of thermal shock, power plants often close down or re-start slowly, reducing or increasing temperature in a waterway gradually rather than all at once.

One inevitable result of thermal pollution is a reduction in the amount **dissolved oxygen** in water. The amount of any gas that can be dissolved in water varies inversely with the temperature. As water is warmed, therefore, it is capable of dissolving less and less oxygen. Organisms that need oxygen to survive will, in such cases, be less able to survive.

Water temperatures can have other, less expected effects also. As an example, trout can swim less rapidly in water above 66°F (19°C) making them less efficient predators. Organisms may become more subject to disease in warmer water too. The bacterium *Chondrococcus columnaris* is harmless to fish at temperatures of less then 50°F (10°C). Between temperatures of 50°-70°F (10°-21°C), however, it is able to invade through wounds in a fish's body. And at temperatures above 70°F (21°C) it can even attack healthy tissue.

The loss of a single aquatic species or the change in the structure of an aquatic community can have far-reaching effects. Each organism is part of a **food chain/web**. Its loss may mean the loss of other organisms farther up the web who depend on it as a source of food.

The water heated by thermal pollution has a number potential useful applications. For example, it may be possible to establish aquatic farms where commercially desirable fish and shellfish can be raised. The Japanese have been especially successful in pursuing this option. Some experts have also suggested using this water to heat buildings, to remove snow, to fill swimming pools, to use for **irrigation**, to de-ice canals, and to operate industrial processes that have modest heat requirements.

The fundamental problem with most of these suggestions is that waste heat has to be used where it is produced. It might not be practical to build a factory close to a nuclear power plant solely for the purpose of using heat generated by the plant. As a result, few of the suggested uses for waste heat have actually been acted upon.

There are no easy solutions to the problems of thermal pollution. To the extent that industries and utilities use less energy or begin to use it more efficiently, a reduction in thermal pollution should result as a fringe benefit.

The other option most often suggested is to do a better job of cooling water before it is returned to a river, lake, or the ocean. This goal could be accomplished by enlarging the cooling towers that most plants already have. However, those towers might have to be as tall as a 30-story building, in which case they would create new problems. In cold weather, for example, the water vapor released from such towers could condense to produce fog, creating driving hazards over an extended area.

Another approach is to divert cooling water to large artificial ponds where it can remain until its temperature has dropped sufficiently. Such cooling ponds are in use in some locations, but they are not a very attractive alternatives since they require so much space. A one megawatt plant, for example, would require a cooling pond with 1,000-2,000 acres (405-810 hectares) of surface area. In many areas, the cost of using land for this purpose would be too great to justify the procedure.

Some people have also used the term thermal pollution to describe changes in the earth's climate that may result from human activities. The large quantities of fossil fuels burned each year release a correspondingly large amount of **carbon dioxide** to the earth's atmosphere. This carbon dioxide, in turn, may increase the amount of heat trapped in the atmosphere through the **greenhouse effect**. One possible result of this change could be a gradual increase in the earth's annual average temperature. A warmer climate might, in turn, have possibly far-reaching and largely unknown effects on agriculture, rainfall, sea levels, and other phenomena around the world. *See also* Alternative energy sources; Industrial waste treatment

[*David E. Newton*]

FURTHER READING

Harrison, R. M., ed. *Pollution: Causes, Effects, and Control.* Cambridge, Royal Society of Chemistry, 1990.

Hudson, J., and J. B. Cravens. "Thermal Effects." *Water Environment Research* 64 (June 1992): 570-81.

Langford, T. E., ed. *Ecological Effects of Thermal Discharges.* New York: Elsevier Science, 1990.

Thermal stratification (water)

The development of relatively stable, warmer and colder layers within a body of water. Thermal stratification is related to incoming heat, water depth and degree of water column mixing. Deep, large lakes such as the **Great Lakes** receive insufficient heat to warm the entire water column and lack adequate physical turnover or mixing of the water for uniform temperature distribution. Thus, they have an upper layer of water that is warmed by surface heating (epilimnion) and a lower layer of much colder water (hypolimnion), separated by a layer called the thermocline in which the temperature decreases rapidly with depth. Both daily and seasonal variations in heat input can promote thermal stratification. Stratification in summer followed by mixing in the fall is a phenomenon commonly observed in temperate lakes of moderate depths (> 33 ft or 10 m).

Thermodynamics, Laws of

One way of understanding the **environment** is to understand the way matter and energy flow through the natural world. For example, it helps to know that a fundamental law of **nature** is that matter can be neither created nor destroyed. That law describes how humans can never really "throw something away." When wastes are discarded, they do not

Thermal stratification of a deep lake.

just disappear. They may change location or change into some other form. But they still exist and are likely to have some impact on the environment.

Perhaps the most important laws involving energy are the laws of thermodynamics. These laws were first discovered in the nineteenth century by scientists studying heat engines. Eventually, it became clear that the laws describing energy changes in these engines apply to all forms of energy.

The first law of thermodynamics says that energy can be changed from one form to another, but it can be neither created nor destroyed. Energy can occur in a variety of forms such as thermal (heat), electrical, magnetic, nuclear, kinetic, or chemical. The conversion of one form of energy to another is familiar to everyone. For example, the striking of a match involves two energy conversions. In the first conversion, the kinetic energy involved in rubbing a match on a scratch pad is converted into a chemical change in the match head. That chemical change results in the release of chemical energy that is then converted into heat and light energy.

Most energy changes on the earth can be traced back to a single common source: the sun. The following describes the movement of energy through a common environmental pathway, the production of food in a green plant:

Solar energy reaches the earth and is captured by the leaves of a green plant. Individual cells in the leaves then make use of solar energy to convert **carbon dioxide** and water to carbohydrates in the process known as **photosynthesis**. The solar energy is converted to a new form, chemical energy, that is stored within carbohydrate molecules.

"Stored" energy is called *potential energy*. The term potential means that energy is available to do work, but it is not currently doing so. A rock sitting at the top of a hill has potential energy because it has the capacity to do work. Once it starts rolling down the hill, it uses a different type of energy to push aside plants, other rocks, and other objects.

Chemical energy stored within molecules is another form of potential energy. When chemical changes occur, that energy is released to do some kind of work.

Energy that is actually being used is called *kinetic energy*. The term kinetic refers to motion. A rock rolling down the hill converts potential energy into the energy of motion, kinetic energy. The first law of thermodynamics says that, theoretically, all of the potential energy stored in the rock can be converted into kinetic energy, without any loss of energy at all.

One can follow, therefore, the movement of solar energy through all parts of the environment and show how it is eventually converted into the chemical energy of carbohydrate molecules, then into the chemical energy of molecules in animals who eat the plant, then into the kinetic energy of animal movement, and so on.

Environmental scientists sometimes put the first law into everyday language by saying that "there is no such thing as a free lunch." By that expression they mean that in order to produce energy, energy must be used. For many years, for example, scientists have known that vast amounts of oil are to be found in rock-like formations known as **oil shale**. But the amount of energy needed to extract that oil by any known process is much greater than the energy that could be obtained from it.

Scientists apply the first law of thermodynamics to an endless variety of situations. A nuclear engineer, for example, can calculate the amount of heat energy that can be obtained from a reactor using nuclear materials (nuclear energy) and the amount of electrical energy that can be obtained from that heat energy.

However, in all such calculations, the engineer has to take into consideration the second law of thermodynamics also. This law states that in any energy conversion, there is always some decrease in the amount of usable energy.

A familiar example of that law is the incandescent light bulb. Light is produced in the bulb when a thin wire inside is heated until it begins to glow. Electrical energy is converted into both heat energy and light energy in the wire.

As far as the bulb is concerned, the desired conversion is electrical energy to light energy. The heat that is produced, while necessary to get the light, is really "waste" energy. In fact, the incandescent light bulb is a very inefficient device. More than 90% of the electrical energy that goes into the bulb comes out as heat. Less than 10% is used for the intended purpose, making light.

Examples of the second law can be found everywhere in the natural and human-made environment. And, in many cases, they are the cause of serious problems.

If one follows the movement of solar energy through the environment again, the amazing observation is how much energy is wasted at each stage. Although green plants do convert solar energy to chemical energy, they do not achieve 100% efficiency. Some of the solar energy is used to heat a plant's leaf and is converted, therefore, to heat energy. As far as the plant is concerned, that heat energy is wasted. By the time solar energy is converted to the kinetic energy used by a school child in writing a test, more than 99% of the original energy received from the sun has been wasted.

Some people use the second law of thermodynamics to argue for less meat-eating by humans. They point out how much energy is wasted in using grains to feed cattle. If humans would eat more plants, they say, less energy would be wasted and more people could be fed with available resources.

The second law explains other environmental problems as well. In a nuclear **power plant**, energy conversion is relatively low, around 30%. That means that about 70% of the nuclear energy stored in radioactive materials is eventually converted not to electricity, but to waste heat. Large cooling towers have to be built to remove that waste heat. Often, the waste heat is carried away into lakes, rivers, and other bodies of water. The waste heat raises the temperature of this water, creating problems of **thermal pollution**.

Scientists often use the concept of *entropy* in talking about the second law. Entropy is a measure of the disorder or randomness of a system and its surroundings. A beautiful glass vase is an example of a system with low entropy since the atoms of which it is made are carefully arranged in a highly structured system. If the vase is broken, the structure is destroyed and the atoms of which it was made are more randomly distributed.

The second law says that any system and its surroundings tends naturally to have increasing entropy. Things tend to spontaneously "fall apart" and become less organized. In some respects, the single most important thing that humans do to the environment is to appear to reverse that process. When they build new objects from raw materials, they tend to introduce order where none appeared before. Instead of iron ore being spread evenly through the earth, it is brought together and arranged into a new automobile, a new building, a piece of art, or some other object.

But the apparent decrease in entropy thus produced is really misleading. In the process of producing this order, humans have also brought together, used up, and then dispersed huge amounts of energy. In the long run, the increase in entropy resulting from energy use exceeds the decrease produced by construction. In the end, of course, the production of order in manufactured goods is only temporary since these objects eventually wear out, break, fall apart, and return to the earth.

For many people, therefore, second law of thermodynamics is a very gloomy concept. It suggests that the universe is "running down." Every time an energy change occurs, it results in less usable energy and more wasted heat.

People concerned about the environment do well, therefore, to know about the law. It suggests, that humans think about ways of using waste heat. Perhaps there would be a way, for example, of using the waste heat from a **nuclear power** plant to heat homes or commercial buildings. Techniques for making productive use of waste heat are known as **cogeneration**.

Another way to deal with the problem of waste heat in energy conversions is to make such conversions more efficient or to find more efficient methods of conversion. The average efficiency rate for power plants using **fossil fuels** is only 33%. Two-thirds of the chemical energy stored in **coal**, oil, and **natural gas** is, therefore, wasted. Methods for improving the efficiency of such plants would obviously provide a large environmental and economic benefit.

New energy conversion devices can also help. Fluorescent light builds, for example, are far more efficient at converting electrical energy into light energy than are incandescent bulbs. Experts point out that simply replacing existing incandescent light bulbs with fluorescent lamps would make a significant contribution in reducing the nation's energy expenditures. *See also* Alternative energy sources; Energy and the environment; Energy flow; Environmental science; Pollution

[*David E. Newton*]

FURTHER READING

Joesten, M. D., et al. *World of Chemistry*. Philadelphia: Saunders, 1991.

Miller, F., Jr. *College Physics*. 6th ed. New York: Harcourt Brace Jovanovich, 1987.

Miller, G. T., Jr. *Energy and Environment: The Four Energy Crises*. 2nd ed. Belmont, CA: Wadsworth, 1980.

———. *Living in the Environment*. 7th ed. Belmont, CA: Wadsworth, 1992.

Thermoplastics

A thermoplastic is any material that can be heated and cooled a number of times. Some common thermoplastics are polystyrene, polyethylene, the acrylics, the polyvinyl **plastics**, and polymeric derivatives of cellulose. Thermoplastics are attractive commercial and industrial materials because they can be molded, shaped, extruded, and otherwise formed while they are molten. A few of the products made from thermoplastics are bottles, bags, toys, packing materials, food wrap, adhesives, yarns, and electrical insulation. The ability to be reshaped is also an **environment**al benefit. Waste thermoplastics can be separated from other solid wastes and recycled by reforming them into new products. *See also* Recyclables; Recycling; Solid waste; Solid waste recycling and recovery; Solid waste volume reduction

Thermosetting polymers

Thermosetting polymers are compounds that solidify, or "set," after cooling from the molten state and then cannot be remelted. Some typical thermosetting polymers are the epoxys, alkyds, polyurethanes, furans, silicones, polyesters, and phenolic **plastics**. Products made from thermosetting polymers include: radio cases, buttons, dinnerware, glass substitutes, paints, synthetic rubber, insulation, and synthetic body parts. Because they cannot be recycled and do not readily decompose, thermosetting polymers pose a serious **environment**al hazard. They contribute significantly, therefore, to the problem of **solid waste** disposal and, in some cases, pose a threat to **wildlife** who swallow or become ensnared in plastic materials. *See also* Solid waste incineration; Solid waste recycling and recovery; Solid waste volume reduction

Third World

The unofficial but common term *Third World* refers to the world's less wealthy and **less developed countries**. In the decades after World War II, the term was developed in recognition of the fact that these countries were emerging from colonial control and were prepared to play an independent role in world affairs. In academic discussions of the world as a single, dynamic system, or world systems theory, the term Third World distinguishes smaller, nonaligned countries from powerful capitalist countries (the **First World**) and from the now disintegrating communist bloc (the **Second World**). In more recent usage, the term has come to designate the world's less developed countries or "underdeveloped," which are understood to share a number of characteristics including low levels of industrial activity, low per capita income and literacy rates, and relatively poor health care that leads to high infant mortality rates and short life expectancies. Often these conditions accompany inequitable distribution of land, wealth, and political power and an economy highly dependent on exploitation of **natural resources**.

Third World pollution

As the countries of the **Third World** struggle with **population growth**, poverty, **famine**s, and wars, their residents are discovering the environmental effects of these problems, in the form of increasing air, water and land pollution. **Pollution** is almost unchecked in many developing nations, where Western nations dump toxic wastes and untreated sewage flows into rivers. Many times, the choice for Third World governments is between poverty or poison, and basic human needs like food, clothing, and shelter take precedence.

Industrialized nations often dump wastes in developing countries where there is little or no environmental regulation, and governments may collect considerable fees for accepting their **garbage**. In 1991, *World Watch* magazine reported that Western companies dumped more than 24 million tons (22 million metric tons) of **hazardous waste** in Africa alone during 1988.

Companies can also export industrial hazards by moving their plants to countries with less restrictive **pollution control** laws than industrialized nations. This was the case with Union Carbine, which moved its chemical manufacturing plant to **Bhopal, India**, to manufacture a product it was not allowed to make in the United States. As Western nations enact laws promoting environmental and worker safety, more manufacturers have moved their hazardous and polluting factories to less developed countries, where there are little or no environmental or occupations laws, or no enforcement agencies. Hazardous industries such as textile, **petrochemical**, and chemical production, as well as smelting and electronics, have migrated to Latin America, Africa, Asia, and Eastern Europe.

For example, IBM, General Motors, and Sony have established manufacturing plants in Mexico, and some of these have created severe environmental problems. At least 10 million gallons (38 million liters) of the factories' raw sewage is discharged into the Tijuana River daily. Because pollution threatens San Diego beaches, most of the cleanup is paid for by the United States and California governments.

Although consumers pay less for goods from these companies, they are paying for their manufacture in the form of higher taxes for environmental cleanup.

Industries with shrinking markets in developed countries due to environmental concerns have begun to advertise vigorously in the Third World. For example, **DDT** production, led by United States and Canadian companies, is at an all-time high even though it is illegal to produce or use the **pesticide** in the United States or Europe since the 1970s. DDT is widely used in the Third World, especially in Latin America, Africa, and on the Indian subcontinent.

Industrial waste is handled more recklessly in underdeveloped countries. The New River, for example, which flows from northern Mexico into southern California before dumping into the Pacific Ocean, is generally regarded as the most polluted river in North America due to lax enforcement of environmental standards in Mexico.

Industrial pollution in Third World countries is not their only environmental problem. Now, in addition to worrying about the environmental implications of **deforestation**, **desertification**, and soil **erosion**, developing countries are facing threats of pollution that come from development, industrialization, poverty, and war.

The number of **gasoline**-powered vehicles in use worldwide is expected to double to one billion in the next forty years, adding to **air pollution** problems. Mexico City, for example, has had air pollution episodes so severe that the government temporarily closed schools and factories. Much of the auto-industry growth will take place in developing countries, where the **automobile** population is expected to increase by more than 200% by the end of this century.

In the Third World the effects of **water pollution** are felt in the form of high rates of death from **cholera**, typhoid, dysentery, and diarrhea from viral and bacteriological sources. More than 1.7 billion people in the Third World have an inadequate supply of safe drinking water. In India, for example, 114 towns and cities dump their human waste and other untreated sewage directly into the Ganges River. Of 3,119 Indian towns and cities, only 209 have partial **sewage treatment**, and only eight have complete treatment.

Zimbabwe's industrialization has created pollution problems in both urban and rural areas. Several lakes have experienced eutrophication because of the **discharge** of untreated sewage and industrial waste. In Bangladesh, degradation of water and **soil** resources is widespread, and flood conditions result in the spread of polluted water across areas used for fishing and rice cultivation. Heavy use of pesticides is also a concern there.

In the Philippines, air and soil pollution poses increasing health risks, especially in urban areas. Industrial and toxic waste disposals have severely polluted thirty-eight river systems.

Widespread poverty and political instability has exacerbated Haiti's environmental problems. Haiti, the poorest country in the Western Hemisphere, suffers from deforestation, land degradation, and water pollution. While the country has plentiful **groundwater**, less than 40% of the population has access to safe drinking water.

As 117 world leaders and their representatives met at the **United Nations Earth Summit** in 1992, some of these concerns were addressed as poorer Third World countries sought the help of richer industrialized nations to preserve the **environment**. Almost always, environmental cleanup in the Third World is an economic issue, and the countries cannot afford to spend more on it.

Another issue affecting Third World pollution control is the role of transnational corporations (TNCs) in global environmental problems. A Third World Network economist cited TNCs for their responsibility for water and air pollution, toxic wastes, hazardous **chemicals** and unsafe working conditions in Third World countries. None of the Earth Summit documents, however, regulated transnational corporations, and the United Nations has closed its Center for Transnational Corporations, which had been monitoring TNC activities in the Third World.

There is a growing environment awareness in Third World nations, and many are trying to correct the problems. In Madras, India, sidewalk vendors sell rice wrapped in banana leaf; the leaf can be thrown to the ground and is consumed by one of the free-roaming cows on Madras' streets. In Bombay, India, tea is sold in a brown clay cup which can be crushed into the earth when empty. The Chinese city of Shanghai produced all its own vegetables, fertilizes them with human waste, and exports a surplus.

Environmentalists worldwide are calling for a strengthened **United Nations Environment Programme** (UNEP) that enact sanctions and keep polluters out of the Third World. It could also enforce the "polluter pays" principle, eventually affecting Western governments and companies that dump on the Third World. Already, UNEP and the **World Bank** provide location advice and environmental **risk assessment** when the host country is not able to do so, and the World Health Organization and the International Labor Organization provide some guidance on occupational health and safety to developing countries. *See also* Drinking-water supply; Environmental policy; Environmental racism; Flooding; Hazardous material; Industrial waste treatment; Marine pollution; Watershed management

[*Linda Rehkopf*]

FURTHER READING

Barber, B. "Lessons from the Third World." *Omni* (January 1992): 25.

Collins, C., and C. Darch. "Summit Sets a Rich Table, but Africa Gets the Crumbs." *National Catholic Reporter* 29 (3 July 1992): 12.

Kumar, P. "Stop Dumping on the South." *World Press Review* (June 1992): 12-13.

LaDou, J. "Deadly Migration: Hazardous Industries' Flight to the Third World." *Technology Review* (July 1991): 47.

"Pollution and the Poor." *Economist* 322 (15 February 1992): 18-19.

Thomas, Lee M. (1944-)

Environmental Protection Agency administrator

If the 1960s and 1970s have become known as decades of growing concern about environmental causes, the 1980s will probably be remembered as a decade of stagnation and retreat on many environmental issues. Presidents Ronald Reagan and George Bush held very different beliefs about many environmental problems than did their immediate predecessors, both Democrat and Republican. Reagan and Bush both argued that environmental concerns had resulted in costly overregulation that acted as a brake on economic development and contributed to the expansion of government bureaucracy.

One of the key offices through which these policies were implemented was the **Environmental Protection Agency (EPA)**. In 1985, President Reagan nominated Lee M. Thomas to be Administrator of that agency. Thomas had a long record of public service before his selection for this position. Little of his service had anything to do with environmental issues, however. Thomas began his political career as a member of the Town Council in his hometown of Ridgeway, South Carolina. He then moved on to a series of posts in the South Carolina state government.

The first of these positions was as executive director of the State Office of Criminal Justice Programs, a post he assumed in 1972. In that office, Thomas was responsible for developing criminal justice plans for the state and for administering funds from the Law Enforcement Assistance Administration.

Thomas left this office in 1977 and spent two years working as an independent consultant in criminal justice. Then, in 1979, he returned to state government as director of Public Safety Programs for the state of South Carolina. In addition to his responsibilities in public safety, Thomas served as chairman of the Governor's Task Force on Emergency Response Capabilities in Support of Fixed Nuclear Facilities. The purpose of the task force was to assess the role of various state agencies and local governments in dealing with emergencies at nuclear installations in the state.

Thomas's first federal appointment came in 1981, when he was appointed executive deputy director and associate director for State and Local Programs and Support of the Federal Emergency Management Agency (FEMA). His responsibilities covered a number of domestic programs, including Disaster Relief, Floodplain Management, Earthquake Hazard Reduction, and Radiological Emergency Preparedness. While working at FEMA, Thomas also served as chairman of the U.S./Mexican Working Group on Hydrological Phenomena and Geological Phenomena.

In 1983, President Reagan appointed Thomas assistant administrator for Solid Waste and Emergency Response of the EPA. In this position, Thomas was responsible for two of the largest and most important of EPA programs, the **Comprehensive Environmental Response Compensation and Liability Act** (Superfund) and the **Resource Conservation and Recovery Act**. Two years later, Thomas was confirmed by the Senate as administrator of the EPA, a position he held until Reagan left office.

[*David E. Newton*]

FURTHER READING

Thomas, Lee M. "The Business Community and the Environment: An Important Partnership," *Business Horizons* (March-April 1992): 21-24.

———. "Trends Affecting Corporate Environmental Policy: The Real Estate Perspective," *Site Selection and Industrial Development* 35 (October 1990): 1(1183)-3(1185).

Thoreau, Henry David (1817-1862)

American writer and natural philosopher

Thoreau was a member of the group of radical Transcendentalists who lived in New England, especially Concord, Massachusetts, around the mid-nineteenth century. He is known worldwide for two written works, both still widely read and influential today: *Walden*, a book, and a tract entitled "Civil Disobedience." All of his works are still in print, but most noteworthy is his fourteen-volume *Journal*, which some critics think contains his best writing. Contemporary readers interested in **conservation**, **environmentalism**, **ecology**, natural history, the human **species**, or philosophy can gain great understanding and wisdom from reading Thoreau.

Today, Thoreau would be considered not only a philosopher, a humanist, and a writer, but also an ecologist (though that word was not coined until after his death). His status as a writer, naturalist, and conservationist has been secure for decades; in conservation circles, he is recognized as what *Backpacker* magazine calls one of the "elders of the tribe."

Trying to trace any idea through Thoreau's work is a complicated task, and that is true of his ecology as well. One straightforward example of Thoreau's sophistication as an ecologist is his essay on "The Succession of Forest Trees." Thoreau found the same unity in nature that present-day ecologists study, and he often commented on it: "The birds with their plumage and their notes are in harmony with the flowers." Only humans, he felt, find such connections difficult: "**Nature** has no human inhabitants who appreciate her." Thoreau did appreciate his surroundings, both natural and human, and studied them with a scientist's eye. The linkages he made showed an awareness of **niche** theory, hierarchical connections, and trophic structure: "The perch swallows the grub-worm, the pickerel swallows the perch, and the fisherman swallows the pickerel; and so all the chinks in the scale of being are filled."

Much of Thoreau's philosophy was concerned with **human ecology**, as he was perhaps most interested in how human beings relate to the world around them. Often characterized as a misanthrope, he should instead be recognized for how deeply he cared about people and about how they related to each other and to the natural world. As Walter Harding notes, Thoreau believed that humans "Antaeus-like, derived [their] strength from contact with nature." When Thoreau insists, as he does, for example, in his journal, that "I assert no independence," he is claiming relationship,

Henry David Thoreau.

not only to "summer and winter...life and death," but also to "village life and commercial routine." He flatly asserts that "we belong to the community." Present-day humans could not more urgently ask the questions he asked: "Shall I not have intelligence with the earth? Am I not partly leaves and vegetable mold myself?"

The essence of Thoreau's message to present-day citizens of the United States can be found in his dictum in *Walden* to "simplify, simplify." That is a straightforward message, but one he elaborates and repeats over and over again. It is a message that many critics of today's materialism believe American citizens need to hear over and over again. Right after those two words in his chapter on "What I Lived For" is a directive on how to achieve simplicity. "Instead of three meals a day, if it be necessary eat but one; instead of a hundred dishes, five; and reduce other things in proportion," he asserts. The message is repeated in different ways, making a major theme, especially in *Walden*, but also in his other writings: "A man is rich in proportion to the number of things he can afford to let alone." Thoreau's preference for simplicity is clear in the fact that he had only three chairs in his house: "one for solitude, two for friendship, three for society." Thoreau is often quoted as stating "I would rather sit on a pumpkin and have it all to myself than be crowded on a velvet cushion."

Hundreds of writers have joined Thoreau in censuring the materialist root of current environmental problems, but reading Thoreau may still be the best literary antidote to that materialism. Consider the stressed commuter/city worker who does not realize that the "cost of a thing is the amount of...life which is required to be exchanged for it, immediately or in the long run." In the pursuit of fashion, ponder his

admonition to "beware of all enterprises that require new clothes."

Thoreau firmly believed that the rich are the most impoverished: "Give me the poverty that enjoys true wealth." The enterprises he thought important were intangible, like being present when the sun rose, or, instead of spending money, spending hours observing a heron on a pond. Working for "treasures that moth and rust will corrupt and thieves break through and steal...is a fool's life." As Thoreau noted, too many of us make ourselves sick so that we "may lay up something against a sick day." To him, most of the luxuries, and many of the so-called comforts of life, are not only dispensable, "but positive hindrances to the elevation of mankind." For most possessions, Thoreau's forthright answer was "it costs more than it comes to."

Thoreau was a humanist, an abolitionist, and a strong believer in egalitarian social systems. One of his criticisms of materialism was that, in the race for more and more money and goods, "a few are riding, but the rest are run over." He recalled that, before the modern materialist state, it was less unfair: "In the savage state every family owns a shelter as good as the best." Thoreau was anti-materialistic and believed that the relentless pursuit of "things" divert people from the real problems at hand, including destruction of the **environment**: "Our inventions are wont to be pretty toys, which distract our attention from serious things." In this same vein, he claimed that "the greater part of what my neighbors call good I believe in my soul to be bad."

In modern life, stress is a major contributor to illness and death. And, much of that stress is generated by the constant acquisitive quest for more and more material goods. Thoreau asks "why should we be in such desperate haste to succeed and in such desperate enterprises?" He notes that "from the desperate city you go into the desperate country" with the result that "the mass of men lead lives of silent desperation." This passage was written in the nineteenth century, but still echoes through the twentieth.

Simplification of lifestyle is now widely taught as a practical antidote to the environmental and personal consequences of the materialist cultures of the urban/industrial twentieth century. And that kind of simplification is central to Thoreau's thought. But readers must remember that Thoreau was unmarried, childless, and often dependent on friends and family for room and board. Thoreau lived on and enjoyed the land around Walden Pond, for example, but he did not own it or have to pay taxes or upkeep on it; he "borrowed" it from his friend Ralph Waldo Emerson (1803–1882). It is not realistic for most people to try to emulate Thoreau directly or to take his suggestions literally. And he agreed, saying "I would not have anyone adopt my mode of living on any account." Still, he did figure out that by working only six weeks a year, he could support himself and so free the other forty-six to live as he saw fit.

Often characterized as an impractical dreamer, Thoreau's wisdom is repeated widely today, a wisdom that is commonly of direct applicability and down to earth. **Aldo Leopold**, for example, is credited with the axiom that wood you cut yourself warms you twice, but it can be found almost a hundred years earlier in Thoreau's chapter on "House-Warming." In 1850, he was an advocate of **national forest** preserves, writing eloquently on the subject in his essay "Chesuncook" in *The Maine Woods*. He also predicted the devastation wreaked on the shad runs by **dams** built on the Concord River.

Thoreau was first and finally a writer. His greatest contribution remains that his writing still raises the consciousness of the reader, causing people who come in contact with his work to be more aware of themselves and of the world around them. As he said "only that day dawns to which we are awake." A raised consciousness means an increase in humility because, as Thoreau teaches, "the universe is wider than our views of it." He remained convinced "that to maintain one's self on this earth is not a hardship but a pastime." *See also* Environmental education; Food chain/web; Trophic level

[*Gerald L. Young*]

FURTHER READING

Fritzell, P. A. "Walden and Paradox: Thoreau as Self-Conscious Ecologist." In *Nature Writing and America: Essays Upon a Cultural Type.* Ames: Iowa State University Press, 1990.

Johnson, W. C., Jr. "Thoreau's Language of Ecology." In *Wilderness Tapestry: An Eclectic Approach to Preservation*, edited by S. I. Zeveloff, L. M. Vause, and W. H. McVaugh. Reno: University of Nevada Press, 1992.

Thoreau, H. D. *Walden.* New York: A. L. Burt, 1902.

Threatened species
See **Endangered species**

Three Gorges Dam (China)

A dam being built on China's longest river, the Chang Jiang (Yangtze River), in west-central China. When completed the Three Gorges Dam will be the largest in the world, spanning 1.2 mi (2.0 km), standing 377 ft (115 m) above the current river level, and holding back a reservoir 400 mi (644 km) long. Designed to control floods, ease navigation, and provide electricity, the Three Gorges dam is expected to produce more than 18,000 **megawatt**s of electricity—equal to a third of the country's supply—to support industrialization and modernization in the region. The reservoir will flood a major agricultural river valley, displacing some 1.3 million people and at least 160 towns and cities.

Proponents of the project argue that China needs the project's electricity for modernization. With locks and the smooth water of the reservoir, river transportation would be far easier than it is now. With reliable reservoir storage, aqueducts could be built to carry Yangtze water to the dry regions in the north (a proposal with unknown ecological consequences). Furthermore, annual flooding on the river has caused thousands of deaths in recent years. An end to flooding could save many lives and prevent economic losses.

In addition, the towns built for resettlement may have better water treatment facilities and other infrastructure to replace outdated and inadequate facilities in the old cities and towns.

The Three Gorges Dam was proposed as early as 1919, and Sun Yat-sen, revolutionary and founder of the Chinese republic, promoted the idea. Since then the project's prohibitive cost, engineering difficulties, political events, and recently an unusual amount of public outcry on the part of Chinese scholars have stalled the project. Construction is now in progress, however, and the dam is scheduled to be completed in 2009, with the reservoir—to be filled in stages—reaching maximum level by 2019. The first 150 million people were relocated in 1996 and 1997. Financial assistance is being provided by foreign investors, mainly from the United States, Canada, and Japan, who are expected to cover 20% of the cost of the project ($3-5 billion).

Environmentalists criticize the dam on the grounds that it will reduce fish stocks, eliminate 78,049 acres (32,000 ha) of important agricultural lands, and threaten habitats of critically endangered species such as the Yangtze river dolphin, Chinese sturgeon, finless porpoise, and Yangtze alligator. The reservoir will also fill one of China's most valuable historical and cultural regions, destroying archeological sites and historic monuments. In addition, the environmental consequences of resettling a million people are uncertain.

Sediment and **silt** accumulation is an additional problem to be solved, since tremendous volumes of sediment will accumulate as the silt- and sand-laden Yangtze River slows in the reservoir. Elsewhere in China silt and sand accumulation has decreased reservoir storage capacity nationwide by 14%. Simply controlling river-bottom gravel may require dredging as much as 200,000 m² of material each year. To reduce silt accumulation, dam operators plan to let spring floods, which carry much of the annual sediment load, flow through from the dam unimpeded. Critics argue, though, that this will largely eliminate any expected flood control benefits from the project. Furthermore, the reservoir will overlie several seismic faults, and the mass of impounded water could trigger earthquakes.

Critics argue that government estimates of the project's costs are vastly underestimated and that costs are only likely to increase over the 15-year construction process. Because the Chang Jiang valley produces 70% of the country's rice, displaced farmers will need to clear more land elsewhere, but both land and housing are chronically short in China. Other critics argue that any failures of the lock system will obstruct, not improve, navigation on the river and that alternative energy sources, including efficiency improvements, smaller turbines, and compost-generated methane, would be cheaper and much quicker ways to provide electricity. Certainly the time and costs of the dam have increased beyond initial expectations. In 1992 the expected completion cost was $11 billion. By 1997 the estimated cost had risen to between $15 and $25 billion. Flood control, argue dam opponents, could be better provided with tree planting and erosion control projects upstream, and a series of smaller dams would cause less ecological and social disruption than a large dam. Finally, the Three Gorges section of the river is

Aerial view of Three Mile Island Nuclear Reactor in Harrisburg, Pennsylvania.

one of China's most valued national symbols, and its loss would be a cultural tragedy.

[*Mary Ann Cunningham*]

FURTHER READING

Gottschang, T. R. "The Economy's Continued Growth." *Current History* 37 (1992): 268-72.

Leopold, Luna. *Sediment Problems at Three Gorges Dam.* Berkeley, CA: International Rivers Network, 1996.

Ryder, Grainne, ed. *Damming the Three Gorges: What the Dam Builders Don't Want You to Know.* Toronto: Probe International, 1990.

Sullivan, L.R. "The Three Gorges Project: Dammed If They Do?" *Current History* vol. 94 (1995): 266-70.

Weiner, R. "China on the Ecological Edge." *E Magazine* vol. 3 (1992): 20-23.

Three Mile Island Nuclear Reactor (Harrisburg, Pennsylvania)

The 1970s were a decade of great optimism about the role of **nuclear power** in meeting world and national demands for energy. Warnings about the declining reserves of **coal**, **petroleum**, and **natural gas**, along with concerns for the environmental hazards posed by **power plant**s run on **fossil fuels**, fed the hope that nuclear power would soon have a growing role in energy production. Those expectations were suddenly and dramatically dashed on the morning of March 28, 1979.

On that date, an unlikely sequence of events resulted in a disastrous accident at the Three Mile Island (TMI) Nuclear Reactor at Harrisburg, Pennsylvania. As a result of the accident, radioactive water was released into the Susquehanna River, radioactive steam escaped into the **atmosphere**, and a huge bubble of explosive **hydrogen** gas filled the reactor's cooling system. For a period of time, there existed a very real danger that the reactor core might melt.

News of the accident produced near panic among residents of the area. Initial responses by government and industry officials downplayed the seriousness of the accident and, in some cases, were misleading and self-serving.

The first official study of the TMI accident was carried out by the President's Commission on the Accident at Three Mile Island. Chaired by John G. Kemeny, then president of Dartmouth College, the Commission attempted to reconstruct the events that led to the accident. It found that the accident was initiated during a routine maintenance operation in which a water purifier used in the system was replaced. Apparently air was accidentally introduced into the system along with the purified fresh water.

Normally the presence of a foreign material in the system would be detected by safety devices in the reactor. However, a series of equipment malfunctions and operator errors negated the plant's monitoring system and eventually resulted in the accident.

At one point, for example, operators turned off emergency cooling pumps when faulty pressure gauges showed that the system was operating normally. Also, tags which hung on water pumps indicating that they were being repaired blocked indicator lights showing an emergency condition inside the reactor.

The Kemeny Commission placed blame for the TMI accident in a number of places. They criticized the nuclear industry and the **Nuclear Regulatory Commission** for being too complacent about reactor safety. They suggested that workers needed better training. The Commission also found that initial reactions to the accident by government and industry officials were inadequate.

No one was killed in the TMI accident, and a 1990 study showed that there were no statistically significant increases in cancers for residents downwind of the accident. A study completed in the mid-1990s, however, refutes those findings stating that "cancer incidence, specifically, lung cancer and leukemia, increased more following the TMI accident in areas estimated to have been in the pathway of radioactive plumes than in other areas." This study also indicates that the radiation levels may have been higher than originally reported, and that cancer rates (lung/leukemia) were 2-10 times higher than upwind rates. Clean-up operations at the plant took over six years to complete and with a $1 billion price tag, cost more than the plant's original construction.

Probably the greatest effect of the TMI accident was the nation's loss of confidence in nuclear power as a source of energy. Since the accident, not one new nuclear power plant has been ordered, and existing plans for sixty-five others were eventually canceled. *See also* Carcinogen; Radiation exposure; Radioactive waste; Radioactivity

[*David E. Newton*]

FURTHER READING

Booth, W. "Post-Mortem on Three Mile Island," *Science* (December 4, 1987): 1342-1345.

Dresser, P. D. *Nuclear Power Plants Worldwide.* Detroit, MI: Gale Research, 1993.

Ford, D. *Three Mile Island: Thirty Minutes to Meltdown.* New York: Penguin, 1983.

Gray, M., and I. Rosen. *The Warming: Accident at Three Mile Island.* New York: W.W. Norton, 1982.

Moss, T. H., and D. L. Sills, eds. *The Three Mile Island Nuclear Accident: Lessons and Implications.* New York: Academy of Sciences, 1981.

President's Commission on the Accident at Three Mile Island. *Report of the President's Commission on the Accident at Three Mile Island.* Washington, DC: U. S. Government Printing Office, 1979.

Stranahan, S. Q. "Three Mile Island: It's Worse Than You Think." *Science Digest* (June 1985): 54-57+.

Threshold dose

In radiology, the threshold dose is the smallest dose of radiation that will produce a specified effect. In the larger context of toxic exposure, threshold dose refers to the dose below which no harm is done. There is a threshold be-

low which relatively little damage occurs from exposure, and above which the damage increases dramatically. For noncarcinogenic toxins, there does seem to be a safe dose for some substances, a threshold dose below which no harm is done. With **carcinogen**s, however, just one change in the genetic materials of one cell may be enough to cause a malignant transformation that can lead eventually to **cancer**. Although there is some evidence that repair mechanisms or surveillance by the immune system may reduce the incidence of some cancers, it is generally considered prudent to assume that no safe or threshold dose exists for carcinogens.

Tidal power

In looking for **alternative energy sources** to meet future needs, some common physical phenomena are obvious candidates. One of these is tidal power. Twice each day on every coastline in the world, bodies of water are pulled onto and off of the shore as a result of gravitational forces exerted by the moon and sun. Only on ocean coasts is this change large enough to notice, however, and therefore, to take advantage of as energy source.

The potential of tidal power as an energy source is clearly demonstrated. Pieces of wood are carried onto a beach and then off again every time the tide comes in or goes out. In theory, the energy that moves this wood could also push against a turbine blade and turn a generator.

In fact, the number of places on the earth where tides are strong enough to spin a turbine is relatively small. The simple back-and-forth movement seen on any shoreline does not contain enough energy by itself. Geographical conditions must concentrate and focus tidal action in a limited area. In such places, tides do not move in and out at a leisurely pace, but rush in and out with the force of a small river.

One of the few commercial tidal power stations in operation is located at the mouth of La Rance River in France. Tides at this location reach a maximum of 44 feet (13.5 meters). Each time the tide comes in, a dam at the La Rance station holds water back until it reaches its maximum depth. At that point, gates in the dam are opened and water is forced to flow into the river, driving a turbine and generator in the process. Gates in the dam are then closed, trapping the water inside the dam. At low tide, the gates open once again, allowing water to flow out of the river, back into the ocean. Again the power of moving water is used to drive a turbine and generator.

Hence the plant produces electricity only four times each day, during each of two high tides and each of two low tides. Although it generates only 250 **megawatt**s daily, the plant's 25% efficiency rate is about equal to that of a **power plant** operated on **fossil fuels**.

One area where tides are high enough to make a power plant feasible is on Canada's Bay of Fundy. Experiments suggest that plants with capacities of one to twenty megawatts could be located at various places along the bay. So far, however, the cost of building such plants is significantly greater than the cost of building conventional power plants of similar capacity. Still, optimists suggest that serious development of tidal power could provide up to a third of the electrical energy now obtained from hydropower worldwide at some time in the future.

Despite the drawbacks and expense of tidal power, China is one country that has used it extensively. Since energy needs are often modest in China, low capacity plants are more feasible. As of the late 1980s, therefore, the Chinese had built more than 120 tidal power plants to provide electricity for small local regions. *See also* Dams; Energy and the environment; Wave power

[*David E. Newton*]

FURTHER READING

Greenburg, D. A. "Modeling Tidal Power." *Scientific American* 257 (November 1987): 128-135.

Holloway, T. "Tidal Power." *Sea Frontiers* 35 (March-April 1989): 114-9.

"The Potential of Tidal Power—Still All At Sea." *New Scientist* 126 (19 May 1990): 52.

Webb, J. "Tide of Optimism Ebbs Over Underwater Windmill." *New Scientist* 138 (24 April 1993): 10.

Tigers (*Panthera tigris*)

Tigers are the largest living members of the family Felidae, which includes all cats. Siberian tigers (*P. t. altaica*) are the largest and most massive of the eight recognized subspecies. They normally reach a weight of 660 lb (300 kg), with a record male that reached 845 lb (384 kg). Several of the subspecies have had their populations totally decimated and are probably extinct, mostly through direct human actions. The **species**' range, overall, has been greatly reduced in historic times. Currently, tigers are found in isolated regions of India, Bangladesh, Nepal, Bhutan, southeast Asia, Manchuria, China, Korea, Russia, and Indonesia. Tigers are designated "endangered" by the U. S. **Fish and Wildlife Service** and by **IUCN—The World Conservation Union**. They are also listed in Appendix I of the **Convention on International Trade in Endangered Species of Fauna and Flora**.

Unlike their relatives, the lion and the cheetah, tigers are not found in open habitats. They tend to be solitary hunters, stalking medium- to large-sized prey (such as pigs, deer, antelope, buffalo, and gaur) in moderately dense cover of a variety of forest habitats, including **tropical rain forest**, moist coniferous and deciduous forests, dry forests, or **mangrove swamp**s. Within their **habitat** both males and females establish home ranges that do not overlap with members of their own sex. Home ranges average 8 sq mi (2,072 ha) for females, but vary from 25-40 sq mi (6,475-10,360 ha) for males depending on prey availability and to allow for the inclusion of several females in his range. Tigers that live in areas of prime habitat raise more offspring than can establish ranges within that habitat, therefore, several are forced to the periphery to establish territories and live. This creates an important condition in that this series of peripheral

individuals helps promote genetic mixing in the breeding population.

Tigers are often labeled "maneaters." Although most tigers shy away from humans, some have been provoked into attack. Others, having been encountered unexpectedly, attack people as a defense, and a very few are thought to hunt humans consciously. An estimated 60-120 people fall victim to tigers each year. Tigers' typical prey includes larger mammals such as deer and buffalo, and the cats will actively search for this prey, instead of waiting in ambush. Tigers hunt alone, and, even though they are highly skilled predators, are rarely successful more than once in every 15 attempts. With a scarcity of habitat for large prey and reduced cover, many tigers will opportunistically attack domesticated livestock, thus, themselves becoming targets of humans.

Population pressures from humans, habitat loss, **poaching**, and **overhunting** have led to the **extinction** or probable extinction of four subspecies and large reductions in the populations of the other four subspecies of tiger. The Balinese tiger (*P. t. balica*) has been extinct for several decades. The South China tiger (*P. t. amoyensis*), which was the target of an extermination campaign, may be extinct in the wild. There has been only one unconfirmed report of the Caspian tiger (*P. t. virgata*) in the last 30 years, thus it is probably extinct. The Javan tiger (*P. t. sondiaca*) is also probably extinct, as its population was reduced to four or five individuals, and there has not been a confirmed sighting since the late 1970s. Little is known of the population levels of the Indochinese tiger (*P. t. corbetti*) since hostilities in that region, having gone on for over 40 years, have prevented accurate estimates. The Sumatran tiger (*P. t. sumatrae*) has a population in the wild of about 500 individuals. The Siberian tiger, whose population dropped to 20-30 individuals in 1940, has a population today of over 300 in the wild. The Bengal tiger (*P. t. tigris*) has been the target of renewed poaching efforts since mid-1990. The bones of these tigers bring a handsome price on the black market. Tiger bones are ground up, dissolved in a liquid, and used in Chinese medicine. Early estimates are that 500 or more Bengal tigers have been poached in the last three years for this purpose. *See also* Endangered species

[*Eugene C. Beckham*]

FURTHER READING

Grzimek, B., ed. *Grzimek's Encyclopedia of Mammals*. Vol. 4. New York: McGraw-Hill, 1990.

Luoma, J. R. "The State of the Tiger." *Audubon* 89 (1987): 61-63.

Nowak, R. M. *Walker's Mammals of the World*. 5th ed. 2 vols. Baltimore, MD: Johns Hopkins University Press, 1991.

Tilth

Tilth is the ability of the **soil** to facilitate tillage, resist weeds, and allow plants to take root. It can also refer to the act of tilling, or cultivating soil. Some have related soil tilth to the physical condition of the soil created by integrating the effects of all physical, chemical, and biological processes occurring within a soil matrix. Soil tilth is usually used as a general descriptive term (good, moderate, or poor) rather than a precisely defined scientific quotient. *See also* Agricultural chemicals; Arable land; Soil fertility

Timberline

The elevational or latitudinal extent of forests. Above upper timberline, either at high elevations or at the Arctic or Antarctic limits, atmospheric and **soil** temperatures are too cold for forest development. Below lower timberline, conditions are too dry to support forests. Timberlines are more common and pronounced in the western than in the eastern United States because of more extreme topographic and climatic conditions in the West.

Times Beach, Missouri

More than 2,000 residents of this Missouri town, located about 30 miles (48 kilometers) southwest of St. Louis, were evacuated after it was contaminated with **dioxin**. In 1971, chemical wastes containing dioxin were mixed with oil and sprayed along the streets of Times Beach to keep down the dust. The spraying was done by Russell M. Bliss, whose company collected and disposed of waste oils and **chemicals** from service stations and industrial plants. Much of this toxic waste oil was sprayed on roads throughout Missouri.

Shortly after the spraying around Times Beach, horses on local farms began dying mysteriously. At one breeding stable, from 1971 to 1973, 62 horses died, as well as several dogs and cats. **Soil** samples were sent to the **Centers for Disease Control** (CDC) in Atlanta for analysis, and after three years of testing, the agency determined that dangerous levels of dioxin were present in the soil.

A decade after the spraying, the town experienced the worst **flooding** in its history. On December 5th, 1982, the Meramec River flooded its banks and inundated the town, submerging homes and contaminating them and almost everything else in Times Beach with dioxin. This compound binds tightly to soil and degrades very slowly, so it was still present in significantly high levels ten years after being used on the roads as a dust suppressant. Following a CDC warning that the town had become uninhabitable, most of the families were temporarily evacuated. The U.S. **Environmental Protection Agency (EPA)** eventually agreed to buy out the town for about $33 million and to relocate its inhabitants.

At the time, the CDC considered soil dioxin levels of one **part per billion** (ppb) and above to be potentially hazardous to human health. Levels found in some areas of Times Beach reached 100 to 300 ppb and above. Dioxin is considered a very toxic chemical. Exposure to this chemical has been linked to **cancer**, miscarriages, genetic **mutation**s, liver and nerve damage, and other health effects, including death, in humans and animals.

Indeed, the contamination seemed to take a serious toll on the health of Times Beach residents. Town officials

claimed that virtually every household in Times Beach experienced health disorders, ranging from nosebleeds, depression, and chloracne (a severe skin disorder) to cancer and heart disease. And almost all of the residents tested for dioxin contamination by the CDC showed abnormalities in their blood, liver, and kidney functions.

By 1983, federal and state officials had located about 100 other sites in Missouri where dioxin wastes had been improperly dumped or sprayed, with levels of the compound reaching as high as 1,750 ppb in some areas.

A decade after the evacuation of Times Beach, debate over dioxin's dangers continues, and some CDC officials now say that the agency overreacted and that the town should not have been abandoned. But by then, Times Beach had become a household name, joining **Love Canal, New York**, and **Seveso, Italy**, on the list of municipalities that were ruined by toxic chemical contamination. *See also* Carcinogen

[*Lewis G. Regenstein*]

FURTHER READING

"Dioxin Cleanup: Status and Opinions." *Science News* 141 (11 January 1992): 30.

Felton, E. "The Times Beach Fiasco." *Insight* 7 (12 August 1991): 12-19.

Gorman, C. "The Double Take on Dioxin." *Time* 138 (26 August 1991): 52.

Kemezis, P. "Times Beach Cleanup Begins." *ENR* 225 (2 August 1990): 37-8.

Tipping fee

The fee charged by the owner or operator of a **landfill** for the acceptance of a unit weight or volume of **solid waste** for disposal, usually done by the truckload. The tipping fee is passed back along the chain of waste acceptor to hauler to generator in the form of fees or taxes. Tipping fees rise as the volume of available landfill space is depleted, or as it becomes harder to open new landfills due to public opposition and stricter environmental regulations. *See also* Garbage; Municipal waste; Transfer station; Waste management; Waste stream

Tobacco

Tobacco, *Nicotiana tabacum*, is an herbaceous plant cultivated around the world for its leaves, which can be rolled into cigars, shredded for cigarettes and pipes, processed for chewing, or ground into snuff. Tobacco leaves are the source of commercial nicotine, a component of many **pesticide**s. The tobacco plant is fast-growing with a stem from 4-8 ft (1-2 m) in height.

Native to the Americas, tobacco was cultivated by Native Americans, and Christopher Columbus found them using it in much the same manner as today. American Indians believed it to possess medicinal properties, and it was important in the ceremonies of the plains tribes.

Tobacco was introduced into Europe in the mid-1500s on the basis of its purported medicinal qualities. Tobacco culture by European settlers in America began in

1612 at Jamestown, and it soon became the chief commodity exchanged by colonists for articles manufactured in Europe.

The leading tobacco-growing countries in the world today are China and the United States, followed by India, Brazil, and Turkey, as well as certain countries in the former Soviet Union. Although about one-third of the annual production in the United States is exported, the country also imports about half as much tobacco as it exports. The leading tobacco-growing state is North Carolina, followed by Kentucky, South Carolina, Tennessee, Virginia, and Georgia.

Nicotine occurs in tobacco along with related alkaloids and organic acids such as malic and citric. Nicotine content is determined by the **species**, variety, and strain of tobacco; it is also affected by the growing conditions, methods of culture and cure, and the position on the plant from which the leaves are taken. Tobacco is high in ash content, which can range from 15-25% of the leaf. Flue-cured tobacco is rich in sugar, and cigar tobaccos are high in nitrogenous compounds but almost free of starch and sugars.

Most tobacco products are manufactured by blending various types of leaves, as well as leaves of different origins, grades, and crop years. Cigarette manufacturers usually add sweetening preparations and other flavorings, but the preparation of tobaccos for pipe smoking and chewing is as varied as the assortment of products themselves. Snuff is made by fermenting fire-cured leaves and stems and grinding them before adding salts and other flavorings. Cigars are made by wrapping a binder leaf around a bunch of cut filler leaf and overwrapping with a fine wrapper leaf.

In the United States and elsewhere, stems and scraps of tobacco are used for nicotine extractions. They can also be ground down and made into reconstituted sheet in a process like papermaking, which is used as a substitute cigar binder or wrapper or cut to supplement the natural tobacco in cigarettes. *See also* Agricultural chemicals; Cigarette smoke; Respiratory diseases

[*Linda Rehkopf*]

FURTHER READING

Chandler, W. U. *Banishing Tobacco*. Washington, DC: Worldwatch Institute, 1986.

Heise, L. "Unhealthy Alliance: With U. S. Government Help, Tobacco Firms Push Their Goods Overseas." *World Watch* (Sept-Oct 1988): 19-28.

National Academy of Sciences. *Environmental Tobacco Smoke: Measuring Exposures and Assessing Health Effects*. Washington, DC: National Academy Press, 1986.

Toilets

The origin of the indoor toilet for the disposal of human wastes goes far back in history. Archaeologists found in the palace of King Minos on Crete an indoor latrine that had a wooden seat and may have worked like a modern flush toilet; they also discovered a water-supply system of terra cotta pipes to provide water for the toilet. Between 2500 and 1500 B.C., cities in the Indus Valley also had indoor toilets that were flushed with water. The wastewater was carried to street drains through brick-lined pits. In 1860, Reverend Henry Moule invented the earth closet, a wooden seat over a bucket and a hopper filled with dry earth, charcoal, or ashes. The user of the toilet pulled a handle to release a layer of earth from the hopper over the wastes in the bucket. The container was emptied periodically. During the eighteenth and nineteenth centuries in Europe, human wastes were deposited in pan closets or jerry pots. After use, the pots were emptied or concealed in commodes. The contents of the jerry pots were often collected by nearby farmers who used the wastes as organic **fertilizer**. However, as cities grew larger, transportation of the wastes to farms became uneconomical, and the wastes were dumped into communal cesspits or into rivers. The flush toilet common in use today was supposedly invented by Thomas Crapper in the nineteenth century; Wallace Rayburn wrote a biography of Crapper, titled *Flushed with Pride*, in 1969.

The development of the flush toilet was primarily responsible for the development of the modern sanitary system, consisting of a maze of underground pipes, pumps, and centralized treatment systems. Modern sanitary systems are efficient in removing human and other wastes from human dwellings but are costly in terms of capital investment in the infrastructure, operational requirements, and energy requirements. The treated **wastewater** is usually disposed of in rivers and lakes, sometimes causing adverse impacts upon the receiving waters.

Sanitary systems require an abundant supply of water, and the flush toilet is responsible for the largest use of water in the home. Each flush of a conventional water-carriage toilet uses between four and seven gallons (15 and 26 liters) of water, depending on the model and water supply pressure. The average amount of water used per flush is 4.3 gallons (16 liters). Since each person flushes the toilet an average of 3.5 times per day, the average daily flow per person is approximately 16 gallons (60 liters) for a yearly flow of 5,840 gallons (22,104 liters).

To reduce the volume of water used for flushing, a variety of devices are available for use with a conventional flush toilet. These devices include:

(1) Tank insert - a displacement device placed in storage tank of conventional toilets to reduce the volume (but not the height) of stored water;

(2) Dual flush toilet - devices used with conventional toilets to enable the user to select from two flush volumes, based on the presence of solid or liquid waste materials;

(3) Water-saving toilet - variation of conventional toilet with redesigned flushing rim and priming jet that allows the initiation of the siphon flush in a smaller trapway with less water;

(4) Pressurized and compressed air (assisted flush toilet) - variation of conventional toilet designed to utilize compressed air to aid in flushing by propelling water into the bowl at increased velocity; and

(5) Vacuum-assisted flush toilet - variation of conventional toilet in which the fixture is connected to a

vacuum system that is used to assist a small amount of water in flushing.

In addition to modifications to conventional flush toilets, non-water carriage toilets are available to reduce the amount of water required. They are also used for disposing of toilet wastes. Types of non-water carriage toilet systems include:

(1) **Composting** toilet - self-contained units that accept toilet wastes and utilize the addition of heat in combination with **aerobic** biological activity to stabilize human excreta; larger units may accept other organic wastes in addition to toilet wastes; requires disposal of residuals periodically;

(2) Incinerating toilet - small self-contained units that utilize a burning assembly or heating element to volatilize the organic components of human waste and evaporate the liquids; requires disposal of residuals periodically; and

(3) Oil-recycle toilets - self-contained unit that uses a mineral oil to transport human excreta from a toilet fixture to a storage tank; oil is purified and reused for flushing; requires removal and disposal of excreta from storage tank periodically (usually yearly).

The wastes from toilets are referred to as "blackwater." If the wastes from toilets are segregated and handled separately using alternative non-water carriage toilets from the wastewaters generated from other fixtures in the home (referred to as "graywater"), significant quantities of pollutants, especially suspended solids, **nitrogen**, and pathogenic organisms, can be eliminated from the total wastewater flow. Graywater, though it still may contain significant numbers of pathogenic organisms, may be simpler to manage than total residential wastewater due to a reduced flow volume. *See also* Municipal solid waste; Sewage treatment

[*Judith Sims*]

FURTHER READING

Love, S. "An Idea in Need of Rethinking: The Flush Toilet." *Smithsonian* 6 (1975): 61-66.

Rodale, R. "Goodbye to the Flush Toilet." *Compost Science* 12 (1971): 24-25.

U. S. Environmental Protection Agency. *Design Manual: Onsite Wastewater Treatment and Disposal Systems.* Cincinnati, OH: Municipal Environmental Research Laboratory, U. S. Environmental Protection Agency, 1980.

Tolerance level

Tolerance level refers to the maximum allowable amount of chemical residue, such as a **pesticide**, legally permitted in food. Tolerance levels are determined by government agencies such as the **Environmental Protection Agency (EPA)** and the **Food and Drug Administration** (FDA), and are based on the results of testing, primarily animal testing. This testing determines the dosage level at which few or no effects are observed. This dose is then adjusted to a human equivalency dose with a margin of error built in for added safety.

While pesticides play an important role in modern society, and are used for a variety of purposes, not until recent decades was it clear how dangerous and persistent many pesticides are. The EPA monitors only a small fraction of pesticides, and in many cases their probable effects on the **environment** are unknown. Pesticide tolerance levels are particularly important worldwide, since pesticides are found in the tissues of people living even in very remote areas of the world. For example, as a result of environmental contamination, the concentration of pesticides in human breast milk has, at certain times in some areas, exceeded the tolerance level for cow's milk.

To establish tolerance levels, scientists conduct a **risk assessment**, or an evaluation of the hazards to the environment, including human health, from exposure to the substance. Data on the toxicity of the substance are combined with data about exposure. The calculation assesses the theoretical maximum residue contribution, or the amount of a chemical that would be present in the average daily diet if all foods treated by that chemical had amounts at the tolerance level. The highest concentration allowable is called the maximum acceptable tolerance concentration. For drinking water, tolerance levels are called the National Primary Drinking Water Requirements. For **air pollution** standards, tolerance levels are called the permissible exposure level.

Environmentalists who criticize the government's tolerance levels charge that standards are not safe enough either for the general population or for workers exposed to toxins. Critics also claim that tolerance levels do not take into account either the cumulative effect of residues from a variety of sources in the environment, the duration of exposure, or the unanticipated effects of two or more **chemicals** combined. Tolerance levels also are criticized for not recognizing threats to at-risk populations such as children, the elderly, and pregnant women. **Animal rights** activists have criticized the use of animals to determine tolerance levels, and advocate the use of computer models or *in vitro* testing (testing on tissue cultures) to make determinations of toxicity or safety of chemicals. *See also* Pesticide residue; Toxic substance

[*Linda Rehkopf*]

FURTHER READING

Harte, John, et al. *Toxics A to Z.* Berkeley: University of California Press, 1991.

Top predator
See **Predator-prey relationships**

Topography

The relief or surface configuration of an area. Topographic studies are valuable because they show how lands are being developed and give insight into the history and relative age of mountains or plains. Topographic features are developed by physical and chemical processes. Physical processes include the relatively long-term tectonic actions and continental movement that lead to subduction of lands in some cases or to the development of high elevation mountains. Earth surface forms are usually altered more quickly by the action of water, ice, and wind, leading to the development of deep canyons, leveling of mountains, and filling of valleys. Chemical processes include oxidation, reduction, carbonation, solution, and hydrolysis. These reactions lead to the alteration of organic and mineral materials that also influence the topographic forms of the earth.

Topsoil

The upper portion of the **soil** that is used by plants for obtaining water and **nutrient**s, often referred to as the *A horizon*. Higher levels of organic matter in topsoil cause it to be darker and richer than **subsoil** and give it greater potential for crop production. The loss of topsoil is a critical problem worldwide. The net effect of this widespread topsoil **erosion** is a reduction in crop production equivalent to removing about one percent of the world's cropland each year. Soil material that can be purchased to add to existing surface soils is also referred to as topsoil. This kind of topsoil may or may not be from the surface of a soil. Often it is a dark colored soil that is high in organic matter and in some cases may be more organic soil than mineral soil.

Tornado and cyclone

A tornado is a vortex or powerful whirling wind, often visible as a funnel-shaped cloud hanging from the base of a thunderstorm. It can be very violent and destructive as it moves across land in a fairly narrow path, usually a few hundred meters in width. Wind speeds are most often too strong to measure with instruments and are often estimated from the damages they cause. Winds have been estimated to exceed 350 mph (563 kph). Very steep pressure gradients are also associated with tornados and contribute to their destructiveness. Sudden changes in atmospheric pressure taking place as the storm passes sometimes cause walls and roofs of buildings to explode or collapse.

In some places such storms are referred to as cyclones. Tornados most frequently occur in the United States in the central plains where maritime polar and maritime tropical air masses often meet, producing highly unstable atmospheric conditions conducive to the development of severe thunderstorms. Most tornados occur between noon and sunset, when late afternoon heating contributes to atmospheric instability.

Torrey Canyon

The grounding in 1967 of the supertanker *Torrey Canyon* on protruding granite rocks near the Scilly Isles off the southwest coast of England introduced the world to a new hazard: immense **oil spills**, especially from supertankers. It exposed current technology's inability to handle such massive quantities of spilled oil and the need for ship design that would help prevent them.

Although oil spills are tragic, each incident provides insight into the progress being made to prevent them. The *Torrey Canyon* accident pointed out needed research in the area of oil spills. These include the efficacy of storm waves, oil-consuming microbes, and time to heal the **environment**.

This wreck demonstrated the inadequacies of existing international marine law, especially questions of responsibility and liability. The international aspects of the *Torrey Canyon* case were complex. This American-owned vessel was registered in Liberia, sailed with a crew of mixed nationals, and grounded in United Kingdom waters, also contaminating the Brittany coast of France. The British government set precedent by ordering the bombing of the wreck in a futile effort to torch the remaining oil.

Efforts to salvage the spilled oil quickly proved useless, as the escaping oil rapidly thinned and became widespread. It was later learned that the most volatile parts of the oil evaporated within several days. Fortunately, this amounted to a large percentage of the total spill.

A number of crucial lessons were learned as a result of abatement efforts. Dispersants, which break the oil into tiny droplets were inadequate and applied too little, too late. Once "mousse" (the term for water encased in the oil) forms under wave action, little can be done to break up this ecologically hazardous muck. One of the first actions in response to the 1993 grounding of the *Braer* near the Shetland Islands was the aerial spraying of dispersants on the rapidly thinning oil.

Use of detergents on the intertidal zone of England's resort beaches proved deadly to grazing organisms. The most effective treatment of oil-tainted water and beaches was discovered to be **nature**'s storm action combined with metabolic breakdown by microorganisms. Efforts to clean oiled seabirds proved largely futile, as they succumbed to hypothermia, stress, and poisoning from ingested oil.

The French discovered an effective emergency tactic to lessen the damage. They used straw and other absorbent materials to sop up the incoming oil. They also protected a 100-year-old research section at Roscoff by making a long boom out of burlap stuffed with straw and wood cuttings, an operation dubbed "Big Sausage." To compensate for inadequate anchoring, students physically held the boom in place while the tide rolled in, with new troops periodically relieving those chilled in the cold water. *See also Amoco Cadiz*, Clean Water Act; *Exxon Valdez*

[*Nathan H. Meleen*]

FURTHER READING

Cowan, E. *Oil and Water: The Torrey Canyon Disaster*. Philadelphia: Lippincott, 1968.

Office of Technology Assessment. *Coping With Oiled Environments*. Washington, DC: U. S. Government Printing Office, 1989.

Petrow, R. *In the Wake of Torrey Canyon*. New York: David McKay, 1968.

Walsh, J. "Pollution: The Wake of the Torrey Canyon." *Science* 160 (12 April 1968): 167-169.

Williams, A. S. *Saving Oiled Seabirds*. Rev. ed. Washington, DC: American Petroleum Institute, 1987.

Toxaphene

Toxaphene was once the nation's most heavily used **pesticide** and accounted for one-fifth of all pesticide use in the United States. It was used mainly on cotton and dozens of food crops and on livestock to kill **parasites**. It is severely toxic to fish and **wildlife** and has been implicated in massive kills of fish, ducks, pelicans, and other waterfowl. Because of this and its ability to cause **cancer**ous tumors and genetic abnormalities in animals, and fears that it may be similarly dangerous to humans, all sale and use of toxaphene have been banned except for already existing stocks. However, this **chlorinated hydrocarbon** pesticide is extremely persistent. Years after application, it has been found in fish, water, wildlife, and the **food chain/web**, posing a continuing potential threat to the **environment** and human health.

Toxic Chemicals Release Inventory (EPA)

A public database containing the total amounts of toxic **chemicals** that are routinely released into the air, water, and **soil** each year from about 30,000 industrial, particularly manufacturing, facilities in the United States. Firms that use or emit any of about 360 listed chemicals in quantities over specified thresholds are required to provide the U.S. **Environmental Protection Agency (EPA)**, states, and the public with estimates of the amount of each chemical stored or used at the firm, the amount emitted, including permitted releases, and other information. This inventory is required under the **Superfund Amendments and Reauthorization Act** of 1986 and has been compiled annually since 1987. It excludes, however, federal facilities; oil, gas, and mining industries; agricultural activities; and small firms. The most recent inventory lists about 20 billion pounds (9.1 billion kg) of **emission**s annually, roughly five percent of the U.S. total toxic emissions as estimated by the U.S. Office of Technology Assessment. The inventory has not been verified using independent sources. The Toxic Chemicals Release Inventory has helped to support new legislation (e.g., pollution prevention programs), provide data for agency projects (**cancer** studies); track toxic chemical estimates; regulate toxic chemicals; and screen environmental risks.

Toxic substance

Substances that are poisonous to living organisms. There are hundreds of thousands of artificial and natural toxic substances, also known as toxins, that are found in solid, liquid, or gaseous form. Toxic substances damage living tissues or organs by interfering with specific functions of cells, membranes, or organs. Some destroy cell membranes, others prevent important cell processes from occurring. Many cause cells to mutate, or make mistakes when they replicate themselves. Some of the most common and dangerous **anthropogenic** (human-made) toxic substances in our **environment** are **chlorinated hydrocarbons**, including **DDT (dichlorodiphenyl-trichloroethane)** and **polychlorinated biphenyl (PCB)**. Many of these are produced by **pesticide** manufacturers and other chemical industries specifically because of their ability to kill pests. **Petroleum** products, produced and used in oil refining, **plastics** manufacturing, industrial solvents, and household cleaning agents, are also widespread and highly toxic agents. **Heavy metals**, including **cadmium**, chromium, **lead**, **mercury**, and **nickel**, and radioactive substances such as **uranium** and **plutonium** are also dangerous toxic agents. Once a toxic substance is released into the environment plants may absorb it along with water and **nutrient**s through their roots or through pores or tissues in their leaves and stems. Animals, including humans, take up environmental toxic substances by eating, drinking, breathing, absorbing them through the skin, or by direct transmission from mother to egg or fetus.

The toxicity (the potential danger) of all toxic materials depends upon dosage. Some toxins are deadly in very small doses; others can be tolerated at relatively high levels before an observable reaction occurs. All chemical substances can become toxic in high enough concentrations, but even very toxic **chemicals** may cause no reaction in very small amounts. If you eat an extremely large dose of table salt (sodium chloride), you will suffer severe reactions, possibly even death. On the other hand, in moderate doses table salt is not toxic. On the contrary, it is essential for your body to continue functioning normally. Likewise, more unusual **trace elements** such as selenium are important to us in extremely minute amounts, but high concentrations have been observed to cause severe **birth defects** and high **mortality** among birds.

One of the most important characteristics that determines a substance's toxicity is the way the substance moves through the environment and through our bodies. Most chemicals and minerals move most effectively when they are dissolved by water or by an oil-based liquid. Generally compounds of mineral substances, including sodium chloride, selenium, zinc, **copper**, lead, cadmium, and the like, dissolve best in water. Organic chemicals (those containing **carbon**), including chlorinated hydrocarbons, **benzene**, toluene, chloroform, and others, dissolve most readily in oily solvents, including **gasoline**, acetone, and the fatty tissues in our bodies. In the environment, inorganic substances are often mobilized when ground is disturbed and watered, as in the case of irrigated agriculture or mining, or when waste dumps become wet and their soluble contents move with **runoff** into **groundwater** or surface water systems. Animals and plants readily take up these substances once they are mobilized and widely distributed in natural water systems. Organic chemicals mainly move through the environment when human activity releases them through pesticide spraying, by allowing aging storage barrels to leak, or by accidental spills. Natural surface and groundwater systems further distribute these compounds. Animals that ingest these compounds also store and distribute toxic organic substances in their bodies.

Once we ingest or breathe a toxic substance, its mobility in our body depends upon its solubility and upon its molecular shape. As they enter our bodies through the tissues lining our lungs or intestines or more rarely through our skin, fat soluble compounds can be picked up and stored by fatty tissues, or lipids, in our cells. Proteins and enzymes in our blood, organs, tissues, and bones recognize and bond with molecules whose shape fits those proteins and enzymes. In most cases our bodies have mechanisms to break down, or metabolize, foreign substances into smaller components. When possible, our bodies metabolize foreign substances and turn them into simpler, water soluble compounds. These are easier for our bodies to eliminate by excretion in feces, urine, sweat, or saliva.

Not all substances are easy to metabolize, however. Some persistent compounds such as DDT simply accumulate in tissues, a process known as **bioaccumulation**. If gradual accumulation goes on long enough, toxic dosages are reached and the animal will suffer a severe reaction or death. Furthermore, the by-products (metabolites) of some substances are more dangerous than the original toxin and more difficult to excrete. Toxic metabolites accumulate in our tissues along with persistent toxins. Although accumulation can occur in bones, fat reserves, blood, and many organs, the most common locations for toxins to accumulate is in the liver and kidneys. These organs have the primary responsibility of removing foreign substances from the blood stream, so any substance that the body cannot excrete tends to collect here.

The parts of our bodies that are most easily damaged by exposure to toxic substances, however, are areas where cells and tissues are reproducing and growing. Brain cells, bones, and organs in children are especially susceptible, and improper cell replication is magnified as growth proceeds. Serious developmental defects can result—a widespread example is the accumulation of lead in children's brains, causing permanent retardation. In adults any tissue that reproduces, repairs, or replaces itself regularly is likely to exhibit the effects of toxicity. Linings of the lungs and intestines, bone marrow, and other tissues that regularly reproduce cells can all develop defective growths, including **cancer**, when exposed to toxic substances. An individual's susceptibility to a toxic substance depends upon exposure— usually workers who handle chemicals are the first to exhibit reactions—and upon the person's genetic resistance, age, size, gender, general health, and previous history of exposures.

Toxins that cause an immediate response, usually a health crisis occurring within a few days, are said to have **acute effects**. Subacute toxic effects appear more gradually, over the course of weeks or months. **Chronic effects** may begin more subtly, and they may last a lifetime. General classes of toxic substances with chronic effects include the following:

1) **Neurotoxin**s, which disable portions of the nervous system, including the brain. Because nerves regulate body functions and because nerve cells are not replaced after an individual reaches maturity, damage is especially critical.
2) **Mutagen**s which cause genetic alterations so that cells are improperly reproduced. These can lead to birth defects or tumors. Compounds that specifically affect embryos are called **teratogen**s.
3) **Carcinogen**s which cause cancer by altering cell reproduction and causing excessive growth, which becomes a tumor.
4) *Tumerogen*s are substances that cause tumors, but if tumors are benign, they are not considered cancer.
5) *Irritant*s which damage cells on contact and also make them susceptible to infection or other toxic effects.

Natural toxins occur everywhere, and many are extremely toxic. Some, such as peroxides and nitric oxide, even occur naturally within our bodies. Many people avoid potatoes, peppers, tomatoes, and other members of the nightshade family because they are sensitive to the alkaloid *solanine* that they contain. Mushrooms and molds contain innumerable toxic substances that can be lethal to adults in minute quantities. Ricin, a protein produced by castor beans, can kill a mouse with a dose of just three ten-billionths (3/ 10,000,000,000) of a gram. Ricin is one of the most toxic organic substance known. Usually we encounter these natural substances in small enough doses that we do not suffer from them, and in many cases our bodies are equipped to metabolize and eliminate them. Except for toxic minerals and heavy metals released by agriculture and mining, most people rarely worry too much about naturally occurring toxic substances, even though they include some of the most toxic agents known.

The most problematic environmental toxic substances are anthropogenic materials that we produce in large quantities for industrial processes and for home use. These are dangerous first because most of them are organic and thus bond readily with our tissues and second because their production and distribution occurs rapidly and is poorly controlled. Every year hundreds of new substances are developed, but the testing process is time-consuming and expensive. The National Institute of Safety and Health has listed 99,585 different toxic and hazardous substances, but there are over 700,000 different chemicals in commercial use, and of these only 20 percent have been thoroughly tested for toxic effects. One-third have not been tested at all. Once these substances are manufactured, their sale, transportation, and especially disposal are often inadequately monitored. Of the more than over 265 million metric tons of toxic and hazardous materials produced every year the United States, about 200 million tons are used or disposed of properly by **recycling**, chemical conversion to non-toxic substances, **incineration**, or permanent storage. About 60 million tons are inappropriately disposed of, mostly in **landfill**s, with nontoxic **solid waste**. Of course, significant amounts of substances that are properly used also freely enter the environment—including pesticides applied to fields, benzene, gasoline, and other **volatile organic compound**s that evaporate and enter the **atmosphere**, and paints and solvents that evaporate or gradually break down after use.

National efforts to control toxic substances in the United States began with the National Environmental Policy Act, passed by Congress in 1969. This act required the establishment of standardized rules governing the identification, testing, and regulation of toxic and hazardous substances. The law setting out those rules finally appeared in 1976 **Resource Conservation and Recovery Act (RCRA)**. This law sets up standard policy for regulating toxic and hazardous substances from the time of production to disposal. Efforts to deal with new and historic environmental problems associated with toxic substances began with the 1980 **Comprehensive Environmental Response, Compensation, and Liability Act (CERCLA)**. This act provided for setting up a multi-billion dollar Superfund to pay clean up costs at the hundreds of abandoned toxic waste sites around the country. Unfortunately Superfund money is proving woefully inadequate in meeting real clean up expenses.

International trade in toxic waste remains a dire problem that has not yet been adequately addressed. In many developing countries pesticides, organic solvents, heavy metals associated with mining, and other noxious materials are regularly released to the environment. Systems for monitoring their release are often completely non-existent. Workers handling these substances frequently suffer terrible diseases and pass on genetic disabilities to their children. Because many of the most dangerous toxins are produced in the United States and Europe for sale to developing regions, wealthier nations stand in a position to force some efforts at regulation. Thus far, however, neither regulation nor worker education has been an international priority.

[*Mary Ann Cunningham*]

FURTHER READING

Cunningham, W. P. *Environmental Science: A Global Concern*. Dubuque, IA: William C. Brown, 1992.

Kamrin, M. A. *Toxicology*. Chelsea, MI: Lewis Publishers, 1988.

Toxic Substances Control Act (1976)

The Toxic Substances Control Act (TSCA), passed in 1976, is a key law for regulating **toxic substance**s in the United States. The Act authorizes the **Environmental Protection Agency (EPA)** to study the health and environmental effects of **chemicals** already on the market and new chemicals proposed for commercial manufacture. If the EPA finds these health and **environment**al effects to be unreasonable risks, it can regulate, or even ban, the chemical in question.

The initiative to regulate toxic substances began in the early 1970s. In 1971 the Council on Environmental Quality completed a report on toxic substances that concluded that such substances were not being adequately regulated by existing health and **environmental law**. The report concluded by advocating a new comprehensive law to deal with

toxic substances. Among the problem substances that had helped to focus national concern on toxic substances were **asbestos, chlorofluorocarbons (CFCs), Kepone** (a **pesticide**), **mercury, polychlorinated biphenyl (PCB)**s, and **vinyl chloride**. Research proved these substances caused significant health and environmental problems, yet they were unregulated.

Congressional debate on regulating toxic substances began in 1971. The Senate passed bills in 1972 and 1973 that were strongly supported by environmentalists and labor, but the House approach to the issue was more limited and had the support of the chemical industry. The key difference between the approaches was how much pre-market review would be required before new chemicals were introduced on the market. Although neither the chemical industry, environmentalists, nor labor was entirely happy with the compromise bill of 1976, all three groups supported it.

The approach adopted in TSCA is pre-market notification, rather than the more rigorous pre-market testing that is required before new drugs are introduced on the market. When a new chemical is to be manufactured, or an existing chemical is to be used in a substantially different way, the manufacturer of the chemical must provide the EPA with "pre-manufacture notification" data at least ninety days before the chemical is to be produced commercially. The EPA then examines this data and makes a determination if regulation is necessary for the new chemical or new use of the existing chemical. The agency can require additional testing by manufacturers if it deems the existing data insufficient. Until such data is available, the EPA can ban or limit the manufacture, distribution, use, or disposal of the chemical. For these new chemicals, the producer must demonstrate that the chemical does not represent an unreasonable risk. The EPA can act quickly and with limited burden to prevent such new chemicals from being produced.

Between July 1979, when TSCA went into effect for new chemicals, and September 1990, the EPA received 18,076 new chemical notices. The agency determined that no action was necessary for nearly 90 percent of these chemicals. Of the 1,615 chemicals that required further action, 742 were never produced commercially due to EPA concerns. The remaining 873 chemicals were controlled through formal actions or negotiated agreements.

As of September 1990, there were nearly 70,000 chemicals within the purview of TSCA (including the 18,000 new chemicals). Although the law requires that the EPA examine each of these chemicals for its potential health and environmental risk, the volume of chemicals and lack of EPA resources has made such a task virtually impossible. Through 1990, the agency had examined almost 500 existing chemicals. Of this grouping, the EPA determined that 250 chemicals required no further action. This was because either the chemical was no longer being manufactured, it was already being studied by another federal agency or industry, adequate data on the chemical existed, or exposure to the chemical was limited. The EPA had issued rules to regulate 106 of these chemicals. The remaining chemicals were in various stages of testing and review.

In order to help the agency set priorities, TSCA created an Interagency Testing Committee (ITC). The ITC designates which existing chemicals should be examined first. Once designated by the ITC, the EPA has one year to act on the chemical. The agency had difficulty meeting this one-year limit. Indeed, the EPA was sued over its failure to meet the deadline and worked under a court schedule to test these identified chemicals.

The EPA also identifies specific chemicals already in use for review. Unlike the policy with new chemicals, the EPA must demonstrate that existing chemicals warrant toxicity testing. Furthermore, if the EPA desires to regulate the chemical once it has been tested, it must pursue another complex course of action. Clearly, the regulation of existing chemicals, by design, is a lengthy and complicated process.

If the EPA concludes that either a new or existing chemical presents "an unreasonable risk of injury to health or the environment," it can: 1) prohibit the manufacture of the chemical by a rule or a court injunction; 2) limit the amount of the chemical produced or the concentration at which the chemical is used; 3) ban or limit uses of the chemical; 4) regulate the disposal of the chemical; 5) require public notification of its use; and 6) require labeling and record keeping for the chemical. The EPA is required to use the least burdensome of these regulatory approaches for chemicals already in use.

There are several other important components to TSCA. First, the law requires strict reporting and record keeping by the manufacturers and processors of the chemicals regulated under the law. In addition to keeping track of the chemicals, these records also include data on environmental and health effects. Second, TSCA is one of the few federal environmental laws that require a balancing of environmental and health benefits with economic and societal costs in the regulatory process. The act states that the regulation of toxic substances should only take place when an unreasonable risk is present. Although "unreasonable risk" is not clearly defined, it does incorporate a concern for balancing costs and benefits.

Third, PCBs received special treatment in the legislation. Manufacture of PCBs was prohibited by 1979, but fewer than one percent of all PCBs in use up to that time would be phased out. Despite this ban, a significant PCB problem has remained. One major problem is how to handle the millions of pounds of PCBs abandoned by firms that went bankrupt in the 1980s. These is also concern that the disposal of PCBs in use could lead to problems. Environmentalists argued that PCB treatment required new legislation, but the EPA decided to issue stricter regulation under the same act to deal with the transportation and final disposal of PCBs.

Fourth, TSCA contained citizen suit provisions: private citizens could sue companies for violation of the law and the EPA for failure to implement TSCA. And finally, certain materials are not covered by TSCA: ammunition and firearms; nuclear materials; tobacco; and chemicals used exclusively in cosmetics, drugs, food and food additives, and pesticides, since these chemicals are already regulated by other laws.

Although the authorization of TSCA expired in 1983 and Congress has not acted to re-authorize the law, it has continued to fund the program. The scope of the law was expanded in 1986 by an amendment requiring asbestos hazards to be reduced in schools, in 1988 by an amendment providing grants and technical assistance to state programs that reduce indoor **radon** and assigning the regulation of genetically engineered organisms to TSCA.

Evaluations of the law have revealed three chief problems. First, the amount of data generated on chemicals is less than expected. A 1984 study by the National Academy of Sciences indicated that only four percent of the major chemicals in the TSCA inventory had studies showing data on possible chronic toxicity. Toxicity data was absent for 78 percent of the chemicals produced at over 1 million pounds (454,000 kilograms) per year and for 76 percent of chemicals that were produced at less than 1 million pounds per year. The lack of data is due to early EPA uncertainty over how to implement the law, and the requirement that any regulation must follow rule-making procedures. Such rule-making procedures are slow and costly; the process can sometimes cost more than the testing.

Second, in terms of existing chemicals, as of 1986, only the use of CFCs as **aerosol** propellants had been banned by the EPA. Part of the lack of action may be due to the costs involved in beginning such a complex new regulatory program. It is also difficult to determine unreasonable risk in light of inadequate data and more general uncertainties. And third, most pre-market notifications for new chemicals are not accompanied by test data. Rather, the EPA identifies potentially harmful chemicals by comparing the new chemical to existing chemicals for which data exists. If the EPA were to require more data for most new chemicals, in many cases the new chemicals may not be produced since the test costs would exceed the expected profit.

The chemical industry and environmentalists have evaluated TSCA differently. The chemical industry has argued that the EPA has required more testing than is scientifically needed and that the regulatory approach for new chemicals is overly burdensome. Environmentalists have criticized the EPA for its slow progress in examining existing chemicals, for requiring no health data for new chemicals, and for withholding much of the data for new chemicals to comply with manufacturers' desire for confidentiality. *See also* Chronic effects; Radioactive waste; Risk analysis

[*Christopher McGrory Klyza*]

FURTHER READING

Druley, R.M. *The Toxic Substances Control Act.* Washington, DC: Bureau of National Affairs, 1981.

Shapiro, M. "Toxic Substances Policy." In: *Public Policies for Environmental Protection,* edited by P. R. Portney. Washington, DC: Resources for the Future, 1990.

Toxic Substances Control Act: Law and Explanation. Chicago: Commerce Clearing House, 1977.

The Toxic Substances Control Act: Overview and Evolution. Austin: The University of Texas Press, 1982.

"Toxic Substances Control Bill Cleared." *Congressional Quarterly Almanac* 32 (1976): 120-25.

Toxic waste

See **Hazardous waste**

Toxics use reduction legislation

In recent years, disasters resulting from toxic **chemicals** such as those at **Love Canal, New York**, and in **Bhopal, India**, have increased awareness of the hazards associated with their use. In response to such concerns, "right to know" statutes and regulations have been enacted on both the state and federal levels. In 1990, Congress passed the **Pollution Prevention Act**, but the provisions of this legislation are relatively limited when compared to the toxics use reduction (TUR) statutes that have been enacted in at least 26 states since 1989.

State TUR statutes, sometimes called **pollution** prevention statutes, are designed to motivate businesses to reduce their use of toxic chemicals. Most such statutes set specific overall goals, such as a 50 percent reduction in the use of toxic chemicals, with that reduction being phased in over a specified number of years. A comprehensive TUR statute usually covers planning requirements, reporting requirements, and protection of trade secrets. It encourages worker and community involvement, provides technical assistance and research, institutes enforcement mechanisms and penalties for non-compliance, and designates funding.

The Massachusetts Toxics Use Reduction Act (MTURA) is considered one of the strongest existing TUR laws, and it is often used as a model for such legislation in other states. The stated goals of the MTURA are to reduce toxic waste by fifty percent statewide by 1997, while continuing to sustain and promote the competitive advantages of Massachusetts' businesses. Companies subject to MTURA are called large quantity toxics users, and each of these are now required to develop an inventory of the toxic chemicals flowing both in and out of every production process at its facilities. The company must then develop a plan for reducing the use of toxic chemicals in each of these production processes. The inventory and a summary of this plan must be filed with a designated state agency, and the company must submit an annual report for each **toxic substance** manufactured or used at that facility. To accommodate concerns about trade secrets, the MTURA allows companies to report amounts of a chemical substance using an index/matrix format, instead of absolute amounts. In other states, TUR laws address such concerns by allowing companies to withhold information they believe would reveal trade secrets except on court order.

Plans filed under the MTURA are not available to the public, but any ten residents living within ten miles (16.09 kilometers) of a facility required to prepare such a plan may petition to have the Massachusetts Department of Environmental Protection examine both the plan and the supporting data. Summaries of these plans must be filed every two years and these are available to Massachusetts residents, as well as the annual reports these companies must issue. Large quantity toxics users must notify their employees of new plans as well as updating existing plans, and management is required to solicit suggestions from all employees on options for reducing the use of toxic substances.

To encourage toxics use reduction, MTURA has established the Office of Toxics Use Reduction Assistance Technology, which provides technical assistance to industrial toxics users. The act also established a Toxics Use Reduction Institute at the University of Lowell, which develops training programs, conducts research on toxics use reduction methods, and provides technical assistance to individual firms seeing to adopt pollution prevention techniques.

Enforcement of MTURA is overseen by the Administrative Council on Toxics Use Reduction, but there are also provisions in the act for court action by groups of ten or more Massachusetts citizens. Civil penalties up to $25,000 for each day of the violation can be assessed, and for willful violations a court can impose fines between $2,500 and $25,000 per violation or imprisonment for up to one year, or both.

Administration of MTURA is funded through a toxics users fee imposed on companies subject to the act. Fees are determined according to the number of employees at each facility and the number of toxic substances reported by the facility.

Those drafting TUR laws in other states have chosen a variety of mechanisms to achieve their goals. One issue on which states differ is whether the reduction of toxics, which focuses on pollution prevention, should be the sole emphasis of the statute, or whether the statute should include other objectives. These other objectives are usually means of **pollution control**, which can include **waste reduction**, waste minimization, and what is called "out-of-process" **recycling**, which occurs when chemical wastes are taken from the production site, transported to recycling equipment, and then returned. Analysts refer to those statutes which promote toxics-use reduction exclusively or almost exclusively as having a pure focus. Those statutes which explicitly combine toxics-use reduction with pollution control are labeled as having a mixed focus. Statutes in Massachusetts are categorized as pure, while toxics use reduction legislation in Oregon, for example, is considered to have a mixed focus.

The Oregon and Massachusetts statutes are considered by many to be the strongest toxics use reduction legislation in the United States, and most states have adopted less stringent provisions. For example, the United States General Accounting Office issued a report in June of 1992, which lists only ten states out of twenty-six with such laws, as having legislation that "clearly promotes" programs to reduce the use of toxic chemicals.

Over the past two decades, Congress has enacted various laws aimed at pollution control. These include the **Resource Conservation and Recovery Act** (1976), the **Toxic Substances Control Act** (1976), and the **Superfund Amendments and Reauthorization Act** (1986). Pollution-control laws such as these are primarily considered source-reduction laws. These laws are designed to reduce waste after it has been generated, while TUR laws are designed to restrict hazardous waste before generation, by reducing or eliminating the toxic chemicals that enter the production processes.

TUR laws have continued the goals of right-to-know legislation by moving away from reactive enforcement of **environmental law**s toward hazard prevention. TUR laws are also different in their "multi-media" approach to regulation. Previous environmental and occupational and health and safety statutes have divided enforcement between various agencies, such as the **Environmental Protection Agency (EPA)**, the **Occupational Safety and Health Administration**, and the **Consumer Product Safety Commission**. Even under the jurisdiction of a single agency, moreover, current environmental laws often require different approaches to regulation of toxics depending on where they are found—air, water, or land. In contrast, TUR laws require comprehensive reports and plans for the reduction of toxics discharged into all media. TUR laws have been supported by coalitions of environmentalists and labor representatives precisely because of this comprehensive, multi-media approach.

Reactions by industry, however, have been mixed. In some instances, businesses have saved money once they began purchasing substitute chemicals, or when changing production processes improved efficiency. But some firms have hesitated to make the capital investments needed to change their industrial processes because the cost-benefit ratio of such changes remains uncertain. Some firms have judged the costs of alternatives chemicals or processes to be prohibitively expensive, and in other cases alternative technologies or less hazardous chemicals have not been developed and are simply not available at any price. The EPA has found, however, that some companies do not take advantage of available technology for reducing or eliminating toxic chemicals because they are unaware of its existence. *See also* Chemical spills; Emergency Planning and Community Right-to-Know Act; Environmental liability; Hazardous material; Hazardous Substances Act; International trade in toxic wastes; NIMBY; Waste management

[*Paulette L. Stenzel*]

FURTHER READING

Massachusetts Toxics Use Reduction Act. Mass. Gen. L. ch 21I, §§ 1-23 (Supp. 1991).

Stenzel, P. L. "Toxics Use Reduction: An Important 'Next Step' After Right to Know." *Utah Law Review* (1993): 707-48.

U. S. General Accounting Offices. *Toxic Substances: Advantages of and Barriers to Reducing the Use of Toxic Chemicals.* A report to the Honorable G. Sikorski, House of Representatives. GAO/RCED-92-212. Washington, DC, June 1992.

Toxins

Toxins are chemicals or physical agents that exert a toxic effect on living organisms. Toxic means poisonous; that is, causing a reaction with cellular components that disrupts essential metabolic processes. At some level of exposure, all chemicals, whether natural or synthetic, are toxic. They all can either cause death or damaging effects soon after expo-

sure; or can cause some other disease (such as **cancer** or birth defects) after longer term exposure.

Although many people think toxins are mainly **pesticide**s or industrial chemicals, they also include the poisons of marine animals, spiders, snakes, plants, and the extremely toxic botulinum toxins that can kill a human being with a single minuscule dose. Toxins can exert their effects on many different organs. The nervous system, the brain, the lungs, the skin, and the eyes are only some of the organs that can be damaged by toxins. Toxicologists use reports, epidemiology, and laboratory studies to characterize both the lethal doses of toxins and the doses of certain chemicals that can cause disease over the long term. Environmental laws regulate exposures to certain human-made toxins.

Trace element/micronutrient

A micro**nutrient** is an element that plants need in small quantities for growth and **metabolism**. Common micronutrients are iron, **copper**, zinc, boron, molybdenum, manganese, and **chlorine**. Some plants may benefit from small amounts of sodium, silicon, and/or cobalt as well. Additional micronutrients may be added to the list as scientists are better able to detect minute quantities and plant requirements. Micronutrients often act as catalyst in plant chemical reactions. Historically, when **animal waste** was used as **fertilizer**, there were few micronutrient deficiencies detected. However, with the use of large amounts of chemical fertilizer, higher yields, and use of **monoculture**, micronutrient deficiencies in crop plants are becoming more evident. Several plant disorders such as beet canker, cracked stem of celery, and stem end of russet in tomatoes can be related to the lack of certain micronutrients. On the other hand, excess of micronutrients in plants may lead to plant toxicity.

Trade in pollution permits

Trade in pollution permits augments the traditional approach to environmental regulation by using market principles to control **pollution**. Since its inception, the program has been criticized as unfair and unfeasible. Yet the concept of trading pollution permits continues to spread.

Most **environmental law**s limit the amount of waste or pollution each regulated facility can emit to air, water, or land. These limits are then written into permits. Regulators monitor the facility to make sure the permits are followed. Any facility exceeding the permitted level of **emission**s may be fined or otherwise penalized. This method of controlling pollution is known as command and control.

In 1990, Title IV of the **Clean Air Act** Amendments became the first federal law to codify a market-based approach to **pollution control**. The title regulated **sulfur dioxide** emissions in an effort to reduce acid rain. It set a goal of a 10-million-pound (4.5 million kilogram) reduction in **power plants** emissions of sulfur dioxide. The law granted each power plant the right to a certain level of pollution. Companies that emit less than they are allowed can sell the remainder of their pollution allowance to other companies.

Title IV redefined pollution as a commodity, like pork bellies or soybean futures. One of the largest trade in pollution transactions took place between two utilities, the **Tennessee Valley Authority** (TVA) and Wisconsin Power and Light. The TVA, one of the largest emitters of sulfur dioxide, paid several million dollars to one of the cleanest utilities in the country, Wisconsin Power, for the right to emit an additional 10,000 pounds (4,500 kilograms) of the compound. Despite its obvious success, financial analysts and utility industry executives are still skeptical about the fledgling market's future.

If the market does become established, critics fear that trades like the one between the TVA and Wisconsin Power will only become more common. Because the market maximizes profit, certain utilities that are already highly polluting may spend money buying the right to pollute rather than to clean up their production processes. Other, cleaner utilities may continue to provide the extra pollution allowances. Certain parts of the country will have more pollution than others.

Proponents of the market-based approach respond that simply reaching the goal of reducing sulfur dioxide emissions by 10 million pounds (4.5 million kilograms) will benefit the country as a whole. They also see an advantage in making pollution costly, for then businesses will have an economic interest in reducing it.

The debate about the feasibility and fairness of pollution trading continues. Other regional and local authorities, such as the Southern California Air Quality Management District, have considered adopting such measures for their jurisdictions. *See also* Agricultural pollution; Air pollution; Air pollution control; Air quality; Environmental economics; Green politics; Green tax; Industrial waste treatment; Marine pollution; Pollution control costs and benefits; Radioactive waste management; Sewage treatment; Solid waste volume reduction; Solid waste recycling and recovery; Toxic use reduction; Waste management; Waste reduction; Water pollution

[*Alair MacLean*]

FURTHER READING

Allen, F. E. "Tennessee Valley Authority Is Buying Pollution Rights from Wisconsin Power." *Wall Street Journal* (11 May 1992): A12.

Mann, E. "Market Driven Environmentalism: The False Promise." *GREEN: Grantmakers Network on the Economy and the Environment* 1 (Winter 1992): 1-3.

Portney, P. "Market-Driven Environmentalism: Tomorrow's Success." *GREEN: Grantmakers Network on the Economy and the Environment* 1 (Winter 1992): 1, 3-5.

Tragedy of the Commons

A term referring to the theory that, when a group of people collectively own a resource, individuals acting in their person-

Overgrazing by domestic animals destroys the grassland and contributes to the tragedy of the commons.

al self-interest will inevitably overtax and destroy the resource. According to the commons theory, each individual gains much more than she or he loses by overusing a commonly held resource, so its destruction is simply an inevitable consequence of normal and rational behavior. In the study of economics, this idea is known as the **free rider** problem. Human population growth is the issue in which the commons idea is most often applied: each individual gains personal security and wealth by producing many children. Even though each additional child taxes the global community's food, water, energy, and material resources, each family theoretically gains more than it loses for each additional child produced. Although the theory was first published in the nineteenth century, **Garrett Hardin** introduced it to modern discussions of **population growth** in a 1968 article published in the journal *Science*. Since that time, the idea of the tragedy of the commons has been a central part of population theory. Many people insist that the logic of the commons is irrefutable; others argue that the logic is flawed and the premises questionable. Despite debates over its validity, the theory of the commons has become an important part of modern efforts to understand and project population growth.

In its first published version, the idea of the commons was a scenario mapped out in mathematical logic and concerning common pasture land in an English village. In his 1833 essay, William Forster Lloyd described the demise of a common pasture through overuse. Up to that time, many English villages had a patch of shared pasture land, collectively owned, on which villagers could let their livestock graze. At the time of Lloyd's writing, however, many of these commons were being ruined through **overgrazing**. This destruction, he proposed, resulted from unchecked population growth and from the persistence of collectively held, rather than private, lands. In previous ages, said Lloyd, wars and plagues kept human and animal populations well below the maximum number the land could support. By the nineteenth century, however, England's population was climbing. More people were looking for room to graze more cattle, and they used common pasture because the resource was essentially free. Free use of a common resource, Lloyd concluded, leads directly to the ruin of that resource.

In his 1968 article, Garrett Hardin applied the same logical argument to a variety of natural amenities that we depend upon. Cattle, grazing on public lands in the American West, directly consume a common pasture owned by all Americans. Normal pursuit of increased capital leads ranchers to add as many cattle as they can, and much of the country's public lands are now severely denuded, gullied, and eroded from overgrazing. **National park**s such as **Yosemite National Park** and **Yellowstone National Park** are commonly held lands to which all Americans have free access. Each individual naturally wishes to maximize her or his vacation time, so that the collective result is congestion and pollution in the parks. The oceans represent the ultimate world commons. Private corporations and individual countries maximize their profit by catching as many fish as possible. In **whaling**, we have seen this practice effectively eliminate some **species** within a few decades. Other fisheries currently stand in danger of the same end.

Extrapolating his reasoning to arguments for population control, Hardin pointed out that if each family produces as many children as it can, then the inevitable collective result will be wholesale depletion of food, clean water, energy resources, and living space. Worldwide, quality of life will then diminish. Because we cannot increase the world's supply of water, energy, and space, argues Hardin, the only way to avoid this chain of events is to prevent population increases. Ideally, we need worldwide agreements to moderate individual childbearing activity, so that the cumulative demand on world resources will not exceed resource availability.

Critics dispute Hardin's thesis on a number of levels. The most important objection is that Lloyd and Hardin condemned the idea of the commons but that their examples did not involve real community resources. A commons, maintained over generations by a group of people for the benefit of the group, lasts because members of the group accept a certain amount of self-restraint in the interest of the community and because they know that self-restraint ensures the resource's survival. Peer pressure, respect for elders and taboos, fear of recrimination from neighbors, and consideration of neighbors' needs all reinforce individual restraint in a commons. All of these restraints rely upon a stable social structure and an understanding of commons management. In a stable society, individual survival depends upon the prosperity of one's neighbors, and every parent has an interest in ensuring that future generations will have access to necessary resources. Many such commons exist around the world today, especially in traditional villages in the developing world, where generational rules dictate the protection of grazing lands, **water resources**, fields, and forests.

In Lloyd's case study, industrialization, widespread eviction of tenant farmers to make way for sheep, and the introduction of capitalism had all disrupted the traditional social fabric of English villages. Uprooted families moving from village to village did not observe traditional rules. More important, many common pastures were being privatized by large landowners, leaving fewer acres of public land for village livestock to squeeze onto. The problem described in Lloyd's essay was, in fact, one of uncontrolled free access to a resource whose collective ownership had broken down. Likewise, ocean fisheries have generally been uncontrolled, unowned resources with no collectively enforced rules of restraint. American public grazing lands have rules of restraint, but they fail because they are poorly enforced and inadequately developed.

Many people also object to the implication of commons logic that a system of private property is superior to one of collectively held property. In criticizing village commons, Lloyd defended the actions of powerful landholders who could, on a whim, evict a community of tenant farmers. Commons logic holds that private landowners make better guardians of resources because they can see that their personal interest is directly served by careful management. However, evidence abounds that private owners frequently exploit and destroy resources much faster than groups do. Nineteenth century landowners, after removing farmers who had husbanded their land for generations, overstocked the country with sheep and clear-cut forests for lumber. Gullied pastures, lost **wildlife habitat**, and other environmental costs resulted. In the American timber industry, virtually all private **old-growth forest**s have been cleared, their capital liquidated. Publicly held old growth, because it is expected to serve other needs beyond lumber production (wildlife habitat, **recreation, watershed** for communities, biological resources), has survived better than private forests. As a community, the people of the United States have imposed some rules and limitations on forest use that private landholders have not had. In a capitalist society, private landowners often benefit most by quickly liquidating **natural resources**, which allows them to move on to another area and another resource.

Where resources are precious or irreplaceable, collective guardianship is often the only way to ensure their maintenance. In villages from India to Zaire to the Philippines, community councils monitor the use of forests, water supplies, and crop lands. In developed countries, common and highly valued resources such as schools, public roadways, and parks have long been monitored and controlled by rules that restrain individual behavior and prevent destruction of those resources. Generally everybody agrees not to block roads, to burn schools, or to vandalize parks because these resources benefit everybody in some way. At the same time, no private individual could adequately maintain such resources. Collective responsibility and respect are necessary.

Finally, some critics argue that it is simplistic to assume that depletion results from population size, rather than uneven distribution of resources. Garrett Hardin chooses to direct his commons logic at large numbers of people using limited amounts of resources without considering the amount of resources used per person. Residents of the world's poorer regions counter that each of their children uses only 5 percent of the resources that an American child uses. The world can afford a great number of these children, they argue, and it could afford even more of them if people in wealthy countries drove fewer cars, ate less beef, and polluted less of the world's air and water. The deduction that breeding causes shortages, not rates of consumption, is hotly contested by those whose survival depends on the labor of their children.

Defenders of poorer segments of the world's population point out that social stability, including a fair distribution of resources, is more likely than population control to deter a global tragedy of the commons. As long as war and **famine** exist, and as long as the rich continue to exploit the labor and resources of the poor (an example of which is American support of the Guatemalan military structure so that we might buy coffee for three dollars a pound and bananas for 50 cents), reliable social structures cannot be rebuilt and responsible guardianship of the world's resources cannot be reestablished.

In the end, arguments for and against commons logic are based upon examples and interpretation. Logical proof, which the scenario set out to establish, remains elusive because the real world is very complex and because one's acceptance of both premises and conclusions depends upon one's political, economic, and social outlook.

[*Mary Ann Cunningham*]

FURTHER READING

Hardin, Garrett. "The Tragedy of the Commons." *Science* 162 (13 December 1968): 1243-48.

"Whose Common Future?" *Ecologist* 22 (July/August 1992).

Trail Smelter arbitration

The Trail Smelter arbitration of 1938 and 1941 was a landmark decision about a dispute over **environmental degradation** between the United States and Canada. This was the first decision to recognize international liability for damages caused to another nation, even when no existing treaty created an obligation to prevent such damage.

A tribunal was set up by Canada and the United States to resolve a dispute over timber and crop damages caused by a **smelter** on the Canadian side of the border. The tribunal decided that Canada had to pay the United States for damages, and further that it was obliged to abate the **pollution**. In delivering their decision, the tribunal made an historic and often-cited declaration:

> [U]nder the principles of international law, as well as of the law of the United States, no State has the right to use or permit the use of its territory in such a manner as to cause injury by fumes in or to the territory of another or the properties or persons therein, when the case is of

serious consequence and the injury is established by clear and convincing evidence . . . .

The case was a landmark because it was the first to challenge historic principles of international law which subordinated international environmental duty to nationalistic claims of sovereignty and free-market methods of unfettered industrial development. The Trail Smelter decision has since become the primary precedent for international **environmental law**, which protects the **environment** through a process known as the "web of treaty law." International environmental law is based on individual governmental responses to discrete international problems, such as the Trail Smelter issue. Legal decisions over environmental disputes between nations are made in reference to a growing body of treaties, conventions, and other indications of "state practices."

The Trail Smelter decision has shaped the core principle underlying international environmental law. According to this principle, a country which creates transboundary pollution or some other environmentally hazardous effect is liable for the harm this causes, either directly or indirectly, to another country. A much older precedent for this same principle is rooted both in Roman Law and Common Law: *sic utere ut alienum non laedas*—use your own property in such a manner as not to injure that of another. Prior to the twentieth century, this principle was not relevant to international law because actions within a nation's borders rarely conflicted with the rights of another. *See also* Acid rain; Environmental Law Institute; Environmental liability; Environmental policy; United Nations Earth Summit

[*Kevin Wolf*]

Train, Russell E. (1920-)

American environmentalist

Concern about environmental issues is a relatively recent phenomenon worldwide. Until the 1960s, citizens were not interested in air and water **pollution**, waste disposal, and **wetlands** destruction.

An important figure in bringing these issues to public attention was Russell Eroll Train. He was born in Jamestown, Rhode Island, on June 4, 1920, the son of a rear admiral in the United States Navy. He attended St. Alban's School and Princeton University, from which he graduated in 1941. After serving in the United States Army during World War II, Train entered Columbia Law School, where he earned his law degree in 1948.

Train's early career suggested that he would follow a somewhat traditional life of government service. He took a job as counsel to the Congressional Joint Committee on Revenue and Taxation in 1948 and five years later, became clerk of the House Ways and Means Committee. In 1957, Train was appointed a judge on the Tax Court of the United States.

This pattern was disrupted, however, because of Train's interest in **conservation** programs. In 1961, he founded the African Wildlife Leadership Foundation and became its first head. He gradually began to spend more time on conservation activities and finally resigned his judgeship to become president of the Conservation Foundation.

Train's first environmental-related government appointment came in 1968, when President Lyndon Johnson asked him to serve on the National Water Commission. The election of Republican Richard Nixon late that year did not end Train's career of government service, but instead provided him with even more opportunities. One of Nixon's first actions after the presidential election was his appointment of a 20-member inter-governmental task force on **natural resources** and the **environment**. The task force's report criticized the government's failure to fund anti-pollution programs adequately, and it recommended the appointment of a special advisor to the President on environmental matters.

In January 1969, Nixon offered Train another assignment. The President had been sharply criticized by environmentalists for his appointment of Alaska Governor Walter J. Hickel as Secretary of the Interior. To blunt that criticism, Nixon chose Train to serve as Under Secretary of the Interior, an appointment widely praised by environmental groups. In his new position, Train was faced with a number of difficult and controversial environmental issues, the most important of which were the proposed **Trans-Alaska pipeline** project and the huge new airport planned for construction in Florida's **Everglades** National Park. When Congress created the **Council on Environmental Quality** in 1970 (largely as a result of Train's urging), he was appointed chairman by President Nixon. The Council's first report identified the most important critical environmental problems facing the nation and encouraged the development of a "strong and consistent federal policy" to deal with these problems.

Train reached the pinnacle of his career in September 1973, when he was appointed administrator of the federal government's primary environmental agency, the **Environmental Protection Agency (EPA)**. During the three and a half years he served in this post, he frequently disagreed with the President who had appointed him. He often felt that Nixon's administration tried to prevent the enforcement of **environmental law**s passed by Congress. Some of his most difficult battles involved energy issues. While the administration preferred a *laissez-faire* approach in which the marketplace controlled energy use and prices, Train argued for more controls that would help conserve energy resources and reduce air and water pollution.

With the election of Jimmy Carter in 1976, Train's tenure in office was limited. He resigned his position at EPA in March 1977 and returned to the Conservation Foundation. *See also* Air pollution; Energy and the environment; Environmental policies, National; Environmental policy; National park; Water pollution

[*David E. Newton*]

FURTHER READING

Durham, M.S. "Nice Guy in a Mean Job." *Audubon* (January 1974): 97-104.

Schoenbaum, E.W. "Russell E. Train." In: *Political Profiles*. New York: Facts on File, 1979.

Trans-Alaska pipeline

The discovery in March 1968 of oil on the Arctic slope of Alaska's Prudhoe Bay ignited an ongoing controversy over the handling of the Arctic slope's abundant energy resources. Of all the options considered for transporting the huge quantities found in North America's largest field, the least hazardous and most suitable was deemed a pipeline to the ice-free southern port of Valdez.

Plans for the pipeline began immediately. Labeled the Trans-Alaskan Pipeline System (TAPS) its cost was estimated at $1.5 billion, a pittance compared to the final cost of $7.7 billion. The total development cost for Prudhoe Bay oil was likely over $15 billion, the most expensive project ever undertaken by private industry. Antagonists, aided by the nascent environmental movement, succeeded in temporarily halting the project. Legislation that created the **Environmental Protection Agency (EPA)** and required environmental impact statements for all federally-related projects added new, critically important requirements to TAPS. Approval came with the 1973 Trans-Alaskan Authorization Act, spurred on by the 1973 OPEC embargo, the world's first severe energy crisis. Construction quickly resumed.

The pipeline is an engineering marvel, having broken new ground in dealing with **permafrost** and mountainous Arctic conditions. The northern half of the pipeline is elevated to protect the permafrost, but river crossings and portions threatened by avalanches are buried for protection. A system was developed to keep the oil warm for 21 days in the event of a shutdown, to prevent TAPS from becoming the "world's largest tube of chapstick." Especially notable is Thompson Pass near the southern end, where descent angles up to 45 degrees severely taxed construction workers, especially welders.

Everything about TAPS is colossal: 799 miles (1,286 km) of 48-inch (122-cm) diameter vanadium alloy pipe; 78,000 support columns; 65,000 welds; 15,000 trucks; peak employment of more than 20,000 workers. TAPS has an operations control center linked to each of the twelve pump stations, with computer controlled flow rates and status checks every ten seconds.

The severe restrictions that the enabling act imposed have paid off in an enviable safety record and few problems. The worst problem thus far was caused by local sabotage of an above-ground segment. In spite of its good record, however, TAPS remains controversial. As predicted, it delivers more oil than West Coast refineries can handle, and efforts continue to allow exports to Japan.

Barring development of the **Arctic National Wildlife Refuge**, by the year 2000, TAPS will be flowing at only 25 percent of capacity. Utilitarian conservationists and altruistic preservationists are at loggerheads over energy development in Alaska, while most native Eskimos consider this an

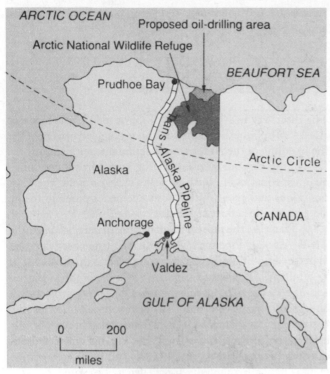

The route of the Trans-Alaska pipeline

opportunity to solidify their growing involvement in the American economy. *See also* Oil drilling; Oil embargo

[*Nathan H. Meleen*]

FURTHER READING

Dixon, M. *What Happened to Fairbanks?: The Effects of the Trans-Alaska Oil Pipeline on the Community of Fairbanks, Alaska.* Boulder, CO: Westview Press, 1978.

Hodgson, B. "The Pipeline: Alaska's Troubled Colossus." *National Geographic* 150 (November 1976): 684-707.

Lee, D. B. "Oil in the Wilderness: An Arctic Dilemma." *National Geographic* 174 (December 1988): 858-871.

Roscow, J. P. *800 Miles to Valdez: the Building of the Alaska Pipeline.* Englewood Cliffs, NJ: Prentice Hall, 1977.

Trans-Amazonian highway

The Trans Amazonian highway begins in northeast Brazil and crosses the states of Para and Amazonia. The earth road, known as BR-230 on travel maps, was completed in the 1970s during the military regime that ruled Brazil from 1964 until 1985. The highway was intended to further **land reform** by drawing landless peasants to the area, especially from the poorest regions of northern Brazil. More than 500,000 people have migrated to Transamazonia since the early 1970s. Many of the colonists feel that the government enticed them there with false promises.

The road has never been paved, so it is nothing but dust in the dry season and an impassable swamp during the wet season. Farmers struggle to make a living, with the highway as their only means of transporting produce to market. When the rains come, large segments of the highway wash away entirely, leaving the farmers with no way to transport their crops. Small farmers live on the brink of survival. Farmer José Ribamar Ripardo says, "People grow crops only to see them rot for lack of transport. It's really an animal's life." To survive in Amazonia, the colonists say, they require a paved road to transport their produce.

The goal of repairing and paving the highway is viewed with disfavor by many environmentalists. Roads through Amazonia are perceived as being synonymous with destruction of the **rain forest**s. Many environmental groups fear that improved roads will bring more people into the area and lead to increased devastation.

The Movement For Survival, spearheaded by José Geraldo Torres da Silva, claims that "If farmers could have technical help to invest in **nature**, they will be able to support their families with just one third of their land lots, avoiding **deforestation**, the indiscriminate killing of numerous animal and plant **species**." Farmers in the region say that they can survive on the land base that they have already acquired. They have proposed preserving some natural vegetation by growing a mixture of rubber and cacoa trees, which grow best in shaded areas, so they will not have to devastate the forest. Efforts are currently underway to establish extractivist preserves to harvest rubber, brazil nuts, and other native products. Such proposals for the use of the forest are a viable option, but they are not enough. The environmentally friendly plans must also take into account fluctuations in the market place. Brazil nuts, for instance, are harvested in the unspoiled forest. When nut prices fall on the international market, the gatherers must have other means of income to fall back on, without having to relocate to a different part of the country.

Many residents of the area fear that if small farmers do not have a reliable road to get produce to market, they will have to leave the region. There is a real danger that their lots will be sold to cattle ranchers, loggers, and investors. Small farmers have a track record of utilizing the land in ways that are more environmentally sound than those who follow in their wake.

[*Debra Glidden*]

FURTHER READING

Babbitt, B. E. "Amazon Grace." *New Republic* 202 (25 June 1990): 18-19.

Fearnside, P. M. "Rethinking Continuous Cultivation in Amazonia: The 'Yurimaguas Technology' May Not Provide the Bountiful Harvest Predicted by its Originators." *Bioscience* 37 (March 1987): 209.

Néto, R. B. "The Transamazonian Highway." *Buzzworm* 4 (November-December 1992): 28-29.

Simpson, J. "To the Beginning of the World." *World Monitor* 6 (January 1993): 34-41.

Vesilind, P. J. "Brazil Moment of Promise and Pain." *National Geographic* 171 (March 1987): 372-373.

Transboundary pollution

The most common interpretation of transboundary pollution is that it is **pollution** not contained by a single nation state, but rather travels across national borders at varying rates. The concept of the global commons is important to an understanding of transboundary pollution. As both population and production increase around the globe, the potential for pollution to spill from one country to another increases. Transboundary pollution can take the form of contaminated water or the deposition of air borne pollutants across national borders. Transboundary pollution can be caused by catastrophic events such as the **Chernobyl** nuclear explosion. It can also be caused by the creeping of industrial discharge that eventually has a measurable impact on adjacent countries. It is possible that pollution can cross state lines within a country and would indeed be referred to as transboundary pollution. This type of case is seldom held up as a serious policy problem since national controls can be brought to bear on the responsible parties and problems can be solved within national borders. It is good to understand how interstate environmental problems might develop and to have knowledge as to those regulatory units of national government that have jurisdiction.

Federalism is important in issues of national environmental pollution in large part because pollution can spread across several states before it is contained. Within the United States, it is the **Environmental Protection Agency** (EPA) that writes the regulations that are enforced by the states. The general rule is that states may enact environmental regulations that are more strict than what the EPA has enacted, but not less strict. In some cases interstate compacts are designated by the EPA to deal with issues of pollution control. An example of this is the regional compacts for the management of low level radioactive waste materials. These interstate compacts meet and make policy for the siting and management of facilities, the transport of materials and the long term planning for adequate and safe storage of low level **radioactive waste** until its radioactivity has been exhausted. Other jurisdictions such as this in the U.S. deal with transboundary issues of **air quality**, **wildlife management**, fisheries, **endangered species**, **water quality**, and **solid waste** management. Federalism has been manifested in specific legislation. The **National Environmental Policy Act** (NEPA) is an attempt to clarify and monitor environmental quality regardless of state boundaries. NEPA provides for a council to monitor trends. The Council on Environmental Quality is a three member council appointed by the President of the United States to collect data at the national level on environmental quality and management, regardless of jurisdiction. This picture at a national level is vastly complicated when moved to a global level.

There is increasing demand for dialogue and support for institutions that can address impacts on the global commons. The issue of "remedies" for transboundary pollution is usually near the top of the agenda. Remedies frequently take the form of payments to rectify a wrong, but more often take the form of fines or other measures to assure compliance with best practices. The problem with this approach is that charges have to be high enough to offset the cost of controlling "creeping" pollution that might cross national borders or the cost of monitoring production processes to prevent predictable disasters. Marine pollution is an excellent example of a transboundary pollution problem that involves many nation states and unlimited point sources of pollution. Marine pollution can be the result of on-shore industrial processes that use the ocean as a waste disposal site. Ships at sea find the ocean just too convenient as a sewer system, and surface ocean activities such as oil drilling are a constant source of pollution due to unintentional discharges. Accidents at sea are well documented, the most famous in recent years being the **Exxon Valdez** oil spill off of Alaska in Prince William Sound in 1989. Earlier, in 1969 an international conference on marine pollution was held. As a result of this conference two treaties were developed and signed that would respond to oil pollution on the high seas. These treaties were not fully ratified until 1975. The Convention on the Prevention of Marine Pollution by Dumping of Wastes and Other Matter and The Convention for the Prevention of Marine Pollution by Dumping from Ships and Aircraft site specific pollutants that are considered extremely detrimental to marine environments. These pollutants are organohalogenic compounds, and **mercury**, as well as slightly less harmful compounds such as **lead**, **arsenic**, **copper**, and **pesticide**s. The specificity of those treaties that deal with ocean environments indicate a rising commitment to the control of transboundary pollution carried by the ocean's currents and helped resolve the question of remedies in the *Valdez* catastrophe.

Acid rain is a clear example of how air currents can carry destructive pollution from one nation state to another, and indeed, around the globe. Air as a vector of pollution is particularly insidious because air patterns, although known, can change abruptly confounding a country's attempt to monitor where pollutants come from. Acid deposition has been an international issue for many years. The residuals from the burning of **fossil fuels** and the byproducts from radiation combine in the upper **atmosphere** with water vapor and precipitate down as acid rain. This precipitation is damaging to lakes and streams as well as to forests and buildings in countries that may have little sulfur and **nitrogen** generation of their own. The negative justice of this issue is that it is the most industrialized nations that are producing these pollutants due to increased production and too often the pollution rains down on developing countries that have neither the resources nor the technical expertise to clean up the mess. Only recently, due to international agreements between nation states, has there been significant reduction in the deposition of acid rain. The **Clean Air Act** Amendments of 1990 in the United States helped to reduce **emission**s from **coal**-burning plants. In Europe, sulfur emissions are being reduced due to an agreement among eight countries. The European Community in 1992 agreed to implement automobile emission standards similar to what the United States agreed to in the early 1980s. In 1994 all large automobiles in Europe were required to reduce emissions with the installation of catalytic converters. These measures are all aimed at reducing transboundary pollution due to air emissions.

Probably the most famous case of transboundary river pollution is that of the Rhine River with its point of incidence in Basel, Switzerland. This was a catastrophe of great proportions. The source of pollution was an explosion at a chemical plant. In the process of putting out the fire, great volumes of water were used. The water mixed with the chemicals at the plant (mercury, insecticides, fungicides, herbicides and other agricultural chemicals), creating a highly toxic discharge. This lethal mixture washed into the Rhine River and coursed its way to the Baltic Sea, affecting every country along the way. Citizens of six sovereign nations were affected and damage was extensive. There was further consternation when compensation for damage was found to be difficult to obtain. Although the chemical company volunteered to pay some compensation it was not enough. It was possible that each affected nation state could try the case in their own national court system, but how would collection for damages take place? "In transboundary cases, if there is no treaty or convention in force, by what combination of other international law principles can the rules of liability and remedy be determined?" (Plater, Abrams, Goldfarb, 1992, pg. 1010) It becomes problematic to institute legal action against another country if there is no precedent. Since there is no history of litigation between nation states in cases of environmental damage there is no precedent to determine outcome. Historically, legal disputes have been resolved (albeit, extremely slowly) through negotiations and treaties. There is no "polluter pays" statute in international law doctrine.

The authority that can be brought to bear on issues of transboundary pollution is weak and confusing. The only mechanism that is currently available to compensate injury is private litigation between parties and that is difficult due to a lack of agreements to enforce civil judgments. If, in fact, the polluter is the national government, as in the case of the Chernobyl disaster, it may be nearly impossible to gain compensation for damages.

Transboundary pollution takes many forms and can be perpetrated by both private industry and government activities. It is difficult if not impossible to litigate on an international scale. It is in fact sometimes difficult to determine who the polluter is when the pollution is "creeping" and not a catastrophic incidence. Airborne transboundary pollution is extremely difficult to track due to the pervasive nature of the practices that produce it. Global solutions to transboundary pollution can only be successful if all nations agree to implement controls to reduce known pollutants and to take responsibility for accidents that damage the environmental quality of other nations.

[*Cynthia Fridgen*]

FURTHER READING

Bernauer, T. and P. Moser. "Reducing Pollution of the River Rhine: The Influence of International Cooperation in The Journal of Environment & Development." *Sage Periodicals Press* 5, no. 4 (December 1996).

Buck, S.J., *Understanding Environmental Administration and Law.* Washington D.C. and California: Island Press, 1996.

Plater, Z.J.B., R.H. Abrams, W. Goldfarb. *Environmental Law and Policy: Nature, Law, and Society.* St. Paul, MN: West Publishing Co, 1992.

"Choosing a Sustainable Future: The Report of the National Commission on the Environment," by the World Wildlife Fund. Washington D.C. and California: Island Press, 1993.

Transfer station

The regional disposal of **solid waste** requires a multi-stage system of collection, transport, consolidation, delivery, and ultimate disposal. Many states and counties have established transfer stations, where solid waste collected from curbsides and other local sources by small municipal garbage trucks is consolidated and transferred to a larger capacity vehicle, such as a refuse transfer truck, for transportation to a disposal facility. Typically, municipal garbage trucks have a capacity of twenty cubic yards and refuse transfer trucks may have a capacity of eighty or one hundred cubic yards. The use of transfer stations reduces hauling costs and promotes a regional approach to **waste management**. *See also* Garbage; Landfill; Municipal waste; Tipping fee; Waste stream

Transmission lines

Transmission lines are used to transport electricity from places where it is generated to places where it is used. Almost all electricity in North America is generated in fossil-fueled, nuclear-fueled, or hydroelectric generating stations. These are located some distance away from the factories, businesses, institutions, and homes where the electricity is actually used, in some cases hundreds of miles away, so that the electricity must be transmitted from the generating stations to these diverse locations.

Transmission lines are strung between tall, well-spaced towers and are linear features that appropriate long, narrow areas of land. Most transmission lines carry a high voltage of alternating current, typically ranging from about 44 kilovolts (kV) to as high as 750 or more kV; (some transmission lines carry a direct current, but this is uncommon). Transmission lines typically feed into lower-voltage distribution lines, which typically have voltage levels less than about 35 kV and an alternating current (in North America) of 60 Hertz (Hz; this is equivalent to 60 cycles of positive to negative per second), and is usually 50 Hz in Europe.

Electrical fields are generated by transmission lines (and by all electrical appliances), with the strength of the field being a function of the voltage level of the current being carried by the powerline. The flow of electricity in transmission lines also generates a magnetic field. Electric fields are strongly distorted by conducting objects (including the human body), but magnetic fields are little affected and freely pass through biomass and most structures. Electric and magnetic fields both induce extremely weak electrical currents in the bodies of humans and other animals. These electrical current are, however, several million times weaker than those induced by the normal functions of certain cells in the human body.

Transmission lines are controversial for various reasons. These include their poor aesthetics, the fact that they can destroy and fragment large areas of natural lands or take large areas out of other economically productive land-uses, and the belief of many people that there are low-level health risks associated with living in the vicinity of these structures.

Aesthetics of Transmission Lines

Transmission lines are very long, tall, extremely prominent, linear features. Transmission lines have an unnatural appearance and their very presence disrupts the visual aesthetics of natural landscapes, as viewed from the ground or the air. As such, transmission lines represent a type of "visual **pollution**" that detracts from otherwise pleasing natural or pastoral landscapes. These aesthetic damages are an important environmental impact of almost all rural transmission lines. Similarly, above-ground transmission lines in urban and suburban areas are not regarded as having good aesthetics.

Damages to Natural Values

Apart from difficult crossings of major rivers and mountainous areas, transmission lines tend to follow the shortest routes between their origin and destination. Often, this means that intervening natural areas must be partially cleared to develop the right-of-way for the transmission line. This can result in permanent losses of natural **habitat**, as typically happens when forests are cleared to develop a powerline right-of-way. Moreover, it is not feasible to allow trees to regenerate beneath a transmission line because they can interfere with the operation and servicing of the powerline.

For these reasons, vegetation is cleared beneath and to the sides of transmission lines (for a width of about one tree-height). This can be done by periodically cutting shrubby vegetation and young trees or by the careful use of herbicides, which can kill shrubs and trees while allowing the growth of grasses and other herbaceous plants.

These sorts of management practices result in the conversion of any original, natural habitats along a transmission right-of-way into artificial habitats. The ecological effects include a net loss of natural habitats and fragmentation of the remainder into smaller blocks. In addition, roads associated with the construction and maintenance of transmission lines may provide relatively easy access for hunters, fishers, and other outdoor recreationalists to previously remote and isolated natural areas. This can result in increased stress for certain wild species, especially hunted ones, as well as other ecological damages.

Some studies of transmission lines have found that hypothesized ecological damages did not occur or were unimportant. For example, naturalists suggested that the construction of extensive hydroelectric transmission lines in the boreal forest of northern Quebec would impede the movements of woodland caribou. In fact, this did not occur, and caribou were sometimes observed to use the relatively open transmission corridors during their migrations and as resting places. Similar observations have been made elsewhere for moose, white-tailed deer, and other ungulates. Predators of these animals, such as wolves and coyotes, will also freely move along transmission corridors, unless they are frequently disturbed by hunters, recreationalists, or maintenance crews.

Certain birds of prey, particularly osprey, may use transmission poles or pylons as a platform upon which to build their bulky nests which may be used for many years. In some cases the birds are considered a management problem, especially if their nests get large enough to potentially short out the powerlines or if the parent birds aggressively defend their nests against linesmen attempting to repair or maintain the transmission line. Fortunately, it is relatively easy to move the nests during the nonbreeding season and to place them on a "dummy" pole located for the purpose beside the transmission line. In most cases, the ospreys will readily use the relocated nest in subsequent years.

Transmission lines also pose lethal risks for certain kinds of birds, especially larger species that may inadvertently collide with wires, severely injuring themselves. There have also been cases of raptors and other large birds being electrocuted by settling on transmission lines, particularly if they somehow span adjacent wires with their wings.

Disruption of Land-use

Some economically important land-uses can occur beneath transmission lines, for example, forestry and some types of agriculture. Other land-uses, however, are not compatible with the immediate proximity of high-voltage transmission lines, particularly residential land-uses. In cases of land-use conflicts, opportunities are lost to engage in certain economically productive uses of the land, a context that detracts from benefits that are associated with the construction and operation of the transmission line.

Many people, including some highly qualified scientists, believe that low-level health risks may be associated with longer-term exposures to the electric and magnetic fields that are generated by transmission lines. These increased risks mean that people living or working in the vicinity of these industrial structures may have an increased risk of developing certain diseases or of suffering other damages to their health.

Although people are routinely exposed to **electromagnetic fields** through the operation of electrical appliances in the home or at work, those exposures are typically intermittent. In contrast, continuous electromagnetic fields are generated by transmission lines, so longer-term exposures can be relatively high. It must be understood, however, that the scientific knowledge in support of the low-level health risks associated with transmission lines is incomplete and equivocal and therefore highly controversial.

In particular, some studies have suggested that long-term exposure to electromagnetic fields generated by high-voltage transmission lines may be associated with an elevated incidence of certain types of **cancers**. The strongest suggestions have been for increased risks of childhood **leukemia**. There is weaker evidence of increased risks of cancers of the lymphatic and nervous systems and of adult leukemia. It must be remembered, however, that not all epidemiological studies of transmission lines have reported these statistical relationships and that the increased risks are rather small when they are found. Studies have also been made of possible increases in the incidences of migraine headaches, mental depression, and reproductive problems associated with longer-term exposures to electromagnetic fields near transmission lines. The results of all these studies are inconsistent and equivocal.

Some researchers who have assessed the medical problems potentially associated with high-voltage transmission lines have concluded that it would be prudent to not have people living in close proximity to these industrial structures. Even though there is no strong and compelling evidence that medical problems are actually occurring, the precautionary approach to environmental management dictates that the potential risks should be avoided to the degree possible. It would therefore be sensible for people to avoid living within about 54.5 yd (50 m) or so of a high-voltage transmission line, and they should avoid frequently using the right-of-way as travel corridors.

[*Bill Freedman*]

FURTHER READING

Alonso, J.C., J.A. Alonso, and R. Munoz-Pulido. "Mitigation of Bird Collisions with Transmission Lines through Ground-wire Marking," *Biology Conservation*, 67 (1994): 129-134.

Carpenter, D.O., and S. Ayrapetyan. *Biological Effects of Electric and Magnetic Fields*. vols. 1 & 2. San Diego: Academic Press, 1994.

Coleman, M.P., et al. "Leukemia and Residence Near Electricity Transmission Equipment: a Case-control Study," *Brit. J. Cancer* 60 (1989): 793-798.

Feychting, M., and A. Ahlbom. "Magnetic Fields and Cancer in Children Residing Near Swedish High-voltage Power Lines," *American Journal of Epidemiology* 138 (1993): 467-481.

Levallois, P., and D. Gauvin. *Risks Associated with Electromagnetic Fields Generated by Electrical Transmission and Distribution Lines*. Great Whale Environmental Assessment: Background Paper No. 9, Part 1. Montreal, PQ: Great Whale Public Review Support Office. 1994.

London, S.J., et al. "Exposure to Residential Electric and Magnetic Fields and Risk of Childhood Leukemia," *American Journal of Epidemiology*, 134 (1991): 923-927.

Steenhof, K., M.A. Kochert, and J.A. Roppe. "Nesting by Raptors and Common Ravens on Electrical Transmission Line Towers," *Journal of Wildlife Management*, 57 (1993): 271-281.

Transpiration

Transpiration is the process by which plants give off water vapor from their leaves to the **atmosphere**. The process is an important stage in the water cycle, often more important in returning water to the atmosphere than is evaporation from rivers and lakes. A single acre of growing corn, for example, transpires an average of 3,500 gallons (13,248 liters) of water per acre of land per day. Transpiration is, therefore, an important mechanism for moving water through the **soil**, into plants, and back into the atmosphere. When plants are removed from an area, soil retains more moisture and is unable to absorb rain water. As a consequence, **runoff** and loss of **nutrient**s from the soil is likely to increase. *See also* Erosion; Flooding; Soil conservation; Soil fertility

Trash

See **Solid waste**

Treespiking

See **Monkey-wrenching**

Trihalomethanes

Trihalomethanes (THMs) are organic **chemicals** composed of three halogen atoms (primarily **chlorine** and bromine) and one **hydrogen** atom bound to a single **carbon** atom. They are commonly used as solvents in a variety of applications, and trichloromethane (or chloroform) was once used by medical doctors as an anesthetic. In 1974, Johannes Rook of the Netherlands discovered the presence of THMs in chlorinated drinking water. He and other researchers subsequently demonstrated that minute quantities of THMs are formed during **water treatment**. Chlorine, when added to disinfect the water, reacts with naturally occurring organic matter present in the water. **Groundwater** can also be contaminated with THMs if people use them improperly, release them accidentally, or dispose of them unsuitably. Since high dosages of chloroform had been found to produce **cancer** in mice and rats, the United States **Environmental Protection Agency (EPA)** amended the drinking water standards in 1979 to limit the concentration of THMs to a sum total of 100 µg/L. A more stringent limit is thought to be forthcoming. *See also* Carcinogen; Drinking-water supply; Water quality standards

Trophic level

One way of analyzing the biological relationships within an **ecosystem** is to describe who eats whom within the system, also called a functional analysis. Each feeding level in an ecosystem is called a trophic level. In the **grasslands**, for example, plants are considered primary producers, forming the first trophic level. The second trophic level consists of primary consumers, such as deer, mice, seed and fruit-eating birds, and other animals, depending completely on the primary producers for their food. Carnivores and predators, such as hawks, are the secondary consumers. Often, the same **species** may fit into several categories. Bears, for example, are considered both primary and secondary consumers, for they feed on plant matter as well as on meat. Bacteria and **fungi** that decompose dead organic matter are called the decomposers. Thus, on the basis of food source and feeding behavior, a complex **food chain/web** exists within any ecosystem and every species belongs to one or more of several trophic levels.

In **environmental science**, the concept of trophic levels is often used to assess the potential for transfer of pollutants through an ecosystem. Since each trophic level is dependent on all the other levels, positive or negative changes in the composition or abundance of any one trophic level will ultimately affect all other levels. In ecosystems that normally have stable, complex trophic levels within the food web, **pollution** can lead to fluctuations and simplification of the trophic levels. Contaminants that are taken up by plants from the **soil** may be transferred to primary and secondary consumers through their feeding patterns. This is known as trophic level transfer.

A classic example of trophic level transfer was the release of **DDT** in the **environment**. DDT is an insecticide commonly used in the United States during the 1950s and early 1960s. DDT ran off treated fields into lakes and rivers, where it accumulated in the fatty tissues of primary consumers such as fish and shellfish. The **chemicals** were then transferred into secondary consumers, such as eagles, which fed on the primary consumers. While the concentrations of DDT were rarely high enough to kill the birds, it did cause them to lay eggs with thin shells. The thin eggshells led to decreased hatching success and thus caused a decline in the eagle population.

Trophic level analysis is a commonly used method of environmental assessment. A pollutant or disturbance is assessed in terms of its effects on each trophic level. If significant amounts of **nutrient**s are brought into a lake receiving fertilizer runoff from fields, a spurt in the growth of algae (primary producers) in the lake may be triggered. However the increased growth might actually be dominated by certain algal groups, such as blue-green algae, which may not constitute desirable food sources for the **zooplankton** and fish (primary consumers) which normally depend on algae for food. In this case, even though the environmental conditions might appear to stimulate increased growth in one trophic level, the nature of the change does not necessarily prove advantageous to other trophic levels within the same system. *See also* Agricultural pollution; Algal bloom; Aquatic weed control; Balance of nature; Bald eagle; Decomposition; Environmental stress; Predator control; Predator-prey interactions

[*Usha Vedagiri*]

FURTHER READING

Connell, D. W., and G. J. Miller. *Chemistry and Ecotoxicology of Pollution.* New York: Wiley, 1984.

Smith, R. L. *Ecology and Field Biology.* New York: Harper and Row, 1980.

Tropical rain forest

The richest and most productive biological communities in the world are in the tropical forests. These forests have been reduced to less than half of their former extent by human activities and now cover only about seven percent of Earth's land area. In this limited area, however, is about two-thirds of the vegetation mass and about half of all living **species** in the world.

The largest, lushest, and most biologically diverse of the remaining tropical moist forests are in the **Amazon Basin** of South America, the Congo River basin of central Africa, and the large islands of southeast Asia (Sumatra,

The layered communities of a tropical rain forest are directly related to the gradual lessening of light, from the brightness of the canopy to the dense shade of the forest floor.

Borneo, and Papua, New Guinea). Whereas the forests of mainland southeast Asia, western Africa, and Central America are strongly seasonal, with wet and dry seasons, the South American and central African forests are true **rain forest**s. Rainfall is generally over 160 inches (406 centimeters) per year and falls more or less evenly throughout the year. It is said that such rain forests "make their own rain," because about half the rain that falls in the forests comes from condensation of water vapor released by **transpiration** from the trees themselves. Rain forests at lower elevations are hot and humid year-round. At higher elevations, tropical mountains intercept moisture-laden clouds, so the forests that blanket their slopes are cool, wet, and fog-shrouded. They are aptly and poetically called "cloud forests." Tropical forests are generally very old. Unlike **temperate rain forest**s, they have not been disturbed by **glaciation** or mountain-building for hundreds of millions of years. This long period of **evolution** under conditions of ample moisture and stable temperatures has created an incredible diversity of organisms of amazing shapes, colors, sizes, habits, and specialized **adaptation**s.

Habitats in a tropical rain forest are stratified into three to five distinct layers from ground level to the tops of the tallest trees. Hundreds of tree species grow together in lush profusion, their crowns interlocking to form a dense, dappled canopy about 120 feet (37 meters) above the forest floor. These unusually tall trees are supported by relatively thin trunks reinforced by wedge-shaped buttresses that attach to a thick mat of roots just under the **soil** surface. A few emergent trees rise above the seemingly solid canopy into a world of sunlight, wind, and open space. Numerous species of birds, insects, reptiles, and small mammals live exclusively in the forest canopy, never descending below the crowns of the trees.

The forest understory is composed of small trees and shrubs growing between the trunks of the major trees, as well as climbing woody vines (lianas) and many epiphytes—mainly orchids, bromeliads, and arboreal ferns—that attach themselves to the trees. Some of the larger trees may support fifty to one hundred different species of epiphytes and an even larger population of animals that are specialized to live in the many habitats they create. These understory layers are a world of bright but filtered light abuzz with animal activity.

By contrast, the forest floor is generally dark, humid, quiet, and rather open. Few herbaceous plants can survive in the deep shade created by the layered canopy of the forest trees and their epiphytes. The most numerous animals are ants and termites that scavenge on the detritus raining down from above. A few rodent species gather fallen fruits and nuts. Rare predators such as leopards, jaguars, smaller cats, and large snakes hunt both on the ground and in the understory.

A tropical rain forest may produce as much as 90 tons of **biomass** per hectare per year, and one might think that the soil that supports this incredible growth is rich and fertile. However, the soil is old, acidic, and **nutrient** poor. Ages of incessant tropical rains and high temperatures have depleted minerals, leaving an iron- and **aluminum**-rich podzol. Tropical forests have only about 10 percent of their organic material and nutrients in the soil, compared to boreal forests, which may have 90 percent of their organic material in litter and **sediment**s.

The interactions of decomposers and living plant roots in the soil are, literally, the critical base that maintains the rain forest **ecosystem**. Tropical rain forests are able to maintain high productivity only through rapid **recycling** of nutrients. The constant rain of detritus and litter that falls to the ground is quickly decomposed by populations of **fungi** and bacteria that flourish in the warm, moist **environment**. Some of these decomposers have symbiotic relationships with the roots of specific trees. Trees have broad, shallow root systems to capitalize on this surface nutrient source; an individual tree might create a dense mat of superficial roots 328 feet (100 meters) in diameter and three feet (one meter) thick. In this way, nutrients are absorbed quickly and almost entirely and are reused almost immediately to build fresh plant growth, the necessary base to the trophic pyramid of this incredible ecosystem. *See also* Biodiversity

[*William P. Cunningham*]

FURTHER READING

Caufield, C. *In the Rainforest*. New York: Knopf, 1985.

Hecht, S., and A. Cockburn. *Fate of the Forest*. New York: Harper Collins, 1991.

Myers, N. *The Primary Source: Tropical Forests and Our Future*. New York: Norton, 1992.

Repetto, R. "Deforestation in the Tropics." *Scientific American* 262 (April 1990): 36-42.

Revkin, A. *The Burning Season: The Murder of Chico Mendes and the Fight for the Amazon Rain Forest*. New York: Houghton Mifflin, 1991.

Tropopause

The tropopause is the upper boundary of the **troposphere**, a layer of the earth's **atmosphere** near the ground. In the troposphere, the temperature generally decreases with increasing altitude, with restricted exceptions called **inversion**s. However, at a height of about six miles (ten kilometers) at the poles to nine miles (15 kilometers) at the equator, the temperature abruptly becomes constant with increasing altitude. This isothermal region is called the **stratosphere**, and the interface between it and the troposphere is called the tropopause. Mixing of air across the tropopause is slow, occurring on a time scale of weeks on the average, while tropospheric mixing is more rapid.

The existence of the stratosphere is largely caused by the absorption of **solar energy**, mostly ultraviolet light, by oxygen to form **ozone**. The balance of the heating is caused by absorption of other parts of the solar spectrum by other trace gases. *See also* Ultraviolet radiation

Troposphere

From the Greek word *tropos*, meaning turning, troposphere is the zone of moisture-laden storms between the surface and the **stratosphere** above. Because ice crystals must form before precipitation can begin, the troposphere rises to 10-12 miles (16-19 kilometers) over the equator but grades downward to 5-6 miles (8-9 kilometers) over the poles. It is marked by a sharp drop in temperature vertically, averaging 3.5 degrees per 1000 feet (305 meters) because of exponentially decreasing density of air molecules. Actual "lapse" rates vary enormously, ranging from inversions, where temperatures rise and trap pollutants, to steep lapse rates with warm surface air topped by very cold polar air; the latter produces dangerous storms.

Tsunamis

Tsunamis are large seismic sea waves that can cause major destruction in coastal regions. *Tsunamis*, Japanese for "wave in bay," are caused by underwater seismic activity, such as earthquakes.

While tsunamis are commonly called "tidal waves," this is an erroneous term; these potentially catastrophic waves have nothing to do with the tides. Tides are the up and down movements of the sea surface at the shore, caused by the gravitational attraction of the moon and sun on our marine waters. Tsunamis are caused by the movements of Earth's crustal plates. Tides rarely cause major damage unless they are associated with a storm, while tsunamis can cause major loss of life and property.

It has been known for several hundred years that tsunamis are caused by seismic movements of the ocean floor. This occurs most commonly during submarine earthquakes, underwater landslides, and perhaps volcanoes, all of which release large amounts of energy. The sudden movement of the Earth's crust caused by an underwater earthquake, for example, displaces or moves the water above it. This causes a high energy wave to form, which is passed rapidly through the water.

Tsunamis are very long waves, with a period (the time for one complete wave to pass a fixed point) ranging from 6-60 minutes. These waves typically travel 450 mi/h (200 m/s or 720 km/h). Therefore, an earthquake in the Gulf of Alaska could result in a tsunami hitting Hawaii less than five hours later.

It is almost impossible to feel a tsunami out at sea in deep water, however, the form of the wave changes when it reaches shallow water. Since the water is shallower, the bottom of the wave begins to "feel" the ocean bottom. The friction that results causes the wave to slow down from about 450 mi/h (200 m/s) in very deep ocean water to 49 mi/h (22 m/s) in water 164 ft (50 m) deep. While the front part of the wave has been reduced in speed, the part at sea is still moving in quickly. As a result, the energy of the wave is compressed. As the wave enters shallow water, like that in a bay, the crest rises. It quickly builds up vertically as the wave moves onto the shore. This wall of water can be more than a hundred feet high, in extreme cases. Since gravity is acting on this huge wall of water, it cannot support itself and crashes or breaks onto the land, similar to a normal breaker in the surf zone of a beach. However, the huge amounts of energy released by a breaking tsunami are many times greater and more destructive than an ordinary breaker at the beach and the tsunami can literally destroy anything in its path.

In Japan, where some of the most destructive tsunamis have occurred, there have been cases in which whole fishing villages were devastated. However, the fishermen, who were at sea plying their trade, did not feel the wave, which passed right under them. They did not discover the disaster until they returned home and found their homes and villages destroyed. Because these villages were often located within shallow bays, and the fishermen, being at sea, did not experience the wave, they assumed that the tsunami arose within the bay. Therefore, these waves were called tsunamis or "wave in bay."

While scientists are not yet able to predict submarine seismic activity with much accuracy, they can easily measure such events when they occur. Scientists use this information about the causes of tsunamis to predict when these destructive sea waves will occur. This is extremely important in reducing loss of life and property. After the destructive 1946 tsunami that hit Hawaii, a group of tsunami early warning stations was set up to monitor seismic activity throughout the Pacific Ocean. The geographical and administrative center of this monitoring system is in Honolulu, Hawaii. When an earthquake, or underwater volcano or landslide is sensed, its location is pinpointed. If a wave is generated and a change in the water height is measured at a nearby tide-measuring station, scientists can then accurately calculate the speed of the wave to determine when the wave will make landfall. The appropriate agencies can be alerted, and if necessary, evacuations and other preparations can be made. This early warning system has been very successful in reducing damage caused by tsunamis. For example, there were no deaths from a tsunami in Hawaii in 1957 because of an early warning, even though the tsunami was over 26 ft (8 m) tall.

Before the warning systems existed, the first indication of an approaching tsunami was the rapid movement of water in a bay out to sea. This exposed areas of the bay bottom that were rarely or never exposed. The water that rushed offshore rose to build the huge crest of the wave that would crash down a few minutes later.

Despite the success of the early warning systems, there are some problems. For example, not all seismic activity generates tsunamis; they more commonly result from shallow focus earthquakes, where the actual point of crustal movement is closer to the surface. It is during these earthquakes that major crustal movement is most likely. Deep focus earthquakes, which can be very strong, but often result in less crustal movement, are less likely to trigger tsunamis. It has been estimated that only one out of ten large underwater earthquakes causes damage. In addition, the chances of a tsunami hitting any one spot directly and causing major damage are relatively small because the energy in the form of the tsunami is not passed along equally in all directions. Finally, there may be other factors that reduce or enhance chances of a tsunami striking. For example, major tsunamis are rare in regions with wide continental shelves, such as the Atlantic coast of the United States. A wide continental shelf is thought to both reflect the wave (with the energy being sent back out to sea) and absorb some of the energy of the wave through friction as it drags along the bottom. Thus, the early warning system, while essential, often gives false alarms.

Tsunamis are more common in the Pacific Ocean than other oceans of the world, primarily because there is so much seismic activity at the perimeter of the Pacific Ocean, where crustal plates meet. Thus, this region is where some of the world's most damaging tsunamis have occurred. For example, one of the most dramatic and destructive tsunamis occurred on August 27, 1883, when the volcanic island of Krakatoa, located in the Pacific Ocean, between Sumatra and Java, exploded and disappeared. The wall of water reached over 98 ft (30 m) in height and left catastrophic damage to coastal areas in the Sundra Strait in its wake. Over 36,000 people lost their lives. The energy from the tsunami was still measurable after it crossed the Indian Ocean, moved around the southern part of Africa, and headed north through the Atlantic Ocean into the English Channel. In addition to the tsunami, the sound of the explosion was heard 3,000 mi (4,827 km) away, and the dust that entered the atmosphere caused unusual sunsets for almost a year.

In 1896 there was a major tsunami in Japan that killed 27,000 people along the coast. In 1964, there was an earthquake in Alaska and the resulting tsunami caused major damage in some ports such as Kodiak and Seward. In addition, the tsunami traveled to the south, where four and a half hours later, despite warnings, it killed additional people and did major damage in Cresent City, California. A total of 119 people died and damage to property amounted to over $100 million.

Tsunamis also occur along the chain of Caribbean islands and in the Mediterranean. Both of these places, like the Pacific, are at the edges of Earth's crustal plates where earthquakes and other seismic activity are common.

[*Max Strieb*]

FURTHER READING

Knauss, J.A. *Introduction to Physical Oceanography.* Englewood Cliffs, New Jersey: Prentice-Hall, Inc., 1978.

Neshyba, S. *Oceanography: Perspectives on a Fluid Earth.* New York: John Wiley and Sons, 1987.

Tumor

See **Cancer; Neoplasm**

Tundra

Tundra is a generic term for a type of low-growing **ecosystem** found in climatically stressed environments. Latitudinal tundra occurs in the Arctic and Antarctic, **environment**s with cool and short growing seasons. Altitudinal tundra occurs at the top of mountains, where the growing season is cool, although it can be long. A major environmental factor affecting tundra communities is the availability of moisture. Wet meadows are dominated by hydric sedges and grasses, while mesic sites are dominated by dwarf shrubs and herbaceous **species** and dry sites by cushion plants and **lichens**.

Turnover time

Turnover time refers to the period of time during which certain materials remain within a particular system. For example, the protein that we eat in food is broken down by enzymes in our bodies and then resynthesized in a different form. The time during which any one protein molecule survives unchanged in the body is called the turnover time for that molecule. Each component of an **environment**al system also has a turnover time. On an average, for example, a molecule of water remains in the **atmosphere** for a period of 11.4 days before it falls to the earth as precipitation. *See also* Chemicals

Turtle excluder device (TED)

Sea turtles of several **species** are often accidentally caught in a variety of fishing gear in many areas of the world, including the southwest Atlantic and the shallow waters of the Gulf of Mexico. Up to 12,500 turtles died annually as a result of entanglement in shrimp trawl fishery alone. This became a concern for the **commercial fishing** industry and environmentalists alike, and the turtle excluder device (TED) was developed in an effort to prevent turtles from entering nets designed to catch other marine animals.

TED designs began as barrier nets preventing turtles from being caught in the main net, then modified to gate-like attachments. Three main within-net designs are currently used. The model designed by the National Marine Fisheries Service (NMFS) consists of an addition in the throat of the trawl net, where the diameter narrows toward the end where the catch is held. The addition includes a diagonal deflator grid, that, once encountered by a turtle, forces the animal upwards and out through a door in the top of the net. A second grid deflects other fish out an opening in the side of the net. Several other TEDs are approved that are lighter and less expensive than the NMFS design, all ejecting turtles and other by-catch through either the top or bottom of the net. Few shrimp are lost in this process, while the capture of turtles and other by-catch is reduced significantly.

Although TEDs are required by law on Mexican shrimp fleets in the Pacific and the Gulf of Mexico, doing so on United States fishing boats has been a struggle. A law mandating their use on shrimp trawlers operating between March 1 and November 30 was to have gone into effect in 1988, but the State of Louisiana obtained an injunction against the order. Continued challenges brought by Louisiana and Florida, as well as political lobbying and civil disobedience in the fishing community, delayed implementation even further. In March 1993 the final regulations were announced, making TEDs mandatory in inshore waters, and in all waters by December 1994. By 1997, even with the required TEDs, some 10,000 animals were killed annually during shrimp trowling. The National Wildlife Federation has called for additional TED requirements. *See also* Dolphins; Environmental law; Environmental politics; Fish and Wildlife Service

[*David A. Duffus*]

FURTHER READING

Hillestad, H. O., et al. "Worldwide Incidental Capture of Sea Turtles." In *Biology and Conservation of Sea Turtles,* edited by K. A. Bjorndal. Washington, DC: Smithsonian Institution Press, 1981.

Hinman, K. "The Real Cost of Shrimp on Your Plate." *Sea Frontiers* 38 (February 1992): 14-19.

Seidel, W. O. and C. McVea. "Development of a Sea Turtle Excluder Shrimp Trawl in the Southeast U.S. Penaeid Shrimp Trawl." In *Biology and Conservation of Sea Turtles,* edited by K. A. Bjorndal. Washington, DC: Smithsonian Institution Press, 1981.

Williams, T. "The Exclusion of Sea Turtles." *Audubon* 92 (January 1990): 24-30.

2,4-D

One of the nation's most popular weed killers, the **herbicide** 2,4-D has been widely used by homeowners, timber companies, government agencies, farmers, and power companies to eliminate unwanted vegetation from lawns and golf courses, forests, rangelands, rights-of-way, pastures, highways, and even farmlands. Scientists and environmentalists have warned for years of the chemical's toxic effects, and **Rachel Carson**'s classic book *Silent Spring* described its dangers to human health and the **environment**. Subsequent studies have linked 2,4-D to **cancer**, miscarriage, and **birth defects** in animals and humans who have been exposed to it. **Agent Orange**, a defoliant used during the Vietnam War, was a 50/50 mixture of 2,4-D and a similar herbicide, **2,4,5-T**.

For years environmentalists have urged that 2,4-D be banned or strictly controlled, but the U.S. **Environmental Protection Agency (EPA)** has so far not acted to do so. *See also* Carcinogen

2,4,5-T

A broad-leaf **herbicide**, now banned for use in the United States. Its full name is 2,4,5-trichlorophenoxyacetic acid. After postemergence treatment it is readily absorbed by foliage and roots and translocated throughout the plant. This herbicide gained much notoriety during and after the Vietnam War because it was a component in the defoliant **Agent Orange**, which has been implicated in **cancer** occurrence in some war veterans. The **carcinogen** 2,3,7,8-TCDD is formed as a byproduct in the manufacture of 2,4,5-T. The **Environmental Protection Agency (EPA)** restricted the use of 2,4,5-T in 1971, and suspended usage in 1979 following concerns that it caused miscarriages in women living in areas where application of 2,4,5-T had occurred. *See also* Carson, Rachel; Dioxin

U

Ultraviolet radiation

Radiation of the sun including ultraviolet A (UV-A, 320-400 nanometers) and ultraviolet B (UV-B, 280-320 nanometers). Exposure to UV-A radiation, which is utilized in tanning booths, damages dermal elastic tissue and the lens of the eye, and causes **cancer** in hairless mice. Exposure to UV-B induces breaks and other mutations in **DNA** and is associated with basal and squamous cell carcinoma as well as melanoma. The **ozone** layer of the earth's **atmosphere** provides protection from ultraviolet radiation, but this protective layer is becoming depleted due to the release of **chlorofluorocarbons** and other causes. *See also* Ozone layer depletion; Radiation exposure

Underground storage tank

See **Leaking underground storage tank**

Union of Concerned Scientists (Cambridge, Massachusetts)

Founded in 1969 by faculty and students at the Massachusetts Institute of Technology, the Union of Concerned Scientists (UCS) promotes four core objectives: nuclear arms reduction, a rational national security policy, safe **nuclear power**, and energy reform. UCS utilizes research, public education, and lobbying and litigation to achieve these goals. UCS also operates a speakers' bureau and publishes various informational materials, including a quarterly magazine addressing various energy and nuclear power issues.

UCS has engaged in a variety of programs targeting a wide range of people. One of the organization's first large-scale programs was the 1971 **Atomic Energy Commission** hearings, in which UCS revealed major weaknesses in nuclear plant system designs. Throughout the 1980s, UCS sponsored an annual Week of Education focusing on the nuclear arms race. The program was targeted at college students throughout the United States. In 1984 the group conducted a study that revealed technical mistakes, high costs, and other flaws in the United States Strategic Defense Initiative (SDI).

In 1989 the organization operated a Voter Education Project which resulted in a television special focusing on what Americans expected from their next president. The show was broadcast in both the United States and the Soviet Union. That same year, UCS participated in the International Scientific Symposium on a Nuclear Test Ban. The organization also conducts research for the U.S. **Nuclear Regulatory Commission**.

UCS has also been involved in projects of a more political nature. Most notable are its lobbying and litigation programs which lobby Congress on various issues. The organization also provides expert testimony to congressional committees and participates in legislative coalitions. In 1991 legal action brought by UCS resulted in the closing of the Yankee Rowe Nuclear Power Plant in western Massachusetts, the oldest commercial nuclear power plant in the United States. While the plant closed voluntarily, UCS was instrumental in pressuring the plant to shut down. UCS litigators have also targeted the Kozloduy nuclear reactors in Bulgaria, citing safety concerns. Legislative programs have focused on the United States' B-2 Stealth bomber and SDI. The organization claimed a victory at the end of 1991 when the United States Congress voted to cut back on both the B-2 and SDI projects.

While the core of UCS consists of field experts, the group also maintains a strong volunteer base. UCS is made up of three core groups: the Scientists' Action Network, the Legislative Alert Network, and the Professionals' Coalition for Nuclear Arms Control. The Scientists' Network focuses on public education and lobbying, the Legislative Network informs UCS members of upcoming elections and laws, and the Professionals' Coalition promotes arms control education and legislation. The Scientists' Action Network relies on volunteers to carry out its programs on the local level. Likewise the Legislative Alert Network utilizes volunteer support in letter-writing and phone-call campaigns to members of Congress. The Professionals' Coalition for Nuclear Arms Control, too, works with physicians, lawyers, and design professionals throughout the United States to promote arms control education and legislation. Contact: Union of Concerned Scientists, 26 Church Street, Cambridge, MA 02238. Internet: http://www.ucsusa.org/. *See also* Nuclear weapons

[*Kristin Palm*]

United Nations Commission on Sustainable Development

A committee of 53 nations created by the United Nations General Assembly for the purpose of implementing recommendations made during the 1992 **United Nations Earth Summit** in Rio de Janeiro. Its overriding goal is to develop economies around the world while preserving the **environment** and existing **natural resources**. Major issues of interest include **water quality**, **desertification**, forest and **species** protection, toxic **chemicals**, and atmospheric and oceanic **pollution**.

Chaired by Malaysian representative Razalie Ismail, the commission endeavors to put into action the specific policies of *Agenda 21*, a United Nations plan aimed at stopping—or at least slowing down—global **environmental degradation**. The United States has taken a strong leadership role in supporting the commission's objectives. Under President Bill Clinton and Vice President **Albert Gore**, the **President's Council on Sustainable Development** was created to balance environmental policies with sound economic development within this country.

With the formation of the commission, several developing countries have raised concerns that the group will withhold financial aid to them based on their environmental practices. Likewise, the **more developed countries (MDC)** worry that money and technology allotted to the **less developed countries (LDC)** will go toward other needs rather than towards protecting the environment. The commission has no legal authority to enforce any of its policies but relies on publicity and international pressure to achieve its goals.

United Nations Conference on Environment and Development

See **United Nations Earth Summit**

United Nations Conference on the Human Environment (1972) Stockholm, Sweden

Held in Stockholm in 1972, the United Nations Conference on the Human Environment was the first global environmental conference and the precursor to the 1992 **United Nations Earth Summit** in Rio de Janeiro, Brazil.

The purpose of the conference was not to discuss scientific or technological approaches to environmental problems but to coordinate international policy. A 27-nation committee held four meetings in the two years preceding the conference, and in the months leading up to it they issued a report calling for "a major reorientation of man's values and redeployment of his energies and resources." In their prelimi-

nary report, the committee emphasized their political priorities: "The very nature of environmental problems—that is to say, their intricate interdependence—is such as to require political choices."

There was a remarkable lack of divisiveness, once the conference began, on most issues under consideration. The Soviet Union and the Eastern bloc did not attend because East Germany, which was not a member of the United Nations, had been denied full representation. But 114 of the 132 member countries of the United Nations were there, and the sessions were distinguished by what the *New York Times* called a "groundswell of unanimity." A number of resolutions passed without a dissenting vote.

Many believe the most important result of the conference was the precedent it set for international cooperation in addressing **environmental degradation**. The nations attending agreed that they shared responsibility for the quality of the **environment**, particularly the oceans and the **atmosphere**, and they signed a declaration of principles, after extensive negotiations, concerning their obligations. The conference also approved an environmental fund and an "action program," which involved 200 specific recommendations for addressing such problems as global climatic change, **marine pollution**, **population growth**, the dumping of **toxic waste**s, and the preservation of **biodiversity**. A permanent environmental unit was established for coordinating these and other international efforts on behalf of the environment; the organization that became the **United Nations Environmental Programme** was formally approved by the General Assembly later that same year and its base established in Nairobi, Kenya. This organization has not only coordinated action but monitored research, collecting and disseminating information, and it has played an ongoing role in international negotiations about environmental issues.

The conference in Stockholm accomplished almost everything the preparatory committee had planned. It was widely considered successful, and many observers were almost euphoric about the extent of agreement. In a speech to the nations gathered in Stockholm, the anthropologist Margaret Mead called the event "a revolution in thought fully comparable to the Copernican revolution by which, four centuries ago, men and women were compelled to revise their whole sense of the earth's place in the cosmos. Today we are challenged to recognize as great a change in our concept of man's place in the **biosphere**."

There were, however, some dissenting voices. Shirley Temple Black and others formally protested the fact that women were not fully represented at the gathering; only 11 delegations of the 114 nations represented included even one woman. A large "counterconference" was held in Stockholm, consisting of a number of scientific and political organizations, and environmentalists such as **Barry Commoner** argued that the official conference, though valuable, had failed to address the subjects that were most important to solving the current environmental crisis, particularly poverty and what he called "ecologically sound ways of producing goods."

[*Douglas Smith*]

United Nations Division for Sustainable Development

This United Nations division serves as the secretariat, or the research staff, of the **U.N. Commission on Sustainable Development**, whose representatives meet periodically to develop policies for **sustainable development** in 40 countries. The division comprises 30 program officers working in specific sectors: health, human settlements, freshwater resources, toxic **chemicals**, **hazardous waste**s, **solid waste**s, and **radioactive waste**s. According to André Vasilyev, First Officer, it prepares studies and analytical reports and conducts research to support the work of the Commission. It also measures the progress of and makes recommendations for development programs. The division's stated mission is to contribute to sustainable development worldwide by working to implement Agenda 21, the Rio Declaration on Environment and Development, the Forest Principles (a United Nations statement of principles for a global consensus on the management, **conservation**, and sustainable development of all types of forests), and the Global Programme of Action for Sustainable Development of Small Island Developing States (SIDS). The division carries out multi-year work programs on sustainable development indicators, changing consumption and production patterns, and the transfer of environmentally sustainable technology.

The Commission was established in 1992 as an adjunct to Agenda 21, the plan of action for environmental sustainability adopted at the United Nations Conference on Environment and Development (UNCED) in Rio de Janeiro. Its charge is to ensure that decisions made at UNCED are carried out at national, regional and international levels, and to further international cooperation and decision-making on these issues.

The full Commission meets once a year. Ad hoc working groups meet periodically to address specific issues, including trade and environmental development, consumption patterns, financial resources, and technology transfer. Open-ended working groups address such issues as integrated management of land resources, forests, combating **desertification**, sustainable mountain development, **sustainable agriculture**, rural development, and biological diversity.

In recent years, the Commission has examined numerous strategies to promote sustainable development: trading debt for sustainable development, creating environmental user charges for air transport, implementing the Convention on Biological Diversity and the Convention to Combat Desertification, and developing tools for integrated land management. In the spring of 1997, the full commission met to conduct a five-year review of the results of UNCED. Contact: The United Nations Division for Sustainable Development, United Nations Department for Policy Coordination and Sustainable Development, Division for Sustainable Development, United Nations Plaza, Rm. DC2-2270, New York, N.Y. 10017. Website: http://www.un.org/dpcsd.

[*Carol Steinfeld*]

United Nations Earth Summit (1992) Rio de Janeiro, Brazil

For 12 days in June 1992, more than 35,000 environmental activists, politicians, and business representatives, along with 9,000 journalists, 25,000 troops, and uncounted vendors, taxi drivers, and assorted others converged on Rio de Janeiro, Brazil for the United Nations Conference on Environment and Development. Known as the Earth Summit, this was the largest environmental conference in history; in fact, it was probably the largest non-religious meeting ever held. Like a three-ring environmental circus, this conference brought together everyone from pin-striped diplomats to activists in bluejeans and indigenous Amazonian people in full ceremonial regalia. One cannot say yet whether the conventions and treaties discussed at this summit meeting will be effective, but they have the potential to make this the most important environmental meeting ever held.

The first **United Nations Conference on the Human Environment** met in Stockholm in 1972, exactly 20 years before the Rio de Janeiro meeting. Called by the industrialized nations of Western Europe primarily to discuss their worries about transboundary **air pollution**, the Stockholm conference had little input from **less developed countries** and almost no representation from **nongovernmental organization**s (NGOs). Some major accomplishments came out of this conference, however, including the **United Nations Environment Programme**, the **Global Environmental Monitoring System**, the **Convention on International Trade in Endangered Species (CITES)**, and the World Heritage Biosphere Reserve Program, which identifies particularly valuable areas of biological diversity. A companion book to the Stockholm Conference entitled *Only One Earth* was written by **René Dubos** and Barbara Ward.

In 1983 the United Nations established an independent commission to address the issues raised at the Stockholm conference and to propose new strategies for global environmental protection. Chaired by Norwegian Prime Minister **Gro Harlem Bruntdland**, the commission spent four years in hearings and deliberations. A significantly greater voice for the developing world was heard as it became apparent that environmental problems affected the poor more than the rich. The commission's final report, published in 1987 as *Our Common Future*, is notable for coining the term "**sustainable development**" and for linking environmental problems to social and economic systems.

In 1990 preparations for the Earth Summit began. Maurice Strong, the Canadian environmentalist who chaired the Stockholm conference, was chosen to lead once again. A series of four working meetings called PrepComs were scheduled to work out detailed agendas and agreements to be ratified in Rio de Janeiro. The first PrepCom met in Nairobi,

Kenya, in August 1990. The second and third meetings were in Geneva, Switzerland, in March and August 1991. The fourth and final PrepCom convened in New York City, in March 1992. Twenty-one issues were negotiated at these conferences including **biodiversity**, **climate** change, **deforestation**, **environmental health**, marine resources, **ozone**, poverty, toxic wastes, and urban environments. Notably, population crisis was barely mentioned in the documents because of opposition by religious groups.

Intense lobbying and jockeying for power marked the two-year PrepCom process. As the date for the Rio de Janeiro conference neared, it appeared that several significant treaties would be ratified in time for presentation to the world community. Among these were treaties on climate change, biological diversity, forests, and a general Earth Charter, which would be an environmental bill of rights for all people. A comprehensive 400-page document called *Agenda 21* presented a practical action plan spelling out policies, laws, institutional arrangements, and financing to carry out the provisions of these and other treaties and conventions. Chairman Strong estimated that it would take $125 billion per year in aid to help the poorer nations of the world protect their **environment**.

In the end, however, the United States refused to accept much of the PrepCom work. During PrepCom IV in New York City, for instance, 139 nations voted for mandatory stabilization of **greenhouse gases** at 1990 levels by the year 2000, laying the groundwork for what promised to be the showcase treaty of the Earth Summit. Only the United States delegation opposed it, but after behind-the-scenes arm twisting and deal-making, the targets and compulsory aspects of the treaty were stripped away, leaving only a weak shell to take to Rio de Janeiro. Many environmentalists felt betrayed. Similarly, the United States, alone among the industrialized world, refused to sign the biodiversity treaty, the forest protection convention, or the promise to donate 0.7 percent of Gross Domestic Product to less developed countries for environmental protection. The nation's excuse was that these treaties were too restrictive for American businesses and might damage the American economy. The United States did, subsequently, sign the biodiversity treaty on June 4, 1993, and President Bill Clinton has also pledged that the U.S. will reduce emissions of heat-trapping gases like **carbon dioxide** to 1990 levels by the year 2000.

Many environmentalists went to Rio de Janeiro intending to denounce United States intransigence. Even **Environmental Protection Agency** chief **William Reilly**, head of the United States delegation, wrote a critical memo to his staff saying that the Bush administration was slow to engage crucial issues, late in assembling a delegation, and unwilling to devote sufficient resources to the meeting. *Newsweek* magazine entitled one article about the summit: "The Grinch of Rio," saying that to much of the world, the Bush administration represented the major obstacle to environmental protection.

Not all was lost at the Rio de Janeiro meeting, however. Important contacts were made and direct negotiations begun between delegates from many countries. Great strides were made in connecting poverty to environmental destruction. Issues such as sustainable development and justice had a prominent place on the negotiating table for the first time. Furthermore, this meeting provided a unique forum for discussing the disparity between the rich industrialized northern nations and the poor, underdeveloped southern nations. Many bilateral—nation to nation—treaties and understandings were reached.

Perhaps more important than the official events at the remote and heavily guarded conference center was the "shadow assembly," or Global Forum of NGOs, held in Flamingo Park along the beach front of Guanabara Bay. Eighteen hours a day, the park pulsed and buzzed as thousands of activists debated, protested, traded information, and built informal networks. In one tent, a large TV screen tracked nearly three dozen complex agreements being negotiated by official delegates at Rio Centrum. In other tents, mini-summits discussed alternative issues such as the role of women, youth, **indigenous peoples**, workers, and the poor. Specialized meetings focused on topics ranging from sustainable energy to **endangered species**. In contrast to Stockholm, where only a handful of citizen groups attended the meetings and almost all were from the developed world, more than 9,000 NGOs sent delegates to Rio de Janeiro. There were over 700 from Brazil alone. The contacts made in these informal meetings may prove to be the most valuable part of the Earth Summit.

[*William P. Cunningham*]

FURTHER READING

French, H. *After the Earth Summit: The Future of Environmental Governance.* World Watch Paper 107. Washington, DC: World Watch Institute, 1992.

Haas, P. M., et al. "Appraising the Earth Summit: How Should We Judge UNCED's Success?" *Environment* 34 (October 1992): 6.

Hinrichsen, D. "The Rocky Road to Rio." *The Amicus Journal* 14 (Winter 1992): 15.

Hildyard, N. "Green Dollars, Green Menace." *The Ecologist* 22 (May-June 1992): 82-84.

United Nations Environment Programme

Formed in 1973 after the **United Nations Conference on the Human Environment**, the U.N. Environment Programme (UNEP) coordinates environmental policies of various nations, **nongovernmental organization**s, and other U.N. agencies in an effort to protect the environment from further degradation. Sometimes dubbed the "environmental conscience of the U.N.," UNEP describes its goal as follows: "to protect the environment by distributing education materials and by serving as a coordinator and catalyst of environmental initiatives."

Some of UNEP's major areas of concern are the **ozone layer**, waste disposal, **toxic substance**s, water and air **pollution**, **deforestation**, **desertification**, and energy resources. The ways in which UNEP addresses these concerns can be best seen in the various programs it oversees or administers. The Earthwatch program—which includes **Global Environmental Monitoring System** (GEMS); **INFOTERRA**; and **International Register of Potentially Toxic Chemicals** (IRPTC)—monitors environmental problems worldwide and shares its information database with interested individuals and groups. UNEP's Regional Seas Program seeks to protect the life and integrity of the Caribbean, Mediterranean, South Pacific, and the Persian Gulf. The **International Geosphere-Biosphere Programme** (IGBP) promotes awareness and preservation of **biogeochemical cycles**. The Industry and Environment Office (IEO) advises industries on environmental issues such as pollution standards, industrial hazards, and clean technology.

In addition to administering these programs, UNEP has also sponsored several key environmental policies in the last few decades. For example they initiated the **Convention on International Trade in Endangered Species of Wild Fauna and Flora (CITES)**, **Convention on the Conservation of Migratory Species of Wild Animals**, and the Vienna Convention for the Protection of the Ozone Layer. Most recently, UNEP was responsible for planning the 1992 **United Nations Earth Summit** in Rio de Janeiro, Brazil.

UNEP is headquartered in Nairobi, Kenya. The organization is headed by Mostafa Kamal Tolba, who assumed the position of Executive Director in 1976 after the departure of Maurice Strong.

U.S. Department of Agriculture

The U.S. Department of Agriculture (USDA) had its origin in the U.S. Patent Office, one of the first federal offices. In 1837, an employee of the Patent Office, Henry L. Ellsworth, began to distribute seeds to American farmers that he had received from overseas. By 1840, Ellsworth had obtained a grant of $1,000 from Congress to establish an Agricultural Division within the Patent Office. This division was charged with collecting statistics on agriculture in the United States and carrying out research, as well as distributing seeds.

Over the next two decades, the Agricultural Division continued to expand within the Patent Office, until Congress created the Department of Agriculture on May 15, 1862. The officer in charge of the department was initially called the Commissioner of Agriculture, but the Department was raised to cabinet level on February 9, 1889, and the Commissioner was renamed the Secretary of Agriculture.

The USDA today is a mammoth executive agency which manages dozens of programs. Its overall goals include the improvement and maintenance of farm incomes, and the development of overseas markets for domestic agricultural products. The department is also committed to reducing poverty, hunger, and malnutrition; protecting **soil**, water, forests, and other **natural resources**; and maintaining standards of quality for agricultural products. The activities of the USDA are subdivided into seven major categories: Small Community and Rural Development, Marketing and

Inspection Services, Food and Consumer Services, International Affairs and Commodity Programs, Science and Education, Natural Resources and Environment, and Economics.

Small Community and Rural Development oversees many of the programs which provide financial assistance to rural citizens. It administers emergency loans as well as loans for youth projects, farm ownership, rural housing, **watershed** protection, and flood prevention. It also underwrites federal crop insurance, and the Rural Electrification Administration is part of this division.

Marketing and Inspection Services is responsible for all activities relating to the inspection and maintenance of health standards for all foods produced in the United States. The Agricultural Cooperative Service, which many consider one of the USDA's most important functions, is part of the division. Food and Consumer Services helps educate consumers about good nutritional practices and provides the means by which people can act on that information. The division administers the Food Stamp program, as well as the School Breakfast, Summer Food Service, Child Care Food, and Human Nutrition Information programs.

The main functions of the International Affairs and Commodity Programs are to promote the sale and distribution of American farm products abroad and to maintain crop yields and farm income at home. The Science and Education division consists of a number of research and educational agencies including the **Agricultural Research Service**, the Extension Service, and the National Agricultural Library.

Some of the USDA's best known services are located within the Natural Resources and Environment Division. The **Forest Service** and **Soil Conservation Service** are the two largest of these. The Economics Division is responsible for collecting, collating, and distributing statistical and other economic data on national agriculture. The Economic Research Service, National Agricultural Statistics Service, Office of Energy, and World Agricultural Outlook Board are all part of this division. *See also* Agricultural Stabilization and Conservation Service

[*Lawrence H. Smith*]

FURTHER READING

Petulla, J. M. *American Environmental History*. San Francisco: Boyd & Fraser, 1977.

The United States Government Manual, 1992/93. Washington, DC: U.S. Government Printing Office, 1992.

U.S. Department of Commerce
See **National Oceanic and Atmospheric Administration**

U.S. Department of Defense
See **Army Corps of Engineers**

U.S. Department of Energy

For most of its history, the United States has felt little concern for its energy needs. The country has had huge reserves of **coal**, **petroleum**, and **natural gas**. In addition, the United States had always been able to buy all the additional **fossil fuels** it needed from other nations. As late as 1970, automotive and home heating fuels sold for about $0.20-$0.30 per gallon ($0.05-$0.08 per liter).

That situation changed dramatically in 1973 when members of the **Organization of Petroleum Exporting Countries** (OPEC) placed an embargo on the oil it shipped to nations around the world, including the United States. It took only a few months for the United States and other oil-dependent countries to realize that it was time to rethink their national energy strategies. The late 1970s saw, therefore, a flurry of activity by both the legislative and executive arms of government to formulate a new **energy policy** for the United States.

Out of that upheaval came a number of new laws and executive orders including the **Energy Reorganization Act** of 1973, the Federal Non-Nuclear Energy Research and Development Act of 1974, the Energy Policy and Conservation Act of 1976, the Energy Conservation and Production Act of 1976, the National Energy Act of 1978 and President Jimmy Carter's National Energy Plan of 1977.

One of the major features of both legislative and executive actions was the creation of a new Department of Energy (DOE). DOE was established to provide a central authority to develop and oversee national energy policy and research and development of energy technologies. The new department replaced or absorbed a number of other agencies previously responsible for one or another aspect of energy policy, including primarily the Federal Energy Administrations and the **Energy Research and Development Administration**. Other agencies transferred to DOE included the **Federal Power Commission**, the five power administrations responsible for production, marketing and transmission of electrical power (Bonnevile, Southeastern, Alaska, Southwestern, and Western Area Power Administrations), and agencies with a variety of other functions previously housed in the Departments of the Interior, Commerce, Housing and Urban Development, and the Navy.

DOE's mission is to provide a framework for a comprehensive and balanced national energy plan by coordinating and administering a variety of Federal energy functions. Among the Department's specific responsibilities are research and development of long-term, high-risk energy technologies, the marketing of power produced at Federal facilities, promotion of **energy conservation**, administration of energy regulatory programs, and collection and analysis of data on energy production and use. In addition, the department has primary responsibility for the nation's **nuclear weapons** program.

DOE is divided into a number of offices, agencies, and other divisions with specific tasks. For example, the Office of Energy Research manages the Department's programs in basic energy sciences, high energy physics, and **nuclear**

fusion energy research. It also funds university research in mathematical and computational sciences and other energy-related research. Another division, the Energy Information Administration, is responsible for collecting, processing, and publishing data on energy reserves, production, demand, consumption, distribution, and technology. *See also* Energy taxes; Federal Energy Regulatory Commission; Hanford Nuclear Reservation; Oak Ridge, Tennessee; Office of Civilian Radioactive Waste Management; Waste Isolation Pilot Plant; Yucca Mountain

[*David E. Newton*]

FURTHER READING

The United States Government Manual, 1992/93. Washington, DC: U.S. Government Printing Office, 1992.

U.S. Department of Health and Human Services

The U.S. Department of Health and Human Services (HHS) is responsible for the welfare, safety, and health of United States citizens. Among other programs, HHS administers drug safety standards, prevents epidemics, and offers assistance to those who are economically disadvantaged.

The **Public Health Service**, a division of HHS, helps state and city governments with health problems. The service studies ways of controlling infectious diseases, works to immunize children, and operates quarantine programs. The agency also operates the **Centers for Disease Control (CDC)**, where most of the nation's health problems are studied. These include occupational health and safety, the dangers of cigarette smoking, and childhood injuries, as well as **communicable disease**s and the epidemic of urban violence. In addition to investigating these problems, the CDC is charged with making policy suggestions on their management. HHS also administers the Social Security and Medicare programs, as well as the Head Start Program.

New **lead**-content standards for paint and other consumer items grew out of CDC studies. The agency conducts energy related epidemiologic research for the **U.S. Department of Energy**, including studies on **radiation exposure**. Through the CDC, the HHS runs the National Center for Health Statistics, an **AIDS** Hotline, an international disaster relief team, and programs to monitor influenza epidemics worldwide.

The **Food and Drug Administration** is another agency of HHS. It is charged with responding to new drug research by drug development companies and approving new drugs for use in the United States. Along with the **U.S. Department of Agriculture**, the FDA is responsible for maintaining the safety of the nation's food and drug supply. HHS also administers the **Agency for Toxic Substances and Disease Registry**, which carries out the health-related responsibilities of the Superfund legislation.

[*Linda Rehkopf*]

FURTHER READING

The United States Government Manual, 1992/93. Washington, DC: U.S. Government Printing Office, 1992.

U.S. Department of the Interior

The U.S. Department of the Interior was founded by an Act of Congress on March 3, 1849. A wide variety of functions were assigned to the "Home Department" as it was called at the time, including administration of the General Land Office which passed large tracts of western lands to home-steaders (294 million acres/119 million hectares), to railroads (94 million acres/38 million hectares), and to colleges and universities. In the twentieth century, the Department of the Interior has become the custodian of **public land**s and **natural resources**, and is now America's primary governmental **conservation** agency. The **National Park Service, Bureau of Land Management, Bureau of Reclamation, Fish and Wildlife Service, Geological Survey, Office of Surface Mining, Reclamation and Enforcement**, and **Bureau of Mines** are part of the Department. In addition the Department is responsible for American Indian reservation communities and for people living in island territories administered by the United States.

The Department's mandate is very broad, including such duties as: 1) administration of over 500 million acres (200 million ha) of federal public lands; 2) development and conservation of mineral and water resources; 3) conservation and utilization of fish and **wildlife** resources; 4) coordination of federal and state **recreation** programs; 5) administration and preservation of America's scenic and historic areas; 6) reclamation of western **arid** lands through **irrigation**; and 7) management of hydroelectric power systems.

Although many Department activities and programs have generated environmental controversy over the years, it is probably these last two activities that have been most contentious. In pursuit of these mandates, the Bureau of Reclamation, working with the **Army Corps of Engineers**, has constructed massive **dams** on rivers in the West. These dams are designed to provide water storage and electricity for western cities and farms, as well as to reduce down-steam **flooding**. However, these dams also have had severe impacts on **ecosystem**s, significantly altering and, at times, devastating riverine **habitat**s.

On balance, however, the programs and practices of the Department of the Interior probably do more environmental good than harm. Among the Department's positive actions and accomplishments during the past several years are: 1) establishment of 23 new refuges and waterfowl production areas in Florida and in Louisiana; 2) initiation of "Refuges 2003," a Fish and Wildlife Service effort aimed at planning management programs and policies for the next 10-15 years on the nation's 472 national **wildlife refuge**s; 3) implementation of the North American Wetlands Conservation Act to restore declining waterfowl populations and to conserve **wetlands**; 4) addition of 131 species to the List of Endangered and Threatened Species in the period January

1989 to September 1991; 5) development and beginning implementation of a mitigation and enhancement plan to restore California's Kesterson Reservoir, which was closed due to high concentrations of selenium; 6) tripling the Coastal Barrier Resources System to 1.25 million acres (500,000 ha) over 1,200 miles (1931 km) of shoreline including the Florida Keys, **Great Lakes**, Puerto Rico and the Virgin Islands; 7) Establishment of a new Office of Surface Mining Reclamation and Enforcement office in Ashland, Kentucky, for rapid response to abandoned mine land problems in need of reclamation on an emergency basis; 8) participation in filing 120 natural resource damage assessments in the period 1988-1991, the largest being the assessment of the **Exxon Valdez** accident in **Prince William Sound, Alaska**. The $1.1 billion settlement of this accident enabled the Federal Government to proceed with cleanup and restoration efforts. *See also* Kesterson National Wildlife Refuge

[*Malcolm T. Hepworth*]

FURTHER READING

The United States Government Manual, 1992/93. Washington, DC: U.S. Government Printing Office, 1992.

Utley, R., and B. MacKintosh. *The Department of Everything Else, Highlights of Interior History.* Washington, DC: U.S. Government Printing Office, 1989.

U.S. Department of State
See **Bureau of Oceans and International Environmental and Scientific Affairs**

U.S. Public Interest Research Group (PIRG) (Washington, D.C.)

Formally founded in 1983 by consumer advocate **Ralph Nader**, the Public Interest Research Group (PIRG) is an outgrowth of Nader's Center for the Study of Responsive Law. PIRG aims to heighten consumer awareness and focuses on such environmental issues as clean air, toxic waste cleanup, protection of the **atmosphere**, **pesticide** control, and **solid waste** reduction. While PIRG did not convene as a national organization until 1983, its roots date back to 1970, when Nader began to establish state PIRGs throughout the United States. The national umbrella organization was founded to lobby for the state units.

PIRG has been vital in bringing about several important environmental regulations. In 1986, the organization led an aggressive campaign that resulted in the strengthening of the federal Superfund program, a $9-billion venture that identifies and provides for the cleanup of sites contaminated by **hazardous waste**. That same year, PIRG was successful in influencing the United States legislature to pass the **Safe Drinking Water Act** (SDWA). The SDWA imposes limits and prohibitions on the amounts and types of **chemicals** allowable in drinking water supplies and provides for regular testing to assure that the limits imposed by the SDWA are being met. In 1987, PIRG proved instrumental in the strengthening of the **Clean Water Act** which requires cleanup of United States waterways. The CWA also imposes limits and prohibitions on chemicals which are discharged into the water system. Several state PIRGs have also met with success when suing major polluters. As the result of PIRG legal action, many polluters have been ordered to pay fines and clean up contaminated areas.

PIRG also educates the general public on various issues. Its current projects are outlined in a quarterly newsletter, *Citizen Agenda*, and some of its key concerns are detailed in such reports as *Toxic Truth and Consequences: The Magnitude of and the Problems Resulting from America's Use of Toxic Chemicals*; *Presumed Innocent: A Report on 69 Cancer-Causing Chemicals Allowed in Our Food*; and *As the World Burns: Documenting America's Failure to Address the Ozone Crisis*.

Ongoing PIRG projects address similar issues. Although successful with the Superfund program, the organization continues to work for the cleanup of toxic waste and actively supports the notion that "polluters pay"—requiring those who cause contamination to fund the subsequent cleanup. PIRG also conducts research into energy efficiency in an effort to curb **carbon monoxide emission**s. Through its lobbying efforts, the group also supports legislation requiring a ban on carcinogenic **pesticide**s in food, preventing **groundwater** contamination, halting **garbage incineration**, and initiating bottle-**recycling** programs in all 50 states. The organization is also involved in a Clean Water Campaign, seeking to further strengthen state and federal water regulations.

PIRG achieves these goals through a balance of professional and volunteer action. PIRG volunteers are utilized in fundraising efforts, letter-writing campaigns, and election drives. Members were once asked to send **aluminum** cans to Congress to show support of PIRG's bottle-recycling campaign. Contact: U.S. Public Interest Research Group, 215 Pennsylvania Avenue, Washington, D.C. 20003. Internet: http://www.pirg.org/pirg/.

[*Kristin Palm*]

Upwellings

Upwellings are highly productive areas along the edges of continents or continental shelves where waters are drawn up from the ocean depths to the surface. Rich in **nutrient**s, these waters nourish algae, which in turn support an abundance of fish and other aquatic life. The most common locations for upwellings are the western edge of continents, such as Peru and southern California in the Pacific, northern and southwestern Africa in the Atlantic, and around **Antarctica**.

In order for upwellings to occur, there must be deep currents flowing close to the continental margin. There must also be prevailing winds that push the surface waters away from the coast—as the surface waters move offshore, the cold, nutrient-rich bottom waters move up to replace them.

The Pacific upwelling near Peru is the result of the northward flow of the cold Humboldt current and the prevailing offshore wind pattern. Every seven to ten years, there is a shift in the prevailing wind pattern off the shore of Peru, a condition known as **El Niño**. The prevailing wind in the eastern Pacific shifts direction, causing the cold Humboldt current to be replaced by warm equatorial waters. This prevents upwelling, and the **ecological productivity** of the ocean in this area falls dramatically.

In oceans, the majority of nutrients sink to the sea bed, leaving the surface waters poor in nutrients. In marine **ecosystem**s, the primary producers are microscopic planktonic algae known as **phytoplankton**, and these are only found in surface waters, where there is enough sunlight for **photosynthesis**. The lack of nutrients limits their growth and thus the productivity of the entire system, and most open oceans have the same low levels of ecological productivity as **tundra** or **desert** ecosystems. In upwellings, the water is cold and oxygen poor but it carries a tremendous amount of **nitrates** and phosphates, which fertilize the phytoplankton in the surface waters. These producers increase dramatically, showing high levels of net primary productivity, and they become the foundation of a biologically rich and varied oceanic **food web**, teeming with fish and bird life.

The high productivity of the upwelling area off Peru supports one of the richest sardine and anchovy fisheries in the world. In addition, the large population of seabirds associated with the Peruvian upwelling deposit equally large quantities of phosphate and **nitrogen** rich droppings called **guano** on rocky islands and the mainland. Until oil-based **fertilizer**s were developed, Peruvian guano was the principle source for agricultural fertilizers.

In the Antarctic upwelling zone, the nutrient-rich waters support food webs at the base of which are massive populations of large marine shrimp, called **krill**. These invertebrates support a wide array of squid, **whales, seals**, penguins, cormorants, boobies, and sea ducks. Commercial fisheries in the Antarctic upwelling zone are now exploiting the krill harvest, an act which endangers all of the members of this unique and complex cold-water food web. *See also* Commercial fishing

[*Neil Cumberlidge*]

FURTHER READING

Ainley, D. G., and R. J. Boekelheide. *Seabirds of the Farallon Islands: Ecology, Dynamics, and Structure of an Upwelling-System Community*. Stanford, CA: Stanford University Press, 1990.

Glantz, M. H., and J. D. Thompson. *Resource Management and Environmental Uncertainty: Lessons from Coastal Upwelling Fisheries*. New York: Wiley, 1981.

Uranium

Uranium is a dense, silvery metallic element with the highest atomic mass of any naturally occurring element. It is the forty-seventh most abundant element in the Earth's crust.

All of the **isotope**s of uranium are radioactive, which accounts for a portion of the **background radiation** that is a natural part of the **environment**. In the 1930s, scientists discovered that one isotope of uranium, uranium-235, could be fissioned, or split. This information brought about a revolution in human society. The potential for **nuclear fission** is demonstrated by the fact that it has made possible not only the world's most destructive weapons, but also the generation of energy in a new way. Regardless of the purpose for which it is used, nuclear fission has created severe waste disposal problems which the world is struggling to solve. *See also* High-level radioactive waste; Nuclear power; Nuclear weapons; Radioactive waste; Radioactivity

Urban contamination

In urban areas where there has been extensive reshaping of the land surface, disturbance from building and road construction, land-filling, and additions of a variety of chemicals and minerals, there are many sources, causes, and types of urban contamination. Urban contamination is of concern from two perspectives: when new land is developed which previously was under agriculture or other rural land use and when the central core industrial areas are redeveloped. Sources of contamination can be summarized in three very broad categories: agricultural, urban, and industrial.

Agricultural-sourced contamination affects urban areas in several ways. Use of some **pesticide**s in agricultural or gardening situations has increased by significant amounts the levels of **copper, arsenic**, and **mercury** in soils. Long term use of **phosphorus** fertilizers can lead to a buildup of cadmium—a contaminant in many **fertilizer**s—in **soil**s. Synthetic organic pesticides used in agriculture can also contribute to contamination. Organochlorine insecticides are persistent and accumulate in food chains. Examples of these types of compounds are **DDT**, aldrin, and dieldrin. Use of these insecticides has been discontinued since their negative impacts on the environment have been well documented. However, these compounds do not readily decompose and are very persistent in soils and sediment. Former agricultural areas that have become urbanized have residues of these chemicals and others that result in a risk for contamination of water supplies as well as soils. This is especially true for very localized areas where pesticides were stored, spilled, or that were regularly used to clean or load spray equipment.

Urban activities past and present also contribute to contamination. The most common and largest volume of contamination sources comes from construction or demolition debris. Much of the debris is made up of nonhazardous materials; however, some of the debris may contain **asbestos**, high levels of trace **metals**, or other problem-causing substances. Asbestos is of particular concern because it causes cancer in humans when ingested through air or water.

Long-term use of **lead**-based paints and **gasoline** has led to considerable contamination. In 1976, the amount of lead used in gasoline in the United States was approximately 210 million tons. This has dropped to less than 50 million tons per year since the use of unleaded gasoline has replaced leaded fuel. Air emissions and deposition of lead from automobile exhaust near roads and highways have contaminated numerous urban areas.

Disposal of domestic wastes containing trace metals and other hazardous materials by land application or in landfills are also large sources of contamination. Smoke stacks from incineration plants for wastes often contain high levels of trace metals. Polyaromatic hydrocarbons (PAHs) have been deposited in urban areas as the result of combustion of fossil fuels (**coal, peat**, etc.) for generating electrical power. Other urban activities that can lead to contamination include land application of soot, coal ash, **sewage** sludge, and corrosion from metals and buildings.

In addition to agricultural and general urban sources, industrial activities such as mining and smelting contribute significantly to localized soil metal contamination. Atmospheric transport of the emissions can contaminate surrounding areas. Many industries have contributed a number of different kinds of toxic materials to the urban environment and as those industries close or move away they have left the areas contaminated, making it difficult to use the sites for other purposes without expensive clean-up. Examples of toxic materials that are found in former industrial sites include asbestos, chromium, arsenic, and boron. Asbestos is found most often in areas that were formerly railroad lands, shipyards, or asbestos factories. Leather tanning industries or areas used for battery production leave residues of chromium and arsenic.

Locations near chemical manufacturing companies or storage and distribution centers are also places where there is considerable contamination. One of the extreme examples where such a site was redeveloped after which major problems arose is **Love Canal** in the state of New York. Up to 248 different industrial chemicals were deposited and buried at the site before 1953. People living there following redevelopment were evacuated after many serious health problems were reported and confirmed.

Many toxic solvents are used in chemical, paint, and dye industries, and frequently these solvents can be found in soils of former industrial sites. In the Silicon Valley of California, solvent leakages into soils from computer chip manufacturing have resulted in both soil and groundwater contamination. Trichloroethylene and chloroethylene are common solvents used in paper making, metal plating, electrical engineering, laundries, dry cleaners, and as degreasing agents. These solvents have caused not only soil contamination, but also groundwater contamination in numerous locations. These sites are very difficult and expensive to clean up after the industries leave.

Contamination by power stations arises from pulverized fuel or **fly ash**, which is alkaline (**pH** 10-12) and contains soluble salts, in particular boron, aluminum, copper, and arsenic. The ash results from burning coal and is extracted from the chimneys to prevent **air pollution**. Its extremely fine particle size makes it difficult to handle and dispose.

Demolition debris from these sites often contains asbestos residues, trace metals, combustible materials, oil spillages, and **polychlorinated biphenyls (PCBs)**.

This urban contamination is a major problem worldwide in industrialized countries. In the Netherlands alone there have been confirmed at least 10,000 contaminated sites, with 50% of them in residential areas, with total clean up costs estimated to be $25 billion. Western Germany has identified over 50,000 potentially contaminated sites. The **Environmental Protection Agency (EPA)** in the United States has identified 32,000 potentially hazardous waste sites, with an estimated clean-up cost of $750 billion. There can be large impacts on the growth of plants and on the health of humans and animals that come in contact with the contamination at the site through either the air, water, or soil. There are three main pathways by which the contaminants can enter the plants: direct uptake from soil, vapor uptake through the air, and sorption on plant surfaces. For organic types of contaminants the predominant pathways are through the roots or air vapors. In general, organic contaminants (including pesticides) can affect plant growth resulting in everything from depressed growth and reproduction rates to death.

The ability of the plant to take up metals and transmit them to animals or humans that eat the plants varies by plant and by metal. Since there are likely to be high concentrations of lead either from **petroleum** products or paint in contaminated sites, there is concern for backyard vegetable gardens or urban gardens where redevelopment has taken place. There are similar concerns for other metals such as zinc and **cadmium**. These metals are usually associated with electroplating industries or battery production and where municipal waste sludges have been land applied. High concentrations of trace metals can cause visible injury to plants and inhibit their growth.

The high concentrations of trace metals in many urban soils in inner city and highly industrialized areas gives rise to concerns about potential human health effects. Lead is a trace metal of particular concern, and two predominant pathways for the uptake of lead have been identified in humans: soil and dust ingestion, and consumption of home grown foods. Depending on the extent of exposure, individuals may develop symptoms of acute or chronic lead poisoning. Symptoms or results of exposure include severe **anemia**, acute nervousness, kidney damage, irreversible brain damage, or death. Preschool children and women of child-bearing age are especially at risk. It has also been reported that people exposed to lead and cadmium in drinking water suffered from increased chronic kidney disease, skin cancer, heart disease, and anemia.

It is estimated that greater than 60% of human cancer is caused by contacting environmental chemicals containing PAHs. However, these compounds can be ingested through contaminated drinking water, but dietary intake of plant based food is the largest single route of exposure.

Urban development and various industrial activities have resulted in extensive contamination in most industrial countries. When urban redevelopment or expansion is considered, the potential impacts of this contamination on plants, animals, and humans needs to be evaluated. Before the development occurs contaminated sites need to be cleaned up, which can be very expensive. Urban populations that live in or near these sites already may be exposed to a wide-range of contaminants that can have both acute and chronic health effects. As we push to revitalize our cities, this is an issue that will become increasingly important. *See also* Brownfields

[*James L. Anderson*]

FURTHER READING

Air Pollution, People and Plants. St. Paul, MN: Sagar Krupa, The American Phytopathological Society, 1977.

Berrow, M.L. "An Overview of Soil Contamination Problems," in J.M. Lester (ed.) *Chemicals in the Environment.* Lisbon, 1986.

Thornton, I. "Metal Contamination of Soils in Urban Areas," in P. Bullock, and P.J. Gregory (eds.) *Soils in the Urban Environment.* Boston: Blackwell Scientific Publications, 1991.

Urban design and planning

Urban design can be expressed as the three-dimensional relationship between buildings, open spaces, and streets within a given area. This visual expression of urban zones (combined with a specific plan that details where and what kind of development should occur) can determine the character of the community.

Currently, prevalent thinking on the subject of urban design is that the new communities should be compact, mixed in both housing and commercial development, affordable, and pedestrian—a move back to living in compact, relatively self-sufficient communities and neighborhoods. It is a move back to a traditional community design in which communities and neighborhoods have affordable housing, jobs, and retail markets within easy walking distance for its residents.

This concept from the past is being promoted as the urban design and planning wave of the future. It addresses some of the ills that were brought about by the rapid suburban expansion after World War II: segregation of housing from workplace and retail areas, high housing costs, traffic congestion, long commutes, decay of community life, and negative environmental consequences (including air pollution and water pollution, inefficient use of energy and materials, etc.).

Proponents suggest that the move back to traditional urban design is good not only from the standpoint of promoting lost community values, but also positive for the environment. In fact, they submit that the environmental factors (such as the desire for clean air) will move the United States toward adopting this "new" approach. As the country addresses the issues of environmental quality, problems such as traffic congestion and affordable housing will become increasingly important to community design and planning, and will aid in the continuing evolution of urban design.

Urban heat island

An urban area where the temperature is commonly 5-10°F (–15 to –12°C) warmer than the surrounding countryside. Effects include reduced heating but higher air conditioning bills. Within cities, this warmth causes spring to arrive one to two weeks earlier and fall foliage to appear one to two weeks later. The chief cause is the high energy use within cities, which ultimately ends up in the atmosphere as waste heat. Also important, however, are the darker surfaces within cities, which absorb more heat, the relative absence of vegetative cooling through **transpiration** because of fewer trees, and less wind because of building obstructions.

Urban runoff

Urbanization causes fundamental changes in the local **hydrologic cycle**, mainly increased speed of water movement through the system, and degraded **water quality**. They are expressed through reduced **groundwater** recharge, faster and higher **storm runoff**, and factors that affect aquatic **ecosystem**s, particularly **sediment**, dissolved solids, and temperature. The resultant problems have encouraged municipalities to reduce negative impacts through storm water management.

Important research on these issues was spearheaded by the U.S. **Geological Survey** (USGS) during the early phases of the current environmental revolution. A sampling of titles used for the USGS Circular 601 series indicates the scope of these efforts: *Urban Sprawl and Flooding in Southern California* (C601-B); *Flood Hazard Mapping in Metropolitan Chicago* (C601-C); *Water as an Urban Resource and Nuisance* (C601-D); *Sediment Problems in Urban Areas* (C601-E); and *Extent and Development of Urban Flood Plains* (C601-J). Also relevant are *Washington D.C.'s Vanishing Springs and Waterways* (C752), and *Urbanization and Its Effects on the Temperature of the Streams on Long Island, New York* (USGS Professional Paper 627-D).

Most of these works cite a 1968 publication written by Luna Leopold, *Hydrology for Urban Land Planning*. Describing a research frontier, Leopold anticipated many of the concerns currently embodied in stormwater management efforts. He identified four separate but interrelated effects of **land use** changes associated with urban runoff: 1) changes in peak flow characteristics, 2) changes in total **runoff**, 3) changes in water quality, and 4) aesthetic or amenities issues.

Urbanization transforms the physical **environment** in a number of ways that affect runoff. Initially construction strips off the vegetation cover, which results in significantly increased **erosion**. Local comparisons with farms and woodlands show that sediment from construction and highway sites may increase 20,000-40,000 times. Furthermore, as slope angles steepen, the erosion rate increases even faster; and above a 10 percent slope (10 ft rise in 100 ft/3 m rise in 30 m) no restraints remain to hold back this sediment. On a larger scale, a Maryland study comparing relatively unurbanized and urbanized basins found a fourfold erosion increase.

Pavement and rooftops cover many permeable areas so that runoff occurs at a greater rate. **Storm sewer**s are built which by their very nature speed up runoff. Estimates range from a two- to six-fold increase in runoff amounts from fully urbanized areas. Even more important, however, is that peak discharge (the key element in **flooding**) is higher and comes more quickly. This makes flash floods more likely, and increases the frequency of runoff events which exceed bank capacity.

This increased flooding causes much channel erosion and altered geometry, as the channels struggle to reach a new equilibrium. Less water infiltrates into groundwater **reservoir**s, which diminishes the base flow (the seepage of groundwater into humid-region channels) and causes springs to dry up. The **urban heat island** effect, combined with reduced baseflow, exposes aquatic ecosystems to higher heat stress and reduced flow in summer, and to colder temperatures in winter. Summer is especially difficult, as rainwater flows from hot streets into channels exposed to direct sunlight. As a consequence, sustaining life becomes more difficult, and sensitive organisms must adapt or die.

Water quality changes increase **cultural eutrophication**, as **fertilizer** and **pesticide residue**s wash from lawns and gardens to join the oil, rubber, pet manure, brake lining dust, and other degrading elements comprising urban drainage. When these are combined with the **effluent** from industrial waste and treated sewage, especially heavy metals, the riverine environment becomes a health concern.

Under **arid** conditions, the damage from mudflows may be increased because the land that once absorbed the sliding mud is now covered with streets and buildings. This situation can be seen in southern California, where hillside development has increased the threat of **landslide**s.

Increasing attention is now being given to stormwater management around the United States. For example, Seattle, Washington has focused on water quality, whereas Tulsa, Oklahoma is primarily concerned with flooding. Both cities have responded to serious local problems.

By the 1950s, Seattle's **Lake Washington** and the adjacent water of Puget Sound had become so polluted that beaches had to be closed. **Sewage treatment** plants around Lake Washington and raw sewage dumping in Puget Sound were the fundamental causes. The residents of the area voted to form a regional water-quality authority to deal with the problems. As a result, all sewage treatment was removed from Lake Washington, and dumping of raw sewage into Puget Sound was halted. The environmental result was dramatic. As **nitrate** and phosphate levels dropped sharply, cultural eutrophication in these waters was greatly reduced, and beaches were reopened. The regional agency continues to seek better ways to improve the water quality of stormwater runoff.

Tulsa's efforts are a response to a series of devastating floods. Between 1970 and 1985, Tulsa led the country in numbers of federal flood declarations; these floods caused 17 deaths and $300 million in damages. Conditions in Tulsa are such that 6.3 inches (16 cm) of rain within six hours is sufficient to produce what hydrologists call a 100-year flood.

In May 1984, 10 inches (25 cm) of rain fell during a seven-hour period, which was a rainfall frequency of about 200 years.

A leader in flood control, Tulsa has taken a multi-faceted approach to stormwater management. During the 1970s, then Congressman James R. Jones sponsored legislation to buy out and tear down houses in the severely flood-prone Mingo Creek Basin; some had qualified seven times for flood disaster aid, with payments far exceeding market value. In a joint venture, Tulsa and the **Army Corps of Engineers** have spent $60 million and $100 million respectively to channelize Mingo Creek in its lower reaches and create detention ponds in the middle portions of the basin. Expected benefits include a $26.9 million reduction in annual flood damage. Continuing flood control efforts have incorporated the use of a state-of-the-art computerized flood warning system.

Recreational possibilities are being exploited in Tulsa's overall stormwater management program. Access roads are being used as running tracks; athletic fields double as detention reservoirs during flood conditions. Since existing parks have been modified to meet the flood program needs, the facilities have benefitted from the improvements, and the water authority leaves the maintenance to the parks department. Using existing parks also eliminates the need to buy out houses and disrupt existing neighborhoods.

Although the Tulsa plan has been successful, more heavily developed floodplains require different measures. Often land costs are so high that it may be cheaper to spend money on flood-proofing or tearing down existing buildings. In any event, urban runoff is an expensive problem to solve. *See also* Heavy metals and heavy metal poisoning; Industrial waste treatment; Land-use control; Water treatment

[*Nathan H. Meleen*]

FURTHER READING

Howard, A. D., and I. Remson. *Geology in Environmental Planning.* New York: McGraw-Hill, 1978.

Leopold, L. B. *Hydrology for Urban Land Planning: A Guidebook on the Hydrologic Effects of Urban Land Use.* USGS Circular 554. Washington, DC: U.S. Government Printing Office, 1968.

Mrowka, J. P. "Man's Impact on Stream Regimen and Quality." In *Perspectives on Environment,* edited by I. R. Manners and M. W. Mikesell. Washington, DC: Association of American Geographers, 1974.

Urban sprawl

Urban sprawl is the process by which an urban area grows outward from a central city, expanding the limits of the city itself and surrounding it with suburbs. Largely a phenomenon of the post-World War II era, urban sprawl is characteristic of regions experiencing economic growth.

Two major factors have made urban sprawl possible. The first of these is prosperity. As individual and family incomes have increased, people have been able to move out of the crowded central core of a city into more desirable rural settings. In response to this change of lifestyle, developers have bought up large tracts of farmland for the construction of suburban housing development and shopping areas. Suburbs eventually became nearly self-sufficient with their own schools, recreation centers and other urban features. Residents may need to travel to the core city only for work or an occasional social outing.

The second factor making urban sprawl possible has been the **automobile**. Cars make it easy for people to travel many miles between home and work. As car ownership has grown, so have the number of highways, making it possible, in turn, for another increase in automotive travel.

Urban sprawl has made possible the development of huge megalopolises—extended metropolitan areas that include several major cities and cover hundreds of square miles. The corridors between Chicago and Detroit, between New York and Boston, and between San Francisco, San Jose and Oakland are examples of the extremes to which the phenomenon has progressed.

Urban sprawl has come about in response to the human desire for a better way of life. The suburban environment is often considered a more pleasant place to live than the city core itself. At the same time, however, urban sprawl has created a myriad of new social, economic, personal, and environmental problems and issues.

For example, huge amounts of productive farmland have been lost as they are converted into highways, shopping centers, or housing developments. In many locations, valuable **wetlands**, hiking trails, camping sites, and other recreational areas have also been destroyed by urban sprawl. The huge increase in automotive traffic that accompanies the spread also increases **pollution** levels and uses up large amounts of valuable **fossil fuels**.

A number of suggestions have been made for controlling urban sprawl. Zoning is one popular method. States, counties, and local communities can exert control over the way land is used by zoning it for farming, **recreation**, or other non-growth purposes. Tax policy can also be used. Farmers may receive special credits, for example, for continuing to use their land for agriculture rather than selling it for development. Purchase of land by organizations such as the **Nature Conservancy** is another approach. This land can then be set aside for recreational purposes or maintained in a natural state. Finally, communities can develop a set of slow-growth policies that will limit urban sprawl. *See also* Land-use control; Sustainable development

[*David E. Newton*]

FURTHER READING

Brown, L. R., and J. Jacobson. *The Future of Urbanization: Facing the Ecological and Economic Restraints.* Washington, DC: Worldwatch Institute, 1987.

Hart, J. *Saving Cities, Saving Money: Environmental Strategies That Work.* Sausalito, CA: Resource Renewal Institute, 1992.

Kemp, R. L., ed. *America's Cities: Strategic Planning for the Future.* New York: Interstate, 1988.

Ryn, S. van der, and P. Calthorpe. *Sustainable Communities: A New Design Synthesis for Cities, Suburbs, and Towns.* San Francisco: Sierra Club, 1986.

Walter, B., L. Arkin, and R. Crenshaw, eds. *Sustainable Cities: Concepts and Strategies for Eco-City Development.* Los Angeles: Eco-Home Media, 1992.

USLE

See **Erosion**

Utilitarianism

According to the ethical theory of utilitarianism, an action is right if it promises to produce better results than—or maximize the expected utility of—other action possible in the circumstances. Although there are earlier examples of utilitarian reasoning, the English philosopher Jeremy Bentham (1748-1832) gave utilitarianism its first full formulation. "Nature has placed mankind under two sovereign masters," Bentham declared, "pain and pleasure. It is for them alone to point out what we ought to do, as well as to determine what we shall do." The ethical person, then, will act to increase the amount of pleasure (or utility) in the world and decrease the amount of pain by following a single principle: Promote the greatest happiness of the greatest number.

As later utilitarians discovered, this principle is not as straightforward as it seems. The very notion of happiness is problematical. Are all pleasures intrinsically equal, as Bentham suggested? Or are some inherently better or "higher" than others, as John Stuart Mill (1806-1873), the English philosopher and political economist, insisted? A related problem is the difficulty—some say the impossibility—of making interpersonal comparisons of utility. If people want to promote the greatest happiness (or good or utility) of the greatest number, they need a way to measure utility. But there is no ruler that can assess the utility of various actions in the way that weight, height, or distance are quantified.

Another problem is the ambiguity of "the greatest happiness of the greatest number." Stressing "the greatest number" implies that the utilitarian should bow to the majority. But "the greatest happiness" may mean that the intense preferences of the minority may override an equivocal majority. Utilitarians have typically taken the second tack by reformulating the principle as "maximize aggregate utility."

Either interpretation seems to call for an ever-increasing population. The more people there are, the more happiness there will be. This has led some utilitarians to argue that people should try to promote average rather than total utility. Since the average amount of happiness could decline in an overcrowded world even as the total amount increased, the "average utilitarian" could consistently argue for population control.

Finally, who counts when happiness or utility is calculated? Everyone counts equally, Bentham said, but does "everyone" include only those people living in this place at this time? The expansive view is that "everyone" embraces all those who may be affected by one's actions, even people who may not yet be born. If so, should today's people count the preferences of **future generations** equally with those presently living? For that matter, should they restrict their concern to people? According to Bentham, the test of inclusion should not be: "Can they reason? nor Can they talk? but, Can they suffer?" This emphasis on sentience has led some contemporary utilitarians to advocate "animal liberation," including **vegetarianism**, as part of a consistent attempt to promote utility. *See also* Animal rights; Environmental ethics; Intergenerational justice

[*Richard K. Dagger*]

FURTHER READING

Bentham, J. *An Introduction to the Principles of Morals and Legislation.* New York: Hafner, 1948 (originally published 1789).

Mill, J. S. "Utilitarianism." In *Utilitarianism, Liberty, Representative Government.* New York: Dutton, 1951.

Smart, J. J. C., and B. Williams. *Utilitarianism: For and Against.* Cambridge: Cambridge University Press, 1973.

V

Vadose zone

The unsaturated zone between the land surface and the **water table**. The vadose zone (from the Latin *vadosus* meaning shallow) includes the soil-water zone, intermediate vadose zone, and capillary fringe. The pore space contains air, water, and other fluids under pressure, which is less than atmospheric pressure. Thus, the water is held to the **soil** particles by forces that are greater than the force of gravity. Saturated zones, such as perched **groundwater** aquifers, may exist in the vadose zone and water pressure within these zones is greater than atmospheric pressure. *See also* Recharge zone; Zone of saturation

Valdez Principles

In March 1989 the ***Exxon Valdez*** ran aground in **Prince William Sound** in Alaska, spilling 11 million gallons (41 million liters) of crude oil. During the international outcry over the environmental consequences of the spill, environmentalists criticized a number of the structural features of the **petroleum** industry and the operational practices of the supertanker transport of oil.

In this climate new approaches were suggested to motivate not only oil companies but all industries to support the protection of the **environment**. The Valdez Principles are perhaps the most important of the approaches suggested during this period. They were developed by the Coalition for Environmentally Responsible Economics (CERES), which was a consortium of 14 environmental groups and the Social Investment Forum, an organization of 325 socially concerned bankers, investors, and brokers. CERES was founded by Boston money manager Joan Bavaria, and it has the support of several major environmental groups, including the **Sierra Club** and the **National Wildlife Federation**.

The Valdez Principles were modelled on the Sullivan Principles, which had been developed to discourage investment in South Africa as a protest against apartheid. Members of CERES controlled $150 billion in both pension and mutual funds. The goal of the Valdez Principles was to reward the behavior that was environmentally sound and punish behavior that was not by investing or withholding funds controlled by CERES members. Corporations were also asked to sign the Valdez Principles in the hopes that the financial incentives provided by CERES would encourage companies to develop environmentally sound practices.

The Valdez Principles support a wide range of environmental issues. Protection of the **biosphere** is one of its objectives, and it encourages industries to minimize or eliminate the **emission** of pollutants. The principles are also devoted to protecting **biodiversity** and insuring the **sustainable development** of land, water, forests, and other **natural resources**. The principles advocate the use of **recycling** whenever possible, support safe disposal methods, and encourage the use of safe and sustainable energy sources. **Energy efficiency** is also a goal, as well as the marketing of products that have minimal **environmental impact**. The principles also call for corporations to have at least one board member qualified to represent environmental interests and a senior executive responsible for environmental affairs. Other goals include damage compensation, disclosure of accidents and hazards, and the creation of independent environmental audit procedures. Many major corporations have indicated an interest in these principles, but few have signed them. Some executives have observed that many aspects of the Valdez Principles are already required by government regulations and internal policies.

Perhaps then the most significant feature of the Valdez Principles is not what they have accomplished but the circumstances of their origin. A major disaster often engenders a social and political climate that is, at least temporarily, receptive to reform. In this case it was a rare coalition between financial investors and environmental groups. Many have argued that the principles had unrealistic goals, but some see in their development hope for the future.

[*Usha Vedagiri and Douglas Smith*]

FURTHER READING

Ohnuma, K. "Missed Manners." *Sierra* 75 (March-April 1990): 24-26.
"The Valdez Principles." *Audubon* 91 (November 1989): 6.

Vapor recovery system

At one time vapors that are potentially harmful to the **environment** or to human health were simply allowed to escape into the **atmosphere**. Each time an **automobile** consumer filled the gas tank, for example, gasoline vapors escaped into the air. As the hazards of these **emission**s became more evident, the use of closed systems of pipes, valves, compressors, and other components became more prevalent. In most systems, those vapors are compressed to a liquid and returned to their original source. Vapor recovery systems not only protect the environment, but conserve resources that might otherwise be wasted.

Vascular plant

A plant that possesses specialized conducting tissue (xylem and phloem) for the purpose of transporting water and solutes within the root-stem-leaf system. Although aquatic forms exist, most vascular plants are terrestrial and include herbs, shrubs and trees. The development of vascular transport allowed plants to become larger, leading to their eventual domination of terrestrial **ecosystem**s. The uptake and translocation of soluble pollutants from the **soil** into the plant occurs through the roots and the conducting tissue. Adverse effects of such **pollution** on vascular plants include stunted growth and death of all or part of the plant.

Vegan

The strictest type of vegetarians, refraining from eating not only meat and fish, but also eggs, dairy products, and all other food containing or derived from animals, often including honey. A vegan diet contains no cholesterol and very little fat, so it is quite healthy as long as sufficient **nutrient**s are obtained, especially vitamins B_{12} and D, calcium, and quality protein. Most vegans also avoid wearing or using animal products of any kind, including fur, leather, and even wool. Vegans are motivated primarily by a humane and ethical concern for the welfare of animals and by a desire to avoid unhealthy food products, as well as by the realization that raising livestock and other food animals damage the natural **environment** and contributes, through its wastefulness and lack of efficiency, to world hunger. *See also* Animal rights; Environmental ethics; Vegetarianism

Vegetarianism

Vegetarians refrain from consuming animals and animal products, including meat, poultry, and fish. Lacto-ovo vegetarians will eat eggs, cheese, yogurt, and other dairy products. However, total vegetarians (**vegan**s) avoid these animal products completely, including foods such as honey. On the whole, vegetarians emphasize the impact of dietary choice on health, on the fate of animals and the planet, and on humanity, including future generations.

Vegetarians avoid meat for many reasons, including concerns for animals, the **environment**, general health, and worldwide food shortages. Some cultures and religions, such as Buddhism and Hinduism, also advocate vegetarianism. Vegetarians emphasize that the overwhelming majority of food animals are raised on "factory farms," where they spend their entire lives in cramped, overcrowded conditions, lacking sunshine, exercise, and the ability to engage in natural behavior.

A vegetarian diet can also be much healthier than one that is meat-centered. Meat contains high amounts of saturated fat and cholesterol, which—in excess amounts—contribute to heart disease, **cancer**, and other degenerative diseases. While poultry and fish are lower in fat and cholesterol than red meat, they also carry health risks. Chicken is a major source of salmonella contamination and other dangerous bacteria, and fish (especially shellfish) are often heavily contaminated with **pesticide**s, **heavy metals**, and toxic **chemicals**.

Vegetarians often cite the massive environmental damage caused by raising food animals. Consider the following illustrations. Livestock occupy and graze on half of the world's land mass. Cattle alone use a quarter of the earth's land. This can result in **water pollution**, clearing of forests, **soil erosion**, and **desertification**. More food could be produced and more people could be fed if resources were not used to produce meat. For example, the amount of land required to feed one meat-eater could theoretically feed 15 to 20 vegetarians. One acre of agricultural land can produce about 165 pounds of beef or 20,000 pounds of potato.

Moreover, the world's cattle eat enough grain to feed everyone on earth, and most of that grain is wasted. A cow must eat 16 pounds of grain and soybeans to produce one pound of feedlot beef—a 94 percent waste of food. A pig has to eat 7.5 pounds of protein to produce one pound of pork protein. Ninety-five percent of all grain grown in the United States is used to feed livestock, as does 97 percent of all legumes (beans, peas, and lentils), and 66 percent of the fish caught in American waters. Over half of all the water used in the United States goes for livestock production, and it takes 100 to 200 times more water to produce beef than wheat.

[*Lewis G. Regenstein*]

FURTHER READING

Amato, P. R., and S. A. Partridge. *The New Vegetarians: Promoting Health and Protecting Life.* New York: Plenum, 1989.

Brown, E. H. *With the Grain: The Essentially Vegetarian Way.* New York: Carroll and Graf, 1990.

Giehl, D. *Vegetarianism: A Way of Life.* New York: Harper & Row, 1979.

Mitra, A. *Food for Thought: The Vegetarian Philosophy.* Willow Springs, MO: Nucleus, 1991.

Robbins, J. *Diet for a New America.* Walpole, NH: Stillpoint Publishing, 1987.

Victims' compensation

Traditionally, legal remedies for environmental problems have been provided by common law (judge-created law developed through private lawsuits). Common law provides remedies including compensation to victims injured by another's negligence. For example, if appropriate care is not taken in the disposal of a **toxic substance** and this substance enters a farm pond, killing or injuring the farmer's livestock, the farmer can sue the polluter for damages.

U. S. proposals for reforming victims' compensation fall into two general categories: 1) an approach that combines administrative relief with common law tort (a tort is a wrong actionable in civil court) reform; and 2) proposals that provide administrative relief, but eliminate tort remedies. The first approach was developed by a Study Group consisting of 12 attorneys designated by the American Bar Association, American Trial Lawyer's Association, the Association of State Attorneys General, and the American Law Institute. In 1980, Congress asked this Study Group to consider the hazardous substance personal injury problem in conjunction with the **Comprehensive Environmental Response, Compensation and Monitoring Act** (Superfund). The Study Group recommended a "two-tier" approach. The first tier, which would be the primary remedy for injured persons, would consist of administrative relief. This part of the system would operate in a manner similar to workmen's compensation. Within three years after the discovery of an injury or disease, an applicant would make a claim based on proof of exposure, existence of the disease or injury, and compensable damages. The applicant, without having to show fault, would receive medical costs and two-thirds of earnings minus the amounts that could be obtained from other government programs. The money for this victims' compensation fund would come from industry sources through a tax on hazardous activities or some other means of eliciting contributions.

Most claims would be dealt with through the administrative system without resort to the courts. However, the second tier in the program would preserve existing tort law. Plaintiffs who chose this option would have to submit to the costs and delays of legal proceedings. However, a plaintiff able to win in the courts would have the right to collect unlimited damages, including full loss of earnings and compensation for pain and suffering.

A second proposal that combines administrative relief with traditional tort remedies originated at the **Environmental Law Institute**. Its director, Jeffrey Trauberman, published an extensive article that appeared in the *Harvard Environmental Law Review* in 1983 proposing a "Model Statute." The approach was different from the Attorneys' Study Group because it emphasized common law tort reform as the primary remedy, with the victims' compensation fund serving as "a residual or secondary source of compensation" in instances when the responsible party could not be identified, had become insolvent, or had gone out of business.

The major common law problem that Trauberman addressed was that of causation. Traditionally, the courts have been reluctant to accept probabilistic evidence as proof of causation. Trauberman, however, argued that evidence from **epidemiology**, animal and human toxicology, and other sources on the "frontiers of scientific knowledge" should be admitted. When a plaintiff was unable to demonstrate a "substantial" case of harm, Trauberman would permit "fractional recovery." By "fractional recovery" he meant that if a **hazardous waste** dump increased the total number of cancers in an area from eight to ten percent, then the

increased incidence of cancer brought on by the dump was 25 percent; in these cases, victims should be able to recover 25 percent of their costs. Recovery for pain and suffering, which was not available to fund claimants, would be available through litigation. These balanced proposals are to be distinguished from bills introduced in the U. S. Congress that would create an administrative compensation system but preclude tort remedies.

In contrast to the U.S., Japan has adopted an approach that combines administrative relief with tort justice. The 1973 Law for the Compensation of Pollution-Related Health Injury, which replaced a simpler 1969 law, established an administrative system to oversee compensation payments. Upon certification by a council of medical, legal, and other experts, victims of designated diseases are eligible for medical expenses, lost earnings, and other expenses; but they receive no allowance for non-economic losses such as pain and suffering. Companies pay the entire cost of this compensation. There has been an administrative review system, but in no case does this system prohibit recourse to the courts. In the U. S., the institutions responsible for developing victims' compensation policy have not, as yet, forged such a comprehensive policy. *See also* Ashio, Japan; Itai-Itai disease; Minamata disease; Yokkaichi asthma

[*Alfred A. Marcus*]

FURTHER READING

Marcus, A. A. *Business and Society*. Homewood, IL: Irwin Press, 1992.

Video display terminal (VDT)
See **Electromagnetic fields**

Vinyl chloride

A colorless, flammable, and toxic liquid when under pressure but a gas under ordinary conditions. Polymerized vinyl chloride, called polyvinyl chloride, is an ubiquitous **plastic** produced in enormous quantities. While vinyl chloride has been detected at some waste sites, exposure has been much greater in the factories that produced it. However, significant efforts were exerted by industry to reduce occupational exposure. Chronic exposure resulted in "vinyl chloride disease" with liver, nerve, and circulatory damage. Epidemiological studies associated **cancer** of the liver (particularly angiosarcoma) and possibly the brain with occupational exposure, and thus vinyl chloride is considered to be a human **carcinogen**.

Virus

A virus is a submicroscopic particle that contains either **RNA (ribonucleic acid)** or **DNA (deoxyribonucleic acid)**. Viruses are not capable of performing metabolic functions outside of a host cell upon which the virus depends for replication. Viruses are found in the **environment** in a wide range of sizes, chemical composition, shape, and host cell specificity. Viruses can cause disease or genetic damage to host cells and can infect many living things including plants, animals, bacteria, and **fungi**.

Bacteriophages are viruses which use bacteria as hosts. Of particular interest in the aquatic environment are coliphages, viruses that infect *Escherichia coli*, a bacteria that commonly grows in the colons of mammals. *E. coli* is an important bacterial indicator of fecal pollution of water. However, coliphages tend to survive much longer in the environment than *E. coli*, and their detection in water in the absence of *E. coli* tends to be a more sensitive indicator of former fecal contamination than coliform bacteria.

Human intestinal viruses are the most commonly encountered viruses in **wastewater** and water supplies since they are shed in large numbers by humans (10^9 viruses per gram of feces from infected individuals) and are largely unaffected by wastewater treatment before discharge to the environment. Viruses cannot replicate in the environment, but they can survive for long periods of time in surface water and **groundwater**. Viruses are difficult to isolate from the environment and, once collected, are difficult to culture and identify because of their small size, numerous types, low concentrations in water, association with suspended particles, and the limitations in viral identification methods.

There are more than 100 types of known enteric viruses, and there are many others yet to be found. Enteric viruses include polioviruses, coxackieviruses A and B, echoviruses, and probably hepatitis A virus. Waterborne transmission of the poliovirus in developed countries is rare. Of more consequence are the coxackieviruses and hepatitis A virus, with hepatitis A virus being a leading etiological agent in waterborne disease. Other viruses of concern include the gastroenteritis virus group, a poorly understood family of viruses which are probably a subset of the enteric viruses. The important members of this group include the Norwalk agent, rotaviruses, coronaviruses, caliciviruses, the W agent, and the cockle virus.

Preventing the transmission of viruses through water supplies depends upon adequate chemical disinfection of the water. Resistance of viruses to disinfectants is due largely to their biological simplicity, their tendency to clump together or aggregate, and protection afforded by association with other forms or organic material present. Proper **chlorination** of water is usually sufficient for inactivation of viruses. **Ozone** has been used for inactivation of viruses in drinking water because of its superior virucidal properties. France has been a leader in the use of ozone for inactivation of waterborne viruses.

[*Gordon R. Finch*]

FURTHER READING

Feachem, R. G., et al. *Sanitation and Disease. Health Aspects of Excreta and Wastewater Management.* New York: Wiley, 1983.

Foliguet, J. M., P. Hartemann, and J. Vial. "Microbial Pathogens Transmitted by Water." *Journal of Environmental Pathology, Toxicology, and Oncology* 7 (1987): 39–114.

Greenberg, A. E., L. S. Clesceri, and A. D. Eaton, eds. *Standard Methods for the Examination of Water and Wastewater.* 18th ed. Washington, DC: American Public Health Association, American Water Works Association, Water Environment Federation, 1982.

Visibility

Visibility generally refers to the quality of vision through the **atmosphere**. Technically, this term denotes the greatest distance in a given direction that an observer can just see a prominent dark object against the sky at the horizon with the naked eye. Visibility is a measure commonly used in weather-observing in the United States. In this context, surface visibility refers to visibility determined from a point on the ground, control tower visibility refers to visibility observed from an airport control tower, and vertical visibility refers to the distance that can be seen vertically into a ground-obscuring medium such as fog or snow.

Visibility is affected by the presence of **aerosol**s or **haze** in the atmosphere. In the ideal case of a black target on a white background, the target can be seen at close range because it reflects no light to the eye, while the background reflects a great deal of light to the eye. As the distance between the observer and the target object increases, the light from the white background is scattered by the intervening particles, blurring to some degree the edge between the target and the surroundings, since light from the background is now scattered into the line of sight to the black target. In addition, the whiteness of the background is decreased by the scattering of light out of the direct line from the background to the eye, and by the absorption of some of the light by dark particles, principally carbon (soot). Finally, particles in the line between the target and the eye scatter light to the eye, decreasing the blackness of the target as seen from the distance. At any distance greater than the visibility, then, all these actions degrade the contrast between the object and its background so that the eye can no longer pick out the object.

Some light is scattered even by air molecules, so visibility through the atmosphere is never infinite. It can be great enough to require correction for the curvature of the earth, and the consequent fact that atmospheric density is less (fewer scattering molecules per unit of distance) at the end of the sight path than at the location of the observer.

Air pollutants now produce a haze that circles the globe, significantly reducing visibility even in places as remote as the Arctic. In areas of industrial concentration, haze may consistently reduce visibility by as much as 40 percent. In addition, gaseous molecules scatter light, and some gases, most notably nitrogen dioxide, absorb light in the visible range, thus changing the apparent color of the background. The effects of **air pollution** on visibility are quite well understood, unlike some other effects of this **pollution** on human health and the **environment**. *See also* Arctic haze; Photochemical smog; Smog

[*James P. Lodge, Jr.*]

FURTHER READING

Lodge, J. P., Jr., et al. "Non-Health Effects of Airborne Particulate Matter." *Atmospheric Environment* 15 (1981): 449-458.

Middleton, W. E. K. *Vision Through the Atmosphere.* Toronto: University of Toronto Press, 1952.

VOC

See **Volatile organic compound**

Vogt, William (1902-1968)

American ecologist and ornithologist

An ecologist and ornithologist whose work has influenced many disciplines, William Vogt was born in 1902 in Mineola, New York. Convalescing from a childhood illness, Vogt became a voracious reader, consuming the works of poets, playwrights, and naturalists. One naturalist in particular, Ernest Thompson Seton, greatly influenced him, cultivating his interest in ornithology. Vogt graduated with honors in 1925 from St. Stephens (now Bard) College in New York, where he had studied romance languages, edited the school literary magazine, and won prizes for his poetry.

After receiving his degree, Vogt worked for two years as assistant editor at the New York Academy of Sciences, and he went on to act as curator of the Jones Beach State Bird Sanctuary from 1933 to 1935. As field naturalist and lecturer at the National Association of Audubon Societies from 1935 to 1939, he edited *Bird Lore* magazine and contributed articles to other related professional periodicals. Perhaps his most important efforts while with the association were his compilation of *Thirst for Land*, which discussed the urgent need for **water conservation**, and his editing of the classic *Birds of America*.

Vogt's chief accomplishment, however, was to make the world more fully aware of the imbalanced relationship between the rapidly growing world population and the food supply. He developed a strong interest in Latin America in the late 1930s. During World War II he acted as a consultant to the United States government on the region, and in 1942 he travelled to Chile to conduct a series of climatological studies, during which he began to realize the full scope of the depletion of **natural resources** and its consequences for world population. As he compiled the results of his studies, Vogt became increasingly interested in the relationship between the **environment** and both human and bird populations. He was appointed chief of the **conservation** section of the Pan American Union in 1943, and he remained at this post until 1950, working to disseminate information on and develop solutions for the problems he had identified.

Vogt's popularity soared in 1948 when he published *Road to Survival*, which closely examined the discrepancy between the world population and food supplies. A bestseller, the book was eventually translated into nine languages. It was also a major influence on **Paul R. Ehrlich**, author of *The Population Bomb* and a key proponent of **zero population growth** theories.

Following the publication of *Road to Survival*, Vogt won Fulbright and Guggenheim grants to study population trends and problems in Scandinavia. Soon after returning to the United States, he was appointed national director of Planned Parenthood Federation of America, an organization wholly concerned with limiting population growth.

During the last seven years of his life, Vogt again turned his attentions to conservationism, and he became secretary of the Conservation Foundation, an organization created to "initiate and advance research and education in the entire field of conservation," which was recently absorbed by the **World Wildlife Fund**. Vogt died in New York City on July 11, 1968. *See also* Family planning; International Council on Bird Preservation; Population biology; Population Institute; Sustainable agriculture; Sustainable development

[*Kimberley A. Peterson*]

FURTHER READING

Squire, C. B. *Heroes of Conservation.* New York: Fleet Press, 1974.

Vogt, W. *Road to Survival.* New York: W. Sloane Associates, 1948.

———. *People! Challenge to Survival.* New York: W. Sloane Associates, 1960.

Volatile organic compound

In environmental science, the term volatile organic compound usually refers to the **hydrocarbons**, especially those found in **air pollution**. In 1988, the five most abundant of these hydrocarbons in urban air were isopentane, n-butane, toluene, propane, and ethane; each of these compounds has unburned **gasoline** as its primary source. In the presence of sunlight, hydrocarbons react with **ozone**, **nitrogen oxides**, and other components of polluted air to form compounds that are hazardous to plants, animals, and humans. In 1989, volatile organic compounds ranked fourth behind **carbon monoxide**, sulfur oxides, and nitrogen oxides in annual pollutant emissions in the United States. *See also* Air pollution control; Air quality

Volcano

Volcanoes have been called the thermostat of the planet. They wreak havoc, but also spawn far-ranging benefits for **soil** and air. Some earth scientists now say that the vast swath of destruction from a volcanic eruption can be a crucible of creation.

Most land volcanoes erupt along plate edges where ocean floors plunge deep under continents and melting rock rises to the surface as magma. The earth's fragmented crust pulls apart and the edges grind past or slide beneath each other at a speed of up to eight inches (20 cm) per year. But just as our blood carries **nutrient**s that feed our body parts, volcanoes do the same for the skin of the earth.

Magma contains elements required for plant growth, such as **phosphorus**, potassium, magnesium and sulfur. When this volcanic material is blasted out as ash, the fertilizing process that moves the nutrients into the soil can occur within months. Java, one of the most volcano-rich spots on the earth, is one of the world's most fertile areas.

Magma also yields energy: it heats underground water which is tapped by wells to warm most of the homes in Iceland. Natural steam drives turbines that provide 7 percent of New Zealand's electric power, and it accounts for 1 percent of U.S. energy needs.

Atmospheric after-effects of a volcanic eruption can last for years, as the eruption of **Mount Pinatubo** in the Philippines on June 15, 1991, has shown. While water vapor is the main gas in magma, there are smaller amounts of hydrogen chloride, **sulfur dioxide**, and **carbon dioxide**. Sulfur dioxide, blasted 25 miles (40 km) into the **stratosphere** after Mount Pinatubo erupted, combined with moisture to create a thin **aerosol** cloud that girdled the globe in 21 days. Scientists calculated that 2 percent of the earth's incoming sunlight was deflected, leading to slightly lower temperatures on worldwide average. These light sulfur dioxides can circle the globe for years and possibly damage the **ozone** layer.

Recently, scientists mapping the sea floor in the South Pacific have found what they call the greatest concentration of active volcanoes on earth. More than 1,000 seamounts and volcanic cones, some as high as 7,000 feet (2,135 m) with peaks 5,000 feet (1,525 m) beneath the ocean surface, are located in an area the size of New York state. One potential benefit of eruptions is that they generate new mineral deposits, including **copper**, iron, sulfur, and gold. The discovery is likely to intensify debate over whether volcanic activity could change water temperatures enough to affect weather patterns in the Pacific. Scientists speculate that periods of extreme volcanic activity underwater could trigger **El Niño**, a weather system that alters weather patterns around the world. *See also* Geothermal energy; Ozone layer depletion; Plate tectonics

[*Linda Rehkopf*]

FURTHER READING

Findley, R. "Mount St. Helens Aftermath: The Mountain That Was and Will Be." *National Geographic* 180 (December 1991): 713.

Grove, N. "Volcanoes: Crucibles of Creation." *National Geographic* 182 (December 1992): 5-41.

Powell, C. S. "Greenhouse Gusher." *Scientific American* 265 (October 1991): 20.

"Volcano Could Cool Climate, Reduce Ozone." *Science News* 140 (6 July 1991): 7.

Vollenweider, Richard (1922-)

Swiss limnologist

Vollenweider is one of the world's most renowned authorities on eutrophication, the process by which lakes mature and are gradually converted into swamps, bogs, and finally meadows. Eutrophication is a natural process that normally takes place over hundreds or even thousands of years, but human activities can accelerate the rate at which it occurs. The study of these human effects has been an important topic of environmental research since the 1960s.

Richard A. Vollenweider was born in Zurich, Switzerland, on June 27, 1922. He received his diploma in biology from the University of Zurich in 1946 and his Ph.D. in biology from the same institution in 1951. After teaching at various schools in Lucerne for five years, in 1954 he was appointed a fellow in **limnology** (the study of lakes) at the Italian Hydrobiological Institute in Palanza, Italy. A year later, he accepted a similar appointment at the Swiss-Swedish Research Council in Uppsala.

Vollenweider has also worked for two international scientific organizations, the United Nations Economic, Scientific, and Cultural Organization (UNESCO), and the Organization for Economic Cooperation and Development (OECD). From 1957 to 1959, he was stationed in Egypt for UNESCO, working on problems of lakes and fisheries. Between 1966 and 1968, he was a consultant on **water pollution** for OECD in Paris.

In 1968, Vollenweider moved to Canada to take a position as chief limnologist and head of the fisheries research board of the Canada Centre for Inland Waters (CCIW). In 1970 he was promoted to chief of the Lakes Research Division and in 1973 to the position of senior scientist at CCIW.

Perhaps the peak of Vollenweider's career came in 1978 when he was awarded the Premio Internazionale Cervia Ambiente by Italian environmentalists for his contributions to research on the **environment**. The award was based largely on Vollenweider's work on eutrophication of lakes and waterways in the Po River region of Italy. Although the area was one of the few in Italy with sophisticated water and **sewage treatment** plants, there was abundant evidence of advanced eutrophication.

Vollenweider found a number of factors contributing to eutrophication in the area. Most importantly the treatment plants were not removing **phosphorus**, which is a major contributor to eutrophication. In addition, pig farming was widely practiced in the area, causing huge quantities of phosphorus contained in pig wastes to enter the surface water.

Vollenweider recommended a wide range of changes to reduce eutrophication. These included the addition of tertiary stages in sewage treatment plants to remove phosphorus, special treatment of wastes from pig farms, and agreements from manufacturers of **detergents** to reduce the amount of phosphorus contained in their products. *See also* Aquatic chemistry; Experimental Lakes Area; Feedlot runoff; Organic waste; Phosphorus removal

[*David E. Newton*]

FURTHER READING

Davey, T. "CCIW Scientist Wins Top Italian Environmental Award."
Water and Pollution Control (January 1979): 23.

Volume reduction, solid waste

See **Solid waste volume reduction**

War, environmental effects of

War and similar conflicts have long been an activity of humans. War is referred to in the earliest historical records, including the Bible. Wars involving hunter-gatherer and early agricultural cultures included clashes between clans and village groups. This sometimes led to the deaths of some participants, as has been observed in the present century in such places as New Guinea and Borneo. In marked contrast, modern warfare involving advanced technological societies can wreak a truly awesome destruction—about 84 million people have been killed during the wars of the twentieth century.

The conflict that has been most destructive of human lives was World War II of 1939-1945, during which about 38 million people died. World War I of 1914-1918 resulted in about 20 million deaths, the Korean War of 1950-1953 about 3.0 million, and the Viet Nam War of 1961-1975, about 2.4 million.

In addition to having awful consequences for people and their civilizations, modern warfare also causes terrible environmental damages. These include the destruction caused by conventional weapons, effects of the military use of poisonous gases and herbicides, and **petroleum** spills. In addition, the potential consequences of nuclear warfare are horrific—a nuclear holocaust would kill billions of people and might also result in climate changes that could cause a collapse of biospheric processes. These environmental effects of warfare are discussed in the following sections.

Destruction By Conventional Warfare

Enormous amounts of explosive munitions are used during modern wars. An estimated 21 million metric tons of explosives were expended during World War II, 36% of that by U.S. forces, 42% by the Germans, and 22% by other combatants (Westing, 1985). About 3 million metric tons were used during the Korean War, 90% of that by U.S. and Allied forces. About 14 million metric tons were used during the Viet Nam War, 95% of that by U.S. and South Viet Namese forces. During the Gulf Conflict, several months of bombardment by U.S.-led coalition forces resulted in 0.12 million metric tons of explosives being used. Although not well documented, the explosion of such enormous quantities of munitions during these wars caused great damages to people, buildings, and **ecosystem**s.

Much of World War I, for example, was waged in an area of coastal lowland in Belgium and France known as the Western Front. This was a terrible theater of war, which involved virtually static confrontations between huge armies that fought back-and-forth over a well-defended landscape webbed with intricate trenchworks. Territorial gains could only be made by extraordinarily difficult frontal assaults, which resulted in enormous casualty of men and wasted material. Battles were preceded by intense artillery bombardments, which devastated the agricultural lands and woodlands of the battlefields.

One observer described the ruined terrain of an area of Belgium known as Flanders in this way: "In this landscape nothing existed but a measureless bog of military rubble, shattered houses, and tree stumps. It was pitted with shell craters containing fetid water. Overhead hung low clouds of smoke and fog. The very ground was soured by poison gas." (cited in Freedman, 1995). Another passage described the destruction of a forest (or copse) by an artillery bombardment: "When a copse was caught in a fury of shells the trees flew uprooted through the air like a handful of feathers; in a flash the area became, as in a magicians trick, as barren as the expanse around it." These were common observations, and they typified the damages caused by explosions, machines, and the mass movements of men at war.

About half of the 14 million metric tons of munitions used during the Viet Nam War was delivered by aircraft, half by artillery, and less than 1% from offshore ships. United States forces dropped about 20 million aerial bombs of various sizes, fired 230 million artillery shells, used more than 100 million grenades, and additional millions of rockets and mortar shells. Of course, these caused enormous physical destruction to the built environment of cities and towns, and to agricultural and natural environments. During 1967 and 1968, for example, about 2.5 million craters were formed by 500- and 750-lb (227- and 341-kg) bombs dropped in saturation patterns by high-flying B-52 bombers. Each plane sortie produced a bombed-out area of about 161 acres (65 ha). Eventually about 21.6 million acres (8.1 million ha) or 11% of the landscape of Indochina was affected in this way (this includes Laos and Viet Nam). Craters were about 16 yd (15 m) wide and 13 yd (12 m) deep, and they usually filled with fresh water. In addition, the explosions often started forest or grassland fires, which caused extensive secondary damages.

Some animals have been brought to the brink of extinction through warfare. For instance, the last wild Pere David's deer (*Elaphurus diavidianus*) were killed during the Boxer War of 1898-1900 in China. The European bison (*Bison bonasus*) was almost rendered extinct by hunting during World War I to provide meat for troops. More recently, warfare has led to lawlessness in much of Africa, allowing well-armed gangs of poachers to cause white **rhinos** (*Ceratotherium simum*), black rhinos (*Diceros bicornis*), **elephants** (*Loxodontia africana*), and other species to become critically endangered over much of their range. These animals are hunted for their horns, tusks, and other valuable body parts.

Although the effects of war on wild animals have mostly been damaging, there have been a few exceptions. Usually this happened because of decreased exploitation— men were too busy trying to kill each other to bother with **hunting** other species. For example, the abundance of gamebirds in Britain increased markedly during both World Wars because of decreased hunting pressures. So did fish stocks in the North Atlantic, because fishing boats were subject to attacks.

The Legacy Of Unexploded Munitions

Many aerial bombs and artillery shells do not explode, and they cause a lingering hazard on the landscape. These problems are made much worse by the use of explosive mines in warfare, because few of these buried devices are recovered after the hostilities cease, and they continue to be an explosive hazard for people and domestic and wild animals for decades. Modern anti-personnel mines are extremely difficult to find, largely because they can contain as little as one gram of metal, which makes it hard to detect them magnetically.

Chemical Weapons in Warfare

Antipersonnel chemical warfare occurred on a large scale during World War I, when more than 100 million kg of lethal agents were used. These were devastating lung poisons such as **chlorine**, phosgene, trichloromethyl chloroformate, and chloropicrin, and the dermal agent known as mustard gas. These poisons caused about 1.3 million casualties, including 100 thousand deaths.

Lethal gases were also used during the Iran-Iraq War of 1981-1987, mostly by Iraqi forces. The most famous incident involved the Kurdish town of Halabja in northern Iraq, which had rebelled against the central government and was aerially gassed with the nerve agents sabin and tabun, causing about 5,000 deaths.

The nonlethal "harassing agent" CS (or o-chlorobenzolmalononitrile) was used by the U.S. military during the Viet Nam War. About 20 million lb (9 million kg) of CS was sprayed over more than 2.5 million acres (one million ha) of South Viet Nam, rendering treated places uninhabitable by humans, and likely wild animals, for up to 45 days.

In addition, extensive areas of View Nam were treated with herbicides by U.S. forces to deprive their enemy of forest cover and food production. More than 3.5 million acres (1.4 million ha) were sprayed at least once, equivalent to about one-seventh the area of South Viet Nam. Most of the treated area was mangrove or upland forest, with about 247 thousand acres (100 thousand ha) being cropland. The most commonly used herbicide was a 50:50 mixture of **2,4,5-T** plus **2,4-D**, known as **Agent Orange**. More than 55 million lb (25 million kg) of 2,4-D and 47 million lb (21 million kg) of 2,4,5-T were sprayed in this military program. Because the intention was to achieve a longer-term defoliation, the application rates were relatively high, equivalent to about ten times the rate normally used in forestry.

The herbicide spraying caused great ecological damages, with effects so severe that critics of the practice labeled it "ecocide," i.e., the intentional use of anti-environmental actions over a large area, carried out as a tactical component of a military strategy. The damages included losses of agricultural lands for many rural people, as well as extensive **deforestation**, which caused severe but almost undocumented effects on the native **biodiversity** of Viet Nam.

Because the 2,4,5-T used in the herbicide spraying was contaminated by a **dioxin** chemical known as TCDD (2,3,7,8-tetrachlorodibenzo-*p*-dioxin), there was also a great deal of controversy about the potential effects on humans. As much as 357 lb (162 kg) of TCDD was sprayed with herbicides onto Viet Nam. Although there have been claims of damages caused to exposed populations, including U.S. military personnel, the scientific studies have not demonstrated convincing linkages. Although the subject remains controversial, it seems likely that the specific effects of TCDD were small in comparison with the overall ecological effects of the use of herbicides in the Viet Nam War.

Effects of Nuclear Warfare

Nuclear weapons have an enormous capability for destruction of humans, their civilization, and natural ecosystems. This was recognized by John F. Kennedy during a speech to the United Nations in 1961: "Mankind must put an end to war, or war will put an end to mankind."

The world's nuclear arsenal peaked during the 1980s, when the explosive yield of all weapons was about 18 thousand megatons (Mt) of TNT-equivalent. This was more than one thousand times larger than the combined yield of all conventional explosives used during World War II (6.0 Mt), the Korean War (0.8 Mt), and the Second Indochina War (4.1 Mt). The late-1980s nuclear arsenal was equivalent to 3-4 tons of TNT per person on Earth.

Thankfully, the cessation of the Cold War has led to substantial reductions in the world's nuclear weaponry, which has declined from a total explosive yield of about 18 thousand megatons in the 1980s to about eight thousand in the mid-1990s. There were about 64 thousand strategic and tactical devices in 1983, but 27 thousand in 1993, and planned reductions to 11-19 thousand in 2003.

Nuclear weapons have twice been used in warfare. This involved bombs dropped by U.S. forces on Japan, in an action that brought World War II to an earlier end than would have occurred otherwise. The first bomb had an explosive yield equivalent to 0.015 Mt of TNT and was dropped on **Hiroshima** on August 6, 1945, and the second (0.021 Mt) was dropped on **Nagasaki** a few days later. The Hiroshima bomb killed about 140 thousand people, while the Nagasaki device killed 74 thousand. The combined effects of blast and heat destroyed about two-thirds of the buildings in Hiroshima, and one-fourth of those in Nagasaki. Although enormous in comparison with conventional bombs, these nuclear devices were "small" in comparison to the typical yield of modern strategic warheads, which average about 0.6 Mt and range to 6 Mt.

Not surprisingly, people are concerned about the likely consequences of a large-scale nuclear exchange. One commonly used scenario of a nuclear war is for a limited exchange of 5-6 thousand megatons, most of which would be exploded in the Northern Hemisphere. The predicted effects on people include the deaths of about 20% of the world's population, including as much as 75% of the population of the United States. The principal cause of death would be thermal radiation, but effects of blast, fire, and ionizing radiation would also be important. Virtually all survivors would be injured by these same forces. Such an overwhelming loss of human life, coupled with the physical devastation, would transform civilization.

It has also been suggested that a nuclear war could result in a global deterioration of **climate**, which would cause additional severe damages. The climatic effects might be caused by various influences of nuclear explosions, but especially the injection of large quantities of sooty smoke, inorganic particulates, and gases into the **atmosphere**. These could interfere with the planet's absorption of solar energy and its re-emission of infrared energy. These potential consequences of nuclear warfare have been studied using computer models of the type that are used to model the effects of emissions of **carbon dioxide** and **methane** on Earth's **greenhouse effect**. In general, the predictions are that nuclear war could cause a global cooling, or a "nuclear winter," which would cause widespread damages to agriculture and natural ecosystems. The longer-term climatic damages would add to the enormous destructions that were caused by blast, thermal radiation, fire, and ionizing radiation within a short time of the nuclear exchange.

Humans have probably engaged in warfare throughout their history, and regrettably we appear likely to continue to do so into the future. Fortunately, the catastrophic effects of modern technological warfare are being increasingly recognized, and many nations have been making progress in avoiding conflicts, particularly amongst the world's most heavily armed nations. Because nuclear war has especially horrific consequences, recent treaties on non-proliferation of nuclear weapons and nuclear arms reductions provide real prospects in this regard.

Hope for a war-less future springs eternal, and can be exemplified by the following quotation from the Bible: "They shall beat their swords into plowshares, and their spears into pruninghooks: nation shall not lift up sword against nation, neither shall they learn war any more." (Isa. 2:4).

[*Bill Freedman*]

FURTHER READING

Barnaby, F. "The Environmental Impact of the Gulf War," *Ecologist*, 21 (1991): 166-172.

Freedman, B. *Environmental Ecology*, 2nd ed. San Diego: Academic Press, 1995.

Grover, H.D., and M.A. Harwell. "Biological effects of nuclear war. II. Impact on the biosphere," *Bioscience* 35 (1985): 576-583.

Grover, H.D., and G.F. White. "Toward understanding the effects of nuclear war," *Bioscience*, 35 (1985): 52-556.

Harwell, M.A., and H.D. Grover. "Biological effects of nuclear war. I. Impact on humans," *Bioscience* 35 (1985): 570-575.

Sivard, R.L. *World Military and Social Expenditures, 1996.* Washington, D.C.: World Priorities, 1996.

Warner, F. "The environmental consequences of the Gulf War," *Environment* 33, no. 5 (1991): 7-26.

Westing, A.H. (ed.). *Herbicides in War: The Long-term Ecological Consequences.* London: Taylor & Francis, 1984.

———. *Explosive Remnants of War. Mitigating the Environmental Impacts.* London: Taylor & Francis, 1985.

Warbler

See **Kirtland's warbler**

Waste exchange

Getting rid of industrial waste poses many problems for those who generate it. With environmental restraints enforced by fines, companies must minimize waste at its source, recycle it within the company, or transport it for off-site **recycling**, treatment or disposal.

The concept of waste exchange, begun in Canada in the 1980s, involves moving one institution's overstock, obsolete, damaged, contaminated, or post-dated materials to another site that might be able to use it. Waste exchange companies sprang up to meet this need, but the need for effective and rapid communication between these companies soon became apparent, because much of the waste involved in the program had to be dealt with on a timely basis. **Hazardous waste**s, for example, must be disposed of within ninety days.

In 1991 the **Environmental Protection Agency (EPA)** gave a $350,000 grant to the Pacific Materials Exchange in Spokane, Washington, to develop a free computer online network. Servicing about thirty waste exchange companies in the United States and Canada, the National Materials Exchange Network acts like "an industrial dating service," according to director Robert Smee. The service is easily accessible by an 800 number [800-858-6625] to anyone with a computer and a modem. Smee estimates that the computer network in its first year of operation saved companies $27 million in disposal fees.

While protecting the identity of companies generating waste, the network publishes a want list and an available source list of laboratory **chemicals**, paints, acids, and other wastes. Some are hazardous, but others are innocuous, such as one company's scrap wood, which was bought by another to be ground up for air freshener. *See also* Industrial waste treatment; Solid waste; Waste management

[*Stephanie Ocko*]

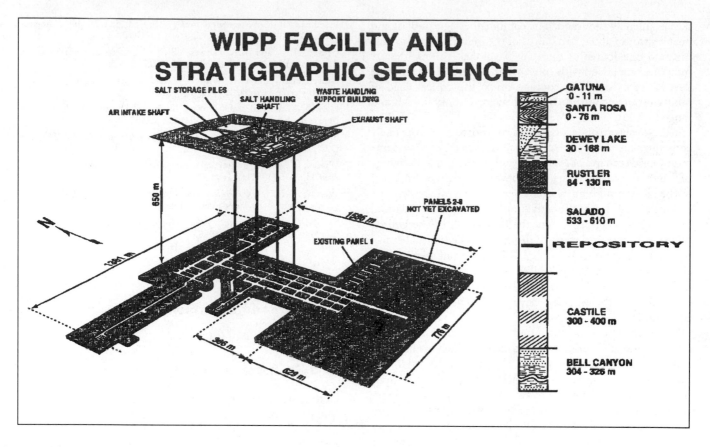

WIPP FACILITY AND STRATIGRAPHIC SEQUENCE

Schematic representation of the Waste Isolation Pilot Plant.

FURTHER READING

Manning, S. "Waste Exchanges: Why Dump When You Can Deal?" *PEM: Plant Engineering & Maintenance* (June 1990): 32-41.

Schwartz, E. I. "A Data Base That Truly Is 'Garbage In, Garbage Out'." *Business Week* (17 September 1990): 92.

Waste Isolation Pilot Plan (WIPP)

Developing a safe and reliable method for disposing of **radioactive waste**s is one of the chief obstacles to broader applications of **nuclear power**. A half century after the world's first nuclear reactor was opened, the United States still has no permanent method for the isolation and storage of wastes that may remain dangerously radioactive for thousands of years. Scientific disputes, technical problems, and political controversies have slowed the pace at which waste disposal systems could be studied and built. The history of the Waste Isolation Pilot Plan (WIPP), located near Carlsbad, New Mexico, is an example of how difficult the solution to this challenge can be.

WIPP was designed by the **U. S. Department of Energy** (DOE) in the 1970s to test methods for isolating and storing low- and intermediate-level and transuranic radioactive wastes. Researchers decided that the most promising disposal system was to seal the wastes in steel containers and bury these in deep caves built into natural salt beds. They knew that salt beds could absorb the heat produced by radioactive waste, and that they were usually located in earthquake-free zones. In addition, salt bed caves were attractive because scientists believed they were dry, which prevented wastes from **leaching** out of their tanks. Also salt would tend to "creep" into openings, thus sealing the drums for thousands of years.

Between the 1970s and 1990s, the DOE spent more than $1 billion building huge caves 2,100 feet (640 meters) underground near Carlsbad. The plan was to bury 800,000 drums of nuclear waste and study its behavior over a number of years. But it was soon discovered that some salt beds contain layers of brine (salt water), indicating that such beds are not always dry. Concern about the damages caused by radioactive materials became so intense that today the WIPP is regulated as carefully as a nuclear power plant, providing regular reports to twenty-eight different governmental agencies. Salt in the caves has begun to "creep," as expected, but controversy has prevented waste drums from ever being buried there, and the caves are now in danger of collapsing.

In October 1991, Secretary of Energy James Watkins announced that the DOE could wait no longer, and wastes that had been stored at ten sites around the nation for two decades awaiting disposal were to be shipped to WIPP. Environmentalists and some government officials in New Mexico reacted strongly to the announcement. They pointed out that Congress was required to give specific approval before any wastes could actually be buried at WIPP. Since that approval had not been given, a federal judge ruled that

Watkins could not carry out his plan until Congress acted, and the experimental tests at WIPP were once again put on hold. *See also* Energy policy; Hazardous waste siting; Low-level radioactive waste; Nuclear fission; Nuclear Regulatory Commission; Radioactive waste management; Storage and transport of hazardous materials

[*David E. Newton*]

FURTHER READING

Charles, D. "Will America's Nuclear Waste Be Laid To Rest?" *New Scientist* (14 December 1991): 16-17.

Lippman, T. W. "Nuclear Waste Plan Still Aborning a Decade Later," *Washington Post* (9 February 1992): A8.

Pool, R. "WIPP Put On Hold," *Nature* (17 October 1991): 523.

———. "DOE Won't Wait on WIPP," *Nature* (10 October 1991): 487.

Waste management

The way that we manage our waste materials is a sign of the times. In our agrarian past, throwing **garbage** out into the street for roving pigs to eat seemed like a perfectly reasonable method of waste management since most of what we threw away was organic material that increased the bulk of the pig and eliminated residuals we did not want. As manufacturing became a larger part of industry and materials had potential for **recycling** we saw the advent of the another kind of scavenger, the "junk man," who pulled from the **waste stream** those materials that had value. This practice increased during the Great Depression and even more so during World War II. During the war there were shortages of metals and cloth as many raw materials were diverted from domestic use to war needs. People got into the habit of **conservation**. Things were not thrown away unless they had no further use either as is or in a remanufactured state. The situation has changed in modern times.

As Jim Hightower points out in the forward to *War on Waste* (1989), "Every year we toss into city dumps 50 million tons of paper, 41 million tons of food and yard waste, 13 million tons of metals, 12 million tons of glass, and 10 million tons of plastic." In addition he points out that the **Environmental Defense Fund** has calculated that, as a nation, we throw away enough iron and steel to supply domestic automakers continuously; enough glass to fill the twin towers of New York City's World Trade Center every two weeks; enough **aluminum** to rebuild our commercial air fleet every three months; and enough office and writing paper to build a 12-foot Great Wall coast to coast every year. The examples go on and on. The opportunity to manage this tremendous resource through careful waste management practices is urgent. Waste is indeed a renewable resource. This renewable resource if managed well could provide us with the ability to reserve our natural non-renewable resources until we really need them.

Most states and major metropolitan areas have a hierarchy of waste management options that guide state and local planning. Although there are refinements of this list in some areas, the standard hierarchy, in order of preference, is: reduce, **reuse**, recycle, compost, waste-to-energy (**incineration**), and **landfill**. Looking at each of these options individually gives a better understanding of an integrated waste management system.

Managing waste through a process of reduction is almost always the first line of defense and viewed as most desirable by waste management professionals. Reduction is an attempt not to generate waste in the first place. This means making certain consumer decisions that eliminate the potential for waste generation. Buying produce in bulk so that packaging is kept at a minimum is one simple consumer decision that can have a profound effect, since over 40 percent of the waste stream is packaging material. To further reduce waste, consumers can bypass disposable items, such as disposable razors and cameras, and have small appliances repaired rather than buy new ones. Using cloth dishtowels and diapers eliminates paper towels and **disposable diapers** from the waste stream.

Reuse is often the second line of defense. This is the small area between avoiding waste and recycling post-consumer materials. A creative way to support reuse of materials is to make them available to those who can use them. Some cities have put in place a center where containers and various post-consumer materials that have been cleaned and source-separated are available to elementary school teachers for art projects. Another example of reuse is consignment shops. These stores will take clothing and small household items on consignment from people and then sell them and divide the profit with the owner.

Recycling is on the increase. Goals of recycling 15, 25, and even 50 percent of waste material have been called for in cities all across the United States. Many believe recycling is a major waste management solution. Industries in the United States are able to recycle quite a variety of materials. Paper, glass, metals, **plastics**, yard and food waste, motor oil, batteries, tires, asphalt, car bumpers, and all manner of scrap metal can be recycled. There is truly little that cannot be recycled, but in some cases, industry is not ready. Manufacturing equipment has not yet been retrofitted to accommodate the heterogenous nature of the waste stream. Also, communities are a dispersed source of "raw" material for manufacturers, and the cost of gathering sufficient tonnage of glass, tin, or other "raw" material for manufacturing is prohibitive. Probably the single most restrictive obstacle to full scale recycling is human behavior. As we look at recycling as a closed loop waste management process we realize that we must source-separate and clean post-consumer waste materials, then we must get them to the point where they can be used and made into a new product. To close the loop, someone must buy that product. All of these activities demand a behavioral change on the part of consumers and manufacturers.

Composting is the biological breakdown of organic matter under **aerobic** conditions. Composting is seen as a major waste management option for large and small communities. The most common form of composting is the layering of leaves, grass and twigs and sometimes kitchen waste in a backyard compost bin. This very simple technology can also be done at the municipal level, as a community picks up leaves and other yard waste at the curb and trucks it to a central location where it is composted in long tent-shaped piles of refuse called windrows, or inside buildings where mechanical systems speed the compost process. Like recycling, composting requires a behavioral change on the part of homeowners. People must prepare the material and get it to the curb on the appropriate day. Some drawbacks to composting are that the process can generate unpleasant odors if the compost pile is not managed well. This means turning the pile frequently and maintaining aerobic conditions so that decomposition proceeds rapidly.

Incineration is not really a new waste management option. Incineration of **solid waste** was practiced in the early 1900s. However, not until the early 1970s did we began to look seriously at **solid waste incineration** with energy recovery as a major goal. There really are two types of waste-to-energy systems. One is a **mass burn** technology which does very little to the waste stream before it reaches the furnace. The other system is a **refuse-derived fuel** (RDF) in which waste is shredded before being delivered to the furnaces. Drawbacks to this system are ash disposal and control of air **emission**s. Concerns over **dioxin**s in stack emissions has caused many supporters to think twice about waste-to-energy. In addition the issue of where to dispose of the sometimes toxic ash residue must be dealt with.

Landfills are still the most common waste management option. Between 75 and 85 percent of the nation's waste still goes to landfills. Three types of landfills are constructed for different types of waste materials.

Type III landfills are the least expensive to build and can accommodate construction debris and other inert material. Most common are sanitary Type II landfills. These are constructed according to the criteria in subtitle D of the **Resource Conservation and Recovery Act** (RCRA). Newer municipal solid waste landfills are usually equipped with synthetic liners, leachate collection systems, monitoring wells and in some cases **methane** wells to draw off the gas that collects in landfills. Type II landfills will take any waste except hazardous waste. **Hazardous waste** can only be disposed of in a Type I landfill. These landfills are constructed in a more rigorous manner and are used primarily for contained **chemicals** and such waste as **asbestos**.

The biggest challenge surrounding modern landfills is the issue of siting. Not in my backyard (**NIMBY**) is a well-known syndrome. Current landfill construction has slowed and many of the old landfills have closed or are slated for closure. There are currently about 3,000 Type II landfills in the continental United States. As more landfills close, the life span of those remaining is shortened. Large multinational companies in the waste management business are attempting to site large regional landfills. In some cases large companies are offering very attractive incentive packages to communities that are willing to site a landfill within their jurisdictions. Whatever method of disposal is used, the process of managing waste must bring into play a cooperative effort between manufacturers, merchants, citizens, and waste management experts if it is to be successful. *See also* Renewable resources; Source separation

[*Cynthia Fridgen*]

FURTHER READING

Blumberg, L., and R. Gottlieb. *War on Waste*. Covelo, CA: Island Press, 1989.

Kharbanda, O. P., and E. A. Stallworthy. *Waste Management: Toward a Sustainable Society*. Westport, CT: Auburn House/Greenwood, 1990.

Underwood, J., et al. *Garbage: Practices, Problems, Remedies*. New York: INFORM, 1988.

Waste reduction

Waste reduction aims to reduce environmental **pollution** by minimizing the generation of waste. It is also often an economically viable option because it requires an efficient use of raw materials. Waste-reduction methods include modifying industrial processes to reduce the amount of waste residue, changing raw materials, or **recycling** or reusing waste sources.

It is more difficult to alter existing industrial processes than it is to incorporate waste-reduction technologies into new operations. Large-scale changes in production equipment are essential to achieving waste reduction. Proper handling of materials and **fugitive emissions** reduction, as well as plugging leaks and preventing spills, all help in waste reduction. Process equipment must be checked on a regular basis for corrosion, vibrations, and leaks. Increases in automation and the prevention of vapor losses also help reduce waste generation.

Changes in what an industry puts into a process can be used to reduce the amount of waste generated. One example is the substitution of raw materials, such as water to clean a part instead of solvents. End-products can also be modified to help reduce waste. Another aspect of waste reduction is the control of fugitive emissions by placing a floating roof on open tanks, for example. Other waste-reduction options include the installation of condensers, automatic tank covers, and increasing tank heights. But these and other decisions on waste reduction very much depend on the size and structure of a company. *See also* Industrial waste treatment; Recyclables; Reuse; Toxic use reduction legislation; Waste management; Waste stream

[*James W. Patterson*]

FURTHER READING

Robinson, W. D., ed. *The Solid Waste Handbook*. New York: Wiley, 1986.

Underwood, J. D., et al. *Garbage: Practices, Problems, and Remedies*. New York: INFORM, 1988.

Waste Minimization: Environmental Quality With Economic Benefits. Washington, DC: U. S. Environmental Protection Agency, Office of Solid Waste and Emergency Response, 1987.

Waste stream

Streams of gas, liquid, or solids which are the by-products of a treatment operation or industrial process. The term has also been used to describe the flow of **solid waste** from various sources, including individual homes. The term is often used in **pollution** prevention strategies and **industrial waste treatment** initiatives. Many industries are now required to pretreat their wastes and seek ways to minimize waste production.

Wastewater

Water used and discharged from homes, commercial establishments, industries, **pollution control** devices, and farms. The term wastewater is now more commonly used than sewage, although, for the most part, the terms are synonymous. Domestic or sanitary wastewater refers to waters used during the course of residential life or those discharged from restrooms. Industrial wastewaters refer to those generated by an industry. Municipal wastewaters are waters used by a municipality, so they would likely include both sanitary and industrial wastewaters. Combined wastewater refers to a mixture of sanitary or municipal wastewaters and stormwaters created by rainfall.

Wastewater treatment

See **Sewage treatment**

Water allocation

Agriculture and fishing have different needs for water, as do manufacturing industries, cities, and **wildlife**. Water allocation is the process of distributing water supplies to meet the various requirements of a community.

Determining how to allocate water supplies requires the consideration of certain factors, including the source of the water and methods for obtaining it. The cost of the water supply and **water treatment** systems are also taken into account, and the intended uses are reviewed. Water use is classified by whether it is an instream or a withdrawal use and by whether it is a consumptive or nonconsumptive use. Instream uses include navigation, hydroelectric power, and fish and wildlife **habitat**s, while withdrawal uses remove water from the source. Consumptive uses make the water unavailable, either through evaporation or **transpiration**, or through incorporation into products or saltwater bodies. Water withdrawn but not consumed can be treated and returned to the water supply for **reuse** downstream.

The demand for water is determined by combining the sum of the amount of water required for instream needs with the sum of the amount of water needed for withdrawal uses. This sum is compared to the amount in the water supply. If it is equal to or greater than the sum, then the supply will meet the demand, but if this is not the case, measures to reduce consumption or increase the water supply need to taken.

About 70 percent of water supplies worldwide go to food production. Industry uses 23 percent and cities use about seven percent of water supplies. In the western United States, for example, about 85 percent of the water supplies are currently used by farming operations at government-subsidized rates. Cities and industry, as well as populations of fish and wildlife split the remaining 15 percent. Some politicians and environmentalists consider this division unfair, and assert that water allocation should be controlled by environmental awareness. They suggest seeking new ways of getting more water to more people while protecting wildlife and **wetlands**.

Government agencies own most of the water supplies in the western United States, and they own about 65 percent of the supplies in the east. Those who control the water supplies govern its use, though regulations on ownership vary by state. In western states, supplies are on a first-owned, first-served basis, even if others later run short. The distribution of supplies and shortages is shared more equally in the east.

Some water allocation programs look towards **conservation** to meet water needs. Certain ordinances, in California for example, restrict and limit water usage. One method of enforcing compliance that has been used there is publishing the names of people who do not abide by the ordinances to embarrass them. Another method uses a special section of the police force for checking water use. These officers give first-time offenders information on water conservation. They fine repeat offenders.

Wells, dams, reservoirs, conveyance systems, and artificial ponds physically control water supplies. Wells draw out **groundwater**. The other constructions manage surface water. Some areas use **desalinization** techniques to get fresh water from sea water.

A well taps groundwater through a hole sunk to an **aquifer**. An aquifer is a **permeable** layer of rock containing water trapped by layers of impermeable rock. If the pressure is sufficient, the water will come to the surface under its force, a type of well known as an **artesian well**. If the pressure is not sufficient for an artesian well, a pump is used to mechanically drag the water to the surface.

Dams are constructed to halt some or all of a river's flow. The region behind the dams, where water collects, is called an impounding, or water collecting, reservoir. Each dam is designed for a specific use, though dam types may be combined depending on the river and the community's needs. Storage dams hold water during times of surplus for periods of deficit, such as holding the spring **runoff** for the summer dry season. Along with providing a water supply, storage dams can improve (or harm) habitats for fish and wildlife, create electricity, and help in **irrigation** and flood control. Diversion dams affect the course of a river, preventing it from flowing forward so that a conveyance system can redirect it to irrigate fields or to fill a distant storage reservoir. These are often used in the western United States, resulting in damage to downstream areas. Lack of water can destroy fisheries and wildfowl habitats, and shorelines and deltas erode when no **sediment** comes downstream to replace what the ocean washes away. Detention dams control floods and trap sediment. Floods are controlled to prevent destruction of communities and habitats downstream from the dam. Trapping sediment causes the downstream portion of the river to be cleaner.

Conveyance systems divert streams so they flow where humans most need them. Conveyance systems include ditches, canals, and aqueducts (also known as transmission stations). Artificial ponds store water that is pumped in using a conveyance system. Aqueducts consist of closed conduits or pipes. A closed system helps to prevent contamination. A pump system helps the flow when the water level is not high enough for gravity to take over. Consumer demand for water varies by day and by season, and enclosed ground reservoirs and water towers may be used to store treated water and meet peak demands.

Only about one third of the earth's water is fresh, and only about five percent is available for use as surface water and groundwater. The rest is in the unusable form of glacial ice. The amount of freshwater is not increasing with the global population, and about a third of the people in the world now live in countries with water problems. These facts make the equitable allocation of water more difficult, and the need for wise water management more acute. Worldwide shortages also make it important for water management to control the quality of water. Farming runoff, urbanization, and industry all reduce **water quality**, which causes health and environmental problems, including **algal bloom**s caused by **nitrogen**-rich **fertilizer**s, and **acid rain**. One survey done by the **Environmental Protection Agency (EPA)** found that over half of the rivers, lakes, and streams in use in the United States have been nearly or totally destroyed by **pollution**. Pollutants have also made it difficult and expensive to recover and purify groundwater. Purification treatments in general can be expensive or difficult to obtain, and this causes poor water quality in many parts of the world.

Competing needs have also created severe problems; including lowered water pressure, decreased stream flow, land subsidence and increased **salinity**. Additionally, **overgrazing**, **deforestation**, loss of water-retaining **topsoil**, and **strip mining** decrease the amount of available water.

Treating sewage before returning it to the water supply and properly disposing of **chemicals** can improve water quality and increase the amount of usable water available. Reducing consumption can prevent water shortages. Households and industries can lower their water consumption by employing devices that decrease the amount of water used in, for example, showers, **toilets**, and dishwashers. Farmers can lower their water consumption by growing **drought**-resistant crops instead of ones requiring large quantities of water, such as alfalfa, and by using more efficient watering techniques. These methods not only stabilize water supplies, they also reduce the cost to the consumer. Another method for use in water shortages is desalinization of sea water. Desalinization plants remove the salt from sea water and purify it. Although such plants can be expensive, the expense can prove to be less

than attempting to pipe fresh water in from sources already strained. *See also* Aquifer restoration; Drinking-water supply; Groundwater pollution; Safe Drinking Water Act; Water quality standards

[*Nikola Vrtis*]

FURTHER READING

"California Drought Cops." *Newsweek* (30 April 1990): 27.

Davis. P. A. "Senate Energy Keeps Spigot on for California Agribusiness." *Congressional Quarterly Weekly Report* (21 March 1992): 723.

Kent, M. M. "New Report Studies Population, Water Supply." *Population Today* (December 1992): 4-5.

O'Reilly, B. "Water: How Much Is There and Whose Is It?" *Fortune* (25 March 1991): 12.

"The U.S. No Water to Waste." *Time* (20 August 1990): 61.

Water conservation

Seventy-one percent of the earth's surface is covered by water—an area called the hydrosphere, which makes up all of the oceans and seas of the world. Only 3 percent of the earth's entire water is freshwater. This includes Arctic and Antarctic ice, **groundwater**, and all the rivers and freshwater lakes. The amount of usable freshwater is only about 0.003 percent of the total. To put this small percentage in perspective, if the total water supply is equal to one gallon, the volume of the usable freshwater supply would be less than one drop. This relatively small amount of freshwater is recycled and purified by the **hydrologic cycle**, which includes evaporation, condensation, precipitation, **runoff**, and **percolation**. Since most of life on earth depends on the availability of freshwater, one can say "water is life."

Worldwide, agricultural **irrigation** uses about 80 percent of all freshwater. Cooling water for electrical power plants, domestic, and other industry use the remaining 20 percent. This figure varies widely from place to place. For example, China uses 87 percent of its available water for agriculture. The United States uses 40 percent for agriculture, 40 percent for electrical cooling, 10 percent for domestic consumption, and 10 percent for industrial use.

Water conservation may be accomplished by improving crop water utilization efficiency and by decreasing the use of high water demanding crops and industrial products. The table shows the amount of water, in pounds, required to produce one pound of selected crops and industrial products (one gallon = 7.8 pounds).

Freshwater sources are either surface water (rivers and lakes) or groundwater. Water that flows on the surface of the land is called surface runoff. The relationship between surface runoff, precipitation, evaporation, and percolation is shown in the following equation:

Surface runoff = precipitation – (evaporation + percolation)

When surface runoff resulting from rainfall or snow melt is confined to a well-defined channel it is called a river or stream runoff.

Groundwater is surface water that has permeated through the soil particles and is trapped among porous soils and rock particles such as sandstone or shale. The upper zone of saturation, where all pores are filled with water, is the **water table**. It is estimated that the groundwater is equal to forty times the volume of all earth's freshwater including all the rivers and freshwater lakes of the world.

The movement of groundwater depends on the porosity of the material that holds the water. Most groundwater is held within sedimentary **aquifer**s. Aquifers are underground layers of rock and soil that hold and produce an appreciable amount of water and can be pumped economically.

Water utilization efficiency is measured by water withdrawal and water consumption. Water withdrawal is water that is pumped from rivers, **reservoir**s, or groundwater wells, and is transported elsewhere for use. Water consumption is water that is withdrawn and returned to its source due to evaporation or transpiration.

Water consumption varies greatly throughout the world. A conservative figure for municipal use in the United States is around 150 gallons (568 l) per person per day. This includes home use for bathing, waste disposal, and landscape in addition to commercial and industrial use. The total water demand per person is around 4,500 gallons (17,032 l) per person per day when one accounts for the production of food, fiber, and fuel. The consumptive use world wide is considerably less than that for the United States.

According to the United Nations World Health Organization (WHO) five gallons (18 l) per person per day is considered a minimum water requirement. The majority of the people in the undeveloped world are unable to obtain the five gallon (18 l) per day minimum requirement. The WHO estimates that nearly two billion people in the world risk consuming contaminated water. Water-born diseases such as polio, typhoid, dysentery, and **cholera** kill nearly 25 million people per year. In order to meet this demand for freshwater, conservation is an obvious necessity.

Since irrigation consumes 80 percent of the world's usable water, improvements in agricultural use is the logical first step in water conservation. This can be accomplished by lining water delivery systems with concrete or other impervious materials to minimize deep percolation or by using drip irrigation systems to minimize evaporation losses. Drip irrigation systems have been successfully used on fruit trees, shrubs, and landscape plants.

Subsurface irrigation is an emerging technology with extremely high water utilization efficiency. Subsurface irrigation uses a special drip irrigation tubing that is buried six to eight inches (15 to 20 cm) underground with 12 to 24 inches (26 to 50 cm) between lines. The tubing contains emitters, or drip outlets, that deliver water and dissolved nutrients at the plant's root zone at a desired rate. In addition to water conservation, subsurface irrigation has several advantages that overhead sprinklers do not: no overwatering, no disease or aeration problems, no runoff or **erosion**, no weeds, and no vandalism. Subsurface irrigation in California has been used on trees, field crops, and lawns with up to 50 percent water savings.

Crop	Pounds of Water
1 lb. cotton	16,000
1 lb. beef	6,400
1 lb. rice	4,400
1 lb. loaf of bread	1,200

Industrial Product	Pounds of Water
1 automobile	800,000
1 lb. aluminum	8,000
1 lb. paper	800
1 gallon gasoline	80

Xeriscape, the use of low water consuming plants, is a most suitable landscape to conserve water, especially in dry, hot urban regions such as the Southwestern United States, where approximately 50 percent of the domestic water consumption is used by lawns and non-**drought** tolerant landscape. Plants such as cacti and succulents, ceanothus, arctostaphylos, which is related to foothill manzanita, trailing rosemary (*Rosemarinus officinale*), and white rock rose (*Cistus cobariensis*) adapt well to hot, dry **climate**s and help conserve water.

In addition to improving irrigation techniques, water conservation can be accomplished by improving domestic use of water. Such a conservation practice is the installation of the ultra-low-flush (ULF) toilets in homes and commercial buildings. A standard toilet uses five to seven gallons of water per flush, while the ultra-low-flush toilet uses 1.5 gallons. Research in Santa Monica, California, shows that replacing a standard toilet with an ULF saves 30 to 40 gallons of water per day, which is equivalent to 10,000 to 16,000 gallons per year.

Another way to conserve the freshwater supply is to extract freshwater from sea water by **desalinization**. Desalinization, the removal of soluble salts and other impurities from sea water by distillation or reverse **osmosis** (RO), is becoming an increasingly acceptable method to provide high quality pure water for drinking, cooking, and other home uses. It is estimated that the 1993 world production of desalinated water is about 3.5 billion gallons per day (13 billion liters). Most desalinated water is produced in Saudi Arabia, Persian Gulf Nations, and, more recently, in California. The cost of desalinated water depends upon the cost of energy. In the United States, it is about three dollars per thousand gallons, which is four to five times the cost paid by urban consumers and over a hundred times the cost paid by farmers for irrigation water. The idea of using desalinated water for irrigation is, currently, cost prohibitive.

Water has played a vital role in the rise and fall of human cultures throughout history. The availability of usable water has always been a limiting factor for a region's ecological carrying capacity. It is important that humans learn to live within the limit of available natural resources. Conservation of water alone will not extend the natural carrying capacity for an indefinite period of time. Since the supply of available and usable water is finite, the consumption per person must be reduced. A permanent solution to the water shortage problem can be accomplished by living within the **ecosystem** carrying capacity or by reducing the number of consumers through effective control of **population growth**.

[*Muthena Naseri*]

FURTHER READING

Buzzelli, B. *How to Get Water Smart: Products and Practices for Saving Water in the Nineties.* Santa Barbara, CA: Terra Firma Publishing, 1991.

Clarke, R. *Water: The International Crisis.* Cambridge: MIT Press, 1993.

Postel, S. "Plug the Leak, Save the City." *International Wildlife* 23 (January-February 1993): 38-41.

Yudelman. M., et al. *New Vegetative Approaches to Soil and Water Conservation.* Washington, DC: World Wildlife Fund, 1990.

Water cycle

See **Hydrologic cycle**

Water Environment Federation (Alexandria, Virginia)

Dedicated to "the preservation and enhancement of water quality worldwide," the Water Environment Federation (WEF) is an international professional organization of **water quality** experts. WEF is made up of 38,000 water professionals, including engineers, biologists, government officials, treatment plant managers and operators, laboratory technicians, equipment manufacturers and distributors, and educators.

WEF was founded in 1928 as the Federation of Sewage Works Associations and served as the publisher of the *Sewage Works Journal.* The organization has also been known as the Water Pollution Control Federation. Its scope has broadened significantly since its inception, and WEF currently publishes a variety of materials relating to the water industry. WEF also sponsors seminars, conferences, and briefings; offers technical training and education; produces informational videos for students; and provides input on environmental legislation and regulations to government bodies.

The publications issued by WEF cover a multitude of topics and are geared toward a variety of readers. Technical publications, including manuals developed by WEF's Technical Practice Committee, brief water-quality professionals on design, operation, and management innovations in the field. Periodicals and newsletters address such issues as industry trends, research findings, water analysis topics, job safety, regulatory and legislative developments, and job openings in the profession.

WEF's technical training and educational programs are geared toward both professionals and students. Audio-visual training courses and study guides are available on such topics as **wastewater** treatment, waste stabilization ponds,

and wastewater facility management. The federation also distributes health and safety videos developed by municipalities. For students, WEF offers *The Water Environment Curriculum,* a series of videos and guides outlining water quality issues geared toward children in fifth through ninth grades. *The Water Environment Curriculum* includes lessons on surface water, **groundwater**, wastewater, and **water conservation**. WEF also publishes guides on water quality issues for the general public.

WEF's major event is its annual conference, the largest water quality and **pollution control** exposition in North America. The conference features technical sessions, expert speakers, and exhibits run by companies in the water quality industry. The federation also holds specialty conferences on such topics as toxicity, **landfill**s, and surface water quality. Two other noteworthy briefings are WEF's Pacific Rim Conference and the Washington Briefing. The Pacific Rim Conference gathers representatives from Pacific Rim countries to discuss environmental problems in that area. The Washington Briefing convenes government officials and water quality experts to discuss current issues affecting the industry.

In addition to its publications, educational tools, and conferences, WEF sponsors an affiliate, the Water Environment Research Foundation, which works to develop and implement water quality innovations. The research foundation's programs strive to find ways to enhance water quality, develop broad-based approaches to water quality that encompass all aspects of the **environment**, use new technology, and promote interaction among individuals involved in the water quality profession.

WEF is also associated with Water Quality 2000, a cooperative effort involving a variety of professional and scientific organizations, industry representatives, environmental groups, academic institutions, and government officials working to develop **water quality standards** and goals for the United States for the twenty-first century. Contact: Water Environment Federation, 601 Wythe Street, Alexandria, VA 22314-1994. Internet: http://www.wef.org/.

[*Kristin Palm*]

Water hyacinth (*Eichhornia crassipes*)

The water hyacinth is an aquatic plant commonly found in the southern United States, including Florida, Texas, the Gulf Coast, and California. As an introduced **species**, it has spread rapidly and is now viewed as a noxious weed. Like other aquatic weeds, water hyacinth can grow rapidly and clog waterways, damaging underwater equipment and impairing navigational and recreational facilities. It is also viewed as a weed in many tropical parts of the world.

Water hyacinths can be either free-floating or rooted, depending on the depth of the water. The plant height may vary from a few inches to three feet. The leaves, growing in rosettes, are glossy green and may be up to eight inches (20 cm) long and six inches (15 cm) wide. The showy attractive

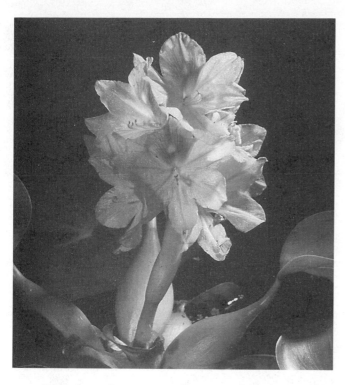

Water hyacinth.

FURTHER READING

Hammer, Donald A. *Constructed Wetlands for Waste Treatment*. Chelsea, MI: Lewis Publishers, Inc., 1989.

Schmidt, James C. *How to Identify and Control Water Weeds and Algae*. Milwaukee, WI: Applied Biochemists, Inc., 1987.

Water pollution

Among the many environmental problems that offend and concern us, perhaps none is as powerful and dramatic as water pollution. Ugly, scummy water full of debris, **sludge**, and dark foam is surely one of the strongest and most easily recognized symbols of our misuse of the **environment**.

What is **pollution**? The verb pollute is derived from the Latin *polluere*: to foul or corrupt. Our most common meaning is to make something unfit or harmful to living things especially by the addition of waste matter or sewage. A broader definition might include any physical, biological, or chemical change in **water quality** that adversely affects living organisms or makes water unsuitable for desired uses.

Paradoxically, however, a change that adversely affects one organism may be advantageous to another. **Nutrient**s that stimulate oxygen consumption by bacteria and other decomposers in a river or lake, for instance, may be lethal to fish but will stimulate a flourishing community of decomposers. Whether the quality of the water has suffered depends on your perspective. There are natural sources of water contamination, such as poison springs, oil seeps, and **sedimentation** from **erosion**, but most discussions of water pollution focus on human-caused changes that affect water quality or usability.

The most serious water pollutants in terms of human health worldwide are pathogenic organisms. Altogether, at least 25 million deaths each year are blamed on these water-related diseases, including nearly two-thirds of the mortalities of children under five years old. The main source of these **pathogen**s is from untreated or improperly treated human wastes. In the more developed countries, **sewage treatment** plants and other **pollution control** techniques have reduced or eliminated most of the worst sources of pathogens in inland surface waters. The United Nations estimates that 90 percent of the people in high-income countries have adequate sewage disposal, and 95 percent have clean drinking water.

For poor people, the situation is quite different. The United Nations estimates that three-quarters of the population in less developed countries have inadequate sanitation, and that less than half have access to clean drinking water. Conditions are generally worse in remote, rural areas where sewage treatment is usually primitive or nonexistent, and purified water is either unavailable or too expensive to obtain. In the thirty-three poorest countries, 60 percent of the urban population have access to clean drinking water but only 20 percent of rural people do.

This lack of pollution control is reflected in surface and **groundwater** quality in countries that lack the resources or political will to enforce pollution control. In Poland, for example, 95 percent of all surface water is unfit to drink. The

flowers may be blue, violet, or white and grow in spikes of several flowers. The leaf blades are inflated with air sacs, which enables the plants to float in water. The seeds are very long-lived. Studies show that seeds that have been buried in mud for many years remain viable under the right conditions, leading to reinfestation of lakes long after chemical treatment.

Weed harvesting methods to control water hyacinth growth are expensive and not very effective. The weight and volume of the harvested material usually adds greatly to the costs of hauling and disposal. Attempts to use the harvested material as **soil fertilizer** or enhancer have failed because of the low mineral and nutritive content of the plant's tissue. Chemical methods to control water hyacinth usually require careful and repeated applications. Commonly used **herbicide**s include Rodeo and Diquat.

In some situations, aquatic weeds serve beneficial purposes. Aquatic plants can be integral components of **wastewater** treatment, particularly in warm climates. Wastewater is routed through lagoons or ponds with dense growths of water hyacinth. In waters containing excess **nutrient**s (**nitrates** and phosphates) and turbidity, water hyacinth plants have been shown to improve **water quality** by taking up the excess nutrients into the plant and by settling the suspended solids which cause turbidity. They also add oxygen to the water through **photosynthesis**. Oxygen is an essential requirement for the **decomposition** of wastewater, and oxygen deficiency is a common problem in waste treatment systems. Water hyacinth has been used successfully in California and Florida, and more states are exploring the possibility of using water hyacinth in waste treatment systems.

[*Usha Vedagiri*]

Vistula River, which winds through the country's most heavily industrialized region, is so badly polluted that more than half the river is utterly devoid of life and unsuited even for industrial use. In Russia, the lower Volga River is reported to be on the brink of disaster due to the 300 million tons of **solid waste** and 20 trillion liters (5 trillion gal) of liquid **effluent** dumped into it annually.

The less developed countries of South America, Africa, and Asia have even worse water quality than do the poorer countries of Europe. Sewage treatment is usually either totally lacking or woefully inadequate. Low technological capabilities and little money for pollution control are made even worse by burgeoning populations, rapid urbanization, and the shift of heavy industry from developed countries where pollution laws are strict to less developed countries where regulations are more lenient.

In Malaysia, forty-two of fifty major rivers are reported to be "ecological disasters." Residues from palm oil and rubber manufacturing, along with heavy erosion from logging of **tropical rain forest**s, have destroyed all higher forms of life in most of these rivers. In the Philippines, domestic sewage makes up 60 to 70 percent of the total volume of Manila's Pasig River. Thousands of people use the river not only for bathing and washing clothes, but also as their source of drinking and cooking water. China treats only two percent of its sewage. Of seventy-eight monitored rivers in China, fifty-four are reported to be seriously polluted. Of forty-four major cities in China, forty-one use "contaminated" water supplies, and few do more than rudimentary treatment before it is delivered to the public.

Pollution control standards and regulations usually distinguish between point and nonpoint pollution sources. Factories, **power plants**, sewage treatment plants, underground coal mines, and oil wells are classified as **point source**s because they discharge pollution from specific locations, such as drain pipes, ditches, or sewer outfalls. These sources are discrete and identifiable, so they are relatively easy to monitor and regulate. It is generally possible to divert effluent from the **waste stream**s of these sources and treat it before it enters the environment.

In contrast, **nonpoint source**s of water pollution are scattered or diffused, having no specific location where they discharge into a particular body of water. Nonpoint sources include **runoff** from farm fields, golf courses, lawns and gardens, construction sites, logging areas, roads, streets, and parking lots. Multiple origins and scattered locations make this pollution more difficult to monitor, regulate, and treat than point sources.

Desert soils often contain high salt concentrations that can be mobilized by **irrigation** and concentrated by evaporation, reaching levels that are toxic for plants and animals. Salt levels in the San Joaquin River in central California rose about 50 percent between 1930 to 1970 as a result of agricultural runoff. **Salinity** levels in the Colorado River and surrounding farm fields have become so high in recent years that millions of hectares of valuable croplands have had to be abandoned. The United States is building a huge desalination plant at Yuma, Arizona, to reduce salinity

in the river. In northern states, millions of tons of sodium chloride and calcium chloride are used to melt road ice in the winter. The corrosive damage to highways and **automobile**s and the toxic effects on vegetation are enormous. **Leaching** of road salts into surface waters has a similarly devastating effect on aquatic **ecosystem**s.

Acids are released by mining and as by-products of industrial processes, such as leather tanning, metal smelting and plating, **petroleum** distillation, and organic chemical synthesis. **Coal** mining is an especially important source of acid water pollution. Sulfides in coal are solubilized to make sulfuric acid. Thousands of kilometers of streams in the United States have been poisoned by acids and metals, some so severely that they are essentially lifeless.

Thousands of different natural and synthetic organic **chemicals** are used in the chemical industry to make **pesticide**s, **plastics**, pharmaceuticals, pigments, and other products that we use in everyday life. Many of these chemicals are highly toxic. Exposure to very low concentrations can cause **birth defects**, genetic disorders, and **cancer**. Some synthetic chemicals are resistant to degradation, allowing them to persist in the environment for many years. Contamination of surface waters and groundwater by these chemicals is a serious threat to human health.

Hundreds of millions of tons of hazardous organic wastes are thought to be stored in dumps, **landfill**s, lagoons, and underground tanks in the United States. Many, perhaps most, of these sites are leaking toxic chemicals into surface waters or groundwater or both. The **Environmental Protection Agency (EPA)** estimates that about 26,000 **hazardous waste** sites will require cleanup because they pose an imminent threat to public health, mostly through water pollution.

Although the oceans are vast, unmistakable signs of human abuse can be seen even in the most remote places. **Garbage** and human wastes from coastal cities are dumped into the ocean. **Silt, fertilizer**s, and pesticides from farm fields smothered **coral reef**s, coastal spawning beds, and overfertilize estuaries. Every year millions of tons of plastic litter and discarded fishing nets entangle aquatic organisms, dooming them to a slow death. Generally coastal areas, where the highest concentrations of sea life are found and human activities take place, are most critically affected.

The amount of oxygen dissolved in water is a good indicator of water quality and of the kinds of life it will support. Water with an oxygen content above 8 **parts per million** (ppm) will support game fish and other desirable forms of aquatic life. Water with less than 2 ppm oxygen will support only worms, bacteria, **fungi**, and other decomposers. Oxygen is added to water by diffusion from the air, especially when turbulence and mixing rates are high, and by **photosynthesis** of green plants, algae, and cyanobacteria. Oxygen is removed from water by **respiration** and chemical processes that consume oxygen.

In spite of the multitude of bad news about water quality, some encouraging pollution control stories are emerging. One of the most outstanding examples is the Thames River in London. Since the beginning of the Industrial

Pollutant	Source	Effects
Nutrients, including nitrogen compounds	Fertilizers, sewage, acid raid from motor vehicles and power plants	Creates algae blooms, destroys marine life
Chlorinated hydrocarbons: pesticides, DDT, PCBs	Agricultural runoff, industrial waste	Contaminates and harms fish and shellfish
Petroleum hydrocarbons	Oil spills, industrial discharge, urban runoff	Kills or harms marine life, damages ecosystems
Heavy metals: arsenic, cadmium, copper, lead, zinc	Industrial waste, mining	Contaminates and harms fish
Soil and other particulate matter	Soil erosion from construction and farming; dredging, dying algae	Smothers shellfish beds, blocks light needed by marine plant life
Plastics	Ship dumping, household waste, litter	Strangles, mutilates wildlife, damages natural habitats

Major pollutants of coastal waters around the United States.

Revolution, the Thames had been little more than an open sewer, full of vile and toxic waste products from domestic and industrial sewers. In the 1950s, however, England undertook a massive cleanup of the Thames. More than $250 million in public funds plus millions more from industry were spent to curb pollution. By the early 1980s, the river was showing remarkable signs of rejuvenation. Oxygen levels had rebounded and some ninety-five **species** of fish had returned, including the pollution-sensitive **salmon**, which had not been seen in London for three hundred years. Perhaps we can bring about similar improvements elsewhere with a little effort, care, and concern for our environment.

[*William P. Cunningham*]

FURTHER READING

Mayberck, M. *Global Freshwater Quality: A First Assessment.* Oxford, UK: Blackwell Reference, 1990.

Protecting Our Future Today. Washington, DC: Environmental Protection Agency, 1991.

Water quality

Water quality encompasses a wide range of water characteristics, including biological, chemical, and physical descriptions of water clarity or contamination. Water quality assessment is typically based on the examination of certain attributes, conditions or properties of a lake, river, bay, **aquifer**, or other water body. The most important of these attributes are pollutants that demand oxygen or cause disease, nutrients that stimulate excessive plant growth, synthetic organic and inorganic **chemicals**, mineral substances, **sediment**s, radioactive substances, and temperature. Since the 1950s, routine tests for water quality have evaluated temperature, turbidity, color, odor, total solids after evaporation, hardness (**pH**), and concentrations of **carbon dioxide**, iron, **nitrogen**, chloride, active **chlorine**, microorganisms, **coliform bacteria**, and amorphous matter. In recent years increasing contamination and growing public concern over water quality have led to the addition of a number of additional parameters, including algal growth, **chemical oxygen demand**, and the presence of **hydrocarbons**, metals, and other **toxic substance**s.

Water quality is evaluated through a set of sample taken from a cross-section of a body of water. Because quality conditions change continually, each set of samples is understood to represent conditions at the time of sampling. Long-term water quality monitoring requires periodic data collection at regular sampling stations. In order to ensure that quality measurements are consistent at different times and locations, standards are legally set for various water uses and contaminant levels. There are two general types of standards for measuring water quality. "Water quality based standards" are set to ensure that a water body is clean enough for its expected uses, e.g., fishing, swimming, industrial use, or drinking. "Technology based standards" are set for **wastewater** entering a water body so that overall water conditions remain acceptable. These standards have been developed worldwide. In the United States, the **Environmental Protection Agency (EPA)** is responsible for developing water quality standards and criteria for surface, ground and marine waters.

Water quality standards, ambient conditions of a water body that meet expected uses, are based upon water quality criteria. These criteria designate acceptable levels of specific pollutants, clarity, or oxygen content. Usually acceptable levels of these criteria are measured in **parts per million** (ppm) of each contaminant or **nutrient**. These measurements allow scientists to assess whether or not a body of water meets the prescribed water quality standards. If standards are not met, then local governing bodies or industries must develop and implement cleanup strategies that target specific criteria. In the United States and many other countries, national water quality criteria have been developed for most conventional, toxic, and non-conventional pollutants. **Conventional pollutants** include **suspended solids**, **biochemical oxygen demand (BOD)**, **pH** (acidity or alkalinity), fecal coliform bacteria, oil, and grease. Toxic **priority pollutant**s include metals and organic chemicals. Non-conventional pollutants are any other contaminants that harm humans or marine resources and require regulation.

Drinking water must meet especially high standards to be safe for human consumption, and its quality is strictly monitored in the United States and most heavily populated regions of the world. Most governments have a legal responsibility to maintain acceptable drinking water quality. Until 1974, efforts to maintain acceptable levels of drinking water quality in the United States were limited to preventing the spread of contagious diseases. The **Safe Drinking Water Act** of 1974 expanded the government's regulatory role to cover all substances that may adversely affect human health or a water body's odor or appearance. This act established national regulations for acceptable levels of various contaminants.

Both point and **nonpoint source**s of pollution affect water quality. **Point source**s are discrete locations that discharge pollutants, mainly industrial outflow pipes or sewage treatment plants. Nonpoint sources are more diffuse, and include **storm runoff** and **runoff** from farming, logging, construction, and other **land use** activities.

In the United States, over 50 percent of the population relies on underground sources for drinking water. Because **groundwater** receives an enormous range of agricultural, industrial, and urban pollutants, groundwater quality is an issue of growing concern. Preventing **groundwater pollution** is especially important because remedial action in an **aquifer** is expensive and technologically difficult. Major sources of groundwater pollution include nitrate contamination from septic systems, organic pollutants from leaking fuel tanks and other storage containers, and an array of contaminants leached from **landfill**s.

In rivers, the most extensive causes of water quality impairment are usually **siltation**, nutrient concentration

(nitrogen and **phosphorus**), fecal coliform bacteria, and low **dissolved oxygen** levels caused by high organic content (sewage, grass clippings, pasture and **feedlot runoff**, etc.). Agricultural runoff including **pesticide**s, **fertilizer**s, and sediments is the largest source of river pollution, followed by municipal sewage discharge. Estuaries, rich **ecosystem**s of mixed salt and fresh water where rivers enter a sea or ocean, often have serious water quality problems. Estuarine contaminants are usually the same as those in rivers—high organic content and low oxygen, disease-causing **pathogen**s, organic **chemicals**, and municipal sewage discharge.

In most lakes, water quality is affected primarily by nitrogen and phosphorus loading, siltation and low dissolved oxygen. Like rivers, lakes suffer from agricultural runoff, habitat modification, storm runoff, and municipal sewage **effluent**. Lakes especially suffer from eutrophication (the excessive growth of aquatic algae and other plants) caused by high levels of nutrients. This burst of growth, also called an **algal bloom**, feeds on concentrated nutrients. Thick mats of algae and other aquatic plants clog water systems, increase turbidity, and suffocate aquatic animals so that an entire ecosystem is disrupted. Of the lakes assessed by the U.S. Environmental Protection Agency's 1988 National Water Quality Inventory, one-third were affected by eutrophication. In some lakes, especially the **Great Lakes**, the presence of persistent toxic substances is an additional concern. Most of these toxins originate in the industrial regions that surround these lakes or in the heavy shipping traffic between lakes.

Water quality degradation affects the stability of aquatic ecosystems as well as human health. Much is still unknown about the effects of specific pollutants on ecosystem health. However, fish and other aquatic organisms exposed to elevated levels of pollutants may have lowered reproduction and growth rates, diseases, and, in severe cases, high death rates. *See also* Cultural eutrophication

[*Marci L. Bortman*]

FURTHER READING

Becker, C. D., ed. *Water Quality in North American River Systems.* Columbus, OH: Battelle Press, 1992.

Cotruvo, J. A., and E. Bellack. "Maintaining Drinking Water Quality." In *Perspectives on Water*, edited by D. H. Speidel, et al. New York: Oxford University Press, 1988.

Eckenfelder, W. W., Jr. *Principles of Water Quality Management.* Boston: CBI Publishing, 1980.

U. S. Environmental Protection Agency. *National Water Quality Inventory 1988 Report to Congress.* Washington, DC: U.S. Government Printing Office, 1990.

U. S. Environmental Protection Agency. *The Quality of Our Nation's Water.* Washington, DC: U.S. Government Printing Office, 1990.

Water quality standards

The development of **water quality** standards is a process first mandated by the Water Quality Act of 1965 and continued by requirements in the Federal Water Pollution Control Act of 1972 (PL 92-500), with amendments in 1977, 1982, and 1987 (collectively referred to as the **Clean**

Water Act). The process is used to establish standards for stream water quality by taking into account the use and value of a stream for public water supplies, propagation of fish and **wildlife**, recreational purposes, as well as agricultural, industrial, and other legitimate uses. Water quality standards are enforceable by law and are applicable to all navigable waters. The goals of water quality standards are to protect public health and the **environment**, and to maintain a standard of water quality consistent with its designated uses. Water quality standards provide the "teeth" for water quality legislation and also the yardstick by which performance may be evaluated.

To establish water quality standards for a water body, officials (1) determine the designated beneficial water use; (2) adopt suitable water quality criteria to protect and maintain that use; and (3) develop a plan for implementing and enforcing the water quality criteria. Both uses and criteria constitute water quality standards, and water quality is evaluated based on how well the designated uses are supported.

Appropriate water use is designated by analyzing the existing use of the water as well as the potential to attain other uses based on an assessment of the physical, chemical, biological, and hydrological characteristics of the water and the economic cost and impact of achieving particular uses. The Clean Water Act requires that, whenever possible, water quality standards should ensure the protection and propagation of fish, shellfish, and wildlife and should provide for **recreation** in and on the stream. States have primary responsibility for designating stream segment uses, so stream uses may vary from state to state. However, stream use as designated by one state must not result in the violation of another state's use of the same stream.

Water quality criteria are most often expressed as numeric constituent concentrations or levels, but may be narrative statements if numeric values are not available or known. Each criterion is based on scientific information available concerning the effect of the pollutant on human health, aquatic life, and aesthetics.

Before the passage of the Clean Water Act, **water pollution** control efforts were considered successful if they achieved water quality standards. However, under the act, the accepted measurements of successful water **pollution control** is whether the **effluent** from **point source**s, specifically Publicly Owned Treatment Works (POTWs), meets technology-based effluent standards. These standards are based on what can be done with available technology rather than what is required to achieve water quality standards.

Water quality standards were retained, however, as part of the overall strategy to control water pollution. Rather than using water quality standards as the highest goal for determining water quality, the state and federal authorities consider water quality control standards to be the lowest acceptable level of water quality. In addition, point sources may be subjected to more stringent requirements than the use of **Best Available Control Technology (BAT)** if necessary to meet water quality standards. For example, in stream segments that do not meet water quality standards, states can establish a "total maximum daily load" of pollutants that will achieve water quality standards and assign a permissible share to individual dischargers. State water quality programs must also include provisions to prevent degradation of existing water quality when necessary to maintain existing uses and certain high quality waters.

The attainment of water quality standards is also affected by control of **pollution** from **nonpoint source**s, such as agricultural practices that result in the addition of **sediment**s, **nutrient**s, **pesticide**s, and other contaminants to water bodies. The 1987 amendments to the Clean Water Act required states to identify water not meeting its standards due to nonpoint source pollution, identify general and specific nonpoint sources causing the problems, and develop management plans for the control of the these sources.

In 1988, state governments compiled a water quality report for the **Environmental Protection Agency (EPA)**. The report indicated that of 519,412 river miles (835,734 km) assessed (out of a total of 1.8 million miles [2.9 million km] in the United States) 10 percent did not support their designated uses, 20 percent partially supported their uses, and 70 percent fully supported their uses. For lakes, of 16,313,962 acres (6,525,585 ha) assessed (out of a total of 39,400,000 acres [15,760,000 ha] in the United States), 10 percent did not support their designated uses, 17 percent partially supported their uses, and 74 percent fully supported their uses. *See also* Agricultural pollution; Agricultural runoff; Criteria pollutant; Marine pollution; Thermal pollution

[*Judith Sims*]

FURTHER READING

Abron, L. A., and R. A. Corbitt. "Air and Water Quality Standards." In *Standard Handbook of Environmental Engineering*, edited by R. A. Corbitt. New York: McGraw-Hill, 1990.

The Universities Council on Water Resources. "The Clean Water Act." *Water Resources Update* 84. Carbondale, IL: Southern Illinois University, 1991.

Water reclamation

The term "water reclamation" can be defined in different ways. In the early and mid-1900s, water reclamation referred primarily to supplying potable water to **arid** areas where water was not readily available, through the development of water projects such as dams and canals. Water reclamation can also mean collecting used water (i.e., **wastewater**) and treating it for reuse for **irrigation** and other purposes.

The federal agency primarily responsible for water reclamation projects that provided a source of water to arid lands is the Bureau of Reclamation, in the Department of the Interior. Formed in 1902 as the Reclamation Service and later renamed the Bureau of Reclamation in 1923, the agency's mission was "the construction and maintenance of irrigation works for the storage, diversion, and development of water for the reclamation of arid and semi-arid lands." This federal agency built **dams**, **reservoir**s, and other water development projects in the 17 western states of the United States. The mission of the Bureau of Reclamation in the early

1900s was to serve the irrigation needs of farms of 160 acres (65 ha) or less. By the 1930s the bureau's constituency expanded to larger farms, towns, and cities. The **Army Corps of Engineers** and the Department of Agriculture Soil Conservation Service (now called the Natural Resources Conservation Service) are also responsible for providing irrigation water in addition to providing flood control, drainage, and navigation.

During the early 1900s, water reclamation projects were a means of providing an opportunity for people to settle in western U.S. The projects provided inexpensive, government-subsidized water used for transportation, farming, industry, and by municipalities for drinking water and electricity. During the Depression era of the 1930s, the Bureau of Reclamation and the Public Works Administration worked together on water projects, which became an important part of the nation's economic recovery program.

In 1959, a Senate Select Committee on National Water Resources was formed to determine whether more water projects were necessary. After two years of investigations, the committee highlighted three main concerns: possible water shortages in the future, decreasing **water quality**, and possible flooding. Some of the recommendations made by the committee to address these concerns included increased regulation of stream flows by reservoirs, improved **groundwater** use, improvements in water use efficiency, and increased use of desalination and weather modification.

As a follow-up to the recommendations by the Select Committee on Natural Water Resources, President Kennedy created a Water Resources Council headed up by the Secretaries of the Interior, Health, Education and Welfare, and the Army to make biennial nationwide water project studies and to develop uniform regulations for evaluating water projects. With the advent of the environmental movement during the 1960s and the lowered unemployment relative to the 1930s, water reclamation projects became less of a national priority. By the 1970s, President Carter proposed that the costs of water projects be shared by the local water users. President Carter also proposed that water reclamation projects be evaluated based on economic, environmental, and safety criteria. During President Reagan's tenure, the criteria used to evaluate the feasibility of water projects were relaxed; however, President Reagan continued support of local cost sharing.

Over the years, there have been numerous water reclamation projects. A year after the formation of the Bureau of Reclamation, the agency was working on six projects. By 1907, it was participating in the development of 27 water projects. From 1905-1991, the Bureau of Reclamation built over 493 reservoirs and diversion dams, 7,670 mi (12,341 km) of irrigation canals, 1,440 mi (2,317 km) of pipelines and tunnels, and 53 hydroelectric power plants. All the larger rivers in the U.S. have been altered in some way by water reclamation projects. For example, the Columbia River has 28 dams. Some of the larger water reclamation projects include the Central Arizona Project (a massive canal system that diverts over 1.2 million acre-feet of water per year from the Colorado River), Bonneville Dam in Oregon, Grand Coulee Dam in Washington, Marshall Ford Dam in Texas, Teton Dam in Idaho, Garrison Dam in North Dakota, **Tellico Dam** in Tennessee, Hoover Dam in Nevada, Glen Canyon Dam in Arizona, Imperial Dam in California, and the Central Valley Project in California. Costs of these projects were large. For example, the California Central Valley Project cost over $950 million. The farmers, large and small, have paid only a small portion of overall costs of water reclamation projects. An estimated 4% of the total cost of the California Central Valley Project, equal to about $38 million, was repaid by the farmers who benefitted from the water project.

Important wildlife **habitat** and **wildlife** were lost as a result of these efforts to create massive dams. Dam building along the **Colorado River** has led to the decline of eight species of fish that are now considered endangered of becoming extinct. Habitat loss can result from **flooding** areas to create reservoirs or from cutting off water and nutrients from naturally occurring periodic flooding. During dam construction, stream-side habitat communities can be altered and destroyed from diverting the course of the river and excavation and dredging activities related to dam building. The **ecology** of these areas typically changes from that of a river to that commonly found along lakes and reservoirs.

Another ecological change occurs from dams cutting off sediment suspended in rivers from flowing downstream. As a result, sediment builds up in dams, reducing their volume and lowering their life expectancy. For example, the volume of Lake Waco in Texas was reduced by half over a 34-year period. When dams trap silt and sediment, erosion can result down stream. Below the Hoover Dam, millions of cubic yards of sediment were eroded over a 100 mi (160 km) stretch of the Colorado River.

Water reclamation projects continue on a much smaller scale today. Another method in which to obtain water for irrigation purposes is using water twice—once for domestic purposes and a second time for irrigation of lands such as farms and golf courses. Reclaiming used water occurs in the U.S. and throughout the world. Israel reclaims over 70% of its used water, or waste water, to irrigate over 47,000 acres (19,000 ha) of farm land. By the end of the 1990s, Israel plans to supply over 16% of its total water needs by reclaiming waste water. The city of Los Angeles, California, reuses its treated waste water to recharge its underground aquifers, which it taps for drinking water. In Arizona, the city of Tucson plans to reuse water to meet over 19% of its total water needs while Phoenix receives over 70,640 ft^3 (2,119 m^3) of fresh water from the Bureau of Reclamation in exchange for every 105,960 ft^3 (3,179 m^3) of reclaimed water used by the nearby irrigation district. The city of St. Petersburg, Florida, has a unique system in which it provides two sources of water; one source is potable water used for drinking, cooking, washing, etc. and the other source of water is reclaimed water from wastewater that is reused for irrigating parks, median strips along roads, and residential lawns. Because the treated wastewater contains nutrients such as **nitrogen** and **phosphorus**, less fertilizer is needed when used for irrigation.

Securing sufficient amounts of water while sustaining a healthy environment can be accomplished in many ways using all types of water reclamation projects including waste water reuse. Water conservation, efficiency of use, and reuse will likely be playing larger roles in ensuring adequate water supplies in the future.

[*Marci L. Bortman*]

FURTHER READING

Gottlieb, R. *A Life of Its Own, The Politics and Power of Water*. New York: Harcourt Brace Jovanovich, 1988.

Hunt, C.E., and V. Huser. *Down by the River, the Impact of Federal Water Projects and Policies on Biological Diversity*. Washington, D.C.: Island Press, 1988.

Outwater, A. *Water, A Natural History*. New York: Basic Books, 1996.

Postel, S. *Last Oasis, Facing Water Scarcity*. The Worldwatch Environmental Alert Series. New York: W.W. Norton & Company, 1992.

Water resources

Water resources represent one of the most serious environmental issues of the twentieth century. Water is abundant globally, yet millions of people have inadequate fresh water, and **drought**s plague rich and poor countries alike. **Water pollution** compounds the scarcity of usable fresh water and threatens the health of millions of people each year. At the same time, the ravages of **flooding** and catastrophes associated with excessive rainfall or snowmelt cause death and destruction of property. To cope with these problems, water resource management has become a high priority worldwide.

Concerns about water scarcity seem unwarranted considering that there are 1.36 billion cubic kilometers of water on earth. Although 99 percent of this water is either unusable (too salty) or unavailable (ice caps and deep **groundwater** storage), the remaining 1 percent can meet all future water needs. The total volume of fresh water on earth is not the problem. Scarcity of fresh water results from the unequal distribution of water on earth and water pollution that renders water unusable.

Fresh water is not always available where or when it is needed the most. In Africa, Chile, for example, no rainfall was measured for 14 consecutive years, from 1903 to 1918. At the other extreme, Mount Waialeale, Kauai, Hawaii, averages 460 inches (11,680 mm) of rainfall per year. Even such extremes in annual precipitation do not tell the complete story of water scarcity. For example, in the tropics, storms in the rainy season can deposit from 16 to over 39 inches (400 to 1,000 mm) of rainfall in two to three days, often resulting in widespread flooding. However, the same areas can experience negligible rainfall for two to three months during the dry season.

The demand for water vary worldwide, with wealthier countries consuming an average of about 264,000 gallons (1,000 cubic m) per person, per year. In contrast, over one-half of the population in the developing countries of North Africa and the Middle East live on a fraction of this amount.

Population growth and droughts have forced people to use water more efficiently. However, **water conservation** alone will not solve water scarcity problems.

Increasing demands for water and the disparity of water distribution have sparked the imagination of hydrologists and engineers. Grandiose schemes have emerged, including towing icebergs from polar regions to the lower latitudes, **desalinization** of ocean water, cloud seeding, and transporting water thousands of kilometers from water-rich to water-poor regions. Although many of these ideas are fraught with environmental, economic, and political concerns, they have placed water supply issues in the international spotlight.

Historically, more conventional, large public investment water development schemes have been a vehicle for economic development. As a result, about 75 percent of the fresh water used worldwide is used for **irrigation**, with 90 percent used for this purpose in some developing countries. Much of this water is being wasted. Poorer countries do not have the technology to irrigate efficiently, using twice as much water to produce one-half the crop yields of wealthier countries.

Multi-purpose **reservoir** projects that generate hydroelectric power, control flood, provide recreational benefits, and supply water have become commonplace worldwide. Hydroelectric power has fostered both municipal and industrial development. Since 1972, 45 percent of the dams constructed with **World Bank** support were primarily for hydropower, in contrast to 55 percent for irrigation and/or flood control. Although the pace of dam construction has slowed worldwide, large projects are still being constructed. For example, the proposed **Three Gorges Dam** on the Yangtze River, China, will cost at least $10 billion and will be the largest hydroelectric power project in the world. It will generate one-eighth of the *total* electrical power that was generated in China in 1991.

Dams and water transfer systems constructed for economic benefit often carry with them environmental costs. **Wildlife** habitat is flooded by reservoir pools, and streamflow volumes and patterns are altered, affecting aquatic **ecosystem**s. The modification of flow by dams in the Columbia River of the United States has either eliminated or severely reduced natural spawning runs of **salmon** in much of the river. The reservoir created by the Three Gorges Dam will flood one of China's most scenic spots and will force over one million people to relocate. Already there are concerns that high rates of **soil erosion** and **sediment** deposition behind the dam will threaten the usefulness of the project. The relocation of people in response to water resource development can also bring unwanted environmental consequences. In developing countries, relocated people seek new land to cultivate, graze livestock, or build new villages, often accelerating **deforestation** and land degradation.

Small-scale projects offer environmentally attractive alternatives to large **dams** and reservoirs. Mini-hydroelectric power projects, which do not necessarily require dams, provide electricity to many small villages. Rainfall harvesting methods in drylands provide fresh water for drinking, livestock, and crops. **Flood plain** management is environmentally and economically preferable to large flood control dams in most instances.

Groundwater provides large volumes of fresh water in many regions of the world. A proposed $25 billion irrigation project in Libya would pump nearly 980 million cubic yards (750 million cubic meters) of groundwater per year in the Sahara to be transported 1,180 miles (1,900 km) north. Groundwater supplies in the Sahara are thought to be nearly 20 trillion cubic yards (15 trillion cubic meters). However, there is concern that such pumping will drop water levels 8-20 inches (20-50 cm) per year, eventually causing water that is too salty for irrigation to intrude. Groundwater mining occurs if water is pumped faster than it is replenished. Such mining is occurring in many parts of the world and cannot provide sustainable sources of water.

Water requirements for urban areas pose formidable challenges in the coming years. With 90 percent of the population growth expected to occur in urban areas over the next few decades, competition for fresh water between rural agricultural areas and cities will become severe. With urban areas able to pay higher prices for water than rural areas, legal and political battles over **water rights** and subsidy issues will likely ensue. In many cities, however, finding sufficient sources of fresh water will be difficult. For example, Mexico City is expected to reach a population of 30 million by the year 2000. Fresh water from lakes and springs have already been exhausted. Groundwater is being mined three times faster than the rate of recharge. Also, a daily discharge of 29 million pounds (13 million kg) of sewage plus industrial wastes threaten groundwater quality. Furthermore, groundwater pumping is causing land to subside around the city. Unfortunately, many other large cities around the world are faced with equally challenging problems of water supply and pollution.

Flooding and droughts are global concerns that lead to **famine** in the poorer countries and will persist until solutions are found. Flood avoidance or flood plain management are not commonplace in many such countries because people have no alternative places to live and farm. The recurring floods and devastation in Bangladesh, and the droughts of North Africa emphasize the dilemma of the poorest of countries.

In contrast to problems of water quantity, water pollution accounts for over 5 million deaths per year, largely the result of drinking water that is contaminated by human and livestock waste. Inadequate **sewage treatment** and a lack of alternative fresh water supplies can be blamed. These problems can be solved but will require that **water quality** issues become a high priority in terms of policies, institutions, and financial support.

Water pollution plagues rich and poor countries alike. Municipalities and industries pollute streams and groundwater with toxic chemicals, sewage, disease-causing agents, oil, heavy metals, **thermal pollution**, and **radioactive waste**. Polluted water from municipalities and industries can and should be treated before it is discharged. **Environmental law**s and enforcement can ensure that this happens.

Agricultural development has made significant strides in solving food problems in the world, but it has also contributed to water pollution. Water supplies have become polluted as a result of heavy **fertilizer** and **pesticide** use. The focus on sustainable agricultural practices that do not rely so heavily upon fertilizers and pesticides offer some promise. Sensible use of **chemicals** and the adoption of "best management practices" also offer a means of meeting food requirements of growing populations without contaminating water supplies.

Just as food security issues attracted global attention through the 1950s to 1970s, similar efforts will be needed to provide for water security in the twenty-first century. Long-term, holistic, and interdisciplinary solutions are needed. The crises management approach of the past—that of attempting to deal with droughts, floods, and contaminated water only when they are upon us—cannot continue.

We currently have the technology to solve most water resource problems. Implementing solutions are often constrained by inadequate policies, institutions, financial resources, and political instability. In many ways, people management is more critical than water resource management. With human populations continuing to grow, water scarcity, flooding, and disease and death from contaminated drinking water will become even more pronounced.

[*Kenneth N. Brooks*]

FURTHER READING

Anton, D. "Thirsty Cities." *IDRC Reports* 18 (No. 4).

Brooks, K. N., et al. *Hydrology and the Management of Watersheds.* Ames: Iowa State University Press, 1991.

"The First Commodity." *The Economist* 322 (1992): 11-12.

Jackson, I. J. *Climate, Water and Agriculture in the Tropics.* 2nd ed. Essex, England: Longman Scientific & Technical, 1989.

Opportunities in the Hydrologic Sciences. Committee on Opportunities in the Hydrologic Sciences, Water Sciences Technology Board. National Research Council. Washington, DC: National Academy Press, 1991.

Van der Leeden, F., F. L. Troise, and D. K. Todd. *The Water Encyclopedia.* 2nd ed. Chelsea, MI: Lewis Publishers, 1990.

Winkler, P. "Qaddafi Challenges the Desert." *World Press Review* (April 1992): 47.

Water rights

Pure, potable water is an essential resource, second only to breathable air in importance for life on earth. But it has other valuable attributes as well. It powers industry, provides **recreation**, irrigates agriculture, and is a highway for ships. It also takes many forms, from oceans, rivers, and lakes to **groundwater** and even atmospheric moisture. Given this vital significance, water rights have been contended throughout history.

One area of frequent dispute is jurisdiction. If a water right is a right to use water, then who has the authority to grant or withhold that right? The obvious answer is the government that has jurisdiction over the territory in which the water is found. But water pays no attention to boundaries. A river that begins in one jurisdiction flows into another.

Problems arise when people in the first jurisdiction deprive people in the other of a sufficient quantity or quality of water from the river. Such a situation forced the United States, which uses the **Colorado River** to irrigate several western states, to build a plant to remove excess salt from the Colorado before it flows into Mexico.

Impossible as it seems, jurisdiction over the water cycle has also been litigated. From atmospheric moisture comes rain and snow, which replenish groundwater and form streams that flow into rivers, which flow in turn into lakes and oceans. Surface water thus forms an interconnected system. International law has focused on rights to "international drainage basins" and, more recently, "international **water resources** systems" that include atmospheric and frozen water.

When jurisdiction is not at issue, water rights are usually established in one of three ways. The first was set out in the Institutes of Justinian (533-34 A.D.), which codified Roman law. This holds that flowing water is a *res communes omnium*—a thing common to all, at least when it is navigable. It cannot be owned or used exclusively by anyone. The second and third approaches have been developed in the United States, where the doctrines of **riparian rights** and prior appropriation predominate in the eastern and western states respectively. In a riparian system, landowners whose land borders a waterway have a special, if not exclusive, right to the water. In the **arid** western states, however, water rights derive from first use, not ownership, as in the "first in time, first in right" rule. *See also* Environmental law; Hydrologic cycle; Irrigation; Land-use control; Riparian land

[*Richard K. Dagger*]

FURTHER READING

Caponera, D. A., ed. *The Law of International Water Resources*. Rome: Food and Agricultural Organization of the United Nations: 1980.

Goldfarb, W. *Water Law*. 2nd ed. New York: Lewis, 1988.

Matthews, O. P. *Water Resources, Geography and Law*. Washington, DC: Resource Publications in Geography, 1984.

Sax, J. *Water Law: Cases and Commentary*. Boulder, CO: Pruett Press, 1965.

Water table

The top or upper surface of the saturated zone of water that occurs underground, except where it is confined by an overlying impermeable layer. This surface separates the zone of **aeration**—the layer of **soil** or rock that is unsaturated most of the time—from the zone of saturation below. The water table is the level at which water rises in a well that is situated in a **groundwater** body but not confined by a layer of **impervious material**. In **wetlands**, the water table can be at the soil surface or a few centimeters below the soil surface, but in drylands it can be several hundred meters below the soil surface. Perched water tables occur where there is a shallow impervious layer (such as a clay layer) that prevents water from percolating downward to the more persistent, regional groundwater zone. As a result, water tables can occur at different depths within a region. Generally, if water tables are close to the soil surface, groundwater is

susceptible to **pollution** from human activities. *See also* Percolation

Water table draw-down

A measurement of how a particular water level is affected by the withdrawal of **groundwater**. It is made by establishing the vertical distance at a given point between the original water level and the pumping water level. The **water table** of an unconfined **aquifer** or the potentiometric surface of a confined aquifer is lowered when a **well** is pumped, and inverted cone of depressions develops around the pumping well.

Changes of drawdown at different distances from the well are shown with a drawdown curve. Specific capacity is the rate of **discharge** of water from the well divided by the drawdown within the well. The drawdown within a well divided by the discharge rate of water from the well—inverse of specific capacity—is called specific drawdown.

Water treatment

Water treatment—or the purification and sanitation of water—varies as to the source and kinds of water. Municipal waters, for example, consist of surface water and **groundwater**, and their treatment is to be distinguished from that of industrial water supplies.

Municipal water supplies are treated, by public or private water utilities, to make the water potable (safe to drink) and palatable (aesthetically pleasing) and to insure an adequate supply of water to meet the needs of the community at a reasonable cost. Except in exceedingly rare instances, the entire supply is treated to drinking **water quality** for three reasons: it is generally not feasible to supply water of more than one quality; it is difficult to control public access to water not treated to drinking water quality; and a substantial amount of treatment may be required even if the water is not intended for human consumption.

Raw (untreated) water is withdrawn from either a surface water supply (such as a lake or stream) or from an underground **aquifer** (by means of **wells**). The water flows or is pumped to a central treatment facility. Large municipalities may utilize more than one source and may have more than one treatment facility. The treated water is then pumped under pressure into a distribution system, which typically consists of a network of pipes (water mains) interconnected with ground-level or elevated storage facilities (**reservoir**s).

As it is withdrawn from the source, surface water is usually screened through steel bars, typically about one inch thick and about two inches apart, to prevent large objects such as logs or fish from entering the treatment facility. Finer screens are sometimes employed to remove leaves. If the water is highly turbid (cloudy or muddy), it may be pretreated in a large basin known as a presedimentation basin to allow time for sand and the larger **silt** particles to settle out.

All surface waters have the potential to carry pathogenic (disease-causing) microorganisms and must be disinfected prior to human consumption. Since the adequacy of disinfection cannot be assured in the presence of turbidity, it is first necessary to remove the suspended solids causing the water to be turbid. This is accomplished by a sequence of treatment processes that typically includes coagulation, flocculation, **sedimentation**, and **filtration**.

Coagulation is accomplished by adding chemical coagulants, usually **aluminum** or iron salts, to neutralize the negative charge on the surfaces of the particles (suspended solids) present in the water, thereby eliminating the repulsive forces between the particles and enabling them to aggregate. Coagulants are usually dispersed in the water by rapid mixing. Other **chemicals** may be added at the same time, including powdered-activated **carbon** (to adsorb taste- and odor-causing chemicals or to remove synthetic chemicals); chemical oxidants such as **chlorine**, **ozone**, chlorine dioxide, or potassium permanganate (to initiate disinfection, to oxidize organic contaminants, to control taste and odor, or to oxidize inorganic contaminants such as iron, manganese, and sulfide); and acid or base (to control **pH**).

Coagulated particles are aggregated into large rapidly settling "floc" particles by flocculation, accomplished by gently stirring the water using paddles, turbines, or impellers. This process typically takes 20 to 30 minutes. The flocculated water is then gently introduced into a sedimentation basin, where the floc particles are given about two to four hours to settle out. After sedimentation, the water is filtered, most commonly through 24 to 30 inches (61-76 cm) of sand or anthracite having an effective diameter of about 0.5 mm. When the raw water is low in turbidity, coagulated or flocculated water may be taken directly to the **filters**, bypassing sedimentation; this practice is referred to as direct filtration.

Once the water has been filtered, it can be satisfactorily disinfected. Disinfection is the elimination of pathogenic microorganisms from the water. It does not render the water completely sterile but does make it safe to drink from a microbial standpoint. Most water treatment plants in the United States rely primarily on chlorine for disinfection. Some utilities utilize ozone, chlorine dioxide, chloramines (formed from chlorine and ammonia), or a combination of chemicals added at different points during treatment. There are important advantages and disadvantages associated with each of these chemicals, and the optimum choice for a particular water requires careful study and expert advice.

Chemical disinfectants react not only with microorganisms but also with naturally occurring organic matter present in the water, producing trace amounts of contaminants collectively referred to as disinfection byproducts (DBPs). The most well known DBPs are the **trihalomethanes**. Although DBPs are not known to be toxic at the concentrations found in drinking water, some are known to be toxic at much higher concentrations. Therefore, prudence dictates that reasonable efforts be made to minimize their presence in drinking water.

The most effective strategy for minimizing DBP formation is to avoid adding chemical disinfectants until the water has been filtered and then to add only the amount required to achieve adequate disinfection. Some DBPs can be minimized by changing to another disinfectant, but all chemical disinfectants form DBPs. Regardless of which chemical disinfectant is used, great care must be exercised to ensure adequate disinfection, since the health risks associated with pathogenic microorganisms greatly outweigh those associated with DBPs.

There are a number of other processes that may be employed to treat water, depending on the quality of the source water and the desired quality of the treated water. Processes that may be used to treat either surface water or groundwater include: 1) lime softening, which involves the addition of lime during rapid mixing to precipitate calcium and magnesium **ion**s; 2) stabilization, to prevent corrosion and scale formation, usually by adjusting the pH or alkalinity of the water or by adding scale inhibitors; 3) activated carbon **adsorption**, to remove taste- and odor-causing chemicals or synthetic organic contaminants; and 4) fluoridation, to increase the concentration of fluoride to the optimum level for the prevention of dental cavities.

Compared to surface waters, groundwaters are relatively free of turbidity and pathogenic microorganisms, but they are more likely to contain unacceptable levels of dissolved gases (**carbon dioxide**, **methane**, and hydrogen sulfide), hardness, iron and manganese, **volatile organic compound**s (VOCs) originating from **chemical spills** or improper waste disposal practices, and dissolved solids (**salinity**).

High quality groundwaters do not require filtration, but they are usually disinfected to protect against contamination of the water as it passes through the distribution system. Small systems are sometimes exempted from disinfection requirements if they are able to meet a set of strict criteria. Groundwaters withdrawn from shallow wells or along river banks may be deemed to be "under the influence of surface water," in which case they are normally required by law to be filtered and disinfected.

Hard groundwaters may be treated by lime softening as are many hard surface waters, or by **ion exchange** softening, in which calcium and magnesium ions are exchanged for sodium ions as the water passes through a bed of ion-exchange resin. Groundwaters having high levels of dissolved gases or VOCs are commonly treated by air stripping, achieved by passing air over small droplets of water to allow the gases to leave the water and enter the air.

Many groundwaters—approximately one quarter of those used for public water supply in the United States—are contaminated with naturally occurring iron and manganese, which tend to dissolve into groundwater in their chemically reduced forms in the absence of oxygen. Iron and manganese are most commonly removed by oxidation (accomplished by **aeration** or by adding a chemical oxidant, such as chlorine or potassium permanganate) followed by sedimentation and filtration; by filtration through an adsorptive media; or by lime softening.

Groundwaters high in dissolved solids may be treated using reverse **osmosis**, in which water is forced through a membrane under high pressure, leaving the salt behind. Membrane processes are rapidly evolving, and membranes suitable for removing hardness, dissolved organic matter, and turbidity from both ground and surface waters have recently been developed.

Industrial water treatment differs from municipal in the specified quality of the treated water. Many industries use water supplied by a local municipality, while others secure their own source of water. Those securing water from a private source often treat it using the same processes used by municipalities. However, industries must often provide additional treatment to provide water suitable for their special needs, which may include process water, boiler feed water, or cooling water.

Process water is water used by an industry in a particular process or for a group of processes. The quality of water required depends on the nature of the process. For example, water used to make white paper must be free of color. In some instances, water of relatively poor quality may be acceptable, e.g., water used to granulate steelmaking slags, while other uses require water of the very highest purity, e.g., ultrapure water used in the manufacture of silicon chips.

Water used in boilers for thermoelectric or **nuclear power** generation must be very low in dissolved solids and must be treated to prevent both corrosion and scale formation in the boilers, turbines, and condensers. High purity process waters and boiler feed waters are typically produced using ion-exchange demineralization and special filters designed to remove sub-micron sized particles.

Cooling water may be used once (single-pass system) or many times (closed-loop system). Cooling water used only once may receive little treatment, typically continuous or intermittent disinfection to reduce slime growths and perhaps stabilization to control corrosion and scale formation. Water entering a closed-loop system may not only be stabilized and disinfected, but may also be treated to remove **nutrient**s (**nitrogen** and **phosphorus**) or dissolved solids. Additional treatment is usually provided in the loop to remove dissolved solids that accumulate as a result of evaporation. *See also* Safe Drinking Water Act

[*Stephen J. Randtke*]

FURTHER READING

Peavy, H. S., D. R. Rowe, and G. Tchobanoglous. *Environmental Engineering.* New York: McGraw-Hill, 1985.

"Recommended Standards for Water Works." Great Lakes Upper Mississippi River Board of State Public Health and Environmental Managers. Albany, NY: Health Education Services, 1992.

Water Treatment Plant Design. 2nd ed. New York: McGraw-Hill, 1990.

Waterless toilets
See **Toilets**

Waterlogging

Saturation of **soil** with water, usually through **irrigation**, resulting in a condition under which most crop plants cannot grow. Although naturally wet soils are extremely common, human-caused waterlogging occurring on active croplands has created the most concern. Where fields are irrigated regularly, some means of drainage is usually necessary to let excess water escape, but if drainage is inadequate, water gradually accumulates, filling pore spaces in the soil. Once the oxygen in these pores is displaced by water, plant roots and soil microorganisms die. Waterlogging frequently occurs where **flooding** has been used. There are two main reasons for flooding: it is a simple, low-technology method of irrigation and in some cases it reduces harmful mineral concentrations in soils. Ideally, flood waters seep through the soil and into **groundwater** or stream channels, but in many agricultural regions impermeable layers of clay block downward drainage, so that irrigation water collects in the soil. Farmers who can afford it avoid this problem by installing some means of field drainage, such as perforated pipes below ground, but the expense of this procedure is prohibitive in many regions. *See also* Soil conservation; Soil eluviation

Watershed

A catchment or drainage basin which is the total area of land that drains into a water body. It is usually a topographically delineated area that is drained by a stream system. River basins are large watersheds that contribute to water flow in a river. The watershed of a lake is the total land area that drains into the lake. In addition to being hydrologic units, watersheds are useful units of land for planning and managing multiple **natural resources**. By using the watershed as a planning unit, management activities and their effects can be determined for the land area that is directly affected by management. The hydrologic effects of land management downstream can be evaluated as well. Sometimes **land use** and management can alter the quantity and quality of water that flows to downstream communities. By considering a watershed, many of these environmental effects can be taken into consideration. *See also* Watershed management

Watershed management

Watershed management is planning, guiding, and organizing **land use** so that desired goods and services are produced from a **watershed** without harming **soil** productivity and **water resources**. Goods and services produced from watersheds include food, forage for livestock and **wildlife**, wood and other forest products, outdoor **recreation**, wildlife **habitat**, scenic beauty, and water. Essential to watershed management is the recognition that production must be accompanied by environmental protection.

The specific objectives of watershed management depend on human needs in a particular area and can include: (1) the rehabilitation of degraded lands; (2) the protection of soil and water resources under land use systems that produce multiple products of the land; and (3) the enhancement of water quantity and quality. Rehabilitating degraded lands is sometimes mistakenly thought of as the only role of watershed management. Rehabilitation requires that both the productivity and hydrologic function of degraded lands be restored. This usually entails the construction of engineering structures, such as gully control **dams**, followed by vegetation establishment, protection, and management, all of which are needed to achieve long-term healing of the landscape.

Most fundamental to watershed management is the prevention of land and water resource degradation in the first place. To achieve this goal, land use must adhere to **conservation** practices that avoid land degradation. The greatest potential for degradation arises from road construction, mining, crop cultivation, logging, and **overgrazing** by livestock in steep terrain. When management guidelines are not followed, soils erode and land productivity is diminished. The loss of soil and vegetative cover reduces the effectiveness of watersheds in moderating the flow of water, **sediment**, and other water borne substances. As a result, damage to aquatic **ecosystem**s and human communities can occur in areas that are positioned downslope or downstream. To achieve sustainable land use, the development of and adherence to land use guidelines and conservation practices must become commonplace.

Preventing degradation of **wetlands** and **riparian land** is of particular environmental concern. These soil-vegetation communities require special management and protection because the wet soils are susceptible to excessive **erosion**. Furthermore, riparian vegetation provides valuable wildlife habitat and plays a critical role in protecting **water quality**.

In some parts of the world, watershed management can be aimed at enhancing water resources. In some instances vegetative cover can be altered to increase water yield or to change the pattern of water flow for beneficial purposes. No matter what the specific objectives, watershed management recognizes that human use of land is usually aimed at producing a variety of goods and services, of which water is one product. By following the principles of soil and **water conservation**, land and natural resources can be managed for sustainable production with environmental protection. *See also* Sustainable agriculture; Sustainable development

[*Kenneth N. Brooks*]

FURTHER READING

Black, P. E. *Watershed Hydrology.* Englewood Cliffs: Prentice Hall, 1991.

Brooks, K. N., et al. *Hydrology and the Management of Watersheds.* Ames: Iowa State University Press, 1991.

Brooks, K. N., et al. "Watershed Management: A Key to Sustainability." In *Managing the World's Forests*, edited by N. P. Sharma. Dubuque, IA: Kendall/Hunt, 1992.

Satterlund, D. R. and P. W. Adams. *Wildland Watershed Management.* 2nd ed. New York: Wiley, 1992.

Watt, James Gaius (1938-)

Secretary of the Interior

Watt was born in Lusk, Wyoming, and raised in nearby Wheatland, a town one of his critics described as "a place frozen in amber decades ago—the 1890s plus electricity and TV." President Ronald Reagan's first Secretary of the Interior, Watt was heavily criticized for his position on **conservation**.

Watt came to the **U.S. Department of the Interior** from a position as head of the Mountain States Legal Foundation in Denver, considered by many critics to have an anti-environmental stance. Within months of his appointment, environmentalists began to criticize his conservative policies. He maintained his actions were for the good of the people and the free enterprise system.

During his tenure as Secretary of the Interior, Watt cut funds for environmental programs, such as those protecting **endangered species**, and reorganized the department to put less regulatory power on the federal level. He favored the elimination of the Land and Water Conservation Fund, which increased the land holdings of **national forest**s, **national wildlife refuge**s, and **national park**s and made matching grants to state governments to do the same, all using money gained from the sale of offshore oil and gas leases. Watt also favored opening extensive shorelands and **wilderness** areas for oil and gas leases, speeding the sale of **public land**s to private interests and doing so at bargain prices.

Watt's stay was marked by heavy and repeated criticisms of his policies, even by fellow Republicans. In April of 1981, the **Sierra Club** and others began a "Dump Watt" petition drive and in October of that year presented Congress with 1.1 million signatures supporting his dismissal. Even the relatively conservative **National Wildlife Federation** called for Watt's removal within six months of his taking office, stating that Watt "places a much higher priority on development and exploitation than on conservation."

His actions and derogatory remarks about Senate members earned him a number of enemies, and when Watt resigned his position as Secretary of the Interior on October 9, 1983, the Senate was drafting a resolution calling for his dismissal. *See also* Environmental policy; National lakeshore; National seashore

[*Gerald L. Young*]

FURTHER READING

Bratton, S. P. "The Ecotheology of James Watt." *Environmental Ethics* 5 (Fall 1983): 225-236.

Coggins, G. C., and D. K. Nagel. "'Nothing Beside Remains': The Legal Legacy of James G. Watts' Tenure as Secretary of the Interior on Federal Land Law and Policy." *Boston College Environmental Affairs Law Review* 17 (Spring 1990): 473-550.

Wave power

The oceans are an enormous reservoir of energy. One form in which that energy appears is waves. The energy in waves is derived from the **wind energy** which generates them. Since wind currents are produced by **solar energy**, wave energy is a renewable source of energy.

Humans have invented devices for capturing the power of waves at least as far back as the time of Leonardo da Vinci. The first modern device for generating electricity from wave power was patented by two French scientists in 1799. In the United States, more than 150 patents for wave power machines have been granted.

Harnessing the energy of wave motion presents many practical problems, however. For example, while the total amount of wave energy in the oceans is very great, the quantity available at any one specific point is usually quite small. For purposes of comparison, an eight-foot tall wave contains the same potential energy as a hydroelectric **dam** eight feet high.

One technical problem inventors face, therefore, is to find a way to magnify the energy of waves in an area. A second problem is to design a machine that will work efficiently with waves of different sizes. Over a period of days, weeks, or months, a region of the sea may be still, it may experience waves of moderate size, or it may be hit by a huge storm. A wave power machine has to be able to survive and to function under all these conditions.

Wave power has been seriously studied as an alternative energy source in the United States since the early 1970s. An experimental device constructed at the Scripps Institute of Oceanography, for example, consisted of a buoy to which was attached a long pipe with a trap near its top. As the buoy moved up and down in the waves, water entered the pipe and was captured in the trap. After a certain number of waves had occurred, enough water had been captured to drive a small turbine and electrical generator. One of the first Scripps devices consisted of a pipe eight inches (20 cm) in diameter and 320 feet (98 m) long. It was able to generate fifty watts of electricity. Scripps researchers hoped eventually to construct a machine with a pipe fifteen feet (4.5 m) in diameter and 300 feet (91.5 m) long. They expected such a machine to produce 300 kilowatts of energy in eight-foot waves.

Research on wave power in the United States essentially died out in the early 1980s, as did research on most other forms of **alternative energy sources**. That research has continued in other countries, however, especially in Japan, Great Britain, and Norway. The Norwegians have had the greatest success. By 1989, they had constructed two prototype wave machines on the coast west of Bergen. The machines were located on the shore and operated by using air pumped into a large tower by the rise and fall of waves. The compressed air was then used to drive a turbine and generator. Unfortunately, one of the towers was destroyed by a series of severe storms in December 1989. The Norwegians appear to be convinced about the potential value of wave power, however, and their research on wave machines continues.

Great Britain has had a more checkered interest in wave power. One of the most ambitious wave machines, known as Salter's Duck, was first proposed in the early 1970s. In this device, the riding motion of waves is used to force water through small pipes. The high-pressure water is then used to drive a turbine and generator.

The British government was so impressed with the potential of wave power that it outlined plans in April 1976 for a 2,000 **megawatt** station. Only six years later, the government changed its mind, however, and abandoned all plans to use wave power. **Fossil fuels** and **nuclear power** had, meanwhile, regained their position as the major—and perhaps only—-energy sources in the nation's future.

Then, in 1989, the British government changed its mind yet again. It announced a new review of the potential of wave power with the possibility of constructing plants off the British coast. One of the designs to be tested was a modification of a Norwegian device, the Tapchan (for "tapered channel"). The Tapchan is designed to be installed on a shoreline where waves can flow into a large chamber filled with air. As waves enter the chamber, they compress the air, which then flows though a valve and into a turbine. The compressed air rotates the turbine and drives a generator. The prototype for this machine was installed at Islay, Scotland, in the early 1990s.

Wave power has many obvious advantages. The raw materials (water and wind) are free and abundant, no harmful pollutants are released to the **environment** and land is not taken out of use. However, the technology for using wave power is still not well developed. It can be used only along coasts, and it is still not economically competitive with traditional energy sources. *See also* Alternative energy sources; Hydrogeology; Land use; Renewable resources

[*David E. Newton*]

FURTHER READING

Charlier, R. H. *Tidal Energy.* New York: Van Nostrand Reinhold, 1982.
Fisher, A. "Wave Power." *Popular Science* (May 1975): 68-73+.
Hersh, S. L. "Waves of Power." *Sea Frontiers* (February 1991): 7.
"Norway Waves Goodbye to Wave Power Machine." *New Scientist* (14 January 1989): 31.
Ross, D. "On the Crest of a Wave." *New Scientist* (19 May 1990): 50-52.

Weather

See **Climate; Meteorology; Milankovitch weather cycles; Weather modification**

Weather modification

When Mark Twain said that everybody talks about the weather, but nobody does anything about it, he was wrong. In fact, the rain falling on his California roof at that moment might have been generated by secret **chemicals** being diffused into clouds by a hired rainmaker named Charles Hatfield. Hatfield got rich selling rain to farmers in the San

Joaquin Valley until he was run out of the state of California by angry San Diegoans who accused him of triggering a flood.

Experiments in rainmaking flourished in the early 1900s in American farmlands where **drought** meant not only hunger but poverty. A little like snake-oil salesmen, early rainmakers sold their ability to make it rain, but it was always ambiguous: when it worked, they were paid. More often, it was hard to tell if they had performed their promised service. Lawsuits were abundant when rain intended for an **arid** area fell across the statelines or caused floods; or when barley growers, pressured by beer companies, paid for rain that coincidentally wiped out other crops of neighboring farmers.

Controlling weather raises myriad questions. Is there an accurate scientific way of measuring human intervention in weather? Who is legally responsible if it rains in the wrong place? Does the community feel that augmenting rainfall is good for everyone? If it rains too much, can the rainmaker be sued? How much does local intervention affect global **climate**? Should regulations be in the hands of the state, the federal government, or a world organization?

For better or worse, people can modify weather both intentionally and inadvertently. Weather responds sensitively to any changes in the global **atmosphere** because it is a complex collection of energy systems powered by the sun. Modest rises in sea surface temperature in the Atlantic Ocean, for example, brought about by ocean circulation shifts or global warming, suppresses rainfall in the African Sahel and contributes to drought.

Sensitive climate changes are also caused by such human activities as cutting down forests or failing to let farmfields lie fallow, which, with **overgrazing** by cattle, sheep, and goats, cause **desertification**, a condition that results when **topsoil** blows away and exposes bare, unplantable land. This increases **albedo**, the reflective quality of the surface of the earth, sends back solar radiation into space, and lowers temperature. With less heat rising, fewer clouds are formed, and rainfall is reduced.

Cities, with their clustered buildings and canyons of thoroughfares, absorb infrared heat and inadvertently modify weather because their shape alters the flow of winds. Because they are localized islands of heat, cities increase cloudiness. **Aerosol**s, microscopic dust particles, given off in industrial **smoke**, bond with water vapor and create city **haze** and **smog**. When the aerosols contain **sulfur dioxide** and **nitrogen oxides**, they cause **acid rain**. Increased urban traffic raises levels of **carbon monoxide** and **carbon dioxide**. In the sky, jet trails contribute to the formation of clouds.

Fossil fuels, which are ancient organic matter, release CO_2 when they are burned. This collects in the greenhouse band, a protective shield that circles the earth. Naturally composed of CO_2, **methane, chlorofluorocarbons**(CFCs), nitrous oxide, and water vapor, the greenhouse layer processes infrared heat sent back into space by earth and regulates the temperature of the earth. When it is too full to allow infrared heat from earth to pass through into space, the temperature rises on earth, affecting local, regional, and global weather.

Intentional weather modification involves taking advantage of the energy contained within weather systems and turning it toward a specific goal. To "make" rain, a scientist mimics the natural process by introducing extra water droplets or ice crystals in clouds. However, he needs the right-shaped clouds with the right internal temperature and the right winds, headed in the direction of his target.

Rainmaking became a serious science in 1950 when physicist Bernard Vonnegut at General Electric devised a way to vaporize silver iodide to let it rise on heated air currents into clouds where it solidified and bonded onto water droplets to create ice crystals. Previous attempts at rainmaking involved dropping dry ice (solid CO_2) onto clouds from planes, but this was expensive. Vonnegut chose silver iodide because its molecular structure most closely matches that of ice crystals.

In California, where the Southern California Edison Company regularly sends out planes to seed rain clouds over the dry San Joaquin Valley farmland, silver iodide is shot from rockets mounted on the leading edge of the wings. It is also vaporized into clouds from ground generators at higher altitudes in the Sierra Mountains. In rainmaking projects, the purpose is to avoid droughts, increase food productivity, and augment water supplies for drinking or hydroelectric plants. But gathering accurate data on successful seeding and subsequent precipitation has been difficult. Currently most scientists agree with a longterm analysis that seasonal cloud seeding has increased precipitation by at least 10 percent, possibly as much as 20 percent. Clouds, which are ever-moving collections of water vapor, regulators of heat, and generators of tremendous internal winds, remain mysterious. Yet they are major players in earth's climate.

Other weather modification projects include dissipating cold fogs, done routinely at major airports around the world. In the former Soviet Union damaging hailstorms were successfully broken up to protect ripening crops. However, statistics from attempts at hail suppression in the United States have been inconclusive, and research is ongoing. In the 1950s and 1960s, scientists experimented with seeding **hurricane**s to diminish the storms' severity and alter their path. Similarly, attempts were made to "explode" tornadoes by firing artillery into the oncoming storms. In both cases, natural energies far exceeded any attempts at control.

"We don't have the capability to turn the weather around," said Bill Blackmore of **National Oceanic and Atmospheric Administration (NOAA)**'s Weather Modification Reporting Program. "If we could modify the weather a hundred percent then we could predict the weather a hundred percent. What we need is a lot more understanding of its complexity."

NOAA funds the Federal State Coop Program, a six-state research group. The Atmospheric Modification Program at NOAA's Wave Propagation Lab in Boulder, Colorado, coordinates and evaluates state projects. Research there and at the Institute for Atmospheric Science at the South Dakota School of Mines and Technology involves doing remote sensing of clouds, computer modelling of clouds, and releasing tracers in convective clouds to better understand the dynamics of thunderstorms.

A new way of collecting rainwater is cloud "milking." Researchers have been collecting fog on the mountains of Chile by stringing 50 nylon mesh nets—39 feet long by 13 feet wide (12 m by 4 m)—at regular intervals on the mountainside. As the windblown fogs hit the net, they trap water particles. These are then collected into containers. On average, the system "milks" 2,500 gallons (9,475 liters) of drinking water a day.

Most rainmaking activities in the United States take place in the western states and are sponsored by water departments or districts and conducted by private and commercial companies. The mistakes made earlier in the history of altering the weather have been dealt with by regulations in each state. Internationally, the World Meteorological Organization (WMO) oversees weather modification; and the Treaty of War and Environmental Weather, signed at the Geneva Arms Limitation Talks in 1977, forbids uncontrolled military weather modification.

In 1971 the United States created Public Law 92-205 which requires states to file all weather modification activity with the NOAA's Weather Modification Reporting Program. Typically, about a dozen states file annually.

Two private organizations, the American Meteorological Society in Boston, Massachusetts, and the Weather Modification Association of Fresno, California, keep records on weather modification. The *Journal of Weather Modification* is an annual publication of the Institute for Atmospheric Science at the South Dakota School of Mines and Technology. *See also* Deforestation; Greenhouse effect; Ozone; Ozone layer depletion

[*Stephanie Ocko*]

FURTHER READING

Arnett, D. S. *Weather Modification by Cloud Seeding.* New York, Academic Press, 1980.

Blackmore, W. H. *A Summary of Weather Modification Activities Reported in the United States During 1991.* Silver Spring, MD: National Oceanic and Atmospheric Administration, 1991.

Breuer, G. *Weather Modification: Prospects and Problems.* New York: Cambridge University Press, 1979.

"Planned and Inadvertent Weather Modification." *Bulletin of the American Meteorological Society* (March 1992): 331-337.

Strauss, S. "To Catch a Cloud." *Technology Review* (May-June 1991): 18-19.

WEE

See **Erosion**

Wells

A well is a hydraulic structure for withdrawal of **groundwater** from **aquifer**s. A well field is an area containing two or more wells. Most wells are constructed to supply water for municipal, industrial, or agricultural use. However, wells are also used for **remediation** of the subsurface (extraction wells), recording water levels and pressure changes (observation wells), water—quality monitoring and protection (monitoring wells), artificial recharge of aquifers (**injection well**s), and the disposal of liquid waste (**deep-well injection**). Vacuum extraction system is a new technology for removing volatile contaminant from the unsaturated zone, in which vapor transport is induced by withdrawing or injecting air through wells screened in the **vadose zone**.

Well construction consists of several operations: (1) drilling, (2) installing the casing, (3) installing a well screen and filter pack, (4) grouting, (5) well development.

Various well drilling technologies have been developed because geologic conditions can range from hard rock such as granite to soft unconsolidated geologic formation such as alluvial **sediment**s.

Selection of a drilling method also depends on the type of the well that will be installed in the borehole, such as a water-supply well or a monitoring well. The two most widely used drilling methods are cable-tool and rotary drilling. The cable-tool percussion method is a relatively simple drilling method developed in China more than 4,000 years ago. Drilling rigs operate by lifting and dropping a string of drilling tools into the borehole. The drill bit crushes and loosens rock into small fragments which form a **slurry** when mixed with water. When the slurry has accumulated so the drilling process is significantly slowed down, it is removed from the borehole with a bailer. In rotary drilling, the borehole is drilled by a rotating bit, and the cuttings are removed from the borehole by continuous circulation of drilling fluid. Boreholes are drilled much faster with this method, and at a greater depth than with the cable-tool method. Other drilling methods include air drilling systems, jet drilling, earth augers, and driven wells.

Though well design depends on hydrogeologic conditions and the purpose of the well, every well has two main elements: the casing and the intake portion or screen. A filter pack of gravel is often placed around the screen to assure good porosity and hydraulic conductivity. After placing the screen and the gravel filter pack, the annular space between the casing and the borehole wall is filled with a slurry of cement or clay. The last phase in well construction is well development. The objective is to remove fine particles around the screen so hydraulic efficiency is improved.

A well is fully penetrating if it is drilled to the bottom of an **aquifer** and is constructed in such a way that it withdraws water from the entire thickness of the aquifer.

Wells are also used for conducting tests to determine aquifer and well characteristics. During an aquifer test, a well is pumped at a constant discharge rate for a period of time, and observation wells are used to record the changes in hydraulic head, also known as **drawdown**. The radius of influence of a pumping well is the radial distance from the center of a well to the point where there is no lowering of the water table or potentiometric surface (the edge of its cone of depression). The collected data are then analyzed to determine hydraulic characteristics. A pumping test with a variable discharge is often used to determine the capacity and the efficiency of the well. A slug test is a simple method for estimating the hydraulic conductivity of an aquifer, a rapid water level change is produced in a piezometer or monitoring well, usually by introducing or withdrawing a "slug" of water. The rise or decline in the water level with time is monitored. The data can be analyzed to estimate hydraulic conductivity of the aquifer.

The predominant tool for extracting vapor or contaminated groundwater from the subsurface is a vertical well. In many situations where environmental remediation is necessary, however, a horizontal well offers a better choice, considering aquifer geometry, groundwater flow patterns, and the geometry of contaminant **plume**s. Extraction of contaminated groundwater is often more efficient with horizontal wells; a horizontal well placed through the core of a plume can recover higher concentrations of contaminants at a given flow rate than a vertical well. In other cases horizontal wells may be the only option, as contaminants are often found directly beneath buildings, **landfill**s, and other obstacles to remedial operations. *See also* Aquifer restoration; Drinking-water supply; Groundwater monitoring; Groundwater pollution; Water table; Water table draw-down

[*Milovan S. Beljin*]

FURTHER READING

Campbell, M., and J. H. Lehr. *Water Well Technology*. New York: McGraw-Hill, 1973.

Driscoll, F. G. *Groundwater and Wells*. St. Paul: Johnson Filtration Systems, 1986.

Nielsen, D. A., and A. I. Johnson. *Ground Water and Vadose Zone Monitoring*. Philadelphia: ASTM, 1990.

Werbach, Adam (1972-)

Environmentalist

Adam Werbach was born in Tarzana, California, the second son of a psychiatrist father and therapist mother. His strong environmental conscience was nurtured by his parents, who were both activists in the **Sierra Club**. Werbach became a Sierra Club member himself at age 13 and formed the Sierra Student Coalition (SSC) at age 19, composed of 300,000 members. He served two years on the Sierra Club's Board of Directors as a member of the Club's national membership committee and volunteer development committee. Then on May 18, 1996, at the age of only 23, Werbach was elected president of the Sierra Club.

It was **David Ross Brower**, 60 years older than Werbach, who ran the campaign for Werbach to be elected president by the 15-member board, which in turn is elected by the Sierra Club membership at large. As the youngest president ever to lead the Sierra Club, Werbach works with the executive director and other staff to manage an organization of about 600,000 members and a $44 million annual budget. The average age of Sierra Club members is around 47, emphasizing the fact that younger generations are currently under-represented in the environmental fields. One of Werbach's goals is to recruit this younger group by appealing

to what interests them—the present and how it will affect their personal future.

Werbach believes: "The **environment** is the primary issue that prompts this generation, my generation, to take social and political action. Our job is to get the word out to them and to give them a place to act on their anxieties and convictions. My goal is to make that place the Sierra Club."

As a high school student, Werbach founded and served as the first director of the Sierra Club's national student program, the Sierra Student Coalition, which has trained, registered, and involved thousands of students in all states with Sierra Club conservation campaigns. He also organized a conference of environmental youth leaders from 20 countries for the first *World Youth Leadership Camp* in 1996. During this same year he earned a B.A. from Brown with a double major in Political science and Modern culture and media.

Werbach has many hobbies, including music, and has toured the United States, Europe, and Asia, singing baritone and playing the guitar with a men's vocal group at Brown University. He has also written several journal articles and a novel entitled *Whirled*, and has worked on several films concerning both natural- and socially-constructed environments.

[*Nicole Beatty*]

Wet scrubber

Devices used to remove pollutants from **flue gas**es. They consist of tanks in which flue gases are allowed to mix with some liquid. If the pollutant to be removed is soluble in water, water alone can be used as the scrubbing agent. However, most scrubbers are used to remove **sulfur dioxide**, which is not sufficiently soluble in water. The liquid used in such cases, therefore, is one that will chemically react with the sulfur dioxide. A solution of sodium carbonate is such a solution. When sulfur dioxide reacts with sodium carbonate, it forms sodium sulfite, which can be drawn off at the bottom of the tank. *See also* Flue-gas scrubbing

Wetlands

During the last four decades, several definitions of the term wetland have been offered by different sources. Today's legal and jurisdictional delineations were published in the *Corps of Engineers Wetlands Delineation Manual* and revised in 1989. It states that wetlands are "those areas that are inundated or saturated by surface or ground water at a frequency and duration sufficient to support, and that under usual circumstances support a prevalence of vegetation typically adapted for life in saturated soil conditions."

For an area to be a wetland, it must have certain **hydrology**, **soil**s, and vegetation. Vegetation is dominated

Wetlands with blue geese and snow geese.

by **species** tolerant of saturated soil conditions. They exhibit a variety of **adaptation**s that allow them to grow, compete, and reproduce in standing water or waterlogged soils lacking oxygen. Soils are wet or have developed under permanent or periodic saturation. The **hydrologic cycle** produces **anaerobic** soils, excluding a strictly upland plant community.

There are seven major types of wetlands that can be divided into two major groups: coastal and inland. Coastal wetlands are those that are influenced by the ebb and flow of tides and include tidal salt marshes, tidal freshwater marshes, and **mangrove swamp**s.

Salt marshes exist in protected coastlines in the middle to high latitudes. Plant and animals in these areas are adapted to **salinity**, periodic **flooding**, and extremes in temperature. These marshes are prevalent along the east and Gulf coast of the United States as well as narrow belts on the west coast and along the Alaskan coastline.

Tidal freshwater marshes occur inland from the tidal salt marshes and host a variety of grasses and perennial broad-leaved plants. They are found primarily along the middle and south Atlantic coasts and along the coasts of Louisiana and Texas.

Mangrove swamps occur in subtropical and tropical regions of the world. Mangrove refers to the type of salt-tolerant trees that dominate the vegetation of this wetland. In the United States these wetlands are only found in a few places. The largest areas in the United States are found in the southern tip of Florida.

Inland wetlands, which constitute the majority of wetlands in the United States, occur across a variety of climatic zones. They can be divided into four types: northern peatlands, southern deep water swamps, freshwater marshes, and riparian **ecosystem**s.

Freshwater marshes represent a variety of different inland wetlands. They have shallow water, peat accumulation, and grow cattails, arrowheads, and different species of grasses and sedges. Major freshwater marshes include the Florida **Everglades**, **Great Lakes** coastal marshes, and areas of Minnesota and the Dakotas.

Southern deepwater swamps are freshwater woody wetlands with standing water for most of the growing season. The most recognizable type of vegetation is cypress. They are either fed by rainwater or occur in alluvial positions that are annually flooded. These wetlands are found in the southeast United States.

Northern peatlands consist of deep accumulation of peat. Primary locations are Minnesota, Wisconsin, Michigan, areas of the Northeast that have been affected by the last **glaciation**, and some mountain and coastal bays in the southeast. Bogs are marshes or swamps that lack contact with local **groundwater** and are acidified by organic acids from plants. They are noted for **nutrient** deficiency and water-logged conditions with vegetation adapted to conserve nutrients in this **environment**.

Riparian forested wetlands, occurring along rivers and streams, are occasionally flooded but generally dry for a large part of the growing season. The most common type of wetland in the United States, they are often productive because of the periodic addition of nutrients with **sediment** deposited during floods.

Wetlands are valuable in several ways. Because of their appearance and **biodiversity** alone, wetlands are a valuable resource. Many types of **wildlife**, including **endangered species** such as the **whooping crane** and the **alligator**, inhabit or use wetlands. Over 50 percent of the 800 species of protected migratory birds rely on wetlands. Wetlands are valuable for **recreation**, attracting hunters of ducks and geese. Over 95 percent of the fish and shellfish that are taken commercially depend on wetland **habitat** in their life cycles.

Forest wetlands are an important source of lumber, and other wetland vegetation, such as cattails or woody shrubs, could someday be harvested for energy production. Peat is used in potted plants, and as a soil amendment, particularly to grow grass sod.

Wetlands intercept and store storm waters reducing the peak runoff and slowing stream discharges, reducing flood damage. In coastal areas wetlands act as buffers to reduce the energy of ocean storms before they reach more populated areas and cause severe damage. Although most wetlands do not, some may recharge underlying groundwater. Wetlands can improve surface **water quality** by the removal of nutrients and toxic materials as water runs over or through it. Most importantly, wetlands may play a significant role in the global cycling of **nitrogen**, sulfur, **methane** and **carbon dioxide**.

The current movement of conservation has encouraged the "reconstruction" of wetlands that have been destroyed through a no-net-loss policy. Wetlands are restored to protect coastlines, improve water quality, and replace lost habitat. *See also* Commercial fishing; Convention on the Conservation of Migratory Species of Wild Animals; Convention on Wetlands of International Importance; Riparian land; Soil eluviation

[*James L. Anderson*]

FURTHER READING

A Citizen's Guide to Protecting Wetlands. Washington, DC: National Wildlife Federation, 1989.

IUCN Environmental Law Centre staff, eds. *The Legal Aspects of the Protection of Wetlands.* Gland, Switzerland: IUCN—The World Conservation Union, 1989.

Kusler, J. A., and M. E. Kentula, eds. *Wetland Creation and Restoration: The Status of the Science.* Covelo, CA: Island Press, 1990.

Mitsch, W. J., and J. G. Gorselink. *Wetlands.* New York: Van Norstrand Reinhold, 1993.

Williams, M., ed. *Wetlands: A Threatened Landscape.* Cambridge, MA: Basil Blackwell, 1990.

Wetlands Convention

See **Convention on Wetlands of International Importance (1971)**

Whales

Whales are aquatic mammals of the order Cetacea. The term is now applied to about 80 **species** of baleen whales and "toothed" whales, which include **dolphins**, porpoises, and non-baleen whales, as well as extinct whales. Cetaceans range from the largest known animal, the blue whale (*Baleanoptera musculus*), at a length up to 102 feet (31 m) to the diminutive vaquita (*Phoceona sinus*) at five feet (1.5 m).

Whales evolved from land animals and have lived exclusively in the aquatic **environment** for at least 50 million years, developing fish-like bodies with no rear limbs, powerful tails, and blow holes for breathing through the top of their heads. They have successfully colonized the seas from polar regions to the tropics, occupying ecological **niche**s from the water's surface to ocean floor.

Baleen whales, such the right whale (*Balaena glacialis*), the blue whale (*Balaenoptera musculus*), and the minke whale (*Balaenoptera acutorostrata*), differ considerably from the toothed whales in their morphology, behavior, and feeding ecology. To feed, a baleen whale strains seawater through baleen plates in the roof of its mouth, capturing **plankton** and small fish. Only the gray whale (*Eschrichtius robustus*) sifts ocean **sediment**s for bottom-dwelling invertebrates. Baleen whales migrate in small groups and travel up to 5,000 miles (8,000 km) to winter feeding grounds in warmer seas.

The toothed whales, such as the killer whale (*Orcinus orca*) and the pilot whale (*Globicephala* spp), feed on a variety of fish, cephalopods, and other marine mammals through a variety of active predatory methods. They travel in larger groups that appear to be matriarchal. Some are a nuisance to **commercial fishing** because they target catches and damage equipment.

Large whales have virtually no natural predators besides humans, and nearly all baleen whales are now listed as **endangered species**, mostly due to commercial whaling. In the southern hemisphere, the blue whale has been reduced from 250,000 at the beginning of the century to its current level of a few hundred. The International Whaling Commission (IWC), which has been setting limits on whaling operations since its inception in 1946, has little power over whaling nations, such as Japan and Norway, who continue to catch hundreds of whales a year under an exemption allowing whaling for scientific research. *See also* American Cetacean Society; Dolphins; International Convention for the Regulation of Whaling

[*David A. Duffus*]

FURTHER READING

Baker, M. L. *Whales, Dolphins, and Porpoises of the World.* Garden City, NY: Doubleday, 1987.

Dolphins, Porpoises, and Whales of the World: The IUCN Red Data Book. Gland, Switzerland: IUCN—The World Conservation Union, 1991.

Ellis, R. *Men and Whales.* New York: Knopf, 1991.

Evans, G. H. *The Natural History of Whales and Dolphins.* New York: Facts on File, 1987.

U. S. National Marine Fisheries Service, Humpback Whale Recovery Team. *Final Recovery Plan for the Humpback Whale (Megaptera novaeangliae).* Silver Spring, MD: U. S. National Marine Fisheries Service, 1991.

Humpback whale breaching.

U. S. National Marine Fisheries Service, Right Whale Recovery Team. *Final Recovery Plan for the Northern Right Whale (Eubaleana glacialis).* Silver Spring, MD: U. S. National Marine Fisheries Service, 1991.

Whaling

Although subsistence whaling by aboriginal peoples has been carried on for thousands of years, it is mainly within about the last one thousand years that humans have pursued whales for commercial gain. The history of whaling may be divided into three periods: the historical whaling era, from 1000 A.D. to 1864-1871; the modern whaling era, from 1864-1871 to the 1970s; and the decline of whaling, from the 1970s to the present.

The Basques of northern Spain were the earliest commercial whalers. Concentrating on the capture of right whales (*Baleana glacialis*), Basque whaling spread over most of the north Pacific Ocean as local populations dwindled from **overhunting**. Like many whales that were later hunted to near **extinction**, the right whale was slow-moving and coastal.

Commercial whaling is considered to have begun when the Basques took their whaling across the Atlantic to Newfoundland and Labrador from about 1530, where between 25,000 and 40,000 whales were taken in the next eighty years. The search for bowhead whale (*Baleana mysticetus*) in the Arctic Ocean and the sperm whale (*Physeter catadon*) in the Atlantic and Pacific provided useful whale oil, waxes, and whalebone, actually the baleen from the whale's mouth. The oil proved to be an excellent lubricant and was used as fuel for lighting. Waxes from body tissues made household candles. A digestive chemical was employed as a fixative in perfumes. Baleen served the same purposes as many plastics and light metals do today. Umbrella ribs, corset stays, and buggy whips all used the material.

The first **species** targeted were slow swimmers that stayed close to the coasts, making them easy prey. Whalers used sail and oar-powered vessels and threw harpoons to capture their prey, then dragged it back to the mainland. As technology improved and the slow-swimming whales began to disappear, whalers sought the larger and faster-swimming whales.

The historical whaling period ended for several reasons. At the end of the nineteenth century, **petroleum** was discovered to be a good substitute for whale oil in lamps. Also, the whales that were so easily caught were becoming scarce. The technology required to take advantage of larger and faster whales was first used by a Norwegian sealing captain, Svend Foyn. Between 1864 and 1871 he combined the steam-powered boat, cannon-fired harpoon, grenade tipped harpoon head, and a rubber compensator to absorb the shock on harpoon lines to catch the whales. A steam-powered winch brought the catch in. Although the American whaler, Thomas Welcome Roys, was responsible for much of the development of the rocket harpoon, it was Foyn and the

Norwegians that packaged the technology that would dominate whaling for the next century.

Modern whaling expanded in two sequences. In the earlier period, whaling was dominated by the spread of whaling stations in the European Arctic and around Iceland, Greenland, Newfoundland. At the same time, it spread on the Pacific coast of Canada and the United States, around South Africa, Australia, and most significantly, Antarctica. Before 1925 whaling was tied to shore processing stations, and whaling could still be regulated from the shore. After 1925 that system broke down as the stern-slipway floating factory was developed, making it unnecessary for whalers to come ashore.

During the modern whaling period, many populations were brought near extinction as no international quotas or regulations existed. Sperm whales once numbered in the millions, and between 1804 and 1876, United States whalers alone killed an estimated 225,000. The gray whale (*Eschrichtius robustus*), has disappeared in the North Atlantic due to early whaling, although the Pacific populations have rebounded significantly. The blue whale (*Balaenoptera musculus*), the largest mammal on earth, was preferred by whalers for its size after improved technology enabled them to be captured. Though protected since 1966, the blue whale has been slow to regain its numbers, and there may be less than 1,000 of these creatures left in the world. Also slow to recover has been the fin whale (*Balaenoptera physalus*), which was hunted intensively after blue whales became less numerous.

As more whales were hunted and populations diminished, the need for an international regulatory agency became apparent. The **International Convention for the Regulation of Whaling** of 1946 formed the International Whaling Commission (IWC) consisting of 38 member nations for this purpose, but the group was largely ineffectual for about 20 years. Growing environmental and political pressure during the 1960s and 1970s resulted in the establishment of the New Management Procedure (NMP) that scientifically assessed whale populations to determine safe catch limits. In 1982 IWC decided to suspend all commercial whaling as of 1986, to reopen in 1996, or when populations had rebounded enough to maintain a **sustained yield**.

However, as of 1993, some whaling nations, Japan and Norway in particular, threatened to leave the commission and resume commercial whaling. Iceland has already left the association. Meanwhile, the IWC is looking forward to new projects, including the protection of **dolphins** and porpoises.

Today, whaling is permitted by aboriginal groups in Canada, the United States, the Caribbean, and Siberia. Unregulated "pirate whalers" continue to kill and market whale meat, and scientific whaling continues to supply meat products primarily to the Japanese market. At the same time, various scientific specialty groups are working on comprehensive population assessments.

Because of migratory habits and the difficulty in sighting deep ocean whales, it is difficult to accurately estimate their population levels. In many cases, it is impossible to ascertain whether or not a species is in danger. It is clear, though, that the world's whales cannot sustain hunting at anywhere near the rates they had been harvested in the past. *See also* American Cetacean Society; Environmental law; Migration

[*David A. Duffus*]

FURTHER READING

Credlund, A. G. *Whales and Whaling*. New York: Seven Hills Books, 1983.

Holy, S. J. "Whale Mining, Whale Saving." *Marine Policy* (July 1985): 192-213.

M'Gonigle, R. M. "The 'Economizing' of Ecology: Why Big, Rare Whales Still Die." *Ecology Law Quarterly* 9 (1980): 119-237.

Tonnessen, J. N. and A. O. Johnsen. *The History of Modern Whaling*. London: Hurst and Co., 1982.

White, Gilbert (1720-1793)

English naturalist

Gilbert White was born in 1720 in the village of Selborne, Hampshire, England. The eldest of eight children, he was expected to attend college and join the priesthood. He earned his bachelor's degree at Oxford in 1743 and his master's degree in 1746. A fair student, White was well known for his rambunctious and romantic exploits.

White developed a fuller sense of religious identity after college. He was ordained a priest three years after leaving Oxford and was subsequently assigned to a parish near his family home in Hampshire, known as "The Wakes." His religious perspective played an important role throughout the rest of his life, and this is reflected in the beauty and gentleness of his writings.

It was at The Wakes that White began studying **nature** and recording his observations in letters and daily diary notations, which also provide an interesting look at various aspects of local life. He was highly susceptible to carriage sickness and rarely traveled, and his writings therefore focused solely on his immediate **environment**—the gardens in the village of Selborne. He organized his observations in what he called his "Garden Kalendar," and in 1789, these notes, letters, and memos were combined to comprise *The Natural History and Antiquities of Selborne*, now considered a classic of English literature.

White's ability to write in a clear and unpretentious poetic style is evident throughout the book. He closely watched leaf warblers, cuckoos, and swallows, and unlike his contemporaries, he describes not just the anatomy and plumage of the birds, but their habits and **habitat**s. He was the first to identify the harvest mouse, Britain's smallest mammal, and sketched its physical traits as well as noting its

As the Japanese whaling fleet factory ship *Nisshin Maru* hauls a whale aboard in the ocean off Antarctica, a Greenpeace inflatable protests against whaling.

behaviors. *The Natural History* also presents descriptive passages of insect biology and wild flowers White found at Selborne.

After a brief illness, White died alone in his family home at the age of 72.

[*Kimberley A. Peterson*]

FURTHER READING

Lockley, R. M. *Gilbert White*. London: H. F. and G. Witherby, 1954.

Jenkins, A. C. *The Naturalists: Pioneers of Natural History*. New York: Mayflower Books, 1978.

White House Office on Environmental Policy

See **Council on Environmental Quality**

White, Lynn Townsend, Jr. (1907-1987)

American historian

For most readers interested in environmental issues, White is known by only one article: "The Historical Roots of Our Ecological Crisis," first published in *Science* in 1967, and widely reprinted. That article, like most of White's work, grew out of his professional interest in medieval technology, including technology's role in "dominating **nature**." Born in San Francisco, schooled at Stanford and the Union Theological Seminary, White received a doctorate in history from Harvard University in 1934. He taught at Princeton and Stanford Universities, spent fifteen years as the President of Mills College (1943-1958), and retired from his position of univeristy professor of history at the University of California in Los Angeles in 1974.

White received most of the honors his profession could bestow. He was a founding member of the Society for the History of Technology, served as its president, and was also elected president of the History of Science Society, president of the American Historical Association, and a Fellow of the American Academy of Arts and Sciences. Perhaps the best introduction to his work can be obtained from two collections of articles, *Machina ex Deo: Essays in the Dynamism of Western Culture* (1968) and *Medieval Religion and Technology: Collected Essays* (1978).

White's article on the ecological crisis traced that crisis back to "modern science [as] an extrapolation of natural

theology." The modern technology that emerged from that science "is at least partly to be explained as an Occidental voluntarist realization of the Christian dogma of man's transcendence of, and rightful mastery over, nature." White then concluded that, since modern science and technology have led us into an ecological crisis, "Christianity bears a huge burden of guilt." Numerous articles over many years either picked up on White's argument or took issue with it, a debate White extended by "Continuing the Conversation" in 1973, and a debate that continues today.

Although White's article received widespread attention, his more significant contributions may have been achieved through his extensive research on technology and its relationship to culture and society. Of particular importance has been his establishment of connections between religion and the way a culture perceives technology. Such perceptions have profound implications for human relationships to the **environment**. White also embraced the cause of women's rights, using his presidency at Mills College as a pulpit to advance those rights, especially in higher education. Feminist issues, such as reproduction or status, also have profound implications for human-environment relationships, and his writings in this area are still worth reading today. *See also* Ecology; Environmental education

[*Gerald L. Young*]

FURTHER READING

Eckberg, D. L., and T. J. Blocker. "Varieties of Religious Involvement and Environmental Concerns: Testing the Lynn White Thesis." *Journal for the Scientific Study of Religion* 28 (December 1989): 509-517.

Hall, B. S. "Lynn Townsend White, Jr. (1907-1987)." *Technology and Culture* 30 (January 1989): 194-213.

Shaiko, R. G. "Religion, Politics, and Environmental Concern: A Powerful Mix of Passions." *Social Science Quarterly* 68 (June 1987): 244-262.

White, L. T., Jr. "The Historical Roots of Our Ecological Crisis." *Science* 155 (10 March 1967): 1203-7.

Whooping crane (*Grus americana*)

The whooping crane has long been considered the symbol for **wildlife conservation** in the United States. This large, white, wading bird of the family Gruidae is our tallest North American bird, standing nearly 5 feet (1.5 m) tall and having a wingspan of seven and a half feet (2.3 m). Whooping cranes have been threatened with **extinction** for most of this century. **Overhunting** in the latter part of the nineteenth and early twentieth centuries, as well as **habitat** loss—primarily due to the conversion of prairie **wetlands** into agricultural land—have been major contributors to this decline. In modern times, the number one cause of death in fledged birds has been collision with high power lines.

In 1937 the federal government established the Arkansas National Wildlife Refuge on the south Texas coast, which is the wintering grounds for the whooping crane, in order to protect this **species**' dwindling population. At the time the refuge was established, the population was at an all time low of 12 birds with a probable founding group of only six to eight birds. There were 31 birds found during a 1950 census and 36 were located in 1960. The year 1961 marked the first captive breeding program for the whooping crane.

Whooping cranes usually reach maturity at four years of age. After that they establish a lifelong mate with whom they will typically nest once a year, although a pair will skip a nesting season if resources are scarce, or, in some cases for no reason whatsoever. Even though two eggs are usually laid, the parents will only raise one of the chicks. With this in mind, part of the captive breeding program involved the removal of one of the eggs from the whopping cranes' nest for mechanical incubation. In 1967, 50 eggs were removed for incubation at the Patuxent Wildlife Research Center in Laurel, Maryland. There were 48 birds at the end of 1967, the same year the Whooping crane was listed as a federally **endangered species**.

Several years of egg removal and artificial incubation followed. Beginning in 1975, eggs from whooping crane nests in their primary nesting area, Wood Buffalo National Park, as well as captive-bred eggs, were placed in the nests of sandhill cranes of Grays Lake, Idaho. This cross-fostering experiment was done to get the more numerous sandhill cranes to help raise whooping cranes to adulthood, and thus increase the population at a faster rate. The experiment has been successful and by 1977, the whooping crane population increased to 120 birds. Today there are nearly 300 in the wild and in captivity.

A flock of 14 captive-raised birds was reintroduced to the Kissimmee Prairie in Florida during the winter of 1993. Nineteen more were released within the year, however, 70% of these released birds were lost due to bobcat predation. Nearly 50 additional whooping cranes are scheduled to be released at this site by the turn of the millennium. An additional facility in Calgary, Canada, has accepted over 30 birds since 1992 in order to establish a third captive flock. *See also* Captive propogation and reintroduction

[*Eugene C. Beckham*]

FURTHER READING

Ehrlich, P., D. Dobkin, and D. Wheye. *The Birder's Handbook*. New York: Simon & Schuster, 1988.

———. *Birds In Jeopardy*. Stanford: Stanford University Press, 1992.

May, Peter and David Henry. A Whooping Crane Reintroduction Project on the Canadian Prairies: Identifying Relevant Issues Using Expert Consultation. Endangered Species Update, vol. 12, no. 7: (1995).

Temple, S., ed. *Endangered Birds: Management Techniques for Preserving Threatened Species*. Madison: University of Wisconsin Press, 1977.

U.S. Fish and Wildlife Service report. Whooping crane (*Grus americana*) population and habitat viability assessment.

Wild and Scenic Rivers Act (1968)

The Wild and Scenic Rivers Act was passed in 1968, during the same week as the National Trails System Act, in the shadow of the **Wilderness Act (1964)**, and in the aftermath of a heated controversy involving **dams** in the Grand Canyon. The main focus of the law is to prevent designated rivers from being dammed.

The act establishes three categories of rivers: wild, scenic, and recreational. *Wild rivers* are completely undeveloped and accessible only by trail. *Scenic rivers* are mainly undeveloped but are accessible by roads. *Recreational rivers* have frequent road access and may have been developed in some ways. As was the case in the Wilderness Act, there would be no transfer of lands from one agency to another after designations were made. That is, designated rivers in national forests are managed by the **Forest Service**, designated rivers in the **Bureau of Land Management** jurisdiction are managed by the BLM, etc. Even state agencies could manage designated rivers. The law provides for the preservation of land at least one-quarter mile wide on both sides of designated rivers. The act emphasizes the use of easements on private lands, rather than acquisition, to achieve this purpose.

The first wild rivers bill, based primarily on studies done by the Agriculture and Interior Departments, was introduced in 1965 by Senator Frank Church of Idaho. The main controversy of the bill focused on which rivers to protect. In order to lessen opposition, only rivers with the support of home state senators would be immediately designated. The Senate passed the bill in early 1966. A wild rivers bill was not seriously considered in the House that year, so the process began again in 1967. The Senate passed a modified version of Church's bill in August 1967. There was some concern that the House would not pass a bill before the end of the session, but under the leadership of Representative John Saylor of Pennsylvania, it did so in September 1968. The House and Senate worked out a compromise bill in conference, and the law was signed by President Lyndon Johnson in October.

Due to the compromise involving home state approval for each designated river, only eight rivers were designated immediately by the act, totaling 773 miles (1,244 kilometers). Twenty-seven rivers were designated for further study. The law allows for the study and potential inclusion of rivers not listed in the original act. Additionally, rivers could be added if

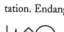

states request the federal government to designate a river in the state as part of the system (this has happened for two rivers in Ohio and one in Maine). This system encompasses rivers throughout the country. For example, the first group of designated rivers were in California, Idaho, Minnesota, Missouri, New Mexico, and Wisconsin. As of 1990, 9,318 miles (14,993 kilometers) had been designated under the act, with 26 additional river segments designated by the **Alaska National Interest Lands Conservation Act** of 1980.

[*Christopher McGrory Klyza*]

FURTHER READING

Allin, C. W. *The Politics of Wilderness Preservation*. Westport, CT: Greenwood Press, 1982.

Dana, S. T., and S. K. Fairfax. *Forest and Range Policy*. 2nd ed. New York: McGraw-Hill, 1980.

Palmer, T. *Endangered Rivers and the Conservation Movement*. Berkeley: University of California Press, 1986.

Wild river

By the mid-1960s, many rivers in the United States had been dammed or otherwise manipulated for flood control, **recreation**, and other water development projects. There was a growing concern that rivers in their natural state would soon disappear. By 1988, for example, roughly 600,000 miles (965,400 kilometers), 17 percent of all the rivers that once were free-running, rivers—had been trapped behind 60,000 **dams**.

In 1968, Congress passed the **Wild and Scenic Rivers Act**, establishing a program to study and protect outstanding, free-flowing rivers. Federal land management agencies such as the **Forest Service** and the **National Park Service** (NPS) were directed to identify rivers on their lands for potential inclusion in the National Wild and Scenic Rivers System. In 1982, the NPS published the National Rivers Inventory (NRI), a list of 1,524 river segments eligible under the act, though budgetary constraints prevented them from including all eligible rivers.

Eligible river segments must be undammed and have at least one outstanding resource—a **wildlife** habitat, or other recreational, scenic, historic, or geological feature. Rivers can be added to the national system through an act of Congress or by order of the **U.S. Department of the Interior** upon official request from an individual state. Congress intended all types of free-flowing rivers to be included, remote rivers as well as those that flow through urban areas, provided they meet the established criteria. Both designated rivers and rivers being studied for inclusion in the

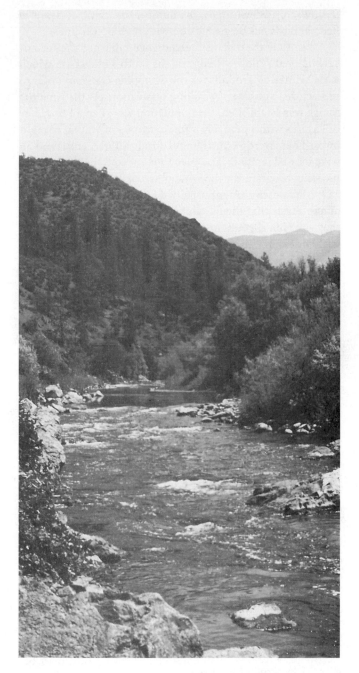

The Klamath River in northern California, designated a wild river under the Wild and Scenic Rivers Act.

system receive numerous protections. The act prohibits the building of hydroelectric or other water development projects and limits mineral extraction in a designated or study river corridor.

The act also mandates the development of a land management plan, covering an average of 320 acres per river mile and roughly one quarter mile on either side of the river, which must include measures to conserve the riverside land and resources. If the land is federally owned, the responsible agency is required to specify allowable activities on the land, depending on whether the river is classified as wild, scenic, or recreational. If it is privately owned, federal and state agencies will coordinate with local governments and landowners to specify appropriate **land use**s within the corridor using zoning and other ordinances.

Identifying a potential wild and scenic river often stirs controversy within local communities, usually among riparian landowners concerned that such a designation will curtail the use of their property. There is no federal power to zone private land, and although the act allows federal agencies to purchase land in a designated corridor, there are strict limitations. Generally, these agencies prefer to assist state, local and private interests in developing a cooperative plan to conserve the river's resources.

Aware of the importance of riverways for local economic development, and concerned about the issue of property rights, Congress made the Wild and Scenic Rivers Act flexible. Riparian landowners are not forced to move from their land, and designation does not affect existing land uses along the river, such as farming, mining, and logging. Designation can lead to some restrictions on new development, but most development will be allowed as long as it occurs in a manner that does not adversely affect the character of the river. These questions are addressed on a site-specific basis in the management plan, which is developed by all affected and interested parties, including landowners.

Currently, there are 152 rivers designated, for a total of 10,516 miles (16,920 kilometers). Some of the segments included are the American and Klamath rivers in California, the Rio Grande in Texas, the upper and middle Delaware in New York, New Jersey and Pennsylvania, and the Bluestone in West Virginia. *See also* Ecotourism; Federal Land Policy and Management Act; Land-use control; Riparian land; Riparian rights

[*Cathryn McCue*]

FURTHER READING

Coyle, K. J. *The American Rivers Guide to Wild and Scenic River Designation: A Primer on National River Conservation.* Washington, DC: American Rivers, 1988.

Wilderness

Wilderness is land that humans neither inhabit nor cultivate. Through the ages of western culture, as the human relation to land has changed, the meaning and perception of wilderness also has changed. At first wilderness was to be either conquered or shunned. At times, it was the place for contrition or banishment, as in the biblical account of the Israelites condemned to wander 40 years in the wilderness. To European settlers of North America, wilderness was the untamed land entered only by the adventurous or perhaps the foolhardy. But the wilderness also held riches, making it new land to be exploited, tamed, and ultimately managed. Few saw wilderness as having value in its own right.

The idea of wilderness as land deserving of protection and preservation for its own sake is largely a product of late nineteenth and twentieth century North American thinking. Rapidly expanding cultivation and industry not only created

wealth, but it also increased the nonconsumptive, intrinsic values of wilderness. Gradually, people began to perceive the wilderness as a land of enjoyment and welcome solitude through intimacy with **nature**. For some, it became an important link to their cultural past, providing assurance that some part of the earth would be left in its primeval condition for future generations, and to many their image of the wilderness is as important as its physical reality.

This relatively new attitude toward wild lands has been fostered by scientific considerations. Such lands can hold a tremendous store of unadulterated native genetic material that may be important in maintaining diversity within and among **species**. Wilderness also can support nondestructive, unobtrusive research projects, which serve as references from which to gauge ecological effects in other areas.

The value of wilderness was promoted from roughly the mid–nineteenth century to mid–twentieth century by many influential people, including George Catlin, **Henry David Thoreau**, **John Muir**, and most notably **Aldo Leopold** and Robert Marshall. Their ideas were ultimately incorporated into the platforms of two major organizations: the **Wilderness Society** and the **Sierra Club**. With the creation of these groups, a formal movement had begun to convince the public and lawmakers that wilderness should be preserved and protected. A significant event in this movement occurred in 1951 at the Sierra Club's second Wilderness Conference when Howard Zahniser of the Wilderness Society proposed the idea of a federal wilderness protection bill. Zahniser's work came to fruition 13 years later, four months after his death.

In 1964, the United States Congress passed the **Wilderness Act**, establishing the National Wilderness Preservation System (NWPS). The act grew out of a concern that an expanding population, with its accompanying settlement and mechanization, would leave no lands in the United States or its possessions in their natural condition. Congress intended to preserve areas of federal lands "to secure for the American people of present and future generations the benefits of an enduring resource of wilderness." The act defines wilderness as follows: "A wilderness, in contrast with those areas where man and his own works dominate the landscape, is hereby recognized as an area where the earth and its community of life are untrammeled by man, where man himself is a visitor who does not remain." Further, wilderness is to "be protected and managed so as to preserve its natural conditions," unimpaired for future use and enjoyment.

The National Wilderness Preservation System began with 54 wilderness areas totaling a little over 9 million acres (3.6 million ha), which were administered by the **Forest Service** in the **U.S. Department of Agriculture**. In the first three decades after passage of the Wilderness Act, the system has grown to nearly 500 units covering almost 95 million acres (38.5 million ha), which is about the size of Montana. These units are administered by the Forest Service, and by the **National Park Service**, **Fish and Wildlife Service**, and **Bureau of Land Management**, in the **U.S. Department of the Interior**. The System is expected to increase to about 100 million acres (40.5 million ha), the size of California, following the passage of the California Desert Protection Act.

The years of greatest growth for the wilderness system were from 1978 to 1984. In 1980, 83 units comprising more than 61 million acres (24.7 million ha) were added to this system; most of this land (56 million acres [22.7 million ha] in 35 units) was added in Alaska with passage of **Alaska National Interest Land Conservation Act**. All but six states, in the northeast and midwest, have wilderness areas. The western United States, with about 20 percent of the nation's population (11 percent in California) has almost 95 percent of NWPS lands. However, the largest tracts of wilderness are in Alaska, which contains nearly two–thirds of the wilderness system acreage.

Although the Wilderness Act generally defines the minimum size for wilderness as 5,000 acres (2,025 ha), it permits land "of sufficient size as to make practicable its preservation and use in an unimpaired condition." Consequently, wilderness areas range in size from the nearly 9-million-acre (3.6-million-ha) Wrangell–Saint Elias Wilderness in Alaska to the 6-acre (2.4-ha) Pelican Island Wilderness in Florida.

In 1989, 25 years after its establishment, the wilderness system contained examples of 157 (60 percent) of the 261 types of **ecosystem**s identified in the United States. Most wildernesses are in Alaska and in moderate to high elevation regions of the western conterminous states; low elevation **grasslands** and coastal systems, **deciduous forests**, **deserts**, and the basin and range province are poorly represented. Ecosystem representation will increase to more than 80 percent with passage of the California Desert Protection Act.

In addition to designated wilderness areas in the NWPS, Congress has established the National Scenic Trails System and the Wild and Scenic Rivers System. Also, several states have designated their own form of wilderness areas, the most notable of which is the Adirondack Forest Preserve in northern New York. These state systems, which are of various types and purity, help broaden the diversity of protected ecosystems and their allowable uses.

Despite the wilderness movement, not everyone agrees that wilderness preservation is a good idea. Opponents object to the restrictions imposed by the Wilderness Act, arguing that they "lock up" huge tracts of land, greatly limiting their use and value to society. The act prohibits roads, use of motorized vehicles or equipment, mechanical means of transport, structures, and commercial enterprises, including timber harvesting. Some low impact uses, such as hiking, hunting, and fishing are allowed, as are limited livestock grazing and mining.

Before passage of the Wilderness Act, the debate over wilderness concerned whether or not it should be preserved. However, after 1964 the debate shifted to two major questions: How much is enough, and how should wilderness be managed? The first question will be nearly settled, at least in law, with passage of the California Desert Protection Act. This will probably be the last sizable addition to the wilderness areas in the United States. The second question may seem oxymoronic, but it presents a substantial challenge to the federal agencies charged with overseeing the health and welfare of these areas. As population pressures increase, decisions become more difficult. For example, wilderness and resource experts must determine an acceptable level of grazing; they must also decide what role fire should play; and, perhaps most importantly, the amount of recreational activity to be allowed.

These management issues are dynamic, and the concept of wilderness likely will change in the future as society's values change. Moreover, decisions regarding management of adjacent lands will influence the management of wilderness areas. Finally, ecosystems themselves change—that which is preserved today will not be what exists tomorrow, as fires, storms, volcanic eruptions, and ecological **succession** reshape the landscape.

Concerns, challenges, and emotional debate over preservation of native ecosystems have arisen in other parts of the world, including Europe and the **Amazon Basin**. Although international concepts of wilderness are different from that in the United States, other countries are studying the American model for possible adaptation to their own situations. Apart from certain differences, concepts of wildernesses around the globe have some strong commonalities: Wilderness is the antithesis of industry; it exists in the body of the earth and in the mind of humanity; and in wilderness lies the ballast of civilization. *See also* Adirondack Mountains; Biodiversity; Frontier economy; National park; National forest; National wildlife refuge; Old-growth forest; Overgrazing; Wild and Scenic Rivers Act; Wild river; Wilderness Study Area; Wildfire; Wildlife; Wildlife management

[*Ronald D. Taskey*]

FURTHER READING

Hendee, J. C., G. H. Stankey, and R. C. Lucas. *Wilderness Management.* Golden, CO: North American Press, 1990.

Journal of Forestry 91 (February 1993).

U. S. Forest Service. *The Principal Laws Relation to Forest Service Activities.* Agriculture Handbook No. 453. Washington, DC: U. S. Government Printing Office, 1978.

Wilderness Act (1964)

The Wilderness Act of 1964 established the National Wilderness Preservation System, an area of land that now encompasses over 95 million acres (38.5 million ha). According to the law, **wilderness** is "an area where the Earth and its community of life are untrammeled by man, where man himself is a visitor who does not remain.... land retaining its primeval character and influence, without permanent improvements or human habitation, which is protected and managed so as to preserve its natural conditions." This law represents the core idea of preservation: the need to preserve large amounts of land in its natural condition. This idea, which arose in the late 1800s, is in stark contrast to the desire to control **nature** and exploit the resources of nature for economic gain.

The early preservation movement focused on protecting natural areas through their designation as **national park**s. The birth of the wilderness system, however, can be traced back to the period around 1920. In 1919, Arthur Carhart, a landscape architect, recommended that the area around Trapper's Lake in the White Mountain National Forest of Colorado be kept roadless, a recommendation that was followed. A few years later, he recommended that a roadless area be established in the Superior National Forest of Minnesota, a recommendation that was also followed (this area was later named the **Boundary Waters Canoe Area**). In 1921, **Aldo Leopold**, then a **Forest Service** employee in New Mexico, proposed that large areas of land be set aside as wilderness in the national forests. For Leopold, wilderness would be an area large enough to absorb a two-week pack trip, "devoid of roads, artificial trails, cottages, or other works of man." He recommended that such an area be established in the Gila National Forest in New Mexico. The next year, Leopold's superiors acted on his recommendation and established a 574,000-acre (232,400-ha) wilderness area.

The first attempt to establish a more general wilderness policy by the Forest Service came in 1929 when the agency issued Regulation L-20. This directed the Chief of the Forest Service to establish a series of "primitive areas" in which primitive conditions would be maintained. Instructions on implementing this regulation, however, indicated that timber, forage, and **water resources** could still be developed in these areas. This effort was plagued by unclear directives and the lack of support of many foresters, who favored the use of resources, not their preservation.

The issue of Forest Service wilderness designation increased in importance in the 1930s, primarily due to the concern of the Forest Service that all of its scenic areas would be transferred to the National Park Service for management. Robert Marshall, head of the Recreation and Lands Division in the Forest Service, led the fight within the agency to increase wilderness designation on Forest Service lands. He and his supporters argued that increased wilderness designation was wise because: 1) it would demonstrate to Congress that the Forest Service could protect its scenic resources and that transfer of these lands to the National Park Service was unnecessary; 2) it would be several years before these resources might be needed, so they could be protected until they were needed; 3) wilderness and its recreation, research, and preservation uses were suitable for national forest lands. These arguments led to the adoption of the U-Regulations in 1939, which were more precise and restrictive than Regulation L-20.

Three new wild land classifications were established by these regulations. "Wilderness" areas were to be at least 100,000 acres (40,500 ha) in size, designated by the Secretary of Agriculture, and contain no roads, motorized transportation, timber harvesting, or occupation. "Wild" areas would be from 5,000-100,000 acres (2,025-40,500 ha) in size and were to be under the same management restrictions as wilderness areas with the exception that they would be

designated by the Chief of the Forest Service. Lastly, the regulations created "**recreation**" areas, which were to be of 100,000 or more acres and were to be managed "substantially in their natural condition." In such areas, road-building and timber harvesting, among other activities, could take place at the Chief's discretion. Lands that had been classified as "primitive" under the L-20 Regulation were to be reviewed and re-classified under the U-Regulations.

The wilderness movement lost much momentum inside the Forest Service with the death of Marshall in 1939. Following World War II, preservationist groups began to discuss the need for statutory protection of wilderness due to controversies over the re-classification of primitive lands and the desire for stronger protection. The proposal for such legislation was first made in 1951 by Howard Zahniser, director of the **Wilderness Society**, at the **Sierra Club**'s Biennial Wilderness Conference. This legislative proposal was put on hold during the battle over the proposed Echo Park dam, but in 1956 preservationists convinced Senator Hubert Humphrey to introduce the first wilderness bill. This original bill, drafted by a group of preservation and conservation groups, would apply not only to **national forest**s, but also to national parks, national monuments, **wildlife refuge**s, and Indian reservations. Within these areas, no farming, logging, grazing, mining, road building, or motorized vehicle use would be allowed. No new agency would be created; rather existing agencies would manage the wilderness lands under their jurisdiction. All Forest Service wilderness, wild, and recreation lands would be immediately designated as wilderness, as well as 49 national parks and 20 wildlife refuges. The expansion (or reduction) of the National Wilderness Preservation System would rest primarily with the executive branch: it would make recommendations that would take affect unless either chamber of Congress passed a motion against the designation within 120 days.

By 1964, when the Wilderness Act was passed, this original bill had changed substantially. Sixty-five different bills had been introduced and nearly 20 congressional hearings were held on these bills. The chief opposition to the wilderness system came from commodity and development interests, especially the timber, mining, and livestock industries. The wilderness bill met with greater success in the Senate, where a bill was passed in 1961. The House proved a more difficult arena, as Wayne Aspinall of Colorado, chair of the Interior and Insular Affairs Committee, opposed the wilderness bill. In the end, the preservationists had to compromise or risk having no law at all. The final law allowed established motorboat and aircraft use to continue; permitted control of fires, insects, and diseases; allowed established grazing to continue; allowed the President to approve water developments; and allowed the staking of new mineral claims under the Mining Law of 1872 through December 31, 1983, and development of legitimate claims indefinitely. The act designated 9.1 million acres (3.7 million ha) as wilderness immediately (Forest Service lands classified as wilderness, wild, or canoe). National park lands and wildlife refuges would be studied for potential designations, and primitive lands were to be protected until Congress determined if they should be designated as wilderness. The act also directed that future designations of wilderness be made through the legislative process.

Since the passage of the Wilderness Act, most of the attention on expanding the wilderness system has focused on Forest Service lands and Alaska lands. In 1971, the Forest Service undertook the Roadless Area Review and Evaluation (RARE I) to analyze its holdings for potential inclusion in the wilderness system. It surveyed 56 million acres (22.7 million ha) in a process that included tremendous public involvement. Based on the review, the agency recommended 12 million additional acres (4.9 million ha) be designated as wilderness. This recommendation did not satisfy preservationists, and the Sierra Club initiated legal action challenging the RARE I process. In an out-of-court settlement, the Forest Service agreed not to alter any of the 56 million acres under study and to undertake a **land use** plan and **environmental impact statement**.

In response to RARE I, Congress passed the Eastern Wilderness Act (1975), which created 16 eastern wilderness areas and directed the Forest Service to alter its methods so that it considered areas previously affected by humans. In 1977, the Forest Service launched RARE II. Over 65 million acres (26.3 million ha) of land were examined, and the Forest Service recommended that 15 million acres (6 million ha) be declared wilderness. Preservationist groups were still not satisfied but did not challenge this process. Based upon these recommendations, additional wilderness has been designated on a state-by-state basis. The Forest Service recommendations have been the starting ground for the political process typically involving commodity groups opposed to more wilderness and preservationist groups favoring designations beyond the Forest Service's recommendations. Thus far, RARE II additions have been made for all but a few states. The completion of RARE II designations will not mean the end of the designation process, however, as preservationists will continue to fight for more wilderness land. The **Alaska National Interest Conservation Land Act** (1980) led to more than a doubling of the wilderness system. The act designated 57 million acres (23 million ha) as wilderness, primarily in national parks and wildlife refuges.

As of 1992, 95.3 million acres (38.6 million ha) of land are designated as wilderness. The Forest Service manages 386 areas of 34 million acres (13.8 million ha), the **National Park Service** 41 areas of 39.1 million acres (15.8 million ha), and the **Fish and Wildlife Service** 75 areas of 20.6 million acres (8.3 million ha). The lands managed by the **Bureau of Land Management** (BLM) were not included in the Wilderness Act, but the **Federal Land Policy and Management Act** of 1976 directed the agency to review its lands for wilderness designation. The BLM now manages 66 areas of 1.6 million acres (648,000 ha), but this figure will increase as the wilderness review and designation process is completed. Ironically, as more lands are designated wilderness by law, de facto wilderness in the nation has been steadily declining.

[*Christopher McGrory Klyza*]

FURTHER READING

Allin, C. W. *The Politics of Wilderness Preservation*. Westport, CT: Greenwood Press, 1982.

Dana, S. T., and S. K. Fairfax. *Forest and Range Policy*. 2nd ed. New York: McGraw-Hill, 1980.

Nash, R. *Wilderness and the American Mind*. 3rd ed. New Haven, CT: Yale University Press, 1982.

Wilderness Society (Washington, D.C.)

This national **conservation** organization focuses on protecting **national park**s, forests, **wildlife refuge**s, seashores, and **recreation** areas and lands administered by the Interior Department's **Bureau of Land Management** (BLM), which total almost a million square miles. The Society has played a leading role on many environmental issues in the last half of the century involving **public land**s, including protecting 84 million acres of land as **wilderness** areas since 1964.

The Society was founded in 1935 by naturalist **Aldo Leopold** and other conservationists, in part to formulate and promote a **land ethic**, a conviction that land is a precious resource "to be cherished and used wisely as an inheritance." One of the Society's proudest accomplishments was the passage of the landmark **Wilderness Act** (1964), which recognized for the first time that the nation's wild areas had a value and integrity that was worthy of protection and should remain places where "man is a visitor who does not remain."

The Society has played an important role in other major legislative victories, including passage of the National Wild and Scenic Rivers Act (1968); the National Trails System Act (1968); the **National Forest Management Act** (1976); the Omnibus Parks Act (1978); the **Alaska National Interest Conservation Land Act** (1980); the Land and Water Conservation Fund Reauthorization (1989); and the Tongass Timber Reform Act (1990).

The Society's agenda for the future is to prevent **oil drilling** in Alaska's **Arctic National Wildlife Refuge**; to double the size of the National Wilderness System by 2015; to eliminate **national forest** timber sales that lose money for the government; and to expand the number of wild and scenic rivers.

One of the group's major projects is to save the last remaining **old-growth forest**s in the Pacific northwest area of the United States, some 90 percent or more of which have already been cut. These ancient forests, found in Washington, Oregon, and northern California, harbor some of the world's oldest and largest trees, as well as such **endangered species** as the **northern spotted owl**. Some of these trees, such as the western hemlock, Douglas fir, cedar, and Sitka spruce, were alive when the Magna Carta was signed over 700 years ago; some now tower 250 feet (76 m) in the air. These forests are home to over 200 **species** of **wildlife**. A single tree can harbor over 100 different species of plants, and a stand of trees can provide **habitat** for over 1,500 species of invertebrates. The Society is fighting plans by the U.S. **Forest Service** to allow the logging, often by **clear-cut-**

ting, of most of the remaining ancient forest. The Society estimates that these forests are being cut at a rate of 170 acres (69 ha) a day—the equivalent of 129 football fields every 24 hours.

The Wilderness Society stresses professionalism and has a full-time staff of over 130 people, including ecologists, biologists, foresters, resource managers, lawyers, and economists. Its main activities consist of public education on the need to protect public lands; testifying before Congress and meeting with legislators and their staff, as well as with federal agency officials, on issues concerning public lands; mobilizing citizens across the nation on conservation campaigns; and sponsoring workshops, conferences, and seminars on conservation issues. The Society publishes a quarterly magazine, *Wilderness*, as well as a variety of brochures, fact sheets, press releases, and member alerts warning of impending environmental threats. Contact: The Wilderness Society, 900 17th Street, NW, Washington, DC 20006-2596. Internet: http://www.wilderness.org/.

[*Lewis G. Regenstein*]

Wilderness Study Area

A Wilderness Study Area is an area of **public land** that is a candidate for official Wilderness Area designation by the United States Government. Federally recognized Wilderness Areas, created by Congress and included in the National Wilderness Preservation System (NWPS), are legally protected from development, road building, motorized access, and most resource exploitation as dictated by the **Wilderness Act** (1964).

The process of identifying, defining, and confirming the areas included in the NWPS is, however, long and slow. In preparation for Wilderness Area designation, states survey their public lands and identify Wilderness Study Areas (WSAs). These areas are parcels of undeveloped and undisturbed land that meet **wilderness** qualifications and on which Congress can later vote for inclusion in the NWPS. Out of over 300 million acres of federally held roadless areas, about 23 million acres, comprising 861 different study areas, were identified as WSAs between 1976 and 1991. Of these WSAs, only a small percentage have been finally recommended to Congress for Wilderness Area status.

Nearly all WSAs are on lands currently administered by the **Bureau of Land Management** (BLM) or the **Forest Service**, and all are in western states. Relatively little undisturbed land remains in eastern states, and most eastern Wilderness Areas were established relatively quickly in 1975 by the Eastern Wilderness Bill. But at the time of this bill adequate surveys of the West had not been completed. The Wilderness Act had ordered western surveys back in 1964, but initial efforts were hasty and incomplete, and the West was excluded from the 1975 Eastern Wilderness Bill.

In 1976 Congress initiated a second attempt to identify western wilderness areas with the **Federal Land Policy and Management Act**. According to this act, each state was to carefully survey its BLM, Forest Service, and **National Park Service** lands. All roadless areas of 5,000 acres or more were to be identified and their wilderness, recreational, and scenic assets assessed. Each state legislature was then required to create a policy and management plan for these public lands, identifying which lands could be considered Wilderness Study Areas and which were best used for development, logging, or intensive livestock grazing. This public lands survey was known as the Second Roadless Area Review and Evaluation (RARE II). Although RARE II recommendations from business-minded BLM and Forest Service administrators did not satisfy most conservationists, the survey's WSA lists represented a substantial improvement over previous wilderness identification efforts.

As potential Wilderness Areas, WSAs require a number of basic "wilderness" attributes. As stressed in the 1964 Wilderness Act, these areas must possess a distinctive "wilderness character" and allow visitors an "unimpaired" wilderness experience. Set aside expressly for their wildness, these areas' intended use is mainly low-impact, short-term **recreation**. Ideally, human presence should be invisible and their impact negligible. Roadless areas are the focus of wilderness surveys precisely because of their relative inaccessibility. However, because all federal laws involve compromise, wilderness designation does not exclude livestock grazing, an extremely common use of public lands in the West. Mineral exploration and exploitation, a potentially disastrous activity in a wilderness, is also legal in Wilderness Areas.

Long and bitter conflicts between **conservation** and development interests have accompanied every state wilderness bill. Some western state legislatures, steered by business interests, have recommended less than ten percent of their roadless areas for inclusion in the NWPS. Once recommendations are made, further study can continue on each WSA until Congress votes, usually considering just a few areas at a time, to include it in the NWPS or to exclude it from consideration. *See also* Ecosystem; Environmental policy; Habitat; Land-use control

[*Mary Ann Cunningham*]

FURTHER READING

Allin, C. W. *The Politics of Wilderness Preservation.* Westport, CT: Greenwood Press, 1982.

Stegner, P. "Backcountry Pilgrimage." *Wilderness* 49 (1986): 12-17+.

U. S. Forest Service. *Final Environmental Statement: Roadless Area Review and Evaluation.* Washington, DC: U. S. Department of Agriculture, 1979.

Wildfire

Few natural forces match fire for its range of impact on the human consciousness, with a roaring forest fire at one extreme and a warming and comforting campfire or cooking

A stand of trees bursts into flames in Grand Teton National Forest in 1988.

flame at the other. Along with earth, water, and air, fire is one of the original "elements" once thought to comprise the universe, and it has frightened and fascinated people long before the beginning of modern civilization. In **nature**, fire both destroys and renews.

Fire is an oxidation process that rapidly transforms the potential energy stored in chemical bonds of organic compounds into the kinetic energy forms of heat and light. Like the much slower oxidation process of **decomposition**, fire destroys organic matter, creating a myriad of gases and **ion**s, and liberating much of the **carbon** and **hydrogen** as **carbon dioxide** and water. A large portion of the remaining organic matter is converted to ash which may go up in the smoke, blow or wash away after the fire, or, like the **humus** created by decomposition, be incorporated into the **soil**.

Although fire often is considered bad and was once thought to destroy natural **ecosystem**s, modern scientists have recognized the importance of fire in ecological succession and in sustaining certain types of plant communities. Fires can help maintain seral successional stages, prolonging the time for the community to reach **climax** stage. Some ecosystems depend on recurring fire for their sustainability; these include many **prairie**s, the chaparral of mediterranean climatic regions, pine **savanna**s of the Southeastern United States, and long–needle pine forests of the American West. Fire controls competing vegetation, such as brush in **grasslands**, prepares new seed beds, and kills harmful insects and disease organisms. Nonetheless, diseases sometimes increase

after fire because of increased susceptibility of partially burned, weakened trees.

The effects of fire on an ecosystem are highly variable, and they depend on the nature of the ecosystem, the fire and its fuel, and weather conditions. In climatic regions where natural fires occur seasonally, grasslands usually are the first ecosystems to burn because the fuel they supply has a large surface area to volume ratio, which allows it to dry rapidly and ignite easily. Grassland fires tend to burn quickly, but they release little energy compared to fires with heavier fuel types. As a result, the effect on soil properties normally is minor and short–lived. The intense greening of a grassland as it recovers from a burn is due largely to the flush of **nutrient**s released from mature and dead plants and made available to new growth. Grassland fires have been set intentionally for many generations in the name of forage improvement.

Naturally caused brushland fires, including the infamous chaparral fires of the southwestern United States, usually start somewhat later in the season than the first grass fires, and they normally have more intense, longer lasting impacts. These fires burn very rapidly but with far more thermal output than grassland fires, because fuel loading is five to fifty times greater.

The season for forest fires normally begins somewhat later than that for grass or brush fires. The fuel in a mature forest, which may be 100 times greater than that of a medium density brushland, requires more time to dry and become available for combustion. When the forest burns, the ground may or may not be intensely heated, depending on the arrangement of fuels from the ground to the forest canopy. Under a hot burn with the heavy ground fuel found in some forests, heat can penetrate mineral soil to a depth of 12 inches (30 cm) or more, significantly altering the physical, chemical, and biological properties of the soil. When the soil is heated, water is driven out; soil structure, which is the small aggregations of sand, **silt**, clay, and organic matter, may be destroyed, leaving a massive soil condition to a depth of several inches.

Forest and brushland soils often become hydrophobic, or water repellent. A hydrophobic layer a few inches thick commonly develops just below the burned surface. This condition is created when the fire's heat turns **soil organic matter** into gas and drives them deeper into the soil, where they then condense on cooler particle surfaces. Under severe conditions, water simply beads and runs off this layer, like water applied to a freshly waxed car. Soil above the hydrophobic layer is highly susceptible to sheet and rill **erosion** during the first rains after a fire. Fortunately, it is soon broken up by insects and burrowing animals, which have survived the fire by going underground; they penetrate the layer, allowing water to soak through it.

Forest fires decrease soil acidity, often causing **pH** to increase by three units (e.g., from 5 to 8) before and after the fire. Normally, conditions return to prefire levels in less than a decade. Fires also transform soil nutrients, most notably converting nutritive **nitrogen** into gaseous forms that go up in the smoke. Some of the first plants to recolonize a hotly burned area are those whose roots support specialized bacteria that replenish the nutritive nitrogen through a process called nitrogen fixation. Large amounts of other nutrients, including **phosphorus**, potassium, and calcium, remain on the site, contributing to the so-called "ashbed effect." Plants that colonize these fertile ashbeds tend to be more vigorous than those growing outside of them. When heating has bee prolonged and intense in areas such as those under burning logs, stumps, or debris piles, soil color can change from brown to reddish. Fires hot enough to cause these color changes are hot enough to sterilize the soil, prolonging the time to recovery.

In the absence of heavy ground fuels, so much of the energy of an intense forest fire may be released directly to the **atmosphere** that soils will be only moderately affected. This was the case in the great fires at **Yellowstone National Park** in 1988, after which soil scientists mapped the entire burn area as low or medium intensity with respect to soil effects. Although soils on some sites did suffer intense heating, these were too small and localized to be mapped or to be of substantial ecological consequence, and most of the areas recovered quickly after the fires.

Although fire is vital to the long-term health and sustainability of many ecosystems, wildfires take numerous human lives and destroy millions of dollars of property each year. Controlling these destructive fires means fighting them aggressively. Fire suppression efforts arc based on the fact that any fire requires three things: heat, fuel, and oxygen. Together, these make up the three legs of the so-called "fire triangle" known to all fire fighters. The strategy in all fire

fighting is to extinguish the blaze by breaking one of the legs of this triangle. An entire science has developed around fire behavior and the effects of changing weather, **topography**, and fuels on that behavior.

Competing conceptions of the costs and benefits of wildfires have led to conflicting fire management and suppression objectives, most notably in the **national park**s and **national forest**s. The debate over which fires should be allowed to burn and which should be suppressed undoubtedly will continue for some time. *See also* Biomass; Biomass fuel; Deforestation; Ecological productivity; Forest management; Forest Service; Old-growth forest; Soil survey

[*Ronald D. Taskey*]

FURTHER READING

Barbour, M. G., J. H. Burk, and W. D. Pitts. *Terrestrial Plant Ecology.* Menlo Park, CA: Benjamin/Cummings, 1980.

Greater Yellowstone Post–Fire Resource Assessment Committee, Burned Area Survey Team. *Preliminary Burned Area Survey of Yellowstone National Park and Adjoining National Forests,* 1988.

Lotan, J. E., et al. *Effects of Fire on Flora.* Forest Service General Technical Report WO–16. Washington, DC: U. S. Government Printing Office, 1981.

National Wildfire Coordinating Group. *Firefighters Guide.* NFES 1571/PMS 414-1. Boise, ID: Boise Interagency Fire Center, 1986.

Wells, C. G., et al. *Effects of Fire on Soil.* Forest Service General Technical Report WO–7. Washington, DC: U. S. Government Printing Office, 1979.

Wildlife

It was once customary to consider all undomesticated **species** of vertebrate animals as wildlife. Birds and mammals still receive the greatest public interest and concern, consistently higher than those expressed for reptiles and amphibians. Most concern over fishes results from interest in sport and commercial value. The tendency in recent years has been to include more life-forms under the category of wildlife. Thus, mollusks, insects, and plants are all now represented on national and international lists of threatened and **endangered species**.

People find many reasons to value wildlife. Virtually everyone appreciates the aesthetic value of natural beauty or artistic appeal present in animal life. **Giant panda**s, **bald eagle**s, and infant harp seals are familiar examples of wildlife with outstanding aesthetic value. Wild species offer recreational value, the most common examples of which are sport hunting and bird watching.

Less obvious, perhaps, is ecological value, resulting from the role an individual species plays within an **ecosystem**. **Alligator**s, for example, create depressions in swamps and marshes. During periods of droughts, these "alligator holes" offer critical refuge to water-dependent life-forms. Educational and scientific values are those that serve in teaching and learning about biology and scientific principles.

Wildlife also has utilitarian value which results from its practical uses. Examples of utilitarian value range from genetic **reservoir**s for crop and livestock improvement to diverse biomedical and pharmaceutical uses. A related category, commercial value, includes such familiar examples as the sale of furs and hunting leases.

Shifts in human lifestyle have been accompanied by changes in attitudes toward wildlife. Societies of hunter-gatherers depend directly on wild species for food, as many plains Indian tribes did on the **bison**. But as people shift from hunting and gathering to agriculture, wildlife comes to be viewed as more of a threat because of potential crop or livestock damage. In modern developed nations, people's lives are based less on rural ways of life and more on business and industry in cities. Urbanites rarely if ever feel threatened economically by wild animals. They have the leisure time and mobility to visit **wildlife refuge**s or parks, where they appreciate seeing native wildlife as a unique, aesthetic experience. They also sense that wildlife is in decline and therefore favor greater protection.

The most obvious threat to wildlife is that of direct exploitation, often related to commercial use. Exploitation helped bring about the **extinction** of the **passenger pigeon** (*Ectopistes migratorius*), the great auk, Stellar's sea cow, and the sea mink, as well as the near extinction of the American bison. In the late nineteenth and early twentieth century, state and federal laws were passed to help curb exploitation. These were successful for the most part, and they continue to play a crucial role in **wildlife management**.

Introductions of **exotic species** represent another threat to wildlife. Insular or island-dwelling species of wildlife are especially vulnerable to the impacts of exotic plants and animals. Beginning in the seventeenth century, sailors deliberately placed goats and pigs on ocean islands, intending to use their descendants as food on future voyages. As the exotic populations grew, the native vegetation proved unable to cope, creating drastic **habitat** changes. Other species, such as rats, mice, and cats, jumped ship and devastated island-dwelling birds, which had evolved in the absence of mammalian predators and had few or no defenses.

Pollution is yet another threat to wildlife. Bald eagles, ospreys, **peregrine falcon**s (*Falco peregrinus*), and **brown pelican**s (*Pelecanus occidentalis*) experienced serious and sudden population declines in the 1950s and 60s. Studies showed that these fish eaters were ingesting heavy doses of **pesticide**s, including **DDT**. The pesticides left the shells of their eggs so thin that they cracked under the weight of incubating parents, and numbers declined due to reproductive failure. Populations of these birds in the United States rebounded after regulatory laws curbed the use of these pesticides. However, thousands of other **chemicals** still enter the air, water, and **soil** every year, and the effects of most of them on wildlife are unknown.

By far the most critical threat to wildlife is habitat alteration. Unfortunately, it is also more subtle than direct exploitation, and thus often escapes public attention. As the twenty-first century approaches, human activities are altering some of the most biologically rich habitats in the world on a scale unprecedented in history. **Tropical rain forest**s, for example, originally covered only about 7 percent of the earth's land surface, yet they are thought to contain half the planet's wild species. Other rich habitats undergoing rapid changes

include tropical dry forests and **coral reef**s. As extensive areas of natural habitat are irrevocably changed, many of the native species that once occurred there will become extinct, even those with no commercial value.

Any species of wild animal has a set of habitat requirements. These begin with food requirements, adequate amounts of available food for each season. Cover requirements are structural components that are used for nesting, roosting, or watching, or that offer protection from severe weather or predators. Water is habitat requirement that affects wildlife directly, by providing drinking water, and indirectly, by influencing local vegetation. The final habitat requirement is space. Biologists can now calculate a minimum area requirement to sustain a particular species of a given size.

Even in the absence of human activities, populations of wild animals change as a result of variations in birth and death rates. When a population is sparse relative to the number that can be supported by local habitat conditions, birth rates tend to be high. In such circumstances, natural mortality, including predation, disease, and starvation, tends to be low. As populations increase, birth rates decline and death rates rise. These trends continue until the population reaches carrying capacity, the number of animals of a particular species that can be sustained within a given area.

Carrying capacity, though, is difficult to define in practice. Variations in winter severity or in summer rainfall can, between years, alter the carrying capacity for a particular area. In addition, carrying capacity changes as forests grows older, **grasslands** mature, or **wetlands** fill in through natural **siltation**. Despite these limitations, the concept of carrying capacity illustrates an important biological principle: living wild animals cannot be stockpiled beyond the practical limits that local habitat conditions can support.

While all populations vary, some undergo extreme fluctuations. When they occur regularly, such fluctuation are called cycles. Cyclical populations fall into two categories, the three- to four-year cycle typical of lemmings and voles, and the eight- to eleven-year cycle known in snowshoe hares and lynx of the Western Hemisphere. The mechanisms that keep cycles going are complex and not completely understood, but the existence of cycles is widely accepted. Extreme populations fluctuations that occur at irregular intervals are called population irruptions. Local populations of deer tend to be irruptive, suddenly showing substantial changes at unpredictable intervals.

There are more species of wild plants and animals in tropical **rain forest**s than on arctic **tundra**s. Such patterns illustrate variations in the complexities of life-forms due to climatic conditions. Measurement of **biodiversity** usually focuses on a particular group of organisms such as trees or birds. The most basic indication of species richness is the total number of species in a certain area or habitat. A measure of species evenness is more valuable because it indicates the relative abundance of each species. As diversity includes richness and evenness, an area with many species uniformly distributed would have a high overall diversity.

Biodiversity is important to wildlife **conservation** as well as to basic **ecology**. Comparisons of species diversity patterns indicate the extent to which natural conditions have been affected by human activities. They also help establish priorities for acquiring new protected areas. *See also* Predator-prey interactions; Wildlife refuge; Wildlife rehabilitation

[*James H. Shaw*]

FURTHER READING

Caughley, G. *Analysis of Vertebrate Populations.* New York: John Wiley & Sons, 1977.

Kellert, S. *Trends in Animal Use and Perception in 20th Century America.* Washington, DC: U. S. Department of the Interior, Fish and Wildlife Service, 1981.

Matthiessen, P. *Wildlife in America.* 2nd ed. New York: Viking Books, 1987.

McCullough, D. *The George Reserve Deer Herd.* Ann Arbor, MI: University of Michigan Press, 1979.

Wildlife management

Wildlife laws are enforced by state and federal agencies, usually known as wildlife departments or fish and game commissions. In the United States, principal responsibility for laws protecting migratory **species** and threatened and **endangered species** rests with the **Fish and Wildlife Service**.

Various **nongovernmental organizations** (NGOs) have grown in membership and influence since the 1960s. NGOs include private conservation groups such as the **National Audubon Society**, the **National Wildlife Federation**, and the **World Wildlife Fund**. Although they have no direct legal powers, NGOs have achieved considerable influence over wildlife management through fund raising, lobbying, and other kinds of political action, as well as by filing lawsuits concerning wildlife-related issues.

Depletion of native wildlife during the late nineteenth century in the United States and Canada led to passage of federal and state laws regulating the harvest and possession of resident species. Congress passed the Lacey Act in 1900, which made interstate shipment of wild animals a federal offense if taken in violation of state laws, and so curbed market hunting. A few years later, the Migratory Bird Treaty Act was passed, establishing federal authority over migratory game and insectivorous birds. This treaty was signed by Great Britain on behalf of Canada in 1916 and became effective two years later.

Other protective measures soon outlawed market hunting and regulated sport hunting. Hunters are now required to purchase hunting licenses, the proceeds of which help pay salaries of game wardens, and game harvests are now regulated chiefly through hunting seasons and bag limits. These are imprecise tools, but the resulting harvests are generally conservative and excessive ones are rare.

In 1973, the **Endangered Species Act** conferred federal protection on listed species, resident as well as migratory. Three years later, the United States became one of the first nations to sign the **Convention on International Trade in Endangered Species** (CITES), which more than 100 nations pledged to regulate commercial trade in threatened species and to effectively outlaw trade in endangered ones.

Although laws regulating the taking or possession of wild animals are essential, they are not sufficient by themselves. Wildlife populations can only be sustained if adequate measures are taken to manage the **habitat**s they require. Habitat management can take three basic approaches: preservation, enhancement, and restoration. Preservation seeks to protect natural habitats that have not been significantly affected by human activity. The principal tactic of preservation is exclusion of mining, grazing by livestock, timber harvesting, oil and gas exploration, and environmentally damaging recreational practices. Federally-designated **wilderness** areas and **national park**s use habitat preservation as their principal strategy.

Habitat enhancement is designed to increase both wildlife numbers and **biodiversity** through practices that improve food production, cover, water, and other habitat components. Enhancement differs from preservation because improvements are often achieved through artificial means, such as nest boxes, the cultivation of food plants, and the installation of devices to regulate water levels. Most state wildlife management areas and many **national wildlife refuge**s practice enhancement.

Habitat restoration seeks to reestablish the original conditions of an area that have been substantially altered by human use, such as farming. Most **land use** practices result in a simpler **biological community**, so many of the original species must be reintroduced. Although not a precise science, in the future this kind of restoration will likely be more widely used to expand rare types of habitat. Costa Rica is using restoration to create more tropical dry forests, and the **Nature Conservancy** in the United States has used it to reestablish tallgrass **prairie** habitat.

Although the strategies used in wildlife management usually involve regulation of harvests and manipulation of habitats, the objectives of most management plans are defined in terms of population levels. Most game management, for example, seeks to increase production of game. Many people assume that game production rises with game populations. In reality, game production is maximized by improving habitat conditions so as to raise the **carrying capacity** for a particular game species. Rather than let populations reach that, modern wildlife managers harvest enough game to keep the population below it, and this practice results in healthier populations with lower rates of natural mortality and higher rates of reproduction. Hunters may take more animals from a population managed at a population level below carrying capacity than they can from one managed at it.

Some wildlife populations are managed to minimize the damage they can inflict upon crops or livestock. Some animal-damage control is done by reducing the wildlife population, usually through poisoning. But just as game populations become more productive when reduced below carrying capacity, so animals that inflict crop or livestock damage often compensate for population reductions with higher rates of reproduction, as well as higher survival rates for their young. This compensatory response to control, together with increased public pressures against uses of poisons, has led to refinements in animal-damage control. The trend in recent years has been toward methods that prevent damage, such as special fencing or other protective measures, and away from widespread population reductions. When lethal measures are taken, wildlife managers have tended to endorse selective removal of offending individuals, particularly in large carnivorous species.

For **rare species**, those endangered, threatened, or declining, managers attempt to increase numbers, establish new populations, and above all, preserve each rare species' **gene pool**. Legal protection and habitat improvement are important means for managing rare species, just as they are for game animals, but in addition, rare species are helped by **captive propagation** done under cooperative agreements between zoos and the U.S. Fish and Wildlife Service. Although expensive, captive propagation can increase numbers quickly by using new technologies such as artificial insemination and embryo transfers. Once the numbers in captivity have been built up, some of the population can then be reintroduced into suitable habitat. Wildlife managers prepare wild animals bred in captivity for reintroduction through acclimation, training, and by selecting favorable age and sex combinations.

Rare species often face long-term problems resulting from reductions in their gene pools. When any species is reduced to a small fraction of its original numbers, certain genes are lost because not enough animals survive to ensure their perpetuation. This loss is known as the bottleneck effect. Rare species typically exist in small, isolated populations, and they lose even more of their gene pools through the resulting inbreeding. The **Florida panther**, a nearly extinct subspecies of cougar, exhibits loss of size, vigor, and reproductive success, clear indications of a depleted gene pool, the result of the bottleneck effect and inbreeding.

Managers try to minimize the loss of gene pools by striving to prevent severe numerical reductions from occurring in the first place. They also use population augmentation to systematically transfer selected individuals from other populations, wild or captive, to encourage outbreeding and can replenish local gene pools.

Modern wildlife managers tend not to concentrate on perpetuating one species, focusing instead maintaining entire communities with all their diverse species of plant and animal life. Maintenance of biodiversity is important because wild species exist as ecologically interdependent communities. If enough of these communities can be maintained on a sufficiently large scale, the long-term survival of all of its species may be assured.

From a practical standpoint, there are simply not enough resources or time to develop management plans for each of the earth's 4,100 species of mammals or 9,000 species of birds, not to mention the other, more diverse life-forms. The tedious process of listing threatened and endangered species is slow and often achieved only after the species is on the brink of **extinction**. Recovery becomes expensive and despite heroic efforts, may still fail.

If biodiversity management succeeds, it may reduce the loss of wild species through proactive, as opposed to reactive, measures. Many North American songbirds, particularly those of the eastern woodlands and the prairie regions, are experiencing steady declines. Even familiar game species including the northern bobwhite quail and several species of duck are becoming less abundant. The causes are complex and elusive, but they probably relate to our failure to stabilize habitat conditions on a sufficient enough scale. If wildlife managers can reverse this trend, they may stop and ultimately reverse these declines. *See also* Defenders of Wildlife; Migration; Overhunting; Predator control; Restoration ecology; Wildlife refuge; Wildlife rehabilitation

[*James H. Shaw*]

FURTHER READING

Kohm, K. A., ed. *Balancing on the Brink of Extinction: The Endangered Species Act and Lessons for the Future.* Washington, D.C.: Island Press, 1991.

Matthiessen, P. *Wildlife in America.* 2nd ed. New York: Viking Books, 1987.

Shaw, J. H. *Introduction to Wildlife Management.* New York: McGraw-Hill Book Co., 1985.

Soule, M. and B. A. Wilcox, eds. 1980. *Conservation Biology.* Sunderland, MA: Sinauer Associates, 1980.

Wildlife refuge

When President **Theodore Roosevelt** issued an executive order making Pelican Island, Florida, a federal bird reservation, he introduced the idea of a **national wildlife refuge**. Nearly 90 years later, Roosevelt's action has expanded to a system of more than 400 national wildlife refuges with a combined area of over 90 million acres (36 million hectares).

Roosevelt's action was aimed at protecting birds that used the islands. Market hunters had relentlessly killed egrets, herons, and other aquatic birds for their feathers or plumes to adorn women's fashions. The first national wildlife refuge, like other **conservation** practices of the early twentieth century, emerged in reaction to unregulated market hunting. Pelican Island became a sanctuary where wild animals, protected from gunfire, would multiply and then disperse to repopulate adjacent countryside.

States followed suit, establishing protected areas known variously as game preserves, sanctuaries, or game refuges. They were expected to function as breeding grounds to repopulate surrounding countryside. Although protected populations usually persisted within the boundaries of such refuges, they seldom repopulated areas outside those boundaries. Migratory waterfowl enjoyed some success in repopulating because they could fly over unsuitable **habitat**s and find others that met their needs. Nonmigratory or resident **species** often found themselves surrounded by inhospitable tracts of farmlands, highways, and pastures. Dispersal chances were limited. Resident populations, particularly those of deer and other large herbivores, built up to unhealthy levels, depleting natural foods, becoming infested with heavy parasite loads, and starving. In short, refuges proved to be too small and too scattered to compensate for changes in the overall landscapes imposed by expanding human populations.

Yet elements of the refuge idea proved to be sound, even critical, under some conditions. The U.S. **Fish and Wildlife Service** administers the National Wildlife Refuge System and, in keeping with its legal responsibilities, designed the system to provide crucial habitat reserves for migratory waterbirds. Roughly 80 percent of the refuges in this system were established to provide breeding grounds, wintering grounds, or migration stopover sites for aquatic migrants. To this mission has been added the task of providing critical habitat for threatened and **endangered species**, another area of federal commitment.

As wildlife researchers learned more about habitat needs, survival rates, and dispersal abilities of birds and mammals, wildlife managers began to redefine refuges more in terms of meeting habitat needs than in providing sanctuary from hunters. Without considering habitat quality both on the refuge itself and along its boundaries, no level of protection from gunfire could ensure perpetuation of native **wildlife**.

Refuges as Islands. Pelican Island is a true island off the Florida coast. Other refuges are, or soon will be, habitat islands surrounded by a sea of farms, ranches, forest plantations, shopping malls, and suburbs. There is increasing evidence that even those refuges providing the highest quality habitat may simply be too small to sustain many of their wild species under conditions of isolation.

But how much is enough? How large must a habitat refuge be to ensure that its populations will survive? Nature provides a clue through an experiment that began 10,000-11,000 years ago at the end of the last **ice age**. As the glacial ice melted, sea levels rose. Coastal peninsulas in the Caribbean and elsewhere became chains of islands as the rising waters covered lower portions of the peninsulas.

The original peninsulas presumably had about the same number of vertebrate species as did the adjacent mainland. By comparing the numbers of birds, mammals, reptiles, and amphibians present on the islands within historical times with those on adjacent mainlands, biologists have found that the islands contain consistently fewer species. Furthermore, the number of species that a given island maintained was correlated directly to island size and inversely to distance from the mainland.

The most likely explanation for this pattern is that the smaller the island, the less likely that species will survive in isolation over long periods of time. The greater the distance, the less likely that wild animals will re-colonize the island by making it across from the mainland.

But is this analogy realistic? After all, most refuges are surrounded by land, not water. Several studies from **national parks** in the American West, areas protected from both hunting and habitat alterations, have compared the number of large mammal species surviving in the parks. These studies show consistently that the bigger the park, the greater the number of surviving species of large mammals.

Large carnivores such as wolves, bears, lions, tigers, and jaguars need the largest expanses of protected areas. Because they attack livestock and occasionally humans, large carnivores have long been subjected to persecution. But there are biological reasons for their rarity as well. Any given level in the **food chain/web** can exist at only a tiny fraction of the abundance of the level beneath it. It may take 100 or more moose to support a single wolf or 1,000 Thompson's gazelles to sustain one lion. These conditions mean that large carnivores occur at low levels of abundance and range over large areas. Simulation models that take into account the areas needed for long-term perpetuation of lions or bears suggest that even the largest national parks and other protected areas may be too small. Either the protected areas themselves will need to be expanded substantially or the populations will have to be aided by reintroduction of individuals from outside the protected zones. Although large carnivores remain controversial, they also offer popular appeal to a growing segment of the public. Refuges, parks, and other protected sites large enough to support a population of tigers or wolves, even for a short time, will almost certainly be large enough to meet the needs of other wild species as well. Thus Project Tiger in India helped sambar and chital deer populations by defining areas as tiger preserves.

In the United States and Canada, people tend to think of national parks as scenic areas for tourism and **recreation**. But national parks also act as refuges by protecting wildlife from direct exploitation and by attempting to keep the original habitat conditions. The **grizzly bear** once ranged from the western prairies to the Pacific Ocean. By the end of World War II, the only grizzly bear populations in the lower 48 states occurred in and around two large national parks: **Yellowstone National Park** and Glacier. Had it not been for these parks, the grizzly bear would have become completely extinct in the United States, exclusive of Alaska, during the first half of the twentieth century.

International Standards. Worldwide standards for refuges, parks, and other protected areas have been developed by the United Nations (UN) and the **IUCN—The World Conservation Union**. These agencies compile listings every 5 years according to three general criteria. To be included, an area must be at least 2,500 acres (1,000 hectares), have effective legal protection and adequate *de facto* protection, and be managed by the highest appropriate level of government.

The 1990 tally by the IUCN/UN is 6,931 protected areas with a total area of 1.6 billion acres (651 million hectares), roughly 4.8 percent of the earth's land surface. Of the 193 major habitat types, 183 are represented by at least one protected area.

The Future of Protected Areas. The number of internationally recognized areas of protected habitats grew from about 1,800 in 1970 to nearly 7,000 by 1990. This expansion resulted from improved cooperation between nations and from the growing realization that without protected areas, the earth's wildlife will have no future. During the next quarter century, the list of protected areas will continue to grow, especially in developing nations. They will become increasingly valued for tourism and for national prestige. The effectiveness of refuges in the more distant future will depend on **population growth** and on how quickly people shift from extractive to sustainable **land use** practices. The currcnt tendency to view habitat protection as the antithesis to economic development will fade as people recognize the importance, both ecologically and economically, of maintaining the world's wildlife.

[*James H. Shaw*]

FURTHER READING

1990 United Nations List of National Parks and Protected Areas. Gland, Switzerland: IUCN—The World Conservation Union, 1990.

Shafer, C. L. *Nature Reserves: Island Theory and Conservation Practice.* Washington, DC: Smithsonian Institution Press, 1990.

Western, D., and M. C. Pearl. *Conservation for the Twenty First Century.* New York: Oxford University Press, 1989.

World Resources Institute. *World Resources 1992-93.* New York: Oxford University Press, 1992.

Wildlife rehabilitation

Wildlife rehabilitation is the practice of saving injured, sick, or orphaned **wildlife** by taking them out of their **habitat** and nursing them back to health. Rehabilitated animals are returned to the wild whenever possible. Although precise estimates of the numbers of wild animals rehabilitated are impossible to obtain, the practice seems to be expanding in nations such as the United States and Canada. The National Wildlife Rehabilitators Association (NWRA), formed in the early 1980s, estimates that its members take in half a million wild animals annually, with at least twice that number of telephone inquiries.

Wildlife rehabilitation differs from **wildlife management** in the fact that rehabilitators focus their attention on the survival of individual animals, often without regard to whether it is a member of a **rare species**. Wildlife managers are principally concerned with the health and well-being of wildlife populations, with rarely concentrate on individuals.

Wayne Marion, formerly of the University of Florida, has summarized the advantages and disadvantages of wildlife rehabilitation. Rehabilitation facilities give the public a place to bring injured or orphaned wild animals while giving veterinary students the opportunity to treat them. They also save the lives of many animals who would otherwise die, and experience gained through the handling and care of common **species** may be put to use when rarer animals need emergency care. But rehabilitation, according to Marion, is expensive, and common species constitute the large majority of animals saved. Rehabilitated wildlife also lose their fear of humans and risk catching diseases from other animals. Besides routine care for injured or orphaned animals, rehabilitation groups often organize rescues of wild animals following catastrophes. When the oil tanker **Exxon Valdez** ran aground in 1989, spilling 11 million gallons of crude oil into **Prince William Sound**, the International Bird Rescue Research Center (IBRRC) directed a rescue operation involving 143 boats. Over 1,600 birds representing 71 species were rescued alive. Survival rates varied by species, but overall roughly half of the birds were eventually returned to the wild. Rehabilitators also recovered 334 live sea otters from areas affected by the spill, cleaned and treated them, and returned 188 to the wild.

Wildlife rehabilitation should become more integrated with conventional wildlife management in the future, especially when catastrophes threaten **endangered species**. Meanwhile, an important role of rehabilitators is in education. Rehabilitated animals who have lost all fear of humans or who are permanently injured cannot be returned to the wild. Such individuals can be used to teach school children and civic groups about the plight of wildlife by bringing rare animals, such as the **bald eagle** or **peregrine falcon** to display at talks. *See also* Game animal; Nongame wildlife; Nongovernmental organizations

[*James H. Shaw*]

FURTHER READING

Maki, A. W. "The Exxon Valdez Wildlife Rescue and Rehabilitation Program." *North American Wildlife and Natural Resources Conference Transactions* 55 (1990): 193-201.

Marion, W. R. "Wildlife Rehabilitation: Its Role in Future Resource Management." *North American Wildlife and Natural Resources Conference Transactions* 54 (1989): 476-82.

Willingness to pay
See **Shadow pricing**

Wilson, Edward Osborne (1929-)
American behavioral and evolutionary biologist

Edward Osborne Wilson was born on June 10, 1929, in Birmingham, Alabama, and is one of the foremost authorities on the **ecology**, systematics, and **evolution** of the ant.

Wilson developed an interest in **nature** and the outdoors at an early age. Growing up in rural, south Alabama, near the border of Florida, young Wilson earned the nickname "Snake" Wilson by having collected most of the forty snake **species** found in that part of the country. He began studying ants after an accident impaired his vision and has been studying them for over fifty years, having progressed from amateur to expert with relative swiftness. His formal training in the biological sciences resulted in his receiving the Bachelor of Science degree in 1949 and Master of Science in 1950 from the University of Alabama. He received his Ph.D. in 1955 from Harvard University.

Wilson's work on ants has taken him all over the world on numerous scientific expeditions. He has discovered several new species of these social insects, whose current tally of named species numbers nearly 9,000. Wilson estimates, however, that there are probably closer to 20,000 species in the world, and those species are comprised of over a million billion individuals. Much of his work on this fascinating

Edward O. Wilson.

group of insects have been synthesized and published in a monumental book he co-authored with Bert Hölldobler in 1990, simply entitled *The Ants*.

Besides hundreds of scientific papers and articles, Wilson has published several other books that have been the focus of much attention in the scientific community. In 1967, Robert H. MacArthur, a renowned ecologist, and Wilson published *The Theory of Island Biogeography*, a work dealing with island size and the number of species that can occur on them. The book also examines the evolutionary equilibrium reached by those populations, the implications of which have been more recently applied to the loss of species through tropical **deforestation**. In 1975, Wilson published his most controversial book, *Sociobiology: The New Synthesis*, in which he discussed human behavior based on the social structure of ants. His book *On Human Nature*, also relating sociobiology and human evolution, earned him a Pulitzer Prize for General Nonfiction in 1979. *Biophilia* won him popular acclaim in 1984, as have his more recent books dealing with the threats to the vast diversity of species on earth, *Biodiversity*, published in 1988, and *The Diversity of Life*, published in 1992.

[*Eugene C. Beckham*]

FURTHER READING

Hölldobler, B., and E. Wilson. *The Ants.* Cambridge: Belknap Press, 1990.

Lessen, D. "Dr. Ant." *International Wildlife* 21 (1991): 30-34.

Wilson, Edward O. *Biophilia.* Cambridge: Harvard University Press, 1984.

———. *The Diversity of Life.* Cambridge: Harvard University Press, 1992.

———. *Insect Societies.* Cambridge: Belknap Press, 1971.

———. *Sociobiology: The New Synthesis.* Cambridge: Belknap Press, 1975.

Wind energy

The ultimate source of most energy used by humans is the sun. **Fossil fuels**, for example, are merely substances in which **solar energy** has been converted and stored as plants or animals that have died and decayed. When energy experts look for **alternative energy sources**, they often search for new ways to use solar energy, and one of the most obvious of these is harnessing wind power.

When sunlight strikes the earth, it heats objects such as land, water, and plants, but it heats them differentially. Dark-colored objects absorb more heat than light-colored ones and rough surfaces absorb more heat than smooth ones. As these materials absorb more or less heat, they also transmit that heat to the air above them. When air is warmed, it rises and is replaced by cooler air, and this movement of air results in winds. For these reasons, some types of topography and some geographic regions are more likely to experience windy conditions than others, and from the standpoint of energy production, these areas are reserves from which solar energy can be extracted.

Devices used for capturing the energy of winds are known as windmills. The wind strikes the blades of a windmill, causing them to turn, and the solar energy stored in wind is converted to the kinetic energy of moving blades. That energy, in turn, is used to turn an axle, to power a pump, to run a mill, or to perform some other function. The amount of power that can be converted by a windmill depends primarily on two factors: the area swept out by the windmill blade and the wind speed. One goal in windmill design, therefore, is to produce a machine with very large blades. But, the power generated by a windmill depends on the cube of the wind speed, and so in any operating windmill natural wind patterns are by far the most important consideration.

Farmers have been using windmills to draw water from wells and to operate machinery for centuries, and the technology has been traced back to the seventh century A.D. In the early twentieth century, windmills were a familiar sight on American farms. More than six million of them existed, and some were used to generate electricity on a small scale. As other sources of power became available, however, that number declined until the late 1970s, when no more than 150,000 were still in use.

In the 1970s, windmills were not considered part of the nation's energy equation. Fossil fuels had long been cheap and readily available, and **nuclear power** was widely regarded as the next best alternative. The 1973 **oil embargo** by the **Organization of Petroleum Exporting Countries** (OPEC) and the **Three Mile Island** nuclear disaster in 1979 changed these perceptions and caused experts to begin thinking once more about wind power as an alternative energy source.

During the 1970s, both governmental agencies and private organizations stepped up their research on wind power. The National Aeronautics and Space Administration (NASA), for example, designed a number of windmills, ranging from designs with huge, broad-blade fans, to ones with thin, airplane-like propellers. The largest of these

Wind turbines at Tehachapi Pass, California.

machines consists of blades 300 feet (100 meters) long and weighing 100 tons, which rotate on top of towers 200 feet (60 meters) tall. At winds of 15 to 45 miles per hour (25 to 70 kilometers per hour) these windmills can generate 2.5 **megawatt**s of electricity. Under the best circumstances, modern windmills achieve an energy-conversion efficiency of 30 percent, comparable or superior to any other form of energy conversion.

As a result of changing economic conditions and technological advances, windmills became an increasingly popular energy source for both individual homes and large energy-producing corporations. With dependable winds of 10 to 12 miles per hour (16 to 20 kph) a private home can generate enough electricity to meet its own needs. The 1978 Public Utilities Regulatory Policies Act requires **electric utilities** to purchase excess electricity from private citizens who produce more than they can use by alternative means, such as wind power. "Wind farms" consisting of hundreds of individual windmills are able to generate enough electricity to meet the needs of small communities. By the late 1980s, more than seventy wind farms existed in Vermont, New Hampshire, Oregon, Montana, Hawaii, and California.

The greatest number of wind farms are found in California, and the greatest concentration of them are located at Altamont Pass east of San Francisco. The wind farms at Altamont Pass date to the early 1980s, when a state study declared it the most promising site for windmills, and a 25 percent state and federal tax credit encouraged eleven differ-

ent developers to build 3,800 windmills there. By the time those credits expired, wind power had proved itself to be an inexpensive source of electricity for northern California. In 1993, wind-generated electricity sold for about five cents per kilowatt-hour, approximately equal to the price of electricity generated at fossil-fueled plants. In 1993, a single company, U. S. Windpower, operated 4,200 windmills at Altamont Pass, dependably generating 420 megawatts of electrical energy. This company was recently retained by the Ukrainian government to construct a 500-megawatt wind farm to replace the power lost after the destruction of the **Chernobyl Nuclear Power Station** in 1986.

In the United States, some authorities claim that wind power can meet between 10 and 20 percent of the nation's electrical needs by the year 2000. These estimates are higher in other countries, rising to 20 and 30 percent. Given the limited economic and environmental impact of windmills, such estimates are encouraging, a few experts see even more promise in wind power. In coastal urban areas, they suggest, wind farms could be built off shore on floating platforms. The electricity generated could be sent back to land on large cables or used on the platforms to generate **hydrogen** from seawater, which could then be shipped to land and used as a fuel.

Like any energy source, wind power has some disadvantages, and these are some of the reasons why wind power has not already become far more popular as an energy source in the United States and other parts of the world. The most obvious disadvantage is that it can be used only in locations that have enough wind over an extended part of the day. Storage of energy is also a problem. Wind is strongest in spring and autumn when power is least needed and weakest in summer and winter when demand is greatest. Other drawbacks include controversies over the appearance of wind farms and the claim that they spoil the natural beauty of an area. Concerns have also been raised about the noise they produce and the electromagnetic fields they create.

Probably the single most important reason for the lack of more extended use of wind power, however, is the present state of technology. Although the basic principles of wind-mill construction are well known, more research is needed to develop machines for both home and wind-farm use. This kind of research has often been funded by governments, as the United States did in the 1970s. But during the 1980s, the Reagan and Bush administrations both took a different view about the development of alternative energy sources. Both presidents believed that the federal government should have little or no role in this type of research, and relatively modest progress has been made during the past decade in the development of wind power. *See also* Energy and the environment; Energy policy; Energy Research and Development Administration

[*David E. Newton*]

FURTHER READING

Lamarre, L. "A Growth Market in Wind Power." *EPRI Journal* (December 1992): 4-15.

Marier, D. *Wind Power*. Emmaus, PA: Rodale Press, 1981.

Mohs, M. "Blowin' in the Wind." *Discover* 6 (June 1985): 68.

Moretti, P., and L. Divone. "Modern Windmills." *Scientific American* 254 (June 1986): 110.

Shea, C. P. "Harvesting the Wind." *World Watch* (March-April 1988): 12-18.

Wade, N. "Windmills: The Resurrection of an Ancient Energy Technology." In *Energy: Use, Conservation and Supply*, by P. H. Abelson. Washington, DC: American Association for the Advancement of Science, 1974.

White, L., Jr. "Medieval Uses of Air." *Scientific American* 223 (August 1970): 92.

Windscale (Sellafield) plutonium reactor, England

The Windscale nuclear reactor was built near Sellafield, a remote farm area of northern England, to supply **nuclear power** to the region. This early reactor was designed with a large graphite block in which were embedded cans containing the **uranium** fuel. The graphite served to slow down fast-moving **neutron**s produced during **nuclear fission**, allowing the reactor to operate more efficiently.

Graphite behaves in a somewhat unusual way when bombarded with neutrons. Water, its modern counterpart, becomes warmer inside the reactor and circulates to transfer heat away from the core. Graphite, on the other hand, increases in volume and begins to store energy. At some point above 572°F (300°C), it may then suddenly release that stored energy in the form of heat.

A safety system that allowed this stored energy to be released slowly was installed in the Windscale reactor. On October 7, 1957, however, a routine procedure designed to release energy stored in the graphite cube failed, and a huge amount of heat was released in a short period of time. The graphite moderator caught fire, uranium metal melted, and radioactive gases were released to the **atmosphere**. The fire burned for two days before it was finally extinguished with water.

Fortunately, the area around Windscale is sparsely populated, and no immediate deaths resulted from the accident. Shortly after the accident, however, quantities of radiation exceeding safe levels were observed in Norway, Denmark, and other countries east of the British islands. British authorities estimate that thirty or more **cancer** deaths since 1957 can be attributed to **radioactivity** released during the accident. In addition, milk from cows contaminated with radioactive **iodine-131** had to be destroyed. The British government eventually decided to close down and seal off the damaged nuclear reactor.

Four decades after the accident, Sellafield is still in the news. In 1991 the Radioactive Waste Management Advisory Committee recommended that Sellafield be chosen as the site for burying Britain's high-, low- and intermediate-level **radioactive waste**s. A complex network of tunnels 2500 feet (800 m) below ground level would be ready to accept wastes by the year 2005, according to the committee's plan.

Although some environmental groups object to the plan, many citizens do not seem to be very concerned. In spite of the high levels of radiation buried in the old plant, Sellafield has become one of the most popular vacation spots for Britons. *See also* High-level radioactive waste; Liquid metal fast breeder reactor; Low-level radioactive waste; Radiation exposure; Radiation sickness

[*David E. Newton*]

FURTHER READING

Dickson, D. "Doctored Report Revives Debate on 1957 Mishap." *Science* (5 February 1988): 556-557.

Dresser, P. D., ed. *Nuclear Power Plants Worldwide*. Detroit, MI: Gale Research, 1993.

Goldsmith, G., et al. "Chernobyl: The End of Nuclear Power?" *The Economist* 16 (1986): 138-209.

Herbert, R. "The Day the Reactor Caught Fire." *New Scientist* (14 October 1982): 84-87.

Howe, H. "Accident at Windscale: World's First Atomic Alarm." *Popular Science* (October 1958): 92-95+.

Pearce, F. "Penney's Windscale Thoughts." *New Scientist* (7 January 1988): 34-35.

Urquhart, J. "Polonium: Windscale's Most Lethal Legacy." *New Scientist* (31 March 1983): 873-875.

Winter range

Winter range is an area that animals use in winter for food and cover. Generally winter range contains a food source and thermal cover that together maintain the organism's energy balance through the winter, as well as some type of protective cover from predators. Although some **species** of animals have special adaptations, such as hibernation, to survive winter **climate**s, many must migrate from their summer ranges when conditions there become too harsh. Elk (*Cervus elaphus*) inhabiting mountainous regions, for example, often move from higher ground to lower in the fall, avoiding the early snow cover at higher elevations. Nothern populations of caribou or reindeer (*Rangifer tarandus*) often travel over 600 miles (965 km) between their summer ranges on the tundra and their winter ranges in northern woodlands. Still more extreme, the summer and winter ranges of some animals are located on different continents. North American birds known as **neotropical migrants** (including many species of songbirds such as warblers) simply fly to Central or South America in the fall, inhabiting winter ranges many thousands of miles from their summer breeding grounds.

Wise use movement

The wise use movement developed in the late 1980s as a response to the environmental movement and increasing government regulation. A grassroots environmental movement came about because of perceived impotence of federal regulatory agencies to either regulate the continuing flow of untested toxics into the **environment** or clean up the massive mountain of accumulating waste through the Superfund law. The wise use movement has begun to address the same issues but basically from a financial standpoint.

Recognizing that clean-up is far more costly than anticipated and persisting in the belief that **public land** should be available for business use, the wise use movement has begun to garner a growing constituency. One of the major new themes, for example, is that low exposures to **chemicals** and radiation are not harmful to humans or **ecosystem**s, or at least not harmful enough to warrant the billions of dollars needed to protect the environment and clean it up. Some companies, rather than changing manufacturing processes or doing research on less toxic chemicals, have chosen to continue doing business as usual and are among the leaders in the wise use movement.

The oil, mining, ranching, fishing, farming, and **off-road vehicles** industries—which are most affected by wetland regulation and restrictions on **land use**—also form a constituency for the wise use movement. The fight for control over land is an old one. Traditionally, the timber and mining companies have sought unrestricted access to public lands. Environmental groups such as the **Wilderness Society**, the **National Audubon Society**, the **Sierra Club**, and the **Nature Conservancy** have fought to restrict access. This controversy has been in open debate since at least 1877. At that time, Carl Schurz, then Secretary of the Interior, proposed the idea of **national forest**s, which would be rationally managed instead of exploited. Today, the debate between the environmental and wise use movements represents little more than the longstanding controversy over the best use of public lands—the 29.2 percent of the total area of the United States owned by the federal government.

At present, the wise use movement is most active in the western states with regard to the debate over land use, but it is moving into the East as well, where the movement is championed by developers who want to abolish **wetlands** regulations.

At this point, several thousand small groups and countless individuals identify to some degree with the wise use movement. They claim they are the only true environmentalists and label traditional environmentalists "preservationists who hate humans." The wise use aim is to gut all environmental legislation on the theory that regulation has ruined America by curtailing the rights of property owners. Many wise use advocates avoid complexity by simply denying the existence of many problems. For example, some wise use leaders insist that the **ozone layer depletion** problem was manufactured by the National Aeronautics and Space Administration (NASA) and isn't a real threat.

The philosophy of the wise use movement is based on a book by Ron Arnold and Alan Gottlieb, *The Wise Use Agenda* (1988). The movement took a major step forward after a conference held in Reno, Nevada, in August of 1988, sponsored by the Center for the Defense of Free Enterprise. Funding for the conference came from large corporations along with a number of right-wing business, political, and religious organizations. The conference was attended by roughly 300 people from across the United States and Canada, representing those industries that feel most threatened by current regulation. These people became the activist founders of the wise use movement. Calling themselves the "new environmentalists," they moved on to organize grassroots support.

The wise use movement has developed a 25-point agenda, seeking to foster business use of **natural resources**. Wise use goals are considered environmentally damaging and are opposed by the traditional environmentalist movement. The wise use movement pursues the development of **petroleum** resources in the **Arctic National Wildlife Refuge** in Alaska. It advocates **clear-cutting** of **old-growth forest** and replanting of public lands with baby trees, the latter at government expense. It wants to open all public lands, including **wilderness** and **national park**s, to mining and **oil drilling**. It seeks to rescind all federal regulation of those water resources originating in or passing through the states, favoring state regulation exclusively. The wise use movement further advocates the use of national parks for recreational purposes and a stop to all regulation that may exclude park visitors for protective purposes. It opposes any further restrictions on **rangelands** as livestock grazing areas. It advocates the prevention and immediate extinction of all **wildfire**s to protect timber for commercial harvesting.

The above is but a sampling of the agenda of wise use groups in the United States and abroad. The movement is using established corporate structures as a base, which provide training and support to activists. Corporations are now being joined by timber and logger associations, chambers of commerce, farm bureaus, and local organizations. The wise use movement is growing because of grassroots support.

Small farmers and ranchers and small mining and logging operations have come under tremendous financial pressure. Resources are dwindling, and costs are going up. With increased mechanization, small business owners and their livelihoods are threatened. To give one example, government scientists, after conducting five separate scientific studies, are recommending that timber harvests in the Pacific Northwest's ancient forests be reduced by 60 percent from what they were in the mid-1980s. Loggers would not be able to cut more than two billion board feet of wood a year from national forests in Oregon and Washington. That is substantially below the five billion-plus board feet the industry harvested on those lands annually from 1983 to 1987, before the dispute over protection of the **northern spotted owl** (*Strix occidentalis caurina*) and old-growth forests wound up in court. Jobs are lost, and people are frightened. The wise use movement is one effort to rally behind what these people see as their enemy—**environmentalism**.

In a strange irony, the grassroots activists of both the environmental movement and the wise use movement have much in common. The rank and file in the wise use movement represent the same kinds of grassroots concerns for environmental justice. Both sides see their well-being threatened, whether in terms of property values, livelihoods, or health, and have organized in self-defense. *See also* Environmental ethics

[*Liane Clorfene Casten and Marijke Rijsberman*]

FURTHER READING

Gottlieb, A. M., and R. Arnold. *The Wise Use Agenda*. Bellevue, WA: Free Enterprise Press, 1989.

Mendocino Environmental Center Newsletter 12 (Summer/Fall 1992).

Rachel's Hazardous Waste News (Environmental Research Foundation). Nos. 332, 335.

Wolman, Abel (1892-1989)

American engineer and educator

Born June 10, 1892 in Baltimore, the fourth of six children of Polish-Jewish immigrants, Wolman became one of the world's most highly respected leaders in the field of sanitary engineering, which evolved into what is now known as **environmental engineering**. His contributions in the areas of water supply, water and **wastewater** treatment, public health, nuclear reactor safety, and engineering education helped to significantly improve the health and prosperity of people not only in the United States but also around the world.

Wolman attended Johns Hopkins University, earning a bachelor's degree in 1913 and another bachelor's in engineering in 1915. He was one of four students in the first graduating class in the School of Engineering. In 1937, having already made major contributions in the field of sanitary engineering, he was awarded an honorary doctorate

Abel Wolman.

by the school. That same year he helped establish the Department of Sanitary Engineering in the School of Engineering and the School of Public Health, and served as its Chairman until his retirement in 1962. As a professor emeritus from 1962 to 1989, he remained active as an educator in many different arenas.

From 1914 to 1939, Wolman worked for the Maryland State Department of Health, serving as Chief Engineer from 1922 to 1939. It was during his early years there that he made what is regarded as his single most important contribution. Working in cooperation with a chemist, Linn Enslow, he standardized the methods used to chlorinate a municipal **drinking-water supply**.

Although **chlorine** was already being applied to drinking water in some locations, the scientific basis for the practice was not well understood and many utilities were reluctant to add a poisonous substance to the water. Wolman's technical contributions and his persuasive arguments regarding the potential benefits of chlorination encouraged many municipalities to begin chlorinating their water supplies. Subsequently, the death rates associated with water-borne communicable diseases plummeted and the average life span of Americans increased dramatically. He assisted many other countries in making similar progress.

During the course of his long and illustrious career, spanning eight decades, Wolman held over 230 official positions in the fields of engineering, public health, public works, and education. He served as a consultant to numerous utilities, state and local governments and agencies, and federal agencies, including the U.S. **Public Health Service**, the National Resources Planning Board, the **Tennessee Valley Authority**, the **Atomic Energy Commission**, the

U.S. **Geological Survey**, the National Research Council, the National Science Foundation, the Department of Defense, the Army, the Navy, and the Air Force.

On the international scene, Wolman served as an advisor to more than 50 foreign governments. For many years he served as an advisor to the World Health Organization (WHO), and he was instrumental in convincing the agency to broaden its focus to include water supply, sanitation, and sewage disposal. He also served as an advisor to the Pan American Health Organization.

Wolman was an active member of a broad array of professional societies, including the National Academy of Sciences, the National Academy of Engineering, the American Public Health Association, the American Public Works Association, the American Water Works Association, the Water Pollution Control Federation, and the American Society of Civil Engineers. His leadership in these organizations is exemplified by his service as President of the American Public Health Association in 1939 and the American Water Works Association in 1942.

Known as an avid reader and a prolific writer, Wolman authored four books and more than 300 professional articles. For 16 years (from 1921-1937) he served as editor-in-chief of the *Journal of the American Water Works Association*. He also served as Associate Editor of the *American Journal of Public Health* (1923-1927) and editor-in-chief of *Municipal Sanitation* (1929-1935).

Wolman was the recipient of more than 60 professional honors and awards, including the Albert Lasker Special Award (American Public Health Association, 1960), the National Medal of Science (presented by President Carter, 1975), the Tyler Prize for Environmental Achievement (1976), the Environmental Regeneration Award (Rene Dubos Center for Human Environments, 1985), and the Health for All by 2000 Award (WHO, 1988). He was an Honorary Member of 17 different national and international organizations, some of which named prestigious awards in his honor.

He was greatly admired for his outstanding integrity and widely known for the help and encouragement he gave to others, for his keen mind and sharp wit (even at the age of 96), for his willingness to change his mind when confronted with new information, and for his devotion to his family. His wife of 65 years, Anne Gordon, passed away in 1984. Wolman's son, Gordon, is Chairman of the Department of Geography and Environmental Science at Johns Hopkins University. *See also* Environmental education; Nuclear power; Sewage treatment; Water conservation; Water quality standards; Water treatment

[*Stephen J. Randtke*]

FURTHER READING

APWA Reporter 56 (October 1989): 24-5.

National Academy of Engineering of the United States of America. *Memorial Tributes* 5. Washington, DC: National Academy Press, 1992.

ReVelle, C. "Abel Wolman, 1892-1989." *EOS* 70 (29 August 1989).

Wolman, Abel. *Water, Health and Society: Selected Papers,* edited by G. F. White. Ann Arbor, MI: Books on Demand.

Wolves

Persecuted by humans for centuries, these members of the dog family (Canidae) are among nature's most maligned and least understood creatures. Yet they are intelligent, highly-evolved, sociable animals that play a valuable role in maintaining the **balance of nature**. Many conservationists consider the presence of wolves to be essential to a true **wilderness**.

Fairy tales such as "Little Red Riding Hood" and "The Three Little Pigs" notwithstanding, healthy, unprovoked wolves do not attack humans. Rather, they avoid them whenever possible. Wolves do prey on rabbits, rodents, and especially on hoofed animals like deer, elk, moose, and caribou. By seeking out the slowest and weakest animals, those that are easiest to catch and kill, wolves tend to cull out the sick and the lame, very old and young, and the unwary, less intelligent, biologically inferior members of the herd. In this way, wolves help ensure the "survival of the fittest" and prevent overpopulation, starvation, and the spread of diseases in the prey **species**.

Wolves have a disciplined, well-organized social structure. They live in packs, share duties, and cooperate in hunting large prey and rearing pups. Members of the pack, often an extended family composed of several generations of wolves, appear to show great interest in and affection for the pups and for each other, and have been known to bring food to a sick or injured companion. It is thought that the orderly and complex social structure of wolf society, especially the submission of members of the pack to the leaders, made it possible for early humans to socialize and domesticate a small variety of wolf that evolved into today's dogs. The famous howls in which wolves seem to delight appear to be more than a way of establishing territory or locating each other. Howling seems to be part of their social culture, often done seemingly for the sheer pleasure of it.

Nevertheless, few animals have withstood such universal, intense, and long-term persecution as have wolves, and with little justification. Bounties on wolves have existed for well over two thousand years and were recorded by the early Greeks and Romans. One of the first actions taken by the colonists settling in New England was to institute a similar system, which was later adopted throughout the United States. Sport and commercial hunting and trapping, along with federal poisoning and trapping programs—referred to as "predator control"—succeeded in eliminating the wolf from all of its original range in the contiguous forty-eight states excepting Minnesota.

The **U.S. Department of the Interior**, at the urging of conservationists, has proposed attempts to reestablish wolf populations in suitable areas, like **Yellowstone National Park**. (In 1995, the first wolves were released to roam the park; the group adapted extremely well and multiplied quickly. By 1997, nearby ranchers began to express concern that the wolves could become a threat to their livestock. It is possible that the dozen wolves most recently released into the park could be the last.) There are still, however, periodic

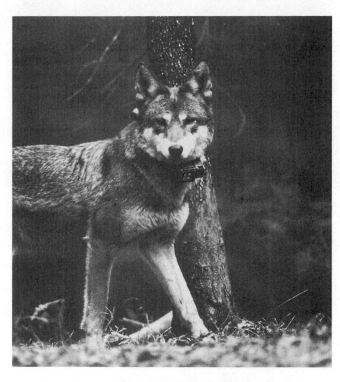

Red wolf, Smoky Mountains National Park.

reports of wolf sightings in Montana and other western states. Recovery programs for the red wolf (*Canis rufus*) are planned or underway in North and South Carolina, Florida, and elsewhere in the southeastern United States. But wolves remain controversial and western sheep and cattle ranchers strongly oppose efforts to bring them back, fearing that their livestock will be threatened.

American timber wolves continue to be hunted and trapped, legally and illegally, in their last remaining refuges in Minnesota and Alaska. Alaska has periodically allowed and even promoted the aerial hunting and shooting of wolves and has proposed plans to shoot wolves from airplanes in order to increase the numbers of moose and caribou for out-of-state sport hunters. One such proposal announced in late 1992 was postponed and then cancelled after **conservation** and **animal rights** groups threatened to launch a tourist boycott of the state.

In Minnesota, wolves are generally protected under the federal **Endangered Species Act**, but poaching persists because many consider wolves to be livestock killers. In Canada, they are frequently hunted, trapped, poisoned, and intentionally exterminated, sometimes to increase the numbers of moose, caribou, and other game animals, especially in the provinces of Alberta and British Columbia, and the Yukon Territory.

The most common type of wolf is the gray wolf (*Canis lupus*) which includes the timber wolf and the Arctic-dwelling tundra wolf. The **Fish and Wildlife Service** lists the gray wolf as an **endangered species** throughout its former range in Mexico and the continental United States, except in Minnesota, where it is "threatened." As many as 1,300 wolves may remain in the wilds of Minnesota, six to ten thousand in

Alaska, and thousands more in Canada. A population ranging from one or two dozen also lives on Isle Royale, Michigan.

The red wolf, a smaller type of wolf once found in the southeastern United States, is extinct or virtually so in the wild except for those released as part of recovery programs. The maned wolf (*Chryocyon brachyurus*) is considered endangered throughout its entire range of Argentina, Bolivia, Brazil, Peru, and Uruguay. *See also* Captive propogation and reintroduction; Extinction; Overhunting; Predator-prey interactions; Wildlife management

[*Lewis G. Regenstein*]

FURTHER READING

Mech, L. D. *The Wolf.* Garden City, New York: The Natural History Press, 1970.

Rutter, R. J. and D. H. Pimlott. *The World of the Wolf.* Philadelphia: J. B. Lippincott, 1968.

Woodpecker
See **Ivory-billed woodpecker**

Woodwell, George M. (1928-)
American biologist

A highly respected but controversial **biosphere** ecologist and biologist, Woodwell was born in Cambridge, Massachusetts. With his parents, who were both educators, Woodwell spent most of his summers on the family farm in Maine, where he was able to learn firsthand about biology, **ecology**, and the **environment**.

Woodwell graduated from Dartmouth College in 1950 with a bachelor's degree in zoology. Soon after graduation, he joined the Navy and served for three years on oceanographic ships. After returning to civilian life, he took advantage of a scholarship to pursue graduate studies and earned both a master's degree (1956) and a doctorate (1958) from Duke University. He began teaching at the University of Maine and was later appointed a faculty member and guest lecturer at Yale University. Throughout most of the 1960s and the early 1970s, Woodwell worked as senior ecologist at the Brookhaven National Laboratory. It was there that he conducted the innovative studies on environmental toxins which earned him a reputation as a nonconformist ecologist. In 1985, he founded the Woods Hole Research Center, a leading facility for ecological research.

A pioneer in the field of biospheric **metabolism**, Woodwell has worked to determine the effects of various toxins on the environment. One of the many studies he conducted examined the effects of **radiation exposure** on forest **ecosystem**s. He used a fourteen-acre combination pine and oak forest as his testing area, and found that the time needed to destroy an ecosystem is far less than that which is necessary to rejuvenate it. He continues to investigate the effects of nuclear **emission**s on the environment.

Beginning in the 1950s, Woodwell worked with the Conservation Foundation—now part of the **World Wildlife Fund**—in investigating the **pesticide** DDT. Woodwell and his colleagues were the first to study the catastrophic effects of the chemical on **wildlife** and, in 1966, were the first to take legal action against its producers. **DDT** was banned in the United States in 1972.

Much of Woodwell's work has focused on the hazards of the **greenhouse effect**. He has provided valuable information for hearings on environmental issues, and has been instrumental in developing similar data for the United States and foreign government agencies. Not only is Woodwell concerned about radiation, **chemicals**, and global warming, but like **Paul R. Ehrlich**, he warns that **population growth** must be kept in balance with any ecosystem development.

While he does publish articles in professional journals, Woodwell produces a number of works for more publications with a broader audience. He considers it imperative that the general population play a key role in saving the planet, and his work has appeared in periodicals such as *Ecology*, *Scientific American*, and the *Christian Science Monitor*.

Woodwell maintains membership in the National Academy of Sciences and is a past president of the Ecological Society of America. He is also a member of the **Environmental Defense Fund** and **Natural Resources Defense Council**. *See also* Biotic community; Family planning; Radioactivity; Zero population growth

[*Kimberley A. Peterson*]

FURTHER READING

Gareffa, P. M., ed. *Contemporary Newsmakers - 1987 Cumulation*. Detroit, MI: Gale Research, 1988.

Grady, D., and T. Levenson. "George Woodwell: Crusader for the Earth." *Discover* (May 1984): 44-6+.

Houghton, R. A., and G. M. Woodwell. "Global Climatic Change." *Scientific American* 260 (April 1989): 36-44.

Woodwell, George M., ed. *Earth in Transition: Patterns and Processes of Biotic Impoverishment*. New York: Cambridge University Press, 1991.

———, et al. *Ecological and Biological Effects of Air Pollution*. New York: Irvington, 1973.

———. "On Causes of Biotic Impoverishment." *Ecology* 70 (February 1989): 14-15.

World Bank

Affiliated with the United Nations, the World Bank was formally established in 1946 to finance projects to spur the economic development of member nations, most notably those in Europe and the **Third World**. The bank has been strongly criticized by environmental and human rights groups in recent years for funding Third World projects that destroy **rain forest**s, damage the **environment**, and harm villagers and **indigenous peoples**.

The bank is headquartered in Washington, D.C. It is administered by a board of governors and a group of executive directors. The board of governors is composed principally of the world's finance ministers and convenes annually. There are twenty-one executive directors who carry out policy matters and approve all loans. The World Bank usually makes loans directly to governments or to private enterprises with their government's guarantee when private capital is not available on reasonable terms. Generally, the Bank lends only for imported materials and equipment and services obtained from abroad. The interest rate charged depends primarily on the cost of borrowing to the Bank. The subscribed capital of the bank exceeds $30 billion, and the voting power of each nation is proportional to its capital subscription.

The 1970s represented a period of extensive growth for the World Bank, both in the volume of lending and the size of its staff. The staff was pressured to disperse money quickly, and little real support for grassroots development ever materialized within the institution. Local populations were hardly ever consulted and rarely taken into account for the majority of the enterprises the bank funded during this period. As a result, billions of dollars of bank money was managed ineffectively by domestic public institutions that were often unrepresentative. The stated purpose of the loans was to promote modernization and open economics, but the lending network further supported the elite in the Third World and prevented the poor from playing a meaningful role in the policies that were so markedly reshaping their environments.

The international debt crisis during this decade also changed the bank, beginning its evolution into a debt-management institution when it lifted the restrictions on non-project lending which had been established by its founders. In an effort to expedite its loan development, the bank underwent a major reorganization in 1986. It consolidated its activities under four senior vice presidents, but many consider the net results of these changes to be far from successful.

The most notable critics of the World Bank have been in the global environmental movement, but defects within the bank's operations complex have largely restricted their campaigns from effecting major changes. The bank has repeatedly withheld the majority of the information it generates in the preparation and implementation of projects, and many environmentalists continue to charge that it has become an institution fundamentally lacking the accountability and responsibility necessary for **sustainable development**.

The way the World Bank handled the controversial Narmada River Sandar Sarovar Dam project in India has been called a case in point. According to the **Environmental Defense Fund**, the history of bank involvement with the project reveals an institution whose primary agenda is to transfer money quickly, no matter what the cost in "systematic violation of its own environmental, economic and social policies and deception of its senior management and Board of Executive Directors." United States Executive Director E. Patrick Coady accused bank management and staff of a cover-up in relation to the Sandar Sarovar Dam, and he directly challenged the bank's credibility, noting that "no matter how egregious the situation, no matter how flawed the project, no matter how many policies have been violated, and no matter how dear the remedies prescribed, the bank will go forward on its own terms." Despite support from Germany, Japan, Canada, Australia, and the Scandinavian countries,

Coady's accusations were ignored. Bank management continued to finance the dam until early 1993, when criticism of the project became so intense that India decided to finance the project itself. There is no plan to resettle the 250,000 people who will be displaced.

Many argue that the failures of policies at the World Bank are illustrated by other case studies in Brazil, Costa Rica, and Ghana. In Brazil, International Monetary Fund (IMF) stabilization programs have hit the poor particularly hard and depleted the country's **natural resources**. Although these structural programs were designed to manage Brazil's tremendous foreign debt, critics argue they have been socially, economically, and environmentally catastrophic. The "economic miracle" of the 1970s never materialized for Brazil's masses, despite the fact that between 1955 and 1980 the economy grew more than any other country in the world. Due largely to ill-conceived IMF and World Bank advice and ineffective leadership by the Brazilian government, development decisions in Brazil have leaned toward extravagant and poorly implemented projects. Many major projects have failed miserably, only adding to lost investments, and the environmental devastation caused by such projects has been enormous, and much of it irreversible, involving massive destruction of the **tropical rain forest**.

The Tucurui Dam project, for example, was part of the Brazilian government's plan to build some 200 new hydroelectric power dams, most of them in the Amazonian region. This project has destroyed thousands of acres of tropical rain forest and degraded **water quality** in the **reservoir** and downstream, further lowering the income and affecting the health of communities below the dam. For environmentalists, Tucurui is representative of the problems inherent in building large **dams** in tropical regions: "Opening of forest areas leads to **migration** of landless people, **deforestation** of reservoir margins, **erosion** and **siltation** causing destruction of power-generating equipment and reduction of its useful lifespan; spread of waterborne disease to human and **wildlife** populations; and the permanent destruction of fish and wildlife **habitat**s, eliminating previously existing local economic activity and unknown numbers of **species** of plants and animals."

Ghana is usually touted by the World Bank and IMF as a particularly successful example of structural adjustment programs in Africa, but many believe that a closer examination reveals something different. The goal of the current adjustment program was to reduce the fiscal deficit, inflation, and external deficits by reducing domestic demand. A large portion of this plan was "to reverse the decline in agricultural production, restore overseas confidence in the Ghanian economy, increase foreign-exchange earnings, restore acceptable living standards, control inflation, reform prices and reestablish production incentives for cocoa." Although cocoa production had increased 20 percent by 1988 as a result of incentives in agricultural sector reform, with the income for cocoa production increasing by as much as 700 percent in some cases, cocoa farmers make up only 18 percent of Ghana's farming population. Furthermore, in recent decades a growing inequity within the cocoa-producing population

has been documented. Half of the land cultivated for cocoa today is owned by the top seven percent of Ghana's cocoa producers, while 70 percent own farms of less than six acres.

The timber industry in Ghana was also identified by the IMF and World Bank as an additional source of foreign exchange, and this led to the steady destruction of Ghana's forests. If timber production is maintained at its current rate and without appropriate environmental controls, many environmentalists and others believe that the Ghanian countryside will be stripped bare by the year 2000. The fishing industry is also threatened. Rising costs have caused the price of fish to increase while real wages have fallen. Ghanians receive 60 percent of their protein from the products of ocean fisheries, and decreased fish consumption in considered one of the leading factors in the rise of malnutrition in the country.

While mounting public pressure might cause the bank to reconsider some of its programs, reforms are possible only if supported by those nations controlling more than half of the bank's voting shares. And no matter what direction is taken, many experts believe that internal contradictions will continue to trouble the bank for years, further lowering the morale of the staff. As long as the bank continues to place priority on its debt-management functions, it will fail to change its policy of making large-scale loans for questionable and destructive projects. Overall quality will be further diminished as developing nations continue to give up natural resources for the rapid earning of foreign exchange. Debt management will force the bank to support large-scale, poorly-organized, and poorly-supervised projects, while the staff will be pressed harder to address wider development problems which will continue to be exacerbated by other aspects of bank lending.

The World Bank's dismal record of ignoring the interests of the poor and the environment clearly raises fundamental questions about the future of the institution. Environmentalists, human rights groups, and other critics of the Bank have offered the following suggestions for improving its operations. While there are obvious reasons for keeping some information confidential, they argue, the bank has abused this right. Greater freedom of information is necessary, for participation with population groups in the development process is impossible without public access. Critics also argue for the establishment within the bank of an independent appeals commission, maintaining that there is a clear need for a body that would hear and act on complaints of environmental and social abuses. It has been suggested that this commission could be made up of environmentalists, academics, church representatives, human rights groups, and others who would encourage the bank to emphasize sustainable development and eliminate environmentally destructive projects. And finally, it has been widely suggested that project quality should be the first priority of the World Bank, with the United Nations taking the lead in demanding this. In short, many believe the bank should no longer be allowed to function as a money-moving machine to address macroeconomic imbalances. *See also* Economic growth and the environment; Environmental economics; Environmental policy; Environmental stress; Green politics; Greens; United Nations Earth Summit; United Nations Environment Programme

[*Roderick T. White, Jr.*]

FURTHER READING

Le Prestre, P. G. *The World Bank and the Environmental Challenge.* London: Associated University Presses, 1989.

Payer, C. *The World Bank: A Critical Analysis.* New York: Monthly Review Press, 1982.

World Commission on Environment and Development

*See **Our Common Future***

World Conservation Strategy

The World Conservation Strategy (WCS): Living Resource Conservation for Sustainable Development is contained in a report published in 1980 and prepared by the International Union for Conservation of Nature and Natural Resources (now called **IUCN—The World Conservation Union**). Assistance and collaboration was received from the **United Nations Environment Programme** (UNEP), the **World Wildlife Fund** (WWF), the Food and Agriculture Organization of the United Nations (FAO), and the United Nations Educational, Scientific and Cultural Organization (UNESCO).

The three main objectives of the WCS are: (1) to maintain essential ecological processes and life-support systems on which human survival and development depend. Items of concern include **soil** regeneration and protection, the **recycling** of **nutrient**s, and protection of **water quality**; (2) to preserve genetic diversity on which depend the functioning of many of the above processes and life-support systems, the breeding programs necessary for the protection and improvement of cultivated plants, domesticated animals, and microorganisms, as well as much scientific and medical advance, technical innovation, and the security of the many industries that use living resources; (3) to ensure the sustainable utilization of **species** and **ecosystem**s which support millions of rural communities as well as major industries.

The WCS believes humans must recognize that the world's **natural resources** are limited, with limited capacities to support life, and must consider the needs of **future generations**. The object, then, is to conserve the natural resources, sustain development, and to support all life. Humans have great capacities for creation of wants or needs and also have great powers of destruction and annihilation. Human action has global consequences, and thus global responsibilities are crucial. The WCS aim is to provide an intellectual framework as well as practical implementation guidelines for achieving its three primary objectives.

The WCS has been endorsed by numerous leaders, organizations, and governments, and has formed the basis for preparation of National Conservation Strategies in over fifty countries.

The World Conservation Monitoring Centre (WCMC) mission is to support conservation and **sustainable development** by providing information on the world's **biodiversity**. It is a joint venture between the three main cooperators of WCS, IUCN, UNEP, and WWF.

The WCS has been supplemented and restated in a document called *Caring for The Earth: A Strategy for Sustainable Living*, published in 1991. This new document restates current thinking about **conservation** and development and suggests practical actions. It establishes targets for change and urges a concerted effort in personal, national, and international relations. It stresses measuring achievements against the objectives of actions.

The WCS of 1980 and the 1991 update have done much to bring attention to the need for sustainable management of the world's natural resources. It outlines problems, suggests needed changes, and stresses the need to quantitate the progress in meeting the needs of a sustainable world. *See also* Environmental education; Environmental ethics; Environmental monitoring; Sustainable biosphere

[*William E. Larson*]

FURTHER READING

Caring for the Earth: A Strategy for Sustainable Living. Gland, Switzerland: IUCN—The World Conservtion Union, 1991.

World Conservation Strategy. Gland, Switzerland: International Union for the Conservation of Nature and Natural Resources, 1980.

World Resources Institute (Washington, D.C.)

An international environmental and resource management policy center, the World Resources Institute researches ways to meet human needs and foster economic growth while conserving **natural resources** and protecting the **environment**. WRI's primary areas of concern are the economic effects of environmental deterioration and the demands on energy and the environment posed by both industrial and developing nations. Since its inception in 1982, WRI has provided governments, organizations, and individuals with information, analysis, technical support, and policy analysis on the interrelated areas of environment, development, and resource management.

WRI conducts various policy research programs and operates the Center for International Development and Environment, formerly the North American arm of the International Institute for Environment and Development. The institute aids governments and non-federal organizations in developing countries, providing technical assistance and policy recommendations, among other services. To promote public education of the issues with which it is involved, WRI also publishes books, reports, and papers; holds briefings, seminars, and conferences; and keeps the media abreast of developments in these areas.

WRI's research projects include programs in biological resources and institutions; economies and population; **climate**, energy, and **pollution**; technology and the environment; and resource and environmental information. In collaboration with the Brookings Institution and the Santa Fe Institute, WRI is also involved in a program called the 2050 Project, which seeks to provide a sustainable future for coming generations. As part of the program, studies will be conducted on such topics as food, energy, **biodiversity**, and the elimination of poverty.

The Center for International Development and Environment assists developing countries assess and manage their natural resources. The center's four main programs are: natural resources management strategies and assessments; natural resource information management; community planning and nongovernmental organization support; and sectoral resource policy and planning.

WRI's other programs are equally innovative. As part of the Biological Resources and Institutions project, WRI has developed a Global Biodiversity Strategy in collaboration with the World Conservation Union and the **United Nations Environment Programme**. The strategy, developed in 1992, outlines 85 specific actions required in the following decade to slow the decline in biodiversity worldwide. The program has also researched ways to reform forest policy in an attempt to halt **deforestation**.

The program on climate, energy, and pollution strives to develop new and different transportation strategies. In so doing, WRI staff have explored the use of **hydrogen**- and electric-powered vehicles and proposed policies that would facilitate their use in modern society. The program also researches renewable **alternative energy sources**, including solar, wind, and biomass power.

WRI is funded privately, by the United Nations, and by national governments. It is run by a 40-member international Board of Directors. Contact: World Resources Institute, 1709 New York Avenue, NW, Suite 700, Washington, DC 20006. Internet: http://www.wri.org/wri/index.html.

[*Kristin Palm*]

World Wildlife Fund (Washington, D.C.)

The World Wildlife Fund (WWF) is an international **conservation** organization founded in 1961, and known internationally as the World Wide Fund for Nature. The World Wildlife Fund acts with other U.S. organizations in a network to conserve the natural **environment** and ecological processes essential to life. Particular attention is paid to **endangered species** and to natural **habitat**s important for human welfare. In hundreds of projects conducted or supported around the world, WWF helps protect endangered wildlife and habitats and helps protect the earth's **biodiversity** through fieldwork, scientific research, institutional development, wildlife trade monitoring, public policy initiatives, technical assistance and training, **environmental education**, and communications.

WWF has articulated nine goals that guide its work:

1) to protect habitat;
2) to protect individual **species**;
3) to promote ecologically sound development;
4) to support scientific investigation;
5) to promote education in developing countries;
6) to provide training for local **wildlife** professionals;
7) to encourage self-sufficiency in developing countries;
8) to monitor international wildlife trade;
9) to influence public opinion and the policies of governments and private institutions.

Toward these goals, WWF monitors international trade in wild plants and animals through its TRAFFIC (Trade Records Analysis of Flora and Fauna in Commerce) program, part of an international network in cooperation with **IUCN—The World Conservation Union**. TRAFFIC focuses on the trade regulations of the **Convention on International Trade in Endangered Species of Wild Fauna and Flora** (CITES), tracking and reporting on traded wildlife species; helping governments comply with CITES provisions; developing training materials and enforcement tools for wildlife-trade enforcement officers; pressing for stronger enforcement under national wildlife trade laws; and seeking protection for newly threatened species.

Other recent WWF projects have included programs to save the African **elephant**, especially through banning ivory imports under CITES legislation. The organization also has undertaken projects to preserve **tropical rain forest**s; to identify conservation priorities in the earth's biogeographical regions; to halt overexploitation of **renewable resources**; and to create new parks and wildlife preserves to conserve species before they become endangered or threatened. Based on WWF's conservation efforts, The Charles Darwin Foundation for the Galapagos Islands awarded WWF an institutional seat on their Board of Directors.

WWF also funded a study of more than 2,000 projects or activities reviewed by the U.S. **Fish and Wildlife Service** between 1986 and 1991. The study found that only 18 of these projects were blocked or withdrawn because of detrimental effects to human populations. The study also showed that the Northwest lost more timber jobs to automation of timber cutting and milling, increased exports of raw logs, and a shift of the industry to the Southeastern United States, than it may lose from the listing of the **northern spotted owl** (*Strix occidentalis caurina*) as an endangered species.

WWF has been credited with saving some 30 endangered animal species from **extinction**, most notably the **giant panda**, which has become the group's logo. Using Georgraphic Information Systems satellite technology, WWF has identified regions where conservation of distinct animal and plant species are most needed. By overlaying these areas with existing parks and projects, WWF is able to see where it needs to concentrate conservation programs. The organization publishes a wide variety of materials, including the periodicals *WWF Letter*, *TRAFFIC*, and *Tropical Forest Conservation*. Booklets produced include "Speaker and News Media Sourcebook: A Guide to Experts in Domestic and International Environmental Issues," for news media, policymakers, and organizations. Educational materials, research papers, and books jointly published include *The Gaia Atlas of Future Worlds: Challenge and Opportunity in an Age of Change* (by Norman Myers); *Options for Conservation: The Different Roles of Nongovernmental Conservation Organizations* (by Sarah Fitzgerald); *WWF Atlas of the Environment* (By Geoffrey Lean, et al.); and *The Official World Wildlife Fund Guide to Endangered Species of North America*. In 1996 the WWF produced a nationwide environmental program, Windows on the Wild, for educators concerning the challenges of global conservation. Contact: World Wildlife Fund-U.S., 1250 12th Street, NW, Washington, DC 20037. Internet: http://www.wwf.org/.

[*Linda Rehkopf*]

Worldwatch Institute (Washington, D.C.)

Worldwatch Institute, a research organization based in Washington, D.C., compiles and publishes information on worldwide environmental problems; it also suggests solutions and alternative courses of action. The Institute was founded in 1975 by **Lester R. Brown**, with financial assistance from the Rockefeller Brothers Fund. Brown is now its president and director of research; chairman of the board is former Secretary of Agriculture Orville Freeman. Membership is $25 annually. The fee helps support the Institute's research and publications, which members receive, but there are no avenues for membership participation within the Institute.

The Institute has published the *State of the World* report annually since 1984; sales in recent years reached 200,000. It is issued in 26 languages and is used as a textbook in over 600 colleges in the United states alone. The publication examines such topics as **global warming**, water and **air quality**, and the environmental impact of social policies. In 1990, *State of the World* was produced as a 10-part series on public television, a joint venture with the producers of *Nova*. The 1992 edition describes "a planet at risk" and warned that "the policy decisions we make during this decade will determine" the quality of life for **future generations**.

Six to eight other Worldwatch papers are published each year, and over a hundred monographs have been issued on specific subjects. *Worldwatch* magazine is published in several languages, and the *Environmental Alert* series targets particular environmental issues. Worldwatch's newest publication is a handbook of statistical indicators, *Vital Signs: The Trends That Are Shaping Our Future*, covering the **environment**, economy, and society. Contact: Worldwatch Institute, 1776 Massachusetts Avenue, NW, Washington, DC 20036. Internet: http://www.worldwatch.org/.

[*Lewis G. Regenstein and Amy Strumolo*]

X ray

Discovered in 1895 by German physicist Wilhelm K. Roentgen, x rays are a form of electromagnetic radiation, widely used in medicine, industry, metal detectors, and scientific research. X rays are most commonly used by doctors and dentists to make pictures of bones, teeth, and internal organs in order to find breaks in bones, evidence of disease, and cavities in teeth.

Since x rays are a form of **ionizing radiation**, they can be very dangerous. They penetrate into, and are absorbed by, plants and animals and can age, damage, and destroy living tissue. They can also cause skin burns, genetic **mutation**s, **cancer**, and death at high levels of exposure. The effects of ionizing radiation tend to be cumulative, and every dose adds to the possibility of further damage.

Some authorities feel that people should try to minimize their exposure to such radiation and avoid being x-rayed unless absolutely necessary. This is especially true of pregnant women, since studies show a much higher rate of childhood **leukemia** and other diseases among children who were exposed to x rays in utero. Ironically, fear of malpractice suits has prompted many doctors to increase the number of x rays performed while examining patients for disease. *See also* Radiation exposure

Xenobiotic

Designating a foreign and usually harmful substance or organism in a biological system. Xenobiotic, derived from the Greek roots *xeno*, meaning "stranger" or "foreign," and *bio*, meaning "life," describes some **toxic substance**s, **parasites**, and symbionts. Food, drugs, and poisons are examples of xenobiotic substances in individual organisms, and their toxicity is linked to the level of consumption. In communities or **species**, xenobiosis happens when two distinct species, such as different kinds of ants, share living space like nests. At the **ecosystem** level, toxic waste, when bioaccumulated in the **food chain/web**, is xenobiotic. *See also* Bioaccumulation; Hazardous waste; Symbiosis

Xeriscaping
See **Arid landscaping**

Xylene

The term xylene refers to any of three **benzene** derivative isomers that share the same chemical formula, $C_6H_4(CH_3)_2$, but differ in their molecular structure. They are useful as solvents, as additives to improve the **octane rating** of aviation fuels, and as raw materials in the manufacture of fibers, films, dyes, and other synthetic products. Because of their high volatility they are classified as aromatic **hydrocarbons** (volatile compounds containing only carbon and **hydrogen** atoms). Xylene fractions were first isolated from coal tar in the mid-nineteenth century in Germany. Coal tar is the thick liquid product of the carbonization, or destructive distillation, of coal, a process in which **coal** is heated without air to temperatures above 1,600°F (862°C). Benzene and toluene, two aromatic hydrocarbons similar to xylene, are formed in the same process. Coal tar remained the source for xylene until industrial demand outgrew the supply. Later, techniques were developed to obtain xylene from **petroleum** refining, and today petroleum is a major source.

The three isomeric xylenes are classified by the arrangement of the methyl (CH_3) groups substituting for hydrogen atoms on the benzene ring. In each case, the methyl groups replace two of the hydrogens attached to the six-carbon benzene ring, but the structure and chemical properties of each isomer depend on which hydrogens are replaced. Ortho-xylene (o-xylene) has methyl groups on two adjacent carbons in the benzene ring structure, while in meta- xylene (m-xylene) the methyl-containing carbons are separated by a hydrogen-containing carbon. In para-xylene (p-xylene) two hydrogen-bearing carbons separate the methyl-containing carbons, placing the methyl groups at opposite ends of the molecule. Ortho-xylene, the least volatile of the three forms, serves as raw material for the manufacture of coatings and plastics. Para-xylene is used to manufacture polyesters. Meta-xylene, less useful than the other forms, is used to make coatings, plastics, and dyes. A commercial xylene mixture in the form of a colorless, flammable, non-viscous, toxic liquid is used as a solvent for lacquers and rubber cements. Emulsified xylene has been used as an economical and effective way of controlling aquatic weeds in **irrigation** systems, but concentrations must be carefully controlled to avoid harming plants and fish exposed to the residues.

Xylene's volatility leads to its easy escape into the **atmosphere**. Unless care is taken, its fumes soon permeate the air in laboratories where it is used. Although its solubility in water is quite limited, xylene, (along with benzene and toluene), is classified as one of the primary components of the "water-soluble" fraction of petroleum. The widespread use of xylene in manufacturing has resulted in significant releases of the chemical into the air and water of the environment. Xylene's toxicity in water is influenced by salinity, temperature, and the presence of other toxic materials. It affects cell permeability and acts as a neurotoxin for fish and other animals. At high concentrations of xylene, fish exhibit a series of behavioral changes including restlessness (rapid and erratic swimming), loss of equilibrium, paralysis, and death. Although each of the three forms of xylene can be detoxified by microorganisms, para-xylene is more difficult to detoxify, and therefore a more persistent threat.

[*Douglas C. Pratt*]

FURTHER READING

Buikema, L., and A.C. Hendricks. *Benzene, Xylene, and Toluene in Aquatic Systems: A Review.* Washington, D.C.: American Petroleum Institute, 1980.

Hancock, E.G., ed. *Toluene, the Xylenes, and Their Industrial Derivatives.* Amsterdam; New York: Elsevier, 1982.

Parmeggiani, L. Technical ed. *Encyclopaedia of Occupational Health and Safety*, 3rd ed. Geneva: International Labour Office, 1983.

Walsh, D. F., ed. *Residues of Emulsified Xylene in Aquatic Weed Control and Their Impact on Rainbow Trout, Salmo gairdneri.* Denver, CO: U.S. Dept. of the Interior [Bureau of Reclamation, Engineering and Research Center, Division of General Research, Applied Sciences Branch], 1977.

Yard waste

As the field of solid **waste management** becomes more developed and specialized, the categories into which **solid waste** is sorted and managed become more numerous. Yard waste—often called vegetative waste—includes leaves, grass clippings, tree trimmings, and other plant materials that are typically generated in outdoor residential settings. Depending on the season and the neighborhood, leaves may account for 5-30% of the total municipal solid waste stream, grass clippings may comprise 10-20%, and wood may form about 5-10%. Yard waste does not include food and **animal waste**s except, possibly, as impurities. Yard waste is usually perceived as the *cleanest* type of solid waste, in contrast to household refuse or industrial and commercial trash.

Since yard waste is almost entirely vegetative in nature, it lends itself easily to **composting**. Composting is the natural breakdown of organic matter, in the presence of oxygen, by microbes to form a stable end product called compost. In the management of yard waste, this natural process decreases the need for **landfill** space and produces **soil** amendment as an end product.

Beneficial use and composting of yard waste may be practiced in the homeowner's backyard or in the waste management areas set up by townships and municipalities. Not all forms of yard waste lend themselves equally well to composting. In fact woody materials such as tree trunks may be better managed and used by shredding into wood chips or saw dust, since wood is very resistant to composting. Leaves are most suitable for composting and provide the richest and most stable base of material and **nutrient**s. With sufficient oxygen, water, and turnover, leaves can usually be broken down in a matter of weeks. Grass clippings decompose so quickly that they need to be mixed with slower degrading materials such as leaves in order to slow down and regulate the rate of **decomposition**. Control over the decomposition process is essential because of the potential for problems such as obnoxious odors. If the decomposition process is too rapid and proceeds without sufficient oxygen, the process becomes **anaerobic** and generates odors that can be highly unpleasant. In seasons other than fall, when the volume of leaves in yard waste is relatively small, many experts recommend that grass clippings be used as **mulch** rather than as compost to avoid the potential for odor.

In urban and mixed **land use** neighborhoods, yard waste may inadvertently contain **plastics**, papers, and other non-degradable materials. In some areas, the *bagging* of yard waste may involve the use of plastic bags. Depending on the efficiency of separation at the waste management area, these inert materials may find their way into the final compost product and lower the esthetics and usefulness of the compost.

[*Usha Vedagiri*]

FURTHER READING

Strom, P. F. and M. S. Finstein. *Leaf Composting and Yard Waste Management for New Jersey Municipalities.* New Jersey Department of Environmental Protection and Energy, 1993.

Yellowstone National Park, Wyoming

Yellowstone National Park has the distinction of being the world's first **national park**. With an area of 3,472 square miles (8,992 sq km), Yellowstone is the largest national park in the lower 48 states. This is an area larger than Rhode Island and Delaware combined. Although primarily in Wyoming (91%), 7.6% of the park is in Montana and the remaining 1.4% is in Idaho.

John Colter, a member of the Lewis and Clark expedition from 1803-1806, was probably the first white man to visit and report on the Yellowstone area. At that time the only Native Americans living year-round in the area were a mixed group of Bannock and Shoshone known as *sheepeaters*. In 1859, the legendary trapper and explorer Jim Bridger, who had been reporting since the 1830s about the wonders of the region, led the first government expedition into the area. The discovery of gold in the Montana Territory in the 1860s brought more expeditions. In 1870, the Washburn-Langford-Doane expedition came to verify the reports about the wonders of the area. They spent four weeks naming the features, including Old Faithful, the most famous geyser in the world. Legend states that while the 19 members of this expedition sat around a campfire, reflecting on the beauty of the area, they came up with the idea of turning the region into a national park. The truth of the legend is debatable. Yet there is no doubt that it was the lecturing and writing of these men that prompted the United States **Geological Survey**

Map of the Yellowstone ecosystem complex or biogeographical region, which extends far beyond the boundaries of the park.

to send a follow-up group to the park in 1871. Reports and photographs from the U.S. Geological Survey expedition stimulated the drafting of legislation to create the first national park. Because of the prevalent utilitarian philosophy and the country's poor economic condition, the battle for the park was difficult and hard-fought. Eventually the park proponents were successful, and on March 1, 1872, President Ulysses S. Grant signed the bill establishing the park.

Because Congress did not allocate any money for park maintenance or protection, the early years of the park were marked by vandalism, **poaching**, the deliberate setting of forest fires, and other destructive behaviors. Eventually, in 1886, the U.S. Army took responsibility for the park. They remained in the role of park managers until the **National Park Service** was formed in 1916.

Water covers about 10% of the park. The largest body of water is Yellowstone Lake with a surface area of 136 square miles (352 sq km). It is one of the largest, highest, and coldest lakes in North America. The park has one of the highest waterfalls in the United States (Lower Yellowstone Falls, 308 feet; 93.87 meters) and the top three trout fishing streams in the world. Approximately 10,000 thermal features can be found in the park. In fact, there are more geysers (200–250) and hot springs in the park than in the rest of the world put together.

The park has a great abundance and diversity of **wildlife**. It has the largest concentration of mammals in the lower 48 states. There are 58 **species** of mammals in the park, including two species of bears and seven species of ungulates. It is one of the last strongholds of the **grizzly**

bear and is the only place where a bison herd has survived continuously since primitive times. Yellowstone is noted also for having the largest concentration of elk to be found anywhere in the world. Besides mammals, the park is home for 279 species of birds, 18 species of fish, 5 species of reptiles, and 4 species of amphibians.

However, one of the continuing difficulties at Yellowstone and other national parks is that Yellowstone is not a self-contained **ecosystem**. Its boundaries were established through a variety of political compromises, and lands around the park that once provided a buffer against outside events are being developed. Airsheds, watersheds, and animal migration routes extend far beyond park boundaries yet they dramatically affect conditions within the park. Yellowstone is but one example of the need to manage entire biogeographical areas to preserve natural conditions within a national park.

[*Ted T. Cable*]

FURTHER READING

Frome, M. *National Park Guide.* 19th ed. Chicago: Rand McNally, 1985.
Yellowstone Fact Sheet. National Park Service, U. S. Department of Interior, 1992.

Yokkaichi asthma

Nowhere is the connection between industrial development and environmental and human health deterioration more graphically demonstrated than at Yokkaichi, Japan. An international port located on the Ise Bay, Yokkaichi was a major textile center by 1897. The shipping business shifted to nearby Nagoya in 1907, and Yokkaichi filled in its coastal lowlands in a successful bid to attract modern industries, especially chemical processing, steel production, and oil and **gasoline** refining.

Spurred by both the World War II demand and the postwar recovery effort, several more **petrochemical** companies were added through the 1950s, creating an oil refinery complex called the Yokkaichi Kombinato. In 1959 it began 24-hour operations, and the sparkle of hundreds of electric lights became known as the "million-dollar night view." Although citizens took pride in the growing industrial complex, their enthusiasm waned when **air pollution** and **noise pollution** created human health problems. As early as 1953 the central government sent a research group to try to discover the cause, but no action was taken. Instead, the petrochemical complex was expanded.

As citizens began to complain about breathing difficulties, scientists documented a high correlation between airborne **sulfur dioxide** concentrations and bronchial **asthma** in schoolchildren and chronic **bronchitis** in individuals over forty. Despite this knowledge a second industrial complex was opened in 1963. In the Isozu district of Yokkaichi the average concentration of sulfur dioxide was eight times that of unaffected districts. Taller smokestacks spread **pollution** over a wider area but did not resolve the problem; increased production also added to the volume discharged. Despite resistance, a third industrial complex was added in

1973, one of the largest **petroleum** refining and ethylene producing facilities in Japan.

As the petrochemical industries continued to expand, local citizens' quality of life deteriorated. In the early years, heavy **smoke** was emitted by coal **combustion**, and parents worried about the exposure of schoolchildren whose playground was close to the **emission**s source. Switching from **coal** to oil in the 1960s seemed to be an improvement; but the now-invisible stack gases still contained large quantities of sulfur oxides, and more people developed **respiratory diseases**. By 1960 fish from the local waterways had developed such a bad taste that they were unsalable, and fishermen demanded compensation for their lost livelihood. By 1961 48% of children under six, 30% of people over sixty, and 19% of those in their twenties had respiratory abnormalities. In 1964 a pollution-free room was established in the local hospital where victims could take refuge and breath freely.

Even so, in 1966 two desperate people committed suicide, and 12 Yokkaichi residents who had been trying to resolve the problem by negotiation finally filed a damage suit against the Shiohama Kombinato in 1967. In 1972, the judge awarded the plaintiffs $286,000 in damages to be paid jointly by the six companies. This was the first case in which a group of Japanese companies were forced to pay damages, making other kombinatos vulnerable to similar suits. As a consequence of the successful litigation by the Yokkaichi victims, the Japanese government enacted a basic antipollution law in 1967. Two years later, the Law Concerning Special Measures for the Relief of Pollution-Related Patients was enacted. It applied to chronic bronchitis/bronchial asthma victims not only from Yokkaichi but also Kawasaki and Osaka. In addition, national air-pollution standards were strengthened to require that oil refineries adhere to air pollution abatement policies.

By 1975, the annual mean sulfur dioxide levels had decreased by a factor of three, below the target level of 0.017 **parts per million** (ppm). The harmful effects on residents of Yokkaichi also decreased. In 1973 the Law Concerning Compensation for Pollution-Related Health Damages and Other Measures aided sufferers of chronic bronchitis and bronchial asthma from the other affected areas of Japan, especially Tokyo. As of December, 1991, 97,276 victims throughout Japan, including 809 from Yokkaichi, were eligible for compensation. *See also* Air-pollutant transport; Environmental law; Industrial waste treatment; Tall stacks

[*Frank M. D'Itri*]

FURTHER READING

"Diseases By Air Pollution." In *Quality of the Environment in Japan*. Tokyo, Japan: Environmental Agency, Government of Japan, 1990.

Huddle, N., and M. Reich. *Island of Dreams: Environmental Crisis in Japan*. Tokyo, Japan: Autumn Press, 1975.

Yosemite National Park, California

Yosemite National Park is a 748,542-acre (303,160-ha) park, located on the western slope of the Sierra Nevadas in northern California. The name Yosemite comes from the name of an Indian tribe, the *U-zu-ma-ti*, who were massacred in 1851 by soldiers sent by the governor of California for refusing to attend a reservation agreement meeting.

By the mid-1800s Yosemite had become a thriving tourist attraction. As word of Yosemite's wonders spread back to the East Coast, public pressure led Congress to declare that the Yosemite Valley and the Mariposa Grove of giant sequoias be held "inalienable for all time." President Abraham Lincoln signed this law on June 30, 1864, turning this land over to the state of California and thereby giving Yosemite the distinction of being the first *state park*. Concern about sheep **overgrazing** in the high meadows led to the designation of the high country as a **national park** in 1890.

The person most strongly associated with the protection of Yosemite and its designation as a national park is naturalist and philosopher **John Muir**. Muir, sometimes called the "Thoreau of the West," first came to Yosemite in 1868. He devoted the next 40 years of his life to ensuring that the ecological integrity of the region was maintained. In 1892, Muir founded the **Sierra Club** to organize efforts to gain national park status for the Yosemite Valley.

Yosemite National Park is famous for its awesome and inspiring scenery. Geologic wonders include the mile-wide Yosemite valley surrounded by granite walls and peaks such as "El Capitan" (7,569 feet [2,307 meters] above sea level; 3,593 feet [1,095 meters] from base) and "Half Dome" (8,842 feet [2,695 meters] above sea level; 4,733 feet [1,443 meters] from base). Spectacular waterfalls include Yosemite Falls (Upper 1,430 feet [436 meters], Middle 675 feet [206 meters], Lower 320 feet [98 meters]), Ribbon Falls (1,612 feet [491 meters]), Bridalveil Falls (620 feet [189 meters]), Sentinel Falls (2,000+ feet [610 meters]), Horsetail Falls (1,000+ feet [305 meters]), and Vernal Falls (317 feet [97 meters]).

The park supports an abundance of plant and animal life. Eleven **species** of fish, 29 species of reptiles and amphibians, 242 species of birds, and 77 species of mammals can be found in the park. There are approximately 1,400 species of flowering plants, including 37 tree species. The most famous of the tree species found here is the giant sequoia (*Sequoiadendron giganteum*). The park has three groves of giant sequoias, the largest being the Mariposa Grove with 500 mature trees, 200 of which exceed 10 feet (3 meters) in diameter.

Because of the high degree of development and the congestion from the large numbers of visitors (over 3.5 million in 1991), some have disparagingly referred to the Valley as "Yosemite City." Yosemite has become a focal point in the controversy of whether we are "loving our parks to death." People management has become as critical as traditional resource management. At Yosemite, balancing the public's needs and desires with the protection of the **natural resources** is the **National Park Service**'s greatest challenge as they plan for the twenty-first century.

[*Ted T. Cable*]

FURTHER READING

Frome, M. *National Park Guide.* 19th ed. Chicago: Rand McNally, 1985.

Yosemite 1992 Fact Sheet. National Park Service, U. S. Department of Interior, 1992.

Yucca Mountain, Nevada

Yucca Mountain is a barren desert ridge about 100 mi (161 km) southeast of Las Vegas, Nevada. The **United States Department of Energy** plans to build its first, and apparently only, high-level nuclear waste storage facility there in an extensive series of tunnels deep beneath the **desert** surface. Choosing this site was a long and divisive process. And although ten years and more than $1 billion have been spent designing and testing the storage facility, it is still not clear whether it will remain dry and stable for the thousands of years it will take for natural decay processes make the wastes less radioactive.

Most of the nuclear waste to be stored at Yucca Mountain will come from **nuclear power** plants. As radioactive uranium[235] is consumed in fission reactions, the fuel becomes depleted and accumulating waste products reduce energy production. Every year about one-third of the fuel in a typical reactor must be removed and replaced with a fresh supply. The spent (depleted) fuel must be handled and stored very carefully because it contains high concentrations of toxic radioactive elements, such as cesium[134], **iodine[131]**, plutonium[239], strontium[89] and ruthenium[106], in addition to natural **uranium**, thorium, and **radon isotope**s. Some of these materials have very long half-lives, requiring storage for at least 10,000 years before their **radioactivity** is reduced to harmless levels by natural decay processes.

Originally, the United States intended to reprocess spent fuel to extract and purify unused uranium and **plutonium** as fuel for advanced breeder reactors. Reprocessing plants released unacceptable amounts of radioactivity, however, and breeder reactors proved to be too expensive and dangerous to serve as civilian power sources. For a time in the 1950s, nuclear wastes were dumped in the ocean, but that practice was stopped when it was discovered that the corroding metal waste containers allow toxins to dissolve in sea water.

In 1982, the U.S. Congress ordered the **U.S. Department of Energy** (DOE) to build tow sites for permanent **radioactive waste** disposal on land by 1998. Understandably, no one wanted this toxic material in their backyard. In 1987, after a long and highly contentious process, DOE announced that it could only find one acceptable site: Yucca Mountain.

The storage facility would be a honeycomb of tunnels more than 1,000 ft (303.3 m) below the surface. When finished, the total length of the tunnels would be more than 112 mi (km)—approximately the size of the world's largest subway system in New York City. Altogether, the tunnels would have room for more than 60,000 tons of nuclear waste packed in corrosion-resistant metal canisters. Because Yucca Mountain is located in one of the driest areas in the U.S. and the bedrock is composed of highly stable volcanic tuff (compacted ash) DOE hopes that storage areas will remain intact and free of leaks for the thousands of years it will take for the wastes to decay to harmless state. Total costs for this facility are estimated to be somewhere between $10-35 billion dollars.

Ever since its designation as the nation's sole repository for high-level nuclear waste, Yucca Mountain has been embroiled in both scientific and political controversy. Citizens of Nevada feel they were ganged up on by all the other states and that they were chosen only because they don't have the political clout to resist. Ironically, Nevada doesn't even have a nuclear power plant. State officials and the Nevada Congressional delegation have vowed to do everything in their power to try to stop construction and operation of the nuclear waste facility.

Scientists are divided about the safety of the site. Although some studies suggest that Yucca Mountain has been geologically stable for thousands of years, others show a history of fairly recent volcanic activity and large earthquakes in the area. Fractures and faults have been discovered in the bedrock that could allow ground water to seep into storage vaults if the climate changes. One hydrologist suggests that **groundwater** levels, while low now, could rise suddenly and fill the tunnels with water.

Although more than $1 billion has been spent on exploratory studies and trial drilling at Yucca Mountain, the DOE announced in 1986 that it could not meet the 1998 deadline imposed by Congress. The earliest date by which the repository might be operational is now 2010. States and power companies, having already paid more than $12 billion to DOE to build the repository, are threatening to sue if it doesn't open as originally promised. Some utilities have begun to negotiate privately with Indian tribes and foreign countries to take their nuclear wastes.

While underground storage of nuclear wastes is fraught with problems and uncertainties, none of the alternatives now available to us appears clearly better. Nevertheless, we have to do something with the wastes we already have generated. Currently, about 30,000 tons of spent fuel is sitting at more than 100 nuclear power plants in 34 states. Most of this waste is being stored in deep water-filled pools inside the plants. These pools were never intended for long-term storage and are now over-crowded. Many power plants have no more room for spent fuel storage and will be forced to shut down in the next ten years unless some form of long-term storage is approved. In 1997, DOE asked Congress for $100 million to purchase large steel casks in which power companies can stockpile spent fuel assemblies in outdoor storage yards. Neighbors who live near these storage sites worry about the possibility of leakage and accidents. Nevertheless, several utilities have already begun on-site dry cask storage.

Waste storage at Yucca Mountain is a complex, expensive, and potentially highly risky problem that exemplifies the unexpected complications of many environmental issues. It also demonstrates the difficulty of making democratic decisions in issues with consequences that affect large geographical areas and future generations in ways that we can neither predict nor control to the degree that we would like.

[*William P. Cunningham*]

FURTHER READING

Flynn, J., R.E. Kaserson, H. Kunreuther, and P. Slovic. "Overcoming Tunnel Vision: Redirecting the U.S. High-Level Nuclear Waste Program." *Environment* 39, no. 3 (April 1997):pp. 6-11.

Kerr, R.A. "A New Way to Ask the Experts: Rating Radioactive Waste Risks." *Science* 274, no. 5289 (8 November 1996): 913.

Poole, W. "Gambling With Tomorrow." *Sierra* 77, no. 5 (Sept/Oct 1992): 50.

Roush, W., and R.F. Service. "Can Nuclear Waste Keep Yucca Mountain Dry—and Safe?" *Science* 270, no. 5243 (15 December 1995): 1761.

Whipple, C.G. "Can Nuclear Waste be Stored Safely at Yucca Mountain?" *Scientific American* 274, no. 6: pp. 72-77.

Z

Zebra mussel (*Dreissena polymorpha*)

The zebra mussel is a small bivalve mollusk native to the freshwater rivers draining the Caspian and Black Seas of western Asia. This **species** of shellfish, which gets its name from the dark brown stripes on its tan shell, was introduced into the **Great Lakes** of the United States and Canada and became established sometime between 1985 and 1988.

The zebra mussel was first discovered in North America in June of 1988 in the waters of Lake St. Clair. The introduction probably took place two or three years prior to the discovery, and it is believed that a freighter dumped its ballast water into Lake St. Clair, flushing the zebra mussel out in the process. By 1989 this mussel had spread west through Lake Huron into Lake Michigan and east into **Lake Erie**. Within three years it had spread to all five of the Great Lakes.

Unlike many of its other freshwater relatives, which burrow into the sand or **silt** substrate of their **habitat**, the zebra mussel attaches itself to any solid surface. This was the initial cause for concern among environmentalists as well as the general public; these mollusks were attaching themselves to boats, docks, and water intake pipes. Zebra mussels also reproduce quickly, and they can form colonies with densities of up to 100,000 individuals per square meter. The city of Monroe, Michigan, lost its water supply for two days because its intake pipes were plugged by a huge colony of zebra mussels, and Detroit Edison spent half a million dollars cleaning them from the cooling system of its Monroe power plant. Ford Motor Company was forced to close its casting plant in Windsor, Ontario, in order to remove a colony from the pipes which send cooling water to their furnaces.

Although the sheer number of these filter feeders has actually improved **water quality** in some areas, they still pose threats to the ecological stability of the aquatic **ecosystem** in this region. Zebra mussels are in direct **competition** with native mussel species for both food and oxygen. Several colonies have become established on the spawning grounds of commercially important species of fish, such as the walleye, reducing their reproductive rate. The zebra mussel feeds on algae, and this may also represent direct competition with several species of fishes.

The eradication of the zebra mussel is widely considered an impossible task, and environmentalists maintain that

Zebra mussels on native clam on beach. [Photo from GLSGN Exotic Species Library.]

this species will now be a permanent member of the Great Lakes ecosystem. Most officials in the region agree that money would be wasted battling the zebra mussel, and they believe that it is more reasonable to accept their presence and concentrate on keeping intake pipes and other structures clear of the creatures. The zebra mussel has very few natural predators, and since it is not considered an edible species, it has no commercial value to man. One enterprising man from Ohio has turned some zebra mussel shells into jewelry, but currently the supply far exceeds the demand. *See also* Commercial fishing; Great Lakes Water Quality Agreement; Introduced species

[*Eugene C. Beckham*]

FURTHER READING

Griffiths, R. W., et al. "Distribution and Dispersal of the Zebra Mussel (*Dreissena polymorpha*) in the Great Lakes Region." *Canadian Journal of Fisheries and Aquatic Science* 48 (1991): 1381-1388.

Holloway, M. "Musseling In." *Scientific American* 267 (October 1992): 30-36.

Schloesser, D. W., and W. P. Kovalak. "Infestation of Unionids by *Dreissena polymorpha* in a Power Plant Canal in Lake Erie." *Journal of Shellfish Research* 10 (1991): 355-359.

Walker, T. "*Dreissena* Disaster." *Science News* 139 (4 May 1991): 282-284.

The Zebra Mussel, Dreissena polymorpha: A Synthesis of European Experiences and a Preview for North America. Ottawa: Ontario Environment, 1990.

Zebras

Zebras are striped members of the horse family (*Equidae*) native to Africa. These grazing animals stand 4-5 feet (1.2 to 1.5 meters) high at the shoulders and are distinctive because of their striking white and black or dark brown stripes running alternately throughout their bodies. These stripes actually have important survival value for zebras, for when they are in a herd, the stripes tend to blend together in the bright African sunlight, making it hard for a lion or other predator to concentrate on a single individual and bring it down.

The zebra's best defense is flight, and it can outrun any of its enemies. It is thus most comfortable grazing and browsing in groups on the flat open plains and **grasslands**. Zebras are often seen standing in circles, their tails swishing away flies, each one facing in a different direction, alert for lions or other predators hiding in the tall grass.

Most zebras live on the grassy plains of East Africa, but some are found in mountainous areas. They live in small groups led by a stallion, and mares normally give birth to a colt every spring. Zebras are fierce fighters, and a kick can kill or cripple predators (lions, leopards, cheetahs, jackals, hyenas, and wild dogs). These predators usually pursue newborn zebras, or those that are weak, sick, injured, crippled, or very old, as those are the easiest and safest to catch and kill. Such predation helps keep the gene pool strong and healthy by eliminating the weak and diseased and ensuring the "survival of the fittest."

Zebras are extremely difficult to domesticate, and most attempts to do so have failed. They are often found grazing with wildebeest, hartebeest, and gazelle, since they all have separate nutritional requirements and do not compete with each other. Zebras prefer the coarse, flowering top layer of grasses, which are high in cellulose. Their trampling and grazing are helpful to the smaller wildebeest, who eat the leafy middle layer of grass that is higher in protein. And the small gazelles feed on the protein-rich young grass, shoots, and herb blossoms found closest to the ground.

One of the most famous African **wildlife** events is the seasonal 800-mile (1,287-km) **migration** in May and November of over a million zebras, wildebeest, and gazelles, sweeping across the Serengeti plains, as they have done for centuries, "in tides that flow as far as the eye can see." But it is now questionable how much longer such scenes will continue to take place.

Zebras were once widespread throughout southern and east Africa, from southern Egypt to Capetown. But hunting for sport, meat, and hides has greatly reduced the zebra's range and numbers, though it is still relatively numerous in the parks of East Africa. One **species**, once found in South Africa, the quagga (*Equus quagga quagga*) is already extinct, wiped out by colonists in search of hides to make grain sacks.

Several other species of zebra are threatened or endangered, such as Grevy's zebra (*Equus grevyi*) in Kenya, Ethiopia, and Somalia; Hartmann's mountain zebra (*Equus zebra hartmannae*) in Angola and Namibia; and the mountain

zebra (*Equus zebra zebra*) in South Africa. The Cape mountain zebra has adapted to life on sheer mountain slopes and ravines where usually only wild goats and sheep can survive. In 1964, only about 25 mountain zebra could be found in the area, but after two decades of protection, the population had increased to several hundred in Cradock National Park in the Cape Province's Great Karroo area.

Probably the biggest long-term threat to the survival of the zebra is the exploding human population of Africa, which is growing so rapidly that it is crowding out the wildlife and intruding on the continent's parks and refuges. Political instability and the proliferation of high powered rifles in many countries also represent a threat to the survival of Africa's wildlife. *See also* Endangered species; Serengeti National Park

[*Lewis G. Regenstein*]

FURTHER READING

D'Alessio, V. "Born-Again Quagga Defies Extinction." *New Scientist* 132 (30 November 1991): 14.

Groves, C. P. *Horses, Asses, and Zebras in the Wild.* Hollywood, FL: Ralph Curtis Books, 1974.

Grubb, P. "*Equus burchelli.*" *Mammalian Species,* no. 157, 1981.

Miller, J. A. "Telling a Quagga By Its Stripes." *Science News* 128 (3 August 1985): 70.

Penzhorn, B. L. "*Equus zebra,*" *Mammalian Species,* no. 314, 1988.

Zero discharge

The goal of eliminating discharges of pollutants by industry, government, and other agencies to air, water, and land with a view to protecting both public health and the integrity of the **environment**. Such a goal is difficult to achieve except where there are **point source**s of **pollution**, and even then the cost of removing the last few percent of a given pollutant may be prohibitive. However, the goal is attainable in many specific cases (e.g. the electroplating industry), and it is particularly urgent in the case of extremely toxic pollutants such as **plutonium** and **dioxin**s. In other cases, it may be desirable as a goal even though it is not likely to be completely attained.

Zero discharge was actually proposed in the early 1970s by the United States Senate as an attainable goal for the Federal Water Pollution Control Acts Amendments of 1972. However, industry, the White House, and other branches of government lobbied intensely against it, and it did not survive the legislative process. *See also* Air quality criteria; Pollution control; Water quality standards

Zero population growth

Zero populations growth (also called the replacement level of fertility) refers to stabilization of a population at its current level. A **population growth** rate of zero means that people are just replacing themselves, and the birth and death rates over several generations are in balance. In **more developed**

countries (MDC), where infant **mortality** rates are low, a fertility rate of about 2.2 children per couple results in zero population growth. This rate is slightly more than two because the extra fraction includes infant deaths, infertile couples, and couples who choose not to have children. In **less developed countries (LDC)**, the replacement level of fertility is often as high as six children per couple.

Zero Population Growth is also the name of a national, non-profit organization, founded in 1968 by **Paul R. Ehrlich**, that works to achieve a sustainable balance between population, resources, and the **environment** worldwide. Contact: Zero Population Growth, 1400 16th Street, NW, Suite 320, Washington, DC 20036. *See also* Family planning

Zero risk

A concept allied to, but less stringent than, that of **zero discharge**. Zero risk permits the release to air, water, and land of those pollutants that have a **threshold dose** below which public health and the **environment** remain undamaged. Such thresholds are often difficult to determine. They may also involve a time element, as in the case of damage to vegetation by **sulfur dioxide** in which less severe fumigations over a longer period are equivalent to more severe exposures over a shorter period. *See also* Air quality criteria; Pollution control; Water quality standards

Zone of saturation

In discussions of **groundwater**, a zone of saturation is an area where water exists and will flow freely to a **well**, as it does in an **aquifer**. The thickness of the zone varies from a few feet to many hundreds of feet, determined by local geology, availability of pores in the formation, and the movement of water from recharge to points of discharge.

Saturation can also be a transient condition in the **soil profile** or **vadose zone** during times of high precipitation or infiltration. Such saturation can vary in duration from a few days or weeks to several months. In **soil**s, the saturated zone will continue to have unsaturated conditions, both above and below it, and when a device to measure saturation, called a piezometer is placed in this zone, water will enter and rise to the depth of saturation. During these periods, the soil pores are filled with water, creating reducing conditions due to lowered oxygen levels. This reduction, as well as the movement of iron and manganese, creates distinctive soil patterns which allow the identification of saturated conditions even when the soil is dry. *See also* Artesian well; Drinking-water supply

Zoo

Zoos are institutions for exhibiting and studying wild animals. Many contemporary zoos have also made **environmental education** and the **conservation** of **biodiversity**

part of their mission. Zoo is a term derived from the Greek *zoion* meaning "living being." As a prefix it indicates the topic of animals, such as in zoology (knowledge of animals) or zoogeography (the distribution and evolutionary **ecology** of animals). As a noun it is a popular shorthand for all zoological gardens and parks.

Design and Operation

Zoological gardens and parks are complex institutions involving important factors of design, staffing, economics, and politics. The *design* of a zoo is a compromise between the needs of the animals (e.g., light, temperature, humidity, cover, feeding areas, opportunities for natural behavior), the requirements of the staff (e.g., offices, libraries, research and veterinary laboratories, garages, storage sheds), and amenities for visitors (e.g., information, exhibitions, restaurants, rest areas, theaters, transportation).

Zoos range in size from as little as two acres to as much as 3,000 acres. So too, the animal enclosures from small cages to fenced-in fields. The proper size for each enclosure is determined by many factors, including the kind and number of **species** being exhibited, and the extent of the enclosure's natural or naturalistic landscaping. In small zoos, space is at a premium. They often use cages and paddocks arranged into taxonomic or zoogeographic pavilions, with visitors walking among the exhibits. As a collection of animals in a confined and artfully arranged space, these zoos are termed *zoological gardens*. In larger zoos, more space is generally available. Enclosures may be bigger, the landscaping more elaborate, and cages fewer in number. Nonpredatory species such as hoofed mammals may roam freely within the confines of the zoo's outer perimeter. Visitors may walk along raised platforms or ride monorail trains through the zoo. Lacking the confinement and precise arrangement of a garden, these zoos are called *zoological parks*. Some zoos take things a step farther and model themselves after Africa's **national park**s and game preserves. Visitors drive cars or ride buses through these *safari parks*, observing animals from vehicles or blinds.

A zoo's many functions are reflected in its *staff*, which is responsible for the animals' well-being, exhibitions, environmental education, and conservation programs. There are several job categories: administrators, office personnel, and maintenance staff tend to the management of the institution. Curators are trained **wildlife** biologists responsible for animal acquisition and transfer, as well as maintaining high standards of animal care. Keepers perform the routine care of the animals and the upkeep of their enclosures. Veterinarians focus on preventive and curative medicine, guard against contagious disease, heal stress-induced ailments or accidental injuries, and preside over births and autopsies. Well-trained volunteers serve as guides and guards, answering questions and monitoring visitor conduct. Educators and scientists may also be present for the purpose of environmental education and research.

Zoos are expensive undertakings, and their *economy* enables or constrains their resources and practices. Few good zoos produce surplus revenue; their business is service, not profit. Most perpetually seek new sources of capital from both public and private sectors, including government subsidies, admission charges, food and merchandise sales, concessionaire rental fees, donations, bequests, and grants. The funds are used for a variety of purposes, such as daily operations, animal acquisitions, renovations, expansion, public education, and scientific research. The precise mixture of public and private funds is situational. As a general rule, public money provide the large investments needed to start, renovate, or expand a zoo. Private funds are better suited for small projects and exhibit startup costs.

A variety of public and private interests claim a stake in a zoo's mission and management. Those concerned with the *politics* of zoos include units of government, regulatory agencies, commercial enterprises, zoological societies, nonprofit foundations, activist groups, and scholars. They influence the availability and use of zoo resources by holding the purse strings and affecting public opinion. Conflict between the groups can be intense, and ongoing disputes over the use of zoos as entertainment, the acquisition of "charismatic megafauna" (big cute animals), and the humane treatment of wildlife are endemic.

History and Purposes

Zoos are complex cultural phenomena. Menageries, unsystematic collection of animals that were the progenitors of zoos, have a long history. Particularly impressive menageries were created by ancient societies. The Chinese emperor Wen Wang (circa 1000 B.C.) maintained a 1,500 acre "Garden of Intelligence." The Greek philosopher Aristotle (384-322 B.C.) studied animal taxonomy from a menagerie stocked largely through the conquests of Alexander the Great (356-323 B.C.). Over 1,200 years later, the menagerie of the Aztec ruler Montezuma (circa A.D. 1515) rivaled any European collection of the sixteenth century.

In the main, these menageries had religious, recreational, and political purposes. Ptolemy II of Egypt (300-251 B.C.) sponsored great processions of exotic animals for religious festivals and celebrations. The Romans maintained menageries of bears, **crocodiles**, **elephants**, and lions for entertainment. Powerful lords maintained and exchanged wild and exotic animals for diplomatic purposes, as did Charlemagne (A.D. 768-814), the medieval king of the Franks. Dignitaries gawked at tamed cheetahs strolling the **botanical garden**s of royal palaces in Renaissance Europe. Indeed, political and social prestige accrued to the individual or community capable of acquiring and supporting an elaborate and expensive menagerie.

In Europe, zoos replaced menageries as scholars turned to the scientific study of animals. This shift occurred in the eighteenth century, the result of European voyages of discovery and conquest, the founding of natural history museums, and the donation of private menageries for public display. Geographically representative species were collected and used to study natural history, taxonomy, and physiology. Some of these zoos were directed by the outstanding minds of the day. The French naturalist Georges Leopold Cuvier (1769-1832) was the zoological director of the Jardin de Plants de Paris (founded in 1793), and the German geographer Alexander von Humboldt (1769-1859) was the first director of the Berlin Zoological Garden (founded in 1844).

The first zoological garden for expressly scientific purposes was founded by the Zoological Society of London in 1826; its establishment marks the advent of modern zoos.

Despite their scientific rhetoric, zoological gardens and parks retained their recreational and political purposes. Late nineteenth century visitors still baited bears, fed elephants, and marveled at the exhausting diversity of life. In the United States, zoos were regarded as a cultural necessity, for they reacquainted harried urbanites with their **wilderness** frontier heritage and proved the natural and cultural superiority of North America. As if **recreation**, politics, and science were not enough, an additional element was introduced in North American zoos: conservation. North Americans had succeeded in decimating much of the continent's wildlife, driving the **passenger pigeon** (*Ectopistes migratorius*) to **extinction**, the American **bison** (*Bison bison*) to endangerment, and formerly common wildlife into rarity. It was believed that zoos would counteract this wasteful slaughter of animals by promoting their wise use. At present, zoos claim similar purposes to explain and justify their existence, namely recreation, education, and conservation.

Evaluating Zoos

Critics of zoos contend they are antiquated, counterproductive, and unethical. Field ecology and **wildlife management** make them unnecessary to the study and conservation of wildlife. Zoos distort the public's image of **nature** and animal behavior, imperil rare and endangered wildlife for frivolous displays, and divert attention from saving natural **habitat**. Finally, they violate humans' moral obligations to animals by incarcerating them for a trivial interest in recreation. Advocates counter these claims by insisting that most zoos are modern, necessary, and humane. They offer a form of recreation that is benign to animal and human alike and are often the only viable place from which to conduct sustained behavioral, genetic, and veterinary research.

Zoos are an important part of environmental education. Indeed, some advocates have proposed "bioparks" that would integrate aquariums, botanical gardens, natural history museums, and zoos. Finally, advocates claim that animals in zoos are treated humanely. By providing for their nutritional, medical, and security needs, zoo animals live long and dignified lives, free from hunger, disease, fear, and predation.

The arguments of both critics and advocates have merit, and in retrospect, zoos have made substantial progress since the turn of the century. In the 1900s many zoos collected animals like postage stamps, placing them in cramped and barren cages, with little thought to their comfort. Today, zoos increasingly use large naturalistic enclosures and house social animals in groups. They often specialize in zoogeographic regions, permitting the creation of habitats which plausibly simulate the **climate**, **topography**, **flora**, and **fauna** of a particular **environment**. Additionally, many zoos contribute to the protection of biodiversity by operating captive-breeding programs, propagating **endangered species**, and restoring destroyed species to suitable habitat.

This progress notwithstanding, zoos have limitations. Statements that zoos are "arks" of biodiversity, or that zoos teach people how to manage the "megazoo" called nature, greatly overstate their uses and lessons. Zoos simply cannot save, manage, and reconstruct nature once its genetic, species, and habitat diversity is destroyed. That said, the promotion by zoos of environmental education and biodiversity conservation is an important role in the defense of the natural world.

[*William S. Lynn*]

FURTHER READING

Foose, T. J. "Erstwild & Megazoo." *Orion Nature Quarterly* 8 (Spring 1989): 60-63.

McKenna, V., W. Travers, and J. Wray, eds. *Beyond the Bars: The Zoo Dilemma*. Northamptonshire, UK: Thorsons Publishing Group, 1987.

Page, J. *Zoo: The Modern Ark*. New York: Facts On File, 1990.

Robinson, M. H. "Beyond the Zoo: The Biopark." *Defenders* 62 (November-December 1987): 10-17.

Stott, J. R. "The Historical Origins of the Zoological Park in American Thought." *Environmental Review* 5 (Fall 1981): 52-65.

Zooplankton

Aquatic animals and protozoans whose movements are largely dependent upon currents. This diverse assemblage includes organisms that feed on bacteria, **phytoplankton**, other zooplankton, as well as organisms that may not feed at all. Zooplankton may be divided into *holoplankton*, organisms which spend their entire lives as **plankton**, such as **krill**, and *meroplankton*, organisms which exist in the plankton for only part of their lives, such as crab larvae. Fish may live their entire lives in the water column, but they are only classified as zooplankton while in their embryonic and larval stages.

Historical Chronology

1798 *Essay on the Principle of Population* published by Thomas Robert Malthus, in which he warned about the dangers of unchecked population growth.

1849 U.S. Department of the Interior established.

1854 Henry David Thoreau publishes *Walden*, a work that inspired many people to live simply and in harmony with nature.

1864 Yosemite in California becomes the first state park in the U.S.

1864 George Perkins Marsh publishes *Man and Nature*, described by some environmentalists as the fountainhead of the conservation movement.

1869 Ernst Haeckel coins the term ecology to describe "the body of knowledge concerning the economy of nature."

1872 Yellowstone in Wyoming becomes the first national park.

1875 American Forestry Association founded to encourage wise forest management.

1879 U.S. Geological Survey established.

1890 Yosemite becomes a national park.

1892 John Muir founds the Sierra Club to preserve the Sierra Nevada mountain chain.

1892 Henry S. Salt publishes *Animal Rights Considered in Relation to Social Progress*, a landmark work on animal rights and welfare.

1892 Adirondack Park established by New York State Constitution, which mandated that the region remain forever wild.

1898 Rivers and Harbors Act established in an effort to control pollution of navigable waters.

1900 Lacey Act regulating interstate shipment of wild animals in the U.S. is passed.

1902 U.S. Bureau of Reclamation established.

1905 National Audubon Society formed.

1908 Chlorination is used extensively in U.S. water treatment plants for the first time.

1913 Construction of Hetch-Hetchy Valley Dam approved to provide water to San Francisco; however, the dam also floods areas of Yosemite National Park.

1914 Martha, the last passenger pigeon, dies in the Cincinnati Zoo.

1916 U.S. National Park Service established.

1918 Save-the-Redwoods League founded.

1918 U.S. and Canada sign treaty restricting the hunting of migratory birds.

1920 Mineral Leasing Act enacted to regulate mining on federal land.

1922 Izaak Walton League founded.

1924 Gila National Forest in New Mexico is designated the first wilderness area.

1930 Dust Bowl.

1933 Tennessee Valley Authority created to assess impact of hydropower on the environment.

1934 Taylor Grazing Act enacted to regulate grazing on federal land.

1935 U.S. Soil Conservation Service established to study and curb soil erosion.

1935 Wilderness Society founded by Aldo Leopold.

1936 National Wildlife Federation established.

1943 Alaska Highway completed, linking lower U.S. and Alaska.

1944 Norman Borlaug begins his work on high-yielding crop varieties.

1946 U.S. Bureau of Land Management created.

1946 Atomic Energy Commission established to study the applications of nuclear power. It was later dissolved in 1975, and its responsibilities were transferred to the Nuclear Regulatory Commission and Energy Research and Development Administration.

1947 Defenders of Wildlife founded, superseding Defenders of Furbearers and the Anti-Steel-Trap League, to protect wild animals and their habitat.

1949 Aldo Leopold publishes *A Sand County Almanac*, in which he sets guidelines for the conservation movement and introduces the concept of a land ethic.

1952 Oregon becomes first state to adopt a significant program to control air pollution.

1954 Humane Society founded in U.S.

1956 Construction of Echo Park Dam on the Colorado River is aborted, due in large part to the efforts of environmentalists.

1959 St. Lawrence Seaway is completed, linking the Atlantic Ocean to the Great Lakes.

1961 Agent Orange is sprayed in Southeast Asia, exposing nearly 3 million American servicemen to dioxin, a probable carcinogen.

1962 *Silent Spring* published by Rachel Carson to document the effects of pesticides on the environment.

1963 First Clean Air Act passed in the U.S.

1963 Nuclear Test Ban Treaty signed by U.S. and U.S.S.R. to stop atmospheric testing of nuclear weapons.

1964 Wilderness Act passed, which protects wild areas in the U.S.

1965 Water Quality Act passed, establishing federal water quality standards.

1966 Eighty people die in New York City due to pollution-related causes.

1967 Supertanker *Torrey Canyon* spills oil off the coast of England.

1967 Environmental Defense Fund established to save the osprey from DDT.

1967 American Cetacean Society founded to protect whales, dolphins, porpoises, and other cetaceans. Considered the oldest whale conservation group in the world.

1968 Wild and Scenic Rivers Act and National Trails System Act passed to protect scenic areas from development.

1969 Greenpeace founded.

1970 First Earth Day celebrated on April 22.

1970 National Environmental Policy Act passed, requiring environmental impact statements for projects funded or regulated by federal government.

1970 Environmental Protection Agency created.

1971 Consultative Group on International Agricultural Research (CGIAR) founded to improve food production in developing countries.

1972 U.N. Conference on the Human Environment held in Stockholm to address environmental issues on a global level.

1972 Clean Water Act passed.

1972 Use of DDT is phased out in the U.S.

1972 Coastal Zone Management Act and Marine Protection, Research, and Sanctuaries Act passed.

1972 Oregon becomes first state to enact bottle-recycling law.

1972 *Limits to Growth* published by the Club of Rome, calling for population control.

1973 Convention on International Trade in Endangered Species of Wild Fauna and Flora (CITES) signed to prevent the international trade of endangered or threatened animals and plants.

1973 Endangered Species Act passed.

1973 Arab members of the Organization of Petroleum Exporting Countries (OPEC) institute an embargo preventing shipments of oil to the U.S.

1973   Cousteau Society founded by Jacques-Yves Cousteau and his son to educate the public and conduct research on marine-related issues.

1973   E.F. Schumacher publishes *Small Is Beautiful*, which advocates simplicity, self-reliance, and living in harmony with nature.

1974   Safe Drinking Water Act passed, requiring EPA to set quality standards for the nation's drinking water.

1975   Atlantic salmon is found in the Connecticut River after a 100-year absence.

1975   *The Monkey Wrench Gang* published by Edward Abbey, who advocates radical and controversial methods for protecting the environment, including "ecotage."

1976   Resource Conservation and Recovery Act passed, giving EPA authority to regulate municipal solid and hazardous waste.

1976   Poisonous gas containing 2,4,5-TCP and dioxin is released from a factory in Seveso, Italy, causing massive animal and plant death. Although no human life was lost, a sharp increase in deformed births was reported.

1976   Land Institute founded by Wes and Dana Jackson to encourage more natural and organic agricultural practices.

1978   Residents of Love Canal, New York, are evacuated after Lois Gibbs discovers that the community was once the site of a chemical waste dump.

1978   Oil tanker *Amoco Cadiz* runs aground, spilling 220,000 tons of oil.

1979   Three Mile Island Nuclear Reactor almost undergoes nuclear melt-down when the cooling water systems fail. Since this accident no new nuclear power plants have been built in the U.S.

1980   Mount St. Helens explodes with a force comparable to 500 Hiroshima-sized bombs.

1980   Comprehensive Environmental Response, Compensation, and Liability Act (Superfund) enacted to clean up abandoned toxic waste sites.

1980   *Global 2000 Report* published, documenting trends in population growth, natural resource depletion, and the environment.

1980   Alaska National Interest Lands Conservation Act enacted, setting aside millions of acres of land as wilderness.

1980   Thomas Lovejoy proposes the idea of debt-for-nature swap, which helps developing countries alleviate national debt by implementing policies that protect the environment.

1981   Earth First! founded by Dave Foreman, with the slogan "No compromise in the defense of Mother Earth."

1982   Bioregional Project founded to promote the aims of the bioregional movement in North America.

1984   Emission of poisonous *methyl isocyanate* vapor, a chemical by-product of agricultural insecticide production, from the Union Carbide plant kills more than 2800 people in Bhopal, India.

1985   Rainforest Action Network founded.

1985   Ozone hole observed over Antarctica.

1986   Chernobyl Nuclear Power Station undergoes nuclear core melt-down, spreading radioactive material over vast parts of the Soviet Union and northern Europe.

1986   Evacuation of Times Beach, Missouri, due to high levels of dioxin.

1987   Montreal Protocol on Substances that Deplete the Ozone Layer signed by 24 nations, declaring their promise to decrease production of chlorofluorocarbons (CFCs).

1987   Yucca Mountain designated the first permanent repository for radioactive waste by the U.S. Department of Energy.

1987   *Ecodefense: A Field Guide to Monkeywrenching* published by Dave Foreman, in which he describes spiking trees and other "environmental sabotage" techniques.

1987   *Our Common Future* (The Brundtland Report) is published.

1988   Ocean Dumping Ban Act established.

1988   Global ReLeaf program inaugurated with the motto "Plant a tree, cool the globe" to address the problem of global warming.

1989 Oil tanker *Exxon Valdez* runs aground in Prince William Sound, Alaska, spilling 11 million gallons of oil.

1990 Oil Pollution Act signed, setting liability and penalty system for oil spills as well as a trust fund for clean up efforts.

1990 Clean Air Act amended to control emissions of sulfur dioxide and nitrogen oxides.

1991 Mount Pinatubo in Philippines erupts, shooting sulfur dioxide 25 mi (40 km) into the atmosphere.

1991 Persian Gulf War begins.

1991 Train containing the pesticide *meta sodium* falls off the tracks near Dunsmuir, California, releasing chemicals into the Sacramento River. Plant and aquatic life for 43 mi (69 km) downriver die as a result.

1991 Over 4,000 people die from cholera in Latin American epidemic.

1992 U.N. Earth Summit held in Rio de Janeiro, Brazil.

1992 Mexico City, Mexico, shuts down as a result of incapacitating air pollution.

1992 Captive-bred California condors and black-footed ferrets reintroduced into the wild.

1992 United Nations calls for an end to global driftnet fishing by the end of 1992.

1992 April brings the birth of Blue Devil—the first aye-aye to be born in captivity—at Duke University, North Carolina.

1993 *Braer* oil tanker runs aground in the Shetland Islands, Scotland, spilling its entire cargo into the sea.

1993 Forest Summit convened in Portland, Oregon, by President Bill Clinton, who met with loggers and environmentalists concerned with the survival of the northern spotted owl.

1993 Norway resumes hunting of minke whales in defiance of a ban on commercial whaling instituted by the International Whaling Commission.

1993 Eight people from *Biosphere 2* emerge after living two years in a self-sustaining, glass dome.

1993 President Clinton and Vice President Gore issue their "Climate Change Action Plan."

1994 Scientists discover that acid rain is a threat to songbirds in Dutch forests. Surveys showed that of the three species of titmouse studied (in 60 forests) 30-50% of females were laying eggs with defective shells. The shells were defective due to a calcium deficiency—caused the scientists surmised, by acid rain.

1994 North American Free Trade Agreement—NAFTA, an international trade agreement between the United States, Canada, and Mexico. Pursuant to NAFTA, most tariffs among the three countries are phased out over 15 years. NAFTA includes side agreements on the environment, labor, and dealing with import surges.

1996 At the age of 23, Adam Werbach is elected president of the Sierra Club.

1996 ISO 14000, a series of environmental management standards, is adapted by the International Organization for Standardization.

1996 Ten years after the Chernobyl Nuclear Power Station tragedy, researchers are beginning to see the long-term effects of the nuclear accident, including increased thyroid cancer in children and the passage of genetic damage (in both local wildlife and humans) to the next generation.

1996 In an effort to rejuvenate the stagnating beaches and marshes of the Grand Canyon, the Bureau of Reclamation opened the Glen Canyon Dam for a week which released some 117 billion gallons of water into the canyon. Periodic flooding of this type keeps the canyon from degenerating.

1997 French oceanographer, Jacques-Yves Cousteau dies in Paris, France.

Environmental Legislation in the United States

1862 **Homestead Act** makes free homesteads on unappropriated land available on a vast scale, speeding settlement of the Plains states and destruction of the region's prairie ecosystem.

1872 **Mining Law** allows any person finding mineral deposits on public land to file a claim which grants him free access to that site for mining or similar development.

1891 **Forest Reserve Act** authorizes the President to create forest reserves from the public domain.

1899 **Refuse Act** authorizes the Army Corps of Engineers to issue discharge permits.

1900 **Lacey Act** makes interstate shipment of wild animals a federal offense if taken in violation of state laws.

1902 **Reclamation Act** (Irrigation of Arid Lands) provides funding for the "reclamation" of drylands in the western United States through irrigation and damming of rivers.

1916 **National Park Service Act** establishes the National Park Service, an agency in the U.S. Department of the Interior, the first such agency in the world.

1918 **Migratory Bird Treaty Act** establishes federal authority over migratory game and insectivorous birds.

1920 **Mineral Leasing Act** regulates the exploitation of fuel and fertilizer minerals on public lands.

1934 **Migratory Bird Hunting Stamp Act** provides funding for waterfowl reserves.

1934 **Taylor Grazing Act** establishes federal management policy on public grazing lands, the last major category of public lands to come under the active supervision of the government.

1935 **Soil Conservation Act** (P.L. 74-46) establishes the Soil Conservation Service to aid in combating soil erosion following the Dust Bowl.

1938 **Food, Drug and Cosmetics Act** sets extensive standards for the quality and labeling of foods, drugs, and cosmetics.

1938 **Natural Gas Act** gives the Federal Power Commission the right to control prices and limit new pipelines from entering the market.

1948 **Water Pollution Control Act** is the first statute to provide state and local governments with the funding to address water pollution.

1954 **Atomic Energy Act** grants the federal government exclusive regulatory authority over nuclear-power facilities.

1955 **Air Pollution Control Act** grants funds to assist the states in their air pollution control activities.

1956 **Federal Water Pollution Control Act** (amended 1965 [P.L. 89-234], 1966 [P.L. 89-753], 1970 [P.L. 91-224; P.L. 91-611], 1972 [P.L. 92-240; P.L. 92-500]) increases federal funding to state and local governments to address water quality issues and calls for the development of water quality standards by the newly-created Federal Water Pollution Control Administration.

1957 **Price-Anderson Act** (Atomic Energy Damages Act, P.L. 85-256) limits the liability of civilian producers of nuclear power in the case of a catastrophic nuclear accident.

1960 **Hazardous Substances Act** (amended 1966) authorizes the Secretary of the Department of Health, Education, and Welfare (HEW) to require warning labels for household substances deemed hazardous.

1960 **Multiple Use-Sustained Yield Act** (P.L. 86-517) mandates that management of the national forests be balanced between ecological and economic interests.

1963 **Clean Air Act** (P.L. 88-206) (amended 1970 [P.L. 91-604], 1977 [P.L. 95-95; P.L. 95-190], 1990 [P.L. 101-549]) serves as the backbone of efforts to control air pollution in the United States.

1964 **Classification and Multiple Use Act** instructs the Bureau of Land Management to inventory its lands and classify them for disposal or retention, the first such inventory in the United States.

1964 **Public Land Law Review Commission Act** establishes a commission to examine the body of public land laws and make recommendations as to how to proceed in this policy area.

1964 **Wilderness Act** (P.L. 88-577) creates the National Wilderness Preservation System to preserve wilderness areas for present and future generations of Americans.

1965 **Solid Waste Disposal Act** (P.L. 89-272) (amended 1970 [P.L. 91-512], 1976 [P.L. 94-580]) addresses inadequate solid waste disposal methods. It was amended by the **Resource Recovery Act** and the **Resource Conservation and Recovery Act**.

1966 **Animal Welfare Act** (P.L. 89-544) designates U. S. Department of Agriculture as responsible for the humane care and handling of warm-blooded and other animals used for biomedical research and calls for inspection of research facilities to insure that adequate food, housing, and care are provided.

1966 **Laboratory Animal Welfare Act** (P.L. 89-544) (amended 1970 [P.L. 91-579], 1976 [P.L. 94-279], 1985 [99-198], 1990 [101-624]) regulates the use of animals in medical and commercial research.

1968 **Wild and Scenic Rivers Act** (P.L. 90-542) creates three categories of rivers—wild, scenic, and recreational—and provides for safeguards against degradation of wild and scenic rivers.

1969 **Coal Mine Health and Safety Act** addresses safety problems in the mining industry.

1969 **National Environmental Policy Act** (NEPA) (P.L. 91-190) ushers in a new era of environmental awareness in the United States, requiring all federal agencies to take into account the environmental consequences of their plans and activities.

1970 **Mining and Minerals Policy Act** (P.L. 91-631) directs the Secretary of the Interior to follow a policy that encourages the private mining sector to develop a financially viable mining industry while conducting research to further "wise and efficient use" of these minerals.

1970 **Occupational Safety and Health Act** (OSHA) (P.L. 91-596) requires employers to provide each of their employees with a workplace that is free from recognized hazards, which may cause death or serious physical harm.

1970 **Resource Recovery Act** (P.L. 91-512), an amendment to **Solid Waste Disposal Act**, funds recycling programs and mandates an extensive assessment of solid waste disposal practices.

1972 **Clean Water Act** (P.L. 92-240; P.L. 92-500) (amended 1977 [P.L. 95-217], 1987 [P.L. 100-4; P.L. 100-202]), which replaced the language of the **Federal Water Pollution Control Act**, is the farthest reaching of all federal water legislation, setting as a national goal the attainment of "fishable and swimmable" quality for all surface waters in the United States.

1972 **Coastal Zone Management Act** (P.L. 92-583) establishes a federal program to help states in planning and managing the development and protection of coastal areas.

1972 **Federal Insecticide, Fungicide, and Rodenticide Act** (P.L. 92-516) regulates the registration, marketing and use of pesticides.

1972 **Marine Mammals Protection Act** (P.L. 92-522) protects, conserves and encourages research on marine animals. It places a moratorium on harassing, hunting, capturing, killing or importing marine mammals with some exceptions (e.g. subsistence hunting by Eskimos).

1972 **Marine Protection, Research and Sanctuaries Act** (P.L. 92-532) (amended 1990 [P.L. 101-593; P.L. 101-596; P.L. 101-605) (also known as the **Ocean Dumping Act**) regulates ocean dumping, authorizes marine pollution research, and establishes regional marine research programs. It also establishes a process for designating marine sanctuaries of significant ecological, aesthetic, historical, or recreational value. The **Ocean Dumping Ban Act** amends the law, prohibiting sewage sludge and industrial wastes from being dumped at sea after December 31, 1991.

1972　Ports and Waterways Safety Act (P.L. 92-340) regulates oil transport and the operation of oil handling facilities.

1973　Endangered Species Act (P.L. 93-205) empowers the Secretary of the Interior to designate any plant or animal (including subspecies, races and local populations) "endangered" (imminent danger of extinction) or "threatened" (significant decline in numbers and danger of extinction in some regions). The act protect habitats critical to the survival of endangered species and prohibits hunting, killing, capturing, selling, importing or exporting products from endangered species.

1974　Federal Non-Nuclear Research and Development Act (P.L. 93-577) focuses government efforts on non-nuclear research.

1974　Forest and Rangeland Renewable Resources Planning Act (P.L. 93-378) establishes a process for assessing the nation's forest and range resources every ten years. It also stipulates that every five years the Forest Service provide a plan for the use and development of these resources based on the assessment.

1974　Safe Drinking Water Act (P.L. 93-523) requires minimum safety standards for every community water supply, regulating such contaminants as bacteria, nitrates, arsenic, barium, cadmium, chromium, fluoride, lead, mercury, silver, and pesticides.

1974　Solar Energy Research, Development and Demonstration Act (P.L. 93-473) establishes a federal policy to "pursue a vigorous and viable program of research and resource assessment of solar energy as a major source of energy for our national needs." The act also establishes two programs: the Solar Energy Coordination and Management Project and the Solar Energy Research Institute.

1975　Eastern Wilderness Act creates 16 eastern wilderness areas and directs the Forest Service to alter its methods so that it considered areas previously affected by humans.

1975　Hazardous Materials Transportation Act (P.L. 92-633; P.L. 94-56) establishes minimum standards of regulation for the transport of hazardous materials by air, ship, rail, and motor vehicle.

1976　Energy Policy and Conservation Act (P.L. 94-364), an amendment to **The Motor Vehicle Information and Cost Savings Act** (P.L. 92-513), outlines provisions intended to decrease fuel consumption. The most significant provisions are the Corporate Average Fuel Economy (CAFE) standards, which set fuel economy standards for passenger cars and light trucks.

1976　Federal Land Policy and Management Act (P.L. 94-579) gives the Bureau of Land Management the authority and direction for managing the lands under its control. The act also sets policy for the grazing, mining and preservation of public lands.

1976　National Forest Management Act (P.L. 94-588) grants the Forest Service significant administrative discretion in managing the logging of national forests based on the general philosophies of multiple use and sustained yield.

1976　Resource Conservation and Recovery Act (RCRA) (P.L. 94-580), an amendment to the **Solid Waste Disposal Act**, regulates the storage, shipping, processing, and disposal of hazardous substances and sets limits on the sewering of toxic chemicals.

1976　Toxic Substances Control Act (TSCA) (P.L. 94-469) categorizes toxic and hazardous substances and regulates the use and disposal of poisonous chemicals.

1977　Surface Mining Control and Reclamation Act (P.L. 95-87) limits the scarring of the landscape, erosion and water pollution associated with surface mining. It empowers the Department of the Interior to develop regulations that impose nationwide environmental standards for all surface-mining operations.

1978　Energy Tax Act (P.L. 95-618) creates a "Gas Guzzler" tax on passenger cars whose individual fuel economy value fall below a certain threshold, starting in 1980.

1978　Port and Tanker Safety Act (P.L. 95-474) empowers the U.S. Coast Guard to supervise vessel and port operations and to set standards for the handling of dangerous substances.

1978　Public Utility Regulatory Policies Act (P.L. 95-617) promotes the development of renewable energy and requires that utilities purchase power at "just" rates from producers who use such alternative sources as wind and solar.

1980　Alaska National Interest Lands Conservation Act (P.L. 96-487) protects 44 million ha (109 million acres) of land in Alaska, establishing 11 new parks, 12 new wildlife refuges and setting aside wilderness areas comprising 22.7 million ha (56 million acres).

1980   **Comprehensive Environmental Response, Compensation, and Liability Act** (Superfund) (P.L. 96-510) (amended 1986, P.L. 99-499) permits direct federal response to remedy the improper disposal of hazardous waste. It establishes a multibillion dollar cash pool (Superfund) to finance government clean-up actions.

1980   **Low-Level Radioactive Waste Policy Act** (P.L. 96-573) (amended 1985, P.L. 99-240) places responsibility for disposal of low-level radioactive waste on generating states and encourages those states to create compacts to develop centralized regional waste sites.

1980   **Nongame Wildlife Act** provides limited federal aid to state wildlife agencies.

1982   **Nuclear Waste Policy Act** (P.L. 97-425) (amended 1987, P.L. 100-203) instructs the Department of Energy to develop a permanent repository for high-level nuclear wastes by 1998.

1983   **International Environment Protection Act of 1983** (P.L. 98-164) authorizes the President to assist other countries in wildlife and plant protection efforts in order to preserve biological diversity.

1986   **Emergency Planning and Community Right-to-Know Act** (P.L. 99-499) requires federal, state and local governments and industry to work together in developing plans to deal with chemical emergencies and community right-to-know reporting on hazardous chemicals.

1986   **Emergency Wetlands Resources Act of 1986** (P.L. 99-645) authorized the purchase of wetlands from Land and Water Conservation Fund monies, removing a prior prohibition on such acquisitions. Required the establishment of a National Wetlands Priority Conservation Plan, and that states include wetlands in their Comprehensive Outdoor Recreation Plans, and transferred to the Migratory Bird Conservation Fund amounts equal to the import duties on arms and ammunition.

1987   **Marine Plastic Pollution Research and Control Act** (P.L. 100-220) prohibits the dumping of plastics at sea, severely restricts the dumping of other ship-generated garbage in the open ocean or in U.S. waters, and requires all ports to have adequate garbage disposal facilities for incoming vessels.

1987   **National Appliance Energy Conservation Act** (P.L. 100-12) sets minimum efficiency standards for heating and cooling systems in new homes as well as for such new appliances as refrigerators and freezers.

1988   **Alternative Motor Fuels Act** (P.L. 100-494) encourages automobile manufactures to design and build cars that can burn alternative fuels such as methanol and ethanol.

1988   **Medical Waste Tracking Act** (P.L. 100-582) creates a "cradle-to-grave" tracking system based on detailed shipping records, similar to the program in place for hazardous waste.

1990   **Coastal Wetlands Planning, Protection, and Restoration Act** (P.L. 101-646) (amended 1991, P.L. 102-212 and 1994, P.L. 103-375) allocates federal monies to states for coastal restoration.

1990   **National Environmental Education Act** (P.L. 101-619) (amended 1994, P.L. 103-382) calls on the Environmental Protection Agency to provide national leadership to increase environmental literacy.

1990   **Oil Pollution Act** (P.L. 101-380; P.L. 101-537; P.L. 101-646), passed in response to the *Exxon Valdez* disaster, initiates a comprehensive federal liability system for all oil spills. It also establishes a federal trust fund to help pay for cleanups, strengthens civil and criminal penalties against parties involved in spills, and requires companies to have spill contingency and readiness plans.

1990   **Pollution Prevention Act** (P.L. 101-508) creates a new EPA office intended to help industry limit pollution through information collection, assistance in technology transfer, and financial assistance to state pollution prevention programs.

1992   **Federal Facility Compliance Act** (P.L. 102-386) requires the military to clean up its nuclear waste sites.

1992   **Wild Bird Conservation Act of 1992** (P.L. 102-440) establishes a new federal system to limit or prohibit U.S. imports of exotic bird species.

1996   **Food Quality Protection Act of 1996** (P.L. 104-170) requires the EPA to develop a screening program to determine whether pesticides or other substances cause effects in humans similar to effects produced by naturally occurring estrogens.

1996   **Magnuson-Stevens Fishery Conservation and Management Act** (P.L. 94-265) works in conjunction with the Migratory Bird Act, the Endangered Species Act of 1973, and the Marine Mammals protection Act of 1972 (amended 1994) to manage fishing bycatch.

General Index

A

Abbey, Edward **1**, 425, 482, 662, 861, 984
Abies alba 427
Ablation 464
Abortion 400
Absorption **1**, 797, 1048
Abu Simbel, colossi of 70
Abyssopelagic zone 775
Acaricide 782
Acclimation **2**
Accounting for nature **3**
Acer saccharum 427
Acetaldehyde 630, 655
Acetylcholine 185
Acetylcholinesterase 754
Achondroplasia 124
Acid and base **3**, 7, 63, 144, 505, 776, 789, 985
Acid deposition **3**, 5, 378, 768, 1043
Acid drainage 999
Acid formers 43
Acid mine drainage **3**, 54, 60, 297, 413, 657, 860
Acid precipitation 3, 631
Acid rain 3-4, **5**, 9, 25, 49, 53, 73, 79, 114, 178, 190, 197, 199, 232, 255, 267, 282, 284, 295, 311, 335, 350, 352, 370, 393, 395, 412, 467, 480, 535, 630, 637, 649, 676, 692, 697, 705, 707, 735, 768, 780, 821, 830, 889, 947, 952, 954, 988, 995-996, 1012, 1040, 1043, 1082, 1098
Acid Rain Bill 349
Acid waste 284
Acidification 3, 5-6, **7**, 348, 378, 392, 427, 808, 952, 995
Acidity 789
Acrocephalus sechellensis 553
Acrolein 187
Acrostichum danaeifolium 388
Actinomycetes 10
Action Alerts 857
Activated charcoal 174
Activated sludge **7**, 11, 942, 952, 968
Acute effects **8**, 186, 252, 1033
Acute radiation syndrome 844

Adams, Ansel **8**, 985
Adaptation 3, **9**, 55, 118, 307, 319, 333, 382, 392, 626, 749, 1007, 1047, 1101
Adaptive fitness 654
Adaptive radiation 445
Addis Ababa, Ethiopia 943
Addition polymers 800
Adirondack Mountains 7, **9**, 525, 641, 768, 1110
Adjudication 351
Administrative Procedures Act 368, 738
Adsorption **9**, 188, 234, 512-513, 760, 810, 937, 978, 1094
Advancement of Learning, The 84
Advection 28
Adventure tourism 317
Aechmorphorus occidentalis 784
Aeration 7, **10**, 11, 202, 219, 412, 489, 736, 1093
Aerobic 7, 10, **10**-11, 58, 116, 123, 198, 204, 218, 246, 255, 324, 408, 640, 647, 670, 759, 774, 781, 810, 860, 937, 942, 951, 1030, 1079
Aerobic sludge digestion 10, **10**, 43, 670, 942, 951
Aerobic/anaerobic systems **10**
Aeromonas hydrophila 412
Aerosol 6, **11**, 25, 60, 72, 84, 409, 511, 532, 635, 661, 664, 813, 833, 849, 881, 1035, 1070, 1072, 1098
Aerosol spray 833
Aestivate 36
Aflatoxin **12**
Africa 1020
African forest elephant 325
African Wildlife Foundation (Washington, D.C.) **12**
African Wildlife Leadership Foundation 1040
Africanized bees (*Apis mellifera scutellata*) **12**, 391
Agano River 656
Agency for Toxic Substances and Disease Registry **13**, 170, 597, 644, 686, 835, 997, 1058

Agenda 21 1054, 1056
Agent Orange **14**, 258, 268, 517, 546, 671, 784, 1051, 1076
Agglomeration **16**
Agitation dredging 275
Agrarian reform 588
Agricola, Georgius 128
Agricultural chemicals **16**, 21, 29, 165, 174, 198, 260, 297, 475, 518, 575, 651, 656, 784, 1028-1029
Agricultural Cooperative Service 1057
Agricultural pollution 17, **18**, 21, 131, 193, 244, 260, 277, 297, 386, 475, 489, 491, 526, 576, 588, 695, 707, 758, 784, 865, 908, 989, 1038, 1047, 1089
Agricultural Research Service **19**, 21, 1057
Agricultural research station 587
Agricultural revolution 17, **19**, 122, 132, 198, 226, 453-454, 817, 950
Agricultural runoff 476, 1089
Agricultural Stabilization and Conservation Service **20**, 22, 758, 1057
Agricultural technology 17, 20-22, 226, 950, 989
Agriculture 704, 1002, 1081
Agriculture Adjustment Act of 1938 423
Agriculture, aquatic 50
Agriculture, sustainable 50, 422
Agroecology **21**, 22, 139, 587, 589, 758, 950
Agroforestry **21**, 21
Aguajes 864
Ahimsa 180
AIDS **22**, 170, 212, 330, 362, 383, 399, 595, 644, 652, 773, 1058
Ailuropoda melanoleuca 460
Air and Waste Management Association (Pittsburgh, Pennsylvania) **23**, 497
Air conditioning systems 184
Air pollutant transport 954
Air pollution 16, 18, 23, **23**, 25-28, 33, 35, 64, 68, 73-74, 77, 85, 93, 137, 158, 163, 170, 184,

189, 200, 208, 232, 238, 255, 268, 270, 284, 292, 296, 310, 328, 335, 341, 350-351, 368, 370, 394, 418, 426, 433, 435, 451, 460, 465, 480, 486, 497, 511, 528, 532, 544, 550, 555, 609, 619, 637, 642, 645, 676, 679, 692, 707, 710, 735, 767, 770, 780, 788, 793, 796, 808, 811, 829, 871, 874, 880-881, 934, 946, 954, 970, 972, 995, 1003, 1005, 1015-1016, 1030, 1038, 1041, 1055, 1061-1062, 1071, 1136

Air pollution control   24, **25**, 34, 78, 93, 166, 184, 189, 201, 232, 282, 373, 416-417, 532, 652, 676-677, 873, 956, 982, 1012, 1038, 1071

Air Pollution Control Act   27, 189

Air pollution index   **26**, 27-28, 677, 811, 829, 831, 1016

Air quality   24, 26, **27**, 28, 73, 76-77, 137, 187, 190, 201, 238, 242, 295, 345, 349-351, 378-379, 465, 483, 511, 515, 532, 616, 619, 642, 651, 761, 780, 793, 829, 835, 882, 953, 995, 999, 1012, 1038, 1043, 1071, 1132

Air Quality Control Region (AQCR)   27, **28**, 242, 676, 831

Air quality criteria   27, **28**-28, 93, 191, 242, 511, 652, 677, 811, 829, 831, 1142-1143

Air quality standards   93

Air-pollutant transport   28, 232, 1137

Airshed   28, **28**, 190

Alamagardo bomb   520

Alar   **28**

Alaska   60, 856

Alaska Coalition   30

Alaska Highway   **29**

Alaska Lands Act   30

Alaska National Interest Conservation Act   947

Alaska National Interest Lands Conservation Act (1980)   **30**, 61, 695, 1108, 1110, 1112

Alaska Native Claims Settlement Act   30

Albedo   **31**, 195, 1098

Albert, Eddie   873

Albert Schweitzer Medal   47

Albinism   124

Albright, Horace   691

Alca impennis   758

Alcohol   1015

Alcohol Policies Project   169

Alcyone   242

Alder   706

Aldrin   754

Alfonso, Juan Perez   741

Algae   10, 437, 452

Algal bloom   **31**, 76, 131, 178, 252, 271, 386, 392, 412, 493, 525, 540, 585, 630, 645, 703-704, 864, 1047, 1082, 1088

Algal turf mariculture   733

Algicide   31, **32**, 393, 784

Alihan, Milla   958

Aliphatic (open-chain) hydrocarbons   788

Alkali and Works Act of 1863   26

Alkalinity   789

Alkylmercury poisoning   655

Allelochemicals   217

Allelopathy   **32**

Allergen   **32**, 69, 97, 137, 881

Allied Chemical Corporation   574

Alligator, American (*Alligator mississippiensis*)   **32**, 243, 388-389, 411, 1102, 1115

Allochthonous   332

Allopatric species   980

Alnus   706

Alosa pseudoharengus   412

Alosa sapidissima   178, 525

Alpha interferon   122

Alpha particle   **33**, 94, 448, 830, 843-844, 853

Alpha radiation   853

Alpha rays   850

Alternating current   322

Alternative agriculture   587

Alternative energy sources   **33**, 99, 114, 206, 210, 292, 322, 334, 339, 341, 460, 465, 486, 504, 619, 649, 717, 733, 742, 753, 796, 822, 970, 1018, 1020, 1026, 1097, 1121, 1131

Alternative fuels   77, 99, 201, 292, 322, 339, 386, 451, 460, 649-650, 743, 753, 788, 796, 956, 1009

Altruism   960

Alum   792

Aluminosilicate minerals   34

Aluminosilicates   188

Aluminum   **34**, 54, 188, 208, 227, 279, 321, 393, 427, 479, 808, 850, 861, 953, 974, 978, 986, 995, 1048, 1060, 1079, 1094

Aluminum clays   34

Aluminum phosphates   34

Aluminum sulfate   792

Alvarez, Walter   635

Alveoli   137

Alzheimer's disease   622

Amazon basin   **34**, 537, 855, 1005,1047, 1110

Amazon River   34

Amazona brasiliensis   553

Amazona imperialis   553

Ambient air   26-28, **35**, 74, 355, 511, 643, 676

Ambystoma jeffersonianum   526

Amchitka Island   925

Amenity value   **35**

American Academy of Environmental Engineers (AAEE)   357

American Association of the Green Cross   478

American box turtle   **35**

American Cetacean Society (San Pedro, California)   **36**, 1102, 1104

American Committee for International Conservation (Washington, D.C.)   **36**

American Conference of Governmental Industrial Hygienists (ACGIH)   639

American Farmland Trust (Washington, D.C.)   **37**, 38, 589

American Fisheries Society   874

American Forestry Association (Washington, D.C.)   **37**, 466, 719, 747

American Heritage Trust Act   692

American Indian Environmental Office (Washington, D.C.)   **38**

American Journal of Public Health   1126

American Museum of Natural History   147

American Oceans Campaign (Santa Monica, California)   **39**

American Ornithology   75

American shad   178, 525

American Society of State Highway Transportation Officials (ASHTO)   214

American Society of Testing Materials (ASTM)   214

American Water Resources Association   874

American Wildlands (Lakewood, Colorado)   **40**

Americans for Safe Food   169

Ames, Bruce N.   41

Ames test   **41**, 183, 813

Amino acid   776

Aminocarb   185, 784

Ammonia   237, 460, 707, 924

Ammonium nitrate   704

Amoco Cadiz   **41**, 744, 1031

Amory, Cleveland   **42**, 442

Amosite   63

Anabaena   412, 706

Anaerobic   10-11, **42**, 43, 54, 116, 218, 246, 266, 407, 520, 627, 647, 649, 670, 696, 706, 759, 781, 810, 888, 937, 942, 996, 1101, 1135

Anaerobic digestion   **43**, 113, 341, 649, 942, 951

Anchistea virginica   388

Anderson, Clinton   828

Anderson, Warren   95

Andrus, Cecil   30

Anemia   **43**, 1062

Aneuploidy   124

Animal cancer tests   **44**, 47, 98

Animal cruelty   299
Animal dealers   45
Animal feed   424
Animal Legal Defense Fund (San
        Rafael, California)   42, 44,
        45, 47
Animal Liberation   45, 776, 948
Animal liberation movement   868
Animal research   46
Animal rights   42, 44-45, **45**, 361,
        381, 408, 470, 558, 710, 775,
        868, 912, 948, 981, 1030, 1065,
        1068, 1127
*Animal Rights and Human
        Obligations*   868
Animal testing   713, 775, 1030
Animal waste   18, **47**, 99, 113, 129,
        246, 408-409, 644, 668, 707,
        1002, 1037, 1135
Animal Welfare Act of 1966   44, 45
Animal Welfare Institute (Washington,
        D.C.)   **47**, 44, 47, 770
Animals' Advocate, The   45
Animals and Their Legal Rights   47
Anions   2
Annona glabra   388
*Annotated Bibliography on Planning and
        Management for Urban-Suburban
        Wildlife, An*   685
Anodorhynchus hyacinthinus   231
Anopheles   212, 623
Ant   1120
Antarctic and Southern Ocean
        Coalition (ASOC)   49
Antarctic Treaty (1961)   **48**
Antarctica   48, **48**-49, 463, 487, 537,
        541, 802, 1060
Antarctica Project (Washington,
        D.C.)   **49**
Anthracite   199, 433
Anthracosis   25, 128
Anthropocentric   246, 360
Anthropogenic   **49**, 99, 195, 338, 349,
        371, 512, 584, 647, 808,
        892, 1032
Antibiotics   782
Antimony   511
Antiquities Act   30
Aphanizomenon   412, 706
Apis mellifera scutellata   12, 391
Apostle Islands National
        Lakeshore   686
Appalachia   990, 998
Application factor (AF)   186
Aquaculture   **50**, 129, 731
Aquarium   386
Aquarium trade   **51**
Aquatic chemistry   **53**, 94, 131, 183,
        186, 386, 393, 413, 513, 525,
        559, 586, 662, 774, 1072
Aquatic microbiology   **54**
Aquatic toxicology   **55**
Aquatic weed   386

Aquatic weed control   **56**, 131, 386,
        707, 1047
Aquifer   19, 53, 56, **56**, 63, 71, 116,
        145, 244, 257, 269, 280, 296,
        310, 350, 358, 387, 408, 433,
        458, 489-490, 548, 606, 669,
        717, 776, 780, 845, 905, 909,
        913, 992, 999, 1081, 1083, 1087-
        1088, 1099, 1143
Aquifer restoration   **56**, 56, 257, 281,
        489-491, 776, 1082, 1100
Aquila chrysaetos   86
Arable land   20, 22, **58**, 198, 215,
        282, 287, 384, 611, 876, 911,
        962, 1028
Aral Sea   **58**, 562, 910
Arbitration   351
ARCO   857
Arco, Idaho   **59**
ARCO Solar   796
Arctic   60, 745
Arctic Council (Oslo, Norway)   **60**
Arctic haze   **60**, 1070
Arctic National Wildlife Refuge,
        Alaska   **60**, 696-697, 1041,
        1112, 1124
Arctocephalus townsendi   930
Area mining   990
Arid   8, 53, 62, **62**, 114, 226, 249,
        262-263, 310, 524, 537, 562,
        575, 645, 662, 686, 749, 821,
        859, 876, 889, 900, 906, 909-
        910, 992, 1059, 1063, 1089,
        1093, 1098
Arid landscaping   **62**
Aristotle   547, 649
Armillaria mellea   427
Army Corps of Engineers   29, **63**, 110,
        192, 244, 276, 365, 379, 388,
        632, 1059, 1064, 1090
Aromatic (benzene-based)
        hydrocarbons   788
Arrowhead   388
Arrowsmith, William   932
Arsenic   33, **63**, 67, 186-187, 232,
        506, 508, 511, 538, 561, 650,
        679, 783, 830, 1043, 1061
Artesian well   56, **63**, 489, 1081, 1143
*As the World Burns: Documenting
        America's Failure to Address the
        Ozone Crisis.*   1060
Asbestos   25, **63**, 66, 79, 93, 163,
        323, 358, 409, 506, 542, 679,
        830, 870, 875, 891, 947, 1034,
        1061, 1080
Asbestos Hazard Emergency Response
        Act (AHERA)   67
Asbestos removal   **64**
Asbestosis   64, **66**, 409, 882
Ash   849
Ashbed effect   1115
Ashio, Japan   **67**, 284, 513, 1069
Ashio Mining Company   67
Asian elephants   325

Asian tiger mosquito   212
Asiatic black bear   **68**
Asiatic clam   907
Aspinall, Wayne   599, 1111
Assateague Island   694
Asset Management Program   832
Assimilative capacity   **68**
Association of American
        Geographers   874
Asthenosphere   803
Asthma   25, 32, 59, **69**, 73, 187, 296,
        329, 543, 881, 946, 1136
Aston, Francis   637
Aswan High Dam, Egypt   **70**, 212,
        562, 876
Atabrine   461
Atlantic cod   414
Atlantic Richfield Oil Company   796
Atmosphere   3, 5, 10-11, 23, 31, 33,
        35, 53, 56, 60, 69, **72**, 83, 85,
        114, 116-117, 173, 175, 183-
        184, 195, 197, 208, 221, 242,
        254, 259, 266, 270-271, 281-
        282, 321, 338, 341-342, 378-
        379, 412, 416, 433, 448, 484,
        486-487, 497, 511, 532, 578,
        617, 631, 635, 642, 647, 649,
        654-655, 661, 665, 705, 708,
        724-725, 795, 813, 821, 829,
        850-851, 876, 891, 902-903,
        954, 956, 966, 968, 987, 995-
        996, 1016, 1025, 1034, 1046,
        1048, 1050, 1053-1054, 1067,
        1070, 1098, 1115, 1123
Atmospheric (air) pollutants   **73**
Atmospheric Environment Service   344
Atmospheric gas balance   883
Atmospheric inversion   28, **73**, 616,
        661, 1003
Atmospheric pollutants   513
Atmospheric pollution   723
Atmospheric pressure   1031
Atmospheric science   649
Atomic bomb   176, 719, 721, 724,
        844-845
Atomic Bomb Casualty
        Commission   520, 676
Atomic Energy Act (1954)   848
Atomic Energy Commission
        (AEC)   59, **74**, 341, 342, 373,
        500, 552, 723, 902, 970,
        1053, 1125
Atrazine   **74**, 516, 784, 797
Attainment area   27-28, **74**, 831
Atterberg limits   964
Attorneys for Animal Rights   45
Attu Island   925
Audubon, John James   **74**, 678,
        771, 787
Auger process   999
Augmentation reintroduction   155
Auklets   463
Australia   **75**, 583, 658
Australian pine   389

Australopithecus 603, 604
Autecology **77**
Autochthonous 332
Autoclaving 644
Automobile 3, 5, 24, 26, 34, 53, **77**,
  78, 205, 237-238, 328, 335, 337,
  394, 433, 450-451, 484, 497,
  528, 551, 579, 611, 615, 631,
  637, 649, 673, 691, 707, 741,
  792-793, 830, 854, 859, 889-
  890, 952, 955, 971, 979, 986,
  1016, 1021, 1064, 1067, 1086
Automobile emissions 78, **78**, 114,
  167, 190, 237, 350, 709, 882
Autotroph **79**, 123, 420
Avalanche **79**
Avicennia germinans 626
Avicide 17, 782
AWI Quarterly 47
Azolla 706
Azotobacter 706
AZT (azidothymidine) 22
Aztecs 652

B

Babbitt, Bruce 243, 770
Bacillus anthracis 212
Bacillus thuringiensis **83**, 547, 781, 784
Back-to-the-land movement 698
Background radiation **83**, 91, 701,
  844, 852, 1061
Backyard Wildlife Habitat
  Program 694
Bacon, Sir Francis **84**, 802
Bacopa caroliniana 388
Bacteria 10, 115, 199, 561
Bacterial agents 358
Bacteriophages 1070
Baekeland, Leo 174, 800
Baeyer, Adolf von 174
Bag trawls 463
Bagasse 341
Baghouse 26, **85**, 248, 410, 442, 538,
  810, 952, 972
Bahia Parasio 49
Baikal Watch 294
Baird, Spencer Fullerton 578
Bakelite 174, 800
Balaena glacialis 1102, 1103
Balaena mysticetus 101, 1103
Balaenoptera acutorostrata 1102
Balaenoptera musculus 101, 1102, 1104
Balaenoptera physalus 1104
Balance of nature **85**, 243, 445, 573,
  1047, 1126
Bald eagle (*Haliaeetus
  leucocephalus*) **86**, 331, 348, 359,
  396, 411, 473, 526, 695, 784,
  824, 831, 856, 925, 1047,
  1115, 1120
Baleen whales 1102
Baltic Sea 296
Bamboo 460

Bang, Oluf 162
Bangkok, Thailand 27
Bangladesh 664, 1021
Barnwell, South Carolina 620
Barriads 943
Barrier island **87**, 583, 694
Barrios 943
Basel Convention **87**
Bases 3
*Basic Guide to Pesticides: Their
  Characteristics and Hazards* 842
Basques 1103
Bathypelagic zone 775
BATNEEC 26
Bats **89**, 445, 493, 841
Batteries 539, 557
Bavaria, Joan 1067
Bays 414
bear, black 61
bear, polar 61
Beattie, Mollie 90, **90**
Beatty, Nevada 620
Becquerel, Henri 850
Bedrock contamination 510
Beef 855
Beer Institute 227
Behn, Mira 180
Behn, Sarala 180
Belarus 296
Belgrade Charter 354
Below Regulatory Concern **90**
Ben and Jerry's 482
Beni Biosphere Reserve 120
Bennet, Hugh Hammond **91**,
  962, 963
Bentham, Jeremy 45, 360, 868,
  948, 1065
Benthic community 276
Benthic macroinvertebrates 107
Benthic storms 928
Benzene 43, 78, **92**, 163, 181, 187,
  228, 266, 352, 432, 606, 679,
  788, 793, 812, 830, 946,
  1032, 1133
Benzo(a)pyrene [B(a)P] 78, **92**, 162,
  671, 812-813
Bergius process 1008
Bernard, Claude 522
Berry, Wendell **92**, 548, 569, 587,
  588-589, 936, 984
Beryllium 830
Best Available Control Technology
  (BACT) **93**, 129, 191-192,
  619, 676, 973, 1089
Best available techniques not entailing
  excessive costs (BATNEEC) 26
Best Practical Technology
  (BPT) **93**, 192
Beta particle **94**, 171, 448, 830, 843,
  844, 852
Beta rays 850
Bethe, Hans 720
Betula 1011
Betula alleghaniensis 426

Beyond the Limits 611
Bhopal, India **94**, 174, 220, 327, 352,
  508, 556, 782, 944, 1020, 1036
Bicycle 528
bidonvillas 943
Big-game hunting 531
Bikini Atoll **96**, 235
Bioaccumulation 54, **97**, 105, 111,
  182, 265, 270, 338, 413, 475,
  512, 517, 565, 575-576, 730,
  781, 812-813, 865, 1033, 1133
Bioaerosols **97**
Bioassay **97**, 107, 265, 276, 596
Biocentrism 292, 361
Biochemical oxygen demand
  (BOD) 7, 11, 69, 93, **98**, 173,
  233, 413, 630, 643, 940, 1088
Biocide 713
Bioconcentration 111
Biodegradable 11, 43, 63, 69, 98, **99**,
  113, 116, 123, 173, 175, 234,
  271, 278, 450, 458, 477, 482-
  483, 670, 761, 793, 810
Biodegradation 229
Biodiversity 21, 35, 60, 76, 90, **99**,
  106, 110, 121, 123, 132, 152,
  156, 167, 249, 255-257, 300,
  303, 306, 317, 319, 330, 333,
  349, 396, 411, 445, 465, 467,
  480, 487, 498, 502, 525, 537-
  538, 623-624, 637, 666, 682,
  703, 711, 752, 756, 828, 854,
  870, 883, 959, 966, 982, 994,
  1002, 1005, 1015, 1048, 1054,
  1056, 1067, 1076, 1102, 1110,
  1116-1117, 1131, 1143
Biodiversity Project 293
Biofilms **102**
Biofiltration **103**
Biofouling **104**, 645, 907
Biogas 753
Biogenic Law 499
Biogenic salts 726
Biogeochemical cycles 21, 99, 113,
  173, 197, 266, 519, 640,
  874, 1057
Biogeochemistry **104**
Biogeography **105**, 333, 804, 914
Biohydrometallurgy **106**
Bioindicator **107**, 540
Biological community 107, **108**, 255,
  445, 607, 719, 992, 1117
Biological controls 21
Biological degradation 43
Biological diversity 195, 594, 628
Biological ecology 594
Biological fertility **109**, 576, 994
Biological legacy 666
Biological methylation **109**, 513,
  648, 650
Biological Resources Division (formerly
  National Biological Service)
  (Washington, D.C.) **109**

Biological response modifiers
　　(BRMs)　154
Biology　579
Bioluminescence　**111**
Biomagnification　54, 68, 105, **111**,
　　266, 276, 338, 348, 413, 422,
　　513, 576, 656, 1013
Biomass　11, 22, 34, 43, 99, 105, **112**,
　　113, 117, 193, 196-197, 208,
　　246, 267, 273, 304, 314, 334,
　　341, 346, 378, 421, 429, 443,
　　473, 520, 619, 650, 653, 782,
　　809, 860, 942, 953, 969, 1001,
　　1006, 1008, 1014, 1048, 1115
Biomass fuel　**113**, 520, 619, 1115
Biome　100, 108, 112, **114**, 118, 262,
　　308, 537, 625, 993
Biomonitors　108
Biomphalaria　921
Bioparks　1144
Bioregion　115
Bioregional Project (Brixley,
　　Missouri)　**115**, 482
Bioregionalism　115, 115, 299, 312,
　　361, 481, 697, 699, 710, 901,
　　908, 959, 984
Bioremediation　11, **115**, 123, 492,
　　510, 560, 649, 685, 796,
　　873, 942
Biosequence　**117**
Biosphere　106, 108, 113-114, **117**,
　　156, 242, 255, 299, 302, 396,
　　484, 522, 554, 565, 617, 774,
　　851, 877, 996, 1002, 1004, 1054,
　　1067, 1127
Biosphere reserve　**119**, 225, 476, 624
Biosynthesis　304
Biosystems theory　594
Biotechnology　109, **121**, 422,
　　455, 458
Biotic community　3, 102, 106, 118,
　　121, **123**, 302, 314, 361, 445,
　　464, 537, 608, 729, 808, 877,
　　898, 982, 1128
Biotic pollination　806
Biotic potential　624
Bioventing　116, **123**
Bird and Bough　147
Bird Conservation International　553
Bird Lore　1071
Bird populations　699
Bird Red Data Books　553
Bird watching　787
Birds　575
Birds of America　75, 1071
Birth control　179, 399
Birth control pills　399
Birth defects　91, **124**, 170, 175, 296,
　　454, 518, 575, 593, 616, 648,
　　651, 656, 671, 679, 771, 785,
　　842-843, 1015, 1032,
　　1051, 1086
Birth rates　665
Biscayne Bay　387

Bismuth　648
Bison　**125**, 153-154, 448, 474, 524,
　　530, 637, 695, 758, 823, 874,
　　918, 1116, 1144
Bison bison　101, 125, 758
Bison bison athabascae　126
Bison bonasus　126
Bituminous coal　199
Black bear　315, 389
Black lung disease　25, **128**, 199,
　　409, 882
Black-footed ferret (*Mustela
　　nigripes*)　**127**, 155
Blackout/brownout　**128**
Blackstone, Sir William　889
Bladderwort　388
Bligh Reef　832
Block, John R.　37
Blow-out　**129**
Blue Angel (Germany)　**129**, 477
Blue crab　178
Blue pike　585
Blue Plan　645
Blue revolution (fish
　　farming)　**129**, 1006
Blue topaz　843
Blue whale　1102, 1104
Blue-baby syndrome　**129**, 279
Blue-green algae　652, 706
Blue-green bacteria　652
Blueprint for a Green School　311
Body Shop　482
Bogs　559, 829, 1101
Bolivia　253
Bombay, India　943
Bonobos　179
Bookchin, Murray　**131**, 482, 958
Boomer v. Atlantic Cement Co.　369
Bordeaux mixture　783
Borlaug, Norman E.　**132**
Borneo　749
Boron　575
Boston Harbor clean up　**133**, 630
Botanical garden　**134**, 1144
Bottom ash　538
Bottoming cycle　205
Botulism　561
Boulder Canyon Project　145
Boulding, Kenneth　**135**, 979
Boundary Waters Canoe Area
　　(Minnesota)　**136**, 1111
Boundary Waters Treaty of 1909　555
Bowhead whale　1103
Bracken Cave　89
Bracken fern　388
Brackish　**136**, 261, 385-386, 703
Braer　744
Brain cancer　844
Brain tumors　322
Brasilia　592
Bravo　96
Brazilian pepper　389
Breaking New Ground　798
Breast cancer　162

Breast-feeding　179
Breeder reactor　612
Brevetoxin　864
Bridger, Jim　1135
Bridges　913
Brine flies　662
Brine shrimp　662
British Central Electricity Generating
　　Board　340
British Gas Corporation　340
British National Coal Board　340
British National Oil Company　340
British Petroleum　477
British Royal Navy　180
British Thermal Unit (Btu)　968
Broinowski, Helen　149
Bronchitis　59, 128, **136**, 187, 296,
　　780, 881, 995, 1136
Bronchospasm　69
Brooks Range　61
Brother Eagle, Sister Sky　931
Broward, Napoleon Bonaparte　388
Brower, David Ross　**137**, 293, 438,
　　482, 1100
Brown Decades, The　632
Brown, Harrison　521
Brown, Jr., George E.　404
Brown, Lancelot "Capability"　869
Brown, Lester R.　**138**, 364,
　　1101, 1132
Brown pelican　338, 348, 447, 695,
　　784, 1116
Brown pelican (*Pelecanus
　　occidentalis*)　**139**
Browner, Carol　**140**, 142, 367, 372
Brownfields　**141**, 1062
Brown-headed cowbird　578
Brownian motion　409
Browning, Iben　702
Brucellosis　126
Bruguiera　626
Bruntdland Commission　1004
Bruntdland, Gro Harlem　**143**, 755,
　　1004, 1055
Bryan, William Jennings　37
Btu (British Thermal Unit)　**144**, 199,
　　342, 972
Btu tax　342
B-2 Stealth bomber　1053
Bubulcus ibis　106
Buddhism　712, 871
Budgies　769
Buffer　3, 6-7, **144**, 789
Bulgaria　296
Bulinus　921
Bulk density　**144**
Bullitt Foundation　504
Bunchgrasses　823
Bunker Hill　63
Burden of proof　**144**
Bureau of Chemistry and Soils　963
Bureau of Forestry　668, 798, 900
Bureau of Land Management
　　(BLM)　40, **144**, 242, 315, 405,

424, 473, 592, 669, 688, 718,
758, 832, 836, 856, 947, 1013,
1059, 1107, 1109, 1112-1113
Bureau of Mines 5, **145**, 688, 1059
Bureau of Oceans and International
Environmental and Scientific
Affairs (OES) **145**
Bureau of Outdoor Recreation 518
Bureau of Reclamation 137, **145**, 465,
562, 576, 633, 820, 859,
1059, 1089
Bureau of Soils 963
Bureau of Sport Fisheries and
Wildlife 330
Burford, Anne Gorsuch 221
Burford, Anne McGill 989
Burger King 857
Buried soil **146**
Burke, William 882
Burkina Faso 179
Burning, controlled 826
Burning, prescribed 826
Burroughs, John **146**, 641, 899
Buses 637
Bush elephants 325
Bush, George 123, 190, 718, 743,
870, 919
Bustard Studies 553
bustees 943
Buttonbush 388
buttons, "vegetable ivory" 1004
Bycatch Reduction Devices
(BRDs) **147**
Byrd, Robert 190
Bythotrephes cederstroemi 907

C

Cabot, Samuel 578
Cactoblastis cactorum 518
Cactus Crater 97
Cadmium 24, **149**, 228, 232, 234,
295, 358, 443, 482, 508, 512,
514, 564, 631, 648, 703, 721,
730, 781, 794-795, 830, 973,
988, 1008, 1032, 1062
Calcareous soil **149**
Calcium 845
Calcium carbonate 149
Calcium hydroxide 792
Calcium silicate 66
Calder, Nigel 979
Caldicott, Helen **149**
Caldicott, William 149
Caldwell, Lynton Keith **150**, 367
Caliciviruses 1070
California condor (*Gymnogyps
californianus*) **151**, 871
California Desert Protection Act 1110
California gulls 662
California Marine Debris Action
Plan 168
California spotted owl 717

California Water Resource Control
Board 576
Callicott, John Baird **152**, 361,
556, 608
Callinectes sapidus 178
Callorhinus ursinus 930
Calothrix 706
Calvaria major 272
Calypso 241-242
Calypso Log 241
Campephilus principalis 566
*Camping and Tramping with
Roosevelt* 147
Camptorhynchus labradorium 101
Canada 344, 557, 664
Canada Wildlife Act 153
*Canada's Green Plan for a Healthy
Environment* 344
Canadian Department of Fisheries and
Oceans 392
Canadian Parks Service **152**, 153, 345
Canadian Wildlife Service **153**,
153, 777
Cancer 12, 22, 25, 29, 44, 59, 63,
66, 73, 78, 84, 91, 149, **153**,
162, 170, 175, 177, 181, 183,
187, 220, 256, 259, 269, 279,
296, 303, 323, 330, 350, 352,
358, 362, 383, 400, 424, 439,
455, 494, 505, 520, 528, 560,
574, 593, 595, 609, 616, 659,
661, 671, 676-679, 699, 705,
724, 727, 773, 785, 813, 830,
838, 842-844, 852-853, 875,
881, 891-892, 947, 983, 988,
1003, 1026, 1028, 1032-1033,
1045-1046, 1053, 1068-1069,
1123, 1133
Canidae 1126
Canine distemper 127
Canis lupus 1127
Canis rufus 1127
Cannon, Walter Bradford 522
Cape Cod National Seashore 694
Cape Hatteras National Seashore 694
Capelin 463
Captive breeding 415, 777, 1107,
1144
Captive propagation and
reintroduction 151, **154**, 415,
461, 750, 777, 814, 1107,
1118, 1127
Carbamates 185, 784
Carbaryl 94, 185, 784
Carbofuran 784
Carbohydrates 198
Carbon 53, 55, 58, 78-79, 112, 115,
156, **156**, 158, 181, 183, 198-
200, 217, 234, 255, 259, 269,
324, 392, 418, 432, 436, 451,
484, 486, 511, 519, 532, 540,
564, 647, 659, 664, 721, 767,
788, 792, 801, 810, 844, 850-

852, 942, 952, 956, 973, 1008,
1012, 1032, 1046, 1094, 1114
Carbon cycle 113-114, **156**, 265, 851
Carbon dioxide 5, 7, 10-11, 57, 72,
79, 113, 115, 118, 121, 137, 149,
156, 158, **158**, 166, 175, 195-
199, 208, 217, 229, 235, 252,
254-255, 271, 320, 328, 336,
338, 379, 381, 412, 417, 433,
441, 484, 486, 492, 532, 549,
561, 571, 613, 640, 649, 652,
655, 659, 670, 708, 741, 759,
763, 788, 791, 794, 796, 810,
813, 829, 851, 855, 858, 869,
881, 933, 946, 956, 968, 982,
1002, 1018, 1056, 1072, 1077,
1087, 1094, 1098, 1102, 1114
Carbon monoxide 24, 27, 44, 74, 78,
113, 156, **158**, 166, 174, 187,
189, 191, 200, 208, 350, 417,
450, 542, 634, 643, 676, 709,
788, 830, 858, 946, 972, 1008,
1012, 1060, 1071, 1098
Carbon offsets **158**
Carbon tax **160**
Carbon tetrachloride 25, 181,
197, 830
Carbon-14 94, 844, 851
Carbon-12 851
Carbonic acid 3
Carboxydismutase 381
Carcharodon charcharias 241
Carcinogen 12, 17-18, 41, 44, 63, 74,
78, 92, 153, **162**, 171, 175, 178,
183, 186-187, 269, 280, 404,
508, 532, 595, 609, 659, 671-
672, 786, 813, 842, 882, 891,
946, 956, 1026, 1028, 1033,
1046, 1051, 1069
Caretta caretta 389, 926
Carhart, Arthur 1111
Caribou 61, 609
Carmageddon 293
Carnivore 123
Carolina Environmental Study
Group 829
Carolina parakeet 101, 770
Carolina Power and Light 322
Carp 585
Carrying capacity **163**, 267, 304, 353,
401, 414, 435, 492, 502, 515,
526, 573, 607, 613, 747, 814,
816, 984, 1116-1117
Carson, Rachel 87, 131, 140, **164**,
251, 257, 364, 617, 641, 809,
842, 1051, 1051
Carter, Jimmy 30, 239, 463, 617,
1041, 1058
Cascades Volcano Observatory 665
Case for Animal Rights, The 776, 868
Cash crop 58, 71, **166**
Casuarina equisetifolia 389
Catalytic converter 26, 79, **166**,
451, 956

Catalytic reforming 451
Cataracts 763
Catastomus commersoni 393
Catharantus roseus 101
Cation 1
Catlin, George 1109
Catskill Mountains 525
Cattail marsh 576
Cattails 559, 839
Cattle 757
Cattle egret 106
Cattle ranching 35, 855
Ceanothus 706
Cellular telephone 322
Cellulose 113
Cenotes 949
Center for Community Pesticide and
    Alternatives Information 678
Center for the Defense of Free
    Enterprise 1124
Center for Environmental Health and
    Injury Control 170
Center for Environmental Philosophy
    (Denton, Texas) **167**
Center for Field Research 295
Center for Infectious Diseases 170
Center for Marine Conservation
    (Washington, D.C.) **167**
Center for Prevention Services 170
Center for Respect of Life and
    Environment (Washington,
    D.C.) **168**
Center for Risk Management 880
Center for Rural Affairs (Walthill,
    Nebraska) **169**
Center for Science in the Public
    Interest (Washington,
    D.C.) **169**, 422, 673
Center for Study of Responsive
    Law 673, 1059
Center for Transnational
    Corporations 1021
Centers for Disease Control and
    Prevention 13, **170**, 187, 212,
    270, 375, 382, 644, 684, 686,
    835, 997, 1028, 1058
Central American avian 870
Central Park, New York 747
Central and Southern Florida Project
    for Flood Control & Other
    Purposes 388
Central Treaty Organization 151
Century 667
Cephalanthus accidentalis 388
Ceratotherium simum 884
Ceriops 626
Cervical cancer 162
Cervus elaphus 1124
Cesium 561
Cesium 137 97, **171**, 501, 560, 609
Cetacea 1102
CFC-11 661
CFC-113 184
Chain fern 388

Chain pickerel 525
Chain reaction **171**, 208, 701,
    719-721
Channel catfish 207
Chaos, theory of 195
Chaparral 114
Chaparral fires 1114
Char 867
Chase, Chevy 311
Chase, Jayni 311
Chelate **171**
Chelonia mydas 926
Chelyabinsk, Russia **172**, 848
Chemical 34, 475
Chemical bond **172**, 182, 266, 304,
    323, 793
Chemical contamination 842
Chemical Corps 896
Chemical destruction 510
Chemical extraction 510
Chemical oxygen demand 7, 43,
    173, 1087
Chemical Release Forms 327
Chemical residue 1030
Chemical spills 170, **173**, 297, 328,
    413, 476, 507, 533, 749, 997,
    1037, 1094
Chemical synthesis gas 201
Chemical warfare 1076
Chemicals 15-16, 20, 53, 97, 104,
    111, 124, 130-131, 145, 162,
    165, 170, 173, **174**, 178, 182,
    185-186, 201, 208, 210, 217,
    220, 232, 246-247, 265, 280-
    281, 318, 352, 358, 378, 404,
    416, 418, 420, 427, 433, 449,
    451, 458, 467, 475, 482, 487,
    490, 493, 506, 528, 532, 545,
    556, 558, 584, 593, 606, 616,
    620, 639, 650, 661, 664, 671-
    672, 704, 726, 735, 750, 781,
    785, 788, 800, 804, 807, 810,
    814, 824, 830, 838, 842, 848,
    880, 884, 886, 890-891, 912,
    921, 937, 939, 946, 951, 962,
    972, 975, 978, 983, 988, 997,
    1003, 1008, 1021, 1028, 1030,
    1032, 1034, 1036, 1046, 1050,
    1059, 1068, 1077, 1080, 1082,
    1086-1088, 1116, 1124, 1128
Chemicals, synthetic 174
Chemiosorption 1
Chemophobia 668
Chemosynthesis 628
Chemotherapy 44, 154, 844
Chen caerulescens 61
Chernobyl Nuclear Power Station
    (Ukraine) 43, 94, 125, 171-
    172, **175**, 296, 334, 560, 720,
    797, 822, 844-845, 1122
Chesapeake Bay **177**, 252, 385-386,
    567, 574, 631, 981
Chesapeake Bay Agreement 178
Chickaree 866

Child survival revolution **179**,
    260, 609
Chile 864
Chilkat Bald Eagle Preserve 87
Chimpanzees **179**, 329, 462, 468, 471,
    555, 750
China 1024
Chipko Andolan movement **180**
Chisso Company 655
Chloracne 269, 940
Chloramination 183
Chlordane 175, **181**, 181, 546, 754,
    784, 838, 896
Chlorinated di-benzo-p-dioxins 634
Chlorinated hydrocarbons 24, 54, **181**,
    233, 307, 526, 700, 728, 783,
    968, 1032
Chlorinated organic compounds 228
Chlorination **182**, 461, 886, 1070
Chlorine 16, 24, 57, 79, 111, 174,
    178, 181-183, 278, 296, 433,
    436, 487, 532, 634, 643, 647,
    659, 661, 759-761, 810, 812,
    837, 882, 909, 917, 924, 942,
    988, 1037, 1046, 1076, 1087,
    1094, 1125
Chlorine gas 182
Chlorine monoxide **183**
Chlorine nitrate 761
Chlorofluorocarbons (CFCs) 25, 175,
    183, 190, 197, 210, 350, 364,
    436, 467, 482, 484, 486-487,
    532, 549, 613, 617, 661, 664, 697,
    708, 760-761, 813, 870, 902,
    988, 1034, 1053, 1098
Chlorofluoromethane 183
Chloroform 181-182
Chloromethane 183
Chlorophylls 794
Cholera 179, **184**, 206, 212, 251,
    261, 362, 461, 835, 916, 944,
    1021, 1083
Cholinesterase inhibitor **185**, 267,
    754, 784
Chondrococcus columnaris 1017
Christianity 871
Chromatography **185**, 618, 884
Chromium 512, 575, 648, 759, 1032
Chronic effects 8, 129, **186**, 252, 781,
    1033, 1035
Chronic Obstructive Pulmonary Disease
    (COPD) 881
Chronic toxicity testing 186
Chryocyon brachyurus 1127
Chrysanthemum cinerariaefolium 783
Chrysobalanus icacao 388
Cigarette smoke 44, 125, 137, 162,
    170, **187**, 329, 705, 813, 882,
    946, 956, 1029
Cigarette smoking 162
Cinnabar 647
Cinnamon fern 388
Circadian 794
Citicorp 120

Citizen Action   140
Citizen Agenda   1060
Citizen's Clearinghouse for Hazardous
      Wastes   463
Citizens for a Better Environment
      (Chicago, Illinois)   **188**
Citizens to Preserve Overton Park v.
      Volpe   369
Civil engineering   357
Civil rights   150
Civilian Conservation Corps   222
Cladium effusum   387
Cladium jamaicense   388
Clamshell Alliance   929
Clark, William P.   870
Classification and Multiple Use
      Act   405
Clawson, Marion   880
Clay minerals   144, **188**, 560
Clay mining   883
Clay-hard pan   **189**
Clean Air Act   26-28, 93, 141, 188,
      189, 191, 238, 290, 340, 368,
      372, 449, 619, 676, 679-680,
      702, 709, 811, 829, 833, 868,
      870, 879, 888, 934, 947, 972,
      1012, 1037, 1043
Clean Air and Future Energy   922
Clean Air Scientific Advisory
      Committee   676
Clean coal technology   5, **191**
Clean Water Act   42, 69, 93, 130,
      133, **191**, 247, 277, 290, 319,
      340, 567, 574, 631, 703, 733,
      800, 811, 830, 832, 872-873,
      889, 971, 1031, 1060, 1089
Clean Water Act Reauthorization   830
Clean Water Action   380
Clean Water Action Project   673
Clean Water Campaign   1060
Clear-cutting   1, 60, 106, **193**, 259,
      370, 372, 425, 428-429, 517,
      525, 538, 571, 681, 798, 856,
      935, 959, 1015, 1113, 1124
Clements, Frederic E.   197
Cleveland, Grover   667, 798
Climate   2, 20, 76, 106, 114, 157, **195**,
      197, 214, 228, 238, 255, 259,
      281, 294, 303, 313, 321, 333,
      345, 370, 375, 379, 382, 391,
      396, 414, 427, 440, 446, 464-
      465, 473, 486, 490, 537, 549,
      553, 562, 591, 622, 635, 649,
      653, 655, 659, 664, 688, 713,
      725, 748, 751, 758, 823, 854,
      889, 962, 964, 967, 1003, 1009,
      1014, 1016, 1056, 1098, 1131
Climate change   708, 1075
Climate control   1001
Climate Protection Institute   294
Climax   316, 980, 1114
Climax (ecological)   **197**, 994
Climax species   980

Clinton, Bill   342, 372, 680, 719, 856,
      895, 1054, 1056
Clod   **197**
Cloning   439
Cloning vector   455
Closed system   748
Closed-in-vessel composting   670
Clostridium   706
Cloud chemistry   173, 196, **197**, 649,
      664, 988
Cloud-seeding   221
Club of Rome   **198**, 610, 920
C:N ratio   **198**, 217, 393
Cnidarians   235
Coal   3, 5, 23, 25, 33, 128, 145, 149,
      156-158, 174, 191, **199**, 200,
      202, 205, 208, 238, 249, 295,
      321, 329, 334-335, 340, 342,
      376, 417, 432, 434, 438, 442,
      458, 467, 472, 486, 611, 619,
      647-648, 651, 657-658, 710,
      738, 741, 753, 756, 788, 799,
      813, 821, 859, 867, 869, 881,
      920, 952, 954, 956, 962, 968,
      990, 995, 997, 999, 1008, 1015-
      1016, 1025, 1043, 1058, 1061,
      1086, 1133, 1137
Coal gasification   191, 199, **200**, 206,
      812, 997, 1008
Coal liquefaction   1008
Coal Mine Health and Safety Act   340
Coal mining   238
Coal tar   162
Coal washing   191, 199, 201, **202**
Coal-fired furnaces   829
Coalition for Environmentally
      Responsible Economics
      (CERES)   381, 1067
Coase theorem   **202**
Coast Guard   506, 743
Coast redwood   865
Coastal Barrier Resources
      System   1059
Coastal forests   627
Coastal Society, The (Gloucester,
      Massachusetts)   **202**
Coastal wetlands   1101
Coastal Zone Management Act
      (1972)   **203**, 232, 592, 694
Coastlines   686
Cobalt   512
Coca-Cola   857
Cocaine   855
Cockatiels   769
Cockatoos   769
Cockle virus   1070
Co-composting   **204**
Cocoplum   388
Code of Federal Regulations   832
Code of Federal Regulations   878
Coelacanth   333
Coevolution   **205**, 209, 308, 445
Coffea arabica   135
Cofrentes nuclear power plant   846

Cogeneration   **205**, 211, 336, 341,
      1019
Coke oven emissions   830
Cold War   1076
Coleoptera   100
Coliform bacteria   **206**, 234, 342, 461,
      730, 831, 1087
Coliphages   1070
Colonias   943
Colorado River   146, **206**, 249, 458,
      464, 472, 562, 615, 820, 876,
      909, 1090, 1093
Colorado River Compact   206
Colorado squawfish   206
Colter, John   1135
Columbia River   846
Columbus, Christopher   19
Column chromatography   185
Combined Sewer Overflows
      (CSO)   **207**
Combustion   3, 5, 11, 23, 77-78, 113,
      144, 158, 167, 182, 191, 199-
      200, **208**, 266, 281, 300, 324,
      335, 337, 341, 378, 416-417,
      451, 497, 512, 538, 615, 634,
      676, 707, 788, 810, 812, 821,
      849, 858, 874, 956, 971-972,
      1016, 1137
Comephorus baicalensis   583
Cometabolism   **208**, 265
Commensalism   **208**, 307, 1007
Commentaries on the Laws of
      England   889
Commercial fishing   47, 59, 72, 131,
      147, **209**, 232, 253, 277, 318,
      321, 386, 414, 463, 474, 562,
      584, 632, 645, 669, 710, 757,
      769, 780, 890, 907, 1003, 1050,
      1060, 1102, 1141
Commercial or retail waste   634
Commercial whaling   552, 1103
Commission for Environmental
      Cooperation   **209**
Committee for Humane Legislation v.
      Richardson   629
Committee for the National Institute
      for the Environment   682
Committee on Rare and Endangered
      Wildlife Species   330
Commodities   832
Common law   368, 1068
Commoner, Barry   **210**, 269, 1054
Commonwealth Edison   322
Communicable diseases   170, 179, **211**,
      280, 1058
Community Discussion Guide, The   467
Community ecology   **213**
Compaction   **214**, 569, 668, 856, 975
Comparative risk   **215**
Competition   32, 106, 199, 206, 213,
      217, 307, 382, 613, 625, 703,
      746, 748, 758, 782, 816, 865,
      930, 1007, 1141
Compost   10, 408

Composting   99, 103, 199, 204, **217**, 449, 592, 619, 668, 670, 704, 731, 752, 810, 864, 880, 898, 951, 971, 973-975, 1079, 1135

Comprehensive Environmental Response, Compensation, and Liability Act (CERCLA)   13, 141, **220**, 228, 327, 350, 357, 372, 375, 507, 509, 593, 606, 692, 868, 870, 872, 877, 989, 997, 1022, 1034, 1058

Comprehensive Environmental Response, Compensation and Monitoring Act   1069

Comprehensive Test Ban Treaty (CTBT)   723

Computer models   1030

Computer terminal   322

Concrete   657

Condensation nuclei   12, **221**

Condensation polymer   801

Condom   399

Condorcet, Marquis de   624

Conducting polymers   801

Conference on the Fate of the Earth   293

Conference on the Law of the Sea   231

Confucianism   713

Congenital abnormality   1015

Congress on Renewable Natural Resources   874

Coniferous forest   114, 118, **221**, 687, 717, 856, 1014

Connate water   489

Connecticut Plan   239

Connecticut River   846

Conocarpus erectus   626

CONOCO   857

Conquest of Paradise: Christopher Columbus and the Columbian Legacy   908

Conservation   8, 12, 21, 36-37, 47, 49, 61, 75, 87, 90-91, 135, 152, 167, 192, 202, **221**, 225-226, 240, 242, 250, 253, 262, 281, 286, 290, 293, 295, 310, 317, 319, 322, 326, 339, 342, 345, 353, 360, 364, 367, 395, 411, 429, 435, 437, 447-448, 486, 492, 527, 537, 553, 555, 560, 565, 567, 586, 594, 607, 622, 624-625, 632, 639, 666, 669, 674, 677, 685, 687, 689, 691, 694, 699, 717, 741, 753, 758-759, 798, 820, 824, 842, 854, 858, 871, 874, 880, 897-899, 919, 922, 925, 927, 931, 946, 959, 962-963, 1000, 1002, 1013-1014, 1040, 1055, 1059, 1071, 1079, 1081, 1096, 1106, 1112-1113, 1118, 1127, 1130-1131

Conservation biology   **223**, 498

Conservation Directory, The   695

Conservation Education Association   354, 714

Conservation Foundation   369, 755, 870, 1041, 1071

Conservation International (Washington, D.C.)   120, **225**, 253, 714, 1004

Conservation and Protection Service   345

Conservation Reserve   963

Conservation tillage   21, 197, **226**, 282, 287, 587, 963

Conservation, whale   558

Conservatism   754

Conserving America   695

Conserving Natural Value   899

Consolidated Edison   322, 986

Construction Grant Amendments   192

Consultative Group on International Agricultural Research (CGIAR) (Washington, D.C.)   **226**

Consumer advocacy   169

Consumer boycott   857

Consumer Product Safety Commission   507, 1037

Consumer protection   422

Contact metamorphism   804

Contact System   692

Container deposit legislation   **227**, 479, 864, 880

Contaminated sediment   276

Contaminated soil   58, 68, 99, 115, 123, 141, 174, **228**, 277, 297, 489-491, 520, 565, 617, 749, 951, 965, 977, 989, 995

Contamination   640, 859

Continental drift   803

Continental shelf   1060

Contour mining   990

Contour plowing   18, **230**, 587, 963, 989

Control Commission of West Germany   922

Control inventory   96

Controlled burning   580, 826

Conuropsis carolinensis   101, 770

Convention on the Conservation of Antarctic Marine Living Resources (CCAMLR)   48, 49

Convention on the Conservation of Migratory Species of Wild Animals (1979)   **230**, 1057, 1102

Convention on International Trade in Endangered Species of Wild Fauna and Flora (1975)   47, 126, 153, **231**, 330, 462, 556, 749, 759, 770, 805, 1027, 1055, 1057, 1117, 1131

Convention on the Law of the Sea (1982)   **231**, 928

Convention on Long-Range Transboundary Air Pollution (1979)   **232**

Convention on the Prevention of Marine Pollution by Dumping of Waste and Other Matter (1972)   **232**, 728, 731, 928

Convention on the Regulation of Antarctic Mineral Resource Activities   48

Convention on Wetlands of International Importance (1971)   153, **233**, 1102

Conventional pollutant   192, **233**, 1088

Cook, Captain James   831

Cool Water Integrated Gasification Combined Cycle   201

Coolidge, Calvin   567

Coots   575

Copper   16, 67, 106, 121, 166, 232, **234**, 284, 451, 458, 512, 514, 561, 631, 648, 703, 783, 794-795, 861, 974, 986, 994, 1008, 1032, 1037, 1043, 1061, 1072

Copper pollution   67

Coprecipitation   **234**, 234, 513

Coral reef   40, 52, 75, **235**, 305, 307, 317, 502, 583, 628, 689, 731, 780, 787, 1086, 1116

Corbicula fluminea   907

Cordova Island   832

Coregonus clupeaformis   585

Corn   113, 122, 450

Coronaviruses   1070

Corporate Average Fuel Economy standards (CAFE)   **236**, 341, 484

Corporate Environmental Affairs   345

Corrosion and material degradation   **237**, 759

Cosmetics   422

Cosmids   455

Costa Rica   225

Costal conservation   202

Cost-benefit analysis   26, **238**, 254, 302, 351, 868

Costle, Douglas M.   **239**, 870

Cotton   70

Council on Environmental Quality (CEQ)   **239**, 354, 467, 637, 679, 870, 1041

Cousin Island   553

Cousteau, Jacques-Yves   **240**, 241

Cousteau, Jean-Michel   241

Cousteau Society, The (Chesapeake, Virginia)   **241**

Covalent bond   172

Coxackieviruses   1070

Cracking   451

Cracking corrosion   237

Cradle-to-grave   878

Crapper, Thomas   1029

Crassostrea virginica   178

Crater Lake   585

Crayfish   393

Creosote   358

Cretaceous period   635

Creutzfeldt-Jakob Disease (CJD)   621
Crick, Francis   271
Crisis in Our Cities   131
Criteria pollutant   26, 189, **242**, 676, 709, 830, 1012, 1089
Critical habitat   121, 135, 194, **242**, 331, 411, 718, 750, 1014
Critical load   69
Crocodiles   76, **243**, 472, 1144
Crocodylidae   243
Crocodylus acutus   244
Cronkite, Walter   923
Crop rotation   423
Cross-breeding   122
Cross-compliance   423
Cross-Florida Barge Canal   **244**
Crude oil   788
Crustaceans   331
Cubatao, Brazil   **245**
Cullet   974
Cultural eutrophication   **245**, 393, 409, 437, 525, 585-586, 792, 809, 1063, 1088
Curie, Irène   850
Currents   321
Cuvier, Georges Leopold   1144
Cuyahoga River, Ohio   142, **247**, 365, 475
Cyanide   759
Cyanuric acid   858
Cyclical populations   1116
Cyclodiene insecticides   181
Cyclodienes   181
Cyclone collector   26, 85, **248**, 418, 809, 822
Cyclopentadiene pesticide   754
Cyperaceae   474
Cypress   1101
Cyprinus carpio   585
Cytomegalovirus   124
Czech Republic   296

D

da Silva, Darci Pereia   646
da Silva, Darli Alves   646
Da Vinci III   529
Daedalus 88   528
Dahoon holly   388
Dairy industry   812
Daly, Herman   983
Dams   59, 137, 145, 206, 214, 242, 244, **249**, 292, 334, 365, 414, 464, 519, 526, 562, 570, 619, 645, 666, 674, 717, 876, 890, 893, 909, 921, 969, 989, 1011, 1013, 1015, 1024, 1027, 1059, 1081, 1089, 1091, 1096-1097, 1108, 1129
Dandelion   748
Danube River   296
Daphnia   186
Darling, Jay Norwood "Ding"   **250**

Darwin, Charles Robert   **250**, 389, 445, 499, 501, 624
Darwin's finches   446
Dawn redwood   865
DDD   54, 783
DDT (dichlorodiphenyl-trichloroethane)   16, 18, 54, 59, 87, 105, 139, 151, 175, 181, 187, 208, **251**, 301, 338, 349, 372, 413, 422, 456, 475, 496, 517, 526, 546, 557, 574, 623, 631, 699, 700, 754, 777, 782, 809, 838, 891, 893, 896, 1021, 1032, 1047, 1061, 1116, 1128
Dead zones   **252**
Deaeration   237
Dean, Norman L.   483
d'Eaubonne, Francoise   298
Debt for nature swap   120, **253**, 609, 625, 698
Deccan Traps   635
Deciduous forest   114, 118, **254**, 305, 537, 622, 686, 699, 856, 918, 1015, 1110
Decline spiral   35, **255**, 493, 525
Decomposers   255
Decomposition   10, 43, 118, 123, 156, 178, 184, 197-198, 255, **255**, 267, 271, 301, 407, 412, 443, 493, 519, 630, 707, 710, 789-790, 797, 856, 911, 964, 974, 1047, 1085, 1114, 1135
Deconstruction   819
Deep ecology   131, **256**, 292, 299, 312, 361, 380, 481, 488, 673, 697, 819, 984
Deep Sea Drilling Project   645
Deep-well injection   58, 174, **256**, 490, 545, 872, 1099
Defenders of Wildlife (Washington, D.C.)   **257**, 499, 710, 714, 759, 1118
Defense Logistics Agency (DLA)   987
Defense Writers Group   924
Defoliant   269
Defoliation   **258**, 782, 1076
Deforestation   22, 35, 157, 212, **259**, 263, 281, 310, 350, 468, 471, 496, 498, 512, 525, 537, 553, 567, 570, 578, 584, 623, 633, 637, 646, 664, 681-682, 750, 753, 798, 854, 874, 889, 918, 1006, 1015, 1021, 1042, 1056, 1076, 1082, 1091, 1099, 1115, 1121, 1129, 1131
Deglaciation   915
Delaney Clause   238, **259**
Delnav   1008
Delphi Prize   897
Demographic transition   179, **260**
Dendroica kirtlandii   578
Denitrification   **260**, 705, 759, 942
Density separation   202

Deoxyribose nucleic acid (DNA)   439, 456
Department of Agriculture   900
Department of Energy   895
Department of Energy Organization Act   403
Department of Fisheries and Oceans (DFO), Canada   414
Dermochelys coriacea   926
Desalinization   **261**, 281, 562, 734, 780, 910, 1081, 1083, 1091
Descartes, René   45, 868
Desert   1, 31, 58, 60, 62, 75, 106, 112, 114-115, 196, 262, **262**-263, 284, 305, 308, 333, 382, 401, 415, 434, 474, 500, 540, 562, 716, 738, 748, 757, 780, 858, 910, 939, 1060, 1086, 1110
Desert Solitaire   1
Desert tortoise   257
Desert tortoise (*Gopherus agassizii*)   257, **262**
Desertification   21, 62, 119, 226, 259, 262, **263**, 281-282, 287, 321, 434, 445, 467, 537, 758, 855, 906, 1021, 1054-1056, 1098
Deserts on the March   931
Design for disassembly   **264**
Destruction and removal efficiency (DRE)   983
Detergents   5, 63, 93, 174, 178, 246-247, **265**, 372, 477, 482, 584, 707, 744, 788, 791, 880, 933, 1072
Deterministic model   660
Detoxification   74, 186, 252, **265**
Detritivores   123, 255, **267**, 577
Detroit River   474
Deuterium   720
Developing countries, pollution in   27
Devils Hole   655
Devonian period   635
Dew point   221, **267**, 533, 760
Diabetes   843
Diatometer   774
Diatoms of the United States   774
Diazinon   267, 754, 784, 797
Dibenzofurans   634
Diceros bicornis   12, 885
Dichlorodiphenyl-trichloroethane   359
Dichloromethane   181
Didermocerus sumatrensis   884
Dieback   6, **267**, 393, 426, 816
Dieldrin   54, 181, 526, 754, 781
Dielectric fluids   812
Die-off   69, **267**, 412, 930
Diesel fuels   77
Diethylstilbestrol (DES)   17, 162
Dietz, Thomas   526
Dillard, Annie   **268**, 936
Dingell, John   190
Dingo   841
Di-nitrogen monoxide   708
Dinoflagellates   864

Dinosaur National Monument 137
Dinosaurs 635
Dioxin 16, 24, 54, 79, 174, 258, **268**, 328, 346, 372, 487, 518, 634, 644, 771, 775, 838, 849, 917, 940, 973, 983, 1028, 1051, 1076, 1080, 1142
Dipeptide 776
Diplococcus pneumoniae 454
Dipodomys ingens 332
Direct runoff 986
Dirty Dozen Campaign 785
Disappearing Species: The Social Challenge 396
Discharge 3, 7, 24, 54, 58, 68-69, 97-98, 177, 182, 192, 246, **270**, 275, 319, 386, 411, 526, 539-540, 645, 659, 681, 733, 809, 830, 948, 1008, 1021, 1093
Disinfectants 735
Disinfection byproducts 1094
Dispersants 744
Displaced farmers 1024
Disposable diapers **270**, 477, 669, 879, 976, 978, 1079
Dissolved air flotation 416
Dissolved oxygen 4, 58, 69, 252, **271**, 386, 512, 586, 630, 831, 1016-1017
Dissolved solids **271**
Disston, Hamilton 387
Disturbed ecosystems 838
DNA (deoxyribose nucleic acid) 41, 44, 84, 122, 153, 162, 180, 182, 255, **271**, 323, 439, 453, 454, 457, 561, 652, 671, 705, 726, 773, 894, 1053, 1069
DNA polymerase 454
Dobzhansky, Theodosius 390
Dodo (*Raphus cucullatus*) 99, **272**, 396
Dolphin Log 241
Dolphins 36, 45, 47, 147, 167, 209, 241-242, **272**, 277, 294, 331, 442, 463, 483, 487, 527, 553, 629, 631, 689, 757, 864, 1013, 1050, 1102, 1104
Dominance **273**
Donora, Pennsylvania 27
Dose response 186, **274**, 305, 362, 596, 891
Douglas fir 717, 1014
Douglas, Marjory Stoneman **274**
Douglas Point, Canada 846
Douglas squirrel 866
Douglas, William O. 515
Dounreay 847
Dow Chemical Company 661, 895
Down the River 1
Down's syndrome 124
Downwelling 628
DPD (N,N-Diethyl-p-phenylenediamine) 183
Dpn 454

Draft Resolution on a National Policy for the Environment, A 150
Drainage **274**
Drainage water 576
Drake, Edwin 788
Drawdown 1099
Dredging 56, 203, **275**, 373, 475, 512, 627, 632, 656-657, 872, 928
Dreissena polymorpha 391, 907, 1141
Drepanididae 102
Drift 464
Drift nets **277**, 294, 380, 413, 629, 689, 710, 926
Driftnet Fishery Conservation Act 47
Drinking-water supply 56, 58, 74, 129, 182-183, 261, **278**, 434, 489-491, 643, 663, 705, 717, 776, 829, 906, 988, 1021, 1046, 1082, 1100, 1125, 1143
Drip irrigation 62, **280**, 536
Drought 20, 62, 70, 75, 146, 195-197, 254, 263, **280**, 286, 316, 321, 401, 427, 453, 458, 468, 473, 489, 535, 613, 664, 749, 751, 758, 823, 855, 906, 918, 962, 1009, 1082-1083, 1098
Drugs 422, 1133
Drury, Newton 919
Dry alkali injection 191, **281**, 416
Dry deposition **282**, 953, 995
Dry steam fields 459
Dry steam well 459
Dryland farming **282**
Drymarchon corais couperi 389
Du Pont Chemical Company 764, 857, 902, 919
du Pont, Eleuthère Irénée 174
Dubos, Rene Jules **282**, 579, 632, 1055
Duck-billed platypus 870
Ducks 386
Ducks Unlimited (Canada) 283
Ducks Unlimited (Long Grove, Illinois) 153, 222, **283**, 447, 698
Ducks Unlimited de Mexico 283
Ducktown, Tennessee **284**, 513
Duke Power 322
Duluth, Minnesota 64
Dunes and dune erosion **284**
Dunsmuir, California 173
Dust Bowl 18, 281, 283, **286**, 524, 931, 963
Dust storm 511
Dwellers in the Land 908
Dyspnea 67

E

E. coli See Escherichia coli
E_H **320**
E horizon 964
E Source 897
Earth Action Month 694
Earth in the Balance 470

Earth Charter **289**
Earth Day 138, 227, **290**, 372-373, 483, 504, 699
Earth First! (Missoula, Montana) 1, 256, **292**, 298, 380, 424, 481, 488, 710, 719
Earth Island Institute (San Francisco, California) 137, 277, **293**, 380, 710
Earth Island Journal 293
Earth Pledge Foundation (New York, New York) **294**
Earth Summit 710, 1055
EarthCorps 295
Earthquake 79, 595, 651, 702, 750, 848, 1049
Earthwatch (Watertown, Massachusetts) 277, **295**, 318, 710
East Germany 296
Eastern European pollution 28, **295**, 849
Eastern indigo snake 389
Eastern lowland gorilla 471
Eastern philosophy 299
Eastern Wilderness Act 1112
Eastman, George 174
Echidnas 841
Echo Park dam 1111
Echolocation 272
Eckholm, Eric 396
Eco 454
Ecoanarchism **297**
Ecocatastrophe 255
Ecocide **298**, 518, 1076
Ecodefense: A Field Guide to Monkeywrenching 662
Ecofeminism **298**, 361, 481
Ecofeminist philosophy 298
Ecofeminists 488
Ecoglasnost 296
Ecojustice 168, **299**, 361, 1056
Ecological (biological) integrity **300**
Ecological consumers **302**, 305
Ecological economics 345
Ecological (environmental) economics **302**
Ecological and environmental justice 300
Ecological literacy 754
Ecological productivity 273, **304**, 493, 994, 1060, 1115
Ecological psychology 958
Ecological risk assessment **305**, 892
Ecological Society of America (Washington, D.C.) **306**, 736, 1003
Ecological succession 1114
Ecology 22, 56, 77, 81, 106, 115, 118, 121, 135, 164, 213, 223, 256, 289, 292, 295, 305, **306**, 309, 326, 333, 343, 370, 378, 382, 435, 445-446, 487, 492, 499, 501, 521, 526, 552, 566, 589,

612, 632, 648, 659, 678, 703, 736, 738, 769, 774, 798, 814-815, 931, 958-960, 1022, 1090, 1106, 1116, 1120, 1127, 1143

Ecomark 129, **309**, 477

EcoNet (San Francisco, California) **309**

Economic Benefits of Rails-to-Trails Conversions to Local Economies, The 854

Economic development 330

Economic Development Administration 239

Economic growth and the environment 121, **309**, 322, 341, 367, 435, 515, 519, 591, 609, 755-756, 922, 959, 1064, 1129

Ecophilosophy 674

Eco-School, Project (Pacific Palisades, California **311**

Ecosophy 256, **312**, 674, 697

Ecosphere 118

Ecosystem 3, 20-21, 38, 46, 48, 54-55, 87, 90, 100, 104, 106-108, 114-115, 119, 130, 135, 144, 146, 152, 163, 165, 167, 194-195, 209, 213, 225, 235, 242, 246, 251, 255, 259, 261, 263, 265, 267, 274, 276, 282, 293, 300, 304-307, **312**, 314-315, 318, 325, 330, 334, 338, 345, 357, 361, 365, 370-371, 380, 385, 387, 391, 396, 413, 420, 428, 445, 474, 481, 492, 499, 512, 516, 525-527, 535, 537, 541, 546, 555, 559, 562, 569, 571, 575, 580, 585, 587, 622, 624, 627, 629, 646-647, 666, 678, 687, 691, 697, 700, 703, 706, 717-718, 739, 745, 748-749, 767, 769, 775, 777, 780-781, 796, 808, 814, 824-826, 858, 860, 872, 876-877, 888-889, 898, 906-907, 920, 935, 938, 952, 958-959, 982, 985, 990, 993, 995, 999, 1001, 1004, 1006, 1009, 1011, 1014, 1046, 1048, 1050, 1059-1060, 1068, 1075, 1084, 1088, 1091, 1096, 1101, 1110, 1113-1115, 1127, 1130, 1133, 1136, 1141

Ecosystem approach in environmental policy 372

Ecosystem health **314**

Ecosystem management **315**, 826

Ecosystem model 659

Ecosystem variation 683

Ecotage 298, 662

Ecoterrorism 298

Ecoteurs 425

Ecotone **317**

Ecotourism 30, 41, 49, 254, **317**, 446, 623, 625, 691, 1109

Ecotoxicology **318**, 517, 596, 851

Ecotype 105, **319**

Ecover 482

Ectomycorrhiza 671

Ectopistes migratorius 101, 758, 771, 1116, 1144

Edaphic **319**

Edaphology **319**, 775

Edey, Marion 599

EDF Letter 349

Edge effect 317

Edge of the Sea 164

Edmonson, W. T. 586

Education for the Future 922

Edward Abbey (ship) 926

Effective concentration (EC) 98

Effective dosage (ED) 98

Effective dose 596

Effluent 24, 93, 97, 182, 192, 232, 234, 245, 247-248, 296, 318-319, **319**, 413, 513, 559, 574, 630, 655, 659, 728, 733, 761, 838, 940, 1063, 1086, 1088-1089

Effluent tax **319**

EG&G, Inc 895

Ehrenfeld, David 528

Ehrlich, Paul **320**, 364, 755, 816, 922, 1071, 1128, 1143

Eichhornia crassipes 1084

El Niño 209, 252, 281, **321**, 664, 864, 1060, 1072

Elaeagnus 706

Electric blanket 322

Electric power tool 322

Electric razor 322

Electric utilities 5, 33, 128, 205, 211, **321**, 341, 403, 407, 441, 619, 697, 930, 971, 986, 1122

Electrical energy 646

Electricity 205, 459, 723, 1015, 1044

Electricity, generation of 23

Electromagnetic field (EMF) 237, **322**, 844, 1044

Electromagnetic radiation 842, 850, 1133

Electron acceptor and donor 116, 320, **324**, 759

Electronics 1020

Electrons 850

Electrostatic precipitation 26, 85, 248, **324**, 410, 416-418, 1012

Electrostatic precipitator 822

Elemental analysis **325**, 637

Eleocharis cellulosa 388

Elephant 1131

Elephantidae 325

Elephants 12, 41, 231, 292, **325**, 329, 332, 487, 527, 758, 805, 816, 1076, 1144

Elephas maximus 231, 325, 332

Ellerman, Vilhelm 162

Ellsworth, Henry L. 1057

Elton, Charles **325**, 420

Embryo transfer 154

Emergency Petroleum Allocation Act 339

Emergency Planning and Community Right-to-Know Act (1986) 96, **327**, 556, 887, 997, 1037

Emerson, Ralph Waldo 146, 712

Emigration 665

Emiliani, Cesare 655

Emission 14, 24, 26, 28, 53, 60, 77-78, 93, 114, 160, 199, 227, 232, 237, 245, 282, 296, 310, 328, **328**, 349-351, 372-373, 379, 384, 393-394, 449, 451, 484, 486, 510-512, 535, 538, 609, 634, 637, 643-644, 681, 702, 709, 735, 761, 769, 782, 793, 797, 804-805, 809, 829, 870, 879, 881, 891, 952, 955, 972, 978, 982, 995, 1003, 1006, 1012, 1016, 1032, 1037, 1060, 1067-1068, 1137

Emission controls 598

Emission standards 26, 189, **328**, 356, 539, 615, 619, 643, 677, 679, 702, 709, 789, 811, 830

Emphysema 73, 128, 137, 187, **329**, 780, 881

Empirical science 85

End moraine 464

Endangered species 36, 45-46, 89, 109-110, 123, 126, 128, 135, 140, 151, 154, 167, 194, 206, 231, 242, 244, 255, 257, 275, 283, 317, **329**, 330, 333, 369, 389, 396, 411, 415, 442, 453, 461-462, 480, 483, 488, 498, 503, 527, 537, 553, 556, 560, 566-567, 579, 629, 637, 659, 681, 689, 692, 695, 697-698, 747, 750, 755, 759, 770-771, 805, 814, 824, 856, 871, 927, 956-957, 1014-1015, 1043, 1056, 1059, 1096, 1102, 1107, 1112, 1115, 1117, 1119-1120, 1131, 1142, 1144

Endangered Species Act (1973) 32, 47, 109, 126, 128, 148, 151, 155, 231, 242, 329, **330**, 368, 372, 556, 578, 695, 718, 759, 770, 787, 927, 956, 1014, 1117, 1127

Endangered Species Committee 242, 331

Endangered Species Conservation Act 331

Endangered Species Handbook, The 47

Endangered Species Preservation Act of 1966 330

Endemic 100, 981

Endemic species 206, **332**, 426, 446, 503, 584, 804

Endomycorrhiza 671

Endosymbionts 1007

Endrin   140, 526, 754, 830

Energy   646, 742

Energy conservation   21, 34, 206, 322, **335**, 339, 342, 452, 468, 742, 1058

Energy Conservation and Production Act of 1976   335, 1058

Energy efficiency   34, 73, 161, 206, 237, 294-295, 335, **336**, 338, 341, 487, 646, 734, 870, 946, 1067

Energy and the environment   34, 161, 322, **334**, 339, 341, 619, 646, 796, 970, 1015, 1020, 1027, 1041, 1123

Energy flow   **338**, 1020

Energy industry   339

Energy Information Administration   1058

Energy path, hard vs. soft   322, **338**, 341, 619

Energy policy   34, 158, 206, 311, 322, **339**, 341-342, 796, 930, 970, 1058, 1079, 1123

Energy Policy and Conservation Act of 1976   236, 335, 1058

Energy Rationalization Law   340

Energy recovery   **341**, 879, 971

Energy Reorganization Act (1973)   **341**, 723, 742, 1058

Energy Research and Development Administration   74, 341, **342**, 1058, 1123

Energy Research and Development Agency (ERDA)   723

Energy Supply and Environmental Coordination Act   340

Energy Tax Act   237

Energy taxes   237, 339, **342**, 1058

English common law   836

Enhanced recovery technique   933

Enhydra lutris   168, 463, 745, 925

Eniwetok Atoll   96

Enslow, Linn   1125

Enteric bacteria   **342**

Enterobacteriaceae   342

Entropy   1019

Enviroethics   556

Environment   2-3, 23, 46, 53, 67-69, 83-84, 99, 104, 106-108, 119, 124, 130-131, 143, 146, 156, 163, 168, 170, 173-174, 182, 185, 191, 198, 206, 208, 211-212, 222, 227-228, 233, 234, 237, 239-241, 247, 249, 256, 265, 270, 277, 280, 282, 289, 292-293, 297-299, 309, 312, 318-319, 329, 332, 334, 341-342, **343**, 345, 349, 353, 355, 357, 361, 365, 375, 378-381, 390, 394-395, 403, 408, 414-415, 433, 438, 444-445, 453, 458, 465-466, 477, 479, 481-483, 487, 490, 496-497, 504-

505, 511-512, 517, 526, 528, 537-538, 544-545, 551, 557, 559, 561-562, 573-574, 586-589, 609, 611-613, 618, 638-639, 642, 648-649, 656, 659, 668, 679, 688, 691, 696-697, 706, 709-710, 737, 744, 748-749, 754, 756-757, 779, 781, 791, 794, 799, 801, 808-809, 814, 819, 821, 824, 829, 835, 838, 842, 845, 847, 850, 852, 857, 859, 866, 869, 873, 876-877, 892, 894, 898, 902, 907, 913, 918, 922, 940, 946, 950, 952-953, 976, 983-985, 1000, 1002, 1005, 1008-1009, 1012, 1016, 1018, 1020-1021, 1030-1032, 1040-1041, 1050, 1054, 1056, 1061-1063, 1068, 1070-1072, 1085, 1089, 1097, 1101-1102, 1106, 1124, 1127-1128, 1132, 1142-1143

Environment Association   309

Environment Canada   153, **344**, 430

Environmental accounting   **345**

Environmental advertising and marketing   129

Environmental aesthetics   **345**

Environmental assessment   683

Environmental attitudes/values   283, 482, 697, 899

Environmental auditing   **346**, 367

Environmental chemistry   **346**

Environmental Choice   129

Environmental consciousness   574

Environmental consumers   479

Environmental controls   563

Environmental Defense Fund (New York, New York)   **349**

Environmental degradation   21, 42, 92, 114, 121, 143, 226, 236, 238, 253, 297, 300, 302, 310, 320, 342, **349**, 353, 361, 363, 369, 382, 385, 394, 438, 444, 467, 480, 482, 484, 551, 585, 599, 610, 618, 645, 716, 754, 869, 908, 936, 938, 944, 963, 981, 1040, 1054, 1079, 1128

Environmental dispute resolution   **350**

Environmental economics   3, 152, 191, 238, 311, 342, **351**, 367, 375, 484, 486, 515, 551, 638, 664, 719, 756, 799, 876, 893, 959, 1015, 1038, 1129

Environmental education   121, 152, 292, 294, 311, **353**, 373, 378, 435, 444, 504, 608, 632, 710, 714, 899, 1024, 1084, 1106, 1126, 1130-1131

Environmental Education Act   354

Environmental enforcement   **355**

Environmental engineering   **357**, 378, 869, 1125

Environmental estrogens   **358**

Environmental ethics   152, **167**, 168, 256, 289, 294, 298, 300, 312, 354, **360**, 378, 435, 444, 479, 488, 522, 556, 586, 589, 608, 674, 697, 699, 710, 712, 773, 819, 868, 898, 899, 901, 947, 959, 980, 981, 1065, 1068, 1125, 1130

Environmental Ethics: Values in and Duties to the Natural World   898

Environmental Forum   370

Environmental health   94, **361**, 555, 597, 683, 736, 781, 784, 1005, 1015, 1056

Environmental history   **363**

Environmental impact   131, 1067

Environmental impact assessment   **365**, 367, 681

Environmental Impact Statement   150, 239, 365, **366**, 368, 373, 465, 630, 680, 719, 1014, 1112

Environmental Investments: The Cost of a Clean Environment   370

Environmental law   68, 121, 191, 204, 220, 231, 290, 311, 351, 356, **368**, 369, 373, 375, 405, 435, 507, 519, 558, 563, 565-566, 656, 682, 688, 697, 719, 737, 743, 829, 856, 870, 1034, 1037, 1040-1041, 1092-1093, 1137

Environmental Law Institute (Washington, D.C.)   **369**, 1040, 1069

Environmental Law Reporter   370

Environmental Leadership Conference   873

Environmental legislation   888

Environmental liability   829, 1037, 1040

Environmental management   660

Environmental Management System (EMS)   563

Environmental monitoring   121, 297, 328, **370**, 710, 756, 774, 1003, 1130

Environmental Monitoring and Assessment Program   328, 367, 371, **371**

Environmental policy   92, 121, 150, 153, 188, 191, 193, 204, 231-232, 309, 311, 356, 367, **371**, 444, 467-468, 483, 486, 519, 526, 558, 563, 674, 682, 688, 710, 756, 774, 828, 870, 873, 876, 890, 956, 1021, 1040-1041, 1096, 1113, 1130

Environmental policy, national   344, 373, 471, 1041

Environmental politics   1050

Environmental protection   714

Environmental Protection Agency (EPA)   2, 13, 16, 27-28, 63, 74, 93, 95, 98, 116, 129, 133, 140-141, 168, 174, 178, 181-

182, 187, 192, 220, 227-228,
239, 247, 257, 269, 277-278,
290, 305, 323, 327, 352, 355,
358, 367, 370-372, **373**, 379,
381, 403, 411, 428, 449, 451,
462, 475, 477, 484, 493, 501,
506, 508-508, 513, 518, 532,
541, 545, 550-551, 560, 563,
574, 593, 597, 606, 616-617,
630, 632, 634, 643, 647, 659,
669, 673, 676, 679-680, 688,
692, 695, 697, 702, 709, 714,
730, 738, 743-744, 763, 770,
774, 785, 811, 829, 832-833,
842-843, 848, 850, 862, 868,
872, 875, 877, 879, 888, 891-
892, 895, 902, 905, 917, 945-
946, 971-972, 975, 977-978,
985, 989, 997, 1022, 1028, 1030,
1032, 1034, 1037, 1041, 1043,
1046, 1051, 1056, 1077, 1082,
1086, 1088-1089
Environmental Quality Report   239
Environmental racism   142, 300, 361,
374, 1021
Environmental refugees   **375**
Environmental resistance   816
Environmental resources   **376**
Environmental Review   188
Environmental science   121, 175, **378**,
445, 499, 521, 613, 618, 632,
642, 820, 1020, 1046
Environmental Side Agreement   715
Environmental stewardship   92
Environmental stress   197, 266, 268,
300, 314, 370, **378**, 392, 502,
703, 749, 756, 809, 876-877,
1047, 1130
Environmental Stress Index
(ZPG)   **379**
Environmental Success Index   873
Environmental terrorism   745, 780
Environmental theology   871
Environmental Working Group
(Washington D.C.)   **379**
Environmentalism   137, 164, 292, 298,
300, 349, 353, 361, 374, **380**,
435, 444-445, 488, 504, 697-
698, 712, 773, 879, 901, 947,
959, 1022, 1125
Environmentally responsible
investing   311, **380**
Environment-related diseases   683
Enzyme   7, 44, 114, 122, 154, 182,
185, 234, 251, 255, 266-267,
329, **381**, 454, 457, 512,
754, 844
Ephemeral species   **382**
Epidemiology   170, **382**, 624,
844, 1069
Epidemiology Program Office   170
Epilobium angustifolium   749
Epipelagic zone   775
Equidae   1142

Equus caballus   333
Equus grevyi   1142
Equus quagga quagga   1142
Equus zebra hartmannae   1142
Equus zebra zebra   1142
Eretmochelys imbricata   926
Erodible   **384**, 963
Erosion   18, 20-21, 35, 37, 62, 70,
91, 101, 129, 178, 189, 194, 203,
219, 222, 226, 230, 236, 245,
249, 259, 263, 282, 284-286,
384, **384**, 392, 423, 428, 459,
463-464, 472, 495, 510, 512,
516, 534, 538, 559, 561, 567,
569, 573, 580, 587, 623, 625,
645, 657, 664, 667-668, 694,
738, 749, 751, 758, 780-781,
791, 848, 855, 860, 869, 876,
889, 893-894, 906, 935, 945,
947, 949-950, 961-965, 989-
990, 1000, 1002, 1005, 1011,
1021, 1031, 1046, 1063, 1068,
1083, 1085, 1096, 1115, 1129
Erosion-corrosion   237
Erwin, Terry   100
Escherichia   342
Escherichia coli   206, 342, 455,
830, 1070
Eschrichtius robustus   654, 1102, 1104
Eskimo curlew   99
Essay on the Principle of Population   624
Estuary   40, 130, 136, 177, 275, 350,
385, 526, 535, 574, 628, 631,
654, 694, 731, 736
Ethane   1071
Ethanol   34, 77, 79, 113, 211, **386**,
517, 814, 867
Ethnobotany   225
Ethology   960
Ethyl alcohol   386, 450
Ethylene   788
Ethylenediaminetetraacetic acid
(EDTA)   171
Eubalaena glacialis   101
Eugenics   961
Eukaryotic cells   1007
Eumetopias jubatus   930
Euphausiacea   579
Eurasian milfoil (*Myriophyllum
spicatum*)   **386**, 392
European Economic Community
(EEC)   **386**, 557, 763, 830
Eutectic   **387**
Eutrophication   408, 475, 704,
789, 917
Evapotranspiration   387, **387**, 533,
620, 768, 938, 962
Everglades   140, 244, 274, **387**, 415,
567, 691, 804, 1041, 1101
Evolution   9, 84, 155, 180, 213, 217,
250, 306, **389**, 396, 445, 452-
453, 468, 499, 521, 537, 579,
586, 623-624, 665, 697, 782,
804, 825, 960, 1047, 1120

Evolutionary biology   960
Evolutionary equilibrium   1121
Ex situ treatment   510
Exchanges   692
Exclusive Economic Zone (EEZ)   232
Exercise-induced asthma   69
Exosymbionts   1007
Exotic animals   1144
Exotic birds   770
Exotic species   56, 231, 255, 326, 389,
391, 580, 907, 980, 1116
Experimental Lakes Area   7, **392**,
525, 1072
Experimental reintroduction   155
Experimental Rural Clean Waters
Program   963
Exponential growth   311, **393**, 493,
610, 613, 814, 816
Exposure assessment   891
Externality   202, 351, **394**, 484, 550,
638, 769
Extinction   32, 35, 47, 89, 99, 118-
119, 156, 205, 209, 217, 231,
243, 259, 272, 329-330, **395**,
431, 446, 453-454, 503, 530,
537-538, 552, 567, 571, 585,
625, 635, 665, 695, 719, 749-
750, 769, 771, 787, 805, 854,
871, 884, 925, 927, 942, 981,
1014, 1027, 1076, 1103, 1106,
1116, 1118, 1127, 1131, 1144
Extremely Low Frequency   323
Extrinsic asthma   69
Exxon Valdez   42, 168, 241, 255,
396, 504, 688, 696, 743-744,
832, 870, 925, 103, 1043, 1059,
1067, 1120

F

Facilitation   883
Factory emissions   27
Factory farming   46, 775, 1068
Facts about Furs   47
Fagus sylvatica   427
Falco peregrinus   338, 776, 784, 1116
Fallout   845
Family farm   169
Family planning   **399**, 467, 755, 815,
817-818, 984, 1005, 1071,
1128, 1143
Famine   132, 139, 198, 263, 321, 399,
400, 816, 898, 906, 1092
Farmland   587, 589, 1064
Farmland Update   37
Fathead minnow   393
Fauna   115, 119, 197, 255, 265, 333,
371, **402**, 415, 445, 464, 503,
775, 802, 823-824, 980,
999, 1014
favelas   943
Fayoumi chicken   453
Fecal contamination   342
Fecundity   109, **402**, 461, 538, 814

Federal Aviation Administration 506
Federal Emergency Management
Agency (FEMA) 1022
Federal Energy Administrations 1058
Federal Energy Regulation Study
Team 403
Federal Energy Regulatory
Commission **403**, 1058
Federal Facility Compliance Act
(1992) 848
Federal Highway Administration 506
Federal Insecticide, Fungicide and
Rodenticide Act (1972) **403**,
507, 678, 784, 786, 889
Federal Land Policy and Management
Act (1976) 144, **405**, 906,
1013, 1109, 1112-1113
Federal Non-Nuclear Energy Research
and Development Act 1058
Federal Non-Nuclear Research and
Development Act 339
Federal Oil Spill Liability Trust
Fund 743
Federal Power Commission 339, 403,
407, 515, 970, 1058
Federal Railroad Administration 506
Federal Register 878
Federal Trade Commission 477
Federal Water Pollution Act 631
Federal Water Pollution Control
Act 1088
Federal Water Pollution Control
Administration 191
Federal Water Power Act 407
Federation of Sewage Works
Associations 1084
Feedlot runoff 17, 131, **407**, 408, 491,
526, 758, 1072, 1088
Feedlots 18, 113, 247, 358, 407, **408**,
710, 758, 791
Feinberg, Joel 46
Feline leukemia 22
Felis concolor coryi 389, 415
Felis pardalis 758
Fenitrothion 784
Fermentation 113, 121
Ferric oxide 235
Ferries 637
Ferrihydrite 561
Fertility 109, 575, 1142
Fertilizer 6, 11, 16, 18, 21, 41, 70, 89,
113, 116, 122-123, 132, 134,
198, 218, 229, 245-246, 271,
280, 284, 310, 377, 394, 401,
407, **408**, 423, 428, 449, 490,
492-493, 512, 533, 546, 559,
569, 574, 585, 587, 596, 630,
649, 657-658, 704-705, 708,
745, 751, 753, 790-791, 859-
860, 908-909, 951-952, 971,
990, 1000, 1002, 1015, 1029,
1037, 1060-1061, 1082, 1085-
1086, 1092

Fertilizer runoff 129, 526, 695,
705, 707
Fetal alcohol syndrome 124
Fibrosis 128, **409**, 882
Field capacity **409**
Fifth Gospel 931
Fight for Conservation, The 799
Filho, Francisco Alvo Mendes 646
Filters 26, 85, 279, 281, **409**, 410,
822, 972, 1094
Filtration 280, 409, **410**, 461, 506,
905, 1094
Fin whale 1104
Finding of no significant impact
(FONSI) 680
Fire 1114
Fire ants **410**, 496, 560, 659
Fire Island 694
Fire triangle 1115
First World 401, **411**, 664, 933, 1020
Fish farming 1002
Fish hawk 526
Fish kills 31, 51, 271, 297, **411**, 585,
735, 794, 917, 940
Fish and Wildlife Service 61, 87, 90,
151, 164, 231, 242, 277, 315,
330, 371, **411**, 415, 446, 460,
465, 488, 560, 695, 718, 750,
759, 804, 836, 956, 981, 1014,
1027, 1050, 1059, 1109, 1112,
1117, 1119, 1127, 1131
Fisheries and Oceans Canada **413**
Fisherman's Guarantee Fund 145
Fishing 625, 1081
Fitness maximization 960
Flame spectroscopy 325
Flash flood 414, 1063
Flesh-eating disease 653
Floating heart 388
Flood control 145, 414, 1015
Flood irrigation 576
Flooding 67, 70, 194, 249, 253, 259,
263, 275, 321, 385, 387, 392,
414, **414**, 534-535, 592, 664,
681, 749, 855, 876, 888-889,
903, 988, 1011, 1015, 1021,
1028, 1046, 1059, 1063, 1090-
1091, 1101
Floodplain 70, 384, **414**, 562, 1092
Floodplain management 966
Flora 115, 119, 135, 197, 206, 255,
333, 382, **415**, 445, 464, 503,
704, 802, 823-824, 999, 1014
Florida 864
Florida Bay 387
Florida panther (*Felis concolor
coryi*) 257, 389, **415**, 1118
Flotation **416**
Flue gas 26, 191, 200, 206, 416, **416**,
486, 538, 995, 1100
Flue-gas scrubbing 191, 201, **416**,
924, 953, 1100
Fluid injection 933
Fluidized bed combustion 191, **417**

Fluoride 490
Fluorine 183, 760
Fly ash 24, 182, 324, 417, **417**,
434, 538, 634, 956, 972, 976,
1012, 1061
Flying Fish 529
Flyway **418**, 695, 703
Foam separation 416
Food additives **418**, 886
Food and Agriculture Organization of
the United Nations (FAO) 147,
223, 226, 277, 453, 465,
785, 1130
Food chain/web 6, 18, 50, 54-56,
97, 111, 199, 213, 252, 265,
269, 276, 304, 307, 312, 338,
382, 385, 388, 412, **420**, 452,
475, 493, 512, 517, 570, 575-
576, 609, 637, 648, 656, 659,
663, 700, 707, 718, 762, 777,
781, 794, 796, 800, 824-825,
838, 882, 1007,1013, 1017, 1024,
1032, 1046, 1060, 1119, 1133
Food chemistry 886
Food contaminants 169
Food and Drug Administration 17,
64, 162, 170, 260, 363, 373, **422**,
493, 507, 560-561, 598, 705,
833, 835, 865, 1030, 1058
Food, Drug, and Cosmetics Act 422
Food labelling practices 169
Food poisoning 653
Food policy **422**
Food processing industry 424
Food production 576, 610
Food safety 169
Food service industry 424
Food waste 114, 218, **424**, 669
For Earth's Sake 138
Foraminifera 655
Forbs 474
Forced ventilation 416
Forced-air system 219
Ford Foundation 880
Ford, Gerald 339, 405, 515
Ford, Henry 854
Foreign policy 145
Forel, F. A. 611
Foreman, Dave 1, 256, 292, **424**,
482, 662
Forest 5, 538
Forest and Rangeland Renewable
Resources Planning Act
(1974) **425**, 719
Forest decline 6, 135, **426**, 430, 682,
719, 799
Forest fire 511-512
Forest management 37, 90, 113, 152,
193, 222, 426, 428, **428**, 430,
519, 538, 578, 682, 719, 799,
869, 881, 900, 949, 959, 1115
Forest products industry 330
Forest Service 40, 110, 136, 144, 221,
242, 315, 369, 372, 405, 424-

425, **429**, 525, 573, 607, 633, 668, 682, 696, 718, 746, 798, 832, 836, 856, 900, 980, 1015, 1057, 1107-1109, 1112-1113
Forestry   669, 959
Forestry Canada   **429**
Formaldehyde   25, 79, 187, 671
Forman, Richard   595
Forrester, Jay   610
Fossey, Dian   **430**, 471, 601
Fossil fuel combustion   995
Fossil fuels   5, 23, 25, 34, 79, 92, 99, 113, 118, 156-157, 196-197, 199, 208, 211, 221, 232, 259, 263, 281, 295, 304, 321, 334-335, 342, 347, 417, **432**, 447, 460, 467, 484, 486-487, 512, 528, 532-533, 548-549, 613, 618-619, 631, 641, 655, 676, 696, 707-708, 720, 722, 741, 743, 756, 778, 788, 795, 797, 812, 821, 867, 874, 920, 956, 968, 992, 996, 1009, 1012, 1016, 1019, 1025-1026, 1058, 1064, 1097-1098
Fossil water   **433**, 740
Fouling   104
Four Corners   **434**
Foyn, Svend   1103
Frameshift mutation   671
Francis of Assisi, St.   **434**
Free radicals   561, 843
Free riders   394, **435**, 1038
Freedom of speech   150
French Atomic Energy Commission   340
Frenchman Flat   701
Freon   **436**, 661
Fresh water ecology   **436**
Freshwater   774, 1082
Freshwater marsh   575, 1101
Friends of the Ancient Forest   294
Friends of the Earth (Washington, D.C.)   137, 424, **437**, 599, 618, 664
Frémont, John   585
Frogs   **438**
Frogs, abnormal   439
Frogs, biomedical research   439
Frontier economy   **440**, 1110
Frost heaving   **440**
Frost point   267
Froth flotation   202
Fuel cells   34, 78, **440**
Fuel loading   1114
Fuel switching   34, **442**, 650
Fuel Use Act   340
Fugitive emissions   24, **442**, 540, 1080
Fuller, R. Buckminster   979
Fumaroles   459
Fumigation   379, **442**
Fund for Animals (New York, New York)   42, 126, **442**
Fund resources   696

Fungi   10, 12, 17, 32, 54, 111, 118, 156, 208, 212, 255, 268, 307, 312, 412, 419, 428, 443, **443**, 449, 456, 474, 512, 519, 536, 609, 650, 672, 706, 735, 768, 773, 784, 800, 865, 992, 1007, 1046, 1048, 1070, 1086
Fungicide   17, 443, **443**, 546, 574, 647, 650, 782
Fur trade   530
Furan   775
Furrowing   883
Future generations   143, 221, 238, 342, 345, 351, 361, 380, 396, **443**, 515, 547, 589, 618, 679, 690, 747, 901, 942, 1004-1005, 1130, 1132

G

Gadus callarias   414
Gaia hypothesis   **445**, 466, 617, 1002
Galápagos Biosphere Reserve   120
Galápagos giant tortoise   445
Galápagos Islands   121, 217, 317, **445**, 503
Gambusia   624
Game animal   **446**, 447, 710, 804, 823-824, 1117, 1120
Game birds   531
Game conservation   222
Game preserves   **447**
Gamma ray   94, 323, **448**, 560-561, 843-844, 852
Gandhi, Mohandas Karamchand   180, **448**, 912
Ganges River   1021
Garbage   34, 145, 206, 341, 424, **449**, 450, 477, 479, 484, 493, 545, 650, 669, 812, 858, 862, 879, 916, 944, 970, 972-973, 1003, 1020, 1028, 1044, 1060, 1079, 1086
Garbage decomposition   858
Garbage Project   **449**, 450
Garbology   **450**
Gardening   62
Gas Guzzler tax   237
Gas-liquid chromatography (GC)   185
Gasohol   34, 114, 341, 386, **450**, 451, 867, 1016
Gasoline   26, 34, 78, 92, 99, 114, 116, 123, 170, 190, 205, 211, 229, 237-238, 342, 386, 394, 410, 435, 450, **450**-451, 484, 512, 532, 596-597, 615, 650-651, 697, 734, 741, 788, 796, 867, 924, 985, 1008, 1016, 1021, 1032, 1061, 1071, 1136
Gasoline tax   **451**
Gastroenteritis   1070
Gastropods   **452**
Gates, David   521
geese, snow   61

Geiger counters   642
Gel permeation chromatography (GPC)   185
Gene bank   **453**, 454, 456, 458, 814
Gene pool   13, 205, 390, 453, **453**, 456, 458, 468, 498, 538, 625, 671, 805, 814, 980, 1118
Gene splicing   457
Gene therapy   457
General Accounting Office   14, 404
General circulation model   661
General Electric   988
General fertility rate   109
General Motors   484
General Public Utilities   322
General Sherman tree   866
Genetic code   671
Genetic diversity   99, 119
Genetic engineering   17, 20-21, 117, 122, 422, 453-454, **454**, 671, 814
Genetic reciprocity   960
Genetic resistance (or genetic tolerance)   **456**
Genetically engineered organism   123, 457, **457**, 560, 671
Genetics   390
Genetics and the Origin of Species   390
Genoa Declaration   645
Genome   454
Genomic DNA   894
Geochelone elephantopus   445
Geochemistry   458
Geodegradable   **458**
Geological Survey   **458**, 655, 665, 688, 820, 990, 1059, 1063, 1126, 1135
Geophysics   458
Geopressurized zones   460
GeoProducts Corporation   460
Geosphere   **459**, 804
Geothermal energy   33, 322, 339, **459**, 665, 742, 823, 1072
Geothermal well   459
Germanium   511
Germinal tissue   671
Germplasm   226
Getches, David H.   889
Geysers   459
Giant panda (*Ailuropoda melanoleuca*)   **460**, 981, 1115, 1131
Giant reedgrass   108, 540
Giant sequoia   865
Giardia   **461**
Giardia intestinalis   461
Giardiasis   461
Gibberellins   17
Gibbons   **462**, 471, 555, 750
Gibbs, Lois   **462**, 616
Gibbsite   189
Gift of Good Land, The   92
Gila National Forest   607, 1111
Gill nets   272, 277, **463**
Gillied land   385

Ginkgo biloba   333
Ginkgo tree   333
Glacial events   667
Glacial flour   464
Glaciation   **463**, 537, 561, 655, 668, 687, 870, 1047, 1101
Glacier National Park   87, 946
Glen Avon, California   988
Glen Canyon Dam   137, 146, 207, **464**, 985
Global 2000 Report, The   239, 395, **467**, 486, 637, 329
Global Change   923
Global Ecology Handbook, The   467
Global Environment and Basic Human Needs, The   396
Global Environment Monitoring System   **465**, 556, 1055, 1057
Global Forum (New York, New York)   **465**
Global Forum on Environment and Development   466
Global Forum of NGOs   1056
Global Issues Resource Centers   467
Global Releaf (Washington, D.C.)   **466**
Global Rivers Environmental Education Network (GREEN)   355
Global Tomorrow Coalition (Washington, D.C.)   37, **466**, 486
Global warming   486, 768, 855, 870, 1132
Globe Fur Dyeing Corporation v. United States   629
Globicephala   1102
Gloeotrichia   706
Glyphosate   784
Gobi Desert   914
God Committee   331
Goddard Space Flight Center   762
Goethite   561
Goiter   **468**
Gold   657, 855
Golden eagle   86
Golden hamster   2
Golden Horn   631
Goldman, Ben   374
Goldrush   529
Golomyanka   583
Gombe Stream National Park   180
Gondwanaland   802
Gonyaulax tamarensis   412, 707, 864
Goodall, Jane   180, 431, **468**, 555, 601
Goodyear, Charles   174
Gopeshwar   180
Gopher tortoise   389
Gopherus agassizii   262
Gopherus polyphemus   389
Gorbachev, Mikhail S.   59, 479
Gordon, Anne   1126
Gore, Albert, Jr.   140, 372, 464, **470**, 486, 1054
Gorilla gorilla berengei   12

Gorillas   12, 180, 325, 430, 462, **471**, 537, 555
Gorillas in the Mist   471
Gorsuch, Anne Burford   903
Gould, Stephen Jay   703, 961
Gradualism   1
Grain alcohol   386
Grameen   1004
Grand Canyon   137, 317, 464
Grand Canyon National Game Preserve   573
Grand Staircase - Escalante National Monument   **472**
Grant, Ulysses S.   1136
Grapevine   311
Grasses   473, 823
Grasslands   114, 118, 214, 259, 263, 308, 317, 325, 333, 420, 429, **473**, 488, 498, 686, 700, 823, 827, 858, 918, 939, 963, 982, 993, 1046, 1110, 1114, 1116, 1142
Gray bat   89
Gray whale   654, 1102, 1104
Grazing   405
Grazing Service and the General Land Office (GLO)   144
Great apes   749
Great auk   99, 101, 758
Great Britain's National Coal Board   922
Great Chain of Life, The   579
Great Lakes   203, 248, 270, 285, 305, 359, 392, 411, 436, **474**, 475, 555, 559, 583-584, 659, 686, 717, 907, 947, 980, 1018, 1059, 1088, 1101, 1141
Great Lakes Critical Programs Act   475
Great Lakes Water Quality Agreement (1978)   **475**, 555, 1141
Great Plains   823
Great Plains Conservation Program   963
Great Slave Lake   126
Great Smoky Mountains   317, **476**
Great Western Desert   914
Great white shark   241
Greater Yellowstone   697
Grebe, western   784
Grebes   575, 662
Green advertising and marketing   273, **477**, 479, 482-483
Green belt/greenway   **478**, 590, 807
Green congress   115
Green Consumer Guide, The   477
Green Cross   129, 289, **478**
Green Cross Certification Company   479
Green labeling   477
Green for Life   138
Green Movement   115, 480
Green packaging   309, 477, **479**, 793, 824, 862

Green Party   481, 487
Green Plan   344, 430
Green plans   **479**
Green politics   256, 292, 294, 298, **480**, 487, 600, 710, 756, 799, 901, 947, 980, 1038, 1130
Green products   273, 309, 381, 438, 477, 479, 482, **482**, 793, 824
Green Revolution   19, 122, 132, 226, 401
Green sea turtle   926
Green Seal (Palo Alto, California)   129, 139, **482**, 504
Green taxes   161, 435, **483**, 1038
Greenhouse effect   25, 35, 38, 72, 79, 114, 157-158, 195-196, 254, 335, 338, 353, 433, 465-466, 480, **484**, 486, 497, 532, 534, 554, 613, 637, 641, 649, 655, 661, 664-665, 758, 763, 789, 828-829, 869, 890, 1005, 1018, 1077, 1099, 1128
Greenhouse gases   76, 79, 158, 334, 338, 342, 465, **486**, 532, 549, 637, 643, 649, 661, 688, 708, 835, 1006, 1056
Greenhouse Gas-ette   294
Greenpeace (Washington, D.C.)   298, 380, 481, **487**, 488, 710, 714, 920, 925, 983
Greens   256, 298, 481, **487**, 600, 710, 799, 1130
Griffin, Susan   298
Grizzlies   823
Grizzly bear (*Ursus arctos*)   61, 257, 293, 331, 395, 443, 448, **488**, 805, 856, 1119, 1136
Grizzly Bear Task Force   293
Grotius, Hugo   231
Ground moraine   464
Groundwater   10, 18, 53, 56, 63, 115, 129, 134, 173, 228, 244, 249, 274, 278, 281, 295-296, 368, 408, 434, 438, 449, 460, 474, 489, **489**-490, 506, 509, 511- 512, 535, 544-545, 567, 587, 592, 596, 606, 649, 669, 678, 701, 704, 740, 750, 776, 780, 788, 791, 810, 820, 838, 848, 859, 868, 872-873, 879, 889, 891-893, 896, 905, 908, 913, 935, 937, 949, 964, 971, 973- 975, 986, 991, 997, 999-1000, 1021, 1032, 1046, 1060, 1063, 1067, 1070, 1081-1082, 1085, 1088, 1090-1093, 1099, 1101, 1138, 1143
Groundwater monitoring   257, **489**, 491, 545, 593, 607, 938, 1100
Groundwater pollution   257, 280, **490**, 545, 558, 576, 593, 607, 649, 701, 740, 789, 880, 913, 917, 989, 1061, 1082, 1088, 1100
Growth curve   **491**

Growth limiting factors **492**, 613, 749, 984, 994
Grus americana 1106
Guadeloupe fur seal 930
Guanacaste dry forest 883
Guano 89, **493**, 1060
Guerrilla theater 292
Guess What's Coming to Dinner: Contaminants in Our Food 170
Guide For the Perplexed, A 922
Guide to Urban Wildlife Management, A 685
Guillemots 463
Gulf of California 206
Gulf of Mexico 744
Gulf of St. Lawrence 474
Gulf War Syndrome **493**
Gullied land **495**
Gushers 788
Gymnocephalus cernuus 907
Gymnodinium 412, 864
Gymnodinium breve 864
Gymnogyps californianus 151
Gypsy moth (*Portheria dispar*) 252, 258, 378, 410, **496**, 560, 782

H

Haagen-Smit, Arie Jan **497**, 955
Habitat 3, 9, 29, 34, 36, 40, 48, 56, 61, 78, 87, 89, 100, 106, 108, 118-119, 140, 151, 153, 155, 163, 168, 177, 180, 184, 198, 206, 212, 225, 235, 241-244, 255-257, 262, 267, 283, 295-296, 307, 313, 318-319, 329, 331, 333, 344, 349, 351, 370, 372, 380, 383, 385, 388, 394-395, 412-413, 445-446, 460, 462, 469, 471, 479, 487-488, **497**, 498, 502, 517, 538, 546, 553, 560, 566, 570, 576, 578-579, 612, 623, 625, 629-630, 654, 663, 678, 681, 686, 689, 694-695, 698, 703-704, 718, 746, 749-750, 758, 769, 777, 782, 787, 808, 815, 823, 831, 839, 854-855, 861, 874, 876-877, 911, 930, 934, 950, 956, 980, 982, 990, 992, 999, 1003, 1005, 1012, 1027, 1039, 1047, 1059, 1081, 1095, 1104, 1106, 1112-1113, 1117-1118, 1129, 1131, 1141, 1144
Habitat destruction 699
Habitat fragmentation **498**, 807, 1045
Habitat loss 883
Hackensack River Meadowlands 883
Haeckel, Ernst 306, **499**
Haemophilus influenzae 454
Hair dryer 322
Hair, Jay D. 695

Haiti 557, 1021
Hale, George Ellery 693
Half-life 458, **500**, 574, 612, 647, 655, 781, 804, 845, 850-852
Haliaeetus leucocephalus 86, 526, 784
Halogenated solvents 186
Halons 763
Hamlet, North Carolina 886
Hanford Engineering Works 500
Hanford Nuclear Reservation (near Richland, Washington) 384, **500**, 620, 844, 846, 848, 1058
Harbor seal 930
Hardin, Garrett 435, **501**, 515, 1038
Hardwood forests 888
Hatfield, Charles 1097
Hawaiian hoary bat 89
Hawaiian honeycreepers 102
Hawaiian Islands 101, 235, 332, 392, 426, **502**
Hawksbill turtle 926
Hawley, Amos 526
Hayden, Ferdinand 458
Hayduke Lives! 1
Hayes, Denis 292, 483, **504**
Hayes, Randall 857
Hazard assessment 891
Hazard Communication Standard 163
Hazard Ranking System 509
Hazardous Chemical Inventory 327
Hazardous chemicals 639
Hazardous material 18, 66, 95, 154, 174-175, 221, 296, 327, 358, 462, 475, **505**, 506-507, 513, 596, 606, 657, 876, 880, 888, 971, 976, 985, 997, 1021, 1037
Hazardous materials transportation 506
Hazardous Materials Transportation Act (1975) 174, 221, 328, **506**, 507, 977, 985
Hazardous Materials Transportation Control Act 506
Hazardous Materials Transportation Uniform Safety Act 507
Hazardous and Solid Waste Amendments (HSWA) 877, 977
Hazardous substance 63, 1033
Hazardous Substances Act (1960) 96, 174, 221, **507**, 985, 997, 1037
Hazardous waste 87, 91, 141, 154, 175, 182, 201, 220, 235, 257, 262, 270, 277, 280, 297, 300, 305, 346, 352, 356, 368, 374, 379, 458, 462, 484, 487, 505-507, **508**, 511, 538, 544, 557, 592, 616, 634, 643, 692, 701, 704, 727, 779, 788, 812, 851, 859, 870, 877, 880, 891, 895, 970, 975, 977, 982, 985, 988, 997, 1020, 1055, 1059, 1069, 1077, 1080, 1086, 1133
Hazardous waste incinerator 368

Hazardous waste site remediation 117, 174, 221, 257, 458, 491, **509**, 617, 692, 737, 779, 983, 989
Hazardous waste siting 163, 221, 237, 257, 280, 375, 434, 458, 490-491, 510, **511**, 556, 558, 617, 692, 779, 876, 928, 983, 985, 989, 1079
Hazardous waste transportation 507
Hazardous waste treatment 872
Haze 26, 60, **511**, 1070, 1098
Hearing loss 709
Heat sink 772
Heat transfer fluids 812
Heat-recovery techniques 539
Heavy metal contamination 512
Heavy metals 145, 229, 511, 538, 700, 703, 710, 930, 971, 983, 999, 1032, 1068
Heavy metals and heavy metal poisoning 68, 107, 162, 170, 186, 234, 381, 428, 475-476, **511**, 514, 565, 597, 599, 631, 651, 656, 677, 704, 781, 811, 882, 1064
Heavy metals precipitation 513, **513**, 576, 983
Heidegger, Martin 299
Heilbroner, Robert L. **514**
Helium nuclei 850
Hells Canyon **515**
Hematite 561
Hemophiliacs 22
Hempstead, Long Island 341
Henderson, Hazel **515**
Hepatitis 644
Hepatitis A virus 1070
Heptachlor epoxide 181, 754
Herbicide 14, 16, 18, 29, 56, 74, 130, 174, 182, **193**, 218, 226, 255, 258, 268, 273, 305, 386, 403, 428, **516**, 525, 546, 569, 587, 589, 627, 748, 751, 771, 782, 785, 797, 830, 839, 890, 934, 1013, 1051, 1076, 1085
Herbivore 123
HERBS TAPES 16
Heritage Conservation and Recreation Service **518**
Hetch Hetchy Reservoir 364, **518**, 570, 668, 798
Heterogenous processes 764
Heterotroph 123, **519**
Hevea 135
Hexachlorobenzene 181
Hexachlorocyclohexanes 181
Hexachlorophene 940
Hexagenia 584
Hexazinone 784
Hickel, Walter J. 1041
High density polyethylene 974
High pressure liquid chromatography (HPLC) 185
High sulfur coal 924

High voltage power line 322
High-grading (mining, forestry) **519**, 991
High-level radioactive waste 97, 232, 500, **519**, 620, 737, 847-848, 850, 896, 927, 1061, 1123
High-occupancy vehicle 638
High-solids reactor **519**
Highway-Wildlife Relationships: A State-of-the-Art Report 685
Himalayas 196
Hin 454
Hinduism 712, 871
Hinkley Point 847
Hiroshima, Japan 162, 172, **520**, 676, 845, 1076
Hirsch, Fred 819
Hitchcock, Dian 617
HIV (human immunodeficiency virus) 22, 212
Hölldobler, Bert 1121
Hoagland, Edward 667
Hodel, Donald 62, 519
Hoffman-LaRoche 940
Holistic approach 300, 438, **521**, 589
Holon 521
Holoplankton 1145
Homeostasis 308, 316, 358, **522**, 618
Homestead Act (1862) **523**
Homo erectus 601, 603
Homo sapiens 600
Honeybees 807
Hooker Chemical Corporation 616
Hoover Dam 207
Hopper dredge 275
Hordeum vulgare 516
Horizon 117, **524**, 964, 992
Hormones 162
Hornaday, William Temple 126
Horses 333
Horton, R. E. 893
Host 209, 1070
House mice 748
House sparrow 748
Housefly 748
Household appliances 322
Household waste 634
How to Get Involved with the Rails-to-Trails Movement 854
Hubbard Brook Experimental Forest 53, **525**
Hudson, Mount 762
Hudson River 9, **525**, 559, 702, 717, 986
Hughes Aircraft 988
Hughes, Wilson 450
Human blood fluke disease 921
Human Dimensions of Global Change Program 527
Human ecology 164, 346, **526**, 614, 641, 931, 944, 958, 1022
Human evolution 1121
Human Genome Project 453
Human growth hormone 122

Human Health Risk Assessments 890
Human immunodeficiency syndrome (HIV) 652
Human Nature and the Human Condition 579
Human-Dominated Systems Program 527
Humane Slaughter Act 47
Humane Society of the United States (Washington, D.C.) 44, 47, 126, 330, 504, **527**, 770
Humanism 361, **528**, 697
Humanitarianism 912
Human-powered vehicles **528**
Humboldt, Alexander von 802, 1144
Humboldt current 1060
Hume, David 444
Hume's Intentions 772
Humpback whales 168
Humphrey, Hubert 425, 682, 1111
Humus 199, 217, 255, 266, 449, 474, 513, **530**, 934, 950-951, 1114
Hundred Years of Philosophy, A 772
Hungary 296
Hunter Lovins 897
Hunting and trapping 46, 68, 447, 473, **530**, 577, 700, 758, 1076
Hurricane 370, 414, 466, 503, **531**, 688, 1098
Hutchinson, G. E. 118
Huxley, Thomas Henry 389
Hyacinth macaw 231
Hyatt, John Wesley 800
Hybridization 122
Hydraulic dredging 275
Hydraulic fluids 812
Hydrocarbons 23, 42, 54, 78, 92, 99, 115, 123, 166, 183, 190, 200, 228, 245, 266, 328, 341, 347, 432, 441, 450-451, 497, 532, **532**, 643, 676, 709, 730, 734, 760, 780, 784, 788, 797, 834, 924, 927, 933, 956, 1008, 1071, 1087, 1133
Hydrochlorofluorocarbons (HCFCs) 175, 184, 190, **532**, 664, 764, 818, 833
Hydrodamalis stelleri 101
Hydroelectric power 407, 464, 619, 753
Hydrofracturing 460
Hydrogen 3, 43, 53, 113, 156, 172, 181, 183, 200, 208, 217, 237, 320, 324, 334, 432, 440, 501, 503, 530, 532, **533**, 560, 578, 701, 720, 724, 759, 789, 794, 851, 908, 968, 977, 1008, 1025, 1046, 1114, 1122, 1131, 1133
Hydrogen bomb 96, 724
Hydrogen bonds 173
Hydrogen chloride 761, 924
Hydrogen cyanide 174, 187
Hydrogen fluoride 829
Hydrogen sulfide 460, 924

Hydrogen-1 852
Hydrogen-2 852
Hydrogen-3 852
Hydrogeology 56, 116, 274, 510, **533**, 1097
Hydrologic cycle 274, 281, 387, 433, 489, **533**, 554, 649, 663, 774, 855, 893, 1063, 1082, 1093, 1101
Hydrology 228, 312, 366, 408, 458, 490, 533, **535**, 538, 544, 660, 986, 1100
Hydrometeorological Information Center 688
Hydroponics **535**
Hydropower 403, 619
Hydrosphere 851
Hylobates 462
Hypericum perforatum 518
Hypertension 843
Hypertonic 755
Hypertrophic 54
Hypochlorite 324
Hypotonic 755
Hypoxemia 67

I

Ice 912
Ice age 196, 333, 463, 537, **537**, 635, 654, 686, 1119
Ice age refugia **537**, 637, 655
Ice cream species 980
Iceland 1104
Ichthyophonus hoferia 412
Ichthyophthirius multifiliis 412
If You Love This Planet: A Plan to Heal the Earth 150
Ignis fatuus 208
Ilex cassine 388
Illegal dumping 506
Illinois Central Railroad Co. v. Illinois 836
Illinois Sustainable Agriculture Society 37
Illite 189
Imboden, Christopher 553
Imbrie, John 655
Immigration 665, 870
Immune system 212, 269
Immunization 179
Immunotherapy 154
Imperial Metal Industries (IMI) 867
Imperial parrot 553
Impermeable cap 510
Impervious material **538**, 1093
Important Bird Areas in Europe 553
Improvement cutting **538**
In Human Scale 908
In situ air sparging 510
In situ bioremediation 510
In situ solidification 510
In situ vitrification 458, 501, 849

In the Hemlocks　146
In vitro testing　1030
Inbreeding　415, **538**
Inbreeding depression　538
Incineration　24, 99, 103, 229, 233,
　　266, 358, 449, 510, **538**, 558,
　　592, 634, 644, 647, 669, 731,
　　801, 810, 812, 849, 863, 880,
　　924, 951-952, 972-973, 978,
　　982, 1033, 1060, 1079
Incinerator　188, 538, 830
India　663
Indian elephant　325
Indiana bat　89
Indiana Dunes National
　　Lakeshore　686
Indicator organism　107-108, 267,
　　540, 610, 719, 749, 980
Indicator species　718
Indigenous cultures　571
Indigenous peoples　30, 115, 119, 169,
　　293, 334, 360, **540**, 609, 625,
　　681, 855, 857, 950, 1056, 1128
Indirect takings　837
Indoor air quality　25, 28, 188,
　　541, 945
Induced ventilation　416
Industrial Biotechnology
　　Association　121
Industrial ecology　610
Industrial growth　657
Industrial Revolution　157
Industrial waste　424, 789
Industrial waste treatment　8, 94, 183,
　　193, 234, 319, 475, 514, 526,
　　543, 558, 759-760, 890, 942,
　　951, 1018, 1021, 1038, 1064,
　　1077, 1080-1081
Industrialization　610, 1021
Infant cyanosis　129
Infant mortality　179
Infiltration　71, 229, 414, **544**
INFORM (New York, New
　　York)　**544**
INFOTERRA (U.N. Environment
　　Programme)　**545**, 556, 1057
Infrared radiation　323
Infrared spectrometry　642
Inhibiting concentration (IC)　98
Injection well　57, 117, 257, **545**, 1099
Inoculate　**545**
In-place vitrification
　　(glassification)　229
Insecticide　63, 83, 574, 659, 754,
　　782, 1008
Insects　561, 855
Institute for Global
　　Communications　309
Institute for Social Ecology　959
Institute for Wildlife Research　694
Institutional waste　634
Instrumental value　360
Insulin　122

Integrated pest management　21, 165,
　　405, 443, 518, **545**, 781,
　　784, 1000
Intelligent Vehicle Highway
　　Systems　638
Interaction principle　960
Inter-American Development
　　Bank　855
Intergenerational justice　238, 361,
　　444, **547**, 591, 1065
Intergovernmental Panel on Climate
　　Change　**549**
Intermediate Technology Development
　　Group　922
Internalizing costs　202, 395, 484, **550**
International Agricultural Research
　　Centers (IARCs)　226
International Atomic Energy Agency
　　(UNESCO)　**551**
International Bacteriological Code of
　　Nomenclature　980
International Bird Rescue Research
　　Center (IBRRC)　1120
International Board for Plant Genetic
　　Resources　226
International Convention for the
　　Regulation of Whaling
　　(1946)　**552**, 926, 1102, 1104
International Council for Bird
　　Preservation (Washington,
　　D.C.)　**553**, 567, 578, 755, 1071
International Council of Scientific
　　Unions　725
International Dolphin Conservation
　　Act, the　47
International drainage basins　1093
International Environmental Education
　　Workshop　354
International Fisheries
　　Commissions　145
International Geophysical Year　48
International Geosphere-Biosphere
　　Programme (U.N. Environmental
　　Programme)　121, **553**, 756,
　　1057
International Great Lakes Water
　　Quality Agreement　475
International Great Lakes Water
　　Quality Board　475
International Green Circle　138, 294
International Green Cross and Green
　　Crescent　479
International Institute for Sustainable
　　Development (Winnipeg, MB,
　　Canada)　**554**
International Joint Commission
　　(Washington, D.C.)　204,
　　475, **555**, 717
International Maritime
　　Organization　233
International Monetary Fund　855
International Network for
　　Environmental Policy　467

International Organization for
　　Standardization (ISO)　562
International Primate Protection League
　　(Summerville, South
　　Carolina)　**555**
International Register of Potentially
　　Toxic Chemicals (U. N.
　　Environment
　　Programme)　**556**, 1057
International Rules of Botanical
　　Nomenclature　980
International Rules of Zoological
　　Nomenclature　980
International Seabed Authority
　　(ISA)　232
International Society for Environmental
　　Ethics (College Park,
　　Maryland)　**556**
International trade in toxic waste　556,
　　557, 593, 1034, 1037
International Tropical Timber
　　Organization (ITTO)　857
International Union for Conservation of
　　Nature and Natural Resources *See*
　　IUCN
International Whaling Commission
　　(IWC)　168, 552, 926,
　　1102, 1104
International Wildlife　695
International Wildlife Coalition　**558**
Intertidal zone　613, 744
Intrauterine devices　400
Intrinsic asthma　69
Intrinsic value　256, 292, 298, 312,
　　360, 380, **559**, 675, 898,
　　943, 948
Introduced species　56, 333, 392, 410,
　　446, 496, **559**, 839, 842, 907,
　　994, 1141
Inversion　955, 1048
In-vessel system　219
Iodine　850
Iodine 131　**560**, 845, 1123
Ion　3-4, 9, 53, 58, 83, 104, 136,
　　172, 182, 197, 234, 237, 320,
　　324, 441, 512, 514, 530, **560**,
　　637, 700, 792-793, 908, 927,
　　977, 1114
Ion exchange　58, 129, 144, 188, 520,
　　560, **560-561**, 1094
Ion exchange chromatography　185
Ionic bond　172
Ionizing radiation　43, 83, 91, 323,
　　448, 560, **560-561**, 671, 843-
　　844, 1015, 1133
Irish potato blight　663
Iron　512, 561, 767, 954
Iron minerals　189, **561**, 623
Iron triangles　372
Irradiation of food　420, **561**
Irrigation　1, 20, 58, 70, 145, 249, 261,
　　263, 271, 275, 281-282, 377,
　　394, 401, 423, 464, 489, 502,
　　519, 533, **562**, 565, 620, 633,

717, 751, 791, 816, 820, 859,
876, 889, 893, 897, 908-909,
917, 921, 965, 969, 971, 1017,
1059, 1081-1082, 1089, 1091,
1093, 1095
Irrigation systems   1134
Irritant   1033
Islam   711, 871
Island biogeography   106
ISO 14000: International
    Environmental Management
    Standards   **562**
ISO 9000   563
Isocyanic acid   858
Isolated system   748
Isopentane   1071
Isotope   97, 171, 560, 562, **564**, 655,
    719-721, 804, 844-845, 851-
    852, 1061
Itai-itai disease   149, 513-514,
    564, 1069
Italy   632
Itrik Island   96
IUCN—The World Conservation
    Union (Gland, Switzerland)   36,
    49, 126, 223, 460, 462, **565**, 759,
    770, 858, 1001, 1027, 1119,
    1130-1131
Ivory   325, 804
Ivory-billed woodpecker (*Campephilus
    principalis*)   99, **566**
Ixtacihuatl   651
Ixtoc I   744
Izaak Walton League (Arlington,
    Virginia)   222, 250, **567**, 682
Izaak Walton League v. Butz   682

J

J. B. S. Haldane   453
Jackson, Dana   569
Jackson, Henry   405
Jackson Hole National
    Monument   946
Jackson, Wes   **569**, 587, 589
Jacobson, Michael   169
Jainism   712
James Bay hydropower project   334,
    570, 717, 1004
Janzen, D. H.   101
Japan   557, 655, 664, 855, 1104
Japanese Environment Agency   309
Japanese logging   **570**
Japanese-Americans, internment of
    during World War II   8
Jeffers, Susan   931
Jefferson salamander   526
Jefferson, Thomas   688
Jennings, W. S.   388
Jeremy Bentham   238
Jet Propulsion Laboratory   765
Jet stream   321, 988
John Burroughs Association   147
Johns Hopkins University   1125

Johnson, Lyndon   484, 1041
Johnston, David   665
Joliot, Frèdèric   850
Jones v. Gordon   630
Jordan, Bill   882
Journal of Forestry   669
*Journal of the American Water Works
    Association*   1126
Judaism   871
Jus publicum   836
Just v. Marinette County   369

K

Kaibab Plateau   163
Kamerlingh-Onnes, Heike   996
Kaolinite   189
Kapirowitz Plateau   **573**
Kaposi's sarcoma   22
Karst topography   949, 992
Kazakhstan   58
Kemeny, John G.   1025
Kemp's Ridley turtle   926
Kennedy, John F.   1004
Kent, William   919
Kepone   178, 270, **574**, 631, 659, 754,
    784, 1034
Kerogene   743
Kerosene   450, 1008
Kesterson National Wildlife
    Refuge   **575**, 695, 1059
*Key Forests for Threatened Birds in
    Africa*   553
Keystone herbivore   577
Keystone species   214, 255, 325,
    576, 981
Khian Sea   557
Killer bee   12
Killer whale   1102
Kinetic energy   1114
King, Clarence   222, 458
King, Ynestra   298
Kings Canyon National Park   8, 946
Kirtland, Jared P.   578
Kirtland's warbler (*Dendroica
    kirtlandii*)   **578**
Kissimmee River   63, 883
Kjeldahl test   643
Klebsiella   342
Klinefelter's syndrome   124
Kneese, Allen   880
Koala   332
Koch, Robert   212
Korean War   1075
Kow   111
Kozloduy nuclear reactors   1053
Krakatau   992
Krakatoa   **578**, 987
Krill   48, **579**, 763, 1060, 1145
Krupp, Fredric D.   349
Krutch, Joseph Wood   **579**
Krutilla, John   880
Kudzu   392, **580**
Kuru   622

Kwashiorkor   **581**
Kyushu Island   655

L

La Amistad Biosphere Reserve   120
La Mettrie, Julien Offroy de   960
L4   893
Laboratory Animal Welfare Act   47
Laboratory animals   47
Labrador duck   101
Lacassagne   162
Lacey Act   47, 1117
Lagoon   87, 228, **583**
Laguncularia racemosa   626
Lahars   665
Lake Baikal, Russia   58, 138, 294, 333,
    436, **583**, 635
Lake Erie   247, 474, 525, **584**, 1141
Lake herring   585
Lake Huron   474
Lake Mead   207
Lake Michigan   474
Lake Nasser   71
Lake Okeechobee   387
Lake Okeechobee Flood Control
    District   388
Lake Ontario   474, 584, 659
Lake Powell   464
Lake St. Clair   474, 1141
Lake Superior   64, 474, 584, 947
Lake Tahoe   247, 436, **585**
Lake Tahoe Area Council   585
Lake Tanganyika   333
Lake Tenochititlán   652
Lake trout   393, 585
Lake Washington   **586**, 883, 1063
Lake white fish   585
Lakes   5, 53, 56, 414, 612
Lamarck, Jean-Baptiste   389
lamblia   461
Lamprey   907
Land and Water Conservation
    Fund   138, 946, 1096
Land development   589, 633
Land ethic   152, 299, **586**, 588,
    607, 1112
Land Institute (Salina, Kansas)   569,
    587, 589
Land management   21, 778
Land reform   **587**, 1042
Land stewardship   361, 587, **588**-589,
    608, 641
Land Stewardship Project (Marine,
    Minnesota)   587, **589**
Land trusts   589
Land use   9, 21, 110, 141, 145,
    164, 203, 283, 285, 366, 371,
    406, 414-415, 510-511, 585-
    586, **591**, 592, 608, 637, 758,
    799, 962, 964-965, 1063, 1095,
    1097, 1109, 1112, 1117, 1119,
    1124, 1135

Landfill 34, 57, 91, 103, 174-175, 219-220, 271, 276, 292, 341, 352, 354, 374, 424, 449-450, 479, 484, 490, 506, 512, 538, 557, 574, 590, **592**, 596, 634, 644, 649, 669-670, 697, 704, 731, 752, 793, 801, 810, 814, 824, 848, 858, 862-863, 868, 872, 879, 890, 898, 940, 951-952, 971-975, 978, 983, 1003, 1016, 1028, 1033, 1044, 1079, 1084, 1086, 1088, 1100, 1135

Landsberg, Hans 880
Landscape architecture 594, 640
Landscape design 747
Landscape ecology **594**
Landscape planning 594
Landslide 180, 412, 458, **595**, 876, 1063
Land-use 21, 820, 962
Land-use control 9, 203, 591, **592**, 608, 1064, 1093, 1109, 1113
Land-use planning 591
Larderello, Italy 459
Largemouth bass 525
Lasiurus cenereus semotus 89
Latency 238, 269, **595**
Latin America 855
Latvia 296
Laurasia 802
Laurel Ridge Conservation Center 695
Lavelle, Rita 221, 989
Law for the Compensation of Pollution-Related Health Injury 1069
Law Concerning Compensation for Pollution-Related Health Damages and Other Measures 67, 1137
Law Concerning Special Measures for the Relief of Pollution-Related Patients 1137
Law of Environmental Protection 370
Law of Octaves 172
Law of thermodynamics 338
Lawrence Livermore National Laboratory 848
Laws of thermodynamics 337
LD 274, 517
LD$_{50}$ 98, 186, 277, **596**, 640
Leachate 228
Leaching 18, 67, 172, 269, 276, 296, 475, 490, 512, 517, 535, 539, 558, 560, 593, **596**, 617, 620, 649, 657, 781, 849, 859, 908, 910, 945, 962, 964, 1004, 1011, 1078, 1086
Lead 25, 27, 43, 79, 87, 106, 170-171, 189, 228, 232, 276, 278, 295, 300, 313, 325, 352, 358, 362, 370, 378, 394, 451, 503, 506, 508, 512, 514, 538, 557, 561, 575, **596**, 597, 599, 642,

648, 650, 676, 684, 697, 700, 703, 709, 734, 771, 781, 783, 794, 804, 808, 830, 850, 880, 905, 953, 973, 986, 988, 1016, 1032, 1043, 1058, 1061
Lead Contamination Control Act of 1988 598
Lead, effects of 597
Lead management **597**
Lead poisoning 597, 599, 648
Lead pollutants 597
Lead shot 87, 151, 597, **599**, 809
Lead sources 597
Lead toxicity 648
Lead-210 187
League of Conservation Voters (Washington, D.C.) **599**
League to Save Lake Tahoe 585
Leakey, Louis 431, 468, **600**, 602, 939
Leakey, Mary 600, **602**, 604, 939
Leakey, Richard E. 600, 604, **604**
Leaking underground storage tank 141, 596, **606**
Leather leaf fern 388
Leatherback turtle 926
Leeuwenhoek, Antoni van 461
Legionella 25
Legionella pneumophila 542
Legionnaire's disease 653
Legumes 706
Lemurs 623
Lentic 612
Leopard 1016
Leopold, Aldo 152, 163, 167, 223, 299, 345, 353, 360, 481, 573, 586, **607**, 633, 641, 824, 826, 882, 936, 1023, 1109, 1111-1112
Lepidochelys kempii 926
Lepidocrocite 561
Leptonycteris nivalis 89
Leptonycteris sanborni 89
Less developed countries (LDC) 17, 195, 261, 311, 557, **608**, 664, 733, 753, 922, 943, 1020, 1054, 1055, 1143
Lethal concentration (LC) 98, 596
Lethal dosage (LD) 98
Leucichthys artedi 585
Leucophoyx thula 758
Leukemia 92, 154, 162, 177, 181, 187, 296, 322, 520, **609**, 844, 1045, 1133
Lewontin, Richard 961
L'homme-machine 960
Liability 828
Libby, Willard F. 851
Lichens 5, 48, 307, 427, 443, 474, **609**, 706, 1050
Life cycle assessment 98, 367, 477, 563, **610**
Life Science Products Company 574
Life table 1000
Light Within Us, The 923

Lignite 199
Lime 792
Limestone 149
Limited Test Ban Treaty 96
Limits of the Earth, The 755
Limits to Growth (1972) and *Beyond the Limits* (1992) 198, **610**, 816, 920
Limnology 271, 436, **611**, 774, 884, 1072
Lincoln, Abraham 1137
Lindane 830
Lindeman, Raymond 421
Lipids 111
Liquefied natural gas 340
Liquid metal fast breeder reactor **612**, 1123
Liquid sodium 612
Liquid wastes 368
Liquid-solid chromatography (LC) 185
Liquified natural gas **613**, 696
Liquified petroleum gas (LPG) 933
Lithology **613**
Lithosphere 459, 851
Litigation 358
Little Ice Age 967
Littoral zone **613**, 775
Lizards tail 388
Lloyd, William Forster 1038
Loading **613**
Loblaw 482
Local Environmental Control Project 678
Local fallout 845
Logarithm 750
Loggerhead turtle 926
Loggers 718
Logging 662, 855
Logistic growth **613**, 814
London 954
London forces 173
Long Island Lighting 322
Lopez, Barry **614**
Lorikeets 769
Los Alamos National Laboratory 848
Los Angeles Basin 79, 497, 511, **614**, 652, 663, 780, 793, 811, 830, 954
Lotic 612
Love Canal Homeowners Association 616
Love Canal: My Story 462
Love Canal, New York 125, 163, 170, 220, 228, 365, 372, 462, 508, 593, **616**, 671, 1028, 1036, 1061
Lovebirds 769
Lovejoy, Thomas 253
Lovelock, James H. 445, 466, 725, 1002
Lovelock, Sir James Ephraim **617**
Lovins, Amory B. 33, 338-339, **618**, 1001
Lowest Achievable Emission Rate **619**

Lowest Achievable Emission Rate (LAER)   93, 329, 677
Lowest observed effect concentration (LOEC)   186
Low-head hydropower   **619**
Low-level radiation   322
Low-level radioactive waste   91, 501, 519, **620**, 728, 737, 847, 850, 1079, 1123
Low-Level Radioactive Waste Policy Act (1980)   848
Low-Level Radioactive Waste Policy Amendments Act (1985)   848
Loxodonta africana   12, 231, 325, 332
Luanda, Angola   943
Lujan, Manuel   465, 718
Lung cancer   843
Lungfishes   870
Lurgi pressure gasifier   200
Luzon   665
Lymantria dispar   782
Lyme disease   383
Lymphoma   163
Lynx canadensis   492
Lysimeter   **620**
Lythrum salicaria   838

M

MacArthur, Robert H.   106, 1121
Macaws   769
Machina ex Deo: Essays in the Dynamism of Western Culture   1106
Mackenzie, Roderick D.   526
Mackerel   1006
Macrofouling   104
Macronutrient   726
Mad cow disease   **621**
Madagascar   101, **622**, 804
Magma   665
Magnesium silicate   66
Magnetic separation   **623**
Magnolia virginiana   388
Maidencane   388
Maize   19, 122
Making Less Garbage: A Planning Guide for Communities   545
Malacosoma disstria   427
Malaria   71, 170, 174, 212, 251, 279, 362, 456, **623**, 773, 782
Malathion   185, 754, 784, 1008
Malayan elephants   325
Malignant melanoma   763
Malnutrition   581
Malthus, Thomas Robert   198, 353, 364, **624**, 816
Malthusian dilemma   624
Mammary cancer   162
Man and Nature: Physical Geography as Modified by Human Action   632
Man and the Biosphere Program   119, 145, 527, **624**
Manatees   101, 244, **625**
Mangal   626

Manganese   512, 648, 658, 767
Mangrove forests   14
Mangrove fox squirrel   389
Mangrove swamp   **626**, 780, 1027, 1101
Manhattan Project   63, 96, 724, 727
Man's Responsibility for Nature   772
Mantle   803
Manure   407
Manville Corporation   64
Marasmus   **627**
March for Parks   692
Mare liberum   231
Margulis, Lynn   617
Mariculture   50, 732
Marine debris   168
Marine Debris Information   168
Marine ecology and biodiversity   **628**
Marine environment   628
Marine Habitat Program   168
Marine Mammal Events Program   242
Marine Mammals Protection Act (MMPA) (1972)   47, 148, 242, 442, **629**, 716, 805, 930
Marine microbiology   102
Marine pollution   42, 131, 167, 204, 233, 350, 627, **630**, 632, 656, 689, 700, 703, 707, 865, 927-928, 1038, 1054, 1089
Marine Protection, Research and Sanctuaries Act (1972)   233, 277, **632**, 728, 730, 927, 928
Marlin   1006
Marlstone   743
Marmot Island Rookery   930
Marone saxatilis   178
MARPOL   631
Mars   617
Marsh, George Perkins   222, 353, 364, **632**
Marshall Islands   96
Marshall, Robert   **633**, 1109, 1111
Marshes   829
Marsupials   841
Martin Marietta Corporation   727
Mass burn   **634**, 1080
Mass extinction   100, 329, 395, 537, **635**
Mass spectrometry   325, **637**
Mass transit   78-79, 616, **637**, 697
Massachusetts Institute of Technology   1053
Massachusetts Water Resources Authority   630
Mastogloia smithii v. lacustris   388
Material Safety Data Sheets (MSDS)   **639**, 891
Materials balance approach   **639**
Materials Policy Commission   880
Materials Recovery Facility (MRF)   862
Materials Recycling Facility (MRF)   863
Mather, Stephen T.   691, 919

Matrix species   883
Matters of Life and Death   868
Maunder, E. Walter   967
Maunder minimum   967
Maxey Flats, Kentucky   846
Maximum acceptable tolerance concentration   1030
Maximum acceptable toxicant concentration (MATC)   186
Maximum contaminant levels (MCLs)   234, 830
Maximum permissible concentration   **640**, 850
Mayak   172
Mayfly   540
Mayfly larvae   584
McCarthy, James   554
McDonalds Corporation   349, 479
McDonnell-Douglas   988
McHarg, Ian   594, **640**
McKibben, Bill   **641**
Meadow   750
Meadows, Dennis   610
Measles   212
Measurement and sensing   637, **642**
Mechanical dredging   275
Media Resource Service (MRS)   923
Mediation   350
Medical waste   540, 632, 634, **643**, 670, 731, 852, 877
Medical Waste Tracking Act   644
Medieval Religion and Technology: Collected Essays   1106
Mediterranean Action Plan   645
Mediterranean fruit fly   391
Mediterranean Sea   232, 631, **645**
Medium-Btu gas   201
Megaptera novaeangliae   168
Megawatt (MW)   503, 619, **646**, 1017, 1024, 1097, 1122
Megazoo   1144
Melaleuca quinquenervia   389
Melanoma skin cancer   163
Mellon Foundation   694
Menageries   1144
Mendel, Gregor   122, 390
Mendes, Chico   35, **646**
Merchant, Carolyn   298
Mercury   33, 109, 111, 125, 173, 228, 232, 260, 265, 276; 307, 313, 334, 362, 372, 378, 380, 413, 422, 443, 475, 482, 503, 512, 514, 539, 570, 630, **647**, 648, 650, 655, 679, 700, 727, 730, 783, 808, 830, 880, 902, 920, 1006, 1032, 1034, 1043, 1061
Meroplankton   1145
Merriam, John   919
Mesocricetus auratus   2
Mesopelagic zone   775
Mesosphere   72
Mesothelioma   66
Mesotrophic   54
Messenger RNA (mRNA)   894

Metabolism   4, 56, 112, 129, 265, 370, **648**, 773, 785, 794, 845, 1037, 1127
Metabolites   1033
Metallic bonds   173
Metallic ores   657
Metalloid   511
Metals, as contaminants   **648**, 685, 796, 813, 1061
Metam sodium   173, 298
Metamorphosis   438
Metasequoia glyptostroboides   865
Meteorologica   649
Meteorology   579, **649**, 664
Methane   11, 34, 43, 113, 118, 134, 156, 158, 182-183, 196, 200, 208, 211, 334, 338, 341, 379, 432, 449, 484, 486, 520, 619, 649, **649**, 696, 708, 810, 933, 942, 975, 1009, 1077, 1080, 1094, 1098, 1102
Methane digester   43, 114, 134, **649**, 1002
Methane formers   43
Methanobacterium   649
Methanoccus   649
Methanogenes   649
Methanol   26, 34, 77, 79, 113, 334, 341, 441, 451, **650**, 696, 867
Methanosarcina   649
Methemoglobinemia   129
Methoxychlor   54, 783, 830
Methyl bromide   764
Methyl chloroform   197, 764
Methyl isocyanate (MIC)   94, 174
Methylation   265, 475, **650**
Methylene chloride   181
Methylmercury   109, 125, 655, 783
Methylmercury seed dressings   443, 513, **650**, 656, 784
Methyl-t-butyl ether (MTBE)   451
Metrosideros polymorpha   426
Meuse River Valley   27
Mexican long-nosed bat   89
Mexican spotted owl   717
Mexico   557, 1020
Mexico City, Mexico   27, 73-74, **651**, 943
Miami River   387
Mice   841
Micelles   265
Michigan   812
Michigan Department of Health   887
Michigan Department of Labor   887
Microbes (microorganisms)   **652**
Microclimate   **653**, 654, 718
Microcystis   412
Microfouling   104
Micro-habitat   497
Micronutrient   54, 726
Microorganisms   107, 174, 652, 790
Microwave oven   323
Microwave radiation   323

Mid-Century Conference on Resources for the Future   880
Middle Atlantic Bight   702
Migration   242, 281, 287, 391, 411, 418, 553, **654**, 662, 696, 700, 794, 856, 911, 925, 938, 999, 1104, 1118, 1129, 1142
Migratory Bird Campaign   553
Migratory Bird Convention Act   695
Migratory Bird Hunting Stamp Act   695
Migratory Bird Treaty Act   695, 1117
Migratory birds   699
Migratory Birds Convention Act   153
Migros   477, 479
Milan, Italy   341
Milankovitch, Milutin   654
Milankovitch weather cycles   **654**
Mill, John Stuart   360, 1004, 1065
Mills College   1106
Minamata disease   109, 125, 413, 443, 513-514, 648, 651, **655**, 1069
Mine safety   145
Mine spoil waste   3, 67, 284, 297, 565, **657**, 756, 860, 991
Mineral King Valley   369
Mineral Leasing Act (1920)   406, 592, **657**
Mineralization   229
Minerals   613
Minerals Convention, Antarctic   49
Mining   145, 405, 687, 1032
Mining Law of 1870   657
Mining Law of 1872   405, 658, 1111
Mining, undersea   **658**
Minitrial   351
Mink   525, 531
Minke whale   1102
Mirex   **659**, 754
Miscarriage   323, 940, 1051
Missile Envy   150
Mississippi River   702
Mitchell, George   190
Mitsubishi Corporation   571, 857
Mittermeier, Russell   225
Mixing zones   **659**
Mobil Chemical   477, 793
Mobile link species   981
Modeling (computer applications)   **659**
Modern technology   579
Modern Temper, The   579
Modular combustion systems   972
Molina, Mario   549, **661**, 683, 761, 902
Molluscicide   782
Mollusks   331
Molybdenum   512, 575, 850
Monachus monachus   930
Mongolian wild horse   154
Monitor organisms   108
Monk seal   930
Monkey Wrench Gang   1, 662
Monkeys   787

Monkey-wrenching   1, 292, 298, 380, 424, 481, **662**
Mono Basin National Forest Scenic Area   663
Mono Lake, California   **662**
Mono Lake Tufa State Reserve   663
Monoclonal antibodies   123
Monoculture   50, 130, 310, 587, 589, **663**, 752, 784, 1037
Monofill   975
Monongahela National Forest   682
Monsoon   20, 473, 485, **663**
Monsoon winds   663
Montmorillonite   189
Montreal Protocol Multilateral Fund   664
Montreal Protocol on Substances That Deplete the Ozone Layer (1987)   184, 436, **664**, 763
Montrose Chemical   988
Moraine   464
More developed country (MDC)   608, **664**, 1054, 1143
Mortality   370, 378-379, 400, 508, 559, **665**, 787, 814, 1000, 1032, 1143
Morton, Rogers   30
Mosquito   623, 782
Mosquito Coast, The   857
Mother Teresa   479
Motor vehicle emissions   28
Mougeotia   393
Moule, Henry   1029
Mount Pinatubo, Philippines   196, 321, 579, **665**, 666, 1072
Mount St. Helens, Washington   383, 579, **665**
Mountain gorilla   471
Mountain lion   415
Mountain sheep   654
Mountain States Legal Foundation   1096
Mueller-Dombois, D.   426
Muhlenbergia filipes   388
Muir, John   147, 222, 353, 519, 633, 641, **666**, 747, 798, 900, 946, 1109, 1137
Mulch   41, 63, 282, 286, **668**, 751, 1135
Mule   121
Mule deer   573
Multiple chemical sensitivity   **668**
Multiple Use-Sustained Yield Act (1960)   429, **668**, 719
Mumford, Lewis   632, 901
Municipal Sanitation   1126
Municipal solid waste   182, 204, 227, 310, 357, 424, 449-450, 479, 520, 634, 644, **669**, 862, 864, 970, 973, 974, 978, 1030
Municipal solid waste composting   545, **670**, 952
Municipal waste   1028, 1044
Municipal Waste Combustor   634

Murres   463
Mus musculus   748
Musa paradisiaca   135
Musca domestica   748
Musée Oceanographique   645
Muskie, Edmund   189
Muskox   61
Muskrat   525
Mustard gas   671, 1076
Mustela nigripes   127
Mutagen   41, 171, 175, 508, **670**, 671,
    1015, 1033
Mutation   41, 83, 124, 153, 183, 390,
    453, 498, 671, **671**, 1028, 1133
Mutualism   106, 1007
Mycobacterium tuberculosis   212
Mycorrhiza   545, **671**, 1008
mycorrhizae   443
Mycotoxin   **672**
Mycteria americana   389
Myers, Norman   395
Myotis grisescens   89
Myotis sodalis   89
Myrica cerifera   388
Myriophyllum spicatum   386, 392
Mysid shrimp   186
Mysidopsis   186
Mysis relicta   393
Mysticism of Paul the Apostle, The   923
Myths & Texts   958

N

Nader, Ralph   **673**, 774, 1059
Naess, Arne   256, 312, 361, 380,
    673, 712
Nagasaki, Japan   520, **675**, 845, 1077
Nasal polyps   69
National Academy of
    Sciences   725, 1126
National Aeronautics and Space
    Administration (NASA)   339,
    554, 762
National Air Toxics Information
    Clearinghouse   **676**
National Ambient Air Quality Standard
    (NAAQS)   28, 74, 93, 189,
    242, 643, **676**, 679, 709,
    829, 996
National Association for Environmental
    Education   354
National Association for Plastic
    Container Recovery   227
National Audubon Society (New York,
    New York)   37, 75, 151, 222,
    274, **677**, 714, 1117, 1124
National Center for Food and
    Agricultural Policy   880
National Center for Health
    Statistics   1058
National Coalition Against the Misuse
    of Pesticides (Washington,
    D.C.)   405, **678**, 784

National Commission on Water
    Quality   192
National Conservation Achievement
    Awards   695
National Consortium for Environmental
    Education and Training
    (NCEET)   355
National Critical Materials Act   688
National Critical Materials
    Council   688, 987
National Emission Standards for
    Hazardous Air Pollutants   328,
    679
National Energy Act of
    1978   335, 1058
National Environmental Policy Act
    (1969)   150, 239, 340, 365, 366,
    368, 372-373, **679**, 889, 946,
    1014, 1034, 1043
National Environmental Satellite, Data
    and Information Service
    (NESDIS)   688
National Environmental Scorecard   599
National forest   30, 222, 372, 406,
    425, 429, 515, 608, 633, 663,
    668, 681, **681**, 689, 697, 718,
    747, 798, 856, 900, 980, 1024,
    1096, 1110-1112, 1124
National Forest Commission   798
National Forest Management Act
    (1976)   426, **681**, 719, 747,
    1112
National Forest Products
    Association   372
National Geographic Society   469
National Heritage Program   518
National Historic Preservation
    Act   694
National Institute for the
    Environment   **682**
National Institute of Environmental
    Health Sciences (Research
    Triangle Park, North
    Carolina)   **683**
National Institute of Occupational
    Safety and Health
    (NIOSH)   64, 170, 597, 684,
    686, 946
National Institute for Urban Wildlife
    (Columbia, Maryland)   **685**
National lakeshore   204, **686**, 691,
    1096
National Law Journal   374
National Marine Fisheries Service
    (NMFS)   45, 331, 374, 629,
    689, 1050
National Materials Exchange
    Network   1077
National Materials and Minerals Policy,
    Research and Development
    Act   687
National Mining and Minerals Act
    (1970)   **687**
National Ocean Service   688

National Oceanic and Atmospheric
    Administration (NOAA)   110,
    203, 331, 371, 632,
    688731, , 1098
National park   8-9, 30, 63, 93, 119,
    126, 137, 152, 190, 222, 317,
    377, 476, 579, 583, 585, 591-
    592, 674, **689**, 690-691, 798,
    837, 901, 946, 1039, 1041, 1096,
    1110-1112, 1117, 1119, 1124,
    1135, 1137, 1143
National Park Service   1, 61, 126-127,
    315, 318, 442, 465, 472, 476,
    518, 592, 686, 689, **690**, 694,
    696, 836, 919, 946, 1059, 1108-
    1109, 1113, 1136-1137
National Park Service Act   690
National Park Trust Fund   692
National Parks   692
National Parks and Conservation
    Association (Washington,
    D.C.)   37, 687, **691**
National Pesticide Forum   678
*National Policy on Recycling and Policy
    Resolutions*   693
National pollutant discharge elimination
    system (NPDES)   192
National Primary Drinking Water
    Requirements   1030
National Priorities List   13, 142, 220,
    228, 374, 449, 509, **692**, 997
National Recycling Coalition
    (Washington, D.C.)   **692**
National Recycling Congress and
    Exposition   693
National Research Council Committee
    on Human Dimensions of Global
    Change   527
National Research Council
    (Washington, D.C.)   148, **693**
National resource   869
National Safe Workplace Institute   882
National Safety Council   882
National seashore   137, 686, 691, **694**,
    946, 1096
National Seashore Act   694
National Soft Drink Association   227
National Solid Wastes Management
    Association   973
National Weather Service (NWS)   688
National Wetlands Newsletter   370
National Wetlands Protection
    Hotline   370
National Wilderness Preservation
    System (NWPS)   137, 946,
    1109, 1110
National Wildlife   695
National Wildlife Federation
    (Washington, D.C.)   36, 242,
    250, 411, 504, **694**, 714, 1067,
    1096, 1117
National wildlife refuge   60, 250, 331,
    411, 576, 625, 668, **695**, 900,
    1096, 1110, 1117-1118

National Wildlife Refuge
Administration Act   696
National Wildlife Rehabilitators
Association (NWRA)   1120
National Wildlife Week   694
Natural capital   3
Natural gas   24, 33, 77, 113, 157-158,
191, 199-200, 334-335, 341,
376, 403, 407, 432, 442, 458-
459, 493, 548, 592, 613, 615,
619, 649, 658, **696**, 740-741,
813, 822, 920, 933, 962, 1016,
1019, 1025, 1058
Natural Gas Act of 1938   339, 403
Natural gas pipeline   613
Natural habitat   1045
Natural history   666
*Natural History and Antiquities of
Selborne, The*   1104
Natural resources   3, 12, 35-37, 63,
139, 150, 174, 177, 198, 204,
221, 226-227, 302-303, 315,
353, 360, 366, 368, 377, 380-
381, 402, 411, 438, 440, 448,
458, 502, 514, 518, 555-556,
567, 586, 588, 608, 610, 668,
688-689, 694, **696**, 697, 725,
755, 758, 798, 832, 842, 863,
871-874, 898-899, 908, 920,
934, 962, 966, 1020, 1039, 1041,
1054, 1057, 1059, 1067, 1071,
1095, 1124, 1129-1130
Natural Resources Conservation
Service   1090
Natural Resources Defense Council
(New York, New York)   29, 37,
696, 714, 1128
*Natural Resources Defense Council v.
EPA*   676
Natural selection   306-307
Nature   41, 59, 70, 84, 89, 115, 119,
131, 139, 164, 221, 244, 256,
292, 298-299, 312, 326, 345,
351, 353, 361, 363, 378, 380,
394, 402, 435, 443, 445, 471,
480, 503-504, 527, 565, 569,
579, 585, 587, 607, 623, 632,
641, 674, 678-679, 695, **697**,
698, 710, 772, 818-819, 898,
912, 958, 1018, 1022, 1031,
1042, 1104, 1106, 1109, 1111,
1120, 1144
Nature Conservancy (Arlington,
Virginia)   37, 110, 222, 225,
255, 380, 448, 481, 589, **698**,
714, 827, 874, 1064, 1117, 1124
NatureQuest   695
NatureScope   695
Navajo   19
Navigation   1015
N-butane   1071
Nearing, Scott   **698**
Negative feedback loop   610
Negligence   368

Negotiation   350
Nellis Air Force Base   701
Nelson, Gaylord   290
Nematicide   17, 782
Neolithic   19, 961
Neo-Malthusian   624
Neoplasm   **699**
Neotropical migrants   **699**
Neritic zone   613, **700**, 775
Nerpa   333, 583
Nervous system   185, 754
Nesoenas mayeri   553
Net primary production   119
Neurotoxin   270, 280, **700**, 1033
Neutron   33, 171, 612, **701**, 719, 721,
724, 844, 850-851
Nevada Proving Ground   701
Nevada Test Site (Mercury,
Nevada)   **701**, 737, 843
Nevado del Ruiz   665
New Atlantis, The   85
New Caledonia   333
New Farm, The   898
New Madrid, Missouri   **702**
New Management Procedure   1104
New Resource Economics (NRE)   832
New Source Performance
Standard   93, 189, 328, 677, **702**
New York Bight   31, **702**, 728
New York City   703
New York Harbor   108
New York State Constitution of
1892   9
New York Zoological Society   755
Newcastle disease   770
Newkirk, Ingrid   775
Nexrad   688
Niagara Falls, New York   474, 616
Niagara Falls State Reservation   748
Niagara River   474
Niche   106, 217, 307, 326, 333, 382,
445, 460, 474, 503, 526, 578,
607, 635, **703**, 994, 1002,
1022, 1102
Nickel   106, 149, 166, 433, 512, 514,
648, **704**, 797, 808, 988,
994, 1032
Nicosia Charter   645
Nicotiana tabacum   1028
Nicotine sulfate   783
Nile River   70
NIMBUS-7   762
NIMBY (Not In My Backyard)   593,
670, **704**, 779, 880, 973, 983,
985, 1037, 1080
Nitrates and nitrites   31, 53, 129, 228,
246, 260, 271, 279, 386, 392,
419, **704**, 705, 707, 831, 911,
938, 956, 1060, 1063 1085
Nitric acid   3
Nitric oxide   208, 707
Nitrification   705, **705**, 937, 942
Nitrobacter   706
Nitrococcus   706

Nitrogen   3, 16, 18, 54, 72-73, 123,
156, 166, 178, 191, 197-198,
217, 234, 246, 252, 255, 260,
276, 282, 304, 313, 384, 392,
407-408, 436, 450, 456-457,
490, 492-493, 532, 559, 574,
586-587, 643, 703-705, **705**,
709, 726, 759, 776, 779, 781,
788, 792-793, 812, 821, 850-
851, 864, 882, 921, 934, 937,
940, 951, 964, 988, 1000, 1011-
1012, 1043, 1060, 1082, 1087,
1090, 1095, 1102, 1115
Nitrogen cycle   31, 79, 105, 158, 260,
282, 386, 540, 652, 705, **705**
Nitrogen cyle   525
Nitrogen dioxide   187, 189, 412, 497,
707, 792
Nitrogen fixation   1115
Nitrogen oxides   3, 5, 9, 23, 26, 27,
74, 79, 158, 190-191, 208, 296,
334, 350, 416-417, 497, 511,
535, 542, 634, 643, 651, 676,
705, **707**, 725, 761, 788, 793,
821, 829-830, 881, 924, 956,
973, 988, 1012, 1071, 1098
Nitrogen waste   705, 707, **707**
Nitrosamines   705
Nitrosococcus   705-706
Nitrosomas   705
Nitrosomonas   706
Nitrous oxide   **708**
Nixon, Richard   189, 191, 236, 239,
244, 373, 425, 484, 870,
902, 1041
No Nature   958
NOAA Corps   688
Nocturnal jets   28
Noise pollution   78, 368, 637, 643,
708, 736, 1136
Nonachlor   754
Nonattainment area   27-28, 190,
709, 831
Noncriteria pollutant   **709**
Nondegradable pollutant   645, **710**
Nongame wildlife   **710**, 1120
Nongame Wildlife Act   710
Nongovernmental organization
(NGO)   36, 153, 253, 479, 554,
565, **710**, 715, 784, 1055-1056,
1117, 1120
Nonpoint source   18, 94, 178, 192,
204, 247, 408, 475, 489-490,
703, **710**, 805, 1086, 1088-1089
Nonrenewable resources   143, 302,
344, 611, 649, **710**, 822
Non-target organisms   784
Non-Western environmental
ethics   **711**, 872
No-observable-adverse-effect-level
(NOAEL)   **713**
North   611, **713**
North American Agreement on
Environmental Cooperation   715

North American Association for Environmental Education (Troy, Ohio) **714**
North American avifauna 870
North American Bioregional Congress 115
North American Conference on Christianity and Ecology 479
North American Free Trade Agreement (NAFTA) 367, 554, 697, **714**
North American Water and Power Alliance **716**
North American Waterfowl Management Plan 283
North American Wetlands Conservation Act 1059
North American wood warbler 578
North Atlantic Fisheries Organization 413
Northern flying squirrel 717
Northern hemisphere 713
Northern peatlands 1101
Northern pike 525
Northern spotted owl (*Strix occidentalis caurina*) 106, 194, 243, 330, 428-429, 710, **717**, 746, 856, 1112, 1125, 1131
Northrop 988
Norwalk agent 1070
Norway 1104
Nostoc 706
Notes on Walt Whitman as a Poet and Person 147
Notestein, Frank 260
No-till farming 966
Nouakchott, Mauritania 943
Novum Organum 84
Nubians 71
Nuclear accident 828
Nuclear disarmament 723
Nuclear energy 34, 570
Nuclear fission 96, 171, 409, 564, 612, 701, **719**, 720-721, 724, 737, 804, 822, 829, 845, 847, 851, 896, 930, 991, 1061, 1079, 1123
Nuclear fuel cycle 845
Nuclear fusion 96, 171, 719-720, **720**, 724, 800, 822, 851, 896, 968, 1058
Nuclear Madness: What You Can Do 150
Nuclear magnetic resonance (NMR) 325
Nuclear power 33, 59, 74, 91, 150, 171-172, 249, 255, 321, 334, 338-342, 486-487, 519, 547, 552, 564, 612, 618, 701, 720, **721**, 723, 725, 737, 753, 795, 804, 822, 828, 845, 847, 850, 852, 890, 928, 1015-1016, 1025, 1053, 1061, 1078, 1095, 1097, 1121, 1123, 1126
Nuclear power plant 1138

Nuclear reaction 721
Nuclear reactor 612, 1123
Nuclear Regulatory Commission (NRC) 74, 91, 341, 552, 612, **723**, 846-848, 929, 985, 1026, 1053, 1079
Nuclear safety 723
Nuclear test ban **723**
Nuclear testing, atmospheric 845
Nuclear testing in Polynesia, French 149
Nuclear waste 63, 1138
Nuclear Waste Fund 737
Nuclear Waste Policy Act (1982) 848, 851
Nuclear Waste Policy Amendments Act (1987) 848
Nuclear waste repository 737
Nuclear weapons 59, 83, 91, 96, 137, 150, 171-172, 438, 448, 487, 500, 551, 560, 685, 697, 701, 720, 723, **724**, 725, 727, 737, 804, 844-845, 851, 894, 918, 923, 991, 1053, 1058, 1061, 1076
Nuclear winter 60, 196, 723, **725**, 780, 844, 851, 1077
Nucleic acid 156, 271, 304, 652, **726**, 844, 894
Nucleotides 894
Numenius borealis 101
Nuphar luteum 388
Nurse species 883
Nutrient 6, 16, 18, 31-32, 43, 47-48, 56-57, 101, 104, 114, 123, 149, 178, 184, 192, 197, 206, 208, 218, 235, 246, 252, 255, 265, 280, 286, 301, 305, 307, 313, 318, 370, 378, 385, 392, 407-408, 426, 443, 460, 474-475, 497, 516, 525, 530, 535, 545, 559, 562, 570, 584, 587, 596, 609, 627, 630, 645, 671, 700, 704-705, **726**, 733, 748, 751, 771, 781-782, 796, 808, 810, 816, 825, 860, 864, 884, 890, 893, 909, 937, 940, 945, 947, 950-951, 992, 1002, 1007, 1011, 1031-1032, 1046-1048, 1068, 1085, 1088-1089, 1101, 1114, 1130, 1135
Nutrient loading 630
Nutrition 169
Nutrition Action Newsletter. 170
Nutrition Project 169
Nylon 801
Nymphaea odorata 388
Nymphoides aquatica 388

O

Oak Ridge National Laboratories 727
Oak Ridge, Tennessee 91, **727**, 848, 1058
Oaks 526

Occupational Safety and Health Act (1970) 327, 686, **728**, 946
Occupational Safety and Health Administration (OSHA) 64, 94, 163, 541, 598, 639, 644, 673, 686, 709, 728, **728**, 886, 891, 946, 948, 1037
Ocean 413, 630, 775
Ocean dumping 40, 63, 232, 276, 558, 632, 645, 697, 703, **728**, 730, 847, 849, 928
Ocean Dumping Ban Act (1988) 40, 233, 632, 728, **730**, 928
Ocean farming **731**
Ocean outfalls **733**
Ocean ranching 732
Ocean thermal energy conversion 33, **733**, 823
Ocelot 758
Octane number 451, 734
Octane rating **734**, 1133
Odén, Svante **734**
Odocoileus hemionus 573
Odocoileus virginianus 415
Odor 368, 407
Odor control 183, 408, 410, **735**
Odum, Eugene P. **736**
Office of Civilian Radioactive Waste Management (OCRWM) **737**, 847, 1058
Office of Coastal Zone Management (OCZM) 203
Office of Energy Research 1058
Office of Information and Regulatory Affairs (OIRA) 738, 869
Office of Management and Budget (OMB) **737**, 869
Office of Oceanic and Atmospheric Research 688
Office of Science and Technology Policy 725
Office on Smoking and Health 170
Office of Solid Waste and Emergency Response 879
Office of Solid Wastes Directives System 878
Office of Surface Mining, Reclamation and Enforcement **738**, 1059
Office of Technology Assessment 701
Off-road vehicles 136, 262, 285, **738**, 1124
Ogallala Aquifer 56, 562, 717, **739**
Oil 743, 788
Oil drilling 204, 232, 242, 339, 616, 632, 692, 696-697, **740**, 789, 857, 1042, 1112, 1124
Oil dumping 780
Oil embargo 150, 199, 236, 336-337, 353, 403, **741**, 753, 822, 879, 1042, 1058, 1121
Oil fires 780
Oil mousse 744
Oil pipeline 403, 745
Oil Placer Act of 1897 657

Oil pollution   1043
Oil Pollution Act (1990)   248, 741, **743**, 745
Oil refining   450, 1032
Oil reserves   62
Oil shale   342, 432, 434, 657, **743**, 1008, 1019
Oil spills   36, 41, 49, 54, 174, 236, 241, 247, 350, 352, 358, 396, 433, 476, 493, 631, 645, 688, 741, 743, **743**, 780, 789, 809, 813, 832, 870, 925, 930, 1031
Oil tanker   743
Oil wells   743
Old-growth forest   1, 9, 38, 49, 159, 193, 243, 294, 426, 428-429, 525, 697, 710, 718, **745**, 856, 980, 982, 993, 1039, 1110, 1112, 1115, 1124
Oligopeptide   776
Oligotrophic   54
Olin Corporation   616
Olmsted, Frederick Law, Sr.   **747**
Olympic National Park   946
On the Beach   149
On the Origin of Species   250, 445
Onchocerca volvulus   893
Onchocerciasis   893
Onchomelania   921
Onchomouse   455
1,1,1-trichloroethane   830
1,1-dichloroethylene   830
1,2-dichlorobenzene   830
1,2-dichloroethane   830
Only One Earth   1055
Open system   **748**
Open-pit mining   999
Operating Manual for Spaceship Earth   979
Operation Castle   96
Operation Crossroads   96
Operation Ranger   701
Opportunistic organism   382, 392, **748**
Opuntia   518
Oral contraception   399
Oral rehydration therapy (ORT)   179
Orangutan (*Pongo pygmaeus*)   462, 471, 555, **749**
Orcinus orca   272, 1102
Orconectes virilis   393
Order of magnitude   **750**
Ordovician period   635
Oregon silverspot butterfly (*Speyeria zerene hippolyta*)   **750**
Organic Agriculture: What the States Are Doing   170
Organic compounds   198
Organic gardening and farming   17, 22, 29, 135, 219, 699, **750**, 898, 922, 1002
Organic Gardening and Farming   898
Organic material   851
Organic solvents   1034

Organic waste   34, 130, 192, 204, 219, 490, 649, 729, **752**, 971, 1072
Organization of Petroleum Exporting Countries (OPEC)   335, 337, 403, 741, **753**, 822, 1058, 1121
Organochloride   105, 182, 270, 475, 754, **754**, 781, 784, 812
Organochlorine   269, 574, 754
Organophosphate   185, 265, 267, 494, 700, 754, **754**, 784, 1008
Organotins   178
Origins of Continents and Oceans, The   802
Ornithology   787
Ornithoptera alexandrae   231
Ornithoptera solitarius   272
Ornithorhynchus anatinus   871
Oropouche fever   212
Orr, David W.   **754**
Orthophosphates   790
Oryza sativa   516
Osborn, Henry Fairfield   **755**
O'Shaughnessy Dam   519
Osmerus mordax   585
Osmosis   58, 129, 261, **755**, 910, 1083, 1095
Osmunda regalis   388
Our Common Future (Brundtland Report)   143, 223, 344, 527, **755**, 1004, 1055
Our Plundered Planet   755
Out of My Life and Thought   923
Outdoor Ethics   567
Outdoor Recreation Resources Review   138
Outlook   669
Overburden   3, 107, 657, **756**, 799, 860, 981, 990, 997
Overfishing   48, 140, 209, 232, 386, 411, 422, 463, 474, 487, **756**, 874, 911, 930
Overgrazing   8, 263, 281, 287, 293, 401, 573, 633, 668, **757**, 824, 858, 874, 980, 1039, 1082, 1096, 1098, 1110, 1137
Overharvesting   428, 1006
Overhunting   47, 68, 101, 126, 395, 411, 418, 422, 553, **758**, 770-771, 874, 1027, 1103, 1106, 1118, 1127
Overpopulation   401
Overshoot   267
Ovibos moschatus   61
Ovis canadensis   654
Ovis dalli   61
Oxidation   237, 759
Oxidation reduction reactions   111, 129, 208, 237, 266, 440, 519, **759**, 781
Oxidizing agent   57, 129, 324, 759, **759**, 780, 968
Oxygen   34, 98, 130, 183, 704, 759-760
Oyster   178

Ozark big-eared bat   89
Ozark Community Congress (OACC)   115
Ozarks Resource Center   115
Ozonation   **760**, 761, 988
Ozone   6, 27, 57, 72, 74, 163, 175, 181, 183-184, 196-197, 267, 279, 296, 300, 378, 416, 426-427, 467, 482, 484, 486-487, 528, 532, 542, 549, 613, 637, 642, 651, 661, 664-665, 688, 707-709, 759, **760**-761, 792-793, 810, 830, 833, 838, 876, 881, 902, 955, 968, 981, 988, 1003, 1006, 1008, 1048, 1053, 1056, 1070-1072, 1099
Ozone "hole," Antarctic   761
Ozone layer   184, 190, 350, 642, 1056
Ozone layer depletion   25, 72, 76, 150, 163, 175, 183-184, 197, 210, 311, 320, 352, 372, 395, 438, 465, 468, 480, 484, 532, 554, 643, 655, 661, 664-665, 760, **761**, 833, 870, 902, 988, 1003, 1053, 1072, 1099, 1124
Ozonosphere   760

P

Pacheco, Alex   775
Pacific Gas and Electric   322
Pacific Materials Exchange   1077
Pacific Northwest   330, 855, 1014
Pacific Ocean   321
Pacific yew   856
Packwood-Magnuson Amendment   47
Padre Island National Seashore   946
Paleoanthropology   600, 602
Paleoecology/paleolimnology   **767**
Paleolimnology   767
Paleomagnetism   804
Paley, William   880
Palmer Station   49
Palouse   473
Pampas   473
Pan troglodytes   179
Pandion haliaetus   526
Pangaea   802
Panicum hemitomon   388
Panthera pardus   1016
Panthera tigris   1027
Panthera tigris tigris   758
Panthera uncia   759
Parakeets   769
Paralytic shellfish poisoning   707, 864
Paraquat   891
Parasites   54, 130, 205, 212, 243, 302, 307, 312, 412, 461, 518, 546, 578, 623, 749, **768**, 782, 893, 907, 921, 1008, 1016, 1032, 1133
Parasitism   1007
Parathion   8, 185, 754, 784
Pareto optimality (Maximum social welfare)   **769**

Pareto, Vilfredo   769
Park, Robert Ezra   526
Park Watchers Program   692
Parrots and parakeets   272, **769**, 787
Particulate   7, 11-12, 27, 72, 74, 85,
       93, 158, 189, 191, 196, 200, 221,
       245, 296, 324, 410, 483, 512,
       538, 642, 647, 651, 676, 709,
       725, **770**, 822, 829-830, 881-
       882, 952, 972, 1012
Parts per billion (ppb)   16, 184-185,
       279, 643, 750, **771**, 1028
Parts per million(ppm)   16, 72, 156,
       246, 279, 325, 372, 484, 511,
       565, 574, 643, 750, 761, **771**,
       909, 1086, 1088
Parts per thousand   136
Parts per trillion (ppt)   269, 643, **771**
Passenger pigeon (*Ectopistes
       migratorius*)   99, 222, 395, 530,
       758, **771**, 1116, 1144
Passer domesticus   748
Passive solar design   **772**, 970
Passmore, John A.   **772**
Pathogen   43, 56, 130, 134, 183-
       184, 211, 218, 260, 271, 274,
       307, 342, 361, 382, 412, 426,
       456, 595, 643, 672, 730, 751,
       773, 782, 809, 911, 917, 951,
       1085, 1088
Pathogenic bacteria   342
Patrick, Ruth   **773**
PCB   24, 54, 358, 372, 838, 891, 1062
P-dichlorobenzene   830
Pearl dace   393
Pease, Charles   578
Peat   956, 1061
Peat soils   388, 774, **774**
Peatlands   312, 774, **774**
Peccei, Aurelio   610
Pedology   **775**
Pedon   961
Peer Match Program   692
Pelagic zone   613, 700, **775**
Pelecanus occidentalis   139, 338,
       784, 1116
Pelican Island   695, 900
Pentachlorophenol (PCP)   110, 181,
       228, 269, **775**, 783, 968
People for the Ethical Treatment of
       Animals (Washington,
       D.C.)   42, 44-45, **775**, 948
Peptides   246, **776**
Perca flavescens   585
Percina tanasi   243, 956, 1014
Percolation   68, 620, **776**, 962,
       1082, 1093
Pere David's deer   154
Peregrine falcon (*Falco peregrinus*)   155,
       338, 348, 473, 477, **776**, 784,
       1116, 1120
Peregrine Fund   777
Pereia, Jerdeir   646
Perez de Cuellar, Javier   479

Perfectibility of Man, The   772
Periophthalmus   627
Periphyton   388
Perk test   776
Perkin, William Henry   174
Permaculture   **778**
Permafrost   29, **779**, 1011, 1041
Permanent retrievable storage   **779**
Permeable   63, 281, **780**, 911, 1081
Permian period   635
Permissible dose   640
Permissible exposure level   1030
Permissible Exposure Limit
       (PEL)   639
Peroxide   324
Peroxyacetyl nitrate (PAN)   25, **780**
Peroxybenzoyl nitrate   79
Perry, Ted   932
Persa borbonia   388
Perseus   765
Persian Gulf War   493, 725, 743, **780**
Persistent compound   266, **781**, 784
Person/Planet   901
Pest   17, 21, 32, 83, 251, 256, 272,
       331, 392, 430, 516, 545, 749,
       751, **781**, 782
Pest control   559
Pest species   882
Pesticide   9, 16, 18, 20-21, 43, 59, 63,
       87, 89, 94, 104, 111, 113, 115,
       122, 132, 139-140, 162, 164,
       170, 173, 175, 178, 181, 185-
       186, 228, 232, 251, 255, 257-
       259, 269, 271, 274, 280, 292,
       297-298, 307, 309-310, 320,
       338, 346, 352, 354, 360, 370,
       373, 378-379, 386, 394, 401,
       403, 408, 410, 418, 423, 456,
       467, 475, 477, 484, 487, 490,
       493, 496, 502, 507, 516, 526,
       533, 542, 545, 569, 574, 587,
       589, 596, 617, 621, 624, 630,
       641, 648, 659, 678, 697, 699-
       700, 764, 777, 781, **782**, 784-
       785, 796-797, 808, 812, 829-
       830, 859, 889, 891, 896, 898,
       934-935, 963, 968, 981, 988,
       1000, 1002, 1008, 1013, 1021,
       1028, 1030, 1032, 1034, 1037,
       1043, 1059-1061, 1086, 1088-
       1089, 1116, 1128
Pesticide Action Network (North
       American Regional Center, San
       Francisco, California)   405, **784**
Pesticide Education Action
       Project   785
Pesticide residue   21, 29, 181, 270,
       297, 547, 750, 784, **785**, 1000,
       1030, 1063
Pesticides and You   678
PET (polyethylene terephthalate)   974
Pet Theft Act   47
Pet trade   262, 462, 556, 750, 769,
       786

Peterson, Roger Tory   **787**
Petrochemical   145, 211, 234, 257,
       270, 296, 497, 618, 749, 788,
       788, 1020, 1136
Petrography   613
Petroleum   54, 62, 77-78, 174, 191,
       220, 231, 234, 237, 310, 338,
       340-342, 352, 403, 411, 417,
       432, 450, 460, 467, 497, 532-
       533, 606, 618, 630, 657, 696,
       703, 725, 730, 740-741, 753,
       780, 788, **788**, 797, 801, 809,
       812-813, 859, 907, 924, 933,
       955, 970, 1005, 1008, 1025,
       1032, 1058, 1062, 1067, 1086,
       1103, 1124, 1133, 1137
Petroleum spills   1075
Petrology   613
Petromyzon marinus   907
Pezophaps solitarius   272
pH   3-5, 9, 11, 43, 53, 57, 63,
       93, 116, 130, 144, 184, 197,
       218, 233, 235, 237, 319-320,
       393, 412, 427, 505, 508, 512-
       513, 530, 561, 631, 704, 750,
       768, 781, **789**, 791, 808, 814,
       892, 908, 951, 1061, 1087-
       1088, 1115
Phalaropes   662
Phenol   788
Philae, temple at   70
Philco-Ford   988
Philippines   665, 1021
Philosophy Gone Wild   899
Phoca sibirica   583
Phoca vitulina   930
Phoceona sinus   1102
Phocomelia   124, 1015
Phosdrin   754
Phosgene   174
Phosphamidon   784
Phosphates   475, 658, **789**, 791
Phosphorite   658
Phosphorus   9, 11, 16, 18, 116, 178,
       197, 217, 246, 252, 304-305,
       392, 407-408, 492, 559, 561,
       584, 643, 703, 706, 726, 767,
       771, 781, 791, **791**, 809-810,
       852, 864, 883, 937, 940, 951,
       1011, 1061, 1072, 1088, 1090,
       1095, 1115
Phosphorus removal   **791**, 1072
Photic zone   775, **792**
Photochemical reaction   24, 69, 173,
       265, 760, 765, **792**, 988
Photochemical smog   24, 78, 497, 511,
       614, 649, 676, 780, 792, **793**,
       954, 1070
Photodegradable plastic   **793**, 801
Photodegradable plastics   801
Photomethylation   650
Photoperiod   **794**
Photosynthesis   4, 55, 74, 114, 118,
       156, 158, 195, 219, 234, 246,

255, 304, 307, 313, 412, 436, 492, 609, 628, 652, 700, 726, 763, 792, **794**, 797, 851, 855, 864, 881-882, 970, 1018, 1060, 1085-1086

Photovoltaic cell   33, 211, 335, 339, 795, **795**, 969

Phragmites australis   108, 540

Phymatodes nitidus   866

Physeter catadon   1103

Physicians for Social Responsibility (PSR)   150

Physics   649

Phytoplankton   48, 54, 71, 112, 178, 252, 393, 422, 436, 584, 706, 730-731, 775, 792, **796**, 800, 809, 864, 1060, 1145

Phytoremediation   **796**

Phytotoxicity   **797**, 995

Picea abies   427, 1011

Picea glauca   1011

Picea mariana   1011

Picea rubens   427

Picea sitchensis   1014

Picoides borealis   244, 389

Pictured Rocks National Lakeshore   686

Piezometer   1143

Pilot whale   1102

Pimephales promelas   393

Pinatubo, Mount   762

Pinchot, Gifford   221, 360, 429, 607, 632, 668, 696, **798**, 899, 959

Pinguinus impennis   101

Pink pigeon   553

Pinket, Harold   900

Pinnipedia   930

Pinus ponderosa   427

Pioneer species   992

Pipeline dredge   275

Piperonyl butoxide,   1008

Pitchblende   850

Placer mining   **799**

Plague   782

Plains buffalo   99

Plains Indians   126

Plankton   130, 252, 380, 413, 645, 748, 775, 796, **800**, 907, 1102, 1145

Planned Parenthood   1071

Planning for Urban Fishing and Waterfront Recreation   685

Planning for Wildlife in Cities and Suburbs   685

Plant diseases   782

Plant pathology   186, 651, **800**

Plant succession   767

Plasma   **800**

Plasmodium   623

Plasmodium falciparum   623

Plasmodium vivax   623

Plasticizers   801

Plastics   24, 56, 78, 99, 145, 149, 163, 168, 174-175, 219, 232, 257,

358, 449-450, 479, 519, 534, 538, 548, 574, 631, 659, 669-670, 710, 725, 788, 793, **800**, 814, 861, 863, 867, 880, 943, 964, 971, 973-975, 978, 1032, 1069, 1079, 1086, 1135

Plastron   36

Plate tectonics   583, 665, **802**, 1072

Platypuses   841

Playfair, John   893

Playfair's law   893

Playing with Fire   983

Plecotus townsendii ingens   89

Plecotus townsendii virginianus   89

Pleistocene era   655, 961

Plow pan   **804**

Plume   57, 228, 280, 328, 490, 501, **804**, 952, 1100

Plumwood, Val   298

Plutonium   269, 500, 612, 618, 721, 723-724, **804**, 848, 895, 918, 1032, 1138, 1142

Plutonium and Uranium Extraction Plant (PUREX)   500

Pneumatophores   627

Pneumocystis carinii   22

Poachers, elephant   45

Poaching   102, 231, 325, 430, 460, 471, 530, 567, 690, 749, 759, 770, 787, **804**, 885, 925, 1027, 1136

Point Reyes National Seashore   694, 946

Point source   28, 93, 130, 178, 247, 319, 329, 358, 372, 379, 475, 555, 584, 677, 707, 710, 804, **805**, 808, 953, 995, 1086, 1088-1089

Poisons   1133

Poland   296

Poliovirus   1070

Polish Ecological Club   296

Pollination   89, **806**

Pollutant   997

Pollutant standard index (PSI)   26

Pollution   47, 67-68, 107, 130, 143, 150, 158, 161, 170, 178, 188, 191, 198, 202, 204, 206, 209-210, 236, 238-239, 247, 255, 274, 295, 310, 314, 318, 328-329, 343, 346-347, 351, 354, 356-357, 370-371, 378, 386, 389, 394, 408, 411, 426, 435, 438, 440, 450, 452-453, 475, 477, 480, 483-484, 490, 512, 525, 532, 540, 551, 555-556, 583-584, 593, 606, 610, 614, 627, 630, 637, 651, 659, 674, 676, 684, 688-689, 692, 696-697, 704, 708-710, 732-733, 749, 758, 769, 774, 780, 786, 794, 800, 805, **807**, 811, 829-830, 855, 861, 863, 870-871, 880, 892, 917, 925-926, 937,

942, 947, 954, 971, 981, 987-989, 1006, 1017, 1020, 1036-1037, 1043, 1046, 1054, 1056, 1064, 1068, 1070, 1080-1082, 1093, 1116, 1131, 1136, 1142

Pollution control   23, 27-28, 158, 189, 191, 235, 245, 307, 309, 319, 370, 372, 416, 468, 475, 484, 486, 492, 532, 585, 681, 703, 717, 736, 774, **809**, 811, 830, 880, 892, 934, 947, 952, 978, 1020, 1036-1037, 1084-1085, 1142-1143

Pollution control costs and benefits   238, 484, **811**, 1038

Pollution Prevention Act (1990)   372, **811**, 1036

Pollution research   676

Polonium-210   187

Polyaromatic hydrocarbons (PAHs)   1061

Polybrominated biphenyls (PBBs)   **812**

Polychlorinated biphenyls (PCBs)   57, 115, 125, 181, 228, 265, 346, 359, 374, 380, 475, 487, 509, 526, 539, 630, 703, 779, 781, **812**, 930, 968, 988, 1032, 1034, 1062

Polychlorinated dibenzofurans (PCDFs)   182

Polychlorinated dibenzo-p-dioxins (PCDDs)   182

Polycyclic aromatic hydrocarbons (PAHs)   78, 92, 178, 187, 703, 730, 781, **812**, 813

Polycyclic organic compounds   **813**

Polymerase chain reaction   455

Polymers   800, 894

Polypedon   961

Polypeptide   776

Polyphosphates   790

Polystyrene   349, **813**

Polyvinyl chloride (PVC)   181, 269, 793, **814**, 1069

Pond apple   388

Pondweeds   56

Pongo pygmaeus   471

Popocatepetl   651

Population   651

Population biology   109-110, 769, 781, **814**, 815, 825, 877, 982, 1071

Population Bomb, The   320, 816

Population control   624

Population Council (New York, New York)   260, 400, **815**

Population density   492

Population explosion   624

Population Explosion, The   320

Population growth   19, 35, 109, 135, 139, 164, 179, 198, 226, 233, 255, 260, 263, 292, 312, 393, 400-402, 454, 467-468, 492, 502, 515, 535, 546, 608, 610,

613-614, 624, 652, 665, 696, 755-756, 814, **815**, 828, 908, 920, 922, 950, 984, 988, 1020, 1038, 1054, 1084, 1091, 1119, 1128, 1142

Population Institute (Washington, D.C.)   400, 922, **818**, 922, 1071

Population size   665

Population theory   624

Populus   1011

Porpoise   630, 831, 1102

Porter, Eliot Furness   **818**

Portheria dispar   496

Positional goods   **819**

Positive feedback loop   610

Post Consumer Materials (PCMs)   863

Postmodernism and environmental ethics   **819**

Potassium   850

Potassium-40   94, 844

Potential energy   1114

Potomac Electric Power   322

Pough, Dick   698

Poverty   1056

Powell, John Wesley   222, 458, 472, **820**

Power lines   322

Power plants   83, 128, 145, 161, 178, 189, 191, 200, 205, 297, 322, 337, 350, 376, 378, 403, 410, 417, 434, 441, 459, 497, 570, 609, 619, 643, 646, 659, 677, 721, 723, 734, **821**, 828, 881, 1012, 1015-1017, 1019, 1025, 1037, 1086

Practical Guide to Environmental Management   370

Practice of the Wild, The   958

Prairie   250, 255, 282-283, 386-387, 497, 524, 569, 654, **823**, 826, 874, 882, 914, 918, 982, 992, 1114, 1117

Prairie CARE   283

Prairies, role of fire in   882

Precipitation   513, 759, 951

Precycling   309, **824**, 975

Predation   77, 106

Predator   267, 576, 1141

Predator control   222, 394, 573, 674, **824**, 874, 1047, 1118

Predator Project   293

Predator-prey interactions   106, 205, 213, 392, 573, 769, 814, **825**, 1047, 1117, 1127

PrepComs   1055

Prescribed burning   580, 826, **826**

Prescribed natural fire zone   827

Preservation   1110

Preservationists   222

Presidential Scorecard   600

President's Advisory Council on Executive Organization   239

President's Council on Environmental Quality   239

President's Council on Sustainable Development   **828**, 1005, 1054

President's Regulatory Review Council   238

Pressure pans   804

Presumed Innocent: A Report on 69 Cancer-Causing Chemicals Allowed in Our Food   1060

Prevention of significant deterioration (PSD)   93, 190

Pribilof fur seal   930

Price, Melvin   828

Price-Anderson Act (1957)   723, **828**

Primary pollutant   24, **829**

Primary standards   189, 242, 811, **829**, 934

Prime mover   205

Prince William Sound, Alaska   396, 743-744, 780, **831**, 925, 1059, 1067, 1120

Priority pollutant   830, **832**, 1088

Priority Toxic Pollutant list   832

Private nuisance   368

Private property rights   837

Private sector   832

Privatization movement   316, 687, **832**

Procarcinogen   44

Procter & Gamble   270, 479

Program in Social Ecology (University of California, Irvine)   958

Project CLIMAP   655

Project Ocean Search   241

Project on the Predicament of Mankind   610

Project Ranch Hand   14

Project SPECMAP   655

Project WILD   355

Prokaryotic cells   1007

Propane   1071

Propellants   184, 708, **833**

Propylene   788

Protein   381, 894

Proterorhinus marmoratus   907

Protocol on Environmental Protection   48

Prudhoe Bay   832

Pseudomonas   706

Pseudotsuga menziesii   1014

Psittaciformes   769

Psittacosis   770

Pteridium aquilinium   388

Public health   212, 639, 723, 853, 879, 916, 1125

Public Health Service   170, 422, 686, **835**, 1058, 1125

Public interest group   349, 372, 438, **835**

Public land   1, 9, 40, 62, 91, 144, 222, 353, 394, 405, 442, 523, 567, 657, 668, 681, 688, 746, 758, 824, 836, **836**, 861, 1013, 1059, 1096, 1112-1113

Public Land Law Review Commission (PLLRC) Act   405

Public Lands Council (Washington, D.C.)   669, **836**

Public Law Education Institute   369

Public nuisance   368

Public sanitation   886

Public trust   145, **836**

Public Utilities Holding Company Act   403

Public Utilities Regulatory Act   206

Public Utility Regulatory Policy Act (PURPA)   973

Publicly Owned Treatment Works   192, 1089

Pueraria lobata   391

Puffins   463

Puget Sound   586

Pulp and paper manufacturing   775

Pulp and paper mills   182, 270, 775, **837**

Pump-and-treat systems   229, 510

Purple loosestrife (*Lythrum salicaria*)   559, **838**

Purse seines   463

Pygmy chimpanzees   179

Pyrethrum   783

Pyrite Canyon   988

Pyrolysis   341

Q

Quad   144

Quartan malaria   623

Queen Alexandria's birdwing butterfly   231

Quercus   427

Quest of the Historical Jesus, The   923

Quickflow   986

Quinine   623

R

Rabbits in Australia   560, **841**

Race to Save the Planet   467

Race to Save the Planet Environmental Education Activity Guide, The   467

Rachel Carson Council (Chevy Chase, Maryland)   **842**

Rachel Carson Trust for the Living Environment   842

Radar equipment   322

Radiation   561, 671, 676, 701, 727, 844, 847, 850, 852, 876, 1123

Radiation burn   843

Radiation damage   520

Radiation ecology   736

Radiation Effects Research Foundation (RERF)   520, 676

Radiation exposure   43, 83, 91, 97, 125, 163, 170, 177, 187, 274, 422, 448, 453, 520, 561-562, 701, 720, 723-724, 737, **842**, 844-845, 851, 853, 896, 1026, 1053, 1058, 1123, 1127, 1133

Radiation sickness   44, 84, 96, 154,
    163, 172, 177, 520, 561, 609,
    723-724, **844**, 849, 851,
    896, 1123
Radioactive decay   97, 177, 459, 500,
    519, 701, **844**, 845, 847-848,
    852-853
Radioactive dust   177
Radioactive fallout   83, 97, 149, 172,
    176, 448, 609, 701, 724, 844,
    844, 851, 896
Radioactive pollution   97, 172, 177,
    501, 519, 720, 811, 844, **845**,
    849, 851, 853, 896, 919, 928
Radioactive substances   830
Radioactive waste   48, 91, 97, 172,
    176, 458, 487, 500, 507, 547,
    552, 558, 590, 606, 618, 620,
    701, 720, 722-723, 728, 737,
    822, 829, 831, 835, 847, **847**,
    859, 876, 896, 919, 927, 935,
    1026, 1035, 1043, 1055, 1061,
    1078, 1092, 1123, 1138
Radioactive waste management   60, 91,
    172, 177, 501, 519, 552, 558,
    612, 720, 722, 847, **847**, 851-
    852, 1038, 1079
Radioactive Waste Management
    Advisory Committee   1123
Radioactivity   33, 44, 60, 83, 94, 172,
    175, 279, 334, 338, 500, 507,
    519, 552, 560-562, 612, 620,
    637, 642, 701, 701, 720, 829,
    842, 844-845, 850, **850**, 852-
    853, 927, 1026, 1061, 1123,
    1128, 1138
Radiocarbon dating   564, 637, 643,
    655, **851**
Radioisotope   781, **851**, 927
Radiology   640
Radionuclides   830
Radiotherapy   154
Radiotracer   **852**
Radium   852
Radium-226   844
Radon   25, 28, 33, 84, 163, 170, 187,
    278, 352, 370, 542, 843-845,
    852, **852**, 1035
Radon Gas and Indoor Air Quality Act
    of 1986   27
Radon isotope   1138
Radon progeny   853
Ragweed   559
Rails-to-Trails Conservancy
    (Washington, D.C.)   **853**
Rain forest   35, 75, 106, 193, 212,
    225, 241, 300, 350, 415, 480,
    499, 541, 570, 622, 646, 667,
    708, 749, **854**, 857, 870, 950,
    981, 1042, 1047, 1116, 1128
Rain Forest Health Alliance   294
Rain forest wood   571
Rain shadow   197, 662, **857**, 952
Rainbow smelt   585

Rainforest Action Groups   857
Rainforest Action Guide, The   857
Rainforest Action Network (San
    Francisco, California)   35, 571,
    647, **857**
Rainforest Catalogue, The   857
Raker Act   519
Ralph M. Parson Company   716
Ramsar Convention   233
Rana temporaria   2
Ranching, ocean   732
Ranching Task Force   293
Rancho Seco   846
Randolph, Jennings   682
Rangelands   17-18, 58, 625, 757, 824,
    836, bold<858, 981, 1124
Ranger Rick   695
Rangifer tarandus   61, 609, 1124
Raphus cucullatus   101, 272
Rapid Assessment Program
    (RAP)   225
Rapid rail   637
Raprenox (nitrogen scrubbing)   26, **858**
Rare species   120, 126, 154, 330, 333,
    461, 578, 637, 770-771, 856,
    858, 871, 1118, 1120
Rathje, William   450, **858**
Rats   841
Raup, David M.   635
Raven, Peter   396
Rawls, John   548
Raymond, Richard L.   116
*Rays of Hope: The Transition to a Post-
    Petroleum World*   504
Reagan, Ronald   30, 190, 339, 870,
    1009, 1096
Recession   742
Recharge zone   244, 776, 780,
    859, 1067
Reclamation   300, 387, 562, 656-657,
    668, 756, **859**, 981, 990,
    998-999
Reclamation Fund   658
Recombinant DNA research   122
Recreation   9, 146, 153, 163, 203,
    206, 222, 236, 376, 380, 385,
    411, 429, 518-519, 592, 632,
    668, 674, 681-682, 690, 856,
    861, 900, 1059, 1064, 1089,
    1092, 1095, 1102, 1108, 1111-
    1113, 1144
Recumbent vehicles   529
Recyclables   228, 265, 477, **861**, 863,
    884, 971, 975, 978, 1020, 1080
Recycling   55, 62, 78, 88, 91, 99,
    115, 175, 219, 227, 264, 292,
    303, 307, 309, 311, 336, 345,
    352, 357, 372, 409, 424, 435,
    449-450, 479, 484, 487, 545,
    557-558, 610-611, 669, 692,
    704, 710-711, 753, 793, 801,
    824, 862, **862**, 870, 873, 879,
    884, 892, 898, 922, 931, 944,
    952, 971, 973-975, 1020, 1033,

    1036, 1048, 1060, 1067, 1077,
    1079-1080
Recycling Advisory Council
    (RAC)   692
Red bay   388
Red Sea   864
Red tide   31, 412, 630, 653, 707, 732,
    864, 917
Red-cockaded woodpecker   389
Redox reaction   759
Reducing agent   759
Reduction   759
Redwood National Park   866, 946
Redwood Summer   293
Redwoods   38, 293, 332, 425, 718,
    856, **865**, 919, 946, 1014
Reestablishment reintroductions   154
Reflection coefficient   31
Reforestation   259, 919
Refrigerants   764
Refrigerators   184
Refuge waters   575
Refuse Act   192
Refuse-derived fuels (RDF)   114, 634,
    866, 972, 1080
Regan, Tom [Thomas Howard]   46,
    775, **868**, 948
Regulation L-20   1111
Regulatory review   738, **868**
Rehabilitation   **869**
Reilly, William K.   764, 811,
    870, 1056
Reindeer moss   609
Relict species   151, 332-333, **870**, 980
Religion and the environment   **871**
Religious humanism   528
Remediation   76, 229, 685, 872,
    872, 1099
Renew America (Washington,
    D.C.)   **873**
Renewable Natural Resources
    Foundation (Bethesda,
    Maryland)   **874**
Renewable resources   34, 113, 344,
    376, 394, 447, 460, 504, 710,
    863, 874, **874**, 897, 1001, 1003,
    1080, 1097, 1131
Renewable Resources Journal   874
Renewal time   884
Re-odorization   736
Reproduction   109
Reproductive failure   267
Reserve Mining Corporation   64,
    875, 948
Reservoir   146, 206, 249, 259, 321,
    384, 386, 392, 414, 459, 464,
    489, 519, 562, 570, 591, 733,
    740, 744, 859, **876**, 910-911,
    935, 957, 986, 988, 1013, 1063,
    1081, 1083, 1089, 1091, 1093,
    1115, 1129
Residence time   313, 539, **876**, 884
Resilience   283, 749, **876**, 877
Resistance (inertia)   **877**

Resource Conservation and Recovery
　　Act　229, 350, 368, 372-373,
　　449, 505-506, 508-509, 704,
　　868, 872, **877**, 970, 973, 977,
　　985, 1022, 1034, 1036, 1080
Resource recovery　623, **879**, 971, 975
Resource Recovery Act　877
Resources for the Future (Washington,
　　D.C.)　874, **880**
Respiration　10, 43, 118, 137, 156,
　　158, 235, 252, 301, 304, 324,
　　421, 630, 640, 705, 794, **881**,
　　882, 888, 1016, 1086
Respiratory diseases　25, 64, 67, 70,
　　128, 137, 287, 296, 329, 409,
　　881, **881**, 946, 956, 1029, 1137
Restoration ecology　255, 294, 305,
　　386, 493, 625, 747, 860, 869,
　　882, 994, 1118
Restriction enzymes　454
Retention time　11, **884**
Retinoic acid　1015
Reuse　94, 192, 227, 265, 309, 358,
　　545, 669, 824, 879, **884**, 951,
　　971, 975, 1079-1081
Rhinoceros sondaicus　884
Rhinoceros unicornis　884
Rhinoceroses　12, 120, 758, 805,
　　884, 1076
Rhizobium　706
Rhizophora mangle　626
Rhizosphere　796
Rhone-Poulenc　477
Rhynchocephalian reptiles　870
Ribbon weeds　56
Ribosomal RNA (rRNA)　894
Richards, Ellen Henrietta
　　Swallow　**885**
Ricin　1033
Rift Valley fever　212
Rifts　803
Right of Way Act　519
Right whale　1102
Right-to-Act legislation　728, **886**
Right-to-know　639, **888**
Ring of Fire　665, 803
Ringelmann scale　642
Rio Blanco　883
Rio de Janeiro, Brazil　1055
Riparian forested wetlands　1101
Riparian land　385, 465, 757, 876, **888**,
　　889, 1093, 1096, 1102, 1109
Riparian rights　592, **889**, 1081,
　　1093, 1109
*Rise of Urbanization and the Decline of
　　Citizenship, The*　131
Risk analysis　238, 367, 405, 639,
　　889, 1035
Risk assessment　238, 352, 366, 509,
　　640, 890, 1021, 1030
Risk Assessment Process　891
Risk assessment (public health)　**890**
Risk assessors　352, **892**
Risk characterization　891

Risk Management and Risk
　　Reduction　891
River basins　35, 234, 876, **893**
River blindness　**893**
Rivers　53, 56, 414, 612
RNA (ribonucleic acid)　22, 44, 271,
　　454, 457, 561, 652, 671, 705,
　　726, 773, **894**, 1069
Road to Survival　1071
Roadless Area Review and Evaluation
　　(RARE I)　1112
Roast bed　953, 994
Rocks　613
Rockwell-International　988
Rocky Flats nuclear plant (near Denver,
　　CO)　97, 846, 848, **894**
Rocky Mountain Arsenal, Colorado
　　(RMA)　**896**
Rocky Mountain Institute (Old
　　Snowmass, Colorado)　**897**
Rodale Institute (Emmaus,
　　Pennsylvania)　873, **898**
Rodale, J. I.　898
Rodale, Robert　873
Rodenticide　63, 782
Roentgen, Wilhelm K.　162, 1133
Rolston, Holmes　361, 556, **898**
Roman Catholic theology　922
Roman civil law　836
Rongelap Island　96
Rook, Johannes　1046
Roosevelt, Franklin D.　222, 963,
　　1013, 1015
Roosevelt, Theodore　147, 222, 364,
　　429, 472, 573, 668, 695, 798,
　　899, 1118
Rostrhamus sociabilis　389
Rosy periwinkle　101
Roszak, Theodore　**901**
Rotaviruses　1070
Rotenone　1008
Rous, Peyton　162
Rowland, Frank Sherwood　661, 761,
　　902
Royal fern　388
Royal Swedish Academy of
　　Sciences　554
Roys, Thomas Welcome　1103
Rubber　646, 855
Rubella　124
Ruckleshaus, William　**902**
Ruether, Rosemary Radford　298
Ruffes　907
Runoff　18, 59, 62, 67, 94, 116,
　　134, 178, 192, 246, 259, 263,
　　269, 277, 279, 296, 303, 307,
　　318, 350, 368, 384, 387, 408,
　　413-414, 460, 475, 525, 533,
　　538, 545, 562, 570, 575, 584,
　　611, 630, 645, 647, 706, 751,
　　779, 790, 813, 860, 864, 890,
　　903, 909, 911, 949, 962, 989-
　　990, 1032, 1046, 1063, 1081-
　　1082, 1088

Rural Enterprise Reporter　169
Rural Recycling Council　692
Rural Sociology　958
Rural Workers Union　646
Russell, Bertrand　587
Russian Taiga　856

S

Sacculina　769
Sacramento River　173, 298
Safari parks　1143
Safe Drinking Water Act (1974)　40,
　　58, 230, 278, 360, 489, 545, 695,
　　831, 872, **905**, 934, 1059, 1082,
　　1088, 1095
Safe Drinking Water Reauthorization
　　Act　830
Sagan, Carl　780
Sagebrush　758
Sagebrush Rebellion　407, 758, 832,
　　906
Sagittaria lancifolia　388
Sagoff, Mark　444
Sahara Desert　914
Sahel　263, 281, 581, 664, **906**
Sailfish　1006
St. Clair River　474
St. Helena　333
St. Lawrence River　474
St. Lawrence Seaway　63, 686, **907**
Sale, Kirkpatrick　**907**
Saline lake　58
Saline soil　**908**, 910
Salinity　48, 59, 76, 106, 235, 261,
　　271, 382, 386, 512, 626, 663,
　　748, 780, 814, 908, **908**, 913,
　　962-963, 1086, 1094, 1101
Salinization　21, 71, 280, 562, 908,
　　909, 910, 913, 965
Salinization of soils　59, 72, 910, **910**
Salleh, Ariel　298
Salmon　129, 146, 194, 209, 272, 277,
　　396, 411-412, 474, 488, 832,
　　856, **911**, 1006, 1015, 1017,
　　1087, 1091
Salmonella　342, 561
Salt　575, 912, 977
Salt, Henry S.　**912**
Salt marshes　1101
Salt (road)　**912**
Salt water intrusion　**913**
Salter's Duck　1097
Saltwater intrusion　72, 311
Salvelinus namaycush　393, 585
San Andreas Fault　615, 803
San Joaquin Valley　575
Sanborn's long-nosed bat　89
Sand County Almanac, A　607
Sand dune ecology　**914**
Sand dune vegetation　914
Sandhill crane　560
Sandia National Laboratory　848
Sanitary engineering　357, 1125

Sanitary landfill   593
Sanitation   212, 357, **916**, 1126
Santa Barbara oil spill   744
São Paulo, Brazil   943
Sargent, Charles   667
Satellites   643
Saturated soil   1101
Satyagraha   180
Saururus cernuus   388
Savanna   101, 114, 255, 325, 474,
        537, 757, 823, 858, 884, **918**,
        939, 1114
Savannah River Site, South
        Carolina   91, 846, 848, 896**918**
Save Our Streams   567
Save-the-Redwoods League (San
        Francisco, California)   755, 865,
        919
Save the Whales (Washington,
        D.C.)   47, **920**
Sawgrass   387
Saxotoxin   707
Scaphiopus multiplicatus   382
Scarcity   440, **920**
Scarlet fever   212
Scavenger   749, 824, **921**
Scenic Hudson Preservation
        Conference   986
Schaller, George   471
Scheuer, James H.   404
Schindler, D. W.   392
Schinus terebinthifolius   389
Schistosoma haematobium   921
Schistosoma japonicum   921
Schistosoma mansoni   921
Schistosomiasis   71, 562, 773, 782, **921**
Schizothrix calcicola   388
Schneider, Claudine   873
Schultze, Charles   483
Schumacher, Ernst Friedrich   **922**
Schweitzer, Albert   165, 299, 587, **923**
*Science and Religion: A Critical
        Survey*   899
Scientific Certification Systems,
        Inc.   479
Scientific Committee on Problems of
        the Environment   725
Scientists' Institute for Public
        Information (New York, New
        York)   **923**
Sciurus niger avicennia   389
Scott Paper   857
Scott, Sir Peter   566
Scrap iron   623
Scrubbers   26, 94, 191, 200, 206, 416,
        538, 634, 810, 822, 858, 879,
        924, 972, 1012
Scytonema hoffmani   388
Sea Around Us, The   164
Sea birds   463, 744
Sea lions   831
Sea otter (*Enhydra lutris*)   168, 213,
        396, 442, 463, 577, 745, 805,
        831, **925**

Sea pencil   626
Sea Shepherd   926
Sea Shepherd Conservation Society
        (Santa Monica, California)   1,
        256, 277, 298, 380, 481-482,
        488, 710, **925**
Sea sturgeon   525
Sea Turtle Restoration Project   294
Sea turtles   147, 167, 209, 257, 277,
        293, 389, 757, 463, 487, 625,
        645, 688, 694, **926**, 1050
Sea waves   1048
Seabed disposal   233, 237, **927**
Seabed Working Group   927
Seabrook Nuclear Reactor (Seabrook,
        New Hampshire)   239, **928**
Seals and sea lions   42, 48, 112, 130,
        147, 167, 209, 277, 442, 463,
        531, 805, 831, 920, 925-926,
        930, 1060
Sears, Paul B.   **930**
Seasons   663
Seattle, Noah   **931**
Seattle, Washington   1063
Seawater   53
Secchi disk   **932**
Second World   411, **933**, 1020
Secondary recovery technique   **933**
Secondary standards   189, 242, 490,
        811, 829, **934**
Secretary of the Interior   242, 1096
*Secretary of the Interior v.
        California*   204
Secular humanism   528
Secure landfills   593
Sedges   474
Sediment   41, 56, 59, 70, 87, 107, 146,
        178, 188, 192, 245-246, 271,
        275, 286, 307, 318, 320, 377,
        384, 396, 412, 432, 464, 475,
        509, 512, 535, 540, 574-575,
        631, 645, 655, 657, 659, 703,
        706, 729, 813, 860, 876, 925,
        927, 932, 934, **934**, 947, 961,
        968, 988, 990, 1011, 1048, 1063,
        1082, 1087, 1089, 1091, 1096,
        1099, 1102
Sediment plume   276
Sedimentation   18, 29, 277, 565, 583-
        584, 855, 876, **934**, 942, 950,
        1085, 1094
Seed bank   135, 453, **935**
Seed for the Future   37
Seed germination   668
Seepage   54, 71, 249, 280, 297, **935**
Selection cutting   35, 538, **935**
Selenium   511, 575, 1032
Self purification   69
Self-reliance   922
Semotilus margarita   393
Senate Committee on Interior and
        Insular Affairs   150
Sense of place   **936**
Septic systems   949

Septic tank   2, 43, 129, 490, 649, 917,
        937
Sequoia   866
Sequoia National Park   866
Sequoia sempervirens   332, 865, 1014
Sequoiadendron giganteum   865, 1137
Seral stages   992
Serengeti National Park   12, **938**, 1142
Serpentine   704
Sesquioxides   34
Settling basin   565
Seventh Generation   482
Seveso, Italy   270, 508, **939**, 1028
Sevin   94
Sewage   177, 341, 513, 583, 630,
        645, 707, 871, 886, 916, 949,
        1061, 1081
Sewage disposal   474
Sewage treatment   11, 43, 55, 94,
        99, 107, 123, 133, 173, 178,
        183, 193, 234-235, 247, 253,
        297, 343, 386, 410, 413, 461,
        475, 490, 520, 526, 540, 574,
        583, 586, 630, 703, 708, 730,
        733, 759, 791-792, 831, 865,
        884, 890, 893, 909, 937, **940**,
        951, 951, 970, 973, 1003, 1021,
        1030, 1038, 1063, 1072, 1085,
        1092, 1126
Sewage Works Journal   1084
Seychelles brush warbler   553
Shadow pricing   35, 380, 559, **942**
Shaking tables   202
Shale   998
Shanty towns   609, **943**
Sharing Success   873
Shark, mako   1006
Shaw, George Bernard   912
sheep, Dall's   61
sheep, fat-tailed   20
Sheepherding   667
Sheffield, Illinois   846
Shell Oil Company   896
Shepard, Paul   **944**
Shifting cultivation   **945**, 950
Shigella   342
Shiva, Vandana   298
Short-nosed sturgeon   525
Shovellers   575
Showa Denko Corporation   656
Shrimp trawlers   1050
Shroud of Turin   851
Shrub steppe   473
Shumacher, E. F.   755
Shute, Nevil   149
Sial   803
Siberia   856
Siberian Traps   635
Sick Building Syndrome   170, 541,
        882, **945**
Sidenstecker I, Maris   920
Sidenstecker II, Maris   920
Siemens Solar Industries (SSI)   796
Sierra Club Foundation   137

Sierra Club v. Morton   369
Sierra Club v. Ruckelshaus, 1972   190
Sierra Club (San Francisco,
    California)   8, 130, 137, 222,
    369, 379-380, 428, 481-482,
    504, 515, 585, 599, 669, 710,
    714, 719, 856, **946**, 984, 1067,
    1096, 1100, 1109, 1111,
    1124, 1137
Sierra Nevada   657, 662, 697
Sierra (pirate whaling ship)   926
Sierra Student Coalition   1100
Silent Spring   131, 164, 251, 842, 1051
Silent World, The   241
Silicon   34
Silicon Valley   1061
Silt   70, 146, 236, 249, 259, 276, 286,
    584, 934, 947, **947**, 964, 1024,
    1086, 1094, 1115, 1141
Siltation   35, 70, 259, 428, 584, 856,
    934, **947**, 1088, 1116, 1129
Silver   512
Silver Back Humpback Whale
    Sanctuary   168
Silver Bay, Minnesota   64, **947**
Silverbacks   471
Silverberry   706
Sima   803
Simazine   784
Simon, Julian   921
Simulium   893
Singer, Peter   42, 45, 775, 868,
    948, 981
Sinkholes   859, **949**
Sinkholes, anthropogenic   949
Site containment   510
Site index   **949**
Sitka spruce   1014
Skidding   **949**
Skin cancer   763
Slash   193, **949**
Slash and burn agriculture   622, 647,
    945, **950**
Sleeping Bear Dunes National
    Lakeshore   686
Slovakia   296
Sludge   7-8, 43, 133, 174, 192, 204,
    218, 232, 416, 509, 512, 514,
    520, 630, 632, 649-650, 669,
    697, 728, 730, 753, 759, 792,
    810, 812, 928, 937, 940, **950**,
    951, 970, 973, 982, 1085
Sludge treatment and disposal   8, 43,
    942, 950, **951**, 972
Slums   943
Slurry   8, 57, 116, 275, 281, 510, 950,
    952, 972, 1099
Slurry walls   229
*Small Is Beautiful: Economics as if People
    Mattered*   922
Smallmouth bass   525
Smallpox   212
Smectite   189
Smee, Robert   1077

Smelter   68, 145, 284, 379, 513, 558,
    565, 630, 704, 797, 808, **952**,
    995, 1040
Smelting   1020
Smith, Henry A.   931
Smith, Robert Angus   735, **954**
Smog   25-28, 189, 197, 232, 350,
    450, 511, 528, 707, 709, 761,
    793, 829, 882, **954**, 956, 1003,
    1070, 1098
Smoke   23, 25, 35, 78, 92, 137,
    189, 295, 324, 328, 369, 417,
    433, 541, 615, 725, 780, 804,
    821, 829, 882, 954, **956**, 1012,
    1098, 1137
Smoke detectors   843
Smuts, Jan   521
Snail darter (*Percina tanasi*)   243, 331,
    369, **956**, 1014
Snail kite   389
Snake River   515
Snapping turtles   525
Snow leopard   759, **957**
Snowy egret   758
Snowy plovers   662
Snyder, Gary   **958**
Social ecology   131-132, 481, **958**
Social Ecology of Change   958
Social insects   960
Social Investment Forum   1067
Society of American Foresters
    (Bethesda, Maryland)   799, **959**
Society for Animal Protective
    Legislation (SAPL)   47
Society for Conservation Biology
    (Seattle, Washington)   **959**
Society for Ecological Restoration   882
Sociobiology   **960**
Sociobiology: The New Synthesis   960
Sodium chloride   1032
Sodium hypochlorite   182
Soil   5, 7, 9-10, 18, 20-21, 34-35,
    43, 47, 49, 53-54, 62, 67, 71,
    91, 99, 103, 106, 114-115, 123,
    129, 144, 146, 149, 176, 188-
    189, 197-198, 212, 214, 219,
    223, 226, 228, 230, 249, 255,
    259-260, 263, 265, 269, 282,
    284, 286, 295, 307, 312, 318-
    320, 352, 358, 366, 377, 382,
    384, 387, 394, 408-409, 415,
    424, 426, 440, 443, 449, 464-
    465, 474, 484, 486, 489-490,
    495, 498, 501, 509, 511-512,
    524-525, 533, 535, 537-538,
    545, 560-562, 569-570, 575,
    589, 591-592, 596, 608-609,
    620, 626, 633, 643, 647, 649-
    650, 667-668, 672, 696, 702,
    704, 706, 708, 727, 745, 749,
    751, 753, 756, 771, 774-776,
    780-781, 795, 797, 804, 808,
    810, 813-814, 823, 838, 844,
    852, 854, 860, 866, 872, 876,

888, 891-893, 900, 903, 906,
    908-910, 918, 934-935, 945,
    947, 949-950, **961**, 963-964,
    967, 970-971, 981, 989-990,
    995, 1000, 1002, 1007, 1015,
    1021, 1027-1028, 1032, 1046-
    1047, 1067-1068, 1085, 1093,
    1095, 1100, 1114, 1116, 1130,
    1135, 1143
Soil acidification   996
Soil Bank   963
Soil body   961
Soil compaction   10, 189, 215, 804,
    866, 945, 962, **962**, 964, 989
Soil conservation   18, 37, 91, 189, 423,
    858, 911, 947, 962, **962**-965,
    1046, 1095
Soil Conservation Act   963
Soil Conservation and Domestic
    Allotment Act   963
Soil Conservation Service   91, 222,
    284, 287, 580, 962, **963**, 965,
    989, 1057
Soil consistency   189, 947, **964**
Soil eluviation   281, 287, 385, 911,
    964, 1095, 1102
Soil erosion   442, 570, 1091
Soil Erosion Service   962-963
Soil fertility   35, 114, 707, 1002,
    1028, 1046
Soil illuviation   911, **964**
Soil liner   **964**
Soil loss tolerance   **964**, 989
Soil organic matter   114, 226, 385,
    668, 945, 963, **964**, 1115
Soil profile   313, 495, 544, 561, 780,
    909, 911, 947, 961, **964**,
    965, 1143
Soil salinization   76, 554
Soil science   544
Soil sealants   174
Soil survey   962-963, **964**
Soil texture   285, 385, 495, 497, 561,
    668, 964-965, **966**
Soil washing/flushing   510
Soil and Water Conservation Society
    (Ankeny, Iowa)   37, 874, 963,
    966
Soil, Water and Related Resources
    Act   385
Solanine   1033
Solar architecture   1001
Solar constant cycle   **966**
Solar detoxification   **967**
Solar energy   33, 60, 118, 195, 197,
    211, 262, 281, 302, 304, 307,
    322, 335, 342, 387, 483, 486,
    503-504, 615, 619, 661, 711,
    733, 742, 753, 772, 795, 823,
    874, 922, 967, **968**, 970, 988,
    1001, 1018, 1048, 1097, 1121
Solar Energy Coordination and
    Management Project   970

Solar Energy Information Data
Bank   970
Solar Energy Research, Development
and Demonstration Act
(1974)   **970**
Solar Energy Research Institute   504,
519, 968, 970
Solar Maximum (Solar Max)
Mission   966
Solar Research, Development, and
Demonstration Act   504
Solid waste   18, 43, 49, 63, 99, 121,
175, 261, 270, 342, 349, 354,
357, 410, 416, 479, 484, 506,
508, 519, 538, 545, 558, 592,
623, 630, 634, 644, 670, 704,
731, 752, 788, 793, 801, 810,
813, 824, 847, 852, 859, 862-
863, 873, 877, 879, 890, 952,
970, 972-975, 1020, 1028, 1033,
1044, 1055, 1059, 1077, 1080-
1081, 1135
Solid Waste Disposal Act   877
Solid waste incineration   520, 540,
558, 634, 670, 862, 880, 972,
972, 976, 1020, 1080
Solid waste landfilling   972, **973**
Solid waste management   670, 884
Solid waste recycling and
recovery   520, 558, 670, 864,
972, **974**, 1020, 1038
Solid waste volume reduction   520,
540, 558, 864, 880, 972, **975**,
1020, 1038
Solidification and stabilization (S/S)
methods   976
Solidification of hazardous
materials   507, 510, **976**
Sonic boom   **977**
Soot   1070
Sorcerer's Apprentice   225
Sorption   8, 103, 266, 928, 968, 976,
978
Source reduction   971
Source separation   863, 972, 975,
978, 1080
South   375, 609, 611, **979**
South America   854
South Pole   48
Southern California Edison   322
Southern deepwater swamps   1101
Spaceship Earth   502, **979**
Spadefoot toad   382
Spatterdock   388
Special use permit   **980**
Species   17, 31-32, 47-48, 62, 87, 89,
100, 104, 106-108, 112, 115,
117, 119, 135, 146, 154, 164,
178, 185-186, 197, 205-206,
217, 221-222, 231, 234-235,
242-243, 251, 254-257, 267,
272, 276-277, 295, 299, 306,
318-319, 330, 332, 344, 351,
370, 376-378, 385, 388-389,

395, 402, 411-412, 428, 442-
446, 454, 460, 462, 464-465,
474, 480, 487, 492, 496-497,
516, 519, 522, 525, 537-538,
541, 545, 551-552, 566, 575,
579, 583, 585-586, 609, 613,
622, 624-626, 645, 647, 662,
672, 677, 682, 687, 695, 697-
698, 704, 706, 717, 739, 746,
748, 751, 757-758, 771, 773,
775, 782, 786, 794, 802, 805,
814-815, 824-825, 838, 841,
854, 858, 864-865, 874, 877,
884, 888, 892-893, 898, 907-
908, 918, 927, 930, 935, 938,
948, 950, 953, 956, **980**, 981-
982, 995, 999, 1003, 1006-1007,
1014-1015, 1022, 1029, 1039,
1042, 1047, 1050, 1054, 1084,
1087, 1101-1102, 1112, 1115,
1117-1118, 1124, 1126, 1129-
1131, 1137, 1141-1143
Speciesism   42, 46, 152, 361, 697, 775,
948, **981**
Spectrometry   642
Spent nuclear fuel   737
Sperm whale   1103
Spermicides   399
Speyeria zerene hippolyta   750
Sphenodon   870
Spikerush   388
Spiny water flea   907
Spoil   **981**, 997
Spoil banks   981
Spontaneous combustion   208
Spotted owl   *See* Northern spotted owl
Spring Valley Water Company   518
Spruce budworm   782
Squamous-cell skin cancer   163
Sri Lankan elephants   325
Stability   308, 313, **982**
Stack emissions   297, 416-417, 540,
982
Stakeholder analysis   **983**
Standard City Planning Enabling
Act   592
Standard State Zoning Act   592
Stapp, William   354
Starvation   267
State Emergency Response
Commission   327
State of the Environment
Reporting   345
State Implementation Plans
(SIPs)   190, 677
State of the States   873
State of the World   1132
Staten Island, New York   341
Static aerated compost pile
composting   670
Steady-State Economics   984
Steady-state economy   352, **983**
Steam soak method   934
Stegner, Wallace   608, 821, **984**

Stellar sea lion   930
Steller's sea cow   101
Stenella longirostris   272
Steroid hormone   270
Stevens, Christine   47
Stevenson, Adlai   979
Stewardship   361, 588, 773
Stilts   575
Stizostedion vitreum glaucum   585
Stochastic change   **985**
Stochastic model   660
Stomata   387
Stone, Christopher   46
Storage and transport of hazardous
material   174, 507, 558, 593,
607, 617, 977, **985**, 989, 1079
Storage tank   606
Storm King Mountain, New York   **986**
Storm runoff   108, 193, 540, 703, 903,
986, **986**, 1063, 1088
Storm sewer   **986**, 1063
Stormflow   986
Strahler, Arthur   893
Strategic Defense Initiative   1053
Strategic minerals   688, **986**
Stratification   252, 584, **987**, 988
Stratosphere   72, 175, 183-184, 350,
532, 579, 613, 642, 661, 665,
688, 760-761, **987**, 1072
Stratospheric clouds   764
Stratospheric fallout   845
Stratton Commission   203
Stream channelization   **988**
Stream order   893
Strentzel, Louise   667
Stringfellow Acid Pits (Glen Avon,
California)   508, 617, **988**
Stringfellow, James   988
Strip cropping   423
Strip mining   1, 3, 107, 201, 256,
297, 380, 424, 442, 519, 657,
662, 695, 753, 859, 869, 981,
989, 1082
Striped bass   178
Strip-farming   963, **989**, 1002
Strix occidentalis caurina   243, 717,
1125, 1131
Stroke   843
Strong, Maurice   289, 1055
Strontium   727
Strontium 90   94, 501, 560, 609, 845,
991
Student Environmental Action
Coalition (Chapel Hill, North
Carolina)   **991**
Studies in the Sierra   667
Styrofoam   764
Subacute toxic effects   1033
Subbituminous coal   199
Subsidence   615, 652, 860, 909, **991**
Subsidy   828
Subsistence whaling   1103
Subsoil   189, 280, 524, 652, 860, 964,
992, 1031

Substitute natural gas 201
Suburbs 579, 1064
Succession 103-104, 197, 213, 273, 308, 503, 746, 915, 935, 981, **992**, 1110
Sucralose 170
Sudbury, Ontario 284, 348, 513, 704, 806, 953, **994**
Sulfate particles **995**
Sulfite 324
Sulfur 767, 995
Sulfur aerosols 764
Sulfur cycle 282, 652, **996**
Sulfur dioxide 5, 23, 26-27, 93, 184, 189-191, 201, 245, 281, 284, 296, 300, 334, 347, 370, 378, 416-417, 426, 433, 460, 497, 511, 538, 609, 634-635, 652, 665, 676, 709, 762, 788, 806, 808, 821, 830, 870, 881, 924, 952, 954, 972, 995-996, **996**, 1012, 1037, 1072, 1098, 1100, 1136, 1143
Sulfuric acid 3, 107, 284
Sumatra 749
Sumatran elephants 325
Summary jury trial 351
Summit of the Years, The 147
Sunkist Growers 988
Sunspot 967
Superconductivity **996**
Superfund Amendments and Reauthorization Act (SARA) (1986) 13, 141, 220, 228, 327, 346, 357, 372, 506, 606, 684, 692, 811, 872, 877, **997**, 1032, 1034, 1036, 1059, 1124
Superior National Forest 1111
Superstack 953
Supertanker 743
Supreme Court 829
Surface corrosion 237
Surface mining 107, 201, 284, 434, 657, 756, 799, 869, 991, **997**
Surface Mining Control and Reclamation Act (1977) 5, 340, 738, 859, 869, 981, **999**
Surfactant 265, 933
Surgical sterilization 400
Survivorship **999**
Survivorship curve 1000
Suspended solid 233, 257, 492, 514, 799, 937, 940, **1000**, 1088
Sustainable agriculture 17, 20-21, 92, 114-115, 169, 226, 311, 409, 448, 468, 547, 587-589, 751, 755, 860, 898, 922, 963, 966, 984, **1000**, 1002, 1055, 1071, 1096
Sustainable architecture **1000**
Sustainable biosphere 197, 311, 445, 589, **1002**, 1130
Sustainable Biosphere Initiative 527, 1003

Sustainable development 76, 119, 143, 164, 223, 289, 294, 297, 300, 304, 311, 344, 367, 466-467, 479, 526, 554, 588-589, 607, 609, 611, 613, 625, 645, 647, 657, 682, 710, 713, 755, 814, 828, 922, 984, 1003, **1004**, 1055, 1064, 1067, 1071, 1096, 1128, 1130
Sustainable forestry **1005**
Sustainable society 696
Sustainable use 624
Sustained yield 406, 647, 682, 1104
Swamp bay 388
Swidden agriculture 945
Swordfish 277, **1006**
Sybille Wildlife Research Institute 127
Symbiosis 77, 105, 205, 209, 272, 307, 443, 545, 610, 672, 749, **1007**, 1133
Symbiote 209
Sympatric species 980
Syndets 265
Synecology 77
Synergism 277, **1008**
Synfuels 1008
Syngas 113
Synthetic fuels 34, 114, 788, **1008**
Synthetic gas 113
Synthetic natural gas (SNG) 1008
System Dynamics model 610
Systemic **1009**

T

Taconite 64, 875
Tadpoles 438
Taft, William Howard 657
Tahoe Regional Planning Agency 585
Taiga 193, 221, **1011**
Tailings 64, 145, 565, 657, 756, 947, 1011, **1011**
Tailings pond 67, 434, 948, **1011**
Tailings, uranium 846
Takings **1011**
Tall stacks 26, 538, 924, **1012**, 1137
Tamarin, golden lion 155
Tamaulipas, Mexico 926
Tamiasciurus douglasii 866
Tanning booths 1053
Taoism 712
Tapchan 1097
Taraxacum officinale 748
Target species 185, 463, **1013**
Task Force on Land Use and Urban Growth 870
Taxol 856
Taylor, Frank B. 802
Taylor Grazing Act (1934) 144, 405, 758, **1013**
Taylor, Paul 361
TCDD 269

Technetium-99 850
Technical Advisory Committee (TAC) 226
Technology 1106
Technology-based standards 1088
Television 322
Tellico Dam 243, 331, 956, **1013**, 1090
Tellurium 511
Temperate rain forest 193, 221, 672, 854, **1014**, 1047
Ten Thousand Islands 387
Tennessee Valley Authority 222, 284, 331, 893, 956, 1013, **1015**, 1038, 1125
Tennessee Valley Authority v. Hill 369
Tennessee Walking Horses 47
Teratogen 124, 171, 175, 440, 508, 648, 651, 655, **1015**, 1033
Terracing 989, 1002, **1015**
Territoriality 106, **1015**
Tertian malaria 623
Tertiary recovery techniques 933
Tethys Sea 645
Tetrachlorodibenzo-p-dioxin 269
Tetrachloroethane 181
Tetrachloroethylene 181
Tetraethyl lead 79, 451, **1016**
Texaco 857
Texas Railroad Commission 339
Thalidomide 124, 1015
Thallium 648
Thames River 883
Thea sinensis 135
Theodore Roosevelt: The Making of a Conservationist 899
Therapeutic index (TI) 98
Thermal desorption 229, 510
Thermal plume **1016**, 1017
Thermal pollution 319, 335, 341, 417, 1016, **1016**, 1019, 1089, 1092
Thermal radiation 1077
Thermal stratification (water) 436, 734, **1018**
Thermodynamics, Laws of **1018**
Thermometers 642
Thermonuclear reactions 720
Thermoplastic polymer 800
Thermoplastics **1020**
Thermosetting polymers 800, **1020**
Thermosphere 72
Thin layer chromatography (TLC) 185
Think About Land 922
Thiobacillus ferrooxidans 107
Third World 27, 166, 211, 247, 294, 401, 411, 453, 486-487, 556, 581, 609, 622, 624, 664, 786, 855, 927, 933, 943, 1020, **1020**, 1128
Third World pollution 609, **1020**
Thirst for Land 1071
Thomas, Lee M. 870, 903, **1021**

Thoreau, Henry David   146, 180, 345,
    353, 699, 712, 912, 936,
    1022, 1109
Thorium   850
Thousand Mile Walk to the Gulf, A   667
Three Gorges Dam (China)   249, 876,
    1024, 1091
Three Mile Island Nuclear Reactor
    (Harrisburg, Pennsylvania)   94,
    150, 177, 372, 720, 722-723,
    822, 846, 930, **1025**, 1121
Threshold dose   640, 844, **1026**, 1143
Threshold Limit Value
    (TLV)   639, 891
Thrush (yeast infection)   22
Thuja plicata   1014
Thunderstorm   531
Thyroxine   439
Tidal power   33, 284, 823, **1026**
Tidal waves   1048
Tigers (*Panthera tigris*)   120, 329, 758,
    1027
Tile drainage   576
Till   464
Tillage pans   804
Tilth   47, 226, 282, 287, 962, **1027**
Timber harvesting   682
Timber industry   425, 718
Timberline   **1028**
Times Beach, Missouri   16, 174, 270,
    372, **1028**
Tin   512
Tinnitus   709
Tipping fee   670, **1028**, 1044
Tissue plasminogen activator   122
Title III   327
T-lymphocytes   22
Tobacco   92, 149, 162, 170, 187, 507,
    541, 812-813, 956, **1028**
Toilets   271, 281, 937, 946, **1029**,
    1082-1083
Tokamak reactor   721
Tolerance level   98, 314, **1030**
Tolerance limits (TL)   98
Tolstoy, Leo   180
Toluene   79, 1071, 1133
Tongass National Forest   856
Topical   579
Topography   28, 58, 197, 285, 307,
    313, 366, 385, 408, 464, 537,
    666, 751, 804, 859, 888, 893,
    938, 961, 964, 992, **1030**, 1115
Topping cycle   205
Topsoil   18, 37, 259, 263, 281, 284,
    286, 401, 428, 569, 587, 657,
    668, 750, 756, 860, 906, 962,
    989-990, **1031**, 1082, 1098
Topsoil erosion   548
Tornado and cyclone   531-532, **1031**
Torrey Canyon   744, **1031**
Total fertility rate   109
Total suspended solids (TSS)   1000
Tourism   317
Toxaphene   830, 838, **1032**

Toxic ash   334
Toxic chemicals   807
Toxic Chemicals Release Inventory
    (EPA)   327, 379, **1032**
Toxic substance   11, 13, 69, 96, 108,
    163, 170, 175, 186, 188, 192,
    221, 235, 265, 267, 270, 274,
    277, 280, 297, 318, 328, 362,
    370, 380, 413, 426, 439, 475,
    487, 503, 538, 558, 596, 606,
    609, 612, 617, 630, 643, 659,
    679, 697, 781, 812, 831, 976,
    986, 997, 1016, 1030, **1032**,
    1034, 1036, 1056, 1068,
    1087, 1133
Toxic Substances Control Act
    (1976)   163, 328, 368, 506, 509,
    539, 607, 889, 986, 997,
    1034, 1036
*Toxic Truth and Consequences: The
    Magnitude of and the Problems
    Resulting from America's Use of
    Toxic Chemicals*   1060
Toxic use reduction   1038
Toxic use reduction legislation   96,
    779, 983, 986, 997, 1080
Toxic waste   557, 1054
Toxic-waste dumping   557
Toxicity Characteristic Leaching
    Procedure (TCLP)   977
Toxicology   14
Toxics Characteristic Leaching
    Procedure   230
Toxics use reduction legislation   328,
    886, **1036**
Toxins   1032, **1037**
Toyon   706
Trace element/micronutrient   60, 409,
    492, 511, 575, 726, 1032, **1037**
Trade in pollution permits   191, 353,
    395, **1037**
Traffic congestion   528, 637
Traffic and Motor Vehicle Safety
    Act   673
Traffic pans   804
Tragedy of the Commons   49, 310,
    353, 394, 435, 588, **1038**
Trail Smelter arbitration   284, **1040**
Trailblazer   854
Train, Russell E.   **1040**
Trans-Alaska pipeline   29, **1041**, 1041
Trans-Amazonian highway   **1042**
Transboundary pollution   **1043**
Transfer RNAs (tRNA)   894
Transfer station   864, 1028, **1044**
Transmissible spongiform
    encephalopathies (TSEs)   621
Transmission lines   **1044**
Transmission lines, health
    threats   1045
Transpiration   160, 854, **1046**, 1047,
    1063, 1081
Transportation   506, 528, 637
Transuranic waste   847

Trapper's Lake   1111
Trapping   46
Treatment, storage and disposal
    facilities (TSDFs)   878
Treaty of Rome   387
Tree mining   222
Tree spiking   293
Trefethen, James B.   573
Triassic period   635
Tribal peoples   540
Tributyltin   178
Trichechus manatus   101
Trichloroethane   181
Trichloroethylene   181, 830
Triethylenemelamine   671
Trihalomethanes   182, 280, 830,
    1046, 1094
Tripeptide   776
Triticum aestivum   516
Tritium   720, 727, 919
Trombe wall   772
Trophic level   106, 111, 267, 389, 420,
    608, 647, 718, 1024, **1046**
Tropical cyclone   531
Tropical rain forest   34, 89, 100, 112,
    114, 118-119, 254, 256, 273,
    292-295, 305, 307, 317, 325,
    329, 333, 350, 377, 395, 466-
    467, 483-484, 537, 548, 553,
    578, 609, 623, 637, 646, 672,
    750, 854, 857, 950, 982, 993,
    1015, 1027, **1047**, 1086, 1116,
    1129, 1131
Tropopause   661, 987, **1048**
Troposphere   72-73, 661, 1048, **1048**
Tropospheric fallout   845
Truman, Harry S.   96, 701, 880
Truth about Where You Live, The   374
Trypanosomiasis   782
Tsuga heterophylla   1014
Tsunamis   414, **1048**
Tsuruga nuclear power plant   846
Tsvett, Mikhail   185
Tubenose gobies   907
Tuberculosis   212
Tubificid worms   540
Tufa towers   662
Tulsa, Oklahoma   1063
Tumerogen   1033
Tumors   1033
Tuna   629, 1006
Tuna boycotts   273
Tuna fishery and dolphin
    mortality   294
Tundra   30, 61, 114, 118, 305, 308,
    474, 488, 540, 609, 674, 808,
    858, 957, 982, 993, **1050**,
    1060, 1116
Tuolumne River   518
Turbidity   830
Turbines   77
Turgios   943
Turkey   632
Turner's syndrome   124

Turnover time   **1050**
Tursiops truncatus   272
Turtle   1050
Turtle excluder device (TED)   148, 168, 463, 689, 926, **1050**
Turtle Island   958
Tuttle, Merlin   89
TVA v. Hill   331
Twain, Mark   1097
Twelve Seasons, The   579
Two Forks Dam   870
2,4-D   14, 268, 386, 516, 546, 781, 784, 830, **1051**, 1076
2,4,5-T   14, 182, 268, 516, 781, 784, 830, 1051, **1051**, 1076
2,4,5-trichlorophenol (2,4,5-TCP)   182, 940
2,3,7,8-tetrachlorodibenzo-p-dioxin (2,3,7,8-TCDD)   182, 940
Typhoid fever   782
Typhoon   531
Typhus   212

U

Udall, Morris   30
Ukraine   296
Ultra-low-flush toilet   1083
Ultrasound   16
Ultraviolet light   843
Ultraviolet radiation   54, 58, 72, 76, 163, 175, 184, 197, 266-267, 323, 350, 436, 532, 549, 642, 661, 664, 671, 760, 793, 810, 843, 981, 1003, 1048, **1053**
Ultraviolet (UV) radiation   195
Ultraviolet-B   762
Under the Apple Trees   147
Underwood, Joanna   544
Underwriters Laboratory (UL)   483
Union Carbide   94, 174, 727, 1020
Union of Concerned Scientists (Cambridge, Massachusetts)   **1053**
United Kingdom Clean Air Act (1956)   26, 955
United Nations   119
United Nations Commission on Sustainable Development   **1054**
United Nations Conference on Environment and Development   527, 1055
United Nations Conference on the Human Environment (1972) Stockholm, Sweden   354, 552, 710, 1005, **1054**
United Nations Development Program (UNDP)   226
United Nations Division for Sustainable Development   **1055**
United Nations Earth Summit (1992) Rio de Janeiro, Brazil   121, 123, 289, 294, 550, 555, 563, 710,

756, 828, 856, 979, 1005, 1021, 1040, **1055**, 1057, 1130
United Nations Educational, Scientific and Cultural Organization (UNESCO)   70, 119, 624, 1130
United Nations Environment Programme   121, 223, 231, 295, 375, 465, 499, 545, 549, 556-557, 645, 756, 1021, 1054-1055, **1056**, 1130-1131
United Nations Food and Agriculture Organization   855
U.S. Agency for International Development   855
U.S. Army Corps of Engineers   713
U.S. Birdwatch   553
U.S. Coast and Geodetic Survey   688
U.S. Department of Agriculture   13, 19, 21, 44, 50, 91, 110, 139, 163, 367, 371, 373, 385, 423-424, 453, 496, 622, 752, 770, 786, 798, 859, 947, 962-963, 965, 989, **1057**, 1058, 1109
U.S. Department of Commerce   239, 331, 688
U.S. Department of Defense   836
U.S. Department of Energy   60, 91, 170, 201, 339, 341-342, 407, 442, 500, 550, 727, 737, 811, 829, 846, 848, 872, 919, 968, 970, **1058**, 1078, 1138
U.S. Department of Health and Human Services   13, 187, 373, 598, 686, 835, **1058**
U.S. Department of Health, Education, and Welfare (HEW)   189
U.S. Department of the Interior   59, 61, 89, 109, 126, 144-145, 203, 243, 330, 373, 407, 411, 429, 434, 443, 462, 465, 472, 518-519, 658, 669, 687, 689-690, 695, 755, 758, 770, 774, 798, 824, 962-963, 999 **1059**, 1096, 1108-1109
U.S. Department of Labor   728
U.S. Department of State   145
U.S. Department of Transportation   369, 506, 985
U.S. Engineering Manpower Commission   357
U.S. Office of Technology Assessment   49
U.S. Patent Office   1057
U.S. Public Interest Research Group (PIRG) (Washington, D.C.)673, 714, **1059**
U.S. Steel   239
United States Synthetic Fuels Corporation   1009
Universal Soil Loss Equation (USLE)   385
University of California   661
Unsafe at Any Speed   673
Unsaturated zone   776

Unsettling of America, The   92
Upwellings   253, 628, 658, 707, 731, **1060**
Uranium   33, 59, 83, 106, 149, 171, 176, 321, 334, 338, 341-342, 416, 434, 458-459, 551, 612, 648, 658, 701, 721, 724, 727, 737, 804, 808, 843-844, 847, 850, 852-853, 1032, **1060**, 1123, 1138
Uranium mill tailings   847
Uranium Mill Tailings Radiation Control Act (1978)   848
Uranium-235   520, 1061
Urban contamination   **1061**
Urban design and planning   **1062**
Urban factor   163
Urban Habitat Program   294
Urban heat island   1016, 1063, **1063**
Urban runoff   54, 193, 275, 277, 297, 414, 559, 707, **1063**
Urban sprawl   37, 141, 297, 478, 589, 638, 874, **1064**
Urban Wetlands for Stormwater Control and Wildlife Enhancement   685
Urban Wildlife Manager's Notebook   685
Urban Wildlife News   685
Urban Wildlife Research Center   685
Urbanization   1063
U-Regulations   1111
Ursus americanus   61
Ursus americanus floridanus   389
Ursus arctos   61, 488
Ursus maritimus   61
Use Book   668
Utilitarianism   45, 238, 360, 691, 948, **1065**
Utility   190, 206
Utricularia   388
Uzbekistan   58

V

Vaccination   652
Vacuum extraction   510
Vacuum extraction system   1099
Vadose zone   10, 489, 510, 776, 780, **1067**, 1099, 1143
Vaginal diaphragm   399.
Valdez Principles   381, 504, **1067**
Van de Kamp, John   585
Vanadium   512
Vapor extraction   229, 510
Vapor recovery system   117, 123, 510, **1067**
Varta   482
Vascular plant   101, 792, **1068**
Vegan   1068, **1068**
Vegetarianism   361, 449, 699, 912, 948, 1065, 1068, **1068**
Vermont   632
Vermont Yankee power plant   846

Vibrio cholerae   184, 212
Victims' compensation   **1068**
Victoriornis imperialis   272
Video display terminal   322
Videotape Referral Service (VRS)   923
Viet Nam War   269, 1051, 1075
Vinyl chloride   163, 175, 181, 671, 679, 830, 968, 1034, **1069**
Viola adunca   750
Violet, western blue   750
Viral diseases   652
Virginia big-eared bat   89
Virunga Volcanoes National Park   471
Virus   54, 69, 162, 182, 192, 212, 383, 391, 411, 455, 542, 726, 748, 768, 773, 784, 800, 810, 937, 946, 1015, **1069**
Visibility   26, 60, 287, 350, 511, 954, **1070**
Vistula River   296
Vitamin A   1015
Vitamins   561
Vogt, William   755, **1071**
Voice of the Desert, The   579
Volatile organic compound   24, 43, 79, 103, 123, 158, 229, 245, 350, 433, 542, 606, 788, 946, 1034, **1071**, 1094
Volatile organic compounds (VOCs)   793, 988
Volcano   5, 79, 146, 158, 170, 197, 235, 319, 321, 328, 370, 379, 382, 458, 503, 512, 579, 637, 651, 665, 725, 803, 808, 889-890, 988, 992, 996, **1071**
Volcano Hazards Program   665
Vollenweider, Richard   **1072**
Vonnegut, Bernard   1098

W

W agent   1070
Wairakei, New Zealand   459
Wake-Robin   147
Wallace, Alfred Russell   389
Walleye   585
Wal-Mart   482
Walt Disney Enterprises   369
Wankel engines   77
War, environmental effects of   520, 675, **1075**
War on Waste   1079
Ward, Barbara   979
Warfarin   124
Warren, Karren   298
Waste   903
Waste disposal   557
Waste exchange   **1077**
Waste haulers   557
Waste heat   1063
Waste Isolation Pilot Plan (WIPP)   849, 1058, **1078**

Waste management   2, 8, 23, 63, 87, 173, 204, 229, 237, 257, 265, 350, 373, 393, 449, 458, 466, 491, 514, 520, 538, 544, 558, 586, 623, 634, 640, 644, 657, 670, 693, 704, 759, 778, 824, 862, 864, 877, 942, 951, 952, 971-972, 975, 982, 985, 1028, 1037-1038, 1077, **1079**, 1080, 1135
Waste ore   106
Waste reclamation   1001
Waste reduction   78, 265, 309, 311, 328, 435, 479, 558, 670, 862, 864, 879, 884, 978, 1036, 1038, **1080**
Waste stream   99, 227, 358, 545, 669, 861-862, 884, 908, 975, 1028, 1044, 1079-1080, **1081**
Waste treatment   43
Wastestream   514
Waste-to-energy   880
Wastewater   2, 7, 10, 34, 43, 94, 97-98, 133, 173, 178, 182, 192, 234, 247, 257, 269-270, 296, 319, 357, 372, 379, 413, 416, 424, 492, 513, 526, 540, 559, 565, 576, 659, 669, 703, 707, 733, 752, 759-761, 792, 810, 909, 916, 937, 940, 950-951, 1000, 1029, 1070, **1081**, 1084-1085, 1089, 1125
Wastewater treatment   10, 938, 1001
Watarase River   67
Water allocation   468, 663, 889, **1081**
Water Bank Program   963
Water chestnut   525
Water conservation   62, 94, 202, 226, 281, 387, 544, 751, 810, 889, 937, 963, 1071, **1082**, 1084, 1091, 1096, 1126
Water, Earth, and Man   893
Water Environment Curriculum, The   1084
Water Environment Federation (Alexandria, Virginia)   **1084**
Water Environment Research Foundation   1084
Water fern   706
Water fleas   186
Water hyacinth (*Eichhornia crassipes*)   266, 559, **1084**
Water hyssop   388
Water infiltration   668
Water logging   562
Water management   1082
Water milfoils   56
Water pollution   34-35, 54, 68, 94, 161, 183, 191, 204, 222, 234, 238-239, 247, 255-257, 280, 296, 310, 317, 319, 351, 354, 368, 373, 393, 407, 413, 460, 475, 480, 484, 512, 535, 540,

544, 565, 567, 576, 585-586, 643, 645, 648, 656, 692, 710, 767, 774, 791, 810-811, 864, 874, 891, 907, 938, 954, 995, 1021, 1038, 1041, 1062, 1068, 1072, **1085**, 1089, 1091
Water Pollution Control Act   191
Water Pollution Control Amendments of 1972, Federal   69
Water Pollution Control Federation   1084
Water Pollution Prevention and Control Act   193
Water quality   4, 31, 56, 58, 70-71, 98, 129, 183, 192, 194, 234, 247-249, 296, 319, 355, 372, 377-378, 407, 413, 428, 434, 465, 475, 489-491, 560, 567, 586, 630, 642, 730, 774, 830, 865, 883, 906, 909, 911, 917, 932, 934-935, 966, 1003, 1008, 1054, 1063, 1082, 1084-1085, **1087**, 1090, 1092-1093, 1102, 1129-1130
Water Quality Act   191-192
Water quality standards   58, 94, 129, 131, 183, 191, 280, 490-491, 774, 811, 830, 832, 906, 909, 1008, 1046, 1082, 1084, 1088, **1088**, 1126, 1142-1143
Water Quality 2000   1084
Water reclamation   **1089**
Water resources   63, 72, 221, 263, 280-281, 349, 535, 555, 615, 663, 717, 889, 966, 1039, **1091**, 1093, 1095, 1111
Water rights   261, 663, 889, 1092, **1092**
Water sanitation   886
Water supply   387
Water table   57, 123, 199, 228, 244, 249, 387, 434, 544-545, 593, 616, 717, 776, 859, 888, 890, 892, 908, 911, 913, 962, 999, 1067, 1083, 1093, **1093**, 1100
Water table draw-down   58, 76, 489, 717, 776, 889, **1093**, 1100
Water treatment   10, 58, 94, 129, 183-184, 297, 385, 416, 491, 760, 916, 980, 1046, 1064, 1081, **1093**, 1126
Water use   1081
Waterfowl   599, 654
Waterfowl conservation   283
Waterlogging   280, **1095**
Waters, Joe   765
Watershed   28, 35, 53, 55, 115, 181, 194, 253, 259, 312, 314, 355, 385, 414, 434, 525, 534, 584, 591, 668, 716, 767, 858-859, 920, 963, 986, 1002, 1057, 1095, **1095**
Watershed management   717, 1021, 1095, **1095**

Watkins, James D.   271, 895, 919
Watson, Paul   925
Watson, Dr. Robert   763
Watt, James Gaius   832, 870, 906,
   947, **1096**
Wave power   34, 334, 619, 711, 742,
   1027, **1097**
Wavelengths   850
Wax myrtle   388
Waxman, Henry   190
Weather modification   197, **1097**
Weather patterns   854
Web of treaty law   1040
Webster Industries   793
Weeding   538
Wegener, Alfred   802
Weicker, Lowell   227
Wells   129, 280, 459, 652, 739, 741,
   744, 788, 906, 913, 933, 1080-
   1081, 1093, **1099**, 1143
Werbach, Adam   **1100**
West Valley, New York   846
Western hemlock   717, 1014
Western lowland gorilla   471
Western red cedar   1014
Western yellow-billed cuckoo   257
Westinghouse Corporation   848
Wet scrubber   26, 85, 191, 809, **1100**
Wet steam fields   459
Wetlands   4-5, 40, 49, 63, 76, 87,
   108, 118, 140, 178, 192, 222,
   233, 244, 267, 274, 283, 308,
   310, 318, 369-370, 385, 387,
   411, 418, 436, 486, 511, 527,
   540, 554, 559, 567, 575, 627,
   681, 685, 689, 694-695, 699,
   713, 767, 780, 791, 823, 837-
   838, 882, 888, 959, 963, 966,
   988, 1003, 1012, 1040, 1059,
   1064, 1081, 1093, 1096, **1100**,
   1106, 1116, 1124
Wetlands Convention   233
Wetlands Watch   567
Whales   36, 42, 47-48, 112, 147, 167,
   242, 277, 303, 329, 331, 380,
   396, 442, 487, 527, 552, 579,
   629, 689, 758, 763, 831, 920,
   926, 942, 1060, **1102**
Whaling   47, 143, 487, 527, 552, 920,
   926, 1039, **1103**
W.   .ass   758
W.   .rge   458
Vl.   **1104**
           .n Environmental

           .35, 528,

Whooping crane (*Grus americana*)   75,
   99, 153, 329, 447, 560, 695,
   1102, **1106**
Wild Bird Conservation Act   47
Wild Horse Act   47
Wild horses   406
Wild river   55, 303, 465, 515, 527,
   691, **1108**, 1110
Wild and Scenic Rivers Act
   (1968)   515, **1107**, 1108, 1110
Wilderness   1, 8-9, 30, 40, 48, 61, 93,
   136-137, 152, 190, 225, 292,
   299, 361, 406, 424-425, 429,
   476, 488, 504, 527, 560, 607,
   624, 633, 666, 675, 681, 687,
   695, 747, 799, 808, 819, 825,
   832, 835-836, 981, 990, 1096,
   1109, 1110, 1112-1113, 1124,
   1126, 1144
Wilderness Act (1964)   9, 136, 144,
   406, 633, 946, 1107, 1109, **1110**,
   1112-1113
Wilderness protection   633
Wilderness Society, (Washington,
   D.C.)   222, 268, 424, 607, 633,
   856, 1109, 1111, **1112**, 1124
Wilderness Study Area   696, 1110,
   1113
Wildfire   76, 300, 314, 316, 370,
   378, 681, 746, 826, 935, 1110,
   1113, 1124
Wildlife   12, 36-37, 47, 61, 63, 87,
   90, 97, 101, 112, 120, 153,
   181, 192, 206, 221, 231, 243,
   250, 252, 257, 270, 284, 317,
   325-326, 349, 355, 359, 371,
   377, 386, 388, 395, 402-403,
   415, 418, 429, 446-447, 465,
   469, 478, 483, 492, 503, 517,
   525, 527, 559, 562, 565, 567,
   576, 589, 592, 608, 624, 667-
   668, 681, 685, 688-689, 692,
   694-695, 710, 713, 727, 738,
   755, 757-758, 793, 804, 809,
   815, 824, 836, 838-839, 854,
   856, 858, 860-861, 889, 896,
   925, 939, 990, 999, 1003-1005,
   1013, 1020, 1032, 1039, 1059,
   1081, 1089-1091, 1102, 1106,
   1108, 1110, 1112, **1115**, 1117,
   1119-1120, 1129, 1131, 1136,
   1142-1143
Wildlife habitat   1090
*Wildlife Habitat Conservation Teacher's
   PAC*   685
Wildlife management   12, 126, 151-
   153, 163, 230-231, 295, 411,
   560, 567, 573, 578, 607, 625,
   633, 685, 696, 719, 750, 759,
   770, 787, 814, 824, 1043, 1110,
   1116, **1117**, 1120, 1127, 1144
Wildlife refuge   30, 61, 119, 128, 257,
   364, 411, 447, 573, 576, 578,

591, 625, 695, 1059, 1111-1112,
   1117-1118, **1118**
Wildlife rehabilitation   128, 156, 411,
   558, 759, 869, 1117-1118, **1120**
Wildlife Society   874
Wildlife trade   231
William Morris Davis   893
Wilson, Alexander   75
Wilson, Edward Osborne   106, 329,
   395, 637, 960**1120**
Wilson, Woodrow   519
Wind energy   33-34, 284, 314, 322,
   335, 339, 349, 619, 742, 753,
   823, 874, 1097, **1121**
Wind Erosion Equation (WEE)   385
Windmills   874
Windrow composting   670
Windrow turners   219
Windrows   219, 1080
Windscale (Sellafield) plutonium
   reactor, England   843, 846, **1123**
Winograd, Isaac   655
Winter range   **1123**
Winter Sunshine   147
Wise Use Agenda, The   1124
Wise use movement   906, **1124**
Wisent   126
"With the Birds"   146
Wolman, Abel   **1125**
Wolves   126, 257, 329, 331, 395, 474,
   527, 573, 804, 823-824, **1126**
Women's rights   1106
Wood alcohol   650
Wood bison   126
Wood Bison National Park   126
Wood, Norman   578
Wood preservative   775
Wood stork   389
Woods Hole Oceanographic
   Institution   928
Woodwell, George M.   **1127**
Work in Progress   138
Worker-management committees   887
Worksite safety and health plan   887
World Association of Soil and Water
   Conservation   963
World Bank   226, 245, 310, 609, 623,
   645, 756, 818, 855, 857, 944,
   1021, 1091, **1128**
World Bird Club   553
World Birdwatch   553
World Commission on Environment
   and Development   143, 755,
   1004
World Conservation Strategy   **1130**
World Conservation Union   289
World Health Organization   261,
   894, 1126
World Heritage Biosphere Reserve
   Program   1055
World Heritage Site   387
World Meteorological
   Organization   725

World Rainforest Report 857
World Resources Institute 303, 396, 499, 637
World Resources Institute (Washington, D.C.) 303, 396, 499, 637, **1130**
World War I 1075
World War II 1075
World Wide Fund for Nature 1131
World Wildlife Federation 774
World Wildlife Fund (Washington, D.C.) 12, 36, 60, 153, 223, 370, 380, 477, 755, 870, 1071, 1117, 1128, 1130, **1131**
World3 610
Worldwatch Institute (Washington, D.C.)138, 396, 516, **1132**
WOW! (Whales On Wheels) 920
Wrangell–Saint Elias Wilderness 1110
Wyoming Fish and Game Department 127

X

X ray 69, 137, 162, 323, 400, 520, 560-561, 724, 843-844, **1133**
Xenobiotic 68, 439, 513, 648, 651, 656, 684, **1133**
Xeriscaping 62
Xiphias gladius 1006

Xylene **1133**

Y

Yangtze River 713, 1024
Yankee Rowe Nuclear Power Plant 1053
Yard waste 219, 539, 669, 971, 973, 976, 978, **1135**
Yasuni Biosphere Reserve 120
Yellow fever 782
Yellow perch 585
Yellowfin tuna 629
Yellowstone National Park, Wyoming 9, 63, 106, 126, 257, 315, 317, 448, 476, 515, 592, 689-690, 938, 1039, 1115, 1119, 1126, **1135**
Yeltsin, Boris 919
Yersinia 342
Yokkaichi asthma 70, 882, 1069, **1136**
Yosemite Grant of 1864 690
Yosemite National Park, California 8, 138, 317, 476, 518, 668, 691, 747, 798, 827, 946, **1137**, 1039
Young, Ruth 958
Your Big Backyard 695
Yttrium-98 845
Yucca Flat 701
Yucca Mountain, Nevada 849, 701, 737, 847, 1058, **1138**

Yugoslavia 296

Z

Zahniser, Howard 1109, 1111
Zea mays 113, 516
Zebra mussel (*Dreissena polymorpha*) 391, 410, 474, 496, 559, 907, 980, **1141**
Zebras 333, **1142**
Zeldovich cycle 208
Zero discharge 192, 838, **1142**, 1143
Zero population growth 312, 613, 624, 665, 710, 755, 817, 922, 984, 1071, 1128, **1142**, 1143
Zero risk **1143**
Zero Waste Lunch 311
Zimbabwe 1021
Zinc 512, 514
Zobell, L. E. 102
Zone of saturation 10, 433, 489, 776, 780, 1067, **1143**
Zoning regulations 592
Zoo 154, 461, **1143**
Zoological Society of London 1144
Zooplankton 112, 393, 412, 422, 579, 630, 762, 767, 775, 800, 1047, **1145**